FOR REFERENCE

Do Not Take From This Room

ProQuest Statistical Abstract of the United States 2023

ProQuest Statistical Abstract of the United States 2023

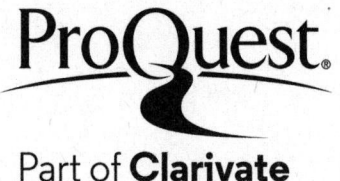

Part of **Clarivate**

Published by Rowman & Littlefield
A wholly owned subsidiary of The Rowman & Littlefield Publishing Group, Inc.
4501 Forbes Boulevard, Suite 200, Lanham, Maryland 20706
www.rowman.com, 800-462-6420
86-90 Paul Street, London, EC2A 4NE

ISBN 13: 978-1-63671-086-0

Suggested Citation:
ProQuest LLC. ProQuest Statistical Abstract of the United States, 2023. (11th ed.) 2022

Preface

The *Statistical Abstract of the United States,* published since 1878, is the best-known statistical reference publication in the country. As a comprehensive collection of statistics on the social, political, and economic conditions of the United States, it is a snapshot of America and its people. In the spring of 2011, the Census Bureau terminated their Statistical Compendia program and production of the *Statistical Abstract.* Since 2012, ProQuest, now part of Clarivate, has taken responsibility for curating the data found in this valuable statistical reference tool and publishing it in this print edition and an expanded online edition.

The *ProQuest Statistical Abstract of the United States* is designed to serve as a convenient volume for statistical reference and as a guide to other statistical publications and sources. The latter function is served by the introductory text to each section; source citations appearing below each table; and Appendix I, which is comprised of the Guide to Sources of Statistics, including a list of international statistical abstracts, and the Guide to State Statistical Abstracts.

Contents—This volume includes a selection of data from many statistical sources, both government and private, as indicated in the source citations at the bottom of every table. Data are obtained from a variety of resources, including PDF documents, Excel data packages, and complex databases. Publications cited as source reports usually contain additional statistical detail and more comprehensive discussions of definitions and concepts. Data not available in written publications issued by the contributing agency but obtained from data files available on the internet or unpublished records are also identified in the source notes. More information on the subjects covered in the tables may generally be obtained from the source.

Except as indicated, figures are for the United States as presently constituted. Although emphasis in the *ProQuest Statistical Abstract* is primarily given to national data, many tables present data for regions and individual states and a smaller number for metropolitan areas and cities. "Appendix II, Metropolitan and Micropolitan Statistical Areas: Concepts, Components, and Population," presents explanatory text, a complete current listing, and 2021 population data for metropolitan and micropolitan areas delineated as of March 2020. Statistics for the Commonwealth of Puerto Rico and for Island Areas of the United States are included in many state tables and are supplemented by information in Section 29.

Statistics in this edition are generally for the most recent year or period available, as of early September 2022. Each year over 1,400 tables are reviewed and evaluated, new tables of current interest are added, continuing series are updated, and less timely data are condensed or eliminated. Text notes and appendices are revised as appropriate.

Changes in this edition—This year ProQuest introduces approximately 40 new tables presenting data on topics that include individual income taxes, IRS audits, school shootings, COVID-19 related changes to school instruction, employment of undergraduate students, energy distribution system reliability, air pollution by metropolitan statistical area, COVID-19 deaths, disability rates, health status and access to health care, abortions, space-related industries employment, nonimmigrant admissions, Puerto Rico GDP and trade, foreign military sales, and federal agriculture subsidies. For a complete list of new tables, see "New Tables," p. xi.

The *Statistical Abstract* generally presents data on an annual basis. Coverage of the coronavirus disease (COVID-19) pandemic is an exception to this. For example, Table 117 in Section 2: Births, Deaths, Marriages, and Divorces shows cumulative data on COVID-19 deaths; and Tables 176 and 205 in Section 3: Health and Nutrition show weekly data on coronavirus cases, testing, hospitalizations, and vaccinations. The data presented here are intended as an illustration of the progression of the pandemic in the U.S. and to provide information on where to find statistics related to the pandemic. Please refer to the table source notes as a guide to accessing revised and up-to-date data.

Online edition—*ProQuest Statistical Abstract* is also available in an electronic format. This dynamic edition features table-specific capabilities for narrowing results by source, data date, subject, and type of data breakdown. The online edition is updated with new statistical content on a monthly basis, enabling users to access new and revised data in advance of the annual publication of this printed edition. The online product functions as a repository for additional historical trends that cannot fit into the print publication. Users will find spreadsheets that correspond to each table in the book. In many cases, these spreadsheets present expanded coverage of the data shown in print. The online edition is available as a stand-alone product or as a part of ProQuest's Statistical Premium Collection (see inside back cover for details).

Limitations of the data—The contents of this volume were taken from many sources. All data from censuses, surveys, and administrative records are subject to error arising from a number of factors including the following: sampling variability (for statistics based on samples), reporting errors in the data for individual units, incomplete coverage, nonresponse, and imputation and processing errors (see also Appendix III). ProQuest cannot accept responsibility for the accuracy or limitations of the data presented here; however, selection of the material and its proper presentation is the responsibility of ProQuest.

For additional information on data presented—Please consult the source publications available in local libraries and on the internet, or contact the agency or organization indicated in the source notes.

Contents

[Numbers following subject are page numbers]

New and Deleted Tables for the 2023 Edition

New Tables for 2023

Tables Deleted Since the 2022 Edition of the Statistical Abstract

[Tables are deleted for several reasons, including: source data have been discontinued, source data were monographic and new data are not available, data are no longer reliable, and data were previously unpublished and cannot be replicated. Some tables have been replaced with tables illustrating similar content. Where applicable, please see reference to new table number]

2022 Table	Section and Table Title	Replaced by...
	Section 2: Births, Deaths, Marriages, and Divorces	
Table 98........	Adults Reporting Sexual Contact with Opposite- and Same-Sex Partners by Sex, Age, and Race/Ethnicity: 2011 to 2013	
Table 99........	Sexual Attraction and Orientation by Sex, Age, and Race/Ethnicity: 2011 to 2013	
Table 102......	Percent of Babies Breastfed by Selected Characteristics of Mother: 1986 to 2013	
	Section 3: Health and Nutrition	
Table 163......	Health Insurance Coverage Status and Plan Type: 1970 to 2018	
Table 164......	Health Insurance Enrollment in High Deductible Health Plans (HDHP) and Health Savings Accounts: 2010 to 2018	
Table 182......	Health Care Sources Used Most Often—Percent Distribution of Persons Age 18 and Over by Selected Characteristics: 2018	
Table 190......	Hospital Overnight Stays by Selected Characteristics: 2018	
Table 208......	Disability Prevalence Among Adults Age 18 and Over by Type of Disability: 2014	Table 208
Table 211.......	Respiratory Diseases Among Persons Age 18 and Over by Selected Characteristics: 2018	
Table 212......	Selected Diseases and Conditions Among Persons Age 18 and Over by Selected Characteristics: 2018	Table 211
Table 214......	Migraine Headaches and Pain in the Neck, Lower Back, Face or Jaw Among Persons Age 18 and Over by Selected Characteristics: 2018	
Table 229......	Leisure-Time Aerobic and Muscle-Strengthening Activity Among Adults Age 18 and Over by Selected Characteristics: 2018	
Table 232......	Sleep—Percent Distribution of Adults Age 18 and Over by Hours of Sleep by Selected Characteristics: 2011 to 2014	
Table 234......	Children With Allergies by Type and Selected Characteristics: 2018	
Table 235......	Learning Disability and Attention Deficit Hyperactivity Disorder Among Children Age 3 to 17: 2018	
Table 236......	Autism and Other Developmental Disability Prevalence Among Children Age 3 to 17: 2014 to 2016	Table 233
	Section 4: Education	
Table 283......	Counselors, Psychologists, and Social Workers in Public Schools by Selected Characteristics: 2015 to 2016	
Table 291......	Career and Technology Education (CTE) Programs in Public School Districts by District Characteristics: 2017	
Table 307......	Active Duty Military Personnel and Veterans Enrolled in Higher Education: 2012 and 2016	
Table 312......	Average Total Price of Attendance of Undergraduate Education: 2016	
Table 314......	Average Out-of-Pocket Net Price of Attendance for Undergraduates: 2016	
	Section 5: Law Enforcement, Courts, and Prisons	
Table 382......	Suspects Arrested by Drug Enforcement Administration by Type of Drug and Arrestee Characteristics: 2016	Table 377
	Section 9: Federal Government Finances and Employment	
Table 522......	Individual Income Tax Returns Filed—Audits Coverage: 1995 to 2019	Table 530
Table 529......	Federal Individual Income Tax Returns—Number, Income Tax, and Average Tax by Size of Adjusted Gross Income: 2015 and 2016	Table 527
	Section 10: National Security and Veterans Affairs	
Table 544......	Department of Defense Property—Sites, Land, and Assets: 2017	
Table 553......	U.S. Military Sales and Assistance to Foreign Governments: 1990 to 2017	
Table 554......	U.S. Military Sales Deliveries by Selected Country: 2000 to 2017	Table 552
Table 573......	Customs and Border Protection (CBP)—Processed and Cleared Passengers, Planes, Vehicles, and Containers: 2008 to 2015	
	Section 13: Income, Expenditures, Poverty, and Wealth	
Table 734......	Annual Expenditures Per Child by Married-Couple Families by Family Income and Expenditure Type: 2015	
	Section 18: Forestry, Fishing, and Mining	
Table 937......	Domestic Fish and Shellfish Catch and Value by Major Species Caught: 2000 to 2019	
Table 940......	Canned, Fresh, and Frozen Fishery Products—Production and Value: 1990 to 2019	
	Section 21: Manufactures	
Table 1065.....	Pharmaceutical Preparations—Value of Shipments: 2010 to 2016	
Table 1066.....	Household Appliances Manufacturing—Value of Shipments: 2010 to 2016	
Table 1067.....	Communications Equipment Manufacturing—Value of Shipments: 2010 to 2016	
Table 1068.....	Computers and Peripheral Equipment Manufacturing—Value of Shipments: 2010 to 2016	
Table 1069.....	Semiconductors, Electronic Components, and Other Electronic Component Manufacturing Equipment—Value of Shipments: 2010 to 2016	
	Section 23: Transportation	
Table 1112.....	Ferry Operators, Vessels, Terminals, Route Distance, and Boarding Counts by State and Island Area: 2015	
Table 1149.....	Household Daily Travel Trips and Trip Length by Trip Purpose: 1969 to 2017	
	Section 26: Arts, Recreation, and Travel	
Table 1286.....	Domestic and International Travel Expenditures by State: 2017	
	Section 30: International Statistics	
Table 1375.....	Indexes of Living Costs Abroad by Selected City: 2019	
Table 1416.....	Terrorism Incidents, Fatalities, and Injuries for Top Countries and Perpetrator Groups: 2019	

Guide to Tabular Presentation

Example of Table Structure

Table 1287. Top 20 U.S. Gateway Airports for Nonstop International Air Travel Passengers: 2021

[94,943 represents 94,943,000. International passengers are residents of any country traveling nonstop to and from the United States on U.S. and foreign carriers. The data cover all passengers arriving and departing from U.S. airports on nonstop commercial international flights with 60 seats or more]

Gateway airport	Airport code	Passengers (1,000)	Gateway airport	Airport code	Passengers (1,000)
Total, all airports...............	**(X)**	**94,943**	Fort Lauderdale, FL.....................	FLL	4,035
Total, top 20 airports..............	(X)	86,417	Washington, DC (Dulles)..............	IAD	3,299
Top 20, percentage of total..............	(X)	91.0	San Francisco, CA......................	SFO	3,291
			Boston, MA.............................	BOS	2,088
New York, NY...........................	JFK	12,812	Charlotte, NC...........................	CLT	2,043
Miami, FL................................	MIA	11,954	Orlando, FL.............................	MCO	1,913
Los Angeles, CA........................	LAX	7,887	Denver, CO.............................	DEN	1,866
Houston, TX.............................	IAH	6,502	Seattle, WA............................	SEA	1,542
Newark, NJ..............................	EWR	6,464	Phoenix, AZ............................	PHX	1,230
Dallas/Fort Worth, TX....................	DFW	5,894	Philadelphia, PA........................	PHL	1,020
Atlanta, GA.............................	ATL	5,566	Detroit, MI.............................	DTW	968
Chicago, IL.............................	ORD	5,278	Las Vegas, NV..........................	LAS	765

X Not applicable.

Source: U.S. Department of Transportation, Research and Innovative Technology Administration, Bureau of Transportation Statistics, Office of Airline Information, "T-100 International Segment data," <www.transtats.bts.gov/Fields.asp?gnoyr_VQ=FJE>, accessed June 2022.

Headnotes immediately below table titles provide information important for correct interpretation or evaluation of the table as a whole or for a major segment of it.

Footnotes below the bottom rule of tables give information relating to specific items or figures within the table.

Unit indicators show the *specified quantities* in which data items are presented. They are used for two primary reasons. Sometimes data are not available in absolute form and are estimates (as in the case of many surveys). In other cases we round the numbers in order to save space to show more data.

When a table presents data with more than one unit indicator, they are found in the headnotes and column headings (Tables 5 and 23), spanner (Table 37), stub (Table 27), or unit column (Table 250). When the data in a table are shown in the same unit indicator, it is shown as the first part of the headnote (Table 2). If no unit indicator is shown, data presented are in absolute form (Table 1).

Vertical rules are used to separate independent sections of a table (Table 1), or in tables where the stub is continued into one or more additional columns (Table 2).

Averages—An average is a single number or value that is often used to represent the "typical value" of a group of numbers. It is regarded as a measure of "location" or "central tendency" of a group of numbers.

The *arithmetic mean* is the type of average used most frequently. It is derived by summing the individual item values of a particular group and dividing the total by the number of items. The arithmetic mean is often referred to as simply the "mean" or "average."

The *median* of a group of numbers is the middle number or value when each item in the group is arranged according to size (lowest to highest or vice versa); it generally has the same number of items above it as well as below it. If there is an even number of items in the group, the median is taken to be the average of the two middle numbers.

Per capita (or per person) quantities—a per capita figure represents an average computed for every person in a specified group (or population). It is derived by taking the total for an item (such as income, taxes, or retail sales) and dividing it by the number of persons in the specified population.

Index numbers—An index number is the measure of difference or change, usually expressed as a percent, relating one quantity (the variable) of a specified kind to another quantity of the same kind. Index numbers are widely used to express changes in prices over periods of time, but may also be used to express differences between related subjects for a single point in time.

To compute a price index, a base year or period is selected. The base year price (of the commodity or service) is then designated as the base or reference price to which the prices for other years or periods are related. Many price indexes use the year 1982 as the base year; in tables, this is shown as "1982 = 100." A method expressing the price relationship is: The price of a set of one or more items for a related year (e.g. 1990) **divided by** the price of the same set of items for the base year (e.g. 1982). The result multiplied by 100 provides the index number. When 100 is subtracted from the index number, the result equals the percent change in price from the base year.

Average annual percent change—Unless otherwise stated in the *Abstract* (as in Section 1, Population), average annual percent change is computed by use of a *compound interest formula*. This formula assumes that the rate of change is constant throughout a specified compounding period (1 year for average annual rates of change). The formula is similar to that used to compute the balance of a savings account that receives compound interest. According to this formula, at the end of a compounding period the amount of accrued change (e.g., school enrollment or bank interest) is added to the amount that existed at the beginning of the period. As a result, over time (e.g., with each year or quarter), the same rate of change is applied to a larger and larger figure.

The *exponential formula,* which is based on continuous compounding, is often used to measure population change. It is preferred by population experts because they view population and population-related subjects as changing without interruption, ever ongoing. Both exponential and compound interest formulas assume a constant rate of change. The former, however, applies the amount of change continuously to the base rather than at the end of each compounding period. When the average annual rates are small (e.g., less than 5 percent), both formulas give virtually the same results. For an explanation of these two formulas as they relate to population, see U.S. Census Bureau, *The Methods and Materials of Demography,* Vol. 2, 3d printing (rev.), 1975.

Current and constant dollars—Statistics in some tables in a number of sections are expressed in both current and constant dollars (see, e.g., Table 719 in Section 13, Income, Expenditures, Poverty, and Wealth). Current dollar figures reflect actual prices or costs prevailing during the specified year(s). Constant dollar figures are estimates representing an effort to remove the effects of price changes from statistical series reported in dollar terms. In general, constant dollar series are derived by dividing current dollar estimates by the appropriate price index for the appropriate period (e.g., the Consumer Price Index). The result is a series as it would presumably exist if prices were the same throughout, as in the base year—in other words, as if the dollar had constant purchasing power. Any changes in this constant dollar series would reflect only changes in real volume of output, income, expenditures, or other measure.

Explanation of Symbols

The following symbols, used in the tables throughout this book, are explained in condensed form in footnotes to the tables where they appear:

— Represents zero or rounds to less than half the unit of measurement shown.

B Base figure too small to meet statistical standards for reliability of a derived figure.

D Figure withheld to avoid disclosure pertaining to a specific organization or individual.

NA Data not enumerated, tabulated, or otherwise available separately.

P Data are preliminary or projected.

S Figure does not meet publication standards for reasons other than that covered by symbol B, above.

X Figure not applicable because column heading and stub line make entry impossible, absurd, or meaningless.

Z Entry would amount to less than half the unit of measurement shown.

In many tables, details will not add to the totals shown because of rounding.

Section 1
Population

This section presents statistics on the growth, distribution, and characteristics of the U.S. population. The principal source of these data is the U.S. Census Bureau, which conducts a decennial census of population, a monthly population survey, a program of population estimates and projections, and a number of other periodic surveys.

Decennial censuses—The U.S. Constitution provides for a census of the population every 10 years, primarily to establish a basis for apportionment of members of the House of Representatives among the states. For over a century after the first census in 1790, the census organization was a temporary one, created only for each decennial census. In 1902, the Census Bureau was established as a permanent federal agency, responsible for enumerating the population and also for compiling statistics on other population and housing characteristics. Data in this 2023 Edition of the *Statistical Abstract of the United States* begin to incorporate results of the 2020 Census. As of fall 2022, apportionment results and redistricting data have been released. Due to COVID-19 pandemic-related delays in operations, the Census Bureau continues to develop and release 2020 Census data products. Selected demographic profiles and demographic and housing characteristics files are planned for release in May 2023 with detailed files to follow in August 2023 and beyond.

Historically, the enumeration of the population has been a complete (100 percent) count. That is, an attempt is made to account for every person, for each person's residence, and for other characteristics (sex, age, family relationships, etc.). In the twentieth century, the questions were divided between a "short" and "long" form. Only a subset of the population was required to answer the long-form questions. Starting in 2010, the census consisted only of a short form, which included basic questions about age, sex, race, Hispanic origin, household relationship, and owner/renter status. After the 2000 Census, the long form became the American Community Survey (ACS) and continues to collect long-form-type information. The ACS includes not only the basic short-form questions, but also detailed questions about population and housing characteristics. It is a nationwide, continuous sample survey designed to provide communities with reliable and timely demographic, housing, social, and economic data every year. Since its start, the ACS has been providing a continuous stream of updated information for states and local areas. Sample data may be used with confidence where large numbers are involved and assumed to indicate trends and relationships where small numbers are involved.

Current Population Survey (CPS)—The CPS sample is a probability sample designed primarily to produce national and state estimates of labor force characteristics of the civilian non-institutional population 16 years of age and older. The sample consists of independent samples in each state and the District of Columbia, and each state sample is specifically tailored to the demographic and labor market conditions that prevail in that particular state.

About 60,000 housing units are required in order to meet the national and State reliability criteria, drawn from 824 sample areas.

The CPS also serves as a vehicle for inquiries on other subjects. Using CPS data, the Census Bureau issues a series of publications under the general title of *Current Population Reports*.

Estimates of population characteristics based on the CPS will not agree with the counts from the census because the CPS and the census use different procedures for collecting and processing the data for racial groups, the Hispanic population, and other topics. Caution should also be used when comparing estimates for various years because of the periodic introduction of changes into the CPS. Beginning in January 1994, a number of changes were introduced into the CPS that affect all data comparisons with prior years. These changes included the results of a major redesign of the survey questionnaire and collection methodology and the introduction of 1990 census population controls, adjusted for the estimated undercount. Beginning with the 2001 CPS Annual Demographic Supplement, the independent estimates used as control totals for the CPS are based on civilian population benchmarks consistent with Census 2000. In 2003, the name of the March supplement was changed to Annual Social and Economic Supplement (ASEC). Beginning with the 2012 March CPS supplement, the estimates are based on Census 2010 population controls. These changes in population controls had relatively little impact on derived measures such as means, medians, and percent distribution, but did have a significant impact on levels.

In 2002, the ASEC incorporated a significant sample expansion. The sample was expanded primarily to improve state estimates of children's health insurance coverage (CHIP). This sample increase of 19,000 households added to the regular sample of 72,500 households and the Hispanic sample of 6,500 gives a total sample size of about 98,000 households. The 2014 CPS ASEC included redesigned questions for income and health insurance coverage. All of the approximately 98,000 addresses were selected to receive the improved set of health insurance coverage items. The improved income questions were implemented using a split panel design. Approximately 68,000 addresses were selected to receive a set of income questions similar to those used in the 2013 CPS ASEC. The remaining 30,000 addresses were selected to receive the redesigned income questions.

Population estimates and projections—The Census Bureau produces and publishes estimates of the population for the nation, states, counties, state/county equivalents, and Puerto Rico. With each annual release of population estimates, the Population Estimates Program (PEP) revises and updates the entire time series of estimates from April 1, 2020 to July 1 of the current year, which is referred to as the vintage year. "Vintage" denotes an entire time series created with a consistent population starting point and methodology. The release of a new vintage of estimates supersedes any previous series and incorporates the most up-to-date input data and methodological improvements. PEP annually utilizes current data on births, deaths, and migration to calculate population change since the most recent decennial census and produce a time series of estimates of population, demographic components of change, and housing units. The annual time series of estimates begins with the most recent decennial census data and extends to the vintage year.

Registered births and deaths are estimated from data supplied by the National Center for Health Statistics and the Federal-State Cooperative for Population Estimates (FSCPE). The net international migration component consists of four parts: (1) the net international migration of the foreign born, (2) the net migration of natives to and from the United States, (3) the net migration between the United States and Puerto Rico, and (4) the net overseas movement of the Armed Forces population. Data from the ACS are used to estimate the annual net migration of the foreign-born population. The estimated net migration of the native-born population is produced using the foreign-census method which utilizes data from over 80 countries. This work compares estimates of the U.S.-born or U.S. citizen population living overseas measured by population registers and censuses in other countries at two consecutive time periods. The residual was used to develop estimates of net native migration. Estimates for net migration between Puerto Rico and the U.S. are derived from the ACS and the Puerto Rico Community Survey. Estimates of the net overseas movement of the Armed Forces are derived from data collected by the Defense Manpower Data Center.

Estimates for state and county areas are based on the same components of change data and sources as the national estimates with the addition of net internal migration. Estimates of net internal migration are derived from federal income tax returns from the Internal Revenue Service; group quarters data from the branches of the military, the Department of Veterans Affairs, and the FSCPE; and Medicare data from the Centers for Medicare and Medicaid Services.

Population estimates and projections are available on the Census Bureau Web site, see <www.census.gov>. These estimates and projections are consistent with official decennial census figures with no adjustment for estimated net census coverage. For details on methodology, see "Methodology for the United States Population Estimates: Vintage 2021," <www.census.gov/programs-surveys/popest/ technical-documentation/methodology.html>.

Immigration—Immigration (migration to a country) is one component of international migration; the other component is emigration (migration *from* a country). In its simplest form, international migration is defined as any movement across a national border. In the United States, federal statistics on international migration are produced primarily by the U.S. Census Bureau and the Office of Immigration Statistics of the U.S. Department of Homeland Security (DHS).

The Census Bureau collects data used to estimate international migration through its decennial censuses and numerous surveys of the U.S. population.

The Office of Immigration Statistics publishes immigration data in annual flow reports and the *Yearbook of Immigration Statistics*. Data for these publications are collected from several administrative data sources including the DS-230 *Application for Immigrant Visa and Alien Registration*, the DS-260 *Electronic Application for Immigrant Visa and Alien Registration* of the U.S. Department of State (used by applicants living abroad), and the I-485 *Application to Register Permanent Residence or Adjust Status* of U.S. Citizenship and Immigration Services (USCIS) for applicants living in the United States.

An immigrant, or lawful permanent resident (LPR), is a foreign national who has been granted lawful permanent residence in the United States. New arrivals are foreign nationals living abroad who apply for an immigrant visa at a consular office of the Department of State, while individuals adjusting status are already living in the United States and file an application for adjustment of status to lawful permanent residence with USCIS. Individuals adjusting status include refugees, asylees, and various classes of nonimmigrants. A refugee is a person outside his or her country of nationality who is unable or unwilling to return to his or her country of nationality because of persecution or a well-founded fear of persecution. An asylee is a person who meets the definition of refugee and is already present in the United States or is seeking admission at a port of entry. Refugees are required to apply for LPR ("green card") status one year after being admitted, and asylees may apply for green card status one year after their grant of asylum.

Nonimmigrants are foreign nationals granted temporary entry into the United States. The major activities for which nonimmigrant admission is authorized include temporary visits for business or pleasure, academic or vocational study, temporary employment, and to act as a representative of a foreign government or international organization. DHS collects information on the characteristics of a proportion of nonimmigrant admissions, those recorded on the I-94/I-94W arrival and departure records.

U.S. immigration law gives preferential immigration status to persons with a close family relationship with a U.S. citizen or legal permanent resident, persons with needed job skills, persons who qualify as refugees or asylees, and persons who are from countries with relatively low levels of immigration to the United States (diversity immigrants). Immigration to the United States can be divided into two general categories: (1) classes of admission subject to the annual worldwide limitation and (2) classes of admission exempt from worldwide limitations. Numerical limits are imposed on visas issued and not on admissions. In 2021, the annual limit for family-sponsored preferences was 226,000 and the limit for employment-based preferences was 140,000 plus any unused visas in the family-sponsored preference classes from the previous year, of which there were 122,288 from 2020.

The Diversity Visa Program is available to nationals of countries with fewer than 50,000 persons granted LPR status during the preceding five years in the employment-based and family-sponsored preferences and immediate relative classes of admission. In 2021, the diversity visa limit was 54,850.

The number of persons who may be admitted to the United States as refugees each year is established by the President in consultation with Congress. The ceiling was set at 62,500 in 2021. There is no numerical limit on the number of persons who can be granted asylum status in a year.

Classes of admission exempt from the worldwide limitation include immediate relatives of U.S. citizens, refugees and asylees adjusting to permanent residence, and other various classes of special immigrants.

Metropolitan and micropolitan areas—Metropolitan and micropolitan statistical areas (metro and micro areas) are geographic entities delineated by the U.S. Office of Management and Budget (OMB) for use by Federal statistical agencies in collecting, tabulating, and publishing Federal statistics. These areas are the result of the application of published standards to Census Bureau data. Generally, the areas are delineated using the most recent set of standards following each decennial census. Between censuses, the delineations are updated annually to reflect the most recent Census Bureau population estimates. Areas based on the 2010 standards and Census Bureau data were last delineated in March 2020. As of fall 2022, delineations based on the 2020 Census are not available.

The term "Core Based Statistical Area" (CBSA) is a collective term for both metro and micro areas. A metro area contains a core urban area of 50,000 or more population, and a micro area contains an urban core of at least 10,000 (but less than 50,000) population. Each metro or micro area consists of one or more counties and includes the counties containing the core urban area, as well as any adjacent counties that have a high degree of social and economic integration (as measured by commuting to work) with the urban core.

Urban and rural—The Census Bureau's urban-rural classification is fundamentally a delineation of geographical areas, identifying both individual urban areas and the rural areas of the nation. The Census Bureau's urban areas represent densely developed territory, and encompass residential, commercial, and other non-residential urban land uses.

The 2020 Census introduced major changes to the definition of urban areas that include the use of housing unit density instead of population density when delineating urban areas. Urban areas represent densely developed territory, and encompass residential, commercial, and other nonresidential urban land uses. For the 2020 Census, each urban area must encompass at least 2,000 housing units or at least 5,000 people. This is a change from the previous minimum of 2,500 persons which had been in place since 1910. Urban areas are defined primarily based on housing unit density measured at the census block level. In addition to the change in minimum thresholds for qualification and the change to use of housing unit density, the Census Bureau will no longer distinguish between urbanized areas of 50,000 or more people and urban clusters of less than 50,000 people. "Rural" encompasses all population, housing, and territory not included within an urban area.

Residence—In determining residence, the Census Bureau counts each person as an inhabitant of a usual place of residence (i.e., the place where one lives and sleeps most of the time). While this place is not necessarily a person's legal residence or voting residence, the use of these different bases of classification would produce the same results in the vast majority of cases.

Race—Beginning with Census 2000, collection and presentation of data on race and ethnicity adhere to federal standards established by the OMB in October

1997. The OMB requires federal agencies to use a minimum of five race categories: White, Black or African American, American Indian or Alaska Native, Asian, and Native Hawaiian or Other Pacific Islander. Additionally, to collect data on individuals of mixed race parentage, respondents were allowed to select one or more races. For respondents who did not identify with any of these five race categories, the OMB approved and included a sixth category—"Some other race" on Census 2000, 2010, and 2020 questionnaires. The OMB standard requires two separate questions, one for Hispanic or Latino origin and one for race. The 2020 Census implemented improvements to the two questions design and updated data processing and coding procedures to enable a more thorough and accurate depiction of how people self-identify. The response categories and write-in answers for the race question can be combined to create the five minimum OMB race categories plus "Some other race." People who responded to the question on race by indicating only one race are referred to as the *race alone* population, or the group that reported only one race category. Six categories make up this population: White alone, Black or African American alone, American Indian and Alaska Native alone, Asian alone, Native Hawaiian and Other Pacific Islander alone, and Some other race alone. Individuals who chose more than one of the six race categories are referred to as the *Two or More Races* population, or as the group that reported more than one race. Additionally, respondents who reported one race together with those who reported the same race plus one or more other races are combined to create the *race alone or in combination* categories. For example, the *White alone or in combination* group consists of those respondents who reported only White or who reported White combined with one or more other race groups, such as "White and Black or African American," or "White and Asian and American Indian and Alaska Native." Another way to think of the group who reported *White alone or in combination* is as the total number of people who identified entirely or partially as White. This group is also described as people who reported White, whether or not they reported any other race.

The *alone or in combination* categories are tallies of *responses* rather than *respondents*. That is, the alone or in combination categories are not mutually exclusive. Individuals who reported two races were counted in two separate and distinct alone or in combination race categories, while those who reported three races were counted in three categories, and so on. Consequently, the sum of all alone or in combination categories equals the number of races reported, which exceeds the total population.

The racial categories included in the census questionnaire generally reflect a social definition of race recognized in this country and not an attempt to define race biologically, anthropologically, or genetically. It is also recognized that the categories of the race item include racial and national origin or sociocultural groups. For example, data are available for the American Indian and Alaska Native tribes. A detailed explanation of race can be found at <www.census.gov/topics/population/race/about.html>.

In the CPS and other household sample surveys conducted through personal interview, respondents are asked to classify their race as: (1) White; (2) Black or African American; (3) American Indian or Alaska Native; (4) Asian; or (5) Native Hawaiian or Other

Pacific Islander. Beginning January 2003, respondents were allowed to report more than one race to indicate their mixed racial heritage.

Hispanic population—People who identify with the terms "Hispanic" or "Latino" are those who classify themselves in one of the specific Hispanic or Latino categories listed on the decennial census questionnaire and various Census Bureau survey questionnaires – "Mexican, Mexican American, Chicano" or "Puerto Rican" or "Cuban" – as well as those who indicate that they are "another Hispanic, Latino, or Spanish origin." Origin can be viewed as the heritage, nationality group, lineage, or country of birth of the person or the person's ancestors before their arrival in the United States.

Traditional and current data collection and classification treat race and Hispanic origin as two separate and distinct concepts in accordance with guidelines from the OMB. People who are Hispanic may be of any race and people in each race group may be either Hispanic or Not Hispanic. Also, each person has two attributes, their race (or races) and whether or not they are Hispanic. The overlap of race and Hispanic origin is the main comparability issue. For example, Black Hispanics (Hispanic Blacks) are included in both the number of Blacks and in the number of Hispanics.

Foreign-born and native populations—The Census Bureau separates the U.S. resident population into two groups based on whether or not a person was a U.S. citizen or U.S. national at the time of birth. Anyone born in the United States, Puerto Rico, or a U.S. Island Area (such as Guam), or born abroad to a U.S. citizen parent is a U.S. citizen at the time of birth and consequently included in the *native population*. The term *foreign-born population* refers to anyone who is not a U.S. citizen or a U.S. national at birth. This includes naturalized U.S. citizens, legal permanent resident aliens (immigrants), temporary migrants (such as foreign students), humanitarian migrants (such as refugees), and people illegally present in the United States. The Census Bureau provides a variety of demographic, social, economic, geographic, and housing information on the foreign-born population in the United States at <www.census.gov/topics/population/foreign-born.html>.

Mobility status—The U.S. population is classified according to mobility status on the basis of a comparison between the place of residence of each individual at the time of the survey or census and the place of residence at a specified earlier date. Nonmovers are all persons who were living in the same house or apartment at the end of the period as at the beginning of the period. Movers are all persons who were living in a different house or apartment at the end of the period than at the beginning of the period. Movers are further classified as to whether they were living in the same or different county, state, or region, or were movers from abroad. Movers from abroad include all persons whose place of residence was outside the United States (including Puerto Rico, other U.S. Island Area, or a foreign country) at the beginning of the period.

Living arrangements—Living arrangements refer to residency in households or in group quarters. A "household" comprises all persons who occupy a "housing unit," that is, a house, an apartment or other group of rooms, or a single room that constitutes "separate living quarters." A household includes the related family members and all the unrelated persons, if any, such as lodgers, foster children, or employees who share the housing unit. A person living alone or a group of unrelated persons sharing the same housing unit is also counted as a household. See text, Section 20, Construction and Housing, for definition of housing unit.

All persons not living in housing units are classified as living in group quarters. These individuals may be institutionalized, e.g., under care or custody in juvenile facilities, jails, correctional centers, hospitals, or nursing homes; or they may be residents in noninstitutional group quarters such as college dormitories, group homes, or military barracks.

Householder—The householder is the person, or one of the people, in whose name the home is owned, being bought, or rented. If a home is owned or rented jointly by a married couple, either spouse may be listed first. Two types of householders are distinguished: a family householder and a nonfamily householder. A family householder is a householder living with one or more people related to him or her by birth, marriage, or adoption. The householder and all people in the household related to him or her are family members. A family household may contain people not related to the householder, but those people are not included as part of the householder's family in census tabulations. Thus, the number of family households is equal to the number of families, but family households may include more members than do families.

Nonfamily—A nonfamily householder is a householder living alone or with nonrelatives only.

Subfamily—A subfamily is a married couple with or without children, or a single parent with one or more own never-married children under 18 years old, who does not maintain their own household, but lives in the home of someone else (the householder). Subfamilies are divided into "related" and "unrelated" subfamilies. A related subfamily is related to, but does not include, the householder or the spouse of the householder. Members of a related subfamily are also members of the family with whom they live. The number of related subfamilies, therefore, is not included in the count of families. An unrelated subfamily may include persons such as guests, lodgers, or resident employees and their spouses and/or children; none of whom is related to the householder. The number of unrelated subfamily members is included in the total number of household members, but is not included in the count of family members.

Married couple—A married couple live together in the same household, with or without children and other relatives.

Statistical reliability—For a discussion of statistical collection and estimation, sampling procedures, and measures of statistical reliability applicable to Census Bureau data, see Appendix III.

Percent Change in Resident Population for the 50 States, the District of Columbia, and Puerto Rico: 2010 to 2020

Percent Change

Twice the U.S. percent change — 14.9 to 18.4
7.5 to 14.8
U.S. percent change (7.4) — 0 to 7.4
No change — -7.4 to -0.1
-11.8 to -7.5

ME 2.6
NH 4.6
MA 7.4
RI 4.3
CT 0.9
NJ 5.7
DE 10.2
MD 7.0
DC 14.6
VT 2.8
NY 4.2
PA 2.4
VA 7.9
WV -3.2
NC 9.5
SC 10.7
FL 14.6
GA 10.6
OH 2.3
KY 3.8
TN 8.9
AL 5.1
MI 2.0
IN 4.7
IL -0.1
MS -0.2
WI 3.6
MO 2.8
AR 3.3
LA 2.7
MN 7.6
IA 4.7
ND 15.8
SD 8.9
NE 7.4
KS 3.0
OK 5.5
TX 15.9
MT 9.6
WY 2.3
CO 14.8
NM 2.8
ID 17.3
UT 18.4
AZ 11.9
WA 14.6
OR 10.6
NV 15.0
CA 6.1
AK 3.3
HI 7.0
PR -11.8

Median Center of Population for the United States: 1880 to 2020

Table 1. Population and Area: 1790 to 2020

[Area figures represent area on indicated date including in some cases considerable areas not then organized or settled, and not covered by the census. Area data include Alaska beginning in 1870 and Hawaii beginning in 1900. Total area figures for 1790 to 1970 have been recalculated on the basis of the remeasurement of states and counties for the 1980 census, but not on the basis of subsequent censuses. The land and water area figures for past censuses have not been adjusted and are not strictly comparable with the total area data for comparable dates because the land areas were derived from different base data, and these values are known to have changed with the construction of reservoirs, draining of lakes, etc. Density figures are based on land area measurements as reported in earlier censuses]

| Census date | Resident population | | | | Area (square miles) | | |
| | Number | Per square mile of land area | Increase over preceding census | | Total | Land | Water [1] |
			Number	Percent			
1790 (Aug. 2).......	3,929,214	4.50	(X)	(X)	891,364	864,746	24,065
1800 (Aug. 4).......	5,308,483	6.10	1,379,269	35.1	891,364	864,746	24,065
1810 (Aug. 6).......	7,239,881	4.30	1,931,398	36.4	1,722,685	1,681,828	34,175
1820 (Aug. 7).......	9,638,453	5.50	2,398,572	33.1	1,792,552	1,749,462	38,544
1830 (June 1)......	12,866,020	7.40	3,227,567	33.5	1,792,552	1,749,462	38,544
1840 (June 1)......	17,069,453	9.80	4,203,433	32.7	1,792,552	1,749,462	38,544
1850 (June 1)......	23,191,876	7.90	6,122,423	35.9	2,991,655	2,940,042	52,705
1860 (June 1)......	31,443,321	10.60	8,251,445	35.6	3,021,295	2,969,640	52,747
1870 (June 1)......	[2] 39,818,449	[2] 11.2	8,375,128	26.6	3,612,299	3,540,705	68,082
1880 (June 1)......	50,189,209	14.20	10,370,760	26.0	3,612,299	3,540,705	68,082
1890 (June 1)......	62,979,766	17.80	12,790,557	25.5	3,612,299	3,540,705	68,082
1900 (June 1)......	76,212,168	21.50	13,232,402	21.0	3,618,770	3,547,314	67,901
1910 (Apr. 15).....	92,228,531	26.00	16,016,363	21.0	3,618,770	3,547,045	68,170
1920 (Jan. 1)......	106,021,568	29.90	13,793,037	15.0	3,618,770	3,546,931	68,284
1930 (Apr. 1).......	123,202,660	34.70	17,181,092	16.2	3,618,770	3,554,608	60,607
1940 (Apr. 1).......	132,165,129	37.20	8,962,469	7.3	3,618,770	3,554,608	60,607
1950 (Apr. 1).......	151,325,798	42.60	19,160,669	14.5	3,618,770	3,552,206	63,005
1960 (Apr. 1).......	179,323,175	50.60	27,997,377	18.5	3,618,770	3,540,911	74,212
1970 (Apr. 1).......	203,211,926	57.50	23,888,751	13.3	3,618,770	3,536,855	78,444
1980 (Apr. 1).......	226,545,805	64.10	23,333,879	11.5	3,618,770	3,539,289	79,481
1990 (Apr. 1).......	248,709,873	70.40	22,164,068	9.8	[3] 3,717,796	3,536,278	[3] 181,518
2000 (Apr. 1).......	281,421,906	79.70	32,712,033	13.2	3,794,083	3,537,438	256,645
2010 (Apr. 1).......	308,745,538	87.40	27,323,632	9.7	3,796,742	3,531,905	264,837
2020 (Apr. 1).......	331,449,281	93.80	22,703,743	7.4	(NA)	(NA)	(NA)

X Not applicable. NA Not available. [1] Data for 1790 to 1980 cover inland water only. Data for 1990 comprise Great Lakes, inland, and coastal water. Data for 2000 and 2010 comprise Great Lakes, inland, territorial, and coastal water. [2] Revised to include adjustments for underenumeration in southern states; unrevised number is 38,558,371 (10.9 per square mile). [3] Data reflect corrections made after publication of the results.

Source: U.S. Census Bureau, *Areas of the United States: 1940*; Area data for 1990: unpublished data from TIGER ®; and "Fast Facts," <www.census.gov/history/www/through_the_decades/fast_facts/>, and "Historical Population Change Data (1910-2020)" and "Historical Population Density Data (1910-2020)," <www.census.gov/programs-surveys/decennial-census/data/tables.2020.html>, accessed August 2021.

Table 2. Population: 1970 to 2021

[In thousands (205,052 represents 205,052,000). Estimates as of July 1. Civilian population excludes Armed Forces. Estimates for 2010-2019 are based on the 2010 Census; beginning 2020, estimates are developed from a base that incorporates the 2020 Census, Vintage 2020 estimates, and 2020 Demographic Analysis estimates]

Year	Resident population, including Armed Forces overseas	Resident population	Civilian population	Year	Resident population, including Armed Forces overseas	Resident population	Civilian population
1970........	205,052	203,984	201,895	1998........	276,115	275,854	274,633
1975........	215,973	215,465	213,789	1999........	279,295	279,040	277,841
1976........	218,035	217,563	215,894	2000........	(NA)	282,162	(NA)
1977........	220,239	219,760	218,106	2001........	(NA)	284,969	(NA)
1978........	222,585	222,095	220,467	2002........	(NA)	287,625	(NA)
1979........	225,055	224,567	222,969	2003........	(NA)	290,108	(NA)
1980........	227,726	227,225	225,621	2004........	(NA)	292,805	(NA)
1981........	229,966	229,466	227,818	2005........	(NA)	295,517	(NA)
1982........	232,188	231,664	229,995	2006........	(NA)	298,380	(NA)
1983........	234,307	233,792	232,097	2007........	(NA)	301,231	(NA)
1984........	236,348	235,825	234,110	2008........	(NA)	304,094	(NA)
1985........	238,466	237,924	236,219	2009........	(NA)	306,772	(NA)
1986........	240,651	240,133	238,412	2010........	309,747	309,327	308,092
1987........	242,804	242,289	240,550	2011........	312,001	311,583	310,366
1988........	245,021	244,499	242,817	2012........	314,214	313,878	312,638
1989........	247,342	246,819	245,131	2013........	316,361	316,060	314,817
1990........	250,132	249,623	247,983	2014........	318,662	318,386	317,160
1991........	253,493	252,981	251,370	2015........	320,975	320,739	319,542
1992........	256,894	256,514	254,929	2016........	323,291	323,072	321,869
1993........	260,255	259,919	258,446	2017........	325,343	325,122	323,932
1994........	263,436	263,126	261,714	2018........	327,075	326,838	325,651
1995........	266,557	266,278	264,927	2019........	328,566	328,330	327,143
1996........	269,667	269,394	268,108	2020........	331,745	331,501	330,405
1997........	272,912	272,647	271,394	2021........	332,141	331,894	330,784

NA Not available.

Source: U.S. Census Bureau, Population Division, data prior to 2010, <www.census.gov/programs-surveys/popest.html>; National Population by Characteristics: 2010 to 2020, "Monthly National Population Estimates by Age, Sex, Race, Hispanic Origin, and Population Universe for the United States: April 1, 2010 to December 1, 2020," <www.census.gov/programs-surveys/popest/technical-documentation/research/evaluation-estimates/2020-evaluation-estimates.html>; and National Population by Characteristics: 2020-2021, "Monthly Population Estimates for the United States: April 1, 2020 to December 1, 2022 (NA-EST2021-POP)," <www.census.gov/data/tables/time-series/demo/popest/2020s-national-detail.html>, accessed February 2022.

Table 3. Resident Population Projections and Components of Change: 2020 to 2060

[In thousands, except as indicated (332,639 represents 332,639,000). As of July 1. The 2017 National Projections are based on the July 1, 2016 population estimates, which are based on the 2010 Census. The projections were produced using a cohort-component method and are based on assumptions about future births, deaths, and net international migration. More information on methodology and assumptions is available at <www.census.gov/programs-surveys/popproj/technical-documentation/methodology.html>]

| Year | Population | | | Components of change | | | |
	Total	Numeric change	Percent change [1]	Natural increase	Births	Deaths	Net international migration [2]
2020................	332,639	2,370	0.7	1,360	4,112	2,752	1,010
2025................	344,234	2,271	0.7	1,241	4,156	2,915	1,030
2030................	355,101	2,093	0.6	1,028	4,162	3,134	1,064
2035................	364,862	1,859	0.5	774	4,166	3,391	1,085
2040................	373,528	1,657	0.5	558	4,196	3,638	1,098
2045................	381,390	1,529	0.4	424	4,243	3,819	1,106
2050................	388,922	1,503	0.4	394	4,304	3,910	1,110
2055................	396,557	1,548	0.4	437	4,359	3,922	1,112
2060................	404,483	1,609	0.4	491	4,397	3,906	1,118

[1] Percent change from immediate preceding year. For 2020, change from 2019. [2] Net international migration includes the international migration of both native and foreign-born populations.

Source: U.S. Census Bureau, 2017 National Population Projections Tables, "Table 1. Projected population size and births, deaths, and migration: 2016 to 2060 (NP2017-T1)," September 2018, <www.census.gov/programs-surveys/popproj/data/tables.html>, accessed April 2020.

Table 4. Resident Population Projections and Components of Change Under High, Low, and Zero Immigration Scenarios: 2025 to 2060

[In thousands. 344,234 represents 344,234,000. As of July 1. Data are from the 2017 National Population Projections Project, and are based on the 2010 Census and official population estimates through 2016. For more information, see <www.census.gov/programs-surveys/popproj/technical-documentation/methodology.html>]

Year and scenario	Population	Births	Deaths	Natural increase	Net international migration	Year and scenario	Population	Births	Deaths	Natural increase	Net international migration
MAIN SERIES [1]						HIGH IMMIGRATION					
2025..............	344,234	4,156	2,915	1,241	1,030	2025..............	351,287	4,332	2,929	1,403	1,706
2030..............	355,101	4,162	3,134	1,028	1,064	2030..............	366,552	4,421	3,157	1,264	1,736
2035..............	364,862	4,166	3,391	774	1,085	2035..............	380,999	4,484	3,426	1,058	1,755
2040..............	373,528	4,196	3,638	558	1,098	2040..............	394,536	4,564	3,686	878	1,766
2050..............	388,922	4,304	3,910	394	1,110	2050..............	420,202	4,794	3,994	800	1,767
2060..............	404,483	4,397	3,906	491	1,118	2060..............	446,866	5,027	4,039	988	1,763
LOW IMMIGRATION						ZERO IMMIGRATION					
2025..............	339,532	4,039	2,906	1,133	579	2025..............	330,128	3,805	2,887	917	-322
2030..............	347,467	3,990	3,118	871	616	2030..............	332,198	3,645	3,087	557	-279
2035..............	354,104	3,953	3,368	585	638	2035..............	332,587	3,529	3,323	206	-256
2040..............	359,522	3,951	3,606	345	653	2040..............	331,510	3,461	3,542	-81	-237
2050..............	368,068	3,978	3,855	123	671	2050..............	326,358	3,324	3,743	-419	-206
2060..............	376,226	3,977	3,817	160	687	2060..............	319,706	3,135	3,639	-504	-174

[1] Current expected projections.

Source: U.S. Census Bureau, Population Division, "2017 National Population Projections Tables: Alternative Scenarios," <www.census.gov/data/tables/2017/demo/popproj/2017-alternative-summary-tables.html>, accessed February 2020.

Table 5. Components of Population Change: 2020 to 2021

[In thousands except as indicated (331,449 represents 331,449,000). Resident population. Estimates base incorporates the 2020 Census, Vintage 2020 estimates, and 2020 Demographic Analysis estimates. See <www.census.gov/programs-surveys/popest/technical-documentation/methodology.html> for details]

| Period | Population as of beginning of period | Net increase | | Births | Deaths | Net international migration [2] | Population as of end of period |
		Total	Percent [1]				
April 1, 2020 to July 1, 2021......................	331,449	444	0.1	4,475	4,287	257	331,894
July 1, 2020 to July 1, 2021......................	331,501	393	0.1	3,582	3,434	245	331,894

[1] Net increase as percent of population at beginning of period. [2] Net international migration includes the international migration of both native and foreign-born populations. Specifically, it includes: (a) the net international migration of the foreign born, (b) the net migration between the United States and Puerto Rico, (c) the net migration of natives to and from the United States, and (d) the net movement of the Armed Forces population between the United States and overseas.

Source: U.S. Census Bureau, Population Division, National Population Totals and Components of Change: 2020-2021, "Annual Population Estimates, Estimated Components of Resident Population Change, and Rates of the Components of Resident Population Change for the United States, States, District of Columbia, and Puerto Rico: April 1, 2020 to July 1, 2021 (NST-EST2021-ALLDATA)," <www.census.gov/data/tables/time-series/demo/popest/2020s-national-total.html>, accessed February 2022.

Table 6. Resident Population by Sex, Race, and Hispanic Origin: 2000 to 2021

[281,425 represents 281,425,000. Data shown are modified race counts; see text, this section. Estimates for 2020-2021 are developed from a base that incorporates the 2020 Census, Vintage 2020 estimates, and 2020 Demographic Analysis estimates]

Characteristic	Number (1,000)					Percent change	
	2000 [1] (April)	2010 [1] (April)	2015 (July)	2020 [3] (April)	2021 (July)	2000 to 2010	2010 to 2020
BOTH SEXES							
Total	**281,425**	**308,758**	**320,739**	**331,449**	**331,894**	**9.7**	**7.3**
One race	277,527	301,774	312,468	321,925	322,104	8.7	6.7
White	228,106	241,945	247,206	251,824	251,462	6.1	4.1
Black or African American	35,705	40,254	42,595	44,826	45,061	12.7	11.4
American Indian and Alaska Native	2,664	3,740	4,028	4,312	4,368	40.4	15.3
Asian	10,589	15,160	17,877	20,115	20,350	43.2	32.7
Native Hawaiian and Other Pacific Islander	463	675	760	848	863	45.9	25.6
Two or more races	3,898	6,984	8,271	9,524	9,790	79.2	36.4
Race alone or in combination with one or more races:							
White	(NA)	248,076	254,524	260,298	260,183	(NA)	4.9
Black or African American	(NA)	43,217	46,261	49,193	49,586	(NA)	13.8
American Indian and Alaska Native	(NA)	6,139	6,638	7,115	7,207	(NA)	15.9
Asian	(NA)	17,677	20,903	23,628	23,962	(NA)	33.7
Native Hawaiian and Other Pacific Islander	(NA)	1,333	1,507	1,678	1,710	(NA)	25.9
Not Hispanic	246,118	258,279	264,621	269,739	269,247	4.9	4.4
One race	242,712	252,675	258,011	262,157	261,456	4.1	3.8
White	195,577	197,326	197,902	197,925	196,833	0.9	0.3
Black or African American	34,314	37,926	39,878	41,704	41,859	10.5	10.0
American Indian and Alaska Native	2,097	2,263	2,366	2,443	2,452	7.9	7.9
Asian	10,357	14,662	17,308	19,468	19,686	41.6	32.8
Native Hawaiian and Other Pacific Islander	367	497	558	617	626	35.4	24.1
Two or more races	3,406	5,605	6,610	7,582	7,791	64.5	35.3
Race alone or in combination with one or more races:							
White	(NA)	202,237	203,743	204,668	203,772	(NA)	1.2
Black or African American	(NA)	40,287	42,785	45,153	45,433	(NA)	12.1
American Indian and Alaska Native	(NA)	4,042	4,264	4,445	4,472	(NA)	10.0
Asian	(NA)	16,795	19,872	22,443	22,743	(NA)	33.6
Native Hawaiian and Other Pacific Islander	(NA)	1,020	1,146	1,267	1,288	(NA)	24.2
Hispanic [2]	35,306	50,479	56,118	61,710	62,647	43.0	22.3
One race	34,815	49,099	54,457	59,769	60,648	41.0	21.7
White	32,530	44,619	49,305	53,900	54,628	37.2	20.8
Black or African American	1,391	2,328	2,717	3,121	3,202	67.4	34.1
American Indian and Alaska Native	566	1,476	1,662	1,870	1,916	160.6	26.6
Asian	232	498	570	647	665	114.2	30.0
Native Hawaiian and Other Pacific Islander	95	177	203	231	237	85.9	30.0
Two or more races	491	1,380	1,661	1,942	2,000	180.8	40.7
Race alone or in combination with one or more races:							
White	(NA)	45,839	50,780	55,630	56,411	(NA)	21.4
Black or African American	(NA)	2,930	3,476	4,040	4,153	(NA)	37.9
American Indian and Alaska Native	(NA)	2,097	2,374	2,670	2,734	(NA)	27.4
Asian	(NA)	881	1,031	1,185	1,220	(NA)	34.4
Native Hawaiian and Other Pacific Islander	(NA)	312	361	410	422	(NA)	31.5
MALE							
Total	**138,056**	**151,789**	**157,907**	**164,193**	**164,385**	**9.9**	**8.2**
One race	136,146	148,362	153,824	159,464	159,522	9.0	7.5
White	112,478	119,703	122,492	125,592	125,387	6.4	4.9
Black or African American	16,972	19,208	20,389	21,592	21,703	13.2	12.4
American Indian and Alaska Native	1,333	1,890	2,032	2,179	2,205	41.8	15.3
Asian	5,128	7,219	8,525	9,670	9,788	40.8	34.0
Native Hawaiian and Other Pacific Islander	235	343	386	431	439	45.8	25.8
Two or more races	1,910	3,426	4,082	4,728	4,862	79.4	38.0
Race alone or in combination with one or more races:							
White	(NA)	122,721	126,114	129,810	129,730	(NA)	5.8
Black or African American	(NA)	20,635	22,175	23,737	23,928	(NA)	15.0
American Indian and Alaska Native	(NA)	3,055	3,304	3,552	3,596	(NA)	16.3
Asian	(NA)	8,468	10,035	11,431	11,600	(NA)	35.0
Native Hawaiian and Other Pacific Islander	(NA)	668	756	845	861	(NA)	26.6
Not Hispanic	119,894	126,169	129,549	132,936	132,669	5.2	5.4
Hispanic [2]	18,162	25,620	28,358	31,257	31,716	41.1	22.0
FEMALE							
Total	**143,368**	**156,969**	**162,832**	**167,257**	**167,509**	**9.5**	**6.6**
One race	141,381	153,411	158,643	162,461	162,581	8.5	5.9
White	115,628	122,242	124,714	126,232	126,074	5.7	3.3
Black or African American	18,733	21,047	22,206	23,234	23,358	12.4	10.4
American Indian and Alaska Native	1,331	1,850	1,996	2,133	2,162	39.0	15.3
Asian	5,461	7,941	9,353	10,445	10,562	45.4	31.5
Native Hawaiian and Other Pacific Islander	227	332	374	416	424	45.9	25.4
Two or more races	1,987	3,558	4,189	4,796	4,928	79.0	34.8
Race alone or in combination with one or more races:							
White	(NA)	125,355	128,409	130,488	130,453	(NA)	4.1
Black or African American	(NA)	22,582	24,086	25,456	25,659	(NA)	12.7
American Indian and Alaska Native	(NA)	3,084	3,334	3,563	3,611	(NA)	15.5
Asian	(NA)	9,209	10,868	12,196	12,362	(NA)	32.4
Native Hawaiian and Other Pacific Islander	(NA)	665	750	832	848	(NA)	25.2
Not Hispanic	126,224	132,110	135,072	136,803	136,578	4.7	3.6
Hispanic [2]	17,144	24,859	27,760	30,454	30,931	45.0	22.5

NA Not available. [1] The April 1, 2000 and 2010 population estimates base reflect changes to the Census 2000 and 2010 population from the Count Question Resolution program and geographic program revisions. [2] Persons of Hispanic origin may be of any race. [3] Estimates base.

Source: U.S. Census Bureau, Population and Housing Unit Estimates Tables, National Population by Characteristics: 2020-2021, "Annual Estimates of the Resident Population by Sex, Race, and Hispanic Origin for the United States: April 1, 2020 to July 1, 2021 (NC-EST2021-SR11H)," June 2022 and earlier releases, <www.census.gov/programs-surveys/popest/data/tables.html>.

Table 7. Resident Population Projections by Sex and Age: 2020 to 2060

[In thousands, except as indicated (332,639 represents 332,639,000). As of July 1. The 2017 National Projections are based on the July 1, 2016 population estimates, which are based on the 2010 Census. The projections were produced using a cohort-component method and are based on assumptions about future births, deaths, and net international migration. More information on methodology and assumptions is available at <www.census.gov/programs-surveys/popproj/technical-documentation/methodology.html>]

Age	2020			2025			2030	2040	2050	2060	Percent distribution				
	Total	Male	Female	Total	Male	Female					2020	2030	2040	2050	2060
Total	332,639	163,904	168,735	344,234	169,738	174,497	355,101	373,528	388,922	404,483	100.0	100.0	100.0	100.0	100.0
FIVE-YEAR AGE GROUPS															
Under 5 years	20,439	10,446	9,993	20,868	10,662	10,205	20,976	21,106	21,610	22,144	6.1	5.9	5.7	5.6	5.5
5 to 9 years	20,200	10,325	9,875	20,721	10,587	10,135	21,163	21,311	21,653	22,261	6.1	6.0	5.7	5.6	5.5
10 to 14 years	20,770	10,604	10,166	20,489	10,476	10,013	21,019	21,599	21,761	22,288	6.2	5.9	5.8	5.6	5.5
15 to 19 years	21,038	10,732	10,306	21,221	10,836	10,385	20,960	21,974	22,159	22,527	6.3	5.9	5.9	5.7	5.6
20 to 24 years	21,899	11,199	10,701	21,910	11,175	10,735	22,146	22,510	23,168	23,384	6.6	6.2	6.0	6.0	5.8
25 to 29 years	23,512	12,029	11,483	22,792	11,627	11,165	22,863	22,978	24,115	24,387	7.1	6.4	6.2	6.2	6.0
30 to 34 years	22,979	11,649	11,330	24,147	12,337	11,810	23,480	23,919	24,412	25,155	6.9	6.6	6.4	6.3	6.2
35 to 39 years	21,922	10,990	10,932	23,326	11,805	11,522	24,527	24,041	24,268	25,470	6.6	6.9	6.4	6.2	6.3
40 to 44 years	20,430	10,168	10,262	22,063	11,027	11,036	23,501	24,129	24,664	25,218	6.1	6.6	6.5	6.3	6.2
45 to 49 years	20,105	9,947	10,157	20,412	10,133	10,279	22,061	24,760	24,382	24,680	6.0	6.2	6.6	6.3	6.1
50 to 54 years	20,510	10,110	10,401	19,855	9,775	10,080	20,197	23,336	24,064	24,681	6.2	5.7	6.2	6.2	6.1
55 to 59 years	21,772	10,599	11,173	20,100	9,831	10,269	19,506	21,562	24,327	24,087	6.5	5.5	5.8	6.3	6.0
60 to 64 years	21,011	10,092	10,919	21,105	10,168	10,937	19,565	19,478	22,664	23,525	6.3	5.5	5.2	5.8	5.8
65 to 69 years	18,030	8,492	9,538	19,978	9,471	10,507	20,144	18,312	20,460	23,269	5.4	5.7	4.9	5.3	5.8
70 to 74 years	14,759	6,837	7,922	16,662	7,701	8,960	18,542	17,567	17,744	20,884	4.4	5.2	4.7	4.6	5.2
75 to 79 years	10,053	4,502	5,551	13,001	5,857	7,144	14,768	16,827	15,592	17,725	3.0	4.2	4.5	4.0	4.4
80 to 84 years	6,508	2,765	3,743	8,136	3,491	4,645	10,609	13,690	13,317	13,779	2.0	3.0	3.7	3.4	3.4
85 to 89 years	3,943	1,529	2,414	4,496	1,785	2,711	5,695	8,707	10,252	9,808	1.2	1.6	2.3	2.6	2.4
90 to 94 years	2,017	684	1,333	2,105	744	1,361	2,455	4,269	5,817	5,957	0.6	0.7	1.1	1.5	1.5
95 to 99 years	649	184	465	729	221	508	784	1,257	2,106	2,666	0.2	0.2	0.3	0.5	0.7
100 years and over	92	21	71	120	30	89	140	196	386	589	(Z)	(Z)	0.1	0.1	0.1
SPECIAL AGE CATEGORIES															
5 to 13 years	36,780	18,789	17,992	37,074	18,947	18,128	38,051	38,568	39,049	40,090	11.1	10.7	10.3	10.0	9.9
14 to 17 years	16,748	8,545	8,203	16,712	8,535	8,177	16,625	17,457	17,566	17,903	5.0	4.7	4.7	4.5	4.4
18 to 24 years	30,380	15,526	14,854	30,554	15,591	14,962	30,612	31,369	32,126	32,467	9.1	8.6	8.4	8.3	8.0
16 years and over	267,049	130,396	136,653	278,019	135,900	142,118	287,784	305,159	319,519	333,323	80.3	81.0	81.7	82.2	82.4
18 years and over	258,672	126,125	132,547	269,580	131,593	137,987	279,449	296,397	310,697	324,346	77.8	78.7	79.4	79.9	80.2
15 to 44 years	131,781	66,768	65,013	135,459	68,806	66,653	137,476	139,551	142,786	146,140	39.6	38.7	37.4	36.7	36.1
55 years and over	98,834	45,705	53,129	106,432	49,299	57,131	112,208	121,865	132,665	142,289	29.7	31.6	32.6	34.1	35.2
65 years and over	56,052	25,014	31,037	65,226	29,301	35,926	73,138	80,827	85,675	94,676	16.9	20.6	21.6	22.0	23.4
75 years and over	23,262	9,685	13,577	28,587	12,128	16,458	34,451	44,946	47,470	50,524	7.0	9.7	12.0	12.2	12.5
85 years and over	6,701	2,418	4,283	7,450	2,780	4,670	9,074	14,430	18,561	19,019	2.0	2.6	3.9	4.8	4.7
Median age (years)[1]	38.5	37.2	39.8	39.3	38.0	40.6	40.1	41.5	42.3	42.9	(X)	(X)	(X)	(X)	(X)

X Not applicable. Z Less than 0.05 percent. [1] For definition of median, see Guide to Tabular Presentation.

Source: U.S. Census Bureau, 2017 National Population Projections Tables, "Table 2. Projected age and sex composition of the population" and "Table 3. Detailed age and sex composition of the population," September 2018, <www.census.gov/programs-surveys/popproj/data/tables.html>, accessed April 2020.

Table 8. Resident Population by Race, Hispanic Origin, and Age: 2020 to 2021

[In thousands, except as indicated (331,449 represents 331,449,000). 2020 data are estimates base as of April 1. 2021 data are as of July 1. Estimates are developed from a base that incorporates the 2020 Census, Vintage 2020 estimates, and 2020 Demographic Analysis estimates. For definition of median, see Guide to Tabular Presentation]

Age	Total 2020	Total 2021	White alone 2020	White alone 2021	Black or African American alone 2020	Black or African American alone 2021	American Indian, Alaska Native alone 2020	American Indian, Alaska Native alone 2021	Asian alone 2020	Asian alone 2021	Native Hawaiian, Other Pacific Islander alone 2020	Native Hawaiian, Other Pacific Islander alone 2021	Two or more races 2020	Two or more races 2021	Hispanic origin[1] 2020	Hispanic origin[1] 2021	Not Hispanic White alone 2020	Not Hispanic White alone 2021
Total	331,449	331,894	251,824	251,462	44,826	45,061	4,312	4,368	20,115	20,350	848	863	9,524	9,790	61,710	62,647	197,925	196,833
FIVE-YEAR AGE GROUPS																		
Under 5 years	19,393	18,827	13,532	13,075	3,025	2,975	352	351	1,172	1,133	71	70	1,240	1,223	5,015	4,902	9,408	9,074
5 to 9 years	20,359	20,292	14,388	14,294	3,118	3,110	348	349	1,205	1,225	68	70	1,232	1,244	5,205	5,186	10,025	9,965
10 to 14 years	21,738	21,448	15,684	15,389	3,299	3,270	348	346	1,165	1,171	65	65	1,179	1,206	5,615	5,569	10,857	10,625
15 to 19 years	21,547	21,565	15,771	15,757	3,205	3,197	332	337	1,197	1,187	61	62	981	1,024	5,227	5,340	11,225	11,124
20 to 24 years	21,469	21,524	15,685	15,719	3,263	3,270	321	324	1,286	1,266	60	60	854	885	4,864	4,962	11,437	11,390
25 to 29 years	22,893	22,392	16,530	16,198	3,641	3,515	339	332	1,567	1,507	68	65	749	775	4,873	4,859	12,269	11,945
30 to 34 years	22,823	23,103	16,713	16,797	3,385	3,527	322	330	1,737	1,742	73	73	594	634	4,664	4,726	12,633	12,670
35 to 39 years	22,211	22,299	16,560	16,578	3,068	3,095	303	306	1,700	1,728	70	71	510	522	4,598	4,611	12,514	12,525
40 to 44 years	20,568	21,105	15,436	15,821	2,836	2,920	275	283	1,529	1,562	59	63	432	456	4,284	4,384	11,651	11,955
45 to 49 years	20,436	19,782	15,539	14,944	2,743	2,671	258	256	1,482	1,491	51	52	362	368	3,914	3,973	12,041	11,401
50 to 54 years	20,771	20,907	16,165	16,215	2,718	2,726	244	248	1,283	1,341	48	49	314	329	3,430	3,555	13,092	13,032
55 to 59 years	22,107	21,567	17,572	17,039	2,779	2,750	243	242	1,172	1,194	45	45	296	296	2,963	3,074	14,915	14,284
60 to 64 years	20,998	21,236	16,934	17,092	2,512	2,554	211	218	1,047	1,067	37	39	257	266	2,329	2,457	14,845	14,888
65 to 69 years	17,899	18,394	14,691	15,040	1,946	2,026	158	168	883	924	28	30	193	206	1,715	1,834	13,142	13,387
70 to 74 years	14,447	15,272	12,093	12,731	1,394	1,506	113	123	686	739	20	22	140	152	1,227	1,323	10,978	11,531
75 to 79 years	9,617	9,905	8,152	8,367	861	891	69	73	435	466	12	13	88	94	786	842	7,433	7,599
80 to 84 years	6,128	6,301	5,195	5,326	543	559	42	44	287	307	7	8	54	58	519	545	4,719	4,827
85 years and over	6,045	5,976	5,184	5,078	491	500	34	37	280	301	6	7	49	52	481	506	4,739	4,611
SPECIAL AGE CATEGORIES																		
Under 18 years	74,385	73,566	53,044	52,241	11,341	11,281	1,248	1,253	4,254	4,237	241	243	4,257	4,313	19,005	18,920	36,979	36,321
Under 5 years	19,393	18,827	13,532	13,075	3,025	2,975	352	351	1,172	1,133	71	70	1,240	1,223	5,015	4,902	9,408	9,074
5 to 13 years	37,768	37,306	26,920	26,479	5,769	5,705	627	624	2,140	2,160	120	122	2,192	2,216	9,720	9,609	18,682	18,373
14 to 17 years	17,225	17,433	12,592	12,687	2,546	2,601	270	277	941	943	50	51	825	874	4,270	4,410	8,889	8,874
18 to 64 years	202,927	202,479	153,465	152,679	28,250	28,298	2,648	2,669	13,288	13,377	533	540	4,743	4,916	37,977	38,678	119,934	118,558
18 to 24 years	30,200	30,089	22,015	21,994	4,568	4,540	453	456	1,772	1,746	84	84	1,229	1,270	6,922	7,039	15,974	15,857
25 to 44 years	88,495	88,899	65,240	65,395	12,930	13,057	1,239	1,250	6,533	6,539	269	272	2,285	2,387	18,419	18,580	49,068	49,095
45 to 64 years	84,312	83,492	66,211	65,290	10,752	10,701	956	964	4,984	5,092	180	185	1,229	1,260	12,637	13,058	54,893	53,606
65 years and over	54,137	55,848	45,315	46,542	5,235	5,482	416	446	2,573	2,737	74	80	524	561	4,728	5,049	41,012	41,954
85 years and over	6,045	5,976	5,184	5,078	491	500	34	37	280	301	6	7	49	52	481	506	4,739	4,611
16 years and over	265,666	266,971	205,088	205,537	34,750	35,054	3,197	3,251	16,337	16,590	631	645	5,663	5,895	44,802	45,876	165,431	164,964
18 years and over	257,064	258,327	198,780	199,221	33,485	33,780	3,064	3,115	15,861	16,114	607	620	5,267	5,477	42,705	43,727	160,946	160,512
15 to 44 years	131,511	131,988	96,695	96,872	19,397	19,523	1,893	1,911	9,016	8,992	390	393	4,120	4,296	28,510	28,882	71,730	71,609
Median age (years)	38.5	38.8	40.3	40.6	34.2	34.5	31.7	32.1	37.1	37.7	32.2	32.7	20.7	21.1	30.1	30.5	43.6	43.8

[1] Hispanic origin is considered an ethnicity, not a race. Persons of Hispanic origin may be of any race.

Source: U.S. Census Bureau, National Population by Characteristics: 2020-2021, "Annual Estimates of the Resident Population by Sex, Age, Race, and Hispanic Origin for the United States: April 1, 2020 to July 1, 2021 (NC-EST2021-ASR6H)," <www.census.gov/data/tables/time-series/demo/popest/2020s-national-detail.html>, accessed July 2022.

Table 9. Resident Population by Race, Hispanic Origin, and Single Years of Age: 2021

[In thousands (331,894 represents 331,894,000). As of July 1. Estimates are developed from a base that incorporates the 2020 Census, Vintage 2020 estimates, and 2020 Demographic Analysis estimates]

Age	Total	Race White alone	Race Black or African American alone	Race American Indian, Alaska Native alone	Race Asian alone	Race Native Hawaiian and Other Pacific Islander alone	Race Two or more races	Hispanic origin [1]	Non-Hispanic White alone
Total......................	331,894	251,462	45,061	4,368	20,350	863	9,790	62,647	196,833
Under 5 years old............	18,827	13,075	2,975	351	1,133	70	1,223	4,902	9,074
Under 1 year old.............	3,564	2,463	574	69	207	14	238	943	1,702
1 year old....................	3,703	2,578	582	69	218	14	242	959	1,798
2 years old...................	3,767	2,617	597	71	224	14	244	985	1,814
3 years old...................	3,857	2,677	611	71	236	14	248	999	1,859
4 years old...................	3,936	2,741	611	71	249	15	250	1,017	1,902
5 to 9 years old..............	20,292	14,294	3,110	349	1,225	70	1,244	5,186	9,965
5 years old...................	4,040	2,843	615	70	245	14	253	1,042	1,975
6 years old...................	4,077	2,865	625	70	250	14	253	1,043	1,996
7 years old...................	4,065	2,863	625	70	244	14	250	1,033	2,001
8 years old...................	4,052	2,853	622	69	248	14	246	1,029	1,992
9 years old...................	4,059	2,871	622	71	238	13	243	1,038	2,001
10 to 14 years old............	21,448	15,389	3,270	346	1,171	65	1,206	5,569	10,625
10 years old..................	4,103	2,920	626	68	233	13	243	1,064	2,020
11 years old..................	4,189	2,997	636	68	232	13	245	1,095	2,062
12 years old..................	4,279	3,072	654	68	231	13	241	1,110	2,121
13 years old..................	4,443	3,196	679	71	240	13	243	1,153	2,205
14 years old..................	4,433	3,205	674	71	235	13	234	1,147	2,218
15 to 19 years old............	21,565	15,757	3,197	337	1,187	62	1,024	5,340	11,124
15 years old..................	4,356	3,167	653	70	232	13	222	1,114	2,205
16 years old..................	4,310	3,143	638	69	236	13	212	1,084	2,205
17 years old..................	4,333	3,173	636	67	240	12	206	1,066	2,247
18 years old..................	4,293	3,146	630	66	242	12	196	1,046	2,237
19 years old..................	4,272	3,129	640	66	238	12	189	1,031	2,230
20 to 24 years old............	21,524	15,719	3,270	324	1,266	60	885	4,962	11,390
20 years old..................	4,347	3,176	656	66	249	12	187	1,031	2,277
21 years old..................	4,347	3,174	665	66	247	12	183	1,016	2,288
22 years old..................	4,279	3,132	649	64	245	12	177	985	2,273
23 years old..................	4,271	3,117	651	64	256	12	171	969	2,270
24 years old..................	4,280	3,120	649	64	269	12	167	961	2,281
25 to 29 years old............	22,392	16,198	3,515	332	1,507	65	775	4,859	11,945
25 years old..................	4,309	3,141	649	63	281	12	162	957	2,304
26 years old..................	4,387	3,184	678	64	289	13	159	963	2,341
27 years old..................	4,481	3,235	710	66	301	13	156	973	2,383
28 years old..................	4,555	3,281	732	68	311	13	150	977	2,424
29 years old..................	4,660	3,357	746	70	325	14	148	989	2,492
30 to 34 years old............	23,103	16,797	3,527	330	1,742	73	634	4,726	12,670
30 years old..................	4,731	3,409	754	69	342	15	142	977	2,558
31 years old..................	4,745	3,430	747	68	351	15	134	969	2,586
32 years old..................	4,612	3,343	709	65	355	15	125	931	2,531
33 years old..................	4,532	3,316	670	64	349	14	119	929	2,504
34 years old..................	4,482	3,300	648	63	345	14	114	921	2,492
35 to 39 years old............	22,299	16,578	3,095	306	1,728	71	522	4,611	12,525
35 years old..................	4,493	3,326	635	62	345	15	109	926	2,513
36 years old..................	4,490	3,334	628	61	347	14	106	925	2,521
37 years old..................	4,397	3,267	606	60	347	14	103	909	2,468
38 years old..................	4,463	3,325	613	62	346	14	103	925	2,512
39 years old..................	4,456	3,326	612	60	343	14	100	926	2,511
40 to 44 years old............	21,105	15,821	2,920	283	1,562	63	456	4,384	11,955
40 years old..................	4,392	3,289	605	59	327	13	98	910	2,488
41 years old..................	4,373	3,267	614	59	322	14	97	914	2,463
42 years old..................	4,194	3,138	585	56	312	12	90	862	2,379
43 years old..................	4,099	3,082	562	55	301	12	87	854	2,328
44 years old..................	4,047	3,045	553	54	300	12	83	844	2,298
45 to 49 years old............	19,782	14,944	2,671	256	1,491	52	368	3,973	11,401
45 years old..................	3,908	2,939	529	52	298	11	79	824	2,208
46 years old..................	3,952	2,980	533	52	301	11	75	814	2,255
47 years old..................	3,875	2,925	520	51	298	10	72	788	2,220
48 years old..................	3,927	2,964	534	50	297	10	71	776	2,271
49 years old..................	4,119	3,136	554	51	296	10	71	771	2,447
50 to 54 years old............	20,907	16,215	2,726	248	1,341	49	329	3,555	13,032
50 years old..................	4,366	3,362	578	53	290	10	73	768	2,676
51 years old..................	4,298	3,321	562	51	283	10	70	743	2,657
52 years old..................	4,136	3,213	529	49	270	10	65	702	2,585
53 years old..................	4,047	3,141	530	48	258	9	61	684	2,528
54 years old..................	4,060	3,177	528	47	239	9	59	659	2,586
55 to 59 years old............	21,567	17,039	2,750	242	1,194	45	296	3,074	14,284
55 years old..................	4,120	3,218	544	48	241	9	59	649	2,636
56 years old..................	4,280	3,362	559	49	240	9	60	642	2,787
57 years old..................	4,383	3,465	557	49	244	9	60	619	2,910
58 years old..................	4,385	3,477	548	48	244	9	59	592	2,947
59 years old..................	4,399	3,517	543	48	225	9	58	571	3,004

See footnotes at end of table.

Table 9. Resident Population by Race, Hispanic Origin, and Single Years of Age: 2021-Continued.

See headnote on page 12.

Age	Total	Race						Hispanic origin [1]	Non-Hispanic White alone
		White alone	Black or African American alone	American Indian, Alaska Native alone	Asian alone	Native Hawaiian and Other Pacific Islander alone	Two or more races		
60 to 64 years old............	21,236	17,092	2,554	218	1,067	39	266	2,457	14,888
60 years old.................	4,391	3,526	535	47	218	8	57	541	3,041
61 years old.................	4,313	3,447	532	46	223	8	56	528	2,974
62 years old.................	4,229	3,401	512	43	211	8	53	488	2,964
63 years old.................	4,190	3,386	493	42	211	7	51	460	2,973
64 years old.................	4,113	3,331	482	40	203	7	49	441	2,935
65 to 69 years old............	18,394	15,040	2,026	168	924	30	206	1,834	13,387
65 years old.................	3,928	3,182	455	38	200	7	47	417	2,808
66 years old.................	3,834	3,117	434	36	196	6	45	398	2,759
67 years old.................	3,695	3,023	407	34	185	6	41	365	2,694
68 years old.................	3,537	2,909	376	31	177	6	39	339	2,603
69 years old.................	3,399	2,808	354	29	168	5	35	315	2,524
70 to 74 years old............	15,272	12,731	1,506	123	739	22	152	1,323	11,531
70 years old.................	3,230	2,664	342	27	158	5	33	298	2,395
71 years old.................	3,076	2,529	323	26	161	5	32	282	2,274
72 years old.................	2,988	2,482	299	24	149	5	30	260	2,246
73 years old.................	2,917	2,444	278	23	139	4	28	247	2,220
74 years old.................	3,061	2,611	264	23	131	4	28	237	2,395
75 to 79 years old............	9,905	8,367	891	73	466	13	94	842	7,599
75 years old.................	2,158	1,806	202	17	108	3	21	198	1,627
76 years old.................	2,060	1,727	193	16	101	3	20	182	1,561
77 years old.................	1,993	1,686	178	15	93	3	19	167	1,534
78 years old.................	1,998	1,709	170	14	85	2	18	157	1,566
79 years old.................	1,696	1,439	148	12	80	2	15	139	1,312
80 to 84 years old............	6,301	5,326	559	44	307	8	58	545	4,827
80 years old.................	1,508	1,274	135	11	72	2	14	128	1,157
81 years old.................	1,366	1,149	124	10	68	2	13	119	1,040
82 years old.................	1,254	1,063	110	9	61	2	11	109	963
83 years old.................	1,156	980	101	8	56	1	10	100	888
84 years old.................	1,017	860	89	7	50	1	9	89	778
85 to 89 years old............	3,579	3,036	311	23	174	4	31	311	2,749
85 years old.................	922	780	82	6	45	1	8	81	705
86 years old.................	809	686	71	5	39	1	7	71	621
87 years old.................	705	599	61	4	34	1	6	61	543
88 years old.................	608	517	51	4	30	1	5	52	469
89 years old.................	535	454	46	3	27	1	5	46	411
90 to 94 years old............	1,737	1,488	136	10	86	2	15	145	1,353
90 years old.................	466	399	37	3	22	1	4	39	362
91 years old.................	412	353	32	2	21	(Z)	4	35	320
92 years old.................	346	296	27	2	18	(Z)	3	29	268
93 years old.................	283	242	22	2	14	(Z)	2	24	220
94 years old.................	232	198	18	1	12	(Z)	2	18	181
95 to 99 years old............	561	475	44	3	33	1	5	43	436
95 years old.................	182	155	14	1	10	(Z)	2	14	142
96 years old.................	141	120	11	1	8	(Z)	1	11	110
97 years old.................	107	91	8	1	6	(Z)	1	8	83
98 years old.................	78	66	6	(Z)	5	(Z)	1	6	61
99 years old.................	53	44	4	(Z)	4	(Z)	1	4	40
100 years old and over.......	98	79	9	1	9	(Z)	1	6	73

Z Less than 500. [1] Persons of Hispanic origin may be of any race.

Source: U.S. Census Bureau, National Population by Characteristics: 2020-2021, "Monthly Population Estimates by Age, Sex, Race and Hispanic Origin for the United States: April 1, 2020 to July 1, 2021 (NC-EST2021-ALLDATA)," <www.census.gov/data/tables/time-series/demo/popest/2020s-national-detail.html>, accessed July 2022.

Table 10. Resident Population by Sex and Age: 2000 to 2021

[In thousands, except as indicated (281,425 represents 281,425,000). Census years as of April 1; all others as of July 1. Estimates for 2020-2021 are developed from a base that incorporates the 2020 Census, Vintage 2020 estimates, and 2020 Demographic Analysis estimates. Excludes Armed Forces overseas]

Age	2000 [1]			2010 [1]			2020, estimates base			2021		
	Total	Male	Female	Total	Male	Female	Total	Male	Female	Total	Male	Female
Total	281,425	138,056	143,368	308,758	151,789	156,969	331,449	164,193	167,257	331,894	164,385	167,509
Under 5 years	19,176	9,811	9,365	20,201	10,319	9,882	19,393	9,915	9,478	18,827	9,624	9,203
5 to 9 years	20,550	10,523	10,026	20,349	10,390	9,959	20,359	10,419	9,940	20,292	10,376	9,915
10 to 14 years	20,528	10,520	10,008	20,677	10,580	10,097	21,738	11,130	10,608	21,448	10,988	10,460
15 to 19 years	20,219	10,391	9,828	22,042	11,305	10,737	21,547	11,011	10,536	21,565	11,023	10,542
20 to 24 years	18,963	9,688	9,275	21,588	11,015	10,572	21,469	10,947	10,521	21,524	10,973	10,551
25 to 29 years	19,382	9,799	9,583	21,103	10,637	10,467	22,893	11,621	11,273	22,392	11,379	11,013
30 to 34 years	20,511	10,322	10,189	19,963	9,997	9,966	22,823	11,550	11,274	23,103	11,674	11,428
35 to 39 years	22,707	11,319	11,388	20,180	10,043	10,138	22,211	11,214	10,997	22,299	11,264	11,035
40 to 44 years	22,442	11,130	11,313	20,892	10,395	10,497	20,568	10,314	10,254	21,105	10,594	10,511
45 to 49 years	20,093	9,890	10,203	22,709	11,210	11,500	20,436	10,220	10,216	19,782	9,876	9,906
50 to 54 years	17,586	8,608	8,978	22,299	10,934	11,365	20,771	10,362	10,409	20,907	10,436	10,471
55 to 59 years	13,469	6,509	6,961	19,665	9,524	10,141	22,107	10,892	11,215	21,567	10,630	10,937
60 to 64 years	10,806	5,137	5,669	16,818	8,078	8,741	20,998	10,209	10,788	21,236	10,333	10,902
65 to 74 years	18,391	8,303	10,088	21,714	10,097	11,617	32,346	15,258	17,088	33,666	15,869	17,797
75 to 84 years	12,361	4,879	7,482	13,062	5,477	7,585	15,745	6,959	8,786	16,206	7,169	9,038
85 years and over	4,240	1,227	3,013	5,495	1,790	3,705	6,045	2,172	3,873	5,976	2,176	3,800
5 to 13 years	37,026	18,964	18,062	36,860	18,834	18,026	37,768	19,335	18,433	37,306	19,093	18,213
14 to 17 years	16,093	8,285	7,808	17,121	8,792	8,329	17,225	8,807	8,418	17,433	8,919	8,514
18 to 24 years	27,141	13,873	13,268	30,674	15,663	15,011	30,120	15,366	14,754	30,089	15,348	14,741
18 years and over	209,130	100,996	108,133	234,576	113,843	120,733	257,064	126,136	130,928	258,327	126,748	131,579
55 years and over	59,267	26,055	33,212	76,755	34,966	41,789	97,241	45,490	51,751	98,651	46,177	52,474
65 years and over	34,992	14,410	20,582	40,271	17,364	22,907	54,137	24,389	29,748	55,848	25,214	30,634
75 years and over	16,601	6,106	10,495	18,557	7,267	11,290	21,790	9,131	12,660	22,182	9,344	12,837
Median age (years)	35.3	34.0	36.5	37.2	35.8	38.5	38.5	37.4	39.5	38.8	37.7	39.8

[1] The April 1, 2000 and April 1, 2010 population estimates bases reflect changes to the Census 2000 and Census 2010 population from the Count Question Resolution program and geographic program revisions.

Source: U.S. Census Bureau, Current Population Reports, P25-1095; "Intercensal Estimates of the United States Population by Age and Sex, 1990-2000: All Months," September 2002, <www.census.gov/data/tables/time-series/demo/popest/intercensal-national.html>; National Population by Characteristics: 2010-2020, "Annual Estimates of the Resident Population by Single Year of Age and Sex: April 1, 2010 to July 1, 2020," <www.census.gov/programs-surveys/popest/technical-documentation/research/evaluation-estimates/2020-evaluation-estimates.html>; and National Population by Characteristics: 2020-2021, "Annual Estimates of the Resident Population for Selected Age Groups by Sex for the United States: April 1, 2020 to July 1, 2021 (NC-EST2021-AGESEX)," <www.census.gov/data/tables/time-series/demo/popest/2020s-national-detail.html>, accessed July 2022.

Table 11. Resident Population Projections for Native and Foreign-Born Populations by Age Group: 2020 to 2060

[In thousands (332,639 represents 332,639,000). As of July 1. The 2017 National Projections are based on the July 1, 2016 population estimates, which are based on the 2010 Census. The projections were produced using a cohort-component method and are based on assumptions about future births, deaths, and net international migration. More information on methodology and assumptions is available at <www.census.gov/programs-surveys/popproj/technical-documentation/methodology.html>]

Nativity and age group	2020	2025	2030	2035	2040	2045	2050	2055	2060
Total population	332,639	344,234	355,101	364,862	373,528	381,390	388,922	396,557	404,483
Under 18 years	73,967	74,654	75,652	76,664	77,131	77,561	78,225	79,148	80,137
Under 5 years	20,439	20,868	20,976	20,993	21,106	21,319	21,610	21,914	22,144
5 to 13 years	36,780	37,074	38,051	38,453	38,568	38,715	39,049	39,532	40,090
14 to 17 years	16,748	16,712	16,625	17,217	17,457	17,527	17,566	17,701	17,903
18 to 64 years	202,621	204,354	206,311	210,201	215,571	220,995	225,023	227,794	229,670
18 to 24 years	30,380	30,554	30,612	30,519	31,369	31,943	32,126	32,229	32,467
25 to 44 years	88,843	92,328	94,370	95,368	95,067	96,054	97,459	98,727	100,230
45 to 64 years	83,398	81,472	81,329	84,314	89,135	92,998	95,437	96,838	96,973
65 years and over	56,052	65,226	73,138	77,997	80,827	82,835	85,675	89,615	94,676
Native population	285,936	293,965	301,318	307,758	313,372	318,497	323,612	329,123	335,150
Under 18 years	71,353	72,145	73,115	74,088	74,469	74,825	75,425	76,294	77,235
Under 5 years	20,153	20,592	20,689	20,697	20,801	21,006	21,292	21,591	21,815
5 to 13 years	35,462	35,780	36,770	37,123	37,194	37,303	37,603	38,059	38,592
14 to 17 years	15,738	15,772	15,656	16,268	16,475	16,516	16,530	16,644	16,828
18 to 64 years	166,549	166,622	167,354	170,136	174,634	179,178	182,350	184,223	185,264
18 to 24 years	27,225	27,470	27,588	27,433	28,233	28,732	28,837	28,873	29,053
25 to 44 years	72,200	75,428	77,224	77,935	77,366	78,041	79,107	79,984	81,113
45 to 64 years	67,124	63,740	62,542	64,767	69,036	72,404	74,406	75,367	75,098
65 years and over	48,034	55,182	60,849	63,535	64,268	64,494	65,838	68,606	72,652
Foreign-born population	46,703	50,270	53,783	57,104	60,156	62,894	65,310	67,434	69,333
Under 18 years	2,614	2,509	2,537	2,576	2,662	2,736	2,800	2,854	2,902
Under 5 years	285	275	286	296	305	312	319	324	329
5 to 13 years	1,319	1,294	1,280	1,330	1,374	1,413	1,446	1,473	1,498
14 to 17 years	1,010	940	970	949	982	1,011	1,036	1,057	1,075
18 to 64 years	36,072	37,717	38,957	40,066	40,936	41,817	42,673	43,571	44,406
18 to 24 years	3,155	3,084	3,024	3,086	3,136	3,211	3,289	3,356	3,415
25 to 44 years	16,643	16,900	17,146	17,433	17,701	18,013	18,352	18,744	19,117
45 to 64 years	16,273	17,732	18,787	19,547	20,099	20,593	21,031	21,472	21,875
65 years and over	8,017	10,044	12,289	14,462	16,559	18,341	19,837	21,009	22,024

Source: U.S. Census Bureau, 2017 National Population Projections Tables, "Table 2. Projected age and sex composition of the population," "Table 9. Age composition of the native-born population," and "Table 10. Age composition of the foreign-born population," September 2018, <www.census.gov/programs-surveys/popproj/data/tables.html>, accessed April 2020.

Table 12. Resident Population Projections by Race, Hispanic Origin, and Age: 2025

[In thousands (344,234 represents 344,234,000). As of July 1. The 2017 National Projections are based on the July 1, 2016 population estimates, which are based on the 2010 Census. The projections were produced using a cohort-component method and are based on assumptions about future births, deaths, and net international migration. More information on methodology and assumptions is available at <www.census.gov/programs-surveys/popproj/technical-documentation/methodology.html>]

Age group	Total	White alone	Black or African American alone	American Indian/ Alaska Native alone	Asian alone	Native Hawaiian/ Other Pacific Islander alone	Two or more races	Hispanic origin[1]	Not Hispanic, White alone
Total	344,234	258,778	46,906	4,452	22,181	865	11,053	68,484	198,751
Under 5 years	20,868	14,437	3,276	320	1,243	54	1,537	5,414	9,853
5 to 9 years	20,721	14,523	3,227	319	1,228	56	1,368	5,245	10,074
10 to 14 years	20,489	14,628	3,097	325	1,185	63	1,192	5,426	9,988
15 to 19 years	21,221	15,261	3,183	336	1,230	63	1,147	5,607	10,429
20 to 24 years	21,910	15,916	3,192	332	1,427	62	980	5,538	11,076
25 to 29 years	22,792	16,481	3,385	331	1,656	62	877	5,424	11,709
30 to 34 years	24,147	17,338	3,765	349	1,853	69	773	5,367	12,610
35 to 39 years	23,326	17,034	3,425	324	1,866	73	604	4,905	12,720
40 to 44 years	22,063	16,426	3,017	297	1,748	69	507	4,628	12,342
45 to 49 years	20,412	15,288	2,793	270	1,570	59	431	4,296	11,484
50 to 54 years	19,855	15,060	2,647	249	1,492	50	356	3,875	11,591
55 to 59 years	20,100	15,614	2,596	233	1,304	45	308	3,373	12,586
60 to 64 years	21,105	16,750	2,616	229	1,181	43	287	2,924	14,124
65 to 69 years	19,978	16,122	2,347	196	1,031	35	247	2,304	14,051
70 to 74 years	16,662	13,701	1,776	143	835	26	181	1,668	12,192
75 to 79 years	13,001	10,903	1,224	98	633	18	125	1,158	9,849
80 to 84 years	8,136	6,913	708	55	377	10	73	701	6,271
85 to 89 years	4,496	3,830	390	29	205	5	38	393	3,469
90 to 94 years	2,105	1,813	175	12	86	2	16	175	1,652
95 to 99 years	729	636	57	4	26	1	5	55	585
100 years and over	120	104	10	1	4	(Z)	1	8	97
SPECIAL CATEGORIES									
5 to 13 years	37,074	26,178	5,702	580	2,183	107	2,325	9,560	18,048
14 to 17 years	16,712	11,989	2,518	263	954	50	938	4,444	8,166
18 to 24 years	30,554	22,161	4,479	469	1,934	88	1,424	7,813	15,353
16 years and over	278,019	212,226	36,685	3,422	18,288	680	6,718	51,295	162,820
18 years and over	269,580	206,174	35,410	3,289	17,801	654	6,252	49,066	162,684
16 to 64 years	212,792	158,204	29,998	2,886	15,091	583	6,032	44,833	118,654
55 years and over	106,431	86,386	11,899	999	5,682	185	1,281	12,758	74,875
65 years and over	65,226	54,022	6,688	537	3,197	97	686	6,461	48,165
75 years and over	28,586	24,199	2,565	197	1,331	36	258	2,490	21,923
85 years and over	7,450	6,383	633	45	321	8	60	630	5,802

Z Less than 500. [1] Hispanic origin is considered an ethnicity, not a race. Persons of Hispanic origin may be of any race.

Source: U.S. Census Bureau, 2017 National Population Projections Datasets, "Table 1. Projected Population by Single Year of Age, Sex, Race, and Hispanic Origin for the United States: 2016 to 2060," September 2018, <www.census.gov/programs-surveys/popproj/data/datasets.html>, accessed April 2020.

Table 13. Resident Population Projections by Race and Hispanic Origin: 2020 to 2060

[In thousands, except as indicated (332,639 represents 332,639,000). As of July 1. Data shown are modified race counts; see text, this section. The 2017 National Projections are based on the July 1, 2016 population estimates, which are based on the 2010 Census. The projections were produced using a cohort-component method and are based on assumptions about future births, deaths, and net international migration. More information on methodology and assumptions is available at <www.census.gov/programs-surveys/popproj/technical-documentation/methodology.html>]

Characteristic	2020	2025	2030	2035	2040	2045	2050	2060
Total	**332,639**	**344,234**	**355,101**	**364,862**	**373,528**	**381,390**	**388,922**	**404,483**
One race	323,069	333,181	342,432	350,454	357,252	363,105	368,473	379,228
White	253,280	258,778	263,453	267,057	269,578	271,249	272,486	275,014
Black or African American	44,734	46,906	49,009	51,002	52,919	54,814	56,725	60,690
American Indian and Alaska Native	4,232	4,452	4,663	4,859	5,038	5,199	5,341	5,583
Asian	20,009	22,181	24,394	26,579	28,718	30,806	32,850	36,815
Native Hawaiian/Other Pacific Islander	813	865	913	958	999	1,038	1,071	1,125
Two or more races	9,570	11,053	12,669	14,408	16,276	18,285	20,450	25,255
Race alone or in combination: [1]								
White	261,811	268,702	274,901	280,151	284,447	288,035	291,344	298,488
Black or African American	49,137	52,177	55,248	58,303	61,383	64,550	67,855	74,984
American Indian and Alaska Native	7,052	7,485	7,910	8,316	8,699	9,060	9,404	10,059
Asian	23,522	26,253	29,074	31,916	34,764	37,614	40,476	46,250
Native Hawaiian/Other Pacific Islander	1,642	1,784	1,928	2,073	2,220	2,368	2,518	2,823
Not Hispanic	**270,326**	**275,750**	**280,293**	**283,632**	**285,912**	**287,564**	**289,125**	**293,267**
One race	262,710	266,968	270,242	272,225	273,055	273,150	273,030	273,450
White	198,571	198,751	197,992	196,105	193,210	189,671	185,954	179,162
Black or African American	41,702	43,548	45,322	46,978	48,550	50,098	51,664	54,949
American Indian and Alaska Native	2,445	2,514	2,575	2,623	2,659	2,683	2,701	2,722
Asian	19,393	21,516	23,678	25,810	27,895	29,928	31,917	35,779
Native Hawaiian/Other Pacific Islander	599	639	676	710	741	769	795	839
Two or more races	7,616	8,783	10,051	11,407	12,857	14,415	16,094	19,816
Race alone or in combination: [1]								
White	205,358	206,638	207,078	206,480	204,970	202,923	200,821	197,620
Black or African American	45,184	47,720	50,263	52,759	55,247	57,798	60,462	66,233
American Indian and Alaska Native	4,457	4,645	4,822	4,978	5,112	5,233	5,347	5,572
Asian	22,366	24,959	27,630	30,308	32,975	35,630	38,285	43,607
Native Hawaiian/Other Pacific Islander	1,246	1,351	1,456	1,559	1,662	1,763	1,865	2,071
Hispanic [2]	**62,313**	**68,484**	**74,807**	**81,230**	**87,616**	**93,826**	**99,798**	**111,216**
One race	60,359	66,214	72,189	78,229	84,197	89,956	95,442	105,777
White	54,709	60,026	65,461	70,952	76,367	81,578	86,532	95,852
Black or African American	3,033	3,358	3,687	4,024	4,368	4,715	5,060	5,740
American Indian and Alaska Native	1,787	1,938	2,088	2,236	2,380	2,515	2,640	2,862
Asian	616	666	716	769	823	878	933	1,036
Native Hawaiian/Other Pacific Islander	214	226	237	248	259	268	277	286
Two or more races	1,954	2,270	2,618	3,000	3,419	3,871	4,355	5,439
Race alone or in combination: [1]								
White	56,454	62,064	67,823	73,671	79,477	85,112	90,523	100,869
Black or African American	3,953	4,457	4,985	5,545	6,135	6,753	7,393	8,751
American Indian and Alaska Native	2,594	2,840	3,089	3,339	3,587	3,827	4,057	4,487
Asian	1,156	1,294	1,444	1,608	1,789	1,984	2,191	2,642
Native Hawaiian/Other Pacific Islander	396	433	472	514	558	605	653	752
PERCENT DISTRIBUTION								
Total	**100.0**	**100.0**	**100.0**	**100.0**	**100.0**	**100.0**	**100.0**	**100.0**
One race	97.1	96.8	96.4	96.1	95.6	95.2	94.7	93.8
White	76.1	75.2	74.2	73.2	72.2	71.1	70.1	68.0
Black or African American	13.5	13.6	13.8	14.0	14.2	14.4	14.6	15.0
American Indian and Alaska Native	1.3	1.3	1.3	1.3	1.4	1.4	1.4	1.4
Asian	6.0	6.4	6.9	7.3	7.7	8.1	8.5	9.1
Native Hawaiian/Other Pacific Islander	0.2	0.3	0.3	0.3	0.3	0.3	0.3	0.3
Two or more races	2.9	3.2	3.6	4.0	4.4	4.8	5.3	6.2
Not Hispanic	**81.3**	**80.1**	**78.9**	**77.7**	**76.5**	**75.4**	**74.3**	**72.5**
One race	79.0	77.6	76.1	74.6	73.1	71.6	70.2	67.6
White	59.7	57.7	55.8	53.8	51.7	49.7	47.8	44.3
Black or African American	12.5	12.7	12.8	12.9	13.0	13.1	13.3	13.6
American Indian and Alaska Native	0.7	0.7	0.7	0.7	0.7	0.7	0.7	0.7
Asian	5.8	6.3	6.7	7.1	7.5	7.9	8.2	8.9
Native Hawaiian/Other Pacific Islander	0.2	0.2	0.2	0.2	0.2	0.2	0.2	0.2
Two or more races	2.3	2.6	2.8	3.1	3.4	3.8	4.1	4.9
Hispanic [2]	**18.7**	**19.9**	**21.1**	**22.3**	**23.5**	**24.6**	**25.7**	**27.5**
One race	18.2	19.2	20.3	21.4	22.5	23.6	24.5	26.2
White	16.5	17.4	18.4	19.5	20.4	21.4	22.3	23.7
Black or African American	0.9	1.0	1.0	1.1	1.2	1.2	1.3	1.4
American Indian and Alaska Native	0.5	0.6	0.6	0.6	0.6	0.7	0.7	0.7
Asian	0.2	0.2	0.2	0.2	0.2	0.2	0.2	0.3
Native Hawaiian/Other Pacific Islander	0.1	0.1	0.1	0.1	0.1	0.1	0.1	0.1
Two or more races	0.6	0.7	0.7	0.8	0.9	1.0	1.1	1.3

[1] In combination with one or more other races. The sum of the five race groups adds to more than the total population because individuals may report more than one race. The original race data from Census 2010 are modified to eliminate the "some other race" category. [2] Persons of Hispanic origin may be of any race.

Source: U.S. Census Bureau, 2017 National Population Projections Datasets, "Table 1. Projected Population by Single Year of Age, Sex, Race, and Hispanic Origin for the United States: 2016 to 2060," September 2018, <www.census.gov/programs-surveys/popproj/data/datasets.html>, accessed April 2020.

Table 14. Resident Population by Region and State: 1990 to 2021

[In thousands (248,791 represents 248,791,000). 1990, 2000, 2010, and 2020 data as of April 1; data for other years as of July 1. Data for 2010-2019 are based on the 2010 Census; beginning 2020, estimates are developed from a base that incorporates the 2020 Census, Vintage 2020 estimates, and 2020 Demographic Analysis estimates. Insofar as possible, population shown for all years is that of present area of state. See Appendix III]

State and region	1990, (April) estimates base [1]	2000, (April) estimates base [2]	2010, (April) estimates base [3]	2015 (July)	2018 (July)	2019 (July)	2020, (April) estimates base	2020 (July)	2021 (July)
United States	**248,791**	**281,425**	**308,758**	**320,739**	**326,838**	**328,330**	**331,449**	**331,501**	**331,894**
Northeast	50,828	53,595	55,318	56,053	56,085	56,003	57,609	57,526	57,160
Midwest	59,669	64,397	66,930	67,886	68,263	68,340	68,985	68,935	68,841
South	85,456	100,235	114,563	121,049	124,649	125,687	126,266	126,409	127,225
West	52,837	63,199	71,947	75,751	77,841	78,300	78,589	78,631	78,667
Alabama	4,040	4,447	4,780	4,855	4,892	4,908	5,024	5,025	5,040
Alaska	550	627	710	738	737	734	733	732	733
Arizona	3,665	5,130	6,392	6,833	7,164	7,292	7,152	7,178	7,276
Arkansas	2,351	2,673	2,916	2,980	3,012	3,021	3,012	3,012	3,026
California	29,811	33,872	37,255	38,904	39,437	39,438	39,538	39,500	39,238
Colorado	3,294	4,302	5,029	5,454	5,697	5,758	5,774	5,784	5,812
Connecticut	3,287	3,406	3,574	3,589	3,575	3,566	3,606	3,600	3,606
Delaware	666	784	898	942	967	977	990	992	1,003
District of Columbia	607	572	602	677	704	708	690	690	670
Florida	12,938	15,983	18,805	20,219	21,255	21,492	21,538	21,570	21,781
Georgia	6,478	8,187	9,689	10,183	10,519	10,628	10,712	10,726	10,800
Hawaii	1,108	1,211	1,360	1,423	1,423	1,416	1,455	1,452	1,442
Idaho	1,007	1,294	1,568	1,652	1,752	1,789	1,839	1,848	1,901
Illinois	11,431	12,420	12,832	12,860	12,725	12,667	12,813	12,785	12,671
Indiana	5,544	6,081	6,484	6,611	6,698	6,731	6,786	6,786	6,806
Iowa	2,777	2,927	3,047	3,123	3,150	3,160	3,190	3,189	3,193
Kansas	2,478	2,689	2,853	2,911	2,913	2,913	2,938	2,936	2,935
Kentucky	3,687	4,042	4,339	4,429	4,464	4,472	4,506	4,504	4,509
Louisiana	4,222	4,469	4,534	4,667	4,664	4,658	4,658	4,651	4,624
Maine	1,228	1,275	1,328	1,329	1,340	1,346	1,362	1,362	1,372
Maryland	4,781	5,297	5,774	5,989	6,042	6,055	6,177	6,173	6,165
Massachusetts	6,016	6,349	6,548	6,797	6,886	6,895	7,030	7,022	6,985
Michigan	9,295	9,939	9,884	9,934	9,987	9,985	10,077	10,068	10,051
Minnesota	4,376	4,920	5,304	5,484	5,609	5,640	5,706	5,707	5,707
Mississippi	2,575	2,845	2,968	2,990	2,983	2,978	2,961	2,957	2,950
Missouri	5,117	5,597	5,989	6,075	6,126	6,140	6,155	6,154	6,168
Montana	799	902	989	1,031	1,062	1,070	1,084	1,086	1,104
Nebraska	1,578	1,711	1,826	1,892	1,926	1,933	1,962	1,961	1,964
Nevada	1,202	1,998	2,701	2,869	3,031	3,091	3,105	3,114	3,144
New Hampshire	1,109	1,236	1,316	1,337	1,355	1,361	1,378	1,378	1,389
New Jersey	7,748	8,415	8,792	8,870	8,892	8,891	9,289	9,280	9,267
New Mexico	1,515	1,819	2,059	2,090	2,094	2,100	2,118	2,118	2,116
New York	17,991	18,977	19,378	19,657	19,544	19,463	20,201	20,155	19,836
North Carolina	6,632	8,046	9,536	10,037	10,391	10,501	10,439	10,457	10,551
North Dakota	639	642	673	756	760	764	779	779	775
Ohio	10,847	11,353	11,537	11,622	11,681	11,697	11,799	11,791	11,780
Oklahoma	3,146	3,450	3,752	3,911	3,943	3,961	3,959	3,962	3,987
Oregon	2,842	3,422	3,831	4,019	4,184	4,216	4,237	4,242	4,246
Pennsylvania	11,883	12,281	12,703	12,790	12,809	12,799	13,003	12,990	12,964
Rhode Island	1,003	1,048	1,053	1,057	1,059	1,058	1,097	1,096	1,096
South Carolina	3,486	4,012	4,625	4,896	5,092	5,158	5,118	5,131	5,191
South Dakota	696	755	814	855	879	887	887	887	895
Tennessee	4,877	5,689	6,346	6,595	6,778	6,830	6,911	6,920	6,975
Texas	16,986	20,851	25,146	27,469	28,625	28,987	29,146	29,218	29,528
Utah	1,723	2,233	2,764	2,984	3,155	3,203	3,272	3,282	3,338
Vermont	563	609	626	626	625	624	643	642	646
Virginia	6,189	7,079	8,001	8,367	8,511	8,557	8,631	8,632	8,642
Washington	4,867	5,894	6,725	7,167	7,527	7,614	7,705	7,719	7,739
West Virginia	1,793	1,808	1,853	1,843	1,806	1,795	1,794	1,790	1,783
Wisconsin	4,892	5,364	5,687	5,763	5,809	5,825	5,894	5,892	5,896
Wyoming	454	494	564	586	579	580	577	577	579

[1] The April 1, 1990 census counts include corrections processed through August 1997, results of special censuses and test censuses, and do not include adjustments for census coverage errors. [2] The April 1, 2000 population estimates base reflects changes to the Census 2000 population from the Count Question Resolution program, legal boundary updates, and other geographic program revisions. [3] The April 1, 2010 population estimates base reflects changes to the Census 2010 population from the Count Question Resolution program and geographic program revisions.

Source: U.S. Census Bureau, 1990 Census of Population and Housing, Population and Housing Unit Counts (CPH-2); Current Population Reports, P25-1106; "Table CO-EST2001-12-00 - Time Series of Intercensal State Population Estimates: April 1, 1990 to April 1, 2000," April 2002, <www2.census.gov/programs-surveys/popest/tables/1990-2000/intercensal/st-co/co-est2001-12-00.pdf>; "Table 1. Intercensal Estimates of the Resident Population for the United States, Regions, States, and Puerto Rico: April 1, 2000 to July 1, 2010 (ST-EST00INT-01)," September 2011, <www.census.gov/data/tables/time-series/demo/popest/intercensal-2000-2010-state.html>; "Annual Estimates of the Resident Population for the United States, Regions, States, and the District of Columbia: April 1, 2010 to July 1, 2020 (NST-EST2020)," December 2020, <www.census.gov/programs-surveys/popest/technical-documentation/research/evaluation-estimates. html>; and "Annual Estimates of the Resident Population for the United States, Regions, States, District of Columbia, and Puerto Rico: April 1, 2020 to July 1, 2021 (NST-EST2021-POP)," December 2021, <www.census.gov/data/tables/time-series/demo/popest/2020s-national-total. html>.

Table 15. State Population—Rank, Percent Change, and Population Density: 2000 to 2021

[As of April 1, except 2021 as of July 1. Insofar as possible, population shown for all years is that of present area of state. For land area by State, see Table 406. Minus sign (-) indicates decrease. See Appendix III]

State	Rank				Percent change			Population per square mile of land area [1]		
	2000	2010	2020	2021	2000 to 2010	2010 to 2020 [2]	2020 to 2021	2010	2020	2021
United States.........	(X)	(X)	(X)	(X)	**9.7**	**7.3**	**0.1**	**87.4**	**93.8**	**94.0**
Alabama..................	23	23	24	24	7.5	5.1	0.3	94.4	99.2	99.5
Alaska....................	48	47	48	48	13.3	3.3	-0.1	1.2	1.3	1.3
Arizona..................	20	16	14	14	24.6	11.9	1.7	56.3	63.0	64.1
Arkansas.................	33	32	33	33	9.1	3.3	0.5	56.0	57.9	58.2
California................	1	1	1	1	10.0	6.1	-0.8	239.1	253.8	251.9
Colorado.................	24	22	21	21	16.9	14.8	0.7	48.5	55.7	56.1
Connecticut..............	29	29	29	29	4.9	0.9	(Z)	738.1	744.7	744.6
Delaware.................	45	45	45	45	14.6	10.2	1.4	460.8	508.0	514.9
District of Columbia....	(X)	(X)	(X)	(X)	5.2	14.6	-2.8	9,856.2	11,294.8	10,975.4
Florida..................	4	4	3	3	17.6	14.5	1.1	350.6	401.6	406.2
Georgia..................	10	9	8	8	18.3	10.6	0.8	168.4	186.3	187.8
Hawaii...................	42	40	40	40	12.3	7.0	-0.9	211.8	226.6	224.4
Idaho....................	39	39	38	38	21.1	17.3	3.4	19.0	22.3	23.0
Illinois.................	5	5	6	6	3.3	-0.1	-1.1	231.1	230.8	228.2
Indiana..................	14	15	17	17	6.6	4.6	0.3	181.0	189.4	190.0
Iowa.....................	30	30	31	31	4.1	4.7	0.1	54.5	57.1	57.2
Kansas...................	32	33	35	35	6.1	3.0	-0.1	34.9	35.9	35.9
Kentucky.................	25	26	26	26	7.4	3.8	0.1	109.9	114.1	114.2
Louisiana................	22	25	25	25	1.4	2.7	-0.7	104.9	107.8	107.0
Maine....................	40	41	42	42	4.2	2.6	0.7	43.1	44.2	44.5
Maryland.................	19	19	18	19	9.0	7.0	-0.2	594.8	636.4	635.1
Massachusetts............	13	14	15	15	3.1	7.4	-0.6	839.4	901.3	895.5
Michigan.................	8	8	10	10	-0.6	2.0	-0.3	174.8	178.2	177.8
Minnesota................	21	21	22	22	7.8	7.6	(Z)	66.6	71.7	71.7
Mississippi..............	31	31	34	34	4.3	-0.2	-0.4	63.2	63.1	62.9
Missouri.................	17	18	19	18	7.0	2.8	0.2	87.1	89.5	89.7
Montana..................	44	44	44	43	9.7	9.6	1.8	6.8	7.4	7.6
Nebraska.................	38	38	37	37	6.7	7.4	0.1	23.8	25.5	25.6
Nevada...................	35	35	32	32	35.1	15.0	1.3	24.6	28.3	28.6
New Hampshire...........	41	42	41	41	6.5	4.6	0.8	147.0	153.9	155.1
New Jersey...............	9	11	11	11	4.5	5.7	-0.2	1,195.5	1,263.1	1,260.1
New Mexico...............	36	36	36	36	13.2	2.8	-0.1	17.0	17.5	17.4
New York.................	3	3	4	4	2.1	4.2	-1.8	411.2	428.7	420.9
North Carolina..........	11	10	9	9	18.5	9.5	1.1	196.1	214.7	217.0
North Dakota............	47	48	47	47	4.7	15.8	-0.5	9.7	11.3	11.2
Ohio.....................	7	7	7	7	1.6	2.3	-0.2	282.3	288.8	288.3
Oklahoma.................	27	28	28	28	8.7	5.5	0.7	54.7	57.7	58.1
Oregon...................	28	27	27	27	12.0	10.6	0.2	39.9	44.1	44.2
Pennsylvania.............	6	6	5	5	3.4	2.4	-0.3	283.9	290.6	289.7
Rhode Island............	43	43	43	44	0.4	4.2	-0.2	1,018.1	1,061.5	1,059.8
South Carolina..........	26	24	23	23	15.3	10.7	1.4	153.9	170.3	172.7
South Dakota............	46	46	46	46	7.9	8.9	1.0	10.7	11.7	11.8
Tennessee................	16	17	16	16	11.5	8.9	0.9	153.9	167.6	169.2
Texas....................	2	2	2	2	20.6	15.9	1.3	96.3	111.6	113.0
Utah.....................	34	34	30	30	23.8	18.4	2.0	33.6	39.8	40.6
Vermont..................	49	49	49	49	2.8	2.8	0.4	67.9	69.8	70.0
Virginia.................	12	12	12	12	13.0	7.9	0.1	202.6	218.6	218.8
Washington...............	15	13	13	13	14.1	14.6	0.4	101.2	115.9	116.4
West Virginia...........	37	37	39	39	2.5	-3.2	-0.6	77.1	74.6	74.2
Wisconsin................	18	20	20	20	6.0	3.6	(Z)	105.0	108.8	108.9
Wyoming..................	50	50	50	50	14.1	2.3	0.3	5.8	5.9	6.0

X Not applicable. Z less than 0.05 percent. [1] Persons per square mile were calculated on the basis of land area data from the 2010 Census. [2] Based on 2010 population estimates base that reflects changes to the Census 2010 population from the Count Question Resolution program and geographic program revisions.

Source: U.S. Census Bureau, *2000 Census of Population and Housing, PHC-3-1, United States Summary*, 2004, <www.census.gov/prod/cen2000/phc3-us-pt1.pdf>; *2010 Census Briefs, Population Distribution and Change: 2000 to 2010,* March 2011, <www.census.gov/prod/cen2010/briefs/c2010br-01.pdf>; and "Annual and Cumulative Estimates of Resident Population Change for the United States, Regions, States, District of Columbia, and Puerto Rico and Region and State Rankings: April 1, 2020 to July 1, 2021 (NST-EST2021-CHG)," December 2021, <www.census.gov/data/tables/time-series/demo/popest/2020s-state-total.html>.

Table 16. State and Region Resident Population—Components of Change: 2020 to 2021

[Covers period April 1, 2020 to July 1, 2021. Minus sign (-) indicates net decrease or net outflow]

State and region	Numeric population change [1]	Births	Deaths	Natural increase (births minus deaths)	Net migration Total	Net migration Inter-national [2]	Net migration Domestic
United States...........	**444,464**	**4,474,986**	**4,287,391**	**187,595**	**256,869**	**256,869**	**(X)**
Northeast.................	-449,310	715,659	749,773	-34,114	-413,021	59,360	-472,381
Midwest...................	-144,010	939,107	955,021	-15,914	-132,534	39,513	-172,047
South.....................	959,222	1,761,946	1,704,397	57,549	904,530	118,947	785,583
West......................	78,562	1,058,274	878,200	180,074	-102,106	39,049	-141,155
Alabama...................	15,598	69,730	81,016	-11,286	26,717	1,242	25,475
Alaska....................	-718	11,687	7,025	4,662	-5,365	547	-5,912
Arizona...................	124,814	94,533	94,005	528	124,295	4,645	119,650
Arkansas..................	14,367	43,575	47,706	-4,131	18,458	854	17,604
California................	-300,387	529,290	414,075	115,215	-415,522	13,861	-429,383
Colorado..................	38,355	75,917	59,823	16,094	21,750	1,716	20,034
Connecticut...............	-347	40,961	47,074	-6,113	5,222	4,996	226
Delaware..................	13,436	12,719	14,304	-1,585	15,039	652	14,387
District of Columbia......	-19,495	10,868	7,939	2,929	-22,143	1,179	-23,322
Florida...................	242,941	260,946	319,149	-58,203	305,218	41,260	263,958
Georgia...................	87,658	150,732	130,940	19,792	67,437	7,458	59,979
Hawaii....................	-13,718	19,906	18,421	1,485	-15,059	1,115	-16,174
Idaho.....................	61,817	26,829	21,368	5,461	56,851	412	56,439
Illinois..................	-141,039	167,169	162,805	4,364	-145,656	5,856	-151,512
Indiana...................	20,457	96,817	96,570	247	19,609	4,994	14,615
Iowa......................	2,710	45,004	44,543	461	2,025	3,186	-1,161
Kansas....................	-3,298	42,122	39,388	2,734	-6,356	1,396	-7,752
Kentucky..................	3,558	63,181	71,410	-8,229	11,496	1,216	10,280
Louisiana.................	-33,710	69,279	68,795	484	-34,074	2,780	-36,854
Maine.....................	9,888	14,248	22,142	-7,894	17,912	909	17,003
Maryland..................	-12,095	83,750	76,782	6,968	-19,312	7,354	-26,666
Massachusetts.............	-45,194	83,111	87,784	-4,673	-40,686	13,653	-54,339
Michigan..................	-26,520	129,524	146,786	-17,262	-10,254	4,462	-14,716
Minnesota.................	896	79,493	66,981	12,512	-11,734	4,213	-15,947
Mississippi...............	-11,314	43,234	47,987	-4,753	-6,685	447	-7,132
Missouri..................	13,274	86,276	91,907	-5,631	18,604	3,071	15,533
Montana...................	20,046	13,285	15,072	-1,787	22,062	579	21,483
Nebraska..................	2,188	29,623	24,254	5,369	-3,378	1,069	-4,447
Nevada....................	39,377	42,076	39,702	2,374	36,605	2,325	34,280
New Hampshire.............	11,463	14,327	18,817	-4,490	15,977	1,302	14,675
New Jersey................	-21,864	119,434	112,573	6,861	-29,149	10,805	-39,954
New Mexico................	-1,645	27,543	28,890	-1,347	-364	1,557	-1,921
New York..................	-365,336	264,380	238,584	25,796	-387,397	18,860	-406,257
North Carolina............	111,774	142,020	144,561	-2,541	114,080	7,196	106,884
North Dakota..............	-4,146	12,436	9,704	2,732	-6,828	291	-7,119
Ohio......................	-19,431	160,886	181,233	-20,347	-97	7,518	-7,615
Oklahoma..................	27,286	58,736	60,920	-2,184	29,192	1,603	27,589
Oregon....................	8,899	50,302	55,926	-5,624	14,491	1,165	13,326
Pennsylvania..............	-38,644	160,565	199,108	-38,543	-590	7,906	-8,496
Rhode Island..............	-1,769	12,201	15,003	-2,802	938	647	291
South Carolina............	72,280	68,052	77,654	-9,602	82,142	3,330	78,812
South Dakota..............	8,709	13,724	11,671	2,053	6,650	1,084	5,566
Tennessee.................	64,378	96,408	106,817	-10,409	75,259	1,787	73,472
Texas.....................	382,436	450,827	308,742	142,085	239,792	28,503	211,289
Utah......................	66,359	56,780	27,872	28,908	37,304	1,220	36,084
Vermont...................	2,493	6,432	8,688	-2,256	4,752	282	4,470
Virginia..................	10,881	116,274	105,578	10,696	210	11,504	-11,294
Washington................	33,411	102,270	88,479	13,791	19,195	9,787	9,408
West Virginia.............	-10,757	21,615	34,097	-12,482	1,704	582	1,122
Wisconsin.................	2,190	76,033	79,179	-3,146	4,881	2,373	2,508
Wyoming...................	1,952	7,856	7,542	314	1,651	120	1,531
Puerto Rico...............	-22,290	23,086	40,034	-16,948	-5,342	-5,342	(X)

X Not applicable. [1] Total population change includes a residual. This residual represents the change in population that cannot be attributed to any specific demographic component. [2] Net international migration for the United States includes the international migration of both native and foreign-born populations. Specifically, it includes: (a) the net international migration of the foreign born, (b) the net migration of natives to and from the United States, (c) the net migration between the United States and Puerto Rico, and (d) the net movement of the Armed Forces population between the United States and overseas.

Source: U.S. Census Bureau, Population Division, State Population Totals and Components of Change: 2020-2021, "Annual and Cumulative Estimates of the Components of Resident Population Change for the United States, Regions, States, District of Columbia, and Puerto Rico: April 1, 2020 to July 1, 2021 (NST-EST2021-COMP)," December 2021, <www.census.gov/data/tables/time-series/demo/popest/2020s-state-total.html>.

Table 17. Resident Population by Age and State: 2021

[In thousands (331,894 represents 331,894,000), unless otherwise noted. As of July 1. Estimates are developed from a base that incorporates the 2020 Census, Vintage 2020 estimates, and 2020 Demographic Analysis estimates]

State	Total	Under 5 years	5 to 14 years	15 to 24 years	25 to 34 years	35 to 44 years	45 to 54 years	55 to 64 years	65 to 74 years	75 to 84 years	85 years and over	Median age (years)	Percent 65 years old and over
United States	**331,894**	**18,827**	**41,739**	**43,089**	**45,495**	**43,404**	**40,688**	**42,803**	**33,666**	**16,206**	**5,976**	**38.8**	**16.8**
Alabama	5,040	292	634	653	656	621	622	672	542	262	85	39.6	17.6
Alaska	733	48	102	96	114	102	83	90	66	24	7	35.6	13.3
Arizona	7,276	402	923	975	1,001	915	848	880	783	416	134	38.6	18.3
Arkansas	3,026	182	398	402	394	379	358	385	315	159	54	38.6	17.5
California	39,238	2,217	5,002	5,110	5,840	5,406	4,928	4,778	3,558	1,722	677	37.6	15.2
Colorado	5,812	313	706	752	909	840	710	702	559	240	81	37.5	15.1
Connecticut	3,606	178	412	480	453	452	460	521	379	190	80	41.1	18.0
Delaware	1,003	54	118	121	128	121	117	144	124	59	19	41.6	20.1
District of Columbia	670	41	69	81	146	110	71	66	51	25	11	34.9	12.8
Florida	21,781	1,104	2,428	2,485	2,766	2,717	2,703	2,980	2,591	1,471	536	42.7	21.1
Georgia	10,800	633	1,435	1,482	1,494	1,429	1,399	1,343	988	455	141	37.5	14.7
Hawaii	1,442	83	174	166	194	191	170	181	163	81	39	40.2	19.6
Idaho	1,901	114	270	258	249	249	216	229	197	90	28	37.4	16.6
Illinois	12,671	707	1,587	1,650	1,714	1,680	1,581	1,651	1,260	601	240	39.0	16.6
Indiana	6,806	408	898	940	894	858	819	874	682	317	116	38.1	16.4
Iowa	3,193	189	417	446	398	404	362	412	336	160	69	38.6	17.7
Kansas	2,935	178	401	417	378	376	328	366	294	137	58	37.4	16.7
Kentucky	4,509	265	573	593	589	563	558	599	476	221	74	39.2	17.1
Louisiana	4,624	285	613	598	626	609	535	595	471	216	74	38.0	16.5
Maine	1,372	62	142	154	167	165	171	213	183	84	30	44.7	21.7
Maryland	6,165	355	772	765	822	827	784	838	604	289	110	39.3	16.3
Massachusetts	6,985	347	766	936	984	897	875	965	727	346	142	39.9	17.4
Michigan	10,051	548	1,215	1,319	1,317	1,208	1,226	1,394	1,118	517	188	40.1	18.1
Minnesota	5,707	338	749	729	748	767	665	756	577	269	110	38.7	16.7
Mississippi	2,950	177	391	402	381	368	356	381	304	143	47	38.4	16.8
Missouri	6,168	360	781	801	813	785	721	823	649	315	119	39.1	17.6
Montana	1,104	58	135	141	143	141	121	148	135	60	21	40.1	19.6
Nebraska	1,964	126	274	275	253	256	218	241	194	90	38	37.1	16.4
Nevada	3,144	178	399	373	455	431	397	392	322	154	43	38.7	16.5
New Hampshire	1,389	62	145	172	177	168	177	219	167	73	27	43.0	19.3
New Jersey	9,267	519	1,142	1,135	1,189	1,216	1,217	1,282	921	459	186	40.3	16.9
New Mexico	2,116	115	272	283	281	268	235	269	239	115	38	38.8	18.5
New York	19,836	1,099	2,303	2,454	2,805	2,548	2,460	2,688	2,038	1,011	429	39.7	17.5
North Carolina	10,551	589	1,302	1,399	1,413	1,332	1,348	1,374	1,101	521	172	39.3	17.0
North Dakota	775	51	105	113	111	100	79	92	74	34	17	35.7	16.1
Ohio	11,780	674	1,470	1,513	1,554	1,457	1,424	1,590	1,278	594	227	39.6	17.8
Oklahoma	3,987	246	550	549	537	519	455	486	388	190	66	37.1	16.2
Oregon	4,246	213	496	511	598	593	519	528	490	224	74	40.0	18.6
Pennsylvania	12,964	681	1,513	1,614	1,702	1,607	1,571	1,812	1,465	707	292	40.9	19.0
Rhode Island	1,096	54	117	149	153	136	133	155	118	56	24	40.3	18.1
South Carolina	5,191	283	637	661	673	640	632	697	601	282	84	40.2	18.6
South Dakota	895	59	125	120	113	112	94	116	98	41	18	37.7	17.5
Tennessee	6,975	402	869	887	963	883	872	914	728	346	111	39.1	17.0
Texas	29,528	1,905	4,270	4,151	4,258	4,120	3,627	3,321	2,409	1,098	370	35.4	13.1
Utah	3,338	237	542	547	489	466	357	311	242	111	36	31.8	11.7
Vermont	646	28	67	88	78	78	78	96	83	38	13	42.9	20.6
Virginia	8,642	491	1,065	1,129	1,179	1,160	1,086	1,126	853	412	141	38.8	16.3
Washington	7,739	434	958	936	1,173	1,095	933	953	783	352	121	38.2	16.2
West Virginia	1,783	89	205	218	213	214	225	249	226	107	36	42.8	20.7
Wisconsin	5,896	320	723	781	738	746	701	830	649	296	113	40.1	17.9
Wyoming	579	32	76	76	74	77	64	75	66	28	10	38.9	17.9

Source: U.S. Census Bureau, State Population by Characteristics: 2020–2021, "Annual Estimates of the Resident Population for Selected Age Groups by Sex: April 1, 2020 to July 1, 2021 (SC-EST2021-AGESEX)," <www.census.gov/data/tables/time-series/demo/popest/2020s-state-detail.html>, accessed July 2022.

Table 18. Age Dependency Ratios by State: 2010 to 2021

[As of April, except 2021 as of July. Estimates for 2020 and 2021 are developed from a base that incorporates the 2020 Census, Vintage 2020 estimates, and 2020 Demographic Analysis estimates]

State	Age dependency ratio [1]			Child dependency ratio [2]			Old-age dependency ratio [3]		
	2010	2020	2021	2010	2020	2021	2010	2020	2021
United States.........	**58.9**	**63.3**	**63.9**	**38.2**	**36.7**	**36.3**	**20.7**	**26.7**	**27.6**
Alabama.................	59.9	65.6	66.4	37.9	37.1	37.1	22.0	28.5	29.3
Alaska...................	51.8	59.8	60.8	40.0	39.6	39.4	11.7	20.3	21.4
Arizona.................	64.7	68.1	68.1	42.0	38.0	37.3	22.7	30.1	30.8
Arkansas...............	63.4	68.3	68.6	39.9	39.5	39.2	23.5	28.9	29.4
California...............	57.1	59.6	60.1	39.2	36.2	35.8	17.9	23.4	24.3
Colorado...............	54.6	57.5	57.6	37.7	34.5	33.7	16.9	23.0	23.8
Connecticut............	58.8	61.5	61.9	36.3	33.2	32.8	22.5	28.3	29.2
Delaware...............	59.5	67.9	69.1	36.6	35.4	35.1	23.0	32.5	34.0
District of Columbia....	39.3	44.1	46.2	23.3	26.5	27.5	15.9	17.6	18.7
Florida.................	62.9	68.2	68.9	34.7	33.5	33.3	28.2	34.7	35.7
Georgia.................	57.2	61.1	61.4	40.4	38.2	37.7	16.7	22.9	23.7
Hawaii.................	57.9	67.2	68.6	35.3	35.7	35.6	22.7	31.5	33.0
Idaho..................	66.1	70.4	70.3	45.5	42.8	42.0	20.6	27.6	28.3
Illinois.................	58.6	62.4	63.1	38.7	36.4	36.1	19.9	26.0	27.1
Indiana.................	60.7	65.3	65.8	39.9	38.9	38.7	20.9	26.4	27.2
Iowa...................	63.3	68.3	68.8	39.0	39.2	38.9	24.3	29.1	29.9
Kansas.................	63.0	68.0	68.5	41.5	40.8	40.4	21.5	27.2	28.1
Kentucky...............	58.5	64.9	65.6	37.4	37.4	37.3	21.1	27.5	28.3
Louisiana...............	58.6	65.3	66.4	39.1	39.0	39.0	19.5	26.3	27.4
Maine..................	57.6	66.1	66.7	32.6	31.1	30.6	25.0	35.0	36.1
Maryland...............	55.5	61.5	62.3	36.4	36.1	35.9	19.1	25.4	26.4
Massachusetts..........	54.9	57.7	58.5	33.6	31.2	30.9	21.4	26.5	27.6
Michigan...............	60.0	64.6	65.5	37.9	35.7	35.4	22.0	29.0	30.0
Minnesota..............	59.0	65.4	66.2	38.5	38.6	38.4	20.5	26.8	27.8
Mississippi.............	62.0	66.7	67.3	41.2	39.5	39.3	20.8	27.2	28.0
Missouri................	60.8	66.0	66.7	38.3	37.6	37.4	22.5	28.5	29.3
Montana................	59.8	68.8	69.2	36.1	36.4	36.0	23.7	32.3	33.2
Nebraska...............	63.0	68.9	69.4	41.0	42.0	41.7	22.0	26.9	27.8
Nevada.................	57.8	62.9	63.2	38.9	36.8	36.3	19.0	26.1	26.9
New Hampshire........	54.7	60.0	60.6	33.8	30.2	29.6	20.9	29.8	30.9
New Jersey.............	58.7	62.6	63.2	37.3	36.0	35.6	21.4	26.7	27.6
New Mexico............	62.4	68.8	69.2	40.9	38.5	37.8	21.5	30.2	31.3
New York...............	55.8	60.7	62.0	34.8	33.6	33.6	21.1	27.0	28.4
North Carolina..........	58.4	63.1	63.4	37.9	36.0	35.6	20.5	27.0	27.8
North Dakota...........	58.2	65.5	66.8	35.2	39.8	40.0	22.9	25.7	26.8
Ohio....................	60.6	65.7	66.5	38.0	36.9	36.8	22.6	28.8	29.7
Oklahoma..............	62.1	67.2	67.5	40.2	40.6	40.4	21.9	26.6	27.1
Oregon.................	57.6	63.1	63.5	35.6	33.7	33.2	21.9	29.4	30.4
Pennsylvania...........	59.8	64.9	65.7	35.1	34.3	34.2	24.6	30.5	31.5
Rhode Island...........	55.5	58.8	59.2	33.1	30.8	30.4	22.5	27.9	28.9
South Carolina.........	58.8	66.4	67.1	37.1	36.2	36.0	21.7	30.2	31.1
South Dakota..........	64.5	71.9	72.7	41.0	42.7	42.5	23.6	29.3	30.2
Tennessee.............	58.8	63.7	64.2	37.4	36.5	36.3	21.4	27.2	27.9
Texas..................	60.4	62.5	62.5	43.8	41.8	41.1	16.6	20.7	21.3
Utah...................	68.2	67.8	66.8	53.0	48.7	47.3	15.2	19.0	19.4
Vermont................	54.3	62.4	63.3	31.9	30.0	29.6	22.5	32.4	33.7
Virginia................	54.7	60.8	61.5	35.9	35.4	35.2	18.9	25.4	26.3
Washington............	55.8	60.5	61.0	36.6	35.3	34.9	19.2	25.2	26.1
West Virginia...........	58.6	68.3	69.1	33.2	34.1	34.0	25.5	34.2	35.0
Wisconsin..............	59.3	64.7	65.4	37.5	36.1	35.8	21.8	28.6	29.7
Wyoming...............	57.4	67.9	69.0	37.8	39.0	38.7	19.6	29.0	30.3

[1] The age dependency ratio is derived by dividing the sum of populations age under 18 and age 65 and over by the population age 18-64, and multiplying by 100. [2] The child dependency ratio is derived by dividing the population under age 18 by the population age 18-64, and multiplying by 100. [3] The old-age dependency ratio is derived by dividing the population age 65 and over by the population age 18-64, and multiplying by 100.

Source: U.S. Census Bureau, Census 2010 Briefs, "Age and Sex Composition: 2010," May 2011; and State Population by Characteristics: 2020-2021, "Annual Estimates of the Resident Population for Selected Age Groups by Sex: April 1, 2020 to July 1, 2021 (SC-EST2021-AGESEX)," <www.census.gov/data/tables/time-series/demo/popest/2020s-state-detail.html>, accessed July 2022.

Table 19. Resident Population by Hispanic Origin and State: 2021

[In thousands, except as indicated (331,894 represents 331,894,000). As of July 1. The estimates are developed from a base that incorporates the 2020 Census, Vintage 2020 estimates, and 2020 Demographic Analysis estimates. Hispanic origin is considered an ethnicity, not a race. Persons of Hispanic origin may be of any race]

State	Number (1,000)				Percent of total		
	Total population	Hispanic or Latino	Total Non-Hispanic	Non-Hispanic White alone	Hispanic or Latino	Total Non-Hispanic	Non-Hispanic White alone
United States......	**331,894**	**62,647**	**269,247**	**196,833**	**18.9**	**81.1**	**59.3**
Alabama.............	5,040	241	4,799	3,270	4.8	95.2	64.9
Alaska..............	733	55	678	435	7.5	92.5	59.3
Arizona.............	7,276	2,351	4,925	3,873	32.3	67.7	53.2
Arkansas...........	3,026	251	2,775	2,157	8.3	91.7	71.3
California...........	39,238	15,755	23,483	13,815	40.2	59.8	35.2
Colorado...........	5,812	1,293	4,519	3,893	22.3	77.7	67.0
Connecticut........	3,606	637	2,968	2,330	17.7	82.3	64.6
Delaware...........	1,003	101	902	608	10.1	89.9	60.6
District of Columbia....	670	77	593	250	11.5	88.5	37.3
Florida.............	21,781	5,831	15,950	11,468	26.8	73.2	52.7
Georgia............	10,800	1,105	9,695	5,510	10.2	89.8	51.0
Hawaii.............	1,442	160	1,281	308	11.1	88.9	21.4
Idaho..............	1,901	252	1,649	1,541	13.3	86.7	81.1
Illinois.............	12,671	2,282	10,389	7,597	18.0	82.0	60.0
Indiana............	6,806	523	6,283	5,276	7.7	92.3	77.5
Iowa..............	3,193	215	2,978	2,686	6.7	93.3	84.1
Kansas............	2,935	374	2,560	2,192	12.7	87.3	74.7
Kentucky...........	4,509	188	4,321	3,766	4.2	95.8	83.5
Louisiana..........	4,624	258	4,366	2,676	5.6	94.4	57.9
Maine.............	1,372	27	1,345	1,270	2.0	98.0	92.5
Maryland...........	6,165	684	5,481	3,021	11.1	88.9	49.0
Massachusetts......	6,985	897	6,087	4,895	12.8	87.2	70.1
Michigan...........	10,051	562	9,489	7,463	5.6	94.4	74.2
Minnesota..........	5,707	333	5,374	4,458	5.8	94.2	78.1
Mississippi.........	2,950	103	2,847	1,653	3.5	96.5	56.0
Missouri...........	6,168	287	5,881	4,854	4.7	95.3	78.7
Montana...........	1,104	48	1,056	944	4.3	95.7	85.5
Nebraska..........	1,964	236	1,728	1,519	12.0	88.0	77.4
Nevada............	3,144	941	2,203	1,465	29.9	70.1	46.6
New Hampshire......	1,389	61	1,328	1,238	4.4	95.6	89.1
New Jersey.........	9,267	1,992	7,275	4,961	21.5	78.5	53.5
New Mexico.........	2,116	1,059	1,057	760	50.1	49.9	35.9
New York...........	19,836	3,868	15,968	10,859	19.5	80.5	54.7
North Carolina......	10,551	1,078	9,473	6,529	10.2	89.8	61.9
North Dakota.......	775	34	741	645	4.4	95.6	83.2
Ohio..............	11,780	509	11,271	9,150	4.3	95.7	77.7
Oklahoma..........	3,987	467	3,519	2,545	11.7	88.3	63.8
Oregon............	4,246	597	3,650	3,148	14.0	86.0	74.1
Pennsylvania.......	12,964	1,085	11,879	9,701	8.4	91.6	74.8
Rhode Island.......	1,096	188	908	771	17.1	82.9	70.4
South Carolina......	5,191	330	4,861	3,290	6.4	93.6	63.4
South Dakota.......	895	41	854	724	4.6	95.4	80.8
Tennessee.........	6,975	426	6,549	5,097	6.1	93.9	73.1
Texas.............	29,528	11,857	17,671	11,885	40.2	59.8	40.3
Utah..............	3,338	494	2,844	2,578	14.8	85.2	77.2
Vermont...........	646	14	631	595	2.2	97.8	92.2
Virginia............	8,642	882	7,760	5,214	10.2	89.8	60.3
Washington.........	7,739	1,059	6,680	5,111	13.7	86.3	66.0
West Virginia.......	1,783	34	1,749	1,632	1.9	98.1	91.5
Wisconsin..........	5,896	443	5,453	4,727	7.5	92.5	80.2
Wyoming...........	579	61	518	482	10.6	89.4	83.3

Source: U.S. Census Bureau, State Population by Characteristics: 2020-2021, Datasets, "Age, Sex, Race, and Hispanic Origin - 6 race groups," <www.census.gov/data/tables/time-series/demo/popest/2020s-state-detail.html>, accessed July 2022.

Table 20. Resident Population by Race and State: 2021

[331,894 represents 331,894,000. As of July 1. The estimates are developed from a base that incorporates the 2020 Census, Vintage 2020 estimates, and 2020 Demographic Analysis estimates]

State	Number (1,000)							Percent distribution					
	Total population	White[1]	Black[1]	American Indian[1,2]	Asian[1]	Native Hawaiian[1,3]	Two or more races	White[1]	Black[1]	American Indian[1,2]	Asian[1]	Native Hawaiian[1,3]	Two or more races
U.S.	331,894	251,462	45,061	4,368	20,350	863	9,790	75.8	13.6	1.3	6.1	0.3	2.9
AL	5,040	3,473	1,353	36	78	5	94	68.9	26.8	0.7	1.6	0.1	1.9
AK	733	473	27	115	48	12	58	64.5	3.6	15.7	6.6	1.6	7.9
AZ	7,276	5,969	395	384	278	21	229	82.0	5.4	5.3	3.8	0.3	3.1
AR	3,026	2,380	475	33	54	13	71	78.6	15.7	1.1	1.8	0.4	2.3
CA	39,238	27,902	2,548	675	6,250	205	1,657	71.1	6.5	1.7	15.9	0.5	4.2
CO	5,812	5,027	272	98	209	13	194	86.5	4.7	1.7	3.6	0.2	3.3
CT	3,606	2,843	457	24	182	4	95	78.8	12.7	0.7	5.1	0.1	2.6
DE	1,003	687	237	7	42	1	29	68.4	23.6	0.7	4.2	0.2	2.9
DC	670	307	307	4	30	1	20	45.9	45.8	0.6	4.5	0.1	3.0
FL	21,781	16,749	3,711	117	664	27	513	76.9	17.0	0.5	3.0	0.1	2.4
GA	10,800	6,418	3,559	59	493	15	255	59.4	33.0	0.5	4.6	0.1	2.4
HI	1,442	364	31	6	530	151	360	25.3	2.2	0.4	36.8	10.5	25.0
ID	1,901	1,764	18	33	31	4	51	92.8	0.9	1.7	1.6	0.2	2.7
IL	12,671	9,668	1,867	80	771	9	277	76.3	14.7	0.6	6.1	0.1	2.2
IN	6,806	5,733	695	30	185	5	158	84.2	10.2	0.4	2.7	0.1	2.3
IA	3,193	2,875	138	18	88	6	67	90.1	4.3	0.6	2.8	0.2	2.1
KS	2,935	2,523	182	36	94	4	96	86.0	6.2	1.2	3.2	0.1	3.3
KY	4,509	3,926	389	14	77	5	98	87.1	8.6	0.3	1.7	0.1	2.2
LA	4,624	2,887	1,525	38	87	3	85	62.4	33.0	0.8	1.9	0.1	1.8
ME	1,372	1,292	25	10	19	1	26	94.2	1.8	0.7	1.4	(Z)	1.9
MD	6,165	3,561	1,938	40	427	8	191	57.8	31.4	0.7	6.9	0.1	3.1
MA	6,985	5,577	651	37	525	8	187	79.8	9.3	0.5	7.5	0.1	2.7
MI	10,051	7,936	1,420	75	343	4	273	79.0	14.1	0.7	3.4	(Z)	2.7
MN	5,707	4,736	424	79	307	5	157	83.0	7.4	1.4	5.4	0.1	2.8
MS	2,950	1,734	1,120	19	33	2	42	58.8	38.0	0.6	1.1	0.1	1.4
MO	6,168	5,096	727	37	139	11	158	82.6	11.8	0.6	2.2	0.2	2.6
MT	1,104	980	7	73	11	1	33	88.7	0.6	6.6	1.0	0.1	3.0
NE	1,964	1,722	105	32	55	3	48	87.7	5.3	1.6	2.8	0.1	2.4
NV	3,144	2,287	334	54	286	27	155	72.8	10.6	1.7	9.1	0.9	4.9
NH	1,389	1,289	27	4	43	1	26	92.8	1.9	0.3	3.1	0.1	1.8
NJ	9,267	6,594	1,420	65	957	12	220	71.1	15.3	0.7	10.3	0.1	2.4
NM	2,116	1,721	57	237	40	4	58	81.3	2.7	11.2	1.9	0.2	2.7
NY	19,836	13,711	3,499	205	1,846	29	546	69.1	17.6	1.0	9.3	0.1	2.8
NC	10,551	7,392	2,350	169	359	15	266	70.1	22.3	1.6	3.4	0.1	2.5
ND	775	672	27	44	13	1	19	86.7	3.5	5.7	1.7	0.1	2.4
OH	11,780	9,560	1,560	35	313	8	303	81.2	13.2	0.3	2.7	0.1	2.6
OK	3,987	2,917	313	387	98	10	262	73.2	7.8	9.7	2.5	0.2	6.6
OR	4,246	3,660	97	80	210	20	179	86.2	2.3	1.9	5.0	0.5	4.2
PA	12,964	10,502	1,586	56	512	11	296	81.0	12.2	0.4	3.9	0.1	2.3
RI	1,096	910	97	13	40	2	33	83.1	8.8	1.2	3.7	0.2	3.0
SC	5,191	3,562	1,383	30	100	5	110	68.6	26.7	0.6	1.9	0.1	2.1
SD	895	754	22	80	15	1	23	84.2	2.5	9.0	1.7	0.1	2.6
TN	6,975	5,458	1,184	35	141	7	150	78.2	17.0	0.5	2.0	0.1	2.2
TX	29,528	23,012	3,895	314	1,617	46	644	77.9	13.2	1.1	5.5	0.2	2.2
UT	3,338	3,013	51	53	90	38	94	90.3	1.5	1.6	2.7	1.1	2.8
VT	646	607	9	3	13	(Z)	13	94.0	1.5	0.4	2.0	(Z)	2.1
VA	8,642	5,942	1,729	49	621	11	290	68.8	20.0	0.6	7.2	0.1	3.4
WA	7,739	5,996	348	153	775	63	403	77.5	4.5	2.0	10.0	0.8	5.2
WV	1,783	1,660	66	5	16	1	35	93.1	3.7	0.3	0.9	(Z)	2.0
WI	5,896	5,107	399	72	187	4	128	86.6	6.8	1.2	3.2	(Z)	2.2
WY	579	535	7	16	6	1	14	92.4	1.2	2.8	1.1	0.1	2.4

Z Less than 500 or 0.05 percent. [1] Data shown for each race alone. [2] Includes Alaska Natives. [3] Includes Other Pacific Islanders.

Source: U.S. Census Bureau, State Population by Characteristics: 2020-2021, Datasets, "Age, Sex, Race, and Hispanic Origin - 6 race groups," <www.census.gov/data/tables/time-series/demo/popest/2020s-state-detail.html>, accessed July 2022.

Table 21. Large Metropolitan Statistical Areas—Population: 2010 to 2021

[Covers metropolitan statistical areas with population of 250,000 and over in 2021, as delineated by the U.S. Office of Management and Budget as of March 2020. All geographic boundaries for 2010 to 2021 population estimates are defined as of January 1, 2020. Estimates for 2020 and 2021 are developed from a base that incorporates the 2020 Census, Vintage 2020 estimates, and 2020 Demographic Analysis estimates. For definitions and components of all metropolitan and micropolitan areas, see Appendix II. Minus sign (-) indicates decrease]

Metropolitan statistical area	2010, estimates base [1] (April)	2020, estimates base [1] (April)	2020 (July)	2021 (July)	Change 2020 to 2021 (July) Number	Change 2020 to 2021 (July) Percent	Rank, 2021
Akron, OH	703,215	702,219	701,305	700,015	-1,290	-0.2	85
Albany-Schenectady-Troy, NY	870,713	899,262	898,561	899,286	725	0.1	63
Albuquerque, NM	887,056	916,528	917,179	918,259	1,080	0.1	61
Allentown-Bethlehem-Easton, PA-NJ	821,095	861,889	861,705	865,310	3,605	0.4	68
Amarillo, TX	251,937	268,691	268,820	269,703	883	0.3	182
Anchorage, AK	381,233	398,328	398,097	398,807	710	0.2	137
Ann Arbor, MI	345,417	372,258	371,656	369,390	-2,266	-0.6	148
Asheville, NC	424,864	469,015	469,454	472,341	2,887	0.6	120
Atlanta-Sandy Springs-Alpharetta, GA	5,286,689	6,089,815	6,101,146	6,144,050	42,904	0.7	8
Atlantic City-Hammonton, NJ	274,532	274,534	274,191	274,966	775	0.3	179
Augusta-Richmond County, GA-SC	564,893	611,000	611,720	615,933	4,213	0.7	96
Austin-Round Rock-Georgetown, TX	1,716,307	2,283,371	2,299,125	2,352,426	53,301	2.3	28
Bakersfield, CA	839,619	909,235	909,997	917,673	7,676	0.8	62
Baltimore-Columbia-Towson, MD	2,710,601	2,844,510	2,841,691	2,838,327	-3,364	-0.1	20
Baton Rouge, LA	825,944	870,569	870,178	871,905	1,727	0.2	66
Beaumont-Port Arthur, TX	388,751	397,565	396,958	395,419	-1,539	-0.4	139
Birmingham-Hoover, AL	1,061,038	1,115,289	1,114,710	1,114,262	-448	(-Z)	50
Boise City, ID	616,566	764,718	769,581	795,268	25,687	3.3	75
Boston-Cambridge-Newton, MA-NH	4,552,598	4,941,632	4,936,511	4,899,932	-36,579	-0.7	11
Boulder, CO	294,560	330,758	330,811	329,543	-1,268	-0.4	157
Bremerton-Silverdale-Port Orchard, WA	251,143	275,611	275,660	274,314	-1,346	-0.5	180
Bridgeport-Stamford-Norwalk, CT	916,910	957,419	955,895	959,768	3,873	0.4	59
Brownsville-Harlingen, TX	406,214	421,017	421,191	423,029	1,838	0.4	131
Buffalo-Cheektowaga, NY	1,135,608	1,166,902	1,165,506	1,162,336	-3,170	-0.3	49
Canton-Massillon, OH	404,408	401,574	401,046	400,525	-521	-0.1	136
Cape Coral-Fort Myers, FL	618,761	760,822	764,679	787,976	23,297	3.0	77
Cedar Rapids, IA	257,947	276,520	276,446	275,435	-1,011	-0.4	178
Charleston, WV	278,000	258,859	257,840	255,020	-2,820	-1.1	191
Charleston-North Charleston, SC	664,647	799,636	802,961	813,052	10,091	1.3	74
Charlotte-Concord-Gastonia, NC-SC	2,243,952	2,660,329	2,669,665	2,701,046	31,381	1.2	22
Chattanooga, TN-GA	528,131	562,647	563,599	567,641	4,042	0.7	101
Chicago-Naperville-Elgin, IL-IN-WI	9,461,540	9,618,502	9,601,605	9,509,934	-91,671	-1.0	3
Cincinnati, OH-KY-IN	2,137,718	2,256,884	2,257,667	2,259,935	2,268	0.1	30
Clarksville, TN-KY	273,942	320,535	321,607	328,304	6,697	2.1	159
Cleveland-Elyria, OH	2,077,270	2,088,251	2,085,357	2,075,662	-9,695	-0.5	34
College Station-Bryan, TX	228,665	268,248	268,864	272,041	3,177	1.2	181
Colorado Springs, CO	645,616	755,105	756,573	762,793	6,220	0.8	79
Columbia, SC	767,478	829,470	830,767	838,250	7,483	0.9	72
Columbus, GA-AL	308,481	328,883	329,141	327,536	-1,605	-0.5	160
Columbus, OH	1,902,012	2,138,926	2,141,042	2,151,017	9,975	0.5	32
Corpus Christi, TX	405,015	421,933	421,862	422,778	916	0.2	132
Crestview-Fort Walton Beach-Destin, FL	235,868	286,973	287,664	293,324	5,660	2.0	169
Dallas-Fort Worth-Arlington, TX	6,366,541	7,637,387	7,662,325	7,759,615	97,290	1.3	4
Davenport-Moline-Rock Island, IA-IL	379,692	384,324	383,526	381,568	-1,958	-0.5	147
Dayton-Kettering, OH	799,280	814,049	813,475	813,516	41	(Z)	73
Deltona-Daytona Beach-Ormond Beach, FL	590,283	668,921	670,869	685,344	14,475	2.2	88
Denver-Aurora-Lakewood, CO	2,543,597	2,963,821	2,969,289	2,972,566	3,277	0.1	19
Des Moines-West Des Moines, IA	606,478	709,466	710,843	719,146	8,303	1.2	82
Detroit-Warren-Dearborn, MI	4,295,968	4,392,041	4,385,748	4,365,205	-20,543	-0.5	14
Duluth, MN-WI	290,635	291,638	291,278	290,780	-498	-0.2	171
Durham-Chapel Hill, NC	564,205	649,903	651,192	654,012	2,820	0.4	92
El Paso, TX	804,110	868,859	869,289	871,234	1,945	0.2	67
Erie, PA	280,586	270,876	270,427	269,011	-1,416	-0.5	183
Eugene-Springfield, OR	351,705	382,971	382,940	383,189	249	0.1	146
Evansville, IN-KY	311,551	314,049	313,930	313,946	16	(Z)	164
Fargo, ND-MN	208,772	249,843	250,219	252,136	1,917	0.8	192
Fayetteville, NC	481,037	520,378	520,354	524,588	4,234	0.8	108
Fayetteville-Springdale-Rogers, AR	440,118	546,725	549,566	560,709	11,143	2.0	102
Flint, MI	425,790	406,211	405,648	404,208	-1,440	-0.4	135
Fort Collins, CO	299,628	359,066	359,686	362,533	2,847	0.8	150
Fort Wayne, IN	388,626	419,601	420,208	423,038	2,830	0.7	130
Fresno, CA	930,503	1,008,654	1,008,966	1,013,581	4,615	0.5	55
Gainesville, FL	305,084	339,247	339,663	341,756	2,093	0.6	153
Grand Rapids-Kentwood, MI	993,655	1,087,592	1,088,203	1,091,620	3,417	0.3	51
Greeley, CO	252,836	328,981	331,358	340,036	8,678	2.6	154
Green Bay, WI	306,241	328,268	328,323	329,490	1,167	0.4	158
Greensboro-High Point, NC	723,943	776,566	776,761	778,848	2,087	0.3	78
Greenville-Anderson, SC	824,023	928,195	930,165	940,774	10,609	1.1	60
Gulfport-Biloxi, MS	388,605	416,259	416,312	418,082	1,770	0.4	133
Hagerstown-Martinsburg, MD-WV	269,153	293,844	294,277	298,227	3,950	1.3	167
Harrisburg-Carlisle, PA	549,457	591,712	592,361	596,305	3,944	0.7	97
Hartford-East Hartford-Middletown, CT	1,212,434	1,213,531	1,211,505	1,211,906	401	(Z)	48
Hickory-Lenoir-Morganton, NC	365,807	365,276	365,235	366,441	1,206	0.3	149
Houston-The Woodlands-Sugar Land, TX	5,920,485	7,122,240	7,137,747	7,206,841	69,094	1.0	5

See footnotes at end of table.

Table 21. Large Metropolitan Statistical Areas—Population: 2010 to 2021-Continued.

See headnote on page 24.

Metropolitan statistical area	2010, estimates base [1] (April)	2020, estimates base [1] (April)	2020 (July)	2021 (July)	Change 2020 to 2021 (July) Number	Change 2020 to 2021 (July) Percent	Rank, 2021
Huntington-Ashland, WV-KY-OH.	370,886	359,862	359,100	356,581	-2,519	-0.7	151
Huntsville, AL.	417,587	491,723	494,018	502,728	8,710	1.8	113
Indianapolis-Carmel-Anderson, IN.	1,888,078	2,111,040	2,113,700	2,126,804	13,104	0.6	33
Jackson, MS.	587,116	591,978	590,626	587,202	-3,424	-0.6	99
Jacksonville, FL.	1,345,594	1,605,848	1,611,388	1,637,666	26,278	1.6	39
Kalamazoo-Portage, MI.	250,327	261,670	261,629	261,108	-521	-0.2	189
Kansas City, MO-KS.	2,009,353	2,192,035	2,193,578	2,199,490	5,912	0.3	31
Kennewick-Richland, WA.	253,328	303,622	304,306	308,293	3,987	1.3	166
Killeen-Temple, TX.	405,327	475,367	476,784	486,101	9,317	2.0	115
Kingsport-Bristol, TN-VA.	309,493	307,614	307,406	308,661	1,255	0.4	165
Knoxville, TN.	815,035	879,773	881,628	893,412	11,784	1.3	64
Lafayette, LA.	466,732	478,384	478,077	479,212	1,135	0.2	118
Lakeland-Winter Haven, FL.	602,068	725,046	729,233	753,520	24,287	3.3	80
Lancaster, PA.	519,443	552,984	552,597	553,652	1,055	0.2	104
Lansing-East Lansing, MI.	534,687	541,297	540,737	540,281	-456	-0.1	106
Laredo, TX.	250,304	267,114	267,234	267,945	711	0.3	186
Las Vegas-Henderson-Paradise, NV.	1,951,278	2,265,461	2,273,386	2,292,476	19,090	0.8	29
Lexington-Fayette, KY.	472,095	516,811	517,028	517,846	818	0.2	109
Lincoln, NE.	302,157	340,217	340,515	342,117	1,602	0.5	152
Little Rock-North Little Rock-Conway, AR.	699,781	748,031	748,434	750,936	2,502	0.3	81
Longview, TX.	280,005	286,184	286,153	287,868	1,715	0.6	173
Los Angeles-Long Beach-Anaheim, CA.	12,828,904	13,200,998	13,173,266	12,997,353	-175,913	-1.3	2
Louisville/Jefferson County, KY-IN.	1,202,686	1,285,439	1,285,058	1,284,566	-492	(-Z)	45
Lubbock, TX.	290,917	321,368	322,123	325,245	3,122	1.0	161
Lynchburg, VA.	252,654	261,593	261,408	262,258	850	0.3	188
Madison, WI.	605,477	680,796	681,484	683,183	1,699	0.2	89
Manchester-Nashua, NH.	400,706	422,937	422,705	424,079	1,374	0.3	129
McAllen-Edinburg-Mission, TX.	774,734	870,781	872,204	880,356	8,152	0.9	65
Memphis, TN-MS-AR.	1,316,108	1,337,779	1,337,311	1,336,103	-1,208	-0.1	43
Merced, CA.	255,797	281,202	281,726	286,461	4,735	1.7	174
Miami-Fort Lauderdale-Pompano Beach, FL.	5,566,285	6,138,333	6,126,441	6,091,747	-34,694	-0.6	9
Milwaukee-Waukesha, WI.	1,555,954	1,574,731	1,573,598	1,566,487	-7,111	-0.5	40
Minneapolis-St. Paul-Bloomington, MN-WI.	3,333,623	3,690,261	3,692,421	3,690,512	-1,909	-0.1	16
Mobile, AL.	430,719	430,197	429,546	428,220	-1,326	-0.3	128
Modesto, CA.	514,451	552,878	552,710	552,999	289	0.1	105
Montgomery, AL.	374,528	386,047	385,738	385,798	60	(Z)	144
Myrtle Beach-Conway-North Myrtle Beach, SC-NC.	376,565	487,722	491,582	509,794	18,212	3.7	111
Naples-Marco Island, FL.	321,514	375,752	377,079	385,980	8,901	2.4	141
Nashville-Davidson-Murfreesboro-Franklin, TN.	1,646,183	1,989,519	1,995,343	2,012,476	17,133	0.9	35
New Haven-Milford, CT.	862,476	864,835	863,498	863,700	202	(Z)	69
New Orleans-Metairie, LA.	1,189,901	1,271,845	1,270,366	1,261,726	-8,640	-0.7	47
New York-Newark-Jersey City, NY-NJ-PA.	18,896,285	20,140,470	20,096,413	19,768,458	-327,955	-1.6	1
North Port-Sarasota-Bradenton, FL.	702,306	833,716	837,107	859,760	22,653	2.7	70
Norwich-New London, CT.	274,076	268,555	268,248	268,805	557	0.2	184
Ocala, FL.	331,296	375,908	377,370	385,915	8,545	2.3	142
Ogden-Clearfield, UT.	597,162	694,863	696,620	706,696	10,076	1.4	83
Oklahoma City, OK.	1,252,989	1,425,695	1,428,709	1,441,647	12,938	0.9	42
Olympia-Lacey-Tumwater, WA.	252,260	294,793	295,729	297,977	2,248	0.8	168
Omaha-Council Bluffs, NE-IA.	865,353	967,604	968,493	971,637	3,144	0.3	58
Orlando-Kissimmee-Sanford, FL.	2,134,401	2,673,376	2,677,687	2,691,925	14,238	0.5	23
Oxnard-Thousand Oaks-Ventura, CA.	823,446	843,843	842,921	839,784	-3,137	-0.4	71
Palm Bay-Melbourne-Titusville, FL.	543,376	606,612	608,007	616,628	8,621	1.4	95
Pensacola-Ferry Pass-Brent, FL.	449,003	509,905	511,557	516,388	4,831	0.9	110
Peoria, IL.	416,253	402,391	401,160	398,224	-2,936	-0.7	138
Philadelphia-Camden-Wilmington, PA-NJ-DE-MD.	5,965,874	6,245,051	6,241,983	6,228,601	-13,382	-0.2	7
Phoenix-Mesa-Chandler, AZ.	4,193,137	4,845,832	4,867,925	4,946,145	78,220	1.6	10
Pittsburgh, PA.	2,356,291	2,370,930	2,367,293	2,353,538	-13,755	-0.6	27
Port St. Lucie, FL.	424,108	487,657	489,804	503,521	13,717	2.8	112
Portland-South Portland, ME.	514,103	551,740	552,089	556,893	4,804	0.9	103
Portland-Vancouver-Hillsboro, OR-WA.	2,226,002	2,512,859	2,516,230	2,511,612	-4,618	-0.2	25
Poughkeepsie-Newburgh-Middletown, NY.	670,267	697,221	697,064	701,637	4,573	0.7	84
Providence-Warwick, RI-MA.	1,601,209	1,676,579	1,675,401	1,675,774	373	(Z)	38
Provo-Orem, UT.	526,885	671,185	674,967	697,141	22,174	3.3	86
Raleigh-Cary, NC.	1,130,479	1,413,982	1,420,225	1,448,411	28,186	2.0	41
Reading, PA.	411,569	428,849	428,694	429,342	648	0.2	126
Reno, NV.	425,442	490,596	491,494	497,535	6,041	1.2	114
Richmond, VA.	1,186,611	1,314,434	1,315,734	1,324,062	8,328	0.6	44
Riverside-San Bernardino-Ontario, CA.	4,224,957	4,599,839	4,605,504	4,653,105	47,601	1.0	12
Roanoke, VA.	308,668	315,251	315,057	314,496	-561	-0.2	163
Rochester, NY.	1,079,702	1,090,135	1,088,776	1,084,973	-3,803	-0.3	52
Rockford, IL.	349,431	338,798	338,184	336,278	-1,906	-0.6	155
Sacramento-Roseville-Folsom, CA.	2,149,151	2,397,382	2,399,351	2,411,428	12,077	0.5	26
St. Louis, MO-IL.	2,787,786	2,820,253	2,818,267	2,809,299	-8,968	-0.3	21
Salem, OR.	390,745	433,353	434,065	436,283	2,218	0.5	125
Salinas, CA.	415,058	439,035	438,500	437,325	-1,175	-0.3	124

See footnotes at end of table.

Metropolitan statistical area	2010, estimates base[1] (April)	2020, estimates base[1] (April)	2020 (July)	2021 (July)	Change 2020 to 2021 (July) Number	Change 2020 to 2021 (July) Percent	Rank, 2021
Salisbury, MD-DE.............................	373,751	418,046	419,397	429,223	9,826	2.3	127
Salt Lake City, UT.............................	1,087,808	1,257,936	1,259,517	1,263,061	3,544	0.3	46
San Antonio-New Braunfels, TX....................	2,142,525	2,558,143	2,566,683	2,601,788	35,105	1.4	24
San Diego-Chula Vista-Carlsbad, CA...............	3,095,352	3,298,634	3,297,252	3,286,069	-11,183	-0.3	17
San Francisco-Oakland-Berkeley, CA..............	4,335,608	4,749,008	4,739,649	4,623,264	-116,385	-2.5	13
San Jose-Sunnyvale-Santa Clara, CA..............	1,836,945	2,000,468	1,995,105	1,952,185	-42,920	-2.2	36
San Luis Obispo-Paso Robles, CA..................	269,599	282,424	282,231	283,159	928	0.3	175
Santa Cruz-Watsonville, CA......................	262,345	270,861	270,353	267,792	-2,561	-0.9	187
Santa Maria-Santa Barbara, CA....................	423,947	448,229	448,096	446,475	-1,621	-0.4	123
Santa Rosa-Petaluma, CA.........................	483,866	488,863	488,345	485,887	-2,458	-0.5	116
Savannah, GA...................................	347,608	404,798	405,053	410,008	4,955	1.2	134
Scranton-Wilkes-Barre, PA.......................	563,635	567,559	566,574	567,750	1,176	0.2	100
Seattle-Tacoma-Bellevue, WA.....................	3,439,808	4,018,762	4,024,730	4,011,553	-13,177	-0.3	15
Shreveport-Bossier City, LA......................	398,614	393,406	392,525	389,155	-3,370	-0.9	140
Sioux Falls, SD.................................	228,268	276,730	277,458	281,958	4,500	1.6	176
South Bend-Mishawaka, IN-MI....................	319,201	324,501	324,112	323,695	-417	-0.1	162
Spartanburg, SC................................	284,329	327,997	329,364	335,864	6,500	2.0	156
Spokane-Spokane Valley, WA.....................	514,752	585,784	587,266	593,466	6,200	1.1	98
Springfield, MA................................	693,059	699,162	697,960	695,305	-2,655	-0.4	87
Springfield, MO................................	436,756	475,432	476,128	481,483	5,355	1.1	117
Stockton, CA...................................	685,298	779,233	780,517	789,410	8,893	1.1	76
Syracuse, NY...................................	662,634	662,057	660,894	658,281	-2,613	-0.4	91
Tallahassee, FL.................................	368,762	384,298	384,546	385,776	1,230	0.3	145
Tampa-St. Petersburg-Clearwater, FL.............	2,783,491	3,175,275	3,183,385	3,219,514	36,129	1.1	18
Toledo, OH....................................	651,434	646,604	645,819	644,217	-1,602	-0.2	94
Trenton-Princeton, NJ...........................	367,485	387,340	386,759	385,898	-861	-0.2	143
Tucson, AZ....................................	980,266	1,043,433	1,045,599	1,052,030	6,431	0.6	53
Tulsa, OK.....................................	937,521	1,015,331	1,016,589	1,023,988	7,399	0.7	54
Tuscaloosa, AL.................................	239,225	268,674	268,711	268,191	-520	-0.2	185
Urban Honolulu, HI.............................	953,203	1,016,508	1,013,227	1,000,890	-12,337	-1.2	56
Utica-Rome, NY................................	299,320	292,264	291,702	290,211	-1,491	-0.5	172
Vallejo, CA....................................	413,343	453,491	453,274	451,716	-1,558	-0.3	122
Virginia Beach-Norfolk-Newport News, VA-NC.....	1,713,955	1,799,674	1,800,081	1,803,328	3,247	0.2	37
Visalia, CA....................................	442,176	473,117	473,736	477,054	3,318	0.7	119
Waco, TX.....................................	252,761	277,547	277,984	280,428	2,444	0.9	177
Washington-Arlington-Alexandria, DC-VA-MD-WV.................................	5,649,698	6,385,162	6,385,714	6,356,434	-29,280	-0.5	6
Wichita, KS....................................	623,061	647,610	647,921	647,919	-2	(-Z)	93
Wilmington, NC................................	254,878	285,905	286,623	291,833	5,210	1.8	170
Winston-Salem, NC.............................	640,489	675,966	676,369	681,438	5,069	0.7	90
Worcester, MA-CT..............................	916,764	978,529	977,701	978,447	746	0.1	57
Yakima, WA...................................	243,240	256,728	256,533	256,035	-498	-0.2	190
York-Hanover, PA..............................	435,016	456,438	456,389	458,696	2,307	0.5	121
Youngstown-Warren-Boardman, OH-PA...........	565,782	541,243	539,686	538,069	-1,617	-0.3	107

Z Less than 0.05%. [1] The April 1, 2010 population estimates base reflects changes to the Census 2010 population from the Count Question Resolution program and geographic program revisions.

Source: U.S. Census Bureau, Metropolitan and Micropolitan Statistical Areas Totals: 2010-2020, "Annual Resident Population Estimates and Estimated Components of Resident Population Change for Metropolitan and Micropolitan Statistical Areas and their Geographic Components: April 1, 2010 to July 1, 2020," <www.census.gov/programs-surveys/popest/technical-documentation/research/evaluation-estimates.html>; and Metropolitan and Micropolitan Statistical Areas Totals: 2020-2021, "Annual Resident Population Estimates and Estimated Components of Resident Population Change for Metropolitan and Micropolitan Statistical Areas and Their Geographic Components: April 1, 2020 to July 1, 2021 (CBSA-EST2021-ALLDATA)," <www.census.gov/programs-surveys/popest/data/tables.html>, accessed March 2022.

Table 22. The 50 Largest Metropolitan Statistical Areas in 2021—Components of Population Change: 2020 to 2021

[Covers period April 1, 2020 to July 1, 2021. Covers metropolitan statistical areas (MSAs) as delineated by the U.S. Office of Management and Budget as of March 2020. Top 50 MSAs ranked by July 2021 population. Estimates developed from a base that incorporates the 2020 Census, Vintage 2020 estimates, and 2020 Demographic Analysis estimates. For definitions and components of all metropolitan and micropolitan areas, see Appendix II. Minus sign (-) indicates decrease]

| Metropolitan statistical area | Number | | | | | | | Percent change |
| | Total change [1] | Natural increase | | | Net migration | | | |
		Total	Births	Deaths	Total	International	Domestic migration	
Atlanta-Sandy Springs-Alpharetta, GA..........	54,235	22,551	84,897	62,346	31,328	6,082	25,246	0.9
Austin-Round Rock-Georgetown, TX...........	69,055	14,111	31,835	17,724	55,084	2,448	52,636	3.0
Baltimore-Columbia-Towson, MD................	-6,183	-93	38,623	38,716	-6,398	2,090	-8,488	-0.2
Birmingham-Hoover, AL.......................	-1,027	-1,291	15,597	16,888	222	275	-53	-0.1
Boston-Cambridge-Newton, MA-NH............	-41,700	1,844	59,909	58,065	-43,461	11,316	-54,777	-0.8
Buffalo-Cheektowaga, NY.....................	-4,566	-3,827	14,168	17,995	-935	713	-1,648	-0.4
Charlotte-Concord-Gastonia, NC-SC..........	40,717	6,203	37,478	31,275	34,416	2,885	31,531	1.5
Chicago-Naperville-Elgin, IL-IN-WI.............	-108,568	14,879	125,780	110,901	-123,457	4,342	-127,799	-1.1
Cincinnati, OH-KY-IN.........................	3,051	1,224	32,552	31,328	1,576	1,591	-15	0.1
Cleveland-Elyria, OH.........................	-12,589	-6,212	26,188	32,400	-6,432	1,276	-7,708	-0.6
Columbus, OH................................	12,091	6,461	32,375	25,914	5,513	2,650	2,863	0.6
Dallas-Fort Worth-Arlington, TX...............	122,228	44,306	116,898	72,592	78,337	9,197	69,140	1.6
Denver-Aurora-Lakewood, CO.................	8,745	10,853	40,265	29,412	-2,438	1,126	-3,564	0.3
Detroit-Warren-Dearborn, MI.................	-26,836	-5,231	58,334	63,565	-22,170	2,390	-24,560	-0.6
Hartford-East Hartford-Middletown, CT........	-1,625	-2,596	13,674	16,270	792	1,570	-778	-0.1
Houston-The Woodlands-Sugar Land, TX......	84,601	47,083	112,367	65,284	37,397	12,997	24,400	1.2
Indianapolis-Carmel-Anderson, IN.............	15,764	5,270	31,254	25,984	10,494	2,280	8,214	0.7
Jacksonville, FL..............................	31,818	818	22,270	21,452	31,186	1,124	30,062	2.0
Kansas City, MO-KS..........................	7,455	4,603	31,771	27,168	2,503	1,194	1,309	0.3
Las Vegas-Henderson-Paradise, NV...........	27,015	3,944	31,589	27,645	22,616	2,171	20,445	1.2
Los Angeles-Long Beach-Anaheim, CA........	-203,645	29,743	163,963	134,220	-232,818	4,708	-237,526	-1.5
Louisville/Jefferson County, KY-IN.............	-873	-1,365	17,873	19,238	386	645	-259	-0.1
Memphis, TN-MS-AR..........................	-1,676	1,520	20,970	19,450	-3,364	279	-3,643	-0.1
Miami-Fort Lauderdale-Pompano Beach, FL...	-46,586	-3,414	77,291	80,705	-42,960	24,029	-66,989	-0.8
Milwaukee-Waukesha, WI......................	-8,244	914	22,559	21,645	-9,157	1,002	-10,159	-0.5
Minneapolis-St. Paul-Bloomington, MN-WI.....	251	13,957	52,321	38,364	-13,701	2,997	-16,698	(Z)
Nashville-Davidson-Murfreesboro-Franklin, TN.	22,957	5,256	29,243	23,987	18,021	937	17,084	1.2
New Orleans-Metairie, LA......................	-10,119	82	18,140	18,058	-10,033	1,299	-11,332	-0.8
New York-Newark-Jersey City, NY-NJ-PA......	-372,012	50,686	270,043	219,357	-418,337	24,842	-443,179	-1.8
Oklahoma City, OK............................	15,952	2,587	21,238	18,651	13,229	546	12,683	1.1
Orlando-Kissimmee-Sanford, FL................	18,549	5,443	34,807	29,364	13,241	6,521	6,720	0.7
Philadelphia-Camden-Wilmington, PA-NJ-DE-MD.	-16,450	-3,768	80,582	84,350	-13,023	4,448	-17,471	-0.3
Phoenix-Mesa-Chandler, AZ....................	100,313	9,716	66,390	56,674	90,467	3,273	87,194	2.1
Pittsburgh, PA...............................	-17,392	-13,424	27,480	40,904	-4,019	919	-4,938	-0.7
Portland-Vancouver-Hillsboro, OR-WA.........	-1,247	2,272	30,461	28,189	-3,676	1,198	-4,874	(-Z)
Providence-Warwick, RI-MA....................	-805	-4,200	19,001	23,201	3,218.0	1,133	2,085	(-Z)
Raleigh-Cary, NC.............................	34,429	6,189	19,299	13,110	28,184	1,644	26,540	2.4
Richmond, VA................................	9,628	218	17,499	17,281	9,408	1,397	8,011	0.7
Riverside-San Bernardino-Ontario, CA........	53,266	15,568	67,389	51,821	37,100	-957	38,057	1.2
Sacramento-Roseville-Folsom, CA.............	14,046	4,531	31,542	27,011	9,195	1,484	7,711	0.6
Salt Lake City, UT............................	5,125	9,270	20,242	10,972	-4,323	760	-5,083	0.4
San Antonio-New Braunfels, TX...............	43,645	10,213	38,355	28,142	33,118	1,036	32,082	1.7
San Diego-Chula Vista-Carlsbad, CA..........	-12,565	13,614	46,391	32,777	-26,554	606	-27,160	-0.4
San Francisco-Oakland-Berkeley, CA..........	-125,744	12,373	58,634	46,261	-136,602	5,263	-141,865	-2.6
San Jose-Sunnyvale-Santa Clara, CA.........	-48,283	9,461	25,836	16,375	-57,128	3,567	-60,695	-2.4
Seattle-Tacoma-Bellevue, WA.................	-7,209	13,877	54,021	40,144	-21,498	7,743	-29,241	-0.2
St. Louis, MO-IL..............................	-10,954	-4,082	37,714	41,796	-7,038	1,505	-8,543	-0.4
Tampa-St. Petersburg-Clearwater, FL..........	44,239	-11,685	38,023	49,708	56,245	3,878	52,367	1.4
Virginia Beach-Norfolk-Newport News, VA-NC.	3,654	3,039	25,919	22,880	578	1,226	-648	0.2
Washington-Arlington-Alexandria, DC-VA-MD-WV.	-28,728	32,949	91,297	58,348	-61,338	13,530	-74,868	-0.4

Z Represents less than .05%. [1] Total population change includes residual. This residual represents the change in population that cannot be attributed to any specific demographic component of change.

Source: U.S. Census Bureau, Metropolitan and Micropolitan Statistical Areas Totals: 2010-2020, "Annual and Cumulative Estimates of the Components of Resident Population Change for Metropolitan Statistical Areas in the United States: April 1, 2020 to July 1, 2021 (CBSA-MET-EST2021-COMP)" and "Annual and Cumulative Estimates of Resident Population Change for Metropolitan Statistical Areas in the United States and Puerto Rico and Metropolitan Statistical Area Rankings: April 1, 2020 to July 1, 2021 (CBSA-MET-EST2021-CHG)," <www.census.gov/programs-surveys/popest/data/tables.html>, accessed March 2022.

Table 23. Population by Core Based Statistical Area (CBSA) Status and State: 2021

[331,894 represents 331,894,000. As of July 1. Covers core based statistical areas (metropolitan and micropolitan statistical areas) as delineated by the U.S. Office of Management and Budget as of March 2020. Estimates were developed from a base that incorporates the 2020 Census, Vintage 2020 estimates, and 2020 Demographic Analysis estimates. For definitions and components of all metropolitan and micropolitan statistical areas, see Appendix II. Minus sign (-) indicates decrease]

State	Total population, 2021 (1,000)	Inside Core-Based Statistical Area (metropolitan or micropolitan statistical area), 2021				Outside CBSA, 2021		Percent change, 2020–2021		
		Total		Metropolitan (1,000)	Micropolitan (1,000)	Number (1,000)	Percent	Metropolitan	Micropolitan	Outside CBSAs
		Number (1,000)	Percent							
United States.........	**331,894**	**313,892**	**94.6**	**286,473**	**27,420**	**18,001**	**5.4**	**0.1**	**0.2**	**0.2**
Alabama.................	5,040	4,634	91.9	3,853	780	406	8.1	0.5	0.1	-0.8
Alaska..................	733	540	73.7	494	46	193	26.3	0.1	-1.0	-0.3
Arizona.................	7,276	7,185	98.7	6,936	249	91	1.3	1.8	1.0	-0.8
Arkansas...............	3,026	2,540	83.9	1,941	599	486	16.1	0.9	-0.2	-0.2
California..............	39,238	38,957	99.3	38,375	582	281	0.7	-0.8	0.4	0.7
Colorado...............	5,812	5,503	94.7	5,094	409	309	5.3	0.6	0.6	1.0
Connecticut............	3,606	3,606	100.0	3,421	185	–	–	(-Z)	-0.1	(X)
Delaware...............	1,003	1,003	100.0	1,003	–	–	–	1.4	(X)	(X)
District of Columbia....	670	670	100.0	670	–	–	–	-2.8	(X)	(X)
Florida.................	21,781	21,459	98.5	21,091	367	323	1.5	1.1	0.7	1.0
Georgia.................	10,800	10,027	92.8	8,985	1,042	773	7.2	0.8	0.8	0.6
Hawaii..................	1,442	1,441	100.0	1,165	276	(Z)	(Z)	-1.4	0.9	–
Idaho...................	1,901	1,755	92.3	1,408	347	146	7.7	3.6	2.5	3.0
Illinois................	12,671	12,073	95.3	11,262	812	598	4.7	-1.1	-0.8	-0.8
Indiana.................	6,806	6,398	94.0	5,337	1,060	408	6.0	0.4	-0.2	-0.2
Iowa....................	3,193	2,437	76.3	1,967	470	756	23.7	0.5	-0.5	-0.5
Kansas..................	2,935	2,553	87.0	2,048	505	382	13.0	0.1	-0.6	-0.7
Kentucky................	4,509	3,606	80.0	2,690	916	903	20.0	0.1	0.3	-0.2
Louisiana...............	4,624	4,342	93.9	3,910	432	282	6.1	-0.7	-1.0	-0.9
Maine...................	1,372	945	68.9	821	124	427	31.1	0.7	0.7	0.8
Maryland................	6,165	6,084	98.7	6,014	70	81	1.3	-0.2	0.1	0.1
Massachusetts..........	6,985	6,970	99.8	6,949	21	14	0.2	-0.7	2.4	1.7
Michigan................	10,051	9,246	92.0	8,238	1,008	805	8.0	-0.4	0.2	0.4
Minnesota...............	5,707	5,187	90.9	4,446	742	520	9.1	(-Z)	0.3	(Z)
Mississippi.............	2,950	2,394	81.1	1,439	955	556	18.9	0.1	-0.9	-0.8
Missouri................	6,168	5,351	86.8	4,658	693	817	13.2	0.2	0.1	0.5
Montana.................	1,104	742	67.2	391	351	362	32.8	1.2	2.9	1.6
Nebraska................	1,964	1,622	82.6	1,294	328	341	17.4	0.4	-0.5	-0.3
Nevada..................	3,144	3,112	99.0	2,849	263	32	1.0	1.2	1.8	1.1
New Hampshire..........	1,389	1,337	96.3	873	464	52	3.7	0.6	1.0	2.8
New Jersey.............	9,267	9,267	100.0	9,267	–	–	–	-0.2	(X)	(X)
New Mexico.............	2,116	2,048	96.8	1,416	632	68	3.2	0.2	-0.7	-0.6
New York...............	19,836	19,443	98.0	18,476	968	393	2.0	-1.9	-0.5	0.1
North Carolina.........	10,551	9,988	94.7	8,628	1,361	563	5.3	1.2	0.4	0.1
North Dakota...........	775	581	75.0	394	187	194	25.0	0.6	-2.1	-1.3
Ohio....................	11,780	11,337	96.2	9,480	1,857	443	3.8	-0.1	-0.4	-0.3
Oklahoma................	3,987	3,441	86.3	2,695	746	546	13.7	0.9	0.2	0.1
Oregon..................	4,246	4,140	97.5	3,550	590	106	2.5	0.1	0.7	1.5
Pennsylvania...........	12,964	12,598	97.2	11,529	1,068	366	2.8	-0.3	-0.5	-0.4
Rhode Island...........	1,096	1,096	100.0	1,096	–	–	–	-0.2	(X)	(X)
South Carolina.........	5,191	4,911	94.6	4,469	443	279	5.4	1.7	-0.1	-0.7
South Dakota...........	895	682	76.1	441	241	214	23.9	1.9	0.3	-0.1
Tennessee..............	6,975	6,371	91.3	5,468	903	604	8.7	0.9	1.1	0.8
Texas...................	29,528	28,171	95.4	26,453	1,718	1,357	4.6	1.4	0.6	1.0
Utah....................	3,338	3,192	95.6	2,996	196	146	4.4	2.0	3.1	1.6
Vermont.................	646	472	73.1	227	246	173	26.9	0.5	0.3	0.3
Virginia................	8,642	7,844	90.8	7,592	251	799	9.2	0.2	-1.1	0.3
Washington.............	7,739	7,553	97.6	6,945	609	185	2.4	0.3	1.5	2.3
West Virginia..........	1,783	1,451	81.4	1,162	289	332	18.6	-0.3	-1.0	-1.2
Wisconsin..............	5,896	5,151	87.4	4,389	762	745	12.6	(-Z)	0.1	0.5
Wyoming................	579	435	75.2	180	255	144	24.8	(-Z)	0.2	1.0

– Represents zero. Z less than 500 or .05 percent. X Not applicable.

Source: U.S. Census Bureau, Metropolitan and Micropolitan Statistical Areas Totals: 2020-2021, "Annual Resident Population Estimates and Estimated Components of Resident Population Change for Metropolitan and Micropolitan Statistical Areas and their Geographic Components: April 1, 2020 to July 1, 2021," <www.census.gov/programs-surveys/popest/data/tables.html>, accessed July 2022.

Table 24. Population of Incorporated Places With 175,000 or More Inhabitants in 2021: 2020 to 2021

[Number except as noted. Estimates are based on the 2020 Census and reflect changes to the April 1, 2020 population due to geographic program revisions and the application of disclosure avoidance to protect confidentiality (DRB clearance number CBDRB-FY22-054). For population estimates methodology statements, see <www.census.gov/programs-surveys/popest/technical-documentation/methodology.html>. Geographic boundaries as of January 1, 2021. Minus sign (-) indicates decrease. See Appendix III]

City or place	Population			Population change, 2020 to 2021		Rank, 2021
	2020 (April) (estimates base)	2020 (July)	2021 (July)	Number	Percent	
Akron, Ohio....................................	190,534	190,164	189,347	-1,187	-0.6	136
Albuquerque, New Mexico....................	564,563	564,648	562,599	-1,964	-0.3	32
Amarillo, Texas.................................	200,904	200,897	201,234	330	0.2	120
Anaheim, California...........................	347,015	347,089	345,940	-1,075	-0.3	55
Anchorage municipality, Alaska............	291,247	290,637	288,121	-3,126	-1.1	73
Arlington, Texas...............................	394,218	393,985	392,786	-1,432	-0.4	50
Atlanta, Georgia..............................	498,602	499,586	496,461	-2,141	-0.4	38
Augusta-Richmond County, Georgia [1].....	202,123	201,850	201,196	-927	-0.5	121
Aurora, Colorado..............................	386,241	386,580	389,347	3,106	0.8	51
Aurora, Illinois.................................	180,688	180,355	179,266	-1,422	-0.8	144
Austin, Texas..................................	959,549	963,121	964,177	4,628	0.5	11
Bakersfield, California........................	402,907	403,401	407,615	4,708	1.2	48
Baltimore, Maryland..........................	585,708	583,132	576,498	-9,210	-1.6	30
Baton Rouge, Louisiana......................	225,128	224,480	222,185	-2,943	-1.3	101
Birmingham, Alabama........................	200,763	200,133	197,575	-3,188	-1.6	124
Boise City, Idaho..............................	235,670	235,829	237,446	1,776	0.8	94
Boston, Massachusetts.......................	676,216	674,272	654,776	-21,440	-3.2	24
Brownsville, Texas............................	186,611	186,762	187,831	1,220	0.7	137
Buffalo, New York.............................	278,302	277,908	276,807	-1,495	-0.5	78
Cape Coral, Florida...........................	194,979	196,290	204,510	9,531	4.9	116
Cary, North Carolina..........................	174,754	175,389	176,987	2,233	1.3	148
Chandler, Arizona.............................	276,330	277,556	279,458	3,128	1.1	76
Charlotte, North Carolina....................	874,541	876,747	879,709	5,168	0.6	16
Chattanooga, Tennessee.....................	181,234	181,624	182,113	879	0.5	142
Chesapeake, Virginia.........................	249,422	249,679	251,269	1,847	0.7	89
Chicago, Illinois...............................	2,747,231	2,741,730	2,696,555	-50,676	-1.8	3
Chula Vista, California........................	276,025	276,466	277,220	1,195	0.4	77
Cincinnati, Ohio...............................	310,242	310,113	308,935	-1,307	-0.4	65
Cleveland, Ohio...............................	373,091	372,032	367,991	-5,100	-1.4	54
Colorado Springs, Colorado.................	479,260	480,213	483,956	4,696	1.0	40
Columbus, Georgia...........................	206,922	206,960	205,617	-1,305	-0.6	115
Columbus, Ohio...............................	905,672	905,860	906,528	856	0.1	14
Corpus Christi, Texas.........................	317,929	317,852	317,773	-156	(-Z)	60
Dallas, Texas..................................	1,304,442	1,303,234	1,288,457	-15,985	-1.2	9
Denver, Colorado.............................	715,522	717,630	711,463	-4,059	-0.6	19
Des Moines, Iowa.............................	214,137	213,699	212,031	-2,106	-1.0	107
Detroit, Michigan.............................	639,614	638,176	632,464	-7,150	-1.1	27
Durham, North Carolina......................	283,547	284,400	285,527	1,980	0.7	74
El Paso, Texas.................................	678,587	678,598	678,415	-172	(-Z)	22
Elk Grove, California..........................	177,145	177,632	178,997	1,852	1.0	145
Eugene, Oregon...............................	174,753	174,802	175,096	343	0.2	151
Fayetteville, North Carolina.................	208,871	208,576	208,778	-93	(-Z)	113
Fontana, California...........................	208,766	208,810	210,761	1,995	1.0	109
Fort Lauderdale, Florida.....................	182,817	182,789	181,668	-1,149	-0.6	143
Fort Wayne, Indiana..........................	263,852	264,169	265,974	2,122	0.8	84
Fort Worth, Texas.............................	918,377	922,592	935,508	17,131	1.9	13
Fremont, California...........................	232,084	231,673	227,514	-4,570	-2.0	97
Fresno, California.............................	542,161	542,159	544,510	2,349	0.4	33
Frisco, Texas..................................	200,675	202,786	210,719	10,044	5.0	110
Garland, Texas................................	246,132	245,478	242,035	-4,097	-1.7	93
Gilbert town, Arizona.........................	268,302	269,206	273,136	4,834	1.8	80
Glendale, Arizona.............................	248,345	248,797	249,630	1,285	0.5	91
Glendale, California...........................	196,841	196,208	192,366	-4,475	-2.3	133
Grand Prairie, Texas..........................	196,272	196,331	197,347	1,075	0.5	126
Grand Rapids, Michigan......................	198,487	198,173	197,416	-1,071	-0.5	125
Greensboro, North Carolina.................	297,899	297,808	298,263	364	0.1	69
Henderson, Nevada...........................	317,521	319,055	322,178	4,657	1.5	57
Hialeah, Florida...............................	223,017	222,153	220,490	-2,527	-1.1	102
Houston, Texas................................	2,302,792	2,300,027	2,288,250	-14,542	-0.6	4
Huntington Beach, California................	199,140	198,707	196,652	-2,488	-1.2	129
Huntsville, Alabama..........................	214,372	215,043	216,963	2,591	1.2	106
Indianapolis, Indiana [1].....................	887,752	887,382	882,039	-5,713	-0.6	15
Irvine, California..............................	305,313	306,389	309,031	3,718	1.2	64
Irving, Texas..................................	256,793	256,873	254,198	-2,595	-1.0	88
Jacksonville, Florida..........................	949,577	950,463	954,614	5,037	0.5	12
Jersey City, New Jersey......................	292,412	291,927	283,927	-8,485	-2.9	75
Kansas City, Missouri.........................	507,969	507,932	508,394	425	0.1	37
Knoxville, Tennessee.........................	190,011	190,594	192,648	2,637	1.4	132
Laredo, Texas.................................	255,181	255,336	256,153	972	0.4	87
Las Vegas, Nevada............................	641,825	643,292	646,790	4,965	0.8	25
Lexington-Fayette urban county, Kentucky..	322,570	322,403	321,793	-777	-0.2	59
Lincoln, Nebraska.............................	291,114	291,383	292,657	1,543	0.5	71
Little Rock, Arkansas.........................	202,514	202,484	201,998	-516	-0.3	118
Long Beach, California........................	466,302	464,759	456,062	-10,240	-2.2	43
Los Angeles, California.......................	3,893,986	3,889,834	3,849,297	-44,689	-1.1	2
Louisville/Jefferson County, Kentucky [1]..	632,689	632,037	628,594	-4,095	-0.6	28
Lubbock, Texas...............................	257,180	257,882	260,993	3,813	1.5	85
Madison, Wisconsin..........................	268,414	268,846	269,196	782	0.3	81

See footnotes at end of table.

City or place	Population			Population change, 2020 to 2021		Rank, 2021
	2020 (April) (estimates base)	2020 (July)	2021 (July)	Number	Percent	
McKinney, Texas....................	195,057	197,122	202,690	7,633	3.9	117
Memphis, Tennessee................	632,207	631,326	628,127	-4,080	-0.6	29
Mesa, Arizona......................	504,500	505,860	509,475	4,975	1.0	36
Miami, Florida.....................	442,265	441,889	439,890	-2,375	-0.5	44
Milwaukee, Wisconsin...............	577,235	576,301	569,330	-7,905	-1.4	31
Minneapolis, Minnesota.............	428,403	429,014	425,336	-3,067	-0.7	46
Mobile, Alabama....................	186,833	186,411	184,952	-1,881	-1.0	138
Modesto, California................	218,471	218,459	218,771	300	0.1	104
Montgomery, Alabama...............	200,567	200,006	198,665	-1,902	-0.9	123
Moreno Valley, California...........	208,865	209,213	211,600	2,735	1.3	108
Nashville-Davidson, Tennessee [1]...	689,504	689,248	678,851	-10,653	-1.5	21
New Orleans, Louisiana.............	383,997	383,282	376,971	-7,026	-1.8	53
New York, New York................	8,804,190	8,772,978	8,467,513	-336,677	-3.8	1
Newark, New Jersey................	310,876	310,350	307,220	-3,656	-1.2	66
Newport News, Virginia.............	186,247	185,916	184,587	-1,660	-0.9	139
Norfolk, Virginia...................	238,005	237,591	235,089	-2,916	-1.2	95
North Las Vegas, Nevada............	262,678	264,216	274,133	11,455	4.4	79
Oakland, California.................	439,349	439,341	433,823	-5,526	-1.3	45
Oklahoma City, Oklahoma...........	681,387	682,760	687,725	6,338	0.9	20
Omaha, Nebraska..................	490,627	491,168	487,300	-3,327	-0.7	39
Ontario, California.................	175,518	175,945	177,963	2,445	1.4	146
Orlando, Florida...................	307,674	307,603	309,154	1,480	0.5	63
Overland Park, Kansas.............	197,295	197,587	197,106	-189	-0.1	127
Oxnard, California.................	202,185	202,242	201,879	-306	-0.2	119
Peoria, Arizona....................	191,052	191,985	194,917	3,865	2.0	131
Philadelphia, Pennsylvania.........	1,603,797	1,601,005	1,576,251	-27,546	-1.7	6
Phoenix, Arizona...................	1,607,739	1,611,345	1,624,569	16,830	1.0	5
Pittsburgh, Pennsylvania...........	303,160	302,777	300,431	-2,729	-0.9	68
Plano, Texas......................	285,900	286,668	288,253	2,353	0.8	72
Port St. Lucie, Florida..............	204,913	206,752	217,523	12,610	6.2	105
Portland, Oregon..................	652,089	652,388	641,162	-10,927	-1.7	26
Providence, Rhode Island...........	190,284	190,101	189,692	-592	-0.3	135
Raleigh, North Carolina.............	467,592	467,425	469,124	1,532	0.3	41
Rancho Cucamonga, California.......	174,628	174,572	175,142	514	0.3	150
Reno, Nevada.....................	263,436	264,116	268,851	5,415	2.1	82
Richmond, Virginia.................	226,610	226,670	226,604	-6	(-Z)	98
Riverside, California................	314,347	314,655	317,261	2,914	0.9	61
Rochester, New York...............	211,233	210,943	210,606	-627	-0.3	111
Sacramento, California..............	522,754	523,416	525,041	2,287	0.4	35
Salem, Oregon....................	175,432	175,806	177,723	2,291	1.3	147
Salt Lake City, Utah...............	198,746	199,587	200,478	1,732	0.9	122
San Antonio, Texas................	1,434,270	1,438,227	1,451,853	17,583	1.2	7
San Bernardino, California..........	221,898	221,784	222,203	305	0.1	100
San Diego, California...............	1,385,922	1,385,394	1,381,611	-4,311	-0.3	8
San Francisco, California...........	873,965	870,014	815,201	-58,764	-6.7	17
San Jose, California................	1,014,545	1,010,908	983,489	-31,056	-3.1	10
Santa Ana, California...............	310,538	309,888	309,441	-1,097	-0.4	62
Santa Clarita, California............	229,213	228,487	224,593	-4,620	-2.0	99
Santa Rosa, California..............	178,155	177,882	176,938	-1,217	-0.7	149
Scottsdale, Arizona................	241,488	241,933	242,753	1,265	0.5	92
Seattle, Washington................	735,157	738,172	733,919	-1,238	-0.2	18
Shreveport, Louisiana..............	187,993	187,338	184,021	-3,972	-2.1	141
Sioux Falls, South Dakota...........	192,683	193,233	196,528	3,845	2.0	130
Spokane, Washington...............	228,831	228,850	229,071	240	0.1	96
St. Louis, Missouri.................	301,578	300,528	293,310	-8,268	-2.7	70
St. Paul, Minnesota................	311,448	310,942	307,193	-4,255	-1.4	67
St. Petersburg, Florida.............	258,277	258,658	258,201	-76	(-Z)	86
Stockton, California................	320,759	320,745	322,120	1,361	0.4	58
Tacoma, Washington...............	219,025	219,383	219,205	180	0.1	103
Tallahassee, Florida...............	196,068	196,342	197,102	1,034	0.5	128
Tampa, Florida....................	382,769	383,980	387,050	4,281	1.1	52
Tempe, Arizona...................	179,765	180,823	184,118	4,353	2.4	140
Toledo, Ohio......................	270,726	270,041	268,508	-2,218	-0.8	83
Tucson, Arizona...................	541,349	541,859	543,242	1,893	0.3	34
Tulsa, Oklahoma..................	412,458	412,629	411,401	-1,057	-0.3	47
Urban Honolulu CDP, Hawaii [2].....	350,943	349,800	345,510	-5,433	-1.5	56
Vancouver, Washington.............	190,810	191,071	192,169	1,359	0.7	134
Virginia Beach, Virginia.............	459,470	459,373	457,672	-1,798	-0.4	42
Washington, District of Columbia....	689,545	690,093	670,050	-19,495	-2.8	23
Wichita, Kansas...................	397,070	397,117	395,699	-1,371	-0.3	49
Winston-Salem, North Carolina......	249,443	249,349	250,320	877	0.4	90
Worcester, Massachusetts..........	206,601	206,242	205,918	-683	-0.3	114
Yonkers, New York.................	211,237	210,970	209,530	-1,707	-0.8	112

Z represents less than 0.05%. [1] Represents the portion of a consolidated city that is not within one or more separately incorporated places. [2] CDP=Census Designated Place.

Source: U.S. Census Bureau, City and Town Population Totals: 2020-2021, "Annual Estimates of the Resident Population for Incorporated Places of 50,000 or More, Ranked by July 1, 2021 Population: April 1, 2020 to July 1, 2021 (SUB-IP-EST2021-ANNRNK)," <www.census.gov/data/tables/time-series/demo/popest/2020s-total-cities-and-towns.html>, accessed July 2022.

Table 25. Incorporated Places by Population Size: 2000 to 2021

[173.5 represents 173,500,000. See Appendix III]

Population size	Number of incorporated places				Population (mil.)				Percent of total			
	2000	2010	2020	2021	2000	2010	2020	2021	2000	2010	2020	2021
Total.................	19,452	19,540	19,494	19,494	173.5	192.0	209.1	208.9	100.0	100.0	100.0	100.0
1,000,000 or more........	9	9	10	9	22.9	23.6	26.1	24.6	13.2	12.3	12.5	11.8
500,000 to 999,999.......	20	24	27	28	12.9	16.1	18.8	19.7	7.4	8.4	9.0	9.4
250,000 to 499,999.......	37	40	51	53	13.3	14.0	17.3	17.7	7.7	7.3	8.3	8.5
100,000 to 249,999.......	172	200	236	238	25.5	30.2	34.6	34.5	14.7	15.7	16.6	16.5
50,000 to 99,999..........	363	432	473	470	24.9	30.1	33.0	32.7	14.4	15.7	15.8	15.7
25,000 to 49,999..........	644	723	756	762	22.6	25.2	26.3	26.5	13.0	13.1	12.6	12.7
10,000 to 24,999..........	1,435	1,542	1,586	1,593	22.6	24.2	25.0	25.1	13.0	12.6	11.9	12.0
Under 10,000..............	16,772	16,570	16,355	16,341	28.7	28.7	28.1	28.1	16.5	14.9	13.4	13.4

Source: U.S. Census Bureau, *1990 Census of Population and Housing, Population and Housing Unit Counts (CPH-2-1); Census 2000 PHC-3, Population and Housing Unit Counts; 2010 Census Redistricting Data (Public Law 94-171) Summary File*; and City and Town Population Totals: 2020-2021, "Subcounty Resident Population Estimates: April 1, 2020 to July 1, 2021 (SUB-EST2021)," <www.census.gov/data/tables/time-series/demo/popest/2020s-total-cities-and-towns.html>, accessed August 2022.

Table 26. Urban and Rural Population by State: 2000 and 2010

[222,361 represents 222,361,000. As of April 1. Resident population. Based on current urban definitions, see text, this section]

State	2000		2010			State	2000		2010		
			Urban						Urban		
	Urban (1,000)	Rural (1,000)	Number (1,000)	Percent	Rural (1,000)		Urban (1,000)	Rural (1,000)	Number (1,000)	Percent	Rural (1,000)
U.S......	222,361	59,061	249,253	80.7	59,492	MO.........	3,883	1,712	4,218	70.4	1,771
AL........	2,466	1,981	2,822	59.0	1,958	MT.........	488	414	553	55.9	436
AK........	411	216	469	66.0	241	NE.........	1,194	518	1,336	73.1	491
AZ.........	4,524	607	5,741	89.8	651	NV.........	1,829	170	2,544	94.2	157
AR........	1,404	1,269	1,638	56.2	1,278	NH.........	732	503	794	60.3	523
CA........	31,990	1,882	35,374	95.0	1,880	NJ.........	7,939	475	8,324	94.7	468
CO........	3,633	668	4,333	86.2	696	NM.........	1,364	456	1,594	77.4	465
CT........	2,988	418	3,145	88.0	429	NY.........	16,603	2,374	17,028	87.9	2,350
DE........	628	156	748	83.3	150	NC.........	4,849	3,200	6,302	66.1	3,234
DC........	572	0	602	100.0	0	ND.........	359	283	403	59.9	270
FL.........	14,270	1,712	17,140	91.2	1,661	OH.........	8,782	2,571	8,990	77.9	2,547
GA........	5,864	2,322	7,272	75.1	2,416	OK.........	2,255	1,196	2,485	66.2	1,266
HI.........	1,108	103	1,250	91.9	110	OR.........	2,694	727	3,104	81.0	727
ID.........	859	434	1,106	70.6	461	PA.........	9,464	2,817	9,991	78.7	2,711
IL.........	10,910	1,510	11,354	88.5	1,477	RI.........	953	95	955	90.7	98
IN.........	4,304	1,776	4,697	72.4	1,787	SC.........	2,427	1,585	3,068	66.3	1,558
IA.........	1,787	1,139	1,950	64.0	1,096	SD.........	391	363	461	56.7	353
KS........	1,921	768	2,117	74.2	736	TN.........	3,620	2,069	4,213	66.4	2,133
KY........	2,254	1,788	2,533	58.4	1,806	TX.........	17,204	3,648	21,298	84.7	3,848
LA........	3,246	1,223	3,318	73.2	1,216	UT.........	1,970	263	2,504	90.6	260
ME........	513	762	514	38.7	815	VT.........	232	376	243	38.9	382
MD........	4,559	738	5,034	87.2	739	VA.........	5,170	1,909	6,037	75.5	1,964
MA........	5,801	548	6,022	92.0	526	WA.........	4,831	1,063	5,652	84.1	1,073
MI.........	7,419	2,519	7,370	74.6	2,514	WV.........	833	976	903	48.7	950
MN........	3,490	1,429	3,886	73.3	1,418	WI.........	3,664	1,700	3,990	70.2	1,697
MS........	1,387	1,457	1,464	49.4	1,503	WY.........	321	172	365	64.8	199

Source: U.S. Census Bureau, 2000 Census of Population and Housing, *Population and Housing Unit Counts PHC-3*; 2010 Census of Population and Housing, *Population and Housing Unit Counts, CPH-2-1, United States Summary*; and "Percent Urban and Rural in 2010 by State," <www.census.gov/programs-surveys/geography/guidance/geo-areas/urban-rural/2010-urban-rural.html>, accessed March 2013.

Table 27. Population in Coastal Watershed Counties: 1970 to 2019

[3,537 represents 3,537,000. Data for 1960 to 2010 as of April 1; 2019 data as of July 1. Data for 1960 through 2000 are based on 675 counties in areas as defined by U.S. National Oceanic and Atmospheric Administration, 1992. Beginning 2010, data cover 678 counties and equivalent areas in a coastal watershed. See Appendix III]

Year		Counties in coastal regions					Balance of U.S.
	Total	Total	Atlantic	Gulf of Mexico	Great Lakes	Pacific	
Land area, 2010 (1,000 sq. mi.)......	3,537	888	147	116	115	510	2,649
POPULATION							
1970 (millions)............................	203.3	110.0	51.1	10.0	26.0	22.9	93.3
1980 (millions)............................	226.5	119.8	53.7	13.1	26.0	27.0	106.7
1990 (millions)............................	248.7	133.4	59.0	15.2	25.9	33.2	115.3
2000 (millions)............................	281.4	148.3	65.2	18.0	27.3	37.8	133.1
2010 (millions)............................	308.7	159.7	70.2	20.9	27.2	41.4	149.0
2019 (millions)............................	328.2	168.9	73.9	23.4	27.2	44.4	159.4
1970 (percent)............................	100.0	54.0	25.0	5.0	13.0	11.0	46.0
1980 (percent)............................	100.0	53.0	24.0	6.0	11.0	12.0	47.0
1990 (percent)............................	100.0	53.6	23.7	6.1	10.4	13.3	46.4
2000 (percent)............................	100.0	53.0	23.0	6.0	10.0	13.0	47.0
2010 (percent)............................	100.0	51.7	22.7	6.8	8.8	13.4	48.3
2019 (percent)............................	100.0	51.4	22.5	7.1	8.3	13.5	48.6

Source: U.S. Census Bureau, U.S. Census of Population: 1960 and 1970; 1980 Census of Population, Vol. 1, Chapter A (PC80-1-A-1), U.S. Summary; 1990 Census of Population and Housing (CPH1); "Annual Estimates of the Resident Population for Counties: April 1, 2000 to July 1, 2009," March 2010 <www2.census.gov/programs-surveys/popest/datasets/2000-2009/counties/totals/>; and "County Population Totals: 2010-2019," <www.census.gov/programs-surveys/popest/data/tables.html>, accessed July 2020.

Table 28. Geographic Mobility Status of the Population by Selected Characteristics: 1950 to 2021

[Numbers in thousands (148,400 represents 148,400,000). For persons 1 year old and over. Based on comparison of place of residence in year of survey vs. 1 year earlier. Movers are all people who were living in a different home at the end of the period rather than at the beginning. Excludes members of the Armed Forces except those living off post or with their families on post. Movers from Puerto Rico and the United States Island Areas are counted as movers from abroad. Based on Current Population Survey, Annual Social and Economic Supplement. See text, this section and Appendix III]

Mobility period	Number (1,000)			Percent distribution					
						Movers (different house in U.S.)			
								Different county		Movers from abroad
	Total persons	Non-movers	Movers	Non-movers	Total movers	Same county	Same state	Different state	
1950-1951.............	148,400	116,936	31,464	78.8	21.2	13.9	3.6	3.5	0.2
1960-1961.............	177,354	140,821	36,533	79.4	20.6	13.7	3.1	3.2	0.6
1970-1971.............	201,506	163,800	37,705	81.3	18.7	11.4	3.1	3.4	0.8
1975-1976.............	208,069	171,276	36,793	82.3	17.7	10.8	3.4	3.0	0.6
1980-1981.............	221,641	183,442	38,200	82.8	17.2	10.4	3.4	2.8	0.6
1985-1986.............	232,998	189,760	43,237	81.4	18.6	11.3	3.7	3.0	0.5
1990-1991.............	244,884	203,345	41,539	83.0	17.0	10.3	3.2	2.9	0.6
1995-1996.............	260,406	217,868	42,537	83.7	16.3	10.3	3.1	2.5	0.5
2000-2001 [1]........	275,611	236,605	39,007	85.8	14.2	8.0	2.7	2.8	0.6
2001-2002.............	278,160	237,049	41,111	85.2	14.8	8.5	2.9	2.8	0.6
2002-2003.............	282,556	242,463	40,093	85.8	14.2	8.3	2.7	2.7	0.4
2003-2004 [2]........	284,367	245,372	38,995	86.3	13.7	7.9	2.8	2.6	0.4
2004-2005 [3]........	287,148	247,261	39,888	86.1	13.9	7.9	2.7	2.6	0.6
2005-2006.............	289,781	249,945	39,837	86.3	13.7	8.6	2.8	2.0	0.4
2006-2007.............	292,749	254,068	38,681	86.8	13.2	8.6	2.5	1.7	0.4
2007-2008.............	294,851	259,685	35,167	88.1	11.9	7.8	2.1	1.6	0.4
2008-2009.............	297,182	260,077	37,105	87.5	12.5	8.4	2.1	1.6	0.4
2009-2010 [4]........	300,419	262,975	37,445	87.5	12.5	8.6	2.1	1.4	0.3
2010-2011 [4]........	302,640	267,602	35,038	88.4	11.6	7.7	1.9	1.6	0.4
2011-2012.............	304,924	268,436	36,488	88.0	12.0	7.7	2.2	1.7	0.4
2012-2013.............	307,243	271,325	35,918	88.3	11.7	7.5	2.3	1.6	0.3
2013-2014 [5]........	309,601	273,920	35,681	88.5	11.5	7.6	2.1	1.5	0.4
2014-2015.............	312,295	275,971	36,324	88.4	11.6	7.3	2.1	1.6	0.5
2015-2016.............	314,992	279,854	35,138	88.8	11.2	6.9	2.4	1.5	0.4
2016-2017.............	316,550	281,647	34,902	89.0	11.0	6.8	2.1	1.7	0.4
2017-2018.............	319,319	286,967	32,352	89.9	10.1	6.2	2.0	1.5	0.4
2018-2019.............	320,667	289,296	31,371	90.2	9.8	5.9	2.1	1.5	0.4
2019-2020.............	321,620	291,840	29,780	90.7	9.3	5.4	2.2	1.3	0.3
2020-2021.............	322,607	295,547	27,059	91.6	8.4	4.9	1.9	1.4	0.2

[1] Population controls consistent with 2000 Census. [2] The migration question wording changed in 2004. Before 2004, it asked about Residence on March 1 of the previous year. As of 2004, it asked about residence one year ago. See <www.census.gov/topics/population/migration/guidance/user-notes.html> for more information. [3] Caution should be used when comparing numbers/rates of movers within the same county and from a different county between the 1999-2000 to 2004-2005 period with other periods. For more information see <www.census.gov/topics/population/migration/guidance/impact-of-processing-on-cps-interstate-migration-rates.html>. [4] Population controls consistent with 2010 Census. [5] The source of 2014 data for this table is the CPS ASEC sample of 98,000 addresses. The 2014 CPS ASEC included redesigned questions for income and health insurance coverage. For more information, see <www.census.gov/topics/population/migration/guidance/user-notes.html>.

Source: U.S. Census Bureau, "CPS Historical Migration/Geographic Mobility Tables," November 2021, <www.census.gov/data/tables/time-series/demo/geographic-mobility/historic.html>.

Table 29. Movers by Type of Move and Reason for Moving: 2021

[27,059 represents 27,059,000. As of March. For persons 1 year old and over. Based on comparison of place of residence in 2021 vs. 2020. Excludes members of the Armed Forces except those living off post or with their families on post. Based on Current Population Survey, Annual Social and Economic Supplement. See text, this section and Appendix III]

Reason for move	All movers	Intra-county	Inter-county	From abroad	Reason for move	All movers	Intra-county	Inter-county	From abroad
Total (1,000).....................	27,059	15,805	10,644	611	**Housing–related reasons......**	**45.7**	**55.3**	**33.2**	**18.0**
					Wanted to own home/not rent.....	7.5	9.1	5.4	0.8
PERCENT DISTRIBUTION					New/better/larger housing [1].......	17.2	22.7	9.8	4.7
Total..............................	100.0	100.0	100.0	100.0	Better neighborhood/less crime...	6.0	6.2	5.8	3.6
Family–related reasons........	**24.6**	**23.5**	**26.6**	**15.7**	Cheaper housing.....................	8.9	9.9	7.4	8.8
Change in marital status...........	4.8	4.7	5.0	2.5	Foreclosure/eviction.................	0.5	0.4	0.6	–
To establish own household.......	10.6	12.3	8.7	2.1	Other housing........................	5.7	6.9	4.2	–
Other family reasons..............	9.2	6.6	12.9	11.1	**Other reasons...................**	**13.9**	**11.9**	**16.2**	**25.7**
Work–related reasons..........	**15.8**	**9.3**	**24.0**	**40.6**	Unmarried partner relationship. ..	3.9	3.9	3.9	4.7
New job/job transfer...............	8.8	2.5	16.7	33.7	Attend/leave college...............	3.0	2.3	4.2	3.1
To look for work/lost job...........	1.5	0.8	2.2	5.2	Change of climate..................	0.7	0.3	1.4	0.3
Closer to work/easier commute...	4.3	5.2	3.3	–	Health reasons.....................	1.6	1.6	1.7	0.2
Retired.............................	0.8	0.5	1.4	–	Natural disaster.....................	0.3	0.2	0.4	0.7
Other job–related reason..........	0.3	0.2	0.4	1.6	Other reason.......................	4.3	3.6	4.5	16.7

– Represents or rounds to zero. [1] In 2020, this category was expanded from "wanted new or better house/apartment" to "wanted newer/better/larger house or apartment."

Source: U.S. Census Bureau, "Geographic Mobility: 2020 to 2021," November 2021, <www.census.gov/topics/population/migration/data/tables.html>.

Table 30. Geographic Mobility Status of the Population by Selected Characteristics: 2020 to 2021

[322,607 represents 322,607,000. As of March. For persons 1 year old and over, unless otherwise noted. Based on comparison of place of residence in year shown vs. previous year. Excludes members of the Armed Forces except those living off post or with their families on post. Based on Current Population Survey, Annual Social and Economic Supplement. See text, this section and Appendix III. For composition of regions, see map, inside front cover]

Mobility period and characteristic	Total persons (1,000)	Percent distribution by geographic mobility						
		Non–movers	Movers (different house in United States)					Movers from abroad
			Total	Same county	Different county			
					Total	Same state	Different state	
2020 to 2021, total.....................	**322,607**	**91.6**	**8.2**	**4.9**	**3.3**	**1.9**	**1.4**	**0.2**
By age:								
1 to 4 years old..............................	15,504	87.8	11.9	7.5	4.4	2.6	1.7	0.3
5 to 9 years old..............................	20,194	91.6	8.2	5.0	3.2	1.9	1.3	0.2
10 to 14 years old...........................	20,651	93.0	6.8	4.3	2.5	1.2	1.3	0.2
15 to 19 years old...........................	20,655	92.0	7.8	4.8	3.0	1.9	1.1	0.3
20 to 24 years old...........................	21,022	81.7	18.0	10.3	7.7	4.9	2.8	0.3
25 to 29 years old...........................	22,592	82.2	17.5	11.1	6.4	3.9	2.5	0.3
30 to 44 years old...........................	64,695	89.7	10.1	6.0	4.1	2.4	1.7	0.3
45 to 64 years old...........................	81,455	94.6	5.2	3.0	2.3	1.4	0.9	0.1
65 to 74 years old...........................	33,040	97.2	2.8	1.4	1.3	0.6	0.7	–
75 to 84 years old...........................	16,804	97.9	2.1	1.4	0.7	0.4	0.3	–
85 years old and over.......................	5,992	97.2	2.8	1.6	1.2	0.6	0.6	–
By region:								
Northeast.....................................	54,224	92.7	7.1	4.1	3.0	2.1	1.0	0.1
Midwest.......................................	66,796	91.5	8.4	5.1	3.3	2.2	1.1	0.1
South..	124,208	91.3	8.4	4.8	3.6	2.1	1.5	0.3
West...	77,379	91.3	8.5	5.5	3.0	1.3	1.6	0.2
By housing tenure:								
Owner occupied units.......................	220,338	95.1	4.8	2.6	2.1	1.3	0.8	0.1
Renter occupied units.......................	102,268	84.0	15.6	9.8	5.8	3.3	2.5	0.4
Persons 16 years old and over...........	**262,084**	**91.7**	**8.1**	**4.8**	**3.3**	**2.0**	**1.3**	**0.2**
Civilian labor force...........................	159,944	90.3	9.6	5.8	3.8	2.3	1.5	0.2
Employed......................................	149,966	90.5	9.4	5.7	3.7	2.3	1.4	0.2
Unemployed...................................	9,978	87.6	12.1	7.1	5.0	2.5	2.5	0.3
Armed Forces.................................	1,089	77.2	19.7	8.1	11.7	1.9	9.7	3.0
Not in labor force.............................	101,051	94.1	5.7	3.2	2.5	1.4	1.1	0.2
By occupation:								
Employed civilians, 16 years old and over...	149,966	90.5	9.4	5.7	3.7	2.3	1.4	0.2
Management, business, and financial.......	27,518	91.2	8.7	4.9	3.8	2.1	1.6	0.1
Professional.................................	36,778	89.3	10.5	6.3	4.2	2.5	1.7	0.2
Service.......................................	23,435	89.8	10.0	6.3	3.7	2.5	1.2	0.2
Sales...	14,232	91.3	8.5	5.2	3.3	2.0	1.3	0.1
Office and administrative support...........	15,850	91.0	9.0	5.8	3.2	2.0	1.2	0.1
Farming, fishing, and forestry..............	997	92.1	7.9	4.7	3.2	2.8	0.4	–
Construction and extraction.................	7,584	91.0	8.9	5.6	3.3	2.2	1.1	0.1
Installation, maintenance, and repair.......	4,861	93.0	7.0	4.1	2.9	1.9	1.0	–
Production....................................	7,676	90.4	9.5	5.7	3.8	2.6	1.1	0.2
Transportation and material moving.........	11,036	90.3	9.4	5.9	3.6	2.5	1.0	0.3

– Represents or rounds to zero.

Source: U.S. Census Bureau, "Geographic Mobility: 2020 to 2021," November 2021, <www.census.gov/topics/population/migration/data/tables.html>.

Table 31. Geographic Mobility Status of Households by Household Income: 2021

[129,943 represents 129,943,000. As of March. Covers householders 15 years old and over. Based on comparison of place of residence in 2021 vs. 2020. Excludes members of the Armed Forces except those living off post or with their families on post. Based on Current Population Survey, Annual Social and Economic Supplement. See text, this section and Appendix III]

Household income in 2020	Total (1,000)	Percent distribution						
		Non–movers	Movers (different house in United States)					Movers from abroad
			Total	Same county	Different county			
					Total	Same state	Different state	
Householders, 15 years and over......	**129,943**	**91.5**	**8.4**	**5.0**	**3.4**	**2.0**	**1.4**	**0.2**
Under $10,000 or loss......................	7,137	88.4	11.0	6.7	4.2	2.5	1.8	0.6
$10,000 to $19,999.........................	10,778	91.9	7.9	4.9	3.0	1.8	1.2	0.2
$20,000 to $29,999.........................	10,795	91.1	8.9	5.0	3.8	2.6	1.2	–
$30,000 to $39,999.........................	10,615	90.7	9.2	5.4	3.9	2.2	1.7	0.1
$40,000 to $49,999.........................	9,787	91.4	8.4	5.6	2.8	1.6	1.2	0.2
$50,000 to $59,999.........................	9,364	90.6	9.3	5.5	3.8	2.5	1.3	0.1
$60,000 to $69,999.........................	8,086	90.3	9.5	5.8	3.7	1.7	2.0	0.2
$70,000 to $84,999.........................	11,143	90.7	9.1	5.4	3.7	2.0	1.7	0.2
$85,000 to $99,999.........................	8,635	92.4	7.5	4.6	2.9	1.6	1.2	0.1
$100,000 and over..........................	43,602	92.6	7.3	4.1	3.2	1.9	1.3	0.1

– Represents less than 0.05%.

Source: U.S. Census Bureau, "Geographic Mobility: 2020 to 2021," November 2021, <www.census.gov/topics/population/migration/data/tables.html>.

Table 32. Geographic Mobility Status of Resident Population by State: 2020

[In percent, except as indicated (325,951 represents 325,951,000). Based on comparison of place of residence in 2020 vs. 2019. Data are based on 2020 American Community Survey (ACS) 1-year experimental estimates. The coronavirus disease 2019 (COVID-19) pandemic impacted 2020 ACS data collection and quality, and standard estimates did not meet statistical quality standards. The Census Bureau does not recommend comparing experimental estimates to standard ACS estimates. For more information, see <www.census.gov/programs-surveys/acs/data/experimental-data.html>. The ACS universe includes the household population and the population living in institutions, college dormitories, and other group quarters. Based on a sample and subject to sampling variability. See text, this section and Appendix III]

| State | Population 1 year old and over (1,000) | Same house in 2019 | Different house in United States in 2019 | | Different county | | | Abroad in 2019 |
			Total	Same county	Total	Same state	Different state	
United States.............	**325,951**	**87.6**	**11.9**	**6.5**	**5.3**	**3.1**	**2.2**	**0.5**
Alabama....................	4,868	88.3	11.3	6.3	5.1	2.9	2.2	0.3
Alaska.....................	722	84.1	15.2	8.3	6.9	3.1	3.8	0.7
Arizona....................	7,351	84.8	14.8	9.4	5.4	1.8	3.6	0.5
Arkansas..................	2,998	87.4	12.4	6.5	5.9	3.6	2.3	0.2
California.................	38,951	88.9	10.5	6.6	3.9	2.8	1.1	0.6
Colorado..................	5,749	84.2	15.4	7.3	8.1	4.6	3.5	0.4
Connecticut...............	3,527	89.1	10.3	5.7	4.6	2.0	2.6	0.6
Delaware..................	978	89.6	10.1	5.4	4.6	1.1	3.5	0.4
District of Columbia........	706	80.6	18.2	10.2	8.0	(X)	8.0	1.1
Florida....................	21,511	85.9	13.3	7.2	6.1	3.1	3.0	0.8
Georgia...................	10,589	87.3	12.3	5.3	7.0	4.5	2.5	0.4
Hawaii....................	1,389	87.9	11.2	6.8	4.4	0.8	3.6	0.9
Idaho.....................	1,811	83.8	15.9	8.1	7.8	3.5	4.3	0.3
Illinois....................	12,451	88.8	10.8	6.8	4.0	2.4	1.6	0.4
Indiana...................	6,684	87.3	12.5	6.8	5.6	3.6	2.0	0.2
Iowa......................	3,126	87.3	12.5	6.6	5.8	3.8	2.1	0.3
Kansas...................	2,880	85.5	14.1	7.6	6.5	3.4	3.1	0.4
Kentucky..................	4,426	87.4	12.3	6.5	5.8	3.5	2.3	0.3
Louisiana.................	4,593	88.7	11.0	6.2	4.8	3.1	1.7	0.3
Maine.....................	1,340	88.5	11.0	5.6	5.4	2.7	2.7	0.6
Maryland..................	5,994	88.0	11.4	5.9	5.5	2.7	2.8	0.6
Massachusetts............	6,825	88.5	10.9	5.7	5.2	2.8	2.4	0.6
Michigan..................	9,864	88.8	10.9	6.1	4.7	3.4	1.4	0.3
Minnesota................	5,589	87.9	11.8	5.8	6.0	4.2	1.8	0.3
Mississippi...............	2,930	89.0	10.8	5.4	5.4	3.2	2.2	0.2
Missouri..................	6,078	87.4	12.3	6.5	5.8	3.4	2.5	0.3
Montana..................	1,072	86.8	12.9	6.6	6.3	2.9	3.4	0.3
Nebraska.................	1,915	86.5	13.1	7.1	6.0	3.7	2.3	0.4
Nevada...................	3,108	85.4	14.2	9.2	5.0	0.6	4.4	0.4
New Hampshire............	1,355	87.5	12.3	5.2	7.1	2.5	4.6	0.3
New Jersey................	8,782	89.9	9.5	4.8	4.7	2.6	2.0	0.6
New Mexico...............	2,083	88.3	11.2	5.8	5.4	2.2	3.2	0.5
New York..................	19,125	90.4	9.0	5.1	3.9	2.6	1.3	0.6
North Carolina.............	10,491	87.3	12.2	5.8	6.4	3.4	3.0	0.4
North Dakota..............	755	86.1	13.6	7.2	6.4	3.4	3.0	0.3
Ohio......................	11,562	88.1	11.6	7.0	4.6	3.1	1.5	0.3
Oklahoma.................	3,939	86.0	13.6	7.3	6.3	3.8	2.5	0.4
Oregon...................	4,203	85.5	14.0	7.3	6.7	3.5	3.2	0.5
Pennsylvania..............	12,659	89.2	10.4	5.9	4.5	2.7	1.8	0.3
Rhode Island..............	1,047	89.3	10.1	5.0	5.1	1.9	3.2	0.7
South Carolina............	5,166	87.3	12.3	5.7	6.6	3.2	3.4	0.3
South Dakota..............	881	87.6	12.2	5.5	6.7	3.8	2.9	0.3
Tennessee................	6,812	86.9	12.9	6.8	6.0	3.0	3.0	0.2
Texas....................	29,011	86.2	13.3	7.5	5.8	4.0	1.8	0.6
Utah.....................	3,204	86.3	13.3	7.9	5.3	2.7	2.6	0.5
Vermont..................	618	86.8	12.7	5.9	6.7	1.9	4.9	0.5
Virginia...................	8,509	86.8	12.5	5.0	7.5	4.6	2.9	0.7
Washington...............	7,607	85.7	13.7	8.3	5.4	2.7	2.8	0.6
West Virginia..............	1,768	89.2	10.6	5.7	4.9	2.7	2.2	0.2
Wisconsin................	5,774	88.4	11.3	6.3	5.0	3.3	1.8	0.3
Wyoming..................	575	83.9	15.8	8.9	6.8	2.4	4.5	0.4

X Not applicable.

Source: U.S. Census Bureau, 2020 ACS 1-Year Experimental Data Tables, "Table XK200701. Geographical Mobility in the Past Year in the United States," <www.census.gov/programs-surveys/acs/data/experimental-data.html>, accessed July 2022.

Table 33. Persons 65 Years Old and Over—Characteristics by Sex: 2000 to 2021

[In percent except as noted (32.6 represents 32,600,000). As of March, except as noted. Covers civilian noninstitutional population. Excludes members of Armed Forces except those living off post or with their families on post. Data for 2000 based on 1990 Census population controls; data for 2010 based on 2000 Census population controls; and data for 2020 and 2021 based on 2010 Census population controls. Beginning 2005, data based on an expanded sample of households. Based on Current Population Survey. See text, this section]

Characteristic	Total				Male				Female			
	2000	2010	2020	2021	2000	2010	2020	2021	2000	2010	2020	2021
Total (million)...............	**32.6**	**38.6**	**54.6**	**55.8**	**13.9**	**16.8**	**24.9**	**25.2**	**18.7**	**21.8**	**29.7**	**30.6**
PERCENT DISTRIBUTION												
Marital status:												
Never married..................	3.9	4.3	5.8	6.1	4.2	4.1	6.0	6.2	3.6	4.5	5.6	6.0
Married......................	57.2	57.6	60.5	59.4	75.2	74.5	72.5	71.6	43.8	44.5	50.2	49.3
Spouse present...............	54.6	55.2	58.1	57.1	72.6	71.7	69.9	69.0	41.3	42.4	48.2	47.2
Spouse absent [1]............	2.6	2.4	2.4	2.3	2.6	2.8	2.6	2.6	2.5	2.1	2.0	2.1
Widowed....................	32.1	28.1	20.9	21.3	14.4	12.7	10.4	10.9	45.3	39.9	29.7	29.8
Divorced....................	6.7	10.0	12.9	13.3	6.1	8.7	11.1	11.3	7.2	11.1	14.5	14.9
Educational attainment:												
Less than 9th grade............	16.7	10.2	5.2	4.8	17.8	10.2	5.0	4.8	15.9	10.1	5.3	4.9
Completed 9th to 12th grade, but no high school diploma...........	13.8	10.3	6.3	6.0	12.7	9.7	5.7	5.9	14.7	10.8	6.7	6.1
High school graduate..............	35.9	36.4	30.5	31.2	30.4	32.0	27.9	28.0	39.9	39.8	32.6	33.8
Some college or associate's degree......................	18.0	20.6	25.3	25.1	17.8	19.7	24.2	24.1	18.2	21.2	26.2	25.9
Bachelor's or advanced degree........	15.6	22.5	32.8	32.8	21.4	28.4	37.1	37.2	11.4	18.0	29.1	29.3
Labor force status: [2]												
Employed....................	12.4	16.2	18.0	18.0	16.9	20.5	22.3	22.3	9.1	12.9	14.5	14.5
Unemployed..................	0.4	1.2	1.5	0.8	0.6	1.6	1.6	1.0	0.3	0.9	1.3	0.7
Not in labor force..............	87.2	82.6	80.6	81.1	82.5	77.9	76.1	76.6	90.6	86.2	84.2	84.8
Percent below poverty level [3]............	9.7	8.9	8.9	9.0	6.9	6.6	7.2	7.6	11.8	10.7	10.3	10.1

[1] Includes separated. [2] Annual averages of monthly figures. Source: U.S. Bureau of Labor Statistics, "Labor Force Statistics from the Current Population Survey," <www.bls.gov/cps/tables.htm>. [3] Poverty status based on income in preceding year.

Source: Except as noted, U.S. Census Bureau, Current Population Reports, P20-546, and earlier reports; series P-23, No. 59; series P-60, No. 226; "The Older Population in the United States: March 2002 Detailed Tables (PPL-167)," May 2003; and "Educational Attainment," <www.census.gov/topics/education/educational-attainment.html>, "America's Families and Living Arrangements," <www.census.gov/topics/families/families-and-households/data/tables.html>, and "Poverty," <www.census.gov/data/tables/time-series/demo/income-poverty/cps-pov.html>, accessed March 2022.

Table 34. Persons 65 Years Old and Over by Living Arrangement: 2010 to 2019

[In thousands (40,434 represents 40,434,000), except as indicated. Based on the American Community Survey (ACS). Based on a sample and subject to sampling variability; see text, this section and Appendix III]

Relationship by household type	2010		2015		2018		2019	
	Number	Percent distribution	Number	Percent distribution	Number	Percent distribution	Number	Percent distribution
Total...................	**40,434**	**100.0**	**47,732**	**100.0**	**52,423**	**100.0**	**54,074**	**100.0**
In households..............	38,869	96.1	46,232	96.9	50,905	97.1	52,561	97.2
In family households..............	26,809	66.3	32,232	67.5	35,597	67.9	36,512	67.5
Householder..................	13,379	33.1	15,801	33.1	17,481	33.3	17,967	33.2
Spouse......................	9,563	23.7	11,707	24.5	13,090	25.0	13,483	24.9
Parent......................	2,208	5.5	2,637	5.5	2,704	5.2	2,680	5.0
Parent-in-law.................	661	1.6	766	1.6	811	1.5	803	1.5
Other relatives...............	807	2.0	1,030	2.2	1,165	2.2	1,218	2.3
Nonrelatives.................	191	0.5	291	0.6	345	0.7	362	0.7
In nonfamily households........	12,060	29.8	14,000	29.3	15,308	29.2	16,050	29.7
Householder..................	11,495	28.4	13,199	27.7	14,362	27.4	15,029	27.8
Male.......................	3,417	8.5	4,244	8.9	4,789	9.1	5,104	9.4
Living alone...............	3,124	7.7	3,851	8.1	4,314	8.2	4,560	8.4
Female.....................	8,078	20.0	8,955	18.8	9,572	18.3	9,925	18.4
Living alone...............	7,784	19.3	8,563	17.9	9,108	17.4	9,424	17.4
Nonrelatives.................	565	1.4	801	1.7	946	1.8	1,021	1.9
In group quarters..................	1,565	3.9	1,500	3.1	1,518	2.9	1,513	2.8

Source: U.S. Census Bureau, American Community Survey, B09020, "Relationship by Household Type (Including Living Alone) for the Population 65 Years and Over," <data.census.gov>, accessed November 2020.

Table 35. Persons 65 Years Old and Over with a Disability by Type and Sex: 2019

[In thousands (17,671 represents 17,671,000). Based on data from the American Community Survey (ACS). Disability data limited to civilian noninstitutionalized population. Based on a sample and subject to sampling variability; see text in this section, and Appendix III]

Type of disability	Number					Percent				
	Total age 65 and over	Males		Females		Total age 65 and over	Males		Females	
		Age 65 to 74	Age 75 and over	Age 65 to 74	Age 75 and over		Age 65 to 74	Age 75 and over	Age 65 to 74	Age 75 and over
Persons with any disability...	**17,671**	**3,719**	**4,130**	**3,804**	**6,019**	**33.5**	**25.6**	**45.7**	**22.8**	**48.1**
With a hearing difficulty...........	7,227	1,772	2,341	909	2,204	13.7	12.2	25.9	5.4	17.6
With a vision difficulty.............	3,164	604	719	668	1,174	6.0	4.2	7.9	4.0	9.4
With a cognitive difficulty...........	4,358	779	1,010	827	1,741	8.3	5.4	11.2	5.0	13.9
With an ambulatory difficulty.....	11,268	1,954	2,351	2,656	4,306	21.3	13.5	26.0	15.9	34.4
With a self-care difficulty.........	3,983	602	922	704	1,755	7.5	4.1	10.2	4.2	14.0
With an independent living difficulty.........................	7,291	950	1,603	1,352	3,386	13.8	6.5	17.7	8.1	27.0

Source: U.S. Census Bureau, 2019 American Community Survey, Tables B18101, B18102, B18103, B18104, B18105, B18106, and B18107, <data.census.gov>, accessed November 2020.

Table 36. Selected Characteristics of Racial Groups and Hispanic or Latino Population: 2019

[In thousands (224,899 represents 224,899,000), except as indicated. The American Community Survey universe includes the household population and the population living in institutions, college dormitories, and other group quarters. Based on a sample and subject to sampling variability; see text, this section and Appendix III]

Characteristic	Total population	White alone	Black or African American alone	American Indian, Alaska Native alone	Asian alone	Native Hawaiian and Other Pacific Islander alone	Some other race alone	Two or more races	Hispanic or Latino origin [1]	White alone, not Hispanic or Latino
EDUCATIONAL ATTAINMENT										
Persons 25 years old and over, total	224,899	167,334	27,337	1,802	13,381	395	9,753	4,896	34,949	144,203
Less than 9th grade	10,875	6,462	977	119	988	22	2,087	220	5,949	2,825
9th to 12th grade, no diploma	14,744	9,598	2,560	214	647	32	1,382	311	4,377	6,822
High school graduate (includes equivalency)	60,482	45,168	8,733	568	1,932	140	2,842	1,100	9,854	38,699
Some college, no degree	44,914	33,605	6,518	452	1,503	90	1,579	1,166	6,225	29,439
Associate's degree	19,382	14,887	2,385	160	877	39	568	466	2,380	13,256
Bachelor's degree	45,730	35,600	3,811	187	4,126	49	927	1,031	4,200	32,610
Graduate degree	28,771	22,015	2,353	103	3,309	23	367	602	1,964	20,552
OCCUPATION										
Employed civilian population, 16 years old and over, total	158,759	116,195	19,025	1,176	9,860	300	7,994	4,209	28,205	97,731
Management, business, science, and arts occupations	63,267	48,524	5,845	334	5,385	83	1,490	1,606	6,718	43,786
Management, business, and financial occupations	25,587	20,278	2,147	140	1,740	34	637	612	2,839	18,262
Computer, engineering, and science occupations	10,182	7,207	711	37	1,730	13	202	281	906	6,575
Education, legal, community service, arts, and media occupations	17,741	13,850	1,887	110	932	24	453	485	2,085	12,389
Healthcare practitioners and technical occupations	9,757	7,189	1,100	47	983	12	198	227	888	6,560
Service occupations	28,094	18,443	4,629	280	1,645	67	2,151	880	6,874	14,161
Sales and office occupations	32,355	24,051	4,074	234	1,608	66	1,422	899	5,490	20,358
Natural resources, construction, and maintenance occupations	14,041	10,947	952	149	273	27	1,387	306	4,323	8,187
Farming, fishing, and forestry occupations	997	738	38	15	15	1	172	19	516	414
Construction and extraction occupations	8,181	6,311	522	95	115	16	953	169	2,874	4,494
Installation, maintenance, and repair occupations	4,863	3,897	392	39	144	11	262	118	934	3,280
Production, transportation, and material moving occupations	21,002	14,229	3,524	180	949	57	1,544	518	4,799	11,238
Production occupations	8,872	6,188	1,231	72	512	22	657	190	2,013	4,935
Transportation occupations	6,260	4,269	1,160	53	236	13	377	152	1,265	3,452
Material moving occupations	5,870	3,773	1,133	55	201	22	510	176	1,521	2,852
FAMILY INCOME IN THE PAST 12 MONTHS										
Total families	79,594	60,304	9,085	619	4,405	125	3,398	1,657	12,483	51,914
Less than $10,000	2,648	1,565	656	45	109	5	186	82	615	1,179
$10,000 to $19,999	3,652	2,269	804	54	161	6	258	100	885	1,692
$20,000 to $29,999	5,066	3,345	957	70	204	9	359	122	1,229	2,539
$30,000 to $39,999	5,728	3,998	931	60	234	11	367	128	1,276	3,159
$40,000 to $49,999	5,812	4,218	822	53	228	10	352	129	1,201	3,432
$50,000 to $59,999	5,684	4,266	711	51	229	9	302	116	1,071	3,548
$60,000 to $74,999	8,187	6,247	956	63	336	14	411	161	1,416	5,321
$75,000 to $99,999	11,481	9,046	1,129	79	533	21	451	223	1,693	7,892
$100,000 to $124,999	9,009	7,227	757	52	500	14	285	176	1,125	6,456
$125,000 to $149,999	6,215	5,035	480	34	371	9	166	121	692	4,551
$150,000 to $199,999	7,305	5,915	489	31	563	10	155	142	684	5,427
$200,000 or more	8,807	7,174	393	28	938	8	107	159	596	6,718
Median family income in the past 12 months (in dollars) [2]	80,944	85,878	54,938	54,920	107,233	73,656	55,378	74,072	59,590	90,471
POVERTY STATUS IN THE PAST 12 MONTHS [3]										
Persons below poverty level	39,490	23,828	8,557	634	1,761	100	2,935	1,674	10,201	17,352
Families below poverty level	6,830	4,072	1,581	114	288	15	557	203	1,865	2,871
HOUSING TENURE										
Total householders	122,803	93,145	15,382	952	6,052	170	4,422	2,678	16,682	81,930
Owner-occupied	78,725	64,910	6,457	520	3,667	68	1,794	1,309	8,020	59,103
Renter-occupied	44,078	28,235	8,926	432	2,385	102	2,629	1,369	8,662	22,828

[1] Persons of Hispanic origin may be of any race. [2] For definition of median, see Guide to Tabular Presentation. [3] For explanation of poverty level, see text, Section 13.

Source: U.S. Census Bureau, 2019 American Community Survey, Tables B15002, B17001, B17010, B19101, B19113, B24010, and B25003, <data.census.gov>, accessed December 2020.

Table 37. Hispanic Population Social and Economic Characteristics: 2019

[60,095 represents 60,095,000, except as noted. As of March, except labor force status is annual average. Excludes members of the Armed Forces except those living off post or with their families on post. Based on Current Population Survey, Annual Social and Economic Supplement; see text, this section and Appendix III]

Characteristic	Number (1,000)						Percent distribution					
	His-panic, total[1]	Mexi-can	Puerto Rican	Cuban	Central Ameri-can[2]	South Ameri-can	His-panic, total[1]	Mexi-can	Puerto Rican	Cuban	Central Ameri-can[2]	South Ameri-can
Total persons	**60,095**	**37,447**	**5,156**	**2,484**	**5,585**	**3,972**	**100.0**	**100.0**	**100.0**	**100.0**	**100.0**	**100.0**
Under 5 years old	5,166	3,421	396	140	444	334	8.6	9.1	7.7	5.6	8.0	8.4
5 to 14 years old	10,583	7,126	796	293	868	551	17.6	19.0	15.5	11.8	15.6	13.9
15 to 44 years old	27,732	17,416	2,324	957	2,905	1,739	46.3	46.6	45.2	38.5	52.0	43.8
45 to 64 years old	12,070	7,142	1,107	638	1,087	964	20.0	19.0	21.5	25.7	19.5	24.3
65 years old and over	4,545	2,342	535	458	280	383	7.6	6.2	10.3	18.4	5.0	9.7
EDUCATIONAL ATTAINMENT												
Persons 25 years old and over	**34,575**	**20,500**	**3,180**	**1,759**	**3,394**	**2,550**	**100.0**	**100.0**	**100.0**	**100.0**	**100.0**	**100.0**
Less than high school graduate	9,761	6,776	489	234	1,408	194	28.2	33.1	15.4	13.3	41.5	7.6
High school graduate	10,848	6,643	1,020	584	981	658	31.4	32.4	32.1	33.2	28.9	25.8
Some college or associate degree	7,455	4,301	863	371	501	629	21.6	21.0	27.1	21.1	14.8	24.7
Bachelor's degree or more	6,512	2,780	808	570	505	1,069	18.8	13.6	25.4	32.4	14.9	41.9
NATIVITY AND CITIZENSHIP STATUS												
Total	**60,095**	**37,447**	**5,156**	**2,484**	**5,585**	**3,972**	**100.0**	**100.0**	**100.0**	**100.0**	**100.0**	**100.0**
Native	39,205	25,697	5,123	1,047	2,275	1,500	65.2	68.6	99.4	42.1	40.7	37.8
Foreign born	20,890	11,750	33	1,438	3,310	2,472	34.8	31.4	0.6	57.9	59.3	62.2
Naturalized citizen	7,890	3,862	24	797	1,080	1,182	13.1	10.3	0.5	32.1	19.3	29.8
Not a citizen	13,000	7,888	9	640	2,230	1,290	21.6	21.1	0.2	25.8	39.9	32.5
LABOR FORCE STATUS[3]												
Civilians 16 years old and over	**43,507**	**26,251**	**3,941**	**2,043**	**(NA)**	**(NA)**	**100.0**	**100.0**	**100.0**	**100.0**	**(NA)**	**(NA)**
Civilian labor force	29,053	17,611	2,448	1,304	(NA)	(NA)	66.8	67.1	62.1	63.8	(NA)	(NA)
Employed	27,805	16,836	2,325	1,265	(NA)	(NA)	63.9	64.1	59.0	62.0	(NA)	(NA)
Unemployed	1,248	775	124	39	(NA)	(NA)	2.9	3.0	3.1	1.9	(NA)	(NA)
Not in labor force	14,454	8,640	1,493	738	(NA)	(NA)	33.2	32.9	37.9	36.1	(NA)	(NA)
HOUSEHOLDS[4]												
Total	**17,758**	**10,244**	**1,861**	**955**	**1,578**	**1,348**	**100.0**	**100.0**	**100.0**	**100.0**	**100.0**	**100.0**
Family households	13,271	8,032	1,181	608	1,241	928	74.7	78.4	63.5	63.7	78.6	68.9
Married-couple families	8,444	5,098	672	428	798	670	47.5	49.8	36.1	44.9	50.5	49.7
Male householder, no spouse present	1,579	1,012	139	57	166	69	8.9	9.9	7.5	5.9	10.5	5.2
Female householder, no spouse present	3,249	1,922	370	123	278	189	18.3	18.8	19.9	12.9	17.6	14.0
Nonfamily households[5]	4,487	2,212	680	346	337	419	25.3	21.6	36.5	36.3	21.4	31.1
Male householder	2,323	1,221	326	157	175	226	13.1	11.9	17.5	16.5	11.1	16.8
Female householder	2,164	991	354	189	162	193	12.2	9.7	19.0	19.8	10.3	14.3
MONEY INCOME IN 2018												
Total families	**13,271**	**8,032**	**1,181**	**608**	**1,241**	**928**	**100.0**	**100.0**	**100.0**	**100.0**	**100.0**	**100.0**
Under $5,000	326	186	47	16	17	28	2.5	2.3	4.0	2.7	1.4	3.0
$5,000 to $9,999	233	141	36	13	13	10	1.8	1.8	3.0	2.1	1.0	1.0
$10,000 to $14,999	341	181	33	21	34	32	2.6	2.3	2.8	3.5	2.7	3.4
$15,000 to $19,999	529	304	52	27	53	32	4.0	3.8	4.4	4.4	4.3	3.5
$20,000 to $24,999	716	469	57	28	60	39	5.4	5.8	4.8	4.6	4.9	4.2
$25,000 to $34,999	1,395	833	107	73	137	101	10.5	10.4	9.1	12.0	11.1	10.9
$35,000 to $49,999	2,086	1,352	185	69	163	136	15.7	16.8	15.6	11.3	13.1	14.6
$50,000 to $74,999	2,677	1,680	200	117	274	159	20.2	20.9	16.9	19.2	22.1	17.2
$75,000 to $99,999	1,850	1,191	155	69	190	109	13.9	14.8	13.1	11.3	15.3	11.7
$100,000 and over	3,119	1,694	309	176	300	283	23.5	21.1	26.1	28.9	24.1	30.5
POVERTY STATUS IN 2018												
Total persons[6]	**59,957**	**37,368**	**5,135**	**2,480**	**5,573**	**3,965**	**100.0**	**100.0**	**100.0**	**100.0**	**100.0**	**100.0**
Below poverty level	10,526	6,903	970	342	934	511	17.6	18.5	18.9	13.8	16.8	12.9
At or above poverty level	49,431	30,465	4,165	2,137	4,640	3,455	82.4	81.5	81.1	86.2	83.2	87.1

NA Not available. [1] Includes other Hispanic groups not shown separately. [2] Central American totals exclude Mexican and Cuban. [3] Source: U.S. Bureau of Labor Statistics, "Labor Force Statistics from the Current Population Survey," <www.bls.gov/cps/tables.htm>. [4] Shown by the Hispanic origin of the householder. [5] Nonfamily households include a single householder living alone or sharing a home with unrelated persons. [6] Persons for whom poverty level determined. Excludes unrelated individuals under 15 years old.

Source: U.S. Census Bureau, "The Hispanic Population in the United States: 2019," <www.census.gov/topics/population/hispanic-origin/data/tables.html>, accessed May 2020.

Table 38. Native and Foreign-Born Population by State: 2020

[329,484 represents 329,484,000. The term foreign-born refers to anyone who is not a U.S. citizen at birth. This includes naturalized U.S. citizens, legal permanent residents (immigrants), temporary migrants (such as foreign students), humanitarian migrants (such as refugees), and persons illegally present in the United States. Data are based on 2020 American Community Survey (ACS) 1-year experimental estimates. The coronavirus disease 2019 (COVID-19) pandemic impacted 2020 ACS data collection and quality, and standard estimates did not meet statistical quality standards. The Census Bureau does not recommend comparing experimental estimates to standard ACS estimates. For more information, see <www.census.gov/programs-surveys/acs/data/experimental-data.html>. The ACS universe includes the household population and the population living in institutions, college dormitories, and other group quarters. Based on a sample and subject to sampling variability; see text, this section and Appendix III]

State	Total population (1,000)	Native population (1,000)	Foreign-born population Number (1,000)	Foreign-born population Percent of total population	State	Total population (1,000)	Native population (1,000)	Foreign-born population Number (1,000)	Foreign-born population Percent of total population
U.S.	329,484	285,968	43,517	13.2	MO	6,152	5,913	238	3.9
AL	4,922	4,748	173	3.5	MT	1,081	1,060	20	1.9
AK	731	674	57	7.8	NE	1,938	1,791	146	7.5
AZ	7,421	6,495	926	12.5	NV	3,138	2,545	593	18.9
AR	3,031	2,885	145	4.8	NH	1,366	1,285	81	5.9
CA	39,368	29,053	10,315	26.2	NJ	8,882	6,857	2,026	22.8
CO	5,808	5,289	518	8.9	NM	2,106	1,927	179	8.5
CT	3,557	3,043	514	14.4	NY	19,337	15,078	4,259	22.0
DE	987	904	83	8.4	NC	10,601	9,782	819	7.7
DC	713	622	91	12.8	ND	765	730	35	4.6
FL	21,733	17,265	4,468	20.6	OH	11,693	11,155	538	4.6
GA	10,710	9,624	1,086	10.1	OK	3,981	3,747	233	5.9
HI	1,407	1,168	239	17.0	OR	4,242	3,847	394	9.3
ID	1,827	1,726	101	5.5	PA	12,783	11,902	882	6.9
IL	12,588	10,867	1,721	13.7	RI	1,057	904	153	14.5
IN	6,755	6,395	360	5.3	SC	5,218	4,956	262	5.0
IA	3,164	2,999	164	5.2	SD	893	860	33	3.7
KS	2,914	2,725	189	6.5	TN	6,887	6,558	329	4.8
KY	4,477	4,308	169	3.8	TX	29,361	24,633	4,728	16.1
LA	4,645	4,470	175	3.8	UT	3,250	2,998	252	7.7
ME	1,350	1,299	51	3.8	VT	623	596	27	4.3
MD	6,056	5,131	925	15.3	VA	8,591	7,546	1,045	12.2
MA	6,894	5,725	1,169	17.0	WA	7,694	6,576	1,118	14.5
MI	9,967	9,305	661	6.6	WV	1,785	1,756	28	1.6
MN	5,657	5,222	435	7.7	WI	5,833	5,556	277	4.7
MS	2,967	2,905	62	2.1	WY	582	560	22	3.8

Source: U.S. Census Bureau, 2020 ACS 1-Year Experimental Data Tables, "Table XK200503. Place of Birth in the United States," <www.census.gov/programs-surveys/acs/data/experimental-data.html>, accessed July 2022.

Table 39. Nativity and Place of Birth of Resident Population—25 Largest Cities: 2019

[The American Community Survey universe includes the household population and the population living in institutions, college dormitories, and other group quarters. Based on a sample and subject to sampling variability; see text, this section and Appendix III. See headnote, Table 38]

City	Total population	Native population Total	Native population Born in United States	Native population Born outside United States [1]	Foreign born Total Number	Foreign born Total Percent of total population	Foreign born Entered 2010 or later Number	Foreign born Entered 2010 or later Percent of foreign-born population
Austin, TX	979,263	786,966	770,567	16,399	192,297	19.6	70,727	36.8
Boston, MA	694,295	505,272	480,780	24,492	189,023	27.2	68,131	36.0
Charlotte, NC	885,707	734,969	723,258	11,711	150,738	17.0	61,499	40.8
Chicago, IL	2,693,959	2,146,254	2,099,796	46,458	547,705	20.3	106,045	19.4
Columbus, OH	902,073	781,891	767,659	14,232	120,182	13.3	51,705	43.0
Dallas, TX	1,343,565	1,004,299	989,489	14,810	339,266	25.3	114,610	33.8
Denver, CO	727,211	631,692	617,812	13,880	95,519	13.1	20,132	21.1
Detroit, MI	670,052	629,041	623,869	5,172	41,011	6.1	15,172	37.0
El Paso, TX	681,729	537,434	520,054	17,380	144,295	21.2	24,674	17.1
Fort Worth, TX	913,656	752,645	737,296	15,349	161,011	17.6	36,823	22.9
Houston, TX	2,316,797	1,661,692	1,628,007	33,685	655,105	28.3	219,122	33.4
Indianapolis, IN [2]	870,340	786,285	777,905	8,380	84,055	9.7	28,574	34.0
Jacksonville, FL	911,528	805,258	778,755	26,503	106,270	11.7	35,990	33.9
Los Angeles, CA	3,979,537	2,529,538	2,478,883	50,655	1,449,999	36.4	247,673	17.1
Nashville–Davidson, TN [2]	668,580	575,948	569,271	6,677	92,632	13.9	37,273	40.2
New York, NY	8,336,817	5,315,734	5,000,206	315,528	3,021,083	36.2	697,400	23.1
Oklahoma City, OK	655,158	575,833	566,665	9,168	79,325	12.1	22,226	28.0
Philadelphia, PA	1,584,064	1,362,602	1,296,822	65,780	221,462	14.0	72,360	32.7
Phoenix, AZ	1,680,988	1,343,636	1,320,391	23,245	337,352	20.1	68,423	20.3
San Antonio, TX	1,547,250	1,329,001	1,288,858	40,143	218,249	14.1	53,494	24.5
San Diego, CA	1,423,852	1,065,415	1,038,966	26,449	358,437	25.2	80,451	22.4
San Francisco, CA	881,549	584,580	564,530	20,050	296,969	33.7	68,197	23.0
San Jose, CA	1,021,786	601,865	583,720	18,145	419,921	41.1	98,101	23.4
Seattle, WA	753,655	605,964	592,058	13,906	147,691	19.6	59,308	40.2
Washington, DC	705,749	620,416	605,792	14,624	85,333	12.1	30,250	35.4

[1] Includes persons born in Puerto Rico, Guam, the Northern Marianas, or the U.S. Virgin Islands, as well as those born abroad of at least one U.S. citizen parent. [2] Represents the portion of a consolidated city that is not within one or more separately incorporated places.

Source: U.S. Census Bureau, 2019 American Community Survey, C05002, "Place of Birth by Nativity"; and C05005, "Period of Entry by Nativity and Citizenship Status in the United States"; <data.census.gov>, accessed December 2020.

Table 40. Native and Foreign-Born Populations by Selected Characteristics: 2019

[In thousands (324,356 represents 324,356,000). As of March. The foreign-born population includes anyone who is not a U.S. citizen at birth. This includes legal permanent residents (immigrants), temporary migrants (such as foreign students), humanitarian migrants (such as refugees), and persons illegally present in the United States. Based on Current Population Survey, Annual Social and Economic Supplement, which includes the civilian noninstitutional population plus Armed Forces living in housing units on or off post with at least one other civilian adult; see text, this section, and Appendix III]

Characteristic	Total population	Native population	Foreign-born population Total	Naturalized citizen	Not a U.S. citizen	Year of entry: 2010 or later
Total.	**324,356**	**278,536**	**45,820**	**22,296**	**23,524**	**11,619**
Under 5 years old.	19,736	19,400	336	69	267	336
5 to 9 years old.	20,212	19,487	725	112	613	721
10 to 14 years old.	20,827	19,933	894	235	659	676
15 to 19 years old.	20,849	19,530	1,319	411	907	698
20 to 24 years old.	21,254	18,903	2,351	718	1,633	1,226
25 to 29 years old.	23,277	19,760	3,516	1,120	2,396	1,776
30 to 34 years old.	21,932	17,596	4,336	1,407	2,929	1,687
35 to 39 years old.	21,443	16,687	4,756	1,777	2,978	1,315
40 to 44 years old.	19,584	14,811	4,773	2,168	2,606	908
45 to 49 years old.	20,345	15,512	4,833	2,431	2,402	697
50 to 54 years old.	20,355	16,160	4,195	2,330	1,865	431
55 to 59 years old.	21,163	17,496	3,667	2,280	1,387	388
60 to 64 years old.	20,592	17,511	3,082	2,012	1,069	294
65 to 69 years old.	17,356	15,047	2,309	1,607	702	185
70 to 74 years old.	14,131	12,315	1,817	1,356	460	133
75 to 79 years old.	9,357	8,089	1,268	961	307	77
80 to 84 years old.	6,050	5,164	886	682	204	44
85 years and over.	5,893	5,134	759	620	139	28
Median age (years).	38	36	45	52	39	31
MARITAL STATUS						
Persons 15 years old and over.	**263,581**	**219,717**	**43,865**	**21,880**	**21,985**	**9,886**
Married.	132,856	105,261	27,595	14,386	13,209	5,641
Widowed.	14,908	12,882	2,025	1,394	631	201
Divorced.	25,480	22,422	3,057	1,955	1,102	320
Separated.	4,928	3,745	1,184	470	714	207
Never married.	85,410	75,407	10,003	3,675	6,328	3,517
EDUCATIONAL ATTAINMENT						
Persons 25 years old and over.	**221,478**	**181,283**	**40,195**	**20,751**	**19,444**	**7,963**
Not high school graduate.	21,975	12,187	9,788	3,283	6,506	1,326
High school graduate.	62,259	52,024	10,235	5,263	4,972	1,845
Some college or associate's degree.	57,428	51,183	6,246	4,040	2,205	1,014
Bachelor's degree.	49,937	41,686	8,250	5,036	3,214	2,145
Advanced degree.	29,880	24,203	5,677	3,130	2,547	1,632
EMPLOYMENT STATUS						
Persons 16 years old and over.	**162,709**	**133,896**	**28,813**	**13,983**	**14,830**	**6,383**
Employed.	156,416	128,621	27,795	13,542	14,253	6,114
Unemployed.	6,293	5,275	1,018	441	577	269
EARNINGS IN 2018 [1]						
Persons 15 years old and over with earnings.	**118,000**	**96,579**	**21,421**	**10,792**	**10,628**	**4,411**
$1 to $14,999 or loss.	3,698	2,908	790	266	524	190
$15,000 to $29,999.	19,847	14,743	5,104	1,904	3,200	1,172
$30,000 to $39,999.	18,351	14,669	3,681	1,672	2,010	737
$40,000 to $49,999.	15,235	12,809	2,427	1,254	1,173	452
$50,000 to $74,999.	28,148	23,969	4,180	2,470	1,710	785
$75,000 to $99,999.	13,511	11,530	1,981	1,219	762	444
$100,000 and over.	19,210	15,951	3,259	2,008	1,250	632
Median earnings (dollars).	50,653	51,323	42,317	51,122	36,825	41,208
HOUSEHOLD SIZE [2]						
Total households.	**128,579**	**108,560**	**20,019**	**11,043**	**8,976**	**3,841**
One person.	36,479	32,627	3,852	2,404	1,448	692
Two people.	44,373	39,080	5,292	3,155	2,138	1,018
Three people.	19,374	15,732	3,642	1,944	1,698	789
Four people.	16,413	12,647	3,766	1,907	1,859	780
Five or more people.	11,940	8,474	3,467	1,633	1,833	561
INCOME IN 2018 [2]						
Total family households.	**83,482**	**68,388**	**15,094**	**8,287**	**6,808**	**2,702**
$1 to $14,999 or loss.	4,400	3,459	941	381	559	231
$15,000 to $29,999.	7,354	5,492	1,863	822	1,040	349
$30,000 to $39,999.	6,307	4,899	1,408	670	738	285
$40,000 to $49,999.	5,909	4,708	1,201	553	649	203
$50,000 to $74,999.	14,587	11,870	2,717	1,429	1,288	492
$75,000 to $99,999.	12,029	10,035	1,994	1,138	856	346
$100,000 and over.	32,896	27,926	4,971	3,293	1,678	795
Median income (dollars).	80,663	83,368	68,182	79,762	56,002	61,025
POVERTY STATUS IN 2018 [3]						
Persons below poverty level.	38,146	31,828	6,317	2,215	4,103	2,142
Persons at or above poverty level.	285,702	246,223	39,479	20,080	19,399	9,455
HOUSEHOLD TENURE [2]						
Total households.	**128,578**	**108,560**	**20,019**	**11,044**	**8,976**	**3,841**
Owner occupied unit.	82,953	72,664	10,289	6,999	3,290	989
Renter occupied unit [4].	45,627	35,896	9,730	4,045	5,686	2,852

[1] Covers only year-round full-time workers. [2] Based on citizenship of householder. [3] Persons for whom poverty status is determined. Excludes unrelated individuals under 15 years old. [4] Includes occupiers who paid no cash rent.

Source: U.S. Census Bureau, "Foreign Born CPS Data Tables," <www.census.gov/topics/population/foreign-born/data/tables.html>, accessed May 2020.

Table 41. Foreign-Born Population—Selected Characteristics by Region of Origin: 2019

[In thousands (45,820 represents 45,820,000). As of March. The term foreign-born refers to anyone who is not a U.S. citizen at birth. This includes naturalized U.S. citizens, legal permanent residents (immigrants), temporary migrants (such as foreign students), humanitarian migrants (such as refugees), and persons illegally present in the United States. Based on Current Population Survey, Annual Social and Economic Supplement; see text, this section and Appendix III]

Characteristic	Total foreign-born	Asia	Europe	Latin America Total	Mexico	Other Latin America	Other areas [1]
Total..	**45,820**	**13,864**	**4,522**	**23,718**	**12,060**	**11,658**	**3,716**
Under 5 years old.................................	336	83	36	142	46	96	75
5 to 9 years old....................................	725	207	73	269	92	177	176
10 to 14 years old.................................	894	276	63	408	118	290	147
15 to 19 years old.................................	1,319	387	85	703	280	423	144
20 to 24 years old.................................	2,351	728	149	1,236	613	622	238
25 to 29 years old.................................	3,516	1,146	271	1,736	869	867	363
30 to 34 years old.................................	4,336	1,327	370	2,304	1,278	1,025	335
35 to 39 years old.................................	4,756	1,363	387	2,648	1,450	1,198	357
40 to 44 years old.................................	4,773	1,324	299	2,777	1,529	1,248	373
45 to 49 years old.................................	4,833	1,392	396	2,663	1,519	1,143	381
50 to 54 years old.................................	4,195	1,168	408	2,330	1,303	1,027	289
55 to 59 years old.................................	3,667	1,117	388	1,920	971	948	242
60 to 64 years old.................................	3,082	1,068	297	1,521	750	772	195
65 to 69 years old.................................	2,309	800	294	1,073	466	606	142
70 to 74 years old.................................	1,817	662	316	744	306	438	95
75 to 79 years old.................................	1,268	373	291	534	222	312	70
80 to 84 years old.................................	886	264	180	399	154	245	43
85 years old and over............................	759	180	217	312	91	220	50
Median age (years) [2]............................	44.9	45.3	51.6	44.3	44.2	44.5	40.3
EDUCATIONAL ATTAINMENT							
Persons 25 years old and over................	**40,195**	**12,184**	**4,115**	**20,960**	**10,910**	**10,050**	**2,936**
Not a high school graduate.....................	9,788	1,214	244	8,056	5,572	2,484	274
High school graduate.............................	10,235	2,338	956	6,313	3,264	3,049	627
Some college or associate's degree..........	6,246	1,709	843	3,066	1,107	1,960	627
Bachelor's degree.................................	8,250	3,822	1,079	2,491	735	1,756	857
Advanced degree..................................	5,677	3,100	992	1,034	232	802	551
INCOME IN 2018							
Total family households.........................	**15,094**	**4,554**	**1,449**	**7,960**	**4,180**	**3,780**	**1,132**
$1 to $14,999 or loss.............................	941	237	67	577	295	282	59
$15,000 to $29,999...............................	1,863	357	57	1,340	764	576	109
$30,000 to $39,999...............................	1,408	275	76	957	582	375	101
$40,000 to $49,999...............................	1,201	235	80	810	466	343	77
$50,000 to $74,999...............................	2,717	594	218	1,686	895	791	219
$75,000 to $99,999...............................	1,994	567	244	1,047	568	479	136
$100,000 and over................................	4,971	2,289	707	1,544	610	934	432
Median income (dollars) [2].....................	68,182	100,258	97,941	52,539	49,420	57,899	75,124
POVERTY STATUS IN 2018 [3]							
Persons below poverty level....................	6,317	1,525	355	3,947	2,184	1,763	491
Persons at or above poverty level.............	39,479	12,339	4,163	19,751	9,871	9,881	3,225

[1] Africa, Oceania, Northern America, and born at sea. [2] For definition of median, see Guide to Tabular Presentation. [3] Persons for whom poverty status is determined. Excludes unrelated individuals under age 15.

Source: U.S. Census Bureau, "Foreign Born CPS Data Tables," <www.census.gov/topics/population/foreign-born/data/tables.html>, accessed May 2020.

Table 42. Foreign-Born Population by Citizenship Status and Place of Birth: 2019

[The term foreign-born refers to anyone who is not a U.S. citizen at birth. This includes naturalized U.S. citizens, legal permanent residents (immigrants), temporary migrants (such as foreign students), humanitarian migrants (such as refugees), and persons illegally present in the United States. The American Community Survey universe includes the household population and the population living in institutions, college dormitories, and other group quarters. Based on a sample and subject to sampling variability; see text, this section and Appendix III]

Region and country	Foreign-born population, total	Naturalized citizens	Not a U.S. citizen Number	Percent of foreign-born
Total [1]..	**44,932,901**	**23,182,917**	**21,749,984**	**48.4**
Latin America......................................	22,588,239	9,584,684	13,003,555	57.6
Caribbean [2].....................................	4,494,211	2,812,050	1,682,161	37.4
Cuba...	1,359,990	(NA)	(NA)	(NA)
Central America................................	14,714,249	4,969,021	9,745,228	66.2
Mexico..	10,931,939	3,696,568	7,235,371	66.2
Other Central America [2]....................	3,782,310	1,272,453	2,509,857	66.4
El Salvador...................................	1,412,101	(NA)	(NA)	(NA)
South America...................................	3,379,779	1,803,613	1,576,166	46.6
Asia [2]..	14,099,479	8,533,827	5,565,652	39.5
China, excluding Hong Kong and Taiwan....	2,250,230	(NA)	(NA)	(NA)
India...	2,688,075	(NA)	(NA)	(NA)
Korea..	1,038,885	(NA)	(NA)	(NA)
Philippines......................................	2,045,248	(NA)	(NA)	(NA)
Vietnam...	1,383,779	(NA)	(NA)	(NA)
Europe..	4,665,173	3,116,657	1,548,516	33.2
Africa...	2,475,118	1,415,959	1,059,159	42.8
North America.....................................	804,602	405,410	399,192	49.6
Oceania..	300,188	126,278	173,910	57.9

NA Not available. [1] Includes persons born at sea. [2] Includes other countries not shown separately.

Source: U.S. Census Bureau, 2019 American Community Survey, B05002, "Place of Birth by Nativity and Citizenship Status"; B05006, "Place of Birth for the Foreign-Born Population in the United States"; and B05007, "Place of Birth by Year of Entry by Citizenship Status for the Foreign-Born Population"; <data.census.gov>, accessed December 2020.

Table 43. American Indian Reservations and Alaska Native Village Statistical Areas With Largest American Indian and Alaska Native Populations: 2010

[As of April. Rankings of the American Indian reservations and Alaska Native village statistical areas are based on the American Indian and Alaska Native alone-or-in-combination population]

| Area | Total population | American Indian and Alaska Native | | | Not American Indian and Alaska Native alone or in combination [1] |
		Alone or in combination [1]	Alone	In combin- ation [1]	
AMERICAN INDIAN RESERVATION					
Navajo Nation Reservation and Off-Reservation Trust Land, AZ–NM–UT..........	173,667	169,321	166,824	2,497	4,346
Pine Ridge Reservation, SD–NE.................	18,834	16,906	16,580	326	1,928
Fort Apache Reservation, AZ....................	13,409	13,014	12,870	144	395
Gila River Indian Reservation, AZ................	11,712	11,251	10,845	406	461
Osage Reservation, OK........................	47,472	9,920	6,858	3,062	37,552
San Carlos Reservation, AZ....................	10,068	9,901	9,835	66	167
Rosebud Indian Reservation and Off-Reservation Trust Land, SD................	10,869	9,809	9,617	192	1,060
Tohono O'odham Nation Reservation and Off-Reservation Trust Land, AZ..........	10,201	9,278	9,139	139	923
Blackfeet Indian Reservation and Off-Reservation Trust Land, MT..............	10,405	9,149	8,944	205	1,256
Flathead Reservation, MT......................	28,359	9,138	7,042	2,096	19,221
ALASKA NATIVE VILLAGE STATISTICAL AREA					
Knik Alaska Native village statistical area.........	65,768	6,582	3,529	3,053	59,186
Bethel Alaska Native village statistical area........	6,080	4,334	3,953	381	1,746
Kenaitze Alaska Native village statistical area......	32,902	3,417	2,001	1,416	29,485
Barrow Alaska Native village statistical area........	4,212	2,889	2,577	312	1,323
Ketchikan Alaska Native village statistical area......	12,742	2,605	1,692	913	10,137
Kotzebue Alaska Native village statistical area......	3,201	2,585	2,355	230	616
Nome Alaska Native village statistical area.........	3,681	2,396	1,994	402	1,285
Chickaloon Alaska Native village statistical area.....	23,087	2,373	1,369	1,004	20,714
Dillingham Alaska Native village statistical area.....	2,378	1,583	1,333	250	795
Sitka Alaska Native village statistical area.........	4,480	1,240	855	385	3,240

[1] In combination with one or more other race groups.

Source: U.S. Census Bureau, 2010 Census Briefs, *The American Indian and Alaska Native Population: 2010*, January 2012. See also <www.census.gov/about/partners/cic/resources/data-links/aian.html>.

Table 44. American Indian and Alaska Native Population by Selected Tribal Groupings: 2010

[As of April. Data shown for American Indian and Alaska Native tribes alone or in combination of tribes or races]

Tribal grouping	American Indian and Alaska Native tribal grouping alone or in any combination [1]	Tribal grouping	American Indian and Alaska Native tribal grouping alone or in any combination [1]
Total [2]............................	**5,220,579**	Navajo...........................	332,129
AMERICAN INDIAN TRIBES		Osage............................	18,576
Apache...........................	111,810	Ottawa...........................	13,033
Arapaho..........................	10,861	Paiute...........................	13,767
Blackfeet.........................	105,304	Pima............................	26,655
Canadian and French American Indian.....	14,822	Potawatomi.......................	33,771
Central American Indian..............	27,844	Pueblo...........................	62,540
Cherokee.........................	819,105	Puget Sound Salish.................	20,260
Cheyenne.........................	19,051	Seminole.........................	31,971
Chickasaw........................	52,278	Shoshone.........................	13,002
Chippewa.........................	170,742	Sioux............................	170,110
Choctaw..........................	195,764	South American Indian..............	47,233
Colville..........................	10,549	Spanish American Indian.............	19,951
Comanche.........................	23,330	Tohono O'odham...................	23,478
Cree............................	7,983	Ute.............................	11,491
Creek............................	88,332	Yakama...........................	11,527
Crow............................	15,203	Yaqui............................	32,595
Delaware..........................	18,264	Yuman...........................	10,089
Hopi............................	18,327	**ALASKA NATIVE TRIBES**	
Houma...........................	10,768	Alaskan Athabascan.................	22,484
Iroquois..........................	81,002	Aleut............................	19,282
Kiowa...........................	13,787	Inupiat...........................	33,360
Lumbee...........................	73,691	Tlingit-Haida......................	26,080
Menominee........................	11,133	Tsimshian.........................	3,755
Mexican American Indian..............	175,494	Yup'ik...........................	33,889

[1] The numbers by American Indian and Alaska Native tribal grouping do not add to the total American Indian and Alaska Native population. This is because the American Indian and Alaska Native tribal groupings are tallies of the number of American Indian and Alaska Native responses rather than the number of American Indian or Alaska Native respondents. Respondents reporting several American Indian or Alaska Native groups are counted several times. [2] Includes other tribal groupings not shown separately.

Source: U.S. Census Bureau, 2010 Census Briefs, *The American Indian and Alaska Native Population: 2010*, January 2012. See also <www.census.gov/about/partners/cic/resources/data-links/aian.html>.

Table 45. Refugee Arrivals and Individuals Granted Asylum by Country of Nationality: 2011 to 2020

[For year ending September 30. Ranked by 2020 country of nationality. Data shown provide information on the number of persons admitted to the U.S. as refugees or granted asylum in the United States in the year shown. For definitions of refugee and asylee, see text, this section. Refugee data were derived from data on refugee admissions that are maintained in the Worldwide Refugee Admissions Processing System (WRAPS) of the Bureau of Population, Refugees, and Migration (PRM) of the U.S. Department of State. Asylee data were derived from data obtained from Global, a cloud-based platform of the U.S. Citizenship and Immigration Services (USCIS) of the U.S. Department of Homeland Security that replaced the Refugee, Asylum, and Parole System (RAPS), and also data obtained from the Executive Office for Immigration Review (EOIR) of the U.S. Department of Justice]

Country of nationality	2011	2012	2013	2014	2015	2016	2017	2018	2019	2020
REFUGEE ARRIVALS										
Total	56,384	58,179	69,909	69,975	69,920	84,989	53,691	22,405	29,916	11,840
Congo, Democratic Republic	962	1,849	2,545	4,502	7,823	16,279	9,325	7,841	12,875	2,863
Burma	16,970	14,159	16,295	14,578	18,323	12,294	5,047	3,525	4,928	2,112
Ukraine	435	377	235	493	1,454	2,526	4,254	2,637	4,432	1,935
Afghanistan	411	450	622	758	914	2,743	1,315	802	1,197	603
Iraq	9,345	12,057	19,331	19,651	12,608	9,837	6,857	140	462	541
Syria	41	31	48	132	1,693	12,583	6,566	62	560	486
Eritrea	1,988	1,329	1,763	1,445	1,576	1,924	1,912	1,260	1,750	475
El Salvador	0	0	0	0	0	364	1,124	724	311	362
Moldova	326	257	115	141	323	464	293	197	116	352
Sudan	335	1,059	2,137	1,307	1,576	1,444	962	74	376	258
Guatemala	5	0	0	0	0	8	50	42	117	249
Colombia	46	125	214	243	504	523	231	127	298	219
Russia	186	224	162	147	301	487	377	442	198	190
Pakistan	54	274	155	239	159	546	347	444	266	169
Somalia	3,145	4,915	7,579	9,011	8,852	9,032	6,122	257	230	149
Iran	2,025	1,760	2,579	2,833	3,099	3,736	2,575	41	198	135
Ethiopia	608	639	859	754	646	1,147	791	387	258	119
ASYLEES										
Total	23,631	27,912	24,866	23,083	25,813	20,165	26,218	37,511	46,130	31,429
China	8,192	9,668	8,561	7,885	6,160	4,462	5,551	6,798	7,448	4,804
Venezuela	1,068	1,067	678	405	489	343	545	5,824	6,701	4,239
El Salvador	236	292	252	369	2,157	2,137	3,453	2,914	3,195	2,012
Guatemala	437	504	380	477	2,058	1,904	2,950	2,319	2,585	1,876
Turkey	40	51	[1] 26	[1] 6	31	[1] 12	28	501	1,774	1,622
Egypt	1,006	2,854	3,374	2,833	1,670	834	1,154	1,565	2,271	1,444
India	308	343	403	480	476	471	671	1,302	2,256	1,337
Honduras	117	207	198	237	1,401	1,475	2,041	1,996	1,815	1,269
Cuba	32	30	30	18	17	11	[2] 62	[2] 161	721	1,242
Mexico	257	416	356	569	854	905	1,027	1,346	1,585	1,207
Russia	621	643	527	323	400	287	345	874	1,396	985
Cameroon	405	407	290	204	184	147	289	490	920	749
Nigeria	53	93	93	108	162	136	193	505	958	562
Nicaragua	30	34	22	23	51	39	57	67	670	552
Syria	52	359	804	935	995	748	775	702	636	348

[1] Asylum affirmatively granted only. [2] Asylum defensively granted only.

Source: U.S. Department of Homeland Security, Office of Immigration Statistics, *Fiscal Year 2020 Refugees and Asylees Annual Flow Report*, March 2022; and "2020 Yearbook of Immigration Statistics," <www.dhs.gov/immigration-statistics/yearbook>, accessed July 2022.

Table 46. Immigrant Orphans Adopted by U.S. Citizens by Sex, Age, Region, and Country of Birth: 2010 and 2020

[For year ending September 30]

Region and country of birth	2010, total	2020					
			Sex		Age		
		Total	Male	Female	Under 1 year old	1 to 4 years old	5 years old and over
Total [1]	11,100	1,648	810	838	40	706	902
REGION							
Africa	3,156	236	110	126	7	91	138
Asia	5,409	685	350	335	21	452	212
Europe	1,721	368	184	184	–	82	286
North America	433	181	92	89	(D)	42	(D)
Oceania	28	8	3	5	(D)	3	(D)
South America	335	170	71	99	8	36	126
COUNTRY [2]							
Ukraine	445	209	106	103	–	31	178
China	3,361	203	96	107	(D)	128	(D)
South Korea	875	183	136	47	–	183	–
Colombia	233	134	50	84	8	33	93
India	249	106	27	79	(D)	83	(D)

– Represents zero. D Data withheld to limit disclosure. [1] Includes countries not shown separately. [2] Data ranked for countries with 100 or more immigrant orphans in 2020.

Source: U.S. Department of Homeland Security, Office of Immigration Statistics, "2020 Yearbook of Immigration Statistics," <www.dhs.gov/immigration-statistics/yearbook>, accessed March 2022.

Table 47. Nonimmigrant Admissions by Class of Admission: 2013 to 2020

[In thousands (173,100 represents 173,100,000). Fiscal years ending September 30. Nonimmigrants are foreign nationals granted temporary admission to the United States. Admissions represent counts of events, i.e., arrivals, not unique individuals; multiple entries of an individual on the same day are counted as one admission. The majority of short-term admissions from Canada and Mexico are excluded. The major purposes for which nonimmigrant admissions are authorized include temporary visits for business or pleasure, academic or vocational study, temporary employment, and to act as a representative of a foreign government or international organization. The U.S. Department of Homeland Security (DHS) collects information regarding nonimmigrant admissions at ports of entry and from DHS Form I-94/I-94W arrival records]

Class of admission	2013	2014	2015	2016	2017	2018	2019	2020
Total all admissions [1]	173,100	180,500	181,300	178,700	181,100	186,200	186,200	86,100
Total I-94 admissions	61,052	74,931	76,638	77,112	77,643	81,280	81,563	37,176
Temporary workers and families	2,997	3,399	3,723	3,938	3,969	3,920	4,106	2,573
Temporary workers and trainees	1,854	2,095	2,307	2,446	2,447	2,379	2,559	1,792
Intracompany transferees	724	836	918	965	977	993	988	471
Treaty traders and investors	373	422	450	478	497	503	516	292
Representatives of foreign information media	46	46	48	48	49	44	44	19
Students	1,669	1,838	1,991	1,992	1,940	1,958	1,907	918
Academic students (F1 visa)	1,578	1,738	1,887	1,893	1,846	1,863	1,818	876
Spouses and children of F1 (F2 visa)	71	78	83	79	74	75	70	32
Vocational students (M1 visa)	19	21	20	19	19	19	18	9
Spouses and children of M1 (M2 visa)	1	1	1	1	1	1	1	(Z)
Exchange visitors	493	558	576	586	594	611	620	226
Diplomats and other representatives	373	421	438	442	450	458	454	219
Temporary visitors for pleasure	48,346	59,785	61,017	61,029	61,600	64,820	64,865	28,732
Temporary visitors for business	6,300	7,734	8,009	8,291	8,456	8,967	9,060	4,209
Transit aliens	629	1,005	690	635	498	454	463	252
Commuter students [2]	105	110	100	68	35	19	9	3
Alien fiancé(e)s of U.S. citizens and children	30	42	35	44	41	29	40	23
Legal Immigration Family Equity (LIFE) Act	3	2	2	1	1	1	(Z)	(Z)
Other	(Z)	(Z)	(Z)	(Z)	(Z)	(Z)	(Z)	(Z)
Unknown	108	37	57	86	58	44	39	21

Z represents less than 500. [1] Estimated admission totals rounded to the nearest hundred thousand. Excludes sea and air crew admissions (D1 and D2 visas). [2] Canadian or Mexican national academic and vocational commuter students.

Source: U.S. Department of Homeland Security, Office of Immigration Statistics, *Fiscal Year 2020 U.S. Nonimmigrant Admissions Annual Flow Report*, October 2021; and "2020 Yearbook of Immigration Statistics," <www.dhs.gov/immigration-statistics/yearbook>, accessed April 2022.

Table 48. Immigrants Obtaining Legal Permanent Resident Status: 1820 to 2020

[In thousands, except rate (152 represents 152,000). For fiscal years ending in year shown, except as noted. For 1820-1867, alien passengers arriving; 1868-1891 and 1895-1897, immigrants arriving; 1892-1894 and 1898 to the present, persons obtaining legal permanent residence. Rates based on Census Bureau estimates as of July 1 for resident population through 1929, and for total population thereafter (excluding Alaska and Hawaii prior to 1959)]

Period/year	Number (1,000)	Rate [1]	Period/year	Number (1,000)	Rate [1]
1820 to 1830 [2]	152	1.2	2000	841	3.0
1831 to 1840 [3]	599	3.9	2002	1,059	3.7
1841 to 1850 [4]	1,713	8.4	2003	704	2.4
1851 to 1860 [4]	2,598	9.3	2004	958	3.3
1861 to 1870 [5]	2,315	6.4	2005	1,122	3.8
1871 to 1880	2,812	6.2	2006	1,266	4.2
1881 to 1890	5,247	9.2	2007	1,052	3.5
1891 to 1900	3,688	5.3	2008	1,107	3.6
1901 to 1910	8,795	10.4	2009	1,131	3.7
1911 to 1920	5,736	5.7	2010	1,043	3.4
1921 to 1930	4,107	3.5	2011	1,062	3.4
1931 to 1940	528	0.4	2012	1,032	3.3
1941 to 1950	1,035	0.7	2013	991	3.1
1951 to 1960	2,515	1.5	2014	1,017	3.2
1961 to 1970	3,322	1.7	2015	1,051	3.3
1971 to 1980	4,399	2.0	2016	1,184	3.7
1981 to 1990	7,256	3.0	2017	1,127	3.5
1991 to 2000	9,081	3.4	2018	1,097	3.4
2001 to 2010	10,501	3.5	2019	1,032	3.1
2011 to 2020	10,298	3.2	2020	707	2.1

[1] Annual rate per 1,000 U.S. population. Rate computed by dividing sum of annual immigration totals by sum of annual U.S. population totals for same number of years. [2] October 1, 1819, to September 30, 1830. [3] October 1, 1830, to December 31, 1840. [4] Calendar years. [5] January 1, 1861, to June 30, 1870.

Source: U.S. Department of Homeland Security, Office of Immigration Statistics, "2020 Yearbook of Immigration Statistics," <www.dhs.gov/immigration-statistics/yearbook>, accessed March 2022.

Table 49. Petitions for Naturalization Filed, Persons Naturalized, and Petitions Denied: 1920 to 2020

[For years ending September 30. Naturalizations refer to immigrants aged 18 and over who become citizens of the United States]

| Year | Petitions filed | Persons naturalized | | | | Petitions denied |
		Total	Civilian	Military	Not reported	
1920............	218,732	177,683	125,711	51,972	–	15,586
1930............	113,151	169,377	167,637	1,740	–	9,068
1940............	278,028	235,260	232,500	2,760	–	6,549
1950............	66,038	66,346	64,279	2,067	–	2,276
1960............	127,543	119,442	117,848	1,594	–	2,277
1970............	114,760	110,399	99,783	10,616	–	1,979
1980............	192,230	156,627	152,073	4,554	–	4,370
1990............	233,843	267,586	245,410	1,618	20,558	6,516
1995............	959,963	485,720	472,518	3,855	9,347	46,067
2000............	460,916	886,026	812,579	836	72,611	399,670
2005............	602,972	604,280	589,269	4,614	10,397	108,247
2008............	525,786	1,046,539	1,032,281	4,342	9,916	121,283
2009............	570,442	743,715	726,043	7,100	10,572	109,832
2010............	710,544	619,913	604,410	9,122	6,381	56,994
2011............	756,008	694,193	677,385	8,373	8,435	57,065
2012............	899,162	757,434	745,932	7,257	4,245	65,874
2013............	772,623	779,929	769,073	6,652	4,204	83,112
2014............	773,824	653,416	642,431	7,468	3,517	66,767
2015............	783,062	730,259	720,645	7,234	2,380	75,810
2016............	972,151	753,060	742,090	8,885	2,085	86,033
2017............	986,851	707,265	695,718	6,883	4,664	83,176
2018............	837,168	761,901	750,771	4,495	6,635	92,631
2019............	830,560	843,593	823,490	3,760	16,343	97,789
2020............	967,755	628,254	615,773	2,588	9,893	80,609

– Represents zero.

Source: U.S. Department of Homeland Security, Office of Immigration Statistics, "2020 Yearbook of Immigration Statistics," <www.dhs.gov/immigration-statistics/yearbook>, accessed March 2022.

Table 50. Estimated Unauthorized Immigrants by Selected Country of Birth and State of Residence: 2000 to 2018

[In thousands (8,460 represents 8,460,000). As of January. The unauthorized resident immigrant population is defined as all foreign-born non-citizens who are not legal U.S. residents; most entered the U.S. without inspection or were admitted temporarily and stayed past the date they were required to leave. Unauthorized immigrants applying for adjustment to legal permanent resident status under the Immigration and Nationality Act are unauthorized until they have been granted lawful permanent residence, though they may have been authorized to work. These estimates were calculated using a "residual method," whereby estimates of the legally resident foreign-born population were subtracted from the total foreign-born population. All of these component populations were resident in the United States on January 1 and entered during the period from 1980 to the year prior to the year shown. Persons who entered the U.S. prior to 1980 were assumed to be legally resident. Estimates of the legally resident foreign-born population were based primarily on administrative data of the Department of Homeland Security, while estimates of the total foreign-born population were obtained from the American Community Survey of the U.S. Census Bureau]

Country of birth	2000	2005	2010 [1]	2011	2012	2013	2014	2015	2016	2017	2018
United States, total...	**8,460**	**10,490**	**11,590**	**11,510**	**11,430**	**11,210**	**11,460**	**11,440**	**11,750**	**11,410**	**11,390**
By country of birth:											
Mexico.................	4,680	5,970	6,830	6,800	6,720	6,450	6,450	6,200	5,970	5,860	5,420
El Salvador.............	430	470	670	660	690	690	670	720	750	750	730
Guatemala.............	290	370	520	520	560	590	620	600	610	610	620
India....................	120	280	270	240	260	320	390	450	560	490	540
Honduras...............	160	180	380	380	360	390	390	420	430	500	450
China..................	190	230	300	280	210	190	230	320	420	410	410
Philippines.............	200	210	290	270	310	340	330	350	410	300	370
Colombia..............	100	110	120	130	130	160	130	130	140	130	210
Brazil.................	100	170	150	150	130	110	110	100	110	150	200
Venezuela.............	(NA)	(NA)	50	50	60	50	40	80	100	120	190
Other countries........	2,180	2,500	2,020	2,030	2,010	1,920	2,090	2,080	2,260	2,090	2,260
By State of residence:											
California..............	2,510	2,770	2,910	2,830	2,820	2,780	2,730	2,760	2,860	2,790	2,610
Texas..................	1,090	1,360	1,780	1,790	1,830	1,750	1,850	1,860	1,910	1,870	1,940
Florida.................	800	850	730	740	730	740	710	540	610	610	660
New York...............	540	560	690	630	580	610	570	630	630	620	520
New Jersey.............	350	380	440	420	430	410	450	420	420	450	460
Illinois.................	440	520	550	550	540	520	530	440	520	440	450
Georgia................	220	470	430	440	400	390	410	370	400	400	380
North Carolina.........	260	360	390	400	360	400	390	370	360	320	350
Arizona................	330	480	350	360	350	350	350	360	330	340	330
Washington.............	170	(NA)	260	260	270	240	280	260	280	280	290
Other states...........	1,750	2,750	3,040	3,100	3,110	3,010	3,190	3,420	3,430	3,300	3,390

NA Not available. [1] Revised to be consistent with estimates derived from the 2010 Census.

Source: U.S. Department of Homeland Security, Office of Immigration Statistics, *Estimates of the Unauthorized Immigrant Population Residing in the United States, January 2015-January 2018*, January 2021. See also <www.dhs.gov/immigration-statistics#>.

Table 51. Immigrants Obtaining Legal Permanent Resident Status by Class of Admission: 2000 to 2020

[For years ending September 30. For definition of immigrants, see text, this section]

Class of admission	2000	2005	2010	2015	2019	2020
Total	**841,002**	**1,122,257**	**1,042,625**	**1,051,031**	**1,031,765**	**707,362**
New arrivals	407,279	383,955	476,049	505,031	453,718	268,153
Adjustments	433,723	738,302	566,576	546,000	578,047	439,209
Immediate relatives of U.S. citizens	346,350	436,115	476,414	465,068	505,765	321,148
Spouses	196,405	259,144	271,909	265,367	304,334	195,718
Children [1]	82,638	94,858	88,297	66,740	61,303	37,379
Parents	67,307	82,113	116,208	132,961	140,128	88,051
Family-sponsored preferences	235,092	212,970	214,589	213,910	204,139	121,560
Unmarried sons/daughters of U.S. citizens and their children	27,635	24,729	26,998	24,533	24,497	11,383
Spouses, children, and unmarried sons/daughters of alien residents	124,540	100,139	92,088	104,892	93,398	51,701
Married sons/daughters of U.S. citizens [2]	22,804	22,953	32,817	24,271	25,213	13,930
Brothers or sisters of U.S. citizens age 21 and older [2]	60,113	65,149	62,686	60,214	61,031	44,546
Employment-based preferences [2]	106,642	246,865	148,343	144,047	139,458	148,959
Priority workers [2]	27,566	64,731	41,055	41,688	39,471	47,388
Professionals with advanced degrees or aliens of exceptional ability [2]	20,255	42,597	53,946	44,344	39,506	43,666
Skilled workers, professionals, unskilled workers [2]	49,589	129,070	39,762	37,243	41,787	43,218
Special immigrants [2]	9,014	10,121	11,100	10,584	9,609	10,704
Employment creation (investors) [2]	218	346	2,480	10,188	9,085	3,983
Diversity (lottery) [3]	50,920	46,234	49,763	47,934	43,463	25,028
Refugees	56,091	112,676	92,741	118,431	80,908	44,404
Asylees	6,837	30,286	43,550	33,564	26,003	19,471
Parolees	3,162	7,715	1,592	23	16	13
Children born abroad to alien residents	(NA)	571	716	403	60	30
Nicaraguan Adjustment and Central American Relief Act	20,364	1,155	248	49	(NA)	(NA)
Haitian Refugee Immigration Fairness Act (HRIFA)	435	2,820	386	9	(NA)	(NA)
Certain Iraqis and Afghans employed by U.S. Government [2]	(NA)	(NA)	2,575	7,048	8,081	9,727
Cancellation of removal	12,154	20,785	8,180	4,713	4,033	3,685
Victims of human trafficking	(NA)	(NA)	511	970	818	866
Victims of crimes and their spouses and children	(NA)	(NA)	2,165	14,138	18,442	11,937
Other	2,955	4,065	852	724	579	534

NA Not available. [1] Includes orphans. [2] Includes spouses and children. [3] The Diversity Visa Program is a lottery available to nationals of countries with fewer than 50,000 persons granted legal permanent residency status within family- and employment-based categories during the preceding 5 years. Includes categories of immigrants admitted under three laws intended to diversify immigration: P.L. 99-603, P.L. 100-658, and P.L. 101-649. Additional rules and adjustments apply; see source for more information.

Source: U.S. Department of Homeland Security, Office of Immigration Statistics, "2020 Yearbook of Immigration Statistics," <www.dhs.gov/immigration-statistics/yearbook>, accessed March 2022.

Table 52. Immigrants Obtaining Legal Permanent Resident Status by Selected Country of Birth and Selected Characteristics: 2020

[For year ending September 30]

Age, marital status, occupation, class of admission	All countries [1]	Mexico	India	China	Dominican Republic	Vietnam	Philippines	El Salvador	Brazil
Total	**707,362**	**100,325**	**46,363**	**41,483**	**30,005**	**29,995**	**25,491**	**17,907**	**16,746**
AGE									
Under 18 years old	117,860	9,223	6,148	4,133	7,980	6,288	4,274	2,124	2,567
18 to 24 years old	74,907	10,779	2,789	2,594	4,051	4,447	2,632	2,891	1,414
25 to 34 years old	177,079	21,652	9,276	13,417	6,238	5,611	6,312	2,980	4,473
35 to 44 years old	153,114	24,519	15,771	8,663	4,923	4,561	5,254	4,356	4,703
45 to 54 years old	98,066	23,281	5,700	5,556	3,782	5,321	3,221	3,680	2,156
55 to 64 years old	52,991	7,675	3,186	4,053	2,109	2,894	2,396	1,281	984
65 years old and over	33,344	3,196	3,493	3,067	922	872	1,402	595	449
MARITAL STATUS									
Married	435,758	69,341	34,428	30,361	14,084	17,149	16,055	9,539	12,107
Single	230,043	23,290	9,753	8,831	14,368	11,550	8,367	6,774	3,867
Other	33,182	4,988	2,002	2,026	1,455	1,255	930	928	586
Unknown	8,379	2,706	180	265	98	41	139	666	186
OCCUPATION [2]									
Management, professional, and related	107,321	7,855	12,617	10,213	1,369	2,088	4,252	1,171	3,648
Service	34,219	6,876	683	2,393	745	540	1,714	1,960	1,100
Sales and office	35,177	3,930	1,859	3,134	1,220	3,507	1,317	679	890
Farming, fishing, and forestry	6,942	(D)	765	601	173	933	99	(D)	19
Construction, extraction, maintenance and repair	10,681	4,849	(D)	(D)	261	(D)	(D)	725	279
Production, transportation, and material moving	30,115	10,619	772	1,044	920	469	398	1,721	472
MAJOR CLASS OF ADMISSION									
Immediate relatives of U.S. citizens	321,148	66,579	12,945	14,660	16,107	9,556	14,890	10,287	8,448
Family-sponsored preferences	121,560	14,064	7,077	7,738	13,337	18,393	5,152	3,181	555
Employment-based preferences	148,959	7,933	24,883	14,018	363	1,865	5,087	(D)	7,427
Diversity program (lottery)	25,028	3	14	10	0	0	(D)	(D)	5
Refugees and asylees	63,875	1,026	1,146	4,956	61	64	(D)	2,006	150
Other	26,792	10,720	298	101	137	117	343	1,146	161

D Data withheld to avoid disclosure. [1] Includes other countries not shown separately. [2] Those in the military, without an occupation or not working outside of home (e.g. home makers, students), and unknown occupation are not shown.

Source: U.S. Department of Homeland Security, Office of Immigration Statistics, "Profiles on Lawful Permanent Residents: Fiscal Year 2020," <www.dhs.gov/profiles-lawful-permanent-residents>, accessed March 2022.

Table 53. Immigrants Obtaining Legal Permanent Resident Status by Country of Birth: 1991 to 2020

[In thousands (9,080.5 represents 9,080,500). For years ending September 30]

Region and country of birth	1991-2000	2001-2010	2011-2019	2020	Region and country of birth	1991-2000	2001-2010	2011-2019	2020
All countries [1]	**9,080.5**	**10,501.1**	**9,590.8**	**707.4**	Vietnam	420.8	306.1	303.9	30.0
Europe	**1,226.0**	**1,263.9**	**766.7**	**69.0**	Yemen	16.3	24.6	40.9	5.9
Albania	26.2	50.5	40.6	3.5	**Africa**	**382.5**	**860.4**	**964.9**	**76.6**
France	27.4	39.6	39.9	4.1	Cameroon	5.8	23.2	39.0	2.8
Germany	67.6	77.7	48.2	3.9	Congo, Dem. Rep. of the	2.5	7.9	53.1	7.5
Italy	22.5	26.5	29.8	3.2	Egypt	46.7	73.1	91.8	6.2
Poland	169.5	116.8	50.1	3.3	Ethiopia	49.3	109.7	114.5	6.3
Romania	57.5	53.6	29.6	2.0	Ghana	35.6	65.3	75.3	4.6
Russia	[2] 127.8	139.7	82.2	8.0	Kenya	14.0	59.7	59.9	4.0
Spain	13.7	15.8	25.0	2.6	Liberia	16.0	45.2	33.6	1.7
Ukraine	[2] 140.1	149.3	84.1	9.9	Morocco	20.0	44.4	34.3	2.9
United Kingdom	135.6	153.5	106.3	9.7	Nigeria	67.2	111.2	121.4	12.4
Asia	**2,973.2**	**3,784.6**	**3,780.5**	**272.6**	Somalia	20.1	64.2	51.1	2.0
Afghanistan	17.4	24.3	79.4	11.4	South Africa	22.6	32.9	25.8	2.7
Armenia	[2] 26.6	29.9	27.6	2.1	Sudan	12.6	32.9	26.3	1.9
Bangladesh	66.0	106.7	136.0	9.3	**Oceania**	**47.9**	**58.1**	**46.2**	**4.0**
Bhutan	(Z)	7.0	53.9	1.1	Australia	17.9	26.4	25.4	2.5
Burma	11.0	45.0	109.6	4.0	**North America**	**3,910.1**	**3,605.1**	**3,298.6**	**222.3**
Cambodia	18.5	35.6	25.4	1.6	Canada	137.2	168.2	108.7	9.5
China	424.4	662.7	672.0	41.5	Cuba	178.7	318.4	452.2	16.4
India	383.0	662.5	585.3	46.4	Dominican Republic	340.8	329.1	451.2	30.0
Iran	112.5	125.9	109.2	8.8	El Salvador	217.3	252.8	196.5	17.9
Iraq	40.7	65.0	145.3	2.3	Guatemala	103.0	160.7	109.0	7.8
Israel	31.9	46.6	35.7	3.7	Haiti	181.7	213.8	181.5	9.3
Japan	61.4	76.1	47.7	3.9	Honduras	66.7	65.4	93.7	8.3
Jordan [3]	39.7	38.7	42.9	3.1	Jamaica	173.4	180.7	183.7	12.8
Korea, South [4]	171.1	221.5	181.5	16.2	Mexico	2,250.5	1,693.2	1,380.6	100.3
Lebanon	43.4	39.5	26.0	2.1	Nicaragua	94.6	60.9	29.1	2.6
Malaysia	14.8	20.5	25.6	1.9	Trinidad and Tobago	63.2	61.8	34.6	1.7
Nepal	3.6	33.1	106.4	7.8	**South America**	**539.3**	**906.0**	**720.9**	**62.2**
Pakistan	124.5	157.0	146.7	10.5	Argentina	24.3	50.5	35.4	3.0
Philippines	505.3	587.2	470.9	25.5	Brazil	52.2	123.8	120.1	16.7
Syria	26.1	25.9	47.9	3.2	Colombia	130.8	251.3	174.1	12.0
Taiwan	106.3	87.9	47.3	4.8	Ecuador	76.3	112.5	96.1	6.2
Thailand	48.4	68.3	65.2	4.2	Guyana	73.8	76.2	51.8	3.0
Turkey	26.3	41.1	41.4	4.4	Peru	105.6	145.7	101.0	5.6
Uzbekistan	[2] 22.9	36.0	39.0	1.3	Venezuela	29.9	84.4	95.8	12.1

Z Less than 500. [1] Includes other countries not shown separately. [2] Covers years 1992–2000. [3] Prior to 2003, includes Palestine; beginning in 2003, Palestine included in Unknown (not shown separately). [4] Prior to 2009, includes a small number of cases from North Korea.

Source: U.S. Department of Homeland Security, Office of Immigration Statistics, "2020 Yearbook of Immigration Statistics," <www.dhs.gov/immigration-statistics/yearbook>, accessed March 2022.

Table 54. Refugees and Asylees Obtaining Legal Permanent Resident Status by Country of Birth: 1991 to 2020

[For years ending September 30]

Country of birth	1991-2000	2001-2010	2011-2019	2020	Country of birth	1991-2000	2001-2010	2011-2019	2020
All countries [1]	**1,016,820**	**1,325,365**	**1,321,189**	**63,875**	Cameroon	299	7,564	7,738	296
Europe	**425,047**	**296,794**	**40,127**	**6,013**	Congo, Dem. Rep. of the	922	5,643	28,363	5,168
Moldova	[2] 10,150	10,813	3,890	325	Congo, Rep. of	25	5,243	3,490	88
Russia	[2] 54,488	32,819	6,151	771	Cote d'Ivoire	119	4,404	2,787	78
Soviet Union [3]	117,783	6,794	2,920	207	Egypt	419	7,987	18,317	853
Spain	438	610	3,030	148	Eritrea	608	4,534	12,274	1,281
Ukraine	[2] 96,974	57,186	12,423	3,832	Ethiopia [4]	17,829	31,900	32,191	1,661
Asia	**350,702**	**389,469**	**580,465**	**19,361**	Gambia, The	53	1,221	2,016	85
Afghanistan	9,711	13,533	7,299	743	Guinea	50	4,467	4,247	104
Armenia	1,794	12,408	2,981	230	Kenya	1,438	15,351	15,239	731
Bhutan	(D)	6,762	53,414	1,045	Liberia	3,836	28,808	5,876	233
Burma	721	32,904	95,924	2,976	Rwanda	389	2,939	6,079	744
China	7,577	111,632	120,509	4,956	Somalia	16,737	59,069	40,097	883
India	2,538	24,010	8,819	1,146	South Africa	194	201	2,101	82
Indonesia	201	7,618	2,136	85	Sudan	5,174	23,580	11,204	490
Iran	24,251	45,515	30,878	561	Tanzania	16	3,503	8,373	1,921
Iraq	22,488	40,789	115,285	922	Uganda	439	2,482	6,305	1,075
Jordan	331	1,013	4,391	149	**Oceania**	**291**	**1,453**	**341**	**20**
Malaysia	383	1,125	12,182	773	**North America**	**183,251**	**326,846**	**438,874**	**17,660**
Nepal	32	6,000	41,234	1,616	Cuba	142,571	276,331	390,684	12,148
Pakistan	1,649	8,339	7,306	884	El Salvador	4,072	4,061	[5] 8,212	2,006
Sri Lanka	353	1,852	2,385	137	Guatemala	2,029	7,399	10,250	1,358
Syria	2,119	2,223	24,258	807	Haiti	9,354	29,824	11,670	120
Thailand	22,716	22,405	26,446	842	Honduras	1,047	1,684	4,981	727
Uzbekistan	[2] 17,991	14,047	2,745	105	Mexico	415	2,780	7,725	1,026
Vietnam	206,530	36,990	3,150	64	**South America**	**5,840**	**65,912**	**30,235**	**2,724**
Africa	**51,469**	**242,839**	**230,406**	**18,080**	Colombia	1,129	40,321	9,543	448
Burundi	148	3,387	3,870	958	Venezuela	1,390	10,726	11,287	1,757

D Data withheld to avoid disclosure. [1] Includes other countries and unknown not shown separately. [2] Covers years 1992-2000. [3] Data are for unknown republics only. [4] Prior to 1993, data include Eritrea. [5] Omits data for 2017 that was withheld to avoid disclosure.

Source: U.S. Department of Homeland Security, Office of Immigration Statistics, "2020 Yearbook of Immigration Statistics," and earlier releases, <www.dhs.gov/immigration-statistics/yearbook>, accessed March 2022.

Table 55. Population by Selected Ancestry Group and Region: 2019

[In thousands (328,240 represents 328,240,000), except percent. Covers single and multiple ancestries; includes all people who reported each ancestry. Ancestry refers to a person's ethnic origin, heritage, descent, or "roots," which may reflect their place of birth or that of previous generations of their family. The American Community Survey universe includes the household population and the population living in institutions, college dormitories, and other group quarters. Based on a sample and subject to sampling variability; see text, this section]

Ancestry group	Total, (1,000)	North-east	Mid-west	South	West	Ancestry group	Total, (1,000)	North-east	Mid-west	South	West
Total population [1]	**328,240**	**17**	**21**	**38**	**24**	Irish	30,353	26	25	31	18
Afghan	156	11	5	31	53	Israeli	145	32	10	29	29
Albanian	200	49	28	17	6	Italian	16,147	42	17	24	17
American	20,071	12	18	56	14	Latvian	86	26	25	24	26
Arab [1]	2,098	23	25	30	22	Lithuanian	632	37	25	21	17
Egyptian	280	33	13	30	24	Northern European	618	12	19	28	42
Iraqi	177	9	35	29	27	Norwegian	4,296	6	47	14	33
Jordanian	93	14	36	30	20	Pennsylvania					
Lebanese	482	25	27	29	19	German	291	54	27	14	6
Moroccan	118	32	14	38	16	Polish	8,970	31	37	20	12
Palestinian	139	15	31	33	21	Portuguese	1,371	43	4	17	36
Syrian	179	34	19	25	21	Romanian	465	24	25	23	28
Arab	289	16	30	30	24	Russian	2,433	34	17	22	26
Armenian	458	20	8	10	62	Scandinavian	1,057	8	29	24	39
Assyrian [3]	94	3	66	3	29	Scotch-Irish	2,925	12	17	51	20
Australian	94	19	14	30	38	Scottish	5,131	15	20	39	26
Austrian	646	27	24	26	23	Serbian	185	20	42	19	20
Belgian	340	11	50	19	20	Slavic	130	26	23	26	25
Brazilian	499	43	6	35	16	Slovak	654	41	32	18	9
British	2,458	13	17	40	29	Slovene	179	15	52	15	18
Bulgarian	101	21	27	26	26	Sub-Saharan					
Cajun	110	5	4	83	9	African [1]	4,018	19	19	45	16
Canadian	608	25	17	29	28	Cape Verdean	101	85	1	10	4
Croatian	402	21	38	16	25	Ethiopian	322	7	17	42	34
Czech	1,295	11	44	29	16	Ghanaian	162	42	14	36	9
Czechoslovakian	298	19	35	28	19	Kenyan	91	14	27	35	24
Danish	1,216	8	29	16	47	Nigerian	462	20	16	52	12
Dutch	3,578	15	38	24	23	Somali	183	8	56	9	28
Eastern European	1,139	33	19	26	22	African	2,127	16	18	51	15
English	23,593	16	21	38	25	Swedish	3,536	13	38	17	32
European	6,918	10	20	37	33	Swiss	905	16	34	20	30
Finnish	653	12	44	16	28	Turkish	212	32	11	32	25
French						Ukrainian	1,010	35	19	21	24
(except Basque)	7,116	23	23	34	20	Welsh	1,956	17	22	34	27
French						West Indian [1,2]	3,067	42	4	49	5
Canadian	1,995	41	19	25	14	Haitian	1,084	37	3	58	2
German	40,364	16	39	26	19	Jamaican	1,172	44	5	46	5
Greek	1,247	32	22	26	20	Trinidadian and					
Guyanese	232	74	4	18	3	Tobagonian	219	51	3	41	5
Hungarian	1,323	31	30	22	17	West Indian	278	55	4	36	6
Iranian	469	11	7	27	55	Yugoslavian	233	20	31	22	26

[1] Includes other groups, not shown separately. [2] Excludes Hispanic-origin groups. [3] Assyrian, Chaldean, and Syriac.

Source: U.S. Census Bureau, 2019 American Community Survey, B04006, "People Reporting Ancestry," <data.census.gov>, accessed November 2020.

Table 56. Language Spoken at Home and English Speaking Ability: 2019

[308,835 represents 308,835,000. See headnote, Table 55]

Language	Number of speakers of language at home (1,000)	Percent who speak English less than "very well"	Language	Number of speakers of language at home (1,000)	Percent who speak English less than "very well"
Total population 5 years old and over	**308,835**	**(X)**	Bengali	369	41.1
			Nepali, Marathi, or other Indic	417	37.5
Speak only English	241,032	(X)	Other Indo-European	576	28.2
Spanish	41,757	38.6	Telugu	420	19.0
French (including Cajun)	1,172	20.5	Tamil	294	15.7
Haitian	925	35.0	Malayalam, Kannada, or other Dravidian	266	19.8
Italian	540	24.6	Chinese (including Mandarin, Cantonese)	3,495	52.0
Portuguese	846	36.2	Japanese	455	38.5
German	895	15.0	Korean	1,075	51.0
Yiddish, Pennsylvania Dutch [1]	560	28.9	Hmong	230	36.8
Greek	264	22.8	Vietnamese	1,571	56.9
Russian	941	41.2	Khmer	193	48.2
Polish	510	36.2	Thai, Lao, or other Tai-Kadai	315	51.0
Serbo-Croatian	243	32.8	Tagalog (including Filipino)	1,764	29.6
Ukrainian or other Slavic languages	322	36.1	Ilocano, Samoan, Hawaiian [2]	486	33.3
Armenian	237	40.5	Arabic	1,260	35.0
Persian (including Farsi, Dari)	457	35.3	Hebrew	211	11.7
Gujarati	455	31.7	Amharic, Somali, or other Afro-Asiatic	590	39.4
Hindi	893	17.7	Yoruba, Twi, Igbo [3]	589	20.9
Urdu	520	26.7	Swahili and other African [4]	299	33.3
Punjabi	322	38.5	Navajo	171	25.5

X Not applicable. [1] Includes other West Germanic. [2] Includes other Austronesian. [3] Includes other West African. [4] Other languages of Central, Eastern, and Southern Africa.

Source: U.S. Census Bureau, 2019 American Community Survey, B16001, "Language Spoken at Home by Ability to Speak English for the Population 5 Years and Over," <data.census.gov>, accessed November 2020.

Table 57. Language Spoken at Home by State: 2019

[In thousands (308,835 represents 308,835,000), except percent. The American Community Survey universe includes the household population and the population living in institutions, college dormitories, and other group quarters. Based on a sample and subject to sampling variability; see text, this section, and Appendix III]

State	Population 5 years old and over (1,000)	English only (1,000)	Language other than English — Number (1,000)	Language other than English — Percent of population 5 years and over	State	Population 5 years old and over (1,000)	English only (1,000)	Language other than English — Number (1,000)	Language other than English — Percent of population 5 years and over
U.S.	**308,835**	**241,032**	**67,802**	**22.0**	MO	5,772	5,393	379	6.6
AL	4,617	4,361	255	5.5	MT	1,010	969	41	4.0
AK	681	570	111	16.3	NE	1,805	1,593	212	11.8
AZ	6,851	4,988	1,863	27.2	NV	2,896	1,992	904	31.2
AR	2,834	2,619	216	7.6	NH	1,296	1,187	109	8.4
CA	37,134	20,617	16,518	44.5	NJ	8,370	5,677	2,693	32.2
CO	5,431	4,526	906	16.7	NM	1,980	1,308	672	34.0
CT	3,385	2,623	762	22.5	NY	18,334	12,710	5,624	30.7
DE	920	791	129	14.0	NC	9,892	8,677	1,214	12.3
DC	660	554	106	16.1	ND	711	675	36	5.1
FL	20,347	14,190	6,156	30.3	OH	11,002	10,177	825	7.5
GA	9,978	8,542	1,436	14.4	OK	3,706	3,301	405	10.9
HI	1,331	960	371	27.8	OR	3,994	3,373	621	15.5
ID	1,671	1,490	181	10.8	PA	12,106	10,686	1,420	11.7
IL	11,929	9,151	2,778	23.3	RI	1,005	776	229	22.7
IN	6,318	5,761	557	8.8	SC	4,859	4,496	363	7.5
IA	2,964	2,700	264	8.9	SD	826	778	48	5.8
KS	2,730	2,401	329	12.1	TN	6,422	5,936	486	7.6
KY	4,195	3,941	253	6.0	TX	27,014	17,410	9,604	35.6
LA	4,356	4,018	338	7.8	UT	2,960	2,486	474	16.0
ME	1,281	1,205	76	5.9	VT	595	562	33	5.5
MD	5,687	4,583	1,104	19.4	VA	8,036	6,683	1,353	16.8
MA	6,537	4,920	1,617	24.7	WA	7,160	5,694	1,466	20.5
MI	9,419	8,476	943	10.0	WV	1,701	1,656	45	2.6
MN	5,290	4,641	649	12.3	WI	5,495	5,015	481	8.7
MS	2,797	2,685	112	4.0	WY	546	510	36	6.6

Source: U.S. Census Bureau, 2019 American Community Survey, C16005, "Nativity by Language Spoken at Home by Ability to Speak English for the Population 5 Years and Over," <data.census.gov>, accessed November 2020.

Table 58. Language Spoken at Home—25 Largest Cities: 2019

[In thousands (922 represents 922,000), except percent. Data shown for population aged 5 and over. The American Community Survey universe includes the household population and the population living in institutions, college dormitories, and other group quarters. Based on a sample and subject to sampling variability; see text, this section, and Appendix III]

City	Popula-tion 5 years old and over (1,000)	English only (1,000)	Language other than English, total [1] — Number (1,000)	Language other than English, total [1] — Percent	Speak English less than "very well" (1,000)	Spanish (1,000)	Other Indo-European languages [2] (1,000)	Asian and Pacific Island languages [2] (1,000)
Austin, TX	922	636	286	31.0	105	197	36	44
Boston, MA	662	418	244	36.9	104	109	72	49
Charlotte, NC	826	646	179	21.7	77	106	29	31
Chicago, IL	2,531	1,636	895	35.4	363	597	150	106
Columbus, OH	838	693	146	17.4	53	41	35	27
Dallas, TX	1,244	708	536	43.1	250	458	27	25
Denver, CO	685	521	164	23.9	53	122	16	14
Detroit, MI	625	554	71	11.4	33	40	12	3
El Paso, TX	635	200	435	68.5	190	421	7	5
Fort Worth, TX	841	544	297	35.3	104	239	25	20
Houston, TX	2,145	1,099	1,046	48.8	481	843	72	88
Indianapolis, IN [3]	807	702	105	13.0	50	57	18	20
Jacksonville, FL	850	715	135	15.8	54	64	32	30
Los Angeles, CA	3,752	1,535	2,217	59.1	942	1,575	270	312
Nashville–Davidson, TN [3]	624	510	114	18.3	59	58	20	15
New York, NY	7,816	4,041	3,775	48.3	1,733	1,864	988	710
Philadelphia, PA	1,481	1,124	358	24.1	166	165	77	83
Phoenix, AZ	1,567	973	593	37.9	195	478	43	42
Portland, OR	621	503	118	19.0	39	45	25	39
San Antonio, TX	1,445	831	614	42.5	184	552	21	30
San Diego, CA	1,343	819	524	39.0	181	289	59	153
San Francisco, CA	842	486	356	42.3	161	87	51	207
San Jose, CA	965	394	570	59.1	224	215	74	266
Seattle, WA	720	560	160	22.2	54	30	28	79
Washington, DC	660	554	106	16.1	34	59	22	14

[1] Includes other language groups, not shown separately. [2] Beginning 2016, data are not comparable with data from previous years due to changes in language classifications; for more information, see <www.census.gov/content/dam/Census/programs-surveys/acs/tech-doc/user-notes/2016_Language_User_Note.pdf>. [3] Represents the portion of a consolidated city that is not within one or more separately incorporated places.

Source: U.S. Census Bureau, 2019 American Community Survey, C16005, "Nativity by Language Spoken at Home by Ability to Speak English for the Population 5 Years and Over," <data.census.gov>, accessed November 2020.

Table 59. Marital Status of the Population by Sex, Race, and Hispanic Origin: 2000 to 2021

[In millions, except percent (213.8 represents 213,800,000). As of March. Data are shown for persons aged 15 years and over. Excludes members of Armed Forces except those living off post or with their families on post. Beginning 2005 based on an expanded sample of households. Data for 2010 based on population controls from Census 2000. 2020 and 2021 data based on population controls from Census 2010. Based on Current Population Survey; see text, this section and Appendix III]

Marital status, race and Hispanic origin	Total				Male				Female			
	2000	2010	2020	2021	2000	2010	2020	2021	2000	2010	2020	2021
Total [1]	**213.8**	**242.0**	**264.7**	**266.1**	**103.1**	**117.7**	**128.5**	**129.3**	**110.7**	**124.4**	**136.2**	**136.8**
Never married	60.0	74.2	86.8	89.2	32.3	40.2	46.0	47.4	27.8	34.0	40.9	41.8
Married [2]	120.2	129.7	137.8	135.9	59.7	64.5	68.4	67.5	60.5	65.2	69.3	68.3
Widowed	13.7	14.3	14.7	15.2	2.6	3.0	3.5	3.6	11.1	11.4	11.3	11.6
Divorced	19.9	23.7	25.3	25.9	8.6	10.0	10.7	10.8	11.3	13.8	14.7	15.1
Percent of total	100.0	100.0	100.0	100.0	100.0	100.0	100.0	100.0	100.0	100.0	100.0	100.0
Never married	28.1	30.7	32.8	33.5	31.3	34.2	35.8	36.6	25.1	27.4	30.0	30.6
Married [2]	56.2	53.6	52.0	51.1	57.9	54.8	53.2	52.2	54.7	52.4	50.9	49.9
Widowed	6.4	5.9	5.6	5.7	2.5	2.5	2.7	2.8	10.0	9.1	8.3	8.5
Divorced	9.3	9.8	9.6	9.7	8.3	8.5	8.3	8.4	10.2	11.1	10.8	11.0
White, total [3]	**177.6**	**195.5**	**204.9**	**205.7**	**86.4**	**96.2**	**100.6**	**101.1**	**91.1**	**99.3**	**104.2**	**104.5**
Never married	45.3	54.7	60.5	62.3	25.1	30.6	32.9	34.0	20.2	24.1	27.6	28.3
Married [2]	104.2	109.6	112.2	110.3	51.9	54.7	56.2	55.3	52.3	54.8	56.1	55.0
Widowed	11.5	11.8	11.8	12.2	2.2	2.5	2.9	3.0	9.3	9.3	8.9	9.2
Divorced	16.5	19.4	20.3	20.8	7.2	8.3	8.7	8.9	9.3	11.1	11.6	12.0
Percent of total	100.0	100.0	100.0	100.0	100.0	100.0	100.0	100.0	100.0	100.0	100.0	100.0
Never married	25.5	28.0	29.5	30.3	29.1	31.8	32.7	33.6	22.1	24.3	26.5	27.1
Married [2]	58.7	56.1	54.8	53.6	60.0	56.9	55.8	54.7	57.4	55.2	53.8	52.6
Widowed	6.5	6.0	5.8	5.9	2.5	2.6	2.8	2.9	10.2	9.3	8.6	8.8
Divorced	9.3	9.9	9.9	10.1	8.4	8.7	8.7	8.8	10.2	11.2	11.1	11.5
Black, total [3]	**25.9**	**29.4**	**33.9**	**34.2**	**11.7**	**13.3**	**15.6**	**15.7**	**14.2**	**16.0**	**18.3**	**18.5**
Never married	11.3	13.7	16.7	17.1	5.2	6.5	8.0	8.1	6.0	7.2	8.7	8.9
Married [2]	10.1	10.6	11.8	11.7	5.0	5.2	5.8	5.8	5.1	5.4	5.9	5.9
Widowed	1.7	1.8	1.9	1.9	0.3	0.4	0.4	0.4	1.4	1.5	1.5	1.5
Divorced	2.8	3.2	3.6	3.5	1.1	1.2	1.3	1.4	1.7	2.0	2.2	2.1
Percent of total	100.0	100.0	100.0	100.0	100.0	100.0	100.0	100.0	100.0	100.0	100.0	100.0
Never married	43.5	46.8	49.3	49.9	44.9	48.8	51.4	51.7	42.4	45.2	47.5	48.3
Married [2]	39.2	36.1	34.7	34.2	42.8	39.4	37.3	36.8	36.2	33.4	32.4	32.0
Widowed	6.6	6.2	5.6	5.7	2.8	2.7	2.6	2.6	9.6	9.1	8.1	8.3
Divorced	10.7	10.9	10.5	10.3	9.5	9.1	8.6	8.9	11.8	12.4	12.1	11.5
Asian, total [3]	**8.4**	**11.2**	**16.7**	**16.7**	**4.0**	**5.3**	**7.9**	**7.8**	**4.4**	**5.9**	**8.8**	**8.9**
Never married	2.8	3.2	5.0	5.0	1.5	1.7	2.6	2.7	1.3	1.4	2.3	2.4
Married [2]	4.9	7.0	10.4	10.2	2.3	3.3	4.9	4.8	2.6	3.7	5.5	5.5
Widowed	0.3	0.5	0.7	0.7	0.0	0.1	0.1	0.1	0.3	0.5	0.6	0.5
Divorced	0.4	0.5	0.7	0.7	0.1	0.2	0.2	0.2	0.2	0.3	0.4	0.5
Percent of total	100.0	100.0	100.0	100.0	100.0	100.0	100.0	100.0	100.0	100.0	100.0	100.0
Never married	33.1	28.3	29.8	30.1	37.7	32.8	33.4	34.1	28.8	24.2	26.7	26.6
Married [2]	58.6	62.8	62.1	61.5	57.8	62.6	62.0	61.1	59.4	62.9	62.3	61.8
Widowed	4.0	4.7	4.1	4.0	1.2	1.3	1.5	1.6	6.6	7.7	6.4	6.1
Divorced	4.3	4.3	4.0	4.4	3.2	3.3	3.1	3.2	5.3	5.2	4.7	5.4
Hispanic, total [4]	**22.8**	**34.3**	**45.0**	**45.8**	**11.3**	**17.7**	**22.5**	**22.9**	**11.5**	**16.6**	**22.6**	**23.0**
Never married	7.5	13.3	18.9	19.5	4.2	7.7	10.3	10.6	3.3	5.6	8.6	8.8
Married [2]	12.7	17.2	21.2	21.5	6.2	8.6	10.3	10.5	6.5	8.6	10.9	11.0
Widowed	0.9	1.2	1.4	1.5	0.2	0.3	0.3	0.4	0.7	0.9	1.1	1.1
Divorced	1.6	2.6	3.5	3.3	0.7	1.1	1.5	1.4	1.0	1.5	2.0	2.0
Percent of total	100.0	100.0	100.0	100.0	100.0	100.0	100.0	100.0	100.0	100.0	100.0	100.0
Never married	33.1	38.7	42.0	42.5	37.5	43.4	46.0	46.6	28.9	33.7	38.1	38.4
Married [2]	55.9	50.1	47.0	46.9	55.1	48.7	45.7	45.8	56.6	51.7	48.3	48.1
Widowed	3.9	3.5	3.2	3.3	1.5	1.7	1.5	1.6	6.2	5.4	4.8	4.9
Divorced	7.1	7.7	7.8	7.3	5.9	6.2	6.8	6.0	8.3	9.2	8.8	8.6

[1] Includes persons of other races not shown separately. [2] Includes persons who are married with spouse present, married with spouse absent, and separated. Beginning 2019, estimates for married individuals include same-sex married couples. [3] Beginning 2003, data represent persons who selected this race group only and exclude persons reporting more than one race. Prior to 2003, the CPS allowed respondents to report only one race group. See also comments on race in the text for this section. [4] Hispanic persons may be of any race.

Source: U.S. Census Bureau, Families and Living Arrangements, Historical Marital Status Tables, "Table MS-1. Marital Status of the Population 15 Years Old and Over, by Sex, Race and Hispanic Origin: 1950 to Present," <www.census.gov/data/tables/time-series/demo/families/marital.html>, accessed January 2022.

Table 60. Marital Status of the Population by Sex and Age: 2021

[129,300 represents 129,300,000. As of March. Data are shown for population aged 15 and older. Excludes members of Armed Forces except those living off post or with their families on post. Population controls based on Census 2010. Based on Current Population Survey; see text, this section, and Appendix III]

Sex and age	Number of persons (1,000)					Percent distribution				
	Total	Never married	Married [1]	Widowed	Divorced	Total	Never married	Married [1]	Widowed	Divorced
MALE										
Total..................	**129,300**	**47,351**	**67,544**	**3,582**	**10,824**	**100.0**	**36.6**	**52.2**	**2.8**	**8.4**
15 to 17 years old..............	6,497	6,383	78	12	24	100.0	98.2	1.2	–	–
18 years old and over.........	122,804	40,968	67,466	3,570	10,799	100.0	33.4	54.9	2.9	8.8
18 to 19 years old............	3,972	3,922	45	–	6	100.0	98.7	1.1	–	–
20 to 24 years old............	10,570	9,806	703	8	54	100.0	92.8	6.7	–	0.5
25 to 29 years old............	11,483	8,522	2,747	13	200	100.0	74.2	23.9	–	1.7
30 to 34 years old............	11,352	5,476	5,439	9	428	100.0	48.2	47.9	–	3.8
35 to 39 years old............	10,738	3,369	6,638	45	686	100.0	31.4	61.8	–	6.4
40 to 44 years old............	10,069	2,366	6,695	42	966	100.0	23.5	66.5	–	9.6
45 to 49 years old............	9,518	1,868	6,395	78	1,177	100.0	19.6	67.2	0.8	12.4
50 to 54 years old............	9,899	1,503	6,835	154	1,407	100.0	15.2	69.0	1.6	14.2
55 to 64 years old............	20,023	2,572	13,946	473	3,031	100.0	12.8	69.6	2.4	15.1
65 to 74 years old............	15,326	1,141	11,262	915	2,008	100.0	7.4	73.5	6.0	13.1
75 to 84 years old............	7,552	351	5,412	1,065	723	100.0	4.6	71.7	14.1	9.6
85 years old and over........	2,303	74	1,347	768	113	100.0	3.2	58.5	33.3	4.9
FEMALE										
Total..................	**136,835**	**41,808**	**68,331**	**11,612**	**15,085**	**100.0**	**30.6**	**49.9**	**8.5**	**11.0**
15 to 17 years old..............	6,341	6,238	87	5	11	100.0	98.4	1.4	–	–
18 years old and over.........	130,494	35,570	68,244	11,607	15,074	100.0	27.3	52.3	8.9	11.6
18 to 19 years old............	3,843	3,762	67	7	7	100.0	97.9	1.7	–	–
20 to 24 years old............	10,449	9,177	1,179	24	69	100.0	87.8	11.3	–	0.7
25 to 29 years old............	11,106	6,974	3,769	48	314	100.0	62.8	33.9	–	2.8
30 to 34 years old............	11,335	4,269	6,394	47	626	100.0	37.7	56.4	–	5.5
35 to 39 years old............	10,865	2,607	7,204	98	957	100.0	24.0	66.3	0.9	8.8
40 to 44 years old............	10,324	1,911	6,973	142	1,299	100.0	18.5	67.5	1.4	12.6
45 to 49 years old............	9,881	1,392	6,796	185	1,508	100.0	14.1	68.8	1.9	15.3
50 to 54 years old............	10,366	1,232	6,997	319	1,817	100.0	11.9	67.5	3.1	17.5
55 to 64 years old............	21,738	2,413	13,780	1,613	3,931	100.0	11.1	63.4	7.4	18.1
65 to 74 years old............	17,690	1,259	10,377	3,070	2,984	100.0	7.1	58.7	17.4	16.9
75 to 84 years old............	9,239	432	3,992	3,559	1,255	100.0	4.7	43.2	38.5	13.6
85 years old and over........	3,657	141	715	2,495	306	100.0	3.9	19.6	68.2	8.4

– Represents or rounds to zero. [1] Includes persons who are married with spouse present, married with spouse absent, and separated.

Source: U.S. Census Bureau, America's Families and Living Arrangements, Adult (A table series), "Table A1. Marital Status of People 15 Years and Over, by Age, Sex, and Personal Earnings: 2021," <www.census.gov/data/tables/2021/demo/families/cps-2021.html>, accessed December 2021.

Table 61. Living Arrangements of Persons 18 Years Old and Over by Age and Sex: 2021

[In thousands (253,298 represents 253,298,000), except percent. As of March. Excludes members of Armed Forces except those living off post or with their families on post. Population controls based on Census 2010 and an expanded sample of households. Based on Current Population Survey (CPS); see text, this section, and Appendix III]

Living arrangement	Total	18 to 24 years old	25 to 34 years old	35 to 64 years old	65 to 74 years old	75 years old and over
NUMBER (1,000)						
Total.................................	**253,298**	**28,836**	**45,275**	**123,421**	**33,016**	**22,751**
Male..................................	122,804	14,543	22,834	60,246	15,326	9,855
Female...............................	130,495	14,293	22,441	63,175	17,690	12,896
PERCENT DISTRIBUTION						
Male, total.......................	**100.0**	**100.0**	**100.0**	**100.0**	**100.0**	**100.0**
Alone................................	(NA)	4.8	11.7	13.5	18.5	23.7
With spouse [1].....................	(NA)	4.3	33.1	63.4	70.7	66.3
Child of householder [2].............	(NA)	59.2	19.7	5.0	(NA)	(NA)
Living with partner..................	(NA)	7.0	16.6	7.5	3.4	2.7
Other relatives......................	(NA)	14.1	10.8	7.8	[3] 5.9	[3] 6.0
Nonrelatives........................	(NA)	10.6	8.2	2.9	1.5	1.2
Female, total.....................	**100.0**	**100.0**	**100.0**	**100.0**	**100.0**	**100.0**
Alone................................	(NA)	4.6	9.1	11.9	25.7	42.8
With spouse [1].....................	(NA)	7.4	42.0	61.7	56.2	34.9
Child of householder [2].............	(NA)	54.5	12.3	2.7	(NA)	(NA)
Living with partner..................	(NA)	11.7	17.0	6.3	2.6	1.3
Other relatives......................	(NA)	13.3	15.0	15.7	[3] 14.2	[3] 19.6
Nonrelatives........................	(NA)	8.5	4.6	1.6	1.3	1.3

NA Not available. [1] Includes only adults who are married, spouse present in the household. This living arrangement supersedes the others shown in the table. For example, people living with their parents and a spouse are counted as living with a spouse, not as a child of the householder. [2] Children of the householder are not living with a spouse or unmarried partner, and are residing in the household of a parent. In CPS, unmarried college students living in dormitories are counted as living in the parental home. [3] Includes children of the householder who are not living with a spouse or unmarried partner, and are residing in the household of a parent.

Source: U.S. Census Bureau, America's Families and Living Arrangements, Historical Living Arrangements of Adults, "Table AD-3. Living Arrangements of Adults 18 and Over, 1967 to Present," <www.census.gov/data/tables/time-series/demo/families/adults.html>, accessed December 2021.

Table 62. Households, Families, Subfamilies, and Married Couples: 1990 to 2021

[In thousands (93,347 represents 93,347,000), except as indicated. As of March. Excludes members of the Armed Services except those living off post or with their families on post. Beginning 2001, based on an expanded sample of households. Population controls for 2010 based on Census 2000; beginning 2012, population controls based on Census 2010. Based on Current Population Survey (CPS), see text, this section and Appendix III. Minus sign (-) indicates decrease]

Type of unit	1990	2000	2010	2015	2020	2021	Percent change		
							1990 to 2000	2000 to 2010	2010 to 2020
Households	**93,347**	**104,705**	**117,538**	**124,587**	**128,451**	**129,931**	**12.2**	**12.3**	**9.3**
Persons per household	2.63	2.62	2.59	2.54	2.53	2.51	(X)	(X)	(X)
White [1]	80,163	87,671	95,489	98,679	100,568	101,582	9.4	8.9	5.3
Black [1]	10,486	12,849	14,730	16,437	17,054	17,358	22.5	14.6	15.8
Asian [1]	(NA)	(NA)	4,687	6,040	6,853	6,987	(NA)	(NA)	46.2
Hispanic [2]	5,933	9,319	13,298	16,239	17,667	18,349	57.1	42.7	32.9
Family households	66,090	72,025	78,833	81,716	83,677	83,907	9.0	9.5	6.1
Married couple	52,317	55,311	58,410	60,010	62,342	61,454	5.7	5.6	6.7
Male householder [3]	2,884	4,028	5,580	6,162	6,503	6,963	39.7	38.5	16.5
Female householder [3]	10,890	12,687	14,843	15,544	14,832	15,490	16.5	17.0	-0.1
Nonfamily households	27,257	32,680	38,705	42,871	44,774	46,024	19.9	18.4	15.7
Male householder	11,606	14,641	18,263	20,143	21,304	21,781	26.2	24.7	16.7
Female householder	15,651	18,039	20,442	22,728	23,470	24,244	15.3	13.3	14.8
One person	22,999	26,724	31,399	34,866	36,198	36,972	16.2	17.5	15.3
Families	**66,090**	**72,025**	**78,833**	**81,716**	**83,677**	**83,907**	**9.0**	**9.5**	**6.1**
Persons per family	3.17	3.17	3.16	3.14	3.15	3.13	(X)	(X)	(X)
With own children under age 18	32,289	34,605	35,218	34,979	33,464	33,579	7.2	1.8	-5.0
Without own children under age 18	33,801	37,420	43,615	46,737	50,213	50,328	10.7	16.6	15.1
Married couple	52,317	55,311	58,410	60,010	62,342	61,454	5.7	5.6	6.7
With own children under age 18	24,537	25,248	24,575	24,040	23,618	23,089	2.9	-2.7	-3.9
Without own children under age 18	27,780	30,062	33,835	35,970	38,724	38,365	8.2	12.6	14.4
Male householder [3]	2,884	4,028	5,580	6,162	6,503	6,963	39.7	38.5	16.5
With own children under age 18	1,153	1,786	2,224	2,388	2,374	2,661	54.9	24.5	6.7
Without own children under age 18	1,731	2,242	3,356	3,774	4,130	4,302	29.5	49.7	23.1
Female householder [3]	10,890	12,687	14,843	15,544	14,832	15,490	16.5	17.0	-0.1
With own children under age 18	6,599	7,571	8,419	8,551	7,472	7,829	14.7	11.2	-11.2
Without own children under age 18	4,290	5,116	6,424	6,993	7,359	7,661	19.3	25.6	14.6
Unrelated subfamilies [4]	**534**	**571**	**484**	**566**	**372**	**397**	**6.9**	**-15.2**	**-23.1**
Married couple	68	37	93	76	70	83	(B)	(B)	(B)
Male reference persons [3]	45	57	44	63	47	64	(B)	(B)	(B)
Female reference persons [3]	421	477	347	428	255	250	13.3	-27.3	-26.5
Related subfamilies [4]	**2,403**	**2,984**	**4,300**	**4,508**	**4,697**	**4,478**	**24.2**	**44.1**	**9.2**
Married couple	871	1,149	1,881	2,144	2,437	2,311	31.9	63.7	29.6
Father-child [3]	153	201	313	308	506	464	31.4	55.7	61.7
Mother-child [3]	1,378	1,634	2,106	2,056	1,754	1,702	18.6	28.9	-16.7
Married couples	**53,256**	**56,497**	**60,384**	**62,230**	**64,849**	**63,848**	**6.1**	**6.9**	**7.4**
With own household	52,317	55,311	58,410	60,010	62,342	61,454	5.7	5.6	6.7
Without own household	939	1,186	1,974	2,220	2,507	2,394	26.3	66.4	27.0
Percent without own household	1.8	2.1	3.2	3.6	3.9	3.7	(X)	(X)	(X)

B Base less than 75,000. NA Not available. X Not applicable. [1] Beginning with the 2003 CPS, respondents could choose more than one race. Beginning in 2003, data represent persons who selected this race group only and exclude persons reporting more than one race. The CPS in prior years allowed respondents to report only one race group. See also comments on race in text for this section. [2] Persons of Hispanic origin may be of any race. [3] No spouse present. [4] A subfamily is a married couple or parent/child group that does not maintain its own household. A subfamily may be related to the householder, or unrelated to the householder.

Source: U.S. Census Bureau, America's Families and Living Arrangements, Tables F1, FG7, and H1, and Historical Households Tables, Table HH-6, <www.census.gov/topics/families/families-and-households.html>, accessed December 2021, and earlier releases.

Table 63. Interracially Married Couples by Race and Hispanic Origin of Spouses: 1980 to 2021

[In thousands (49,714 represents 49,714,000), except percent. As of March. Persons 15 years old and over. Data shown for opposite-sex married couples only. Persons of Hispanic origin may be of any race. Population controls for 2010 based on Census 2000; beginning 2012, based on Census 2010. Based on Current Population Survey; see headnote, Table 62 and Appendix III]

Race and origin of spouses	1980	1990	2000	2010	2015	2019	2020	2021
Married couples, total [1]	**49,714**	**53,256**	**56,497**	**60,384**	**62,230**	**63,882**	**64,248**	**63,131**
Interracial married couples, total	**651**	**964**	**1,464**	**2,478**	**3,010**	**3,255**	**3,395**	**3,547**
Interracial married couples, percent	1.3	1.8	2.6	4.1	4.8	5.1	5.3	5.6
White [2] and Black [2]	167	211	363	558	562	697	691	742
Black husband and White wife	122	150	268	390	383	391	385	477
White husband and Black wife	45	61	95	168	179	306	306	265
White [2] and other race [3]	450	720	1,051	1,723	2,171	2,246	2,379	2,506
Black [2] and other race [3]	34	33	50	132	187	239	244	209
Other [4]	(NA)	(NA)	(NA)	65	90	73	81	90
HISPANIC ORIGIN								
Hispanic and Hispanic	1,906	3,085	4,739	6,166	7,176	7,726	7,533	7,657
Hispanic and other origin (not Hispanic)	891	1,193	1,743	2,289	2,830	3,284	3,483	3,529
All other couples (not of Hispanic origin)	46,917	48,979	50,015	51,928	52,224	52,872	53,232	51,946

NA Not available. [1] Includes other married couples not shown separately. [2] See footnote 1, Table 62. [3] "Other race," is any race other than White or Black, such as Asian; beginning 2003, "other race" includes Asian alone and other single race alone (excluding black and white) or any combination of races. [4] One spouse is Asian only and the other spouse is any other race (excluding black and white) or combination of races.

Source: U.S. Census Bureau, Families & Households, Historical Marital Status Tables, "Table MS-3. Interracial Married Couples: 1980 to 2002"; and America's Families and Living Arrangements, Family groups (FG table series), "Table FG3. Opposite-Sex Married Couple Family Groups, By Presence Of Own Children Under 18, And Age, Earnings, Education, And Race And Hispanic Origin Of Both Spouses," <www.census.gov/topics/families/families-and-households.html>, accessed December 2021, and earlier releases.

Table 64. Households and Persons Per Household by Type of Household: 2010 to 2021

[117,538 represents 117,538,000. As of March. See headnote, Table 62]

Type of household	Households						Persons per household		
	Number (1,000)			Percent distribution					
	2010	2020	2021	2010	2020	2021	2010	2020	2021
Total households..............	117,538	128,451	129,931	100.0	100.0	100.0	2.59	2.53	2.51
Family households.....................	78,833	83,677	83,907	67.1	65.1	64.6	3.24	3.22	3.20
Married couple family.................	58,410	62,342	61,454	49.7	48.5	47.3	3.24	3.20	3.18
Male householder, no spouse present........	5,580	6,503	6,963	4.7	5.1	5.4	3.24	3.21	3.22
Female householder, no spouse present.....	14,843	14,832	15,490	12.6	11.5	11.9	3.23	3.29	3.28
Nonfamily households.....................	38,705	44,774	46,024	32.9	34.9	35.4	1.26	1.25	1.25
Living alone.......................	31,399	36,198	36,972	26.7	28.2	28.5	1.00	1.00	1.00
Male householder......................	18,263	21,304	21,781	15.5	16.6	16.8	1.35	1.31	1.31
Living alone.......................	13,971	16,256	16,654	11.9	12.7	12.8	1.00	1.00	1.00
Female householder...................	20,442	23,470	24,244	17.4	18.3	18.7	1.18	1.19	1.20
Living alone.......................	17,428	19,942	20,318	14.8	15.5	15.6	1.00	1.00	1.00

Source: U.S. Census Bureau, Current Population Reports, P20-537, 2001, and earlier reports; and America's Families and Living Arrangements, "Table AVG1" and "Table H1," <www.census.gov/data/tables/2021/demo/families/cps-2021.html>, accessed December 2021, and earlier releases.

Table 65. Households by Age of Householder and Size of Household: 1990 to 2021

[In millions (93.3 represents 93,300,000). As of March. Based on Current Population Survey; see headnote, Table 62]

Age of householder and size of household	1990	2000	2005	2010	2015	2017	2018	2019	2020	2021
Total.....................	93.3	104.7	113.3	117.5	124.6	126.2	127.6	128.6	128.5	129.9
15 to 24 years old.........	5.1	5.9	6.7	6.2	6.4	6.2	6.2	6.2	5.4	5.5
25 to 29 years old.........	9.4	8.5	9.2	9.4	9.4	9.5	9.5	10.0	9.5	9.4
30 to 34 years old.........	11.0	10.1	10.1	9.8	10.7	10.6	10.7	10.6	10.9	11.2
35 to 44 years old........	20.6	24.0	23.2	21.5	21.1	21.5	21.6	21.4	21.4	22.1
45 to 54 years old........	14.5	20.9	23.4	24.9	23.6	22.8	22.5	22.1	21.7	21.7
55 to 64 years old........	12.5	13.6	17.5	20.4	23.5	23.8	24.0	24.2	24.6	24.3
65 to 74 years old........	11.7	11.3	11.5	13.2	16.9	18.2	19.0	19.7	20.0	20.5
75 years old and over.....	8.4	10.4	11.6	12.1	13.1	13.6	14.0	14.5	14.9	15.2
One person................	23.0	26.7	30.1	31.4	34.9	35.3	35.7	36.5	36.2	37.0
Male......................	9.0	11.2	12.8	14.0	15.5	15.8	16.0	16.5	16.3	16.7
Female....................	14.0	15.5	17.3	17.4	19.4	19.5	19.7	20.0	19.9	20.3
Two persons...............	30.1	34.7	37.4	39.5	41.9	43.5	44.0	44.4	44.7	45.5
Three persons.............	16.1	17.2	18.3	18.6	19.3	19.5	19.3	19.4	19.3	19.5
Four persons..............	14.5	15.3	16.4	16.1	16.5	16.2	16.5	16.4	16.3	16.1
Five persons..............	6.2	7.0	7.2	7.4	7.5	7.3	7.4	7.4	7.4	7.6
Six persons...............	2.1	2.4	2.5	2.8	2.8	2.8	2.9	2.9	2.9	2.6
Seven persons or more...	1.3	1.4	1.4	1.7	1.7	1.6	1.7	1.6	1.5	1.6

Source: U.S. Census Bureau, Current Population Reports, P20-537, and earlier reports; and America's Families and Living Arrangements, "Households (H table series)," <www.census.gov/data/tables/2021/demo/families/cps-2021.html>, accessed December 2021.

Table 66. Family Households With Own Children Under 18 Years of Age by Type of Family, 2000 to 2021, and by Age of Householder, 2021

[34,605 represents 34,605,000. As of March. See headnote, Table 67]

Age of householder	Family households with children		Married couple households with children		Male householder with children [1]		Female householder with children [1]	
	Number (1,000)	Percent of all family households	Number (1,000)	Percent of all married couple households	Number (1,000)	Percent of all male house-holder families [1]	Number (1,000)	Percent of all female house-holder families [1]
2000, total.................	34,605	48	25,248	46	1,786	44	7,571	60
2010, total.................	35,218	45	24,575	42	2,224	40	8,419	57
2015, total.................	34,979	43	24,040	40	2,388	39	8,551	55
2020, total.................	33,464	40	23,618	38	2,374	37	7,472	50
2021, total.................	33,579	40	23,089	38	2,661	38	7,829	51
15 to 24 years old.......	874	34	329	46	104	13	442	44
25 to 34 years old.......	8,485	66	5,059	63	778	49	2,648	83
35 to 44 years old.......	13,826	80	9,923	80	955	69	2,947	83
45 to 54 years old.......	8,165	50	6,086	51	602	47	1,478	49
55 to 64 years old.......	1,787	11	1,386	11	186	18	215	10
65 years old and over...	442	2	306	2	36	4	100	4

[1] No spouse present.

Source: U.S. Census Bureau, Current Population Reports, P20-537, 2001; and America's Families and Living Arrangements, Family households (F table series), "Table F1. Family Households, by Type, Age of Own Children, Age of Family Members, and Age of Householder," <www.census.gov/data/tables/2021/demo/families/cps-2021.html>, accessed January 2022, and earlier releases.

Table 67. Family Groups With Children Under 18 Years of Age by Race and Hispanic Origin: 2000 to 2021

[In thousands (37,496 represents 37,496,000). As of March. Family groups are family households, related subfamilies, and unrelated subfamilies; each married couple or parent/child group is counted separately, even if they reside in the same household. Excludes members of Armed Forces except those living off post or with their families on post. Beginning 2005, based on an expanded sample of households. Data for 2010 based on Census 2000 population controls. Beginning 2012, data based on Census 2010 population controls. Based on Current Population Survey, Annual Social and Economic Supplement, see text, this section and Appendix III]

Race and Hispanic origin of householder or reference person	Number (1,000)					Percent distribution				
	2000	2010	2015	2020	2021	2000	2010	2015	2020	2021
All races, total [1]	37,496	39,947	39,934	37,891	37,881	100	100	100	100	100
Two-parent family groups [2]	25,771	27,082	26,862	26,062	25,696	69	68	67	69	68
One-parent family groups	11,725	11,686	11,780	10,719	11,016	31	29	29	28	29
Maintained by mother	9,681	9,924	9,891	8,625	8,765	26	25	25	23	23
Maintained by father	2,044	1,762	1,889	2,094	2,251	5	4	5	6	6
Grandparent householder [3]	(NA)	1,179	1,292	1,110	1,169	(NA)	3	3	3	3
White, total [4]	30,079	30,933	30,131	28,265	28,078	100	100	100	100	100
Two-parent family groups [2]	22,241	22,457	21,664	20,632	20,309	74	73	72	73	72
One-parent family groups	7,838	7,729	7,639	6,901	6,999	26	25	25	24	25
Maintained by mother	6,216	6,396	6,177	5,341	5,362	21	21	21	19	19
Maintained by father	1,622	1,333	1,462	1,560	1,637	5	4	5	6	6
Grandparent householder [3]	(NA)	747	828	732	770	(NA)	2	3	3	3
Black, total [4]	5,530	5,903	5,837	5,544	5,664	100	100	100	100	100
Two-parent family groups [2]	2,135	2,275	2,209	2,255	2,241	39	39	38	41	40
One-parent family groups	3,396	3,280	3,262	2,976	3,098	61	56	56	54	55
Maintained by mother	3,060	2,977	2,971	2,622	2,682	55	50	51	47	47
Maintained by father	335	303	291	354	416	6	5	5	6	7
Grandparent householder [3]	(NA)	348	366	313	325	(NA)	6	6	6	6
Asian, total [4]	1,469	2,025	2,443	2,586	2,532	100	100	100	100	100
Two-parent family groups [2]	1,184	1,694	2,071	2,286	2,194	81	84	85	88	87
One-parent family groups	285	292	340	285	313	19	14	14	11	12
Maintained by mother	236	235	291	229	242	16	12	12	9	10
Maintained by father	49	57	49	56	71	3	3	2	2	3
Grandparent householder [3]	(NA)	39	32	15	25	(NA)	2	1	1	1
Hispanic, total [5]	5,503	7,572	8,345	8,258	8,419	100	100	100	100	100
Two-parent family groups [2]	3,625	4,856	5,407	5,381	5,467	66	64	65	65	65
One-parent family groups	1,877	2,499	2,688	2,674	2,708	34	33	32	32	32
Maintained by mother	1,565	2,186	2,338	2,234	2,240	28	29	28	27	27
Maintained by father	313	313	350	440	468	6	4	4	5	6
Grandparent householder [3]	(NA)	217	250	203	244	(NA)	3	3	2	3
Non-Hispanic White, total [4]	24,847	23,911	22,657	20,885	20,637	100	100	100	100	100
Two-parent family groups [2]	18,750	17,911	16,738	15,760	15,440	75	75	74	75	75
One-parent family groups	6,096	5,457	5,317	4,576	4,647	25	23	23	22	23
Maintained by mother	4,766	4,404	4,171	3,400	3,417	19	18	18	16	17
Maintained by father	1,331	1,053	1,146	1,176	1,230	5	4	5	6	6
Grandparent householder [3]	(NA)	543	602	549	550	(NA)	2	3	3	3

NA Not available. [1] Includes other race/ethnicities, not shown separately. [2] Beginning 2007, includes children living with married and unmarried parents. [3] With grandchild(ren) under age 18. [4] Beginning with the 2003 Current Population Survey (CPS), respondents could choose more than one race. Beginning 2003, data represent persons who selected this race group only and exclude persons reporting more than one race. The CPS prior to 2003 allowed respondents to report only one race group. [5] Hispanic persons may be of any race.

Source: U.S. Census Bureau, Families and Living Arrangements, Current Population Reports, P20-537, 2001; and America's Families and Living Arrangements, Family groups (FG table series), "Table FG10. Family Groups: 2021," <www.census.gov/data/tables/2021/demo/families/cps-2021.html>, accessed January 2022, and earlier releases.

Table 68. Parents and Children in Stay-At-Home Parent Family Groups: 1995 to 2021

[In thousands (22,973 represents 22,973,000), except percent. Family groups with children include those families that maintain their own household (family households with own children); those that live in the home of a relative (related subfamilies); and those that live in the home of a nonrelative (unrelated subfamilies). Stay-at-home family groups are opposite-sex married-couple family groups with children under age 15 where one parent is in the labor force all of the previous year and the other parent is out of the labor force for the entire year with the reason 'taking care of home and family.' Only opposite-sex married couples with children under age 15 are included. Based on Current Population Survey; see Appendix III]

Year	Married-couple family groups with children under 15 years old					Children under 15 years old in married-couple family groups				
	Number		Percent			Number		Percent		
	Total	With stay-at-home mothers	With stay-at-home fathers	With stay-at-home mothers	With stay-at-home fathers	Total	With stay-at-home mothers	With stay-at-home fathers	With stay-at-home mothers	With stay-at-home fathers
1995	22,973	4,440	64	19.3	0.3	41,008	9,106	125	22.2	0.3
2000	22,953	4,785	93	20.8	0.4	41,860	10,087	180	24.1	0.4
2005	23,305	5,584	142	24.0	0.6	41,111	11,224	247	27.3	0.6
2010	22,138	5,020	154	22.7	0.7	41,026	10,833	287	26.4	0.7
2015	21,586	5,210	199	24.1	0.9	39,621	10,758	368	27.2	0.9
2017	21,330	4,965	267	23.3	1.3	39,659	10,427	503	26.3	1.3
2018	21,361	5,061	190	23.7	0.9	39,813	10,574	336	26.6	0.8
2019	21,328	4,944	191	23.2	0.9	40,197	10,365	390	25.8	1.0
2020	21,327	4,777	215	22.4	1.0	40,403	10,176	404	25.2	1.0
2021	20,763	4,397	204	21.2	1.0	39,326	9,394	411	23.9	1.0

Source: U.S. Census Bureau, Families and Households, Historical Families Tables, "Table SHP-1. Parents and Children in Stay-At-Home Parent Family Groups: 1994 to Present," <www.census.gov/data/tables/time-series/demo/families/families.html>, accessed December 2021.

Table 69. Children Under 18 Years of Age by Presence of Parents: 2000 to 2021

[72,012 represents 72,012,000. As of March. Excludes persons under 18 years old who maintained households or family groups and their spouses. Based on Current Population Survey; see headnote, Table 67]

Race, Hispanic origin, and year	Number (1,000)	Both parents [1]	Mother only					Father only	Neither parent
			Total	Divorced	Married, spouse absent [2]	Never married	Widowed		
ALL RACES [3]									
2000	72,012	69.1	22.4	7.9	4.5	9.2	1.0	4.2	4.2
2005	73,494	67.3	23.4	7.9	4.6	10.1	0.8	4.8	4.5
2010	74,718	69.4	23.1	7.1	5.1	10.1	0.8	3.4	4.1
2015	73,623	69.2	23.1	6.6	4.4	11.3	0.8	3.7	3.9
2020	72,901	70.4	21.0	6.1	3.8	10.4	0.8	4.5	4.1
2021	72,568	69.7	21.5	6.1	3.6	11.0	0.8	4.9	3.8
WHITE [4]									
2000	56,455	75.3	17.3	(NA)	(NA)	(NA)	(NA)	4.3	3.1
2005	56,234	73.5	18.4	7.9	4.0	5.8	0.7	4.7	3.4
2010	56,416	74.9	18.3	6.9	4.5	6.1	0.8	3.5	3.4
2015	53,621	74.9	18.2	6.6	4.0	6.7	0.8	3.7	3.2
2020	52,652	75.8	16.3	6.0	3.5	6.0	0.8	4.5	3.4
2021	51,600	74.9	17.0	6.2	3.1	6.9	0.7	4.8	3.3
BLACK [4]									
2000	11,412	37.6	49.0	(NA)	(NA)	(NA)	(NA)	4.2	9.2
2005	11,293	35.0	50.2	8.7	8.1	32.0	1.3	5.0	9.8
2010	11,272	39.2	49.7	8.6	8.4	31.5	1.2	3.6	7.5
2015	11,091	38.7	49.4	7.6	6.7	33.9	1.1	4.2	7.7
2020	10,913	41.2	46.3	7.7	5.2	32.4	1.1	4.5	8.0
2021	11,075	42.6	44.8	6.5	6.0	31.3	1.1	5.8	6.8
ASIAN [4]									
2005	2,843	83.6	10.2	4.0	2.3	2.7	1.3	3.6	2.5
2010	3,300	85.5	10.1	3.8	3.7	2.1	0.6	2.2	2.1
2015	3,736	85.7	10.6	2.8	3.4	3.9	0.5	2.0	1.7
2020	3,908	88.9	7.8	2.2	2.7	2.1	0.8	1.9	1.4
2021	4,174	87.3	8.7	3.7	2.3	2.2	0.5	2.6	1.4
HISPANIC [5]									
2000	11,613	65.1	25.1	(NA)	(NA)	(NA)	(NA)	4.4	5.4
2005	14,241	64.7	25.4	6.1	7.1	11.4	0.8	4.8	5.2
2010	16,941	67.0	26.3	5.8	8.1	11.7	0.7	2.7	4.0
2015	17,981	67.0	25.9	5.3	7.1	13.0	0.6	3.0	4.1
2020	18,655	67.9	24.0	5.4	6.0	12.0	0.6	4.1	4.0
2021	18,472	67.6	24.7	5.9	5.5	12.7	0.7	4.3	3.4
NON-HISPANIC WHITE [4]									
2005	43,106	75.9	16.4	8.5	3.1	4.2	0.7	4.8	2.9
2010	41,089	77.5	15.5	7.5	3.1	4.2	0.8	3.8	3.1
2015	38,084	77.5	15.5	7.2	2.7	4.7	0.8	4.1	2.9
2020	36,515	78.6	13.4	6.3	2.5	3.8	0.9	4.7	3.2
2021	35,958	77.6	14.0	6.3	2.2	4.7	0.7	5.1	3.3

NA Not available. [1] Beginning in 2007, includes children living with married and unmarried parents. [2] Includes separated. [3] Includes other races and non-Hispanic groups, not shown separately. [4] Beginning with the 2003 Current Population Survey (CPS), respondents could choose more than one race. Data represents persons who selected this race group only and exclude persons reporting more than one race. Prior to 2003, the CPS allowed respondents to report only one race group. See also comments on race in the text for this section. [5] Hispanic persons may be of any race.

Source: U.S. Census Bureau, America's Families and Living Arrangements, Children (C table series), "Table C3. Living Arrangements of Children Under 18 Years and Marital Status of Parents, by Age, Sex, Race, and Hispanic Origin and Selected Characteristics of the Child for All Children: 2021," <www.census.gov/data/tables/2021/demo/families/cps-2021.html>, accessed January 2022, and earlier releases.

Table 70. Grandparents Living With Grandchildren by Race, Hispanic Origin, and Sex: 2019

[In thousands (7,048 represents 7,048,000), except percent. Covers both grandparents living in own home with grandchildren present and grandparents living in grandchildren's home. The American Community Survey universe includes the household population and the population living in institutions, college dormitories, and other group quarters. Based on a sample and subject to sampling variability; see Appendix III]

Race, Hispanic origin, and sex	Grandparents living with own grandchildren, total	Grandparents responsible for grandchildren		
		Total	30 to 59 years old	60 years old and over
Grandparents living with own grandchildren under 18 years old (1,000)	**7,048**	**2,335**	**1,225**	**1,110**
PERCENT DISTRIBUTION				
Total	100.0	100.0	100.0	100.0
One race	97.9	97.8	97.5	98.1
White alone	62.8	65.8	64.6	67.1
Black or African American alone	16.7	20.4	21.3	19.3
American Indian and Alaska Native alone	1.5	2.1	2.1	2.2
Asian alone	8.8	3.5	2.1	5.2
Native Hawaiian and Other Pacific Islander alone	0.4	0.3	0.4	0.2
Some other race alone	7.8	5.7	7.0	4.2
Two or more races	2.1	2.2	2.5	1.9
Hispanic origin [1]	26.1	19.8	24.1	15.1
White alone, not Hispanic	45.8	53.0	49.2	57.2
Male	36.1	36.7	33.5	40.3
Female	63.9	63.3	66.5	59.7

[1] Persons of Hispanic origin may be of any race.

Source: U.S. Census Bureau, 2019 American Community Survey, S1002, "Grandparents," <data.census.gov>, accessed November 2020.

Table 71. Group Quarters Population by Type of Group Quarter and Selected Resident Characteristics: 2019

[In percent, except as indicated. The American Community Survey universe includes the household population and the population living in institutions, college dormitories, and other group quarters. Based on a sample and subject to sampling variability]

Characteristic	Total group quarters population [1]	Institutionalized group quarters population			Noninstitutionalized group quarters population	
		Total [1]	Adult correctional facilities	Nursing facilities/ skilled nursing facilities	Total [1]	College/ university housing
Total population................	**8,084,362**	**3,868,023**	**2,166,192**	**1,479,899**	**4,216,339**	**2,723,749**
PERCENT DISTRIBUTION						
Male............................	61.1	69.7	90.5	38.6	53.3	45.3
Female..........................	38.9	30.3	9.5	61.4	46.7	54.7
Under 15 years old.............	0.7	1.1	(X)	(X)	0.4	(X)
15 to 17 years old.............	1.6	2.3	0.2	(X)	1.0	1.0
18 to 24 years old.............	40.9	7.2	10.8	0.1	71.9	96.8
25 to 34 years old.............	12.6	18.7	32.4	0.6	7.0	1.8
35 to 44 years old.............	10.1	16.3	27.8	1.2	4.5	0.3
45 to 54 years old.............	7.7	11.2	17.0	3.7	4.4	0.1
55 to 64 years old.............	7.6	10.0	9.1	11.7	5.5	–
65 to 74 years old.............	5.8	9.3	2.4	20.5	2.6	–
75 to 84 years old.............	5.7	10.4	0.4	26.6	1.4	(X)
85 years old and over..........	7.2	13.7	–	35.6	1.3	(X)
Median age (years).............	30.1	48.7	37.1	80.0	20.5	19.6
One race.......................	100.0	100.0	100.0	100.0	100.0	100.0
White..........................	67.0	63.2	52.4	79.4	70.6	72.9
Black..........................	23.1	29.0	37.7	15.9	17.6	14.3
American Indian and Alaska Native.........	1.3	1.6	2.4	0.6	0.9	0.6
Asian..........................	4.8	1.4	1.0	2.1	7.9	10.2
Native Hawaiian/Pacific Islander............	0.3	0.2	0.3	0.1	0.3	0.2
Some other race................	3.6	4.6	6.3	2.0	2.7	1.9
Hispanic origin [2]................	13.9	15.1	20.9	6.1	12.8	10.9
Not Hispanic...................	86.1	84.9	79.1	93.9	87.2	89.1
White alone, not Hispanic......	55.9	52.3	37.7	74.9	59.3	62.3

– Represents or rounds to zero. X Not applicable or not available. [1] Includes other types of group quarters, not shown separately. [2] Persons of Hispanic origin may be of any race.

Source: U.S. Census Bureau, 2019 American Community Survey, S2601A, "Characteristics of the Group Quarters Population"; and S2602, "Characteristics of the Group Quarters Population by Group Quarters Type (3 Types)"; <data.census.gov>, accessed November 2020.

Table 72. Population in Group Quarters by State: 2000 to 2020

[In thousands (7,780 represents 7,780,000). Census years, as of April. All persons not living in housing units are classified as living in group quarters. These individuals may be institutionalized, e.g., under care or custody in juvenile facilities, jails, correctional centers, hospitals, or nursing homes; or they may be residents in noninstitutional group quarters such as college dormitories, group homes, or military barracks]

State	2000 [1]	2010 [2]	2019 (July)	2020 [3]	State	2000 [1]	2010 [2]	2019 (July)	2020 [3]
United States........	**7,780**	**7,999**	**8,063**	**7,761**	Missouri.............	164	174	171	158
Alabama................	115	116	117	115	Montana.............	25	29	29	27
Alaska.................	19	26	27	26	Nebraska............	51	51	51	48
Arizona................	110	140	162	146	Nevada..............	34	36	37	35
Arkansas...............	74	79	83	76	New Hampshire.....	36	40	40	39
California..............	820	820	828	816	New Jersey..........	195	187	181	183
Colorado...............	103	116	121	113	New Mexico.........	36	43	43	41
Connecticut............	108	118	111	109	New York............	581	586	564	570
Delaware...............	25	24	25	24	North Carolina.......	254	257	283	261
District of Columbia....	36	40	38	37	North Dakota........	24	25	25	24
Florida.................	389	425	430	412	Ohio................	299	306	315	301
Georgia................	234	254	268	253	Oklahoma...........	112	112	110	102
Hawaii.................	36	43	42	42	Oregon..............	77	87	89	85
Idaho..................	31	29	31	29	Pennsylvania........	433	427	415	411
Illinois.................	322	302	297	289	Rhode Island........	39	43	41	42
Indiana................	178	187	190	182	South Carolina.....	135	139	134	122
Iowa...................	104	99	96	92	South Dakota.......	28	34	34	32
Kansas................	82	79	79	75	Tennessee..........	148	154	158	150
Kentucky...............	115	126	133	125	Texas...............	561	582	591	562
Louisiana..............	136	128	130	122	Utah................	40	46	49	47
Maine..................	35	36	36	35	Vermont.............	21	25	26	26
Maryland...............	134	139	140	138	Virginia.............	231	240	245	235
Massachusetts........	221	239	248	247	Washington.........	136	139	148	144
Michigan...............	250	230	223	212	West Virginia.......	43	49	47	44
Minnesota.............	136	135	129	124	Wisconsin...........	156	151	144	138
Mississippi.............	95	93	94	84	Wyoming............	14	14	14	13

[1] The April 1, 2000, population estimates base reflects changes to the Census 2000 population from the Count Question Resolution program and geographic program revisions. [2] The April 1, 2010 population estimates base reflects changes to the Census 2010 population from the Count Question Resolution program and geographic program revisions. [3] Estimates for 2020 are developed from a base that incorporates the 2020 Census, Vintage 2020 estimates, and 2020 Demographic Analysis estimates. Due to complications in group quarters data as a result of the COVID-19 pandemic, Vintage 2021 estimates remain the same as 2020 data and are not repeated here.

Source: U.S. Census Bureau, "CO-EST2009-ALLDATA" and "CO-EST2020-ALLDATA," <www2.census.gov/programs-surveys/popest/datasets/>; and "Annual Resident Population Estimates, Estimated Components of Resident Population Change, and Rates of the Components of Resident Population Change for States and Counties: April 1, 2020 to July 1, 2021 (CO-EST2021-ALLDATA)," <www.census.gov/data/tables/time-series/demo/popest/2020s-counties-total.html>, accessed May 2022.

Table 73. Opposite-Sex and Same-Sex Couple Households by Selected Characteristics: 2019

[In percent, except as indicated (57,803 represents 57,803,000). The American Community Survey universe includes the household population and the population living in institutions, college dormitories, and other group quarters. Based on a sample and subject to sampling variability. See text, this section and Appendix III]

Characteristic	Married opposite-sex couples	Unmarried opposite-sex couples	Married and unmarried same-sex couples Total	Male-male couples	Female-female couples	Married same-sex couples
Total households (1,000).............................	57,803	7,645	980	462	518	568
Age of householder:						
15 to 24 years old......................................	1.1	10.6	5.2	3.4	6.7	2.4
25 to 34 years old......................................	12.6	34.5	23.7	21.3	25.7	18.2
35 to 44 years old......................................	19.7	20.9	20.2	20.2	20.2	21.6
45 to 54 years old......................................	20.5	15.0	20.2	21.4	19.1	22.4
55 to 64 years old......................................	21.3	11.2	18.8	20.8	17.1	21.5
65 years old and over.................................	24.8	7.8	12.0	12.9	11.2	13.9
Average age of householder (years).................	52.8	40.3	45.9	47.2	44.6	48.4
Average age of spouse/partner (years)...............	52.1	39.5	44.5	45.0	44.0	47.3
Race of householder:						
White alone..	80.6	76.3	80.2	82.4	78.3	82.0
Black or African American alone.....................	7.2	10.8	8.8	6.3	11.1	6.9
American Indian or Alaska Native alone............	0.6	1.1	1.0	0.9	1.1	0.9
Asian alone..	6.2	2.8	3.3	4.0	2.7	3.7
Native Hawaiian or Pacific Islander alone...........	0.1	0.2	0.2	0.1	0.2	0.2
Some other race alone.................................	3.5	5.4	2.9	3.0	2.9	2.8
Two or more races......................................	1.8	3.4	3.6	3.3	3.8	3.4
Percent of couples interracial........................	7.8	15.0	18.3	21.5	15.4	16.6
Hispanic origin of householder:						
Hispanic [1]..	13.4	18.9	13.9	14.5	13.3	13.1
White alone, not Hispanic.............................	71.3	64.2	70.5	72.1	69.1	72.9
Children in the household:						
Children in the household [2]...........................	38.1	36.2	16.1	7.2	24.0	18.9
Own children in the household.......................	38.0	34.0	15.0	6.6	22.5	18.5
Household income:						
Less than $35,000.......................................	10.4	17.2	10.3	7.8	12.5	8.9
$35,000 to $49,999.....................................	8.9	12.7	8.4	6.7	9.9	7.0
$50,000 to $74,999.....................................	16.7	22.0	16.6	14.5	18.5	14.8
$75,000 to $99,999.....................................	15.7	16.8	15.4	14.0	16.7	15.1
$100,000 or more.......................................	48.4	31.3	49.3	57.0	42.5	54.1
Median household income (dollars).................	96,932	72,401	98,613	114,182	87,289	107,210
Housing tenure:						
Owner occupied...	80.4	46.0	61.8	64.3	59.5	69.7
Renter occupied...	19.6	54.0	38.2	35.7	40.5	30.3

[1] Persons of Hispanic origin may be of any race. [2] Includes biological children, stepchildren, adopted children, and nonrelatives of the householder under 18 years old.

Source: U.S. Census Bureau, 2019 American Community Survey, "Characteristics of Same-Sex Couple Households: 2005 to Present," <www.census.gov/topics/families/same-sex-couples/data/tables.html>, accessed November 2020.

Table 74. Opposite Sex Unmarried Couples by Presence of Biological Children, Sex, and Age: 2021

[In thousands (9,640 represents 9,640,000), except percent. As of March. Excludes members of Armed Forces except those living off post or with their families on post. All opposite-sex unmarried couples are included, regardless of householder status. Unmarried couples of the opposite sex with children under 18 years old are included in the estimates if either partner had at least one never-married biological child living with them. Population controls based on Census 2010. Based on Current Population Survey; see text, this section and Appendix III]

Sex and age of partner	Unmarried couples, total	Without children under 18 years old	With children under 18 years old Number	Percent of total
Total...	9,640	6,554	3,086	32.0
Age of male partner:				
15 to 24 years old.......................................	983	726	258	26.2
25 to 29 years old.......................................	1,930	1,364	567	29.4
30 to 34 years old.......................................	1,677	988	688	41.0
35 to 39 years old.......................................	1,079	516	563	52.2
40 to 44 years old.......................................	893	401	492	55.1
45 to 49 years old.......................................	632	420	212	33.5
50 to 54 years old.......................................	676	494	182	26.9
55 to 64 years old.......................................	1,014	911	103	10.2
65 years old and over..................................	755	734	21	2.8
Age of female partner:				
15 to 24 years old.......................................	1,595	1,213	382	23.9
25 to 29 years old.......................................	2,185	1,426	759	34.7
30 to 34 years old.......................................	1,442	740	702	48.7
35 to 39 years old.......................................	996	447	549	55.1
40 to 44 years old.......................................	735	353	381	51.8
45 to 49 years old.......................................	602	416	187	31.1
50 to 54 years old.......................................	567	474	93	16.4
55 to 64 years old.......................................	911	887	24	2.6
65 years old and over..................................	606	598	8	1.3

Source: U.S. Census Bureau, America's Families and Living Arrangements, Unmarried couples (UC table series), "Table UC3. Opposite Sex Unmarried Couples by Presence of Biological Children under 18, and Age, Earnings, Education, and Race Send Hispanic Origin of Both Partners," <www.census.gov/data/tables/2021/demo/families/cps-2021.html>, accessed December 2021.

Table 75. Opposite and Same-Sex Coupled Households by Marital Status and Region: 2019

[122,803 represents 122,803,000. The American Community Survey universe includes the household population and the population living in institutions, college dormitories, and other group quarters. For composition of regions, see map inside front cover. Based on a sample and subject to sampling variability; see text, this section and Appendix III]

Household type	Total (1,000s)					Percent distribution				
	Total	North-east	Midwest	South	West	Total	North-east	Mid-west	South	West
Total households................	**122,803**	**21,665**	**27,106**	**46,382**	**27,650**	**100.0**	**100.0**	**100.0**	**100.0**	**100.0**
Married couple households..............	58,371	9,994	12,744	22,016	13,617	47.5	46.1	47.0	47.5	49.2
Opposite-sex....................	57,803	9,886	12,650	21,818	13,449	47.1	45.6	46.7	47.0	48.6
Same-sex....................	568	108	94	197	168	0.5	0.5	0.3	0.4	0.6
Male householder and male spouse....................	265	53	40	89	82	0.2	0.2	0.1	0.2	0.3
Female householder and female spouse....................	303	55	54	108	86	0.2	0.3	0.2	0.2	0.3
Cohabiting couple households..........	8,057	1,449	1,874	2,766	1,968	6.6	6.7	6.9	6.0	7.1
Opposite-sex....................	7,645	1,376	1,796	2,610	1,863	6.2	6.3	6.6	5.6	6.7
Same-sex....................	412	73	78	157	105	0.3	0.3	0.3	0.3	0.4
Male householder and male partner....................	198	35	36	73	54	0.2	0.2	0.1	0.2	0.2
Female householder and female partner....................	215	38	42	84	51	0.2	0.2	0.2	0.2	0.2
All other households....................	56,375	10,223	12,487	21,600	12,065	45.9	47.2	46.1	46.6	43.6

Source: U.S. Census Bureau, 2019 American Community Survey, B11009, "Coupled Households by Type," <data.census.gov>, accessed November 2020.

Table 76. Young Adults Living in Parental Home by Sex and Age: 1990 to 2021

[In thousands (12,450 represents 12,450,000), except percent. As of March. Excludes members of Armed Forces except those living off post or with their families on post. Unmarried college students living in dormitories are counted as living in the home of their parent(s). Beginning 2005, based on an expanded sample of households. Population controls for 2005 to 2010 based on Census 2000; beginning 2012, population controls based on Census 2010. Based on Current Population Survey; see text, this section and Appendix III]

Year	Male young adults			Female young adults		
		Child of householder living at home			Child of householder living at home	
	Total	Number	Percent of total	Total	Number	Percent of total
18 TO 24 YEARS OLD						
1990....................	12,450	7,232	58.1	12,860	6,135	47.7
1995....................	12,545	7,328	58.4	12,613	5,896	46.7
2000....................	13,291	7,593	57.1	13,242	6,232	47.1
2005....................	14,060	7,448	53.0	13,933	6,413	46.0
2010....................	14,824	8,501	57.3	14,469	7,123	49.2
2015....................	15,123	8,808	58.2	14,893	7,714	51.8
2020....................	14,634	8,792	60.1	14,418	8,122	56.3
2021....................	14,542	8,717	59.9	14,292	7,879	55.1
25 TO 34 YEARS OLD						
1990....................	21,462	3,213	15.0	21,779	1,774	8.1
1995....................	20,589	3,166	15.4	20,800	1,759	8.5
2000....................	18,563	2,387	12.9	19,222	1,602	8.3
2005....................	19,656	2,660	13.5	19,632	1,597	8.1
2010....................	20,685	3,387	16.4	20,383	2,133	10.5
2015....................	21,417	3,896	18.2	21,574	2,613	12.1
2020....................	22,778	5,021	22.0	22,451	3,011	13.4
2021....................	22,835	4,725	20.7	22,441	2,963	13.2

Source: U.S. Census Bureau, Families and Households, Historical Living Arrangements of Adults, "Table AD-1. Young Adults, 18-34 Years Old, Living At Home: 1960 to Present," <www.census.gov/data/tables/time-series/demo/families/adults.html>, accessed December 2021.

Table 77. Children in Households by Relationship to Householder: 2010 to 2019

[In thousands (73,904 represents 73,904,000). Data shown for population under age 18 in households, excluding householders, spouses, and unmarried partners. Based on a sample and subject to sampling variability; see text this section and Appendix III]

Type of relationship	2010	2013	2014	2015	2016	2017	2018	2019
NUMBER								
Total children in households..............	**73,904**	**73,336**	**73,325**	**73,386**	**73,399**	**73,403**	**73,106**	**72,746**
Own child....................	65,472	64,595	64,426	64,445	64,392	64,367	63,987	63,307
Biological child....................	61,540	60,766	60,628	60,632	60,564	60,518	60,180	59,488
Adopted child....................	1,582	1,496	1,447	1,423	1,428	1,439	1,440	1,422
Stepchild....................	2,351	2,332	2,351	2,391	2,400	2,410	2,367	2,396
Grandchild....................	5,397	5,712	5,830	5,887	5,964	5,957	6,038	6,179
Other relatives....................	1,826	1,738	1,792	1,793	1,762	1,803	1,807	1,842
Foster child or other unrelated child.......	1,209	1,292	1,277	1,261	1,280	1,276	1,274	1,419
PERCENT DISTRIBUTION								
Total children in households................	100.0	100.0	100.0	100.0	100.0	100.0	100.0	100.0
Own child....................	88.6	88.1	87.9	87.8	87.7	87.7	87.5	87.0
Biological child....................	83.3	82.9	82.7	82.6	82.5	82.4	82.3	81.8
Adopted child....................	2.1	2.0	2.0	1.9	1.9	2.0	2.0	2.0
Stepchild....................	3.2	3.2	3.2	3.3	3.3	3.3	3.2	3.3
Grandchild....................	7.3	7.8	8.0	8.0	8.1	8.1	8.3	8.5
Other relatives....................	2.5	2.4	2.4	2.4	2.4	2.5	2.5	2.5
Foster child or other unrelated child.......	1.6	1.8	1.7	1.7	1.7	1.7	1.7	2.0

Source: U.S. Census Bureau, American Community Survey, B09018, "Relationship to Householder for Children Under 18 in Households," <data.census.gov>, accessed November 2020.

Table 78. Religious Adherents and Jewish Population—States: 2010 to 2011

[137,450 represents 137,450,000. Adherents were defined as "all members, including full members, their children and others who regularly attend services." The Jewish population includes Jews who define themselves as Jewish by religion as well as those who define themselves as Jewish in cultural or ethnic terms. Data on Jewish population are based on both scientific studies and informant estimates provided by local Jewish communities]

State	Number (1,000)			Percent of population [3]		
	Christian adherents, [1] 2010	Other religious adherents, [2] 2010	Jewish population, 2011	Christian adherents, [1] 2010	Other religious adherents, [2] 2010	Jewish population, 2011
United States...............	**137,450**	**10,890**	**6,588**	**44.5**	**3.5**	**2.1**
Alabama..........	2,948	52	9	61.7	1.1	0.2
Alaska..........	200	40	6	28.1	5.7	0.9
Arizona..........	1,894	466	106	29.6	7.3	1.7
Arkansas..........	1,573	40	2	53.9	1.4	0.1
California..........	15,021	1,530	1,220	40.3	4.1	3.3
Colorado..........	1,684	199	91	33.5	4.0	1.8
Connecticut..........	1,735	48	116	48.6	1.3	3.2
Delaware..........	349	22	15	38.9	2.5	1.7
District of Columbia..........	298	16	28	49.6	2.7	4.7
Florida..........	6,829	400	639	36.3	2.1	3.4
Georgia..........	4,702	186	128	48.5	1.9	1.3
Hawaii..........	421	140	7	31.0	10.3	0.5
Idaho..........	384	417	2	24.5	26.6	0.1
Illinois..........	6,529	486	298	50.9	3.8	2.3
Indiana..........	2,793	69	17	43.1	1.1	0.3
Iowa..........	1,592	46	6	52.3	1.5	0.2
Kansas..........	1,375	61	18	48.2	2.1	0.6
Kentucky..........	2,182	49	11	50.3	1.1	0.3
Louisiana..........	2,688	50	11	59.3	1.1	0.2
Maine..........	345	19	14	26.0	1.4	1.0
Maryland..........	2,214	118	238	38.3	2.0	4.1
Massachusetts..........	3,546	122	278	54.2	1.9	4.2
Michigan..........	3,910	211	82	39.6	2.1	0.8
Minnesota..........	2,894	69	46	54.6	1.3	0.9
Mississippi..........	1,709	33	2	57.6	1.1	0.1
Missouri..........	2,806	123	59	46.9	2.0	1.0
Montana..........	326	50	1	33.0	5.0	0.1
Nebraska..........	974	38	6	53.3	2.1	0.3
Nevada..........	725	196	74	26.8	7.3	2.8
New Hampshire..........	444	14	10	33.7	1.1	0.8
New Jersey..........	4,321	272	504	49.1	3.1	5.7
New Mexico..........	940	87	12	45.6	4.2	0.6
New York..........	8,529	611	1,635	44.0	3.2	8.4
North Carolina..........	4,372	140	31	45.9	1.5	0.3
North Dakota..........	443	8	(Z)	65.9	1.2	0.1
Ohio..........	4,861	146	148	42.1	1.3	1.3
Oklahoma..........	2,148	75	5	57.3	2.0	0.1
Oregon..........	998	187	41	26.1	4.9	1.1
Pennsylvania..........	6,530	206	295	51.4	1.6	2.3
Rhode Island..........	558	10	19	53.1	0.9	1.8
South Carolina..........	2,337	70	13	50.5	1.5	0.3
South Dakota..........	464	13	(Z)	57.0	1.6	(Z)
Tennessee..........	3,425	82	20	54.0	1.3	0.3
Texas..........	13,062	872	140	51.9	3.5	0.6
Utah..........	256	1,929	6	9.3	69.8	0.2
Vermont..........	199	9	5	31.8	1.4	0.9
Virginia..........	3,206	351	97	40.1	4.4	1.2
Washington..........	1,945	364	46	28.9	5.4	0.7
West Virginia..........	635	22	2	34.3	1.2	0.1
Wisconsin..........	2,973	62	28	52.3	1.1	0.5
Wyoming..........	158	65	1	28.0	11.5	0.2

Z Fewer than 500 or less than 0.05 percent. [1] Comprises evangelical Protestants, Black Protestants, mainline Protestants, Orthodox and Catholic groups. [2] Includes counts of Jain, Shinto, Sikh, Tao, National Spiritualist Association, Church of Jesus Christ of Latter Day Saints, Unitarian Universalist, Jehovah's Witnesses, Church of Christ Scientist, Bahá'í, three Buddhist groupings, four Hindu groupings, Muslims, and Zoroastrians. Excludes four Judaism groups. [3] Based on U.S. Census Bureau data for resident population enumerated as of April 1, 2010 and estimated as of July 2012.

Source: Religious adherents: Clifford Grammich, Kirk Hadaway, Richard Houseal, Dale E. Jones, Alexei Krindatch, Richie Stanley, and Richard H. Taylor, *2010 U.S. Religion Census: Religious Congregations & Membership Study* ©, 2012, Association of Statisticians of American Religious Bodies. See also <www.asarb.org>. Jewish population: Ira M. Sheskin and Arnold Dashefsky, University of Miami and University of Connecticut, *Jewish Population of the United States, 2011,* published by the Mandell L. Berman North American Jewish Data Bank in cooperation with the Association for the Social Scientific Study of Jewry and the Jewish Federations of North America, see also <www.jewishdatabank.org>

Table 79. Religious Adherents by Metropolitan Area Status and Religious Groups: 2010

[Groups shown have 500,000 adherents or more. Adherents were defined as all members, including full members, their children and the estimated number of other participants who are not considered members. Based on a study of 236 religious bodies sponsored by the Association of Statisticians of American Religious Bodies. Participants included 217 Christian denominations, associations, or communions (including Latter-day Saints, Messianic Jews, and Unitarian/Universalist groups); counts of Jain, Shinto, Sikh, Tao, and National Spiritualist Association congregations, and counts of congregations and individuals for Bahá'í, three Buddhist groupings, four Hindu groupings, four Jewish groupings, Muslims, and Zoroastrians. For definition of metropolitan and micropolitan areas, see Appendix II]

Religious group	Total adherents (1,000)	Percent		
		In metropolitan area	In micropolitan area	Outside metro/micro area
U.S. population, total...............................	308,746	83.7	10.0	6.3
Total adherents....................................	**150,686**	**83.5**	**10.0**	**6.5**
Catholic..	58,929	90.5	6.2	3.3
Southern Baptist Convention....................	19,897	69.3	17.2	13.5
Non-denominational Christian Churches........	12,241	88.7	7.8	3.5
United Methodist Church..........................	9,948	73.6	15.3	11.1
Church of Jesus Christ of Latter-day Saints.....	6,145	82.8	11.6	5.6
Evangelical Lutheran Church in America........	4,181	70.4	16.0	13.6
Assemblies of God..................................	2,945	82.7	11.0	6.3
Muslim, estimate....................................	2,600	97.4	2.0	0.6
Presbyterian Church (U.S.A.).....................	2,452	82.5	11.4	6.1
Lutheran Church—Missouri Synod...............	2,271	72.7	13.7	13.6
Episcopal...	1,952	88.2	8.1	3.7
National Baptist Convention, USA, Inc..........	1,881	90.3	7.0	2.7
Churches of Christ...................................	1,584	69.8	17.1	13.1
American Baptist Churches in the USA.........	1,561	83.8	9.8	6.4
Christian Churches and Churches of Christ.....	1,453	72.6	15.9	11.5
United Church of Christ............................	1,284	79.3	13.5	7.2
Seventh-day Adventist Church....................	1,195	87.7	8.2	4.1
Church of God (Cleveland, Tennessee).........	1,110	72.2	17.5	10.3
African Methodist Episcopal Church.............	1,010	77.7	12.3	10.0
Orthodox Judaism..................................	947	99.6	0.0	0.4
Church of the Nazarene............................	894	76.2	15.6	8.2
Christian Church (Disciples of Christ)...........	786	70.3	17.7	12.0
Reform Judaism.....................................	766	98.3	1.3	0.4
Mahayana Buddhism...............................	733	92.8	6.8	0.4
Church of God in Christ............................	624	87.8	7.3	4.9
Conservative Judaism.............................	502	99.5	0.4	0.1

Source: Clifford Grammich, Kirk Hadaway, Richard Houseal, Dale E. Jones, Alexei Krindatch, Richie Stanley, and Richard H. Taylor. *2010 U.S. Religion Census: Religious Congregations & Membership Study*, 2012 ©. Association of Statisticians of American Religious Bodies.

Births, Deaths, Marriages, and Divorces

This section presents vital statistics data on births, mortality, marriages, and divorces, as well as factors that help explain fertility, such as use of contraception, sexual activity, and prevalence of abortions and fetal deaths. Vital statistics are collected and disseminated for the nation through the National Vital Statistics System by the National Center for Health Statistics (NCHS) and published annually in *Vital Statistics of the United States, National Vital Statistics Reports (NVSR),* and other selected publications. Reports are also issued by various state bureaus participating in the National Vital Statistics System. Factors influencing fertility are collected in NCHS's National Survey of Family Growth and the U.S. Census Bureau's American Community Survey and Current Population Reports (published in *Fertility of American Women*).

Additionally, data on births, deaths, and other public health topics can be accessed via the Centers for Disease Control's (CDC) WONDER Online databases at <wonder.cdc.gov/>. Data on abortions are collected by CDC's Abortion Surveillance System and published in selected issues of *Morbidity and Mortality Weekly Report (MMWR) Surveillance Summaries.*

Registration of vital events—The registration of births, deaths, fetal deaths, and other vital events in the United States is primarily a state and local function. There are 57 vital registration jurisdictions in the United States: the 50 states, five territories (Puerto Rico, etc.), District of Columbia, and New York City. Each of the 57 jurisdictions has a direct statistical reporting relationship with NCHS. Vital events occurring to U.S. residents outside the United States are not included in the data.

Births and deaths—The live-birth, death, and fetal-death statistics prepared by NCHS are based on vital records filed in the registration offices of all states, New York City, and the District of Columbia. The annual collection of death statistics on a national basis began in 1900 with a national death-registration area of ten states and the District of Columbia; a similar annual collection of birth statistics for a national birth-registration area began in 1915, also with ten reporting states and the District of Columbia. Since 1933, the birth- and death-registration areas have comprised the entire United States, including Alaska (beginning 1959) and Hawaii (beginning 1960). National statistics on fetal deaths were first compiled for 1918 and annually since 1922. Prior to 1951, birth statistics came from a complete count of records received in the Public Health Service (now received in NCHS). From 1951 through 1971, they were based on a 50-percent sample of all registered births (except for a complete count in 1955 and a 20- to 50-percent sample in 1967). Beginning in 1972, they have been based on a complete count for states participating in the Vital Statistics Cooperative Program (VSCP) (for details, see the technical appendix in *U.S. Vital Statistics System: Major Activities and Developments, 1950-95*) and on a 50-percent sample of all other areas. Since 1986, all reporting areas participated in the VSCP. Mortality data have been based on a complete count of records for each area (except for a 50-percent sample in 1972). Beginning in 1970, births to and deaths of nonresident aliens of the United States and U.S. citizens outside the United States have been excluded from the data. Fetal deaths and deaths among Armed Forces abroad are excluded. Data based on samples are subject to sampling error; for details, see annual issues of *National Vital Statistics Reports.*

Mortality statistics by cause of death are compiled in accordance with World Health Organization regulations according to the *International Classification of Diseases* (ICD). The ICD is revised approximately every 10 years. The tenth revision of the ICD was employed beginning in 1999. Deaths for prior years were classified according to the revision of the ICD in use at the time. Each revision of the ICD introduces a number of discontinuities in mortality statistics; for a discussion of those between the ninth and tenth revisions of the ICD, see *Deaths: Final Data for 2019, National Vital Statistics Report,* Vol. 70, No. 8. Information on tests of statistical significance, differences between death rates, and standard errors can also be found in the aforementioned report.

Some of the tables present age-adjusted death rates in addition to crude death rates. Age-adjusted death rates shown in this section were prepared using the direct method, in which age-specific death rates for a population of interest are applied to a standard population distributed by age. Age adjustment eliminates the differences in observed rates between points in time or among compared population groups that result from age differences in population composition.

Fertility and life expectancy—The total fertility rate, defined as the number of births that 1,000 women would have in their lifetime if at each year of age they experienced the birth rates occurring in the specified year, is compiled and published by NCHS. See *Births: Final Data for 2020, National Vital Statistics Reports,* Vol. 70, No.17. Data on life expectancy, the average remaining lifetime in years for persons who attain a given age, are also computed and published by NCHS. See *Deaths: Final Data for 2019, National Vital Statistics Reports,* Vol. 70, No. 8 and <www.cdc.gov/nchs/nvss/deaths.htm>for details.

Marriage and divorce—In 1957 and 1958 respectively, the National Office of Vital Statistics established marriage- and divorce-registration areas consisting of an increasing number of States over time. Procedures for estimating the number of marriages and divorces in the registration States are discussed in *Vital Statistics of the United States, Vol. III—Marriage and Divorce.* Total counts of events for registration and nonregistration states are gathered by collecting already summarized data on marriages and divorces reported by state offices of vital statistics and by county offices of registration. The collection and publication of detailed marriage and divorce statistics was suspended beginning in January 1996. For additional information, visit the National Center for Health Statistics online at <www.cdc.gov/nchs/nvss/marriage-divorce.htm>.

With the suspension of detailed data collection by the NCHS, data on marriage and divorce can be found in the Census Bureau's American Community Survey data tables. See <www.census.gov/programs-surveys/acs/> for information and data access.

Vital statistics rates—Except as noted, vital statistics rates computed by NCHS are based on decennial census population figures as of April 1 for 1960, 1970, 1980, 1990, 2000, and 2010; and on midyear population figures for other years, as estimated by the Census Bureau (see text, Section 1).

Race—Data by race for births, deaths, marriages, and divorces from NCHS are based on information contained in the certificates of registration. The Census Bureau's Current Population Survey obtains information on race by asking respondents to classify their race as (1) White, (2) Black, (3) American Indian or Alaska Native, (4) Native Hawaiian or Other Pacific Islander, or (5) Asian. Beginning with the 1989 data year, NCHS has tabulated birth data primarily by race of the mother. In 1988 and prior years, births were tabulated by race of the child, which was determined from the race of the parents as entered on the birth certificate. Trend data by race shown in this section are by race of mother beginning with the 1980 data. Persons of Hispanic origin may be of any race; therefore, Hispanic origin of the mother is reported and tabulated independently of race. The majority of women of Hispanic origin are reported as White.

Race categorizations found in the *National Vital Statistics Reports* are variously shown according to either 1977 or 1997 Office of Management and Budget (OMB) standards. States reporting multiple-race data according to new 1997 OMB standards has varied widely. In some cases, to provide a comparison of data by race between the 1977 and 1997 OMB standards, the responses of those reporting more than one race were "bridged" to a single race. See headnotes of individual tables and respective source reports for additional information.

Statistical reliability—For a discussion of statistical collection, estimation, and sampling procedures and measures of reliability applicable to data from NCHS and the Census Bureau, see Appendix III.

Table 80. Live Births, Deaths, Marriages, and Divorces: 1960 to 2020

[4,258 represents 4,258,000. Beginning 1970, excludes births to and deaths of nonresidents of the United States. See Appendix III]

Year	Number (1,000)					Rate per 1,000 population				
		Deaths		Mar-			Deaths		Mar-	
	Births	Total	Infant [1]	riages [2]	Divorces [3]	Births	Total	Infant [1]	riages [2]	Divorces [3]
1960	4,258	1,712	111	1,523	393	23.7	9.5	26.0	8.5	2.2
1965	3,760	1,828	93	1,800	479	19.4	9.4	24.7	9.3	2.5
1970	3,731	1,921	75	2,159	708	18.4	9.5	20.0	10.6	3.5
1971	3,556	1,928	68	2,190	773	17.2	9.3	19.1	10.6	3.7
1972	3,258	1,964	60	2,282	845	15.6	9.4	18.5	10.9	4.0
1973	3,137	1,973	56	2,284	915	14.8	9.3	17.7	10.8	4.3
1974	3,160	1,934	53	2,230	977	14.8	9.1	16.7	10.5	4.6
1975	3,144	1,893	51	2,153	1,036	14.6	8.8	16.1	10.0	4.8
1976	3,168	1,909	48	2,155	1,083	14.6	8.8	15.2	9.9	5.0
1977	3,327	1,900	47	2,178	1,091	15.1	8.6	14.1	9.9	5.0
1978	3,333	1,928	46	2,282	1,130	15.0	8.7	13.8	10.3	5.1
1979	3,494	1,914	46	2,331	1,181	15.6	8.5	13.1	10.4	5.3
1980	3,612	1,990	46	2,390	1,189	15.9	8.8	12.6	10.6	5.2
1981	3,629	1,978	43	2,422	1,213	15.8	8.6	11.9	10.6	5.3
1982	3,681	1,975	42	2,456	1,170	15.9	8.5	11.5	10.6	5.1
1983	3,639	2,019	41	2,446	1,158	15.6	8.6	11.2	10.5	5.0
1984	3,669	2,039	40	2,477	1,169	15.6	8.6	10.8	10.5	5.0
1985	3,761	2,086	40	2,413	1,190	15.8	8.8	10.6	10.1	5.0
1986	3,757	2,105	39	2,407	1,178	15.6	8.8	10.4	10.0	4.9
1987	3,809	2,123	38	2,403	1,166	15.7	8.8	10.1	9.9	4.8
1988	3,910	2,168	39	2,396	1,167	16.0	8.9	10.0	9.8	4.8
1989	4,041	2,150	40	2,403	1,157	16.4	8.7	9.8	9.7	4.7
1990	4,158	2,148	38	2,443	1,182	16.7	8.6	9.2	9.8	4.7
1991	4,111	2,170	37	2,371	1,187	16.2	8.6	8.9	9.4	4.7
1992	4,065	2,176	35	2,362	1,215	15.8	8.5	8.5	9.3	4.8
1993	4,000	2,269	33	2,334	1,187	15.4	8.7	8.4	9.0	4.6
1994	3,953	2,279	31	2,362	1,191	15.0	8.7	8.0	9.1	4.6
1995	3,900	2,312	30	2,336	1,169	14.6	8.7	7.6	8.9	4.4
1996	3,891	2,315	28	2,344	1,150	14.4	8.6	7.3	8.8	4.3
1997	3,881	2,314	28	2,384	1,163	14.2	8.5	7.2	8.9	4.3
1998	3,942	2,337	28	2,244	[4] 1,135	14.3	8.5	7.2	8.4	[4] 4.2
1999	3,959	2,391	28	2,358	(NA)	14.2	8.6	7.1	8.6	[4] 4.1
2000	4,059	2,403	28	2,315	[5] 944	14.4	8.5	6.9	8.2	[5] 4.0
2001	4,026	2,416	28	2,326	[5] 940	14.1	8.5	6.9	8.2	[5] 4.0
2002	4,022	2,443	28	2,290	[6] 955	14.0	8.5	7.0	8.0	[6] 3.9
2003	4,090	2,448	28	2,245	[7] 927	14.1	8.4	6.9	7.7	[7] 3.8
2004	4,112	2,398	28	2,279	[8] 879	14.0	8.2	6.8	7.8	[8] 3.7
2005	4,138	2,448	28	2,249	[9] 847	14.0	8.3	6.9	7.6	[9] 3.6
2006	4,266	2,426	29	[10] 2,193	[9] 872	14.3	8.1	6.7	[10] 7.5	[9] 3.7
2007	4,316	2,424	29	2,197	[9] 856	14.3	8.0	6.8	7.3	[9] 3.6
2008	4,248	2,472	28	2,157	[9] 844	14.0	8.1	6.6	7.1	[9] 3.5
2009	4,131	2,437	26	2,080	[9] 840	13.5	7.9	6.4	6.8	[9] 3.5
2010	3,999	2,468	25	2,096	[9] 872	13.0	8.0	6.2	6.8	[9] 3.6
2011	3,954	2,515	24	2,118	[9] 877	12.7	8.1	6.1	6.8	[9] 3.6
2012	3,953	2,543	24	2,131	[9] 851	12.6	8.1	6.0	6.8	[9] 3.4
2013	3,932	2,597	23	[11] 2,081	[12] 832	12.4	8.2	6.0	[11] 6.8	[12] 3.3
2014	3,988	2,626	23	[11] 2,140	[12] 814	12.5	8.2	5.8	[11] 6.9	[12] 3.2
2015	3,978	2,713	23	2,222	[12] 801	12.4	8.4	5.9	6.9	[12] 3.1
2016	3,946	2,744	23	2,251	[13] 776	12.2	8.5	5.9	7.0	[13] 3.0
2017	3,856	2,814	22	2,236	[14] 787	11.8	8.6	5.8	6.9	[14] 2.9
2018	3,792	2,839	21	2,133	[14] 782	11.6	8.7	5.7	6.5	[14] 2.9
2019	3,748	2,855	21	2,016	[14] 747	11.4	8.7	5.6	6.1	[14] 2.7
2020	3,614	3,384	20	1,677	[14] 631	11.0	10.3	5.4	5.1	[14] 2.3

NA Not available. [1] Infant mortality rate; infants under 1 year, excluding fetal deaths. [2] Marriages and marriage rates are by place of occurrence. Beginning 1991, data are provisional. Includes estimates for some States through 1965 and for 1976-1977, and marriage licenses for some states for all years except 1973 and 1975. Beginning 1978, includes nonlicensed marriages in California. [3] Divorces and divorce rates are by place of occurrence. Includes reported annulments and some estimated state figures for all years. Beginning 1991, data are provisional. [4] Excludes data for California, Colorado, Indiana, and Louisiana. [5] Excludes data for California, Indiana, Louisiana, and Oklahoma. [6] Excludes data for California, Indiana, New York City, and Oklahoma. [7] Excludes data for California, Hawaii, Indiana, and Oklahoma. [8] Excludes data for California, Georgia, Hawaii, Indiana, and Louisiana. [9] Excludes data for California, Georgia, Hawaii, Indiana, Louisiana, and Minnesota. [10] Excludes data for Louisiana. [11] Excludes data for Georgia. [12] Excludes data for California, Georgia, Hawaii, Indiana, and Minnesota. [13] Excludes data for California, Georgia, Hawaii, Indiana, Minnesota, and New Mexico. [14] Excludes data for California, Hawaii, Indiana, Minnesota, and New Mexico.

Source: U.S. National Center for Health Statistics, *Births: Final Data for 2020*, Vol. 70, No. 17, February 2022; and CDC WONDER Online Database, "Multiple Cause of Death, 1999-2020," <wonder.cdc.gov/>, and "National Marriage and Divorce Rate Trends," <www.cdc.gov/nchs/nvss/marriage-divorce.htm>; accessed March 2022.

Table 81. Births, Birth Rates, and Fertility Rates by Sex and Mother's Race and Age: 1980 to 2020

[Births in thousands (3,612 represents 3,612,000). Beginning 2016, all States and the District of Columbia reported race data according to 1997 Office of Management and Budget (OMB) standards. To maintain comparability of 2016 data with earlier data, data for mothers reporting multiple-race were bridged to single-race categories. Beginning with 2003, data shown here for race/ethnicity of mother are from the CDC WONDER database and are calculated differently than in other natality published reports. In computing birth and fertility rates by race and Hispanic origin, the National Center for Health Statistics includes births with origin of mother not stated with non-Hispanic births, according to the race of mother. See Technical Notes, source. For population bases used to derive these data, see text this section, and Appendix III]

Item	1980	1990	2000	2005	2010	2015	2016	2017	2018	2019	2020
Live births [1]	**3,612**	**4,158**	**4,059**	**4,138**	**3,999**	**3,978**	**3,946**	**3,856**	**3,792**	**3,748**	**3,614**
Male	1,853	2,129	2,077	2,119	2,047	2,036	2,018	1,973	1,938	1,917	1,848
Female	1,760	2,029	1,982	2,019	1,952	1,942	1,928	1,883	1,854	1,830	1,766
Males per 100 females (sex ratio)	105	105	105	105	105	105	105	105	105	105	105
Race/ethnicity of mother:											
Non-Hispanic	(NA)	(NA)	(NA)	(NA)	3,027	3,022	2,991	2,924	2,872	2,825	2,713
White alone	(NA)	(NA)	(NA)	(NA)	(NA)	(NA)	2,056	1,992	1,956	1,916	1,843
Black or African American alone	(NA)	(NA)	(NA)	(NA)	(NA)	(NA)	559	561	552	548	530
American Indian or Alaska Native alone	(NA)	(NA)	(NA)	(NA)	(NA)	(NA)	31	30	29	28	27
Asian alone	(NA)	(NA)	(NA)	(NA)	(NA)	(NA)	254	249	241	239	219
Native Hawaiian or Other Pacific Islander alone	(NA)	(NA)	(NA)	(NA)	(NA)	(NA)	9	9	9	10	10
Hispanic	(NA)	595	816	986	945	924	918	899	886	886	867
Bridged race estimates: [2]											
White	2,936	3,290	3,194	3,229	3,069	3,013	2,946	2,858	2,835	2,790	(NA)
Black	568	684	623	633	636	640	654	658	634	635	(NA)
American Indian or Alaska Native	29	39	42	45	47	44	44	42	42	42	(NA)
Asian or Pacific Islander	74	142	201	231	247	281	302	298	281	281	(NA)
Age of mother:											
Under 20 years old	562	533	478	421	372	232	212	196	182	173	160
20 to 24 years old	1,226	1,094	1,018	1,040	952	851	804	765	726	704	666
25 to 29 years old	1,108	1,277	1,088	1,132	1,134	1,152	1,149	1,124	1,099	1,078	1,024
30 to 34 years old	550	886	929	951	962	1,095	1,111	1,092	1,091	1,089	1,070
35 to 39 years old	141	318	452	483	465	528	547	555	567	573	564
40 to 44 years old	(NA)	(NA)	90	105	107	112	113	115	117	120	121
45 to 54 years old	(NA)	(NA)	4	6	8	9	9	9	10	10	9
Mean age of mother at first birth (years)	22.7	24.2	24.9	25.2	25.4	26.4	26.6	26.8	26.9	27.0	27.1
Birth rate per 1,000 population	**15.9**	**16.7**	**14.4**	**14.0**	**13.0**	**12.4**	**12.2**	**11.8**	**11.6**	**11.4**	**11.0**
Race/ethnicity of mother:											
Non-Hispanic	(NA)	(NA)	(NA)	(NA)	11.7	11.4	11.3	11.0	10.7	10.6	10.1
White alone	(NA)	(NA)	(NA)	(NA)	(NA)	(NA)	10.4	10.1	9.9	9.7	9.4
Black or African American alone	(NA)	(NA)	(NA)	(NA)	(NA)	(NA)	13.9	13.8	13.5	13.3	12.8
American Indian or Alaska Native alone	(NA)	(NA)	(NA)	(NA)	(NA)	(NA)	13.2	12.5	12.0	11.7	11.0
Asian alone	(NA)	(NA)	(NA)	(NA)	(NA)	(NA)	14.3	13.6	12.9	12.6	11.3
Native Hawaiian or Other Pacific Islander alone	(NA)	(NA)	(NA)	(NA)	(NA)	(NA)	16.5	16.3	16.2	16.4	15.7
Hispanic	23.5	26.7	23.1	22.9	18.7	16.3	16.0	15.3	14.8	14.6	14.1
Bridged race estimates: [2]											
White	15.1	15.8	13.9	13.6	12.5	12.0	11.7	11.3	11.1	10.9	(NA)
Black	21.3	22.4	17.0	16.1	15.1	14.3	14.4	14.3	13.7	13.6	(NA)
American Indian or Alaska Native	20.7	18.9	14.0	12.6	11.0	9.7	9.4	8.9	8.9	8.7	(NA)
Asian or Pacific Islander	19.9	19.0	17.1	15.9	14.5	14.0	14.8	14.0	13.0	12.9	(NA)
Age of mother:											
10 to 14 years old	1.1	1.4	0.9	0.6	0.4	0.2	0.2	0.2	0.2	0.2	0.2
15 to 19 years old	53.0	59.9	47.7	39.7	34.2	22.3	20.3	18.8	17.4	16.7	15.4
20 to 24 years old	115.1	116.5	109.7	101.8	90.0	76.8	73.8	71.0	68.0	66.6	63.0
25 to 29 years old	112.9	120.2	113.5	116.5	108.3	104.3	102.1	98.0	95.3	93.7	90.2
30 to 34 years old	61.9	80.8	91.2	96.7	96.5	101.5	102.7	100.3	99.7	98.3	94.9
35 to 39 years old	19.8	31.7	39.7	46.4	45.9	51.8	52.7	52.3	52.6	52.8	51.8
40 to 44 years old	3.9	5.5	8.0	9.1	10.2	11.0	11.4	11.6	11.8	12.0	11.8
45 to 54 years old [3]	0.2	0.2	0.5	0.6	0.7	0.8	0.9	0.9	0.9	0.9	0.9
Fertility rate per 1,000 women [4]	**68.4**	**70.9**	**65.9**	**66.7**	**64.1**	**62.5**	**62.0**	**60.3**	**59.1**	**58.3**	**56.0**
Race/ethnicity of mother:											
Non-Hispanic	(NA)	(NA)	(NA)	(NA)	59.8	59.6	59.1	57.7	56.6	55.7	53.4
White alone	(NA)	(NA)	(NA)	(NA)	(NA)	(NA)	58.1	56.6	55.7	54.6	52.6
Black or African American alone	(NA)	(NA)	(NA)	(NA)	(NA)	(NA)	62.8	62.7	61.5	60.9	58.6
American Indian or Alaska Native alone	(NA)	(NA)	(NA)	(NA)	(NA)	(NA)	62.0	58.9	56.9	55.4	51.9
Asian alone	(NA)	(NA)	(NA)	(NA)	(NA)	(NA)	60.1	56.9	54.2	53.7	49.4
Native Hawaiian or Other Pacific Islander alone	(NA)	(NA)	(NA)	(NA)	(NA)	(NA)	71.6	71.4	71.1	72.2	70.5
Hispanic	95.4	107.7	95.9	96.4	80.2	71.7	70.6	67.6	65.9	65.3	63.1
Bridged race estimates: [2]											
White	65.6	68.3	65.3	66.8	64.4	63.1	61.8	59.8	59.2	58.2	(NA)
Black	84.7	86.8	70.0	68.5	66.3	64.0	65.1	64.9	62.2	61.9	(NA)
American Indian or Alaska Native	82.7	76.2	58.7	53.6	48.6	43.9	42.8	40.8	40.7	40.0	(NA)
Asian or Pacific Islander	73.2	69.6	65.8	63.0	63.0	59.2	58.5	62.1	59.3	55.2	54.9	(NA)

NA Not available. [1] Includes other races not shown separately. [2] Bridged race categories consistent with 1977 Office of Management and Budget standards. [3] Birth rates computed by relating births to women age 45 and over (includes mothers up to age 64) to women age 45-49. [4] Number of live births per 1,000 women, 15 to 44 years old in specified group.

Source: U.S. National Center for Health Statistics, National Vital Statistics Reports, *Births: Final Data for 2020*, Vol. 70, No. 17, February 2022, and earlier reports; and CDC WONDER Online Database, "Natality for 2007-2020," <wonder.cdc.gov/natality.html>, accessed February 2022.

Table 82. Births—Number and Rate by Race/Ethnicity and State and Island Area: 2020

[For registered births by place of residence. Excludes births to nonresidents of the United States. Based on race and Hispanic origin of mother. Race categories are consistent with 1997 Office of Management and Budget standards; see Technical Notes in source. Race alone is defined as only one race reported on the birth certificate. See Appendix III]

State and Island Area	All races [1]	White alone [2]	Black alone [2]	American Indian or Alaska Native alone [2]	Asian alone [2]	Native Hawaiian or Other Pacific Islander alone [2]	Hispanic [3]	Birth rate [4]	Fertility rate [5]
United States [6]	**3,613,647**	**1,843,432**	**529,811**	**26,813**	**219,068**	**9,626**	**866,713**	**11.0**	**56.0**
Alabama	57,647	32,672	17,746	133	836	40	5,233	11.7	60.6
Alaska	9,469	4,770	281	1,797	524	325	734	13.0	65.7
Arizona	76,947	30,854	4,389	3,551	2,624	203	32,999	10.4	54.0
Arkansas	35,251	22,106	6,834	183	825	449	3,939	11.6	60.7
California	420,259	115,543	21,350	1,391	58,543	1,617	194,295	10.7	52.4
Colorado	61,494	34,924	3,146	338	2,519	169	18,111	10.6	51.5
Connecticut	33,460	17,785	4,056	35	1,992	7	8,861	9.4	49.9
Delaware	10,392	4,949	2,722	18	617	3	1,768	10.5	57.0
District of Columbia	8,874	2,947	3,992	8	393	2	1,349	12.4	46.1
Florida	209,671	88,080	45,585	229	6,539	145	66,156	9.6	53.4
Georgia	122,473	52,717	42,373	115	5,579	127	18,415	11.4	55.7
Hawaii	15,785	3,060	383	25	3,940	1,577	2,623	11.2	61.1
Idaho	21,533	16,463	265	206	327	64	3,687	11.8	60.9
Illinois	133,298	70,550	22,293	79	8,505	39	28,808	10.6	53.8
Indiana	78,616	56,290	9,848	56	2,335	62	8,480	11.6	59.8
Iowa	36,114	27,542	2,685	143	1,067	234	3,725	11.4	60.4
Kansas	34,376	23,663	2,412	162	1,146	81	5,970	11.8	61.1
Kentucky	51,668	40,726	5,154	53	1,099	75	3,472	11.5	60.8
Louisiana	57,328	28,635	21,552	245	1,037	30	5,016	12.3	62.2
Maine	11,539	10,231	514	85	195	3	258	8.5	49.2
Maryland	68,554	28,060	20,869	79	4,595	29	13,034	11.3	57.7
Massachusetts	66,428	37,357	6,580	71	5,826	22	14,080	9.6	47.6
Michigan	104,074	70,426	19,341	410	4,260	50	6,985	10.4	55.6
Minnesota	63,443	42,099	8,074	873	5,026	59	5,320	11.2	58.3
Mississippi	35,473	17,648	15,155	252	451	22	1,679	12.0	61.0
Missouri	69,285	50,190	10,156	163	1,610	249	4,469	11.3	58.7
Montana	10,791	8,639	62	1,063	112	11	569	10.0	54.3
Nebraska	24,291	16,433	1,631	284	870	40	4,393	12.5	64.7
Nevada	33,653	11,602	4,533	234	2,467	358	12,763	10.7	54.8
New Hampshire	11,791	10,075	256	10	428	7	797	8.6	47.7
New Jersey	97,954	44,709	12,951	41	10,451	30	27,205	11.0	58.6
New Mexico	21,903	5,872	403	2,434	410	14	12,406	10.4	54.6
New York	209,338	104,581	30,057	360	21,074	54	47,904	10.8	54.6
North Carolina	116,730	60,518	27,228	1,351	4,718	141	19,449	11.0	56.2
North Dakota	10,059	7,199	659	771	250	26	672	13.1	67.4
Ohio	129,191	92,033	21,447	102	3,995	89	7,669	11.0	58.3
Oklahoma	47,623	26,290	3,944	4,367	1,282	274	7,561	12.0	61.0
Oregon	39,820	26,256	973	378	2,112	278	7,923	9.4	47.8
Pennsylvania	130,693	85,956	17,118	83	6,074	45	16,741	10.2	54.9
Rhode Island	10,101	5,495	805	36	476	3	2,927	9.6	48.7
South Carolina	55,704	30,465	16,309	106	1,148	62	5,993	10.7	55.9
South Dakota	10,960	7,740	390	1,501	215	8	660	12.3	66.7
Tennessee	78,689	50,668	15,413	85	1,767	62	8,928	11.4	58.5
Texas	368,190	120,329	46,643	638	19,064	543	175,940	12.5	60.2
Utah	45,702	33,145	576	341	1,146	518	8,160	14.1	64.1
Vermont	5,133	4,646	108	15	137	(NA)	132	8.2	44.7
Virginia	94,749	51,120	19,622	146	6,945	116	14,806	11.0	55.8
Washington	83,086	46,199	3,841	1,002	8,429	1,231	16,020	10.8	54.0
West Virginia	17,323	15,698	603	16	160	2	373	9.7	55.3
Wisconsin	60,594	42,715	6,429	573	2,870	25	6,438	10.4	55.4
Wyoming	6,128	4,762	55	176	58	6	818	10.5	56.4
Puerto Rico	18,933	298	43	2	27	–	18,542	6.0	31.2
Virgin Islands	876	(NA)	(NA)	(NA)	(NA)	(NA)	(NA)	8.2	46.5
Guam	2,935	147	25	6	690	1,854	27	17.4	89.6
American Samoa	(NA)	(NA)	(NA)	(NA)	(NA)	(NA)	(NA)	(NA)	(NA)
Northern Marianas	628	5	1	1	222	373	–	12.1	69.7

– Represents zero. NA Not available. [1] Includes persons of other racial/ethnic groups, not shown separately. [2] Non-Hispanic. [3] Persons of Hispanic origin may be of any race. [4] Per 1,000 estimated population. [5] Number of births per 1,000 women aged 15 to 44 years. [6] Does not include data for the Island Areas.

Source: U.S. National Center for Health Statistics, National Vital Statistics Reports, *Births: Final Data for 2020*, Vol. 70, No. 17, February 2022. See also <www.cdc.gov/nchs/nvss/births.htm>.

Table 83. Births, Twin Births, and Triplet and Higher-order Multiple Births by Race and Hispanic Origin of Mother: 2010 to 2020

[Represents registered births. Excludes births to nonresidents of the United States. Data are based on Hispanic origin and race of mother. Persons of Hispanic origin may be of any race. Race categories are consistent with 1997 Office of Management and Budget standards; see source for details. See Appendix III]

Year and race and Hispanic origin	Number			Rate		
	Total births	Twin births	Triplet and higher-order births	Multiple births, total [1]	Twin births [2]	Triplet and higher-order births [3]
All races and origins: [4]						
2010	3,999,386	132,562	5,503	34.5	33.1	137.6
2015	3,978,497	133,155	4,123	34.5	33.5	103.6
2017	3,855,500	128,310	3,917	34.3	33.3	101.6
2018	3,791,712	123,536	3,525	33.5	32.6	93.0
2019	3,747,540	120,291	3,286	33.0	32.1	87.7
2020	3,613,647	112,437	2,875	31.9	31.1	79.6
White alone, non-Hispanic :						
2017	1,992,461	70,704	2,324	36.7	35.5	116.6
2018	1,956,413	67,203	1,996	35.4	34.4	102.0
2019	1,915,912	64,011	1,865	34.4	33.4	97.3
2020	1,843,432	60,082	1,664	33.5	32.6	90.3
Black alone, non-Hispanic:						
2017	560,715	22,982	671	42.2	41.0	119.7
2018	552,029	22,502	658	42.0	40.8	119.2
2019	548,075	22,397	589	41.9	40.9	107.5
2020	529,811	21,554	521	41.7	40.7	98.3
Hispanic: [5]						
2017	898,764	22,041	614	25.2	24.5	68.3
2018	886,210	21,654	573	25.1	24.4	64.7
2019	886,467	21,811	590	25.3	24.6	66.6
2020	866,713	20,709	488	24.5	23.9	56.3

[1] Number of live births in all multiple deliveries per 1,000 live births. [2] Number of births in twin deliveries per 1,000 live births. [3] Number of births in greater than twin deliveries per 100,000 live births. [4] Includes other races not shown separately. [5] Persons of Hispanic origin may be of any race.

Source: U.S. National Center for Health Statistics, National Vital Statistics Reports, *Births: Final Data for 2020*, Vol. 70, No. 17, February 2022. See also <www.cdc.gov/nchs/nvss/births.htm>.

Table 84. Births by Method of Delivery and Race and Hispanic Origin: 2010 to 2020

[In thousands (3,999 represents 3,999,000), except rate. Race categories are consistent with 1997 Office of Management and Budget standards. Data are based on race and Hispanic origin of mother. Persons of Hispanic origin may be of any race. See Appendix III]

Method of delivery	2010	2015	2016	2017	2018	2019	2020			
							Total [1]	White alone, non-Hispanic	Black alone, non-Hispanic	Hispanic
Births, total	**3,999**	**3,978**	**3,946**	**3,856**	**3,792**	**3,748**	**3,614**	**1,843**	**530**	**867**
Vaginal	2,681	2,704	2,685	2,621	2,582	2,559	2,463	1,276	337	594
Cesarean	1,309	1,273	1,259	1,232	1,208	1,186	1,149	567	192	272
Not stated	9	2	2	2	2	2	2	1	(Z)	(Z)
Cesarean delivery rate [2]	32.8	32.0	31.9	32.0	31.9	31.7	31.8	30.8	36.3	31.4
Rate of vaginal birth after previous Cesarean [3]	(NA)	(NA)	12.4	12.8	13.3	13.8	13.9	14.0	13.7	13.4

Z Represents less than 500. NA Not available. [1] Includes other races, not shown separately. [2] Percent of all live births by cesarean delivery. [3] Number of births to women having a vaginal delivery per 100 births to women with a previous cesarean delivery.

Source: U.S. National Center for Health Statistics, National Vital Statistics Reports, *Births: Final Data for 2020*, Vol. 70, No. 17, February 2022, and earlier reports. See also <www.cdc.gov/nchs/nvss/births.htm>.

Table 85. Births Delivered by Physicians, Midwives, and Other Attendants by Place of Delivery: 2020

[Number, except as noted]

Place of delivery	Total births [1]	Physician			Midwife			Other
		Total	Doctor of medicine	Doctor of osteopathy	Total	Certified nurse midwife	Other midwife	
Total	**3,613,647**	**3,171,753**	**2,853,659**	**318,094**	**410,388**	**372,991**	**37,397**	**29,732**
Percent	100.0	87.8	79.0	8.8	11.4	10.3	1.0	0.8
In hospital [2]	3,541,612	3,168,755	2,850,976	317,779	355,615	349,243	6,372	16,767
Not in hospital	71,870	2,914	2,608	306	54,750	23,741	31,009	12,925
Freestanding birthing center	21,884	781	686	95	19,841	11,546	8,295	1,229
Clinic or doctor's office	595	125	99	26	454	295	159	12
Residence	45,646	1,500	1,361	139	33,068	11,582	21,486	10,118
Other	3,745	508	462	46	1,387	318	1,069	1,566
Not specified	165	84	75	9	23	7	16	40

[1] Includes unspecified attendants, not shown separately. [2] Includes births occurring en route to or upon arrival at hospital.

Source: U.S. National Center for Health Statistics, National Vital Statistics Reports, *Births: Final Data for 2020, Supplemental Tables*, Vol. 70, No. 17, February 2022. See also <www.cdc.gov/nchs/nvss/births.htm>.

Table 86. Total Fertility Rate by Race and Hispanic Origin: 2010 to 2020

[Based on race of mother. Excludes births to nonresidents of United States. The total fertility rate estimates the number of births that a hypothetical cohort of 1,000 women would have if they experienced throughout their childbearing years the same age-specific birth rates observed in a given year. The rate can be expressed as the average number of children that would be born per woman. A total fertility rate of 2,100 represents "replacement level" fertility for the total population under current mortality conditions (assuming no net immigration). Race categories are consistent with 1997 Office of Management and Budget standards. See Appendix III]

Race and Hispanic origin	2010	2014	2015	2016	2017	2018	2019	2020
Total	**1,931**	**1,863**	**1,844**	**1,821**	**1,766**	**1,730**	**1,706**	**1,641**
Non-Hispanic:								
White alone	(NA)	(NA)	(NA)	1,719	1,667	1,640	1,611	1,552
Black alone	(NA)	(NA)	(NA)	1,833	1,825	1,792	1,776	1,714
American Indian or Alaska Native alone	(NA)	(NA)	(NA)	1,795	1,702	1,651	1,612	1,517
Asian alone	(NA)	(NA)	(NA)	1,691	1,597	1,525	1,511	1,385
Native Hawaiian or other Pacific Islander alone	(NA)	(NA)	(NA)	2,077	2,086	2,107	2,178	2,142
Hispanic [1]	2,350	2,131	2,124	2,093	2,007	1,959	1,940	1,876

NA Not available. [1] Persons of Hispanic origin may be of any race.

Source: U.S. National Center for Health Statistics, National Vital Statistics Reports, *Births: Final Data for 2020*, Vol. 70, No. 17, February 2022. See also <www.cdc.gov/nchs/nvss/births.htm>.

Table 87. Teenagers—Births and Birth Rates by Age, Race, and Hispanic Origin: 2010 to 2020

[Birth rates per 1,000 women in specified group. Based on race and Hispanic origin of mother. Race categories are consistent with 1997 Office of Management and Budget (OMB) standards. See source for details]

Age, race, and Hispanic origin	Number of births				Birth rates			
	2010	2018	2019	2020	2010	2018	2019	2020
All races, 15 to 19 years [1]	**367,678**	**179,871**	**171,674**	**158,043**	**34.2**	**17.4**	**16.7**	**15.4**
15 to 17 years	109,173	44,291	41,081	38,587	17.3	7.2	6.7	6.3
18 to 19 years	258,505	135,580	130,593	119,456	58.2	32.3	31.1	28.9
Non-Hispanic:								
White alone	(NA)	64,917	60,484	54,426	(NA)	12.1	11.4	10.4
Black alone	(NA)	37,715	36,696	34,147	(NA)	26.3	25.8	24.4
American Indian or Alaska Native alone	(NA)	2,578	2,516	2,189	(NA)	29.7	29.2	25.7
Asian alone	(NA)	1,444	1,357	1,127	(NA)	2.8	2.7	2.3
Native Hawaiian or other Pacific Islander alone	(NA)	516	520	452	(NA)	26.5	26.2	22.6
Hispanic [2]	(NA)	65,122	62,654	58,752	(NA)	26.7	25.3	23.5

NA Not available. [1] Includes other racial/ethnic groups, not shown separately. [2] Persons of Hispanic origin may be of any race.

Source: U.S. National Center for Health Statistics, National Vital Statistics Reports, *Births: Final Data for 2020*, Vol. 70, No. 17, February 2022. See also <www.cdc.gov/nchs/nvss/births.htm>.

Table 88. Births to Unmarried Women by Age, Race, and Hispanic Origin: 2020

[Data are based on Hispanic origin and race of mother. Race categories are consistent with 1997 Office of Management and Budget standards; see source for details. See also Appendix III]

Race/ethnicity of mother		Age of mother						
	Total	Under 15 years old	15 to 19 years old	20 to 24 years old	25 to 29 years old	30 to 34 years old	35 to 39 years old	40 years and over
NUMBER								
Total	**1,464,121**	**1,762**	**144,957**	**450,641**	**423,015**	**274,427**	**133,942**	**35,377**
Non-Hispanic:								
White alone	523,347	379	47,855	166,375	149,256	98,605	48,408	12,469
Black alone	373,130	512	33,497	111,942	115,848	72,045	31,637	7,649
American Indian or Alaska Native alone	18,659	31	2,084	5,815	5,283	3,578	1,568	300
Asian alone	26,777	12	877	4,335	7,671	7,582	4,781	1,519
Native Hawaiian or other Pacific Islander alone	5,007	4	412	1,718	1,446	889	443	95
Hispanic [1]	457,978	730	53,635	140,750	126,963	81,679	42,367	11,854
PERCENT OF TOTAL BIRTHS								
Total	**40.5**	**99.8**	**91.7**	**67.7**	**41.3**	**25.6**	**23.7**	**27.3**
Non-Hispanic:								
White alone	28.4	100.0	87.9	56.6	28.3	16.3	16.0	20.5
Black alone	70.4	100.0	98.1	89.6	74.0	56.8	46.4	41.1
American Indian or Alaska Native alone	69.6	100.0	95.2	80.5	66.9	59.5	54.9	49.6
Asian alone	12.2	(S)	77.8	36.6	16.1	8.5	8.5	11.7
Native Hawaiian or other Pacific Islander alone	52.0	(S)	91.2	70.4	49.1	39.0	37.1	30.4
Hispanic [1]	52.8	99.7	91.3	70.7	50.7	39.0	36.2	37.8

S Figure does not meet standards of reliability. [1] Persons of Hispanic origin may be of any race.

Source: U.S. National Center for Health Statistics, National Vital Statistics Reports, *Births: Final Data for 2020*, Vol. 70, No. 17, February 2022. See also <www.cdc.gov/nchs/nvss/births.htm>.

Table 89. Percent of Births to Teenage Mothers, Unmarried Women, and Births with Low Birth Weight by State: 2010 and 2020

[In percent. By place of residence. Excludes nonresidents of the United States]

State	Births to teenage mothers [1]		Births to unmarried women		Births with low birth weight [2]		State	Births to teenage mothers [1]		Births to unmarried women		Births with low birth weight [2]	
	2010	2020	2010	2020	2010	2020		2010	2020	2010	2020	2010	2020
U.S...........	9.2	4.4	40.8	40.5	8.1	8.2	MO.............	10.0	5.1	40.2	41.1	8.2	8.7
AL.............	12.2	6.6	41.9	48.4	10.3	10.8	MT.............	9.4	3.8	36.4	33.9	7.5	7.7
AK.............	8.3	4.0	37.6	36.5	5.7	6.6	NE.............	7.6	4.1	33.6	33.4	7.1	7.4
AZ.............	10.7	5.1	44.9	45.2	7.1	7.4	NV.............	9.5	4.5	44.3	48.8	8.3	9.0
AR.............	13.6	7.6	45.3	46.8	8.8	9.6	NH.............	5.6	2.3	33.2	32.1	6.9	6.8
CA.............	8.5	3.2	40.5	38.6	6.8	6.9	NJ.............	5.4	2.5	35.4	33.9	8.2	7.7
CO.............	8.2	3.6	23.9	23.2	8.8	9.3	NM.............	13.9	6.8	52.3	53.2	8.7	8.9
CT.............	6.0	2.6	37.4	38.1	8.0	7.8	NY.............	6.2	2.7	41.7	38.1	8.2	8.2
DE.............	8.6	4.2	47.4	48.1	8.9	8.9	NC.............	10.1	5.0	42.0	41.9	9.1	9.5
DC.............	10.4	3.4	54.8	46.7	10.2	9.6	ND.............	7.2	3.2	32.7	32.8	6.7	6.9
FL.............	8.9	4.3	47.5	47.2	8.7	8.7	OH.............	9.9	5.0	43.8	43.6	8.6	8.5
GA.............	10.7	5.4	45.8	46.3	9.7	9.9	OK.............	12.2	6.8	41.8	44.4	8.4	8.4
HI.............	7.1	3.0	37.8	39.4	8.3	8.1	OR.............	7.7	3.0	35.7	36.7	6.3	6.5
ID.............	8.0	4.2	26.5	27.7	6.8	6.9	PA.............	8.3	3.7	41.5	40.9	8.3	8.3
IL.............	9.0	4.0	40.5	40.5	8.3	8.3	RI.............	8.0	3.2	45.0	44.7	7.7	7.7
IN.............	10.3	5.2	43.0	43.6	8.0	8.1	SC.............	11.7	5.5	47.6	46.6	9.9	9.8
IA.............	7.8	3.8	34.2	36.3	7.0	6.9	SD.............	8.3	4.9	37.6	36.0	6.8	6.9
KS.............	9.5	5.1	37.8	36.8	7.1	7.2	TN.............	11.6	6.1	44.1	44.6	9.0	8.9
KY.............	12.0	6.4	41.2	43.1	9.0	8.5	TX.............	12.4	6.1	42.4	41.7	8.4	8.2
LA.............	12.3	6.4	53.3	54.5	10.7	10.9	UT.............	5.8	3.0	19.2	19.3	7.0	7.0
ME.............	7.1	3.4	41.2	38.4	6.3	7.5	VT.............	6.4	2.7	39.2	38.9	6.1	7.0
MD.............	7.3	3.5	41.9	40.8	8.8	8.5	VA.............	7.2	3.7	35.5	35.8	8.2	8.3
MA.............	5.4	2.0	34.7	33.0	7.7	7.4	WA.............	6.9	3.0	33.0	31.6	6.3	6.7
MI.............	9.5	4.0	41.8	41.2	8.4	8.9	WV.............	12.7	6.6	43.9	46.8	9.2	9.3
MN.............	5.9	2.5	33.2	32.6	6.4	6.7	WI.............	7.4	3.5	36.7	37.9	7.0	7.7
MS.............	15.2	7.6	54.8	55.8	12.1	11.8	WY.............	9.6	5.3	34.0	34.1	9.0	9.7

[1] Defined as teenage mothers aged 15-19. [2] Less than 2,500 grams (5 pounds, 8 ounces).

Source: U.S. National Center for Health Statistics, National Vital Statistics Reports, *Births: Final Data for 2020, Supplemental Tables*, Vol. 70, No. 17, February 2022, and earlier reports; and CDC WONDER Online Database, "Natality for 2007-2020," <wonder.cdc.gov>, accessed February 2022. See also <www.cdc.gov/nchs/nvss/births.htm>.

Table 90. Rate of Pregnancy Risk Factors, Labor and Delivery Characteristics, and Birth Defects by Age of Mother: 2020

[Rates are number of live births with specified risk factor, procedure, or characteristic per 1,000 live births in specified group, except as noted; birth defects are per 100,000 live births. In 2020, total number of births to residents in reporting areas is 3,613,647]

Factor/characteristic	Births with factor reported (number)	Rates by age						
		All ages	Under 20 years	20 to 24 years	25 to 29 years	30 to 34 years	35 to 39 years	40 to 54 years
RISK FACTORS IN CURRENT PREGNANCY								
Diabetes:								
Prepregnancy (diagnosis prior to pregnancy)......	38,093	10.6	4.4	6.9	8.9	10.9	15.9	24.1
Gestational (diagnosis in current pregnancy)......	281,789	78.1	25.0	44.6	66.2	88.3	117.5	153.2
Hypertension:								
Prepregnancy (chronic)..............................	91,528	25.4	9.1	16.0	21.1	26.8	38.4	57.6
Gestational (pregnancy-induced, preeclampsia)...	304,293	84.3	87.6	85.9	82.3	81.1	86.5	104.7
Eclampsia [1]......................................	9,981	2.8	3.6	3.1	2.6	2.5	2.8	4.0
Previous preterm birth...............................	133,516	37.0	8.1	26.4	36.8	40.0	48.1	55.0
Pregnancy resulted from infertility treatment.........	73,206	20.3	0.2	2.3	9.1	23.1	43.8	99.8
Mother had previous cesarean delivery [2]............	557,895	225.7	94.7	159.3	206.7	239.5	274.3	295.0
LABOR AND DELIVERY CHARACTERISTICS								
Induction of labor....................................	1,133,627	313.9	356.1	341.6	317.5	298.8	291.9	311.0
Breech presentation (rate per 100 live births)........	146,676	4.1	2.6	2.9	3.7	4.5	5.2	6.4
BIRTH DEFECTS (CONGENITAL ANOMALIES)								
Anencephaly...	332	9.2	16.3	8.3	10.1	6.2	12.1	10.8
Meningomyelocele or spina bifida....................	489	13.6	11.3	14.6	13.4	13.4	13.5	13.9
Cyanotic congenital heart disease....................	2,287	63.4	56.4	56.3	59.5	61.4	74.0	108.8
Gastroschisis..	744	20.6	87.7	42.0	18.6	8.4	6.9	4.6
Cleft lip with or without cleft palate..................	1,787	49.5	50.7	53.1	47.6	47.2	50.6	59.4
Down syndrome......................................	1,954	54.1	28.2	27.4	28.7	38.9	102.6	338.8

[1] Excludes data for South Carolina and Tennessee. [2] Excludes women who have not had a previous pregnancy and from whom total birth order is unknown.

Source: U.S. National Center for Health Statistics, National Vital Statistics Reports, *Births: Final Data for 2020, Supplemental Tables*, Vol. 70, No. 17, February 2022. See also <www.cdc.gov/nchs/nvss/births.htm>.

Table 91. Percent of Premature Births by Whether Early or Late Preterm and by Age, Race, and Hispanic Origin of Mother: 2020

[Preterm/premature births are those with less than 37 completed weeks of gestation based on obstetric estimates. Based on race and Hispanic origin of mother. Race categories are consistent with 1997 Office of Management and Budget standards. See source for details]

Characteristic	Total births (number)	Percent preterm				
		Total under 37 weeks	Early preterm			Late preterm
			Under 28 weeks	28 to 31 weeks	32 to 33 weeks	34 to 36 weeks
Total [1]	**3,613,647**	**10.1**	**0.6**	**0.9**	**1.2**	**7.4**
Age of mother:						
Under 15 years	1,765	15.5	2.2	1.8	1.9	9.6
15 to 19 years	158,043	10.3	0.9	1.0	1.2	7.2
20 to 24 years	665,595	9.7	0.7	0.9	1.1	7.1
25 to 29 years	1,024,402	9.5	0.6	0.8	1.1	7.0
30 to 34 years	1,069,984	9.8	0.6	0.9	1.1	7.2
35 to 39 years	564,059	11.1	0.7	1.0	1.3	8.2
40 to 44 years	120,570	13.7	0.8	1.2	1.6	10.1
45 to 54 years	9,229	20.6	1.4	2.0	2.5	14.8
Race and Hispanic origin of mother:						
White alone, non-Hispanic	1,843,432	9.1	0.4	0.7	1.0	6.9
Black alone, non-Hispanic	529,811	14.4	1.5	1.6	1.8	9.5
Hispanic [2]	866,713	9.8	0.6	0.8	1.1	7.3

[1] Total includes those with gestational age not stated; and races other than White and Black, not shown separately. [2] Persons of Hispanic origin may be of any race.

Source: U.S. National Center for Health Statistics, *Births, Final Data for 2020*, Vol. 70, No. 17, February 2022. See also <www.cdc.gov/nchs/nvss/births.htm>.

Table 92. Women Who Had a Birth in the Past 12 Months by Selected Characteristics: 2019

[For women aged 15 to 50 years old. Based on the 2019 American Community Survey (ACS). The ACS sample includes the household population and the population living in institutions, dormitories, and other group quarters. Based on a sample and subject to sampling variability. See Appendix III for details]

Characteristic	Total women (number)	Women who had a birth in the past 12 months			
		Number	Percent distribution	Rate per 1,000 women	Percent unmarried
Total, aged 15 to 50 years	**76,879,571**	**3,877,882**	**(X)**	**50**	**32.8**
Age:					
15 to 19 years	10,449,871	110,459	2.8	11	86.4
20 to 34 years	32,933,396	2,773,193	71.5	84	34.9
35 to 50 years	33,496,304	994,230	25.6	30	20.9
Race/ethnicity:					
One race	74,179,173	3,743,194	96.5	50	32.5
White	52,648,175	2,628,122	67.8	50	26.8
Black or African American	10,908,109	567,631	14.6	52	62.9
American Indian and Alaska Native	708,275	35,367	0.9	50	58.9
Asian	5,281,751	252,552	6.5	48	10.0
Native Hawaiian and Other Pacific Islander	172,393	10,025	0.3	58	50.5
Some other race	4,460,470	249,497	6.4	56	41.1
Two or more races	2,700,398	134,688	3.5	50	40.7
Hispanic origin:					
Hispanic or Latino origin (of any race)	15,869,681	864,844	22.3	54	40.4
White alone, not Hispanic or Latino	42,308,780	2,066,688	53.3	49	23.6
Nativity:					
Native	64,041,016	3,144,037	81.1	49	35.7
Foreign born [1]	12,838,555	733,845	18.9	57	20.2
Education:					
Less than high school graduate	12,354,406	423,188	10.9	34	52.1
High school graduate (includes equivalency)	16,058,268	899,106	23.2	56	50.1
Some college or associate's degree	23,726,891	1,176,144	30.3	50	39.2
Bachelor's degree	16,023,912	848,593	21.9	53	12.2
Graduate or professional degree	8,716,094	530,851	13.7	61	6.8
Poverty status in past 12 months:					
Women 15 to 50 years old with poverty status determined	75,108,636	3,865,281	(X)	51	32.6
Below 100 percent of poverty level	10,710,505	792,565	20.5	74	67.5
100 to 199 percent of poverty level	12,757,677	777,748	20.1	61	41.3
200 percent or more above poverty level	51,640,454	2,294,968	59.4	44	17.6
Labor force status:					
In labor force [2]	55,265,605	2,548,687	65.8	46	33.2
Public assistance income in past 12 months:					
Women 15 to 50 years old with public assistance status determined	76,879,571	3,877,882	(X)	50	32.8
Received public assistance income	1,339,850	149,594	3.9	112	70.3
Did not receive public assistance income	75,539,721	3,728,288	96.1	49	31.3

X Not applicable. [1] Excludes persons born outside of the United States to a parent who is a U.S. citizen. [2] Data are shown for women aged 16 to 50 years old.

Source: U.S. Census Bureau, 2019 American Community Survey, S1301, "Fertility," <data.census.gov>, accessed November 2020.

Table 93. Women by Number of Children Ever Born by Age, Marital Status, and Race/Ethnicity: 2018

[76,414 represents 76,414,000. As of June. Data shown are for women aged 15 to 50. Based on the Current Population Survey; for more information, see <www.census.gov/programs-surveys/cps.html>]

Characteristic	Total women (1,000)	Percent distribution by number of children ever born						
		None	One	Two	Three	Four	Five and six	Seven or more
Total women: [1]	**76,414**	**44.2**	**16.8**	**21.7**	**10.7**	**4.3**	**1.9**	**0.4**
By age:								
15 to 19 years old	10,294	96.9	2.1	0.8	0.1	–	0.1	–
20 to 24 years old	10,607	78.6	14.0	6.0	1.0	0.3	0.2	–
25 to 29 years old	11,476	54.2	20.4	16.2	6.5	2.1	0.5	0.1
30 to 34 years old	10,889	33.6	22.3	24.6	12.8	4.4	1.9	0.3
35 to 39 years old	10,727	20.0	19.2	32.6	17.4	7.3	3.2	0.4
40 to 44 years old	9,896	15.0	18.7	34.6	18.6	8.7	3.8	0.7
45 to 50 years old	12,524	15.4	19.8	35.4	17.3	7.4	3.6	1.2
By marital status:								
Women ever married	41,451	17.5	21.6	33.8	16.6	6.8	3.0	0.6
Women never married	34,963	75.8	11.1	7.5	3.6	1.4	0.6	0.1
By race and Hispanic origin:								
White alone	56,229	44.4	16.1	22.1	11.1	4.2	1.8	0.4
White alone, non-Hispanic	42,373	45.7	16.1	22.8	10.1	3.5	1.5	0.4
Black alone	11,258	40.8	19.8	20.1	10.4	5.6	2.8	0.5
Asian alone	5,519	45.5	18.1	25.0	7.7	2.4	1.0	0.4
Hispanic [2]	15,674	40.2	16.7	19.9	13.7	6.3	2.7	0.5

– Represents or rounds to zero. [1] Includes women of other races, not shown separately. [2] Persons of Hispanic origin may be of any race.

Source: U.S. Census Bureau, "Fertility of Women in the United States: 2018," <www.census.gov/topics/health/fertility/data/tables.html>, accessed June 2019.

Table 94. Women's Relationship Status and Age at First Birth by Current Age and Race/Ethnicity: 2018

[In percent, except as noted (42,670 represents 42,670,000). As of June. Data are from the Current Population Survey; for more information, see <www.census.gov/programs-surveys/cps.html>]

Current age and race/ethnicity	Total mothers, 1,000	Married at first birth			Not married at first birth					
					Living with unmarried partner			Neither married nor living with unmarried partner		
		Under age 20 at first birth	Age 20 to 25 at first birth	Over age 25 at first birth	Under age 20 at first birth	Age 20 to 25 at first birth	Over age 25 at first birth	Under age 20 at first birth	Age 20 to 25 at first birth	Over age 25 at first birth
TOTAL										
15 to 50 years old	**42,670**	**5.9**	**21.9**	**34.7**	**6.7**	**9.9**	**4.6**	**6.4**	**7.3**	**2.5**
15 to 19 years old	321	6.7	(X)	(X)	52.3	(X)	(X)	41.0	(X)	(X)
20 to 24 years old	2,274	10.4	15.4	(X)	18.1	22.0	(X)	16.4	17.6	(X)
25 to 29 years old	5,258	6.6	22.1	10.9	12.7	19.5	3.3	9.8	12.7	2.4
30 to 34 years old	7,230	6.7	20.5	32.0	7.8	12.1	5.9	5.7	6.7	2.6
35 to 39 years old	8,583	6.0	21.6	38.3	5.6	8.9	5.6	6.1	5.4	2.5
40 to 44 years old	8,411	5.6	21.8	43.3	4.9	6.3	4.9	5.7	4.9	2.7
45 to 50 years old	10,593	4.1	25.1	47.0	1.6	5.2	4.5	3.0	6.5	3.0
WHITE ALONE										
15 to 50 years old	31,275	6.3	24.3	37.4	6.4	9.4	4.3	4.9	5.3	1.8
15 to 19 years old	252	8.2	(X)	(X)	51.9	(X)	(X)	39.9	(X)	(X)
20 to 24 years old	1,533	12.3	19.0	(X)	20.0	20.7	(X)	12.6	15.5	(X)
25 to 29 years old	3,644	8.2	26.1	12.3	12.3	18.9	2.7	7.7	9.8	2.0
30 to 34 years old	5,269	7.3	23.2	33.0	7.8	11.9	5.5	4.8	4.6	1.9
35 to 39 years old	6,315	5.7	23.0	41.4	5.3	8.4	5.6	4.7	3.9	2.1
40 to 44 years old	6,237	6.1	24.1	45.5	4.3	6.5	4.3	3.8	3.5	1.8
45 to 50 years old	8,025	4.2	27.0	50.3	1.5	4.6	4.1	2.1	4.5	1.8
BLACK ALONE										
15 to 50 years old	6,666	4.4	11.5	14.4	9.3	13.7	7.1	15.3	18.4	6.0
15 to 19 years old	42	–	(X)	(X)	45.1	(X)	(X)	54.9	(X)	(X)
20 to 24 years old	492	4.1	3.6	(X)	12.4	21.9	(X)	30.9	27.1	(X)
25 to 29 years old	1,078	2.2	7.7	3.1	16.3	21.2	5.2	17.8	23.1	3.5
30 to 34 years old	1,146	3.7	8.8	15.6	9.3	16.5	9.0	12.5	18.6	6.1
35 to 39 years old	1,286	6.5	13.3	15.1	8.9	13.7	7.3	14.8	14.3	6.1
40 to 44 years old	1,181	5.2	12.1	19.2	8.8	7.7	10.6	16.2	13.2	7.0
45 to 50 years old	1,439	4.2	17.4	22.5	2.5	8.3	6.7	8.9	20.2	9.3
HISPANIC [1]										
15 to 50 years old	9,376	9.8	25.5	21.4	10.2	11.9	5.4	6.9	6.7	2.2
15 to 19 years old	83	3.9	(X)	(X)	64.7	(X)	(X)	31.4	(X)	(X)
20 to 24 years old	663	12.7	13.2	(X)	25.4	16.1	(X)	17.5	15.2	(X)
25 to 29 years old	1,329	11.0	21.1	5.9	15.2	18.9	3.7	11.5	11.0	1.8
30 to 34 years old	1,660	11.7	21.5	17.8	13.8	15.6	5.6	6.9	5.1	2.0
35 to 39 years old	1,803	10.3	25.3	22.7	8.1	11.1	6.9	7.8	5.1	2.9
40 to 44 years old	1,794	9.0	28.9	29.9	6.3	10.0	6.0	4.3	3.8	1.9
45 to 50 years old	2,044	7.0	33.9	33.6	2.2	5.9	6.5	1.2	6.6	3.3

– Represents or rounds to zero. X Not applicable. [1] Persons of Hispanic origin may be of any race.

Source: U.S. Census Bureau, "Fertility of Women in the United States: 2018," <www.census.gov/topics/health/fertility/data/tables.html>, accessed June 2019.

Table 95. Women Who Had a Birth in the Past Year Who Are in the Labor Force by Educational Attainment: 2010 to 2017

[In thousands (2,562 represents 2,562,000), except percent. For women aged 16 to 50 years old. Based on the American Community Survey (ACS). The ACS universe includes the household population and population living in institutions, college dormitories, and other group quarters. Based on a sample and subject to sampling variability, see Appendix III]

Year	Number of women who had a birth in the past year who are in the labor force					Percent of women who had a birth in the past year who are in the labor force				
	Total	Less than high school diploma	High school diploma or GED	Some college	Bachelor's degree or higher	Total	Less than high school diploma	High school diploma or GED	Some college	Bachelor's degree or higher
2010.........	2,562	278	589	859	836	61.6	39.7	57.9	66.4	72.7
2013.........	2,418	221	513	805	879	61.7	38.8	56.4	64.4	73.8
2014.........	2,436	203	508	815	909	61.8	38.2	55.4	64.9	73.7
2015.........	2,447	196	508	816	927	62.4	38.2	56.0	65.1	74.2
2016.........	2,493	194	526	804	970	63.3	39.6	57.2	65.3	74.7
2017.........	2,534	182	532	794	1,027	63.5	39.6	56.7	64.3	75.4

Source: U.S. Census Bureau, "Fertility: Historical Time Series Tables," <www.census.gov/topics/health/fertility/data/tables.html>, accessed June 2019.

Table 96. Women Who Had a Birth in the Past 12 Months by Nativity, Educational Attainment, and Poverty Status by State: 2019

[In percent, except for total. For women 15 to 50 years old. Based on 2019 American Community Survey (ACS). See headnote, Table 95]

State	Total (number)	Nativity		Educational attainment					Below poverty [3]
		Native born	Foreign born [1]	Less than high school graduate	High school graduate [2]	Some college or associate's degree	Bachelor's degree	Graduate or professional degree	
United States......	3,877,882	81.1	18.9	10.9	23.2	30.3	21.9	13.7	20.5
Alabama..............	58,542	94.5	5.5	13.4	27.5	32.4	18.4	8.4	24.5
Alaska...............	10,502	90.1	9.9	14.2	21.0	28.6	21.5	14.7	18.1
Arizona..............	89,019	82.8	17.2	15.7	26.6	33.3	16.8	7.6	22.8
Arkansas............	35,370	92.3	7.7	10.7	29.3	35.3	16.6	8.1	31.3
California............	450,971	68.0	32.0	11.9	20.2	31.3	22.9	13.7	16.4
Colorado.............	64,252	86.1	13.9	10.6	19.7	28.9	25.8	15.1	14.0
Connecticut..........	30,781	71.5	28.5	5.1	17.3	25.2	25.7	26.7	15.6
Delaware.............	8,580	85.9	14.1	13.1	32.1	26.5	18.0	10.3	21.8
District of Columbia...	8,375	72.2	27.8	7.6	19.2	16.1	26.7	30.4	14.1
Florida...............	205,856	72.2	27.8	10.5	27.3	30.1	20.8	11.3	21.3
Georgia..............	134,809	84.3	15.7	12.3	24.7	29.8	20.3	12.8	21.4
Hawaii...............	18,431	74.6	25.4	5.3	23.8	31.5	25.4	14.0	15.4
Idaho................	27,171	84.2	15.8	7.3	20.4	39.8	25.2	7.3	19.9
Illinois..............	147,037	82.0	18.0	11.1	20.2	27.5	24.1	17.0	18.9
Indiana..............	81,658	93.0	7.0	8.6	29.4	31.7	21.2	9.2	21.2
Iowa.................	37,815	87.6	12.4	9.7	18.0	33.7	26.2	12.4	19.1
Kansas..............	41,058	86.6	13.4	10.9	22.1	31.0	23.5	12.5	22.3
Kentucky............	47,407	94.9	5.1	11.1	25.8	32.8	17.2	13.1	28.3
Louisiana............	57,992	94.0	6.0	13.4	33.6	26.8	19.0	7.1	30.6
Maine...............	14,130	92.1	7.9	6.9	21.3	37.6	21.5	12.6	26.0
Maryland............	73,824	71.7	28.3	8.1	20.9	24.6	22.3	24.2	14.0
Massachusetts.......	69,139	75.8	24.2	7.5	15.5	24.5	26.1	26.5	11.4
Michigan............	115,459	89.5	10.5	10.6	24.6	32.5	19.7	12.6	22.3
Minnesota...........	71,159	84.0	16.0	10.4	14.1	31.5	26.9	17.2	11.7
Mississippi..........	35,965	97.3	2.7	12.2	23.9	42.2	14.2	7.4	37.5
Missouri.............	76,428	94.1	5.9	9.1	23.1	31.8	23.8	12.2	23.7
Montana.............	12,267	97.2	2.8	10.6	23.4	31.4	27.7	6.9	18.9
Nebraska............	26,897	88.1	11.9	11.1	15.9	30.6	27.0	15.4	16.9
Nevada..............	37,443	70.6	29.4	13.7	29.4	32.1	16.5	8.2	20.1
New Hampshire.......	11,966	88.2	11.8	2.8	23.5	19.3	30.3	24.1	7.0
New Jersey..........	95,678	67.8	32.2	7.6	20.0	23.2	26.7	22.6	15.4
New Mexico..........	26,945	84.0	16.0	16.0	25.0	35.7	16.3	6.9	33.5
New York............	217,713	73.7	26.3	11.4	20.7	23.4	22.5	22.0	20.3
North Carolina.......	129,358	83.6	16.4	10.8	23.4	34.0	19.2	12.6	27.0
North Dakota........	13,098	85.5	14.5	10.6	24.3	29.5	26.8	8.8	17.9
Ohio................	150,899	90.0	10.0	12.1	25.0	30.2	21.1	11.6	26.1
Oklahoma............	55,049	90.0	10.0	11.1	32.0	32.7	16.5	7.8	24.0
Oregon..............	42,254	87.8	12.2	12.3	22.8	28.7	22.1	14.1	15.9
Pennsylvania........	148,956	88.8	11.2	10.6	27.1	25.1	20.4	16.9	21.5
Rhode Island........	7,968	77.1	22.9	2.7	21.8	22.9	31.6	20.9	8.9
South Carolina.......	63,576	90.1	9.9	10.8	26.4	34.8	16.4	11.5	22.6
South Dakota........	12,568	90.8	9.2	8.1	22.1	32.4	23.4	14.0	18.6
Tennessee...........	78,042	89.9	10.1	9.5	24.9	32.6	22.8	10.2	26.2
Texas...............	390,925	76.5	23.5	13.5	23.9	32.3	19.8	10.5	22.4
Utah................	45,033	89.6	10.4	6.6	18.9	38.8	29.7	6.1	12.6
Vermont.............	6,553	84.1	15.9	9.4	18.4	30.2	24.5	17.5	17.1
Virginia.............	98,004	78.3	21.7	8.5	19.4	28.5	25.7	17.9	18.1
Washington..........	98,105	74.5	25.5	8.8	23.3	31.4	24.4	12.1	15.7
West Virginia........	21,275	97.3	2.7	9.2	29.4	33.8	17.1	10.5	27.7
Wisconsin...........	68,675	90.4	9.6	7.1	21.0	32.0	27.3	12.6	17.0
Wyoming............	6,905	94.9	5.1	7.1	29.0	32.9	19.6	11.3	10.9

[1] Foreign born excludes people born outside the U.S. to a parent who is a U.S. citizen. [2] Includes equivalency. [3] The population universe used when determining poverty status excludes people institutionalized, in military group quarters, and in college dormitories, and unrelated individuals under 15 years old.

Source: U.S. Census Bureau, 2019 American Community Survey, Tables B13008, B13010, and B13014, <data.census.gov>, accessed November 2020.

Table 97. Women Who Had a Birth in the Past 12 Months by Household Income and Marital Status: 2017

[In thousands (3,412.3 represents 3,412,300), except percent. Data shown for women aged 15 to 50 years old; does not include women living in group quarters. Based on the American Community Survey (ACS). Based on a sample and subject to sampling variability]

Annual household income	Total women	Women with a birth in the past 12 months			Percent of total women	Percent of women with a birth in the past 12 months		
		Total	Married [1]	Unmarried [2]		Total	Married [1]	Unmarried [2]
Under $10,000...............	3,412.3	226.7	60.2	166.5	4.6	5.7	2.3	11.9
$10,000-$14,999.............	1,912.2	113.9	35.0	78.9	2.6	2.9	1.4	5.6
$15,000-$24,999.............	4,861.7	299.4	120.3	179.2	6.5	7.5	4.7	12.8
$25,000-$34,999.............	5,530.4	334.3	166.5	167.8	7.4	8.4	6.5	12.0
$35,000-$49,999.............	8,520.1	494.1	286.0	208.1	11.4	12.4	11.1	14.8
$50,000-$74,999.............	13,210.4	705.1	470.1	235.0	17.7	17.8	18.3	16.8
$75,000-$99,999.............	10,813.8	559.0	411.1	147.9	14.5	14.1	16.0	10.5
$100,000-$149,999...........	13,829.4	670.6	533.8	136.8	18.5	16.9	20.8	9.8
$150,000-$199,999...........	6,262.7	283.3	236.6	46.7	8.4	7.1	9.2	3.3
$200,000 or more............	6,454.4	283.5	248.1	35.4	8.6	7.1	9.7	2.5

[1] Includes women who are married, spouse present. [2] Includes women who are widowed, divorced, separated, and never married.

Source: U.S. Census Bureau, "Fertility of Women in the United States: 2018," <www.census.gov/topics/health/fertility/data/tables.html>, accessed June 2019.

Table 98. Sexually Active High School Students and Birth Control Use by Sex, Race/Ethnicity, and Grade: 2019

[In percent. For public and private school students in grades 9 to 12. Current sexual activity defined as having had sexual intercourse with at least one person during the 3 months before the survey. Based on the Youth Risk Behavior Survey; see source for details]

Item	Total	Race/ethnicity			Grade level			
		White [1]	Black [1]	Hispanic	9th	10th	11th	12th
TOTAL								
Ever had sexual intercourse................	38.4	38.0	42.3	41.8	19.2	33.6	46.5	56.7
Currently sexually active....................	27.4	27.5	29.0	29.7	11.7	23.1	34.3	42.3
Condom use [2]..............................	54.3	55.8	48.2	56.2	61.3	55.4	56.3	50.3
Birth control use [3]........................	30.9	39.5	19.7	18.2	14.2	22.7	33.4	38.1
No pregnancy prevention method [2].......	11.9	8.4	23.0	13.3	15.3	12.0	11.2	11.4
MALE								
Ever had sexual intercourse................	39.2	36.7	50.1	43.6	21.6	35.4	46.6	56.3
Currently sexually active....................	26.3	25.2	32.4	29.2	12.5	22.0	32.7	40.6
Condom use [2]..............................	60.0	60.9	51.8	62.3	69.0	64.2	60.7	53.4
Birth control use [3]........................	25.9	33.0	18.7	16.7	11.2	16.5	29.4	33.7
No pregnancy prevention method [2].......	10.1	6.3	21.0	10.6	14.0	9.6	10.1	9.0
FEMALE								
Ever had sexual intercourse................	37.6	39.2	34.0	40.3	16.7	31.8	46.6	56.8
Currently sexually active....................	28.4	29.9	25.4	30.3	10.8	24.3	35.9	43.8
Condom use [2]..............................	49.6	51.6	44.5	50.9	51.8	47.8	52.3	47.8
Birth control use [3]........................	35.2	45.2	21.2	19.6	17.8	28.6	36.9	42.1
No pregnancy prevention method [2].......	13.4	10.1	24.1	15.6	16.9	14.2	12.1	13.3

[1] Non-Hispanic. [2] During last sexual intercourse. [3] Includes use of birth control pills, an IUD or implant, or a shot, patch, or birth control ring.

Source: U.S. Centers for Disease Control and Prevention, Youth Risk Behavior Surveillance System (YRBSS), "YRBS Explorer," <yrbs-explorer.services.cdc.gov/#/>, accessed August 2020. See also <www.cdc.gov/healthyyouth/data/yrbs/>.

Table 99. Contraceptive Use Among Women by Age, Race/Ethnicity, Educational Attainment, and Method: 2017 to 2019

[In units, as indicated (72,672 represents 72,672,000). Data are based primarily on responses of 6,141 women to a National Survey of Family Growth question about contraceptive use status during the month of interview; interviews were conducted during the 2017-2019 period. Women currently using more than one contraceptive method are classified according to the method most effective in preventing pregnancy]

Characteristic	Total women (1,000)	Percent currently using contraception by method				
		Any contraceptive method [1]	Female sterilization	Oral contraceptive pill	Male condom	Long acting reversable [2]
Women aged 15 to 49 [3]..................	**72,672**	**65.3**	**18.1**	**14.0**	**8.4**	**10.4**
AGE						
15 to 19 years old..........................	9,439	38.7	(S)	19.5	5.1	5.8
20 to 29 years old..........................	21,392	60.9	2.9	21.6	10.4	13.7
30 to 39 years old..........................	21,581	72.3	21.2	10.9	9.7	12.7
40 to 49 years old..........................	20,260	74.8	39.1	6.5	6.5	6.6
RACE/ETHNICITY						
White, Non-Hispanic........................	40,420	69.2	18.5	17.8	7.0	10.9
Black, Non-Hispanic........................	9,805	61.4	17.6	8.1	11.0	10.9
Hispanic [4]................................	15,133	60.5	19.9	7.9	10.5	10.3
EDUCATION [5]						
No high school diploma nor GED [6].......	4,744	71.2	39.9	5.7	8.7	9.3
High school diploma or GED [6]............	14,530	70.0	31.5	6.8	9.3	7.9
Some college, no bachelor's degree......	17,631	71.3	22.2	10.8	8.7	12.5
Bachelor's degree or higher................	22,371	69.1	12.1	18.1	8.6	13.1

S Figure does not meet standards of reliability or precision. [1] Includes other methods not shown separately. [2] Includes contraceptive implants and intrauterine devices. [3] Includes women of other or multiple races, not shown separately. [4] Persons of Hispanic origin may be of any race. [5] Data shown for women aged 22 to 49 years old. [6] GED is general equivalency diploma.

Source: U.S. National Center for Health Statistics, *Current Contraceptive Status Among Women Aged 15–49: United States*, NCHS Data Brief No. 388, October 2020. See also <www.cdc.gov/nchs/nsfg/index.htm>.

Table 100. Abortions Reported and Rates by Age: 2010 to 2019

[Data on abortions are voluntarily provided to the CDC by the central health agencies of 48 reporting areas (New York City and 47 states, excluding California, the District of Columbia, Maryland, and New Hampshire). Data by age are from 44 reporting areas (excludes California, District of Columbia, Florida, Maine, Maryland, New Hampshire, Vermont, and Wyoming that did not report, did not report by age, or did not meet reporting standards for 1 year or more)]

Age	2010	2013	2014	2015	2016	2017	2018	2019	Percent change, 2010 to 2019
Total (number) [1]	762,755	661,874	649,849	636,902	623,471	609,095	614,820	625,346	-18.0
Rate per 1,000 women aged 15-44	14.4	12.4	12.1	11.8	11.6	11.2	11.3	11.4	-20.8
BY AGE									
Total (number)	672,271	579,406	565,691	553,596	542,922	528,308	533,557	539,634	-19.7
Percent distribution:									
Under 15 years old	0.5	0.3	0.3	0.3	0.3	0.2	0.2	0.2	-60.0
15 to 19 years old	14.6	11.4	10.4	9.8	9.4	9.1	8.8	8.7	-40.4
20 to 24 years old	32.9	32.7	32.1	31.1	30.0	29.3	28.5	27.8	-15.5
25 to 29 years old	24.5	25.9	26.8	27.6	28.5	29.0	29.4	29.3	19.6
30 to 34 years old	15.3	16.8	17.2	17.7	18.0	18.3	18.8	19.4	26.8
35 to 39 years old	8.9	9.2	9.7	10.0	10.3	10.5	10.7	10.8	21.3
40 years old and over	3.4	3.6	3.6	3.6	3.6	3.6	3.5	3.7	8.8
Abortion rate: [2]									
Under 15 years old	1.0	0.6	0.5	0.5	0.4	0.4	0.4	0.4	-60.0
15 to 19 years old	11.7	8.2	7.3	6.7	6.2	5.9	5.8	5.8	-50.4
20 to 24 years old	26.8	21.9	20.9	19.9	19.0	18.4	18.2	18.1	-32.5
25 to 29 years old	20.2	18.2	18.1	17.9	17.7	17.3	17.6	17.8	-11.9
30 to 34 years old	13.2	11.8	11.7	11.7	11.6	11.5	11.9	12.3	-6.8
35 to 39 years old	7.6	7.0	7.1	7.0	6.9	6.7	6.8	7.0	-7.9
40 years old and over	2.8	2.5	2.5	2.5	2.5	2.5	2.5	2.6	-7.1

[1] Data shown for continuously reporting areas during 2010-2019 period. [2] Number of abortions obtained by women in a given age group per 1,000 women in that same age group. Adolescents aged 13–14 years were used as the denominator for the group of women aged under 15 years, and women aged 40–44 years were used as the denominator for the group of women aged 40 and older. Abortions for women of unknown age were distributed according to the distribution of abortions among women of known age.

Source: U.S. Centers for Disease Control and Prevention, *Morbidity and Mortality Weekly Report, Surveillance Summaries*, 70:9, November 26, 2021, "Abortion Surveillance—United States, 2019." See also <www.cdc.gov/mmwr/index.html>.

Table 101. Abortions Reported and Those Obtained by Out-of-State Residents by State and Reporting Area of Occurrence: 2019

[Data are presented by the State or reporting area in which abortions were performed, not by residence of the person obtaining the abortion. Data are voluntarily provided to the CDC by the central health agencies of 49 reporting areas (New York City, the District of Columbia, and 47 states, excluding California, Maryland, and New Hampshire)]

State and area of occurrence	Abortions reported Total	Abortions per 1,000 women age 15-44	Abortions per 1,000 live births	Abortions obtained by out-of-state residents	State and area of occurrence	Abortions reported Total	Abortions per 1,000 women age 15-44	Abortions per 1,000 live births	Abortions obtained by out-of-state residents
Total [1]	629,898	(NA)	(NA)	(NA)	Montana	1,568	8.0	142	169
					Nebraska	2,068	5.5	84	267
Alabama	6,009	6.3	103	1,040	Nevada	8,414	14.0	240	434
Alaska	1,270	8.8	129	19	New Jersey [2]	22,178	13.2	223	1,309
Arizona	13,097	9.4	165	67	New Mexico	3,942	9.9	172	939
Arkansas	2,963	5.1	81	338	New York	78,587	20.3	355	6,989
Colorado	9,002	7.6	143	946	New York City	49,784	27.2	472	4,668
Connecticut	9,202	13.7	269	334	New York State	28,803	14.1	248	2,321
Delaware	2,042	11.3	193	277	North Carolina	28,450	13.8	240	5,079
District of Columbia	4,552	23.9	501	3,126	North Dakota	1,121	7.6	107	289
Florida	71,914	18.5	327	2,256	Ohio	20,102	9.1	150	1,186
Georgia	36,907	16.9	292	6,500	Oklahoma	4,995	6.4	102	407
Hawaii	2,003	7.6	119	49	Oregon	8,688	10.5	208	795
Idaho	1,513	4.4	69	78	Pennsylvania	31,018	13.0	231	2,222
Illinois	46,517	18.6	332	7,534	Rhode Island	2,099	10.1	206	274
Indiana	7,637	5.8	94	618	South Carolina	5,101	5.2	89	312
Iowa	3,566	6.0	95	490	South Dakota	414	2.6	36	82
Kansas	6,894	12.3	195	3,372	Tennessee	9,719	7.3	121	1,823
Kentucky	3,664	4.3	69	643	Texas	57,275	9.5	152	1,303
Louisiana	8,144	8.8	138	1,358	Utah	2,922	4.2	62	146
Maine	2,021	8.7	172	107	Vermont	1,195	10.4	223	265
Massachusetts	18,593	13.3	269	631	Virginia	15,601	9.2	160	867
Michigan	27,339	14.6	253	1,435	Washington	17,262	11.4	203	848
Minnesota	9,940	9.2	151	888	West Virginia	1,183	3.8	65	168
Mississippi	3,194	5.5	87	335	Wisconsin	6,511	6.0	103	139
Missouri	1,471	1.2	20	128	Wyoming	31	0.3	5	5

NA Not available. [1] Includes those with known and unknown residence status. [2] Reporting to the central health agency is not required. Data are requested from hospitals and licensed ambulatory care facilities only.

Source: U.S. Centers for Disease Control and Prevention, *Morbidity and Mortality Weekly Report, Surveillance Summaries*, 70:9, November 26, 2021, "Abortion Surveillance—United States, 2019." See also <www.cdc.gov/mmwr/index.html>.

Table 102. Assisted Reproductive Technology (ART) Procedures and Outcomes: 2000 to 2020

[Covers ART procedures with the intent to transfer at least one embryo; excludes freezing/banking cycles. In 1996, Centers for Disease Control (CDC) initiated data collection regarding Assisted Reproductive Technology (ART) procedures performed in the United States, as mandated by the Fertility Clinic Success Rate and Certification Act. ARTs include those infertility treatments in which both eggs and sperm are handled in the laboratory for the purpose of establishing a pregnancy (i.e., in vitro fertilization and related procedures)]

Year	Procedures started [1]	Number of pregnancies [2]	Live birth deliveries [3]	Live born infants	Year	Procedures started [1]	Number of pregnancies [2]	Live birth deliveries [3]	Live born infants
2000	99,629	30,557	25,228	35,025	2014	173,198	68,988	57,323	70,354
2005	134,260	47,651	38,910	52,041	2015	186,157	72,870	60,778	72,913
2009	146,244	56,399	45,870	60,190	2016	197,737	80,971	65,969	76,897
2010	147,260	57,773	47,090	61,564	2017	196,454	84,340	68,908	78,052
2011	151,923	59,132	47,818	61,610	2018	203,119	89,688	73,831	81,478
2012	157,662	62,977	51,267	65,160	2019	209,687	95,030	77,998	83,946
2013	163,209	65,580	54,323	67,996	2020 (P)	203,164	(NA)	75,023	79,942

P Preliminary. NA Not available. [1] Excludes procedures for which new treatments were being evaluated. [2] Beginning in 2012, excludes pregnancies from procedures performed in U.S. territories other than Puerto Rico; and, beginning in 2013, excludes pregnancies resulting from oocyte thaw procedures. [3] A live birth delivery is defined as the delivery of one or more live born infants.

Source: U.S. Centers for Disease Control and Prevention, *2019 Assisted Reproductive Technology, Fertility Clinic and National Summary Report,* 2021 and earlier reports; *Assisted Reproductive Technology Surveillance - United States, 2019,* MMWR Surveillance Summaries, Vol. 71, No. 4, February 2022 and earlier reports; and Assisted Reproductive Technology, "Preliminary 2020 Data," <www.cdc.gov/art/artdata/index.html#preliminary>, accessed July 2022.

Table 103. Life Expectancy at Birth, 1940 to 2020, and Projected, 2030 to 2060

[In years. Beginning 2001, life table data are based on revised life table methodology. Race and Hispanic-origin categories are consistent with 1977 Office of Management and Budget (OMB) standards. From 2003-2017, the number of states reporting multiple-race data according to new 1997 OMB standards varied widely. To provide a comparison of data by race between the 1977 and 1997 OMB standards, those reporting more than one race were "bridged" to single-race categories. For more information, see Technical notes, source]

Year	Total [1] Total	Total [1] Male	Total [1] Female	White, non-Hispanic [2] Total	White, non-Hispanic [2] Male	White, non-Hispanic [2] Female	Black, non-Hispanic [2] Total	Black, non-Hispanic [2] Male	Black, non-Hispanic [2] Female	Hispanic [2,3] Total	Hispanic [2,3] Male	Hispanic [2,3] Female
1940	62.9	60.8	65.2	(NA)	(NA)	(NA)	(NA)	(NA)	(NA)	(NA)	(NA)	(NA)
1950	68.2	65.6	71.1	(NA)	(NA)	(NA)	(NA)	(NA)	(NA)	(NA)	(NA)	(NA)
1960	69.7	66.6	73.1	(NA)	(NA)	(NA)	(NA)	(NA)	(NA)	(NA)	(NA)	(NA)
1970	70.8	67.1	74.7	(NA)	(NA)	(NA)	(NA)	(NA)	(NA)	(NA)	(NA)	(NA)
1980	73.7	70.0	77.4	(NA)	(NA)	(NA)	(NA)	(NA)	(NA)	(NA)	(NA)	(NA)
1990	75.4	71.8	78.8	(NA)	(NA)	(NA)	(NA)	(NA)	(NA)	(NA)	(NA)	(NA)
2000	76.8	74.1	79.3	(NA)	(NA)	(NA)	(NA)	(NA)	(NA)	(NA)	(NA)	(NA)
2010	78.7	76.2	81.0	78.8	76.4	81.1	74.7	71.5	77.7	81.7	78.8	84.3
2019	78.8	76.3	81.4	78.8	76.4	81.3	75.0	71.6	78.2	81.9	79.1	84.4
2020	77.0	74.2	79.9	77.5	74.9	80.2	71.9	68.1	75.6	77.9	74.6	81.3
Projections: [4]												
2030	81.7	79.6	83.7	82.1	80.2	84.0	(NA)	(NA)	(NA)	82.6	80.6	84.5
2040	83.0	81.2	84.8	83.5	81.7	85.2	(NA)	(NA)	(NA)	83.5	81.7	85.2
2050	84.4	82.7	86.0	84.8	83.2	86.4	(NA)	(NA)	(NA)	84.8	83.2	86.4
2060	85.6	84.0	87.1	86.0	84.5	87.4	(NA)	(NA)	(NA)	86.0	84.5	87.4

NA Not available. [1] Includes races and origins not shown separately. [2] Based on death rates adjusted for misclassification; see Technical notes, source. [3] Persons of Hispanic origin may be of any race. [4] Based on mortality assumptions; for details, see source: U.S. Census Bureau, 2014 National Population Projections, "Table 17: Projected Life Expectancy at Birth by Sex, Race, and Hispanic Origin for the United States: 2015 to 2060 (NP2014-T17)," December 2014.

Source: Except as noted. U.S. National Center for Health Statistics, National Vital Statistics Reports (NVSR), *United States Life Tables, 2020,* Vol. 71, No. 1, August 2022. See also <www.cdc.gov/nchs/nvss/life-expectancy.htm>.

Table 104. Life Expectancy by Sex, Age, and Race and Hispanic Origin: 2020

[Average number of years of life remaining. Excludes deaths of nonresidents of the United States. Race categories are consistent with 1997 Office of Management and Budget (OMB) standards; see source for details]

Age	Total [1] Total	Total [1] Male	Total [1] Female	White alone, Non-Hispanic [2] Total	White alone, Non-Hispanic [2] Male	White alone, Non-Hispanic [2] Female	Black alone, Non-Hispanic [2] Total	Black alone, Non-Hispanic [2] Male	Black alone, Non-Hispanic [2] Female	Hispanic [2,3] Total	Hispanic [2,3] Male	Hispanic [2,3] Female
0	77.0	74.2	79.9	77.4	74.8	80.1	71.5	67.8	75.4	77.9	74.6	81.3
1	76.4	73.6	79.3	76.7	74.2	79.4	71.3	67.5	75.1	77.3	74.0	80.7
5	72.5	69.7	75.3	72.8	70.2	75.5	67.4	63.7	71.2	73.4	70.0	76.7
10	67.5	64.7	70.4	67.8	65.3	70.5	62.5	58.7	66.2	68.4	65.1	71.8
15	62.6	59.8	65.4	62.9	60.3	65.5	57.6	53.8	61.3	63.4	60.1	66.8
20	57.7	55.0	60.5	58.0	55.5	60.6	52.9	49.3	56.5	58.6	55.3	61.9
25	53.0	50.5	55.7	53.3	50.9	55.8	48.4	45.0	51.7	53.9	50.7	57.1
30	48.4	45.9	50.9	48.6	46.3	51.0	44.0	40.8	47.0	49.2	46.1	52.2
35	43.8	41.5	46.2	44.1	41.9	46.3	39.5	36.5	42.4	44.5	41.6	47.4
40	39.3	37.0	41.5	39.5	37.4	41.6	35.2	32.4	37.9	39.9	37.1	42.6
45	34.8	32.7	36.9	35.0	33.1	37.0	31.0	28.3	33.5	35.3	32.7	37.9
50	30.4	28.4	32.4	30.6	28.8	32.5	26.9	24.3	29.2	30.9	28.4	33.3
55	26.2	24.3	28.0	26.4	24.7	28.1	23.0	20.6	25.1	26.6	24.2	28.8
60	22.2	20.5	23.8	22.4	20.8	23.9	19.4	17.2	21.3	22.6	20.4	24.5
65	18.5	17.0	19.8	18.6	17.2	19.9	16.2	14.3	17.8	18.8	16.9	20.4
70	14.9	13.7	15.9	14.9	13.8	16.0	13.2	11.6	14.5	15.3	13.6	16.5
75	11.6	10.6	12.4	11.6	10.6	12.4	10.5	9.2	11.4	11.9	10.6	12.9
80	8.6	7.8	9.2	8.6	7.8	9.2	8.0	7.0	8.6	8.9	7.9	9.5
85	6.1	5.5	6.5	6.1	5.5	6.5	5.9	5.2	6.3	6.4	5.6	6.7
90	4.2	3.7	4.4	4.1	3.7	4.3	4.3	3.8	4.4	4.4	3.8	4.5
95	2.8	2.5	2.9	2.8	2.5	2.9	3.1	2.8	3.2	3.0	2.6	3.0
100	2.0	1.8	2.0	2.0	1.8	2.0	2.3	2.1	2.3	2.1	1.9	2.1

[1] Includes other races and origins not shown separately. [2] Based on death rates adjusted for misclassification. [3] Persons of Hispanic origin may be of any race.

Source: U.S. National Center for Health Statistics, National Vital Statistics Reports (NVSR), *United States Life Tables, 2020,* Vol. 71, No. 1, August 2022. See also <www.cdc.gov/nchs/nvss/life-expectancy.htm>.

Table 105. Life Expectancy at Birth by Sex, Race, and State: 1989 to 2001

[Average number of years of life remaining. Excludes deaths of nonresidents of the United States. Decennial life tables are based on population data from a decennial census and reported deaths of the 3-year period surrounding the census year; the census year is the middle year. The annual tables are based on deaths in a single year, and except for census years, on postcensal population estimates]

State	Total, 1989–1991	1999-2001						
		Total	Male			Female		
			Total	White	Black	Total	White	Black
United States...............	**75.37**	**76.83**	**74.10**	**74.74**	**68.08**	**79.45**	**79.97**	**75.12**
Alabama........................	73.64	74.80	71.32	72.85	66.42	78.34	79.14	74.94
Alaska..........................	74.83	76.63	74.18	75.45	(B)	79.41	80.10	(B)
Arizona........................	76.10	78.15	75.25	75.51	70.95	81.16	81.64	77.70
Arkansas......................	74.33	75.43	72.05	73.17	67.30	78.99	79.59	73.58
California......................	75.86	78.80	76.02	76.11	69.97	81.63	81.36	76.67
Colorado.......................	76.96	78.72	76.29	76.23	71.71	81.16	81.31	76.59
Connecticut...................	76.91	78.90	76.13	76.73	71.73	81.63	81.92	77.71
Delaware......................	74.76	77.04	74.24	75.05	70.27	79.78	80.55	75.21
District of Columbia..........	67.99	73.09	68.57	78.94	64.59	77.59	84.31	74.46
Florida.........................	75.84	78.10	74.97	75.64	68.98	81.40	82.14	75.53
Georgia........................	73.61	75.27	72.28	73.88	68.29	78.22	79.53	76.16
Hawaii.........................	78.21	80.23	77.17	78.40	(B)	83.65	83.31	(B)
Idaho..........................	76.88	78.29	76.18	76.46	(B)	80.50	80.53	(B)
Illinois.........................	74.90	77.06	73.91	75.33	66.81	80.26	80.78	74.20
Indiana........................	75.39	76.47	73.55	74.24	67.47	79.45	79.69	76.55
Iowa...........................	77.29	78.76	76.11	76.19	70.81	81.39	81.35	75.16
Kansas.........................	76.76	77.78	74.84	75.46	68.47	80.88	81.00	75.02
Kentucky......................	74.37	75.20	72.25	72.73	69.01	78.20	78.42	74.46
Louisiana......................	73.05	74.28	71.12	73.47	66.45	77.44	79.41	75.30
Maine..........................	76.35	77.46	75.23	75.59	(B)	79.63	80.88	(B)
Maryland.......................	74.79	76.36	73.55	75.58	68.41	79.08	80.66	75.78
Massachusetts................	76.72	78.76	75.79	76.35	73.14	81.68	81.63	79.33
Michigan.......................	75.04	76.90	73.98	75.26	67.38	79.83	80.59	75.95
Minnesota.....................	77.76	79.26	76.74	77.03	71.59	81.80	82.61	76.60
Mississippi....................	73.03	73.88	70.30	72.25	66.72	77.62	79.13	73.68
Missouri........................	75.25	76.52	73.59	74.29	67.22	79.46	79.93	74.50
Montana.......................	76.23	77.74	75.18	75.07	(B)	80.56	81.24	(B)
Nebraska......................	76.92	78.37	76.00	76.17	69.15	80.78	81.14	74.67
Nevada........................	74.18	76.05	73.34	73.49	70.56	79.24	78.97	74.75
New Hampshire...............	76.72	78.79	76.24	76.46	(B)	81.40	81.30	(B)
New Jersey....................	75.42	77.58	74.77	75.82	68.85	80.32	81.32	75.54
New Mexico....................	75.74	77.26	74.52	75.19	71.63	80.06	80.69	74.37
New York......................	74.68	78.20	75.13	75.78	70.13	81.16	81.49	77.84
North Carolina................	74.48	76.27	73.05	74.27	66.33	79.56	80.34	76.68
North Dakota..................	77.62	79.06	75.96	76.65	(B)	82.61	82.67	(B)
Ohio...........................	75.32	76.49	73.94	74.58	68.60	78.95	80.01	74.91
Oklahoma.....................	75.10	75.61	72.75	73.00	68.97	78.59	78.75	74.34
Oregon........................	76.44	78.09	75.82	75.72	70.67	80.37	80.20	78.24
Pennsylvania..................	75.38	77.02	74.09	75.03	67.26	79.90	80.65	75.34
Rhode Island..................	76.54	78.65	75.83	76.06	72.18	81.42	81.60	77.39
South Carolina................	73.51	75.04	71.68	73.76	67.34	78.49	79.77	75.41
South Dakota.................	76.91	78.34	75.19	76.35	(B)	81.79	82.61	(B)
Tennessee....................	74.32	75.29	71.98	73.31	66.86	78.66	79.28	74.16
Texas..........................	75.14	77.04	74.12	74.74	69.18	80.05	80.35	74.76
Utah...........................	77.70	78.89	76.84	76.95	(B)	80.95	80.93	(B)
Vermont.......................	76.54	78.24	76.18	76.30	(B)	80.29	80.90	(B)
Virginia........................	75.22	76.95	74.48	75.62	69.37	79.34	80.69	76.20
Washington...................	76.82	78.64	76.18	76.10	71.90	81.14	80.98	77.11
West Virginia..................	74.26	75.28	72.75	72.75	69.87	77.84	78.36	72.65
Wisconsin.....................	76.87	78.56	75.61	76.12	68.41	81.64	81.87	74.34
Wyoming.......................	76.21	76.64	74.83	75.33	(B)	78.55	80.41	(B)

B Base figure too small to meet statistical standards for reliability.

Source: U.S. National Center for Health Statistics, National Vital Statistics Reports (NVSR), *U.S. Decennial Life Tables for 1999-2001: State Life Tables*, Vol. 60, No. 9, September 2012, and earlier reports. See also <www.cdc.gov/nchs/products/life_tables.htm>.

Table 106. Life Expectancy at Birth and Age 65 By Sex and State: 2020

[Average number of years of life remaining, except rank. Life expectancies shown are rounded; rankings are based on unrounded life expectancies. Excludes deaths of nonresidents of the United States. Based on state-specific final numbers of deaths for 2020 collected from death certificates filed in state vital statistics offices and reported to the National Center for Health Statistics (NCHS)]

State	Life expectancy at birth				Life expectancy at age 65			
	Rank	Average years			Rank	Average years		
		Total	Male	Female		Total	Male	Female
United States.................	(X)	**77.0**	**74.2**	**79.9**	(X)	**18.5**	**17.0**	**19.8**
Alabama.........................	48	73.2	70.1	76.4	50	16.6	15.1	17.9
Alaska...........................	29	76.6	74.3	79.2	15	18.8	17.6	20.1
Arizona..........................	33	76.3	73.4	79.5	19	18.5	17.1	19.8
Arkansas........................	45	73.8	71.1	76.6	46	16.9	15.5	18.1
California........................	4	79.0	76.2	82.0	2	19.5	17.9	20.9
Colorado........................	12	78.3	75.8	80.9	9	19.0	17.8	20.2
Connecticut.....................	10	78.4	75.6	81.3	11	19.0	17.6	20.2
Delaware........................	27	76.7	73.9	79.5	22	18.4	17.2	19.5
District of Columbia...........	39	75.3	71.7	78.7	38	17.7	15.8	19.3
Florida..........................	19	77.5	74.6	80.5	6	19.2	17.7	20.6
Georgia.........................	37	75.6	72.8	78.3	41	17.4	16.0	18.7
Hawaii...........................	1	80.7	77.6	83.8	1	21.0	19.0	22.7
Idaho............................	11	78.4	76.1	80.8	14	18.8	17.6	20.1
Illinois...........................	26	76.8	73.8	79.8	32	18.0	16.6	19.4
Indiana..........................	41	75.0	72.3	77.9	43	17.3	15.9	18.5
Iowa.............................	21	77.5	74.9	80.1	29	18.2	16.8	19.4
Kansas..........................	31	76.4	73.8	79.2	34	17.9	16.4	19.2
Kentucky........................	47	73.5	70.6	76.5	47	16.9	15.6	18.0
Louisiana........................	49	73.1	69.9	76.4	48	16.6	15.2	18.0
Maine............................	14	77.8	74.9	80.7	10	19.0	17.8	20.1
Maryland........................	24	76.8	73.8	79.7	23	18.4	17.0	19.6
Massachusetts..................	5	79.0	76.4	81.5	12	18.9	17.6	20.1
Michigan........................	36	76.0	73.4	78.8	36	17.8	16.4	19.0
Minnesota.......................	3	79.1	76.8	81.4	8	19.1	17.9	20.2
Mississippi......................	51	71.9	68.6	75.2	51	16.1	14.6	17.5
Missouri.........................	40	75.1	72.1	78.1	42	17.4	16.0	18.7
Montana.........................	23	76.8	74.2	79.6	20	18.4	17.1	19.9
Nebraska........................	16	77.7	75.2	80.3	26	18.3	16.9	19.6
Nevada..........................	34	76.3	73.5	79.2	35	17.8	16.4	19.1
New Hampshire.................	6	79.0	76.5	81.5	7	19.1	17.9	20.3
New Jersey......................	20	77.5	74.6	80.5	28	18.2	16.7	19.6
New Mexico.....................	43	74.5	71.3	77.8	25	18.3	17.0	19.5
New York........................	15	77.7	74.8	80.7	21	18.4	16.8	19.9
North Carolina..................	35	76.1	73.3	79.0	33	18.0	16.7	19.2
North Dakota....................	22	76.9	74.2	80.0	27	18.2	16.8	19.7
Ohio.............................	38	75.3	72.5	78.1	40	17.5	16.1	18.7
Oklahoma.......................	44	74.1	71.5	76.9	49	16.6	15.3	17.8
Oregon..........................	8	78.8	76.3	81.3	5	19.3	18.0	20.5
Pennsylvania....................	25	76.8	74.0	79.6	30	18.1	16.7	19.4
Rhode Island....................	13	78.2	75.5	80.9	16	18.6	17.1	19.9
South Carolina..................	42	74.8	71.7	78.0	37	17.7	16.3	19.0
South Dakota...................	28	76.7	74.2	79.4	24	18.3	16.8	19.9
Tennessee.......................	46	73.8	70.7	77.0	45	17.0	15.5	18.3
Texas............................	30	76.5	73.7	79.3	39	17.7	16.2	19.0
Utah.............................	9	78.6	76.7	80.6	13	18.8	17.9	19.8
Vermont.........................	7	78.8	76.1	81.4	3	19.5	18.2	20.6
Virginia..........................	18	77.6	75.1	80.1	17	18.6	17.2	19.7
Washington......................	2	79.2	76.9	81.6	4	19.5	18.2	20.6
West Virginia....................	50	72.8	69.8	76.1	44	17.0	15.6	18.3
Wisconsin........................	17	77.7	75.2	80.3	18	18.5	17.2	19.8
Wyoming........................	32	76.3	74.0	78.9	31	18.1	17.0	19.3

X Not applicable.

Source: U.S. National Center for Health Statistics, National Vital Statistics Reports (NVSR), *U.S. State Life Tables, 2020*, Vol. 71, No. 2, August 2022. See also <www.cdc.gov/nchs/products/life_tables.htm>.

Table 107. Survivors Out of 100,000 Population Born Alive by Age, Sex, and Race/Ethnicity: 2020

[Number of persons from the original hypothetical cohort of 100,000 live births who survive to the beginning of each age interval. Data are based on final numbers of deaths for the year 2020: July 1, 2020 population estimates based on the 2010 Census; and age-specific death and population counts for black and white Medicare beneficiaries aged 66–99 for the year 2020 from the Centers for Medicare & Medicaid Services. Excludes deaths of nonresidents of the United States. Race categories are consistent with 1997 Office of Management and Budget standards. See Technical Notes, source]

Age	All races Total	All races Male	All races Female	White, non-Hispanic Total	White, non-Hispanic Male	White, non-Hispanic Female	Black, non-Hispanic Total	Black, non-Hispanic Male	Black, non-Hispanic Female	American Indian or Alaska Native, non-Hispanic Total	American Indian or Alaska Native, non-Hispanic Male	American Indian or Alaska Native, non-Hispanic Female	Asian, non-Hispanic Total	Asian, non-Hispanic Male	Asian, non-Hispanic Female	Hispanic Total	Hispanic Male	Hispanic Female
SURVIVORS																		
Age 0	100,000	100,000	100,000	100,000	100,000	100,000	100,000	100,000	100,000	100,000	100,000	100,000	100,000	100,000	100,000	100,000	100,000	100,000
Age 1	99,461	99,415	99,508	99,562	99,526	99,600	98,967	98,884	99,052	99,241	99,168	99,316	99,689	99,671	99,708	99,532	99,493	99,573
Age 5	99,377	99,313	99,429	99,480	99,425	99,538	98,794	98,705	98,906	99,002	98,898	99,111	99,638	99,621	99,657	99,460	99,415	99,508
Age 10	99,323	99,254	99,381	99,431	99,366	99,500	98,689	98,596	98,819	98,877	98,790	98,972	99,606	99,593	99,622	99,415	99,369	99,465
Age 15	99,242	99,155	99,317	99,355	99,265	99,448	98,551	98,431	98,727	98,716	98,585	98,855	99,560	99,539	99,582	99,344	99,291	99,403
Age 20	98,952	98,741	99,157	99,111	98,921	99,304	97,970	97,547	98,459	98,079	97,779	98,383	99,400	99,382	99,479	99,080	98,921	99,249
Age 25	98,415	97,961	98,876	98,646	98,273	99,039	96,936	95,995	97,964	96,925	96,250	97,610	99,135	99,082	99,350	98,602	98,219	99,015
Age 30	97,725	96,994	98,479	97,984	97,369	98,633	95,828	94,418	97,351	95,047	93,789	96,351	98,889	98,754	99,222	98,002	97,332	98,726
Age 35	96,856	95,815	97,933	97,107	96,191	98,070	94,477	92,563	96,510	92,276	90,539	94,103	98,613	98,388	99,071	97,291	96,337	98,333
Age 40	95,794	94,420	97,215	96,031	94,801	97,320	92,799	90,333	95,362	88,798	86,372	91,330	98,264	97,881	98,865	96,418	95,102	97,851
Age 45	94,471	92,731	96,266	94,722	93,154	96,362	90,658	87,635	93,746	85,128	81,962	88,437	97,782	97,203	98,554	95,297	93,549	97,191
Age 50	92,680	90,497	94,928	92,976	91,027	95,015	87,851	84,131	91,592	79,925	75,635	84,417	97,012	96,133	98,042	93,695	91,444	96,132
Age 55	90,115	87,332	92,979	90,449	88,016	93,094	84,012	79,438	88,571	73,946	68,906	79,320	96,133	94,434	97,221	91,325	88,384	94,516
Age 60	86,376	82,736	90,111	86,906	83,646	90,302	78,572	72,901	84,200	66,875	60,578	73,514	93,991	91,910	96,041	87,768	83,770	92,084
Age 65	81,181	76,439	86,039	81,945	77,663	86,395	71,104	64,034	78,108	59,059	52,078	66,470	91,202	87,964	94,206	82,693	77,408	88,345
Age 70	74,466	68,491	80,574	75,531	70,099	81,164	61,788	53,210	70,247	50,767	42,836	59,262	86,892	82,298	91,037	75,945	68,979	83,244
Age 75	65,565	58,588	72,737	66,755	60,346	73,419	51,101	41,552	60,589	41,271	33,305	50,051	80,678	74,712	86,165	67,055	58,488	75,942
Age 80	53,346	45,661	61,298	54,434	47,242	61,940	38,680	29,200	48,213	30,807	23,623	38,925	71,468	64,046	78,165	55,278	45,707	65,134
Age 85	37,700	30,276	45,424	38,463	31,358	45,884	25,336	17,281	33,536	20,376	14,955	26,586	57,178	48,731	64,816	39,857	30,344	49,467
Age 90	20,447	14,824	26,271	20,779	15,321	26,448	12,856	7,605	18,298	11,145	7,779	14,906	37,395	29,498	44,377	22,489	15,009	29,682
Age 95	6,889	4,216	9,599	6,867	4,239	9,510	4,422	2,172	6,724	4,549	3,010	6,072	16,399	11,372	20,370	8,143	4,343	11,374
Age 100	1,142	549	1,727	1,088	514	1,646	892	352	1,403	1,271	805	1,608	3,760	2,182	4,715	1,523	583	2,155
PERCENT SURVIVING																		
Age 0	100.0	100.0	100.0	100.0	100.0	100.0	100.0	100.0	100.0	100.0	100.0	100.0	100.0	100.0	100.0	100.0	100.0	100.0
Age 1	99.5	99.4	99.5	99.6	99.5	99.6	99.0	98.9	99.1	99.2	99.2	99.3	99.7	99.7	99.7	99.5	99.5	99.6
Age 5	99.4	99.3	99.4	99.5	99.4	99.5	98.8	98.7	98.9	99.0	98.9	99.1	99.6	99.6	99.6	99.5	99.4	99.5
Age 10	99.3	99.3	99.4	99.4	99.4	99.5	98.7	98.6	98.8	98.9	98.8	99.0	99.6	99.6	99.6	99.4	99.4	99.5
Age 15	99.2	99.2	99.3	99.4	99.3	99.4	98.6	98.4	98.7	98.7	98.6	98.9	99.6	99.5	99.6	99.3	99.3	99.4
Age 20	99.0	98.7	99.2	99.1	98.9	99.3	98.0	97.5	98.5	98.1	97.8	98.4	99.4	99.4	99.5	99.1	98.9	99.2
Age 25	98.4	98.0	98.9	98.6	98.3	99.0	96.9	96.0	98.0	96.9	96.3	97.6	99.1	99.1	99.2	98.6	98.2	99.0
Age 30	97.7	97.0	98.5	98.0	97.4	98.6	95.8	94.4	97.4	95.0	93.8	96.4	98.9	98.8	99.2	98.0	97.3	98.7
Age 35	96.9	95.8	97.9	97.1	96.2	98.1	94.5	92.6	96.5	92.3	90.5	94.1	98.6	98.4	99.1	97.3	96.3	98.3
Age 40	95.8	94.4	97.2	96.0	94.8	97.3	92.8	90.3	95.4	88.8	86.4	91.3	98.3	97.9	98.9	96.4	95.1	97.9
Age 45	94.5	92.7	96.3	94.7	93.2	96.4	90.7	87.6	93.7	85.1	82.0	88.4	97.8	97.2	98.6	95.3	93.5	97.2
Age 50	92.7	90.5	94.9	93.0	91.0	95.0	87.9	84.1	91.6	79.9	75.6	84.4	97.0	96.1	98.0	93.7	91.4	96.1
Age 55	90.1	87.3	93.0	90.5	88.0	93.1	84.0	79.4	88.6	73.9	68.9	79.3	96.1	94.4	97.2	91.3	88.4	94.5
Age 60	86.4	82.7	90.1	86.9	83.6	90.3	78.6	72.9	84.2	66.9	60.6	73.5	94.0	91.9	96.0	87.8	83.8	92.1
Age 65	81.2	76.4	86.0	81.9	77.7	86.4	71.1	64.0	78.1	59.1	52.1	66.5	91.2	88.0	94.2	82.7	77.4	88.3
Age 70	74.5	68.5	80.6	75.5	70.1	81.2	61.8	53.2	70.2	50.8	42.8	59.3	86.9	82.3	91.0	75.9	69.0	83.2
Age 75	65.6	58.6	72.7	66.8	60.3	73.4	51.1	41.6	60.6	41.3	33.3	50.1	80.7	74.7	86.2	67.1	58.5	75.9
Age 80	53.3	45.7	61.3	54.4	47.2	61.9	38.7	29.2	48.2	30.8	23.6	38.9	71.5	64.0	78.2	55.3	45.7	65.1
Age 85	37.7	30.3	45.4	38.5	31.4	45.9	25.3	17.3	33.5	20.4	15.0	26.6	57.2	48.7	64.8	39.9	30.3	49.5
Age 90	20.4	14.8	26.3	20.8	15.3	26.4	12.9	7.6	18.3	11.1	7.8	14.9	37.4	29.5	44.4	22.5	15.0	29.7
Age 95	6.9	4.2	9.6	6.9	4.2	9.5	4.4	2.2	6.7	4.5	3.0	6.1	16.4	11.4	20.4	8.1	4.3	11.4
Age 100	1.1	0.5	1.7	1.1	0.5	1.6	0.9	0.4	1.4	1.3	0.8	1.6	3.8	2.2	4.7	1.5	0.6	2.2

Source: U.S. National Center for Health Statistics, National Vital Statistics Reports (NVSR), *United States Life Tables, 2020*, Vol. 71, No. 1, August 2022. See also <www.cdc.gov/nchs/products/life_tables.htm>.

Table 108. Deaths and Death Rates by Sex, Race, and Hispanic Origin: 1970 to 2020

[Deaths in thousands (1,921 represents 1,921,000). Rates are per 100,000 population for specified groups. Excludes deaths of nonresidents of the United States and fetal deaths. Rates are based on population enumerated as of April 1 for census years and estimated as of July 1 for all other years. Data for Hispanic origin and specified races other than White and Black should be interpreted with caution because of inconsistent reporting of race and Hispanic origin on death certificates and censuses and surveys]

Sex and race	1970	1980	1990	2000	2010	2015	2016	2017	2018	2019	2020
Deaths [1]	**1,921**	**1,990**	**2,148**	**2,403**	**2,468**	**2,713**	**2,744**	**2,814**	**2,839**	**2,855**	**3,384**
Male [1]	1,078	1,075	1,113	1,178	1,232	1,373	1,400	1,439	1,458	1,474	1,770
Female [1]	843	915	1,035	1,226	1,236	1,339	1,344	1,374	1,381	1,381	1,614
White, non-Hispanic [2]	(NA)	(NA)	(NA)	1,960	1,970	2,124	2,133	2,180	2,188	2,190	2,491
Male	(NA)	(NA)	(NA)	945	972	1,064	1,077	1,103	1,112	1,119	1,282
Female	(NA)	(NA)	(NA)	1,015	998	1,060	1,056	1,077	1,077	1,071	1,209
Black, non-Hispanic [2]	(NA)	(NA)	(NA)	283	283	315	327	336	343	349	452
Male	(NA)	(NA)	(NA)	143	144	162	169	174	179	182	239
Female	(NA)	(NA)	(NA)	139	140	153	158	161	164	166	213
American Indian or Alaska Native, non-Hispanic [2]	(NA)	(NA)	(NA)	11	15	18	19	19	19	20	27
Male	(NA)	(NA)	(NA)	6	8	10	10	11	11	11	15
Female	(NA)	(NA)	(NA)	5	7	8	8	9	9	9	12
Asian or Pacific Islander, non-Hispanic [2]	(NA)	(NA)	(NA)	34	50	65	68	73	75	77	100
Male	(NA)	(NA)	(NA)	19	26	33	35	37	39	40	52
Female	(NA)	(NA)	(NA)	16	24	32	33	35	37	38	47
Hispanic origin [3]	(NA)	(NA)	(NA)	107	144	179	188	197	205	212	306
Male	(NA)	(NA)	(NA)	60	80	98	104	109	113	118	176
Female	(NA)	(NA)	(NA)	47	65	81	85	89	92	95	130
Death rates [1]	**945**	**878**	**864**	**854**	**800**	**844**	**849**	**864**	**868**	**870**	**1,027**
Male [1]	1,090	977	918	853	812	868	880	897	905	912	1,091
Female [1]	808	785	812	855	787	821	819	831	832	829	965
White, non-Hispanic [2]	(NA)	(NA)	(NA)	993	984	1,055	1,060	1,083	1,088	1,090	1,242
Male	(NA)	(NA)	(NA)	979	988	1,073	1,086	1,111	1,121	1,129	1,297
Female	(NA)	(NA)	(NA)	1,007	981	1,039	1,035	1,056	1,056	1,052	1,189
Black, non-Hispanic [2]	(NA)	(NA)	(NA)	806	719	755	776	788	800	807	1,036
Male	(NA)	(NA)	(NA)	860	765	809	836	854	870	880	1,143
Female	(NA)	(NA)	(NA)	757	677	704	720	726	736	739	937
American Indian or Alaska Native, non-Hispanic [2]	(NA)	(NA)	(NA)	470	578	671	686	703	710	712	967
Male	(NA)	(NA)	(NA)	517	640	747	773	784	808	800	1,094
Female	(NA)	(NA)	(NA)	425	518	597	602	626	616	628	845
Asian or Pacific Islander, non-Hispanic [2]	(NA)	(NA)	(NA)	301	310	342	350	360	366	373	468
Male	(NA)	(NA)	(NA)	338	337	365	375	386	394	401	514
Female	(NA)	(NA)	(NA)	267	286	320	328	336	341	348	426
Hispanic origin [3]	(NA)	(NA)	(NA)	304	286	317	328	335	342	351	499
Male	(NA)	(NA)	(NA)	331	311	343	357	365	374	385	568
Female	(NA)	(NA)	(NA)	275	261	290	298	304	309	316	428
Age-adjusted death rates [1,4]	**1,223**	**1,039**	**939**	**869**	**747**	**733**	**729**	**732**	**724**	**715**	**835**
Male [1]	1,542	1,348	1,203	1,054	887	863	861	865	856	847	998
Female [1]	971	818	751	731	635	624	618	620	611	603	695
White, non-Hispanic [2]	(NA)	(NA)	(NA)	856	755	753	749	755	746	737	831
Male	(NA)	(NA)	(NA)	1,035	893	881	880	885	874	865	981
Female	(NA)	(NA)	(NA)	722	643	644	637	643	634	625	700
Black, non-Hispanic [2]	(NA)	(NA)	(NA)	1,137	920	876	883	881	880	871	1,102
Male	(NA)	(NA)	(NA)	1,422	1,132	1,070	1,081	1,083	1,085	1,075	1,376
Female	(NA)	(NA)	(NA)	941	771	731	734	728	724	715	893
American Indian or Alaska Native, non-Hispanic [2]	(NA)	(NA)	(NA)	801	819	806	800	800	781	767	1,008
Male	(NA)	(NA)	(NA)	956	966	950	954	944	937	911	1,206
Female	(NA)	(NA)	(NA)	679	697	680	668	674	642	641	834
Asian or Pacific Islander, non-Hispanic [2]	(NA)	(NA)	(NA)	507	426	396	394	395	392	385	471
Male	(NA)	(NA)	(NA)	625	513	469	467	470	468	457	572
Female	(NA)	(NA)	(NA)	417	361	340	337	336	332	327	389
Hispanic origin [3]	(NA)	(NA)	(NA)	666	559	525	526	525	524	524	724
Male	(NA)	(NA)	(NA)	818	678	629	632	632	633	633	904
Female	(NA)	(NA)	(NA)	546	463	438	436	434	432	431	570

NA Not available. [1] Includes other races not shown separately. [2] Multiple-race data reported according to 1997 OMB standards were bridged to single-race categories of 1977 OMB standards; see Technical Notes in source for details. [3] Persons of Hispanic origin may be of any race. [4] Age-adjusted death rates are better indicators than crude death rates for showing changes in the risk of death over time when the age distribution of the population is changing, and for comparing the mortality of population subgroups that have different age compositions. All age-adjusted death rates are standardized to the year 2000 population.

Source: U.S. National Center for Health Statistics, National Vital Statistics Reports (NVSR), *Deaths: Final Data*, annual; and CDC WONDER Online Database, "Multiple Cause of Death, 1999-2020," <wonder.cdc.gov>, accessed August 2022. See also <www.cdc.gov/nchs/nvss/deaths.htm>.

Table 109. Death Rates by Age, Sex, and Race: 1970 to 2020

[Rates per 100,000 population]

Characteristic	All ages [1]	Under 1 year	1 to 4 years	5 to 14 years	15 to 24 years	25 to 34 years	35 to 44 years	45 to 54 years	55 to 64 years	65 to 74 years	75 to 84 years	85 years and over
MALE												
Total:												
1970	1,090	2,410	93	51	189	215	403	959	2,283	4,874	10,010	17,822
1980	977	1,429	73	37	172	196	299	767	1,815	4,105	8,817	18,801
1990	918	1,083	52	29	147	204	310	610	1,553	3,492	7,889	18,057
2000	853	807	36	21	115	139	255	543	1,231	2,980	6,973	17,501
2010	812	680	30	15	98	142	213	506	1,076	2,275	5,694	15,414
2019	870	603	25	15	100	177	257	490	1,112	2,179	5,074	14,230
2020	1,027	569	26	16	122	221	326	602	1,323	2,582	5,937	16,355
White:												
1990	931	896	46	26	131	176	268	549	1,467	3,398	7,845	18,268
2000	888	668	33	20	106	124	234	497	1,163	2,906	6,933	17,716
2010	866	584	27	14	92	136	207	492	1,033	2,232	5,704	15,640
2015	933	542	25	14	92	157	221	487	1,071	2,160	5,427	15,203
2019	978	503	23	14	91	172	251	477	1,079	2,140	5,124	14,726
2020	1,153	487	23	15	107	209	313	576	1,261	2,482	5,920	16,794
Black:												
1990	1,008	2,112	86	41	252	431	700	1,261	2,618	4,946	9,130	16,955
2000	834	1,568	55	28	181	261	453	1,018	2,080	4,254	8,486	16,791
2010	725	1,207	43	20	143	217	308	716	1,662	3,206	6,722	14,715
2015	765	1,150	46	21	151	229	326	678	1,613	3,042	6,205	13,066
2019	830	1,126	39	23	162	252	380	707	1,616	3,096	5,900	12,639
2020	1,075	1,031	41	26	220	341	497	920	2,037	4,012	7,581	15,958
Asian or Pacific Islander: [2]												
1990	334	605	45	21	76	80	131	287	789	2,041	5,009	12,446
2000	333	529	23	13	55	55	105	250	642	1,661	4,328	12,125
2010	327	434	19	8	43	53	84	214	519	1,226	3,439	10,825
2015	355	438	15	10	49	56	85	205	508	1,131	3,092	9,406
2019	390	426	17	10	48	66	97	221	530	1,123	2,994	8,490
2020	499	308	13	9	51	75	128	282	691	1,511	3,725	10,447
American Indian or Alaska Native: [2]												
1990	476	1,057	77	33	220	256	365	620	1,211	2,462	5,389	11,244
2000	416	700	45	20	136	179	295	520	1,090	2,478	5,351	10,726
2010	398	543	34	18	116	156	258	496	951	1,971	4,452	10,268
2015	455	486	35	15	101	191	281	544	994	1,841	4,171	8,277
2019	488	463	29	17	111	221	304	520	970	1,787	3,723	7,222
2020	649	377	27	16	132	309	448	710	1,310	2,362	4,698	8,800
FEMALE												
Total:												
1970	808	1,864	75	32	68	102	231	517	1,099	2,580	6,678	15,518
1980	785	1,142	55	24	58	76	159	413	934	2,145	5,440	14,747
1990	812	856	41	19	49	74	138	343	879	1,991	4,883	14,274
2000	855	663	29	15	43	64	143	313	772	1,921	4,815	14,719
2010	787	564	23	11	36	64	129	311	644	1,528	4,138	13,219
2019	829	500	21	12	38	79	142	297	670	1,402	3,711	12,666
2020	965	478	20	11	45	96	171	349	773	1,627	4,261	14,560
White:												
1990	847	690	36	18	46	62	117	309	823	1,924	4,839	14,401
2000	912	551	26	14	41	55	126	281	731	1,868	4,785	14,891
2010	857	488	22	11	36	61	123	295	618	1,505	4,165	13,419
2015	899	455	20	11	38	72	132	307	640	1,444	4,028	13,443
2019	905	411	18	11	37	78	138	289	651	1,391	3,765	13,115
2020	1,040	409	18	11	41	91	163	333	736	1,580	4,267	14,957
Black:												
1990	748	1,736	68	28	69	160	299	639	1,453	2,866	5,688	13,310
2000	733	1,280	45	20	58	122	272	588	1,227	2,690	5,697	13,941
2010	643	994	33	15	43	93	199	481	972	2,021	4,581	12,590
2015	666	970	32	15	46	93	192	447	970	1,864	4,310	11,741
2019	697	966	35	17	52	104	207	430	961	1,844	4,102	11,168
2020	881	870	32	16	69	138	264	533	1,182	2,350	5,144	13,974
Asian or Pacific Islander: [2]												
1990	234	518	32	13	29	38	70	183	483	1,089	3,128	10,254
2000	262	434	20	12	22	28	66	156	391	996	2,882	9,052
2010	277	342	16	8	17	27	49	128	299	789	2,446	8,590
2015	311	358	15	7	19	26	51	128	288	705	2,264	8,142
2019	338	334	17	8	19	29	50	125	287	684	2,095	7,910
2020	413	248	12	7	24	31	58	148	345	845	2,492	9,482
American Indian or Alaska Native: [2]												
1990	330	689	38	26	69	102	156	381	806	1,679	3,073	8,201
2000	346	492	40	18	59	85	172	285	772	1,900	3,850	9,118
2010	332	366	24	11	44	86	147	326	624	1,482	3,392	9,278
2015	376	431	27	14	47	105	171	354	622	1,360	3,193	7,637
2019	395	386	32	9	54	124	206	341	626	1,217	2,806	6,621
2020	518	289	20	13	57	186	285	465	858	1,566	3,607	7,925

[1] Figures for age not stated are included in "All ages" but not distributed among age groups. [2] The death rates for specified races other than White and Black should be interpreted with caution because of inconsistencies between reporting race on death certificates and censuses and surveys.

Source: U.S. National Center for Health Statistics, *Health, United States*, annual; and CDC WONDER Online Database, "Multiple Cause of Death, 1999-2020," <wonder.cdc.gov>, accessed March 2022. See also <www.cdc.gov/nchs/nvss/deaths.htm>.

Table 110. Deaths and Death Rates by Age, Sex, Race, and Hispanic Origin: 2020

[Rates per 100,000 population in specified group; see Technical Notes. Race and Hispanic-origin categories are consistent with 1977 Office of Management and Budget (OMB) standards. Multiple-race data reported according to 1997 OMB standards were bridged to single-race categories of 1977 OMB standards. Data for specified race or Hispanic-origin groups other than non-Hispanic White and non-Hispanic Black should be interpreted with caution because of inconsistencies in reporting these items on death certificates and surveys; see Technical Notes, source]

Age	Total[1]			White, non-Hispanic			Black, non-Hispanic			American Indian or Alaska Native, non-Hispanic			Asian or Pacific Islander, non-Hispanic			Hispanic[2]		
	Total	Male	Female	Total	Male	Female	Total	Male	Female	Total	Male	Female	Total	Male	Female	Total	Male	Female
DEATHS																		
All ages	3,383,729	1,769,884	1,613,845	2,491,026	1,282,214	1,208,812	451,792	239,016	212,776	26,755	14,827	11,928	99,574	52,442	47,132	305,708	175,585	130,123
Under 1 year	19,582	10,859	8,723	8,250	4,567	3,683	6,014	3,314	2,700	224	130	94	655	370	285	4,238	2,366	1,872
1 to 4 years	3,529	2,026	1,503	1,614	940	674	966	553	413	70	41	29	132	71	61	742	418	324
5 to 9 years	2,210	1,245	965	1,019	585	434	594	343	251	41	19	22	87	44	43	468	253	215
10 to 14 years	3,413	2,117	1,296	1,645	1,030	615	813	535	278	57	35	22	121	73	48	772	440	332
15 to 19 years	12,278	8,951	3,327	5,505	3,889	1,616	3,389	2,618	771	215	144	71	344	211	133	2,803	2,076	727
20 to 24 years	23,538	17,533	6,005	11,060	7,963	3,097	6,461	4,943	1,518	416	293	123	660	469	191	4,906	3,837	1,069
25 to 29 years	32,696	23,554	9,142	16,994	11,923	5,071	8,224	6,019	2,205	748	500	248	823	588	235	5,844	4,476	1,368
30 to 34 years	40,790	28,278	12,512	22,877	15,673	7,204	9,234	6,398	2,836	1,007	611	396	1,035	709	326	6,559	4,835	1,724
35 to 39 years	48,081	32,066	16,015	27,654	18,150	9,504	10,035	6,541	3,494	1,122	691	431	1,355	918	437	7,793	5,679	2,114
40 to 44 years	56,409	36,428	19,981	31,829	20,388	11,441	12,181	7,467	4,714	1,092	681	411	1,694	1,097	597	9,459	6,693	2,766
45 to 49 years	76,431	48,154	28,277	44,011	27,389	16,622	15,956	9,652	6,304	1,354	850	504	2,550	1,595	955	12,327	8,505	3,822
50 to 54 years	114,711	71,690	43,021	70,098	43,483	26,615	22,653	13,573	9,080	1,709	1,004	705	3,478	2,163	1,315	16,325	11,149	5,176
55 to 59 years	183,228	113,660	69,568	118,561	73,219	45,342	34,888	20,751	14,137	2,331	1,416	915	4,822	3,032	1,790	21,864	14,677	7,187
60 to 64 years	257,321	157,467	99,854	172,951	105,968	66,983	47,705	28,152	19,553	2,723	1,539	1,184	6,850	4,291	2,559	26,035	16,738	9,297
65 to 69 years	306,388	182,736	123,652	213,293	127,655	85,638	52,283	29,957	22,326	2,723	1,580	1,143	8,635	5,214	3,421	28,266	17,471	10,795
70 to 74 years	368,119	209,263	158,856	272,400	155,214	117,186	51,417	28,249	23,168	2,828	1,564	1,264	10,254	5,828	4,426	29,973	17,576	12,397
75 to 79 years	398,191	215,751	182,440	307,170	167,790	139,380	46,204	23,371	22,833	2,592	1,376	1,216	11,004	6,141	4,863	30,243	16,414	13,829
80 to 84 years	423,893	213,107	210,786	332,508	169,152	163,356	43,351	19,849	23,502	2,250	1,063	1,187	12,978	6,753	6,225	31,988	15,798	16,190
85 years and over	1,012,805	394,920	617,885	831,544	327,209	504,335	79,412	26,725	52,687	3,253	1,290	1,963	32,096	12,874	19,222	65,092	26,173	38,919
DEATH RATES																		
All ages	1,027.0	1,090.8	965.1	1,242.4	1,296.9	1,189.4	1,035.7	1,143.4	936.7	967.1	1,094.3	845.1	467.8	513.8	425.5	498.6	567.8	428.2
Under 1 year	524.3	569.1	477.5	433.5	469.2	396.1	1,019.6	1,101.7	934.2	648.5	742.0	552.3	276.3	304.2	246.8	436.7	478.2	393.6
1 to 4 years	22.7	25.5	19.7	20.3	23.1	17.4	39.8	45.0	34.6	48.4	55.8	40.7	12.8	13.3	12.2	18.4	20.4	16.4
5 to 9 years	10.9	12.0	9.8	9.8	11.0	8.5	19.7	21.8	16.4	20.7	(S)	22.7	6.6	6.5	6.7	9.0	9.6	8.5
10 to 14 years	16.4	20.0	12.8	15.3	18.7	11.7	25.7	33.3	17.8	27.8	33.8	21.6	9.8	11.6	7.9	14.4	16.1	12.6
15 to 19 years	58.6	83.7	32.4	48.8	67.3	29.4	109.1	166.2	50.3	105.7	139.9	70.7	27.1	33.1	21.0	54.9	79.8	29.0
20 to 24 years	109.0	158.9	56.9	93.5	131.4	53.7	198.0	299.1	94.3	198.7	276.9	118.8	47.5	66.9	27.8	100.0	152.7	44.6
25 to 29 years	140.7	198.3	80.5	133.4	182.9	81.6	227.2	328.8	123.2	330.6	434.7	223.0	48.8	69.6	27.9	117.8	174.5	57.1
30 to 34 years	178.6	244.4	111.0	178.1	240.9	113.6	280.9	395.6	169.9	493.3	595.3	390.2	56.4	79.3	34.7	140.6	197.4	77.8
35 to 39 years	220.3	293.2	147.1	221.5	289.1	153.2	347.6	472.7	232.5	622.4	779.2	470.5	76.8	109.3	47.3	172.7	242.1	97.5
40 to 44 years	277.8	360.4	195.9	273.1	348.2	197.3	454.5	590.0	333.3	670.0	850.9	495.4	107.2	148.6	70.9	223.6	308.6	134.2
45 to 49 years	382.7	487.7	280.0	371.6	461.8	281.1	617.7	799.2	458.3	867.1	1,120.4	628.7	167.3	223.3	117.9	319.2	437.4	199.3
50 to 54 years	562.4	713.2	415.9	541.4	674.5	409.4	881.0	1,130.2	662.7	1,080.1	1,316.7	860.0	261.4	348.8	185.1	481.8	652.7	308.1
55 to 59 years	848.2	1,081.2	627.2	809.3	1,016.9	608.6	1,320.1	1,699.3	994.4	1,354.3	1,735.6	1,010.7	398.1	541.2	274.9	747.1	1,012.9	486.4
60 to 64 years	1,237.1	1,578.2	922.6	1,169.9	1,476.1	880.8	1,961.6	2,553.2	1,470.9	1,696.4	2,068.4	1,355.0	625.5	863.8	427.6	1,117.7	1,488.2	771.8
65 to 69 years	1,714.2	2,177.9	1,303.9	1,616.9	2,028.5	1,241.5	2,744.1	3,618.8	2,072.1	2,140.3	2,711.0	1,657.9	933.7	1,277.2	662.3	1,638.5	2,176.0	1,170.6
70 to 74 years	2,508.4	3,080.5	2,015.3	2,432.0	2,942.0	1,977.8	3,690.8	4,818.5	2,871.5	2,951.7	3,543.8	2,446.1	1,399.8	1,810.1	1,078.0	2,391.1	3,110.7	1,800.6
75 to 79 years	3,987.2	4,822.7	3,309.2	3,959.4	4,741.0	3,303.8	5,276.1	6,691.4	4,337.1	4,364.2	5,170.2	3,709.7	2,323.4	2,944.5	1,834.7	3,687.5	4,687.9	2,942.2
80 to 84 years	6,557.0	7,750.5	5,673.7	6,643.8	7,810.1	5,754.1	7,743.9	9,548.1	6,678.1	6,247.2	6,940.9	5,734.0	4,109.5	4,926.3	3,483.0	5,833.9	7,068.8	4,984.2
85 years and over	15,210.9	16,354.9	14,560.0	15,887.0	17,029.8	15,224.1	14,905.5	16,335.9	14,271.7	10,058.1	10,666.4	9,694.8	9,893.4	10,482.4	9,534.6	12,172.0	13,436.2	11,447.7

S Does not meet standards of reliability. [1] Includes deaths for origin not stated. [2] Persons of Hispanic origin may be of any race.

Source: U.S. National Center for Health Statistics, National Vital Statistics Reports (NVSR), *Deaths: Final Data*, annual; and CDC WONDER Online Database, "Multiple Cause of Death, 1999-2020," <wonder.cdc.gov>, accessed March 2022. See also <www.cdc.gov/nchs/nvss/deaths.htm>.

Table 111. Deaths and Death Rates by State: 1990 to 2020

[2,148 represents 2,148,000. By state of residence. Excludes deaths of nonresidents of the United States. Caution should be used in comparing death rates by state; rates are affected by the population composition of the area. See also Appendix III]

State	Number of deaths (1,000)						Death rate per 1,000 population [1]						Age-adjusted rate, 2020 [1,2]
	1990	2000	2010	2015	2019	2020	1990	2000	2010	2015	2019	2020	
United States	2,148	2,403	2,468	2,713	2,855	3,384	8.6	8.5	8.0	8.4	8.7	10.3	8.3
Alabama	39	45	48	52	54	65	9.7	10.1	10.1	10.7	11.0	13.2	10.6
Alaska	2	3	4	4	5	5	4.0	4.6	5.2	5.8	6.3	7.1	7.7
Arizona	29	41	47	54	60	76	7.9	7.9	7.3	8.0	8.3	10.2	8.0
Arkansas	25	28	29	32	33	38	10.5	10.6	9.9	10.6	10.9	12.6	10.0
California	214	230	234	259	270	320	7.2	6.8	6.3	6.6	6.8	8.1	7.0
Colorado	22	27	31	36	39	47	6.6	6.3	6.3	6.7	6.8	8.1	7.5
Connecticut	28	30	29	31	32	38	8.4	8.8	8.0	8.5	8.9	10.6	7.7
Delaware	6	7	8	9	9	11	8.7	8.8	8.6	9.1	9.6	11.2	8.4
District of Columbia	7	6	5	5	5	6	12.0	10.5	7.8	7.2	7.0	8.7	8.6
Florida	134	164	174	192	207	240	10.4	10.3	9.2	9.5	9.6	11.0	7.3
Georgia	52	64	71	80	86	103	8.0	7.8	7.4	7.8	8.1	9.6	9.0
Hawaii	7	8	10	11	12	12	6.1	6.8	7.1	7.7	8.2	8.6	5.9
Idaho	7	10	11	13	14	16	7.4	7.4	7.3	7.9	8.1	9.0	7.8
Illinois	103	107	100	107	109	133	9.0	8.6	7.8	8.3	8.6	10.5	8.5
Indiana	50	55	57	63	66	78	8.9	9.1	8.8	9.5	9.8	11.6	9.7
Iowa	27	28	28	30	31	36	9.7	9.6	9.1	9.5	9.8	11.4	8.5
Kansas	22	25	25	27	28	32	9.0	9.2	8.6	9.2	9.5	11.0	8.8
Kentucky	35	40	42	47	49	56	9.5	9.8	9.7	10.5	11.0	12.5	10.3
Louisiana	38	41	41	44	46	57	8.9	9.2	9.0	9.4	9.9	12.2	10.4
Maine	11	12	13	14	15	16	9.0	9.7	9.6	10.9	11.2	11.7	7.9
Maryland	38	44	43	47	51	60	8.0	8.3	7.5	7.9	8.4	9.9	8.2
Massachusetts	53	57	53	58	59	68	8.8	8.9	8.0	8.5	8.5	9.9	7.6
Michigan	79	87	88	95	99	117	8.5	8.7	8.9	9.6	9.9	11.7	9.1
Minnesota	35	38	39	43	46	52	7.9	7.7	7.3	7.8	8.1	9.3	7.4
Mississippi	25	29	29	32	33	40	9.8	10.1	9.8	10.6	11.1	13.5	11.4
Missouri	50	55	55	60	62	74	9.8	9.8	9.2	9.8	10.2	12.0	9.4
Montana	7	8	9	10	10	12	8.6	9.0	8.9	9.6	9.7	11.1	8.4
Nebraska	15	15	15	17	17	20	9.4	8.8	8.3	8.8	8.8	10.1	8.2
Nevada	9	15	20	23	26	31	7.8	7.6	7.3	7.9	8.3	9.8	8.5
New Hampshire	8	10	10	12	13	14	7.7	7.8	7.7	9.0	9.4	10.0	7.4
New Jersey	70	75	69	72	75	96	9.1	8.9	7.9	8.1	8.4	10.8	8.4
New Mexico	11	13	16	18	20	24	7.0	7.4	7.7	8.5	9.3	11.3	9.1
New York	169	158	146	154	156	203	9.4	8.3	7.6	7.8	8.0	10.5	8.0
North Carolina	57	72	79	89	96	109	8.6	8.9	8.3	8.9	9.1	10.3	8.6
North Dakota	6	6	6	6	7	8	8.9	9.1	8.8	8.2	8.8	10.5	8.5
Ohio	99	108	109	118	124	144	9.1	9.5	9.4	10.2	10.6	12.3	9.5
Oklahoma	30	35	37	39	41	48	9.7	10.2	9.7	10.1	10.3	12.0	10.1
Oregon	25	30	32	36	37	40	8.8	8.6	8.3	8.9	8.9	9.5	7.4
Pennsylvania	122	131	125	133	134	156	10.3	10.7	9.8	10.4	10.5	12.2	8.7
Rhode Island	10	10	10	10	10	12	9.5	9.6	9.1	9.6	9.7	11.2	8.1
South Carolina	30	37	42	47	51	61	8.5	9.2	9.0	9.6	9.9	11.7	9.4
South Dakota	6	7	7	8	8	10	9.1	9.3	8.7	9.0	9.3	11.0	8.7
Tennessee	46	55	60	67	72	84	9.5	9.7	9.4	10.1	10.5	12.2	10.1
Texas	125	150	167	190	203	250	7.4	7.2	6.6	6.9	7.0	8.5	8.6
Utah	9	12	15	17	19	21	5.3	5.5	5.3	5.8	5.8	6.6	7.6
Vermont	5	5	5	6	6	6	8.2	8.4	8.6	9.5	9.5	10.4	7.4
Virginia	48	56	59	66	70	81	7.8	8.0	7.4	7.8	8.2	9.4	7.9
Washington	37	44	48	55	58	63	7.6	7.5	7.2	7.6	7.7	8.2	7.1
West Virginia	19	21	21	23	23	26	10.8	11.7	11.5	12.3	13.1	14.6	10.6
Wisconsin	43	46	47	51	54	63	8.7	8.7	8.3	8.9	9.3	10.8	8.3
Wyoming	3	4	4	5	5	6	7.1	7.9	7.9	8.2	8.8	10.3	8.4

[1] Rates based on enumerated resident population as of April 1 for 1990, 2000, and 2010; estimated resident population as of July 1 for all other years. [2] Age-adjusted death rates are better indicators than crude death rates for showing changes in the risk of death over time when the age distribution of the population is changing, and for comparing the mortality of population subgroups that have different age compositions. See text this section.

Source: U.S. National Center for Health Statistics, CDC WONDER Online Database, "Multiple Cause of Death, 1999-2020," <wonder.cdc.gov>, accessed April 2022; and National Vital Statistics Reports (NVSR), *Deaths: Final Data*, annual report.

Table 112. Deaths and Death Rates by Urban-Rural Status and Sex: 2000 to 2020

[Rates per 100,000 population. Rates are based on population numerated as of April 1 for 2000 and 2010 and estimated as of July 1 for all other years]

Year	Number		Crude rate		Age-adjusted rate [1]	
	Urban	Rural	Urban	Rural	Urban	Rural
2000	1,931,159	472,192	816.1	1,054.4	858.3	918.1
2005	1,972,266	475,751	788.8	1,046.1	800.3	885.7
2010	1,989,099	479,336	757.9	1,035.4	728.7	837.6
2015	2,196,111	516,519	797.9	1,118.8	711.6	846.0
2016	2,227,271	516,977	804.0	1,121.2	707.9	840.0
2017	2,285,463	528,040	817.3	1,145.9	710.7	845.8
2018	2,308,265	530,940	821.3	1,151.7	702.5	837.5
2019	2,320,231	534,607	822.3	1,160.6	693.4	834.0
2020	2,763,553	620,176	975.0	1,347.5	(NA)	(NA)

NA Not available. [1] See footnote 1, Table 124.

Source: U.S. National Center for Health Statistics, *Trends in Death Rates in Urban and Rural Areas: United States, 1999–2019*, NCHS Data Brief, No. 417, September 2021; and CDC WONDER Online Database, "Multiple Cause of Death, 1999-2020," <wonder.cdc.gov>, accessed April 2022. See also <www.cdc.gov/nchs/nvss/deaths.htm>.

Table 113. Fetal and Infant Deaths: 1990 to 2019

[The term "fetal death," defined on an all inclusive basis to end confusion arising from the use of such terms as stillbirth, spontaneous abortion, and miscarriage, has been adopted by the National Center for Health Statistics (NCHS) as the nationally recommended standard. Fetal deaths do not include induced terminations of pregnancy. In 2014, the NCHS transitioned to the use of the obstetric estimate of gestational age (OE) rather than the last normal menses (LMP) estimate, introducing a discontinuity in perinatal measures for earlier years]

Year	Fetal deaths [1,6]			Infant deaths		Fetal mortality rate [2,6]			Perinatal mortality rate [6]	
	Total [1]	20 to 27 weeks [3]	28 weeks or more [3]	Less than 7 days	Less than 28 days	Total [1]	20 to 27 weeks [3]	28 weeks or more [3]	Defi- nition I [4]	Defi- nition II [5]
1990.....	31,386	13,427	17,959	19,439	23,591	7.5	3.2	4.3	9.0	13.1
1995.....	27,294	13,043	14,251	15,483	19,186	7.0	3.3	3.6	7.6	11.8
2000.....	27,003	13,497	13,506	14,893	18,733	6.6	3.3	3.3	7.0	11.2
2001.....	26,373	13,122	13,251	14,622	18,275	6.5	3.2	3.3	6.9	11.0
2002.....	25,943	13,072	12,871	15,020	18,791	6.4	3.2	3.2	6.9	11.1
2003.....	26,004	13,348	12,656	15,152	18,935	6.3	3.3	3.1	6.8	10.9
2004.....	26,001	13,068	12,933	14,836	18,602	6.3	3.2	3.1	6.7	10.8
2005.....	25,894	13,326	12,568	15,013	18,782	6.2	3.2	3.0	6.6	10.7
2006.....	25,972	13,269	12,703	15,148	19,041	6.1	3.1	3.0	6.5	10.5
2007.....	26,593	13,822	12,771	15,138	19,094	6.1	3.2	3.0	6.4	10.5
2008.....	26,335	13,347	12,988	14,649	18,238	6.2	3.1	3.0	6.5	10.4
2009.....	24,872	12,813	12,059	13,767	17,261	6.0	3.1	2.9	6.2	10.1
2010.....	24,258	12,388	11,870	12,901	16,193	6.0	3.1	3.0	6.2	10.1
2011.....	24,289	12,432	11,857	12,959	16,065	6.1	3.1	3.0	6.3	10.1
2012.....	24,073	12,334	11,739	12,911	15,887	6.1	3.1	3.0	6.2	10.0
2013.....	23,595	11,874	11,721	12,900	15,893	6.0	3.0	3.0	6.2	10.0
2014.....	23,980	12,579	11,263	12,772	15,737	6.0	3.1	2.8	6.0	9.9
2015.....	23,776	12,351	11,317	12,578	15,672	5.9	3.1	2.8	6.0	9.9
2016.....	23,880	12,422	11,336	12,353	15,303	6.0	3.1	2.9	6.0	9.9
2017.....	22,827	11,792	10,903	11,971	14,844	5.9	3.0	2.8	5.9	9.7
2018.....	22,459	11,782	10,559	11,577	14,328	5.9	3.1	2.8	5.8	9.6
2019.....	21,478	11,159	10,209	11,124	13,834	5.7	3.0	2.7	5.7	9.4

[1] Fetal deaths with stated or presumed gestation of 20 weeks or more. [2] Rate per 1,000 live births and fetal deaths in specified age group. [3] Prior to 2014, not stated gestational age proportionally distributed. Beginning 2014, unknown gestational age not shown. [4] Infant deaths of less than 7 days and fetal deaths with stated or presumed period of gestation of 28 weeks or more, per 1,000 live births and fetal deaths. [5] Infant deaths of less than 28 days and fetal deaths with stated or presumed period of gestation of 20 weeks or more per 1,000 live births and fetal deaths. [6] Prior to 2014, based on LMP (last normal menses) measure of gestational age. Beginning 2014, based on the OE (obstetric measure) of gestational age.

Source: U.S. National Center for Health Statistics, National Vital Statistics Reports (NVSR), *Fetal and Perinatal Mortality, United States, 2013*, Vol. 64. No. 8, July 2015; and CDC WONDER Online Database, "Linked Birth / Infant Death Records for 2007-2019," and "Fetal Deaths for 2014-2019 (expanded)," <wonder.cdc.gov/>, accessed June 2022.

Table 114. Infant, Neonatal, and Pregnancy-Related Mortality Rates by Race: 1980 to 2020

[Deaths per 1,000 live births, except as noted. Data based on death certificates, fetal death records, and birth certificates. Excludes deaths of nonresidents of the United States. Race categories are consistent with 1977 Office of Management and Budget (OMB) standards. Multiple-race data reported according to 1997 OMB standards were bridged to the single-race categories of 1977 OMB standards. See also Appendix III]

Race and year	Infant [1]	Neonatal [1]		Post- neonatal [1]	Pregnancy- related mortality rate [2]
		Under 28 days	Under 7 days		
ALL RACES					
1980....................	12.6	8.5	7.1	4.1	(NA)
1990....................	9.2	5.8	4.8	3.4	10.0
2000....................	6.9	4.6	3.7	2.3	14.5
2005....................	6.9	4.5	3.6	2.3	15.4
2010....................	6.1	4.0	3.2	2.1	16.7
2015....................	5.9	3.9	3.2	2.0	17.2
2018....................	5.7	3.8	3.0	1.9	17.3
2019....................	5.6	3.7	3.0	1.9	(NA)
2020....................	5.4	3.6	2.9	1.9	(NA)
WHITE [3]					
1980....................	10.9	7.4	6.1	3.5	(NA)
1990....................	7.6	4.8	3.9	2.8	(NA)
2000....................	5.7	3.8	3.0	1.9	(NA)
2005....................	5.7	3.8	3.0	1.9	(NA)
2010....................	5.2	3.5	2.7	1.7	(NA)
2015....................	4.9	3.3	2.7	1.6	(NA)
2018....................	4.7	3.2	2.6	1.5	(NA)
2019....................	4.7	3.1	2.5	1.5	(NA)
2020....................	(NA)	(NA)	(NA)	(NA)	(NA)
BLACK [3]					
1980....................	22.2	14.6	12.3	7.6	(NA)
1990....................	18.0	11.6	9.7	6.4	(NA)
2000....................	14.1	9.4	7.6	4.7	(NA)
2005....................	13.7	9.1	7.3	4.7	(NA)
2010....................	11.6	7.5	6.0	4.1	(NA)
2015....................	11.4	7.4	6.0	4.0	(NA)
2018....................	10.7	6.8	5.5	3.8	(NA)
2019....................	10.6	6.7	5.4	3.9	(NA)
2020....................	(NA)	(NA)	(NA)	(NA)	(NA)

NA Not available. [1] Infant (under 1 year of age), neonatal (under 28 days), early neonatal (under 7 days), and postneonatal (28 days–11 months). [2] Number of pregnancy-related deaths per 100,000 live births. [3] Infant deaths are tabulated by race of decedent.

Source: U.S. National Center for Health Statistics, "Health, United States—Data Finder," <www.cdc.gov/nchs/hus/index.htm>; CDC WONDER Online database, "Multiple Cause of Death, 1999-2020," <wonder.cdc.gov/>; and "Pregnancy Mortality Surveillance System," <www.cdc.gov/reproductivehealth/maternal-mortality/index.html>; accessed August 2022.

Table 115. Infant Deaths and Mortality Rates by Race, Hispanic Origin, and State: 2019

[Rates are for infant (under 1 year old) deaths per 1,000 live births in specified group. Infant deaths are based on race or Hispanic origin of decedent; live births are based on race or Hispanic origin of mother. Race and Hispanic-origin categories are consistent with 1997 Office of Management and Budget (OMB) standards. See Technical Notes in source for more detail]

State	Total [1]		White alone, non-Hispanic		Black alone, non-Hispanic		Hispanic	
	Number	Rate	Number	Rate	Number	Rate	Number	Rate
United States.........	**20,921**	**5.6**	**8,366**	**4.4**	**6,092**	**11.1**	**4,607**	**5.2**
Alabama...............	449	7.7	186	5.6	219	12.0	36	7.3
Alaska.................	48	4.9	13	(B)	2	(B)	4	(B)
Arizona................	429	5.4	124	3.9	49	10.8	192	5.7
Arkansas..............	251	6.9	137	5.9	79	11.3	23	5.6
California..............	1,879	4.2	410	3.4	212	9.5	994	4.9
Colorado..............	306	4.9	120	3.3	32	10.5	122	6.7
Connecticut...........	153	4.5	62	3.4	38	9.0	46	5.3
Delaware..............	66	6.3	16	(B)	32	11.4	8	(B)
District of Columbia....	44	4.9	4	(B)	37	9.0	3	(B)
Florida................	1,330	6.1	420	4.5	499	10.5	333	4.9
Georgia...............	888	7.0	282	5.1	471	10.8	100	5.4
Hawaii................	85	5.1	13	(B)	6	(B)	25	9.7
Idaho.................	97	4.4	69	4.1	2	(B)	19	(B)
Illinois................	794	5.7	299	4.0	258	11.1	160	5.3
Indiana................	525	6.5	338	5.8	114	11.1	53	6.3
Iowa..................	189	5.0	126	4.3	29	10.3	19	(B)
Kansas................	201	5.7	113	4.6	28	11.4	39	6.4
Kentucky..............	266	5.0	186	4.4	49	9.7	17	(B)
Louisiana..............	468	7.9	160	5.4	260	11.8	38	7.6
Maine.................	63	5.4	51	4.9	5	(B)	2	(B)
Maryland..............	413	5.9	116	4.0	199	9.3	66	5.1
Massachusetts..........	254	3.7	111	2.8	47	6.9	67	4.7
Michigan...............	690	6.4	321	4.4	246	12.1	57	8.0
Minnesota.............	302	4.6	144	3.2	65	7.9	32	6.2
Mississippi.............	322	8.8	118	6.5	186	11.8	11	(B)
Missouri...............	433	6.0	259	4.9	124	11.8	22	5.0
Montana...............	54	4.9	35	4.0	–	(B)	4	(B)
Nebraska..............	125	5.1	70	4.1	20	12.1	26	6.0
Nevada................	201	5.7	55	4.4	49	10.9	73	5.5
New Hampshire........	37	3.1	31	3.1	1	(B)	1	(B)
New Jersey............	428	4.3	146	3.2	126	9.4	116	4.2
New Mexico...........	129	5.6	24	3.9	8	(B)	76	5.9
New York..............	955	4.3	355	3.3	295	9.2	188	3.7
North Carolina..........	808	6.8	287	4.6	353	12.7	107	5.6
North Dakota...........	77	7.4	49	6.5	6	(B)	4	(B)
Ohio..................	930	6.9	493	5.2	337	14.9	46	6.0
Oklahoma..............	343	7.0	156	5.7	66	16.1	43	5.6
Oregon................	203	4.9	120	4.3	8	(B)	51	6.2
Pennsylvania...........	788	5.9	392	4.4	235	13.4	97	5.8
Rhode Island...........	61	6.0	24	4.3	12	(B)	16	(B)
South Carolina.........	391	6.9	136	4.3	211	12.6	28	4.9
South Dakota..........	80	7.0	50	6.1	5	(B)	4	(B)
Tennessee.............	563	7.0	266	5.1	215	13.5	61	7.2
Texas.................	2,075	5.5	570	4.6	505	10.7	908	5.1
Utah..................	249	5.3	159	4.8	2	(B)	62	7.6
Vermont...............	15	(B)	14	(B)	–	(B)	1	(B)
Virginia...............	570	5.9	221	4.2	205	10.1	77	5.3
Washington............	365	4.3	178	3.8	44	11.5	78	4.8
West Virginia...........	112	6.2	96	5.8	12	(B)	2	(B)
Wisconsin..............	371	5.9	200	4.5	89	13.0	46	7.1
Wyoming..............	46	7.0	41	8.0	–	(B)	4	(B)

– Represents zero. B Base figure too small to meet statistical standards for reliability. [1] Includes other races, not shown separately.

Source: U.S. National Center for Health Statistics, National Vital Statistics Reports (NVSR), *Deaths: Final Data for 2019*, Vol. 70, No. 8, July 2021. See also <www.cdc.gov/nchs/deaths.htm>.

Table 116. Maternal Mortality—Number and Rate by Race, Hispanic Origin, and Age: 2018 to 2020

[Rates per 100,000 live births. Maternal mortality is deaths of women that occur while pregnant or within 42 days of being pregnant, from any cause related to or aggravated by the pregnancy or its management, but not from accidental or incidental causes. Data are shown for maternal causes using the International Classification of Diseases, Tenth Revision (ICD-10)]

Race/ethnicity and age	2018 Live births (number)	2018 Maternal deaths (number)	2018 Maternal mortality rate	2019 Live births (number)	2019 Maternal deaths (number)	2019 Maternal mortality rate	2020 Live births (number)	2020 Maternal deaths (number)	2020 Maternal mortality rate
Total [1]...............	**3,791,712**	**658**	**17.4**	**3,747,540**	**754**	**20.1**	**3,613,647**	**861**	**23.8**
Under 25 years old.......	907,782	96	10.6	877,803	111	12.6	825,403	114	13.8
25 to 39 years old.........	2,756,974	458	16.6	2,739,976	544	19.9	2,658,445	607	22.8
40 years and over..........	126,956	104	81.9	129,761	98	75.5	129,799	140	107.9
White alone, non-Hispanic.............	1,956,413	291	14.9	1,915,912	343	17.9	1,843,432	352	19.1
Under 25 years old.......	391,829	41	10.5	374,129	49	13.1	348,666	40	11.5
25 to 39 years old.........	1,504,888	207	13.8	1,480,595	248	16.8	1,433,839	253	17.6
40 years and over..........	59,696	43	72.0	61,188	46	75.2	60,927	59	96.8
Black alone, non-Hispanic.............	552,029	206	37.3	548,075	241	44.0	529,811	293	55.3
Under 25 years old.......	176,243	27	15.3	169,853	32	18.8	159,541	46	28.8
25 to 39 years old.........	358,276	137	38.2	360,206	179	49.7	351,648	198	56.3
40 years and over..........	17,510	42	239.9	18,016	30	166.5	18,622	49	263.1
Hispanic [2]...............	886,210	105	11.8	886,467	112	12.6	866,713	158	18.2
Under 25 years old.......	275,553	21	7.6	270,948	23	8.5	258,635	20	7.7
25 to 39 years old.........	579,553	72	12.4	584,109	71	12.2	576,690	111	19.2
40 years and over..........	31,104	12	(S)	31,410	18	(S)	31,388	27	86

S Data do not meet publication standards. [1] Includes race/ethnicities not shown separately. [2] Persons of Hispanic origin may be of any race.

Source: U.S. National Center for Health Statistics, *Maternal Mortality Rates in the United States, 2020*, February 2022. See also <www.cdc.gov/nchs/maternal-mortality/index.htm>.

Table 117. Coronavirus Disease 2019 (COVID-19) Deaths by Sex and State: Through August 27, 2022

[Data are provisional for the period January 1, 2020 through August 27, 2022, reported as of August 31, 2022; counts are continually revised as more records are received and processed by the National Center for Health Statistics (NCHS). Number of deaths reported in this table are the total number of deaths received and coded as of the date of analysis and do not represent all deaths that occurred in that period. Data during this period are incomplete because of the lag in time between when the death occurred and when the death certificate is completed, submitted to NCHS, and processed for reporting purposes. This delay can range from 1 to 8 weeks or more. COVID-19 deaths are identified using a new International Classification of Diseases, Tenth Revision (ICD–10) code. When COVID-19 is reported as a cause of death, or when it is listed as a "probable" or "presumed" cause, the death is coded as U07.1. This can include cases with or without laboratory confirmation]

State and jurisdiction	Total	Female	Male	State and jurisdiction	Total	Female	Male
United States [1]........	**1,042,093**	**466,327**	**575,766**	Montana...............	3,658	1,576	2,082
Alabama..................	19,945	9,212	10,733	Nebraska...............	5,142	2,198	2,944
Alaska...................	1,355	550	805	Nevada.................	11,459	4,439	7,020
Arizona..................	28,085	11,516	16,569	New Hampshire.........	2,610	1,214	1,396
Arkansas.................	11,556	5,360	6,196	New Jersey.............	32,987	14,963	18,024
California................	99,417	41,026	58,391	New Mexico............	8,118	3,502	4,616
Colorado.................	13,890	5,945	7,945	New York [2]...........	37,790	17,876	19,914
Connecticut..............	11,351	5,562	5,789	New York City..........	35,891	15,345	20,546
Delaware.................	3,054	1,447	1,607	North Carolina.........	30,573	14,399	16,174
District of Columbia.....	2,066	901	1,165	North Dakota...........	2,868	1,219	1,649
Florida..................	74,225	32,317	41,908	Ohio...................	44,955	21,033	23,922
Georgia..................	33,590	15,443	18,147	Oklahoma..............	16,720	7,531	9,189
Hawaii...................	1,607	645	962	Oregon.................	7,885	3,504	4,381
Idaho....................	5,180	2,152	3,028	Pennsylvania..........	47,990	22,783	25,207
Illinois..................	35,621	16,051	19,570	Rhode Island...........	3,738	1,857	1,881
Indiana..................	24,570	11,515	13,055	South Carolina.........	18,882	8,633	10,249
Iowa.....................	9,953	4,607	5,346	South Dakota..........	3,153	1,418	1,735
Kansas...................	9,237	4,146	5,091	Tennessee..............	27,338	12,463	14,875
Kentucky.................	17,651	8,470	9,181	Texas..................	97,867	41,308	56,559
Louisiana................	16,456	7,503	8,953	Utah...................	5,377	2,097	3,280
Maine....................	2,671	1,271	1,400	Vermont................	722	333	389
Maryland.................	16,219	7,700	8,519	Virginia...............	20,436	9,604	10,832
Massachusetts...........	19,056	9,254	9,802	Washington............	13,052	5,647	7,405
Michigan.................	33,340	15,103	18,237	West Virginia..........	7,333	3,422	3,911
Minnesota................	13,428	6,114	7,314	Wisconsin..............	15,295	6,912	8,383
Mississippi..............	13,727	6,597	7,130	Wyoming...............	1,680	765	915
Missouri.................	21,324	9,879	11,445	Puerto Rico............	4,976	2,190	2,786

[1] U.S. total does not include Puerto Rico. [2] Excludes New York City.

Source: U.S. National Center for Health Statistics, "COVID-19 Death Data and Resources," <www.cdc.gov/nchs/nvss/covid-19.htm>, and "Provisional COVID-19 Death Counts by Sex and Age," <www.cdc.gov/nchs/covid19/covid-19-mortality-data-files.htm>, accessed August 2022.

Table 118. Age-Adjusted Death Rates by Major Cause: 1960 to 2020

[Age-adjusted rates per 100,000 population. Age-adjusted death rates were prepared using the direct method, in which age specific death rates for a population of interest are applied to a standard population distributed by age. Age adjustment eliminates the differences in observed rates between points in time or among compared population groups that result from age differences in population composition. Beginning 1999, deaths classified according to International Classification of Diseases, Tenth Revision (ICD-10); for earlier years, causes of death were classified according to the revisions then in use. Changes in classification of causes of death due to these revisions may result in discontinuities in cause-of-death trends. See Appendix III]

Year	Diseases of the heart	Malignant neoplasms (cancer)	Coronavirus disease 2019, COVID-19	Accidents[1]	Cerebrovascular diseases	Chronic lower respiratory diseases	Alzheimer's disease	Diabetes mellitus	Influenza and pneumonia	Nephritis, nephrotic syndrome and nephrosis
1960	559.0	193.9	(X)	63.1	177.9	12.5	(NA)	22.5	53.7	10.6
1970	492.7	198.6	(X)	62.2	147.7	21.3	(NA)	24.3	41.7	5.5
1980	412.1	207.9	(X)	46.4	96.4	28.3	(NA)	18.1	31.4	9.1
1990	321.8	216.0	(X)	36.3	65.3	37.2	6.3	20.7	36.8	9.3
1995	293.4	209.9	(X)	34.4	63.1	40.1	8.4	23.2	33.4	9.5
2000	257.6	199.6	(X)	34.9	60.9	44.2	18.1	25.0	23.7	13.5
2001	249.5	196.5	(X)	35.7	58.4	43.9	19.3	25.4	22.2	14.1
2002	244.6	194.3	(X)	37.1	57.2	43.9	20.8	25.6	23.2	14.4
2003	236.3	190.9	(X)	37.6	54.6	43.7	22.1	25.5	22.6	14.7
2004	221.6	186.8	(X)	38.1	51.2	41.6	22.6	24.7	20.4	14.5
2005	216.8	185.1	(X)	39.5	48.0	43.9	24.0	24.9	21.0	14.7
2006	205.5	181.8	(X)	40.2	44.8	41.0	23.7	23.6	18.4	14.8
2007	196.1	179.3	(X)	40.4	43.5	41.4	23.8	22.8	16.8	14.9
2008	192.1	176.4	(X)	39.2	42.1	44.7	25.8	22.0	17.6	15.1
2009	182.8	173.5	(X)	37.5	39.6	42.7	24.2	21.0	16.5	15.1
2010	179.1	172.8	(X)	38.0	39.1	42.2	25.1	20.8	15.1	15.3
2011	173.7	169.0	(X)	39.1	37.9	42.5	24.7	21.6	15.7	13.4
2012	170.5	166.5	(X)	39.1	36.9	41.5	23.8	21.2	14.4	13.1
2013	169.8	163.2	(X)	39.4	36.2	42.1	23.5	21.2	15.9	13.2
2014	167.0	161.2	(X)	40.5	36.5	40.5	25.4	20.9	15.1	13.2
2015	168.5	158.5	(X)	43.2	37.6	41.6	29.4	21.3	15.2	13.4
2016	165.5	155.8	(X)	47.4	37.3	40.6	30.3	21.0	13.5	13.1
2017	165.0	152.5	(X)	49.4	37.6	40.9	31.0	21.5	14.3	13.0
2018	163.6	149.1	(X)	48.0	37.1	39.7	30.5	21.4	14.9	12.9
2019	161.5	146.2	(X)	49.3	37.0	38.2	29.8	21.6	12.3	12.7
2020	168.2	144.1	85.0	57.6	38.8	36.4	32.4	24.8	13.0	12.7

NA Not available. X Not applicable. [1] Unintentional injuries.

Source: U.S. National Center for Health Statistics, National Vital Statistics Reports (NVSR), *Deaths: Final Data*, annual report; and CDC WONDER Online Database, "Multiple Cause of Death, 1999-2020," <wonder.cdc.gov>, accessed February 2022. See also <www.cdc.gov/nchs/nvss/deaths.htm>.

Table 119. Deaths by Leading Cause, Race, and Hispanic Origin: 2020

[Rank based on number of deaths. Race and Hispanic origin are reported separately on death certificates. Persons of Hispanic origin may be of any race. Data for Hispanic persons are not tabulated by race; data for non-Hispanic persons are tabulated by race. Data for racial and ethnic groups other than non-Hispanic White and non-Hispanic Black should be interpreted with caution because of misreporting of Hispanic origin and race on the death certificate. Cause of death based on International Classification of Diseases, Tenth Revision (ICD-10). See Appendix III]

Cause of death	White, Non-Hispanic Rank	White, Non-Hispanic Deaths	Black, Non-Hispanic Rank	Black, Non-Hispanic Deaths	American Indian or Alaska Native, Non-Hispanic Rank	American Indian or Alaska Native, Non-Hispanic Deaths	Asian or Pacific Islander, Non-Hispanic Rank	Asian or Pacific Islander, Non-Hispanic Deaths	Hispanic Rank	Hispanic Deaths
All causes	(X)	2,491,026	(X)	451,792	(X)	26,755	(X)	99,574	(X)	305,708
Diseases of heart	1	530,355	1	93,320	2	3,868	2	18,992	2	48,323
Malignant neoplasms (cancer)	2	463,160	2	70,963	3	3,385	1	19,869	3	43,942
Coronavirus disease 2019 (COVID-19)	3	209,606	3	56,528	1	4,436	3	13,597	1	65,237
Accidents (unintended injuries)	4	141,335	4	29,133	4	2,670	6	3,927	4	23,152
Chronic lower respiratory diseases	5	130,947	8	12,361	7	861	8	2,176	9	5,949
Cerebrovascular diseases	6	116,752	5	22,404	8	848	4	6,655	5	13,370
Alzheimer's disease	7	109,316	9	10,893	11	436	7	3,574	7	9,867
Diabetes mellitus	8	64,098	6	19,495	6	1,356	5	4,123	6	12,832
Influenza and pneumonia	9	39,003	12	6,885	10	451	9	2,169	10	4,875
Chronic liver disease and cirrhosis	10	36,919	14	4,082	5	1,522	15	943	8	8,049
Intentional self-harm (suicide)	11	35,716	15	3,415	9	663	12	1,502	12	4,571
Nephritis, nephrotic syndrome and nephrosis	12	35,008	10	10,581	13	381	11	1,777	11	4,701
Parkinson disease	13	34,423	18	2,059	16	125	13	1,163	16	2,462
Septicemia	14	28,803	13	6,832	14	308	14	1,001	15	3,018
Essential hypertension and hypertensive renal disease	15	27,951	11	8,051	15	266	10	1,841	14	3,674
Assault (homicide)	20	6,256	7	13,594	12	382	18	373	13	3,920

X Not applicable.

Source: U.S. National Center for Health Statistics, National Vital Statistics Reports (NVSR), *Deaths: Leading Causes*, annual; and CDC WONDER Online database, "Multiple Cause of Death, 1999-2020," <wonder.cdc.gov>, accessed February 2022. See also <www.cdc.gov/nchs/nvss/deaths.htm>.

Table 120. Deaths and Death Rates by Selected Causes: 2019 and 2020

[Rates per 100,000 population. Figures are weighted data rounded to the nearest individual, so categories may not add to total or subtotal. Excludes deaths of nonresidents of the United States. Deaths classified according to the International Classification of Diseases, Tenth Revision (ICD-10). See also Appendix III]

Cause of death	2019			2020		
	Number	Rate	Age-adjusted rate [1]	Number	Rate	Age-adjusted rate [1]
All causes [2]	**2,854,838**	**869.7**	**715.2**	**3,383,729**	**1,027.0**	**835.4**
Major cardiovascular diseases [2]	869,883	265.0	213.4	923,237	280.2	223.0
Diseases of heart	659,041	200.8	161.5	696,962	211.5	168.2
Acute rheumatic fever and chronic rheumatic heart disease	3,647	1.1	0.9	3,876	1.2	0.9
Hypertensive heart disease	55,355	16.9	13.7	65,701	19.9	16.0
Hypertensive heart and renal disease	10,193	3.1	2.5	12,389	3.8	3.0
Ischemic heart disease	360,900	110.0	88.0	382,820	116.2	91.8
Acute myocardial infarction	104,280	31.8	25.5	109,199	33.1	26.3
Other heart diseases	228,946	69.7	56.4	232,176	70.5	56.5
Heart failure	86,177	26.3	21.0	85,855	26.1	20.7
Essential (primary) hypertension and hypertensive renal disease	36,524	11.1	8.9	41,907	12.7	10.1
Cerebrovascular diseases	150,005	45.7	37.0	160,264	48.6	38.8
Atherosclerosis	4,417	1.3	1.1	4,757	1.4	1.1
Malignant neoplasms (cancer) [2]	599,601	182.7	146.2	602,350	182.8	144.1
Malignant neoplasms of lip, oral cavity, and pharynx	10,492	3.2	2.5	10,835	3.3	2.6
Malignant neoplasms of esophagus	15,962	4.9	3.8	15,673	4.8	3.7
Malignant neoplasms of stomach	11,092	3.4	2.8	11,233	3.4	2.8
Malignant neoplasms of colon, rectum and anus	52,986	16.1	13.1	53,095	16.1	12.9
Malignant neoplasms of liver and intrahepatic bile ducts	27,959	8.5	6.6	28,227	8.6	6.6
Malignant neoplasms of pancreas	45,886	14.0	11.0	46,774	14.2	11.1
Malignant neoplasms of trachea, bronchus and lung	139,682	42.6	33.4	136,166	41.3	31.9
Malignant melanoma of skin	8,092	2.5	2.0	8,214	2.5	2.0
Malignant neoplasm of breast	42,748	13.0	10.7	42,765	13.0	10.5
Malignant neoplasm of ovary	13,445	4.1	3.3	13,438	4.1	3.2
Malignant neoplasm of prostate	31,638	9.6	7.7	32,707	9.9	7.8
Malignant neoplasms of kidney and renal pelvis	14,021	4.3	3.4	14,441	4.4	3.4
Malignant neoplasms of bladder	16,796	5.1	4.1	16,682	5.1	4.0
Malignant neoplasms of meninges, brain and other parts of central nervous system	17,233	5.3	4.3	18,034	5.5	4.5
Malignant neoplasms of lymphoid, hematopoietic and related tissue [2]	57,460	17.5	14.2	57,742	17.5	14.0
Non-Hodgkin's lymphoma	20,270	6.2	5.0	20,171	6.1	4.9
Leukemia	23,170	7.1	5.8	23,422	7.1	5.8
Accidents (unintentional injuries)	173,040	52.7	49.3	200,955	61.0	57.6
Transport accidents [2]	41,949	12.8	12.3	45,162	13.7	13.3
Motor vehicle accidents	39,107	11.9	11.5	42,339	12.9	12.5
Nontransport accidents [2]	131,091	39.9	37.0	155,793	47.3	44.3
Falls	39,443	12.0	9.8	42,114	12.8	10.3
Accidental discharge of firearms	486	0.1	0.2	535	0.2	0.2
Accidental drowning and submersion	3,692	1.1	1.1	4,177	1.3	1.3
Accidental exposure to smoke, fire and flames	2,692	0.8	0.7	2,951	0.9	0.8
Accidental poisoning and exposure to noxious substances	65,773	20.0	20.2	87,404	26.5	26.9
Chronic lower respiratory diseases [2]	156,979	47.8	38.2	152,657	46.3	36.4
Bronchitis, chronic and unspecified	448	0.1	0.1	457	0.1	0.1
Emphysema	7,272	2.2	1.8	7,425	2.3	1.7
Asthma	3,524	1.1	1.0	4,145	1.3	1.1
Pneumonitis due to solids and liquids	19,184	5.8	4.7	18,327	5.6	4.4
Coronavirus disease 2019 (COVID-19)	(X)	(X)	(X)	350,831	106.5	85.0
Influenza and pneumonia [2]	49,783	15.2	12.3	53,544	16.3	13.0
Influenza	5,902	1.8	1.5	5,943	1.8	1.5
Pneumonia	43,881	13.4	10.8	47,601	14.4	11.6
Septicemia (blood poisoning)	38,431	11.7	9.5	40,050	12.2	9.7
Viral hepatitis	4,285	1.3	1.0	3,943	1.2	0.9
Human immunodeficiency virus (HIV) disease	5,044	1.5	1.4	5,115	1.6	1.4
Anemias	5,254	1.6	1.3	5,633	1.7	1.4
Diabetes mellitus	87,647	26.7	21.6	102,188	31.0	24.8
Nutritional deficiencies	11,570	3.5	2.8	14,682	4.5	3.5
Malnutrition	11,252	3.4	2.7	14,337	4.4	3.4
Parkinson's disease	35,311	10.8	8.8	40,284	12.2	9.9
Alzheimer's disease	121,499	37.0	29.8	134,242	40.7	32.4
Chronic liver disease and cirrhosis	44,358	13.5	11.3	51,642	15.7	13.3
Alcoholic liver disease	24,110	7.3	6.4	29,505	9.0	7.9
Nephritis, nephrotic syndrome, and nephrosis [2]	51,565	15.7	12.7	52,547	15.9	12.7
Renal failure	50,534	15.4	12.4	51,478	15.6	12.5
Intentional self-harm (suicide)	47,511	14.5	13.9	45,979	14.0	13.5
Intentional self-harm (suicide) by discharge of firearms	23,941	7.3	6.8	24,292	7.4	7.0
Assault (homicide)	19,141	5.8	6.0	24,576	7.5	7.8
Assault (homicide) by discharge of firearms	14,414	4.4	4.6	19,384	5.9	6.2
Events of undetermined intent	5,683	1.7	1.7	6,042	1.8	1.8
Complications of medical and surgical care	5,329	1.6	1.3	5,361	1.6	1.3
Enterocolitis due to Clostridium difficile [3]	4,533	1.4	1.1	4,069	1.2	1.0
Drug-induced deaths [3]	74,511	22.7	22.8	96,096	29.2	29.5
Alcohol-induced deaths [3]	39,043	11.9	10.4	49,061	14.9	13.1
Injury by firearms [3]	39,707	12.1	11.9	45,222	13.7	13.6

[1] See text, this section. [2] Includes other causes, not shown separately. [3] Also included in selected other categories.

Source: U.S. National Center for Health Statistics, National Vital Statistics Reports, *Deaths: Final Data*, annual report; and CDC WONDER Online database, "Multiple Cause of Death, 1999-2020," <wonder.cdc.gov>, accessed February 2022. See also <www.cdc.gov/nchs/nvss/deaths.htm>.

Table 121. Deaths by Age and Selected Cause: 2020

Table 121. Deaths by Age and Selected Cause: 2020

[Deaths are classified according to the International Classification of Diseases, Tenth Revision (ICD-10). See Appendix III]

Cause of death	All ages[1]	Under 1 year	1 to 4 years	5 to 14 years	15 to 24 years	25 to 34 years	35 to 44 years	45 to 54 years	55 to 64 years	65 to 74 years	75 to 84 years	85 years and over
All causes[2]	3,383,729	19,582	3,529	5,623	35,816	73,486	104,490	191,142	440,549	674,507	822,084	1,012,805
Septicemia	40,050	117	43	35	106	386	770	979	2,510	6,242	9,656	9,530
Human immunodeficiency virus (HIV) disease[2]	5,115	2	0	0	53	468	770	1,165	1,542	833	242	40
Malignant neoplasms (cancer)[2]	602,350	54	307	792	1,306	3,573	10,730	34,589	110,243	175,464	162,876	102,413
Malignant neoplasm of esophagus	15,673	0	0	0	3	28	216	1,016	3,694	5,328	3,660	1,728
Malignant neoplasms of colon, rectum, and anus	53,095	1	0	0	46	408	1,523	4,800	10,544	13,337	12,241	10,195
Malignant neoplasms of liver and intrahepatic bile ducts	28,227	4	15	14	38	97	321	1,424	6,806	9,988	6,591	2,929
Malignant neoplasms of pancreas	46,774	0	0	0	9	56	458	2,447	8,695	15,072	13,227	6,810
Malignant neoplasms of trachea, bronchus, and lung	136,166	0	1	5	13	126	756	5,058	26,664	45,572	40,513	17,458
Malignant neoplasms of breast	42,765	0	0	0	5	377	1,769	4,555	8,648	10,750	9,195	7,464
Malignant neoplasm of ovary	13,438	0	0	4	14	96	285	1,065	2,837	4,014	3,478	1,645
Malignant neoplasms of prostate	32,707	0	0	0	1	1	32	326	2,944	8,083	10,944	10,375
Malignant neoplasms of kidney and renal pelvis	14,441	2	15	22	25	61	210	893	2,690	4,302	3,828	2,393
Malignant neoplasms of bladder	16,682	0	0	0	1	18	65	342	1,696	3,800	5,372	5,388
Malignant neoplasms of meninges, brain and other parts of central nervous system	18,034	10	73	310	237	414	862	1,830	4,158	5,275	3,441	1,424
Malignant neoplasms of lymphoid, hematopoietic and related tissue[2]	57,742	20	88	187	324	546	977	2,355	7,036	14,711	18,645	12,852
Non-Hodgkins lymphoma	20,171	0	3	14	44	144	319	759	2,495	5,184	6,591	4,617
Leukemia	23,422	20	85	171	261	346	541	956	2,616	5,685	7,405	5,336
Diabetes mellitus	102,188	0	5	56	312	1,168	2,904	7,546	18,002	27,213	25,445	19,536
Parkinson's disease	40,284	0	0	0	1	3	6	85	873	6,187	17,323	15,806
Alzheimer's disease	134,242	0	0	0	0	0	7	100	1,393	9,300	37,728	85,713
Major cardiovascular diseases[2]	923,237	363	171	252	1,135	4,922	15,300	42,859	110,555	174,090	226,698	346,865
Diseases of heart[2]	696,962	242	112	167	870	3,984	12,177	34,169	88,551	134,827	167,346	254,492
Hypertensive heart disease	65,701	11	4	3	53	613	2,076	4,948	10,550	11,863	12,434	23,161
Ischemic heart diseases	382,820	6	2	3	86	997	5,133	18,668	53,125	81,703	95,669	127,398
Acute myocardial infarction	109,199	10	11	3	35	407	1,962	6,822	18,101	26,220	27,429	28,208
Heart failure	85,855	10	11	9	50	212	675	1,904	5,554	11,881	21,343	44,206
Essential (primary) hypertension and hypertensive renal disease	41,907	10	5	7	23	149	576	1,830	4,983	7,766	9,915	16,663
Cerebrovascular diseases	160,264	104	55	76	188	600	2,008	5,686	14,153	26,363	43,252	67,777
Influenza and pneumonia	53,544	125	84	105	185	578	1,148	2,511	6,295	10,460	13,832	18,219
Influenza	5,943	14	36	42	70	179	256	516	1,043	1,206	1,247	1,301
Pneumonia	47,601	111	48	63	115	399	892	1,995	5,252	9,254	12,585	16,918
Chronic lower respiratory diseases[2]	152,657	8	19	147	220	400	793	3,538	18,816	38,559	49,363	40,790
Pneumonitis due to solids and liquids[2]	18,327	7	3	12	41	119	246	587	1,652	3,229	4,957	7,473
Chronic liver disease and cirrhosis[2]	51,642	0	0	4	47	1,631	4,938	9,503	16,151	11,895	5,676	1,796
Alcoholic liver disease	29,505	0	0	0	29	1,375	3,904	6,786	10,198	5,524	1,472	216
Nephritis, nephrotic syndrome, and nephrosis[2]	52,547	44	12	10	68	321	859	2,344	6,213	11,461	14,696	16,518
Renal failure	51,478	42	7	8	62	304	825	2,284	6,090	11,249	14,401	16,205
Accidents (unintentional injuries)[2]	200,955	1,194	1,153	1,566	15,117	31,315	31,057	27,819	28,915	18,609	18,646	25,541
Transport accidents[2]	45,162	77	363	957	7,149	8,460	6,643	6,059	6,856	4,532	2,843	1,220
Motor vehicle accidents	42,339	74	349	892	6,922	8,117	6,228	5,629	6,223	4,089	2,637	1,176
Nontransport accidents[2]	155,793	1,117	790	609	7,968	22,855	24,414	21,760	22,059	14,077	15,803	24,321
Falls	42,114	7	12	28	152	359	625	1,282	3,140	5,925	11,176	19,407
Accidental poisoning and exposure to noxious substances	87,404	17	37	61	6,664	20,938	21,943	18,078	15,030	3,891	522	205
Intentional self-harm (suicide)	45,979	0	0	601	6,062	8,454	7,314	7,249	7,160	4,716	3,032	522
Assault (homicide)	24,576	246	311	454	6,466	7,125	4,482	2,542	1,753	742	329	124
Assault (homicide) by discharge of firearms	19,384	10	75	309	5,966	6,158	3,540	1,783	992	353	152	45
Coronavirus disease 2019 (COVID-19)	350,831	35	19	49	501	2,254	6,079	16,964	42,090	76,277	97,030	109,529

[1] Includes persons with age not stated, not shown separately. [2] Includes other causes, not shown separately.

Source: U.S. National Center for Health Statistics, National Vital Statistics Reports (NVSR), Deaths: Final Data, annual report; and CDC WONDER Online Database, "Multiple Cause of Death, 1999-2020," <wonder.cdc.gov>, accessed February 2022. See also <www.cdc.gov/nchs/nvss/deaths.htm>.

Table 122. Deaths and Death Rates by Leading Cause and Age: 2020

[Rates per 100,000 population in specified group. Data are based on the International Classification of Diseases, Tenth Revision (ICD-10)]

Age and cause of death	Number	Rate	Age and cause of death	Number	Rate
ALL AGES [1]			**25 TO 34 YEARS (continued)**		
All causes............................	3,383,729	1,027.0	Malignant neoplasms (cancer).................	3,573	7.8
Diseases of heart........................	696,962	211.5	COVID-19.................................	2,254	4.9
Malignant neoplasms (cancer)............	602,350	182.8	Chronic liver disease and cirrhosis..........	1,631	3.5
Coronavirus disease, 2019 (COVID-19)........	350,831	106.5	Diabetes mellitus........................	1,168	2.5
Accidents (unintentional injuries)........	200,955	61.0	Cerebrovascular diseases.................	600	1.3
Cerebrovascular diseases................	160,264	48.6	Pregnancy, childbirth and the puerperium.......	594	1.3
Chronic lower respiratory diseases........	152,657	46.3	**35 TO 44 YEARS**		
Alzheimer's disease.....................	134,242	40.7	All causes............................	104,490	248.0
Diabetes mellitus.......................	102,188	31.0	Accidents (unintentional injuries).........	31,057	73.7
Influenza and pneumonia................	53,544	16.3	Diseases of heart.......................	12,177	28.9
Nephritis, nephrotic syndrome and nephrosis. ..	52,547	15.9	Malignant neoplasms (cancer)............	10,730	25.5
1 TO 4 YEARS			Intentional self-harm (suicide)............	7,314	17.4
All causes............................	3,529	22.7	COVID-19.................................	6,079	14.4
Accidents (unintentional injuries)........	1,153	7.4	Chronic liver disease and cirrhosis..........	4,938	11.7
Congenital malformations [2].............	382	2.5	Assault (homicide)......................	4,482	10.6
Assault (homicide)......................	311	2.0	Diabetes mellitus.......................	2,904	6.9
Malignant neoplasms (cancer)............	307	2.0	Cerebrovascular diseases.................	2,008	4.8
Diseases of heart.......................	112	0.7	Influenza and pneumonia................	1,148	2.7
Influenza and pneumonia................	84	0.5	**45 TO 54 YEARS**		
Cerebrovascular diseases................	55	0.4	All causes............................	191,142	473.5
Conditions originating in the perinatal period....	54	0.3	Malignant neoplasms (cancer)............	34,589	85.7
Septicemia............................	43	0.3	Diseases of heart.......................	34,169	84.6
In situ and benign neoplasms and neoplasms			Accidents (unintentional injuries)........	27,819	68.9
of uncertain or unknown behavior.........	35	0.2	COVID-19.................................	16,964	42.0
5 TO 9 YEARS			Chronic liver disease and cirrhosis..........	9,503	23.5
All causes............................	2,210	10.9	Diabetes mellitus.......................	7,546	18.7
Accidents (unintentional injuries)........	685	3.4	Intentional self-harm (suicide)............	7,249	18.0
Malignant neoplasms (cancer)............	382	1.9	Cerebrovascular diseases.................	5,686	14.1
Congenital malformations [2].............	171	0.8	Chronic lower respiratory diseases........	3,538	8.8
Assault (homicide)......................	169	0.8	Assault (homicide)......................	2,542	6.3
Diseases of heart.......................	56	0.3	**55 TO 64 YEARS**		
Influenza and pneumonia................	55	0.3	All causes............................	440,549	1,038.9
Chronic lower respiratory diseases........	54	0.3	Malignant neoplasms (cancer)............	110,243	260.0
Cerebrovascular diseases................	32	0.2	Diseases of heart.......................	88,551	208.8
In situ and benign neoplasms and neoplasms			COVID-19.................................	42,090	99.3
of uncertain or unknown behavior..............	28	0.1	Accidents (unintentional injuries)........	28,915	68.2
Intentional self-harm (suicide)............	20	0.1	Chronic lower respiratory diseases........	18,816	44.4
10 TO 14 YEARS			Diabetes mellitus.......................	18,002	42.5
All causes............................	3,413	16.4	Chronic liver disease and cirrhosis..........	16,151	38.1
Accidents (unintentional injuries)........	881	4.2	Cerebrovascular diseases.................	14,153	33.4
Intentional self-harm (suicide)............	581	2.8	Intentional self-harm (suicide)............	7,160	16.9
Malignant neoplasms (cancer)............	410	2.0	Influenza and pneumonia................	6,295	14.8
Assault (homicide)......................	285	1.4	**65 to 74 YEARS**		
Congenital malformations [2].............	150	0.7	All causes............................	674,507	2,072.3
Diseases of heart.......................	111	0.5	Malignant neoplasms (cancer)............	175,464	539.1
Chronic lower respiratory diseases........	93	0.4	Diseases of heart.......................	134,827	414.2
Diabetes mellitus.......................	50	0.2	COVID-19.................................	76,227	234.3
Influenza and pneumonia................	50	0.2	Chronic lower respiratory diseases........	38,559	118.5
Cerebrovascular diseases................	44	0.2	Diabetes mellitus.......................	27,213	83.6
15 TO 19 YEARS			Cerebrovascular diseases.................	26,363	81.0
All causes............................	12,278	58.6	Accidents (unintentional injuries)........	18,609	57.2
Accidents (unintentional injuries)........	4,654	22.2	Chronic liver disease and cirrhosis..........	11,895	36.5
Assault (homicide)......................	2,572	12.3	Nephritis, nephrotic syndrome and nephrosis. ..	11,461	35.2
Intentional self-harm (suicide)............	2,216	10.6	Influenza and pneumonia................	10,460	32.1
Malignant neoplasms (cancer)............	549	2.6	**75 TO 84 YEARS**		
Diseases of heart.......................	294	1.4	All causes............................	822,084	4,997.0
Congenital malformations [2].............	184	0.9	Diseases of heart.......................	167,346	1,017.2
COVID-19.................................	118	0.6	Malignant neoplasms (cancer)............	162,876	990.0
Diabetes mellitus.......................	93	0.4	COVID-19.................................	97,030	589.8
Chronic lower respiratory diseases........	90	0.4	Chronic lower respiratory diseases........	49,363	300.1
Cerebrovascular diseases................	75	0.4	Cerebrovascular diseases.................	43,252	262.9
20 TO 24 YEARS			Alzheimer's disease.....................	37,728	229.3
All causes............................	23,538	109.0	Diabetes mellitus.......................	25,445	154.7
Accidents (unintentional injuries)........	10,463	48.5	Accidents (unintentional injuries)........	18,646	113.3
Assault (homicide)......................	3,894	18.0	Parkinson's disease.....................	17,323	105.3
Intentional self-harm (suicide)............	3,846	17.8	Nephritis, nephrotic syndrome and nephrosis. ..	14,696	89.3
Malignant neoplasms (cancer)............	757	3.5	**85 YEARS AND OVER**		
Diseases of heart.......................	576	2.7	All causes............................	1,012,805	15,210.9
COVID-19.................................	383	1.8	Diseases of heart.......................	254,492	3,822.1
Diabetes mellitus.......................	219	1.0	COVID-19.................................	109,529	1,645.0
Congenital malformations [2].............	200	0.9	Malignant neoplasms (cancer)............	102,413	1,538.1
Pregnancy, childbirth and the puerperium.......	155	0.7	Alzheimer's disease.....................	85,713	1,287.3
Chronic lower respiratory diseases........	130	0.6	Cerebrovascular diseases.................	67,777	1,017.9
25 TO 34 YEARS			Chronic lower respiratory diseases........	40,790	612.6
All causes............................	73,486	159.5	Accidents (unintentional injuries)........	25,541	383.6
Accidents (unintentional injuries)........	31,315	68.0	Diabetes mellitus.......................	19,536	293.4
Intentional self-harm (suicide)............	8,454	18.4	Influenza and pneumonia................	18,219	273.6
Assault (homicide)......................	7,125	15.5	Essential hypertension and		
Diseases of heart.......................	3,984	8.6	hypertensive renal disease......................	16,663	250.3

[1] Includes deaths under 1 year of age. [2] Congenital malformations, deformations and chromosomal abnormalities.

Source: U.S. National Center for Health Statistics, *Deaths: Leading Causes*, annual; and CDC WONDER Online database, "Multiple Cause of Death, 1999-2020," <wonder.cdc.gov>, accessed February 2022. See also <www.cdc.gov/nchs/nvss/deaths.htm>.

Table 123. Age-Adjusted Death Rates for Major Causes of Death by State: 2020

[Age-adjusted rates per 100,000 resident population as of July 1. Excludes nonresidents of the United States. Causes of death classified according to the International Classification of Diseases, Tenth Revision (ICD-10)]

State	All causes of death	Diseases of heart	Malig- nant neo- plasms (cancer)	Corona- virus disease 2019, (COVID-19)	Accidents Total	Motor vehicle acci- dents	Cerebro- vascular diseases	Chronic lower respira- tory disease	Alz- heimer's disease	Diabetes mellitus	Inten- tional self- harm (suicide)
U.S.	**835.4**	**168.2**	**144.1**	**85.0**	**57.6**	**12.5**	**38.8**	**36.4**	**32.4**	**24.8**	**13.5**
AL.	1,057.8	237.5	161.6	103.6	59.6	19.9	54.5	52.9	50.8	23.6	16.0
AK.	769.4	139.8	143.7	35.7	65.5	11.0	34.2	31.0	26.8	24.8	27.5
AZ.	800.3	144.8	127.7	87.6	69.1	13.6	32.7	36.6	32.7	26.5	17.6
AR.	1,002.4	222.5	163.8	90.2	58.0	22.5	43.5	60.4	45.6	33.8	19.0
CA.	705.3	144.0	130.3	68.7	44.1	10.9	39.1	28.1	40.6	25.4	10.0
CO.	754.2	128.1	127.2	69.6	60.5	11.3	35.9	39.3	36.9	18.0	21.5
CT.	769.1	138.4	133.8	112.3	63.5	8.9	28.4	24.4	20.3	17.5	9.3
DE.	835.6	159.6	151.1	73.4	70.9	12.0	52.5	32.7	35.1	23.8	12.3
DC.	862.3	187.7	138.1	117.0	77.1	6.1	37.9	20.4	12.3	24.3	5.5
FL.	735.7	143.1	136.3	56.4	67.7	15.7	43.5	33.4	19.8	22.8	13.2
GA.	902.1	183.7	147.6	81.7	50.8	16.3	43.0	41.6	45.9	23.9	13.7
HI.	588.0	125.0	123.8	16.8	39.4	5.8	38.4	17.8	22.8	17.0	12.9
ID.	784.4	151.9	136.5	63.9	50.8	13.2	37.4	39.4	36.7	22.7	23.2
IL.	850.7	171.4	150.9	99.2	53.4	10.2	42.3	34.0	28.7	22.2	10.5
IN.	967.1	183.9	162.7	103.2	66.9	13.8	40.3	53.7	34.3	29.6	15.0
IA.	848.6	172.9	147.8	99.0	45.7	11.4	31.9	39.4	31.9	24.7	18.0
KS.	882.2	167.0	151.4	90.5	53.4	14.1	36.7	43.9	25.3	28.5	18.4
KY.	1,031.6	204.5	177.3	74.2	87.5	18.9	42.4	56.2	32.3	27.7	17.7
LA.	1,044.7	221.5	159.9	118.0	79.4	18.2	46.6	41.6	45.8	33.1	13.7
ME.	787.2	146.2	161.5	20.2	76.9	13.1	33.0	41.5	27.9	23.9	16.4
MD.	820.5	168.3	142.3	80.9	44.4	10.2	42.5	27.7	15.8	23.9	9.2
MA.	756.7	126.9	135.2	100.2	54.3	5.1	24.4	27.8	18.6	17.2	8.4
MI.	907.7	205.0	157.3	85.9	56.8	11.8	44.5	41.9	36.9	26.0	14.0
MN.	739.6	118.1	138.7	71.9	52.6	8.5	32.1	30.6	35.0	21.0	13.1
MS.	1,138.7	245.6	176.0	123.5	73.0	28.6	54.5	59.2	58.0	41.0	13.9
MO.	937.6	196.7	157.9	87.1	68.4	16.8	40.3	47.0	34.9	23.1	18.2
MT.	839.4	162.7	141.5	75.5	61.9	19.6	31.0	42.4	23.8	23.5	26.1
NE.	817.2	143.8	147.6	84.4	42.3	11.9	36.1	43.4	32.2	26.2	14.9
NV.	853.3	201.3	144.1	88.4	53.5	11.1	40.3	44.9	28.7	24.2	18.2
NH.	737.8	146.5	145.0	40.9	58.1	8.1	29.8	33.4	26.1	19.2	16.4
NJ.	834.4	166.3	133.4	141.6	50.3	6.6	31.8	25.0	22.1	21.2	7.1
NM.	912.5	152.7	129.8	106.2	85.5	20.0	34.6	41.3	26.6	29.3	24.2
NY.	797.1	183.9	128.8	139.1	41.7	6.0	24.8	25.5	14.0	21.2	8.0
NC.	856.4	156.2	148.4	60.4	67.1	16.3	44.4	38.5	37.5	26.9	13.2
ND.	848.8	147.3	139.5	121.9	51.9	13.3	32.1	34.6	39.7	24.3	18.2
OH.	953.9	196.9	159.1	87.3	78.2	11.5	45.3	44.6	38.0	28.3	13.8
OK.	1,011.6	244.1	171.1	100.3	62.0	17.7	41.0	60.1	38.2	32.8	21.9
OR.	741.2	134.0	145.8	26.0	52.0	11.8	40.5	34.6	37.0	24.5	18.3
PA.	866.0	175.7	153.2	88.1	69.0	9.3	36.7	32.8	23.2	23.6	12.6
RI.	806.6	150.5	141.6	104.3	65.6	6.2	26.7	29.5	31.9	23.2	8.5
SC.	937.6	170.9	153.9	77.7	77.8	21.3	43.5	43.6	40.4	28.5	16.3
SD.	868.1	155.2	148.1	127.0	58.5	16.8	35.5	36.9	39.7	29.2	21.0
TN.	1,015.1	212.0	164.4	80.3	86.5	18.2	43.6	51.2	44.4	30.1	17.2
TX.	862.1	173.9	139.8	105.2	44.2	13.8	41.1	36.2	44.6	26.7	13.3
UT.	765.3	155.6	119.5	48.6	49.4	10.2	34.1	32.7	42.9	27.3	20.8
VT.	737.7	167.1	152.2	16.0	67.1	9.5	28.3	37.4	31.0	17.5	18.1
VA.	792.8	152.0	146.6	56.3	52.5	10.4	39.9	32.8	28.7	24.7	13.5
WA.	711.2	134.6	138.7	36.7	51.3	8.6	34.7	29.6	42.9	22.7	15.2
WV.	1,055.8	197.8	177.0	56.2	122.2	16.3	36.7	59.5	35.9	41.3	19.4
WI.	828.4	162.2	148.7	70.2	71.5	11.6	36.4	35.6	33.2	22.0	14.5
WY.	842.0	160.4	136.3	63.1	60.4	18.8	30.6	53.5	32.1	20.7	30.5

Source: U.S. National Center for Health Statistics, National Vital Statistics Reports (NVSR), *Deaths: Final Data*, annual; and CDC WONDER Online database, "Multiple Cause of Death, 1999-2020," <wonder.cdc.gov>, accessed February 2022.

Table 124. Death Rates For Heart Disease by Selected Characteristics: 1980 to 2020

[Rates per 100,000 population. Excludes deaths of nonresidents of the United States. Beginning 1999, deaths classified according to the International Classification of Diseases, Tenth Revision (ICD-10); for earlier years, causes of death were classified according to the revisions then in use. Changes in classification of causes of death due to these revisions may result in discontinuities in cause-of-death trends. See Appendix III]

Characteristic	1980	1990	2000	2005	2010	2015	2018	2019	2020
All ages, age-adjusted [1]	**412.1**	**321.8**	**257.6**	**216.8**	**179.1**	**168.5**	**163.6**	**161.5**	**168.2**
All ages, crude rate	**336.0**	**289.5**	**252.6**	**220.7**	**193.6**	**197.2**	**200.3**	**200.8**	**211.5**
Under 1 year	22.8	20.1	13.0	8.9	8.3	7.3	7.5	7.1	6.5
1 to 4 years	2.6	1.9	1.2	0.9	1.0	0.9	0.7	0.8	0.7
5 to 14 years	0.9	0.9	0.7	0.6	0.5	0.5	0.4	0.4	0.4
15 to 24 years	2.9	2.5	2.6	2.6	2.4	2.3	2.1	2.0	2.0
25 to 34 years	8.3	7.6	7.4	8.3	7.8	8.0	7.8	7.6	8.6
35 to 44 years	44.6	31.4	29.2	29.2	25.8	25.6	25.5	25.2	28.9
45 to 54 years	180.2	120.5	94.2	89.7	81.6	79.3	77.4	76.2	84.6
55 to 64 years	494.1	367.3	261.2	212.8	186.6	188.1	191.7	190.4	208.8
65 to 74 years	1,218.6	894.3	665.6	512.3	409.2	389.5	392.4	388.8	414.2
75 to 84 years	2,993.1	2,295.7	1,780.3	1,458.5	1,172.0	1,071.6	1,008.3	991.2	1,017.2
85 years and over	7,777.1	6,739.9	5,926.1	5,188.3	4,285.2	3,986.5	3,844.8	3,798.3	3,822.1
MALE									
All ages, age-adjusted [1]	**538.9**	**412.4**	**320.0**	**268.2**	**225.1**	**211.8**	**207.5**	**204.8**	**214.2**
White	539.6	409.2	316.7	264.8	222.9	211.2	206.3	203.9	211.3
Black	561.4	485.4	392.5	338.8	280.6	258.6	259.5	256.0	284.5
American Indian, Alaska Native	320.5	264.1	222.2	191.7	158.7	148.0	141.0	137.9	144.0
Asian, Pacific Islander	286.9	220.7	185.5	149.4	127.2	109.7	110.2	106.0	116.5
Hispanic origin [2]	(NA)	270.0	238.2	210.5	165.1	146.4	143.0	141.9	157.5
Non-Hispanic, White [2]	(NA)	413.6	319.9	267.9	226.9	216.3	212.3	209.8	216.5
All ages, crude rate	**368.6**	**297.6**	**249.8**	**222.3**	**202.5**	**211.7**	**220.0**	**221.3**	**235.9**
Under 1 year	25.5	21.9	13.3	9.6	9.8	7.5	7.6	7.6	6.1
1 to 4 years	2.8	1.9	1.4	1.0	1.1	1.0	0.7	0.9	0.7
5 to 14 years	1.0	0.9	0.8	0.6	0.5	0.5	0.4	0.4	0.4
15 to 24 years	3.7	3.1	3.2	3.5	3.2	3.0	2.8	2.4	2.5
25 to 34 years	11.4	10.3	9.6	11.2	10.7	10.3	10.1	10.0	11.4
35 to 44 years	68.7	48.1	41.4	41.3	36.0	35.1	35.1	34.6	39.7
45 to 54 years	282.6	183.0	140.2	131.6	117.8	112.1	110.1	109.0	120.8
55 to 64 years	746.8	537.3	371.7	303.9	269.5	269.4	276.3	272.7	301.1
65 to 74 years	1,728.0	1,250.0	898.3	680.1	553.0	529.7	541.9	537.2	571.3
75 to 84 years	3,834.3	2,968.2	2,248.1	1,815.1	1,475.7	1,354.4	1,282.2	1,261.2	1,301.0
85 years and over	8,752.7	7,418.4	6,430.0	5,713.2	4,833.6	4,495.1	4,358.7	4,302.4	4,325.4
FEMALE									
All ages, age-adjusted [1]	**320.8**	**257.0**	**210.9**	**177.5**	**143.3**	**133.6**	**127.9**	**126.2**	**130.2**
White	315.9	250.9	205.6	173.2	140.4	132.4	126.6	125.3	127.8
Black	378.6	327.5	277.6	234.5	185.3	165.7	162.2	158.5	175.1
American Indian, Alaska Native	175.4	153.1	143.6	129.3	103.5	94.0	85.1	79.9	83.6
Asian, Pacific Islander	132.3	149.2	115.7	97.5	81.2	68.5	65.2	63.6	69.1
Hispanic origin [2]	(NA)	177.2	163.7	139.9	107.8	93.0	87.6	86.4	94.3
Non-Hispanic, White [2]	(NA)	252.6	206.8	174.8	142.5	135.6	130.3	129.1	131.2
All ages, crude rate	**305.1**	**281.8**	**255.3**	**219.0**	**184.9**	**183.1**	**181.3**	**180.9**	**187.9**
Under 1 year	20.0	18.3	12.5	8.2	6.8	7.2	7.4	6.5	6.9
1 to 4 years	2.5	1.9	1.0	0.9	0.9	0.9	0.7	0.8	0.7
5 to 14 years	0.9	0.8	0.5	0.6	0.4	0.5	0.4	0.5	0.4
15 to 24 years	2.1	1.8	2.1	1.7	1.5	1.5	1.4	1.7	1.5
25 to 34 years	5.3	5.0	5.2	5.3	4.9	5.6	5.4	5.2	5.8
35 to 44 years	21.4	15.1	17.2	17.2	15.6	16.2	16.0	15.9	18.1
45 to 54 years	84.5	61.0	49.8	49.1	46.5	47.4	45.5	44.2	49.4
55 to 64 years	272.1	215.7	159.3	128.0	109.3	112.3	112.8	113.6	122.5
65 to 74 years	828.6	616.8	474.0	369.5	284.2	266.2	261.4	258.9	276.9
75 to 84 years	2,497.0	1,893.8	1,475.1	1,213.8	952.7	855.9	795.2	780.5	795.0
85 years and over	7,350.5	6,478.1	5,720.9	4,955.1	4,020.3	3,717.6	3,561.6	3,515.0	3,535.8

NA Not available. [1] Age-adjusted death rates were prepared using the direct method, in which age-specific death rates for a population of interest are applied to a standard population distributed by age. Age adjustment eliminates the differences in observed rates between points in time or among compared population groups that result from age differences in population composition. [2] Persons of Hispanic origin may be of any race. Prior to 1997, excludes data from states lacking a Hispanic-origin item on their death certificates. See text, this section.

Source: U.S. National Center for Health Statistics, *Health, United States*, annual; and CDC WONDER Online database, "Multiple Cause of Death, 1999-2020," <wonder.cdc.gov>, accessed April 2022. See also <www.cdc.gov/nchs/nvss/deaths.htm>.

Table 125. Death Rates For Cerebrovascular Diseases (Stroke) by Sex and Age: 1990 to 2020

[Rates per 100,000 population. Excludes deaths of nonresidents of the United States. Beginning 1999, deaths classified according to the International Classification of Diseases, Tenth Revision (ICD-10); for earlier years, causes of death were classified according to the revisions then in use. Changes in classification of causes of death due to these revisions may result in discontinuities in cause-of-death trends. For explanation of age adjustment, see text, this section]

Age	Total				Male				Female			
	1990	2000	2010	2020	1990	2000	2010	2020	1990	2000	2010	2020
All ages, age-adjusted [1]	65.3	60.9	39.1	38.8	68.5	62.4	39.3	39.8	62.6	59.1	38.3	37.4
All ages, crude rate	57.8	59.6	41.9	48.6	46.7	46.9	34.5	42.9	68.4	71.8	49.1	54.2
Under 1 year	3.8	3.3	3.3	2.8	4.4	3.8	3.2	2.9	3.1	2.7	3.4	2.7
1 to 4 years	0.3	0.3	0.3	0.4	0.3	(B)	0.3	0.4	0.3	0.4	0.3	0.3
5 to 14 years	0.2	0.2	0.2	0.2	0.2	0.2	0.3	0.2	0.2	0.2	0.2	0.2
15 to 24 years	0.6	0.5	0.4	0.4	0.7	0.5	0.5	0.4	0.6	0.5	0.4	0.5
25 to 34 years	2.2	1.5	1.3	1.3	2.1	1.5	1.3	1.4	2.2	1.5	1.2	1.2
35 to 44 years	6.4	5.8	4.6	4.8	6.8	5.8	5.0	5.7	6.1	5.7	4.2	3.8
45 to 54 years	18.7	16.0	13.1	14.1	20.5	17.5	14.9	16.6	17.0	14.5	11.4	11.6
55 to 64 years	47.9	41.0	29.3	33.4	54.3	47.2	34.7	40.8	42.2	35.3	24.3	26.4
65 to 74 years	144.2	128.6	81.7	81.0	166.6	145.0	92.0	93.0	126.7	115.1	72.8	70.5
75 to 84 years	498.0	461.3	288.3	262.9	551.1	490.8	295.2	277.8	466.2	442.1	283.4	251.3
85 years and over	1,628.9	1,589.2	993.8	1,017.9	1,528.5	1,484.3	892.0	911.8	1,667.6	1,632.0	1,043.0	1,078.3

B Figure too small to meet statistical standards for reliability. [1] See footnote 1, Table 124.

Source: U.S. National Center for Health Statistics, *Health, United States*, annual; and CDC WONDER Online database, "Multiple Cause of Death, 1999-2020," <wonder.cdc.gov>, accessed April 2022. See also <www.cdc.gov/nchs/nvss/deaths.htm>.

Table 126. Death Rates For All and Selected Types of Malignant Neoplasms (Cancer) by Age: 1990 to 2020

[Rates per 100,000 population. Excludes deaths of nonresidents of the United States. Beginning 1999, deaths classified according to the International Classification of Diseases, Tenth Revision (ICD-10); for earlier years, causes of death were classified according to the revisions then in use. Changes in classification of causes of death due to these revisions may result in discontinuities in cause-of-death trends. For explanation of age adjustment, see text, this section. See Appendix III]

Item	1990	2000	2005	2010	2015	2018	2019	2020
ALL MALIGNANT NEOPLASMS								
All ages, age-adjusted [1]	216.0	199.6	185.1	172.8	158.5	149.1	146.2	144.1
All ages, crude rate	203.2	196.5	189.3	186.2	185.4	183.2	182.7	182.8
Under 1 year	2.3	2.4	1.9	1.6	1.3	1.3	1.5	1.4
1 to 4 years	3.5	2.7	2.4	2.1	2.2	2.0	1.8	2.0
5 to 14 years	3.1	2.5	2.5	2.2	2.1	2.1	1.9	1.9
15 to 24 years	4.9	4.4	4.0	3.7	3.4	3.2	3.3	3.1
25 to 34 years	12.6	9.8	9.2	8.8	8.4	8.1	7.8	7.8
35 to 44 years	43.3	36.6	33.5	28.8	26.9	25.8	25.7	25.5
45 to 54 years	158.9	127.5	118.6	111.6	99.7	89.6	87.1	85.7
55 to 64 years	449.6	366.7	323.9	300.1	284.1	269.6	263.3	260.0
65 to 74 years	872.3	816.3	733.2	666.1	594.3	554.4	543.3	539.1
75 to 84 years	1,348.5	1,335.6	1,272.8	1,202.2	1,100.8	1,031.5	1,005.9	990.0
85 years old and over	1,752.9	1,819.4	1,778.2	1,729.5	1,628.6	1,577.7	1,571.0	1,538.1
MALIGNANT NEOPLASM OF BREAST FOR FEMALES								
All ages, age-adjusted [1]	33.3	26.8	24.2	22.1	20.3	19.7	19.4	19.1
All ages, crude rate	34.0	29.2	27.4	26.1	25.4	25.6	25.4	25.3
Under 25 years	(B)	(B)	(B)	(B)	(B)	(B)	(B)	(B)
25 to 34 years	2.9	2.3	1.8	1.6	1.8	1.8	1.9	1.7
35 to 44 years	17.8	12.4	11.4	9.8	9.0	8.7	9.2	8.4
45 to 54 years	45.4	33.0	28.7	25.7	23.7	21.9	22.2	22.1
55 to 64 years	78.6	59.3	54.0	47.7	43.3	40.5	40.4	39.1
65 to 74 years	111.7	88.3	78.5	73.9	66.7	63.9	62.1	61.1
75 to 84 years	146.3	128.9	119.6	109.1	101.7	103.4	96.9	98.2
85 years old and over	196.8	205.7	191.2	185.8	173.3	176.1	173.5	173.9
MALIGNANT NEOPLASM OF TRACHEA, BRONCHUS, AND LUNG								
All ages, age-adjusted [1]	59.3	56.1	52.7	47.6	40.5	34.8	33.4	31.9
All ages, crude rate	56.8	55.3	53.9	51.3	47.9	43.5	42.6	41.3
Under 25 years	(Z)	(Z)	(Z)	(Z)	(Z)	(Z)	(Z)	(B)
25 to 34 years	0.7	0.5	0.3	0.4	0.3	0.3	0.2	0.3
35 to 44 years	6.8	6.1	5.3	3.3	2.5	1.9	1.9	1.8
45 to 54 years	46.8	31.6	29.7	26.9	20.5	15.1	13.6	12.5
55 to 64 years	160.6	122.4	102.4	85.4	76.8	68.5	64.8	62.9
65 to 74 years	288.4	284.2	256.3	223.9	181.0	150.9	144.3	140.0
75 to 84 years	333.3	370.8	375.0	357.2	306.4	267.9	260.9	246.3
85 years old and over	242.5	302.1	328.2	332.4	316.1	286.2	281.3	262.2

B Base figure too small to meet statistical standards for reliability of a derived figure. Z Less than 0.05. [1] Age-adjusted death rates were prepared using the direct method, in which age specific death rates for a population of interest are applied to a standard population distributed by age. Age adjustment eliminates the differences in observed rates between points in time or among compared population groups that result from age differences in population composition.

Source: U.S. National Center for Health Statistics, *Health, United States*, annual; and CDC WONDER Online database, "Multiple Cause of Death, 1999-2020," <wonder.cdc.gov>, accessed April 2022. See also <www.cdc.gov/nchs/nvss/deaths.htm>.

Table 127. Deaths and Death Rates for Coronavirus Disease 2019 (COVID-19) by Sex, Age, and Race/Ethnicity: 2020

[Rates per 100,000 population; based on resident population as of July 1. Data shown for underlying cause of death classified as U07.1 (COVID-19) under the International Classification of Diseases, Tenth Revision (ICD-10)]

Characteristic	Number			Crude rate			Age-adjusted rate [1]		
	Total	Male	Female	Total	Male	Female	Total	Male	Female
Total [2].....................	**350,831**	**192,512**	**158,319**	**106.5**	**118.6**	**94.7**	**85.0**	**107.7**	**66.6**
AGE									
Under 1 year.............................	35	23	12	0.9	1.2	(B)	(X)	(X)	(X)
1 to 4 years.............................	19	11	8	(B)	(B)	(B)	(X)	(X)	(X)
5 to 14 years...........................	49	28	21	0.1	0.1	0.1	(X)	(X)	(X)
15 to 24 years.........................	501	309	192	1.2	1.4	0.9	(X)	(X)	(X)
25 to 34 years.........................	2,254	1,466	788	4.9	6.3	3.5	(X)	(X)	(X)
35 to 44 years.........................	6,079	4,068	2,011	14.4	19.3	9.5	(X)	(X)	(X)
45 to 54 years.........................	16,964	11,385	5,579	42.0	57.1	27.3	(X)	(X)	(X)
55 to 64 years.........................	42,090	26,997	15,093	99.3	131.8	68.9	(X)	(X)	(X)
65 to 74 years.........................	76,277	47,014	29,263	234.3	309.6	168.5	(X)	(X)	(X)
75 to 84 years.........................	97,030	54,719	42,311	589.8	757.5	458.5	(X)	(X)	(X)
85 years and over......................	109,529	46,489	63,040	1,645.0	1,925.3	1,485.5	(X)	(X)	(X)
RACE/ETHNICITY									
Non-Hispanic:									
White...................................	209,606	110,300	99,306	104.5	111.6	97.7	66.3	81.7	54.1
Black...................................	56,528	29,946	26,582	129.6	143.2	117.0	140.0	182.8	111.0
Asian or Pacific Islander.............	13,597	8,060	5,537	63.9	79.0	50.0	63.7	86.8	45.4
American Indian or Alaska Native. ..	4,436	2,424	2,012	160.4	178.9	142.5	165.4	199.6	136.8
Hispanic [3].............................	65,237	40,830	24,407	106.4	132.0	80.3	155.5	214.5	107.5

X Not applicable. B Figure too small to meet statistical standards for reliability. [1] See footnote 1, Table 124. [2] Total counts and rates include deaths for persons with age and race/ethnicity "not stated." [3] Persons of Hispanic origin may be of any race.

Source: U.S. National Center for Health Statistics, CDC WONDER Online database, "Multiple Cause of Death, 1999-2020," <wonder.cdc.gov>, accessed April 2022. See also <www.cdc.gov/nchs/nvss/deaths.htm>.

Table 128. Firearm Deaths and Death Rates by Sex and Race/Ethnicity: 2010 to 2020

[Rates are age-adjusted, per 100,000 population, and based on populations enumerated as of April 1 for census years and as of July 1 for all other years. Deaths are those attributable to injury by firearms. Race and Hispanic-origin categories are consistent with 1977 Office of Management and Budget (OMB) standards. Prior to 2018, the number of states reporting multiple-race data according to new 1997 OMB standards varied widely. To provide a comparison of data by race between the 1977 and 1997 OMB standards, those reporting more than one race were "bridged" to single-race categories; see Technical notes, source]

Sex and race/ethnicity	Number of deaths					Age-adjusted rates				
	2010	2015	2018	2019	2020	2010	2015	2018	2019	2020
Total [1].............................	**31,672**	**36,252**	**39,740**	**39,707**	**45,222**	**10.1**	**11.1**	**11.9**	**11.9**	**13.6**
Male...................................	27,356	31,032	33,955	34,041	38,981	17.9	19.4	20.7	20.7	23.8
Female.................................	4,316	5,220	5,785	5,666	6,241	2.7	3.2	3.4	3.4	3.8
Non-Hispanic:										
White...................................	20,513	23,026	24,789	24,151	24,870	9.5	10.6	11.3	11.0	11.6
Male...................................	17,350	19,208	20,860	20,340	21,000	16.6	18.0	19.4	18.9	19.8
Female.................................	3,163	3,818	3,929	3,811	3,870	3.0	3.6	3.7	3.6	3.7
Black...................................	7,330	8,904	9,801	10,395	14,119	17.8	20.7	22.4	23.6	31.8
Male...................................	6,607	8,068	8,640	9,277	12,530	33.4	38.6	40.5	43.1	57.5
Female.................................	723	836	1,161	1,118	1,589	3.4	3.8	5.2	5.0	7.1
American Indian/Alaska Native..	293	353	427	385	522	11.2	13.3	15.6	14.1	18.7
Male...................................	246	301	356	315	450	18.7	23.0	26.4	23.3	32.9
Female.................................	47	52	71	70	72	3.9	4.0	5.3	5.1	5.0
Asian or Pacific Islander.........	383	504	618	640	627	2.2	2.5	2.9	2.9	2.9
Male...................................	329	426	503	532	531	4.1	4.4	4.9	5.1	5.0
Female.................................	54	78	115	108	96	0.6	0.8	1.0	0.9	0.8
Hispanic [2].............................	3,008	3,332	4,018	4,058	5,003	5.9	5.8	6.6	6.6	7.9
Male...................................	2,694	2,912	3,521	3,503	4,395	10.5	10.1	11.6	11.2	13.8
Female.................................	314	420	497	555	608	1.3	1.5	1.7	1.9	1.9

[1] Includes deaths for other races and those not stated, not shown separately. [2] Persons of Hispanic origin may be of any race.

Source: U.S. National Center for Health Statistics, *Deaths: Final Data, Supplemental Tables*, annual; and CDC WONDER Online database "Multiple Cause of Death, 1999-2020," <wonder.cdc.gov>, accessed April 2022. See also <www.cdc.gov/nchs/nvss/deaths.htm>.

Table 129. Death Rates For Suicide by Selected Characteristics: 1990 to 2020

[Rates per 100,000 population. Excludes deaths of nonresidents of the United States. Beginning 1999, deaths classified according to the International Classification of Diseases, Tenth Revision (ICD-10). See Appendix III]

Characteristic	1990	2000	2005	2010	2015	2017	2018	2019	2020
All ages, age-adjusted [1]	**12.5**	**10.4**	**10.9**	**12.1**	**13.3**	**14.0**	**14.2**	**13.9**	**13.5**
All ages, crude rate	**12.4**	**10.4**	**11.0**	**12.4**	**13.7**	**14.5**	**14.8**	**14.5**	**14.0**
5 to 14 years	0.8	0.7	0.7	0.7	1.0	1.3	1.5	1.3	1.5
15 to 24 years	13.2	10.2	9.9	10.5	12.5	14.5	14.5	13.9	14.2
15 to 19 years	11.1	8.0	7.5	7.5	9.8	11.8	11.4	10.5	10.6
20 to 24 years	15.1	12.5	12.4	13.6	15.1	17.0	17.4	17.3	17.8
25 to 34 years	15.2	12.0	12.7	14.0	15.7	17.5	17.6	17.5	18.4
35 to 44 years	15.3	14.5	15.1	16.0	17.1	17.9	18.2	18.1	17.4
45 to 54 years	14.8	14.4	16.5	19.6	20.3	20.2	20.0	19.6	18.0
55 to 64 years	16.0	12.1	13.7	17.5	18.9	19.0	20.2	19.4	16.9
65 to 74 years	17.9	12.5	12.4	13.7	15.2	15.6	16.3	15.5	14.5
75 to 84 years	24.9	17.6	16.8	15.7	17.9	18.0	18.7	18.6	18.4
85 years and over	22.2	19.6	18.3	17.6	19.4	20.1	19.1	20.1	20.9
AGE-ADJUSTED RATES [1]									
Male	**21.5**	**17.7**	**18.1**	**19.8**	**21.1**	**22.4**	**22.8**	**22.4**	**22.0**
White	22.8	19.1	19.8	22.0	23.6	25.1	25.5	24.9	24.3
Black	12.8	10.0	9.2	9.1	9.6	11.0	11.6	11.8	12.4
Asian, Pacific Islander	9.6	8.6	7.3	9.5	9.1	9.7	10.4	10.7	10.1
American Indian, Alaska Native	20.1	16.0	17.3	15.5	18.8	20.4	20.9	20.3	22.5
Hispanic [2]	13.7	10.3	9.6	9.9	9.9	11.2	12.1	11.6	12.3
Non-Hispanic, White [2]	23.5	20.2	21.4	24.2	26.6	28.2	28.4	27.9	27.0
Female	**4.8**	**4.0**	**4.4**	**5.0**	**6.0**	**6.1**	**6.2**	**6.0**	**5.5**
White	5.2	4.3	4.9	5.6	6.9	6.9	7.0	6.8	6.1
Black	2.4	1.8	1.8	1.8	2.0	2.7	2.8	2.8	2.8
Asian, Pacific Islander	4.1	2.8	3.2	3.4	4.0	3.8	3.8	3.8	3.8
American Indian, Alaska Native	3.6	3.8	4.2	6.1	6.5	6.6	6.6	6.9	6.6
Hispanic [2]	2.3	1.7	1.8	2.1	2.6	2.6	2.8	3.0	2.8
Non-Hispanic, White [2]	5.4	4.7	5.3	6.2	7.8	7.9	8.0	7.6	6.9

[1] Age-adjusted death rates were prepared using the direct method, in which age-specific death rates for a population of interest are applied to a standard population distributed by age. Age adjustment eliminates the differences in observed rates between points in time or among compared population groups that result from age differences in population composition. [2] Persons of Hispanic origin may be of any race. Excludes data from states lacking a Hispanic-origin item on their death certificates.

Source: U.S. National Center for Health Statistics, *Health, United States*, annual; and CDC WONDER Online database, "Multiple Cause of Death, 1999-2020," <wonder.cdc.gov>, accessed April 2022. See also <www.cdc.gov/nchs/nvss/deaths.htm>.

Table 130. Suicide Deaths by Age, Sex, and Method: 2020

[It is generally accepted that children under 5 years of age cannot commit suicide. Deaths based on the International Classification of Diseases, Tenth Revision (ICD-10)]

Method	Total	Age								
		5-14 years	15-24 years	25-34 years	35-44 years	45-54 years	55-64 years	65-74 years	75-84 years	85+ years
Total [1]	**45,979**	**601**	**6,062**	**8,454**	**7,314**	**7,249**	**7,160**	**4,716**	**3,032**	**1,389**
MEN										
Total [1]	**36,551**	**390**	**4,859**	**6,882**	**5,723**	**5,514**	**5,539**	**3,743**	**2,645**	**1,255**
Knife or other sharp object	751	–	36	125	150	134	147	86	43	30
Drowning	328	1	50	65	53	42	58	30	19	10
Fall or jump from high place	820	3	133	181	140	112	118	81	29	23
Fire/flame	125	–	8	23	27	28	15	15	5	3
Firearm	21,180	189	2,820	3,366	2,700	2,877	3,308	2,740	2,179	1,001
Poisoning	2,834	4	244	485	438	557	587	274	160	85
Hanging, suffocation, strangulation	9,753	188	1,413	2,455	2,080	1,645	1,201	483	194	94
WOMEN										
Total [1]	**9,428**	**211**	**1,203**	**1,572**	**1,591**	**1,735**	**1,621**	**973**	**387**	**134**
Knife or other sharp object	156	–	4	21	24	37	36	21	8	5
Drowning	170	1	19	23	22	33	39	17	12	4
Fall or jump from high place	254	–	41	39	44	45	46	22	11	6
Fire/flame	50	1	3	3	13	12	8	8	2	–
Firearm	3,112	35	353	535	515	541	581	367	158	27
Poisoning	2,694	30	232	304	406	583	578	364	137	60
Hanging, suffocation, strangulation	2,742	142	501	608	517	441	292	156	58	27

– Represents zero. [1] Includes other methods not shown separately and deaths with age not stated.

Source: U.S. National Center for Health Statistics, CDC WONDER Online database, "Multiple Cause of Death, 1999-2020," <wonder.cdc.gov>, accessed April 2022.

Table 131. Drug Overdose/Poisoning Deaths and Those Involving Opioids: 1999 to 2020

[Rates are age-adjusted and per 100,000 population. Deaths may involve more than one drug and are classified according to the International Classification of Diseases, Tenth Revision (ICD-10). Opioids include opium, heroin, natural and semisynthetic opioids, methadone, synthetic opioids other than methadone, and other and unspecified narcotics]

Year	Total [1]		Opioids					
			Total [1]		Heroin		Synthetic opioids including fentanyl [2]	
	Number	Rate	Number	Rate	Number	Rate	Number	Rate
1999	16,849	6.1	8,050	2.9	1,960	0.7	730	0.3
2000	17,415	6.2	8,407	3.0	1,842	0.7	782	0.3
2001	19,394	6.8	9,496	3.3	1,779	0.6	957	0.3
2002	23,518	8.2	11,920	4.1	2,089	0.7	1,295	0.4
2003	25,785	8.9	12,940	4.5	2,080	0.7	1,400	0.5
2004	27,424	9.4	13,756	4.7	1,878	0.6	1,664	0.6
2005	29,813	10.1	14,918	5.1	2,009	0.7	1,742	0.6
2006	34,425	11.5	17,545	5.9	2,088	0.7	2,707	0.9
2007	36,010	11.9	18,516	6.1	2,399	0.8	2,213	0.7
2008	36,450	11.9	19,582	6.4	3,041	1.0	2,306	0.8
2009	37,004	11.9	20,422	6.6	3,278	1.1	2,946	1.0
2010	38,329	12.3	21,089	6.8	3,036	1.0	3,007	1.0
2011	41,340	13.2	22,784	7.3	4,397	1.4	2,666	0.8
2012	41,502	13.1	23,166	7.4	5,925	1.9	2,628	0.8
2013	43,982	13.8	25,052	7.9	8,257	2.7	3,105	1.0
2014	47,055	14.7	28,647	9.0	10,574	3.4	5,544	1.8
2015	52,404	16.3	33,091	10.4	12,989	4.1	9,580	3.1
2016	63,632	19.8	42,249	13.3	15,469	4.9	19,413	6.2
2017	70,237	21.7	47,600	14.9	15,482	4.9	28,466	9.0
2018	67,367	20.7	46,802	14.6	14,996	4.7	31,335	9.9
2019	70,630	21.6	49,860	15.5	14,019	4.4	36,359	11.4
2020	91,799	28.3	68,630	21 4	13,165	4.1	56,516	17.8

[1] Includes deaths due to other drug types not shown separately. [2] Synthetic opioids other than methadone. Includes drugs such as fentanyl, fentanyl analogs, and tramadol.

Source: U.S. National Center for Health Statistics, *Drug Overdose Deaths in the United States, 1999-2020*, December 2021; and CDC WONDER Online database, "Multiple Cause of Death, 1999-2020," <wonder.cdc.gov>, accessed April 2022.

Table 132. Drug Overdose Deaths and Age-adjusted Death Rates Involving Opioids, Benzodiazepines, and Stimulants by Drug: 2012 to 2017

[Age-adjusted rates per 100,000 population. Deaths may involve other drugs in addition to the referent drug. Deaths involving more than one drug are counted in all relevant categories. Deaths are classified according to the International Classification of Diseases, Tenth Revision (ICD-10). See Appendix III]

Drug	Deaths						Age-adjusted death rates					
	2012	2013	2014	2015	2016	2017	2012	2013	2014	2015	2016	2017
Total	41,502	43,982	47,055	52,404	63,632	70,237	13.1	13.8	14.7	16.3	19.8	21.7
OPIOIDS												
Fentanyl	1,615	1,919	4,223	8,251	18,335	27,299	0.5	0.6	1.3	2.6	5.9	8.7
Heroin	6,155	8,418	10,882	13,318	15,961	15,982	2.0	2.7	3.5	4.3	5.1	5.0
Hydrocodone	3,037	3,113	3,299	3,051	3,199	3,072	1.0	1.0	1.0	0.9	1.0	0.9
Methadone	4,087	3,700	3,498	3,376	3,493	3,286	1.3	1.2	1.1	1.1	1.1	1.0
Morphine	3,513	3,772	4,024	4,226	5,014	4,874	1.1	1.2	1.2	1.3	1.5	1.5
Oxycodone	5,178	4,967	5,431	5,792	6,199	6,053	1.7	1.6	1.7	1.8	1.9	1.8
BENZODIAZEPINES												
Alprazolam	3,803	3,724	4,237	4,801	6,209	6,647	1.2	1.2	1.3	1.5	2.0	2.1
Diazepam	1,577	1,618	1,748	1,796	2,022	2,025	0.5	0.5	0.5	0.5	0.6	0.6
STIMULANTS												
Cocaine	4,780	5,319	5,892	7,324	11,316	14,948	1.5	1.7	1.8	2.3	3.6	4.6
Methamphetamine	2,267	3,194	3,747	5,092	6,762	9,356	0.7	1.0	1.2	1.6	2.1	2.9

Source: National Center for Health Statistics, National Vital Statistics Reports, *Drugs Most Frequently Involved in Drug Overdose Deaths: United States, 2011-2016*, Vol. 67, No. 9, December 2018; and *Regional Differences in the Drugs Most Frequently Involved in Drug Overdose Deaths: United States, 2017*, Vol. 68, No. 12, October 2019. See also <www.cdc.gov/nchs/products/nvsr.htm>.

Table 133. Drug Overdose Death Rates by Sex, Age, and Race/Ethnicity: 2000 to 2020

[Rates per 100,000 resident population. Drug overdose deaths include those resulting from accidental or intentional overdose of a drug, being given the wrong drug, taking the wrong drug in error, taking a drug inadvertently, or other misuses of drugs. These deaths are from all manners and intents, including unintentional, suicide, homicide, legal intervention, operations of war, and undetermined intent. Deaths classified according to the International Classification of Diseases, Tenth Revision (ICD-10). Beginning with 2018 data, all States and the District of Columbia reported race according to 1997 OMB standards and presented single-race estimates (only one race was reported on the death certificate). Data for 2003–2017 were tabulated according to the 1977 standards, and race data were bridged to retain comparability across states as they transitioned from 1977 to 1997 standards. Single-race estimates for 2018-2020 are not completely comparable with bridged-race estimates for earlier years. See source for details]

Characteristic	2000	2005	2010	2014	2015	2016	2017	2018 [3]	2019 [3]	2020 [3]
ALL PERSONS										
All ages, age-adjusted [1]	**6.2**	**10.1**	**12.3**	**14.7**	**16.3**	**19.8**	**21.7**	**20.7**	**21.6**	**28.3**
All ages, crude	**6.2**	**10.1**	**12.4**	**14.8**	**16.3**	**19.7**	**21.6**	**20.6**	**21.5**	**27.9**
Under 15 years old	0.1	0.2	0.2	0.2	0.2	0.2	0.2	0.2	0.3	0.4
15 to 24 years old	3.7	6.9	8.2	8.6	9.7	12.4	12.6	10.8	11.2	16.7
25 to 34 years old	7.9	13.6	18.4	23.1	26.9	34.6	38.4	35.5	35.6	47.3
35 to 44 years old	14.3	19.6	20.8	25.0	28.3	35.0	39.0	38.3	40.5	53.9
45 to 54 years old	11.6	21.1	25.1	28.2	30.0	34.5	37.7	35.3	36.9	46.9
55 to 64 years old	4.2	9.0	15.0	20.3	21.8	25.6	28.0	28.3	30.4	37.3
65 to 74 years old	2.0	3.2	4.7	6.9	7.2	8.2	9.2	10.2	11.3	13.2
75 to 84 years old	2.4	3.1	3.4	3.6	3.6	3.4	3.6	3.9	4.2	4.0
85 years old and over	4.4	4.1	4.7	4.1	4.4	4.0	4.0	3.8	3.6	3.9
AGE-ADJUSTED RATES [1]										
MALE										
Total	**8.3**	**12.8**	**15.0**	**18.3**	**20.8**	**26.2**	**29.1**	**27.9**	**29.6**	**39.5**
White	8.4	13.6	16.8	20.4	23.2	28.8	31.6	30.1	31.4	41.0
Black	10.8	12.8	10.1	13.8	16.8	24.0	29.7	31.5	36.8	52.9
American Indian, Alaska Native	6.1	10.8	11.8	15.9	16.0	17.7	19.7	20.3	22.7	31.3
Asian or Pacific Islander	1.4	2.2	2.5	3.3	4.1	4.7	5.2	(NA)	(NA)	(NA)
Hispanic [2]	7.1	8.4	7.6	9.3	10.9	13.9	15.9	16.6	19.5	27.3
Non-Hispanic, White	8.6	14.7	19.0	23.2	26.2	32.7	35.8	33.8	34.5	44.5
Non-Hispanic, Black	10.9	13.0	10.5	14.2	17.3	24.7	30.8	32.4	37.7	54.8
Non-Hispanic, Asian	(NA)	(NA)	(NA)	(NA)	(NA)	(NA)	(NA)	4.4	5.2	7.2
FEMALE										
Total	**4.1**	**7.3**	**9.6**	**11.1**	**11.8**	**13.4**	**14.4**	**13.6**	**13.7**	**17.1**
White	4.3	8.0	10.9	12.7	13.6	15.2	16.3	15.3	15.2	18.5
Black	4.1	6.0	5.7	7.0	7.5	10.0	11.2	11.2	12.9	18.2
American Indian, Alaska Native	3.7	8.6	9.7	11.2	11.3	13.1	12.7	13.1	15.8	21.3
Asian or Pacific Islander	0.8	1.3	1.5	1.7	1.5	1.8	2.0	(NA)	(NA)	(NA)
Hispanic [2]	2.0	3.0	3.6	4.1	4.4	5.0	5.1	5.2	5.7	7.5
Non-Hispanic, White	4.5	8.8	12.5	14.6	15.8	17.7	19.1	18.0	17.6	21.5
Non-Hispanic, Black	4.2	6.2	5.9	7.3	7.7	10.4	11.7	11.6	13.4	18.9
Non-Hispanic, Asian	(NA)	(NA)	(NA)	(NA)	(NA)	(NA)	(NA)	1.8	1.6	2.2

NA Not available. [1] Age-adjusted rates are calculated using the year 2000 standard population and were prepared using the direct method, in which age specific death rates for a population of interest are applied to a standard population distributed by age. Age adjustment eliminates the differences in observed rates between points in time or among compared population groups that result from age differences in population composition. [2] Persons of Hispanic origin may be of any race. [3] Data based on single-race estimates. Data by race not strictly comparable to bridged-race estimates from prior years; see source for details.

Source: U.S. National Center for Health Statistics, "Health, United States—Data Finder," <www.cdc.gov/nchs/hus/index.htm>; and CDC WONDER Online Database, "Multiple Cause of Death, 2018-2020," <wonder.cdc.gov>; accessed August 2022.

Table 134. Percent of First Marriages Reaching Stated Anniversary by Sex and Year of Marriage: 2014

[In percent except number of marriages (6,609 represents 6,609,000). For currently married couples aged 15 years and over. Based on the 2014 Social Security Administration Supplement to the Survey of Income and Program Participation (SIPP)]

Sex and year of marriage	Marriages (1,000)	Anniversary						
		5th	10th	15th	20th	25th	30th	35th
MEN								
1970 to 1974	6,609	86.4	73.6	64.3	58.0	54.8	51.1	50.0
1975 to 1979	6,668	84.9	71.3	63.4	57.4	52.3	50.7	(X)
1980 to 1984	7,133	88.1	74.3	62.7	57.2	54.6	(X)	(X)
1985 to 1989	6,683	84.3	69.2	59.3	54.1	(X)	(X)	(X)
1990 to 1994	7,996	83.9	70.9	62.1	(X)	(X)	(X)	(X)
1995 to 1999	7,678	88.2	73.6	(X)	(X)	(X)	(X)	(X)
2000 to 2004	7,174	87.0	(X)	(X)	(X)	(X)	(X)	(X)
WOMEN								
1970 to 1974	7,526	86.4	71.5	64.2	56.5	52.3	48.7	46.6
1975 to 1979	7,122	82.9	70.4	63.0	57.6	52.8	49.7	(X)
1980 to 1984	8,081	84.1	73.2	62.4	58.0	52.8	(X)	(X)
1985 to 1989	7,503	85.0	69.0	57.8	50.8	(X)	(X)	(X)
1990 to 1994	7,705	85.8	73.5	67.2	(X)	(X)	(X)	(X)
1995 to 1999	7,711	88.3	75.6	(X)	(X)	(X)	(X)	(X)
2000 to 2004	7,653	87.5	(X)	(X)	(X)	(X)	(X)	(X)

X Not applicable.

Source: U.S. Census Bureau, Current Population Reports, *Number, Timing, and Duration of Marriages and Divorces: 2016*, P70-167, April 2021. See also <www.census.gov/newsroom/press-releases/2021/marriages-and-divorces.html>.

Table 135. People Who Got Married and Divorced in the Past 12 Months by State: 2019

[For 12-month period prior to interview date, which occurred for each month in calendar year. For example, a person interviewed in January 2019 could report they got married between January 2018 and January 2019. Data shown for persons 15 years old and over. Vital event is counted in state in which respondent lived at the time of survey. Based on 2019 American Community Survey (ACS). The ACS universe includes the household population and the group quarters population. Based on a sample and subject to sampling variability. See Appendix III]

State	People who got married in the past 12 months				People who got divorced in the past 12 months			
	Males	Marriage rate per 1,000 men	Females	Marriage rate per 1,000 women	Males	Divorce rate per 1,000 men	Females	Divorce rate per 1,000 women
United States.............	2,261,617	17.3	2,231,263	16.3	933,988	7.1	1,042,174	7.6
Alabama..................	32,426	17.0	31,765	15.2	16,299	8.5	19,059	9.1
Alaska....................	6,430	21.3	4,900	17.7	1,663	5.5	1,899	6.9
Arizona...................	48,699	16.6	46,807	15.6	22,454	7.7	24,599	8.2
Arkansas.................	22,283	18.9	20,716	16.5	11,433	9.7	13,514	10.7
California.................	259,807	16.4	251,700	15.5	90,565	5.7	104,935	6.5
Colorado.................	50,155	21.1	49,026	20.9	14,744	6.2	18,639	7.9
Connecticut..............	19,086	13.2	19,018	12.4	9,865	6.8	10,871	7.1
Delaware.................	5,316	13.8	4,918	11.7	4,119	10.7	3,952	9.4
District of Columbia......	7,324	26.4	6,771	21.4	1,027	3.7	1,501	4.8
Florida...................	144,226	16.6	141,275	15.2	74,471	8.6	74,952	8.1
Georgia..................	72,899	17.8	76,748	17.3	33,422	8.1	39,301	8.9
Hawaii...................	8,918	15.4	9,045	15.5	3,184	5.5	3,889	6.6
Idaho....................	14,005	19.8	13,373	18.9	8,176	11.5	5,634	8.0
Illinois...................	82,007	16.3	83,916	15.8	29,693	5.9	32,978	6.2
Indiana...................	47,678	18.0	47,051	16.9	24,798	9.3	25,116	9.0
Iowa.....................	20,242	16.0	20,164	15.6	8,065	6.4	8,148	6.3
Kansas...................	21,904	19.0	21,491	18.2	7,932	6.9	10,829	9.2
Kentucky.................	31,568	17.8	31,895	17.1	15,427	8.7	18,831	10.1
Louisiana................	27,638	15.3	27,239	14.1	13,172	7.3	14,108	7.3
Maine....................	10,776	19.5	11,795	20.0	4,008	7.2	2,806	4.8
Maryland.................	39,512	16.7	40,050	15.6	19,247	8.1	18,166	7.1
Massachusetts...........	44,932	16.2	46,122	15.3	15,334	5.5	19,207	6.4
Michigan.................	66,787	16.6	66,745	15.9	30,397	7.6	31,205	7.4
Minnesota...............	39,537	17.6	40,710	17.7	14,079	6.3	15,352	6.7
Mississippi...............	19,741	17.3	19,804	15.8	7,633	6.7	10,880	8.7
Missouri..................	45,821	18.9	47,031	18.3	22,084	9.1	23,366	9.1
Montana.................	7,801	17.7	6,856	15.6	2,852	6.5	3,820	8.7
Nebraska................	13,696	18.0	14,534	18.8	5,071	6.7	5,312	6.9
Nevada..................	22,962	18.4	22,346	17.8	10,769	8.6	12,740	10.2
New Hampshire...........	8,530	15.0	8,643	14.8	2,367	4.2	4,802	8.2
New Jersey...............	57,051	16.2	52,650	14.0	17,022	4.8	23,570	6.3
New Mexico..............	12,037	14.4	12,298	14.2	6,369	7.6	8,805	10.2
New York................	130,553	16.9	119,456	14.3	41,635	5.4	51,468	6.1
North Carolina............	66,442	16.1	70,586	15.8	31,180	7.6	35,797	8.0
North Dakota.............	6,646	21.4	5,862	19.5	2,247	7.2	2,599	8.6
Ohio.....................	76,171	16.4	78,342	15.9	33,766	7.3	40,717	8.3
Oklahoma................	30,383	19.6	31,370	19.5	14,257	9.2	16,798	10.4
Oregon..................	29,913	17.4	29,117	16.3	16,561	9.6	14,790	8.3
Pennsylvania.............	84,199	16.3	82,158	15.0	33,717	6.5	33,320	6.1
Rhode Island.............	6,113	14.1	5,709	12.4	3,777	8.7	3,051	6.6
South Carolina...........	33,708	16.7	33,375	15.1	11,661	5.8	14,619	6.6
South Dakota............	5,884	16.7	6,032	17.2	2,534	7.2	2,099	6.0
Tennessee...............	47,812	17.8	49,573	17.2	25,675	9.5	24,457	8.5
Texas....................	220,268	19.6	210,648	18.2	88,772	7.9	99,315	8.6
Utah.....................	25,336	20.9	25,226	20.7	8,196	6.7	11,459	9.4
Vermont..................	3,256	12.4	3,366	12.5	1,732	6.6	1,831	6.8
Virginia..................	63,755	18.7	63,459	17.7	26,397	7.8	28,432	7.9
Washington..............	64,729	20.9	65,458	20.9	22,130	7.1	24,437	7.8
West Virginia.............	11,523	15.7	11,904	15.6	6,493	8.8	6,410	8.4
Wisconsin................	36,803	15.6	37,128	15.3	13,908	5.9	15,505	6.4
Wyoming.................	6,329	26.6	5,092	22.3	1,609	6.8	2,284	10.0

Source: U.S. Census Bureau, 2019 American Community Survey, B12501, "Marriage in the Last Year by Sex by Marital Status for the Population 15 Years and Over," and B12503, "Divorces in the Last Year by Sex by Marital Status for the Population 15 Years and Over"; <data.census.gov>, accessed November 2020.

Table 136. Marriage and Divorce Rates by State: 1990 to 2020

[Rate per 1,000 population residing in area. Population enumerated as of April 1 for 1990, 2000, and 2010; estimated as of July 1 for all other years. Rates are based on provisional counts by state of occurrence. See Appendix III]

State	Marriage rates						Divorce rates [1]					
	1990	2000	2005	2010	2015	2020	1990	2000	2005	2010	2015	2020
United States [2]	**9.8**	**8.2**	**7.6**	**6.8**	**6.9**	**5.1**	**4.7**	**4.0**	**3.6**	**3.6**	**3.1**	**2.3**
Alabama	10.6	10.1	9.2	8.2	7.4	7.2	6.1	5.5	4.9	4.4	3.9	3.7
Alaska	10.2	8.9	8.2	8.0	7.4	5.7	5.5	3.9	4.3	4.7	4.1	3.2
Arizona	10.0	7.5	6.6	5.9	5.9	4.9	6.9	4.6	4.2	3.5	3.6	2.9
Arkansas	15.3	15.4	12.9	10.8	10.0	7.8	6.9	6.4	6.0	5.7	4.8	3.6
California [3]	7.9	5.8	6.4	5.8	6.2	3.2	4.3	(NA)	(NA)	(NA)	(NA)	(NA)
Colorado	9.8	8.3	7.6	6.9	6.8	6.7	5.5	4.7	4.4	4.3	3.7	2.9
Connecticut	7.9	5.7	5.8	5.6	5.3	4.3	3.2	3.3	3.0	2.9	3.1	1.6
Delaware	8.4	6.5	5.9	5.2	5.7	4.4	4.4	3.9	3.8	3.5	3.1	2.3
District of Columbia	8.2	4.9	4.1	7.6	8.2	6.5	4.5	3.2	2.0	2.8	2.8	2.1
Florida	10.9	8.9	8.9	7.3	8.2	5.7	6.3	5.1	4.6	4.4	4.0	3.0
Georgia	10.3	6.8	7.0	7.3	6.2	5.1	5.5	3.3	(NA)	(NA)	(NA)	1.9
Hawaii	16.4	20.6	22.6	17.6	15.9	7.4	4.6	3.9	(NA)	(NA)	(NA)	(NA)
Idaho	13.9	10.8	10.5	8.8	8.2	7.3	6.5	5.5	5.0	5.2	4.1	3.4
Illinois	8.8	6.9	5.9	5.7	5.9	3.9	3.8	3.2	2.6	2.6	2.2	1.6
Indiana	9.6	7.9	6.9	6.3	6.9	5.8	(NA)	(NA)	(NA)	(NA)	(NA)	(NA)
Iowa	9.0	6.9	6.9	6.9	6.3	4.9	3.9	3.3	2.7	2.4	1.2	2.1
Kansas	9.2	8.3	6.8	6.4	5.9	4.9	5.0	3.6	3.1	3.7	2.8	1.8
Kentucky	13.5	9.8	8.7	7.4	7.2	4.9	5.8	5.1	4.6	4.5	3.7	3.1
Louisiana	9.6	9.1	8.0	6.9	6.8	3.4	(NA)	(NA)	(NA)	(NA)	2.8	1.4
Maine	9.7	8.8	8.2	7.1	7.6	5.8	4.3	5.0	4.1	4.2	3.4	2.4
Maryland	9.7	7.5	6.9	5.7	6.2	4.3	3.4	3.3	3.1	2.8	2.6	1.7
Massachusetts	7.9	5.8	6.2	5.6	5.5	4.0	2.8	2.5	2.2	2.5	2.6	1.0
Michigan	8.2	6.7	6.1	5.5	6.0	4.2	4.3	3.9	3.4	3.5	3.0	2.1
Minnesota	7.7	6.8	6.0	5.3	5.6	4.4	3.5	3.2	(NA)	(NA)	(NA)	(NA)
Mississippi	9.4	6.9	5.8	4.9	7.0	5.7	5.5	5.0	4.4	4.3	3.4	3.3
Missouri	9.6	7.8	7.0	6.5	6.8	5.6	5.1	4.5	3.6	3.9	3.2	2.7
Montana	8.6	7.3	7.4	7.4	8.0	10.4	5.1	4.2	4.5	3.9	3.4	2.3
Nebraska	8.0	7.6	7.0	6.6	6.4	5.0	4.0	3.7	3.3	3.6	3.2	2.8
Nevada	99.0	72.2	57.4	38.3	31.0	21.0	11.4	9.9	7.4	5.9	4.6	3.0
New Hampshire	9.5	9.4	7.3	7.3	6.9	6.1	4.7	4.8	3.9	3.8	3.3	2.4
New Jersey	7.6	6.0	5.7	5.1	5.6	4.1	3.0	3.0	2.9	3.0	2.8	1.7
New Mexico	8.8	8.0	6.6	7.7	6.2	3.4	4.9	5.1	4.6	4.0	3.3	(NA)
New York	8.6	7.1	6.8	6.5	7.1	4.5	3.2	3.0	2.9	2.9	2.7	1.8
North Carolina	7.8	8.2	7.3	6.6	7.0	5.5	5.1	4.5	4.1	3.8	3.1	2.8
North Dakota	7.5	7.2	6.8	6.5	6.2	5.3	3.6	3.4	2.9	3.1	2.8	2.4
Ohio	9.0	7.8	6.5	5.8	5.9	4.8	4.7	4.2	3.5	3.4	3.1	2.5
Oklahoma	10.6	(NA)	7.3	7.2	7.4	5.9	7.7	(NA)	5.6	5.2	4.4	3.5
Oregon	8.9	7.6	7.3	6.5	6.9	5.2	5.5	4.8	4.2	4.0	3.4	2.6
Pennsylvania	7.1	6.0	5.8	5.3	5.7	4.6	3.3	3.1	2.3	2.7	2.6	2.3
Rhode Island	8.1	7.6	7.0	5.8	6.4	4.5	3.7	2.9	3.0	3.2	3.0	1.9
South Carolina	15.9	10.6	8.3	7.4	7.5	5.7	4.5	3.8	2.9	3.1	2.8	2.0
South Dakota	11.1	9.4	8.4	7.3	7.2	6.0	3.7	3.5	2.8	3.4	2.6	2.5
Tennessee	13.9	15.5	10.9	8.8	8.5	7.3	6.5	5.9	4.6	4.2	3.7	3.2
Texas	10.5	9.4	7.8	7.1	7.2	5.3	5.5	4.0	3.3	3.3	2.6	1.5
Utah	11.2	10.8	9.8	8.5	8.1	8.4	5.1	4.3	4.1	3.7	3.6	3.3
Vermont	10.9	10.0	8.9	9.3	8.1	6.0	4.5	4.1	3.6	3.8	3.1	2.1
Virginia	11.4	8.8	8.2	6.8	7.0	5.3	4.4	4.3	4.0	3.8	3.3	2.6
Washington	9.5	6.9	6.5	6.0	6.2	4.8	5.9	4.6	4.3	4.2	3.4	2.8
West Virginia	7.2	8.7	7.4	6.7	6.6	5.6	5.3	5.1	5.1	5.1	4.0	3.1
Wisconsin	7.9	6.7	6.1	5.3	5.6	4.5	3.6	3.2	2.9	3.0	2.6	2.0
Wyoming	10.7	10.0	9.3	7.6	7.3	6.8	6.6	5.8	5.2	5.1	4.1	3.8

NA Not available. [1] Includes annulments. Includes divorce petitions filed or legal separations for some counties or States. [2] Beginning 2000, rates based solely on the combined counts and populations for reporting states and the District of Columbia. [3] Marriage data includes nonlicensed marriages registered.

Source: U.S. National Center for Health Statistics, National Vital Statistics System, "Marriages and Divorces, Detailed State Tables," <www.cdc.gov/nchs/nvss/marriage-divorce.htm>, accessed March 2022.

Table 137. People Who Got Married or Divorced in the Past 12 Months by Selected Characteristics: 2019

[In units, as indicated (267,721 represents 267,721,000). For 12-month period prior to interview date, which occurred for each month in calendar year. For example, a person interviewed in January 2019 could report they got married between January 2018 and January 2019. Persons 15 years and over. Based on the 2019 American Community Survey (ACS). The ACS universe includes the household population and the group quarters population. Based on a sample and subject to sampling variability. See Appendix III]

Characteristic	Total population	Married in the past 12 months		Divorced in the past 12 months	
		Males	Females	Males	Females
Population 15 years old and over (1,000)...............	**267,721**	**2,262**	**2,231**	**934**	**1,042**
AGE					
Median age........................	45.9	32.1	30.4	45.6	43.6
EDUCATIONAL ATTAINMENT					
Population 18 years and over (1,000).................	255,272	2,233	2,202	932	1,040
Bachelor's degree or higher (percent)...............	30.6	35.1	41.3	26.5	31.8
LABOR FORCE PARTICIPATION					
Population 16 years and over (1,000).................	263,534	2,247	2,217	934	1,042
In labor force (percent).............................	63.6	89.2	79.0	78.9	78.0
Not in labor force (percent)........................	36.4	10.8	21.0	21.1	22.0
POVERTY STATUS IN PAST 12 MONTHS					
Population for whom poverty status is determined (1,000).........	260,816	2,227	2,223	905	1,036
Below poverty (percent).............................	11.2	5.9	7.0	10.6	18.0
PRESENCE OF OWN CHILD UNDER 18 YEARS					
Population in households (1,000).......................	259,697	2,222	2,221	900	1,034
With own child under 18 years (percent).............	22.8	28.2	30.6	18.3	36.9
HOUSING TENURE					
Population 15 years and over in occupied housing units (1,000)...	259,697	2,222	2,221	900	1,034
Owner-occupied housing units (percent)............	67.7	52.6	52.9	58.0	52.5
Renter-occupied housing units (percent)...........	32.3	47.4	47.1	42.0	47.5

Source: U.S. Census Bureau, 2019 American Community Survey, S1251, "Characteristics of People with a Marital Event in the Last 12 Months," <data.census.gov>, accessed November 2020.

Table 138. Marital Status of Population and Number of Times Married by Sex and Median Duration of Marriage: 2010 to 2019

[248,056 represents 248,056,000. Data shown are for the population age 15 years and over. Based on the American Community Survey (ACS). The ACS universe includes the household population and the group quarters population. Based on a sample and subject to sampling variability. See Appendix III]

Characteristic	2010	2013	2014	2015	2016	2017	2018	2019
NUMBER (1,000)								
Population aged 15 years and over......	**248,056**	**255,017**	**257,771**	**260,415**	**262,140**	**264,697**	**266,322**	**267,721**
Male...............................	120,743	124,380	125,665	127,013	127,864	129,186	129,974	130,629
Never married....................	42,741	45,175	45,865	46,677	47,195	47,654	48,052	48,481
Ever married.....................	78,001	79,205	79,800	80,336	80,669	81,532	81,921	82,148
Once...........................	58,734	59,667	60,106	60,648	60,898	61,580	61,927	62,106
Two times......................	15,183	15,284	15,406	15,381	15,438	15,592	15,635	15,649
Three or more times............	4,085	4,253	4,287	4,307	4,333	4,359	4,359	4,393
Female...........................	127,313	130,637	132,106	133,402	134,277	135,511	136,349	137,092
Never married....................	36,899	39,145	39,944	40,667	41,143	41,442	41,880	42,292
Ever married.....................	90,414	91,492	92,162	92,734	93,134	94,070	94,469	94,800
Once...........................	68,330	69,185	69,723	70,088	70,419	71,248	71,413	71,632
Two times......................	17,449	17,533	17,642	17,776	17,838	17,945	18,110	18,191
Three or more times............	4,636	4,774	4,796	4,871	4,876	4,876	4,945	4,977
PERCENT DISTRIBUTION								
Male:								
Never married....................	35.4	36.3	36.5	36.7	36.9	36.9	37.0	37.1
Ever married.....................	64.6	63.7	63.5	63.3	63.1	63.1	63.0	62.9
Once...........................	48.6	48.0	47.8	47.7	47.6	47.7	47.6	47.5
Two times......................	12.6	12.3	12.3	12.1	12.1	12.1	12.0	12.0
Three or more times............	3.4	3.4	3.4	3.4	3.4	3.4	3.4	3.4
Female:								
Never married....................	29.0	30.0	30.2	30.5	30.6	30.6	30.7	30.8
Ever married.....................	71.0	70.0	69.8	69.5	69.4	69.4	69.3	69.2
Once...........................	53.7	53.0	52.8	52.5	52.4	52.6	52.4	52.3
Two times......................	13.7	13.4	13.4	13.3	13.3	13.2	13.3	13.3
Three or more times............	3.6	3.7	3.6	3.7	3.6	3.6	3.6	3.6
Median duration of marriage (years) [1]........	19.0	19.5	19.5	19.6	19.7	19.7	19.7	19.8

[1] Data shown for current marriage.

Source: U.S. Census Bureau, American Community Survey, B12504, "Median Duration of Current Marriage in Years By Sex By Marital Status for the Married Population 15 years and Over," and B12505, "Number of Times Married by Sex By Marital Status for the Population 15 Years and Over"; <data.census.gov>, accessed November 2020.

Section 3
Health and Nutrition

This section presents statistics on numerous indicators of the nation's health care system, the health care industry and its institutions, and the health of the population. Data in this section cover national and personal health expenditures, health insurance coverage, Medicare and Medicaid, medical personnel, hospitals, nursing homes and other health care facilities, injuries, diseases, vaccinations, disability status, substance use (including alcohol, tobacco, and illicit drug use), exercise, food consumption, and nutrition. This section also includes data on selected health conditions and indicators among children.

Also appearing in this section are data on weekly trends in cases of and hospitalizations due to the coronavirus disease, COVID-19, and vaccinations against COVID-19, as available during the time of production of this *Abstract*. The data presented here are an illustration of the progression of the pandemic and of vaccinations in the U.S.; please see the sources noted in the relevant tables for revised and up-to-date data.

Data on national health expenditures, medical costs, and insurance coverage are compiled by the U.S. Centers for Medicare & Medicaid Services (CMS) and are available at <www.cms.gov/Research-Statistics-Data-and-Systems/Research-Statistics-Data-and-Systems>. Medicare data are available on the CMS website under "CMS Program Statistics." Internet users can find data on Medicare enrollment, utilization, and expenditures, and also data on Medicare-certified institutional and noninstitutional health care providers. Another key source of information on Medicare is the annual report to Congress from the Boards of Trustees for Medicare. The Trustees' report covers the financial operations and actuarial status of Medicare. Selected data on Medicaid and the Children's Health Insurance Program (CHIP) are available from <Medicaid.gov>, the U.S. National Center for Health Statistics (NCHS), and the Medicaid and CHIP Payment and Access Commission, a nonpartisan legislative branch agency that provides analysis to the states, Congress, and the Secretary of the Department of Health and Human Services.

Summary statistics showing recent trends in health care and health indicators of the population, and discussions of selected health issues are published annually by the NCHS in *Health, United States*. Statistics on health insurance are collected by surveys conducted by the Census Bureau. The NCHS also collects health insurance data and other detailed data on the population's health status annually in its National Health Interview Survey. Data from past and the most recent National Health Interview Surveys are available in online data tools and various reports, including the Early Release Program, accessible at <www.cdc.gov/nchs/nhis/index.htm>.Please note that the NHIS went through a questionnaire redesign that was implemented in 2019; therefore users should exercise caution in comparing trends before and after the questionnaire redesign. NCHS also operates the National Health and Nutrition Examination Survey to track various health indicators, such as food and nutrition, exercise, body weight, and incidence of

conditions such as diabetes, high blood cholesterol, and blood pressure (hypertension).

Statistics on hospitals are published annually by the Health Forum, LLC, an affiliate of the American Hospital Association (AHA), in *AHA Hospital Statistics*. As a proxy for actual food consumption, the U.S. Dept of Agriculture's Economic Research Service provides data on food availability online at <www.ers.usda.gov/data-products/food-availability-per-capita-data-system/>. Available from the USDA's Agricultural Research Service are data on nutrient and energy consumption, compiled by the Food Surveys Research Group for the *What We Eat In America* program.

National health expenditures—CMS compiles estimates of national health expenditures (NHE) to measure spending for health care in the United States. The NHE accounts are structured to show spending by type of expenditure: hospital care, physician and clinical care, dental care, and other professional care; home health care; retail sales of prescription drugs; durable medical equipment, and other nondurable medical goods; nursing home care and other personal health expenditures; other expenditures such as public health activities, administration, and the net cost of private health insurance; and medical sector investment, which is the sum of noncommercial medical research and capital formation in medical sector structures and equipment. The NHE also shows spending by source of funding (e.g., private health insurance, Medicare, Medicaid, out-of-pocket payments, and other third party payers and programs).

Data used to estimate health expenditures come from numerous public and private sources. The expenditure type estimates rely upon statistics produced by such groups as the AHA, the Census Bureau, and the U.S. Department of Health and Human Services (HHS). Funding source estimates are constructed using administrative and statistical records from the Medicare and Medicaid programs, the U.S. Department of Defense and Veterans Affairs medical programs, the Social Security Administration, the Census Bureau, state and local governments, other HHS agencies, and other nongovernment sources.

The Health Care Satellite Account (HCSA), developed by the Bureau of Economic Analysis (BEA), is a tool that measures health care spending as the cost to treat specific diseases and medical conditions (such as cancer, or diseases of the circulatory system), as opposed to spending on specific types of health care services and goods (such as doctor's visits and prescription drugs). The HCSA can help answer questions regarding whether changes in medical expenditures are due to changes in costs of treatments or changes in number of persons receiving care, which medical conditions account for larger portions of spending, and which medical conditions experience the greatest changes in treatment costs. The BEA presents two versions of the HCSA. One version, the "MEPS Account," uses data from the Medical Expenditure Panel Survey; the other version, the "Blended Account," combines data from multiple sources, including large claims databases that cover millions of health insurance enrollees and billions of claims. The table in this section presents data from the Blended Account. See <www.bea.gov/data/special-topics/health-care> for detailed information about how the Health Care Satellite Account is constructed.

Medicare, Medicaid, and Children's Health Insurance Program (CHIP)—The Original Medicare program has two components: Medicare Part A, Hospital Insurance; and Medicare Part B, Medical Insurance. Medicare Part A helps pay for in-patient hospital stays, care in a skilled nursing facility, hospice care, and home health care after hospital stays. Medicare Part B is optional; it helps pay for physician and outpatient care services, durable medical equipment, and preventive services. An additional component of Medicare, Part D, provides subsidized access to prescription drug insurance coverage on a voluntary basis for all beneficiaries, with premium and cost-sharing subsidies for low-income enrollees. Participants in Parts B and D pay monthly premiums. In addition to covering persons age 65 and older, Medicare covers persons under age 65 with a disability and who have been receiving for the past 24 months disability benefits from Social Security or the Railroad Retirement Board; persons of any age with ALS (Amyotrophic Lateral Sclerosis, also known as Lou Gehrig's disease); and persons of any age with end-stage renal disease. Medicare's Hospital Insurance and Supplementary Medical Insurance have separate trust funds, sources of revenue, and categories of expenditures.

Medicare also has an alternative option to Original Medicare coverage, the Medicare Advantage Plan (also known as Part C). Medicare Advantage plans are offered by private companies and organizations, are required to provide at least services covered by Medicare Parts A and B (except hospice services), and are financed from both Medicare's Hospital Insurance (HI) trust fund and the Part B account within the Supplementary Medical Insurance (SMI) trust fund in proportion to the relative weights of Part A and Part B benefits to the total benefits paid by the Medicare program.

Medicaid is a health insurance program for certain low-income people, families and children, pregnant women, the elderly, and people with disabilities. There are special rules for those who live in nursing homes and for disabled children living at home. Medicaid is funded and administered through a federal-state partnership. Although there are broad federal requirements for Medicaid, states have a wide degree of flexibility to design their programs. Eligibility criteria for Medicaid varies from state to state.

The Children's Health Insurance Program Reauthorization Act of 2009 (CHIPRA or Public Law 111-3) reauthorized CHIP, which was originally signed into law in 1997. The program went into effect on April 1, 2009. CHIP replaced the State Children's Health Insurance Program (SCHIP). It preserves coverage for the millions of children who rely on CHIP, and provides the resources for states to reach millions of additional children who would otherwise be without health insurance coverage. CHIP is a federal-state partnership, similar to Medicaid, that expands health insurance to children whose families earn too much money to be eligible for Medicaid, but not enough money to purchase private health insurance. CHIPRA also gives states the option to provide prenatal, delivery, and postpartum care to low-income pregnant women without health insurance. Under CHIP, states can operate their programs as an expansion of Medicaid or as a program entirely separate from Medicaid, or a combination of both approaches. Most states have either expanded Medicaid or run a combination of both types of programs. Only two states, Connecticut and Washington, run separate programs without Medicaid expansions.

Health care resources and utilization—Hospital statistics based on data from AHA's yearly survey are published annually in *AHA Hospital Statistics* and cover all hospitals accepted for registration by the Association. Up until fiscal year 2016, the AHA used its own detailed criteria for recognizing hospitals for registration. Beginning with fiscal year 2017, the AHA uses the following definition: an institution is a hospital if it is licensed as a general or specialty hospital by the appropriate state agency and accredited by one of the following organizations: The Joint Commission, Healthcare Facilities Accreditation Program (HFAP), DNV Health Accreditation, Center for Improvement in Healthcare Quality Accreditation, or Medicare certified as a provider of acute services under Title 18 of the Social Security Act.

Ambulatory care data, including emergency room visits, are presented here from the National Hospital Ambulatory Medical Care Survey (NHAMCS). Data on physicians generally come from the professional organizations that collect data on medical school graduates and physicians. Statistics on patient visits to health care providers come from the National Health Interview Survey and the National Ambulatory Medical Care Survey.

Disability and illness, mental health, and substance use—General health statistics, including morbidity, disability, injuries, preventive care, and findings from physiological testing are collected by NCHS in its National Health Interview Survey and its National Health and Nutrition Examination Surveys. The Centers for Disease Control and Prevention in Atlanta, Georgia collects and publishes data on nationally notifiable diseases. Data are collected from State health departments and territories under the National Notifiable Diseases Surveillance System (NNDSS), which is operated by the CDC in collaboration with the Council of State and Territorial Epidemiologists. The list of diseases is revised annually. The Substance Abuse and Mental Health Services Administration, an agency within HHS, studies and provides data regarding mental health disorders and treatment (including mental health treatment facilities and clients), and substance use (including tobacco, alcohol, and prescription and illicit drugs).

Statistical reliability—For discussions of statistical collections, including methodologies and sources of information on measures of reliability and other technical issues for data from the NCHS and CMS, see Appendix III.

Table 139. National Health Expenditures by Type of Service: 1960 to 2020

[In billions of dollars (27.1 represents $27,100,000,000). Excludes Puerto Rico and Island Areas. For definitions, methodology, and related information, see <www.cms.gov/files/document/definitions-sources-and-methods.pdf>]

Year	Total expenditures [1]	Health consumption expenditures, total [2]	Personal health care expenditures									
			Total [3]	Hospital care	Physician and clinical services	Dental services	Other professional services [4]	Home health care [5]	Nursing care facilities [6]	Prescription drugs	Durable medical equipment [7]	Nondurable medical equipment [8]
1960....	27.1	24.6	23.1	9.0	5.6	2.0	0.4	0.1	0.8	2.7	0.7	1.5
1961....	29.1	26.2	24.6	9.8	5.8	2.1	0.4	0.1	0.8	2.7	0.8	1.6
1962....	31.8	28.3	26.5	10.4	6.3	2.2	0.4	0.1	0.9	3.0	0.9	1.8
1963....	34.6	30.8	29.0	11.5	7.1	2.4	0.5	0.1	1.0	3.2	0.9	1.8
1964....	38.2	33.9	31.8	12.5	8.1	2.6	0.5	0.1	1.2	3.3	1.0	1.9
1965....	41.6	36.9	34.4	13.5	8.6	2.8	0.5	0.1	1.4	3.7	1.1	1.9
1966....	45.8	40.8	38.0	15.3	9.3	3.0	0.6	0.1	1.7	4.0	1.2	2.0
1967....	51.2	46.0	43.0	17.8	10.4	3.4	0.6	0.2	2.2	4.2	1.1	2.0
1968....	58.0	52.2	48.6	20.5	11.3	3.7	0.6	0.2	2.9	4.7	1.3	2.2
1969....	65.4	58.4	54.9	23.4	12.7	4.2	0.7	0.3	3.4	5.1	1.5	2.3
1970....	74.1	66.3	62.4	27.2	14.3	4.7	0.7	0.2	4.0	5.5	1.7	2.6
1971....	82.4	73.6	68.7	30.2	15.9	5.2	0.8	0.2	4.6	5.9	1.8	2.7
1972....	92.4	82.5	76.4	33.8	17.7	5.6	0.9	0.2	5.2	6.3	2.0	2.9
1973....	102.7	92.2	85.3	37.9	19.6	6.4	1.0	0.3	6.0	6.8	2.2	3.1
1974....	116.3	104.9	97.8	44.1	22.2	7.2	1.2	0.4	6.9	7.4	2.5	3.5
1975....	132.7	119.9	112.1	51.2	25.3	8.0	1.3	0.6	8.0	8.1	2.8	3.8
1976....	152.0	138.0	128.1	59.4	28.7	9.0	1.6	0.9	9.1	8.7	3.0	4.2
1977....	172.7	158.3	145.1	67.0	33.1	10.1	2.1	1.1	10.3	9.2	3.2	4.5
1978....	194.0	178.1	162.4	75.6	35.8	11.0	2.4	1.6	11.8	9.9	3.4	5.3
1979....	219.7	202.2	184.9	86.2	41.2	12.0	2.8	1.9	13.3	10.7	3.8	6.2
1980....	253.2	232.7	214.3	100.5	47.7	13.3	3.5	2.4	15.3	12.0	4.1	7.1
1981....	293.6	270.1	248.6	117.5	55.6	15.7	4.3	2.9	17.3	13.4	4.3	8.1
1982....	330.9	304.2	279.5	133.6	61.6	17.0	4.9	3.5	19.5	15.0	4.6	9.0
1983....	364.8	335.5	308.0	144.7	68.7	18.3	5.7	4.2	21.7	17.3	5.3	10.1
1984....	401.9	371.0	337.9	154.4	77.4	19.9	7.3	5.1	23.7	19.6	6.1	11.2
1985....	439.9	408.7	372.6	164.6	90.9	21.7	8.1	5.6	26.2	21.8	7.1	12.2
1986....	472.3	440.0	405.4	175.8	100.7	23.2	9.3	6.4	28.6	24.3	8.1	13.4
1987....	514.5	478.8	444.4	189.7	112.9	25.3	11.3	6.6	30.6	26.9	9.5	14.7
1988....	576.6	536.8	495.1	206.5	128.6	27.4	13.7	8.4	34.2	30.6	11.1	15.7
1989....	642.2	598.5	547.0	226.0	143.3	29.4	14.5	10.2	38.6	34.8	11.9	17.0
1990....	718.8	670.2	612.0	250.4	159.0	31.6	17.3	12.5	44.7	40.3	13.8	18.5
1991....	786.1	734.0	672.7	275.8	176.6	33.4	18.6	15.1	49.2	44.4	13.1	19.2
1992....	852.4	795.3	728.4	298.5	191.3	37.2	20.9	18.7	52.8	47.0	13.5	19.1
1993....	915.1	854.2	775.7	315.7	202.7	39.0	23.0	22.7	55.8	49.6	14.1	19.4
1994....	966.7	903.1	818.0	328.4	212.7	41.6	24.0	27.3	58.4	53.0	15.3	19.8
1995....	1,020.6	955.1	866.8	339.3	222.2	44.6	26.7	32.3	64.2	59.8	15.9	20.4
1996....	1,074.0	1,006.9	915.0	350.8	230.8	47.0	28.9	35.7	69.2	68.1	17.4	21.1
1997....	1,133.4	1,061.8	966.1	363.4	241.6	50.3	31.3	36.9	74.1	77.6	19.2	21.6
1998....	1,198.9	1,120.4	1,019.7	374.9	256.5	53.6	33.4	34.1	79.1	88.5	21.3	22.5
1999....	1,273.7	1,189.3	1,079.2	393.6	269.5	57.3	34.6	32.8	80.6	105.3	22.2	24.1
2000....	1,365.7	1,280.0	1,157.0	415.5	288.2	62.1	36.6	32.3	85.0	122.0	26.0	25.2
2001....	1,483.1	1,393.1	1,257.1	449.4	312.7	67.7	40.3	34.3	90.8	140.6	25.4	26.1
2002....	1,630.6	1,529.2	1,366.1	486.5	337.7	73.6	43.3	36.5	94.5	159.8	29.7	27.9
2003....	1,769.9	1,661.3	1,476.5	525.9	364.3	76.3	46.5	40.2	100.1	179.7	30.7	30.3
2004....	1,894.1	1,777.2	1,583.0	565.3	384.6	82.2	50.2	44.6	105.1	195.6	33.2	32.7
2005....	2,025.9	1,900.4	1,694.4	608.6	409.8	87.2	52.8	49.3	111.4	208.6	36.2	35.5
2006....	2,164.4	2,031.4	1,807.0	651.2	433.0	91.8	55.3	52.1	115.9	228.1	39.7	38.7
2007....	2,305.0	2,158.8	1,922.2	691.9	457.3	97.7	60.1	57.5	124.9	239.3	43.4	41.7
2008....	2,402.0	2,245.7	2,008.0	721.6	481.5	102.8	64.5	62.2	130.4	244.3	42.7	45.3
2009....	2,492.5	2,345.3	2,106.2	771.0	497.5	103.4	67.0	67.0	135.2	254.3	41.4	47.6
2010....	2,589.4	2,437.3	2,181.3	808.8	512.4	105.9	69.9	70.5	140.5	253.4	40.0	51.8
2011....	2,676.2	2,517.4	2,254.7	833.2	535.8	108.0	72.8	74.6	145.3	256.3	40.6	56.6
2012....	2,782.8	2,619.6	2,347.0	878.0	557.1	109.7	76.4	78.1	147.3	257.0	43.3	61.2
2013....	2,855.8	2,692.7	2,405.7	906.8	567.9	111.4	78.1	80.9	148.6	259.4	44.9	63.2
2014....	3,001.4	2,841.9	2,527.3	940.5	597.7	114.7	82.4	84.6	152.3	290.6	46.6	65.5
2015....	3,163.6	3,000.6	2,674.1	989.0	636.4	120.0	87.5	89.6	156.4	312.2	48.7	69.3
2016....	3,305.6	3,139.5	2,795.3	1,035.4	675.3	126.2	92.2	93.7	161.6	313.3	50.6	71.9
2017....	3,446.5	3,266.3	2,905.2	1,077.6	709.4	131.1	96.9	99.4	163.4	315.9	51.9	74.5
2018....	3,604.5	3,415.9	3,021.8	1,122.6	736.9	137.5	104.5	105.6	167.6	324.2	54.4	77.5
2019....	3,759.1	3,564.2	3,175.2	1,193.7	767.9	143.2	111.3	113.0	174.2	338.1	57.0	81.1
2020....	4,124.0	3,931.3	3,357.8	1,270.1	809.5	142.4	117.4	123.7	196.8	348.4	54.9	85.7

[1] Includes Health Consumption Expenditures plus, not shown here, expenditures for noncommercial medical research, and medical structures and equipment. [2] Includes Personal Health Expenditures plus, not shown, expenditures for government administration, net cost of health insurance, and government public health activities. [3] Includes items shown here, and also other health, residential, and personal services. [4] Includes health practitioners other than physicians and dentists, such as, but not limited to, chiropractors, optometrists, physical, occupational, and speech therapists, podiatrists, and private-duty nurses. [5] Services delivered by freestanding home health care facilities only. [6] Care provided in nursing care facilities (NAICS 6231), continuing care retirement communities (623311), state and local government nursing facilities, and nursing facilities operated by the Department of Veterans Affairs. [7] Retail sales of items such as contact lenses, eyeglasses and other ophthalmic products, surgical and orthopedic products, medical equipment rental, oxygen, and hearing aids. Durable products generally last over 3 years. [8] Non-prescription drugs and sundry medical items.

Source: U.S. Centers for Medicare and Medicaid Services, Office of the Actuary, National Health Statistics Group, "National Health Expenditure Data, Historical," <www.cms.gov/Research-Statistics-Data-and-Systems/Statistics-Trends-and-Reports/NationalHealthExpend Data/index>, accessed January 2022.

Table 140. National Health Expenditures by Source of Funds: 1990 to 2020

[In billions of dollars (718.8 represents $718,800,000,000), except percent. Excludes Puerto Rico and Island Areas. For definitions and related information, see <www.cms.gov/files/document/definitions-sources-and-methods.pdf>]

Source of funds	1990	2000	2005	2010	2015	2018	2019	2020 [8]
National health expenditure, total.........	**718.8**	**1,365.7**	**2,025.9**	**2,589.4**	**3,163.6**	**3,604.5**	**3,759.1**	**4,124.0**
Annual percent change [1]......................	11.9	7.2	7.0	3.9	5.4	4.6	4.3	9.7
Percent of gross domestic product...........	12.1	13.3	15.5	17.2	17.4	17.6	17.6	19.7
Consumer out of pocket......................	133.7	193.5	264.4	301.3	352.9	386.5	403.7	388.6
Health insurance............................	431.1	901.8	1,383.8	1,832.3	2,287.6	2,613.3	2,726.4	2,809.3
Private health insurance....................	225.9	440.8	670.8	819.9	975.6	1,131.0	1,165.6	1,151.4
Medicare..................................	110.2	224.8	339.8	519.5	647.9	749.4	801.4	829.5
Medicaid (Title XIX).......................	73.7	200.4	309.4	397.4	543.0	596.4	614.4	671.2
CHIP (Title XIX and Title XXI)................	(X)	3.0	7.6	11.5	14.7	18.6	19.9	21.3
Department of Defense.....................	10.4	13.7	26.5	38.3	41.6	41.7	42.8	43.8
Department of Veterans Affairs.............	10.9	19.1	29.8	45.7	64.7	76.2	82.3	92.2
Other third party payers and programs........	85.4	141.7	194.9	227.9	274.6	316.3	329.2	509.7
Worksite health care.......................	2.2	3.5	4.3	4.7	6.2	7.2	7.6	5.4
Other private revenues [2]...................	37.5	74.1	96.6	124.2	153.8	190.3	200.7	204.9
Indian health services......................	1.0	1.9	2.4	3.5	3.7	4.1	4.2	4.6
Workers' compensation.....................	17.5	26.5	41.5	36.5	48.1	48.5	47.5	44.6
General assistance........................	5.0	3.9	6.3	7.1	6.7	6.1	6.3	6.5
Maternal and Child health..................	1.7	3.2	3.4	3.9	3.8	3.9	3.8	3.9
Vocational rehabilitation...................	0.3	0.4	0.5	0.6	0.6	0.6	0.6	0.6
Other federal programs [3].................	1.6	4.5	6.4	7.7	12.6	12.8	14.0	193.9
Substance Abuse and Mental Health Services Administration.....................	1.4	2.6	3.2	3.4	3.5	5.6	5.6	5.6
Other state and local programs [4]...........	15.9	18.7	26.9	32.1	30.8	31.5	33.0	34.1
School health.............................	1.3	2.5	3.4	4.3	4.8	5.6	5.8	5.6
Public health activity [5]......................	20.0	43.1	57.3	75.7	85.5	99.7	105.0	223.7
Investment................................	**48.6**	**85.7**	**125.5**	**152.1**	**163.1**	**188.6**	**194.9**	**192.7**
Research [6]...............................	12.7	25.5	40.3	49.1	46.4	53.6	56.2	60.2
Structures & equipment [7].................	35.9	60.2	85.2	103.0	116.7	135.0	138.7	132.5

X Not applicable. [1] Average percent change from prior year. [2] Mostly philanthropy, from individuals, philanthropic fundraising organizations, foundations, and corporations. [3] Includes federal general hospital/medical; pre-existing conditions insurance plans (2010-2014) created under the Affordable Care Act; and the Provider Relief Fund and the Paycheck Protection Program, both established under the Coronavirus Aid, Relief and Economic Security (CARES) Act of 2020. [4] Includes temporary disability insurance, and state and local subsidies to providers. [5] Government health services such as epidemiological surveillance, inoculations, immunization/vaccination services, disease prevention programs, and public health laboratories. In the National Health Expenditure Accounts, spending for these activities is reported in government public health activity. [6] Non-profit or government entities. Excludes R&D expenditures by drug and medical supply and equipment manufacturers. [7] Structures are defined as the value of new construction by the medical sector. Equipment includes the value of new capital equipment (including software). Includes establishments that provide health care, and excludes retail establishments that sell non-durable or durable medical goods. Excludes maintenance and repairs. [8] For information on federal spending during the COVID-19 pandemic, see <www.cms.gov/files/document/accounting-federal-covid-expenditures-national-health-expenditure-accounts.pdf>.

Source: U.S. Centers for Medicare and Medicaid Services, Office of the Actuary, National Health Statistics Group, "National Health Expenditure Data, Historical," <www.cms.gov/Research-Statistics-Data-and-Systems/Statistics-Trends-and-Reports/NationalHealthExpend Data/index>, accessed January 2022.

Table 141. National Health Expenditure Projections by Source of Funds and Type of Expenditure: 2021 to 2029

[In billions of dollars (4,297.1 represents $4,297,100,000,000). For calendar years. Projections take into account legislative impacts and the effects of the coronavirus 2019 (COVID-19) pandemic. See source methodology available at <www.cms.gov/NationalHealthExpendData/Downloads/ProjectionsMethodology.pdf>. Excludes Puerto Rico and Island areas]

Funding source and expenditure type	2021	2022	2023	2024	2025	2026	2027	2028	2029
Total........................	**4,297.1**	**4,496.6**	**4,720.5**	**4,962.1**	**5,231.0**	**5,510.8**	**5,802.4**	**6,120.9**	**6,450.9**
SOURCE OF FUNDS									
Consumer out-of-pocket.................	406.5	431.3	455.0	478.8	501.2	522.6	543.4	565.2	587.5
Health insurance.......................	3,064.7	3,276.9	3,457.3	3,657.7	3,875.9	4,101.7	4,335.2	4,590.8	4,855.1
Private health insurance [1].............	1,224.2	1,326.2	1,420.7	1,508.5	1,589.8	1,668.0	1,743.0	1,823.7	1,909.3
Medicare............................	923.0	991.9	1,050.4	1,123.6	1,207.3	1,298.9	1,393.7	1,495.1	1,601.7
Medicaid............................	740.8	783.2	803.9	836.5	879.1	923.6	975.8	1,037.4	1,097.0
Other health insurance programs [2]....	176.7	175.6	182.2	189.1	199.7	211.3	222.6	234.5	247.1
Other third party payers and programs [3]...............	405.0	377.0	399.1	420.2	442.5	464.3	485.8	508.5	532.0
TYPE OF EXPENDITURE									
Health consumption expenditures [4].......................	4,088.3	4,272.5	4,483.4	4,712.5	4,968.3	5,234.6	5,512.1	5,816.5	6,131.9
Personal health care...................	3,520.5	3,719.8	3,929.3	4,150.1	4,387.1	4,629.9	4,878.2	5,148.8	5,427.6
Hospital care.......................	1,342.1	1,435.2	1,516.3	1,601.1	1,695.6	1,791.9	1,890.2	2,002.4	2,113.6
Physician and clinical services.......	850.4	903.0	959.0	1,016.3	1,077.0	1,139.5	1,202.1	1,267.5	1,337.2
Dental services.....................	166.4	165.6	173.2	182.2	190.5	198.5	206.2	214.0	222.1
Other professional services [5].......	127.6	132.2	140.1	148.5	156.6	165.2	173.7	182.6	191.9
Home health care [6]................	121.6	129.1	139.1	148.9	159.9	171.6	184.2	198.0	212.7
Nursing care facilities and continuing care retirement communities................	181.6	188.1	197.6	207.9	217.9	227.9	238.6	250.3	262.1
Prescription drugs..................	364.8	380.4	398.2	418.6	440.0	462.4	485.9	511.3	538.5
Durable medical equipment..........	57.1	59.5	62.5	65.6	69.6	73.3	76.9	80.7	84.4
Nondurable medical products........	88.5	95.0	99.7	104.4	109.5	114.7	120.0	125.6	131.3
Other health, residential, and personal care [7]......	220.4	231.8	243.7	256.7	270.7	285.1	300.3	316.4	333.8
Government public health activity [8]...................	212.1	187.3	172.0	155.8	148.7	146.0	147.8	152.0	157.2
Research [9]........................	65.8	70.3	73.8	77.5	81.6	85.8	90.1	94.7	99.4
Structures [10]......................	67.3	72.9	77.6	81.5	85.7	90.1	94.6	99.2	103.9
Equipment [10]......................	75.7	80.9	85.8	90.6	95.4	100.4	105.5	110.6	115.7

[1] Includes employer sponsored insurance and other private insurance, which also includes marketplace plans. [2] Children's Health Insurance Program (Titles XIX and XXI), Department of Defense, and Department of Veterans' Affairs. [3] See Table 140. [4] See footnote 2, Table 139. [5] See footnote 4, Table 139. [6] See footnote 5, Table 139. [7] See footnote 4, Table 142. [8] See footnote 5, Table 140. [9] See footnote 6, Table 140. [10] See footnote 7, Table 140.

Source: U.S. Centers for Medicare and Medicaid Services, Office of the Actuary, National Health Statistics Group, "National Health Expenditure Data, Projected," <www.cms.gov/nationalhealthexpenddata>, accessed April 2022.

Table 142. Health Consumption Expenditures—Per Capita Spending by Type of Expenditure: 2000 to 2020

[In dollars, except percent. Based on U.S. Census Bureau estimates of total U.S. resident population. Health consumption expenditures include all personal health care spending, government administration and the net cost of private health insurance, and public health activities. Excludes investment in research, structures, and equipment. Excludes Puerto Rico and Island Areas]

Type of expenditure	2000	2005	2010	2015	2016	2017	2018	2019	2020
Total [1]	**4,540**	**6,444**	**7,888**	**9,364**	**9,727**	**10,057**	**10,462**	**10,867**	**11,945**
Annual percent change [2]	(NA)	6.0	3.0	4.8	3.9	3.4	4.0	3.9	9.9
Hospital care	1,474	2,064	2,618	3,086	3,208	3,318	3,438	3,640	3,859
Physician and clinical services	1,022	1,390	1,658	1,986	2,092	2,184	2,257	2,341	2,459
Dental services	220	296	343	374	391	404	421	437	433
Other professional services [3]	130	179	226	273	286	298	320	339	357
Other health, residential, and personal care [4]	227	322	415	515	542	570	585	597	634
Home health care	115	167	228	280	290	306	323	345	376
Nursing care facilities and continuing care retirement communities	302	378	455	488	501	503	513	531	598
Prescription drugs	433	707	820	974	971	972	993	1,031	1,059
Durable medical equipment [5]	92	123	129	152	157	160	166	174	167
Other nondurable medical products [6]	89	120	168	216	223	229	237	247	261
Public health activities [7]	153	194	245	267	279	296	305	320	680

NA Not available. [1] Includes other items, not shown separately. [2] Average annual growth from previous year. [3] See footnote 4, Table 139. [4] Mostly services in non-traditional settings, including school health, worksite health care, Medicaid home and community based waivers, some ambulance services, residential mental health and substance abuse facilities, and residential intellectual and developmental disability facilities. [5] See footnote 7, Table 139. [6] See footnote 8, Table 139. [7] See footnote 5, Table 140.

Source: U.S. Centers for Medicare and Medicaid Services, Office of the Actuary, National Health Statistics Group, "National Health Expenditure Data, Historical," <www.cms.gov/Research-Statistics-Data-and-Systems/Statistics-Trends-and-Reports/NationalHealthExpend Data/index>, accessed January 2022.

Table 143. Health Consumption Expenditures by Type of Expenditure and Source of Funds: 2020

[In billions of dollars (3,931.3 represents $3,931,300,000,000). Excludes Puerto Rico and Island Areas. Excludes investment in research, structures, and equipment]

Type of expenditure	Total	Out-of-pocket	Health insurance Total	Private health insurance	Medicare	Medicaid	Other health insurance programs [1]	Other third party payers and programs [2]
Total	**3,931.3**	**388.6**	**2,809.3**	**1,151.4**	**829.5**	**671.2**	**157.2**	**509.7**
Personal health care [3]	3,357.8	388.6	2,491.1	1,000.2	754.5	586.9	149.4	478.1
Hospital care	1,270.1	32.5	1,029.5	409.0	319.3	220.8	80.4	208.2
Physician and clinical services	809.5	59.4	624.3	300.6	194.7	86.8	42.2	125.7
Dental services	142.4	53.2	78.7	59.7	2.6	12.6	3.8	10.5
Other health, residential, and personal care [4]	208.8	6.8	143.4	14.1	4.4	121.9	2.9	58.7
Home health care	123.7	12.6	98.1	15.7	41.6	40.2	0.6	13.0
Nursing care facilities and continuing care retirement communities	196.8	45.3	116.1	16.7	39.6	53.2	6.5	35.5
Prescription drugs	348.4	46.5	297.6	140.9	109.9	34.5	12.3	4.4
Durable medical equipment	54.9	23.3	30.5	10.6	11.2	8.5	0.2	1.1
Government administration [5]	48.4	(X)	45.8	(X)	11.6	28.8	5.2	2.5
Net cost of health insurance [5]	301.4	(X)	272.4	151.1	63.4	55.5	2.4	29.0
Public health activities [6]	223.7	(X)	(X)	(X)	(X)	(X)	(X)	(X)

X Not applicable. [1] Includes Children's Health Insurance Program (CHIP) Titles XIX and XXI, Department of Defense, and Department of Veterans Affairs. [2] Includes worksite health care, other private revenues, Indian Health Service, workers' compensation, general assistance, maternal and child health, vocational rehabilitation, other federal programs (includes COVID-19 Paycheck Protection Program loans and the Provider Relief Fund), Substance Abuse and Mental Health Services Administration, other state and local programs, and school health. [3] Comprises all medical goods and services that are rendered to treat or prevent a specific disease or condition in a specific person. Includes expenditures for items not shown separately. [4] See footnote 4, Table 142. [5] See source for definitions. [6] See footnote 5, Table 140.

Source: U.S. Centers for Medicare and Medicaid Services, Office of the Actuary, National Health Statistics Group, "National Health Expenditure Data, Historical," <www.cms.gov/Research-Statistics-Data-and-Systems/Statistics-Trends-and-Reports/NationalHealthExpend Data/index>, accessed January 2022.

Table 144. Personal Health Care Expenditures by Source of Funds: 2000 to 2020

[In billions of dollars (1,157.0 represents $1,157,000,000,000). Excludes Puerto Rico and Island Areas]

Source of funds	2000	2005	2010	2015	2016	2017	2018	2019	2020
Personal health care expenditures	**1,157.0**	**1,694.4**	**2,181.3**	**2,674.1**	**2,795.3**	**2,905.2**	**3,021.8**	**3,175.2**	**3,357.8**
Out-of-pocket	193.5	264.4	301.3	352.9	365.6	372.6	386.5	403.7	388.6
Health insurance	832.7	1,261.3	1,669.9	2,075.0	2,169.0	2,257.2	2,349.1	2,472.1	2,491.1
Private health insurance	394.6	586.9	725.1	869.1	917.7	956.7	990.9	1,036.1	1,000.2
Medicare	216.3	326.3	488.8	606.2	628.9	659.0	696.6	744.9	754.5
Medicaid	186.9	287.6	365.7	484.5	503.4	516.1	531.8	553.0	586.9
Other health insurance [1]	34.9	60.5	90.3	115.2	119.0	125.4	129.9	138.2	149.4
Other third party payers and programs [2]	130.8	168.7	210.1	246.2	260.8	275.4	286.1	299.4	478.1

[1] Includes Children's Health Insurance Program (Titles XIX and XXI), Department of Defense, and Department of Veterans Affairs. [2] See footnote 2, Table 143.

Source: U.S. Centers for Medicare and Medicaid Services, Office of the Actuary, National Health Statistics Group, "National Health Expenditure Data, Historical," <www.cms.gov/Research-Statistics-Data-and-Systems/Statistics-Trends-and-Reports/NationalHealthExpend Data/index>, accessed January 2022.

Table 145. National Health Expenditures by Sponsor: 2000 to 2020

[In billions of dollars (1,365.7 represents $1,365,700,000,000). Excludes Puerto Rico and Island Areas. Type of sponsor is defined as the entity that is ultimately responsible for financing the health care bill. These sponsors pay health insurance premiums and out-of-pocket costs, or finance health care through dedicated taxes and/or general revenues. See source for sponsor inclusion and exclusion details]

Type of sponsor	2000	2005	2010	2015	2017	2018	2019	2020 [5]
Total	1,365.7	2,025.9	2,589.4	3,163.6	3,446.5	3,604.5	3,759.1	4,124.0
Business, households and other private revenues	876.9	1,221.8	1,430.6	1,709.7	1,881.5	1,966.9	2,050.2	2,037.3
Private business [1]	335.5	468.4	510.9	595.1	654.2	686.6	712.5	690.5
Household [2]	437.3	616.1	745.7	900.8	977.5	1,021.7	1,067.0	1,078.3
Other private revenues	104.1	137.2	174.0	213.8	249.7	258.7	270.7	268.6
Governments	488.8	804.1	1,158.8	1,454.0	1,565.0	1,637.6	1,708.9	2,086.7
Federal government [3]	263.2	456.5	739.7	916.2	988.8	1,041.2	1,102.3	1,498.7
State and local government [4]	225.5	347.6	419.0	537.8	576.3	596.4	606.6	588.0

[1] Includes employer contributions to employer-sponsored health insurance premiums, employer Medicare Hospital Insurance (HI) Trust Fund payroll taxes, workers' compensation, temporary disability insurance, and worksite health care. [2] Includes employee contributions to employer-sponsored health insurance premiums, directly purchased health insurance, the medical portion of property and casualty insurance premiums, employee and self-employment payroll taxes and premiums paid to the Medicare HI Trust Fund, premiums paid to the Medicare Supplementary Medical Insurance (SMI) Trust Fund, premiums paid for the Pre-existing Condition Insurance Program (PCIP) for 2010-2014, and out-of-pocket health spending. [3] Includes employer contributions to employer-sponsored health insurance premiums, employer Medicare HI payroll taxes, federal general revenue and Medicare net Trust Fund expenditures, federal Medicaid expenditures, the federal portion of Medicaid buy-ins for the Medicare premiums of people eligible for both Medicaid and Medicare (dual eligibles), Medicare Retiree Drug Subsidy (RDS) payments to private business and state and local government employer plans beginning in 2006, Marketplace tax credits and subsidies, and other federal health programs. [4] Includes employer contributions to employer-sponsored health insurance premiums, employer Medicare HI payroll taxes, state and local Medicaid expenditures, the state and local portion of Medicaid buy-ins for the Medicare premiums of people eligible for both Medicaid and Medicare (dual eligibles), and other programs. [5] For information on federal spending during the COVID-19 pandemic, see <www.cms.gov/files/document/accounting-federal-covid-expenditures-national-health-expenditure-accounts.pdf>.

Source: U.S. Centers for Medicare and Medicaid Services, Office of the Actuary, National Health Statistics Group, "National Health Expenditure Data, Historical," <www.cms.gov/Research-Statistics-Data-and-Systems/Statistics-Trends-and-Reports/NationalHealthExpend Data/index>, accessed January 2022.

Table 146. Hospital Care, Physician and Clinical Services, Nursing Care Facilities and Continuing Care Retirement Communities, and Prescription Drug Expenditures by Source of Funds: 2000 to 2020

[In billions of dollars (415.5 represents $415,500,000,000). Excludes Puerto Rico and Island Areas]

Expense type and payment source	2000	2005	2010	2016	2017	2018	2019	2020 [3]
Hospital care, total	415.5	608.6	808.8	1,035.4	1,077.6	1,122.6	1,193.7	1,270.1
Out-of-pocket	13.3	19.5	27.0	31.6	32.8	34.3	37.1	32.5
Health insurance	355.5	528.1	698.6	903.2	938.3	977.1	1,034.1	1,029.5
Private health insurance	138.2	212.1	284.3	372.9	389.8	407.9	434.7	409.0
Medicare	123.5	176.6	220.8	273.9	286.5	300.5	318.0	319.3
Medicaid	70.9	103.8	142.2	190.1	192.2	197.9	207.1	220.8
CHIP [1]	0.9	2.7	3.2	4.4	4.6	4.6	5.1	5.2
Dept. of Defense	7.6	12.0	16.5	16.2	16.7	16.3	16.8	17.0
Veterans Affairs	14.3	20.8	31.7	45.8	48.4	49.8	52.5	58.2
Other third party payers and programs [2]	46.7	61.0	83.2	100.6	106.5	111.3	122.4	208.2
Physician and clinical services, total	288.2	409.8	512.4	675.3	709.4	736.9	767.9	809.5
Out-of-pocket	31.5	40.6	47.6	57.9	59.4	60.8	61.7	59.4
Health insurance	216.8	318.5	406.2	540.1	567.8	591.6	624.1	624.3
Private health insurance	131.7	190.0	223.7	282.4	297.0	300.6	308.6	300.6
Medicare	59.1	86.4	118.2	154.5	164.1	178.1	193.8	194.7
Medicaid	19.3	30.1	43.4	73.1	74.9	78.3	83.4	86.8
CHIP [1]	0.7	1.7	3.1	3.9	4.3	4.4	4.7	4.7
Dept. of Defense	4.7	7.9	12.1	15.3	15.6	16.4	17.2	17.5
Veterans Affairs	1.3	2.5	5.8	10.9	12.0	13.9	16.3	20.0
Other third party payers and programs [2]	40.0	50.7	58.6	77.4	82.2	84.5	82.1	125.7
Nursing care facilities and continuing care retirement communities, total	85.0	111.4	140.5	161.6	163.4	167.6	174.2	196.8
Out-of-pocket	26.9	32.4	37.1	42.9	41.7	43.7	45.8	45.3
Health insurance	51.9	71.6	93.3	106.6	108.2	110.3	113.1	116.1
Private health insurance	7.2	6.9	10.6	13.8	14.1	15.5	16.8	16.7
Medicare	10.9	20.5	32.3	37.0	37.4	37.6	38.0	39.6
Medicaid	31.9	41.3	46.3	50.7	51.3	51.5	52.2	53.2
Veterans Affairs	1.9	2.8	4.0	5.0	5.4	5.7	6.0	6.5
Other third party payers and programs [2]	6.3	7.4	10.1	12.1	13.4	13.6	15.3	35.5
Prescription drugs, total	122.0	208.6	253.4	313.3	315.9	324.2	338.1	348.4
Out-of-pocket	34.7	55.8	47.7	50.3	47.3	47.4	48.5	46.5
Health insurance	83.4	146.5	200.1	258.6	264.2	272.3	285.0	297.6
Private health insurance	59.9	99.5	114.3	129.1	130.4	133.8	137.7	140.9
Medicare	1.6	3.2	56.3	89.9	93.5	97.2	104.5	109.9
Medicaid	19.8	36.5	20.4	29.3	29.4	30.4	31.7	34.5
CHIP [1]	0.3	1.1	1.4	1.8	2.0	2.0	2.1	2.2
Dept. of Defense	0.7	3.6	4.7	4.9	4.9	4.9	4.9	5.3
Veterans Affairs	1.1	2.7	3.0	3.6	3.9	4.0	4.1	4.8
Other third party payers and programs [2]	3.9	6.3	5.5	4.4	4.4	4.5	4.6	4.4

[1] Children's Health Insurance Program (Titles XIX and XXI), effective beginning 1998. [2] Includes worksite health care, other private revenues, Indian Health Service, workers' compensation, general assistance, maternal and child health, vocational rehabilitation, other federal programs (including the Provider Relief Fund and the Paycheck Protection Program, both established under the Coronavirus Aid, Relief and Economic Security (CARES) Act of 2020), Substance Abuse and Mental Health Services Administration, other state and local programs, and school health. [3] For information on federal spending during the COVID-19 pandemic, see <www.cms.gov/files/document/accounting-federal-covid-expenditures-national-health-expenditure-accounts.pdf>.

Source: U.S. Centers for Medicare and Medicaid Services, Office of the Actuary, National Health Statistics Group, "National Health Expenditure Data, Historical," <www.cms.gov/Research-Statistics-Data-and-Systems/Statistics-Trends-and-Reports/NationalHealthExpend Data/index>, accessed January 2022.

Table 147. Medical Care Consumer Price Indexes: 1990 to 2021

[Indexes with base of 1982-1984=100. Indexes are annual averages of monthly data based on components of consumer price index for all urban consumers; for explanation, see text, Section 14 and Appendix III]

Year	Medical care, total	Medical care services					Medical care commodities		Annual percent change [3]		
		Total [1]	Professional services			Hospital and related services	Total [2]	Pre-scription drugs	Medical care, total	Medical care services	Medical care com-modities
			Total [1]	Physi-cians	Dental						
1990.......	162.8	162.7	156.1	160.8	155.8	178.0	163.4	181.7	9.0	9.3	8.4
1995.......	220.5	224.2	201.0	208.8	206.8	257.8	204.5	235.0	4.5	5.1	1.9
2000.......	260.8	266.0	237.7	244.7	258.5	317.3	238.1	285.4	4.1	4.3	3.2
2005.......	323.2	336.7	281.7	287.5	324.0	439.9	276.0	349.0	4.2	4.8	2.5
2010.......	388.4	411.2	328.2	331.3	398.8	607.7	314.7	407.8	3.4	3.5	3.1
2013.......	425.1	454.0	349.5	354.2	431.8	701.3	335.1	442.6	2.5	3.1	0.4
2014.......	435.3	464.8	355.2	359.1	441.0	733.8	343.4	458.3	2.4	2.4	2.5
2015.......	446.8	476.2	361.5	366.1	452.2	761.9	354.6	479.3	2.6	2.4	3.3
2016.......	463.7	494.8	371.5	378.1	465.0	795.1	366.8	502.5	3.8	3.9	3.4
2017.......	475.3	506.8	375.1	380.1	472.6	831.7	377.0	519.6	2.5	2.4	2.8
2018.......	484.7	517.8	378.4	380.5	485.5	866.9	381.4	528.0	2.0	2.2	1.2
2019.......	498.4	536.1	382.6	383.2	496.2	885.2	381.3	526.8	2.8	3.5	–
2020.......	518.9	562.7	389.9	389.9	511.1	921.1	383.2	532.1	4.1	4.9	0.5
2021.......	525.3	573.1	401.9	406.5	522.5	950.0	377.1	522.4	1.2	1.9	-1.6

– Represents or rounds to zero. [1] Includes other services not shown separately. [2] Includes other commodities not shown separately. [3] Percent change from the immediate prior year.

Source: U.S. Bureau of Labor Statistics, "Consumer Price Index Databases," <www.bls.gov/cpi/data.htm>, accessed January 2022.

Table 148. Consumer Expenditures per Consumer Unit for Health Care: 2020

[In dollars, except percent. Expenditures are direct out-of-pocket expenditures. Consumers units may be all members in a housing unit (families), a person living alone or sharing a household with others and financially independent, or 2 or more unrelated persons living together who share expenses. See also text for Section 13, and source. For composition of regions, see map, inside front cover]

Consumer characteristic	Health care, total		Health insur-ance	Medical services	Drugs and medical sup-plies [1]	Percent distribution		
	Amount	Percent of total expendi-tures				Health insur-ance	Medical services	Drugs and medical sup-plies [1]
Total...........................	**5,177**	**8.4**	**3,667**	**864**	**646**	**70.8**	**16.7**	**12.5**
Age of reference person:								
Under 25 years old...........................	1,350	3.5	941	219	190	69.7	16.2	14.1
25 to 34 years old...........................	3,320	5.8	2,412	589	319	72.7	17.7	9.6
35 to 44 years old...........................	4,579	6.2	3,225	852	501	70.4	18.6	10.9
45 to 54 years old...........................	5,465	7.3	3,771	1,083	611	69.0	19.8	11.2
55 to 64 years old...........................	5,684	8.8	3,897	1,077	710	68.6	18.9	12.5
65 years old and older...........................	6,668	14.0	4,854	835	978	72.8	12.5	14.7
Race of reference person:								
White and other [2]...........................	5,460	8.6	3,819	944	696	69.9	17.3	12.7
Asian...........................	4,924	7.3	3,714	752	458	75.4	15.3	9.3
Black...........................	3,511	7.4	2,706	404	401	77.1	11.5	11.4
Origin of reference person:								
Hispanic...........................	3,284	6.3	2,371	565	348	72.2	17.2	10.6
Non-Hispanic...........................	5,490	8.7	3,881	913	695	70.7	16.6	12.7
Region of residence:								
Northeast...........................	5,006	7.3	3,613	784	609	72.2	15.7	12.2
Midwest...........................	5,739	9.6	3,994	1,017	729	69.6	17.7	12.7
South...........................	5,098	9.1	3,709	773	617	72.8	15.2	12.1
West...........................	4,916	7.4	3,331	938	648	67.8	19.1	13.2
Size of consumer unit:								
One person...........................	3,202	8.2	2,203	530	470	68.8	16.6	14.7
Two or more persons...........................	6,016	8.5	4,289	1,006	721	71.3	16.7	12.0
Two persons...........................	6,287	9.9	4,517	958	812	71.8	15.2	12.9
Three persons...........................	5,778	8.3	4,218	907	653	73.0	15.7	11.3
Four persons...........................	6,103	7.3	4,240	1,230	635	69.5	20.2	10.4
Five persons or more...........................	5,369	6.6	3,711	1,024	633	69.1	19.1	11.8
Income before taxes, by quintile:								
Lowest 20 percent...........................	2,775	9.7	2,032	330	413	73.2	11.9	14.9
Second 20 percent...........................	4,146	10.4	2,951	584	611	71.2	14.1	14.7
Third 20 percent...........................	4,964	9.6	3,568	780	616	71.9	15.7	12.4
Fourth 20 percent...........................	6,087	8.5	4,276	1,161	649	70.2	19.1	10.7
Highest 20 percent...........................	7,931	6.9	5,520	1,469	942	69.6	18.5	11.9
Education:								
Less than a high school graduate...........	2,605	7.7	1,778	302	525	68.3	11.6	20.2
High school graduate...........................	3,645	9.3	2,741	468	437	75.2	12.8	12.0
High school graduate with some college....	4,313	8.6	3,045	708	560	70.6	16.4	13.0
Associate's degree...........................	4,616	8.3	3,376	734	505	73.1	15.9	10.9
Bachelor's degree...........................	5,705	8.1	4,069	897	739	71.3	15.7	13.0
Master's, professional, or doctoral degree...	7,698	8.5	5,244	1,560	894	68.1	20.3	11.6

[1] Includes prescription, vitamins, and nonprescription drugs. [2] Other races includes Native Hawaiian or other Pacific Islander, American Indian or Alaska Native, and approximately 2 percent reporting more than one race.

Source: U.S. Bureau of Labor Statistics, Consumer Expenditure Surveys, "Calendar year means, shares across all items, and coefficients of variation by demographic characteristics, 2020," <www.bls.gov/cex/tables.htm>, accessed November 2021.

Table 149. Medical Expenditures by Health Condition in Current and Chained (2012) Dollars and Per Capita: 2010 and 2019

[In billions of dollars (2,078.10 represents $2,078,100,000,000), except as noted. For 2000 through 2014, health conditions are classified according to the International Classification of Diseases, 9th revision (ICD-9). Beginning 2015, health conditions are classified according to ICD-10. Users should exercise caution when comparing estimates before and after 2015. Users should exercise caution when comparing trends across time. Based on Bureau of Economic Analysis' Health Care Satellite Account, Blended Account. The Blended Account combines data from multiple sources, including large claims databases. The BEA also has available health expenditure data based on the Medical Expenditure Panel Survey. See source for details]

Health expense item	Current dollars (billions)		Chained (2012) billion dollars		Per capita (dollars)	
	2010	2019	2010	2019	2010	2019
Total health	**2,078.10**	**3,073.87**	**2,166.08**	**2,574.63**	**6,745.19**	**9,398.70**
Health services	1,973.87	2,921.11	2,061.37	2,424.77	6,406.87	8,931.62
Medical services by disease	1,714.32	2,587.18	1,790.99	2,140.97	5,564.41	7,910.59
Infectious and parasitic diseases	66.76	143.03	71.55	98.47	216.69	437.33
Neoplasms	111.81	169.58	117.59	153.15	362.92	518.51
Endocrine, nutritional, and metabolic diseases and immunity disorders	116.60	182.25	121.77	146.45	378.47	557.25
Mental illness	74.21	134.56	74.48	108.65	240.87	411.43
Diseases of the nervous system and sense organs	120.96	207.31	130.06	159.72	392.62	633.87
Diseases of the circulatory system	233.60	291.36	229.10	248.84	758.23	890.87
Diseases of the respiratory system	144.67	192.81	152.81	161.85	469.58	589.54
Diseases of the digestive system	94.59	138.91	101.52	110.54	307.02	424.73
Diseases of the genitourinary system	106.74	132.29	111.81	128.16	346.46	404.49
Complications of pregnancy, childbirth, and the puerperium	38.32	54.11	39.86	44.70	124.38	165.45
Diseases of the skin and subcutaneous organs	41.96	67.99	44.67	52.70	136.20	207.89
Diseases of the musculoskeletal system and connective tissue	169.86	252.72	173.20	206.86	551.34	772.72
Injury and poisoning	112.41	151.15	116.04	118.91	364.87	462.16
Symptoms, signs, and ill-defined conditions	212.78	365.85	224.80	302.47	690.65	1,118.63
Other diseases	69.07	103.26	81.96	100.65	224.19	315.73
Diseases of blood and blood-forming organs	20.23	28.09	31.02	37.20	65.66	85.89
Congenital anomalies	7.66	8.61	7.35	6.40	24.86	26.33
Conditions originating in perinatal period	6.85	11.58	8.77	7.20	22.23	35.41
Residual codes, unclassified, all E codes [1]	34.32	54.98	35.95	51.82	111.40	168.11
Medical services by provider	259.55	333.93	270.39	283.14	842.46	1,021.03
Dental services	104.46	139.70	109.35	117.53	339.06	427.15
Nursing homes	155.10	194.22	161.05	165.43	503.43	593.85
Proprietary and government nursing homes	102.36	133.43	106.29	113.65	332.24	407.98
Nonprofit nursing homes services to households	52.73	60.79	54.76	51.78	171.15	185.87
Medical products, appliances and equipment	104.22	152.76	104.85	151.20	338.28	467.08
Pharmaceutical and other medical products	51.82	81.10	51.59	82.58	168.20	247.97
Pharmaceutical products (excl. prescription drugs) [2]	47.82	74.66	47.54	76.23	155.22	228.28
Nonprescription drugs	47.82	74.66	47.54	76.23	155.22	228.28
Other medical products	4.00	6.44	4.06	6.34	12.98	19.69
Therapeutic appliances and equipment	52.40	71.66	53.28	68.71	170.08	219.11
Corrective eyeglasses and contact lenses	29.84	38.54	30.38	36.21	96.86	117.84
Therapeutic medical equipment	22.56	33.12	22.90	32.61	73.23	101.27

[1] E codes cover external causes of injury or poisoning. [2] Excludes prescription drugs; prescription drug expenses have been allocated by health condition.

Source: U.S. Bureau of Economic Analysis, Health Care Satellite Account, "Blended Account, 2000-2019," <www.bea.gov/data/special-topics/health-care>, accessed January 2022.

Table 150. Federal Budget Outlays For Health Programs: 1980 to 2022

[In billions of dollars (65.4 represents $65,400,000,000), except percent. For fiscal years ending September 30]

Year	Total [1]	Defense health program	Medicare (excluding premiums)	Medicaid	Veterans medical care	Federal employee health benefits	Health insurance assistance	Other health	Health program outlays as percent of:	
									Total outlays	GDP
1980	65.4	3.7	35.0	14.0	6.5	3.6	(NA)	9.2	11.1	2.3
1990	180.4	12.4	109.7	41.1	12.1	11.0	(NA)	17.8	14.4	3.1
1995	307.1	15.4	180.1	89.1	16.4	15.9	(NA)	26.6	20.3	4.1
2000	388.9	17.8	219.0	117.9	19.5	19.6	(NA)	36.7	21.7	3.8
2005	614.1	36.1	336.9	181.7	28.8	29.6	0.1	70.5	24.8	4.8
2010	916.3	49.8	516.8	272.8	45.7	39.0	4.1	93.1	26.5	6.2
2011	960.8	52.6	555.3	275.0	50.1	40.6	5.8	94.7	26.7	6.2
2012	922.5	53.3	544.6	250.5	50.6	42.6	3.8	94.5	26.2	5.7
2013	955.3	46.7	575.1	265.4	52.5	43.9	2.4	92.6	27.7	5.7
2014	1,026.3	48.9	592.4	301.5	56.2	46.1	13.7	94.5	29.3	5.9
2015	1,138.4	48.0	629.6	349.8	61.9	48.4	27.3	104.7	30.8	6.3
2016	1,218.8	47.7	684.9	368.3	65.2	50.1	30.9	112.9	31.6	6.6
2017	1,249.2	49.0	696.9	374.7	69.7	50.6	39.2	121.6	31.4	6.5
2018	1,264.4	50.5	700.1	389.2	73.9	53.2	46.0	117.3	30.8	6.2
2019	1,366.7	50.6	770.8	409.4	80.3	55.3	48.7	127.0	30.7	6.5
2020	1,667.8	53.4	904.4	458.5	90.6	56.1	51.5	238.2	25.4	8.0
2021	1,644.4	51.7	830.8	520.6	99.9	59.0	64.7	210.8	24.1	7.4
2022 [2]	1,788.7	55.7	915.1	561.8	103.5	60.0	72.5	235.4	30.6	7.4

NA Not available. [1] Total outlays are net of Medicare premiums and income from Federal employee health benefits, not shown separately. [2] Estimated.

Source: U.S. Office of Management and Budget, *Budget of the U.S. Government, Fiscal Year 2023: Historical Tables*, March 2022. See also <www.whitehouse.gov/omb/budget>.

Table 151. Medicare Enrollment by State: 2019 and 2020

[In thousands (61,514.5 represents 61,514,500). Covers Medicare beneficiaries enrolled in either Hospital Insurance and/or Supplementary Medical Insurance. Enrollment counts are determined by using a person-year methodology; for each calendar year, total person-year counts are determined by summing the total number of months that each beneficiary is enrolled during the year and dividing by 12 (see source for more information). Numbers may not add to totals because of rounding]

State	2019 Total Medicare	2019 Original Medicare [1]	2019 Medicare Advantage [2]	2020 Total Medicare	2020 Original Medicare [1]	2020 Medicare Advantage [2]
Total.............	**61,514.5**	**38,577.0**	**22,937.5**	**62,849.9**	**37,785.8**	**25,064.1**
United States [3].............	**60,242.6**	**37,898.5**	**22,344.1**	**61,561.6**	**37,103.9**	**24,457.7**
Alabama.....................	1,046.6	605.6	441.0	1,062.5	576.7	485.9
Alaska.....................	100.3	98.6	1.7	104.5	102.7	1.8
Arizona....................	1,325.8	789.2	536.6	1,370.4	788.3	582.1
Arkansas..................	637.6	468.5	169.1	647.0	454.1	193.0
California..................	6,277.2	3,528.5	2,748.6	6,413.0	3,505.8	2,907.2
Colorado..................	911.5	530.7	380.9	939.1	528.0	411.1
Connecticut...............	680.4	398.8	281.6	692.1	382.2	309.9
Delaware.................	208.3	174.5	33.8	215.8	174.9	40.9
District of Columbia.......	94.1	75.6	18.4	94.1	73.3	20.8
Florida....................	4,556.6	2,455.8	2,100.8	4,680.9	2,412.7	2,268.2
Georgia...................	1,727.4	1,040.1	687.3	1,773.4	1,012.3	761.1
Hawaii....................	274.1	148.1	125.9	281.3	148.2	133.0
Idaho.....................	334.4	220.1	114.4	349.2	219.6	129.6
Illinois....................	2,233.2	1,623.8	609.4	2,266.1	1,582.8	683.3
Indiana...................	1,260.6	857.1	403.5	1,284.2	823.8	460.4
Iowa......................	625.2	483.6	141.7	637.5	477.5	160.0
Kansas...................	534.9	435.0	100.0	546.5	429.9	116.6
Kentucky..................	928.9	612.7	316.2	943.4	579.0	364.4
Louisiana.................	869.8	534.5	335.3	884.1	512.8	371.3
Maine....................	339.4	217.1	122.3	347.6	202.7	144.9
Maryland..................	1,037.0	909.4	127.5	1,058.4	920.3	138.1
Massachusetts............	1,331.3	997.2	334.0	1,352.9	989.6	363.3
Michigan..................	2,064.9	1,198.8	866.1	2,100.7	1,097.0	1,003.7
Minnesota................	1,021.8	555.4	466.4	1,046.6	540.1	506.4
Mississippi...............	601.6	479.4	122.3	609.8	464.5	145.3
Missouri..................	1,227.5	771.0	456.5	1,248.5	748.5	500.1
Montana..................	230.3	185.9	44.4	237.8	189.0	48.8
Nebraska.................	346.2	288.1	58.0	353.8	282.6	71.2
Nevada...................	531.6	331.6	200.0	549.6	329.5	220.1
New Hampshire...........	298.7	243.1	55.7	307.6	240.2	67.4
New Jersey...............	1,615.2	1,133.4	481.8	1,637.5	1,109.7	527.8
New Mexico...............	422.0	267.9	154.1	432.5	262.1	170.5
New York.................	3,629.6	2,118.6	1,511.1	3,673.3	2,070.3	1,603.0
North Carolina............	1,985.3	1,246.7	738.5	2,035.8	1,211.6	824.2
North Dakota.............	131.0	106.8	24.2	134.3	107.6	26.7
Ohio.....................	2,340.0	1,323.4	1,016.6	2,381.6	1,279.7	1,101.9
Oklahoma.................	738.9	577.1	161.7	753.6	563.4	190.2
Oregon...................	863.7	470.2	393.4	886.4	468.9	417.5
Pennsylvania..............	2,732.8	1,567.9	1,165.0	2,776.4	1,540.1	1,236.3
Rhode Island..............	220.5	120.1	100.5	224.8	117.5	107.2
South Carolina............	1,075.1	752.5	322.7	1,106.1	738.0	368.1
South Dakota.............	175.6	138.2	37.4	180.2	138.7	41.5
Tennessee................	1,356.7	812.7	544.0	1,385.4	797.0	588.4
Texas....................	4,158.9	2,493.5	1,665.3	4,286.9	2,457.0	1,829.9
Utah.....................	401.0	250.9	150.0	415.0	248.9	166.1
Vermont..................	147.2	129.4	17.8	151.3	129.5	21.9
Virginia...................	1,509.5	1,176.6	332.9	1,545.7	1,157.4	388.3
Washington...............	1,362.0	898.6	463.5	1,399.3	889.2	510.0
West Virginia..............	438.6	289.8	148.8	442.7	275.0	167.7
Wisconsin.................	1,172.0	661.5	510.5	1,200.7	645.6	555.1
Wyoming..................	110.0	105.0	4.9	113.8	108.2	5.6
American Samoa...........	4.6	4.4	0.2	4.7	4.4	0.3
Guam.....................	17.4	17.3	0.1	17.8	17.7	0.1
Northern Mariana Islands......	2.5	(NA)	([4])	2.7	2.6	(Z)
Puerto Rico...............	749.9	160.9	589.0	749.4	148.2	601.2
U.S. Virgin Islands.........	19.9	19.5	0.4	20.1	19.6	0.5
Foreign and other outlying areas......................	477.0	473.4	3.5	493.3	489.1	4.3

NA Not available. Z Less than 50. [1] Original Medicare consists of Part A (Hospital Insurance) and Part B (Supplementary Medical Insurance). Enrollment in Original Medicare includes beneficiaries enrolled in either Part A and/or Part B. [2] Medicare Advantage and other health plans are also known as Medicare Part C. Medicare Part C includes both Part A and Part B coverage. Medicare Advantage and other health plan enrollees are Medicare beneficiaries who are enrolled in health plans offered by private companies approved by Medicare. [3] U.S. total excludes territories, possessions, foreign countries or outlying areas, and unknown. [4] Enrollee counts of 1 to 10 are suppressed.

Source: U.S. Centers for Medicare and Medicaid Services, CMS Program Statistics, <data.cms.gov/collection/cms-program-statistics>, accessed November 2021.

Table 152. Medicare Enrollment by Type: 2014 to 2020

[In thousands (54,013 represents 54,013,000), except as noted. Based on person-year methodology; see source for details. Medicare Advantage, an alternative option to traditional Medicare, allows beneficiaries to receive health care services through private sector health plans. Medicare Advantage plans are required to provide at least services covered by Medicare Parts A and B (except hospice services), and are financed from both Medicare's Hospital Insurance (HI) trust fund and the Part B account within the Supplementary Medical Insurance (SMI) trust fund in proportion to the relative weights of Part A and Part B benefits to the total benefits paid by the Medicare program. Numbers and percentages may not add to totals because of rounding]

Enrollment by type	2014	2015	2016	2017	2018	2019	2020
Total Medicare enrollment [1]	**54,013**	**55,496**	**56,981**	**58,457**	**59,990**	**61,515**	**62,840**
Aged	45,217	46,631	48,143	49,678	51,304	52,991	54,532
Disabled [2]	8,796	8,865	8,838	8,779	8,686	8,523	8,308
Part A, Hospital insurance	53,675	55,153	56,639	58,115	59,650	61,167	62,499
Aged	44,879	46,289	47,802	49,338	50,964	52,644	54,191
Disabled [2]	8,796	8,865	8,837	8,778	8,686	8,523	8,308
Part B, Medical insurance	49,412	50,758	52,086	53,350	54,690	56,002	57,308
Aged	41,475	42,741	44,074	45,394	46,813	48,269	49,732
Disabled [2]	7,937	8,017	8,012	7,956	7,877	7,732	7,576
Original Medicare enrollment [1]	**37,790**	**38,025**	**38,610**	**38,668**	**38,665**	**38,577**	**37,776**
Percent of total	70.0	68.5	67.8	66.2	64.5	62.7	60.1
Aged	31,110	31,479	32,204	32,471	32,745	33,046	32,753
Disabled [2]	6,681	6,547	6,406	6,197	5,920	5,531	5,024
Part A, Hospital insurance	37,477	37,708	38,288	38,348	38,352	38,258	37,465
Aged	30,796	31,162	31,883	32,152	32,432	32,728	32,442
Disabled [2]	6,680	6,546	6,406	6,196	5,919	5,531	5,023
Part B, Medical insurance	33,190	33,287	33,715	33,562	33,366	33,077	32,246
Aged	27,368	27,589	28,136	28,188	28,255	28,333	27,954
Disabled [2]	5,822	5,698	5,580	5,374	5,111	4,745	4,291
Medicare Advantage enrollment [1]	**16,223**	**17,471**	**18,371**	**19,789**	**21,325**	**22,937**	**25,064**
Percent of total	30.0	31.5	32.2	33.9	35.6	37.3	39.9
Part A, Hospital insurance	16,198	17,445	18,351	19,768	21,298	22,908	25,034
Aged	14,082	15,127	15,919	17,186	18,532	19,917	21,749
Disabled [2]	2,116	2,319	2,432	2,582	2,766	2,992	3,285
Part B, Medical insurance	16,222	17,471	18,370	19,788	21,324	22,924	25,063
Aged	14,107	15,152	15,939	17,206	18,558	19,937	21,778
Disabled [2]	2,116	2,318	2,432	2,582	2,766	2,988	3,285

[1] Enrollment in Medicare Part A and/or Part B. [2] Persons enrolled due to end stage renal disease-only are included in the disabled enrollee counts.

Source: U.S. Centers for Medicare & Medicaid Services, CMS Program Statistics, <data.cms.gov/collection/cms-program-statistics>, accessed February 2022.

Table 153. Medicare Utilization—Persons Utilizing Medicare, Program Payments, and Cost Sharing: 2015 to 2020

[38,025 represents 38,025,000. Covers all Original Medicare (also known as "fee-for-service"), which consists of Part A (Hospital Insurance), and Part B (Medical Insurance). Persons utilizing Medicare do not include beneficiaries who received services but for whom no program payments were reported. Amounts do not sum to totals because beneficiaries may have used more than one type of service during a year, and for payments and costs, due to rounding]

Item	2015	2016	2017	2018	2019	2020
ORIGINAL MEDICARE ENROLLEES (1,000)						
Total, Part A and/or Part B	**38,025**	**38,610**	**38,668**	**38,665**	**38,577**	**37,776**
Part A	37,708	38,288	38,348	38,352	38,258	37,465
Part B	33,287	33,715	33,562	33,366	33,077	32,246
UTILIZATION (1,000)						
Medicare Part A and/or Part B	**34,398**	**34,827**	**34,790**	**34,822**	**34,335**	**33,406**
Part A	7,656	7,680	7,719	7,627	7,491	6,904
Inpatient hospital services	6,630	6,619	6,609	6,460	6,264	5,391
Skilled nursing facility services	1,845	1,803	1,764	1,705	1,624	1,468
Hospice services [1]	1,395	1,441	1,505	1,564	1,622	1,728
Home health agency services	1,671	1,642	1,610	1,572	1,515	1,373
Part B	33,824	34,241	34,170	34,168	33,654	32,682
Physician and other medical services	33,311	33,713	33,609	33,601	33,184	32,163
Outpatient services	25,283	25,711	25,715	25,687	25,357	23,334
Home health agency services	1,954	1,982	1,953	1,964	1,932	1,833
PAYMENTS AND COSTS (mil. dol.)						
Medicare Part A and/or Part B	**360,096**	**368,728**	**376,979**	**389,526**	**400,240**	**379,601**
Part A	182,146	185,493	188,093	190,702	193,251	187,446
Inpatient hospital services	130,168	133,380	135,274	136,996	138,525	130,157
Skilled nursing facility services	29,152	28,409	28,064	27,652	27,132	28,555
Hospice services [1]	15,892	16,847	17,922	19,251	20,899	22,445
Home health agency services	6,934	6,857	6,833	6,802	6,695	6,288
Part B	177,950	183,235	188,886	198,824	206,989	192,156
Physician and other medical services	102,235	103,806	105,610	109,928	114,813	106,549
Outpatient services	64,445	68,169	72,278	77,764	81,021	74,813
Home health agency services	11,270	11,260	10,998	11,132	11,156	10,794
BENEFICIARY COST SHARING [2] (mil. dol.)						
Medicare Part A and/or Part B	**61,391**	**63,045**	**64,488**	**66,402**	**67,866**	**61,742**
Part A	16,302	16,210	16,171	15,908	15,525	14,360
Part B	45,089	46,835	48,317	50,493	52,340	47,382

[1] The total Medicare Part A enrollee counts are based on enrollees in Original Medicare and Medicare Advantage/Other Health Plans (also known as Part C), combined, because once a beneficiary enrolled in a Medicare Advantage/Other Health Plan elects the hospice benefit, his or her Medicare benefits revert to fee-for-service. [2] Includes costs for copayments, coinsurance, deductibles, and out-of-pocket payments for balanced billing (the difference between Medicare allowed charges and physicians' submitted charges). Excludes monthly premium for Part B coverage, Part D coverage, voluntary hospital insurance coverage, and other supplemental insurance.

Source: U.S. Centers for Medicare and Medicaid Services, CMS Program Statistics, <data.cms.gov/collection/cms-program-statistics>, accessed February 2022.

Table 154. Medicare and Medicaid Dual Enrollment by Type of Eligibility: 2011 to 2020

[In thousands (8,972.1 represents 8,972,100). Covers Medicare beneficiaries who have low incomes and limited resources who also receive Medicaid program benefits. Services that are covered by Medicare are paid for by the Medicare program first before any payments are made by Medicaid. Based on person-year methodology; see source for details. See headnote, Table 152. Numbers may not sum to totals due to rounding]

| Year | Total Medicare-Medicaid dual enrollment | Type of eligibility | | | | | | | |
| | | Full benefit enrollment | | | | Partial benefit enrollment | | | |
		Total	Qualified Medicare beneficiary plus [1]	Specified low-income Medicare beneficiary plus [2]	Other full-benefit enrollee with Medicaid	Total	Qualified Medicare beneficiary [1]	Specified low-income Medicare beneficiary [2]	Qualified disabled & working individual [3]
Total Medicare:									
2011	8,972.1	6,603.6	4,829.3	230.5	1,543.7	2,368.5	1,096.3	821.8	450.3
2012	9,329.6	6,769.1	4,958.0	242.6	1,568.5	2,560.5	1,184.0	879.7	496.7
2013	9,586.4	6,902.3	5,080.4	245.2	1,576.7	2,684.1	1,255.4	911.1	517.5
2014	9,913.8	7,131.2	5,188.1	251.1	1,691.9	2,782.6	1,329.1	922.7	530.7
2015	10,192.6	7,317.9	5,302.7	256.9	1,758.3	2,874.7	1,383.0	940.6	551.0
2016	10,415.7	7,464.6	5,394.7	263.1	1,806.8	2,951.1	1,447.9	961.8	541.4
2017	10,632.6	7,602.3	5,491.3	270.5	1,840.6	3,030.3	1,520.4	976.8	533.0
2018	10,822.7	7,709.7	5,612.8	286.3	1,810.6	3,112.9	1,552.5	1,002.5	558.0
2019	10,959.8	7,787.5	5,740.9	290.8	1,755.8	3,172.2	1,567.4	1,023.9	580.9
2020	11,218.0	7,959.9	5,916.8	304.3	1,738.8	3,258.1	1,654.2	1,026.5	577.4
Original Medicare:									
2011	7,165.9	5,527.5	4,019.6	195.9	1,312.1	1,638.4	828.8	537.2	272.3
2012	7,260.4	5,546.9	4,033.0	202.1	1,311.8	1,713.5	862.9	557.0	293.6
2013	7,219.8	5,494.4	4,002.0	200.5	1,292.0	1,725.4	875.1	555.1	295.1
2014	7,178.2	5,453.4	3,911.9	200.3	1,341.2	1,724.8	890.1	541.3	293.4
2015	7,025.4	5,312.3	3,777.7	196.6	1,338.0	1,713.1	889.6	529.7	293.9
2016	6,994.9	5,296.6	3,753.8	196.6	1,346.2	1,698.3	900.5	520.2	277.6
2017	6,889.5	5,222.5	3,689.1	195.4	1,338.0	1,667.0	898.4	506.4	262.3
2018	6,675.7	5,083.3	3,611.2	199.9	1,272.2	1,592.5	845.1	487.9	259.5
2019	6,342.0	4,861.8	3,477.1	191.4	1,193.2	1,480.2	771.3	458.7	250.2
2020	5,942.9	4,609.6	3,305.4	184.9	1,119.3	1,333.2	713.8	400.7	218.7
Medicare Advantage:									
2011	1,806.1	1,076.0	809.7	34.7	231.6	730.1	267.5	284.6	178.0
2012	2,069.2	1,222.2	925.0	40.5	256.7	847.0	321.1	322.7	203.2
2013	2,366.6	1,407.9	1,078.5	44.7	284.7	958.7	380.3	356.0	222.4
2014	2,735.6	1,677.8	1,276.2	50.9	350.8	1,057.8	439.0	381.4	237.3
2015	3,167.2	2,005.6	1,524.9	60.3	420.3	1,161.5	493.4	411.0	257.2
2016	3,420.8	2,168.0	1,640.8	66.5	460.6	1,252.8	547.5	441.6	263.8
2017	3,743.0	2,379.8	1,802.2	75.1	502.6	1,363.2	622.0	470.5	270.7
2018	4,146.9	2,626.5	2,001.7	86.4	538.3	1,520.5	707.4	514.6	298.5
2019	4,617.8	2,925.8	2,263.8	99.4	562.6	1,692.1	796.1	565.2	330.8
2020	5,275.2	3,350.3	2,611.4	119.3	619.5	1,924.9	940.4	625.8	358.7

[1] A qualified Medicare beneficiary (QMB) has Medicare Part A, income less than or equal to 100 percent of the Federal poverty level, and resources below twice the value allowed under supplemental security income (SSI). For those who qualify, the Medicaid program pays Medicare Part A premiums (if applicable), Part B premiums, and Medicare deductibles and coinsurance amounts for Medicare covered services depending on the Medicaid state plan. An individual qualifying for full Medicaid benefits is sometimes referred to as "QMB plus." [2] A specified low-income Medicare beneficiary (SLMB) has Medicare Part A, income above 100 percent but less than 120 percent of the Federal poverty level, and resources below twice the value allowed under SSI. For those who qualify, the Medicaid program pays only the Medicare Part B premium. An individual who qualifies for full Medicaid benefits is sometimes referred to as "SLMB plus." [3] Data are combined for qualified disabled and working individuals (QDWIs) and qualifying individuals; total counts for QDWIs are less than 100. For QDWIs, Medicaid pays Medicare Part A premiums for certain disabled individuals who lost Medicare coverage because they returned to work. These individuals have incomes below 200 percent of the Federal Poverty Level, resources not more than twice the value allowed under SSI, and are not otherwise eligible for Medicaid. Qualifying individuals are entitled to Medicare Part A, have income of at least 120% but less than 135% of the Federal Poverty Level, resources that do not exceed twice the limit for SSI eligibility, and are not otherwise eligible for Medicaid. Medicaid pays their Medicare Part B premiums only. There is an annual cap on the amount of money available, which may limit the number of individuals in the group.

Source: U.S. Centers for Medicare and Medicaid Services, CMS Program Statistics, <data.cms.gov/collection/cms-program-statistics>, accessed February 2022.

Table 155. Medicare Hospital Insurance and Supplementary Medical Insurance—Average Costs per Beneficiary: 1970 to 2031

[In dollars. See headnote, Table 156]

Year	Total	Hospital Insurance	SMI Part B	SMI Part D	Year	Total	Hospital Insurance	SMI Part B	SMI Part D
1970........	385	270	115	(X)	2010........	11,902	5,193	4,901	1,808
1980........	1,352	929	423	(X)	2011........	12,165	5,275	5,032	1,858
1990........	3,334	1,979	1,355	(X)	2012........	12,204	5,195	5,169	1,839
1991........	3,569	2,125	1,443	(X)	2013........	12,199	5,155	5,170	1,874
1992........	3,941	2,411	1,530	(X)	2014........	12,433	5,010	5,392	2,031
1993........	4,259	2,648	1,611	(X)	2015........	12,737	5,028	5,556	2,153
1994........	4,678	2,948	1,730	(X)	2016........	12,925	5,095	5,674	2,156
1995........	5,061	3,194	1,867	(X)	2017........	13,134	5,145	5,870	2,120
1996........	5,378	3,424	1,954	(X)	2018........	13,578	5,220	6,219	2,139
1997........	5,649	3,616	2,033	(X)	2019........	14,183	5,393	6,615	2,175
1998........	5,602	3,468	2,134	(X)	2020........	14,359	5,475	6,686	2,198
1999........	5,561	3,306	2,255	(X)	2021........	15,309	5,667	7,414	2,228
2000........	5,844	3,348	2,496	(X)	2022 (P).....	16,192	6,049	7,920	2,224
2001........	6,370	3,610	2,760	(X)	2023 (P).....	17,042	6,312	8,419	2,311
2002........	6,788	3,813	2,975	(X)	2024 (P).....	17,899	6,581	8,911	2,407
2003........	7,144	3,922	3,221	(X)	2025 (P).....	18,818	6,885	9,452	2,481
2004........	7,722	4,162	3,561	(X)	2026 (P).....	19,864	7,204	10,087	2,574
2005........	8,278	4,439	3,839	(X)	2027 (P).....	20,893	7,527	10,692	2,673
2006........	10,179	4,602	4,116	1,461	2028 (P).....	21,960	7,851	11,327	2,782
2007........	10,702	4,759	4,313	1,630	2029 (P).....	23,120	8,182	12,040	2,899
2008........	11,232	4,996	4,574	1,662	2030 (P).....	24,183	8,483	12,676	3,023
2009........	11,696	5,174	4,792	1,730	2031 (P).....	25,383	8,829	13,399	3,154

X Not applicable. P Projected.

Source: U.S. Centers for Medicare and Medicaid Services, Trustees Report & Trust Funds, "2022 Expanded and Supplementary Tables and Figures," June 2022, <www.cms.gov/oact/tr/2021>.

Table 156. Medicare Insurance Trust Funds: 1990 to 2021

[In billions of dollars (126.3 represents $126,300,000,000), on cash basis, for calendar years. The Medicare program has two components: Medicare Part A Hospital Insurance (HI); and Supplementary Medical Insurance (SMI), consisting of Part B Medical Insurance, and Part D Prescription Drug Coverage. See text, this section, for details]

Type of trust fund	1990	2000	2005	2010	2015	2018	2019	2020	2021
TOTAL MEDICARE									
Total income [1]	126.3	257.1	357.5	486.1	644.4	755.8	794.7	899.9	887.6
Total expenditures	111.0	221.8	336.4	522.9	647.6	740.7	796.1	925.8	839.3
Net change in assets	15.3	35.3	21.0	-36.8	-3.2	15.1	-1.4	-25.9	48.3
Assets, end of year	114.4	221.5	309.8	344.0	263.2	304.7	303.3	277.4	325.7
HOSPITAL INSURANCE, PART A									
Net contribution income [2]	71.9	155.5	183.3	199.5	265.3	296.8	313.5	335.0	332.4
Interest and other income [3,4]	8.5	11.7	16.1	16.1	10.1	9.8	9.0	6.7	5.1
Benefit payments [4,5]	66.2	128.5	180.0	244.5	273.4	303.0	322.8	397.7	323.6
Trust fund balance, end of year	98.9	177.5	285.8	271.9	193.8	200.4	194.6	134.1	142.7
SMI, PART B									
Premiums from enrollees [1]	11.3	20.6	37.5	52.0	69.4	93.3	99.4	111.2	111.0
Government contributions [1,6]	33.0	65.9	118.1	153.5	203.9	253.2	268.2	336.0	318.6
Interest and other income [3,4]	1.6	3.5	1.4	3.3	5.7	7.1	5.9	5.1	6.0
Benefit payments [1,4,5]	42.5	88.9	149.2	209.7	275.8	333.0	365.7	414.1	400.5
Trust fund balance, end of year	15.5	44.0	24.0	71.4	68.2	96.3	99.6	133.3	163.3
SMI, PART D									
Premiums from enrollees [7]	(X)	(X)	–	6.5	12.7	15.9	15.7	15.8	17.0
Government contributions [8]	(X)	(X)	1.1	51.1	68.4	67.8	70.2	77.7	85.3
Transfers from states [9]	(X)	(X)	(X)	4.0	8.9	11.7	12.3	11.6	12.1
Interest and other income	(X)	(X)	–	(Z)	(Z)	0.1	0.5	0.7	0.3
Benefit payments [10]	(X)	(X)	1.1	61.7	89.4	94.7	97.1	104.6	104.4
Trust fund balance, end of year	(X)	(X)	–	0.7	1.3	8.0	9.2	10.0	19.7

– Represents zero. X Not applicable. Z Less than $50 million. [1] Includes adjustments for benefit checks issued at the end of the year instead of the following January; see source for details on this and other adjustments. [2] Includes income from payroll taxes, taxation of benefits, railroad retirement account transfers, reimbursement for uninsured persons, premiums from voluntary enrollees, and payments for military wage credits. [3] Includes recoveries of amounts reimbursed from the trust fund, receipts from fraud and abuse control program, and other miscellaneous income. [4] Values after 2005 include additional premiums for Medicare Advantage (MA) plans that are deducted from beneficiaries' Social Security checks; see source for details. [5] Includes monies transferred to the SMI trust fund in 1998-2003 for home health agency costs. [6] Matching payments from the general fund, plus certain interest-adjustment items. See also footnote 1. [7] Premiums include both amounts withheld from Social Security benefit checks (and other certain Federal benefit payments) and amounts paid directly to Part D plans. [8] Includes, net of transfers from States, all government transfers required to fund benefit payments, administrative expenses, and State expenses for making low-income eligibility determinations. [9] With the availability of Part D drug coverage and low-income subsidies beginning in 2006, Medicaid is no longer the primary payer for full-benefit dual Medicare and Medicaid eligibles. States are subject to a contribution requirement and must pay the Part D account in the SMI trust fund a portion of their estimated forgone drug costs for this population. Starting in 2006, States must pay 90 percent of the estimated costs, with this percentage phasing down over a 10-year period, to 75 percent in 2015 and later. [10] Includes payments to plans, subsidies to employer-sponsored retiree prescription drug plans, payments to States for making low-income eligibility determinations, Part D drug premiums collected from beneficiaries and transferred to Medicare Advantage plans and private drug plans, and premium amounts paid directly by enrollees to plans. Includes amounts for transitional assistance benefits in 2004-2007.

Source: U.S. Centers for Medicare and Medicaid Services, Trustees Report & Trust Funds, "2022 Expanded and Supplementary Tables and Figures," June 2022, <www.cms.gov/OACT/TR/2021>.

Table 157. Medicaid Benefit Spending by Source of Funds and Per Enrollee by State and Island Area: 2020

[In units as indicated (652,931.2 represents $652,931,200,000). For the fiscal year 2020. Data exclude spending for program administration and Medicaid-expansion Children's Health Insurance Program enrollees. Data are based on analysis of administrative data submitted to the Centers for Medicare & Medicaid Services (CMS) via CMS-64 records, as of June 28, 2021 for expenditures and as of October 22, 2021 for enrollment. All states had certified their CMS-64 financial management report (FMR) submissions as of June 28, 2021. Data may change if states revise their expenditure data after this date]

State and Island Area	Medicaid benefit spending (million dollars)			Medicaid full year enrollees [1] (1,000)	Total spending per enrollee (dollars)
	Total	Federal funds	State funds		
Total [2]	**652,931.2**	**441,421.8**	**211,509.4**	**76,670.6**	**8,516**
U.S. total [3]	**649,886.6**	**438,701.8**	**211,184.8**	**75,385.9**	**8,621**
Alabama	6,096.2	4,678.1	1,418.0	1,069.6	5,699
Alaska	2,019.3	1,528.8	490.5	219.7	9,192
Arizona	14,380.1	11,442.2	2,937.8	1,933.1	7,439
Arkansas	6,619.7	5,310.6	1,309.0	851.6	7,773
California	97,209.6	61,466.3	35,743.3	12,476.8	7,791
Colorado	9,571.1	5,820.7	3,750.5	1,249.2	7,662
Connecticut	8,488.1	5,297.3	3,190.8	970.7	8,744
Delaware	2,376.2	1,643.4	732.8	218.8	10,862
District of Columbia	3,116.5	2,402.5	713.9	261.7	11,908
Florida	25,287.5	16,822.8	8,464.7	3,948.4	6,405
Georgia	11,298.6	8,147.0	3,151.6	2,049.5	5,513
Hawaii	2,330.9	1,573.9	756.9	328.1	7,105
Idaho	2,486.1	1,915.1	571.0	343.7	7,233
Illinois	22,388.0	14,076.2	8,311.7	2,724.3	8,218
Indiana	14,269.0	10,699.1	3,569.9	1,421.7	10,036
Iowa	5,822.6	4,097.5	1,725.1	618.8	9,410
Kansas	3,829.9	2,450.3	1,379.6	365.0	10,493
Kentucky	11,905.6	9,606.3	2,299.3	1,351.1	8,812
Louisiana	12,559.5	9,603.0	2,956.4	1,663.6	7,549
Maine	3,209.0	2,276.5	932.4	296.1	10,838
Maryland	11,901.6	7,511.2	4,390.4	1,278.0	9,313
Massachusetts	17,967.4	10,681.4	7,285.9	1,717.2	10,463
Michigan	19,110.8	14,066.7	5,044.1	2,473.8	7,725
Minnesota	13,611.7	8,306.7	5,304.9	1,083.6	12,562
Mississippi	5,596.3	4,570.8	1,025.5	685.2	8,167
Missouri	10,905.1	7,728.6	3,176.5	883.4	12,345
Montana	1,992.9	1,583.6	409.3	245.9	8,103
Nebraska	2,290.9	1,364.6	926.3	244.0	9,387
Nevada	4,119.5	3,201.7	917.8	616.0	6,688
New Hampshire	2,252.9	1,365.9	886.9	188.1	11,974
New Jersey	16,411.7	10,224.0	6,187.8	1,631.8	10,057
New Mexico	6,287.1	5,184.5	1,102.6	850.0	7,397
New York	70,674.2	45,261.6	25,412.6	6,236.8	11,332
North Carolina	14,778.3	10,607.8	4,170.5	2,211.8	6,682
North Dakota	1,274.3	810.6	463.8	93.8	13,586
Ohio	25,194.5	18,231.2	6,963.2	2,909.3	8,660
Oklahoma	4,971.3	3,601.8	1,369.5	682.1	7,288
Oregon	10,660.6	7,980.0	2,680.7	1,007.6	10,581
Pennsylvania	34,964.9	21,953.1	13,011.8	2,906.4	12,030
Rhode Island	2,810.0	1,796.2	1,013.8	296.6	9,475
South Carolina	6,651.7	5,013.5	1,638.2	1,294.7	5,137
South Dakota	926.2	617.1	309.1	105.6	8,772
Tennessee	11,538.3	8,059.8	3,478.5	1,597.7	7,222
Texas	41,798.9	27,533.3	14,265.5	4,314.6	9,688
Utah	3,085.0	2,313.4	771.5	319.5	9,655
Vermont	1,617.0	1,021.0	596.0	168.9	9,572
Virginia [4]	13,512.4	8,560.7	4,951.7	1,392.3	9,705
Washington	13,616.1	8,834.9	4,781.2	1,774.7	7,672
West Virginia	4,146.0	3,397.0	749.0	529.1	7,836
Wisconsin	9,345.3	6,113.8	3,231.5	1,228.7	7,606
Wyoming	610.6	347.5	263.2	57.2	10,681
American Samoa	48.4	44.3	4.0	35.0	1,382
Guam	131.3	121.0	10.4	34.1	3,854
Northern Mariana Islands	41.9	38.6	3.3	16.2	2,582
Puerto Rico	2,745.4	2,444.3	301.1	1,168.2	2,350
Virgin Islands	77.6	71.8	5.8	31.2	2,489

[1] Full year equivalent enrollment; may also be referred to as average monthly enrollment. [2] Total includes 50 states, DC, and Island Areas. [3] Includes 50 states and DC. [4] Virginia did not report enrollment for October 2019–March 2020 on its enrollment reports ending September 30, 2020, or December 31, 2020. Shown here are data for October–December 2019 enrollment as reported in the CMS-64 enrollment report for the period ending December 31, 2019, and January–March 2020 enrollment as reported in the CMS-64 enrollment report for the period ending March 31, 2020.

Source: Medicaid and CHIP Payment and Access Commission, "MACStats," <www.macpac.gov/macstats/>, accessed February 2022.

Table 158. Children's Health Insurance Program (CHIP) by State—Expenditures and Enrollment: 2019 and 2020

[18,600.4 represents $18,600,400,000. For fiscal year. Components may not add to total due to rounding. CHIP is a federal-state program that provides health benefits coverage to children without health insurance and living in families whose incomes are too high to qualify for Medicaid. States may create CHIP programs as an expansion of Medicaid, a program separate from Medicaid, or a combination of both approaches. Based on analysis of CHIP data from the Centers for Medicare & Medicaid Services; see source for details. Minus (-) sign indicates negative spending; see source for details]

| State | Expenditures [1] (million dollars) | | | | | | Children enrolled [2] (number) | |
| | 2019 | | | 2020 | | | | |
	Total	Federal	State [3]	Total	Federal	State [3]	2019	2020
United States	**18,600.4**	**17,532.5**	**1,067.8**	**19,664.8**	**17,004.6**	**2,660.2**	**9,656,259**	**9,062,750**
Alabama	391.4	391.4	–	366.7	348.5	18.3	219,923	210,081
Alaska	37.0	32.5	4.4	30.7	24.4	6.4	22,580	21,029
Arizona	234.4	234.4	(-Z)	251.2	235.7	15.5	129,236	120,401
Arkansas	189.5	189.5	(-Z)	211.2	198.2	13.1	104,055	104,865
California	3,650.6	3,212.4	438.2	3,865.9	3,167.8	698.1	1,946,764	1,811,755
Colorado	360.1	316.9	43.3	336.0	265.4	70.6	174,310	164,505
Connecticut	47.9	99.6	-51.7	46.4	69.7	-23.3	23,706	21,609
Delaware	42.2	39.4	2.8	44.7	35.5	9.2	14,073	13,573
District of Columbia	55.3	55.3	–	61.1	57.3	3.8	17,203	18,186
Florida	841.5	804.6	36.9	840.6	737.1	103.5	471,886	461,726
Georgia	434.6	434.6	(-Z)	431.8	397.3	34.5	251,194	251,620
Hawaii	58.6	53.3	5.4	63.8	52.5	11.3	30,522	27,611
Idaho	87.1	87.1	–	85.8	80.7	5.1	40,319	44,319
Illinois	430.5	379.9	50.7	635.3	508.7	126.5	328,981	330,376
Indiana	235.7	233.8	1.9	284.5	258.3	26.2	137,504	123,134
Iowa	144.6	137.4	7.3	180.2	158.1	22.2	104,915	101,719
Kansas	150.8	140.2	10.6	161.7	139.0	22.7	69,810	68,955
Kentucky	228.1	228.0	0.1	253.5	240.5	13.0	108,297	101,275
Louisiana	401.4	395.4	6.0	408.2	373.7	34.5	184,650	176,621
Maine	36.8	36.1	0.7	38.0	33.9	4.1	29,398	32,127
Maryland	384.6	338.4	46.2	340.2	270.8	69.4	148,152	131,725
Massachusetts	780.8	687.2	93.6	805.3	645.3	160.0	233,372	219,055
Michigan	303.5	297.8	5.6	284.5	254.5	30.0	87,945	71,853
Minnesota	16.2	129.4	-113.2	18.5	108.8	-90.3	3,514	3,363
Mississippi	264.5	264.5	–	260.7	257.0	3.6	86,489	84,459
Missouri	287.0	283.5	3.5	341.4	310.0	31.3	114,802	117,301
Montana	114.7	113.5	1.3	91.6	82.2	9.4	42,680	[4] 40,927
Nebraska	94.1	84.5	9.5	93.3	77.5	15.8	60,837	62,225
Nevada	81.2	79.9	1.3	85.4	77.9	7.5	73,122	65,832
New Hampshire	33.9	45.5	-11.5	42.4	45.4	-3.0	17,742	17,115
New Jersey	621.4	546.5	74.9	728.7	582.7	146.0	269,392	262,080
New Mexico	102.4	102.4	0.1	114.5	109.5	5.0	12,805	9,613
New York	1,655.6	1,456.9	198.7	1,895.7	1,522.3	373.4	790,829	751,094
North Carolina	558.9	558.9	(Z)	576.5	527.0	49.5	317,326	309,267
North Dakota	29.2	25.7	3.5	21.8	17.3	4.5	6,139	(NA)
Ohio	539.9	523.8	16.1	556.7	494.6	62.1	242,786	211,086
Oklahoma	258.0	249.5	8.6	273.3	249.2	24.2	210,825	219,541
Oregon	446.6	432.5	14.2	461.5	407.8	53.7	196,984	[5] 187,285
Pennsylvania	767.8	687.8	80.0	812.5	659.9	152.6	372,821	357,620
Rhode Island	113.7	102.0	11.7	89.2	71.8	17.4	37,149	32,526
South Carolina	203.2	203.2	–	208.4	196.4	12.0	113,535	111,645
South Dakota	32.9	30.5	2.4	33.0	27.9	5.1	19,903	16,552
Tennessee	210.6	208.7	1.9	317.7	287.6	30.1	77,564	73,668
Texas	1,549.9	1,452.6	97.3	1,467.9	1,281.8	186.1	1,080,313	905,469
Utah	128.1	128.2	(-Z)	130.2	120.7	9.5	55,872	49,592
Vermont	13.8	27.9	-14.1	13.6	19.7	-6.1	5,333	4,748
Virginia	429.0	377.5	51.5	449.1	358.8	90.2	242,834	239,439
Washington	218.9	273.0	-54.1	208.9	234.1	-25.2	90,139	80,322
West Virginia	75.4	75.4	–	77.0	74.8	2.2	39,897	36,869
Wisconsin	211.4	230.6	-19.3	253.8	237.4	16.4	188,794	172,724
Wyoming	14.7	13.0	1.8	14.5	11.6	2.9	7,038	6,129

– Represents zero. Z represents an amount between $0.05 million and -$0.05 million that rounds to zero. [1] Expenditure data for FY2019 as of July 2020, and for FY2020 as of July 2021. [2] Enrollment data for FY2019 and FY2020 as of June 2021 and subject to revision. [3] Section 2105(g) of the Social Security Act permits 11 qualifying states to use CHIP funds to pay the difference between the regular Medicaid matching rate and the enhanced CHIP matching rate for Medicaid-enrolled, Medicaid-financed children whose family income exceeds 133 percent of the federal poverty level. Although these are CHIP funds, they effectively reduce state spending on children in Medicaid and do not require a state match within the CHIP program. In cases where the sum of 2105(g) federal CHIP spending (for Medicaid enrollees) and regular federal CHIP spending (for CHIP enrollees) exceeds total spending for CHIP enrollees, states are shown in this table as having negative state CHIP spending. [4] Montana FY2020 enrollment totals contain duplicates and are artificially high. [5] Oregon FY2020 enrollment data are artificially low due to missing data.

Source: Medicaid and CHIP Payment and Access Commission, "MACStats: Program Enrollment and Spending, CHIP," <www.macpac.gov/macstats/>; and U.S. Centers for Medicare & Medicaid Services, CHIP Reports & Evaluations, "Annual Enrollment Reports," <www.medicaid.gov/chip/reports-and-evaluations/index.html>; accessed February 2022.

Table 159. Medicaid Managed Care Enrollment by State and Other Areas: 2000 to 2019

[In thousands except as noted (33,690 represents 33,690,000). Through 2010, for year ending June 30; beginning with 2013, as of July 1. Medicaid managed care provides Medicaid health benefits and additional services through contracted arrangements between state Medicaid agencies and managed care entities. The unduplicated Medicaid enrollment figures include dual Medicare-Medicaid enrollees. The unduplicated managed care enrollment figures include enrollees in any Medicaid managed care program, including comprehensive managed care organizations (MCOs), limited benefit plans such as prepaid inpatient and ambulatory health plans, primary care case management (PCCM) programs, and PCCM entities]

| State and other areas | Total enroll-ment | Managed care enrollment | | State and other areas | Total enroll-ment | Managed care enrollment | | State and other areas | Total enroll-ment | Managed care enrollment | |
		Number	Percent of total			Number	Percent of total			Number	Percent of total
2000......	33,690	18,786	55.8	GA[4].......	1,918	1,466	76.5	NM........	832	668	80.3
2010......	54,612	39,020	71.5	HI..........	328	328	100.0	NY.........	6,140	4,705	76.6
2013......	62,507	45,923	73.5	ID..........	291	289	99.2	NC.........	2,174	1,621	74.6
2014......	72,050	55,459	77.0	IL...........	3,001	2,123	70.7	ND.........	89	46	51.7
2015......	77,847	62,373	80.1	IN..........	1,462	1,075	73.5	OH........	2,823	2,372	84.0
2016......	80,185	65,006	81.1	IA..........	642	603	93.9	OK........	790	645	81.6
2017......	80,243	65,796	82.0	KS..........	398	342	85.9	OR........	1,080	870	80.5
2018......	79,899	66,164	82.8	KY..........	1,353	1,224	90.5	PA.........	2,827	2,627	92.9
2019				LA..........	1,622	1,501	92.5	RI..........	312	293	93.9
Total[1]...	**78,738**	**65,745**	**83.5**	ME........	259	242	93.8	SC.........	1,253	1,253	100.0
U.S......	77,406	64,413	83.2	MD........	1,458	1,191	81.7	SD.........	122	90	73.9
AL.........	1,040	870	83.7	MA........	1,829	1,188	64.9	TN.........	1,565	1,438	91.8
AK[2]......	207	–	–	MI..........	4,713	4,650	98.7	TX.........	3,879	3,742	96.5
AZ.........	1,875	1,581	84.3	MN........	1,085	850	78.3	UT.........	290	258	89.1
AR........	952	823	86.5	MS........	673	436	64.8	VT.........	166	109	65.5
CA........	12,780	10,395	81.3	MO........	858	841	98.0	VA.........	1,460	1,276	87.4
CO[3]......	1,232	1,183	96.0	MT........	254	207	81.5	WA........	1,743	1,743	100.0
CT[2]......	837	–	–	NE........	248	247	99.6	WV........	508	387	76.2
DE.........	237	209	87.9	NV........	654	575	87.9	WI.........	1,195	813	68.0
DC.........	267	249	93.2	NH........	193	173	89.5	WY........	60	(Z)	0.2
FL.........	3,813	3,097	81.2	NJ..........	1,613	1,499	93.0	PR.........	1,332	1,332	100.0

– Represents zero. Z Less than 500. [1] Includes enrollment for Puerto Rico. [2] Alaska and Connecticut total Medicaid enrollment as of July 1, 2019 was taken from the Medicaid Budget and Expenditure System, accessed June 16, 2021. [3] Colorado reported plan level enrollment as 0 for plans that had less than 30 beneficiaries. [4] Georgia's total Medicaid enrollment in any type of managed care does not include enrollees in Georgia's Non-Emergency Medical Transportation (NEMT) program.

Source: U.S. Centers for Medicare and Medicaid Services, "Medicaid Managed Care Enrollment Report: 2019 Medicaid Managed Care Enrollment Summary," <www.medicaid.gov/medicaid/managed-care/enrollment/index.html>, Summer 2021, and earlier releases and reports.

Table 160. Medicaid Benefit Spending by Service Category: 2014 to 2020

[In millions of dollars (469,683 represents $469,683,000,000). For fiscal years. Covers the 50 states, DC, and the territories. Includes federal and state funds. Service category definitions and spending amounts shown here may differ from other Centers for Medicare & Medicaid (CMS) sources. Data shown here are subject to revisions because States may revise their expenditure data after an initial submission date]

Spending category	2014	2015	2016	2017	2018	2019	2020
Total benefit spending...........................	**469,683**	**526,159**	**550,880**	**572,244**	**588,213**	**597,385**	**652,931**
Fee for service:							
Hospital services...........................	85,537	92,745	88,607	77,790	78,862	79,077	81,939
Physician and surgical services..............	13,973	11,189	9,935	8,752	8,968	8,113	8,645
Dental services............................	3,960	4,218	3,929	3,951	3,420	4,305	3,739
Other practitioner services..................	1,913	2,150	2,599	1,892	1,784	1,848	1,799
Clinic and health centers...................	10,216	11,180	10,624	11,134	11,156	12,648	12,499
Other acute services[1].....................	38,294	38,905	36,541	45,622	45,430	40,968	43,138
Drugs[2]...................................	8,059	10,535	8,480	3,218	9,981	4,727	4,210
Institutional long-term services and supports (LTSS)[3]......	65,692	59,552	60,070	58,001	56,652	56,505	55,486
Home and community LTSS[4].................	55,796	58,107	62,052	63,987	71,485	76,622	84,129
Managed care and premium assistance...........	179,089	230,220	258,551	285,653	288,219	301,727	347,756
Medicare premiums and coinsurance............	15,094	15,428	17,159	19,209	19,884	20,599	21,890
Collections[5]...............................	-7,940	-8,070	-7,667	-6,966	-7,628	-9,754	-12,299

[1] Other acute services include laboratory or x-ray services; early periodic screening, diagnostic, and treatment (EPSDT) screenings; emergency services for unauthorized aliens; physical, occupational, speech, and hearing therapy; prosthetics, dentures, and eyeglasses; preventive services and vaccines; school-based services; rehabilitative services; hospice; and various other services. [2] Spending for drugs are net of rebates. [3] Institutional LTSS includes nursing facility, intermediate care facility for individuals with intellectual disabilities, and mental health facility. [4] Home- and community-based LTSS includes home health, waiver and state plan services, personal care, and certified community behavioral health clinic. [5] Collections includes third-party liability, estate, and other recoveries.

Source: Medicaid and CHIP Payment and Access Commission, "MACStats, Program Enrollment and Spending: Medicaid Benefits," <www.macpac.gov/macstats/>, accessed February 2022; and *MACStats: Medicaid and CHIP Data Book*, December 2020, and previous editions. See also <www.macpac.gov/macstats/>.

Table 161. Medicare Hospital Insurance and Supplemental Medical Insurance Expenditures, Total and as a Percent of GDP: 1990 to 2040

[In millions of dollars (5,963,145 represents $5,963,145,000,000), except percent. Incurred amounts relate to expenditures for services performed in a given year, even if payment for those expenditures occurs in a later year. The Medicare program has two components: Medicare Part A Hospital Insurance (HI); and Supplementary Medical Insurance (SMI), consisting of Part B Medical Insurance, and Part D Prescription Drug Coverage. See text in this section for details]

Year	GDP	Medicare expenditures				Medicare expenditures as percent of GDP			
		Total	HI Part A	SMI Part B	SMI Part D	Total	HI Part A	SMI Part B	SMI Part D
ACTUAL									
1990............	5,963,145	110,903	66,785	44,118	(X)	1.86	1.12	0.74	(X)
2000............	10,250,952	224,629	131,449	93,180	(X)	2.19	1.28	0.91	(X)
2010............	15,048,970	523,912	245,985	215,070	62,857	3.48	1.63	1.43	0.42
2011............	15,599,732	548,501	256,104	226,018	66,379	3.52	1.64	1.45	0.43
2012............	16,253,970	571,683	262,571	240,227	68,885	3.52	1.62	1.48	0.42
2013............	16,843,196	590,102	268,913	247,896	73,294	3.50	1.60	1.47	0.44
2014............	17,550,688	618,128	269,441	266,434	82,253	3.52	1.54	1.52	0.47
2015............	18,206,023	649,720	277,779	281,993	89,949	3.57	1.53	1.55	0.49
2016............	18,695,106	677,732	289,021	295,570	93,141	3.63	1.55	1.58	0.50
2017............	19,479,622	708,152	300,162	313,714	94,276	3.64	1.54	1.61	0.48
2018............	20,527,159	749,517	311,508	340,048	97,960	3.65	1.52	1.66	0.48
2019............	21,372,582	803,136	329,981	370,546	102,609	3.76	1.54	1.73	0.48
2020............	20,893,746	832,512	342,359	383,174	106,979	3.98	1.64	1.83	0.51
2021............	22,989,423	903,311	359,200	432,815	111,297	3.93	1.56	1.88	0.48
PROJECTED [1]									
2022............	24,951,102	975,930	390,840	470,577	114,514	3.91	1.57	1.89	0.46
2023............	26,193,835	1,053,694	417,848	512,953	122,892	4.02	1.60	1.96	0.47
2024............	27,364,655	1,137,115	447,096	557,787	132,233	4.16	1.63	2.04	0.48
2025............	28,537,909	1,226,225	479,172	606,709	140,344	4.30	1.68	2.13	0.49
2026............	29,719,718	1,326,546	513,407	663,579	149,560	4.46	1.73	2.23	0.50
2030............	34,924,021	1,746,279	652,373	903,678	190,227	5.00	1.87	2.59	0.54
2035............	42,674,064	2,423,573	875,271	1,299,599	248,702	5.68	2.05	3.05	0.58
2040............	51,968,150	3,131,252	1,107,463	1,709,609	314,179	6.03	2.13	3.29	0.60

X Not applicable. [1] Projections are a projected baseline, and are based on current law; that is, they assume that laws on the books will be implemented and adhered to with respect to scheduled taxes, premium revenues, and payments to providers and health plans. The one exception is that the projections disregard payment reductions that would result from the projected depletion of the Medicare Hospital Insurance trust fund (Part A), thus allowing the size of deficits to become apparent. To date, Congress has not allowed the assets of the Medicare Hospital Insurance trust fund to become depleted.

Source: U.S. Centers for Medicare and Medicaid Services, Trustees Report & Trust Funds, "2022 Expanded and Supplementary Tables and Figures," June 2022, <www.cms.gov/OACT/TR/2021>.

Table 162. Persons With and Without Health Insurance Coverage by State: 2020

[295,794 represents 295,794,000. Data are based on 2020 American Community Survey (ACS) 1-year experimental estimates. The coronavirus disease 2019 (COVID-19) pandemic impacted 2020 ACS data collection and quality, and standard estimates did not meet statistical quality standards. The Census Bureau does not recommend comparing experimental estimates to standard ACS estimates. For more information, see <www.census.gov/programs-surveys/acs/data/experimental-data.html>. Data are based on a sample of the civilian noninstitutionalized population. The American Community Survey (ACS) measures population without health insurance coverage at the time of the interview. See source for more information]

State	Total persons covered (1,000)	Total persons not covered		Children not covered [1]		State	Total persons covered (1,000)	Total persons not covered		Children not covered [1]	
		Number (1,000)	Percent of total	Number (1,000)	Percent of total			Number (1,000)	Percent of total	Number (1,000)	Percent of total
U.S.........	**295,794**	**28,553**	**8.8**	**4,177**	**5.4**	MO...........	5,432	609	10.1	100	6.8
AL...........	4,372	470	9.7	39	3.4	MT...........	971	93	8.7	17	7.1
AK...........	620	81	11.6	15	8.2	NE...........	1,755	154	8.1	26	5.2
AZ...........	6,501	817	11.2	161	9.2	NV...........	2,727	371	12.0	61	8.3
AR...........	2,724	251	8.5	31	4.2	NH...........	1,268	82	6.1	8	2.8
CA...........	36,099	2,747	7.1	319	3.4	NJ...........	8,111	663	7.6	88	4.3
CO...........	5,228	482	8.4	70	5.3	NM...........	1,865	201	9.7	29	5.9
CT...........	3,346	163	4.6	21	2.8	NY...........	18,115	989	5.2	104	2.5
DE...........	909	62	6.3	8	3.7	NC...........	9,288	1,099	10.6	129	5.3
DC...........	679	24	3.5	2	1.5	ND...........	694	54	7.2	12	6.5
FL...........	18,755	2,644	12.4	319	7.1	OH...........	10,749	772	6.7	129	4.7
GA...........	9,134	1,370	13.0	197	7.4	OK...........	3,302	595	15.3	95	9.4
HI...........	1,298	53	3.9	10	3.2	OR...........	3,924	276	6.6	33	3.6
ID...........	1,631	174	9.6	30	6.3	PA...........	11,789	791	6.3	165	5.9
IL...........	11,526	881	7.1	89	3.0	RI...........	1,002	38	3.7	6	3.0
IN...........	6,159	497	7.5	100	6.1	SC...........	4,577	535	10.5	67	5.7
IA...........	2,967	152	4.9	20	2.7	SD...........	789	86	9.8	14	6.2
KS...........	2,602	252	8.8	39	5.4	TN...........	6,089	691	10.2	96	6.0
KY...........	4,141	255	5.8	46	4.4	TX...........	23,821	5,062	17.5	908	11.6
LA...........	4,161	372	8.2	50	4.4	UT...........	2,949	273	8.5	69	7.1
ME...........	1,236	99	7.5	14	5.5	VT...........	592	26	4.1	1	1.0
MD...........	5,612	340	5.7	49	3.5	VA...........	7,749	605	7.2	85	4.3
MA...........	6,642	180	2.6	24	1.7	WA...........	7,095	477	6.3	53	3.1
MI...........	9,343	520	5.3	61	2.7	WV...........	1,637	116	6.6	11	2.8
MN...........	5,321	277	4.9	48	3.5	WI...........	5,439	324	5.6	60	4.5
MS...........	2,557	339	11.7	40	5.5	WY...........	507	65	11.3	11	7.8

[1] Children under age 19, who are eligible for health insurance coverage under Medicaid and the Children's Health Insurance Program.

Source: U.S. Census Bureau, 2020 ACS 1-Year Experimental Data Tables, "Table XK202701. Age by Health Insurance Coverage Status," <www.census.gov/programs-surveys/acs/data/experimental-data.html>, accessed February 2022.

Table 163. Health Insurance Coverage Status by Selected Characteristics: 2020

[325,638 represents 325,638,000. Data for coverage during all or part of 2020; people not covered had no health insurance for the entire year. Based on the Current Population Survey, Annual Social and Economic Supplement (CPS ASEC); see text, Section 1, and Appendix III. Private health insurance includes coverage provided through an employer or union, coverage purchased directly from an insurance company or through a federal or state marketplace, or TRICARE (formerly known as Civilian Health and Medical Program of the Uniformed Services). Public (government) health insurance coverage includes Medicaid, Medicare, CHAMPVA (Civilian Health and Medical Program of the Department of Veterans Affairs), and care provided by the Department of Veterans Affairs and the military. People covered only through the Indian Health Service are considered uninsured. The Census Bureau recommends data users consider the impact of the coronavirus disease 2019 (COVID-19) pandemic on the CPS ASEC. See source for more information]

	Number (1,000)							Percent			
		Not covered by health insurance	Covered by private or public health insurance					Not covered by health insurance		Employer based coverage	Medicaid coverage
Characteristic				Private		Public					
	Total persons		Total [1]	Total	Employer based	Medi-care	Medi-caid		Total cov-ered [1]		
Total.............	**325,638**	**27,957**	**297,680**	**216,532**	**177,175**	**59,844**	**57,921**	**8.6**	**91.4**	**54.4**	**17.8**
Sex:											
Male.................	159,691	15,304	144,386	106,915	88,030	27,077	27,109	9.6	90.4	55.1	17.0
Female...............	165,947	12,653	153,294	109,616	89,145	32,767	30,812	7.6	92.4	53.7	18.6
Race:											
White alone [2].........	247,763	20,631	227,132	169,847	137,623	49,435	38,459	8.3	91.7	55.5	15.5
Black alone [2].........	43,427	4,523	38,904	23,693	20,097	6,540	12,373	10.4	89.6	46.3	28.5
Asian alone [2].........	20,125	1,180	18,945	14,571	12,360	2,668	3,177	5.9	94.1	61.4	15.8
Hispanic origin [3].......	61,160	11,192	49,968	30,515	25,178	5,473	17,324	18.3	81.7	41.2	28.3
Age:											
Under 19 years......	76,156	4,291	71,865	47,393	41,459	300	26,478	5.6	94.4	54.4	34.8
19 to 25 years........	29,269	4,210	25,059	20,320	17,194	416	4,948	14.4	85.6	58.7	16.9
26 to 34 years........	40,916	5,809	35,107	28,791	25,099	867	6,612	14.2	85.8	61.3	16.2
35 to 44 years........	42,004	5,224	36,780	30,952	27,393	961	5,960	12.4	87.6	65.2	14.2
45 to 64 years........	81,457	7,860	73,596	61,374	52,487	5,115	10,400	9.6	90.4	64.4	12.8
65 years and over....	55,836	563	55,273	27,702	13,542	52,185	3,523	1.0	99.0	24.3	6.3
Household income:											
Less than $25,000....	41,274	5,942	35,332	9,994	5,264	14,116	17,830	14.4	85.6	12.8	43.2
$25,000–$49,999.....	55,310	6,945	48,366	25,201	16,875	15,168	16,470	12.6	87.4	30.5	29.8
$50,000–$74,999.....	52,757	6,000	46,757	32,879	25,294	10,029	10,575	11.4	88.6	47.9	20.0
$75,000-$99,999.....	42,567	3,394	39,173	31,788	26,512	6,326	5,730	8.0	92.0	62.3	13.5
$100,000-$124,999...	34,538	2,364	32,174	27,749	23,931	4,349	3,090	6.8	93.2	69.3	8.9
$125,000-$149,999...	24,031	1,220	22,811	20,532	17,822	2,839	1,425	5.1	94.9	74.2	5.9
$150,000 or more....	75,160	2,094	73,067	68,389	61,478	7,018	2,802	2.8	97.2	81.8	3.7
Below poverty.........	37,156	6,396	30,761	8,629	5,302	6,611	19,083	17.2	82.8	14.3	51.4

[1] Includes other private and public insurance, not shown separately. Persons with coverage counted only once in total, even if covered by more than one type of policy. [2] Refers to people who reported specified race and no other race category. [3] Persons of Hispanic origin may be of any race.

Source: U.S. Census Bureau, *Health Insurance Coverage in the United States: 2020,* Current Population Reports, P60-274, September 2021; and "Current Population Survey Tables for Health Insurance Coverage, Health Insurance: Tables 2018-forward," Table H-01, <www.census.gov/topics/health/health-insurance/data/tables.html>, accessed November 2021.

Table 164. People Without Health Insurance for the Entire Year by Age, Sex, Race/Ethnicity, and Marital Status: 2019 and 2020

[In thousands, except as noted (324,550 represents 324,550,000). Based on the Current Population Survey, Annual Social and Economic Supplement (CPS ASEC); see text, Section 1. The Census Bureau recommends data users consider the impact of the coronavirus disease 2019 (COVID-19) pandemic on the CPS ASEC. See source for more information]

	2019			2020		
		Uninsured persons			Uninsured persons	
Characteristic	Total persons	Number	Percent of total persons	Total persons	Number	Percent of total persons
Total [1]....................................	**324,550**	**26,111**	**8.0**	**325,638**	**27,957**	**8.6**
Male..	159,103	14,029	8.8	159,691	15,304	9.6
Female......................................	165,446	12,082	7.3	165,947	12,653	7.6
White alone [2]...............................	247,869	19,381	7.8	247,763	20,631	8.3
Black alone [2]...............................	42,991	4,118	9.6	43,427	4,523	10.4
Asian alone [2]...............................	19,905	1,240	6.2	20,125	1,180	5.9
Hispanic [3].................................	60,517	10,122	16.7	61,160	11,192	18.3
Under age 19 [4]............................	76,636	3,994	5.2	76,156	4,291	5.6
Age 19 to 25 [4]............................	29,605	4,202	14.2	29,269	4,210	14.4
Age 26 to 34 years..........................	40,511	5,379	13.3	40,916	5,809	14.2
Age 35 to 44 years..........................	41,412	4,716	11.4	42,004	5,224	12.4
Age 45 to 64 years..........................	81,744	7,227	8.8	81,457	7,860	9.6
Age 65 and older...........................	54,642	594	1.1	55,836	563	1.0
Married.....................................	100,795	7,629	7.6	98,821	8,425	8.5
Widowed....................................	3,319	447	13.5	3,304	401	12.1
Divorced....................................	18,290	2,196	12.0	18,486	2,431	13.2
Separated..................................	3,802	724	19.0	3,738	756	20.2
Never married..............................	67,065	10,528	15.7	69,297	11,090	16.0

[1] Includes other races not shown separately. [2] Refers to people who reported specified race and did not report any other race category. [3] Persons of Hispanic origin may be of any race. [4] Children under age 19 may be eligible for Medicaid/CHIP (Children's Health Insurance Program). Individuals age 19-25 may be eligible to participate as a dependent on a parent's health insurance plan.

Source: U.S. Census Bureau, *Health Insurance Coverage in the United States: 2020,* Current Population Reports, P60-274, September 2021; and "Current Population Survey Tables for Health Insurance Coverage, Health Insurance: Tables 2018-forward," Table H-01, <www.census.gov/topics/health/health-insurance/data/tables.html>, accessed November 2021.

Table 165. Health Insurance Coverage—Public, Private, and Exchange-Based Coverage by Selected Characteristics: 2019 to 2021

[In percent, except as noted (10.0 represents 10,000,000). Covers persons age 18 to 64, except as noted. Based on the National Health Interview Survey. Data are estimates that have been released prior to final data editing and final weighting; see source for details. Data are based on a sample of the civilian noninstitutionalized population and are subject to sampling error. In 2019, the NCHS redesigned the NHIS questionnaire and made other methodological changes]

Year and characteristic	No insurance [1]	Public health plan [2]	Private health insurance [3]	Exchange-based private health insurance [4] Total (millions)	Exchange-based private health insurance [4] Percent
Total age 64 and under:					
2019	12.1	26.0	63.7	10.0	3.7
2020 [8]	11.5	26.4	64.1	10.1	3.8
2021	11.0	27.7	63.2	11.6	4.3
Age 17 and under:					
2019	5.1	41.4	55.2	1.3	1.7
2020 [8]	5.1	42.2	54.9	1.5	2.1
2021	4.1	44.3	53.8	1.5	2.1
Age 18 to 64:					
2019	14.7	20.4	66.8	8.7	4.4
2020 [8]	13.9	20.5	67.5	8.6	4.4
2021	13.5	21.7	66.6	10.1	5.1
Male:					
2019	16.3	18.1	67.5	4.7	3.5
2020 [8]	14.8	18.6	68.4	4.2	3.1
2021	15.8	18.4	67.5	5.2	3.9
Female:					
2019	13.1	22.6	66.1	5.3	3.9
2020 [8]	13.0	22.4	66.6	5.9	4.4
2021	11.3	24.8	65.7	6.5	4.8
White only, non-Hispanic:					
2019	10.5	17.0	74.5	5.5	3.6
2020 [8]	9.2	16.9	76.0	5.7	3.7
2021	8.7	18.5	74.8	6.4	4.2
Black only, non-Hispanic:					
2019	14.7	34.3	53.7	1.0	2.9
2020 [8]	14.6	33.1	54.9	0.9	2.6
2021	14.1	32.6	55.4	1.3	3.9
Hispanic or Latino: [5]					
2019	29.7	22.5	48.8	2.1	3.8
2020 [8]	29.3	23.0	48.6	2.4	4.2
2021	30.1	23.7	47.4	2.5	4.4
Poor: [6]					
2019	25.8	52.3	23.6	1.1	3.0
2020 [8]	25.3	56.3	20.7	0.6	1.9
2021	24.5	54.1	22.9	1.2	3.6
Near poor: [6]					
2019	26.8	35.4	40.1	2.8	5.3
2020 [8]	25.0	38.8	39.0	2.4	4.8
2021	23.7	39.0	40.1	3.3	6.4
Not poor: [6]					
2019	9.0	10.4	82.4	5.8	3.2
2020 [8]	8.7	10.4	82.5	6.9	3.7
2021	8.4	11.1	82.0	6.9	3.8
In states with Medicaid expansion [7]					
2019	11.0	23.4	67.6	5.7	3.3
2020 [8]	10.2	22.5	69.2	6.2	3.5
2021	10.1	23.8	67.8	7.2	4.0
In states without Medicaid expansion [7]					
2019	21.2	15.1	65.3	4.3	4.3
2020 [8]	20.8	16.7	64.3	3.9	4.1
2021	20.4	17.4	64.1	4.4	4.9

[1] Also includes persons with only Indian Health Service coverage or only a private plan covering one type of service, such as accidents or dental care. [2] Includes Medicaid, Children's Health Insurance Program (CHIP), state-sponsored or other government-sponsored health plan, Medicare, and military plans. A small number of persons covered by both public and private plans are included in both categories. [3] Includes plans obtained through an employer, purchased directly, purchased through local or community programs, or purchased through the Health Insurance Marketplace or a state-based exchange. Excludes plans that cover only one type of service, such as accidents or dental care. A small number of persons covered by both public and private plans are included in both categories. [4] For persons under age 65, except for the age groups below. Covers persons who purchased a private health insurance plan through the Health Insurance Marketplace or state-based exchanges established under the Affordable Care Act of 2010. These persons are also included under "private health insurance." [5] Persons of Hispanic or Latino origin may be of any race or combination of races. [6] Based on family size and income using the U.S. Census Bureau's poverty thresholds. "Poor" persons have incomes below the poverty threshold; "Near poor" persons have incomes at 100% to less than 200% of the poverty threshold; and "Not poor" persons have incomes at or above 200% of the poverty threshold. Excludes persons with unknown poverty status. Poverty categories are based the family's income in the previous calendar. [7] The Affordable Care Act gave states the option to expand Medicaid coverage to adults with incomes up to and including 138 percent of the federal poverty level. As of 2019, Medicaid had been expanded in 33 states and DC. States with no Medicaid expansion included Alabama, Florida, Georgia, Idaho, Kansas, Mississippi, Missouri, Nebraska, North Carolina, Oklahoma, South Carolina, South Dakota, Tennessee, Texas, Utah, Wisconsin, and Wyoming. In 2020, Idaho and Utah expanded Medicaid. In 2021, Nebraska expanded Medicaid. [8] Due to the coronavirus disease (COVID-19) pandemic, the NHIS data collection switched to a telephone-only mode beginning March 19, 2020. Personal visits resumed in September 2020. For April-December, response rates were lower and respondent characteristics were different, which may have impacted the estimates for 2020 when compared to earlier years.

Source: U.S. National Center for Health Statistics, National Health Interview Survey Early Release Program, *Health Insurance Coverage: Early Release of Estimates From the National Health Interview Survey, 2021,* May 2022. See also <www.cdc.gov/nchs/nhis/releases.htm>.

Table 166. Worker Participation in Employer-Sponsored Health Insurance and Benefit Programs, and Participant Contributions: 2021

[Based on the March 2021 National Compensation Survey; survey drew responses from 6,007 private industry establishments of all sizes, representing about 114.52 million workers. Excludes federal government workers, the military, agricultural workers, private household workers, and the self-employed. For more information, see Appendix III, and the Bureau of Labor Statistics (BLS) Handbook of Methods, National Compensation Measures, online at <www.bls.gov/opub/hom/ncs/home.htm>]

Characteristic	Percent of workers participating				Single coverage medical plans		Family coverage medical plans	
	Medical care	Dental care	Vision care	Out-patient prescription drug coverage	Percent of employees required to contribute to premium	Average monthly contribution [1] (dol.)	Percent of employees required to contribute to premium	Average monthly contribution [1] (dol.)
Total.............................	**47**	**31**	**21**	**46**	**89**	**147.12**	**95**	**601.59**
Management, professional, and related...	63	46	28	62	92	144.32	97	598.94
Management, business, and financial...	70	52	31	69	92	156.35	98	634.49
Professional and related...................	59	43	26	58	91	136.11	96	574.52
Service......................................	22	13	9	22	84	158.61	95	705.96
Sales and office...........................	45	28	18	44	91	145.27	97	615.59
Sales and related.........................	34	19	13	33	92	149.89	97	636.59
Office and administrative support........	52	35	22	51	90	142.95	97	605.21
Natural resources, construction, and maintenance................................	55	30	22	53	85	156.16	90	585.23
Production, transportation, and material moving...........................	54	37	27	53	89	144.19	92	532.91
Production...................................	59	40	30	57	92	140.26	95	508.35
Transportation, and material moving....	50	34	24	49	85	148.82	89	562.20
Full-time [2].................................	59	39	25	58	90	147.01	96	602.17
Part-time [2].................................	11	8	6	11	80	149.09	87	591.05
Union [3]....................................	78	61	48	75	77	162.47	80	437.46
Nonunion....................................	44	29	18	44	91	145.22	97	621.78
Average hourly wage percentile: [4]								
Lowest 25 percent.........................	21	11	7	20	90	148.85	98	657.76
Lowest 10 percent.........................	11	5	4	11	86	158.85	98	737.56
Second 25 percent.........................	47	30	20	45	90	149.28	95	625.58
Third 25 percent............................	60	39	25	58	89	145.72	95	593.94
Highest 25 percent.........................	69	52	33	67	89	146.14	94	569.64
Highest 10 percent.........................	72	58	37	71	88	141.50	95	571.84

[1] The average is for all workers with medical care benefits, and covers plans that have a flat monthly cost. [2] Employees are classified as working either a full-time or part-time schedule based on the definition used by each establishment. [3] Union workers are those whose wages are determined through collective bargaining. [4] Tenth percentile, $11.74; 25th, $15.00; 50th (median), $20.00; 75th, $32.20; and 90th, $50.78. See "Technical Note" in source, <www.bls.gov/ncs/ebs/benefits/2021/home.htm>.

Source: U.S. Bureau of Labor Statistics, Annual Bulletin on Benefit Coverage, *National Compensation Survey: Employee Benefits in the United States, March 2021*, September 2021. See also <www.bls.gov/ncs/ebs/home.htm>.

Table 167. Employer-Sponsored Health Insurance Enrollment by Type of Plan and Employer Size: 2019

[In millions (183.0 represents 183,000,000). Based on the Current Population Survey, Annual and Social Economic Supplement, and Agency for Healthcare Research and Quality's Medical Expenditure Panel Surveys. For persons and their dependents covered by health insurance sponsored by a current or former employer. Abbreviations: HMO = health maintenance organization; PPO = preferred provider organization; POS = point-of-service plan; and HDED = high deductible health plan (including but not limited to IRS-qualified high deductible health plans)]

Employer sector and size	Total					Self-insured plans [1]					Fully insured plans [2]				
	Total	HMO	PPO	POS	HDED	Total	HMO	PPO	POS	HDED	Total	HMO	PPO	POS	HDED
TOTAL															
Total employee size.....	**183.0**	**33.2**	**88.4**	**10.0**	**51.4**	**108.2**	**12.8**	**57.1**	**2.5**	**35.9**	**74.8**	**20.5**	**31.3**	**7.5**	**15.6**
Less than 50..............	29.4	5.9	11.4	4.5	7.6	4.0	0.5	2.0	0.3	1.2	25.3	5.4	9.4	4.2	6.4
50 to 99...................	10.9	2.2	4.5	1.5	2.7	2.1	0.3	1.1	0.1	0.6	8.8	1.9	3.5	1.4	2.1
100 to 499................	23.4	3.6	10.2	1.5	8.1	10.5	0.7	5.7	0.3	3.9	12.9	2.9	4.5	1.2	4.2
500 to 999................	13.1	1.8	6.2	0.9	4.2	6.7	0.5	3.7	0.3	2.3	6.3	1.3	2.6	0.6	1.9
1,000 or more............	106.2	19.8	56.0	1.6	28.8	84.8	10.8	44.7	1.5	27.8	21.4	9.0	11.3	0.1	1.0
PRIVATE SECTOR [3]															
Total employee size.....	**139.3**	**24.4**	**64.0**	**9.1**	**41.8**	**86.1**	**10.4**	**45.0**	**2.2**	**28.5**	**53.2**	**14.0**	**19.0**	**6.9**	**13.2**
Less than 50..............	28.3	5.7	11.0	4.3	7.3	3.9	0.5	1.9	0.3	1.2	24.4	5.3	9.1	4.0	6.1
50 to 99...................	9.8	1.9	4.1	1.4	2.4	1.9	0.2	1.0	0.1	0.6	7.9	1.7	3.1	1.3	1.8
100 to 499................	19.9	3.1	8.7	1.4	6.8	9.3	0.6	5.0	0.3	3.4	10.6	2.5	3.6	1.1	3.4
500 to 999................	10.2	1.4	4.9	0.7	3.3	5.5	0.4	3.0	0.2	1.9	4.7	0.9	1.9	0.5	1.4
1,000 or more............	71.0	12.3	35.4	1.3	22.0	65.5	8.6	34.1	1.2	21.5	5.5	3.6	1.3	0.1	0.5

[1] Self-insured plans are those in which the employer directly assumes some or all medical claim and administrative costs. [2] Fully insured plans are those in which the employer contracts with another organization to assume financial responsibility for the enrollees' medical claims and administrative costs. [3] Private sector includes self-employed.

Source: U.S. Department of Labor, Employee Benefits Security Administration, *Health Insurance Coverage Bulletin: Abstract of Auxiliary Data for the March 2020 Annual Social and Economic Supplement to the Current Population Survey*, September 2021. See also <www.dol.gov/agencies/ebsa/researchers/data/auxiliary-data>.

Table 168. Revenue for Health Care Industries: 2018 to 2020

[In millions of dollars (2,636,270 represents $2,636,270,000,000). For all employer firms, and taxable employer firms. Data are based on the 2012 North American Industry Classification System (NAICS). Estimates have been adjusted using results of the 2017 Economic Census where applicable. In some instances, results from the 2017 Economic Census may reflect revisions based on additional analytical review following the release of the 2017 Geographic Area Statistics. For a description of benchmarking methods and exceptions, see <www.census.gov/programs-surveys/sas/technical-documentation/methodology/benchmarkprocess.html>. Based on Service Annual Survey and administrative data; see Appendix III]

Kind of business	NAICS code [1]	Total, all firms [2]			Taxable employer firms		
		2018	2019	2020	2018	2019	2020
Health care and social assistance [3]	**62**	**2,636,270**	**2,786,127**	**2,828,912**	**1,311,362**	**1,376,084**	**1,379,341**
Ambulatory health care services [3]	**621**	**1,076,451**	**1,129,986**	**1,131,847**	**963,851**	**1,010,968**	**1,008,505**
Offices of physicians (except mental health specialists)	621111	486,131	505,567	503,327	486,131	505,567	503,327
Offices of physicians, mental health specialists	621112	6,351	6,965	7,568	6,351	6,965	7,568
Offices of dentists	6212	132,139	138,468	125,487	132,139	138,468	125,487
Offices of chiropractors	62131	14,137	14,935	14,546	14,137	14,935	14,546
Offices of optometrists	62132	16,135	16,668	15,689	16,135	16,668	15,689
Offices of mental health practitioners (except physicians)	62133	10,105	11,465	12,849	10,105	11,465	12,849
Offices of PT/OT/speech therapists and audiologists [4]	62134	34,095	35,455	32,951	34,095	35,455	32,951
Offices of podiatrists	621391	4,878	5,123	4,912	4,878	5,123	4,912
Outpatient care centers	6214	176,857	186,530	193,330	99,799	105,561	109,108
Family planning centers	62141	3,143	3,300	3,219	1,369	1,455	1,296
Outpatient mental health and substance abuse centers	62142	23,090	24,812	25,969	8,142	9,305	10,005
HMO medical centers [5]	621491	36,788	39,324	40,901	23,852	25,590	26,660
Kidney dialysis centers	621492	26,563	28,132	28,903	24,962	26,372	27,009
Freestanding ambulatory surgical and emergency centers	621493	31,829	33,314	34,440	27,465	28,833	29,754
All other outpatient care centers	621498	55,444	57,648	59,898	14,009	14,006	14,384
Medical and diagnostic laboratories	6215	54,164	55,607	60,736	54,164	55,607	60,736
Home health care services	6216	89,420	97,225	102,723	68,815	74,782	79,745
Ambulance services	62191	15,543	16,115	15,989	12,100	12,643	12,528
Blood and organ banks	621991	12,500	13,622	14,095	4,405	4,981	(S)
Hospitals	**622**	**1,115,638**	**1,191,917**	**1,213,236**	**131,663**	**136,194**	**136,783**
General medical and surgical hospitals, government	622118	216,903	231,135	244,853	(X)	(X)	(X)
General medical and surgical hospitals, private	622119	827,685	885,877	890,462	107,139	110,925	110,196
Psychiatric and substance abuse hospitals, government	622218	12,362	12,690	13,336	(X)	(X)	(X)
Psychiatric and substance abuse hospitals, private	622219	12,574	13,425	13,798	7,393	7,937	8,254
Specialty hospitals, government	622318	8,900	9,816	10,139	(X)	(X)	(X)
Specialty hospitals, private	622319	37,214	38,974	40,648	17,131	17,332	18,333
Nursing and residential care facilities [3]	**623**	**242,367**	**252,503**	**263,015**	**155,305**	**162,798**	**170,744**
Nursing care facilities (skilled nursing facilities)	6231	120,267	124,102	130,126	97,231	101,028	106,599
Residential intellectual/developmental disability facilities	62321	29,098	29,605	31,127	9,558	9,729	10,401
Residential mental health and substance abuse facilities	62322	17,013	18,078	19,367	7,390	7,732	8,692
Continuing care retirement communities	623311	36,783	39,445	40,310	13,022	14,521	14,890
Assisted living facilities for the elderly	623312	31,310	33,133	33,638	26,849	28,471	28,858

S Figure does not meet publication standards. X Not applicable. [1] 2012 North American Industry Classification System (NAICS); see text, Section 15. [2] Includes taxable and tax-exempt employer firms. [3] Includes other kinds of business, not shown separately. See Table 611, for data on NAICS 624 Social assistance industries. [4] Offices of physical, occupational, and speech therapists, and audiologists. [5] HMO is health maintenance organization.

Source: U.S. Census Bureau, Service Annual Survey, "Service Annual Survey Latest Data (NAICS-basis): 2020," <www.census.gov/programs-surveys/sas/data.html>, accessed December 2021.

Table 169. Revenue for Selected Health Care Industries by Source: 2020

[In millions of dollars (510,895 represents $510,895,000,000). For all employer firms regardless of tax status. See headnote, Table 168. Based on Service Annual Survey and administrative data; see Appendix III]

Source of revenue	Offices of physicians (NAICS 6211)	Offices of dentists (NAICS 6212)	Outpatient care centers (NAICS 6214)	Home health care services (NAICS 6216)	Hospitals (NAICS 622)	Nursing and residential care facilities (NAICS 623) [1]
Revenue, total	**510,895**	**125,487**	**193,330**	**102,723**	**1,213,236**	**263,015**
Medicare [2]	85,457	(S)	23,736	(NA)	271,800	37,929
Medicaid (fee for service only)	20,087	(S)	20,347	19,795	101,682	80,866
Workers' compensation	4,509	(S)	2,481	564	6,236	(S)
All other government programs	9,542	1,609	11,203	5,520	43,865	17,940
Revenue from health care providers for patient care	34,842	3,012	4,313	2,756	8,263	(NA)
Private health insurance [3]	227,387	54,915	60,257	21,061	570,112	29,945
Property, auto, and casualty insurance	1,662	(S)	499	(S)	2,972	220
Patient out-of-pocket from patients and their families	40,167	51,243	(S)	4,976	25,371	46,373
All other sources of revenue for patient care	50,082	(S)	35,318	4,233	57,879	20,976
Contributions, gifts, and grants received	(NA)	(NA)	10,878	734	28,876	5,848
Investment and property income	(NA)	(NA)	681	194	18,669	1,780
Revenue from health care providers for non-patient care [4]	17,134	(S)	5,294	(S)	8,818	(NA)
All other non-patient care revenue	16,522	(S)	(S)	738	68,386	17,013

NA Not available. S Figure does not meet publication standards. [1] Total revenue for NAICS 623 also includes $2,940 million in revenue from social security benefits—direct payments of social security on behalf of patients. [2] Fee for service, Medicare Part A hospital insurance, Part B medical insurance, and Part D prescription drug coverage. [3] Includes Medicare Part C (Medicare Advantage plans providing coverage from private insurance companies), and Medicaid managed care plans. [4] Includes revenue from medical administration and other administrative services, incentive payments, management fees, medical director fees, etc.

Source: U.S. Census Bureau, Service Annual Survey, "Service Annual Survey Latest Data (NAICS-basis): 2020," <www.census.gov/programs-surveys/sas/data.html>, accessed December 2021.

Table 170. Employment in the Health Service Industries: 2000 to 2021

[In thousands (12,861 represents 12,861,000). Covers persons on establishment payrolls who worked or received pay for any part of the pay period that includes the 12th day of the month. Excludes proprietors, the unincorporated self-employed, unpaid volunteer or family employees, farm employees, domestic employees, and military personnel. Based on the 2017 North American Industry Classification System (NAICS)]

Industry	NAICS code	2000	2010	2015	2017	2018	2019	2020	2021
Health care and social assistance [1]	**62**	**12,861**	**16,820**	**18,557**	**19,520**	**19,923**	**20,421**	**19,796**	**20,084**
Health care	**621,2,3**	**10,858**	**13,777**	**15,042**	**15,717**	**15,964**	**16,269**	**15,850**	**16,024**
Ambulatory health care services [1]	621	4,320	5,975	6,856	7,297	7,477	7,704	7,498	7,875
Offices of physicians	6211	1,801	2,264	2,471	2,581	2,616	2,673	2,632	2,739
Office of physicians, except mental health	621111	1,764	2,218	2,420	2,527	2,560	2,615	2,574	2,676
Office of mental health physicians	621112	37	46	51	55	56	58	58	63
Offices of dentists	6212	688	828	905	936	951	974	889	994
Offices of other health practitioners	6213	438	671	813	889	929	974	926	1,012
Outpatient care centers	6214	425	649	806	897	931	969	970	997
Medical and diagnostic laboratories	6215	162	228	260	269	275	283	282	306
Home health care services	6216	633	1,085	1,315	1,420	1,467	1,519	1,495	1,514
Hospitals	622	3,954	4,679	4,896	5,072	5,130	5,190	5,137	5,126
General medical and surgical hospitals	6221	3,745	4,357	4,498	4,669	4,713	4,767	4,715	4,703
Psychiatric and substance abuse hospitals	6222	86	109	138	140	150	152	153	150
Other hospitals	6223	123	213	260	263	267	271	270	273
Nursing and residential care facilities [1]	623	2,583	3,124	3,291	3,348	3,357	3,375	3,214	3,023
Nursing care facilities	6231	1,514	1,657	1,648	1,627	1,607	1,596	1,499	1,375

[1] Includes other industries, not shown separately.

Source: U.S. Bureau of Labor Statistics, Current Employment Statistics, "Employment, Hours, and Earnings—National," <www.bls.gov/ces/data/>, accessed March 2022.

Table 171. Physicians by Sex, Osteopathic Physicians, and International Medical Graduates by Specialty: 2019

[Covers federal and nonfederal physicians working 20 or more hours per week in specialties in which there are over 2,500 active physicians. Active physicians include those working in direct patient care, administration, medical teaching, research, or other non-patient care activities. Physicians selected their specialties on the American Medical Association's Census of Physicians]

Specialty	Total [1]	By sex			By type		
		Male	Female	Percent female	Patient care physicians	Osteopathic physicians	International graduates [2]
Total	**938,980**	**596,236**	**340,018**	**36.3**	**816,922**	**77,265**	**232,190**
Allergy & immunology	4,900	2,889	2,009	41.0	4,221	174	1,119
Anatomic/clinical pathology	12,643	7,774	4,860	38.5	8,711	328	3,893
Anesthesiology	42,267	31,275	10,948	25.9	39,377	2,896	8,772
Cardiovascular disease	22,521	19,146	3,356	14.9	20,430	896	6,973
Child & adolescent psychiatry	9,787	4,500	5,282	54.0	8,670	560	3,026
Critical care medicine	13,093	9,568	3,508	26.8	11,146	709	5,388
Dermatology	12,516	6,133	6,372	51.0	11,747	735	591
Emergency medicine	45,202	32,382	12,787	28.3	41,466	5,255	2,965
Endocrinology [3]	7,994	3,890	4,092	51.3	6,439	235	3,286
Family medicine/general practice	118,198	69,329	48,693	41.3	108,984	19,230	28,569
Gastroenterology	15,469	12,534	2,916	18.9	14,007	633	4,495
General surgery	25,564	19,915	5,629	22.0	21,949	1,166	4,894
Geriatric medicine	5,974	2,755	3,213	53.8	5,029	331	3,057
Hematology & oncology	16,274	10,673	5,582	34.3	13,506	489	6,031
Infectious disease	9,687	5,609	4,064	42.0	7,448	337	3,387
Internal medicine	120,171	73,560	46,401	38.7	105,736	6,869	47,840
Internal medicine/pediatrics	5,509	2,581	2,926	53.1	4,924	299	583
Interventional cardiology	4,407	4,049	350	8.0	3,956	181	2,009
Neonatal-perinatal medicine	5,919	2,789	3,126	52.8	5,008	255	2,245
Nephrology	11,407	8,098	3,296	28.9	9,964	500	5,755
Neurological surgery	5,748	5,207	537	9.3	5,246	112	695
Neurology	14,146	9,769	4,363	30.9	11,896	740	4,450
Neuroradiology	4,089	3,285	798	19.5	3,496	175	581
Obstetrics & gynecology	42,720	17,523	25,160	58.9	39,825	2,991	5,987
Ophthalmology	19,312	14,156	5,146	26.7	17,859	475	1,320
Orthopedic surgery	19,069	17,965	1,099	5.8	18,097	1,069	925
Otolaryngology	9,777	7,987	1,784	18.3	9,140	391	568
Pain medicine & pain management	5,871	4,745	1,113	19.0	5,459	577	1,565
Pediatric anesthesiology	2,571	1,249	1,315	51.3	2,127	159	458
Pediatric cardiology	2,966	1,864	1,098	37.1	2,414	70	776
Pediatric critical care medicine	2,639	1,350	1,287	48.8	2,118	125	722
Pediatric hematology/oncology	3,079	1,381	1,695	55.1	2,251	104	769
Pediatrics	60,618	21,642	38,923	64.3	54,764	2,903	14,981
Physical medicine & rehabilitation	9,767	6,254	3,486	35.8	8,920	1,402	2,231
Plastic surgery	7,317	6,053	1,261	17.2	6,938	121	753
Preventive medicine	6,675	4,322	2,349	35.2	4,218	579	875
Psychiatry	38,792	23,199	15,571	40.2	33,776	1,818	11,800
Pulmonary disease	5,106	4,478	627	12.3	4,490	200	1,555
Radiation oncology	5,306	3,848	1,455	27.4	4,854	92	562
Radiology & diagnostic radiology	28,025	20,595	7,413	26.5	24,748	1,105	3,060
Rheumatology	6,265	3,360	2,892	46.3	5,333	342	2,182
Sports medicine	2,897	2,103	787	27.2	2,624	548	469
Sports medicine (orthopedic surgery)	2,903	2,702	201	6.9	2,737	190	121
Thoracic surgery	4,479	4,119	360	8.0	4,105	103	894
Urology	10,201	9,226	971	9.5	9,593	260	1,053
Vascular & interventional radiology	3,877	3,497	379	9.8	3,425	136	516
Vascular surgery	3,943	3,366	575	14.6	3,586	161	694

[1] Includes active physicians with unknown sex and type of medical degree. [2] All physicians, including U.S. citizens, who completed their medical education in a school outside the U.S., Puerto Rico, and Canada. [3] Includes diabetes and metabolism specialties.

Source: Association of American Medical Colleges, *2020 Physician Specialty Data Report* ©. See also <www.aamc.org/data-reports/workforce-studies>.

Table 172. Physicians, Doctors of Osteopathy, and Female Physicians by State: 2020

[As of year end. Rates per 100,000 resident population, based on U.S. Census Bureau estimates as of July 1, 2019. Covers active federal and nonfederal physicians who work at least 20 hours per week]

| State | Active physicians [1] | | | Active physicians in patient care | | | | | | |
| | Total (number) | Female | | Total [3] | | Osteopathic physicians | | Primary care physicians [4] | |
		Number	Percent [2]	Number	Rate	Number	Rate	Number	Rate
U.S. [5]	940,254	344,329	36.7	812,492	247.5	68,910	21.0	277,466	84.5
AL	10,983	3,212	29.3	9,853	201.0	550	11.2	3,563	72.7
AK	2,101	806	38.4	1,945	265.9	252	34.4	812	111.0
AZ	18,343	6,003	33.2	16,787	230.6	2,074	28.5	5,452	74.9
AR	6,500	1,885	29.0	5,843	193.6	346	11.5	2,328	77.1
CA	113,718	44,030	38.8	98,607	249.6	5,514	14.0	35,136	88.9
CO	16,956	6,723	39.7	15,562	270.2	1,591	27.6	5,217	90.6
CT	12,977	5,033	38.8	11,092	311.1	480	13.5	3,414	95.8
DE	2,850	1,138	40.0	2,532	260.0	329	33.8	880	90.4
DC	6,147	2,967	48.3	4,449	630.4	113	16.0	1,304	184.8
FL	58,822	18,604	31.7	52,947	246.5	5,017	23.4	17,508	81.5
GA	25,072	9,177	36.6	22,140	208.5	1,098	10.3	7,818	73.6
HI	4,557	1,651	36.3	3,965	280.0	221	15.6	1,546	109.2
ID	3,504	949	27.1	3,285	183.8	484	27.1	1,235	69.1
IL	37,122	14,567	39.3	31,194	246.2	2,294	18.1	11,182	88.2
IN	15,918	5,205	32.7	14,456	214.7	1,157	17.2	5,088	75.6
IA	7,056	2,383	33.8	6,239	197.7	1,290	40.9	2,503	79.3
KS	6,874	2,335	34.0	6,224	213.6	752	25.8	2,409	82.7
KY	10,528	3,385	32.2	9,718	217.5	718	16.1	3,286	73.6
LA	12,557	4,076	32.5	11,082	238.4	255	5.5	3,664	78.8
ME	4,459	1,691	38.0	4,103	305.2	714	53.1	1,599	119.0
MD	23,791	9,984	42.0	18,707	309.4	742	12.3	5,927	98.0
MA	32,116	13,885	43.3	24,956	362.1	854	12.4	7,947	115.3
MI	30,040	10,820	36.1	25,841	258.8	4,969	49.8	9,049	90.6
MN	17,617	6,711	38.1	15,342	272.0	822	14.6	5,502	97.6
MS	5,857	1,653	28.3	5,316	178.6	426	14.3	1,859	62.5
MO	18,297	6,051	35.1	14,806	241.2	2,143	34.9	4,900	79.8
MT	2,750	899	32.7	2,620	245.1	267	25.0	988	92.4
NE	4,820	1,609	33.4	4,309	222.8	257	13.3	1,590	82.2
NV	6,731	1,956	29.8	5,859	190.2	781	25.4	2,031	65.9
NH	4,391	1,637	37.3	3,990	293.4	370	27.2	1,343	98.8
NJ	27,832	10,487	37.8	24,409	274.8	2,869	32.3	7,860	88.5
NM	5,269	2,096	39.8	4,586	218.7	307	14.6	1,771	84.5
NY	75,749	30,131	39.8	60,446	310.7	3,558	18.3	18,799	96.6
NC	27,650	10,138	36.7	24,113	229.9	1,435	13.7	8,305	79.2
ND	1,826	571	31.3	1,655	217.2	94	12.3	618	81.1
OH	35,333	12,630	35.8	29,798	254.9	4,005	34.3	9,887	84.6
OK	8,293	2,548	30.8	7,548	190.8	1,627	41.1	2,717	68.7
OR	13,127	5,269	40.2	11,720	277.9	950	22.5	4,288	101.7
PA	42,051	15,484	36.9	35,571	277.9	5,351	41.8	11,425	89.2
RI	4,063	1,723	42.4	3,505	330.9	236	22.3	1,139	107.5
SC	12,197	3,901	32.0	10,844	210.6	728	14.1	3,814	74.1
SD	2,214	713	32.2	2,028	229.2	180	20.3	777	87.8
TN	17,687	5,552	31.4	15,638	229.0	859	12.6	5,325	78.0
TX	67,182	24,199	36.1	59,332	204.6	4,542	15.7	19,578	67.5
UT	7,198	1,821	25.4	6,631	206.8	643	20.1	2,038	63.6
VT	2,410	1,031	42.8	2,106	337.5	91	14.6	810	129.8
VA	22,874	8,768	38.4	20,038	234.8	1,306	15.3	7,000	82.0
WA	21,731	8,643	39.8	19,099	250.8	1,327	17.4	7,057	92.7
WV	4,914	1,507	30.7	4,198	234.2	715	39.9	1,606	89.6
WI	15,975	5,770	36.1	14,289	245.4	1,070	18.4	5,117	87.9
WY	1,225	322	26.3	1,169	202.0	137	23.7	455	78.6
PR	9,813	3,717	38.0	8,059	252.3	2	0.1	3,396	106.3

[1] Active physicians work in direct patient care, administration, medical teaching, research, or other nonpatient care activities. [2] Excludes physicians whose sex was not reported. [3] Includes physicians with Doctor of Medicine degrees, and unknown degree type. [4] Primary care physicians include physicians in the following specialties: adolescent medicine (pediatrics), family medicine, general practice, geriatric medicine (family practice and internal medicine), internal medicine, and pediatrics. [5] U.S. totals exclude Puerto Rico (PR).

Source: Association of American Medical Colleges, *2021 State Physician Workforce Data Report*, January 2022 ©. See also <www.aamc.org/data-reports>.

Table 173. Registered Nurses, Nurse Practitioners, and Licensed Practical and Vocational Nurses by State: 2021

[Covers nurses working in the health care and social assistance industry (North American Industry Classification System code 62), as of May. Rates per 100,000 resident population, based on U.S. Census Bureau estimates as of July 1 for year shown]

State	Registered nurses (RNs)		Nurse practitioners		Licensed practical and vocational nurses (LPNs, VPNs)	
	Total	Rate [2]	Total	Rate [2]	Total	Rate [2]
United States [1].....................	**2,626,050**	**791.2**	**213,450**	**64.3**	**551,670**	**166.2**
Alabama..........................	43,120	855.6	3,700	73.4	8,870	176.0
Alaska............................	5,100	696.1	640	87.4	270	36.9
Arizona...........................	49,750	683.7	4,640	63.8	4,990	68.6
Arkansas.........................	22,670	749.2	2,490	82.3	9,370	309.7
California.........................	276,150	703.8	14,760	37.6	61,590	157.0
Colorado.........................	46,140	793.9	3,380	58.2	3,990	68.7
Connecticut......................	28,920	802.1	2,420	67.1	7,620	211.3
Delaware.........................	10,430	1,039.5	880	87.7	2,070	206.3
District of Columbia.............	10,080	1,504.4	630	94.0	880	131.3
Florida...........................	165,610	760.3	14,050	64.5	33,250	152.7
Georgia..........................	67,880	628.5	6,490	60.1	18,020	166.9
Hawaii............................	9,650	669.4	460	31.9	770	53.4
Idaho.............................	12,620	663.9	890	46.8	1,920	101.0
Illinois............................	115,380	910.5	6,800	53.7	15,220	120.1
Indiana...........................	61,690	906.4	6,210	91.2	12,500	183.7
Iowa..............................	28,570	894.7	2,010	62.9	5,270	165.0
Kansas...........................	25,210	859.1	2,530	86.2	5,770	196.6
Kentucky.........................	37,640	834.7	4,210	93.4	7,950	176.3
Louisiana.........................	38,110	824.2	3,740	80.9	16,370	354.0
Maine.............................	12,430	905.8	1,290	94.0	930	67.8
Maryland..........................	44,140	716.0	3,120	50.6	7,760	125.9
Massachusetts....................	77,690	1,112.3	6,810	97.5	13,370	191.4
Michigan..........................	92,560	920.9	5,630	56.0	8,510	84.7
Minnesota........................	60,980	1,068.4	4,100	71.8	12,440	218.0
Mississippi........................	24,600	833.9	3,400	115.3	7,390	250.5
Missouri..........................	58,990	956.4	5,720	92.7	11,580	187.7
Montana..........................	8,290	750.7	670	60.7	1,350	122.3
Nebraska.........................	17,500	891.2	1,580	80.5	4,360	222.0
Nevada...........................	21,270	676.5	1,500	47.7	2,710	86.2
New Hampshire...................	10,990	791.2	1,320	95.0	1,780	128.2
New Jersey.......................	67,930	733.0	6,470	69.8	14,510	156.6
New Mexico.......................	13,520	639.0	1,180	55.8	1,550	73.3
New York.........................	152,660	769.6	13,080	65.9	32,710	164.9
North Carolina....................	88,790	841.5	6,280	59.5	13,600	128.9
North Dakota......................	10,150	1,309.8	600	77.4	2,370	305.8
Ohio..............................	114,920	975.6	9,740	82.7	32,030	271.9
Oklahoma.........................	26,220	657.7	2,040	51.2	9,910	248.6
Oregon...........................	29,140	686.3	1,800	42.4	2,760	65.0
Pennsylvania.....................	128,660	992.4	7,360	56.8	32,190	248.3
Rhode Island.....................	9,340	852.5	970	88.5	1,010	92.2
South Carolina....................	37,120	715.1	2,690	51.8	7,870	151.6
South Dakota.....................	12,370	1,381.5	730	81.5	1,810	202.1
Tennessee........................	54,290	778.3	10,080	144.5	19,860	284.7
Texas.............................	183,840	622.6	16,220	54.9	56,230	190.4
Utah..............................	20,970	628.2	1,910	57.2	990	29.7
Vermont..........................	5,680	879.8	710	110.0	830	128.6
Virginia...........................	56,160	649.8	5,920	68.5	15,550	179.9
Washington.......................	54,330	702.1	3,300	42.6	5,820	75.2
West Virginia.....................	16,640	933.3	1,740	97.6	5,270	295.6
Wisconsin.........................	55,360	939.0	4,190	71.1	5,410	91.8
Wyoming..........................	3,800	656.5	370	63.9	520	89.8
Puerto Rico.......................	15,320	469.4	(NA)	(NA)	2,800	85.8

NA Not available. [1] U.S. total excludes Puerto Rico. [2] Rates are calculated using data from the U.S. Census Bureau, "Annual Estimates of the Resident Population for the United States, Regions, States, District of Columbia, and Puerto Rico: April 1, 2020 to July 1, 2021 (NST-EST2021-POP)," <www.census.gov/data/tables/time-series/demo/popest/2020s-state-total.html>, accessed May 2022. The population estimates are developed from a base that incorporates the 2020 Census.

Source: U.S. Bureau of Labor Statistics, Occupational Employment Statistics, "OES Data: Research Estimates by State and Industry," <www.bls.gov/oes/home.htm>, accessed May 2022.

Table 174. Physician Use of Electronic Medical or Health Record System by Physician Specialty: 2015 and 2017

[In percent. Data are from the National Electronic Health Records Survey of nonfederal office-based patient care physicians; survey excludes anesthesiologists, radiologists, and pathologists. Using any electronic health record/electronic medical record system was defined by physicians answering "yes" to use of an electronic health record system at the reporting location. Having a certified system was defined by physicians answering "yes" to having a current system that "meet meaningful use criteria defined by the Department of Health and Human Services." For more information on certified systems and meaningful use (renamed "promoting interoperability") criteria, see <www.cms.gov/ehrincentiveprograms>]

Physician specialty	2015		2017	
	Any electronic medical/health record system	Certified system	Any electronic medical/health record system	Certified system
All physicians............................	**86.9**	**77.9**	**85.9**	**79.7**
Primary care..............................	89.6	80.9	88.5	83.5
Non-primary care.........................	84.4	75.1	83.6	76.0
Surgical..................................	84.5	77.0	84.2	77.3
Medical..................................	84.4	74.0	83.1	75.1
BY SPECIALTY				
Cardiovascular disease...................	95.6	83.2	(S)	(S)
Dermatology..............................	70.2	62.3	80.0	79.5
General surgery...........................	93.8	77.6	95.8	94.2
General/family practice...................	92.7	84.0	86.1	81.5
Internal medicine.........................	88.2	81.4	84.9	81.6
Neurology................................	94.5	89.9	(S)	(S)
Obstetrics/gynecology....................	89.2	80.6	95.7	90.7
Ophthalmology...........................	72.7	70.0	(S)	(S)
Orthopedic surgery.......................	93.2	86.6	96.7	(S)
Otolaryngology...........................	89.4	82.7	94.6	(S)
Pediatrics................................	87.4	76.3	92.1	84.9
Psychiatry................................	61.3	40.8	(S)	(S)
Urology..................................	94.0	92.6	88.7	86.7
Other....................................	86.4	78.6	89.3	81.1

S Estimate does not meet standards of reliability.

Source: U.S. National Center for Health Statistics, Ambulatory Health Care Data, NAMCS and NHAMCS Web Tables, "NEHRS Specialty and Overall Physicians Electronic Health Record Adoption Summary Tables," <www.cdc.gov/nchs/ahcd/web_tables.htm>, accessed March 2019.

Table 175. Medical Record Confidentiality Breaches Reported—Incidents and Persons Affected by Type and Location of Breach: 2018 to 2021

[Individuals affected in thousands (14,162 represents 14,162,000). Data for breaches by date of submission to the Secretary of Health and Human Services (HHS), affecting 500 or more individuals. As required by section 13402(e)(4) of the Health Information Technology for Economic and Clinical Health (HITECH) Act, the Secretary of HHS must post a list of breaches of unsecured protected health information affecting 500 or more individuals. The Privacy Rule of the Health Insurance Portability and Accountability Act of 1996 (HIPAA) provides federal protections for individually identifiable health information held by covered entities and their business associates. Covered entities include health care providers, health plans, and health care clearinghouses. Data are subject to revision]

Item	2018		2019		2020		2021	
	Incidents (number)	Individuals affected (1,000)	Incidents (number)	Individuals affected (1,000)	Incidents (number)	Individuals affected (1,000)	Incidents (number)	Individuals affected (1,000)
Total..............................	368	14,162	512	44,959	663	34,346	715	49,840
TYPE OF BREACH								
Hacking/information technology incident.....	165	10,218	313	40,874	456	30,327	534	47,783
Improper disposal............................	10	342	6	26	16	585	5	191
Loss.......................................	13	30	15	1,319	14	58	10	33
Theft......................................	41	685	38	364	39	812	24	108
Unauthorized access/disclosure..............	139	2,887	140	2,375	138	2,563	142	1,725
LOCATION OF INFORMATION BREACHED [1]								
Desktop computer..........................	32	534	33	542	19	479	19	746
Electronic medical record.....................	20	169	29	355	32	409	33	505
E-mail.....................................	114	3,777	207	5,481	234	11,156	200	6,122
Laptop computer...........................	19	76	18	157	11	702	8	64
Network server............................	65	7,051	116	35,972	255	20,244	384	41,908
Other portable electronic device.............	15	43	11	1,387	10	101	9	29
Paper/films................................	77	1,199	54	166	85	1,005	46	177
Other [2].................................	26	1,313	44	900	17	251	16	288

[1] Location of information breaches can include a combination of other locations within the categories specified. For example, incidents involving desktop computers can also include electronic medical record, network server, email, and other locations. Incidents are categorized according to the first type as given in the source. [2] Other locations of information breaches can include incidents involving mailings (postal and electronic), storage facilities, mobile applications, file transfers, computer systems and software, computer hard drives, web sites and web portals, and other materials and locations.

Source: U.S. Department of Health and Human Services, Office for Civil Rights, HIPAA for Professionals—Breach Notification Rule, "Breaches Affecting 500 or More Individuals," <www.hhs.gov/hipaa/for-professionals/breach-notification/index.html>, accessed June 2022.

Table 176. Coronavirus Disease 2019 (COVID-19) Cases, Testing, and Hospitalizations by Week: 2021 to 2022

[Counts of COVID-19 caused by SARS-CoV-2 (severe acute respiratory syndrome coronavirus 2) have been reported to the Centers for Disease Control and Prevention (CDC) since January 21, 2020. CDC data may differ from data from other sources due to differences in timing and reporting of data, and differences in processes for validating and confirming data. Data are provisional or preliminary; CDC continually updates data. Data are presented here as an illustration of the progression of COVID-19 in the U.S.]

Week ending	Week number	Cases [1]			New test results reported [2]		Hospitalizations per 100,000 population [3]	
		New cases each week	Daily 7-day moving average	Cumulative total	Total tests	Positive tests	Cumulative	Weekly
July 3, 2021............	26	97,380	13,911	33,537,080	3,961,293	107,794	586.8	1.7
July 10, 2021............	27	139,188	19,884	33,832,053	3,819,359	149,682	589.0	2.3
July 17, 2021............	28	235,038	33,576	34,067,422	4,451,344	250,288	592.0	3.0
July 24, 2021............	29	381,695	54,527	34,450,498	5,340,208	410,607	596.2	4.2
July 31, 2021............	30	576,704	82,386	35,028,255	6,349,521	623,341	602.5	6.3
August 7, 2021............	31	779,319	111,331	35,816,404	7,855,502	809,442	610.9	8.4
August 14, 2021........	32	912,169	130,309	36,729,680	9,021,889	946,078	621.2	10.3
August 21, 2021........	33	1,027,498	146,785	37,761,186	9,772,906	1,012,369	632.7	11.5
August 28, 2021........	34	1,109,198	158,456	38,871,962	11,238,757	1,113,045	644.9	12.2
September 4, 2021......	35	1,138,845	162,692	40,013,102	11,804,588	1,099,074	657.3	12.4
September 11, 2021...	36	1,036,018	148,002	41,052,518	11,162,261	970,857	668.8	11.5
September 18, 2021...	37	1,006,114	143,730	42,062,097	12,016,080	935,674	679.0	10.2
September 25, 2021...	38	824,110	117,730	42,889,865	11,743,532	800,830	688.7	9.7
October 2, 2021........	39	739,696	105,670	43,633,179	11,195,748	706,333	697.5	8.8
October 9, 2021........	40	658,208	94,029	44,304,382	10,972,159	635,698	706.4	8.9
October 16, 2021......	41	571,574	81,653	44,879,711	10,335,716	553,001	714.8	8.4
October 23, 2021......	42	479,460	68,494	45,361,466	10,212,060	506,895	722.6	7.8
October 30, 2021......	43	502,618	71,802	45,887,535	9,693,355	480,604	730.6	8.0
November 6, 2021.....	44	502,834	71,833	46,400,118	9,737,401	514,953	738.6	8.1
November 13, 2021....	45	573,843	81,977	46,992,151	10,157,478	586,323	748.1	9.5
November 20, 2021....	46	644,269	92,038	47,647,469	10,587,929	646,782	758.1	10.0
November 27, 2021....	47	597,433	85,347	48,245,959	7,633,745	568,675	768.8	10.7
December 4, 2021.....	48	768,962	109,851	49,015,349	11,421,540	828,643	781.1	12.3
December 11, 2021....	49	832,118	118,874	49,847,467	11,206,396	791,242	794.4	13.3
December 18, 2021....	50	929,095	132,727	50,780,474	11,861,572	1,054,078	807.5	13.0
December 25, 2021....	51	1,479,204	211,314	52,260,299	12,409,987	1,931,489	823.3	15.8
January 1, 2022........	52	2,954,920	422,131	55,215,219	13,001,600	3,479,584	850.6	27.4
January 8, 2022........	1	4,918,005	702,572	60,133,224	18,176,612	5,294,515	885.7	35.0
January 15, 2022......	2	5,676,176	810,882	65,855,971	17,506,226	4,802,495	918.9	33.3
January 22, 2022......	3	4,937,787	705,398	70,793,758	15,852,512	4,074,850	946.2	27.3
January 29, 2022......	4	3,702,828	528,975	74,496,586	12,039,724	2,510,656	967.2	21.0
February 5, 2022......	5	2,068,537	295,505	76,578,704	9,969,737	1,445,235	981.9	14.7
February 12, 2022.....	6	1,184,075	169,153	77,773,279	8,942,490	844,491	993.0	11.1
February 19, 2022.....	7	686,726	98,103	78,460,681	8,563,660	510,443	1,000.4	7.4
February 26, 2022.....	8	447,283	63,897	78,907,964	6,912,214	310,254	1,006.3	5.8
March 5, 2022..........	9	295,643	42,234	79,231,731	6,818,814	207,314	1,010.6	4.4
March 12, 2022........	10	230,303	32,900	79,466,251	6,152,028	140,453	1,013.8	3.2
March 19, 2022........	11	186,012	26,573	79,675,743	6,307,987	134,871	1,016.4	2.6
March 26, 2022........	12	182,596	26,085	79,875,431	5,981,939	139,119	1,018.9	2.5
April 2, 2022............	13	179,497	25,642	80,073,632	5,625,660	151,960	1,021.0	2.1
April 9, 2022............	14	207,240	29,605	80,283,818	5,540,982	193,905	1,023.5	2.4
April 16, 2022..........	15	254,605	36,372	80,540,115	4,876,607	246,699	1,026.7	3.2
April 23, 2022..........	16	326,817	46,688	80,868,661	4,516,613	248,362	1,030.5	3.8
April 30, 2022..........	17	405,487	57,926	81,277,388	5,897,193	398,372	1,035.1	4.7
May 7, 2022............	18	498,986	71,283	81,777,441	5,600,084	465,471	1,040.9	5.8
May 14, 2022..........	19	636,772	90,967	82,416,386	5,998,499	590,720	1,047.9	6.9
May 21, 2022..........	20	769,235	109,890	83,194,243	6,360,484	695,379	1,055.4	7.5
May 28, 2022..........	21	771,548	110,221	83,965,791	5,963,174	671,675	1,062.7	7.3
June 4, 2022............	22	713,881	101,983	84,679,679	5,020,313	606,395	1,070.2	7.5
June 11, 2022..........	23	757,239	108,177	85,436,918	4,399,893	538,224	1,077.4	7.3
June 18, 2022..........	24	692,270	98,895	86,129,188	4,345,308	594,407	1,084.7	7.3
June 25, 2022..........	25	744,083	106,297	86,873,271	3,991,207	606,918	1,092.8	8.1
July 2, 2022............	26	794,936	113,562	87,670,896	3,605,496	601,728	1,100.9	8.2
July 9, 2022............	27	766,698	109,528	88,437,594	3,913,347	714,206	1,109.9	9.0
July 16, 2022..........	28	912,710	130,387	89,350,304	4,233,073	779,387	1,119.1	9.3
July 23, 2022..........	29	900,828	128,689	90,275,442	4,158,381	772,854	1,128.5	9.5
July 30, 2022..........	30	862,677	123,239	91,230,257	3,913,549	713,518	1,138.0	9.5
August 6, 2022........	31	805,405	115,057	92,035,662	3,907,575	670,493	1,147.2	9.2
August 13, 2022.......	32	719,844	102,834	92,755,506	3,692,883	586,219	1,155.8	8.7
August 20, 2022.......	33	656,328	93,761	93,417,907	3,598,639	528,926	1,163.1	7.4
August 27, 2022.......	34	622,533	88,933	94,040,101	3,597,201	499,101	1,167.3	4.2
September 3, 2022....	35	561,748	80,249	94,603,730	2,522,848	345,177	(NA)	(NA)

NA Not available. [1] Total cases are based on aggregate counts of COVID-19 cases reported by state and territorial jurisdictions to the CDC. Numbers are confirmed and probable COVID-19 cases as reported by U.S. states, U.S. territories, New York City, and the District of Columbia from the previous day. [2] Represents viral COVID-19 laboratory test results from over 1,000 laboratories and testing locations in the U.S. Data shown are for laboratory test totals, not individual people, and exclude antibody and antigen tests. Data are provisional. [3] The Coronavirus Disease 2019 (COVID-19)-Associated Hospitalization Surveillance Network (COVID-NET) conducts population-based surveillance for laboratory-confirmed COVID-19-associated hospitalizations in children under age 18 years and adults. The current network covers nearly 100 counties in the 10 Emerging Infections Program (EIP) states (CA, CO, CT, GA, MD, MN, NM, NY, OR, and TN) and four additional states through the Influenza Hospitalization Surveillance Project (IA (IA removed after May 2022), MI, OH, and UT) and represents approximately 10% of U.S. population.

Source: U.S. Centers for Disease Control and Prevention, COVID Data Tracker, "Cases, Deaths, and Testing" and "Health Care Settings, COVID-NET Hospitalization Surveillance Network," <covid.cdc.gov/covid-data-tracker>, accessed September 7, 2022. See also "COVID-19 Diagnostic Laboratory Testing (PCR Testing) Time Series," <healthdata.gov/>; and "Laboratory-Confirmed COVID-19-Associated Hospitalizations," <gis.cdc.gov/grasp/COVIDNet/COVID19_3.html>.

Table 177. Long-Term Care Facilities, Staff, and Clients by Provider Type and Selected Characteristics: 2018

[Data for 2018 except as noted. Based on the National Study of Long-Term Care Providers. Long-term care services assist the needs of frail older people and other adults with limited capacity for self-care due to chronic illness, injury, disability, or other health-related conditions. Percentages may not add to 100 because of rounding; percentages are based on unrounded numbers]

Item	Facilities by provider type				
	Adult day services center	Home health agency	Hospice	Nursing home	Residential care community
Number of providers	**4,200**	**11,500**	**4,700**	**15,600**	**31,400**
Number of beds or licensed maximum capacity [1]	283,200	(X)	(X)	1,655,400	1,183,600
Average capacity [1]	68	(NA)	(NA)	106	38
Average number of people served [2]	65	458	356	85	32
Provider ownership type (percent):					
For profit	42.3	82.0	66.4	70.0	79.2
Not for profit	52.8	14.3	21.3	23.2	18.8
Government and other	4.8	3.7	12.3	6.8	2.0
Services provided (percent):					
Social work	50.2	81.7	100.0	63.8	62.8
Mental health or counseling	37.7	(NA)	97.3	63.6	62.0
Therapy [3]	45.4	95.8	97.9	71.7	71.7
Skilled nursing or nursing	62.0	100.0	100.0	71.6	70.8
Pharmacy or pharmacist	30.9	4.5	(NA)	70.1	84.5
Hospice	12.6	5.4	(X)	83.0	66.8
Distinct unit for dementia special care	(NA)	(NA)	(NA)	13.4	19.4
Total nursing and social work employee FTEs [4]	**24,300**	**139,200**	**91,300**	**660,000**	**474,200**
Percent of total nursing employee FTEs:					
Registered nurse	26.6	51.5	48.4	12.1	14.7
Licensed practical nurse or licensed vocational nurse	8.6	21.3	8.7	23.3	14.1
Aide	55.6	24.7	31.6	62.8	70.0
Clients [2]	**251,100**	**4,940,270**	**1,562,524**	**1,321,200**	**918,700**
Percent by age:					
Under 65	39.4	17.3	5.2	16.9	7.5
65 and over	60.6	82.7	94.8	83.1	92.5
65 to 74	17.8	27.5	17.6	19.5	12.1
75 to 84	24.1	29.9	29.2	27.2	25.5
85 and over	18.6	25.2	48.0	36.4	54.9
Percent by sex:					
Men	43.5	39.4	41.6	36.7	32.6
Women	56.5	60.6	58.4	63.3	67.4
Percent with selected conditions:					
Diagnosed with Alzheimer's or other dementia	27.8	35.5	46.3	49.1	33.7
Diagnosed with depression	21.8	40.5	23.7	48.8	27.5

NA Not available. X Not applicable. [1] For adult day services, capacity is based on licensed maximum capacity. For nursing homes and residential care communities, capacity is based on number of licensed or certified beds. [2] For adult day services, nursing homes, and residential care communities, data are daily average or totals for 2018. For home health agencies, data are total discharges in 2017. For hospices, data are total patients served in 2017. [3] Physical, occupational, or speech therapy. [4] FTE is full-time equivalent.

Source: U.S. Centers for Disease Control and Prevention, National Center for Health Statistics, *Post-acute and Long-term Care Providers and Services Users in the United States, 2017–2018*, Vital and Health Statistics, Series 3, No. 47, May 2022. See also www.cdc.gov/nchs/npals/index.htm>.

Table 178. Mental Health Treatment Facilities, Clients, and Beds by Service Setting and Facility Type: 2020

[Based on the National Mental Health Services Survey (N-MHSS), a census of all known facilities, public and private, that provide mental health treatment services in the 50 states, the District of Columbia, American Samoa, Guam, Northern Mariana Islands, Puerto Rico, and the U.S. Virgin Islands. Facilities can offer treatment in more than one service setting. Client data are collected every other year and represent clients for an average day or month. Excludes: (1) Department of Defense (DoD) military treatment facilities, (2) individual private practitioners or small group practices not licensed as a mental health clinic or center, and (3) jails or prisons]

Facility type	24-hour hospital inpatient care			24-hour residential care			Outpatient, day treatment, or partial hospitalization	
	Facilities	Clients [1]	Beds [1]	Facilities	Clients [1]	Beds [1]	Facilities	Clients [2]
Total [3]	**1,756**	**77,622**	**85,948**	**1,905**	**43,744**	**46,828**	**10,051**	**3,593,843**
Psychiatric hospitals	661	51,951	57,192	111	5,252	5,844	292	54,000
Public	203	29,822	30,786	25	1,995	1,986	27	11,772
Private	458	22,129	26,406	86	3,257	3,858	265	42,228
General hospitals [4]	958	21,046	24,682	23	476	368	396	94,054
Residential treatment centers for children	6	459	596	586	14,502	16,487	109	3,986
Residential treatment centers for adults	1	253	251	799	12,007	11,199	66	938
Other types of residential facilities	0	0	0	60	2,386	2,686	20	1,035
Veterans Affairs medical centers	102	1,852	2,337	85	1,947	2,844	552	334,711
Community mental health centers	22	866	628	35	620	1,039	2,540	1,124,082
Certified community behavioral health clinics	2	49	58	3	86	114	335	223,786
Partial hospitalization or day treatment facilities	0	25	0	6	39	108	429	19,207
Outpatient mental health facilities	0	1,047	133	7	140	545	4,941	1,621,510
Multi-setting mental health facilities [5]	2	66	61	189	6,272	5,578	369	115,066

[1] On April 30, 2020. [2] For the month of April 2020, and enrolled on April 30, 2020. [3] Total includes data for other unspecified type of facilities not shown separately. [4] Nonfederal general hospitals with separate psychiatric units. [5] Includes non-hospital residential, plus either outpatient and/or partial hospitalization/day treatment.

Source: U.S. Substance Abuse and Mental Health Services Administration, *National Mental Health Services Survey (N-MHSS): 2020, Data on Mental Health Treatment Facilities* 2021. See also <www.samhsa.gov/data/data-we-collect/n-mhss-national-mental-health-services-survey>.

Table 179. Mental Health Treatment Facilities by Type: 2020

[Based on the National Mental Health Services Survey (N-MHSS), a census of all known facilities, public and private, that provide mental health treatment services in the 50 states, the District of Columbia, American Samoa, Guam, Puerto Rico, Northern Mariana Islands, and the U.S. Virgin Islands. Excludes: (1) Department of Defense (DoD) military treatment facilities, (2) individual private practitioners or small group practices not licensed as a mental health clinic or center, and (3) jails or prisons]

Characteristic	Total [1]	Psychiatric hospitals	General hospitals [2]	RTCs, total [3]	Veterans Affairs medical centers	Community centers [4]	PHP/day treatment facilities [5]	Outpatient facilities [6]	Multi-setting facilities [7]
Total (number)	**12,275**	**668**	**967**	**1,462**	**552**	**2,548**	**429**	**4,941**	**369**
Percent	100.0	5.4	7.9	11.9	4.5	20.8	3.5	40.3	3.0
SERVICE SETTING [8]									
24-hour hospital inpatient	1,756	661	958	7	102	22	0	0	2
24-hour residential	1,905	111	23	1,445	85	35	6	7	189
Less than 24-hour day treatment or partial hospitalization	1,806	227	218	113	55	304	408	247	208
Less than 24-hour outpatient	9,634	240	338	142	552	2,522	225	4,935	346
FACILITY CONTROL									
Private for-profit	2,589	312	160	394	0	174	160	1,278	93
Private non-profit	7,402	151	712	987	0	1,815	231	2,995	252
Public [9]	2,284	205	95	81	552	559	38	668	24
AGE OF PATIENTS ACCEPTED [8]									
All ages	3,645	62	56	5	1	1,371	7	1,877	89
Children age 5 and younger	4,701	91	85	57	1	1,560	55	2,512	137
Children age 6 to 12	6,990	216	172	359	1	2,009	142	3,614	212
Children age 13 to 17	7,964	312	246	621	2	2,125	214	3,916	252
Young adults age 18 to 25	10,777	573	779	838	552	2,449	318	4,585	354
Adults age 26 to 64	10,299	594	869	809	552	2,336	282	4,239	306
Senior adults age 65 and older	9,831	585	869	704	552	2,282	247	4,017	273

[1] Total includes other types of facilities not shown separately. [2] Nonfederal general hospitals with separate psychiatric units. [3] Residential treatment centers. [4] Community mental health centers provide outpatient services, 24-hour emergency care, day treatment or partial hospitalization or psychosocial rehabilitation services, or patient screening for admission to state facilities. [5] Partial hospitalization program and day treatment facilities provide services to ambulatory patients in 3 or more hour sessions. [6] Outpatient mental health facilities provide services to clients, usually in under 3 hours per visit. [7] Includes non-hospital residential, plus either outpatient and/or partial hospitalization/day treatment. [8] Sums to more than the total because a facility could offer treatment in more than one service setting and to more than one age group. [9] Includes facilities operated by state mental health and other agencies, local/county/municipal governments, tribal governments, Indian Health Service, and Department of Veterans Affairs.

Source: U.S. Substance Abuse and Mental Health Services Administration, *National Mental Health Services Survey (N-MHSS): 2020, Data on Mental Health Treatment Facilities*, 2021. See also <www.samhsa.gov/data/>.

Table 180. Mental Health Care Client Characteristics by Treatment Setting: 2020

[Data are for patients receiving inpatient or residential services on April 30, 2020, and for clients who were receiving outpatient services at least once during April 2020 and were enrolled in treatment on April 30, 2020. Not all facilities reported demographic data for all clients. See headnote, Table 178]

Client characteristic	24-hour hospital inpatient treatment		24-hour residential treatment		Outpatient, day treatment, or partial hospitalization [1]	
	Number	Percent	Number	Percent	Number	Percent
Total clients	**77,622**	**100.0**	**43,744**	**100.0**	**3,593,843**	**100.0**
SEX						
Male	46,191	61.9	26,097	61.2	1,721,380	50.3
Female	28,467	38.1	16,554	38.8	1,703,035	49.7
AGE						
17 years old and under	8,388	11.2	25,269	45.2	912,482	26.7
18 to 64 years old	56,279	75.0	27,552	49.3	2,145,897	62.8
65 years old and over	10,393	13.8	3,101	5.5	358,183	10.5
RACE						
American Indian or Alaska Native	565	0.8	736	1.7	38,746	1.1
Asian	1,411	1.9	521	1.2	50,711	1.5
Black or African American	16,179	21.9	8,718	20.5	539,115	15.8
Native Hawaiian or Other Pacific Islander	331	0.4	247	0.6	13,052	0.4
White	31,581	42.8	20,264	47.7	1,750,361	51.4
Two or more races	1,664	2.3	1,787	4.2	153,113	4.5
Unknown or not collected	22,105	29.9	10,178	24.0	862,308	25.3
HISPANIC ORIGIN [2]						
Hispanic or Latino	6,023	8.0	4,117	9.7	412,569	12.1
Not Hispanic or Latino	43,093	57.5	27,304	64.5	2,067,392	60.6
Unknown or not collected	25,843	34.5	10,920	25.8	933,306	27.3
LEGAL STATUS [3]						
Voluntary	31,122	42.3	39,307	71.6	3,244,808	96.2
Involuntary, non-forensic	26,405	35.9	10,467	19.1	80,596	2.4
Involuntary, forensic	16,051	21.8	5,142	9.4	47,554	1.4

[1] Less than 24-hour care provided to ambulatory patients. Outpatient care typically involves care for less than 3 hours per visit. Day treatment and partial hospitalization programs typically involve care lasting more than 3 hours per visit, on a regular schedule. [2] Persons of Hispanic origin may be of any race. [3] Clients may voluntarily admit themselves to receive mental health treatment, or be admitted involuntarily with a forensic (criminal) or non-forensic (noncriminal) status.

Source: U.S. Substance Abuse and Mental Health Services Administration, *National Mental Health Services Survey (N-MHSS): 2020, Data on Mental Health Treatment Facilities*, 2021. See also <www.samhsa.gov/data/data-we-collect/n-mhss-national-mental-health-services-survey>.

Table 181. Opioid Treatment and Medication-Assisted Therapy—Clients and Facilities: 2020

[As of March 31, 2020. Based on the National Survey of Substance Abuse Treatment Services, a census of all known public and private facilities providing substance abuse treatment in the U.S. and associated jurisdictions. Medication-assisted opioid therapy includes the use of methadone or buprenorphine to treat opioid addiction or dependence, and the use of naltrexone for preventing a relapse in opioid addiction. Methadone is available only at opioid treatment programs (OTPs) certified by the Substance Abuse and Mental Health Services Administration (SAMHSA). Buprenorphine is prescribed by medical practitioners who have Drug Addiction Treatment Act of 2000 (DATA 2000) specific training and a waiver to prescribe the medication for treating opioid use disorder. Naltrexone is prescribed by any medical practitioner with prescribing privileges. Data for 2020 are based on responses from 16,066 eligible facilities (88.4 percent of survey universe)]

Facilities by type of therapy	Total	Private non-profit	Private for-profit	Local, county, or community government	State government	Federal government [1]	Tribal government
Clients receiving medication-assisted opioid therapy, total [2]	**509,008**	**163,702**	**314,328**	**11,564**	**8,014**	**9,156**	**2,244**
Methadone [3]	311,531	103,707	191,625	7,121	6,312	1,735	1,031
Buprenorphine [4]	176,152	50,978	113,040	3,647	1,470	5,966	1,051
Naltrexone [4]	21,325	9,017	9,663	796	232	1,455	162
Substance abuse treatment facilities [5]	**16,066**	**8,004**	**6,535**	**670**	**285**	**323**	**249**
Facilities offering detoxification from opioids	3,459	1,300	1,872	86	57	130	14
Facilities providing medication-assisted therapy	8,250	3,740	3,709	308	149	258	86
Buprenorphine	7,066	3,154	3,268	235	114	234	61
Injectable naltrexone	6,016	2,920	2,440	249	103	240	64
Opioid treatment program (OTP) [6]	**1,754**	**543**	**1,085**	**44**	**35**	**37**	**10**
Outpatient treatment	1,602	460	1,029	40	27	36	10
Regular	1,291	388	806	33	22	34	8
Intensive	517	212	252	11	14	25	3
Day treatment or partial hospitalization	106	45	47	2	3	8	1
Detoxification	734	162	525	9	7	27	4
Methadone/buprenorphine maintenance or injectable naltrexone treatment	1,570	453	1,004	40	27	36	10
Residential, non-hospital	165	75	63	4	8	15	0
Hospital inpatient	134	66	42	5	5	15	1

[1] Includes Department of Veteran's Affairs, Department of Defense, Indian Health Service, and other, not shown separately. [2] Client data are for a point in time (reference date noted above), and are not annual totals. [3] Clients in facilities SAMHSA certified to use methadone. [4] Clients in all substance abuse treatment facilities that provide opioid medication-assisted therapy. Excludes clients of independent physicians. [5] For additional data on substance abuse treatment facilities, see Table 220. [6] Facilities that have opioid treatment programs certified by SAMHSA. Methadone is available only at these facilities.

Source: U.S. Substance Abuse and Mental Health Services Administration, *National Survey of Substance Abuse Treatment Services (N-SSATS): 2020, Data on Substance Abuse Treatment Facilities*, June 2021. See also <www.samhsa.gov/data/data-we-collect/n-ssats-national-survey-substance-abuse-treatment-services>.

Table 182. Community Health Centers, Patients, and Medical Personnel: 2020

[Patient and patient visit data in thousands (28,591 represents 28,591,000). Community health centers are community-based and patient-directed organizations that provide primary health care services to underserved populations with limited access to health care. Populations served include low-income persons, the uninsured, those with limited English proficiency, migratory and seasonal agricultural workers and their families, people experiencing homelessness, and residents of public housing. Most health centers receive Health Center Program federal grant funding. Some health centers that meet all Health Center Program requirements do not receive Federal award funding; these are called health center program look-alikes]

Item	Health Center Program grantees	Health Center Program look-alikes	Item	Health Center Program grantees	Health Center Program look-alikes
Health centers, total (number)	**1,375**	**87**	Insurance source:		
PATIENTS (1,000s)			None/uninsured	6,240	83
Total patients	28,591	679	Regular Medicaid (Title XIX)	13,125	351
Male	12,141	291	CHIP Medicaid [2]	120	7
Female	16,450	388	Dual eligible (Medicare and Medicaid)	1,120	32
Age 17 and under	7,872	186	Medicare [3]	2,973	85
Age 18 to 64	17,787	418	Other public insurance [4]	254	5
Age 65 and older	2,932	76	Private insurance	5,878	148
			PERSONNEL (FTEs) [5]		
Non-Hispanic, total [1]	16,610	443	Total physicians [6]	14,317	424
White	10,049	233	Family, general practice, and internist	9,250	280
Black/African American	4,856	123	Obstetrician/gynecologists	1,317	55
American Indian/Alaska native	240	3	Pediatricians	3,125	68
Asian	951	44	Nurse practitioners	11,086	258
Native Hawaiian/Other Pacific Islander	190	2	Physician assistants	3,479	96
Multiracial	325	8	Certified nurse midwives	705	11
Hispanic	10,002	200	PATIENT VISITS (1,000s) [7]		
Unreported race and ethnicity	1,399	37	By type of practitioner seen:		
			Total physicians [6]	38,788	999
Income as percent of poverty level:			Family, general practice, and internist	25,124	676
100% and under	13,168	260	Obstetrician/gynecologists	3,435	82
101 to 150%	2,884	69	Pediatricians	8,362	201
151 to 200%	1,511	33	Nurse practitioners	26,348	619
Over 200%	1,817	49	Physician assistants	9,395	265
Unknown	9,212	267	Certified nurse midwives	1,424	28

[1] Includes unknown/unreported race, not shown separately. [2] CHIP, Children's Health Insurance Program. [3] Includes dual eligible and other Title XVIII beneficiaries. [4] CHIP and non-CHIP. [5] FTE, full-time equivalent. [6] Includes data for other specialty physicians not shown separately. [7] Includes clinic and virtual visits.

Source: U.S. Health Resources & Services Administration, Bureau of Primary Health Care, "Health Center Data & Reporting," <bphc.hrsa.gov/datareporting/index.html>, accessed February 2022.

Table 183. Health Care Visits—Percent Distribution by Selected Patient Characteristics: 2010 and 2018

[Covers visits to hospital emergency departments, home health care visits, and visits to doctor's offices, clinics, or some other place during a 12-month period. Excludes dental visits. Based on the National Health Interview Survey. See source, and Appendix III]

Characteristic	Percent distribution of health care visits							
	None		1–3 visits		4–9 visits		10 or more visits	
	2010	2018	2010	2018	2010	2018	2010	2018
All persons [1,2]	**15.6**	**14.5**	**45.4**	**49.2**	**25.8**	**23.4**	**13.2**	**12.9**
SEX [2]								
Male	20.4	18.7	46.4	49.7	22.7	21.2	10.5	10.3
Female	10.9	10.3	44.4	48.8	28.8	25.6	15.9	15.4
AGE								
Under 18 years	8.1	7.4	55.6	60.3	28.2	25.4	8.2	6.9
Under 6 years	3.7	4.9	48.9	52.7	36.8	33.9	10.6	8.4
6 to 17 years	10.4	8.6	59.1	63.9	23.6	21.4	6.9	6.2
18 to 44 years	24.2	21.9	43.9	47.6	20.6	18.7	11.3	11.7
45 to 64 years	14.8	14.2	42.8	45.5	26.1	24.7	16.4	15.7
65 years and over	5.3	5.5	33.8	38.0	36.7	32.5	24.2	24.0
75 years and over	4.1	4.1	31.0	34.8	38.0	33.6	27.0	27.6
RACE [2,3]								
White	15.3	14.0	44.9	48.5	26.1	24.0	13.7	13.4
Black or African American	15.7	13.8	47.2	51.9	24.7	22.1	12.4	12.2
American Indian or Alaska Native	19.4	16.5	40.3	41.5	28.1	25.9	12.2	16.1
Asian	20.4	19.9	49.9	53.3	22.1	18.8	7.6	8.0
Native Hawaiian or Other Pacific Islander only	(B)	20.9	(B)	53.2	(B)	15.7	(B)	(B)
Two or more races	13.9	15.3	42.3	47.1	25.2	23.5	18.6	14.1
HISPANIC ORIGIN AND RACE [2,3,4]								
Hispanic or Latino	23.5	20.3	43.2	48.1	22.6	21.0	10.7	10.6
Not Hispanic or Latino	14.0	13.1	45.8	49.4	26.5	24.0	13.7	13.5
White, non-Hispanic	13.2	12.1	45.3	48.5	27.1	25.1	14.4	14.3
Black, non-Hispanic	15.6	13.7	47.3	51.8	24.9	22.2	12.2	12.3
HEALTH INSURANCE STATUS [5,6]								
Insured	12.3	13.0	48.5	51.8	26.1	23.1	13.1	12.1
Private	12.4	13.2	51.0	53.6	25.5	22.7	11.1	10.4
Medicaid	10.9	12.2	38.2	44.5	28.0	24.3	23.0	19.0
Uninsured	37.2	36.8	42.2	44.9	15.2	13.2	5.4	5.1
Insured continuously 12 months prior to interview	12.1	12.9	48.6	51.9	26.2	23.1	13.0	12.1
Uninsured for any period up to 12 months prior to interview	18.5	21.2	47.8	48.4	22.0	20.9	11.6	9.5
Uninsured more than 12 months prior to interview	43.8	45.3	39.7	41.6	12.6	9.9	3.9	3.1

B Estimates are considered unreliable. [1] Includes other categories not shown separately. [2] Age adjusted to the year 2000 standard population. [3] Race groups include persons of Hispanic and non-Hispanic origin. Race-specific estimates are for persons reporting one race only. [4] Persons of Hispanic or Latino origin may be of any race. [5] For persons under age 65, at time of interview. Estimates are age-adjusted to the year 2000 standard population. [6] Health insurance categories are mutually exclusive. Persons who reported both Medicaid and private coverage are classified as having private coverage. Medicaid coverage includes State-sponsored health plans and the Children's Health Insurance Program (CHIP). The insured category also includes military plans, other government-sponsored health plans, and Medicare, not shown separately. Persons not covered by private insurance, Medicaid, CHIP, state-sponsored or other government-sponsored health plans, Medicare, or military plans are considered to have no health insurance coverage. Persons with only Indian Health Service coverage are considered to have no health insurance coverage.

Source: U.S. National Center for Health Statistics, *Health, United States, 2019*, March 2021. See also <www.cdc.gov/nchs/hus/index.htm>.

Table 184. Physician Office Visits by Leading Reason for Visit by Patient Sex: 2018

[860,386 represents 860,386,000. Based on the 2018 National Ambulatory Medical Care Survey (NAMCS). NAMCS is an annual nationally representative sample survey of visits to nonfederal office-based patient care physicians, excluding anesthesiologists, radiologists, and pathologists. The sampling frame for the 2018 NAMCS was composed of all physicians contained in the master files maintained by the American Medical Association and the American Osteopathic Association. Data are subject to sampling and nonsampling errors]

Leading reason for visit	Number of visits (1,000)	Percent distribution		Leading reason for visit	Number of visits (1,000)	Percent distribution	
		Male [1]	Fe-male [2]			Male [1]	Fe-male [2]
All visits [3]	**860,386**	**100.0**	**100.0**	Gynecological examination	11,494	(X)	2.3
Progress visit [4]	151,669	19.4	16.4	Symptoms referable to throat	11,066	1.2	1.3
General medical examination	54,456	6.7	6.1	Preoperative visit for surgery	[5] 10,836	0.9	1.5
Postoperative visit	[5] 26,785	2.3	([5])	Sleep disturbances	[5] 10,672	([5])	1.0
For test results	[5] 19,637	2.4	2.2	Well-baby examination	10,530	2.0	0.7
Prenatal examination, routine	19,380	(X)	3.8	Anxiety and nervousness	10,154	1.2	1.2
Knee symptoms	18,666	1.8	2.4	Diabetes mellitus	9,866	1.4	1.0
Cough	18,469	2.6	1.9	Stomach/abdominal pain	9,460	0.8	1.3
Medication	16,824	2.2	1.8	Pregnancy & puerperium complications	9,391	(X)	1.9
Hypertension	16,466	2.1	1.8	Vision dysfunctions	8,634	1.2	0.9
Counseling [4]	15,448	1.7	1.9	All other reasons	400,481	48.7	45.0

X Not applicable. [1] Based on 353,263,000 visits made by males. [2] Based on 507,122,000 visits made by females. [3] Numbers may not sum to totals due to rounding. [4] Not otherwise specified. [5] Estimate does not meet NCHS standards of reliability.

Source: U.S. National Center for Health Statistics, *National Ambulatory Medical Care Survey: 2018 National Summary Tables*, July 2021. See also <www.cdc.gov/nchs/ahcd/index.htm>.

Table 185. Hospital Emergency Department (ER) Visits by Wait Time and Total Time Spent: 2015 to 2019

[136,943 represents 136,943,000. Based on the National Hospital Ambulatory Medical Care Survey (NHAMCS). Data cover visits to hospital emergency departments; excludes federal, military, and Veterans Administration hospitals]

Visit characteristic	Number of visits (1,000)			Percent distribution of visits		
	2015	2018	2019	2015	2018	2019
Total visits [1]	**136,943**	**129,974**	**150,650**	**100.0**	**100.0**	**100.0**
WAIT TIME TO SEE MEDICAL PROFESSIONAL [2]						
Fewer than 15 minutes	48,540	56,588	64,345	35.4	43.5	42.7
15 to 59 minutes	43,925	39,759	41,217	32.1	30.6	27.4
1 hour, but less than 2 hours	13,228	12,180	11,983	9.7	9.4	8.0
2 hours, but less than 3 hours	3,894	3,841	4,721	2.8	3.0	3.1
3 hours, but less than 4 hours	1,496	1,609	2,069	1.1	1.2	1.4
4 hours, but less than 6 hours	1,028	872	1,468	0.8	0.7	1.0
6 hours or more	870	682	999	0.6	0.5	0.7
TIME SPENT IN EMERGENCY DEPARTMENT						
Less than 1 hour	15,361	12,103	14,868	11.2	9.3	9.9
1 hour, but less than 2 hours	30,987	27,688	30,942	22.6	21.3	20.5
2 hours, but less than 4 hours	45,699	45,238	52,104	33.4	34.8	34.6
4 hours, but less than 6 hours	19,462	20,604	21,833	14.2	15.9	14.5
6 hours, but less than 10 hours	9,410	10,896	12,532	6.9	8.4	8.3
10 hours, but less than 14 hours	2,093	2,369	2,484	1.5	1.8	1.6
14 hours, but less than 24 hours	1,902	2,174	2,567	1.4	1.7	1.7
24 hours or more	1,093	1,717	2,274	0.8	1.3	1.5

[1] Totals include nonresponse and nonapplicable categories. [2] Medical professional may be a physician, physician assistant, or advanced practice registered nurse.

Source: U.S. National Center for Health Statistics, *National Hospital Ambulatory Medical Care Survey: 2019 Emergency Department Summary Tables*, August 2022 and earlier reports. See also <www.cdc.gov/nchs/ahcd/index.htm>.

Table 186. Ambulatory Care Visits to Physician Offices and Emergency Departments by Patient and Other Characteristics: 2018 and 2019

[860,386 represents 860,386,000. Covers nonfederal office-based patient care physicians and emergency departments (EDs) in noninstitutional general and short-stay hospitals, excluding Federal, military, and Veterans Administration hospitals. Based on the National Ambulatory Medical Care Survey (NAMCS) and the National Hospital Ambulatory Medical Care Survey (NHAMCS), and subject to sampling error; see sources for details]

Characteristic	Physician office visits, 2018		Emergency department visits, 2019	
	Number (1,000)	Per 100 persons [1]	Number (1,000)	Per 100 persons [1]
Total	**860,386**	**267.1**	**150,650**	**46.6**
PATIENT AGE				
Under 15 years old	109,930	180.7	30,003	49.6
15 to 24 years old	58,754	139.9	19,840	47.6
25 to 44 years old	158,770	186.9	39,477	46.1
45 to 64 years old	251,488	302.5	33,582	40.7
65 years and over	281,444	550.2	27,748	52.6
65 to 74 years old	147,017	485.7	13,462	43.1
75 years old and over	134,427	643.8	14,286	66.4
PATIENT SEX				
Male	353,263	224.3	68,415	43.3
Female	507,122	308.1	82,235	49.8
PATIENT RACE/ETHNICITY [2]				
White	722,966	293.1	107,781	43.6
Black or African American	72,623	171.0	36,598	85.6
Other	64,796	196.5	6,271	18.8
Hispanic or Latino	127,972	216.1	26,162	43.7
EXPECTED PAYMENT SOURCE [3]				
Private insurance	490,463	(X)	44,232	(X)
Medicare	238,047	(X)	29,815	(X)
Medicaid/CHIP/state-based program [4]	110,571	(X)	55,991	(X)
Medicare and Medicaid [5]	12,196	(X)	5,590	(X)
No insurance: [6]	[7] 54,373	(X)	12,578	(X)
Self pay	[7] 50,644	(X)	12,178	(X)
No charge/charity	[7] 4,088	(X)	416	(X)
Worker's compensation	4,948	(X)	1,116	(X)

X Not applicable. [1] Rates are based on July 1 Census Bureau estimates of the civilian noninstitutional population for the same year as data are shown. [2] Race groups White, Black or African American, and Other include persons of Hispanic origin. Persons of Hispanic origin may be of any race. See source for information on missing and imputed data. [3] Estimates include all expected sources of payment. Other and unknown sources are not shown separately. [4] Children's Health Insurance Program (CHIP). [5] Visits for patients with dual Medicare and Medicaid coverage are also included in the Medicare and Medicaid/CHIP/state-based program categories. [6] "No insurance" is having only "self-pay" or "no charge/charity" as payment sources. [7] Figure does not meet standards of reliability or precision.

Source: U.S. National Center for Health Statistics, Ambulatory Health Care Data, "NAMCS and NHAMCS Web Tables: 2018 and 2019," <www.cdc.gov/nchs/ahcd/web_tables.htm>, accessed August 2022.

Table 187. Medicare-Certified Hospitals, Institutions, and Physicians by Provider Type: 2010 to 2020

[Inpatient hospitals and other institutional providers are active and Medicare-certified in the reporting year. Physician provider counts originate from Medicare fee-for-service Part B claims, and reflect services provided by participating and non-participating physicians]

Providers by type	2010	2015	2016	2017	2018	2019	2020
INPATIENT HOSPITALS							
Total hospitals [1]	**6,169**	**6,140**	**6,146**	**6,123**	**6,072**	**6,023**	**6,214**
Beds	927,535	931,951	933,209	934,197	931,555	932,559	927,342
Beds per 1,000 enrollees [2]	19.6	16.9	16.5	16.1	15.6	15.2	14.8
Short stay	3,566	3,436	3,419	3,392	3,334	3,283	3,481
Psychiatric units	1,180	1,118	1,113	1,092	1,063	1,027	998
Rehabilitation units	938	908	911	890	864	840	832
Swing bed hospitals	510	488	474	467	455	445	662
Psychiatric	511	560	570	586	598	604	613
Rehabilitation	235	266	277	282	296	306	314
Children's	77	100	99	97	96	95	93
Long term care	438	426	420	401	382	367	347
Critical access	1,325	1,336	1,343	1,347	1,351	1,353	1,351
SELECTED INSTITUTIONAL PROVIDERS							
Skilled nursing facilities	15,084	15,236	15,274	15,268	15,218	15,103	15,015
Beds	1,572,511	1,600,752	1,607,056	1,605,515	1,602,222	1,592,041	1,588,755
Beds per 1,000 enrollees [2]	33.2	29.0	28.4	27.6	26.9	26.0	25.4
Home health agencies	10,914	12,149	11,956	11,593	11,317	11,157	11,221
Hospices	3,509	4,302	4,473	4,650	4,775	4,970	5,260
Independent and clinical labs	224,684	252,044	254,133	258,473	262,524	265,057	284,414
Outpatient physical therapy/speech pathology	2,536	2,130	2,080	2,043	2,016	2,032	2,044
End stage renal disease	5,631	6,558	6,843	7,082	7,429	7,629	7,755
Rural health clinics	3,845	4,104	4,153	4,233	4,402	4,482	4,736
Ambulatory surgical centers	5,316	5,470	5,529	5,598	5,718	5,812	5,905
Federally qualified health centers	4,308	7,022	7,723	8,289	8,836	9,467	10,000
PHYSICIAN PROVIDERS							
All physician specialties [1, 3]	**595,783**	**656,195**	**665,772**	**675,579**	**684,790**	**692,846**	**698,164**
Primary care	212,849	227,370	228,907	229,946	227,587	227,255	225,008
Family practice	84,982	92,830	93,893	94,703	95,031	95,358	95,263
General practice	13,401	9,985	9,492	9,225	8,849	8,648	8,215
Internal medicine	106,343	114,420	115,335	115,792	113,155	112,362	110,443
Pediatric medicine	8,123	10,135	10,187	10,226	10,552	10,887	11,087
Surgical specialties	108,093	111,272	111,439	112,390	112,839	113,541	113,522
Radiology	36,656	38,156	38,736	39,419	39,903	40,434	40,828
Obstetrics/gynecology	32,881	34,890	35,092	35,439	35,556	35,605	35,433
Psychiatry	27,550	28,139	28,150	28,224	28,200	28,277	27,925

[1] Includes other provider types not shown separately. [2] Beds per 1,000 enrollees based on Medicare Part A enrollee counts. [3] Physicians may be counted in more than one specialty.

Source: U.S. Centers for Medicare & Medicaid Services, CMS Program Statistics, <data.cms.gov/collection/cms-program-statistics>, accessed February 2022.

Table 188. Nursing Homes, Beds, Residents, and Occupancy Rate by State: 2016

[Based on a census of certified nursing facilities. Annual numbers of nursing homes, beds, and residents are based on the Centers for Medicare & Medicaid Services' reporting cycle. Starting with 2013 data, a new editing rule was used for number of beds. For the U.S., the number of beds decreased by less than 1%. For most states, this caused little or no change in the data. The change in the number of beds also caused a change in some occupancy rates. Because of the methodology change, interpret trends with caution]

State	Nursing homes	Beds	Residents	Occupancy rate [1]	State	Nursing homes	Beds	Residents	Occupancy rate [1]
U.S.	**15,647**	**1,690,304**	**1,346,941**	**79.7**	MO	513	55,120	38,279	69.4
AL	229	26,702	22,554	84.5	MT	78	6,614	4,385	66.3
AK	18	693	591	85.3	NE	214	15,750	11,718	74.4
AZ	147	16,535	11,480	69.4	NV	58	6,649	4,967	74.7
AR	229	24,649	17,707	71.8	NH	75	7,471	6,655	89.1
CA	1,205	118,666	101,744	85.7	NJ	366	52,784	44,598	84.5
CO	221	20,904	16,267	77.8	NM	75	7,198	5,713	79.4
CT	225	27,252	23,224	85.2	NY	624	115,542	104,187	90.2
DE	45	4,807	4,206	87.5	NC	425	45,537	36,654	80.5
DC	19	2,766	2,494	90.2	ND	81	6,169	5,562	90.2
FL	690	83,823	73,183	87.3	OH	963	90,547	74,844	82.7
GA	358	39,905	33,324	83.5	OK	304	28,517	18,729	65.7
HI	46	4,385	3,564	81.3	OR	137	11,419	7,462	65.3
ID	78	5,858	3,892	66.4	PA	701	88,263	78,042	88.4
IL	742	94,923	68,188	71.8	RI	84	8,720	7,829	89.8
IN	546	61,604	38,884	63.1	SC	189	19,948	16,932	84.9
IA	440	31,624	24,106	76.2	SD	110	6,867	6,234	90.8
KS	340	25,685	17,810	69.3	TN	320	36,902	27,486	74.5
KY	291	27,119	23,442	86.4	TX	1,216	137,028	92,737	67.7
LA	279	34,642	26,300	75.9	UT	98	8,479	5,443	64.2
ME	103	6,918	6,142	88.8	VT	37	3,174	2,603	82.0
MD	228	28,090	24,534	87.3	VA	288	32,783	27,713	84.5
MA	412	47,779	40,065	83.9	WA	221	21,109	16,652	78.9
MI	446	47,285	38,847	82.2	WV	126	10,866	9,446	86.9
MN	378	29,816	25,279	84.8	WI	386	33,079	25,766	77.9
MS	205	18,389	16,100	87.6	WY	38	2,950	2,378	80.6

[1] Percentage of beds occupied (number of nursing home residents per 100 nursing home beds).

Source: U.S. National Center for Health Statistics, *Health, United States, 2017*, September 2018. See also <www.cdc.gov/nchs/hus/index.htm>.

Table 189. Hospital Emergency Department Visits by Leading Reason for Visit by Patient Age and Sex: 2019

[150,650 represents 150,650,000. Based on the annual National Hospital Ambulatory Medical Care Survey and subject to sampling error; see source for details. Data may not sum due to rounding]

Principal reason for visit	Visits (1,000)	Percent of visits	Principal reason for visit	Visits (1,000)	Percent of visits
Total, all ages............................	**150,650**	**100.0**	Back symptoms.................................	1,408	1.5
			Shortness of breath...........................	1404	1.5
Stomach & abdominal pain, cramps, spasms....	13,142	8.7	Cough...	1,345	1.4
Chest pain and related symptoms [1]..............	8,043	5.3	Problems of pregnancy........................	1,173	1.3
Fever...	6,516	4.3	Symptoms referable to throat................	1,105	1.2
Cough..	5,404	3.6	Nausea...	980	1.1
Shortness of breath...........................	4,429	2.9	All other reasons [4]..........................	32,303	34.8
Headache, pain in head.......................	3,856	2.6	**Male**...	**40,326**	**43.4**
Back symptoms.................................	3,435	2.3	Stomach & abdominal pain, cramps, spasms....	3,106	3.3
Pain [2].......................................	3,212	2.1	Chest pain and related symptoms [1]..............	2,750	3.0
Vomiting.......................................	2,987	2.0	Back symptoms.................................	1,086	1.2
Injury [3].....................................	2,590	1.7	Pain [2].......................................	1,045	1.1
All other reasons [4]..........................	97,035	64.4	Headache, pain in head.......................	1,031	1.1
Patients under age 15 years	**30,003**	**100.0**	Shortness of breath...........................	**1,021**	**1.1**
Female.......................................	**13,689**	**45.6**	Cough...	921	1.0
Fever...	2,307	7.7	Related to psychological & mental disorders.....	867	0.9
Cough..	1,100	3.7	Foot and toe symptoms........................	747	0.8
Stomach & abdominal pain, cramps, spasms....	921	3.1	Leg symptoms.................................	731	0.8
Skin rash.......................................	508	1.7	All other reasons [4]..........................	27,021	29.1
Vomiting.......................................	473	1.6	**Patients age 65 years and over**	**27,748**	**100.0**
Injury [3].....................................	425	1.4	**Female**.......................................	**15,973**	**57.6**
Earache or ear infection.......................	368	1.2	Chest pain and related symptoms [1].............	1,100	4.0
Headache, pain in head.......................	348	1.2	Stomach & abdominal pain, cramps, spasms....	1,065	3.8
Nasal congestion..............................	(B)	0.8	Shortness of breath...........................	909	3.3
Symptoms referable to throat..................	239	0.8	General weakness.............................	633	2.3
All other reasons [4]..........................	6,760	22.5	Accident, not otherwise specified..............	612	2.2
Male...	**16,313**	**54.4**	Vertigo—dizziness............................	579	2.1
Fever...	2,643	8.8	Leg symptoms.................................	476	1.7
Cough..	1,529	5.1	Back symptoms.................................	472	1.7
Skin rash.......................................	801	2.7	Related to psychological & mental disorders.....	430	1.6
Stomach & abdominal pain, cramps, spasms....	711	2.4	Hypertension..................................	378	1.4
Injury [3].....................................	654	2.2	All other reasons [4]..........................	9,318	33.6
Vomiting.......................................	652	2.2	**Male**...	**11,775**	**42.4**
Earache or ear infection.......................	561	1.9	Shortness of breath...........................	803	2.9
Symptoms referable to throat..................	375	1.2	Chest pain and related symptoms [1]..............	775	2.8
Headache, pain in head.......................	311	1.0	Stomach & abdominal pain, cramps, spasms....	723	2.6
Labored or difficult breathing (dyspnea)..........	283	0.9	Related to psychological & mental disorders.....	365	1.3
All other reasons [4]..........................	7,795	26.0	Back symptoms.................................	343	1.2
Patients age 15 to 64 years	**92,899**	**100.0**	Vertigo—dizziness............................	**332**	**1.2**
Female.......................................	**52,574**	**56.6**	General weakness.............................	319	1.2
Stomach & abdominal pain, cramps, spasms....	6,615	7.1	Accident, not otherwise specified..............	281	1.0
Chest pain and related symptoms [1]..............	3,149	3.4	Leg symptoms.................................	277	1.0
Headache, pain in head.......................	1,641	1.8	Pain [2].......................................	276	1.0
Pain [2].......................................	1,451	1.6	All other reasons [4]..........................	7,281	26.2

[1] Not referable to body systems. [2] Site not referable to a specific body system. [3] Injury, other and unspecified type—head, neck, and face. [4] Includes all other reasons not listed above, and unknown and blank responses.

Source: U.S. National Center for Health Statistics, *National Hospital Ambulatory Medical Care Survey, 2019 Emergency Department Summary Tables*, August 2022. See also <www.cdc.gov/nchs/ahcd/index.htm>.

Table 190. Hospital Utilization Rates by Type of Hospital: 1990 to 2020

[In units, as indicated (21.9 represents 21,900,000)]

Type of hospital	1990	2000	2005	2010	2016	2017 [4]	2018	2019	2020
Community hospitals: [1]									
Admissions per 1,000 population [2]...............	125	117	119	114	105	105	105	104	95
Admissions per bed...........................	34	40	44	44	43	43	43	43	40
Average length of stay (days) [3]...............	7.2	7.4	5.6	5.4	5.5	5.4	5.4	5.4	5.6
Outpatient visits per admission...............	9.7	15.8	16.6	18.5	22.2	22.3	22.4	23.0	22.8
Outpatient visits per 1,000 population [2]..........	1,207	1,852	1,976	2,108	2,342	2,352	2,343	2,392	2,177
Surgical operations (million)......................	21.9	26.1	27.5	27.3	28.2	28.2	28.2	28.4	25.0
Number per admission......................	0.7	0.8	0.8	0.8	0.8	0.8	0.8	0.8	0.8
Nonfederal psychiatric:									
Admissions per 1,000 population [2]...............	2.9	2.4	2.5	2.5	2.5	3.7	3.7	3.8	3.6
Days in hospital per 1,000 population [2]..........	190	93	89	77	65	77	77	78	73

[1] See headnote, Table 192. [2] Based on Census Bureau estimated resident population as of July 1. Data for 1990, 2000, and 2010 based on enumerated resident population as of April 1. [3] Number of inpatient days divided by number of admissions. [4] See footnote 8, Table 191.

Source: Health Forum LLC, an affiliate of the American Hospital Association, Chicago, IL, *AHA Hospital Statistics 2022 Edition* ©, and previous editions. See also <guide.prod.iam.aha.org/stats/>.

Table 191. Hospitals—Summary Characteristics: 2000 to 2020

[In units indicated (984 represents 984,000). Covers hospitals accepted for registration by the American Hospital Association; see text, this section. Short-term hospitals have an average patient stay of less than 30 days; long-term, an average stay of longer duration]

Item	2000	2005	2010	2015	2016	2017 [8]	2018	2019	2020
NUMBER									
All hospitals	5,810	5,756	5,754	5,564	5,534	6,210	6,146	6,090	6,093
With 100 beds or more	3,102	2,942	2,832	2,682	2,659	2,763	2,730	2,692	2,672
Nonfederal [1]	5,565	5,530	5,541	5,352	5,325	6,002	5,937	5,882	5,886
Community hospitals [2]	4,915	4,936	4,985	4,862	4,840	5,262	5,198	5,141	5,139
Nongovernmental nonprofit	3,003	2,958	2,904	2,845	2,849	2,968	2,937	2,946	2,960
For profit	749	868	1,013	1,034	1,035	1,322	1,296	1,233	1,228
State and local government	1,163	1,110	1,068	983	956	972	965	962	951
Long term general and special	131	115	109	77	76	106	109	102	98
Psychiatric	496	456	435	401	397	620	616	625	645
Tuberculosis	4	3	2	2	2	2	2	2	2
Federal	245	226	213	212	209	208	209	208	207
BEDS (1,000) [3]									
All hospitals	984	947	942	898	895	931	924	920	921
Rate per 1,000 population [4]	3.5	3.2	3.0	2.8	2.8	2.9	2.8	2.8	2.8
Beds per hospital	169	165	164	160	162	150	150	151	151
Nonfederal [1]	931	901	897	859	857	893	887	882	884
Community hospitals [2]	824	802	805	782	780	799	792	788	789
Rate per 1,000 population [4]	2.9	2.7	2.6	2.4	2.4	2.5	2.4	2.4	2.4
Nongovernmental nonprofit	583	561	556	531	533	545	543	546	548
For profit	110	114	125	135	134	142	140	131	130
State and local government	131	128	125	117	113	111	110	110	112
Long term general and special	18	15	15	8	8	11	11	9	9
Psychiatric	87	82	76	68	68	82	82	84	87
Federal	53	46	45	39	38	38	38	38	37
AVERAGE DAILY CENSUS (1,000) [5]									
All hospitals	650	656	627	588	589	614	612	611	600
Community hospitals [2]	526	540	520	497	499	510	508	507	485
Nongovernmental nonprofit	382	388	368	346	349	357	356	358	340
For profit	61	68	71	77	78	81	81	78	75
State and local government	83	85	80	74	72	72	71	71	70
EXPENSES (bil. dol.) [6]									
All hospitals	395.4	570.5	750.6	936.5	991.5	1,061.0	1,112.2	1,161.0	1,213.9
Nonfederal [1]	371.5	533.7	698.2	872.0	923.0	993.0	1,037.2	1,083.7	1,131.9
Community hospitals [2]	356.6	515.7	678.0	851.5	902.9	966.0	1,010.0	1,056.5	1,102.3
Nongovernmental nonprofit	267.1	386.0	510.7	636.0	677.0	721.0	755.8	794.7	830.0
For profit	35.0	51.8	67.2	88.8	94.0	105.0	108.0	106.9	106.8
State and local government	54.5	77.9	100.1	126.7	132.1	140.0	146.0	154.9	165.5
Long term general and special	2.8	3.6	4.2	3.2	2.9	3.9	4.1	3.6	4.1
Psychiatric	11.9	13.9	15.8	16.8	17.2	22.5	22.2	23.0	24.9
Federal	23.9	36.8	52.4	64.5	68.1	67.6	75.0	77.4	82.0
PERSONNEL (1,000) [7]									
All hospitals	4,454	4,790	5,184	5,397	5,562	5,841	5,903	5,989	6,002
Nonfederal [1]	4,157	4,479	4,825	5,056	5,184	5,459	5,484	5,563	5,562
Community hospitals [2]	3,911	4,260	4,600	4,859	4,992	5,216	5,239	5,315	5,317
Nongovernmental nonprofit	2,919	3,154	3,388	3,562	3,681	3,841	3,848	3,929	3,927
For profit	378	421	474	534	551	591	594	573	560
State and local government	614	681	738	762	759	783	797	813	830
Long term general and special	41	38	39	23	21	28	32	27	28
Psychiatric	200	182	182	172	169	212	211	218	215
Federal	297	311	359	341	379	382	419	426	440
OUTPATIENT VISITS (mil.)									
Total	592.7	673.7	750.4	832.3	863.7	880.4	879.6	900.7	834.0
Emergency visits	106.9	118.9	131.5	145.3	146.7	150.2	147.4	147.5	126.9

[1] Includes hospital units of institutions; and tuberculosis hospitals, not shown separately. [2] Short-term (average stay less than 30 days) general and specialty (e.g., obstetrics and gynecology, rehabilitation, etc. except psychiatric, tuberculosis, alcoholism, and chemical dependency). Excludes hospital units of institutions. [3] Number of beds at end of reporting period. [4] See footnote 2, Table 190. [5] The average number of people served on an inpatient basis on a single day during the reporting period. [6] Excludes new construction. [7] Includes full-time equivalents of part-time personnel. [8] Beginning with the 2019 edition of *AHA Hospital Statistics* presenting data from the 2017 annual survey, the AHA discontinued using its own methodology to classify hospitals as registered and began including hospitals under a more generally known and accepted definition, which resulted in an increase in the number of hospitals covered in *AHA Hospital Statistics*.

Source: Health Forum LLC, an affiliate of the American Hospital Association, Chicago, IL, *AHA Hospital Statistics 2022 Edition* ©, and previous editions. See also <guide.prod.iam.aha.org/stats/>.

Table 192. Community Hospital Summary Data by State: 2010 and 2020

[In units indicated (804.9 represents 804,900). Community hospitals are defined as all nonfederal, short-term general, and other specialty hospitals. Other specialty hospitals include obstetrics and gynecology; eye, ear, nose, and throat; rehabilitation; orthopedic; and other individually described specialty services. Community hospitals include academic medical centers or other teaching hospitals if they are nonfederal short-term hospitals. Excluded are hospitals not accessible by the general public, such as prison hospitals or college infirmaries. Beginning with the 2019 edition of *AHA Hospital Statistics* presenting data from the 2017 annual survey, the AHA discontinued using its own methodology to classify hospitals as registered and began including hospitals under a more generally known and accepted definition, which resulted in an increase in the number of hospitals covered in *AHA Hospital Statistics*]

State	Number of hospitals		Beds (1,000)		Patients admitted (1,000)		Average daily census [1] (1,000)		Outpatient visits (mil.)		Average cost per day (dol.)	
	2010	2020	2010	2020	2010	2020	2010	2020	2010	2020	2010	2020
United States	4,985	5,139	804.9	789.4	35,149	31,393	519.5	484.5	651.4	717.2	1,910	2,873
Alabama	105	101	15.1	15.4	642	589	9.2	9.6	8.8	7.8	1,372	1,786
Alaska	22	20	1.5	1.6	57	37	0.9	1.0	1.8	1.7	2,020	2,233
Arizona	73	81	13.4	14.3	712	623	8.7	8.8	8.1	8.0	2,173	3,131
Arkansas	85	90	9.5	9.5	370	343	5.2	4.9	5.0	5.7	1,477	1,947
California	343	353	70.4	72.6	3,424	3,100	47.8	46.2	51.7	52.5	2,566	4,098
Colorado	80	91	10.2	11.1	449	419	6.1	6.2	8.3	8.7	2,190	3,302
Connecticut	34	31	8.1	7.5	407	356	6.3	5.6	8.3	7.9	2,154	3,290
Delaware	7	7	2.2	2.2	102	95	1.6	1.5	1.8	2.0	2,227	3,364
District of Columbia	11	10	3.5	3.2	132	114	2.5	2.4	2.3	2.4	2,434	3,648
Florida	210	214	53.3	55.0	2,452	2,435	33.4	34.8	24.2	27.7	1,837	2,586
Georgia	154	144	25.5	25.1	961	971	16.8	17.4	14.3	19.1	1,338	2,100
Hawaii	26	22	3.1	2.7	111	108	2.3	1.9	2.2	2.7	1,755	2,945
Idaho	41	46	3.4	3.5	131	134	1.7	1.7	3.2	6.3	1,748	2,683
Illinois	189	184	33.3	31.8	1,543	1,218	20.7	17.7	32.6	34.2	1,983	2,939
Indiana	125	129	17.8	18.4	718	686	10.3	10.1	18.7	20.4	1,964	2,814
Iowa	118	116	10.1	9.1	342	287	5.7	4.8	11.0	12.0	1,288	1,786
Kansas	130	135	10.0	9.4	305	299	5.4	4.9	6.7	8.7	1,304	2,191
Kentucky	106	104	14.2	14.3	609	506	8.6	8.0	10.4	14.4	1,546	2,303
Louisiana	126	159	15.4	15.1	625	541	9.2	8.2	12.4	10.7	1,561	2,371
Maine	37	34	3.6	3.5	146	117	2.2	2.3	6.0	6.8	2,077	2,902
Maryland	47	49	11.7	11.2	708	509	8.7	7.6	8.4	8.0	2,383	3,336
Massachusetts	79	74	15.7	15.8	823	716	11.4	11.1	21.8	21.6	2,419	3,462
Michigan	156	141	25.6	24.5	1,208	1,013	17.0	14.8	30.3	34.2	1,959	2,681
Minnesota	133	125	15.3	13.8	592	489	9.9	8.4	11.1	11.8	1,731	2,568
Mississippi	96	97	12.9	11.8	403	347	7.0	6.7	4.6	6.9	1,154	1,311
Missouri	122	118	18.7	18.5	821	718	11.5	10.9	19.8	24.8	1,981	2,668
Montana	48	56	3.7	3.8	97	91	2.3	1.9	3.5	4.4	1,190	2,050
Nebraska	88	93	7.2	6.6	209	189	4.0	3.5	4.6	5.7	1,516	2,473
Nevada	36	46	5.2	6.5	241	263	3.6	4.2	2.7	3.0	1,885	2,397
New Hampshire	28	28	2.9	2.8	120	115	1.7	1.7	4.8	5.5	2,164	3,247
New Jersey	73	81	21.1	21.9	1,067	958	14.9	13.8	16.0	13.3	2,179	3,232
New Mexico	36	42	4.0	3.8	186	181	2.3	2.3	4.6	3.6	2,058	3,150
New York	185	162	59.5	50.7	2,510	1,970	47.2	36.3	53.7	53.3	1,883	3,676
North Carolina	117	112	23.0	21.7	1,038	971	16.0	14.5	18.3	19.5	1,633	2,528
North Dakota	41	41	3.3	3.4	94	88	2.0	1.8	3.1	3.0	1,342	1,808
Ohio	183	193	34.3	32.2	1,517	1,284	20.8	18.3	35.8	41.3	2,138	3,226
Oklahoma	113	122	11.2	11.1	429	402	6.4	6.1	5.7	7.5	1,499	2,207
Oregon	58	61	6.4	7.0	321	324	3.8	4.2	9.2	12.2	2,818	3,986
Pennsylvania	196	186	39.9	35.4	1,810	1,416	26.8	21.7	38.6	38.0	1,906	2,810
Rhode Island	11	11	2.5	2.2	123	105	1.7	1.5	2.7	2.0	2,325	3,019
South Carolina	67	73	12.5	11.2	523	490	8.2	7.4	6.4	10.0	1,788	2,341
South Dakota	53	57	4.1	4.3	101	102	2.6	2.4	2.0	3.1	1,113	1,642
Tennessee	134	111	20.8	19.2	833	785	12.5	12.0	11.4	12.9	1,462	2,350
Texas	426	523	61.4	66.6	2,580	2,632	36.5	38.7	38.3	41.7	1,943	2,923
Utah	44	53	5.1	5.9	224	236	2.7	3.2	5.5	8.4	2,233	3,350
Vermont	14	14	1.3	1.3	49	47	0.8	0.8	3.4	2.9	1,656	3,114
Virginia	89	95	17.7	18.2	777	727	11.8	11.4	13.8	16.2	1,736	2,549
Washington	86	91	11.5	12.2	589	504	7.2	7.6	11.8	15.5	2,810	3,945
West Virginia	56	52	7.3	6.3	278	223	4.4	3.9	6.7	7.3	1,323	2,104
Wisconsin	124	133	13.5	12.2	589	480	8.1	6.9	14.6	18.5	1,953	2,732
Wyoming	24	28	2.0	1.9	50	40	1.1	1.0	1.0	1.3	1,103	1,466

[1] The average number of people served on an inpatient basis on a single day during the reporting period.

Source: Health Forum LLC, an affiliate of the American Hospital Association, Chicago, IL, *AHA Hospital Statistics 2022 Edition* ©, and previous editions. See also <guide.prod.iam.aha.org/stats/>.

Table 193. Average Cost to Community Hospitals Per Patient: 1990 to 2020

[In dollars, except percent. Covers non-federal short-term general or specialty hospitals (excluding psychiatric or tuberculosis hospitals and hospital units of institutions). Total cost per patient based on total hospital expenses (payroll, employee benefits, professional fees, supplies, etc.). Data have been adjusted for outpatient visits]

Type of expense and hospital	1990	2000	2005	2010	2015	2016	2017 [2]	2018	2019	2020
Average cost per day, total	687	1,149	1,522	1,910	2,271	2,338	2,424	2,517	2,607	2,873
Annual percent change [1]	7.8	4.2	5.0	3.1	2.7	2.9	3.7	3.8	3.6	10.2
Nongovernmental nonprofit	692	1,182	1,585	2,025	2,413	2,488	2,574	2,653	2,738	3,032
For profit	752	1,057	1,412	1,629	1,831	1,889	1,996	2,093	2,149	2,301
State and local government	635	1,064	1,329	1,625	2,013	2,013	2,129	2,260	2,372	2,606
Average cost per stay, total	4,947	6,649	8,793	10,313	12,359	12,777	13,126	13,542	14,101	16,190
Nongovernmental nonprofit	5,001	6,717	8,670	10,652	12,755	13,182	13,504	13,883	14,446	16,524
For profit	4,727	5,642	7,351	8,336	9,510	9,698	10,273	10,684	10,764	12,543
State and local government	4,838	7,106	8,793	10,283	13,070	13,720	14,015	14,591	15,518	17,717

[1] Change from immediate prior year. [2] Beginning with *AHA Hospital Statistics 2019 Edition* presenting data from the 2017 annual survey, the AHA discontinued using its own methodology to classify hospitals as registered and began including hospitals under a more generally known and accepted definition, which resulted in an increase in the number of hospitals covered.

Source: Health Forum LLC, an affiliate of the American Hospital Association, Chicago, IL, *AHA Hospital Statistics 2022 Edition* ©, and previous editions. See also <guide.prod.iam.aha.org/stats/>.

Table 194. Household Medical Debt—Incidence and Value by Selected Characteristics: 2017

[In units as indicated. Based on the Survey of Income and Program Participation, a survey of a sample of households and subject to sampling variability. Presence of medical debt was determined by asking respondents whether they had medical bills that they were unable to pay in full]

Characteristic	Percent with medical debt	Median value of medical debt (dollars)	Mean value of medical debt (dollars)	Characteristic	Percent with medical debt	Median value of medical debt (dollars)	Mean value of medical debt (dollars)
Total [1]	**19.0**	**2,000**	**12,430**	Highest education in household:			
				No high school diploma	19.0	2,000	10,210
Race/ethnicity of householder:				High school graduate only	22.3	2,000	17,760
White alone	17.9	2,000	12,330	Some college, no degree	26.2	2,000	11,120
White alone, not Hispanic	17.2	2,081	12,310	Associate's degree	23.0	2,700	13,480
Black alone	27.9	2,000	13,250	Bachelor's degree	15.5	2,000	8,955
Asian alone	9.7	1,000	10,800	Graduate/professional degree	10.9	1,800	10,270
Other race group	23.3	2,100	11,390				
Hispanic origin [2]	21.7	1,840	11,560	Household poverty status:			
Not of Hispanic origin	18.6	2,000	12,600	Below poverty threshold	19.0	2,000	15,290
				Above poverty threshold	19.0	2,000	12,050
Age of householder:							
Less than 35 years	19.4	2,000	9,982	Health insurance coverage:			
35 to 44 years	22.4	2,000	12,250	Coverage for all of household			
45 to 54 years	22.9	2,500	17,120	all year	16.2	2,000	11,130
55 to 64 years	22.0	2,000	10,310	No coverage for part or all of			
65 years and over	11.3	2,000	12,300	household during the year	30.8	3,000	15,390

[1] Includes persons of other race groups not shown separately. [2] Persons of Hispanic origin may be of any race.

Source: U.S. Census Bureau, America Counts: Stories Behind the Numbers, "Who Had Medical Debt in the United States," April 2021, <www.census.gov/library/stories/2021/04/who-had-medical-debt-in-united-states.html>; and "Wealth, Asset Ownership, & Debt of Households Detailed Tables: 2017," <www.census.gov/data/tables/2017/demo/wealth/wealth-asset-ownership.html>, accessed April 2021.

Table 195. Medical and Mental Health Care Delay or Nonreceipt During the Past 12 Months Due to Cost: 2019 and 2020

[Data shown as percent of population. For adults age 18 and over except as noted. Based on the National Health Interview Survey, a sample survey of the civilian noninstitutionalized population. Respondents reported delaying or not getting needed medical and mental health care due to cost in the past 12 months, and for those taking prescription medications, not taking medication as prescribed to save money in the past 12 months. Unknowns were not included in the denominators when calculating percentages. The NHIS questionnaire was redesigned in 2019. Due to changes in weighting and design methodology, direct comparisons between estimates for 2019 and beyond to earlier years should be made with caution, as the impact of these changes has not been fully evaluated at this time. In 2020, the NHIS switched data collection from personal visits to telephone mode during the coronavirus disease 2019 (COVID-19) pandemic. For more information, see *Technical Notes for Interactive Summary Health Statistics—2019-2020: National Health Interview Survey* at <wwwn.cdc.gov/NHISDataQueryTool/SHS_adult/SHS_Tech_Notes.pdf>]

Characteristic	Delayed medical care 2019	Delayed medical care 2020	Did not get needed medical care 2019	Did not get needed medical care 2020	Did not get needed mental health care 2019	Did not get needed mental health care 2020	Did not take medication as prescribed [1] 2019	Did not take medication as prescribed [1] 2020
Total	**9.1**	**7.5**	**8.3**	**6.6**	**4.4**	**4.3**	**9.6**	**8.3**
Sex:								
Male	7.8	6.3	6.9	5.6	2.6	2.7	7.9	7.0
Female	10.3	8.7	9.5	7.6	6.0	5.8	10.9	9.3
Age group:								
18 to 34 years	10.5	9.1	9.1	7.6	6.6	7.0	11.0	9.8
35 to 49 years	10.9	8.8	10.0	7.9	5.1	5.2	13.3	10.8
50 to 64 years	10.3	8.6	9.8	8.0	3.5	3.0	10.1	9.5
65 years and over	3.4	2.7	3.4	2.3	1.3	1.1	5.3	4.3
Race and Hispanic origin: [2]								
White alone	8.8	7.3	7.8	6.2	4.4	4.4	9.1	7.6
Black or African American alone	10.6	8.3	11.1	7.9	4.4	4.4	13.0	11.1
American Indian/Alaska Native alone	10.5	6.1	11.2	8.3	6.6	(B)	11.6	11.6
Asian alone	3.5	3.5	3.6	3.5	1.9	1.6	5.1	5.0
Hispanic or Latino	13.2	10.8	12.2	9.5	4.7	5.1	11.8	12.4
Not Hispanic or Latino	8.2	6.9	7.5	6.1	4.3	4.1	9.3	7.7
Health insurance status: [3]								
Private	6.3	5.7	5.5	4.7	4.0	4.3	8.6	6.9
Medicaid or other public	8.9	7.4	7.9	7.2	6.1	5.3	12.6	11.5
Other coverage	9.9	9.2	10.1	9.6	5.7	5.5	14.4	13.6
Uninsured	32.2	26.1	30.3	23.4	10.0	9.5	29.3	30.9
Disability status: [4]								
With disability	15.1	13.1	14.8	13.1	7.1	7.5	16.3	14.7
Without disability	8.4	7.0	7.6	6.0	4.1	4.0	8.7	7.4

B Estimate does not meet standards of reliability. [1] Respondents who reported taking prescribed medicine in the past 12 months were asked in separate questions if during the past 12 months any of the following were true: they skipped medication doses to save money, they took less medication to save money, they delayed filling a prescription to save money. [2] Race groups refer to persons who indicated only a single race group, regardless of Hispanic or Latino origin. Persons of Hispanic or Latino origin may be of any race or combination of races. [3] For adults age 18 to 64, at time of interview. Based on a hierarchy of mutually exclusive categories. Adults with more than one type of health insurance were assigned to the first appropriate category in the following hierarchy: private, Medicaid or other public, other coverage, or uninsured. "Uninsured" includes adults who had no coverage as well as those who had only Indian Health Service coverage or had only a private plan that paid for one type of service such as dental or vision care. [4] Respondents considered to have a disability reported "a lot of difficulty" or "cannot do at all" regarding at least one of six functioning domains: seeing (even if wearing glasses), hearing (even if wearing hearing aids), mobility (walking or climbing stairs), communication (understanding or being understood by others), cognition (remembering or concentrating), and self-care (such as washing all over or dressing).

Source: U.S. National Center for Health Statistics, National Health Interview Survey, "Interactive Summary Health Statistics for Adults," <www.cdc.gov/nchs/nhis/SHS.htm>, accessed May 2022.

Table 196. Cosmetic Plastic Surgical and Nonsurgical Procedures: 2018 and 2019

[Data are projected to reflect nationwide statistics. Data cover procedures performed only by plastic surgeons who are certified by the American Board of Plastic Surgery. Previous surveys included procedures performed by physicians from specialties other than plastic surgery. For more information, see March 2018 press release, <www.theaestheticsociety.org/media/press-releases/american-society-aesthetic-plastic-surgery-reports-modern-cosmetic-procedures>]

Procedure	2018, Total	2019 Total	2019 Women	2019 Men
Total surgical procedures	**1,533,640**	**1,469,752**	**1,366,914**	**102,838**
Breast augmentation	329,914	280,692	280,692	0
Breast implant removal	49,834	66,982	66,982	(X)
Breast lift	158,964	146,711	146,711	(X)
Breast reduction, female	84,599	86,543	86,543	(X)
Brow lift	21,868	23,305	21,373	1,932
Buttock augmentation	26,774	35,880	35,800	80
Buttock lift	5,257	7,780	7,642	138
Chin augmentation	7,149	6,641	5,710	932
Ear surgery	10,724	11,989	7,814	4,175
Eyelid surgery	115,508	113,229	94,478	18,751
Facelift	73,174	68,983	64,912	4,071
Fat transfer: breast	23,340	24,892	24,892	0
Fat transfer: face	39,461	43,177	41,159	2,018
Labiaplasty (excluding vaginal rejuvenation)	12,756	12,903	12,903	(X)
Liposuction	289,261	270,670	237,843	32,827
Lower body lift	6,098	7,797	7,314	483
Male breast reduction (treats gynecomastia)	24,672	21,407	(X)	21,407
Neck lift	27,475	30,688	25,668	5,020
Nose surgery	41,213	39,692	34,655	5,037
Thigh lift	9,743	9,815	9,746	69
Tummy tuck	157,492	140,381	134,550	5,831
Upper arm lift	18,364	19,596	19,527	69
Total nonsurgical procedures	**3,315,888**	**3,121,439**	**2,818,219**	**303,221**
Total injectables	2,671,130	2,525,279	2,283,900	241,379
Botulinum toxin [1]	1,801,033	1,712,994	1,541,305	171,689
Calcium hydroxylapatite [2]	31,821	34,776	29,153	5,624
Hyaluronic acid [3]	810,240	749,409	687,102	62,307
Poly-L-Latic acid [4]	28,036	28,100	26,341	1,760
Total facial rejuvenation	341,619	276,017	248,642	27,376
Chemical peel	129,596	78,971	74,020	4,951
Full field ablative (laser skin resurfacing)	37,849	31,033	27,893	3,140
Micro-ablative resurfacing (fractional resurfacing)	38,550	66,275	57,029	9,246
Photorejuvenation (IPL, intense pulsed light)	135,624	99,740	89,700	10,040
Total other nonsurgical procedures	303,139	320,143	285,677	34,466
Hair removal (laser or pulsed light)	118,592	180,332	162,029	18,302
Nonsurgical fat reduction [5]	174,244	129,686	113,522	16,163
Sclerotherapy	10,303	10,126	10,126	0

X Not applicable. [1] Includes Botox, Dysport, and Xeomin. [2] Radiesse. [3] Includes Juvederm Ultra, Ultra Plus, Voluma, Restylane Lyft, Restylane, and Belotero. [4] Sculptra. [5] Includes CoolSculpting, Vaser Shape, and Liposonix.

Source: The American Society for Aesthetic Plastic Surgery, *2019 Aesthetic Plastic Surgery National Data Bank Statistics* ©. See also <www.theaestheticsociety.org/media/procedural-statistics>.

Table 197. Cancer Survival Rates by Type/Body Site and Race and Year of Diagnosis: 1999 to 2018

[For invasive cancer, unless otherwise noted. For top 15 cancers ranked by incidence rates per 100,000 persons for 2015-2019 period. Based on follow-up of patients into 2019. The 5-year relative survival rate represents the proportion of patients alive 5 years after their cancer diagnosis, compared to similar persons among the general population without cancer. Based on information collected as part of the National Cancer Institute's Surveillance, Epidemiology and End Results (SEER) program, from a collection of population-based registries in 8 areas]

Cancer type	White 1999 to 2001	White 2002 to 2004	White 2005 to 2007	White 2008 to 2011	White 2012 to 2018	Black 1999 to 2001	Black 2002 to 2004	Black 2005 to 2007	Black 2008 to 2011	Black 2012 to 2018
All types [1]	**66.8**	**68.0**	**69.6**	**70.3**	**70.8**	**58.3**	**60.2**	**63.3**	**65.1**	**66.4**
Female breast	90.4	91.1	92.1	92.2	92.5	79.4	79.5	81.0	83.2	84.6
Prostate	98.6	99.0	99.0	98.7	96.8	96.2	97.2	98.1	97.5	96.2
Lung and bronchus	15.1	16.2	17.9	19.5	24.5	12.3	13.8	13.9	18.0	23.8
Colon and rectum	66.0	66.4	67.2	67.2	66.6	54.1	55.7	60.2	60.1	63.1
Corpus and uterus	85.4	85.2	85.6	85.0	84.9	63.5	61.1	66.8	66.2	67.1
Melanoma of skin	91.7	92.4	93.0	93.6	95.3	69.9	76.5	75.5	67.4	71.7
Non-Hodgkin's lymphoma [3]	65.0	71.0	72.3	74.5	76.9	56.1	63.3	61.8	68.8	73.3
Urinary bladder [2]	79.6	79.8	79.3	77.8	79.7	64.6	64.6	66.9	68.0	65.0
Kidney and renal pelvis	64.3	68.8	73.9	74.0	77.5	67.1	63.4	74.2	75.7	78.9
Thyroid	96.7	97.1	98.0	98.5	98.4	92.4	97.3	96.7	97.7	95.7
Leukemia [3]	52.3	59.3	63.9	66.6	69.1	46.4	52.2	57.8	58.1	65.4
Pancreas	5.0	5.6	7.4	8.3	12.1	6.1	5.0	6.0	7.8	11.7
Oral cavity and pharynx	62.2	65.8	67.6	69.9	72.2	45.3	51.0	47.1	53.7	57.2
Ovary	43.6	43.5	44.4	47.4	50.1	36.5	39.9	39.3	38.4	43.0
Liver & intrahepatic bile duct	10.7	13.8	16.8	17.9	20.9	6.9	9.1	12.7	14.3	22.8

[1] Includes other sites, not shown separately. [2] Invasive and in situ. [3] All types combined.

Source: U.S. National Institutes of Health, National Cancer Institute, Surveillance Epidemiology and End Results Program, "Cancer Query System: SEER Survival Statistics," <seer.cancer.gov/canques/survival.html>, accessed April 2022.

Table 198. Top 15 Cancers Among Men and Women by Race/Ethnicity: 2015 to 2019

[Rates per 100,000 population, age-adjusted to the 2000 U.S. standard population. Includes top 15 cancers for each racial/ethnic group. Cancer incidence measures the number of newly diagnosed cases occurring in a specified population during a year. Data are for cancers diagnosed during 2015 to 2019 period, based on cancer registries in 22 areas monitored by the Surveillance, Epidemiology, and End Results (SEER) Program. See source for more information]

Cancer by site, and sex	All race/ethnicities Rank	Rate	White, non-Hispanic Rank	Rate	Black, non-Hispanic Rank	Rate	Asian/Pacific Islander, non-Hispanic Rank	Rate	Hispanic [1] Rank	Rate
TOTAL										
All sites...............	(X)	**445.5**	(X)	**476.3**	(X)	**459.0**	(X)	**308.3**	(X)	**354.3**
Prostate [2]...............	1	112.7	1	110.0	1	183.4	1	59.6	1	88.6
Breast...................	2	68.6	2	72.5	2	73.7	2	58.4	2	53.1
Lung and bronchus............	3	52.0	3	58.4	3	56.1	3	35.4	4	27.4
Colon and rectum............	4	37.7	4	38.1	4	44.3	4	30.7	3	34.4
Corpus and uterus, NOS [2,3]...	5	27.8	6	28.0	5	29.3	5	22.6	5	26.1
Lymphoma.................	6	21.6	7	23.3	7	17.3	7	15.0	6	19.7
Melanoma of the skin..........	7	21.5	5	31.1	26	0.9	24	1.3	21	4.4
Non-Hodgkin lymphoma........	8	19.0	9	20.4	9	14.6	8	13.6	8	17.5
Urinary bladder.............	9	18.7	8	22.4	11	11.2	14	8.6	14	10.3
Kidney and renal pelvis........	10	17.3	10	17.7	6	18.8	13	8.7	7	18.5
Thyroid.................	11	14.6	11	15.8	17	8.6	6	15.9	10	13.8
Leukemia................	12	14.1	12	15.4	12	11.1	16	8.2	12	11.0
Pancreas................	13	13.3	13	13.5	8	16.1	10	10.0	11	12.0
Oral cavity and pharynx........	14	11.5	14	13.4	18	8.6	15	8.6	17	7.1
Ovary [2,4]...............	15	10.6	15	11.0	15	9.1	12	9.4	13	10.3
Liver and IBD [5].............	16	9.5	17	7.5	13	11.0	9	12.5	9	15.1
Myeloma................	18	7.2	20	6.4	10	14.5	18	4.0	18	6.8
Stomach................	19	7.1	21	5.4	14	10.1	11	9.7	15	10.1
MEN										
All sites...............	(X)	**484.7**	(X)	**514.8**	(X)	**535.1**	(X)	**308.3**	(X)	**374.6**
Prostate.................	1	112.7	1	110.0	1	183.4	1	59.6	1	88.6
Lung and bronchus............	2	58.9	2	64.0	2	71.6	2	44.4	3	33.5
Colon and rectum............	3	43.4	3	43.5	3	52.4	3	36.5	2	41.1
Urinary bladder.............	4	32.4	5	38.5	6	18.9	7	15.3	8	17.6
Melanoma of the skin..........	5	27.6	4	38.6	23	1.0	21	1.5	18	4.6
Lymphoma................	6	25.9	6	28.0	5	20.5	5	18.1	5	22.9
Kidney and renal pelvis........	7	23.6	8	24.3	4	26.2	9	12.3	4	24.1
Non-Hodgkin lymphoma........	8	23.0	7	24.8	9	17.4	6	16.5	7	20.2
Leukemia................	9	18.0	10	19.8	11	13.8	12	10.3	9	13.3
Oral cavity and pharynx........	10	17.4	9	20.3	13	13.2	10	12.2	12	10.4
Pancreas................	11	15.1	11	15.7	8	17.7	11	11.0	10	12.8
Liver and IBD [5].............	12	14.4	12	11.3	7	18.1	4	19.4	6	22.2
Stomach................	13	9.3	17	7.6	12	13.5	8	12.8	11	12.3
Myeloma................	14	8.8	16	8.1	10	17.0	14	5.1	13	8.1
Thyroid.................	15	7.7	13	8.9	18	3.8	13	7.9	14	6.0
Brain & other nervous system..............	16	7.4	14	8.8	16	4.9	15	4.6	15	5.8
Esophagus...............	17	7.2	15	8.4	15	5.7	16	3.7	17	4.9
Larynx.................	19	4.9	19	5.1	14	7.1	18	2.0	19	4.1
WOMEN										
All sites...............	(X)	**419.9**	(X)	**450.8**	(X)	**408.7**	(X)	**312.5**	(X)	**346.5**
Female breast...............	1	128.3	1	137.6	1	129.6	1	106.9	1	99.9
Lung and bronchus............	2	46.8	2	54.3	2	45.6	2	28.5	4	23.0
Colon and rectum............	3	32.9	3	33.3	3	38.6	3	26.0	2	29.0
Corpus and uterus, NOS [3].....	4	27.8	4	28.0	4	29.3	5	22.6	3	26.1
Thyroid.................	5	21.3	6	22.7	9	12.8	4	23.0	5	21.6
Lymphoma................	6	18.0	7	19.4	6	14.8	6	12.5	6	17.2
Melanoma of the skin..........	7	17.0	5	25.5	24	0.9	21	1.2	18	4.5
Non-Hodgkin lymphoma........	8	15.8	8	16.7	10	12.4	7	11.3	7	15.3
Kidney and renal pelvis........	9	11.9	9	11.9	7	13.3	14	5.8	8	13.9
Pancreas................	10	11.8	11	11.7	5	14.9	9	9.2	9	11.3
Leukemia................	11	11.0	10	11.8	11	9.2	12	6.5	12	9.2
Ovary [4]................	12	10.6	12	11.0	12	9.1	8	9.4	10	10.3
Urinary bladder.............	13	8.0	13	9.5	15	6.1	16	3.5	16	4.8
Cervix uteri..............	14	7.8	15	7.1	13	9.0	13	6.3	11	10.0
Oral cavity and pharynx........	15	6.4	14	7.2	17	5.0	15	5.7	19	4.3
Myeloma................	16	5.9	17	5.0	8	12.9	17	3.2	15	5.9
Stomach................	18	5.3	19	3.7	14	7.8	10	7.3	14	8.4
Liver and IBD [5].............	19	5.2	18	4.1	16	5.5	11	6.9	13	9.0

X Not applicable. [1] Persons of Hispanic origin may be of any race. [2] For cancer sites that occur in only one sex, the sex-specific population (e.g., females for cervical cancer) is used. [3] NOS, not otherwise specified. [4] Ovary excludes borderline cases or histologies 8442, 8451, 8462, 8472, and 8473. [5] IBD, intrahepatic bile duct.

Source: National Institutes of Health, National Cancer Institute, Surveillance, Epidemiology, and End Results Program, "Cancer Query Systems: SEER Incidence Statistics," <seer.cancer.gov/canques/>, accessed April 2022.

Table 199. Cancer Incidence for Total and Top 5 Cancers by State: 2018

[For invasive cancer sites. Top five cancers are ranked by total number of new cases. Data are produced by the Centers for Disease Control and Prevention (CDC) and the National Cancer Institute]

State	Total cancer cases (number)	Rate per 100,000 population					
		All cancers [1]	Prostate	Breast [1]	Lung and bronchus	Colon and rectum	Melanoma of the skin
Total [2]	1,725,233	527.8	133.8	79.4	67.1	43.7	25.7
Alabama	27,125	555.0	158.0	78.9	81.0	50.0	27.5
Alaska	2,990	406.7	102.2	62.7	46.8	40.0	15.0
Arizona	32,863	459.1	92.0	70.7	54.4	37.7	37.0
Arkansas	18,349	609.7	161.8	79.4	99.6	53.7	28.6
California	171,748	435.2	100.9	70.9	41.6	37.3	25.2
Colorado	24,550	431.4	109.3	74.8	41.7	33.4	22.5
Connecticut	20,734	580.5	159.8	92.0	71.7	44.4	23.5
Delaware	5,890	610.1	171.6	95.3	83.1	45.2	37.0
District of Columbia	2,881	410.7	124.7	74.1	43.3	36.5	8.4
Florida	131,409	618.6	123.4	84.7	82.2	47.8	34.2
Georgia	53,748	511.3	146.5	78.5	63.9	43.0	27.5
Hawaii	7,552	531.6	149.2	92.9	56.9	46.7	31.6
Idaho	8,761	500.5	138.4	76.5	54.3	39.6	31.5
Illinois	69,403	545.5	137.7	82.8	73.5	48.3	25.7
Indiana	34,396	513.7	115.0	78.3	75.2	45.3	23.7
Iowa	18,715	594.4	150.4	85.2	77.3	49.1	34.2
Kansas	15,346	527.1	141.3	80.1	65.2	45.9	28.5
Kentucky	27,778	622.7	138.2	82.5	107.7	57.8	33.2
Louisiana	26,935	578.0	181.6	81.8	74.2	51.8	21.5
Maine	9,134	682.1	158.6	91.7	107.4	48.3	39.9
Maryland	32,389	536.6	164.5	82.9	62.9	42.9	27.9
Massachusetts	36,637	532.3	142.2	82.4	70.2	38.1	19.0
Michigan	56,095	561.8	144.8	83.6	80.0	43.9	24.7
Minnesota	30,944	552.0	137.4	81.9	64.0	42.4	42.8
Mississippi	17,037	571.5	170.5	79.2	89.7	58.8	19.9
Missouri	33,143	541.4	118.1	79.5	88.3	48.2	20.5
Montana	6,412	604.5	198.0	93.1	65.0	44.2	36.0
Nebraska	10,798	560.8	169.8	81.0	67.0	49.0	33.9
Nevada	(NA)	(NA)	(NA)	(NA)	(NA)	(NA)	(NA)
New Hampshire	8,511	628.8	170.3	95.4	82.2	46.0	36.1
New Jersey	53,194	598.6	174.0	89.3	67.6	46.5	25.6
New Mexico	9,202	439.7	103.3	71.1	42.6	40.0	18.8
New York	114,373	585.6	165.7	87.4	72.2	44.7	21.7
North Carolina	58,056	559.2	153.0	89.4	78.9	42.7	29.2
North Dakota	3,789	499.8	149.7	71.6	68.1	41.3	24.1
Ohio	68,371	585.6	149.7	84.9	85.8	49.8	29.1
Oklahoma	20,480	519.8	118.1	75.0	80.2	46.2	23.4
Oregon	21,413	512.0	115.1	87.2	62.9	38.5	26.9
Pennsylvania	78,426	612.7	142.2	88.2	84.4	49.4	26.9
Rhode Island	6,242	589.8	151.3	97.4	82.7	43.9	26.9
South Carolina	27,906	548.9	137.7	85.4	80.0	44.5	28.1
South Dakota	4,824	549.0	155.8	74.7	68.1	46.5	34.8
Tennessee	38,007	561.3	147.9	79.2	90.4	47.1	22.8
Texas	120,013	419.2	103.3	62.8	47.3	38.8	13.6
Utah	11,588	367.5	107.5	53.9	23.4	25.7	36.5
Vermont	3,852	617.0	158.6	89.2	81.2	46.0	47.2
Virginia	40,108	471.8	113.9	77.4	62.1	39.9	24.0
Washington	38,055	505.8	122.7	78.6	58.7	38.3	28.6
West Virginia	12,210	676.7	152.1	86.1	112.4	61.4	29.9
Wisconsin	33,727	580.8	157.0	86.3	75.6	42.9	26.7
Wyoming	2,812	486.8	162.1	70.8	48.1	40.7	32.2
Puerto Rico	16,312	510.8	225.5	75.8	23.8	55.9	4.4

Not available. [1] Excludes data for in situ breast cancers. [2] Total includes States, District of Columbia, and Puerto Rico.

Source: U.S. Centers for Disease Control and Prevention, CDC WONDER Online Database, "Cancer Incidence 1999-2018," <wonder.cdc.gov/cancer.html>, accessed February 2022.

Table 200. Selected Notifiable Diseases—Cases Reported: 1990 to 2019

[In thousands only where indicated (690 represents 690,000). Interpret figures with caution. Although reporting of some of these diseases is incomplete, the figures are of value in indicating trends of disease incidence. Includes cases imported from outside the U.S.]

Disease	1990	2000	2005	2010	2015	2016	2017	2018	2019 [13]
Babesiosis..........................	(1)	(1)	(1)	(1)	2,100	1,910	2,368	2,160	2,420
Botulism [3].......................	92	138	135	112	195	201	177	225	196
Campylobacteriosis..............	(1)	(1)	(1)	(1)	54,556	60,120	67,537	70,200	71,509
Chikungunya virus................	(1)	(1)	(1)	(1)	896	247	156	117	192
Coccidioidomycosis..............	(1)	2,867	6,542	(1)	11,072	11,829	14,364	15,611	18,407
Cryptosporidiosis.................	(1)	3,128	5,659	8,944	9,735	13,453	11,414	12,533	13,975
Dengue virus infections [4].........	(1)	(1)	(1)	700	951	953	437	424	1,414
Giardiasis..........................	(1)	(1)	19,733	19,811	14,485	16,310	15,193	15,548	14,860
Haemophilus influenza...........	(1)	1,398	2,304	3,151	4,138	4,895	5,548	5,573	6,143
Hepatitis virus, acute: A.........	31,441	13,397	4,488	1,670	1,390	2,007	3,365	12,474	18,846
Hepatitis virus, acute: B.........	21,102	8,036	5,119	3,374	3,370	3,218	3,409	3,322	3,544
Hepatitis virus, acute: C.........	2,553	3,197	652	849	2,447	2,942	4,225	4,768	5,479
HIV diagnoses [2].................	41,595	40,758	41,120	35,741	33,817	34,775	33,938	32,999	31,723
Invasive pneumococcal disease [5].......	(X)	(X)	(X)	16,569	16,163	17,626	19,780	19,857	19,951
Legionellosis......................	1,370	1,127	2,301	3,346	6,079	6,141	7,458	9,933	8,890
Listeriosis.........................	(1)	755	896	821	768	786	887	864	928
Lyme disease......................	(1)	17,730	23,305	30,158	38,069	36,429	42,743	33,666	34,945
Malaria.............................	1,292	1,560	1,494	1,773	1,390	1,955	2,056	1,748	1,936
Measles............................	27,786	86	66	63	188	85	120	375	1,275
Meningococcal disease..........	2,451	2,256	1,245	833	372	375	353	327	371
Mumps.............................	5,292	338	314	2,612	1,329	6,369	6,109	2,515	3,780
Pertussis (whooping cough).....	4,570	7,867	25,616	27,550	20,762	17,972	18,975	15,609	18,617
Rabies, animal....................	4,826	6,934	5,915	4,331	5,491	4,609	4,423	4,984	4,645
Rubella [6].........................	1,125	176	11	5	5	1	7	4	6
Salmonella Typhi infection [12].....	552	377	324	467	367	376	419	401	409
Salmonellosis [7]..................	48,603	39,574	45,322	54,424	55,108	53,850	54,285	60,999	58,371
Shiga toxin-producing E. coli (STEC).........	(1)	(1)	(1)	5,476	7,059	8,169	8,672	15,996	16,939
Shigellosis [8]....................	27,077	22,922	16,168	14,786	23,590	21,097	14,912	16,333	18,574
Spotted fever rickettsiosis.......	(1)	495	1,936	1,985	4,198	4,269	6,248	5,544	5,207
Streptococcal toxic-shock syndrome.........	(1)	83	129	142	335	283	372	371	416
Tetanus............................	64	35	27	26	29	34	33	23	26
Toxic-shock syndrome...........	322	135	90	82	64	40	30	33	44
Tuberculosis [9]..................	25,701	16,377	14,097	11,182	9,557	9,272	9,105	9,025	8,916
Varicella (chickenpox) morbidity [10].....	173,099	27,382	32,242	15,427	9,789	8,953	8,775	8,201	8,297
West Nile virus, neuroinvasive [4]......	(1)	(1)	1,309	629	1,455	1,308	1,425	1,657	636
West Nile virus, nonneuroinvasive [4].....	(1)	(1)	1,691	392	720	841	672	989	338
Zika virus disease and infections [11]...........	(1)	(1)	(1)	(1)	(1)	6,118	1,177	334	205
Sexually transmitted diseases:									
Chlamydia (1,000)...............	(1)	702	976	1,308	1,527	1,598	1,709	1,759	1,809
Gonorrhea (1,000)...............	690	359	340	309	395	469	556	583	616
Syphilis (1,000).................	134	32	33	46	75	88	102	115	130

X Not applicable. [1] Disease was not notifiable. [2] Human immunodeficiency virus diagnoses, including cases of AIDS (classified as HIV stage III). Cases reported to the Division of HIV/AIDS Prevention, National Center for HIV/AIDS, Viral Hepatitis, STD, and TB Prevention. In 2008, CDC revised the HIV case definition to cover HIV infection and AIDS into a single case definition. [3] Includes foodborne, infant, wound, and unspecified cases. [4] Totals reported to the Division of Vector-Borne Diseases (DVBD), National Center for Emerging and Zoonotic Infectious Diseases (NCEZID) (ArboNET Surveillance). [5] Data for 2010, 2011, and 2015 reported as Streptococcus pneumoniae invasive disease. [6] German measles, excluding congenital syndrome. [7] Excludes typhoid fever. Beginning 2018, excludes paratyphoid fever. [8] Bacillary dysentery. [9] Totals reported to the Division of Tuberculosis Elimination, NCHHSTP. [10] Varicella (chickenpox) was removed from the nationally notifiable disease list in 1981; it became notifiable again in 2003. [11] Includes Zika virus diseases and infections, congenital and noncongenital. [12] Prior to 2019, cases were reported as typhoid fever. Beginning January 2019, cases reported as Salmonella Typhi infection. [13] Numerous states and other jurisdictions may have reported incomplete data due to the COVID-19 pandemic.

Source: U.S. Centers for Disease Control and Prevention, "Summary of Notifiable Infectious Diseases and Conditions—United States, 2015," *Morbidity and Mortality Weekly Report*, 64:53, August 11, 2017, and earlier reports; and "WONDER Annual Tables of Infectious Diseases and Conditions (2016 to present)," <www.cdc.gov/nndss/data-statistics/infectious-tables/index.html>, accessed June 2021.

Table 201. HIV Diagnoses and Chlamydia and Lyme Disease Cases Reported by State: 2019

[Numerous states and other jurisdictions may have reported incomplete data due to the coronavirus disease 2019 (COVID-19) pandemic]

State	HIV [1]	Chlamydia [1]	Lyme disease [2]	State	HIV [1]	Chlamydia [1]	Lyme disease [2]	State	HIV [1]	Chlamydia [1]	Lyme disease [2]
U.S. [3]...	31,723	1,808,703	34,945	KY........	232	20,911	22	ND.............	31	3,880	38
AL.......	536	31,228	66	LA........	901	36,131	8	OH.............	821	65,393	467
AK.......	27	6,254	3	ME.......	30	3,989	2,167	OK.............	188	23,518	(6)
AZ.......	646	43,058	10	MD.......	783	37,779	1,417	OR.............	186	19,279	65
AR.......	265	17,196	18	MA.......	437	31,622	7	PA.............	928	61,694	8,998
CA.......	3,533	236,719	144	MI........	652	50,104	413	RI.............	54	5,718	971
CO.......	431	29,821	8	MN.......	265	24,470	1,528	SC.............	665	35,950	47
CT.......	165	15,290	1,233	MS.......	421	25,303	4	SD.............	19	4,547	10
DE.......	88	5,864	641	MO.......	470	34,416	17	TN.............	723	41,089	45
DC.......	233	9,327	100	MT.......	25	4,753	8	TX.............	3,069	129,075	41
FL........	4,341	110,794	162	NE.......	78	9,291	10	UT.............	126	11,075	19
GA.......	1,969	67,720	18	NV.......	442	17,827	17	VT.............	10	1,718	1,064
HI........	57	8,093	(5)	NH.......	27	3,577	1,710	VA.............	806	48,169	1,199
ID........	21	6,863	14	NJ........	860	37,591	3,619	WA.............	483	37,795	43
IL.........	1,108	81,012	395	NM.......	121	14,283	7	WV.............	122	5,609	885
IN........	466	35,430	189	NY [4].....	594	48,696	3,487	WI.............	194	29,080	2,178
IA........	92	16,044	303	NYC [4]....	1,511	75,926	756	WY.............	13	2,189	5
KS.......	119	15,286	35	NC........	1,339	70,257	334	Island Areas...	345	6,918	(6)

[1] Total diagnoses reported to the National Center for HIV/AIDS, Viral Hepatitis, STD, and TB Prevention. [2] Confirmed and probable. [3] Excludes Island areas. [4] New York City (NYC). Data for New York state excludes NYC. [5] Not reportable. [6] No cases reported.

Source: U.S. Centers for Disease Control and Prevention, National Notifiable Diseases Surveillance System, "WONDER Annual Tables of Infectious Diseases and Conditions (2016 to present)," <www.cdc.gov/nndss/data-statistics/index.html>, accessed June 2021.

Table 202. HIV (Human Immunodeficiency Virus) Infection Diagnoses and Persons Living With HIV by Selected Characteristics: 2017 to 2020

[For all HIV infections, regardless of stage of disease. Data reported to the Centers for Disease Control and Prevention's National HIV Surveillance System as of December 31, 2021. Covers the 50 states, the District of Columbia, and 6 U.S. dependent areas. As of April 2008, all jurisdictions had implemented confidential name-based HIV infection reporting. Data may not be representative of all persons with HIV. The completeness of HIV infection reporting is estimated to be at least 85% in all but 1 jurisdiction. See source for more information. Data for 2020 should be interpreted with caution due to the impact of the coronavirus disease 2019 (COVID-19) pandemic on access to HIV testing, care-related services, and case surveillance activities in state and local jurisdictions]

Characteristic	Diagnoses [11]				Persons living with HIV			
	2017	2018	2019	2020	2017	2018	2019	2020 (P)
Total [1]	**38,881**	**37,955**	**36,997**	**30,692**	**1,013,886**	**1,036,586**	**1,058,669**	**1,072,051**
SEX AND GENDER IDENTITY								
Male, assigned at birth	30,825	30,098	29,277	24,515	762,324	780,831	798,709	810,267
Female, assigned at birth	7,394	7,164	6,998	5,480	240,574	244,164	247,754	249,044
Transgender female [2]	614	629	654	640	10,413	10,949	11,499	11,985
Transgender male [2]	33	49	45	40	391	439	481	512
Additional gender identity [2]	15	15	23	17	184	203	226	243
AGE AT DIAGNOSIS								
Under 13 years	105	87	57	57	2,066	1,900	1,674	1,447
13 to 14 years	25	20	21	12	675	674	654	643
15 to 19 years	1,798	1,736	1,654	1,256	4,581	4,400	4,264	3,800
20 to 24 years	6,532	6,171	6,026	4,867	28,677	27,216	26,232	24,403
25 to 29 years	7,786	7,788	7,461	6,103	71,045	71,504	69,966	66,068
30 to 34 years	5,734	5,731	5,730	5,233	83,595	88,485	93,936	97,943
35 to 39 years	4,312	4,243	4,179	3,445	92,903	94,664	96,491	97,688
40 to 44 years	3,015	3,012	3,013	2,540	97,393	97,974	99,438	101,775
45 to 49 years	2,971	2,824	2,612	2,094	131,864	125,006	118,722	110,929
50 to 54 years	2,687	2,504	2,342	1,883	165,360	159,981	152,961	147,624
55 to 59 years	1,907	1,871	1,869	1,599	146,606	155,114	162,572	165,411
60 to 64 years	1,106	1,066	1,131	901	97,654	105,941	113,927	122,308
65 years and over	903	902	902	702	91,467	103,727	117,832	132,012
RACE/ETHNICITY [3]								
American Indian/Alaska Native	200	173	205	201	2,850	2,978	3,126	3,250
Asian [4]	933	872	746	637	13,964	14,856	15,626	16,266
Black/African American	16,283	15,794	15,508	12,859	406,513	415,886	425,003	430,332
Native Hawaiian/other Pacific Islander	52	63	70	66	809	858	912	968
White	9,648	9,451	9,075	7,843	295,085	299,526	303,536	306,048
Multiple races	1,378	1,214	1,106	792	52,710	52,856	52,916	52,447
Hispanic/Latino	10,387	10,388	10,287	8,294	241,218	248,889	256,817	262,007
TRANSMISSION CATEGORY [5]								
Males age 13 and over, total [6]	31,407	30,701	29,920	25,145	771,920	791,050	809,615	821,785
Male-to-male sexual contact	25,580	24,810	24,204	20,758	554,845	573,263	591,073	604,590
Injection drug use	1,326	1,431	1,406	1,198	71,657	70,889	70,228	69,099
Male-to-male sexual contact and injection drug use	1,483	1,477	1,536	1,109	57,919	57,945	58,120	57,629
Heterosexual contact [7]	2,987	2,947	2,734	2,051	79,709	81,079	82,192	82,394
Perinatal [8]	14	16	20	9	4,963	5,058	5,183	5,265
Other [9]	17	21	19	20	2,827	2,817	2,820	2,808
Females age 13 and over, total [6]	7,369	7,167	7,020	5,490	239,900	243,636	247,380	248,819
Injection drug use	1,095	1,107	1,160	857	49,985	49,792	49,670	49,114
Heterosexual contact [7]	6,216	6,008	5,805	4,575	182,568	186,307	189,994	191,832
Perinatal [8]	51	46	47	51	5,655	5,829	5,984	6,126
Other [9]	7	7	7	7	1,692	1,708	1,732	1,747
Children under age 13 at diagnosis	105	87	57	57	2,066	1,900	1,674	1,447
Perinatal	88	68	46	44	1,710	1,554	1,377	1,197
Other [9]	17	19	11	13	356	346	297	250
REGION								
Northeast	5,987	5,565	5,312	4,271	232,022	234,097	235,593	235,337
Midwest	5,115	4,940	4,748	4,127	118,984	122,094	124,872	126,929
South	19,725	19,412	19,181	15,689	449,534	461,779	474,316	482,479
West	7,594	7,587	7,344	6,316	196,814	202,225	207,410	210,858
U.S. dependent areas [10]	460	451	412	289	16,532	16,391	16,478	16,448

P Preliminary [1] Total may include persons whose racial/ethnic category is unknown (not shown separately). [2] Transgender female persons were assigned "male" sex at birth but have ever identified as "female" gender. Transgender male persons were assigned "female" sex at birth but have ever identified as "male" gender. Additional gender identity include "bi-gender," "gender queer," and "two-spirit." [3] Persons by race are not Hispanic or Latino, but may include persons whose Hispanic ethnicity was not reported. Persons of Hispanic/Latino ethnicity can be of any race. [4] For persons living with HIV, the Asian category includes Asian/Pacific Islander legacy cases. See source for more information. [5] Transmission category is classified based on a hierarchy of the risk factors most likely responsible for HIV transmission; see technical notes in source for details. Data for persons age 13 and over have been statistically adjusted to account for missing transmission category; therefore, values may not sum to column subtotals and total. [6] Data based on sex at birth and include transgender persons. [7] Heterosexual contact with a person known to have, or be at high risk for, HIV infection. [8] Persons were age 13 and over at the time of diagnosis of HIV infection. [9] Includes hemophilia, blood transfusion, and risk factor not reported or not identified. [10] American Samoa, Guam, Northern Mariana Islands, Puerto Rico, Republic of Palau, and the U.S. Virgin Islands. [11] Numbers less than 12 should be interpreted with caution.

Source: U.S. Centers for Disease Control and Prevention, *HIV Surveillance Report: Diagnoses of HIV Infection in the United States and Dependent Areas, 2020*, Vol. 33, May 2022. See also <www.cdc.gov/hiv/library/reports/hiv-surveillance.html>.

Table 203. AIDS Diagnoses and Persons Living with HIV Infection Ever Classified as Stage 3 (AIDS) by Selected Characteristics: 2017 to 2020

[Covers persons age 13 and over. Data reported to the Centers for Disease Control and Prevention's National HIV Surveillance System as of December 31, 2021. HIV infection is classified as stage 3 (AIDS) when the immune system of a person infected with human immunodeficiency virus becomes severely compromised (CD4 cell count drops below 200 cells/mm or if they develop certain opportunistic illnesses). Data cover the 50 states, the District of Columbia, and 5 U.S. dependent areas. Data may not be representative of all persons with HIV (not all persons are tested, and anonymous testing is excluded). The completeness of HIV infection reporting is estimated to be at more than 85%. 2020 data should be interpreted with caution due to the impact of the COVID-19 pandemic]

Characteristic	AIDS diagnoses				Persons living with HIV ever classified as stage 3			
	2017	2018	2019	2020	2017	2018	2019	2020 (P)
Total [1]	17,745	17,142	16,450	14,288	522,274	526,889	530,956	531,441
SEX [2]								
Male	13,480	13,040	12,630	11,038	398,241	401,820	404,942	405,481
Female	4,265	4,102	3,820	3,250	124,033	125,069	126,014	125,960
AGE								
13 to 24 years	1,375	1,275	1,104	908	6,058	5,310	4,696	4,061
25 to 34 years	4,782	4,749	4,643	4,026	44,887	44,690	44,166	42,557
35 to 44 years	4,168	4,047	3,990	3,417	85,059	83,349	81,906	80,631
45 to 54 years	4,116	3,851	3,342	2,948	172,202	162,268	151,638	141,234
55 years and over	3,304	3,220	3,371	2,989	214,068	231,272	248,550	262,958
RACE/ETHNICITY [3]								
American Indian/Alaska Native	74	60	64	79	1,387	1,413	1,432	1,457
Asian [4]	337	333	268	266	6,296	6,565	6,761	6,961
Black/African American	8,174	7,903	7,412	6,365	211,124	213,617	215,738	216,132
Native Hawaiian/Other Pacific Islander	22	19	20	15	384	394	403	408
White	4,224	4,009	3,916	3,479	150,871	151,002	151,065	150,478
Multiple races	885	791	761	648	30,016	29,903	29,774	29,374
Hispanic/Latino	4,029	4,027	4,009	3,436	122,159	123,958	125,747	126,595
TRANSMISSION CATEGORY [5]								
Male transmission:								
Heterosexual contact	1,902	1,790	1,728	1,397	46,852	47,403	47,814	47,781
Injection drug use	935	895	893	727	45,275	44,470	43,742	42,661
Male-to-male sexual contact	9,736	9,507	9,094	8,172	266,622	270,900	274,596	276,871
Male-to-male sexual contact and injection drug use	838	761	836	687	34,998	34,549	34,278	33,680
Female transmission:								
Heterosexual contact	3,407	3,265	2,982	2,605	90,374	91,633	92,773	93,217
Injection drug use	766	751	765	585	29,706	29,419	29,174	28,665

P Preliminary. [1] HIV prevalence data may include persons whose racial/ethnic category is unknown (not shown separately). [2] Sex as assigned at birth. [3] Race categories are non-Hispanic. Persons of Hispanic/Latino origin may be of any race. [4] For persons living with HIV ever classified as stage 3 (AIDS), the Asian category includes Asian/Pacific Islander legacy cases. [5] Data have been statistically adjusted to account for missing transmission category; therefore, values may not sum to column subtotals and total.

Source: U.S. Centers for Disease Control and Prevention, National Center for HIV, Viral Hepatitis, STD, and TB Prevention, "NCHHSTP AtlasPlus," <www.cdc.gov/nchhstp/atlas/index.htm>, accessed May 2022.

Table 204. Youth and Adult Vaccinations by Selected Type: 2010 to 2020

[In percent. Data for youth are from the National Immunization Survey-Teen, which monitors vaccines received by adolescents age 13-17 across the U.S. and its territories. Vaccination coverage estimates are based on provider-reported information, except for the influenza vaccination, which is parent-reported. Beginning in 2014, vaccination coverage estimates are not directly comparable to those for 2013 and previous years due to a change in the definition of adequate provider data. Data for adults are from the Behavioral Risk Factor Surveillance Survey, and excludes U.S. territories. Abbreviations: Td = tetanus diphtheria toxoid vaccine; Tdap = tetanus, diphtheria, and acellular pertussis vaccine; MenACWY = quadrivalent meningococcal conjugate vaccine; HPV = human papillomavirus]

Vaccine	2010	2013	2014	2015	2016	2017	2018	2019	2020
YOUTH, AGE 13 to 17									
Tdap, ≥ 1 dose	68.7	86.0	87.6	86.4	88.0	88.7	88.9	90.2	90.1
MenACWY, ≥ 1 dose	62.7	77.8	79.3	81.3	82.2	85.1	86.6	88.9	89.3
HPV vaccine:									
Total, ≥ 1 dose	(NA)	(NA)	(NA)	(NA)	60.4	65.5	68.1	71.5	75.1
Total, up-to-date [1]	(NA)	(NA)	(NA)	(NA)	43.4	48.6	51.1	54.2	58.6
Males, ≥ 1 dose	1.4	34.6	41.7	49.8	56.0	62.6	66.3	69.8	73.1
Males, ≥ 3 doses	(NA)	13.9	21.6	28.1	31.5	34.8	32.1	26.6	(NA)
Males, up-to-date [1]	(NA)	(NA)	(NA)	(NA)	37.5	44.3	48.7	51.8	56.0
Females, ≥ 1 dose	48.7	57.3	60.0	62.8	65.1	68.6	69.9	73.2	77.1
Females, ≥ 3 doses	32.0	37.6	39.7	41.9	43.0	44.0	37.9	28.5	(NA)
Females, up-to-date [1]	(NA)	(NA)	(NA)	(NA)	49.5	53.1	53.7	56.8	61.4
Influenza [2]	34.5	46.4	46.6	46.8	48.8	47.3	52.1	53.3	50.8
ADULTS									
Pneumococcal (pneumonia) vaccine:									
Age 18 to 64 at increased risk [3]	27.0	31.2	31.2	33.5	33.3	36.1	30.1	33.2	29.2
Age 65 and over	68.0	68.4	69.3	71.9	72.4	74.7	71.8	71.7	70.3
Tetanus (Td or Tdap) vaccine [4]									
Age 18 and over	(NA)	57.5	(NA)	(NA)	60.3	(NA)	(NA)	70.5	(NA)
Age 65 and over	(NA)	48.9	(NA)	(NA)	48.7	(NA)	(NA)	65.1	(NA)
Herpes zoster (shingles) vaccine [5]									
Age 60 and over	(NA)	(NA)	31.8	(NA)	(NA)	39.4	(NA)	(NA)	40.5
Age 65 and over	(NA)	(NA)	35.9	(NA)	(NA)	44.4	(NA)	(NA)	45.7
Influenza, age 18 and over [2]	40.5	42.2	43.6	41.7	43.3	37.1	45.3	48.4	50.2

NA Not available. [1] HPV up-to-date measure assesses completion of the HPV vaccine series. Beginning 2016, includes those with ≥3 doses, and those with 2 doses when the first HPV vaccine dose was initiated before age 15, and there was at least 5 months minus 4 days between the 1st and 2nd dose. [2] For the season beginning in the year shown. Excludes U.S. territories. [3] Self-reported. [4] Tetanus vaccination is determined by asking respondents if they received a tetanus shot in the past 10 years. During 2013-2017, tetanus vaccination was determined by asking respondents if they had received a tetanus shot since 2005. [5] Recommended for all adults age 60 and over.

Source: U.S. Centers for Disease Control and Prevention, Vaccines & Immunizations, "TeenVaxView," "AdultVaxView," and "FluVaxView," <www.cdc.gov/vaccines/vaxview/index.html>, accessed February 2022.

Table 205. Coronavirus Disease 2019 (COVID-19) Vaccinations by Week: 2021 to 2022

[Data are as of August 31, 2022. Data are updated weekly and subject to change over time as historical data are reported to the CDC. The CDC determines the number of people receiving at least one dose of the COVID-19 vaccine, and the number of people who are fully vaccinated based on information that state, territorial, tribal, and local public health agencies and federal entities report to CDC on dose number, dose manufacturer, administration date, recipient identification, and date of submission. Because the method used to determine dose numbers needs to be applied across multiple jurisdictions with different reporting practices, CDC's dose number estimates might differ from those reported by jurisdictions and federal entities. See source for more information. Data are subject to change. Data are presented here as an illustration of the progress in vaccinating people in the U.S. against COVID-19]

Week ending	Week number	People receiving 1st dose, weekly	People receiving 1 or more doses, cumulative [1]	People fully vaccinated each week [2]	People fully vaccinated, cumulative [2]	People receiving booster dose each week	People receiving booster dose, cumulative
June 5, 2021	22	2,639,708	175,701,254	4,361,943	150,510,372	602	9,460
June 12, 2021	23	2,459,833	178,161,087	5,076,656	155,587,028	405	9,865
June 19, 2021	24	2,119,784	180,280,871	3,783,391	159,370,419	346	10,211
June 26, 2021	25	1,965,530	182,246,401	2,556,239	161,926,658	308	10,519
July 3, 2021	26	1,794,063	184,040,464	2,039,898	163,966,556	416	10,935
July 10, 2021	27	1,609,692	185,650,156	1,762,483	165,729,039	216	11,151
July 17, 2021	28	1,827,080	187,477,236	1,691,903	167,420,942	169	11,320
July 24, 2021	29	2,439,800	189,917,036	1,606,525	169,027,467	200	11,520
July 31, 2021	30	3,044,502	192,961,538	1,527,391	170,554,858	275	11,795
August 7, 2021	31	3,399,624	196,361,162	1,618,226	172,173,084	340	12,135
August 14, 2021	32	3,254,553	199,615,715	1,946,285	174,119,369	52,704	64,839
August 21, 2021	33	3,001,959	202,617,674	2,423,021	176,542,390	644,890	709,729
August 28, 2021	34	2,889,074	205,506,748	2,744,832	179,287,222	649,220	1,358,949
September 4, 2021	35	2,568,163	208,074,911	2,652,822	181,940,044	670,666	2,029,615
September 11, 2021	36	2,059,821	210,134,732	2,349,602	184,289,646	494,748	2,524,363
September 18, 2021	37	2,006,213	212,140,945	2,483,387	186,773,033	481,665	3,006,028
September 25, 2021	38	1,693,159	213,834,104	2,185,082	188,958,115	909,072	3,915,100
October 2, 2021	39	1,776,894	215,610,998	1,910,510	190,868,625	3,226,826	7,141,926
October 9, 2021	40	1,531,476	217,142,474	1,662,078	192,530,703	3,016,076	10,158,002
October 16, 2021	41	1,398,643	218,541,117	1,458,254	193,988,957	2,691,230	12,849,232
October 23, 2021	42	1,380,806	219,921,923	1,272,471	195,261,428	3,252,164	16,101,396
October 30, 2021	43	1,788,021	221,709,944	1,267,242	196,528,670	6,417,802	22,519,198
November 6, 2021	44	2,164,785	223,874,729	1,198,888	197,727,558	6,311,258	28,830,456
November 13, 2021	45	3,517,184	227,391,913	1,042,582	198,770,140	5,734,689	34,565,145
November 20, 2021	46	3,238,326	230,630,239	1,042,135	199,812,275	6,492,815	41,057,960
November 27, 2021	47	2,123,353	232,753,592	932,786	200,745,061	4,769,975	45,827,935
December 4, 2021	48	2,591,688	235,345,280	2,647,065	203,392,126	7,289,502	53,117,437
December 11, 2021	49	2,451,147	237,796,427	2,289,100	205,681,226	7,022,880	60,140,317
December 18, 2021	50	2,344,044	240,140,471	1,548,277	207,229,503	6,601,417	66,741,734
December 25, 2021	51	1,990,557	242,131,028	1,028,774	208,258,277	5,167,218	71,908,952
January 1, 2022	52	1,995,946	244,126,974	1,123,335	209,381,612	4,529,492	76,438,444
January 8, 2022	1	2,271,485	246,398,459	1,361,032	210,742,644	5,149,779	81,588,223
January 15, 2022	2	2,092,537	248,490,996	1,130,251	211,872,895	4,694,244	86,282,467
January 22, 2022	3	1,510,469	250,001,465	1,002,828	212,875,723	3,277,738	89,560,205
January 29, 2022	4	1,244,562	251,246,027	1,084,125	213,959,848	2,556,781	92,116,986
February 5, 2022	5	919,025	252,165,052	1,004,262	214,964,110	1,725,915	93,842,901
February 12, 2022	6	818,949	252,984,001	906,999	215,871,109	1,407,946	95,250,847
February 19, 2022	7	632,880	253,616,881	709,280	216,580,389	1,116,753	96,367,600
February 26, 2022	8	540,711	254,157,592	577,619	217,158,008	941,869	97,309,469
March 5, 2022	9	438,527	254,596,119	467,224	217,625,232	759,565	98,069,034
March 12, 2022	10	352,731	254,948,850	372,074	217,997,306	568,605	98,637,639
March 19, 2022	11	332,650	255,281,500	324,646	218,321,952	544,860	99,182,499
March 26, 2022	12	325,580	255,607,080	281,795	218,603,747	498,080	99,680,579
April 2, 2022	13	377,609	255,984,689	344,943	218,948,690	556,428	100,237,007
April 9, 2022	14	411,263	256,395,952	399,739	219,348,429	577,051	100,814,058
April 16, 2022	15	395,769	256,791,721	376,906	219,725,335	553,714	101,367,772
April 23, 2022	16	347,671	257,139,392	327,187	220,052,522	478,870	101,846,642
April 30, 2022	17	328,100	257,467,492	314,717	220,367,239	462,855	102,309,497
May 7, 2022	18	305,679	257,773,171	288,069	220,655,308	423,416	102,732,913
May 14, 2022	19	309,385	258,082,556	281,912	220,937,220	431,683	103,164,596
May 21, 2022	20	326,519	258,409,075	288,681	221,225,901	476,349	103,640,945
May 28, 2022	21	314,685	258,723,760	275,998	221,501,899	552,292	104,193,237
June 4, 2022	22	249,683	258,973,443	213,581	221,715,480	440,256	104,633,493
June 11, 2022	23	269,682	259,243,125	222,921	221,938,401	460,616	105,094,109
June 18, 2022	24	247,760	259,490,885	202,680	222,141,081	403,866	105,497,975
June 25, 2022	25	371,127	259,862,012	185,000	222,326,081	375,066	105,873,041
July 2, 2022	26	414,937	260,276,949	176,650	222,502,731	346,032	106,219,073
July 9, 2022	27	332,156	260,609,105	156,918	222,659,649	289,994	106,509,067
July 16, 2022	28	407,591	261,016,696	207,797	222,867,446	394,466	106,903,533
July 23, 2022	29	409,327	261,426,023	254,237	223,121,683	413,965	107,317,498
July 30, 2022	30	362,194	261,788,217	243,544	223,365,227	370,050	107,687,548
August 6, 2022	31	322,848	262,111,065	207,916	223,573,143	328,620	108,016,168
August 13, 2022	32	292,363	262,403,428	196,916	223,770,059	295,432	108,311,600
August 20, 2022	33	266,754	262,670,182	179,490	223,949,549	261,812	108,573,412
August 27, 2022	34	211,129	262,881,311	145,333	224,094,882	207,379	108,780,791

[1] Cumulative totals include data for individuals who had received 1 or more doses of vaccine by December 14, 2020. [2] Represents total number of people who have received the 2nd dose of a two-dose vaccine, or one dose of a single-shot vaccine.

Source: U.S. Centers for Disease Control and Prevention, COVID Data Tracker, "Vaccination Delivery and Coverage," <covid-data-tracker/#datatracker-home>, accessed September 7, 2022.

Table 206. Coronavirus Disease 2019 (COVID-19) Vaccinations by State, Territory, and Federal Entity: Through September 7, 2022

[Data shown by state or jurisdiction of residence. People are fully vaccinated if they received 2 doses on different days of the 2-dose mRNA or protein-based series or received 1 dose of a single-dose vaccine. Persons who received a 1st booster dose includes anyone who is fully vaccinated who has received another dose of COVID-19 vaccine since August 13, 2021; persons with a first booster (either original or updated) may include people who received additional doses. Data are based on information reported by state, territorial, tribal, and local public health agencies and federal entities. Estimates are capped at 95% to avoid potential over-estimates. See source for additional information on data sources, limitations, and updates. Data are subject to revision]

State, territory, and federal entity	Population fully vaccinated		Population age 5 and over fully vaccinated		Population age 18 and over fully vaccinated		Population fully vaccinated with 1st booster dose	
	Total	Percent	Total	Percent	Total	Percent	Total	Percent
United States	**224,367,691**	**67.6**	**224,000,330**	**71.7**	**199,737,504**	**77.4**	**108,953,688**	**48.6**
Alabama	2,558,655	52.2	2,558,156	55.5	2,372,961	62.2	970,025	37.9
Alaska	463,635	63.4	462,480	68.0	408,246	74.0	218,463	47.1
Arizona	4,597,005	63.2	4,592,904	67.1	4,074,152	72.3	2,074,232	45.1
Arkansas	1,678,989	55.6	1,677,223	59.3	1,514,803	65.4	706,277	42.1
California	29,060,326	73.5	28,973,312	78.0	25,375,052	82.9	16,219,949	55.8
Colorado	4,125,180	71.6	4,116,219	75.9	3,646,561	81.0	2,281,706	55.3
Connecticut	2,881,218	80.8	2,876,340	85.0	2,538,950	89.5	1,546,518	53.7
Delaware	690,769	70.9	690,230	75.1	621,168	80.7	335,056	48.5
District of Columbia	557,746	79.0	553,549	83.8	501,427	86.8	246,812	44.3
Florida	14,648,767	68.2	14,640,977	72.0	13,461,268	78.0	6,219,011	42.5
Georgia	5,952,421	56.1	5,949,251	59.7	5,385,336	66.4	2,433,453	40.9
Hawaii	1,129,082	79.7	1,127,092	84.7	990,746	88.8	647,078	57.3
Idaho	985,999	55.2	985,265	59.0	889,086	66.4	452,950	45.9
Illinois	8,824,657	69.6	8,803,578	73.8	7,719,795	78.3	4,837,240	54.8
Indiana	3,827,605	56.9	3,824,960	60.6	3,462,353	67.0	1,864,408	48.7
Iowa	1,987,296	63.0	1,985,102	67.1	1,785,898	73.5	1,095,348	55.1
Kansas	1,846,220	63.4	1,844,187	67.6	1,642,377	74.2	857,535	46.4
Kentucky	2,610,361	58.4	2,608,427	62.2	2,374,708	68.5	1,210,823	46.4
Louisiana	2,527,881	54.4	2,526,673	58.1	2,324,234	65.3	1,054,346	41.7
Maine	1,092,647	81.3	1,091,399	85.2	984,662	89.9	638,741	58.5
Maryland	4,677,823	77.4	4,665,139	82.1	4,069,273	86.4	2,546,819	54.4
Massachusetts	5,573,783	80.9	5,553,456	85.0	4,897,778	88.4	2,990,928	53.7
Michigan	6,105,673	61.1	6,101,761	64.8	5,513,315	70.3	3,443,927	56.4
Minnesota	3,970,631	70.4	3,958,369	74.9	3,469,091	80.0	2,400,243	60.4
Mississippi	1,577,047	53.0	1,576,663	56.5	1,443,259	63.4	628,146	39.8
Missouri	3,519,315	57.3	3,515,506	60.9	3,187,977	66.9	1,577,712	44.8
Montana	618,651	57.9	618,146	61.3	562,974	67.0	308,514	49.9
Nebraska	1,253,360	64.8	1,250,853	69.4	1,106,265	75.9	668,802	53.4
Nevada	1,909,521	62.0	1,908,651	65.9	1,729,493	72.4	780,894	40.9
New Hampshire	984,548	72.4	983,526	75.9	892,503	80.8	476,691	48.4
New Jersey	6,854,030	77.2	6,843,436	81.8	6,051,061	87.1	3,421,594	49.9
New Mexico	1,527,044	72.8	1,525,164	77.2	1,341,733	82.8	800,749	52.4
New York	15,272,806	78.5	15,251,884	83.2	13,631,166	88.4	7,216,366	47.2
North Carolina	6,662,127	63.5	6,651,764	67.3	6,009,109	73.4	1,912,053	28.7
North Dakota	431,979	56.7	431,629	61.0	391,948	67.4	196,539	45.5
Ohio	6,935,957	59.3	6,927,904	63.0	6,273,023	68.9	3,789,579	54.6
Oklahoma	2,320,862	58.7	2,319,414	62.7	2,105,446	70.1	916,344	39.5
Oregon	2,983,101	70.7	2,979,962	74.7	2,669,939	79.7	1,679,916	56.3
Pennsylvania	9,036,682	70.6	9,014,850	74.5	8,132,869	80.0	4,032,052	44.6
Rhode Island	900,147	85.0	898,800	89.4	795,015	93.0	505,296	56.1
South Carolina	3,005,004	58.4	3,001,750	61.8	2,740,821	67.9	1,280,777	42.6
South Dakota	563,880	63.7	563,620	68.4	504,003	75.5	249,427	44.2
Tennessee	3,785,061	55.4	3,782,428	58.9	3,477,219	65.4	1,753,967	46.3
Texas	18,004,022	62.1	17,987,237	66.6	15,709,317	72.7	6,709,062	37.3
Utah	2,097,731	65.4	2,095,198	70.8	1,789,011	78.6	991,813	47.3
Vermont	517,353	82.9	515,674	86.7	454,418	89.1	327,478	63.3
Virginia	6,372,093	74.7	6,354,633	79.1	5,572,546	83.5	3,258,155	51.1
Washington	5,619,512	73.8	5,601,932	78.3	4,965,075	83.4	3,132,856	55.7
West Virginia	1,051,642	58.7	1,050,764	61.8	972,330	67.9	502,555	47.8
Wisconsin	3,882,982	66.7	3,877,468	70.6	3,474,534	76.3	2,274,365	58.6
Wyoming	300,396	51.9	300,165	55.2	275,793	62.0	135,914	45.2
American Samoa	42,318	89.3	42,318	95.0	29,902	95.0	24,437	57.7
Federated States of Micronesia	65,708	64.2	65,697	70.8	48,106	72.1	30,523	46.5
Guam	141,796	84.2	141,777	92.8	119,754	95.0	72,781	51.3
Marshall Islands	32,753	42.1	32,655	47.2	24,986	52.6	13,887	42.4
Northern Mariana Islands	43,603	84.1	43,584	90.6	34,272	95.0	22,486	51.6
Puerto Rico	2,702,788	84.6	2,702,148	87.8	2,338,865	89.2	1,656,560	61.3
Republic of Palau	18,347	85.2	18,339	90.0	15,797	95.0	12,063	65.7
Virgin Islands	57,711	54.3	57,684	57.9	53,506	65.6	18,302	31.7
Bureau of Prisons [1]	137,922	(NA)	137,921	(NA)	137,921	(NA)	51,747	37.5
Department of Defense [1]	3,424,148	(NA)	3,424,067	(NA)	3,172,692	(NA)	848,996	24.8
Indian Health Service [1]	891,884	42.8	891,406	(NA)	772,840	(NA)	306,725	34.4
Veterans Health [1]	2,983,298	(NA)	2,983,227	(NA)	2,981,812	(NA)	1,211,916	40.6

NA Not available. [1] Data for federal entities are also incorporated into their respective jurisdictional totals.

Source: U.S. Centers for Disease Control and Prevention, Covid Data Tracker, "Vaccination Distribution & Coverage: Vaccinations in the U.S., States, and Jurisdictions," <covid.cdc.gov/covid-data-tracker/#vaccine-delivery-coverage>, as of September 7, 2022.

Table 207. Organ Transplants: 1990 to 2021

[As of year end. Based on Organ Procurement and Transplantation Network data; data are from work supported in part by Health Resources and Services Administration contract HHSH250-2019-00001C]

Organ [1]	1990	1995	2000	2005	2010	2015	2018	2019	2020	2021
NUMBER OF TRANSPLANTS										
Total [2]..............................	**15,001**	**19,396**	**23,274**	**28,119**	**28,668**	**30,974**	**36,530**	**39,719**	**39,036**	**41,355**
Kidney..............................	9,416	11,084	13,631	16,485	16,900	17,878	21,167	23,401	22,817	24,670
Liver...............................	2,690	3,934	5,001	6,444	6,291	7,127	8,250	8,896	8,906	9,236
Pancreas...........................	69	109	439	542	349	228	192	143	135	143
Kidney-pancreas....................	459	919	915	903	828	719	835	872	827	820
Heart..............................	2,107	2,363	2,199	2,125	2,332	2,804	3,408	3,552	3,658	3,817
Lung...............................	203	872	959	1,406	1,769	2,057	2,530	2,714	2,539	2,524
Heart-lung.........................	52	69	48	35	42	15	32	45	58	45
Intestine...........................	5	46	82	178	151	141	104	81	91	96
Multiple organ [3]..................	71	127	222	522	559	891	1,017	1,073	1,200	1,258
PATIENTS ON WAITLIST [4]										
Total...............................	**20,481**	**41,203**	**74,078**	**90,526**	**110,375**	**122,071**	**114,155**	**113,226**	**108,605**	**106,937**
Kidney..............................	16,833	29,603	47,758	64,833	87,757	100,916	95,119	94,971	91,760	90,483
Liver...............................	1,232	5,649	16,832	17,356	16,146	14,832	13,511	12,902	12,049	11,611
Pancreas...........................	464	283	1,025	1,686	1,418	1,033	871	849	883	848
Kidney-pancreas....................	(NA)	1,210	2,466	2,502	2,224	1,956	1,628	1,698	1,689	1,806
Heart..............................	1,780	3,460	4,148	2,994	3,189	4,170	3,806	3,747	3,526	3,502
Lung...............................	302	1,887	3,636	3,162	1,805	1,529	1,432	1,396	983	1,051
Heart-lung.........................	217	205	207	141	70	49	48	48	42	41
Intestine...........................	(NA)	83	150	205	265	262	245	226	219	200
Pancreas-Islet......................	(NA)	35	172	317	200	188	75	77	77	82
Vascular Composite Allograft (VCA)..	(NA)	(NA)	(NA)	(NA)	(NA)	10	24	22	20	19

NA Not available. [1] Kidney-pancreas and heart-lung transplants are each counted as one procedure. All other multi-organ transplants are included in the multi-organ row. [2] Total may include other types of organ transplants not shown separately. [3] Excludes kidney-pancreas and heart-lung transplants. [4] Number of patients on the National Transplant Waiting List, at year end, December 31; data as of January 1, 2022. Some patients are listed for more than one organ.

Source: U.S. Department of Health and Human Services, Health Resources and Services Administration, Organ Procurement and Transplantation Network (OPTN), <optn.transplant.hrsa.gov/data/>, accessed June 2022; and unpublished data, based on OPTN data as of January 2022.

Table 208. Disability Rates by Type of Disability and Selected Characteristics: 2020

[As percent of total population. Data are from the Behavioral Risk Factor Surveillance System, a state-based telephone survey of noninstitutionalized adults age 18 and over in the 50 states, DC, Puerto, Guam, and the U.S. Virgin Islands. Disability is defined as having serious difficulty with cognition (concentration, memory, making decisions), hearing, mobility, vision, self-care activities (such as dressing or bathing), and independent living activities (such as doing errands alone). Estimates are age-adjusted to the 2000 U.S. standard population, except for estimates stratified by age. Survey respondents could report more than one type of disability]

Characteristic	No disability	Any disability	Cognitive disability	Hearing disability	Mobility disability	Vision disability	Self-care disability	Indepen- dent living disability
Total...........................	**75.2**	**24.8**	**10.9**	**5.7**	**11.1**	**4.9**	**3.0**	**6.4**
Male...............................	76.5	23.5	9.5	7.2	9.6	4.4	3.0	4.8
Female.............................	73.8	26.2	12.3	4.4	12.5	5.3	3.1	7.9
Age 18 to 44.......................	81.6	18.4	11.8	2.3	4.1	3.4	1.5	4.8
Age 45 to 64.......................	73.3	26.7	10.2	6.1	15.3	6.1	4.6	7.2
Age 65 and over....................	58.4	41.6	9.3	15.9	25.5	7.3	5.2	9.6
Non-Hispanic:								
White..............................	76.5	23.5	10.6	5.9	10.1	3.6	2.5	6.1
Black..............................	72.9	27.1	11.8	4.3	14.4	6.8	4.3	7.5
Asian..............................	85.5	14.5	5.1	2.7	6.0	3.1	1.1	2.5
Native Hawaiian or Other Pacific Islander....................	70.6	29.4	12.6	6.9	15.3	7.6	3.4	6.4
American Indian or Alaska Native.............................	60.9	39.1	18.3	9.9	17.8	9.7	6.1	13.3
Other/multiracial.................	67.2	32.8	15.7	7.6	15.1	5.9	5.4	10.7
Hispanic...........................	69.6	30.4	13.4	5.8	14.2	8.8	4.5	7.6
Veteran............................	70.2	29.8	12.4	11.2	12.9	4.1	4.3	7.2
Non-veteran.......................	75.7	24.3	10.8	5.0	11.0	5.0	2.9	6.4
Have health care coverage.....	87.8	83.6	83.4	83.4	85.5	77.4	(NA)	(NA)
No health care coverage........	12.2	16.4	16.6	16.6	14.5	22.6	(NA)	(NA)

NA Not available.

Source: U.S. Centers for Disease Control and Prevention, Disability and Health Data System, "Comparison Report," <www.cdc.gov/ncbddd/disabilityandhealth/dhds/index.html>, accessed May 2022.

Table 209. Population With a Disability by Age Group and State: 2020

[In thousands (42,071 represents 42,071,000). Data are based on 2020 American Community Survey (ACS) 1-year experimental estimates. The coronavirus disease 2019 (COVID-19) pandemic impacted 2020 ACS data collection and quality, and standard estimates did not meet statistical quality standards. The Census Bureau does not recommend comparing experimental estimates to standard ACS estimates. For more information, see <www.census.gov/programs-surveys/acs/data/experimental-data.html>. Disability data limited to civilian noninstitutionalized population. Covers children under age 5 with a hearing or vision difficulty. Covers children age 5 to 14 with a hearing, vision, cognitive, ambulatory, or self-care difficulty. For people age 15 and older, also covers independent living difficulty. American Community Survey (ACS) disability data should not be compared with disability estimates from Census 2000, and more detailed measures of disability from sources such as the National Health Interview Survey and the Survey of Income and Program Participation. Based on a sample and subject to sampling variability; see Appendix III]

State	Total	Under age 18	18 to 64 years	65 years and over	State	Total	Under age 18	18 to 64 years	65 years and over
U.S.	42,071	3,412	20,787	17,873	Missouri	856	66	438	353
Alabama	802	53	421	328	Montana	153	9	74	71
Alaska	87	8	43	36	Nebraska	215	16	100	98
Arizona	1,007	83	480	444	Nevada	406	30	198	178
Arkansas	551	48	288	215	New Hampshire	172	13	87	73
California	4,261	335	1,996	1,929	New Jersey	940	65	441	434
Colorado	632	46	335	251	New Mexico	343	24	170	148
Connecticut	408	35	194	179	New York	2,237	167	1,058	1,012
Delaware	140	15	67	59	North Carolina	1,419	110	725	584
District of Columbia	69	5	43	21	North Dakota	81	8	40	34
Florida	2,961	229	1,293	1,438	Ohio	1,644	137	833	674
Georgia	1,373	121	726	525	Oklahoma	677	52	353	273
Hawaii	158	9	65	84	Oregon	631	47	317	268
Idaho	255	21	126	108	Pennsylvania	1,746	146	849	751
Illinois	1,452	114	698	639	Rhode Island	144	12	72	60
Indiana	928	84	495	349	South Carolina	758	59	365	334
Iowa	380	27	190	163	South Dakota	100	6	47	46
Kansas	379	34	194	151	Tennessee	1,063	82	536	445
Kentucky	780	61	429	289	Texas	3,439	359	1,752	1,327
Louisiana	723	62	375	286	Utah	332	38	179	114
Maine	212	16	107	89	Vermont	81	4	43	34
Maryland	662	57	328	278	Virginia	1,004	85	483	436
Massachusetts	816	71	399	345	Washington	999	78	508	413
Michigan	1,408	99	736	573	West Virginia	333	20	170	143
Minnesota	620	51	309	261	Wisconsin	668	51	319	298
Mississippi	490	40	257	193	Wyoming	77	4	37	36

Source: U.S. Census Bureau, 2020 ACS 1-Year Experimental Data Tables, "Table XK201801. Disability Status by Age," <www.census.gov/programs-surveys/acs/data/experimental-data.html>, accessed February 2022.

Table 210. Yoga, Meditation, and Chiropractor Use Among Children and Adults: 2017

[In percent. Covers use within the past 12 months. Data are from the National Health Interview Survey of the civilian noninstitutional population. Data are age-adjusted using the projected 2000 U.S. population as the standard population and age groups 4-11 and 12-17 for children, and age groups 18-44, 45-64, and 65 and over for adults. Data shown by age are not age-adjusted]

Characteristic	Children			Characteristic	Adults		
	Yoga	Medi-tation	Chiro-practor		Yoga	Medi-tation	Chiro-practor
Total	8.4	5.4	3.4	Total	14.3	14.2	10.3
				Men	8.6	11.8	9.4
Boys	5.6	4.9	3.0	Women	19.8	16.3	11.1
Girls	11.3	6.0	3.7	Age 18 to 44	17.9	13.4	9.9
Age 4 to 11	8.7	4.7	2.1	Age 45 to 64	12.2	15.9	11.4
Age 12 to 17	8.0	6.5	5.1	Age 65 and over	6.7	13.4	9.5
White, non-Hispanic	10.5	5.9	5.1	White, non-Hispanic	17.1	15.2	12.7
Black, non-Hispanic	4.6	4.7	1.0	Black, non-Hispanic	9.3	13.5	5.5
Hispanic	5.9	4.7	1.4	Hispanic	8.0	10.9	6.6

Source: U.S. National Center for Health Statistics, *Use of Yoga, Meditation, and Chiropractors Among U.S. Children Aged 4–17 Years*, NCHS Data Brief No. 324, November 2018; and *Use of Yoga, Meditation, and Chiropractors Among U.S. Adults Aged 18 and Over*, NCHS Data Brief No. 325, November 2018. See also <www.cdc.gov/nchs/nhis/nhis_db.htm>.

Table 211. Diabetes, Chronic Kidney Disease, and End-Stage Renal Disease by Selected Characteristics: 2015 to 2020

[37.1 represents 37,100,000. Data on diabetes and chronic kidney disease are for adults age 18 and over and are based on the National Health and Nutrition Examination Survey (NHNES), which involves interviews, physical examinations, and laboratory testing. Data on end-stage renal disease (ESRD) cover all persons with ESRD in treatment; a person is identified as having ESRD when a physician certifies the disease on the Medical Evidence form, when there is other evidence of chronic dialysis that meets the criteria of ESRD, or upon registering as a candidate for kidney transplant through the Organ Procurement and Transplantation Network (OPTN)]

Characteristic	Diabetes, 2017-2020 [1]						Percent with chronic kidney disease, 2015-2018 [3]	Rate of persons with end-stage renal disease, 2019 [5, 6]
	Number (millions) [2]			Percent				
	Total	Diag-nosed	Undiag-nosed	Total	Diag-nosed	Undiag-nosed		
Total..................	37.1	28.5	8.5	14.7	11.3	3.4	[4] 15.0	2,302.4
By age:								
18 to 44 years.........	5.6	3.5	2.1	4.8	3.0	1.9	6.0	930.5
45 to 64 years.........	15.5	11.8	3.8	18.9	14.5	4.5	12.4	4,169.0
65 years and over.....	15.9	13.3	2.6	29.2	24.4	4.7	38.1	([7])
By sex:								
Men.....................	19.1	15.4	3.6	15.4	12.6	2.8	12.4	(NA)
Women..................	18.0	13.1	4.9	14.1	10.2	3.9	14.3	(NA)
By race/ethnicity:								
White, non-Hispanic...	22.2	17.8	4.3	13.6	11.0	2.7	12.7	1,500.2
Black, non-Hispanic...	5.4	3.9	1.5	17.4	12.7	4.7	16.3	6,423.3
Asian, non-Hispanic...	2.7	1.8	0.9	16.7	11.3	5.4	12.9	2,354.1
Hispanic................	6.5	4.7	1.8	15.5	11.1	4.4	13.6	3,394.7

NA Not available. [1] Covers January 2017 through March 2020. Diagnosed diabetes is based on self-report. Undiagnosed diabetes is based on fasting plasma glucose and A1C levels among people self-reporting no diabetes. [2] Estimated numbers were derived from percentages for January 2017–March 2020 applied to July 1, 2019 U.S. resident population estimates from the Census Bureau. [3] Percent of adults with chronic kidney disease (CKD) stages 1 to 4 using data from the 2015-2018 NHNES and the CKD Epidemiology Collaboration (CKD-EPI) equation. Excludes CKD stage 5 (kidney failure). Estimates are based on a single measure of albuminuria or serum creatinine, and do not account for persistence of albuminuria or levels of creatinine that are higher than normal as indicated by the Kidney Disease Improving Global Outcomes recommendations. Estimates might be overestimated. [4] Data are rounded. [5] Prevalence of end-stage renal disease per one million population. Data are adjusted to the age, sex, race, and Hispanic ethnicity distribution of the 2015 U.S. population; rates omit patients with unknown sex and other/unknown race/ethnicity. [6] Total persons with end-stage renal disease is 809,103. [7] Prevalence for population age 65-74 is 7,419.25 per million; prevalence for persons age 75 and over is 7,472.85 per million.

Source: U.S. Centers for Disease Control and Prevention, "National Diabetes Statistics Report," <www.cdc.gov/diabetes/data/statistics-report/index.html>; "Chronic Kidney Disease in the United States, 2021," <www.cdc.gov/kidneydisease/publications-resources/ckd-national-facts.html>; and U.S. Renal Data System, "2021 USRDS Annual Data Report," <adr.usrds.org/2021>; accessed June 2022.

Table 212. Circulatory Diseases Among Persons Age 18 and Over by Selected Characteristics: 2019 and 2020

[In percent. Based on the National Health Interview Survey (NHIS), a household survey of a sample of the civilian noninstitutionalized population. In separate questions, respondents were asked if they had ever been told by a doctor or other health professional that they had: hypertension (or high blood pressure), coronary heart disease, angina (or angina pectoris), or heart attack (or myocardial infarction). A person may be represented in more than one column. Unknowns were not included in the denominators when calculating percentages. The NHIS questionnaire was redesigned in 2019. Due to changes in weighting and design methodology, direct comparisons between estimates for 2019 and beyond to earlier years should be made with caution, as the impact of these changes has not been fully evaluated at this time]

Characteristic	2019				2020 [5]			
	Hyper-tension [1]	Coronary heart disease	Angina	Heart attack	Hyper-tension [1]	Coronary heart disease	Angina	Heart attack
Total..........................	27.0	4.6	1.7	3.1	26.6	4.6	1.5	3.0
SEX								
Male................................	27.2	5.9	1.7	4.1	27.0	5.9	1.6	4.0
Female..............................	26.9	3.4	1.6	2.2	26.2	3.5	1.3	2.1
AGE								
18 to 44 years....................	7.4	0.5	0.5	0.3	6.9	0.4	0.3	0.3
45 to 64 years....................	34.3	4.4	1.7	3.3	33.7	4.1	1.5	3.1
65 to 74 years....................	54.9	10.5	3.4	7.4	54.0	10.7	3.1	7.3
75 years and over................	64.5	19.2	5.7	11.6	63.0	20.0	5.1	10.8
RACE/ETHNICITY								
Single race: [2]								
White..............................	27.1	5.0	1.8	3.6	26.7	5.2	1.6	3.5
Black or African American..........	34.6	4.4	1.4	2.7	34.6	4.0	1.4	2.6
American Indian or Alaska Native..........	31.3	5.4	1.7	3.9	27.7	(B)	(B)	3.0
Asian..............................	19.7	2.8	1.1	0.9	20.6	2.9	0.9	0.9
Native Hawaiian or Other Pacific Islander......................	28.0	(B)	(B)	(B)	22.6	(B)	(B)	(B)
Hispanic or Latino [3].............	20.2	2.8	1.5	1.4	18.3	2.2	0.7	1.1
Not Hispanic or Latino.............	28.4	5.0	1.7	3.5	28.3	5.1	1.6	3.4
DISABILITY								
With disability [4]................	56.1	17.0	6.4	11.2	54.2	16.6	5.7	11.8
Without disability................	24.2	3.4	1.2	2.3	23.9	3.5	1.0	2.2

B Estimate does not meet NCHS standards of reliability. [1] Among respondents who had ever been told on two or more different physician visits that they had high blood pressure, respondents classified as having diagnosed hypertension were told they had hypertension or were taking prescription medication for high blood pressure, within the past 12 months. [2] Persons who indicated only a single race group, regardless of Hispanic or Latino origin. [3] Persons of Hispanic or Latino origin may be of any race or combination of races. [4] Represents adults who responded "a lot of difficulty" or "cannot do at all" to questions regarding at least one of six functional areas: seeing (even if wearing glasses), hearing (even if wearing hearing aids), mobility (walking or climbing stairs), communication (understanding or being understood by others), cognition (remembering or concentrating), and self-care (such as washing all over or dressing). [5] The NHIS switched data collection from personal visits to telephone mode during the coronavirus disease 2019 (COVID-19) pandemic. For more information, see *Technical Notes for Interactive Summary Health Statistics— 2019-2020: National Health Interview Survey.*

Source: U.S. National Center for Health Statistics, National Health Interview Survey, "Interactive Summary Health Statistics for Adults," <www.cdc.gov/nchs/nhis/SHS.htm>, accessed May 2022.

Table 213. Selected Indicators of Health Status and Access to Health Care Among Adults: 2019 to 2021

[In percent. Covers experiences in the past 12 months, for adults age 18 and over. The National Health Interview Survey (NHIS) surveys a sample of the civilian noninstitutionalized population living in households and group quarters (e.g. homeless shelters, group homes), in the 50 states and DC. Unknowns were not included in the denominators when calculating percentages. The NHIS questionnaire was redesigned in 2019. Due to changes in weighting and design methodology, direct comparisons between estimates for 2019 and beyond to earlier years should be made with caution. For more information, see <www.cdc.gov/nchs/nhis/2019_quest_redesign.htm>. See also Appendix III]

Indicator	2019	2020 [8]	2021 (P)
HEALTH STATUS			
Having a disability [1]	9.0	8.8	9.3
Missing 6 or more workdays due to illness, injury, or disability	11.2	11.9	15.8
Asthma episode	3.4	3.5	3.3
Hypertension (high blood pressure) diagnosis	27.0	26.6	27.4
Chronic pain, regularly	20.5	21.8	21.7
Feelings of worry, nervousness, or anxiety, regularly [2]	11.1	11.2	11.7
Feelings of depression, regularly [2]	4.7	4.4	4.8
HEALTH CARE SERVICES USED			
Doctor visit	84.9	83.4	82.1
Hospital emergency department visit	21.8	19.0	18.5
Counseling with a mental health professional	9.5	10.1	10.9
Dental exam or cleaning	65.3	63.0	(NA)
Blood pressure check	88.1	(NA)	83.8
Receipt of influenza vaccination	46.8	47.9	47.8
HEALTH CARE ACCESS			
Did not get needed medical care due to cost	8.3	6.6	6.3
Did not get needed mental health care due to cost	4.4	4.3	4.2
Did not take medication as prescribed to save money [3]	9.6	8.3	7.1
HEALTH INSURANCE [4]			
No health insurance at time of interview [5]	14.5	13.9	13.5
Covered by private health insurance at time of interview [6]	67.5	67.7	66.6
Covered by public health insurance at time of interview [7]	20.4	20.7	21.7
HEALTH BEHAVIORS			
Current cigarette smoking	14.0	12.5	12.6
Current electronic cigarette (e-cigarette) use	4.5	3.7	4.7

NA Not available. P Preliminary. [1] Represents adults who responded "a lot of difficulty" or "cannot do at all" to questions regarding at least one of six functional areas: seeing (even if wearing glasses), hearing (even if wearing hearing aids), mobility (walking or climbing stairs), communication (understanding or being understood by others), cognition (remembering or concentrating), and self-care (such as bathing or dressing). [2] Adults responded having these feelings a) daily and describing the level of these feelings as "somewhere in between a little and a lot" or "a lot," or b) weekly and describing the level of these feelings as "a lot." [3] Skipping doses of medication, taking less medicine, or delaying filling a prescription, to save money. [4] For persons age 18-64 only. A small number of people covered by both public and private plans are included in both categories. [5] No health insurance includes persons covered by only Indian Health Service or only a private plan that paid for one type of service, such as dental or vision care. [6] Includes any comprehensive private insurance plan obtained through an employer, or purchased directly, through local or community programs, or through the Health Insurance Marketplace or a state-based exchange. Excludes plans that pay for only one type of service, such as dental or vision care. [7] Includes Medicaid, Children's Health Insurance Program (CHIP), state-sponsored or other government-sponsored health plan, Medicare, and military plans. [8] Due to the coronavirus disease (COVID-19) pandemic, NHIS data collection switched from in-person interviews to a telephone-only mode beginning March 19, 2020. Personal visits resumed in all areas in September 2020. See "Technical Notes" in source for more information.

Source: U.S. National Center for Health Statistics, National Health Interview Survey, "Interactive Summary Health Statistics for Adults," <www.cdc.gov/nchs/nhis/SHS.htm>, accessed May 2022; and "National Health Interview Early Release Program," *Early Release of Selected Estimates Based on Data From the 2021 National Health Interview Survey*, April 2022, <www.cdc.gov/nchs/nhis/erkeyindicators.htm>.

Table 214. Nonfatal Injury and Poisoning Episodes by Cause, Sex, and Age: 2020

[Data are from the National Electronic Injury Surveillance System–All Injury Program, which collects data on nonfatal injuries and poisonings treated in participating hospital emergency departments]

Cause of injury	Total Number [1]	Total Percent	Male	Female	Under age 1	Age 1 to 14	Age 15 to 24	Age 25 to 64	Age 65 and over
Total [2]	22,887,137	100.0	12,758,195	10,127,702	157,372	2,897,235	3,275,553	12,215,192	4,334,126
UNINTENTIONAL									
Fall	6,841,044	29.9	3,133,657	3,707,336	83,049	1,038,270	459,348	2,396,983	2,862,925
Struck by or against [3]	2,252,101	9.8	1,356,978	895,123	17,162	515,498	414,720	1,070,222	234,265
Poisoning	1,796,671	7.9	1,206,159	590,027	3,827	50,317	218,200	1,387,931	135,250
Motor vehicle occupant	1,696,165	7.4	825,266	870,785	2,041	80,995	416,916	1,045,733	149,811
Cut/pierce/stab	1,542,027	6.7	992,329	549,673	4,605	193,096	283,908	919,340	141,077
Overexertion	1,512,124	6.6	766,401	745,723	4,158	159,205	260,798	910,330	177,633
Bite or sting excl. dog bites [4]	552,495	2.4	269,903	282,592	4,143	108,749	64,636	296,750	78,194
Foreign object [5]	447,969	2.0	264,919	183,050	8,326	152,661	46,475	186,976	53,532
Dog bite	316,421	1.4	159,207	157,214	1,587	84,910	46,495	155,941	27,488
Fire/burn/smoke inhalation	276,092	1.2	147,775	128,316	5,116	49,802	42,054	153,626	25,488
VIOLENCE RELATED									
Assault (all)	1,419,151	6.2	874,141	544,959	4,201	70,199	322,490	976,702	42,761
Self-harm	483,084	2.1	196,012	286,954	(X)	53,746	171,280	242,686	15,326
Legal intervention	82,769	0.4	69,346	13,423	(S)	(S)	15,403	65,468	(S)

S Estimate is unstable due to small sample size or coefficient of variation is greater than 30 percent. X Not applicable. [1] Total number may include injuries with unknown age of victim. [2] Total includes injuries from various other causes not shown separately and for injuries with unknown age of victim. [3] Injury from being struck, hit, or crushed by, or hitting against, another person, animal, object or force; excludes vehicles and machinery. [4] Include bites and stings from another person or any insect, animal, or plant; excludes dogs. [5] Injury resulting from the entrance of a foreign object into or through the eye or other natural body opening; excludes objects blocking an airway or causing suffocation.

Source: U.S. Centers for Disease Control and Prevention, National Center for Injury Prevention and Control, "WISQARS (Web-based Injury Statistics Query and Reporting System)," <www.cdc.gov/injury/wisqars/index.html>, accessed February 2022.

Table 215. Injuries Associated With Selected Consumer Products: 2020

[Estimates are based on a national probability sample of hospitals in the U.S. and its territories. Patient information is collected from each participating hospital for every emergency visit involving an injury associated with consumer products. From this sample, the total number of product-related injuries treated in hospital emergency rooms nationwide is estimated. A person's injury may be represented in up to three product groups. Products are associated with injuries, not necessarily the cause of injuries]

Product type	Number	Rate [1]	Product type	Number	Rate [1]
Items for infants/children:			**Housewares:**		
All nursery equipment	73,783	22.4	Cans, other containers	244,646	74.2
Baby strollers	8,021	(NA)	Cleaning equipment,		
High chairs	9,848	(NA)	noncaustic detergents	43,556	13.2
Toys	164,715	49.9	Drinking glasses, cups, mugs	68,056	(NA)
Sports & recreational equipment:			Knives (not elsewhere classified)	303,694	(NA)
All terrain vehicles, mopeds,			Soaps, detergents	41,353	12.5
minibikes, etc	229,974	69.7	**Tools & garden equipment:**		
Baseball, softball	70,209	21.3	Chain saws	29,416	8.9
Basketball	214,847	65.1	Hand garden tools	40,128	12.2
Bicycles & accessories	425,910	129.1	Lawn and garden equipment	78,886	23.9
Exercise, exercise equipment	377,939	114.6	Lawn mowers	67,215	20.4
Football	122,181	37.0	Power home workshop saws	83,141	25.2
Lacrosse, rugby, misc. ball games	29,134	8.8	Workshop manual tools	107,285	32.5
Playground equipment	120,829	36.6	**Household appliances:**		
Skateboards, scooters, hoverboards	217,646	66.0	Cooking ranges, ovens, etc	44,509	13.5
Skating (excluding in-line)	51,331	15.6	Heating stoves, space heaters	22,899	6.9
Snowskiing, snowboarding	42,137	12.8	Refrigerators, freezers	47,814	14.5
Soccer	81,452	24.7	Small kitchen appliances	53,050	16.1
Swimming, pools, equipment	129,708	39.3	**Home furnishings & fixtures:**		
Trampolines	106,358	32.2	Bathroom structures & fixtures	478,017	144.9
Home entertainment equipment:			Beds, mattresses, pillows	815,908	247.3
Sound recording equipment	53,065	16.1	Carpets, rugs	194,455	58.9
Television sets & stands	34,168	10.4	Chairs, sofas, sofa beds	545,070	165.2
Personal use items:			Desks, cabinets, shelves, racks	230,520	69.9
Clothing	340,521	103.2	Glass doors, windows, panels	109,309	33.1
Grooming devices	40,340	12.2	Ladders, stools	228,840	69.4
Razors, shavers, razor blades	37,014	11.2	Tables [2]	284,327	86.2

NA Not available. [1] Estimated rates are calculated using the Census Bureau's July 1, 2020 U.S. resident population estimates. [2] Excludes baby-changing tables, billiard or pool tables, and television tables or stands.

Source: Consumer Product Safety Commission, National Electronic Injury Surveillance System (NEISS), *2020 NEISS Data Highlights: Overview—All Products;* and "NEISS Estimates Query Builder," <www.cpsc.gov/cgibin/NEISSQuery/home.aspx>, accessed February 2022. See also <www.cpsc.gov/Research--Statistics/NEISS-Injury-Data/>.

Table 216. Food Security Status of Households and Households with Children: 2000 to 2020

[106,043 represents 106,043,000. Food security status of households is measured through a series of questions about experiences and behaviors that characterize households having difficulty meeting basic food needs. All questions refer to the previous 12 months and remind respondents to report only conditions resulting from inadequate financial resources; survey excludes voluntary fasting and dieting to lose weight. *Food-secure* households report 0-2 food-insecure conditions. *Food-insecure* households report 3 or more conditions. Low and very low food security differ in the extent and character of the adjustments the household makes to its eating patterns and food intake. Households classified as having *low food security* report multiple indications of food access problems, but typically report few, if any, indications of reduced food intake. Households classified as having *very low food security* report multiple indications of reduced food intake and disrupted eating patterns due to inadequate resources for food. Prior to 2006, households with very low food security were described as "food insecure with hunger." The omission of homeless persons biases the statistics downward. Data are from the Food Security Supplement to the Current Population Survey (CPS); for details about the CPS, see text, Section 1 and Appendix III]

Household status	Number (1,000)					Percent distribution				
	2000	2010	2018	2019	2020	2000	2010	2018	2019	2020
Households, total [1]	**106,043**	**118,756**	**129,245**	**129,621**	**130,459**	**100.0**	**100.0**	**100.0**	**100.0**	**100.0**
Food-secure	94,942	101,527	114,934	115,959	116,705	89.5	85.5	88.9	89.5	89.5
Food-insecure	11,101	17,229	14,311	13,662	13,754	10.5	14.5	11.1	10.5	10.5
With low food security	7,786	10,872	8,730	8,340	3,613	7.3	9.1	6.8	6.4	6.6
With very low food security	3,315	6,357	5,581	5,322	5,141	3.1	5.4	4.3	4.1	3.9
Adult members [2]	**201,922**	**229,129**	**249,443**	**250,956**	**251,953**	**100.0**	**100.0**	**100.0**	**100.0**	**100.0**
In food-secure households	181,586	196,505	223,390	226,481	225,388	89.9	85.8	89.6	90.2	89.5
In food-insecure households	20,336	32,624	26,053	24,475	26,565	10.1	14.2	10.4	9.8	10.5
With low food security	14,763	21,357	16,576	15,495	17,174	7.3	9.3	6.6	6.2	6.8
With very low food security	5,573	11,267	9,477	8,980	9,391	2.8	4.9	3.8	3.6	3.7
Child members [2,3]	**71,763**	**74,905**	**73,562**	**73,279**	**72,837**	**100.0**	**100.0**	**100.0**	**100.0**	**100.0**
In food-secure households	58,867	58,697	62,388	62,547	61,115	82.0	78.4	84.8	85.4	83.9
In food-insecure households	12,896	16,208	11,174	10,732	11,722	18.0	21.6	15.2	14.6	16.1
With very low food security among children	562	976	540	361	584	0.8	1.3	0.7	0.5	0.8

[1] Total excludes households for which food security status is unknown. [2] The food security survey measures food security status at the household level. Not all individuals and children residing in food-insecure households were directly affected by the households' food insecurity. Similarly, not all individuals and children in households classified as having very low food security were subject to the reductions in food intake and disruptions in eating patterns that characterize this condition. Young children, in particular, are often protected from effects of the households' food insecurity. [3] Percents among only households with children.

Source: U.S. Department of Agriculture, Economic Research Service, *Household Food Security in the United States in 2020*, Economic Research Report Number 298, September 2021. See also <www.ers.usda.gov/topics/food-nutrition-assistance/food-security-in-the-us.aspx>.

Table 217. Mammography Use Among Women Age 40 and Over by Patient Characteristics: 2000 to 2019

[Percent of women having a mammogram within the past 2 years. Covers civilian noninstitutional population. Based on National Health Interview Survey; see Appendix III]

Characteristic	2000	2003	2005	2008	2010	2013	2015	2018	2019[7]
Women age 40 and over, total [1]	**70.4**	**69.7**	**66.8**	**67.6**	**67.1**	**66.8**	**65.3**	**66.7**	**69.1**
AGE									
40 to 49 years	64.3	64.4	63.5	61.5	62.3	59.6	58.3	61.5	60.2
50 to 64 years	78.7	76.2	71.8	74.2	72.6	71.4	71.3	71.8	75.7
65 years and over	67.9	67.7	63.8	65.5	64.4	66.9	63.3	64.8	68.1
65 to 74 years	74.0	74.6	72.5	72.6	71.9	75.3	72.2	75.0	78.1
75 years and over	61.3	60.6	54.7	57.9	55.7	56.5	51.5	50.6	54.2
RACE AND ETHNICITY [2]									
White only	71.4	70.1	67.4	67.9	67.4	66.8	65.3	67.3	69.2
Black only	67.8	70.4	64.9	68.0	67.9	67.1	69.8	68.1	71.1
American Indian or Alaska Native only	47.4	63.1	72.8	62.7	71.2	62.6	51.5	65.3	61.3
Asian only	53.5	57.6	54.6	66.1	62.4	66.6	59.7	57.8	63.7
Two or more races	69.2	65.3	63.7	55.2	51.4	65.4	62.7	59.8	65.6
Hispanic or Latina [3]	61.2	65.0	58.8	61.2	64.2	61.4	60.9	62.7	69.4
Not Hispanic or Latina	71.1	70.1	67.5	68.3	67.4	67.5	65.9	67.3	69.1
EDUCATION									
No high school diploma nor GED [4]	57.7	58.1	52.8	53.8	53.0	53.6	51.7	54.0	59.8
High school diploma or GED	69.7	67.8	64.9	65.2	64.4	63.4	60.1	63.2	65.7
Some college or more	76.2	75.1	72.7	73.4	72.1	71.6	70.5	70.9	72.7
POVERTY STATUS [5]									
Below 100% poverty	54.8	55.4	48.5	51.4	51.4	49.9	52.2	51.7	59.0
100% to 199% poverty	58.1	60.8	55.3	55.8	53.8	56.7	54.9	56.8	61.3
200% to 399% poverty	68.8	69.9	67.2	64.4	66.2	66.0	63.4	65.3	66.7
400% and over poverty	81.5	77.7	76.6	79.0	78.1	77.2	74.7	75.4	77.3
HEALTH INSURANCE STATUS [6]									
Insured	76.0	75.1	72.5	73.4	74.1	72.1	69.7	71.1	73.3
Private insurance	77.1	76.3	74.5	74.2	75.6	73.4	72.2	73.2	74.4
Medicaid	61.7	63.5	55.6	64.2	64.4	63.5	57.7	58.0	66.6
Uninsured	40.7	41.5	38.1	39.7	36.0	37.3	30.0	37.5	40.6

[1] Includes other races not shown separately and unknown education, poverty, and health insurance status. [2] Race groups include persons of Hispanic and non-Hispanic origin. [3] Persons of Hispanic origin may be of any race. [4] GED is General Educational Development high school equivalency diploma. [5] Poverty as percent of Federal poverty level based on family income and family size and composition using U.S. Census Bureau poverty thresholds. [6] Health insurance status at time of interview, only for women age 40 to 64. Health insurance categories are mutually exclusive. Persons who reported both Medicaid and private coverage are classified as having private coverage. Persons with only Indian Health Service coverage are considered to have no health insurance coverage. [7] In 2019, the NHIS questionnaire was redesigned and other changes were made to weighting and design methodology. Data have not been fully evaluated for comparability with earlier years.

Source: U.S. National Center for Health Statistics, "Health, United States—Data Finder," <www.cdc.gov/nchs/hus/index.htm>, accessed August 2022.

Table 218. Current Cigarette Smoking Among Adults: 2000 to 2019

[In percent. A current smoker is a person who has smoked at least 100 cigarettes and who now smokes every day or some days. Excludes unknown smoking status. Race groups White and Black include persons of Hispanic and non-Hispanic origin. For definition of age adjustment, see text, Section 2. Based on National Health Interview Survey; for details, see Appendix III]

Sex, age, and race	2000	2010	2015	2019[4]	Sex, age, and race	2000	2010	2015	2019[4]
Total smokers, age-adjusted [1]	**23.1**	**19.3**	**15.3**	**14.2**	Black, total	26.2	24.3	20.6	17.2
Male	25.2	21.2	16.8	15.5	18 to 24 years	20.9	18.8	[3] 15.9	(B)
Female	21.1	17.5	13.8	13.0	25 to 34 years	23.2	25.7	26.0	21.5
					35 to 44 years	30.7	22.6	17.9	23.6
					45 to 64 years	32.2	31.8	22.8	21.0
White male	25.4	21.4	16.8	15.6	65 years and over	14.2	10.0	16.0	9.4
Black male	25.7	23.3	20.3	17.7	**Female, total**	**20.9**	**17.3**	**13.6**	**12.7**
					18 to 24 years	24.9	17.4	11.0	8.2
White female	22.0	18.3	14.8	14.5	25 to 34 years	22.3	20.6	15.0	14.4
Black female	20.7	16.6	13.2	12.8	35 to 44 years	26.2	19.0	16.5	14.7
					45 to 64 years	21.7	19.1	16.1	16.2
Total smokers [2]	**23.2**	**19.3**	**15.1**	**14.0**	65 years and over	9.3	9.3	7.3	7.3
Male, total	**25.6**	**21.5**	**16.7**	**15.3**	White, total	21.4	17.9	14.3	14.0
18 to 24 years	28.1	22.8	15.0	7.8	18 to 24 years	28.5	18.4	11.2	9.0
25 to 34 years	28.9	26.1	21.3	19.1	25 to 34 years	24.9	22.0	16.3	16.4
35 to 44 years	30.2	22.5	18.3	18.5	35 to 44 years	26.6	20.5	18.3	17.2
45 to 64 years	26.4	23.2	17.9	17.9	45 to 64 years	21.4	19.5	17.1	17.9
65 years and over	10.2	9.7	9.7	9.4	65 years and over	9.1	9.4	7.5	7.5
White, total	25.7	21.4	16.5	15.3	Black, total	20.8	17.0	13.1	12.9
18 to 24 years	30.4	23.8	15.6	9.0	18 to 24 years	14.2	14.2	[3] 8.6	(B)
25 to 34 years	29.7	26.6	20.9	19.6	25 to 34 years	15.5	19.3	14.9	14.0
35 to 44 years	30.6	23.1	19.1	17.9	35 to 44 years	30.2	17.2	15.4	15.5
45 to 64 years	25.8	22.5	17.3	17.9	45 to 64 years	25.6	19.8	14.5	14.5
65 years and over	9.8	9.6	9.3	9.4	65 years and over	10.2	9.4	9.7	9.6

B Estimates are considered unreliable. [1] Data are age-adjusted to the year 2000 standard population using five age groups: 18–24 years, 25–34 years, 35–44 years, 45–64 years, 65 years and over. Includes persons of unknown race and sex. [2] Crude, not age-adjusted. Includes persons of unknown race and sex. [3] Estimate has a relative standard error of 20%–30%. [4] In 2019, the NHIS questionnaire was redesigned and other changes were made to weighting and design methodology. Data for 2019 have not been fully evaluated for comparability with earlier years. For more information, see <www.cdc.gov/nchs/nhis/2019_quest_redesign.htm>.

Source: U.S. National Center for Health Statistics, "Health, United States—Data Finder," <www.cdc.gov/nchs/hus/index.htm>, accessed August 2022.

Table 219. Current Cigarette Smoking by Sex and State: 2020

[In percent. Current cigarette smoking is defined as persons age 18 and older who reported having smoked 100 or more cigarettes during their lifetime and who currently smoke every day or some days. Based on the Behavioral Risk Factor Surveillance System (BRFSS), a telephone survey of health behaviors of the civilian, noninstitutionalized U.S. population, age 18 and over]

State	Total	Male	Female	State	Total	Male	Female	State	Total	Male	Female
U.S. [1]...	**15.5**	**(NA)**	**(NA)**	KY.......	21.4	22.3	20.5	OH.......	19.3	19.8	18.8
AL........	18.5	20.5	16.6	LA........	18.3	20.5	16.3	OK.......	19.1	20.6	17.6
AK.......	18.0	17.9	18.1	ME.......	16.5	17.3	15.8	OR.......	13.4	14.6	12.1
AZ.......	13.1	15.9	10.4	MD.......	10.9	13.2	8.8	PA.......	15.8	16.7	14.8
AR.......	20.5	22.2	18.8	MA.......	11.1	12.8	9.5	RI........	13.5	14.1	12.9
CA.......	8.9	11.1	6.7	MI........	18.4	19.7	17.2	SC.......	18.1	20.2	16.2
CO......	12.4	13.4	11.4	MN.......	13.9	15.0	12.8	SD.......	17.8	17.6	17.9
CT.......	11.9	13.3	10.5	MS.......	20.1	23.4	17.1	TN.......	19.5	20.5	18.5
DE......	15.1	18.0	12.6	MO......	17.8	18.6	16.9	TX.......	13.2	17.2	9.3
DC......	11.3	11.6	11.2	MT.......	16.4	16.6	16.2	UT.......	8.2	9.4	7.0
FL........	14.7	17.6	12.0	NE.......	13.9	15.6	12.4	VT.......	13.3	14.8	11.8
GA.......	15.8	18.3	13.5	NV.......	14.2	16.6	11.9	VA.......	13.6	16.1	11.3
HI........	11.6	12.1	11.1	NH.......	13.9	15.1	12.7	WA.......	11.5	12.3	10.7
ID........	13.7	14.3	13.0	NJ........	10.8	13.2	8.7	WV.......	22.6	22.7	22.5
IL........	12.7	14.0	11.5	NM.......	16.1	18.9	13.4	WI........	15.5	17.2	13.8
IN........	19.4	20.8	18.1	NY.......	12.0	14.2	10.0	WY.......	18.5	19.4	17.5
IA........	15.8	17.1	14.5	NC.......	16.5	18.8	14.4	GU [2].....	20.0	24.7	15.2
KS.......	16.6	18.2	15.1	ND.......	17.4	18.9	15.8	PR [2].....	9.9	14.2	6.2

NA Not available. [1] Represents median value among the states and DC. For definition of median, see Guide to Tabular Presentation. [2] GU is Guam. PR is Puerto Rico.

Source: U.S. Centers for Disease Control and Prevention, Behavioral Risk Factors Data Portal, "Behavioral Risk Factor Surveillance System: Table of Tobacco Use (updated September 14, 2021)," <chronicdata.cdc.gov/browse?category=Behavioral+Risk+Factors>, accessed February 2022.

Table 220. Substance Abuse Treatment Facilities and Clients: 2010 to 2020

[As of the last weekday in March. Based on the National Survey of Substance Abuse Treatment Services, a census of all known public and private facilities that provide substance abuse treatment in the United States and associated jurisdictions. Selected missing data for responding facilities were imputed. Beginning 2013, the full survey on facilities and clients is administered in odd-numbered years. An alternate survey collecting facility data, and occasionally a limited amount of client data, is administered in even-numbered years; in 2020 an exception was made to field the full survey to measure the effect of the coronavirus disease 2019 (COVID-19) pandemic on services]

Facility characteristic	Number of facilities				Number of clients [1]			
	2010	2018	2019	2020	2010	2017	2019	2020
Total.............................	**13,339**	**14,809**	**15,961**	**16,066**	**1,175,462**	**1,356,015**	**1,460,706**	**1,090,357**
FACILITY OPERATIONAL STRUCTURE								
Private non-profit.............................	7,683	7,642	8,043	8,004	625,321	658,896	726,238	504,780
Private for-profit.............................	3,985	5,584	6,327	6,535	372,525	550,992	591,442	485,411
Local, county, or community government.......	751	690	694	670	70,963	66,577	59,708	39,571
State government............................	380	304	310	285	47,203	28,529	27,081	19,601
Federal government.........................	348	327	333	323	47,676	34,435	41,848	30,589
Dept. of Veterans Affairs......................	218	219	222	228	39,157	29,619	36,951	26,825
Dept. of Defense..........................	91	76	69	57	7,035	3,618	2,065	2,278
Indian Health Service.......................	36	23	31	29	1,431	1,103	842	502
Other...................................	3	9	11	9	53	95	1,990	984
Tribal government...........................	192	262	254	249	11,774	16,586	14,389	10,405
TYPE OF CARE OFFERED/RECEIVED [2]								
Outpatient..................................	10,753	12,243	13,044	13,161	1,056,532	1,238,654	1,355,024	1,021,185
Regular...................................	9,914	11,394	12,114	12,249	593,077	599,290	642,554	459,157
Intensive..................................	5,990	6,868	7,325	7,243	138,188	133,850	130,343	83,073
Detoxification..............................	1,227	1,505	1,752	1,869	13,216	11,839	21,460	13,445
Day treatment/partial hospitalization...........	1,678	2,051	2,255	2,277	22,458	23,310	19,973	14,112
Medication-assisted treatment [3]...............	1,137	4,087	5,256	5,829	289,593	470,365	540,694	451,398
Residential (non-hospital).......................	3,452	3,500	3,794	3,825	103,692	99,881	91,592	58,952
Detoxification..............................	893	1,140	1,410	1,412	7,549	10,938	8,629	5,377
Short-term treatment (30 days or fewer).......	1,691	2,039	2,386	2,427	26,014	32,156	33,698	20,440
Long-term treatment (more than 30 days).....	2,801	2,770	2,958	2,972	70,129	56,787	49,265	33,135
Hospital inpatient............................	748	785	898	861	15,238	17,480	14,090	10,220
Detoxification..............................	666	721	806	784	6,476	7,551	6,258	4,776
Treatment.................................	548	588	680	658	8,762	9,929	7,832	5,444
TREATMENT FOR SUBSTANCE ABUSE								
Both alcohol and drug............................	(NA)	(NA)	(NA)	(NA)	498,671	500,948	476,065	333,526
Drug abuse only...............................	(NA)	(NA)	(NA)	(NA)	459,069	642,713	743,828	569,522
Alcohol abuse only.............................	(NA)	(NA)	(NA)	(NA)	215,101	211,460	205,402	146,710
Both substance abuse and mental health disorders...	(NA)	(NA)	(NA)	(NA)	479,699	683,810	702,914	531,105

NA Not available. [1] Client data are for the last weekday in March of the year shown, and are not annual totals. Inpatient and residential clients received treatment services on the reference date in March. Outpatient clients received services at least once during the month of March and were still enrolled on the reference date in 2018. Client data were not collected in 2018. [2] Number of facilities can sum to more than the total because a facility could provide more than one type of care. [3] Methadone/buprenorphine maintenance or injectable naltrexone treatment. Methadone is available only at facilities that have opioid treatment programs certified by the Substance Abuse and Mental Health Services Administration.

Source: U.S. Substance Abuse and Mental Health Services Administration, *National Survey of Substance Abuse Treatment Services (N-SSATS): 2020, Data on Substance Abuse Treatment Facilities,* June 2021, and earlier reports. See also <www.samhsa.gov/data/data-we-collect/n-ssats-national-survey-substance-abuse-treatment-services>.

Table 221. Drug Use by Type of Drug and Age Group: 2015 to 2020

[In percent. Data comes from the National Survey on Drug Use and Health (NSDUH). Based on a representative sample of the U.S. population age 12 and older, including persons living in households, in noninstitutional group quarters such as dormitories and homeless shelters, and civilians on military bases. Estimates are based on computer-assisted self-interviewing and personal interviewing of a target sample of approximately 67,500 respondents. The NSDUH was redesigned in 2015, and therefore data from previous surveys for several survey items are not comparable to data from the 2015 NSDUH and subsequent surveys; see source for more information. Subject to sampling variability]

Age and type of drug	Lifetime (ever) use			Past year use			Past month use		
	2015	2019	2020 [5]	2015	2019	2020 [5]	2015	2019	2020 [5]
AGE 12 YEARS AND OLDER									
Any illicit drug [1]	48.8	50.2	50.0	17.8	20.8	21.4	10.1	13.0	13.5
Marijuana	44.0	46.2	45.7	13.5	17.5	17.9	8.3	11.5	11.8
Cocaine	14.5	15.1	14.2	1.8	2.0	1.9	0.7	0.7	0.7
Heroin	1.9	2.1	2.3	0.3	0.3	0.3	0.1	0.2	0.2
Hallucinogens	15.3	16.0	15.9	1.8	2.2	2.6	0.5	0.7	0.6
Inhalants	9.6	9.1	9.7	0.7	0.8	0.9	0.2	0.3	0.3
Methamphetamine	5.4	5.8	5.6	0.6	0.7	0.9	0.3	0.4	0.6
Opioids [2]	(NA)	(NA)	(NA)	4.7	3.7	3.4	1.5	1.1	1.0
Illicit drugs other than marijuana	(NA)	(NA)	(NA)	9.2	8.6	8.7	3.5	3.4	3.4
Tobacco products [3]	63.9	61.0	57.8	29.2	26.2	23.3	23.9	21.1	18.7
Cigarettes	58.5	55.0	52.5	23.1	20.2	18.4	19.4	16.7	15.0
Smokeless tobacco	16.3	15.5	13.5	4.7	4.2	3.3	3.4	3.1	2.5
Cigars	32.8	31.2	29.5	9.1	8.1	7.1	4.7	4.3	3.8
Pipe tobacco	12.5	11.4	9.8	(NA)	(NA)	(NA)	0.8	0.7	0.7
Nicotine vaping	(NA)	(NA)	12.5	(NA)	(NA)	6.5	(NA)	(NA)	3.8
Alcohol	81.0	80.3	79.5	65.7	65.1	64.2	51.7	50.8	50.0
"Binge" alcohol use [4]	(NA)	(NA)	(NA)	(NA)	(NA)	(NA)	24.9	23.9	22.2
AGE 12 TO 17 YEARS									
Any illicit drug [1]	25.3	24.5	20.9	17.5	17.2	13.8	8.8	8.7	6.7
Marijuana	15.7	15.8	12.4	12.6	13.2	10.1	7.0	7.4	5.9
Cocaine	0.8	0.6	0.4	0.6	0.4	0.3	0.2	0.1	–
Hallucinogens	3.1	2.5	2.3	2.1	1.8	1.5	0.5	0.6	0.3
Inhalants	9.1	8.8	9.3	2.7	3.0	2.7	0.7	0.9	0.4
Methamphetamine	0.3	0.3	0.2	0.2	0.2	0.1	0.1	–	–
Opioids [2]	(NA)	(NA)	(NA)	3.9	2.3	1.6	1.1	0.7	0.4
Tobacco products [3]	17.3	12.8	9.3	11.6	8.3	5.6	6.0	3.8	2.4
Cigarettes	13.2	9.0	7.2	8.1	5.4	3.9	4.2	2.3	1.4
Smokeless tobacco	5.5	4.0	2.4	3.5	2.5	1.4	1.5	1.0	0.6
Cigars	7.2	5.1	3.8	5.1	3.6	2.4	2.1	1.4	0.8
Nicotine vaping	(NA)	(NA)	12.6	(NA)	(NA)	9.5	(NA)	(NA)	5.1
Alcohol	28.4	26.7	22.8	22.7	21.2	18.5	9.6	9.4	8.2
"Binge" alcohol use [4]	(NA)	(NA)	(NA)	(NA)	(NA)	(NA)	5.8	4.9	4.1
AGE 18 TO 25 YEARS									
Any illicit drug [1]	57.5	55.8	53.4	37.5	39.1	37.0	22.3	24.9	23.9
Marijuana	52.7	51.7	49.6	32.2	35.4	34.5	19.8	23.0	23.1
Cocaine	11.7	11.3	9.1	5.4	5.3	4.3	1.7	1.6	1.3
Heroin	1.8	1.2	0.7	0.6	0.3	0.2	0.3	0.1	0.1
Hallucinogens	18.6	16.6	15.7	7.0	7.2	7.3	1.8	1.9	1.9
Inhalants	9.9	9.2	8.7	1.4	1.7	1.5	0.4	0.5	0.5
Methamphetamine	3.3	2.7	1.6	0.9	0.8	0.5	0.4	0.3	0.2
Opioids [2]	(NA)	(NA)	(NA)	8.7	5.3	4.1	2.5	1.3	0.9
Tobacco products [3]	61.7	52.7	46.0	43.8	35.2	28.8	33.0	24.3	19.2
Cigarettes	53.3	43.5	38.4	35.0	25.8	21.6	26.7	17.5	13.9
Smokeless tobacco	19.6	16.7	13.4	9.0	7.7	6.0	5.4	4.9	3.9
Cigars	36.3	31.0	25.7	19.5	16.3	12.3	8.9	7.7	5.9
Nicotine vaping	(NA)	(NA)	26.8	(NA)	(NA)	18.1	(NA)	(NA)	11.7
Alcohol	82.4	78.9	75.4	75.5	72.0	69.5	58.3	54.3	51.5
"Binge" alcohol use [4]	(NA)	(NA)	(NA)	(NA)	(NA)	(NA)	39.0	34.3	31.4
AGE 26 YEARS AND OLDER									
Any illicit drug [1]	50.1	52.2	52.8	14.6	18.3	19.9	8.2	11.6	12.6
Marijuana	46.0	48.8	48.9	10.4	15.2	16.3	6.5	10.2	10.8
Cocaine	16.6	17.3	16.5	1.3	1.7	1.7	0.6	0.7	0.6
Heroin	2.1	2.4	2.8	0.3	0.3	0.4	0.1	0.2	0.2
Hallucinogens	16.2	17.5	17.5	0.8	1.5	2.0	0.2	0.5	0.5
Inhalants	9.6	9.1	9.8	0.3	0.4	0.5	0.1	0.2	0.3
Methamphetamine	6.4	6.9	6.8	0.6	0.8	1.1	0.4	0.5	0.8
Opioids [2]	(NA)	(NA)	(NA)	4.2	3.6	3.5	1.3	1.2	1.1
Tobacco products [3]	69.9	67.8	65.2	28.9	26.8	24.4	24.5	22.6	20.4
Cigarettes	64.7	62.0	59.9	22.9	21.0	19.6	20.0	18.2	16.7
Smokeless tobacco	17.0	16.6	14.8	4.1	3.8	3.1	3.2	3.1	2.5
Cigars	35.3	34.3	33.1	7.8	7.3	6.8	4.3	4.0	3.9
Nicotine vaping	(NA)	(NA)	10.2	(NA)	(NA)	4.3	(NA)	(NA)	2.4
Alcohol	87.1	86.7	86.7	69.2	69.1	68.6	55.6	55.0	54.6
"Binge" alcohol use [4]	(NA)	(NA)	(NA)	(NA)	(NA)	(NA)	24.8	24.5	22.9

– Represents or rounds to zero. NA Not available. [1] Illicit drugs include marijuana, cocaine (including crack), heroin, hallucinogens (including LSD, PCP, and Ecstasy), inhalants, methamphetamine, and the misuse of prescription psychotherapeutic drugs. [2] Includes use of heroin and/or misuse of prescription pain relievers. [3] Includes other products not shown separately. Tobacco product use in the past year excludes past year pipe tobacco use, but includes past month pipe tobacco use. [4] Binge alcohol use is defined as drinking five or more drinks (for males) or four or more drinks (for females) on the same occasion (i.e., at the same time or within a couple of hours of each other) on at least 1 day in the past 30 days. [5] Use caution when comparing estimates between 2020 and prior years because of methodological changes for 2020. See the 2020 National Survey on Drug Use and Health: Methodological Summary and Definitions for details.

Source: U.S. Substance Abuse and Mental Health Services Administration, Results from the 2020 National Survey on Drug Use and Health: Detailed Tables, October 2021, and earlier reports. See also <www.samhsa.gov/data/data-we-collect/nsduh-national-survey-drug-use-and-health>.

Table 222. Drug, Alcohol, and Cigarette Estimated Users by State: 2019 and 2020

[In units as indicated (36,556 represents 36,556,000). Data in this table are annual averages for a 2-year period. Data are based on the National Survey on Drug Use and Health (NSDUH). Covers persons age 12 years and over who indicated current use of a substance (use within the 30 days prior to the interview). Based on a representative sample of the U.S. population, including persons living in households, noninstitutional group quarters such as dormitories and homeless shelters, and civilians living on military bases. During the coronavirus disease 2019 (COVID-19) pandemic, 2020 NSDUH data were collected only in the 1st and 4th quarters of 2020; the survey collected data through in-person interviews and via the internet from 36,284 respondents. Across 2019 and 2020 combined, the NSDUH collected data from 103,909 respondents from the 50 states and the District of Columbia. For methodology information, see "2019-2020 National Survey on Drug Use and Health: Guide to State Tables and Summary of Small Area Estimation Methodology" at <www.samhsa.gov/data/report/2019-2020-nsduh-guide-state-tables-and-summary-sae-methodology>]

State	Estimated current users (1,000)					Current users as percent of population				
	Illicit drug use [1]	Mari-juana	Any illicit drug other than mari-juana [2]	Binge alcohol use [3]	Cigarette use	Illicit drug use [1]	Mari-juana	Any illicit drug other than mari-juana [2]	Binge alcohol use [3]	Cigarette use
United States...........	**36,556**	**32,195**	**9,319**	**63,709**	**43,639**	**13.2**	**11.7**	**3.4**	**23.1**	**15.8**
Northeast................	6,597	5,884	1,667	11,303	6,945	13.8	12.3	3.5	23.7	14.6
Midwest..................	7,408	6,547	1,822	14,210	10,256	12.9	11.4	3.2	24.8	17.9
South.....................	11,589	10,005	3,297	23,495	17,816	11.0	9.5	3.1	22.3	16.9
West.....................	10,962	9,760	2,534	14,701	8,622	16.7	14.8	3.8	22.3	13.1
Alabama................	439	343	139	849	865	10.7	8.3	3.4	20.6	21.0
Alaska...................	109	100	24	144	91	18.7	17.1	4.2	24.7	15.7
Arizona..................	868	710	237	1,388	853	14.0	11.5	3.8	22.4	13.8
Arkansas................	298	264	81	539	536	11.9	10.5	3.2	21.5	21.3
California................	5,391	4,798	1,279	7,244	3,942	16.3	14.5	3.9	21.9	11.9
Colorado................	942	923	203	1,208	657	19.3	18.9	4.2	24.8	13.5
Connecticut............	465	413	108	754	382	15.2	13.5	3.5	24.7	12.5
Delaware................	101	86	29	181	134	12.2	10.3	3.5	21.7	16.1
District of Columbia......	124	110	35	214	91	20.5	18.2	5.8	35.5	15.1
Florida...................	2,356	2,152	573	4,204	2,893	12.7	11.6	3.1	22.7	15.6
Georgia.................	882	743	270	1,707	1,370	10.0	8.4	3.0	19.3	15.5
Hawaii...................	138	135	34	247	154	12.0	11.7	2.9	21.5	13.3
Idaho....................	162	145	44	306	215	10.8	9.7	2.9	20.5	14.4
Illinois...................	1,606	1,428	348	2,717	1,731	15.1	13.4	3.3	25.6	16.3
Indiana..................	725	615	175	1,337	1,134	12.9	10.9	3.1	23.8	20.2
Iowa.....................	276	242	77	716	478	10.4	9.2	2.9	27.1	18.1
Kansas..................	291	249	89	603	406	12.2	10.4	3.7	25.2	17.0
Kentucky................	399	354	102	774	831	10.7	9.5	2.7	20.7	22.3
Louisiana...............	426	359	147	949	827	11.2	9.4	3.9	24.8	21.6
Maine....................	220	201	37	239	187	18.7	17.1	3.2	20.4	16.0
Maryland................	681	607	154	1,144	637	13.4	12.0	3.0	22.6	12.6
Massachusetts.........	1,118	1,000	255	1,545	724	18.8	16.8	4.3	26.0	12.2
Michigan................	1,426	1,307	290	1,988	1,569	16.8	15.4	3.4	23.4	18.5
Minnesota..............	470	431	128	1,243	661	9.9	9.1	2.7	26.3	14.0
Mississippi.............	265	207	80	466	544	10.8	8.4	3.3	19.0	22.2
Missouri................	565	491	159	1,197	949	11.0	9.6	3.1	23.3	18.5
Montana................	168	154	29	268	171	18.4	17.0	3.2	29.4	18.8
Nebraska...............	151	133	47	442	256	9.5	8.4	2.9	27.8	16.1
Nevada..................	523	438	118	628	393	20.0	16.8	4.5	24.0	15.0
New Hampshire.........	183	170	39	306	172	15.4	14.3	3.3	25.7	14.5
New Jersey.............	782	717	218	1,851	895	10.4	9.5	2.9	24.6	11.9
New Mexico............	259	216	63	343	291	14.7	12.3	3.6	19.5	16.6
New York...............	2,226	1,971	610	3,636	2,353	13.5	12.0	3.7	22.0	14.3
North Carolina..........	1,041	905	274	1,926	1,631	11.8	10.2	3.1	21.8	18.5
North Dakota...........	58	51	19	173	110	9.2	8.2	3.1	27.7	17.7
Ohio.....................	1,253	1,104	313	2,247	2,006	12.7	11.2	3.2	22.8	20.4
Oklahoma...............	461	436	103	607	674	14.2	13.4	3.2	18.6	20.7
Oregon..................	767	698	154	797	565	21.2	19.3	4.2	22.0	15.6
Pennsylvania...........	1,302	1,131	346	2,607	2,008	12.0	10.4	3.2	24.0	18.5
Rhode Island............	177	161	35	237	143	19.4	17.7	3.8	26.0	15.7
South Carolina...........	410	353	132	952	824	9.4	8.1	3.0	21.8	18.9
South Dakota...........	67	61	20	178	142	9.2	8.4	2.8	24.6	19.6
Tennessee..............	669	607	182	1,245	1,085	11.6	10.5	3.2	21.6	18.9
Texas...................	2,197	1,794	697	5,802	3,496	9.2	7.5	2.9	24.4	14.7
Utah.....................	263	200	93	451	278	10.1	7.7	3.6	17.4	10.7
Vermont................	124	119	19	129	79	22.8	21.9	3.5	23.6	14.5
Virginia..................	672	541	251	1,656	1,040	9.4	7.6	3.5	23.3	14.6
Washington.............	1,326	1,201	244	1,554	924	20.6	18.7	3.8	24.1	14.4
West Virginia............	167	145	48	280	338	10.9	9.5	3.1	18.3	22.1
Wisconsin...............	521	435	157	1,368	813	10.5	8.8	3.2	27.7	16.5
Wyoming................	46	42	14	121	87	9.6	8.8	2.8	25.1	18.0

[1] "Illicit drug use" includes the misuse of prescription psychotherapeutics or the use of marijuana, cocaine (including crack), heroin, hallucinogens, inhalants, or methamphetamine. Misuse of prescription psychotherapeutics is defined as use in any way not directed by a doctor, including use without a prescription of one's own; use in greater amounts, more often, or longer than told; or use in any other way not directed by a doctor. Prescription psychotherapeutics do not include over-the-counter drugs. [2] "Illicit drug use other than marijuana" includes the misuse of prescription psychotherapeutics or the use of cocaine (including crack), heroin, hallucinogens, inhalants, or methamphetamine. Excludes persons who use marijuana only, but includes persons who use marijuana in addition to other illicit drugs. [3] "Binge alcohol use" is defined as drinking 5/more drinks (for males) or 4/more drinks (for females) on the same occasion (i.e., at the same time or within a couple of hours of each other) on at least 1 day in the past 30 days.

Source: U.S. Substance Abuse and Mental Health Services Administration, National Survey on Drug Use and Health, "State Data Tables and Reports From the 2019-2020 NSDUH," <www.samhsa.gov/data/nsduh/state-reports-NSDUH-2020>, accessed April 2022.

Table 223. Prescription Psychotherapeutic Drug Use and Misuse by Drug Type and User Characteristics: 2020

[In percent. Data are from the National Survey on Drug Use and Health, and cover persons age 12 and older. Misuse of prescription drugs is defined as use in any way not directed by a physician, including use without a prescription of one's own; use in greater amounts, more often, or longer than instructed to take a drug; or use in any other way not directed by a physician. Excludes over-the-counter drugs. See also headnote, Table 221. For information on methodological changes for 2020, and on drug types covered, see *2020 National Survey on Drug Use and Health (NSDUH): Methodological Summary and Definitions,* <www.samhsa.gov/data/sites/default/files/reports/rpt35330/2020NSDUHMethodSummDefs091721.pdf>]

User characteristics	Any use in past year				Misuse in past year			
	Pain relievers	Stimu-lants	Tranquil-izers	Seda-tives	Pain relievers	Stimu-lants	Tranquil-izers	Seda-tives
Total............................	**27.2**	**6.6**	**12.6**	**5.5**	**3.3**	**1.8**	**2.0**	**0.4**
SEX								
Male..........................	25.1	6.2	9.7	4.8	3.1	2.0	1.8	0.4
Female........................	29.1	7.1	15.4	6.3	3.5	1.7	2.1	0.5
AGE								
12 to 17 years................	12.3	6.4	2.4	1.7	1.6	1.2	0.8	0.1
18 years and over.............	28.6	6.6	13.7	5.9	3.5	1.9	2.1	0.5
18 to 25 years.............	20.5	11.3	10.0	3.2	4.1	4.8	3.3	0.7
26 years and over...........	29.9	5.9	14.2	6.3	3.4	1.5	1.9	0.4
RACE AND ETHNICITY								
Not Hispanic..................	27.8	7.0	13.6	6.0	3.3	2.0	2.1	0.5
White.......................	28.8	7.8	15.7	6.9	3.3	2.3	2.4	0.5
Black or African American......	29.1	4.3	8.3	3.8	3.6	0.8	1.1	0.3
American Indian or Alaska Native.........	29.0	(B)	10.6	5.1	3.2	1.8	3.1	2.8
Native Hawaiian or Other Pacific Islander....................	(B)	0.6	(B)	0.4	0.6	0.2	0.4	(B)
Asian.......................	13.8	4.4	3.9	0.9	2.4	0.9	0.6	–
Two or more races............	32.3	7.0	14.9	5.8	2.6	2.2	3.5	1.1
Hispanic or Latino.............	24.0	4.9	8.0	3.6	3.6	1.3	1.4	0.2
REGION								
Northeast......................	24.5	6.4	13.7	5.4	3.4	2.2	1.5	0.4
Midwest.......................	26.2	7.1	12.8	5.8	2.9	2.0	2.1	0.5
South.........................	28.8	6.8	13.0	5.5	3.1	1.8	2.0	0.5
West..........................	27.2	6.1	11.1	5.5	4.0	1.6	2.2	0.4
METRO STATUS								
Large metro [1]..............	25.2	6.8	12.3	5.1	3.1	2.0	1.7	0.4
Small metro [2]..............	29.8	6.9	13.5	6.0	3.8	2.0	2.4	0.6
Nonmetro.....................	28.8	5.5	12.1	6.3	3.3	0.9	1.9	0.4

– Represents or rounds to zero. B Figure does not meet standards of reliability or precision. [1] Over 1 million population. [2] Less than 1 million population.

Source: U.S. Substance Abuse and Mental Health Services Administration, *Results From the 2020 National Survey on Drug Use and Health: Detailed Tables,* October 2021. See also <www.samhsa.gov/data/data-we-collect/nsduh-national-survey-drug-use-and-health>.

Table 224. Prescription Drug Use in Past 30 Days by Sex, Race/Ethnicity, and Age: 1999 to 2018

[Data shown as percent of population using prescription drugs in past 30 days. Based on the National Health and Nutrition Examination Survey, covering a sample of the civilian noninstitutionalized population]

Sex, race/ethnicity, and age	Use of 1 or more prescription drugs			Use of 3 or more prescription drugs			Use of 5 or more prescription drugs		
	1999-2002	2007-2010	2015-2018	1999-2002	2007-2010	2015-2018	1999-2002	2007-2010	2015-2018
Both sexes, age adjusted [1,2]............	**45.2**	**47.5**	**45.7**	**17.8**	**20.8**	**21.3**	**7.5**	**10.1**	**11.2**
Male.........................	39.8	42.8	41.7	14.8	19.1	20.0	6.1	9.2	10.8
Female.......................	50.3	52.0	49.5	20.4	22.5	22.6	8.7	11.0	11.6
White alone [3]...................	48.7	52.8	49.7	18.9	22.4	22.8	7.8	10.7	12.0
Male.....................	43.0	47.5	45.5	15.9	20.6	21.4	6.3	9.8	11.7
Female...................	54.3	57.9	53.9	21.8	24.3	24.3	9.2	11.6	12.2
Black or African American alone [3]............	40.1	42.3	43.3	16.5	20.7	21.1	7.7	10.8	12.4
Male.....................	35.4	36.7	39.8	14.5	17.7	19.1	6.4	9.1	10.9
Female...................	43.8	46.8	46.1	18.1	22.9	22.7	8.7	12.0	13.5
Asian alone [3].................	(NA)	(NA)	35.4	(NA)	(NA)	14.7	(NA)	(NA)	6.6
Male.....................	(NA)	(NA)	32.9	(NA)	(NA)	15.4	(NA)	(NA)	6.9
Female...................	(NA)	(NA)	37.6	(NA)	(NA)	14.1	(NA)	(NA)	6.3
Hispanic or Latino [4].............	(NA)	35.2	37.7	(NA)	15.7	17.9	(NA)	8.4	9.0
Male.....................	(NA)	31.7	33.1	(NA)	14.0	17.0	(NA)	7.3	8.3
Female...................	(NA)	38.8	42.3	(NA)	17.4	18.7	(NA)	9.5	9.7
Both sexes, crude.....................	**45.0**	**48.5**	**48.6**	**17.6**	**21.7**	**24.0**	**7.4**	**10.6**	**12.8**
Male.........................	38.6	43.0	43.8	13.9	19.0	21.7	5.6	9.1	11.8
Under 18 years.............	25.7	24.5	23.3	4.3	4.4	3.9	(B)	0.8	1.2
18 to 44 years.............	27.1	29.5	27.0	6.7	7.1	8.2	1.7	2.1	3.4
45 to 64 years.............	55.6	61.3	62.9	23.6	30.4	33.8	9.5	14.4	17.4
65 years and over...........	80.1	88.8	87.9	46.3	66.8	65.5	24.7	39.5	42.0
Female.......................	51.1	53.8	53.1	21.1	24.2	26.1	9.1	12.1	13.7
Under 18 years.............	21.7	23.5	19.6	3.9	3.1	2.9	[5] 0.8	[5] 0.7	0.7
18 to 44 years.............	44.6	47.6	44.2	10.2	12.2	11.9	2.8	4.0	5.0
45 to 64 years.............	72.0	70.8	71.0	37.5	38.1	38.9	16.8	19.1	18.7
65 years and over...........	88.1	90.4	88.9	55.9	66.4	67.1	28.9	39.8	41.9

NA Not available. B Estimate has a relative standard error greater than 30%. [1] Estimates are age-adjusted to the year 2000 standard population using four age groups: under 18 years, 18-44 years, 45-64 years, and 65 years and over. [2] Includes persons of other race/ethnicities not shown separately. [3] Not Hispanic or Latino. [4] Persons of Hispanic or Latino origin may be of any race. [5] Estimate has a relative standard error (RSE) of 20% to 30% and is considered unreliable.

Source: U.S. National Center for Health Statistics, *Health, United States, 2019,* March 2021. See also <www.cdc.gov/nchs/hus/index.htm>.

Table 225. Height of Population Age 20 and Over by Sex, Age, and Race/Ethnicity: 2015 to 2018

[In inches. Data cover the 2015-2018 period. Based on National Health and Nutrition Examination Survey (NHANES), a sample of the civilian noninstitutional population. Data are collected through household interviews, and through health examinations conducted in mobile examination centers by health technicians following a standard protocol. Standing height is measured with a wall-mounted stadiometer and recorded automatically. Measurements are done in the metric system; conversions are made to U.S. customary units. Survey oversampled persons age 80 and over, Hispanic persons, black persons, Asian persons, and persons with low income; see source for more information]

Age and race/ethnicity	Males, height in inches						Females, height in inches					
		Percentile						Percentile				
	Mean	10th	25th	50th	75th	90th	Mean	10th	25th	50th	75th	90th
Total: [1]												
20 years and over......	69.0	65.3	67.0	69.1	71.0	72.7	63.5	60.0	61.6	63.5	65.3	67.0
20–29 years.............	69.2	65.8	67.3	69.3	71.0	72.8	64.0	60.5	62.2	64.1	65.8	67.2
30–39 years.............	69.4	65.6	67.4	69.6	71.4	73.3	64.1	60.7	62.2	64.0	66.0	67.5
40–49 years.............	69.4	65.4	67.5	69.5	71.4	72.8	63.9	60.2	62.1	64.0	65.6	67.5
50–59 years.............	69.0	65.0	67.0	69.0	71.1	72.8	63.5	60.2	61.6	63.4	65.3	67.0
60–69 years.............	68.7	64.9	66.7	68.6	70.4	72.3	63.3	60.1	61.4	63.3	65.1	66.5
70–79 years.............	68.1	64.8	66.4	68.1	69.9	71.8	62.3	59.3	60.6	62.2	64.0	65.3
80 years and over......	67.1	63.4	65.3	67.1	69.0	70.7	61.3	57.9	59.6	61.3	62.9	64.4
White, non-Hispanic:												
20 years and over......	69.5	66.0	67.6	69.6	71.4	73.0	63.9	60.5	62.1	63.9	65.7	67.3
20–39 years.............	70.1	66.7	68.2	70.1	71.7	73.5	64.7	61.6	63.3	64.7	66.4	67.6
40–59 years.............	69.8	66.4	67.9	69.9	71.5	73.0	64.3	60.8	62.6	64.2	65.9	67.4
60 years and over......	68.7	65.4	66.8	68.6	70.3	72.2	62.9	59.8	61.0	62.9	64.7	66.2
Black, non-Hispanic:												
20 years and over......	69.3	65.8	67.4	69.3	71.1	72.8	64.0	60.6	62.3	64.0	65.6	67.1
20–39 years.............	69.4	66.0	67.6	69.2	71.3	72.9	64.3	60.9	62.6	64.4	66.1	67.5
40–59 years.............	69.6	66.2	67.7	69.7	71.2	72.9	64.1	60.7	62.6	64.1	65.6	67.2
60 years and over......	68.4	64.9	66.6	68.5	70.1	71.8	63.2	60.2	61.6	63.0	64.7	66.1
Hispanic:												
20 years and over......	67.1	63.3	65.1	67.0	69.1	70.8	62.0	58.8	60.2	61.8	63.7	65.4
20–39 years.............	67.4	63.7	65.6	67.4	69.3	70.9	62.5	59.3	60.7	62.3	64.3	66.0
40–59 years.............	67.0	63.0	64.9	66.9	69.1	70.7	61.9	58.6	60.1	61.8	63.5	65.2
60 years and over......	66.2	62.8	64.5	66.2	67.8	69.6	60.9	58.1	59.4	60.8	62.3	63.5

[1] Total includes persons of other race/ethnicities not shown separately.

Source: U.S. Centers for Disease Control and Prevention, National Health and Nutrition Examination Survey, *Anthropometric Reference Data For Children and Adults: United States, 2015-2018*, Series 3, No. 46, January 2021. See also <www.cdc.gov/nchs/nhanes/index.htm>.

Table 226. Weight of Population Age 20 and Over by Age, Sex, and Race/Ethnicity: 2015 to 2018

[In pounds. Data are for 2015-2018 period. Based on National Health and Nutrition Examination Survey (NHANES). Weight is measured using a digital floor scale and values are recorded automatically. Measurements are done in the metric system; conversions are made to U.S. customary units. For persons age 20 and over. Excludes pregnant females. See headnote, Table 225]

Age and race/ethnicity	Males, weight in pounds						Females, weight in pounds					
		Percentile						Percentile				
	Mean	10th	25th	50th	75th	90th	Mean	10th	25th	50th	75th	90th
Total: [1]												
20 years and over.......	199.8	146.9	166.1	192.6	224.6	263.2	170.8	118.9	137.1	161.2	195.3	232.1
20–29 years.............	188.6	135.6	152.8	179.1	216.5	255.7	165.0	113.3	128.7	153.2	190.5	236.0
30–39 years.............	208.1	154.9	171.1	197.7	230.6	273.0	174.9	118.6	139.9	161.5	201.6	244.2
40–49 years.............	206.9	154.5	176.2	199.5	229.2	263.6	178.1	125.7	142.4	165.7	203.0	249.5
50–59 years.............	202.5	151.1	169.1	197.5	224.8	273.2	173.5	121.6	140.5	164.4	198.7	231.0
60–69 years.............	201.2	149.1	168.7	197.2	226.8	257.3	172.4	124.5	141.7	165.5	196.9	228.5
70–79 years.............	193.4	147.8	167.0	188.0	216.1	239.7	164.6	119.8	138.4	161.4	184.9	209.6
80 years and over.......	177.5	136.7	152.6	175.6	198.4	218.6	149.7	110.2	126.3	146.2	168.2	190.2
White, non-Hispanic:												
20 years and over.......	203.4	150.3	169.9	197.6	227.6	264.7	170.9	120.3	138.3	161.3	194.7	231.2
20–39 years.............	201.9	142.8	163.2	191.2	230.2	270.4	170.0	116.8	133.0	157.5	194.9	238.1
40–59 years.............	207.5	155.3	175.7	200.7	230.9	269.6	176.1	127.1	144.9	165.3	201.6	235.1
60 years and over.......	200.3	152.1	170.9	195.6	226.2	253.1	166.6	120.3	137.5	161.0	188.1	220.6
Black, non-Hispanic:												
20 years and over.......	200.1	140.7	162.7	190.6	229.0	272.7	188.5	128.9	150.6	180.0	215.3	262.0
20–39 years.............	195.3	138.5	154.2	182.8	216.0	274.3	183.9	120.8	142.8	175.4	212.1	255.8
40–59 years.............	211.8	155.4	176.2	204.1	241.1	277.9	199.4	134.1	157.7	193.5	229.1	278.1
60 years and over.......	189.6	137.7	157.7	184.6	214.4	246.3	179.2	133.1	151.2	170.1	199.0	234.2
Hispanic:												
20 years and over.......	193.7	147.0	165.0	187.6	216.2	245.4	168.0	121.1	138.4	159.1	189.1	224.3
20–39 years.............	193.9	143.4	164.1	188.1	218.7	244.4	169.0	118.4	134.2	156.4	192.4	233.7
40–59 years.............	196.9	151.2	169.0	189.7	218.3	251.6	169.3	126.0	141.9	161.6	191.0	220.7
60 years and over.......	185.3	145.0	159.1	180.5	206.7	233.6	162.9	124.3	138.4	158.0	182.4	207.1

[1] Total includes persons of other race/ethnicities not shown separately.

Source: U.S. Centers for Disease Control and Prevention, National Health and Nutrition Examination Survey, *Anthropometric Reference Data For Children and Adults: United States, 2015-2018*, Series 3, No. 46, January 2021. See also <www.cdc.gov/nchs/nhanes/index.htm>.

Table 227. Body Mass Index of Population Age 20 and Over by Age, Sex, and Race/Ethnicity: 2015 to 2018

[Data are for 2015-2018 period. Body Mass Index (BMI) is a measure that adjusts body weight for height, and is calculated as weight in kilograms divided by the square of height in meters. For both men and women, BMI weight categories are: below 18.5 underweight, 18.5-24.9 normal, 25.0-29.9 overweight, and 30.0 and higher obese. Data are based on National Health and Nutrition Examination Survey (NHANES), a sample of the civilian noninstitutional population. Data are collected through household interviews and health examinations. Measurements are conducted by health technicians following a standard protocol and are recorded automatically. Excludes pregnant women. Survey oversampled persons age 80 and over, Hispanic persons, black persons, Asian persons, and persons with low income; see source for more information]

Age and race/ethnicity	Males, BMI								Females, BMI							
	Mean	Percentile							Mean	Percentile						
		10th	15th	25th	50th	75th	85th	90th		10th	15th	25th	50th	75th	85th	90th
Total:[1]																
20 years and over	29.4	22.4	23.3	25.0	28.5	32.8	35.3	37.1	29.8	21.2	22.1	23.9	28.4	33.9	37.5	40.3
20-29 years	27.6	20.0	21.0	22.6	26.5	31.6	34.4	36.8	28.3	19.6	20.4	21.9	26.2	32.9	37.4	39.6
30-39 years	30.3	23.0	23.8	25.4	28.9	33.7	36.4	38.3	29.9	21.2	22.0	23.6	28.3	34.2	38.2	41.1
40-49 years	30.1	23.5	24.7	26.2	29.1	32.8	35.5	38.1	30.7	22.6	22.8	24.4	28.6	34.8	39.3	43.1
50-59 years	29.8	22.6	24.0	25.2	29.1	33.3	35.3	37.4	30.3	21.5	22.5	24.3	29.1	34.2	37.7	41.5
60-69 years	29.9	23.2	23.9	25.8	28.9	33.3	35.3	37.1	30.3	22.2	23.2	24.9	29.2	34.7	37.2	39.5
70-79 years	29.2	22.9	24.1	25.9	28.2	32.8	34.5	35.6	29.8	22.0	23.3	25.3	28.8	33.3	35.7	37.9
80 years and over	27.6	22.3	22.9	24.3	27.2	30.2	32.3	34.0	28.0	20.8	22.2	23.8	27.5	30.8	33.5	35.5
White, non-Hispanic:																
20 years and over	29.5	22.4	23.3	25.1	28.6	32.9	35.3	37.1	29.4	21.2	22.0	23.6	27.9	33.5	37.1	39.7
20-39 years	28.8	21.2	22.4	23.7	27.3	32.7	36.0	37.9	28.5	19.9	21.0	22.2	26.2	33.0	37.3	39.8
40-59 years	29.9	22.8	24.0	25.6	29.2	32.7	35.3	37.1	30.0	21.8	22.4	24.0	28.4	33.9	38.1	42.2
60 years and over	29.8	23.2	24.1	26.0	28.7	33.3	35.1	36.4	29.6	21.8	22.9	24.6	28.4	33.5	36.1	38.4
Black, non-Hispanic:																
20 years and over	29.2	21.2	22.2	24.2	27.9	33.1	36.2	38.4	32.3	22.2	23.5	26.1	31.1	37.1	40.7	43.6
20-39 years	28.4	20.4	21.2	22.4	26.6	31.9	36.4	38.5	31.1	20.8	21.9	24.0	30.1	36.5	40.0	42.6
40-59 years	30.6	22.8	24.1	26.0	30.0	34.6	36.8	39.1	34.1	23.8	25.1	26.5	32.9	38.8	43.5	46.8
60 years and over	28.4	21.3	22.4	24.2	27.7	31.6	33.8	36.0	31.6	23.2	24.6	26.5	30.2	35.4	38.5	40.4
Asian, non-Hispanic:																
20 years and over	26.1	21.5	22.2	23.3	25.5	28.4	29.7	31.2	25.1	19.8	20.4	21.3	24.2	27.9	30.1	31.8
20-39 years	26.7	21.4	22.4	23.3	25.8	28.9	31	32.1	24.8	19.4	20	20.8	23.9	27.7	30.1	31.9
40-59 years	26.2	21.9	22.5	23.7	25.8	28.5	29.4	30.9	25.1	20.1	20.7	21.8	24.2	28.1	29.7	31.3
60 years and over	24.8	21.0	21.8	22.7	24.2	26.9	28.3	29.1	25.6	20.0	20.8	22.0	24.9	27.9	30.2	31.9
Hispanic:																
20 years and over	30.2	23.8	25.0	26.5	29.2	33.0	35.7	37.1	30.7	22.1	23.4	25.4	29.4	34.5	38.0	40.6
20-39 years	30.0	22.4	24.0	26.1	29.1	33.3	35.5	37.0	30.4	21.1	22.0	24.4	28.5	34.1	38.9	41.4
40-59 years	30.7	25.1	25.9	27.1	29.5	33.0	36.2	37.9	31.0	23.1	24.0	26.2	29.9	34.7	37.4	40.3
60 years and over	29.6	23.9	24.7	26.1	29.0	32.1	34.3	35.8	30.9	23.8	25.0	26.6	29.8	34.7	37.4	39.4
Mexican American:																
20 years and over	30.5	23.7	25.0	26.6	29.9	33.4	35.9	37.2	31.6	23.0	24.2	26.4	30.1	35.9	39.1	41.6
20-39 years	30.4	22.3	24.3	26.4	29.9	33.7	35.9	37.2	31.5	21.6	23.2	25.6	29.7	36.0	39.8	42.7
40-59 years	31.0	25.1	25.9	27.2	30.1	33.2	36.2	38.6	31.8	23.6	24.8	26.8	30.4	36.0	38.9	41.2
60 years and over	29.6	23.9	24.8	26.3	29.2	31.9	34.3	35.7	31.7	24.5	25.3	27.0	30.0	35.2	38.4	40.5

[1] Total includes persons of other race/ethnicities not shown separately.

Source: U.S. Centers for Disease Control and Prevention, National Health and Nutrition Examination Survey, *Anthropometric Reference Data For Children and Adults: United States, 2015-2018,* Series 3, No. 46, January 2021. See also <www.cdc.gov/nchs/nhanes/index.htm>.

Table 228. Overweight and Obesity Prevalence Among Adults Age 20 and Over by Sex, Age, and Race/Ethnicity: 1988 to 2018

[Shown as percent of population age 20 and over. Weight status is determined by body mass index (BMI), which is calculated as weight in kilograms divided by the square of height in meters. Excludes pregnant women. Data are based on the National Health and Nutrition Examination Survey (NHANES). Measurements are conducted by health technicians following a standard protocol and are recorded automatically. Percents do not sum to 100 because data for persons with BMI under 18.5 are not shown, and percent of persons with obesity are included with the overweight. See headnote, Table 227]

Characteristic	Normal weight [1]			Overweight or obese [2]			Obese [3]		
	1988 to 1994	2001 to 2004	2015 to 2018	1988 to 1994	2001 to 2004	2015 to 2018	1988 to 1994	2001 to 2004	2015 to 2018
Total, age-adjusted [4]...............	**41.6**	**32.3**	**26.0**	**56.0**	**66.0**	**72.5**	**22.9**	**31.4**	**41.1**
Male..	37.9	28.3	22.5	60.9	70.5	76.4	20.2	29.5	40.5
Female....................................	45.0	36.1	29.4	51.4	61.6	68.8	25.5	33.2	41.5
Total, crude............................	**42.6**	**32.2**	**25.9**	**54.9**	**66.1**	**72.6**	**22.3**	**31.5**	**41.2**
Male..	39.4	28.4	22.7	59.4	70.4	76.0	19.5	29.5	40.5
Female....................................	45.7	35.8	28.8	50.7	61.9	69.4	25.0	33.3	41.8
White, non-Hispanic..................	43.6	33.2	26.8	53.8	65.1	71.6	21.3	30.9	40.7
Male..	38.2	27.4	22.8	60.6	71.6	76.0	19.8	30.5	41.7
Female....................................	48.8	38.8	30.6	47.4	58.7	67.4	22.7	31.2	39.7
Black or African American, non-Hispanic....	35.9	24.8	22.8	61.8	73.3	75.7	29.5	41.9	48.1
Male..	41.5	31.5	27.3	56.7	66.3	70.9	20.7	30.7	38.7
Female....................................	31.2	19.3	19.0	66.0	79.1	79.6	36.7	51.1	55.9
Asian, non-Hispanic..................	(NA)	(NA)	47.9	(NA)	(NA)	49.6	(NA)	(NA)	15.1
Male..	(NA)	(NA)	41.5	(NA)	(NA)	56.8	(NA)	(NA)	14.2
Female....................................	(NA)	(NA)	53.6	(NA)	(NA)	43.3	(NA)	(NA)	16.0
Hispanic [5]...............................	(NA)	(NA)	17.1	(NA)	(NA)	82.0	(NA)	(NA)	45.8
Male..	(NA)	(NA)	13.8	(NA)	(NA)	85.4	(NA)	(NA)	44.8
Female....................................	(NA)	(NA)	20.5	(NA)	(NA)	78.6	(NA)	(NA)	46.8
Male by age:									
20 to 34 years.........................	51.1	38.3	32.3	47.5	59.0	65.2	14.1	23.2	37.2
35 to 44 years.........................	33.4	26.5	18.7	65.5	72.9	81.0	21.3	33.8	42.5
45 to 54 years.........................	33.6	21.2	16.2	66.1	78.5	83.0	23.2	31.8	42.9
55 to 64 years.........................	28.6	22.2	21.5	70.5	77.3	77.5	27.2	36.0	43.9
65 to 74 years.........................	30.1	23.1	15.6	68.5	76.1	83.7	24.1	32.1	41.9
75 years and over....................	40.9	32.1	24.7	56.5	66.8	74.6	13.2	19.9	31.8
Female by age:									
20 to 34 years.........................	57.9	44.2	36.6	37.0	51.6	60.0	18.5	28.6	35.6
35 to 44 years.........................	47.1	38.3	28.3	49.6	60.1	70.7	25.5	33.3	45.0
45 to 54 years.........................	37.2	31.0	27.1	60.3	67.4	71.3	32.4	38.0	43.1
55 to 64 years.........................	31.5	29.2	25.6	66.3	69.9	72.7	33.7	39.0	46.2
65 to 74 years.........................	37.0	27.0	20.9	60.3	71.5	78.9	26.9	37.9	45.9
75 years and over....................	43.0	34.6	29.0	52.3	63.7	69.9	19.2	23.2	36.1

NA Not available. [1] Normal weight status is a BMI of 18.5 to 24.9. [2] Overweight or obese is a BMI of 25.0 or more. [3] Obese is a BMI of 30.0 or more. [4] Estimates are age-adjusted to the year 2000 standard population using five age groups: 20–34 years, 35–44 years, 45–54 years, 55–64 years, and 65 years and over. [5] Persons of Hispanic origin may be of any race.

Source: U.S. National Center for Health Statistics, *Health, United States, 2019*, March 2021. See also <www.cdc.gov/nchs/hus/index.htm>.

Table 229. Dental Care Visit in the Past Year—Percent of Population by Age and Selected Characteristics: 2000 to 2019

[In percent. Covers civilian noninstitutionalized population who had a dental care visit in the past year. Based on the National Health Interview Survey; see Appendix III]

Characteristic	Age 2 to 17 years				Age 18 to 64 years				Age 65 years and over			
	2000	2010	2018	2019 [5]	2000	2010	2018	2019 [5]	2000	2010	2018	2019 [5]
Total [1].................................	**74.1**	**78.9**	**85.9**	**86.9**	**65.1**	**61.1**	**65.9**	**65.5**	**56.6**	**57.7**	**65.6**	**64.5**
Sex:												
Male.......................................	73.7	78.3	86.1	87.0	60.7	56.8	61.5	61.5	56.1	56.2	64.4	61.5
Female...................................	74.6	79.6	85.7	86.7	69.4	65.4	70.2	69.3	56.9	58.9	66.5	67.0
Race/ethnicity: [2]												
White alone............................	75.8	79.2	85.6	87.0	67.2	62.4	66.6	66.8	58.4	59.3	67.6	67.2
Black or African American alone.....	70.0	79.0	87.5	88.3	57.1	53.1	63.0	61.2	38.2	40.6	54.6	49.8
American Indian/Alaska Native alone...	71.3	73.2	93.5	[6] 83.8	55.0	49.8	56.7	64.9	(B)	72.2	42.9	49.8
Asian alone............................	72.8	74.8	85.5	85.2	65.6	64.6	67.1	70.1	60.6	61.9	59.0	69.8
Two or more races...................	71.4	77.9	84.6	88.2	60.5	54.7	63.2	57.8	57.4	48.1	51.0	47.5
Hispanic or Latino [3].................	60.6	74.8	85.1	85.7	48.6	48.5	58.5	58.7	44.5	42.1	55.9	49.2
Not Hispanic or Latino..............	76.8	80.1	86.2	87.3	67.5	63.4	67.6	67.0	57.2	59.0	66.5	66.0
Percent of poverty level: [4]												
Below 100%...........................	62.4	73.2	83.9	84.0	46.8	41.0	48.8	49.8	33.3	32.8	39.6	36.3
100% to 199%........................	66.1	73.4	82.2	83.6	48.4	44.1	50.0	50.6	43.0	43.8	46.9	45.5
200% to 399%........................	75.5	79.0	85.0	86.5	62.2	59.6	62.9	62.8	62.8	57.9	64.7	64.1
400% or more.........................	85.9	88.0	90.5	91.6	78.5	77.5	78.7	78.8	73.8	77.2	82.3	82.6

B Estimates are considered unreliable. [1] Includes persons of other race and ethnic groups not shown separately, and those with unknown sex. [2] Race groups include persons of Hispanic and non-Hispanic origin. [3] Persons of Hispanic origin may be of any race. [4] Poverty level is based on family income and family size and composition using Census Bureau poverty thresholds. Missing family income data are imputed. [5] In 2019, the NHIS questionnaire was redesigned and other changes were made to weighting and design methodology. Data for 2019 have not been fully evaluated for comparability with earlier years. For more information, see <www.cdc.gov/nchs/nhis/2019_quest_redesign.htm>. Beginning 2019, dental visits in past year were identified by asking respondents "About how long has it been since [child of respondent or adult respondent] last had a dental examination or cleaning?" [6] Estimate meets National Center for Health Statistics (NCHS) standards of reliability, but its complement does not. See source for more information.

Source: U.S. National Center for Health Statistics, "Health, United States—Data Finder," <www.cdc.gov/nchs/hus/index.htm>, accessed August 2022.

Table 230. Depression and Receipt of Mental Health Treatment in the Past Year Among Adults Age 18 and Over by Selected Characteristics: 2019 and 2020

[In thousands (19,357 represents 19,357,000), except percent. Based on the National Survey on Drug Use and Health. Covers adults who had a major depressive episode as defined in the 5th edition of the *Diagnostic and Statistical Manual of Mental Disorders* (DSM-5), which specifies a period of at least 2 weeks when a person experienced a depressed mood or loss of interest or pleasure in daily activities and had a majority of specified depression symptoms. Treatment is defined as seeing or talking to a professional or using prescription medication for depression in the past year; respondents with unknown treatment data were excluded]

Characteristic	Had major depressive episode (MDE)				Those with an MDE who received treatment for depression			
	2019		2020 [1]		2019		2020 [1]	
	Number (1,000)	Percent of population	Number (1,000)	Percent of population	Number (1,000)	Percent	Number (1,000)	Percent
Total............................	19,357	7.8	20,976	8.4	12,824	66.3	13,832	66.0
AGE								
18 to 25 years old..............	5,045	15.2	5,610	17.0	2,565	50.9	3,230	57.6
26 to 49 years old..............	8,914	8.9	9,168	9.1	6,135	68.9	5,937	64.8
50 years old and older..................	5,399	4.7	6,199	5.4	4,124	76.5	4,665	75.3
SEX AND AGE								
Male.............................	7,125	6.0	7,440	6.2	4,041	56.8	4,193	56.4
18 to 25 years old..............	1,841	11.1	1,829	11.1	793	43.1	854	46.8
26 to 49 years old..............	3,271	6.6	3,649	7.3	1,927	59.2	1,978	54.2
50 years old and older..............	2,013	3.8	1,962	3.6	1,321	65.6	(B)	(B)
Female............................	12,233	9.6	13,536	10.5	8,783	71.9	9,639	71.2
18 to 25 years old..............	3,204	19.4	3,781	22.9	1,772	55.3	2,377	62.9
26 to 49 years old..............	5,643	11.1	5,518	10.8	4,208	74.6	3,958	71.7
50 years old and older..............	3,386	5.6	4,236	6.9	2,802	83.0	3,304	78.0
RACE AND HISPANIC ORIGIN								
Not Hispanic or Latino..................	16,588	8.0	18,094	8.7	11,223	67.7	12,386	68.5
White..............................	13,319	8.5	14,840	9.5	9,346	70.2	10,351	69.8
Black or African American..............	1,841	6.3	1,786	6.0	1,096	59.6	(B)	(B)
American Indian or Alaska Native......	129	9.4	58	4.2	(B)	(B)	(B)	(B)
Native Hawaiian or other Pacific Islander................................	34	3.5	(B)	(B)	(B)	(B)	(B)	(B)
Asian.............................	669	4.7	593	4.2	346	51.7	(B)	(B)
Two or more races.....................	595	13.7	737	15.9	359	60.3	(B)	(B)
Hispanic or Latino.....................	2,769	6.8	2,882	7.0	1,601	58.0	1,447	50.2

B Low precision; does not meet statistical standards for reliability of a derived figure. [1] Caution should be used when comparing estimates between 2020 and prior years because of methodological changes for 2020 during the coronavirus disease 2019 (COVID-19) pandemic. See source for details.

Source: U.S. Substance Abuse and Mental Health Services Administration, *Results from the 2020 National Survey on Drug Use and Health: Detailed Tables,* October 2021. See also <www.samhsa.gov/data/data-we-collect/nsduh-national-survey-drug-use-and-health>.

Table 231. Children and Youth With Disabilities Receiving Special Education and Related Services by Type of Disability: 2000 to 2020

[In thousands (5,773.9 represents 5,773,900). As of Fall. For children and youth age 6 to 21 receiving special education and related services under the Individuals with Disabilities Education Act (IDEA) Part B. Includes outlying areas]

Disability	2000	2005	2010	2015	2017	2018	2019	2020 [2]
Total.............................	5,773.9	6,109.6	5,834.9	6,050.7	6,130.6	6,315.2	6,472.1	6,712.0
Autism..............................	79.6	193.6	370.6	550.4	616.2	663.8	704.4	768.2
Deaf-blindness........................	1.3	1.6	1.3	1.3	1.3	1.4	1.5	1.6
Developmental delay [1]..............	28.6	79.1	109.4	149.3	159.5	167.7	178.0	255.8
Emotional disturbance..............	474.3	472.4	388.2	346.5	335.0	344.5	345.2	345.4
Hearing impairment..................	70.8	72.4	69.9	67.4	64.8	64.4	63.4	65.0
Intellectual disability.................	613.4	545.5	445.8	418.5	418.4	423.2	416.1	408.5
Multiple disabilities..................	122.9	133.9	123.8	125.2	122.4	126.7	126.1	123.7
Orthopedic impairment.............	73.0	63.1	55.8	41.2	34.9	33.5	30.9	30.4
Other health impairment...........	294.0	561.0	706.1	907.2	970.0	1,026.0	1,074.2	1,097.3
Specific learning disability..........	2,881.6	2,780.2	2,420.0	2,348.9	2,339.9	2,377.7	2,377.7	2,319.7
Speech or language impairment...	1,093.4	1,157.2	1,093.7	1,044.3	1,018.5	1,036.8	1,043.7	1,183.3
Traumatic brain injury...............	14.9	23.5	24.7	25.5	25.3	25.3	24.9	24.2
Visual impairment....................	26.0	26.0	25.7	24.9	24.4	24.2	23.9	24.0

[1] Beginning 1997, States could include children ages 3 to 9 with a developmental delay among children identified as having a disability. "Developmental delay" applies only to children ages 3 to 9. [2] Data for 2020 are for school-age children age 5 (in kindergarten) to age 21.

Source: U.S. Department of Education, Office of Special Education Programs, "IDEA Section 618 Data Products: State Level Data Files," <ideadata.org/idea-section-618-data-products>, accessed April 2022.

Table 232. Children Under Age 18 Receiving Special Education or Early Intervention Services: 2019 and 2020

[In percent. Based on the National Health Interview Survey (NHIS), a household survey of a sample of the civilian noninstitutionalized population. Receiving special education or early intervention services is based on the question, "Does [child's name] currently have a special education or early intervention plan? (Consider special education or early intervention plans received during the past school year.)" Estimates are based on responses about the sample child, not all children in the family. Unknowns were not included in the denominators when calculating percentages. The NHIS questionnaire was redesigned in 2019. Due to changes in weighting and design methodology, direct comparisons between estimates for 2019 and beyond to earlier years should be made with caution]

Selected characteristic	2019	2020 [6]	Selected characteristic	2019	2020 [6]
Total...........................	**7.8**	**9.9**	FAMILY STRUCTURE [3]		
SEX and AGE			Single parent, never married........................	9.8	7.8
Male...........................	10.2	12.3	Single parent, ever married.........................	12.2	16.3
Female.........................	5.4	7.3	Married parents....................................	6.8	8.9
4 years and under...............	3.3	2.8	Cohabiting parents................................	6.1	5.8
5 to 11 years...................	9.7	12.2	At least 1 related or unrelated adult (not a parent)...	8.0	15.7
12 to 17 years..................	9.4	12.7	DISABILTY STATUS [4]		
RACE AND ETHNICITY			With a disability..................................	38.2	46.1
Single race [1]			Without a disability...............................	5.2	6.4
White.........................	7.9	10.5	HEALTH INSURANCE COVERAGE [5]		
Black or African American.......	9.1	10.7	Private...	6.1	9.0
American Indian or Alaska Native...	10.3	(B)	Medicaid or other public...........................	11.2	11.5
Asian........................	3.3	8.5	Other..	7.4	13.6
Hispanic or Latino [2].............	7.7	8.9	Uninsured..	4.4	5.4
Not Hispanic or Latino...........	7.9	10.2			

B Estimate is considered unreliable. [1] Persons indicating a single race group only, and includes those of Hispanic or Latino origin. [2] Persons of Hispanic or Latino origin may be of any race or combination of races. [3] Refers to parents living in the household. "Parent" can include biological, adoptive, or step. Legal guardians and foster relationships are classified in "At least 1 related or unrelated adult (not a parent)." [4] Based on questions asking the level of difficulty the child has with various types of activities and skills indicating a physical, learning, emotional, or behavioral disability. See source for more information. [5] Based on a hierarchy of mutually exclusive categories. Children with more than one type of health insurance were assigned to the first appropriate category in the following hierarchy: private, Medicaid or other public, other coverage, or uninsured. "Uninsured" includes children with no coverage, with only Indian Health Service coverage, or with only a private plan that paid for one type of service such as dental or vision care. [6] The NHIS switched data collection from personal visits to telephone mode during the COVID-19 pandemic. For more information, see *Technical Notes for Interactive Summary Health Statistics—2019-2020: National Health Interview Survey* at <wwwn.cdc.gov/NHISDataQueryTool/SHS_child/SHS_Tech_Notes.pdf>.

Source: U.S. National Center for Health Statistics, National Health Interview Survey, "Interactive Summary Health Statistics for Children, 2019-2020," <www.cdc.gov/nchs/nhis/shs.htm>, accessed May 2022.

Table 233. Autism Spectrum Disorder Among Children Age 8: 2000 to 2018

[Covers children age 8. Data are from the Centers for Disease Control and Prevention's Autism and Developmental Disabilities Monitoring (ADDM) Network. The ADDM network collects data from health, special education, or administrative or billing records of children living in communities that identify and treat or provide services to children with autism spectrum disorder (ASD). The ADDM method is population-based; the network attempts to identify all children with ASD from the entire population of children within each geographic area. The ADDM is not a representative sample of the United States. More information is available at <www.cdc.gov/ncbddd/autism/addm.html>]

Year	Number of ADDM sites reporting data	Birth year of children	Prevalence of ASD per 1,000 children	Approximate prevalence (1 child in X children)	2018	
					Sex and race/ethnicity	Prevalence of ASD per 1,000 children
2000.......	6	1992	6.7	1 in 150	By sex:	
2006.......	11	1998	9.0	1 in 110	Male..........................	36.5
2008.......	14	2000	11.3	1 in 88	Female........................	8.8
2010.......	11	2002	14.7	1 in 68	By race/ethnicity:	
2012.......	11	2004	14.5	1 in 69	White, non-Hispanic...........	21.2
2014.......	11	2006	16.8	1 in 59	Black, non-Hispanic...........	22.3
2016.......	11	2008	18.5	1 in 54	Asian/Pacific Islander, non-Hispanic...	22.2
2018.......	11	2010	23.0	1 in 44	Hispanic......................	22.5

Source: U.S. Centers for Disease Control and Prevention, "Data & Statistics on Autism Spectrum Disorder," <www.cdc.gov/ncbddd/autism/data.html>, accessed April 2022; and Maenner, Matthew J. et al., *Prevalence and Characteristics of Autism Spectrum Disorder Among Children Aged 8 Years — Autism and Developmental Disabilities Monitoring Network, 11 Sites, United States, 2018*, Morbidity and Mortality Weekly Report, Surveillance Summaries, Vol 70:11, December 3, 2021. See also <www.cdc.gov/ncbddd/autism/new-data.html>.

Table 234. High School Students Who Had a Concussion by Sex, Race/Ethnicity, and Grade: 2017 and 2019

[In percent. Based on the Youth Risk Behavior Survey. Covers students reporting having a concussion one or more times in the past 12 months from playing a sport or being physically active. Survey defined concussion as a blow or jolt to the head that causes problems such as headaches, dizziness, being dazed or confused, difficulty remembering or concentrating, vomiting, blurred vision, or being knocked out]

Characteristic	2017			2019		
	Total	Male	Female	Total	Male	Female
Total........................	**15.1**	**17.1**	**13.0**	**15.1**	**17.0**	**13.3**
Race/ethnicity:						
Asian, non-Hispanic.................	13.0	11.9	14.0	10.2	11.0	9.4
Black, non-Hispanic.................	17.0	20.0	13.9	16.7	19.0	14.5
White, non-Hispanic.................	14.6	16.7	12.6	15.2	16.7	13.6
Multiple race, non-Hispanic..........	14.0	19.0	9.6	13.9	15.0	12.9
Hispanic...........................	14.9	16.5	13.5	14.7	16.9	12.5
Grade:						
9th...............................	17.0	18.6	15.5	15.8	18.2	13.3
10th..............................	15.2	18.6	11.9	14.4	15.2	13.7
11th..............................	15.3	17.1	13.6	16.1	17.9	14.3
12th..............................	12.2	13.9	10.5	13.8	16.6	11.2

Source: U.S. Centers for Disease Control and Prevention, Youth Risk Behavior Surveillance System, "Youth Online Data Analysis Tool," <www.cdc.gov/healthyyouth/data/yrbs/index.htm>, accessed July 2021.

Table 235. Immunization of Children Born in 2017 and 2018 by Vaccine Type and State: 2018 to 2020

[In percent. Data cover children born in 2017 and 2018 who received the recommended doses of each vaccine by age 24 months, except as noted. Based on estimates from the National Immunization Survey (NIS), which includes a survey of the parents and guardians of children age 19-35 months, and a survey of health care providers of the children to verify and/or complete vaccination information. Please note that beginning with the *Morbidity and Mortality Weekly Report* published in October 2019, child vaccination data are reported by birth year of children; previously, data were reported by survey year. Data for the 2017 birth year are from survey years 2018-2020; data for birth year 2018 are considered preliminary and come from survey years 2019-2020. Abbreviations: DTaP = diphtheria and tetanus toxoids, and pertussis vaccine; MMR = measles, mumps, and rubella vaccine; HepB = hepatitis B vaccine; HepA = hepatitis A vaccine; Hib = Haemophilus influenzae type b vaccine; PCV = pneumococcal conjugate vaccine]

State	DTaP, ≥3 doses [1]	DTaP, ≥4 doses [1]	Polio, ≥3 doses	MMR, ≥1 dose [2]	Hib, primary series [3]	Hib, full series [3]	HepB, birth dose [4]	HepB, ≥3 doses	Vari-cella, ≥1 dose	PCV, ≥3 doses	PCV, ≥4 doses	HepA, ≥2 doses [5]	Rota-virus [6]	Com-bined series [7]
U.S.....	93.7	81.6	92.7	91.6	92.9	80.2	78.4	91.9	90.9	92.4	82.3	77.7	75.6	70.5
AL......	95.0	81.5	93.6	93.2	92.4	80.2	78.5	91.9	91.6	94.1	85.5	67.6	72.9	72.1
AK......	89.6	74.3	88.5	86.8	88.7	78.4	70.6	89.0	82.7	85.8	74.7	72.1	62.5	61.2
AZ......	94.6	85.7	94.3	93.8	95.3	81.2	88.5	93.4	93.5	93.4	81.0	77.2	76.6	74.0
AR.....	91.4	71.8	90.8	89.5	90.6	77.4	81.0	93.2	89.6	90.1	79.0	74.5	73.4	66.5
CA.....	94.4	84.0	93.5	89.4	93.0	78.4	76.2	91.3	89.3	93.0	82.1	80.6	76.1	68.6
CO.....	95.5	81.4	95.0	91.8	94.8	82.4	80.3	91.6	90.0	95.1	84.3	79.0	84.1	70.6
CT.....	95.3	88.7	95.3	94.6	95.1	89.3	82.4	92.9	92.9	94.4	91.6	88.7	84.4	81.6
DE.....	95.3	84.5	94.6	91.4	95.7	84.9	81.8	92.0	90.7	95.4	86.0	81.3	81.3	77.1
DC.....	93.7	85.2	92.4	92.7	93.0	78.4	80.4	91.5	91.7	93.1	84.0	83.1	80.7	71.4
FL......	94.2	84.5	92.4	92.8	93.6	80.1	62.2	92.0	92.5	92.2	81.6	69.6	71.3	69.2
GA.....	92.8	74.9	91.1	89.1	91.4	75.0	78.3	92.7	88.7	91.2	78.6	70.4	70.4	65.5
HI......	92.0	77.2	90.3	88.0	91.0	78.8	82.7	90.4	86.8	90.9	78.8	78.3	74.7	72.0
ID......	94.4	82.0	92.3	91.6	92.5	80.1	71.4	94.0	88.2	93.0	84.6	82.1	80.7	71.9
IL......	94.4	81.6	93.9	91.4	93.4	78.6	77.5	93.3	90.8	92.6	82.4	71.5	75.4	70.6
IN......	92.8	78.7	91.1	88.2	91.8	75.3	80.7	92.1	88.5	91.8	81.0	76.9	75.1	68.1
IA......	95.1	81.4	95.0	94.0	93.6	85.9	83.3	95.4	92.8	92.0	85.2	82.6	72.0	73.8
KS.....	94.6	79.0	94.4	93.5	91.8	81.8	79.9	95.3	92.5	93.3	85.3	85.2	80.3	71.2
KY.....	92.3	82.6	92.3	89.2	91.8	82.5	79.8	89.8	88.9	90.8	81.1	78.5	71.9	72.6
LA.....	90.9	75.7	90.5	92.9	92.4	76.1	77.8	92.9	92.1	89.9	78.8	69.8	68.2	64.3
ME.....	94.6	86.2	94.2	92.4	94.2	84.6	72.9	91.1	91.3	92.8	84.5	76.2	77.2	75.8
MD.....	95.3	83.9	94.7	94.0	95.1	84.4	80.1	94.2	94.3	95.2	86.1	80.3	81.2	75.5
MA.....	96.2	88.8	96.2	96.4	97.0	88.3	82.9	94.4	94.2	95.1	87.5	84.2	80.6	79.8
MI......	94.6	83.9	93.4	94.3	94.5	82.0	82.5	94.1	94.0	93.3	84.1	82.3	75.0	73.3
MN.....	94.6	81.2	92.9	92.7	94.8	83.1	80.6	94.6	92.8	93.7	83.3	82.4	79.6	73.0
MS.....	94.4	81.2	93.3	90.6	93.8	80.7	78.8	92.1	88.7	93.5	81.0	60.8	68.4	70.9
MO.....	93.1	80.0	92.2	91.9	93.4	79.4	83.4	93.2	91.9	91.6	81.6	72.9	77.6	73.1
MT.....	95.0	75.6	94.0	91.2	91.9	80.9	77.2	93.6	87.5	91.3	81.4	73.9	70.8	65.3
NE.....	95.2	85.3	94.2	93.0	93.8	83.1	84.0	93.7	92.1	93.4	85.9	81.4	79.5	77.7
NV.....	92.8	78.9	91.3	89.9	91.1	79.8	76.9	90.8	90.3	90.5	77.8	80.3	71.6	67.5
NH.....	97.1	89.1	96.8	95.4	96.3	90.5	83.8	95.3	95.2	96.8	92.6	85.7	87.7	78.6
NJ.....	92.9	78.4	92.3	89.6	92.5	78.9	77.8	91.7	90.0	92.1	82.5	72.7	74.0	68.7
NM.....	94.1	79.4	93.6	95.0	91.4	79.7	74.6	92.6	93.2	93.0	79.9	79.2	77.9	67.1
NY.....	95.3	84.1	94.2	94.6	92.7	82.1	77.1	91.2	92.7	93.0	82.4	78.1	75.0	71.3
NC.....	93.6	83.8	93.6	92.5	94.0	85.6	82.0	93.6	93.0	92.7	86.5	76.7	79.4	75.9
ND.....	94.4	82.2	94.1	95.7	95.3	85.6	85.6	94.5	92.7	95.0	84.4	82.9	81.1	74.1
OH.....	89.8	77.4	88.3	85.6	88.6	77.9	80.7	91.6	85.6	88.1	79.2	79.7	73.2	68.1
OK.....	90.6	75.6	89.7	88.9	91.1	78.6	77.0	88.1	87.5	88.8	79.3	73.9	69.6	66.3
OR.....	94.2	82.9	93.7	94.5	92.4	79.2	81.5	90.4	93.3	91.3	80.0	81.0	76.8	71.1
PA.....	95.2	85.9	94.3	93.9	94.0	84.8	85.5	94.9	93.7	93.7	84.4	83.9	78.5	77.4
RI......	96.1	88.7	96.4	94.5	95.5	86.5	81.7	96.8	94.9	96.9	89.7	82.7	86.2	77.2
SC.....	93.5	78.2	92.8	90.6	93.1	76.6	76.5	91.9	90.4	92.3	82.7	82.1	76.3	68.3
SD.....	96.5	81.7	95.8	94.1	96.3	80.9	84.3	94.8	93.2	95.7	86.2	79.4	79.5	73.4
TN.....	94.4	79.8	93.4	91.7	94.1	82.9	74.0	95.0	92.3	93.9	82.0	84.4	75.9	69.3
TX.....	91.5	77.4	90.6	90.9	91.2	76.0	79.8	88.0	89.6	91.4	79.9	78.0	74.3	65.9
UT.....	94.2	84.8	94.1	91.5	94.2	83.5	79.5	94.6	91.3	94.1	83.6	87.7	83.0	75.8
VT.....	95.0	86.7	92.7	93.9	93.3	86.8	67.2	91.9	91.1	92.6	88.4	76.3	75.6	79.6
VA.....	91.8	79.6	89.4	90.8	91.3	79.9	77.4	88.9	88.9	90.1	83.2	76.5	76.1	70.8
WA.....	95.5	86.5	93.4	93.9	94.3	84.5	77.9	90.4	92.4	94.3	83.9	76.8	77.7	72.9
WV.....	94.5	83.3	94.8	89.6	93.8	80.3	82.6	94.4	89.4	92.7	82.0	80.1	76.0	73.0
WI......	93.3	80.3	91.3	91.1	92.3	80.3	81.5	90.2	89.8	92.5	81.5	66.8	76.7	68.9
WY.....	93.0	76.6	91.3	91.4	93.1	80.4	80.9	91.3	90.2	90.7	80.0	66.2	74.9	68.9

[1] Includes children who might have received diphtheria and tetanus toxoids vaccine or diphtheria, tetanus toxoids, and pertussis vaccine. [2] Includes children who might have received measles, mumps, rubella, and varicella combination vaccine. [3] Hib primary series: receipt of ≥2 or ≥3 doses, depending on product type received. Full series (by age 24 months): primary series and booster dose, which includes receipt of ≥3 or ≥4 doses, depending on product type received. [4] HepB administered from birth through age 3 days. [5] ≥2 doses of Hepatitis A vaccine administered by age 35 months. [6] ≥2 or ≥3 doses of Rotavirus vaccine, depending on product type received, administered through age 8 months. [7] The combined 7 vaccine series (4:3:1:3*:3:1:4) includes ≥4 doses of DTaP, ≥3 doses of poliovirus vaccine, ≥1 dose of measles-containing vaccine, full series of Hib vaccine (≥3 or ≥4 doses, depending on product type), ≥3 doses of HepB, ≥1 dose of varicella vaccine, and ≥4 doses of PCV.

Source: U.S. Centers for Disease Control and Prevention, Immunization Managers, Hill, Holly A. et al, "Vaccination Coverage by Age 24 Months Among Children Born in 2017 and 2018 — National Immunization Survey-Child, United States, 2018-2020," *Morbidity and Mortality Weekly Report,* 70:41, October 15, 2021; and "ChildVaxView Interactive!," <www.cdc.gov/vaccines/imz-managers/coverage/childvaxview/index.html>, accessed February 2022.

Table 236. Immunization of Children Born in 2017 and 2018 by Vaccine, Race/Ethnicity, Poverty Status, and Health Insurance Coverage: 2018 to 2020

[In percent. Data cover children born in 2017 and 2018 who received the recommended doses of each vaccine by age 24 months, except as noted. Based on estimates from the National Immunization Survey (NIS), which includes a survey of the parents and guardians of children age 19-35 months, and a survey of health care providers of the children to verify and/or complete vaccination information. See headnote, Table 235. Abbreviations: DTaP = diphtheria and tetanus toxoids, and pertussis vaccine; MMR = measles, mumps, and rubella vaccine; HepB = hepatitis B vaccine; HepA = hepatitis A vaccine; Hib = Haemophilus influenzae type b vaccine; PCV = pneumococcal conjugate vaccine]

| Vaccination | Total [1] | Race/ethnicity [2] | | | | Poverty [3] | | Health insurance | | |
		White	Black	His-panic	Asian	At or above poverty	Below poverty	Private only	Any Med-icaid	Unin-sured
DTaP, ≥3 doses [4]	93.7	95.0	91.3	92.8	96.3	95.2	90.5	96.3	92.1	85.1
DTaP, ≥4 doses [4]	81.6	84.4	76.1	79.1	86.0	84.5	74.6	87.7	77.7	61.9
Poliovirus, ≥3 doses	92.7	93.8	90.4	91.9	96.1	94.1	89.5	95.4	91.0	83.9
MMR, ≥1 dose [5]	91.6	93.2	89.1	89.5	94.6	92.9	88.0	94.4	89.8	82.3
Hib, Primary series [6]	92.9	94.0	91.0	92.0	96.2	94.7	89.4	95.8	91.2	82.4
Hib, Full series [6]	80.2	83.7	75.4	76.3	85.6	84.1	72.6	86.8	75.8	61.5
HepB, birth dose [7]	78.4	77.2	75.8	81.1	82.9	78.4	78.9	79.4	78.1	76.5
HepB, ≥ 3 doses	91.9	92.8	91.3	90.6	94.3	93.2	89.4	93.6	91.0	84.4
Varicella (chickenpox), ≥1 dose [5]	90.9	92.2	89.3	89.2	94.2	92.1	88.0	93.3	89.6	78.2
PCV, ≥3 doses	92.4	93.6	89.9	91.6	95.4	94.1	88.9	95.3	90.7	83.1
PCV, ≥4 doses	82.3	85.5	76.4	79.6	85.1	85.6	75.3	89.2	77.7	62.2
HepA, ≥1 dose	87.0	87.3	84.9	87.3	91.0	88.4	84.1	89.2	85.9	72.8
HepA, ≥2 doses by age 35 months	77.7	77.6	75.7	78.5	84.9	80.0	71.9	82.4	74.9	(NA)
Rotavirus [8]	75.6	79.4	66.6	72.9	80.7	79.6	66.9	84.7	68.8	55.7
Influenza, ≥ 2 doses [9]	60.6	66.1	45.5	56.9	74.7	66.7	46.7	74.2	49.9	36.4
Combined series [10]	70.5	74.7	64.7	66.3	74.2	74.7	62.5	78.3	65.6	48.3
No vaccinations	1.0	1.0	1.2	0.7	(NA)	0.9	0.9	0.8	1.0	3.3

NA Not available. [1] Includes other racial/ethnic and health insurance coverage categories not shown separately. [2] Children identified as White, Black, and Asian are Non-Hispanic. Children of Hispanic origin may be any race. [3] Poverty level based on 2017-2019 U.S. Census Bureau poverty thresholds. [4] Includes diphtheria and tetanus toxoids vaccine; or diphtheria, tetanus toxoids, and pertussis vaccine. [5] May include measles, mumps, rubella, and varicella vaccine. [6] Hib primary series: receipt of ≥2 or ≥3 doses, depending on product type. Full series: primary series and booster dose, which includes receipt of ≥3 or ≥4 doses, depending on product type. [7] One dose given from birth through age 3 days. [8] Includes ≥2 doses of Rotarix monovalent rotavirus vaccine, or ≥3 doses of RotaTeq pentavalent rotavirus vaccine (RV5). Maximum age for the final dose is 8 months. [9] Doses must be at least 24 days apart, and could be received during two influenza seasons. [10] The combined 7 vaccine series (4:3:1:3*:3:1:4) includes ≥4 doses of DTaP, ≥3 doses of poliovirus vaccine, ≥1 dose of measles-containing vaccine, Hib full series vaccine (≥3 or ≥4 doses, depending on product type), ≥3 doses of HepB, ≥1 dose of varicella vaccine, and ≥4 doses of PCV.

Source: U.S. Centers for Disease Control and Prevention, Immunization Managers, Hill, Holly A. et al, "Vaccination Coverage by Age 24 Months Among Children Born in 2017 and 2018 — National Immunization Survey-Child, United States, 2018-2020," *Morbidity and Mortality Weekly Report,* 70:41, October 15, 2021. See also <www.cdc.gov/vaccines/imz-managers/coverage/childvaxview/pubs-presentations.html>.

Table 237. Asthma Incidence Among Children Under Age 18 by Selected Characteristics: 2019 and 2020

[In percent. Based on the National Health Interview Survey (NHIS), a household survey of a sample of the civilian noninstitutionalized population. Based on the questions: "Has a doctor or other health professional ever told you that [child's name] had asthma?" and "Does [child's name] still have asthma?" Estimates are based on responses about the sample child, not all children in the family. Unknowns were not included in the denominators when calculating percentages. The NHIS questionnaire was redesigned in 2019. Due to changes in weighting and design methodology, direct comparisons between estimates for 2019 and beyond to earlier years should be made with caution, as the impact of these changes has not been fully evaluated at this time]

| Characteristic | Ever told had asthma | | Still have asthma | |
	2019	2020 [3]	2019	2020 [3]
Total	**10.5**	**9.4**	**7.0**	**5.8**
SEX				
Male	12.5	10.4	8.4	5.7
Female	8.5	8.5	5.5	6.0
AGE				
4 years and under	3.2	3.7	2.6	2.0
5 to 11 years	11.9	8.9	8.3	5.9
12 to 17 years	14.8	14.4	8.9	8.6
RACE/ETHNICITY				
Single race: [1]				
White	9.4	8.8	5.9	5.2
Black or African American	17.5	11.1	13.5	8.9
American Indian or Alaska Native	(B)	(B)	(B)	(B)
Asian	7.0	7.7	4.2	3.2
Native Hawaiian or Other Pacific Islander	(B)	(B)	(B)	(B)
Hispanic or Latino [2]	10.0	9.8	6.7	5.6
Not Hispanic or Latino	10.7	9.3	7.1	5.9

B Estimate is considered unreliable. [1] Persons indicating a single race group only, and includes those of Hispanic or Latino origin. [2] Persons of Hispanic or Latino origin may be of any race or combination of races. [3] The NHIS switched data collection from personal visits to telephone mode during the coronavirus disease 2019 (COVID-19) pandemic. For more information, see *Technical Notes for Interactive Summary Health Statistics—2019-2020: National Health Interview Survey* (online at <wwwn.cdc.gov/NHISDataQueryTool/SHS_child/SHS_Tech_Notes.pdf>).

Source: U.S. National Center for Health Statistics, National Health Interview Survey, "Interactive Summary Health Statistics for Children, 2019-2020," <www.cdc.gov/nchs/nhis/shs.htm>, accessed May 2022.

Table 238. Child Obesity by Age, Sex, and Race/Ethnicity: 1976 to 2018

[In percent. For children age 6 to 17. Data are from U.S. National Center for Health Statistics, National Health and Nutrition Examination Surveys, a program of studies that combines interviews and physical examinations to assess the health and nutritional status of adults and children. Children classified as obese have a body mass index (BMI) at or above the 95th percentile]

Selected characteristic	1976 to 1980	1988 to 1994	1999 to 2002	2003 to 2006	2007 to 2010	2011 to 2014	2015 to 2018
Total [1]	**5.7**	**11.2**	**16.0**	**17.3**	**18.6**	**19.5**	**20.0**
RACE AND HISPANIC ORIGIN							
White, non-Hispanic	4.9	10.5	13.2	15.5	16.0	17.1	15.4
Black, non-Hispanic	8.2	14.0	20.7	21.5	24.0	22.5	25.9
Asian, non-Hispanic	(NA)	(NA)	(NA)	(NA)	(NA)	9.8	11.4
Hispanic origin [2,3]	(NA)	(NA)	(NA)	(NA)	23.7	24.3	27.4
Mexican-American [2,3]	(NA)	15.4	23.0	22.7	23.8	25.2	29.6
SEX AND AGE							
Male	5.5	11.8	17.2	18.1	20.4	18.9	21.3
Female	5.8	10.6	14.7	16.3	16.7	20.0	18.7
Ages 6 to 11	6.5	11.3	15.8	17.0	18.8	17.5	19.3
Male	6.7	11.6	16.9	18.0	20.7	17.6	20.9
Female	6.4	11.0	14.7	15.8	16.9	17.5	17.7
Ages 12 to 17	4.9	11.1	16.1	17.5	18.4	21.3	20.7
Male	4.5	12.0	17.5	18.2	20.1	20.1	21.7
Female	5.4	10.2	14.7	16.8	16.6	22.5	19.6

NA Not available. [1] Includes other races not shown separately. [2] Persons of Hispanic and Mexican origin may be of any race. [3] From 1976 to 2006, the survey sample was designed to provide estimates specifically for persons of Mexican origin. Beginning in 2007, the survey allows for reporting of both total Hispanics and Mexican Americans.

Source: Federal Interagency Forum on Child and Family Statistics, "America's Children: Key National Indicators of Well-Being, 2021," <www.childstats.gov/index.asp>, accessed July 2022.

Table 239. High School Students Engaged in Physical Activity by Sex: 2019

[In percent. For students in grades 9 to 12. Based on the Youth Risk Behavior Survey, a biennial survey of students in grades 9-12 conducted in public and private schools, and subject to sampling error; see source for details]

Characteristic	No physical activity for 60+ min. on any day [1]	Physically active for 60+ min. on 5 of last 7 days [2]	Physically active for 60+ min. on all 7 days [2]	Played on at least one sports team [3]	Attended physical education class [4] Total	Attended physical education class [4] Attended daily	Used computers 3 or more hours/ day [5]	Watched TV 3 or more hours/ day [6]
All students	**17.0**	**44.1**	**23.2**	**57.4**	**52.2**	**25.9**	**46.1**	**19.8**
Male	**14.4**	**52.8**	**30.9**	**60.2**	**55.4**	**28.9**	**47.5**	**18.7**
Grade 9	12.6	55.8	34.7	62.3	69.7	36.5	48.5	18.8
Grade 10	14.4	53.9	30.4	61.2	55.8	30.3	48.6	19.5
Grade 11	14.3	50.6	29.5	62.6	48.6	24.4	45.2	17.6
Grade 12	16.3	50.5	28.7	54.3	46.0	23.7	47.7	18.7
Female	**19.6**	**35.3**	**15.4**	**54.6**	**48.6**	**22.8**	**44.6**	**20.8**
Grade 9	14.5	42.0	19.2	61.5	68.0	32.8	44.3	21.3
Grade 10	17.2	37.2	15.4	54.8	48.4	22.5	45.1	22.6
Grade 11	23.7	31.7	15.0	55.5	40.6	19.7	45.5	19.2
Grade 12	23.0	29.7	11.7	45.6	36.7	15.6	43.1	19.7

[1] Did not participate in 60 or more minutes in any physical activity that increased their heart rate and made them breathe hard some of the time for at least 1 day during the 7 days before the survey. [2] Did any kind of physical activity that increased their heart rate and made them breathe hard some of the time, during the 7 days before the survey. [3] Any team run by the school or community groups, during the 12 months before the survey. [4] In an average week when student was in school. [5] Includes time spent playing games, watching videos, texting, or using social media on their smartphone, computer, Xbox, PlayStation, iPad, or other device, for something unrelated to school, on an average school day. [6] On an average school day.

Source: U.S. Centers for Disease Control and Prevention, Youth Risk Behavior Surveillance System (YRBSS), "YRBS Explorer," <www.cdc.gov/healthyyouth/data/yrbs/index.htm>, accessed August 2020.

Table 240. High School Student Use of Tobacco and Nicotine Products by Sex and Race/Ethnicity: 2021

[In percent, except as noted (2,060 represents 2,060,000). Data represent current use of tobacco and nicotine products, defined as use within the past 30 days. Data are based on the National Youth Tobacco Survey, administered to students in public and private middle schools (grade 6-8) and high schools (grades 9-12). During the COVID-19 pandemic, the 2021 survey was administered online. Reported tobacco use might differ by survey setting and thus the 2021 results cannot be directly compared with previous survey results that were primarily conducted on school campuses. The 2021 results are based on responses from 20,413 students attending 279 schools, from a sample of 25,149 students at 508 sampled schools. Results are weighted to represent 11.97 million middle schools students and 15.44 million high school students]

Tobacco and nicotine product	Total Number [1] (1,000)	Total Percent	Sex Male	Sex Female	Race and ethnicity White, non-Hispanic	Race and ethnicity Black, non-Hispanic	Race and ethnicity Other race, non-Hispanic	Race and ethnicity Hispanic [2]
Use of any tobacco product [3]	**2,060**	**13.4**	**13.0**	**13.8**	**16.2**	**11.0**	**9.3**	**9.1**
Electronic cigarettes (vaping)	1,720	11.3	10.7	11.9	14.5	5.9	7.4	7.6
Cigarettes	280	1.9	2.0	1.8	2.2	(B)	(B)	1.6
Cigars	310	2.1	2.6	1.5	2.1	4.4	(B)	1.2
Smokeless tobacco [4]	170	1.2	1.7	(B)	1.5	(B)	(B)	(B)
Hookah	180	1.2	1.2	1.3	0.8	3.2	(B)	1.3
Nicotine pouch	160	1.1	1.6	0.6	1.4	(B)	(B)	(B)
Pipe tobacco	60	0.4	(B)	(B)	0.5	(B)	(B)	(B)
Two or more tobacco products	580	3.8	4.5	3.1	4.4	4.0	(B)	2.6

B Statistically unreliable. Sample size less than 50 or relative standard error greater than 0.3. [1] Estimates are rounded down to nearest 10,000. [2] Persons of Hispanic origin may be of any race. [3] Includes use of bidis and heated tobacco products, not shown separately. [4] Includes chewing tobacco, snuff, dip, snus, and dissolvable tobacco.

Source: U.S. Centers for Disease Control and Prevention, Gentzke, Andrea S. et al., "Tobacco Product Use and Associated Factors Among Middle and High School Students — National Youth Tobacco Survey, United States, 2021," *Morbidity and Mortality Weekly Report,* Vol. 71:5, March 11, 2022. See also <www.cdc.gov/tobacco/data_statistics/fact_sheets/youth_data/tobacco_use/index.htm>.

Table 241. Depression and Receipt of Mental Health Treatment in the Past Year Among Youth Age 12 to 17 by Selected Characteristics: 2005 to 2020

[In percent. Data are from the National Survey on Drug Use and Health. Covers youth age 12 to 17 who had a major depressive episode (MDE) as defined in the 5th edition of the *Diagnostic and Statistical Manual of Mental Disorders* (DSM-5), which specifies a period of at least 2 weeks when a person experienced a depressed mood or loss of interest or pleasure in daily activities and had a majority of specified depression symptoms. Treatment is defined as seeing or talking to a medical doctor or other professional, or using prescription medication in the past year for depression. Respondents with unknown incidence of major depressive episode and unknown treatment data were excluded]

Characteristic	Youth with major depressive episode (MDE)				Youth with an MDE receiving treatment for depression			
	2005	2010	2019	2020 [4]	2005	2010	2019	2020 [4]
Total [1].........	**8.8**	**8.0**	**15.7**	**17.0**	**37.8**	**37.8**	**43.3**	**41.6**
AGE								
12 to 13 years old.........	5.2	4.3	10.5	11.2	32.9	32.5	37.5	(B)
14 to 15 years old.........	9.5	9.0	16.4	18.2	41.1	38.4	43.9	41.5
16 to 17 years old.........	11.5	10.6	20.1	21.9	37.1	39.3	45.6	40.0
SEX								
Male.........	4.5	4.4	8.8	9.2	34.1	32.0	36.8	39.7
Female.........	13.3	11.9	23.0	25.2	39.0	40.1	45.8	42.4
RACE ETHNICITY								
White, non-Hispanic.........	9.1	8.6	15.9	18.7	39.3	41.1	50.3	49.1
Black, non-Hispanic.........	7.6	6.8	11.4	12.9	39.3	23.0	35.6	(B)
American Indian or Alaska Native.........	6.1	7.4	12.2	(B)	(NA)	(NA)	(NA)	(NA)
Asian.........	6.0	5.5	15.1	13.9	(NA)	(NA)	(NA)	(NA)
Two or more races.........	10.5	9.4	20.9	29.9	(NA)	(NA)	(NA)	(NA)
Hispanic [2].........	9.1	7.8	17.3	15.7	31.8	38.4	37.9	36.8
POVERTY STATUS [3]								
Below 100% poverty.........	8.1	7.2	14.0	12.4	37.3	33.8	42.6	(B)
100-199% poverty.........	9.6	9.0	16.0	17.7	32.1	39.1	42.1	32.4
200% poverty and above.........	8.7	7.9	16.2	18.2	40.1	38.4	43.9	46.0

B Data do not meet statistical standards for reliability of a derived figure. NA Not available. [1] Total includes persons of other races, not shown separately. [2] Persons of Hispanic origin may be of any race. [3] Estimates are based on a definition of poverty level that incorporates information on family income, size, and composition and is calculated as a percentage of the U.S. Census Bureau's poverty thresholds. [4] Caution should be used when comparing estimates between 2020 and prior years because of methodological changes for 2020 during the coronavirus disease 2019 (COVID-19) pandemic. See source for details.

Source: U.S. Substance Abuse and Mental Health Services Administration, *Results From the 2020 National Survey on Drug Use and Health: Detailed Tables,* October 2021; see also <www.samhsa.gov/data/data-we-collect/nsduh-national-survey-drug-use-and-health>. Prior to 2016, Federal Interagency Forum on Child and Family Statistics, "America's Children: Key National Indicators of Well-Being, 2017," <www.childstats.gov>, accessed July 2017, and previous editions.

Table 242. Foodborne Disease Outbreaks and Illnesses by Etiology, Food Category, and Location of Food Preparation: 2017

[Data reported as of February 6, 2019. Foodborne disease outbreaks are a nationally notifiable condition. An outbreak involves 2 or more cases of a similar illness resulting from consuming a common food. Public health agencies in all 50 States, D.C., and the U.S. territories voluntarily submit reports of foodborne disease outbreaks that their agencies investigate. Excludes outbreaks on cruise ships that dock in U.S. and international ports and those in which food was eaten outside the U.S. Not all outbreaks are identified, investigated, or reported. Data are subject to change. See source for other limitations]

Item	Out-breaks	Ill-nesses	Hospital-izations	Item	Out-breaks	Ill-nesses
Total [1].........	841	14,481	827	By food category:		
By etiology (cause): [2]				Aquatic animals.........	86	468
Bacterial [1].........	271	5,380	670	Land animals [1].........	83	1,996
Salmonella.........	122	3,061	478	Dairy.........	14	85
Clostridium perfringens.........	41	843	1	Eggs.........	5	81
Campylobacter.........	23	147	14	Beef.........	19	329
Escherichia coli (E. coli) [3].........	21	521	113	Pork.........	13	376
Vibrio parahaemolyticus.........	17	70	4	Chicken.........	23	487
Staphylococcus aureus.........	12	128	0	Turkey.........	4	609
Bacillus cereus.........	11	341	2	Plant products.........	45	1,339
Chemical and toxin [4].........	40	156	6	Other [5].........	627	10,921
Parasitic.........	13	155	5	By location of food preparation:		
Cyclospora.........	7	99	4	Restaurant.........	489	5,533
Cryptosporidium.........	3	35	1	Catering or banquet facility.........	104	3,584
Viral [1].........	325	6,393	67	Private home.........	74	989
Norovirus.........	316	6,340	53	Institutional location.........	24	1,015
Hepatitis A.........	5	35	14	Grocery store.........	13	105
Other [5].........	192	2,397	79	Hospital or nursing home.........	11	239

[1] Includes other categories not shown separately. [2] Includes both confirmed and suspected etiologies. [3] E. coli that produce shiga toxins, known as Shiga toxin-producing E. coli (STEC). These bacteria are also called verocytotoxic-producing E. coli and enterohemorrhagic E. coli. [4] Includes cases involving scombroid toxin/histamine, ciguatoxin, mycotoxins, paralytic and neurotoxic shellfish poison, and other not specified. [5] Other includes incidents that involved multiple categories and unknown or not reported categories.

Source: U.S. Centers for Disease Control and Prevention, *Surveillance for Foodborne Disease Outbreaks, United States, 2017: Annual Report,* 2019. See also <www.cdc.gov/fdoss/index.html>.

Table 243. Fruit and Vegetable Availability for Consumption Per Capita by Commodity: 1980 to 2019

[In pounds, farm weight. Available supply of fresh fruits and vegetables at the farm level or early stage of processing for domestic consumption after subtracting measurable uses such as farm inputs (feed and seed), exports, ending stocks, and industrial uses. Food availability is a proxy for actual food consumption. Based on Census Bureau estimated resident population plus Armed Forces overseas for most commodities]

Commodity	1980	1990	2000	2005	2010	2015	2017	2018	2019
Fruits and vegetables, total [1]	**604.8**	**662.7**	**713.1**	**685.3**	**653.0**	**631.3**	**655.9**	**641.7**	**644.2**
Fruits, total	**266.0**	**271.0**	**288.2**	**270.8**	**255.9**	**251.9**	**252.1**	**240.3**	**236.1**
Fresh fruits	106.4	117.3	128.7	125.3	128.6	136.0	142.1	139.6	138.8
Noncitrus [2]	80.5	95.6	105.3	103.7	107.0	113.3	118.3	115.7	113.1
Apples	19.4	19.8	17.6	16.8	15.4	17.6	18.2	17.0	17.6
Apricots	0.1	0.2	0.2	0.1	0.1	0.1	0.1	0.1	0.1
Avocados	2.1	1.4	2.3	3.5	4.0	7.2	8.1	8.5	7.9
Bananas	20.8	24.3	28.4	25.2	25.6	27.9	28.6	28.3	27.4
Blueberries	0.2	0.1	0.3	0.4	1.1	1.6	1.7	2.0	2.3
Cantaloupes	5.8	9.2	11.1	9.6	8.5	6.8	7.3	7.1	6.1
Cherries	0.7	0.4	0.6	0.9	1.3	1.1	1.5	1.3	1.3
Grapes	4.0	7.9	7.5	8.7	8.0	7.9	8.3	8.1	8.4
Honeydew melons	1.4	2.1	2.3	1.9	1.7	1.7	1.7	1.7	1.4
Kiwifruit	(NA)	0.5	0.6	0.4	0.5	0.6	0.6	0.6	0.7
Mangoes	0.2	0.5	1.8	1.9	2.2	2.6	3.2	3.2	3.3
Papayas	0.2	0.2	0.7	0.9	1.2	1.3	1.4	1.3	1.3
Peaches and nectarines	7.1	5.5	5.3	4.8	4.7	2.9	2.7	2.2	2.1
Pears	2.6	3.3	3.4	2.9	2.9	2.7	2.7	2.9	2.8
Pineapples	1.5	2.0	3.2	4.9	5.7	7.0	7.8	7.8	7.6
Plums and prunes	1.5	1.5	1.2	1.1	0.8	0.6	0.7	0.6	0.6
Raspberries	(NA)	(NA)	0.1	0.1	0.2	0.9	0.9	0.8	0.9
Strawberries	2.0	3.2	4.9	5.8	7.2	7.7	6.8	6.4	5.8
Watermelons	10.7	13.3	13.8	13.5	15.7	14.9	16.2	15.7	15.4
Fresh citrus	25.9	21.7	23.4	21.6	21.6	22.7	23.8	24.0	25.7
Oranges and temples	14.2	12.6	11.6	11.4	9.7	8.7	8.0	8.2	8.5
Tangerines and tangelos	2.1	1.3	2.9	2.5	3.8	5.2	5.8	5.9	6.8
Grapefruit	7.3	4.6	5.1	2.6	2.8	2.2	1.9	1.6	1.4
Lemons	1.9	2.6	2.4	2.9	2.8	3.6	4.3	4.2	4.9
Limes	0.4	0.7	1.4	2.1	2.6	3.0	3.8	4.1	4.1
Processed fruit	159.7	153.6	159.4	145.5	127.3	115.9	109.9	100.7	97.3
Canned fruit [3]	24.6	21.1	17.6	16.7	15.0	14.4	13.4	12.1	12.4
Fruit juice [4]	119.7	115.8	126.5	112.9	97.2	84.8	81.2	80.1	76.3
Frozen fruit [5]	3.3	4.3	4.5	5.2	5.1	5.6	4.7	4.8	4.8
Dried fruit [6]	11.3	12.2	10.5	10.1	9.3	10.2	9.5	3.0	3.1
Vegetables, total	**338.7**	**391.8**	**424.9**	**414.5**	**397.2**	**379.4**	**403.8**	**401.3**	**408.0**
Fresh vegetables [7]	151.8	176.4	200.7	196.4	190.3	186.4	202.8	190.7	195.7
Asparagus	0.3	0.6	1.0	1.1	1.4	1.5	1.6	1.8	1.8
Bell peppers (all uses)	2.9	5.9	8.2	9.2	10.3	10.7	11.3	11.2	11.3
Broccoli	1.4	3.4	5.9	5.3	6.0	7.4	7.1	5.9	6.2
Cabbage	8.0	8.3	8.9	7.8	7.5	6.3	6.2	5.7	6.5
Carrots	6.2	8.3	9.2	8.7	7.8	8.8	7.4	12.2	13.6
Cauliflower	1.1	2.2	1.7	1.8	1.3	1.6	2.4	2.5	3.0
Celery (all uses)	7.4	7.2	6.3	5.9	6.1	5.1	4.7	4.9	5.3
Corn, sweet	6.5	6.7	9.0	8.7	9.2	8.6	7.2	6.8	6.8
Cucumbers	3.9	4.7	6.4	6.2	6.7	7.6	7.4	8.0	8.0
Garlic (all uses)	0.9	1.4	2.2	2.4	2.3	2.4	3.0	2.4	1.9
Kale	(NA)	(NA)	0.4	0.4	0.5	0.6	1.0	1.1	1.1
Lettuce, head	25.6	27.7	23.5	20.9	15.9	13.6	15.2	12.3	12.7
Lettuce, Romaine and leaf	(NA)	3.8	8.4	9.7	12.0	11.9	15.1	12.1	12.4
Mushrooms	1.2	2.0	2.6	2.6	2.6	3.0	3.0	2.8	(NA)
Onions	11.4	15.1	18.9	20.9	19.6	18.3	25.1	20.5	20.4
Potatoes	51.1	46.7	47.1	41.3	36.8	34.2	34.9	33.0	34.2
Pumpkin (all uses)	(NA)	4.4	4.6	4.8	4.4	3.1	6.4	6.3	5.8
Snap beans	1.3	1.1	2.0	1.8	1.9	1.6	1.6	1.6	1.8
Spinach	0.4	0.8	1.4	2.3	1.7	1.7	1.9	1.9	2.5
Squash (all uses)	2.3	3.5	4.4	4.4	4.3	4.6	5.7	5.6	5.9
Sweet potatoes (all uses)	4.4	4.4	4.2	4.5	6.3	7.6	8.0	5.6	7.9
Tomatoes	12.8	15.5	19.0	20.2	20.6	20.6	20.1	20.3	20.3
Processed vegetables	187.0	215.3	224.2	218.0	206.8	193.0	201.1	210.7	212.3
Canned vegetables [8]	102.5	110.3	103.2	104.8	99.4	82.0	84.8	91.1	93.2
Frozen vegetables [9]	51.6	66.7	79.7	76.4	71.0	70.2	73.2	74.2	73.1
Dehydrated vegetables [10]	10.5	14.9	17.3	13.9	13.0	12.9	14.2	13.6	15.4
Chips, potato	16.5	16.3	15.6	16.0	15.0	19.6	17.8	18.1	19.4
Legumes [11]	5.9	7.2	8.5	6.8	8.4	8.3	11.1	13.7	11.1

NA Not available. [1] Excludes wine grapes. [2] Includes other fruits not shown separately. [3] Canned fruit include apples, apricots, cherries, olives, peaches, pears, pineapples, plums, and prunes. [4] Fruit juice includes apple, cranberry, grape, grapefruit, lemon, lime, orange, pineapple, and prune juice. [5] Frozen fruit include apples, apricots, blackberries, blueberries, boysenberries, cherries, loganberries, peaches, plums, prunes, raspberries, strawberries, and other miscellaneous fruit and berries. [6] Dried fruit include apples, apricots, dates, figs, peaches, pears, prunes, and raisins. [7] Includes other vegetables not shown separately. [8] Canned vegetables include asparagus, lima beans, snap beans, beets, cabbage, carrots, sweet corn, cucumbers, mushrooms, green peas, chile peppers, potatoes, spinach, tomatoes, and other miscellaneous vegetables. [9] Frozen vegetables include asparagus, lima beans, snap beans, broccoli, carrots, cauliflower, sweet corn, green peas, potatoes, spinach and other miscellaneous vegetables. [10] Onions and potatoes. [11] Dry peas, beans, and lentils.

Source: U.S. Department of Agriculture, Economic Research Service, "Food Availability (Per Capita) Data System," <www.ers.usda.gov/data-products/food-availability-per-capita-data-system/>, accessed August 2022.

Table 244. Food Availability for Consumption Per Capita by Major Food Commodity: 1980 to 2019

[In pounds, retail weight, except as indicated. Available supply for domestic consumption after subtracting measurable uses, such as farm inputs (feed and seed), exports, ending stocks, and industrial uses. Food availability is a proxy for actual food consumption. Based on Census Bureau estimated resident population plus Armed Forces overseas for most commodities. For commodities not shipped overseas in substantial amounts, such as fluid milk and cream, the resident population is used]

Commodity	Unit	1980	1990	2000	2010	2017	2018	2019
Red meat, total (boneless, trimmed weight) [1]..	Pounds	126.4	112.2	113.7	102.0	102.0	103.0	105.2
Beef.........	Pounds	72.1	63.9	64.5	56.7	54.3	54.6	55.4
Veal.........	Pounds	1.3	0.9	0.5	0.3	0.2	0.2	0.2
Pork.........	Pounds	52.1	46.4	47.8	44.4	46.7	47.4	48.8
Lamb.........	Pounds	1.0	1.0	0.8	0.7	0.8	0.8	0.8
Poultry (boneless, trimmed weight)............	Pounds	40.8	56.3	67.9	70.9	77.1	77.9	79.6
Chicken.........	Pounds	32.7	42.5	54.2	58.0	64.1	65.2	67.0
Turkey.........	Pounds	8.1	13.8	13.7	12.9	13.0	12.8	12.6
Fish and shellfish (boneless, trimmed weight).........	Pounds	12.4	14.9	15.2	15.8	16.1	16.1	(NA)
Eggs.........	Number	271.1	234.1	250.2	246.0	281.9	287.5	292.4
Shell.........	Number	236.2	186.2	178.0	172.1	200.2	204.0	207.1
Processed.........	Number	34.9	47.9	72.2	73.9	81.8	83.5	85.3
Dairy products, total [2].........	Pounds	543.1	568.0	591.1	604.1	644.7	645.8	652.6
Beverage milks [3].........	Gallons	27.6	25.7	22.8	20.6	17.3	16.8	16.4
Plain whole milk.........	Gallons	16.5	10.2	7.8	5.5	5.6	5.7	5.7
Plain reduced-fat milk (2%).........	Gallons	6.3	9.1	7.2	7.2	5.7	5.6	5.4
Plain reduced-fat milk (1%).........	Gallons	1.8	2.3	2.6	2.8	2.4	2.3	2.1
Plain skim milk.........	Gallons	1.3	2.6	3.4	3.1	1.6	1.4	1.2
Flavored whole milk.........	Gallons	0.6	0.3	0.4	0.2	0.2	0.3	0.3
Flavored milk, low-fat and skim............	Gallons	0.6	0.8	1.1	1.5	1.4	1.4	1.3
Buttermilk.........	Gallons	0.5	0.4	0.3	0.2	0.2	0.2	0.2
Yogurt (excl. frozen).........	Gallons	0.3	0.5	0.8	1.6	1.6	1.6	1.5
Sour cream.........	Gallons	0.2	0.3	0.4	0.5	0.5	0.5	0.5
Fluid cream products [4].........	Gallons	0.4	0.5	0.7	(NA)	(NA)	(NA)	(NA)
Butter (product weight).........	Pounds	4.5	4.3	4.5	4.9	5.7	(NA)	(NA)
Condensed and evaporated milks............	Pounds	7.0	7.9	5.8	7.2	6.9	6.8	6.7
Whole milk.........	Pounds	3.8	3.1	2.0	2.0	1.8	1.9	1.9
Skim milk.........	Pounds	3.3	4.8	3.8	5.2	5.1	4.9	4.8
Cheese [5].........	Pounds	17.5	24.6	29.5	32.7	37.0	38.0	38.3
American [6].........	Pounds	9.6	11.1	12.7	13.3	15.1	15.4	15.5
Cheddar.........	Pounds	6.8	9.1	9.9	10.1	11.1	10.3	10.1
Italian [6].........	Pounds	4.4	8.9	11.4	13.5	15.1	15.7	15.9
Mozzarella.........	Pounds	3.0	6.9	9.1	10.6	11.6	12.2	12.5
Other [6].........	Pounds	3.5	4.6	5.4	5.9	6.7	6.9	6.9
Swiss.........	Pounds	1.3	1.3	1.0	1.2	1.0	1.1	1.1
Cream and Neufchatel.........	Pounds	1.0	1.7	2.4	2.3	2.6	2.6	2.6
Cottage cheese, total.........	Pounds	4.4	3.3	2.6	2.3	2.1	2.1	2.1
Low-fat.........	Pounds	0.8	1.2	1.3	1.3	1.1	1.0	1.0
Frozen dairy products [7].........	Pounds	25.8	28.2	27.5	23.9	22.7	22.1	22.4
Ice cream.........	Pounds	17.1	15.4	16.1	14.0	12.3	12.0	12.1
Low-fat ice cream.........	Pounds	6.1	6.6	6.6	6.5	6.7	6.6	6.6
Sherbet.........	Pounds	1.2	1.2	1.1	1.0	0.8	0.7	0.8
Frozen yogurt.........	Pounds	(NA)	2.8	2.0	1.0	1.2	1.0	1.1
Flour and cereal products [8].........	Pounds	146.4	181.1	199.5	194.2	172.5	173.1	173.7
Wheat flour.........	Pounds	116.9	135.6	146.3	134.8	131.8	132.1	131.1
Rice, milled.........	Pounds	11.0	16.2	19.2	20.4	(NA)	(NA)	(NA)
Corn products.........	Pounds	12.9	21.4	28.4	33.1	34.6	34.9	36.5
Oat products.........	Pounds	3.9	6.5	4.4	4.7	4.7	4.7	4.9
Caloric sweeteners, total [9].........	Pounds	120.2	132.3	148.9	131.5	127.9	124.5	123.2
Sugar, refined cane and beet.........	Pounds	83.6	64.4	65.5	65.9	69.3	68.7	68.4
Corn sweeteners [10].........	Pounds	35.3	66.8	81.6	63.9	56.5	53.8	52.7
High-fructose corn syrup.........	Pounds	19.0	49.6	62.5	48.3	40.4	37.7	36.7
Honey.........	Pounds	0.8	0.7	1.1	1.0	1.4	1.4	1.3
Other:								
Cocoa, bean equivalent.........	Pounds	3.4	5.4	5.9	5.5	(NA)	(NA)	(NA)
Coffee, green bean equivalent.........	Pounds	10.3	10.3	10.3	9.2	(NA)	(NA)	(NA)
Tea, dry leaf equivalent.........	Pounds	0.8	0.7	0.8	1.0	(NA)	(NA)	(NA)
Peanuts, total.........	Pounds	5.1	6.5	6.0	7.2	7.6	7.5	(NA)
Tree nuts, total.........	Pounds	1.8	2.5	2.6	3.9	5.1	5.2	(NA)

NA Not available. [1] Excludes edible offal. [2] Milk-fat milk-equivalent basis. Includes fluid milk and cream, sour cream, yogurt, butter, cheese, frozen and dry dairy products, and evaporated and condensed milk. [3] Includes eggnog and other miscellaneous milk products not shown separately. [4] Heavy cream, light cream, and half-and-half. Includes total fluid cream sales and volume consumed where produced. [5] Natural equivalent of cheese and cheese products. Excludes full-skim American, cottage, pot, and baker's cheese. [6] Includes other cheeses, not shown separately. [7] Includes other frozen dairy products made with dairy ingredients, and mellorine mix for 1980 to 1990, not shown separately. Excludes whipped cream products. [8] Includes rye flour and barley products, not shown separately. Excludes wheat not ground into flour. [9] Dry weight. Includes edible syrups (maple, molasses, etc.), not shown separately. [10] Includes glucose and dextrose, not shown separately.

Source: U.S. Department of Agriculture, Economic Research Service, "Food Availability (Per Capita) Data System," <www.ers.usda.gov/data-products/food-availability-per-capita-data-system/>, accessed April 2021.

Table 245. Nutrient Consumption From Food and Beverages by Sex, Age, and Race and Hispanic Origin: 2017 to March 2020

[In units as indicated. Covers population age 2 years and older, except as noted. Data are mean amounts per person estimated from Day 1 dietary recall interviews conducted in the What We Eat in America, National Health and Nutrition Examination Survey (NHANES). The NHANES 2019-2020 cycle was interrupted in March 2020 due to the coronavirus 2019 (COVID-19) pandemic, and is not nationally representative. Data from the 2017-2018 and the 2019-2020 cycles of the NHANES were combined to produce nationally representative data for the 2017 to March 2020 period. Data are based on consumption of food and beverages, including water, and exclude intake from dietary supplements and medications. What We Eat in America is a joint project of the USDA and the U.S. Department of Health and Human Services]

Nutrient	Unit	Total	Male	Female	Age 2 to 19	Age 20 and over	White, non-Hispanic	Black, non-Hispanic	Asian, non-Hispanic	Hispanic
Total energy intake	kcal [1]	**2,089**	**2,379**	**1,812**	**1,911**	**2,144**	**2,097**	**2,055**	**1,921**	**2,107**
Protein	g	77.7	89.2	66.8	66.9	81.0	77.8	72.7	78.3	80.4
Carbohydrate	g	244	275	214	244	244	241	240	242	254
Sugars, total	g	107	119	95	111	105	108	107	86	106
Dietary fiber	g	16.0	17.2	14.9	14.1	16.6	15.7	13.5	19.5	17.8
Fats, total	g	85.4	96.4	75.0	76.5	88.2	87.4	84.7	71.0	83.0
Saturated fat	g	28.1	31.8	24.6	26.4	28.6	29.1	26.7	22.1	27.1
Monounsaturated fat	g	28.9	32.9	25.2	25.0	30.1	29.5	29.0	24.9	28.0
Polyunsaturated fat	g	19.9	22.1	17.8	17.4	20.7	20.2	20.7	16.9	19.3
Cholesterol	mg	294	334	256	229	314	289	292	269	323
Vitamin A, RAE [2]	mcg	613	645	583	562	629	640	518	593	576
Thiamin	mg	1.6	1.8	1.3	1.5	1.6	1.6	1.4	1.6	1.6
Riboflavin	mg	2.0	2.3	1.7	1.8	2.1	2.1	1.6	1.7	1.9
Niacin	mg	24.7	29.3	20.4	21.2	25.8	25.0	23.5	23.3	25.1
Vitamin B6	mg	2.0	2.4	1.7	1.7	2.1	2.1	1.8	1.9	2.1
Folic acid [3]	mcg	165	192	140	187	159	163	155	172	172
Folate [3]	mcg	198	215	182	151	213	197	171	239	209
Choline	mg	316	361	273	248	337	316	290	314	336
Vitamin B12	mcg	4.6	5.6	3.7	4.3	4.8	4.7	4.1	4.0	4.8
Vitamin C	mg	75.9	79.5	72.5	71.4	77.3	71.8	77.9	91.0	85.8
Vitamin D	mcg	4.4	5.0	3.9	4.8	4.3	4.4	3.8	5.1	4.8
Vitamin E [4]	mg	9.0	9.8	8.3	7.8	9.4	9.2	8.5	8.3	8.7
Vitamin K	mcg	113.8	111.9	115.7	72.2	126.7	116.2	115.1	135.3	100.9
Calcium	mg	953	1,059	852	978	945	981	818	814	980
Phosphorus	mg	1,342	1,522	1,171	1,254	1,369	1,362	1,204	1,268	1,381
Magnesium	mg	287	318	259	236	303	291	247	304	295
Iron	mg	13.7	15.5	12.0	13.2	13.9	13.7	12.6	13.8	14.2
Zinc	mg	10.4	12.0	8.9	9.2	10.8	10.5	9.2	9.8	10.8
Copper	mg	1.1	1.2	1.0	0.9	1.2	1.2	1.0	1.3	1.1
Selenium	mcg	108.0	124.8	92.1	93.7	112.5	106.8	104.4	111.6	112.8
Potassium	mg	2,475	2,735	2,229	2,088	2,595	2,515	2,177	2,597	2,509
Sodium	mg	3,346	3,824	2,891	2,968	3,463	3,337	3,259	3,454	3,387
Caffeine	mg	134.9	150.1	120.4	25.7	168.7	169.0	55.6	81.2	88.9

[1] A kilocalorie is equal to the amount of energy (heat) required to raise the temperature of 1 kilogram of water 1 degree centigrade. The "Calorie" commonly used to measure food energy is actually the kilocalorie. One kilocalorie is the same as one Calorie (upper case C), and represents 1,000 true calories of energy. [2] RAE, retinol activity equivalent. [3] Folate occurs naturally in foods, and covers several forms of vitamin B9. Folic acid is the synthetic form of folate and is added in the manufacturing process of food and supplements. [4] Alpha-tocopherol.

Source: U.S. Department of Agriculture, Agricultural Research Service, Food Surveys Research Group: Beltsville, MD, "What We Eat in America, Data Tables," <www.ars.usda.gov/northeast-area/beltsville-md-bhnrc/beltsville-human-nutrition-research-center/food-surveys-research-group/>, accessed August 2022.

Table 246. Energy Consumption from Food and Beverages: 2005 to 2020

[In units as indicated. Data cover population age 2 years and older, except as noted. See Headnote, Table 245]

Energy and component	2005-2006	2007-2008	2009-2010	2011-2012	2013-2014	2015-2016	2017-2018	2017-2020 [4]
Energy (kcal) [1]	**2,157**	**2,070**	**2,081**	**2,139**	**2,079**	**2,048**	**2,093**	**2,089**
GRAMS								
Protein	81.8	78.1	79.5	79.9	80.3	78.8	78.3	77.7
Carbohydrate	265.0	256.0	259.0	266.0	251.0	243.0	247.0	244.0
Sugar	124.0	120.0	119.0	120.0	112.0	106.0	108.0	107.0
Fiber	15.1	15.2	16.2	17.2	16.3	16.5	16.2	16.0
Total fat	81.9	78.3	76.8	80.0	80.0	81.4	85.0	85.4
Saturated fat	27.8	26.3	25.5	26.2	26.3	27.1	28.0	28.1
Monounsaturated fat	30.1	28.8	27.5	28.4	27.6	28.4	28.8	28.9
Polyunsaturated fat	17.0	16.4	16.8	18.9	18.6	18.6	19.9	19.9
Alcohol [2]	(NA)	(NA)	(NA)	12.1	11.0	9.9	10.0	10.6
PERCENT [3]								
Protein	15	15	16	15	16	16	15	15
Carbohydrate	50	50	51	51	49	48	48	47
Total fat	34	33	33	33	34	35	36	36
Saturated fat	11	11	11	11	11	12	12	12
Monounsaturated fat	12	12	12	12	12	12	12	12
Polyunsaturated fat	7	7	7	8	8	8	8	8
Alcohol [2]	(NA)	(NA)	(NA)	3	3	3	3	3

NA Not available. [1] See footnote 1, Table 245. [2] Data for alcohol are shown for population age 20 and over. [3] Percents are estimated as a ratio of each person's energy intake of protein, carbohydrate, fat, and alcohol, divided by the individual's total food energy intake. [4] The NHANES 2019-2020 cycle was interrupted in March 2020 due to the COVID-19 pandemic, and is not nationally representative. Data from the 2017-2018 and 2019-2020 cycles of the NHANES were combined to produce nationally representative data for the 2017 to March 2020 period.

Source: U.S. Department of Agriculture, Agricultural Research Service, Food Surveys Research Group: Beltsville, MD, "What We Eat in America, Data Tables," <www.ars.usda.gov/northeast-area/beltsville-md-bhnrc/beltsville-human-nutrition-research-center/food-surveys-research-group/>, accessed August 2022.

Education

This section presents data primarily concerning formal education as a whole, at various levels, and for public and private schools. Data shown relate to the school-age population and school enrollment, educational attainment, education personnel, and financial aspects of education. In addition, data are shown for charter schools, homeschooling, post-secondary education, security measures used in schools, and academic libraries. The chief sources are the decennial census of population and the Current Population Survey (CPS), both conducted by the U.S. Census Bureau (see text, Section 1, Population); annual, biennial, and other periodic surveys conducted by the National Center for Education Statistics (NCES), a part of the U.S. Department of Education; and surveys conducted by the National Education Association.

The censuses of population have included data on school enrollment since 1840 and on educational attainment since 1940. The CPS has reported on school enrollment annually and on educational attainment periodically since 1947.

The NCES is continuing the pattern of statistical studies and surveys conducted by the U.S. Office of Education since 1870. The annual *Digest of Education Statistics*, found at <nces.ed.gov/programs/digest>, compiles statistics on pupils, staff, finances (including government expenditures), and organization at the elementary, secondary, and higher education levels. It is also a primary source for detailed information on federal funds for education, projections of enrollment, graduates, and teachers. The *Condition of Education*, issued annually and found at <nces.ed.gov/programs/coe>, presents a summary of information on education of particular interest to policymakers. NCES also conducts special studies periodically.

The census of governments, conducted by the Census Bureau every 5 years (for the years ending in "2" and "7"), provides data on school district finances and state and local government expenditures for education. Reports published by the Bureau of Labor Statistics contain data relating civilian labor force experience to educational attainment (see also Tables 627, 655, and 662 in Section 12, Labor Force, Employment, and Earnings).

Types and sources of data—The statistics in this section are of two general types. One type, exemplified by data from the Census Bureau, is based on direct interviews with individuals to obtain information about their own and their family members' education. Data of this type relate to school enrollment and level of education attained, classified by age, sex, and other characteristics of the population. The school enrollment statistics reflect attendance or enrollment in any regular school within a given period; educational attainment statistics reflect the highest grade completed by an individual, or beginning 1992, the highest diploma or degree received.

Beginning in 2012, CPS estimates reflect population controls based on Census 2010. From 2000–2011, the CPS used Census 2000 population controls. From 1994 to 2000, the CPS used 1990 census population

controls plus adjustment for undercount. Also beginning 1994, the survey is conducted through computer-assisted technology rather than by paper forms. For years 1981 through 1993, 1980 census population controls were used; 1971 through 1980, 1970 census population controls had been used. These changes had little impact on summary measures (e.g., medians) and proportional measures (e.g., enrollment rates); however, use of the controls may have significant impact on absolute numbers.

The second type of data, generally exemplified by data from the NCES and the National Education Association, is based on reports from administrators of educational institutions and of state and local agencies having jurisdiction over education. Data of this type relate to enrollment, attendance, staff, and finances for the nation, individual states, and local areas.

Unlike the NCES, the Census Bureau does not regularly include specialized vocational, trade, business, or correspondence schools in its surveys. The NCES includes nursery schools and kindergartens that are part of regular grade schools in their enrollment figures. The Census Bureau includes all nursery schools and kindergartens. At the higher education level, the statistics of both agencies are concerned with institutions granting degrees or offering work acceptable for degree-credit, such as junior colleges.

School attendance—All states require that children attend school. While state laws vary as to the ages and circumstances of compulsory attendance, generally they require that formal schooling begin by age 6 and continue to age 16.

Schools—The NCES defines a school as "a division of the school system consisting of students composing one or more grade groups or other identifiable groups, organized as one unit with one or more teachers to give instruction of a defined type, and housed in a school plant of one or more buildings. More than one school may be housed in one school plant, as is the case when the elementary and secondary programs are housed in the same school plant."

Regular schools are those which advance a person toward a diploma or degree. They include public and private nursery schools, kindergartens, graded schools, colleges, universities, and professional schools.

Public schools are schools controlled and supported by local, state, or federal governmental agencies.

Private schools are those controlled and supported mainly by religious organizations or by private persons or organizations.

The Census Bureau defines *elementary* schools as including grades 1 through 8; *high* schools as including grades 9 through 12; and *colleges* as including junior or community colleges, regular 4-year colleges, and universities and graduate or professional schools. Statistics reported by the NCES and the National Education Association by type of organization, such as elementary level and secondary level, may not be strictly comparable with those from the Census Bureau because the grades included at the two levels vary, depending on the level assigned to the middle or junior high school by the local school systems.

School year—Except as otherwise indicated in the tables, data refer to the school year which, for elementary and secondary schools, generally begins in August or September of the preceding year and ends in June of the year stated. For the most part, statistics concerning school finances are for a 12-month period, usually July 1 to June 30. Enrollment data generally refer to a specific point in time, such as Fall, as indicated in the tables.

Statistical reliability—For a discussion of statistical collection, estimation, and sampling procedures and measures of statistical reliability applicable to the Census Bureau and the NCES data, see Appendix III.

Table 247. Federal Funds for Education and Related Programs: 2010 to 2020

[In millions of dollars (179,560.2 represents $179,560,200,000), except percent. For fiscal years ending in September. Figures represent on-budget funds (appropriations or outlays). Excludes federal support for medical education benefits under Medicare in the U.S. Department of Health and Human Services]

Level, agency, and program	2010	2019	2020
Total, all programs	**179,560.2**	**245,601.5**	**342,466.1**
Percent of federal budget outlays	5.2	5.5	5.2
Elementary/secondary education programs [1]	**75,155.8**	**87,090.7**	**89,917.6**
Department of Education [1]	39,646.5	40,775.2	42,015.7
Education for the disadvantaged	15,864.7	16,543.8	16,996.8
Impact aid program [2]	1,276.2	1,446.1	1,486.1
School improvement programs	6,999.9	6,473.3	6,718.8
Indian education	127.3	180.2	180.7
Special education	12,587.0	13,468.7	13,885.2
Vocational and adult education	2,016.4	1,925.7	1,960.7
Department of Agriculture [1]	18,336.1	24,750.0	25,543.0
Child nutrition programs	16,891.0	23,139.0	23,615.0
Agricultural Marketing Service—commodities [3]	1,053.0	1,403.0	1,708.0
Department of Defense [1]	1,981.3	2,188.7	2,213.8
Junior Reserve Officers Training Corps (JROTC)	359.7	386.0	392.7
Overseas dependents schools	1,186.6	1,250.7	1,235.0
Domestic schools [4]	435.1	552.0	586.1
Department of Health and Human Services	7,234.0	10,063.1	10,613.1
Head Start	7,234.0	10,063.1	10,613.1
Department of Homeland Security	0.5	(NA)	(NA)
Department of the Interior [1]	781.1	1,100.0	1,075.6
Mineral Leasing Act and other funds [5]	73.0	140.9	73.8
Indian Education	707.1	959.1	1,001.8
Department of Justice	137.5	136.7	157.3
Department of Labor	4,845.7	5,270.9	5,354.9
Job Corps	1,017.2	1,718.7	1,743.7
Department of Veterans Affairs	760.5	1,409.3	1,581.2
Vocational rehab for disabled veterans	760.5	1,387.6	1,559.1
Social Security student benefits [1]	1,281.7	1,263.6	1,207.4
Higher education programs [1]	**58,198.9**	**107,465.1**	**199,708.8**
Department of Education [1]	35,518.2	74,809.6	165,579.2
Student financial assistance	24,596.6	31,572.7	31,663.8
Direct loan program [6]	3,481.9	36,528.8	114,143.5
Federal Family Education Loans [6]	4,274.4	3,661.4	16,599.4
Department of Agriculture	80.7	84.7	100.5
Department of Defense	2,550.7	2,482.4	2,569.7
Tuition assistance for military personnel	669.9	561.9	555.7
Service academies	402.6	249.8	256.2
Senior ROTC	885.5	956.1	991.3
Professional development education [1]	592.6	714.6	766.4
Department of Health and Human Services [1]	10,372.6	15,746.6	16,277.7
Health professions training programs	406.0	641.7	734.5
National Health Service Corps scholarships	41.0	38.0	38.0
National Institutes of Health training grants [7]	775.2	889.0	909.9
Department of Homeland Security	45.8	13.8	13.7
Department of the Interior	143.0	100.6	60.0
Shared revenues, Mineral Leasing Act and other receipts—estimated education share [5]	16.3	36.4	19.0
Indian programs	161.4	99.2	75.3
Department of State	657.7	701.0	730.7
Department of Transportation	90.0	433.8	427.7
Department of Veterans Affairs [1]	8,034.5	11,937.1	12,763.4
Post-Vietnam veterans	1.5	0.1	0.1
All-volunteer-force educational assistance	1,854.9	323.5	300.6
National Endowment for the Humanities	47.9	25.0	33.0
National Science Foundation	618.8	985.1	996.4
Other education programs [1]	**9,212.2**	**9,872.7**	**9,824.6**
Department of Education [1]	5,062.7	5,764.4	5,959.1
Administration	1,531.2	2,295.1	2,391.9
Rehabilitative services and disability research	3,506.9	3,438.8	3,534.7
Department of Agriculture	565.4	567.8	618.1
Department of Health and Human Services	339.7	444.5	459.4
Department of Homeland Security	341.1	254.0	351.2
Department of Justice	47.9	(NA)	(NA)
Department of State	143.5	262.2	284.1
Agency for International Development	542.7	454.4	(NA)
Library of Congress	510.9	524.6	551.9
National Archives and Records Administration	339.0	403.2	377.8
National Endowment for the Arts	2.9	2.5	2.9
National Endowment for the Humanities	94.6	66.6	63.1
Research programs at universities and related institutions [1,8]	**36,993.3**	**41,173.1**	**43,015.1**
Department of Agriculture	737.2	911.2	1,025.1
Department of Defense	3,154.3	3,743.4	3,768.7
Department of Energy	3,402.6	4,611.1	5,061.2
Department of Health and Human Services	21,796.2	21,684.8	23,012.9
National Aeronautics and Space Administration	1,585.5	3,242.5	3,012.3
National Science Foundation	4,914.7	5,587.5	5,670.4

NA Not available. [1] Includes other programs and agencies, not shown separately. [2] Includes funds used to support school districts with concentrations of children who reside on Indian lands, military bases, low-rent housing properties, and other federal properties, or who have parents in the uniformed services or employed on eligible federal properties. [3] Purchased under Section 32 of the Agricultural Adjustment Act of 1935 (Public Law 74-320) for use in child nutrition programs. [4] The DoD Domestic Dependent Elementary and Secondary Schools (DDESS) program supports students in military communities in the United States, Guam, and Puerto Rico. [5] Data for 2013 through 2020 are estimated. [6] The U.S. Department of Education periodically reestimates the subsidy costs of the Direct Loan Program and Federal Family Education Loan (FFEL) Program to reflect changes in collection and technical assumptions or other changing circumstances. The Federal Family Education Loan (FFEL) Program eliminated the authorization to originate new FFEL loans after June 30, 2010; all new loans are originated through the Direct Loan Program. [7] Includes alcohol, drug abuse, and mental health training programs. [8] Data for 2020 are estimated.

Source: U.S. National Center for Education Statistics, *Digest of Education Statistics,* "Latest version of all Digest tables," <nces.ed.gov/programs/digest>, accessed April 2022.

Table 248. School Expenditures by Level of Instruction in Current and Constant (2019-2020) Dollars: 1980 to 2020

[In millions of dollars (160,075 represents $160,075,000,000). For school years ending in year shown. Data shown reflect historical revisions. Total expenditures for public elementary and secondary schools include current expenditures, interest on school debt, and capital outlay. Based on survey of state education agencies; see source for details]

Year	Current dollars			Constant 2019-2020 dollars [1]			
	Total	Elementary and second-ary schools	Colleges and universities [2]	Total	Elementary and secondary schools		Colleges and universities [2]
					Total	Public	
1980...............	160,075	103,162	56,914	530,395	341,817	317,960	188,578
1990...............	365,825	231,170	134,656	741,100	468,311	431,035	272,790
2000...............	649,322	412,538	236,784	986,610	626,829	580,182	359,781
2005...............	875,988	540,969	335,019	1,175,481	725,922	670,367	449,559
2006...............	925,249	571,669	353,580	1,196,037	738,976	682,875	457,061
2007...............	984,048	608,495	375,553	1,239,978	766,752	708,410	473,227
2008...............	1,054,901	646,414	408,487	1,281,765	785,430	725,770	496,335
2009...............	1,089,683	658,926	430,757	1,305,794	789,607	731,369	516,187
2010...............	1,100,897	654,418	446,479	1,306,590	776,691	720,434	529,899
2011...............	1,124,352	652,356	471,997	1,308,160	759,002	703,155	549,158
2012...............	1,136,876	648,794	488,083	1,285,078	733,369	680,468	551,708
2013...............	1,153,874	655,013	498,861	1,282,941	728,280	674,689	554,661
2014...............	1,192,886	675,818	517,067	1,305,917	739,855	684,241	566,062
2015...............	1,241,626	706,135	535,491	1,349,449	767,456	707,680	581,993
2016...............	1,296,371	736,905	559,466	1,399,510	795,533	731,515	603,977
2017...............	1,352,197	768,623	583,574	1,433,410	814,786	749,275	618,624
2018...............	1,404,579	798,976	605,603	1,456,115	828,291	761,839	627,823
2019 [3]............	1,468,000	836,000	632,354	1,491,000	849,000	781,000	642,247
2020 [4]............	1,515,000	864,000	651,000	1,515,000	864,000	794,000	651,000

[1] Constant dollars based on the Consumer Price Index, prepared by the Bureau of Labor Statistics, U.S. Department of Labor, adjusted to a school-year basis. [2] Postsecondary data through 1996 are for institutions of higher education; thereafter, data are for degree-granting institutions. See source for details. [3] Data for elementary and secondary education are estimated; data for degree-granting institutions are actual. [4] Estimated.

Source: U.S. National Center for Education Statistics, *Digest of Education Statistics*, "Latest version of all Digest tables," <nces.ed.gov/programs/digest/>, accessed January 2022.

Table 249. School Enrollment: 1990 to 2030

[In thousands (60,683 represents 60,683,000). As of Fall]

Year	All levels			Pre-kindergarten through grade 8		Grades 9 through 12		College [3]	
	Total	Public	Private	Public	Private [1,2]	Public	Private [1]	Public	Private
1990.....................	60,683	52,061	8,622	29,876	4,512	11,341	1,136	10,845	2,974
1995.....................	65,020	55,933	9,087	32,338	4,756	12,502	1,163	11,092	3,169
2000.....................	68,685	58,956	9,729	33,686	4,906	13,517	1,264	11,753	3,560
2001.....................	69,920	59,905	10,014	33,936	5,023	13,736	1,296	12,233	3,695
2002.....................	71,015	60,935	10,080	34,114	4,915	14,069	1,306	12,752	3,860
2003.....................	71,551	61,399	10,152	34,201	4,788	14,339	1,311	12,859	4,053
2004.....................	72,154	61,776	10,379	34,178	4,756	14,618	1,331	12,980	4,292
2005.....................	72,674	62,135	10,539	34,204	4,724	14,909	1,349	13,022	4,466
2006.....................	73,061	62,491	10,570	34,235	4,631	15,081	1,360	13,175	4,579
2007.....................	73,459	62,791	10,667	34,204	4,546	15,086	1,364	13,501	4,757
2008.....................	74,055	63,236	10,818	34,286	4,365	14,980	1,342	13,971	5,111
2009.....................	75,163	64,172	10,991	34,409	4,179	14,952	1,309	14,811	5,503
2010.....................	75,886	64,626	11,260	34,625	4,084	14,860	1,299	15,142	5,877
2011.....................	75,800	64,638	11,162	34,773	3,977	14,749	1,291	15,116	5,894
2012.....................	75,748	64,656	11,092	35,018	4,031	14,753	1,302	14,885	5,760
2013.....................	75,817	64,791	11,026	35,251	4,084	14,794	1,312	14,747	5,630
2014.....................	76,097	64,967	11,130	35,370	4,202	14,943	1,373	14,655	5,554
2015.....................	76,177	65,011	11,166	35,388	4,304	15,050	1,446	14,573	5,415
2016.....................	76,216	65,201	11,015	35,477	4,272	15,138	1,482	14,586	5,261
2017.....................	76,184	65,257	10,926	35,496	4,252	15,190	1,468	14,572	5,206
2018.....................	75,955	65,233	10,722	35,498	4,167	15,196	1,443	14,539	5,112
2019.....................	75,912	65,300	10,612	35,551	4,066	15,246	1,420	14,504	5,127
2020, [4]................	74,361	63,243	11,118	34,059	4,492	15,316	1,502	13,867	5,125
2021, projection...........	76,294	65,047	11,247	34,614	4,383	15,458	1,512	14,975	5,352
2022, projection...........	75,751	64,704	11,047	34,360	4,251	15,575	1,535	14,769	5,261
2023, projection...........	75,267	64,384	10,884	34,160	4,141	15,574	1,542	14,650	5,201
2024, projection...........	74,856	64,149	10,708	33,983	4,026	15,502	1,484	14,664	5,198
2025, projection...........	74,453	63,836	10,617	33,835	3,934	15,285	1,464	14,716	5,218
2026, projection...........	73,609	63,169	10,439	33,347	3,729	15,021	1,458	14,801	5,253
2027, projection...........	73,047	62,703	10,344	32,967	3,602	14,854	1,455	14,882	5,287
2028, projection...........	72,857	62,549	10,308	32,829	3,522	14,760	1,463	14,960	5,322
2029, projection...........	72,648	62,395	10,253	32,494	3,501	14,863	1,397	15,038	5,355
2030, projection...........	72,541	62,354	10,188	32,261	3,496	14,992	1,311	15,101	5,381

[1] Since the biennial Private School Universe Survey (PSS) is collected in the fall of odd numbered years, data for even numbered years are estimated. [2] Excludes preprimary students in private schools that do not offer kindergarten or higher grades. [3] Postsecondary data through 1995 are for institutions of higher education, while later data are for degree-granting institutions. Degree-granting institutions grant associate's or higher degrees and participate in Title IV federal financial aid programs. The degree-granting classification is very similar to the earlier higher education classification, but it includes more 2-year colleges and excludes a few higher education institutions that did not grant degrees. [4] Data for private school enrollment pre-K through 12 are projections.

Source: U.S. National Center for Education Statistics, *Digest of Education Statistics*, "Latest version of all Digest tables," <nces.ed.gov/programs/digest>, accessed August 2022.

Table 250. School Enrollment, Faculty, Graduates, and Finances—Projections: 2020 to 2030

[In units as indicated (55,369 represents 55,369,000). As of the fall for the academic years indicated below, except as noted. Data for higher education are for degree-granting institutions that grant associate's or higher degrees and participate in Title IV federal financial aid programs]

Item	Unit	2020 [1]	2021	2022	2023	2024	2025	2030
ELEMENTARY AND SECONDARY SCHOOLS								
School enrollment, total..........................	1,000	55,369	55,967	55,720	55,416	54,994	54,519	52,059
Pre-kindergarten through grade 8...............	1,000	38,551	38,998	38,611	38,301	38,009	37,769	35,757
Grades 9 through 12.............................	1,000	16,818	16,969	17,109	17,115	16,986	16,750	16,303
Public...	1,000	49,375	50,072	49,935	49,734	49,485	49,120	47,253
Pre-kindergarten through grade 8...............	1,000	34,059	34,614	34,360	34,160	33,983	33,835	32,261
Grades 9 through 12.............................	1,000	15,316	15,458	15,575	15,574	15,502	15,285	14,992
Private...	1,000	5,994	5,895	5,786	5,683	5,510	5,399	4,807
Pre-kindergarten through grade 8...............	1,000	4,492	4,383	4,251	4,141	4,026	3,934	3,496
Grades 9 through 12.............................	1,000	1,502	1,512	1,535	1,542	1,484	1,464	1,311
Classroom teachers, total FTE [2]...............	1,000	3,647	3,664	3,631	3,624	3,617	3,609	3,498
Public...	1,000	3,171	3,186	3,158	3,152	3,146	3,139	3,044
Private...	1,000	476	478	473	472	471	470	454
High school graduates, total..................	1,000	3,669	3,670	3,684	3,733	3,798	3,793	3,549
Public...	1,000	3,338	3,343	3,358	3,343	3,457	3,444	3,216
Private...	1,000	332	327	326	391	341	349	333
Public schools:								
Constant (2020-2021) dollars: [3]								
Current school expenditure....................	Bil. dol.	699.9	717.8	715.2	714.4	713.9	712.6	698.0
Per pupil in fall enrollment...................	Dollar	14,170	14,330	14,330	14,360	14,430	14,510	14,770
HIGHER EDUCATION								
Enrollment, total.............................	1,000	18,992	20,327	20,031	19,851	19,862	19,934	20,482
Full-time.......................................	1,000	11,591	12,387	12,177	12,041	12,041	12,099	12,402
Males..	1,000	4,980	5,472	5,360	5,286	5,280	5,303	5,447
Females..	1,000	6,611	6,914	6,817	6,755	6,761	6,796	6,955
Part-time.......................................	1,000	7,400	7,941	7,854	7,810	7,821	7,835	8,080
Males..	1,000	2,889	3,212	3,164	3,137	3,137	3,141	3,253
Females..	1,000	4,511	4,729	4,690	4,674	4,684	4,694	4,827
Public...	1,000	13,867	14,975	14,770	14,650	14,664	14,716	15,101
Four-year institutions.........................	1,000	9,165	9,418	9,273	9,183	9,187	9,223	9,469
Two-year institutions..........................	1,000	4,703	5,557	5,497	5,467	5,477	5,493	5,632
Private...	1,000	5,125	5,352	5,261	5,201	5,198	5,218	5,381
Four-year institutions.........................	1,000	4,913	5,144	5,056	4,997	4,994	5,013	5,172
Two-year institutions..........................	1,000	211	208	205	204	204	205	209
Undergraduate..................................	1,000	15,852	17,014	16,799	16,683	16,711	16,775	17,146
Postbaccalaureate..............................	1,000	3,140	3,313	3,231	3,168	3,151	3,159	3,336
Full-time equivalent............................	1,000	14,316	15,292	15,050	14,898	14,902	14,966	15,359
Public...	1,000	10,063	10,828	10,666	10,567	10,574	10,619	10,881
2-year...	1,000	2,650	3,146	3,108	3,087	3,091	3,103	3,177
4-year...	1,000	7,413	7,682	7,558	7,481	7,484	7,517	7,704
Private...	1,000	4,253	4,464	4,384	4,331	4,328	4,346	4,478
2-year...	1,000	203	198	195	193	194	195	199
4-year...	1,000	4,051	4,267	4,189	4,137	4,134	4,152	4,279
Degrees conferred, total......................	1,000	4,224	4,358	4,461	4,491	4,531	4,603	5,060
Associate's.....................................	1,000	1,077	1,117	1,156	1,183	1,210	1,241	1,403
Bachelor's......................................	1,000	2,078	2,123	2,166	2,185	2,210	2,247	2,453
Master's..	1,000	876	922	935	912	901	903	983
Doctoral [4].....................................	1,000	193	196	204	211	210	212	221

[1] Data are projected except for public elementary and secondary education enrollment, and higher education enrollment. [2] Full-time equivalent. [3] Based on the Consumer Price Index (CPI) for all urban consumers, U.S. Bureau of Labor Statistics. CPI adjusted to a school year basis by NCES. [4] Doctoral degrees include Ph.D., Ed.D., and comparable degrees at the doctoral level. Includes most degrees formerly classified as first-professional, such as M.D., D.D.S., and law degrees.

Source: U.S. National Center for Education Statistics, *Digest of Education Statistics*, "Latest version of all Digest Tables," <nces.ed.gov/programs/digest/>, accessed August 2022. See also <nces.ed.gov/programs/pes/>.

Table 251. School Enrollment by Control and Level: 1980 to 2022

[In thousands (58,305 represents 58,305,000). As of Fall. Data below college level are for regular day schools and exclude subcollegiate departments of colleges, federal schools, and home-schooled children. Based on survey of state education agencies; see source for details. For more projections, see Table 249 and Table 250]

Control of school and level	1980	1990	2000	2005	2010	2015	2019	2020	2021, proj.	2022, proj.
Total.............................	58,305	60,683	68,685	72,674	75,886	76,177	75,912	74,361	76,294	75,751
Public............................	50,335	52,061	58,956	62,135	64,626	65,011	65,300	63,243	65,047	64,704
Private...........................	7,971	8,622	9,729	10,539	11,260	11,166	10,612	11,118	11,247	11,047
Pre-kindergarten through 8.....	31,639	34,388	38,592	38,928	38,708	39,692	39,617	38,551	38,998	38,611
Public...........................	27,647	29,876	33,686	34,204	34,625	35,388	35,551	34,059	34,614	34,360
Private [1]........................	3,992	4,512	4,906	4,724	4,084	4,304	4,066	4,492	4,383	4,251
Grades 9 through 12............	14,570	12,476	14,781	16,258	16,159	16,496	16,665	16,818	16,969	17,109
Public...........................	13,231	11,341	13,517	14,909	14,860	15,050	15,246	15,316	15,458	15,575
Private [1]........................	1,339	1,136	1,264	1,349	1,299	1,446	1,420	1,502	1,512	1,535
College [2, 3]....................	12,097	13,819	15,312	17,487	21,019	19,988	19,630	18,992	20,327	20,031
Public...........................	9,457	10,845	11,753	13,022	15,142	14,573	14,504	13,867	14,975	14,769
Private...........................	2,640	2,974	3,560	4,466	5,877	5,415	5,127	5,125	5,352	5,261
Not-for-profit..................	2,528	2,760	3,109	3,455	3,854	4,066	4,135	4,101	(NA)	(NA)
For profit......................	112	214	450	1,011	2,023	1,349	991	1,024	(NA)	(NA)

NA Not available. [1] Beginning in fall 1985, data include estimates for an expanded universe of private schools; avoid direct comparisons with data for earlier years. Private school data for even numbered years are estimated; 2020 data are projected. [2] Beginning 2000, reflects new classification system. See footnote 3, Table 249.

Source: U.S. National Center for Education Statistics, *Digest of Education Statistics*, "Latest version of all Digest tables," <nces.ed.gov/programs/digest>, accessed August 2022.

Table 252. School Enrollment by Age: 1970 to 2020

[Enrollment in thousands (60,357 represents 60,357,000); rate as percent of total population in each age group. As of October. Covers civilian noninstitutional population enrolled in nursery school and above. Based on Current Population Survey; see text, Section 1 and Appendix III]

Age	1970	1980	1990	2000	2010	2015	2017	2018	2019	2020
ENROLLMENT (1,000)										
Total, 3 to 34 years old...........	60,357	57,348	60,588	69,560	75,148	77,066	73,883	74,247	73,571	70,868
3 and 4 years old.................	1,461	2,280	3,292	4,097	4,706	4,203	4,319	4,393	4,334	3,189
5 and 6 years old.................	7,000	5,853	7,207	7,648	7,955	7,507	7,516	7,448	7,506	7,268
7 to 13 years old.................	28,943	23,751	25,016	28,296	27,984	28,250	28,152	28,262	28,212	27,573
14 and 15 years old...............	7,869	7,282	6,555	7,885	7,736	8,207	8,082	8,158	8,141	8,159
16 and 17 years old...............	6,927	7,129	6,098	7,341	7,963	7,923	7,933	7,761	7,778	7,671
18 and 19 years old...............	3,322	3,788	4,044	4,926	5,904	5,591	5,606	5,776	5,586	5,484
20 and 21 years old...............	1,949	2,515	2,852	3,314	4,552	4,641	4,570	4,563	4,641	4,621
22 to 24 years old................	1,410	1,931	2,231	2,731	3,602	3,793	3,696	3,598	3,537	3,236
25 to 29 years old................	1,011	1,714	2,013	2,030	3,088	2,880	2,758	2,916	2,517	2,366
30 to 34 years old................	466	1,105	1,281	1,292	1,658	1,398	1,251	1,372	1,319	1,301
35 years old and over............	(NA)	1,290	2,439	2,653	3,372	2,674	2,526	2,592	2,520	2,353
ENROLLMENT RATE										
Total, 3 to 34 years old...........	56.4	49.7	50.2	55.9	56.5	55.2	54.6	54.6	54.1	52.4
3 and 4 years old.................	20.5	36.7	44.4	52.1	53.2	52.7	53.8	54.0	53.7	40.3
5 and 6 years old.................	89.5	95.7	96.5	95.6	94.5	94.2	93.5	93.5	93.6	89.2
7 to 13 years old.................	99.2	99.3	99.6	98.2	98.0	97.7	97.5	97.7	97.8	96.4
14 and 15 years old...............	98.1	98.2	99.0	98.7	98.1	98.0	98.2	98.6	97.9	97.8
16 and 17 years old...............	90.0	89.0	92.5	92.8	96.1	93.7	92.9	92.3	92.7	92.3
18 and 19 years old...............	47.7	46.4	57.3	61.2	69.2	68.5	68.2	69.1	67.3	66.5
20 and 21 years old...............	31.9	31.0	39.7	44.1	52.4	53.3	55.0	54.6	53.5	52.8
22 to 24 years old................	14.9	16.3	21.0	24.6	28.9	28.8	28.4	28.0	28.6	26.6
25 to 29 years old................	7.5	9.3	9.7	11.4	14.6	13.2	12.1	12.7	11.0	10.5
30 to 34 years old................	4.2	6.5	5.8	6.7	8.3	6.6	5.9	6.3	6.0	5.8
35 years old and over............	(NA)	1.6	2.1	1.9	2.1	1.6	1.5	1.5	1.4	1.3

NA Not available.

Source: U.S. Census Bureau, Current Population Reports, P-20, and earlier reports; and "School Enrollment Tables," <www.census.gov/topics/education/school-enrollment/data/tables.html>, accessed January 2022.

Table 253. School Enrollment by Race, Hispanic Origin, and Age: 2000 to 2020

[Enrollment in thousands (54,257 represents 54,257,000); rate as percent of total population in each age group. As of October. Covers civilian noninstitutional population enrolled in nursery school and above. Based on Current Population Survey; see text, Section 1 and Appendix III]

Age	White [1]			Black [1]			Hispanic [2]		
	2000	2010	2020	2000	2010	2020	2000	2010	2020
ENROLLMENT (1,000)									
Total, 3 to 34 years old............	**54,257**	**56,776**	**50,905**	**11,115**	**11,272**	**10,568**	**9,928**	**15,235**	**17,097**
3 and 4 years old......................	3,091	3,439	2,266	725	776	491	518	1,025	674
5 and 6 years old......................	5,959	5,956	5,172	1,219	1,207	1,152	1,390	1,961	1,821
7 to 13 years old......................	22,061	21,201	19,857	4,675	4,108	4,114	4,373	6,241	7,165
14 and 15 years old....................	6,176	5,907	5,913	1,260	1,157	1,224	1,093	1,555	2,075
16 and 17 years old....................	5,845	6,059	5,628	1,106	1,245	1,115	959	1,448	1,815
18 and 19 years old....................	3,924	4,566	3,949	716	837	867	617	1,171	1,289
20 and 21 years old....................	2,688	3,432	3,338	416	678	551	311	582	1,000
22 to 24 years old.....................	2,101	2,720	2,285	393	514	471	309	559	578
25 to 29 years old.....................	1,473	2,289	1,636	353	462	339	198	462	494
30 to 34 years old.....................	939	1,207	861	252	288	244	160	231	186
35 years old and over.................	2,087	2,462	1,603	387	697	445	235	435	426
ENROLLMENT RATE									
Total, 3 to 34 years old............	**55.1**	**55.8**	**51.8**	**59.0**	**58.4**	**52.2**	**51.3**	**55.1**	**53.4**
3 and 4 years old......................	50.2	52.1	40.0	59.9	56.2	40.1	35.9	44.2	32.9
5 and 6 years old......................	95.3	94.2	89.2	96.3	94.4	90.0	94.3	94.3	87.0
7 to 13 years old......................	98.2	97.9	96.4	98.0	98.0	95.9	97.5	97.8	95.8
14 and 15 years old....................	98.4	98.1	97.5	99.6	98.5	98.8	96.2	97.9	98.1
16 and 17 years old....................	92.8	96.2	92.7	91.4	95.5	93.2	87.0	96.0	91.3
18 and 19 years old....................	61.3	70.0	65.1	57.2	62.7	71.6	49.5	66.2	62.7
20 and 21 years old....................	44.9	51.6	53.2	36.6	50.2	41.5	26.1	37.0	47.8
22 to 24 years old.....................	23.7	28.1	25.3	24.2	29.0	26.9	18.2	23.8	21.2
25 to 29 years old.....................	10.4	13.9	10.0	14.3	16.0	9.8	7.4	11.4	10.2
30 to 34 years old.....................	6.0	7.8	5.3	9.6	10.9	7.5	5.6	5.7	4.0
35 years old and over.................	1.8	1.9	1.1	2.6	4.0	2.1	2.0	2.3	1.6

[1] Beginning 2003, data represent persons who selected this race group only and exclude persons reporting more than one race. Before 2003, the CPS permitted respondents to report only one race group. See also comments on race in the text for Section 1, Population. [2] Persons of Hispanic origin may be of any race.

Source: U.S. Census Bureau, Current Population Reports, P-20, and earlier reports; and "School Enrollment Tables," <www.census.gov/topics/education/school-enrollment/data/tables.All.html>, accessed January 2022.

Table 254. Enrollment in Public and Private Schools: 1970 to 2020

[In millions (52.2 represents 52,200,000), except percent. As of October. For civilian noninstitutional population. Prior to 1995, total enrolled does not include the population age 35 and over. For enrollment of population age 35 and over, see Table 252. Based on Current Population Survey]

Year	Public						Private					
	Total	Nursery	Kinder-garten	Elemen-tary	High school	College	Total	Nursery	Kinder-garten	Elemen-tary	High school	College
1970............	52.2	0.3	2.6	30.0	13.5	5.7	8.1	0.8	0.5	3.9	1.2	1.7
1980............	(NA)	0.6	2.7	24.4	(NA)	(NA)	(NA)	1.4	0.5	3.1	(NA)	(NA)
1990 [1]........	51.8	1.2	3.3	26.6	11.8	8.9	8.7	2.2	0.6	2.7	0.9	2.4
2000............	61.2	2.2	3.2	29.4	14.4	12.0	11.0	2.2	0.7	3.5	1.3	3.3
2005............	64.3	2.5	3.3	29.1	15.9	13.4	11.5	2.1	0.6	3.4	1.4	4.0
2006............	64.1	2.5	3.6	29.0	15.6	13.5	11.1	2.2	0.5	3.1	1.5	3.8
2007............	65.2	2.6	3.7	29.1	15.8	14.1	10.8	2.1	0.5	3.1	1.3	3.9
2008............	65.5	2.6	3.6	29.2	15.4	14.7	10.8	2.0	0.5	3.2	1.3	3.9
2009............	66.9	2.7	3.8	29.4	15.3	15.7	10.4	2.0	0.4	2.9	1.2	4.0
2010............	67.9	2.8	3.8	29.8	15.3	16.2	10.6	2.1	0.5	2.8	1.2	4.1
2011............	68.2	2.9	3.7	30.0	15.4	16.1	10.9	2.0	0.5	2.9	1.2	4.3
2012............	67.8	2.7	3.7	29.9	15.7	15.8	10.7	1.9	0.5	2.8	1.3	4.2
2013............	67.4	2.6	3.7	30.2	15.5	15.5	10.3	2.1	0.4	2.7	1.1	4.0
2014............	66.8	2.7	3.6	29.8	15.4	15.3	10.4	2.0	0.5	2.8	1.3	3.9
2015............	67.0	2.6	3.6	30.2	15.4	15.2	10.1	1.9	0.4	2.7	1.2	3.9
2016............	66.7	2.8	3.7	30.0	15.3	15.0	10.5	1.9	0.4	2.6	1.3	4.2
2017............	66.5	2.8	3.5	29.9	15.5	14.8	9.9	1.9	0.4	2.7	1.3	3.6
2018............	66.7	2.8	3.5	29.7	15.5	15.2	10.1	2.1	0.4	2.8	1.2	3.7
2019............	65.9	2.6	3.5	29.8	15.2	14.7	10.2	2.1	0.5	2.9	1.2	3.5
2020............	62.7	2.1	3.1	28.6	15.0	13.9	10.5	1.5	0.6	3.4	1.3	3.8
Percent White:												
1970............	84.5	59.5	84.4	83.1	85.6	90.7	93.4	91.1	88.2	94.1	96.1	92.8
1980............	(NA)	68.2	80.7	80.9	(NA)	(NA)	(NA)	89.0	87.0	90.7	(NA)	(NA)
1990............	79.6	71.7	78.3	78.9	79.3	83.4	87.5	89.6	83.2	88.2	89.4	85.1
2000............	77.0	69.4	77.3	76.7	78.0	78.0	83.5	84.8	82.7	85.9	84.6	79.8
2005 [2]........	75.7	71.3	78.0	75.2	76.0	76.7	81.4	83.6	79.0	83.0	83.6	78.4
2010 [2]........	74.9	71.8	72.9	75.0	75.1	75.4	78.9	81.0	79.4	80.9	84.5	74.7
2015 [2]........	72.3	68.1	72.2	72.2	72.9	72.7	75.5	75.5	79.4	78.7	79.4	71.9
2016 [2]........	72.2	70.7	70.6	72.7	71.9	72.4	74.3	75.3	77.2	74.1	78.7	72.3
2017 [2]........	71.6	67.8	72.8	71.6	72.7	71.1	75.8	75.5	80.1	76.3	75.3	75.2
2018 [2]........	71.2	70.3	71.1	71.5	72.0	70.0	75.9	75.5	84.7	76.8	82.8	72.2
2019 [2]........	70.9	67.2	71.7	71.0	72.8	69.3	74.8	75.5	69.0	78.8	73.3	72.5
2020 [2]........	71.3	68.2	71.5	71.4	72.0	70.9	74.0	77.5	72.5	75.7	77.6	69.9

NA Not available. [1] Beginning 1990, based on a revised edit and tabulation package. [2] Beginning in 2003, represents persons who selected this race group only. See footnote 4, Table 256.

Source: U.S. Census Bureau, Current Population Reports, P-20, and earlier reports; and "School Enrollment: CPS Historical Time Series Tables on School Enrollment," <www.census.gov/topics/education/school-enrollment/data/tables.All.html>, accessed March 2022.

Table 255. School Enrollment by Sex and Level: 1970 to 2020

[In millions (60.4 represents 60,400,000). As of October. For the civilian noninstitutional population. Prior to 1980, data cover persons age 3 to 34; beginning 1980, age 3 and over. Elementary includes kindergarten and grades 1–8; high school, grades 9–12; and college, 2-year and 4-year colleges, universities, and graduate and professional schools. Data for college represent degree-credit enrollment. Based on Current Population Survey; see text, Section 1 and Appendix III]

Year	All levels [1]			Elementary			High school			College		
	Total	Male	Female	Total	Male	Female	Total	Male	Female	Total	Male	Female
1970............	60.4	31.4	28.9	37.1	19.0	18.1	14.7	7.4	7.3	7.4	4.4	3.0
1980............	58.6	29.6	29.1	30.6	15.8	14.9	14.6	7.3	7.3	11.4	5.4	6.0
1990 [2]..........	63.0	31.5	31.5	33.2	17.1	16.0	12.8	6.5	6.4	13.6	6.2	7.4
2000............	72.2	35.8	36.4	36.7	18.9	17.9	15.8	8.1	7.7	15.3	6.7	8.6
2001............	73.1	36.3	36.9	36.9	19.0	17.9	16.1	8.2	7.8	15.9	6.9	9.0
2002............	74.0	36.8	37.3	36.7	18.9	17.8	16.4	8.3	8.0	16.5	7.2	9.3
2003............	74.9	37.3	37.6	36.3	18.7	17.6	17.1	8.6	8.4	16.6	7.3	9.3
2004............	75.5	37.4	38.0	36.5	19.0	17.6	16.8	8.4	8.4	17.4	7.6	9.8
2005............	75.8	37.4	38.4	36.4	18.6	17.7	17.4	8.9	8.5	17.5	7.5	9.9
2006............	75.2	37.2	38.0	36.1	18.5	17.6	17.1	8.8	8.4	17.2	7.5	9.7
2007............	76.0	37.6	38.4	36.3	18.6	17.7	17.1	8.8	8.3	18.0	7.8	10.1
2008............	76.4	37.8	38.6	36.4	18.7	17.7	16.7	8.5	8.2	18.6	8.3	10.3
2009............	77.3	38.0	39.3	36.4	18.6	17.7	16.4	8.4	8.1	19.8	8.6	11.1
2010............	78.5	38.7	39.8	36.8	18.8	18.1	16.6	8.5	8.1	20.3	9.0	11.3
2011............	79.0	39.2	39.8	37.1	19.0	18.1	16.6	8.6	8.1	20.4	9.1	11.3
2012............	78.4	38.5	39.9	36.8	19.0	17.9	17.0	8.6	8.5	19.9	8.6	11.3
2013............	77.8	38.3	39.5	37.0	19.0	18.0	16.6	8.4	8.2	19.5	8.5	10.9
2014............	77.2	38.2	39.0	36.7	18.8	17.9	16.7	8.4	8.2	19.2	8.6	10.5
2015............	77.1	38.2	38.9	36.9	18.9	18.0	16.5	8.4	8.1	19.1	8.5	10.6
2016............	77.2	38.4	38.9	36.6	18.7	17.9	16.7	8.5	8.1	19.2	8.6	10.6
2017............	76.4	37.8	38.6	36.5	18.7	17.8	16.8	8.6	8.3	18.4	8.1	10.3
2018............	76.8	38.0	38.8	36.4	18.6	17.8	16.7	8.6	8.1	18.9	8.4	10.5
2019............	76.1	37.8	38.3	36.7	18.8	17.9	16.4	8.4	8.0	18.3	8.1	10.2
2020............	73.2	35.9	37.3	35.7	18.4	17.4	16.3	8.2	8.1	17.7	7.6	10.1

[1] Includes nursery schools, not shown separately. [2] For data beginning 1990, based on a revised edit and tabulation package.

Source: U.S. Census Bureau, Current Population Reports, P-20, and earlier reports; and "School Enrollment Tables," <www.census.gov/topics/education/school-enrollment/data/tables.All.html>, accessed January 2022.

Table 256. Educational Attainment by Race and Hispanic Origin: 1970 to 2021

[In percent. For persons 25 years old and over. 1970 and 1980 data as of April 1 and based on sample data from the censuses of population. Other years as of March and based on the Current Population Survey; see text, Section 1 and Appendix III. See Table 257 for data by sex]

Year	High school graduate or more [1]					College graduate or more [2]				
	Total [3]	White [4]	Black [4]	Asian [4]	His-panic [5]	Total [3]	White [4]	Black [4]	Asian [4]	His-panic [5]
1970............	55.2	57.4	33.7	(NA)	(NA)	11.0	11.6	4.5	(NA)	(NA)
1975............	62.5	64.5	42.5	(NA)	37.9	13.9	14.5	6.4	(NA)	6.3
1980............	68.6	70.5	51.2	(NA)	45.3	17.0	17.8	7.9	(NA)	7.9
1985............	73.9	75.5	59.8	(NA)	47.9	19.4	20.0	11.1	(NA)	8.5
1990............	77.6	79.1	66.2	(NA)	50.8	21.3	22.0	11.3	(NA)	9.2
1995............	81.7	83.0	73.8	(NA)	53.4	23.0	24.0	13.2	(NA)	9.3
2000............	84.1	84.9	78.5	(NA)	57.0	25.6	26.1	16.5	(NA)	10.6
2005............	85.2	85.8	81.1	87.6	58.5	27.7	28.1	17.6	50.2	12.0
2010............	87.1	87.6	84.2	88.9	62.9	29.9	30.3	19.8	52.4	13.9
2011............	87.6	88.1	84.5	88.6	64.3	30.4	31.0	19.9	50.3	14.1
2012............	87.6	88.1	85.0	88.9	65.0	30.9	31.3	21.2	51.0	14.5
2013............	88.2	88.6	85.1	90.1	66.2	31.7	32.0	21.8	53.2	15.1
2014............	88.3	88.8	85.8	89.5	66.5	32.0	32.3	22.2	52.3	15.2
2015............	88.4	88.8	87.0	89.1	66.7	32.5	32.8	22.5	53.9	15.5
2016............	89.1	89.5	87.1	90.3	68.5	33.4	33.7	23.3	55.9	16.4
2017............	89.6	90.1	87.3	90.9	70.5	34.2	34.5	23.9	54.8	17.2
2018............	89.8	90.2	87.9	90.5	71.6	35.0	35.2	25.2	56.5	18.3
2019............	90.1	90.5	87.9	91.2	71.8	36.0	36.3	26.1	58.1	18.8
2020............	90.9	91.3	89.4	91.6	74.3	37.5	37.5	27.8	61.1	20.8
2021............	91.1	91.2	90.3	92.9	74.2	37.9	37.9	28.1	61.0	20.6

NA Not available. [1] Through 1991, completed 4 years of high school or more. [2] Through 1991, completed 4 years of college or more. [3] Includes other races not shown separately. [4] The 2003 Current Population Survey (CPS) allowed respondents to choose more than one race. Beginning 2003, data represent persons who selected this race group only and exclude persons reporting more than one race. Before 2003, the CPS permitted respondents to report only one race group. See also comments on race in the text for Section 1, Population. [5] Persons of Hispanic origin may be of any race.

Source: U.S. Census Bureau, U.S. Census of Population,1960, 1970, and 1980, Summary File 3; Current Population Reports, P20-550, and earlier reports; and "Educational Attainment in the United States: CPS Historical Time Series Tables," <www.census.gov/topics/education/educational-attainment.html>, accessed March 2022.

Table 257. Educational Attainment by Race, Hispanic Origin, and Sex: 1970 to 2021

[In percent. See Table 256 for headnote and totals for both sexes]

Year	All races [1]		White [2]		Black [2]		Asian [2]		Hispanic [3]	
	Male	Female	Male	Female	Male	Female	Male	Female	Male	Female
HIGH SCHOOL GRADUATE OR MORE [4]										
1970........................	55.0	55.4	57.2	57.6	32.4	34.8	(NA)	(NA)	(NA)	(NA)
1980........................	69.2	68.1	71.0	70.1	51.1	51.3	(NA)	(NA)	46.4	44.1
1990........................	77.7	77.5	79.1	79.0	65.8	66.5	(NA)	(NA)	50.3	51.3
2000........................	84.2	84.0	84.8	85.0	78.7	78.3	(NA)	(NA)	56.6	57.5
2010........................	86.6	87.6	86.9	88.2	83.6	84.6	91.2	87.0	61.4	64.4
2011........................	87.1	88.0	87.4	88.6	83.8	85.0	90.4	87.1	63.6	65.1
2012........................	87.3	88.0	87.6	88.5	84.3	85.5	90.4	87.6	64.0	66.0
2013........................	87.6	88.6	88.0	89.2	84.1	86.0	91.5	89.0	64.6	67.9
2014........................	87.7	88.9	88.0	89.6	85.3	86.2	91.9	87.4	65.1	67.9
2015........................	88.0	88.8	88.3	89.3	86.4	87.6	91.0	87.4	65.5	67.8
2016........................	88.5	89.6	88.8	90.1	86.4	87.7	91.9	89.0	67.2	69.7
2017........................	89.1	90.0	89.5	90.6	86.5	87.9	92.6	89.4	69.5	71.6
2018........................	89.4	90.2	89.6	90.8	87.7	88.1	92.7	88.6	70.7	72.5
2019........................	89.6	90.5	89.9	91.0	87.1	88.6	92.8	89.8	70.8	72.8
2020........................	90.6	91.3	90.8	91.7	88.6	90.0	92.6	90.7	73.8	74.8
2021........................	90.5	91.6	90.5	91.8	89.8	90.7	94.0	91.9	72.6	75.9
COLLEGE GRADUATE OR MORE [4]										
1970........................	14.1	8.2	15.0	8.6	4.6	4.4	(NA)	(NA)	(NA)	(NA)
1980........................	20.9	13.6	22.1	14.0	7.7	8.1	(NA)	(NA)	9.7	6.2
1990........................	24.4	18.4	25.3	19.0	11.9	10.8	(NA)	(NA)	9.8	8.7
2000........................	27.8	23.6	28.5	23.9	16.3	16.7	(NA)	(NA)	10.7	10.6
2010........................	30.3	29.6	30.8	29.9	17.7	21.4	55.6	49.5	12.9	14.9
2011........................	30.8	30.1	31.5	30.5	18.0	21.4	53.4	47.7	13.1	15.2
2012........................	31.4	30.6	31.9	30.8	19.2	22.9	53.7	48.8	13.3	15.8
2013........................	32.0	31.4	32.4	31.6	19.8	23.3	56.1	50.8	13.9	16.2
2014........................	31.9	32.0	32.3	32.3	20.4	23.7	54.7	50.3	14.2	16.1
2015........................	32.3	32.7	32.6	32.9	20.6	24.0	56.8	51.5	14.3	16.6
2016........................	33.2	33.7	33.4	34.0	21.7	24.6	58.8	53.4	15.4	17.4
2017........................	33.7	34.6	34.0	35.0	22.1	25.4	56.6	53.2	15.8	18.6
2018........................	34.6	35.3	34.9	35.5	23.2	26.9	59.3	54.0	16.6	20.1
2019........................	35.4	36.6	35.7	36.8	24.1	27.7	60.4	56.1	16.9	20.8
2020........................	36.7	38.3	36.8	38.2	24.7	30.5	63.0	59.4	19.4	22.3
2021........................	36.6	39.1	36.6	39.1	24.9	30.8	63.5	58.9	18.9	22.3

NA Not available. [1] Includes other races not shown separately. [2] Beginning 2003, for persons who selected this race group only. See footnote 4, Table 256. [3] Persons of Hispanic origin may be of any race. [4] Through 1990, completed 4 years of high school or more and 4 years of college or more.

Source: U.S. Census Bureau, U.S. Census of Population, 1960, 1970, and 1980, Summary File 3; Current Population Reports, P20-550, and earlier reports; and "Educational Attainment in the United States: CPS Historical Time Series Tables," <www.census.gov/topics/education/educational-attainment.html>, accessed March 2022.

Table 258. Educational Attainment by Selected Characteristics: 2021

[224,580 represents 224,580,000. For persons 25 years old and over. As of March. Based on the Current Population Survey; see text, Section 1 and Appendix III]

Characteristic	Population (1,000)	Percent of population—					
		Not a high school graduate	High school graduate	Some college, but no degree	Associate's degree [1]	Bachelor's degree	Advanced degree
Total persons..........................	224,580	8.9	27.9	14.9	10.5	23.5	14.4
Age:							
25 to 34 years old......................	45,283	6.3	26.3	16.2	10.3	28.8	12.1
35 to 44 years old......................	42,004	9.0	23.9	13.9	10.5	25.7	17.0
45 to 54 years old......................	39,679	8.7	26.3	13.6	10.9	24.5	16.1
55 to 64 years old......................	41,776	9.4	30.5	14.8	11.5	21.2	12.7
65 to 74 years old......................	33,040	9.1	29.1	16.6	10.8	19.8	14.6
75 years old or over..................	22,796	13.4	34.2	14.3	7.5	17.0	13.6
Sex:							
Male...................................	108,327	9.5	29.4	15.0	9.5	22.9	13.7
Female..............................	116,253	8.4	26.4	14.8	11.3	24.1	15.0
Race:							
White [2]................................	175,206	8.8	27.7	14.8	10.7	23.9	14.0
Black [2]................................	28,160	9.7	33.4	18.2	10.6	17.2	10.9
Asian [2]................................	14,247	7.1	17.8	7.5	6.7	33.7	27.3
Hispanic origin:							
Hispanic...............................	35,893	25.7	31.5	13.1	9.0	14.5	6.1
Non-Hispanic white..................	143,225	4.9	26.9	15.3	11.1	26.0	15.9
Marital status:							
Never married.........................	49,915	9.8	30.2	15.8	9.4	24.0	10.8
Married, spouse present............	126,013	7.4	25.1	13.8	10.6	25.8	17.3
Married, spouse absent [3]...........	3,456	14.9	31.1	12.7	7.5	20.2	13.6
Separated.............................	4,268	18.4	33.7	16.7	9.2	14.1	8.0
Widowed..............................	15,174	15.0	37.3	15.7	9.0	14.2	8.7
Divorced...............................	25,754	8.7	29.6	18.3	13.3	18.8	11.2
Civilian labor force status:							
Employed..............................	132,290	6.0	24.1	14.2	11.1	27.5	17.1
Unemployed...........................	7,811	10.7	31.8	17.7	11.0	19.7	9.1
Not in the labor force.................	84,479	13.4	33.4	15.7	9.3	17.7	10.5

[1] Includes occupational and academic degrees. [2] For persons who selected this race group only. See footnote 4, Table 256. [3] Excludes those separated.

Source: U.S. Census Bureau, "Educational Attainment in the United States: 2021," <www.census.gov/topics/education/educational-attainment.html>, accessed March 2022.

Table 259. Mean Earnings by Highest Level of Education or Degree and Selected Characteristics: 2020

[In dollars. Persons as of March 2021. For persons 18 years old and over with earnings. Based on Current Population Survey, Annual Social and Economic Supplement; see text, Section 1 and Appendix III. For definition of mean, see Guide to Tabular Presentation]

Characteristic	Mean earnings, total [1]	Mean earnings by highest level of education or degree (dollars)							
		Ninth to twelfth grade, non-graduate	High school graduate only	Some college, no degree	Associate's	Bachelor's	Master's	Professional	Doctorate
All persons [2]..................	58,329	26,815	39,498	41,222	48,753	73,499	92,272	147,236	136,702
Age:									
25 to 34 years old...............	50,248	26,915	36,137	37,823	41,486	61,528	72,665	102,781	102,515
35 to 44 years old...............	67,918	31,710	43,465	51,639	52,204	82,545	97,918	154,049	148,295
45 to 54 years old...............	71,514	32,734	47,160	51,631	56,652	87,868	108,564	160,289	153,439
55 to 64 years old...............	66,778	36,000	45,470	54,879	55,736	82,451	102,509	169,551	141,608
65 years old and over..........	57,025	25,362	39,900	50,129	47,662	66,489	64,167	141,157	118,912
Sex:									
Male..............................	67,964	31,014	45,276	49,611	58,998	88,447	117,617	170,966	155,485
Female..........................	47,655	20,380	31,123	32,241	39,551	58,938	72,568	116,137	113,858
White [3]............................	59,539	27,917	41,082	42,927	50,174	75,123	92,128	151,092	134,289
Male..............................	69,772	32,722	46,923	51,932	60,758	91,238	119,184	175,843	159,867
Female..........................	47,726	20,077	32,130	32,825	40,022	58,895	71,596	115,833	102,418
Black [3]............................	46,149	22,884	33,514	35,877	43,895	61,807	77,406	110,918	128,628
Male..............................	49,682	25,097	38,139	40,138	50,613	68,690	90,470	128,097	131,880
Female..........................	43,036	20,072	28,032	32,177	39,446	56,700	70,404	99,624	126,294
Asian [3]............................	74,487	25,158	35,151	33,176	43,933	75,445	108,205	147,455	147,912
Male..............................	86,756	24,697	40,546	42,072	54,654	86,313	126,071	159,056	147,288
Female..........................	61,050	25,560	29,098	23,451	35,578	64,631	85,149	130,183	148,834
Hispanic [4]........................	41,027	28,032	34,404	35,502	42,950	58,969	76,738	131,122	99,235
Male..............................	45,726	31,226	38,644	41,126	50,681	68,401	92,849	170,486	107,572
Female..........................	34,960	22,323	27,780	29,712	35,995	50,052	63,036	85,206	90,692

[1] Includes those with less than ninth grade education, not shown separately. [2] Includes other races not shown separately. [3] For persons who selected this race group only. See footnote 4, Table 256. [4] Persons of Hispanic origin may be of any race.

Source: U.S. Census Bureau, *Income and Poverty in the United States: 2020*, Current Population Reports, P60-273, September 2021; and "Current Population Survey Tables for Personal Income: Table PINC-04," <www.census.gov/data/tables/time-series/demo/income-poverty/cps-pinc/pinc-04.html>, accessed January 2022.

Table 260. Educational Attainment by State: 2000 to 2019

[In percent. 2000 as of April; 2010 and 2019 represents annual averages for calendar year. For persons 25 years old and over. Based on the 2000 Census of Population, and the American Community Survey, which includes the household population and the population living in institutions, college dormitories, and other group quarters. See text, Section 1 and Appendix III. For margin of error data, see source]

State	2000			2010			2019		
	High school graduate or more	Bachelor's degree or more	Advanced degree or more	High school graduate or more	Bachelor's degree or more	Advanced degree or more	High school graduate or more	Bachelor's degree or more	Advanced degree or more
United States	**80.4**	**24.4**	**8.9**	**85.6**	**28.2**	**10.4**	**88.6**	**33.1**	**12.8**
Alabama	75.3	19.0	6.9	82.1	21.9	8.0	87.1	26.3	10.0
Alaska	88.3	24.7	8.6	91.0	27.9	9.4	93.6	30.2	11.7
Arizona	81.0	23.5	8.4	85.6	25.9	9.2	87.6	30.2	11.3
Arkansas	75.3	16.7	5.7	82.9	19.5	6.3	87.5	23.3	8.3
California	76.8	26.6	9.5	80.7	30.1	11.0	84.0	35.0	13.1
Colorado	86.9	32.7	11.1	89.7	36.4	13.0	92.4	42.7	16.0
Connecticut	84.0	31.4	13.3	88.6	35.5	15.3	90.7	39.8	17.8
Delaware	82.6	25.0	9.4	87.7	27.8	11.3	90.3	33.2	13.7
District of Columbia	77.8	39.1	21.0	87.4	50.1	26.9	91.9	59.7	34.0
Florida	79.9	22.3	8.1	85.5	25.8	9.2	88.4	30.7	11.4
Georgia	78.6	24.3	8.3	84.3	27.3	9.8	87.9	32.5	12.6
Hawaii	84.6	26.2	8.4	89.9	29.5	9.6	92.4	33.6	11.6
Idaho	84.7	21.7	6.8	88.3	24.4	7.7	91.5	28.7	9.9
Illinois	81.4	26.1	9.5	86.9	30.8	11.5	89.8	35.8	14.1
Indiana	82.1	19.4	7.2	87.0	22.7	8.1	89.6	26.9	9.7
Iowa	86.1	21.2	6.5	90.6	24.9	7.9	92.6	29.3	9.5
Kansas	86.0	25.8	8.7	89.2	29.8	10.5	91.8	34.0	12.4
Kentucky	74.1	17.1	6.9	81.9	20.5	8.1	87.2	25.1	10.3
Louisiana	74.8	18.7	6.5	81.9	21.4	7.0	86.0	25.0	8.9
Maine	85.4	22.9	7.9	90.3	26.8	9.5	93.2	33.2	12.4
Maryland	83.8	31.4	13.4	88.1	36.1	16.4	90.4	40.9	19.1
Massachusetts	84.8	33.2	13.7	89.1	39.0	16.7	91.3	45.0	20.3
Michigan	83.4	21.8	8.1	88.7	25.2	9.6	91.4	30.0	11.9
Minnesota	87.9	27.4	8.3	91.8	31.8	10.3	93.6	37.3	12.7
Mississippi	72.9	16.9	5.8	81.0	19.5	7.1	85.3	22.3	8.6
Missouri	81.3	21.6	7.6	86.9	25.6	9.5	90.7	30.2	11.8
Montana	87.2	24.4	7.2	91.7	28.8	9.0	94.2	33.6	10.5
Nebraska	86.6	23.7	7.3	90.4	28.6	9.0	92.0	33.2	11.4
Nevada	80.7	18.2	6.1	84.7	21.7	7.4	86.9	25.7	9.0
New Hampshire	87.4	28.7	10.0	91.5	32.8	12.4	93.3	37.6	14.7
New Jersey	82.1	29.8	11.0	88.0	35.4	13.3	90.3	41.2	16.1
New Mexico	78.9	23.5	9.8	83.3	25.0	10.8	85.9	27.7	12.2
New York	79.1	27.4	11.8	84.9	32.5	14.0	87.6	37.8	16.6
North Carolina	78.1	22.5	7.2	84.7	26.5	8.7	88.6	32.3	11.8
North Dakota	83.9	22.0	5.5	90.3	27.6	7.9	93.5	30.4	8.9
Ohio	83.0	21.1	7.4	88.1	24.6	8.9	90.8	29.3	11.1
Oklahoma	80.6	20.3	6.8	86.2	22.9	7.5	88.4	26.2	9.1
Oregon	85.1	25.1	8.7	88.8	28.8	10.5	91.4	34.5	13.5
Pennsylvania	81.9	22.4	8.4	88.4	27.1	10.4	91.0	32.3	12.8
Rhode Island	78.0	25.6	9.7	83.5	30.2	12.2	89.3	34.8	13.9
South Carolina	76.3	20.4	6.9	84.1	24.5	8.8	88.3	29.6	11.2
South Dakota	84.6	21.5	6.0	89.6	26.3	7.7	92.1	29.7	9.1
Tennessee	75.9	19.6	6.8	83.6	23.1	8.5	88.0	28.7	10.7
Texas	75.7	23.2	7.6	80.7	25.9	8.6	84.6	30.8	10.8
Utah	87.7	26.1	8.3	90.6	29.3	9.4	93.0	34.8	11.3
Vermont	86.4	29.4	11.1	91.0	33.6	13.3	93.1	38.7	16.0
Virginia	81.5	29.5	11.6	86.5	34.2	14.2	90.0	39.6	17.2
Washington	87.1	27.7	9.3	89.8	31.1	11.1	91.7	37.0	14.2
West Virginia	75.2	14.8	5.9	83.2	17.5	6.6	87.1	21.1	8.4
Wisconsin	85.1	22.4	7.2	90.1	24.1	9.0	92.8	31.3	10.7
Wyoming	87.9	21.9	7.0	92.3	22.3	8.4	94.5	29.1	10.4

Source: U.S. Census Bureau, 2000 Census of Population, P37, "Sex by Educational Attainment for the Population 25 Years and Over"; and American Community Survey, S1501, "Educational Attainment," <data.census.gov>, accessed November 2020.

Table 261. Children Who Speak a Language Other Than English at Home by Region: 2019

[In thousands (12,084 represents 12,084,000), except percent. For children 5 to 17 years old. For more on languages spoken at home, see Table 57 and Table 58. Based on the American Community Survey; see text Section 1, and Appendix III. For composition of regions, see map inside front cover]

Item	U.S.	Northeast	Midwest	South	West
Children who speak another language at home.............................	**12,084**	**2,005**	**1,462**	**4,413**	**4,204**
Percent of children 5 to 17 years old..	**22.6**	**23.8**	**13.0**	**21.1**	**32.3**
Speak Spanish..	8,585	1,098	835	3,469	3,183
Speak English "very well"......................................	7,040	905	691	2,748	2,697
Speak English less than "very well"........................	1,545	193	144	721	486
Speak other Indo-European languages...............................	1,583	536	280	454	312
Speak English "very well"......................................	1,281	414	217	389	260
Speak English less than "very well"........................	302	122	63	65	52
Speak Asian and Pacific Island languages.............................	1,268	240	169	319	539
Speak English "very well"......................................	972	182	124	247	419
Speak English less than "very well"........................	296	58	46	72	120
Speak other languages..	649	132	178	171	169
Speak English "very well"......................................	532	110	142	138	141
Speak English less than "very well"........................	117	21	35	33	28
Have difficulty speaking English [1]................................	2,260	395	288	891	686
Language spoken at home in limited English speaking households [2]........	2,476	449	284	999	743
Speak only English..	198	46	29	61	62
Speak Spanish...	1,675	230	143	789	514
Speak other Indo-European languages..................................	223	83	39	59	42
Speak Asian and Pacific Island languages.............................	270	66	39	63	102
Speak other languages...	110	24	34	28	24

[1] Children age 5 to 17 who speak English less than "very well." [2] A household in which no person age 14 or over speaks English at least "very well."

Source: U.S. Census Bureau, 2019 American Community Survey, B16003, "Age by Language Spoken at Home for the Population 5 Years and Over" and B16004, "Age by Language Spoken at Home by Ability to Speak English for the Population 5 Years and Over," <data.census.gov>, accessed November 2020.

Table 262. Preprimary School Enrollment—Summary: 1970 to 2020

[10,949 represents 10,949,000. As of October. Civilian noninstitutional population. Includes public and private preschool (or nursery school) and kindergarten programs. Excludes 5-year-olds enrolled in elementary school. Based on Current Population Survey (CPS). See text, Section 1 and Appendix III]

Item	1970	1980	1990	2000	2010	2015	2018	2019	2020
NUMBER OF CHILDREN (1,000)									
Population, 3 to 5 years old.................	10,949	9,284	11,207	11,858	12,949	11,958	12,109	12,166	11,858
Total enrolled [1]........................	**4,104**	**4,878**	**6,659**	**7,592**	**8,246**	**7,683**	**7,747**	**7,841**	**6,371**
Preschool (or nursery school).............	1,094	1,981	3,378	4,326	4,797	4,475	4,734	4,654	3,488
Public..................................	332	628	1,202	2,146	2,749	2,561	2,687	2,554	2,047
Private.................................	762	1,353	2,177	2,180	2,048	1,914	2,047	2,101	1,441
Kindergarten...............................	3,010	2,897	3,281	3,266	3,449	3,207	3,013	3,187	2,883
Public..................................	2,498	2,438	2,767	2,701	3,079	2,864	2,711	2,763	2,434
Private.................................	511	459	513	565	369	342	302	424	448
White [2]...................................	3,443	3,994	5,389	5,861	6,160	5,515	5,605	5,535	4,600
Black [2]...................................	586	725	964	1,265	1,301	1,193	1,094	1,225	953
Hispanic [3]................................	(NA)	370	642	1,155	1,874	1,810	1,871	1,934	1,468
3 years old................................	454	857	1,205	1,540	1,718	1,513	1,583	1,721	1,143
4 years old................................	1,007	1,423	2,086	2,556	2,988	2,691	2,810	2,612	2,047
5 years old................................	2,643	2,598	3,367	3,496	3,787	3,479	3,354	3,507	3,181
PERCENT ENROLLED									
Total enrolled [1].........................	**37.5**	**52.5**	**59.4**	**64.0**	**63.7**	**64.2**	**64.0**	**64.5**	**53.7**
White [2]..................................	37.8	52.7	59.7	63.2	63.4	63.9	65.1	64.2	53.7
Black [2]..................................	34.9	51.8	57.8	68.5	64.1	65.3	62.7	63.4	53.3
Hispanic [3]...............................	(NA)	43.3	49.0	52.6	56.0	58.7	59.4	61.4	48.1
3 years old................................	12.9	27.3	32.6	39.2	38.2	38.4	39.7	42.8	29.7
4 years old................................	27.8	46.3	56.0	64.9	68.6	66.7	67.7	64.5	50.3
5 years old................................	69.3	84.7	88.8	87.6	88.1	87.3	84.5	85.7	80.6

NA Not available. [1] Includes races not shown separately. [2] Beginning 2003, data represent persons who selected this race group only and exclude persons reporting more than one race. Before 2003, the CPS permitted respondents to report only one race group. See also comments on race in the text for Section 1, Population.. [3] Persons of Hispanic origin may be of any race. The method of identifying Hispanic children was changed in 1980 from allocation based on status of mother to status reported for each child. The number of Hispanic children using the new method is larger.

Source: U.S. Census Bureau, Current Population Reports, P-20, and unpublished data; and "School Enrollment Tables," <www.census.gov/topics/education/school-enrollment.html>, accessed January 2022.

Table 263. Public Elementary and Secondary School Finances by Enrollment-Size Group: 2020

[In units, as indicated (771,111 represents $771,111,000,000). For school fiscal year ending in 2020. Enrollment as of Fall 2019. Data are based on the Annual Government Finance Survey. For details, see source. See also Appendix III]

Item	All school systems	School systems with enrollment of—						
		50,000 or more	25,000 to 49,999	15,000 to 24,999	7,500 to 14,999	5,000 to 7,499	3,000 to 4,999	Under 3,000
TOTAL (millions of dollars)								
General revenue	**771,111**	**172,923**	**94,651**	**72,657**	**108,023**	**66,811**	**83,884**	**172,160**
From federal sources	57,779	13,568	7,677	5,397	7,452	4,053	5,213	14,419
Through state [1]	53,343	12,805	7,223	5,151	6,996	3,815	4,841	12,513
Child nutrition programs	15,553	3,625	2,215	1,595	2,268	1,244	1,537	3,070
Direct	4,435	763	454	246	456	238	373	1,906
From state sources [1]	362,372	70,294	47,869	38,981	54,635	30,807	38,198	81,589
General formula assistance	244,826	44,975	35,184	27,953	38,950	20,529	25,032	52,203
Compensatory programs	6,642	1,908	938	744	928	427	645	1,052
Special education	22,411	5,647	2,668	1,989	2,696	1,714	2,165	5,531
From local sources	350,960	89,061	39,106	28,280	45,936	31,952	40,472	76,153
Taxes [1]	240,601	44,851	28,841	21,221	34,787	24,149	30,408	56,344
Property taxes	229,821	42,162	26,927	20,217	33,351	23,388	29,163	54,613
Contributions from parent government	64,678	34,501	4,813	2,848	5,166	4,181	5,606	7,563
From other local governments	10,282	855	1,638	1,121	1,551	833	1,070	3,214
Current charges [1]	12,853	2,202	1,417	1,112	1,739	1,114	1,375	3,895
School lunch	4,238	613	481	405	669	436	539	1,095
Other	22,546	6,653	2,397	1,977	2,694	1,674	2,014	5,137
General expenditure	**776,387**	**173,906**	**95,346**	**73,697**	**110,109**	**67,295**	**84,448**	**171,587**
Current spending [2]	667,873	148,648	81,541	62,641	93,870	58,205	73,030	149,938
By function:								
Instruction	405,059	95,163	49,029	37,257	56,872	35,657	44,566	86,514
Support services	231,170	46,679	28,393	22,220	32,428	19,991	25,331	56,127
Other current spending [2]	31,645	6,806	4,119	3,164	4,570	2,557	3,133	7,297
By object:								
Total salaries and wages	371,859	80,723	47,449	36,293	53,661	32,438	40,575	80,721
Total employee benefits	163,515	34,005	19,093	15,377	23,428	15,058	18,915	37,639
Capital outlay	84,015	19,387	10,559	8,670	12,628	6,906	9,118	16,748
Interest on debt	20,653	4,738	2,899	2,281	3,166	1,917	2,091	3,561
Payments to other governments	3,846	1,132	348	104	445	266	210	1,341
Debt outstanding	514,785	118,419	69,365	58,806	79,184	44,981	53,334	90,697
Long-term	504,612	115,859	68,168	58,281	77,907	44,151	52,137	88,109
Short-term	10,173	2,561	1,197	525	1,276	829	1,197	2,588
Long-term debt issued	75,040	14,544	10,127	8,232	12,601	7,047	7,762	14,725
Long-term debt retired	55,916	10,991	7,452	5,740	8,403	5,027	6,468	11,834
Fall enrollment (1,000s)	48,008	10,523	6,669	5,008	7,250	4,137	5,086	9,336
PER PUPIL (dollars)								
General revenue	**16,062**	**16,433**	**14,193**	**14,509**	**14,899**	**16,149**	**16,494**	**18,441**
From federal sources	1,204	1,289	1,151	1,078	1,028	980	1,025	1,545
From state sources [1]	7,548	6,680	7,178	7,784	7,536	7,446	7,511	8,739
General formula assistance	5,100	4,274	5,276	5,582	5,372	4,962	4,922	5,592
Special education	467	537	400	397	372	414	426	593
From local sources [1]	7,310	8,464	5,864	5,647	6,336	7,723	7,958	8,157
Taxes [1]	5,012	4,262	4,325	4,238	4,798	5,837	5,979	6,035
Property taxes	4,787	4,007	4,038	4,037	4,600	5,653	5,734	5,850
Contributions from parent government	1,347	3,279	722	569	712	1,011	1,102	810
Current charges [1]	268	209	213	222	240	269	270	417
School lunch	88	58	72	81	92	105	106	117
General expenditure [1]	**15,755**	**15,920**	**13,943**	**14,418**	**14,873**	**15,831**	**16,217**	**17,978**
Current spending [2]	13,494	13,520	11,873	12,210	12,634	13,634	13,972	15,659
By function:								
Instruction	8,176	8,581	7,142	7,297	7,678	8,325	8,511	9,070
Support services	4,815	4,436	4,258	4,437	4,473	4,832	4,981	6,012
By object:								
Total salaries and wages	7,746	7,671	7,115	7,247	7,401	7,841	7,978	8,647
Total employee benefits	3,406	3,232	2,863	3,071	3,231	3,640	3,719	4,032
Capital outlay	1,750	1,842	1,583	1,731	1,742	1,669	1,793	1,794
Interest on debt	430	450	435	456	437	463	411	381
Debt outstanding	10,723	11,254	10,401	11,743	10,921	10,873	10,487	9,715
Long-term	10,511	11,010	10,222	11,638	10,745	10,672	10,252	9,438

[1] Includes other sources not shown separately. [2] Expenditures for adult education, community services, and other non-elementary/secondary programs are included in total "Current spending" and "Other current spending" but excluded under pupil amounts.

Source: U.S. Census Bureau, Annual Survey of School System Finances Tables, "2020 Public Elementary-Secondary Education Finance Data," May 2022, <www.census.gov/programs-surveys/school-finances/data/tables.html>, accessed May 2022.

Table 264. Public Elementary and Secondary School Estimated Finances by State: 2020

[In millions of dollars (771,111 represents $771,111,000,000), except as noted. For the school fiscal year. Includes finances of charter schools whose charters are held directly by a government or government agency; excludes charters schools whose charters are held by nongovernmental entities]

State	Revenue receipts				Expenditures				
		Source					Current expenditures		
						Per capita [2] (dol.)	Total current spending [3]	Average per pupil [4]	
	Total	Federal	State	Local	Total [1]			Amount [5] (dol.)	Rank
Total....................	**771,111**	**57,779**	**362,372**	**350,960**	**776,387**	**2,365**	**667,873**	**13,494**	**(X)**
Alabama....................	8,715	936	4,943	2,836	8,474	1,727	7,688	10,116	42
Alaska....................	2,612	382	1,660	570	2,613	3,561	2,425	18,313	7
Arizona....................	10,103	1,231	4,457	4,415	9,905	1,358	8,394	8,785	49
Arkansas....................	5,636	601	4,241	794	5,851	1,937	4,959	10,345	39
California....................	95,534	7,995	52,444	35,094	95,418	2,419	80,806	14,031	19
Colorado....................	12,919	834	5,353	6,731	13,008	2,259	10,437	11,602	33
Connecticut....................	12,018	470	4,487	7,062	11,587	3,249	10,705	21,346	3
Delaware....................	2,475	149	1,556	770	2,306	2,361	2,137	17,235	10
District of Columbia..........	1,591	131	(X)	1,460	1,650	2,330	1,238	22,856	2
Florida....................	32,718	3,379	12,427	16,912	32,618	1,518	28,711	9,937	44
Georgia....................	23,612	1,824	10,908	10,880	22,903	2,155	20,367	11,707	32
Hawaii....................	3,397	278	3,067	51	3,214	2,271	3,017	16,564	14
Idaho....................	2,835	264	1,838	734	2,687	1,502	2,399	8,272	51
Illinois....................	38,878	2,397	16,476	20,005	37,895	2,992	33,855	17,293	9
Indiana....................	13,340	948	8,341	4,052	13,362	1,985	11,047	10,935	38
Iowa....................	7,403	510	3,931	2,962	7,498	2,373	6,219	11,958	30
Kansas....................	7,254	522	4,857	1,875	7,558	2,595	6,322	12,697	27
Kentucky....................	8,797	994	4,745	3,057	9,048	2,023	7,959	11,397	35
Louisiana....................	8,769	1,000	3,649	4,120	8,210	1,762	7,564	11,843	31
Maine....................	3,118	178	1,233	1,707	3,044	2,262	2,763	14,892	16
Maryland....................	16,890	890	7,294	8,706	16,052	2,651	14,103	15,489	15
Massachusetts....................	18,975	850	8,050	10,075	19,853	2,879	18,243	18,733	6
Michigan....................	20,751	1,806	11,709	7,236	19,963	1,999	17,281	13,072	22
Minnesota....................	13,807	728	8,859	4,220	14,788	2,622	11,755	13,603	21
Mississippi....................	4,991	664	2,504	1,824	5,097	1,711	4,487	9,653	47
Missouri....................	10,981	976	4,717	5,287	11,772	1,917	10,171	11,239	37
Montana....................	2,045	254	878	914	2,172	2,030	1,807	12,101	29
Nebraska....................	4,846	350	1,613	2,883	4,986	2,580	4,264	12,939	23
Nevada....................	5,258	408	3,271	1,578	5,343	1,729	4,414	9,814	46
New Hampshire....................	3,389	160	1,058	2,171	3,217	2,364	3,033	17,900	8
New Jersey....................	32,427	1,203	14,027	17,198	31,858	3,583	29,932	20,670	5
New Mexico....................	4,540	633	3,078	828	4,215	2,007	3,577	11,332	36
New York....................	77,774	3,321	30,933	43,521	77,888	4,002	69,427	25,519	1
North Carolina....................	15,555	1,632	9,583	4,339	16,186	1,541	14,424	9,958	43
North Dakota....................	1,931	193	1,058	680	1,999	2,617	1,673	14,242	18
Ohio....................	25,332	1,738	9,762	13,832	26,850	2,296	23,037	13,805	20
Oklahoma....................	7,203	762	3,430	3,011	7,127	1,800	6,300	9,508	48
Oregon....................	9,198	579	4,915	3,705	10,306	2,444	7,787	12,855	25
Pennsylvania....................	33,725	2,103	13,001	18,621	33,646	2,629	30,014	17,142	11
Rhode Island....................	2,596	198	1,043	1,354	2,575	2,433	2,412	16,857	12
South Carolina....................	10,809	868	5,126	4,816	10,687	2,072	8,833	11,532	34
South Dakota....................	1,734	241	582	911	1,737	1,958	1,447	10,208	41
Tennessee....................	11,115	1,121	5,233	4,761	11,174	1,636	10,110	9,896	45
Texas....................	68,895	6,834	23,549	38,512	71,852	2,479	53,836	10,342	40
Utah....................	6,085	431	3,127	2,527	6,367	1,987	5,146	8,366	50
Vermont....................	2,030	129	1,842	59	1,978	3,169	1,903	20,838	4
Virginia....................	18,153	1,123	7,350	9,680	18,502	2,162	16,814	12,905	24
Washington....................	20,095	1,169	14,182	4,745	21,092	2,770	16,764	14,556	17
West Virginia....................	3,732	432	2,052	1,248	3,563	1,985	3,303	12,375	28
Wisconsin....................	12,700	824	6,971	4,905	12,935	2,221	10,987	12,740	26
Wyoming....................	1,827	138	963	726	1,758	3,030	1,578	16,698	13

X Not applicable. [1] Includes interest on school debt and payments to state and local governments, not shown separately. [2] Based on U.S. Census Bureau estimated resident population, as of July 1, 2019. [3] Includes expenditures for adult education, community services, and other nonelementary-secondary programs. [4] Based on Fall 2019 enrollment, National Center for Education Statistics, Common Core of Data. [5] Per pupil amounts exclude expenditures for payments to other school systems, adult education, community services, and other nonelementary-secondary programs.

Source: U.S. Census Bureau, Annual Survey of School System Finances Tables, "2020 Public Elementary-Secondary Education Finance Data," May 2022, <www.census.gov/programs-surveys/school-finances/data/tables.html>, accessed May 2022.

Table 265. Public Elementary and Secondary Schools—Summary: 1990 to 2022

[In units as indicated (44,949 represents 44,949,000). For school year ending in year shown, except as indicated. Data are estimates]

Item	Unit	1990	2000	2010	2015	2020	2021	2022
School districts, total.............................	**Number**	**15,552**	**15,403**	**16,340**	**16,638**	**16,455**	**16,513**	**16,529**
ENROLLMENT								
Population 5-17 years old [1]........................	1,000	44,949	52,811	53,890	53,691	53,462	54,993	54,739
Percent of resident population..................	Percent	18.2	18.9	17.6	16.9	16.3	16.6	16.5
Fall enrollment [2].................................	**1,000**	**40,527**	**46,577**	**49,104**	**49,901**	**50,176**	**48,847**	**48,778**
Percent of population 5-17 years old............	Percent	90.2	88.2	91.1	92.9	93.9	88.8	89.1
Average daily attendance........................	1,000	37,573	43,313	45,835	46,780	46,823	45,663	45,807
INSTRUCTIONAL STAFF								
Total [3]..	**1,000**	**2,685**	**3,273**	**3,644**	**3,663**	**3,764**	**3,763**	**3,777**
Classroom teachers...............................	1,000	2,362	2,891	3,182	3,157	3,194	3,192	3,196
Average salaries:								
Instructional staff........................	Dollar	32,638	43,837	56,995	59,702	66,038	67,507	68,827
Classroom teachers........................	Dollar	31,367	41,807	55,370	57,758	64,172	65,293	66,397
REVENUES								
Revenue receipts...............................	**Mil. dol.**	**208,656**	**369,754**	**586,995**	**649,654**	**793,156**	**817,694**	**859,924**
Federal..	Mil. dol.	13,184	26,346	75,592	53,888	59,868	71,564	91,941
State...	Mil. dol.	100,787	183,986	258,396	305,510	375,590	382,322	393,409
Local...	Mil. dol.	94,685	159,421	253,006	290,256	357,698	363,808	374,574
Percent of total:								
Federal..	Percent	6.3	7.1	12.9	8.3	7.5	8.8	10.7
State...	Percent	48.3	49.8	44.0	47.0	47.4	46.8	45.7
Local/other....................................	Percent	45.4	43.1	43.1	44.7	45.1	44.5	43.6
EXPENDITURES								
Total..	**Mil. dol.**	**209,698**	**374,782**	**615,210**	**651,243**	**791,694**	**809,925**	**847,135**
Current expenditures...........................	Mil. dol.	186,583	320,954	526,146	571,943	686,458	701,430	733,941
Other current expenditures [4]...................	Mil. dol.	3,341	6,618	10,621	13,624	11,501	12,657	12,831
Capital outlay..................................	Mil. dol.	16,012	37,552	53,052	46,188	70,700	73,331	77,138
Interest on school debt.........................	Mil. dol.	3,762	9,659	25,391	19,487	23,035	22,507	23,224
Percent of total:								
Current expenditures...........................	Percent	89.0	85.6	85.5	87.8	86.7	86.6	86.6
Other current expenditures [4]...................	Percent	1.6	1.8	1.7	2.1	1.5	1.6	1.5
Capital outlay..................................	Percent	7.6	10.0	8.6	7.1	8.9	9.1	9.1
Interest on school debt.........................	Percent	1.8	2.6	4.1	3.0	2.9	2.8	2.7
Current expenditures per pupil enrolled..........	Dollar	4,604	6,891	10,715	11,461	13,681	14,360	15,047

[1] Estimated resident population as of July 1 of the previous year, except 1990, 2000, 2010 and 2020 population enumerated as of April 1. Estimates reflect revisions based on the 2020 Census of Population. Source: U.S. Census Bureau, Population and Housing Estimates, "National Population by Characteristics: 2020-2021," <www.census.gov/programs-surveys/popest/data/tables.html>, accessed August 2022. [2] Enrollment in fall of the previous year. [3] Full-time equivalent. [4] Current expenses for summer schools, adult education, post-high-school vocational education, personnel retraining, and community services; and services to private school pupils, community centers, recreational activities, and public libraries, and so on, when operated by local school districts and not part of regular public elementary and secondary day-school programs.

Source: National Education Association, Washington, DC. Data from *Rankings of the States 2021 and Estimates of School Statistics 2022*, used with permission of the National Education Association © 2022. All rights reserved.

Table 266. Public Elementary and Secondary School Enrollment by Grade: 1980 to 2020

[In thousands (40,877 represents 40,877,000). As of Fall of year shown. Covers the 50 states and DC. Based on survey of state education agencies; see source for details]

Grade	1980	1990	1995	2000	2005	2010	2015	2017	2018	2019	2020 [3]
Pupils enrolled [1]..........	**40,877**	**41,217**	**44,840**	**47,204**	**49,113**	**49,484**	**50,438**	**50,686**	**50,694**	**50,796**	**49,375**
Pre-kindergarten to 8 [1].......	27,647	29,876	32,338	33,686	34,204	34,625	35,388	35,496	35,498	35,551	34,059
Pre-kindergarten [2].........	96	303	637	776	1,036	1,279	1,402	1,471	1,540	1,586	1,234
Kindergarten..................	2,593	3,306	3,536	3,382	3,619	3,682	3,713	3,684	3,681	3,716	3,377
First..........................	2,894	3,499	3,671	3,636	3,691	3,754	3,768	3,667	3,641	3,647	3,522
Second........................	2,800	3,327	3,507	3,634	3,606	3,701	3,842	3,684	3,654	3,638	3,531
Third..........................	2,893	3,297	3,445	3,676	3,586	3,686	3,869	3,788	3,709	3,686	3,554
Fourth........................	3,107	3,248	3,431	3,711	3,578	3,711	3,793	3,859	3,777	3,706	3,607
Fifth..........................	3,130	3,197	3,438	3,707	3,633	3,718	3,733	3,877	3,876	3,801	3,647
Sixth..........................	3,038	3,110	3,395	3,663	3,670	3,682	3,731	3,827	3,893	3,896	3,748
Seventh.......................	3,085	3,067	3,422	3,629	3,777	3,676	3,732	3,777	3,849	3,918	3,861
Eighth........................	3,086	2,979	3,356	3,538	3,802	3,659	3,719	3,772	3,788	3,865	3,889
Ungraded......................	924	541	500	334	205	77	87	89	92	92	89
Grades 9 to 12 [1]..............	13,231	11,341	12,502	13,517	14,909	14,860	15,050	15,190	15,196	15,246	15,316
Ninth.........................	3,377	3,169	3,704	3,963	4,287	4,008	4,019	3,996	4,004	4,044	4,016
Tenth.........................	3,368	2,896	3,237	3,491	3,866	3,800	3,846	3,834	3,849	3,868	3,897
Eleventh......................	3,195	2,612	2,826	3,083	3,454	3,538	3,598	3,677	3,653	3,671	3,700
Twelfth........................	2,925	2,381	2,487	2,803	3,180	3,472	3,537	3,631	3,649	3,621	3,662
Ungraded......................	366	284	247	177	121	42	49	52	41	41	42

[1] Includes unclassified students, not shown separately. [2] Data for 2019 includes imputations for nonreported prekindergarten enrollment in California; data for 2020 includes imputations for California and Oregon. [3] Includes imputations for nonreported enrollment for all grades in Illinois.

Source: U.S. National Center for Education Statistics, *Digest of Education Statistics*, "Latest version of all Digest tables," <nces.ed.gov/programs/digest>, accessed February 2022.

Table 267. Selected Statistics for the Largest Public School Districts: 2019

[For the 50 largest districts by enrollment size. For school year ending in 2019. Data from the Common Core Data Program; see source for details. School district boundaries are not necessarily the same as city or county boundaries]

School district	City	County	Number of students [1]	Number of full-time equivalent (FTE) teachers [2]	Number of schools [3]	Total expenditures per pupil
New York City Public Schools, NY [4]	New York	(X)	960,484	64,988	1,522	35,190
Los Angeles Unified School District, CA	Los Angeles	Los Angeles	495,255	21,981	785	19,043
City Of Chicago School District 299, IL	Chicago	Cook	359,476	21,809	658	19,132
Miami-Dade County Public School District, FL	Miami	Miami-Dade	350,434	18,252	510	11,152
Clark County School District, NV	Las Vegas	Clark	330,225	14,882	374	10,706
Broward County School District, FL	Fort Lauderdale	Broward	270,978	14,345	328	10,952
Hillsborough County School District, FL	Tampa	Hillsborough	220,252	13,191	297	10,303
Houston Independent School District, TX	Houston	Harris	209,772	11,967	280	13,748
Orange County Public Schools, FL	Orlando	Orange	208,203	11,879	258	12,269
Palm Beach County School District, FL	West Palm Beach	Palm Beach	192,533	11,648	234	11,919
Fairfax County Public Schools, VA	Falls Church	Fairfax	187,797	13,000	222	17,276
Hawaii Department of Education, HI	Honolulu	Honolulu	181,278	12,132	292	17,730
Gwinnett County School District, GA	Lawrenceville	Gwinnett	179,758	11,382	138	11,995
Montgomery County Public Schools, MD	Rockville	Montgomery	162,680	11,030	208	19,247
Wake County Schools, NC	Cary	Wake	161,784	10,219	187	11,879
Dallas Independent School District, TX	Dallas	Dallas	155,119	10,001	240	13,484
Charlotte-Mecklenburg Schools, NC	Charlotte	Mecklenburg	147,638	9,112	175	11,913
Prince George's County Public Schools, MD	Upper Marlboro	Prince George's	132,657	9,320	207	17,612
Philadelphia City School District, PA	Philadelphia	Philadelphia	132,520	7,943	217	26,930
Duval County School District, FL	Jacksonville	Duval	130,229	7,067	205	9,787
Cypress-Fairbanks Independent School District, TX	Houston	Harris	116,512	7,262	89	12,049
Baltimore County Public Schools, MD	Towson	Baltimore	113,814	7,395	174	16,283
Shelby County School District, TN	Memphis	Shelby	112,125	6,867	219	12,705
Cobb County School District, GA	Marietta	Cobb	111,854	7,319	111	12,497
Northside Independent School District, TX	San Antonio	Bexar	106,501	6,962	120	11,385
San Diego City Unified School District, CA	San Diego	San Diego	103,194	4,388	176	20,693
Polk County School District, FL	Bartow	Polk	101,408	5,793	163	10,482
Pinellas County School District, FL	Largo	Pinellas	100,948	7,520	157	11,421
DeKalb County School District, GA	Stone Mountain	DeKalb	99,166	7,052	130	14,046
Jefferson County School District, KY	Louisville	Jefferson	97,936	6,184	170	15,403
Fulton County, GA	Atlanta	Fulton	94,491	6,370	107	13,850
Lee County School District, FL	Fort Myers	Lee	94,410	5,267	121	11,094
Denver School District, CO	Denver	Denver	92,039	6,155	206	16,753
Prince William County Public Schools, VA	Manassas	Prince William	90,843	5,594	94	13,917
Albuquerque Public Schools, NM	Albuquerque	Bernalillo	89,788	5,894	173	12,044
Nashville Davidson County Schools, TN	Nashville	Davidson	84,667	5,564	169	14,152
Jefferson County School District, CO	Golden	Jefferson	84,646	4,684	165	12,101
Fort Worth Independent School District, TX	Fort Worth	Tarrant	84,510	5,778	144	12,115
Anne Arundel County Public Schools, MD	Annapolis	Anne Arundel	83,300	5,617	124	17,812
Loudoun County Public Schools, VA	Ashburn	Loudoun	81,906	5,784	92	17,167
Alpine School District, UT	American Fork	Utah	81,715	3,205	87	9,726
Austin Independent School District, TX	Austin	Travis	80,032	5,540	130	21,986
Katy Independent School District, TX	Katy	Fort Bend	79,913	5,274	70	13,662
Baltimore City Public Schools, MD	Baltimore	Baltimore City	79,297	4,931	166	20,661
Greenville County School District, SC	Greenville	Greenville	76,158	4,848	91	11,175
Fort Bend Independent School District, TX	Sugar Land	Fort Bend	76,122	4,662	81	11,692
Milwaukee School District, WI	Milwaukee	Milwaukee	75,431	4,387	161	15,960
Pasco County School District, FL	Land o' Lakes	Pasco	75,048	4,616	102	10,140
Davis School District, UT	Farmington	Davis	74,289	3,033	92	9,027
Brevard County School District, FL	Viera	Brevard	73,734	4,502	113	10,157

X Not applicable. [1] Number of students receiving educational services from the school district. [2] Full-time equivalent is the amount of time required to perform an assignment stated as a proportion of a full-time position. [3] Totals for number of schools may differ from published estimates since they exclude closed, inactive, and future schools. [4] Represents New York City Geographic Districts 1-32. Data for per pupil expenditures are from the NYC Chancellor's Office.

Source: U.S. Department of Education, National Center for Education Statistics, "Elementary/Secondary Information System," <www.nces.ed.gov/ccd/elsi>, accessed March 2022.

Table 268. Public Elementary and Secondary School Enrollment by State: 1990 to 2020

[In thousands (29,876 represents 29,876,000). As of Fall. Includes unclassified/ungraded students. Based on survey of state education agencies; see source for details]

State	Pre-kindergarten through grade 8					Grades 9 through 12				
	1990	2000	2010	2015	2020	1990	2000	2010	2015	2020
United States..............	29,876	33,686	34,625	35,388	34,059	11,341	13,517	14,860	15,050	15,316
Alabama......................	527	539	534	522	518	195	201	222	222	217
Alaska........................	85	94	92	94	92	29	39	40	39	38
Arizona.......................	479	641	752	775	761	161	237	320	334	355
Arkansas....................	314	318	346	350	342	123	132	136	142	144
California....................	3,614	4,407	4,294	4,362	4,093	1,337	1,734	1,996	1,943	1,970
Colorado.....................	420	517	601	638	605	154	208	242	261	279
Connecticut.................	347	406	387	371	345	122	156	173	167	164
Delaware....................	73	81	90	95	95	27	34	39	40	43
District of Columbia...........	61	54	54	65	71	19	15	18	19	19
Florida.......................	1,370	1,760	1,858	1,952	1,929	492	675	785	840	861
Georgia......................	849	1,060	1,202	1,243	1,199	303	385	475	514	531
Hawaii........................	123	132	128	132	124	49	52	52	50	52
Idaho.........................	160	170	194	206	212	61	75	82	86	95
Illinois........................	1,310	1,474	1,455	1,422	1,286	512	575	637	619	606
Indiana.......................	676	703	729	725	710	279	286	318	321	323
Iowa..........................	345	334	348	361	355	139	161	148	147	152
Kansas.......................	320	323	343	353	337	117	147	141	143	145
Kentucky.....................	459	471	480	488	458	177	194	193	199	201
Louisiana....................	586	547	512	520	492	199	197	184	199	201
Maine........................	155	146	129	125	117	60	61	60	56	55
Maryland.....................	527	609	588	627	615	188	244	264	253	268
Massachusetts.............	604	703	666	669	628	230	273	289	295	294
Michigan.....................	1,145	1,222	1,076	1,052	971	440	498	511	484	463
Minnesota...................	546	578	570	599	594	211	277	268	266	278
Mississippi..................	372	364	351	349	313	131	134	140	139	130
Missouri......................	588	645	643	650	614	228	268	276	269	269
Montana......................	111	105	98	103	103	42	50	43	42	44
Nebraska....................	198	195	210	224	227	76	91	88	92	98
Nevada.......................	150	251	307	331	335	51	90	130	137	148
New Hampshire.............	126	147	132	124	114	46	61	63	58	55
New Jersey..................	783	968	981	989	950	306	346	421	420	424
New Mexico.................	208	225	239	239	217	94	95	99	97	100
New York....................	1,827	2,029	1,869	1,870	1,787	771	853	866	842	815
North Carolina..............	783	945	1,058	1,081	1,050	304	348	432	464	464
North Dakota................	85	72	66	78	82	33	37	30	31	33
Ohio..........................	1,258	1,294	1,223	1,195	1,142	514	541	531	522	503
Oklahoma....................	425	445	483	505	498	154	178	176	188	197
Oregon.......................	340	379	393	427	397	132	167	178	182	181
Pennsylvania...............	1,172	1,258	1,210	1,177	1,156	496	556	584	541	548
Rhode Island................	102	114	98	99	94	37	44	46	43	45
South Carolina..............	452	493	516	543	538	170	184	210	221	229
South Dakota...............	95	88	88	97	99	34	41	38	37	41
Tennessee...................	598	668	702	709	690	226	241	286	292	295
Texas........................	2,511	2,943	3,587	3,809	3,762	872	1,117	1,349	1,492	1,611
Utah..........................	325	333	425	464	473	122	148	161	184	208
Vermont......................	71	70	68	62	58	25	32	29	26	24
Virginia.......................	728	816	871	897	856	270	329	380	387	394
Washington..................	613	694	714	750	744	227	310	330	337	343
West Virginia................	224	201	201	197	177	98	85	81	80	77
Wisconsin....................	565	595	598	604	569	232	285	274	264	261
Wyoming.....................	71	60	63	68	65	27	30	26	27	28

Source: U.S. National Center for Education Statistics, *Digest of Education Statistics*, "Latest version of all Digest tables," and earlier releases, <nces.ed.gov/programs/digest>, accessed February 2022.

Table 269. Parent Participation in School-Related Activities by Selected School, Student, and Family Characteristics: 2019

[In percent, except as noted (51,498 represents 51,498,000). For school year ending in year shown. Covers parents with children in kindergarten through grade 12. Homeschooled students are excluded. Based on the Parent and Family Involvement in Education Survey, a component of the National Household Education Surveys Program]

Characteristic	Number of students in grades K through 12 (1,000)	Participation in school activities by parent or other household member				
		Attended a general school or PTO/PTA meeting [1]	Attended regularly scheduled parent-teacher conference	Attended a school or class event	Volunteered or served on school committee	Participated in school fundraising
Total..	**51,498**	**89**	**75**	**79**	**43**	**57**
School type: [2]						
Public, assigned..............................	39,830	88	73	78	39	54
Public, chosen................................	6,036	90	77	79	45	57
Private, religious.............................	3,736	95	86	91	73	79
Private, nonreligious.........................	916	95	91	92	74	75
Student's sex:						
Male...	26,633	88	76	78	41	56
Female..	24,865	89	74	81	45	57
Student's race/ethnicity:						
White, non-Hispanic..........................	24,906	90	76	85	49	64
Black, non-Hispanic..........................	7,032	88	77	76	35	49
Asian or Pacific Islander, non-Hispanic...........	3,166	83	73	70	41	55
Other, non-Hispanic [3].......................	3,268	90	79	83	45	58
Hispanic [4]..................................	13,126	87	73	72	35	46
Student's grade level:						
Kindergarten to 2nd grade..........................	12,229	94	90	83	57	66
3rd to 5th grade..............................	12,173	93	88	86	49	61
6th to 8th grade..............................	12,263	89	72	80	36	53
9th to 12th grade.............................	14,833	80	54	70	32	48
Parents' highest education level:						
Less than high school........................	5,291	82	68	61	25	36
High school graduate or equivalent.............	9,745	82	71	69	28	44
Vocational/technical or some college............	13,082	88	75	79	38	56
Bachelor's degree............................	13,609	92	78	86	54	66
Graduate or professional school..................	9,772	94	80	90	58	68
Parents' language at home:						
Both/only parent(s) speak(s) English..............	43,935	90	76	82	45	59
One of two parents speaks English................	1,932	89	75	76	38	43
No parent speaks English.....................	5,631	81	67	62	26	38

[1] Parent Teacher Organization (PTO) or Parent Teacher Association (PTA) meeting. [2] School type classifies the school currently attended as either public or private. Public schools are further classified according to whether the school was chosen or assigned. Private schools are classified as being religious or nonreligious. [3] Includes persons of all other races and multiple races, non-Hispanic. [4] Persons of Hispanic ethnicity may be of any race.

Source: U.S. Department of Education, National Center for Education Statistics, *Parent and Family Involvement in Education: 2019, First Look*, July 2020, NCES 2020-076. See also <nces.ed.gov/nhes>.

Table 270. School Enrollment Below Postsecondary—Summary by Sex, Race, and Hispanic Origin: 2020

[In thousands (55,548 represents 55,548,000), except percent. As of October. Covers civilian noninstitutional population enrolled in nursery school through high school. Based on Current Population Survey, see text, Section 1 and Appendix III]

Characteristic	Total			Race and Hispanic origin				
				White [2]				
	Number [1]	Male	Female	Total	Non-Hispanic	Black [2]	Asian [2]	Hispanic [3]
All students......................	**55,548**	**28,322**	**27,225**	**40,010**	**27,842**	**8,422**	**3,012**	**13,972**
Nursery..............................	3,545	1,762	1,783	2,553	1,900	512	178	751
Full day...........................	1,923	(NA)	(NA)	1,380	1,013	291	81	424
Part day...........................	1,622	(NA)	(NA)	1,173	887	220	97	326
Public schools.....................	2,094	(NA)	(NA)	1,429	969	382	104	534
Full day...........................	996	(NA)	(NA)	660	432	201	45	264
Part day...........................	1,098	(NA)	(NA)	769	537	181	59	271
Private schools....................	1,451	(NA)	(NA)	1,124	931	130	73	216
Full day...........................	927	(NA)	(NA)	720	581	90	35	161
Part day...........................	524	(NA)	(NA)	404	350	40	38	56
Kindergarten........................	3,698	1,878	1,820	2,651	1,881	597	219	890
Elementary..........................	32,046	16,491	15,554	23,031	15,802	4,811	1,801	8,302
High school.........................	16,259	8,191	8,068	11,775	8,258	2,502	814	4,029
Population 18 to 24 years old.......	29,159	14,593	14,567	21,326	15,333	4,289	1,855	6,868
Percent dropouts [4].................	5.2	6.2	4.1	5.5	4.6	4.1	2.5	7.6
Percent high school graduates. . . .	89.1	87.2	90.9	89.1	90.3	88.0	94.6	86.4
Percent enrolled in college.........	40.0	35.5	44.5	39.4	40.9	36.1	63.3	35.8

NA Not available. [1] Includes other races not shown separately. [2] For persons who selected this race group only. See footnote 4, Table 256. [3] Persons of Hispanic origin may be of any race. [4] For persons not in regular school and who have not completed the 12th grade nor received a general equivalency degree.

Source: U.S. Census Bureau, "School Enrollment," <www.census.gov/topics/education/school-enrollment.html>, accessed February 2022.

Table 271. Elementary and Secondary Schools—Teachers, Enrollment, and Pupil-Teacher Ratio: 1970 to 2020

[In thousands (2,292 represents 2,292,000), except ratios. As of Fall. Data are for full-time equivalent teachers. Based on surveys of state education agencies and private schools; see source for details. Data may not sum due to rounding]

Year	Teachers			Enrollment			Pupil-teacher ratio		
	Total	Public	Private [1]	Total	Public	Private [1]	Total	Public	Private [1]
1970	2,292	2,059	233	51,257	45,894	5,363	22.4	22.3	23.0
1980	2,485	2,184	301	46,208	40,877	5,331	18.6	18.7	17.7
1990	2,759	2,398	361	46,864	41,217	5,648	17.0	17.2	15.6
2000	3,366	2,941	424	53,373	47,204	6,169	15.9	16.0	14.5
2005	3,593	3,143	450	55,187	49,113	6,073	15.4	15.6	13.5
2006	3,622	3,166	456	55,307	49,316	5,991	15.3	15.6	13.2
2007	3,656	3,200	456	55,201	49,291	5,910	15.1	15.4	13.0
2008	3,670	3,222	448	54,973	49,266	5,707	15.0	15.3	12.8
2009	3,647	3,210	437	54,849	49,361	5,488	15.0	15.4	12.5
2010	3,512	3,099	413	54,867	49,484	5,382	15.6	16.0	13.0
2011	3,508	3,103	405	54,790	49,522	5,268	15.6	16.0	13.0
2012	3,517	3,109	408	55,104	49,771	5,333	15.7	16.0	13.1
2013	3,555	3,114	441	55,440	50,045	5,396	15.6	16.1	12.2
2014	3,594	3,132	461	55,888	50,313	5,575	15.6	16.1	12.1
2015	3,633	3,151	482	56,189	50,438	5,751	15.5	16.0	11.9
2016	3,653	3,169	483	56,369	50,615	5,754	15.4	16.0	11.9
2017	3,652	3,170	482	56,406	50,686	5,720	15.4	16.0	11.9
2018	3,652	3,170	[2] 482	56,411	50,694	[2] 5,717	15.4	16.0	[2] 11.9
2019 [2]	3,661	3,176	485	56,350	50,634	5,716	15.4	15.9	11.8
2020 [2]	3,670	3,184	486	56,368	50,654	5,714	15.4	15.9	11.8

[1] Private school data are estimated based on the Private School Universe Survey, biennially 1990-2016. [2] Projected. Projections were made before the coronavirus disease 2019 (COVID-19) pandemic and do not account for the impact of the pandemic.

Source: U.S. National Center for Education Statistics, *Digest of Education Statistics*, "Latest version of all Digest tables," <nces.ed.gov/programs/digest>, accessed January 2022.

Table 272. Private Schools—Number, Students, and Teachers by School Characteristics: 2020

[In thousands where indicated (4,653 represents 4,653,000). For school year ending in year shown. Based on the Private School Survey, conducted every 2 years; see source for details. For composition of regions, see map inside front cover]

Characteristic	Schools (number)	Students (1,000)	Teachers (1,000) [1]	Average enrollment by school level				Student to teacher ratio by school level			
				Total	Elementary & middle [2]	Secondary & high [3]	Combined	Total	Elementary & middle [2]	Secondary & high [3]	Combined
Total	**30,492**	**4,653**	**481**	**152.6**	**106.1**	**257.7**	**215.8**	**9.7**	**10.1**	**10.2**	**9.0**
School type:											
Catholic	6,449	1,743	140	270.3	210.6	502.5	361.2	12.5	12.7	12.4	11.1
Parochial	2,196	493	38	224.6	210.9	359.4	359.5	12.8	13.1	11.8	11.2
Diocesan	3,081	833	65	270.4	218.0	514.2	350.0	12.8	12.9	13.0	10.3
Private	1,172	417	36	355.3	170.4	522.8	369.0	11.5	10.2	11.9	11.5
Other religious	13,794	1,813	186	131.4	81.6	159.8	200.5	9.7	9.7	9.3	9.8
Conservative Christian	3,698	591	58	159.8	100.6	142.6	187.0	10.2	10.0	11.0	10.3
Affiliated	3,134	572	62	182.6	118.8	192.0	313.0	9.3	8.9	8.9	9.7
Unaffiliated	6,962	649	67	93.3	62.3	143.4	162.1	9.8	10.4	9.2	9.3
Nonsectarian	10,249	1,097	155	107.1	53.7	131.9	223.4	7.1	6.5	7.1	7.5
Regular	4,985	750	99	150.5	63.6	196.2	396.5	7.6	7.1	7.1	8.1
Special emphasis	3,470	227	33	65.4	41.8	106.0	181.0	6.9	5.8	8.7	8.4
Special education	1,794	120	23	66.8	53.4	38.8	79.8	5.1	4.9	4.9	5.2
Program emphasis:											
Regular	21,083	4,145	404	196.6	144.7	318.3	250.2	10.3	11.0	10.5	9.4
Montessori	2,566	99	18	38.4	34.3	(B)	103.3	5.6	5.3	(B)	6.9
Special program emphasis	929	150	17	161.1	102.8	171.2	250.3	8.6	7.8	8.0	9.4
Special education	2,025	133	26	65.8	54.4	38.4	77.1	5.2	5.0	4.9	5.3
Vocational/technical	(B)	(B)	(B)	(B)	(B)	(B)	(B)	(B)	(B)	(B)	(B)
Alternative	843	76	8	90.2	45.6	95.1	125.8	9.9	6.9	11.0	10.5
Early childhood	3,033	49	9	16.2	16.2	(X)	(B)	5.7	5.7	(X)	(B)
Enrollment size:											
Less than 50	12,636	271	48	21.4	19.7	23.7	26.9	5.6	5.9	4.4	5.3
50 to 149	8,223	758	95	92.2	93.7	87.5	90.5	7.9	8.7	6.6	7.1
150 to 299	5,271	1,107	109	210.0	206.6	219.4	214.3	10.2	11.2	9.1	8.9
300 to 499	2,460	939	87	381.8	378.4	389.1	382.7	10.8	12.2	9.9	9.6
500 to 749	1,064	644	61	605.3	587.0	607.4	613.9	10.6	13.5	11.3	9.2
750 or more	838	934	81	1,114.4	1,086.9	1,069.6	1,145.5	11.5	13.0	13.3	10.5
Region:											
Northeast	6,739	982	115	145.8	102.4	257.4	190.9	8.6	9.5	9.0	7.2
Midwest	7,057	1,063	97	150.6	115.6	316.2	201.7	10.9	11.5	12.0	9.2
South	10,671	1,696	181	158.9	97.0	223.9	228.7	9.4	9.0	10.3	9.4
West	6,025	912	89	151.4	110.5	252.9	220.1	10.3	10.5	10.3	10.0
Urban/rural status:											
City	10,445	2,058	211	197.0	135.7	304.6	291.0	9.8	10.1	10.7	9.0
Suburban	11,670	1,819	188	155.9	109.7	288.0	220.7	9.7	10.1	10.4	8.9
Town	2,476	269	27	108.7	86.9	143.1	146.2	9.9	10.2	9.3	9.7
Rural	5,901	507	55	85.9	49.4	125.2	135.7	9.2	10.3	7.9	9.0

X Not applicable. B Reporting standards not met. There are fewer than 15 sample cases. [1] Full-time equivalents. [2] Schools enrolling the majority of students in either grades kindergarten to 4 or grades 5 to 8. [3] Schools enrolling the majority of students in grades 9 to 12.

Source: U.S. National Center for Education Statistics, Private School Universe Survey, "Data Tables," <nces.ed.gov/surveys/pss>, accessed April 2022.

Table 273. Public Elementary and Secondary Schools by Type and Size of School: 2020

[Enrollment in thousands (50,438 represents 50,438,000). For school year ending in 2020. Data reported by schools, rather than school districts. Based on the Common Core of Data Survey; see source for details]

Enrollment size of school	Number of schools					Enrollment				
	Total [1]	Elementary	Middle	Secondary	Other [2]	Total [1]	Elementary	Middle	Secondary	Other [2]
Total...........	**98,469**	**52,322**	**16,264**	**23,529**	**4,901**	**50,438**	**23,808**	**9,694**	**15,228**	**1,492**
PERCENT [3]										
Total...........	100.00	100.00	100.00	100.00	100.00	100.00	100.00	100.00	100.00	100.00
Under 100 students.......	9.79	4.31	5.84	19.38	35.13	0.84	0.48	0.48	1.21	3.57
100 to 199 students.......	8.84	7.34	7.11	11.44	16.23	2.51	2.46	1.82	2.44	5.81
200 to 299 students.......	11.33	12.70	9.14	9.57	11.21	5.40	7.07	3.85	3.43	6.81
300 to 399 students.......	14.15	18.16	10.56	8.66	7.86	9.38	13.98	6.17	4.36	6.73
400 to 499 students.......	14.02	19.15	10.23	6.80	4.91	11.89	18.82	7.66	4.40	5.48
500 to 599 students.......	11.44	15.06	10.36	5.35	4.59	11.84	18.05	9.50	4.22	6.22
600 to 699 students.......	8.44	10.23	10.31	4.06	3.59	10.32	14.47	11.21	3.79	5.79
700 to 799 students.......	5.84	6.03	9.47	3.58	2.78	8.25	9.85	11.84	3.86	5.15
800 to 999 students.......	6.59	5.08	14.16	5.43	3.83	11.04	9.77	21.08	7.02	8.52
1,000 to 1,499 students...	5.65	1.81	11.47	10.87	5.21	12.77	4.50	22.50	19.36	15.71
1,500 to 1,999 students...	2.06	0.10	1.20	7.40	2.38	6.72	0.37	3.34	18.55	10.13
2,000 to 2,999 students...	1.53	0.02	0.14	6.30	1.16	6.82	0.09	0.51	21.45	6.76
3,000 or more students. ..	0.32	0.01	0.01	1.16	1.11	2.22	0.07	0.04	5.92	13.32

[1] Excludes special education schools, vocational schools, and alternative schools. Totals include data for prekindergarten schools, not shown separately. [2] Other includes ungraded, and not applicable or not reported. [3] Percent distribution calculations include data only for schools reporting enrollments greater than zero.

Source: U.S. National Center for Education Statistics, *Digest of Education Statistics*, "Latest version of all Digest tables," <nces.ed.gov/programs/digest>, accessed May 2022.

Table 274. Public Elementary and Secondary Schools—Number and Average Salary of Classroom Teachers: 1990 to 2020, and by State, 2021

[Estimates for school year ending in June of year shown]

Year and state	Teachers [1]	Average salary (dollars)	Year and state	Teachers [1]	Average salary (dollars)	Year and state	Teachers [1]	Average salary (dollars)
1990.........	2,361,588	31,367	HI.............	11,227	70,922	NM............	21,434	54,923
2000.........	2,891,071	41,807	ID.............	17,501	51,817	NY............	213,537	90,222
2010.........	3,182,220	55,370	IL.............	132,354	70,705	NC............	93,461	53,458
2015.........	3,152,710	57,748	IN.............	61,069	53,072	ND............	10,360	54,837
2018.........	3,181,421	60,768	IA.............	38,079	58,831	OH............	101,148	63,082
2019.........	3,197,623	62,355	KS.............	35,573	53,619	OK............	42,929	54,762
2020.........	3,194,190	64,172	KY.............	39,977	54,139	OR............	30,813	68,565
2021			LA.............	48,882	52,472	PA............	120,717	71,479
U.S. total. ..	**3,192,309**	**65,293**	ME.............	14,952	57,167	RI............	10,669	75,966
AL............	46,792	54,271	MD.............	62,767	74,006	SC............	52,533	53,188
AK............	7,390	73,061	MA.............	75,147	86,755	SD............	9,848	49,547
AZ............	61,180	52,157	MI.............	81,204	64,262	TN............	64,666	52,871
AR............	31,079	51,668	MN.............	56,426	66,561	TX............	369,478	57,641
CA............	269,850	85,856	MS.............	31,856	46,862	UT............	30,551	57,226
CO............	57,625	58,183	MO.............	75,928	51,557	VT............	8,176	62,483
CT............	41,822	79,742	MT.............	10,647	53,133	VA............	99,783	58,506
DE............	9,838	65,141	NE.............	25,048	56,463	WA............	62,791	79,388
DC............	7,678	80,659	NV.............	22,435	58,167	WV............	18,494	50,261
FL............	142,110	51,009	NH.............	16,710	61,849	WI............	56,446	59,992
GA............	117,204	60,553	NJ.............	116,717	77,677	WY............	7,408	60,234

[1] Full-time equivalent.

Source: National Education Association, Washington, DC. Data from *Rankings of the States 2021 and Estimates of School Statistics 2022*, April 2022, used with permission of the National Education Association © 2022, and earlier reports. All rights reserved.

Table 275. Public School Employment by Occupation, Sex, and Race/Ethnicity: 2018

[In thousands (5,311 represents 5,311,000). Covers all public elementary-secondary school districts with 100 or more full-time employees]

Occupation	Total [1]	Male	Female	White non-Hispanic	Black non-Hispanic	Asian non-Hispanic	Hispanic [2]
All occupations.....................	**5,311**	**1,324**	**3,986**	**3,781**	**649**	**105**	**682**
Officials, administrators....................	105	46	59	79	12	2	11
Principals and assistant principals........	146	61	85	102	24	2	15
Classroom teachers [3].....................	2,797	656	2,142	2,184	238	55	274
Elementary schools......................	1,287	145	1,141	1,004	101	24	137
Secondary schools......................	1,123	429	694	887	93	23	101
Other professional staff..................	505	87	419	361	65	11	58
Teachers' aides [4].........................	651	105	546	409	112	14	103
Clerical, secretarial staff..................	330	14	316	216	37	5	66
Service workers [5]........................	775	356	419	429	160	16	155

[1] Includes other races/ethnicities not shown separately. [2] Persons of Hispanic origin may be of any race. [3] Includes other classroom teachers not shown separately. [4] Includes technicians. [5] Includes craftworkers and laborers.

Source: U.S. Equal Employment Opportunity Commission, "Equal Employment Opportunity, EEO-5 Statistical File–2018, United States Summary," <eeoc.gov/statistics/job-patterns-minorities-and-women-elementary-secondary-public-schools-eeo-5>, accessed May 2020.

Table 276. Public School Teachers, Base Salary, and Additional Income by Selected Characteristics: 2018

[3,323 represents 3,323,000. Salary and income shown in current dollars. For school year ending in 2018. Data shown for regular full-time teachers only; excludes other staff even when they have full-time teaching duties. Based on the 2017-2018 National Teacher and Principal Survey and subject to sampling error; for details, see <nces.ed.gov/surveys/ntps>]

Characteristic	Number of full-time teachers (1,000)	Base teacher salary (dollars)	Total income from school and nonschool sources [1,2] (dollars)	Teachers with additional income					
				Job outside the school system during the school year		Supplemental school system contract during summer [3]		Employed in a non-school job during the summer	
				Percent of teachers	Average income (dollars)	Percent of teachers	Average income (dollars)	Percent of teachers	Average income (dollars)
Total...............	**3,323**	**57,950**	**62,200**	**17.8**	**5,800**	**18.2**	**3,040**	**16.2**	**4,410**
Sex:									
Male...............	794	59,360	66,560	25.1	7,320	21.6	3,880	23.8	5,730
Female...............	2,529	57,500	60,840	15.5	5,030	17.1	2,710	13.9	3,700
Race/ethnicity:									
White...............	2,622	57,900	62,220	18.4	5,690	17.1	2,990	17.4	4,370
Black...............	228	56,480	60,540	17.5	6,020	23.5	3,090	12.4	4,330
Hispanic...............	317	58,310	62,320	13.7	7,030	21.9	3,210	11.0	4,970
Asian...............	71	65,200	68,610	12.2	5,480	20.6	3,230	9.8	5,150
Pacific Islander...............	8	62,980	66,900	15.0	(S)	24.6	(S)	[5] 11.6	(S)
American Indian or Alaska Native...............	17	48,980	54,220	14.9	6,110	26.2	(S)	13.1	5,850
Two or more races...........	60	56,850	61,330	23.8	5,230	20.5	2,610	17.9	3,910
Age:									
Under 30 years old.........	507	45,590	49,790	20.8	4,490	20.2	2,470	25.6	3,510
30 to 39 years old...........	936	53,920	57,970	18.3	5,470	18.7	3,050	17.0	4,090
40 to 49 years old...........	967	61,440	65,540	17.3	6,520	17.9	3,010	14.2	5,350
50 years old or over........	913	65,240	69,900	16.3	6,290	16.9	3,460	12.4	4,760
Years of full- and part-time teaching experience:									
1 year or less...............	231	44,150	48,110	17.7	5,470	16.4	2,860	26.4	4,840
2 to 4 years...............	485	46,870	51,100	20.3	5,310	20.4	2,670	20.2	3,910
5 to 9 years...............	598	50,750	54,780	18.5	5,560	19.6	2,900	17.0	4,030
10 to 14 years...............	647	57,860	61,710	17.4	5,620	18.6	3,140	14.8	4,270
15 to 19 years...............	557	64,980	69,180	17.2	6,360	17.1	3,130	13.8	4,950
20 to 24 years...............	385	68,440	72,680	17.3	6,240	17.0	3,300	14.2	4,350
25 to 29 years...............	238	69,170	73,530	16.3	6,180	15.9	3,250	12.9	5,110
30 years or more...........	184	70,450	77,430	15.7	6,130	17.2	3,550	11.5	5,090
Highest degree held:									
Less than bachelor's........	88	55,250	60,950	19.7	7,800	17.1	3,320	19.6	6,480
Bachelor's...............	1,327	49,890	53,780	16.7	5,550	17.4	2,820	17.5	4,410
Master's...............	1,628	63,120	67,500	18.3	5,740	18.7	3,160	15.3	4,210
Education specialist........	243	66,510	71,100	18.7	5,910	19.0	3,120	14.9	4,490
Doctorate...............	37	69,520	76,070	24.6	9,310	17.3	4,610	14.7	6,650
Instructional level: [4]									
Elementary...............	1,639	56,640	59,690	14.5	5,130	16.8	2,710	13.9	3,920
Secondary...............	1,685	59,220	64,650	21.0	6,250	19.5	3,320	18.5	4,770
School locale:									
City...............	970	59,430	63,630	17.3	5,900	19.9	3,140	14.5	4,370
Suburban...............	1,288	62,820	66,920	17.9	5,720	17.5	3,100	15.8	4,100
Town...............	387	50,590	55,130	18.5	5,980	19.6	2,720	17.0	5,040
Rural...............	679	50,770	55,240	18.0	5,710	16.3	2,980	19.0	4,620

S Figure does not meet publication standards. [1] Includes retirement pension funds paid during the school year. [2] Includes types of income not shown separately. [3] Includes teaching summer sessions and other non-teaching jobs at any school. [4] Teachers were classified as elementary or secondary on the basis of the grades they taught, rather than on the level of the school in which they taught. In general, elementary teachers include those teaching pre-kindergarten through grade 6 and those teaching multiple grades with a preponderance of grades taught being kindergarten through grade 6. In general, secondary teachers include those teaching grades 7 through 12 and those teaching multiple grades with a preponderance of grades taught being grades 7 through 12 and usually no grade taught being lower than grade 5. [5] Interpret data with caution. The coefficient of variation is between 30 and 50 percent.

Source: U.S. National Center for Education Statistics, *Digest of Education Statistics*, "Latest version of all Digest tables," <nces.ed.gov/programs/digest>, accessed May 2020.

Table 277. Education and Teaching Experience of Public Elementary and Secondary School Teachers by Selected Characteristics: 2018

[3,545 represents 3,545,000. For school year ending in 2018. Excludes prekindergarten teachers. Data are based on a head count of full-time and part-time teachers. Based on the National Teacher and Principal Survey (NTPS); see source for details]

Characteristic	Number of teachers (1,000s)	Percent of teachers by highest degree earned					Percent of teachers by years of teaching experience [1]			
		Less than bachelor's	Bachelor's	Master's	Education specialist [2]	Doctor's	Less than 3	3 to 9	10 to 20	Over 20
Total................	**3,545**	**2.7**	**39.3**	**49.2**	**7.6**	**1.2**	**9.0**	**28.3**	**39.9**	**22.8**
Sex:										
Male.........................	834	4.0	39.0	49.6	5.7	1.7	8.9	44.0	40.6	23.2
Female......................	2,712	2.3	39.4	49.1	8.2	1.0	9.0	28.6	39.7	22.7
Race/ethnicity: [3]										
White........................	2,811	2.6	38.6	50.4	7.4	1.0	8.3	27.3	40.1	24.3
Black........................	239	3.0	32.9	50.7	11.3	2.1	10.8	30.3	38.7	20.2
Asian........................	75	1.7	29.0	55.1	11.3	2.8	12.0	31.1	42.1	14.8
Pacific Islander.............	8	(S)	44.2	38.6	[6] 8.7	(S)	[6] 6.7	24.0	44.2	25.1
American Indian/Alaska Native...	18	[6] 5.3	51.6	36.2	6.2	(S)	9.0	20.9	42.5	27.6
Two or more races..........	63	3.2	40.8	47.0	7.8	[6] 1.2	12.5	35.5	34.6	17.4
Hispanic.....................	331	3.6	51.1	37.9	6.1	1.3	11.8	34.0	39.6	14.6
Age:										
Under age 30...............	531	2.7	64.8	30.3	2.1	(S)	37.1	62.8	(S)	(S)
Age 30 to 39...............	991	2.2	37.9	52.9	6.5	0.6	6.7	42.9	50.3	(S)
Age 40 to 49...............	1,028	2.9	33.5	53.3	9.2	1.1	3.4	15.5	58.1	23.0
Age 50 to 59...............	732	2.9	33.4	52.1	9.5	2.1	2.0	9.2	33.5	55.2
Age 60 and over............	263	3.6	32.1	49.2	12.0	3.1	1.7	6.5	28.2	63.6
Level of instruction: [4]										
Elementary...................	1,779	2.1	42.6	47.1	7.6	0.7	9.4	29.2	39.0	22.4
General....................	1,097	2.1	45.0	45.5	6.9	0.5	9.4	28.8	39.9	21.9
Arts/music.................	99	1.4	49.1	42.9	5.5	[6] 1.1	9.1	29.7	37.0	24.2
English....................	117	1.9	35.4	51.3	10.4	[6] 1.0	7.7	25.5	39.0	27.8
ESL/bilingual [5]............	48	[6] 1.8	32.9	51.2	13.3	[6] 0.9	8.8	29.8	39.3	22.1
Health/physical education..	65	5.1	50.2	41.5	3.0	(S)	7.6	24.1	38.9	29.4
Mathematics................	36	[6] 2.7	43.1	48.0	6.2	(S)	7.5	31.2	41.4	19.8
Science....................	23	[6] 4.3	45.8	44.9	[6] 3.8	(S)	[6] 8.6	29.3	42.9	19.2
Special education..........	235	1.2	33.9	53.2	10.3	1.3	11.8	33.6	34.8	19.8
Other elementary..........	60	2.3	32.4	54.2	9.5	[6] 1.4	6.8	29.9	38.9	24.4
Secondary...................	1,766	3.4	36.0	51.3	7.7	1.6	8.6	27.4	40.9	23.2
Arts/music.................	130	3.3	44.8	44.6	5.8	1.4	9.7	28.6	35.9	25.9
English....................	294	1.5	34.1	54.2	8.4	1.8	8.4	27.6	41.2	22.7
ESL/bilingual [5]............	24	(S)	24.0	58.1	14.7	[6] 1.7	6.8	25.8	43.7	23.6
Foreign language...........	85	0.8	31.3	57.5	7.5	2.9	8.7	26.0	43.8	21.5
Health/physical education..	97	2.8	45.0	47.7	4.0	[6] 0.4	5.6	22.3	41.7	30.4
Mathematics................	265	2.5	37.5	53.1	5.8	1.1	8.9	28.3	40.9	21.8
Science....................	220	2.9	33.7	54.5	6.4	2.5	9.1	27.1	42.5	21.3
Social studies.............	214	2.2	35.9	53.3	6.8	1.8	8.0	27.3	42.8	21.9
Special education..........	199	2.6	30.7	50.9	14.6	1.2	9.3	30.6	37.3	22.8
Vocational/technical.......	139	14.4	37.8	40.1	6.0	1.7	9.3	27.6	40.9	22.2
Other secondary...........	98	4.3	37.6	49.0	8.4	[6] 0.7	7.6	23.5	41.4	27.6

S Figure does not meet publication standards. [1] Includes full- and part-time teaching experience. [2] Education specialist degrees or certificates are generally awarded for 1 year of work beyond the master's degree level. Includes certificate of advanced graduate studies. [3] Data for race categories exclude persons of Hispanic origin. [4] Teachers were classified as elementary or secondary on the basis of the grades they taught, rather than on the level of the school in which they taught. Elementary teachers generally include those teaching prekindergarten through grade 5 and those teaching multiple grades with a preponderance of grades taught being kindergarten through grade 6. Secondary teachers generally include those teaching any of grades 7 through 12 and those teaching multiple grades with a preponderance of grades taught being grades 7 through 12. [5] ESL is English as a second language. [6] Interpret data with caution. The coefficient of variation (CV) for this estimate is between 30 and 50 percent.

Source: U.S. National Center for Education Statistics, *Digest of Education Statistics*, "Latest version of all Digest Tables," <nces.ed.gov/programs/digest>, accessed July 2020.

Table 278. Private School Teachers, Base Salary, and Additional Income by Selected Characteristics: 2018

[411.0 represents 411,000. For school year ending in 2018. Data shown for regular full-time teachers only; excludes other staff even when they have full-time teaching duties. Based on the 2017-18 National Teacher and Principal Survey and subject to sampling error; for details, see <nces.ed.gov/surveys/ntps/>]

Characteristic	Number of full-time teachers (1,000)	Base teacher salary (dollars)	Total income [1,2] (dollars)	Teachers with additional income					
				Job outside the school system during the school year		Supplemental school system contract during summer [3]		Employed in a non-school job during the summer	
				Percent of teachers	Average income (dollars)	Percent of teachers	Average income (dollars)	Percent of teachers	Average income (dollars)
Total [4]	411.0	45,320	50,340	20.7	6,690	20.2	3,710	17.1	4,840
SEX									
Male	106.1	51,540	60,190	28.7	8,940	25	4,290	25	6,290
Female	304.8	43,150	46,900	17.8	5,440	18.5	3,440	14.4	3,970
RACE/ETHNICITY									
Non-Hispanic:									
White	350.7	45,410	50,360	20.6	6,340	20	3,600	17	4,570
Black	12.8	41,510	48,680	25.7	12,580	22.1	4,820	20.4	(S)
Asian	10.3	47,730	51,040	20.5	3,590	26.5	3,640	[6] 12.8	(S)
Two or more races	6.0	49,620	57,530	27.7	(S)	22.4	(S)	26.3	(S)
Hispanic	29.3	44,790	49,350	16.7	8,130	20.0	4,290	12.6	4,770
AGE									
Less than 30 years old	72.8	36,820	41,070	25.2	4,240	24.4	3,010	29.3	3,850
30 to 39 years old	101.4	43,810	48,670	22.7	6,730	19.9	4,430	17.7	5,310
40 to 49 years old	92.5	46,240	51,090	20.0	7,790	22.0	3,170	14.5	6,410
50 or more years old	144.3	50,110	55,730	17.3	7,650	17.1	4,070	12.1	4,360
YEARS OF TEACHING EXPERIENCE									
1 year or less	25.4	32,450	36,630	19.0	5,600	21.3	2,920	31.5	4,880
2 to 4 years	65.0	36,340	40,950	25.7	5,400	23.0	3,180	25.7	4,370
5 to 9 years	83.0	42,740	47,210	19.6	6,760	21.1	3,990	16.7	4,770
10 to 14 years	71.7	44,230	48,270	20.8	6,130	18.6	3,790	13.3	4,820
15 to 19 years	51.4	48,180	53,930	22.3	9,000	22.8	4,260	16.2	6,320
20 to 24 years	37.0	52,360	56,630	20.4	7,340	19.3	3,790	16.0	4,590
25 to 29 years	27.6	54,300	58,880	17.8	4,530	18.6	3,630	10.6	3,250
30 or more years	49.8	56,470	64,780	16.5	8,360	15.5	3,680	9.7	5,380
HIGHEST DEGREE HELD									
Less than bachelor's	36.2	30,800	34,750	21.0	4,780	17.2	[6] 3,560	26.5	4,640
Bachelor's	179.6	40,500	44,960	21.0	6,080	19.0	3,560	17.1	4,610
Master's	165.3	52,180	57,690	20.4	7,530	21.8	3,820	15.7	5,100
Education specialist	19.4	49,810	56,860	18.1	6,600	23.0	3,960	11.2	4,580
Doctorate	10.5	60,040	66,910	22.4	10,990	19.6	4,210	16.1	6,350
INSTRUCTIONAL LEVEL [5]									
Elementary	214.0	41,400	45,030	18.5	5,060	19.5	3,210	15.4	3,890
Secondary	196.9	49,600	56,140	22.9	8,140	21.0	4,210	18.8	5,690

S Figure does not meet publication standards. [1] Includes retirement pension funds paid during the school year. [2] Income from school and non-school sources. Includes sources of income not shown separately. [3] Includes teaching summer sessions and other non-teaching jobs at any school. [4] Includes race/ethnicities not shown separately. [5] Teachers were classified as elementary or secondary on the basis of the grades they taught, rather than on the level of the school in which they taught. In general, elementary teachers include those teaching prekindergarten through grade 6 and those teaching multiple grades with a preponderance of grades taught being kindergarten through grade 6. In general, secondary teachers include those teaching any of grades 7 through 12 and those teaching multiple grades with a preponderance of grades taught being grades 7 through 12 and usually with no grade taught being lower than grade 5. [6] Interpret data with caution. The coefficient of variation is between 30 and 50 percent.

Source: U.S. National Center for Education Statistics, *Digest of Education Statistics*, "Latest version of all Digest Tables," <nces.ed.gov/programs/digest/>, accessed June 2022.

Table 279. Public and Private Schools Reporting Changes to Instruction During COVID-19 Pandemic by Selected School Characteristics and Type of Change: 2020

[Percent of schools reporting changes to instruction delivery during spring 2020. Data are preliminary. Respondents could select more than one way in which the pandemic affected instruction. Based on data from the 2020-21 National Teacher and Principal Survey]

Characteristics	All or some classes were cancelled	All or some classes moved to online distance-learning format	All or some classes moved to paper-based distance-learning format	Instruction changed in some other way	No change
PUBLIC SCHOOLS					
Total	9	77	41	9	3
School classification:					
Traditional public	9	77	41	9	3
Charter school	8	82	38	9	4
Region:					
Northeast	6	84	33	11	[1] 1
Midwest	10	76	40	10	4
South	10	73	44	9	3
West	8	80	43	6	2
School level:					
Primary	10	76	47	9	2
Middle	8	80	30	11	2
High	7	81	30	8	2
Combined	10	72	43	10	8
PRIVATE SCHOOLS					
Total	10	73	48	10	5
School classification:					
Catholic	8	84	44	8	3
Other religious	11	64	52	12	6
Nonsectarian	11	78	45	11	6
Region:					
Northeast	11	73	38	13	4
Midwest	8	71	55	10	5
South	9	73	46	9	8
West	13	78	52	11	[1] 3
School level:					
Elementary	11	72	54	10	5
Secondary	6	77	16	11	8
Combined	9	74	48	10	6

[1] Interpret data with caution. The coefficient of variation (CV) for this estimate is between 30 and 50 percent.

Source: U.S. National Center for Education Statistics, *Impact of the Coronavirus (COVID-19) Pandemic on Public and Private Elementary and Secondary Education in the United States (Preliminary Data): Results from the 2020–21 National Teacher and Principal Survey (NTPS) First Look*, February 2022. See also <nces.ed.gov/surveys/ntps/>.

Table 280. Elementary and Secondary Schools—English Language Learner Student Enrollment by Home Language and Grade: 2009 to 2019

[4,647.0 represents 4,647,000. Data cover the academic year beginning with shown year. Data for 2013 and earlier years include all English Language Learner (ELL) students enrolled at any time during the school year; beginning 2014, data shown as of fall. Includes all students identified as English language learners (ELL), both those participating in ELL programs and those not participating in ELL programs. Data exclude U.S. territories, and the Bureau of Indian Education]

Home language and grade	2009 [1]	2011 [1]	2012	2013	2014	2015	2016	2017	2018 [4]	2019
Total	**4,647.0**	**4,635.2**	**4,850.3**	**4,930.0**	**4,813.7**	**4,854.3**	**4,949.4**	**5,010.5**	**5,024.2**	**5,115.9**
HOME LANGUAGE										
Spanish, Castilian	3,577.6	3,562.9	3,718.0	3,770.8	3,709.8	3,741.1	3,790.9	3,749.3	3,777.9	3,872.2
Arabic	71.2	86.2	98.0	109.2	109.2	114.4	129.4	136.5	135.9	131.6
English [2]	77.9	85.2	90.7	91.7	83.2	80.3	70.0	94.9	99.5	105.3
Chinese	80.1	96.5	104.8	107.8	104.3	101.3	104.1	106.5	102.8	100.1
Vietnamese	93.2	89.5	92.6	89.7	85.3	81.2	78.7	77.8	76.5	75.6
Portuguese	15.2	15.7	17.1	19.1	19.8	23.7	28.2	33.3	37.5	44.8
Russian	33.3	32.2	33.7	33.8	32.5	33.1	34.8	36.8	38.2	39.7
Haitian, Haitian Creole	39.7	39.9	38.8	37.4	31.4	30.2	31.6	32.7	32.8	31.5
Hmong	49.7	43.8	41.4	39.9	37.4	34.8	33.1	32.2	31.3	30.8
Korean	39.7	(NA)	34.9	32.4	28.5	27.3	26.1	26.5	26.0	25.8
GRADE										
Kindergarten	615.6	657.4	667.8	667.7	629.0	606.4	600.2	587.5	555.7	555.6
Grade 1	617.6	646.4	665.3	665.6	640.0	621.1	603.8	588.5	571.9	554.6
Grade 2	576.3	585.7	609.8	630.5	614.7	614.8	599.1	574.7	557.8	549.0
Grade 3	511.5	500.0	540.4	558.9	567.1	564.8	576.1	551.3	527.4	521.5
Grade 4	420.1	417.6	428.1	439.5	436.6	461.0	457.5	505.0	494.2	475.8
Grade 5	336.2	338.2	367.1	361.7	364.2	372.8	389.3	400.1	426.3	430.4
Grade 6	278.0	273.5	288.1	293.8	287.8	305.5	318.7	329.3	346.3	372.6
Grade 7	254.8	239.2	255.4	267.4	260.5	267.1	286.3	291.9	308.2	332.9
Grade 8	233.3	214.9	227.8	239.8	242.5	245.6	258.2	265.2	278.7	299.0
Grade 9	258.7	244.3	255.0	261.6	263.1	269.7	286.2	280.4	291.1	326.4
Grade 10	211.7	201.7	202.8	202.4	197.5	214.0	232.7	255.0	251.4	269.6
Grade 11	175.5	162.8	170.8	168.4	157.4	162.3	184.0	202.4	219.0	219.1
Grade 12	148.2	145.4	159.4	161.2	143.2	138.8	146.4	167.1	185.7	199.1
Ungraded [3]	8.7	8.1	11.8	11.4	10.1	10.2	11.0	11.8	10.0	10.5

NA Not available. [1] Includes data for California that reflect ELL students enrolled on a single date, rather than a cumulative count of all ELL students enrolled at any time during the school year. [2] Examples of situations in which English might be reported as an English learner's home language include students who live in multilingual households and students adopted from other countries who speak English at home but also have been raised speaking another language. [3] Includes students reported in grade 13. [4] Data for Vermont were not available.

Source: U.S. National Center for Education Statistics, *Digest of Education Statistics*, "Latest version of all Digest tables," <nces.ed.gov/programs/digest/> and earlier reports, accessed March 2022.

Table 281. Public and Private School Start Times by Selected Characteristics: 2018

[For academic year ending in 2018. Data are from the National Teacher and Principal Survey]

School characteristic	Average start time	Percent distribution of start times				
		Before 7:30 a.m.	7:30 a.m. to 7:59 a.m.	8:00 a.m. to 8:29 a.m.	8:30 a.m. to 8:59 a.m.	9:00 a.m. or later
All schools..............	**8:11**	**3.5**	**24.7**	**43.9**	**20.4**	**7.5**
Public schools..............	**8:10**	**4.3**	**27.5**	**40.3**	**19.8**	**8.2**
School classification:						
Traditional public..............	8:11	4.2	27.6	39.7	20.1	8.4
Charter school................	8:05	4.6	26.1	46.9	16.4	5.9
School level:						
Primary.......................	8:15	1.7	23.5	39.6	25.4	9.9
Middle........................	8:05	6.4	36.3	36.6	13.1	7.7
High..........................	8:03	10.4	32.1	40.0	11.8	5.7
Combined......................	8:05	3.2	26.7	51.0	14.4	4.8
Private schools..............	**8:12**	**1.0**	**14.9**	**56.6**	**22.5**	**4.9**
School classification:						
Catholic.......................	8:03	[1] 1.7	32.6	55.0	9.2	[1] 1.4
Other religious................	8:13	[1] 0.8	9.9	61.4	24.1	3.9
Nonsectarian..................	8:19	[1] 0.9	6.2	49.9	33.0	10.1
School level:						
Elementary....................	8:11	[1] 1.0	15.1	55.0	25.7	3.2
Secondary....................	8:15	2.0	22.2	49.4	17.2	9.3

[1] Interpret data with caution. The coefficient of variation (CV) for this estimate is between 30 percent and 50 percent.

Source: U.S. National Center for Education Statistics, National Teacher and Principal Survey, "2017–2018 NTPS Tables," <nces.ed.gov/surveys/ntps/tables_list.asp>, accessed May 2020.

Table 282. Homeschooled Students by Selected Characteristics: 2012 to 2019

[1,773 represents 1,773,000. For students age 5 to 17 with a grade equivalent of K–12. Homeschoolers are students whose parents reported them to be schooled at home instead of in a public or private school. Excludes students who were enrolled in school for more than 25 hours a week in 2012 and 2016 or for more than 24 hours a week in 2019, or who were homeschooled due to a temporary illness. Based on the Parent and Family Involvement in Education Survey of the National Household Education Surveys Program]

Characteristic	2012 [1]		2016		2019	
	Home-schooled (1,000)	Percent home-schooled	Home-schooled (1,000)	Percent home-schooled	Home-schooled (1,000)	Percent home-schooled
Total....................	**1,773**	**3.4**	**1,690**	**3.3**	**1,457**	**2.8**
Sex:						
Male........................	875	3.3	807	3.0	725	2.7
Female......................	898	3.6	882	3.5	732	2.9
Race/ethnicity: [2]						
White, non-Hispanic..........	1,205	4.5	998	3.8	1,014	4.0
Black, non-Hispanic..........	140	2.0	132	1.9	84	1.2
Hispanic [3].................	265	2.3	444	3.5	250	1.9
Grade equivalent: [4]						
Kindergarten to grade 5........	833	3.2	767	3.0	703	2.8
Kindergarten...............	212	4.0	181	3.5	115	2.6
Grades 1 to 3..............	353	2.9	300	2.4	322	2.7
Grades 4 to 5..............	268	3.2	287	3.4	267	3.2
Grades 6 to 8..............	424	3.5	398	3.3	429	3.4
Grades 9 to 12.............	516	3.8	525	3.8	325	2.3
Number of children in the household:						
One child....................	418	3.4	338	2.7	276	2.2
Two children................	493	2.5	475	2.3	475	2.3
Three or more children........	862	4.5	877	4.7	706	3.9
Number of parents in the household:						
Two parents.................	1,354	3.8	1,358	3.7	1,214	3.3
One parent..................	342	2.5	293	2.3	206	1.6
Nonparental guardians........	[5] 77	[5] 4.0	38	2.0	[5] 37	[5] 2.1
Parent/guardian participation in the labor force:						
Two parents/guardians—both in labor force.	588	2.5	427	1.7	399	1.6
Two parents/guardians—one in labor force.	719	6.2	935	7.2	839	6.6
One parent/guardian in labor force.	247	2.2	189	1.8	127	1.2
No parent/guardian in labor force.	130	4.8	139	4.0	93	3.1
Highest education of parents/guardians:						
High school diploma or less....	560	3.4	510	3.3	330	2.2
Vocational/technical degree or some college.	525	3.4	418	3.1	376	2.9
Bachelor's degree or some graduate school.	434	3.7	501	3.6	449	3.3
Graduate/professional school....	255	3.3	260	3.0	302	3.1
Household income:						
$20,000 or less..............	219	2.9	184	2.9	150	3.0
$20,001 to 50,000............	528	3.8	483	3.7	292	2.5
$50,001 to 75,000............	370	3.9	435	4.8	302	3.6
$75,001 to 100,000..........	288	4.2	268	3.8	223	3.2
$100,000 or more............	367	2.7	319	1.9	490	2.5

[1] The NCES uses a statistical adjustment for estimates of total homeschoolers in 2012; therefore, data will not add to total. [2] Includes other race/ethnicities not shown separately. [3] Persons of Hispanic origin may be of any race. [4] Excludes those ungraded. [5] Interpret data with caution.

Source: U.S. National Center for Education Statistics, *Digest of Education Statistics,* "Latest version of all Digest tables," <nces.ed.gov/programs/digest>, accessed May 2022.

Table 283. Average Class Size in Public and Private Schools by Selected School Characteristics: 2018

[Data are average number of students per class. For school year ending in year shown. In self-contained classes, teachers give instruction to the same group of students all or most of the day in multiple subjects. Departmentalized instruction is instruction to several classes of different students most or all of the day in one or more subjects. Data are from the National Teacher and Principal Survey (NTPS)]

School characteristics	Public schools — Self-contained classes			Public schools — Departmentalized education			School characteristics	Private schools — Self-contained classes		Private schools — Departmentalized education	
	Primary	Middle	High	Primary	Middle	High		Elementary	Secondary	Elementary	Secondary
All schools	**20.9**	**16.6**	**16.3**	**26.2**	**24.9**	**23.3**	**All schools**	**16.7**	**17.8**	**17.6**	**17.7**
School type:							School type:				
Traditional	20.9	16.1	15.8	26.2	24.9	23.4	Catholic	18.4	21.3	19.6	20.2
Charter school	22.1	25.5	25.5	26.1	25.2	21.5					
Community type:							Community type:				
City	21.4	17.6	17.7	28.1	25.3	24.5	City	17.7	19.3	19.5	18.8
Suburban	21.3	15.5	15.3	27.2	25.5	24.3	Suburban	17.6	18.9	17.0	17.5
Town	20.5	18.3	16.8	25.1	23.9	21.3	Town	14.8	11.9	16.4	15.5
Rural	19.5	16.0	15.9	23.2	23.3	20.8	Rural	12.2	14.7	13.0	14.7
Enrollment size:							Enrollment size:				
Less than 100	14.8	(S)	18.3	15.7	17.4	16.0					
100–199	17.7	20.6	17.5	20.1	18.7	15.7	Less than 100	(S)	(S)	(S)	(S)
200–499	20.4	18.6	19.2	24.8	22.5	19.2	100–199	16.4	17.6	16.0	14.7
500–749	21.4	14.5	16.9	27.9	24.6	21.0	200–499	19.8	19.5	20.5	17.2
750–999	22.3	16.3	19.2	28.7	25.7	22.2	500–749	23.0	19.7	23.2	19.6
1,000 or more	22.1	16.5	14.9	26.4	27.1	25.0	750 or more	(S)	(S)	(S)	(S)

S Data does not meet publication standards.

Source: U.S. National Center for Education Statistics, National Teacher and Principal Survey, "2017–2018 NTPS Tables," <nces.ed.gov/surveys/ntps/tables_list.asp>, accessed April 2021.

Table 284. Enrollment in Public Schools by School Type, Level, and Charter, Magnet, and Virtual Status: 2010 to 2019

[As of fall. Covers the 50 states and the District of Columbia. Based on the Common Core of Data, Public Elementary/Secondary School Universe Survey]

School characteristic	2010	2014	2015	2016	2017	2018	2019
Total, all schools	**49,177,617**	**50,009,771**	**50,115,178**	**50,264,883**	**50,330,241**	**50,330,883**	**50,437,821**
School type:							
Regular	48,259,245	49,178,890	49,313,134	49,459,192	49,531,526	49,534,589	49,629,390
Special education	190,910	186,269	180,155	184,261	185,073	180,523	173,348
Vocational	164,013	147,550	146,321	146,601	147,516	158,088	152,961
Alternative [1]	563,449	497,062	475,568	474,829	466,126	457,683	482,122
School level:							
Prekindergarten	159,013	176,494	186,614	190,523	196,914	211,861	217,022
Elementary	23,725,686	24,223,110	24,154,981	24,051,448	24,077,645	23,898,171	23,808,079
Middle	9,391,287	9,439,744	9,392,450	9,366,871	9,531,009	9,603,188	9,693,590
Secondary and high	14,842,780	14,939,874	15,050,043	15,210,764	15,179,513	15,174,601	15,227,541
Other, ungraded, and not applicable	1,058,851	1,230,549	1,331,090	1,445,277	1,345,160	1,443,062	1,491,589
SCHOOL STATUS AND LEVEL							
Charter schools, total [2]	1,787,091	2,721,786	2,845,322	3,008,297	3,143,269	3,290,149	3,431,230
Prekindergarten	5,884	5,315	5,857	5,653	5,449	5,219	5,365
Elementary	771,063	1,196,503	1,235,990	1,289,641	1,376,412	1,443,839	1,512,281
Middle	156,606	232,530	235,177	243,333	246,751	249,027	256,721
Secondary and high	430,332	620,217	657,256	690,159	723,070	747,380	771,361
Other, ungraded, and not applicable	423,206	667,221	711,042	779,511	791,587	844,684	885,502
Magnet schools, total [2]	2,055,133	2,609,104	2,604,145	2,536,520	2,665,820	2,672,473	2,694,281
Prekindergarten	1,488	1,520	1,203	785	757	591	1,184
Elementary	707,591	853,557	838,514	810,267	881,389	882,526	886,750
Middle	374,297	509,944	505,172	495,047	528,151	552,592	560,470
Secondary and high	943,492	1,218,907	1,220,936	1,186,564	1,227,219	1,207,307	1,215,852
Other, ungraded, and not applicable	28,265	25,176	38,320	43,857	28,304	29,457	30,025
Virtual schools, total [2, 3]	(NA)	229,608	234,148	212,311	278,783	289,614	293,689
Prekindergarten	(NA)	–	–	–	–	–	–
Elementary	(NA)	16,503	15,972	9,429	13,293	11,208	12,757
Middle	(NA)	3,780	3,384	5,634	8,143	5,442	7,854
Secondary and high	(NA)	43,556	47,373	45,829	62,363	65,749	64,444
Other, ungraded, and not applicable	(NA)	165,769	167,419	151,419	194,984	207,215	208,634

– Represents zero. NA Not available. [1] Includes schools that provide nontraditional education, address needs of students that typically cannot be met in regular schools, serve as adjuncts to regular schools, or fall outside the categories of regular, special education, or vocational education. [2] Magnet, charter, and virtual schools are also included under regular, special education, vocational, or alternative schools as appropriate. [3] Virtual schools provide instruction during which students and teachers are separated by time and/or location and interact via internet-connected computers or other electronic devices.

Source: U.S. National Center for Education Statistics, *Digest of Education Statistics,* "Latest version of all Digest tables," <nces.ed.gov/programs/digest>, accessed March 2022.

Table 285. Public Charter and Traditional Schools by Selected Characteristics: 2009 and 2019

[49,082 represents 49,082,000. As of Fall. A public charter school is a public school that, in accordance with an enabling state statute, has been granted a charter exempting it from selected state and local rules and regulations]

Characteristic	2009 Total	2009 Traditional	2009 Public charter	2019 Total	2019 Traditional	2019 Public charter
Enrollment (1,000)	**49,082**	**47,471**	**1,610**	**50,438**	**47,007**	**3,431**
PERCENT DISTRIBUTION OF STUDENTS						
Race/ethnicity	100.0	100.0	100.0	100.0	100.0	100.0
White, non-Hispanic	54.1	54.7	37.3	46.5	47.6	30.4
Black, non-Hispanic	16.8	16.3	30.3	15.0	14.2	24.9
Hispanic	22.2	22.0	26.0	27.6	27.1	35.3
Asian	4.9	5.0	3.8	5.3	5.4	4.2
Pacific Islander	0.1	0.1	0.1	0.4	0.4	0.4
American Indian/Alaska Native	1.2	1.2	1.0	0.9	1.0	0.8
Two or more races	0.7	0.7	1.4	4.3	4.3	4.2
Number of teachers (1,000)	3,075	2,990	85	3,144	2,970	174
Pupil/teacher ratio	16.0	15.9	17.3	15.9	15.8	17.8
Total number of schools	**98,817**	**93,865**	**4,952**	**98,469**	**90,922**	**7,547**
PERCENT DISTRIBUTION OF SCHOOLS						
School level	100.0	100.0	100.0	100.0	100.0	100.0
Prekindergarten	1.0	1.0	0.5	1.5	1.6	0.5
Elementary	53.2	53.7	43.6	53.1	53.6	47.0
Middle	16.8	17.1	11.6	16.5	17.0	10.5
Secondary and high	23.8	23.4	30.9	23.9	23.6	27.7
Other	5.2	4.8	13.5	5.0	4.2	14.4
Size of enrollment	100.0	100.0	100.0	100.0	100.0	100.0
Less than 300 students	31.4	29.8	61.5	30.0	28.8	43.6
300 to 499 students	27.6	28.0	20.8	28.2	28.5	24.5
500 to 999 students	32.0	32.9	14.0	32.3	33.0	24.7
1,000 students or more	9.0	9.3	3.7	9.6	9.8	7.1
Region	100.0	100.0	100.0	100.0	100.0	100.0
Northeast	15.5	15.9	9.1	15.1	15.5	10.3
Midwest	26.7	26.8	24.0	25.9	26.4	19.7
South	34.5	34.8	29.5	34.9	35.0	33.9
West	23.3	22.5	37.4	24.1	23.1	36.1

Source: U.S. National Center for Education Statistics, *Digest of Education Statistics*, "Latest version of all Digest tables," <nces.ed.gov/programs/digest>, accessed March 2022.

Table 286. Public Charter Schools and Enrollment by State: 2019

[3,431.2 represents 3,431,200. As of Fall]

State	Number of charter schools	Number of students (1,000)	Charter schools as a percent of public schools	Charter school enrollment as a percent of public school enrollment	State	Number of charter schools	Number of students (1,000)	Charter schools as a percent of public schools	Charter school enrollment as a percent of public school enrollment
United States	**7,547**	**3,431.2**	**7.7**	**6.8**	Missouri	71	24.5	2.9	2.7
Alabama	4	1.2	0.3	0.2	Montana	–	–	–	–
Alaska	29	7.0	5.7	5.3	Nebraska	–	–	–	–
Arizona	557	214.2	24.0	18.7	Nevada	78	56.1	11.0	11.3
Arkansas	83	34.3	7.7	6.9	New Hampshire	40	4.2	8.1	2.4
California	1,321	674.7	12.7	11.0	New Jersey	88	55.6	3.4	4.0
Colorado	261	127.0	13.6	13.9	New Mexico	97	26.6	11.0	8.1
Connecticut	22	10.8	2.2	2.1	New York	316	159.0	6.6	6.0
Delaware	22	16.4	9.9	11.7	North Carolina	196	117.3	7.4	7.5
Dist. of Columbia	114	38.5	49.6	43.3	North Dakota	–	–	–	–
Florida	675	329.2	16.1	11.5	Ohio	313	107.2	8.9	6.3
Georgia	89	65.7	3.9	3.7	Oklahoma	64	46.0	3.6	6.5
Hawaii	37	11.9	12.6	6.6	Oregon	133	38.4	10.6	6.7
Idaho	68	24.4	9.1	7.8	Pennsylvania	179	146.5	6.1	8.6
Illinois	141	63.5	3.2	3.3	Rhode Island	37	10.1	11.7	7.1
Indiana	101	45.0	5.3	4.3	South Carolina	80	39.3	6.3	5.0
Iowa	2	0.1	0.2	(Z)	South Dakota	–	–	–	–
Kansas	9	3.1	0.7	0.6	Tennessee	118	44.0	6.3	4.3
Kentucky	–	–	–	–	Texas	906	391.7	10.1	7.1
Louisiana	146	86.6	10.7	12.2	Utah	132	77.6	12.3	11.3
Maine	12	2.5	2.0	1.4	Vermont	–	–	–	–
Maryland	46	22.7	3.2	2.5	Virginia	8	1.2	0.4	0.1
Massachusetts	81	47.7	4.4	5.1	Washington	10	3.1	0.4	0.3
Michigan	369	146.3	10.4	10.1	West Virginia	–	–	–	–
Minnesota	245	62.8	9.6	7.0	Wisconsin	236	44.7	10.5	5.2
Mississippi	6	2.1	0.6	0.5	Wyoming	5	0.6	1.4	0.7

– Represents zero. Z rounds to less than 0.5 percent.

Source: U.S. National Center for Education Statistics, *Digest of Education Statistics*, "Latest version of all Digest tables," <nces.ed.gov/programs/digest>, accessed February 2022.

Table 287. Proficiency Levels on Selected NAEP Tests for Students in Public Schools by State: 2019

[Represents percent of public school students scoring at or above basic and proficient levels. Basic denotes partial mastery of the knowledge and skills that are fundamental for proficient work at a given grade level. Proficient represents solid academic performance. Students reaching this level demonstrated competency over challenging subject matter. For more detail, see <nationsreportcard.gov>. Based on the National Assessment of Educational Progress (NAEP) tests which are administered to a representative sample of students in public schools, private schools, and Department of Defense schools]

State	Grade 4 Math		Grade 8 Math		Grade 4 Reading		Grade 8 Reading	
	At or above Basic	At or above Proficient	At or above Basic	At or above Proficient	At or above Basic	At or above Proficient	At or above Basic	At or above Proficient
U.S. average.................	**80**	**40**	**68**	**33**	**65**	**34**	**72**	**32**
Alabama....................	71	28	57	21	58	28	64	24
Alaska.....................	73	33	63	29	53	25	63	23
Arizona....................	77	37	68	31	61	31	70	28
Arkansas..................	75	33	63	27	62	31	68	30
California..................	75	34	61	29	63	32	68	30
Colorado..................	80	44	73	37	71	40	77	38
Connecticut...............	82	45	72	39	70	40	78	41
Delaware..................	79	39	65	29	62	33	69	31
District of Columbia........	73	34	55	23	57	30	58	23
Florida....................	87	48	66	31	70	38	72	34
Georgia...................	77	36	67	31	63	32	72	32
Hawaii....................	78	40	65	28	63	34	68	29
Idaho.....................	82	43	74	37	69	37	77	37
Illinois....................	77	38	69	34	64	34	74	35
Indiana...................	84	47	73	37	67	37	75	37
Iowa......................	81	42	72	33	68	35	73	33
Kansas...................	79	40	71	33	66	34	74	32
Kentucky..................	81	40	67	29	67	35	73	33
Louisiana.................	73	29	61	23	55	26	68	27
Maine.....................	81	42	71	34	67	36	75	36
Maryland..................	76	39	65	33	64	35	73	36
Massachusetts............	85	50	78	47	76	45	81	45
Michigan..................	76	36	68	31	64	32	73	31
Minnesota.................	85	53	77	44	69	38	74	34
Mississippi................	84	39	62	24	65	32	67	25
Missouri..................	80	39	70	32	64	34	74	33
Montana..................	82	43	73	36	69	36	76	34
Nebraska.................	84	45	74	37	69	37	74	34
Nevada...................	77	34	62	26	64	31	69	29
New Hampshire............	86	46	77	38	71	38	78	38
New Jersey................	85	48	76	44	72	42	77	43
New Mexico...............	72	29	56	21	53	24	61	23
New York..................	76	37	66	34	66	34	70	32
North Carolina.............	82	41	71	37	67	36	72	33
North Dakota..............	84	44	75	37	69	34	75	32
Ohio......................	82	41	73	38	68	36	75	38
Oklahoma.................	80	35	66	26	63	29	71	26
Oregon...................	75	37	67	31	64	34	73	34
Pennsylvania..............	81	47	70	39	68	40	73	35
Rhode Island..............	81	40	64	29	66	35	71	35
South Carolina............	77	36	64	29	61	32	69	29
South Dakota.............	83	43	76	39	69	36	74	32
Tennessee................	79	40	68	31	66	35	73	32
Texas....................	84	44	68	30	61	30	67	25
Utah.....................	82	46	72	37	72	40	77	38
Vermont..................	81	39	75	38	68	37	77	40
Virginia...................	87	48	75	38	69	38	71	33
Washington...............	79	39	72	40	65	35	74	38
West Virginia..............	74	30	62	24	60	30	67	25
Wisconsin................	80	45	76	41	66	36	76	39
Wyoming..................	87	48	76	37	73	41	75	34

Source: U.S. National Center for Education Statistics, "NAEP Data Explorer," <www.nationsreportcard.gov/ndecore/xplore/nde>, accessed January 2020.

Table 288. School Enrollment Status by Race, Hispanic Origin, and Sex: 2010 and 2020

[17,210 represents 17,210,000. As of October. For persons 18 to 21 years old. For the civilian noninstitutional population. Based on the Current Population Survey; see text, Section 1 and Appendix III]

Characteristic	Total persons 18 to 21 years old (1,000)		Percent distribution							
			Enrolled in high school		High school graduates				Not high school graduates, not enrolled in high school	
					Total		In college			
	2010	2020	2010	2020	2010	2020	2010	2020	2010	2020
Total [1]	**17,210**	**16,995**	**9.9**	**9.4**	**81.5**	**85.3**	**50.6**	**50.0**	**8.4**	**5.3**
White	13,176	12,341	9.7	8.9	82.2	85.5	50.8	50.1	8.0	5.5
Black	2,538	2,538	13.9	12.7	73.0	83.5	41.5	43.2	13.0	3.7
Hispanic [2]	3,339	4,146	13.5	9.8	71.3	83.2	38.9	45.4	15.2	7.0
Male [1]	**8,824**	**8,584**	**11.0**	**10.8**	**79.8**	**83.0**	**46.7**	**44.5**	**9.0**	**6.1**
White	6,867	6,254	10.8	10.2	80.4	83.1	46.6	43.8	8.7	6.6
Black	1,277	1,257	15.5	14.1	69.1	81.1	36.2	39.3	15.4	4.7
Hispanic [2]	1,744	2,026	14.0	11.3	70.0	80.2	35.7	39.0	15.8	8.5
Female [1]	**8,386**	**8,412**	**8.8**	**8.0**	**83.2**	**87.7**	**54.8**	**55.7**	**7.8**	**4.4**
White	6,308	6,087	8.4	7.6	84.1	88.0	55.5	56.5	7.2	4.4
Black	1,261	1,281	12.3	11.3	76.9	85.9	46.9	47.0	10.5	2.8
Hispanic [2]	1,595	2,120	12.9	8.4	72.7	85.9	42.4	51.4	14.4	5.5

[1] Includes other races not shown separately. [2] Persons of Hispanic origin may be of any race.

Source: U.S. Census Bureau, Current Population Reports, P-20, and earlier reports; and "School Enrollment," <www.census.gov/topics/education/school-enrollment/data/tables.All.html>, accessed February 2022.

Table 289. Public High School Graduates by State: 1980 to 2030

[In thousands (2,747.7 represents 2,747,700). For school year ending in year shown. Data include regular diploma recipients, but exclude students receiving a certificate of attendance and persons receiving high school equivalency certificates]

State	1980	1990	2000	2010	2015 (P)	2020 (P)	2025 (P)	2030 (P)
United States	**2,747.7**	[1] **2,320.3**	**2,553.8**	**3,128.0**	**3,187.0**	**3,300.6**	**3,456.9**	**3,210.7**
Alabama	45.2	40.5	37.8	43.2	45.4	46.3	49.1	46.4
Alaska	5.2	5.4	6.6	8.2	7.9	7.7	8.1	8.1
Arizona	28.6	32.1	38.3	61.1	67.2	71.1	76.0	73.1
Arkansas	29.1	26.5	27.3	28.3	30.4	31.6	34.4	32.1
California	249.2	236.3	309.9	405.0	422.8	413.7	411.0	384.3
Colorado	36.8	33.0	38.9	49.3	51.5	57.3	59.7	53.1
Connecticut	37.7	27.9	31.6	34.5	37.2	37.1	37.5	34.6
Delaware	7.6	5.6	6.1	8.1	8.4	9.1	10.1	10.3
District of Columbia [2]	5.0	3.6	2.7	3.6	4.0	4.6	5.6	6.2
Florida	87.3	88.9	106.7	156.1	163.7	175.1	181.5	166.4
Georgia	61.6	56.6	62.6	91.6	97.4	107.0	117.7	104.9
Hawaii	11.5	10.3	10.4	11.0	10.8	11.2	12.0	11.2
Idaho	13.2	12.0	16.2	17.8	18.1	20.0	22.3	20.8
Illinois	135.6	108.1	111.8	139.0	140.5	138.9	148.8	139.0
Indiana	73.1	60.0	57.0	64.6	66.8	67.9	72.6	68.2
Iowa	43.4	31.8	33.9	34.5	32.5	33.3	35.8	33.3
Kansas	30.9	25.4	29.1	31.6	31.9	33.4	34.7	32.1
Kentucky	41.2	38.0	36.8	42.7	42.5	44.8	46.8	38.7
Louisiana	46.3	36.1	38.4	36.6	37.7	41.7	43.2	38.8
Maine	15.4	13.8	12.2	14.1	12.6	12.5	12.5	11.1
Maryland	54.3	41.6	47.8	59.1	57.7	60.1	64.8	62.0
Massachusetts	73.8	55.9	53.0	64.5	65.8	68.6	69.7	64.8
Michigan	124.3	93.8	97.7	110.7	102.0	99.7	95.6	88.5
Minnesota	64.9	49.1	57.4	59.7	56.8	58.1	63.9	62.8
Mississippi	27.6	25.2	24.2	25.5	26.3	26.2	26.6	20.4
Missouri	62.3	49.0	52.8	64.0	60.6	60.5	64.6	55.8
Montana	12.1	9.4	10.9	10.1	9.4	9.2	10.1	9.0
Nebraska	22.4	17.7	20.1	19.4	20.7	22.3	21.7	22.5
Nevada	8.5	9.5	14.6	21.0	23.0	24.7	27.3	25.8
New Hampshire	11.7	10.8	11.8	15.0	13.5	13.0	12.7	11.2
New Jersey	94.6	69.8	74.4	96.2	95.3	97.0	101.3	95.8
New Mexico	18.4	14.9	18.0	18.6	19.5	20.0	21.0	17.8
New York	204.1	143.3	141.7	183.8	179.1	180.6	179.8	166.9
North Carolina	70.9	64.8	62.1	88.7	97.0	105.3	108.5	101.9
North Dakota	9.9	7.7	8.6	7.2	7.0	7.1	8.1	8.2
Ohio	144.2	114.5	111.7	123.4	120.9	122.5	124.6	115.9
Oklahoma	39.3	35.6	37.6	38.5	38.4	41.7	46.4	44.1
Oregon	29.9	25.5	30.2	34.7	34.8	33.6	35.7	33.3
Pennsylvania	146.5	110.5	114.0	131.2	123.6	123.3	126.6	120.5
Rhode Island	10.9	7.8	8.5	9.9	9.9	10.2	10.6	9.5
South Carolina	38.7	32.5	31.6	40.4	42.7	46.4	52.6	50.0
South Dakota	10.7	7.7	9.3	8.2	8.1	8.2	9.7	9.4
Tennessee	49.8	46.1	41.6	62.4	62.0	63.3	67.7	65.0
Texas	171.4	172.5	212.9	280.9	309.3	348.9	385.6	361.7
Utah	20.0	21.2	32.5	31.5	34.1	38.9	45.0	43.5
Vermont	6.7	6.1	6.7	7.2	6.2	5.6	5.6	5.1
Virginia	66.6	60.6	65.6	81.5	82.7	88.0	91.1	82.9
Washington	50.4	45.9	57.6	66.0	68.2	70.7	74.3	67.0
West Virginia	23.4	21.9	19.4	17.7	17.5	17.0	17.8	15.0
Wisconsin	69.3	52.0	58.5	64.7	60.5	60.1	62.6	56.5
Wyoming	6.1	5.8	6.5	5.7	5.6	5.8	6.5	5.8

P Projected. [1] U.S. total includes estimates for nonreporting states. [2] Beginning in 1985-86, graduates from adult programs are excluded.

Source: U.S. National Center for Education Statistics, *Digest of Education Statistics*, "Latest version of all Digest tables," and earlier releases, <nces.ed.gov/programs/digest>, accessed May 2022.

Table 290. High School Dropouts by Selected Characteristics: 2010 to 2019

[3,294 represents 3,294,000. As of October. Data are for status dropouts, who are youth age 16 to 24 that are not enrolled in school and who have not completed a high school program, regardless of when they left school and whether they ever attended school in the United States. People who have received equivalency credentials, such as the GED, are counted as high school completers. Based on the American Community Survey; see Appendix III]

Characteristic	2010	2011	2012	2013	2014	2015	2016	2017	2018	2019
Total (1,000)................	**3,294**	**3,044**	**2,784**	**2,716**	**2,497**	**2,397**	**2,279**	**2,125**	**2,079**	**1,970**
PERCENT										
Total.................	**8.3**	**7.7**	**7.0**	**6.8**	**6.3**	**6.0**	**5.8**	**5.4**	**5.3**	**5.1**
Male................	10.0	9.0	8.2	8.0	7.2	7.0	6.8	6.4	6.2	6.0
Female................	6.6	6.2	5.7	5.6	5.2	5.0	4.7	4.4	4.4	4.2
Race/ethnicity:										
White................	5.3	5.1	4.7	4.7	4.4	4.5	4.5	4.3	4.2	4.1
Black................	10.3	9.6	9.0	9.0	7.9	7.2	7.0	6.5	6.4	5.6
Hispanic................	16.7	14.5	12.8	11.8	10.7	9.9	9.1	8.2	8.0	7.7
Asian................	2.8	2.7	2.6	2.5	2.5	2.4	2.0	2.1	1.9	1.8
Pacific Islander................	4.8	8.8	9.1	5.0	10.6	5.4	6.9	3.9	8.1	8.0
American Indian/Alaska Native......	15.4	13.1	12.8	12.8	11.5	13.2	11.0	10.1	9.5	9.6
Some other race [1]................	9.2	7.9	5.9	5.1	5.6	7.5	5.1	5.2	4.5	3.9
Two or more races................	6.1	6.0	5.6	5.2	5.0	4.7	4.8	4.5	5.2	5.1
Nativity:										
Native-born................	7.0	6.6	6.2	6.1	5.6	5.5	5.3	5.0	5.0	4.7
Foreign-born................	20.3	17.7	15.1	14.1	12.6	11.3	10.5	9.4	9.3	9.5
Disability status: [2]										
With a disability................	17.4	15.8	15.4	15.2	13.9	12.6	12.4	12.1	11.7	10.7
Without a disability................	7.8	7.2	6.5	6.3	5.8	5.6	5.3	5.0	4.9	4.7

[1] Respondents who wrote in some other race that was not included as an option on the questionnaire. [2] Individuals identified as having a disability reported difficulty in at least one of the following: walking, climbing stairs, dressing, bathing, learning, or remembering.

Source: U.S. National Center for Education Statistics, *Digest of Education Statistics*, "Latest version of all Digest tables," <nces.ed.gov/programs/digest>, accessed March 2021.

Table 291. High School Dropouts by Age, Race, and Hispanic Origin: 1980 to 2020

[5,212 represents 5,212,000. As of October. For persons 14 to 24 years old. Dropouts are persons not in regular school and who have not completed the 12th grade nor received a general equivalency degree. Based on Current Population Survey; see text, Section 1 and Appendix III]

Age and race	Number of dropouts (1,000)					Percent of population				
	1980	1990	2000	2010	2020	1980	1990	2000	2010	2020
Total dropouts [1,2]......	**5,212**	**3,854**	**3,883**	**2,952**	**2,161**	**12.0**	**10.1**	**9.1**	**6.4**	**4.7**
16 to 17 years............	709	418	460	227	473	8.8	6.3	5.8	2.7	5.7
18 to 21 years............	2,578	1,921	2,005	1,445	893	15.8	13.4	12.9	8.4	5.3
22 to 24 years............	1,798	1,458	1,310	1,144	614	15.2	13.8	11.8	9.2	5.1
White [2,3]................	**4,169**	**3,127**	**3,065**	**2,232**	**1,671**	**11.3**	**10.1**	**9.1**	**6.3**	**5.0**
16 to 17 years............	619	334	366	181	347	9.2	6.4	5.8	2.9	5.7
18 to 21 years............	2,032	1,516	1,558	1,048	614	14.7	13.1	12.6	8.0	5.5
22 to 24 years............	1,416	1,235	1,040	893	493	14.0	14.0	11.7	9.2	5.5
Black [2,3]................	**934**	**611**	**705**	**498**	**238**	**16.0**	**10.9**	**10.9**	**7.2**	**3.5**
16 to 17 years............	80	73	84	30	49	6.9	6.9	7.0	2.3	4.1
18 to 21 years............	486	345	383	283	95	23.0	16.0	16.0	10.5	3.7
22 to 24 years............	346	185	232	167	79	24.0	13.5	14.3	9.4	4.5
Hispanic [2,4]............	**919**	**1,122**	**1,499**	**1,122**	**693**	**29.5**	**26.8**	**23.5**	**12.8**	**6.3**
16 to 17 years............	92	89	121	40	129	16.6	12.9	11.0	2.7	6.5
18 to 21 years............	470	502	733	506	290	40.3	32.9	30.0	15.2	7.0
22 to 24 years............	323	523	602	543	234	40.6	42.8	35.5	23.2	8.6

[1] Includes other racial/ethnic groups not shown separately. [2] Includes persons age 14 to 15, not shown separately. [3] Beginning 2003, for persons who selected this race only. See footnote 4, Table 256. [4] Persons of Hispanic origin may be of any race.

Source: U.S. Census Bureau, Current Population Reports, series PPL and P-20; and "School Enrollment," <www.census.gov/topics/education/school-enrollment/data/tables.All.html>, accessed February 2022.

Table 292. ACT Program Scores and Characteristics of College-Bound Students: 1990 to 2021

[For academic year ending in year shown. Data based on all ACT tested seniors graduating in year shown. Beginning 1990, not comparable with previous years because a new version of the ACT was introduced]

Type of test and characteristic	Unit	1990	2000	2010	2015	2016	2017	2018	2019	2020	2021
TEST SCORES [1]											
Composite....................	**Point**	**20.6**	**21.0**	**21.0**	**21.0**	**20.8**	**21.0**	**20.8**	**20.7**	**20.6**	**20.3**
Male.....................	Point	21.0	21.2	21.2	21.1	20.9	21.0	20.8	20.6	20.5	20.3
Female................... [2]	Point	20.3	20.9	20.9	21.0	20.9	21.1	20.9	20.8	20.8	20.6
Other responses [2]............	Point	(NA)	(NA)	(NA)	(NA)	(NA)	(NA)	(NA)	(NA)	17.8	18.5
English........................	Point	20.5	20.5	20.5	20.4	20.1	20.3	20.2	20.1	19.9	19.6
Male.....................	Point	20.1	20.0	20.1	20.0	19.8	19.9	19.7	19.6	19.3	19.1
Female...................	Point	20.9	20.9	20.8	20.8	20.6	20.8	20.7	20.6	20.5	20.2
Other responses [2]............	Point	(NA)	(NA)	(NA)	(NA)	(NA)	(NA)	(NA)	(NA)	16.8	17.4
Math...........................	Point	19.9	20.7	21.0	20.8	20.6	20.7	20.5	20.4	20.2	19.9
Male.....................	Point	20.7	21.4	21.6	21.3	21.0	21.2	20.9	20.8	20.6	20.4
Female...................	Point	19.3	20.2	20.5	20.4	20.3	20.4	20.2	20.0	20.0	19.7
Other responses [2]............	Point	(NA)	(NA)	(NA)	(NA)	(NA)	(NA)	(NA)	(NA)	17.8	18.2
Reading [2].....................	Point	(NA)	21.4	21.3	21.4	21.3	21.4	21.3	21.2	21.2	20.9
Male.....................	Point	(NA)	21.2	21.1	21.2	21.0	21.2	21.0	20.7	20.8	20.6
Female...................	Point	(NA)	21.5	21.4	21.6	21.6	21.8	21.7	21.7	21.6	21.5
Other responses [2]............	Point	(NA)	(NA)	(NA)	(NA)	(NA)	(NA)	(NA)	(NA)	18.2	19.0
Science........................	Point	(NA)	21.0	20.9	20.9	20.8	21.0	20.7	20.6	20.6	20.4
Male.....................	Point	(NA)	21.6	21.4	21.3	21.1	21.3	20.9	20.8	20.7	20.6
Female...................	Point	(NA)	20.6	20.5	20.6	20.6	20.8	20.6	20.5	20.5	20.4
Other responses [2]............	Point	(NA)	(NA)	(NA)	(NA)	(NA)	(NA)	(NA)	(NA)	18.0	18.8
PARTICIPANTS [3]											
Total [4].......................	**1,000**	817	1,065	1,569	1,924	2,090	2,030	1,915	1,783	1,670	1,295
Male.....................	Percent	46	43	45	47	46	46	47	46	46	46
White.....................	Percent	73	72	62	55	54	52	52	52	52	54
Black.....................	Percent	9	10	14	13	13	13	13	12	12	12
Obtaining composite scores of:											
27 or above.....................	Percent	12	14	16	18	14	15	15	15	15	14
18 or below.....................	Percent	35	32	35	37	39	38	40	35	42	44

NA Not available. [1] Minimum score, 1; maximum score, 36. [2] Students who chose "another gender, preferred not to indicate a gender, and unknown." [3] Data by race are for those responding to the race question. [4] 817 represents 817,000.

Source: ACT, Inc., Iowa City, IA. Most recent score reported in the *The ACT® Profile Report - National*, annual ©. Reproduced with permission.

Table 293. SAT Scores and Characteristics of High School Graduates: 2021

[Data reflect 2021 high school graduates who took the new SAT during high school. If a student took the SAT more than once, the most recent score and self-reported SAT questionnaire responses are summarized. Maximum total score is 1600]

Characteristic	Test takers		Mean score			Percent with benchmarks met			
	Number	Percent	Total	ERW [1]	Math	Both	ERW [1]	Math	None
Total....................................	**1,509,133**	**(X)**	**1,060**	**533**	**528**	**46**	**67**	**49**	**30**
Took essay [2]....................	687,305	46	1,088	545	543	51	70	53	28
Race/ethnicity:									
White.....................	635,486	42	1,112	562	550	57	80	59	18
Black.....................	168,454	11	934	477	457	22	46	23	53
Hispanic/Latino................	352,094	23	967	490	477	28	52	30	46
Asian.....................	167,208	11	1,239	597	642	78	85	83	10
American Indian/Alaska Native.........	10,288	1	927	468	459	21	42	24	56
Native Hawaiian/Other Pacific Islander....	3,015	(Z)	950	481	469	26	48	28	50
Two or more races....................	54,961	4	1,116	565	551	56	79	58	20
Sex:									
Female.....................	774,684	51	1,054	535	519	44	69	46	29
Male.....................	731,634	48	1,067	530	537	49	65	52	31
First language learned:									
English only.....................	903,402	60	1,078	547	532	50	74	52	25
English and another language..........	311,691	21	1,058	526	531	45	63	48	34
Another language....................	167,125	11	1,072	521	551	48	61	54	33
Highest level of parental education:									
No high school diploma....................	111,318	7	917	459	458	19	38	23	59
High school diploma.....................	348,132	23	981	496	485	30	56	33	42
Associate degree.....................	87,924	6	1,021	518	504	38	66	40	32
Bachelor's degree.....................	440,198	29	1,120	562	559	59	81	62	17
Graduate degree.....................	353,732	23	1,198	599	600	72	87	74	11

X Not applicable. Z Represents less than .05%. [1] Evidence-based reading and writing. [2] Reflects test takers who completed the SAT essay at any point, not necessarily on the most recent test administration date.

Source: The College Board, *2021 SAT Suite of Assessments Annual Report*, © 2021. Reproduced with permission. See also <www.collegeboard.org>.

Table 294. Higher Education—Institutions and Enrollment: 1990 to 2020

[13,819 represents 13,819,000. As of Fall. Covers universities, colleges, professional schools, and junior and teachers' colleges, both publicly and privately controlled, regular session. Includes estimates for institutions not reporting. Data for 1990 cover institutions of higher education; beginning 2000, data cover degree-granting institutions. Degree-granting institutions grant associate's or higher degrees and participate in Title IV federal financial aid programs. The degree-granting classification includes more 2-year colleges and excludes a few higher education institutions that did not grant degrees. Data are based on the Integrated Postsecondary Education Data System. See also Appendix III]

Item	Unit	1990	2000	2010	2015	2018	2019	2020
ALL INSTITUTIONS								
Number of institutions [1]	**Number**	**3,559**	**4,182**	**4,599**	**4,583**	**4,042**	**3,982**	**3,931**
4-year	Number	2,141	2,450	2,870	3,004	2,703	2,679	2,637
2-year	Number	1,418	1,732	1,729	1,579	1,339	1,303	1,294
Instructional staff—								
lecturer or above [2]	**1,000**	**(NA)**	**(NA)**	**(NA)**	**1,552**	**1,543**	**1,549**	**1,489**
Percent full-time	Percent	(NA)	(NA)	(NA)	52	54	54	56
Total enrollment [3]	**1,000**	**13,819**	**15,312**	**21,019**	**19,988**	**19,651**	**19,630**	**18,992**
Male	1,000	6,284	6,722	9,046	8,724	8,445	8,364	7,870
Female	1,000	7,535	8,591	11,974	11,264	11,207	11,266	11,122
4-year institutions	1,000	8,579	9,364	13,336	13,489	13,898	14,039	14,078
2-year institutions	1,000	5,240	5,948	7,684	6,499	5,753	5,591	4,914
Full-time	1,000	7,821	9,010	13,087	12,288	11,990	11,954	11,591
Part-time	1,000	5,998	6,303	7,932	7,701	7,662	7,676	7,400
Public	1,000	10,845	11,753	15,142	14,573	14,539	14,504	13,867
Private	1,000	2,974	3,560	5,877	5,415	5,112	5,127	5,125
Not-for-profit	1,000	2,760	3,109	3,854	4,066	4,132	4,135	4,101
For profit	1,000	214	450	2,023	1,349	980	991	1,024
Undergraduate	1,000	11,959	13,155	18,082	17,047	16,616	16,558	15,852
Men	1,000	5,380	5,778	7,836	7,502	7,228	7,149	6,650
Women	1,000	6,579	7,377	10,246	9,544	9,388	9,408	9,202
Full-time	1,000	6,976	7,923	11,457	10,603	10,266	10,210	9,830
Part-time	1,000	4,983	5,232	6,625	6,444	6,350	6,348	6,022
First-time freshmen [4]	1,000	2,257	2,428	3,157	2,883	2,880	2,857	2,603
Postbaccalaureate	1,000	1,860	2,157	2,937	2,942	3,035	3,073	3,140
Men	1,000	904	944	1,209	1,222	1,216	1,214	1,219
Women	1,000	955	1,213	1,728	1,720	1,819	1,858	1,921
2-YEAR INSTITUTIONS								
Number of institutions [1]	Number	1,418	1,732	1,729	1,579	1,339	1,303	1,294
Public	Number	972	1,076	978	910	868	853	835
Private	Number	446	656	751	669	471	450	459
Instructional staff—								
lecturer or above [2]	1,000	(NA)	(NA)	(NA)	372	327	315	281
Enrollment [3]	1,000	5,240	5,948	7,684	6,499	5,753	5,591	4,914
Public	1,000	4,996	5,697	7,218	6,224	5,556	5,401	4,703
Private	1,000	244	251	466	275	197	190	211
Male	1,000	2,233	2,559	3,266	2,818	2,455	2,374	1,977
Female	1,000	3,007	3,390	4,418	3,681	3,298	3,216	2,936
4-YEAR INSTITUTIONS								
Number of institutions [1]	Number	2,141	2,450	2,870	3,004	2,703	2,679	2,637
Public	Number	595	622	678	710	768	772	752
Private	Number	1,546	1,828	2,192	2,294	1,935	1,907	1,885
Instructional staff—								
lecturer or above [2]	1,000	(NA)	(NA)	(NA)	1,181	1,216	1,234	1,208
Enrollment [3]	1,000	8,579	9,364	13,336	13,489	13,898	14,039	14,078
Public	1,000	5,848	6,055	7,924	8,349	8,983	9,103	9,165
Private	1,000	2,730	3,308	5,412	5,140	4,915	4,937	4,913
Male	1,000	4,051	4,163	5,780	5,906	5,990	5,990	5,892
Female	1,000	4,527	5,201	7,556	7,583	7,909	8,050	8,186

NA Not available. [1] Number of institutions includes count of branch campuses. Includes schools accredited by the National Association of Trade and Technical Schools. [2] Beginning in 2007, includes institutions with fewer than 15 full-time employees; prior to 2007, these institutions did not report staff. [3] Branch campuses counted according to actual status, e.g., 2-year branch in 2-year category. May include unclassified students taking courses for credit but not towards a degree. [4] Students seeking certificates or degrees.

Source: U.S. National Center for Education Statistics, *Digest of Education Statistics*, "Latest version of all Digest tables," and earlier releases, <nces.ed.gov/programs/digest/>, accessed August 2022.

Table 295. Degree-Granting Higher Education Institutions—Number and Enrollment by State and Selected Characteristics: 2019

[19,637 represents 19,637,000. Number of institutions beginning in academic year. Opening Fall enrollment of resident and extension students attending full-time or part-time. Based on data from the Integrated Postsecondary Education Data System (IPEDS)]

State	Num-ber of institu-tions [1]	Enrollment (1,000)							Minority			Non-resi-dent alien
		Total	Male	Female	Public	Private	Full-time	White [2]	Total [3]	Black [2]	His-panic	
United States........	3,982	19,637	8,363	11,275	14,501	5,136	11,966	10,142	8,522	2,474	3,783	974
Alabama...............	62	303	128	175	255	48	205	188	106	77	12	9
Alaska.................	8	23	9	14	22	1	10	13	9	1	2	(Z)
Arizona...............	68	609	235	374	378	231	338	292	299	77	156	17
Arkansas.............	54	159	65	94	142	17	98	107	47	25	12	5
California.............	416	2,715	1,205	1,510	2,247	468	1,507	712	1,857	168	1,144	147
Colorado.............	67	368	158	210	284	85	208	223	133	28	68	12
Connecticut..........	40	194	80	113	111	83	128	106	76	25	32	11
Delaware.............	8	60	23	37	42	18	36	33	23	13	6	4
District of Columbia....	18	99	38	61	4	94	65	42	45	24	10	12
Florida................	176	1,067	438	629	798	269	621	449	572	187	302	46
Georgia...............	113	554	225	329	445	109	341	259	269	167	50	26
Hawaii................	17	60	24	37	50	10	34	10	47	1	8	4
Idaho.................	15	122	52	70	79	43	61	91	24	1	13	7
Illinois................	156	719	303	415	452	266	419	371	306	86	144	41
Indiana...............	74	423	184	239	333	90	268	290	109	43	33	24
Iowa..................	56	218	100	118	164	54	139	164	43	13	17	10
Kansas................	63	209	94	115	177	31	118	138	58	16	23	13
Kentucky..............	59	267	114	153	200	67	158	200	51	23	12	16
Louisiana.............	56	244	95	149	213	31	163	131	106	75	14	7
Maine.................	30	72	30	42	48	23	43	60	11	3	3	2
Maryland..............	52	355	155	199	295	60	184	154	179	98	36	22
Massachusetts.........	107	492	212	281	203	290	347	268	163	43	60	62
Michigan..............	92	525	235	291	455	71	322	359	139	59	31	28
Minnesota.............	84	403	151	252	242	161	217	259	129	61	26	15
Mississippi............	34	167	66	101	148	19	121	93	71	59	5	3
Missouri..............	97	363	153	210	226	137	220	255	91	41	22	16
Montana..............	23	48	22	26	44	4	33	38	9	(Z)	2	1
Nebraska..............	36	136	59	76	100	36	85	98	32	7	15	5
Nevada...............	22	120	50	70	111	9	65	48	69	9	36	2
New Hampshire........	24	169	64	105	37	132	75	117	48	22	16	4
New Jersey............	86	413	187	226	327	86	273	188	203	57	93	22
New Mexico...........	39	122	49	72	118	4	58	38	81	3	60	3
New York..............	299	1,236	534	702	678	557	884	568	559	164	229	109
North Carolina.........	135	569	232	337	463	106	354	324	225	124	53	20
North Dakota...........	20	52	25	27	46	7	35	41	9	2	2	2
Ohio..................	162	656	284	372	512	145	403	471	156	75	32	30
Oklahoma..............	51	193	81	112	168	25	123	110	74	15	20	9
Oregon................	54	226	100	126	190	36	137	143	73	7	34	10
Pennsylvania..........	218	693	299	394	389	304	502	450	198	74	55	46
Rhode Island..........	14	80	34	46	40	40	61	51	25	6	12	5
South Carolina.........	66	242	98	143	198	44	168	152	84	56	14	5
South Dakota..........	22	52	23	29	43	8	32	42	9	2	2	2
Tennessee.............	86	323	132	191	226	97	227	217	98	59	18	8
Texas.................	244	1,658	702	955	1,480	178	860	570	1,025	201	662	64
Utah..................	30	381	161	220	189	192	286	281	93	20	43	7
Vermont...............	19	41	19	23	25	16	30	33	7	2	2	2
Virginia...............	111	557	237	320	384	173	347	311	227	107	53	19
Washington............	74	363	159	204	316	47	251	200	141	17	52	22
West Virginia..........	42	139	68	71	82	57	69	103	32	14	10	4
Wisconsin.............	69	333	146	187	275	58	205	249	72	18	27	12
Wyoming..............	9	32	15	18	32	(Z)	18	26	5	(Z)	3	1
U.S. military [4]..........	5	15	11	4	15	(X)	15	10	5	1	2	(Z)

X Not applicable. Z Fewer than 500. [1] Branch campuses counted as separate institutions. [2] Non-Hispanic. [3] Includes other races not shown separately. [4] Service academies.

Source: U.S. National Center for Education Statistics, *Digest of Education Statistics*, "Latest version of all Digest tables," <nces.ed.gov/programs/digest>, accessed March 2022.

Table 296. Historically Black Colleges and Universities (HBCUs) Enrollment, Degrees Conferred, and Finances by Selected Characteristics: 2020

[In units as indicated (8,997,410 represents $8,997,410,000). Institutions and enrollment for Fall 2020. Degrees conferred and financial statistics for 2019-2020 academic year. Historically Black colleges and universities are degree-granting institutions established prior to 1964 with the principal mission of educating Black Americans. Totals include persons of other races not shown separately. Totals may not sum due to rounding. Data are from the Integrated Postsecondary Education Data System]

Characteristic	Total	Public			Private		
		Total	4-year	2-year	Total	4-year	2-year
Number of Institutions...............	**102**	**53**	**42**	**11**	**49**	**48**	**1**
FALL ENROLLMENT (NUMBER)							
Total enrollment........................	**279,157**	**214,685**	**181,787**	**32,898**	**64,472**	**64,249**	**223**
Male..	99,611	75,438	62,885	12,553	24,173	24,112	61
Black....................................	72,730	52,277	48,190	4,087	20,453	20,399	54
Female....................................	179,546	139,247	118,902	20,345	40,299	40,137	162
Black....................................	139,044	103,955	95,093	8,862	35,089	34,953	136
Full time.................................	209,487	151,945	141,227	10,718	57,542	57,343	199
Male....................................	74,953	53,633	49,149	4,484	21,320	21,263	57
Female..................................	134,534	98,312	92,078	6,234	36,222	36,080	142
Part time.................................	69,670	62,740	40,560	22,180	6,930	6,906	24
Male....................................	24,658	21,805	13,736	8,069	2,853	2,849	4
Female..................................	45,012	40,935	26,824	14,111	4,077	4,057	20
DEGREES CONFERRED (NUMBER)							
Associate's.............................	5,210	4,998	1,185	3,813	212	178	34
Male....................................	1,851	1,746	290	1,456	105	94	11
Black....................................	658	563	135	428	95	85	10
Female..................................	3,359	3,252	895	2,357	107	84	23
Black....................................	1,635	1,538	487	1,051	97	74	23
Bachelor's..............................	33,244	24,272	24,272	(X)	8,972	8,972	(X)
Male....................................	11,698	8,581	8,581	(X)	3,117	3,117	(X)
Black....................................	8,750	6,130	6,130	(X)	2,620	2,620	(X)
Female..................................	21,546	15,691	15,691	(X)	5,855	5,855	(X)
Black....................................	17,573	12,386	12,386	(X)	5,187	5,187	(X)
Master's................................	6,963	5,844	5,844	(X)	1,119	1,119	(X)
Male....................................	2,134	1,766	1,766	(X)	368	368	(X)
Black....................................	1,429	1,133	1,133	(X)	296	296	(X)
Female..................................	4,829	4,078	4,078	(X)	751	751	(X)
Black....................................	3,573	2,953	2,953	(X)	620	620	(X)
Doctorate................................	2,794	1,705	1,705	(X)	1,089	1,089	(X)
Male....................................	1,048	639	639	(X)	409	409	(X)
Black....................................	525	285	285	(X)	240	240	(X)
Female..................................	1,746	1,066	1,066	(X)	680	680	(X)
Black....................................	1,115	644	644	(X)	471	471	(X)
FINANCIAL STATISTICS ($1,000) [1]							
Total revenue........................	**8,997,410**	**5,842,968**	**5,447,431**	**395,537**	**3,154,442**	**3,144,630**	**9,811**
Student tuition and fees..............	1,929,746	1,020,974	976,008	44,966	908,772	904,220	4,552
Federal government [2]...............	2,336,542	1,504,636	1,365,957	138,679	831,906	827,510	4,396
State governments [2]................	2,214,561	2,128,350	1,992,078	136,272	86,210	86,210	–
Local governments [2]...............	131,312	92,622	45,251	47,371	38,690	38,138	553
Private gifts and grants [3]...........	573,278	138,781	135,523	3,257	434,498	434,188	310
Investment return (gain or loss).....	137,712	53,108	51,681	1,427	84,604	84,604	–
Auxiliary enterprises.................	886,332	573,557	567,621	5,936	312,775	312,775	–
Hospitals and other sources.........	787,927	330,941	313,311	17,630	456,986	456,986	–
Total expenditures...................	**8,369,751**	**5,495,847**	**5,114,108**	**381,739**	**2,873,903**	**2,867,156**	**6,748**
Instruction..............................	2,262,327	1,536,308	1,401,541	134,766	726,019	724,064	1,955
Research................................	503,333	348,091	348,091	–	155,243	155,243	–
Academic support......................	697,583	480,085	452,665	27,420	217,498	216,902	596
Institutional support...................	1,565,319	848,553	780,403	68,150	716,766	714,100	2,666
Auxiliary enterprises.................	1,052,214	770,499	762,787	7,712	281,715	280,378	1,337
Other expenditures....................	2,288,975	1,512,312	1,368,622	143,691	776,663	776,469	193

– Represents zero. X Not applicable. [1] Most public institutions reported data using the Government Accounting Standards Board form. Private institutions and some public institutions reported data using the Financial Accounting Standards Board form. Combined totals are approximate. [2] Includes appropriations, grants, and contracts. [3] Includes contributions from affiliated entities.

Source: U.S. National Center for Education Statistics, *Digest of Education Statistics*, "Latest version of all Digest tables," <nces.ed.gov/programs/digest>, accessed May 2022.

Table 297. College Enrollment of Recent High School Completers: 1970 to 2020

[2,758 represents 2,758,000. For persons 16 to 24 years old who graduated from high school in the preceding 12 months. Includes persons receiving General Education Degrees (GEDs). Based on sample surveys and subject to sampling error; data not comparable with that in other tables]

Year	Number of high school completers (1,000)						Percent enrolled in college [5]					
	Total [1]	Male	Female	White [2]	Black [2,3]	Hispanic [3,4]	Total [1]	Male	Female	White [2]	Black [2,3]	Hispanic [3,4]
1970	2,758	1,343	1,415	2,461	(NA)	(NA)	51.7	55.2	48.5	52.0	(NA)	(NA)
1975	3,185	1,513	1,672	2,701	302	132	50.7	52.6	49.0	51.1	41.7	58.0
1980	3,088	1,498	1,589	2,554	350	130	49.3	46.7	51.8	49.8	42.7	52.3
1985	2,668	1,287	1,381	2,104	332	141	57.7	58.6	56.8	60.1	42.2	51.0
1990	2,362	1,173	1,189	1,819	331	121	60.1	58.0	62.2	63.0	46.8	42.7
1991	2,276	1,140	1,136	1,727	310	154	62.5	57.9	67.1	65.4	46.4	57.2
1992	2,397	1,216	1,180	1,724	354	198	61.9	60.0	63.8	64.3	48.2	55.0
1993	2,342	1,120	1,223	1,719	304	201	62.6	59.9	65.2	62.9	55.6	62.2
1994	2,517	1,244	1,273	1,915	316	178	61.9	60.6	63.2	64.5	50.8	49.1
1995	2,599	1,238	1,361	1,861	349	288	61.9	62.6	61.3	64.3	51.2	53.7
1996	2,660	1,297	1,363	1,875	406	227	65.0	60.1	69.7	67.4	56.0	50.8
1997	2,769	1,354	1,415	1,909	384	336	67.0	63.6	70.3	68.2	58.5	65.6
1998	2,810	1,452	1,358	1,980	386	314	65.6	62.4	69.1	68.5	61.9	47.4
1999	2,897	1,474	1,423	1,978	436	329	62.9	61.4	64.4	66.3	58.9	42.3
2000	2,756	1,251	1,505	1,938	393	300	63.3	59.9	66.2	65.7	54.9	52.9
2001	2,549	1,277	1,273	1,834	381	241	61.8	60.1	63.5	64.3	55.0	51.7
2002	2,796	1,412	1,384	1,903	382	344	65.2	62.1	68.4	69.1	59.4	53.6
2003	2,677	1,306	1,372	1,832	327	314	63.9	61.2	66.5	66.2	57.5	58.6
2004	2,752	1,327	1,425	1,854	398	286	66.7	61.4	71.5	68.8	62.5	61.8
2005	2,675	1,262	1,414	1,799	345	390	68.6	66.5	70.4	73.2	55.7	54.0
2006	2,692	1,328	1,363	1,805	318	382	66.0	65.8	66.1	68.5	55.5	57.9
2007	2,955	1,511	1,444	2,043	416	355	67.2	66.1	68.3	69.5	55.7	64.0
2008	3,151	1,640	1,511	2,091	416	458	68.6	65.9	71.6	71.7	55.7	63.9
2009	2,937	1,407	1,531	1,863	415	459	70.1	66.0	73.8	71.3	69.5	59.3
2010	3,160	1,679	1,482	1,937	461	507	68.1	62.8	74.0	70.5	62.0	59.7
2011	3,079	1,611	1,468	1,747	464	623	68.2	64.7	72.2	68.3	67.1	66.6
2012	3,203	1,622	1,581	(NA)	(NA)	(NA)	66.2	61.3	71.3	65.7	56.4	70.3
2013	2,977	1,524	1,453	(NA)	(NA)	(NA)	65.9	63.5	68.4	68.8	56.7	59.8
2014	2,868	1,423	1,445	(NA)	(NA)	(NA)	68.4	64.0	72.6	67.7	70.2	65.2
2015	2,965	1,448	1,516	(NA)	(NA)	(NA)	69.2	65.8	72.5	71.3	55.6	68.9
2016	3,137	1,517	1,620	(NA)	(NA)	(NA)	69.8	67.5	71.9	69.7	57.3	72.0
2017	2,870	1,345	1,525	(NA)	(NA)	(NA)	66.7	61.1	71.7	69.1	59.4	61.0
2018	3,212	1,614	1,598	(NA)	(NA)	(NA)	69.1	66.9	71.4	70.9	64.5	65.4
2019	3,178	1,486	1,693	(NA)	(NA)	(NA)	66.2	62.0	69.8	68.0	49.8	63.4
2020	3,118	1,581	1,537	(NA)	(NA)	(NA)	62.7	59.3	66.2	65.0	57.5	56.2

NA Not available. [1] Includes persons of other racial/ethnic groups, not shown separately. [2] Beginning 2003, for persons of this race group only. See footnote 4, Table 256. [3] Due to small sample size, data are subject to relatively large sampling errors. [4] Persons of Hispanic origin may be of any race. [5] As of October.

Source: U.S. National Center for Education Statistics, *Digest of Education Statistics*, "Latest version of all Digest tables," <nces.ed.gov/programs/digest/>, accessed February 2022.

Table 298. College Enrollment by Sex and Attendance Status: 2000 to 2021

[In thousands (15,312 represents 15,312,000). As of Fall. Includes enrollment at branch campuses, some additional (primarily 2-year) colleges, and excludes a few institutions that did not award degrees. Includes enrollment at institutions that were eligible to participate in Title IV federal financial aid programs. Includes unclassified students (students taking courses for credit, but are not candidates for degrees)]

Sex and age	2000		2010		2015		2019		2021 (P)	
	Total	Part-time	Total	Part-time	Total	Part-time	Total	Part-time	Total	Part-time
Total [1]	**15,312**	**6,303**	**21,019**	**7,932**	**19,988**	**7,701**	**19,630**	**7,676**	**20,327**	**7,941**
Male [1]	**6,722**	**2,611**	**9,046**	**3,207**	**8,724**	**3,165**	**8,364**	**3,088**	**8,685**	**3,212**
Under 18 years old	58	7	94	23	435	352	592	492	595	494
18 to 19 years old	1,464	212	1,820	245	1,955	342	2,002	347	1,949	340
20 to 21 years old	1,411	255	1,948	362	1,849	378	1,812	358	1,860	375
22 to 24 years old	1,222	388	1,723	508	1,541	507	1,372	455	1,441	476
25 to 29 years old	908	498	1,410	695	1,227	545	1,085	496	1,156	513
30 to 34 years old	581	395	731	430	644	348	571	318	637	344
35 years old and over	1,077	855	1,320	944	1,056	683	921	617	1,038	665
Female [1]	**8,591**	**3,692**	**11,974**	**4,725**	**11,264**	**4,535**	**11,266**	**4,587**	**11,643**	**4,729**
Under 18 years old	73	3	108	9	618	495	863	708	866	710
18 to 19 years old	1,794	223	2,237	316	2,387	387	2,509	410	2,449	403
20 to 21 years old	1,593	298	2,155	377	2,230	459	2,251	454	2,304	471
22 to 24 years old	1,378	497	2,036	666	1,784	661	1,676	620	1,750	641
25 to 29 years old	1,136	660	1,844	953	1,552	792	1,490	767	1,565	781
30 to 34 years old	752	520	1,074	630	867	514	832	502	921	540
35 years old and over	1,865	1,491	2,520	1,774	1,802	1,214	1,633	1,118	1,775	1,173

P Projection. [1] Beginning with data for 2015, totals may include data for "age unknown," not shown separately.

Source: U.S. National Center for Education Statistics, *Digest of Education Statistics*, "Latest version of all Digest Tables," <nces.ed.gov/programs/digest>, accessed June 2022.

Table 299. College Enrollment by Selected Characteristics: 1990 to 2020

[In thousands (13,818.6 represents 13,818,600). As of Fall. Nonresident alien students are not distributed among racial/ethnic groups. Beginning in 2000, data reflect a new classification of institutions; this includes more 2-year colleges and excludes a few institutions that did not award degrees. Includes institutions that were eligible to participate in Title IV federal financial aid programs and schools accredited by the National Association of Trade and Technical Schools. Based on data from the Integrated Postsecondary Education Data System (IPEDS)]

Characteristic	1990	2000	2010	2015	2017	2018	2019	2020
Total	**13,818.6**	**15,312.3**	**21,019.4**	**19,988.2**	**19,778.2**	**19,651.4**	**19,630.2**	**18,991.8**
Male	6,283.9	6,721.8	9,045.8	8,723.8	8,571.3	8,444.6	8,363.9	7,869.5
Female	7,534.7	8,590.5	11,973.7	11,264.4	11,206.8	11,206.8	11,266.3	11,122.3
Public	10,844.7	11,752.8	15,142.2	14,572.8	14,571.7	14,539.3	14,503.6	13,867.2
Private	2,973.9	3,559.5	5,877.3	5,415.4	5,206.4	5,112.2	5,126.5	5,124.6
2-year	5,240.1	5,948.4	7,683.6	6,499.5	5,952.6	5,753.0	5,590.7	4,913.8
4-year	8,578.6	9,363.9	13,335.8	13,488.7	13,825.4	13,898.5	14,039.5	14,078.0
Undergraduate	11,959.1	13,155.4	18,082.4	17,046.7	16,773.0	16,616.4	16,557.5	15,851.9
Postbaccalaureate	1,859.5	2,156.9	2,937.0	2,941.5	3,005.1	3,035.0	3,072.6	3,139.9
White [1]	**10,722.5**	**10,462.1**	**12,720.8**	**10,939.2**	**10,517.4**	**10,305.2**	**10,139.8**	**9,797.5**
Male	4,861.0	4,634.6	5,605.8	4,848.5	4,632.2	4,501.8	4,395.5	4,155.9
Female	5,861.5	5,827.5	7,115.0	6,090.7	5,885.2	5,803.4	5,744.3	5,641.6
Public	8,385.4	7,963.4	9,182.1	7,910.6	7,646.3	7,508.1	7,368.8	7,047.6
Private	2,337.0	2,498.7	3,538.7	3,028.5	2,871.1	2,797.1	2,771.0	2,749.9
2-year	3,954.3	3,804.1	4,321.3	3,225.8	2,879.5	2,728.2	2,583.2	2,314.4
4-year	6,768.1	6,658.0	8,399.5	7,713.4	7,637.9	7,577.0	7,556.6	7,483.1
Undergraduate	9,272.6	8,983.5	10,895.9	9,303.8	8,882.8	8,667.6	8,497.8	8,115.2
Postbaccalaureate	1,449.8	1,478.6	1,824.9	1,635.4	1,634.6	1,637.6	1,641.9	1,682.3
Black [1]	**1,247.0**	**1,730.3**	**3,039.0**	**2,681.0**	**2,549.5**	**2,496.1**	**2,467.3**	**2,382.4**
Male	484.7	635.3	1,089.0	998.9	942.0	911.2	894.3	832.6
Female	762.3	1,095.0	1,949.9	1,682.1	1,607.5	1,584.9	1,573.1	1,549.9
Public	976.4	1,319.2	1,988.8	1,775.1	1,725.3	1,715.3	1,695.7	1,604.1
Private	270.6	411.1	1,050.2	906.0	824.2	780.9	771.7	778.4
2-year	524.3	734.9	1,198.9	940.5	844.8	806.1	776.8	669.9
4-year	722.8	995.4	1,840.0	1,740.5	1,704.7	1,690.1	1,690.5	1,712.5
Undergraduate	1,147.2	1,548.9	2,677.1	2,316.5	2,184.0	2,130.7	2,100.2	1,998.5
Postbaccalaureate	99.8	181.4	361.9	364.5	365.5	365.5	367.2	383.9
Hispanic	**782.4**	**1,461.8**	**2,748.8**	**3,297.7**	**3,546.0**	**3,642.5**	**3,785.9**	**3,689.7**
Male	353.9	627.1	1,157.6	1,389.2	1,479.0	1,506.7	1,549.0	1,443.2
Female	428.5	834.7	1,591.2	1,908.5	2,067.0	2,135.8	2,236.9	2,246.4
Public	671.4	1,229.3	2,163.8	2,694.5	2,929.7	3,018.6	3,126.6	2,997.0
Private	111.0	232.5	585.0	603.2	616.3	624.0	659.2	692.6
2-year	424.2	843.9	1,393.0	1,555.6	1,510.2	1,502.3	1,533.8	1,299.9
4-year	358.2	617.9	1,355.9	1,742.1	2,035.7	2,140.2	2,252.1	2,389.8
Undergraduate	724.6	1,351.0	2,551.0	3,055.0	3,270.6	3,351.5	3,478.4	3,348.8
Postbaccalaureate	57.9	110.8	197.8	242.7	275.4	291.0	307.5	340.9
Asian/Pacific Islander [1]	**572.4**	**978.2**	**1,281.6**	**1,284.3**	**1,327.8**	**1,355.2**	**1,378.0**	**1,390.7**
Male	294.9	465.9	600.6	602.9	617.3	626.7	634.6	629.0
Female	277.5	512.3	681.0	681.5	710.5	728.5	743.4	761.7
Public	461.0	770.5	968.7	970.1	1,007.4	1,030.4	1,043.1	1,043.6
Private	111.5	207.7	312.8	314.2	320.4	324.8	334.9	347.0
2-year	215.2	401.9	463.1	401.9	369.0	368.4	358.7	329.0
4-year	357.2	576.3	818.5	882.5	958.8	986.8	1,019.3	1,061.7
Undergraduate	500.5	845.5	1,087.3	1,084.0	1,113.6	1,134.3	1,147.3	1,144.2
Postbaccalaureate	72.0	132.7	194.3	200.3	214.2	220.9	230.7	246.4
American Indian/ Alaska Native [1]	**102.8**	**151.2**	**196.2**	**146.1**	**137.5**	**133.1**	**129.7**	**121.0**
Male	43.1	61.4	78.7	58.2	53.7	51.3	49.2	43.6
Female	59.7	89.7	117.5	88.0	83.7	81.8	80.4	77.5
Public	90.4	127.3	150.8	113.7	107.7	104.5	102.4	93.5
Private	12.4	23.9	45.5	32.5	29.7	28.5	27.2	27.5
2-year	54.9	74.7	87.2	62.8	55.7	52.4	49.3	42.1
4-year	47.9	76.5	109.0	83.4	81.7	80.6	80.3	78.9
Undergraduate	95.5	138.5	179.1	132.2	123.9	119.5	116.2	107.3
Postbaccalaureate	7.3	12.6	17.1	13.9	13.6	13.6	13.4	13.8
Nonresident alien	**391.5**	**528.7**	**707.7**	**982.3**	**1,000.0**	**989.9**	**974.6**	**848.7**
Male	246.3	297.3	379.6	548.6	551.6	541.6	528.6	457.8
Female	145.2	231.4	328.0	433.7	448.4	448.3	446.0	390.9
Public	260.0	343.1	453.0	626.8	623.6	610.2	596.3	511.4
Private	131.4	185.6	254.7	355.5	376.4	379.7	378.3	337.2
2-year	67.1	89.0	99.3	104.2	88.1	86.3	79.1	61.3
4-year	324.3	439.7	608.3	878.1	911.8	903.6	895.5	787.3
Undergraduate	218.7	288.0	398.4	565.1	574.1	565.2	548.6	468.9
Postbaccalaureate	172.7	240.7	309.3	417.2	425.9	424.8	426.1	379.8

[1] Non-Hispanic.

Source: U.S. National Center for Education Statistics, *Digest of Education Statistics*, "Latest version of all Digest tables," and earlier releases, <nces.ed.gov/programs/digest>, accessed March 2022.

Table 300. College Enrollment by Sex, Age, and Race/Ethnicity: 1980 to 2020

[In thousands (11,387 represents 11,387,000). As of October for the civilian noninstitutional population, 14 years old and over. Based on the Current Population Survey; see text, Section 1 and Appendix III]

Characteristic	1980	1990 [1]	1995	2000	2005	2010	2015	2017	2018	2019	2020
Total [2]............................	**11,387**	**13,621**	**14,715**	**15,314**	**17,472**	**20,275**	**19,101**	**18,398**	**18,908**	**18,289**	**17,674**
Male [3].............................	5,430	6,192	6,703	6,682	7,539	9,007	8,484	8,112	8,373	8,067	7,577
18 to 24 years..................	3,604	3,922	4,089	4,342	4,972	5,698	5,694	5,459	5,587	5,442	5,187
25 to 34 years..................	1,325	1,412	1,561	1,361	1,486	2,055	1,803	1,714	1,842	1,641	1,514
35 years old and over...........	405	772	985	918	1,019	1,161	878	854	859	880	785
Female [3]........................	5,957	7,429	8,013	8,631	9,933	11,268	10,617	10,287	10,534	10,223	10,097
18 to 24 years..................	3,625	4,042	4,452	5,109	5,859	6,515	6,460	6,477	6,510	6,492	6,477
25 to 34 years..................	1,378	1,749	1,788	1,846	2,115	2,569	2,372	2,167	2,358	2,104	2,096
35 years old and over...........	802	1,546	1,684	1,589	1,838	2,049	1,672	1,492	1,541	1,477	1,443
White [3, 4].......................	9,925	11,488	12,021	11,999	13,467	15,258	13,859	13,224	13,323	12,783	12,497
18 to 24 years..................	6,334	6,635	7,011	7,566	8,499	9,324	8,969	8,690	8,770	8,602	8,419
25 to 34 years..................	2,328	2,698	2,686	2,339	2,647	3,414	2,966	2,706	2,737	2,411	2,459
35 years old and over...........	1,051	2,023	2,208	1,978	2,206	2,365	1,776	1,672	1,647	1,613	1,522
Male............................	4,804	5,235	5,535	5,311	5,844	6,883	6,253	5,864	5,980	5,661	5,343
Female..........................	5,121	6,253	6,486	6,689	7,624	8,375	7,607	7,360	7,343	7,123	7,154
Black [3, 4].......................	1,163	1,393	1,772	2,164	2,297	3,083	2,826	2,812	3,009	2,848	2,591
18 to 24 years..................	688	894	988	1,216	1,229	1,692	1,637	1,595	1,670	1,587	1,549
25 to 34 years..................	289	258	426	567	520	715	627	674	807	699	573
35 years old and over...........	156	207	334	361	448	642	537	509	517	517	415
Male............................	476	587	710	815	864	1,185	1,147	1,175	1,183	1,171	1,055
Female..........................	686	807	1,062	1,349	1,435	1,898	1,679	1,637	1,826	1,676	1,536
Asian [3, 4].......................	(NA)	(NA)	(NA)	(NA)	1,184	1,322	1,616	1,581	1,691	1,768	1,759
18 to 24 years..................	(NA)	(NA)	(NA)	(NA)	696	811	1,026	1,101	1,079	1,132	1,174
25 to 34 years..................	(NA)	(NA)	(NA)	(NA)	341	354	426	352	466	468	390
35 years old and over...........	(NA)	(NA)	(NA)	(NA)	130	125	143	95	127	133	181
Male............................	(NA)	(NA)	(NA)	(NA)	605	647	752	750	846	870	821
Female..........................	(NA)	(NA)	(NA)	(NA)	579	676	864	831	844	898	938
Hispanic origin [3, 5].............	443	748	1,207	1,426	1,942	2,879	3,374	3,574	3,574	3,555	3,553
18 to 24 years..................	315	435	745	899	1,216	1,814	2,369	2,410	2,431	2,469	2,460
25 to 34 years..................	118	168	250	309	438	652	648	717	780	714	665
35 years old and over...........	(NA)	130	193	195	257	372	315	368	305	332	392
Male............................	222	364	568	619	804	1,302	1,484	1,529	1,613	1,559	1,436
Female..........................	221	384	639	807	1,139	1,576	1,890	2,045	1,960	1,996	2,116

NA Not available. [1] Beginning 1990, based on a revised edit and tabulation package. [2] Includes other races not shown separately. [3] Includes persons 14 to 17 years old not shown separately. [4] Beginning 2003, for persons who selected this race group only. See footnote 4, Table 256. [5] Persons of Hispanic origin may be of any race.

Source: U.S. Census Bureau, Current Population Reports, P-20, and earlier reports; and "School Enrollment," <www.census.gov/topics/education/school-enrollment/data/tables.All.html>, accessed February 2022.

Table 301. College Enrollment by Type of College, Sex, and Selected Characteristics: 2020

[In thousands (17,674 represents 17,674,000). As of October. Covers civilian noninstitutional population 15 years old and over enrolled in colleges and graduate schools. Based on Current Population Survey. See text, Section 1 and Appendix III]

Characteristic	Total				Male		Female	
	Total enrolled	Two-year college	Four-year college	Graduate school	Total enrolled [1]	Four-year college	Total enrolled [1]	Four-year college
Total enrollment [2]...............	**17,674**	**3,742**	**10,083**	**3,849**	**7,577**	**4,442**	**10,097**	**5,641**
Age:								
15 to 19 years old..................	4,208	1,228	2,916	64	1,801	1,199	2,407	1,718
20 to 24 years old..................	7,628	1,347	5,219	1,062	3,478	2,477	4,151	2,741
25 to 34 years old..................	3,610	686	1,251	1,673	1,513	536	2,096	715
35 years old and over.............	2,228	480	698	1,050	785	230	1,443	467
Race/ethnicity:								
White [3]...........................	12,497	2,666	7,180	2,652	5,343	3,152	7,154	4,027
White, non-Hispanic [3]............	9,423	1,630	5,585	2,208	4,119	2,523	5,305	3,062
Black [3]...........................	2,591	598	1,481	513	1,055	624	1,536	856
Asian [3]...........................	1,759	236	985	537	821	457	938	528
Hispanic [4]........................	3,553	1,206	1,856	491	1,436	745	2,116	1,110
Control of school:								
Public..............................	13,917	3,430	8,059	2,427	5,971	3,532	7,946	4,528
Private.............................	3,757	312	2,024	1,422	1,606	910	2,151	1,114
Employment status:								
Employed full-time.................	4,278	850	1,623	1,805	1,730	680	2,548	943
Employed part-time.................	4,647	1,137	2,733	777	1,784	1,056	2,862	1,677
Not employed.......................	8,749	1,756	5,727	1,267	4,062	2,707	4,687	3,021
Enrollment status:								
Full time students.................	13,774	2,548	8,650	2,576	5,994	3,833	7,780	4,817
15 to 19 years old..............	3,867	986	2,818	64	1,624	1,159	2,243	1,657
20 to 24 years old..............	6,566	975	4,717	875	3,001	2,218	3,566	2,500
25 to 34 years old..............	2,377	372	808	1,198	1,011	353	1,366	454
35 years old and over..........	965	216	308	441	359	103	606	205
Part time students.................	3,900	1,193	1,434	1,273	1,583	609	2,317	824
15 to 19 years old..............	341	243	99	–	177	38	164	61
20 to 24 years old..............	1,062	372	502	188	477	260	585	242
25 to 34 years old..............	1,233	315	443	475	503	183	731	261
35 years old and over..........	1,263	264	390	610	427	127	837	262

– Represents or rounds to zero. [1] Includes enrollment in two-year colleges and graduate school, not shown separately. [2] Includes other races not shown separately. [3] For persons who selected this race group only. [4] Persons of Hispanic origin may be of any race.

Source: U.S. Census Bureau, "School Enrollment," <www.census.gov/topics/education/school-enrollment/data/tables.All.html>, accessed February 2022.

Table 302. Foreign (Nonimmigrant) Student Enrollment in U.S. Colleges and Universities by World Region and Selected Country of Origin: 1980 to 2021

[In thousands (286 represents 286,000). For Fall of the previous year]

Region of origin	1980	1990	1995	2000	2005	2010	2013	2014	2015	2016	2017	2018	2019	2020	2021
All regions.........	**286**	**387**	**453**	**515**	**565**	**691**	**820**	**866**	**975**	**1,044**	**1,079**	**1,095**	**1,095**	**1,075**	**914**
Africa [1]...............	36	25	21	30	36	37	36	37	40	43	45	47	47	49	45
Nigeria..............	16	4	2	4	6	7	7	8	9	11	12	13	13	14	13
Asia [1, 2, 3]............	165	245	292	315	356	469	597	655	724	790	827	842	842	823	697
China................	1	33	39	54	63	128	236	274	304	329	351	363	370	373	317
Taiwan.............	18	31	36	29	26	27	22	21	21	21	22	22	23	24	20
Hong Kong..........	10	11	13	8	7	8	8	8	8	8	8	7	7	7	6
India..............	9	26	34	42	80	105	97	103	133	166	186	196	202	193	167
Indonesia.............	2	9	12	11	8	7	8	8	8	9	9	9	8	8	7
Iran...................	51	7	3	2	2	5	9	10	11	12	13	13	12	11	10
Japan...............	12	30	45	47	42	25	20	19	19	19	19	19	18	18	12
Saudi Arabia........	10	4	4	5	3	16	45	54	60	61	53	44	37	31	22
South Korea........	5	22	34	41	53	72	71	68	64	61	59	55	52	50	39
Europe [4]...........	23	46	65	78	72	85	86	87	91	92	93	93	91	90	68
Latin America [1, 5].....	42	48	47	62	68	66	67	72	86	85	80	80	81	80	73
Mexico..............	6	7	9	11	13	13	14	15	17	17	17	15	15	14	13
Venezuela............	10	3	4	5	5	5	6	7	8	8	9	8	8	7	6
North America [6].......	16	19	23	24	29	29	27	28	27	27	27	26	26	26	25
Canada..............	15	18	23	24	28	28	27	28	27	27	27	26	26	26	25
Oceania...............	4	4	4	5	4	5	6	6	6	7	7	7	8	7	6

[1] Includes countries not shown separately. [2] Includes the Middle East. [3] Beginning 2006, excludes Cyprus and Turkey. [4] Beginning 2006, includes Cyprus and Turkey. [5] Includes Mexico, Central America, Caribbean, and South America. Prior to 2011, excludes Bermuda. [6] Prior to 2011, includes Bermuda.

Source: Institute of International Education, New York, NY, *Open Doors Report on International Educational Exchange* ©, annual (2021). See also <opendoorsdata.org>.

Table 303. Higher Education Enrollment in Languages Other Than English: 1970 to 2016

[1,153.2 represents 1,153,200. As of Fall. For credit enrollment]

Item	1970	1980	1986	1990	1995	2006	2009	2013	2016
Registrations [1] (1,000)................	**1,153.2**	**924.3**	**1,003.2**	**1,185.5**	**1,138.8**	**1,575.8**	**1,673.6**	**1,561.1**	**1,417.8**
By selected language (1,000):									
Spanish....................	386.6	379.0	411.4	534.1	606.3	822.1	861.0	789.9	712.2
French......................	358.5	248.3	275.1	273.1	205.4	206.0	215.2	197.7	175.7
American Sign Language..................	(NA)	(NA)	(NA)	1.6	4.3	79.7	92.1	109.6	107.1
German.....................	201.8	127.0	120.9	133.6	96.3	94.1	95.6	86.8	80.6
Japanese....................	6.6	11.5	23.5	45.8	44.7	65.4	72.4	66.8	68.8
Italian......................	34.2	34.8	40.9	49.8	43.8	78.2	80.3	71.0	56.7
Chinese.....................	6.1	11.4	16.9	19.4	26.5	51.4	59.9	61.1	53.1
Arabic......................	1.3	3.5	3.4	3.7	4.4	24.0	35.2	33.5	31.6
Latin.......................	28.4	25.0	25.0	28.2	25.9	32.2	32.4	27.2	24.9
Russian....................	36.4	24.0	33.9	44.5	24.7	24.8	26.7	22.0	20.4
Korean.....................	0.1	0.4	0.9	2.4	3.3	7.1	8.4	12.3	13.9
Hebrew.....................	16.6	19.3	15.7	13.0	13.1	23.8	22.1	19.3	15.1
Index (1965=100).............	111.5	89.3	97.0	114.6	110.1	152.3	161.8	150.9	137.0

NA Not available. [1] Includes other languages, not shown separately.

Source: Modern Language Association, Dennis Looney and Natalia Lusin. *Enrollments in Languages Other Than English in United States Institutions of Higher Education, Summer 2016 and Fall 2016: Final Report*, June 2019 ©. For 1970 to 2009, consult Association of Departments of Foreign Languages (ADFL) Bulletins. For 2002 to 2016 reports, see: <www.mla.org/Resources/Guidelines-and-Data/Reports-and-Professional-Guidelines>.

Table 304. COVID-19 Pandemic Impact on Higher Education Students: 2020

[In percent. Data are based on responses from approximately 61,000 undergraduate students participating in the 2019-2020 National Postsecondary Student Aid Study. Data are preliminary, and cover students attending higher education institutions in the 50 states, DC, and Puerto Rico. Data represent percent of undergraduate students who experienced disruptions at their higher education institute due to the COVID-19 pandemic between January 1 and June 30, 2020]

Student experiences	Total	Public			Private, nonprofit	
		Less than 2-year	2-year	4-year	Less than 4-year	4-year
Experienced enrollment disruption or change..........................	87.5	88.6	87.8	92.2	82.6	85.7
Withdrew from school..................................	4.4	6.9	6.8	2.7	6.3	2.9
Took leave of absence from school...........................	3.8	9.3	4.1	2.5	[2] 5.0	2.7
Some or all classes canceled...........................	9.5	31.7	9.8	9.1	13.6	9.1
School break extended...........................	35.0	25.1	31.7	39.9	(S)	40.4
Some or all in-person classes moved to online only instruction.....	84.1	[2] 73.2	81.5	89.2	75.2	84.8
Experienced housing disruption or change..........................	27.5	[2] 11.0	8.3	34.7	6.9	50.1
Experienced financial disruption or change..........................	39.6	25.2	35.4	43.0	39.0	40.4
Received emergency financial assistance from school..............	14.6	[2] 7.4	10.3	17.6	16.2	16.2
Lost job or lost income due to reduced work hours...................	28.6	18.6	26.4	31.0	23.4	28.8
Received full or partial tuition refund [1]........................	27.3	13.3	26.3	30.6	[2] 28.7	24.0
Received full or partial room and board refund [1]......................	38.3	[2] 8.2	6.1	45.5	(S)	60.3

S Reporting standards not met. [1] Excludes credit for future enrollment costs. Housing refunds include only students who lived on campus or in college-owned housing. [2] Interpret data with caution. Standard error is between 30 and 50 percent.

Source: U.S. National Center for Education Statistics, *2019-20 National Postsecondary Student Aid Study (NPSAS:20): First Look at the Impact of the Coronavirus (COVID-19) Pandemic on Undergraduate Student Enrollment, Housing, and Finances (Preliminary Data)*, June 2021.

Table 305. College Students Reporting Disability Status by Selected Characteristic: 2015 to 2016

[19,308 represents 19,308,000. Students with disabilities are those who reported having deafness or serious difficulty hearing; blindness or serious difficulty seeing; serious difficulty concentrating, remembering, or making decisions because of a physical, mental, or emotional condition; or serious difficulty walking or climbing stairs. For 2015-16, the question about difficulty concentrating, remembering, or making decisions was expanded to include examples of relevant conditions. Specifically, students were instructed to "consider conditions including, but not limited to, a serious learning disability, depression, ADD, or ADHD." Therefore, data for 2015-16 cannot be compared to estimates of the percentages in earlier years. Based on the 2015-2016 National Postsecondary Student-Aid Study; see source for details]

Student characteristic	Undergraduate			Graduate and first-professional		
	All students	Disabled students	Nondisabled students	All students	Disabled students	Nondisabled students
Total students (1,000)............................	**19,308**	**3,755**	**15,554**	**3,547**	**423**	**3,124**
PERCENT DISTRIBUTION						
Total..	**100.0**	**19.4**	**80.6**	**100.0**	**11.9**	**88.1**
Age:						
15 to 23 years old..........................	100.0	17.6	82.4	100.0	8.1	91.9
24 to 29 years old..........................	100.0	21.6	78.4	100.0	11.3	88.7
30 years or older...........................	100.0	22.6	77.4	100.0	13.5	86.5
Sex:						
Male..	100.0	19.2	80.8	100.0	9.9	90.1
Female......................................	100.0	19.6	80.4	100.0	13.3	86.7
Race/ethnicity of student:						
White non-Hispanic.........................	100.0	20.8	79.2	100.0	13.0	87.0
Black non-Hispanic.........................	100.0	17.2	82.8	100.0	10.3	89.7
Hispanic....................................	100.0	18.3	81.7	100.0	14.3	85.7
Asian.......................................	100.0	15.2	84.8	100.0	6.2	93.8
Pacific Islander............................	100.0	23.6	76.4	100.0	[1] 14.9	85.1
American Indian/Alaska Native..............	100.0	27.8	72.2	100.0	[1] 11.8	88.2
Two or more races..........................	100.0	22.1	77.9	100.0	19.7	80.3
Attendance status:						
Full-time, full-year.........................	100.0	17.3	82.7	100.0	12.0	88.0
Part-time or part-year.......................	100.0	20.8	79.2	100.0	11.9	88.1
Student housing status:						
On-campus..................................	100.0	15.8	84.2	(NA)	(NA)	(NA)
Off-campus.................................	100.0	20.6	79.4	(NA)	(NA)	(NA)
With parents or relatives....................	100.0	19.5	80.5	(NA)	(NA)	(NA)
Attended more than one institution..........	100.0	18.7	81.3	(NA)	(NA)	(NA)
Dependency status:						
Dependent..................................	100.0	17.2	82.8	(NA)	(NA)	(NA)
Independent, unmarried.....................	100.0	23.9	76.1	100.0	11.5	88.5
Independent, married.......................	100.0	20.5	79.5	100.0	10.3	89.7
Independent with dependents...............	100.0	20.3	79.7	100.0	13.4	86.6

NA Not available. [1] Interpret data with caution.

Source: U.S. National Center for Education Statistics, *Digest of Education Statistics*, "Latest version of all Digest tables," <nces.ed.gov/programs/digest>, accessed January 2019.

Table 306. College Freshmen—Summary Characteristics: 1980 to 2019

[In percent. As of Fall for first-time full-time freshmen in 4-year colleges and universities. Based on sample survey and subject to sampling error; see source]

Characteristic	1980	1990	2000	2005	2010	2015	2017	2018	2019
Sex:									
Male..	48.8	46.9	45.2	45.0	44.3	43.8	44.8	44.6	45.5
Female......................................	51.2	53.1	54.8	55.0	55.7	56.2	55.2	55.4	54.5
Applied to more than three colleges..................	31.5	42.9	50.5	55.4	64.1	71.9	71.0	69.6	71.9
Average grade in high school:									
A- to A+....................................	26.6	29.4	42.9	46.6	48.4	58.7	57.4	57.6	59.3
B- to B+....................................	58.2	57.0	50.5	48.0	47.5	38.5	39.6	39.3	38.2
C to C+.....................................	14.9	13.4	6.5	5.4	4.1	2.8	3.1	3.1	2.5
D...	0.2	0.2	0.1	0.1	0.1	–	–	0.1	–
Political orientation:									
Liberal......................................	21.0	24.6	24.8	27.1	27.3	29.6	32.2	30.5	32.2
Middle of the road..........................	57.0	51.7	51.9	45.0	46.4	44.9	41.4	43.8	43.6
Conservative...............................	19.0	20.6	18.9	22.6	21.7	19.8	20.4	20.0	17.8
Probable field of study:									
Biological sciences.........................	4.5	4.9	6.6	7.6	10.8	14.9	15.5	14.5	15.4
Business....................................	21.2	21.1	16.7	17.4	13.7	13.4	13.8	14.5	13.4
Education...................................	8.4	10.3	11.0	9.9	7.2	4.2	4.4	4.3	4.2
Engineering.................................	11.2	9.7	8.7	8.3	10.3	13.1	11.5	10.9	9.7
Physical science............................	3.2	2.8	2.6	3.1	2.7	2.7	2.7	2.1	2.2
Social science..............................	8.2	11.0	10.0	10.7	8.9	10.8	11.0	11.1	11.7
Communications [1]..........................	2.4	2.9	2.7	2.0	1.8	1.9	1.6	0.9	0.9
Computer science...........................	2.6	1.7	3.7	1.1	1.0	3.8	4.2	3.8	4.3
Personal objectives—very important or essential:									
Being very well off financially...............	62.5	72.3	73.4	74.5	77.4	81.9	82.5	82.9	84.3
Developing a meaningful philosophy of life...........	62.5	45.9	42.4	45.0	46.9	46.5	48.1	46.5	49.8
Keeping up to date with political affairs...............	45.2	46.6	28.1	36.4	33.2	40.4	48.1	43.5	45.2

– Represents or rounds to zero. [1] Beginning in 2012, the communications field includes journalism majors.

Source: The Higher Education Research Institute, University of California, Los Angeles, CA, *The American Freshman: National Norms Fall 2019* ©, 2020, and earlier editions. See also <heri.ucla.edu/publications-tfs>.

Table 307. Employed Undergraduate Students by Enrollment Status and Selected Characteristics: 2020

[In percent. Students were classified as full time if they were taking at least 12 hours of classes during an average school week and as part time if they were taking fewer hours. Data are from the Current Population Survey; based on sample surveys of the civilian noninstitutionalized population]

Characteristic	Full-time undergraduates						Part-time undergraduates	
	Percent of all full-time under-graduates	Percent employed					Percent of all full-time under-graduates	Percent employed [1]
		Total [1]	Hours worked per week [2]					
			Less than 10	10 to 19	20 to 34	35 or more		
Total..........................	**100.0**	**39.6**	**3.5**	**9.2**	**15.5**	**9.9**	**100.0**	**73.5**
Sex:								
Male..........................	44.1	35.1	2.7	7.9	14.4	8.9	42.5	74.5
Female........................	55.9	43.1	4.1	10.2	16.3	10.7	57.5	72.8
Race/ethnicity: [3]								
White, non-Hispanic...........	53.3	42.3	4.0	11.0	16.0	9.1	47.5	78.1
Black, non-Hispanic...........	13.3	32.6	[6] 2.2	5.8	11.9	11.8	16.3	69.6
Asian, non-Hispanic...........	8.8	27.5	5.4	9.6	9.1	[6] 3.2	6.3	55.6
Two or more races.............	2.7	40.2	(S)	[6] 10.9	12.6	[6] 15.5	1.3	(S)
Hispanic.......................	20.8	42.6	2.4	6.4	20.0	12.6	27.8	73.6
Age:								
16 to 24 years old.............	84.9	36.6	3.8	9.5	15.8	6.4	46.5	70.8
25 to 29 years old.............	7.0	56.1	(S)	10.8	11.1	28.4	16.8	77.9
30 to 39 years old.............	5.4	55.4	(S)	[6] 5.5	16.4	30.1	19.3	80.1
40 to 49 years old.............	2.0	57.7	[6] 6.7	(S)	14.9	30.5	11.4	78.0
50 to 64 years old.............	0.8	61.4	(S)	(S)	[6] 16.9	39.4	6.0	52.3
Level of institution:								
2-year.........................	22.6	46.5	1.7	8.5	21.0	13.4	45.5	67.8
4-year.........................	77.4	37.5	4.0	9.4	13.8	8.9	54.5	78.3
Householder status: [4]								
Non-householder...............	79.0	35.7	3.5	9.7	14.2	7.0	52.7	71.7
Householder...................	21.0	54.1	3.4	7.3	20.2	20.8	47.3	75.6
Presence of own children under 18 in household: [5]								
Child or children present......	6.5	49.2	[6] 3.0	[6] 2.3	14.7	26.3	23.7	72.6
No children present............	93.5	38.9	3.5	9.7	15.5	8.8	76.3	73.8

S Figure does not meet publication standards. [1] Includes those who were employed but not at work during the survey week. [2] Excludes those who were employed but not at work during the survey week; therefore, detail may not sum to total percent employed. [3] Includes other races not shown separately. [4] Householders are persons in whose name the housing unit is owned or rented. Never-married students living away from home in college dormitories are not considered householders. [5] Includes stepchildren and adopted children. [6] Use data with caution. The coefficient of variation for this estimate is between 30 and 50 percent.

Source: U.S. National Center for Education Statistics, *Digest of Education Statistics*, "Latest version of all Digest tables," <nces.ed.gov/programs/digest>, accessed May 2022.

Table 308. Residence and Migration of College Freshmen by State: 2020

[As of Fall. Includes first-time postsecondary students who had graduated from high school in the previous 12 months and were enrolled at public and private nonprofit 4-year degree-granting institutions that participated in Title IV federal financial aid programs. Excludes respondents for whom state residence and/or migration are unknown. Based on data from the Integrated Postsecondary Education Data System (IPEDS). See source for more information]

State	Total freshmen enrollment in institutions located in the state	Ratio of in-state students to freshmen enrollment	Ratio of in-state students to residents enrolled in any state [1]	State	Total freshmen enrollment in institutions located in the state	Ratio of in-state students to freshmen enrollment	Ratio of in-state students to residents enrolled in any state [1]
U.S. [2]......	**1,599,156**	**0.72**	**0.74**	MO..........	25,712	0.65	0.71
AL..........	26,339	0.59	0.83	MT..........	5,462	0.57	0.76
AK..........	1,313	0.91	0.49	NE..........	11,889	0.71	0.79
AZ..........	32,175	0.55	0.79	NV..........	11,941	0.87	0.77
AR..........	15,573	0.68	0.84	NH..........	7,698	0.40	0.44
CA..........	151,569	0.86	0.79	NJ..........	29,602	0.86	0.46
CO..........	28,333	0.72	0.69	NM..........	6,247	0.76	0.72
CT..........	19,738	0.52	0.45	NY..........	110,049	0.70	0.73
DE..........	6,935	0.56	0.64	NC..........	49,137	0.73	0.82
DC..........	8,638	0.05	0.19	ND..........	5,653	0.50	0.77
FL..........	106,349	0.85	0.86	OH..........	68,718	0.76	0.83
GA..........	59,787	0.83	0.80	OK..........	18,263	0.68	0.83
HI..........	4,132	0.59	0.45	OR..........	14,263	0.57	0.66
ID..........	10,095	0.52	0.71	PA..........	78,009	0.62	0.76
IL..........	43,937	0.73	0.52	RI..........	10,759	0.25	0.53
IN..........	44,849	0.66	0.84	SC..........	25,578	0.64	0.82
IA..........	18,337	0.54	0.79	SD..........	5,646	0.55	0.72
KS..........	14,263	0.65	0.74	TN..........	31,255	0.68	0.75
KY..........	23,030	0.71	0.83	TX..........	138,470	0.93	0.84
LA..........	25,629	0.78	0.86	UT..........	21,832	0.64	0.90
ME..........	6,963	0.51	0.62	VT..........	4,998	0.22	0.42
MD..........	18,879	0.68	0.47	VA..........	42,402	0.70	0.72
MA..........	48,596	0.51	0.58	WA..........	28,967	0.78	0.71
MI..........	48,475	0.81	0.85	WV..........	11,044	0.58	0.87
MN..........	23,207	0.73	0.58	WI..........	33,175	0.68	0.76
MS..........	10,180	0.55	0.77	WY..........	1,832	0.62	0.62

[1] Students residing in a particular state when admitted to an institution anywhere, either in their home state or another state. [2] Includes U.S. Service Academies (Air Force Academy, Coast Guard Academy, Merchant Marine Academy, Military Academy, and Naval Academy), not shown separately.

Source: U.S. National Center for Education Statistics, *Digest of Education Statistics*, "Latest version of all Digest tables," <nces.ed.gov/programs/digest>, accessed August 2022.

Table 309. Higher Education Public and Private Institutions—Average Charges: 1985 to 2021

[In current dollars. Estimated. For the entire academic year ending in year shown. Figures are average charges per full-time equivalent student. Room and board are based on full-time students]

Academic control and year	Tuition and required fees [1]			Dormitory room charges			Board rates [2]		
	All institutions	4-yr. institutions	2-yr. institutions	All institutions	4-yr. institutions	2-yr. institutions	All institutions	4-yr. institutions	2-yr. institutions
PUBLIC									
1985...............	971	1,228	584	1,196	1,217	921	1,241	1,237	1,302
1990...............	1,356	1,780	756	1,513	1,557	962	1,635	1,638	1,581
1995...............	2,057	2,681	1,192	1,959	2,023	1,232	1,949	1,967	1,712
2000...............	2,504	3,349	1,348	2,440	2,519	1,549	2,364	2,406	1,834
2005...............	3,629	5,027	1,849	3,304	3,418	2,174	2,931	2,981	2,353
2010...............	4,763	6,717	2,283	4,401	4,564	2,854	3,655	3,755	2,571
2014...............	6,120	8,312	2,881	5,304	5,479	3,448	4,205	4,308	2,955
2015...............	6,370	8,543	2,955	5,504	5,677	3,559	4,313	4,412	3,072
2016...............	6,612	8,778	3,038	5,686	5,850	3,759	4,469	4,576	3,118
2017...............	6,818	8,804	3,156	5,859	6,018	3,823	4,562	4,666	3,111
2018...............	7,051	9,036	3,242	6,060	6,227	3,834	4,682	4,785	3,204
2019...............	7,248	9,212	3,312	6,290	6,459	4,057	4,843	4,927	3,582
2020...............	7,410	9,349	3,377	6,483	6,655	4,105	4,943	5,031	3,578
2021...............	7,638	9,375	3,501	6,630	6,774	4,407	5,107	5,189	3,649
PRIVATE									
1985...............	5,315	5,556	3,485	1,426	1,426	1,424	1,462	1,469	1,294
1990...............	8,147	8,396	5,196	1,923	1,935	1,663	1,948	1,953	1,811
1995...............	11,111	11,481	6,914	2,587	2,601	2,233	2,509	2,520	2,023
2000...............	14,100	14,616	8,225	3,236	3,242	3,067	2,877	2,879	2,753
2005...............	18,154	18,604	12,122	4,178	4,173	4,475	3,485	3,483	3,700
2010...............	21,764	22,269	14,862	5,248	5,248	5,211	4,329	4,329	4,390
2014...............	25,110	25,707	14,170	6,021	6,026	5,489	4,864	4,866	4,211
2015...............	26,182	26,739	14,261	6,221	6,228	5,506	5,019	5,021	4,560
2016...............	27,436	27,942	14,528	6,457	6,464	5,666	5,123	5,128	4,181
2017...............	28,945	29,476	14,589	6,710	6,717	5,949	5,268	5,273	4,350
2018...............	30,274	30,723	14,894	6,961	6,968	6,057	5,437	5,440	4,645
2019...............	31,527	31,883	15,720	7,171	7,179	5,951	5,616	5,608	6,909
2020...............	32,411	32,764	15,831	7,397	7,401	6,326	5,756	5,760	4,587
2021...............	32,444	32,825	15,474	7,573	7,581	5,572	5,903	5,907	4,621

[1] For public institutions, data are for in-state students. [2] Beginning 1990, rates reflect 20 meals per week, rather than meals served 7 days a week.

Source: U.S. National Center for Education Statistics, *Digest of Education Statistics*, "Latest version of all Digest tables," <nces.ed.gov/programs/digest>, accessed May 2022.

Table 310. Federal Student Financial Assistance: 1995 to 2017

[5,472 represents $5,472,000,000. For award years July 1 of year shown to the following June 30. Funds utilized exclude operating costs, and so forth, and represent funds given to students]

Type of assistance	1995	2000	2005	2010	2015	2016	2017
FUNDS UTILIZED (mil. dol.)							
Federal Pell Grants............................	5,472	7,956	12,693	35,677	28,559	26,894	28,672
TEACH Grants [1].............................	(X)	(X)	(X)	121	(NA)	(NA)	(NA)
Federal Supplemental Educational Opportunity Grant......	764	908	1,084	1,013	993	987	1,008
Federal Work-Study............................	764	939	1,050	1,198	1,096	1,086	1,009
Federal Perkins Loan..........................	1,029	1,144	1,594	857	1,045	886	631
Federal Direct Student Loan (FDSL).........................	8,296	10,348	12,930	84,704	(NA)	(NA)	(NA)
NUMBER OF AWARDS (1,000)							
Federal Pell Grants............................	3,612	3,899	5,168	9,308	7,660	7,195	7,112
TEACH Grants [1].............................	(X)	(X)	(X)	39	(NA)	(NA)	(NA)
Federal Supplemental Educational Opportunity Grant......	1,083	1,174	1,419	1,633	1,530	1,484	1,499
Federal Work-Study............................	702	713	711	718	635	617	613
Federal Perkins Loan..........................	688	639	728	461	422	356	256
Federal Direct Student Loan (FDSL).........................	2,339	2,739	2,971	16,647	(NA)	(NA)	(NA)
AVERAGE AWARD (dol.)							
Federal Pell Grants............................	1,515	2,040	2,456	3,833	3,728	3,738	4,031
TEACH Grants [1].............................	(X)	(X)	(X)	3	(NA)	(NA)	(NA)
Federal Supplemental Educational Opportunity Grant......	706	773	764	620	649	665	672
Federal Work-Study............................	1,087	1,318	1,478	1,668	1,726	1,759	1,647
Federal Perkins Loan..........................	1,496	1,790	2,190	1,860	2,479	2,491	2,461
Federal Direct Student Loan (FDSL).........................	3,547	3,778	4,352	5,088	(NA)	(NA)	(NA)

X Not applicable. NA Not available. [1] Teacher Education Assistance for College and Higher Education (TEACH) Grant Program.

Source: U.S. Department of Education, Office of Postsecondary Education, "OPE Program Data," <www2.ed.gov/finaid/prof/resources/data/ope.html>, accessed July 2020.

Table 311. Average Cost of Attendance for Undergraduate Education by Control of Institution, Living Arrangement, and Type of Cost: 2011 and 2021

[In current dollars. For school year ending in year shown. Data shown are for first time, full-time undergraduate students in degree-granting postsecondary institutions. Based on data from the Integrated Postsecondary Education Data System (IPEDS). See source for more information]

Level of institution, living arrangement, and type of cost	2011				2021			
	All institutions	Public, in-State [1]	Private		All institutions	Public, in-State [1]	Private	
			Non-profit	For-profit			Non-profit	For-profit
4-YEAR INSTITUTIONS								
By living arrangement:								
On campus....................	27,589	20,035	39,676	31,897	35,551	25,707	54,501	33,528
Off campus, living with family.........	20,084	12,554	31,689	22,268	24,587	14,949	43,165	23,944
Off campus, not living with family.....	29,142	21,324	40,033	31,000	35,392	25,972	54,593	32,488
By type of cost:								
Tuition and required fees..............	14,596	7,163	26,637	15,191	19,020	9,377	37,641	18,244
Books and supplies....................	1,223	1,196	1,221	1,522	1,226	1,230	1,228	1,065
Room, board, and other expenses								
On campus								
Room and board.....................	8,912	8,497	9,455	9,304	12,057	11,557	12,857	9,092
Other...............................	2,858	3,179	2,363	5,879	3,248	3,543	2,774	5,126
Off campus, living with family								
Other...............................	4,265	4,195	3,832	5,554	4,341	4,342	4,295	4,635
Off campus, not living with family								
Room and board.....................	8,802	8,942	8,202	8,866	10,521	10,914	10,429	8,556
Other...............................	4,521	4,022	3,974	5,421	4,625	4,451	5,294	4,622
2-YEAR INSTITUTIONS								
By living arrangement:								
On campus....................	13,777	12,336	25,763	29,179	16,488	15,862	33,270	27,246
Off campus, living with family.........	8,964	7,843	18,931	19,350	10,089	9,666	23,741	21,396
Off campus, not living with family.....	16,389	15,153	27,458	27,366	19,969	19,577	33,056	30,697
By type of cost:								
Tuition and required fees..............	3,850	2,748	13,832	13,954	4,289	3,862	17,968	15,765
Books and supplies....................	1,302	1,295	1,153	1,407	1,465	1,471	958	1,441
Room, board, and other expenses								
On campus								
Room and board.....................	5,654	5,351	7,806	9,961	7,369	7,111	11,804	8,910
Other...............................	2,971	2,941	2,973	3,857	3,365	3,419	2,541	1,130
Off campus, living with family								
Other...............................	3,812	3,799	3,947	3,989	4,335	4,333	4,816	4,190
Off campus, not living with family								
Room and board.....................	7,478	7,412	7,999	7,889	9,844	9,902	9,558	8,468
Other...............................	3,759	3,698	4,475	4,117	4,370	4,342	4,572	5,023

[1] Tuition and fees at public institutions are the lower of either in-district or in-state tuition and fees.

Source: U.S. National Center for Education Statistics, *Digest of Education Statistics*, "Latest version of all Digest tables," <nces.ed.gov/programs/digest/>, accessed May 2022.

Table 312. Bachelor's Degree Recipients with Loans and Amount Borrowed in Constant (2009) Dollars by Selected Characteristics: 2001 to 2017

[For first-time Bachelor's degree recipients 1 year after they complete their degrees. Estimates cover students who were enrolled in Title IV eligible postsecondary institutions in the 50 states, D.C., and Puerto Rico. Based on Baccalaureate and Beyond Longitudinal Studies]

Characteristic	Percent with loans			Average cumulative amount borrowed for undergraduate education (2009 dollars)		
	2001 [2]	2009	2017	2001 [2]	2009	2017
Total loans.............................	**63.5**	**65.6**	**67.4**	**21,800**	**24,700**	**30,500**
Sex:						
Male..	62.5	62.9	63.7	21,300	23,900	29,800
Female.....................................	64.3	67.6	70.3	22,100	25,200	31,000
Race/ethnicity: [1]						
White.......................................	62.2	64.6	66.8	21,700	24,500	30,500
Black.......................................	78.8	80.3	85.9	25,200	28,700	36,900
Hispanic...................................	66.7	67.0	69.7	19,900	22,800	26,900
Asian......................................	55.5	53.4	45.4	19,100	21,000	24,600
Other......................................	62.8	68.8	70.4	21,500	25,600	30,300
Age at receipt of bachelor's degree:						
18 to 23....................................	60.0	61.0	62.4	20,800	23,700	27,400
24 to 29....................................	71.3	76.8	73.4	23,100	24,900	33,100
30 and older...............................	65.7	72.5	82.0	23,000	28,300	37,700
Institution type:						
2-year or less:						
Public 2-year...........................	67.8	67.5	71.1	21,500	24,500	30,600
Other 2-year or less....................	64.6	85.0	85.6	24,500	31,600	38,300
4-year:						
Public..................................	59.5	62.1	64.1	20,100	21,900	28,600
Private nonprofit.......................	69.0	69.4	66.4	24,100	27,900	31,200
For-profit..............................	77.3	87.7	84.1	27,400	36,000	42,700

[1] Asian includes Pacific Islander and Native Hawaiian and other includes American Indian, Alaska Native, and graduates of two or more races or a race not listed. Excludes persons of Hispanic origin, unless specified. [2] Includes loans from family and friends.

Source: National Center for Education Statistics, *Trends in Debt for Bachelor's Degree Recipients a Year After Graduation: 1994, 2001, and 2009*, December 2012; and *Baccalaureate and Beyond (B&B:16/17): A First Look at the Employment and Educational Experiences of College Graduates, 1 Year Later*, June 2019. See also <nces.ed.gov/surveys/b&b>.

Table 313. Voluntary Financial Support of Higher Education: 1990 to 2021

[9,800 represents $9,800,000,000. For school years ending in years shown. Voluntary support, as defined in Gift Reporting Standards, excludes income from endowment and other invested funds as well as all support received from federal, state, and local governments and their agencies, and contract research]

Item	Unit	1990	2000	2010	2015	2018	2019	2020	2021
Estimated support, total...................	**Mil. dol.**	**9,800**	**23,200**	**28,000**	**40,300**	**46,730**	**49,600**	**49,500**	**52,900**
SOURCES OF SUPPORT									
Individuals, total.............................	Mil. dol.	4,770	12,220	12,020	18,850	20,721	19,500	19,690	21,050
Alumni......................................	Mil. dol.	2,540	6,800	7,100	10,850	12,154	11,200	11,060	12,250
Nonalumni individuals......................	Mil. dol.	2,230	5,420	4,920	8,000	8,567	8,300	8,630	8,800
Organizations, total.........................	Mil. dol.	5,030	10,980	15,675	21,450	26,008	30,100	29,810	31,850
Corporations...............................	Mil. dol.	2,170	4,150	4,730	5,750	6,732	6,800	6,630	7,000
Foundations...............................	Mil. dol.	1,920	5,080	8,400	11,600	14,010	17,000	16,440	17,500
Other organizations........................	Mil. dol.	940	1,750	2,545	4,100	5,266	6,300	6,740	7,350
PURPOSES OF SUPPORT									
Current operations, total....................	Mil. dol.	5,440	11,270	17,000	24,650	27,400	28,500	30,500	32,300
Capital purposes............................	Mil. dol.	4,360	11,930	11,000	15,650	19,330	21,100	19,000	20,600
Institutions reporting support..............	Number	1,056	945	996	983	929	913	873	864
Total support reported.....................	Mil. dol.	8,214	19,419	23,487	35,082	37,221	39,490	38,263	41,481
Private 4-year institutions.................	Mil. dol.	5,072	11,047	12,189	17,944	17,726	21,433	19,709	20,854
Public 4-year institutions..................	Mil. dol.	3,056	8,254	11,114	14,876	19,251	17,834	18,365	20,314
2-year colleges............................	Mil. dol.	85	117	185	192	244	222	189	314

Source: Council for Advancement and Support of Education, Washington, DC, *Voluntary Support of Education* ©, annual. See also <www.case.org>.

Table 314. Undergraduate Students Who Received a Pell Grant by Selected Characteristics: 2004 to 2016

[In units as indicated. For school year ending in year shown. Data shown for students enrolled in Title IV eligible postsecondary institutions in the 50 States, the District of Columbia, and Puerto Rico. Based on the National Postsecondary Student-Aid Study; see source for details]

Institutional and student characteristics	2004		2008		2012 [1]		2016	
	Percent	Average amount (dollars)	Percent	Average amount (dollars)	Percent	Average amount (dollars)	Percent	Average amount (dollars)
Total.........................	**27.2**	**2,400**	**27.8**	**2,500**	**41.3**	**3,400**	**39.1**	**3,700**
AGE								
23 or younger....................	25.5	2,600	25.6	2,700	37.8	3,600	(NA)	(NA)
18 or younger...................	(NA)	(NA)	(NA)	(NA)	(NA)	(NA)	39.7	4,100
19 to 23.........................	(NA)	(NA)	(NA)	(NA)	(NA)	(NA)	36.2	4,000
24 to 29.........................	36.6	2,400	36.1	2,400	48.9	3,200	47.3	3,500
30 or older......................	24.8	2,300	26.9	2,300	43.5	3,200	(NA)	(NA)
30 to 39.........................	(NA)	(NA)	(NA)	(NA)	(NA)	(NA)	42.7	3,400
40 or older......................	(NA)	(NA)	(NA)	(NA)	(NA)	(NA)	33.2	3,300
SEX								
Male.............................	22.3	2,500	21.9	2,600	36.5	3,400	34.0	3,700
Female...........................	30.8	2,400	32.2	2,500	44.8	3,400	43.1	3,700
RACE/ETHNICITY								
White............................	20.7	2,300	20.9	2,400	33.5	3,300	31.5	3,600
Black............................	47.9	2,500	46.0	2,600	61.9	3,400	57.7	3,700
Hispanic.........................	37.5	2,600	39.8	2,700	50.0	3,500	46.9	3,900
Asian/Pacific Islander............	21.9	2,800	23.3	2,800	33.8	3,800	(NA)	(NA)
Asian...........................	(NA)	(NA)	(NA)	(NA)	(NA)	(NA)	30.9	4,200
Pacific Islander..................	(NA)	(NA)	(NA)	(NA)	(NA)	(NA)	35.6	4,100
American Indian..................	31.9	2,400	36.0	2,500	54.0	3,400	51.1	3,500
Other or two or more races........	29.8	2,500	31.1	2,600	45.2	3,500	42.2	3,800
ATTENDANCE STATUS								
Full-time, full-year..............	32.2	3,100	33.6	3,300	47.1	4,400	44.7	4,700
Part-time, full-year..............	(NA)	(NA)	(NA)	(NA)	(NA)	(NA)	44.0	3,500
Part-time or part-year............	23.8	1,900	24.4	1,900	37.6	2,600	(NA)	(NA)
TYPE OF INSTITUTION								
Public 4-year.....................	26.4	2,600	26.2	2,800	38.0	3,800	38.2	4,100
Private nonprofit 4-year...........	27.9	2,600	26.8	2,900	35.8	3,700	36.4	4,000
Public 2-year.....................	22.3	2,200	21.1	2,300	37.7	3,000	33.5	3,300
EMPLOYMENT STATUS [2]								
Not employed.....................	28.8	2,600	31.0	2,700	44.7	3,500	41.7	3,900
Employed part-time...............	28.1	2,500	29.2	2,600	41.4	3,500	38.3	3,800
Employed full-time...............	24.5	2,300	23.4	2,200	36.2	3,000	36.4	3,300

NA Not available. [1] 2012 excludes Puerto Rico. [2] Work-study, assistantships, and traineeships. Full-time work is defined as 35 or more hours per week, and part-time less than 35 hours.

Source: U.S. Department of Education, National Center for Education Statistics, *Trends in Pell Grant Receipt and the Characteristics of Pell Grant Recipients: Selected Years, 1999–2000 to 2011–12*, September 2015; and *Student Financing of Undergraduate Education in 2015-16: Financial Aid by Types and Source*, March 2019. See also <nces.ed.gov/surveys/npsas>.

Table 315. Undergraduate Student Receipt of Financial Aid by Source and Type of Institution Attended: 2016

[In percent. For school year ending in 2016. Covers students enrolled in Title IV eligible postsecondary institutions in the 50 states, DC, and Puerto Rico. Based on the National Postsecondary Student-Aid Study; see source for details]

Type of institution	Total [1]	Source of aid				
		Federal [2]	Non-federal [3]	State [4]	Institu-tional [5]	Employer [6]
Total	**72.3**	**54.5**	**48.8**	**22.4**	**24.6**	**6.3**
Institution attended:						
Public 2-year	57.5	38.9	35.1	23.0	6.6	5.3
Public 4-year	77.1	58.9	57.1	27.6	30.4	6.3
Private nonprofit 4-year	86.3	63.3	71.0	18.1	57.2	9.9
Private for-profit 2-year or more	87.0	76.3	43.8	10.6	28.5	6.7
Private for-profit less-than-2-year	82.9	77.4	24.8	6.7	9.3	1.8

[1] Excludes aid from parents, friends, or relatives, and federal tax credits for education. Includes Direct PLUS Loans to parents and aid from Veterans' benefits and job training grants. [2] Includes federal grants, loans, work-study awards, and federal loans including Direct PLUS loans. Includes aid from programs in Title IV of the Higher Education Act, and aid from other federal sources such as Public Health Service Loans, Bureau of Indian Affairs Grants, and District of Columbia Tuition Assistance Grants. Excludes federal veterans' benefits and education tax credits and tax deduction benefits. [3] Includes grants from states, institutions, and private organizations, and loans from private sources. [4] Includes all grants and scholarships, loans, and work-study provided by state governments, including vocational rehabilitation and job training grants funded by the federal Workforce Investment Opportunity Act (WIA). [5] Includes all institution need- and merit-based grants, scholarships, tuition waivers, loans, and work-study assistance. [6] Excludes tuition waivers to students holding assistantships.

Source: U.S. Department of Education, National Center for Education Statistics, *Trends in Undergraduate Nonfederal Grant and Scholarship Aid by Demographic and Enrollment Characteristics, Selected Years: 2003–04 to 2015–16,* August 2019. See also <nces.ed.gov/surveys/npsas>.

Table 316. Financial Aid for Graduate Students by Degree Type and Source of Aid: 2016

[For school year ending in 2016. Based on the National Postsecondary Student-Aid Study; see source for details. Excludes Puerto Rico]

Degree type	Percent receiving aid by source				Average aid received (dollars)	Tuition and fees (dollars)	Price of atten-dance [4] (dollars)	Out-of-pocket net price [5] (dollars)
	Total [1]	Federal [2]	Institu-tional [3]	Em-ployer				
Total	**72.5**	**42.6**	**30.5**	**12.8**	**22,200**	**15,100**	**29,400**	**13,400**
Master's degree program:								
Business administration (M.B.A.)	71.0	35.0	24.0	21.9	18,700	14,700	27,600	14,600
Education (any master's)	66.9	44.4	20.9	13.3	14,100	8,400	19,300	9,900
M.A. (except in education)	71.1	43.4	29.1	9.9	16,900	11,200	24,100	12,300
M.S. (except in education)	68.7	35.4	28.5	13.4	17,100	12,200	25,300	13,800
Other master's [6]	74.4	47.2	27.4	14.4	19,500	14,000	27,900	13,600
Control of institution:								
Public	66.2	34.3	26.5	14.0	16,000	9,600	22,000	11,500
Private nonprofit	72.9	43.3	25.5	15.4	19,300	15,400	29,200	15,300
For-profit	74.7	52.9	24.5	14.6	14,900	9,400	19,500	8,700
Doctor's degree program - research/scholarship:								
Ph.D. (except in education)	84.8	23.4	66.5	6.9	28,000	19,000	36,900	13,200
Education (any doctorate)	73.6	44.0	33.4	16.3	16,200	9,500	22,300	10,800
Other doctorate	77.1	42.1	34.4	11.7	20,700	15,000	29,300	13,200
Control of institution:								
Public	80.4	18.0	64.3	8.4	21,500	12,800	28,900	11,800
Private nonprofit	82.8	27.2	59.3	9.9	33,700	25,000	44,800	16,900
For-profit	79.9	70.1	17.6	11.5	16,500	10,800	20,500	7,300
Doctor's degree program - professional practice:								
Medicine (M.D. or D.O.)	83.7	73.8	40.9	(S)	53,100	37,400	65,700	21,300
Other health science [7]	86.0	75.7	34.5	(S)	50,600	36,100	59,700	15,900
Law (LL.B. or J.D.)	89.7	71.1	57.8	[8] 1.6	45,700	35,700	58,300	18,400
Control of institution:								
Public	83.0	70.3	47.0	2.7	41,000	28,800	51,300	17,400
Private nonprofit	85.6	69.1	43.8	[8] 4.1	53,100	40,400	65,600	20,200
For-profit	91.8	82.3	37.5	[8] 9.9	43,300	30,300	49,700	10,300

S Figure does not meet publication standards. [1] Financial aid includes all types of financial aid from any source except parents, friends, or relatives. Types of aid such as employer aid, veterans benefits, and job-training grants are included, but federal tax credits for education are not included. [2] Consists of federal loans, federal grants, and federal work-study. Does not include military benefits. [3] Includes all institution need- and merit-based grants, scholarships, tuition waivers, graduate assistantships, loans, and work-study assistance funded by the institution attended. [4] Price of attendance is the total budget (attendance intensity-adjusted) at the institution for students who attended only one institution during the academic year. The budget includes tuition, fees, housing, meals, books, supplies, transportation, and personal expenses. Institutions typically use this value as a student's budget for the purpose of awarding federal financial aid. [5] Out-of-pocket net price is the total price of attendance minus all financial aid received, including Direct PLUS Loans. The total price of attendance includes tuition and fees, room and board, books and supplies, transportation, and personal or miscellaneous expenses. Federal education tax benefits are not included in the calculation. Averages include students who received no aid. [6] Includes M.S.W. (Master of Social Work), M.P.A. (Master of Public Administration), and M.F.A. (Master of Fine Arts). [7] Includes chiropractic (D.C. or D.C.M.), dentistry (D.D.S. or D.M.D.), optometry (O.D.), pharmacy (D.Pharm.), podiatry (Pod.D. or D.P.M.), and veterinary medicine (D.V.M.). [8] Underlying data has a standard error between 30-50%.

Source: U.S. Department of Education, National Center for Education Statistics, *Profile and Financial Aid Estimates of Graduate Students: 2015–16,* January 2019. See also <nces.ed.gov/surveys/npsas>.

Table 317. State and Local Financial Support for Higher Education by State: 2021

[10,600.4 represents 10,600,400. For fiscal year ending in 2021. Educational appropriations include State and local appropriations for general operating expenses of public postsecondary education. Includes state-funded financial aid to students attending in-state public institutions and federal stimulus funds. Excludes appropriations for independent institutions, financial aid for students attending independent institutions, research, hospitals, and medical education]

State	FTE enroll- ment [2] (1,000)	Educational appropri- ations per FTE enrollment [3] (dollars)	Net tuition revenue [4] (million dollars)	State	FTE enroll- ment [2] (1,000)	Educational appropri- ations per FTE enrollment [3] (dollars)	Net tuition revenue [4] (million dollars)
Total U.S. [1]...	10,600.4	9,327	71,264	MO.............	156.5	9,504	993
AL..............	194.9	7,733	2,472	MT.............	33.5	7,646	248
AK..............	13.7	17,497	85	NE.............	72.6	11,113	500
AZ..............	292.2	6,194	2,635	NV.............	75.9	6,490	224
AR..............	105.0	8,886	650	NH.............	32.3	4,370	377
CA..............	1,608.7	9,859	4,956	NJ.............	252.1	7,753	2,124
CO..............	179.7	5,462	2,053	NM.............	65.9	15,134	228
CT..............	74.5	11,287	931	NY.............	494.1	12,428	2,953
DE..............	36.4	6,984	701	NC.............	392.4	11,090	1,772
DC..............	2.7	34,466	20	ND.............	31.9	9,133	335
FL..............	595.4	8,323	1,370	OH.............	374.2	7,567	3,207
GA..............	356.9	9,844	1,624	OK.............	124.0	5,838	923
HI..............	34.2	13,881	221	OR.............	129.8	7,395	1,292
ID..............	53.7	10,612	412	PA.............	309.8	6,097	3,402
IL..............	305.5	18,752	2,257	RI.............	31.4	6,137	330
IN..............	237.6	6,408	2,335	SC.............	164.3	7,624	1,700
IA..............	119.0	6,115	1,175	SD.............	32.0	7,665	254
KS..............	123.2	8,680	848	TN.............	178.6	11,412	1,076
KY..............	137.6	7,931	1,144	TX.............	1,044.7	9,039	5,347
LA..............	163.7	6,209	839	UT.............	129.3	8,717	777
ME..............	32.9	8,724	247	VT.............	19.5	7,370	340
MD..............	213.3	9,050	1,974	VA.............	298.9	7,215	2,676
MA..............	145.9	9,611	1,017	WA.............	214.9	10,296	1,255
MI..............	343.6	8,197	4,591	WV.............	62.0	6,309	453
MN..............	171.3	11,759	1,641	WI.............	198.4	9,107	1,397
MS..............	121.6	8,161	841	WY.............	20.9	26,393	63

[1] The U.S. total does not include data from the District of Columbia. [2] Full-time equivalent enrollment converts student credit hours to full-time, academic year students, but excludes medical students. [3] State and local appropriations for general operating expenses of public postsecondary education. Includes state-funded financial aid to students attending in-state public institutions and federal stimulus funding. Excludes appropriations for independent institutions, financial aid for students attending independent institutions, research, hospitals, and medical education. [4] Net tuition revenue is the gross amount of tuition and fees, less financial aid, tuition waivers or discounts, and medical student tuition and fees. Includes revenue used for capital debt service. Illinois, New Jersey, and Pennsylvania are estimated.

Source: State Higher Education Executive Officers, Boulder, CO, *State Higher Education Finance: FY2021* ©, 2022. See also <shef.sheeo.org/>.

Table 318. Higher Education Price Indexes: 2010 to 2021 ©

[1983=100. For years ending June 30. The Higher Education Price Index (HEPI), calculated for the July-June academic fiscal year, reflects prices paid by colleges and universities for the following eight cost factors: faculty salaries, administrative salaries, clerical and service employees, fringe benefits, miscellaneous services, supplies and materials, and utilities. Minus sign (-) indicates decrease]

Item and year	Total	Personnel compensation					Contracted services, supplies, and equipment		
		Faculty salaries [1]	Admin- istrative salaries	Clerical salaries	Service employ- ees salaries	Fringe benefits [1]	Miscel- laneous services	Supplies and materials	Utilities
INDEXES									
2010......................	281.8	280.6	337.6	255.2	230.0	402.8	255.8	179.3	193.6
2011......................	288.4	284.5	343.2	260.2	233.2	417.6	260.3	193.9	201.5
2012......................	293.2	289.6	352.3	264.8	235.7	425.3	264.6	203.9	191.7
2013......................	297.8	294.6	362.4	269.8	239.4	437.5	269.4	180.0	195.6
2014......................	306.7	301.0	366.4	274.8	242.0	458.3	274.2	200.2	211.4
2015......................	312.9	306.4	381.9	280.4	248.4	484.0	279.8	190.7	183.5
2016......................	317.7	318.2	393.3	289.1	253.3	487.9	285.7	179.5	146.5
2017......................	327.4	326.0	405.2	297.3	262.7	501.6	290.7	180.1	167.8
2018......................	336.1	333.6	414.1	305.9	271.6	516.3	297.8	187.9	170.7
2019......................	346.0	342.2	424.1	316.6	282.5	534.1	304.8	195.6	172.3
2020......................	352.7	351.4	430.3	326.6	293.9	549.6	313.2	188.8	145.3
2021......................	362.3	354.7	437.2	335.7	306.6	572.2	319.3	195.4	167.0
ANNUAL PERCENT CHANGE [2]									
2010......................	0.9	1.2	2.0	1.4	1.4	2.1	1.1	-1.3	-9.5
2011......................	2.3	1.4	1.7	2.0	1.4	3.7	1.8	8.2	4.1
2012......................	1.7	1.8	2.7	1.7	1.1	1.8	1.7	5.2	-4.9
2013......................	1.6	1.7	2.9	1.9	1.6	2.9	1.8	-11.7	2.1
2014......................	3.0	2.2	1.1	1.9	1.1	4.8	1.8	11.2	8.1
2015......................	2.0	1.8	4.2	2.1	2.6	5.6	2.1	-4.8	-13.2
2016......................	1.5	3.8	3.0	3.1	2.0	0.8	2.1	-5.8	-20.2
2017......................	3.0	2.5	3.0	2.8	3.7	2.8	1.7	0.3	14.5
2018......................	2.6	2.3	2.2	2.9	3.4	2.9	2.4	4.3	1.7
2019......................	3.0	2.6	2.4	3.5	4.0	3.5	2.4	4.1	0.9
2020......................	1.9	2.7	1.5	3.2	4.0	2.9	2.8	-3.5	-15.7
2021......................	2.7	1.0	1.6	2.8	4.3	4.1	2.0	3.5	15.0

[1] In 2015, the American Association of University Professors (AAUP) began using a new methodology to calculate salary and total compensation that is not directly comparable with the past. Adjustments were made to FY2020 data and data for fiscal years 2015-2020 have been restated to account for the change and make the data compatible with past reporting.

Source: The Commonfund Institute, Wilton, CT ©. See also <www.commonfund.org>.

Table 319. Average Salaries for College Faculty Members: 2020 to 2022

[In dollars. For academic year ending in year shown. Figures are for 9 months teaching for full-time faculty members in 2-year and 4-year institutions. Data are based the American Association of University Professors (AAUP) Faculty Compensation Survey; the number of institutions reporting salary data varies from year to year.]

Type of control and academic rank	2020	2021	2022	Type of control and academic rank	2020	2021	2022
Public: All ranks	**96,063**	**97,141**	**98,745**	**Private [1]: All ranks**	**124,396**	**124,683**	**127,366**
Professor	131,890	132,199	134,580	Professor	176,885	175,943	181,490
Associate professor	93,579	93,991	95,764	Associate professor	108,032	108,195	110,651
Assistant professor	81,252	82,136	83,562	Assistant professor	93,886	93,999	96,657
Instructor	56,864	57,812	58,064	Instructor	75,893	77,417	74,566

[1] Excludes religiously-affiliated colleges and universities.

Source: American Association of University Professors, Washington, DC, *AAUP Annual Report on the Economic Status of the Profession* © 2022. See also <www.aaup.org>.

Table 320. Employees in Higher Education Institutions by Employment Status, Sex, and Occupation: 2020

[In thousands (3,811.1 represents 3,811,100). As of Fall. Covers institutions that grant associate's or higher degrees and that participate in Title IV federal financial aid programs. Includes institutions with fewer than 15 full-time employees. Detail may not sum to totals because of rounding. Based on Integrated Postsecondary Education Data System data]

Primary occupation	Full-time and part-time		Female		Full-time		Part-time	
	Total	Male	Total	Percent	Male	Female	Male	Female
All institutions	**3,811.1**	**1,695.0**	**2,116.1**	**55.5**	**1,120.8**	**1,423.6**	**574.2**	**692.5**
Faculty	1,489.4	734.6	754.8	50.7	438.8	397.8	295.8	357.0
Instruction	1,363.3	666.2	697.0	51.1	379.2	349.2	287.0	347.8
Research	95.0	53.4	41.6	43.8	47.7	36.1	5.7	5.5
Public service	31.1	15.0	16.2	52.0	11.9	12.5	3.0	3.7
Graduate assistants [1]	377.5	189.0	188.5	49.9	(X)	(X)	189.0	188.5
Librarians, curators, and archivists	38.5	11.4	27.1	70.3	10.2	23.3	1.3	3.8
Student and academic affairs, and other education services	174.3	54.2	120.1	68.9	35.3	88.4	18.8	31.7
Management	263.8	112.0	151.8	57.5	109.5	147.9	2.5	3.8
Business and financial operations	228.2	61.8	166.5	72.9	58.5	157.8	3.2	8.7
Computer, engineering, and science	239.4	142.4	97.0	40.5	134.9	87.4	7.4	9.6
Community, social service, legal, arts, design, entertainment, sports, and media	187.2	81.4	105.8	56.5	67.1	90.2	14.3	15.6
Healthcare practitioners and technicians	115.7	33.7	82.0	70.9	29.4	69.6	4.2	12.4
Service occupations	224.9	128.5	96.4	42.9	112.0	82.3	16.5	14.1
Sales and related occupations	10.6	3.6	6.9	65.7	3.1	5.8	0.5	1.1
Office and administrative support	375.1	64.6	310.5	82.8	48.6	266.2	16.0	44.2
Natural resources, construction, and maintenance	69.3	63.8	5.5	8.0	61.3	4.6	2.5	1.0
Production, transportation, and material moving	17.3	14.2	3.1	18.0	12.1	2.4	2.0	0.7

X Not applicable. [1] By definition, all graduate assistants are part time.

Source: U.S. National Center for Education Statistics, *Digest of Education Statistics*, "Latest version of all Digest tables," <nces.ed.gov/programs/digest>, accessed June 2022.

Table 321. Faculty in Institutions of Higher Education: 1980 to 2020

[In thousands (686 represents 686,000), except percent. As of Fall. Beginning in 1997, data reflect a new classification of institutions; this classification includes some additional, primarily 2-year, colleges and excludes a few institutions that did not award degrees. Includes institutions that were eligible to participate in Title IV federal financial aid programs. Includes schools accredited by the National Association of Trade and Technical Schools. Based on complete census taken every other year; see source]

Year	Total	Employment status		Control		Level		Percent		
		Full-time	Part-time	Public	Private	4-year	2-year or less	Part-time	Public	2-year or less
1980 [1]	686	450	236	495	191	494	192	34	72	28
1985 [1]	715	459	256	503	212	504	211	36	70	30
1991 [2]	826	536	291	581	245	591	235	35	70	28
1995	932	551	381	657	275	647	285	41	70	31
1999	1,038	593	444	719	319	719	318	43	69	31
2001	1,113	618	495	771	342	764	349	44	69	31
2003	1,174	630	544	792	382	814	359	46	67	31
2005	1,290	676	615	841	449	917	373	48	65	29
2007 [3]	1,372	704	668	877	495	992	379	49	64	28
2009	1,439	729	710	914	525	1,038	401	49	63	28
2011	1,524	762	762	954	570	1,116	409	50	63	27
2013	1,545	791	754	969	577	1,152	394	49	63	25
2015	1,552	807	745	971	581	1,181	372	48	63	24
2016	1,546	814	732	974	572	1,197	349	47	63	23
2017	1,546	823	723	973	573	1,209	337	47	63	22
2018	1,543	832	711	982	561	1,216	327	46	64	21
2019	1,549	844	705	984	565	1,234	315	46	64	20
2020	1,489	837	653	941	548	1,208	281	44	63	19

[1] Estimated on the basis of enrollment. [2] Beginning 1987, data are not comparable to prior years. [3] Beginning in 2007, data include institutions with fewer than 15 full-time employees; these institutions did not report staff data prior to 2007.

Source: U.S. National Center for Education Statistics, *Digest of Education Statistics,* "Latest version of all Digest tables," <nces.ed.gov/programs/digest>, accessed March 2022.

Table 322. Starting Salaries for New College Graduates by Degree and Field of Study: 2015 to 2021

[In dollars. Data are actual starting base salaries. Data reported by representative colleges throughout the United States]

Field of study	Bachelor's			Master's [1]			Doctorate		
	2015	2020	2021	2015	2020	2021	2015	2020	2021
Accounting	51,426	54,809	56,103	54,721	56,791	58,703	(NA)	(NA)	(NA)
Business administration/ management [2]	49,494	54,392	56,391	73,951	82,372	84,696	123,162	118,429	[3] 133,344
Marketing	43,678	48,610	49,481	66,537	59,238	58,611	(NA)	(NA)	(NA)
Engineering:									
Civil	57,368	62,249	61,314	58,290	68,415	70,696	[3] 60,464	72,632	[3] 78,130
Chemical	65,782	72,713	70,099	64,140	74,399	[3] 70,673	75,743	95,334	[3] 85,694
Computer	68,820	85,996	88,158	87,546	109,343	113,711	[3] 105,400	134,111	[3] 133,355
Electrical	67,593	80,819	78,148	86,218	99,769	97,808	95,373	115,013	109,728
Mechanical	[3] 62,239	69,278	67,744	66,786	82,459	83,370	79,664	97,206	[3] 82,400
Nuclear [4]	54,351	[3] 68,742	[3] 70,330	[3] 56,643	[3] 82,867	(NA)	[3] 73,480	[3] 100,824	[3] 98,525
Petroleum	74,996	87,989	[3] 75,917	(NA)	[3] 84,600	[3] 100,883	(NA)	[3] 110,000	(NA)
Chemistry	41,832	44,981	[3] 45,430	[3] 51,908	60,485	[3] 60,036	63,091	70,518	78,726
Mathematics	56,440	64,244	66,657	72,976	70,513	[3] 58,588	[3] 79,250	76,050	[3] 62,811
Physics	56,403	63,600	69,420	[3] 65,875	58,715	[3] 107,915	66,601	72,758	[3] 68,502
Humanities	52,990	52,010	45,845	[3] 47,583	66,858	64,286	68,216	[3] 62,579	(NA)
Social sciences [5]	40,964	50,298	52,077	50,705	62,185	64,985	65,101	85,458	72,701
Computer science	75,191	85,766	86,281	90,934	107,193	111,165	100,726	129,821	123,701

NA Not available. [1] Candidates with 1 year or less of full-time nonmilitary employment. [2] For master's degree, starting salaries are after nontechnical undergraduate degree. [3] Fewer than 50 salaries reported. [4] Includes engineering physics. [5] Excludes economics.

Source: National Association of Colleges and Employers, Bethlehem, PA ©. Reprinted with permission from Fall 2010-2014, Spring 2015-2019, and Summer 2020-2022 Salary Surveys. All rights reserved.

Table 323. Degrees Earned by Level and Sex: 1960 to 2020

[In thousands (477 represents 477,000), except percent. Based on data from the Integrated Postsecondary Education Data System (IPEDS)]

Year ending	All degrees		Associate's		Bachelor's		Master's		Doctoral [1]	
	Total	Percent male	Male	Female	Male	Female	Male	Female	Male	Female
1960	477	65.8	(NA)	(NA)	[2] 254	[2] 138	51	24	9	1
1970	1,271	59.2	117	89	451	341	131	83	54	6
1975	1,666	56.0	191	169	505	418	166	131	71	14
1980	1,731	51.1	184	217	474	456	157	148	70	26
1985	1,828	49.3	203	252	483	497	149	144	66	35
1986	1,830	49.0	196	250	486	502	149	146	65	35
1987	1,823	48.4	191	245	481	510	147	149	63	36
1988	1,835	48.0	190	245	477	518	150	156	63	36
1989	1,873	47.3	186	250	483	535	154	163	63	38
1990	1,940	46.6	191	264	492	560	158	172	64	40
1991	2,025	45.8	199	283	504	590	161	182	64	41
1992	2,108	45.6	207	297	521	616	166	192	67	43
1993	2,167	45.5	212	303	533	632	173	202	67	45
1994	2,206	45.1	215	315	532	637	181	212	67	46
1995	2,218	44.9	218	321	526	634	183	221	67	47
1996	2,248	44.2	220	336	522	642	183	229	67	48
1997	2,288	43.6	224	347	521	652	185	240	68	50
1998	2,298	43.2	218	341	520	664	189	247	67	52
1999	2,330	42.7	221	344	520	682	190	256	65	51
2000	2,385	42.6	225	340	530	708	196	267	65	54
2001	2,416	42.4	232	347	532	712	198	276	64	55
2002	2,494	42.2	238	357	550	742	203	285	63	57
2003	2,623	42.1	253	381	573	776	215	304	63	59
2004	2,757	41.8	260	406	596	804	233	331	64	62
2005	2,852	41.6	268	429	613	827	237	343	67	67
2006	2,936	41.3	270	443	631	855	242	358	69	69
2007	3,008	41.2	275	453	650	875	242	368	71	73
2008	3,094	41.2	283	467	668	896	250	381	73	76
2009	3,205	41.3	298	489	685	916	264	399	76	79
2010	3,351	41.2	323	526	707	943	275	418	77	82
2011	3,554	41.3	361	582	734	982	292	439	80	84
2012	3,740	41.3	393	628	766	1,026	302	453	83	88
2013	3,775	41.4	389	618	787	1,053	302	450	85	90
2014	3,807	41.5	391	614	802	1,068	303	452	86	92
2015	3,847	41.6	397	618	813	1,082	307	452	85	94
2016	3,893	41.6	392	616	822	1,099	321	465	84	94
2017	3,948	41.6	394	612	836	1,120	327	478	85	97
2018	3,996	41.4	399	613	845	1,136	327	493	85	98
2019	4,071	41.2	407	629	858	1,155	326	508	86	102
2020	4,090	40.7	393	625	861	1,177	326	518	85	105

NA Not available. [1] Includes Ph.D., Ed.D., and comparable degrees at the doctoral level. Includes most degrees formerly classified as first-professional, such as M.D., D.D.S., and law degrees. [2] Includes some degrees classified as master's or doctor's degrees in later years.

Source: U.S. National Center for Education Statistics, *Digest of Education Statistics*, "Latest version of all Digest tables," <nces.ed.gov/programs/digest>, accessed June 2022.

Table 324. Degrees Earned by Level and Race/Ethnicity: 1990 to 2020

[For school year ending in year shown. Based on Integrated Postsecondary Education Data System surveys; see Appendix III]

Level of degree and race/ethnicity	Total					Percent distribution		
	1990	2000 [1]	2010	2019	2020	2000 [1]	2010	2020
Associate's degrees, total............	**455,102**	**564,933**	**848,856**	**1,036,640**	**1,018,233**	**100.0**	**100.0**	**100.0**
White, non-Hispanic....................	376,816	408,822	552,376	530,675	509,466	72.4	65.1	50.0
Black, non-Hispanic....................	34,326	60,208	113,867	125,205	119,826	10.7	13.4	11.8
Hispanic................................	21,504	51,563	112,403	246,881	254,561	9.1	13.2	25.0
Asian or Pacific Islander..............	13,066	27,778	44,026	63,940	64,582	4.9	5.2	6.3
American Indian/Alaska Native.......	3,430	6,474	10,101	9,064	8,451	1.1	1.2	0.8
Two or more races.....................	(NA)	(NA)	(NA)	36,422	37,768	(NA)	(NA)	3.7
Nonresident alien......................	5,960	10,088	16,083	24,453	23,579	1.8	1.9	2.3
Bachelor's degrees, total............	**1,051,344**	**1,237,875**	**1,649,919**	**2,013,086**	**2,038,431**	**100.0**	**100.0**	**100.0**
White, non-Hispanic....................	887,151	929,102	1,167,322	1,190,080	1,183,959	75.1	70.8	58.1
Black, non-Hispanic....................	61,046	108,018	164,789	196,654	197,444	8.7	10.0	9.7
Hispanic................................	32,829	75,063	140,426	285,024	302,615	6.1	8.5	14.8
Asian or Pacific Islander..............	39,230	77,909	117,391	156,099	161,444	6.3	7.1	7.9
American Indian/Alaska Native.......	4,390	8,717	12,405	9,167	9,151	0.7	0.8	0.4
Two or more races.....................	(NA)	(NA)	(NA)	73,665	77,619	(NA)	(NA)	3.8
Nonresident alien......................	26,698	39,066	47,586	102,397	106,199	3.2	2.9	5.2
Master's degrees, total [2]...........	**(NA)**	**463,185**	**693,313**	**833,792**	**843,449**	**100.0**	**100.0**	**100.0**
White, non-Hispanic....................	(NA)	324,990	445,158	447,433	448,419	70.2	64.2	53.2
Black, non-Hispanic....................	(NA)	36,606	76,472	93,123	92,750	7.9	11.0	11.0
Hispanic................................	(NA)	19,379	43,603	78,876	84,555	4.2	6.3	10.0
Asian or Pacific Islander..............	(NA)	23,523	42,520	52,200	54,668	5.1	6.1	6.5
American Indian/Alaska Native.......	(NA)	2,263	3,965	3,452	3,549	0.5	0.6	0.4
Two or more races.....................	(NA)	(NA)	(NA)	20,544	22,133	(NA)	(NA)	2.6
Nonresident alien......................	(NA)	56,424	81,595	138,164	137,375	12.2	11.8	16.3
Doctoral degrees, total [2, 3].....	**(NA)**	**118,736**	**158,590**	**187,577**	**190,178**	**100.0**	**100.0**	**100.0**
White, non-Hispanic....................	(NA)	82,984	104,419	107,570	107,853	69.9	65.8	56.7
Black, non-Hispanic....................	(NA)	7,078	10,413	15,119	15,725	6.0	6.6	8.3
Hispanic................................	(NA)	5,042	8,085	14,145	14,868	4.2	5.1	7.8
Asian or Pacific Islander..............	(NA)	10,682	16,560	21,035	21,611	9.0	10.4	11.4
American Indian/Alaska Native.......	(NA)	708	952	721	674	0.6	0.6	0.4
Two or more races.....................	(NA)	(NA)	(NA)	5,090	5,497	(NA)	(NA)	2.9
Nonresident alien......................	(NA)	12,242	18,161	23,897	23,950	10.3	11.5	12.6
First-professional degrees, total.....	**70,988**	**80,057**	**94,103**	**(NA)**	**(NA)**	**100.0**	**100.0**	**(NA)**

NA Not available. [1] Beginning 2000, data reflect the new classification of institutions. See headnote, Table 294. [2] Data prior to 2009 have been revised. Revisions for 1990 not available. [3] Includes Ph.D., Ed.D., and comparable degrees at the doctoral level, as well as M.D., D.D.S., and law degrees that were formerly classified as first-professional degrees prior to 2010-2011.

Source: U.S. National Center for Education Statistics, *Digest of Education Statistics*, "Latest version of all Digest tables," <nces.ed.gov/programs/digest>, accessed August 2022.

Table 325. Bachelor's Degrees Earned by Field: 1971 to 2020

[For school year ending in year shown. The new Classification of Instructional Programs was introduced in 2019-20. Data for previous years has been reclassified where necessary to conform to the new classifications. Based on Integrated Postsecondary Education Data System (IPEDS) surveys]

Field of study	1971	1981	1991	2001	2011	2019	2020
Total [1]...	**839,730**	**935,140**	**1,094,538**	**1,244,171**	**1,716,053**	**2,013,086**	**2,038,431**
Agriculture and natural resources...........................	12,674	21,886	13,363	23,766	29,203	41,373	41,848
Architecture and related services...........................	5,570	9,455	9,781	8,480	9,831	8,806	9,045
Area, ethnic, cultural, and gender studies....................	2,579	2,887	4,776	6,160	8,955	7,733	7,767
Biological and biomedical sciences...........................	35,705	43,078	39,482	60,576	89,984	121,233	126,590
Business...	115,396	200,521	249,165	263,515	365,133	390,490	387,851
Communication, journalism, and related programs...........	10,324	29,428	51,650	58,013	83,231	92,528	91,752
Communications technologies...............................	478	1,854	1,397	1,178	4,858	4,444	4,424
Computer and information sciences and support services...	2,388	15,121	25,159	44,142	43,066	88,638	97,047
Education...	176,307	108,074	110,807	105,458	104,008	83,952	85,057
Engineering...	45,034	63,642	62,448	58,209	76,356	126,692	128,332
Engineering technologies...................................	5,148	11,713	17,303	14,660	16,741	19,620	19,788
English language and literature/letters........................	63,914	31,922	51,064	50,569	52,754	39,344	38,036
Family and consumer sciences/human sciences..............	11,167	18,370	13,920	16,421	22,438	23,956	23,245
Foreign languages, literatures, and linguistics...............	20,988	11,638	13,937	16,128	21,705	16,605	16,305
Health professions and related clinical sciences..............	25,221	63,665	59,636	75,537	142,890	250,650	257,282
Homeland security, law enforcement, and firefighting........	2,045	13,707	16,806	25,211	47,600	57,333	57,044
Legal professions and studies...............................	545	776	1,827	1,991	4,429	4,235	4,262
Liberal arts/sciences, general studies, and humanities......	7,481	21,643	30,526	37,962	46,717	44,222	42,903
Mathematics and statistics.................................	24,801	11,078	14,393	11,171	17,182	26,155	27,216
Multi/interdisciplinary studies...............................	6,324	12,986	17,774	26,478	42,473	53,303	55,022
Parks, recreation, leisure, fitness, and kinesiology...........	1,621	5,729	4,315	17,948	35,934	53,540	53,749
Philosophy and religious studies............................	8,149	6,776	7,423	9,442	14,336	11,981	11,889
Physical sciences and science technologies..................	21,410	23,936	16,334	18,025	24,705	31,155	30,738
Psychology..	38,187	41,068	58,655	73,645	100,906	116,550	119,968
Public administration and social services....................	5,466	16,707	14,350	19,447	26,799	35,104	34,356
Social sciences and history.................................	155,324	100,513	125,107	128,036	177,169	160,678	161,164
Theology and religious vocations............................	3,720	5,808	4,799	6,220	7,567	7,061	6,855
Transportation and materials moving.........................	–	263	2,622	3,748	4,941	5,051	5,251
Visual and performing arts.................................	30,394	40,479	42,186	61,148	93,939	89,741	92,332

– Represents zero. [1] Includes other fields of study, not shown separately.

Source: U.S. National Center for Education Statistics, *Digest of Education Statistics*, "Latest version of all Digest tables," <nces.ed.gov/programs/digest>, accessed February 2022.

Table 326. Associate's Degrees by Field of Study and Sex: 2010 to 2020

[For school year ending in year shown. Covers associate's degrees conferred by degree-granting institutions. Data are based on the 2020 Classification of Instructional Programs. Data for previous years has been reclassified where necessary to conform to the new classifications. Based on Integrated Postsecondary Education Data System (IPEDS) survey; see Appendix III]

Field of study	2010	2015	2017	2018	2019	2020		
						Total	Male	Female
Total [1]	**848,856**	**1,014,341**	**1,005,687**	**1,011,696**	**1,036,640**	**1,018,233**	**393,079**	**625,154**
Agriculture and natural resources, total	10,044	13,759	13,686	13,087	13,229	12,738	4,959	7,779
Architecture and related services	553	491	503	539	585	613	389	224
Area, ethnic, cultural, gender, and group studies	199	382	420	559	713	666	276	390
Biological and biomedical sciences	2,664	4,883	5,550	6,391	7,299	7,443	2,234	5,209
Business [1]	133,265	132,374	122,252	117,821	116,799	112,120	45,442	66,678
Business, management, marketing, and support services [1]	116,798	113,681	108,376	105,785	105,588	102,536	42,048	60,488
Accounting and related services	17,925	16,080	13,760	13,022	12,114	11,464	3,238	8,226
Business administration, management, and operations	46,086	52,668	53,930	55,404	56,307	56,268	25,433	30,835
Culinary, entertainment, and personal services	16,467	18,693	13,876	12,036	11,211	9,584	3,394	6,190
Communication, journalism, and related programs	2,841	6,034	7,379	7,785	8,548	9,012	4,002	5,010
Communications technologies	4,418	4,628	4,307	4,196	4,256	4,097	2,596	1,501
Computer and information sciences and support services	32,351	36,420	31,171	31,496	32,001	32,016	25,293	6,723
Education	17,346	17,178	16,603	16,180	16,210	16,177	1,775	14,402
Engineering	2,508	4,875	5,915	6,408	6,367	6,506	5,340	1,166
Engineering technologies	52,893	56,585	53,150	53,309	53,252	49,401	43,992	5,409
English language and literature/letters	1,658	2,324	2,870	3,133	3,340	3,425	1,127	2,298
Family and consumer sciences/human sciences	9,515	8,750	8,871	8,858	9,365	9,261	449	8,812
Foreign languages, literatures, and linguistics	1,683	2,102	2,363	2,607	2,798	2,905	667	2,238
Health professions and related programs	173,129	193,952	180,834	176,076	177,506	172,207	28,204	144,003
Dental assisting	7,063	7,762	7,397	7,072	7,129	5,607	323	5,284
Emergency medical technician (EMT paramedic)	2,413	3,456	3,453	3,413	3,648	3,527	2,363	1,164
Clinical/medical lab science	2,621	3,143	3,062	3,051	3,037	3,116	678	2,438
Medical and other health assisting	25,719	30,825	26,998	23,918	22,689	17,906	3,344	14,562
Nursing and patient care assistant	1	50	56	100	58	79	10	69
Practical nursing	1,973	1,858	1,420	1,105	1,274	1,297	145	1,152
Nursing, registered nurse and other	81,280	82,904	77,051	77,658	81,070	82,859	11,801	71,058
Health sciences, other	52,059	63,954	61,397	59,759	58,601	57,816	9,540	48,276
Homeland security, law enforcement, and firefighting [1]	37,154	43,041	37,362	35,282	35,197	34,892	18,853	16,039
Criminal justice and corrections	32,194	36,213	31,983	29,886	29,758	29,730	14,603	15,127
Legal professions and studies	9,999	9,095	6,904	6,218	5,646	5,534	870	4,664
Liberal arts and sciences, general studies, and humanities	284,954	367,852	386,746	398,002	410,632	402,669	149,030	253,639
Library science	112	170	158	156	195	202	30	172
Mathematics and statistics	1,051	2,697	3,454	4,135	4,632	4,841	3,398	1,443
Military technologies and applied sciences	668	1,229	1,093	1,226	1,202	992	761	231
Multi/interdisciplinary studies	17,279	29,139	30,780	31,102	33,390	33,655	13,884	19,771
Parks, recreation, leisure, fitness, and kinesiology	2,006	4,669	5,037	5,098	5,634	5,668	2,995	2,673
Philosophy and religious studies	256	697	1,384	1,357	1,417	1,625	1,000	625
Physical sciences and science technologies	4,141	7,568	9,223	10,119	10,557	10,744	5,998	4,746
Physical sciences	2,378	5,040	5,838	6,692	7,066	6,753	3,818	2,935
Science technologies/technicians	1,763	2,528	3,385	3,427	3,491	3,991	2,180	1,811
Precision production	2,794	4,382	5,251	5,334	5,386	4,748	4,324	424
Psychology	6,582	8,780	11,283	12,499	14,486	16,202	3,735	12,467
Public administration and social services	4,522	8,436	7,591	7,140	6,822	6,321	845	5,476
Social sciences and history	10,649	17,916	21,392	23,692	25,974	28,212	10,348	17,864
Social sciences	10,108	16,631	19,636	21,552	23,561	25,710	8,831	16,879
History	541	1,285	1,756	2,140	2,413	2,502	1,517	985
Theology and religious vocations	613	1,135	1,164	1,127	1,131	1,079	506	573
Transportation and materials moving	1,444	1,810	1,547	1,610	1,926	1,720	1,473	247
Visual and performing arts	19,565	20,988	19,444	19,154	20,145	20,542	8,284	12,258
Fine and studio arts	2,277	2,866	3,315	3,767	4,060	4,257	1,360	2,897
Music and dance	1,335	1,886	1,993	2,309	2,621	2,641	1,641	1,000
Visual and performing arts, other	15,953	16,236	14,136	13,078	13,464	13,644	5,283	8,361

[1] Includes other fields of study, not shown separately.

Source: U.S. National Center for Education Statistics, *Digest of Education Statistics*, "Latest version of all Digest tables," <nces.ed.gov/programs/digest>, accessed February 2022.

Table 327. Education Certificates Awarded by Field of Study and Sex: 2020

[For school year ending in 2020. Covers certificates below the associate's degree level based on postsecondary curriculums of less than 4 years in degree- and nondegree-granting institutions of higher education. Based on Integrated Postsecondary Education Data System (IPEDS) survey; see Appendix III]

Field of study	Less than 1-year awards			1- to less than 4-year awards		
	Total	Male	Female	Total	Male	Female
Total..	**512,799**	**240,906**	**271,893**	**450,531**	**176,633**	**273,898**
Agriculture and natural resources............................	6,444	3,333	3,111	4,676	1,638	3,038
Agricultural, animal, plant, veterinary science, and related fields..	5,211	2,635	2,576	4,443	1,478	2,965
Natural resources and conservation............................	1,233	698	535	233	160	73
Architecture and related services............................	213	115	98	83	49	34
Area, ethnic, cultural, gender, and group studies...................	2,188	462	1,726	118	17	101
Biological and biomedical sciences............................	1,275	323	952	282	88	194
Business, management, marketing, and support services..........	81,230	31,861	49,369	20,398	6,505	13,893
Accounting and related services............................	12,241	3,560	8,681	4,545	1,177	3,368
Business/commerce, general............................	2,528	1,061	1,467	1,682	808	874
Business administration, management, and operations............	28,206	12,372	15,834	5,388	1,805	3,583
Management information systems and services................	754	501	253	76	53	23
Business operations support and assistant services...............	9,534	2,994	6,540	4,236	884	3,352
Business and management, other............................	27,967	11,373	16,594	4,471	1,778	2,693
Culinary, entertainment, and personal services....................	44,750	4,397	40,353	57,821	9,334	48,487
Communication, journalism, and related programs................	2,975	1,327	1,648	1,586	934	652
Communications technologies............................	3,007	1,886	1,121	2,600	1,818	782
Computer and information sciences and support services..........	35,616	27,367	8,249	10,102	7,850	2,252
Education............................	9,526	927	8,599	3,620	428	3,192
Engineering............................	1,200	928	272	518	410	108
Engineering technologies [1]............................	75,195	68,228	6,967	67,554	63,179	4,375
English language and literature/letters..........................	1,771	534	1,237	513	185	328
Family and consumer sciences/human sciences.................	15,758	1,221	14,537	3,592	145	3,447
Foreign languages, literatures, and linguistics....................	2,487	579	1,908	672	156	516
Health professions and related programs.......................	121,361	23,633	97,728	134,227	17,269	116,958
Dental assisting............................	4,308	340	3,968	9,058	681	8,377
Emergency medical technician (EMT paramedic)..................	15,615	9,350	6,265	5,752	4,152	1,600
Clinical/medical lab science............................	8,086	967	7,119	1,139	175	964
Medical assisting............................	7,773	525	7,248	36,949	2,624	34,325
Pharmacy assisting............................	1,936	376	1,560	3,533	696	2,837
Other allied health assisting............................	5,624	1,841	3,783	813	185	628
Nursing and patient care assistant..........................	34,625	3,906	30,719	1,128	114	1,014
Practical nursing............................	4,754	516	4,238	43,656	4,251	39,405
Nursing, registered nurse and other..........................	1,273	140	1,133	2,475	368	2,107
Health sciences, other............................	37,367	5,672	31,695	29,724	4,023	25,701
Homeland security, law enforcement, and firefighting..............	26,454	18,517	7,937	6,923	4,430	2,493
Criminal justice and corrections............................	18,251	11,880	6,371	5,751	3,477	2,274
Fire control and safety............................	6,544	5,859	685	930	850	80
Homeland security and related protective services, other..........	953	574	379	76	55	21
Security science and technology............................	706	204	502	166	48	118
Legal professions and studies............................	2,093	401	1,692	2,367	425	1,942
Liberal arts and sciences, general studies, and humanities.........	11,969	3,986	7,983	97,414	38,107	59,307
Library science............................	169	28	141	40	2	38
Mathematics and statistics............................	388	281	107	33	23	10
Military technologies and applied sciences.....................	117	88	29	13	13	0
Multi/interdisciplinary studies............................	3,537	1,276	2,261	3,161	1,438	1,723
Parks, recreation, leisure, fitness, and kinesiology..................	1,503	712	791	554	307	247
Philosophy and religious studies............................	242	35	207	444	21	423
Physical sciences and science technologies......................	1,670	719	951	1,436	833	603
Physical sciences............................	390	226	164	47	10	37
Science technologies/technicians............................	1,280	493	787	1,389	823	566
Precision production............................	29,619	27,140	2,479	17,248	15,823	1,425
Psychology............................	335	60	275	56	8	48
Public administration and social services.......................	1,755	328	1,427	552	93	459
Social sciences and history............................	1,995	885	1,110	328	166	162
Social sciences............................	1,943	861	1,082	326	166	160
History............................	52	24	28	2	0	2
Theology and religious vocations............................	370	186	184	664	304	360
Transportation and materials moving..........................	17,574	15,423	2,151	1,011	924	87
Visual and performing arts............................	8,013	3,720	4,293	9,925	3,711	6,214
Fine and studio arts............................	630	206	424	5,816	1,981	3,835
Music and dance............................	489	279	210	308	159	149
Visual and performing arts, other [2]............................	6,894	3,235	3,659	3,801	1,571	2,230

[1] Includes engineering-related fields; construction trades; and mechanic and repair technologies/technicians. [2] Includes design and applied arts, drama and theatre arts, film and photographic arts, and all other arts not included under "Fine and studio arts" or "Music and dance."

Source: U.S. National Center for Education Statistics, *Digest of Education Statistics*, "Latest version of all Digest tables," <www.nces.ed.gov/programs/digest>, accessed June 2022.

Table 328. Master's and Doctoral Degrees Earned by Field: 1971 to 2020

[For school years ending in years shown. Data are based on the 2020 Classification of Instructional Programs. Data for previous years has been reclassified where necessary to conform to the new classifications. Based on data from the Integrated Postsecondary Education Data System (IPEDS)]

Field of study	1971	1981	1991	2001	2011	2019	2020
MASTER'S DEGREES							
Total [1]	**235,564**	**302,637**	**342,863**	**473,502**	**730,922**	**833,792**	**843,449**
Agriculture and natural resources	2,546	4,150	3,402	4,430	6,023	7,544	7,393
Architecture and related services	1,705	3,153	3,490	4,302	7,788	7,311	6,796
Area, ethnic, cultural, gender, and group studies	1,032	802	1,233	1,555	1,913	1,593	1,527
Biological and biomedical sciences	5,625	5,766	4,834	7,017	11,324	18,092	18,776
Business	26,490	57,888	78,255	115,602	187,178	197,074	197,422
Communication, journalism, and related programs	1,770	2,896	4,123	5,218	8,302	10,463	10,588
Communications technologies	86	209	204	427	502	535	539
Computer and information sciences and support services	1,588	4,218	9,324	16,911	19,516	45,671	51,521
Education	87,666	96,713	87,352	127,829	185,127	146,429	146,975
Engineering	16,813	16,893	24,454	25,174	38,664	49,701	47,266
Engineering technologies	134	323	996	2,013	4,515	6,232	6,219
English language and literature/letters	10,441	5,742	6,784	6,763	9,475	8,217	7,862
Family and consumer sciences/human sciences	1,452	2,570	1,541	1,838	2,918	3,287	3,280
Foreign languages, literatures, and linguistics	5,480	2,934	3,049	3,035	3,727	3,081	2,930
Health professions and related programs	5,241	16,029	21,247	43,465	75,314	131,391	135,324
Homeland security, law enforcement, and firefighting	194	1,538	1,108	2,514	7,433	10,303	10,606
Legal professions and studies	955	1,832	2,057	3,829	6,475	9,487	10,002
Liberal arts and sciences, general studies, and humanities	885	2,375	2,213	3,193	3,997	2,109	1,990
Library science	7,001	4,859	4,763	4,727	7,729	5,164	4,959
Mathematics and statistics	5,191	2,567	3,549	3,209	5,866	11,382	12,039
Parks, recreation, leisure, fitness, and kinesiology	218	643	483	2,354	6,546	8,963	9,108
Philosophy and religious studies	1,326	1,231	1,471	1,534	2,257	2,280	2,178
Physical sciences and science technologies	6,336	5,246	5,281	5,134	6,386	7,121	6,976
Psychology	5,717	10,223	11,349	16,539	25,062	29,136	29,763
Public administration and social services	7,785	17,803	17,905	25,268	38,614	48,883	49,712
Social sciences and history	16,539	11,945	12,233	13,791	21,085	20,303	19,507
Theology and religious vocations	7,747	11,061	10,498	9,728	12,752	12,842	12,646
Transportation and materials moving	–	–	406	756	1,390	774	631
Visual and performing arts	6,675	8,629	8,657	11,404	16,277	17,119	16,517
DOCTORAL DEGREES							
Total [1]	**64,998**	**98,016**	**105,547**	**119,585**	**163,827**	**187,577**	**190,178**
Agriculture and natural resources	2,384	3,062	3,319	3,483	4,028	4,954	4,886
Architecture and related services	36	93	135	153	205	255	252
Area, ethnic, cultural, gender, and group studies	143	161	159	216	278	370	334
Biological and biomedical sciences	3,603	3,640	4,152	5,225	7,693	7,978	7,885
Business	774	808	1,185	1,180	2,286	3,640	3,443
Communication, journalism, and related programs	145	171	259	368	577	583	602
Computer and information sciences and support services	128	252	676	768	1,588	2,224	2,414
Education	6,041	7,279	6,189	6,284	9,642	13,020	13,051
Engineering	3,687	2,598	5,316	5,485	8,369	11,136	11,141
English language and literature/letters	1,554	1,040	1,056	1,330	1,344	1,274	1,285
Foreign languages, literatures, and linguistics	1,084	931	889	1,078	1,158	1,212	1,162
Health professions and related programs	14,690	27,600	27,708	36,663	57,439	79,556	82,492
Legal professions and studies	17,441	36,391	38,035	38,190	44,853	34,387	34,471
Mathematics and statistics	1,199	728	978	997	1,586	2,003	2,020
Philosophy and religious studies	555	411	464	612	835	712	694
Physical sciences and science technologies	4,324	3,105	4,248	3,968	5,295	6,298	5,968
Psychology	2,144	3,576	3,932	5,091	5,851	6,215	6,346
Public administration and social services	174	362	430	574	851	1,287	1,409
Social sciences and history	3,660	3,122	3,012	3,930	4,390	4,544	4,436
Theology and religious vocations	312	1,273	1,076	1,449	2,343	1,937	1,981
Visual and performing arts	621	654	838	1,167	1,646	1,845	1,716

– Represents zero. [1] Includes other fields of study, not shown separately.

Source: U.S. National Center for Education Statistics, *Digest of Education Statistics*, "Latest version of all Digest tables," <nces.ed.gov/programs/digest>, accessed February 2022.

Table 329. First Professional Degrees Earned in Selected Professions: 1970 to 2020

[First professional degrees include degrees which require at least 6 years of college work for completion (including at least 2 years of preprofessional training). Based on Integrated Postsecondary Education Data System surveys; see Appendix III]

Type of degree and sex of recipient	1970	1980	1990	2000	2010	2015	2017	2018	2019	2020
Medicine (M.D.):										
Institutions conferring degrees	86	112	124	118	120	127	131	133	134	137
Degrees conferred, total	8,314	14,902	15,075	15,286	16,356	18,302	18,698	19,142	19,423	19,773
Percent to women	8.4	23.4	34.2	42.7	48.2	47.8	47.4	47.5	48.2	49.7
Dentistry (D.D.S. or D.M.D.):										
Institutions conferring degrees	48	58	57	54	55	60	63	63	63	64
Degrees conferred, total	3,718	5,258	4,100	4,250	5,062	5,816	6,388	6,267	6,321	6,537
Percent to women	0.9	13.3	30.9	40.1	45.8	47.9	47.9	49.5	50.7	51.0
Law (LL.B. or J.D.):										
Institutions conferring degrees	145	179	182	190	205	212	214	211	211	209
Degrees conferred, total	14,916	35,647	36,485	38,152	44,346	40,024	34,894	34,128	34,133	34,212
Percent to women	5.4	30.2	42.2	45.9	47.3	48.0	49.6	49.7	51.6	52.4
Theological (B.D., M.Div., M.H.L.):										
Institutions conferring degrees	(NA)	(NA)	(NA)	198	(NA)	(NA)	(NA)	(NA)	(NA)	(NA)
Degrees conferred, total	5,298	7,115	5,851	6,129	5,825	6,300	5,830	5,842	5,774	5,670
Percent to women	2.3	13.8	24.8	29.2	(NA)	31.4	31.8	30.1	31.6	31.8

NA Not available.

Source: U.S. National Center for Education Statistics, *Digest of Education Statistics*, "Latest version of all Digest tables," <nces.ed.gov/programs/digest>, accessed August 2022.

Table 330. Graduate and Undergraduate Students Taking Online Classes and Degree Programs by Selected Characteristics: 2016

[In thousands (19,308 represents 19,308,000), except percent. For school year ending in 2016]

Student characteristics	Undergraduate students				Graduate students			
	Number of students		Percent of students taking—		Number of students		Percent of students taking—	
	Total enroll-ment	Students taking any online classes	Any online classes	Entire degree program online [1]	Total enroll-ment	Students taking any online classes	Any online classes	Entire degree program online [1]
Total................................	**19,308**	**8,319**	**43.1**	**10.8**	**3,547**	**1,617**	**45.6**	**27.3**
Sex:								
Male....................	8,406	3,340	39.7	9.2	1,446	591	40.8	24.6
Female....................	10,903	4,979	45.7	12.1	2,101	1,026	48.9	29.3
Race/ethnicity:								
White....................	10,276	4,671	45.5	11.1	2,105	942	44.8	26.0
Black....................	3,006	1,278	42.5	14.9	504	315	62.5	45.3
Hispanic....................	3,723	1,431	38.4	7.7	326	161	49.5	31.2
Asian....................	1,399	544	38.9	7.8	500	138	27.5	10.8
Pacific Islander....................	83	35	42.2	12.0	8	5	64.1	[2] 33.4
American Indian or Alaska Native....................	160	76	47.5	12.2	17	8	43.9	33.1
Two or more races....................	661	283	42.8	10.4	88	49	55.6	33.8
Age:								
15 to 23 years old....................	11,368	4,157	36.6	3.5	466	130	27.9	8.0
24 to 29 years old....................	3,536	1,793	50.7	17.5	1,387	525	37.8	16.8
30 years old and over....................	4,404	2,369	53.8	24.9	1,695	962	56.8	41.6
Attendance status:								
Exclusively full-time....................	7,239	2,789	38.5	6.0	1,279	408	31.9	15.2
Exclusively part-time....................	5,059	2,398	47.4	14.7	850	453	53.3	36.7
Mixed full-time and part-time....................	7,010	3,131	44.7	13.2	1,418	756	53.3	33.1
Field of study:								
Business/management....................	2,973	1,525	51.3	17.0	592	320	54.1	36.7
Education....................	841	384	45.7	9.7	605	352	58.2	34.3
Engineering....................	1,140	380	33.3	5.1	(NA)	(NA)	(NA)	(NA)
Health....................	3,438	1,547	45.0	13.3	694	325	46.8	26.6
Humanities....................	3,083	1,274	41.3	7.8	281	99	35.3	18.2
Law....................	(NA)	(NA)	(NA)	(NA)	132	21	15.9	8.0
Social/behavioral sciences....................	1,323	556	42.0	9.1	245	112	45.7	29.0
Vocational/technical....................	594	188	31.7	6.0	(NA)	(NA)	(NA)	(NA)

NA Not available. [1] Excludes students not in a degree or certificate program. [2] Interpret data with caution. The coefficient of variation (CV) for this estimate is between 30 and 50 percent.

Source: U.S. National Center for Education Statistics, *Digest of Education Statistics*, "Latest version of all Digest tables," <nces.ed.gov/programs/digest>, accessed May 2019.

Table 331. College and University Libraries by Selected Characteristics: 2015 to 2017

[In units as indicated (778,357 represents 778,357,000). As of Fall of year shown. Data shown for degree-granting postsecondary institution libraries. FTE is full-time equivalent. Based on data from the Integrated Postsecondary Education Data System (IPEDS)]

Item	Unit	2015	2016	2017			
				Total	Public	Private non-profit	Private for-profit
Number of libraries....................	Number	3,999	3,944	3,710	1,557	1,592	561
Percent of institutions with libraries....................	Percent	91.7	91.4	91.8	95.2	95.7	75.6
Circulation transactions....................	1,000	778,357	772,169	684,318	430,045	211,103	43,169
Physical transaction....................	1,000	67,796	58,199	52,923	31,233	21,180	510
Electronic transaction....................	1,000	710,561	713,970	631,395	398,812	189,923	42,659
Circulation transactions per FTE student....................	Number	52	52	46	41	61	52
ENROLLMENT							
Total enrollment....................	1,000	19,988	19,847	19,778	14,572	4,108	1,098
FTE enrollment....................	1,000	15,079	14,938	14,884	10,569	3,480	835
COLLECTIONS							
Total number of physical and electronic materials....................	1,000	1,985,142	2,208,941	2,220,810	1,229,563	870,127	121,120
Number of books....................	1,000	1,573,341	1,650,727	1,638,949	895,176	664,182	79,591
Physical books....................	1,000	824,767	799,192	753,816	449,893	301,200	2,723
Electronic books....................	1,000	748,575	851,536	885,133	445,283	362,982	76,868
Number of media (includes audiovisual materials)....................	1,000	410,274	557,267	580,621	333,928	205,501	41,192
Number of databases [1]....................	1,000	1,527	947	1,239	459	444	336
OPERATING EXPENDITURES (CURRENT DOLLARS)							
Total operating expenditures [2, 3]....................	1,000 dol.	8,085,556	8,243,595	8,319,149	4,901,850	3,344,487	72,812
Salaries and wages [4]....................	1,000 dol.	3,455,940	3,504,446	3,532,353	2,192,542	1,310,179	29,632
Fringe benefits....................	1,000 dol.	759,363	784,747	799,696	498,300	298,541	2,856
Information resources....................	1,000 dol.	3,083,854	3,126,900	3,160,845	1,788,419	1,340,572	31,855
Operating expenditures per FTE student....................	Dol.	536	552	559	464	961	87

[1] Electronic databases only. [2] Excludes capital outlay. Expenditure data are reported only by degree-granting institutions with total expenditures over $100,000. [3] Includes other expenditures not shown separately. [4] Includes student hourly wages.

Source: U.S. National Center for Education Statistics, *Digest of Education Statistics*, "Latest version of all Digest tables," <nces.ed.gov/programs/digest>, accessed March 2021.

Table 332. College Campus Crime—Incidents and Rates by Type of Crime and Institution: 2001 to 2019

[For school year ending in year shown. Data are from Department of Education's Campus Safety and Security Reporting System. Data are for degree-granting institutions, which are institutions that grant associate's or higher degrees and participate in Title IV federal financial aid programs. Some institutions that report data as mandated by the Clery Act, specifically, non-degree-granting institutions and institutions outside of the 50 states and the District of Columbia, are excluded from this table. Crimes, arrests, and referrals include incidents involving students, staff, and on-campus guests. Excludes off-campus crimes and arrests even if they involve college students or staff]

Control and level of institution and type of crime	Total, in residence halls and other locations						2019		
	2001	2006	2011	2016	2017	2018	Total	In residence halls	At other locations
NUMBER OF INCIDENTS									
Selected crimes against persons and property	**41,596**	**44,492**	**30,407**	**28,239**	**29,034**	**28,587**	**27,334**	**12,837**	**14,497**
Murder [1]	17	8	16	15	22	12	20	6	14
Negligent manslaughter [2]	2	–	1	2	3	2	5	1	4
Sex offenses, forcible [3]	2,201	2,670	3,375	8,908	10,481	12,376	11,767	7,375	4,392
Sex offenses, nonforcible [4]	461	43	46	60	82	63	74	42	32
Robbery	1,663	1,547	1,285	1,080	1,034	833	806	167	639
Aggravated assault	2,947	2,817	2,239	2,156	2,257	2,235	2,154	692	1,462
Burglary	26,904	31,260	19,472	11,918	11,098	9,583	8,991	4,304	4,687
Motor vehicle theft	6,221	5,231	3,334	3,506	3,448	3,070	3,061	33	3,028
Arson [5]	1,180	916	639	594	609	413	456	217	239
Arrests [5]	40,348	50,187	54,285	38,992	37,875	32,349	27,731	14,168	13,563
Illegal weapons possession	1,073	1,316	1,023	1,198	1,241	1,177	1,145	244	901
Drug law violations	11,854	13,952	20,729	19,226	19,837	18,190	14,097	6,747	7,350
Liquor law violations	27,421	34,919	32,533	18,568	16,797	12,982	12,489	7,177	5,312
Referrals for disciplinary action [5]	18,710	218,040	249,694	228,802	215,288	199,819	187,331	173,015	14,316
Illegal weapons possession	1,277	1,871	1,282	1,402	1,290	1,231	1,056	718	338
Drug law violations	23,900	27,251	51,562	55,373	57,602	53,569	46,313	40,170	6,143
Liquor law violations	130,024	188,918	196,850	172,027	156,396	145,019	139,962	132,127	7,835
INCIDENTS PER 10,000 FTE STUDENTS [6, 7]									
Selected crimes against persons and property	**35.6**	**33.4**	**20.0**	**19.3**	**19.9**	**19.5**	**18.7**	**23.9**	**5.6**
By type of crime:									
Murder [1]	(Z)	(Z)	(Z)	(Z)	(Z)	(Z)	(Z)	(Z)	(Z)
Negligent manslaughter [2]	(Z)	–	(Z)	(Z)	(Z)	(Z)	(Z)	(Z)	–
Sex offenses, forcible [3]	1.9	2.0	2.2	6.1	7.2	8.5	8.0	10.7	1.3
Sex offenses, nonforcible [4]	0.4	(Z)	(Z)	(Z)	0.1	(Z)	0.1	0.1	(Z)
Robbery	1.4	1.2	0.8	0.7	0.7	0.6	0.6	0.7	0.3
Aggravated assault	2.5	2.1	1.5	1.5	1.5	1.5	1.5	1.7	0.9
Burglary	23.0	23.4	12.8	8.1	7.6	6.6	6.1	7.9	1.9
Motor vehicle theft	5.3	3.9	2.2	2.4	2.4	2.1	2.1	2.5	1.2
Arson	1.0	0.7	0.4	0.4	0.4	0.3	0.3	0.4	0.1
By type of institution:									
Public 4-year	36.2	35.5	22.0	19.8	20.6	21.1	21.0	22.6	7.7
Nonprofit 4-year	57.4	57.7	33.2	32.7	32.5	30.9	27.0	29.2	8.3
For-profit 4-year	19.1	9.6	6.0	3.9	5.0	5.1	5.2	22.0	1.8
Public 2-year	19.9	15.4	10.0	8.0	8.2	6.7	6.7	11.9	5.4
Nonprofit 2-year	64.0	81.9	45.5	21.8	14.6	8.7	7.2	29.3	3.2
For profit-2-year	25.4	18.2	7.5	7.6	6.0	6.4	5.5	13.4	5.4
Arrests [5]	**34.6**	**37.6**	**35.8**	**26.6**	**25.9**	**22.1**	**18.9**	**25.4**	**3.0**
Illegal weapons possession	0.9	1.0	0.7	0.8	0.8	0.8	0.8	0.9	0.4
Drug law violations	10.2	10.5	13.7	13.1	13.6	12.4	9.6	12.7	1.9
Liquor law violations	23.5	26.2	21.4	12.7	11.5	8.9	8.5	11.7	0.7
By type of institution:									
Public 4-year	60.1	68.7	67.2	44.2	42.0	34.9	29.6	32.6	4.5
Nonprofit 4-year	24.5	21.0	16.8	13.3	12.2	10.6	8.2	8.8	2.9
For-profit 4-year	0.4	0.8	2.0	1.8	2.1	2.7	6.7	37.7	0.3
Public 2-year	7.8	10.9	9.0	8.1	9.7	9.5	8.6	29.4	3.1
Nonprofit 2-year	27.9	22.0	16.0	21.8	11.4	6.2	8.0	24.4	5.0
For profit-2-year	8.8	1.8	0.7	2.2	1.8	2.1	1.2	13.4	1.0
Referrals for disciplinary action [5]	**132.9**	**163.4**	**164.5**	**156.2**	**147.3**	**136.6**	**127.9**	**178.6**	**2.2**
Illegal weapons possession	1.1	1.4	0.8	1.0	0.9	0.8	0.7	0.9	0.2
Drug law violations	20.5	20.4	34.0	37.8	39.4	36.6	31.6	43.9	1.1
Liquor law violations	111.3	141.6	129.7	117.4	107.0	99.1	95.5	133.7	0.9
By type of institution:									
Public 4-year	153.1	184.6	194.0	166.1	154.3	141.1	132.2	148.0	1.4
Nonprofit 4-year	275.5	353.9	341.4	302.8	280.9	258.4	237.3	263.0	8.3
For-profit 4-year	12.0	7.6	9.7	10.5	17.2	13.9	17.1	99.0	0.4
Public 2-year	10.3	16.1	19.7	20.6	21.0	19.9	20.8	91.4	2.1
Nonprofit 2-year	160.9	176.0	110.8	163.4	118.7	89.5	77.4	506.8	–
For profit-2-year	15.4	13.9	4.9	6.8	6.2	4.6	1.9	50.3	0.9

– Represents zero. Z Less than .05%. [1] Excludes suicides, fetal deaths, traffic fatalities, accidental deaths, and justifiable homicide (such as the killing of a felon by a law enforcement officer in the line of duty). [2] Defined as the killing of another person through gross negligence (excludes traffic fatalities). [3] Any sexual act directed against another person forcibly and/or against that person's will. [4] Includes only statutory rape or incest. [5] If an individual is both arrested and referred to college officials for disciplinary action for a single offense, only the arrest is counted. [6] FTE is full-time equivalent. Although crimes, arrests, and referrals include incidents involving students, staff, and campus guests, they are expressed as a ratio to FTE students because comprehensive FTE counts of all these groups are not available. [7] Data on incidents per 10,000 FTE students are shown for institutions with and without residence halls.

Source: U.S. National Center for Education Statistics, *Digest of Education Statistics*, "Latest version of all Digest tables," <nces.ed.gov/programs/digest>, accessed March 2022.

Table 333. Public Schools Reporting Incidents of Crime by Incident Type and Selected School Characteristics: 2020

[For school year ending in 2020. Includes incidents that happen in school buildings, on school grounds, on school buses, and at places that hold school-sponsored events or activities. Based on the School Survey on Crime and Safety (SSOCS). Based on sample; see source for details]

School characteristic	Total number of schools	Number of incidents		Percent of schools with—		Rate per 1,000 students	
		Violent incidents [1]	Serious violent incidents [2]	Violent incidents [1]	Serious violent incidents [2]	Violent incidents [1]	Serious violent incidents [2]
All public schools.................	**83,100**	**938,500**	**62,800**	**70.2**	**25.4**	**19.2**	**1.3**
Level: [3]							
Elementary..........................	49,200	408,300	24,700	58.4	19.2	17.5	1.1
Middle................................	14,600	276,500	14,800	91.0	32.5	28.4	1.5
High school........................	16,000	237,300	21,600	89.6	37.5	16.4	1.5
Combined..........................	3,300	16,300	1,800	60.3	27.1	12.5	1.3
Enrollment size:							
Less than 300....................	17,700	97,500	9,000	55.8	20.8	24.3	2.2
300 to 499........................	25,600	207,800	14,600	66.4	21.9	19.6	1.4
500 to 999........................	30,900	401,900	22,700	75.2	26.0	19.1	1.1
1,000 or more....................	8,800	231,300	16,600	92.5	42.2	17.4	1.3
Percent minority enrollment:							
Zero to 25 percent..............	27,600	195,900	12,800	65.5	20.2	14.4	0.9
26 to 50 percent.................	17,700	167,600	15,300	67.8	27.0	14.8	1.4
51 to 75 percent.................	16,000	225,500	15,100	74.5	27.9	22.1	1.5
76 percent or more..............	21,800	349,500	19,600	74.9	28.7	25.5	1.4

[1] Violent incidents include rape, sexual battery other than rape, physical attack or fight with or without a weapon, threat of physical attack with or without a weapon, and robbery with or without a weapon. [2] Serious violent incidents include rape, sexual battery other than rape, physical attack or fight with a weapon, threat of physical attack with a weapon, and robbery with or without a weapon. [3] Elementary schools are defined as schools that enroll more students in grades K through 4 than in higher grades. Middle schools are defined as schools that enroll more students in grades 5 through 8 than in higher or lower grades. High schools are defined as schools that enroll more students in grades 9 through 12 than in lower grades. Combined schools include all other combinations of grades, including K–12 schools.

Source: U.S. National Center for Education Statistics, *Digest of Education Statistics*, "Latest version of all Digest tables," <nces.ed.gov/programs/digest>, accessed May 2022; and *Indicators of School Crime and Safety*, annual. See also <nces.ed.gov/surveys/ssocs>.

Table 334. Disciplinary Problems Reported at Public Schools by Selected School Characteristics: 2020

[In percent. For school year ending in 2020. "At school" includes activities that happen in school buildings, on school grounds, on school buses, and at places that hold school-sponsored events or activities. Based on the School Survey on Crime and Safety (SSOCS); responses were provided by the principal or the person most knowledgeable about crime and safety issues at the school. Respondents to the survey had the option of either completing the survey on paper and mailing it back, or completing the survey online. Based on sample; see source for details]

School characteristic	Happens at least once a week						Happens at all
	Student racial tensions	Student bullying	Student sexual harassment of other students [1]	Student verbal abuse of teachers	Widespread disorder in classrooms	Student acts of disrespect for teachers	Gang activities [2]
All public schools.........	**3.8**	**14.6**	**1.6**	**9.8**	**4.1**	**15.3**	**14.0**
Level: [3]							
Elementary....................	2.9	11.4	(S)	8.9	3.3	13.6	6.0
Middle..........................	6.5	24.6	3.9	12.8	6.3	21.2	23.5
Secondary/high school.......	4.1	16.1	2.5	10.4	4.1	15.8	31.6
Combined.....................	(S)	[4] 10.0	(S)	[4] 6.4	[4] 6.2	[4] 11.2	[4] 5.7
Enrollment size:							
Less than 300.................	(S)	8.7	(S)	8.9	[4] 2.8	13.7	8.8
300 to 499.....................	3.6	13.1	[4] 1.1	10.1	2.8	13.2	8.2
500 to 999.....................	4.4	17.3	2.2	9.8	5.6	17.4	14.1
1,000 or more.................	7.0	21.0	4.4	10.3	5.0	17.2	40.4
Percent minority enrollment:							
Zero to 25 percent...........	[4] 1.7	11.2	[4] 1.0	3.8	2.0	11.0	3.6
26 to 50 percent.............	4.5	13.8	[4] 1.8	7.1	2.2	14.1	10.5
51 to 75 percent.............	6.8	19.1	2.9	15.3	5.1	19.8	18.9
76 percent or more..........	3.5	16.1	1.5	15.5	7.5	18.3	26.4

S Figure does not meet publication standards. [1] Defined as conduct that is unwelcome, sexual in nature, and denies or limits a student's ability to participate in or benefit from a school's education program. The conduct can be carried out by school employees, other students, and non-employee third parties. Both male and female students can be victims of sexual harassment, and the harasser and the victim can be of the same sex. The conduct can be verbal, nonverbal, or physical. [2] Gang includes an "ongoing loosely organized association of three or more persons, whether formal or informal, that has a common name, signs, symbols or colors, whose members engage, either individually or collectively, in violent or other forms of illegal behavior." [3] Elementary schools are defined as schools that enroll more students in grades K through 4 than in higher grades. Middle schools are defined as schools that enroll more students in grades 5 through 8 than in higher or lower grades. Secondary or high schools are defined as schools that enroll more students in grades 9 through 12 than in lower grades. Combined schools include all other combinations of grades, including K–12 schools. [4] Interpret data with caution.

Source: U.S. National Center for Education Statistics, *Digest of Education Statistics*, "Latest version of all Digest tables," <nces.ed.gov/programs/digest>, accessed May 2022; and *Indicators of School Crime and Safety*, annual. See also <nces.ed.gov/surveys/ssocs>.

Table 335. Students Who Reported Being Threatened or Injured With a Weapon on School Property by Selected Student Characteristics: 2005 to 2019

[In percent. Based on the Centers for Disease Control and Prevention's Youth Risk Behavior Surveillance System, which surveys students in public and private schools, in grades 9 to 12. Data are for previous 12 months. "On school property" was not defined for survey respondents. "Weapon" was defined as a gun, knife, or club for survey respondents]

Characteristic	2005	2007	2009	2011	2013	2015	2017	2019
Total	**7.9**	**7.8**	**7.7**	**7.4**	**6.9**	**6.0**	**6.0**	**7.4**
Sex:								
Male	9.7	10.2	9.6	9.5	7.7	7.0	7.8	8.0
Female	6.1	5.4	5.5	5.2	6.1	4.6	4.1	6.5
Race/ethnicity: [1]								
White	7.2	6.9	6.4	6.1	5.8	4.9	5.0	7.1
Black	8.1	9.7	9.4	8.9	8.4	7.9	7.8	8.8
Hispanic	9.8	8.7	9.1	9.2	8.5	6.6	6.1	6.9
Asian	4.6	[2] 7.6	5.5	7.0	5.3	[2] 3.6	4.3	3.2
Pacific Islander/Native Hawaiian	[2] 14.5	[2] 8.1	12.5	11.3	[2] 8.7	[2] 20.5	[2] 7.0	[2] 12.3
American Indian/Alaska Native	9.8	5.9	16.5	8.2	18.5	[2] 8.2	13.7	12.6
More than one race	10.7	13.3	9.2	9.9	7.7	8.0	8.0	11.4
Grade:								
9th	10.5	9.2	8.7	8.3	8.5	7.2	7.2	8.1
10th	8.8	8.4	8.4	7.7	7.0	6.2	6.2	8.0
11th	5.5	6.8	7.9	7.3	6.8	5.5	5.5	7.1
12th	5.8	6.3	5.2	5.9	4.9	4.4	4.4	5.9
Sexual orientation: [3]								
Heterosexual	(NA)	(NA)	(NA)	(NA)	(NA)	5.1	5.4	6.3
Gay, lesbian, or bisexual	(NA)	(NA)	(NA)	(NA)	(NA)	10.0	9.4	11.9
Not sure	(NA)	(NA)	(NA)	(NA)	(NA)	12.6	11.1	12.9

NA Not available. [1] Race categories exclude persons of Hispanic ethnicity. [2] Interpret data with caution. [3] Students were asked which sexual orientation, "heterosexual (straight)," "gay or lesbian," "bisexual," or "not sure," which best described them.

Source: U.S. National Center for Education Statistics, *Digest of Education Statistics,* "Lastest version of all Digest tables," <nces.ed.gov/programs/digest>, accessed July 2021; and *Indicators of School Crime and Safety,* annual. See also <nces.ed.gov/surveys/ssocs>.

Table 336. Public Schools Using Selected Safety and Security Measures by Type: 2000 to 2020

[In percent. For school year ending in year shown. Based on the School Survey on Crime and Safety and subject to sampling error; see source for details]

Measure	2000	2010	2014 [1]	2016	2018	2020 [6]
Controlled access during school hours:						
Buildings (locked or monitored doors)	74.6	91.7	93.3	94.1	95.4	97.1
Grounds (locked or monitored gates)	33.7	46.0	42.7	49.9	50.8	58.9
Visitors required to sign or check in and wear badges [2]	96.6	99.3	98.6	93.5	94.6	98.1
Classrooms equipped with doors that lock from the inside	(NA)	(NA)	(NA)	66.7	64.8	73.1
Student dress, IDs, and school supplies:						
Required students to wear uniforms	11.8	18.9	20.4	21.5	19.8	18.8
Enforced a strict dress code	47.4	56.9	58.5	53.1	48.8	43.7
Required students to wear badges or picture IDs	3.9	6.9	8.9	7.0	9.2	10.1
Required faculty and staff to wear badges or picture IDs	25.4	62.9	68.0	67.9	69.9	76.8
Required clear book bags or banned book bags on school grounds	5.9	5.5	6.3	3.9	3.5	4.4
Provided school lockers to students	46.5	52.1	49.9	50.4	49.0	49.4
Drug testing:						
Students participating in athletics or other extracurricular activities	(NA)	6.2	6.7	7.7	8.9	9.5
Athletes	(NA)	6.0	6.6	7.2	(NA)	(NA)
Students in non-athletic extracurricular activities	(NA)	4.6	4.3	6.0	(NA)	(NA)
Any other students	(NA)	3.0	3.5	(NA)	(NA)	(NA)
Metal detectors and sweeps:						
Random metal detector checks on students	7.2	5.2	4.2	4.5	4.9	6.0
Students required to pass through metal detectors daily	0.9	1.4	2.0	1.8	2.2	2.7
Random sweeps for contraband [3]	25.3	27.7	28.2	28.2	27.4	28.7
Communications systems and technology:						
Provided telephones in most classrooms	44.6	74.0	78.7	79.3	(NA)	(NA)
Provided electronic notification system for school wide emergencies	(NA)	63.1	81.6	73.0	71.6	70.4
Provided structured anonymous threat reporting system [4]	(NA)	35.9	46.5	43.9	49.3	65.7
Had silent alarms directly connected to law enforcement	(NA)	(NA)	(NA)	27.1	29.1	40.0
Used security cameras to monitor the school	19.4	61.1	75.1	80.6	83.5	91.1
Provided two-way radios to any staff	(NA)	73.3	74.2	73.3	77.8	83.2
Limited access to social networking sites from school computers	(NA)	93.4	91.9	89.1	(NA)	(NA)
Prohibited non-academic use of cell phones or smartphones [5]	(NA)	90.9	75.9	65.8	70.3	76.9

NA Not available. [1] Data for 2013-2014 were collected using the Fast Response Survey System. The 2013-2014 survey was designed to allow comparisons with School Survey on Crime and Safety (SSOCS) data. However, respondents to the 2013-2014 survey could choose either to complete the survey by mail or online, whereas respondents to SSOCS did not have the online option. The 2013-2014 survey also relied on a smaller sample. These differences may have impacted 2013-2014 results. [2] Prior to the 2015-2016 survey, the survey asked only if visitors were required to sign or check in, and did not include the requirement to wear badges. [3] May include locker checks and/or random dog sniffs for items such as drugs and weapons. [4] For example, a system for reporting threats through online submission, telephone hotline, or written submission via drop box. [5] Prior to the 2017-2018 survey, the survey asked about prohibiting the use of cell phones and text messaging devices during school hours, and did not refer to "non-academic" use of such devices, nor the use of smartphones. [6] The coronavirus pandemic affected 2020 data collection activities. Use caution when comparing 2020 estimates with those from earlier years.

Source: U.S. National Center for Education Statistics, *Digest of Education Statistics,* "Latest version of all Digest tables," <nces.ed.gov/programs/digest>, accessed May 2022; and *Indicators of School Crime and Safety,* annual. See also <nces.ed.gov/surveys/ssocs>.

Table 337. Students Who Reported Being Bullied at School or Cyber-Bullied by Student Characteristics: 2019

[In percent. For school year ending in 2019. For students aged 12 through 18. "At school" includes the school building, on school property, on a school bus, or going to and from school. Based on the Bureau of Justice Statistics' School Crime Supplement to the National Crime Victimization Survey. The 2019 survey was conducted with a split sample design. Estimates in this table are based on the 60 percent of the 2019 sample that received a questionnaire consistent with prior years. See source for more information]

Characteristic	Bullied at school						
	Total bullying at school [1]	Made fun of, called names, or insulted	Subject of rumors	Threatened with harm	Purposefully excluded	Pushed, shoved, tripped, or spit on	Online or by text
Total.................	**22.2**	**13.8**	**15.3**	**4.5**	**6.0**	**5.2**	**15.8**
Sex:							
Male..................	19.1	11.8	11.9	4.7	3.7	6.2	7.6
Female...............	25.5	15.9	18.9	4.3	8.5	4.1	22.4
Race/ethnicity: [2]							
White..................	24.6	16.6	16.6	5.0	7.1	5.0	17.2
Black..................	22.2	10.7	16.1	4.2	[3] 4.1	7.2	[3] 9.6
Hispanic..............	18.0	10.5	12.8	4.2	5.4	3.9	16.6
Asian..................	13.5	9.3	9.4	(S)	(S)	[3] 3.1	(S)
Two or more races.....	37.1	19.0	23.2	[3] 6.6	[3] 10.0	11.4	[3] 12.1
Grade:							
6th.....................	28.1	18.4	15.4	3.9	7.0	8.2	(S)
7th.....................	28.0	20.3	20.3	5.9	9.0	6.9	10.0
8th.....................	26.7	17.4	18.9	6.5	7.6	8.3	22.7
9th.....................	18.9	13.2	12.7	4.8	3.5	5.5	[3] 9.7
10th....................	18.7	10.7	11.0	3.9	4.5	3.3	20.4
11th....................	21.7	9.5	17.0	4.2	5.5	[3] 2.1	21.6
12th....................	15.8	8.6	12.0	[3] 1.7	5.5	[3] 2.8	21.5

S Reporting standards not met. [1] In the total for students bullied at school, students who reported more than one type of bullying were counted only once. [2] Race categories exclude persons of Hispanic ethnicity. [3] Interpret data with caution.

Source: U.S. National Center for Education Statistics, *Digest of Education Statistics*, "Latest version of all Digest tables," <nces.ed.gov/programs/digest>, accessed July 2021; and *Indicators of School Crime and Safety*, annual. See also <nces.ed.gov/surveys/ssocs>.

Table 338. Cyberbullying Among Students in Grades 9 to 12 by Student Characteristics: 2011 to 2019

[In percent. Covers students in grades 9 to 12 who reported being electronically bullied during the previous 12 months. Data are based on the U.S. Centers for Disease Control and Prevention's Youth Risk Behavior Surveillance System. Electronic bullying, or cyberbullying, for 2011-2015 includes "being bullied through e-mail, chat rooms, instant messaging, websites, or texting," and for 2017 and 2019, "being bullied through texting, Instagram, Facebook, or other social media"]

Student characteristic	2011	2013	2015	2017	2019
Total............................	**16.2**	**14.8**	**15.5**	**14.9**	**15.7**
Sex:					
Male............................	10.8	8.5	9.7	9.9	10.9
Female..........................	22.1	21.0	21.7	19.7	20.4
Race/ethnicity: [1]					
White...........................	18.6	16.9	18.4	17.3	18.6
Black...........................	8.9	8.7	8.6	10.9	8.6
Asian...........................	14.4	12.9	13.9	10.0	12.1
Pacific Islander.................	19.6	15.7	[2] 11.8	15.0	[2] 19.0
American Indian/Alaska Native.......	16.2	18.0	18.7	13.2	[2] 21.3
Two or more races..............	21.0	18.9	20.4	16.0	19.2
Hispanic ethnicity..............	13.6	12.8	12.4	12.3	12.7
Sexual orientation:					
Heterosexual....................	(NA)	(NA)	14.2	13.3	14.1
Gay, lesbian, or bisexual...........	(NA)	(NA)	28.0	27.1	26.6
Not sure........................	(NA)	(NA)	22.5	22.0	19.4
Grade:					
9th.............................	15.5	16.1	16.5	16.7	16.5
10th............................	18.1	14.5	16.6	14.8	16.0
11th............................	16.0	14.9	14.7	14.2	14.4
12th............................	15.0	13.5	14.3	13.5	15.4

NA Not available. [1] Race categories exclude persons of Hispanic ethnicity. [2] Interpret data with caution. The coefficient of variation (CV) for this estimate is between 30 and 50 percent.

Source: U.S. National Center for Education Statistics, *Digest of Education Statistics*, "Latest version of all Digest tables," <nces.ed.gov/programs/digest>, accessed July 2021. See also *Indicators of School Crime and Safety: 2020*, <nces.ed.gov/surveys/ssocs>.

Table 339. Violent Deaths Occurring at Schools by Type; and Homicides and Suicides of Youth Aged 5 to 18, Total and School-Associated: 2000 to 2018

[For school year ending in year shown. A school-associated violent death is defined as a homicide, suicide, or legal intervention (involving a law enforcement officer) in which the fatal injury occurred on the campus of a functioning elementary or secondary school in the United States, including while the victim was on the way to or from regular sessions at school or while the victim was attending or traveling to or from an official school-sponsored event. Victims include students, staff members, and others who are not students. Data from school year 2000 onward are subject to change until interviews with school and law enforcement officials have been completed. The details learned during interviews can occasionally change the classification of a case. Based on data from U.S. Centers for Disease Control and Prevention, and Federal Bureau of Investigation and Bureau of Justice Statistics]

Year	School-associated violent deaths				Homicides of youth aged 5 to 18		Suicides of youth aged 5 to 18	
	Total[1]	Homicides	Suicides[2]	Legal inter-ventions	Total	At school	Total[2]	At school
2000	37	26	11	0	1,694	14	1,420	8
2001	34	26	7	1	1,636	14	1,451	6
2002	36	27	8	1	1,593	16	1,343	5
2003	36	25	11	0	1,658	18	1,264	10
2004	45	37	7	1	1,620	23	1,411	5
2005	52	40	10	2	1,720	22	1,484	8
2006	44	37	6	1	1,859	21	1,311	3
2007	63	48	13	2	1,906	32	1,243	9
2008	48	39	7	2	1,858	21	1,256	5
2009	44	29	15	0	1,720	18	1,425	7
2010	35	27	5	3	1,551	19	1,441	2
2011	32	26	6	0	1,436	11	1,559	3
2012	45	26	14	5	1,360	15	1,541	5
2013	53	41	11	1	1,310	31	1,608	6
2014	48	26	20	1	1,160	12	1,638	8
2015	47	28	17	2	1,273	20	1,882	9
2016	38	30	7	1	1,478	18	1,941	3
2017	42	28	13	1	1,587	18	2,186	6
2018	56	46	9	1	1,502	35	2,408	8

[1] Total includes unintentional firearm-related deaths and undetermined violent deaths, not shown separately. [2] Excludes self-inflicted deaths among children age 5 to 9. The number of self-inflicted deaths among children age 5 to 9 was generally less than 7 per year during the period covered by this table.

Source: U.S. National Center for Education Statistics, *Digest of Education Statistics*, "Latest version of all Digest tables," <nces.ed.gov/programs/digest>, accessed January 2022; and *Indicators of School Crime and Safety*, annual. See also <nces.ed.gov/surveys/ssocs>.

Table 340. School Shootings and Casualties by Type of Casualty and School Level: 2001 to 2021

[For school year ending in year shown. School shootings include all incidents in which a gun is brandished or fired or a bullet hits school property for any reason, regardless of the number of victims (including zero), time, day of the week, or reason (e.g., planned attack, accidental, domestic violence, gang-related). Deaths and injuries include both shooters and victims. Data are from the School Shooting Database Project of the Department of Defense, Naval Postgraduate School's Center for Homeland Defense and Security]

Year	Casualties			School shootings							
					Type of casualty			School level[1]			
	Total	Deaths	Injuries	Total	With deaths	With injuries only	With no casualties	Elem-entary schools	Middle or junior high schools	High schools[2]	Other[3]
2001	47	18	29	30	16	7	7	4	3	23	0
2002	18	5	13	17	5	8	4	2	1	14	0
2003	29	13	16	24	12	7	5	2	6	16	0
2004	45	16	29	34	12	16	6	5	3	26	0
2005	63	22	41	44	12	27	5	9	1	32	2
2006	55	13	42	51	12	30	9	5	6	39	0
2007	91	28	63	64	21	35	8	9	12	42	1
2008	23	10	13	16	8	6	2	2	2	11	1
2009	61	19	42	52	19	22	11	11	6	31	4
2010	15	5	10	15	5	6	4	1	2	12	0
2011	32	8	24	18	7	10	1	4	2	12	0
2012	21	9	12	16	6	8	2	3	3	9	1
2013	55	42	13	26	14	8	4	7	5	13	1
2014	55	19	36	46	15	22	9	7	3	32	4
2015	65	20	45	43	15	20	8	13	4	24	2
2016	45	9	36	38	8	19	11	7	4	25	2
2017	60	13	47	47	12	26	9	8	8	31	0
2018	185	52	133	89	22	37	30	14	8	64	3
2019	116	34	82	115	33	45	37	35	14	60	4
2020[4]	124	32	92	114	27	50	37	32	11	69	2
2021[4]	118	46	72	146	43	50	53	59	21	57	8

[1] Schools that had multiple shootings in a single year are counted only once in that year's total. [2] Includes other school types which end in grade 12. [3] Includes schools for which school-level information was unknown or unspecified as well as those whose school level was "other." [4] Due to school closures caused by the COVID-19 pandemic, caution should be used when comparing 2020 and 2021 data with data from earlier years.

Source: U.S. National Center for Education Statistics, *Digest of Education Statistics*, "Latest release of all Digest tables," <nces.ed.gov/programs/digest>, accessed February 2022.

Section 5
Law Enforcement, Courts, and Prisons

This section presents data on crimes committed, victims of crimes, arrests, and data related to criminal violations and the criminal justice system. The major sources of these data are the Bureau of Justice Statistics (BJS), the Federal Bureau of Investigation (FBI), and the Administrative Office of the U.S. Courts. BJS issues many reports—see our Guide to Sources for a complete listing. The Federal Bureau of Investigation's major annual reports are *Crime in the United States, Law Enforcement Officers Killed and Assaulted*, and *Hate Crimes*, which present data on reported crimes as gathered from state and local law enforcement agencies.

Legal jurisdiction and law enforcement—Law enforcement is, for the most part, a function of state and local officers and agencies. The U.S. Constitution reserves general police powers to the states. By act of Congress, federal offenses include only offenses against the U.S. government and against or by its employees while engaged in their official duties, and offenses which involve the crossing of state lines or an interference with interstate commerce. Excluding the military, there are 52 separate criminal law jurisdictions in the United States: one in each of the 50 states, one in the District of Columbia, and the federal jurisdiction. Each of these has its own criminal law and procedure and its own law enforcement agencies. While the systems of law enforcement are quite similar among the states, there are often substantial differences in the penalties for like offenses.

Law enforcement can be divided into three parts: Investigation of crimes and arrests of persons suspected of committing them; prosecution of those charged with crime; and the punishment or treatment of persons convicted of crime.

Crime—The U.S. Department of Justice administers two statistical programs to measure the magnitude, nature, and impact of crime in the nation: the Uniform Crime Reporting (UCR) Program and the National Crime Victimization Survey (NCVS). Each of these programs produces valuable information about aspects of the nation's crime problem. Because the UCR and NCVS programs are conducted for different purposes, use different methods, and focus on somewhat different aspects of crime, the information they produce together provides a more comprehensive panorama of the nation's crime problem than either could produce alone.

Uniform Crime Reports (UCR)—The FBI's UCR Program, which began in 1929, collects information on the following crimes reported to law enforcement authorities: Part 1 offenses, for which detailed data is reported—murder and nonnegligent manslaughter, rape, robbery, aggravated assault, burglary, larceny-theft, motor vehicle theft, and arson; and Part 2 offenses, 20 additional crime categories for which law enforcement agencies report only arrest data. The latest UCR releases are available on the FBI's Crime Data Explorer. UCR definitions of criminal offenses (including those listed) can be found at <crime-data-explorer.fr.cloud.gov/>.

Beginning in 2013, the UCR program implemented a revised definition of rape. Not all state and local agencies have been able to effect the change in their records management systems and some agencies currently can report the offense based on only the legacy definition. Therefore, rape data collected under both definitions are used in the *Crime in the United States* report. In 2016, the FBI Director approved the recommendation to discontinue the reporting of rape data using the UCR legacy definition beginning in 2017. However, to maintain the availability of 20-year trend data, national estimates for rape under the legacy definition are provided along with estimates under the revised definition for 2017.

The UCR Program compiles data from monthly law enforcement reports or individual crime incident records transmitted directly to the FBI or to centralized state agencies that then report to the FBI. The Program thoroughly examines each report it receives for reasonableness, accuracy, and deviations that may indicate errors. Large variations in crime levels may indicate modified records procedures, incomplete reporting, or changes in a jurisdiction's boundaries. To identify any unusual fluctuations in an agency's crime counts, the Program compares monthly reports to previous submissions of the agency and with those for similar agencies.

The UCR Program presents crime counts for the nation as a whole, as well as for regions, states, counties, cities, towns, tribal law enforcement, and colleges and universities. This permits studies among neighboring jurisdictions and among those with similar populations and other common characteristics.

The UCR Program annually publishes its findings online in a preliminary release in the spring of the following calendar year, followed by a detailed report, *Crime in the United States*, issued in the fall. In addition to crime counts and trends, this report includes data on crimes cleared, persons arrested (age, sex, and race), law enforcement personnel (including the number of sworn officers killed or assaulted), and the characteristics of homicides (including age, sex, and race of victims and offenders; victim-offender relationships; weapons used; and circumstances surrounding the homicides). Other periodic reports are also available from the UCR Program.

National Crime Victimization Survey (NCVS)—A second perspective on crime is provided by this survey of the Bureau of Justice Statistics (BJS). The NCVS is an annual data collection (interviews of persons aged 12 or older), conducted by the U.S. Census Bureau for the BJS. As an ongoing survey of households, the NCVS measures crimes of violence and property both reported and not reported to police. It produces national rates and levels of personal and property victimization. No attempt is made to validate the information against police records or any other source.

The NCVS measures rape/sexual assault, robbery, assault, pocket-picking, purse snatching, burglary, and motor vehicle theft. Murder and kidnaping are not covered. The so-called victimless crimes, such as drunkenness, drug abuse, and prostitution, also are excluded, as are crimes for which it is difficult to identify knowledgeable respondents or to locate data records.

Crimes of which the victim may not be aware also cannot be measured effectively. Buying stolen property may fall into this category, as may some instances of embezzlement. Attempted crimes of many types probably are under-recorded for this reason. Events in which the victim has shown a willingness to participate in illegal activity also are excluded.

In any encounter involving a personal crime, more than one criminal act can be committed against an individual. For example, a rape may be associated with a robbery, or a household property offense, such as a burglary, can escalate into something more serious in the event of a personal confrontation. Each criminal incident has been counted only once, by the most serious act that took place during the incident, and ranked in accordance with the seriousness classification system used by the FBI. The order of seriousness for crimes against persons is as follows: rape, robbery, assault, and larceny. Personal crimes take precedence over household offenses.

A *victimization*, the basic measure of the occurrence of crime, is a specific criminal act as it affects a single victim. The number of victimizations is determined by the number of victims of such acts. Victimization counts serve as key elements in computing rates of victimization. For crimes against persons, the rates are based on the total number of individuals aged 12 and over or on a portion of that population sharing a particular characteristic or set of traits. As general indicators of the danger of having been victimized during the reference period, the rates are not sufficiently refined to represent true measures of risk for specific individuals or households.

An *incident* is a specific criminal act involving one or more victims; therefore the number of incidents of personal crimes is lower than that of victimizations.

Courts—Statistics on criminal offenses and the outcome of prosecutions are incomplete for the country as a whole, although data are available for many states individually.

State courts handle the majority of civil and criminal litigation in the country. Only when the U.S. Constitution and acts of Congress specifically confer jurisdiction upon the federal courts may civil or criminal litigation be heard and decided by them. Generally, the federal courts have jurisdiction over the following types of cases: suits or proceedings by or against the United States; civil actions between private parties arising under the Constitution, laws, or treaties of the United States; civil actions between private litigants who are citizens of different states; civil cases

involving admiralty, maritime, or private jurisdiction; and all matters in bankruptcy.

There are several types of courts with varying degrees of legal jurisdiction. These jurisdictions include original, appellate, general, and limited or special. A court of original jurisdiction is one having the authority initially to try a case and pass judgment on the law and the facts; a court of appellate jurisdiction is one with the legal authority to review cases and hear appeals; a court of general jurisdiction is a trial court of unlimited original jurisdiction in civil and/or criminal cases, also called a "major trial court"; a court of limited or special jurisdiction is a trial court with legal authority over only a particular class of cases, such as probate, juvenile, or traffic cases.

The 94 federal courts of original jurisdiction are known as the U.S. district courts. One or more of these courts is established in every state and one each in the District of Columbia, Puerto Rico, the Virgin Islands, the Northern Mariana Islands, and Guam. Appeals from the district courts are taken to intermediate appellate courts of which there are 13, known as U.S. courts of appeals and the United States Court of Appeals for the Federal Circuit. The Supreme Court of the United States is the final and highest appellate court in the federal system of courts.

Juvenile offenders—For statistical purposes, the FBI and most states classify as juvenile offenders persons under the age of 18 years who have committed a crime or crimes.

Delinquency cases are all cases of youths referred to a juvenile court for violation of a law or ordinance or for seriously "antisocial" conduct. Several types of facilities are available for those adjudicated delinquents, ranging from short-term physically unrestricted to long-term very restrictive supervision.

Prisoners and jail inmates—BJS started to collect annual data in 1979 on prisoners in federal and state prisons and reformatories. Adults convicted of criminal activity may be given a prison or jail sentence. A *prison* is a confinement facility having custodial authority over adults sentenced to confinement of more than 1 year. A *jail* is a facility, usually operated by a local law enforcement agency, holding persons detained pending adjudication and/or persons committed after adjudication for 1 year or less.

Data on inmates in local jails were collected by the BJS for the first time in 1970. Jail censuses are taken periodically. For details, see <bjs.ojp.gov/data-collection/census-jails-coj>.

Statistical reliability—For discussion of statistical collection, estimation and sampling procedures, and measures of statistical reliability pertaining to the National Crime Victimization Survey and Uniform Crime Reporting Program, see Appendix III.

Table 341. Crimes and Crime Rates by Type of Offense: 1980 to 2020

[13,408 represents 13,408,000. Data include offenses reported to law enforcement, and offense estimations for nonreporting and partially reporting agencies within each state. Rates are based on Census Bureau estimated resident population as of July 1, except 1980, 1990, 2000, and 2010, which are enumerated as of April 1. See source for details]

Item and year	All crimes	Violent crime						Property crimes			
		Total	Murder[1]	Rape[2]	Rape legacy def.[2]	Robbery	Aggravated assault	Total	Burglary	Larceny/ theft	Motor vehicle theft
NUMBER OF OFFENSES (1,000)											
1980	13,408	1,345	23.0	(NA)	83.0	566	673	12,064	3,795	7,137	1,132
1990	14,476	1,820	23.4	(NA)	102.6	639	1,055	12,655	3,074	7,946	1,636
2000	11,608	1,425	15.6	(NA)	90.2	408	912	10,183	2,051	6,972	1,160
2003	11,827	1,384	16.5	(NA)	93.9	414	859	10,443	2,155	7,027	1,261
2004	11,679	1,360	16.1	(NA)	95.1	401	847	10,319	2,144	6,937	1,238
2005	11,565	1,391	16.7	(NA)	94.3	417	862	10,175	2,155	6,783	1,236
2006	11,455	1,435	17.3	(NA)	94.5	449	874	10,020	2,195	6,626	1,198
2007	11,305	1,423	17.1	(NA)	92.2	447	866	9,882	2,190	6,592	1,100
2008	11,169	1,394	16.5	(NA)	90.8	444	844	9,774	2,229	6,586	959
2009	10,663	1,326	15.4	(NA)	89.2	409	813	9,337	2,203	6,338	796
2010	10,364	1,251	14.7	(NA)	85.6	369	782	9,113	2,168	6,205	740
2011	10,259	1,206	14.7	(NA)	84.2	355	752	9,053	2,185	6,151	717
2012	10,219	1,217	14.9	(NA)	85.1	355	762	9,002	2,110	6,169	723
2013	9,820	1,168	14.3	113.7	82.1	345	727	8,652	1,932	6,019	700
2014	9,362	1,153	14.2	118.0	84.9	323	731	8,209	1,713	5,809	687
2015	9,223	1,199	15.9	126.1	91.3	328	764	8,024	1,588	5,723	713
2016	9,179	1,250	17.4	132.4	97.0	333	803	7,929	1,516	5,645	767
2017	8,931	1,248	17.3	135.7	99.7	321	810	7,683	1,397	5,513	773
2018	8,429	1,210	16.4	143.8	101.4	281	811	7,219	1,235	5,232	752
2019	8,205	1,210	16.7	143.2	103.1	268	822	6,995	1,118	5,152	725
2020	7,730	1,278	21.6	126.4	91.0	244	922	6,452	1,035	4,606	810
RATE PER 100,000 POPULATION											
1980	5,950	597	10.2	(NA)	36.8	251	299	5,353	1,684	3,167	502
1990	5,803	730	9.4	(NA)	41.1	256	423	5,073	1,232	3,185	656
2000	4,125	507	5.5	(NA)	32.0	145	324	3,618	729	2,477	412
2003	4,067	476	5.7	(NA)	32.3	143	295	3,591	741	2,417	434
2004	3,977	463	5.5	(NA)	32.4	137	289	3,514	730	2,362	422
2005	3,901	469	5.6	(NA)	31.8	141	291	3,432	727	2,288	417
2006	3,826	479	5.8	(NA)	31.6	150	292	3,347	733	2,213	400
2007	3,748	472	5.7	(NA)	30.6	148	287	3,276	726	2,185	365
2008	3,673	459	5.4	(NA)	29.8	146	278	3,215	733	2,166	315
2009	3,473	432	5.0	(NA)	29.1	133	265	3,041	718	2,065	259
2010	3,350	405	4.8	(NA)	27.7	119	253	2,946	701	2,006	239
2011	3,292	387	4.7	(NA)	27.0	114	242	2,905	701	1,974	230
2012	3,256	388	4.7	(NA)	27.1	113	243	2,868	672	1,965	230
2013	3,103	369	4.5	35.9	25.9	109	230	2,734	611	1,902	221
2014	2,936	362	4.4	37.0	26.6	101	229	2,574	537	1,822	215
2015	2,874	374	4.9	39.3	28.4	102	238	2,501	495	1,784	222
2016	2,838	387	5.4	40.9	30.0	103	248	2,452	469	1,745	237
2017	2,747	384	5.3	41.7	30.7	99	249	2,363	430	1,696	238
2018	2,580	370	5.0	44.0	31.0	86	248	2,210	378	1,602	230
2019	2,499	369	5.1	43.6	31.4	82	250	2,131	341	1,569	221
2020	2,346	388	6.5	38.4	27.6	74	280	1,958	314	1,398	246

NA Not available. [1] Includes nonnegligent manslaughter. [2] Beginning 2013, the FBI introduced a revised definition of rape. For more information, see <ucr.fbi.gov/recent-program-updates/new-rape-definition-frequently-asked-questions>.

Source: U.S. Department of Justice, Federal Bureau of Investigation, "Crime Data Explorer," <crime-data-explorer.app.cloud.gov>, accessed January 2022.

Table 342. Crimes and Crime Rates by Offense Type and Geographic Area: 2020

[In thousands (894.1 represents 894,100), except rate. Rate per 100,000 population. For area definitions, see <ucr.fbi.gov/crime-in-the-u.s/2019/crime-in-the-u.s.-2019/topic-pages/area-definitions>. See headnote, Table 341]

Type of crime	Cities		Metropolitan counties[1]		Nonmetropolitan counties[1]		Suburban areas[2]	
	Total	Rate	Total	Rate	Total	Rate	Total	Rate
Violent crime	894.1	469.4	166.4	265.0	46.2	227.5	271.8	250.4
Murder[3]	14.1	7.4	2.5	4.0	1.0	4.8	3.9	3.6
Rape[4]	80.2	42.1	19.8	31.6	7.9	38.9	33.3	30.7
Robbery	185.4	97.4	20.2	32.2	2.1	10.2	37.6	34.7
Aggravated assault	614.5	322.7	123.8	197.2	35.3	173.7	196.9	181.5
Property crime	4,293.5	2,254.0	809.4	1,289.1	201.5	991.7	1,616.7	1,489.8
Burglary	658.7	347.1	144.8	231.6	55.1	272.2	251.0	231.3
Larceny-theft	3,060.0	1,686.7	559.5	906.9	121.0	610.5	1,181.9	1,089.1
Motor vehicle theft	574.7	301.8	105.1	167.4	25.4	125.2	183.8	169.4

[1] Includes state police agencies that report aggregately for the entire state. [2] Suburban areas include law enforcement agencies in cities with less than 50,000 inhabitants and county law enforcement agencies within a Metropolitan Statistical Area. Excludes all metropolitan agencies associated with a principal city. Agencies associated with suburban areas also appear in other groups within this table. [3] Includes nonnegligent manslaughter. [4] Estimated using the revised FBI Uniform Crime Reporting (UCR) definition of rape. For more information, see <ucr.fbi.gov/recent-program-updates/new-rape-definition-frequently-asked-questions>.

Source: U.S. Department of Justice, Federal Bureau of Investigation, "Crime Data Explorer," <crime-data-explorer.app.cloud.gov>, accessed January 2022.

Table 343. Crime Rates by State, 2019 and 2020, and by Type, 2020

[For year ending December 31. Rates per 100,000 population. Offenses reported to law enforcement. Based on Census Bureau estimated resident population as of July 1]

State	Violent crime						Property crime				
	2019, total	2020					2019, total	2020			
		Total	Murder	Rape [1]	Robbery	Aggravated assault		Total	Burglary	Larceny/ theft	Motor vehicle theft
United States............	380.8	398.5	6.5	38.4	73.9	279.7	2,130.6	1,958.2	314.2	1,398.0	246.0
Alabama [3].................	504.7	453.6	9.6	32.7	54.2	357.1	2,622.8	2,136.8	399.5	1,515.3	222.0
Alaska....................	865.0	837.8	6.7	154.8	97.4	578.9	2,902.5	2,260.5	379.5	1,611.7	269.3
Arizona..................	447.1	484.8	6.9	44.0	83.7	350.2	2,436.0	2,227.7	330.0	1,656.0	241.7
Arkansas.................	580.8	671.9	10.6	73.5	52.0	535.8	2,847.7	2,613.4	523.1	1,828.5	261.8
California................	442.1	442.0	5.6	34.2	113.6	288.7	2,335.8	2,138.9	369.7	1,341.7	427.6
Colorado.................	384.6	423.1	5.1	62.9	68.3	286.9	2,614.6	2,833.8	400.3	1,909.3	524.3
Connecticut..............	184.6	181.6	3.9	16.7	57.2	103.8	1,432.3	1,565.1	187.1	1,141.2	236.8
Delaware.................	422.7	431.9	7.4	26.4	70.9	327.1	2,245.6	1,961.4	254.2	1,538.5	168.7
District of Columbia [2].....	1,045.2	999.8	28.2	43.6	332.9	595.1	4,351.4	3,493.0	275.5	2,740.7	476.8
Florida...................	378.2	383.6	5.9	35.4	62.2	280.1	2,144.8	1,769.4	240.6	1,352.7	176.1
Georgia..................	326.2	400.1	8.8	31.9	65.5	293.8	2,774.0	2,007.4	290.7	1,478.5	238.2
Hawaii...................	264.5	254.2	2.9	40.4	61.6	149.2	2,869.2	2,411.4	329.1	1,702.5	379.8
Idaho....................	232.6	242.6	2.2	45.5	9.5	185.3	1,243.3	1,111.9	204.2	810.9	96.7
Illinois..................	415.3	425.9	9.1	40.4	97.4	278.9	1,855.1	1,559.4	246.4	1,143.5	169.5
Indiana..................	371.5	357.7	7.5	34.8	62.4	253.0	1,947.7	1,783.2	280.4	1,274.3	228.5
Iowa [3]..................	287.6	303.5	3.5	40.7	29.8	229.4	1,849.8	1,698.2	371.1	1,130.1	197.1
Kansas...................	405.5	425.0	3.4	43.3	31.8	346.4	2,276.5	2,199.1	331.4	1,619.6	248.1
Kentucky.................	220.7	259.1	7.2	30.6	52.9	168.3	1,909.2	1,779.5	344.1	1,178.6	256.8
Louisiana................	559.7	639.4	15.8	46.0	80.7	497.0	3,186.3	2,884.4	510.1	2,107.3	266.9
Maine....................	116.1	108.6	1.6	36.0	12.6	58.4	1,247.7	1,156.2	148.8	943.5	63.8
Maryland [3].............	454.4	399.9	9.1	28.6	118.5	243.7	1,950.3	1,609.8	252.0	1,184.9	172.9
Massachusetts............	328.7	308.8	2.3	26.9	43.7	235.9	1,180.6	1,053.2	149.7	804.3	99.2
Michigan.................	438.6	478.0	7.6	60.9	44.5	365.1	1,585.6	1,360.9	233.1	943.3	184.5
Minnesota................	237.5	277.5	3.4	39.1	68.5	166.5	2,091.7	2,124.9	307.0	1,567.8	250.0
Mississippi [4]............	261.2	291.2	10.6	38.7	47.8	194.0	2,341.2	2,101.6	488.3	1,408.3	205.0
Missouri.................	499.6	542.7	11.8	43.3	74.4	413.3	2,658.1	2,531.0	378.8	1,759.1	393.2
Montana.................	417.9	469.8	5.0	55.3	25.8	383.7	2,236.1	2,120.8	270.1	1,603.0	247.6
Nebraska................	304.6	334.1	3.6	60.0	41.2	229.3	2,046.7	1,909.2	229.9	1,418.7	260.5
Nevada..................	496.1	460.3	5.7	59.0	88.7	306.8	2,330.4	1,926.6	368.8	1,221.4	336.4
New Hampshire...........	158.1	146.4	0.9	39.7	20.5	85.3	1,216.4	1,098.9	103.3	919.1	76.4
New Jersey...............	206.7	195.4	3.7	14.4	49.4	127.9	1,334.3	1,158.2	146.2	896.3	115.7
New Mexico..............	824.0	778.3	7.8	55.5	99.0	615.9	3,178.8	2,841.9	648.8	1,765.5	427.6
New York................	361.0	363.8	4.2	28.3	90.6	240.7	1,386.1	1,410.7	165.5	1,143.6	101.7
North Carolina [4].........	378.7	419.3	8.0	27.6	69.2	314.5	2,391.4	2,226.5	471.2	1,561.7	193.6
North Dakota.............	301.4	329.0	4.2	51.7	19.7	253.4	1,999.4	2,124.1	417.6	1,435.5	271.0
Ohio [4]..................	296.0	308.8	7.0	43.2	66.9	191.6	2,056.5	1,850.5	318.8	1,359.8	171.7
Oklahoma................	436.3	458.6	7.4	52.8	59.1	339.3	2,865.8	2,705.6	613.3	1,714.3	378.0
Oregon [4]...............	293.7	291.9	2.9	36.9	51.4	200.6	2,788.5	2,659.0	339.2	1,928.8	391.0
Pennsylvania [3]..........	306.0	389.5	7.9	33.1	83.9	264.6	1,403.8	1,644.1	248.6	1,274.5	121.0
Rhode Island.............	222.7	230.8	3.0	38.5	31.8	157.5	1,541.5	1,245.5	166.8	935.9	142.7
South Carolina............	510.1	530.7	10.5	40.0	59.8	420.3	2,946.5	2,721.1	448.0	1,991.0	282.1
South Dakota.............	397.1	501.4	4.5	67.1	30.7	399.1	1,768.2	1,956.7	340.1	1,357.3	259.3
Tennessee................	598.9	672.7	9.6	38.9	81.0	543.2	2,661.7	2,492.8	384.5	1,802.0	306.4
Texas....................	421.8	446.5	6.6	46.0	91.4	302.5	2,405.6	2,245.0	370.7	1,587.3	287.0
Utah.....................	236.9	260.7	3.1	55.7	41.9	159.9	2,168.6	2,464.4	290.6	1,857.3	316.6
Vermont..................	207.2	173.4	2.2	34.2	10.3	126.7	1,437.1	1,217.0	154.2	1,020.5	42.4
Virginia..................	209.4	208.7	6.1	26.5	34.3	141.7	1,647.2	1,456.4	133.5	1,196.6	126.3
Washington..............	303.3	293.7	3.9	34.8	67.4	187.6	2,725.7	2,732.4	522.1	1,854.2	356.1
West Virginia.............	318.9	355.9	6.6	46.6	20.7	282.1	1,522.2	1,399.4	273.3	998.9	127.2
Wisconsin................	297.1	323.4	5.3	34.6	52.8	230.6	1,473.0	1,485.7	218.5	1,106.1	161.0
Wyoming.................	215.0	234.2	3.1	57.2	11.3	162.6	1,568.1	1,610.6	210.4	1,234.7	165.5
Puerto Rico...............	202.9	164.5	16.7	4.7	37.3	105.8	702.7	419.1	93.4	263.1	62.6

[1] Beginning in 2013, the FBI has revised the definition of rape as used in Uniform Crime Reporting (UCR) Program. For more information, see <ucr.fbi.gov/recent-program-updates/new-rape-definition-frequently-asked-questions>. [2] Includes offenses reported by the Metro Transit Police and the District of Columbia Fire and Emergency Medical Services: Arson Investigation Unit. [3] Limited data for 2020 were available. [4] Submitted rape data according to the legacy UCR definition of rape.

Source: U.S. Department of Justice, Federal Bureau of Investigation, "Crime Data Explorer," <crime-data-explorer.app.cloud.gov>, accessed January 2022.

Table 344. Crime Rates by Type—Selected Large Cities: 2020

[For year ending December 31. Rates per 100,000 population. Offenses reported to law enforcement]

Cities ranked by population size, 2020	Violent crime					Property crime			
	Total	Murder	Rape [1]	Robbery	Aggra-vated assault	Total	Burglary	Larceny/ theft	Motor vehicle theft
New York, NY..............	577.8	5.6	27.1	158.8	386.2	1,558.5	167.6	1,279.4	111.5
Los Angeles, CA................	721.9	8.8	49.6	200.3	463.3	2,148.0	344.3	1,274.6	529.2
Chicago, IL.....................	986.9	28.6	50.0	292.1	616.2	(NA)	320.9	(NA)	373.2
Houston, TX.....................	1,256.3	17.1	48.5	373.3	817.5	4,178.9	672.9	2,875.9	630.0
Phoenix, AZ.....................	798.5	10.9	62.5	191.8	533.3	2,989.5	433.4	2,121.4	434.7
Las Vegas, NV [2]..............	527.7	5.7	63.1	100.8	358.1	2,210.6	416.8	1,390.7	403.0
San Antonio, TX [2]............	735.4	8.3	75.5	137.5	514.2	3,626.8	503.4	2,679.8	443.7
San Diego, CA..................	368.9	3.9	33.7	84.0	247.3	1,691.8	231.2	1,116.0	344.5
Dallas, TX......................	844.7	17.3	41.8	241.5	544.2	3,446.3	727.6	1,955.7	763.1
San Jose, CA...................	425.0	3.9	55.0	115.1	251.0	2,316.3	392.9	1,237.2	686.2
Austin, TX......................	467.0	4.4	47.8	110.1	304.7	3,631.2	477.3	2,747.3	406.6
Charlotte-Mecklenburg, NC.....	836.3	12.4	25.6	184.0	614.4	3,240.2	449.9	2,478.9	311.4
Fort Worth, TX.................	541.0	11.8	48.0	93.3	388.0	2,733.2	366.9	1,988.9	377.4
Jacksonville, FL...............	697.9	15.2	49.5	100.8	532.3	2,871.5	419.3	2,129.5	322.7
Columbus, OH..................	555.6	19.1	89.5	197.1	250.0	3,130.4	609.1	2,180.6	340.7
Indianapolis, IN [2]............	870.7	24.3	64.3	243.2	538.9	3,569.9	580.6	2,376.9	612.5
San Francisco, CA.............	544.1	5.5	22.5	270.9	245.3	4,394.4	845.4	2,872.2	676.8
Seattle, WA....................	626.3	6.7	39.0	190.7	389.9	4,872.6	1,351.5	2,884.6	636.5
Denver, CO.....................	857.9	13.2	90.8	165.1	588.9	4,648.7	708.0	2,800.8	1,139.9
Washington, DC................	957.9	27.8	43.1	309.8	577.3	3,431.3	275.4	2,683.2	472.8
Boston, MA [2]..................	624.4	8.3	26.4	131.8	457.9	1,866.4	243.5	1,439.4	183.6
Nashville, TN [2]...............	1,155.7	16.4	56.0	253.2	830.1	4,073.0	544.3	3,086.9	441.9
El Paso, TX [2].................	316.2	4.1	38.1	42.2	231.9	1,241.4	123.6	1,057.2	60.6
Oklahoma City, OK [2]..........	726.0	9.5	84.2	123.1	509.2	3,895.5	881.3	2,444.3	569.9
Portland, OR...................	522.7	8.0	39.5	121.7	353.4	4,738.9	567.0	3,211.0	960.9
Detroit, MI.....................	2,178.5	49.7	102.5	280.2	1,746.2	3,210.7	661.1	1,703.9	845.6
Memphis, TN....................	2,352.0	44.4	63.1	327.4	1,917.1	5,560.8	895.8	3,982.6	682.4
Milwaukee, WI..................	1,596.8	32.4	73.2	326.8	1,164.5	2,728.6	578.5	1,388.2	761.8
Albuquerque, NM...............	1,343.6	14.2	78.5	256.0	994.9	5,012.1	902.9	3,225.8	883.4
Tucson, AZ.....................	698.2	11.1	84.1	177.7	425.3	3,620.9	381.0	2,898.7	341.2
Fresno, CA.....................	664.8	14.4	27.6	166.0	456.8	3,076.7	567.0	2,014.9	494.9
Mesa, AZ [2]....................	371.7	3.6	44.6	72.1	251.4	1,846.4	302.8	1,350.9	192.7
Sacramento, CA................	683.4	8.1	24.1	169.4	481.8	2,745.0	546.0	1,715.3	483.8
Kansas City, MO...............	1,585.9	35.3	76.5	257.3	1,216.8	4,119.5	615.2	2,595.1	909.2
Colorado Springs, CO..........	597.0	7.4	82.5	77.5	429.6	3,379.6	533.5	2,344.8	501.4
Raleigh, NC....................	392.1	4.4	34.2	97.0	256.5	2,020.7	270.0	1,468.3	282.4
Omaha, NE......................	631.3	7.7	73.1	96.6	453.9	3,174.5	316.7	2,227.2	630.7
Miami, FL......................	555.6	12.8	19.7	128.1	394.9	2,749.8	305.2	2,104.0	340.7
Long Beach, CA................	506.4	7.8	52.3	155.8	290.5	2,746.5	552.0	1,593.6	600.9
Virginia Beach, VA............	98.7	3.8	13.3	27.5	54.1	1,511.8	110.7	1,262.7	138.4
Oakland, CA....................	1,290.9	23.3	82.7	566.1	618.8	5,165.8	579.3	3,053.7	1,532.7
Minneapolis, MN................	1,154.9	18.2	83.0	409.6	644.2	4,558.1	899.8	2,747.1	911.3
Tampa, FL......................	520.2	10.1	24.8	79.8	405.6	1,365.2	227.1	980.2	157.9
Arlington, TX..................	531.9	5.7	60.6	89.6	376.0	2,550.5	300.7	1,935.9	313.9
Tulsa, OK......................	1,132.6	17.9	94.0	184.3	836.5	5,111.6	1,095.8	3,045.0	970.7
New Orleans, LA................	1,324.4	51.0	180.8	280.9	811.6	4,539.6	506.4	3,138.3	894.9
Bakersfield, CA...............	516.9	11.3	27.3	155.6	322.7	4,022.8	807.2	2,229.4	986.2
Aurora, CO.....................	900.4	10.1	102.9	200.9	586.4	3,390.8	456.3	1,915.9	1,018.6
Cleveland, OH..................	1,656.7	42.2	103.7	420.2	1,090.7	4,070.7	973.8	2,321.2	775.7
Anaheim, CA....................	352.6	4.6	37.8	117.1	193.2	2,519.1	349.2	1,675.7	494.2
Riverside, CA..................	445.9	6.0	45.5	117.8	276.6	2,984.7	490.2	1,930.8	563.8
Santa Ana, CA.................	429.0	4.5	43.5	120.4	260.6	2,079.2	341.0	1,224.2	514.0
Corpus Christi, TX [2].........	842.4	10.3	70.5	145.3	616.3	3,266.1	620.6	2,377.8	267.7
Henderson, NV [2]..............	207.9	4.0	31.7	54.0	118.3	1,426.3	188.7	1,071.8	165.8
Lexington, KY..................	320.1	8.6	54.6	102.8	154.1	2,871.6	445.0	2,108.3	318.2
Stockton, CA...................	1,277.2	17.8	60.0	288.6	910.9	2,981.5	486.7	2,019.8	475.0
St. Paul, MN...................	748.7	9.7	74.9	233.3	430.8	3,802.7	692.6	2,197.1	913.0
Cincinnati, OH.................	892.9	30.2	70.6	246.1	546.1	3,683.3	762.0	2,427.1	494.2
Greensboro, NC.................	901.7	19.7	31.7	193.7	656.6	3,611.4	737.6	2,501.9	371.8
St. Louis, MO..................	2,016.3	88.1	78.4	416.2	1,433.5	5,830.3	855.2	3,895.8	1,079.3
Irvine, CA.....................	51.2	0.3	12.1	16.5	22.2	1,498.6	278.7	1,123.0	97.0
Orlando, FL....................	860.4	10.6	57.6	172.8	619.4	3,803.5	408.4	3,003.8	391.3
Plano, TX......................	155.4	1.0	34.7	39.2	80.5	1,645.2	211.8	1,282.0	151.3
Anchorage, AK..................	1,212.3	6.3	194.8	194.8	816.4	3,447.1	504.2	2,541.7	401.2
Durham, NC.....................	858.8	12.6	43.9	219.7	582.6	3,737.8	669.0	2,730.2	338.7
Newark, NJ.....................	528.6	19.8	41.1	130.0	337.7	1,618.1	189.6	823.8	604.8
Chula Vista, CA................	329.5	3.6	22.7	108.6	194.6	1,171.5	171.2	726.9	273.4
Fort Wayne, IN.................	412.8	14.3	35.6	90.0	272.9	2,246.7	240.6	1,818.8	187.3
Toledo, OH.....................	1,006.1	19.5	78.5	181.8	726.3	2,893.8	655.2	1,867.0	371.6
St. Petersburg, FL............	662.0	5.6	41.1	102.7	512.5	2,555.6	331.4	1,985.5	238.7
Laredo, TX.....................	323.5	4.5	33.9	58.8	226.4	1,444.7	235.8	1,127.6	81.4
Chandler, AZ...................	205.6	3.4	46.6	39.4	116.3	1,854.8	191.2	1,498.1	165.5
Jersey City, NJ................	443.3	6.5	22.4	129.1	285.3	1,496.6	189.9	1,141.0	165.6
Scottsdale, AZ.................	178.7	2.7	41.4	36.9	97.7	1,880.2	259.7	1,506.8	113.7
Madison, WI....................	320.5	3.8	28.2	62.8	225.7	2,778.8	497.5	2,034.7	246.6

NA Not available. [1] Beginning in 2013, the FBI has revised the definition of rape as used in Uniform Crime Reporting (UCR) Program. For more information, see <ucr.fbi.gov/recent-program-updates/new-rape-definition-frequently-asked-questions>. [2] Because of changes in the state/local agency's reporting practices, figures are not comparable to previous years' data.

Source: U.S. Department of Justice, Federal Bureau of Investigation, "Crime Data Explorer," <crime-data-explorer.app.cloud.gov>, accessed January 2022.

Table 345. Homicide Trends: 1990 to 2020

[Based on Federal Bureau of Investigation's Uniform Crime Reports Supplementary Homicide Reports. Homicide includes murder and nonnegligent manslaughter, which is the willful killing of one human being by another. Excludes deaths caused by negligence, suicide, or accident; justifiable homicides; and attempts to murder. Justifiable homicides based on the reports of law enforcement agencies are analyzed separately. Deaths from the terrorist attacks of September 11, 2001 are not included. Data based on criminal homicides handled by state and local law enforcement, and as determined solely by police investigation, and not by the determination of a court, medical examiner, coroner, jury, or other non-law enforcement body. Excludes homicides handled by Federal law enforcement]

| Year | Number of victims | | | | | | | Rate [1] | | | | | | |
	Total [2]	Male	Female	White	Black	American Indian/ Alaskan Native	Asian [3]	Total [2]	Male	Female	White	Black	American Indian/ Alaska Native	Asian [3]
1990...	23,438	18,303	5,115	11,278	11,487	150	250	9.4	15.0	4.0	5.4	37.5	7.3	3.3
1995...	21,606	16,549	5,021	10,374	10,442	160	421	8.1	12.7	3.7	4.7	30.9	6.6	4.4
1998...	16,974	12,756	4,140	8,391	7,933	141	252	6.2	9.4	2.9	3.7	22.3	5.2	2.3
1999...	15,522	11,704	3,800	7,777	7,139	160	298	5.6	8.6	2.7	3.4	19.7	5.6	2.6
2000...	15,586	11,818	3,733	7,560	7,425	119	280	5.5	8.6	2.6	3.3	20.3	4.0	2.4
2001...	16,037	12,232	3,775	7,884	7,522	105	319	5.6	8.7	2.6	3.4	20.2	3.4	2.6
2002...	16,229	12,429	3,770	7,796	7,770	130	308	5.6	8.8	2.6	3.3	20.6	4.1	2.4
2003...	16,528	12,792	3,707	7,944	7,883	117	351	5.7	9.0	2.5	3.4	20.6	3.5	2.6
2004...	16,148	12,553	3,555	7,939	7,570	134	282	5.5	8.7	2.4	3.4	19.5	3.9	2.0
2005...	16,740	13,149	3,565	8,045	8,016	131	312	5.7	9.1	2.4	3.4	20.4	3.7	2.2
2006...	17,309	13,605	3,661	8,063	8,548	123	343	5.8	9.3	2.4	3.4	21.4	3.3	2.3
2007...	17,128	13,411	3,678	8,017	8,450	104	302	5.7	9.1	2.4	3.3	20.9	2.7	1.9
2008...	16,465	12,844	3,573	7,953	7,860	124	250	5.4	8.6	2.3	3.3	19.1	3.1	1.6
2009...	15,399	11,846	3,535	7,450	7,374	119	290	5.0	7.9	2.3	3.0	17.7	2.9	1.7
2010...	14,722	11,371	3,328	6,851	7,322	117	260	4.8	7.5	2.1	2.8	17.4	2.7	1.5
2011...	14,661	11,354	3,281	6,786	7,277	111	284	4.7	7.4	2.1	2.7	17.1	2.6	1.6
2012...	14,856	11,518	3,318	6,834	7,481	101	285	4.7	7.5	2.1	2.8	17.3	2.3	1.6
2013...	14,319	11,116	3,178	6,519	7,268	104	257	4.5	7.1	2.0	2.6	16.6	2.3	1.4
2014...	14,164	10,939	3,188	6,421	7,196	122	249	4.4	7.0	2.0	2.6	16.2	2.7	1.3
2015...	15,883	12,499	3,354	6,938	8,293	183	253	4.9	7.9	2.1	2.8	18.5	4.0	1.3
2016...	17,413	13,648	3,719	7,628	9,084	169	298	5.4	8.6	2.3	3.0	20.0	3.6	1.5
2017...	17,294	13,545	3,695	7,574	8,922	214	302	5.3	8.4	2.2	3.0	19.4	4.6	1.4
2018...	16,374	12,618	3,722	7,117	8,516	184	289	5.0	7.8	2.2	2.8	18.4	3.9	1.3
2019...	16,669	13,061	3,573	6,912	8,971	199	304	5.1	8.1	2.1	2.7	19.3	4.2	1.4
2020...	21,570	17,185	4,341	8,526	12,035	293	328	6.5	10.6	2.6	3.3	25.5	6.0	1.5

[1] Rate is per 100,000 inhabitants. [2] Includes unknown sex, race, or ethnicity. [3] Includes Native Hawaiian and Pacific Islanders.

Source: U.S. Department of Justice, Office of Justice Programs, "Easy Access to the FBI's Supplementary Homicide Reports (EZASHR)," <ojjdp.gov/ojstatbb/ezashr/>; and U.S. Centers for Disease Control and Prevention, WONDER Online Database, "Multiple Cause of Death, 1999-2020," <wonder.cdc.gov/>; accessed May 2022.

Table 346. Homicide Victims by Race and Sex: 1990 to 2020

[Excludes deaths to nonresidents of United States. Effective with data for 1999, causes of death are classified by the International Classification of Diseases, Tenth Revision (ICD-10), replacing the Ninth Revision (ICD-9) used for 1979–1998 data. In ICD-9, the category Homicide also includes death as a result of legal intervention. ICD-10 differentiates between homicides due to assault and deaths due to legal intervention. Some caution should be used in comparing data. See text, Section 2]

| Year | Homicide victims | | | | | Homicide rate [2] | | | | |
| | Total [1] | White | | Black | | Total [1] | White | | Black | |
		Male	Female	Male	Female		Male	Female	Male	Female
1990...	24,932	9,147	3,006	9,981	2,163	10.0	9.0	2.8	69.2	13.5
1995...	22,895	8,336	3,028	8,847	1,936	8.7	7.8	2.7	56.3	11.1
1998...	18,272	6,707	2,534	6,873	1,547	6.8	6.1	2.2	42.1	8.6
1999...	16,889	6,162	2,466	6,214	1,434	6.1	5.5	2.1	36.1	7.6
2000...	16,765	5,925	2,414	6,482	1,385	6.0	5.2	2.1	37.2	7.2
2001...	20,308	8,254	3,074	6,780	1,446	7.1	7.2	2.6	38.2	7.4
2002...	17,638	6,282	2,403	6,896	1,391	6.1	5.4	2.0	38.4	7.0
2003...	17,732	6,337	2,372	7,083	1,309	6.1	5.5	2.0	38.9	6.5
2004...	17,357	6,302	2,341	6,839	1,296	5.9	5.4	2.0	37.0	6.4
2005...	18,124	6,457	2,313	7,412	1,257	6.1	5.5	1.9	39.6	6.1
2006...	18,573	6,514	2,346	7,677	1,355	6.2	5.5	1.9	40.4	6.5
2007...	18,361	6,541	2,373	7,584	1,286	6.1	5.5	1.9	39.3	6.1
2008...	17,826	6,556	2,337	7,148	1,187	5.9	5.5	1.9	36.5	5.5
2009...	16,799	5,983	2,340	6,715	1,159	5.5	4.9	1.9	33.8	5.3
2010...	16,259	5,648	2,215	6,704	1,114	5.3	4.7	1.8	33.4	5.1
2011...	16,238	5,569	2,199	6,739	1,119	5.2	4.6	1.8	33.0	5.0
2012...	16,688	5,639	2,197	7,129	1,112	5.3	4.6	1.8	34.5	4.9
2013...	16,121	5,393	2,130	6,937	1,122	5.1	4.4	1.7	33.1	4.9
2014...	15,872	5,304	2,093	6,823	1,080	5.0	4.3	1.7	32.1	4.7
2015...	17,793	5,798	2,209	8,021	1,152	5.5	4.6	1.7	37.3	4.9
2016...	19,362	6,325	2,343	8,650	1,345	6.0	5.1	1.8	39.8	5.7
2017...	19,510	6,274	2,496	8,776	1,297	6.0	5.0	1.9	39.8	5.4
2018...	18,830	6,050	2,374	8,254	1,449	5.8	4.8	1.8	37.2	6.0
2019...	19,141	5,921	2,286	8,808	1,379	5.8	4.7	1.8	39.4	5.7
2020...	24,576	7,400	2,568	11,935	1,845	7.5	5.9	2.0	52.7	7.5

[1] Includes other races not shown separately. [2] Rates per 100,000 resident population in specified group. Based on enumerated population figures as of April 1 for 1990, 2000, and 2010; estimated resident population as of July 1 for other years.

Source: U.S. National Center for Health Statistics, through 2014, National Vital Statistics Reports (NVSR), *Deaths: Final Data for 2014*, Vol. 65, No. 4, June 2016 and earlier reports; thereafter, CDC WONDER Online Database, "Multiple Cause of Death, 1999-2020," <wonder.cdc.gov/>, accessed May 2022.

Table 347. Criminal Victimizations and Victimization Rates: 2010 to 2020

[4,936 represents 4,936,000. A victimization refers to a single victim or household that experienced a criminal incident. Includes victimizations reported and not reported to the police. Criminal incidents or crimes are distinguished from victimizations in that one criminal incident may have multiple victims or victimizations. Based on the National Crime Victimization Survey (NCVS). See source for more information]

Type of crime	Number of victimizations (1,000)				Victimization rates [1]			
	2010	2015	2019	2020	2010	2015	2019	2020
Violent victimization [2].........	**4,936**	**5,007**	**5,813**	**4,558**	**19.3**	**18.6**	**21.0**	**16.4**
Not Injured..........	3,646	3,703	4,548	3,397	14.2	13.7	16.4	12.2
Injured:								
Treated........	591	622	526	365	2.3	2.3	1.9	1.3
Not treated..........	696	678	733	794	2.7	2.5	2.6	2.9
Serious violent victimization [3].........	1,695	1,827	2,013	1,569	6.6	6.8	7.3	5.6
Rape/sexual assault...........	269	432	459	320	1.0	1.6	1.7	1.2
Robbery........	569	579	534	437	2.2	2.1	1.9	1.6
Not Injured..........	370	370	398	265	1.4	1.4	1.4	1.0
Injured:								
Treated........	97	100	85	92	0.4	0.4	0.3	0.3
Not treated..........	101	108	51	81	0.4	0.4	0.2	0.3
Aggravated assault...........	858	817	1,019	812	3.4	3.0	3.7	2.9
Not Injured..........	538	526	706	556	2.1	1.9	2.5	2.0
Injured:								
Treated........	192	173	238	118	0.8	0.6	0.9	0.4
Not treated..........	127	116	73	136	0.5	0.4	0.3	0.5
Simple assault........	3,241	3,179	3,800	2,989	12.7	11.8	13.7	10.7
Not Injured..........	2,619	2,534	3,249	2,451	10.2	9.4	11.7	8.8
Injured:								
Treated........	198	271	169	120	0.8	1.0	0.6	0.4
Not treated..........	420	374	380	418	1.6	1.4	1.4	1.5
Personal theft/larceny [4]........	138	89	110	77	0.5	0.3	0.4	0.3
Property crimes...........	**15,412**	**14,611**	**12,818**	**12,085**	**125.4**	**110.7**	**101.4**	**94.5**
Motor vehicle theft...........	607	564	496	546	4.9	4.3	3.9	4.3
Theft [5]...........	11,628	11,142	10,144	9,798	94.6	84.4	80.2	76.6
Burglary........	2,338	2,021	1,485	1,211	19.0	15.3	11.7	9.5
Trespassing........	838	884	694	531	6.8	6.7	5.5	4.1

[1] Per 1,000 persons age 12 or older for violent victimization and personal theft/larceny; per 1,000 households for property crime. [2] Excludes homicide because the NCVS is based on interviews with victims and therefore cannot measure murder. [3] Includes rape, sexual assault, personal robbery, and aggravated assault, attempted and completed crimes. [4] Includes pocket picking, completed purse snatching, and attempted purse snatching. [5] The taking or attempted unlawful taking of property or cash without personal contact with the victim. Incidents involving theft of property from within a household are classified as theft if the offender has a legal right to be in the house (such as a maid, delivery person, or guest).

Source: U.S. Department of Justice, Bureau of Justice Statistics, "National Crime Victimization Survey (NCVS) Dashboard (N-DASH) Tool," <ncvs.bjs.ojp.gov/>, accessed February 2022.

Table 348. Victimization Rates by Type of Crime and Characteristics of the Victim: 2020

[Rate per 1,000 persons age 12 years or older. Based on the National Crime Victimization Survey. See text, this section and Appendix III]

Victim characteristics	Violent victimization						Personal theft [2]
	Total	Serious violent victim-ization [1]	Rape/ sexual assault	Robbery	Aggravated assault	Simple assault	
Total.......	**16.4**	**5.6**	**1.2**	**1.6**	**2.9**	**10.7**	**0.3**
Male.......	16.6	5.1	[4] 0.2	1.7	3.2	11.5	0.4
Female.......	16.2	6.2	2.1	1.4	2.7	10.0	[4] 0.1
12 to 14 years old.......	16.5	3.0	[4] 0.2	[4] 1.4	[4] 1.3	13.5	(Z)
15 to 17 years old.......	18.3	8.5	[4] 2.7	[4] 0.9	[4] 4.9	9.8	[4] 0.5
18 to 20 years old.......	30.5	13.6	4.8	5.8	3.0	16.9	[4] 2.5
21 to 24 years old.......	28.9	10.5	3.6	[4] 3.2	3.8	18.4	[4] 0.6
25 to 34 years old.......	21.4	9.0	1.4	2.4	5.2	12.5	[4] 0.2
35 to 49 years old.......	18.3	5.5	0.9	1.2	3.4	12.8	[4] 0.1
50 to 64 years old.......	14.6	4.0	0.5	1.1	2.4	10.6	[4] 0.1
65 years old and over.......	4.5	1.6	[4] 0.2	0.6	0.8	2.9	[4] 0.2
White, non-Hispanic.......	16.2	5.3	1.3	1.2	2.9	10.9	0.1
Black, non-Hispanic.......	17.5	7.5	1.1	2.6	3.8	10.0	[4] 1.0
Hispanic.......	15.9	5.5	1.0	1.4	3.1	10.4	[4] 0.3
Other [3].......	17.0	5.7	[4] 0.8	3.1	1.8	11.3	[4] 0.3
Household income:							
Less than $7,500.......	24.7	15.3	[4] 1.9	7.9	5.5	9.4	(Z)
$7,500 to $14,999.......	38.6	16.8	4.0	3.2	9.7	21.8	[4] 0.3
$15,000 to $24,999.......	21.9	6.7	[4] 1.4	2.0	3.3	15.2	(Z)
$25,000 to $34,999.......	17.9	6.4	0.7	[4] 1.7	4.0	11.5	[4] 0.5
$35,000 to $49,999.......	16.7	5.4	0.9	1.5	3.1	11.3	[4] 0.2
$50,000 to $74,999.......	16.0	5.5	1.3	1.6	2.6	10.5	[4] 0.1
$75,000 or more.......	12.3	3.6	0.9	0.9	1.8	8.7	[4] 0.4

Z Rounds to less than .05 victimizations per 1,000. [1] Includes rape, sexual assault, personal robbery, and aggravated assault, attempted and completed crimes. [2] Includes pocket picking and purse snatching. [3] Includes American Indians and Alaska Natives, Asians, Native Hawaiians, other Pacific Islanders, and persons of two or more races. [4] Based on 10 or fewer sample cases or the coefficient of variation is greater than 50%.

Source: U.S. Department of Justice, Bureau of Justice Statistics, "National Crime Victimization Survey (NCVS) Dashboard (N-DASH) Tool," <ncvs.bjs.ojp.gov>, accessed February 2022.

Table 349. Murder Victims—Circumstances and Weapons Used or Cause of Death: 2000 to 2020

[For year ending December 31. The FBI's Uniform Crime Reporting (UCR) Program defines murder and nonnegligent manslaughter as the willful (nonnegligent) killing of one human being by another. The classification of this offense is based solely on police investigation as opposed to the determination of a court, medical examiner, coroner, jury, or other judicial body. The UCR Program does not include the following situations in this offense classification: deaths caused by negligence, suicide, or accident; justifiable homicides; and attempts to murder, which are scored as aggravated assaults]

Characteristic	2000	2010	2015	2016	2017	2018	2019	2020
Murders, total [1]	**13,230**	**13,164**	**13,847**	**15,367**	**15,220**	**14,486**	**14,391**	**17,754**
CIRCUMSTANCES								
Felonies, total [1]	2,229	1,974	1,930	2,137	2,266	2,211	2,088	1,933
Rape [2]	58	41	14	21	20	14	11	19
Robbery	1,077	803	596	694	691	559	522	514
Burglary	76	85	87	81	86	92	86	100
Larceny-theft	23	21	18	13	22	25	31	46
Motor vehicle theft	25	35	34	58	33	62	40	51
Arson	81	35	19	32	75	66	77	91
Prostitution and commercialized vice	6	5	7	15	15	13	15	7
Other sex offenses	10	14	15	4	8	5	9	11
Narcotic drug laws	589	474	452	472	549	610	625	540
Gambling	12	7	5	11	10	6	3	6
Suspected felony type	60	68	103	97	149	211	141	63
Other than felony type [1]	6,871	6,485	5,831	6,405	6,694	6,438	6,275	7,704
Domestic violence	122	90	103	111	112	138	92	99
Child killed by babysitter	30	36	42	37	32	32	20	10
Brawl due to influence of alcohol	188	122	117	97	85	67	47	33
Brawl due to influence of narcotics	99	60	72	130	65	20	32	63
Argument over money or property	206	187	181	196	202	203	133	131
Other arguments	3,589	3,280	2,932	3,132	3,202	3,344	3,524	4,035
Gangland killings	65	181	181	478	374	315	282	486
Juvenile gang killings	653	675	576	411	380	309	294	415
Institutional killings	10	17	24	17	27	26	32	28
Unknown	4,070	4,637	5,983	6,728	6,111	5,626	5,887	8,054
TYPE OF WEAPON OR CAUSE OF DEATH [1]								
Total firearms	8,661	8,874	9,143	10,403	11,020	10,484	10,537	13,620
Handguns	6,778	6,115	6,194	6,783	7,054	6,699	6,543	8,017
Rifles	411	367	215	300	389	304	375	454
Shotguns	485	366	248	247	263	238	215	203
Other guns	53	93	152	172	178	164	51	112
Firearms, type not stated	934	1,933	2,334	2,901	3,136	3,079	3,353	4,834
Knives or cutting instruments	1,782	1,732	1,533	1,562	1,605	1,539	1,525	1,732
Blunt objects (club, hammer, etc.)	617	549	438	466	476	454	413	392
Personal weapons (hands, fists, feet, pushed, etc.)	927	769	651	670	717	715	639	657
Fire	134	78	63	78	93	78	85	106
Narcotics	20	45	70	119	114	101	108	113
Drowning	15	10	12	9	8	9	7	5
Strangulation	166	122	96	97	90	75	66	58
Asphyxiation	92	98	105	93	112	93	94	71

[1] Includes items not shown separately. [2] Rape figures in this table are an aggregate total of data submitted using both the revised and legacy UCR definitions.

Source: U.S. Department of Justice, Federal Bureau of Investigation, "Crime Data Explorer," <crime-data-explorer.app.cloud.gov>, accessed January 2022.

Table 350. Murder Victims by Age, Sex, and Race/Ethnicity: 2020

[See headnote, Table 349]

Age	Total [1]	Sex		Race			Ethnicity [2]	
		Male	Female	White	Black	Other [3]	Hispanic or Latino	Not Hispanic or Latino
Murders, total [1]	**17,754**	**14,146**	**3,573**	**7,029**	**9,913**	**497**	**2,847**	**11,347**
Percent of total [4]	100.0	79.7	20.1	39.6	55.8	2.8	17.6	70.1
Under 18 years old [1]	1,472	1,092	378	591	807	34	275	882
18 years old and over [1]	16,146	12,966	3,160	6,397	9,045	459	2,559	10,396
Infant (under 1 year old)	137	87	49	64	63	4	18	84
1 to 4 years old	239	132	107	104	118	11	39	144
5 to 8 years old	115	59	56	55	51	6	12	80
9 to 12 years old	115	85	30	59	48	6	18	73
13 to 16 years old	484	401	83	176	289	5	107	284
17 to 19 years old	1,474	1,271	200	497	937	14	294	876
20 to 24 years old	2,858	2,421	437	855	1,894	68	487	1,811
25 to 29 years old	2,836	2,395	439	844	1,896	69	424	1,873
30 to 34 years old	2,334	1,946	386	840	1,392	70	382	1,492
35 to 39 years old	1,894	1,523	370	805	992	67	337	1,231
40 to 44 years old	1,320	1,055	265	612	659	34	237	820
45 to 49 years old	980	736	241	470	456	33	169	610
50 to 54 years old	782	566	209	392	343	27	111	515
55 to 59 years old	724	528	196	388	300	26	79	480
60 to 64 years old	521	377	144	297	190	22	51	364
65 to 69 years old	337	224	113	202	116	11	33	224
70 to 74 years old	194	118	76	129	52	8	19	123
75 years old and over	274	134	137	199	56	12	17	194

[1] Includes unknown victim categories not shown separately. [2] Not all agencies provide ethnicity data; therefore, data will not sum to total. [3] Includes American Indian or Alaska Native, Asian, and Native Hawaiian or Pacific Islander. [4] Percentages rounded, may not add to 100.

Source: U.S. Department of Justice, Federal Bureau of Investigation, "Crime Data Explorer," <crime-data-explorer.app.cloud.gov>, accessed January 2022.

Table 351. Violent Crime Between Intimate Partners by Sex of Victims: 1993 to 2020

[Intimate partners are defined as current and former spouses, boyfriends, and girlfriends. Based on the National Crime Victimization Survey (NCVS); see text this section, and source]

Year	Female victims				Male victims			
	Total intimate partner violence	Rate per 1,000 [1]			Total intimate partner violence	Rate per 1,000 [1]		
		Overall intimate partner violence	Serious violence [3]	Simple assault [4]		Overall intimate partner violence	Serious violence [3]	Simple assault [4]
1993............	1,689,687	15.5	5.7	9.9	347,924	3.4	1.5	1.9
1994............	1,843,713	16.8	6.1	10.7	258,990	2.5	0.7	1.8
1995............	1,727,462	15.5	3.7	11.8	285,907	2.8	1.0	1.8
1996............	1,626,516	14.5	4.7	9.8	194,647	1.9	0.8	1.1
1997............	1,661,683	14.7	4.8	9.8	176,651	1.7	0.5	1.2
1998............	1,336,585	11.7	3.6	8.0	228,793	2.1	0.6	1.5
1999............	1,164,554	10.0	3.5	6.5	230,230	2.1	0.5	1.6
2000............	783,762	6.7	1.9	4.8	116,152	1.1	[5] 0.2	0.9
2001............	981,671	8.3	2.9	5.4	108,740	1.0	0.5	0.5
2002............	797,805	6.7	2.0	4.7	131,956	1.2	[5] 0.5	0.7
2003............	906,628	7.4	3.6	3.8	133,657	1.2	0.5	0.7
2004............	816,139	6.6	2.3	4.3	215,582	1.8	0.5	1.4
2005............	621,041	4.9	1.6	3.4	194,966	1.6	[5] 0.9	0.7
2006 [2]........	1,063,775	8.4	3.2	5.2	241,475	2.0	1.1	0.9
2007............	780,979	6.1	2.1	4.0	124,831	1.0	[5] 0.4	0.7
2008............	914,422	7.1	2.5	4.6	188,970	1.5	0.7	0.9
2009............	914,529	7.0	1.6	5.4	125,121	1.0	0.3	0.7
2010............	636,770	4.9	1.7	3.2	136,663	1.1	0.4	0.7
2011............	604,645	4.6	1.6	3.0	246,127	2.0	[5] 0.4	1.6
2012............	682,417	5.1	1.7	3.4	128,378	1.0	0.4	0.6
2013............	619,357	4.6	2.1	2.5	129,438	1.0	0.6	0.4
2014............	500,920	3.7	1.4	2.2	133,692	1.0	0.6	0.5
2015............	741,645	5.4	2.2	3.1	64,403	0.5	[5] 0.2	0.3
2016............	513,494	3.7	1.6	2.0	83,705	0.6	0.3	0.4
2017............	602,902	4.3	1.7	2.6	63,407	0.5	0.2	0.2
2018............	754,842	5.3	2.4	2.9	92,384	0.7	0.3	0.4
2019............	627,635	4.4	2.0	2.4	67,424	0.5	[5] 0.1	0.4
2020............	408,038	2.9	1.3	1.6	76,789	0.6	0.3	0.3

[1] Rates are per 1,000 persons age 12 and older. [2] Due to methodological changes, use caution when comparing 2006 National Crime Victimization Survey criminal victimization estimates to other years. See *Criminal Victimization, 2007*, NCJ 224390. [3] Rape or sexual assault, robbery, and aggravated assault. [4] Attack or attempted attack without a weapon that results in no injury, minor injury, or an undetermined injury requiring less than two days of hospitalization. [5] Interpret data with caution.

Source: U.S. Department of Justice, Bureau of Justice Statistics, "National Crime Victimization Survey (NCVS) Dashboard (N-DASH) Tool," <ncvs.bjs.ojp.gov/>, accessed February 2022.

Table 352. Stalking Victimization by Type of Stalking and Selected Victim Characteristics: 2019

[Data shown for persons age 16 or older who experienced stalking victimization in the past year. Stalking is repeated unwanted contacts or behaviors that either cause the victim to experience fear or substantial emotional distress or that would cause a reasonable person to experience fear or substantial emotional distress]

Characteristic	Number of victims	Percent of all persons	Characteristic	Number of victims	Percent of all persons
Total stalking victims [1].............	**3,419,710**	**1.3**	SEX		
Traditional stalking [2]...................	2,300,830	0.9	Male....................................	982,080	0.8
Traditional stalking only...............	681,240	0.3	Female.................................	2,437,630	1.8
Stalking with technology [3]...........	2,738,470	1.1	MARITAL STATUS		
Stalking with technology only.........	1,118,890	0.4	Never married........................	1,394,440	1.7
Both traditional and with technology...	1,619,580	0.6	Married................................	973,100	0.8
			Widowed..............................	126,680	0.8
AGE			Divorced..............................	719,900	2.5
			Separated............................	197,250	3.8
16 to 19 years old.....................	239,650	1.5	RACE AND ETHNICITY		
20 to 24 years old.....................	426,840	2.0	White [4]...............................	2,188,360	1.3
25 to 34 years old.....................	796,270	1.7	Black [4]...............................	342,430	1.1
35 to 49 years old.....................	942,610	1.5	Hispanic..............................	515,110	1.2
50 to 64 years old.....................	690,500	1.1	Asian/Native Hawaiian/Other Pacific Islander [4].....	179,840	1.1
65 years old and over.................	323,830	0.6	American Indian/Alaska Native [4].....................	48,940	3.3
			Two or more races..................	145,030	3.9

[1] Victims may experience more than one type of stalking. [2] Includes the following unwanted behaviors: following; sneaking into, waiting at, or showing up at a place; leaving or sending unwanted items; and harassing friends or family about the victim's whereabouts. [3] Includes the following unwanted behaviors: making unwanted phone calls, leaving voice messages, or sending text messages; spying using technology; tracking the victim's whereabouts with an electronic tracking device or application; posting or threatening to post unwanted information on the internet; sending emails or messages using the internet; and monitoring activities using social media. [4] Non-Hispanic.

Source: U.S. Department of Justice, Bureau of Justice Statistics, *Stalking Victimization, 2019*, NCJ 301735, February 2022. See also <bjs.ojp.gov/library>.

Table 353. Hate Crimes—Number of Incidents, Offenses, Victims, and Known Offenders by Bias Motivation: 2000 to 2020

[2,267 law enforcement agencies submitted data on hate crimes. 15,136 law enforcement agencies covering over 306 million people participated in the Hate Crime Statistics Program in 2020. Hate crime offenses cover incidents motivated by race, ethnicity/national origin, religion, sexual orientation, gender identity, and disability. See source and Appendix III]

Bias motivation	Incidents reported	Offenses	Victims [1]	Known offenders [2]
2000	8,213	9,619	10,117	7,690
2010	6,628	7,699	8,208	6,008
2020, total [3]	**7,759**	**10,532**	**10,861**	**6,431**
Race/ethnicity/ancestry, total	**4,939**	**6,319**	**6,512**	**4,137**
Anti-White	773	923	952	741
Anti-Black or African American	2,755	3,675	3,769	2,233
Anti-American Indian/Alaska native	79	86	89	64
Anti-Asian	274	324	336	235
Anti-Native Hawaiian or Other Pacific Islander	14	14	17	11
Anti-multiple races, group	191	245	256	106
Anti-Arab	69	83	85	51
Anti-Hispanic or Latino	507	650	679	517
Anti-Other race/ethnicity/ancestry	277	319	329	179
Religion, total [3]	**1,174**	**1,331**	**1,408**	**775**
Anti-Jewish	676	787	824	401
Anti-Catholic	68	72	75	46
Anti-Protestant	19	20	20	19
Anti-Islamic (Muslim)	104	119	124	121
Anti-Sikh	67	71	71	47
Sexual orientation, total	**1,051**	**2,115**	**2,158**	**997**
Anti-gay (male homosexual)	649	745	766	667
Anti-lesbian (female homosexual)	99	1,016	1,021	82
Anti-lesbian, gay, bisexual, or transgender	279	327	343	227
Anti-heterosexual	8	9	10	7
Anti-bisexual	16	18	18	14
Disability, total	**83**	**103**	**104**	**86**
Anti-physical	38	45	45	37
Anti-mental	45	58	59	49
Gender identity	**236**	**261**	**268**	**256**
Anti-transgender	196	217	223	214
Anti-gender non-conforming	40	44	45	42
Multiple bias [4]	**205**	**326**	**333**	**119**

[1] "Victim" may refer to an individual, business/financial institution, government entity, religious organization, or society/public as a whole. [2] "Known offender" does not imply that the identity of the suspect is known, but only that an attribute of the suspect has been identified which distinguishes him/her from an unknown offender. [3] Includes other motivation types not shown separately. [4] Incident in which one or more offense types are motivated by two or more biases.

Source: U.S. Department of Justice, Federal Bureau of Investigation, "Hate Crime Statistics 2020," <crime-data-explorer.app.cloud.gov>, accessed September 2021.

Table 354. Hate Crimes by Bias Motivation and Location of Incident: 2020

[See headnote, Table 353]

Location	Total incidents	Race/ ethnicity/ ancestry	Religion	Sexual orientation	Disability	Gender	Gender identity	Multiple-bias incidents [1]
Total [2]	**7,759**	**4,939**	**1,174**	**1,051**	**83**	**71**	**236**	**205**
Air/bus/train terminal	117	76	9	20	2	–	6	4
Bar/nightclub	74	36	4	24	2	1	4	3
Church/synagogue/temple/mosque	276	46	213	10	–	–	–	7
Commercial office building	173	108	35	19	1	5	1	4
Community center	31	22	5	3	–	–	–	1
Construction site	31	22	8	–	–	–	–	1
Convenience store	186	141	14	21	1	–	5	4
Cyberspace	103	57	19	10	3	2	5	7
Department/discount store	98	71	9	13	–	–	4	1
Drug store/doctor's office/hospital	92	66	7	7	2	2	2	6
Field/woods	58	34	13	9	–	–	–	2
Government/public building	118	92	13	6	1	1	2	3
Grocery/supermarket	114	87	12	9	1	1	3	1
Highway/road/alley/street/sidewalk	1,544	1,073	134	233	9	6	60	29
Hotel/motel/etc	88	63	11	7	–	–	4	3
Jail/prison/penitentiary/corrections facility	62	44	3	14	–	1	–	–
Park/playground	283	174	48	32	1	2	11	15
Parking/drop lot/garage	505	375	39	64	2	5	11	9
Residence/home	2,195	1,368	255	371	45	30	73	53
Restaurant	195	142	12	33	–	1	2	5
School/college [3]	27	17	6	3	–	–	–	1
School-college/university	113	67	22	16	–	1	4	3
School-elementary/secondary	205	118	39	24	6	–	3	15
Service/gas station	87	58	10	10	–	2	5	2
Specialty store (TV, fur, etc.)	75	52	9	9	1	–	3	1
Other/unknown	909	530	225	84	6	11	28	25

– Represents zero. [1] See footnote 4, Table 353. [2] Includes other locations not shown separately. [3] The location designation school/college has been retained for agencies that have not updated their records to include the new location designations of school, which allow for more specificity in reporting.

Source: U.S. Department of Justice, Federal Bureau of Investigation, "Hate Crime Statistics 2020," <crime-data-explorer.app.cloud.gov>, accessed September 2021.

Table 355. Rape and Sexual Assault Rates Among College-Age Females: 1998 to 2013

[Estimated victimization rates per 1,000 females, based on 3-year rolling averages centered on the most recent year. Data from the National Crime Victimization Survey]

Year	Students 18 to 24 years old [1]	Nonstudents 18 to 24 years old [2]	Not college-age females [3]	Year	Students 18 to 24 years old [1]	Nonstudents 18 to 24 years old [2]	Not college-age females [3]
1998	7.8	8.9	3.1	2006	5.4	5.5	1.7
1999	6.0	11.2	3.5	2007	5.5	5.4	1.7
2000	7.1	12.2	2.8	2008	5.2	6.7	1.9
2001	8.8	11.2	3.0	2009	3.7	8.3	1.6
2002	8.9	10.0	2.2	2010	[4] 4.1	8.4	1.6
2003	7.6	8.8	2.2	2011	4.6	7.1	1.4
2004	6.5	7.0	1.8	2012	5.9	4.1	1.3
2005	4.7	5.6	1.6	2013	4.4	4.3	1.4

[1] Includes female victims age 18 to 24 enrolled part time or full time in a post-secondary institution (i.e., college or university, trade school, or vocational school). [2] Includes female victims age 18 to 24 not enrolled in a post-secondary institution. [3] Includes females age 12 to 17 and age 25 or older. [4] Interpret with caution, subject to sampling error.

Source: U.S. Bureau of Justice Statistics, *Rape and Sexual Assault Victimization Among College-Age Females, 1995–2013*, NCJ 248471, December 2014. See also <bjs.ojp.gov/library>.

Table 356. Internet Crime Complaints—Victims and Value of Loss by Crime Type: 2019 to 2021

[Data shown are suspected criminal internet activities reported by victims to the FBI's Internet Crime Complaint Center (IC3). Victims are encouraged and often directed by law enforcement to file a complaint online at <www.ic3.gov> along with documentation and other information necessary to support the complaint. Complaints are reviewed by an IC3 analyst and categorized according to crime type. See source for full description of crime types and additional information]

Crime	2019		2020		2021	
	Victims (number)	Loss (dollars)	Victims (number)	Loss (dollars)	Victims (number)	Loss (dollars)
Phishing/vishing/smishing/pharming	114,702	57,836,379	241,342	54,241,075	323,972	44,213,707
Non-payment/non-delivery	61,832	196,563,497	108,869	265,011,249	82,478	337,493,071
Personal data breach	38,218	120,102,501	45,330	194,473,055	51,829	517,021,289
Identity theft	16,053	160,305,789	43,330	219,484,699	51,629	278,267,918
Extortion	43,101	107,498,956	76,741	70,935,939	39,360	60,577,741
Confidence/romance fraud	19,473	475,014,032	23,751	600,249,821	24,299	956,039,740
Tech support	13,633	54,041,053	15,421	146,477,709	23,903	347,657,432
Investment	3,999	222,186,195	8,788	336,469,000	20,561	1,455,943,193
BEC/EAC [1]	23,775	1,776,549,688	19,369	1,866,642,107	19,954	2,395,953,296
Spoofing	25,789	300,478,433	28,218	216,513,728	18,522	82,169,806
Credit card fraud	14,378	111,491,163	17,614	129,820,792	16,750	172,998,385
Employment	14,493	42,618,705	16,879	62,314,015	15,253	47,231,023
Terrorism & threats of violence [2]	61	49,589	65	–	12,346	4,390,720
Real estate/rental property	11,677	221,365,911	13,638	213,196,082	11,578	350,328,166
Government impersonation	13,873	124,292,606	12,827	109,938,030	11,335	142,643,253
Advanced fee	14,607	100,602,297	13,020	83,215,405	11,034	98,694,137
Overpayment	15,395	55,820,212	10,988	51,039,922	6,108	33,407,671
Lottery/sweepstakes/inheritance	7,767	48,642,332	8,501	61,111,319	5,991	71,289,089
Intellectual property rights, copyright and counterfeit	3,892	10,293,307	4,213	5,910,617	4,270	16,365,011
Ransomware [3]	2,047	8,965,847	2,474	29,157,405	3,729	49,207,908
Crimes against children	1,312	975,311	3,202	660,044	2,167	198,950
Corporate data breach	1,795	53,398,278	2,794	128,916,648	1,287	151,568,225
Civil matter	908	20,242,867	968	24,915,958	1,118	85,049,939
Denial of service (DoS)/telephony DoS	1,353	7,598,198	2,018	512,127	1,104	217,981
Computer Intrusion	(NA)	(NA)	(NA)	(NA)	979	19,603,037
Malware/scareware/virus	2,373	2,009,119	1,423	6,904,054	810	5,596,889
Health care related	657	1,128,838	1,383	29,042,515	578	7,042,942
Re-shipping	929	1,772,692	883	3,095,265	516	631,466
Gambling	262	1,458,118	391	3,961,508	395	1,940,237
Misrepresentation	5,975	12,371,573	24,276	19,707,242	(NA)	(NA)
Harassment/threats of violence [2]	15,502	19,866,654	20,604	6,547,449	(NA)	(NA)
False charity	407	2,214,383	659	4,428,766	(NA)	(NA)
Hacktivist	39	129,000	52	50	(NA)	(NA)
Other	10,842	66,223,160	10,372	101,523,082	12,346	75,837,524

NA Not available. – Represents or rounds to zero. [1] Business email compromise/email account compromise are scams carried out in order to conduct unauthorized transfer of funds. [2] Beginning 2021, harassment/threats of violence is included with terrorism. [3] Does not include estimates of lost business, time, wages, files, or equipment, or any third party remediation services acquired by a victim. In some cases victims do not report any loss amount to the FBI, thereby creating an artificially low overall ransomware loss rate. Represents what victims report to the FBI via the IC3 and does not account for victim direct reporting to FBI field offices and agents.

Source: U.S. Department of Justice, Federal Bureau of Investigation, *2021 Internet Crime Report*, and earlier reports. See also <www.ic3.gov>.

Table 357. Property Crime by Selected Household Characteristics: 2019

[126,434 represents 126,434,000. For crimes against households (burglary/trespassing, theft, and motor vehicle theft), each household affected by a crime is counted as a single victimization. Based on National Crime Victimization Survey (NCVS); see text, this section and Appendix III]

Characteristic	Number of house-holds (1,000)	Property crimes							
		Number of victimizations (1,000)				Victimization rate per 1,000 households			
		Total	Burglary/tres-passing [1]	Motor vehicle theft	Theft	Total	Burglary	Motor vehicle theft	Theft
Total	**126,434**	**12,818**	**2,178**	**496**	**10,144**	**101.4**	**17.2**	**3.9**	**80.2**
Race:									
White	98,581	9,612	1,596	351	7,664	97.5	16.2	3.6	77.7
Black	17,017	1,908	344	95	1,469	112.1	20.2	5.6	86.3
Other [2]	10,835	1,298	238	50	1,011	119.8	22.0	4.6	93.3
Ethnicity:									
Hispanic	17,803	2,069	307	116	1,646	116.2	17.2	6.5	92.4
Non-Hispanic	108,631	10,749	1,872	380	8,498	99.0	17.2	3.5	78.2
Household income:									
Less than $7,500	4,179	719	112	26	580	172.0	26.9	6.3	138.7
$7,500 to $14,999	6,064	1,042	302	48	692	171.8	49.9	7.9	114.1
$15,000 to $24,999	8,488	1,089	273	48	768	128.3	32.2	5.7	90.5
$25,000 to $34,999	9,592	1,037	182	33	822	108.1	19.0	3.4	85.7
$35,000 to $49,999	14,009	1,538	257	64	1,217	109.8	18.3	4.6	86.9
$50,000 to $74,999	16,575	1,672	217	67	1,388	100.9	13.1	4.1	83.7
$75,000 or more	33,433	3,236	396	111	2,729	96.8	11.8	3.3	81.6
Unknown	34,094	2,485	438	98	1,949	72.9	12.9	2.9	57.2
Number of persons in household:									
1	42,863	3,996	920	99	2,977	93.2	21.5	2.3	69.4
2 or 3	60,865	5,789	896	271	4,622	95.1	14.7	4.5	75.9
4 or 5	19,611	2,519	323	96	2,100	128.5	16.5	4.9	107.1
6 or more	3,094	513	39	29	445	165.9	12.6	9.5	143.9

[1] Formerly called "burglary." Burglary/trespassing includes unlawful or forcible entry or attempted entry of places, including a permanent residence, other residence (e.g., a hotel room or vacation residence), or other structure (e.g., a garage or shed). Includes victimizations where the offender stole, attempted to steal, or did not attempt to steal. Does not include trespassing on land. [2] Includes American Indians and Alaska Natives, Asians, Native Hawaiians and Other Pacific Islanders, other races, and persons of two or more races.

Source: U.S. Department of Justice, Bureau of Justice Statistics, "National Crime Victimization Survey (NCVS)Dashboard (N-DASH) Tool," <ncvs.bjs.ojp.gov/>, accessed January 2021.

Table 358. Robbery and Property Crimes by Type, Location, and Average Value Lost: 2010 to 2020

[300.3 represents 300,300. Data are from the FBI's Uniform Crime Reporting (UCR) Program]

Characteristic of offense	Number of offenses (1,000)				Average value lost (dol.)			
	2010	2018	2019	2020	2010	2018	2019	2020
Robbery, total	**300.3**	**230.6**	**211.1**	**198.9**	**1,239**	**2,119**	**1,797**	**1,834**
Location of crime:								
Street or highway	129.6	83.8	74.1	63.7	908	1,739	1,529	1,719
Commercial house	39.7	37.0	34.8	33.6	1,858	1,546	1,772	1,497
Gas or service station	7.0	7.3	6.7	7.2	939	1,028	1,248	1,469
Convenience store	15.7	16.1	14.4	14.7	782	961	1,006	1,005
Residence	51.9	37.2	33.7	34.8	1,491	4,600	2,560	2,236
Bank	6.5	3.7	3.0	2.2	4,410	4,303	4,213	4,339
Miscellaneous	49.9	45.6	44.3	42.7	1,115	1,662	1,864	2,161
Burglary, total	**1,898.0**	**1,047.4**	**917.5**	**859.6**	**2,119**	**2,799**	**2,661**	**2,692**
Location and time of burglary:								
Residence (dwelling)	1,402.2	685.8	576.6	477.4	2,137	8,407	8,290	7,937
Night	389.9	218.0	195.9	183.1	1,868	2,123	2,345	2,140
Day	722.2	346.3	290.9	232.6	2,158	2,401	2,507	2,321
Unknown	290.1	121.4	89.8	61.7	2,445	3,833	3,439	3,477
Nonresidence (store, office, etc.)	495.7	361.6	340.9	382.1	2,070	10,183	8,781	9,779
Night	204.6	161.8	157.3	183.6	1,765	2,833	2,667	2,974
Day	168.9	128.1	125.6	145.6	2,010	3,199	2,510	2,822
Unknown	122.2	71.7	58.0	52.9	2,662	4,151	3,604	3,982
Larceny-theft, total [1]	**5,391.6**	**4,390.4**	**4,132.6**	**3,800.5**	**988**	**1,153**	**1,162**	**1,482**
Type of larceny:								
Pocket-picking	21.1	22.9	24.0	15.6	526	1,169	1,235	1,233
Purse-snatching	24.5	16.9	15.1	11.6	400	718	651	634
Shoplifting	925.1	937.0	905.0	795.5	174	304	338	306
From motor vehicles (except accessories)	1,423.9	1,183.6	1,121.1	1,046.2	704	994	1,012	1,053
Motor vehicle accessories	477.8	272.1	264.7	324.3	681	648	690	873
Bicycles	179.6	131.8	125.1	130.5	351	546	569	724
From buildings	607.9	448.4	404.7	322.0	1,406	1,610	1,663	1,616
From coin-operated machines	17.6	9.7	9.2	7.3	365	851	829	816
All others	1,714.0	1,368.0	1,263.7	1,147.5	1,654	1,890	1,888	2,926
Larceny-theft by value:								
Over $200	2,443.1	2,052.4	1,956.5	1,831.7	2,089	2,407	2,395	3,026
$50 to $200	1,235.1	939.8	877.1	768.7	111	107	107	101
Under $50	1,713.3	1,398.1	1,298.9	1,200.2	17	15	14	10
Motor vehicle theft, total	**641.9**	**660.3**	**612.2**	**692.5**	**6,152**	**8,407**	**8,886**	**9,166**

[1] Excludes motor vehicles.

Source: U.S. Department of Justice, Federal Bureau of Investigation, "Crime Data Explorer," <crime-data-explorer.app.cloud.gov>, accessed January 2022.

Table 359. Fraud and Identity Theft—Consumer Complaints by State: 2021

[Rate per 100,000 population. As of December 31. Rates based on U.S. Census Bureau's 2019 population estimates. The Consumer Sentinel Network is a secure online database of consumer complaints available only to law enforcement. Based on unverified complaints reported by consumers. Excludes complaints from state-specific data contributors]

State	Fraud and other complaints		Identity theft victims		State	Fraud and other complaints		Identity theft victims	
	Number	Rate	Number	Rate		Number	Rate	Number	Rate
AL........	59,669	1,217	19,691	402	MO......	58,485	953	13,372	218
AK........	8,458	1,156	896	122	MT......	8,612	806	1,130	106
AZ........	77,534	1,065	28,108	386	NE......	13,475	697	2,409	125
AR........	24,176	801	6,358	211	NV......	43,339	1,407	17,985	584
CA........	391,517	991	133,119	337	NH......	12,429	914	2,205	162
CO........	64,464	1,119	33,572	583	NJ........	98,316	1,107	31,857	359
CT........	32,686	917	6,666	187	NM......	18,613	888	4,611	220
DE........	13,726	1,410	5,449	560	NY......	210,749	1,083	109,466	563
DC........	12,004	1,701	4,072	577	NC......	108,698	1,036	30,318	289
FL........	294,328	1,370	110,675	515	ND......	4,637	608	999	131
GA........	150,898	1,421	65,666	618	OH......	114,140	976	50,421	431
HI........	12,051	851	2,993	211	OK......	30,996	783	6,850	173
ID........	14,464	809	2,719	152	OR......	40,908	970	8,016	190
IL........	136,640	1,078	117,056	924	PA......	154,313	1,205	54,460	425
IN........	57,988	861	11,866	176	RI........	11,289	1,066	30,270	2,857
IA........	20,071	636	3,758	119	SC......	59,177	1,149	17,642	343
KS........	24,615	845	39,461	1,355	SD......	4,854	549	673	76
KY........	35,544	796	10,416	233	TN......	79,012	1,157	20,254	297
LA........	55,456	1,193	34,043	732	TX......	313,044	1,080	146,095	504
ME........	11,035	821	2,239	167	UT......	26,373	823	6,060	189
MD........	85,568	1,415	29,778	493	VT......	5,292	848	825	132
MA........	67,515	980	16,566	240	VA......	93,763	1,099	19,214	225
MI........	87,996	881	20,556	206	WA......	77,128	1,013	12,917	170
MN........	45,599	809	9,457	168	WV......	14,287	797	2,845	159
MS........	26,958	906	9,906	333	WI........	46,755	803	11,253	193
					WY......	4,230	731	620	107

Source: U.S. Federal Trade Commission, *Consumer Sentinel Network Data Book 2021,* February 2022. See also <www.ftc.gov/enforcement/consumer-sentinel-network/reports>.

Table 360. Victims of Identity Theft by Type of Account and Selected Victim Characteristics: 2018

[Data shown are for persons age 16 or older who experienced at least one identity theft incident during the past 12 months. Excludes respondents who discovered the most recent incident prior to the reference period. Estimates are based on the most recent identity theft incident. Includes successful and attempted identity theft, regardless of whether the victim experienced a loss. Details do not sum to totals because persons could experience more than one type of identity theft. Based on the National Crime Victimization Survey's Identity Theft Supplement]

Theft type and victim characteristics	Number of victims	Percent of all persons [1]	Theft type and victim characteristics	Number of victims	Percent of all persons [1]
Total.....	**23,183,020**	**9.0**	By sex:		
By type of theft:			Male.....	**11,219,660**	**9.0**
Misused only one type of existing account...	19,663,220	7.6	Female.....	11,963,360	9.0
Credit card.....	9,650,050	3.7	By race/Hispanic origin:		
Bank.....	8,467,070	3.3	White, non-Hispanic.......	16,560,830	10.1
Other.....	1,546,110	0.6	Black, non-Hispanic.......	2,100,740	6.8
Opened new account only.....	996,000	0.4	Hispanic.....	2,719,120	6.4
Misused personal information only.....	634,780	0.2	Asian, non-Hispanic.......	1,192,880	7.8
Misused multiple types.....	1,889,010	0.7	Other, non-Hispanic [2]......	609,440	10.3
Existing account only.....	1,295,940	0.5	By age:		
Other.....	593,070	0.2	16 to 17 years old.....	99,310	1.2
By household income:			18 to 24 years old.....	1,759,310	5.9
$24,999 or less.....	2,847,190	6.0	25 to 34 years old.....	4,410,270	9.8
$25,000–$49,999.....	4,323,590	6.5	35 to 49 years old.....	6,772,500	11.0
$50,000–$74,999.....	4,211,840	8.8	50 to 64 years old.....	6,478,060	10.3
$75,000 or more.....	11,800,400	12.2	65 years or older.....	3,663,570	7.2

[1] For data by characteristic, percent based on number of persons in specified category. [2] Includes Native Hawaiians, Other Pacific Islanders, American Indians, Alaska Natives, and persons of two or more races.

Source: U.S. Department of Justice, Bureau of Justice Statistics, *Victims of Identity Theft, 2018,* NCJ 256085, April 2021. See also <bjs.ojp.gov/library/publications/victims-identity-theft-2018>.

Table 361. Firearm Violence Victimizations by Selected Characteristics: 2010 to 2020

[In units as indicated. Includes violent crimes in which the offender possessed, showed, or used a firearm. Data are from the National Crime Victimization Survey]

Characteristic	2010	2013	2014	2015	2016	2017	2018	2019	2020
Total violent victimizations (number).....	4,935,983	6,126,423	5,359,570	5,006,615	5,353,816	5,612,667	6,385,515	5,813,408	4,558,154
Firearm victimizations (number) [1]............	**415,003**	**332,951**	**466,113**	**284,910**	**486,591**	**456,269**	**470,843**	**481,947**	**350,458**
Rate of firearm victimization [2]...	1.6	1.3	1.7	1.1	1.8	1.7	1.7	1.7	1.3
By race/ethnicity:									
White, non-Hispanic..........	1.1	1.0	1.4	0.7	1.6	1.4	1.4	1.3	1.2
Black, non-Hispanic..........	3.2	3.0	2.9	2.8	3.1	2.0	2.6	2.9	3.2
Hispanic......................	2.3	1.5	1.9	1.2	2.1	2.4	2.0	2.5	0.6
Firearm victimizations reported to police:									
Number........................	211,383	250,580	381,659	217,850	314,502	254,913	310,306	290,785	212,475
Percent........................	50.9	75.3	81.9	76.5	64.6	55.9	65.9	60.3	60.6

[1] Each victimization represents one person involved in an incident. [2] Rate is per 1,000 persons age 12 or older.

Source: U.S. Department of Justice, Bureau of Justice Statistics, "National Crime Victimization Survey (NCVS) Dashboard (N-DASH) Tool," <ncvs.bjs.ojp.gov>, accessed February 2022.

Table 362. Nonfatal Firearm and Nonfirearm Violence by Victim-Offender Relationship and Location of Crime: 2014 to 2018

[Data are for victimizations and whether the offender did or did not have, show, or use a firearm. Covers period from 2014 to 2018. Detail may not sum to total due to rounding. Data from National Crime Victimization Survey]

Characteristic	Total nonfatal violence		Firearm violence		Nonfirearm violence	
	Number	Percent	Number	Percent	Number	Percent
RELATIONSHIP TO VICTIM						
Any.............................	**9,179,700**	**100.0**	**1,907,300**	**100.0**	**7,272,400**	**100.0**
Nonstranger.......................	5,211,900	56.8	768,800	40.3	4,443,100	61.1
Intimate [1].......................	1,517,800	16.5	175,300	9.2	1,342,600	18.5
Other relative......................	716,600	7.8	125,900	6.6	590,700	8.1
Friend/acquaintance.................	2,977,500	32.4	467,600	24.5	2,509,800	34.5
Stranger............................	3,967,800	43.2	1,138,500	59.7	2,829,300	38.9
LOCATION						
Any.............................	**10,032,400**	**100.0**	**2,164,700**	**100.0**	**7,867,600**	**100.0**
Victim's home or lodging.............	2,660,200	26.5	372,600	17.2	2,287,600	29.1
Near victim's home..................	1,495,400	14.9	453,800	21.0	1,041,500	13.2
In, at, or near a friend, neighbor, or relative's home......	1,009,000	10.1	218,500	10.1	790,500	10.0
Commercial place...................	811,200	8.1	189,300	8.7	621,900	7.9
Parking lot or garage................	704,700	7.0	239,600	11.1	465,000	5.9
School [2].........................	611,300	6.1	[3] 33,700	[3] 1.6	577,600	7.3
Open area, on street, or public transportation.............	1,877,200	18.7	503,400	23.3	1,373,900	17.5
Other location......................	863,400	8.6	153,800	7.1	709,600	9.0

[1] Includes current or former spouses, boyfriends, or girlfriends. [2] Includes inside a school building or on school property. [3] Interpret with caution. Estimate based on 10 or fewer sample cases, or coefficient of variation is greater than 50%.

Source: Department of Justice, Bureau of Justice Statistics, *Trends and Patterns in Firearm Violence, 1993-2018*, NCJ 251663, April 2022. See also <bjs.ojp.gov/library>.

Table 363. Active Shooter Incidents and Casualties: 2000 to 2021

[The Federal Bureau of Investigation (FBI) defines active shooters as "one or more individuals actively engaged in killing or attempting to kill people in a populated area." This definition encompasses shootings that happen in schools, workplaces, and other public spaces. A shooting can be categorized as an active shooter incident even if no one is killed or wounded. Excluded from this report are gang- and drug-related shootings and gun-related incidents that appeared not to have put other people in peril (e.g., the accidental discharge of a firearm in a bar)]

Year and location	Active shooter incidents	Casualties		
		Total	Fatal	Injury
2000	3	18	16	2
2010	27	91	38	53
2015	20	134	56	78
2016	20	214	83	131
2017	31	734	143	591
2018	30	225	86	139
2019	30	258	103	155
2020	40	164	38	126
2021	61	243	103	140
BY LOCATION 2000-2021				
Place of commerce	203	1,294	559	735
Education facility	64	433	183	250
Open space	79	992	203	789
Government	36	209	97	112
Residence	19	114	51	63
Place of worship	16	147	80	67
Health care facility	16	67	29	38
Other location	1	2	1	1

Source: U.S. Department of Justice, Federal Bureau of Investigation, Office of Partner Engagement, "Active Shooter Resources," <www.fbi.gov/about/partnerships/office-of-partner-engagement/active-shooter-resources#FBI-Resources>, accessed June 2022.

Table 364. Persons Experiencing Nonfatal Threats or Use of Force During Police Contact: 2015 and 2018

[Data shown for persons age 16 and older. Includes persons reporting threats or use of force during the most recent contact or any earlier contacts with police in the last 12 months. Details may not sum to totals due to rounding. Data from the Police-Public Contact Survey]

Characteristics	2015			2018		
	Persons with any police contact	Experienced threats or use of force		Persons with any police contact	Experienced threats or use of force	
		Number	Percent		Number	Percent
Total	**53,469,300**	**985,300**	**1.8**	**61,542,300**	**1,254,300**	**2.0**
SEX						
Male	27,038,300	735,100	2.7	30,467,400	917,900	3.0
Female	26,431,000	250,200	0.9	31,074,900	336,400	1.1
RACE/ETHNICITY						
White, non-Hispanic	37,334,200	485,700	1.3	42,525,700	647,100	1.5
Black, non-Hispanic	6,146,400	201,100	3.3	6,545,700	250,700	3.8
Hispanic	6,680,700	203,100	3.0	8,238,400	280,100	3.4
Other [1]	3,307,900	95,500	2.9	4,232,500	76,300	1.8
AGE						
16 to 17 years old	1,188,300	[2] 24,300	[2] 2.0	1,143,500	39,200	3.4
18 to 24 years old	8,248,000	261,100	3.2	8,859,700	280,000	3.2
25 to 44 years old	19,998,800	473,100	2.4	23,518,700	625,500	2.7
45 to 64 years old	17,290,700	222,900	1.3	19,160,700	274,400	1.4
65 years or older	6,743,400	[2] 4,000	[2] 0.1	8,859,600	35,200	0.4

[1] Includes non-Hispanic Asians, Native Hawaiians, other Pacific Islanders, American Indians, Alaska Natives, and persons of two or more races. [2] Interpret with caution. Estimate is based on 10 or fewer sample cases, or coefficient of variation is greater than 50%.

Source: Department of Justice, Bureau of Justice Statistics, *Contacts Between Police and the Public, 2018 - Statistical Tables*, NCJ 255730, December 2020. See also <bjs.ojp.gov/library>.

Table 365. Background Checks for Firearm Transfers: 2008 to 2018

[In thousands (10,131 represents 10,131,000), except as noted. The Brady Handgun Violence Prevention Act (Brady Act) P.L. 103–159, 1993 requires a background check on an applicant for a firearm purchase from a dealer who is a Federal Firearms Licensee. The period beginning November 30, 1998 is the effective date for the Brady Act. The National Instant Criminal Background Check System (NICS) began operations in 1998. Checks on handgun and long gun transfers are conducted by the FBI, and by state and local agencies. Totals combine Firearm Inquiry Statistics (FIST) estimates for state and local agencies with transactions and denials reported by the FBI]

Inquiries and rejections	2008	2009	2010	2011	2012	2013	2014	2015	2016	2017	2018
Applications received	10,131	11,071	10,643	12,135	15,718	17,602	14,993	16,610	19,203	17,144	16,765
Applications denied	147	150	153	160	192	193	193	226	265	236	230
Denied (percent)	*1.5*	*1.4*	*1.5*	*1.3*	*1.2*	*1.1*	*1.3*	*1.4*	*1.4*	*1.4*	*1.4*
Selected reasons for rejection: [1]											
Felony indictment/conviction	77	67	62	(NA)	82	(NA)	82	100	111	108	108
Other	70	83	91	(NA)	110	(NA)	111	126	154	129	122
Felony denials per 1,000 applications	7.2	6.2	6.0	(NA)	5.2	(NA)	5.5	6.0	5.8	6.3	6.4

NA Not available. [1] Beginning in 2008, the FBI instituted a new classification system; therefore, data prior to 2008 aren't comparable to previously published estimates.

Source: U.S. Department of Justice, Bureau of Justice Statistics, *Background Checks for Firearm Transfers, 2018*, NCJ 301318, October 2021. See also <bjs.ojp.gov/library>.

Table 366. Denials of Firearm Transfer Applications by Reason and Agency Type: 2016 to 2018

[In percent. Reasons for denials are based on The Brady Handgun Violence Prevention Act, pursuant to 18 U.S.C. 922 and state laws. Denial occurs when an applicant is prohibited from receiving a firearm or a permit that can be used to receive a firearm because a disqualifying factor was found during a background check. Application for firearm transfer is information submitted by a person to a state or local checking agency to purchase a firearm or obtain a permit that can be used for a purchase. Information may be submitted directly to a checking agency or forwarded by a prospective seller. Totals were based on federal and state agencies that reported counts on reasons for denial. Reasons for denial for local agencies were estimated]

Reason for denial	2016 FBI	2016 State	2016 Local	2017 FBI	2017 State	2017 Local	2018 FBI	2018 State	2018 Local
Felony indictment/conviction..............	46.4	28.2	19.7	52.4	28.3	16.8	53.0	27.7	23.5
Felony indictment/information...........	5.3	1.8	3.2	7.0	2.3	3.2	7.9	6.8	8.6
Felony conviction.........................	41.1	26.4	16.5	45.4	26.0	13.6	45.1	20.9	14.9
Felony arrest with no disposition........	(X)	10.8	2.2	(X)	13.3	1.7	(X)	14.5	2.5
Fugitive....................................	20.3	8.9	4.3	6.6	5.3	3.0	5.8	3.8	3.3
Domestic violence........................	10.0	10.1	21.8	11.3	11.3	14.6	10.6	10.5	16.1
Misdemeanor conviction...............	7.3	6.3	16.2	8.3	5.7	11.9	7.6	5.4	12.9
Protection/restraining order..........	2.7	3.8	5.6	3.0	5.6	2.7	3.0	5.1	3.2
Drug user/addict..........................	9.4	5.2	4.7	12.2	7.0	6.3	13.7	7.5	6.6
Mental health commitment/adjudication.......	4.7	5.8	7.0	5.9	6.9	6.6	6.1	6.8	6.1
Illegal/unlawful alien....................	2.6	2.0	0.8	3.2	1.6	0.4	3.0	1.5	1.0
State law prohibition [1]...................	6.4	17.7	20.5	8.1	17.6	34.6	7.5	16.7	17.1
Local law prohibition [1]..................	(X)	(X)	2.7	(X)	(X)	3.6	(X)	(X)	3.7
Other prohibitions [2]....................	0.2	11.3	16.2	0.2	8.7	12.5	0.2	11.0	20.2

X Not applicable. [1] State and local laws may impose prohibitions based on juvenile offense records, adjudications of delinquency, misdemeanor convictions for an offense other than domestic violence, and mental health orders that do not cause a federal prohibition. [2] Includes juveniles, persons dishonorably discharged from the Armed Services, persons who have renounced their U.S. citizenship, and other unspecified persons.

Source: U.S. Department of Justice, Bureau of Justice Statistics, *Background Checks For Firearm Transfers, 2018*, NCJ 301318, October 2021, and earlier reports. See also <bjs.ojp.gov/library>.

Table 367. Employment by State and Local Law Enforcement Agencies by Type of Agency and Employee: 2008

[As of September 30. Based on census of all state and local law enforcement agencies operating nationwide, conducted every 4 years]

Type of agency	Number of agencies	Full-time employees (number) Total	Full-time employees (number) Sworn	Full-time employees (number) Civilian	Part-time employees (number) Total	Part-time employees (number) Sworn	Part-time employees (number) Civilian
Total [1]..........................	**17,985**	**1,133,905**	**765,237**	**368,668**	**100,340**	**44,062**	**56,278**
Local police...........................	12,501	593,003	461,054	131,949	58,129	27,810	30,319
Sheriffs' offices.......................	3,063	353,461	182,979	170,482	26,052	11,334	14,718
Primary State.........................	50	93,148	60,772	32,376	947	54	893
Special jurisdiction..................	1,733	90,262	56,968	33,294	14,681	4,451	10,230
Constable/marshal..................	638	4,031	3,464	567	531	413	118

[1] Excludes agencies with less than one full-time officer or the equivalent in part-time officers.

Source: U.S. Bureau of Justice Statistics, *Census of State and Local Law Enforcement Agencies, 2008.* See also <bjs.ojp.gov/library>.

Table 368. State and Local Government Criminal Justice Expenditures Per Capita by State: 2019

[In dollars. Based on Census Bureau's Annual Survey of State and Local Government Finances]

State	Total justice system	Police protec- tion	Judicial and legal	Correc- tions	State	Total justice system	Police protec- tion	Judicial and legal	Correc- tions
Total...................	**777**	**375**	**152**	**250**	Missouri.................	576	321	96	159
Alabama.................	530	277	82	171	Montana................	761	328	191	242
Alaska...................	1,315	522	331	461	Nebraska...............	662	275	102	285
Arizona..................	745	351	140	253	Nevada..................	890	454	174	262
Arkansas................	491	239	79	174	New Hampshire.........	647	353	132	162
California................	1,142	527	233	381	New Jersey.............	839	407	183	249
Colorado................	787	370	166	252	New Mexico.............	891	366	169	356
Connecticut.............	722	349	192	181	New York...............	1,101	553	228	320
Delaware................	956	382	207	368	North Carolina..........	616	334	81	202
District of Columbia.....	1,534	928	243	363	North Dakota...........	683	298	152	233
Florida...................	786	440	123	223	Ohio.....................	701	347	162	192
Georgia..................	616	268	144	203	Oklahoma...............	564	284	90	190
Hawaii...................	759	358	230	171	Oregon..................	902	359	203	340
Idaho....................	655	271	133	252	Pennsylvania............	784	337	152	295
Illinois...................	756	449	119	188	Rhode Island............	865	471	157	238
Indiana..................	493	229	96	168	South Carolina..........	514	276	81	157
Iowa.....................	539	273	122	145	South Dakota...........	585	252	113	220
Kansas..................	629	321	120	188	Tennessee..............	634	327	132	176
Kentucky................	515	184	129	203	Texas...................	641	302	117	221
Louisiana................	684	343	147	193	Utah.....................	608	291	133	185
Maine....................	511	244	89	179	Vermont.................	723	340	152	230
Maryland................	981	488	169	324	Virginia..................	753	301	123	329
Massachusetts..........	745	350	162	233	Washington.............	698	307	153	237
Michigan................	676	278	140	258	West Virginia............	608	237	150	221
Minnesota...............	777	422	147	208	Wisconsin...............	720	338	122	259
Mississippi..............	531	263	97	171	Wyoming................	992	390	216	387

Source: U.S. Census Bureau, "2019 State and Local Government Finance Historical Datasets and Tables," <www.census.gov/programs-surveys/gov-finances.html>, accessed April 2022; and "Annual Estimates of the Resident Population for the United States, Regions, States, the District of Columbia, and Puerto Rico: April 1, 2010 to July 1, 2019; April 1, 2020; and July 1, 2020 (NST-EST2020)," July 2021, <www.census.gov/programs-surveys/popest/technical-documentation/research/evaluation-estimates.html>.

Table 369. Equal Employment Opportunity Commission (EEOC) Charges Filed by Type and Litigation: 2010 to 2021

[Number, except as noted (85.1 represents $85,100,000). For fiscal years ending in year shown. The EEOC enforces federal laws making it illegal to discriminate against a job applicant or employee for charges listed below. Most employers with at least 15 employees, labor unions, and employment agencies are covered by EEOC laws. If the EEOC does not resolve charges through conciliation or other informal methods, the Commission may pursue litigation against private sector employers, employment agencies, labor unions and, in cases alleging age discrimination or equal pay violations, against state and local governments. The number for total charges reflects the number of individual charge filings. Charge data do not sum to total because individuals often file charges claiming multiple types of discrimination. See <www.eeoc.gov> for more information]

Charges and litigation	2010	2015	2016	2017	2018	2019	2020	2021
CHARGES FILED								
Total charges filed with EEOC.........	**99,922**	**89,385**	**91,503**	**84,254**	**76,418**	**72,675**	**67,448**	**61,331**
Race.........................	35,890	31,027	32,309	28,528	24,600	23,976	22,064	20,908
Sex...........................	29,029	26,396	26,934	25,605	24,655	23,532	21,398	18,762
National origin................	11,304	9,438	9,840	8,299	7,106	7,009	6,377	6,213
Religion......................	3,790	3,502	3,825	3,436	2,859	2,725	2,404	2,111
Color (skin complexion)........	2,780	2,833	3,102	3,240	3,166	3,415	3,562	3,516
Retaliation, all statutes........	36,258	39,757	42,018	41,097	39,469	39,110	37,632	34,332
Retaliation, Title VII only [1]......	30,948	31,893	33,082	32,023	30,556	30,117	27,997	25,121
Age...........................	23,264	20,144	20,857	18,376	16,911	15,573	14,183	12,965
Disability (ADA) [2]...............	25,165	26,968	28,073	26,838	24,605	24,238	24,324	22,843
Equal Pay Act.................	1,044	973	1,075	996	1,066	1,117	980	885
GINA [3]........................	201	257	238	206	220	209	440	242
LITIGATION [4]								
Suits filed....................	271	174	114	201	217	157	97	124
Resolutions...................	315	171	171	125	156	180	176	140
Monetary benefits (mil. dol.)...	85.1	65.3	52.2	42.4	53.6	39.1	106.1	34.0

[1] Title VII of the Civil Rights Act of 1964. [2] Americans with Disabilities Act. [3] Genetic Information Non-Discrimination Act. [4] Suits filed and resolved in federal district courts.

Source: U.S. Equal Employment Opportunity Commission, "Enforcement and Litigation Statistics," <www.eeoc.gov/eeoc/statistics/enforcement/index.cfm>, accessed March 2022.

Table 370. Asset Forfeiture Fund—Net Deposits by State: 2019 to 2021

[In thousands of dollars (2,227,068 represents $2,227,068,000). For fiscal years ending September 30. Transactions to or from the Department of Justice Asset Forfeiture Fund (AFF), which encompasses the seizure and forfeiture of assets that represent the proceeds of or were used to facilitate federal crimes. They do not reflect total forfeiture activity for any jurisdiction. See source for more details. Minus (-) sign indicates refunds]

State or territory	2019	2020	2021	State or territory	2019	2020	2021
Total.....................	**2,227,068**	**1,758,166**	**1,411,408**	Montana...................	11	–	91
				Nebraska.................	4,432	4,603	6,307
Investment income [1]......	156,615	68,865	7,607	Nevada...................	3,338	8,068	27,018
Alabama..................	8,019	2,846	4,029	New Hampshire..........	513	699	671
Alaska...................	795	329	181	New Jersey..............	64,784	32,125	27,461
Arizona..................	9,605	5,874	4,488	New Mexico.............	2,532	2,076	2,241
Arkansas.................	2,944	2,703	3,327	New York................	305,404	72,729	230,375
California................	283,079	718,338	330,247	North Carolina...........	16,270	15,073	23,234
Colorado.................	12,622	22,516	20,740	North Dakota............	157	72	15
Connecticut..............	6,308	5,548	5,103	Ohio.....................	16,610	20,914	17,115
Delaware.................	–	–	26	Oklahoma...............	3,384	2,339	2,901
District of Columbia.......	240,403	356,894	59,635	Oregon..................	4,322	5,295	6,461
Florida...................	83,486	59,339	98,258	Pennsylvania............	24,349	23,018	36,052
Georgia..................	13,654	10,259	18,744	Rhode Island............	–	2	9
Hawaii...................	–	7	1,565	South Carolina..........	7,092	2,851	5,620
Idaho....................	–	–	–	South Dakota............	–	–	–
Illinois...................	58,331	28,803	24,519	Tennessee...............	5,597	6,859	10,109
Indiana..................	5,255	4,772	5,179	Texas....................	79,908	43,306	207,741
Iowa.....................	500	21	27	Utah.....................	2,581	2,788	4,190
Kansas..................	7,107	4,964	4,634	Vermont.................	558	2,023	2,820
Kentucky.................	9,501	7,582	11,191	Virginia..................	664,453	65,959	41,957
Louisiana................	2,090	7,652	8,055	Washington..............	8,749	9,281	5,762
Maine....................	–	36	91	West Virginia............	1,590	464	2
Maryland.................	15,696	18,319	15,748	Wisconsin...............	8,727	11,212	5,590
Massachusetts............	30,519	20,923	14,686	Wyoming................	–	-1	–
Michigan.................	17,423	15,909	35,201	Guam....................	1,413	123	134
Minnesota................	27,274	5,638	7,981	Puerto Rico..............	5,157	25,461	33,823
Mississippi...............	3,747	24,294	34,343	Virgin Islands............	246	33	–
Missouri.................	15,980	21,890	15,199	Other [2]..................	-16,063	-13,529	-17,096

– Represents or rounds to zero. [1] Idle funds invested in U.S. Treasury Securities. [2] Comprised of transactions made to the AFF where a district has not been identified, where Federal reimbursements were made for services rendered, or summary estimates for financial reporting purposes where details by state were not available.

Source: U.S. Department of Justice, Asset Forfeiture Program, "Annual Reports to Congress," <www.justice.gov/afp>, accessed February 2022.

Table 371. Arrests by Type of Offense, Sex, and Age: 2020

[5,292.1 represents 5,292,100. For year ending December 31. Based on Uniform Crime Reporting Program. Arrests reported by 10,466 agencies with a total population of 228,864,358 as estimated by the FBI. Some persons may be arrested more than once during a year; therefore, in some cases, the data in this table could represent multiple arrests of the same person]

Offense charged	Total			Male			Female		
	Total	Under 18 years old	18 years and over	Total	Under 18 years old	18 years and over	Total	Under 18 years old	18 years and over
Total.........	5,292.1	297.1	4,995.1	3,891.3	210.5	3,680.7	1,400.8	86.5	1,314.3
Violent crime.........	338.4	24.7	313.8	267.9	20.0	248.0	70.5	4.7	65.8
Murder and nonnegligent manslaughter...	8.7	0.7	8.0	7.6	0.6	7.0	1.1	0.1	1.0
Rape [1].........	14.5	2.1	12.4	14.1	2.0	12.1	0.4	0.1	0.3
Robbery.........	48.0	8.5	39.5	40.7	7.5	33.3	7.3	1.0	6.3
Aggravated assault.........	267.2	13.4	253.8	205.5	9.9	195.6	61.7	3.5	58.2
Property crime.........	611.7	52.6	559.1	402.8	37.5	365.3	208.9	15.1	193.8
Burglary.........	104.5	10.6	94.0	84.5	9.1	75.3	20.1	1.4	18.7
Larceny-theft.........	442.0	32.9	409.1	267.6	21.0	246.5	174.5	11.9	162.5
Motor vehicle theft.........	58.3	8.3	50.1	45.4	6.6	38.7	13.0	1.6	11.3
Arson.........	6.9	0.9	6.0	5.4	0.7	4.7	1.4	0.1	1.3
Other assaults.........	633.7	50.1	583.6	452.4	31.0	421.3	181.3	19.1	162.2
Forgery and counterfeiting.........	22.6	0.3	22.2	15.3	0.3	15.1	7.2	0.1	7.2
Fraud.........	54.8	1.8	52.9	35.6	1.2	34.4	19.1	0.6	18.5
Embezzlement.........	6.6	0.3	6.3	3.4	0.2	3.2	3.2	0.1	3.1
Stolen property (buying, receiving, possessing).........	61.9	5.8	56.1	48.9	4.9	44.0	12.9	0.9	12.0
Vandalism.........	121.4	16.4	105.0	93.2	12.9	80.3	28.2	3.5	24.8
Weapons (carrying, possessing, etc.).........	115.8	7.8	108.0	105.0	7.2	97.8	10.8	0.6	10.2
Prostitution and commercialized vice.........	11.8	0.1	11.7	4.9	(Z)	4.9	6.8	(Z)	6.8
Sex offenses except rape & prostitution....	22.1	2.8	19.3	20.8	2.5	18.3	1.3	0.3	1.0
Drug abuse violations.........	801.5	29.4	772.2	601.0	22.0	579.0	200.6	7.4	193.2
Gambling.........	1.2	0.1	1.1	0.8	(Z)	0.8	0.4	(Z)	0.3
Offenses against family and children.......	40.5	1.6	38.9	27.4	0.9	26.5	13.1	0.7	12.4
Driving under the influence.........	531.8	4.0	527.8	396.7	3.0	393.7	135.2	1.0	134.1
Liquor laws.........	70.9	12.4	58.5	49.8	7.3	42.5	21.0	5.1	16.0
Drunkenness.........	135.7	1.7	134.0	105.4	1.1	104.3	30.3	0.6	29.7
Disorderly conduct.........	156.5	17.0	139.5	109.9	10.7	99.2	46.6	6.3	40.2
Vagrancy.........	9.8	0.2	9.6	7.5	0.1	7.3	2.3	0.1	2.3
All other offenses (except traffic).........	1,535.0	59.8	1,475.2	1,136.9	42.3	1,094.6	398.0	17.5	380.6
Suspicion.........	0.2	(Z)	0.2	0.2	(Z)	0.1	0.1	(Z)	0.1
Curfew and loitering law violations.........	8.2	8.2	(X)	5.4	5.4	(X)	2.8	2.8	(X)

X Not applicable. Z Less than 50. [1] Data are an aggregate total of the data submitted using both the revised and legacy Uniform Crime Reporting definitions. For more information, see <ucr.fbi.gov/recent-program-updates/new-rape-definition-frequently-asked-questions>.

Source: U.S. Department of Justice, Federal Bureau of Investigation, "Crime Data Explorer," <crime-data-explorer.app.cloud.gov>, accessed January 2022.

Table 372. Arrests by Offense and Race/Ethnicity: 2020

[Arrests reported by 10,466 agencies with an estimate total population of 228,864,358. See headnote, Table 371. Totals provided in this table reflect only those persons arrested by law enforcement agencies that provided race information to the UCR program]

Offense charged	Total	White	Black	Hispanic or Latino [1]	American Indian/ Alaska Native	Asian	Native Hawaiian/ other Pacific Islander
Total.........	5,213,213	3,648,470	1,356,208	928,437	129,815	64,863	13,857
Violent crime.........	334,923	201,322	118,971	78,577	8,068	5,289	1,273
Murder and nonnegligent manslaughter......	8,618	3,968	4,394	1,633	123	110	23
Rape [2].........	14,181	10,011	3,606	3,509	286	227	51
Robbery.........	47,674	22,688	23,519	10,887	712	501	254
Aggravated assault.........	264,450	164,655	87,452	62,548	6,947	4,451	945
Property crime.........	603,810	413,096	170,218	91,320	12,463	6,705	1,328
Burglary.........	103,568	71,826	28,603	19,591	1,659	1,251	229
Larceny-theft.........	435,625	295,929	124,867	55,986	9,396	4,578	855
Motor vehicle theft.........	57,823	40,394	15,237	14,473	1,244	727	221
Arson.........	6,794	4,947	1,511	1,270	164	149	23
Other assaults.........	625,158	409,055	190,453	107,191	15,330	8,771	1,549
Forgery and counterfeiting.........	22,289	15,304	6,350	3,332	229	374	32
Fraud.........	53,968	35,568	16,385	6,896	1,111	816	88
Embezzlement.........	6,490	3,942	2,351	828	71	115	11
Stolen property (buying, receiving, possessing).........	61,086	38,267	20,856	10,875	988	825	150
Vandalism.........	119,655	81,656	33,131	21,209	3,020	1,573	275
Weapons (carrying, possessing, etc.).........	114,690	59,798	52,094	23,456	1,226	1,243	329
Prostitution and commercialized vice.........	11,692	6,209	4,792	2,725	52	582	57
Sex offenses except rape & prostitution.........	21,774	16,090	4,664	5,754	457	504	59
Drug abuse violations.........	791,450	572,858	195,695	155,970	12,010	9,051	1,836
Gambling.........	1,174	777	258	468	6	123	10
Offenses against the family and children.......	39,583	27,000	9,318	5,542	2,870	342	53
Driving under the influence.........	516,965	417,593	77,366	123,406	11,419	8,898	1,689
Liquor laws.........	68,586	53,638	9,290	9,496	4,642	892	124
Drunkenness.........	134,508	102,205	18,957	31,408	11,706	1,371	269
Disorderly conduct.........	153,881	100,607	44,284	16,711	7,267	1,353	370
Vagrancy.........	9,710	6,394	2,775	1,608	396	129	16
All other offenses (except traffic).........	1,513,490	1,081,163	375,977	229,968	36,219	15,830	4,301
Suspicion.........	264	166	42	22	53	2	1
Curfew and loitering law violations.........	8,067	5,762	1,981	1,675	212	75	37

[1] Persons of Hispanic origin may be of any race. [2] See footnote 1, Table 371.

Source: U.S. Department of Justice, Federal Bureau of Investigation, "Crime Data Explorer," <crime-data-explorer.app.cloud.gov>, accessed January 2022.

Table 373. Law Enforcement Officers Killed and Assaulted: 1990 to 2020

[The statistics presented in this table are based on information collected by the staff of the FBI's Law Enforcement Officers Killed and Assaulted Program from law enforcement agencies throughout the U.S. and U.S. Territories. It contains statistics on line-of-duty felonious deaths, accidental deaths, and assaults of duly sworn local, state, tribal, and federal law enforcement officers]

Item	1990	2000	2010	2014	2015	2016	2017	2018	2019	2020
OFFICERS KILLED										
Total killed	**132**	**134**	**127**	**96**	**86**	**118**	**94**	**107**	**89**	**93**
By region and area:										
Northeast	13	13	11	16	9	9	9	10	4	3
Midwest	20	32	24	12	11	25	20	23	17	18
South	68	67	61	36	48	54	51	53	49	53
West	23	19	28	27	14	26	12	19	17	19
Puerto Rico	8	3	3	5	4	4	2	2	2	–
Island Areas	–	–	–	–	–	–	–	–	–	–
Total feloniously killed	**65**	**51**	**55**	**51**	**41**	**66**	**46**	**57**	**48**	**46**
By type of weapon:										
Firearms	56	47	54	46	38	62	42	52	44	41
Handgun	47	33	38	33	29	37	32	39	34	21
Rifle	8	10	15	10	7	23	9	10	7	10
Shotgun	1	4	1	3	1	1	1	2	1	–
Multiple firearms [1]	(NA)	(NA)	(NA)	–	–	1	–	–	–	–
Type of firearm unknown	(NA)	(NA)	–	–	1	–	–	–	1	1
Firearm type not reported	–	–	–	–	–	–	–	1	1	9
Knife/cutting instrument [2]	3	1	–	–	–	–	1	–	–	–
Knife [2]	(NA)	(NA)	(NA)	–	–	–	1	–	–	–
Other cutting instrument [2]	(NA)	(NA)	(NA)	–	–	–	–	–	–	–
Personal weapons [3]	2	–	–	1	–	–	–	1	–	1
Vehicle	1	3	1	4	3	4	3	4	4	4
Other	3	–	–	–	–	–	–	–	–	–
Total accidentally killed	**67**	**83**	**72**	**45**	**45**	**52**	**48**	**50**	**41**	**47**
OFFICERS ASSAULTED										
Population covered (1,000) [4]	197,426	204,599	248,727	246,681	251,555	269,401	269,608	250,651	219,848	235,546
Number of:										
Reporting agencies	9,343	8,940	11,826	11,235	12,102	12,293	12,198	11,788	9,457	9,895
Officers employed	410,131	452,531	557,884	543,331	547,398	593,097	596,604	546,247	475,848	505,212
Total assaulted	**72,091**	**58,398**	**56,491**	**48,988**	**50,991**	**58,011**	**60,211**	**58,866**	**56,034**	**60,105**
By type of weapon:										
Firearm	3,651	1,749	1,925	1,976	2,050	2,388	2,677	2,116	2,141	2,744
Knife/cutting instrument	1,647	1,015	918	966	921	1,107	1,083	1,163	1,037	1,180
Other dangerous weapon	7,423	8,132	7,413	6,976	7,705	9,201	10,209	8,889	8,440	11,760
Personal weapons [3]	59,370	47,502	46,235	39,070	40,315	45,315	46,242	46,698	44,416	44,421

– Represents zero. NA Not available. [1] Multiple firearms used by offender(s), unable to determine which caused fatal injury. [2] Prior to 2011, the type of weapon categories Knife and Other cutting instrument were combined. [3] Includes hands, fists, feet, etc. [4] Represents the number of persons covered by reporting agencies.

Source: U.S. Department of Justice, Federal Bureau of Investigation, "Law Enforcement Officers Killed and Assaulted, 2020," and previous reports, <ucr.fbi.gov>, accessed November 2021.

Table 374. Presidential Pardons and Commutations: 1961 to 2022

[For fiscal years shown. Not shown are petitions pending at the beginning of the fiscal year, or in the case of a change of administration, the number of cases pending at the time of the new President's inauguration]

Period	President	Petitions received	Petitions granted [1]			Petitions denied or closed without Presidential Action
			Pardon	Commutation	Remission	
1961 to 2022 [2]	**Total**	**91,495**	**4,622**	**2,410**	**17**	**67,460**
1961 to 1964	John F. Kennedy	1,749	472	100	3	831
1964 to 1969	Lyndon B. Johnson	4,537	960	226	1	2,830
1969 to 1975	Richard M. Nixon	2,591	863	60	3	2,614
1975 to 1977	Gerald R. Ford	1,527	382	22	5	900
1977 to 1981	Jimmy Carter	2,627	534	29	3	2,056
1981 to 1989	Ronald W. Reagan	3,404	393	13	–	2,804
1989 to 1993	George H.W. Bush	1,466	74	3	–	1,621
1993 to 2001	William J. Clinton	7,489	396	61	2	4,554
2001 to 2009	George W. Bush	11,074	189	11	–	11,914
2009 to 2017	Barack Obama	36,544	212	1,715	–	25,217
2017 to 2021	Donald J. Trump	12,078	144	94	–	8,303
2021 to 2022 [2]	Joseph R. Biden	6,409	3	76	–	3,816

– Represents zero. [1] Petitions granted are taken from a count of clemency warrants maintained by the Office of the Pardon Attorney. Cases in which multiple forms of relief were granted are counted in only one category. Cases in which clemency was granted to a person who did not file an application with the Office of the Pardon Attorney are counted as "petitions granted" but have not been counted as "petitions pending" or "petitions received" since at least FY1990. Excludes individual members of a class of persons granted pardons by proclamation. [2] As of August 31, 2022.

Source: U.S. Department of Justice, Office of the Pardon Attorney, "Clemency Statistics," <www.justice.gov/pardon/clemency-statistics>, accessed August 2022.

Table 375. Forensic Services Requests and Backlog by Type of Request: 2014

[Numbers are rounded to the nearest hundred. Census of 409 laboratories, with a 88% return rate. Totals exclude requests outsourced to other laboratories. Request is classified as backlogged if it has been submitted to a crime lab, but has not yet been examined and reported to the submitting agency within 30 days. Estimates based on imputations for labs that did not report backlog data, see source for details]

Type of request	Received		Completed		Backlogged requests	
	Number	Percent	Number	Percent	Number	Percent
All requests..	**3,783,000**	**100**	**3,646,000**	**100**	**570,100**	**100**
Controlled substances.......................................	1,265,000	33	1,197,000	33	213,700	37
Crime scene..	171,000	5	170,000	5	(X)	(X)
Digital evidence..	25,000	1	24,000	1	7,800	1
Firearms/toolmarks..	154,000	4	142,000	4	51,100	9
Forensic biology:						
Casework [1]...	333,000	9	296,000	8	107,800	19
Convicted offender/arrestee samples [1]...............	908,000	24	904,000	25	64,800	11
Impressions...	7,000	(Z)	7,000	(Z)	2,400	(Z)
Latent prints..	295,000	8	301,000	8	69,400	12
Questioned documents.....................................	9,000	(Z)	9,000	(Z)	800	(Z)
Toxicology..	566,000	15	554,000	15	40,000	7
Trace evidence...	49,000	1	41,000	1	12,200	2

X Not applicable. Z Less than 0.5%. [1] Includes biology screening and DNA analysis.

Source: U.S. Bureau of Justice Statistics, *Publicly Funded Forensic Crime Laboratories: Resources and Services, 2014*, NCJ 250151, November 2016. See also <bjs.ojp.gov/library>.

Table 376. Freedom of Information Act (FOIA) Requests Received, Processed, Granted and Denied by Federal Department and Selected Agency: 2021

[For year ending September 30. Freedom of Information Act (FOIA) provides the public the right to request access to records from any executive federal agency. Agencies are required to disclose any information requested under the FOIA unless it falls under one of nine exemptions; see <www.foia.gov/faq.html#exemptions> for full listing. Each agency is required to file an annual report with the Department of Justice detailing their administration of the FOIA. Data are compiled from those reports]

Department or agency	Requests pending from prior year	Requests received	Requests processed	Requests pending at year end	Disposition		
					Requests granted in full	Requests granted in part	Full denials [2]
Total [1]..	**222,676**	**838,164**	**838,668**	**222,172**	**165,847**	**336,135**	**336,686**
Department of Agriculture............................	6,857	20,956	21,815	5,998	16,829	2,433	2,553
Department of Commerce............................	1,169	2,274	2,195	1,248	501	352	1,342
Department of Defense...............................	22,283	52,805	50,703	24,385	12,681	16,502	21,520
Department of Education..............................	961	2,151	2,292	820	293	1,160	839
Department of Energy.................................	708	1,492	1,408	792	273	319	816
Department of Health and Human Services........	11,230	33,158	32,952	11,436	11,103	4,324	17,525
Department of Homeland Security..................	83,594	442,650	467,347	58,897	40,491	249,515	177,341
Department of Housing and Urban Development...	1,373	1,734	2,093	1,014	253	334	1,506
Department of Justice.................................	36,957	97,490	75,511	58,936	25,709	10,292	39,510
Department of Labor...................................	2,620	13,560	14,022	2,158	2,246	5,335	6,441
Department of State....................................	14,877	10,683	9,505	16,055	258	4,401	4,846
Department of the Interior.............................	4,764	6,302	5,774	5,292	1,335	1,521	2,918
Department of the Treasury...........................	2,872	10,820	10,755	2,937	3,027	2,334	5,394
Department of Transportation........................	5,572	15,740	14,754	6,558	4,833	5,136	4,785
Department of Veterans Affairs......................	5,781	27,762	30,227	3,316	10,375	9,121	10,731
Central Intelligence Agency..........................	2,895	2,837	2,870	2,862	160	360	2,350
Chemical Safety and Hazard Investigation Board..	31	179	134	76	2	–	132
Consumer Financial Protection Bureau.............	137	255	366	26	41	175	150
Consumer Product Safety Commission.............	543	596	548	591	92	149	307
Environmental Protection Agency...................	2,358	6,485	6,943	1,900	3,038	1,129	2,776
Equal Employment Opportunity Commission.......	2,003	15,320	16,048	1,275	1,481	10,495	4,072
Federal Communications Commission..............	52	534	537	49	85	226	226
Federal Deposit Insurance Corporation............	34	312	295	51	37	66	192
Federal Reserve System..............................	53	637	654	36	272	96	286
Federal Trade Commission...........................	38	1,385	1,375	48	494	412	469
General Services Administration.....................	454	1,349	1,294	509	201	580	513
Merit Systems Protection Board......................	55	172	171	56	44	50	77
National Aeronautics and Space Administration....	84	759	775	68	126	165	484
National Archives and Records Administration.....	3,511	7,725	6,867	4,369	5,276	61	1,530
National Labor Relations Board......................	47	1,436	1,411	72	256	928	227
National Railroad Passenger Corporation (AMTRAK)...	138	164	27	275	15	3	9
National Science Foundation.........................	368	293	257	404	23	158	76
National Transportation Safety Board...............	296	453	584	165	54	154	376
Nuclear Regulatory Commission.....................	92	239	229	102	56	60	113
Occupational Safety and Health Review Commission..	6	143	148	1	47	10	91
Office of Management and Budget...................	668	280	278	670	21	24	233
Office of Personnel Management....................	422	640	842	220	239	125	478
Office of the Director of National Intelligence.......	709	441	651	499	69	225	357
Pension Benefit Guaranty Corporation.............	189	3,517	3,481	225	2,724	358	399
Securities and Exchange Commission..............	641	12,363	12,171	833	3,883	787	7,501
Small Business Administration.......................	1,595	18,127	15,238	4,484	7,288	737	7,213
Social Security Administration.......................	1,908	13,440	14,662	686	8,064	3,577	3,021
Tennessee Valley Authority...........................	36	213	215	34	77	73	65
U.S. Agency for International Development.........	399	329	297	431	27	122	148
United States Postal Service.........................	396	4,864	4,905	355	734	745	3,426

– Represents zero. [1] Includes other agencies not shown below. [2] Denials due to FOIA exemptions and other nonexemption reasons, including no records available, incorrect agency, duplicate, and not reasonably descriptive.

Source: U.S. Department of Justice, Office of Information Policy, "Annual FOIA Reports – FY 2021," <www.justice.gov/oip/annual-foia-reports-fy-2021>, accessed March 2022. See also <www.foia.gov>.

Table 377. Federal and State Arrests by the Drug Enforcement Administration by Type of Drug: 2010 to 2020

[For fiscal year ending in year shown. Data are from Drug Enforcement Administration's (DEA) Defendant Statistical System]

Fiscal year	Total arrested	Drug type						
		Powder cocaine	Crack cocaine	Heroin [1]	Other opioids [2]	Marijuana	Metham-phetamine	Other nonopioids [3]
2010.........	31,517	8,231	2,640	3,029	1,582	8,215	5,527	2,293
2011...........	32,379	7,664	2,726	3,575	2,379	7,723	5,547	2,765
2012.........	31,628	7,386	2,653	3,664	2,269	6,787	6,000	2,869
2013.........	30,532	6,346	2,113	4,181	2,227	5,862	6,858	2,945
2014.........	29,548	5,582	1,782	4,852	2,048	5,082	7,005	3,197
2015.........	31,538	6,017	1,567	6,340	1,918	4,741	8,023	2,932
2016.........	29,486	5,484	1,455	5,926	1,553	4,213	8,068	2,787
2017.........	27,223	5,495	1,152	5,452	1,790	3,541	7,280	2,513
2018.........	27,348	5,198	1,103	5,078	2,170	3,266	8,088	2,445
2019.........	27,543	4,899	970	4,837	2,598	2,597	9,076	2,566
2020.........	26,696	4,474	1,217	3,707	2,925	2,576	8,783	3,014

[1] Includes heroin, morphine, and opium base. [2] Synthetic compounds that emulate the effects of natural compounds found in the opium poppy. [3] Includes nonopioid pharmaceutical controlled substances, other depressants, sedatives, ephedrine, pseudoephedrine, hallucinogens, synthetic cannabinoids, other steroids, equipment to manufacture controlled substances, and drug-use paraphernalia. Also includes drug diversion arrests where drug type is not indicated.

Source: U.S. Department of Justice, Bureau of Justice Statistics, *Federal Justice Statistics 2020*, NCJ 304314, May 2022. See also <bjs.ojp.gov/library>.

Table 378. Missing Person Reports by Selected Characteristics: 2019 to 2021

[Data shown are missing person records entered into the National Crime Information Center's (NCIC) Missing Person File during the year shown and does not include records removed (canceled, cleared, and located). The NCIC contained 93,718 active missing person records remaining in the database as of December 31, 2021; this figure includes entries from earlier years. For more information, see source]

Characteristic	2019			2020			2021		
	All ages	Under age 18	Age 18 and older	All ages [7]	Under age 18	Age 18 and older	All ages [7]	Under age 18	Age 18 and older
Total missing person entries...................	**609,275**	**421,394**	**187,881**	**543,018**	**365,348**	**177,316**	**521,705**	**337,195**	**184,068**
By type:									
Juvenile (under age 21) [1]..........	401,875	398,250	3,625	346,230	345,012	1,218	317,869	316,757	1,112
Endangered [2]......................	44,840	9,580	35,260	41,693	8,629	32,999	41,855	8,632	33,137
Involuntary [3]......................	14,479	4,828	9,651	13,236	4,479	8,733	13,621	4,680	8,907
Disability [4].......................	32,058	4,988	27,070	29,204	4,106	25,057	29,393	4,093	25,253
Catastrophe [5].....................	280	59	221	279	55	221	346	75	264
Other (over age 21)...............	115,743	3,689	112,054	112,376	3,067	109,088	118,621	2,958	115,395
By sex:									
Female.............................	298,190	221,636	76,554	268,884	197,486	71,258	257,385	183,684	73,541
Male...............................	311,008	199,701	111,307	274,057	167,807	106,036	264,160	153,383	110,495
Unknown...........................	77	57	20	77	55	22	160	128	32
By race/ethnicity:									
White [6]...........................	359,768	237,469	122,299	321,859	207,424	114,213	305,249	186,321	118,639
Black...............................	205,802	154,589	51,213	182,548	133,045	49,422	177,530	126,607	50,815
Asian..............................	12,671	6,700	5,971	10,776	5,360	5,412	10,805	5,040	5,763
American Indian...................	10,447	7,858	2,589	9,575	7,062	2,503	9,572	6,630	2,938
Unknown...........................	20,587	14,778	5,809	18,260	12,457	5,766	18,549	12,597	5,913

[1] A person under the age of 21 or not emancipated by state of residence, who is missing and does not meet any of the entry criteria set forth in the other categories. [2] Indicating that physical safety may be in danger. [3] Disappearance may not have been voluntary, i.e. abduction or kidnapping. [4] Proven physical/mental disability or senile and subjecting themselves or others to personal and immediate danger. [5] Person missing after a catastrophe. [6] Includes Hispanic ethnicity or origin. [7] Includes persons of unknown age.

Source: U.S. Department of Justice, Federal Bureau of Investigation, "2021 NCIC Missing Person and Unidentified Person Statistics," and earlier releases, <www.fbi.gov/services/cjis/ncic>, accessed February 2022.

Table 379. Federal Prosecutions of Public Corruption by Prosecution Status: 2000 to 2020

[As of December 31. Prosecution of persons who have corrupted public office in violation of Federal Criminal Statutes]

Type of official	2000			2010			2019			2020		
	Charged	Con-victed	Await-ing trial	Charged	Con-victed	Await-ing trial	Charged	Con-victed	Await-ing trial	Charged	Con-victed	Await-ing trial
Total....................	**1,000**	**938**	**327**	**1,184**	**1,036**	**554**	**780**	**734**	**451**	**628**	**469**	**561**
Federal officials.........	441	422	92	422	397	103	300	307	131	242	207	154
State officials...........	92	91	37	168	108	105	60	63	46	55	30	48
Local officials...........	211	183	89	296	280	146	213	199	111	135	110	129
Others involved [1].......	256	242	109	298	251	200	207	165	163	196	122	230

[1] Includes individuals who are neither public officials nor employees, but were involved with public officials or employees in violating the law.

Source: U.S. Department of Justice, Criminal Division, *Report to Congress on the Activities and Operations of the Public Integrity Section for 2020*, and earlier reports. See also <www.justice.gov/criminal/pin>.

Table 380. U.S. Supreme Court—Cases on Docket, Disposed of, and Remaining: 2000 to 2020

[Statutory term of court begins first Monday in October. Often the Court grants or denies cases after the Court recesses but before the next statutory term]

Action	2000	2005	2010	2015	2016	2017	2018	2019	2020
NUMBER OF CASES ON DOCKET									
Total	**8,965**	**9,608**	**9,066**	**7,535**	**7,334**	**7,390**	**7,626**	**6,534**	**6,129**
Original	9	8	4	8	7	8	9	10	10
Paid	2,305	2,025	1,895	1,839	1,850	2,062	1,915	1,818	2,137
In Forma Pauperis	6,651	7,575	7,167	5,688	5,477	5,320	5,702	4,706	3,982
CASES DISPOSED OF									
Total	**7,762**	**8,240**	**7,827**	**6,506**	**6,258**	**6,192**	**6,528**	**5,712**	**5,226**
Original	2	4	2	1	1	1	2	2	6
Paid	2,024	1,703	1,580	1,539	1,505	1,728	1,583	1,509	1,747
In Forma Pauperis	5,736	6,533	6,245	4,966	4,752	4,463	4,943	4,201	3,473
NUMBER REMAINING ON DOCKET									
Total	**1,203**	**1,368**	**1,239**	**1,029**	**1,076**	**1,198**	**1,094**	**822**	**903**
Original	7	4	2	7	6	7	7	8	4
Paid	281	322	315	300	345	334	327	309	390
In Forma Pauperis	915	1,042	922	722	725	857	760	505	509
Cases argued during term	86	90	86	82	71	69	73	73	72
Number disposed of by full opinions	83	82	83	70	68	63	69	69	69
Number disposed of by per curiam opinions	4	5	3	12	1	6	2	4	3
Number set for re-argument next term	0	3	0	0	2	0	2	0	0
Total cases granted plenary review	99	78	90	81	75	78	86	60	72
Cases reviewed and decided without oral argument	127	105	84	145	66	103	56	105	91
Total cases available for argument at start of next term	49	31	43	31	32	38	50	37	31

Source: Administrative Office of the U.S. Courts, "Judicial Business of the United States Courts, Table A-1–Supreme Court of the United States Judicial Business," September 2021, and earlier reports, <www.uscourts.gov/data-table-topics/us-supreme-court>. See also <www.supremecourt.gov/orders/journal.aspx>.

Table 381. Federal Judiciary Caseloads: 2000 to 2021

[For 12-month periods ending June 30]

Judicial caseload	2000	2010	2015	2017	2018	2019	2020	2021
U.S. Courts of Appeals: [1]								
Cases filed	54,642	56,097	53,032	52,028	49,220	47,783	49,044	45,790
Cases terminated	56,509	59,343	53,934	56,709	50,804	47,832	48,514	47,842
Cases pending	40,815	46,816	40,913	40,040	38,481	38,433	38,973	36,921
U.S. District Courts Civil:								
Cases filed	263,049	289,630	280,037	271,721	281,202	293,520	421,082	374,250
Cases terminated	260,277	295,908	273,562	299,002	248,093	325,920	281,742	272,609
Cases pending	247,973	285,071	340,401	364,117	395,685	363,532	503,329	604,970
U.S. District Courts Criminal (includes transfers):								
Cases filed	62,523	78,213	60,866	58,121	67,257	72,926	64,853	59,500
Defendants filed	84,147	100,031	79,154	75,235	84,827	90,411	79,122	75,407
Cases terminated	57,543	77,633	61,299	57,610	61,287	66,307	66,034	48,912
Cases pending	46,796	80,506	72,094	72,454	78,869	84,687	82,894	93,437
U.S. Bankruptcy Courts:								
Cases filed	1,276,922	1,572,597	879,736	796,037	775,578	773,361	682,363	462,309
Cases terminated	1,271,300	1,441,419	1,024,504	869,448	825,364	791,523	760,297	609,855
Cases pending	1,396,916	1,659,399	1,316,672	1,100,309	1,050,476	1,032,572	954,786	807,243
Post-conviction supervision:								
Persons under supervision	99,577	126,642	133,428	135,947	131,036	128,649	127,680	124,249
Pretrial services:								
Total cases activated	86,067	110,666	95,538	87,517	97,144	106,019	90,069	77,065
Pretrial services cases activated	84,107	109,711	94,757	86,974	96,718	105,579	89,685	76,709
Pretrial diversion cases activated	1,960	955	781	543	426	440	384	356
Total released on supervision	31,607	29,748	24,429	22,960	23,474	25,392	23,357	26,867
Pretrial supervision	31,927	28,440	23,368	22,190	22,843	24,738	22,779	26,290
Diversion supervision	2,166	1,308	1,061	770	631	654	578	577

[1] Excludes the U.S. Court of Appeals for the Federal Circuit.

Source: Administrative Office of the United States Courts, "Statistical Tables for the Federal Judiciary," <www.uscourts.gov/statistics-reports/analysis-reports/statistical-tables-federal-judiciary>, accessed November 2021.

Table 382. U.S. District Courts—Civil Cases Filed by Basis of Jurisdiction and Nature of Suit: 2010 to 2021

[For 12-month periods ending June 30]

Type of case	2010	2015	2017	2018	2019	2020	2021
Total cases filed [1]	**285,215**	**280,037**	**271,721**	**281,202**	**293,520**	**421,082**	**374,250**
BASIS OF JURISDICTION							
U.S. cases:							
U.S. plaintiff	8,427	6,182	5,014	4,705	4,237	3,630	3,322
U.S. defendant	34,306	35,651	41,677	38,235	37,135	41,278	43,803
Private cases:							
Federal question	137,776	151,330	149,577	149,243	151,513	142,089	136,546
Diversity of citizenship	104,703	86,865	75,449	89,018	100,629	234,084	190,578
Local jurisdiction	3	9	4	1	6	1	1
NATURE OF SUIT							
Contract actions [1]	31,461	26,506	23,678	26,100	25,216	26,012	26,661
Insurance	9,236	9,923	8,774	10,374	10,749	11,071	13,294
Recovery of overpayments [2]	3,079	2,307	1,515	1,114	1,043	743	534
Real property actions [1]	6,809	8,963	8,202	7,018	6,966	5,689	3,325
Foreclosure	3,836	4,043	4,070	3,176	2,983	2,324	1,035
Tort actions	87,256	69,875	57,007	68,776	81,089	213,392	169,073
Personal injury	82,057	62,318	53,030	64,545	77,297	209,489	165,253
Personal injury product liability	66,958	41,607	35,340	47,335	53,456	188,878	147,013
Other personal injury [1]	15,099	20,711	17,690	17,210	23,841	20,611	18,240
Medical malpractice	1,120	1,097	1,243	1,169	1,209	1,069	1,120
Personal property damage	5,199	7,557	3,977	4,231	3,792	3,903	3,820
Actions under statutes [1]	159,683	174,693	182,834	179,308	180,249	175,989	175,191
Bankruptcy suits	2,615	2,688	2,141	2,132	2,233	2,146	1,984
Civil rights [1]	34,427	37,015	39,056	40,617	43,223	42,053	43,272
Employment	14,343	12,258	12,198	12,387	12,572	12,252	11,264
Environmental matters	826	578	1,160	1,965	659	439	489
Prisoner petitions	52,450	52,844	61,031	53,626	54,445	56,823	49,658
Forfeiture and penalty	2,297	1,620	1,110	1,205	1,148	1,024	1,138
Labor laws	18,878	19,047	17,887	17,816	16,840	15,479	14,039
Immigration	1,262	1,244	1,907	1,696	2,017	2,387	3,971
Protected property rights [3]	8,519	14,145	11,060	11,845	13,185	10,178	11,161
Securities, commodities, and exchanges	1,442	1,012	1,353	1,527	1,655	1,835	2,301
Social security laws	13,725	19,102	18,953	19,115	17,903	18,259	23,615
Tax suits	1,171	1,005	993	948	773	587	528
Freedom of information	315	481	602	859	819	799	690
Cases terminated	**295,909**	**273,562**	**299,002**	**248,093**	**325,920**	**281,742**	**272,609**
Cases pending	**285,071**	**340,401**	**364,117**	**395,685**	**363,532**	**503,329**	**604,970**

[1] Includes other types not shown separately. [2] Includes enforcement of judgments in student loan cases, and overpayments of veterans' benefits. [3] Includes copyright, patent, and trademark rights.

Source: Administrative Office of the United States Courts, "Statistical Tables for the Federal Judiciary," <www.uscourts.gov/statistics-reports/analysis-reports/statistical-tables-federal-judiciary>, accessed November 2021.

Table 383. U.S. District Courts—National Petit and Grand Juror Service: 2010 to 2021

[For years ending September 30. Includes data on jury selection days only. Data on juror service after the selection day are not included]

Juror service	2010	2015	2016	2017	2018	2019	2020	2021
PETIT JUROR SERVICE								
Jurors present for jury selection or orientation	262,376	195,206	194,211	184,019	189,504	192,595	102,531	104,270
Percent selected	22.7	22.6	22.5	22.8	22.0	22.0	21.9	23.7
Percent challenged	38.5	40.6	39.5	39.8	40.5	39.4	38.4	36.9
Percent not selected or challenged	38.7	36.8	38.0	37.5	37.5	38.6	39.8	39.4
Voir Dire [1]	24.9	23.7	25.2	25.0	24.0	24.8	25.0	26.3
Non-Voir Dire [2]	13.9	13.1	12.8	12.4	13.4	13.8	14.8	13.1
Total juries selected	5,332	4,149	3,887	3,708	3,660	3,718	1,916	2,098
GRAND JUROR SERVICE								
Juries serving	784	749	743	755	755	749	651	698
Sessions convened	9,277	8,087	8,249	8,124	8,258	8,374	5,449	5,686
Jurors in session	186,020	161,493	164,733	161,759	163,859	167,310	107,489	110,954
Average per session	20.1	20.0	20.0	19.9	19.8	20.0	19.7	19.5
Hours in session	44,845	36,098	36,621	35,823	36,458	36,706	24,940	27,086
Average hours per session	4.8	4.5	4.4	4.4	4.4	4.4	4.6	4.8
Proceedings filed by indictment:								
Cases	49,654	(NA)	(NA)	(NA)	(NA)	(NA)	(NA)	(NA)
Defendants	70,433	56,164	55,227	55,818	63,877	70,078	55,233	57,816
Average defendants indicted per session	7.6	6.9	6.7	6.9	7.7	8.4	10.1	10.2

NA Not available. [1] Jurors who completed pre-screening questionnaires or were in the courtroom during the conducting of voir dire. [2] Other jurors not selected or challenged who were not called to the courtroom or otherwise did not participate in the actual voir dire.

Source: Administrative Office of the United States Courts, "Judicial Business of the United States Courts 2021," <www.uscourts.gov/Statistics/JudicialBusiness.aspx>, accessed March 2022.

Table 384. U.S. Courts of Appeals—Nature of Suit or Offense in Cases Arising from the U.S. District Courts: 2010 to 2021

[For 12-month periods ending June 30. Excludes data for the U.S. Court of Appeals for the Federal Circuit. Includes appeals reopened, remanded, and reinstated (after being terminated due to procedural defaults) as well as original appeals]

Nature of suit and offense	2010	2015	2016	2017	2018	2019	2020	2021
Total cases	**43,880**	**40,234**	**39,506**	**38,594**	**37,487**	**36,596**	**36,186**	**34,141**
Criminal cases	12,863	10,902	11,945	10,216	9,614	9,895	9,577	10,756
Civil cases	31,017	29,332	27,561	28,378	27,873	26,701	26,609	23,385
U.S cases	7,772	7,471	6,586	7,609	7,660	6,778	6,634	5,779
U.S. plaintiff	435	353	321	305	261	206	226	182
U.S. defendant	7,337	7,118	6,265	7,304	7,399	6,572	6,408	5,597
Private cases	23,245	21,861	20,975	20,769	20,213	19,923	19,975	17,606
Federal question	20,599	18,821	18,005	17,918	17,423	17,133	16,865	15,049
Diversity of citizenship	2,646	3,040	2,969	2,851	2,790	2,789	3,109	2,557
General local jurisdiction	–	–	1	–	–	1	1	–
Criminal cases	12,863	10,902	11,945	10,216	9,614	9,895	9,577	10,756
Violent offenses	621	483	477	570	512	523	546	661
Property offenses	1,624	1,420	1,403	1,271	1,212	1,241	931	950
Drug offenses	5,066	3,843	4,844	3,578	3,207	3,371	3,562	4,292
Firearms and explosives offenses	1,927	1,560	1,806	1,860	1,888	1,967	2,011	2,298
Sex offenses	651	786	736	769	762	765	746	874
Justice system offenses	142	169	129	147	134	133	140	133
Immigration offenses	1,787	1,491	1,342	957	897	929	725	548
General offenses	411	289	261	253	235	279	231	261
Other [1]	634	861	947	811	767	687	685	739

– Represents or rounds to zero. [1] Other includes regulatory, traffic, and unclassified offenses.

Source: Administrative Office of the United States Courts, "Statistical Tables for the Federal Judiciary," <www.uscourts.gov/statistics-reports/analysis-reports/statistical-tables-federal-judiciary>, accessed November 2021.

Table 385. Total Incoming Caseloads in State Trial Courts by Case Category: 2020

[States reporting incomplete data or data not conforming to reporting guidelines are not shown. Represents new filings, plus reopened and reactivated cases when provided, as reported to the Court Statistics Project. Since state court caseload statistics should only be viewed in the context of each state's court structure, comparisons of the data reported here should not be made without additional information. See source for state court structures and characteristics]

State	Total	Civil [1]	Domestic relations [2]	Criminal [3]	Juvenile [4]	Traffic/other violations [5]
Alabama	772,834	148,388	48,988	204,595	31,527	339,336
Alaska	111,387	18,111	9,812	28,958	2,861	51,645
Arizona	1,637,570	292,510	81,080	425,973	12,705	825,302
California	5,520,639	917,227	309,767	979,485	70,164	3,243,996
Colorado	714,345	272,467	37,177	254,909	12,065	137,727
Connecticut	422,291	170,445	43,397	80,805	13,368	114,276
Delaware	327,857	53,967	27,895	72,155	3,849	169,991
District of Columbia	40,826	21,409	7,264	11,128	1,025	([6])
Florida	2,691,798	956,136	195,914	513,900	33,754	992,094
Georgia	2,009,110	549,169	104,072	1,220,526	37,984	97,359
Hawaii	459,622	34,909	11,649	111,381	6,841	294,842
Idaho	326,014	65,497	21,278	84,695	6,488	148,056
Illinois	1,657,966	331,170	104,722	210,714	16,721	994,639
Indiana	1,000,644	315,867	86,857	262,887	42,004	293,029
Iowa	590,639	110,155	29,645	108,477	8,770	333,592
Kentucky	697,677	172,105	54,596	242,541	23,030	205,405
Louisiana	912,839	148,696	52,951	191,353	18,790	501,049
Maine	119,175	17,448	11,777	36,516	1,955	51,479
Maryland	1,345,364	603,997	79,232	200,255	7,559	454,321
Massachusetts	418,264	177,489	59,479	119,168	9,695	52,433
Michigan	2,229,653	476,473	85,315	632,186	20,020	1,015,659
Minnesota	894,715	129,946	48,383	157,763	20,547	538,076
Missouri	1,187,327	237,258	100,616	177,616	9,837	662,000
Montana	251,735	51,141	13,591	59,790	2,953	124,260
Nebraska	368,099	108,396	25,720	127,663	14,513	91,807
Nevada	736,959	130,581	48,141	179,824	8,523	369,890
New Hampshire	117,032	43,796	11,124	29,186	3,235	29,691
New Jersey	4,978,114	604,899	137,042	600,303	19,319	3,616,551
New Mexico	291,652	65,143	27,919	116,268	3,065	79,257
New York	1,709,666	748,557	299,619	264,896	41,956	354,638
North Carolina	2,104,977	381,284	110,932	1,257,498	15,499	339,764
Ohio	2,227,610	438,032	160,205	574,603	62,861	991,909
Pennsylvania	2,341,801	276,864	338,124	364,008	23,991	1,338,814
Rhode Island	132,992	43,248	8,432	27,166	3,366	50,780
Texas	8,271,694	1,335,166	316,159	1,913,975	34,092	4,672,302
Utah	677,094	93,323	38,035	201,808	14,335	329,593
Vermont	97,696	14,845	6,540	13,533	2,006	60,772

[1] Includes tort, contract, real property, small claims, probate/estate, mental health, and civil appeals cases. [2] Includes divorce/dissolution, paternity, custody, support, visitation, adoption, and civil protection/restraining order cases. [3] Includes felony, misdemeanor, and appeals from limited jurisdiction courts. [4] Includes delinquency, dependency, and status offense petitions. [5] Includes non-criminal traffic violations (infractions), parking violations, and ordinance violations. [6] Data are not applicable because the reporting unit does not have jurisdiction over the case type or case category.

Source: National Center for State Courts, Court Statistics Project, "CSP Stat, Trial Court Caseload Overview ©," <www.courtstatistics.org>, accessed July 2022.

Table 386. U.S. Sentencing Commission Summary—Cases Reviewed by Disposition and Primary Offense: 2021

[In numbers, except as noted. For fiscal year ending in year shown. Covers federal felony and Class A misdemeanor cases reported to the U.S. Sentencing Commission by federal courts as required under the Sentencing Reform Act. See source for details]

Characteristic	Total [1]	Immi-gration	Drug traffick-ing	Firearms	Fraud, theft, embezzle-ment	Robbery	Child porn-ography	Money laun-dering	All other
Total cases...................	**57,287**	**16,937**	**17,608**	**8,151**	**4,571**	**1,300**	**1,215**	**1,028**	**6,477**
CASES INVOLVING PRISON									
Total receiving prison...............	**52,301**	**16,164**	**16,990**	**7,676**	**3,202**	**1,275**	**1,199**	**908**	**4,887**
Prison only..............................	50,648	15,897	16,307	7,515	2,982	1,245	1,179	867	4,656
Prison term ordered:									
Up to 12 months........................	13,306	9,091	1,311	567	889	31	21	147	1,249
13 to 60 months........................	23,318	6,628	7,023	4,941	1,771	346	325	413	1,871
61 to 120 months......................	8,709	170	5,023	1,659	256	477	463	168	493
Over 120 months.......................	5,315	8	2,950	348	66	391	370	139	1,043
Prison & alternatives [2]..................	1,653	267	683	161	220	30	20	41	231
Mean sentence (in months) [3]...........	48	13	74	48	20	104	108	57	63
Median sentence (in months) [3].........	24	8	60	37	12	90	90	30	15
CASES INVOLVING PROBATION									
Total receiving probation...............	**4,576**	**772**	**618**	**473**	**1,315**	**25**	**16**	**120**	**1,237**
Probation only.........................	3,527	573	450	370	1,014	20	12	88	1,000
Probation & alternatives [2]...............	1,049	199	168	103	301	5	4	32	237
CASES INVOLVING FINES & RESTITUTION									
Total receiving fines & restitution.........	[4] 9,766	395	1,020	646	3,511	803	570	343	2,478
Median amount (in dollars)................	10,000	1,000	1,500	1,500	89,011	3,235	10,000	277,827	(NA)
Fine only.................................	410	1	–	2	54	–	–	–	353

NA Not available. – Represents zero. [1] Details may not sum to total due to rounding. [2] Includes additional conditions of a term of community confinement, home detention, or intermittent confinement. [3] Sentences greater than 470 months are included in these calculations as 470 months. [4] 1,087 cases are excluded due to missing information.

Source: U.S. Sentencing Commission, "2021 Annual Report and Sourcebook of Federal Sentencing Statistics," <www.ussc.gov/research/sourcebook-2021>, accessed March 2022.

Table 387. Mandatory Minimum Sentencing Summary: 2015 to 2021

[For fiscal year ending in year shown for cases reported to the U.S. Sentencing Commission (USSC). Relief from mandatory minimum sentencing may be provided through a safety valve provision and/or by providing the government with substantial assistance; see source]

Item	2015	2016	2017	2018	2019	2020	2021
Cases reported to USSC (number).....................	71,003	67,742	66,873	69,425	76,538	64,565	57,287
Cases involving a mandatory minimum penalty (number)...........	14,138	13,604	13,577	16,228	18,819	15,274	16,439
Percent subject to mandatory minimum penalties..................	22.2	21.9	21.8	24.7	26.1	25.2	29.9
Percent receiving relief.............................	39.2	38.7	37.3	40.6	44.3	44.1	46.5
Percent not receiving relief.........................	60.8	61.3	62.7	59.4	55.7	55.9	53.5
Percent remaining subject to mandatory minimum at sentencing.........	13.5	13.4	13.7	14.2	14.1	13.7	15.7
Offenders convicted of an offence carrying a mandatory minimum sentence by race/ethnicity (percent distribution):							
White..	27.2	27.2	26.9	27.3	27.6	29.5	30.1
Black..	28.9	29.7	29.5	27.4	27.6	26.4	25.0
Hispanic.....................................	41.5	40.4	41.0	42.7	41.8	41.2	41.7
Other..	2.4	2.7	2.6	2.6	3.0	2.9	3.2

Source: U.S. Sentencing Commission, *Quick Facts: Mandatory Minimum Penalties*, June 2022 and earlier reports. See also <www.ussc.gov/research/quick-facts>.

Table 388. Delinquency Cases Disposed by Juvenile Courts by Type of Offense: 1990 to 2019

[In thousands (1,304 represents 1,304,000), except rate. A delinquency offense is an act committed by a juvenile for which an adult could be prosecuted in a criminal court. Disposition of a case involves taking a definite action such as waiving the case to criminal court, dismissing the case, placing the youth on probation, placing the youth in a facility for delinquents, or actions such as fines, restitution, and community service. Data are developed and maintained by the National Center for Juvenile Justice]

Type of offense	1990	1995	2000	2005	2010	2013	2014	2015	2016	2017	2018	2019
All delinquency offenses......	**1,304**	**1,800**	**1,692**	**1,648**	**1,321**	**999**	**930**	**866**	**815**	**788**	**738**	**723**
Case rate [1]...............	50.8	62.7	55.0	51.3	41.9	31.9	29.5	27.5	25.8	24.9	23.3	22.7
Person offenses [2]............	251	405	398	430	335	261	248	241	234	232	230	237
Criminal homicide............	2	3	1	1	1	1	1	1	1	1	1	1
Rape................	6	9	9	11	9	8	8	7	7	8	8	8
Robbery............	25	37	22	26	25	20	19	18	19	20	19	19
Aggravated assault...........	44	63	48	47	34	24	24	25	25	25	25	26
Simple assault...........	135	233	257	278	220	173	164	159	153	148	146	153
Property offenses [2].........	767	909	702	606	489	347	322	297	273	258	224	215
Burglary............	144	147	117	100	85	60	56	52	51	51	42	39
Larceny-theft............	344	437	328	272	239	174	161	144	124	111	97	90
Motor vehicle theft...........	65	53	36	33	16	11	12	13	15	16	15	15
Arson............	6	10	8	7	5	4	3	3	3	2	2	2
Drug law violations............	68	164	184	182	159	133	124	110	104	104	100	96
Public order offenses [2].........	218	322	408	430	338	258	236	218	204	193	183	175
Obstruction of justice...........	85	131	207	194	160	125	118	109	102	97	89	81
Disorderly conduct...........	55	90	102	130	99	73	64	58	55	50	48	48
Weapons offenses...........	29	46	34	42	30	23	20	19	18	17	16	16
Liquor law violations...........	13	11	16	15	13	7	6	6	5	5	4	4
Nonviolent sex offenses...........	10	8	13	12	11	10	10	11	11	11	11	12

[1] Number of cases disposed per 1,000 juveniles ages 10 to upper age of juvenile court jurisdiction. The upper age of juvenile court jurisdiction is defined by statute in each state. [2] Total includes other offenses not shown.

Source: U.S. Department of Justice, Office of Juvenile Justice and Delinquency Prevention, "Delinquency Case Rates by Offense, Sex, and Race (1985-2019)," <www.ojjdp.gov/ojstatbb/court/data.html>; and "Easy Access to Juvenile Court Statistics, Detailed Offenses," <www.ojjdp.gov/ojstatbb/ezajcs>; accessed July 2021.

Table 389. Delinquency Cases Disposed by Juvenile Courts by Type of Offense, Sex, and Race: 2005 to 2019

[See headnote, Table 388. Data are developed and maintained by the National Center for Juvenile Justice]

Item	Number of cases disposed				Case rate [1]			
	2005	2010	2015	2019	2005	2010	2015	2019
Male, total.............	**1,193,671**	**952,427**	**627,548**	**522,293**	**72.5**	**59.0**	**39.0**	**32.1**
Person............	300,960	232,587	167,614	163,973	18.3	14.4	10.4	10.1
Property............	438,463	343,995	216,777	160,494	26.6	21.3	13.5	9.9
Drugs............	145,788	130,857	85,951	71,657	8.9	8.1	5.3	4.4
Public order............	308,460	244,987	157,206	126,169	18.7	15.2	9.8	7.8
Female, total............	**453,997**	**368,471**	**238,780**	**200,332**	**29.0**	**24.0**	**15.5**	**12.8**
Person............	128,533	102,633	73,804	73,043	8.2	6.7	4.8	4.7
Property............	167,561	144,531	79,851	53,992	10.7	9.4	5.2	3.5
Drugs............	36,552	28,590	24,160	24,755	2.3	1.9	1.6	1.6
Public order............	121,351	92,716	60,965	48,542	7.8	6.0	4.0	3.1
White, total [2]............	**792,665**	**595,008**	**374,866**	**310,152**	**40.9**	**33.1**	**21.6**	**18.3**
Person............	189,412	141,015	98,258	97,849	9.8	7.8	5.7	5.8
Property............	317,928	230,921	128,601	89,358	16.4	12.8	7.4	5.3
Drugs............	103,186	88,313	60,562	51,487	5.3	4.9	3.5	3.0
Public order............	182,138	134,759	87,446	71,458	9.4	7.5	5.0	4.2
Black, total [2].............	**546,488**	**441,829**	**305,061**	**254,782**	**108.4**	**92.4**	**65.7**	**53.9**
Person............	172,552	133,860	95,860	90,236	34.2	28.0	20.6	19.1
Property............	176,822	154,359	108,302	82,094	35.1	32.3	23.3	17.4
Drugs............	43,446	32,528	20,670	18,227	8.6	6.8	4.5	3.9
Public order............	153,668	121,082	80,229	64,225	30.5	25.3	17.3	13.6
Hispanic, total............	**262,477**	**247,440**	**162,949**	**136,143**	**45.5**	**37.5**	**22.7**	**17.6**
Person............	57,285	52,445	41,805	42,294	9.9	8.0	5.8	5.5
Property............	91,616	87,842	50,751	36,059	15.9	13.3	7.1	4.7
Drugs............	31,012	34,122	25,214	23,233	5.4	5.2	3.5	3.0
Public order............	82,565	73,032	45,179	34,557	14.3	11.1	6.3	4.5
American Indian, total [3]........	**23,817**	**19,447**	**13,968**	**12,864**	**44.6**	**33.7**	**24.0**	**21.5**
Person............	5,530	4,503	3,331	4,000	10.4	7.8	5.7	6.7
Property............	9,703	7,588	5,271	4,210	18.2	13.1	9.1	7.0
Drugs............	2,791	2,589	2,285	2,192	5.2	4.5	3.9	3.7
Public order............	5,793	4,767	3,081	2,462	10.8	8.3	5.3	4.1
Asian/Native Hawaiian/Pacific Islander, total [2]............	**22,220**	**17,173**	**9,484**	**8,685**	**15.9**	**11.0**	**5.4**	**4.6**
Person............	4,714	3,399	2,165	2,638	3.4	2.2	1.2	1.4
Property............	9,955	7,817	3,702	2,765	7.1	5.0	2.1	1.5
Drugs............	1,904	1,895	1,381	1,273	1.4	1.2	0.8	0.7
Public order............	5,647	4,063	2,235	2,009	4.0	2.6	1.3	1.1

[1] Cases per 1,000 juveniles ages 10 to upper age of juvenile court jurisdiction. The upper age of juvenile court jurisdiction is defined by statute in each state. [2] Non-Hispanic. [3] Data do not always allow for identification of Hispanic ethnicity for cases involving American Indian youth. The American Indian group includes an unknown proportion of Hispanic youth.

Source: U.S. Department of Justice, Office of Juvenile Justice and Delinquency Prevention, "Delinquency Case Rates by Offense, Sex, and Race (1985-2019)," <www.ojjdp.gov/ojstatbb/court/data.html>; and "Easy Access to Juvenile Court Statistics, Analyze Delinquency Cases," <www.ojjdp.gov/ojstatbb/ezajcs/>; accessed August 2021.

Table 390. Child Victims of Abuse and Neglect—Total and First-Time Victims by State: 2020

[For fiscal years ending in year shown. Data are unique counts, which count a child once, regardless of the number of reports concerning that child. Based on available State submissions to National Child Abuse and Neglect Data System (NCANDS) of alleged child abuse and neglect. States reporting 95 percent or more first-time victims are excluded due to potential issues with data quality. NCANDS collects case level data on children who received child protective services response in the form of an investigative or alternative response. Each state has its own definition of child abuse and neglect based on standards set by federal law. Child abuse is defined as any recent act or failure to act on the part of a parent or caretaker which results in death, serious physical or emotional harm, sexual abuse or exploitation; or an act or failure to act which presents an imminent risk or serious harm. See source for details]

| State | Total child population | Victims | First-time victims | | State | Total child population | Victims | First-time victims | |
			Number	Rate per 1,000 children				Number	Rate per 1,000 children
Total........	73,368,194	618,399	422,217	5.9	MO..........	1,371,429	4,449	3,866	2.8
AL............	1,087,283	11,663	9,391	8.6	MT...........	229,683	3,777	3,009	13.1
AK............	178,731	3,212	2,120	11.9	NE...........	475,015	2,376	1,881	4.0
AZ............	1,646,423	9,954	8,166	5.0	NV...........	697,580	5,016	3,316	4.8
AR............	699,714	9,241	7,705	11.0	NH...........	253,134	1,182	946	3.7
CA............	8,791,234	60,317	47,931	5.5	NJ............	1,934,535	3,655	2,902	1.5
CO............	1,250,035	11,615	8,225	6.6	NM...........	472,491	7,050	4,949	10.5
CT............	718,952	6,346	4,611	6.4	NY...........	3,988,354	59,126	34,462	8.6
DE............	204,656	1,200	1,010	4.9	NC...........	2,306,400	22,399	(NA)	(NA)
DC............	129,588	1,568	1,013	7.8	ND...........	181,629	1,614	1,130	6.2
FL............	4,250,732	28,268	12,765	3.0	OH...........	2,568,641	23,691	17,381	6.8
GA............	2,499,950	8,690	7,156	2.9	OK...........	953,520	14,685	11,374	11.9
HI............	295,818	1,294	1,004	3.4	OR...........	860,778	11,487	7,472	8.7
ID............	451,043	1,958	1,602	3.6	PA...........	2,620,757	4,582	4,331	1.7
IL............	2,777,968	35,437	23,628	8.5	RI............	201,849	2,743	1,849	9.2
IN............	1,566,439	22,648	16,032	10.2	SC...........	1,117,925	14,263	10,083	9.0
IA............	725,559	10,600	7,132	9.8	SD...........	218,479	1,570	1,238	5.7
KS............	696,746	2,386	2,142	3.1	TN...........	1,513,401	8,687	4,306	2.8
KY............	1,001,917	16,748	10,732	10.7	TX...........	7,435,132	65,116	52,650	7.1
LA............	1,081,280	6,859	5,437	5.0	UT...........	929,276	9,694	6,722	7.2
ME............	248,168	4,726	3,099	12.5	VT...........	113,166	530	433	3.8
MD............	1,333,919	7,242	4,661	3.5	VA...........	1,866,420	5,658	5,315	2.8
MA............	1,341,523	22,538	12,466	9.3	WA...........	1,665,794	3,967	1,851	1.1
MI............	2,126,813	26,932	16,859	7.9	WV...........	356,267	6,116	5,029	14.1
MN............	1,301,219	6,647	6,044	4.6	WI............	1,258,524	4,177	3,519	2.8
MS............	693,133	8,136	7,145	10.3	WY...........	133,091	992	768	5.8

NA Not available.

Source: U.S. Department of Health and Human Services, Administration for Children and Families, Statistics and Research, *Child Maltreatment 2020*, January 2022. See also <www.acf.hhs.gov/cb/data-research/child-maltreatment>.

Table 391. Child Abuse and Neglect Victims by Type of Maltreatment and Age and Sex of Victim: 2010 to 2020

[For fiscal years ending in year shown. Data are unique counts, which count a child once, regardless of the number of reports concerning that child. Based on available State submissions to National Child Abuse and Neglect Data System (NCANDS) of alleged child abuse and neglect. NCANDS collects case level data on children who received child protective services response in the form of an investigative or alternative response. Each state has its own definition of child abuse and neglect based on standards set by federal law. Child abuse is defined as any recent act or failure to act on the part of a parent or caretaker which results in death, serious physical or emotional harm, sexual abuse or exploitation; or an act or failure to act which presents an imminent risk or serious harm]

Item	2010	2015	2016	2017	2018	2019	2020
Victims, total [1]............................	688,251	683,487	671,622	673,830	677,529	656,243	618,399
SEX OF VICTIM							
Male..	333,864	332,464	326,707	327,373	328,281	316,972	297,352
Female..	352,174	348,087	342,203	343,949	346,957	337,163	319,230
Unknown..	2,213	2,936	2,712	2,508	2,291	2,108	1,817
AGE OF VICTIM							
1 year and younger...........................	136,910	144,354	145,976	147,300	149,828	142,290	136,600
2 to 5 years old...............................	180,271	172,337	166,930	166,392	165,016	158,946	150,673
6 to 9 years old...............................	145,354	153,019	149,514	146,435	143,389	136,784	125,593
10 to 13 years old............................	119,555	115,153	113,788	116,980	122,299	122,585	114,410
14 to 17 years old............................	103,764	95,134	92,921	93,955	94,361	93,049	88,989
18 years old and over [2].....................	490	(NA)	(NA)	(NA)	(NA)	(NA)	(NA)
Unknown [3].....................................	979	3,490	2,493	2,768	2,636	2,589	2,134
TYPES OF MALTREATMENT [4, 5]							
Neglect..	499,691	514,500	502,615	504,545	411,969	399,992	470,297
Physical abuse.................................	118,502	117,772	122,067	123,065	72,814	67,678	101,961
Sexual abuse..................................	62,057	57,286	57,329	58,114	47,124	47,205	57,963
Psychological or emotional..................	53,426	42,549	37,859	38,635	15,605	15,672	39,652
Medical neglect...............................	15,711	15,169	14,028	15,160	5,720	5,614	12,287
Sex trafficking.................................	(NA)	(NA)	(NA)	(NA)	339	439	953
Multiple maltreatment types.................	(NA)	(NA)	(NA)	(NA)	105,322	101,973	(NA)
Other and unknown...........................	68,590	47,514	46,394	47,747	18,636	17,670	36,935

NA Not available. [1] Total victims is the sum for states contributing data to the Child File. The number of states not contributing data varies by year. [2] Beginning in 2011, data included in unknown. [3] Includes unborn, unknown age, and, beginning 2011, victims age 18–21. [4] Data for 2010-2017 and 2020 are counts of the number of distinct victims of the specified types of maltreatment. A child may be a victim of more than one type of maltreatment; therefore, the sum of types is greater than the count of victims. For 2018 and 2019, if a victim is reported with two or more maltreatment types, the victim is counted in the multiple maltreatment category once. [5] Not all states use this taxonomy, nor do states define the categories in the same way.

Source: U.S. Department of Health and Human Services, Administration for Children and Families, Statistics and Research, *Child Maltreatment 2020*, January 2022 and earlier editions, and unpublished data. See also <www.acf.hhs.gov/cb/data-research/child-maltreatment>.

Table 392. Prisoners Under Jurisdiction of Federal or State Correctional Authorities—Summary by State: 2000 to 2020

[For years ending December 31. Jurisdiction refers to the legal authority over a prisoner, regardless of where held. Multiple states reported large changes in prison populations, admissions, and releases between 2019 and 2020 due to criminal justice reforms enacted to address the COVID-19 pandemic. Occasionally, states do not submit data in a given year and estimates are imputed; see source for details]

State	2000	2010	2012	2013	2014	2015	2016	2017	2018	2019	2020
U.S.	1,394,231	1,613,803	1,570,397	1,576,950	1,562,319	1,526,603	1,508,129	1,489,189	1,464,385	1,430,165	1,215,821
Federal [1]	145,416	209,771	217,815	215,866	210,567	196,455	189,192	183,058	179,898	175,116	152,156
State [2]	1,248,815	1,404,032	1,352,582	1,361,084	1,351,752	1,330,148	1,318,937	1,306,131	1,284,487	1,255,049	1,063,665
AL	26,406	31,764	32,431	32,381	31,771	30,810	28,883	27,608	26,841	28,304	25,328
AK [3]	4,173	5,391	5,633	5,081	5,794	5,338	4,434	4,399	4,380	4,475	4,578
AZ	26,510	40,209	40,080	41,177	42,259	42,719	42,320	42,030	42,005	42,441	37,731
AR	11,915	16,204	14,654	17,235	17,874	17,707	17,537	18,070	17,799	17,759	16,094
CA	163,001	165,062	134,534	135,981	136,085	129,593	130,084	131,039	128,625	122,687	97,328
CO	16,833	22,815	20,462	20,371	20,646	20,041	19,981	19,946	20,372	19,785	16,168
CT [3]	18,355	19,321	17,530	17,563	16,636	15,816	14,957	14,040	13,681	12,823	9,559
DE [3]	6,921	6,615	6,914	7,004	6,955	6,654	6,585	6,443	6,067	5,692	4,710
DC [4]	10,352	(NA)	(NA)	(NA)	(NA)	(NA)	(NA)	(NA)	(NA)	(NA)	(NA)
FL	71,319	104,306	101,930	103,028	102,870	101,424	99,974	98,504	97,538	96,009	81,027
GA	44,232	56,432	55,457	54,004	52,949	52,193	53,627	53,667	53,647	54,816	47,141
HI [3]	5,053	5,912	5,831	5,632	5,866	5,879	5,602	5,630	5,375	5,279	4,171
ID	5,535	7,431	7,985	8,242	8,117	8,052	8,252	8,579	8,664	9,437	8,171
IL	45,281	48,418	49,348	48,653	48,278	46,240	43,657	41,427	39,965	38,259	29,729
IN	20,125	28,028	28,831	29,913	29,271	27,355	25,546	26,024	26,877	27,180	23,944
IA	7,955	9,455	8,733	8,697	8,838	8,849	9,031	9,024	9,419	9,282	8,307
KS	8,344	9,051	9,682	9,763	9,877	9,857	9,920	10,015	10,218	10,177	8,779
KY	14,919	20,544	22,110	21,030	21,657	21,701	23,022	23,543	23,431	23,082	18,552
LA	35,207	39,445	40,172	39,299	38,030	36,377	35,682	33,739	32,397	31,609	26,964
ME	1,679	2,154	2,108	2,173	2,242	2,279	2,404	2,404	2,425	2,185	1,714
MD	23,538	22,645	21,522	21,335	21,011	20,764	19,994	19,367	18,856	18,595	15,623
MA	10,722	11,313	11,308	10,950	10,713	9,922	9,403	9,133	8,692	8,205	6,762
MI	47,718	44,165	43,636	43,759	43,390	42,628	41,122	39,666	38,761	38,053	33,617
MN	6,238	9,796	9,938	10,289	10,637	10,798	10,592	10,708	10,101	9,982	8,148
MS	20,241	21,067	22,319	21,969	18,793	18,911	19,192	19,103	19,275	19,417	17,577
MO [7]	27,543	30,623	31,247	31,537	31,942	32,330	32,461	32,601	30,369	26,044	23,062
MT [7]	3,105	3,716	3,609	3,642	3,699	3,685	3,814	3,698	3,765	4,723	3,927
NE	3,895	4,587	4,705	5,026	5,441	5,372	5,302	5,313	5,491	5,682	5,306
NV	10,063	12,653	12,883	13,056	12,537	13,071	13,757	13,721	13,641	12,840	11,422
NH	2,257	2,761	2,790	3,018	2,963	2,897	2,818	2,750	2,722	2,691	2,352
NJ	29,784	25,007	23,225	22,452	21,590	20,489	19,786	19,585	19,362	18,613	12,830
NM [2]	5,342	6,763	6,727	6,931	7,021	7,104	7,055	7,276	7,030	6,723	5,500
NY	70,199	56,656	54,210	53,550	52,518	51,727	50,716	49,461	46,636	43,500	34,128
NC [2]	31,266	40,382	37,136	36,922	37,096	36,617	35,697	36,394	34,899	34,079	29,461
ND [2]	1,076	1,487	1,512	1,576	1,718	1,795	1,791	1,723	1,695	1,794	1,401
OH	45,833	51,712	50,876	51,729	51,519	52,233	52,175	51,478	50,431	50,338	45,036
OK [5]	23,181	26,252	25,225	27,547	27,650	28,547	29,916	28,143	26,956	25,033	22,462
OR [2]	10,580	14,876	14,840	15,517	15,075	15,245	15,166	15,218	15,268	14,961	12,753
PA	36,847	51,264	51,125	51,422	50,694	49,858	49,244	48,333	47,239	45,702	39,357
RI [3]	3,286	3,357	3,318	3,361	3,359	3,248	3,103	2,861	2,767	2,740	2,227
SC	21,778	23,578	22,388	22,060	21,401	20,929	20,858	19,906	19,033	18,608	16,157
SD	2,616	3,434	3,650	3,682	3,608	3,564	3,831	3,970	3,948	3,801	3,250
TN	22,166	27,451	28,411	28,521	28,769	28,172	28,203	28,980	26,321	26,349	22,685
TX	166,719	173,649	166,372	168,280	166,043	163,909	163,703	162,523	163,628	158,429	135,906
UT [6]	5,637	6,807	6,962	7,077	7,031	6,495	6,175	6,219	6,651	6,671	5,446
VT [3]	1,697	2,079	2,034	2,078	1,979	1,750	1,735	1,546	1,659	1,608	1,284
VA	30,168	37,638	37,044	36,982	37,544	38,403	37,813	37,158	36,660	36,091	31,838
WA	14,915	18,235	17,271	17,984	18,120	18,284	19,104	19,656	19,523	19,261	15,724
WV	3,856	6,681	7,070	6,824	6,896	7,118	7,162	7,092	6,775	6,800	6,044
WI	20,754	22,729	22,600	22,471	22,597	22,975	23,377	23,945	24,064	23,956	20,298
WY	1,680	2,112	2,204	2,310	2,383	2,424	2,374	2,473	2,543	2,479	2,087

NA Not available. [1] Includes adult prisoners held in nonsecure community corrections facilities and adults and persons age 17 or younger held in privately operated facilities. [2] Total and state estimates for 2018 and 2019 include imputed counts for Oregon and estimates for 2017 include imputed data for New Mexico and North Dakota. Imputed data counts should not be compared to other years' data. [3] Data include both total jail and prison population. Prisons and jails form one integrated system. [4] As of December 31, 2001, sentenced felons from the District of Columbia are the responsibility of the Federal Bureau of Prisons. [5] 2016-2020 counts includes persons who were waiting in county jails to be moved to state prison. [6] Data for 2018 are not comparable to data for previous years. Total counts of the prisoner population from 2018 include an undetermined number of offenders excluded from counts in 2017 due to a change in legal-status requirements for a program for parole violators that was instituted in 2018. [7] Montana implemented a change in prisoner tracking software at the end of 2018, which has rendered counts between 2018 and 2020 incomparable.

Source: U.S. Department of Justice, Bureau of Justice Statistics, "Corrections Statistical Analysis Tool," <bjs.gov/index.cfm?ty=nps>, accessed April 2021; and *Prisoners in 2020 - Statistical Tables*, NCJ 302776, December 2021.

Table 393. Jail Inmates by Sex, Race, and Hispanic Origin: 2010 to 2020

[Based on the number of inmates on the last weekday in June, except as noted. Data adjusted for nonresponse and rounded to the nearest 100. See source for methodology, and impact of COVID-19 pandemic. Does not include offenders supervised outside of jail facilities. Based on the Annual Survey of Jails, and Census of Jails]

Characteristic	2010	2014	2015 [1]	2016 [1]	2017	2018	2019	2020
Total inmates.	**748,700**	**744,600**	**727,400**	**740,700**	**745,200**	**738,400**	**734,500**	**549,100**
Incarceration rate per 100,000 U.S. residents.	242	234	227	229	229	226	224	167
Adults.	741,200	740,400	723,800	736,800	741,600	735,000	731,600	546,800
Male.	649,300	631,600	620,300	629,700	628,200	620,500	621,100	(NA)
Female.	91,900	108,800	103,500	107,100	113,400	114,500	110,500	(NA)
Juveniles [2].	7,600	4,200	3,600	3,900	3,600	3,400	2,900	2,300
Held as adult [3].	5,600	3,700	3,200	3,200	3,200	2,700	2,200	2,000
Held as juvenile.	1,900	500	400	700	300	700	700	300
White, non-Hispanic.	331,600	352,800	351,600	356,100	370,100	368,500	362,900	262,100
Black, non-Hispanic.	283,200	263,800	255,200	254,600	250,100	242,300	247,100	192,600
American Indian or Alaska Native non-Hispanic.	9,900	10,400	9,000	9,000	8,800	9,700	10,200	6,700
Asian, non-Hispanic.	4,400	5,400	5,200	5,200	4,800	4,800	4,700	3,700
Native Hawaiian/Other Pacific Islander non-Hispanic.	700	(NA)	900	700	1,000	1,000	800	600
Two or more races.	800	(NA)	1,700	2,300	2,000	2,800	1,900	1,500
Hispanic/Latino [4].	118,100	110,600	103,900	112,700	108,400	109,300	106,900	81,900
Rated capacity [5].	866,800	890,500	901,400	915,400	915,100	907,000	907,700	913,700

NA Not available. [1] In 2015 and 2016, the Annual Survey of Jails collected demographic data on the inmate population at year-end instead of midyear. Jails typically hold fewer inmates at year-end than at midyear. The inmate populations were adjusted for seasonal variation and represent estimated midyear counts, see source for Methodology. [2] Juveniles age 17 or younger at midyear. [3] Includes juveniles who were tried or awaiting trial as adults. [4] Persons of Hispanic origin may be of any race. [5] Maximum number of beds or inmates assigned by a rating official to a facility, excluding separate temporary holding areas.

Source: U.S. Department of Justice, Bureau of Justice Statistics, *Jail Inmates in 2020 – Statistical Tables*, NCJ 303308, December 2021, and earlier releases. See also <bjs.ojp.gov/library>.

Table 394. Prisoners Under Federal and State Jurisdiction by Sex, Race, and Hispanic Origin: 1980 to 2020

[As of December 31. Represents prisoners sentenced to more than one year under jurisdiction of federal or state authorities. Jurisdiction refers to the legal authority of state or federal correctional officials over a prisoner, regardless of where the prisoner is held. Federal prisoners includes inmates held in nonsecure privately operated community corrections facilities and juveniles held in contract facilities. From the National Prisoner Statistics Program. See source for methodology]

Year	Total [1]		Sex		Race/ethnicity			Jurisdiction	
	Number [1]	Rate [2]	Male	Female	White [3,4]	Black [3,4]	Hispanic [3]	Federal	State
1980.	315,974	139	303,643	12,331	(NA)	(NA)	(NA)	20,611	295,363
1990.	739,980	297	699,416	40,564	(NA)	(NA)	(NA)	50,403	689,577
1991.	789,610	313	745,808	43,802	(NA)	(NA)	(NA)	56,696	732,914
1992.	846,277	332	799,776	46,501	(NA)	(NA)	(NA)	65,706	780,571
1993.	932,074	359	878,037	54,037	(NA)	(NA)	(NA)	74,399	857,675
1994.	1,016,691	389	956,566	60,125	(NA)	(NA)	(NA)	79,795	936,896
1995.	1,085,022	411	1,021,059	63,963	(NA)	(NA)	(NA)	83,663	1,001,359
1996.	1,137,722	427	1,068,123	69,599	(NA)	(NA)	(NA)	88,815	1,048,907
1997.	1,195,498	445	1,121,663	73,835	(NA)	(NA)	(NA)	94,987	1,100,511
1998.	1,245,402	461	1,167,802	77,600	(NA)	(NA)	(NA)	103,682	1,141,720
1999.	1,304,074	476	1,221,611	82,463	(NA)	(NA)	(NA)	114,275	1,189,799
2000.	1,334,174	5 470	1,249,130	85,044	(NA)	(NA)	(NA)	125,044	1,209,130
2001.	1,345,217	470	1,260,033	85,184	(NA)	(NA)	(NA)	136,509	1,208,708
2002.	1,380,516	477	1,291,450	89,066	(NA)	(NA)	(NA)	143,040	1,237,476
2003.	1,408,361	483	1,315,790	92,571	(NA)	(NA)	(NA)	151,919	1,256,442
2004.	1,433,728	487	1,337,730	95,998	(NA)	(NA)	(NA)	159,137	1,274,591
2005.	1,462,866	492	1,364,178	98,688	(NA)	(NA)	(NA)	166,173	1,296,693
2006.	1,504,598	501	1,401,261	103,337	507,100	590,300	313,600	173,533	1,331,065
2007.	1,532,851	506	1,427,088	105,763	499,800	592,900	330,400	179,204	1,353,647
2008.	1,547,742	506	1,441,384	106,358	499,900	592,800	329,800	182,333	1,365,409
2009.	1,553,574	504	1,448,239	105,335	490,000	584,800	341,200	187,886	1,365,688
2010.	1,552,669	500	1,447,766	104,903	490,500	568,500	338,500	190,641	1,362,028
2011.	1,538,847	492	1,435,141	103,706	480,400	554,400	341,300	197,050	1,341,797
2012.	1,512,430	480	1,411,076	101,354	470,900	536,600	336,100	196,574	1,315,856
2013.	1,520,403	479	1,416,102	104,301	469,800	530,100	343,100	195,098	1,325,305
2014.	1,507,781	472	1,401,685	106,096	463,800	516,800	339,500	191,374	1,316,407
2015.	1,476,847	459	1,371,879	104,968	450,600	496,400	335,800	178,688	1,298,159
2016 [6].	1,459,948	450	1,354,109	105,839	440,700	484,600	342,100	171,482	1,288,466
2017 [7].	1,439,877	442	1,334,828	105,049	436,800	473,000	338,800	166,203	1,273,674
2018 [8].	1,413,370	431	1,309,194	104,176	430,500	461,500	332,900	163,653	1,249,717
2019 [8].	1,379,786	419	1,278,484	101,302	422,900	449,900	322,700	158,498	1,221,288
2020.	1,182,166	358	1,102,651	79,515	358,900	389,500	275,300	142,028	1,040,138

NA Not available. [1] Includes persons of two or more races and other race groups not shown separately. [2] Rate per 100,000 estimated population. Based on U.S. Census Bureau estimated resident population. [3] Rounded to the nearest 100. [4] Excludes persons of Hispanic or Latino origin and persons of two or more races. [5] Decrease in incarceration rate from 1999 to 2000 due to use of new Census numbers. [6] Total and state estimates include imputed counts for North Dakota, which did not submit data. [7] Total and state estimates include imputed counts for New Mexico and North Dakota, which did not submit 2017 NPS data. [8] Estimates for 2018 and 2019 include imputed counts for Oregon, which did not submit 2018 or 2019 data. 2019 includes imputed counts for Vermont, which provided total jurisdiction counts but could not break down the population by sentence length.

Source: U.S. Department of Justice, Bureau of Justice Statistics, *Prisoners in 2020 – Statistical Tables*, NCJ 302776, December 2021, and earlier reports. See also <bjs.ojp.gov/library>.

Table 395. Prisoners Executed Under Civil Authority by State: 1977 to 2021

[Alaska, Colorado, Connecticut, District of Columbia, Hawaii, Illinois, Iowa, Maine, Maryland, Massachusetts, Michigan, Minnesota, New Hampshire, New Jersey, New Mexico, North Dakota, Rhode Island, Vermont, West Virginia, and Wisconsin are jurisdictions without a death penalty. Delaware, New York, and Washington state courts invalidated death penalty statue but the penalty is not legislatively repealed]

State	1977 to 2021	2000	2010	2019	2020	2021 (P)
United States [1]	1,540	85	46	22	17	11
Alabama	68	4	5	3	1	1
Arizona	37	3	1	–	–	–
Arkansas	31	2	–	–	–	–
California	13	1	–	–	–	–
Colorado	1	–	–	–	–	–
Connecticut	1	–	–	–	–	–
Delaware	16	1	–	–	–	–
Florida	99	6	1	2	–	–
Georgia	76	–	2	3	1	–
Idaho	3	–	–	–	–	–
Illinois	12	–	–	–	–	–
Indiana	20	–	–	–	–	–
Kentucky	3	–	–	–	–	–
Louisiana	28	1	1	–	–	–
Maryland	5	–	–	–	–	–
Mississippi	22	–	3	–	–	1
Missouri	91	5	–	1	1	1
Montana	3	–	–	–	–	–
Nebraska	4	–	–	–	–	–
Nevada	12	–	–	–	–	–
New Mexico	1	–	–	–	–	–
North Carolina	43	1	–	–	–	–
Ohio	56	–	8	–	–	–
Oklahoma	114	11	3	–	–	2
Oregon	2	–	–	–	–	–
Pennsylvania	3	–	–	–	–	–
South Carolina	43	1	–	–	–	–
South Dakota	5	–	–	1	–	–
Tennessee	13	1	–	3	1	–
Texas	573	40	17	9	3	3
Utah	7	–	1	–	–	–
Virginia	113	8	3	–	–	–
Washington	5	–	1	–	–	–
Wyoming	1	–	–	–	–	–

P Preliminary – Represents zero. [1] Includes persons executed within the Federal system.

Source: Through 1978, U.S. Law Enforcement Assistance Administration; thereafter, U.S. Department of Justice, Bureau of Justice Statistics, *Capital Punishment, 2020: Statistical Tables*, NCJ 302729, December 2021, and earlier reports. See also <bjs.ojp.gov/library>.

Table 396. Prisoners Executed Under Civil Authority by Sex and Race: 1930 to 2021

[Excludes executions by military authorities. See source for more information]

Period or year	Total [1]	Male	Female	White [2]	Black [2]	His-panic
1930 to 1939	1,667	1,656	11	827	816	(NA)
1940 to 1949	1,284	1,272	12	490	781	(NA)
1950 to 1959	717	709	8	336	376	(NA)
1960 to 1967	191	190	1	98	93	(NA)
1968 to 1976 [3]	–	–	–	–	–	–
1977	1	1	–	1	–	–
1978	–	–	–	–	–	–
1979	2	2	–	2	–	–
1980	–	–	–	–	–	–
1981	1	1	–	1	–	–
1982	2	2	–	1	1	–
1983	5	5	–	4	1	–
1984	21	20	1	13	8	–
1985	18	18	–	9	7	2
1986	18	18	–	9	7	2
1987	25	25	–	11	11	3
1988	11	11	–	6	5	–
1989	16	16	–	6	8	2
1990	23	23	–	16	7	–
1991	14	14	–	6	7	1
1992	31	31	–	17	11	2
1993	38	38	–	19	14	4
1994	31	31	–	19	11	1
1995	56	56	–	31	22	2
1996	45	45	–	29	14	2
1997	74	74	–	41	26	5
1998	68	66	2	40	18	8
1999	98	98	–	53	33	9
2000	85	83	2	43	35	6
2001	66	63	3	45	17	3
2002	71	69	2	47	18	6
2003	65	65	–	41	20	3
2004	59	59	–	36	19	3
2005	60	59	1	38	19	3
2006	53	53	–	25	20	8
2007	42	42	–	22	14	6
2008	37	37	–	17	17	3
2009	52	52	–	24	21	7
2010	46	45	1	28	13	5
2011	43	43	–	22	16	5
2012	43	43	–	25	11	7
2013	39	38	1	23	13	3
2014	35	33	2	12	18	5
2015	28	(NA)	(NA)	11	10	7
2016	20	(NA)	(NA)	16	2	2
2017	23	(NA)	(NA)	13	8	2
2018	25	(NA)	(NA)	14	6	5
2019	22	22	–	14	7	1
2020	17	17	–	10	5	1
2021 (P)	11	10	1	5	6	–

– Represents zero. NA Not available. P Preliminary. [1] Includes American Indians, Alaska Natives, Asians, Native Hawaiians, and other Pacific Islanders, not shown separately. [2] Excludes persons of Hispanic or Latino origin. In 2017, two of the white prisoners executed in Texas were of Hispanic or Latino origin. [3] In 1972, the U.S. Supreme Court invalidated capital punishment statutes in several states, effecting a moratorium on executions. Executions resumed in 1977 when the Supreme Court found revisions to several state statutes had effectively addressed the issues previously held as unconstitutional.

Source: Through 1978, U.S. Law Enforcement Assistance Administration; thereafter, U.S. Department of Justice, Bureau of Justice Statistics, *Capital Punishment, 2020: Statistical Tables*, NCJ 302729, December 2021. See also <bjs.ojp.gov/library>.

Table 397. Prisoners Under Death Sentence by Race: 1980 to 2020

[As of December 31. Excludes prisoners under sentence of death who remained within local correctional systems pending exhaustion of appellate process or who had not been committed to prison. Data from the National Prisoner Statistics Program]

Year	Total	White [1]	Black [1]	Other [2]	Year	Total	White [1]	Black [1]	Other [2]
1980	692	424	264	4	2001	3,577	1,968	1,538	71
1982	1,066	613	441	12	2002	3,562	1,939	1,551	72
1983	1,209	692	505	12	2003	3,377	1,882	1,417	78
1984	1,420	806	598	16	2004	3,320	1,856	1,390	74
1985	1,575	896	664	15	2005	3,245	1,802	1,366	77
1986	1,800	1,013	762	25	2006	3,233	1,806	1,353	74
1987	1,967	1,128	813	26	2007	3,215	1,806	1,338	71
1988	2,117	1,235	848	34	2008	3,210	1,795	1,343	72
1989	2,243	1,308	898	37	2009	3,173	1,779	1,318	76
1990	2,346	1,368	940	38	2010	3,139	1,743	1,309	87
1991	2,465	1,449	979	37	2011	3,065	1,721	1,274	70
1992	2,580	1,511	1,031	38	2012	3,011	1,684	1,258	69
1993	2,727	1,575	1,111	41	2013	2,983	1,670	1,251	62
1994	2,905	1,653	1,203	49	2014	2,942	1,647	1,233	62
1995	3,064	1,732	1,284	48	2015	2,872	1,606	1,202	64
1996	3,242	1,833	1,358	51	2016	2,797	1,553	1,179	65
1997	3,328	1,864	1,408	56	2017	2,703	1,508	1,129	66
1998	3,465	1,917	1,489	59	2018	2,626	1,470	1,091	65
1999	3,540	1,960	1,515	65	2019	2,563	1,443	1,057	63
2000	3,601	1,989	1,541	71	2020	2,469	1,394	1,015	60

[1] Includes persons of Hispanic origin. [2] Includes Asians, Native Hawaiians, Other Pacific Islanders, American Indians, Alaska Natives, and persons for whom only ethnicity was identified.

Source: U.S. Department of Justice, Bureau of Justice Statistics, *Capital Punishment, 2020: Statistical Tables*, NCJ 302729, December 2021. See also <bjs.ojp.gov/library>.

Table 398. Prisoners—Firearm Possession and Use During Offense That Led to Imprisonment by Type of Controlling Offense: 2016

[For sentenced prisoners and those awaiting sentencing with one offense, that offense is the controlling offense. For sentenced prisoners with multiple offenses and sentences, the controlling offense is the one with the longest sentence. For sentenced prisoners with multiple offenses and one sentence and those awaiting sentencing with multiple offenses, the controlling offense is the most serious offense. Data are from the Survey of Prison Inmates]

Controlling offense	State prisoners			Federal prisoners		
		Percent who—			Percent who—	
	Number [1]	Possessed a firearm [1]	Used a firearm [2]	Number [1]	Possessed a firearm [1]	Used a firearm [2]
Total	**1,211,200**	**20.9**	**13.9**	**170,400**	**20.0**	**5.0**
Violent	667,300	29.1	23.0	20,900	36.2	25.3
Homicide [3]	191,400	43.6	37.2	3,800	35.9	28.4
Rape/sexual assault	144,800	2.0	0.8	2,400	(B)	(B)
Robbery	149,600	43.3	31.5	10,700	46.3	32.1
Assault	149,400	25.0	20.6	2,900	29.0	18.1
Other violent [4]	32,200	17.0	12.6	1,200	34.1	(B)
Property	186,100	[9] 4.9	[9] 2.0	12,000	[9] 2.6	(B)
Burglary	88,100	6.7	3.2	300	(B)	(B)
Other property [5]	98,000	3.3	1.0	11,800	2.4	(B)
Drug	180,800	[9] 8.4	[9] 0.8	80,500	[9] 12.3	[9] 0.6
Trafficking [6]	130,500	9.4	0.9	72,300	12.9	0.7
Possession	45,900	6.1	(B)	3,500	(B)	(B)
Other/unspecified drug	4,300	(B)	(B)	4,700	(B)	(B)
Public order	158,300	[9] 21.5	[9] 5.6	52,900	30.2	[9] 5.3
Weapons [7]	43,800	67.2	15.7	22,200	66.9	11.3
Other public order [8]	114,400	4.0	1.7	30,700	3.6	(B)
Other	3,900	(B)	(B)	1,800	(B)	(B)
Unknown	14,900	[9] 4.3	(B)	2,200	(B)	(B)

B Not calculated. Too few cases to provide a reliable estimate, or coefficient of variation is greater than 50%. [1] Data are estimates. Excludes prisoners who were missing responses on firearm possession; includes prisoners who were missing responses on firearm use. [2] Excludes prisoners who were missing responses on firearm use. [3] Includes murder and negligent and non-negligent manslaughter. [4] Includes kidnapping, blackmail, extortion, hit-and-run driving with bodily injury, child abuse, and criminal endangerment. [5] Includes larceny, theft, motor vehicle theft, arson, fraud, stolen property, destruction of property, vandalism, hit-and-run driving with no bodily injury, criminal tampering, trespassing, entering without breaking, and possession of burglary tools. [6] Includes possession with intent to distribute. [7] Includes being armed while committing a crime; possession of ammunition, concealed weapons, firearms and explosive devices; selling or trafficking weapons; and other weapons offenses. [8] Includes commercialized vice, immigration crimes, DUI, violations of probation/parole, and other public-order offenses. [9] Difference with comparison group (total violent offenders) is significant at the 95% confidence level across main categories, and no testing was done on subcategories (e.g., homicide).

Source: U.S. Department of Justice, Bureau of Justice Statistics, *Source and Use of Firearms Involved in Crimes: Survey of Prison Inmates, 2016*, NCJ 251776, January 2019. See also <bjs.ojp.gov/library>.

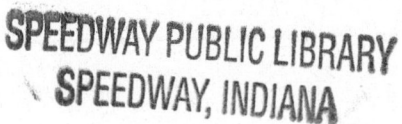

Table 399. Adults Under Community Supervision, Probation, and Parole by State: 2020

[As of December 31, 2020. Rates computed using the estimated U.S. adult resident population in each jurisdiction on January 1, 2021. Counts may not be actual as reporting agencies may provide estimates on some or all detailed data; see source. From Annual Survey of Probation and Parole]

Area	Community supervision [1]		Probation		Parole	
	Number	Rate per 100,0000	Number	Rate per 100,0000	Number	Rate per 100,0000
United States, total.........	**3,890,400**	**1,511**	**3,053,742**	**1,186**	**862,113**	**335**
Federal......................	120,300	47	12,394	5	107,922	42
States.......................	3,770,100	1,465	3,041,348	1,181	754,191	293
Alabama.....................	55,400	1,440	47,407	1,233	8,245	214
Alaska [3]...................	3,400	623	2,438	442	1,003	182
Arizona.....................	79,800	1,366	72,946	1,249	6,887	118
Arkansas...................	64,900	2,775	39,871	1,705	25,852	1,106
California [3]...............	293,700	960	183,334	599	[2] 110,349	361
Colorado [3]................	90,800	1,980	78,562	1,712	12,284	268
Connecticut [3].............	35,600	1,253	31,473	1,110	4,080	144
Delaware...................	10,500	1,336	10,150	1,289	373	47
District of Columbia........	5,900	1,015	3,495	598	2,547	436
Florida [3]..................	183,900	1,046	179,594	1,021	4,280	24
Georgia [3].................	357,500	4,331	341,434	4,136	19,447	236
Hawaii......................	18,800	1,698	17,291	1,559	1,544	139
Idaho.......................	33,400	2,394	27,418	1,966	5,967	428
Illinois.....................	113,600	1,161	88,894	908	24,744	253
Indiana.....................	105,900	2,036	99,763	1,918	6,136	118
Iowa [3]....................	31,800	1,302	24,839	1,018	7,261	297
Kansas.....................	21,300	959	15,874	715	5,428	244
Kentucky [3]...............	69,900	2,008	55,460	1,593	14,429	414
Louisiana..................	48,000	1,348	27,898	783	21,566	605
Maine......................	6,000	541	5,966	540	18	2
Maryland...................	66,000	1,398	56,551	1,197	9,490	201
Massachusetts [3]..........	35,900	647	34,624	624	1,316	24
Michigan [3]................	132,200	1,686	118,778	1,514	13,461	172
Minnesota.................	92,600	2,121	85,254	1,952	7,359	169
Mississippi................	39,500	1,738	29,024	1,276	10,510	462
Missouri....................	59,500	1,241	38,749	809	20,729	433
Montana [3]................	11,200	1,309	9,524	1,113	1,683	197
Nebraska..................	12,600	860	11,454	781	1,156	79
Nevada....................	18,400	749	9,222	374	9,222	374
New Hampshire.............	4,600	412	2,723	244	1,882	168
New Jersey.................	128,000	1,843	112,507	1,619	15,516	223
New Mexico [3].............	11,700	712	11,682	712	2,725	166
New York...................	120,300	786	76,323	499	43,979	287
North Carolina.............	79,000	946	65,808	788	13,419	161
North Dakota...............	6,600	1,124	5,845	1,000	724	124
Ohio [3]....................	224,200	2,455	201,455	2,206	22,769	249
Oklahoma..................	25,300	831	23,027	758	2,237	74
Oregon....................	59,600	1,753	35,732	1,052	23,832	702
Pennsylvania [3]...........	200,700	1,974	112,440	1,106	88,263	868
Rhode Island [3]...........	18,400	2,152	17,805	2,080	619	72
South Carolina.............	30,800	746	26,389	639	4,638	112
South Dakota..............	11,200	1,659	7,550	1,116	3,673	543
Tennessee [3]..............	73,000	1,350	60,550	1,120	12,407	230
Texas......................	442,100	2,000	334,353	1,513	110,437	500
Utah.......................	14,700	625	10,231	436	4,433	189
Vermont....................	4,000	790	3,125	612	909	178
Virginia....................	66,300	984	64,280	954	2,017	30
Washington [3].............	73,700	1,215	72,181	1,191	14,536	240
West Virginia..............	9,900	696	6,243	438	3,682	258
Wisconsin [3]..............	61,600	1,343	38,385	837	23,174	505
Wyoming...................	6,400	1,415	5,427	1,204	954	212

[1] Community supervision counts are rounded to nearest hundred. December 31, 2020 population excludes 13,669 offenders under community supervision who were on both probation and parole. [2] In California, includes post-release community supervision and mandatory supervision parolees. [3] Includes estimates for nonreporting agencies; see source for explanatory notes.

Source: U.S. Department of Justice, Bureau of Justice Statistics, *Probation and Parole in the United States, 2020*, NCJ 303102, December 2021. See also <bjs.ojp.gov/library>.

Table 400. Rate of Adults Under Community Supervision, Probation, and Parole: 2000 to 2020

[As of December 31. From the Annual Survey of Probation and Parole. Probation is a court-ordered period of correctional supervision in the community, generally as an alternative to incarceration. Probation can be a combined sentence of incarceration followed by a period of community supervision. Parole is a period of conditional supervised release in the community following a prison term. Parolees include persons released through discretionary or mandatory supervised release from prison]

Year	Rate per 100,000 population			U.S. residents on—		
	Community supervision [1,2]	Probation	Parole	Community supervision [1]	Probation	Parole
2000	2,162	1,818	344	1 in 46	1 in 55	1 in 291
2001	2,184	1,842	342	1 in 46	1 in 54	1 in 292
2002	2,198	1,849	349	1 in 45	1 in 54	1 in 287
2003	2,219	1,865	354	1 in 45	1 in 55	1 in 282
2004	2,226	1,875	351	1 in 45	1 in 53	1 in 285
2005	2,215	1,864	351	1 in 45	1 in 54	1 in 285
2006	2,228	1,875	353	1 in 45	1 in 53	1 in 283
2007	2,237	1,878	361	1 in 45	1 in 53	1 in 277
2008	2,202	1,847	357	1 in 45	1 in 54	1 in 280
2009	2,148	1,797	353	1 in 47	1 in 56	1 in 283
2010	2,067	1,715	356	1 in 48	1 in 58	1 in 281
2011	2,017	1,663	358	1 in 50	1 in 60	1 in 279
2012	1,984	1,634	356	1 in 50	1 in 61	1 in 281
2013	1,949	1,606	349	1 in 51	1 in 62	1 in 287
2014	1,916	1,572	349	1 in 52	1 in 64	1 in 287
2015	1,873	1,527	351	1 in 53	1 in 66	1 in 285
2016	1,811	1,466	349	1 in 55	1 in 68	1 in 287
2017	1,786	1,444	347	1 in 56	1 in 69	1 in 289
2018	1,729	1,391	345	1 in 58	1 in 72	1 in 290
2019	1,701	1,363	343	1 in 59	1 in 73	1 in 291
2020	1,511	1,186	335	1 in 66	1 in 84	1 in 299

[1] Adults on probation or parole. [2] Beginning 2008, detail does not sum to total because the community supervision rate was adjusted to exclude parolees who were also on probation.

Source: U.S. Department of Justice, Bureau of Justice Statistics, *Probation and Parole in the United States, 2020*, NCJ 303102, December 2021, and earlier reports. See also <bjs.ojp.gov/library>.

Table 401. Prisoner Recidivism by Selected Characteristics: 2012 to 2017

[Data are shown for state prisoners released in 2012 across 34 states (except as noted) who were arrested for a new crime from 2012 to 2017. See source for details]

Characteristic	Number of released prisoners	Percent		
		Arrested within 5 years of release	Arrested and convicted within 5 years of release [1]	Returned to prison within 5 years of release [2]
Total	**408,300**	**70.8**	**54.4**	**45.8**
SEX				
Male	363,200	71.7	55.4	47.2
Female	45,100	63.1	46.5	34.0
RACE/HISPANIC ORIGIN				
White alone, non-Hispanic	179,000	69.5	53.5	45.5
Black alone, non-Hispanic	147,700	74.0	56.7	48.0
Hispanic	66,500	66.9	51.7	42.3
American Indian/Alaska Native, non-Hispanic	6,200	78.9	63.0	51.2
Asian/Native Hawaiian/Other Pacific Islander, non-Hispanic	2,700	64.8	39.2	28.4
Other [3]	6,100	67.8	56.7	41.0
AGE AT RELEASE				
24 years old and under	66,200	81.0	65.2	56.8
25 to 39 years old	203,600	74.4	58.2	48.8
40 years and older	138,400	60.5	43.8	36.3
40 to 54 years old	116,100	63.8	46.8	38.8
55 to 64 years old	19,100	46.3	30.5	24.5
65 years old and over	3,100	25.6	13.0	14.4
MOST SERIOUS COMMITMENT OFFENSE				
Violent	112,300	65.2	(NA)	(NA)
Property	115,600	78.3	(NA)	(NA)
Drug	103,900	69.8	(NA)	(NA)
Public order	76,500	68.9	(NA)	(NA)
NUMBER OF PRIOR ARRESTS [4]				
4 or fewer	104,500	54.5	(NA)	(NA)
2 or fewer	47,300	47.6	(NA)	(NA)
3 to 4	57,300	60.3	(NA)	(NA)
5 to 9	127,100	70.0	(NA)	(NA)
10 or more	176,600	81.0	(NA)	(NA)

NA Not available. [1] Estimates are based on prisoners released across the 31 states that could provide necessary court data. [2] Estimates are based on prisoners released across the 21 states that could provide necessary data on persons returned to prison for a probation or parole violation or an arrest that led to a new sentence. [3] Includes non-Hispanic persons of two or more races or other unspecified races. [4] Includes arrests in the prisoners' criminal history and the arrest that resulted in the imprisonment.

Source: U.S. Department of Justice, Bureau of Justice Statistics, *Recidivism of Prisoners Released in 34 States in 2012: A 5-Year Follow-Up Period (2012–2017)*, NCJ 255947, July 2021. See also <bjs.ojp.gov/library>.

Table 402. The U.S. Fire Service: Departments, Personnel, and Responses by Type: 1990 to 2019

[In thousands (1,025.7 represents 1,025,700), except where noted. A fire department is a public or private organization that provides fire prevention, fire suppression, and associated emergency and non-emergency services to a jurisdiction such as a county, municipality, or organized fire district]

Items	1990	2000	2005	2010	2015	2016	2017	2018	2019
FIRE DEPARTMENTS (NUMBER)									
Total departments	**30,391**	**30,339**	**30,300**	**30,125**	**29,727**	**29,710**	**29,819**	**29,705**	**29,537**
All career	1,949	2,178	2,087	2,495	2,651	2,775	2,785	3,009	2,789
Mostly career	1,338	1,667	1,766	1,860	1,893	2,048	2,316	2,368	2,533
Mostly volunteer	4,000	4,523	4,902	5,290	5,421	5,451	5,405	5,206	5,148
All volunteer	23,104	21,971	21,575	20,480	19,762	19,436	19,313	19,122	19,067
By whether Emergency Medical Service (EMS) provided:									
Provide EMS service only	(NA)	(NA)	12,900	13,440	13,500	(NA)	13,631	(NA)	(NA)
Provide EMS service and advance life support	(NA)	(NA)	4,260	4,515	4,617	(NA)	4,629	(NA)	(NA)
No EMS service	(NA)	(NA)	13,170	12,170	11,610	(NA)	11,559	(NA)	(NA)
FIRE DEPARTMENT PERSONNEL (1,000)									
Total personnel	**1,025.7**	**1,064.2**	**1,136.7**	**1,103.3**	**1,160.5**	**1,090.1**	**1,056.2**	**1,115.0**	**1,080.8**
Career [1]	253.0	286.8	313.3	335.2	345.6	361.1	373.6	370.0	358.0
Volunteer [2]	772.7	777.4	823.7	768.2	814.9	729.0	682.6	745.0	722.8
RESPONSES BY TYPE (1,000)									
Total responses	**13,708**	**20,520**	**23,252**	**28,205**	**33,603**	**35,320**	**34,684**	**36,747**	**37,272**
Fires	2,019	1,708	1,602	1,332	1,346	1,342	1,320	1,319	1,292
Medical aid	7,650	12,251	14,374	18,522	21,500	22,751	22,341	23,552	24,481
False alarms	1,476	2,127	2,134	2,187	2,567	2,622	2,547	2,889	2,893
Malicious mischievous	442	300	241	163	166	173	141	172	(NA)
System malfunctions	593	884	746	709	828	837	752	889	(NA)
Unintentional calls	318	714	838	992	1,200	1,226	1,286	1,379	(NA)
Other [3]	124	230	310	324	374	387	369	451	(NA)
Mutual aid/assistance	487	864	1,091	1,190	1,493	1,515	1,353	1,513	1,487
Hazardous material	210	319	375	402	442	425	424	426	440
Other hazardous [4]	423	544	667	660	643	685	693	707	744
All other [5]	1,443	2,708	3,009	3,913	5,646	5,981	6,006	6,343	5,936

NA Not available. [1] Includes full-time uniform firefighters regardless of assignment (i.e., suppression, administrative, prevention/inspection, etc.). Does not include firefighters who work for the state or federal government or in private fire brigades. [2] Volunteer firefighters include any active part-time (call or volunteer) firefighters. [3] Bomb scares, etc. [4] Arcing wires, bomb removal, power line down, biological hazard, etc. [5] Smoke scares, lock-outs, animal rescue, unauthorized burning, severe weather, etc.

Source: National Fire Protection Association, Quincy, MA, *U.S. Fire Department Profile 2019 Supporting Tables ©*, and *Fire Loss in the United States During 2018 ©*, and earlier reports. See also <www.nfpa.org/News-and-Research>.

Table 403. Firefighter On-Duty Fatalities and Injuries: 2010 to 2020

[Number, unless otherwise noted. On-duty refers to involvement in operations at the scene of an emergency, whether it is a fire or nonfire incident; responding to or returning from an incident; performing other officially assigned duties including training; and being on call]

Item	2010	2013	2014	2015	2016	2017	2018	2019	2020
Total fatalities [1]	**89**	**110**	**97**	**90**	**92**	**93**	**85**	**65**	**[4] 102**
Fatalities per 100,000 fires (rate)	2.33	4.84	2.39	2.45	2.01	(NA)	(NA)	(NA)	(NA)
Emergency duty deaths (percent)	55.6	70	45.4	47.8	41.3	48.4	52.9	61.5	70.6
By incident characteristic:									
Wildland related fatalities	12	31	11	12	15	10	10	7	13
Incidents with multiple fatalities	4	4	2	3	3	1	2	0	3
Training fatalities	12	7	10	7	9	12	9	5	7
Cause of fatal injury:									
Stress/overexertion [2]	56	40	62	61	44	54	37	37	37
Vehicle collision	12	10	12	5	19	12	13	7	15
Total nonfatal Injuries [3]	**71,875**	**65,880**	**63,350**	**68,085**	**62,085**	**58,835**	**58,250**	**60,825**	**64,875**
Fireground injuries	32,675	29,760	27,015	29,130	24,325	24,495	22,975	23,825	22,450
Injuries at nonfire emergencies	13,355	12,535	14,595	14,320	12,780	12,240	11,625	14,150	13,650
Nature of injury:									
Burns (fire or chemical)	2,585	1,975	1,810	2,020	1,900	1,310	1,550	1,775	1,475
Smoke or gas inhalation	1,500	1,895	1,980	1,645	2,355	2,135	3,150	3,075	2,700
Other respiratory distress	940	915	855	1,060	800	850	975	1,075	1,400
Burns and smoke inhalation	635	195	585	535	880	1,525	1,450	1,350	825
Wound, cut, bleeding, bruise	11,110	10,530	9,705	10,205	9,450	9,470	8,075	9,000	7,675
Dislocation, fracture	1,820	1,900	1,995	1,685	1,850	1,330	1,300	1,700	1,675
Heart attack or stroke	810	620	905	920	575	550	825	575	750
Strain, sprain, muscular pain	40,385	37,565	35,015	37,945	32,650	30,970	29,550	30,500	29,725
Thermal stress (frostbite, heat exhaustion)	3,195	2,080	2,245	2,860	2,475	2,095	2,875	3,000	2,375
Other	8,895	8,205	8,255	9,210	9,150	8,600	8,500	8,775	16,275
Fire department vehicle collisions	14,200	12,350	14,910	16,600	15,430	15,425	14,425	15,350	15,675
Injuries	775	730	550	1,150	700	1,005	575	575	550
Personal vehicle collisions	1,000	830	620	700	850	795	700	800	725
Injuries	75	185	90	50	175	75	50	10	200

NA Not available. [1] Includes causes not shown, such as struck by object, caught/trapped, structural collapse, fall, violence, lost/disoriented, and unknown. [2] Stress/overexertion include all firefighter deaths that are cardiac or cerebrovascular in nature such as heart attacks, strokes, and other events such as extreme climatic thermal exposure (heat exhaustion). [3] Includes other types of nonfatal injuries not shown separately. [4] Includes 36 deaths due to exposure to COVID-19.

Source: Fatalities: U.S. Department of Homeland Security, Federal Emergency Management Agency, U.S. Fire Administration, *Firefighter Fatalities in the United States in 2020*, March 2022, and earlier reports. See also <www.usfa.fema.gov/data/statistics/ff_fatality_reports.html>. Nonfatal Injuries: National Fire Protection Association, *United States Firefighter Injuries in 2020 ©*, December 2021, and earlier reports. See also <nfpa.org/News-and-Research>.

Table 404. Fires—Number and Loss by Type and Property Use: 2017 to 2020

[Number of fires in thousands (1,320 represents 1,320,000); property loss in millions of dollars (23,000 represents $23,000,000,000). Based on annual sample survey of fire departments. No adjustments were made for unreported fires and losses]

Type and property use	Number (1,000)				Direct property loss (mil. dol.) [1]			
	2017	2018	2019	2020	2017 [7]	2018 [8]	2019	2020 [9]
Fires, total	**1,320**	**1,319**	**1,292**	**1,389**	**23,000**	**25,600**	**14,820**	**21,866**
Structure	499	499	482	491	10,700	11,066	12,287	12,107
Outside of structure [2]	74	71	71	84	137	139	206	210
Brush and rubbish	458	439	422	502	–	–	(NA)	(NA)
Vehicle [3]	198	213	223	210	2,044	1,876	2,229	5,170
Other	91	98	95	103	136	176	98	179
Structure fires by property use:								
Residential	379	387	362	380	7,900	8,286	7,976	8,703
1-2 family homes [4]	263	277	265	271	6,141	6,493	6,428	6,771
Apartments	95	87	75	86	1,600	1,529	1,339	1,629
Other residential [5]	23	24	22	23	162	264	209	303
Non-residential	120	112	120	111	2,807	2,780	4,311	3,404
Public assembly	15	16	(NA)	(NA)	285	384	(NA)	(NA)
Educational	6	5	(NA)	(NA)	51	109	(NA)	(NA)
Institutional	7	7	(NA)	(NA)	40	44	(NA)	(NA)
Stores and offices	18	18	(NA)	(NA)	763	778	(NA)	(NA)
Storage	28	27	(NA)	(NA)	834	833	(NA)	(NA)
Industry, utility, defense [6]	9	11	(NA)	(NA)	503	508	(NA)	(NA)
Special structures	39	30	(NA)	(NA)	331	124	(NA)	(NA)

– Represents zero. NA Not available. [1] Direct property damage figures do not include indirect losses (such as business interruption and temporary shelter costs) and adjustments for inflation. [2] Includes outside storage, crops, timber, etc. [3] Includes highway and other vehicles (trains, boats, ships, aircraft, and farm and construction vehicles). [4] Includes manufactured homes. [5] Includes hotels and motels, college dormitories, boarding houses, etc. [6] Data underreported as some incidents were handled by private fire brigades or fixed suppression systems which do not report. [7] Includes $10 billion estimated property loss for Northern California Wildfires. [8] Includes $12.4 billion in losses from major California Wildfires. [9] Includes losses of $4.2 billion from California fires in the Wildland Urban Interface (WUI) and a blaze that destroyed a naval ship ($3 billion).

Source: National Fire Protection Association, Quincy, MA, *Fire Loss in the United States During 2020* ©, September 2021, and earlier reports. See also <www.nfpa.org/News-and-Research>.

Table 405. Fires and Property Loss for Incendiary and Suspicious Fires and Civilian Fire Deaths and Injuries by Selected Property Type: 2010 to 2020

[In thousands (482 represents 482,000), except as indicated. Based on sample survey of fire departments]

Characteristic	2010	2013	2014	2015	2016	2017	2018	2019	2020
NUMBER (1,000)									
Structure fires, total	**482**	**488**	**494**	**502**	**476**	**499**	**499**	**482**	**491**
Structure fires that were intentionally set	28	23	19	23	20	23	26	(NA)	(NA)
PROPERTY LOSS (mil. dol.) [1]									
Structure fires, total	**9,716**	**9,526**	**9,846**	**10,280**	**7,898**	**10,700**	**11,066**	**12,287**	**12,107**
Structure fires that were intentionally set	585	577	613	460	473	582	593	(NA)	(NA)
CIVILIAN FIRE DEATHS									
Deaths, total [2]	**3,120**	**3,240**	**3,275**	**3,280**	**3,390**	**3,400**	**3,655**	**3,740**	**3,500**
Residential property	2,665	2,785	2,795	2,605	2,800	2,710	2,820	2,870	2,630
One- and two-family dwellings	2,200	2,430	2,345	2,155	2,410	2,290	2,360	2,390	2,230
Apartments	440	325	400	405	325	340	360	380	350
Vehicles [3]	310	320	345	500	355	430	560	644	630
CIVILIAN FIRE INJURIES									
Injuries, total [2]	**17,720**	**15,925**	**15,775**	**15,700**	**14,650**	**14,670**	**15,200**	**16,600**	**15,200**
Residential property	13,800	12,575	12,175	11,575	11,125	10,910	11,600	12,700	11,900
One- and two-family dwellings	9,400	8,300	8,025	8,050	7,375	7,470	7,800	8,800	8,600
Apartments	3,950	3,900	3,800	3,025	3,375	3,130	3,400	3,400	2,900
Vehicles [3]	1,590	1,050	1,450	1,875	1,225	1,610	1,500	2,000	1,700

NA Not available. [1] Direct property loss only. [2] Includes deaths or injuries from other types of fires, not shown separately. [3] Includes highway vehicles, and trains, boats, ships, farm vehicles, and construction vehicles.

Source: National Fire Protection Association, Quincy, MA, *Fire Loss in the United States During 2020* ©, September 2021, and earlier reports. See also <www.nfpa.org/News-and-Research>.

Section 6
Geography and Environment

This section presents a variety of information on the physical environment of the United States, starting with basic area measurement data and ending with climatic data for selected weather stations around the country. The subjects covered between those points are mostly concerned with environmental trends but include related subjects such as land use, water consumption, air pollutant emissions, toxic releases, oil spills, hazardous waste sites, municipal waste and recycling, threatened and endangered wildlife, and the environmental industry.

The information in this section is selected from a wide range of federal agencies that compile the data for various administrative or regulatory purposes, such as the Environmental Protection Agency (EPA), U.S. Geological Survey (USGS), National Oceanic and Atmospheric Administration (NOAA), and the Natural Resources Conservation Service (NRCS).

Area—Land and water area measurements were calculated by computer based on the information contained in a single, consistent geographic database, the Topologically Integrated Geographic Encoding & Referencing system (TIGER®) database, a national geographic and cartographic database prepared by the Census Bureau. The 2018 area measurements may be found in Table 406.

Geography—The USGS conducts investigations, surveys, and research in the fields of geography, geology, topography, geographic information systems, mineralogy, hydrology, and geothermal energy resources as well as natural hazards. The USGS provides United States cartographic data through the Earth Sciences Information Center and water resources data through the *Water Resources of the United States* at <water.usgs.gov>. In a joint project with the U.S. Census Bureau, during the 1980s, the USGS provided the basic information on geographic features for input into the TIGER® database. Since then, using a variety of sources, the Census Bureau has updated these features and their related attributes (names, descriptions, etc.) and inserted current information on the boundaries, names, and codes of legal and statistical geographic entities. The measures of land and water area, including their classifications, reflect base feature updates made in the Master Address File (MAF)/TIGER® database showing the names and boundaries of entities and are available on a current basis.

An inventory of the nation's land resources by type of use/cover was conducted by the NRCS every 5 years from 1977 through 1997. Since 2000, data have been gathered annually, though major releases of these data continue to be reported at 5-year intervals. The most recent survey results, covered all nonfederal land for the contiguous 48 states. See <nrcs.usda.gov/wps/portal/nrcs/main/national/technical/nra/nri/>.

Environment—The principal federal agency responsible for pollution abatement and control activities is the EPA. It is responsible for establishing and monitoring national air quality standards, water quality activities, solid and hazardous waste disposal, and control of toxic substances. Many of these series

now appear in the "Envirofacts" portion of the EPA website at <enviro.epa.gov/>.

The Clean Air Act, which was last amended in 1990, requires the EPA to set National Ambient Air Quality Standards (NAAQS) (40 CFR part 50) for pollutants considered harmful to public health and the environment. The Clean Air Act established two types of national air quality standards. *Primary standards* set limits to protect public health, including the health of "sensitive" populations such as asthmatics, children, and the elderly. *Secondary standards* set limits to protect public welfare, including protection against decreased visibility and damage to animals, crops vegetation, and buildings. See <epa.gov/criteria-air-pollutants/naaqs-table> for more information. The EPA Office of Air Quality Planning and Standards (OAQPS) has set standards for six principal pollutants, which are called "criteria" pollutants. These pollutants are: carbon monoxide, lead, nitrogen dioxide, particulate matter, ozone, and sulfur dioxide. NAAQS are periodically reviewed and revised to include any additional or new health or welfare data. Table 421 gives some of the health-related standards for the six air pollutants having NAAQS. Data gathered from state networks are periodically submitted to EPA. For details, see "Air Trends" on the EPA website at <epa.gov/air-trends/>.

The Toxics Release Inventory (TRI), a database published by the EPA, is a valuable source of information on 770 chemicals that are being used, manufactured, treated, transported, or released into the environment. Sections 313 of the Emergency Planning and Community Right-to-Know Act (EPCRA) and 6607 of the Pollution Prevention Act (PPA) mandate that a publicly-accessible toxic chemical database be developed and maintained by the EPA. The TRI contains information concerning waste management activities and the release of toxic chemicals by facilities that manufacture, process, or otherwise use said materials. Data on the release of these chemicals are collected from about 21,000 facilities that have the equivalent of 10 or more full time employees and meet the established thresholds for manufacturing, processing, or "other use" of listed chemicals. Facilities must report their releases and other waste management quantities. More information can be found at <epa.gov/toxics-release-inventory-tri-program>.

Climate—NOAA, through the National Weather Service and the National Environmental Satellite, Data, and Information Service, is responsible for collecting climate data. NOAA maintains about 8,000 weather stations, of which a portion produce precipitation measurement records, some take hourly readings of a series of weather elements, and the remainder record data once a day. These data are reported using the Storm Events Database (see <ncdc.noaa.gov/stormevents/>, and hourly, daily, and monthly data from nearly 2,400 locations within the U.S., surrounding territories, and other selected areas is viewable at Local Climatological Data <www.ncdc.noaa.gov/cdo-web/datatools>(published by location for major cities). Data can be found in tables 442–446.

Table 406. Land and Water Area of States and Other Entities: 2018

[One square mile = 2.59 square kilometers. The area measurements were derived from the Census Bureau's Master Address File/Topologically Integrated Geographic Encoding and Referencing (MAF/TIGER®) database. The boundaries of the states and equivalent areas are as of January 1, 2018. The land and water areas, including their classifications, reflect base feature updates made in the MAF/TIGER® database through May 2018. For more details, see <www.census.gov/geographies/mapping-files/time-series/geo/tiger-line-file.html>]

State and other areas [2]	Total area Sq. mi.	Total area Sq. km.	Land area [1] Sq. mi.	Land area [1] Sq. km.	Water area [1] Total Sq. mi.	Water area [1] Total Sq. km.	Inland (sq. mi.)	Coastal (sq. mi.)	Great Lakes (sq. mi.)	Territorial (sq. mi.)
Total [3]	3,806,358	9,858,422	3,536,641	9,159,859	269,717	698,563	85,076	42,390	60,093	82,157
United States [4]	3,797,173	9,834,633	3,532,614	9,149,429	264,559	685,204	84,961	42,355	60,093	77,150
Alabama	52,420	135,767	50,647	131,174	1,773	4,593	1,057	517	–	200
Alaska	665,764	1,724,321	570,983	1,478,840	94,781	245,482	18,983	26,139	–	49,658
Arizona	113,987	295,226	113,591	294,199	397	1,027	397	–	–	–
Arkansas	53,179	137,732	52,035	134,769	1,144	2,963	1,144	–	–	–
California	163,695	423,968	155,794	403,504	7,901	20,464	2,818	245	–	4,838
Colorado	104,095	269,605	103,639	268,423	456	1,182	456	–	–	–
Connecticut	5,544	14,358	4,843	12,542	701	1,816	171	530	–	–
Delaware	2,489	6,446	1,948	5,046	541	1,400	92	355	–	94
District of Columbia	68	177	61	158	7	19	7	–	–	–
Florida	65,757	170,310	53,649	138,949	12,109	31,361	5,002	1,349	–	5,757
Georgia	59,423	153,905	57,715	149,482	1,708	4,423	1,211	47	–	450
Hawaii	10,970	28,412	6,422	16,634	4,547	11,778	42	9	–	4,496
Idaho	83,569	216,442	82,645	214,050	923	2,392	923	–	–	–
Illinois	57,914	149,995	55,514	143,781	2,400	6,215	826	–	1,574	–
Indiana	36,420	94,327	35,826	92,789	594	1,538	361	–	232	–
Iowa	56,273	145,745	55,854	144,661	419	1,084	419	–	–	–
Kansas	82,278	213,099	81,759	211,755	519	1,344	519	–	–	–
Kentucky	40,407	104,655	39,490	102,279	917	2,375	917	–	–	–
Louisiana	52,375	135,651	43,204	111,898	9,171	23,754	4,562	2,876	–	1,733
Maine	35,380	91,634	30,845	79,887	4,535	11,747	2,312	591	–	1,633
Maryland	12,406	32,131	9,711	25,151	2,695	6,980	765	1,820	–	111
Massachusetts	10,554	27,335	7,801	20,205	2,753	7,130	483	1,176	–	1,093
Michigan	96,713	250,487	56,603	146,601	40,111	103,886	1,937	–	38,174	–
Minnesota	86,940	225,174	79,625	206,229	7,315	18,945	4,769	–	2,546	–
Mississippi	48,441	125,460	46,924	121,534	1,516	3,927	768	620	–	129
Missouri	69,707	180,540	68,746	178,051	961	2,489	961	–	–	–
Montana	147,040	380,832	145,546	376,963	1,494	3,869	1,494	–	–	–
Nebraska	77,347	200,328	76,818	198,957	530	1,372	530	–	–	–
Nevada	110,571	286,377	109,780	284,330	790	2,047	790	–	–	–
New Hampshire	9,350	24,216	8,953	23,189	396	1,027	328	–	–	69
New Jersey	8,723	22,593	7,354	19,048	1,369	3,545	437	427	–	505
New Mexico	121,593	314,925	121,312	314,196	281	729	281	–	–	–
New York	54,555	141,296	47,123	122,049	7,431	19,247	1,992	976	3,986	478
North Carolina	53,819	139,390	48,619	125,924	5,199	13,466	4,050	–	–	1,149
North Dakota	70,699	183,111	68,999	178,708	1,700	4,403	1,700	–	–	–
Ohio	44,826	116,098	40,861	105,829	3,965	10,269	474	–	3,491	–
Oklahoma	69,899	181,038	68,596	177,663	1,303	3,375	1,303	–	–	–
Oregon	98,379	254,799	95,988	248,607	2,391	6,192	1,068	72	–	1,251
Pennsylvania	46,054	119,279	44,743	115,884	1,311	3,395	562	–	748	–
Rhode Island	1,545	4,001	1,034	2,678	511	1,324	182	64	–	266
South Carolina	32,023	82,940	30,064	77,865	1,960	5,075	1,061	109	–	790
South Dakota	77,116	199,730	75,810	196,347	1,306	3,383	1,306	–	–	–
Tennessee	42,144	109,153	41,237	106,803	907	2,350	907	–	–	–
Texas	268,596	695,659	261,257	676,653	7,338	19,006	5,590	401	–	1,347
Utah	84,898	219,885	82,196	212,886	2,702	6,999	2,702	–	–	–
Vermont	9,616	24,905	9,218	23,874	398	1,030	398	–	–	–
Virginia	42,775	110,786	39,482	102,258	3,293	8,529	1,289	1,565	–	438
Washington	71,302	184,672	66,453	172,113	4,849	12,559	1,715	2,467	–	668
West Virginia	24,230	62,756	24,041	62,266	189	489	189	–	–	–
Wisconsin	65,496	169,635	54,166	140,290	11,330	29,345	1,989	–	9,341	–
Wyoming	97,810	253,326	97,089	251,459	721	1,868	721	–	–	–
Puerto Rico	5,325	13,791	3,424	8,869	1,901	4,922	76	13	–	1,812
Island Areas:	3,860	9,998	603	1,562	3,257	8,436	39	22	–	3,196
American Samoa	581	1,505	76	198	505	1,307	8	–	–	497
Guam	571	1,478	210	544	361	934	8	1	–	352
Northern Mariana Islands	1,976	5,117	182	472	1,793	4,644	6	5	–	1,782
U.S. Virgin Islands	733	1,898	134	348	599	1,550	17	16	–	565

– Represents or rounds to zero. [1] Water area calculations in this table include only perennial water. All other water (intermittent, glacier, and marsh/swamp) is included in this table as part of land area calculations. [2] This table does not include area calculations for the U.S. Minor Outlying Islands. [3] Includes all 50 states, the District of Columbia, Puerto Rico, and the Island Areas. [4] Includes all 50 states and the District of Columbia.

Source: U.S. Census Bureau, unpublished data from the MAF/TIGER® database. See <tigerweb.geo.census.gov>.

Table 407. Great Lakes Profile

[The Great Lakes contain the largest supply of freshwater in the world, holding about 21% of the world's total freshwater and about 84% of the United States' total freshwater. The Lakes are a series of five interconnecting large lakes, one small lake, four connecting channels, and the St. Lawrence Seaway. Combined, the lakes cover an area of over 94,000 square miles (245,000 square kilometers) and contain over 5,400 cubic miles (23,000 cubic kilometers) of water]

Characteristics	Unit	Lake Superior	Lake Michigan	Lake Huron	Lake Erie	Lake Ontario
Volume.	Cubic miles	2,900	1,180	850	116	393
Water surface area [1]	Square miles	31,700	22,300	23,000	9,910	7,340
Land drainage area.	Square miles	49,300	45,600	[4] 51,700	[5] 30,140	[6] 24,720
Shoreline length [2]	Miles	2,726	1,638	3,827	871	712
Depth:						
Average.	Feet	483	279	195	62	283
Maximum.	Feet	1,332	925	750	210	802
Retention/replacement time [3]	Years	191	99	22	3	6

[1] Includes surface area in both U.S. and Canada. [2] Greater than the sum of the shoreline length for the lakes because it includes the connecting channels (but not the St. Lawrence River). [3] The amount of time it takes for lakes to get rid of pollutants. [4] Includes St. Marys River. [5] Includes the St. Clair-Detroit system. [6] Includes the Niagara River.

Source: U.S. Environmental Protection Agency, The Great Lakes, "Physical Features of the Great Lakes," <www.epa.gov/greatlakes>, accessed August 2022.

Table 408. Great Lakes Length of Shoreline in Separate Basin

[In statute miles]

Shorelines	Total	Canada	U.S.	MI	MN	WI	IL	IN	OH	PA	NY
Total	**10,368**	**5,127**	**5,241**	**3,288**	**189**	**820**	**63**	**45**	**312**	**51**	**473**
Lake Superior	2,980	1,549	1,431	917	189	325	–	–	–	–	–
St. Marys River	297	206	91	91	–	–	–	–	–	–	–
Lake Michigan	1,661	–	1,661	1,058	–	495	63	45	–	–	–
Lake Huron	3,350	2,416	934	934	–	–	–	–	–	–	–
St. Clair River	128	47	81	81	–	–	–	–	–	–	–
Lake St. Clair	160	71	89	89	–	–	–	–	–	–	–
Detroit River	107	43	64	64	–	–	–	–	–	–	–
Lake Erie	860	366	494	54	–	–	–	–	312	51	77
Niagara River	99	34	65	–	–	–	–	–	–	–	65
Lake Ontario	726	395	331	–	–	–	–	–	–	–	331

– Represents zero.

Source: State of Michigan, Department of Environment Quality, "Great Lakes, Shorelines of the Great Lakes," and U.S. Lake Survey, File no. 3-3284 corrected to 1952, <www.michigan.gov/egle>.

Table 409. Largest Lakes in the United States

[The list of lakes include manmade lakes and those that are only partially within the United States]

Lake	Location	Area in sq. mi.	Lake	Location	Area in sq. mi.
Lake Superior	MI-MN-WI-Ontario	31,700	Lake Pontchartrain	Louisiana	631
Lake Huron	MI-Ontario	23,000	Lake Sakakawea [1]	North Dakota	520
Lake Michigan	IL-IN-MI-WI	22,300	Lake Champlain	NY-VT-Quebec	490
Lake Erie	MI-NY-OH-PA-Ontario	9,910	Becharof Lake	Alaska	453
Lake Ontario	NY-Ontario	7,340	Lake St. Clair	MI-Ontario	430
Great Salt Lake	Utah	2,117	Red Lake	Minnesota	427
Lake of the Woods	MN-Manitoba-Ontario	1,485	Selawik Lake	Alaska	404
Iliamna Lake	Alaska	1,014	Fort Peck Lake [1]	Montana	393
Lake Oahe [1]	ND-SD	685	Salton Sea	California	347
Lake Okeechobee	Florida	662	Rainy Lake	MN-Ontario	345

[1] Manmade lakes.

Source: U.S. Geological Survey, 2003, and National Oceanic and Atmospheric Administration, "Great Lakes, 2002" and The National Atlas of the United States of America, *Lakes*, <www.usgs.gov/core-science-systems/national-geospatial-program/small-scale-data>.

Table 410. Coastline Counties Most Frequently Hit by Hurricanes: 1960 to 2008

[Hurricane is a type of tropical cyclone, an intense tropical weather system of strong thunderstorms with a well-defined surface circulation and maximum sustained winds of 74 miles per hour or higher. See <coast.noaa.gov/digitalcoast/> for more info]

County and State	Coastline region	Number of hurricanes	Percent change in population 1960 to 2008	Percent change in population 2000 to 2008	Percent change in housing units 1960 to 2008	Percent change in housing units 2000 to 2008
Monroe County, FL	Gulf of Mexico	15	50.8	-9.2	221.8	4.3
Lafourche Parish, LA	Gulf of Mexico	14	67.2	2.9	151.5	8.9
Carteret County, NC	Atlantic	14	104.3	6.4	366.4	12.4
Dare County, NC	Atlantic	13	465.9	12.1	709.6	22.8
Hyde County, NC	Atlantic	13	-10.1	-11.1	83.7	5.8
Jefferson Parish, LA	Gulf of Mexico	12	108.9	-4.2	201.4	-3.5
Palm Beach County, FL	Atlantic	12	454.7	11.9	616.9	15.2
Miami-Dade County, FL	Atlantic	11	156.5	6.4	180.6	14.9
St. Bernard Parish, LA	Gulf of Mexico	11	17.2	-43.9	-2.6	-67.9
Cameron Parish, LA	Gulf of Mexico	11	4.8	-27.6	87.7	-8.1
Terrebonne Parish, LA	Gulf of Mexico	11	78.7	3.9	179.4	11.0

Source: U.S. National Oceanic and Atmospheric Administration (NOAA), Coastal Services Center, Historical Hurricane Tracks: 1851 to 2008; U.S. Census Bureau, Current Population Reports, P25-1139, Population Estimates and Projections, "Coastline Population Trends in the United States: 1960 to 2008," May 2010. See also <www.census.gov/topics/preparedness/about/coastal-areas.html>.

Table 411. U.S.–Canada and U.S.–Mexico Border Lengths

[In statute miles. Each statute mile equals one mile]

State	Length of international border	State	Length of international border
United States–Canada total...............	**5,525**	Ohio..	146
Alaska..	1,538	Pennsylvania...................................	42
Idaho...	45	Vermont...	90
Maine...	611	Washington......................................	427
Michigan..	721		
Minnesota...	547	**United States–Mexico total**...............	**1,933**
Montana...	545	Arizona...	373
New Hampshire.................................	58	California..	140
New York..	445	New Mexico......................................	180
North Dakota.....................................	310	Texas...	1,241

Source: U.S.–Canada lengths: International Boundary Commission, 2003; U.S. Mexico lengths: U.S. Geological Survey; and The National Atlas of the United States, 1976, "Borders," <www.usgs.gov/core-science-systems/national-geospatial-program>.

Table 412. Coastline and Shoreline of the United States by State

[In statute miles. Each statute mile equals one mile. The term coastline is used to describe the general outline of the seacoast. For the table below, United States coastline measurements were made from small-scale maps, and the coastline was generalized. The coastlines of large sounds and bays were included. Measurements were made in 1948. Shoreline is the term used to describe a more detailed measure of the seacoast. The tidal shoreline figures in the table below were obtained in 1939-1940 from the largest-scale charts and maps then available. Shoreline of the outer coast, offshore islands, sounds, and bays was included, as well as the tidal portion of rivers and creeks. Only States with coastline or shoreline are included in the following table]

State	General coastline	Tidal shoreline	State	General coastline	Tidal shoreline
United States.................	**12,383**	**88,633**	Mississippi......................	44	359
Alabama..........................	53	607	New Hampshire..............	13	131
Alaska.............................	6,640	33,904	New Jersey.....................	130	1,792
California.........................	840	3,427	New York........................	127	1,850
Connecticut......................	–	618	North Carolina................	301	3,375
Delaware.........................	28	381	Oregon...........................	296	1,410
Florida.............................	1,350	8,426	Pennsylvania..................	–	89
Georgia...........................	100	2,344	Rhode Island..................	40	384
Hawaii.............................	750	1,052	South Carolina................	187	2,876
Louisiana.........................	397	7,721	Texas.............................	367	3,359
Maine..............................	228	3,478	Virginia...........................	112	3,315
Maryland..........................	31	3,190	Washington.....................	157	3,026
Massachusetts.................	192	1,519			

– Represents zero.

Source: National Oceanic Atmospheric Administration, 1975 and The National Atlas of the United States, "Coastline and Shoreline," <www.usgs.gov/core-science-systems/national-geospatial-program/small-scale-data>. See also <shoreline.noaa.gov/>.

Table 413. Flows of Largest U.S. Rivers—Length, Discharge, and Drainage Area

[A flow of 1,000 cubic ft. per second is equal to 646 million gallons per day, 724,000 acre-feet per year, or 28.3 cubic meters per second. One acre-foot is the volume of water that would cover 1 acre to a depth of 1 foot]

River	Location of mouth	Source stream (name and location)	Length (miles) [1]	Average discharge at mouth (1,000 cubic feet per second)	Drainage area (1,000 sq. miles)
Missouri.................	Missouri	Red Rock Creek, MT	[2] 2,540	76.2	[3] 529
Mississippi..............	Louisiana	Mississippi River, MN	2,340	[4] 593	[3,5] 1,150
Yukon....................	Alaska	McNeil River, Canada	1,980	225	[3] 328
St. Lawrence............	Canada	North River, MN	1,900	348	[3] 396
Rio Grande.............	Mexico-Texas	Rio Grande, CO	1,900	([6])	336
Arkansas................	Arkansas	East Fork Arkansas River, CO	1,460	41	161
Colorado................. [7]	Mexico	Colorado River, CO	1,450	([6])	246
Atchafalaya [7]............	Louisiana	Tierra Blanca Creek, NM	1,420	58	95
Ohio......................	Illinois-Kentucky	Allegheny River, PA	1,310	281	203
Red [7]....................	Louisiana	Tierra Blanca Creek, NM	1,290	56	93
Brazos...................	Texas	Blackwater Draw, NM	1,280	([6])	46
Columbia................	Oregon-Washington	Columbia River, Canada	1,240	265	[3] 258
Snake....................	Washington	Snake River, WY	1,040	56.9	108
Platte....................	Nebraska	Grizzly Creek, CO	990	([6])	85
Pecos....................	Texas	Pecos River, NM	926	([6])	44
Canadian................	Oklahoma	Canadian River, CO	906	([6])	47
Tennessee..............	Kentucky	Courthouse Creek, NC	886	68	41

[1] From source to mouth. [2] The length from the source of the Missouri River to the Mississippi River and thence to the Gulf of Mexico is about 3,710 miles. [3] Drainage area includes both the United States and Canada. [4] Includes about 167,000 cubic feet per second diverted from the Mississippi into the Atchafalaya River but excludes the flow of the Red River. [5] Excludes the drainage areas of the Red and Atchafalaya Rivers. [6] Less than 15,000 cubic feet per second. [7] In east-central Louisiana, the Red River flows into the Atchafalaya River, a distributary of the Mississippi River. Data on average discharge, length, and drainage area include the Red River, but exclude all water diverted into the Atchafalaya from the Mississippi River.

Source: U.S. Geological Survey, *Largest Rivers in the United States*, September 2005, <pubs.usgs.gov/of/1987/ofr87-242/>.

Table 414. Extreme and Mean Elevations by State and Other Areas

[One foot = .305 meter. There are 2,130 square miles of the United States below sea level (Death Valley is the lowest point). There are 20,230 square miles above 10,000 feet (Denali is the highest point in the United States). Minus sign (-) indicates below sea level]

State and other areas	Highest point Name	Elevation Feet	Elevation Meters	Lowest point Name	Elevation Feet	Elevation Meters	Approximate mean elevation Feet	Approximate mean elevation Meters
U.S.........	**Denali (AK)** [1]	**20,310**	**6,190**	**Death Valley (CA)**	**-282**	**-86**	**2,500**	**763**
AL............	Cheaha Mountain	2,407	734	Gulf of Mexico	([2])	([2])	500	153
AK...........	Denali [1]	20,310	6,190	Pacific Ocean	([2])	([2])	1,900	580
AZ............	Humphreys Peak	12,633	3,853	Colorado River	70	21	4,100	1,251
AR............	Magazine Mountain	2,753	840	Ouachita River	55	17	650	198
CA............	Mount Whitney	14,494	4,419	Death Valley	-282	-86	2,900	885
CO...........	Mount Elbert	14,433	4,402	Arikaree River	3,315	1,011	6,800	2,074
CT............	Mount Frissell on south slope	2,380	726	Long Island Sound	([2])	([2])	500	153
DE............	Ebright Road [3]	448	137	Atlantic Ocean	([2])	([2])	60	18
DC............	Tenleytown at Reno Reservoir	410	125	Potomac River	1	(Z)	150	46
FL............	Britton Hill	345	105	Atlantic Ocean	([2])	([2])	100	31
GA...........	Brasstown Bald	4,784	1,459	Atlantic Ocean	([2])	([2])	600	183
HI............	Pu'u Wekiu, Mauna Kea	13,796	4,208	Pacific Ocean	([2])	([2])	3,030	924
ID............	Borah Peak	12,662	3,862	Snake River	710	217	5,000	1,525
IL............	Charles Mound	1,235	377	Mississippi River	279	85	600	183
IN............	Hoosier Hill	1,257	383	Ohio River	320	98	700	214
IA............	Hawkeye Point	1,670	509	Mississippi River	480	146	1,100	336
KS...........	Mount Sunflower	4,039	1,232	Verdigris River	679	207	2,000	610
KY...........	Black Mountain	4,145	1,264	Mississippi River	257	78	750	229
LA............	Driskill Mountain	535	163	New Orleans	-8	-2	100	31
ME...........	Mount Katahdin	5,268	1,607	Atlantic Ocean	([2])	([2])	600	183
MD...........	Hoye Crest	3,360	1,025	Atlantic Ocean	([2])	([2])	350	107
MA...........	Mount Greylock	3,491	1,065	Atlantic Ocean	([2])	([2])	500	153
MI............	Mount Arvon	1,979	604	Lake Erie	571	174	900	275
MN...........	Eagle Mountain	2,301	702	Lake Superior	601	183	1,200	366
MS...........	Woodall Mountain	806	246	Gulf of Mexico	([2])	([2])	300	92
MO...........	Taum Sauk Mountain	1,772	540	St. Francis River	230	70	800	244
MT...........	Granite Peak	12,799	3,904	Kootenai River	1,800	549	3,400	1,037
NE............	Panorama Point	5,424	1,654	Missouri River	840	256	2,600	793
NV............	Boundary Peak	13,140	4,007	Colorado River	479	146	5,500	1,678
NH...........	Mount Washington	6,288	1,918	Atlantic Ocean	([2])	([2])	1,000	305
NJ............	High Point	1,803	550	Atlantic Ocean	([2])	([2])	250	76
NM...........	Wheeler Peak	13,161	4,014	Red Bluff Reservoir	2,842	867	5,700	1,739
NY............	Mount Marcy	5,344	1,630	Atlantic Ocean	([2])	([2])	1,000	305
NC...........	Mount Mitchell	6,684	2,039	Atlantic Ocean	([2])	([2])	700	214
ND...........	White Butte	3,506	1,069	Red River of the North	750	229	1,900	580
OH...........	Campbell Hill	1,550	473	Ohio River	455	139	850	259
OK...........	Black Mesa	4,973	1,517	Little River	289	88	1,300	397
OR...........	Mount Hood	11,239	3,428	Pacific Ocean	([2])	([2])	3,300	1,007
PA............	Mount Davis	3,213	980	Delaware River	([2])	([2])	1,100	336
RI............	Jerimoth Hill	812	248	Atlantic Ocean	([2])	([2])	200	61
SC............	Sassafras Mountain	3,560	1,086	Atlantic Ocean	([2])	([2])	350	107
SD...........	Harney Peak	7,242	2,209	Big Stone Lake	966	295	2,200	671
TN............	Clingmans Dome	6,643	2,026	Mississippi River	178	54	900	275
TX............	Guadalupe Peak	8,749	2,668	Gulf of Mexico	([2])	([2])	1,700	519
UT............	Kings Peak	13,528	4,126	Beaverdam Wash	2,000	610	6,100	1,861
VT............	Mount Mansfield	4,393	1,340	Lake Champlain	95	29	1,000	305
VA............	Mount Rogers	5,729	1,747	Atlantic Ocean	([2])	([2])	950	290
WA...........	Mount Rainier	14,411	4,395	Pacific Ocean	([2])	([2])	1,700	519
WV...........	Spruce Knob	4,863	1,483	Potomac River	240	73	1,500	458
WI............	Timms Hill	1,951	595	Lake Michigan	579	177	1,050	320
WY...........	Gannett Peak	13,804	4,210	Belle Fourche River	3,099	945	6,700	2,044
Other areas:								
Puerto Rico........	Cerro de Punta	4,390	1,339	Atlantic Ocean	([2])	([2])	1,800	549
American Samoa.....	Lata Mountain	3,160	964	Pacific Ocean	([2])	([2])	1,300	397
Guam........	Mount Lamlam	1,332	406	Pacific Ocean	([2])	([2])	330	101
U.S. Virgin Islands.....	Crown Mountain	1,556	475	Atlantic Ocean	([2])	([2])	750	229

Z Less than .5 meter. [1] Formerly Mount McKinley. The mountain's name was changed on August 28, 2015. [2] Sea level. [3] At DE–PA state line.

Source: For highest and lowest points, see U.S. Geological Survey, "Elevations and Distances in the United States," <pubs.er.usgs.gov/publication/70037974>, released April 2005. For mean elevations, see *Elevations and Distances in the United States*, 1983 edition.

Table 415. Acres of Land Cover by Type and Use: 1997 to 2017

[In millions of acres (1,944 represents 1,944,000,000), except percent. Excludes Alaska and District of Columbia. For inventory-specific glossary of key terms, see <nrcs.usda.gov/wps/portal/nrcs/main/national/technical/nra/nri/processes>]

Year	Total surface area [1]	Nonfederal rural land							Devel-oped land	Water areas	Federal land
		Rural land total	Crop-land	CRP land [2]	Pasture-land	Range-land	Forest land	Other rural land			
Land											
1997........................	1,944	1,395	376	33	120	408	416	41	96	51	403
2002........................	1,944	1,384	368	31	120	407	416	41	105	51	404
2007........................	1,944	1,377	359	32	121	407	416	43	111	52	405
2012........................	1,944	1,373	362	24	123	405	416	43	114	52	405
2017........................	1,944	1,370	367	16	122	404	417	44	116	52	406
Percent of total land											
1997........................	100.0	71.7	19.4	1.7	6.2	21.0	21.4	2.1	4.9	2.6	20.7
2002........................	100.0	71.2	18.9	1.6	6.2	21.0	21.4	2.1	5.4	2.6	20.8
2007........................	100.0	70.8	18.5	1.7	6.2	20.9	21.4	2.2	5.7	2.7	20.8
2012........................	100.0	70.6	18.6	1.2	6.3	20.8	21.4	2.2	5.8	2.7	20.8
2017........................	100.0	70.5	18.9	0.8	6.3	20.8	21.5	2.3	6.0	2.7	20.9

[1] Includes Puerto Rico and Virgin Islands. [2] Conservation Reserve Program (CRP) land. CRP is a federal program established under the Food Security Act of 1985 to assist private landowners to convert highly erodible cropland to vegetative cover for 10 years.

Source: U.S. Department of Agriculture, Natural Resources Conservation Service, *Summary Report: 2017 National Resources Inventory*, September 2020. See also <www.nrcs.usda.gov/technical/NRI>.

Table 416. Wetlands on Nonfederal Land and Water Areas by Land Cover Type for Top 10 States: 2017

[In thousands of acres (111,228 represents 111,228,000). Covers both palustrine (nontidal) and estuarine (tidal) wetlands; see source for details]

Top 10 States	Total	Crop-land [1]	Forest land	Range-land	Other rural land	Developed land	Water area
Wetlands, total [2].................	**111,228**	**17,426**	**65,984**	**7,877**	**14,802**	**1,487**	**3,653**
Minnesota............................	10,636	1,955	6,862	–	1,707	42	70
Louisiana............................	9,747	1,970	4,996	155	2,385	79	163
Florida..............................	9,010	393	5,133	978	2,156	162	188
Georgia..............................	6,555	217	5,600	–	462	123	153
Michigan.............................	6,023	265	4,647	–	977	74	61
Wisconsin............................	5,553	933	3,456	–	1,040	48	75
Texas................................	5,301	983	2,498	762	406	154	498
Maine................................	5,124	73	4,706	–	287	36	22
North Carolina.......................	4,733	60	4,280	–	265	43	87
Mississippi..........................	4,614	620	3,642	–	92	73	187

– Represents zero. [1] Cultivated and non-cultivated. Includes pastureland and Conservation Reserve Program (CRP) lands. [2] Includes other States and Caribbean areas not shown below.

Source: U.S. Department of Agriculture, Natural Resources Conservation Service, *Summary Report: 2017 National Resources Inventory*, September 2020. See also <www.nrcs.usda.gov/wps/portal/nrcs/main/national/technical/nra/nri/>.

Table 417. Acres of Federal and Non-Federal Land Cover by Type and State: 2017

[In thousands of acres (1,944,146 represents 1,944,146,000), except percent. Excludes Alaska and District of Columbia]

State	Total surface area [1]	Selected nonfederal rural land, percent of total			State	Total surface area [1]	Selected nonfederal rural land, percent of total		
		Crop-land	Range-land	Forest land			Crop-land	Range-land	Forest land
United States [2]....	**1,944,146**	**18.9**	**20.8**	**21.5**	Montana...........	94,110	16.3	39.1	6.3
Alabama..............	33,424	6.8	0.1	65.3	Nebraska..........	49,510	41.1	45.9	1.7
Arizona..............	72,964	1.2	46.0	5.8	Nevada............	70,763	0.9	12.4	0.5
Arkansas.............	34,037	20.9	0.1	44.1	New Hampshire...	5,941	1.9	–	63.6
California............	101,510	9.2	19.0	13.9	New Jersey.......	5,216	9.1	–	31.2
Colorado.............	66,625	12.0	36.9	5.3	New Mexico.......	77,823	1.9	52.9	7.2
Connecticut.........	3,195	5.2	–	50.0	New York..........	31,409	15.8	–	55.9
Delaware.............	1,534	25.4	–	22.9	North Carolina....	33,709	15.0	–	46.5
Florida..............	37,534	7.1	6.6	35.2	North Dakota......	45,251	56.0	23.6	1.0
Georgia..............	37,741	11.8	–	57.7	Ohio..............	26,445	42.5	–	27.0
Hawaii...............	4,123	1.9	27.7	35.6	Oklahoma..........	44,738	19.5	29.7	18.1
Idaho................	53,488	10.1	12.7	7.6	Oregon............	62,161	5.8	14.6	19.9
Illinois.............	36,059	66.4	–	11.3	Pennsylvania......	28,995	17.0	–	54.1
Indiana..............	23,158	57.5	–	17.0	Rhode Island......	813	2.2	–	44.2
Iowa.................	36,017	72.1	–	6.8	South Carolina....	19,939	10.5	–	56.2
Kansas...............	52,661	50.0	29.6	3.6	South Dakota.....	49,358	36.8	45.3	1.2
Kentucky.............	25,863	21.5	–	42.4	Tennessee........	26,974	17.8	–	44.4
Louisiana............	31,377	15.6	0.6	41.7	Texas.............	171,052	13.8	53.3	9.3
Maine................	20,966	1.7	–	83.2	Utah..............	54,339	2.8	20.4	4.3
Maryland.............	7,870	18.1	–	29.3	Vermont...........	6,154	8.4	–	65.7
Massachusetts.......	5,339	3.9	–	47.7	Virginia..........	27,087	10.6	–	49.1
Michigan.............	37,349	21.3	–	44.8	Washington........	44,039	14.2	13.6	27.9
Minnesota............	54,010	39.9	–	30.3	West Virginia.....	15,508	4.1	–	67.9
Mississippi..........	30,527	15.3	–	57.1	Wisconsin.........	35,920	29.0	–	41.2
Missouri.............	44,614	34.0	0.2	28.5	Wyoming...........	62,603	3.1	42.9	1.7

– Represents or rounds to zero. [1] Total surface area includes both Federal and non-Federal land. [2] Includes Puerto Rico and U.S. Virgin Islands, not shown separately.

Source: U.S. Department of Agriculture, Natural Resources Conservation Service, *Summary Report, 2017 National Resources Inventory*, September 2020. See also <www.nrcs.usda.gov/technical/NRI>.

Table 418. U.S. Wetland Resources and Deepwater Habitats by Type: 2004 and 2009

[In thousands of acres (153,121.4 represents 153,121,400). Wetlands and deepwater habitats are defined separately because the term wetland does not include permanent water bodies. Deepwater habitats are permanently flooded land lying below the deepwater boundary of wetlands. Deepwater habitats include environments where surface water is permanent and often deep, so that water, rather than air, is the principal medium within which the dominant organisms live, whether or not they are attached to the substrate. As in wetlands, the dominant plants are hydrophytes; however, the substrates are considered nonsoil because the water is too deep to support emergent vegetation. In general terms, wetlands are lands where saturation with water is the dominant factor determining the nature of soil development and the types of plant and animal communities living in the soil and on its surface. The single feature that most wetlands share is soil or substrate that is at least periodically saturated with or covered by water. Wetlands are lands transitional between terrestrial and aquatic systems where the water table is usually at or near the surface or the land is covered by shallow water. For more information on wetlands, see the "Classification of Wetlands and Deepwater Habitats of the United States" at <www.fws.gov/wetlands/documents/classwet/index.html>]

Wetland or deepwater category	Estimated area, 2004	Estimated area, 2009	Change, 2004 to 2009
All wetlands and deepwater habitats, total................	**153,121.4**	**153,206.4**	**85.0**
All deepwater habitats, total.....................................	42,999.4	43,146.6	147.2
Lacustrine [1]	16,786.0	16,859.6	73.6
Riverine [2]	7,517.9	7,510.5	-7.4
Estuarine Subtidal [3]	18,695.4	18,776.5	81.1
All wetlands, total......................	110,122.1	110,059.8	-62.3
Intertidal wetlands [4]	5,869.3	5,785.2	-84.1
Marine intertidal....................................	219.2	227.8	8.5
Estuarine intertidal nonvegetated.............................	999.4	1,017.7	18.3
Estuarine intertidal vegetated..........................	4,650.7	4,539.7	-110.9
Freshwater wetlands....................................	104,252.7	104,274.6	21.9
Freshwater nonvegetated..........................	6,502.1	6,709.3	207.2
Freshwater vegetated..........................	97,750.6	97,565.3	-185.3
Freshwater emergent [5]	27,162.7	27,430.5	267.8
Freshwater forested [6]	52,256.5	51,623.3	-633.1
Freshwater shrub [7]	18,331.4	18,511.5	180.1

[1] The lacustrine system includes deepwater habitats with all of the following characteristics: (1) situated in a topographic depression or a dammed river channel; (2) lacking trees, shrubs, persistent emergents, emergent mosses or lichens with greater than 30 percent coverage; and (3) total area exceeds 20 acres (8 hectares). [2] The riverine system includes deepwater habitats contained within a channel, with the exception of habitats with water containing ocean derived salts in excess of 0.5 parts per thousand. [3] The estuarine system consists of deepwater tidal habitats and adjacent tidal wetlands that are usually semi-enclosed by land but have open, partly obstructed, or sporadic access to the open ocean, and in which ocean water is at least occasionally diluted by freshwater runoff from the land. Subtidal is where the substrate is continuously submerged by marine or estuarine waters. [4] Intertidal is where the substrate is exposed and flooded by tides. Intertidal includes the splash zone of coastal waters. [5] Emergent wetlands are characterized by erect, rooted, herbaceous hydrophytes, excluding mosses and lichens. This vegetation is present for most of the growing season in most years. These wetlands are usually dominated by perennial plants. [6] Forested wetlands are characterized by woody vegetation that is 20 feet tall or taller. [7] Shrub wetlands include areas dominated by woody vegetation less than 20 feet tall. The species include true shrubs, young trees, and trees or shrubs that are small or stunted because of environmental conditions.

Source: U.S. Fish and Wildlife Service, *Status and Trends of Wetlands in the Conterminous United States, 2004 to 2009*, September 2011. See also <www.fws.gov/wetlands/Status-And-Trends-2009/index.html>.

Table 419. U.S. Water Withdrawals Per Day by End Use: 1950 to 2015

[In billions of gallons of water per day (180 represents 180,000,000,000). Includes the District of Columbia, Puerto Rico and U.S. Virgin Islands, as noted. Withdrawal signifies water physically withdrawn from a source. Includes fresh and saline water; excludes water used for hydroelectric power. For information on changes in data collection and presentation methods, see source report]

Year	Total with-drawals	Public supply	Rural domestic and livestock Self supplied domestic	Live-stock	Irri-gation	Thermo-electric power	Other Self supplied industrial	Mining	Com-mercial	Aqua-culture
1950 [1].........	180	14	2.1	1.5	89	40	37.0	(5)	(5)	(5)
1955 [2].........	240	17	2.1	1.5	110	72	39.0	(5)	(5)	(5)
1960 [3].........	270	21	2.0	1.6	110	100	38.0	(5)	(5)	(5)
1965 [4].........	310	24	2.3	1.7	120	130	46.0	(5)	(5)	(5)
1970 [4].........	370	27	2.6	1.9	130	170	47.0	(5)	(5)	(5)
1975 [3].........	420	29	2.8	2.1	140	200	45.0	(5)	(5)	(5)
1980 [3].........	430	33	3.4	2.2	150	210	45.0	(5)	(5)	(5)
1985 [3].........	397	37	3.3	2.2	135	187	25.8	3.4	1.2	2.2
1990 [3].........	404	39	3.4	2.3	134	194	22.4	4.9	2.4	2.2
1995 [3].........	398	40	3.4	2.3	130	190	21.6	3.6	2.9	3.3
2000 [3].........	413	43	3.6	2.4	139	195	19.5	4.1	(NA)	5.8
2005 [3].........	410	44	3.7	2.2	127	201	18.1	3.8	(NA)	8.8
2010 [3].........	354	42	3.5	2.0	116	162	16.2	4.0	(NA)	9.0
2015 [3].........	322	39	3.3	2.0	118	133	14.8	4.0	(NA)	7.6

NA Not available. [1] Population covered: 48 states, District of Columbia (D.C.), and Hawaii. [2] Population covered: 48 states and D.C. [3] Population covered: 50 states, D.C., Puerto Rico, and the Virgin Islands. [4] Population covered: 50 states, D.C., and Puerto Rico. [5] Included in "self-supplied industrial."

Source: U.S. Geological Survey, *Estimated Use of Water in the United States in 2015*, circular 1441, 2018. See also <pubs.er.usgs.gov/publication/cir1441>.

Table 420. Marine Economy Value Added and Gross Output by Activity: 2015 to 2020

[In millions of current dollars (366,398 represents $366,398,000,000). Measures contributions to the U.S. economy of activities related to the nation's oceans, seaports, and the Great Lakes]

Activity	Value added (mil. dol.)				Gross output (mil. dol.)			
	2015	2018	2019	2020	2015	2018	2019	2020
Marine economy, total.	**366,398**	**387,767**	**400,642**	**361,361**	**614,479**	**660,537**	**686,968**	**610,295**
Living resources, marine.	12,247	13,800	14,390	15,066	23,754	26,954	27,878	29,298
Commercial harvest, seafood markets, & processing.	11,370	12,382	12,546	12,281	22,219	24,531	24,763	24,614
Commercial harvest & seafood markets.	7,076	8,092	7,994	7,745	10,599	12,167	12,051	11,665
Seafood processing.	4,294	4,291	4,552	4,536	11,620	12,364	12,713	12,949
Fish-based animal foods.	61	69	70	73	164	157	163	169
Pharmaceuticals, marine-based.	815	1,349	1,774	2,712	1,372	2,266	2,951	4,515
Construction, coastal & marine.	3,283	3,948	5,020	5,222	5,689	6,276	7,992	8,047
Conservation.	1,945	2,587	2,778	2,968	3,667	4,238	4,615	4,689
Dredging.	147	212	506	443	287	359	879	730
Recreation facilities.	1,192	1,149	1,735	1,811	1,735	1,678	2,497	2,627
Research & education, marine.	6,502	6,952	7,519	8,330	8,852	9,769	10,667	12,010
Scientific research.	3,900	4,586	4,890	5,613	5,441	6,679	7,309	8,539
National defense R&D.	112	109	113	112	145	143	149	160
Federal nondefense R&D.	1,184	1,455	1,539	1,507	1,526	1,910	2,043	2,162
State and local R&D.	1,450	1,654	1,665	1,607	1,870	2,171	2,211	2,307
Nonacademic R&D.	1,153	1,368	1,574	2,388	1,901	2,455	2,906	3,910
Educational programs & courses.	2,397	2,146	2,389	2,505	3,061	2,724	2,971	3,126
Vocational training.	153	166	183	161	293	307	325	290
Laboratories.	51	54	56	50	57	60	62	55
Transportation and warehousing, marine.	25,444	26,711	27,472	23,908	59,833	69,422	70,539	57,514
Freight transportation.	17,610	18,089	18,313	17,775	38,578	41,593	40,865	39,680
Passenger transportation.	6,383	6,363	6,718	3,548	18,666	24,380	25,993	14,042
Warehousing and storage.	1,451	2,260	2,441	2,586	2,589	3,449	3,682	3,792
Professional & technical services, marine.	3,537	3,304	3,295	3,440	6,391	6,644	6,872	7,058
Minerals, offshore.	53,806	53,316	52,740	34,970	95,848	89,275	92,599	67,334
Oil & gas.	52,292	51,468	51,006	33,316	92,899	85,874	89,338	64,362
Sand & gravel.	1,163	1,523	1,409	1,380	2,354	2,840	2,701	2,504
Support services.	352	325	324	275	596	561	560	469
Utilities, coastal.	8,221	8,284	8,661	8,211	14,195	14,256	14,360	12,994
Traditional power generation.	8,221	8,284	8,661	8,211	14,195	14,256	14,360	12,994
Ship & boat building, nonrecreational.	7,962	6,794	7,115	7,761	16,689	15,887	16,384	16,447
Ship building [1].	6,508	5,506	5,884	6,610	13,515	12,716	13,458	13,935
Barges & other nonpropelled ships.	89	68	62	50	186	158	141	106
Military ships.	6,080	5,144	5,543	6,332	12,631	11,881	12,680	13,348
Other ships.	338	294	279	228	698	677	637	481
Boat building [2].	1,455	1,287	1,231	1,151	3,174	3,171	2,926	2,512
Fishing boats.	64	30	28	23	131	69	65	49
Tugboats & towboats.	259	255	243	198	535	589	555	418
Outboard motorboats.	132	90	65	68	306	231	159	153
Inboard motorboats.	380	419	406	421	872	1,112	1,006	950
Other boats.	621	494	489	439	1,330	1,170	1,140	942
Tourism and recreation, coastal & offshore.	131,145	148,316	153,753	125,246	211,192	243,381	248,316	195,650
Guided tours.	6,841	8,494	7,902	4,300	14,708	18,023	16,856	11,477
Water guided tours.	4,045	4,971	4,870	2,305	8,796	10,486	10,325	6,343
Other scenic tours.	2,796	3,524	3,032	1,996	5,912	7,537	6,531	5,134
Recreational fishing, offshore.	1,600	2,418	2,417	2,462	3,267	5,062	5,006	4,918
Boating & paddling, offshore.	23,166	24,950	25,685	20,829	44,541	50,059	50,142	38,806
Sailing.	1,161	1,263	1,397	1,034	2,101	2,319	2,524	1,852
Motorboating.	15,811	16,986	17,619	14,457	29,942	33,646	33,969	26,883
Canoeing.	37	41	49	49	62	69	82	83
Kayaking.	132	146	154	191	186	205	216	314
Other boating & paddling [3].	6,025	6,514	6,466	5,097	12,249	13,820	13,351	9,674
Other water activities [4].	1,858	1,911	2,178	2,563	3,208	3,283	3,674	4,462
Other coastal recreation.	16,028	17,108	17,656	14,999	29,001	31,377	31,936	26,515
Maritime museums & cultural institutions.	902	1,081	1,054	966	1,747	1,906	1,922	1,635
Beachgoing.	132	136	148	133	237	255	280	263
Amusement parks.	1,612	1,900	1,943	1,172	2,520	2,987	3,034	1,934
Hiking & camping.	795	845	1,007	1,044	1,422	1,576	1,841	1,874
RVing.	5,209	5,705	5,892	5,165	9,295	10,435	10,491	8,348
Photography.	252	163	168	190	347	240	243	271
Other general expenses.	7,126	7,278	7,444	6,329	13,434	13,979	14,125	12,189
Trips & travel, coastal.	81,652	93,434	97,914	80,093	116,468	135,577	140,702	109,473
Eating & drinking places.	11,245	13,398	14,154	11,230	18,924	22,386	23,683	19,002
Hotel & lodging places.	54,356	60,582	63,637	57,971	67,218	75,415	78,669	68,960
Travel arrangement services.	1,527	1,888	1,938	661	3,248	4,356	4,645	2,168
Transportation services.	14,523	17,566	18,186	10,230	27,077	33,421	33,706	19,342
National defense & public administration.	114,252	116,343	120,678	129,207	172,036	178,674	191,361	203,942
National defense & coast guard.	108,016	109,019	113,104	121,056	162,745	167,962	180,226	191,529
Federal public administration.	5,849	6,886	7,108	7,697	8,290	9,560	9,922	11,193
State & local public administration.	386	438	466	455	1,002	1,152	1,213	1,220

[1] Government and commercial vessels built in shipyards including (but not limited to): naval surface combatants, cargo ships, barges, oil drilling platforms, passenger ships, tugboats, research vessels, submarines, and fishing vessels. [2] Government and commercial vessels not built in shipyards including (but not limited to): commercial fishing boats, motorboats (inboard and outboard), inflatables, tour boats, sailboats, and underwater remote operated vehicles. Activity associated with the manufacture of boats and other water craft used for recreational purposes is included in tourism and recreation sector. [3] Hovercraft, personal watercrafts, pontoon boats, life rafts and associated expenses such as repair services, insurance, fuel, etc. [4] Swimming, snorkeling, SCUBA diving, surfing, and related water activities.

Source: U.S. Bureau of Economic Analysis, *Marine Economy Satellite Account, 2014-2020*, June 2022. See also <www.bea.gov/data/special-topics/marine-economy>.

Table 421. National Ambient Air Pollutant Concentrations by Type of Pollutant: 2010 to 2020

[Data represent composite averages across monitoring stations meeting minimum data completeness requirements for the trend period. Carbon monoxide is based on the second-highest, nonoverlapping, 8-hour average; ozone, the fourth-highest maximum 8-hour value; particulates (PM-10) on the second highest daily 24-hour average; fine particulates (PM2.5) annual average on the weighted annual mean of daily 24-hour averages; and lead on the maximum rolling three-month average. Based on data from the Air Quality System. µg/m ^{3} = micrograms of pollutant per cubic meter of air; ppm = parts per million; ppb = parts per billion]

Pollutant	Unit	Monitoring stations, number	Air quality standard [1]	2010	2014	2015	2016	2017	2018	2019	2020
Carbon monoxide	ppm	181	[2] 9	1.41	1.25	1.23	1.20	1.21	1.21	1.07	1.24
Ozone	ppm	1,090	[3] 0.070	0.071	0.066	0.067	0.067	0.067	0.068	0.064	0.064
Sulfur dioxide	ppb	246	[4] 75	44.2	28.0	24.1	18.7	14.5	14.0	13.0	11.4
Particulates (PM-10)	µg/m ^{3}	476	[5] 150	78.7	73.8	73.3	71.5	83.7	78.7	65.2	85.7
Fine particulates (PM2.5) annual average	µg/m ^{3}	609	[6] 12	9.8	8.7	8.4	7.6	8.0	8.2	7.5	8.0
Nitrogen dioxide	ppb	192	[7] 100	41.4	37.9	36.6	34.8	35.0	34.9	34.1	32.6
Lead	µg/m ^{3}	83	[8] 0.15	0.23	0.08	0.04	0.05	0.05	0.04	0.03	0.03

[1] Refers to the primary National Ambient Air Quality Standard. See <epa.gov/criteria-air-pollutants/naaqs-table>. [2] Based on 8-hour standard of 9 ppm. [3] Based on 8-hour standard of 0.070 ppm. On December 28, 2015, EPA revised the level of the primary and secondary 8-hour ozone standards to 0.070 ppm. [4] Based on a 1-hour daily maximum concentration of 75 ppb. [5] Based on 24-hour (daily) standard of 150 µg/m ^{3}. The particulates (PM-10) standard replaced the previous standard for total suspended particulates in 1987. In 2006, EPA revoked the annual PM-10 standard. [6] Based on annual standard of 12 µg/m ^{3}. The PM-2.5 national monitoring network was deployed in 1999. [7] Based on a 1-hour daily maximum concentration of 100 ppb. [8] Based on 3-month rolling average of 0.15 µg/m ^{3}.

Source: U.S. Environmental Protection Agency, "Air Trends," <www.epa.gov/air-trends>, accessed March 2022.

Table 422. Selected Air Pollutant Emissions: 1990 to 2021

[In thousands of tons (4,320 represents 4,320,000). For documentation regarding the data, see <www.epa.gov/air-emissions-inventories/national-emissions-inventory-nei>]

Year	Ammonia	Carbon monoxide	Nitrogen oxide	PM-10 [1]	PM-2.5 [1]	Sulfur dioxide	VOCs [2]
1990	4,320	154,188	25,527	27,753	7,560	23,077	24,108
2000	4,907	114,467	22,598	23,747	7,288	16,347	17,512
2010	4,271	73,771	14,846	20,823	5,964	7,732	17,835
2011	4,032	73,762	14,519	20,723	6,100	6,479	18,154
2012	3,823	71,758	13,879	19,970	5,940	5,079	17,872
2013	3,813	69,755	13,239	19,217	5,780	4,873	17,590
2014	3,571	65,537	12,589	18,183	5,381	4,674	16,883
2015	3,764	63,516	11,682	17,526	5,229	3,945	16,330
2016	3,955	58,904	10,304	16,830	5,060	3,204	15,459
2017	4,297	66,605	9,838	17,035	5,681	2,539	17,185
2018	4,933	62,283	9,211	16,395	5,419	2,438	16,435
2019	4,864	52,118	8,569	15,082	4,533	1,984	13,678
2020	4,864	51,256	8,050	15,071	4,520	1,782	13,567
2021	4,864	50,393	7,710	15,060	4,507	1,882	13,456

[1] PM = Particular Matter; PM-10 is equal to or less than ten microns in diameter; PM-2.5 to or less than 2.5 microns effective diameter. [2] Volatile organic compounds.

Source: U.S. Environmental Protection Agency, "National Emissions Inventory (NEI) Air Pollutant Emissions Trends Data, 1970-2021," <www.epa.gov/air-emissions-inventories/air-pollutant-emissions-trends-data>, accessed April 2022.

Table 423. Air Pollutant Emissions by Selected Pollutant and Source: 2021

[In thousands of tons (4,864 represents 4,864,000). See headnote, Table 422]

Source	Ammonia	Carbon monoxide	Nitrogen oxide	PM-10 [1]	PM-2.5 [1]	Sulfur dioxide	VOCs [2]
Total emissions	**4,864**	**50,393**	**7,710**	**15,060**	**4,507**	**1,882**	**13,456**
Fuel combustion, stationary sources	87	3,965	2,317	701	617	1,289	512
Electric utilities	17	468	784	115	95	916	31
Industrial	16	830	1,038	245	186	332	118
Other fuel combustion	54	2,666	496	342	336	41	363
Industrial and other processes	88	3,010	1,043	1,131	588	417	6,717
Chemical and allied product manufacturing	23	115	38	18	14	96	75
Metals processing	1	478	59	50	33	64	23
Petroleum and related industries	2	670	546	27	22	91	2,671
Other	37	436	313	769	298	136	371
Solvent utilization	–	2	1	4	4	–	2,696
Storage and transport	4	8	5	35	14	1	702
Waste disposal and recycling	22	1,301	81	227	203	28	177
Highway vehicles	103	15,114	2,239	206	79	14	1,014
Off highway [3]	3	11,420	1,851	117	109	27	1,039
Miscellaneous [4]	4,583	16,886	260	12,906	3,114	136	4,174

– Rounds to zero. [1] See footnote 1, Table 422. [2] Volatile organic compounds. [3] Includes emissions from farm tractors and other farm machinery, construction equipment, industrial machinery, recreational marine vessels, and small general utility engines such as lawn mowers. [4] Includes emissions from forest fires and other kinds of burning, various agricultural activities, fugitive dust from paved and unpaved roads, other construction and mining activities, and natural sources.

Source: U.S. Environmental Protection Agency, "National Emissions Inventory (NEI) Air Pollutant Emissions Trends Data, 1970-2021," <www.epa.gov/air-emissions-inventories/air-pollutant-emissions-trends-data>, accessed April 2022.

Table 424. Greenhouse Gas Emissions by Type and Source: 1990 to 2020

[In millions of metric tons of carbon dioxide equivalent (MMT CO2 Eq.). 6,453.5 represents 6,453,500,000. MMT CO2 Eq. weights each gas by its global warming potential (GWP) value. GWP is a quantified measure of the globally averaged relative radiative forcing impacts of a particular greenhouse gas. The reference gas used is CO2; therefore, GWP-weighted emissions are measured in MMT CO2 Eq. See source for details]

Type and/or source	1990	2000	2010	2015	2017	2018	2019	2020
Total emissions	**6,453.5**	**7,327.6**	**7,007.4**	**6,689.0**	**6,501.0**	**6,687.5**	**6,571.7**	**5,981.4**
BY SOURCE								
Energy	5,341.1	6,195.6	5,884.1	5,543.1	5,372.7	5,539.4	5,409.8	4,854.7
Industrial processes and product use [1]	346.2	395.1	362.8	375.9	369.4	373.4	379.5	376.4
Sulfur hexafluoride (SF6)	28.8	16.6	7.3	5.5	5.9	5.7	5.9	5.4
Hydrofluorocarbons (HFCs)	46.5	118.1	155.4	168.0	171.1	171.0	175.9	178.8
Perfluorocarbons (PFCs)	24.3	15.9	4.8	5.2	4.2	4.8	4.6	4.4
Agriculture	551.9	553.6	592.8	613.5	603.2	616.7	622.9	594.7
Waste	214.2	183.3	167.8	156.5	155.7	157.9	159.6	155.6
Land use, land-use change, and forestry [2]	31.4	37.4	30.4	48.9	45.5	39.8	30.3	53.2
Net flux from land use, land use change, and forestry [3]	-860.6	-825.2	-761.0	-700.1	-781.2	-769.3	-730.5	-758.9
Net emissions (sources and sinks) [4]	5,592.8	6,502.4	6,246.4	5,988.9	5,719.8	5,918.2	5,841.2	5,222.4
BY TYPE AND SOURCE								
Carbon dioxide (CO2), total	**5,122.5**	**6,016.4**	**5,681.4**	**5,376.6**	**5,211.0**	**5,376.7**	**5,259.1**	**4,715.7**
Energy	4,902.4	5,790.3	5,500.5	5,194.0	5,038.3	5,204.3	5,080.4	4,544.5
Fossil fuel combustion	4,731.2	5,609.0	5,345.7	5,006.5	4,853.3	4,989.3	4,852.3	4,342.7
Transportation	1,468.9	1,792.2	1,696.8	1,718.2	1,780.0	1,812.8	1,813.8	1,572.0
Electricity	1,820.0	2,296.2	2,258.6	1,900.6	1,732.0	1,752.9	1,606.1	1,439.0
Industrial	853.7	869.9	796.4	797.3	790.4	814.1	816.1	766.3
Residential	338.6	371.7	334.8	317.3	293.4	338.2	341.4	315.8
Commercial	228.3	236.5	224.5	244.6	232.0	245.8	250.7	226.8
Biomass (wood) [5]	215.2	218.1	215.5	224.7	211.9	220.0	217.6	202.1
Industrial processes and product use	213.0	218.5	172.4	174.2	164.7	165.1	171.2	163.6
Agriculture	7.1	7.5	8.6	8.4	8.0	7.3	7.6	7.7
Land use, land-use change, and forestry (sink)	-892.0	-862.6	-791.4	-748.9	-826.7	-809.0	-760.8	-812.2
Methane (CH4), total	**780.8**	**718.1**	**705.3**	**666.7**	**663.8**	**671.1**	**668.8**	**650.4**
Energy	368.6	320.9	317.9	296.2	285.4	287.3	284.0	269.1
Industrial processes and product use	0.3	0.3	0.1	0.2	0.3	0.3	0.4	0.3
Agriculture	214.7	234.7	242.0	238.0	247.8	251.1	250.3	250.9
Land use, land-use change, and forestry	27.2	29.4	25.4	36.0	34.0	30.7	25.5	38.1
Waste management	197.3	162.1	145.3	132.3	130.3	132.4	134.1	130.0
Nitrous oxide (N2O), total	**450.5**	**442.3**	**452.7**	**466.5**	**444.6**	**457.7**	**456.8**	**426.1**
Energy	70.1	84.4	65.7	53.0	49.0	47.9	45.3	41.1
Industrial processes and product use	33.3	25.0	22.4	22.2	22.7	26.0	21.1	23.3
Agriculture	330.1	311.3	342.2	367.1	347.5	358.4	365.0	336.1
Land use, land-use change, and forestry	4.2	8.0	5.0	12.9	11.5	9.1	4.8	15.2
Waste management	16.9	21.2	22.5	24.1	25.4	25.5	25.4	25.6

[1] Total includes items not shown separately. [2] Land use, land-use change, and forestry (LULUCF) emissions of CH4 and N2O are reported separately from gross emissions totals. [3] The net LULUCF flux total includes CH4 and N2O emissions plus net LULUCF carbon stock changes. [4] Net emissions total includes emissions and sinks from removals from LULUCF. [5] Emissions from wood biomass consumption are not included specifically in summing energy sector totals. Net carbon fluxes from changes in biogenic carbon reservoirs are accounted for in the estimates for land use, land-use change, and forestry.

Source: U.S. Environmental Protection Agency, *Inventory of U.S. Greenhouse Gas Emissions and Sinks, 1990-2020*, April 2022. See also <www.epa.gov/ghgemissions/inventory-us-greenhouse-gas-emissions-and-sinks>.

Table 425. Carbon Dioxide Emissions from Fossil Fuel Combustion by Fuel Type and Sector: 1990 to 2020

[In millions of metric tons of carbon dioxide equivalent (MMT CO2 Eq.); 4,731.2 represents 4,731,200,000. See source for details on methodology]

Fuel and sector	1990	2000	2010	2015	2017	2018	2019	2020
Total [1]	**4,731.2**	**5,609.0**	**5,345.7**	**5,006.5**	**4,853.3**	**4,989.3**	**4,852.3**	**4,342.7**
Coal	**1,719.8**	**2,065.2**	**1,931.2**	**1,427.6**	**1,270.0**	**1,211.6**	**1,028.2**	**835.6**
Residential	3.0	1.1	–	–	–	–	–	–
Commercial	12.0	8.8	6.6	3.0	2.0	1.8	1.6	1.4
Industrial	157.8	128.5	94.2	70.0	58.7	54.4	49.5	43.0
Electricity generation	1,546.5	1,926.4	1,827.3	1,351.4	1,207.1	1,152.9	973.5	788.2
Natural gas	**1,000.0**	**1,219.8**	**1,274.0**	**1,454.9**	**1,434.6**	**1,592.0**	**1,648.8**	**1,610.7**
Residential	237.8	270.8	258.9	252.7	241.5	273.8	275.5	256.4
Commercial	142.0	172.5	168.0	175.4	173.2	192.5	192.9	173.9
Industrial	408.8	459.4	407.9	459.1	469.5	494.0	501.6	485.5
Transportation	36.0	35.7	38.2	39.4	42.3	50.9	58.9	58.1
Electricity generation	175.4	280.8	399.5	525.2	505.6	577.4	616.0	634.3
Petroleum	**2,010.9**	**2,323.5**	**2,140.1**	**2,123.6**	**2,148.3**	**2,185.3**	**2,175.0**	**1,895.9**
Residential	97.8	99.8	75.8	64.6	51.9	64.4	65.9	59.5
Commercial	74.3	55.3	49.9	66.2	56.8	51.5	56.2	51.6
Industrial	287.1	282.1	294.4	268.2	262.2	265.7	265.0	237.8
Transportation	1,432.9	1,756.6	1,658.6	1,678.8	1,737.7	1,761.8	1,754.8	1,514.0
Electricity generation	97.5	88.5	31.4	23.7	18.9	22.2	16.2	16.2

– Represents zero. [1] Includes data for geothermal energy-related carbon dioxide emissions and U.S. territories, not shown separately.

Source: U.S. Environmental Protection Agency, *Inventory of U.S. Greenhouse Gas Emissions and Sinks, 1990-2020*, April 2022. See also <www.epa.gov/ghgemissions/inventory-us-greenhouse-gas-emissions-and-sinks>.

Table 426. Air Pollution—Air Quality Index Days at Unhealthy Levels by Selected Metropolitan Statistical Area: 1980 to 2020

[Number of days with AQI (Air Quality Index) values greater than 100 at monitoring sites. AQI integrates information on 6 major pollutants (particulate matter (the term for solid or liquid particles found in the air) less than 10 microns in diameter, particulate matter less than 2.5 microns in diameter, sulfur dioxide, carbon monoxide, ozone, and nitrogen dioxide) across an entire monitoring network into a single number that represents the worst daily air quality experienced in an urban area. Data for 1999 to 2009 include particulate matter 2.5 micron in diameter (PM 2.5). An AQI greater than 100 indicates that at least 1 criteria pollutant exceeded air quality standards on a given day; therefore, air quality would be in the unhealthful range on that day. Based on data from the Environmental Protection Agency's Air Quality System database]

Metropolitan statistical area	1980	1990	2000	2005	2010	2015	2016	2017	2018	2019	2020
Albany-Schenectady-Troy, NY	87	28	8	20	9	2	3	0	3	0	3
Albuquerque, NM	51	26	35	26	5	4	3	4	24	4	10
Allentown-Bethlehem-Easton, PA	104	34	35	39	31	6	11	6	5	4	1
Atlanta-Sandy Springs-Roswell, GA	118	146	117	71	47	16	32	11	10	19	3
Austin-Round Rock, TX	19	20	35	18	10	10	1	4	9	2	2
Bakersfield, CA	162	177	204	169	125	122	116	139	130	95	129
Baltimore-Columbia-Towson, MD	142	86	61	63	53	15	24	15	16	13	3
Baton Rouge, LA	76	81	105	117	45	17	9	8	19	9	6
Birmingham-Hoover, AL	63	66	124	69	30	6	11	10	8	18	3
Boston-Cambridge-Newton, MA-NH	126	98	22	36	10	4	7	5	5	1	0
Bradenton-Sarasota-Venice, FL	3	17	35	20	6	1	0	3	2	2	0
Bridgeport-Stamford-Norwalk, CT	227	70	31	36	29	30	23	16	21	21	13
Buffalo-Cheektowaga-Niagara Falls, NY	281	143	102	52	9	4	6	1	3	0	2
Charleston-North Charleston, SC	41	17	21	16	2	1	5	1	0	1	1
Charlotte-Concord-Gastonia, NC-SC	167	82	82	71	38	11	9	5	10	18	2
Chicago-Naperville-Joliet, IL-IN-WI	301	200	126	94	43	14	28	25	26	17	28
Cincinnati-Middletown, OH-KY-IN	245	223	107	110	50	13	18	10	13	20	8
Cleveland-Elyria, OH	176	213	93	120	96	20	24	7	15	7	15
Columbia, SC	84	79	59	35	12	0	5	2	1	2	1
Columbus, OH	92	45	42	50	23	5	10	3	3	1	3
Dallas-Fort Worth-Arlington, TX	107	67	126	99	28	44	18	24	36	29	24
Denver-Aurora-Lakewood, CO	166	46	53	41	38	26	29	40	57	22	34
Detroit-Warren-Dearborn, MI	195	123	107	100	33	20	22	16	23	13	23
El Paso, TX	133	196	42	42	16	7	6	23	17	13	18
Fresno, CA	166	138	195	115	87	102	105	120	98	66	98
Grand Rapids-Wyoming, MI	85	32	14	38	5	3	10	0	4	0	8
Hartford-West Hartford-East Hartford, CT	96	30	24	26	15	16	16	9	10	8	2
Hilo, HI	(NA)	46	55	110	344	304	311	301	170	0	11
Houston-Sugarland-Baytown, TX	189	157	103	116	44	45	23	25	35	31	24
Indianapolis-Carmel, IN	218	128	120	93	32	5	12	9	16	5	7
Jacksonville, FL	89	85	84	31	21	1	0	1	7	1	6
Kansas City, MO-KS	186	39	60	76	41	41	7	7	13	1	5
Knoxville, TN	170	135	134	130	40	2	14	1	2	3	0
Las Vegas-Paradise, NV	121	73	56	64	33	23	26	29	49	5	25
Los Angeles-Long Beach-Anaheim, CA	288	235	178	139	115	134	108	122	110	91	141
Louisville/Jefferson County, KY-IN	311	120	128	105	63	14	19	6	11	4	7
Madison, WI	88	7	8	18	4	1	3	0	2	0	5
Memphis, TN-MS-AR	230	114	76	92	24	5	8	4	11	5	4
Miami-Fort Lauderdale-West Palm Beach, FL	90	9	26	12	6	1	6	8	4	2	2
Milwaukee-Waukesha-West Allis, WI	161	67	27	41	14	5	9	8	9	3	7
Minneapolis-St. Paul-Bloomington, MN-WI	190	117	27	27	12	6	5	1	5	3	3
Nashville-Davidson-Murfreesboro-Franklin, TN	221	205	96	55	28	1	6	1	7	1	2
New Haven-Milford, CT	75	76	27	36	18	16	14	12	14	14	13
New Orleans-Metairie, LA	40	38	77	43	72	8	11	2	6	2	0
New York-Newark-Jersey City, NY-NJ-PA	295	131	71	76	61	38	30	19	27	16	11
Oklahoma City, OK	32	21	36	33	11	2	3	7	12	2	5
Omaha-Council Bluffs, NE-IA	94	8	17	30	13	5	4	2	5	0	2
Orlando-Kissimmee-Sanford, FL	12	23	33	21	8	1	1	3	3	6	0
Oxnard-Thousand Oaks-Ventura, CA	161	139	84	62	18	13	9	33	17	9	26
Philadelphia-Camden-Wilmington, PA-NJ-DE-MD	242	167	87	86	48	30	20	22	19	16	8
Phoenix-Mesa-Scottsdale, AZ	211	108	167	91	59	70	75	95	85	54	230
Pittsburgh, PA	303	288	166	151	83	32	30	32	25	16	14
Portland-Vancouver-Hillsboro, OR-WA	78	19	12	15	3	7	2	16	10	3	14
Providence-Warwick, RI-MA	134	99	31	29	20	11	6	7	13	2	4
Raleigh, NC	98	57	68	46	11	3	3	0	0	0	1
Richmond, VA	104	122	40	54	25	3	4	1	2	0	0
Riverside-San Bernardino-Ontario, CA	245	251	205	178	162	169	161	175	173	145	176
Sacramento-Arden-Arcade-Roseville, CA	110	124	105	92	42	40	59	56	57	20	50
Salt Lake City, UT	228	197	52	62	24	27	28	48	43	17	21
San Antonio, TX	34	17	23	27	11	14	6	6	11	6	10
San Diego-Carlsbad, CA	210	191	97	55	25	41	42	62	35	25	49
San Francisco-Oakland-Hayward, CA	57	21	29	21	14	14	15	16	19	9	23
San Jose-Sunnyvale-Santa Clara, CA	56	48	50	24	13	7	6	12	18	4	22
San Juan-Carolina-Caguas, PR	45	58	34	2	2	3	27	7	14	19	19
Seattle-Tacoma-Bellevue, WA	150	33	28	25	3	18	3	24	16	2	14
St. Louis, MO-IL	308	285	162	169	103	16	19	12	19	10	11
Tampa-St. Petersburg-Clearwater, FL	181	156	140	68	20	5	6	4	5	6	3
Toledo, OH	128	38	19	40	8	1	5	4	10	1	8
Tucson, AZ	190	30	23	18	5	1	4	7	11	2	13
Tulsa, OK	121	111	46	49	9	2	3	2	11	2	2
Washington-Arlington-Alexandria, DC-VA-MD-WV	124	96	70	63	50	14	16	8	10	11	3
Wichita, KS	14	12	27	16	13	0	1	0	0	0	6
Youngstown-Warren-Boardman, OH	120	54	30	47	17	5	6	4	5	0	4

NA Not available.

Source: U.S. Bureau of Transportation Statistics, "National Transportation Statistics," <www.bts.gov/topics/national-transportation-statistics>, accessed March 2022.

Table 427. Municipal Solid Waste Generation, Materials Recovery, Recycling, Combustion With Energy Recovery, and Discards: 1980 to 2018

[In millions of tons (151.6 represents 151,600,000), except as indicated. Covers post-consumer residential, commercial, and institutional solid wastes that comprise the major portion of typical municipal collections. Excludes mining, agricultural and industrial processing, demolition and construction wastes, sewage sludge, junked autos, and obsolete equipment wastes. Based on material-flows estimating procedure and wet weight as generated]

Item and material	1980	1990	2000	2010	2015	2017	2018
Waste generated	**151.6**	**208.3**	**243.5**	**251.1**	**262.1**	**268.7**	**292.4**
Per person per day (lb.)	3.7	4.6	4.7	4.5	4.5	4.5	4.9
Total materials recovery	**14.5**	**33.2**	**69.5**	**85.4**	**91.0**	**94.0**	**94.0**
Per person per day (lb.)	0.4	0.7	1.4	1.5	1.6	1.6	1.6
Recovery for recycling	14.5	29.0	53.0	65.3	67.6	67.0	69.1
Per person per day (lb.)	0.4	0.6	1.0	1.2	1.2	1.1	1.2
Recovery for composting [1]	(Z)	4.2	16.5	20.2	23.4	27.0	24.9
Per person per day (lb.)	(Z)	0.1	0.3	0.4	0.4	0.5	0.4
Combustion with energy recovery	2.8	29.8	33.7	29.3	33.6	34.2	34.6
Per person per day (lb.)	0.1	0.7	0.7	0.5	0.6	0.6	0.6
Discards to landfill, other disposal	134.4	145.3	140.3	136.3	137.6	140.5	146.1
Per person per day (lb.)	3.2	3.2	2.7	2.4	2.4	2.4	2.4
PERCENT DISTRIBUTION OF GENERATION							
Materials in products	**71.8**	**70.3**	**73.4**	**70.9**	**70.1**	**70.3**	**64.9**
Paper and paperboard	36.4	34.9	36.0	28.4	26.0	24.9	23.1
Glass	10.0	6.3	5.2	4.6	4.4	4.6	4.2
Metals	10.2	7.9	7.8	8.9	9.1	9.4	8.8
Plastics	4.5	8.2	10.5	12.5	13.2	13.2	12.2
Rubber and leather	2.8	2.8	2.7	3.1	3.3	3.4	3.1
Textiles	1.7	2.8	3.9	5.3	6.1	6.3	5.8
Wood	4.6	5.9	5.6	6.3	6.2	6.8	6.2
Other	1.7	1.5	1.6	1.9	1.8	1.7	1.5
Other waste	**28.2**	**29.7**	**26.6**	**29.1**	**29.9**	**29.7**	**35.1**
Food waste	8.6	11.5	12.6	14.2	15.2	15.1	21.6
Yard trimmings	18.1	16.8	12.5	13.3	13.2	13.1	12.1
Miscellaneous inorganic wastes	1.5	1.4	1.4	1.5	1.5	1.5	1.4

Z Less than 5,000 tons or 0.05 percent. [1] Composting of yard trimmings, food scraps, and other municipal solid waste organic material. Does not include backyard composting.

Source: U.S. Environmental Protection Agency, *Advancing Sustainable Materials Management: 2018 Tables and Figures*, December 2020. See also <www.epa.gov/smm>.

Table 428. Generation and Recovery of Selected Materials in Municipal Solid Waste: 1980 to 2018

[In millions of tons (151.6 represents 151,600,000), except as indicated. Covers post-consumer residential, commercial, and institutional solid wastes that comprise the major portion of typical municipal collections. Excludes mining, agricultural and industrial processing, demolition and construction wastes, sewage sludge, and junked autos and obsolete equipment wastes. Based on material-flows estimating procedure and wet weight as generated. Material recovered includes material recycled and composted]

Item and material	1980	1990	2000	2010	2015	2017	2018
Waste generated, total [1]	**151.6**	**208.3**	**243.5**	**251.1**	**262.1**	**268.7**	**292.4**
Paper and paperboard	55.2	72.7	87.7	71.3	68.1	67.0	67.4
Glass	15.1	13.1	12.8	11.5	11.5	12.3	12.3
Ferrous metals	12.6	12.6	14.2	16.9	18.2	18.9	19.2
Aluminum	1.7	2.8	3.2	3.5	3.7	3.8	3.9
Other nonferrous metals	1.2	1.1	1.6	2.0	2.0	2.5	2.5
Plastics	6.8	17.1	25.6	31.4	34.5	35.4	35.7
Food waste	13.0	23.9	30.7	35.7	39.7	40.7	63.1
Yard trimmings	27.5	35.0	30.5	33.4	34.7	35.2	35.4
Materials recovered, total [1]	**14.5**	**33.2**	**69.5**	**85.4**	**91.0**	**94.0**	**94.0**
Paper and paperboard	11.7	20.2	37.6	44.6	45.3	44.2	46.0
Glass	0.8	2.6	2.9	3.1	3.2	3.1	3.1
Ferrous metals	0.4	2.2	4.7	5.8	6.1	6.2	6.4
Aluminum	0.3	1.0	0.9	0.7	0.7	0.6	0.7
Other nonferrous metals	0.5	0.7	1.1	1.4	1.3	1.7	1.7
Plastics	(Z)	0.4	1.5	2.5	3.1	3.0	3.1
Food waste [2]	(Z)	(Z)	0.7	1.0	2.1	2.6	2.6
Yard trimmings	(Z)	4.2	15.8	19.2	21.3	24.4	22.3
Percent of generation recovered, total [1]	**9.6**	**16.0**	**28.5**	**34.0**	**34.7**	**35.0**	**32.1**
Paper and paperboard	21.3	27.8	42.8	62.5	66.6	65.9	68.2
Glass	5.0	20.1	22.6	27.2	27.8	25.0	25.0
Ferrous metals	2.9	17.6	33.1	34.3	33.4	32.7	33.1
Aluminum	17.9	35.9	27.0	19.4	18.3	15.7	17.2
Other nonferrous metals	46.6	66.4	66.3	71.3	64.2	68.1	67.3
Plastics	0.3	2.2	5.8	8.0	9.0	8.5	8.7
Food waste [2]	(Z)	(Z)	2.2	2.7	5.3	6.3	4.1
Yard trimmings	(Z)	12.0	51.7	57.5	61.3	69.4	63.0

Z Less than 5,000 tons or 0.05 percent. [1] Includes other types of materials not shown separately. [2] Includes collection of other municipal solid waste organic materials for composting.

Source: U.S. Environmental Protection Agency, *Advancing Sustainable Materials Management: 2018 Tables and Figures*, December 2020. See also <www.epa.gov/smm>.

Table 429. Municipal Solid Waste—Generation, Recycling, and Landfill Disposal by Selected Type of Product: 2018

[67,390 represents 67,390,000. See headnote, Table 428]

Type of product	Generation (1,000 tons)	Recycling Volume recycled (1,000 tons)	Recycling Percent of generation	Landfill disposal (1,000 tons)
Paper and paperboard products [1]	**67,390**	**45,970**	**68.2**	**17,220**
Nondurable goods	25,490	12,080	47.4	10,780
Newspapers/mechanical papers	5,050	3,270	64.8	1,430
Other paper nondurable goods	20,440	8,810	43.1	9,350
Containers and packaging	41,900	33,890	80.9	6,440
Corrugated boxes	33,260	32,090	96.5	940
Other paper and paperboard packaging	8,640	1,800	20.8	5,500
Glass products [1]	**12,250**	**3,060**	**25.0**	**7,550**
Containers and packaging	9,790	3,060	31.3	5,420
Beer and soft drink bottles	4,650	1,840	39.6	2,260
Wine and liquor bottles	1,810	720	39.8	880
Other bottles and jars	3,330	500	15.0	2,280
Metal products [1]	**25,600**	**8,720**	**34.1**	**13,930**
Metals in durable goods	21,250	6,420	30.2	12,280
Ferrous	16,990	4,730	27.8	10,060
Aluminum	1,750	(NA)	(NA)	1,480
Other nonferrous	800	(Z)	(Z)	720
Metals in containers and packaging	4,130	2,300	55.7	1,470
Plastics [1]	**35,680**	**3,090**	**8.7**	**26,970**
Plastics in durable goods	13,690	930	6.8	11,020
Plastics in nondurable goods	7,460	180	2.4	5,860
Plastics in containers and packaging	14,530	1,980	13.6	10,090
Rubber and leather [1]	**9,160**	**1,670**	**18.2**	**4,990**
Durable goods	7,980	1,670	20.9	4,040
Rubber in tires	4,180	1,670	40.0	780
Other durables	3,800	(Z)	(Z)	3,260
Nondurable goods	1,180	(Z)	(Z)	950
Clothing and footwear	900	(Z)	(Z)	720
Other nondurables	280	(Z)	(Z)	230

NA Not available. Z Less than 5,000 tons or .05 percent. [1] Includes products not shown separately.

Source: U.S. Environmental Protection Agency, *Advancing Sustainable Materials Management: 2018 Tables and Figures,* December 2020. See also <www.epa.gov/smm>.

Table 430. Environmental Industry—Revenues and Employment by Industry Segment: 2010 to 2021

[319.1 represents $319,100,000,000. Employment data are rounded to the nearest hundredth. Covers approximately 30,000 private and public companies engaged in revenue-generating environmental activities]

Industry segment	Revenue (billion dollars) 2010	2015	2020	2021	Employment 2010	2015	2020	2021
Industry total	**319.1**	**362.1**	**427.3**	**447.2**	**1,656,400**	**1,719,700**	**1,792,800**	**1,831,600**
SERVICES								
Analytical services [1]	1.9	1.9	2.0	2.1	17,000	16,100	15,800	16,000
Wastewater treatment works [2]	52.0	51.9	64.9	66.3	194,200	175,500	203,000	206,200
Solid waste management [3]	53.4	59.0	65.6	68.6	278,000	290,800	293,200	302,600
Hazardous waste management [4]	10.0	10.9	10.3	10.8	48,500	49,400	44,800	46,200
Remediation/industrial services	12.4	13.5	13.7	14.1	105,000	101,300	94,400	98,800
Consulting and engineering	26.8	29.7	34.6	36.4	240,500	234,800	240,800	230,700
EQUIPMENT								
Water equipment and chemicals	26.9	30.7	32.3	33.1	160,100	169,900	162,200	164,700
Instrument manufacturing	5.4	6.7	8.2	8.6	37,100	43,000	50,100	52,700
Air pollution control equipment [5]	14.9	16.3	15.8	15.6	96,400	97,300	86,200	84,900
Waste management equipment [6]	12.7	14.7	15.4	15.9	86,600	92,500	92,100	94,200
RESOURCES								
Water utilities [7]	52.8	66.2	80.0	82.7	208,900	246,600	268,900	275,900
Resource recovery [8]	28.5	26.1	23.0	24.5	102,600	84,200	71,800	76,000
Clean energy systems and power [9]	21.4	34.6	61.4	68.4	81,500	118,300	169,500	182,700

[1] Covers environmental laboratory testing and services. [2] Mostly revenues collected by municipal entities for sewage or wastewater plants. [3] Covers public & private sector collection, transportation, transfer stations, disposal, landfill ownership and management for solid waste and recyclables. [4] Transportation and disposal of hazardous, medical, and nuclear waste. [5] Includes stationary and mobile sources. [6] Equipment for handling, storing or transporting solid, liquid or hazardous waste. Includes recycling/remediation equipment. [7] Revenues generated from the sale of water, majority in public sector. [8] Revenues generated from the sale of recovered metals, paper, plastic, etc. [9] Revenues generated from the sale of equipment and systems and electricity.

Source: Environmental Business International, Inc., San Diego, CA, publisher of *Environmental Business Journal*; © 2022 EBI Inc. See also <ebionline.org>.

Table 431. Toxic Chemical Releases and Transfers by Media: 2011 to 2020

[In millions of pounds (4,117.7 represents 4,117,700,000), except as indicated. Based on reports filed to the Toxic Release Inventory (TRI) Program, as required by Section 313 of the Emergency Planning and Community Right-to-Know Act (EPCRA). The Pollution Prevention Act (PPA) of 1990 mandates collection of data on toxic chemicals that are treated on-site, recycled, and combusted for energy recovery. Owners and operators of facilities within specific North American Industry Classification System industries that have 10 or more full-time employees, and that manufacture, process, or otherwise use any listed toxic chemical in quantities greater than the established threshold in the course of a calendar year are covered and required to report. For trend analysis, a 2011 core list of must-be-reported chemicals is used. Includes carcinogens; persistent, bioaccumulative, toxic (PBT) chemicals; and dioxin and dioxin-like compounds. Does not include off-site disposal or other releases transferred to other TRI program facilities that reported the amounts as on-site disposal or other releases]

Media	2011	2014	2015	2016	2017	2018	2019	2020
Total facilities reporting (number)	**21,920**	**22,369**	**22,376**	**22,187**	**22,001**	**21,999**	**21,760**	**21,124**
Total on- & off-site disposal or other releases	**4,117.7**	**3,961.4**	**3,676.8**	**3,541.4**	**3,901.1**	**3,661.7**	**3,345.9**	**3,020.4**
On-site releases	3,701.7	3,508.3	3,199.5	3,137.5	3,511.7	3,242.2	2,923.2	2,667.7
Air emissions [1]	808.5	742.2	677.5	600.1	597.6	604.8	583.2	532.2
Surface water discharges	222.9	218.7	199.2	192.5	191.4	194.4	200.5	193.4
Underground injection class I	197.8	202.0	209.2	198.4	197.4	210.3	177.0	167.6
Underground injection class II-V	0.2	0.9	0.8	2.0	1.9	2.0	1.8	1.5
RCRA subtitle C landfills [2]	3.7	3.7	2.5	4.8	4.5	5.1	3.5	3.0
Other landfills	273.6	287.4	283.7	268.6	295.1	281.8	230.5	193.3
Land treatment/application farming	15.0	13.3	14.3	12.4	14.8	16.1	13.7	13.7
Surface impoundments	884.9	758.8	800.7	887.8	881.3	851.4	758.5	728.7
Other land disposal	1,229.5	1,226.9	935.6	884.9	1,246.2	991.9	885.8	764.1
Off-site releases	416.0	453.1	477.4	403.9	389.4	419.5	422.7	352.7
Total transfers offsite for further waste management	**3,724.2**	**3,676.0**	**3,657.3**	**3,609.0**	**3,701.8**	**3,867.8**	**3,717.4**	**3,380.5**
Transfers to recycling	2,370.5	2,236.8	2,202.7	2,228.8	2,350.3	2,440.6	2,336.0	2,037.7
Transfers to energy recovery	354.7	422.4	412.6	425.2	404.2	418.3	434.4	455.4
Transfers to treatment	550.2	524.6	525.2	514.6	511.6	542.4	486.1	491.3
Transfers to POTWs (treatment) [3]	242.0	216.7	212.9	212.9	228.7	207.3	192.3	178.7
Transfers to POTWs (other releases) [3]	0.8	25.8	30.4	32.3	31.9	53.8	56.6	54.7
Transfers off-site for disposal or other releases	447.8	466.0	485.9	407.5	403.1	410.6	402.5	339.0
Total production-related waste managed	**22,714.0**	**28,683.3**	**27,872.0**	**27,609.5**	**28,331.1**	**30,884.2**	**29,613.3**	**27,650.5**
Recycled on-site	6,295.0	11,806.4	11,359.7	11,534.4	11,840.2	14,408.2	13,853.9	13,253.3
Recycled off-site	2,367.0	2,235.0	2,201.9	2,225.7	2,348.5	2,439.1	2,334.5	2,037.1
Energy recovery on-site	2,110.7	2,560.0	2,451.8	2,431.0	2,458.2	2,582.1	2,459.8	2,311.8
Energy recovery off-site	354.9	421.3	411.7	423.1	402.6	417.6	434.0	454.8
Treated on-site	6,899.7	7,146.4	7,221.0	6,911.4	6,832.8	6,791.9	6,665.7	6,044.0
Treated off-site	523.9	522.7	524.4	511.9	510.3	541.4	486.1	489.0
Quantity disposed or otherwise release of on-/off-site	4,162.8	3,991.4	3,701.6	3,572.0	3,938.5	3,703.7	3,379.3	3,060.4
Non-production-related waste managed	14.6	13.6	17.2	14.1	13.5	7.8	7.3	7.3

[1] Air emissions include both fugitive and point source. [2] RCRA=Resource Conservation and Recovery Act. [3] POTW (Publicly Owned Treatment Work) is a wastewater treatment facility that is owned by a state or municipality.

Source: U.S. Environmental Protection Agency, Toxic Release Inventory (TRI) Program, "TRI Explorer, 2020 Updated Dataset (released May 2022)," <enviro.epa.gov/triexplorer/tri_release.chemical>, accessed July 2022.

Table 432. Industrial Pollution—Toxic Chemical Releases by Industry: 2020

[In millions of pounds (3,020.4 represents 3,020,400,000). Based on 21,154 facilities. See headnote, Table 431]

Industry	NAICS [1] code	Total on- and off-site releases	On-site releases Total [2]	On-site releases Air emissions	On-site releases Other surface impoundments	Off-site releases/ transfers to disposal [3]
Total [4]	**(X)**	**3,020.4**	**2,667.7**	**532.2**	**725.7**	**352.7**
Coal mining	2121	3.5	3.5	(Z)	0.2	(Z)
Metal mining	2122	1,368.6	1,367.9	1.4	647.7	0.7
Electric utilities	2211	215.5	179.7	59.7	19.3	35.9
Food/beverages/tobacco	311/312	162.3	135.8	42.8	0.2	26.5
Textiles	313/314	1.9	1.7	0.8	–	0.3
Leather	316	1.1	(Z)	(Z)	–	1.0
Wood products	321	11.8	9.0	8.8	(Z)	2.8
Paper	322	141.7	135.9	105.2	1.9	5.8
Printing and publishing	323/511	2.0	1.7	1.7	–	0.4
Petroleum	324	68.2	62.9	31.1	(Z)	5.2
Chemicals	325	472.8	399.5	159.7	19.5	73.3
Plastics and rubber	326	35.9	29.8	29.3	(Z)	6.1
Nonmetallic mineral products	327	25.4	19.5	15.9	0.1	5.9
Primary metals	331	257.2	149.6	23.9	35.4	107.6
Fabricated metals	332	41.6	17.3	16.4	(Z)	24.3
Machinery	333	7.0	1.4	1.4	(Z)	5.6
Computers/electronic products	334	5.5	2.5	1.1	–	3.0
Electrical equipment	335	4.4	1.5	1.5	(Z)	2.9
Transportation equipment	336	28.7	22.9	22.8	(Z)	5.9
Furniture	337	3.4	3.3	3.3	–	0.1
Miscellaneous manufacturing	339	3.6	1.2	1.2	–	2.4
Chemical wholesalers	4246	1.8	0.8	0.8	–	1.0
Petroleum bulk terminals	4247	1.6	1.5	1.5	(Z)	0.1
Hazardous waste	562	118.0	93.8	0.4	0.4	24.2

– Represents zero. X Not applicable. Z less than 50,000 lbs. [1] North American Industry Classification System, see text, Section 12. [2] Includes other on-site releases, not shown separately. [3] Includes off-site disposal to underground injection for Class I wells, Class II to V wells, other surface impoundments, land releases, and other releases, not shown separately. [4] Includes other industries not shown separately, and industries with no specific industry identified, and uses a double counting algorithm.

Source: U.S. Environmental Protection Agency, Toxic Release Inventory (TRI) Program, "TRI Explorer, 2020 Updated Dataset (released May 2022)," <enviro.epa.gov/triexplorer/tri_release.industry>, accessed July 2022.

Table 433. Pollution—Toxic Chemical Releases by State and Outlying Area: 2020

[In millions of pounds (3,020.4 represents 3,020,400,000). Based on reports filed as required by Section 313 of the EPCRA. See headnote, Table 431]

State and outlying area	Total on- and off-site releases	On-site releases or other disposal — Total [2]	On-site releases or other disposal — Total air emissions	On-site releases or other disposal — Other surface impoundments	Off-site releases/transfers to disposal	State and outlying area	Total on- and off-site releases	On-site releases or other disposal — Total [2]	On-site releases or other disposal — Total air emissions	On-site releases or other disposal — Other surface impoundments	Off-site releases/transfers to disposal
Total [1]	3,020.4	2,667.7	532.2	725.7	352.7	MO	52.9	47.3	9.3	27.1	5.6
U.S. total	3,015.8	2,664.6	529.9	725.7	351.2	MT	56.5	56.0	1.5	40.8	0.5
AL	68.1	55.8	25.2	0.1	12.3	NE	16.1	13.3	5.0	(Z)	2.8
AK	627.4	626.7	0.4	305.9	0.7	NV	464.8	458.9	0.7	181.9	5.9
AZ	53.7	52.1	1.6	19.2	1.5	NH	0.4	0.1	0.1	–	0.3
AR	29.8	26.1	13.1	0.2	3.6	NJ	11.7	5.3	1.4	(Z)	6.4
CA	30.8	22.4	6.9	0.6	8.3	NM	5.9	4.6	0.8	0.2	1.3
CO	19.8	18.2	1.8	3.2	1.6	NY	15.2	10.6	4.3	1.6	4.6
CT	1.8	0.6	0.6	(Z)	1.2	NC	50.8	34.8	17.2	1.6	16.0
DE	7.7	7.6	0.5	(Z)	0.1	ND	40.2	35.2	19.8	2.3	5.0
DC	(Z)	(Z)	(Z)	(Z)	(Z)	OH	91.0	65.4	31.1	2.0	25.6
FL	48.3	44.4	15.9	0.3	3.9	OK	28.0	25.5	17.9	0.1	2.5
GA	43.2	39.1	26.3	0.5	4.1	OR	16.7	14.0	10.7	(Z)	2.7
HI	2.6	2.3	1.6	(Z)	0.2	PA	48.6	33.0	10.1	(Z)	15.6
ID	39.8	38.5	5.1	9.8	1.2	RI	0.5	0.2	0.2	–	0.3
IL	59.9	39.9	19.2	1.8	19.9	SC	31.9	23.3	18.0	0.2	8.6
IN	104.8	65.1	22.4	0.6	39.7	SD	8.7	8.3	1.7	(Z)	0.4
IA	37.9	25.1	17.9	0.5	12.8	TN	72.4	62.3	19.7	16.3	10.1
KS	23.4	15.3	9.4	1.3	8.1	TX	181.2	155.7	47.1	1.5	25.5
KY	48.0	29.9	14.4	1.0	18.0	UT	183.2	180.3	6.7	74.4	3.0
LA	122.5	119.2	48.3	2.0	3.4	VT	0.4	0.2	0.1	–	0.2
ME	7.4	5.5	2.2	–	2.0	VA	34.0	27.9	14.3	(Z)	6.1
MD	5.6	4.0	1.3	(Z)	1.6	WA	15.0	9.9	6.2	(Z)	5.0
MA	3.0	0.7	0.6	(Z)	2.4	WV	22.5	18.5	11.0	0.7	4.0
MI	61.4	38.2	9.4	7.9	23.2	WI	28.7	14.6	6.8	0.3	14.1
MN	20.1	16.3	8.4	4.6	3.8	WY	18.8	17.9	2.4	2.7	0.8
MS	52.6	48.0	13.0	12.5	4.5	PR	4.0	2.4	1.9	–	1.5

– Represents zero. Z Less than 50,000 lbs. [1] Total includes all states, Puerto Rico, and other outlying areas not shown separately. [2] Includes other types of release, not shown separately.

Source: U.S. Environmental Protection Agency, Toxic Release Inventory (TRI) Program, "TRI Explorer, 2020 Updated Dataset (released May 2022)," <enviro.epa.gov/triexplorer/tri_release.geography>, accessed July 2022.

Table 434. Hazardous Waste Sites on the Superfund National Priority List by State and Outlying Area: 2022

[As of August 2022. Includes final sites listed on the National Priorities List for the Superfund program as authorized by the Comprehensive Environmental Response, Compensation, and Liability Act (CERCLA) of 1980 and the Superfund Amendments and Reauthorization Act (SARA) of 1986. Prior to 2022, data in this table show final and proposed sites. For information on CERCLA and SARA, see <www.epa.gov/superfund/superfund-cercla-overview> and <www.epa.gov/superfund/superfund-amendments-and-reauthorization-act-sara>]

State and outlying area	Total sites	Rank	Percent distribution	Federal	Non-federal	State and outlying area	Total sites	Rank	Percent distribution	Federal	Non-federal
Total [1]	1,329	(X)	(X)	158	1,171	Missouri	33	14	2.5	3	30
United States	1,308	(X)	(X)	156	1,152	Montana	18	23	1.4	–	18
Alabama	12	32	0.9	3	9	Nebraska	17	24	1.3	1	16
Alaska	6	44	0.5	5	1	Nevada	1	48	0.1	–	1
Arizona	9	40	0.7	2	7	New Hampshire	20	20	1.5	1	19
Arkansas	9	40	0.7	–	9	New Jersey	114	1	8.7	6	108
California	96	2	7.3	24	72	New Mexico	15	26	1.1	1	14
Colorado	20	20	1.5	3	17	New York	85	4	6.5	4	81
Connecticut	13	30	1.0	1	12	North Carolina	38	11	2.9	2	36
Delaware	15	26	1.1	1	14	North Dakota	–	51	–	–	–
Dist. of Columbia	1	48	0.1	1	–	Ohio	37	12	2.8	3	34
Florida	52	7	4.0	6	46	Oklahoma	8	42	0.6	1	7
Georgia	17	24	1.3	2	15	Oregon	14	28	1.1	3	11
Hawaii	3	46	0.2	2	1	Pennsylvania	90	3	6.9	6	84
Idaho	6	44	0.5	2	4	Rhode Island	12	32	0.9	2	10
Illinois	45	9	3.4	4	41	South Carolina	28	17	2.1	2	26
Indiana	39	10	3.0	–	39	South Dakota	2	47	0.2	1	1
Iowa	11	36	0.8	1	10	Tennessee	19	22	1.5	3	16
Kansas	14	28	1.1	1	13	Texas	56	6	4.3	4	52
Kentucky	11	36	0.8	1	10	Utah	12	32	0.9	5	7
Louisiana	13	30	1.0	1	12	Vermont	12	32	0.9	–	12
Maine	11	36	0.8	3	8	Virginia	29	16	2.2	11	18
Maryland	21	19	1.6	10	11	Washington	46	8	3.5	13	33
Massachusetts	32	15	2.4	6	26	West Virginia	11	36	0.8	2	9
Michigan	65	5	5.0	–	65	Wisconsin	36	13	2.8	–	36
Minnesota	25	18	1.9	2	23	Wyoming	1	48	0.1	1	–
Mississippi	8	42	0.6	–	8	Puerto Rico	18	(X)	(X)	1	17

– Represents zero. X Not applicable. [1] Total includes areas not shown separately.

Source: U.S. Environmental Protection Agency, "Superfund National Priorities List," <www.epa.gov/superfund>, accessed August 2022.

Table 435. Hazardous Waste Generated, Shipped, and Received by State and Other Areas: 2019

[In thousands of tons (34,932.0 represents 34,932,000). Covers hazardous waste regulated under the Resource Conservation and Recovery Act (RCRA) of 1976 as amended. See source for data exclusions]

State and other area	Hazardous waste quantity			State and other area	Hazardous waste quantity		
	Generated	Shipped	Received		Generated	Shipped	Received
Total	**34,932.0**	**6,246.9**	**6,124.9**	Montana	7.4	7.4	–
United States	**34,913.2**	**6,230.5**	**6,124.5**	Nebraska	24.0	36.3	48.6
Alabama	953.7	243.8	471.2	Nevada	19.9	23.9	96.9
Alaska	1.9	1.9	0.1	New Hampshire	3.9	3.9	–
Arizona	45.9	44.6	9.1	New Jersey	214.1	217.0	150.2
Arkansas	391.2	255.9	297.0	New Mexico	6.6	8.5	3.1
California	255.1	291.6	164.7	New York	489.1	130.8	67.3
Colorado	42.4	53.7	45.1	North Carolina	87.5	99.2	30.1
Connecticut	40.3	40.3	28.1	North Dakota	402.9	1.7	0.1
Delaware	54.6	54.5	0.1	Ohio	1,545.1	515.6	628.7
District of Columbia	1.0	1.0	–	Oklahoma	117.5	94.3	183.8
Florida	236.4	43.6	15.6	Oregon	88.5	81.6	69.8
Georgia	71.1	70.3	0.5	Pennsylvania	256.8	221.3	313.1
Hawaii	531.8	2.5	(Z)	Rhode Island	8.5	17.8	8.7
Idaho	5.6	5.9	7.9	South Carolina	148.4	152.9	207.9
Illinois	610.0	187.2	250.0	South Dakota	2.1	2.2	0.1
Indiana	999.0	413.8	569.6	Tennessee	81.0	46.1	102.8
Iowa	53.5	53.0	0.2	Texas	17,566.7	782.8	699.6
Kansas	1,007.8	95.4	142.7	Utah	54.0	79.4	139.6
Kentucky	124.9	161.8	61.5	Vermont	2.6	3.8	2.4
Louisiana	5,367.0	470.8	362.8	Virginia	73.0	58.2	0.5
Maine	5.3	5.5	0.7	Washington	124.4	103.0	25.5
Maryland	39.8	44.3	46.8	West Virginia	52.8	41.0	11.0
Massachusetts	60.5	72.9	14.3	Wisconsin	274.0	290.3	57.7
Michigan	394.4	345.3	519.2	Wyoming	6.0	5.8	–
Minnesota	89.5	55.3	24.3	Guam	0.2	0.2	0.1
Mississippi	1,577.7	101.3	21.4	Puerto Rico	17.3	14.8	0.3
Missouri	295.8	89.9	224.1	Virgin Islands	1.4	1.4	–

– Represents zero. Z Less than 50.

Source: U.S. Environmental Protection Agency, Office of Resource Conservation and Recovery, RCRAInfo Web, "Biennial Report," <rcrainfo.epa.gov/rcrainfoweb/>, accessed March 2021.

Table 436. Oil Spills in U.S. Waters—Number and Volume: 2000 to 2020

[Based on reported discharges of oil and petroleum based products into U.S. navigable waters, including territorial waters (extending 3 to 12 miles from the coastline), tributaries, the contiguous zone, onto shoreline, or into other waters that threaten the marine environment. Data from the U.S. Coast Guard; see also *Polluting Incidents In and Around U.S. Waters, A Spill/Release Compendium: 1969–2011*]

Spill source	Number of spills					Spill volume (gallons)				
	2000	2010	2018	2019	2020	2000	2010	2018	2019	2020
Total	**8,354**	**3,008**	**2,834**	**2,855**	**2,194**	**1,431,370**	**207,712,793**	**549,914**	**714,416**	**181,275**
Vessel sources, total	5,560	1,508	1,977	1,572	1,284	1,033,643	894,934	342,454	471,039	73,010
Tankship	111	23	18	24	16	608,176	421,583	1,520	47,710	636
Tank barge	229	73	58	62	49	133,540	965	41,360	131,400	17,592
Other vessels [1]	5,220	1,412	1,901	1,414	1,219	291,927	472,386	299,574	291,929	54,782
Nonvessel sources, total	1,645	1,008	687	1,283	910	373,761	206,809,141	206,173	230,093	108,265
Offshore pipelines	4	34	26	17	18	17	4,627	17,306	4,109	548
Onshore pipelines	21	–	–	–	–	17,004	–	–	–	–
Other [2]	1,620	974	491	843	767	356,740	206,804,514	187,579	225,984	107,211
Unknown source	1,149	492	170	153	125	23,966	8,718	1,288	13,284	506

– Represents zero. [1] Commercial vessels, fishing boats, freight barges, freight ships, industrial vessels, oil recovery vessels, passenger vessels, unclassified public vessels, recreational boats, research vessels, school ships, tow and tug boats, mobile offshore drilling units, offshore supply vessels, publicly owned tank and freight ships, and vessels not fitting any particular class (unclassified). [2] Deepwater ports, designated waterfront facilities, nonmarine land facilities, fixed offshore and inshore platforms, mobile facility, municipal facility, aircraft, land vehicles, railroad equipment, bridges, factories, fleeting areas, industrial facilities, intakes, locks, marinas, MARPOL reception facilities, nonvessel common carrier facilities, outfalls, sewers, drains, permanently moored facilities, shipyards, and ship repair facilities.

Source: U.S. Bureau of Transportation Statistics, "National Transportation Statistics," <www.bts.gov/topics/national-transportation-statistics>, accessed November 2021.

Table 437. Petroleum and Hazardous Waste Underground Storage Tanks, Releases, and Corrective Actions: 2010 to 2021

[For year ending September 30. EPA collects data from states and territories regarding Underground Storage Tank (UST) systems storing either petroleum or certain hazardous substances. Approximately 800 substances (excluding radionuclides) are identified as hazardous under the Comprehensive Environmental Response, Compensation, and Liability Act (CERCLA). See <www.epa.gov/ust>]

Year	Active tanks	Closed tanks	Confirmed releases		Cleanups initiated [1]	Cleanups completed		Cleanups remaining
			Current year actions	Cumulative		Current year actions	Cumulative	
2010	597,333	1,748,204	6,328	494,997	470,460	11,591	401,874	93,123
2015	565,956	1,823,543	6,830	528,521	505,468	9,869	456,660	71,861
2017	555,079	1,856,451	5,678	538,193	516,882	8,775	469,898	68,295
2018	550,379	1,871,148	5,654	543,812	522,801	8,128	478,366	65,446
2019	546,192	1,885,633	5,375	550,897	536,957	8,358	493,589	57,308
2020	540,423	1,900,121	4,944	559,900	545,707	7,211	497,407	62,493
2021	539,610	1,905,508	4,991	564,767	550,956	7,271	502,786	61,981

[1] Cleanups initiated are cumulative. Even as a cleanup progresses and is completed, it is still counted in the cleanups initiated category.

Source: Environmental Protection Agency, "Underground Storage Tanks (USTs), UST Performance Measures," <www.epa.gov/ust/ust-performance-measures>, accessed March 2022.

Table 438. Tornadoes, Floods, Tropical Storms, and Lightning: 2000 to 2021

[424 represents $424,000,000]

Weather type	2000	2005	2010	2015	2016	2017	2018	2019	2020	2021
Tornadoes: [1]										
Number	1,072	1,262	1,282	1,177	976	1,429	1,126	1,517	1,082	1,314
Lives lost	41	38	45	36	18	35	10	42	76	104
Injuries	882	537	699	924	325	516	199	537	733	878
Property loss (mil. dol.)	424	422	1,107	317	181	632	670	3,102	2,504	229
Floods and flash floods:										
Lives lost	38	43	103	187	126	136	80	92	57	146
Injuries	47	38	310	50	31	19	21	45	9	60
Property loss (mil. dol.)	1,255	1,538	3,927	2,277	10,708	60,576	1,188	2,418	(NA)	3,013
North Atlantic tropical cyclones and hurricanes [2]	15	27	21	12	16	18	15	18	31	21
Hurricanes	8	15	12	4	7	10	8	6	14	7
Lives lost	–	1,016	–	14	11	43	7	–	333	101
Property loss (mil. dol.)	8	93,064	15	41	3,054	22,383	12,145	24	41,975	79,575
Pacific Basin tropical cyclones [2]	19	15	12	19	22	20	22	18	21	19
Hurricanes	6	7	3	13	13	9	12	7	4	8
Extreme temperature:										
Lives lost	184	182	172	98	125	134	144	98	363	296
Injuries	469	299	593	643	417	179	506	166	80	68
Property and crop loss (mil. dol.)	9.2	142.3	779.0	2.8	0.4	954.1	150.0	1.7	37.2	713.5
Cold:										
Lives lost	26	24	34	53	31	27	36	35	13	106
Injuries	–	1	1	3	6	3	3	1	1	1
Property and crop loss (mil. dol.)	9.2	139.3	775.2	2.8	0.4	954.1	150.0	0.2	31.2	713.4
Heat:										
Lives lost	158	158	138	45	94	107	108	187	350	190
Injuries	469	298	592	640	411	176	503	165	79	67
Property and crop loss (mil. dol.)	–	3.0	4.3	–	–	(Z)	(Z)	1.5	6.0	0.1
Lightning:										
Deaths	51	38	29	27	38	16	20	20	17	11
Injuries	364	309	182	130	120	86	82	100	53	69

NA Not available. – Represents zero. Z Less than $500,000. [1] Source: U.S. National Weather Service, <www.spc.noaa.gov/climo/online/monthly/newm.html>. A violent, rotating column of air descending from a cumulonimbus cloud in the form of a tubular- or funnel-shaped cloud, usually characterized by movements along a narrow path and wind speeds from 100 to over 300 miles per hour. Also known as a "twister" or "waterspout." [2] Tropical cyclones include depressions, storms and hurricanes. Fatalities are assumed to be caused by wind-driven debris or structural failure due to winds. For data on individual hurricanes, see National Hurricane Center (NHC) at <www.nhc.noaa.gov/>.

Source: Except as noted, U.S. National Oceanic and Atmospheric Administration (NOAA), National Weather Service (NWS), Office of Climate, Water, and Weather Services, "Weather Related Fatality and Injury Statistics," <www.weather.gov/hazstat/>, accessed July 2022.

Table 439. Number of Earthquakes in the United States: 2000 to 2012

[For information by region, see <usgs.gov/natural-hazards/earthquake-hazards/information-region>]

Magnitude (Richter seismic scale)	2000	2004	2005	2006	2007	2008	2009	2010	2011	2012	State earthquakes	1974– 2003 [1]
Total	2,342	3,550	3,685	2,783	2,791	3,618	4,262	8,496	5,237	3,365	Total	21,080
8.0 to 9.9	–	–	–	–	–	–	–	–	–	–	AK	[2] 12,053
7.0 to 7.9	–	–	1	–	1	–	–	1	1	–	CA	4,895
6.0 to 6.9	6	2	4	7	9	9	4	8	3	4	HI	1,533
5.0 to 5.9	63	25	47	51	72	85	58	89	51	25	NV	778
4.0 to 4.9	281	284	345	346	366	432	288	631	347	250	WA	424
3.0 to 3.9	917	1,362	1,475	1,213	1,137	1,486	1,492	3,584	1,838	1,096	ID	404
2.0 to 2.9	660	1,336	1,738	1,145	1,173	1,573	2,379	4,132	2,941	1,951	WY	217
1.0 to 1.9	–	1	2	7	11	13	26	39	47	34	MT	186
0.1 to 0.9	–	–	–	1	–	–	1	–	1	–	UT	139
No magnitude	415	540	73	13	22	20	14	12	8	5	OR	73

– Represents zero. [1] The total number represents earthquakes of a magnitude range of 3.5 and greater. [2] Number of earthquakes is underreported since events with magnitude from 3.5 to 4.0 in the in the Aleutian Islands are not recorded on enough seismograph stations to be located.

Source: U.S. Geological Survey, *Earthquake Facts and Statistics*, <earthquake.usgs.gov>, accessed August 2016.

Table 440. Wildland Fires, Number, and Acres: 1970 to 2021

[Acres in thousands (3,278.6 represents 3,278,600). As of December 31. Data are for wildland fires only and do not include prescribed fires. Wildland fire is any nonstructural fire that occurs in the wildland. Includes those that are unplanned and unwanted, and include unauthorized human-caused fires, and escaped prescribed fire projects)]

Year	Total Fires	Total Acres (1,000)	Year	Total Fires	Total Acres (1,000)	State	Top states ranked by wildland acres burned in 2021 Fires	Top states ranked by wildland acres burned in 2021 Acres (1,000)
1970	121,736	3,278.6	2011	74,126	8,711.4	Total	58,985	7,125.6
1975	134,872	1,791.3	2012	67,774	9,326.2	CA	9,280	2,233.7
1980	234,892	5,260.8	2013	47,579	4,319.5	OR	2,202	828.8
1985	82,591	2,896.1	2014	63,612	3,595.6	MT	2,573	747.7
1990	66,481	4,621.6	2015	68,151	10,125.1	WA	1,863	674.2
1995	82,234	1,840.5	2016	67,743	5,510.0	AZ	1,773	524.4
2000	92,250	7,393.5	2017	71,499	10,026.1	ID	1,332	439.6
2005	66,753	8,689.4	2018	58,083	8,767.5	AK	384	253.4
2009	78,792	5,921.8	2019	50,477	4,664.4	TX	5,576	168.3
2010	71,971	3,422.7	2020	58,950	10,122.3	KS	55	164.0

Source: National Interagency Coordination Center, *Wildland Fire Summary and Statistics Annual Report, 2021*, and earlier reports. See also <www.predictiveservices.nifc.gov/intelligence/intelligence.htm>.

Table 441. Major U.S. Weather and Climate Disasters: 2021

[10.6 represents $10,600,000,000. Cost in CPI-adjusted dollars. Covers only weather and climate related disasters costing $1 billion or more. See source for more information]

Event	Description	Time period	Estimated cost (bil. dol.)	Deaths (number)
Western Wildfires............	Severe drought conditions and periods of extreme heat provided conditions favorable for another damaging western wildfire season most focused across CA, CO, OR, WA, ID, MT and AZ. The Dixie Fire consumed over 960,000 acres making it the second-largest wildfire on record in CA while also destroying more than 1,000 structures. CA's Caldor Fire grew rapidly during August, threatening South Lake Tahoe communities and burned over 220,000 acres. Other large wildfires included the Ford Corkscrew Fire (WA), the Bootleg Fire (OR), the Boundary Fire (ID), the Trail Creek Fire (MT) and the Telegraph Fire (AZ), among many others. There was also the Marshall Fire in Boulder County, CO on December 30 that damaged or destroyed more than 1,000 homes and businesses. This wildfire is the most destructive on record in CO. Throughout the wildfire season air quality was also a concern across numerous states, as ash and fine particulates from wildfires obscured the skies and made outdoor activities more hazardous. Over 7.1 million acres burned nationally during the 2021 wildfire season.	June 1 to Dec. 31, 2021	$10.6	8
Western Drought and Heat Wave............	Western drought conditions were persistent throughout 2021, as the drought expanded and intensified across many Western states. A historic heat wave also developed for many days across the Pacific Northwest shattering numerous all-time high temperature records across the region. This prolonged heat dome was maximized over the states of OR and WA and extended well into Canada. These extreme temperatures impacted several major cities and millions of people. For example, Portland reached a high of 116 degrees F while Seattle reached 108 degrees F. These extreme temperatures caused hundreds of direct and indirect heat-related fatalities across OR and WA, not including excess mortality that may be hundreds of additional deaths. This combined drought and heat rapidly dried out vegetation across the West, impacting agriculture. Low water levels also forced the hydroelectric power plant at Lake Oroville in California to shut down for the first time since it opened in 1967.	Jan. 1 to Dec. 31, 2021	$8.9	229
Midwest Derecho and Tornado Outbreak............	A rare, record-breaking December derecho and tornado outbreak caused widespread damage that was focused across KS, NE, IA, MN and WI. There were many reports of hurricane-force thunderstorm wind gusts and more than 50 tornadoes causing widespread damage to homes, vehicles, businesses and infrastructure. This was the first December derecho on record to occur within the United States. This event also produced the first December tornado on record in MN since 1950, with 17 tornadoes reported across southeast MN.	Dec. 15, 2021	$1.8	1
Southeast, Central Tornado Outbreak............	Historic December tornado outbreak across several southeast and central states caused devastating damage across many towns and cities. This outbreak produced two long-tracked EF-4 tornadoes across AR, MO, TN and KY. The longest tornado track was nearly 166 miles across KY and was a U.S. record tornado track length for the month of December. There were over 800 total miles of tornado path length on December 10. The peak intensity from this outbreak was EF-4 rated wind speeds of 190 mph in Mayfield, KY.	Dec. 10, 2022	$3.9	93
Hurricane Nicholas............	Category 1 Hurricane Nicholas made landfall near Sargent Beach, TX on September 14 and moved slowly toward LA over the next several days. This slow progression helped to produce flooding rainfall across regions of the Gulf Coast that were already saturated from Hurricane Ida.	Sept. 14-18, 2021	$1.0	–
Hurricane Ida............	Category 4 Hurricane Ida made landfall near Port Fourchon, LA with maximum sustained winds of 150 mph (240km/h) and a minimum central pressure of 930 mb. Ida was one of three hurricanes in recorded history to make landfall in Louisiana with 150 mph winds. Grand Isle, LA took a direct hit with 100% of its homes damaged and nearly 40% were nearly-to-completely destroyed. There was heavy damage to the energy infrastructure across southern Louisiana causing widespread, long duration power outages to millions of people. Parts of New Orleans were without power for nearly a week due to the widespread damage. As the remnants of Ida moved into the Northeast it merged with a frontal system creating severe weather and flash flooding across a wide region from eastern PA to NY. Flash flood emergencies were declared in NJ and NY for the first time, producing damage to homes, businesses, vehicles and infrastructure while also causing dozens of fatalities.	Aug. 29 to Sept. 1, 2021	$75.0	96
Tropical Storm Fred............	Tropical Storm Fred made landfall near Panama City, FL. As Fred progressed northward it caused torrential flooding across the southern Appalachian Mountains with more than a foot of rainfall reported in some locations of western NC. This flash flooding caused damage to many homes, businesses, vehicles, roads and bridges, in additional to several fatalities. Fred also produced nearly a dozen tornadoes across the Northeast as it moved up the East Coast.	Aug. 16-18, 2021	$1.3	7
North Central Severe Weather. ..	Widespread high wind impacts across numerous North Central states including IL, MI, WI, IN, OH and MO. This multi-day event caused damage to infrastructure, homes, vehicles and businesses.	Aug. 10-13, 2021	$1.3	2

See footnotes at end of table.

Table 441. Major U.S. Weather and Climate Disasters: 2021-Continued.
See headnote on page 274.

Event	Description	Time period	Estimated cost (bil. dol.)	Deaths (number)
Central Severe Storms	Severe storms caused considerable hail damage across numerous Central states including Missouri, NE, IA, SD, ND, NM and TX. There was also widespread high wind damage to homes, vehicles and businesses in many other surrounding states.	July 8-11, 2021	$1.1	–
Tropical Storm Elsa	Tropical Storm Elsa made landfall in Taylor County, FL producing heavy rain, wind, flooding and tornadoes in portions of FL, GA and the Carolinas, as well as flooding across parts of the Northeast. Southern New England and NY's Long Island experienced flash flooding, leading to impassable roads, stranded vehicles and disruption.	July 7-9, 2021	$1.2	1
Central Severe Storms	A combination of thunderstorm high winds, hail and tornadoes affected numerous Central states. The states most affected included MI, IL, IN, OH, MO, KS and TX with damage to homes, businesses, vehicles and agriculture.	June 24-26, 2021	$1.3	–
Ohio Valley Hail Storms	Damaging hail storm and high wind impacts across several states including OH, IL, IN, MI, WI, MN, IA and MO. The hail impacts were most severe in southeastern MN, southern IA, southeastern IN and southwestern OH, with damage to many homes, vehicles and businesses.	June 17-18, 2021	$1.7	–
Louisiana Flooding	Torrential rainfall from thunderstorms across LA and coastal TX caused widespread flooding and resulted in hundreds of water rescues. Baton Rouge and Lake Charles experienced flood damage to thousands of homes, vehicles and businesses, as more than 12 inches of rain fell.	May 17-18, 2021	$1.4	5
Southern Tornadoes and Southeast Severe Weather	Tornadoes and severe storms with widespread high wind and large hail cause damage across many Southern and Southeastern states including MS, TX, AR, AL, GA, SC, NC, and TN. There were over 111 confirmed tornadoes largely clustered in central MS and surrounding states.	May 2-4, 2021	$1.3	4
Texas and Oklahoma Severe Weather	Severe weather including tornadoes, high wind, localized flooding and large hail cause widespread impacts across central TX and OK. There was considerable damage across TX and OK to many homes, vehicles and businesses particularly from hail storms.	Apr. 27-28, 2021	$3.3	–
Texas Hail Storms	A series of hail storms impacted central TX causing damage to many homes, vehicles and businesses. There was considerable hail damage northeast of Austin, west of Georgetown and southwest of The Woodlands.	Apr. 12-15, 2021	$1.5	–
Eastern Severe Weather	Severe weather producing hail, high wind and more than two dozen tornadoes impacted numerous states including AR, AL, GA, MS, SC, NC and VA. TN was also affected with significant flooding in Nashville and surrounding areas that damaged businesses, homes and vehicles. There were also many high wind damage reports across PA, MD and NJ.	Mar. 27-28, 2021	$1.4	8
Southeast Tornadoes and Severe Weather	At least 41 tornadoes impact several states including KY, TN, MS, AL and GA. These included one EF-4, four EF-3s, ten EF-2s and approximately two-dozen EF-1 or EF-0 tornadoes. The strongest of these tornadoes were focused across central AL and western GA with tracks across the entire width of AL. There was widespread damage to homes, businesses, vehicles and infrastructure.	Mar. 24-25, 2021	$1.8	6
Northwest, Central, Eastern Winter Storm and Cold Wave	Historic cold wave and winter storm impacts many northwest, central and eastern states. Temperature departures exceeding 40.0 degrees F (22.2 degrees C) below normal occurred from NE southward to TX. The prolonged arctic air caused widespread power outages in TX, as well as other southern states, with multiple days of sustained below-freezing temperatures. At the peak of the outage, nearly 10 million people were without power. Additional impacts were frozen water pipes, which burst upon thawing causing water damage to buildings. These extreme conditions also caused or contributed to the direct and indirect deaths of more than 210 people in TX alone. There were also snow and ice impacts across numerous states including OK, AK, MO, IL, KY, TN, LA, MS, CO, OR and WA. This is now the costliest U.S. winter storm event on record.	Feb. 10-19, 2021	$24.0	226
California Flooding and Severe Weather	CA was impacted by an atmospheric river in late-January, in which more than 7 inches of rain fell from southern CA to the central CA coast. Rainfall totals exceeded 15 inches in Monterey and San Luis Obispo counties. These heavy rains caused flooding and mudslides in some of the same areas burned by wildfires in late-2020. This combination caused dozens of slides and debris flows damaging homes, vehicles and businesses and infrastructure. Highway 1 south of Big Sur was washed out while the Sierra Nevada range received several feet of snow, closing major highways. In addition to significant rain and snow, high winds also caused extensive power outages across parts the region.	Jan. 24-29, 2021	$1.2	2

– Represents zero.

Source: U.S. National Oceanic and Atmospheric Administration, National Centers for Environmental Information, "Billion-Dollar Weather and Climate Disasters, 1980-2021," <www.ncdc.noaa.gov/billions/events>, accessed February 2022.

Geography and Environment

Table 442. Highest and Lowest Temperatures by State Through 2021

[Data have been evaluated by the National Oceanic and Atmospheric Administration National Climatic Data Center, and/or by the State Climate Extremes Committee and determined to be valid. The data may come from sources other than official NOAA-supervised weather stations, but are archived, officially recognized observations]

State	Highest temperatures			Lowest temperatures		
	Station	Temperature (°F)	Date	Station	Temperature (°F)	Date
U.S.	**Greenland Ranch, CA**	**134**	**July 10, 1913**	**Prospect Creek Camp, AK**	**-80**	**Jan. 23, 1971**
AL	Centreville	112	Sept. 6, 1925	New Market	-27	Jan. 30, 1966
AK	Fort Yukon	100	June 27, 1915	Prospect Creek Camp	-80	Jan. 23, 1971
AZ	Lake Havasu City	128	June 29, 1994	Hawley Lake	-40	Jan. 7, 1971
AR	Ozark	120	Aug. 10, 1936	Gravette	-29	Feb. 13, 1905
CA	Greenland Ranch	134	July 10, 1913	Boca	-45	Jan. 20, 1937
CO	John Martin Dam	115	July 20, 2019	Maybell	-61	Feb. 1, 1985
CT	Danbury	106	[1] July 15, 1995	Coventry	-32	[1] Jan. 22, 1961
DE	Millsboro	110	July 21, 1930	Millsboro	-17	Jan. 17, 1893
FL	Monticello	109	June 29, 1931	Tallahassee	-2	Feb. 13, 1899
GA	Greenville	112	[1] Aug. 20, 1983	CCC Camp F-16	-17	Jan. 27, 1940
HI	Pahala	100	Apr. 27, 1931	Mauna Kea Obs. 111.2	12	May 17, 1979
ID	Orofino	118	July 28, 1934	Island Park Dam	-60	Jan. 18, 1943
IL	East St. Louis	117	July 14, 1954	Mount Carroll	-38	Jan. 31, 2019
IN	Collegeville	116	July 14, 1936	New Whiteland	-36	Jan. 19, 1994
IA	Keokuk	118	July 20, 1934	Elkader	-47	[1] Feb. 3, 1996
KS	Alton	121	[1] July 24, 1936	Lebanon	-40	Feb. 13, 1905
KY	Greensburg	114	July 28, 1930	Shelbyville	-37	Jan. 19, 1994
LA	Plain Dealing	114	Aug. 10, 1936	Minden	-16	Feb. 13, 1899
ME	North Bridgton	105	[1] July 10, 1911	Big Black River	-50	Jan. 16, 2009
MD	Frederick Police Barracks	109	[1] July 10, 1936	Oakland	-40	Jan. 13, 1912
MA	Chester	107	[1] Aug. 2, 1975	Chester	-35	[1] Jan. 12, 1981
MI	Stanwood	112	July 13, 1936	Vanderbilt	-51	Feb. 9, 1934
MN	Beardsley	115	July 29, 1917	Tower	-60	Feb. 2, 1996
MS	Holly Springs	115	July 29, 1930	Corinth	-19	Jan. 30, 1966
MO	Warsaw	118	July 14, 1954	Warsaw	-40	Feb. 13, 1905
MT	Medicine Lake	117	[1] July 5, 1937	Rogers Pass	-70	Jan. 20, 1954
NE	Minden	118	[1] July 24, 1936	Oshkosh	-47	[1] Dec. 22, 1989
NV	Laughlin	125	June 29, 1994	San Jacinto	-50	Jan. 8, 1937
NH	Nashua	106	July 4, 1911	Mt. Washington	-50	Jan. 22, 1885
NJ	Runyon	110	July 10, 1936	River Vale	-34	Jan. 5, 1904
NM	Waste Isolation Pilot Plant	122	June 27, 1994	Gavilan	-50	Feb. 1, 1951
NY	Troy	108	July 22, 1926	Old Forge	-52	Feb. 18, 1979
NC	Fayetteville	110	Aug. 21, 1983	Mt. Mitchell	-34	Jan. 21, 1985
ND	Steele	121	July 6, 1936	Parshall	-60	Feb. 15, 1936
OH	Gallipolis (near)	113	July 21, 1934	Milligan	-39	Feb. 10, 1899
OK	Altus Irig Res	120	[1] Aug. 12, 1936	Nowata	-31	Feb. 10, 2011
OR	Pelton Dam	119	[1] June 29, 2021	Seneca	-54	[1] Feb. 10, 1933
PA	Phoenixville	111	[1] July 10, 1936	Smethport	-42	Jan. 5, 1904
RI	Providence	104	Aug. 2, 1975	Wood River Junction	-28	Jan. 11, 1942
SC	Columbia Univ. of SC	113	June 29, 2012	Caesars Head	-19	Jan. 21, 1985
SD	Fort Pierre	120	[1] July 15, 2006	McIntosh	-58	Feb. 17, 1936
TN	Perryville	113	[1] Aug. 9, 1930	Mountain City	-32	Dec. 30, 1917
TX	Monahans	120	[1] June 28, 1994	Seminole	-23	Feb. 8, 1933
UT	Saint George	117	July 5, 1985	East Portal	-50	Jan. 5, 1913
VT	Vernon	107	July 7, 1912	Bloomfield	-50	Dec. 30, 1933
VA	Balcony Falls	110	[1] July 15, 1954	Mtn. Lake Bio. Stn.	-30	Jan. 21, 1985
WA	Hanford	120	[1] June 29, 2021	Winthrop	-48	[1] Dec. 30, 1968
WV	Martinsburg	112	[1] July 10, 1936	Lewisburg	-37	Dec. 30, 1917
WI	Wisconsin Dells	114	[1] July 13, 1936	Couderay	-55	[1] Feb. 4, 1996
WY	Diversion Dam	115	[1] July 15, 1988	Riverside R.S.	-66	Feb. 9, 1933

[1] Also on earlier dates at the same or other places.

Source: U.S. National Oceanic and Atmospheric Administration, National Climatic Data Center, State Climate Extremes Committee, "Maximum and Minimum Temperature Records," <www.ncei.noaa.gov/access/monitoring/scec/records>, accessed June 2022.

Table 443. Highest Temperature of Record—Selected Cities

[In degrees Fahrenheit. Airport data, except as noted. Data for each city are shown for varying periods of record; see source for date ranges for each location]

State	Station	Jan.	Feb.	Mar.	Apr.	May	June	July	Aug.	Sept.	Oct.	Nov.	Dec.	Annual [1]
AL.....	Mobile	84	84	89	94	100	103	104	105	100	98	88	81	105
AK.....	Juneau	60	57	61	74	80	86	90	84	78	63	56	54	90
AZ.....	Phoenix	88	92	100	105	113	122	121	117	118	107	99	88	122
AK.....	Little Rock	83	85	91	95	98	107	112	114	106	98	86	81	114
CA.....	Los Angeles	95	95	98	106	102	112	108	105	113	108	100	92	113
CA. ...	Sacramento	76	78	88	95	105	115	114	112	109	104	87	74	115
CA. ...	San Diego	88	90	93	98	97	101	99	98	111	107	100	88	111
CA. ...	San Francisco	79	81	87	94	97	103	99	98	106	102	86	76	106
CO. ...	Denver	74	83	84	90	96	104	104	102	99	89	81	75	104
CT.....	Hartford	72	77	89	96	99	101	103	102	101	91	83	76	103
DE. ...	Wilmington	75	78	86	94	96	100	103	101	100	98	85	75	103
DC. ...	Washington Nat'l	79	82	89	95	99	104	105	105	101	98	86	79	105
FL.....	Jacksonville	85	89	94	95	102	103	105	102	100	96	89	85	105
FL.....	Miami	88	89	93	97	98	98	98	98	97	95	91	89	98
GA. ...	Atlanta	79	80	89	93	97	106	105	104	99	98	84	79	106
HI.....	Honolulu	88	88	89	91	93	92	94	95	95	94	93	89	95
ID.....	Boise	63	71	81	92	99	110	111	110	102	94	78	65	111
IL......	Chicago	65	72	88	91	97	104	104	101	99	91	78	71	104
IL......	Peoria	70	74	86	92	97	105	104	103	100	93	81	71	105
IN. ...	Indianapolis	71	77	85	89	95	104	105	102	100	92	81	74	105
IA.....	Des Moines	67	75	91	93	99	103	106	108	101	95	81	69	108
KS.....	Wichita	75	87	89	96	102	110	113	111	108	97	86	83	113
KY.....	Louisville	77	82	86	91	95	105	106	105	104	97	85	76	106
LA.....	New Orleans	83	85	89	92	97	101	101	102	101	97	88	85	102
ME. ...	Portland	67	68	88	92	94	98	100	103	95	88	74	71	103
MD. ...	Baltimore	75	79	89	94	100	103	106	105	100	99	86	77	106
MA. ...	Boston	74	73	89	94	96	100	103	102	100	90	83	76	103
MI.....	Detroit	64	70	86	89	95	104	102	100	98	91	78	69	104
MI.....	Sault Ste. Marie	47	49	83	85	90	93	97	98	95	81	75	62	98
MN. ...	Duluth	48	55	75	88	92	94	97	95	95	86	75	55	97
MN. ...	Minneapolis-St. Paul	58	63	83	95	100	103	105	102	98	90	77	68	105
MS. ...	Jackson	83	86	89	94	99	105	106	107	104	99	88	84	107
MO....	Kansas City	74	79	87	93	95	105	107	109	106	95	82	74	109
MO....	St. Louis	77	85	89	93	98	108	115	107	104	94	85	76	115
MT. ...	Helena	63	69	78	86	93	103	105	105	99	87	76	65	105
NE. ...	Omaha	69	78	91	97	101	105	110	107	103	95	83	69	110
NV. ...	Reno	71	75	83	90	97	104	108	105	102	93	77	71	108
NH. ...	Concord	69	74	89	95	97	98	102	101	98	90	80	73	102
NJ.....	Atlantic City	78	76	87	94	99	106	105	103	99	96	81	77	106
NM. ...	Albuquerque	69	76	85	89	98	107	105	101	100	91	77	72	107
NY. ...	Albany	71	74	89	93	94	99	100	99	100	91	82	72	100
NY. ...	Buffalo	72	71	82	94	93	96	98	99	98	87	80	74	99
NY. ...	NYC Central Park	72	78	86	96	99	101	106	104	102	94	84	75	106
NC. ...	Charlotte	79	82	90	93	100	104	104	104	104	99	85	80	104
NC. ...	Raleigh	80	84	92	95	97	105	105	105	104	100	88	81	105
ND. ...	Bismarck	63	73	81	93	96	111	112	107	105	95	79	65	112
OH. ...	Cincinnati	74	79	84	89	93	102	104	102	102	95	82	75	104
OH. ...	Cleveland	73	77	83	88	93	104	103	102	101	93	82	77	104
OH. ...	Columbus	74	78	85	89	93	101	104	101	100	94	80	76	104
OK. ...	Oklahoma City	80	92	93	100	104	105	110	113	108	96	87	86	113
OR. ...	Portland	66	71	80	90	100	102	107	107	105	92	73	65	107
PA.....	Philadelphia	74	77	87	95	97	100	104	101	100	96	84	73	104
PA.....	Pittsburgh	75	78	83	89	91	98	103	100	97	89	82	74	103
RI.....	Providence	70	72	85	98	96	97	102	104	100	88	81	77	104
SC. ...	Columbia	84	84	91	94	101	109	107	107	101	101	90	83	109
SD. ...	Sioux Falls	66	70	88	94	104	110	110	109	104	94	82	63	110
TN. ...	Memphis	79	81	86	94	99	104	108	107	103	98	86	81	108
TN. ...	Nashville	78	84	87	91	95	109	107	106	105	99	88	79	109
TX. ...	Dallas	88	95	97	100	103	112	112	111	110	100	92	89	112
TX. ...	El Paso	80	85	93	98	105	114	112	108	104	96	87	80	114
TX. ...	Houston	84	91	91	95	99	107	104	109	109	96	89	85	109
UT.....	Salt Lake City	63	69	80	89	99	105	107	106	100	89	75	69	107
VT.....	Burlington	66	72	84	91	95	100	100	101	98	85	75	68	101
VA.....	Norfolk	80	82	88	97	100	101	105	104	99	95	86	82	105
VA.....	Richmond	81	82	91	96	100	104	105	104	103	99	86	81	105
WA....	Seattle	64	70	79	89	93	96	103	99	98	89	74	66	103
WA....	Spokane	62	63	72	90	97	105	108	108	98	87	70	60	108
WV....	Charleston	80	81	89	94	94	103	104	104	102	94	85	80	104
WI.....	Milwaukee	63	71	84	91	95	101	103	103	98	89	77	68	103
WY....	Cheyenne	70	71	76	84	91	100	100	98	95	84	75	69	100
PR. ...	San Juan	92	96	96	97	96	97	95	97	97	98	96	94	98

[1] Represents the highest observed temperature in any month.

Source: U.S. National Oceanic and Atmospheric Administration, *Comparative Climatic Data for the United States Through 2020.* See also <www.ncei.noaa.gov/products/land-based-station/comparative-climatic-data>.

Table 444. Lowest Temperature of Record—Selected Cities

[In degrees Fahrenheit. Airport data, except as noted. Data for each city are shown for varying periods of record; see source for date ranges for each location]

State	Station	Jan.	Feb.	Mar.	Apr.	May	June	July	Aug.	Sept.	Oct.	Nov.	Dec.	Annual [1]
AL......	Mobile	3	11	21	32	43	49	62	59	42	30	22	8	3
AK.....	Juneau	-22	-22	-15	6	25	31	36	27	23	11	-5	-21	-22
AZ.....	Phoenix	17	22	25	34	40	50	61	60	47	34	25	22	17
AR.....	Little Rock	-4	-5	11	28	38	46	54	52	37	28	17	-1	-5
CA.....	Los Angeles	28	29	35	39	43	49	53	51	50	41	38	30	28
CA.....	Sacramento	20	23	26	31	34	41	48	48	42	35	26	18	18
CA.....	San Diego	29	36	39	41	48	50	55	57	51	43	38	34	29
CA.....	San Francisco	30	31	35	40	43	47	47	48	48	43	39	27	27
CO.....	Denver	-25	-25	-10	-2	22	30	43	41	17	3	-10	-25	-25
CT.....	Hartford	-26	-21	-8	9	28	37	44	36	27	17	1	-14	-26
DE.....	Wilmington	-14	-6	2	18	30	41	48	43	36	24	14	-7	-14
DC.....	Washington Nat'l	-5	4	14	24	34	47	54	49	39	29	16	3	-5
FL......	Jacksonville	7	19	23	31	45	47	61	63	48	33	21	11	7
FL......	Miami	30	35	32	42	55	60	69	68	68	53	39	30	30
GA.....	Atlanta	-8	5	10	26	37	46	53	55	36	28	3	0	-8
HI......	Honolulu	52	53	55	56	60	65	66	65	64	61	57	54	52
ID......	Boise	-17	-15	6	19	22	31	35	34	23	11	-3	-25	-25
IL......	Chicago	-27	-19	-8	7	24	36	40	41	28	17	1	-25	-27
IL......	Peoria	-25	-19	-10	14	25	39	47	41	29	19	-2	-23	-25
IN......	Indianapolis	-27	-21	-7	18	27	37	48	41	32	20	-2	-23	-27
IA......	Des Moines	-24	-26	-22	9	28	41	47	40	28	14	-4	-22	-26
KS.....	Wichita	-12	-21	-2	15	31	43	51	48	31	18	1	-16	-21
KY.....	Louisville	-22	-19	-1	22	31	42	50	46	33	23	-1	-15	-22
LA......	New Orleans	14	16	25	32	41	50	60	60	42	35	24	11	11
ME.....	Portland	-26	-39	-21	8	23	33	40	33	23	15	3	-21	-39
MD.....	Baltimore	-7	-3	4	20	32	40	50	45	35	25	13	0	-7
MA.....	Boston	-12	-14	1	16	34	41	50	46	37	25	12	-11	-14
MI.....	Detroit	-21	-15	-4	10	25	36	41	38	29	17	7	-10	-21
MI......	Sault Ste. Marie	-36	-37	-28	-2	18	26	36	29	25	16	-10	-31	-37
MN.....	Duluth	-39	-39	-29	-5	17	27	35	32	23	8	-23	-34	-39
MN.....	Minneapolis-St. Paul	-34	-32	-32	2	18	34	43	39	26	13	-17	-29	-34
MS.....	Jackson	2	10	15	27	36	47	51	54	35	26	17	4	2
MO.....	Kansas City	-17	-19	-10	12	30	42	51	43	31	17	1	-23	-23
MO.....	St. Louis	-18	-12	-5	22	31	43	51	47	32	22	1	-16	-18
MT.....	Helena	-42	-42	-30	1	17	30	36	28	18	-8	-39	-38	-42
NE.....	Omaha	-23	-21	-16	5	27	38	44	43	25	13	-9	-23	-23
NV.....	Reno	-16	-16	0	13	18	25	33	24	20	8	1	-16	-16
NH.....	Concord	-33	-37	-16	4	21	26	33	29	20	10	-5	-22	-37
NJ......	Atlantic City	-10	-11	2	12	25	37	42	40	32	20	10	-2	-11
NM.....	Albuquerque	-17	-7	8	18	28	40	52	50	35	19	-7	-7	-17
NY.....	Albany	-28	-22	-21	10	26	35	40	34	24	16	-11	-22	-28
NY.....	Buffalo	-16	-20	-7	12	26	35	43	38	31	20	7	-10	-20
NY.....	NYC Central Park	-6	-15	3	12	32	44	52	50	39	28	5	-13	-15
NC.....	Charlotte	-5	5	4	21	32	45	53	50	39	24	11	2	-5
NC.....	Raleigh	-9	0	11	23	29	38	48	46	37	19	11	4	-9
ND.....	Bismarck	-44	-43	-31	-12	15	30	35	33	11	-10	-30	-43	-44
OH.....	Cincinnati	-25	-15	-11	15	27	39	47	43	31	16	0	-20	-25
OH.....	Cleveland	-20	-17	-5	10	25	31	41	38	32	19	3	-15	-20
OH.....	Columbus	-22	-13	-6	14	25	35	43	39	31	17	-4	-17	-22
OK.....	Oklahoma City	-4	-5	1	20	32	47	53	50	36	16	11	-8	-8
OR.....	Portland	-2	-3	19	29	29	39	43	44	34	26	13	6	-3
PA......	Philadelphia	-7	-4	7	19	28	44	51	44	35	25	15	1	-7
PA......	Pittsburgh	-22	-12	-5	14	26	34	42	39	31	16	-1	-12	-22
RI......	Providence	-13	-9	1	14	29	41	48	40	32	20	6	-10	-13
SC.....	Columbia	-1	5	4	26	34	44	54	53	40	23	12	4	-1
SD.....	Sioux Falls	-36	-31	-23	4	17	33	38	34	22	9	-17	-28	-36
TN.....	Memphis	-4	-11	12	28	36	48	52	48	36	25	9	-13	-13
TN......	Nashville	-17	-13	2	23	34	42	54	49	36	26	-1	-10	-17
TX......	Dallas	0	7	11	31	39	53	60	56	36	27	17	1	0
TX......	El Paso	-8	1	14	21	31	46	57	56	41	25	1	5	-8
TX......	Houston	12	20	22	31	42	52	62	60	48	29	19	7	7
UT.....	Salt Lake City	-22	-14	2	15	25	35	40	37	27	14	-14	-15	-22
VT......	Burlington	-30	-30	-20	2	24	33	39	35	25	15	-2	-26	-30
VA......	Norfolk	-3	8	18	28	36	45	54	49	45	27	20	7	-3
VA......	Richmond	-12	-8	10	23	31	40	51	47	35	21	14	1	-12
WA.....	Seattle	0	1	11	29	28	38	43	44	35	28	6	6	0
WA.....	Spokane	-24	-24	-10	14	24	33	37	35	22	7	-21	-25	-25
WV.....	Charleston	-16	-12	0	19	26	33	46	41	34	17	6	-12	-16
WI.....	Milwaukee	-26	-26	-10	12	21	33	40	44	28	18	-5	-20	-26
WY.....	Cheyenne	-30	-34	-21	-8	9	25	33	36	8	-1	-21	-28	-34
PR.....	San Juan	61	62	60	64	66	69	69	70	69	67	66	63	60

[1] Represents the lowest observed temperature in any month.

Source: U.S. National Oceanic and Atmospheric Administration, *Comparative Climatic Data for the United States Through 2020.* See also <www.ncei.noaa.gov/products/land-based-station/comparative-climatic-data>.

Table 445. Average Snow, Hail, Ice Pellets, and Sleet—Selected Cities

[Average in inches. Data for each city are shown for varying periods of record; see source for date ranges for each location. T denotes trace. Stations may show snowfall (hail) during the warm months]

State	Station	Jan.	Feb.	Mar.	Apr.	May	June	July	Aug.	Sept.	Oct.	Nov.	Dec.	Annual
AL.....	Mobile	0.1	0.1	0.1	–	–	–	–	–	–	–	–	0.1	0.4
AK.....	Juneau	25.3	18.2	13.6	2.4	–	–	–	–	–	1.0	12.5	20.6	93.6
AZ.....	Phoenix	–	–	–	–	–	–	–	–	–	–	–	–	–
AR.....	Little Rock	2.0	1.5	0.5	–	–	–	–	–	–	–	0.1	0.6	4.7
CA.....	Los Angeles	–	–	–	–	–	–	–	–	–	–	–	–	–
CA.....	Sacramento	–	–	–	–	–	–	–	–	–	–	–	–	–
CA.....	San Diego	–	–	–	–	–	–	–	–	–	–	–	–	–
CA.....	San Francisco	–	–	–	–	–	–	–	–	–	–	–	–	–
CO.....	Denver	7.4	7.7	11.7	7.9	1.6	–	–	–	1.3	4.0	8.1	7.5	57.2
CT.....	Hartford	13.1	12.7	8.9	1.3	–	–	–	–	–	0.3	1.8	10.0	48.1
DE.....	Wilmington	6.5	6.8	3.2	0.2	–	–	–	–	–	–	0.7	3.2	20.6
DC.....	Washington Nat'l	5.3	5.3	2.1	–	–	–	–	–	–	–	0.6	2.7	16.0
FL.....	Jacksonville	–	–	–	–	–	–	–	–	–	–	–	–	–
FL.....	Miami	–	–	–	–	–	–	–	–	–	–	–	–	–
GA...	Atlanta	0.9	0.5	0.4	–	–	–	–	–	–	–	–	0.2	2.0
HI.....	Honolulu	–	–	–	–	–	–	–	–	–	–	–	–	–
ID.....	Boise	6.3	3.5	1.6	0.5	0.1	–	–	–	–	0.1	2.1	5.8	20.0
IL.....	Chicago	11.3	9.2	6.1	1.5	–	–	–	–	–	0.3	1.9	8.2	38.5
IL.....	Peoria	6.9	6.0	3.8	0.7	T	–	–	–	–	0.1	1.8	6.0	25.3
IN.....	Indianapolis	7.8	6.2	3.5	0.4	–	–	–	–	–	0.2	1.4	5.7	25.2
IA.....	Des Moines	8.5	8.4	5.6	1.7	0.1	–	–	–	–	0.4	2.7	7.3	34.7
KS.....	Wichita	3.8	4.1	2.4	0.2	–	–	–	–	–	0.1	1.1	3.3	15.0
KY.....	Louisville	5.1	4.3	2.8	0.1	–	–	–	–	–	0.1	0.8	2.2	15.4
LA.....	New Orleans	–	–	–	–	–	–	–	–	–	–	–	0.1	0.1
ME....	Portland	19.1	17.4	12.9	2.8	0.1	–	–	–	–	0.2	2.8	14.7	70.0
MD....	Baltimore	5.9	6.7	3.4	–	–	–	–	–	–	–	0.6	3.1	19.7
MA....	Boston	13.0	12.4	8.0	1.2	–	–	–	–	–	0.1	1.1	8.0	43.8
MI.....	Detroit	11.9	10.7	6.5	1.6	–	–	–	–	–	0.1	2.5	9.7	43.0
MI.....	Sault Ste. Marie	30.2	20.3	14.1	6.3	0.4	–	–	–	0.1	2.0	15.5	30.4	119.3
MN....	Duluth	17.1	12.9	13.8	7.6	0.8	–	–	–	0.1	1.9	12.2	17.1	83.5
MN....	Minneapolis-St. Paul	10.3	8.8	10.0	3.1	0.1	–	–	–	–	0.6	6.9	10.1	49.9
MS....	Jackson	0.4	0.3	0.1	–	–	–	–	–	–	–	–	0.2	1.0
MO....	Kansas City	5.3	5.5	2.2	0.5	–	–	–	–	–	0.2	1.2	4.1	19.0
MO....	St. Louis	5.5	4.4	3.7	0.3	–	–	–	–	–	–	1.2	3.6	18.7
MT....	Helena	8.1	6.3	6.7	4.3	1.1	0.1	–	0.1	1.2	2.3	6.1	7.9	44.2
NE.....	Omaha	7.0	7.0	5.5	0.9	0.1	–	–	–	–	0.3	2.3	5.8	28.9
NV.....	Reno	5.3	5.0	3.8	1.0	0.6	–	–	–	–	0.2	1.9	4.5	22.3
NH....	Concord	17.7	15.5	11.7	2.4	0.1	–	–	–	–	0.4	3.4	14.0	65.2
NJ.....	Atlantic City	5.9	6.2	2.3	0.3	–	–	–	–	–	–	0.3	2.8	17.8
NM....	Albuquerque	2.1	1.9	1.4	0.5	–	–	–	–	–	0.2	1.0	2.4	9.5
NY....	Albany	16.2	13.8	11.2	2.3	0.1	–	–	–	–	0.2	3.7	13.9	61.4
NY....	Buffalo	24.9	18.2	12.2	2.9	0.2	–	–	–	–	0.5	9.9	23.2	92.0
NY....	NYC Central Park	7.8	8.8	5.0	0.8	–	–	–	–	–	–	0.8	5.5	28.7
NC...	Charlotte	1.9	1.5	0.9	–	–	–	–	–	–	–	0.1	0.5	4.9
NC...	Raleigh	2.5	2.3	1.0	–	–	–	–	–	–	–	0.1	0.8	6.7
ND....	Bismarck	8.3	7.2	8.4	4.1	0.7	–	–	–	0.1	1.7	6.7	8.5	45.7
OH....	Cincinnati	7.3	5.9	4.0	0.5	–	–	–	–	–	0.2	1.6	4.0	23.5
OH....	Cleveland	14.7	13.0	10.4	2.5	–	–	–	–	–	0.4	4.8	12.0	57.8
OH....	Columbus	8.8	6.8	4.3	0.8	–	–	–	–	–	0.1	1.9	5.5	28.2
OK....	Oklahoma City	2.6	2.3	1.2	–	–	–	–	–	–	–	0.5	1.9	8.5
OR....	Portland	2.9	1.3	0.4	–	–	–	–	–	–	–	0.4	1.3	6.3
PA.....	Philadelphia	6.8	7.2	3.7	0.3	–	–	–	–	–	0.1	0.5	3.6	22.2
PA.....	Pittsburgh	12.0	10.1	7.9	1.5	0.1	–	–	–	–	0.3	3.4	8.4	43.7
RI.....	Providence	10.2	10.1	6.8	0.7	0.1	–	–	–	–	0.1	1.0	7.0	36.0
SC.....	Columbia	0.5	0.7	0.2	–	–	–	–	–	–	–	–	0.2	1.6
SD.....	Sioux Falls	7.0	8.5	8.6	3.2	0.1	–	–	–	–	0.7	5.1	7.8	41.0
TN.....	Memphis	1.8	1.2	0.6	–	–	–	–	–	–	–	0.1	0.4	4.1
TN.....	Nashville	3.5	2.6	1.2	–	–	–	–	–	–	–	0.4	1.0	8.7
TX.....	Dallas	0.9	0.7	0.2	–	–	–	–	–	–	–	0.1	0.2	2.1
TX.....	El Paso	1.1	0.7	0.3	0.3	–	–	–	–	–	–	0.9	1.6	4.9
TX.....	Houston	0.1	0.1	–	–	–	–	–	–	–	–	–	0.1	0.3
UT.....	Salt Lake City	13.0	10.1	9.0	4.8	0.6	–	–	–	0.1	1.3	6.6	12.7	58.2
VT.....	Burlington	19.7	17.4	14.0	3.8	0.1	–	–	–	T	0.3	6.4	18.5	80.2
VA.....	Norfolk	3.0	2.6	0.9	–	–	–	–	–	–	–	–	1.0	7.5
VA.....	Richmond	4.9	3.8	2.1	0.1	–	–	–	–	–	–	0.3	1.9	13.1
WA....	Seattle	4.3	2.0	1.1	–	–	–	–	–	–	–	0.8	2.4	10.6
WA....	Spokane	12.9	7.8	3.6	0.6	0.1	–	–	–	–	0.3	5.5	11.7	42.5
WV....	Charleston	10.5	8.5	5.1	0.7	–	–	–	–	–	0.3	1.9	5.0	32.0
WI.....	Milwaukee	13.8	10.6	8.1	1.9	0.1	–	–	–	–	0.2	2.9	10.3	47.9
WY....	Cheyenne	5.9	7.4	11.1	10.4	3.4	0.2	–	–	0.7	4.4	7.2	7.1	57.8
PR.....	San Juan	–	–	–	–	–	–	–	–	–	–	–	–	–

– Represents zero.

Source: U.S. National Oceanic and Atmospheric Administration, *Comparative Climatic Data for the United States Through 2020.* See also <www.ncei.noaa.gov/products/land-based-station/comparative-climatic-data>.

Table 446. Cloudiness, Average Wind Speed, and Average Relative Humidity—Selected Cities

[Airport data, except as noted. Data shown for varying periods of record; see source for date ranges for each location. M = morning. A = afternoon]

State	Station	Cloudiness-average percent of days annually [1]	Average wind speed (miles per hour, m.p.h.)			Average relative humidity (percent)					
			Annual	January	July	Annual		Jan.		July	
						M	A	M	A	M	A
AL.........	Mobile	72.1	7.4	8.5	5.7	87	57	83	60	90	61
AK.........	Juneau	87.9	7.4	7.3	6.6	84	74	84	80	84	72
AZ.........	Phoenix	42.5	6.1	4.9	7.4	46	23	60	33	42	21
AR........	Little Rock	67.7	7.0	7.7	6.1	84	57	80	61	87	56
CA........	Los Angeles	49.0	1.9	1.4	2.1	58	54	52	49	65	59
CA........	Sacramento	48.5	6.3	5.0	7.6	78	45	87	69	71	29
CA........	San Diego	60.0	6.3	5.1	7.0	74	63	69	58	80	67
CA........	San Francisco	56.2	10.5	6.8	13.0	87	69	87	66	91	71
CO........	Denver	68.5	8.0	7.8	7.9	50	43	53	54	46	35
CT........	Hartford	77.5	7.8	8.3	6.7	76	53	73	57	78	51
DE........	Wilmington	73.4	8.5	9.2	7.4	78	55	75	59	78	54
DC........	Washington Nat'l (VA)	74.0	8.9	9.5	8.0	74	53	71	55	76	53
FL.........	Jacksonville	74.2	6.7	7.0	5.8	88	56	87	57	89	59
FL.........	Miami	79.5	8.4	8.6	7.2	82	61	84	59	81	63
GA........	Atlanta	70.1	8.3	9.3	7.1	81	55	79	58	86	58
HI.........	Honolulu	75.3	10.3	8.5	11.9	74	56	79	61	70	53
ID.........	Boise	67.1	7.6	6.5	7.4	64	42	79	70	49	20
IL..........	Chicago	77.0	9.9	11.1	8.2	80	60	78	68	81	55
IL..........	Peoria	73.7	8.3	9.4	6.4	83	61	80	70	86	58
IN.........	Indianapolis	76.2	9.5	10.9	7.6	82	60	81	70	83	58
IA.........	Des Moines	71.5	9.8	10.6	8.3	81	60	78	68	84	58
KS........	Wichita	64.9	11.5	11.1	10.7	80	55	79	61	80	50
KY........	Louisville	74.8	7.8	9.0	6.6	79	56	78	64	81	56
LA........	New Orleans	72.3	8.0	9.1	5.9	87	62	84	65	90	65
ME........	Portland	72.3	7.9	8.1	6.9	78	59	75	59	79	60
MD........	Baltimore	71.2	7.2	7.9	6.2	77	53	73	56	78	52
MA........	Boston	73.2	11.5	12.6	10.2	72	57	69	58	72	56
MI.........	Detroit	79.5	9.4	11.0	7.9	80	59	80	69	80	53
MI.........	Sault Ste. Marie	81.9	7.7	7.8	6.7	84	65	80	73	87	61
MN........	Duluth	79.2	10.0	10.6	8.5	82	63	78	70	86	60
MN........	Minneapolis-St. Paul	74.0	9.6	9.6	8.7	79	59	77	68	81	54
MS........	Jackson	69.6	6.1	7.2	4.6	90	57	85	62	93	58
MO........	Kansas City	67.1	10.3	10.9	8.9	81	60	78	64	85	59
MO........	St. Louis	72.6	9.0	10.0	7.6	81	58	79	65	82	55
MT........	Great Falls	78.4	11.5	14.0	9.1	63	46	65	61	60	30
NE........	Omaha	69.6	10.0	10.3	8.6	81	59	79	66	85	57
NV........	Reno	56.7	6.4	4.6	7.2	63	31	75	51	54	18
NH........	Concord	75.3	6.0	6.6	5.1	80	53	76	58	81	51
NJ........	Atlantic City	74.2	8.7	9.5	7.4	80	56	77	58	81	57
NM........	Albuquerque	54.2	8.2	7.3	8.2	53	29	62	40	54	28
NY........	Albany	81.1	7.9	8.7	6.6	79	57	77	63	79	54
NY........	Buffalo	85.2	10.3	12.4	8.9	79	62	79	72	78	55
NY........	Central Park	71.0	6.1	7.6	4.7	70	54	67	56	73	54
NC........	Charlotte	70.4	6.4	6.6	5.7	81	52	78	54	84	55
NC........	Raleigh	69.9	6.5	6.8	6.1	83	53	79	53	86	56
ND........	Bismarck	74.5	9.4	9.2	8.5	81	58	77	71	85	49
OH........	Cincinnati	77.8	8.3	9.7	6.5	81	59	80	68	84	57
OH........	Cleveland	81.9	9.6	11.4	7.8	79	61	79	70	80	56
OH........	Columbus	80.3	7.6	9.2	6.0	80	58	78	68	82	55
OK........	Oklahoma City	61.9	11.3	11.6	9.8	80	55	78	59	82	51
OR........	Portland	81.1	7.4	9.2	7.1	82	59	84	76	77	44
PA........	Philadelphia	74.5	9.2	9.9	8.3	76	54	73	58	77	52
PA........	Pittsburgh	83.8	7.8	9.2	6.2	79	57	77	66	82	54
RI........	Providence	73.2	9.2	9.7	8.4	75	55	71	57	76	56
SC........	Columbia	68.5	6.1	6.6	5.7	84	50	82	52	86	52
SD........	Sioux Falls	71.2	10.2	10.3	9.1	82	60	77	69	85	55
TN........	Memphis	67.7	8.1	8.9	6.8	80	56	77	62	84	57
TN........	Nashville	71.8	7.0	8.0	5.8	84	56	80	64	87	56
TX........	Dallas	63.0	9.4	8.9	8.9	78	54	76	58	77	49
TX........	El Paso	47.1	8.1	7.4	7.7	50	27	58	34	56	29
TX........	Houston	75.3	7.5	7.9	6.2	89	59	85	62	93	57
UT........	Salt Lake City	65.8	8.4	6.5	9.1	63	43	78	70	47	21
VT........	Burlington	84.1	8.2	9.2	7.0	76	58	74	64	77	53
VA........	Norfolk	71.2	9.5	10.0	8.5	78	57	74	58	80	59
VA........	Richmond	72.9	7.7	8.2	6.9	81	53	78	55	83	55
WA........	Seattle	80.5	7.9	8.4	7.3	82	63	83	76	79	48
WA........	Spokane	76.4	8.7	8.2	8.6	74	52	86	80	59	26
WV........	Charleston	82.2	4.6	5.8	3.5	83	56	78	62	89	58
WI.........	Milwaukee	75.3	10.1	11.0	8.9	79	63	76	68	81	60
WY........	Cheyenne	71.2	12.2	14.3	9.9	61	45	55	51	63	38
PR........	San Juan	80.0	7.9	7.7	9.6	78	66	81	65	78	67

[1] Percent of days that are either partly cloudy or cloudy.

Source: U.S. National Oceanic and Atmospheric Administration, *Comparative Climatic Data For the United States Through 2020*. See also <www.ncdc.noaa.gov/ghcn/comparative-climatic-data>.

Table 447. Drought Conditions—Area and Population Impacted by Level of Drought: 2021

[In percent. For continental United States. Data shown for the last week of each month, as of Tuesday. Dryness and drought conditions are indicated as follows: D0, abnormally dry; D1, moderate drought; D2, severe drought; D3, extreme drought; and D4, exceptional drought. Data are categorical statistics showing percent of the area or population that is in a certain drought category. See source for details, <droughtmonitor.unl.edu/AboutUSDM.aspx>. The U.S. Drought Monitor is jointly produced by the National Drought Mitigation Center at the University of Nebraska-Lincoln, the United States Department of Agriculture, and the National Oceanic and Atmospheric Administration]

Week	Area (percent of continental U.S. square miles)						Population (percent of continental U.S. population)					
	None	D0	D1	D2	D3	D4	None	D0	D1	D2	D3	D4
1/26/2021....	37.68	16.29	13.51	11.41	12.14	8.96	62.95	15.84	7.23	6.70	4.63	2.64
2/23/2021....	36.10	18.34	14.70	12.19	10.22	8.44	62.83	15.62	9.85	5.12	4.28	2.29
3/30/2021....	36.59	19.49	14.31	10.93	9.97	8.71	51.57	20.68	16.32	5.45	3.54	2.44
4/27/2021....	31.73	19.90	15.89	10.76	12.50	9.22	41.85	24.82	15.26	6.05	9.53	2.50
5/25/2021....	38.64	17.94	13.26	8.91	11.02	10.23	43.78	26.82	10.09	6.21	8.54	4.55
6/29/2021....	41.48	11.33	11.47	12.97	13.04	9.71	60.14	13.53	7.34	4.52	9.33	5.14
7/27/2021....	46.46	7.23	7.92	12.91	16.64	8.84	70.64	4.62	4.47	6.82	7.18	6.26
8/31/2021....	44.48	8.89	10.04	12.11	16.56	7.92	69.45	6.38	6.41	4.70	7.07	5.99
9/28/2021....	37.35	14.82	11.24	13.48	15.84	7.27	62.96	11.44	7.76	4.95	7.10	5.79
10/26/2021...	35.79	16.87	13.52	14.74	13.04	6.04	62.56	12.87	7.56	4.93	7.43	4.65
11/30/2021...	30.95	15.63	18.31	17.34	12.44	5.33	57.90	12.92	10.65	6.02	9.12	3.38
12/28/2021...	26.51	18.19	19.03	22.26	12.10	1.90	47.96	19.52	14.22	12.51	5.66	0.13

Source: National Drought Mitigation Center, "United States Drought Monitor," <droughtmonitor.unl.edu>, accessed January 2022.

Table 448. Top 20 Significant Flood Event Losses Covered by the National Flood Insurance Program, as of January 30, 2019

[In nominal dollars. Covers period beginning in 1978. A significant event is one with 1,500 or more paid losses, or occasionally one added for other reasons]

Event	Date	Number of paid losses	Amount paid ($)	Average paid loss ($)
Hurricane Katrina	Aug. 2005	166,790	16,257,744,061	97,474
Hurricane Harvey	Sept. 2017	76,257	8,908,547,689	116,823
Superstorm Sandy	Oct. 2012	132,360	8,804,242,152	66,517
Hurricane Ike	Sept. 2008	46,701	2,702,388,727	57,866
Louisiana severe storms and flooding	Aug. 2016	26,976	2,468,493,541	91,507
Hurricane Ivan	Sept. 2004	28,154	1,607,512,533	57,097
Hurricane Irene	Aug. 2011	44,314	1,345,775,273	30,369
Tropical Storm Allison	June 2001	30,671	1,105,003,344	36,028
Hurricane Irma	Sept. 2017	21,920	1,054,248,877	48,095
Hurricane Matthew	Oct. 2016	16,586	654,394,214	39,455
Hurricane Florence	Sept. 2018	13,754	648,333,990	47,138
Louisiana flood	May 1995	31,343	585,071,593	18,667
Hurricane Isaac	Aug. 2012	12,084	561,527,299	46,469
Hurricane Isabel	Sept. 2003	19,938	500,270,118	25,091
Texas torrential rain	Apr. 2016	7,437	471,517,374	63,402
Texas flooding	May 2015	6,774	468,799,696	69,206
Hurricane Rita	Sept. 2005	9,354	466,223,897	49,842
Tropical Storm Lee	Sept. 2011	9,905	462,459,225	46,689
Hurricane Floyd	Sept. 1999	20,439	462,326,389	22,620
Hurricane Opal	Oct. 1995	10,343	405,527,543	39,208

Source: U.S. Department of Homeland Security, Federal Emergency Management Agency, National Flood Insurance Program Statistics, "Significant Flood Events [since 1978], as of January 31, 2019," <http://www.fema.gov/significant-flood-events>, accessed September 2019.

Table 449. Threatened and Endangered Wildlife and Plant Species: 2022

[As of May 2022. Endangered species: one in danger of becoming extinct throughout all or a significant part of its natural range. Threatened species: one likely to become endangered in the foreseeable future]

Item	Total [1]	Mammals	Birds	Reptiles	Amphibians	Fishes	Snails	Clams	Crustaceans	Insects	Arachnids	Plants
Total listings	2,367	380	337	140	48	207	53	94	30	94	17	942
Endangered species, total	1,869	327	293	87	31	121	39	78	25	79	17	769
United States [2]	1,269	66	76	16	23	94	38	76	25	75	12	768
Foreign	600	261	217	71	8	27	1	2	–	4	5	1
Threatened species, total	498	53	44	53	17	86	14	16	5	15	–	173
United States [2]	402	30	23	29	16	77	13	16	5	15	–	171
Foreign	96	23	21	24	1	9	1	–	–	–	–	2

– Represents zero. [1] Includes other categories not shown separately. Twenty-two animal species (14 in the U.S. and 8 Foreign) are counted more than once, primarily because these animals have distinct population segments (each with its own individual listing status). [2] United States listings include those populations in which the U.S. shares jurisdiction with another nation.

Source: U.S. Fish and Wildlife Service, Environmental Conservation Online System, Threatened & Endangered Species, "Listed Species Summary," <ecos.fws.gov/ecp/>, accessed June 2022.

Section 7
Elections

This section relates primarily to presidential, congressional, and gubernatorial elections. Also presented are summary tables on congressional legislation; state legislatures; minority and female officeholders; population of voting age; voter participation; and campaign finances.

Official statistics on federal elections, collected by the Clerk of the House, are published biennially in *Statistics of the Presidential and Congressional Election* and *Statistics of the Congressional Election*. Federal elections data also appear in the *Congressional Directory* and in official state documents. Data on reported registration and voting for social and economic groups are obtained by the U.S. Census Bureau as part of the Current Population Survey (CPS) and are published in *Current Population Reports*, Series P20 (see text, Section 1).

Almost all federal, state, and local governmental units in the United States conduct elections for political offices and other purposes. The conduct of elections is regulated by state laws or, in some cities and counties, by local charter. An exception is that the U.S. Constitution prescribes the basis of representation in Congress and the manner of electing the president and grants to Congress the right to regulate the times, places, and manner of electing federal officers. Amendments to the Constitution have prescribed national criteria for voting eligibility. The 15th Amendment, adopted in 1870, gave all male citizens the right to vote regardless of race, color, or previous condition of servitude. The 19th Amendment, adopted in 1920, further extended the right to vote to all citizens regardless of sex. The payment of poll taxes as a prerequisite to voting in federal elections was banned by the 24th Amendment in 1964. In 1971, as a result of the 26th Amendment, eligibility to vote in national elections was extended to all citizens, 18 years old and over.

Presidential election—The Constitution specifies how the president and vice president are selected. Each state elects, by popular vote, a group of electors equal in number to its total of members of Congress. The 23rd Amendment, adopted in 1961, grants the District of Columbia three presidential electors, a number equal to that of the least populous state. Subsequent to the election, the electors meet in their respective states to vote for president and vice president. Usually, each elector votes for the candidate receiving the most popular votes in his or her state. A majority vote of all electors is necessary to elect the president and vice president. If no candidate receives a majority, the House of Representatives, with each state having one vote, is empowered to elect the president and vice president, again, with a majority of votes required.

The 22nd Amendment to the Constitution, adopted in 1951, limits presidential tenure to two elective terms of 4 years each or to one elective term for any person who, upon succession to the presidency, has held the office or acted as President for more than 2 years.

Congressional election—The Constitution provides that representatives be apportioned among the states according to their population, that a census of population be taken every 10 years as a basis for apportionment, and that each state have at least one representative. At the time of each apportionment, Congress decides what the total number of representatives will be. Since 1912, the total has been 435, except during 1960 to 1962 when it increased to 437, adding one representative each for Alaska and Hawaii. The total reverted to 435 after reapportionment following the 1960 census. Members are elected for 2-year terms, all terms covering the same period. The District of Columbia, American Samoa, Guam, and the Virgin Islands each elect one nonvoting delegate, and Puerto Rico elects a nonvoting resident commissioner.

The Senate is composed of 100 members, two from each state, who are elected to serve for a term of 6 years. One-third of the Senate is elected every 2 years. Senators were originally chosen by the state legislatures. The 17th Amendment to the Constitution, adopted in 1913, prescribed that senators be elected by popular vote.

Voter eligibility and participation—The Census Bureau publishes estimates of the population of voting age and the percent casting votes in each state for presidential and congressional election years. These voting-age estimates include a number of persons who meet the age requirement but are not eligible to vote, (e.g. aliens and some institutionalized persons). In addition, since 1964, voter participation and voter characteristics data have been collected during November of election years as part of the CPS. Survey data on voting age population estimates includes non-citizens but excludes members of the Armed Forces and institutionalized populations. Data on percent casting votes excludes institutionalized populations, members of the Armed forces and citizens residing outside the U.S. casting absentee ballots.

Statistical reliability—For a discussion of statistical collection and estimation, sampling procedures, and measures of statistical reliability applicable to Census Bureau data, see Appendix III.

Table 450. Participation in Elections for President and U.S. Representatives: 1940 to 2020

[84,728 represents 84,728,000. As of November, except as noted. Estimated resident population 21 years old and over, 1940 to 1970, except as noted, and 18 years old and over thereafter. Includes Armed Forces stationed in the U.S. Prior to 1958, excludes Alaska and prior to 1960, excludes Hawaii. District of Columbia is included in votes cast for President beginning 1964]

Year	Resident population (includes aliens) of voting age [1] (1,000)	Votes cast			
		For President (1,000)	Percent of voting-age population	For U.S. Representa- tives (1,000)	Percent of voting-age population
1940	84,728	49,815	58.8	(NA)	(NA)
1942	86,465	(X)	(X)	28,074	32.5
1944	85,654	48,026	56.1	45,110	52.7
1946	92,659	(X)	(X)	34,410	37.1
1948	95,573	48,834	51.1	46,220	48.4
1950	98,134	(X)	(X)	40,430	41.2
1952	99,929	61,552	61.6	57,571	57.6
1954	102,075	(X)	(X)	42,583	41.7
1956	104,515	62,027	59.3	58,886	56.3
1958	106,447	(X)	(X)	45,719	43.0
1960	109,672	68,836	62.8	64,124	58.5
1962	112,952	(X)	(X)	51,242	45.4
1964	114,090	70,098	61.4	65,879	57.7
1966	116,638	(X)	(X)	52,902	45.4
1968	120,285	73,027	60.7	66,109	55.0
1970	124,498	(X)	(X)	54,259	43.6
1972	140,777	77,625	55.1	71,188	50.6
1974	146,338	(X)	(X)	52,313	35.7
1976	152,308	81,603	53.6	74,259	48.8
1978	158,369	(X)	(X)	54,584	34.5
1980	163,945	86,497	52.8	77,874	47.5
1982	169,643	(X)	(X)	63,881	37.7
1984	173,995	92,655	53.3	82,422	47.4
1986	177,922	(X)	(X)	59,758	33.6
1988	181,956	91,587	50.3	81,682	44.9
1990	185,812	(X)	(X)	62,355	33.6
1992	189,493	104,600	55.2	97,198	51.3
1994	193,010	(X)	(X)	70,494	36.5
1996	196,789	96,390	49.0	90,233	45.9
1998	201,270	(X)	(X)	66,605	33.1
2000	[2] 209,130	105,594	50.5	98,800	47.2
2002	[2] 214,689	(X)	(X)	74,707	34.8
2004	[2] 219,508	122,349	55.7	113,192	51.6
2006	[2] 224,622	(X)	(X)	80,976	36.0
2008	[2] 229,989	131,407	57.1	122,586	53.3
2010	[2] 234,576	(X)	(X)	86,785	37.0
2012	[2] 240,165	129,140	53.8	122,346	50.9
2014	[2] 244,793	(X)	(X)	78,813	32.2
2016	[2] 249,372	136,787	54.9	129,833	52.1
2018	[2] 253,453	(X)	(X)	114,017	45.0
2020	[2] 256,662	158,482	61.7	153,431	59.8

X Not applicable. NA Not available. [1] Population 18 and over in Georgia, 1944-70, and in Kentucky, 1956–70; and 20 and over in Alaska and Hawaii, 1960–70. Source: Through 1990, U.S. Census Bureau, "Table 4. Participation in Elections for President and U.S. Representatives: 1930 to 1992," May 1994, <www.census.gov/population/socdemo/voting/p25-1117/tab03-04.pdf>. For 1992–1998, "Estimates and Projections of the Voting-Age Population, 1992 to 2000, and Percent Casting Votes for President, by State: November 1992 and 1996," July 2000, <www.census.gov/population/socdemo/voting/proj00/tab03.txt>. For 2000-2009, "Annual Estimates of the Resident Population for Selected Age Groups by Sex for the United States, States, Counties, and Puerto Rico Commonwealth and Municipios: April 1, 2000 to July 1, 2009," <www.census.gov/topics/population.html>, accessed June 2015. Starting 2010, "Annual estimates of the resident population by single year of age and sex for the United States: April 1, 2010 to July 1, 2020," <www.census.gov/programs-surveys/popest.html>, accessed June 2021. [2] 2000 and 2010, as of April 1, population estimates base. All other years as of July 1.

Source: Except as noted, U.S. House of Representatives, Office of the Clerk, *Statistics of the Presidential and Congressional Election of November 3, 2020*, February 2021, and earlier reports. See also <clerk.house.gov/Members#ElectionInformation>.

Table 451. Voters by Whether Voting on Election Day or Utilizing Alternative Early Voting: 2000 to 2020

[Percent distribution of persons voting. As of November. Data are from November Voting and Registration Supplements to the Current Population Survey (see text, Section 1, and Appendix III)]

Election Year	Total [1]	On election day [2]	Alternative early voting methods		
			Total	Before election day [2]	By mail
2000 [3]	100.0	86.0	14.0	3.8	10.2
2002	100.0	85.9	14.1	3.4	10.7
2004 [3]	100.0	79.3	20.7	7.8	12.9
2006	100.0	80.4	19.6	5.8	13.7
2008 [3]	100.0	69.3	30.7	14.3	16.4
2010	100.0	73.5	26.5	8.4	18.1
2012 [3]	100.0	67.2	32.8	14.3	18.5
2014	100.0	68.9	31.2	10.3	20.9
2016 [3]	100.0	59.9	40.1	19.1	21.0
2018	100.0	59.6	39.7	16.6	23.1
2020 [3]	100.0	30.4	69.0	26.0	43.0

[1] Includes unknown or did not respond to survey question. [2] Voted in person. [3] Presidential election year.

Source: U.S. Census Bureau, "Voting and Registration in the Election of November 2020," April 2021, <www.census.gov/data/tables/time-series/demo/voting-and-registration/p20-585.html>, and earlier reports.

Table 452. Resident Population of Voting-Age, Total Votes Cast, and Percent Casting Votes—States: 2018 to 2020

[253,768 represents 253,768,000. Votes cast as of November. Estimated population, 18 years old and over. Includes Armed Forces stationed in each state, aliens, and institutional population]

State	Voting-age population (1,000) [1]		Total votes cast (1,000)			Percent casting votes for–		
			Presidential electors	U.S. Representatives		Presidential electors	U.S. Representatives	
	2018	2020	2020	2018	2020	2020	2018	2020
U.S.............	253,768	256,662	158,482	114,017	153,431	61.7	44.9	59.8
AL.................	3,798	3,834	2,323	1,660	2,052	60.6	43.7	53.5
AK.................	554	552	360	282	353	65.1	51.0	63.9
AZ.................	5,529	5,775	3,387	2,341	3,268	58.7	42.3	56.6
AR.................	2,311	2,331	1,219	889	1,179	52.3	38.5	50.6
CA.................	30,567	30,577	17,501	12,185	16,725	57.2	39.9	54.7
CO.................	4,430	4,558	3,257	2,514	3,165	71.5	56.7	69.4
CT.................	2,837	2,838	1,824	1,380	1,773	64.3	48.6	62.5
DE.................	764	782	504	354	488	64.5	46.3	62.4
DC.................	575	583	343	(X)	(X)	58.8	(X)	(X)
FL.................	17,070	17,483	11,067	7,021	10,465	63.3	41.1	59.9
GA.................	8,014	8,210	5,001	3,802	4,884	60.9	47.4	59.5
HI.................	1,117	1,111	571	399	580	51.4	35.7	52.2
ID.................	1,307	1,376	868	596	850	63.1	45.6	61.8
IL.................	9,884	9,810	6,034	4,540	5,877	61.5	45.9	59.9
IN.................	5,124	5,189	3,033	2,256	2,996	58.5	44.0	57.8
IA.................	2,425	2,438	1,700	1,316	1,700	69.7	54.3	69.7
KS.................	2,206	2,217	1,372	1,050	1,359	61.9	47.6	61.3
KY.................	3,460	3,475	2,137	1,570	2,116	61.5	45.4	60.9
LA.................	3,564	3,564	2,148	1,461	1,947	60.3	41.0	54.6
ME.................	1,088	1,102	828	631	828	75.2	58.0	75.2
MD.................	4,703	4,722	3,037	2,286	2,954	64.3	48.6	62.6
MA.................	5,535	5,552	3,658	2,753	3,658	65.9	49.7	65.9
MI.................	7,831	7,840	5,539	4,155	5,423	70.7	53.1	69.2
MN.................	4,309	4,356	3,277	2,577	3,194	75.2	59.8	73.3
MS.................	2,280	2,274	1,314	939	1,228	57.8	41.2	54.0
MO.................	4,750	4,780	3,026	2,418	2,973	63.3	50.9	62.2
MT.................	833	851	604	504	602	70.9	60.6	70.7
NE.................	1,452	1,463	956	697	941	65.4	48.0	64.4
NV.................	2,345	2,441	1,405	961	1,356	57.6	41.0	55.5
NH.................	1,098	1,113	806	571	787	72.4	52.0	70.7
NJ.................	6,955	6,948	4,549	3,099	4,433	65.5	44.6	63.8
NM.................	1,613	1,634	924	693	904	56.6	43.0	55.3
NY.................	15,474	15,348	8,662	6,251	8,604	56.4	40.4	56.1
NC.................	8,083	8,294	5,525	3,381	5,325	66.6	41.8	64.2
ND.................	581	584	362	322	356	62.0	55.3	60.9
OH.................	9,096	9,125	5,922	4,406	5,762	64.9	48.4	63.1
OK.................	2,987	3,027	1,561	1,179	1,551	51.6	39.5	51.2
OR.................	3,317	3,381	2,374	1,848	2,308	70.2	55.7	68.3
PA.................	10,158	10,162	6,915	4,930	6,779	68.0	48.5	66.7
RI.................	852	855	518	373	488	60.5	43.8	57.1
SC.................	3,978	4,100	2,513	1,709	2,505	61.3	43.0	61.1
SD.................	665	674	423	336	398	62.7	50.5	59.0
TN.................	5,264	5,373	3,054	2,160	2,842	56.8	41.0	52.9
TX.................	21,304	21,926	11,315	8,203	11,094	51.6	38.5	50.6
UT.................	2,229	2,321	1,488	1,053	1,432	64.1	47.2	61.7
VT.................	510	510	371	278	371	72.7	54.5	72.7
VA.................	6,648	6,724	4,461	3,313	4,335	66.3	49.8	64.5
WA.................	5,872	6,028	4,088	3,022	3,944	67.8	51.5	65.4
WV.................	1,442	1,429	781	578	761	54.7	40.1	53.3
WI.................	4,537	4,574	3,297	2,572	3,238	72.1	56.7	70.8
WY.................	443	449	279	205	279	62.0	46.3	62.0

X Not applicable. [1] As of July 1. Source: U.S. Census Bureau, "Annual Estimates of the Resident Population for Selected Age Groups by Sex for the United States, States, Counties, and Puerto Rico Commonwealth and Municipios: April 1, 2010 to July 1, 2020," <data.census.gov>, accessed July 2021.

Source: Except as noted, U.S. House of Representatives, Office of the Clerk, *Statistics of the Presidential and Congressional Election*, November 2020, and earlier reports. See also <clerk.house.gov/Members#ElectionInformation>.

Table 453. Voting-Age Population—Reported Registration and Voting by Selected Characteristics: 2008 to 2020

[225.5 represents 225,500,000. As of November. Covers civilian noninstitutional population 18 years old and over. Includes aliens. Figures are based on Current Population Survey (see text, Section 1 and Appendix III) and differ from those in Table 450 based on population estimates and official vote counts]

Characteristic	Voting-age population (mil.) 2008	2010	2012	2014	2016	2018	2020	Registered — Presidential 2008	2012	2016	2020	Registered — Congressional 2010	2014	2018	Voted — Presidential 2008	2012	2016	2020	Voted — Congressional 2010	2014	2018
Total [1]	**225.5**	**229.7**	**235.2**	**239.9**	**245.5**	**249.7**	**252.3**	**64.9**	**65.1**	**64.2**	**66.7**	**59.8**	**59.3**	**61.3**	**58.2**	**56.5**	**56.0**	**61.3**	**41.8**	**38.5**	**49.0**
AGE																					
18 to 20 years old	11.7	12.2	12.3	11.9	11.7	12.0	12.3	49.3	44.2	46.7	52.6	34.4	32.6	40.8	41.0	35.1	36.4	45.5	16.4	14.1	27.2
21 to 24 years old	16.6	16.7	17.6	17.8	13.2	17.0	16.4	56.2	53.1	71.4	58.2	47.2	43.6	49.1	46.6	40.0	55.2	49.9	22.0	17.1	32.1
25 to 34 years old	40.2	41.2	41.1	42.3	43.8	44.8	44.9	56.5	57.0	56.4	61.0	49.8	49.4	52.1	48.5	46.1	46.4	53.7	26.9	24.2	37.0
35 to 44 years old	41.5	39.9	39.6	39.6	39.9	40.8	41.6	61.4	61.7	60.0	62.2	57.3	56.3	57.3	55.2	52.9	51.8	56.4	37.7	32.8	44.2
45 to 64 years old	78.1	80.7	82.1	82.8	83.8	83.3	81.9	70.4	70.4	68.5	69.9	66.6	65.4	66.1	65.0	63.4	61.7	65.5	51.1	46.0	55.0
65 years old and over	37.5	39.0	42.5	45.6	48.7	51.9	55.3	75.0	76.9	75.3	75.8	72.5	73.0	73.3	68.1	69.7	68.4	71.9	58.9	57.5	63.8
SEX																					
Male	109.0	111.1	113.2	115.6	118.5	120.6	121.9	62.6	63.1	62.3	65.1	57.9	57.2	59.5	55.7	54.4	53.8	59.5	40.9	37.2	47.2
Female	116.5	118.6	122.0	124.2	127.0	129.2	130.4	67.0	67.0	66.0	68.2	61.5	61.2	63.0	60.4	58.5	58.1	63.0	42.7	39.6	50.6
RACE/ETHNICITY																					
White [2]	183.2	185.8	187.1	189.3	192.1	194.1	195.2	66.6	66.7	66.3	69.1	61.6	61.3	63.7	59.6	57.6	58.2	63.7	43.4	40.3	51.1
Black [2]	26.5	27.4	28.7	29.7	30.6	31.6	32.2	65.5	68.5	65.3	64.7	58.8	59.7	60.2	60.8	62.0	55.9	58.7	40.7	37.3	48.0
Asian [2]	10.5	11.0	12.5	13.5	14.9	15.7	16.1	37.3	37.2	38.9	45.7	34.1	34.4	37.7	32.1	31.3	33.9	42.8	21.3	19.1	28.9
Hispanic [3]	30.9	32.5	35.2	36.8	39.0	41.0	42.5	37.6	38.9	39.2	44.1	33.8	34.9	37.9	31.6	31.8	32.5	38.8	20.5	18.4	28.5
REGION [4]																					
Northeast	41.5	42.3	42.9	43.5	43.9	44.2	43.6	63.7	65.2	64.0	68.1	59.7	58.3	60.7	57.4	56.6	56.2	62.7	41.6	36.3	48.4
Midwest	49.4	50.1	50.6	51.0	51.6	51.8	52.2	70.6	71.4	70.2	71.7	65.0	65.0	67.5	63.4	62.3	61.4	65.5	45.1	42.3	53.5
South	82.4	84.2	87.1	89.2	92.0	94.5	96.0	65.5	65.3	64.0	65.4	59.4	60.0	60.8	57.7	55.7	54.9	59.4	39.3	38.4	47.3
West	52.2	53.2	54.6	56.1	58.0	59.3	60.4	59.4	58.9	59.3	63.4	55.5	53.7	57.0	54.6	52.3	52.9	59.6	42.7	36.8	48.0
EDUCATIONAL ATTAINMENT																					
8 years or less	11.1	11.1	10.5	9.9	9.8	8.9	8.7	30.1	28.7	24.5	25.3	27.0	24.5	22.9	23.4	21.6	18.3	20.7	15.8	13.2	14.4
High school: Less than high school graduate	19.1	18.8	18.7	18.6	17.7	16.7	15.0	43.2	42.6	39.0	42.8	37.8	37.5	36.6	33.7	32.2	29.3	35.2	20.8	18.2	23.2
High school graduate or GED [5]	70.4	71.0	70.6	70.6	71.3	71.6	73.3	59.5	59.0	57.5	58.4	54.0	53.5	53.1	50.9	48.7	47.4	51.1	35.2	31.5	38.8
College: Some college or Associate's degree	63.8	65.3	67.7	68.8	69.9	69.5	68.8	72.0	71.2	69.8	72.9	65.5	64.0	67.0	65.0	61.5	60.5	66.8	44.4	40.0	52.2
Bachelor's or advanced degree	61.1	63.5	67.8	72.0	76.8	83.1	86.4	76.8	77.2	76.2	77.2	72.5	70.8	72.7	73.3	71.7	71.0	74.2	57.1	52.5	63.9
EMPLOYMENT STATUS																					
Employed	143.2	138.3	142.6	146.2	150.9	156.0	149.2	66.4	67.1	65.9	68.3	61.5	60.4	62.4	60.1	58.6	57.8	63.1	42.5	38.2	49.6
Unemployed	9.5	13.9	11.1	8.4	6.9	5.5	9.9	57.2	56.9	57.0	61.6	52.3	50.7	56.5	48.8	46.1	44.8	52.7	31.6	26.9	40.2
Not in labor force	72.8	77.5	81.6	85.2	87.8	88.2	93.2	62.9	62.8	61.8	64.7	58.0	58.2	59.6	55.5	54.3	53.8	59.4	42.3	40.1	48.4

[1] Includes other races, not shown separately. [2] Data represent persons who selected this race group only and exclude persons reporting more than one race. [3] Persons of Hispanic origin may be of any race. [4] For composition of regions, see map, inside cover. [5] The General Educational Development (GED) Test measures how well a non-high school graduate has mastered the skills and general knowledge that are acquired in a 4-year high school education. Successfully passing the exam is a credential generally considered to be equivalent to a high school diploma.

Source: U.S. Census Bureau, "Voting and Registration in the Election of November 2020," <www.census.gov/topics/public-sector/voting.html>, accessed June 2021, and earlier releases.

Table 454. Persons Reporting Voter Registration and Whether Voted by State: 2020

[252,274 represents 252,274,000. As of November. See headnote, Table 453]

State	Voting-age population (1,000)	Percent of voting-age population Registered	Percent of voting-age population Voted	State	Voting-age population (1,000)	Percent of voting-age population Registered	Percent of voting-age population Voted
United States	**252,274**	**66.7**	**61.3**	Missouri	4,637	73.1	64.5
Alabama	3,769	67.0	59.6	Montana	836	76.6	72.6
Alaska	528	72.6	62.4	Nebraska	1,435	67.7	62.2
Arizona	5,638	68.8	64.7	Nevada	2,402	60.6	56.3
Arkansas	2,283	59.6	51.9	New Hampshire	1,101	76.6	72.4
California	30,342	59.3	55.7	New Jersey	6,801	73.6	68.2
Colorado	4,525	66.2	62.7	New Mexico	1,610	63.9	58.3
Connecticut	2,777	66.6	60.5	New York	15,105	62.0	57.0
Delaware	766	70.8	63.8	North Carolina	8,113	63.6	58.9
District of Columbia	576	80.5	77.8	North Dakota	571	75.2	65.3
Florida	17,244	60.9	56.4	Ohio	8,951	75.2	68.5
Georgia	8,032	65.2	60.9	Oklahoma	2,942	64.0	55.5
Hawaii	1,056	63.8	59.7	Oregon	3,369	76.9	71.3
Idaho	1,370	65.7	61.6	Pennsylvania	9,902	74.1	68.2
Illinois	9,658	68.2	62.7	Rhode Island	840	68.5	61.3
Indiana	5,096	67.0	58.9	South Carolina	4,010	67.7	61.3
Iowa	2,361	73.8	68.5	South Dakota	659	66.3	57.7
Kansas	2,157	64.8	60.1	Tennessee	5,283	70.8	63.3
Kentucky	3,384	72.4	65.3	Texas	21,485	62.1	55.3
Louisiana	3,438	66.5	59.4	Utah	2,320	63.3	59.7
Maine	1,087	76.5	70.5	Vermont	507	72.0	67.5
Maryland	4,606	73.4	68.7	Virginia	6,481	70.1	66.0
Massachusetts	5,514	64.3	58.9	Washington	5,993	67.2	64.3
Michigan	7,790	70.8	64.1	West Virginia	1,397	66.4	55.3
Minnesota	4,339	79.2	74.3	Wisconsin	4,538	74.7	71.7
Mississippi	2,212	79.1	69.2	Wyoming	436	67.9	64.1

Source: U.S. Census Bureau, "Voting and Registration in the Election of November 2020," <www.census.gov/topics/public-sector/voting.html>, accessed June 2021.

Table 455. Reported Voting and Registration Among Native and Naturalized Citizens by Race and Hispanic Origin: 2020

[In thousands, except percent, (231,593 represents 231,593,000). Data shown for population aged 18 years and over. As of November]

Nativity status, race, and Hispanic origin	Total citizen population (1,000)	Reported registered Number (1,000)	Reported registered Percent	Not registered Number (1,000)	Not registered Percent	Reported voted Number (1,000)	Reported voted Percent	Did not vote Number (1,000)	Did not vote Percent
TOTAL									
All races [1]	231,593	168,308	72.7	25,782	11.1	154,628	66.8	40,561	17.5
White alone [2]	181,891	134,889	74.2	19,548	10.7	124,301	68.3	30,888	17.0
White alone, non-Hispanic	154,827	118,389	76.5	14,251	9.2	109,830	70.9	23,413	15.1
Black alone [2]	30,204	20,844	69.0	3,178	10.5	18,922	62.6	5,246	17.4
Asian alone [2]	11,530	7,354	63.8	1,635	14.2	6,881	59.7	2,227	19.3
Hispanic [3]	30,627	18,719	61.1	5,879	19.2	16,459	53.7	8,335	27.2
NATIVE CITIZEN									
All races [1]	210,083	154,035	73.3	22,298	10.6	141,545	67.4	35,737	17.0
White alone [2]	170,332	127,484	74.8	17,497	10.3	117,610	69.0	28,053	16.5
White alone, non-Hispanic	150,195	115,123	76.6	13,706	9.1	106,880	71.2	22,502	15.0
Black alone [2]	27,472	18,864	68.7	2,864	10.4	17,084	62.2	4,798	17.5
Asian alone [2]	4,929	2,799	56.8	631	12.8	2,645	53.7	831	16.9
Hispanic [3]	22,895	14,081	61.5	4,220	18.4	12,245	53.5	6,230	27.2
White alone or in combination [4]	174,191	130,158	74.7	18,111	10.4	119,922	68.8	29,056	16.7
Black alone or in combination [4]	29,399	20,180	68.6	3,196	10.9	18,232	62.0	5,294	18.0
Asian alone or in combination [4]	5,968	3,546	59.4	746	12.5	3,307	55.4	1,025	17.2
NATURALIZED CITIZEN									
All races [1]	21,509	14,273	66.4	3,484	16.2	13,082	60.8	4,824	22.4
White alone [2]	11,560	7,405	64.1	2,051	17.7	6,691	57.9	2,835	24.5
White alone, non-Hispanic	4,632	3,266	70.5	545	11.8	2,949	63.7	912	19.7
Black alone [2]	2,732	1,980	72.5	314	11.5	1,838	67.3	448	16.4
Asian alone [2]	6,602	4,556	69.0	1,005	15.2	4,237	64.2	1,396	21.1
Hispanic [3]	7,732	4,638	60.0	1,659	21.5	4,215	54.5	2,105	27.2
White alone or in combination [4]	11,792	7,552	64.0	2,075	17.6	6,831	57.9	2,866	24.3
Black alone or in combination [4]	2,876	2,061	71.7	339	11.8	1,919	66.7	472	16.4
Asian alone or in combination [4]	6,674	4,611	69.1	1,012	15.2	4,286	64.2	1,410	21.1

[1] Includes other races, not shown separately. [2] Data shown represent persons who selected this race group only and exclude persons reporting more than one race. [3] Persons of Hispanic origin may be of any race. [4] In combination with one or more races.

Source: U.S. Census Bureau, "Voting and Registration in the Election of November 2020," <www.census.gov/topics/public-sector/voting.html>, accessed June 2021.

Table 456. Vote Cast for President by Major Political Party: 1948 to 2020

[In thousands (48,834 represents 48,834,000), except percent and electoral vote. Prior to 1960, excludes Alaska and Hawaii; prior to 1964, excludes DC. Vote cast for major party candidates includes the votes of minor parties cast for those candidates]

Year	Candidates for President — Democratic	Candidates for President — Republican	Total popular vote[1] (1,000)	Democratic Popular vote Number (1,000)	Democratic Popular vote Percent	Democratic Electoral vote	Republican Popular vote Number (1,000)	Republican Popular vote Percent	Republican Electoral vote
1948..........	Truman	Dewey	48,834	24,106	49.4	303	21,969	45.0	189
1952..........	Stevenson	Eisenhower	61,552	27,315	44.4	89	33,779	54.9	442
1956..........	Stevenson	Eisenhower	62,027	26,739	43.1	73	35,581	57.4	457
1960..........	Kennedy	Nixon	68,836	34,227	49.7	303	34,108	49.5	219
1964..........	Johnson	Goldwater	70,098	42,825	61.1	486	27,147	38.7	52
1968..........	Humphrey	Nixon	73,027	30,989	42.4	191	31,710	43.4	301
1972..........	McGovern	Nixon	77,625	28,902	37.2	17	46,740	60.2	520
1976..........	Carter	Ford	81,603	40,826	50.0	297	39,148	48.0	240
1980..........	Carter	Reagan	86,497	35,481	41.0	49	43,643	50.5	489
1984..........	Mondale	Reagan	92,655	37,450	40.4	13	54,167	58.5	525
1988..........	Dukakis	Bush	91,587	41,717	45.5	111	48,643	53.1	426
1992..........	Clinton	Bush	104,600	44,858	42.9	370	38,799	37.1	168
1996..........	Clinton	Dole	96,390	47,402	49.2	379	39,198	40.7	159
2000..........	Gore	Bush	105,594	50,996	48.3	266	50,465	47.8	271
2004..........	Kerry	Bush	122,349	58,895	48.1	251	61,873	50.6	286
2008..........	Obama	McCain	131,407	69,498	52.9	365	59,948	45.6	173
2012..........	Obama	Romney	129,140	65,752	50.9	332	60,670	47.0	206
2016..........	Clinton	Trump	136,787	65,677	48.0	227	62,692	45.8	304
2020..........	Biden	Trump	158,482	80,884	51.0	306	73,920	46.6	232

[1] Include votes for minor party candidates, independents, unpledged electors, and scattered write-in votes.

Source: U.S. House of Representatives, Office of the Clerk, *Statistics of the Presidential and Congressional Election*, February 2021, and earlier reports. See also <clerk.house.gov/Members#ElectionInformation>.

Table 457. Vote Cast for Leading Minority Party Candidates for President: 1948 to 2020

[In thousands (1,169 represents 1,169,000). See headnote, Table 456. Data do not include write-ins, scatterings, or votes for candidates who ran on party tickets not shown, unless otherwise noted]

Year	Candidate	Party	Popular vote[1] (1,000)	Candidate	Party	Popular vote (1,000)
1948..........	Strom Thurmond	States' Rights	1,169	Henry Wallace	Progressive	1,156
1952..........	Vincent Hallinan	Progressive	135	Stuart Hamblen	Prohibition	73
1956 [1]........	T. Coleman Andrews	States' Rights	91	Eric Hass	Socialist Labor	41
1960..........	Eric Hass	Socialist Labor	46	Rutherford Decker	Prohibition	46
1964..........	Eric Hass	Socialist Labor	43	Clifton DeBerry	Socialist Workers	22
1968..........	George Wallace	American Independent	9,446	Henning Blomen	Socialist Labor	52
1972 [1]........	John Schmitz	American	993	Benjamin Spock	People's	9
1976..........	Eugene McCarthy	Independent	680	Roger McBride	Libertarian	172
1980..........	John Anderson	Independent	5,251	Ed Clark	Libertarian	920
1984..........	David Bergland	Libertarian	227	Lyndon H. LaRouche	Independent	79
1988..........	Ron Paul	Libertarian	410	Lenora B. Fulani	New Alliance	129
1992..........	H. Ross Perot	Independent	19,722	Andre Marrou	Libertarian	281
1996..........	H. Ross Perot	Reform	7,137	Ralph Nader	Green	527
2000..........	Ralph Nader	Green	2,530	Pat Buchanan	Reform	324
2004..........	Michael Badnarik	Libertarian	369	Ralph Nader	Independent	156
2008..........	Ralph Nader	Independent	739	Bob Barr	Libertarian	515
2012..........	Gary Johnson	Libertarian	1,216	Jill Stein	Green	401
2016..........	Gary Johnson	Libertarian	4,081	Jill Stein	Green	1,351
2020..........	Jo Jorgensen	Libertarian	1,761	Howie Hawkins	Green	372

[1] Data include write-ins, scatterings, and/or votes for candidates who ran on party tickets not shown.

Source: U.S. House of Representatives, Office of the Clerk, *Statistics of the Presidential and Congressional Election*, February 2021, and earlier reports. See also <clerk.house.gov/Members#ElectionInformation>.

Table 458. Electoral Vote Cast for President by Major Political Party—States: 1980 to 2020

[D = Democratic, R = Republican. For composition of regions, see map, inside front cover]

State	1980	1984	1988 [1]	1992	1996	2000 [2]	2004 [3]	2008 [4]	2012	2016 [5]	2020 [6]
Democratic........	**49**	**13**	**111**	**370**	**379**	**266**	**251**	**365**	**332**	**227**	**306**
Republican........	**489**	**525**	**426**	**168**	**159**	**271**	**286**	**173**	**206**	**304**	**232**
Northeast:											
Democratic..........	4	–	53	106	106	102	101	101	96	75	95
Republican..........	118	113	60	–	–	4	–	–	–	21	1
Midwest:											
Democratic..........	10	10	29	100	100	68	57	97	80	30	57
Republican..........	135	127	108	29	29	61	66	27	38	88	61
South:											
Democratic..........	31	3	8	68	80	15	16	71	58	29	45
Republican..........	138	174	168	116	104	168	173	118	138	165	151
West:											
Democratic..........	4	–	21	96	93	81	77	96	98	93	109
Republican..........	98	111	90	23	26	38	47	28	30	30	19
Alabama..............	R-9	R-9	R-9	R-9	R-9	R-9	R-9	R-9	R-9	R-9	R-9
Alaska...............	R-3	R-3	R-3	R-3	R-3	R-3	R-3	R-3	R-3	R-3	R-3
Arizona..............	R-6	R-7	R-7	R-8	D-8	R-8	R-10	R-10	R-11	R-11	D-11
Arkansas.............	R-6	R-6	R-6	D-6	D-6	R-6	R-6	R-6	R-6	R-6	R-6
California............	R-45	R-47	R-47	D-54	D-54	D-54	D-55	D-55	D-55	D-55	D-55
Colorado.............	R-7	R-8	R-8	D-8	R-8	R-8	R-9	D-9	D-9	D-9	D-9
Connecticut..........	R-8	R-8	R-8	D-8	D-8	D-8	D-7	D-7	D-7	D-7	D-7
Delaware.............	R-3	R-3	R-3	D-3	D-3	D-3	D-3	D-3	D-3	D-3	D-3
District of Columbia...	D-3	D-3	D-3	D-3	D-3	D-2	D-3	D-3	D-3	D-3	D-3
Florida..............	R-17	R-21	R-21	R-25	D-25	R-25	R-27	D-27	D-29	R-29	R-29
Georgia..............	D-12	R-12	R-12	D-13	R-13	R-13	R-15	R-15	R-16	R-16	D-16
Hawaii...............	D-4	D-4	D-4	D-4	D-4	D-4	D-4	D-4	D-4	D-3	D-4
Idaho................	R-4	R-4	R-4	R-4	R-4	R-4	R-4	R-4	R-4	R-4	R-4
Illinois..............	R-26	R-24	R-24	D-22	D-22	D-22	D-21	D-21	D-20	D-20	D-20
Indiana..............	R-13	R-12	R-12	R-12	R-12	R-12	R-11	D-11	R-11	R-11	R-11
Iowa................	R-8	R-8	D-8	D-7	D-7	D-7	R-7	D-7	D-6	R-6	R-6
Kansas..............	R-7	R-7	R-7	R-6	R-6	R-6	R-6	R-6	R-6	R-6	R-6
Kentucky.............	R-9	R-9	R-9	D-8	D-8	R-8	R-8	R-8	R-8	R-8	R-8
Louisiana............	R-10	R-10	R-10	D-9	D-9	R-9	R-9	R-9	R-8	R-8	R-8
Maine...............	R-4	R-4	R-4	D-4	D-4	D-4	D-4	D-4	D-4	D-3	D-3
Maryland.............	D-10	R-10	R-10	D-10	D-10	D-10	D-10	D-10	D-10	D-10	D-10
Massachusetts........	D-14	R-13	D-13	D-12	D-12	D-12	D-12	D-12	D-11	D-11	D-11
Michigan.............	R-21	R-20	R-20	D-18	D-18	D-18	D-17	D-17	D-16	R-16	D-16
Minnesota............	D-10	D-10	D-10	D-10	D-10	D-10	D-9	D-10	D-10	D-10	D-10
Mississippi...........	R-7	R-7	R-7	R-7	R-7	R-7	R-6	R-6	R-6	R-6	R-6
Missouri.............	R-12	R-11	R-11	D-11	D-11	R-11	R-11	R-11	R-10	R-10	R-10
Montana.............	R-4	R-4	R-4	D-3	R-3	R-3	R-3	R-3	R-3	R-3	R-3
Nebraska.............	R-5	R-5	R-5	R-5	R-5	R-5	R-5	R-4	R-5	R-5	R-4
Nevada..............	R-3	R-4	R-4	D-4	D-4	R-4	R-5	D-5	D-6	D-6	D-6
New Hampshire.......	R-4	R-4	R-4	D-4	D-4	R-4	D-4	D-4	D-4	D-4	D-4
New Jersey...........	R-17	R-16	R-16	D-15	D-15	D-15	D-15	D-15	D-14	D-14	D-14
New Mexico..........	R-4	R-5	R-5	D-5	D-5	D-5	R-5	D-5	D-5	D-5	D-5
New York............	R-41	R-36	D-36	D-33	D-33	D-33	D-31	D-31	D-29	D-29	D-29
North Carolina........	R-13	R-13	R-13	R-14	R-14	R-14	R-15	D-15	R-15	R-15	R-15
North Dakota.........	R-3	R-3	R-3	R-3	R-3	R-3	R-3	R-3	R-3	R-3	R-3
Ohio................	R-25	R-23	R-23	D-21	D-21	R-21	R-20	D-20	D-18	R-18	R-18
Oklahoma............	R-8	R-8	R-8	R-8	R-8	R-8	R-7	R-7	R-7	R-7	R-7
Oregon..............	R-6	R-7	D-7	D-7	D-7	D-7	D-7	D-7	D-7	D-7	D-7
Pennsylvania.........	R-27	R-25	R-25	D-23	D-23	D-23	D-21	D-21	D-20	R-20	D-20
Rhode Island.........	D-4	R-4	D-4	D-4	D-4	D-4	D-4	D-4	D-4	D-4	D-4
South Carolina........	R-8	R-8	R-8	R-8	R-8	R-8	R-8	R-8	R-9	R-9	R-9
South Dakota.........	R-4	R-3	R-3	R-3	R-3	R-3	R-3	R-3	R-3	R-3	R-3
Tennessee............	R-10	R-11	R-11	D-11	D-11	R-11	R-11	R-11	R-11	R-11	R-11
Texas................	R-26	R-29	R-29	R-32	R-32	R-32	R-34	R-34	R-38	R-36	R-38
Utah................	R-4	R-5	R-5	R-5	R-5	R-5	R-5	R-5	R-6	R-6	R-6
Vermont..............	R-3	R-3	R-3	D-3	D-3	D-3	D-3	D-3	D-3	D-3	D-3
Virginia..............	R-12	R-12	R-12	R-13	R-13	R-13	R-13	D-13	D-13	D-13	D-13
Washington...........	R-9	R-10	D-10	D-11	D-11	D-11	D-11	D-11	D-12	D-8	D-12
West Virginia.........	D-6	R-6	D-5	D-5	D-5	R-5	R-5	R-5	R-5	R-5	R-5
Wisconsin............	R-11	R-11	D-11	D-11	D-11	D-11	D-10	D-10	D-10	R-10	D-10
Wyoming.............	R-3	R-3	R-3	R-3	R-3	R-3	R-3	R-3	R-3	R-3	R-3

– Represents zero. [1] Excludes one electoral vote cast in West Virginia for Lloyd Bentsen for President. [2] Excludes one electoral vote left blank by a Democratic elector in the District of Columbia. [3] Excludes one electoral vote cast in Minnesota for Democratic vice presidential nominee John Edwards. [4] Excludes one electoral vote cast in Nebraska for Barack Obama. [5] Excludes one electoral vote cast in Hawaii for Bernie Sanders, one electoral vote cast in Maine for Donald J. Trump, one electoral vote each cast in Texas for John Kasich and Ron Paul, and, in Washington, three electoral votes cast for Colin Powell and one electoral vote cast for Faith Spotted Eagle. [6] Excludes one electoral vote cast in Maine for Donald J. Trump and one electoral vote cast in Nebraska for Joe Biden.

Source: U.S. House of Representatives, Office of the Clerk, *Statistics of the Presidential and Congressional Election*, February 2021, and earlier reports. See also <clerk.house.gov/Members#ElectionInformation>.

Table 459. Popular Vote Cast for President by Political Party—States: 2016 and 2020

[In thousands (136,787 represents 136,787,000), except percent]

State	2016			Percent of total vote		2020			Percent of total vote	
	Total [1]	Demo-cratic party	Republi-can party	Demo-cratic party	Republi-can party	Total [1]	Demo-cratic party	Republi-can party	Demo-cratic party	Republi-can party
United States........	**136,787**	**65,677**	**62,692**	**48.0**	**45.8**	**158,482**	**80,884**	**73,920**	**51.0**	**46.6**
Alabama..................	2,123	730	1,318	34.4	62.1	2,323	850	1,441	36.6	62.0
Alaska....................	319	116	163	36.6	51.3	360	154	190	42.8	52.8
Arizona..................	2,573	1,161	1,252	45.1	48.7	3,387	1,672	1,662	49.4	49.1
Arkansas.................	1,131	380	685	33.7	60.6	1,219	424	761	34.8	62.4
California................	14,182	8,754	4,484	61.7	31.6	17,501	11,110	6,006	63.5	34.3
Colorado.................	2,780	1,339	1,202	48.2	43.3	3,257	1,804	1,365	55.4	41.9
Connecticut..............	1,645	898	673	54.6	40.9	1,824	1,081	715	59.3	39.2
Delaware.................	442	236	185	53.4	41.9	504	296	201	58.7	39.8
District of Columbia.....	313	283	13	90.5	4.1	343	317	19	92.6	5.4
Florida...................	9,420	4,505	4,618	47.8	49.0	11,067	5,297	5,669	47.9	51.2
Georgia..................	4,115	1,878	2,089	45.6	50.8	5,001	2,475	2,462	49.5	49.2
Hawaii...................	438	267	129	61.0	29.4	571	366	197	64.2	34.5
Idaho....................	690	190	409	27.5	59.3	868	287	554	33.1	63.8
Illinois..................	5,536	3,091	2,146	55.8	38.8	6,034	3,472	2,447	57.5	40.6
Indiana..................	2,735	1,033	1,557	37.8	56.9	3,033	1,242	1,730	41.0	57.0
Iowa.....................	1,566	654	801	41.8	51.2	1,700	759	898	44.6	52.8
Kansas...................	1,184	427	671	36.1	56.7	1,372	570	771	41.6	56.2
Kentucky.................	1,924	629	1,203	32.7	62.5	2,137	772	1,327	36.2	62.1
Louisiana................	2,029	780	1,179	38.4	58.1	2,148	856	1,256	39.9	58.5
Maine....................	772	358	336	46.3	43.5	828	435	361	52.5	43.6
Maryland.................	2,781	1,678	943	60.3	33.9	3,037	1,985	976	65.4	32.2
Massachusetts...........	3,379	1,995	1,091	59.1	32.3	3,658	2,382	1,167	65.1	31.9
Michigan.................	4,799	2,269	2,280	47.3	47.5	5,539	2,804	2,650	50.6	47.8
Minnesota...............	2,945	1,368	1,323	46.4	44.9	3,277	1,717	1,484	52.4	45.3
Mississippi..............	1,209	485	701	40.1	57.9	1,314	540	757	41.1	57.6
Missouri.................	2,809	1,071	1,595	38.1	56.8	3,026	1,253	1,719	41.4	56.8
Montana.................	495	178	279	35.9	56.5	604	245	344	40.6	56.9
Nebraska................	844	284	496	33.7	58.7	956	375	557	39.2	58.2
Nevada..................	1,125	539	512	47.9	45.5	1,405	703	670	50.1	47.7
New Hampshire..........	744	349	346	46.8	46.5	806	425	366	52.7	45.4
New Jersey..............	3,874	2,148	1,602	55.5	41.4	4,549	2,608	1,883	57.3	41.4
New Mexico.............	798	385	320	48.3	40.0	924	502	402	54.3	43.5
New York................	7,802	4,380	2,527	56.1	32.4	8,662	4,845	2,949	55.9	34.0
North Carolina..........	4,742	2,189	2,363	46.2	49.8	5,525	2,684	2,759	48.6	49.9
North Dakota............	344	94	217	27.2	63.0	362	115	236	31.8	65.1
Ohio.....................	5,496	2,394	2,841	43.6	51.7	5,922	2,679	3,155	45.2	53.3
Oklahoma................	1,453	420	949	28.9	65.3	1,561	504	1,020	32.3	65.4
Oregon..................	2,001	1,002	782	50.1	39.1	2,374	1,340	958	56.5	40.4
Pennsylvania............	6,115	2,926	2,971	47.9	48.6	6,915	3,458	3,378	50.0	48.8
Rhode Island............	464	253	181	54.4	38.9	518	307	200	59.4	38.6
South Carolina..........	2,103	855	1,155	40.7	54.9	2,513	1,092	1,385	43.4	55.1
South Dakota...........	370	117	228	31.7	61.5	423	150	261	35.6	61.8
Tennessee...............	2,508	871	1,523	34.7	60.7	3,054	1,144	1,852	37.5	60.7
Texas....................	8,969	3,878	4,685	43.2	52.2	11,315	5,259	5,890	46.5	52.1
Utah.....................	1,131	311	515	27.5	45.5	1,488	560	865	37.6	58.1
Vermont.................	320	179	95	55.7	29.8	371	243	113	65.5	30.4
Virginia.................	3,983	1,981	1,769	49.8	44.4	4,461	2,414	1,962	54.1	44.0
Washington..............	3,317	1,743	1,222	52.5	36.8	4,088	2,370	1,585	58.0	38.8
West Virginia............	713	189	489	26.5	68.6	781	236	545	30.2	69.8
Wisconsin................	2,976	1,383	1,405	46.5	47.2	3,297	1,631	1,610	49.5	48.8
Wyoming................	259	56	174	21.6	67.4	279	73	194	26.4	69.5

[1] Includes other parties.

Source: U.S. House of Representatives, Office of the Clerk, *Statistics of the Presidential and Congressional Election*, February 2021, and earlier reports. See also <clerk.house.gov/Members#ElectionInformation>.

Table 460. Vote Cast for U.S. Senators, 2018 and 2020, and Incumbent Senators, 2021 by State

[2,384 represents 2,384,000. D = Democrat, R = Republican, I = Independent]

State	2018 Total [2] (1,000)	2018 Percent for leading party	2020 Total [2] (1,000)	2020 Percent for leading party	Incumbent senators and year term expires [1] Name, party, and year	Incumbent senators and year term expires [1] Name, party, and year
Alabama	(X)	(X)	2,316	R-60.1	Richard C. Shelby (R) 2023	Tommy Tuberville (R) 2027
Alaska	(X)	(X)	355	R-53.9	Lisa Murkowski (R) 2023	Dan Sullivan (R) 2027
Arizona	2,384	D-50.0	(X)	(X)	[3] Mark Kelly (D) 2023	Kyrsten Sinema (D) 2025
Arkansas	(X)	(X)	1,193	R-66.5	John Boozman (R) 2023	Tom Cotton (R) 2027
California	11,113	[4] D-100.0	(X)	(X)	Dianne Feinstein (D) 2025	Alex Padilla (D) 2023
Colorado	(X)	(X)	3,236	D-53.5	Michael F. Bennet (D) 2023	John W. Hickenlooper (D) 2027
Connecticut	1,387	D-56.8	(X)	(X)	Richard Blumenthal (D) 2023	Christopher Murphy (D) 2025
Delaware	363	D-60.0	491	D-59.4	Thomas R. Carper (D) 2025	Christopher A. Coons (D) 2027
Florida	8,190	R-50.1	(X)	(X)	Marco Rubio (R) 2023	Rick Scott (R) 2025
Georgia	(X)	(X)	4,600	D-49.3	Jon Ossoff (D) 2027	Raphael G. Warnock (D) 2023
Hawaii	399	D-69.3	(X)	(X)	Mazie K. Hirono (D) 2025	Brian Schatz (D) 2023
Idaho	(X)	(X)	860	R-62.6	Mike Crapo (R) 2023	James E. Risch (R) 2027
Illinois	(X)	(X)	5,969	D- 54.9	Tammy Duckworth (D) 2023	Richard J. Durbin (D) 2027
Indiana	2,283	R-50.7	(X)	(X)	Mike Braun (R) 2025	Todd Young (R) 2023
Iowa	(X)	(X)	1,700	R-50.9	Joni Ernst (R) 2027	Chuck Grassley (R) 2023
Kansas	(X)	(X)	1,368	R-53.2	Roger Marshall (R) 2027	Jerry Moran (R) 2023
Kentucky	(X)	(X)	2,135	R-57.8	Mitch McConnell (R) 2027	Rand Paul (R) 2023
Louisiana	(X)	(X)	2,072	R-61.2	Bill Cassidy (R) 2027	John Kennedy (R) 2023
Maine	646	I-53.3	828	R-50.4	Susan M. Collins (R) 2027	Angus S. King (I) 2025
Maryland	2,300	D-64.9	(X)	(X)	Benjamin L. Cardin (D) 2025	Chris Van Hollen (D) 2023
Massachusetts	2,753	D-59.3	3,658	D-64.5	Edward J. Markey (D) 2027	Elizabeth Warren (D) 2025
Michigan	4,237	D-52.3	5,480	D-49.9	Gary C. Peters (D) 2027	Debbie Stabenow (D) 2025
Minnesota	2,597	D-60.3	3,214	D-48.7	Amy Klobuchar (D) 2025	Tina Smith (D) 2027
Mississippi	936	R-58.5	1,311	R-54.1	Cindy Hyde-Smith (R) 2027	Roger F. Wicker (R) 2025
Missouri	2,442	R-51.4	(X)	(X)	Roy Blunt (R) 2023	Josh Hawley (R) 2025
Montana	504	D-50.3	606	R-55.0	Steve Daines (R) 2027	Jon Tester (D) 2025
Nebraska	699	R-57.7	930	R-62.7	Deb Fischer (R) 2025	Ben Sasse (R) 2027
Nevada	972	D-50.4	(X)	(X)	Catherine Cortez Masto (D) 2023	Jacky Rosen (D) 2025
New Hampshire	(X)	(X)	796	D-56.6	Margaret Wood Hassan (D) 2023	Jeanne Shaheen (D) 2027
New Jersey	3,169	D-54.0	4,440	D-57.2	Cory A. Booker (D) 2027	Robert Menendez (D) 2025
New Mexico	697	D-54.1	917	D-51.7	Martin Heinrich (D) 2025	Ben Ray Luján (D) 2027
New York	6,251	D-60.1	(X)	(X)	Kirsten E. Gillibrand (D) 2025	Charles E. Schumer (D) 2023
North Carolina	(X)	(X)	5,475	R-48.7	Richard Burr (R) 2023	Thom Tillis (R) 2027
North Dakota	326	R-55.1	(X)	(X)	Kevin Cramer (R) 2025	John Hoeven (R) 2023
Ohio	4,411	D-53.4	(X)	(X)	Sherrod Brown (D) 2025	Rob Portman (R) 2023
Oklahoma	(X)	(X)	1,556	R-62.9	James M. Inhofe (R) 2027	James Lankford (R) 2023
Oregon	(X)	(X)	2,321	D-56.9	Jeff Merkley (D) 2027	Ron Wyden (D) 2023
Pennsylvania	5,009	D-55.7	(X)	(X)	Robert P. Casey, Jr. (D) 2025	Patrick J. Toomey (R) 2023
Rhode Island	377	D-61.4	494	D-66.5	Jack Reed (D) 2027	Sheldon Whitehouse (D) 2025
South Carolina	(X)	(X)	2,513	R-54.5	Lindsey Graham (R) 2027	Tim Scott (R) 2023
South Dakota	(X)	(X)	420	R-65.7	Mike Rounds (R) 2027	John Thune (R) 2023
Tennessee	2,244	R-54.7	2,960	R-62.2	Marsha Blackburn (R) 2025	Bill Hagerty (R) 2027
Texas	8,372	R-50.9	11,144	R-53.5	John Cornyn (R) 2027	Ted Cruz (R) 2025
Utah	1,063	R-62.6	(X)	(X)	Mike Lee (R) 2023	Mitt Romney (R) 2025
Vermont	278	I-70.6	(X)	(X)	Patrick J. Leahy (D) 2023	Bernard Sanders (I) 2025
Virginia	3,351	D-57.0	4,405	D-56.0	Tim Kaine (D) 2025	Mark R. Warner (D) 2027
Washington	3,086	D-58.4	(X)	(X)	Maria Cantwell (D) 2025	Patty Murray (D) 2023
West Virginia	586	D-49.6	779	R-70.3	Shelley Moore Capito (R) 2027	Joe Manchin III (D) 2025
Wisconsin	2,661	D-55.4	(X)	(X)	Tammy Baldwin (D) 2025	Ron Johnson (R) 2023
Wyoming	205	R-66.4	279	R-71.1	John Barrasso (R) 2025	Cynthia M. Lummis (R) 2027

X Not applicable. [1] As of April 21, 2021; see <www.senate.gov/pagelayout/reference/three_column_table/Senators.htm>. [2] Includes vote cast for minor parties. [3] Elected in a special election on November 3, 2020, to complete the term left vacant by the death of John McCain. [4] Two Democrats ran for Senate; no Republican challenger.

Source: U.S. House of Representatives, Office of the Clerk, *Statistics of the Presidential and Congressional Election of November 3, 2020*, February 2021, and earlier reports; and ProQuest research. See also <clerk.house.gov/Members#ElectionInformation>.

Table 461. Vote Cast for U.S. House of Representatives by Major Political Party—States: 2016 to 2020

[In thousands (129,833 represents 129,833,000), except percent. R = Republican, D = Democrat, and I = Independent. In each state, totals represent the sum of votes cast in each Congressional District or votes cast for Representative-at-Large in states where only one member is elected. In all years there are numerous districts within the state where either the Republican or Democratic party had no candidate. In some states the Republican and Democratic vote includes votes cast for the party candidate by endorsing parties]

State	2016				2018				2020			
	Total [1]	Demo-cratic	Republi-can	Percent for leading party	Total [1]	Demo-cratic	Republi-can	Percent for leading party	Total [1]	Demo-cratic	Republi-can	Percent for leading party
U.S........	129,833	61,417	62,772	R-48.3	114,017	60,320	50,467	D-52.9	153,431	77,123	72,467	D-50.3
AL..........	1,890	622	1,222	R-64.7	1,660	679	976	R-58.8	2,052	609	1,416	R-69.0
AK..........	308	111	155	R-50.3	282	131	150	R-53.1	353	160	192	R-54.4
AZ..........	2,412	1,035	1,264	R-52.4	2,341	1,179	1,139	D-50.4	3,268	1,629	1,639	R-50.1
AR..........	1,069	111	760	R-71.2	889	313	556	R-62.6	1,179	330	828	R-70.2
CA..........	13,414	8,624	4,682	D-64.3	12,185	8,010	3,973	D-65.7	16,725	11,084	5,641	D-66.3
CO..........	2,701	1,264	1,289	R-47.7	2,514	1,343	1,080	D-53.4	3,165	1,679	1,378	D-53.1
CT..........	1,575	917	558	D-58.2	1,380	809	512	D-58.6	1,773	1,023	677	D-57.7
DE..........	421	234	172	D-55.5	354	227	125	D-64.3	488	281	196	D-57.6
FL [2]........	8,837	3,985	4,734	R-53.6	7,021	3,307	3,675	R-52.3	10,465	4,942	5,469	R-52.3
GA..........	3,773	1,498	2,272	R-60.2	3,802	1,814	1,987	R-52.3	4,884	2,393	2,490	R-51.0
HI..........	438	316	86	D-72.3	399	288	87	D-72.2	580	355	155	D-61.2
ID..........	682	209	448	R-65.7	596	207	368	R-61.8	850	256	561	R-66.1
IL..........	5,242	2,811	2,397	D-53.6	4,540	2,758	1,754	D-60.7	5,877	3,355	2,417	D-57.1
IN..........	2,658	1,053	1,443	R-54.3	2,256	1,000	1,248	R-55.3	2,996	1,195	1,739	R-58.0
IA..........	1,516	674	813	R-53.7	1,316	665	612	D-50.5	1,700	762	859	R-50.5
KS..........	1,174	318	694	R-59.1	1,050	464	563	R-53.6	1,359	557	776	R-57.1
KY..........	1,765	517	1,248	R-70.7	1,570	613	935	R-59.6	2,116	735	1,364	R-64.5
LA [2]........	1,749	530	1,178	R-67.3	1,461	553	836	R-57.2	1,947	727	1,170	R-60.1
ME..........	772	387	357	D-50.1	631	344	250	D-54.4	828	469	340	D-56.6
MD..........	2,708	1,636	962	D-60.4	2,286	1,493	738	D-65.3	2,954	1,913	1,028	D-64.7
MA..........	3,379	2,345	451	D-69.4	2,753	1,944	498	D-70.6	3,658	2,483	699	D-67.9
MI..........	4,671	2,194	2,243	R-48.0	4,155	2,175	1,853	D-52.4	5,423	2,689	2,618	D-49.6
MN..........	2,860	1,435	1,335	D-50.2	2,577	1,421	1,126	D-55.1	3,194	1,554	1,475	D-48.7
MS..........	1,182	450	681	R-57.6	939	399	471	R-50.2	1,228	421	807	R-65.7
MO..........	2,750	1,041	1,601	R-58.2	2,418	1,028	1,331	R-55.0	2,973	1,172	1,724	R-58.0
MT..........	508	206	285	R-56.2	504	233	257	R-50.9	602	262	339	R-56.4
NE..........	788	221	558	R-70.7	697	264	432	R-62.0	941	326	585	R-62.2
NV..........	1,078	508	498	D-47.1	961	491	440	D-51.1	1,356	666	634	D-49.1
NH..........	716	336	316	D-47.0	571	311	249	D-54.5	787	414	354	D-52.6
NJ..........	3,463	1,822	1,542	D-52.6	3,099	1,857	1,199	D-59.9	4,433	2,539	1,843	D-57.3
NM..........	780	437	343	D-56.0	693	404	265	D-58.3	904	496	408	D-54.9
NY..........	7,800	4,202	2,141	D-53.9	6,251	3,761	1,640	D-60.2	8,604	4,717	2,692	D-54.8
NC..........	4,598	2,143	2,447	R-53.2	3,381	1,633	1,707	R-50.5	5,325	2,661	2,631	D-50.0
ND..........	338	80	234	R-69.1	322	114	194	R-60.2	356	98	245	R-69.0
OH..........	5,218	2,155	2,996	R-57.4	4,406	2,083	2,291	R-52.0	5,762	2,452	3,253	R-56.5
OK [2]........	1,133	305	782	R-69.0	1,179	428	731	R-62.0	1,551	476	1,044	R-67.3
OR..........	1,912	1,027	731	D-53.7	1,848	1,061	703	D-57.4	2,308	1,285	967	D-55.7
PA..........	5,744	2,625	3,097	R-53.9	4,930	2,713	2,206	D-55.0	6,779	3,347	3,433	R-50.6
RI..........	432	264	141	D-61.1	373	243	130	D-65.0	488	313	110	D-64.0
SC..........	2,012	768	1,177	R-58.5	1,709	758	927	R-54.3	2,505	1,077	1,413	R-56.4
SD..........	370	133	237	R-64.1	336	121	203	R-60.3	398	(X)	322	R-81.0
TN..........	2,391	814	1,494	R-62.5	2,160	846	1,280	R-59.2	2,842	1,106	1,685	R-59.3
TX..........	8,529	3,161	4,878	R-57.2	8,203	3,853	4,135	R-50.4	11,094	4,897	5,927	R-53.4
UT..........	1,114	356	711	R-63.8	1,053	374	617	R-58.7	1,432	506	873	R-61.0
VT..........	320	264	(X)	D-82.5	278	189	71	D-67.8	371	239	96	D-64.4
VA..........	3,782	1,859	1,843	D-49.2	3,313	1,867	1,409	D-56.4	4,335	2,254	2,048	D-52.0
WA..........	3,141	1,736	1,405	D-55.3	3,022	1,889	900	D-62.5	3,944	2,340	1,545	D-59.3
WV..........	686	224	445	R-64.8	578	235	337	R-58.3	761	247	514	R-67.5
WI..........	2,774	1,380	1,270	D-49.8	2,572	1,367	1,173	D-53.2	3,238	1,567	1,661	R-51.3
WY..........	259	75	156	R-60.3	205	60	128	R-62.3	279	67	186	R-66.7

X Not applicable. [1] Includes votes cast for minor parties. [2] State law does not require tabulation of votes for unopposed candidates.

Source: U.S. House of Representatives, Office of the Clerk, *Statistics of the Presidential and Congressional Election of November 6, 2020*, February 2021. See also <clerk.house.gov/Members#ElectionInformation>.

Table 462. Vote Cast for U.S. House of Representatives by Major Political Party—Congressional Districts: 2020

[As of February 2021. Does not include special elections or votes received from endorsing parties. If multiple candidates from the same party ran in the general election, only the candidate with the leading number of votes is shown]

State and district	Democrat Name	Percent of total	Republican Name	Percent of total
AL.....	(X)	(X)	(X)	(X)
1st...	Averhart	35.5	Carl	64.4
2d.....	Harvey-Hall	34.7	Moore	65.2
3d.....	Winfrey	32.5	Rogers	67.5
4th....	Neighbors	17.7	Aderholt	82.2
5th....	(1)	(1)	Brooks	95.8
6th....	(1)	(1)	Palmer	97.1
7th....	Sewell	97.2	(1)	(1)
AK.....	Galvin	45.3	Young	54.4
AZ.....	(X)	(X)	(X)	(X)
1st....	O'Halleran	51.6	Shedd	48.4
2d.....	Kirkpatrick	55.1	Martin	44.9
3d.....	Grijalva	64.6	Wood	35.4
4th....	DiSanto	30.2	Gosar	69.7
5th....	Greene	41.1	Biggs	58.9
6th....	Tipirneni	47.8	Schweikert	52.2
7th....	Gallego	76.7	Barnett	23.3
8th....	Muscato	40.4	Lesko	59.6
9th....	Stanton	61.6	Giles	38.4
AR.....	(X)	(X)	(X)	(X)
1st....	(1)	(1)	Crawford	100.0
2d.....	Elliott	44.6	Hill	55.4
3d.....	Williams	31.8	Womack	64.3
4th....	Hanson	27.5	Westerman	69.7
CA.....	(X)	(X)	(X)	(X)
1st....	Denney	43.0	LaMalfa	57.0
2d.....	Huffman	75.7	Mensing	24.3
3d.....	Garamendi	54.7	Hamilton	45.3
4th....	Kennedy	44.1	McClintock	55.9
5th....	Thompson	76.1	Giblin	23.9
6th....	Matsui	73.3	Bish	26.7
7th....	Bera	56.6	Patterson	43.4
8th....	Bubser	43.9	Obernolte	56.1
9th....	McNerney	57.6	Amador	42.4
10th...	Harder	55.2	Howze	44.8
11th...	DeSaulnier	73.0	Sharma	27.0
12th...	Pelosi	77.6	(1)	(1)
13th...	Lee	90.4	Piterman	9.6
14th...	Speier	79.3	Petel	20.7
15th...	Swalwell	70.9	Hayden	29.1
16th...	Costa	59.4	Cookingham	40.6
17th...	Khanna	71.3	Tandon	28.7
18th...	Eshoo	63.2	(1)	(1)
19th...	Lofgren	71.7	Aguilera	28.3
20th...	Panetta	76.8	Gorman	23.2
21st...	Cox	49.6	Valadao	50.4
22d...	Arballo	45.8	Nunes	54.2
23d...	Mangone	37.9	McCarthy	62.1
24th...	Carbajal	58.7	Caldwell	41.3
25th...	Smith	50.0	Garcia	50.0
26th...	Brownley	60.6	Baldwin-Kennedy	39.4
27th...	Chu	69.8	Nalbandian	30.2
28th...	Schiff	72.7	Early	27.3
29th...	Cárdenas	56.6	(1)	(1)
30th...	Sherman	69.5	Reed	30.5
31st...	Aguilar	61.3	Gibboney	38.7
32d...	Napolitano	66.6	Scott	33.4
33d...	Lieu	67.6	Bradley	32.4
34th...	Gomez	53.0	(1)	(1)
35th...	Torres	69.3	Cargile	30.7
36th...	Ruiz	60.3	Cruz	39.7
37th...	Bass	85.9	Webber	14.1
38th...	Sánchez	74.3	(1)	(1)
39th...	Cisneros Jr.	49.4	Kim	50.6
40th...	Roybal-Allard	72.7	Delgado	27.3
41st...	Takano	64.0	Smith	36.0
42d...	O'Mara	42.9	Calvert	57.1
43d...	Waters	71.7	Collins	28.3
44th...	Barragán	67.8	(1)	(1)
45th...	Porter	53.5	Raths	46.5
46th...	Correa	68.8	Waters	31.2
47th...	Lowenthal	63.3	Briscoe	36.7
48th...	Rouda	48.9	Steel	51.1
49th...	Levin	53.1	Maryott	46.9
50th...	Campa-Najjar	46.0	Issa	54.0
51st...	Vargas	68.3	Hidalgo Jr.	31.7
52d...	Peters	61.6	DeBello	38.4
53d...	Jacobs	59.5	(1)	(1)
CO.....	(X)	(X)	(X)	(X)
1st.....	DeGette	73.6	Bolling	23.5
2d.....	Neguse	61.5	Winn	35.4
3d.....	Bush	45.2	Boebert	51.4
4th....	McCorkle	36.6	Buck	60.1
5th....	Freeland	37.4	Lamborn	57.6
6th....	Crow	57.1	House	40.0
7th....	Perlmutter	59.1	Stockham	37.6
CT.....	(X)	(X)	(X)	(X)
1st....	Larson	61.0	Fay	35.0
2d.....	Courtney	56.4	Anderson	38.2
3d.....	DeLauro	56.1	Streicker	38.0
4th....	Himes	62.2	Riddle	36.2
5th....	Hayes	52.6	Sullivan	43.5
DE.....	Rochester	57.6	Murphy	40.2
DC.....	(X)	(X)	(X)	(X)
FL......	(X)	(X)	(X)	(X)
1st....	Ehr	34.0	Gaetz	64.6
2d.....	(1)	(1)	Dunn	97.9
3d.....	Christensen	42.9	Cammack	57.1
4th....	Deegan	38.9	Rutherford	61.1
5th....	Lawson Jr.	65.1	Adler	34.9
6th....	Curtis	39.4	Waltz	60.6
7th....	Murphy	55.3	Valentin	43.2
8th....	Kennedy	38.6	Posey	61.4
9th....	Soto	56.0	Olson	44.0
10th...	Demings	63.6	Francois	36.4
11th...	Cottrell	33.3	Webster	66.7
12th...	Walker	37.1	Bilirakis	62.9
13th...	Crist	53.0	Luna	47.0
14th...	Castor	60.3	Quinn	39.7
15th...	Cohn	44.6	Franklin	55.4
16th...	Good	44.5	Buchanan	55.5
17th...	Ellison	34.1	Steube	64.6
18th...	Keith	41.5	Mast	56.3
19th...	Banyai	38.7	Donalds	61.3
20th...	Hastings	78.7	Musselwhite	21.3
21st...	Frankel	59.0	Loomer	39.1
22d...	Deutch	58.6	Pruden	41.4
23d...	Wasserman Shultz	58.2	Spalding	41.8
24th...	Wilson	75.6	Spicer	20.4
25th...	(1)	(1)	Diaz-Balart	(2)
26th...	Mucarsel-Powell	48.3	Gimenez	51.7
27th...	Shalala	48.6	Salazar	51.4
GA.....	(X)	(X)	(X)	(X)
1st...	Griggs	41.7	Carter	58.3
2d...	Bishop Jr.	59.1	Cole	40.9
3d.....	Almonord	35.0	Ferguson	65.0
4th....	Johnson Jr.	80.1	Ezammudeen	19.9
5th....	Williams	85.1	Stanton-King	14.9
6th....	McBath	54.6	Handel	45.4
7th....	Bourdeaux	51.4	McCormick	48.6
8th....	Holliday	35.5	Scott	64.5
9th....	Pandy	21.4	Clyde	78.6
10th...	Johnson-Green	37.7	Hice	62.3
11th...	Barrett	39.6	Loudermilk	60.4
12th...	Johnson	41.6	Allen	58.4
13th...	Scott	77.4	Hites	22.6
14th...	Ausdal	25.3	Greene	74.7
HI......	(X)	(X)	(X)	(X)
1st...	Case	64.7	Curtis	25.1
2d...	Kahele	57.9	Akana	28.4
ID......	(X)	(X)	(X)	(X)
1st...	Soto	28.6	Fulcher	67.8
2d...	Swisher	31.7	Simpson	64.1
IL.......	(X)	(X)	(X)	(X)
1st...	Rush	73.8	White	26.2
2d...	Kelly	78.8	Raborn	21.2
3d.....	Newman	56.4	Fricilone	43.6
4th....	García	84.1	Solorio	15.9
5th....	Quigley	70.8	Hanson	26.6
6th....	Casten	52.8	Ives	45.4
7th....	Davis	80.4	Cameron	13.3
8th....	Krishnamoorthi	73.2	(1)	(1)
9th....	Schakowsky	71.0	Sangari	29.0
10th...	Schneider	63.9	Mukherjee	36.1
11th...	Foster	63.3	Laib	36.7
12th...	Lenzi	39.6	Bost	60.4
13th...	Londrigan	45.5	Davis	54.5
14th...	Underwood	50.7	Oberweis	49.3
15th...	Weaver	26.6	Miller	73.4
16th...	Brzozowski	35.3	Kinzinger	64.7
17th...	Bustos	52.0	King	48.0
18th...	Petrilli	29.6	LaHood	70.4

See footnotes at end of table.

Table 462. Vote Cast for U.S. House of Representatives by Major Political Party—Congressional Districts: 2020-Continued.

See headnote on page 293.

State and district	Democrat Name	Percent of total	Republican Name	Percent of total
IN......	(X)	(X)	(X)	(X)
1st....	Mrvan	56.6	Leyva	40.4
2d.....	Hackett	38.5	Walorski	61.5
3d.....	Coldiron	32.2	Banks	67.8
4th....	Mackey	33.4	Baird	66.6
5th....	Hale	45.9	Spartz	50.0
6th....	Lake	27.8	Pence	68.7
7th....	Carson	62.4	Smith	37.6
8th....	Marsili	29.8	Bucshon	66.9
9th....	Ruff	34.1	Hollingsworth	61.8
IA......	(X)	(X)	(X)	(X)
1st....	Finkenauer	47.5	Hinson	50.0
2d.....	Hart	47.6	Miller-Meeks	47.6
3d.....	Axne	47.6	Young	46.2
4th....	Scholten	36.1	Feenstra	59.1
KS.....	(X)	(X)	(X)	(X)
1st....	Barnett	28.8	Mann	71.2
2d.....	De La Isla	40.6	LaTurner	55.1
3d.....	Davids	53.6	Adkins	43.6
4th....	Lombard	36.3	Estes	63.7
KY.....	(X)	(X)	(X)	(X)
1st....	Rhodes	25.0	Comer	75.0
2d.....	Lindermann	26.3	Guthrie	71.0
3d.....	Yarmuth	62.7	Palazzo	37.3
4th....	Owensby	32.9	Massie	67.1
5th....	Best	15.8	Rogers	84.2
6th....	Hicks	41.0	Barr	57.3
LA.....	(X)	(X)	(X)	(X)
1st....	Dugas	25.3	Scalise	72.2
2d.....	Richmond[3]	74.2	Schilling	19.9
3d.....	Harris	29.5	Higgins	67.8
4th....	Houston	33.3	Johnson	66.7
5th....	Christophe	42.4	Letlow	57.6
6th....	Williams	25.5	Graves	71.0
ME.....	(X)	(X)	(X)	(X)
1st....	Pingree	60.5	Allen	36.8
2d.....	Golden	52.1	Crafts	46.1
MD.....	(X)	(X)	(X)	(X)
1st....	Mason	36.4	Harris	63.4
2d.....	Ruppersberger	67.7	Salling	32.0
3d.....	Sarbanes	69.8	Anthony	30.0
4th....	Brown	79.6	McDermott	20.2
5th....	Hoyer	68.8	Palombi	31.0
6th....	Trone	58.8	Parrott	39.2
7th....	Mfume	71.6	Klacik	28.0
8th....	Raskin	68.2	Coll	31.6
MA.....	(X)	(X)	(X)	(X)
1st....	Neal	73.9	(1)	(1)
2d.....	McGovern	63.4	Lovvorn	33.6
3d.....	Trahan	73.9	(1)	(1)
4th....	Auchincloss	57.8	Hall	36.9
5th....	Clark	71.2	Colarusso	24.5
6th....	Moulton	63.3	Moran	33.3
7th....	Pressley	81.8	(1)	(1)
8th....	Lynch	71.7	(1)	(1)
9th....	Keating	58.9	Brady	34.9
MI.....	(X)	(X)	(X)	(X)
1st....	Ferguson	36.8	Bergman	61.6
2d.....	Berghoef	38.2	Huizenga	59.2
3d.....	Scholten	47.0	Meijer	53.0
4th....	Hilliard	32.4	Moolenaar	65.0
5th....	Kildee	54.5	Kelly	41.8
6th....	Hoadley	40.1	Upton	55.8
7th....	Driskell	41.2	Walberg	58.8
8th....	Slotkin	50.9	Junge	47.3
9th....	Levin	57.7	Langworthy	38.4
10th...	Bizon	33.7	McClain	66.3
11th...	Stevens	50.2	Esshaki	47.8
12th...	Dingell	66.4	Jones	30.7
13th...	Tlaib	78.1	Dudenhoefer	18.6
14th...	Lawrence	79.3	Patrick	18.3
MN.....	(X)	(X)	(X)	(X)
1st....	Feehan	45.5	Hagedorn	48.6
2d.....	Craig	48.2	Kistner	45.9
3d.....	Phillips	55.6	Qualls	44.3
4th....	McCollum	63.2	Rechtzigel	29.0
5th....	Omar	64.3	Johnson	25.8
6th....	Zahradka	34.2	Emmer	65.7
7th....	Peterson	39.8	Fischbach	53.4
8th....	Nystrom	37.6	Stauber	56.8
MS.....	(X)	(X)	(X)	(X)
1st....	Eliason	31.3	Kelly	68.7
2d.....	Thompson	66.0	Flowers	34.0
3d....	Benford	35.3	Guest	64.7
4th....	(1)	(1)	Palazzo	100.0
MO.....	(X)	(X)	(X)	(X)
1st....	Bush	78.8	Rogers	19.0
2d.....	Schupp	45.5	Wagner	51.9
3d.....	Rezabek	28.5	Luetkemeyer	69.4
4th....	Simmons	29.7	Hartzler	67.6
5th....	Cleaver	58.8	Derks	38.6
6th....	Ross	30.8	Graves	67.1
7th....	Montseny	26.6	Long	68.9
8th....	Ellis	21.4	Smith	76.9
MT.....	Williams	43.6	Rosendale	56.4
NE.....	(X)	(X)	(X)	(X)
1st....	Bolz	37.7	Fortenberry	59.5
2d.....	Eastman	46.2	Bacon	50.8
3d.....	Elworth Jr.	17.7	Smith	78.5
NV.....	(X)	(X)	(X)	(X)
1st....	Titus	61.8	Bentley	33.4
2d.....	Ackerman	40.7	Amodei	56.5
3d.....	Lee	48.8	Rodimer	45.8
4th....	Horsford	50.7	Marchant	45.8
NH.....	(X)	(X)	(X)	(X)
1st....	Pappas	51.3	Mowers	46.2
2d.....	Kuster	53.9	Negron	43.7
NJ......	(X)	(X)	(X)	(X)
1st....	Norcross	62.5	Gustafson	37.5
2d.....	Kennedy	46.2	Van Drew	51.9
3d.....	Kim	53.2	Richter	45.5
4th....	Schmid	38.3	Smith	59.9
5th....	Gottheimer	53.2	Pallotta	45.6
6th....	Pallone Jr.	61.2	Onuoha	38.8
7th....	Malinowski	50.6	Kean Jr.	49.4
8th....	Sires	74.0	Mushnick	24.6
9th....	Pascrell Jr.	65.8	Prempeh	31.9
10th...	Payne Jr.	83.3	Zinone	13.9
11th...	Sherrill	53.3	Becchi	46.7
12th...	Coleman	65.6	Razzoli	32.6
NM.....	(X)	(X)	(X)	(X)
1st....	Haaland	58.2	Holmes	41.8
2d.....	Small	46.3	Herrell	53.7
3d.....	Fernandez	58.7	Johnson	41.3
NY.....	(X)	(X)	(X)	(X)
1st....	Goroff	40.4	Zeldin	47.5
2d.....	Gordon	40.4	Garbarino	44.1
3d.....	Suozzi	49.1	Santos	37.0
4th....	Rice	51.9	Tuman	36.2
5th....	Meeks	82.4	(1)	(1)
6th....	Meng	57.8	Zmich	27.1
7th....	Velázquez	66.7	Kelly	12.5
8th....	Jeffries	72.5	Wallace	13.7
9th....	Clarke	68.1	Jean-Pierre	14.0
10th...	Nadler	62.7	Bernstein	21.1
11th...	Rose	44.7	Malliotakis	47.6
12th...	Maloney	78.9	Santiago-Cano	14.6
13th...	Espaillat	75.9	Gwinn	7.4
14th...	Ocasio-Cortez	68.3	Cummings	23.5
15th...	Torres	84.7	Delices	9.5
16th...	Bowman	82.1	(1)	(1)
17th...	Jones	53.4	McArdle-Schulman	34.0
18th...	Maloney	48.0	Farley	36.1
19th...	Delgado	45.4	Van De Water	40.9
20th...	Tonko	52.5	Joy	32.7
21st...	Cobb	37.6	Stefanik	52.1
22d...	Brindisi	42.5	Tenney	43.9
23d...	Mitrano	35.8	Reed	49.9
24th...	Balter	41.9	Katko	44.3
25th...	Morelle	51.0	Mitris	31.6
26th...	Higgins	59.9	Donovan Sr.	27.1
27th...	McMurray	34.4	Jacobs	48.4
NC.....	(X)	(X)	(X)	(X)
1st....	Butterfield	54.2	Smith	45.8
2d.....	Ross	63.0	Swain	34.8
3d.....	Farrow	36.6	Murphy	63.4
4th....	Price	67.3	Thomas	32.7
5th....	Brown	31.1	Foxx	66.9
6th....	Manning	62.3	Haywood	37.7
7th....	Ward	39.6	Rouzer	60.2
8th....	Timmons-Goodson	46.7	Hudson	53.3
9th....	Wallace	44.4	Bishop	55.6
10th...	Parker	31.1	McHenry	68.9
11th...	Davis	42.3	Cawthorn	54.5
12th...	Adams	100.0	(1)	(1)
13th...	Huffman	31.8	Budd	68.2

See footnotes at end of table.

Table 462. Vote Cast for U.S. House of Representatives by Major Political Party—Congressional Districts: 2020-Continued.

See headnote on page 293.

State and district	Democrat Name	Percent of total	Republican Name	Percent of total
ND.....	Raknerud	27.6	Armstrong	69.0
OH.....	(X)	(X)	(X)	(X)
1st....	Schroder	44.6	Chabot	51.8
2d.....	Castle	38.9	Wenstrup	61.1
3d.....	Beatty	70.8	Richardson	29.1
4th....	Freshour	29.3	Jordan	67.9
5th....	Rubando	32.0	Latta	68.0
6th....	Roberts	25.6	Johnson	74.4
7th....	Potter	29.2	Gibbs	67.5
8th....	Enoch	31.0	Davidson	69.0
9th....	Kaptur	63.1	Weber	36.9
10th...	Tims	41.6	Turner	58.4
11th...	Fudge	80.1	Gore	19.9
12th...	Shearer	41.8	Balderson	55.2
13th...	Ryan	52.5	Hagan	44.9
14th...	Mueri	39.9	Joyce	60.1
15th...	Newby	36.6	Stivers	63.4
16th...	Godfrey	36.8	Gonzalez	63.2
OK.....	(X)	(X)	(X)	(X)
1st....	Asaoa-Caesar	32.7	Hern	63.7
2d.....	Lanier	22.0	Mullin	75.0
3d.....	Midyett	21.5	Lucas	78.5
4th....	Brannon	28.8	Cole	67.8
5th....	Horn	47.9	Bice	52.1
OR.....	(X)	(X)	(X)	(X)
1st....	Bonamici	64.6	Christensen	35.2
2d.....	Spenser	36.9	Bentz	59.9
3d.....	Blumenauer	73.0	Harbour	23.5
4th....	DeFazio	51.5	Skarlatos	46.2
5th....	Schrader	51.9	Courser	45.2
PA......	(X)	(X)	(X)	(X)
1st....	Finello	43.4	Fitzpatrick	56.6
2d.....	Boyle	72.5	Torres	27.5
3d.....	Evans	91.0	Harvey	9.0
4th....	Cunnane	59.5	Barnette	40.5
5th....	Scanlon	64.7	Pruett	35.3
6th....	Houlahan	56.1	Emmons	43.9
7th....	Wild	51.9	Scheller	48.1
8th....	Cartwright	51.8	Bognet	48.2
9th....	Wegman	33.7	Meuser	66.3
10th...	DePasquale	46.7	Perry	53.3
11th...	Hammond	36.9	Smucker	63.1
12th...	Griffin	29.2	Keller	70.8
13th...	Rowley	26.5	Joyce	73.5
14th...	Marx	35.3	Reschenthaler	64.7
15th...	Williams	26.5	Thompson Jr.	73.5
16th...	Gnibus	40.7	Kelly Jr.	59.3
17th...	Lamb	51.1	Parnell	48.9
18th...	Doyle Jr.	69.2	Negron	30.8
RI......	(X)	(X)	(X)	(X)
1st....	Cicilline	70.8	(1)	(1)
2d.....	Langevin	58.2	Lancia	41.5
SC.....	(X)	(X)	(X)	(X)
1st....	Cunningham	49.3	Mace	50.6
2d.....	Boroughs	42.6	Wilson	55.7
3d.....	Cleveland	28.7	Duncan	71.2
4th....	Nelson	36.9	Timmons	61.6
5th....	Brown	39.9	Norman	60.1
6th....	Clyburn	68.2	McCollum	30.8
7th....	Watson	38.1	Rice	61.8
SD.....	(1)	(1)	Johnson	81.0
TN.....	(X)	(X)	(X)	(X)
1st....	Walsingham	22.5	Harshbarger	74.7
2d.....	Hoyos	31.1	Burchett	67.6
3d.....	Gorman	30.5	Fleischmann	67.3
4th....	Hale	33.3	DesJarlais	66.7
5th....	Cooper	100.0	(1)	(1)
6th....	Finley	24.0	Rose	73.7
7th....	Sreepada	27.3	Green	69.9
8th....	Pearson	29.5	Kustoff	68.5
9th....	Cohen	77.4	Bergmann	20.1
TX......	(X)	(X)	(X)	(X)
1st....	Gilbert	27.4	Gohmert	72.6
2d.....	Ladjevardian	42.8	Crenshaw	55.6
3d.....	Seikaly	42.9	Taylor	55.1
4th....	Foster	22.6	Fallon	75.1
5th....	Salter	35.9	Gooden	62.0
6th....	Daniel	44.0	Wright	52.8
7th....	Fletcher	50.8	Hunt	47.5
8th....	Hernandez	25.5	Brady	72.5
9th....	Green	75.5	Teague	21.6
10th...	Siegel	45.3	McCaul	52.5
11th...	Hogg	18.3	Pfluger	79.7
12th...	Welch	33.0	Granger	63.7
13th...	Trujillo	18.5	Jackson	79.4
14th...	Bell	38.4	Weber Sr.	61.6
15th...	Gonzalez	50.5	Cruz-Hernandez Armendariz-	47.6
16th...	Escobar	64.7	Jackson	35.3
17th...	Kennedy	40.9	Sessions	55.9
18th...	Lee	73.3	Champion	23.5
19th...	Watson	22.9	Arrington	74.8
20th...	Castro	64.7	Garza	33.1
21st...	Davis	45.4	Roy	52.0
22d...	Kulkarni	44.6	Nehls	51.5
23d...	Jones	46.6	Gonzales	50.6
24th...	Valenzuela	47.5	Van Duyne	48.8
25th...	Oliver	42.1	Williams	55.9
26th...	Iannuzzi	37.3	Burgess	60.6
27th...	De La Fuente	34.9	Cloud	63.1
28th...	Cuellar	58.3	Whitten	39.0
29th...	Garcia	71.1	Blanco	27.4
30th...	Johnson	77.5	Pennie	18.4
31st...	Imam	44.3	Carter	53.4
32d...	Allred	51.9	Collins	45.9
33d...	Veasey	66.8	Vasquez	25.2
34th...	Vela	55.4	Gonzalez	41.8
35th...	Doggett	65.4	Sharon	29.9
36th...	Lewis	24.3	Babin	73.6
UT.....	(X)	(X)	(X)	(X)
1st....	Parry	30.4	Moore	69.5
2d.....	Weston	36.6	Stewart	59.0
3d.....	Thorpe	26.8	Curtis	68.7
4th....	McAdams	46.7	Owens	47.7
VT......	Welch	64.4	Berry	25.8
VA......	(X)	(X)	(X)	(X)
1st....	Rashid	41.7	Wittman	58.1
2d.....	Luria	51.6	Taylor	45.8
3d.....	Scott	68.4	Collick Jr.	31.4
4th....	McEachin	61.6	Benjamin Sr.	38.2
5th....	Webb	47.3	Good	52.4
6th....	Betts	35.3	Cline	64.6
7th....	Spanberger	50.8	Freitas	49.0
8th....	Beyer Jr.	75.8	Jordan	24.0
9th....	(1)	(1)	Griffith	94.0
10th...	Wexton	56.5	Andrews	43.4
11th...	Connolly	71.4	Anantatmula	28.3
WA.....	(X)	(X)	(X)	(X)
1st....	DelBene	58.6	Beeler Sr.	41.3
2d.....	Larsen	63.1	Hazelo	36.7
3d.....	Long	43.4	Beutler	56.4
4th....	McKinley	33.6	Newhouse	66.2
5th....	Wilson	38.5	Rodgers	61.3
6th....	Kilmer	59.3	Kreiselmaier	40.5
7th....	Jayapal	83.0	Keller	16.8
8th....	Schrier	51.7	Jensen	48.1
9th....	Smith	74.1	Basler	25.7
10th...	Strickland	84.9	(1)	(1)
WV.....	(X)	(X)	(X)	(X)
1st....	Cline	31.0	McKinley	69.0
2d.....	Kunkel	36.9	Mooney	63.1
3d.....	Turner	28.6	Miller	71.3
WI.....	(X)	(X)	(X)	(X)
1st....	Polack	40.6	Steil	59.3
2d.....	Pocan	69.7	Theron	30.3
3d.....	Kind	51.3	Van Orden	48.6
4th....	Moore	74.6	Rogers	22.7
5th....	Palzewicz	39.8	Fitzgerald	60.1
6th....	King	40.7	Grothman	59.2
7th....	Zunker	39.2	Tiffany	60.7
8th....	Stuck	35.8	Gallagher	64.2
WY.....	Grey Bull	23.9	Cheney	66.7

X Not applicable. [1] No candidate. [2] According to Florida law, the names of those with no opposition are not printed on the ballot. [3] Richmond resigned from the House of Representatives on January 15, 2021. Troy Carter (D) won the runoff against Karen Peterson (R), April 24th, 2021, and is the current sitting representative.

Source: U.S. House of Representatives, Office of the Clerk, *Statistics of the Presidential and Congressional Election of November 3, 2020*, February 2021, and earlier reports. See also <clerk.house.gov/Members#ElectionInformation>.

Table 463. Apportionment of Membership in House of Representatives by State: 1800 to 2020

[Total membership includes Representatives assigned to newly admitted States after the apportionment acts. Population figures used for apportionment purposes are those determined for States by each decennial census. For more information on apportionment, see <www.census.gov/topics/public-sector/congressional-apportionment/about/historical-perspective.html>]

State	\ Membership based on Census of—																				
---	1800	1830	1840	1850	1860	1870	1880	1890	1900	1910	1920[3]	1930	1940	1950	1960	1970	1980	1990	2000	2010	2020
U.S.	142	242	232	237	243	293	332	357	391	435	435	435	435	437	435	435	435	435	435	435	435
AL	(X)	5	7	7	6	8	8	9	9	10	10	9	9	9	8	7	7	7	7	7	7
AK	(X)	(X)	(X)	(X)	(X)	(X)	(X)	(X)	(X)	(X)	(X)	(X)	(X)	1[1]	1	1	1	1	1	1	1
AZ	(X)	(X)	(X)	(X)	(X)	(X)	(X)	(X)	(X)[2]	(X)[2]	1	1	2	2	3	4	5	6	8	9	9
AR	(X)	(X)	1[2]	2	3	4	5	6	8	7	7	7	7	6	4	4	4	4	4	4	4
CA	(X)	(X)	(X)	2	3	4	6	7	8	11	11	20	23	30	38	43	45	52	53	53	52
CO	(X)	(X)	(X)	(X)	(X)	(X)	1	2	3	4	4	4	4	4	4	5	6	6	7	7	8
CT	7	6	6	4	4	4	4	4	5	5	5	6	6	6	6	6	6	6	5	5	5
DE	1	1	1	1	1	1	1	1	1	1	1	1	1	1	1	1	1	1	1	1	1
FL	(X)	(X)	(X)	1	1	2	2	2	3	4	4	5	6	8	12	15	19	23	25	27	28
GA	4	9	8	8	7	9	10	11	11	12	12	10	10	10	10	10	10	11	13	14	14
HI	(X)	(X)	(X)	(X)	(X)	(X)	(X)	(X)	(X)	(X)	(X)	(X)	(X)	1[1]	2	2	2	2	2	2	2
ID	(X)	(X)	(X)	(X)	(X)	(X)	(X)	1	1	2	2	2	2[2]	2	2	2	2	2	2	2	2
IL	1	3	10	9	14	19	20	22	25	27	27	27	26	25	24	24	22	20	19	18	17
IN	(X)	7	10	11	11	13	13	13	13	13	13	12	11	11	11	11	10	10	9	9	9
IA	(X)	(X)	(X)[2]	2	6	9	11	11	11	11	11	9	8	8	7	6	6	5	5	4	4
KS	(X)	(X)	(X)	(X)	1	3	7	8	8	8	8	7	6	6	5	5	5	4	4	4	4
KY	6	13	10	10	9	10	11	11	11	11	11	9	9	8	7	7	7	6	6	6	6
LA	(X)	3	4	4	5	6	6	6	7	8	8	8	8	8	8	8	8	7	7	6	6
ME	(X)	8	7	6	5	5	4	4	4	4	4	3	3	3	2	2	2	2	2	2	2
MD	9	8	8	6	5	6	6	6	6	6	6	6	6	7	8	8	8	8	8	8	8
MA	17	12	10	11	10	11	12	13	14	16	16	15	14	14	12	12	11	10	10	9	9
MI	(X)	1[1]	3	4	6	9	11	12	12	13	13	17	17	18	19	19	18	16	15	14	13
MN	(X)	(X)	(X)	(X)	2	3	5	7	9	10	10	9	9	9	8	8	8	8	8	8	8
MS	(X)	2	4	5	5	6	7	7	8	8	8	7	7	6	5	5	5	5	4	4	4
MO	(X)	2	5	7	9	13	14	15	16	16	16	13	13	11	10	10	9	9	9	8	8
MT	(X)	(X)	(X)	(X)	(X)	(X)	(X)	1	1	2	2	2	2	2	2	2	2	1	1	1	2
NE	(X)	(X)	(X)	(X)	(X)	1	3	6	6	6	6	5	4	4	3	3	3	3	3	3	3
NV	(X)	(X)	(X)	(X)	(X)	1	1	1	1	1	1	1	1	1	1	2	2	2	3	4	4
NH	4	5	4	3	3	3	2	2	2	2	2	2	2	2	2	2	2	2	2	2	2
NJ	5	6	5	5	5	7	7	8	10	12	12	14	14	14	15	15	14	13	13	12	12
NM	(X)	(X)	(X)	(X)	(X)	(X)	(X)	(X)	(X)[2]	(X)[2]	1	1	2	2	2	2	3	3	3	3	3
NY	17	40	34	33	31	33	34	34	37	43	43	45	45	43	41	39	34	31	29	27	26
NC	12	13	9	8	7	8	9	9	10	10	10	11	12	12	11	11	11	12	13	13	14
ND	(X)[1]	(X)	(X)	(X)	(X)	(X)	(X)	1	2	3	3	2	2	2	2	1	1	1	1	1	1
OH	1	19	21	21	19	20	21	21	21	22	22	24	23	23	24	23	21	19	18	16	15
OK	(X)	(X)	(X)	(X)	(X)	(X)	(X)	(X)	5[1]	8	8	9	8	6	6	6	6	6	5	5	5
OR	(X)	(X)	(X)	(X)	(X)	1	1	2	2	3	3	3	4	4	4	4	5	5	5	5	6
PA	18	28	24	25	24	27	28	30	32	36	36	34	33	30	27	25	23	21	19	18	17
RI	2	2	2	2	2	2	2	2	2	3	3	2	2	2	2	2	2	2	2	2	2
SC	8	9	7	6	4	5	7	7	7	7	7	6	6	6	6	6	6	6	6	7	7
SD	(X)	(X)	(X)	(X)	(X)	(X)	(X)	2	2	3	3	2	2	2	2	2	1	1	1	1	1
TN	3	13	11	10	8	8	10	10	10	10	10	9	10	9	9	8	8	9	9	9	9
TX	(X)	(X)	(X)	2	4	6	11	13	16	18	18	21	21	22	23	24	27	30	32	36	38
UT	(X)	(X)	(X)	(X)	(X)	(X)	(X)	(X)	1	2	2	2	2	2	2	2	3	3	3	4	4
VT	4	5	5	4	3	3	3	2	2	2	2	1	1	1	1	1	1	1	1	1	1
VA	22	21	15	13	11	9	10	10	10	10	10	9	9	10	10	10	10	11	11	11	11
WA	(X)	(X)	(X)	(X)	(X)	(X)	(X)	2	3	5	5	6	6	7	7	7	8	9	9	10	10
WV	(X)	(X)	(X)	(X)	(X)	3	4	4	5	6	6	6	6	6	5	5	4	3	3	3	2
WI	(X)	(X)	(X)[2]	3	6	8	9	10	11	11	11	10	10	10	10	9	9	9	8	8	8
WY	(X)	(X)	(X)	(X)	(X)	(X)	(X)	1	1	1	1	1	1	1	1	1	1	1	1	1	1

X Not applicable. [1] Assigned after apportionment. [2] Included in apportionment in anticipation of statehood. [3] No reapportionment occurred based on 1920 population census.

Source: U.S. Census Bureau, "Congressional Apportionment." <www.census.gov/topics/public-sector/congressional-apportionment.html>, accessed May 2021.

Table 464. Composition of Congress by Political Party Affiliation—States: 2015 to 2021

[Figures are for the beginning of the first session, except as noted. Dem. = Democratic; Rep. = Republican]

State	Representatives 114th Cong.,[1] 2015 Dem.	Rep.	115th Cong., 2017 Dem.	Rep.	116th Cong.,[2] 2019 Dem.	Rep.	117th Cong.,[3] 2021 Dem.	Rep.	Senators 114th Cong.,[4] 2015 Dem.	Rep.	115th Cong.,[4] 2017 Dem.	Rep.	116th Cong.,[4] 2019 Dem.	Rep.	117th Cong.,[4,5] 2021 Dem.	Rep.
U.S.......	188	245	194	241	235	197	222	211	44	54	46	52	45	53	48	50
AL........	1	6	1	6	1	6	1	6	–	2	–	2	1	1	–	2
AK........	–	1	–	1	–	1	–	1	–	2	–	2	–	2	–	2
AZ........	4	5	4	5	5	4	5	4	–	2	–	2	1	1	2	–
AR........	–	4	–	4	–	4	–	4	–	2	–	2	–	2	–	2
CA........	39	14	39	14	46	7	42	11	2	–	2	–	2	–	2	–
CO........	3	4	3	4	4	3	4	3	1	1	1	1	1	1	2	–
CT........	5	–	5	–	5	–	5	–	2	–	2	–	2	–	2	–
DE........	1	–	1	–	1	–	1	–	2	–	2	–	2	–	2	–
FL........	10	17	11	16	13	14	11	16	1	1	1	1	–	2	–	2
GA........	4	10	4	10	5	9	6	8	–	2	–	2	–	2	2	–
HI........	2	–	2	–	2	–	2	–	2	–	2	–	2	–	2	–
ID........	–	2	–	2	–	2	–	2	–	2	–	2	–	2	–	2
IL........	10	8	11	7	13	5	13	5	1	1	2	–	2	–	2	–
IN........	2	7	2	7	2	7	2	7	1	1	1	1	–	2	–	2
IA........	1	3	1	3	3	1	1	3	–	2	–	2	–	2	–	2
KS........	–	4	–	4	1	3	1	3	–	2	–	2	–	2	–	2
KY........	1	5	1	5	1	5	1	5	–	2	–	2	–	2	–	2
LA........	1	5	1	5	1	5	1	4	–	2	–	2	–	2	–	2
ME........	1	1	1	1	2	–	2	–	–	1	–	1	–	1	–	1
MD........	7	1	7	1	7	1	7	1	2	–	2	–	2	–	2	–
MA........	9	–	9	–	9	–	9	–	2	–	2	–	2	–	2	–
MI........	5	9	5	9	7	7	7	7	2	–	2	–	2	–	2	–
MN........	5	3	5	3	5	3	4	4	2	–	2	–	2	–	2	–
MS........	1	2	1	3	1	3	1	3	–	2	–	2	–	2	–	2
MO........	2	6	2	6	2	6	2	6	1	1	1	1	–	2	–	2
MT........	–	1	–	1	–	1	–	1	1	1	1	1	1	1	1	1
NE........	1	2	–	3	–	3	–	3	–	2	–	2	–	2	–	2
NV........	1	3	3	1	3	1	3	1	1	1	1	1	2	–	2	–
NH........	1	1	2	–	2	–	2	–	1	1	2	–	2	–	2	–
NJ........	6	6	7	5	11	1	10	2	2	–	2	–	2	–	2	–
NM........	2	1	2	1	3	–	2	1	2	–	2	–	2	–	2	–
NY........	18	8	18	9	21	6	19	7	2	–	2	–	2	–	2	–
NC........	3	10	3	10	3	8	5	8	–	2	–	2	–	2	–	2
ND........	–	1	–	1	–	1	–	1	1	1	1	1	–	2	–	2
OH........	4	12	4	12	4	12	4	12	1	1	1	1	1	1	1	1
OK........	–	5	–	5	1	4	–	5	–	2	–	2	–	2	–	2
OR........	4	1	4	1	4	1	4	1	2	–	2	–	2	–	2	–
PA........	5	13	5	13	9	8	9	9	1	1	1	1	1	1	1	1
RI........	2	–	2	–	2	–	2	–	2	–	2	–	2	–	2	–
SC........	1	6	1	6	2	5	1	6	–	2	–	2	–	2	–	2
SD........	–	1	–	1	–	1	–	1	–	2	–	2	–	2	–	2
TN........	2	7	2	7	2	7	2	7	–	2	–	2	–	2	–	2
TX........	11	25	11	25	13	23	13	23	–	2	–	2	–	2	–	2
UT........	–	4	–	4	1	3	–	4	–	2	–	2	–	2	–	2
VT........	1	–	1	–	1	–	1	–	1	–	1	–	1	–	1	–
VA........	3	8	4	7	7	4	7	4	2	–	2	–	2	–	2	–
WA........	6	4	6	4	7	3	7	3	2	–	2	–	2	–	2	–
WV........	–	3	–	3	–	3	–	3	1	1	1	1	1	1	1	1
WI........	3	5	3	5	3	5	3	5	1	1	1	1	1	1	1	1
WY........	–	1	–	1	–	1	–	1	–	2	–	2	–	2	–	2

– Represents zero. [1] Two vacancies—one in Mississippi due to the death of Alan Nunnelee, February 6, 2015, and one in New York due to the resignation of Michael G. Grimm, January 5, 2015. [2] Three vacancies—one in Pennsylvania due the resignation of Tom Marino on January 23, 2019; and two in North Carolina, one due to the death of Walter Jones on February 10, 2019, and one due to North Carolina's State Board of Elections and Ethics Reform's refusal to certify the results of the NC-09 election due to irregularities involving absentee ballots. [3] Two vacancies in Louisiana due to the death of Luke Letlow on December 29th, 2020 and the resignation of Cedric L. Richmond on January 15th, 2021. [4] Vermont and Maine had one Independent senator each. [5] Reflects results of the January 5, 2021 runoff elections in Georgia.

Source: U.S. House of Representatives, Office of the Clerk, *Official List of Members*, January 2021, and earlier editions. See also <clerk.house.gov/member_info/>.

Table 465. Members of Congress—Seniority of Senators and Representatives: 1969 to 2021

[Represents the makeup of Congress on the 1st day of the session]

Congress	Senators — Number by length of service				Mean years of service	Representatives — Number by terms served				Mean terms of service
	6 years or less [1]	7-12 years	13-18 years	19+ years		1-3 terms	4-6 terms	7-9 terms	10+ terms	
91st (1969)	32 (14)	32	17	19	11.2	171	126	65	73	5.6
92nd (1971)	25 (10)	24	29	22	11.5	162	122	68	83	5.8
93rd (1973)	40 (13)	20	20	20	11.2	162	128	66	76	5.5
94th (1975)	[2] 36 (12)	22	23	19	11.5	196	100	78	61	5.2
95th (1977)	42 (17)	25	13	20	10.6	219	87	70	59	4.9
96th (1979)	48 (20)	24	10	18	9.6	219	95	65	54	4.8
97th (1981)	55 (18)	20	10	15	8.5	209	121	56	49	4.7
98th (1983)	43 (5)	28	16	13	9.6	210	125	45	54	4.7
99th (1985)	32 (7)	38	18	12	10.1	184	138	58	54	5.1
100th (1987)	26 (13)	44	16	14	9.6	163	143	64	65	5.5
101st (1989)	31 (10)	26	29	14	9.8	120	167	86	60	5.8
102nd (1991)	30 (5)	23	28	19	11.1	133	137	91	74	6.1
103rd (1993)	30 (13)	17	32	21	11.3	192	109	69	65	5.2
104th (1995)	29 (11)	26	20	25	12.3	220	78	78	59	4.9
105th (1997)	40 (15)	24	13	23	11.2	243	71	65	56	4.8
106th (1999)	35 (8)	24	16	25	11.2	185	127	58	65	4.8
107th (2001)	37 (11)	21	19	23	11.5	149	155	54	76	5.6
108th (2003)	30 (10)	29	16	25	12.7	149	158	60	68	5.5
109th (2005)	29 (9)	27	15	29	12.5	137	128	97	72	5.9
110th (2007)	29 (10)	26	14	31	13.1	149	116	99	71	6.0
111th (2009)	[3] 32 (11)	19	20	29	14.0	147	102	106	79	6.2
112th (2011)	42 (13)	17	14	27	12.3	170	97	69	97	6.0
113th (2013)	43 (13)	23	15	19	10.2	196	91	72	74	5.7
114th (2015)	45 (13)	24	11	20	9.4	205	91	51	88	5.5
115th (2017)	36 (7)	34	11	19	10.2	177	118	55	85	5.8
116th (2019)	32 (9)	33	17	18	10.1	184	121	56	73	5.4
117th (2021) [4]	26 (8)	37	18	19	12.0	185	121	54	73	5.5

[1] Numbers in parentheses are number of freshman senators. Senators who are currently in their first full term are listed under "6 years or less." [2] Total includes John Durkin (D-NH). After a contested election in 1974, the Senate declared the seat vacant as of August 8, 1975. Durkin was then elected by special election, September 16, 1975, to fill the vacancy. [3] Total includes Al Franken (D-MN), who, on June 30, 2009, was declared elected after a court challenge brought by his Republican opponent; and Roland Burris (D-IL) who was appointed on December 31, 2008 to fill the seat vacated by Barack Obama. Total also includes Joe Biden (D-DE), who resigned his seat on January 15, 2009, but was present on the first day of the session. [4] Includes Jon Ossoff and Raphael Warnock, who were elected on January 5, 2021, and Kamala Harris, who did not resign from office until January 18th, 2021.

Source: The Brookings Institution, "Vital Statistics on Congress" ©, February 2021, <www.brookings.edu/multi-chapter-report/vital-statistics-on-congress>.

Table 466. Women, Black, Asian, and Hispanic Members of Congress by Party Affiliation: 2001 to 2021

[As of beginning of first session of each Congress. Data do not include delegates or commissioners]

Characteristic	107th (2001)	108th (2003)	109th (2005)	110th (2007)	111th (2009) [1]	112th (2011)	113th (2013) [2]	114th (2015)	115th (2017)	116th (2019)	117th (2021) [3]
Women, total	72	73	79	87	91	93	96	104	104	127	143
Representatives	59	59	65	71	74	76	76	84	83	102	118
Democrat	41	38	42	50	57	52	56	62	62	89	89
Republican	18	21	23	21	17	24	20	22	21	13	29
Senators	13	14	14	16	17	17	20	20	21	25	25
Democrat	10	9	9	11	13	12	16	14	16	17	17
Republican	3	5	5	5	4	5	4	6	5	8	8
Black, total	36	37	41	41	39	42	42	46	50	56	62
Representatives	36	37	40	40	39	42	41	44	47	53	58
Democrat	35	37	40	40	39	40	41	42	45	52	56
Republican	1	0	0	0	0	2	0	2	2	1	2
Senators	0	0	1	1	0	0	1	2	3	3	4
Democrat	0	0	1	1	0	0	0	1	2	2	3
Republican	0	0	0	0	0	0	1	1	1	1	1
Asian, total	7	6	7	8	7	10	11	12	16	16	18
Representatives	5	4	5	6	5	8	10	11	13	13	15
Democrat	5	4	4	5	4	7	10	11	13	13	13
Republican	0	0	1	1	1	1	0	0	0	0	2
Senators	2	2	2	2	2	2	1	1	3	3	3
Democrat	2	2	2	2	2	2	1	1	3	3	3
Republican	0	0	0	0	0	0	0	0	0	0	0
Hispanic, total	19	22	25	26	26	29	31	35	42	45	49
Representatives	19	22	23	23	24	27	28	32	38	41	44
Democrat	16	18	19	20	21	19	23	23	28	34	32
Republican	3	4	4	3	3	8	5	9	10	7	12
Senators	0	0	2	3	2	2	3	3	4	4	5
Democrat	0	0	1	2	1	1	1	1	2	2	3
Republican	0	0	1	1	1	1	2	2	2	2	2

[1] Roland Burris was not seated on the first day of the 111th session. [2] Tim Scott, who was appointed on December 17th to replace outgoing Senator Jim DeMint, is included in the Senate totals. [3] Includes both Jon Ossoff and Raphael Warnock, who were elected on January 5, 2021, and Kamala Harris, who did not resign from office until January 18th, 2021.

Source: The Brookings Institution, "Vital Statistics on Congress" ©, February 2021, <www.brookings.edu/multi-chapter-report/vital-statistics-on-congress>.

Table 467. Composition of Congress by Political Party: 1977 to 2021

[D = Democratic, R = Republican. As of beginning of first session of each Congress unless otherwise noted. Data reflect immediate result of elections. Vacancies and third party candidates are noted]

Year	Party and president	Congress	House Majority party	House Minority party	House Other	Senate Majority party	Senate Minority party	Senate Other
1977 [1]	D (Carter)	95th	D-292	R-143	–	D-61	R-38	1
1979 [1]	D (Carter)	96th	D-277	R-158	–	D-58	R-41	1
1981 [2]	R (Reagan)	97th	D-242	R-192	1	R-53	D-46	1
1983	R (Reagan)	98th	D-269	R-166	–	R-54	D-46	–
1985	R (Reagan)	99th	D-253	R-182	–	R-53	D-47	–
1987	R (Reagan)	100th	D-258	R-177	–	D-55	R-45	–
1989	R (Bush)	101st	D-260	R-175	–	D-55	R-45	–
1991 [3]	R (Bush)	102nd	D-267	R-167	1	D-56	R-44	–
1993 [3]	D (Clinton)	103rd	D-258	R-176	1	D-57	R-43	–
1995 [3]	D (Clinton)	104th	R-230	D-204	1	R-52	D-48	–
1997 [4]	D (Clinton)	105th	R-226	D-207	2	R-55	D-45	–
1999 [3]	D (Clinton)	106th	R-223	D-211	1	R-55	D-45	–
2001 [4]	R (Bush)	107th	R-221	D-212	2	D-50	R-50	–
2003 [2, 5]	R (Bush)	108th	R-229	D-204	1	R-51	D-48	1
2005 [2]	R (Bush)	109th	R-232	D-202	1	R-55	D-44	1
2007 [6]	R (Bush)	110th	D-233	R-202	–	D-49	R-49	2
2009 [5, 6, 7]	D (Obama)	111th	D-256	R-178	–	D-55	R-41	2
2011 [6]	D (Obama)	112th	R-242	D-193	–	D-51	R-47	2
2013 [5, 6]	D (Obama)	113th	R-234	D-200	–	D-53	R-45	2
2015 [6]	D (Obama)	114th	R-247	D-188	–	R-54	D-44	2
2017 [6]	R (Trump)	115th	R-241	D-194	–	R-52	D-46	2
2019 [6, 8]	R (Trump)	116th	R-235	D-197	–	R-53	D-45	2
2021 [6, 9]	D (Biden)	117th	D-222	R-211	–	R-50	D-48	2

– Represents zero. [1] Senate had one Independent. [2] House and Senate each had one Independent. [3] House had one Independent-Socialist. [4] House had one Independent-Socialist and one Independent. [5] House had one vacancy. [6] Senate had two Independents. [7] Senate had two vacancies. [8] House had three vacancies. [9] House had two vacancies.

Source: U.S. House of Representatives, Office of the Clerk, "Member Information," <clerk.house.gov> and *Official List of Members by State*, January 2021 and earlier editions; and U.S. Senate, <www.senate.gov/index.htm>, accessed January 2021.

Table 468. U.S. Congress—Measures Introduced and Enacted and Time in Session: 2005 to 2022

[Excludes simple and concurrent resolutions]

Item	109th Cong., 2005–06	110th Cong., 2007–08	111th Cong., 2009–10	112th Cong., 2011-12	113th Cong., 2013-14	114th Cong., 2015-16	115th Cong., 2017-18	116th Cong., 2019-20	117th Cong., 2021-22 [3]
Measures introduced	10,703	11,228	10,778	10,612	9,097	10,223	13,558	16,603	15,635
Bills	10,560	11,081	10,629	10,439	8,919	10,074	11,201	14,150	13,303
Joint resolutions	143	147	149	173	178	149	215	192	148
Measures enacted	590	460	385	239	296	329	339	283	165
Public [1]	589	460	383	238	296	329	338	283	165
Private [2]	1	0	2	1	0	0	1	0	0
HOUSE OF REPRESENTATIVES									
Number of days	241	283	286	327	295	288	366	365	268
Number of hours	1,917	2,138	2,126	1,718	1,471	1,438	1,515	1,352	1,150
Number of hours per day	8.0	7.6	7.4	5.3	5.0	5.0	4.1	3.7	4.3
SENATE									
Number of days	297	374	349	323	292	333	386	379	301
Number of hours	2,250	2,364	2,495	2,032	2,003	1,855	2,181	1,910	1,726
Number of hours per day	7.6	6.3	7.1	6.3	6.9	5.6	5.7	5.1	5.7

[1] Laws on public matters that apply to all persons. [2] Laws designed to provide legal relief to specified persons or entities adversely affected by laws of general applicability. [3] Current session. Data for January 3, 2021 through July 31, 2022.

Source: U.S. Congress, *Résumé of Congressional Activity*, August 2022, and earlier reports. See also <www.senate.gov/legislative/ResumesofCongressionalActivity1947present.htm>.

Table 469. Congressional Bills Vetoed: 1961 to 2022

Period	President	Total vetoes	Regular vetoes	Pocket vetoes	Vetoes sustained	Bills passed over veto
1961 to 1963	John F. Kennedy	21	12	9	21	0
1963 to 1969	Lyndon B. Johnson	30	16	14	30	0
1969 to 1974	Richard M. Nixon	43	26	17	36	7
1974 to 1977	Gerald R. Ford	66	48	18	54	12
1977 to 1981	Jimmy Carter	31	13	18	29	2
1981 to 1989	Ronald W. Reagan	78	39	39	69	9
1989 to 1993	George H. W. Bush	44	29	15	43	1
1993 to 2001	William J. Clinton	37	36	1	35	2
2001 to 2009	George W. Bush	12	12	0	8	4
2009 to 2017	Barack Obama	12	12	0	11	1
2017 to 2021	Donald J. Trump	10	10	0	9	1
2021 to 2022 [1]	Joe Biden	0	0	0	0	0

[1] For the period January 20, 2021 to August 31, 2022.

Source: U.S. Senate, "Summary of Bills Vetoed," <www.senate.gov/reference/reference_index_subjects/Vetoes_vrd.htm>, accessed August 2022.

Table 470. Number of Governors by Political Party Affiliation: 1975 to 2022

[Reflects figures after inaugurations for each year. State governors only]

Year	Demo-cratic	Republi-can	Inde-pendent/other	Year	Demo-cratic	Republi-can	Inde-pendent/other	Year	Demo-cratic	Republi-can	Inde-pendent/other
1975........	36	13	1	2005........	22	28	–	2017........	16	33	1
1980........	31	19	–	2010........	26	24	–	2018........	16	33	1
1985........	34	16	–	2013........	20	30	–	2019........	23	27	–
1990........	29	21	–	2014........	21	29	–	2020........	24	26	–
1995........	19	30	1	2015........	18	31	1	2021........	23	27	–
2000........	18	30	2	2016........	18	31	1	2022........	22	28	–

– Represents zero.

Source: ProQuest research.

Table 471. Vote Cast for and Governor Elected by State: 2016 to 2020

[D = Democratic, R = Republican, I = Independent]

State	Current governor [1]	Year of election	Total vote [2]	Republican	Democratic	Percent leading party
Alabama............	Kay Ivey	2018	1,719,589	1,022,457	694,495	R-59.5
Alaska............	Mike Dunleavy	2018	283,134	145,631	125,739	R-51.4
Arizona............	Doug Ducey	2018	2,376,441	1,330,863	994,341	R-56.0
Arkansas............	Asa Hutchinson	2018	891,509	582,406	283,218	R-65.3
California............	Gavin Christopher Newsom	2018	12,464,235	4,742,825	7,721,410	D-61.9
Colorado [3]............	Jared Schutz Polis	2018	2,525,062	1,080,801	1,348,888	D-53.4
Connecticut [3]............	Ned Lamont	2018	1,406,803	650,138	694,510	D-50.7
Delaware............	John Carney Jr.	2020	492,635	190,312	292,903	D-59.5
Florida............	Ronald Dion DeSantis	2018	8,220,561	4,076,186	4,043,723	R-49.6
Georgia............	Brian P. Kemp	2018	3,939,328	1,978,408	1,923,685	R-50.2
Hawaii............	David Ige	2018	390,843	131,719	244,934	D-62.7
Idaho............	Brad Little	2018	605,131	361,661	231,081	R-59.8
Illinois............	J.B. Pritzker	2018	4,547,657	1,765,751	2,479,746	D-54.5
Indiana............	Eric Holcomb	2020	3,020,388	1,706,727	968,094	R-51.4
Iowa............	Kim Reynolds	2018	1,327,638	667,275	630,986	R-50.3
Kansas............	Laura Kelly	2018	1,055,566	453,645	506,727	D-48.0
Kentucky............	Andy Beshear	2019	1,446,123	707,754	709,890	D-49.1
Louisiana............	John Bel Edwards	2019	1,508,784	734,286	774,498	D-51.3
Maine............	Janet Trafon Mills	2018	630,667	272,311	320,962	D-50.9
Maryland............	Larry Hogan	2018	1,482,029	855,539	608,810	R-57.7
Massachusetts.....	Charlie Baker	2018	2,674,615	1,781,341	885,770	R-66.6
Michigan............	Gretchen Esther Whitmer	2018	4,250,585	1,859,534	2,266,193	D-53.3
Minnesota............	Timothy James Walz	2018	2,587,287	1,097,705	1,393,096	D-53.8
Mississippi............	Tate Reeves	2019	884,911	459,396	414,368	R-51.9
Missouri............	Michael Parson	2020	3,012,287	1,720,202	1,225,771	R-57.1
Montana............	Greg Gianforte	2020	603,608	328,548	250,860	R-54.4
Nebraska............	Pete Ricketts	2018	697,981	411,812	286,169	R-59.0
Nevada............	Steve Sisolak	2018	971,799	440,320	480,007	D-49.4
New Hampshire....	Chris Sununu	2020	793,260	516,609	264,639	R-65.1
New Jersey.........	Phil Murphy	2017	2,147,415	899,583	1,203,110	D-56.0
New Mexico........	Michelle Lujan Grisham	2018	696,459	298,091	398,368	D-57.2
New York [4]............	Kathleen Courtney Hochul [5]	2018	6,097,362	2,207,602	3,635,340	D-59.6
North Carolina.......	Roy Cooper	2020	5,502,778	2,586,605	2,834,790	D-51.5
North Dakota.......	Doug Burgum	2020	357,859	235,629	90,925	R-65.8
Ohio.................	Mike DeWine	2018	4,429,582	2,231,917	2,067,847	R-50.4
Oklahoma...........	Kevin Stitt	2018	1,186,385	644,579	500,973	R-54.3
Oregon..............	Kate Brown	2016	1,561,819	684,321	796,006	D-51.0
Pennsylvania........	Tom Wolf	2018	5,012,555	2,039,882	2,895,652	D-57.8
Rhode Island.......	Dan McKee	2018	376,401	139,932	198,122	D-52.6
South Carolina.....	Henry McMaster	2018	1,707,569	921,342	784,182	R-54.0
South Dakota.......	Kristi Noem	2018	338,715	172,706	161,171	R-51.0
Tennessee..........	Bill Lee	2018	2,243,294	1,336,106	864,863	R-59.6
Texas...............	Greg Abbott	2018	8,343,443	4,656,196	3,546,615	R-55.8
Utah................	Spencer Cox	2020	1,438,711	918,754	442,754	R-63.9
Vermont............	Phil Scott	2020	370,968	248,412	99,214	R-67.0
Virginia.............	Ralph Northam	2017	2,614,282	1,175,731	1,409,175	D-53.9
Washington.........	Jay Inslee	2020	4,056,454	1,749,066	2,294,243	D-56.6
West Virginia.......	Jim Justice [6]	2020	768,804	497,944	237,024	R-64.8
Wisconsin..........	Anthony Steven Evers	2018	2,672,342	1,295,080	1,324,307	D-49.6
Wyoming............	Mark Gordon	2018	203,238	136,412	55,965	R-67.1

[1] As of March 2021. [2] Includes minor party and scattered votes. [3] In Connecticut, Republican vote total includes 25,388 votes from the Independent party. Democratic vote total includes 17,861 from the Working Families Party. [4] In New York, Democratic vote includes 68,713 from the Independence Party, 27,733 from the Women's Equality Party, and 114,478 from the Working Families Party. The Republican vote includes 253,624 from the Conservative Party and 27,493 from the Reform Party. [5] New York Lt. Gov. Kathleen Hochul was sworn in as governor in Aug. 2021 after Andrew Cuomo resigned. [6] In August 2017, West Virginia Gov. Jim Justice switched from the Democratic party to the Republican party.

Source: The Council of State Governments, Lexington, KY, The Book of the States 2021 ©, and ProQuest research.

Table 472. Political Party Control of State Legislatures by Party: 1990 to 2022

[As of beginning of year. Nebraska has a nonpartisan legislature]

Year	Legislatures under—			Year	Legislatures under—			Year	Legislatures under—		
	Demo-cratic control	Split control or tie	Repub-lican control		Demo-cratic control	Split control or tie	Repub-lican control		Demo-cratic control	Split control or tie	Repub-lican control
1990......	29	11	9	2009......	27	8	14	2016......	11	8	30
1995......	18	12	19	2010......	27	8	14	2017......	14	3	32
2000......	16	15	18	2011......	16	8	25	2018......	13	4	32
2005......	19	10	20	2012......	15	7	27	2019......	18	1	30
2006......	19	10	20	2013......	19	4	26	2020......	19	1	29
2007......	22	12	15	2014......	19	3	27	2021......	18	1	30
2008......	23	14	12	2015......	11	8	30	2022......	17	2	30

Source: National Conference of State Legislatures, Denver, CO, *State & Legislative Partisan Composition* ©, November 2021 and earlier reports. See also <ncsl.org>.

Table 473. Composition of State Legislatures by Political Party Affiliation: 2020 and 2021

[2020 data as of February; 2021 data as of April. Figures reflect immediate results of elections, including holdover members in state houses which do not have all of their members running for reelection. Dem. = Democrat, Rep. = Republican, Vac. = Vacancies. In general, Lower House refers to body consisting of state representatives and Upper House of state senators]

State	2020								2021							
	Lower house				Upper house				Lower house				Upper house			
	Dem.	Rep.	Other	Vac.	Dem.	Rep.	Other	Vac.	Dem.	Rep.	Other	Vac.	Dem.	Rep.	Other	Vac.
US.........	2,582	2,775	32	22	859	1,058	1	5	2,450	2,917	30	14	852	1,057	6	8
AL [2]......	28	77	–	–	8	27	–	–	28	75	–	2	8	26	–	1
AK [1]......	14	22	3	1	7	13	–	–	15	21	4	–	7	13	–	–
AZ [3]......	29	31	–	–	13	17	–	–	29	31	–	–	14	16	–	–
AR [1]......	23	75	–	2	9	26	–	–	22	78	–	–	7	28	–	–
CA [1]......	61	18	1	–	29	10	–	1	58	19	1	2	31	9	–	–
CO [1]......	41	24	–	–	19	16	–	–	41	24	–	–	20	15	–	–
CT [3]......	91	60	–	–	22	14	–	–	96	54	–	1	24	12	–	–
DE [1]......	26	15	–	–	12	9	–	–	26	15	–	–	14	7	–	–
FL [1]......	47	73	–	–	17	23	–	–	42	78	–	–	16	24	–	–
GA [3]......	75	105	–	–	20	35	–	1	77	103	–	–	22	34	–	–
HI [1]......	46	5	–	–	24	1	–	–	47	4	–	–	24	1	–	–
ID [3]......	14	56	–	–	7	28	–	–	12	58	–	–	7	28	–	–
IL [4]......	74	44	–	–	40	19	–	–	72	45	–	1	41	18	–	–
IN [1]......	33	67	–	–	10	40	–	–	29	71	–	–	11	39	–	–
IA [1]......	47	53	–	–	18	32	–	–	41	59	–	–	18	32	–	–
KS [1]......	41	84	–	–	11	29	–	–	39	86	–	–	11	29	–	–
KY [1]......	38	60	–	2	9	29	–	–	25	75	–	–	8	30	–	–
LA [2]......	35	68	2	–	12	27	–	–	35	67	2	1	12	27	–	–
ME [3]......	87	56	6	2	21	14	–	–	80	66	5	–	22	13	–	–
MD [2]......	98	42	–	1	32	15	–	–	99	42	–	–	32	15	–	–
MA [3]......	125	31	1	3	34	4	–	2	128	30	1	1	37	3	–	–
MI [1]......	52	58	–	–	16	22	–	–	52	58	–	–	16	20	–	2
MN [1]......	75	59	–	–	32	35	–	–	70	64	–	–	31	34	2	–
MS [2]......	45	75	2	–	16	36	–	–	46	75	1	–	16	36	–	–
MO [1]......	48	114	–	1	10	24	–	–	48	114	–	1	10	24	–	–
MT [1]......	43	57	–	–	20	30	–	–	33	67	–	–	19	31	–	–
NE [5]......	([5])	([5])	([5])	([5])	([5])	([5])	([5])	([5])	([5])	([5])	([5])	([5])	([5])	([5])	([5])	([5])
NV [1]......	28	13	–	1	13	8	–	–	26	16	–	–	12	9	–	–
NH [3]......	233	162	1	4	14	10	–	–	186	212	–	2	10	14	–	–
NJ [1]......	52	28	–	–	25	15	–	–	52	28	–	–	25	15	–	–
NM [1]......	46	24	–	–	26	16	–	–	45	24	1	–	27	15	–	–
NY [3]......	103	43	1	3	40	23	–	–	106	43	1	–	43	20	–	–
NC [3]......	55	65	–	–	21	29	–	–	51	69	–	–	22	28	–	–
ND [2]......	15	79	–	–	10	37	–	–	14	80	–	–	7	40	–	–
OH [1]......	38	61	–	–	9	24	–	–	35	64	–	–	8	25	–	–
OK [1]......	23	77	–	1	9	38	–	1	19	82	–	–	9	38	–	1
OR [1]......	38	22	–	–	18	12	–	–	37	23	–	–	18	11	1	–
PA [1]......	93	110	–	–	21	28	1	–	90	111	–	2	20	27	1	2
RI [3]......	65	8	1	1	33	5	–	–	65	10	–	–	33	5	–	–
SC [1]......	44	80	–	–	19	27	–	–	43	81	–	–	16	30	–	–
SD [3]......	11	59	–	–	5	30	–	–	8	62	–	–	3	32	–	–
TN [1]......	26	73	–	–	5	28	–	–	26	73	–	–	6	27	–	–
TX [1]......	67	83	–	–	12	19	–	–	68	82	–	–	13	18	–	–
UT [1]......	16	59	–	–	6	23	–	–	17	58	–	–	6	23	–	–
VT [3]......	95	43	12	–	24	6	–	–	92	46	12	–	21	7	2	–
VA [1]......	55	45	–	–	21	19	–	–	55	45	–	–	21	18	–	1
WA [1]......	57	41	–	–	29	20	–	–	57	41	–	–	29	20	–	–
WV [1]......	41	58	1	–	14	20	–	–	23	77	–	–	11	23	–	–
WI [1]......	36	63	–	–	14	19	–	–	38	60	–	1	12	20	–	1
WY [1]......	9	50	1	–	3	27	–	–	7	51	2	–	2	28	–	–

– Represents zero. [1] Upper House members serve 4–year terms and Lower House members serve 2–year terms. [2] Members of both houses serve 4–year terms. [3] Members of both houses serve 2–year terms. [4] In Illinois, members serve 4– and 2–year terms depending on district. [5] Nebraska is the only state to have a nonpartisan unicameral legislature and members serve 4–year terms. For 2020 and 2021, Nebraska legislature has 49 members.

Source: The Council of State Governments, Lexington, KY, *The Book of the States 2021*, and earlier reports ©. See also <www.csg.org>.

Table 474. Women Holding State Public Offices by Office and State: 2022

[As of June]

State	Total	Statewide elective executive office [1]	State legislature Total	State legislature Percent	State	Total	Statewide elective executive office [1]	State legislature Total	State legislature Percent
U.S............	**2,396**	**96**	**2,300**	**31.0**	MO.............	52	1	51	25.9
					MT.............	52	3	49	32.7
AL..............	25	2	23	16.4	NE.............	13	–	13	26.5
AK.............	18	–	18	30.0	NV.............	40	3	37	58.7
AZ.............	45	6	39	43.3	NH.............	149	–	149	35.1
AR.............	33	2	31	23.0	NJ.............	42	1	41	34.2
CA.............	42	4	38	31.7	NM.............	51	3	48	42.9
CO.............	47	2	45	45.0	NY.............	75	2	73	34.3
CT.............	67	3	64	34.2	NC.............	47	3	44	25.9
DE.............	23	4	19	30.6	ND.............	34	3	31	22.0
FL.............	59	3	56	35.0	OH.............	41	–	41	31.1
GA.............	81	1	80	33.9	OK.............	35	4	31	20.8
HI.............	27	–	27	35.5	OR.............	44	4	40	44.4
ID.............	36	3	33	31.4	PA.............	75	1	74	29.2
IL.............	75	2	73	41.2	RI.............	52	2	50	44.2
IN.............	39	4	35	23.3	SC.............	31	2	29	17.1
IA.............	44	1	43	28.7	SD.............	32	2	30	28.6
KS.............	52	2	50	30.3	TN.............	20	–	20	15.2
KY.............	40	2	38	27.5	TX.............	50	1	49	27.1
LA.............	28	–	28	19.4	UT.............	28	1	27	26.0
ME.............	82	1	81	43.5	VT.............	77	2	75	41.7
MD.............	82	–	82	43.6	VA.............	48	1	47	33.6
MA.............	64	4	60	30.0	WA.............	64	2	62	42.2
MI.............	56	3	53	35.8	WV.............	18	–	18	13.4
MN.............	74	2	72	35.8	WI.............	43	2	41	31.1
MS.............	27	1	26	14.9	WY.............	17	1	16	17.8

– Represents zero. [1] Excludes women elected to the judiciary, women appointed to state cabinet-level positions, women elected to executive posts by the legislature, and elected members of university Boards of Trustees or Boards of Education.

Source: Center for American Women and Politics, Eagleton Institute of Politics, Rutgers University, New Brunswick, NJ, "Women in Elective Office," <www.cawp.rutgers.edu/> ©, accessed June 2022.

Table 475. Hispanic Public Elected Officials by Office, 2010 to 2021, and by State, 2021

[As of January or November of year shown]

State	Total [1]	State executives and legislators [2]	County and municipal officials	Judicial and law enforcement	Education and school boards	State	Total [1]	State executives and legislators [2]	County and municipal officials	Judicial and law enforcement	Education and school boards
2010........	5,763	275	2,270	874	2,072	MA......	57	8	28	1	20
2015........	6,124	349	2,334	860	2,342	MI......	18	4	7	4	3
2016........	6,176	347	2,388	859	2,344	MN......	20	6	4	8	2
2017........	6,600	377	2,638	879	2,473	MS......	0	0	0	0	0
2018........	6,749	378	2,733	890	2,496	MO......	3	1	1	0	1
2019........	6,832	389	2,775	882	2,535	MT......	0	0	0	0	0
2020........	6,883	384	2,768	903	2,593	NE......	5	2	1	1	1
						NV......	33	9	9	7	8
2021........	**7,087**	**401**	**2,853**	**913**	**2,668**	NH......	5	3	1	1	0
AL........	0	0	0	0	0	NJ......	169	12	94	1	62
AK........	1	0	1	0	0	NM......	649	52	318	101	138
AZ........	358	28	128	29	167	NY......	186	29	66	60	31
AR........	5	0	1	2	2	NC......	6	1	3	1	1
CA........	1,833	47	625	128	894	ND......	0	0	0	0	0
CO........	156	14	82	16	38	OH......	20	2	11	3	4
CT........	75	14	43	0	18	OK......	4	3	0	0	1
DE........	4	3	0	0	1	OR......	39	5	6	10	17
DC........	0	0	0	0	0	PA......	24	3	16	3	2
FL........	214	25	109	66	14	RI......	35	12	15	0	8
GA........	13	4	5	3	1	SC......	0	0	0	0	0
HI........	4	4	0	0	0	SD......	1	0	1	0	0
ID........	3	0	3	0	0	TN......	3	0	1	1	1
IL........	134	18	80	8	21	TX......	2,808	54	1,094	443	1,164
IN........	31	3	13	3	12	UT......	9	4	2	1	2
IA........	23	1	13	0	9	VT......	2	0	1	0	1
KS........	13	5	6	1	1	VA......	13	5	7	0	1
KY........	2	1	0	0	1	WA......	65	8	40	2	15
LA........	3	0	1	1	1	WV......	4	3	0	1	0
ME........	2	0	1	0	1	WI......	15	2	4	7	2
MD........	11	3	8	0	0	WY......	9	3	4	0	2

[1] Also includes special district officials, not shown separately. [2] Includes U.S. Senators and Representatives, not shown separately.

Source: National Association of Latino Elected and Appointed Officials (NALEO) Educational Fund, Washington, DC, *National Directory of Latino Elected Officials* ©, and earlier reports. See also <www.naleo.org>.

Table 476. Political Action Committees—Financial Activity Summary by Committee Type: 2015 to 2020

[In millions of dollars (4,046.3 represents $4,046,300,000). Covers financial activity during 2-year calendar period indicated]

Committee type	Receipts			Disbursements [1]			Contributions to candidates		
	2015 to 2016	2017 to 2018	2019 to 2020 [2]	2015 to 2016	2017 to 2018	2019 to 2020 [2]	2015 to 2016	2017 to 2018	2019 to 2020 [2]
Total..............................	4,046.3	4,674.2	13,227.9	3,973.3	4,554.1	12,947.1	444.0	465.6	448.8
Corporate............................	405.5	417.2	429.6	385.7	404.8	408.5	182.8	178.1	165.7
Labor................................	342.4	365.8	384.3	331.5	342.2	385.6	46.7	53.8	51.8
Trade................................	159.9	174.3	161.7	148.2	164.1	149.8	82.8	87.3	79.0
Membership........................	159.8	100.4	141.4	152.0	97.6	130.9	40.3	33.0	38.3
Cooperative........................	8.0	9.1	7.8	7.0	8.4	7.3	4.7	5.1	5.1
Corporation without stock.........	15.7	14.3	14.3	14.5	14.4	13.2	7.5	7.4	6.7
Nonconnected......................	2,954.9	3,593.0	12,088.8	2,934.3	3,522.5	11,851.7	79.2	100.8	102.1

[1] Comprises contributions to candidates, independent expenditures, and other disbursements. [2] See footnote 3, Table 478.

Source: U.S. Federal Election Commission, Campaign Finance Statistics, "Political Action Committee (PAC) Data Summary Tables," <www.fec.gov/campaign-finance-data/campaign-finance-statistics/>, accessed May 2021.

Table 477. Congressional Campaign Finances—Receipts and Disbursements: 2009 to 2020

[In millions of dollars (1,103.2 represents $1,103,200,000). Covers all campaign finance activity during 2-year calendar period indicated for primary, general, run-off, and special elections. Data have been adjusted to eliminate transfers between all committees within a campaign. For further information on legal limits of contributions, see Federal Election Campaign Act of 1971, as amended]

Item	House of Representatives					Senate				
	2009 to 2010	2011 to 2012	2015 to 2016	2017 to 2018	2019 to 2020 [3]	2009 to 2010	2011 to 2012	2015 to 2016	2017 to 2018	2019 to 2020 [3]
Total receipts [1]...............	1,103.2	1,136.5	1,049.8	1,740.8	1,959.3	757.2	742.3	594.5	1,033.3	2,046.1
Individual contributions.........	640.6	637.0	546.4	1,063.0	1,330.8	468.0	466.1	424.2	691.4	1,758.1
Contributions from PAC's......	326.2	351.0	354.5	406.1	390.2	87.6	80.9	92.8	84.8	86.5
Candidate contributions & loans...........................	109.6	108.2	107.0	165.5	123.4	149.6	167.3	31.6	188.4	69.5
Democrats.........................	510.3	486.8	476.4	1,034.5	1,026.8	314.7	307.9	313.4	571.5	1,206.8
Incumbents.....................	393.0	249.1	249.9	299.3	656.8	139.5	172.1	67.0	399.2	273.1
Challengers.....................	64.4	174.8	126.7	446.7	266.7	38.8	71.4	176.2	119.5	889.5
Open seats [2]..................	52.9	62.9	99.7	288.6	103.3	136.5	64.4	70.1	52.8	44.1
Republicans.......................	587.5	632.7	559.4	693.1	919.6	427.4	416.1	278.8	430.8	815.3
Incumbents.....................	231.7	436.2	406.7	494.5	498.7	109.5	77.8	201.3	80.4	656.2
Challengers.....................	266.0	125.7	51.5	61.6	292.1	148.9	143.1	29.1	295.0	107.7
Open seats [2]..................	89.8	70.7	101.2	137.0	128.7	169.1	195.3	48.5	55.5	51.4
Others.............................	5.4	17.0	14.0	13.1	12.9	15.0	18.3	2.3	30.9	24.0
Incumbents.....................	1.7	2.2	4.4	0.9	2.5	–	6.3	–	15.6	–
Challengers.....................	3.2	13.5	5.0	8.0	8.3	0.5	8.7	2.1	15.2	23.9
Open seats [2]..................	0.5	1.3	4.6	4.2	2.1	14.5	3.3	0.2	0.2	0.1
Total disbursements........	1,096.3	1,099.3	971.7	1,698.9	1,803.6	737.3	747.9	625.3	1,019.5	1,961.6
Democrats.........................	534.7	479.1	425.1	983.5	937.2	319.3	315.7	316.0	557.8	1,162.2
Republicans.......................	556.6	604.3	533.5	703.0	854.1	403.2	417.7	306.8	436.4	775.6
Others.............................	5.1	15.9	13.1	12.4	12.4	14.9	14.5	2.5	25.3	23.8

– Represents or rounds to zero. [1] Includes other types of receipts, not shown separately. [2] Elections in which an incumbent did not seek reelection. [3] See footnote 3, Table 478.

Source: U.S. Federal Election Commission, Campaign Finance Statistics, "Congressional Candidate Data Summary Tables," <www.fec.gov/campaign-finance-data/campaign-finance-statistics/>, accessed May 2021.

Table 478. Political Action Committees (PAC) Contributions to Congressional Campaigns by Type of Committee: 2017 to 2020

[In millions of dollars (383.9 represents $383,900,000). Covers amounts given to candidates in primary, general, run-off, and special elections during the 2-year calendar period indicated]

Type of committee	Total [1]	Democrats	Republicans	Incumbents	Challengers	Open seats [2]
HOUSE OF REPRESENTATIVES						
2017-2018.........................	383.9	167.7	215.1	328.9	24.5	30.5
2019-2020, total [3]......................	361.6	196.0	165.1	318.9	25.8	16.8
Corporate............................	132.9	63.5	69.3	128.7	1.7	2.5
Trade association [4].......................	97.4	48.0	49.4	89.2	4.0	4.2
Labor................................	46.6	40.9	5.6	39.7	4.5	2.4
Nonconnected [5]...........................	74.3	38.2	35.9	51.5	15.5	7.4
Cooperative........................	4.6	2.5	2.1	4.3	0.1	0.3
Corporation without stock..............	5.7	2.9	2.8	5.5	0.1	0.1
SENATE						
2017-2018.........................	81.5	47.8	32.4	60.5	12.1	8.9
2019-2020, total [3]......................	85.8	28.7	56.7	69.0	10.8	6.0
Corporate............................	32.8	7.3	25.5	30.3	0.8	1.7
Trade association [4].......................	19.6	5.0	14.6	16.7	1.3	1.6
Labor................................	5.1	4.4	0.6	2.6	2.1	0.4
Nonconnected [5]...........................	26.8	11.6	15.0	18.1	6.6	2.2
Cooperative........................	0.5	0.1	0.4	0.4	(Z)	0.1
Corporation without stock..............	0.9	0.3	0.7	0.9	(Z)	(Z)

Z represents less than $50,000. [1] Includes other parties, not shown separately. [2] Elections in which an incumbent did not seek reelection. [3] Due to COVID-19 related office closures, data excludes some reports filed on paper. [4] Includes membership organizations and health organizations. [5] Represents "ideological" groups as well as other issue groups not necessarily ideological in nature.

Source: U.S. Federal Election Commission, Campaign Finance Statistics, "Political Action Committees (PAC) Data Summary Tables," <www.fec.gov/campaign-finance-data/campaign-finance-statistics>, accessed May 2021.

Table 479. Presidential Campaign Receipts and Disbursements by Political Party: 1991 to 2020

[In millions of dollars (348.8 represents $348,800,000). Covers financial activity during 2-year calendar period indicated]

Item	1991 to 1992	1995 to 1996	1999 to 2000 [2]	2003 to 2004 [2]	2007 to 2008 [2]	2011 to 2012 [2]	2015 to 2016	2017 to 2018	2019 to 2020 [3]
RECEIPTS									
Total	**348.8**	**464.0**	**511.9**	**850.8**	**1,550.8**	**1,379.8**	**1,540.1**	**75.3**	**4,073.9**
Republican	115.4	296.4	172.2	362.4	219.6	483.5	673.3	67.6	748.9
Democrat	157.6	123.5	128.4	321.2	747.8	738.5	841.3	7.5	3,298.8
Other	75.8	44.2	26.7	(NA)	(NA)	4.0	25.5	0.2	26.3
DISBURSEMENTS [1]									
Total	**330.4**	**456.0**	**527.2**	**867.5**	**1,645.0**	**1,359.8**	**1,527.5**	**63.1**	**4,071.9**
Republican	111.4	294.7	186.5	355.0	239.7	483.1	667.5	55.9	757.3
Democrat	143.2	119.4	120.3	332.7	760.4	737.1	834.7	7.0	3,289.8
Other	75.7	41.9	(NA)	(NA)	(NA)	3.8	25.3	0.2	24.8

NA Not available. [1] Comprises operating expenses, transfers to other committees, and other disbursements. [2] Party data reflect only the candidate who stood in the general election. [3] Due to COVID-19 related office closures, data excludes some reports filed on paper.

Source: U.S. Federal Election Commission, Campaign Finance Statistics, "Presidential Candidate Data Summary Tables," <www.fec.gov/campaign-finance-data/campaign-finance-statistics/>, accessed February 2022.

State and Local Government Finances and Employment

This section presents data on revenues, expenditures, debt, and employment of state and local governments. Nationwide statistics relating to state and local governments, their numbers, finances, and employment are compiled primarily by the U.S. Census Bureau through a program of censuses and surveys. Every fifth year (for years ending in "2" and "7"), the Census Bureau conducts a census of governments involving collection of data for all governmental units in the United States. In addition, the Census Bureau conducts annual surveys which cover all the state governments and a sample of local governments.

Annually, the Census Bureau releases information on financial data for the federal government, nationwide totals for state and local governments, and state-local data by states. Also released annually is a series on state, city, county, and school finances and on state and local public employment. There is also a series of quarterly data releases covering tax revenue and finances of major public employee retirement systems.

Basic information for Census Bureau statistics on governments is obtained by mail canvass from state and local officials; however, financial data for each state government and for many of the large local governments are compiled from their official records and reports by Census Bureau personnel. In over two-thirds of the states, all or part of local government financial data are obtained through central collection arrangements with state governments. Financial data on the federal government's aid to state and local areas are primarily based on the *Budget of the United States Government* published by the Office of Management and Budget.

Governmental units—The governmental structure of the United States includes, in addition to the federal government and the states, thousands of local governments—counties, municipalities, townships, school districts, and many "special districts." In 2017, 90,075 local governments were identified by the census of governments (see table 480 and table 481). As defined by the census, governmental units include all agencies or bodies having an organized existence, governmental character, and substantial autonomy. While most of these governments can impose taxes, many of the special districts—such as independent public housing authorities and numerous local irrigation, power, and other types of districts—are financed from rentals, charges for services, benefit assessments, grants from other governments, and other non-tax sources. The count of governments excludes semi-autonomous agencies through which states, cities, and counties sometimes provide for certain functions—for example, "dependent" school systems, state institutions of higher education, and certain other "authorities" and special agencies which are under the administrative or fiscal control of an established governmental unit.

Finances—The financial statistics relate to government fiscal years ending June 30 or at some date within the 12 previous months. The following governments are exceptions and are included as though they were part of the June 30 group: the state governments of Alabama and Michigan and the city government of The District of Columbia, with fiscal years ending September 30; the state government of Texas ending August 31; and New York State ending its fiscal year on March 31. The federal government ended the fiscal year June 30 until 1976 when its fiscal year, by an act of Congress, was revised to extend from October 1 to September 30. A 3-month quarter (July 1 to September 30, 1976) bridged the transition.

Nationwide government finance statistics have been classified and presented in terms of uniform concepts and categories, rather than according to the highly diverse terminology, organization, and fund structure utilized by individual governments.

Statistics on governmental finances distinguish among general government, utilities, liquor stores, and insurance trusts. *General government* comprises all activities except utilities, liquor stores, and insurance trusts. *Utilities* include government water supply, electric light and power, gas supply, and transit systems. *Liquor stores* are operated by 17 states and by local governments in 5 states. *Insurance trusts* relate to employee retirement, unemployment compensation, and other social insurance systems administered by the federal, state, and local governments.

Data for cities or counties relate only to municipal or county and their dependent agencies and do not include amounts for other local governments in the same geographic location. Therefore, expenditure figures for "education" do not include spending by the separate school districts which administer public schools within most municipal or county areas. Variations in the assignment of governmental responsibility for public assistance, health, hospitals, public housing, and other functions to a lesser degree also have an important effect upon reported amounts of city or county expenditure, revenue, and debt.

Employment and payrolls—These data are based mainly on mail canvassing of state and local governments. Payroll includes all salaries, wages, and individual fee payments for the month specified. Employment relates to all persons on governmental payrolls during a pay period of the month covered, including paid officials, temporary help, and (unless otherwise specified) part-time as well as full-time personnel. Effective with the 1997 Census of Governments, the reference period for measuring government employment was changed from October of the calendar year to March of the calendar year. As a result, there was no annual survey of government employment covering the October 1996 period. The prior reference month of October was used from 1958 to 1995. Figures shown for individual governments cover major dependent agencies such as institutions of higher education, as well as the basic central departments and agencies of the government.

Statistical reliability—For a discussion of statistical collection and estimation, sampling procedures, and measures of statistical reliability applicable to Census Bureau data, see Appendix III.

Table 480. Number of Governmental Units by Type: 1972 to 2017

Type of government	1972	1977	1982	1987	1992	1997	2002	2007	2012	2017
Total units	**78,269**	**79,913**	**81,831**	**83,237**	**85,006**	**87,504**	**87,576**	**89,527**	**90,107**	**90,126**
U.S. government	1	1	1	1	1	1	1	1	1	1
State governments	50	50	50	50	50	50	50	50	50	50
Local governments	78,218	79,862	81,780	83,186	84,955	87,453	87,525	89,476	90,056	90,075
County	3,044	3,042	3,041	3,042	3,043	3,043	3,034	3,033	3,031	3,031
Municipal	18,517	18,862	19,076	19,200	19,279	19,372	19,429	19,492	19,519	19,495
Township and town	16,991	16,822	16,734	16,691	16,656	16,629	16,504	16,519	16,360	16,253
School district	15,781	15,174	14,851	14,721	14,422	13,726	13,506	13,051	12,880	12,754
Special district	23,885	25,962	28,078	29,532	31,555	34,683	35,052	37,381	38,266	38,542

Source: U.S. Census Bureau, Census of Governments, "2017 Census of Governments Organization Tables," <www.census.gov/programs-surveys/cog.html>, accessed May 2019.

Table 481. Number of Local Governments by Type—States: 2017

[Governments in existence in January. Excludes a few counties and numerous townships and incorporated places existing as areas for which statistics can be presented as to population and other subjects, but lacking any separate organized county, township, or municipal government. See Appendix III]

State	All governmental units [1]	County	Municipal	Township [1]	School district	Special district Total [2]	Natural resources	Fire protection	Housing [3]
United States	**90,075**	**3,031**	**19,495**	**16,253**	**12,754**	**38,542**	**7,253**	**5,975**	**3,344**
Alabama	1,195	67	461	–	137	530	68	13	147
Alaska	179	15	149	–	–	15	–	–	14
Arizona	658	15	91	–	242	310	84	151	–
Arkansas	1,541	75	501	–	235	730	258	73	117
California	4,444	57	482	–	1,011	2,894	484	357	64
Colorado	3,141	62	271	–	180	2,628	168	261	91
Connecticut	625	–	30	149	17	429	1	65	113
Delaware	334	3	57	–	19	255	233	–	4
District of Columbia	2	–	1	–	–	1	–	–	–
Florida	1,712	66	412	–	95	1,139	119	54	92
Georgia	1,380	152	537	–	180	511	37	–	191
Hawaii	21	3	1	–	–	17	16	–	–
Idaho	1,170	44	200	–	118	808	177	156	11
Illinois	6,918	102	1,297	1,429	886	3,204	1,014	838	113
Indiana	2,638	91	567	1,004	289	687	142	2	64
Iowa	1,941	99	943	–	348	551	238	60	27
Kansas	3,792	103	625	1,265	306	1,493	256	1	177
Kentucky	1,322	118	417	–	173	614	126	151	19
Louisiana	516	60	304	–	69	83	8	2	–
Maine	834	16	23	465	98	232	17	–	30
Maryland	344	23	157	–	–	164	128	–	20
Massachusetts	858	5	53	298	85	417	17	11	250
Michigan	2,863	83	533	1,240	571	436	77	24	–
Minnesota	3,643	87	853	1,780	333	590	144	9	153
Mississippi	969	82	298	–	157	432	233	30	52
Missouri	3,768	114	944	283	530	1,897	323	401	135
Montana	1,226	54	129	–	313	730	132	214	13
Nebraska	2,538	93	529	366	269	1,281	87	413	163
Nevada	189	16	19	–	17	137	34	15	3
New Hampshire	541	10	13	221	168	129	11	14	21
New Jersey	1,338	21	324	241	519	233	15	183	–
New Mexico	1013	33	105	–	96	779	561	–	–
New York	3,450	57	601	929	678	1,185	1	885	–
North Carolina	970	100	552	–	–	318	136	–	93
North Dakota	2,664	53	357	1,308	179	767	74	275	38
Ohio	3,897	88	931	1,308	666	904	103	116	81
Oklahoma	1,830	77	590	–	542	621	104	27	128
Oregon	1,510	36	240	–	230	1,004	186	265	19
Pennsylvania	4,830	66	1,013	1,546	514	1,691	5	–	90
Rhode Island	129	–	8	31	4	86	5	31	26
South Carolina	671	46	270	–	81	274	45	64	42
South Dakota	1,916	66	311	902	150	487	105	80	1
Tennessee	906	92	345	–	14	455	105	1	93
Texas	5,343	254	1,218	–	1,073	2,798	435	267	384
Utah	619	29	250	–	41	299	79	12	19
Vermont	729	14	42	237	277	159	14	16	8
Virginia	517	95	228	–	1	193	47	–	–
Washington	1,900	39	281	–	295	1,285	181	368	43
West Virginia	651	55	232	–	55	309	14	–	35
Wisconsin	3,096	72	601	1,251	438	734	272	1	160
Wyoming	794	23	99	–	55	617	134	69	–

– Represents zero. [1] Includes town governments in the six New England States and in Minnesota, New York, and Wisconsin. [2] Includes other special districts not shown separately. [3] Includes community development.

Source: U.S. Census Bureau, Census of Governments, "2017 Census of Governments Organization Tables," <www.census.gov/programs-surveys/cog.html>, accessed May 2019.

Table 482. State and Local Government Current Receipts and Expenditures in the National Income and Product Accounts: 1990 to 2021

[In billions of dollars (730.1 represents $730,100,000,000). For explanation of national income, see text, Section 13. Minus sign (-) indicates net loss]

Item	1990	2000	2010	2015	2017	2018	2019	2020	2021
Current receipts...............	**730.1**	**1,304.3**	**1,993.1**	**2,372.6**	**2,517.6**	**2,650.6**	**2,793.1**	**3,096.6**	**3,519.4**
Current tax receipts....................	519.1	893.2	1,306.4	1,598.4	1,724.7	1,818.4	1,927.0	1,963.6	2,159.6
Personal current taxes....................	122.6	236.7	294.1	407.4	435.4	459.8	496.5	515.9	595.2
Income taxes........................	109.6	217.4	265.8	374.5	399.8	421.8	457.1	476.1	554.2
Other..............................	13.0	19.4	28.3	32.9	35.6	38.0	39.4	39.8	41.0
Taxes on production and imports.........	374.1	621.3	966.3	1,134.8	1,234.7	1,298.1	1,357.6	1,376.6	1,467.4
Sales taxes........................	125.6	221.4	295.1	374.2	405.6	426.9	443.9	448.9	499.5
Excise taxes........................	58.7	95.5	154.8	181.3	196.0	208.7	205.2	202.7	215.1
Property taxes........................	161.5	254.7	438.6	490.4	536.0	555.1	599.6	615.3	632.8
Other..............................	28.2	49.8	77.8	89.0	97.1	107.4	108.9	109.8	119.9
Taxes on corporate income.............	22.5	35.2	46.1	56.2	54.6	60.5	72.9	71.0	97.0
Contributions for government social insurance........................	10.0	10.8	17.8	19.2	19.8	20.4	20.4	19.9	22.1
Income receipts on assets.................	68.5	94.4	82.2	81.5	88.2	94.3	96.8	96.4	98.5
Interest receipts.....................	64.1	86.8	67.8	64.9	71.4	77.4	78.2	76.8	78.4
Dividends..........................	0.2	1.4	3.0	5.4	5.9	6.1	6.6	6.3	6.5
Rents and royalties...................	4.2	6.3	11.4	11.2	10.9	10.9	12.0	13.3	13.6
Current transfer receipts....................	126.4	299.7	604.4	675.5	692.4	725.4	759.6	1,033.5	1,250.9
Federal grants-in-aid.................	104.4	233.1	505.2	533.1	560.5	582.5	609.2	880.5	1,093.8
From business (net).....................	7.1	28.6	40.3	65.9	51.3	55.3	57.6	59.1	61.3
From persons........................	14.9	38.0	58.8	75.9	80.6	86.2	91.4	93.7	95.4
From the rest of the world..............	(NA)	–	–	0.6	0.2	1.5	1.4	0.2	0.5
Current surplus of government enterprises.....................	6.1	6.1	-17.7	-2.0	-7.6	-8.0	-10.7	-16.8	-11.7
Current expenditures...................	**766.3**	**1,345.0**	**2,300.6**	**2,588.4**	**2,748.1**	**2,846.4**	**2,942.1**	**3,020.5**	**3,242.3**
Consumption expenditures.................	544.0	961.9	1,508.1	1,653.8	1,748.0	1,830.0	1,876.5	1,916.5	2,045.4
Government social benefit payments to persons........................	127.7	271.4	523.9	665.3	708.8	729.7	758.7	808.3	902.0
Interest payments.....................	94.3	111.1	267.0	268.7	290.8	286.1	306.2	295.0	291.8
Subsidies........................	0.4	0.5	1.6	0.5	0.6	0.6	0.6	0.6	3.1
Net state and local government saving...................	**-36.2**	**-40.6**	**-307.5**	**-215.8**	**-230.6**	**-195.8**	**-149.0**	**76.1**	**277.1**
Social insurance funds.....................	2.0	2.0	0.9	3.7	5.4	5.5	4.5	3.4	5.0
Other..............................	-38.2	-42.6	-308.4	-219.5	-236.0	-201.2	-153.6	72.8	272.1

NA Not available. – Represents zero.

Source: U.S. Bureau of Economic Analysis, National Income and Product Accounts Tables, "Table 3.3. State and Local Government Current Receipts and Expenditures," <www.bea.gov/itable/>, accessed June 2022.

Table 483. Federal Grants–in–Aid to State and Local Governments: 1990 to 2022

[135,325 represents $135,325,000,000, except as indicated. For fiscal year ending September 30. Minus sign (-) indicates decrease]

Year	Current dollars						Constant (2012) dollars	
	Total grants (mil. dol.)	Annual percent change [1]	Grants to individuals		Grants as percent of—		Total grants (bil. dol.)	Annual percent change [1]
			Total (mil. dol.)	Percent of total grants	Federal outlays	Gross domestic product		
1990...............	135,325	11.0	77,431	57.2	10.8	2.3	239.1	5.9
1995...............	224,991	6.8	145,652	64.7	14.8	3.0	339.1	3.9
2000...............	285,874	6.7	186,534	65.3	16.0	2.8	389.6	3.8
2001...............	318,542	11.4	208,008	65.3	17.1	3.0	422.8	8.5
2002...............	352,895	10.8	231,854	65.7	17.5	3.3	461.2	9.1
2003...............	388,542	10.1	251,235	64.7	18.0	3.4	496.7	7.7
2004...............	407,512	4.9	267,046	65.5	17.8	3.4	506.0	1.9
2005...............	428,018	5.0	278,764	65.1	17.3	3.3	511.4	1.1
2006...............	434,099	1.4	277,559	63.9	16.3	3.2	499.7	-2.3
2007...............	443,797	2.2	289,460	65.2	16.3	3.1	493.6	-1.2
2008...............	461,317	3.9	306,123	66.4	15.5	3.1	493.1	-0.1
2009...............	537,991	16.6	362,031	67.3	15.3	3.7	573.0	16.2
2010...............	608,390	13.1	391,427	64.3	17.6	4.1	637.5	11.3
2011...............	606,770	-0.3	392,713	64.7	16.8	3.9	620.7	-2.6
2012...............	544,573	-10.3	364,095	66.9	15.4	3.4	544.6	-12.3
2013...............	546,178	0.3	379,008	69.4	15.8	3.3	536.3	-1.5
2014...............	576,978	5.6	412,466	71.5	16.5	3.3	556.8	3.8
2015...............	624,357	8.2	463,392	74.2	16.9	3.5	599.4	7.7
2016...............	660,836	5.8	495,711	75.0	17.2	3.6	630.8	5.2
2017...............	674,712	2.1	507,976	75.3	16.9	3.5	632.9	0.3
2018...............	696,507	3.2	525,813	75.5	17.0	3.4	637.9	0.8
2019...............	721,140	3.5	549,313	76.2	16.2	3.4	648.6	1.7
2020...............	829,093	15.0	608,628	73.4	12.7	4.0	734.8	13.3
2021...............	1,245,280	50.2	689,771	55.4	18.3	5.6	1,060.6	44.3
2022, estimate.....	1,229,092	-1.3	759,434	61.8	21.0	5.1	995.8	-6.1

[1] Average annual percent change from previous year.

Source: U.S. Office of Management and Budget, *Budget of the U.S. Government, Fiscal Year 2023: Historical Tables*, March 2022. See also <www.whitehouse.gov/omb/budget>.

Table 484. Federal Outlays for Grants to State and Local Governments—Selected Agencies and Programs: 2000 to 2023

[In millions of dollars (285,874 represents $285,874,000,000). For fiscal year ending September 30. Includes trust funds]

Agency and program	2000	2010	2015	2016	2017	2018	2019	2020	2021	2022 est.	2023 est.
Total outlays for grants	**285,874**	**608,390**	**624,357**	**660,836**	**674,712**	**696,507**	**721,140**	**829,093**	**1,245,280**	**1,229,092**	**1,037,109**
Energy	433	2,656	577	764	774	771	819	824	841	1,111	2,874
Natural resources and environment	4,595	9,132	7,043	6,702	6,155	6,394	6,698	7,211	6,715	8,077	13,477
Environmental Protection Agency[1]	3,490	6,883	4,570	4,270	3,750	3,862	4,103	4,351	4,037	4,038	8,649
Agriculture	724	843	707	806	763	815	828	804	909	890	1,288
Transportation	32,222	60,981	60,835	63,876	64,795	64,836	65,637	69,309	86,603	101,225	105,225
Grants for airports[2]	1,624	3,156	2,988	2,963	3,129	3,036	3,303	3,289	8,663	5,823	4,565
Federal-aid highways[1]	24,711	30,385	41,205	43,035	43,236	43,305	43,768	46,327	43,252	46,389	52,422
Urban mass transportation[1]	5,262	12,939	11,784	12,271	12,124	12,608	13,109	13,038	24,220	34,130	26,159
Community and regional development	8,665	18,908	14,357	15,301	14,797	19,089	15,565	52,499	52,287	53,523	48,205
Rural Community Advancement Program	479	–	–	–	–	–	–	–	–	–	–
Community Development Fund	4,955	7,043	6,548	6,016	5,616	5,889	5,178	5,235	6,759	10,768	10,942
Homeland Security	2,439	8,483	5,924	7,951	7,758	12,038	8,988	45,613	43,624	39,286	32,297
Federal assistance, FEMA	–	–	–	–	84	516	1,350	2,023	2,228	3,016	3,147
State and local programs	192	3,337	2,918	2,683	2,119	1,704	903	273	62	50	–
Operations and support, FEMA	13	–	–	–	–	–	–	–	–	–	–
Natural predisaster mitigation grants	–	–	–	–	–	–	–	–	–	–	–
Disaster relief fund	2,234	5,141	2,919	5,155	5,348	9,715	6,735	43,317	41,334	36,213	29,073
Education, training, employment, social services	36,672	97,586	60,527	60,867	61,553	60,591	63,106	67,890	89,905	117,193	84,246
Education for the disadvantaged[3]	8,511	19,515	15,199	15,570	16,186	15,277	16,203	15,810	16,084	19,623	17,884
School improvement programs	2,394	5,184	4,138	4,224	4,295	4,060	4,616	4,591	4,622	6,903	5,183
Special education	4,696	17,075	12,077	12,357	12,479	12,753	12,978	12,741	12,533	18,366	14,336
Social Services block grant	1,827	2,035	1,832	1,780	1,661	1,587	1,646	1,727	1,655	1,636	1,627
Children and family services programs	5,843	10,473	9,608	10,026	10,232	10,651	11,240	11,892	13,021	14,624	15,100
Training and employment services	2,957	4,592	2,639	2,673	2,783	2,724	2,684	2,782	2,882	3,887	3,182
Health	124,843	290,168	368,026	396,666	406,946	421,117	442,324	493,400	571,967	617,575	585,561
Substance abuse and mental health services[4]	1,931	2,846	2,671	2,927	2,903	3,258	3,679	4,322	4,892	6,597	8,687
Grants to states for Medicaid[4]	117,921	272,771	349,762	368,280	374,682	389,157	409,421	458,468	520,588	561,838	535,893
State children's health insurance fund[4]	1,220	7,887	9,233	14,305	16,224	17,282	17,689	16,880	16,093	16,613	15,938
Income security	68,653	115,156	101,082	104,769	107,400	110,649	112,566	118,222	177,820	195,108	166,947
Supplemental Nutrition Assistance Program (SNAP) (formerly Food Stamp Program)[4]	3,508	5,739	5,100	6,406	6,954	7,485	7,100	8,006	12,268	10,717	10,848
Child nutrition programs[4]	9,060	16,259	20,999	21,952	22,445	22,803	23,247	22,709	25,744	30,771	28,265
Temporary Assistance for Needy Families (TANF)[4]	15,464	17,513	15,940	15,620	15,972	16,414	15,493	16,551	15,380	17,034	16,514
Veterans benefits and services[4]	434	836	1,821	1,829	1,992	2,061	2,050	2,979	2,896	2,512	3,308
Administration of justice	5,263	5,086	3,664	3,536	3,973	4,195	5,161	9,368	5,467	10,063	8,350

– Represents zero. [1] Grants include trust funds. [2] Trust funds. [3] Formerly Accelerating Achievement and Ensuring Equity. [4] Includes grants for payments to individuals.

Source: U.S. Office of Management and Budget, *Budget of the U.S. Government, Fiscal Year 2023: Historical Tables*, March 2022. See also <www.whitehouse.gov/omb/budget>.

Table 485. State and Local Governments—Summary of Finances: 2000 to 2020

[In millions of dollars (1,942,328 represents $1,942,328,000,000). For fiscal year ending in year shown; see text, this section. Local government amounts are estimates subject to sampling variation; see Appendix III and source]

Item	2000	2005	2010	2015	2019	2020
Revenue [1]	**1,942,328**	**2,528,546**	**3,180,023**	**3,416,065**	**4,074,321**	**4,278,593**
From federal government	**291,950**	**438,558**	**623,801**	**658,012**	**761,438**	**911,218**
From state and local sources	**1,650,379**	**2,089,988**	**2,556,222**	**2,758,053**	**3,312,882**	**3,367,375**
General, net intergovernmental	1,249,373	1,587,476	1,887,045	2,262,308	2,704,931	2,713,241
Taxes	872,351	1,098,513	1,278,847	1,563,701	1,863,758	1,861,618
Property	249,178	335,779	443,947	484,251	577,612	599,990
Sales and gross receipts	309,290	384,266	435,571	544,359	643,722	650,980
Individual income	211,661	242,273	261,510	368,862	446,723	424,769
Corporation net income	36,059	43,256	44,108	57,130	67,885	60,620
Other	66,164	92,939	93,710	109,100	127,816	125,260
Charges and miscellaneous	377,022	488,963	608,198	698,607	841,173	851,624
Utility and liquor stores	89,546	119,608	154,758	175,655	190,897	192,143
Water supply system	30,515	37,378	49,327	61,157	72,411	76,071
Electric power system	42,436	59,157	76,492	81,250	83,902	81,776
Gas supply system	3,954	6,937	8,219	7,478	6,755	6,466
Transit system	8,049	10,146	13,003	16,359	17,189	16,504
Liquor stores	4,592	5,990	7,716	9,412	10,640	11,327
Insurance trust revenue [2]	311,460	382,904	514,420	320,090	417,054	461,990
Unemployment compensation	23,366	35,367	75,191	49,303	37,202	44,249
Employee retirement	273,881	316,576	416,536	247,486	355,177	392,118
Direct expenditure	**1,742,914**	**2,363,696**	**3,110,833**	**3,402,229**	**3,978,545**	**4,227,229**
By character and object:						
Current operation	1,288,746	1,760,283	2,228,794	2,561,396	2,996,411	3,131,136
Capital outlay	217,063	278,063	355,437	336,088	413,025	425,006
Construction	161,694	218,691	284,213	271,190	333,102	343,492
Equipment, land, and existing structures	55,369	59,372	71,224	64,898	79,923	81,514
Assistance and subsidies	31,375	37,755	47,636	57,332	66,494	71,736
Interest on debt (general and utility)	80,499	91,859	119,939	122,305	129,708	130,709
Insurance benefits and repayments	125,230	195,735	359,027	325,109	372,908	468,643
Expenditure for salaries and wages [3]	548,796	694,583	844,650	900,861	1,034,940	1,075,072
By function:						
Direct general expenditure [2]	1,502,768	2,007,490	2,537,892	2,841,079	3,348,350	3,494,137
Education [2]	521,612	688,314	860,118	934,353	1,092,416	1,131,609
Higher education	134,352	182,003	243,515	273,935	311,456	320,820
Elementary and secondary	365,181	473,843	573,641	609,926	718,263	742,450
Public welfare	233,350	360,730	456,200	613,502	745,838	791,216
Hospitals	75,976	103,555	145,902	170,198	211,480	222,808
Health	51,366	66,637	81,383	91,810	112,441	122,201
Highways	101,336	126,350	155,912	171,084	202,562	204,258
Police protection	56,798	74,131	95,772	104,807	123,279	128,833
Fire protection	23,102	30,830	41,335	45,967	55,249	58,000
Natural resources	20,235	23,519	28,433	28,560	35,388	35,893
Parks and recreation	25,038	31,925	40,247	39,678	49,050	51,335
Housing and community development	26,590	40,014	53,923	49,754	57,235	59,188
Sanitation and sewerage	45,261	57,940	75,620	75,830	90,438	92,850
Financial administration	29,300	36,695	40,241	43,117	49,921	50,746
Interest on general debt [4]	69,814	81,122	105,715	105,613	113,477	114,045
Utility and liquor stores [4]	114,916	160,470	213,914	236,041	257,288	264,449
Water supply system	35,789	45,695	60,655	66,905	78,881	80,453
Electric power system	39,719	58,612	78,478	79,045	79,996	78,524
Gas supply system	3,724	7,075	8,273	7,457	7,661	6,390
Transit system	31,883	44,203	60,149	74,947	81,937	89,760
Liquor stores	3,801	4,885	6,359	7,687	8,812	9,323
Insurance trust expenditure [2]	125,230	195,735	359,027	325,109	372,908	468,643
Unemployment compensation	18,648	29,849	135,367	33,352	27,080	110,620
Employee retirement	95,679	145,796	204,803	275,406	330,850	341,874
Debt outstanding, year end	**1,451,815**	**2,085,026**	**2,844,190**	**2,988,463**	**3,191,792**	**3,267,238**
Short-term	24,291	30,758	45,088	34,621	35,693	40,262
Long-term	1,427,524	2,054,268	2,799,101	2,953,842	3,156,099	3,226,977
Long-term debt:						
Issued	184,831	323,739	398,962	362,594	347,455	428,385
Retired	121,897	224,639	275,810	370,232	291,004	436,420

[1] Aggregates exclude duplicative transactions between state and local governments; see source. [2] Includes amounts for other items not shown separately. [3] Included in items above. [4] Interest on utility debt included in "utility and liquor stores expenditure." For total interest on debt, see "Interest on debt (general and utility)."

Source: U.S. Census Bureau, Annual Survey of State and Local Government Finances, "Datasets & Tables," <www.census.gov/programs-surveys/gov-finances.html>, accessed August 2022.

Table 486. State and Local Governments—Revenue and Expenditures by Function: 2010 and 2020

[In millions of dollars (3,180,023 represents $3,180,023,000,000). For fiscal year ending in year shown; see text, this section. Local government amounts are estimates subject to sampling variation; see Appendix III and source]

Item	2010 Total	2010 State	2010 Local	2020 Total	2020 State	2020 Local
Revenue [1]...........................	**3,180,023**	**2,039,927**	**1,635,634**	**4,278,593**	**2,724,588**	**2,153,396**
Intergovernmental revenue [1]........................	623,801	575,372	543,967	911,218	845,556	665,052
Total revenue from own sources [1]...................	2,556,222	1,464,555	1,091,667	3,367,375	1,879,032	1,488,343
General revenue from own sources....................	1,887,045	991,835	895,210	2,713,241	1,461,316	1,251,925
Taxes [2]........................	1,278,847	705,929	572,917	1,861,618	1,057,323	804,294
Property........................	443,947	14,454	429,494	599,990	18,941	581,048
Sales and gross receipts....................	435,571	344,522	91,048	650,980	511,645	139,334
General sales.....................	288,499	224,314	64,185	443,441	340,592	102,849
Selective sales [2]...................	147,072	120,208	26,864	207,539	171,053	36,486
Motor fuel........................	37,922	36,632	1,291	52,725	51,111	1,614
Alcoholic beverages....................	6,021	5,511	511	7,530	6,815	715
Tobacco products....................	17,303	16,858	444	18,783	18,464	319
Public utilities....................	28,487	14,653	13,834	27,276	11,929	15,348
Individual income....................	261,510	236,987	24,524	424,769	385,630	39,139
Corporation income....................	44,108	38,006	6,102	60,620	52,169	8,451
Motor vehicle and operators' licenses....................	22,459	20,861	1,598	29,909	27,722	2,186
Charges and miscellaneous [2]................	608,198	285,906	322,293	851,624	403,993	447,631
Current charges [2]................	411,200	169,855	241,345	581,465	245,244	336,221
Education [2]................	121,138	94,530	26,608	135,418	113,968	21,450
Higher education....................	105,515	93,081	12,434	121,605	113,004	8,601
School lunch sales....................	6,600	34	6,567	4,240	25	4,215
Hospitals....................	113,339	42,938	70,401	187,921	81,702	106,219
Highways....................	12,001	6,885	5,116	21,923	12,480	9,443
Airports....................	18,067	1,327	16,740	26,149	1,749	24,400
Sea and inland port facilities....................	3,881	1,038	2,843	6,410	2,075	4,335
Natural resources....................	4,633	2,788	1,845	6,502	4,047	2,455
Parks and recreation....................	9,329	1,516	7,813	11,392	1,694	9,699
Housing and community development................	5,789	622	5,167	7,937	968	6,969
Sewerage....................	43,472	612	42,860	66,549	1,105	65,444
Solid waste management....................	15,738	420	15,317	20,445	232	20,213
Interest earnings....................	59,828	34,523	25,305	73,853	40,595	33,258
Special assessments....................	7,001	165	6,836	11,634	15	11,619
Sale of property....................	2,829	692	2,137	5,289	2,245	3,044
Utility and liquor store revenue....................	154,758	21,617	133,141	192,143	23,122	169,021
Insurance trust revenue....................	514,420	451,103	63,316	461,990	394,593	67,397
Expenditures [1]........................	**3,115,172**	**1,943,523**	**1,666,796**	**4,230,373**	**2,705,136**	**2,146,666**
By character and object:						
Current operation....................	2,228,794	934,322	1,294,473	3,131,136	1,439,526	1,691,610
Capital outlay....................	355,437	118,011	237,426	425,006	148,233	276,773
Construction....................	284,213	100,962	183,251	343,492	125,889	217,604
Equipment, land, and existing structures................	71,224	17,048	54,175	81,514	22,344	59,170
Assistance and subsidies....................	47,636	37,562	10,074	71,736	59,592	12,144
Interest on debt (general and utility)....................	119,939	47,351	72,588	130,709	46,702	84,007
Insurance benefits and repayments....................	359,027	320,721	38,306	468,643	404,088	64,555
Expenditure for salaries and wages [3]	844,650	244,952	599,698	1,075,072	310,142	764,931
Intergovernmental expenditure [1]................	4,339	485,557	13,929	3,144	606,996	17,576
Direct expenditure [1]....................	3,110,833	1,457,965	1,652,867	4,227,229	2,098,140	2,129,089
General expenditure [2]....................	2,537,892	1,108,137	1,429,755	3,494,137	1,652,908	1,841,229
Education [1]....................	860,118	253,758	606,360	1,131,609	350,500	781,109
Elementary and secondary education....................	573,641	7,832	565,809	742,450	7,373	735,077
Higher education....................	243,515	202,964	40,551	320,820	274,788	46,032
Libraries....................	10,991	449	10,542	13,227	442	12,785
Public welfare....................	456,200	403,572	52,627	791,216	728,641	62,575
Hospitals....................	145,902	58,752	87,150	222,808	101,253	121,555
Health....................	81,383	39,971	41,412	122,201	57,163	65,038
Highways....................	155,912	93,127	62,786	204,258	122,100	82,158
Police protection....................	95,772	12,376	83,395	128,833	17,131	111,702
Fire protection....................	41,335	–	41,335	58,000	–	58,000
Corrections....................	73,100	46,095	27,005	86,142	54,704	31,438
Natural resources....................	28,433	19,336	9,097	35,893	24,518	11,374
Parks and recreation....................	40,247	4,912	35,335	51,335	6,372	44,963
Housing and community development....................	53,923	11,487	42,437	59,188	9,494	49,694
Sewerage....................	51,991	1,118	50,873	63,987	1,411	62,575
Solid waste management....................	23,629	2,281	21,348	28,863	1,165	27,699
Governmental administration....................	126,719	52,147	74,572	157,923	66,932	90,991
Interest on general debt....................	105,715	45,260	60,455	114,045	44,110	69,935
Utility....................	207,555	23,864	183,691	255,127	33,204	221,922
Liquor store expenditure....................	6,359	5,244	1,115	9,323	7,940	1,383
Insurance trust expenditure....................	359,027	320,721	38,306	468,643	404,088	64,555

– Represents or rounds to zero. [1] Aggregates exclude duplicative transactions between levels of government; see source. [2] Includes data for other items not shown separately. [3] Included in items shown above.

Source: U.S. Census Bureau, Annual Survey of State and Local Government Finances, "Datasets & Tables," <www.census.gov/programs-surveys/gov-finances.html>, accessed August 2022.

Table 487. State and Local Governments—Capital Outlays: 2000 to 2020

[In millions of dollars (217,063 represents $217,063,000,000), except percent. For fiscal year ending in year shown; see text, this section. Local government amounts are subject to sampling variation; see Appendix III and source]

Level and function	2000	2005	2010	2015	2016	2017	2018	2019	2020
State & local governments, total	**217,063**	**278,063**	**355,437**	**336,088**	**352,195**	**365,479**	**390,866**	**413,025**	**425,006**
Percent of direct expenditure	12.5	11.8	11.4	9.9	10.0	10.0	10.2	10.4	10.1
By function:[1]									
Education[2]	60,968	77,780	93,562	84,148	92,857	98,486	103,987	111,382	119,323
Elementary and secondary	45,150	54,563	60,240	52,892	58,371	63,829	69,611	76,784	84,509
Higher education	15,257	22,735	31,644	30,641	34,024	34,228	33,795	34,011	34,001
Hospitals[3]	5,502	6,100	8,553	8,782	9,074	9,144	8,990	8,990	8,669
Highways	56,439	70,689	89,895	93,810	99,262	101,790	112,140	116,911	115,492
Natural resources	4,347	4,541	5,214	4,697	6,120	5,384	5,181	7,208	6,254
Parks and recreation	6,916	8,136	10,711	8,342	9,261	10,674	10,460	11,770	13,187
Sewerage	10,093	14,081	21,915	17,847	20,042	19,695	22,478	21,880	20,998
Utilities	24,847	34,790	49,258	54,829	50,708	53,470	55,613	57,226	61,846
State governments, total	**76,233**	**95,155**	**118,011**	**128,925**	**130,229**	**132,044**	**142,011**	**149,534**	**148,233**
Percent of direct expenditure	10.1	8.9	8.1	7.9	7.6	7.5	7.7	7.8	7.1
By function:[1]									
Education[2]	14,077	20,585	28,643	28,126	30,915	30,798	30,841	30,732	30,575
Elementary and secondary	521	447	1,066	757	923	806	847	819	714
Higher education	12,995	19,656	25,899	26,753	29,530	29,563	29,413	29,326	29,047
Hospitals[3]	2,228	2,363	2,654	3,562	3,717	3,511	3,768	3,793	4,038
Highways	41,651	52,607	64,755	68,979	72,518	74,694	81,443	87,525	83,844
Natural resources	2,758	2,667	2,337	2,565	3,652	2,630	2,435	3,352	2,905
Parks and recreation	1,044	915	910	851	837	980	926	914	1,238
Sewerage	403	486	488	60	95	147	133	155	126
Utilities	4,232	4,319	5,318	12,747	7,211	8,129	10,026	8,739	11,435
Local governments, total	**140,830**	**182,908**	**237,426**	**207,163**	**221,967**	**233,435**	**248,856**	**263,491**	**276,773**
Percent of direct expenditure	14.3	14.1	14.4	11.7	12.2	12.3	12.6	12.8	13.0
By function:[1]									
Education[2]	46,890	57,195	64,919	56,022	61,942	67,688	73,146	80,650	88,749
Elementary and secondary	44,629	54,116	59,174	52,134	57,448	63,023	68,764	75,965	83,794
Higher education	2,261	3,079	5,745	3,888	4,494	4,665	4,382	4,685	4,954
Hospitals[3]	3,274	3,737	5,899	5,219	5,357	5,632	5,222	5,197	4,631
Highways	14,789	18,083	25,140	24,832	26,744	27,096	30,697	29,386	31,648
Natural resources	1,589	1,873	2,878	2,131	2,468	2,754	2,747	3,856	3,349
Parks and recreation	5,872	7,221	9,802	7,490	8,424	9,693	9,533	10,856	11,950
Sewerage	9,690	13,595	21,426	17,788	19,946	19,549	22,345	21,724	20,872
Utilities	20,615	30,471	43,940	42,083	43,496	45,340	45,587	48,487	50,411

[1] Includes other functions not shown separately. [2] Includes other education, not shown separately. [3] For 2000 only, data include outlays for both health and hospitals.

Source: U.S. Census Bureau, Annual Survey of State and Local Government Finances, "Datasets & Tables," <www.census.gov/programs-surveys/gov-finances.html>, accessed August 2022.

Table 488. State and Local Governments—Expenditures for Public Works: 2000 to 2020

[In millions of dollars (230,569 represents $230,569,000,000), except percent. Represents direct expenditures excluding intergovernmental grants]

Item	Total	Highways	Air trans-portation	Sea and inland port facilities	Sewerage	Solid waste manage-ment	Water supply	Mass transit
2000, total	230,569	101,336	13,160	3,141	28,052	17,208	35,789	31,883
State	74,974	61,942	1,106	863	955	2,347	354	7,407
Local	155,595	39,394	12,054	2,277	27,098	14,861	35,435	24,476
Capital expenditures (percent)	41.9	55.7	51.0	51.5	36.0	8.9	29.5	30.5
2010, total	381,808	155,912	24,209	5,263	51,991	23,629	60,655	60,149
State	111,280	93,127	1,724	1,245	1,118	2,281	378	11,407
Local	270,529	62,786	22,485	4,019	50,873	21,348	60,277	48,742
Capital expenditures (percent)	(NA)	57.7	(NA)	(NA)	42.2	8.9	(NA)	(NA)
2017, total	445,679	181,262	26,001	6,311	57,084	24,978	71,538	78,504
State	134,923	108,987	2,354	2,145	1,253	1,115	497	18,573
Local	310,756	72,275	23,648	4,166	55,832	23,863	71,042	59,931
Capital expenditures (percent)	(NA)	56.2	(NA)	(NA)	34.5	7.7	(NA)	(NA)
2018, total	472,039	194,652	28,607	6,355	60,796	25,955	75,341	80,333
State	144,920	116,836	2,495	2,320	1,244	1,140	437	20,448
Local	327,119	77,816	26,112	4,035	59,552	24,815	74,904	59,885
Capital expenditures (percent)	(NA)	57.6	(NA)	(NA)	37.0	8.9	(NA)	(NA)
2019, total	492,165	202,562	31,383	6,963	62,787	27,651	78,881	81,937
State	152,692	124,423	2,842	2,572	1,316	1,194	482	19,863
Local	339,473	78,139	28,541	4,391	61,471	26,457	78,400	62,073
Capital expenditures (percent)	(NA)	57.7	(NA)	(NA)	34.8	8.3	(NA)	(NA)
2020, total	507,521	204,258	33,308	6,892	63,987	28,863	80,453	89,760
State	154,065	122,100	2,864	2,600	1,411	1,165	522	23,404
Local	353,457	82,158	30,445	4,293	62,575	27,699	79,931	66,356
Capital expenditures (percent)	(NA)	56.5	(NA)	(NA)	32.8	7.7	(NA)	(NA)

NA Not available.

Source: U.S. Census Bureau, Annual Survey of State and Local Government Finances, "Datasets & Tables," <www.census.gov/programs-surveys/gov-finances.html>, accessed August 2022, and unpublished data.

Table 489. State and Local Governments—Indebtedness: 2000 to 2020

[In billions of dollars (1,451.8 represents $1,451,800,000,000). For fiscal year ending in year shown; see text, this section. Local government amounts are estimates subject to sampling variation; see Appendix III and source]

Item	Debt outstanding						Long-term	
	Total	Cash and security holdings	Short-term	Long-term			Debt issued	Debt retired
				Total	Public debt for private purposes	All other		
2000, total.........	1,451.8	3,503.7	24.3	1,427.5	372.6	1,054.9	184.8	121.9
State..............	547.9	2,518.9	6.4	541.5	227.3	314.2	75.0	44.4
Local..............	903.9	984.8	17.9	886.0	145.3	740.7	109.8	77.5
2010, total.........	2,844.2	4,826.0	45.1	2,799.1	625.9	2,173.2	399.0	275.8
State..............	1,115.5	3,323.0	14.7	1,100.8	397.1	703.6	183.7	125.1
Local..............	1,728.7	1,503.0	30.4	1,698.3	228.8	1,469.6	215.2	150.7
2011, total.........	2,923.1	5,265.1	34.7	2,888.4	616.1	2,272.3	364.6	275.1
State..............	1,139.7	3,681.4	5.4	1,134.2	389.1	745.1	138.1	112.4
Local..............	1,783.5	1,583.7	29.3	1,754.2	227.0	1,527.2	226.5	162.7
2012, total.........	2,950.5	5,305.6	43.6	2,906.8	599.4	2,307.4	341.8	333.0
State..............	1,146.7	3,700.9	15.5	1,131.3	373.6	757.7	137.1	138.6
Local..............	1,803.7	1,604.7	28.2	1,775.6	225.8	1,549.7	204.7	194.5
2013, total.........	2,970.0	5,640.4	31.9	2,938.0	600.5	2,337.6	369.5	355.7
State..............	1,138.6	3,952.1	5.7	1,133.0	366.2	766.7	148.5	147.0
Local..............	1,831.3	1,688.4	26.3	1,805.1	234.2	1,570.8	221.0	208.8
2014, total.........	2,980.0	6,095.2	33.7	2,946.3	578.9	2,367.4	303.9	305.8
State..............	1,152.3	4,330.8	8.7	1,143.6	355.6	788.0	130.1	123.7
Local..............	1,827.7	1,764.5	25.0	1,802.7	223.3	1,579.4	173.8	182.1
2015, total.........	2,988.5	6,277.8	34.6	2,953.8	566.1	2,387.8	362.6	370.2
State..............	1,155.1	4,415.6	8.6	1,146.5	354.4	792.1	143.3	144.0
Local..............	1,833.3	1,862.3	26.1	1,807.3	211.7	1,595.6	219.3	226.2
2016, total.........	3,022.5	6,326.4	34.4	2,988.1	555.2	2,432.9	383.4	370.6
State..............	1,170.6	4,416.3	9.0	1,161.6	353.9	807.7	142.4	132.1
Local..............	1,851.9	1,910.0	25.4	1,826.5	201.4	1,625.1	241.1	238.5
2017, total.........	3,064.2	6,935.1	35.6	3,028.7	553.2	2,475.4	409.8	397.3
State..............	1,153.1	4,880.9	7.9	1,145.3	348.2	797.1	153.9	160.1
Local..............	1,911.1	2,054.2	27.7	1,883.4	205.0	1,678.4	256.0	237.2
2018, total.........	3,138.5	7,347.0	33.8	3,104.7	554.8	2,549.9	395.9	347.6
State..............	1,171.3	5,180.6	8.2	1,163.1	352.7	810.3	150.3	135.8
Local..............	1,967.2	2,166.4	25.6	1,941.6	202.0	1,739.6	245.6	211.8
2019, total.........	3,191.8	7,616.0	35.7	3,156.1	553.8	2,602.3	347.5	291.0
State..............	1,166.5	5,353.4	9.2	1,157.3	350.4	806.9	122.2	105.6
Local..............	2,025.3	2,262.5	26.5	1,998.8	203.4	1,795.4	225.3	185.4
2020, total.........	**3,267.2**	**7,858.5**	**40.3**	**3,227.0**	**567.1**	**2,659.9**	**428.4**	**436.4**
State..............	1,184.6	5,501.2	12.0	1,172.6	357.5	815.2	155.6	210.0
Local..............	2,082.6	2,357.3	28.3	2,054.3	209.6	1,844.7	272.8	226.4

Source: U.S. Census Bureau, Annual Survey of State and Local Government Finances, "Datasets & Tables," <www.census.gov/programs-surveys/gov-finances.html>, accessed August 2022.

Table 490. New Security Issues—State and Local Governments: 2000 to 2021

[In billions of dollars (180.4 represents $180,400,000,000)]

Type of issue, issuer, or use	2000	2005	2010	2015	2016	2017	2018	2019	2020	2021
All issues, new and refunding [1].......	**180.4**	**409.6**	**460.8**	**399.6**	**431.0**	**425.6**	**351.2**	**434.1**	**475.0**	**472.3**
By type of issue:										
General obligation..........................	64.5	145.8	137.5	161.1	161.4	152.4	107.6	137.7	168.7	153.0
Revenue.................................	115.9	263.8	323.2	238.7	269.9	273.3	243.6	296.3	306.4	319.3
By type of issuer:										
State....................................	19.9	31.6	55.2	(NA)	(NA)	(NA)	(NA)	(NA)	(NA)	(NA)
Special district or statutory authority [2]....	121.2	298.6	294.9	(NA)	(NA)	(NA)	(NA)	(NA)	(NA)	(NA)
Municipality, county, or township..........	39.3	79.4	86.6	(NA)	(NA)	(NA)	(NA)	(NA)	(NA)	(NA)
Issues for new capital....................	**154.3**	**223.8**	**278.5**	**169.5**	**168.4**	**197.5**	**230.9**	**233.9**	**220.1**	**236.4**
By use of proceeds:										
Education................................	38.7	71.0	60.4	46.5	50.4	57.6	59.1	63.9	57.2	51.7
Transportation...........................	19.7	25.4	32.3	13.9	19.6	20.2	25.7	30.2	29.5	24.6
Utilities and conservation..................	11.9	9.9	22.3	8.5	3.9	7.4	10.9	15.2	15.7	17.5
Industrial aid............................	7.1	18.6	35.7	14.7	14.1	17.7	32.6	27.2	21.0	27.2
Other purposes...........................	47.3	60.6	92.4	56.0	56.7	60.5	64.0	55.6	60.9	58.2

NA Not available. [1] Par amounts of long-term issues based on date of sale. [2] Includes school districts.

Source: Board of Governors of the Federal Reserve System, Business Finance, "New Security Issues, State and Local Governments," <www.federalreserve.gov/data.htm>, accessed June 2022.

Table 491. State and Local Governments—Total Revenue and Expenditures by State: 2000 to 2020

[In millions of dollars (1,942,328 represents $1,942,328,000,000). For fiscal year ending in year shown; see text, this section. These data cannot be used to compute the deficit or surplus for any single government, as these are estimates for all state and local governments within a state area. For further information, see the *2006 Government Finance and Employment Classification Manual* at <www.census.gov/programs-surveys/gov-finances/technical-documentation/classification-manuals.html>]

State	Revenue				Expenditures			
	2000	2010	2019	2020	2000	2010	2019	2020
United States.............	**1,942,328**	**3,180,023**	**4,074,321**	**4,278,593**	**1,746,943**	**3,115,172**	**3,981,749**	**4,230,373**
Alabama....................	25,726	42,189	53,172	55,343	25,319	42,255	50,277	52,647
Alaska.....................	10,525	15,643	13,885	14,035	8,628	14,450	14,935	15,077
Arizona....................	27,778	54,099	71,246	73,442	27,293	53,432	66,575	71,488
Arkansas..................	13,833	24,539	30,678	34,423	12,245	22,798	28,821	28,981
California..................	270,380	453,354	664,586	651,904	236,645	432,363	644,170	678,463
Colorado..................	29,603	49,260	63,701	79,607	26,173	48,630	66,638	74,023
Connecticut...............	25,828	39,427	51,372	51,910	24,011	39,311	43,163	45,286
Delaware..................	6,224	9,831	12,502	14,835	5,153	9,745	12,801	13,312
District of Columbia........	6,383	11,644	16,283	17,429	6,527	13,682	19,963	23,500
Florida....................	92,402	166,817	200,028	208,906	84,301	163,536	199,037	208,234
Georgia...................	49,310	76,370	96,864	103,264	43,517	78,158	92,409	100,472
Hawaii....................	8,488	14,666	20,441	21,256	8,254	14,340	18,774	20,157
Idaho.....................	7,590	12,490	16,331	18,030	6,404	12,054	15,324	16,686
Illinois....................	80,695	126,384	147,098	163,635	74,727	129,518	154,526	165,364
Indiana...................	32,716	54,803	72,014	75,170	31,250	53,247	64,808	69,569
Iowa......................	17,220	31,055	43,606	45,151	17,275	29,537	37,441	40,434
Kansas...................	16,235	26,330	33,416	34,130	14,419	26,536	31,658	33,462
Kentucky..................	25,200	37,560	46,419	50,023	21,473	38,595	46,890	50,421
Louisiana.................	27,109	47,078	50,304	52,700	25,018	48,755	50,952	53,406
Maine.....................	8,554	12,557	15,680	17,243	7,652	12,286	13,957	15,097
Maryland..................	33,949	57,493	75,622	78,311	30,598	57,485	75,577	81,014
Massachusetts............	46,103	76,100	97,923	105,809	44,362	76,679	98,927	108,760
Michigan..................	70,112	93,819	108,163	113,519	61,506	90,935	108,805	115,916
Minnesota................	38,785	57,410	78,188	79,427	35,424	55,975	72,049	78,062
Mississippi................	16,672	28,690	32,343	32,983	15,379	27,216	30,791	32,580
Missouri..................	31,635	51,592	61,564	62,378	27,953	50,040	59,325	62,087
Montana..................	5,643	9,784	11,930	12,082	4,983	9,296	11,306	12,098
Nebraska.................	11,650	20,121	25,104	27,116	10,831	19,315	23,992	25,196
Nevada...................	11,885	22,838	33,912	34,047	11,230	23,856	29,889	33,360
New Hampshire............	6,948	11,581	14,234	15,193	6,222	11,439	13,300	14,181
New Jersey................	62,331	99,751	120,968	119,261	54,590	102,667	114,685	117,269
New Mexico...............	13,073	21,998	29,855	28,619	11,195	22,372	25,762	27,703
New York..................	188,907	313,781	384,383	376,215	171,858	295,467	375,228	387,677
North Carolina.............	50,542	86,699	108,607	110,401	46,135	79,955	102,441	107,765
North Dakota..............	4,495	7,890	12,348	13,207	4,041	6,746	10,253	10,922
Ohio......................	80,074	123,289	130,284	155,504	68,418	113,844	135,718	145,981
Oklahoma.................	18,760	32,939	39,504	41,479	15,962	31,338	36,168	38,217
Oregon...................	28,644	41,031	62,439	60,947	24,086	39,506	60,034	65,714
Pennsylvania..............	80,546	124,379	157,637	169,744	75,624	130,085	160,251	174,154
Rhode Island..............	7,427	11,726	13,499	14,645	6,432	11,303	13,674	14,507
South Carolina.............	23,467	42,509	54,319	55,773	23,436	42,800	53,108	56,241
South Dakota.............	4,277	6,941	8,518	9,837	3,760	6,845	8,271	8,752
Tennessee................	33,625	54,297	69,732	67,702	32,010	53,554	65,802	67,877
Texas....................	120,666	209,930	291,325	333,017	109,634	218,807	294,399	312,359
Utah.....................	14,954	24,149	34,524	39,948	13,044	24,552	35,276	37,874
Vermont..................	4,019	7,016	8,568	9,796	3,766	6,781	8,723	9,568
Virginia...................	44,175	71,093	97,607	100,687	38,092	67,673	90,846	97,890
Washington................	46,372	71,623	106,905	110,941	41,794	75,167	100,678	112,283
West Virginia..............	10,760	16,993	19,217	20,247	9,990	15,685	18,760	20,317
Wisconsin.................	43,003	66,291	55,923	84,836	34,559	55,839	64,592	67,584
Wyoming..................	7,030	10,176	9,553	12,486	3,743	8,720	10,000	10,387

Source: U.S. Census Bureau, Annual Survey of State and Local Government Finances, "Datasets & Tables," <www.census.gov/programs-surveys/gov-finances.html>, accessed August 2022.

Table 492. State and Local Governments—Revenue by State: 2020

[In millions of dollars (4,278,593 represents $4,278,593,000,000). For fiscal year ending in year shown; see text, this section]

State	Total revenue	General revenue: Total	Intergovernmental from federal government	General revenue from own sources	Select taxes: Total[1]	Property	Sales and gross receipt	Individual income	Corporation income	Total	Current charges and miscellaneous revenue: Total[1]	Current charges: Education	Hospitals	Sewerage	Miscellaneous revenue: Total[1]	Interest earnings	Special assessments	Utility and liquor stores	Insurance trust revenue
U.S..	4,278,593	3,624,460	911,218	2,713,241	1,861,618	599,990	650,980	424,769	60,620	851,624	581,465	135,418	187,921	66,549	270,158	73,853	11,634	192,143	461,990
AL...	55,343	48,105	14,728	33,378	18,874	3,177	9,217	4,413	754	14,504	11,731	3,045	6,663	661	2,773	743	30	3,881	3,357
AK...	14,035	12,415	4,757	7,657	3,313	1,667	682	—	163	4,345	1,602	191	409	123	2,743	1,369	3	452	1,169
AZ...	73,442	63,084	22,081	41,003	29,687	8,658	14,895	4,530	523	11,317	7,381	3,350	617	1,012	3,935	1,216	89	5,212	5,147
AR...	34,423	28,627	9,696	18,932	13,061	2,404	6,696	2,915	469	5,870	4,076	1,426	1,385	344	1,794	409	18	1,020	4,775
CA...	651,904	521,560	116,049	405,510	276,550	77,212	84,321	84,412	9,818	128,960	97,935	13,835	32,391	10,288	31,025	9,245	2,963	34,321	96,024
CO...	79,607	62,008	12,681	49,327	32,786	11,315	11,826	7,539	697	16,541	11,477	3,697	2,709	1,265	5,063	1,589	367	3,412	14,187
CT...	51,910	46,238	10,381	35,857	30,416	11,863	7,468	8,177	2,062	5,440	3,463	1,431	487	437	1,977	762	11	784	4,889
DE...	14,835	13,051	4,338	8,714	5,811	1,041	606	1,745	252	2,903	1,574	703	5	194	1,329	191	27	498	1,286
DC...	17,429	14,771	4,819	9,952	8,334	2,927	1,611	2,377	728	1,617	806	36	132	388	811	54	5	804	1,854
FL...	208,906	186,647	41,782	144,866	87,299	33,244	43,334	—	2,482	57,566	35,234	4,510	9,647	4,039	22,332	4,185	3,725	9,927	12,331
GA...	103,264	84,651	19,386	65,265	43,709	14,332	15,343	11,704	984	21,556	16,279	3,108	6,286	2,465	5,277	905	104	4,618	13,995
HI...	21,256	19,546	4,080	15,466	10,861	2,259	5,538	2,359	44	4,605	2,503	409	466	537	2,103	381	14	429	1,281
ID...	18,030	16,043	4,857	11,186	7,528	2,089	2,797	1,913	246	3,658	2,679	534	766	293	979	252	78	464	1,523
IL...	163,635	136,538	29,584	106,954	81,820	29,002	27,368	17,956	3,492	25,134	15,505	4,168	2,237	1,506	9,628	3,007	734	5,438	21,660
IN...	75,170	69,605	19,838	49,766	31,940	7,776	12,743	9,591	759	17,826	13,266	3,861	6,040	1,903	4,561	1,650	18	2,823	2,742
IA...	45,151	40,466	8,977	31,489	17,327	5,759	5,655	4,077	620	14,162	8,240	2,040	4,390	686	5,921	2,420	32	1,610	3,075
KS...	34,130	30,829	6,232	24,597	15,296	5,028	5,819	3,382	434	9,301	6,905	1,610	3,579	553	2,396	460	142	1,593	1,707
KY...	50,023	44,610	16,108	28,502	19,496	4,090	7,341	6,434	804	9,006	7,092	1,768	3,289	762	1,915	432	17	1,881	3,533
LA...	52,700	47,563	17,592	29,972	20,511	4,254	10,838	3,916	451	9,461	6,330	1,734	2,278	572	3,131	685	20	1,254	3,883
ME...	17,243	15,836	4,875	10,962	8,746	3,899	2,409	1,843	216	2,216	1,574	357	117	220	641	192	8	377	1,030
MD...	78,311	71,223	17,286	53,937	42,034	10,768	10,383	17,031	1,325	11,903	8,037	2,583	174	1,470	3,866	884	108	1,518	5,570
MA...	105,809	89,608	22,629	66,979	51,014	18,524	9,932	17,415	2,532	15,965	9,159	2,969	431	1,749	6,806	1,543	11	3,818	12,383
MI...	113,519	97,309	28,454	68,855	42,916	16,045	13,626	9,596	813	25,940	19,075	6,401	5,577	2,335	6,865	1,816	186	4,653	11,557
MN...	79,427	67,148	15,630	51,518	37,137	10,135	11,963	10,923	1,604	14,381	9,524	2,492	2,415	1,257	4,857	1,319	342	3,192	9,087
MS...	32,983	29,974	10,688	19,286	11,739	3,452	5,385	1,861	421	7,547	6,272	1,386	3,844	303	1,276	262	8	1,330	1,679
MO...	62,378	53,714	15,908	37,806	24,413	6,854	9,412	6,324	453	13,393	8,764	2,410	3,374	1,295	4,629	1,364	98	2,504	6,160
MT...	12,082	10,692	3,882	6,811	4,856	1,961	696	1,339	186	1,955	1,241	509	79	149	713	219	89	297	1,092
NE...	27,116	20,951	5,101	15,850	11,087	4,095	3,320	2,446	391	4,764	3,287	1,101	659	370	1,477	380	67	4,318	1,846
NV...	34,047	26,729	6,271	20,458	14,949	3,590	9,371	—	—	5,509	3,549	607	723	563	1,960	778	118	1,437	5,881
NH...	15,193	13,409	3,824	9,586	7,070	4,526	980	123	781	2,515	1,423	587	7	173	1,092	409	2	875	908
NJ...	119,261	109,430	20,026	89,405	70,319	31,839	16,413	15,413	3,565	19,086	11,364	3,918	1,049	1,659	7,722	1,799	5	2,194	7,637
NM...	28,619	26,535	9,176	17,359	10,580	1,904	5,487	1,228	96	6,778	3,052	690	1,424	230	3,726	1,100	13	789	1,296
NY...	376,215	336,539	79,245	257,294	200,443	62,847	48,756	67,964	11,311	56,851	34,737	4,096	12,440	2,996	22,114	6,403	151	16,160	23,517

See footnotes at end of table.

Table 492. State and Local Governments—Revenue by State: 2020-Continued.

See headnote on page 314.

State	Total revenue	General revenue		General revenue from own sources																Utility and liquor stores	Insurance trust revenue
		Total	Intergovernmental from federal government	General revenue from own sources		Select taxes					Current charges and miscellaneous revenue										
				Total	Total¹	Total¹	Property	Sales and gross receipt	Individual income	Corporation income	Total	Current charges				Miscellaneous revenue				
												Total¹	Education	Hospitals	Sewerage	Total¹	Interest earnings	Special assessments		
NC...	110,401	95,906	24,254	71,652	44,012	16,668	11,313	16,668	12,506	662	27,641	21,577	4,064	12,574	1,553	6,064	1,345	18	5,237	9,257
ND...	13,207	11,911	3,391	8,519	5,878	1,881	1,198	1,881	377	81	2,642	1,230	494	3	79	1,412	836	149	310	987
OH...	155,504	119,320	32,584	86,736	57,263	22,741	17,193	22,741	14,291	283	29,473	18,583	5,998	6,110	2,562	10,890	2,638	290	4,810	31,374
OK...	41,479	36,320	10,036	26,285	16,504	7,277	3,499	7,277	3,365	302	9,781	6,084	2,445	1,343	513	3,697	696	20	2,183	2,975
OR...	60,947	51,361	14,133	37,228	22,065	2,643	7,339	2,643	8,636	996	15,163	10,430	2,109	2,928	1,293	4,733	1,115	84	3,003	6,583
PA...	169,744	143,191	40,978	102,213	72,142	22,995	21,359	22,995	18,296	3,100	30,071	21,651	6,840	4,689	3,226	8,420	2,099	105	5,333	21,220
RI...	14,645	13,216	4,357	8,859	6,283	1,907	2,684	1,907	1,242	213	2,576	1,591	539	3	245	985	401	9	240	1,188
SC...	55,773	49,903	12,668	37,235	20,817	6,821	6,740	6,821	5,096	505	16,418	12,884	2,752	7,289	817	3,533	729	63	3,607	2,263
SD...	9,837	8,859	3,243	5,616	3,961	2,114	1,425	2,114	–	37	1,655	909	336	100	116	746	314	20	366	611
TN...	67,702	53,795	15,111	38,684	25,735	15,968	5,847	15,968	58	1,505	12,948	8,659	2,084	3,277	1,144	4,289	1,322	150	9,046	4,862
TX...	333,017	275,510	68,236	207,274	138,615	64,980	64,758	64,980	–	–	68,659	43,743	10,983	15,084	4,964	24,916	7,643	540	17,220	40,287
UT...	39,948	31,970	6,423	25,547	14,659	5,999	3,968	5,999	3,735	360	10,888	8,246	2,432	3,040	617	2,642	737	48	2,521	5,457
VT...	9,796	9,014	3,510	5,504	4,144	1,191	1,837	1,191	763	142	1,360	894	586	–	83	466	121	4	320	462
VA...	100,687	91,344	19,059	72,285	48,312	12,979	15,800	12,979	14,997	1,362	23,974	17,177	4,892	5,944	1,872	6,796	1,478	70	3,181	6,162
WA...	110,941	90,355	17,752	72,603	47,513	29,236	13,332	29,236	–	–	25,090	19,009	3,517	5,633	3,091	6,082	1,986	357	7,896	12,690
WV...	20,247	18,595	6,897	11,697	7,656	2,967	1,794	2,967	1,948	152	4,041	2,792	884	465	291	1,249	277	15	430	1,222
WI...	84,836	58,433	13,648	44,785	31,047	9,317	10,120	9,317	8,514	1,441	13,739	8,942	2,704	2,045	1,215	4,796	1,196	75	2,192	24,211
WY...	12,486	10,001	3,980	6,021	3,090	1,064	1,248	1,064	–	–	2,931	1,928	195	1,306	72	1,003	499	11	365	2,120

– Represents or rounds to zero. ¹ Includes items not shown separately.

Source: U.S. Census Bureau, Annual Survey of State and Local Government Finances, "Datasets & Tables," <www.census.gov/programs-surveys/gov-finances.html>, accessed August 2022.

Table 493. State and Local Governments—Expenditures and Debt by State: 2020

[In millions of dollars (4,230,373 represents $4,230,373,000,000). For fiscal year ending in year shown; see text, this section]

State	Total expenditures	General expenditures — Total[1]	Direct general expenditures — Total[1]	Education[1]	Public welfare	Hospitals	Health	Highways	Police protection	Corrections	Natural resources	Parks and recreation	Housing and community development	Sewerage	Solid waste	Governmental administration	Interest on general debt	Utility and liquor store expenditures	Insurance trust expenditures	Total debt outstanding
U.S...	4,230,373	3,497,281	3,494,137	1,131,609	791,216	222,808	122,201	204,258	128,833	86,142	35,893	51,335	59,188	63,987	28,863	157,923	114,045	264,449	468,643	3,267,238
AL....	52,647	44,407	44,407	15,229	7,806	7,348	954	2,639	1,453	887	250	518	595	479	344	1,797	1,195	3,728	4,512	34,978
AK....	15,077	12,726	12,726	3,086	2,731	437	239	1,361	406	348	470	126	237	147	127	980	331	668	1,682	9,411
AZ....	71,488	58,552	58,552	19,622	17,299	977	1,037	3,049	2,917	1,847	520	959	554	772	522	2,687	1,488	6,437	6,499	43,521
AR....	28,981	25,662	25,661	8,881	7,366	1,517	288	1,836	737	538	302	293	306	299	229	1,230	539	997	2,322	20,257
CA....	678,463	543,866	541,102	159,812	136,899	33,543	32,486	22,788	22,282	16,481	8,417	7,295	9,763	8,597	3,984	20,017	17,496	47,236	87,361	519,537
CO....	74,023	60,912	60,880	19,966	10,781	3,273	923	3,467	2,317	1,505	609	2,035	1,334	1,322	146	3,686	2,719	4,610	8,502	67,061
CT....	45,286	36,728	36,728	14,090	3,935	1,593	1,009	2,099	1,293	716	178	241	717	519	274	2,071	2,123	1,423	7,135	52,999
DE....	13,312	11,638	11,637	4,456	2,816	80	530	725	391	363	82	92	176	227	108	760	309	611	1,063	7,875
DC....	23,500	15,941	15,941	3,318	4,394	282	665	661	681	262	119	352	1,077	386	159	1,018	631	5,481	2,078	19,659
FL....	208,234	179,937	179,937	49,591	30,644	11,340	7,749	12,242	10,100	5,011	4,517	3,912	2,607	4,370	3,041	8,565	3,711	12,234	16,064	130,745
GA....	100,472	81,136	81,136	31,892	13,788	5,840	2,384	5,052	3,042	2,175	648	1,057	1,107	1,473	837	4,447	1,604	6,436	12,900	62,963
HI....	20,157	16,060	16,060	3,718	3,071	537	775	773	543	234	161	298	373	519	344	1,095	372	1,638	2,459	17,247
ID....	16,686	14,774	14,774	4,215	3,273	853	334	1,454	540	488	363	255	236	253	205	1,040	277	409	1,504	6,092
IL....	165,364	130,549	130,534	41,015	27,960	4,530	2,213	8,482	5,678	2,346	613	3,114	2,154	1,620	508	6,432	7,406	8,305	26,509	159,311
IN....	69,569	62,807	62,806	20,062	16,809	5,709	1,038	3,610	1,600	1,140	506	635	904	1,416	326	2,388	1,809	2,740	4,022	52,020
IA....	40,434	35,284	35,284	11,631	7,254	4,529	397	3,295	915	476	548	464	280	837	350	1,285	625	1,591	3,558	20,512
KS....	33,462	29,334	29,334	10,495	5,141	3,804	744	1,839	1,059	552	273	423	219	499	183	1,503	685	1,513	2,615	28,441
KY....	50,421	42,228	42,228	12,988	13,252	2,930	762	2,453	818	923	442	389	440	1,136	244	1,715	1,261	2,087	6,106	53,077
LA....	53,406	45,323	45,323	12,934	13,601	2,957	821	2,182	1,516	928	990	785	554	649	328	1,889	1,181	1,409	6,674	31,148
ME....	15,097	13,217	13,217	3,932	3,913	189	301	1,162	328	244	161	98	304	243	116	780	302	348	1,532	8,853
MD....	81,014	68,621	68,621	23,156	14,844	424	2,984	3,477	3,039	2,054	606	1,250	1,840	1,767	764	3,328	2,387	4,376	8,017	59,070
MA....	108,760	86,784	86,772	24,995	25,682	1,649	2,111	3,333	2,432	1,685	279	533	3,178	1,500	391	3,887	3,275	7,219	14,756	98,337
MI....	115,916	95,704	95,701	33,658	19,533	6,138	4,611	5,774	2,922	2,568	470	1,028	1,071	2,623	609	3,684	2,854	5,197	15,015	81,886
MN....	78,062	66,327	66,327	20,881	18,025	2,232	1,853	5,436	2,414	1,157	871	1,386	1,109	1,157	509	3,311	1,807	3,601	8,135	58,751
MS....	32,580	27,688	27,688	8,714	6,538	4,236	501	1,755	789	539	321	303	324	306	222	1,231	528	1,370	3,523	14,499
MO....	62,087	52,395	52,381	16,640	10,394	4,877	2,555	2,762	2,116	963	421	789	782	1,306	161	2,126	1,745	2,743	6,948	47,755
MT....	12,098	10,402	10,402	3,230	2,464	154	421	1,043	374	275	338	111	89	153	99	748	204	370	1,325	5,801
NE....	25,196	19,182	19,128	7,697	2,932	812	333	1,978	584	597	323	312	278	374	137	784	366	4,461	1,553	15,632
NV....	33,360	27,018	27,015	7,827	4,747	1,167	508	2,354	1,470	857	360	1,713	325	497	37	1,391	994	1,625	4,717	29,401
NH....	14,181	12,255	12,255	4,356	2,585	67	156	801	492	222	52	109	243	245	152	1,114	428	784	1,142	10,095
NJ....	117,269	95,103	95,087	39,212	19,755	2,856	2,360	4,382	3,987	2,149	567	658	1,334	1,631	1,034	4,110	3,468	4,436	17,731	91,472
NM....	27,703	23,701	23,701	6,691	7,385	1,597	654	1,129	765	827	360	321	191	228	214	1,148	611	934	3,068	16,334
NY....	387,677	309,839	309,839	93,490	83,018	18,251	8,096	10,630	11,084	6,510	590	3,366	7,609	4,046	3,609	11,423	15,145	35,646	42,192	368,276

See footnotes at end of table.

Table 493. State and Local Governments—Expenditures and Debt by State: 2020-Continued.
See headnote on page 316.

State	Total expenditures	General expenditures Total [1]	Direct general expenditures Total [1]	Education	Public welfare	Hospitals	Health	Highways	Police protection	Corrections	Natural resources	Parks and recreation	Housing and community development	Sewerage	Solid waste	Governmental administration	Interest on general debt	Utility and liquor store expenditures	Insurance trust expenditures	Total debt outstanding
NC...	107,765	93,667	93,667	29,796	17,003	13,333	4,318	5,926	3,616	2,144	887	1,351	1,886	1,355	888	4,098	2,066	5,888	8,210	47,759
ND...	10,922	9,624	9,624	3,179	1,680	53	217	1,206	257	180	382	269	95	105	83	456	336	433	865	9,722
OH...	145,981	119,031	119,010	39,731	31,464	6,663	3,549	6,395	4,057	2,428	494	1,735	2,177	2,799	609	6,381	3,363	5,368	21,582	93,306
OK...	38,217	32,397	32,350	11,527	7,142	1,490	1,257	2,950	1,139	788	233	589	616	376	285	1,385	486	2,314	3,506	19,393
OR...	65,714	54,724	54,724	17,116	13,110	3,118	1,993	2,473	1,587	1,515	695	839	935	1,186	175	3,237	1,470	3,373	7,617	41,878
PA...	174,154	146,083	145,966	46,778	41,898	5,087	6,154	11,052	4,290	4,222	873	1,108	2,363	2,973	966	7,409	4,439	7,077	20,995	128,442
RI...	14,507	12,061	12,042	3,668	3,207	52	420	730	513	258	88	82	232	162	108	940	523	339	2,106	12,180
SC...	56,241	48,274	48,274	16,801	8,661	7,778	1,549	2,372	1,418	801	277	696	531	784	519	2,226	897	3,410	4,558	37,687
SD...	8,752	7,623	7,623	2,606	1,234	120	215	1,212	229	194	169	166	94	115	61	412	200	383	746	6,566
TN...	67,877	53,925	53,925	15,790	13,212	4,312	1,292	2,957	2,290	1,230	527	660	856	1,001	555	2,961	1,758	9,181	4,770	50,188
TX...	312,359	263,280	263,280	99,600	44,171	22,681	7,072	19,568	9,354	6,519	2,214	3,872	2,776	5,190	1,803	10,263	10,584	21,562	27,517	324,213
UT...	37,874	32,813	32,813	11,758	4,808	3,198	992	2,581	927	626	390	716	438	492	227	2,120	571	2,824	2,238	22,432
VT...	9,568	8,443	8,443	3,618	1,957	23	432	695	219	147	113	72	155	100	41	339	137	355	770	4,744
VA...	97,890	85,244	85,244	29,354	16,837	6,334	2,779	5,607	2,701	2,898	325	1,241	1,064	1,718	699	4,432	2,358	4,313	8,333	69,617
WA...	112,283	89,455	89,455	30,134	14,082	7,594	4,893	5,084	2,542	2,085	1,326	1,518	2,108	2,317	938	3,085	3,061	11,627	11,201	90,236
WV...	20,317	17,792	17,792	5,563	4,993	556	304	1,846	455	426	237	254	169	284	68	1,186	399	491	2,034	15,117
WI...	67,584	57,692	57,692	20,157	14,238	2,434	1,512	4,790	1,922	1,592	710	795	360	1,350	440	2,732	1,463	2,502	7,390	48,603
WY...	10,387	9,052	9,029	2,949	886	1,249	460	788	231	221	227	149	25	81	86	591	55	346	989	2,143

[1] Includes items not shown separately.

Source: U.S. Census Bureau, Annual Survey of State and Local Government Finances, "Datasets & Tables," <www.census.gov/programs-surveys/gov-finances.html>, accessed August 2022.

Table 494. Estimated State and Local Taxes Paid by a Family of Three for Largest City in Selected States: 2020

[Data based on average family of three (two wage earners and one school age child) living in a city where taxes apply. The families in the top four income levels are assumed to own their own home; at the $25,000 income level, the families are assumed to rent and not own their own housing unit. Comprises state and local sales, income, auto, and real estate taxes. Negative number indicates the family would receive a net refund. For definition of median, see Guide to Tabular Presentation]

City	Total taxes paid by gross family income level (dollars)					Total taxes paid as percent of income				
	$25,000	$50,000	$75,000	$100,000	$150,000	$25,000	$50,000	$75,000	$100,000	$150,000
Albuquerque, NM.......	1,553	3,930	6,451	8,982	13,407	6.2	7.9	8.6	9.0	8.9
Atlanta, GA..............	3,594	4,922	7,716	10,599	14,340	14.4	9.8	10.3	10.6	9.6
Baltimore, MD..........	1,555	6,984	10,878	14,740	19,757	6.2	14.0	14.5	14.7	13.2
Boston, MA.............	3,612	3,057	4,893	6,634	11,587	14.4	6.1	6.5	6.6	7.7
Charlotte, NC..........	3,079	4,042	6,669	8,902	13,065	12.3	8.1	8.9	8.9	8.7
Chicago, IL.............	3,846	6,065	9,313	12,323	17,391	15.4	12.1	12.4	12.3	11.6
Columbus, OH..........	3,059	4,934	7,466	10,181	14,925	12.2	9.9	10.0	10.2	9.9
Denver, CO.............	3,260	3,893	6,050	8,102	11,959	13.0	7.8	8.1	8.1	8.0
Detroit, MI.............	2,957	6,322	11,731	15,647	23,078	11.8	12.6	15.6	15.6	15.4
Honolulu, HI............	3,943	3,399	5,663	7,760	11,470	15.8	6.8	7.6	7.8	7.6
Houston, TX............	2,658	3,172	4,482	5,843	7,956	10.6	6.3	6.0	5.8	5.3
Indianapolis, IN........	3,398	5,185	7,720	10,109	14,431	13.6	10.4	10.3	10.1	9.6
Jacksonville, FL........	2,377	3,282	4,987	6,733	9,561	9.5	6.6	6.6	6.7	6.4
Kansas City, MO........	3,332	5,069	8,519	11,284	16,401	13.3	10.1	11.4	11.3	10.9
Las Vegas, NV..........	2,805	3,903	5,506	7,137	9,769	11.2	7.8	7.3	7.1	6.5
Los Angeles, CA........	4,086	5,309	8,184	11,150	17,038	16.3	10.6	10.9	11.2	11.4
Louisville, KY..........	3,181	6,200	9,296	12,060	17,425	12.7	12.4	12.4	12.1	11.6
Milwaukee, WI..........	2,029	4,705	8,487	11,905	18,002	8.1	9.4	11.3	11.9	12.0
Minneapolis, MN.......	433	3,625	6,212	9,023	15,184	1.7	7.2	8.3	9.0	10.1
Nashville, TN..........	3,449	3,479	4,617	5,854	7,383	13.8	7.0	6.2	5.9	4.9
New Orleans, LA.......	3,151	5,071	7,252	9,597	13,605	12.6	10.1	9.7	9.6	9.1
New York, NY..........	3,484	5,022	8,621	11,847	18,037	13.9	10.0	11.5	11.8	12.0
Oklahoma City, OK......	2,678	4,175	6,573	8,899	12,517	10.7	8.3	8.8	8.9	8.3
Philadelphia, PA.......	4,572	5,994	9,004	11,915	17,083	18.3	12.0	12.0	11.9	11.4
Phoenix, AZ.............	2,922	4,874	7,356	9,726	14,080	11.7	9.7	9.8	9.7	9.4
Portland, OR............	3,111	5,407	8,798	11,765	17,528	12.4	10.8	11.7	11.8	11.7
Seattle, WA.............	4,933	3,919	5,637	7,010	9,066	19.7	7.8	7.5	7.0	6.0
Virginia Beach, VA.....	3,136	4,567	7,656	10,095	14,229	12.5	9.1	10.2	10.1	9.5
Washington, DC........	1,548	3,065	5,595	8,159	12,973	6.2	6.1	7.5	8.2	8.6
Wichita, KS.............	2,203	4,067	6,305	8,752	12,136	8.8	8.1	8.4	8.8	8.1
Average [1]..............	**2,733**	**4,427**	**7,068**	**9,564**	**14,156**	**10.9**	**8.9**	**9.4**	**9.6**	**9.4**
Median [1]...............	**2,847**	**4,156**	**6,669**	**9,213**	**14,080**	**11.4**	**8.3**	**8.9**	**9.2**	**9.4**

[1] Based on the largest city in each State and District of Columbia. For complete list of cities, see Table 495.

Source: Government of the District of Columbia, Office of the Chief Financial Officer, *Tax Rates and Tax Burdens in the District of Columbia – A Nationwide Comparison 2020*, April 2022, and earlier reports. See also <cfo.dc.gov/page/tax-burden-studies>.

Table 495. Residential Property Tax Rates for Largest City in Each State: 2020

[The real property tax is a function of housing values, real estate tax rates, assessment levels, and homeowner exemptions and credits. Effective rate is the amount each jurisdiction considers based upon assessment level used. Assessment level is ratio of assessed value to assumed market value. Nominal rates represent the "announced" rates levied by the jurisdiction]

City	Effective tax rate per $100		Assessment level (percent)	Nominal rate per $100	City	Effective tax rate per $100		Assessment level (percent)	Nominal rate per $100
	Rank	Rate				Rank	Rate		
Detroit, MI..............	1	3.26	46.9	6.96	Philadelphia, PA.........	28	1.30	93.2	1.40
Newark, NJ..............	2	3.20	84.2	3.80	Sioux Falls, SD..........	29	1.30	80.0	1.62
Indianapolis, IN.........	3	2.95	99.5	0.03	Minneapolis, MN.........	30	1.25	97.5	1.28
Bridgeport, CT..........	4	2.81	52.1	5.39	Portland, OR.............	31	1.25	50.1	2.49
Milwaukee, WI..........	5	2.81	101.7	[1] 2.76	Wichita, KS.............	32	1.23	10.6	11.68
Des Moines, IA..........	6	2.60	53.8	4.84	Los Angeles, CA.........	33	1.20	100.0	1.20
Houston, TX.............	7	2.35	98.0	2.40	Fargo, ND...............	34	1.19	4.1	29.21
Chicago, IL..............	8	2.23	[2] 10.0	6.91	Charleston, SC...........	35	1.13	4.0	28.20
Baltimore, MD..........	9	2.23	94.4	2.36	Boise, ID................	36	1.12	93.5	1.20
Burlington, VT..........	10	2.21	[3] 74.8	2.96	Las Vegas, NV...........	37	1.12	34.1	3.28
Omaha, NE..............	11	2.11	94.0	2.24	Billings, MT..............	38	0.99	1.4	73.23
Manchester, NH........	12	1.96	79.4	2.47	Boston, MA..............	39	0.95	89.0	1.07
Jackson, MS.............	13	1.91	10.0	19.13	Virginia Beach, VA......	40	0.91	89.7	1.02
Providence, RI..........	14	1.83	74.5	2.46	Nashville, TN...........	41	0.89	21.2	4.22
Portland, ME...........	15	1.79	77.0	2.33	Cheyenne, WY...........	42	0.88	9.5	9.21
Jacksonville, FL........	16	1.78	94.4	18.87	Charlotte, NC............	43	0.85	88.5	0.97
Wilmington, DE.........	17	1.64	28.1	5.86	Charleston, WV..........	44	0.85	54.0	1.58
Phoenix, AZ.............	18	1.55	10.0	15.54	Washington, DC.........	45	0.83	97.8	0.85
Atlanta, GA.............	19	1.53	37.4	4.10	Seattle, WA..............	46	0.82	89.2	0.92
Columbus, OH..........	20	1.53	26.1	5.85	New York City, NY.......	47	0.80	3.6	22.23
Anchorage, AK..........	21	1.52	89.0	1.71	Birmingham, AL.........	48	0.72	10.0	7.25
New Orleans, LA.......	22	1.51	10.0	15.11	Salt Lake City, UT.......	49	0.65	52.9	1.22
Albuquerque, NM.......	23	1.44	30.0	4.80	Denver, CO..............	50	0.53	7.2	74.20
Louisville, KY..........	24	1.43	100.0	1.43	Honolulu, HI.............	51	0.35	100.0	0.35
Little Rock, AR.........	25	1.33	19.0	7.00					
Oklahoma City, OK.....	26	1.31	11.0	11.91	**Unweighted average...**	**(X)**	**1.51**	**55.9**	**8.77**
Kansas City, MO........	27	1.31	16.1	8.12	**Median..................**	**(X)**	**1.31**	**53.8**	**3.28**

X Not applicable. [1] For Milwaukee, WI, the nominal tax rate takes the assessment sales ratio statistic into account. [2] For Chicago, IL, the state equalizer of 3.2 percent was applied to the assessment level of 10 percent to reflect the equalizer's impact on the final rate. [3] For Vermont, the Common Level of Appraisal value for school funding equalization is used in lieu of a sales ratio statistic.

Source: Government of the District of Columbia, Office of the Chief Financial Officer, *Tax Rates and Tax Burdens in the District of Columbia—A Nationwide Comparison 2020*, April 2022. See also <cfo.dc.gov/page/tax-burden-studies>.

Table 496. Gross Revenue From Parimutuel and Amusement Taxes and Lotteries by State: 2020

[In millions of dollars (87,241.5 represents $87,241,500,000). For fiscal years; see text, this section]

State	Total gross revenue	Amuse-ment taxes [1]	Pari-mutuel taxes [2]	Lottery revenue Total [3]	Apportionment of funds Prizes	Adminis-tration	Proceeds available from ticket sales
United States	**87,241.5**	**6,962.2**	**126.3**	**80,152.9**	**53,524.3**	**3,345.0**	**23,384.3**
Alabama	2.2	–	2.2	(X)	(X)	(X)	(X)
Alaska	2.3	2.3	(X)	(X)	(X)	(X)	(X)
Arizona	1,028.1	4.5	0.2	1,023.4	737.9	42.2	243.3
Arkansas	586.5	53.3	1.7	531.4	369.6	44.4	117.4
California	6,637.3	(X)	15.3	6,622.0	4,403.7	314.0	1,904.3
Colorado	697.9	88.7	0.4	608.9	424.6	44.2	140.1
Connecticut	1,478.4	234.8	11.2	1,232.4	822.2	63.3	346.8
Delaware	303.1	(X)	0.1	303.1	189.2	10.8	103.1
Florida	7,258.6	159.9	8.0	7,090.8	5,030.2	189.9	1,870.6
Georgia	4,347.0	(X)	(X)	4,347.0	3,045.6	173.1	1,128.4
Hawaii	(X)	(X)	(X)	(X)	(X)	(X)	(X)
Idaho	256.7	(X)	1.1	255.7	185.8	13.9	55.9
Illinois	3,645.6	797.8	6.1	2,841.7	1,842.2	308.6	691.0
Indiana	1,718.3	427.2	1.7	1,289.4	914.2	72.5	302.7
Iowa	592.4	241.7	3.1	347.6	236.3	30.7	80.6
Kansas	249.6	0.2	(X)	249.3	166.5	17.6	65.2
Kentucky	1,148.6	0.1	16.1	1,132.4	801.2	58.2	273.0
Louisiana	1,058.9	573.4	5.2	480.2	277.9	25.9	176.5
Maine	337.6	43.4	1.0	293.3	213.7	16.8	62.8
Maryland	2,800.1	773.1	1.0	2,026.0	1,369.0	61.5	595.5
Massachusetts	5,436.5	189.7	0.7	5,246.0	3,866.0	101.8	1,278.3
Michigan	3,906.4	57.2	1.7	3,847.5	2,640.0	93.9	1,113.5
Minnesota	704.3	79.2	1.4	623.7	440.2	27.9	155.6
Mississippi	412.9	132.8	(X)	280.1	198.3	9.6	72.2
Missouri	1,711.3	288.3	(X)	1,423.0	1,062.5	54.2	306.4
Montana	117.4	57.5	0.1	59.9	36.8	7.9	15.2
Nebraska	177.9	6.1	0.1	171.7	108.3	20.4	43.0
Nevada	805.3	805.3	(Z)	(X)	(X)	(X)	(X)
New Hampshire	369.9	0.4	0.3	369.2	246.9	22.8	122.6
New Jersey	3,308.4	278.2	(X)	3,030.2	1,969.6	113.2	947.4
New Mexico	194.7	66.8	0.8	127.1	68.3	11.9	38.5
New York	8,349.3	2.0	15.9	8,331.4	4,623.6	393.3	3,314.4
North Carolina	2,753.2	(Z)	(X)	2,753.1	1,957.6	68.1	725.5
North Dakota	37.9	13.4	1.2	23.3	12.7	5.1	5.6
Ohio	3,514.6	272.8	3.8	3,238.0	2,259.3	87.7	978.7
Oklahoma	293.8	24.4	1.5	267.9	166.7	30.4	70.9
Oregon	938.3	8.9	2.0	927.4	223.5	127.7	576.2
Pennsylvania	5,334.1	1,187.2	6.9	4,139.9	2,927.6	106.9	1,105.4
Rhode Island	430.3	(X)	0.8	429.4	156.7	16.7	256.0
South Carolina	1,992.2	34.0	(X)	1,958.2	1,424.2	46.8	487.2
South Dakota	184.0	8.4	0.1	175.5	36.1	10.3	129.0
Tennessee	1,557.1	(X)	(X)	1,557.1	1,092.1	31.6	433.5
Texas	6,378.2	17.8	4.2	6,356.1	4,442.4	239.8	1,674.0
Utah	(X)	(X)	(X)	(X)	(X)	(X)	(X)
Vermont	128.7	(X)	(X)	128.7	91.6	9.7	27.4
Virginia	2,028.0	0.1	(X)	2,027.9	1,318.1	110.9	598.9
Washington	741.5	3.7	1.0	736.8	530.2	26.5	180.1
West Virginia	572.2	27.1	2.9	542.1	127.9	31.1	383.2
Wisconsin	684.6	0.2	–	684.5	453.5	48.8	182.2
Wyoming	29.4	0.3	6.5	22.5	13.8	2.6	6.1

– Represents zero. X Not applicable. Z Less than $50,000. [1] Represents nonlicense taxes. [2] Represents legalized gambling taxes. [3] Excludes commissions.

Source: U.S. Census Bureau, "Annual Survey of State Government Finances," and "Annual Survey of State Government Tax Collections," <www.census.gov/topics/public-sector.html>, accessed April 2022.

Table 497. Lottery Sales—Type of Game and Proceeds: 1990 to 2021

[In millions of dollars (20,137 represents $20,137,000,000). For fiscal years]

Game	1990	2000	2005	2010	2015	2019	2020	2021
Total ticket sales	**20,137**	**37,201**	**47,425**	**54,200**	**66,715**	**82,289**	**82,447**	**98,642**
Instant [1]	5,204	15,387	26,006	30,665	41,653	51,109	53,007	64,933
Three-digit [2]	4,572	5,780	5,858	5,861	5,925	6,282	6,191	7,657
Four-digit [2]	1,302	2,273	2,869	3,419	3,865	4,376	4,593	5,196
Lotto [3]	8,563	9,339	9,828	10,894	10,820	14,227	9,740	12,472
Other [4]	497	4,423	2,864	3,362	4,452	6,295	8,916	8,384
State proceeds (net income) [5]	7,703	11,871	15,792	17,957	21,154	25,330	24,003	27,703

[1] Player scratches a latex section on ticket that reveals instantly whether ticket is a winner. [2] Players choose and bet on three or four digits, depending on game, with various payoffs for different straight order or mixed combination bets. [3] Players typically select six digits out of a large field of numbers. Varying prizes are offered for matching three through six numbers drawn by lottery. [4] Includes break-open tickets, spiel, keno, video lottery, etc. [5] Sales minus prizes and expenses equal net government income.

Source: TLF Publications, Inc. © 2022. All Rights Reserved.

Table 498. State Financial Resources, Expenditures, and Balances: 2020 and 2021

[In millions of dollars (2,284,484 represents $2,284,484,000,000). For fiscal year ending in year shown; see text, this section. General funds exclude special funds earmarked for particular purposes, such as highway trust funds and federal funds; they support most on-going broad-based state services, and are available for appropriation to support any governmental activity. Minus sign (-) indicates deficit]

State	Total, 2020 actual	Expenditures by fund source 2021 estimated			State general fund Resources [2,3]		Expenditures [3]		Balance [4]	
		Total [1]	General fund	Federal fund	2020	2021 (P)	2020	2021 (P)	2020	2021 (P)
United States......	**2,284,484**	**2,654,318**	**923,131**	**1,074,978**	**962,761**	**1,115,977**	**893,040**	**931,697**	**52,728**	**153,212**
Alabama..............	31,638	31,662	9,396	12,793	10,713	11,866	9,308	9,939	820	1,450
Alaska................	11,930	14,920	6,599	6,441	4,522	4,853	4,805	4,638	-1,287	-920
Arizona..............	40,784	45,102	11,464	15,967	11,928	14,475	11,284	13,611	373	864
Arkansas............	27,775	31,222	5,465	12,300	5,753	6,845	5,750	5,900	3	946
California............	357,085	512,850	166,083	277,220	151,270	194,332	146,285	166,083	5,557	28,249
Colorado............	35,641	36,850	11,142	15,539	14,379	16,401	12,716	13,251	1,823	3,150
Connecticut........	34,031	35,704	20,056	7,455	19,194	20,531	19,163	20,051	39	481
Delaware............	11,887	13,285	4,519	3,956	5,473	6,350	4,514	4,516	959	1,833
Florida..............	85,991	92,269	34,751	35,261	40,414	50,024	32,870	33,795	6,352	13,236
Georgia.............	60,767	57,697	28,070	15,691	28,742	31,671	26,119	25,174	2,622	6,496
Hawaii...............	18,134	24,401	8,756	5,251	9,037	10,006	8,035	8,756	1,003	1,250
Idaho................	11,708	15,444	4,357	8,053	4,080	3,861	3,907	3,866	186	140
Illinois..............	77,814	87,503	37,733	24,367	40,387	47,381	41,921	42,741	531	3,206
Indiana..............	37,656	44,698	18,136	20,319	17,144	20,738	16,522	17,732	542	2,621
Iowa.................	26,046	27,577	7,827	9,375	8,126	9,048	7,821	7,809	306	1,239
Kansas..............	19,412	21,251	7,588	6,294	8,017	9,370	7,523	7,267	495	2,103
Kentucky............	38,434	42,070	11,382	21,219	12,349	13,852	11,622	11,508	353	1,629
Louisiana............	31,078	37,698	10,073	18,611	10,471	10,238	10,141	9,871	270	–
Maine................	10,545	12,104	3,755	5,618	4,161	4,774	3,934	3,895	184	155
Maryland............	48,576	56,438	19,259	22,386	19,791	21,904	19,531	18,914	703	3,239
Massachusetts.......	63,085	68,491	32,163	19,339	52,289	58,254	34,185	37,035	4,295	5,980
Michigan............	62,318	72,524	10,982	35,760	11,466	13,334	8,890	10,433	2,535	2,366
Minnesota...........	42,989	50,009	23,978	15,613	27,122	27,898	23,778	23,978	3,344	3,920
Mississippi..........	19,919	23,245	5,586	10,945	5,822	5,699	5,731	5,586	9	10
Missouri.............	27,310	29,778	9,759	11,473	10,014	12,144	9,212	9,789	803	2,354
Montana.............	8,302	11,133	2,390	5,946	2,891	3,404	2,436	2,684	452	720
Nebraska............	12,901	15,067	4,526	5,081	5,386	6,375	4,499	4,526	711	1,849
Nevada..............	15,074	16,290	4,540	5,649	5,118	5,451	4,467	4,562	574	783
New Hampshire......	6,920	7,562	1,606	3,585	1,718	1,793	1,688	1,606	-51	–
New Jersey..........	66,759	75,101	40,461	22,107	40,303	51,616	38,140	44,963	2,163	6,653
New Mexico.........	22,347	25,326	7,274	12,614	10,265	11,821	7,672	8,893	2,514	2,451
New York............	172,981	186,587	74,095	71,685	86,413	83,256	77,469	74,095	8,944	9,161
North Carolina.......	61,655	59,886	24,487	22,267	25,649	31,190	24,062	23,964	1,471	7,224
North Dakota........	7,058	8,403	2,284	2,749	2,615	3,484	2,333	2,362	282	1,123
Ohio.................	74,556	81,216	22,892	34,351	24,460	28,078	23,190	23,357	1,270	4,721
Oklahoma...........	24,799	27,768	5,566	10,784	7,817	8,469	7,493	6,581	324	1,606
Oregon..............	48,807	59,609	10,294	21,260	11,029	15,358	11,006	11,455	23	3,704
Pennsylvania........	96,018	103,778	38,777	41,709	31,356	36,635	35,219	34,013	-2,734	–
Rhode Island........	11,417	15,125	3,983	7,539	4,098	4,474	3,937	4,133	156	332
South Carolina.......	26,949	29,443	8,574	12,035	10,898	12,264	8,633	8,398	1,805	3,615
South Dakota........	4,851	6,710	1,861	3,534	1,741	2,016	1,703	1,888	19	86
Tennessee...........	36,048	46,370	16,716	23,021	17,541	18,127	14,620	15,831	1,991	2,198
Texas................	136,396	143,234	61,379	55,129	57,506	73,053	59,084	58,904	-3,774	11,229
Utah.................	18,155	23,690	8,502	9,119	7,646	9,621	7,298	8,507	304	1,114
Vermont.............	6,175	7,290	1,623	3,262	1,621	2,157	1,607	1,742	–	104
Virginia.............	64,426	75,014	22,590	20,382	23,472	24,612	22,287	22,694	1,185	1,917
Washington..........	54,299	61,812	26,395	19,814	24,620	28,194	23,967	24,828	654	3,366
West Virginia........	18,496	19,058	3,691	5,696	5,061	5,468	4,588	4,775	454	679
Wisconsin............	51,834	59,356	18,276	17,574	19,250	21,932	18,450	19,516	1,172	2,581
Wyoming............	4,708	4,698	1,470	840	1,627	1,284	1,627	1,284	–	–

P Preliminary. – Represents zero. [1] Includes bonds and other state funds, not shown separately. [2] Includes funds budgeted, adjustments, and balances from previous year. [3] May or may not include budget stabilization fund transfers, depending on state accounting practices. [4] Resources less expenditures, minus adjustments.

Source: National Association of State Budget Officers, Washington, DC, *2021 State Expenditure Report: Fiscal Years 2019-2021* ©, 2021; and *Fiscal Survey of States, Fall 2021* ©, 2021. See also <www.nasbo.org>.

Table 499. State Governments—Summary of Finances: 2000 to 2020

[In millions of dollars (1,260,829 represents $1,260,829,000,000). For fiscal year ending in year shown; see text, this section]

Item	2000	2005	2010	2014	2015	2016	2017	2018	2019	2020
Total revenue	**1,260,829**	**1,642,468**	**2,039,927**	**2,357,406**	**2,164,784**	**2,141,692**	**2,591,555**	**2,711,266**	**2,658,088**	**2,802,271**
General revenue	984,783	1,286,899	1,567,207	1,748,172	1,860,023	1,917,520	1,974,050	2,104,133	2,198,568	2,306,872
Intergovernmental revenue	274,382	407,792	575,372	550,390	605,936	641,557	659,241	687,770	708,502	845,556
Total taxes	539,655	650,612	705,929	870,437	911,430	923,259	949,845	1,033,054	1,084,270	1,057,323
General sales and gross receipts taxes	174,461	212,921	224,314	273,899	286,023	291,902	303,553	321,033	335,501	340,592
Selective sales and gross receipts taxes	77,685	99,663	120,208	141,007	144,686	149,255	153,494	165,599	170,405	171,053
License taxes	32,598	42,584	50,429	51,318	52,053	53,909	55,071	57,027	58,768	58,876
Individual income taxes	194,573	221,597	236,987	311,562	336,558	342,376	351,179	393,673	408,935	385,630
Corporation net income taxes	32,522	38,691	38,006	46,492	48,612	45,575	44,617	48,444	59,736	52,169
All other taxes	27,815	35,155	35,985	46,159	43,498	40,241	41,931	47,278	50,924	49,003
Current charges	86,467	123,129	169,855	193,781	201,657	215,373	223,145	234,159	244,920	245,244
Miscellaneous general revenue	84,279	105,367	116,051	133,564	140,999	137,330	141,819	149,151	160,876	158,749
Utility revenue	4,513	14,628	15,122	14,317	14,721	13,828	13,609	14,028	14,374	13,409
Liquor stores revenue	3,895	5,118	6,495	7,615	8,020	7,818	8,338	8,686	9,132	9,713
Insurance trust revenue [1]	267,639	335,822	451,103	587,302	282,020	202,526	595,559	584,419	436,013	472,277
Total expenditure	**1,084,097**	**1,472,542**	**1,943,523**	**2,078,644**	**2,161,620**	**2,244,467**	**2,307,270**	**2,402,120**	**2,504,920**	**2,695,335**
Intergovernmental expenditure	327,070	405,925	485,557	507,163	525,656	542,753	549,867	562,084	586,048	606,996
Direct expenditure	757,027	1,066,617	1,457,965	1,571,481	1,635,964	1,701,714	1,757,403	1,840,036	1,918,872	2,088,339
Current operations	523,114	738,886	934,322	1,067,552	1,140,270	1,192,437	1,241,699	1,299,151	1,359,960	1,439,526
Capital outlay	76,233	95,155	118,011	115,874	128,561	130,532	132,044	142,011	149,534	148,233
Insurance benefits and repayments	105,456	168,200	320,721	296,189	275,454	284,865	288,611	298,637	306,853	394,287
Assistance and subsidies	22,136	28,403	37,562	45,307	45,847	47,966	49,110	51,869	55,039	59,592
Interest on debt	30,089	35,974	47,351	46,559	45,832	45,913	45,939	48,369	47,485	46,702
Exhibit: salaries and wages	154,504	194,907	244,952	248,674	253,951	260,783	272,100	281,093	291,348	301,936
General expenditure	964,723	1,278,434	1,593,694	1,751,941	1,847,037	1,926,373	1,983,579	2,065,129	2,160,625	2,259,904
Intergovernmental general expenditure	327,070	405,925	485,557	507,163	525,656	542,753	549,867	562,084	586,048	606,996
Direct general expenditure	637,653	872,508	1,108,137	1,244,778	1,321,381	1,383,619	1,433,712	1,503,045	1,574,577	1,652,908
General expenditure, by function:										
Education	346,465	454,348	571,147	613,568	644,358	669,623	687,278	707,156	734,971	755,827
Public welfare	238,890	368,765	462,431	547,809	613,061	654,770	679,747	706,650	744,675	792,516
Hospitals	32,578	43,623	64,509	71,787	73,645	79,029	85,797	90,579	96,153	103,507
Health	42,066	48,634	58,245	60,010	56,423	58,300	62,749	65,169	69,091	76,972
Highways	74,415	92,816	111,170	119,629	122,417	127,452	129,200	137,340	147,653	148,201
Police protection	9,788	11,395	13,828	15,029	15,267	15,798	16,617	17,314	17,999	19,082
Correction	35,129	40,562	48,550	49,941	51,171	51,481	51,495	53,370	53,595	57,007
Natural resources	15,967	18,822	21,515	20,777	21,572	23,714	23,946	24,671	27,954	27,943
Parks and recreation	4,676	5,334	5,720	5,496	6,060	6,276	6,639	6,691	7,352	7,473
Governmental administration	35,527	46,464	53,976	67,426	60,366	61,591	65,088	67,057	68,848	69,791
Interest on general debt	29,187	34,242	45,260	44,122	43,336	43,404	43,463	45,752	44,905	44,110
Other and unallocable	100,034	113,427	137,344	90,416	91,670	86,940	117,107	129,141	133,349	143,276
Utility expenditure	10,723	21,827	23,864	35,462	44,043	37,737	37,865	40,710	39,029	42,181
Liquor store expenditure [1]	3,195	4,082	5,244	6,092	6,480	6,506	6,925	7,123	7,527	7,940
Insurance trust expenditure	105,456	168,200	320,721	296,189	275,454	284,865	288,611	298,637	306,853	394,287
Debt outstanding, long term and short term [2]	**547,876**	**810,852**	**1,115,463**	**1,152,282**	**1,155,113**	**1,170,612**	**1,153,147**	**1,171,287**	**1,166,494**	**1,184,617**
Cash and security holdings	**2,518,936**	**3,153,795**	**3,323,047**	**2,915,718**	**2,996,239**	**3,009,115**	**4,833,360**	**5,183,081**	**5,352,777**	**5,504,635**

[1] Within insurance trust revenue, net earnings of state-administered pension systems is a calculated statistic, and thus can be positive or negative. Net earnings is the sum of earnings on investments plus gains on investments minus losses on investments. [2] As of fiscal year 2005, the Census Bureau no longer collects government debt information by the character of long-term debt. For further information, see the 2006 Government Finance and Employment Classification Manual at <www.census.gov/programs-surveys/gov-finances/technical-documentation/classification-manuals.html>.

Source: U.S. Census Bureau, "Annual Survey of State Government Finances," <www.census.gov/programs-surveys/state.html>, accessed April 2022.

Table 500. State Governments—Revenue by State: 2020

[In millions of dollars (2,724,588 represents $2,724,588,000,000). For fiscal year ending in year shown; see text, this section. Includes local shares of state imposed taxes]

State	Total revenue [1,2]	General revenue							Utilities and liquor store revenue	Insurance trust revenue
		Total	Intergovernmental revenue		General revenue from own sources					
			Total [1]	From federal govern-ment	Total	Total taxes	Current charges	Miscel-laneous general revenue		
United States......	**2,724,588**	**2,306,872**	**845,556**	**828,021**	**1,461,316**	**1,057,323**	**245,244**	**158,749**	**23,122**	**394,593**
Alabama..............	36,680	33,149	13,657	13,497	19,492	12,045	5,790	1,658	423	3,108
Alaska................	9,927	8,807	4,476	4,469	4,331	1,318	680	2,333	21	1,098
Arizona..............	49,445	44,621	21,168	20,916	23,453	17,654	3,342	2,457	22	4,802
Arkansas............	28,293	23,601	9,365	9,354	14,236	10,255	2,816	1,165	–	4,692
California............	396,092	315,857	101,432	98,647	214,426	171,964	33,480	8,981	910	79,324
Colorado.............	47,005	33,681	11,566	11,480	22,116	15,074	4,760	2,281	–	13,324
Connecticut..........	37,082	32,781	10,344	9,802	22,437	18,401	2,415	1,622	58	4,243
Delaware............	12,329	11,110	4,309	4,241	6,801	4,555	1,090	1,156	18	1,201
Florida..............	109,500	100,056	36,791	36,473	63,265	43,118	8,648	11,499	26	9,418
Georgia..............	60,062	47,953	17,800	17,770	30,153	23,609	3,910	2,635	–	12,109
Hawaii...............	16,779	15,498	4,205	3,788	11,293	7,708	1,681	1,904	–	1,281
Idaho................	13,241	11,513	4,730	4,693	6,783	5,280	919	584	206	1,522
Illinois..............	97,527	82,822	26,817	26,417	56,005	45,285	5,409	5,312	–	14,705
Indiana..............	51,122	48,685	19,472	19,379	29,214	22,374	4,020	2,820	–	2,437
Iowa.................	31,884	28,451	8,563	8,534	19,887	10,661	4,122	5,104	367	3,066
Kansas..............	22,904	21,545	6,025	5,978	15,519	9,660	4,531	1,328	–	1,360
Kentucky............	38,142	34,688	15,453	15,407	19,235	13,371	4,499	1,366	–	3,454
Louisiana............	36,485	32,998	17,247	16,726	15,751	11,381	2,124	2,246	13	3,474
Maine................	12,299	11,042	4,778	4,732	6,264	4,851	924	489	227	1,030
Maryland............	50,619	46,348	15,701	15,512	30,648	23,883	4,242	2,522	102	4,169
Massachusetts.......	74,160	64,556	21,484	20,908	43,072	31,630	5,859	5,583	836	8,768
Michigan.............	80,111	69,207	26,752	26,561	42,454	28,062	10,280	4,113	1,252	9,652
Minnesota...........	55,692	46,918	14,776	14,550	32,142	26,791	2,877	2,474	104	8,670
Mississippi..........	23,615	21,509	10,177	10,138	11,332	8,100	2,444	788	428	1,679
Missouri.............	39,395	33,907	15,416	15,116	18,491	12,410	3,179	2,902	–	5,488
Montana.............	8,887	7,705	3,589	3,587	4,116	3,168	542	405	117	1,065
Nebraska............	13,917	12,382	4,710	4,676	7,672	5,857	1,082	733	–	1,535
Nevada..............	22,714	16,801	5,758	5,549	11,044	9,453	924	667	52	5,860
New Hampshire......	10,398	8,790	4,168	3,725	4,622	2,858	863	900	740	868
New Jersey..........	78,899	70,460	20,121	19,194	50,340	37,927	6,735	5,678	861	7,578
New Mexico..........	22,547	21,251	8,883	8,631	12,369	7,150	1,959	3,260	–	1,296
New York............	208,104	188,170	70,869	69,676	117,302	92,721	11,692	12,889	8,011	11,922
North Carolina.......	69,723	60,497	22,060	21,878	38,437	28,303	6,627	3,508	1	9,225
North Dakota........	10,126	9,228	3,205	3,145	6,022	4,336	744	942	–	899
Ohio.................	109,992	77,468	30,769	30,152	46,699	30,582	9,782	6,335	1,433	31,090
Oklahoma............	29,043	25,549	9,515	9,377	16,034	10,173	3,128	2,733	627	2,866
Oregon..............	42,845	35,570	13,116	13,081	22,454	12,775	6,455	3,224	739	6,537
Pennsylvania........	115,760	96,757	37,779	37,703	58,978	40,685	13,083	5,211	2,039	16,964
Rhode Island........	10,855	9,808	4,289	4,195	5,520	3,527	1,139	854	22	1,025
South Carolina......	36,364	32,407	12,511	12,185	19,896	11,795	5,810	2,292	1,704	2,253
South Dakota........	6,601	6,060	3,087	3,044	2,974	2,018	379	577	1	540
Tennessee...........	39,354	35,316	14,226	14,126	21,090	16,775	2,122	2,193	–	4,038
Texas...............	196,854	160,726	66,663	62,988	94,063	61,013	17,606	15,444	–	36,129
Utah.................	26,990	21,270	5,801	5,797	15,469	8,731	5,250	1,488	445	5,275
Vermont.............	8,384	7,858	3,422	3,420	4,436	3,420	643	373	88	438
Virginia.............	69,369	63,157	18,494	17,559	44,663	28,064	11,392	5,206	971	5,241
Washington..........	66,732	54,978	16,190	15,780	38,788	29,013	6,407	3,367	–	11,755
West Virginia........	16,086	14,888	6,723	6,613	8,165	5,462	1,682	1,021	120	1,078
Wisconsin............	64,654	41,732	13,305	13,056	28,427	20,115	4,907	3,405	–	22,922
Wyoming.............	8,997	6,740	3,804	3,794	2,937	1,963	253	720	136	2,120

– Represents zero. [1] Includes amounts for categories not shown separately. [2] Duplicate intergovernmental transactions are excluded.

Source: U.S. Census Bureau, Annual Survey of State and Local Government Finances, "Datasets & Tables," <www.census.gov/programs-surveys/gov-finances.html>, accessed August 2022.

Table 501. State Government Tax Collections by State: 2021

[In millions of dollars (1,271,509 represents $1,271,509,000,000). Data are for the state fiscal year; see Narrative, Section 8 for details. Data presented here may differ from data published by state governments; see source for more information]

State	All taxes	Total property taxes	Selective sales and gross receipts — Total	Total general sales and gross receipts	Selective sales tax — Total [1]	Alcoholic beverage sales	Insurance premiums	Motor fuels sales	Public utilities	Tobacco products	License taxes — Total [1]	Corporation	Motor vehicle	Occupation and business n.e.c. [2]	Income taxes — Total	Individual income	Corporation net income	Other taxes — Total [1]	Death and gift	Severance
U.S.	1,271,509	23,331	550,718	370,907	179,810	7,557	26,293	51,477	12,178	19,143	64,892	9,501	30,377	15,697	596,443	506,265	90,179	36,125	6,435	11,804
AL	14,251	468	7,015	3,912	3,102	272	468	878	664	171	606	188	260	70	6,043	4,909	1,134	119	(X)	39
AK	1,053	120	268	(X)	268	41	62	45	4	61	153	(X)	36	75	125	(X)	125	387	(X)	387
AZ	20,818	1,267	11,291	9,185	2,106	89	680	845	22	294	618	28	293	206	7,439	6,533	906	203	–	36
AR	11,727	1,308	5,753	4,187	1,565	68	310	588	(X)	233	424	32	179	145	4,086	3,467	618	156	–	33
CA	248,188	3,151	61,192	41,974	19,218	412	3,117	7,659	653	1,970	11,292	88	5,226	4,841	172,422	146,325	26,097	131	(Z)	131
CO	18,818	(X)	6,573	3,661	2,912	53	348	619	(X)	228	720	26	458	54	11,525	10,247	1,278	–	(X)	–
CT	22,067	(X)	8,148	5,253	2,896	79	181	470	257	323	388	33	223	59	12,866	10,259	2,607	664	286	(X)
DE	5,396	(X)	588	(X)	588	33	123	125	46	116	2,077	1,823	62	162	2,483	2,148	335	248	(Z)	(Z)
DC	8,980	2,995	1,647	1,201	445	6	134	24	167	22	184	37	35	48	3,506	2,643	863	649	32	(X)
FL	49,314	(X)	38,522	29,874	8,648	339	1,492	2,874	1,682	1,100	2,509	536	1,523	160	3,407	(X)	3,407	4,876	(X)	30
GA	27,851	732	10,258	6,948	3,310	228	538	1,782	(X)	243	750	67	407	86	15,972	14,221	1,751	139	–	(X)
HI	8,047	(X)	4,148	3,296	851	45	192	71	125	109	259	2	177	50	3,546	3,355	191	94	31	(X)
ID	6,472	(X)	3,180	2,517	663	11	118	405	2	49	474	5	232	95	2,809	2,458	351	302	(X)	6
IL	55,532	60	23,486	13,429	10,057	312	513	2,384	1,276	917	3,819	401	2,444	589	27,600	21,871	5,730	567	479	(X)
IN	26,646	14	13,848	9,283	4,565	59	235	1,546	208	410	819	12	352	47	11,964	10,579	1,385	1	(Z)	1
IA	11,817	2	5,522	4,002	1,520	30	144	674	79	201	1,101	65	761	160	5,060	4,267	794	131	100	(X)
KS	11,616	816	4,970	3,767	1,203	149	451	445	(Z)	123	458	32	243	101	5,345	4,617	727	28	–	28
KY	14,617	707	7,088	4,558	2,530	174	187	700	81	421	533	116	223	136	6,139	5,213	926	150	62	84
LA	12,257	104	6,854	4,049	2,805	79	1,004	640	9	269	477	238	85	107	4,521	3,933	588	302	–	302
ME	5,452	45	2,630	1,910	720	18	102	232	22	145	326	15	126	131	2,360	2,075	284	93	40	(X)
MD	25,221	893	10,587	5,459	5,128	39	758	1,025	144	388	969	168	521	234	12,027	10,186	1,841	744	241	(X)
MA	36,336	10	10,428	7,785	2,643	93	537	663	(X)	398	1,274	28	472	351	23,356	19,683	3,673	1,267	788	(X)
MI	34,432	2,396	15,926	11,190	4,735	235	349	1,337	38	886	2,179	34	1,456	268	13,496	11,999	1,496	435	–	24
MN	31,793	809	11,204	6,699	4,506	101	650	845	95	626	1,506	16	946	271	17,594	15,171	2,423	680	205	65
MS	9,353	30	5,657	4,230	1,427	46	398	450	2	141	570	214	170	78	3,066	2,516	550	30	–	30
MO	15,091	37	5,945	4,120	1,826	46	448	696	(X)	99	692	–	334	184	8,402	7,716	687	15	(Z)	–
MT	3,880	335	768	(X)	768	46	139	274	41	74	482	7	188	177	2,158	1,889	268	138	(X)	131
NE	6,961	(Z)	3,041	2,382	658	35	70	415	54	56	195	7	118	36	3,702	3,131	571	24	(X)	3
NV	10,416	386	8,393	6,180	2,213	45	489	352	38	185	623	88	210	236	(X)	(X)	(X)	1,014	(X)	279
NH	3,213	401	978	(X)	978	14	139	117	38	251	473	80	94	227	1,159	149	1,010	203	(X)	(X)
NJ	43,683	5	17,872	12,803	5,069	175	639	386	935	602	1,986	518	681	623	22,793	16,833	5,960	1,026	530	(X)
NM	7,472	92	3,823	2,972	851	24	235	230	35	95	343	43	214	50	1,352	1,199	153	1,862	(X)	1,804
NY	93,504	(X)	27,164	15,613	11,551	271	2,079	1,465	793	1,007	1,793	1	1,419	121	59,951	54,997	4,954	4,595	1,537	(X)

See footnotes at end of table.

Table 501. State Government Tax Collections by State: 2021-Continued.

See headnote on page 323.

State	All taxes	Total property taxes	Selective sales and gross receipts — Total	Total general sales and gross receipts	Selective sales tax — Total [1]	Alcoholic beverage sales	Insurance premiums	Motor fuels sales	Public utilities	Tobacco products	License taxes — Total [1]	Corporation	Motor vehicle	Occupation and business n.e.c. [2]	Income taxes — Total	Individual income	Corporation net income	Other taxes — Total [1]	Death and gift	Severance
NC.....	34,712	(X)	14,568	9,718	4,851	534	725	2,113	(Z)	307	2,597	990	995	379	17,424	15,908	1,516	123	(Z)	2
ND.....	3,909	5	1,427	920	507	10	59	173	53	26	210	(X)	118	66	604	449	155	1,662	(X)	1,662
OH.....	34,909	(X)	22,149	14,393	7,755	119	667	2,524	1,037	928	2,029	277	504	894	10,669	10,663	6	63	(Z)	63
OK.....	11,299	(X)	4,976	3,116	1,859	147	449	571	48	463	1,085	56	813	1	4,369	3,768	601	870	(Z)	754
OR.....	17,800	21	2,387	(X)	2,387	18	50	619	19	378	2,484	1,232	796	306	12,480	11,257	1,224	428	410	15
PA.....	49,571	40	24,413	13,718	10,695	445	852	3,031	994	1,292	2,955	15	1,307	1,284	20,023	15,978	4,045	2,140	1,303	–
RI.....	4,344	4	2,132	1,335	797	22	146	130	93	159	137	7	28	81	2,016	1,758	258	56	38	(X)
SC.....	13,286	79	6,120	4,154	1,965	208	274	838	28	28	707	148	303	171	6,197	5,456	740	184	(X)	(X)
SD.....	2,150	(X)	1,784	1,274	510	20	90	190	3	52	301	7	89	137	54	(X)	54	11	(X)	10
TN.....	19,978	(X)	14,493	11,060	3,432	211	1,109	1,211	9	243	2,333	1,382	388	453	2,744	179	2,564	408	1	(Z)
TX.....	65,377	(X)	56,642	40,414	16,228	1,263	2,700	3,597	726	1,397	3,646	260	2,221	586	(X)	(X)	(X)	5,089	(X)	5,089
UT.....	12,632	(X)	4,803	3,629	1,175	18	166	535	55	107	372	(Z)	243	59	7,418	6,673	746	38	(X)	38
VT.....	4,103	1,203	1,248	507	740	12	63	110	10	77	144	3	76	30	1,400	1,233	167	109	27	(X)
VA.....	32,328	43	11,719	6,527	5,192	295	551	1,422	496	288	995	77	504	226	18,646	17,067	1,579	924	324	3
WA.....	32,614	4,350	24,013	19,057	4,957	473	684	1,518	611	387	2,073	50	998	438	(X)	(X)	(X)	2,178	(X)	43
WV.....	6,046	8	2,969	1,537	1,431	17	118	400	126	171	197	1	5	15	2,574	2,254	320	298	(X)	274
WI.....	22,301	96	9,185	6,373	2,811	74	227	1,124	354	604	1,341	29	719	349	11,553	9,036	2,517	127	(Z)	4
WY.....	1,875	296	927	735	192	2	36	111	5	22	212	18	102	45	(X)	(X)	(X)	439	–	435

X Not applicable. Z Less than $500,000. – Represents zero. [1] Includes other items not shown separately. [2] N.e.c. means not elsewhere classified.

Source: U.S. Census Bureau, Annual Survey of State Government Tax Collections, "2021 State Government Tax Tables," <www.census.gov/programs-surveys/stc.html>, accessed June 2022.

Table 502. State Governments—Expenditures and Debt by State: 2020

[In millions of dollars (2,705,136 represents $2,705,136,000,000). For fiscal year ending in year shown; see text, this section]

State	Total expenditures	Inter-govern-mental	Direct expenditures Total	Direct general expenditures Total[1]	Educa-tion	Public welfare	Hospi-tals	Health	High-ways	Police protec-tion	Correc-tions	Parks and recre-ation	Hous-ing and com-munity devel-opment	Sewer-age	Solid waste man-age-ment	Gov-ern-men-tal admin-istra-tion	Inter-est on gen-eral debt	Utility and liquor store	Insur-ance trust	Cash and security holdings	Total debt out-stand-ing
U.S...	2,705,136	606,996	2,098,140	1,652,908	350,500	728,641	101,253	57,163	122,100	17,131	54,704	6,372	9,494	1,411	1,165	66,932	44,110	41,144	404,088	5,501,194	1,184,617
AL...	35,890	8,341	27,549	22,910	6,947	7,765	2,668	508	1,705	190	658	23	39	–	–	716	388	399	4,240	60,238	9,934
AK...	12,029	2,261	9,768	7,988	1,214	2,719	38	159	1,136	139	340	12	102	–	–	663	199	131	1,650	95,078	5,849
AZ..	47,446	9,909	37,537	31,503	8,657	17,130	–	602	1,497	285	1,127	92	92	–	1	639	644	26	6,008	77,490	12,947
AR..	23,686	5,864	17,821	15,546	3,376	7,354	1,333	203	1,233	105	350	71	17	–	11	755	187	–	2,275	45,014	7,565
CA..	423,157	116,459	306,699	233,876	49,277	115,221	16,278	4,235	11,410	2,248	9,829	939	190	501	331	7,173	5,419	1,096	71,726	876,253	144,041
CO...	42,508	8,411	34,097	26,037	7,587	9,821	1,370	463	1,620	292	1,050	105	203	4	8	1,590	855	12	8,049	94,570	20,127
CT...	30,902	6,305	24,597	17,850	4,057	3,849	1,593	919	1,429	246	716	38	167	–	80	1,448	1,723	597	6,151	55,493	41,363
DE..	11,280	2,015	9,265	8,124	2,168	2,813	80	492	559	161	363	59	93	12	73	603	238	180	962	19,015	5,069
FL..	107,679	19,365	88,314	74,837	14,282	29,385	1,651	5,884	8,440	650	2,946	178	213	–	188	2,632	704	241	13,235	257,167	25,013
GA..	60,728	14,859	45,869	34,260	9,260	13,661	1,318	1,359	2,971	456	1,278	204	278	12	11	1,181	575	37	11,573	124,911	14,116
HI..	15,202	323	14,878	12,419	3,718	2,990	537	735	524	53	234	61	187	–	–	670	117	–	2,459	28,896	9,430
ID..	12,128	2,841	9,288	7,626	1,457	3,240	55	213	766	76	339	36	136	–	–	577	166	160	1,502	29,362	3,348
IL...	100,910	23,266	77,645	57,845	8,092	27,342	962	1,250	5,192	526	1,635	97	137	–	7	1,867	4,059	12	19,787	187,069	64,854
IN...	47,089	10,700	36,389	32,503	8,234	16,786	151	696	2,173	263	680	73	394	2	4	850	1,005	–	3,885	70,029	23,841
IA...	26,492	5,633	20,859	17,050	3,322	7,160	2,449	116	1,725	108	306	26	115	1	3	630	227	–	3,552	53,594	6,250
KS...	22,749	5,993	16,756	14,276	2,950	5,125	2,964	402	868	117	355	42	94	–	–	563	191	257	2,480	27,962	6,928
KY...	38,509	4,910	33,598	27,543	5,875	13,208	2,266	405	1,847	190	623	103	251	–	25	1,046	599	–	6,021	51,596	14,635
LA...	39,587	6,837	32,751	26,322	4,837	13,535	364	586	1,491	257	565	313	51	–	–	736	829	34	6,418	71,055	16,858
ME..	10,984	1,522	9,461	7,758	1,081	3,867	106	261	784	97	152	9	162	–	–	520	184	10	1,532	23,746	5,151
MD...	53,606	10,469	43,137	34,569	6,660	14,726	375	2,284	2,396	654	1,567	290	450	218	26	1,756	1,340	171	6,380	79,203	29,359
MA..	77,895	10,420	67,475	50,859	6,933	25,600	748	1,942	2,141	572	1,685	174	1,341	283	1	2,450	2,671	2,188	12,430	107,906	77,321
MI..	86,724	24,755	61,969	47,843	12,813	18,112	5,258	2,033	2,170	532	1,921	145	643	–	6	960	1,287	4,185	13,118	120,906	34,403
MN..	55,700	15,514	40,186	31,702	6,619	16,348	321	1,110	1,999	409	546	231	136	157	11	1,991	609	1,008	7,940	96,659	17,401
MS...	23,958	5,515	18,443	14,492	2,890	6,512	1,615	412	966	143	342	34	23	–	–	509	288	543	3,523	39,443	7,289
MO...	38,553	6,829	31,724	25,614	4,561	10,212	2,707	2,169	1,508	255	758	44	227	–	3	898	819	428	6,105	101,919	18,970
MT..	8,624	1,170	7,454	6,016	1,046	2,419	64	246	782	71	227	18	29	–	–	485	113	114	1,324	22,857	2,726
NE..	12,168	2,882	9,287	8,164	2,334	2,782	197	281	951	90	432	52	1	–	5	344	60	–	1,122	28,077	2,586
NV...	20,174	5,028	15,146	10,405	2,666	4,268	303	317	883	99	349	39	17	–	6	456	160	46	4,694	54,298	3,653
NH...	9,998	1,865	8,134	6,414	1,181	2,300	67	140	505	73	136	25	129	40	36	744	313	603	1,117	16,749	7,543
NJ...	85,563	16,101	69,462	48,346	11,720	18,857	2,581	2,031	3,015	796	1,519	143	609	13	5	2,194	2,444	3,422	17,694	123,817	64,058
NM...	24,097	5,924	18,174	15,103	2,302	7,268	1,356	540	796	137	526	54	70	–	–	626	423	2	3,068	66,412	7,268
NY...	227,411	64,784	162,627	118,123	13,608	69,675	6,475	3,965	4,552	954	3,413	733	793	4	21	5,920	4,309	17,596	26,908	460,657	156,004
NC...	67,979	16,321	51,658	43,463	11,562	15,483	2,717	1,120	5,202	608	1,486	191	286	–	11	2,269	670	43	8,152	145,702	15,099

See footnotes at end of table.

Table 502. State Governments—Expenditures and Debt by State: 2020-Continued.
See headnote on page 325.

State	Total expenditures	Intergovernmental	Direct expenditures Total	Direct general expenditures Total [1]	Education	Public welfare	Hospitals	Health	Highways	Police protection	Corrections	Parks and recreation	Housing and community development	Sewerage	Solid waste management	Governmental administration	Interest on general debt	Utility and liquor store	Insurance trust	Cash and security holdings	Total debt outstanding
ND...	7,957	2,105	5,852	4,975	1,223	1,605	53	128	652	40	119	24	23	–	3	225	129	49	827	35,778	3,018
OH...	98,196	19,306	78,889	56,319	11,416	28,891	4,479	1,305	3,548	487	1,673	99	77	–	26	2,120	911	1,153	21,418	269,977	30,412
OK...	27,014	4,908	22,106	18,021	4,702	7,112	305	934	2,133	197	654	78	174	–	3	735	228	704	3,380	52,528	7,805
OR...	45,149	7,126	38,023	30,127	6,438	12,851	2,658	989	1,194	245	873	86	173	5	11	1,804	370	509	7,387	114,777	14,600
PA...	122,627	24,373	98,254	78,093	13,100	37,754	5,082	2,889	8,060	1,171	2,574	289	162	17	40	3,224	1,668	1,841	18,321	140,793	51,735
RI...	10,555	1,431	9,125	7,413	1,055	3,199	52	400	596	102	236	32	86	57	53	739	411	131	1,580	19,823	9,372
SC...	37,044	6,555	30,489	24,473	6,556	8,627	2,458	1,311	1,965	177	528	160	187	–	–	817	278	1,467	4,549	52,971	12,896
SD...	5,740	923	4,817	4,105	920	1,218	24	179	762	53	127	42	45	–	–	217	127	–	712	18,551	3,856
TN...	37,770	7,774	29,996	26,135	5,422	13,016	394	845	1,865	253	724	91	325	1	37	1,395	370	1	3,861	77,955	6,858
TX...	174,987	35,312	139,675	115,168	30,113	43,210	9,352	3,779	13,024	1,256	3,852	291	59	74	74	2,842	1,963	75	24,433	459,754	57,887
UT...	25,256	4,624	20,632	18,094	5,527	4,624	2,725	468	1,750	196	373	64	122	–	7	1,205	205	321	2,218	48,015	7,594
VT...	7,598	1,969	5,629	4,856	1,126	1,955	23	422	395	95	147	24	90	2	4	209	103	78	695	10,382	3,563
VA...	65,446	13,198	52,247	44,165	10,576	15,142	5,992	1,239	4,079	484	1,578	158	194	–	3	1,973	1,160	982	7,100	115,632	29,341
WA...	69,277	18,306	50,972	40,077	9,662	13,815	4,106	3,138	2,492	340	1,198	138	22	–	13	964	1,435	42	10,853	154,428	29,659
WV...	16,582	2,614	13,968	11,922	2,274	4,982	177	256	1,748	95	374	67	37	4	10	689	322	106	1,940	23,138	11,626
WI...	46,151	11,846	34,305	27,538	6,206	12,241	2,403	406	2,012	45	1,080	49	33	4	–	1,019	585	20	6,747	156,688	22,446
WY...	6,380	1,234	5,146	4,040	897	865	4	396	589	44	142	24	10	–	5	292	27	117	989	36,861	949

– Represents or rounds to zero. [1] Includes other direct general expenditures not shown separately.
Source: U.S. Census Bureau, Annual Survey of State and Local Government Finances, "Datasets & Tables," <www.census.gov/programs-surveys/gov-finances.html>, accessed August 2022.

Table 503. Local Governments—Revenue by State: 2020

[In millions of dollars (2,153,396 represents $2,153,396,000,000). For fiscal year ending in year shown; see text, this section. Minus sign (-) indicates decrease]

State	Total revenue	General revenue, total	Inter-govern-mental revenue	Gen. rev. from own sources – Total	Taxes Total[1]	Property	Sales and gross receipt	Indi-vidual income	Current charges & misc. – Total	Current charges Total[1]	Educa-tion	Hospi-tals	Sewer-age	Misc. Total[1]	Interest earn-ings	Special assess-ment	Utility rev-enue	Liquor store rev-enue	Insur-ance trust rev-enue
U.S. ...	2,153,396	1,916,978	665,052	1,251,925	804,294	581,048	139,334	39,139	447,631	336,221	21,450	106,219	65,444	111,410	33,258	11,619	167,407	1,614	67,397
AL....	25,647	21,939	8,054	13,886	6,829	2,731	3,313	139	7,057	5,941	247	3,996	661	1,115	376	30	3,458	–	250
AK....	5,799	5,299	1,972	3,326	1,994	1,541	413	–	1,332	922	21	407	123	410	210	3	422	9	70
AZ....	33,833	28,299	10,749	17,550	12,033	7,562	4,006	–	5,517	4,040	441	617	1,012	1,478	422	89	5,190	–	345
AR. ..	11,243	10,140	5,444	4,695	2,806	1,197	1,558	–	1,889	1,260	133	162	344	629	209	18	1,020	–	83
CA. ..	378,965	328,854	137,770	191,084	104,586	74,148	21,768	–	86,499	64,455	2,184	18,222	10,288	22,044	7,751	2,963	33,411	–	16,700
CO. ..	40,777	36,502	9,290	27,211	17,712	11,315	5,814	–	9,500	6,718	442	1,519	1,265	2,782	724	367	3,412	–	863
CT....	21,116	19,744	6,325	13,420	12,016	11,863	–	–	1,404	1,049	87	–	437	355	83	11	726	–	645
DE. ..	4,368	3,803	1,890	1,913	1,256	1,041	20	59	657	484	10	–	191	173	44	27	480	–	85
DC. ..	17,677	15,019	5,068	9,952	8,334	2,927	1,611	2,377	1,617	806	36	132	388	811	54	5	804	–	1,854
FL....	122,510	109,696	28,095	81,601	44,182	33,244	8,167	–	37,419	26,587	1,768	8,359	4,039	10,832	2,254	3,725	9,901	–	2,913
GA. ..	57,151	50,647	15,536	35,111	20,100	13,669	5,804	–	15,011	12,369	514	6,006	2,465	2,642	608	104	4,618	–	1,886
HI. ...	5,217	4,788	615	4,173	3,153	2,259	614	–	1,020	822	–	–	537	198	90	2	429	–	–
ID. ...	7,845	7,586	3,183	4,403	2,248	2,089	82	–	2,155	1,761	71	758	293	394	104	78	258	–	1
IL.....	86,554	74,161	23,213	50,948	36,535	28,942	6,718	–	14,413	10,097	1,215	1,343	1,506	4,317	1,073	734	5,438	–	6,955
IN. ...	35,455	32,327	11,774	20,553	9,566	7,762	236	1,288	10,987	9,246	275	6,040	1,903	1,741	469	18	2,823	–	305
IA....	19,244	17,992	6,391	11,602	6,666	5,757	696	117	4,936	4,118	473	2,085	686	818	215	32	1,243	–	9
KS....	16,751	14,810	5,732	9,078	5,636	4,244	1,221	2	3,442	2,373	389	732	553	1,069	233	142	1,593	–	348
KY....	16,562	14,603	5,336	9,266	6,125	3,435	802	1,603	3,141	2,593	132	787	762	549	150	17	1,881	–	79
LA....	22,114	20,465	6,245	14,221	9,130	4,163	4,778	–	5,091	4,206	31	2,269	572	885	205	20	1,241	–	408
ME. ..	6,488	6,338	1,640	4,698	3,895	3,857	7	–	803	651	30	81	220	152	43	8	150	–	–
MD...	36,568	33,751	10,462	23,289	18,151	9,901	873	6,332	5,138	3,794	430	63	1,284	1,344	297	108	1,102	314	1,401
MA. ..	42,557	35,960	12,053	23,907	19,384	18,516	442	–	4,523	3,300	334	390	1,240	1,223	216	11	2,982	–	3,615
MI. ...	54,172	48,866	22,465	26,401	14,854	13,672	217	567	11,548	8,795	1,132	806	2,335	2,752	711	186	3,401	–	1,905
MN. ..	37,569	34,064	14,688	19,376	10,347	9,379	610	–	9,030	6,647	485	2,226	969	2,382	799	342	2,790	297	417
MS. ..	13,995	13,093	5,139	7,954	3,639	3,423	121	–	4,315	3,828	326	2,644	303	488	151	8	902	–	–
MO. ..	29,850	26,674	7,359	19,315	12,003	6,818	3,954	422	7,311	5,585	543	2,282	1,295	1,727	497	98	2,504	–	672
MT. ..	4,613	4,405	1,710	2,695	1,688	1,629	17	–	1,008	699	66	76	149	308	56	89	181	–	27
NE. ..	15,792	11,162	2,984	8,178	5,229	4,095	507	–	2,949	2,205	211	631	370	744	198	67	4,318	–	312
NV. ..	18,141	16,735	7,321	9,414	5,496	3,243	1,776	–	3,918	2,626	22	722	563	1,293	536	116	1,384	–	21
NH. ..	6,871	6,696	1,733	4,964	4,212	4,117	7	–	752	560	37	–	170	192	36	2	135	–	40
NJ....	53,595	52,203	13,138	39,065	32,391	31,834	142	–	6,674	4,629	962	273	1,654	2,044	298	5	1,333	–	59
NM...	10,856	10,068	5,078	4,990	3,430	1,814	1,552	–	1,559	1,093	112	205	230	466	148	13	789	–	–
NY...	224,181	204,438	64,446	139,992	107,722	62,847	20,368	14,305	32,270	23,046	1,094	6,349	2,996	9,225	1,925	151	8,148	–	11,594

See footnotes at end of table.

State	Total revenue	General revenue, total	Inter-govern-mental revenue	General revenue from own sources — Total	Taxes — Total¹	Taxes — Property	Taxes — Sales and gross receipt	Taxes — Indi-vidual income	Current charges and misc general revenue — Total	Current charges — Total¹	Current charges — Educa-tion	Current charges — Hospi-tals	Current charges — Sewer-age	Misc general revenue — Total¹	Misc general revenue — Interest earn-ings	Misc general revenue — Special assess-ment	Utility rev-enue	Liquor store rev-enue	Insur-ance trust rev-enue
NC..	56,721	51,452	18,237	33,215	15,708	11,313	3,828	–	17,507	14,950	459	10,468	1,553	2,556	586	18	4,258	978	32
ND..	5,176	4,778	2,281	2,497	1,541	1,193	316	–	956	486	60	–	79	470	144	149	310	–	88
OH..	63,814	60,154	20,117	40,037	26,681	17,193	2,689	6,006	13,356	8,800	1,161	1,754	2,562	4,556	1,772	290	3,376	–	284
OK..	16,865	15,200	4,949	10,250	6,331	3,499	2,665	–	3,920	2,956	266	1,096	513	964	224	20	1,557	–	109
OR..	26,544	24,234	9,459	14,775	9,290	7,317	715	–	5,485	3,975	461	423	1,293	1,509	663	84	2,264	–	46
PA...	78,396	70,847	27,612	43,235	31,458	21,319	1,550	5,924	11,777	8,568	754	33	3,226	3,209	1,366	105	3,293	–	4,256
RI...	5,263	4,882	1,543	3,339	2,756	2,682	29	–	583	452	41	–	142	131	25	9	218	–	164
SC...	26,157	24,244	6,905	17,339	9,023	6,698	1,439	–	8,316	7,075	200	5,110	817	1,241	275	63	1,904	15	10
SD...	4,171	3,734	1,091	2,643	1,944	1,425	436	–	699	530	47	99	116	169	41	20	350	–	72
TN...	36,416	26,546	8,953	17,594	8,960	5,847	2,748	–	8,633	6,537	455	3,260	1,144	2,097	1,011	150	9,046	–	824
TX...	175,743	154,366	41,154	113,211	77,602	64,758	11,637	–	35,609	26,137	2,020	7,704	4,963	9,472	3,617	540	17,220	–	4,158
UT...	16,988	14,730	4,652	10,079	5,928	3,968	1,772	–	4,151	2,997	164	490	617	1,154	277	48	2,076	–	182
VT...	4,202	3,946	2,877	1,068	724	687	26	–	344	251	33	–	83	93	18	4	233	–	24
VA...	46,048	42,918	15,295	27,623	20,248	15,764	2,912	–	7,375	5,785	231	343	1,872	1,590	481	70	2,210	–	921
WA...	62,568	53,737	19,922	33,815	18,500	9,593	7,477	–	15,316	12,601	259	3,540	3,091	2,714	969	357	7,896	–	935
WV...	6,198	5,744	2,212	3,532	2,195	1,786	148	–	1,338	1,110	21	392	282	227	42	15	310	–	144
WI...	32,834	29,352	12,994	16,358	10,932	10,019	619	–	5,426	4,035	490	22	1,215	1,391	493	75	2,192	–	1,289
WY...	5,213	4,984	1,900	3,084	1,126	952	113	–	1,958	1,675	73	1,306	72	283	64	11	229	–	–

– Represents or rounds to zero. ¹ Includes corporation income, not shown separately.

Source: U.S. Census Bureau, Annual Survey of State and Local Government Finances, "Datasets & Tables," <www.census.gov/programs-surveys/gov-finances.html>, accessed August 2022.

Table 504. Local Governments—Expenditures and Debt by State: 2020

[In millions of dollars (2,146,666 represents $2,146,666,000,000). For fiscal year ending in year shown; see text, this section]

State	Total expenditures [1]	Direct expenditures Total [1]	Direct general expenditures Total [1]	Education [1]	Public welfare	Hospitals	Health	Highways	Police protection	Corrections	Parks and recreation	Housing and community development	Sewerage	Solid waste management	Governmental administration	Interest on general debt	Utility expenditures	Insurance trust expenditures	Debt outstanding
U.S....	2,146,666	2,129,089	1,841,229	781,109	62,575	121,555	65,038	82,158	111,702	31,438	44,963	49,694	62,575	27,699	90,991	69,935	221,922	64,555	2,082,621
AL....	25,118	25,098	21,497	8,283	41	4,680	446	934	1,263	229	495	556	479	344	1,081	806	3,329	273	25,043
AK....	5,308	5,308	4,738	1,872	13	399	80	225	267	7	114	135	147	127	317	132	532	33	3,562
AZ....	34,365	33,951	27,049	10,965	169	977	435	1,553	2,632	721	868	462	772	521	2,048	844	6,411	491	30,574
AR....	11,185	11,159	10,116	5,505	12	184	85	602	632	187	223	288	299	218	474	352	997	47	12,692
CA....	369,642	369,001	307,226	110,535	21,677	17,266	28,251	11,378	20,034	6,652	6,356	9,573	8,097	3,653	12,843	12,077	46,140	15,635	375,496
CO...	39,931	39,894	34,843	12,379	959	1,904	460	1,847	2,024	455	1,929	1,131	1,318	139	2,095	1,864	4,598	453	46,934
CT....	20,691	20,688	18,878	10,033	86	–	89	670	1,047	–	203	550	519	194	624	399	827	984	11,636
DE....	4,047	4,046	3,513	2,288	2	–	38	166	230	–	33	83	215	36	157	70	431	101	2,806
DC....	23,500	23,500	15,941	3,318	4,394	282	665	661	681	262	352	1,077	386	159	1,018	631	5,481	2,078	19,659
FL....	120,220	119,921	105,100	35,309	1,258	9,690	1,865	3,801	9,450	2,065	3,733	2,394	4,370	2,853	5,933	3,007	11,993	2,828	105,732
GA..	54,615	54,603	46,877	22,632	127	4,523	1,026	2,081	2,586	897	853	829	1,461	826	3,266	1,029	6,399	1,327	48,847
HI....	5,279	5,279	3,641	–	81	–	41	249	490	–	237	186	519	344	425	255	1,638	–	7,817
ID.....	7,400	7,399	7,148	2,757	33	798	122	688	464	150	219	100	253	205	463	112	249	2	2,744
IL.....	87,704	87,704	72,689	32,924	618	3,567	963	3,289	5,152	711	3,016	2,017	1,620	501	4,565	3,346	8,293	6,722	94,457
IN.....	33,208	33,179	30,303	11,827	22	5,559	342	1,438	1,336	460	561	510	1,414	322	1,537	804	2,740	137	28,178
IA.....	19,600	19,575	18,234	8,309	94	2,079	281	1,571	808	170	438	165	836	347	655	398	1,334	6	14,262
KS....	16,710	16,706	15,058	7,544	16	841	342	971	942	197	381	125	499	183	940	493	1,513	135	21,513
KY....	16,832	16,823	14,685	7,113	43	664	357	606	628	300	287	189	1,136	219	669	662	2,053	85	38,443
LA....	20,676	20,655	19,001	8,097	66	2,594	236	691	1,259	364	472	503	649	328	1,154	352	1,399	255	14,290
ME....	5,638	5,635	5,459	2,851	47	83	40	378	231	92	90	142	243	116	259	118	177	–	3,702
MD....	37,876	37,876	34,052	16,496	118	49	699	1,081	2,385	487	960	1,390	1,549	739	1,572	1,047	1,914	1,636	29,711
MA....	41,729	41,272	35,912	18,062	83	901	169	1,192	1,860	–	359	1,837	1,217	390	1,438	605	3,034	2,326	21,016
MI....	54,264	53,944	47,858	20,845	1,421	880	2,577	3,604	2,391	647	883	428	2,623	603	2,724	1,567	4,189	1,897	47,483
MN....	37,977	37,876	34,625	14,262	1,677	1,911	743	3,437	2,006	611	1,156	973	1,000	498	1,319	1,198	2,798	195	41,350
MS....	14,138	14,138	13,196	5,825	26	2,621	90	788	645	197	269	300	306	222	722	240	942	–	7,211
MO....	30,350	30,349	26,767	12,079	181	2,171	386	1,254	1,862	205	745	555	1,306	158	1,228	927	2,738	844	28,786
MT....	4,644	4,644	4,386	2,184	45	90	175	261	303	48	92	60	153	99	263	91	256	2	3,075
NE....	15,867	15,856	10,964	5,362	150	615	51	1,028	495	165	260	277	374	132	441	306	4,461	430	13,047
NV....	18,233	18,211	16,610	5,162	479	864	191	1,471	1,371	508	1,674	308	497	30	936	834	1,579	22	25,748
NH....	6,096	6,048	5,841	3,175	285	–	16	296	419	85	84	114	205	115	370	115	181	25	2,551
NJ....	47,929	47,792	46,741	27,492	898	275	329	1,367	3,192	630	515	725	1,618	1,029	1,916	1,024	1,014	36	27,414
NM....	9,550	9,529	8,597	4,389	117	241	114	333	627	301	268	121	228	214	522	188	932	–	9,066
NY....	235,778	235,050	191,716	79,882	13,344	11,777	4,131	6,078	10,131	3,097	2,633	6,816	4,042	3,588	5,503	10,836	18,050	15,284	212,272

See footnotes at end of table.

Table 504. Local Governments—Expenditures and Debt by State: 2020-Continued.

See headnote on page 329.

State	Total expenditures [1]	Direct expenditures Total [1]	Direct general expenditures Total [1]	Education	Public welfare	Hospitals	Health	Highways	Police protection	Corrections	Parks and recreation	Housing and community development	Sewerage	Solid waste management	Governmental administration	Interest on general debt	Utility expenditures	Insurance trust expenditures	Debt outstanding
NC..	56,186	56,107	50,205	18,235	1,520	10,615	3,199	725	3,008	658	1,160	1,600	1,354	877	1,829	1,397	5,014	58	32,660
ND..	5,084	5,070	4,648	1,956	75	1	89	555	218	61	246	72	105	80	231	208	385	37	6,704
OH..	67,645	67,071	62,691	28,315	2,573	2,184	2,244	2,847	3,569	755	1,637	2,100	2,799	583	4,261	2,453	4,215	165	62,894
OK..	16,068	16,064	14,329	6,826	30	1,184	322	817	942	134	511	442	376	282	649	258	1,609	125	11,588
OR..	27,698	27,691	24,597	10,678	259	460	1,004	1,279	1,342	642	753	762	1,181	165	1,433	1,100	2,863	230	27,278
PA...	75,794	75,783	67,873	33,678	4,144	5	3,266	2,993	3,119	1,648	819	2,201	2,956	926	4,185	2,771	5,236	2,674	76,707
RI....	5,363	5,363	4,629	2,613	8	–	20	134	412	22	51	146	105	55	201	112	208	526	2,808
SC....	25,836	25,753	23,801	10,245	33	5,320	238	407	1,240	273	536	344	784	519	1,409	619	1,943	9	24,790
SD....	3,936	3,935	3,518	1,686	17	96	35	450	176	67	124	50	115	61	195	73	370	34	2,710
TN....	37,883	37,881	27,791	10,368	196	3,918	447	1,092	2,037	506	569	530	1,000	517	1,566	1,389	9,181	909	43,329
TX....	175,493	172,683	148,112	69,487	961	13,329	3,293	6,545	8,097	2,667	3,581	2,717	5,116	1,729	7,421	8,621	21,487	3,084	266,326
UT....	17,248	17,242	14,719	6,231	183	473	525	831	731	253	652	316	492	220	915	366	2,503	20	14,838
VT....	3,939	3,939	3,587	2,492	2	–	9	300	124	–	49	65	98	38	130	34	277	75	1,181
VA....	45,984	45,643	41,079	18,778	1,694	342	1,540	1,528	2,217	1,321	1,083	870	1,718	696	2,459	1,198	3,331	1,233	40,276
WA..	61,542	61,311	49,378	20,472	267	3,488	1,756	2,592	2,201	887	1,380	2,086	2,317	925	2,121	1,626	11,585	348	60,577
WV..	6,354	6,349	5,870	3,289	11	380	48	99	361	52	187	132	281	57	496	77	384	94	3,492
WI....	33,297	33,279	30,155	13,951	1,998	31	1,106	2,778	1,877	512	746	327	1,346	440	1,713	878	2,482	643	26,157
WY..	5,219	5,218	4,989	2,053	22	1,246	64	199	188	79	125	15	81	80	299	28	230	–	1,194

– Represents or rounds to zero. [1] Includes other items not shown separately.

Source: U.S. Census Bureau, Annual Survey of State and Local Government Finances, "Datasets & Tables," <www.census.gov/programs-surveys/gov-finances.html>, accessed August 2022.

Table 505. State and Local Government—Employer Costs Per Hour Worked: 2022

[In dollars. As of March. Based on a sample; see source for details]

Occupation and industry	Total compen- sation	Wages and salaries	Benefit cost					
			Total	Paid leave	Supple- mental pay	Insur- ance	Retire- ment and savings	Legally required benefits
Total workers	**55.47**	**34.32**	**21.15**	**4.08**	**0.54**	**6.40**	**7.11**	**3.02**
OCCUPATIONAL GROUP								
Management, professional, and related	66.13	42.29	23.84	4.54	0.42	6.98	8.53	3.37
Professional and related	64.26	41.37	22.89	4.04	0.40	6.95	8.25	3.25
Teachers [1]	72.56	47.94	24.62	3.53	0.29	7.48	9.90	3.43
Primary, secondary, and special education school teachers	72.14	46.94	25.20	3.19	0.27	7.98	10.52	3.23
Sales and office	38.47	22.04	16.43	3.33	0.34	6.04	4.43	2.28
Office and administrative support	38.63	22.07	16.56	3.35	0.34	6.12	4.47	2.28
Service	41.24	23.60	17.64	3.45	0.89	5.09	5.66	2.55
INDUSTRY GROUP								
Education and health services	57.75	36.93	20.82	3.72	0.37	6.55	7.26	2.93
Educational services	59.11	38.01	21.11	3.56	0.28	6.65	7.70	2.92
Elementary and secondary schools	57.46	36.94	20.52	2.93	0.25	6.72	7.86	2.77
Junior colleges, colleges, and universities	63.91	41.11	22.80	5.41	0.35	6.45	7.24	3.35
Health care and social assistance	49.37	30.30	19.07	4.71	0.96	5.90	4.53	2.96
Hospitals	52.30	32.73	19.57	4.97	1.11	5.88	4.48	3.12
Public administration	53.61	30.90	22.71	4.94	0.83	6.35	7.35	3.24

[1] Includes postsecondary teachers; primary, secondary, and special education teachers; and other teachers and instructors.

Source: U.S. Bureau of Labor Statistics, National Compensation Survey, *Employer Costs for Employee Compensation–March 2022*, June 2022. See also <www.bls.gov/ncs/ect/>.

Table 506. State and Local Government—Full-Time Employment and Salary by Sex and Race/Ethnicity: 1980 to 2019

[2,350 represents 2,350,000. As of June 30. Excludes school systems and educational institutions. Based on reports from state governments (42 in 1980; 49 in 1984 through 1987; and 50 from 1989 and thereafter) and a sample of county, municipal, township, and special district jurisdictions. Beginning 1993, only for state and local governments with 100 or more employees. For definition of median, see Guide to Tabular Presentation]

Year and occupation	Employment (1,000)						Median annual salary ($1,000)				
				Minority						Minority	
	Male	Female	White [1]	Total [2]	Black [1]	His- panic [3]	Male	Female	White [1]	Black [1]	His- panic [3]
1980	2,350	1,637	3,146	842	619	163	15.2	11.4	13.8	11.5	12.3
1985	2,789	1,952	3,563	1,179	835	248	22.3	17.3	20.6	17.5	19.2
1986	2,797	1,982	3,549	1,230	865	259	23.4	18.1	21.5	18.7	20.2
1987	2,818	2,031	3,600	1,249	872	268	24.2	18.9	22.4	19.3	21.1
1989	3,030	2,227	3,863	1,394	961	308	26.1	20.6	24.1	20.7	22.7
1990	3,071	2,302	3,918	1,456	994	327	27.3	21.8	25.2	22.0	23.8
1991	3,110	2,349	3,965	1,494	1,011	340	28.4	22.7	26.4	22.7	24.5
1993	2,820	2,204	3,588	1,436	948	341	30.6	24.3	28.5	24.2	26.8
1995	2,960	2,355	3,781	1,534	993	379	33.5	27.0	31.4	26.8	28.6
1997	2,898	2,307	3,676	1,529	973	392	34.6	27.9	32.2	27.4	29.5
1999	2,939	2,393	3,723	1,609	1,012	417	37.0	29.9	34.8	29.6	31.2
2001	3,080	2,554	3,888	1,746	1,077	471	39.8	32.1	37.5	31.5	33.8
2003	3,134	2,610	3,919	1,826	1,097	508	42.2	34.7	40.0	33.6	36.6
2005	3,185	2,644	3,973	1,856	1,100	532	44.1	36.4	41.5	35.3	38.9
2007	3,383	2,823	4,156	(NA)	(NA)	(NA)	(NA)	(NA)	(NA)	(NA)	(NA)
2009	3,239	2,742	3,976	2,004	1,145	601	50.3	41.5	47.6	40.3	44.8
2011	2,924	2,477	3,561	1,839	1,015	570	51.8	43.1	49.1	41.7	47.0
2013	3,055	2,568	3,671	1,952	1,057	634	52.5	43.8	49.9	42.0	46.8
2015	2,969	2,492	3,536	1,926	1,011	634	54.9	46.5	52.2	44.1	49.8
2017	3,031	2,536	3,511	2,056	1,025	698	(NA)	(NA)	54.0	46.2	52.3
2019, total	**2,976**	**2,564**	**3,416**	**2,124**	**1,011**	**738**	**(NA)**	**(NA)**	**57.1**	**48.8**	**54.5**
Officials/administrators	225	205	298	133	55	41	(NA)	(NA)	72.8	72.2	72.4
Professionals	638	933	1,009	563	259	156	(NA)	(NA)	66.9	59.3	66.8
Technicians	238	172	262	147	65	54	(NA)	(NA)	54.0	46.0	52.6
Protective service	924	236	752	408	190	170	(NA)	(NA)	60.8	49.7	63.9
Paraprofessionals	96	252	179	169	94	54	(NA)	(NA)	42.2	37.7	43.3
Administrative support	124	628	428	324	143	132	(NA)	(NA)	41.1	40.8	43.3
Skilled craft	359	18	255	122	54	49	(NA)	(NA)	41.7	52.1	57.8
Service/maintenance	370	120	233	257	150	82	(NA)	(NA)	33.1	43.0	44.1

NA Not available. [1] Non-Hispanic. [2] Includes other minority groups, not shown separately. [3] Persons of Hispanic origin may be of any race.

Source: U.S. Equal Employment Opportunity Commission, "Job Patterns for Minorities and Women in State and Local Government," <www.eeoc.gov/statistics/job-patterns-minorities-and-women-state-and-local-government-eeo-4>, accessed June 2021.

Table 507. State and Local Government Full-Time Equivalent Employment by Selected Function and State: 2021

[In thousands (1,913.6 represents 1,913,600). For March. Local government amounts are estimates subject to sampling variation; see Appendix III and source]

State	Total[1] State	Total[1] Local	Elem./sec. State	Elem./sec. Local	Higher ed. State	Higher ed. Local	Public welfare State	Public welfare Local	Health State	Health Local	Hospitals State	Hospitals Local	Highways State	Highways Local	Police State	Police Local	Fire State	Fire Local	Corrections State	Corrections Local	Parks & rec. State	Parks & rec. Local
U.S.	1,913.6	6,878.8	42.8	6,573.1	1,794.3	305.7	246.1	267.2	200.1	269.4	417.0	610.1	204.9	274.8	104.2	853.3	(X)	381.8	420.4	260.6	34.9	219.6
AL	46.7	94.4	—	94.4	43.6	0.1	4.0	1.0	6.4	6.5	14.9	24.6	4.3	6.2	1.7	13.3	(X)	6.3	4.7	3.3	0.5	3.8
AK	7.8	15.5	3.2	15.4	4.2	—	1.7	0.1	0.9	0.5	0.3	0.9	2.2	0.6	0.6	1.4	(X)	0.9	2.2	0.1	0.1	0.5
AZ	38.2	116.1	—	105.2	36.0	10.9	6.5	1.3	2.4	2.9	0.7	3.7	2.5	3.9	1.9	18.2	(X)	9.9	9.2	5.0	0.2	4.4
AR	26.9	66.7	—	66.7	25.8	—	4.0	0.1	2.9	0.7	7.0	1.3	3.5	3.8	1.4	7.7	(X)	3.2	4.8	2.5	1.2	1.5
CA	172.5	693.3	—	627.8	168.3	65.5	5.9	79.2	17.4	60.0	47.4	75.5	20.0	22.4	10.6	107.9	(X)	43.5	59.5	31.4	3.7	27.1
CO	58.5	112.4	—	111.1	57.7	1.3	2.4	7.8	1.7	5.7	4.1	7.8	3.1	5.6	1.4	15.6	(X)	8.1	7.6	4.3	1.2	7.5
CT	20.9	85.7	—	85.7	17.8	—	5.1	1.4	3.1	1.2	6.0	—	3.1	3.2	1.7	8.0	(X)	4.3	6.3	—	0.4	1.8
DE	8.6	18.6	—	18.6	8.2	—	1.7	(Z)	2.1	0.3	0.9	—	1.5	0.4	1.1	1.6	(X)	0.2	2.8	—	0.4	0.3
DC	(X)	10.6	(X)	9.8	(X)	0.8	(X)	2.4	(X)	2.5	(X)	—	(X)	2.2	(X)	4.6	(X)	2.1	(X)	1.6	(X)	0.9
FL	71.7	375.1	—	349.0	69.0	26.1	8.8	4.2	4.4	6.1	3.9	54.9	5.8	11.7	4.1	60.7	(X)	32.7	22.6	17.4	1.3	18.4
GA	64.4	236.5	—	236.5	61.3	—	6.3	1.4	4.4	7.4	7.4	18.9	3.7	7.3	2.7	25.7	(X)	14.7	12.4	9.7	3.5	5.8
HI	36.0	—	25.1	—	10.8	—	0.4	0.1	1.9	0.4	3.2	—	0.8	0.9	—	4.2	(X)	2.3	2.2	—	0.2	2.1
ID	9.2	35.9	—	34.0	8.8	1.9	1.9	0.1	1.9	1.0	0.6	4.3	1.6	2.0	0.6	4.0	(X)	1.6	2.4	1.7	0.7	1.0
IL	54.7	289.9	—	269.7	52.5	20.2	9.8	3.8	2.1	6.1	11.1	11.8	6.6	10.7	2.9	36.9	(X)	16.7	13.1	10.2	0.7	13.9
IN	56.2	132.1	—	132.1	55.3	—	6.6	0.7	1.7	3.3	1.5	21.9	3.5	5.6	1.7	14.4	(X)	8.3	5.8	7.1	0.1	3.4
IA	23.5	87.1	—	80.5	22.4	6.6	3.3	1.0	0.6	1.6	9.3	13.0	2.3	5.4	0.9	6.4	(X)	2.1	2.7	1.8	0.6	2.0
KS	23.7	91.1	—	83.8	23.2	7.3	2.5	0.7	1.4	3.1	13.1	8.9	2.5	4.3	1.1	8.0	(X)	3.5	3.0	2.6	0.8	1.7
KY	36.5	103.5	—	103.5	34.4	—	6.6	0.3	3.8	4.5	8.3	5.3	4.0	3.0	2.1	8.0	(X)	4.5	3.8	3.8	0.8	3.3
LA	35.8	94.5	(Z)	94.5	33.2	—	5.5	1.0	3.8	1.5	10.5	18.2	1.9	1.7	1.8	15.4	(X)	5.1	5.4	6.3	0.9	0.7
ME	7.1	33.8	(Z)	33.8	6.7	—	2.9	2.5	1.0	0.2	0.6	0.3	1.9	4.6	0.6	2.5	(X)	1.6	1.2	0.7	0.3	3.3
MD	40.4	138.7	—	128.3	38.5	10.4	5.9	2.2	7.7	5.4	3.2	3.4	4.2	5.7	2.2	16.2	(X)	7.7	9.9	3.5	0.5	5.9
MA	33.3	149.5	2.2	149.2	30.0	0.3	8.1	3.9	8.3	3.1	4.6	6.1	2.7	7.6	3.2	17.6	(X)	13.2	11.4	—	0.9	2.5
MI	73.2	165.0	—	154.2	72.5	10.8	10.8	—	6.2	9.6	19.3	4.2	5.1	6.7	3.0	18.2	(X)	7.1	11.1	4.9	0.5	3.3
MN	39.9	131.3	—	131.3	38.3	—	3.1	12.1	3.8	3.5	5.1	19.3	2.9	4.3	1.2	11.9	(X)	3.2	4.2	6.0	0.3	3.8
MS	18.9	72.6	—	66.7	17.2	6.0	3.9	0.4	2.7	0.3	12.2	11.9	5.1	6.0	1.2	8.0	(X)	3.5	2.0	2.3	0.5	1.4
MO	28.7	139.5	0.6	134.4	26.9	5.1	6.0	2.7	2.7	4.0	10.6	11.4	5.1	6.0	2.4	16.1	(X)	7.6	9.6	3.3	0.1	4.6
MT	10.6	22.4	—	22.3	10.1	—	1.6	0.4	0.7	1.3	0.9	2.2	2.0	1.2	0.5	2.2	(X)	0.7	1.3	0.8	0.3	1.0
NE	19.0	53.2	—	49.8	18.5	3.5	2.6	1.0	0.5	0.6	2.1	5.2	2.0	3.2	0.7	4.4	(X)	1.5	3.3	1.8	0.2	1.0
NV	11.0	46.2	—	46.2	10.8	—	2.3	1.5	1.4	1.1	1.3	4.4	1.7	1.0	0.8	7.9	(X)	2.8	3.4	2.7	0.7	2.3
NH	6.7	33.0	—	33.0	6.5	—	1.4	2.1	0.8	0.2	0.6	—	1.5	1.5	0.5	3.5	(X)	2.1	1.0	0.7	0.7	0.5
NJ	47.2	212.6	8.2	203.1	36.8	9.5	8.8	8.0	3.3	4.3	13.0	1.2	5.7	8.5	4.1	31.2	(X)	8.0	8.0	5.6	0.7	5.3
NM	17.3	44.9	—	41.9	16.4	3.0	1.8	0.5	2.6	0.8	8.1	1.1	2.2	1.4	0.5	5.4	(X)	2.8	3.6	2.1	0.5	2.5
NY	61.8	492.1	—	471.2	58.3	21.0	4.2	40.1	8.5	14.5	43.9	49.6	9.5	25.1	6.0	78.4	(X)	25.6	31.0	23.9	3.0	11.6
NC	65.7	204.3	—	185.0	62.7	19.4	1.1	16.9	2.0	17.0	22.9	55.3	7.7	3.4	5.9	25.7	(X)	10.2	18.1	0.7	1.2	5.2
ND	7.9	18.0	—	18.0	7.6	—	0.9	1.0	2.1	0.8	0.7	—	0.9	1.4	0.2	1.9	(X)	0.6	0.9	0.7	0.2	1.2
OH	70.0	234.8	—	230.6	67.8	4.1	2.6	19.6	3.0	12.9	14.3	11.0	5.8	10.6	2.5	28.4	(X)	17.0	12.8	8.7	0.5	8.5
OK	28.9	86.0	—	86.0	27.3	—	6.7	0.2	5.1	1.8	1.1	12.1	2.8	1.9	2.0	9.6	(X)	4.7	5.0	1.6	0.7	1.6
OR	27.6	72.8	—	65.8	26.7	7.0	10.5	1.6	2.1	5.2	9.2	3.1	3.8	3.6	1.4	7.8	(X)	4.4	5.2	3.5	0.4	3.6
PA	62.5	232.3	3.1	223.7	58.5	8.6	11.3	13.8	4.7	5.8	8.1	(Z)	11.8	10.8	6.6	25.6	(X)	6.5	16.6	13.2	1.0	3.0
RI	8.9	16.0	—	16.0	5.3	—	1.4	0.1	1.0	0.1	0.6	—	0.8	2.5	0.3	2.8	(X)	2.5	1.4	—	0.1	0.4
SC	38.5	103.5	—	103.5	35.5	—	5.9	0.3	5.6	2.7	6.5	25.6	3.9	2.5	2.1	12.8	(X)	6.7	6.8	3.2	0.8	3.9
SD	5.6	21.0	—	20.9	5.3	0.1	1.6	0.3	0.6	0.4	0.5	0.5	1.0	1.4	0.4	1.8	(X)	0.6	0.8	0.8	0.2	0.7
TN	36.4	133.3	—	133.3	34.3	—	7.1	1.4	4.0	4.8	2.8	23.2	4.0	6.7	1.7	20.5	(X)	8.5	5.4	6.3	1.0	4.2
TX	147.6	786.3	0.4	742.7	144.5	43.6	24.7	3.8	21.0	32.0	28.1	64.9	12.9	21.6	7.5	73.4	(X)	30.6	36.4	26.7	3.0	17.6
UT	33.1	56.5	—	56.5	31.1	—	3.1	0.6	2.7	4.4	12.1	0.9	1.6	1.9	0.6	5.9	(X)	3.0	3.1	2.2	0.3	3.9
VT	4.8	18.3	—	18.3	4.5	—	1.5	(Z)	0.5	0.1	0.2	—	1.0	1.1	0.6	0.9	(X)	0.3	0.9	—	0.1	0.2
VA	62.0	192.2	3.1	191.0	59.9	1.2	3.2	9.6	6.7	5.8	12.5	2.3	7.6	4.1	3.1	18.7	(X)	12.0	12.7	10.7	1.0	7.2
WA	53.9	122.4	—	122.4	52.5	—	11.5	1.4	9.1	3.8	15.9	21.1	6.6	6.7	2.2	12.7	(X)	10.2	9.6	4.6	0.7	5.2
WV	14.9	39.9	—	39.9	13.7	(Z)	3.6	(Z)	0.8	1.3	1.2	1.8	4.9	1.0	1.0	3.0	(X)	1.0	3.3	0.2	0.6	0.8
WI	34.8	126.7	—	117.4	33.8	9.4	2.0	12.4	1.7	5.9	3.9	1.5	1.3	8.5	0.8	14.9	(X)	5.0	9.0	4.0	0.2	2.7
WY	3.8	20.2	—	18.3	3.6	1.9	0.5	0.1	0.8	0.5	0.6	7.5	1.7	0.7	0.2	1.7	(X)	0.5	1.0	0.7	0.3	0.8

— Represents zero. X Not applicable. Z Less than 50. [1] Includes other categories, not shown separately.

Source: U.S. Census Bureau, "Annual Survey of Public Employment and Payroll Datasets and Tables," <www.census.gov/programs-surveys/apes.html>, accessed July 2022.

Table 508. State and Local Government Employment and Average Monthly Earnings by State: 2010 to 2021

[4,378 represents 4,378,000. As of March. Employment numbers are for full -time equivalent (FTE) employees; average monthly earnings data are for full time employees. Full-time equivalent is a computed statistic representing the number of full-time employees that could have been employed if the reported number of hours worked by part-time employees had been worked by full-time employees. Starting with the 2019 data, this data is calculated using a linear model based on historical data; prior to 2019, data was calculated separately for each function of a government by dividing the "part-time hours paid" by the standard number of hours for full-time employees in the particular government and then adding the resulting quotient to the number of full-time employees. See source for more information]

| State | Full-time equivalent employment (1,000) | | | | | | Average monthly earnings (dol.) | | | | | |
| | State | | | Local [1] | | | State | | | Local [1] | | |
	2010	2020	2021	2010	2020	2021	2010	2020	2021	2010	2020	2021
United States......	4,378	4,499	4,376	12,171	12,372	12,028	4,620	5,960	6,062	4,310	5,329	5,454
Alabama.............	90	97	95	198	192	188	4,099	5,120	5,220	3,240	4,056	4,206
Alaska...............	27	24	24	28	27	26	5,176	6,360	6,186	4,935	5,892	6,072
Arizona.............	67	75	74	225	213	205	4,365	5,537	5,628	4,163	5,012	5,198
Arkansas...........	63	63	61	106	107	105	3,795	4,684	4,724	3,208	3,567	3,692
California............	411	438	429	1,381	1,473	1,405	5,740	8,199	7,807	5,787	7,502	7,716
Colorado............	71	97	94	199	223	217	5,033	6,599	6,749	4,230	5,315	5,417
Connecticut.........	63	60	59	123	122	119	5,632	6,891	7,074	5,063	5,819	6,003
Delaware............	26	27	26	23	25	25	4,113	5,324	5,335	4,484	5,315	5,389
Dist. of Columbia....	(X)	(X)	(X)	44	50	51	(X)	(X)	(X)	5,900	7,579	7,651
Florida..............	184	183	180	727	722	711	3,861	4,816	4,967	3,986	4,651	4,825
Georgia.............	124	126	122	392	399	389	3,795	4,941	5,313	3,439	4,370	4,501
Hawaii..............	58	59	56	15	17	18	3,943	5,236	5,431	5,040	6,493	6,574
Idaho...............	22	25	25	55	62	62	4,280	5,869	5,787	3,341	4,142	4,214
Illinois..............	131	125	122	513	496	478	5,324	6,581	6,838	4,716	5,785	5,980
Indiana..............	90	90	88	254	239	235	4,023	5,205	5,318	3,547	4,293	4,386
Iowa................	51	51	50	124	139	137	5,326	7,078	6,975	3,831	4,720	4,841
Kansas..............	44	56	55	156	147	144	4,178	5,159	5,314	3,361	4,173	4,221
Kentucky............	81	81	79	161	162	156	3,940	4,963	4,997	3,101	3,794	3,885
Louisiana............	89	83	81	187	182	179	4,282	4,671	4,821	3,397	3,834	3,945
Maine................	21	21	21	51	50	49	4,063	5,067	5,311	3,545	4,227	4,435
Maryland............	88	96	94	215	223	215	4,650	6,608	6,161	5,190	6,189	6,287
Massachusetts.......	95	106	102	233	235	228	4,973	6,721	6,827	4,800	5,974	6,158
Michigan............	146	151	142	329	291	278	5,208	6,398	6,611	4,618	5,044	5,176
Minnesota...........	80	85	85	201	219	214	5,338	6,543	6,780	4,447	5,500	5,573
Mississippi...........	57	54	53	136	130	127	3,537	4,536	4,625	2,985	3,567	3,650
Missouri.............	89	83	80	234	234	229	3,518	4,398	4,501	3,502	4,138	4,258
Montana.............	20	23	23	38	36	36	4,016	4,521	4,769	3,476	4,351	4,533
Nebraska............	33	36	35	88	91	90	4,013	5,142	5,245	3,785	5,011	5,161
Nevada..............	28	30	29	86	88	84	4,891	5,857	5,958	5,149	5,827	5,887
New Hampshire......	19	19	18	53	51	50	4,584	5,788	6,007	3,813	4,764	4,956
New Jersey..........	152	145	130	356	335	331	5,767	6,495	6,689	5,449	6,502	6,640
New Mexico..........	48	46	46	80	78	74	3,978	5,190	5,283	3,440	4,103	4,250
New York............	251	257	245	975	978	933	5,484	6,642	6,826	5,315	6,668	6,658
North Carolina.......	146	151	147	402	407	400	3,886	5,480	5,641	3,690	4,407	4,553
North Dakota........	18	18	18	26	29	30	4,103	5,325	5,444	3,550	4,679	4,822
Ohio................	140	134	129	466	447	432	4,995	5,971	6,186	4,101	4,893	5,065
Oklahoma...........	71	64	63	146	146	142	3,864	4,817	4,842	3,119	4,002	4,070
Oregon..............	65	76	76	133	136	132	4,452	5,987	6,360	4,348	5,719	5,928
Pennsylvania.........	168	157	152	429	403	391	4,564	6,037	6,265	4,290	5,338	5,464
Rhode Island.........	19	21	20	31	27	26	5,298	6,435	6,502	4,953	5,998	6,096
South Carolina.......	77	85	82	171	195	190	3,810	4,583	4,810	3,557	4,334	4,342
South Dakota........	14	14	14	31	33	33	3,938	4,959	5,155	3,149	4,079	4,236
Tennessee...........	83	80	77	247	257	253	3,822	5,041	5,131	3,358	4,179	4,238
Texas................	318	323	319	1,134	1,231	1,214	4,280	5,718	5,874	3,604	4,502	4,613
Utah.................	51	65	66	90	98	98	4,409	5,751	5,935	3,706	4,935	5,174
Vermont.............	14	14	13	26	23	24	4,645	6,013	6,277	3,589	5,188	5,140
Virginia..............	125	131	129	319	327	315	4,384	5,747	5,928	3,905	4,863	4,924
Washington..........	123	133	131	226	262	255	4,913	6,477	6,716	5,416	7,280	7,533
West Virginia........	39	39	39	62	61	60	3,554	4,575	4,778	3,219	3,690	3,776
Wisconsin...........	72	66	68	211	215	210	4,901	5,980	6,192	4,239	5,056	5,156
Wyoming............	14	13	13	37	38	37	4,240	4,910	5,218	4,068	5,009	5,047

X Not applicable. [1] Estimates subject to sampling variation; see Appendix III and source.

Source: U.S. Census Bureau, Census of Governments, "Annual Survey of Public Employment and Payroll Datasets and Tables," <www.census.gov/programs-surveys/apes.html>, accessed July 2022.

Table 509. State and Local Government Employment and Payrolls by Function: 2010 to 2021

[Employees in thousands (19,527 represents 19,527,000); payroll in millions of dollars (70,318.9 represents $70,318,900,000). Data are for the month of March. Covers both full-time and part-time employees. Local government data are estimates subject to sampling variation; see Appendix III and source]

Function	Employees (1,000)			Payrolls (mil. dol.)		
	Total	State	Local	Total	State	Local
2010..	19,527	5,326	14,201	70,318.9	19,579.2	50,739.7
2011..	19,302	5,314	13,988	70,483.5	19,971.9	50,511.6
2012..	19,247	5,286	13,961	70,994.7	20,172.8	50,821.9
2013..	19,086	5,282	13,804	71,437.4	20,501.6	50,935.7
2014..	19,229	5,330	13,900	73,157.0	21,120.2	52,036.8
2015..	19,293	5,344	13,949	75,071.7	21,568.4	53,503.3
2016..	19,406	5,368	14,038	77,324.7	22,148.7	55,176.0
2017..	19,574	5,462	14,113	80,755.8	23,109.8	57,645.9
2018..	19,639	5,472	14,167	83,155.2	23,873.7	59,281.5
2019..	19,685	5,497	14,188	86,245.0	24,770.2	61,474.7
2020..	19,741	5,494	14,248	89,589.4	25,845.2	63,744.2
2021, total............................	**18,828**	**5,248**	**13,580**	**89,803.0**	**25,833.0**	**63,970.0**
Financial administration.................	452	173	280	2,397.8	966.0	1,431.8
Other government administration.......	408	58	350	1,564.0	312.6	1,251.4
Judicial and legal.......................	433	180	253	2,506.5	1,137.3	1,369.2
Police protection........................	1,008	105	903	6,485.1	720.7	5,764.4
Fire protection..........................	451	–	451	2,837.4	–	2,837.4
Corrections.............................	690	424	266	3,663.8	2,261.9	1,401.9
Streets and highways....................	495	207	287	2,477.0	1,110.6	1,366.4
Air transportation.......................	53	4	49	321.1	23.4	297.7
Sea and inland port facilities...........	14	5	9	102.6	36.6	66.0
Public welfare...........................	530	249	281	2,472.4	1,133.6	1,338.8
Health..................................	506	209	296	2,536.2	1,060.0	1,476.3
Hospitals...............................	1,116	454	662	6,416.3	2,545.1	3,871.2
Social insurance administration.........	75	74	1	385.0	379.6	5.4
Solid waste management................	113	2	111	490.9	14.3	476.6
Sewerage...............................	131	2	129	700.8	12.8	688.1
Parks and recreation....................	365	39	325	1,064.8	140.7	924.1
Housing and community development....	113	2	111	587.8	12.0	575.8
Natural resources.......................	186	138	48	879.5	668.0	211.5
Water supply............................	190	1	189	1,049.6	4.7	1,044.8
Electric power..........................	77	4	73	668.9	38.4	630.5
Gas supply.............................	12	–	12	65.2	–	65.2
Transit.................................	258	40	219	1,656.3	290.9	1,365.4
Elementary and secondary education...	7,361	49	7,312	31,951.8	231.2	31,720.6
Higher education........................	3,045	2,561	484	13,145.5	11,303.4	1,842.1
Other education.........................	81	81	–	412.8	412.8	–
Libraries...............................	167	1	166	510.0	3.6	506.4
State liquor stores......................	13	13	–	35.6	35.6	–
All other and unallocable...............	484	173	311	2,418.3	977.1	1,441.2

– Represents or rounds to zero.

Source: U.S. Census Bureau, Census of Governments, "Annual Survey of Public Employment and Payroll, Datasets and Tables," <www.census.gov/programs-surveys/apes.html>, accessed July 2022.

Section 9
Federal Government Finances and Employment

This section presents statistics relating to the financial structure and civilian employment of the federal government. The fiscal data cover taxes, other receipts, outlays, and debt. The principal sources of fiscal data are the *Budget of the United States Government* and related documents, published annually by the Office of Management and Budget (OMB), and the U.S. Department of the Treasury's *Combined Statement of Receipts, Outlays, and Balances of the United States Government.* Detailed data on tax returns and collections are published annually by the Internal Revenue Service. Data on staffing, payrolls, and retirements are published by the Office of Personnel Management (OPM). Data on federally owned land and real property are collected by the General Services Administration and presented online at <www.gsa.gov/reference/reports/real-property-reports>.

Budget concept—Under the unified budget concept, all federal monies are included in one comprehensive budget. These monies comprise both federal funds and trust funds. Federal funds are derived mainly from taxes and borrowing and are not restricted by law to any specific government purpose. Trust funds, such as the Unemployment Trust Fund, collect certain taxes and other receipts for use in carrying out specific purposes or programs in accordance with the terms of the trust agreement or statute. Fund balances include both cash balances with the Treasury and investments in U.S. securities. Part of the balance is obligated, part unobligated. Prior to 1985, the budget totals, under provisions of law, excluded some federal activities—including the Federal Financing Bank, the Postal Service, the Synthetic Fuels Corporation, and the lending activities of the Rural Electrification Administration. The Balanced Budget and Emergency Deficit Control Act of 1985 (P.L.99-177) repealed the off-budget status of these entities and placed Social Security (Federal Old-Age and Survivors Insurance and the Federal Disability Insurance Trust Funds) off-budget. Though Social Security is now off-budget and, by law excluded from coverage of the congressional budget resolutions, it continues to be a federal program.

Receipts arising from the government's sovereign powers are reported as governmental receipts and all other receipts, i.e., from business or market-oriented activities, and are offset against outlays. Outlays are reported on a checks-issued (net) basis (i.e., outlays are recorded at the time the checks to pay bills are issued).

Debt concept—For most of U.S. history, the total debt consisted of debt borrowed by the Treasury (i.e., public debt). The present debt series includes both public debt and agency debt. The *gross federal debt* includes money borrowed by the Treasury and by various federal agencies; it is the broadest generally used measure of the federal debt. *Total public debt* is covered by a statutory debt limitation and includes only borrowing by the Treasury.

Treasury receipts and outlays—All receipts of the government, with a few exceptions, are deposited to the credit of the U.S. Treasury regardless of ultimate disposition. Under the Constitution, no money may be withdrawn from the Treasury unless appropriated by the Congress.

The day-to-day cash operations of the federal government clearing through the accounts of the U.S. Treasury are reported in the *Daily Treasury Statement.* Extensive detail on the public debt is published in the *Monthly Statement of the Public Debt of the United States.*

Budget receipts such as taxes, customs duties, and miscellaneous receipts, which are collected by government agencies, and outlays represented by checks issued and cash payments made by disbursing officers as well as government agencies, are reported in the *Monthly Treasury Statement of Receipts and Outlays of the United States Government* and in the Treasury's *Combined Statement of Receipts, Outlays, and Balances of the United States Government.* These deposits in and payments from accounts maintained by government agencies are on the same basis as the unified budget.

The quarterly *Treasury Bulletin* contains data on fiscal operations and related Treasury activities, including financial statements of government corporations and other business-type activities.

Income tax returns and tax collections—Tax data are compiled by the Internal Revenue Service of the Treasury Department. The annual *Internal Revenue Service Data Book* gives a detailed account of tax collections by kind of tax. The agency's annual *Statistics of Income* reports present detailed data from individual income tax returns and corporation income tax returns as well as historical tax data. The quarterly *Statistics of Income Bulletin* presents data on such diverse subjects as tax-exempt organizations, unincorporated businesses, fiduciary income tax and estate tax returns, sales of capital assets by individuals, international income and taxes reported by corporations and individuals, and estate tax wealth.

Employment and payrolls—The Office of Personnel Management collects employment, payroll, and retirement data from all departments and agencies of the federal government, except the Central Intelligence Agency, the National Security Agency, the National Geospatial-Intelligence Agency, and the Defense Intelligence Agency. Employment figures represent the number of persons who occupied civilian positions at the end of the report month shown and who are paid for services rendered to the federal government, regardless of the nature of appointment or method of payment. Federal payrolls include all payments for personnel services rendered during the report month and payments for accumulated annual leave of employees who separate from the service. Since most federal employees are paid on a biweekly basis, the calendar month earnings are partially estimated on the basis of the number of work days in each month where payroll periods overlap.

Federal employment and payroll figures are published by the Office of Personnel Management in the FedScope database system. The OPM also publishes employment data on minority groups, white- and blue-collar workers, employment by geographic area, and salary and wage distribution of federal employees. General schedule is primarily white-collar; wage system primarily blue-collar. Data on federal employment are also issued by the Bureau of Labor Statistics in its *Monthly Labor Review* and *Employment and Earnings Online*.

Table 510. Federal Budget—Receipts and Outlays: 1960 to 2022

[92.5 represents $92,500,000,000. For fiscal years ending in year shown; see text, Section 8. See also headnote, Table 512]

Fiscal year	In current dollars (billion dollars)			In constant (2012) dollars (billion dollars)			As percent of GDP [1]		
	Receipts	Outlays	Surplus or deficit (-)	Receipts	Outlays	Surplus or deficit (-)	Receipts	Outlays	Surplus or deficit (-)
1960...............	92.5	92.2	0.3	697.0	694.7	2.3	17.3	17.3	0.1
1970...............	192.8	195.6	-2.8	1,080.8	1,096.7	-15.9	18.4	18.7	-0.3
1980...............	517.1	590.9	-73.8	1,394.6	1,593.7	-199.1	18.5	21.2	-2.6
1990...............	1,032.0	1,253.0	-221.0	1,756.8	2,133.1	-376.3	17.5	21.2	-3.7
1995...............	1,351.8	1,515.7	-164.0	1,962.2	2,200.2	-238.0	17.9	20.0	-2.2
2000...............	2,025.2	1,789.0	236.2	2,694.5	2,380.2	314.3	20.0	17.7	2.3
2001...............	1,991.1	1,862.8	128.2	2,580.5	2,414.3	166.2	18.9	17.7	1.2
2002...............	1,853.1	2,010.9	-157.8	2,364.9	2,566.2	-201.3	17.1	18.6	-1.5
2003...............	1,782.3	2,159.9	-377.6	2,210.2	2,678.4	-468.2	15.8	19.2	-3.3
2004...............	1,880.1	2,292.8	-412.7	2,271.2	2,769.8	-498.6	15.6	19.1	-3.4
2005...............	2,153.6	2,472.0	-318.3	2,515.3	2,887.1	-371.8	16.8	19.3	-2.5
2006...............	2,406.9	2,655.0	-248.2	2,715.6	2,995.7	-280.0	17.6	19.5	-1.8
2007...............	2,568.0	2,728.7	-160.7	2,818.9	2,995.3	-176.4	18.0	19.1	-1.1
2008...............	2,524.0	2,982.5	-458.6	2,677.4	3,163.8	-486.4	17.1	20.2	-3.1
2009...............	2,105.0	3,517.7	-1,412.7	2,236.3	3,737.0	-1,500.8	14.5	24.3	-9.8
2010...............	2,162.7	3,457.1	-1,294.4	2,257.1	3,607.9	-1,350.8	14.5	23.2	-8.7
2011...............	2,303.5	3,603.1	-1,299.6	2,348.3	3,673.2	-1,324.9	14.9	23.3	-8.4
2012...............	2,450.0	3,526.6	-1,076.6	2,450.0	3,526.6	-1,076.6	15.2	21.9	-6.7
2013...............	2,775.1	3,454.9	-679.8	2,736.3	3,406.5	-670.3	16.7	20.7	-4.1
2014...............	3,021.5	3,506.3	-484.8	2,932.3	3,402.8	-470.5	17.4	20.2	-2.8
2015...............	3,249.9	3,691.8	-442.0	3,137.3	3,563.9	-426.6	18.0	20.4	-2.4
2016...............	3,268.0	3,852.6	-584.6	3,135.0	3,695.9	-560.9	17.6	20.8	-3.2
2017...............	3,316.2	3,981.6	-665.4	3,128.5	3,756.3	-627.8	17.2	20.7	-3.5
2018...............	3,329.9	4,109.0	-779.1	3,071.3	3,789.9	-718.6	16.4	20.2	-3.8
2019...............	3,463.4	4,447.0	-983.6	3,139.1	4,030.6	-891.5	16.4	21.0	-4.7
2020...............	3,421.2	6,553.6	-3,132.4	3,039.1	5,821.8	-2,782.7	16.3	31.3	-15.0
2021...............	4,047.1	6,822.4	-2,775.3	3,502.8	5,904.8	-2,402.1	18.1	30.5	-12.4
2022, estimate......	4,436.6	5,851.6	-1,415.0	3,654.9	4,820.5	-1,165.6	18.3	24.1	-5.8

[1] Gross domestic product; see text, Section 13.

Source: U.S. Office of Management and Budget, *Budget of the U.S. Government, Fiscal Year 2023: Historical Tables*, March 2022. See also <www.whitehouse.gov/omb/budget>.

Table 511. Federal Budget Debt: 1960 to 2022

[290.5 represents $290,500,000,000. As of the end of the fiscal year. See text, Section 8]

Fiscal year	Total (billion dollars)					As percent of GDP [1]				
	Gross federal debt	Federal govern- ment accounts	Held by the public			Gross federal debt	Federal govern- ment accounts	Held by the public		
			Total	Federal Reserve System	Other			Total	Federal Reserve System	Other
1960...............	290.5	53.7	236.8	26.5	210.3	54.4	10.0	44.3	5.0	39.4
1970...............	380.9	97.7	283.2	57.7	225.5	36.4	9.3	27.1	5.5	21.5
1980...............	909.0	197.1	711.9	120.8	591.1	32.6	7.1	25.5	4.3	21.2
1990...............	3,206.3	794.7	2,411.6	234.4	2,177.1	54.4	13.5	40.9	4.0	36.9
1995...............	4,920.6	1,316.2	3,604.4	374.1	3,230.3	65.1	17.4	47.7	4.9	42.7
2000...............	5,628.7	2,218.9	3,409.8	511.4	2,898.4	55.6	21.9	33.7	5.1	28.6
2001...............	5,769.9	2,450.3	3,319.6	534.1	2,785.5	54.8	23.3	31.5	5.1	26.5
2002...............	6,198.4	2,658.0	3,540.4	604.2	2,936.2	57.2	24.5	32.7	5.6	27.1
2003...............	6,760.0	2,846.6	3,913.4	656.1	3,257.3	59.9	25.2	34.7	5.8	28.9
2004...............	7,354.7	3,059.1	4,295.5	700.3	3,595.2	61.1	25.4	35.7	5.8	29.9
2005...............	7,905.3	3,313.1	4,592.2	736.4	3,855.9	61.6	25.8	35.8	5.7	30.0
2006...............	8,451.4	3,622.4	4,829.0	768.9	4,060.0	62.0	26.6	35.4	5.6	29.8
2007...............	8,950.7	3,915.6	5,035.1	779.6	4,255.5	62.6	27.4	35.2	5.4	29.7
2008...............	9,986.1	4,183.0	5,803.1	491.1	5,311.9	67.5	28.3	39.2	3.3	35.9
2009...............	11,875.9	4,331.1	7,544.7	769.2	6,775.5	82.1	29.9	52.2	5.3	46.8
2010...............	13,528.8	4,509.9	9,018.9	811.7	8,207.2	90.9	30.3	60.6	5.5	55.1
2011...............	14,764.2	4,636.0	10,128.2	1,664.7	8,463.5	95.5	30.0	65.5	10.8	54.7
2012...............	16,050.9	4,769.8	11,281.1	1,645.3	9,635.8	99.6	29.6	70.0	10.2	59.8
2013...............	16,719.4	4,736.7	11,982.7	2,072.3	9,910.4	100.3	28.4	71.9	12.4	59.5
2014...............	17,794.5	5,014.6	12,779.9	2,451.7	10,328.2	102.4	28.9	73.6	14.1	59.5
2015...............	18,120.1	5,003.4	13,116.7	2,461.9	10,654.7	100.2	27.7	72.5	13.6	58.9
2016...............	19,539.5	5,371.8	14,167.6	2,463.5	11,704.2	105.4	29.0	76.4	13.3	63.1
2017...............	20,205.7	5,540.3	14,665.4	2,465.4	12,200.0	105.0	28.8	76.2	12.8	63.4
2018...............	21,462.3	5,712.7	15,749.6	2,313.2	13,436.4	105.8	28.1	77.6	11.4	66.2
2019...............	22,669.5	5,868.8	16,800.7	2,113.3	14,687.4	107.2	27.7	79.4	10.0	69.4
2020...............	26,902.5	5,885.8	21,016.7	4,445.5	16,571.2	128.4	28.1	100.3	21.2	79.1
2021...............	28,385.6	6,101.5	22,284.0	5,433.2	16,850.9	127.0	27.3	99.7	24.3	75.4
2022, estimated..	31,291.9	6,455.7	24,836.2	(NA)	(NA)	129.0	26.6	102.4	(NA)	(NA)

NA Not available. [1] Gross domestic product; see text, Section 13.

Source: U.S. Office of Management and Budget, *Budget of the U.S. Government, Fiscal Year 2023: Historical Tables*, May 2022. See also <www.whitehouse.gov/omb/budget>.

Table 512. Federal Budget Outlays by Type: 1990 to 2022

[1,253.0 represents $1,253,000,000,000. For fiscal years ending September 30. Given the inherent imprecision in adjusting outlays for inflation, the data shown in constant dollars present a reasonable perspective, not precision. The deflators and the categories that are deflated are as comparable over time as feasible. Minus sign (-) indicates offset]

Type	Unit	1990	2000	2010	2019	2020	2021	2022, estimate
Current dollar outlays	Bil. dol.	**1,253.0**	**1,789.0**	**3,457.1**	**4,447.0**	**6,553.6**	**6,822.4**	**5,851.6**
National defense [1]	Bil. dol.	299.3	294.4	693.5	686.0	724.6	753.9	779.7
Nondefense, total	Bil. dol.	953.7	1,494.6	2,763.6	3,761.0	5,829.0	6,068.5	5,071.9
Payments for individuals	Bil. dol.	592.4	1,067.4	2,305.9	3,114.7	4,216.7	4,628.9	4,040.6
Direct payments [2]	Bil. dol.	513.5	876.6	1,906.7	2,561.5	3,604.2	3,934.9	3,275.0
Grants to state and local governments	Bil. dol.	78.9	190.7	399.2	553.2	612.5	694.0	765.6
All other grants	Bil. dol.	56.2	95.1	209.2	168.0	216.6	551.3	463.5
Net interest [2]	Bil. dol.	184.3	222.9	196.2	375.2	345.5	352.3	357.1
All other [2]	Bil. dol.	157.4	151.7	134.4	201.3	1,156.5	659.9	442.8
Undistributed offsetting receipts [2]	Bil. dol.	-36.6	-42.6	-82.1	-98.2	-106.4	-123.9	-232.1
Constant (2012) dollar outlays	Bil. dol.	**2,133.1**	**2,380.2**	**3,607.9**	**4,030.6**	**5,821.8**	**5,904.8**	**4,820.5**
National defense [1]	Bil. dol.	542.7	431.6	723.6	626.6	655.1	662.3	658.7
Nondefense, total	Bil. dol.	1,590.2	1,948.6	2,884.2	3,403.9	5,166.6	5,242.4	4,161.7
Payments for individuals	Bil. dol.	944.3	1,369.8	2,406.1	2,831.4	3,785.7	4,042.9	3,332.0
Direct payments [2]	Bil. dol.	818.3	1,124.3	1,989.5	2,328.7	3,236.0	3,436.9	2,700.8
Grants to state and local governments	Bil. dol.	126.0	245.5	416.6	502.7	549.8	605.9	631.1
All other grants	Bil. dol.	112.1	143.2	220.8	146.0	185.2	454.9	364.9
Net interest [2]	Bil. dol.	291.0	286.1	203.8	333.7	303.3	300.1	292.7
All other [2]	Bil. dol.	325.4	214.2	139.5	175.9	982.0	546.0	355.0
Undistributed offsetting receipts [2]	Bil. dol.	-82.4	-64.8	-86.0	-83.3	-89.8	-101.5	-183.1
Outlays as percent of GDP [3]	**Percent**	**21.2**	**17.7**	**23.2**	**21.0**	**31.3**	**30.5**	**24.1**
National defense [1]	Percent	5.1	2.9	4.7	3.2	3.5	3.4	3.2
Nondefense, total	Percent	16.2	14.8	18.6	17.8	27.8	27.1	20.9
Payments for individuals	Percent	10.0	10.6	15.5	14.7	20.1	20.7	16.7
Direct payments [2]	Percent	8.7	8.7	12.8	12.1	17.2	17.6	13.5
Grants to state and local governments	Percent	1.3	1.9	2.7	2.6	2.9	3.1	3.2
All other grants	Percent	1.0	0.9	1.4	0.8	1.0	2.5	1.9
Net interest [2]	Percent	3.1	2.2	1.3	1.8	1.6	1.6	1.5
All other [2]	Percent	2.7	1.5	0.9	1.0	5.5	3.0	1.8
Undistributed offsetting receipts [2]	Percent	-0.6	-0.4	-0.6	-0.5	-0.5	-0.6	-1.0

[1] Includes a small amount of grants to state and local governments and direct payments for individuals. [2] Includes some off-budget amounts; most of the off-budget amounts are direct payments for individuals (social security benefits). [3] Gross domestic product; see text, Section 13.

Source: U.S. Office of Management and Budget, *Budget of the U.S. Government, Fiscal Year 2023: Historical Tables*, March 2022. See also <www.whitehouse.gov/omb/budget>.

Table 513. Federal Budget Outlays by Agency: 1990 to 2022

[In billions of dollars (1,253.0 represents $1,253,000,000,000). For fiscal years ending September 30]

Department or other unit	1990	2000	2010	2015	2019	2020	2021	2022, estimate
Outlays, total	**1,253.0**	**1,789.0**	**3,457.1**	**3,691.9**	**4,447.0**	**6,553.6**	**6,822.4**	**5,851.6**
Legislative branch	2.2	2.9	5.8	4.3	5.0	5.4	5.3	6.0
Judicial branch	1.6	4.1	7.2	7.1	8.0	8.3	8.3	8.8
Agriculture	45.9	75.1	129.5	139.1	150.1	184.2	235.2	260.7
Commerce	3.7	7.8	13.2	9.0	11.3	15.9	13.1	16.6
Defense—Military	289.7	281.0	666.7	562.5	654.0	690.4	717.6	741.0
Education	23.0	33.5	93.7	90.0	104.4	204.4	260.4	222.9
Energy	12.1	15.0	30.8	25.4	28.9	32.0	33.7	38.3
Health and Human Services	175.5	382.3	854.1	1,027.5	1,213.8	1,504.0	1,466.7	1,626.1
Homeland Security	7.2	13.2	44.5	42.6	56.3	92.0	91.1	89.5
Housing and Urban Development	20.2	30.8	60.1	35.5	29.2	33.2	35.1	33.4
Interior	5.8	8.0	13.2	12.3	13.9	16.4	15.8	19.9
Justice	5.9	16.8	29.6	26.9	35.1	39.6	39.3	44.2
Labor	26.1	31.9	173.1	45.2	35.8	477.5	404.8	145.7
State	4.8	6.7	23.8	26.5	28.0	32.9	35.8	35.1
Transportation	25.6	41.6	77.8	75.4	80.7	100.3	104.9	123.8
Treasury	253.9	390.5	444.3	485.6	689.5	1,151.7	1,633.8	942.3
Veterans Affairs	29.0	47.0	108.3	159.2	199.6	218.4	233.8	273.7
Corps of Engineers—Civil Works	3.3	4.2	9.9	6.7	6.5	7.6	7.9	7.0
Other Defense—Civil Programs	21.7	32.8	54.0	63.0	60.9	65.2	58.1	63.9
Environmental Protection Agency	5.1	7.2	11.0	7.0	8.1	8.7	8.3	8.7
Executive Office of the President	0.2	0.3	0.6	0.4	0.4	0.4	0.4	0.5
General Services Administration	-0.2	0.1	0.9	-0.9	-1.1	-0.3	-1.3	-0.3
International Assistance Programs	10.1	12.1	20.0	24.4	23.6	21.7	20.0	24.6
National Aeronautics and Space Administration	12.4	13.4	18.9	18.3	20.2	21.5	22.2	23.4
National Science Foundation	1.8	3.4	6.7	6.8	7.3	7.3	7.4	8.6
Office of Personnel Management	31.9	48.7	69.9	91.7	103.1	105.6	108.6	114.5
Small Business Administration	0.7	-0.4	6.1	-0.7	0.5	577.4	322.7	24.1
Social Security Administration (on-budget)	17.3	45.1	70.8	87.4	93.6	98.0	92.7	111.7
Social Security Administration (off-budget)	245.0	396.2	683.4	856.8	1,008.3	1,055.9	1,099.7	1,171.0
Other independent agencies (on-budget)	68.7	8.8	-7.5	16.0	21.0	21.8	17.2	38.9
Other independent agencies (off-budget)	1.6	2.0	4.7	-1.7	-1.1	-2.4	-2.7	5.1
Undistributed offsetting receipts [1]	-98.9	-173.0	-267.9	-257.6	-247.8	-241.6	-273.4	-378.3

[1] Includes some off-budget amounts; most of the off-budget amounts are direct payments to individuals (social security benefits).

Source: U.S. Office of Management and Budget, *Budget of the U.S. Government, Fiscal Year 2023: Historical Tables*, March 2022. See also <www.whitehouse.gov/omb/budget>.

Table 514. Federal Budget Outlays by Detailed Function: 1990 to 2022

[In billions of dollars (1,253.0 represents $1,253,000,000,000). For fiscal years ending September 30. Minus sign (-) indicates decrease]

Superfunction and function	1990	2000	2010	2015	2018	2019	2020	2021	2022, estimate
Total outlays	**1,253.0**	**1,789.0**	**3,457.1**	**3,691.9**	**4,109.0**	**4,447.0**	**6,553.6**	**6,822.4**	**5,851.6**
National defense [1]	299.3	294.4	693.5	589.7	631.1	686.0	724.6	753.9	779.7
Department of Defense—Military	289.7	281.0	666.7	562.5	600.7	654.0	690.4	717.6	741.0
Military personnel	75.6	76.0	155.7	145.2	145.8	156.3	161.4	172.6	177.8
Operation and maintenance	88.3	105.8	276.0	247.2	256.7	271.7	278.9	286.2	302.6
Procurement	81.0	51.7	133.6	101.3	112.7	124.7	139.1	141.4	134.4
Research, development, test, and evaluation	37.5	37.6	77.0	64.1	77.0	89.3	99.9	105.7	111.6
Military construction	5.1	5.1	21.2	8.1	6.7	7.4	8.9	9.1	11.4
Atomic energy defense activities	9.0	12.1	19.3	18.7	20.9	22.8	24.5	25.8	28.9
International affairs [1]	13.8	17.2	45.2	52.0	49.0	52.7	67.7	46.9	61.6
International development and humanitarian assistance	5.5	6.5	19.0	24.1	25.1	26.3	28.2	33.4	32.0
International security assistance	8.7	6.4	11.4	12.9	11.4	11.2	12.1	9.2	16.6
Conduct of foreign affairs	3.0	4.7	13.6	13.2	12.0	12.6	16.6	15.3	15.6
General science, space, and technology	14.4	18.6	30.1	29.4	31.5	32.4	34.0	35.5	39.1
General science and basic research	2.8	6.2	11.7	11.7	12.4	12.9	13.3	14.0	16.5
Space flight, research, and supporting activities	11.6	12.4	18.4	17.7	19.1	19.5	20.7	21.5	22.6
Energy [1]	3.3	-0.8	11.6	6.8	2.2	5.0	7.1	6.0	5.7
Energy supply	2.0	-1.8	5.8	4.7	1.4	4.1	5.5	4.8	5.3
Natural resources and environment [1]	17.1	25.0	43.7	36.0	39.1	37.8	42.5	44.2	50.5
Water resources	4.4	5.1	11.7	7.8	6.0	7.8	8.9	9.7	11.6
Conservation and land management	4.0	6.8	10.8	10.5	13.4	11.1	13.5	14.8	16.7
Recreational resources	1.4	2.5	3.9	3.5	4.0	3.9	4.2	4.2	5.2
Pollution control and abatement	5.2	7.4	10.8	7.2	8.0	8.2	8.7	8.4	8.7
Agriculture	11.6	36.5	21.4	18.5	21.8	38.3	47.3	47.4	35.3
Farm income stabilization	9.6	33.4	16.5	13.4	16.7	32.9	26.4	16.7	21.5
Agricultural research and services	2.1	3.0	4.9	5.1	5.1	5.4	20.9	30.7	13.8
Commerce and housing credit [1]	67.6	3.2	-82.3	-37.9	-9.5	-25.7	572.1	307.8	-2.4
Mortgage credit	3.8	-3.3	35.8	-35.7	-7.4	-43.5	-26.5	-31.8	-45.8
Postal service	2.1	2.1	-0.7	-1.6	-1.4	-1.0	-2.3	-2.7	5.1
Deposit insurance	57.9	-3.1	-32.0	-12.8	-15.9	-8.0	-7.2	-9.0	-7.0
Transportation [1]	29.5	46.9	92.0	89.5	92.8	95.8	145.6	154.3	141.5
Ground transportation	19.0	31.7	60.8	59.1	61.9	63.1	78.9	81.6	97.3
Air transportation	7.2	10.6	21.4	20.0	20.2	21.2	55.1	59.9	30.2
Water transportation	3.2	4.4	9.4	10.0	10.2	11.0	11.2	12.3	13.5
Community and regional development [1]	8.5	10.6	23.9	20.7	42.2	26.8	81.9	44.7	81.3
Community development	3.5	5.5	9.9	7.8	7.1	6.3	6.4	9.0	21.2
Disaster relief and insurance	2.1	2.6	10.7	9.0	32.3	17.1	71.3	32.3	52.3
Education, training, employment, and social services [1]	37.2	53.8	128.6	122.0	95.5	136.7	237.8	298.4	265.0
Elementary, secondary, and vocational education	9.9	20.6	73.3	40.0	39.5	41.4	51.4	90.5	152.2
Higher education	11.1	10.1	20.9	51.3	24.6	63.1	153.0	172.7	69.7
Research and general education aids	1.6	2.5	3.6	3.5	3.6	3.7	3.9	4.1	4.8
Training and employment	5.6	6.8	9.9	7.1	6.8	6.7	6.6	7.3	8.4
Social services	8.1	12.6	19.2	18.3	19.1	19.9	21.0	21.9	27.8
Health	57.7	154.5	369.1	482.3	551.2	584.8	747.6	796.5	868.4
Health care services	47.6	136.2	330.7	446.4	511.6	542.2	703.8	750.0	817.4
Health research and training	8.6	16.0	34.2	31.4	35.5	37.7	38.8	41.0	44.0
Consumer and occupational health and safety	1.5	2.3	4.1	4.5	4.2	4.9	5.0	5.4	7.0
Medicare	98.1	197.1	451.6	546.2	588.7	651.0	776.2	696.5	760.9
Income security [1]	148.8	253.7	622.1	508.8	495.3	514.8	1,263.6	1,647.7	926.1
General retirement and disability insurance (excluding social security)	5.1	5.2	6.6	7.8	6.3	3.7	2.1	6.2	61.4
Federal employee retirement and disability	52.0	77.1	119.8	139.1	140.7	149.6	153.8	156.1	164.2
Unemployment compensation	18.9	23.0	160.1	35.0	30.9	29.9	475.1	396.2	81.9
Housing assistance	15.9	28.9	58.7	47.8	49.5	50.6	53.0	89.8	89.4
Food and nutrition assistance	24.1	32.5	95.1	104.8	98.1	93.6	115.4	168.4	203.7
Social security	248.6	409.4	706.7	887.8	987.8	1,044.4	1,095.8	1,134.6	1,219.5
Veterans' benefits and services [1]	29.1	47.0	108.5	159.8	178.9	199.8	218.7	234.3	274.0
Income security for veterans	15.3	25.0	49.3	76.4	85.6	101.1	110.1	115.8	142.8
Veterans education, training, and rehabilitation	0.2	1.3	8.1	13.4	12.4	13.1	12.8	12.0	12.7
Hospital and medical care for veterans	12.1	19.5	45.7	61.9	73.9	80.3	90.6	99.9	103.5
Veterans housing	0.5	0.4	0.5	0.7	-1.3	-3.1	-3.4	-3.4	1.7
Administration of justice	10.2	28.5	54.4	51.9	60.4	65.8	72.0	71.4	79.5
Federal law enforcement activities	4.8	12.1	28.7	26.9	31.3	34.2	37.8	38.3	41.0
Federal litigative and judicial activities	3.6	7.8	14.5	14.7	17.0	17.3	17.9	18.4	18.3
Federal correctional activities	1.3	3.7	6.3	7.0	6.8	7.1	7.8	7.7	7.8
Criminal justice assistance	0.5	4.9	4.8	3.2	5.3	7.2	8.5	7.1	12.4
General government	10.5	13.0	23.0	21.0	23.9	23.5	180.1	273.9	140.7
Net interest [1]	184.3	222.9	196.2	223.2	325.0	375.2	345.5	352.3	357.1
Interest on Treasury debt securities (gross)	264.7	361.9	413.9	402.4	521.6	572.9	522.6	562.4	561.8
Interest received by on-budget trust funds	-46.3	-69.3	-67.3	-45.8	-66.3	-67.1	-56.4	-76.3	-78.8
Interest received by off-budget trust funds	-16.0	-59.8	-118.5	-96.0	-83.8	-82.5	-78.8	-73.3	-67.4
Undistributed offsetting receipts [2]	-36.6	-42.6	-82.1	-115.8	-97.9	-98.2	-106.4	-123.9	-232.1

[1] Includes functions not shown separately. [2] Includes some off-budget amounts; most of the off-budget amounts are direct payments for individuals (social security benefits).

Source: U.S. Office of Management and Budget, *Budget of the U.S. Government, Fiscal Year 2023: Historical Tables*, March 2022. See also <www.whitehouse.gov/omb/budget>.

Table 515. Federal Budget Outlays for Payments for Individuals by Category and Major Program: 1990 to 2022

[In billions of dollars (592.4 represents $592,400,000,000). For fiscal years ending September 30]

Category and program	1990	2000	2010	2015	2018	2019	2020	2021	2022, estimate
Total, payments for individuals	**592.4**	**1,067.4**	**2,307.0**	**2,654.9**	**2,894.5**	**3,116.2**	**4,218.4**	**4,630.7**	**4,042.6**
Social security and railroad retirement	253.3	410.7	706.6	890.2	991.2	1,048.0	1,100.1	1,139.5	1,224.4
Social security:									
Old age and survivors insurance	221.9	351.4	576.6	738.0	837.6	892.9	945.1	987.4	1,072.8
Disability insurance	24.4	54.4	123.5	143.4	143.9	145.1	144.3	140.9	140.3
Railroad retirement (excl. social security)	7.0	4.8	6.5	8.9	9.7	10.0	10.7	11.3	11.3
Federal employees' retirement and insurance	64.1	100.4	166.7	211.9	224.0	249.1	263.1	272.0	306.3
Military retirement	21.5	32.8	50.6	56.7	54.5	60.7	62.3	63.1	66.5
Civil service retirement	31.0	45.1	69.5	81.8	85.9	88.8	91.0	92.5	97.3
Veterans service-connected compensation	10.7	20.8	43.5	69.7	80.0	95.6	105.6	112.1	138.1
Other	0.8	1.7	3.2	3.7	3.6	4.0	4.1	4.3	4.4
Unemployment assistance	17.5	21.1	158.3	32.7	28.5	27.4	472.1	387.7	75.7
Medical care [1]	167.4	368.6	876.8	1,111.0	1,264.1	1,366.7	1,564.0	1,582.3	1,726.6
Medicare:									
Hospital insurance	65.9	127.9	245.6	273.5	292.1	318.4	395.8	326.8	344.2
Supplementary medical insurance	41.5	87.2	264.9	348.6	400.1	444.3	500.1	495.3	561.6
State children's health insurance	–	1.2	7.9	9.2	17.3	17.7	16.9	16.1	16.6
Medicaid	41.1	117.9	272.8	349.8	389.2	409.4	458.5	520.6	561.8
Indian health	1.1	2.4	4.4	4.6	4.2	4.6	5.3	8.7	8.4
Hospital and medical care for veterans	12.3	20.1	48.5	63.7	72.9	79.7	90.3	101.0	103.5
Health resources and services	1.4	3.9	7.1	7.7	9.5	9.9	10.5	12.1	15.7
Substance abuse and mental health services	1.2	2.5	3.3	3.1	3.8	4.3	5.2	5.9	8.3
Uniformed Services retiree health care fund	–	–	8.4	10.0	10.1	10.5	10.6	11.2	11.3
Assistance to students	11.2	10.9	55.5	74.7	60.9	84.6	175.7	185.4	106.2
Veterans' education benefits	0.8	1.6	8.8	13.6	12.7	13.4	13.1	12.2	12.9
Student assistance, Department of Education and other	10.4	9.2	46.8	61.1	48.2	71.1	162.6	173.2	93.3
Housing assistance	15.9	28.6	57.6	46.7	48.4	49.4	51.8	54.3	60.5
Food and nutrition assistance	24.0	32.4	95.0	104.6	97.9	93.3	115.0	167.9	203.1
SNAP (including Puerto Rico) [2]	15.9	18.3	70.5	76.1	68.5	63.5	85.6	134.5	165.4
Child nutrition and special milk programs	5.0	9.2	16.4	21.0	22.8	23.3	22.7	25.8	30.9
Supplemental feeding programs (WIC and CSFP [3])	2.1	4.0	6.5	6.3	5.4	5.3	5.0	5.0	4.8
Commodity donations and other	1.0	0.9	1.6	1.1	1.1	1.3	1.6	2.6	2.0
Public assistance and related programs [1]	34.9	88.5	183.2	175.3	169.7	186.5	464.1	826.9	318.7
Supplemental security income program	11.5	29.7	44.0	52.3	47.9	53.1	53.8	53.4	58.5
Family support payments to states and TANF [4]	12.2	18.4	24.8	20.7	21.2	20.2	21.6	20.1	21.8
Low income home energy assistance	1.3	1.5	4.6	3.4	3.4	3.7	3.8	4.4	5.7
Earned income tax credit	4.4	26.1	54.7	60.1	58.6	59.2	57.6	60.8	68.5
Child care assistance for low income families	–	3.3	5.9	5.1	5.9	7.2	10.0	15.3	27.1
Veterans' non-service-connected pensions	3.6	3.0	4.4	5.3	4.8	4.9	4.8	4.2	4.1
Payments to states for foster care/adoption assistance	1.6	5.5	7.0	7.3	8.6	8.6	8.8	9.7	10.9
Child tax credit and child and dependent care tax credit	–	0.8	22.7	20.6	18.6	28.9	27.8	79.0	106.1
U.S. Coronavirus payments and credits	(X)	(X)	(X)	(X)	(X)	(X)	275.4	579.7	15.6
Other public assistance	0.3	0.3	15.2	0.4	0.7	0.7	0.6	0.5	0.5
All other payments for individuals	4.0	6.3	7.3	7.8	9.7	11.2	12.5	14.5	21.0
Coal miners and black lung benefits	1.5	1.5	0.5	0.4	0.5	0.4	0.4	0.3	0.4
Veterans' insurance and burial benefits	1.4	1.4	1.3	1.2	0.6	0.6	0.4	0.5	0.9
Aging services programs	–	0.9	1.5	1.7	1.9	2.0	2.4	2.7	3.8
Energy employees compensation fund	–	–	1.1	1.0	1.4	1.4	1.6	1.7	1.8
September 11th victim compensation	–	–	–	0.1	1.2	1.3	1.5	1.8	2.0
Refugee assistance and other	1.1	2.5	2.9	3.3	4.1	5.4	6.2	7.5	12.2

X Not applicable. – Represents zero. [1] Includes other items not shown separately. [2] Supplemental Nutrition Assistance Program, formerly known as food stamps. [3] WIC is Women, Infants, and Children. CSFP is Commodity Supplemental Food Program. [4] TANF is Temporary Assistance for Needy Families.

Source: U.S. Office of Management and Budget, *Budget of the U.S. Government, Fiscal Year 2023: Historical Tables*, March 2022. See also <www.whitehouse.gov/omb/budget>.

Table 516. Federal Budget Receipts by Source: 1990 to 2022

[In billions of dollars (1,032.0 represents $1,032,000,000,000). For fiscal years ending September 30. Receipts reflect collections. Covers both federal funds and trust funds; see text, this section. Minus sign (-) indicates decrease]

Source	1990	2000	2010	2015	2018	2019	2020	2021	2022, estimate
Total federal receipts..............	**1,032.0**	**2,025.2**	**2,162.7**	**3,249.9**	**3,329.9**	**3,463.4**	**3,421.2**	**4,047.1**	**4,436.6**
(On-budget)...............................	750.3	1,544.6	1,531.0	2,479.5	2,475.2	2,549.1	2,455.7	3,094.8	3,389.4
(Off-budget)..............................	281.7	480.6	631.7	770.4	854.7	914.3	965.4	952.3	1,047.2
Individual income taxes................	466.9	1,004.5	898.5	1,540.8	1,683.5	1,717.9	1,608.7	2,044.4	2,263.4
Corporation income taxes.............	93.5	207.3	191.4	343.8	204.7	230.2	211.8	371.8	382.6
Social insurance and retirement receipts............................	380.0	652.9	864.8	1,065.3	1,170.7	1,243.1	1,310.0	1,314.1	1,445.6
Excise taxes...............................	35.3	68.9	66.9	98.3	95.0	98.9	86.8	75.3	84.1
Other.......................................	56.2	91.7	141.0	201.8	175.9	173.2	203.9	241.5	261.0
Social insurance and retirement receipts...........	**380.0**	**652.9**	**864.8**	**1,065.3**	**1,170.7**	**1,243.1**	**1,310.0**	**1,314.1**	**1,445.6**
Employment and general retirement, total.............	353.9	620.5	815.9	1,010.4	1,121.2	1,197.4	1,261.7	1,251.9	1,381.3
Old–age and survivors insurance (off–budget).........	255.0	411.7	540.0	658.5	691.2	770.3	825.3	814.0	895.2
Disability insurance (off–budget).........	26.6	68.9	91.7	111.8	163.5	144.0	140.1	138.3	152.0
Hospital insurance....................	68.6	135.5	180.1	234.2	260.7	277.6	291.8	294.8	328.6
Railroad retirement/pension fund.........	2.3	2.7	2.3	3.3	3.4	3.3	2.7	2.9	3.1
Unemployment insurance funds...........	21.6	27.6	44.8	51.2	45.0	40.9	43.1	56.6	58.0
Other retirement......................	4.5	4.8	4.1	3.7	4.5	4.8	5.2	5.6	6.4
Federal employees retirement, employee share............	4.4	4.7	4.1	3.6	4.5	4.8	5.2	5.6	6.3
Excise taxes, total.............	**35.3**	**68.9**	**66.9**	**98.3**	**95.0**	**98.9**	**86.8**	**75.3**	**84.1**
Federal funds [1]......................	15.6	22.7	18.3	37.8	30.1	34.8	29.6	18.4	21.1
Alcohol..................................	5.7	8.1	9.2	9.6	10.1	10.0	9.5	10.3	10.6
Tobacco.................................	4.1	7.2	17.2	14.5	12.9	12.5	12.4	12.1	11.5
Telephone..............................	3.0	5.7	1.0	0.6	0.5	0.4	0.4	0.3	0.2
Ozone–depleting chemicals/products....	0.4	0.1	–	–	–	–	–	–	–
Transportation fuels..................	–	0.8	-11.0	-3.4	-1.5	-3.6	-6.5	-6.0	-4.7
Health insurance providers..........	–	–	–	11.3	4.7	9.6	15.3	0.2	–
Indoor tanning services..............	–	–	–	0.1	0.1	0.1	0.1	0.1	0.1
Trust funds [1]............................	19.8	46.2	48.7	60.5	64.9	64.1	57.2	56.9	63.0
Transportation.........................	13.9	35.0	35.0	40.8	42.6	43.7	42.8	43.5	43.1
Airport and airway....................	3.7	9.7	10.6	14.3	15.8	16.0	9.0	8.2	14.4
Black lung disability..................	0.7	0.5	0.6	0.6	0.4	0.2	0.3	0.3	0.2
Inland waterway.......................	0.1	0.1	0.1	0.1	0.1	0.1	0.1	0.1	0.1
Hazardous substance superfund........	0.8	(Z)	–	–	–	–	–	–	0.4
Oil spill liability.......................	0.1	0.2	0.5	0.5	0.5	0.2	0.4	0.6	0.7
Aquatic resources.....................	0.2	0.3	0.6	0.6	0.6	0.6	0.6	0.6	0.6
Leaking underground storage tank.......	0.1	0.2	0.2	0.2	0.2	0.2	0.2	0.2	0.2
Tobacco assessments..................	–	–	0.9	(Z)	(Z)	–	–	(Z)	–
Vaccine injury compensation..........	0.2	0.1	0.2	0.3	0.3	0.3	0.3	0.3	0.3
Supplementary medical insurance.......	–	–	–	3.0	4.1	2.4	3.2	2.8	2.7

– Represents zero. Z less than $50,000,000. [1] Includes other funds, not shown separately.

Source: U.S. Office of Management and Budget, *Budget of the U.S. Government, Fiscal Year 2023: Historical Tables*, March 2022. See also <www.whitehouse.gov/omb/budget>.

Table 517. Federal Trust Fund Income, Outlays, and Balances: 2021 to 2023

[In billions of dollars (22.5 represents $22,500,000,000). For fiscal years ending September 30. Income reflects receipts deposited. Outlays are on a checks-issued basis less refunds collected. Balances reflect funds that have not been spent. See text, this section, for discussion of the budget concept and trust funds]

Fund type	Income			Outlays			Balances [1]		
	2021	2022, estimate	2023, estimate	2021	2022, estimate	2023, estimate	2021	2022, estimate	2023, estimate
Airport and airway trust fund.....................	22.5	14.7	17.9	-16.7	-17.2	-17.6	14.8	12.3	12.6
Civil service retirement and disability fund......	116.6	119.2	115.2	-92.3	-97.5	-103.0	986.4	1,008.1	1,020.4
Federal employees' health benefits fund........	58.7	61.3	63.9	-59.0	-60.0	-63.1	27.8	29.0	29.8
Employee life insurance fund.....................	4.8	4.8	5.0	-3.8	-3.6	-3.7	49.7	50.9	52.3
Foreign military sales trust fund.................	35.9	51.5	49.9	-34.5	-46.8	-47.2	36.3	41.0	43.7
Foreign service retirement and disability fund..	1.4	1.3	1.3	-1.0	-1.1	-1.1	20.3	20.6	20.9
Highway trust fund..............................	57.6	161.7	44.6	-54.2	-58.6	-65.7	21.0	124.2	103.2
Medicare:									
Hospital insurance (HI) trust fund..............	384.4	404.1	400.8	-382.5	-377.8	-413.2	136.3	162.6	150.1
Supplementary insurance trust fund...........	579.1	604.0	648.1	-530.4	-583.9	-626.6	137.6	157.7	179.2
Military retirement fund........................	179.2	199.4	199.8	-63.1	-66.5	-71.6	1,014.2	1,147.1	1,275.4
Railroad retirement trust funds.................	17.8	12.8	12.3	-13.4	-14.8	-14.3	25.6	23.7	21.7
Social security:									
Disability insurance trust fund.................	144.4	159.2	167.2	-143.4	-143.0	-150.6	98.1	114.3	131.0
Old-age and survivors trust fund...............	936.0	1,024.6	1,068.0	-991.4	-1,076.7	-1,168.5	2,755.8	2,703.9	2,603.3
Unemployment trust funds.......................	235.7	61.3	56.8	-231.3	-75.2	-46.5	18.7	4.6	14.9
Other trust funds................................	36.8	32.1	31.1	-33.1	-29.0	-30.5	65.7	68.9	69.6

[1] Balances available on a cash basis (rather than an authorization basis) at the end of the year. Balances are primarily invested in federal debt securities.

Source: U.S. Office of Management and Budget, *Budget of the U.S. Government, Fiscal Year 2023: Analytical Perspectives*, March 2022. See also <www.whitehouse.gov/omb/budget>.

Table 518. Tax Expenditure Estimates Relating to Individual and Corporate Income Taxes by Selected Function: 2021 to 2024

[In millions of dollars (13,940 represents $13,940,000,000). For fiscal years ending September 30. Tax expenditures are defined as revenue losses attributable to provisions of the federal tax laws which allow a special exclusion, exemption, or deduction from gross income or which provide a special credit, a preferential rate of tax, or a deferral of liability. Minus sign (-) indicates decrease]

Function and provision	2021	2022	2023	2024
National defense:				
Exclusion of benefits and allowances to armed forces personnel..............................	13,940	14,500	15,050	15,630
International affairs:				
Exclusion of income earned abroad by U.S. citizens..................................	6,470	6,790	7,130	7,490
Exclusion of certain allowances for Federal employees abroad..........................	280	290	310	320
Reduced tax rate on active income of controlled foreign corporations......................	19,520	33,810	36,350	38,870
General science, space, and technology:				
Expensing of research and experimentation expenditures (normal tax method)...............	6,420	-22,210	-39,660	-28,680
Credit for increasing research activities.................................	18,520	20,400	22,020	23,500
Energy:				
Energy production credit.................................	5,290	5,220	5,510	5,900
Energy investment credit.................................	6,360	7,210	7,010	7,610
Credit for residential energy efficient property.............................	2,590	2,200	1,640	480
Commerce and housing:				
Financial institutions and insurance:				
Exclusion of life insurance death benefits..................................	11,970	12,910	13,400	14,130
Housing:				
Deductibility of mortgage interest on owner–occupied homes........................	29,370	30,340	31,340	33,530
Deductibility of state and local property tax on owner–occupied homes..................	6,740	7,030	7,070	7,290
Capital gains exclusion on home sales..................................	40,900	42,730	44,640	46,410
Exclusion of net imputed rental income..................................	124,100	130,880	135,350	137,800
Exception from passive loss rules for $25,000 of rental loss........................	5,910	5,940	6,200	6,460
Credit for low–income housing investments.................................	8,900	11,280	10,540	10,380
Commerce:				
Capital gains (except agriculture, timber, iron ore, and coal)........................	102,250	107,710	111,640	115,280
Step–up basis of capital gains at death.................................	41,850	43,910	46,060	48,480
Accelerated depreciation of machinery and equipment (normal tax method)...............	31,470	26,180	11,510	-2,550
Allow 20-percent deduction to certain pass-through income..........................	33,780	56070	56700	59150
Transportation:				
Exclusion of reimbursed employee parking expenses..........................	1,460	1,740	2,090	2,150
Education, training, employment, and social services:				
Education:				
Exclusion of scholarship and fellowship income (normal tax method)...................	3,790	4,140	4,280	4,520
Tax credits and deductions for postsecondary education expenses....................	9,250	14,620	14,380	14,320
Exclusion of interest on bonds for private nonprofit educational facilities..............	2,450	2,470	2,400	2,460
Deductibility of charitable contributions (education).............................	6,840	7,270	7,730	8,170
Training, employment, and social services:				
Exclusion of employee meals and lodging (other than military).......................	5,620	7,760	8,120	8,050
Credit for child and dependent care expenses..................................	3,860	5,230	3,480	3,540
Deductibility of charitable contributions, other than education and health..............	52,140	55,500	58,860	62,250
Health:				
Exclusion of employer contributions for medical insurance premiums and medical care..................................	221,460	221,020	225,140	235,300
Self–employed medical insurance premiums..................................	7,690	8,010	8,530	9,080
Medical Savings Accounts/Health Savings Accounts...........................	10,760	10,890	11,150	11,610
Deductibility of medical expenses..................................	8,350	8,820	9,390	10,100
Exclusion of interest on hospital construction bonds.............................	3,510	3,530	3,430	3,520
Refundable Premium Assistance Tax Credit.................................	6,360	5,160	3,690	3,990
Deductibility of charitable contributions (health).............................	9,970	10,570	11,170	11,770
Income security:				
Child credit..................................	72,570	65,240	76,880	77,010
Exclusion of workers' compensation benefits..................................	9,010	9,020	9,030	9,040
Net exclusion of pension contributions and earnings:				
Defined benefit employer plans..................................	70,340	73,370	74,750	77,170
Defined contribution employer plans..................................	100,020	102,850	109,150	111,860
Individual Retirement Accounts (IRAs).................................	20,770	19,890	21,460	22,630
Self-employed plans..................................	32,260	33,170	35,210	36,080
Exclusion of other employee benefits:				
Premiums on group term life insurance..................................	3,190	3,250	3,330	3,450
Earned income tax credit..................................	2,080	2,410	2,780	2,970
Recovery rebate credits..................................	20,480	1,280	20	–
Social security:				
Exclusion of social security benefits:				
Social security benefits for retired and disabled workers, spouses, dependents, and survivors..................................	26,630	27,240	27,570	29,330
Veterans' benefits and services:				
Exclusion of veterans' death benefits and disability compensation..........................	9,770	11,010	11,380	11,720
General purpose fiscal assistance:				
Exclusion of interest on public purpose state and local bonds........................	31,240	31,520	30,520	31,360
Deductibility of nonbusiness state and local tax, other than owner-occupied homes............	7,170	7,670	7,710	7,880
Interest:				
Deferral of interest on U.S. savings bonds..................................	840	830	820	810
Addendum: Aid to state and local governments:				
Deductibility of:				
Property taxes on owner–occupied homes..................................	6,740	7,030	7,070	7,290
Nonbusiness state and local taxes other than on owner–occupied homes..................	7,170	7,670	7,710	7,880
Exclusion of interest on state and local bonds for:				
Public purposes..................................	31,240	31,520	30,520	31,360
Private nonprofit educational facilities..................................	2,450	2,470	2,400	2,460
Hospital construction..................................	3,510	3,530	3,430	3,520

– Represents or rounds to zero.

Source: U.S. Department of the Treasury, "Tax Expenditures," accessed April 2022. See also <home.treasury.gov/policy-issues/tax-policy/tax-expenditures>.

Table 519. Internal Revenue Gross Collections by Type of Tax: 2010 to 2021

[2,345 represents $2,345,000,000,000, except percent. For fiscal years ending September 30. See text, this section, for information on taxes]

Type of tax	Gross collections (bil. dol.)						Percent of total					
	2010	2015	2018	2019	2020	2021	2010	2015	2018	2019	2020	2021
United States, total............	**2,345**	**3,303**	**3,466**	**3,565**	**3,493**	**4,112**	**100.0**	**100.0**	**100.0**	**100.0**	**100.0**	**100.0**
Individual income taxes............	1,164	1,760	1,934	1,942	1,837	2,294	49.6	53.3	55.8	54.5	52.6	55.8
Withheld by employers...........	900	1,241	1,349	1,351	1,270	1,532	38.4	37.6	38.9	37.9	36.3	37.3
Tax payments [1]....................	264	519	585	591	568	762	11.3	15.7	16.9	16.6	16.3	18.5
Estate and trust income tax.......	12	33	39	40	34	54	0.5	1.0	1.1	1.1	1.0	1.3
Employment taxes..................	824	1,022	1,133	1,208	1,268	1,258	35.1	31.0	32.7	33.9	36.3	30.6
Old-age and disability insurance.........................	813	1,007	1,118	1,195	1,257	1,247	34.7	30.5	32.3	33.5	36.0	30.3
Unemployment insurance........	7	9	9	6	6	6	0.3	0.3	0.3	0.2	0.2	0.2
Railroad retirement.............	5	6	6	6	5	5	0.2	0.2	0.2	0.2	0.1	0.1
Business income taxes [2]..........	278	390	263	277	264	419	11.9	11.8	7.6	7.8	7.5	10.2
Estate and gift taxes.............	20	20	24	18	18	28	0.8	0.6	0.7	0.5	0.5	0.7
Excise taxes......................	47	77	74	81	72	58	2.0	2.3	2.1	2.3	2.1	1.4

[1] Includes collections of estimated income tax and payments made in conjunction with individual income tax return filings. Also includes estate and trust income tax for 2005. [2] Includes corporate income tax and tax-exempt organization unrelated business income tax.

Source: U.S. Internal Revenue Service, *IRS Data Book 2021*, May 2022, and earlier editions. See also <www.irs.gov/statistics/soi-tax-stats-irs-data-book>.

Table 520. Individual Income Tax Summary: 1986 to 2019

[In units as indicated (103,045 represents 103,045,000). Based on a sample of returns; see Appendix III]

Year	Total returns filed (1,000)	Taxable returns								
		Number (1,000)	Percent of total returns	Adjusted gross income (less deficit) (bil. dol.)	Total income tax (bil. dol.)	Average tax rate (percent)	Average adjusted gross income (less deficit) per return		Average total income tax per return	
							Current dollars	Constant dollars [1]	Current dollars	Constant dollars [1]
1986.........	103,045	83,967	81.5	2,440	367	15.1	29,062	26,516	4,374	3,991
1987.........	106,996	86,724	81.1	2,701	369	13.7	31,142	27,414	4,257	3,747
1988.........	109,708	87,135	79.4	2,990	413	13.8	34,313	29,005	4,738	4,005
1989.........	112,136	89,178	79.5	3,158	433	13.7	35,415	28,560	4,855	3,915
1990.........	113,717	89,862	79.0	3,299	447	13.6	36,711	28,088	4,976	3,807
1991.........	114,730	88,734	77.3	3,337	448	13.4	37,603	27,609	5,054	3,711
1992.........	113,605	86,732	76.3	3,484	476	13.7	40,168	28,630	5,491	3,914
1993.........	114,602	86,435	75.4	3,564	503	14.1	41,233	28,535	5,817	4,026
1994.........	115,943	87,619	75.6	3,737	535	14.3	42,646	28,776	6,104	4,119
1995.........	118,218	89,253	75.5	4,008	588	14.7	44,901	29,463	6,593	4,326
1996.........	120,351	90,929	75.6	4,342	658	15.2	47,750	30,433	7,239	4,614
1997.........	122,422	93,471	76.4	4,765	731	15.3	50,980	31,763	7,824	4,875
1998.........	124,771	93,048	74.6	5,160	789	15.3	55,458	33,836	8,475	5,171
1999.........	127,075	94,546	74.4	5,581	877	15.7	59,028	35,431	9,280	5,570
2000.........	129,374	96,818	74.8	6,083	981	16.1	62,832	36,488	10,129	5,882
2001.........	130,255	94,764	72.8	5,847	888	15.2	61,702	34,840	9,370	5,291
2002.........	130,076	90,964	69.9	5,641	797	14.1	62,015	34,472	8,762	4,870
2003.........	130,424	88,922	68.2	5,747	748	13.0	64,625	35,122	8,412	4,572
2004.........	132,226	89,102	67.4	6,266	832	13.3	70,318	37,225	9,337	4,943
2005.........	134,373	90,593	67.4	6,857	935	13.6	75,687	38,754	10,319	5,284
2006 [2]......	138,395	92,741	67.0	7,439	1,024	13.8	80,218	39,791	11,041	5,477
2007 [2]......	142,979	96,273	67.3	8,072	1,116	13.8	83,851	40,449	11,588	5,590
2008.........	142,451	90,660	63.6	7,583	1,032	13.6	83,647	38,851	11,379	5,285
2009.........	140,494	81,890	58.3	6,778	866	12.8	82,765	38,579	10,575	4,929
2010.........	142,892	84,476	59.1	7,246	952	13.1	85,778	39,338	11,266	5,166
2011.........	145,370	91,694	63.1	7,693	1,046	13.6	83,901	37,299	11,402	5,069
2012.........	144,928	93,110	64.2	8,442	1,188	14.1	90,669	39,491	12,759	5,557
2013.........	147,351	94,532	64.2	8,426	1,235	14.7	89,133	38,261	13,065	5,608
2014.........	148,607	96,544	65.0	9,103	1,378	15.1	94,285	39,827	14,271	6,028
2015.........	150,493	99,041	65.8	9,551	1,458	15.3	96,433	40,686	14,720	6,211
2016.........	150,272	100,052	66.6	10,226	1,446	14.1	102,206	42,584	14,453	6,022
2017.........	152,903	103,747	67.9	10,395	1,605	15.4	100,197	40,877	15,473	6,312
2018.........	153,774	100,424	65.3	10,850	1,539	14.2	108,042	43,026	15,322	6,102
2019.........	157,797	104,006	65.9	11,210	1,581	14.1	107,783	42,159	15,204	5,947

[1] Constant dollars are calculated using the U.S. Bureau of Labor Statistics' Consumer Price Index, chained to 1982-84 dollars. [2] Total number of returns does not include returns filed by individuals only to receive economic stimulus payment with no other reason to file.

Source: U.S. Internal Revenue Service, *Individual Tax Returns Complete Report 2019*, December 2021. See also <www.irs.gov/statistics/soi-tax-stats-individual-income-tax-return-form-1040-statistics>.

Table 521. Federal Individual Income Tax Returns—Adjusted Gross Income (AGI) by Selected Source of Income and Income Class: 2019

[In millions of dollars ($11,210,097 represents $11,210,097,000,000), except as indicated. For the tax year. Minus sign (-) indicates net loss was greater than net income. Based on a sample of returns; see source and Appendix III]

Item	Total [1]	Under $10,000 [1]	$10,000 to $19,999	$20,000 to $29,999	$30,000 to $39,999	$40,000 to $49,999	$50,000 to $99,999	$100,000 and over
Number of taxable returns (1,000)	104,006	286	7,461	10,853	11,035	10,136	33,426	30,809
Adjusted gross income (AGI) [2]	11,210,097	-8,413	121,365	272,607	385,579	455,155	2,400,798	7,583,005
Salaries and wages	7,447,275	1,012	100,043	225,868	313,620	372,960	1,834,292	4,599,480
Percent of AGI	66.4	-12.0	82.4	82.9	81.3	81.9	76.4	60.7
Interest received	195,349	1,165	750	1,935	2,549	3,194	20,740	165,016
Dividends in AGI	541,654	1,224	1,158	2,530	4,055	5,275	43,127	484,286
Business or profession, net profit less loss	283,983	-240	4,898	7,031	8,793	7,709	47,573	208,220
Sales of property, net gain less loss [3]	841,711	3,666	336	522	1,292	1,884	21,375	812,635
Pensions and annuities in AGI	735,400	160	10,483	22,405	33,968	37,443	231,502	399,441
Rents and royalties, net income less loss [4]	66,434	18	494	236	449	700	3,472	61,065
Number of all returns (1,000)	157,797	21,920	21,127	18,784	16,091	12,503	36,358	31,014
Adjusted gross income [2]	11,966,874	-138,039	313,486	468,538	560,073	560,259	2,589,840	7,612,717
Salaries and wages	8,273,071	106,277	235,529	385,571	471,544	465,548	1,992,453	4,616,149
Interest received	214,829	11,232	3,048	3,691	3,497	3,959	22,634	166,768
Dividends in AGI	579,981	13,683	5,811	6,593	7,003	7,035	50,919	488,939
Business or profession, net profit less loss	354,741	-4,119	38,184	21,929	16,550	14,042	58,285	209,871
Sales of property, net gain less loss [3]	872,846	17,785	1,826	2,194	3,078	3,555	27,332	817,076
Pensions and annuities in AGI	784,498	10,223	26,497	33,446	37,765	39,737	236,249	400,581
Rents and royalties, net income less loss [4]	63,470	-3,638	1,015	791	267	506	3,402	61,128

[1] Includes a small number of returns with no adjusted gross income. [2] Includes other sources, not shown separately. [3] Includes sales of capital assets. [4] Excludes rental passive losses disallowed in the computation of AGI.

Source: U.S. Internal Revenue Service, *Statistics of Income—Individual Income Tax Returns 2019*, December 2021. See also <www.irs.gov/statistics/soi-tax-stats-individual-income-tax-return-form-1040-statistics>.

Table 522. Federal Individual Income Tax Returns—Total and Selected Sources of Adjusted Gross Income: 2018 and 2019

[In units as indicated (153,774 represents 153,774,000). For tax years. Based on a sample of returns; see source and Appendix III. Minus sign (-) indicates decrease]

Item	2018 Number of returns (1,000)	2018 Amount (mil. dol.)	2019 Number of returns (1,000)	2019 Amount (mil. dol.)	Change in amount, 2018-2019 Net change (mil. dol.)	Change in amount, 2018-2019 Percent change
Adjusted gross income (less deficit) [1]	153,774	11,643,439	157,797	11,966,874	323,435	2.8
Salaries and wages	126,830	7,907,551	129,776	8,273,071	365,520	4.6
Taxable interest	46,559	128,583	48,676	153,253	24,671	19.2
Ordinary dividends	28,702	321,070	28,980	331,791	10,720	3.3
Qualified dividends	26,626	243,746	26,758	248,191	4,444	1.8
Business or profession net income (less loss)	26,556	348,746	27,257	354,741	5,995	1.7
Net capital gain	25,426	926,858	25,762	864,735	-62,123	-6.7
Capital gain distributions [2]	14,200	101,059	13,912	70,119	-30,939	-30.6
Sales of property other than capital assets, net gain (less loss)	2,143	19,739	1,994	19,359	-380	-1.9
Sales of property other than capital assets, net gain	1,085	39,800	993	37,870	-1,929	-4.8
Taxable social security benefits	21,793	337,046	22,416	360,039	22,993	6.8
Total rental and royalty net income (less net loss) [3]	10,607	64,777	10,167	63,470	-1,307	-2.0
Partnership and S corporation net income (less loss)	9,035	683,316	8,940	677,154	-6,162	-0.9
Estate and trust net income (less loss)	659	30,554	671	31,352	797	2.6
Farm net income (less loss)	1,768	-23,395	1,729	-23,797	-402	1.7
Farm net income	449	10,814	446	10,882	68	0.6
Unemployment compensation	4,518	21,998	4,364	21,395	-603	-2.7
Taxable pensions and annuities [4]	[4] 34,702	[4] 1,087,228	28,285	784,498	(X)	(X)
Taxable Individual Retirement Account (IRA) distributions	([4])	([4])	15,642	324,972	(X)	(X)
Other net income (less loss) [5]	6,322	44,746	6,462	38,422	-6,324	-14.1
Gambling earnings	1,994	32,919	1,948	35,756	2,837	8.6

X Not applicable. [1] Includes other sources of income not shown separately. [2] Includes both Schedule D and Form 1040 or 1040A capital gain distributions. [3] Includes farm rental net income (less loss). [4] For 2018, taxable Individual Retirement Account (IRA) distributions and taxable pensions and annuities were combined on Form 1040. [5] Other net income (less loss) represents data reported on Form 1040, line 21, except net operating losses, foreign-earned income exclusions, cancellation of debt, taxable health savings account distributions, and gambling earnings.

Source: U.S. Internal Revenue Service, *Statistics of Income—Individual Income Tax Returns 2019*, Publication 1304, December 2021. See also <www.irs.gov/statistics/soi-tax-stats-individual-income-tax-return-form-1040-statistics>.

Table 523. Federal Individual Income Tax Returns—Net Capital Gains, with Capital Gain Distributions from Mutual Funds: 1990 to 2019

[14,288 represents 14,288,000. For tax years. Based on a sample of returns; see source and Appendix III. Minus sign (-) indicates decrease]

Tax year	Net capital gain (less loss)				Capital gain distributions [2]			
	Number of returns (1,000)	Current dollars (mil. dol.)	Constant (1982–1984) dollars [1]		Number of returns (1,000)	Current dollars (mil. dol.)	Constant (1982–1984) dollars [1]	
			Amount (mil. dol.)	Percent change			Amount (mil. dol.)	Percent change
1990	14,288	114,231	87,399	-25.6	5,069	3,905	2,988	-32.4
1991	15,009	102,776	75,460	-13.7	5,796	4,665	3,425	14.6
1992	16,491	118,230	84,269	11.7	5,917	7,426	5,293	54.5
1993	18,409	144,172	99,773	18.4	9,998	11,995	8,301	56.8
1994	18,823	142,288	96,011	-3.8	9,803	11,322	7,640	-8.0
1995	19,963	170,415	111,821	16.5	10,744	14,391	9,443	23.6
1996	22,065	251,817	160,495	43.5	12,778	24,722	15,757	66.9
1997	24,240	356,083	221,859	38.2	14,969	45,132	28,120	78.5
1998	25,690	446,084	273,671	23.4	16,070	46,147	28,311	0.7
1999	27,701	542,758	325,785	19.0	17,012	59,473	35,698	26.1
2000	29,521	630,542	366,168	12.4	17,546	79,079	45,923	28.6
2001	25,956	326,527	184,374	-49.6	12,216	13,609	7,684	-83.3
2002	24,189	238,789	132,734	-28.0	7,567	5,343	2,970	-61.4
2003	22,985	294,354	159,975	20.5	7,265	4,695	2,552	-14.1
2004	25,267	473,662	250,747	56.7	10,733	15,336	8,119	218.2
2005	26,196	668,015	342,046	36.4	13,393	35,581	18,219	124.4
2006	26,668	779,462	386,638	13.0	14,511	59,417	29,473	61.8
2007	27,156	907,656	437,758	13.2	15,714	86,397	41,669	41.4
2008	23,731	469,273	217,959	-50.2	11,544	21,954	10,197	-75.5
2009	20,291	231,548	107,929	-50.5	4,191	2,411	1,124	-89.0
2010	21,315	364,410	167,118	54.8	6,567	6,270	2,875	155.9
2011	22,154	377,037	167,617	0.3	8,859	14,171	6,300	119.1
2012	22,721	622,887	271,299	61.9	10,412	17,829	7,766	23.3
2013	23,993	489,621	210,176	-22.5	12,845	44,774	19,220	147.5
2014	24,268	698,649	295,117	40.4	13,665	79,059	33,396	73.8
2015	24,278	706,515	298,086	1.0	14,056	74,060	31,247	-6.4
2016	24,043	620,975	258,732	-13.2	13,233	42,534	17,722	-43.3
2017	25,400	854,487	348,599	34.7	14,173	73,274	29,893	68.7
2018	25,426	926,858	369,109	5.9	14,200	101,059	40,245	34.6
2019	25,762	864,735	338,240	-8.4	13,912	70,119	27,427	-31.9

[1] Constant dollars were calculated using the U.S. Bureau of Labor Statistics consumer price index for urban consumers (CPI-U, 1982-1984=100). See Table 765. [2] Capital gain distributions are included in net capital gain (less loss). For 1991–1996, and 1999 and later years, capital gain distributions from mutual funds are the sum of the amounts reported on the Form 1040 and Schedule D. For 1997 and 1998, capital gain distributions were reported entirely on the Schedule D.

Source: U.S. Internal Revenue Service, Statistics of Income, "SOI Tax Stats - Individual Statistical Tables by Size of Adjusted Gross Income," <www.irs.gov/statistics/soi-tax-stats-individual-statistical-tables-by-size-of-adjusted-gross-income>, accessed February 2022.

Table 524. Alternative Minimum Tax: 1986 to 2019

[609 represents 609,000. For tax years. Based on a sample of returns; see source and Appendix III]

Tax year	Highest statutory alternative minimum tax rate (percent) [1]	Alternative minimum tax		Tax year	Highest statutory alternative minimum tax rate (percent) [1]	Alternative minimum tax	
		Number of returns (1,000)	Amount (mil. dol.)			Number of returns (1,000)	Amount (mil. dol.)
1986	20	609	6,713	2003	28	2,358	9,470
1987	21	140	1,675	2004	28	3,096	13,029
1988	21	114	1,028	2005	28	4,005	17,421
1989	21	117	831	2006	28	3,967	21,565
1990	21	132	830	2007	28	4,109	24,110
1991	24	244	1,213	2008	28	3,935	25,649
1992	24	287	1,357	2009	28	3,828	22,580
1993	28	335	2,053	2010	28	4,020	27,461
1994	28	369	2,212	2011	28	4,248	30,479
1995	28	414	2,291	2012	28	4,225	32,770
1996	28	478	2,813	2013	28	3,940	27,426
1997	28	618	4,005	2014	28	4,278	28,646
1998	28	853	5,015	2015	28	4,468	31,166
1999	28	1,018	6,478	2016	28	4,634	31,016
2000	28	1,304	9,601	2017	28	5,075	36,404
2001	28	1,120	6,757	2018	28	244	4,023
2002	28	1,911	6,854	2019	28	170	2,793

[1] Beginning 1997, the top rate on most long-term capital gains was 20 percent; beginning 2003, the rate was 15 percent; beginning 2018, the rate returned to 20 percent.

Source: U.S. Internal Revenue Service, Statistics of Income, "SOI Tax Stats - Individual Statistical Tables by Size of Adjusted Gross Income," <www.irs.gov/statistics/soi-tax-stats-individual-statistical-tables-by-size-of-adjusted-gross-income>, accessed February 2022.

Table 525. Federal Individual Income Tax Returns—Sources of Net Losses Included in Adjusted Gross Income: 2018 and 2019

[25,505 represents 25,505,000. For tax years. Based on a sample of returns; see source and Appendix III]

Item	2018 Number of returns (1,000)	2018 Amount (mil. dol.)	2019 Number of returns (1,000)	2019 Amount (mil. dol.)	Percent change in amount, 2018-2019
Total net losses..	**25,505**	**593,818**	**25,352**	**613,567**	**3.3**
Business or profession net loss............................	6,918	81,317	7,184	88,113	8.4
Net capital loss [1]..	7,810	17,106	7,806	16,266	-4.9
Net loss, sales of property other than capital assets........	1,059	20,061	1,001	18,511	-7.7
Total rental and royalty net loss [2]........................	4,058	49,289	3,796	48,858	-0.9
Partnership and S corporation net loss.....................	2,799	169,047	2,773	179,866	6.4
Estate and trust net loss...................................	47	4,416	41	4,861	10.1
Farm net loss..	1,318	34,209	1,284	34,679	1.4
Net operating loss [3].......................................	1,171	209,244	1,145	212,145	1.4
Other net loss [4]...	325	9,129	321	10,267	12.5

[1] As reported on Form 1040, Schedule D. Includes only the portion of capital losses allowable in the calculation of adjusted gross income. Only $3,000 of net capital loss per return ($1,500 for married filing separately) are allowed to be included in negative total income. Any excess is carried forward to future years. [2] Includes farm rental net loss. [3] Net operating loss is a carryover of the loss from a business when taxable income from a prior year was less than zero. [4] Other net loss represents losses reported on Form 1040, line 21, except net operating loss and the foreign-earned income exclusion.

Source: U.S. Internal Revenue Service, Statistics of Income, "SOI Tax Stats - Individual Statistical Tables by Size of Adjusted Gross Income," <www.irs.gov/statistics/soi-tax-stats-individual-statistical-tables-by-size-of-adjusted-gross-income>, accessed February 2022.

Table 526. Federal Individual Income Tax Returns—Adjusted Gross Income, Taxable Income, and Total Income Tax: 2010 to 2019

[142,892 represents 142,892,000. For tax years. Based on a sample of returns; see source and Appendix III]

Year	2010 Number of returns (1,000)	2010 Amount (mil. dol.)	2018 Number of returns (1,000)	2018 Amount (mil. dol.)	2019 Number of returns (1,000)	2019 Amount (mil. dol.)	Percent change in amount, 2018-19
Adjusted gross income (less deficit).........................	**142,892**	**8,089,142**	**153,774**	**11,643,439**	**157,797**	**11,966,874**	**2.8**
Exemptions [1]...............	287,679	1,049,272	[2] 7,986	[2] 31,701	(NA)	(NA)	(NA)
Taxable income.............	107,304	5,502,001	120,916	8,941,445	124,144	9,226,944	3.2
Total income tax............	84,476	951,674	100,424	1,538,749	104,006	1,581,352	2.8
Alternative minimum tax......	4,020	27,461	244	4,023	170	2,793	-30.6

NA Not available. [1] The number of returns represent the number of exemptions. Exemptions suspended for tax years 2018-2025. [2] Data from prior year returns.

Source: U.S. Internal Revenue Service, Statistics of Income, Individual Income Tax Returns Complete Report 2019, December 2021. See also <www.irs.gov/statistics/soi-tax-stats-individual-income-tax-return-form-1040-statistics>.

Table 527. Federal Individual Income Tax Returns—Number, Adjusted Gross Income (AGI), and Income Tax by Size of AGI: 2018 and 2019

[153,774 represents 153,774,000. Based on sample of returns; see Appendix III]

Size of AGI	Number of returns (1,000) 2018	Number of returns (1,000) 2019	AGI (bil. dol.) 2018	AGI (bil. dol.) 2019	Total income tax (bil. dol.) 2018	Total income tax (bil. dol.) 2019	Income tax as a percent of AGI 2018	Income tax as a percent of AGI 2019
Total........................	**153,774**	**157,797**	**11,643**	**11,967**	**1,538.7**	**1,581.4**	**13.2**	**13.2**
Under $1.....................	1,962	2,128	-202	-237	0.1	0.2	(NA)	(NA)
$1 to 9,999..................	19,202	19,793	99	99	0.1	(Z)	0.1	(Z)
$10,000 to $19,999...........	21,641	21,127	321	313	2.8	2.8	0.9	0.9
$20,000 to $29,999...........	18,595	18,784	463	469	12.4	12.6	2.7	2.7
$30,000 to $49,999...........	27,528	28,594	1,079	1,120	49.5	51.7	4.6	4.6
$50,000 to $99,999...........	35,146	36,358	2,507	2,590	186.8	192.9	7.5	7.4
$100,000 to $199,999........	21,147	21,998	2,878	3,004	320.5	333.8	11.1	11.1
$200,000 to $499,999........	6,906	7,298	1,971	2,091	327.8	348.8	16.6	16.7
$500,000 to $999,999........	1,108	1,162	747	782	173.2	181.6	23.2	23.2
$1,000,000 to $1,499,999. ..	242	254	291	306	75.6	80.2	26.0	26.2
$1,500,000 to $1,999,999. ..	99	103	170	177	45.7	47.9	26.9	27.1
$2,000,000 to $4,999,999. ..	142	144	422	425	115.8	117.0	27.5	27.5
$5,000,000 to $9,999,999. ..	35	35	238	238	65.0	64.8	27.3	27.3
$10,000,000 or more.........	22	21	659	590	163.2	146.9	24.8	24.9

NA Not available. Z Represents less than 0.05.

Source: U.S. Internal Revenue Service, Individual Tax Returns Complete Report 2019, December 2021. See also <www.irs.gov/statistics/soi-tax-stats-individual-income-tax-return-form-1040-statistics>.

Table 528. Federal Individual Income Tax Returns—Selected Itemized Deductions and the Standard Deduction: 2018 and 2019

[17,533 represents 17,533,000. For tax years. Based on a sample of returns; see source and Appendix III. Minus sign (-) indicates decrease]

Item	2018 Number of returns [1] (1,000)	2018 Amount (mil. dol.)	2019 Number of returns [1] (1,000)	2019 Amount (mil. dol.)	Percent change, 2018–2019 Number of returns [1] (1,000)	Percent change, 2018–2019 Amount (percent)
Total itemized deductions..................................	**17,533**	**648,882**	**17,349**	**645,103**	**-1.0**	**-0.6**
Medical and dental expenses after Adjusted Gross Income (AGI) limitation......................	4,599	78,497	4,412	79,060	-4.1	0.7
Taxes paid [2]..	17,380	145,908	17,217	138,950	-0.9	-4.8
State and local income taxes..........................	12,621	199,419	12,573	212,116	-0.4	6.4
State and local general sales taxes..................	4,329	10,844	4,175	9,589	-3.6	-11.6
Interest paid [3].......................................	14,194	197,472	14,183	207,442	-0.1	5.0
Home mortgage interest...............................	13,892	175,756	13,878	183,640	-0.1	4.5
Charitable contributions................................	14,845	196,956	14,459	190,114	-2.6	-3.5
Other than cash contributions........................	9,206	83,501	8,752	74,799	-4.9	-10.4
Casualty and theft losses.............................	25	1,060	12	387	-54.7	-63.5
Total unlimited miscellaneous deductions..........	928	26,495	884	27,653	-4.7	4.4
Basic standard deduction..............................	**134,270**	**2,208,537**	**138,308**	**2,307,521**	**3.0**	**4.5**
Additional standard deduction.........................	**22,811**	**44,168**	**23,726**	**46,434**	**4.0**	**5.1**

[1] Returns with no adjusted gross income are excluded from the deduction counts. For this reason, the sum of the number of returns with total itemized deductions and the number of returns with total standard deduction is less than the total number of returns for all filers. [2] Includes real estate taxes, personal property taxes, and other taxes, not shown separately. [3] Includes investment interest, deductible mortgage "points," and qualified mortgage interest premiums, not shown separately.

Source: U.S. Internal Revenue Service, Statistics of Income, "SOI Tax Stats - Individual Statistical Tables by Size of Adjusted Gross Income," <www.irs.gov/statistics/soi-tax-stats-individual-statistical-tables-by-size-of-adjusted-gross-income>, accessed February 2022.

Table 529. Federal Individual Income Tax Returns—Statutory Adjustments: 2018 and 2019

[37,762 represents 37,762,000. For tax years. Based on a sample of returns; see source and Appendix III. Minus sign (-) indicates decrease]

Item	2018 Number of returns (1,000)	2018 Amount (mil. dol.)	2019 Number of returns (1,000)	2019 Amount (mil. dol.)	Percent change in amount, 2018-2019
Total statutory adjustments........................	**37,762**	**141,839**	**39,140**	**144,926**	**2.2**
Payments to an Individual Retirement Account (IRA)...................	2,469	12,503	2,437	12,691	1.5
Educator expenses deduction.........................	3,476	901	3,629	938	4.0
Certain business expenses of reservists, performing artists, etc......	303	2,095	343	2,764	32.0
Moving expenses adjustment..........................	104	322	112	294	-8.8
Student loan interest deduction.......................	12,425	13,435	12,719	14,145	5.3
Tuition and fees deduction.............................	[2] 27	[2] 56	1,286	3,010	(NA)
Health savings account deduction....................	1,953	5,590	2,023	5,729	2.5
Self-employment tax deduction.......................	20,148	32,663	20,461	33,645	3.0
Self-employment health insurance deduction.......	3,926	31,611	3,789	31,385	-0.7
Payments to a self-employed retirement (Keogh) plan.................	985	25,496	951	25,528	0.1
Penalty on early withdrawal of savings..............	496	266	501	243	-8.5
Alimony paid..	578	13,582	491	12,374	-8.9
Domestic production activities deduction [3]........	183	1,721	56	258	-85.0
Other adjustments [1]..................................	164	1,598	197	1,921	20.2

NA Not available. [1] Includes foreign housing adjustment, medical savings accounts deduction, and other adjustments. [2] Data for 2018 is for previous year returns only. [3] Beginning 2018, this deduction was repealed with limited exceptions. For 2019, data only for some specified agricultural and horticultural cooperatives.

Source: U.S. Internal Revenue Service, Statistics of Income, "SOI Tax Stats - Individual Statistical Tables by Size of Adjusted Gross Income," <www.irs.gov/statistics/soi-tax-stats-individual-statistical-tables-by-size-of-adjusted-gross-income>, accessed February 2022.

Table 530. IRS Audits—Individual Income Tax Returns Examined: 2010 to 2018

[In units as indicated (143,114 represents 143,114,000). An IRS audit is a review/examination of an organization's or individual's tax return to determine if income, expenses, and credits are being reported accurately. Includes tax returns selected for examination based on an earned income tax credit claim, and the resulting recommended additional taxes]

Year	Returns filed [1] (1,000)	Returns examined Total (1,000)	Returns examined Closed [2] (1,000)	Returns examined In process [3] (1,000)	Percent examined	Number of returns examined with no change (1,000)	Average recommended additional tax (mil. dol.)
2010..............	143,114	1,439	1,436	3	1.0	216	11,021
2011..............	145,586	1,300	1,296	4	0.9	160	10,402
2012..............	145,143	1,184	1,179	5	0.8	157	9,617
2013..............	147,552	955	947	8	0.6	99	8,208
2014..............	148,797	867	853	14	0.6	80	7,603
2015..............	150,675	871	846	25	0.6	80	6,568
2016..............	150,447	770	736	33	0.5	79	5,023
2017 [4]..........	153,063	663	522	141	0.4	75	2,826
2018 [4]..........	153,928	370	235	136	0.2	41	997

[1] Includes all returns filed for the specified tax year as of December 31, 2020. [2] Includes examinations that were closed as of September 30, 2020. Represents a distinct count of taxpayers by tax year and form type. During the course of an examination, additional related returns within the statute of limitations may require examination; these related return closures are counted by the appropriate tax year and form type. [3] Includes examinations that are in an open examination status. [4] Within the 3-year statute of limitations; therefore, the percentage covered and recommended additional tax will increase in future years as additional examinations are opened.

Source: U.S. Internal Revenue Service, *IRS Data Book 2020*, June 2021. See also <www.irs.gov/statistics/soi-tax-stats-irs-data-book>.

Table 531. Federal Individual Income Tax Returns—Itemized Deductions and Statutory Adjustments by Size of Adjusted Gross Income: 2019

[17,349 represents 17,349,000. Based on a sample of returns; see Appendix III]

Item	Unit	Adjusted gross income class							
		Total [1]	Under $10,000 [1]	$10,000 to $19,999	$20,000 to $29,999	$30,000 to $39,999	$40,000 to $49,999	$50,000 to $99,999	$100,000 and over
RETURNS WITH ITEMIZED DEDUCTIONS									
Number of returns [2]	1,000	17,349	187	338	499	650	806	4,769	10,100
Amount [2,3]	Mil. dol.	4,180,994	1,013	5,227	12,562	22,910	36,443	355,892	3,746,946
Medical and dental expenses: [4]									
Returns	1,000	4,412	143	232	338	358	379	1,650	1,312
Amount	Mil. dol.	79,060	2,157	3,740	5,493	5,596	6,189	27,184	28,701
Taxes paid:									
Returns	1,000	17,217	182	324	475	635	793	4,728	10,081
Amount	Mil. dol.	138,950	789	1,358	2,062	3,226	4,294	32,500	94,721
State and local taxes: [5]									
Returns	1,000	16,824	169	302	451	601	759	4,582	9,961
Amount	Mil. dol.	333,639	1,053	1,537	2,141	3,104	4,444	35,608	285,752
Real estate taxes:									
Returns	1,000	15,277	131	220	318	440	623	4,139	9,405
Amount	Mil. dol.	110,339	750	1,124	1,497	1,976	2,814	19,844	82,334
Interest paid:									
Returns	1,000	14,183	105	187	272	394	565	3,826	8,834
Amount	Mil. dol.	207,442	940	2,151	2,440	3,909	5,750	39,802	152,450
Home mortgage interest:									
Returns	1,000	13,878	100	181	263	380	556	3,780	8,619
Amount	Mil. dol.	183,640	914	2,051	2,271	3,602	5,278	37,245	132,279
Charitable contributions:									
Returns	1,000	14,459	109	206	342	486	599	3,758	8,959
Amount	Mil. dol.	190,114	162	618	1,372	2,291	2,986	19,637	163,047
RETURNS WITH STATUTORY ADJUSTMENTS									
Number of returns [1]	1,000	39,140	3,645	4,924	3,579	3,267	3,119	10,231	10,376
Amount of adjustments [3]	Mil. dol.	144,926	5,131	6,414	6,355	6,446	6,252	27,295	87,034
Payments to IRAs: [6]									
Returns	1,000	2,437	40	116	196	206	210	822	846
Amount	Mil. dol.	12,691	144	371	758	807	857	4,039	5,717
Deduction for self-employment tax:									
Returns	1,000	20,461	2,911	4,002	1,980	1,372	1,142	3,911	5,143
Amount	Mil. dol.	33,645	1,308	3,348	2,256	1,764	1,545	6,139	17,284
Self-employment health insurance:									
Returns	1,000	3,789	260	264	215	231	187	809	1,823
Amount	Mil. dol.	31,385	1,119	824	768	971	868	5,335	21,500
Payments to Keogh plans:									
Returns	1,000	951	[7] 8	[7] 9	[7] 12	19	14	106	782
Amount	Mil. dol.	25,528	[7] 209	[7] 47	[7] 112	145	137	1,193	23,685

[1] For returns with statutory adjustments, includes a small number of taxable returns with no adjusted gross income. [2] After limitations. [3] Includes other deductions and adjustments, not shown separately. [4] After AGI limitation. [5] State and local taxes include income taxes and sales taxes. [6] Individual Retirement Accounts. [7] Includes estimates that should be used with caution due to the small number of sample returns on which they are based.

Source: U.S. Internal Revenue Service, Statistics of Income, "SOI Tax Stats - Individual Statistical Tables by Size of Adjusted Gross Income," <www.irs.gov/statistics/soi-tax-stats-individual-statistical-tables-by-size-of-adjusted-gross-income>, accessed February 2022.

Table 532. Federal Individual Income Tax Returns—Selected Tax Credits: 2018 and 2019

[59,067 represents 59,067,000. For tax years. Based on a sample of returns; see source and Appendix III]

Item	2018		2019		Percent change, 2018-2019	
	Number of returns (1,000)	Amount (mil. dol.)	Number of returns (1,000)	Amount (mil. dol.)	Number of returns (1,000)	Amount (mil. dol.)
Total tax credits [1]	**59,067**	**137,806**	**59,887**	**138,024**	**1.4**	**0.2**
Child care credit	6,461	3,789	6,375	3,779	-1.3	-0.3
Earned income credit [2]	2,483	617	2,553	650	2.8	5.3
Foreign tax credit	9,006	24,925	9,400	25,455	4.4	2.1
General business credit	477	5,357	428	5,101	-10.3	-4.8
Prior-year minimum tax credit	982	2,922	244	1,559	-75.1	-46.6
Child tax credit	39,377	81,496	39,718	83,109	0.9	2.0
Education credit [3]	8,700	8,931	7,880	8,573	-9.4	-4.0
Retirement savings contribution credit	9,259	1,735	9,629	1,837	4.0	5.8
Residential energy credit	756	2,512	1,958	3,515	159.0	39.9

[1] Includes credits not shown separately. [2] Represents portion of credit used to offset income tax before credits. [3] Excludes refundable portion.

Source: U.S. Internal Revenue Service, Statistics of Income, "SOI Tax Stats - Individual Statistical Tables by Size of Adjusted Gross Income," <www.irs.gov/statistics/soi-tax-stats-individual-statistical-tables-by-size-of-adjusted-gross-income>, accessed February 2022.

Table 533. Federal Individual Income Tax Returns by State: 2019

[In units as indicated (157,705 represents 157,705,000). For tax year. Data may not agree with data in other tables due to differing survey methodology used to derive state data]

State	Total number of returns (1,000)	Adjusted gross income (mil. dol.)			Itemized deductions (mil. dol.)				Income tax after credits (mil. dol.)
		Total [1]	Salaries and wages	Net capital gain [2]	Total [1]	State and local income tax	Real estate taxes	Home mortgage interest paid	
United States......	**157,705**	**11,947,410**	**8,255,244**	**864,843**	**638,119**	**212,403**	**109,676**	**178,769**	**1,559,076**
Alabama.............	2,131	129,686	91,655	6,005	6,167	1,258	346	1,334	13,708
Alaska..............	357	26,062	18,054	1,089	820	16	140	267	3,124
Arizona.............	3,289	225,171	152,672	15,608	12,200	2,485	1,216	3,532	26,553
Arkansas...........	1,289	75,768	52,817	3,760	3,574	1,037	219	589	7,861
California...........	18,639	1,647,811	1,148,076	136,127	122,646	63,281	23,912	44,572	241,322
Colorado...........	2,872	238,915	162,200	20,712	13,662	3,756	1,419	4,825	31,444
Connecticut.........	1,794	179,306	120,302	16,000	10,109	5,140	2,337	2,597	28,247
Delaware...........	485	34,638	23,225	1,586	1,711	553	193	537	4,075
District of Columbia..	352	37,632	26,404	3,369	2,885	1,445	371	965	6,382
Florida..............	10,637	787,861	467,799	94,409	40,099	3,592	6,156	8,866	109,172
Georgia.............	4,753	321,505	231,832	18,594	21,669	5,556	2,461	5,241	38,873
Hawaii..............	715	48,908	33,544	2,516	3,194	1,057	271	1,415	5,405
Idaho..............	824	53,777	35,468	4,290	2,701	770	284	701	5,677
Illinois.............	6,174	483,338	337,185	31,913	22,122	7,276	5,545	5,783	64,340
Indiana.............	3,216	200,005	145,657	8,315	6,580	2,067	641	1,372	21,324
Iowa................	1,489	98,952	69,451	4,630	3,706	1,034	500	642	10,373
Kansas.............	1,368	94,211	65,151	5,623	4,110	1,248	502	729	10,768
Kentucky...........	1,967	114,991	83,139	5,130	4,021	1,393	430	933	11,969
Louisiana...........	2,050	121,882	88,481	5,691	5,149	1,129	398	1,129	13,888
Maine..............	678	43,198	29,364	2,425	1,517	544	274	404	4,580
Maryland...........	3,047	254,318	181,024	12,967	21,859	8,434	3,345	7,238	33,300
Massachusetts.......	3,486	351,919	237,033	34,533	18,766	7,410	3,792	5,897	53,619
Michigan...........	4,851	319,389	221,780	16,325	11,787	3,240	1,929	2,653	37,040
Minnesota..........	2,843	221,932	157,983	11,589	10,232	4,764	1,538	2,847	27,308
Mississippi..........	1,281	65,583	47,949	2,049	3,061	561	220	547	6,163
Missouri............	2,872	187,248	129,951	10,532	7,755	2,009	896	1,571	21,315
Montana............	530	33,953	21,261	2,905	1,635	525	190	412	3,747
Nebraska...........	932	63,191	44,417	3,709	2,670	449	356	435	6,927
Nevada.............	1,540	108,302	69,962	10,164	6,647	644	585	1,583	13,958
New Hampshire......	724	60,533	41,903	4,297	2,350	303	604	667	7,872
New Jersey..........	4,513	417,369	299,107	23,181	24,681	10,495	7,634	7,467	61,288
New Mexico.........	963	55,762	36,872	3,626	2,409	469	225	561	5,847
New York...........	9,761	855,064	577,100	75,296	46,386	31,425	11,460	11,916	133,525
North Carolina.......	4,797	322,067	226,242	18,481	15,737	4,689	1,777	4,108	37,434
North Dakota........	372	27,842	18,568	2,046	977	119	88	155	3,302
Ohio................	5,759	369,792	261,209	16,616	12,014	3,746	2,003	2,539	41,668
Oklahoma...........	1,704	104,824	74,455	5,150	5,370	1,048	433	843	11,237
Oregon.............	2,043	145,488	98,657	8,658	8,867	3,846	1,476	2,918	17,035
Pennsylvania........	6,354	460,886	321,406	24,808	18,208	5,311	3,379	4,535	57,284
Rhode Island........	551	39,238	27,621	2,522	1,728	574	354	529	4,788
South Carolina......	2,357	149,689	100,288	8,418	7,320	2,144	667	1,915	16,717
South Dakota........	436	29,073	18,602	2,025	1,126	62	106	159	3,266
Tennessee..........	3,148	205,841	143,348	13,976	8,089	469	765	1,870	24,114
Texas..............	13,334	975,784	699,660	74,785	47,611	1,440	9,334	10,301	128,160
Utah...............	1,431	106,828	74,941	10,052	8,523	2,078	687	2,130	11,997
Vermont............	332	22,419	14,777	1,808	820	310	168	183	2,489
Virginia............	4,063	337,258	237,221	19,757	22,564	6,986	3,427	7,921	44,032
Washington.........	3,758	345,740	238,278	29,889	18,862	702	3,063	6,234	47,463
West Virginia........	781	42,994	31,166	1,026	999	374	70	249	4,149
Wisconsin...........	2,913	202,837	140,573	11,126	7,231	2,603	1,269	1,571	23,415
Wyoming............	281	23,510	13,468	3,091	1,346	131	87	164	3,044
Other [3].............	871	77,122	65,947	11,646	1,845	405	135	217	6,486

[1] Includes other items, not shown separately. [2] Less loss. [3] Includes returns filed from Army Post Office and Fleet Post Office addresses by members of the armed forces stationed overseas; returns filed by other U.S. citizens abroad; and returns filed by residents of Puerto Rico with income from sources outside of Puerto Rico or with income earned as U.S. government employees.

Source: U.S. Internal Revenue Service, Statistics of Income Bulletin, "Historical Data Tables," <www.irs.gov/statistics/soi-tax-stats-historical-data-tables>, accessed February 2022.

Table 534. Federal Tax Refunds Issued by State and Type of Refund: 2021

[In millions of dollars (1,137,821 represents $1,137,821,000,000). Collection and refund data may not be comparable for a given fiscal year because payments made in prior years may be refunded in the current fiscal year. Adjustments to prior-year returns made in FY2021 may result in negative amounts when such adjustments exceed current-year refunds. Classification by state is based on an individual's address or a corporation's principal place of business]

| State | Total federal tax refunds [2] | Business income tax refunds [3] | Individual income tax refunds | | | | Estate and trust income tax refunds | Employ- ment tax refunds [6] | Excise tax refunds [7] |
			Total refunds	Traditional refunds	Economic impact payments [4]	Advance Child Tax Credit pay- ments [5]			
United States [1]	1,137,821	53,087	1,049,901	464,235	539,306	46,360	4,062	27,410	2,413
Alabama	15,426	482	14,679	5,424	8,536	719	20	232	13
Alaska	2,321	35	2,228	920	1,191	117	7	48	2
Arizona	21,632	453	20,769	7,729	11,979	1,062	42	336	22
Arkansas	9,433	187	9,078	3,251	5,365	463	17	139	8
California	117,874	4,373	109,043	44,084	59,653	5,305	357	3,763	129
Colorado	17,803	991	16,202	6,560	8,879	764	46	494	50
Connecticut	11,782	968	10,401	4,727	5,246	428	105	281	12
Delaware	3,791	640	2,874	1,131	1,609	134	147	119	8
District of Columbia	2,153	291	1,728	820	840	69	10	118	4
Florida	71,138	1,530	67,871	28,286	36,765	2,819	310	1,305	37
Georgia	33,595	1,221	31,337	12,142	17,579	1,616	55	852	112
Hawaii	4,350	98	4,111	1,556	2,360	195	13	112	13
Idaho	5,483	42	5,350	1,803	3,241	307	6	79	5
Illinois	42,538	3,036	37,344	15,756	19,856	1,732	401	1,511	214
Indiana	21,842	606	20,743	8,052	11,668	1,023	37	416	32
Iowa	10,207	526	9,422	3,517	5,430	475	11	185	62
Kansas	9,295	483	8,456	3,142	4,870	444	21	282	53
Kentucky	14,529	552	13,653	4,984	8,006	663	19	277	22
Louisiana	15,214	409	14,430	5,794	7,944	691	27	321	15
Maine	4,195	118	4,010	1,449	2,397	164	8	55	3
Maryland	18,003	549	16,863	7,023	9,008	832	92	468	18
Massachusetts	21,524	1,336	19,252	8,666	9,813	773	124	776	30
Michigan	32,364	1,292	30,196	11,962	16,872	1,362	77	757	28
Minnesota	19,956	3,308	16,022	6,052	9,149	821	31	526	59
Mississippi	9,490	112	9,224	3,426	5,332	466	10	138	5
Missouri	19,575	695	18,283	6,860	10,535	888	61	494	15
Montana	3,206	21	3,113	1,065	1,896	152	4	62	2
Nebraska	6,190	277	5,752	2,111	3,328	313	11	139	9
Nevada	10,864	524	9,889	4,118	5,312	460	107	306	22
New Hampshire	4,311	109	4,022	1,668	2,194	160	63	110	7
New Jersey	28,821	2,053	25,638	11,135	13,326	1,178	137	947	19
New Mexico	6,412	37	6,208	2,324	3,578	306	17	141	2
New York	64,649	3,174	58,427	25,253	30,693	2,481	297	2,439	164
North Carolina	31,910	1,061	30,125	11,158	17,470	1,498	72	626	13
North Dakota	2,405	32	2,301	924	1,261	116	2	64	5
Ohio	37,530	1,209	35,203	13,412	20,133	1,658	107	799	201
Oklahoma	14,029	1,655	12,004	4,511	6,868	625	101	220	44
Oregon	12,268	207	11,681	4,234	6,906	541	25	330	12
Pennsylvania	41,734	2,017	38,523	15,707	21,141	1,674	122	1,018	35
Rhode Island	3,365	46	3,226	1,352	1,743	131	13	74	4
South Carolina	15,493	228	14,991	5,359	8,888	743	23	234	13
South Dakota	2,932	42	2,715	1,000	1,574	141	129	44	3
Tennessee	23,542	1,458	21,376	8,415	11,966	995	56	613	28
Texas	103,451	8,571	91,609	38,888	47,941	4,780	442	2,181	589
Utah	10,248	391	9,538	3,499	5,433	605	20	200	96
Vermont	1,972	23	1,874	718	1,082	75	6	67	1
Virginia	25,783	1,084	23,969	9,655	13,146	1,168	77	622	15
Washington	25,385	2,103	22,348	9,444	11,878	1,026	71	772	74
West Virginia	5,563	63	5,436	1,973	3,229	235	5	54	4
Wisconsin	18,963	1,182	17,142	6,424	9,911	807	58	524	45
Wyoming	1,923	16	1,810	727	994	88	41	54	1

[1] Includes refunds not shown separately including Puerto Rico and overseas members of the Armed Services and territories other than Puerto Rico. [2] Includes estate tax, gift tax, overpayment refunds, refunds resulting from examination activity, refundable tax credits, and other refunds required by law. Also includes $3.1 billion in interest, of which $1.1 billion was paid to corporations and $2.0 billion was paid to all others. Excludes refunds credited to taxpayer accounts for tax liability in a subsequent year. [3] Includes refunds of taxes on corporation income (Form 1120 series) and on unrelated business income from tax-exempt organizations (Form 990–T). [4] The Coronavirus Aid, Relief, and Economic Security Act of 2020 (CARES Act), the Coronavirus Response and Relief Supplemental Appropriations Act of 2021 (CRRSAA), and the American Rescue Plan Act of 2021 (ARP Act) included provisions to distribute economic impact payments (EIPs) to qualified taxpayers. These payments are considered advance refundable tax credits for returns to be filed for Tax Year 2020 and 2021, and therefore are classified as refunds issued during FY2021. In FY2021, the IRS disbursed $539.3 billion of payments to eligible taxpayers based upon the criteria in each Act. The CARES Act authorized an EIP for eligible taxpayers of up to $1,200 for individuals and $2,400 for individuals filing a joint tax return, with up to an additional $500 for each eligible child added. The CRRSAA created an additional EIP of up to $600 for individuals and $1,200 for individuals filing a joint tax return, with up to an additional $600 for each eligible child. Additionally, the ARP created an additional EIP of up to $1,400 for individuals, and $2,800 for individuals filing a joint tax return, with up to an additional $1,400 for each qualifying dependent. This includes $3.3 billion in EIPs that were distributed to U.S. possessions through the Recovery Rebate credit in FY2021. [5] Monthly Advance Child Tax Credit Payments to qualified taxpayers occurred from July 2021 through December 2021. These payments are considered advance refundable credits for returns to be filed for Tax Year 2021, and therefore are classified as refunds issued during FY2021. This table includes only those payments issued through September 30, 2021. [6] Includes refunds of self-employment income taxes under the Self-Employment Insurance Contributions Act; railroad retirement taxes under the Railroad Retirement Tax Act; unemployment insurance taxes under the Federal Unemployment Tax Act; and Old-age, Survivors, Disability, and Hospital Insurance (OASDHI) taxes on salaries and wages under the Federal Insurance Contributions Act. [7] Excludes refunds of excise taxes collected by U.S. Customs and Border Protection and the Alcohol and Tobacco Tax and Trade Bureau. Beginning with FY2015, some refunds which had been classified as excise tax refunds in prior years, were reclassified as corporate tax refunds.

Source: U.S. Internal Revenue Service, *IRS Data Book 2021*, May 2022. See also <www.irs.gov/statistics/soi-tax-stats-irs-data-book>.

Table 535. Individuals Due an Unclaimed Income Tax Refund by State: 2018

[1,456,504 represents $1,456,504,000. Data are estimates, and are for unclaimed income tax refunds for taxpayers who did not file a 2018 Form 1040 federal income tax return. Taxpayers have a 3-year window in which to claim a tax refund, after which the money becomes the property of the U.S. Treasury]

State	Total persons (number)	Value of potential refunds ($1,000) [1]	Median potential refund (dol.)	State	Total persons (number)	Value of potential refunds ($1,000) [1]	Median potential refund (dol.)
Total U.S.	**1,514,627**	**1,456,504**	**813**	Missouri	33,858	31,284	783
Alabama	24,474	23,029	796	Montana	4,914	4,561	758
Alaska	5,515	6,186	969	Nebraska	7,647	7,204	809
Arizona	38,182	33,578	718	Nevada	17,919	16,896	792
Arkansas	13,727	12,568	762	New Hampshire	6,755	7,023	920
California	148,938	139,660	776	New Jersey	39,046	39,628	872
Colorado	30,836	28,979	787	New Mexico	9,893	9,613	804
Connecticut	15,020	15,243	864	New York	77,315	79,825	896
Delaware	5,764	5,487	793	North Carolina	50,069	45,991	776
District of Columbia	4,011	3,967	802	North Dakota	4,011	4,140	893
Florida	98,979	94,579	818	Ohio	56,285	51,975	793
Georgia	51,034	46,467	735	Oklahoma	21,529	21,076	824
Hawaii	8,199	8,317	873	Oregon	23,552	20,729	715
Idaho	7,026	5,982	686	Pennsylvania	59,459	58,994	865
Illinois	55,767	54,851	840	Rhode Island	4,011	4,100	893
Indiana	34,770	33,534	839	South Carolina	18,063	16,289	720
Iowa	14,843	14,256	840	South Dakota	3,872	3,719	858
Kansas	14,813	14,125	822	Tennessee	30,693	28,459	788
Kentucky	20,030	19,137	836	Texas	145,616	147,059	856
Louisiana	24,292	23,610	793	Utah	11,644	10,649	757
Maine	5,851	5,241	772	Vermont	3,089	2,906	832
Maryland	30,224	29,637	814	Virginia	41,663	39,286	776
Massachusetts	32,234	33,570	908	Washington	42,272	43,022	863
Michigan	49,252	47,229	812	West Virginia	6,968	7,146	880
Minnesota	22,685	20,921	771	Wisconsin	21,753	19,536	755
Mississippi	13,007	11,754	730	Wyoming	3,258	3,486	912

[1] Excluding credits.

Source: U.S. Internal Revenue Service, News Release, "IRS has $1.5 billion in refunds for people who have not filed a 2018 federal income tax return; April deadline approaches," IR-2022-66, March 2022. See also <www.irs.gov/newsroom>.

Table 536. Federal Employees—Summary Characteristics: 1990 to 2021

[In percent, except as indicated. As of September 30. For civilian employees of executive branch agencies participating in Office of Personnel Management's Central Personnel Data File (CPDF)]

Characteristics	1990	1995	2000	2005	2010	2015	2017	2020	2021
Average age (years) [1]	42.3	44.3	46.3	46.9	46.8	47.4	47.5	47.3	47.3
Average length of service (years)	13.4	15.5	17.1	16.4	14.3	13.7	13.5	13.0	12.9
Retirement eligible:									
Civil Service Retirement System [2]	8.0	10.0	17.0	33.0	57.0	81.1	89.5	96.5	97.3
Bachelor's degree or higher	35.0	39.0	41.0	43.0	46.0	51.0	51.7	52.3	52.8
Sex:									
Male	57.0	56.0	55.0	56.0	55.9	56.8	56.6	55.9	55.6
Female	43.0	44.0	45.0	44.0	44.1	43.2	43.4	44.1	44.4
Race and Hispanic origin:									
Total minorities	27.4	28.9	30.4	31.7	33.3	35.3	36.7	37.6	38.4
Black	16.7	16.8	17.1	17.0	17.5	17.7	18.2	18.1	18.2
Hispanic	5.4	5.9	6.6	7.4	7.7	8.4	8.8	9.3	9.5
Asian/Pacific Islander	3.5	4.2	4.5	5.1	5.6	6.2	6.5	6.7	7.1
American Indian/Alaska Native	1.8	2.0	2.2	2.1	2.1	1.7	1.7	1.6	1.6
Disabled	7.0	7.0	7.0	7.0	7.0	12.5	9.9	10.9	11.0
Veterans preference	30.0	26.0	24.0	22.0	23.1	25.9	26.3	25.9	25.6
Vietnam era veterans	17.0	17.0	14.0	11.0	8.0	3.2	2.2	1.2	0.9
Retired military	4.9	4.2	3.9	5.4	7.0	8.3	8.3	8.1	7.9
Retired officers	0.5	0.5	0.5	1.0	1.6	1.9	1.9	1.9	1.8
Average base salary (dollar) [1]	32,026	41,557	51,618	64,175	76,231	81,249	84,913	91,525	93,075

[1] For full-time permanent employees. [2] Represents full-time permanent employees under the Civil Service Retirement System (excludes hires since January 1984).

Source: U.S. Office of Personnel Management, Office of Workforce Information, *The Fact Book, Federal Civilian Workforce Statistics*, annual. Beginning 2008, Central Personnel Data File, "Profile of Federal Civilian Non-Postal Full-Time Employees," <www.opm.gov/policy-data-oversight/data-analysis-documentation/federal-employment-reports/reports-publications/profile-of-federal-civilian-non-postal-employees/>, accessed February 2022; and unpublished data.

Table 537. Full-Time Federal Civilian Employment—Employees and Average Pay by Pay System: 2010 to 2021

[1,950 represents 1,950,000. As of September 30. Data are shown for all full-time nonseasonal employees. Includes employees in U.S., U.S. territories, foreign countries, and unspecified locations. Excludes postal employees and other selected agencies; see <www.fedscope.opm.gov /datadefn/aboutehri_sdm.asp> for details. See text, this section, for explanation of general schedule and wage system]

Pay system	Employees (1,000)				Average annual pay (dol.)			
	2010	2015	2020	2021	2010	2015	2020	2021
Total, excluding postal	**1,950**	**1,940**	**2,054**	**2,068**	**75,707**	**70,548**	**90,956**	**92,543**
General schedule and equivalently graded	1,410	1,430	1,473	1,485	73,656	67,078	87,964	89,310
Prevailing rate pay plans (blue collar)	195	185	185	180	52,056	53,049	59,959	60,897
Other white collar pay plans	344	325	396	402	97,480	95,893	116,628	118,854

Source: U.S. Office of Personnel Management, "FedScope," <www.fedscope.opm.gov>, accessed February 2022.

Table 538. Federal Government Civilian Employment by State: 2010 to 2021

[As of September 30. For agencies excluded from total, see <www.fedscope.opm.gov/datadefn/aboutehri_sdm.asp>]

State	2010	2015	2016	2017	2018	2019	2020	2021
U.S.[1]	2,061,320	2,029,293	2,054,180	2,045,704	2,056,092	2,087,269	2,134,575	2,144,744
AL	42,267	38,006	38,422	37,939	38,017	38,678	39,474	39,301
AK	14,072	11,606	11,549	10,917	10,962	10,923	11,268	11,299
AZ	42,409	31,421	31,601	31,404	31,195	32,082	33,410	32,707
AR	14,741	13,207	13,015	12,781	13,003	13,110	13,180	13,306
CA	172,547	140,618	142,086	140,467	140,882	143,597	148,734	146,552
CO	40,744	37,208	38,071	37,299	37,058	37,497	38,575	38,744
CT	8,671	8,035	8,020	7,873	7,837	7,969	8,198	8,125
DE	3,425	3,085	3,062	3,120	3,047	3,075	3,278	3,237
DC	167,893	147,050	149,279	146,399	142,576	142,202	144,932	144,738
FL	88,933	76,472	77,984	77,736	79,000	81,610	84,916	85,919
GA	80,229	70,294	71,478	70,869	71,789	73,203	75,788	76,513
HI	25,354	21,919	22,250	22,157	22,490	23,218	23,465	23,723
ID	10,496	9,698	9,595	9,647	9,776	9,703	9,959	9,967
IL	51,136	41,266	41,118	40,385	40,223	40,610	41,828	42,068
IN	24,734	22,156	22,637	22,556	22,939	23,907	24,861	23,746
IA	9,245	8,647	8,683	8,568	8,691	8,538	8,821	8,893
KS	17,792	15,998	16,004	15,873	16,091	16,319	16,561	16,599
KY	26,523	22,500	22,678	22,225	22,054	21,160	21,423	21,609
LA	21,075	17,886	17,993	18,360	18,539	18,789	18,922	18,683
ME	11,132	10,277	10,571	10,566	10,993	11,177	11,568	11,662
MD	128,281	129,005	130,290	129,847	128,746	128,356	132,361	135,385
MA	29,223	25,118	24,743	24,326	24,104	24,596	24,756	24,986
MI	30,023	25,439	25,479	25,207	25,219	25,688	26,005	26,581
MN	18,561	16,097	16,185	16,294	16,323	16,556	16,823	16,936
MS	19,353	17,998	17,944	17,737	17,717	18,101	18,277	18,329
MO	38,351	33,828	34,244	33,804	34,644	35,209	37,220	37,427
MT	12,010	10,350	10,487	10,163	10,158	10,268	10,380	10,749
NE	10,686	9,644	9,812	9,725	9,685	9,718	9,924	9,846
NV	11,475	10,980	11,021	11,374	11,419	11,750	12,246	12,610
NH	4,436	4,354	4,388	4,238	4,373	4,463	4,444	4,412
NJ	30,101	20,511	20,259	19,963	19,970	20,244	20,812	20,975
NM	27,682	22,069	22,140	21,565	21,297	21,746	22,097	22,039
NY	68,202	51,541	51,538	50,063	50,377	50,719	51,125	51,336
NC	43,678	43,007	43,481	43,290	44,279	45,302	46,290	47,239
ND	6,723	5,425	5,557	5,402	5,418	5,453	5,517	5,557
OH	53,014	48,213	49,277	49,132	49,589	50,397	50,916	51,239
OK	39,463	36,863	38,091	37,864	38,788	39,020	39,988	40,441
OR	22,470	20,125	20,438	19,844	20,072	20,144	20,525	20,249
PA	69,792	59,111	60,110	59,312	60,156	61,500	62,386	62,836
RI	7,135	7,228	7,335	7,374	7,422	7,714	7,729	7,867
SC	21,675	20,603	20,595	20,701	21,172	21,967	22,590	22,760
SD	8,849	8,231	8,453	8,398	8,315	8,252	8,482	8,513
TN	28,822	26,186	26,090	25,184	25,867	26,363	27,160	27,696
TX	140,292	110,270	110,801	111,519	112,247	114,377	120,024	121,283
UT	31,051	27,575	28,665	27,810	28,634	30,144	31,372	32,074
VT	4,495	3,194	3,257	3,154	3,162	3,246	3,235	3,120
VA	145,449	133,300	134,567	132,649	134,523	136,486	139,058	139,807
WA	57,894	54,139	54,607	54,032	54,403	54,979	55,607	55,670
WV	16,287	15,034	15,053	15,026	14,857	15,349	16,043	16,161
WI	15,809	15,274	15,387	15,193	15,604	15,738	16,242	16,538
WY	6,640	6,328	6,432	6,226	6,310	6,325	6,479	6,476

[1] Total does not include employees based in U.S. Territories or foreign countries and includes data that has been suppressed for security purposes; see source for details.

Source: U.S. Office of Personnel Management, "FedScope," <www.fedscope.opm.gov>, accessed February 2022.

Table 539. Federal Executive Branch Retirements: 2015 to 2019

[For fiscal years ending September 30. Covers non-seasonal, full-time permanent employees. Data are from the Enterprise Human Resources Integration database, which primarily covers Executive Branch employees excluding the Postal Service and intelligence agencies; for more information, see source]

Characteristic	2015	2016	2017	2018	2019
Total retirements	61,958	59,712	59,183	62,883	63,059
Sex:					
Male	34,525	33,517	33,450	35,489	36,026
Female	27,433	26,195	25,732	27,393	27,032
Race:					
White	43,618	42,180	41,445	43,506	42,989
Black	9,958	9,422	9,670	10,477	11,002
Hispanic	4,031	3,921	3,975	4,376	4,557
Other	4,333	4,181	4,078	4,509	4,500
Retirement type:					
Disability	4,015	2,756	1,686	2,992	3,314
Early out	1,235	900	741	1,129	771
Other	1,441	1,398	1,607	1,456	1,406
Voluntary	55,267	54,658	55,149	57,306	57,568
Average retirement age (years)	61.3	61.7	61.8	61.8	61.8
Average length of service (years)	26.7	26.1	25.7	25.2	24.9

Source: U.S. Office of Personnel Management, *Retirement Statistics and Trend Analysis: Fiscal Year 2015 to Fiscal Year 2019*. See also <www.opm.gov/policy-data-oversight/data-analysis-documentation/federal-employment-reports>.

Table 540. Federal Government Civilian Employees by Agency: 2000 to 2023

[In thousands, except percent (1,814 represents 1,814,000). Shown for fiscal years ending September 30 in the year shown. Data shown for full-time equivalent (FTE) executive branch employees, excluding the U.S. Postal Service]

Fiscal year	Total Executive branch	Department of Defense	Civilian agencies Total	Agriculture	HHS, Education, Social Security [1]	Homeland Security	Interior	Justice	Transportation	Treasury	Veterans Affairs	Other
NUMBER (1,000)												
2000......	1,814	660	1,153	95	128	67	67	95	57	113	203	328
2010......	2,128	741	1,386	96	137	173	71	113	57	112	285	342
2011......	2,102	771	1,331	96	141	180	70	116	57	111	296	264
2012......	2,091	765	1,326	92	138	184	70	115	57	106	301	262
2013......	2,058	738	1,320	88	137	184	67	115	56	102	313	258
2014......	2,033	724	1,310	86	135	183	64	112	54	99	323	252
2015......	2,042	725	1,317	86	139	179	64	114	54	95	335	251
2016......	2,057	725	1,332	87	140	184	64	115	54	93	345	249
2017......	2,062	726	1,336	87	140	182	65	118	55	92	352	245
2018......	2,061	730	1,331	84	138	186	63	113	54	89	363	241
2019......	2,085	742	1,344	81	138	192	62	112	53	88	376	242
2020......	2,180	777	1,403	79	139	198	61	114	53	91	389	279
2021......	2,183	783	1,400	84	142	202	62	116	54	94	403	244
2022 [2]......	2,206	786	1,420	90	144	197	63	117	54	96	407	251
2023 [2]......	2,289	791	1,498	100	149	207	68	123	56	102	436	258
PERCENT												
2000......	100.0	36.4	63.6	5.2	7.0	3.7	3.7	5.3	3.1	6.3	11.2	18.1
2010......	100.0	34.8	65.2	4.5	6.5	8.1	3.3	5.3	2.7	5.3	13.4	16.1
2011......	100.0	36.7	63.3	4.6	6.7	8.5	3.4	5.5	2.7	5.3	14.1	12.6
2012......	100.0	36.6	63.4	4.4	6.6	8.8	3.3	5.5	2.7	5.1	14.4	12.5
2013......	100.0	35.9	64.1	4.3	6.6	8.9	3.3	5.6	2.7	5.0	15.2	12.5
2014......	100.0	35.6	64.4	4.2	6.6	9.0	3.2	5.5	2.7	4.9	15.9	12.4
2015......	100.0	35.5	64.5	4.2	6.8	8.8	3.1	5.6	2.7	4.7	16.4	12.3
2016......	100.0	35.3	64.7	4.2	6.8	8.9	3.1	5.6	2.6	4.5	16.8	12.1
2017......	100.0	35.2	64.8	4.2	6.8	8.8	3.1	5.7	2.7	4.5	17.0	11.9
2018......	100.0	35.4	64.6	4.1	6.7	9.0	3.1	5.5	2.6	4.3	17.6	11.7
2019......	100.0	35.6	64.4	3.9	6.6	9.2	3.0	5.4	2.5	4.2	18.0	11.6
2020......	100.0	35.6	64.4	3.6	6.4	9.1	2.8	5.2	2.5	4.2	17.9	12.8
2021......	100.0	35.9	64.1	3.8	6.5	9.2	2.8	5.3	2.5	4.3	18.5	11.2
2022 [2]......	100.0	35.6	64.4	4.1	6.5	8.9	2.9	5.3	2.5	4.4	18.4	11.4
2023 [2]......	100.0	34.6	65.4	4.4	6.5	9.0	3.0	5.4	2.4	4.4	19.0	11.3

[1] Department of Health and Human Services, Department of Education, and Social Security Administration. [2] Estimate.

Source: U.S. Office of Management and Budget, *Budget of the U.S. Government, Fiscal Year 2023: Historical Tables*, March 2022, <www.whitehouse.gov/omb/historical-tables/>.

Table 541. Area of Federally Owned Buildings by State: 2020

[2,838.6 represents 2,838,600,000. As of September 30. For executive branch departments and agencies subject to the Chief Financial Officers Act of 1990]

State	Total building area (mil. sq. ft.) [2]	Owned building area (mil. sq. ft.)	Leased building area (mil. sq. ft.)	State	Total building area (mil. sq. ft.) [2]	Owned building area (mil. sq. ft.)	Leased building area (mil. sq. ft.)
Total [1].............	2,838.6	2,430.8	288.6	Missouri...........	51.8	37.7	11.5
Alabama.............	60.5	52.1	4.5	Montana...........	16.5	13.5	2.2
Alaska..............	40.8	38.8	1.4	Nebraska..........	16.2	13.6	1.6
Arizona.............	58.4	52.5	4.7	Nevada............	34.4	31.2	2.3
Arkansas...........	24.2	19.5	1.4	New Hampshire...	5.0	3.4	0.6
California...........	274.5	248.5	22.4	New Jersey........	41.9	35.0	4.6
Colorado............	63.4	55.8	6.9	New Mexico........	58.9	54.2	3.3
Connecticut.........	13.8	11.5	1.0	New York..........	87.4	74.9	9.0
Delaware............	6.7	5.5	0.5	North Carolina....	97.3	88.6	6.0
Dist. of Columbia...	90.3	68.9	21.5	North Dakota......	16.4	13.6	0.9
Florida..............	114.9	98.0	12.6	Ohio..............	67.8	59.9	5.2
Georgia.............	118.5	106.4	10.2	Oklahoma.........	61.8	53.7	5.9
Hawaii..............	51.0	48.9	0.9	Oregon............	25.1	19.3	2.8
Idaho...............	17.7	15.0	1.7	Pennsylvania......	81.1	67.6	10.7
Illinois.............	67.6	57.9	5.7	Rhode Island......	9.7	8.6	0.6
Indiana.............	33.7	27.4	3.1	South Carolina....	54.1	49.3	2.5
Iowa................	16.0	10.9	1.9	South Dakota.....	16.7	14.3	0.9
Kansas.............	33.5	28.0	3.2	Tennessee.........	53.0	46.6	3.5
Kentucky............	49.7	44.4	2.9	Texas.............	195.9	169.8	22.4
Louisiana...........	42.3	30.9	3.6	Utah..............	33.9	28.4	3.3
Maine..............	10.8	9.2	0.8	Vermont...........	4.7	2.9	1.2
Maryland...........	139.5	117.8	19.8	Virginia...........	185.7	153.2	30.9
Massachusetts......	33.3	28.4	2.9	Washington.......	86.8	79.4	5.5
Michigan............	27.5	19.1	4.9	West Virginia......	23.8	19.0	2.6
Minnesota...........	18.8	11.6	2.3	Wisconsin.........	22.7	17.1	2.6
Mississippi..........	38.6	30.0	2.1	Wyoming..........	14.5	12.5	0.8

[1] Includes property in U.S. territories, not shown separately. [2] Includes museum trust and state government owned. Non-federal government entities hold title to the real property asset but rights for use have been granted to the Federal Government in a method other than a leasehold arrangement; in the case of a museum trust, the trust holds title but Federal funds may be received to cover operational and maintenance costs.

Source: U.S. General Services Administration, "Federal Real Property Profile (FRPP) Summary Report Library," <www.gsa.gov/policy-regulations/policy/real-property-policy/data-collection-and-reports/frpp-summary-report-library>, accessed February 2022.

National Security and Veterans Affairs

This section displays data for national security (national defense and homeland security) and benefits for veterans. Data are presented on national defense and its human and financial costs; active and reserve military personnel; federally sponsored programs and benefits for veterans; and funding, budget and selected agencies for homeland security. The principal sources of these data are the *Veterans Benefits Administration Annual Benefits Report*, U.S. Department of Veterans Affairs; *Budget-in-Brief*, U.S. Department of Homeland Security; and *The Budget of the United States Government*, Office of Management and Budget.

Department of Defense (DoD)—The U.S. Department of Defense is responsible for providing the military forces of the United States. It includes the Office of the Secretary of Defense, the Joint Chiefs of Staff, the Army, the Navy, the Air Force, and the defense agencies. The President serves as Commander-in-Chief of the Armed Forces; from him, the authority flows to the Secretary of Defense and through the Joint Chiefs of Staff to the commanders of unified and specified commands (e.g., U.S. Strategic Command).

Reserve components—The Reserve components of the Armed Forces consist of the Army National Guard of the United States, Army Reserve, Naval Reserve, Marine Corps Reserve, Air National Guard, Air Force Reserve, and Coast Guard Reserve. They provide trained personnel and units available for active duty in the Armed Forces during times of war or national emergency, and at such other times as national security may require. The National Guard has dual federal/state responsibilities and uses jointly provided equipment, facilities, and budget support. The President is empowered to mobilize the National Guard and to use the Armed Forces as he considers necessary to enforce federal authority in any state. There is in each Armed Force a ready reserve, a standby reserve, and a retired reserve. The Ready Reserve includes the Selected Reserve, which provides trained and ready units and individuals to augment the active forces during times of war or national emergency, or at other times when required; and the Individual Ready Reserve, which is a manpower pool that can be called to active duty during times of war or national emergency and would normally be used as individual fillers for active, guard, and reserve units, and as a source of combat replacements. Most of the Ready Reserve serves in an active status.

Department of Veterans Affairs (VA)—A veteran is someone 18 years and older (there are a few 17-year-old veterans) who is not currently on active duty, but who once served on active duty in the United States Army, Navy, Air Force, Marine Corps, or Coast Guard, or who served in the Merchant Marine during World War II. There are many groups whose active service makes them veterans including: those who incurred a service-connected disability during active duty for training in the Reserves or National Guard even though that service would not otherwise have counted for veteran status, and members of a national guard or reserve component who have been ordered to active duty by order of the President or those who have a full-time military job. The latter are called AGRs (Active Guard and Reserve). No one who has received a dishonorable discharge is a veteran.

The VA administers laws authorizing benefits for eligible former and present members of the Armed Forces and for the beneficiaries of deceased members. Veterans' benefits available under various acts of Congress include compensation for service-connected disability or death; pensions for non-service-connected disability or death; vocational rehabilitation, education and training; home loan insurance; life insurance; health care; special housing and automobiles or other conveyances for certain disabled veterans; burial and plot allowances; and educational assistance to families of deceased or totally disabled veterans, servicemen missing in action, or prisoners of war. Since these benefits are legislated by Congress, the dates they were enacted and the dates they apply to veterans may be different from the actual dates the conflicts occurred. VA estimates of veterans cover all persons discharged from active U.S. military service under conditions other than dishonorable.

Department of Homeland Security (DHS)—The creation of DHS, which began operations in March 2003, represents a fusion of 22 federal agencies from different legacy agencies (the Coast Guard and Secret Service remained intact) to coordinate and centralize the leadership of many homeland security activities under a single department. The largest organizations under DHS include: Customs and Border Protection (CBP), Immigration and Customs Enforcement (ICE), Transportation Security Administration (TSA), Federal Emergency Management Agency (FEMA), and the Coast Guard.

Coast Guard—With more than 218 years of service to the Nation, the Coast Guard is a military, multi-mission, maritime organization that promotes safety and safeguards U.S. economic and security interests throughout the maritime environment. As one of the five Armed Services of the United States, it is the only military organization within the DHS. Unlike its sister services in the Department of Defense (DoD), the Coast Guard is also a law enforcement and regulatory agency with broad domestic authorities.

Federal Emergency Management Agency (FEMA)—FEMA manages and coordinates the federal response to and recovery from major domestic disasters and emergencies of all types in accordance with the Robert T. Stafford Disaster Relief and Emergency Assistance Act. The agency ensures the effectiveness of emergency response providers at all levels of government in responding to terrorist attacks, major disasters, and other emergencies. Through the Disaster Relief Fund, FEMA provides individual and public assistance to help families and communities impacted by declared disasters rebuild and recover. FEMA is also the principal component for preparing state and local governments to prevent or respond to threats or incidents of terrorism and other catastrophic events, through their state and local programs.

The Customs and Border Protection (CBP)—CBP is responsible for managing, securing, and controlling U.S. borders. This includes carrying out traditional border-related responsibilities, such as stemming the tide of illegal drugs and illegal aliens; securing and facilitating legitimate global trade and travel; and protecting the food supply and agriculture industry from pests and disease. CBP is composed of the Border Patrol and Inspections (both moved from Immigration and Naturalization Service) along with Customs (absorbed from the U.S. Department of Treasury) and Animal and Plant Health Inspections Services (absorbed from the U.S. Department of Agriculture).

The Immigration and Customs Enforcement (ICE)—ICE's mission is to protect America and uphold public safety by targeting the people, money, and materials crossing the nation's borders that support terrorist and criminal activities. ICE is the largest investigation arm of DHS. ICE is composed of five law enforcement divisions: Investigations, Intelligence, Federal Protective Service, International Affairs, and Detention and Removal Operations. ICE investigates a wide range of national security, financial, and smuggling violations including drug smuggling, human trafficking, illegal arms exports, financial crimes, commercial fraud, human smuggling, document fraud, money laundering, child pornography/exploitation, and immigration fraud.

The Transportation Security Administration (TSA)—TSA was created as part of the Aviation and Transportation Security Act on November 19, 2001. TSA was originally part of the U.S. Department of Transportation, but was moved to DHS. TSA's mission is to provide security to our nation's transportation systems with a primary focus on aviation security.

Table 542. National Defense Outlays and Veterans' Benefits: 1965 to 2023

[In billions of dollars (56.3 represents $56,300,000,000), except percent. For fiscal year ending in year shown; see text, Section 8. Includes outlays of Department of Defense, Department of Veterans Affairs, and other agencies for activities primarily related to national defense and veterans programs. For explanation of average annual percent change, see Guide to Tabular Presentation. Minus sign (-) indicates decrease]

Year	National defense and veterans' outlays				Annual percent change [1]			Defense outlays, percent of—	
	Total outlays	Defense outlays		Veterans' outlays	Total outlays	Defense outlays	Veterans' outlays	Federal outlays	Gross domestic product [2]
		Current dollars	Constant (2012) dollars						
1965	56.3	50.6	388.5	5.7	-6.8	-7.6	0.7	42.8	7.1
1970	90.4	81.7	498.5	8.7	0.3	-1.0	13.6	41.8	7.8
1975	103.1	86.5	364.2	16.6	11.2	9.0	24.0	26.0	5.4
1980	155.2	134.0	384.5	21.2	13.9	15.2	6.3	22.7	4.8
1981	180.5	157.5	407.5	23.0	16.3	17.6	8.5	23.2	5.0
1982	209.3	185.3	440.1	24.0	15.9	17.6	4.2	24.8	5.6
1983	234.7	209.9	475.2	24.8	12.2	13.3	3.7	26.0	5.9
1984	253.0	227.4	489.5	25.6	7.8	8.3	3.0	26.7	5.8
1985	279.0	252.7	523.7	26.3	10.3	11.1	2.7	26.7	5.9
1986	299.7	273.4	554.0	26.3	7.4	8.2	0.2	27.6	6.0
1987	308.8	282.0	563.2	26.8	3.0	3.2	1.6	28.1	5.9
1988	319.8	290.4	565.7	29.4	3.6	3.0	9.9	27.3	5.7
1989	333.6	303.6	569.4	30.0	4.3	4.5	2.1	26.5	5.5
1990	328.4	299.3	542.7	29.1	-1.6	-1.4	-3.2	23.9	5.1
1991	304.6	273.3	472.3	31.3	-7.2	-8.7	7.7	20.6	4.5
1992	332.5	298.3	507.5	34.1	9.1	9.2	8.9	21.6	4.6
1993	326.8	291.1	490.2	35.7	-1.7	-2.4	4.6	20.7	4.3
1994	319.3	281.6	469.9	37.6	-2.3	-3.2	5.4	19.3	3.9
1995	310.0	272.1	445.2	37.9	-2.9	-3.4	0.8	17.9	3.6
1996	302.8	265.7	425.7	37.0	-2.3	-2.3	-2.4	17.0	3.3
1997	309.8	270.5	426.8	39.3	2.3	1.8	6.3	16.9	3.2
1998	310.0	268.2	415.1	41.8	0.0	-0.9	6.3	16.2	3.0
1999	318.0	274.8	417.0	43.2	2.6	2.5	3.4	16.1	2.9
2000	341.4	294.4	431.6	47.0	7.4	7.1	8.8	16.5	2.9
2001	349.8	304.7	432.0	45.0	2.4	3.5	-4.3	16.4	2.9
2002	399.4	348.5	478.4	51.0	14.2	14.3	13.2	17.3	3.2
2003	461.6	404.7	521.9	56.8	15.6	16.2	11.5	18.7	3.6
2004	515.5	455.8	566.4	59.7	11.7	12.6	5.1	19.9	3.8
2005	565.4	495.3	587.4	70.1	9.7	8.7	17.4	20.0	3.9
2006	591.7	521.8	593.4	69.8	4.6	5.4	-0.4	19.7	3.8
2007	624.1	551.3	606.9	72.8	5.5	5.6	4.3	20.2	3.9
2008	700.8	616.1	653.1	84.7	12.3	11.8	16.3	20.7	4.2
2009	756.6	661.0	702.4	95.5	8.0	7.3	12.8	18.8	4.6
2010	802.0	693.5	723.6	108.5	6.0	4.9	13.5	20.1	4.7
2011	832.8	705.6	715.2	127.3	3.8	1.7	17.3	19.6	4.6
2012	802.5	677.9	677.8	124.7	-3.6	-3.9	-2.0	19.2	4.2
2013	772.5	633.4	629.0	139.0	-3.7	-6.6	11.5	18.3	3.8
2014	753.1	603.5	589.6	149.6	-2.5	-4.7	7.6	17.2	3.5
2015	749.4	589.7	573.8	159.8	-0.5	-2.3	6.8	16.0	3.3
2016	767.9	593.4	575.3	174.6	2.5	0.6	9.2	15.4	3.2
2017	775.3	598.7	572.7	176.6	1.0	0.9	1.2	15.0	3.1
2018	810.0	631.1	588.4	178.9	4.5	5.4	1.3	15.4	3.1
2019	885.8	686.0	626.6	199.8	9.4	8.7	11.7	15.4	3.2
2020	943.3	724.6	655.1	218.7	6.5	5.6	9.4	11.1	3.5
2021	988.2	753.9	662.3	234.3	4.8	4.0	7.1	11.1	3.4
2022, estimate	1,053.6	779.7	658.8	274.0	6.6	3.4	16.9	13.3	3.2
2023, estimate	1,104.0	808.6	668.4	295.4	4.8	3.7	7.8	14.0	3.2
2024, estimate	1,144.3	836.5	677.8	307.8	3.7	3.5	4.2	13.8	3.1
2025, estimate	1,189.1	850.7	675.8	338.4	3.9	1.7	9.9	13.3	3.1
2026, estimate	1,212.9	857.2	667.5	355.7	2.0	0.8	5.1	12.7	3.0
2027, estimate	1,240.1	867.1	662.0	373.0	2.2	1.2	4.9	12.3	2.9

[1] Change from immediate prior year. [2] Represents fiscal year GDP; for definition, see text, Section 13.

Source: U.S. Office of Management and Budget, *Budget of the U.S. Government, Fiscal Year 2023: Historical Tables*, March 2022. See also <www.whitehouse.gov/omb/budget/>.

Table 543. National Defense Budget Authority and Outlays for Defense Functions: 2000 to 2023

[In billions of dollars (304.0 represents $304,000,000,000). For year ending September 30. Data includes defense budget authority and outlays by other departments. Minus sign (-) indicates decrease]

Function	2000	2010	2015	2016	2017	2018	2019	2020	2021	2022 est.	2023 est.
Total budget authority..........	**304.0**	**721.2**	**598.4**	**624.1**	**656.3**	**726.8**	**745.7**	**774.5**	**759.6**	**766.6**	**827.0**
Department of Defense—Military...	290.3	695.6	570.8	595.7	626.2	694.5	712.6	738.8	719.5	727.0	784.0
Military personnel..................	73.8	157.1	145.9	145.4	146.1	150.9	157.3	163.3	172.9	174.3	184.8
Operation and maintenance.......	108.7	293.6	246.6	245.1	258.7	274.1	283.1	301.5	285.6	293.2	310.3
Procurement.......................	55.0	135.8	102.1	118.9	124.3	147.5	146.8	141.0	140.9	143.4	146.2
Research, development, test, and evaluation.....................	38.7	80.2	63.9	69.5	74.1	92.0	95.5	105.2	106.1	107.7	130.5
Military construction...............	5.1	22.6	5.7	6.9	6.9	10.4	11.3	16.7	7.1	7.1	10.2
Family housing....................	3.5	2.3	1.1	1.3	1.3	1.4	1.6	1.5	1.5	1.4	2.0
Other.............................	5.4	4.0	5.6	8.5	14.7	18.3	16.9	9.5	5.4	-0.1	0.2
Atomic energy defense activities. ..	12.4	18.2	19.0	20.1	21.4	23.3	24.0	26.0	29.4	29.5	31.8
Defense-related activities..........	1.3	7.3	8.5	8.3	8.7	9.0	9.1	9.7	10.8	10.1	11.1
Total outlays..................	**294.4**	**693.5**	**589.7**	**593.4**	**598.7**	**631.1**	**686.0**	**724.6**	**753.9**	**779.7**	**808.6**
Department of Defense—Military...	281.0	666.7	562.5	565.4	568.9	600.7	654.0	690.4	717.6	741.0	767.6
Military personnel..................	76.0	155.7	145.2	147.9	144.7	145.8	156.3	161.4	172.6	177.8	183.6
Operation and maintenance.......	105.8	276.0	247.2	243.2	245.2	256.7	271.7	278.9	286.2	302.6	304.7
Procurement.......................	51.7	133.6	101.3	102.7	104.1	112.7	124.7	139.1	141.4	134.4	138.0
Research, development, test, and evaluation.....................	37.6	77.0	64.1	64.9	68.1	77.0	89.3	99.9	105.7	111.6	126.5
Military construction...............	5.1	21.2	8.1	6.7	6.7	6.7	7.4	8.9	9.1	11.4	11.0
Family housing....................	3.4	3.2	1.2	1.3	1.2	1.2	1.2	1.3	1.5	1.6	1.6
Other.............................	1.4	0.1	-4.7	-1.2	-1.1	0.7	3.5	1.0	1.1	1.7	2.3
Atomic energy defense activities. ..	12.1	19.3	18.7	19.4	20.5	20.9	22.8	24.5	25.8	28.9	30.9
Defense-related activities..........	1.2	7.5	8.5	8.6	9.3	9.5	9.3	9.7	10.5	9.8	10.0

Source: U.S. Office of Management and Budget, *Budget of the U.S. Government, Fiscal Year 2023: Historical Tables*, March 2022. See also <www.whitehouse.gov/omb/budget/>.

Table 544. Military Personnel and Families by Selected Characteristics: 2010 to 2020

[In units, as indicated. Reserve and National Guard includes Selected Reserve only, unless otherwise noted. Personnel data primarily from Defense Manpower Data Center (DMDC). Family member data is from the Defense Enrollment and Eligibility Reporting System]

Characteristic	2010 Active Duty	2010 Reserve and Guard	2015 Active Duty	2015 Reserve and Guard	2019 Active Duty	2019 Reserve and Guard	2020 Active Duty	2020 Reserve and Guard
MILITARY PERSONNEL								
Total (number).................	**1,417,370**	**857,261**	**1,301,443**	**826,106**	**1,326,200**	**807,602**	**1,333,822**	**802,248**
Ratio of officers to enlisted members.....	1 to 5.0	1 to 5.7	1 to 4.6	1 to 5.3	1 to 4.7	1 to 5.0	1 to 4.7	1 to 4.9
Separations from duty (number)..........	176,248	133,223	188,276	125,895	164,775	119,216	157,548	121,671
Retired personnel (number) [1].............	1,540,830	716,228	1,573,562	766,658	1,588,636	780,451	1,584,665	786,399
PERCENT								
Male...	85.6	82.1	84.5	81.0	83.1	79.4	82.8	78.9
Female......................................	14.4	17.9	15.5	19.0	16.9	20.6	17.2	21.1
Minority race/ethnicity [2].....................	30.0	24.1	31.3	26.0	32.1	26.4	31.1	27.5
Duty location in the U.S. & territories.....	86.4	99.1	87.5	99.2	87.4	99.3	87.9	99.6
25 years old and under....................	44.2	33.3	43.8	34.0	45.7	32.8	45.0	38.5
With bachelor's degree or higher........	17.7	19.4	21.1	22.7	22.3	24.8	22.5	25.4
Married.....................................	56.4	48.2	54.3	44.7	50.7	43.7	49.9	43.9
In dual-military marriages.................	6.7	2.6	6.4	2.7	6.8	2.7	6.8	2.6
MILITARY FAMILIES								
Family members (number)..............	**1,983,236**	**1,161,631**	**1,728,710**	**1,064,795**	**1,591,042**	**1,039,786**	**1,569,841**	**1,023,295**
Spouses (number)........................	725,877	413,295	641,639	374,621	605,716	363,462	597,737	357,220
Adult dependents (number)..............	9,485	1,961	10,268	1,708	8,135	1,509	7,619	1,473
PERCENT								
With children................................	44.1	43.2	41.1	41.5	36.5	41.0	35.9	40.5
With children age 5 & under.............	42.3	27.9	42	30.5	42.1	31.6	41.4	31.1
Single parents.............................	5.4	9.3	4.5	9.1	4.0	9.1	3.9	8.6
Average age at birth of first child (years).................................	24.9	26.6	25.8	28	25.8	28.2	25.9	28.6

[1] Retired Reserve and Guard includes ready reserve. [2] Black or African American, Asian, American Indian or Alaska Native, Native Hawaiian or Other Pacific Islander, multi-racial, or other/unknown.

Source: U.S. Department of Defense, Office of the Deputy Assistant Secretary of Defense, Military Community and Family Policy, *2020 Demographics Profile of the Military Community*, and earlier reports. See also <www.militaryonesource.mil/reports-and-surveys>.

Table 545. Department of Defense Personnel by Service Branch and Sex: 1960 to 2021

[In thousands (2,475 represents 2,475,000). As of end of fiscal year; see text, Section 8. Includes National Guard, Reserve, and retired regular personnel on extended or continuous active duty. Excludes Coast Guard. Other officer candidates are included under enlisted personnel]

Year	Total[1,2]	Army Total[1]	Army Male Officers	Army Male Enlisted	Army Female Officers	Army Female Enlisted	Navy[2] Total[1]	Navy Male Officers	Navy Male Enlisted	Navy Female Officers	Navy Female Enlisted	Marine Corps Total[1]	MC Male Officers	MC Male Enlisted	MC Female Officers	MC Female Enlisted	Air Force Total[1]	AF Male Officers	AF Male Enlisted	AF Female Officers	AF Female Enlisted
1960	2,475	873	96.7	761.7	4.3	8.3	617	67.3	539.6	2.7	5.4	171	15.9	152.5	0.1	1.5	815	126.3	677.3	3.7	5.7
1965	2,654	969	108.2	846.5	3.8	8.5	670	75.4	582.7	2.6	5.3	190	16.9	171.6	0.1	1.4	825	127.9	685.3	4.1	4.7
1970	3,065	1,323	161.8	1,141.5	5.2	11.5	691	78.1	600.2	2.9	5.8	260	24.7	232.9	0.3	2.1	791	125.3	648.0	4.7	9.0
1975	2,128	784	98.4	640.3	4.6	37.7	535	62.3	448.5	3.7	17.5	196	18.7	174.2	0.3	2.8	613	100.0	477.8	5.0	25.2
1980	2,051	777	91.4	612.3	7.6	61.7	527	58.1	429.9	4.9	30.1	189	17.5	163.8	0.5	6.2	558	89.5	404.1	8.5	51.9
1985	2,151	781	99.2	598.6	10.8	68.4	571	64.1	449.3	6.9	45.7	198	19.3	169.0	0.7	9.0	602	96.1	430.9	11.9	58.1
1986	2,169	781	98.7	597.3	11.3	69.7	581	64.7	456.8	7.3	47.2	200	19.4	169.8	0.6	9.1	608	96.6	433.8	12.4	61.2
1987	2,174	781	96.4	596.4	11.6	71.6	587	64.8	462.3	7.2	47.7	200	19.4	169.9	0.6	9.1	607	94.4	431.8	12.6	63.2
1988	2,138	772	95.3	588.0	11.8	72.0	593	64.7	466.3	7.3	49.7	197	19.3	168.0	0.7	9.0	576	92.1	405.5	12.9	61.5
1989	2,130	770	94.8	583.7	12.2	74.3	593	64.5	463.9	7.5	52.1	197	19.3	168.0	0.7	9.0	571	90.6	399.3	13.4	63.7
1990	2,044	732	91.6	552.8	12.4	71.2	579	64.2	450.9	7.8	52.1	197	19.3	168.3	0.7	8.7	535	86.7	370.2	13.3	60.8
1991	1,986	711	91.5	535.2	12.5	67.8	570	63.0	443.6	8.0	51.4	194	19.3	165.7	0.7	8.3	510	83.7	349.9	13.3	59.1
1992	1,807	610	83.3	449.3	11.7	61.7	542	60.7	417.0	8.3	51.0	185	18.4	157.1	0.6	7.9	470	77.3	319.9	12.7	56.1
1993	1,705	572	76.9	419.8	11.1	60.2	510	57.7	389.7	8.3	49.3	178	17.4	152.8	0.6	7.2	444	71.7	301.5	12.3	54.5
1994	1,610	541	74.1	393.5	10.9	59.0	469	54.0	355.1	8.0	47.9	174	17.4	149.0	0.6	7.0	426	68.7	287.0	12.3	54.0
1995	1,518	509	72.2	364.7	10.8	57.3	435	51.1	324.1	7.9	47.9	175	17.3	149.6	0.7	7.4	400	65.9	265.9	12.1	52.1
1996	1,472	491	70.0	347.5	10.8	59.0	417	49.7	308.2	7.8	46.9	175	17.2	149.1	0.8	7.8	389	64.3	255.8	12.0	52.8
1997	1,439	492	68.9	345.9	10.4	62.4	396	48.4	290.5	7.8	44.8	174	17.0	147.6	0.8	8.5	377	62.0	245.5	12.0	53.8
1998	1,407	484	68.1	339.8	10.4	61.4	382	47.2	280.2	7.8	42.9	173	17.0	146.3	0.9	8.9	368	59.9	237.4	12.0	54.2
1999	1,386	479	66.6	336.6	10.5	61.5	373	45.8	271.3	7.7	43.9	173	17.0	145.5	0.9	9.3	361	58.5	231.5	11.8	54.6
2000	1,384	482	65.9	338.5	10.8	62.9	373	45.7	271.7	7.8	43.8	173	17.0	145.9	0.9	9.5	356	57.2	227.3	11.8	55.0
2001	1,385	481	65.0	336.6	11.0	63.4	378	46.0	273.4	8.0	46.6	173	17.0	145.4	1.0	9.6	354	57.0	224.4	12.0	55.6
2002	1,414	487	66.5	340.8	11.5	63.2	385	46.8	278.7	8.2	47.3	174	17.0	145.5	1.0	9.5	368	59.1	233.4	12.9	58.6
2003	1,434	499	68.0	351.5	12.0	63.5	382	46.8	275.7	8.2	47.3	178	17.9	149.4	1.1	9.6	375	60.5	237.0	13.5	60.0
2004	1,427	500	68.6	357.5	12.3	61.0	373	46.1	272.8	8.1	46.1	178	17.7	149.0	1.1	9.7	377	60.5	242.3	13.6	60.2
2005	1,389	493	69.1	353.1	12.4	57.9	363	45.0	265.5	7.8	44.5	180	17.7	151.2	1.0	9.8	354	59.7	224.7	13.4	55.6
2006	1,385	505	69.0	365.0	12.5	58.5	350	44.0	255.0	7.6	43.2	180	18.0	151.0	1.1	10.0	349	58.0	223.0	12.8	55.8
2007	1,380	522	71.0	379.0	13.0	58.8	338	44.0	244.0	7.6	42.2	186	18.0	156.0	1.1	10.5	333	54.0	214.0	11.8	53.4
2008	1,402	544	74.0	392.0	13.5	59.7	332	44.0	235.0	7.7	41.4	199	19.0	167.0	1.2	11.1	327	53.0	207.0	11.9	51.4
2009	1,419	553	76.0	399.0	14.3	59.4	329	44.0	231.0	7.9	42.2	203	19.0	170.0	1.2	11.7	333	53.0	211.0	12.1	52.0
2010	1,431	566	79.0	407.0	15.1	60.3	328	44.0	228.0	8.2	43.4	202	18.0	169.0	1.3	12.2	334	54.0	212.0	12.4	50.9
2011	1,425	565	82.0	403.0	15.7	60.2	325	44.0	224.0	8.5	44.0	201	21.0	167.0	1.3	12.4	333	53.0	213.0	12.3	50.3
2012	1,400	550	82.4	389.6	16.0	57.4	318	44.2	216.8	8.6	44.3	198	20.4	163.8	1.3	12.6	333	52.5	214.2	12.5	49.8
2013	1,383	532	82.4	373.3	16.2	55.7	324	44.9	219.0	9.0	47.0	196	19.9	161.8	1.4	12.8	330	52.1	212.7	12.7	49.1
2014	1,338	508	81.1	352.7	16.2	53.8	326	45.2	219.1	9.2	48.1	188	19.5	154.2	1.4	12.8	316	49.9	203.4	12.4	46.7
2015	1,314	491	78.7	338.9	15.9	53.4	328	44.8	219.3	9.4	49.9	183	19.2	150.1	1.5	12.6	311	48.6	200.0	12.4	46.3
2016	1,301	475	76.4	325.5	15.7	53.2	325	44.6	215.5	9.8	50.2	184	19.2	149.5	1.5	13.3	318	48.4	204.5	12.6	48.3
2017	1,307	476	75.9	325.5	15.4	54.4	324	44.4	213.6	10.1	51.4	184	19.5	149.4	1.6	13.9	323	48.7	206.9	12.9	50.1
2018	1,317	476	75.9	325.0	16.1	54.6	330	44.4	217.0	10.4	53.6	185	19.7	149.7	1.7	14.3	326	49.3	207.2	13.3	51.8
2019	1,339	484	75.9	330.2	16.5	56.8	337	44.4	221.5	10.7	55.9	186	19.7	149.7	1.8	14.9	332	50.0	209.8	13.9	54.2
2020	1,347	485	76.0	330.3	17.0	57.6	347	44.6	227.8	11.1	58.6	181	19.6	145.2	1.8	14.3	334	49.9	210.1	14.3	55.2
2021	1,348	486	76.2	331.0	17.2	57.6	348	44.6	228.4	11.4	58.8	180	19.7	143.7	2.0	14.3	335	50.2	210.0	14.7	55.6

[1] Includes cadets, midshipmen, and others, not shown separately. [2] Beginning 1980, excludes Navy Reserve personnel on active duty for Training and Administration of Reserves (TARS).

Source: U.S. Department of Defense, Statistical Information Analysis Division, Selected Manpower Statistics, discontinued; and Defense Manpower Data Center, "Active Duty Military Personnel by Service by Rank/Grade," <www.dmdc.osd.mil/appj/dwp/dwp_reports.jsp>, accessed December 2021.

Table 546. Military Personnel on Active Duty by Rank or Grade: 2000 to 2021

[As of September 30]

Rank/grade	2000	2010	2017	2018	2019	2020	2021
Total	1,384,338	1,430,985	1,307,364	1,317,325	1,339,036	1,346,651	1,348,479
Total officers	217,178	234,000	228,972	230,708	232,889	234,336	236,061
General – Admiral	34	39	37	40	37	45	41
Lieutenant General – Vice Admiral	119	150	147	147	142	153	157
Major General – Rear Admiral (U.)	282	310	301	296	295	281	294
Brigadier General – Rear Admiral (L.)	436	482	418	438	409	417	409
Colonel – Captain	11,304	12,160	11,222	10,999	11,080	11,246	11,197
Lieutenant Colonel – Commander	27,461	28,773	27,028	27,126	27,152	27,569	27,800
Major – LT Commander	43,229	45,295	42,630	43,145	43,908	45,066	45,402
Captain – Lieutenant	68,106	74,997	74,838	74,120	73,820	72,602	73,507
1st Lieutenant – Lieutenant (JG)	24,713	25,523	27,642	28,250	29,228	31,411	32,136
2nd Lieutenant – Ensign	26,405	27,128	26,607	28,002	28,590	27,145	26,222
Chief Warrant Officer W-5	473	746	739	783	774	749	736
Chief Warrant Officer W-4	2,029	3,233	2,756	2,761	2,647	2,657	2,748
Chief Warrant Officer W-3	3,824	4,795	5,327	5,225	5,153	4,975	4,802
Chief Warrant Officer W-2	6,674	7,489	6,875	6,737	6,768	7,078	7,463
Warrant Officer W-1	2,089	2,880	2,405	2,639	2,886	2,942	3,122
Total enlisted	1,154,624	1,183,200	1,065,163	1,073,324	1,092,937	1,099,125	1,099,378
E-9	10,240	10,192	10,071	10,369	10,472	10,414	10,438
E-8	26,035	27,331	26,137	26,195	27,477	27,271	26,916
E-7	97,717	97,070	88,408	91,086	92,617	93,945	92,584
E-6	164,857	170,856	154,681	157,265	160,725	167,362	168,739
E-5	229,492	249,981	218,278	221,114	226,193	225,035	227,526
E-4	250,999	279,315	251,734	245,602	253,718	265,000	267,687
E-3	196,276	228,152	186,496	191,054	189,579	192,764	196,229
E-2	98,983	75,177	71,613	70,960	71,703	66,465	66,472
E-1	80,025	45,126	57,745	59,679	60,453	50,867	42,787
Cadets and Midshipmen	12,536	13,785	13,229	13,293	13,210	13,190	13,040

Source: U.S. Department of Defense, Statistical Information Analysis Division, *Atlas/Data Abstract for the United States and Selected Areas*, annual, discontinued; and "Active Duty Military Personnel by Rank/Grade," <dwp.dmdc.osd.mil/dwp/app/dod-data-reports/workforce-reports>, accessed January 2022.

Table 547. Military Retirement System—Disabled and Non-Disabled Personnel and Payments: 2020

[Payment in thousands of dollars (4,835,079 represents $4,835,079,000). As of September 30. The data published in the source report are produced from files maintained by the Defense Manpower Data Center. This report compiles data primarily from the "Retiree Pay and Survivor Pay" files. Any grouping of members by address reflects mailing, not necessarily residence, address. Only those members in plans administered by the Department of Defense (DoD) are included in this table. The data are preliminary because of reporting delays about members who retired or died within one month of the September 30 reporting date. These data were not processed in time to be included in this report. For more information, see Introduction and Overview, source]

State	Retired military personnel [1]			Monthly payment ($1,000)	State	Retired military personnel [1]			Monthly payment ($1,000)
	Total	Disabled [2]	Non-disabled			Total	Disabled [2]	Non-disabled	
Total [3]	2,183,110	294,993	1,888,117	4,835,079	MS	28,078	3,384	24,694	53,730
					MO	39,345	6,081	33,264	75,855
U.S.	2,143,208	289,836	1,853,372	4,755,681	MT	9,884	1,301	8,583	20,669
AL	62,510	7,550	54,960	138,866	NE	14,630	1,588	13,042	33,103
AK	11,099	1,636	9,463	24,464	NV	30,371	3,149	27,222	68,036
AZ	58,586	6,958	51,628	131,021	NH	9,562	1,163	8,399	21,104
AR	25,169	3,537	21,632	48,325	NJ	18,999	3,281	15,718	33,136
CA	149,430	19,385	130,045	330,186	NM	20,806	2,453	18,353	47,357
CO	54,063	7,785	46,278	137,549	NY	40,257	8,114	32,143	65,612
CT	10,118	1,614	8,504	19,742	NC	101,780	14,762	87,018	232,636
DE	9,301	900	8,401	18,917	ND	5,545	560	4,985	10,362
DC	2,337	361	1,976	6,476	OH	48,311	8,099	40,212	95,084
FL	207,332	23,557	183,775	497,473	OK	36,387	5,069	31,318	73,277
GA	101,134	15,102	86,032	216,443	OR	20,800	3,481	17,319	40,680
HI	18,136	1,893	16,243	44,816	PA	51,963	7,504	44,459	100,088
ID	15,169	1,955	13,214	31,964	RI	5,279	712	4,567	11,518
IL	36,471	6,017	30,454	73,423	SC	62,432	7,397	55,035	135,703
IN	27,006	5,026	21,980	46,301	SD	8,859	866	7,993	18,285
IA	13,595	2,157	11,438	23,988	TN	58,326	8,346	49,980	122,029
KS	22,532	3,282	19,250	48,867	TX	220,990	34,997	185,993	504,451
KY	29,014	4,782	24,232	57,630	UT	17,968	2,138	15,830	38,236
LA	26,443	4,330	22,113	52,714	VT	3,950	585	3,365	7,009
ME	11,946	1,544	10,402	23,371	VA	157,977	12,879	145,098	472,331
MD	55,997	5,762	50,235	139,666	WA	74,916	9,027	65,889	170,833
MA	18,101	3,004	15,097	33,131	WV	10,982	1,637	9,345	20,287
MI	31,108	6,196	24,912	52,976	WI	22,668	3,422	19,246	40,168
MN	19,729	2,828	16,901	33,672	WY	5,817	680	5,137	12,121

[1] Represents military personnel (officers and enlisted) receiving and not receiving pay from DoD. [2] A disabled military member is entitled to disability retired pay if the disability is not the result of the member's intentional misconduct or willful neglect, was not incurred during a period of unauthorized absence, and either: (1) the member has at least 20 years of service; or (2) at the time of determination, the disability is at least 30 percent (under a standard schedule of rating disabilities by the Veterans Administration) and one of four additional conditions are met. For details on these conditions and additional information, see Overview, source. [3] Includes states, U.S. territories, and retirees living in foreign countries.

Source: U.S. Department of Defense, Office of the Actuary, *Statistical Report on the Military Retirement System, Fiscal Year Ended September 30, 2020*, September 2021. See also <actuary.defense.gov>.

Table 548. U.S. Active Duty Military Deaths and Personnel Wounded in Action by Conflict and Manner of Death: 2001 to 2022

[As of September 2, 2022. See source for details. Data include deaths where wounding occurred in theater and death occurred elsewhere]

Item	Operation Enduring Freedom (OEF) [1]	Operation Iraqi Freedom (OIF) [2]	Operation New Dawn (OND) [3]	Operation Inherent Resolve (OIR) [4]	Operation Freedom's Sentinel (OFS) [5]
Deaths, total..................	**2,349**	**4,418**	**74**	**107**	**107**
Total hostile deaths........	[6] **1,845**	**3,481**	**38**	**20**	**77**
Killed in action................	1,370	2,676	22	12	51
Died of wounds...............	472	798	16	8	26
Died while missing in action..	(NA)	1	–	–	–
Died while captured.........	(NA)	5	–	–	–
Died while detained..........	(NA)	1	–	–	–
Died of terrorist activities.....	2	–	–	–	–
Total non-hostile deaths...	**504**	**937**	**36**	**87**	**30**
Accident........................	305	570	7	32	19
Illness or injury................	62	97	10	19	2
Homicide.......................	14	37	3	3	1
Self-inflicted...................	112	222	13	32	8
Undetermined.................	10	11	3	1	–
Pending........................	1	–	–	–	–
Wounded in action...........	**20,149**	**31,994**	**298**	**276**	**620**

– Represents zero. NA Not available. [1] OEF October 2001-December 2014 combat operations in Afghanistan and against al Qaeda. [2] OIF March 2003-September 2010 combat operations in Iraq. [3] OND September 2010-December 2011, to advise and train Iraqi security forces in Iraq. [4] OIR August 2014-present, to support Iraqi Security Force operations against the Islamic State of Iraq and the Levant (ISIL). [5] OFS 2015-present, to train, advise, and assist Afghan National Defense and Security Forces in Afghanistan and conduct counterterrorism operations against the remnants of al Qaeda. [6] Includes 1 death not attributed to a manner of death.

Source: U.S. Department of Defense, Defense Manpower Data Center, "Defense Casualty Analysis System, Conflict Casualties," <dcas.dmdc.osd.mil/dcas/app>, accessed September 2022.

Table 549. U.S. Military Personnel on Active Duty Overseas by Selected Country: 2010 to 2021

[As of September 30. Data from Defense Manpower Data Center (DMDC)]

Country	2010	2013	2014	2015	2016	2017	2018 [1]	2019 [1]	2020 [1]	2021 [1]
Total overseas [2]........	**339,360**	**251,737**	**232,790**	**213,067**	**198,557**	**215,249**	[3] **172,370**	[3] **174,253**	[3] **168,766**	[3] **174,711**
Afghanistan.................	81,875	48,807	24,170	9,392	9,027	13,329	([3])	([3])	([3])	([3])
Australia.....................	163	229	1,147	1,201	187	1,239	1,496	2,858	1,085	1,768
Bahrain......................	4,626	6,308	5,502	5,160	5,370	8,610	4,214	4,202	4,004	4,031
Belgium......................	1,157	1,155	1,202	1,202	852	867	1,049	1,046	1,147	1,143
British Indian Ocean Territory....................	484	451	521	486	294	264	299	325	230	223
Canada.......................	131	149	145	146	139	129	144	144	132	143
Cuba (Guantanamo)......	870	978	892	782	797	753	831	776	738	629
Djibouti.......................	990	2,084	1,984	1,970	1,702	3,132	954	88	176	68
Egypt.........................	262	266	304	350	356	375	280	276	269	292
Germany......................	43,911	35,849	36,855	35,216	34,612	34,516	35,116	35,275	33,959	35,468
Greece.......................	380	393	380	371	360	433	410	389	380	429
Honduras.....................	391	376	374	660	397	505	467	474	370	372
Hungary......................	50	65	66	70	207	215	202	194	77	77
Iraq...........................	38,591	138	498	4,231	4,626	7,402	([3])	([3])	([3])	([3])
Italy..........................	8,836	10,686	11,373	11,614	12,090	11,756	12,703	12,902	12,249	12,436
Japan.........................	46,313	52,972	52,518	55,744	38,834	44,562	54,281	55,245	53,732	56,010
Jordan........................	42	1,140	1,386	1,861	1,556	1,862	59	95	254	88
Kenya........................	23	120	104	96	40	208	46	44	52	97
Korea, South................	27,869	30,252	29,074	24,934	24,190	23,635	25,813	26,525	26,416	25,593
Kosovo.......................	52	514	496	87	366	384	(NA)	(NA)	17	14
Kuwait.......................	17,584	8,109	11,377	8,809	5,818	9,241	1,863	1,798	2,169	2,614
Kyrgyzstan...................	5,483	3,222	121	83	67	65	5	2	8	9
Netherlands..................	433	378	411	399	382	407	404	393	415	422
Niger.........................	2	97	119	139	8	510	8	13	16	30
Norway.......................	68	84	81	83	77	344	474	556	733	81
Pakistan......................	268	87	94	116	121	111	35	27	66	67
Philippines...................	546	398	251	234	36	101	145	170	185	126
Poland........................	18	47	51	61	53	173	150	163	165	167
Portugal......................	699	698	653	464	197	192	233	232	252	259
Qatar.........................	12,036	5,919	5,589	5,219	3,216	4,666	783	545	490	487
Romania......................	7	166	675	611	682	451	294	108	124	132
Saudi Arabia.................	325	654	553	515	371	402	323	314	382	1,396
Singapore....................	216	214	217	252	176	206	205	200	206	187
Somalia......................	2	310	53	232	106	285	60	85	73	50
Spain.........................	1,396	1,915	3,095	3,393	3,272	3,940	3,602	3,658	3,169	3,234
Syria.........................	3	1	(NA)	(NA)	(NA)	1,547	([3])	([3])	([3])	([3])
Thailand......................	201	106	110	108	296	309	316	303	100	99
Turkey........................	1,721	1,514	1,595	2,081	2,139	1,950	1,695	1,659	1,685	1,753
United Arab Emirates.....	1,427	3,384	2,045	2,620	1,510	3,455	414	352	195	200
United Kingdom............	8,764	9,045	8,495	8,062	8,404	8,341	9,137	9,254	9,287	9,576
Yemen........................	104	248	161	8	7	14	4	7	4	5
Guam.........................	5,423	5,467	6,337	6,531	3,977	4,590	6,199	5,560	6,140	6,273
Puerto Rico..................	654	667	657	725	142	176	158	161	163	161

NA Not available. [1] As of December 2017, excludes personnel on temporary duty, or deployed in support of contingency operations. [2] Includes items not shown separately, and also personnel in unknown and classified locations. [3] Data are not shown for Afghanistan, Iraq, and Syria. With ongoing operations, questions concerning DoD personnel strength numbers are deferred to OSD Public Affairs/Joint Chiefs of Staff.

Source: U.S. Department of Defense, DoD Personnel, Workforce Reports & Publications, "Military and Civilian Personnel by Service/Agency by State/Country," <www.dmdc.osd.mil/appj/dwp/stats_reports.jsp>, accessed April 2022.

Table 550. Suicides of Military Personnel by Selected Characteristics: 2013 to 2020

[Data are shown for suicides reported in Department of Defense Suicide Event Report (DoDSER). Beginning 2013, covers service members in the active component of the military only. DoDSER standardizes suicide surveillance efforts across the military services to support the DoD's suicide prevention mission. Confirmed suicides are those that have been confirmed by the Armed Forces Medical Examiner System (AFMES)]

Characteristics	Suicides							
	2013	2014	2015	2016	2017	2018	2019	2020
Suicides confirmed/pending confirmation [1]	**256**	**276**	**266**	**280**	**285**	**325**	**344**	**369**
By sex:								
Male	241	256	252	260	269	304	315	342
Female	15	20	14	20	16	21	29	27
By race/ethnicity:								
White	192	199	186	215	220	234	260	276
Black or African American	32	42	44	33	28	42	36	48
Asian or Pacific Islander	8	8	12	9	13	23	22	18
American Indian or Alaska Native	8	3	4	6	2	2	7	8
By Hispanic origin:								
Hispanic or Latino	21	34	29	29	41	50	52	65
Non-Hispanic or Latino	232	240	231	245	236	265	277	303
Unknown	3	2	6	6	8	10	15	1
By age:								
Under 25 years old	108	102	107	127	121	144	161	187
25-29 years old	72	72	62	68	75	74	92	90
30-39 years old	57	83	77	62	60	83	72	70
40 years old and over	19	19	20	23	29	24	19	22
By marital status:								
Never married	106	105	116	120	115	133	151	173
Married	126	145	132	135	141	179	170	175
Legally separated	2	–	–	2	–	–	–	–
Divorced	22	25	17	22	28	13	23	21
Widowed	–	1	1	1	1	–	–	–

– Represents zero. [1] Includes other or unknown race/ethnicity, age, and marital status, not shown separately.

Source: U.S. Department of Defense, Defense Suicide Prevention Office, *Department of Defense Suicide Event Report, Calendar Year 2020 Annual Report*, 2022, and earlier reports. See also <www.dspo.mil>.

Table 551. Sexual Assault in the Military—Incident Reports and Victims by Type of Report and Selected Characteristics: 2018 to 2021

[Data are for fiscal years. Reports of sexual assault (rape, aggravated sexual assault, sexual assault, aggravated sexual contact, abusive sexual contact, wrongful sexual contact, non-consensual sodomy, and attempts to commit these offenses) by or against Service Members. Restricted Reporting allows victim confidential access to medical care and advocacy services. When a victim makes an unrestricted report, the report is also referred to a Military Criminal Investigation Organization for investigation and command is notified]

Item	Unrestricted				Restricted			
	2018	2019	2020	2021	2018	2019	2020	2021
REPORTS [1]								
Total	**5,685**	**5,578**	**5,519**	**6,220**	**1,818**	**2,126**	**2,176**	**2,510**
Service member on service member	2,853	2,830	2,947	3,323	1,006	1,153	1,293	1,456
Service member on non-service member	900	870	833	907	40	50	53	27
Non-service member on service member	178	174	157	185	413	497	416	483
Unidentified subject on service member	913	738	625	780	359	424	412	496
Unknown	841	966	957	1,025	–	2	2	48
VICTIMS IN COMPLETED INVESTIGATIONS [2]								
Total	**5,053**	**5,245**	**5,165**	**5,533**	**(X)**	**(X)**	**(X)**	**(X)**
Service member victims	4,162	4,320	4,208	4,608	(X)	(X)	(X)	(X)
Non-service member victims	891	925	957	925	(X)	(X)	(X)	(X)
VICTIMS [3]								
By sex:								
Male	905	980	960	1,060	366	440	451	559
Female	4,143	4,256	4,201	4,470	1,452	1,685	1,725	1,942
By age:								
0-15 years old	67	44	29	44	150	141	153	201
16-19 years old	1,263	1,350	1,454	1,608	434	567	606	670
20-24 years old	2,157	2,240	2,173	2,371	783	870	924	1,080
25-34 years old	956	938	883	884	360	412	384	465
35-49 years old	205	210	154	169	64	89	82	88
50-64 years old	5	16	12	13	3	7	1	6
65 years and older	86	68	130	99	–	–	–	–
SERVICE MEMBER VICTIMS								
By service branch:								
Army	1,849	1,940	1,934	2,240	569	644	675	(NA)
Navy	1,064	1,005	1,008	1,101	423	553	544	(NA)
Marines	524	522	473	482	347	369	366	(NA)
Air Force	725	849	791	784	438	508	535	(NA)
Coast Guard	–	–	1	–	1	–	–	(NA)

– Represents zero. X Not applicable. NA Not available. [1] Reports of sexual assault during the fiscal year. [2] Victims in investigations completed during the fiscal year. Includes victims of unknown sex, age, and service branch, not shown separately. [3] For unrestricted reports, data shown for victims in investigations completed during the fiscal year.

Source: U.S. Department of Defense, *Annual Report on Sexual Assault in the Military, Fiscal Year 2021*, September 2022, and earlier reports. See also <sapr.mil/reports>.

Table 552. U.S. Foreign Military Sales by Selected Country: 1950 to 2021

[In thousands of dollars (704,759,426 represents $704,759,426,000). For fiscal year ending September 30. Foreign Military Sales (FMS) is a security assistance program authorized by the Arms Export Control Act (AECA) and conducted on the basis of formal contracts and agreements between the U.S. Government and authorized recipient governments or international organizations. Sales numbers include new sales implemented in a given fiscal year and any adjustments (increases or decreases) to existing programs via amendments or modifications implemented that fiscal year. Minus (-) sign indicates negative sales numbers, an indication that the amount of program decreases were more than combined new sales and positive adjustments]

Country	1950 to 2016	2017	2018	2019	2020	2021
Total [1]	704,759,426	41,929,520	55,657,932	55,385,864	50,781,535	34,809,699
Afghanistan	8,020,260	2,525,453	2,698,501	1,576,712	1,071,477	1,263,903
Albania	88,862	5,590	5,331	2,918	42,284	8,760
Argentina	757,623	195,927	24,789	3,396	36,957	6,159
Australia	32,359,755	1,233,621	1,462,956	1,638,806	1,718,362	937,503
Austria	502,726	19,523	32,999	32,116	16,936	42,766
Bahrain	3,124,997	62,463	2,425,463	1,946,173	66,971	452,024
Bangladesh	97,483	4,432	104	35,356	15,616	6,072
Belgium	4,577,690	107,162	47,602	5,456,525	41,778	109,225
Bosnia-Herzegovina	88,923	3,536	6,005	430	40,832	255
Brazil	2,497,153	28,870	30,251	41,767	19,274	101,744
Bulgaria	174,568	4,681	5,123	1,261,030	16,905	28,043
Canada	9,469,754	356,532	193,479	1,074,081	517,415	2,555,819
Chile	1,311,502	9,682	18,976	23,143	39,635	585,584
Colombia	2,908,827	25,690	37,287	35,326	62,880	71,639
Croatia	70,021	7,678	6,131	3,425	85,068	-419
Czechia	209,420	5,634	13,981	72,715	663,996	9,550
Denmark	4,108,184	15,468	82,062	261,842	154,374	35,164
Egypt	38,199,041	307,258	66,184	509,143	783,017	2,027,882
Estonia	137,768	5,438	30,262	35,559	610	37,267
Finland	4,932,944	124,902	20,807	114,043	24,830	90,560
France	5,762,576	190,864	153,118	304,993	246,337	1,516,440
Georgia	349,677	3,597	76,715	40,575	62,880	51,949
Germany	16,965,706	222,722	127,818	1,160,998	501,525	1,097,410
Greece	14,212,328	19,121	1,349,336	39,872	408,137	314,601
Hungary	181,941	4,766	5,021	13,062	13,570	515,135
India	8,449,081	754,497	282,197	6,203	3,363,691	320,196
Indonesia	2,370,514	224,658	81,818	-47,287	8,936	27,639
Iraq	17,192,155	3,139,192	735,887	1,362,267	367,847	386,405
Israel	42,064,771	2,440,937	598,754	1,489,743	1,058,778	1,478,486
Italy	4,484,563	58,110	91,369	53,016	151,648	935,623
Japan	28,554,797	4,117,135	3,498,907	6,880,409	1,982,589	3,903,518
Jordan	6,442,786	249,170	280,671	269,595	197,837	153,551
Kenya	346,078	75,764	75,935	4,081	6,817	5,764
Kuwait	16,520,888	585,189	7,456,131	386,229	908,479	1,256,741
Latvia	87,656	30,155	32,469	204,264	38,193	23,076
Lebanon	1,780,628	72,271	94,384	157,286	109,436	67,119
Lithuania	171,780	15,727	49,210	22,107	136,545	319,585
Macedonia	109,007	769	925	11,013	21,085	84,692
Malaysia	1,624,323	30,938	26,023	24,573	38,957	63,229
Mexico	1,873,347	-1,450	48,828	24,530	-60,133	78,789
Morocco	5,138,970	52,925	11,041	12,401	4,538,590	53,481
Netherlands	13,214,405	331,345	1,689,914	324,402	450,998	522,238
New Zealand	637,255	11,475	1,130,964	11,468	991,810	58,576
Niger	23,952	39,555	1,218	7,386	6,245	12
Nigeria	200,303	1,663	496,414	3,451	2,851	-510
Norway	6,246,419	1,285,189	154,624	202,082	242,354	36,781
Pakistan	10,356,952	22,209	65,596	-10,827	146,151	73,161
Philippines	1,823,442	104,074	96,769	90,669	140,047	90,326
Poland	5,487,991	508,894	4,897,049	673,495	4,709,501	126,642
Portugal	1,834,893	13,887	40,619	33,345	25,914	21,314
Qatar	9,082,907	14,509,250	67,806	661,679	604,415	-68,443
Montenegro	6,782	674	2,366	1,329	38,501	13,623
Romania	704,611	74,968	1,187,680	1,099,099	768,211	986,416
Saudi Arabia	139,883,296	2,560,998	14,274,963	14,971,804	1,175,239	1,564,781
Singapore	9,209,602	192,778	443,227	137,499	1,291,281	24,773
Slovakia	351,116	8,444	519	1,881,342	11,854	119,900
Slovenia	46,936	103	4,709	28,852	23,356	12,015
South Korea	35,598,061	577,102	560,886	2,688,444	2,124,078	1,901,969
Spain	9,754,245	92,923	129,582	1,788,391	140,088	186,487
Sweden	1,133,911	9,129	1,148,715	17,298	96,721	11,154
Switzerland	4,049,713	72,571	176,151	41,665	88,956	36,912
Taiwan	30,019,094	563,513	1,677,158	875,552	11,777,426	2,678,026
Thailand	6,274,164	140,873	50,588	16,710	247,699	297,798
Tunisia	1,375,931	60,292	48,493	67,118	58,740	175,458
Turkey	20,483,720	213,402	37,032	134,780	82,195	256,859
Ukraine	405,796	207,722	250,782	272,465	510,599	333,050
United Arab Emirates	22,896,188	759,534	3,217,015	1,087,905	3,567,997	359,734
United Kingdom	27,640,751	1,132,285	398,873	572,223	440,842	2,861,109
Vietnam	35,020	13,900	11,663	14,373	38,400	20,000
North Atlantic Treaty Organization (NATO)	136,476	105,329	241,444	143,954	218,877	170,328

[1] Includes countries, programs, and classified totals not shown separately.

Source: U.S. Department of Defense, Defense Security Cooperation Agency, *Historical Sales Book, Fiscal Years 1950-2021*. See also <www.dsca.mil/resources/dsca-historical-sales-book>.

Table 553. Veterans by Selected Period of Service, State, and Island Area: 2021

[In thousands (19,163 represents 19,163,000). As of September 30. The Veteran Population Projection Model 2018 (VetPop2018) is the Department of Veterans Affairs (VA) latest official estimate and projection of the veteran population. It is based on tabulations prepared for the VA Office of the Actuary; recent American Community Survey, Internal Revenue Service, and Social Security Administration data; administrative data and projections of service member separations from active duty provided by the Department of Defense, Defense Manpower Data Center and the Office of the Actuary; and VA data on veterans benefits. Data may not sum due to rounding]

State and Island Area	Total [1,2]	Gulf War era [3]	Vietnam era [4]	State and Island Area	Total [1,2]	Gulf War era [3]	Vietnam era [4]
United States [5]	**19,163**	**8,211**	**6,054**	Montana	88	35	31
Alabama	358	169	110	Nebraska	124	56	39
Alaska	67	39	17	Nevada	218	95	71
Arizona	493	199	172	New Hampshire	97	37	33
Arkansas	196	86	65	New Jersey	329	113	107
California	1,616	692	502	New Mexico	148	65	52
Colorado	388	190	114	New York	714	252	226
Connecticut	158	54	53	North Carolina	688	322	212
Delaware	69	26	25	North Dakota	53	26	15
District of Columbia	28	15	5	Ohio	726	272	236
Florida	1,492	594	485	Oklahoma	290	137	93
Georgia	689	349	195	Oregon	290	103	105
Hawaii	113	59	32	Pennsylvania	771	267	260
Idaho	123	50	43	Rhode Island	61	23	21
Illinois	591	226	193	South Carolina	394	180	129
Indiana	402	153	129	South Dakota	64	29	20
Iowa	195	73	64	Tennessee	449	195	143
Kansas	193	92	60	Texas	1,563	796	450
Kentucky	285	122	90	Utah	132	67	40
Louisiana	283	135	83	Vermont	41	14	13
Maine	107	37	39	Virginia	713	410	184
Maryland	378	181	106	Washington	547	255	172
Massachusetts	306	103	99	West Virginia	136	54	47
Michigan	554	191	190	Wisconsin	343	118	119
Minnesota	304	104	104	Wyoming	47	19	17
Mississippi	183	88	51	Puerto Rico	66	21	24
Missouri	414	166	138	Island Areas & Foreign	85	58	32

[1] Veterans serving in more than one period of service are counted only once in the total. [2] Current civilians discharged from active duty, other than for training only without service-connected disability. [3] Service from August 2, 1990 to the present. [4] Service from August 5, 1964 to May 7, 1975. [5] U.S. total includes Puerto Rico and Island Areas & Foreign.

Source: U.S. Department of Veterans Affairs, National Center for Veterans Analysis and Statistics, "The Veteran Population Projection Model 2018 (VetPop2018)," <www.va.gov/vetdata/veteran_population.asp>, accessed July 2022.

Table 554. Veterans Living by Period of Service, Age, and Sex: 2021

[19,163 represents 19,163,000. As of September 30. Includes veterans living outside the United States. Based on the Department of Veterans Affairs' (VA) latest official estimate and projection of the veteran population, the Veteran Population Projection Model 2018 (VetPop2018)]

Period of service and age	Total	Male	Female	Period of service and age	Total	Male	Female
Total	**19,163**	**17,117**	**2,045**	30 to 34 years old	925	753	173
PERIOD OF SERVICE				35 to 39 years old	1,070	869	202
Wartime vets [1]	14,959	13,336	1,624	40 to 44 years old	1,108	898	210
Gulf War Era [2]	8,211	6,853	1,358	45 to 49 years old	1,145	957	188
Vietnam Era [3]	6,054	5,801	253	50 to 54 years old	1,550	1,335	215
Korean conflict [4]	954	927	27	55 to 59 years old	1,758	1,531	227
World War II	240	228	13	60 to 64 years old	1,849	1,621	228
Peacetime	4,203	3,782	422	65 to 69 years old	1,762	1,591	170
AGE				70 to 74 years old	2,354	2,246	108
Under 20 years old	10	7	3	75 to 79 years old	2,067	2,007	60
20 to 24 years old	267	212	55	80 to 84 years old	1,203	1,162	41
25 to 29 years old	613	496	117	85 years old and over	1,483	1,434	49

[1] Veterans who served in more than one wartime period are counted only once in the total. [2] Service from August 2, 1990 to the present. [3] Service from August 5, 1964 to May 7, 1975. [4] Service during period June 27, 1950 to January 31, 1955.

Source: U.S. Department of Veterans Affairs, National Center for Veterans Analysis and Statistics, "The Veteran Population Projection Model 2018 (VetPop2018)," <www.va.gov/vetdata/Veteran_Population.asp>, accessed July 2022.

Table 555. Veterans Benefits—Expenditures by Program and Compensation for Service-Connected Disabilities: 2000 to 2021

[In millions of dollars (47,086 represents $47,086,000,000). For years ending September 30]

Program	2000	2005	2010	2015	2016	2017	2018	2019	2020	2021
Total expenditures...............	**47,086**	**69,667**	**108,635**	**167,210**	**173,686**	**180,591**	**180,604**	**202,405**	**217,954**	**224,122**
Medical programs................	19,637	29,433	42,372	65,561	63,473	69,710	71,303	77,803	86,808	88,218
Construction.......................	466	483	1,618	1,828	1,708	1,467	1,177	1,238	1,531	1,677
General operating expenses........................	1,016	1,294	6,101	8,056	7,898	9,223	9,513	10,117	10,798	8,751
Compensation and pension....................	22,012	34,694	47,785	75,787	84,028	84,138	82,776	97,638	104,566	111,805
Vocational rehabilitation and education....................	1,610	2,937	8,260	13,408	13,838	13,182	13,178	13,811	12,688	11,583
All other [1]........................	2,345	826	2,499	2,570	2,740	2,871	2,656	1,798	1,563	2,088
Compensation for service-connected disabilities............	15,511	24,515	36,486	60,213	64,714	69,991	76,709	84,915	91,426	98,540

[1] Includes insurance, indemnities, and miscellaneous funds and expenditures and offsets from public receipts. Excludes expenditures from personal funds of patients.

Source: U.S. Department of Veterans Affairs, "Geographic Distribution of VA Expenditures (GDX): Summary Expenditures by State," <va.gov/vetdata/Expenditures.asp>, accessed July 2022; and *Annual Benefits Report, Fiscal Year 2021*, June 2022, and earlier reports. See also <benefits.va.gov/REPORTS/abr>.

Table 556. Veterans Compensation and Pension Benefits—Number on Rolls by Period of Service and Status: 1990 to 2021

[In thousands (3,584 represents 3,584,000). As of September 30. Living veterans refers to veterans receiving compensation for disability incurred or aggravated while on active duty, and war veterans receiving pension benefits for non-service connected disabilities and/or who are age 65 and older. Survivors include veterans' spouses, dependent children, and (based on need) dependent parents of veterans]

Period of service and veteran status	1990	2000	2010	2013	2014	2015	2016	2017	2018	2019	2020	2021
Total......................	**3,584**	**3,236**	**4,070**	**4,639**	**4,848**	**5,061**	**5,247**	**5,442**	**5,619**	**5,787**	**5,906**	**5,686**
Living veterans.............	2,746	2,672	3,524	4,051	4,254	4,464	4,645	4,829	5,003	5,183	5,301	5,420
Compensation [1]..........	2,184	2,308	3,210	3,743	3,949	4,169	4,356	4,553	4,743	4,944	5,082	5,225
Pension [2].................	562	364	314	308	305	295	289	277	260	239	220	195
Survivors of veterans......	838	564	546	587	594	597	602	613	616	604	605	600
Compensation [1].........	320	307	347	377	382	390	399	411	423	434	446	461
Pension [2].................	518	257	199	210	212	206	203	201	193	170	159	140
World War I and earlier....	198	34	6	4	4	3	3	2	2	2	2	1
Living veterans...........	18	(Z)	(Z)	(Z)	(Z)	(Z)	(Z)	(Z)	(Z)	(Z)	(Z)	(Z)
World War II..............	1,723	968	529	434	399	357	320	286	249	205	171	135
Living veterans...........	1,294	676	298	215	189	160	135	112	89	69	52	36
Korean conflict [3]..........	390	323	275	271	268	262	256	249	238	221	204	180
Living veterans...........	305	255	209	199	194	186	178	174	158	145	130	110
Vietnam era [4]..............	774	969	1,447	1,660	1,716	1,765	1,803	1,840	1,868	1,890	1,889	1,870
Living veterans...........	685	848	1,261	1,433	1,477	1,514	1,538	1,560	1,572	1,581	1,566	1,531
Gulf War era [5].............	(X)	334	1,140	1,561	1,723	1,915	2,090	2,267	2,441	2,622	2,784	2,976
Living veterans...........	(X)	326	1,117	1,523	1,694	1,883	2,057	2,231	2,403	2,581	2,741	2,929
Peacetime..................	495	607	673	709	738	759	775	797	821	848	856	859
Living veterans...........	444	567	638	683	700	720	737	758	781	806	813	814

X Not applicable. Z Fewer than 500. [1] Compensation is based on military service-connected disability and death. [2] Pension is based on need and includes coverage for veterans with disabilities not connected to military service. [3] Service during period June 27, 1950 to January 31, 1955. [4] Service from August 5, 1964 to May 7, 1975. [5] Service from August 2, 1990 to the present.

Source: U.S. Department of Veterans Affairs, 1990 to 1995, *Annual Report of the Secretary of Veterans Affairs*; 1996 to 2010, *Annual Accountability Report* and unpublished data; and beginning 2011, *Annual Benefits Report, Fiscal Year 2021*, June 2022 and earlier reports. See also <benefits.va.gov/REPORTS/abr>.

Table 557. Veteran Income, Education, Poverty, and Disability Status Compared to Nonveteran Population: 2018 and 2019

[252,806 represents 252,806,000. Data are based on American Community Survey (ACS). The ACS universe includes the civilian household and group quarters population. Based on a sample and subject to sampling variability]

Characteristic	2018			2019		
	Total	Veterans	Nonveterans	Total	Veterans	Nonveterans
Population 18 years old and over (1,000).......	**252,806**	**17,964**	**234,842**	**254,046**	**17,418**	**236,628**
INCOME						
Median income in past 12 months (dollars) [1].......	31,476	41,555	30,883	32,903	44,241	32,098
Male...	(NA)	42,064	37,736	(NA)	45,048	40,403
Female...	(NA)	35,991	25,501	(NA)	37,302	26,892
EDUCATIONAL ATTAINMENT						
Population 25 years old and over...................	222,557	17,714	204,844	224,125	17,196	206,928
Less than high school graduate (percent).........	11.7	5.5	12.2	11.4	5.3	11.9
High school graduate or equivalency (percent)...	26.9	27.7	26.8	26.9	27.7	26.9
Some college or associate's degree (percent)....	28.8	37.5	28.1	28.5	37.5	27.8
Bachelor's degree or higher (percent)............	32.6	29.4	32.9	33.1	29.5	33.4
POVERTY AND DISABILITY STATUS						
Population for whom poverty status is determined..	246,337	17,656	228,681	247,592	17,111	230,481
Below poverty in the past 12 months (percent)...	11.7	6.7	12.1	11.1	6.7	11.4
With any disability (percent).......................	15.2	29.3	14.1	15.3	29.9	14.2

NA Not available. [1] For population with income.

Source: U.S. Census Bureau, American Community Survey, S2101, "Veteran Status," <data.census.gov>, accessed December 2020.

Table 558. Veterans by Sex, Race, and Hispanic Origin: 2018 and 2019

[See headnote, Table 557]

Characteristic	2018			2019		
	Total veterans	18 to 64 years	65 years and over	Total veterans	18 to 64 years	65 years and over
Total.........................	**17,964,242**	**8,973,535**	**8,990,707**	**17,418,351**	**8,647,927**	**8,770,424**
Male.........................	16,311,444	7,656,867	8,654,577	15,781,864	7,350,723	8,431,141
Female.......................	1,652,798	1,316,668	336,130	1,636,487	1,297,204	339,283
White alone...................	14,698,804	6,744,091	7,954,713	14,172,728	6,474,126	7,698,602
Male.........................	13,527,706	5,853,178	7,674,528	13,018,671	5,597,479	7,421,192
Female.......................	1,171,098	890,913	280,185	1,154,057	876,647	277,410
Black or African American alone........	2,150,689	1,465,798	684,891	2,146,395	1,434,240	712,155
Male.........................	1,825,182	1,177,069	648,113	1,814,230	1,144,209	670,021
Female.......................	325,507	288,729	36,778	332,165	290,031	42,134
American Indian/Alaska Native alone..	141,438	85,654	55,784	142,972	85,703	57,269
Male.........................	125,355	72,475	52,880	123,305	69,502	53,803
Female.......................	16,083	13,179	2,904	19,667	16,201	3,466
Asian alone..................	308,983	185,975	123,008	313,348	185,852	127,496
Male.........................	269,031	152,473	116,558	273,575	152,379	121,196
Female.......................	39,952	33,502	6,450	39,773	33,473	6,300
Native Hawaiian and other Pacific Islander alone.........................	41,271	31,247	10,024	35,431	24,242	11,189
Male.........................	33,327	24,317	9,010	28,638	18,111	10,527
Female.......................	7,944	6,930	1,014	6,793	6,131	662
Some other race alone.................	244,340	179,827	64,513	236,595	172,372	64,223
Male.........................	213,175	151,878	61,297	208,234	147,136	61,098
Female.......................	31,165	27,949	3,216	28,361	25,236	3,125
Two or more races......................	378,717	280,943	97,774	370,882	271,392	99,490
Male.........................	317,668	225,477	92,191	315,211	221,907	93,304
Female.......................	61,049	55,466	5,583	55,671	49,485	6,186
Hispanic or Latino origin [1]...............	1,284,854	898,180	386,674	1,255,169	871,802	383,367
Male.........................	1,132,008	762,843	369,165	1,102,542	737,977	364,565
Female.......................	152,846	135,337	17,509	152,627	133,825	18,802

[1] Persons of Hispanic or Latino origin may be of any race.

Source: U.S. Census Bureau, American Community Survey, Tables B21001, C21001A, C21001B, C21001C, C21001D, C21001E, C21001F, C21001G, and C21001I, <data.census.gov>, accessed December 2020.

Table 559. Deferred Action for Childhood Arrivals (DACA) Recipients by Selected Characteristics and Top Country of Birth: 2022

[The active DACA population are individuals who have an approved I-821D Consideration of DACA form with expiration on or after March 31, 2022. Data are estimates. Individuals who have obtained Lawful Permanent Resident Status or U.S. Citizenship are excluded]

Characteristic	Number	Top 20 countries of birth	Number
Total............................	**611,270**	Mexico..	494,350
SEX		El Salvador.....................................	23,700
Female..	328,240	Guatemala.......................................	16,090
Male...	282,600	Honduras...	14,750
Not available.................................	430	Peru..	5,740
AGE [1]		Korea, South....................................	5,670
Under 16 years old..........................	(D)	Brazil...	4,640
16 to 20 years old...........................	17,070	Ecuador..	4,330
21 to 25 years old...........................	193,360	Colombia...	3,800
26 to 30 years old...........................	208,400	Argentina...	3,040
31 to 35 years old...........................	134,450	Philippines.......................................	2,970
36 to 40 years old...........................	57,980	Jamaica..	2,030
		India..	2,000
Median age...................................	28	Venezuela.......................................	1,900
MARITAL STATUS		Dominican Republic...........................	1,760
Single...	431,430	Uruguay..	1,560
Married...	162,800	Trinidad and Tobago..........................	1,320
Divorced.......................................	13,020	Bolivia..	1,300
Widowed.......................................	560	Costa Rica.......................................	1,220
Not available.................................	3,460	Nicaragua..	1,210

D Data withheld; disclosure standards not met. [1] Age as of September 30, 2021.

Source: Department of Homeland Security, U.S. Citizenship and Immigration Services, "Immigration and Citizenship Data," <uscis.gov/tools/reports-studies/immigration-forms-data>, accessed July 2022.

Table 560. Customs and Border Patrol Drug Seizures: 2019 to 2021

[In units, as indicated. For fiscal years ending September 30. Data from U.S. Border Patrol (USBP) and Office of Field Operations (OFO)]

Year	Total	Mari-juana	Metham-phetamine	Cocaine	Heroin	Fentanyl	Ecstasy	LSD	Ket-amine	Khat	Other drugs
SEIZURE EVENTS (number)											
2019....................	60,031	20,366	4,576	2,812	1,532	814	6,902	2,683	1,355	217	25,676
2020....................	66,937	18,070	5,908	3,226	2,563	1,174	6,847	3,744	597	181	29,027
2021....................	81,970	13,865	5,769	3,873	2,276	1,516	4,834	2,221	1,378	537	47,217
SEIZED WEIGHT (pounds)											
2019....................	902,573	556,401	141,970	101,140	6,227	2,804	2,223	560	953	36,257	54,038
2020....................	1,060,641	582,393	177,684	58,002	5,763	4,791	2,120	725	1,134	111,959	116,071
2021....................	914,469	319,448	190,861	97,638	5,400	11,203	1,201	38	10,848	202,820	75,013

Source: Department of Homeland Security, U.S. Customs and Border Protection, "Drug Seizure Statistics," <www.cbp.gov/newsroom/stats/drug-seizure-statistics>, accessed May 2022.

Table 561. Department of Homeland Security Total Budget Authority and Personnel by Organization: 2021 and 2022

[87,816,178 represents $87,816,178,000. For the fiscal year ending September 30. Not all activities carried out by the Department of Homeland Security (DHS) constitute homeland security funding (e.g., Coast Guard search and rescue activities)]

Organization or activity	Budget authority (thousand dollars)		Full-time employees (number)	
	2021 [1]	2022 [1]	2021 [1]	2022 [1]
Total..	**87,816,178**	**90,982,133**	**234,173**	**237,583**
Departmental management and operations [2]..........................	3,896,210	4,479,479	6,037	6,182
Analysis and operations...	298,500	320,620	853	872
Office of the Inspector General.....................................	190,186	205,359	742	760
U.S. Customs & Border Protection..................................	16,347,172	15,948,536	57,660	58,475
U.S. Immigration & Customs Enforcement.........................	8,350,439	8,371,096	21,087	21,257
Transportation Security Administration.............................	8,549,522	8,871,561	56,556	55,169
U.S. Coast Guard...	13,070,820	13,108,293	49,864	50,377
U.S. Secret Service...	2,708,803	2,839,917	7,796	7,961
Cybersecurity and Infrastructure Security Agency [3].................	2,024,976	2,133,630	2,365	2,464
Federal Emergency Management Agency (FEMA)....................	26,452,121	28,795,330	12,284	13,382
FEMA Grants [3]...	3,019,700	3,033,870	([4])	([4])
U.S. Citizenship & Immigration Services...........................	4,908,232	4,828,291	18,676	20,445
Federal Law Enforcement Training Center.........................	340,348	355,636	1,082	1,081
Science & Technology Directorate (S&T)...........................	765,558	822,903	499	511
Countering Weapons of Mass Destruction..........................	402,277	427,461	267	279

[1] Revised enacted. [2] Comprised of the Office of the Secretary & Executive Management, and the Management Directorate, which includes the Under Secretary for Management and its team of chief officers. [3] Includes State and Local Programs, Emergency Management Performance Grants, and Assistance to Firefighters Grants. [4] Employee data are included with FEMA full-time employees.

Source: U.S. Department of Homeland Security, *Budget-in-Brief, Fiscal Year 2023*, March 2022. See also <www.dhs.gov/dhs-budget>.

Table 562. Homeland Security Grants by State and Outlying Area: 2021 and 2022

[In thousands of dollars (1,120,000 represents $1,120,000,000). For years ending September 30. The Homeland Security Grant Program consists of the following: State Homeland Security Program (SHSP), Urban Areas Security Initiative (UASI), and Operation Stonegarden. These programs support activities to prevent, protect against, prepare for and respond to acts of terrorism, and to secure U.S. borders]

State/territory	2021	2022	State/territory	2021	2022	State/territory	2021	2022
Total.........	1,120,000	1,120,000	KS.............	4,603	4,848	OK............	4,603	4,848
			KY.............	4,603	4,848	OR............	8,403	8,648
U.S............	1,109,749	1,109,307	LA.............	5,418	7,027	PA............	25,448	26,587
			ME............	5,533	5,743	RI.............	4,603	4,848
AL.............	4,703	4,948	MD............	11,596	10,875	SC............	4,603	4,848
AK.............	4,603	4,848	MA............	23,328	23,091	SD............	4,603	4,848
AZ.............	28,367	26,483	MI.............	12,548	12,238	TN............	4,603	4,848
AR.............	4,603	4,848	MN............	10,915	11,160	TX............	103,262	103,385
CA.............	206,221	204,513	MS............	4,803	5,098	UT............	4,603	4,848
CO.............	8,503	8,748	MO............	8,403	10,148	VT............	5,103	5,348
CT.............	4,603	4,848	MT............	6,281	6,269	VA............	12,248	11,936
DE.............	4,603	4,848	NE............	4,603	4,848	WA...........	14,285	13,905
DC.............	57,030	56,212	NV............	9,853	10,098	WV............	4,603	4,848
FL.............	34,723	34,446	NH............	4,783	5,028	WI............	4,603	4,848
GA.............	11,741	12,039	NJ............	26,396	25,990	WY............	4,603	4,848
HI.............	8,403	4,848	NM............	7,558	7,803	AS [1]	1,052	1,108
ID.............	4,848	5,021	NY............	251,376	246,667	GU [1]	1,052	1,108
IL.............	82,427	81,077	NC............	9,080	8,885	MP [1]	1,052	1,108
IN.............	4,603	6,348	ND............	6,127	6,348	PR [1]	5,944	6,177
IA.............	4,603	4,848	OH............	7,197	9,944	VI [1]	1,152	1,193

[1] AS—American Samoa, GU—Guam, MP—Northern Mariana Islands, PR—Puerto Rico, VI—Virgin Islands.

Source: U.S. Department of Homeland Security, Federal Emergency Management Agency, *Grant Programs Directorate Information Bulletin*, No. 476, August 2022, and earlier reports. See also <www.fema.gov/grants/preparedness>.

Table 563. Urban Areas Security Initiative (UASI) Grant Program: 2022

[In thousands of dollars (615,000 represents $615,000,000). For year ending September 30. The UASI Program provides financial assistance to address the unique planning, organization, equipment, training, and exercise needs of high-risk urban areas to build capacity to prevent, protect against, prepare for and respond to acts of terrorism]

State	Urban area	Amount	State	Urban area	Amount
Total........	(X)	615,000	MA...........	Boston	16,900
			MI............	Detroit	5,250
AZ............	Phoenix	5,250	MN............	Minneapolis-Saint Paul (Twin Cities)	5,250
CA............	Anaheim/Santa Ana Area	5,250	MO............	Kansas City	1,500
CA............	San Francisco Bay Area	37,049	MO............	St. Louis	3,800
CA............	Los Angeles/Long Beach	67,182	NV............	Las Vegas	5,250
CA............	Riverside	3,900	NJ............	Jersey City/Newark	18,915
CA............	Sacramento	3,800	NY............	New York City	176,599
CA............	San Diego	16,696	NC............	Charlotte	3,800
CO............	Denver	3,900	OH............	Cincinnati	1,500
DC............	National Capital Region	51,127	OH............	Cleveland	1,500
FL............	Miami/Fort Lauderdale	14,750	OR............	Portland	3,800
FL............	Orlando	3,800	PA............	Philadelphia	16,900
FL............	Tampa	3,800	PA............	Pittsburgh	1,500
GA............	Atlanta	6,700	TX............	Dallas/Fort Worth/Arlington	16,900
IL............	Chicago	67,182	TX............	Houston	24,600
IN............	Indianapolis	1,500	TX............	San Antonio	3,800
LA............	New Orleans	1,500	VA............	Hampton Roads Area	3,800
MD...........	Baltimore	3,800	WA...........	Seattle	6,250

X Not applicable.

Source: U.S. Department of Homeland Security, Federal Emergency Management Agency, *Grant Programs Directorate Information Bulletin*, No. 476, August 2022. See also <www.fema.gov/grants/preparedness>.

Table 564. Preparedness Grant Programs: 2010 to 2022

[In millions of dollars (2,968 represents $2,968,000,000. For years ending September 30. Preparedness grants help develop and sustain capabilities at the state and local, tribal and territorial levels and in high-risk transit systems, ports and along our borders to prevent, protect against, respond to, recover from and mitigate terrorism and other high-consequence disasters and emergencies]

Program	2010	2013	2014	2015	2016	2017	2018	2019	2020	2021	2022
Total [1].............................	2,968	1,507	1,616	1,617	1,617	1,622	1,687	1,715	1,780	1,970	1,639
Homeland Security Grant Program [1]....	1,786	968	1,043	1,044	1,037	1,037	1,067	1,095	1,120	1,120	1,120
State Homeland Security Program.....	842	355	401	402	402	402	402	415	415	415	415
Urban Areas Security Initiative..........	833	559	587	587	580	580	580	590	615	615	615
Operation Stonegarden..................	60	55	55	55	55	55	85	90	90	90	90
Emergency Management Performance Grants Program..........	330	332	350	350	350	350	350	350	355	[2] 455	(NA)
Tribal Homeland Security Grant Program......................................	10	10	10	10	10	10	10	10	15	15	15
Nonprofit Security Grant Program.......	19	10	13	13	20	25	60	60	90	180	250
Emergency Operations Center Grant Program...................................	58	(NA)	(NA)	(NA)	(NA)	(NA)	(NA)	(NA)	(NA)	(NA)	49
Transit Security Grant Program..........	253	84	90	87	87	88	88	88	88	88	93
Intercity Passenger Rail Program (AMTRAK)...........................	20	9	10	10	10	10	10	10	10	10	10
Port Security Grant Program.............	288	93	100	100	100	100	100	100	100	100	100
Intercity Bus Security Grant Program. ..	12	(NA)	(NA)	3	3	2	2	2	2	2	2

NA Not available. [1] Includes grant programs not listed separately. [2] American Rescue Plan Act (ARPA) of 2021 provides $100 million in additional funding.

Source: U.S. Department of Homeland Security, Federal Emergency Management Agency, *Grant Programs Directorate Information Bulletin*, No. 476, August 2022, and earlier reports. See also <www.fema.gov/grants/preparedness>.

Table 565. Noncitizens Returned or Removed by Leading Crime Category and Country of Nationality: 2012 to 2020

[For year ending September 30. For definitions of immigration enforcement terms, see source. "Crime categories" and "Countries of nationality" are ranked by data for most recent year]

Crime category and country of nationality	2012	2013	2014	2015	2016	2017	2018	2019	2020
Total noncitizens returned or removed	**646,693**	**611,187**	**568,880**	**454,852**	**438,024**	**387,452**	**487,501**	**519,594**	**406,478**
Returns [1]	231,106	178,975	163,838	129,661	106,454	100,694	159,933	171,126	167,327
Removals [2]	415,587	432,212	405,042	325,191	331,570	286,758	327,568	348,468	239,151
Noncriminal	215,548	233,724	232,639	201,914	215,216	177,163	179,445	178,356	120,794
Criminal [3]	200,039	198,488	172,403	123,277	116,354	109,595	148,123	170,112	118,357
Leading crime category:									
Immigration	47,559	62,033	54,646	37,734	37,052	28,829	41,942	63,176	39,664
Dangerous drugs	42,738	30,692	28,202	22,530	21,610	19,845	18,039	16,809	13,120
Traffic offenses	46,141	29,966	24,725	16,138	15,068	15,807	17,463	18,456	12,232
Assault	12,993	20,192	17,721	13,422	12,117	12,432	12,283	12,501	9,390
Weapon offenses	2,510	5,277	4,588	3,548	3,456	3,258	3,200	3,009	2,480
Sexual assault	3,363	3,168	2,953	2,516	2,486	2,472	2,409	2,368	2,078
Burglary	3,557	5,504	4,750	3,482	3,110	3,065	2,780	2,589	1,966
Fraudulent activities	3,870	5,186	3,940	2,660	2,164	2,951	2,700	2,532	1,843
Larceny	5,419	5,329	4,350	2,851	2,479	2,590	2,575	2,619	1,797
Sex offenses	2,063	2,594	2,424	1,968	1,969	2,133	2,076	1,902	1,682
All other	29,826	28,547	24,104	16,428	14,843	16,213	42,656	44,151	32,105
Leading country of nationality of criminals removed:									
Mexico	151,337	146,170	126,146	89,201	82,803	74,100	90,178	98,679	77,946
Guatemala	13,497	15,426	13,722	10,509	10,601	11,110	19,814	23,017	10,211
Honduras	13,824	16,598	14,064	8,556	8,592	9,282	12,732	17,941	9,543
El Salvador	8,670	9,472	8,952	7,221	6,719	6,489	7,002	8,803	5,001
Colombia	1,057	929	876	795	763	640	2,283	2,611	1,549
Ecuador	708	579	571	488	465	507	888	1,478	1,499
Dominican Republic	2,187	1,821	1,642	1,521	1,485	1,515	1,494	1,627	1,481
Brazil	426	375	281	288	330	407	1,185	1,479	1,324
Jamaica	1,157	999	834	641	620	678	1,003	1,225	1,166
Venezuela	123	87	79	61	55	81	1,300	1,455	706
Nicaragua	729	692	643	440	392	379	568	1,058	622
Canada	385	383	305	264	257	207	557	746	572
India	163	135	107	134	103	160	459	630	546

[1] Returns are the confirmed movement of an inadmissible or deportable noncitizen out of the U.S., not based on an order of removal. [2] Removals are the compulsory and confirmed movement of an inadmissible or deportable noncitizen out of the U.S., based on an order of removal. A noncitizen who is removed has administrative or criminal consequences placed on subsequent reentry. [3] Persons removed based on a criminal charge or those with a criminal conviction.

Source: U.S. Department of Homeland Security, Office of Immigration Statistics, *Immigration Enforcement Actions: 2020*, and "Yearbook of Immigration Statistics, 2020," <www.dhs.gov/immigration-statistics>, accessed March 2022. See also <www.dhs.gov/immigration-statistics/enforcement-actions>.

Table 566. Noncitizens Apprehended or Arrested by Program and Border Patrol Sector: 2000 to 2020

[As of the end of September. Border Patrol apprehensions and Immigration and Customs Enforcement (ICE) administrative arrests]

Program and sector	2000	2010	2015	2018	2019	2020
Total	**1,814,729**	**796,587**	**462,388**	**572,566**	**1,013,539**	**518,597**
Investigations	138,291	18,290	7,288	9,843	10,939	9,974
Enforcement and Removal Operations (ERO) [1]	(X)	314,915	117,983	158,581	143,099	103,603
Border Patrol (apprehensions)	**1,676,438**	**463,382**	**337,117**	**404,142**	**859,501**	**405,020**
All southwest sectors	**1,643,679**	**447,731**	**331,333**	**396,579**	**851,508**	**400,635**
Rio Grande Valley, Texas	133,243	59,766	147,257	162,262	339,135	90,203
Tucson, Arizona	616,346	212,202	63,397	52,172	63,490	66,074
El Paso, Texas	115,696	12,251	14,495	31,561	182,143	54,396
San Diego, California	151,681	68,565	26,290	38,591	58,049	53,277
Laredo, Texas	108,973	35,287	35,888	32,641	38,378	51,425
Del Rio, Texas	157,178	14,694	19,013	15,833	57,269	40,342
El Centro, California	238,126	32,562	12,820	29,230	35,138	27,487
Yuma, Arizona	108,747	7,116	7,142	26,244	68,269	8,804
Big Bend, Texas [2]	13,689	5,288	5,031	8,045	9,637	8,627
All other sectors	**32,759**	**15,651**	**5,784**	**7,563**	**7,993**	**4,385**
Miami, Florida	6,237	4,651	1,752	2,169	1,891	1,302
Swanton, Vermont	1,957	1,422	341	736	1,056	574
New Orleans, Louisiana	6,478	3,171	849	798	1,132	572
Detroit, Michigan	2,057	1,669	637	1,930	1,322	455
Ramey, Puerto Rico	1,731	398	557	280	562	356
Buffalo, New York	1,570	2,422	291	384	537	302
Spokane, Washington	1,324	356	190	347	428	236
Blaine, Washington	2,581	673	282	359	524	227
Grand Forks, North Dakota	562	543	789	461	412	227
Houlton, Maine	489	56	32	52	52	104
Havre, Montana	1,568	290	64	47	77	30
Livermore, California [3]	6,205	(X)	(X)	(X)	(X)	(X)

X Not applicable. [1] Includes arrests of fugitive and nonfugitive noncitizens under the Office of Detention and Removal Operations (DRO), National Fugitive Operations Program. Beginning in 2008, includes all administrative arrests conducted by ICE ERO. [2] Formerly known as Marfa, TX. [3] Livermore sector closed August 31, 2004.

Source: U.S. Department of Homeland Security, Office of Immigration Statistics, "2020 Yearbook of Immigration Statistics," and earlier reports, <www.dhs.gov/immigration-statistics/yearbook>, accessed March 2022.

Table 567. Noncitizens Apprehended or Arrested: 1925 to 2020

[As of the end of September. Prior to 1952, data refer to Border Patrol Apprehensions. Detention and Removal Operations data are included beginning in 2006. Beginning in 2008, includes all administrative arrests conducted by U.S. Immigration and Customs Enforcement (ICE), Office of Enforcement and Removal Operations (ERO). Beginning in 2009, data also include administrative arrests conducted under the 287(g) program (Delegation of Immigration Authority)]

Year	Number	Year	Number	Year	Number	Year	Number
1925.........	22,199	1975..........	766,600	2001..........	1,387,486	2011..........	678,606
1930.........	20,880	1980..........	910,361	2002..........	1,062,270	2012..........	671,327
1935.........	11,016	1985..........	1,348,749	2003..........	1,046,422	2013..........	662,483
1940.........	10,492	1990..........	1,169,939	2004..........	1,264,232	2014..........	679,996
1945.........	69,164	1995..........	1,394,554	2005..........	1,291,065	2015..........	462,388
1950.........	468,339	1996..........	1,649,986	2006..........	1,206,408	2016 [1].........	530,250
1955.........	254,096	1997..........	1,536,520	2007..........	960,673	2017..........	461,540
1960.........	70,684	1998..........	1,679,439	2008..........	1,043,759	2018..........	572,566
1965.........	110,371	1999..........	1,714,035	2009..........	889,212	2019..........	1,013,539
1970.........	345,353	2000..........	1,814,729	2010..........	796,587	2020 [2].........	518,597

[1] The counting methodology for administrative arrests by ICE ERO was revised to align with ICE ERO reporting for 2016; prior to 2016, only one administrative arrest could be counted for the same person on the same day. [2] Includes USBP encounters resulting in expulsions on public health grounds under U.S. Code Title 42 in response to the COVID-19 pandemic.

Source: U.S. Department of Homeland Security, Office of Immigration Statistics, "2020 Yearbook of Immigration Statistics," <www.dhs.gov/immigration-statistics/yearbook>, accessed March 2022.

Table 568. Federal Arrests for Immigration Offenses by Sex, Age, Citizenship Status, and Country and World Region of Citizenship: 1998 to 2018

[For fiscal years ending in year shown. Suspects with more than one arrest are counted separately. Immigration violations subject to federal arrest and prosecution include smuggling, transporting, and harboring aliens; illegal entry and re-entry; and misuse of visas and other violations. Excludes D.C. Superior Court arrests. Based on data from the U.S. Marshals Service's Justice Detainee Information System]

Suspect characteristics	Number				Percent			
	1998	2008	2017	2018	1998	2008	2017	2018
Total......................	**20,942**	**78,033**	**58,031**	**108,667**	**100.0**	**100.0**	**100.0**	**100.0**
SEX								
Male........................	19,100	70,236	53,343	97,473	91.2	90.0	91.9	89.7
Female......................	1,841	7,797	4,684	11,191	8.8	10.0	8.1	10.3
AGE								
17 years old or under...........	60	63	25	49	0.3	0.1	(Z)	0.1
18 to 19 years................	1,508	6,211	3,530	8,889	7.2	8.0	6.1	8.2
20 to 24 years................	5,464	17,607	10,417	24,034	26.1	22.6	18.0	22.1
25 to 29 years................	5,208	17,164	11,162	21,854	24.9	22.0	19.2	20.1
30 to 34 years................	3,819	14,456	10,955	18,639	18.2	18.5	18.9	17.2
35 to 39 years................	2,470	10,177	9,046	14,793	11.8	13.0	15.6	13.6
40 to 44 years................	1,347	6,178	6,325	10,215	6.4	7.9	10.9	9.4
45 to 49 years................	622	3,440	3,592	5,746	3.0	4.4	6.2	5.3
50 to 54 years................	262	1,733	1,790	2,697	1.3	2.2	3.1	2.5
55 years and over.............	172	1,003	1,185	1,747	0.8	1.3	2.0	1.6
Mean age (in years)............	29	30	32	31	(X)	(X)	(X)	(X)
CITIZENSHIP STATUS								
U.S. citizen [1]................	1,072	2,433	2,356	2,913	5.2	3.2	4.1	2.7
Non-U.S. citizen..............	19,556	74,000	55,454	105,748	94.8	96.8	95.9	97.3
COUNTRY AND WORLD REGION								
North America................	19,400	75,137	56,954	106,100	94.0	98.3	98.5	97.6
United States...............	1,072	2,433	2,356	2,913	5.2	3.2	4.1	2.7
Mexico.....................	17,143	61,924	40,884	65,491	83.1	81.0	70.7	60.3
Canada.....................	47	64	26	27	0.2	0.1	(Z)	(Z)
Caribbean Islands............	416	790	506	553	2.0	1.0	0.9	0.5
Central America.............	722	9,926	13,182	37,116	3.5	13.0	22.8	34.2
South America................	166	472	566	1,227	0.8	0.6	1.0	1.1
Asia and Oceania.............	736	476	118	928	3.6	0.6	0.2	0.9
Europe......................	262	261	150	359	1.3	0.3	0.3	0.3
Africa.......................	64	87	22	47	0.3	0.1	(Z)	(Z)

X Not applicable. Z Less than 0.1 percent. [1] Citizenship is defined as the country of citizenship indicated at the time of federal booking.

Source: U.S. Department of Justice, Bureau of Justice Statistics, *Immigration, Citizenship, and the Federal Justice System, 1998-2018*, NCJ 253116, August 2019. See also <bjs.ojp.gov/library>.

Table 569. Foreign Visitor Overstays by Country of Citizenship: 2020

[Data shown for foreign nationals entering the U.S. as nonimmigrant visitors for business or pleasure (except as noted) through an air or sea point of entry. For fiscal year ending Sept. 30. An overstay is a nonimmigrant who was lawfully admitted to the U.S. for an authorized period but stayed or remains in the U.S. beyond the lawful admission period. The Visa Waiver Program (VWP) allows citizens of specific countries to travel to the U.S. for tourism, business, or while in transit for up to 90 days without obtaining a visa. Data are generated from Department of Homeland Security's Arrival and Departure Information System (ADIS)]

Country of citizenship	Expected departures	Overstays (number)			Overstays (percent)	
		Total	Out-of-country [1]	Suspected in-country [2]	Total	Suspected in-country [2]
Total [3]	**46,195,116**	**684,499**	**99,614**	**584,885**	**1.48**	**1.27**
North American, total [3]	**12,437,099**	**135,086**	**9,857**	**125,229**	**1.09**	**1.01**
Canada	9,382,043	57,592	5,253	52,339	0.61	0.56
Mexico	3,055,056	77,494	4,604	72,890	2.54	2.39
VISA WAIVER PROGRAM						
Total [4]	**16,232,821**	**104,621**	**13,037**	**91,584**	**0.64**	**0.56**
United Kingdom	3,374,402	21,443	1,808	19,635	0.64	0.58
Japan	2,237,344	6,022	198	5,824	0.27	0.26
France	1,447,079	11,364	813	10,551	0.79	0.73
Germany	1,435,302	6,785	824	5,961	0.47	0.42
Korea, South	1,050,572	3,645	745	2,900	0.35	0.28
Italy	928,906	7,996	1,175	6,821	0.86	0.73
Australia	909,085	4,364	567	3,797	0.48	0.42
Spain	793,108	13,286	1,891	11,395	1.68	1.44
Netherlands	576,237	2,910	369	2,541	0.51	0.44
Ireland	390,260	1,655	155	1,500	0.42	0.38
Chile	318,878	5,613	735	4,878	1.76	1.53
Sweden	298,747	1,298	211	1,087	0.43	0.36
Taiwan	276,201	1,666	458	1,208	0.60	0.44
Switzerland	265,200	1,348	178	1,170	0.51	0.44
Poland	243,282	2,304	670	1,634	0.95	0.67
New Zealand	231,289	1,226	184	1,042	0.53	0.45
Denmark	210,530	912	87	825	0.43	0.39
Belgium	198,630	1,049	123	926	0.53	0.47
Norway	164,050	637	100	537	0.39	0.33
Austria	143,168	998	83	915	0.70	0.64
Portugal	140,246	3,066	408	2,658	2.19	1.90
Finland	98,103	516	41	475	0.53	0.48
Singapore	95,615	265	56	209	0.28	0.22
Czechia	84,781	656	143	513	0.77	0.61
Hungary	75,714	937	234	703	1.24	0.93
Greece	64,468	1,105	413	692	1.71	1.07
NON-VISA WAIVER PROGRAM						
Total [4]	**13,807,503**	**352,748**	**46,292**	**306,456**	**2.55**	**2.22**
Brazil	1,990,811	48,881	2,170	46,711	2.46	2.35
China	1,863,549	22,885	5,628	17,257	1.23	0.93
India	1,177,135	19,044	4,655	14,389	1.62	1.22
Colombia	918,535	33,540	3,061	30,479	3.65	3.32
Argentina	785,868	5,870	368	5,502	0.75	0.70
Dominican Republic	467,765	14,562	1,032	13,530	3.11	2.89
Ecuador	418,992	10,997	758	10,239	2.62	2.44
Israel	395,727	2,624	240	2,384	0.66	0.60
Venezuela	346,756	33,204	1,605	31,599	9.58	9.11
Costa Rica	333,721	4,087	260	3,827	1.22	1.15
Peru	319,916	7,372	812	6,560	2.30	2.05
Jamaica	305,320	9,981	1,471	8,510	3.27	2.79
Philippines	304,051	5,632	1,011	4,621	1.85	1.52
Bahamas, The	287,876	7,090	412	6,678	2.46	2.32
Guatemala	276,217	7,716	1,275	6,441	2.79	2.33
Russia	236,581	5,420	707	4,713	2.29	1.99
El Salvador	220,226	6,842	3,062	3,780	3.11	1.72
Honduras	215,115	6,452	1,030	5,422	3.00	2.52
Trinidad and Tobago	192,574	1,916	246	1,670	0.99	0.87
Turkey	151,332	2,513	491	2,022	1.66	1.34
Panama	145,936	1,394	207	1,187	0.96	0.81
Nigeria	140,566	11,337	1,264	10,073	8.07	7.17
South Africa	123,848	1,369	207	1,162	1.11	0.94
Haiti	118,791	11,335	1,734	9,601	9.54	8.08
Indonesia	97,384	1,162	81	1,081	1.19	1.11
Vietnam	94,776	2,273	373	1,900	2.40	2.00
Saudi Arabia	92,507	1,025	356	669	1.11	0.72
Thailand	90,372	1,897	235	1,662	2.10	1.84
Romania	89,920	1,255	501	754	1.40	0.84
Ukraine	86,342	1,867	406	1,461	2.16	1.69
Pakistan	85,164	3,320	413	2,907	3.90	3.41
Egypt	80,578	2,791	446	2,345	3.46	2.91
Malaysia	78,806	825	49	776	1.05	0.98
Uruguay	72,808	935	60	875	1.28	1.20
Bolivia	65,339	1,658	128	1,530	2.54	2.34
Nicaragua	65,296	2,560	427	2,133	3.92	3.27
Barbados	61,646	1,875	88	1,787	3.04	2.90
Guyana	53,681	3,603	549	3,054	6.71	5.69

[1] Individuals whose departure was recorded after their lawful admission period expired. [2] Individuals for whom no departure has been recorded. [3] Includes all nonimmigrant visa classes, including students and exchange visitors and other in-scope visitors. See source for more information on visa classes. [4] Includes only business and pleasure visitors. Excludes students, exchange visitors, and other in-scope visitors.

Source: Department of Homeland Security, *Fiscal Year 2020 Entry/Exit Overstay Report*, December 2021. See also <www.dhs.gov/publication/entryexit-overstay-report>.

Table 570. Terrorism Related Deaths, Injuries, and Kidnappings of Private U.S. Citizens by Selected Country: 2013 to 2020

[Private U.S. citizen refers to any U.S. citizen overseas not acting in an official capacity on behalf of the U.S. government. Includes U.S. government employees' households and U.S. citizens working for contractors hired by the U.S. government. Excludes U.S. military personnel while on active duty or employees of the Department of State and other federal agencies while overseas on U.S. government orders]

Incident type and location	2013	2014	2015	2016	2017	2018	2019	2020
DEATHS								
Total [1]	**16**	**24**	**20**	**16**	**7**	**6**	**12**	**2**
Afghanistan	12	10	8	1	–	4	3	–
Israel, Jerusalem, West Bank, Gaza	–	5	3	3	–	–	1	–
Somalia	–	3	1	–	3	–	2	–
Sri Lanka	–	–	–	–	–	–	4	–
United Kingdom	–	–	–	–	1	–	–	1
Yemen	–	–	–	–	–	–	–	1
INJURIES								
Total [1]	**[2] 7**	**8**	**22**	**34**	**8**	**6**	**–**	**–**
Afghanistan	1	2	2	5	1	2	–	–
Belgium	–	–	–	17	–	–	–	–
France	–	–	6	3	–	–	–	–
Germany	–	–	–	2	–	–	–	–
Israel, Jerusalem, West Bank, Gaza	–	5	6	6	1	2	–	–
Kenya	6	–	–	–	–	–	–	–
United Kingdom	–	–	–	–	4	–	–	–
KIDNAPPINGS								
Total [1]	**13**	**3**	**–**	**6**	**3**	**–**	**–**	**–**
Afghanistan	–	2	–	1	–	–	–	–
Colombia	1	–	–	–	3	–	–	–
Nigeria	3	1	–	–	–	–	–	–
Syria	7	–	–	1	–	–	–	–

– Represents zero. [1] Includes countries not shown separately. [2] Excludes 2 citizens held hostage in Algeria; and 48 citizens present, but not medically injured, in Kenya.

Source: U.S. State Department, Bureau of Counterterrorism, "Country Reports on Terrorism 2020," and earlier releases, <www.state.gov/country-reports-on-terrorism>, accessed March 2022.

Table 571. Passengers Screened and Firearms Discovered at TSA Checkpoints: 2017 to 2021

[In units, as indicated (771.6 represents 771,600,000). Firearms are those found in carry-on bags]

Item	2017	2018	2019	2020	2021	Top 5 airports for firearm discoveries	Firearms found in 2021 (number)
Passengers & crew screened (millions)	771.6	813.8	848.1	324.0	585.3	Atlanta (ATL)	507
						Dallas-Fort Worth (DFW)	317
Firearms found (number)	3,957	4,244	4,432	3,257	5,972	Houston (IAH)	245
Percent loaded	84	86	87	83	86	Phoenix (PHX)	196
Airports with firearms discovered (number)	239	249	278	234	268	Nashville (BNA)	163

Source: U.S. Department of Homeland Security, Transportation Security Administration, "TSA highlights the top 21 accomplishments in transportation security to close out 2021," <www.tsa.gov/news/press/releases>, and earlier releases.

Table 572. Value of Counterfeit Goods Seized for Intellectual Property Rights Violations by Commodity and Country of Origin: 2019 and 2020

[In thousands of dollars (1,555,269 represents $1,555,269,000), except as indicated. Customs and Border Protection enforces Intellectual Property Rights (IPR), most visibly by seizing products that infringe IPR such as trademarks, copyrights, and patents. Value of goods seized represent Manufacturer's Suggested Retail Price (MSRP), which is the price at which merchandise is sold at retail to the consumer or what the value of the counterfeit goods would have been at retail had they been genuine. Updates to the CBP seizure database may result in a slight difference in multi-year comparisons]

Commodity	2019	2020	Country of origin	2019	2020
Number of IPR seizures	**27,599**	**26,503**			
Total MSRP value of IPR seizures	**1,555,269**	**1,309,157**	China	1,030,182	660,767
Jewelry, watches, and parts	687,167	435,249	Hong Kong	397,277	428,962
Handbags/wallets/backpacks	212,782	282,702	Turkey	14,241	31,237
Consumer electronics/parts	105,957	162,235	Vietnam	13,556	25,804
Wearing apparel/accessories	343,732	157,227	Korea, South	5,633	25,283
Consumer products	27,908	85,471	India	9,540	12,862
Footwear	37,994	63,146	Thailand	(NA)	12,602
Pharmaceuticals/personal care	48,772	20,415	Taiwan	(NA)	12,144
Labels/tags	(NA)	19,824	Netherlands	(NA)	11,797
Batteries	(NA)	14,432	Pakistan	12,157	(NA)
Computers/technology components	13,217	(NA)	Singapore	10,453	(NA)
Automotive/aerospace	12,143	(NA)	Dominican Republic	9,542	(NA)
All other commodities	65,598	68,455	All other countries	52,689	87,699

NA Not available.

Source: U.S. Department of Homeland Security, Customs and Border Protection, *Intellectual Property Rights Seizure Statistics FY2020*, September 2021, and earlier reports. See also <www.cbp.gov/trade/priority-issues/ipr/statistics>.

Social Insurance and Human Services

This section presents data related to government expenditures for social insurance and human services; the population receiving government assistance; government programs for Old-Age, Survivors, and Disability Insurance (OASDI), commonly known as Social Security; state and local government employee retirement; private retirement savings plans; government unemployment and disability insurance; federal supplemental security income payments and aid to the needy; child and other welfare services; and federal food programs. Also included here are selected data on workers' compensation, child support, child care, homelessness, social assistance organizations, and the nonprofit sector.

A principal source for these data is the Social Security Administration's *Annual Statistical Supplement to the Social Security Bulletin*, which presents current data on many of the programs. Additional sources of data include the Census Bureau's Annual Social and Economic Supplement of the Current Population Survey, and the Survey of Income and Program Participation (conducted as a series of surveys over a period of time spanning several years); and the Department of Health and Human Services' Administration for Children and Families.

Social insurance under the Social Security Act—Programs established by the Social Security Act provide protection against wage loss resulting from retirement, prolonged disability, death, or unemployment, and protection against the cost of medical care during old age and disability. The federal OASDI program provides monthly benefits to retired or disabled insured workers and their dependents, and to survivors of insured workers. To be eligible, a worker must have had a specified period of employment in which OASDI taxes were paid. The age of eligibility for full retirement benefits had been 65 for many years. For persons born in 1938 or later, that age gradually increases until it reaches age 67 for those born in 1960 and later. Reduced benefits may be obtained as early as age 62. The worker's spouse is under the same limitations. Survivor benefits are payable to dependents of deceased insured workers. Disability benefits are payable to an insured worker under full retirement age with a prolonged disability, and to the disabled worker's dependents on the same basis as dependents of retired workers. Disability benefits are provided at age 50 to the disabled widow or widower of a deceased worker who was fully insured at the time of death. Disabled children, age 18 or older, of retired, disabled, or deceased workers are also eligible for benefits. A special lump sum benefit may be payable on the death of an insured worker to a spouse or minor children. For information on the Medicare program, see Section 3, Health and Nutrition.

Retirement, survivors, and disability insurance benefits are funded by a payroll tax on annual earnings (up to a maximum share of earnings set by law) of workers, employers, and the self-employed. The maximum taxable earnings are adjusted annually to reflect increasing wage levels (see Table 578). The Old Age and Survivors Insurance trust fund pays retirement and survivors benefits; the Disability Insurance trust fund pays disability benefits. These two funds are separate entities by law. Special benefits for uninsured persons; hospital benefits for persons age 65 and over with specified amounts of social security coverage less than that required for cash benefit eligibility; and that part of the cost of supplementary medical insurance not financed by contributions from participants are all financed from federal general revenues.

Retirement—Social security benefits are a component of retirement income. This section also includes data on the use of individual retirement savings plans and accounts, including benefits sponsored by employers. The Bureau of Labor Statistics collects detailed data for the National Compensation Survey on the availability of and participation in employer-sponsored defined benefit and defined contribution retirement savings plans. Defined benefit plans are funded by the employer; defined contribution plans require the employee to save for retirement. Additional data on individual retirement savings also come from surveys conducted by the Investment Company Institute.

Unemployment insurance—Unemployment insurance is administered by the U.S. Employment and Training Administration and each state's employment security agency. By agreement with the U.S. Secretary of Labor, state agencies also administer unemployment compensation for eligible former military personnel and federal employees. Under state unemployment insurance laws, benefits related to an individual's past earnings are paid to eligible unemployed workers. State laws vary concerning the length of time benefits are paid and their amount. In most states, benefits are payable for 26 weeks and, during periods of high unemployment, extended benefits are payable under a federal-state program to those who have exhausted their regular state benefits. Some states also supplement the basic benefit with allowances for dependents. Unemployment insurance is financed through Federal and state employer payroll taxes. Generally, employers pay both Federal and state unemployment taxes for workers paid $1,500 or more during any quarter of a calendar year, or if they had at least 1 employee during any day of the week during 20 weeks in a calendar year (weeks need not be consecutive).

Workers' compensation—All states provide protection against work-connected injuries, illnesses, and deaths, although some states exclude certain workers (e.g., domestic workers). Workers' compensation is the only social insurance system run almost entirely by states, with no federal guidelines. Federal laws cover federal employees, private employees in the District of Columbia, and longshoremen and harbor workers. In addition, the Department of Labor administers "black lung" benefit programs for coal miners disabled by pneumoconiosis and for specified dependents and survivors. Specified occupational diseases are compensable to some extent. In most states, benefits are related to the worker's salary. The benefits may or may not be augmented by dependents' allowances or automatically adjusted to prevailing wage levels.

Income support—Income support programs are designed to provide benefits that assist persons with limited income and resources. The Supplemental Security Income (SSI) program and Temporary Assistance for Needy Families (TANF) program are the major programs providing monthly payments. In addition, a number of programs provide money payments or in-kind benefits for special needs or purposes. Several programs offer food and nutritional services. Also, various federal-state programs provide energy assistance, public housing, and subsidized housing to individuals and families with low incomes. General assistance may also be available at the state or local level.

The SSI program, administered by the Social Security Administration, provides income support to persons with low income and few resources who are age 65 and older, or blind or disabled, and children who have limited income and resources. Unlike social security, SSI benefits are not based on a person's work history, and the program is financed by general tax revenues. Eligibility requirements and federal payment standards are nationally uniform. Most states supplement the basic SSI payment for all or selected categories of persons.

The Personal Responsibility and Work Opportunity Reconciliation Act of 1996 contains provisions that replaced the Aid to Families With Dependent Children (AFDC), Job Opportunities and Basic Skills (JOBS), and Emergency Assistance programs with the TANF block grant program. The federal government provides grants to states that use the money to fund monthly cash assistance payments to low-income families with children, and numerous additional services to encourage economic self-sufficiency. This law creating TANF contains strong work requirements, comprehensive child support enforcement, support for families moving from welfare to work, and other features. The TANF program became effective as soon as each state submitted a complete implementation plan, but no later than July 1, 1997.

Federal nutrition assistance—Under the Supplemental Nutrition Assistance Program (SNAP), formerly known as the food stamp program, single persons and those living in households meeting nationwide standards for income and assets may receive benefits to assist in purchasing food. Benefits come on an electronic benefits transfer card that recipients use much like a bank debit card for purchasing eligible food items in retail food stores. The monthly amount of benefits, also known as allotments, is determined by household size and income. Households without income receive the determined monthly cost of a nutritionally adequate diet for their household size. This amount is regularly updated to account for food price increases. Households are expected to spend about 30 percent of their own resources on food, thus for households with income, the program provides a benefit that equals the maximum monthly allotment according to household size minus 30 percent of the household's net monthly income.

The USDA website has detailed information regarding eligibility for SNAP, including income limits and maximum monthly SNAP allotments by household size, at <www.fns.usda.gov/snap/recipient/eligibility>. All households in which all members receive TANF or SSI are categorically eligible for SNAP without meeting these income or resource criteria. Households are certified for varying lengths of time, depending on their income sources and individual circumstances.

Health services—For information about the Medicaid program, see Section 3, Health and Nutrition.

Noncash benefits—The U.S. Census Bureau annually collects data on the characteristics of recipients of noncash (in-kind) benefits to supplement the collection of annual money income data in the Current Population Survey (see text, Section 1, Population, and Section 13, Income, Expenditures, Poverty, and Wealth). Noncash benefits are those benefits received in a form other than money which serve to enhance or improve the economic well-being of the recipient. As for money income, the data for noncash benefits are for the calendar year prior to the date of the interview. The major categories of noncash benefits covered are public transfers (e.g., SNAP, school lunch, public housing, and Medicaid) and employer or union-provided benefits to employees.

Statistical reliability—For discussion of statistical collection, estimation, and sampling procedures and measures of statistical reliability applicable to Census Bureau data, see Appendix III.

Table 573. Government Transfer Payments to Individuals—Summary: 1990 to 2020

[In billions of current dollars (568.1 represents $568,100,000,000)]

Year	Government transfer payments to individuals, total	Retirement and disability insurance benefits	Medical payments	Income maintenance benefits	Unemployment insurance benefits	Veterans benefits	Education and training assistance payments [1]	Other [2]
1990	568.1	263.9	188.8	65.4	18.2	17.7	12.3	1.7
2000	1,032.4	424.5	427.2	110.6	21.0	25.0	21.9	2.3
2005	1,473.5	545.5	655.6	165.9	32.3	36.4	33.0	4.9
2006	1,575.4	576.9	720.4	170.4	30.9	38.9	34.8	3.1
2007	1,679.8	608.8	775.9	180.6	33.4	41.7	36.8	2.6
2008	1,900.5	639.0	825.5	196.0	52.0	45.0	42.5	100.4
2009	2,087.4	698.5	890.4	230.8	132.0	51.5	53.5	30.6
2010	2,260.4	724.9	938.4	256.0	139.7	58.0	64.5	78.8
2011	2,288.7	747.4	970.1	264.1	107.9	63.3	65.0	70.9
2012	2,300.2	796.2	1,001.6	267.6	84.4	70.1	63.7	16.5
2013	2,363.2	832.8	1,040.5	271.2	63.0	79.1	63.8	12.8
2014	2,475.6	870.3	1,117.7	271.0	35.8	84.2	64.7	31.9
2015	2,612.3	908.0	1,197.7	273.7	32.9	92.6	63.4	44.1
2016	2,694.1	930.4	1,250.5	270.7	32.3	96.8	64.1	49.4
2017	2,784.5	959.2	1,292.3	269.7	30.6	111.4	64.9	56.3
2018	2,902.3	1,006.3	1,351.0	262.7	28.2	119.7	68.5	65.9
2019	3,057.8	1,065.5	1,427.2	272.1	28.0	130.9	70.6	63.6
2020	4,050.3	1,113.8	1,504.7	302.6	536.9	145.5	71.9	374.7

[1] See footnote 9, Table 574. [2] See footnote 10, Table 574.

Source: U.S. Bureau of Economic Analysis, Regional Economic Accounts, Annual Personal Income and Employment by State, "Personal Current Transfer Receipts (SAINC35)," <www.bea.gov/data/economic-accounts/regional>, accessed November 2021.

Table 574. Government Transfer Payments to Individuals by Payment Type: 1990 to 2020

[In millions of current dollars (568,060 represents $568,060,000,000)]

Payment type	1990	2000	2005	2010	2018	2019	2020
Total	**568,060**	**1,032,404**	**1,473,518**	**2,260,351**	**2,902,300**	**3,057,831**	**4,050,252**
Retirement & disability insurance benefits	263,888	424,461	545,484	724,895	1,006,324	1,065,496	1,113,849
Social security	244,135	401,393	512,728	690,174	972,412	1,030,743	1,077,928
Railroad retirement & disability	7,221	8,267	9,194	10,779	12,731	13,024	13,126
Workers' compensation (federal & state)	8,618	10,898	15,863	15,505	12,624	12,363	12,102
Other government disability insurance & retirement [1]	3,914	3,903	7,699	8,437	8,557	9,366	10,693
Medical payments	188,808	427,194	655,571	938,402	1,351,012	1,427,227	1,504,739
Medicare	107,638	219,117	332,127	513,390	734,919	785,703	819,202
Public assistance medical care [2]	78,176	205,021	315,189	410,957	601,999	626,648	670,395
Military medical insurance [3]	2,994	3,056	8,255	14,055	14,094	14,876	15,142
Income maintenance benefits	65,441	110,582	165,905	256,034	262,713	272,103	302,583
Supplemental Security Income (SSI)	16,670	31,675	38,261	49,158	56,858	57,716	57,932
Earned income tax credit	6,313	30,423	39,237	59,778	68,459	67,881	67,150
Supplemental Nutrition Assistance Program	14,741	14,565	29,492	66,515	58,138	54,686	83,766
Family assistance [4]	19,187	18,440	18,355	22,421	19,972	20,166	20,926
Other, excluding family assistance [5]	8,530	15,479	40,560	58,162	59,286	71,654	72,809
Unemployment insurance compensation	18,208	20,989	32,277	139,715	28,154	27,952	536,927
State unemployment insurance compensation	17,644	20,223	31,001	137,016	27,296	27,139	535,935
Unemployment compensation for federal civilian employees	215	226	225	535	162	185	223
Unemployment compensation for railroad employees	89	81	72	116	89	100	210
Unemployment compensation for veterans	144	181	446	1,155	160	124	239
Other unemployment compensation [6]	116	278	533	893	447	404	320
Veterans benefits	17,687	25,004	36,389	57,962	119,704	130,899	145,543
Veterans pension & disability	15,550	21,966	32,511	48,455	93,365	102,656	112,009
Veterans readjustment [7]	257	1,322	2,256	7,976	11,424	11,520	10,581
Veterans life insurance benefits	1,868	1,706	1,597	1,442	989	916	821
Other assistance to veterans [8]	12	10	25	89	13,926	15,807	22,132
Federal education & training assistance payments [9]	12,286	21,851	33,015	64,511	68,471	70,564	71,941
Other payments to individuals [10]	1,742	2,323	4,877	78,832	65,922	63,590	374,670

[1] Mostly temporary disability, pension benefit guaranty, black lung, and Panama Canal construction annuity payments. [2] Medicaid and other medical vendor payments. [3] Payments made under TRICARE Program (formerly called CHAMPUS) for medical care of dependents of active duty and retired military personnel and their dependents at nonmilitary medical facilities. [4] Through 1995, Emergency Assistance and Aid to Families with Dependent Children. Beginning 1998, Temporary Assistance for Needy Families benefits. [5] Mostly general assistance; food expenditures under Special Supplemental Nutrition Program for Women, Infants, and Children (WIC); other needs assistance; refugee assistance; foster home care and adoption assistance; Additional Child Tax Credits; and energy assistance. [6] Trade readjustment allowance, Redwood Park benefit, public service employment benefit, and transitional benefit. [7] Mostly veterans' readjustment benefit payments, educational assistance to spouses and children of disabled or deceased veterans, and payments to paraplegics and for autos and conveyances for disabled veterans. [8] Mostly state and local government payments to veterans and Veterans Choice and VA Community Care benefits. [9] Mostly federal fellowship payments (National Science Foundation fellowships and traineeships, subsistence payments to state maritime academy cadets, and other fellowships), interest subsidy on higher education loans, Pell Grants, Job Corps payments, education exchange payments, and state education assistance payments. [10] Mostly other refundable tax credits; Bureau of Indian Affairs payments; Alaska Permanent Fund dividend payments; compensation of survivors of public safety officers; compensation of victims of crime; disaster relief payments; supplemental payments to United Mine Workers health benefits; compensation for Japanese internment; the American Recovery and Reinvestment Act of 2009 funded Federal Additional Compensation for unemployment, COBRA premium reduction; Economic Recovery lump sum payment; Affordable Care Act cost sharing reduction; lost wages assistance during the COVID-19 pandemic; and other special payments to individuals.

Source: U.S. Bureau of Economic Analysis, Regional Economic Accounts, Annual Personal Income and Employment by State, "Personal Current Transfer Receipts (SAINC35)," <www.bea.gov/data/economic-accounts/regional>, accessed November 2021.

Table 575. Government Transfer Payments to Individuals by State: 2010 to 2020

[In millions of current dollars not adjusted for inflation (2,260,351 represents $2,260,351,000,000)]

State	2010, total	2019, total	2020							
			Total	Retire-ment and disability insurance benefits	Medical payments	Income mainte-nance benefits	Unem-ployment insurance benefits	Veterans benefits	Educa-tion and training assis-tance [1]	Other [2]
United States.........	2,260,351	3,057,831	4,050,252	1,113,849	1,504,739	302,583	536,927	145,543	71,941	374,670
Alabama...............	36,885	48,551	58,951	19,551	19,959	5,112	3,819	3,396	1,376	5,738
Alaska...............	5,189	7,786	8,984	1,764	3,235	835	900	759	73	1,419
Arizona...............	46,551	65,097	87,824	25,094	32,874	5,515	10,705	3,687	2,078	7,870
Arkansas...............	23,007	30,818	37,043	11,564	14,441	2,783	2,563	1,795	786	3,111
California...............	259,129	365,176	531,274	113,514	198,475	42,543	108,302	12,734	10,444	45,261
Colorado...............	28,542	44,252	58,629	16,440	21,052	3,270	7,587	3,117	1,445	5,717
Connecticut............	28,329	35,437	45,468	13,133	18,410	2,708	5,871	831	695	3,821
Delaware...............	6,972	10,899	13,193	4,212	5,421	772	887	417	432	1,052
District of Columbia....	5,301	7,029	9,580	1,410	4,505	1,040	1,578	172	255	619
Florida...............	147,547	212,411	265,441	82,722	96,982	19,767	18,511	11,612	4,864	30,984
Georgia...............	59,961	83,720	113,580	32,150	34,699	10,002	15,900	6,209	2,384	12,236
Hawaii...............	9,006	12,341	18,486	4,828	5,628	1,337	3,895	966	192	1,640
Idaho...............	9,921	14,659	18,425	6,395	6,517	1,132	1,020	983	309	2,069
Illinois...............	90,583	109,222	149,260	40,650	55,999	13,483	20,285	3,301	2,353	13,189
Indiana...............	45,972	61,884	78,440	24,721	31,530	5,193	6,135	2,225	1,744	6,893
Iowa...............	21,092	28,437	35,252	11,600	13,016	2,188	3,198	1,127	638	3,485
Kansas...............	18,598	24,332	30,485	10,321	10,855	2,041	2,509	1,230	418	3,112
Kentucky...............	34,555	46,055	59,792	16,759	24,567	4,446	5,679	2,046	1,469	4,825
Louisiana...............	33,352	47,366	61,308	14,960	25,781	5,396	6,506	2,291	1,234	5,139
Maine...............	11,056	14,796	18,494	5,725	7,226	1,051	1,550	939	243	1,760
Maryland...............	37,990	53,520	70,605	19,117	27,358	5,005	9,635	2,538	800	6,152
Massachusetts..........	54,798	70,567	100,085	22,826	38,211	7,922	20,541	1,914	1,077	7,595
Michigan...............	80,630	101,266	140,635	40,560	48,091	9,064	25,672	3,468	2,241	11,538
Minnesota...............	37,924	51,832	67,618	19,283	25,722	4,331	9,165	2,167	1,284	5,668
Mississippi...............	23,427	29,997	37,239	10,897	14,025	3,306	3,282	1,526	733	3,471
Missouri...............	44,332	57,553	70,355	22,640	27,360	4,574	4,823	2,982	1,059	6,918
Montana...............	6,854	10,204	12,780	4,259	4,529	671	1,076	801	161	1,284
Nebraska...............	11,489	15,992	19,644	6,536	6,844	1,251	1,165	1,017	358	2,473
Nevada...............	16,258	25,752	37,959	9,569	11,635	2,622	8,047	1,899	766	3,421
New Hampshire.........	8,864	12,712	16,366	5,752	5,822	638	1,559	660	449	1,487
New Jersey............	68,883	85,126	115,102	32,292	41,570	7,868	19,692	1,770	1,821	10,088
New Mexico............	15,448	21,160	27,687	7,334	11,242	2,585	2,510	1,347	373	2,297
New York...............	178,462	225,425	303,588	66,396	126,278	23,676	55,607	4,004	4,396	23,231
North Carolina..........	68,663	95,419	119,495	37,227	41,538	9,092	9,345	7,009	2,455	12,828
North Dakota...........	4,405	6,185	7,996	2,500	2,875	431	881	387	110	812
Ohio...............	88,300	111,727	145,224	41,260	58,124	10,789	15,955	4,288	2,403	12,405
Oklahoma...............	26,910	35,655	44,315	13,591	14,876	3,539	3,613	3,142	873	4,680
Oregon...............	28,483	41,519	54,499	15,925	21,005	3,517	6,307	2,470	592	4,682
Pennsylvania...........	108,365	141,674	189,855	51,712	72,166	13,134	31,515	4,159	2,130	15,039
Rhode Island...........	9,319	11,615	15,280	4,205	5,780	1,123	2,304	358	271	1,238
South Carolina..........	35,399	49,919	61,911	20,670	21,040	4,290	4,718	3,607	1,597	5,989
South Dakota...........	5,212	7,346	8,891	3,085	3,059	666	340	541	116	1,083
Tennessee...............	49,089	64,882	79,605	25,358	28,699	6,674	5,841	3,894	1,393	7,746
Texas...............	153,344	218,806	292,757	74,536	106,615	25,071	34,746	15,172	4,696	31,920
Utah...............	13,185	19,094	24,605	7,592	8,123	1,788	1,656	929	928	3,589
Vermont...............	5,220	6,897	8,927	2,664	3,356	510	1,166	247	209	776
Virginia...............	47,926	69,491	91,487	28,194	32,158	5,427	9,215	5,624	1,824	9,046
Washington............	48,772	67,183	88,691	27,242	29,845	5,930	12,306	4,047	1,594	7,727
West Virginia...........	16,457	21,204	25,584	8,330	9,712	1,900	1,803	1,227	509	2,103
Wisconsin...............	40,869	52,922	65,404	22,470	23,993	4,311	4,625	2,124	1,215	6,666
Wyoming...............	3,525	4,919	6,154	2,317	1,918	261	419	387	76	776

[1] Mostly federal fellowship payments (National Science Foundation fellowships and traineeships, subsistence payments to state maritime academy cadets, and other federal fellowships), interest subsidy on higher education loans, Pell Grants, Job Corps payments, education exchange payments, and state education assistance payments. [2] Mostly other refundable tax credits; Bureau of Indian Affairs payments; Alaska Permanent Fund dividend payments; compensation of survivors of public safety officers; compensation of victims of crime; disaster relief payments; supplemental payments to United Mine Workers health benefits; compensation for Japanese internment; the American Recovery and Reinvestment Act of 2009 funded Federal Additional Compensation for unemployment, COBRA premium reduction; Economic Recovery lump sum payment; Affordable Care Act cost sharing reductions; lost wages assistance during the COVID-19 pandemic; and other special payments to individuals.

Source: U.S. Bureau of Economic Analysis, Regional Economic Accounts, Annual Personal Income and Employment by State, "Personal Current Transfer Receipts (SAINC35)," <www.bea.gov/data/economic-accounts/regional>, accessed November 2021.

Table 576. Number of Persons With Income by Source of Income: 2020

[In thousands (235,916 represents 235,916,000). Persons age 15 and over as of March of following year. Based on Current Population Survey, Annual Social and Economic Supplement (CPS ASEC); see text, Sections 1 and 13, and Appendix III]

Source of income	Total persons with income	Under 65 years	65 years and over	Men	Women	White [1]	Black [1]	Hispanic origin [2]
Total..........................	**235,916**	**182,064**	**53,852**	**116,965**	**118,951**	**184,403**	**29,436**	**37,169**
Earnings............................	166,847	154,389	12,458	87,599	79,248	129,211	21,009	29,499
Wages and salary.....................	157,832	146,997	10,834	82,313	75,518	121,620	20,272	27,756
Nonfarm self-employment.............	12,302	10,533	1,769	6,949	5,353	10,266	1,130	2,098
Farm self-employment................	1,960	1,683	277	1,130	829	1,634	210	175
Unemployment compensation...........	23,583	21,905	1,677	11,493	12,090	17,522	3,486	4,094
State or local only..................	19,925	18,556	1,369	9,614	10,311	14,836	2,879	3,528
Combinations........................	3,660	3,352	308	1,881	1,779	2,688	607	566
Workers' compensation................	1,377	1,205	172	871	506	1,073	203	228
State payments......................	284	258	26	196	88	212	47	49
Employment insurance................	592	531	61	394	198	472	78	103
Own insurance......................	7	4	4	5	2	5	2	–
Other..............................	709	603	106	414	295	546	107	114
Social Security.......................	55,567	10,562	45,006	25,114	30,453	46,214	6,071	4,960
SSI (Supplemental Security Income).....	5,890	4,523	1,367	2,744	3,146	3,766	1,530	980
Public assistance, total...............	1,552	1,445	107	367	1,185	932	488	389
TANF only [3].......................	992	933	59	195	797	559	345	242
Other assistance only................	522	473	49	172	350	361	121	139
Both...............................	38	38	–	–	38	12	22	8
Veterans' benefits....................	4,355	2,241	2,114	3,536	819	3,427	700	402
Disability only......................	2,999	1,715	1,284	2,605	394	2,345	497	270
Survivors only......................	279	64	215	30	249	228	31	22
Pension only.......................	620	179	441	519	101	501	92	59
Education only......................	82	82	–	65	16	66	6	10
Other only.........................	118	28	89	93	25	95	18	10
Combinations.......................	257	172	85	224	34	192	57	32
Means-tested.......................	554	279	275	463	91	403	109	63
Nonmeans-tested....................	3,801	1,962	1,839	3,074	727	3,024	591	339
Survivors benefits [4].................	3,008	1,038	1,970	770	2,239	2,661	217	202
Company or union..................	1,232	245	987	226	1,005	1,078	101	72
Federal government.................	239	73	165	28	210	201	23	10
Military retirement..................	177	28	150	31	147	150	16	17
State or local government............	278	82	197	44	234	247	19	20
Estates or trusts....................	340	221	120	154	186	320	7	29
Annuities...........................	222	99	122	69	152	201	15	17
Disability benefits [4].................	2,648	2,220	428	1,420	1,228	1,979	454	407
Workers' compensation..............	305	272	32	193	111	226	43	63
Company or union..................	509	438	71	234	275	408	81	87
Federal government.................	190	138	51	95	95	124	47	24
Military retirement..................	176	108	69	163	14	125	43	12
State or local government............	502	441	61	271	231	372	73	75
Accident insurance.................	271	228	44	140	132	212	45	35
Retirement income [4].................	29,377	7,477	21,900	14,836	14,541	25,516	2,393	1,657
Pension income....................	18,128	3,551	14,576	9,912	8,216	15,785	1,553	939
Company or union retirement........	11,884	2,260	9,624	6,647	5,238	10,377	1,022	687
Federal government retirement.......	1,795	519	1,276	975	820	1,494	190	103
Military retirement..................	990	452	538	729	260	790	143	61
State or local government retirement...	6,458	1,868	4,591	2,653	3,806	5,565	593	398
Railroad retirement.................	64	5	60	19	45	55	9	7
Annuities...........................	4,195	758	3,438	1,924	2,271	3,813	203	160
Retirement accounts [5]..............	9,204	1,390	7,814	4,803	4,401	8,326	388	308
Property income......................	146,220	109,521	36,698	71,526	74,694	119,722	13,013	15,764
Interest............................	143,319	107,527	35,792	69,917	73,402	117,386	12,734	15,361
Dividends..........................	35,580	25,034	10,545	19,565	16,014	30,182	1,891	2,002
Rents, royalties, estates or trusts....	11,755	7,447	4,308	6,124	5,631	10,039	704	950
Educational assistance [4].............	7,218	7,206	12	3,114	4,104	5,127	1,104	1,323
Pell grant only.....................	1,916	1,914	2	776	1,140	1,242	440	447
Other government only...............	925	921	4	429	496	631	146	204
Scholarships only...................	2,516	2,516	–	1,119	1,397	1,859	285	353
Child support........................	3,586	3,542	44	321	3,265	2,510	767	679
Financial assistance from outside the household...........................	2,435	2,133	301	1,028	1,406	1,783	311	395
Other income, not elsewhere classified...........	1,719	1,407	313	872	848	1,373	145	165

– Represents or rounds to zero. [1] Refers to people who reported specified race only and no other race category. [2] Persons of Hispanic origin may be of any race. [3] TANF is Temporary Assistance for Needy Families Program. [4] Includes other sources not shown separately. [5] Includes individual retirement account, tax-deferred retirement plan for self-employed and unincorporated businesses, employer-sponsored retirement plan, and other plan types.

Source: U.S. Census Bureau, *Income and Poverty in the United States: 2020*, Current Population Reports, P60-273, September 2021; and "Current Population Survey Tables for Personal Income: Table PINC-09," <www.census.gov/topics/income-poverty/income/data/tables.html>, accessed November 2021.

Table 577. Persons Living in Households Receiving Selected Benefits by Selected Characteristics: 2020

[325,713 represents 325,713,000, except percent. Based on Current Population Survey, Annual Social and Economic Supplement (CPS ASEC); see text of Section 1 and Appendix III. Persons who lived with someone (a nonrelative or a relative) who received aid. Not every person tallied here received the aid themselves. Excludes members of the Armed Forces except those living off post or with their families on post. Population controls are based on Census 2010. SNAP = Supplemental Nutrition Assistance Program]

Characteristic	Total pop-ulation (1,000)	In household receiving means-tested assistance [1]		In household receiving means-tested cash assistance		In household receiving food stamps (SNAP)		In household in which one or more persons are covered by Medicaid		Living in public or authorized housing	
		(1,000)	Percent	(1,000)	Percent	(1,000)	Percent	(1,000)	Percent	(1,000)	Percent
Total.................	325,713	116,556	35.8	18,262	5.6	42,067	12.9	82,703	25.4	11,598	3.6
Under 18 years.................	72,295	38,957	53.9	4,015	5.6	15,033	20.8	27,042	37.4	3,433	4.7
18 to 24 years.................	28,838	11,262	39.1	1,485	5.1	3,598	12.5	8,287	28.7	1,070	3.7
25 to 34 years.................	45,284	16,165	35.7	2,274	5.0	5,948	13.1	12,283	27.1	1,483	3.3
35 to 44 years.................	42,004	16,009	38.1	2,056	4.9	5,240	12.5	10,793	25.7	1,235	2.9
45 to 54 years.................	39,680	12,419	31.3	2,325	5.9	4,039	10.2	8,525	21.5	1,096	2.8
55 to 59 years.................	20,682	5,548	26.8	1,635	7.9	2,103	10.2	4,149	20.1	587	2.8
60 to 64 years.................	21,094	5,579	26.4	1,669	7.9	2,074	9.8	4,500	21.3	699	3.3
65 years and over.................	55,836	10,617	19.0	2,802	5.0	4,031	7.2	7,124	12.8	1,995	3.6
Male.................	159,699	55,711	34.9	8,706	5.5	18,859	11.8	39,230	24.6	4,969	3.1
Female.................	166,014	60,846	36.7	9,556	5.8	23,207	14.0	43,474	26.2	6,629	4.0
White alone [2].................	247,865	80,305	32.4	11,365	4.6	26,615	10.7	56,311	22.7	5,947	2.4
Black alone [2].................	43,355	22,595	52.1	4,786	11.0	10,915	25.2	16,395	37.8	4,304	9.9
Asian alone [2].................	20,155	6,288	31.2	1,042	5.2	1,545	7.7	4,812	23.9	430	2.1
Hispanic [3].................	61,196	34,296	56.0	3,875	6.3	12,048	19.7	25,608	41.8	2,773	4.5
In married couple families.......	194,009	56,192	29.0	7,010	3.6	14,714	7.6	37,018	19.1	2,184	1.1
In families with male house-holder, no spouse present.....	20,248	10,715	52.9	1,653	8.2	3,607	17.8	7,829	38.7	741	3.7
In families with female house-holder, no spouse present.....	48,141	32,159	66.8	5,830	12.1	16,319	33.9	25,494	53.0	4,704	9.8

[1] Means-tested assistance includes means-tested cash assistance, supplemental nutrition assistance program benefits, Medicaid, and public or authorized housing. [2] Refers to people who reported specific race and did not report any other race category. [3] People of Hispanic origin may be of any race.

Source: U.S. Census Bureau, *Income and Poverty in the United States: 2020*, Current Population Reports, P60-273, September 2021; and "Current Population Survey Detailed Tables for Poverty: Table POV-26," <www.census.gov/topics/income-poverty/poverty/data/tables.html>, accessed November 2021.

Table 578. Social Security—Covered Employment, Earnings, and Contribution Rates: 1990 to 2021

[164.3 represents 164,300,000. Includes the Island Areas of the U.S. Represents all reported employment. Data are estimated. OASDI is Old-age, Survivors, and Disability Insurance; SMI is Supplementary medical insurance. All data are subject to revision by source]

Item	Unit	1990	2000	2010	2016	2017	2018	2019	2020	2021
Workers with insured status [1]......	**Million**	**164.3**	**185.4**	**204.3**	**217.4**	**219.9**	**222.5**	**224.9**	**226.2**	**227.6**
Male.................	Million	86.8	95.5	103.5	109.4	110.6	111.7	112.8	113.3	113.9
Female.................	Million	77.5	89.9	100.8	107.9	109.4	110.7	112.1	112.9	113.8
Under 20 years old.................	Million	4.8	4.9	2.5	2.6	2.8	2.9	3.0	2.8	2.8
Age 20 to 24.................	Million	16.6	16.0	16.0	15.9	16.0	16.2	16.4	16.4	16.5
Age 25 to 29.................	Million	20.7	17.5	19.3	20.6	20.6	21.0	21.0	20.7	20.4
Age 30 to 34.................	Million	21.3	19.3	18.7	19.9	20.0	20.4	20.7	21.1	21.4
Age 35 to 39.................	Million	19.4	21.3	18.2	19.2	19.6	19.8	20.0	20.1	20.2
Age 40 to 44.................	Million	17.0	21.4	19.6	17.9	17.9	18.1	18.4	18.9	19.2
Age 45 to 49.................	Million	12.9	19.2	21.2	19.4	19.3	19.0	18.7	18.2	17.8
Age 50 to 54.................	Million	10.1	16.5	20.9	20.3	19.8	19.4	19.1	19.1	19.1
Age 55 to 59.................	Million	8.8	12.2	18.3	20.4	20.5	20.5	20.5	20.1	19.7
Age 60 to 64.................	Million	8.6	9.3	15.5	18.1	18.5	18.8	19.1	19.3	19.5
Age 65 to 69.................	Million	8.0	7.9	11.2	15.2	15.4	15.7	16.2	16.6	17.0
Age 70 to 74.................	Million	6.4	7.1	8.1	10.9	11.7	12.3	12.9	13.6	13.9
Age 75 and older.................	Million	9.9	12.8	14.9	16.9	17.6	18.3	18.9	19.3	20.1
Workers reported with—										
Taxable earnings [2].................	Million	133.0	154.7	157.1	170.7	172.7	175.2	176.5	174.5	179.3
Maximum earnings [2].................	Million	7.6	9.6	9.0	11.0	10.2	10.8	10.9	10.4	11.1
Earnings in covered employment [2]....	Bil. dol.	2,716	4,832	6,294	8,021	8,394	8,810	9,216	9,377	10,154
Reported taxable [2].................	Bil. dol.	2,359	4,008	5,307	6,664	7,006	7,333	7,691	7,755	8,261
Percent of total.................	Percent	86.9	82.9	84.3	83.1	83.5	83.2	83.5	82.7	81.4
Average per worker:										
Total earnings [2].................	Dollars	20,423	31,237	40,074	46,991	48,592	50,279	52,215	53,745	56,644
Taxable earnings [2].................	Dollars	17,737	25,908	33,788	39,043	40,554	41,850	43,574	44,445	46,083
Annual maximum taxable earnings [3].................	Dollars	51,300	76,200	106,800	118,500	127,200	128,400	132,900	137,700	142,800
Contribution rates for OASDI: [4]										
Each employer and employee........	Percent	7.65	7.65	7.65	7.65	7.65	7.65	7.65	7.65	7.65
Self-employed [5].................	Percent	15.30	15.30	15.30	15.30	15.30	15.30	15.30	15.30	15.30
SMI, monthly premium (as of Jan. 1)...	Dollars	28.60	45.50	110.50	121.80	134.00	134.00	135.50	144.60	148.50

[1] Estimated number fully insured for retirement and/or survivor benefits as of end of year. [2] Includes self-employment. Averages per worker computed with unrounded earnings and worker amounts, and may not agree with rounded table amounts. [3] Beginning in 1994, the upper limit on earnings subject to HI taxes was removed. [4] OASDI tax rates for employees and self-employed workers were reduced by 2 percent for 2011 and 2012. This reduction is being made up by transfers from the General Fund of the Treasury to the OASI and DI trust funds. [5] Half of self-employment tax is deductible for income tax purposes and for computing self-employment income subject to social security tax.

Source: U.S. Social Security Administration, *Annual Statistical Supplement to the Social Security Bulletin, 2021* and unpublished data. See also <www.ssa.gov/policy/docs/statcomps/supplement/index.html>.

Table 579. Social Security (OASDI)—Benefits by Type of Beneficiary: 1990 to 2021

[39,832 represents 39,832,000. A person eligible to receive more than one type of benefit is generally classified or counted only once as a retired-worker beneficiary. OASDI = Old-age, survivors, and disability insurance. See also headnote, Table 580]

Type of beneficiary	1990	2000	2010	2016	2017	2018	2019	2020	2021
Number of benefits [1] (1,000)	**39,832**	**45,415**	**54,032**	**60,907**	**61,903**	**62,906**	**64,064**	**64,851**	**65,228**
Retired workers [2]	24,838	28,499	34,593	41,233	42,447	43,721	45,094	46,330	47,293
Disabled workers [3]	3,011	5,042	8,204	8,809	8,695	8,537	8,378	8,151	7,877
Wives and husbands [2,4]	3,367	2,963	2,477	2,506	2,502	2,510	2,544	2,428	2,262
Children	3,187	3,803	4,313	4,222	4,169	4,108	4,051	4,004	3,908
Under age 18	2,497	2,976	3,209	3,007	2,938	2,858	2,798	2,755	2,672
Disabled children [5]	600	729	949	1,085	1,105	1,127	1,141	1,150	1,143
Students [6]	89	98	155	129	125	122	113	99	94
Of retired workers	422	459	580	662	675	690	702	704	687
Of deceased workers	1,776	1,878	1,913	1,893	1,904	1,911	1,916	1,936	1,976
Of disabled workers	989	1,466	1,820	1,667	1,590	1,507	1,434	1,363	1,245
Widowed mothers and fathers [7]	304	203	158	133	128	121	117	115	114
Widows and widowers [2,8]	5,111	4,901	4,286	4,004	3,961	3,908	3,878	3,823	3,774
Parents [2]	6	3	2	1	1	1	1	1	1
Special benefits [9]	7	(Z)	(Z)	(NA)	(NA)	(NA)	(NA)	(NA)	(NA)
AVERAGE MONTHLY BENEFIT, CURRENT DOLLARS									
Retired workers [2]	603	844	1,176	1,360	1,404	1,461	1,503	1,544	1,658
Retired worker and wife [2]	1,027	1,420	1,930	2,296	2,383	2,494	2,583	2,635	2,793
Disabled workers [3]	587	786	1,068	1,171	1,197	1,234	1,258	1,277	1,358
Wives and husbands [2,4]	298	416	561	687	712	744	767	778	820
Children of retired workers	259	395	577	657	675	697	713	730	782
Children of deceased workers	406	550	752	837	858	885	902	918	978
Children of disabled workers	164	228	318	355	366	381	391	399	428
Widowed mothers and fathers [7]	409	595	849	947	975	1,007	1,034	1,054	1,126
Widows and widowers, nondisabled [2]	556	810	1,134	1,301	1,338	1,388	1,423	1,455	1,555
Parents [2]	482	704	998	1,154	1,186	1,232	1,271	1,299	1,393
Special benefits [9]	167	217	276	(NA)	(NA)	(NA)	(NA)	(NA)	(NA)
AVERAGE MONTHLY BENEFIT, CONSTANT (2021) DOLLARS [10]									
Retired workers [2]	1,256	1,353	1,495	1,571	1,588	1,622	1,631	1,653	1,658
Retired worker and wife [2]	2,140	2,275	2,455	2,651	2,695	2,768	2,802	2,820	2,793
Disabled workers [3]	1,223	1,260	1,358	1,352	1,354	1,369	1,365	1,367	1,358
Wives and husbands [2,4]	621	667	714	794	805	825	832	833	820
Children of deceased workers	846	881	956	967	970	982	979	982	978
Widowed mothers and fathers [7]	852	953	1,080	1,094	1,103	1,118	1,122	1,128	1,126
Widows and widowers, nondisabled [2]	1,159	1,298	1,442	1,502	1,514	1,540	1,544	1,558	1,555
Number of benefits awarded (1,000)	**3,717**	**4,290**	**5,697**	**5,456**	**5,520**	**5,597**	**5,700**	**5,761**	**5,400**
Retired workers [2]	1,665	1,961	2,634	2,911	2,975	3,082	3,175	3,368	3,186
Disabled workers [3]	468	622	1,027	706	716	687	679	620	540
Wives and husbands [2,4]	379	385	409	476	452	476	523	435	368
Children	695	777	1,045	776	777	754	721	695	636
Widowed mothers and fathers [7]	58	40	32	24	23	22	21	22	25
Widows and widowers [2,8]	452	505	550	563	577	577	581	621	644
Parents [2]	(Z)	(Z)	(Z)	(Z)	(Z)	(Z)	(Z)	(Z)	(Z)
Special benefits [9]	(Z)	(Z)	(Z)	(NA)	(NA)	(NA)	(NA)	(NA)	(NA)
BENEFIT PAYMENTS DURING YEAR (bil. dol.)									
Total [11]	**247.8**	**407.6**	**701.6**	**911.3**	**941.5**	**988.6**	**1,047.9**	**1,095.9**	**1,133.2**
Monthly benefits [12]	247.6	407.4	701.4	911.1	941.3	988.4	1,047.7	1,095.6	1,132.9
Retired workers [2]	156.8	253.5	443.4	616.0	644.0	686.0	738.0	783.5	822.4
Disabled workers [3]	22.1	49.8	115.1	143.0	134.0	144.0	137.0	135.2	132.4
Wives and husbands [2,4]	14.5	19.4	24.6	30.0	31.0	32.0	34.0	34.5	33.5
Children	12.0	19.3	30.7	33.5	33.9	34.6	35.4	35.9	36.0
Under age 18	9.0	14.1	21.4	22.1	22.1	22.3	22.6	22.8	22.7
Disabled children [5]	2.5	4.6	8.0	10.3	10.6	11.1	11.6	12.0	12.2
Students [6]	0.5	0.7	1.3	1.2	1.2	1.2	1.2	1.1	1.0
Of retired workers	1.3	2.1	4.1	5.4	5.6	5.8	6.1	6.3	6.4
Of deceased workers	8.6	12.5	18.0	19.8	20.0	20.7	21.3	21.8	22.4
Of disabled workers	2.2	4.7	8.5	8.5	8.3	8.2	8.0	7.8	7.1
Widowed mothers and fathers [7]	1.4	1.4	1.6	1.6	1.5	1.5	1.5	1.5	1.5
Widows and widowers [2,8]	40.7	63.9	86.0	95.8	96.7	99.0	102.6	105.0	107.1
Parents [2]	(Z)	(Z)	(Z)	(Z)	(Z)	(Z)	(Z)	(Z)	(Z)
Special benefits [9]	(Z)	(Z)	(Z)	(NA)	(NA)	(NA)	(NA)	(NA)	(NA)
Lump sum	0.2	0.2	0.2	0.2	0.2	0.2	0.2	0.2	0.2

NA Not available. Z Fewer than 500 or less than $50 million. [1] Number of benefit payments in current-payment status, i.e., actually being made at a specified time with no deductions or with deductions amounting to less than a month's benefit. [2] Age 62 and over. [3] Disabled workers under full retirement age. [4] Includes spouse beneficiaries with entitled children in their care and entitled divorced spouses. [5] Age 18 and over. Disability began before age 22. [6] Full-time students age 18 and 19. [7] Includes surviving divorced mothers and fathers with entitled children in their care. [8] Includes widows and widowers and surviving divorced widows and widowers age 60 and over, and disabled widows and widowers age 50 and over. [9] Benefits for persons age 72 and over not insured under regular or transitional provisions of Social Security Act. [10] Constant dollar figures are based on the consumer price index (CPI-U) for December as published by the U.S. Bureau of Labor Statistics. [11] Represents total disbursements of benefit checks by the U.S. Department of the Treasury during the years specified. [12] Distribution by type estimated.

Source: U.S. Social Security Administration, *Annual Statistical Supplement to the Social Security Bulletin, 2022*, and earlier editions. See also <www.ssa.gov/policy/index.html>.

Table 580. Social Security—Beneficiaries, Annual Payments, and Average Monthly Benefit, 2000 to 2021, and by State and Other Areas, 2021

[45,417 represents 45,417,000. Number of beneficiaries in current-payment status, and annual and average monthly benefit as of December. Data for 2000 are based on 10-percent sample of administrative records. All other years are 100 percent data. See also headnote, Table 579]

Year, state, and other area	Number of beneficiaries (1,000)				Annual payments [2] (mil. dol.)				Average monthly benefit (dol.)		
	Total	Retired workers and dependents [1]	Survivors	Disabled workers and dependents	Total	Retired workers and dependents [1]	Survivors	Disabled workers and dependents	Retired workers [3]	Disabled workers	Widows and widowers [4]
2000	45,417	31,761	6,981	6,675	407,431	274,645	77,848	54,938	845	787	810
2010	54,032	37,489	6,358	10,184	701,436	471,505	105,740	124,191	1,176	1,068	1,134
2014	59,007	41,918	6,790	10,931	848,228	592,616	114,037	141,620	1,329	1,165	1,276
2015	59,963	43,073	6,084	10,806	886,012	626,378	116,352	143,282	1,342	1,166	1,286
2016	60,907	44,266	6,031	10,610	911,132	651,280	117,149	142,703	1,360	1,171	1,301
2017	61,903	45,498	5,994	10,411	941,252	680,233	118,279	142,740	1,404	1,197	1,338
2018	62,906	46,803	5,940	10,162	988,373	723,542	121,175	143,656	1,461	1,234	1,388
2019	64,064	48,227	5,912	9,925	1,047,677	777,259	125,369	145,049	1,503	1,258	1,423
2020	64,851	49,358	5,875	9,618	1,095,649	823,868	128,294	143,487	1,544	1,277	1,455
Total, 2021 [5, 6]	**65,228**	**50,146**	**5,864**	**9,218**	**1,132,927**	**861,874**	**131,057**	**139,996**	**1,658**	**1,358**	**1,555**
United States	63,660	48,970	5,649	9,041	1,116,014	850,585	127,808	137,621	(NA)	(NA)	(NA)
Alabama	1,164	801	120	243	19,695	13,562	2,518	3,615	1,621	1,334	1,528
Alaska	110	87	10	13	1,832	1,424	213	195	1,595	1,349	1,540
Arizona	1,449	1,166	118	165	25,840	20,522	2,705	2,613	1,696	1,414	1,607
Arkansas	709	490	69	150	11,563	8,020	1,408	2,135	1,565	1,295	1,483
California	6,166	4,997	516	653	105,711	83,613	11,711	10,387	1,625	1,396	1,518
Colorado	925	750	74	101	16,477	13,147	1,744	1,586	1,692	1,375	1,621
Connecticut	700	559	54	87	13,432	10,697	1,355	1,380	1,833	1,417	1,747
Delaware	229	182	18	29	4,330	3,431	422	477	1,810	1,462	1,718
District of Columbia	83	63	7	13	1,410	1,086	135	189	1,645	1,209	1,436
Florida	4,910	3,917	388	605	85,113	66,946	8,772	9,395	1,648	1,392	1,575
Georgia	1,919	1,426	182	311	32,660	24,135	3,846	4,679	1,623	1,361	1,544
Hawaii	287	243	21	23	5,001	4,172	471	358	1,655	1,400	1,529
Idaho	378	298	30	50	6,442	5,018	696	728	1,632	1,334	1,613
Illinois	2,272	1,773	207	292	40,644	31,215	4,919	4,510	1,687	1,373	1,643
Indiana	1,389	1,035	132	221	24,991	18,584	3,073	3,334	1,716	1,355	1,687
Iowa	669	527	57	86	11,746	9,185	1,323	1,238	1,669	1,292	1,621
Kansas	573	444	51	78	10,298	7,978	1,174	1,146	1,722	1,321	1,664
Kentucky	1,010	687	112	212	16,653	11,229	2,305	3,119	1,574	1,322	1,488
Louisiana	925	631	123	171	15,036	10,041	2,548	2,447	1,541	1,300	1,463
Maine	359	271	28	60	5,880	4,419	607	854	1,569	1,275	1,520
Maryland	1,038	816	88	134	19,294	15,089	2,052	2,153	1,774	1,413	1,655
Massachusetts	1,295	992	99	205	23,308	17,827	2,329	3,152	1,729	1,367	1,635
Michigan	2,253	1,688	203	362	41,229	30,758	4,882	5,589	1,747	1,385	1,704
Minnesota	1,083	870	80	133	19,654	15,745	1,907	2,002	1,741	1,351	1,665
Mississippi	682	469	76	136	10,991	7,560	1,480	1,951	1,540	1,298	1,452
Missouri	1,329	979	124	226	22,704	16,690	2,680	3,334	1,629	1,319	1,589
Montana	249	199	21	29	4,139	3,262	460	417	1,577	1,288	1,569
Nebraska	360	283	31	46	6,314	4,952	718	644	1,677	1,275	1,615
Nevada	572	459	44	69	9,835	7,714	1,014	1,107	1,612	1,430	1,576
New Hampshire	322	247	22	53	5,971	4,619	543	809	1,802	1,401	1,735
New Jersey	1,653	1,316	133	203	31,949	25,148	3,359	3,442	1,835	1,505	1,723
New Mexico	455	345	42	68	7,453	5,607	862	984	1,567	1,281	1,458
New York	3,681	2,860	296	525	65,925	50,669	6,992	8,264	1,708	1,407	1,605
North Carolina	2,203	1,676	183	344	38,282	29,099	3,930	5,253	1,660	1,359	1,565
North Dakota	141	111	14	16	2,385	1,851	308	226	1,608	1,269	1,536
Ohio	2,409	1,787	250	372	41,317	30,230	5,645	5,442	1,622	1,304	1,590
Oklahoma	814	591	84	139	13,803	9,975	1,819	2,009	1,619	1,303	1,556
Oregon	910	731	68	111	16,017	12,711	1,627	1,679	1,663	1,339	1,630
Pennsylvania	2,878	2,196	255	427	52,065	39,467	6,052	6,546	1,720	1,366	1,648
Rhode Island	231	175	16	39	4,096	3,121	387	588	1,708	1,339	1,652
South Carolina	1,216	921	106	189	21,277	16,089	2,265	2,923	1,677	1,387	1,559
South Dakota	189	153	16	21	3,169	2,537	343	289	1,600	1,265	1,514
Tennessee	1,503	1,096	147	260	25,774	18,804	3,105	3,865	1,644	1,325	1,557
Texas	4,476	3,389	472	614	75,905	56,545	10,296	9,064	1,627	1,341	1,507
Utah	439	345	41	53	7,803	6,072	954	777	1,720	1,351	1,709
Vermont	158	122	11	24	2,754	2,155	261	338	1,694	1,280	1,597
Virginia	1,598	1,236	136	226	28,684	22,094	3,128	3,462	1,718	1,371	1,602
Washington	1,413	1,132	107	175	25,891	20,547	2,616	2,728	1,752	1,372	1,680
West Virginia	476	327	57	92	8,090	5,455	1,256	1,379	1,612	1,345	1,539
Wisconsin	1,289	1,017	99	173	23,026	18,084	2,348	2,594	1,703	1,340	1,667
Wyoming	121	96	10	15	2,156	1,685	245	226	1,696	1,366	1,671
American Samoa	6	3	1	2	62	31	15	16	1,007	970	927
Guam	19	15	3	2	231	164	42	25	1,130	1,246	1,056
Northern Mariana Islands	4	2	1	(Z)	33	21	8	4	858	969	804
Puerto Rico	822	567	95	160	9,707	6,132	1,427	2,148	1,080	1,197	956
U.S. Virgin Islands	22	19	2	2	330	271	35	24	1,412	1,366	1,253
Abroad	695	571	113	11	6,541	4,661	1,720	160	870	1,346	893

NA Not available. Z Less than 500. [1] Data for 1990-2006 include special benefits for persons age 72 years and over not insured under regular or transitional provisions of Social Security Act. [2] Unnegotiated checks not deducted. [3] Excludes persons with special benefits. [4] Nondisabled only. [5] Includes those with state or area unknown. [6] 2021 data are preliminary.

Source: U.S. Social Security Administration, *Annual Statistical Supplement to the Social Security Bulletin, 2022*, and earlier reports. See also <www.ssa.gov/policy/index.html>.

Table 581. Social Security Trust Funds: 1990 to 2021

[In billions of dollars (286.7 represents $286,700,000,000). Trust fund operations and asset reserves reflect the 12 months of benefits scheduled for payment in each year]

Type of trust fund	1990	2000	2010	2016	2017	2018	2019	2020	2021
OLD-AGE AND SURVIVORS INSURANCE (OASI)									
Total income [1]	286.7	490.5	677.1	797.5	825.6	831.0	917.9	968.3	942.9
Net payroll tax contributions	266.1	421.4	544.8	678.8	706.5	715.9	805.1	856.0	838.2
Taxation of benefits	4.8	11.6	22.1	31.6	35.9	34.5	34.9	39.0	37.2
Interest received [2]	16.4	57.5	108.2	87.0	83.2	80.7	77.9	73.3	67.5
Total expenditures [1]	227.5	358.3	584.9	776.4	806.7	853.5	911.4	961.0	1,001.9
Benefit payments [3]	223.0	352.7	577.4	768.6	798.7	844.9	902.8	952.4	993.1
Assets, end of year	214.2	931.0	2,429.0	2,801.3	2,820.3	2,797.9	2,804.3	2,811.7	2,752.6
DISABILITY INSURANCE (DI)									
Total income [1]	28.8	77.9	104.0	160.0	171.0	172.3	143.9	149.7	145.5
Net payroll tax contributions	28.4	71.1	92.5	157.4	167.1	169.2	139.4	145.3	142.4
Taxation of benefits	0.1	0.7	1.9	1.2	2.0	0.5	1.6	1.7	0.5
Interest received [2]	0.9	6.9	9.3	1.4	1.9	2.6	2.9	2.8	2.6
Total expenditures [1]	25.6	56.8	127.7	145.9	145.8	146.8	147.9	146.3	142.6
Benefit payments [3]	24.8	55.0	124.2	142.8	142.8	143.7	145.1	143.6	140.1
Assets, end of year	11.1	118.5	179.9	46.3	71.5	97.1	93.1	96.6	99.4

[1] Includes other income or expenses not shown separately. [2] Includes relatively small amounts of gifts to the fund. [3] Includes payments for vocational rehabilitation services furnished to disabled persons receiving benefits because of their disabilities. Amounts reflect deductions for unnegotiated benefit checks.

Source: U.S. Social Security Administration, Office of the Chief Actuary, "Statistical Tables," <www.ssa.gov/oact/STATS/index.html>, accessed May 2022.

Table 582. Retirement Employee Benefit Participation by Worker Characteristics: 2010 to 2021

[In percent. Based on National Compensation Survey (NCS). The March 2021 NCS obtained data from 6,007 private industry establishments of all sizes, representing approximately 114.52 million workers; see Appendix III. Defined benefit plans provide retirement benefits based on employer benefit formulas that may take into account salary, years of service, and age. Defined contribution plans provide benefits based on employer and employee contributions to individual employee accounts and the rate of return on money invested; the retirement benefit depends on the account balance at retirement. See source for more information]

Characteristic	Total [1]				Defined benefit				Defined contribution			
	2010	2019	2020	2021	2010	2019	2020	2021	2010	2019	2020	2021
All workers	**50**	**52**	**51**	**51**	**19**	**12**	**11**	**11**	**41**	**47**	**47**	**47**
Management, professional, and related	68	72	71	72	25	18	16	16	60	69	68	69
Service	23	25	25	24	7	6	5	5	18	21	22	20
Sales and office	53	54	52	51	16	9	9	8	46	51	49	49
Natural resources, construction, and maintenance	51	47	48	50	26	16	17	18	40	40	41	42
Production, transportation, and material moving	51	55	54	55	24	15	14	15	38	48	47	48
Full-time	59	61	61	62	22	15	14	14	50	57	57	57
Part-time	21	22	20	21	8	5	5	5	15	19	17	18
Union	82	82	82	84	67	57	54	56	44	48	51	53
Nonunion	46	49	48	49	13	8	8	8	41	47	47	47

[1] Total is less than the sum of the individual retirement items because many employees participate in both types of plans.

Source: U.S. Bureau of Labor Statistics, *National Compensation Survey: Employee Benefits in the United States, March 2021*, September 2021, and previous editions. See also <www.bls.gov/ncs/ebs/home.htm>.

Table 583. Households Owning Individual Retirement Accounts (IRAs): 2000 to 2021

[In percent. Based on the source's Annual Mutual Fund Shareholder Tracking Survey. Prior to 2014, the survey was based on a sample of landline telephone numbers only. Beginning 2014, the survey reflects revised sampling and weighting methodology, including a sample of landline and cellular telephone numbers. The 2021 survey is based on a sample of 3,001 households. See source for details]

Year and characteristic	Any type of IRA [1]	Traditional IRA	Roth IRA	Employer-sponsored IRA [2]	Year and characteristic	Any type of IRA [1]	Traditional IRA	Roth IRA	Employer-sponsored IRA [2]
2000	35.7	28.7	9.2	6.8	2019 [3]	36.1	28.1	19.4	6.1
2005	37.9	30.0	12.8	7.4	2020 [3]	37.3	28.6	20.5	6.7
2010	41.4	32.8	16.6	8.0	**2021, total [3, 4]**	**36.7**	**28.2**	**21.0**	**6.6**
2014 [3]	33.7	25.3	15.6	6.0	Under 35 years	31.0	17.0	20.0	6.0
2015 [3]	32.3	24.4	16.3	5.4	35 to 44 years	36.0	25.0	25.0	9.0
2016 [3]	33.8	25.5	17.4	5.7	45 to 54 years	39.0	28.0	25.0	6.0
2017 [3]	34.8	27.8	19.7	6.0	55 to 64 years	43.0	37.0	25.0	9.0
2018 [3]	33.4	26.0	17.6	5.9	65 years and over	36.0	32.0	15.0	4.0

[1] Excludes ownership of Coverdell Education Savings Accounts, which were referred to as Education IRAs before July 2001. [2] Employer-sponsored IRAs include SEP IRAs, SAR-SEP IRAs, and SIMPLE IRAs. [3] Beginning 2014, fluctuating incidence likely results in part from a revised sampling methodology. See source for details. [4] Age is based on the age of the sole or co-decision maker for household saving and investing.

Source: Investment Company Institute, Washington, DC, Holden, Sarah, and Daniel Schrass, "Appendix: The Role of IRAs in US Households' Saving for Retirement, 2021," ICI Research Perspective 28, No. 1, January 2022 ©. See also <www.ici.org/research/retirement>.

Table 584. State and Local Government Retirement Systems—Beneficiaries and Finances: 2018 to 2021

[In billions of dollars (221.1 represents $221,100,000,000), except as indicated. For fiscal years closed during the 12 months ending June 30. Covers public employee pension systems classified as defined benefit plans. Based on the Annual Survey of Public Pensions. For state-administered pension plans, each pension fund is treated as a separate unit of analysis rather than as part of a larger system]

Year and level of government	Number of bene-ficiaries (1,000)	Receipts				Benefits and withdrawals			Cash and investment holdings
		Contributions			Earnings on invest-ments	Total benefits paid	Admin-istrative costs	With-drawals	
		Total	Employee	Govern-ment					
2018: All systems.........	11,043	221.1	55.9	165.2	99.7	310.4	19.3	7.6	4,354.2
State-administered......	9,415	173.6	46.8	126.8	79.9	254.5	14.8	6.3	3,541.4
Locally administered....	1,628	47.6	9.1	38.5	19.8	55.9	4.5	1.4	812.8
2019: All systems........	11,239	223.9	56.6	167.3	94.8	323.8	20.4	7.0	4,440.6
State-administered......	9,634	177.2	47.7	129.6	76.4	264.9	16.0	5.7	3,626.4
Locally administered....	1,605	46.7	9.0	37.7	18.4	58.9	4.4	1.3	814.1
2020: All systems.........	11,464	237.7	58.1	179.6	98.8	330.7	21.1	7.0	4,512.2
State-administered......	9,811	189.4	48.6	140.8	80.6	269.5	16.3	5.4	3,665.4
Locally administered....	1,653	48.2	9.4	38.8	18.3	61.2	4.8	1.6	846.8
2021: All systems.......	**11,693**	**244.1**	**58.3**	**185.8**	**113.4**	**338.7**	**25.3**	**7.1**	**5,581.9**
State-administered......	10,021	194.5	48.7	145.8	91.9	274.2	19.5	5.3	4,561.4
Locally administered....	1,672	49.6	9.6	40.0	21.6	64.4	5.8	1.8	1,020.5

Source: U.S. Census Bureau, Annual Survey of Public Pensions, "Annual Survey of Public Pensions: State & Local Tables," <www.census.gov/programs-surveys/aspp.html>, accessed June 2022.

Table 585. Defined Benefit Retirement Plan Participation Among Workers by Plan Status: 2021

[In percent. All workers participating in defined benefit plans = 100 percent. Based on the March 2021 National Compensation Survey; survey drew responses from 6,007 private industry establishments of all sizes, representing about 114.52 million workers. Excludes farm and private households, the self-employed, Federal government, and establishments with no workers in the survey scope. For more information, see Appendix III, and source]

Characteristic	Open plans [1]	Frozen plans [2]			Workers in plans frozen 6 or more years
		All participants accrue benefits	Some participants accrue benefits	No participants accrue benefits [3]	
All workers..........	**57**	**23**	**4**	**15**	**89**
OCCUPATION					
Management, professional, and related............	49	24	6	21	87
Management, business, and financial...............	46	22	6	26	83
Professional and related..........	51	25	7	18	91
Service..........	79	14	(S)	(S)	(NA)
Sales and office..........	48	25	4	24	89
Sales and related..........	45	18	4	33	(NA)
Office and administrative support..........	49	27	3	21	86
Natural resources, construction, and maintenance..........	79	16	1	4	(NA)
Construction, extraction, farming, fishing, and forestry...........	88	10	(S)	(S)	(NA)
Installation, maintenance, and repair..........	64	25	(S)	(S)	(NA)
Production, transportation, and material moving..........	58	29	4	9	88
Production..........	37	39	8	16	(NA)
Transportation and material moving..........	73	21	1	4	(NA)
WORK STATUS					
Full time..........	55	23	5	17	89
Part time..........	74	21	(S)	(S)	(NA)
UNION STATUS					
Union..........	77	17	1	5	95
Nonunion..........	45	26	7	22	87
AVERAGE WAGE PERCENTILE [4]					
Lowest 25 percent..........	62	27	(S)	(S)	(NA)
Lowest 10 percent..........	85	(S)	(S)	(S)	(NA)
Second 25 percent..........	62	22	3	14	89
Third 25 percent..........	55	26	5	15	87
Highest 25 percent..........	56	21	5	17	89
Highest 10 percent..........	47	26	5	23	89
INDUSTRY					
Goods-producing industries..........	49	29	9	13	95
Manufacturing..........	27	42	13	17	(NA)
Service-providing industries..........	60	21	3	16	86
Trade, transportation, and utilities..........	66	28	(S)	(S)	87
Information..........	32	37	(S)	31	(NA)
Financial activities..........	38	21	2	39	78
Professional and business services..........	64	7	6	23	(NA)
Education and health services..........	69	19	4	8	93

NA Not available. S No workers in this category or data do not meet publication standards. [1] Plans open to new participants. [2] New employees are not allowed in the plan. Benefit accruals may continue for existing participants. [3] Participants in these plans stopped accruing benefits on the date the plan was frozen. The benefit the employee receives is calculated as of the day the plan was frozen. [4] Based on the average wage for the occupation, which may include workers with earnings both above and below the threshold. For values, see "Technical Note" in source.

Source: U.S. Bureau of Labor Statistics, *National Compensation Survey: Employee Benefits in the United States, March 2021*, September 2021. See also <www.bls.gov/ncs/ebs/home.htm>.

Table 586. Private Pension Plans—Summary by Type of Plan: 2000 to 2019

[In units as indicated (735.7 represents 735,700). Pension plans include defined benefit plans, and defined contribution plans. A defined benefit plan, funded by the employer, promises a specific monthly benefit at retirement, often determined by a formula that includes factors such as salary, age, and job tenure. A defined contribution plan requires the employee to make contributions to an individual account; employers may add contributions to accounts for each employee. The retirement benefit is dependent upon the account balance at retirement, which will reflect contributions, investment gains or losses, and fees charged to the account. Employee Stock Ownership Plans (ESOP) and 401(k) plans are included among defined contribution plans. Data are based on Form 5500 series reports filed with the Department of Labor and exclude (1) selected pension plans qualified under sections 403(b), 457(b) and 457(f) of the Internal Revenue Code, (2) most SARSEP, SEP and SIMPLE IRA plans, (3) unfunded excess benefit plans, (4) selected church plans, (5) unfunded pension plan for select group of management or highly compensated employees, (6) individual retirement accounts (IRAs), and (7) governmental plans]

Item	Unit	Total				Defined benefit plan				Defined contribution plan			
		2000	2010	2018	2019	2000	2010	2018	2019	2000	2010	2018	2019
Number of plans [1]	1,000	735.7	701.0	721.9	733.7	48.8	46.5	46.9	46.9	686.9	654.5	675.0	686.8
Total participants [2]	Million	103.3	129.7	139.8	141.9	41.6	41.4	34.0	32.8	61.7	88.3	105.8	109.1
Active participants [3]	Million	73.1	90.6	96.4	98.1	22.2	17.2	13.1	12.6	50.9	73.4	83.4	85.5
Assets [4]	Bil. dol.	4,203	6,282	9,233	10,707	1,986	2,448	2,968	3,274	2,216	3,833	6,265	7,433
Contributions [5]	Bil. dol.	232	445	630	673	33	131	98	103	199	314	532	570
Benefits [6]	Bil. dol.	341	457	795	857	128	170	244	258	214	287	551	599

[1] Excludes all plans covering only one participant. [2] Includes active, retired, and separated vested participants not yet in pay status. Also includes double counting of workers in more than one plan. [3] Active participants includes individuals who are eligible to elect to have the employer make payments to a 401(k) type plan (even if individuals are not contributing) and nonvested individuals who are earning or retaining credited service under the plan. [4] Asset amounts shown exclude funds held by life insurance companies under allocated group insurance contracts for payment of retirement benefits. [5] Includes both employer and employee contributions. [6] Includes benefits paid directly from trust funds and premium payments made from plans to insurance carriers. Excludes benefits paid directly by insurance carriers.

Source: U.S. Department of Labor, Employee Benefits Security Administration, Retirement Bulletins, *Private Pension Plan Bulletin Historical Tables and Graphs, 1975-2019,* September 2021. See also <www.dol.gov/agencies/ebsa/researchers/statistics/retirement-bulletins/private-pension-plan>.

Table 587. Characteristics of U.S. Households Owning Individual Retirement Accounts (IRAs): 2021

[Data are based on a 2021 mutual fund shareholder tracking survey of 3,001 households conducted via landline and cellular telephone; and a 2021 IRA owners survey of 3,257 U.S. households owning traditional or Roth IRAs, conducted via a self-administered survey online. See source for details and changes in methodology]

Characteristic	Unit	Households owning IRAs				Households not owning IRAs
		Total	Traditional IRA	Roth IRA	Employer-sponsored [1]	
MEDIAN PER HOUSEHOLD						
Age of household sole or co-decision maker for saving & investing	Years	54	58	51	50	51
Household income [2]	Dollars	100,000	112,500	112,500	125,000	50,000
Household financial assets [3]	Dollars	350,000	450,000	420,000	400,000	45,000
Household financial assets in traditional or Roth IRAs	Dollars	100,000	160,000	105,000	(NA)	(X)
Share of household financial assets in type of IRA indicated	Percent	40	31	15	(NA)	(X)
PERCENT OF HOUSEHOLDS						
Household has defined contribution account or defined benefit plan coverage (total) [4]	Percent	82	84	88	84	42
Defined contribution retirement plan account	Percent	73	75	82	71	32
Defined benefit plan coverage	Percent	38	44	42	42	20
Types of IRAs owned: [4]						
Traditional IRA	Percent	77	100	67	63	(X)
Roth IRA	Percent	57	50	100	55	(X)
Employer-sponsored IRA [1]	Percent	18	15	17	100	(X)

X Not applicable. NA Not available. [1] Employer-sponsored IRAs include SEP IRAs, SAR-SEP IRAs, and SIMPLE IRAs. [2] Total reported is household income before taxes in 2020. [3] Household financial assets include assets in employer-sponsored retirement plans but exclude the household's primary residence. [4] Multiple responses are included.

Source: Investment Company Institute, Washington, DC. Holden, Sarah, and Daniel Schrass, "Appendix: The Role of IRAs in US Households' Saving for Retirement, 2021," *ICI Research Perspective* 28, No. 1, January 2022 ©. See also <www.ici.org/research/retirement>.

Table 588. Households with Assets in Individual Retirement Accounts (IRAs) by Type of IRA: 2020 and 2021

[Shown as percent of households with assets in IRAs, by household asset size group. Data are based on an annual survey of approximately 3,200 U.S. households owning traditional IRAs and Roth IRAs, conducted via a self-administered survey online. The IRA Owners Survey excludes households owning only employer-sponsored IRAs (SEP, SAR-SEP, and SIMPLE IRAs) or Coverdell Education Savings Accounts (education IRAs). See source for details]

Size of assets	Unit	2020			2021		
		Total assets in IRAs	Type of IRA owned		Total assets in IRAs	Type of IRA owned	
			Traditional IRAs	Roth IRAs		Traditional IRAs	Roth IRAs
PERCENT DISTRIBUTION OF HOUSEHOLDS							
Less than $10,000.............................	Percent	13	15	23	13	14	22
$10,000 to $24,999............................	Percent	13	13	19	10	11	19
$25,000 to $49,999............................	Percent	11	13	16	11	12	14
$50,000 to $99,999............................	Percent	15	14	18	14	15	18
$100,000 to $249,999.........................	Percent	18	20	16	19	19	15
$250,000 or more..............................	Percent	30	25	8	33	29	12
TOTAL ASSETS IN IRAs							
Mean...	Dollars	218,400	198,700	83,700	244,790	222,850	98,530
Median..	Dollars	87,500	78,000	35,000	100,000	87,500	40,000

Source: Investment Company Institute, Washington, DC. Holden, Sarah, and Daniel Schrass, "Appendix: The Role of IRAs in US Households' Saving for Retirement, 2021," *ICI Research Perspective* 28, No. 1, January 2022 ©, and previous edition. See also <www.ici.org/research/retirement>.

Table 589. Defined Contribution 401(k) Type Plans, Active Participants, Assets, Contributions, Benefits, and Return Rates: 1990 to 2019

[Participants in thousands (19,466 represents 19,466,000); values in millions of dollars (384,854 represents $384,854,000,000). Excludes "one-participant plans." Based on Form 5500 filings with Department of Labor. See source for methodology]

Year	Number of 401(k) type plans	Active participants [1] (1,000)	Total assets [2] (mil. dol.)	Total contributions [3] (mil. dol.)	Total benefits [4] (mil. dol.)	Investment rates of return [5]
1990................	97,614	19,466	384,854	48,998	32,028	(NA)
2000................	348,053	39,847	1,724,549	169,238	172,211	-3.8
2005................	436,207	54,623	2,395,792	223,533	189,822	6.3
2006................	465,653	58,351	2,768,242	251,233	229,217	12.4
2007................	490,917	59,566	2,981,522	273,235	262,108	7.6
2008................	511,583	59,976	2,230,188	285,773	233,452	-24.9
2009................	512,464	60,285	2,734,064	258,357	208,467	18.8
2010................	518,675	60,510	3,142,141	267,584	245,474	12.0
2011................	513,496	61,371	3,146,851	285,679	252,692	0.1
2012................	516,293	63,088	3,530,122	306,092	284,677	11.2
2013................	527,047	64,495	4,179,351	327,886	328,680	18.3
2014................	533,769	62,651	4,399,891	349,216	365,657	6.7
2015................	546,896	65,307	4,382,033	377,743	385,907	0.1
2016................	560,373	67,121	4,738,481	398,920	391,540	7.6
2017................	571,841	68,187	5,476,365	429,440	425,013	15.8
2018................	588,499	70,335	5,229,194	464,578	473,790	-4.5
2019................	604,424	72,202	6,242,230	499,522	519,038	20.1

NA Not available. [1] Since 2005, includes individuals who are eligible to elect to have the employer make payments to a 401(k) type plan (even if individuals are not contributing), and nonvested individuals who are earning or retaining credited service under the plan. Prior to 2005, active participants were adjusted to exclude individuals who were not contributing to the retirement plan and not entitled to receive benefits. Between 2009 and 2013, all participants reported on the Form 5500-SF were assumed to be active. Since 2014, active participants are separately reported on the Form 5500-SF. [2] Excludes funds held by life insurance companies under allocated group insurance contracts for payment of retirement benefits. [3] Includes both employer and employee contributions. [4] Includes both benefits paid directly from trust funds and premium payments made by plans to insurance carriers. Amounts exclude benefits paid directly by insurance carriers. [5] For plans with 100 or more participants.

Source: U.S. Department of Labor, Employee Benefits Security Administration, Retirement Bulletins, *Private Pension Plan Bulletin Historical Tables and Graphs, 1975-2019*, September 2021. See also <www.dol.gov/agencies/ebsa/researchers/statistics/retirement-bulletins/private-pension-plan>.

Table 590. State Unemployment Insurance—Summary: 2000 to 2020

[In units as indicated (2,110 represents 2,110,000). Includes unemployment compensation for state and local government employees where covered by state law]

Item	Unit	2000	2010	2014	2015	2016	2017	2018	2019	2020
Insured unemployment, average weekly.........	1,000	2,110	4,487	2,574	2,237	2,099	1,948	1,755	1,684	10,099
Percent of covered employment [1]...............	Percent	1.7	3.6	1.9	1.6	1.5	1.4	1.2	1.2	7.4
Percent of civilian unemployed..................	Percent	37.1	30.3	26.8	27.0	27.1	27.9	27.8	28.1	78.0
Unemployment benefits, average weekly........	Dollars	221	299	315	329	344	351	356	369	319
Percent of weekly wage.........................	Percent	32.9	33.7	32.2	32.6	33.7	33.3	32.7	32.7	26.0
Weeks compensated.............................	Million	96.0	203.1	115.1	100.7	94.8	87.6	79.3	76.0	471.6
Beneficiaries, first payments..................	1,000	7,033	10,727	7,043	6,506	6,097	5,696	5,167	5,125	30,829
Average duration of benefits [2]....................	Weeks	13.7	18.9	16.3	15.5	15.5	15.4	15.3	14.8	15.3
Claimants exhausting benefits...................	1,000	2,144	6,365	3,029	2,510	2,324	2,120	1,928	1,760	11,435
Exhaustion rate (percent of first payments) [3]...	Percent	31.8	53.4	40.3	38.0	36.3	35.4	35.5	34.7	43.2
Contributions collected [4].........................	Bil. dol.	19.9	35.9	43.9	41.8	38.9	36.8	34.9	33.6	32.0
Benefits paid....................................	Bil. dol.	19.4	53.9	32.4	29.8	29.5	27.8	25.6	25.5	131.7
Unemployment trust fund reserves [5].............	Bil. dol.	54.1	9.5	30.4	38.8	47.0	55.2	66.6	75.7	24.7
Average employer tax rate [6].....................	Percent	1.8	3.0	2.9	2.7	2.4	2.2	2.0	1.9	1.7

[1] Insured unemployment as percent of average covered employment. [2] Weeks compensated during the year divided by the number of first payments. May include more than one period of continuous unemployment. [3] Percent of claimants who started receiving unemployment insurance benefits who also received the maximum benefits they were entitled to before the end of their benefit year. Based on first payments for 12-month period ending June 30. [4] Contributions collected through unemployment taxes paid by employers and by employees in states that tax workers. [5] Reserves as of December 31 are the funds on deposit in a State's account, as reported by the U.S. Treasury. Trust fund balances are the major portion of reserves. The reserves for all States have been adjusted to contain amounts loaned or advanced from the Federal Unemployment Account. These advances, which can be used only for the payment of unemployment benefits, must be repaid. [6] As percent of taxable wages.

Source: U.S. Department of Labor, Employment and Training Administration, Unemployment Insurance Data, "Benefits and Claims: Annual Program and Financial Data (Handbook 394)," <oui.doleta.gov/unemploy/DataDashboard.asp>, accessed February 2022.

Table 591. State Unemployment Insurance by State and Island Area: 2020

[In units as indicated (30,829 represents 30,829,000). See headnote, Table 590. For state data on insured unemployment, see Table 664. Please note that temporary provisions made during the coronavirus disease 2019 (COVID-19) pandemic may have affected usual unemployment insurance procedures and reporting]

State and Island Area	Beneficiaries, first payments (1,000)	Benefits paid (mil. dol.)	Avg. weekly unemployment benefits (dol.)	Average duration of benefits (weeks)	State and Island Area	Beneficiaries, first payments (1,000)	Benefits paid (mil. dol.)	Avg. weekly unemployment benefits (dol.)	Average duration of benefits (weeks)
Total [1].....	30,829	131,688	319	15.3	MT..........	16	279	363	(NA)
AL..........	363	793	252	9.0	NE..........	86	327	298	14.3
AK..........	73	308	282	16.1	NV..........	459	2,391	357	17.6
AZ..........	423	1,362	238	14.8	NH..........	134	277	259	10.6
AR..........	194	369	229	10.1	NJ..........	812	5,591	417	18.6
CA..........	5,002	25,857	294	18.3	NM..........	156	702	317	17.8
CO..........	512	2,425	380	14.1	NY..........	2,303	12,859	343	19.3
CT..........	339	1,713	313	21.4	NC..........	734	1,573	226	9.9
DE..........	74	284	251	17.4	ND..........	75	363	439	11.9
DC..........	88	610	351	21.9	OH..........	922	3,453	337	13.1
FL..........	1,668	3,138	232	9.3	OK..........	346	1,197	340	11.3
GA..........	1,039	3,808	262	16.0	OR..........	429	2,036	377	13.5
HI..........	196	1,498	454	19.0	PA..........	1,364	6,234	348	15.7
ID..........	96	239	307	10.0	RI..........	145	553	326	13.7
IL..........	1,297	6,144	335	15.5	SC..........	372	965	237	12.4
IN..........	600	1,335	247	11.7	SD..........	38	92	298	10.0
IA..........	316	1,173	349	12.2	TN..........	490	1,371	217	14.1
KS..........	390	723	365	7.1	TX..........	2,060	10,330	367	15.9
KY..........	365	1,847	315	13.3	UT..........	151	587	365	12.0
LA..........	474	1,519	185	17.1	VT..........	80	341	338	15.2
ME..........	134	134	317	13.7	VA..........	1,241	1,814	267	6.8
MD..........	419	1,643	325	13.9	WA..........	578	3,661	444	18.7
MA..........	960	5,531	448	15.3	WV..........	158	522	255	14.5
MI..........	1,284	4,708	315	13.9	WI..........	396	1,428	295	15.2
MN..........	45	3,036	390	(NA)	WY..........	33	174	405	14.0
MS..........	250	550	190	13.9	PR..........	277	689	235	17.0
MO..........	364	1,087	246	13.9	VI..........	8	45	373	17.4

NA Not available. [1] Includes all States, District of Columbia, Puerto Rico, and Virgin Islands.

Source: U.S. Department of Labor, Employment and Training Administration, Unemployment Insurance Data, "Benefits and Claims: Annual Program and Financial Data (Handbook 394)," <oui.doleta.gov/unemploy/DataDashboard.asp>, accessed February 2022.

Table 592. Workers' Compensation Costs and Payments: 2000 to 2019

[In units as indicated (127.1 represents 127,100,000). See headnote, Table 593]

Item	2000	2010	2011	2012	2013	2014	2015	2016	2017	2018	2019
Workers covered (mil.)...............	127.1	124.6	125.9	127.9	130.1	132.8	136	138.5	140.4	142.6	144.4
Covered wages (bil. dol.)...........	4,495	5,834	6,058	6,326	6,835	6,840	7,211	7,432	7,787	8,178	8,560
Employer costs [1] (bil. dol.)............	**62.4**	**74.9**	**81.2**	**87.1**	**91.8**	**96.6**	**99.3**	**100.2**	**100.8**	**101.4**	**100.2**
Private carriers.................	36.9	43.8	47.7	52.5	56.3	58.8	60.9	61.7	62.3	62.0	60.9
State funds.......................	9.2	9.9	10.7	11.4	12.5	13.8	13.7	13.5	12.7	12.6	12.0
Self-insured employers...........	12.7	17.0	18.4	18.8	18.4	19.1	19.2	19.3	19.6	19.8	19.8
Federal programs [2].................	3.6	4.2	4.4	4.5	4.6	4.9	5.4	5.7	6.3	7.0	7.5
Benefits paid [3] (bil. dol.)..............	**47.7**	**58.5**	**61.4**	**62.7**	**63.4**	**63.6**	**62.8**	**62.6**	**62.5**	**62.9**	**63.0**
By private carriers...............	26.9	31.1	33.0	33.9	35.2	35.3	34.8	34.8	34.6	34.9	35.1
From state funds..................	7.4	9.8	9.8	10.0	9.5	9.3	9.1	8.9	8.9	8.9	8.8
Self-insured employers...........	10.5	13.9	14.8	15.0	15.0	15.4	15.2	15.3	15.5	15.8	15.8
Federal programs [2].................	3.0	3.7	3.8	3.8	3.7	3.7	3.7	3.6	3.5	3.5	3.4
Type of benefit:											
Medical........................	20.9	28.7	30.8	31.3	32.3	32.4	31.6	31.5	31.1	31.4	31.3
Cash...........................	26.8	29.8	30.6	31.4	31.2	31.2	31.1	31.1	31.3	31.6	31.8
Per $100 of covered wages: (dol.)											
Employer costs.................	1.39	1.28	1.34	1.38	1.34	1.41	1.38	1.35	1.29	1.24	1.17
Benefits paid..................	1.06	1.00	1.01	0.99	0.93	0.93	0.87	0.84	0.80	0.77	0.74

[1] Estimates of employer costs are equal to the sum of: premiums and deductibles paid to private insurers and state funds; benefits and administrative costs paid by self-insured employers; and assessments paid to special funds (e.g., second-injury funds). [2] Includes benefits paid plus administrative costs. Also includes costs to the Federal government under the Federal Employees' Compensation Act and employer costs associated with the Federal Black Lung Disability Trust fund, and employer costs associated with the Longshore and Harbor Workers' Compensation Act. [3] Benefits are calendar-year payments to injured workers and to providers of their medical care, including benefits paid by employers through deductible policies.

Source: National Academy of Social Insurance, Washington, DC, *Workers' Compensation: Benefits, Costs, and Coverage, 2019*, October 2021 ©. See also <www.nasi.org/research/workers-compensation-2/>.

Table 593. Workers' Compensation Payments by State: 2015 to 2019

[In millions of dollars (62,780 represents $62,780,000,000). Calendar-year data. Workers' compensation provides medical care, rehabilitation, and cash benefits for workers who are injured on the job or who contract work-related illnesses. It also pays benefits to families of workers who die of work-related causes. Workers' compensation benefits are paid by private insurance carriers, by state or federal workers' compensation funds, or by self-insured employers. See source for data estimation methodology]

State	2015	2016	2017	2018	2019	State	2015	2016	2017	2018	2019
Total...................	**62,780**	**62,607**	**62,450**	**62,949**	**63,046**	Missouri..................	924	937	964	978	990
						Montana.................	253	261	254	237	230
Alabama...............	617	601	601	643	670	Nebraska...............	300	312	311	319	323
Alaska.................	240	226	213	226	207	Nevada.................	342	355	354	394	402
Arizona................	740	752	744	748	757	New Hampshire.........	216	206	210	209	210
Arkansas..............	197	207	215	201	208	New Jersey...........	2,338	2,368	2,463	2,417	2,516
California.............	12,029	12,171	12,213	12,303	12,404	New Mexico...........	327	309	297	300	319
Colorado..............	835	800	811	776	833	New York.............	5,895	6,003	6,223	6,288	6,192
Connecticut...........	982	895	911	871	890	North Carolina.........	1,215	1,195	1,122	1,076	1,099
Delaware..............	228	225	221	211	193	North Dakota...........	180	166	157	149	143
District of Columbia.....	160	164	163	174	179	Ohio..................	2,064	2,014	1,881	1,858	1,824
Florida.................	3,528	3,532	3,543	3,586	3,565	Oklahoma.............	707	604	576	545	522
Georgia................	1,315	1,366	1,382	1,445	1,423	Oregon...............	633	631	682	669	699
Hawaii..................	298	306	325	358	382	Pennsylvania..........	2,975	3,124	2,818	2,904	2,892
Idaho..................	263	268	283	292	319	Rhode Island..........	155	149	148	147	156
Illinois................	2,389	2,338	2,329	2,240	2,185	South Carolina.........	896	910	929	979	1,027
Indiana................	567	576	595	581	605	South Dakota..........	106	103	98	107	115
Iowa...................	614	660	653	658	628	Tennessee.............	664	615	599	547	552
Kansas................	423	423	421	406	431	Texas.................	1,554	1,474	1,427	1,522	1,518
Kentucky..............	675	635	606	636	612	Utah..................	269	274	275	281	290
Louisiana..............	982	983	982	1,032	982	Vermont...............	151	140	144	139	144
Maine.................	233	241	255	262	252	Virginia...............	920	947	984	946	916
Maryland..............	965	895	931	1,021	902	Washington............	2,412	2,437	2,465	2,538	2,614
Massachusetts.........	1,090	1,158	1,192	1,231	1,279	West Virginia..........	417	415	396	412	398
Michigan..............	1,078	955	918	910	899	Wisconsin.............	1,167	1,169	1,168	1,195	1,223
Minnesota.............	1,033	1,031	1,017	1,054	1,065	Wyoming..............	178	175	176	165	180
Mississippi............	332	306	318	304	305	**Federal, total [1]**.........	**3,706**	**3,603**	**3,483**	**3,455**	**3,375**

[1] Federal benefits include: those paid under the Federal Employees' Compensation Act for civilian employees; the portion of the black lung benefit program that is financed by employers; and a portion of benefits under the Longshore and Harbor Workers' Compensation Act (LHWCA) that are not reflected in state data, namely, benefits paid by self-insured employers and by special funds under the LHWCA. See Appendix B in source for more information about federal programs.

Source: National Academy of Social Insurance, Washington, DC, *Workers' Compensation: Benefits, Costs, and Coverage, 2019*, October 2021 ©. See also <www.nasi.org/research/workers-compensation-2/>.

Table 594. Supplemental Security Income (SSI)—Recipients and Payments: 1990 to 2020

[In units as indicated (4,817 represents 4,817,000). Recipients and monthly payment as of December. Payments are federally administered, for the calendar year. Includes persons with a federal SSI payment and/or state supplementation]

Program	Unit	1990	2000	2010	2015	2016	2017	2018	2019	2020
Recipients, total...............	**1,000**	**4,817**	**6,602**	**7,912**	**8,310**	**8,251**	**8,228**	**8,129**	**8,077**	**7,960**
Aged..............................	1,000	1,454	1,289	1,184	1,157	1,165	1,176	1,169	1,167	1,136
Blind..............................	1,000	84	79	69	68	68	69	69	69	68
Disabled..........................	1,000	3,279	5,234	6,659	7,084	7,018	6,982	6,891	6,841	6,756
Payments, total [1]...............	**Mil. dol.**	**16,133**	**30,672**	**48,195**	**54,966**	**54,799**	**54,516**	**54,847**	**55,852**	**56,285**
Aged..............................	Mil. dol.	3,559	4,540	5,454	5,729	5,797	5,838	5,924	6,070	6,139
Blind..............................	Mil. dol.	329	386	423	448	455	458	463	476	482
Disabled..........................	Mil. dol.	12,245	25,746	42,317	48,788	48,547	48,220	48,460	49,307	49,664
Average monthly payment.....	**Dollars**	**276**	**379**	**501**	**541**	**542**	**542**	**551**	**566**	**576**
Aged..............................	Dollars	208	300	400	428	429	429	437	449	458
Blind..............................	Dollars	319	413	522	558	560	560	569	583	592
Disabled..........................	Dollars	303	398	518	560	561	561	570	585	595

[1] Totals for Aged, Blind, and Disabled are derived. The derivation creates slight discrepancies summing to total.

Source: U.S. Social Security Administration, *Annual Statistical Supplement to the Social Security Bulletin, 2021*, December 2021; and *SSI Annual Statistical Report, 2020,* October 2021. See also <www.ssa.gov/policy/docs/statcomps/supplement/index.html> and <www.ssa.gov/policy/docs/statcomps/ssi_asr/index.html>.

Table 595. Supplemental Security Income (SSI)—Recipients and Payments by State and Other Area: 2010 to 2020

[In units as indicated (7,912 represents 7,912,000). Recipients as of December; payments for calendar year. Data cover federal SSI payments and/or federally administered state supplementation]

State and other area	Recipients (1,000)		Payments (mil. dol.)			State and other area	Recipients (1,000)		Payments (mil. dol.)		
	2010	2020	2010	2019	2020		2010	2020	2010	2019	2020
Total [1]....	**7,912**	**7,960**	**48,195**	**55,852**	**56,285**	MO..........	134	135	785	907	914
U.S.........	**7,911**	**7,959**	**48,189**	**55,845**	**56,278**	MT..........	18	17	98	114	115
AL..........	172	157	996	1,066	1,067	NE..........	26	29	144	188	194
AK..........	12	12	70	81	82	NV..........	41	56	241	394	401
AZ..........	110	119	644	815	834	NH..........	18	18	103	118	119
AR..........	107	103	603	702	712	NJ..........	169	174	1,001	1,196	1,195
CA..........	1,269	1,194	8,870	9,445	9,417	NM..........	60	61	340	405	407
CO..........	66	72	377	492	491	NY..........	681	602	4,445	4,212	4,208
CT..........	58	67	340	454	465	NC..........	219	228	1,243	1,534	1,559
DE..........	16	17	91	119	122	ND..........	8	8	43	53	54
DC..........	24	25	153	187	187	OH..........	286	306	1,784	2,155	2,182
FL..........	484	575	2,760	3,844	3,922	OK..........	94	96	541	650	667
GA..........	228	258	1,317	1,755	1,780	OR..........	75	88	439	612	621
HI..........	25	22	157	161	161	PA..........	358	348	2,229	2,508	2,521
ID..........	27	31	155	205	208	RI..........	33	32	201	217	220
IL..........	273	260	1,662	1,831	1,838	SC..........	112	114	635	770	778
IN..........	118	127	716	896	908	SD..........	14	15	75	93	96
IA..........	48	52	266	338	345	TN..........	175	173	1,023	1,186	1,195
KS..........	46	47	269	322	325	TX..........	617	633	3,316	4,133	4,182
KY..........	192	168	1,116	1,148	1,148	UT..........	28	31	160	217	219
LA..........	175	170	989	1,177	1,182	VT..........	15	15	87	101	103
ME..........	35	36	196	237	239	VA..........	148	155	832	1,040	1,062
MD..........	107	120	658	863	876	WA..........	137	147	881	1,048	1,062
MA..........	193	179	1,211	1,206	1,219	WV..........	80	69	472	484	480
MI..........	254	266	1,581	1,909	1,913	WI..........	107	116	625	803	810
MN..........	86	93	516	653	665	WY..........	6	7	35	45	46
MS..........	126	114	699	756	760	MP [2]........	1	1	6	8	8

[1] Includes Northern Marianas and recipients whose residence was "unknown." Total may not equal sum due to rounding. [2] Northern Marianas.

Source: U.S. Social Security Administration, *Annual Statistical Supplement to the Social Security Bulletin, 2021*, December 2021, and previous editions. See also <www.ssa.gov/policy/docs/statcomps/supplement/index.html>.

Table 596. Temporary Assistance for Needy Families (TANF)—Families and Recipients: 1980 to 2021

[In thousands (3,712 represents 3,712,000). Average monthly families and recipients for the calendar year through 2018; beginning with 2019, data are shown for the fiscal year ending in September. Prior to TANF, the cash assistance program to families was called Aid to Families with Dependent Children (1980–1996). Under the Personal Responsibility and Work Opportunity Reconciliation Act of 1996, the program became TANF. See text, this section. Includes Puerto Rico, Guam, and Virgin Islands]

Year	Families	Recipients	Year	Families	Recipients	Year	Families	Recipients
1980..........	3,712	10,774	2006..........	1,777	4,148	2014..........	1,476	3,407
1990..........	4,057	11,695	2007..........	1,674	3,897	2015..........	1,300	3,010
2000..........	2,215	5,778	2008..........	1,633	3,795	2016..........	1,174	2,678
2001..........	2,104	5,359	2009..........	1,769	4,154	2017..........	1,075	2,486
2002..........	2,048	5,069	2010..........	1,858	4,403	2018..........	984	2,197
2003..........	2,024	4,929	2011..........	1,846	4,363	2019 [1]........	917	2,045
2004..........	1,979	4,748	2012..........	1,723	4,017	2020 [1]........	894	2,037
2005..........	1,894	4,469	2013..........	1,612	3,713	2021 [1]........	804	1,848

[1] Data are for the fiscal year ending in September of the year shown.

Source: U.S. Department of Health and Human Services, Administration for Children and Families, State TANF Data and Reports, "Caseload Data," <www.acf.hhs.gov/ofa/programs/tanf/data-reports>, accessed April 2022.

Table 597. Temporary Assistance for Needy Families (TANF)—Recipients by State and Island Area: 2010 to 2021

[In thousands (1,858.2 represents 1,858,200). Average monthly families and recipients for the calendar year through 2018; beginning with 2019, data are shown for the fiscal year ending in September. See headnote, Table 596]

State and Island Area	Families			Recipients			State and Island Area	Families			Recipients		
	2010	2020[1]	2021[1]	2010	2020[1]	2021[1]		2010	2020[1]	2021[1]	2010	2020[1]	2021[1]
Total[2]	**1,858.2**	**894.1**	**804.1**	**4,402.9**	**2,036.5**	**1,847.6**	MT	3.7	3.0	2.2	9.4	7.2	4.9
U.S.	1,842.9	889.4	799.2	4,361.3	2,023.6	1,834.4	NE	7.6	4.1	3.5	18.3	9.7	8.0
AL	22.0	7.2	6.3	53.5	16.2	14.1	NV	10.5	7.8	5.7	27.1	20.2	14.5
AK	3.4	2.3	1.8	9.3	6.0	4.7	NH	5.3	3.5	3.0	11.0	7.2	6.1
AZ	27.7	7.8	7.0	60.3	16.2	14.6	NJ	33.9	9.3	8.9	80.7	22.1	21.6
AR	8.5	2.3	1.7	19.3	5.2	3.7	NM	20.3	10.6	11.6	53.5	26.6	29.9
CA	583.9	277.8	237.6	1,437.4	688.4	606.8	NY	121.8	81.3	75.1	272.3	182.9	166.7
CO	11.4	13.9	11.6	29.3	34.2	28.1	NC	23.9	13.9	13.6	45.8	24.3	24.7
CT	17.1	7.3	5.7	34.0	15.3	12.1	ND	2.0	1.0	1.1	5.1	2.4	2.8
DE	5.4	3.0	2.7	15.4	8.3	7.4	OH	103.5	52.0	48.1	238.4	96.8	86.6
DC	8.1	7.4	6.4	18.5	21.6	19.1	OK	9.3	5.6	5.0	21.0	12.6	11.2
FL	57.6	40.5	38.1	105.5	68.7	67.9	OR	28.0	14.6	14.4	72.2	32.6	31.9
GA	20.4	8.5	7.7	37.8	15.5	14.6	PA	53.6	36.1	27.2	130.4	87.7	64.7
HI	9.1	5.0	6.6	25.9	14.4	20.3	RI	7.2	3.5	2.3	16.8	8.6	5.5
ID	1.8	1.9	1.7	2.7	2.8	2.4	SC	18.6	7.8	7.3	43.8	17.5	16.7
IL	23.4	10.7	10.5	66.2	21.2	20.7	SD	3.2	2.8	2.6	6.8	5.6	5.1
IN	35.1	6.3	7.6	86.2	13.7	17.9	TN	61.5	17.3	14.3	157.2	36.5	29.2
IA	17.9	7.2	6.2	45.7	16.9	14.9	TX	51.2	20.8	18.2	116.7	45.5	37.2
KS	14.8	4.1	3.1	38.3	4.1	3.1	UT	6.5	2.8	2.4	17.6	6.4	5.4
KY	30.5	15.6	13.1	62.0	31.3	26.6	VT	2.9	2.1	1.7	6.3	4.2	3.3
LA	10.6	3.6	3.4	23.7	8.6	7.8	VA	35.2	15.6	15.7	79.3	33.0	33.3
ME	11.1	3.4	3.3	26.2	8.1	7.9	WA	66.7	27.4	28.1	161.7	61.6	64.9
MD	24.7	20.4	22.1	59.6	50.3	55.9	WV	10.0	6.1	5.6	22.5	11.8	11.0
MA	49.7	29.4	25.3	97.5	67.2	56.8	WI	22.9	14.4	15.0	53.2	30.6	33.2
MI	68.1	13.6	9.4	178.5	34.9	23.1	WY	0.3	0.5	0.5	0.7	1.2	1.1
MN	23.1	15.1	19.2	49.5	35.2	46.2	GU	1.3	0.4	0.4	3.0	1.0	1.0
MS	12.0	2.6	1.7	25.3	4.8	2.9	PR	13.5	4.3	4.4	37.1	11.6	12.0
MO	35.8	8.6	6.8	86.2	19.7	15.3	VI	0.5	0.1	0.1	1.5	0.3	0.2

[1] Data are for the fiscal year ending in September of the year shown. [2] Includes Puerto Rico (PR), Guam (GU), and the Virgin Islands (VI).

Source: U.S. Department of Health and Human Services, Administration for Children and Families, State TANF Data and Reports, "Caseload Data," <www.acf.hhs.gov/ofa/programs/tanf/data-reports>, accessed April 2022.

Table 598. Household Use of Food Pantries and Emergency (Soup) Kitchens: 2020

[In thousands (130,041 represents 130,041,000), except percent. Based on the 2020 Current Population Survey Food Security Supplement that asked questions about use of food pantries and emergency kitchens among households with incomes below 185 percent of the Federal poverty level, and households above this level that indicated difficulty in meeting food needs. Covers the use of food pantries and emergency kitchens at least once during the 12-month period ended December 2020, for persons occupying housing units. The CPS excludes persons who are homeless, and may also miss persons in tenuous housing arrangements (such as temporarily living with another family); these factors bias the statistics downward]

Category	Food pantries			Emergency (soup) kitchens		
	Total households[1]	Number of users	Percent using	Total households[1]	Number of users	Percent using
All households	**130,041**	**8,695**	**6.7**	**130,084**	**451**	**0.4**
All persons in households	323,616	24,804	7.7	323,798	867	0.3
Adults in households	251,210	16,969	6.8	251,310	724	0.3
Children in households	72,406	7,835	10.8	72,488	143	0.2
Households by food security status:[2]						
Food-secure households	116,420	3,719	3.2	116,465	126	0.1
Food-insecure households	13,561	4,953	36.5	13,578	325	2.4
Households with low food security	8,499	2,648	31.2	8,509	130	1.5
Households with very low food security	5,062	2,305	45.5	5,069	195	3.9

[1] Totals exclude households that did not answer questions about using food pantries and emergency kitchens, and also households that did not answer questions about food security. [2] Food secure households report zero or 1-2 indications, typically anxiety over food sufficiency or supply, with little or no indication of changes in diets or food intake. Households with low food security report reduced quality, variety, or desirability of diet, with little or no indication of reduced food intake. Households with very low food security report multiple indications of disrupted eating patterns and reduced food intake. See also headnote, Table 216.

Source: U.S. Department of Agriculture, Economic Research Service, *Statistical Supplement to Household Food Security in the United States in 2020*, No. 091, September 2021. See also <www.ers.usda.gov/topics/food-nutrition-assistance/food-security-in-the-u-s/>.

Table 599. Temporary Assistance for Needy Families (TANF)—Expenditures by State: Fiscal Years 2000 to 2020

[In millions of dollars (24,781 represents $24,781,000,000). Represents federal and state funds expended in fiscal year. Negative values occur when contracted obligations are fulfilled or terminated and the actual cost for the service is less than the obligated amount. Expenditures on basic assistance includes cash, payments, vouchers, and other forms of benefits designed to meet a family's ongoing basic needs (food, clothing, shelter, utilities, household goods, personal care items, and general incidental expenses)]

State	2000, Total	2010, Total	2020 Total [1]	2020 Expenditures on basic assistance	State	2000, Total	2010, Total	2020 Total [1]	2020 Expenditures on basic assistance
U.S.	24,781	33,255	28,984	7,051	MO.	321	405	350	32
AL.	96	191	176	16	MT.	44	47	38	17
AK.	93	62	78	46	NE.	79	98	87	28
AZ.	261	350	336	45	NV.	69	108	111	33
AR.	139	233	84	4	NH.	73	86	80	34
CA.	6,481	7,239	6,345	2,598	NJ.	321	1,446	1,402	83
CO.	205	323	446	81	NM.	149	237	272	69
CT.	436	500	479	36	NY.	3,512	5,347	4,586	1,444
DE.	55	75	126	12	NC.	440	563	544	35
DC.	157	251	312	185	ND.	33	37	39	4
FL.	781	901	784	134	OH.	995	1,331	1,123	247
GA.	386	563	483	110	OK.	130	179	108	19
HI.	162	378	211	39	OR.	169	392	246	84
ID.	43	35	36	8	PA.	1,327	964	920	131
IL.	879	1,255	1,156	51	RI.	172	149	150	22
IN.	342	344	271	16	SC.	245	180	166	49
IA.	163	194	152	30	SD.	21	31	27	13
KS.	151	207	167	13	TN.	293	338	165	24
KY.	203	281	264	180	TX.	727	908	953	45
LA.	118	264	197	15	UT.	100	132	74	17
ME.	108	141	111	37	VT.	62	78	81	13
MD.	336	564	523	153	VA.	418	299	268	66
MA.	690	1,022	1,014	241	WA.	535	1,494	943	140
MI.	1,264	1,703	1,256	129	WV.	134	199	134	40
MN.	381	475	516	94	WI.	382	524	489	73
MS.	62	106	77	4	WY.	34	29	29	11

[1] In addition to basic assistance, TANF provides funding for numerous additional activities covering work, education and training, work supports (including assistance for transportation, and work-related supplies and fees), financial education, supportive counseling services, child care and early education, child welfare services, prevention of out-of-wedlock pregnancies, and other services, as well as funding for program management.

Source: U.S. Department of Health and Human Services, Administration for Children and Families, State TANF Data and Reports, "Expenditure Data," <www.acf.hhs.gov/ofa/programs/tanf/data-reports>, accessed April 2022.

Table 600. Federal Food Programs: Fiscal Years 1990 to 2021

[20.0 represents 20,000,000, except as noted. For fiscal years ending September 30. Program data include Puerto Rico, Virgin Islands, Guam, American Samoa, Northern Marianas, and the former Trust Territory when a federal food program was operated in these areas. Participation data are average monthly figures except as noted]

Program	Unit	1990	2000	2010	2015	2018	2019	2020	2021 (P)
Supplemental nutrition assistance program: [1]									
Participants	Million	20.0	17.2	40.3	45.8	40.8	35.7	39.9	41.5
Value of benefits	Mil. dol.	14,143	14,983	64,702	69,645	60,917	55,622	74,233	108,637
Average monthly benefit value per recipient	Dollars	59	73	134	127	125	130	155	218
Nutrition assistance program for Puerto Rico: [2]									
Federal grant	Mil. dol.	937	1,268	2,001	1,951	1,920	1,924	1,938	2,038
National school lunch program (NSLP):									
Children participating [3]	Million	24.1	27.3	31.8	30.5	29.7	29.6	22.4	9.5
Total lunches served	Million	4,009	4,575	5,278	5,005	4,866	4,867	3,210	1,349
Free lunches served	Percent	41.5	48.2	55.9	65.4	68.5	68.4	72.0	98.0
Reduced-price lunches served	Percent	6.8	8.9	9.4	7.2	5.9	5.7	4.9	0.3
Federal cost (cash payments)	Mil. dol.	3,214	5,493	9,752	11,696	12,580	12,870	9,021	4,869
School breakfast (SB):									
Children participating [3]	Million	4.1	7.6	11.7	14.0	14.7	14.8	12.3	5.4
Federal cash payments	Mil. dol.	599	1,393	2,859	3,892	4,397	4,546	3,548	2,082
Special supplemental food program for Women, Infants, and Children (WIC): [4]									
Participants	Million	4.5	7.2	9.2	8.0	6.9	6.4	6.2	6.2
Federal cost for food	Mil. dol.	1,637	2,853	4,562	4,176	3,375	3,139	2,884	2,648
Child and adult care (CACFP): [5]									
Participants [6]	Million	1.5	2.7	3.4	4.2	4.6	4.8	4.3	4.8
Federal cash payments	Mil. dol.	719	1,500	2,398	3,009	3,322	3,432	2,764	3,471
Federal cost of food commodities for: [7]									
School food programs [8]	Mil. dol.	617	655	1,128	1,307	1,243	1,331	1,296	964
The Emergency Food Assistance Program (TEFAP) [9]	Mil. dol.	329	225	631	525	630	764	769	1,258

P Preliminary. [1] The program name was changed from Food Stamp to Supplemental Nutrition Assistance (SNAP) in October 2008. [2] Puerto Rico receives a grant in lieu of SNAP benefits. [3] Average participation per day are 9-month averages (excludes summer months). Includes children in public and nonprofit private elementary and secondary schools and in residential child care institutions. [4] WIC serves pregnant and postpartum women, infants, and children up to age 5. [5] CACFP provides year-round subsidies to feed preschool children and elderly and disabled adults in day care centers, and children and youth in emergency shelters for the homeless and eligible afterschool care programs. [6] Average quarterly daily attendance at participating institutions. [7] Includes the federal cost of commodity entitlements, cash-in-lieu of commodities, and bonus foods. [8] National school lunch and breakfast programs, and special milk program. [9] Emergency food assistance is food made available to hunger relief organizations such as food banks and soup kitchens. It is not disaster relief. Participants are not reported.

Source: U.S. Department of Agriculture, Food and Nutrition Service, "Program Data, Overview," <www.fns.usda.gov/pd/overview>, accessed April 2022.

Table 601. Supplemental Nutrition Assistance Program (SNAP) Beneficiaries and Benefits by State: 2010 to 2021

[40,302 represents 40,302,000; 64,702 represents $64,702,000,000. Participation data are average monthly number participating in fiscal year ending September 30. The Food Stamp Program was renamed the Supplemental Nutrition Assistance Program (SNAP) in October 2008]

State	Persons (1,000)			Benefits (mil. dol.)			State	Persons (1,000)			Benefits (mil. dol.)		
	2010	2020	2021	2010	2020	2021		2010	2020	2021	2010	2020	2021
Total [1]	40,302	39,879	41,500	64,702	74,110	108,631	MS.	576	430	418	847	772	1,066
							MO.	901	715	699	1,361	1,325	1,735
U.S.	40,245	39,812	41,436	64,562	73,942	108,418	MT.	114	104	97	177	193	229
AL.	805	731	770	1,226	1,359	1,974	NE.	163	157	157	238	254	357
AK.	76	83	83	159	198	288	NV.	278	449	453	415	923	1,235
AZ.	1,018	833	879	1,588	1,469	2,176	NH.	104	73	69	152	117	175
AR.	467	393	346	686	661	766	NJ.	622	701	826	1,030	1,289	2,169
CA.	3,239	4,312	4,327	5,692	7,819	11,243	NM.	357	469	520	542	904	1,340
CO.	405	483	514	688	913	1,305	NY.	2,758	2,658	2,781	4,985	5,119	7,312
CT.	336	372	372	570	722	980	NC.	1,346	1,318	1,542	2,072	2,392	3,995
DE.	113	120	115	171	215	288	ND.	60	46	50	95	84	113
DC.	118	116	140	196	225	381	OH.	1,607	1,397	1,509	2,734	3,100	3,865
FL.	2,603	3,177	3,356	4,417	6,008	7,924	OK.	582	597	619	900	1,113	1,473
GA.	1,591	1,566	1,641	2,565	2,906	4,086	OR.	705	635	706	1,067	1,171	1,847
HI.	138	165	196	358	564	944	PA.	1,575	1,795	1,766	2,333	3,249	5,170
ID.	194	146	133	300	279	258	RI.	139	146	142	238	279	379
IL.	1,646	1,870	1,930	2,784	3,374	5,070	SC.	797	596	608	1,256	1,102	1,550
IN.	813	601	646	1,291	1,134	1,619	SD.	95	78	75	153	144	178
IA.	340	311	286	526	546	727	TN.	1,224	869	881	1,966	1,774	3,095
KS.	270	200	200	403	337	489	TX.	3,552	3,551	3,408	5,447	6,300	8,752
KY.	778	555	598	1,186	998	1,610	UT.	247	164	163	367	280	413
LA.	826	831	925	1,286	1,576	2,463	VT.	86	69	68	124	117	169
ME.	230	160	158	356	277	410	VA.	786	730	758	1,213	1,331	1,902
MD.	561	701	824	878	1,271	2,146	WA.	956	871	928	1,387	1,598	2,360
MA.	749	821	929	1,166	1,472	2,350	WV.	341	306	302	487	518	772
MI.	1,776	1,254	1,278	2,809	2,297	3,246	WI.	715	647	762	1,000	1,104	1,964
MN.	430	409	453	625	725	1,986	WY.	35	27	29	52	46	73

[1] Includes Guam and the Virgin Islands. Puerto Rico, American Samoa, and the Northern Marianas, which receive nutrition assistance grants in lieu of SNAP.

Source: U.S. Department of Agriculture, Food and Nutrition Service, Supplemental Nutrition Assistance Program (SNAP), "National and/or State Level Monthly and/or Annual Data," <www.fns.usda.gov/pd/supplemental-nutrition-assistance-program-snap>, accessed March 2022.

Table 602. Supplemental Nutrition Assistance Program (SNAP) Households and Participants by Type: 1990 to 2019

[7,811 represents 7,811,000. For fiscal years ending September 30. Data for 1990 exclude Guam and the Virgin Islands. The Food Stamp Program was renamed Supplemental Nutrition Assistance Program (SNAP) in October 2008. Based on a sample of households from the SNAP Quality Control System]

Fiscal year	Households				Participants		
	Total [1] (1,000)	Percent of total with-			Total (1,000)	Percent of total	
		Children	Elderly [2]	Disabled [3]		Children	Elderly [2]
1990.	7,811	60.3	18.1	8.9	20,440	49.6	7.7
1995.	10,883	59.7	16.0	18.9	26,955	51.5	7.1
1996.	10,552	59.5	16.2	20.2	25,926	51.0	7.3
1997.	9,452	58.3	17.6	22.3	23,117	51.4	7.9
1998.	8,246	58.3	18.2	24.4	19,969	52.8	8.2
1999.	7,670	55.7	20.1	26.4	18,149	51.5	9.4
2000.	7,252	54.6	20.4	26.7	16,916	51.6	9.6
2001.	7,276	54.2	19.7	26.6	16,850	51.3	9.3
2002.	8,010	55.1	17.9	25.7	18,608	51.4	8.5
2003.	8,971	55.1	17.1	22.1	20,764	50.8	8.1
2004.	10,069	54.3	17.3	22.7	23,279	50.0	8.2
2005.	10,852	53.7	17.1	23.0	24,794	49.9	8.3
2006.	11,313	52.0	17.9	23.1	25,472	49.1	8.7
2007.	11,561	51.0	17.8	23.8	25,775	48.9	8.8
2008.	12,464	50.6	18.5	22.6	27,607	48.4	9.1
2009.	14,981	49.9	16.6	21.2	32,889	47.5	8.3
2010.	18,369	48.7	15.5	19.8	39,759	46.6	7.9
2011.	20,803	47.1	16.5	20.2	44,148	45.1	8.5
2012.	22,046	45.3	17.2	20.0	46,022	44.5	9.0
2013.	22,802	44.8	17.4	20.3	47,098	44.4	9.3
2014.	22,445	43.6	19.0	20.4	45,874	44.2	10.1
2015.	22,293	42.7	19.6	20.2	45,184	44.0	10.6
2016.	21,511	42.9	21.8	20.3	43,539	44.1	11.8
2017.	20,597	41.7	24.1	20.8	41,491	43.5	13.1
2018.	19,727	41.2	26.0	20.7	39,519	43.7	14.1
2019.	18,802	39.5	28.1	21.1	37,202	42.7	15.6

[1] Total excludes those who are ineligible and those receiving disaster benefits. [2] Persons age 60 and over. [3] Non-elderly individuals with disabilities. The fluctuations in 1995 and 2003 are in part due to changes in the definition of a household with an individual with a disability. Changes involve primarily raising and lowering the age to be considered "nonelderly," and the inclusion of households receiving supplemental security income and/or other government benefits due to a disability. Additional changes in definitions were made in 2015 and 2016. See source, appendix A, for details.

Source: U.S. Department of Agriculture, Food and Nutrition Service, *Characteristics of Supplemental Nutrition Assistance Program Households: Fiscal Year 2019*, Report No. SNAP-20-CHAR, March 2021. See also <www.fns.usda.gov/research-analysis>.

Table 603. Supplemental Nutrition Assistance Program (SNAP) Households and Participants—Summary: 2019

[18,802 represents 18,802,000. For fiscal year ending September 30. Based on a sample of households from the SNAP Quality Control System. Figures are lower than official participation counts because they do not include ineligible participants or those receiving disaster food stamp assistance]

Characteristic	Households Number (1,000)	Households Percent	Characteristic	Participants Number (1,000)	Participants Percent
Total households............................	**18,802**	**100.0**	**Total participants**.......................	**37,202**	**100.0**
With children............................	7,420	39.5	Children..............................	15,871	42.7
Single-parent households...............	4,621	24.6	Under age 5...........................	4,822	13.0
Married-couple households.............	1,155	6.1	Age 5 to 17............................	11,049	29.7
Other [1]...............................	1,643	8.8	Nonelderly adults......................	15,532	41.7
With elderly persons.....................	5,289	28.1	Age 18 to 35..........................	7,246	19.5
Living alone...........................	4,387	23.3	Age 36 to 59..........................	8,285	22.3
Not living alone.......................	902	4.8	Elderly, age 60 and over...............	5,800	15.6
With disabled nonelderly persons..........	3,959	21.1			
Living alone...........................	2,544	13.5	Male.................................	15,813	42.5
Not living alone.......................	1,415	7.5	Female...............................	21,389	57.5
With earned income.....................	5,384	28.6	White, non-Hispanic...................	13,596	36.5
Wages and salaries....................	4,565	24.3	Black, non-Hispanic...................	9,611	25.8
With unearned income...................	11,666	62.0	Hispanic..............................	5,947	16.0
TANF [2]...............................	799	4.2	Asian, non-Hispanic...................	1,221	3.3
Supplemental security income............	4,462	23.7	Native American, non-Hispanic..........	542	1.5
Social security..........................	5,871	31.2	Multiracial, non-Hispanic...............	296	0.8
With no gross income....................	3,480	18.5	Race unknown........................	5,989	16.1

[1] Other households with children include other multiple-adult households and children-only households. [2] Temporary Assistance for Needy Families (TANF) program.

Source: U.S. Department of Agriculture, Food and Nutrition Service, *Characteristics of Supplemental Nutrition Assistance Program Households: Fiscal Year 2019*, Report No. SNAP-20-CHAR, March 2021. See also <www.fns.usda.gov/research-analysis>.

Table 604. Children Under Age 6 in Child Care by Type of Child Care Arrangement by Child and Family Characteristics: 2019

[In percent, except as indicated (21,195 represents 21,195,000). Covers children under age 6 (from birth through age 5) not enrolled in kindergarten who are in a nonparental care arrangement on a weekly basis. Children may have multiple weekly care arrangements, thus a single child may be represented in multiple columns. Based on the Early Childhood Program Participation Survey, a component of the National Household Education Surveys (NHES) Program. The NHES methodology changes over time and users should use caution when comparing results here to previous surveys. Detail may not sum to totals because of rounding]

Selected child or family characteristic	Number of children (1,000)	Children in weekly nonparental care arrangement [1] At least one nonparental care arrangement	Relative	Nonrelative care	Center-based care [2]	Children with no weekly nonparental care
Total children under age 6............	**21,195**	**59**	**38**	**20**	**62**	**41**
Age of child:						
Under 1 year old.........................	4,621	42	58	26	32	58
1 to 2 years old.........................	8,425	55	44	25	47	45
3 to 5 years old.........................	8,149	74	26	14	83	26
Non-Hispanic race of child:						
White..................................	10,420	61	34	23	65	39
Black..................................	2,706	63	45	13	59	37
Asian or Pacific Islander.................	1,181	55	35	12	67	45
Other [3]...............................	1,463	59	32	23	62	41
Hispanic, any race.......................	5,424	56	44	16	57	44
Number of parents in household:						
Two parents............................	17,105	58	35	20	63	42
One parent.............................	4,089	65	50	17	60	35
Highest education of parents/guardians:						
Less than high school....................	1,884	43	49	[6] 18	55	57
High school/GED [4].....................	4,001	49	49	17	56	51
Vocational/technical/some college......	5,061	56	43	17	58	44
Bachelor's degree.......................	5,988	64	34	21	64	36
Graduate/professional degree...........	4,261	75	29	23	70	25
Household income:						
$20,000 or less.........................	2,401	51	43	17	64	49
$20,001 to $50,000......................	5,063	46	45	14	59	54
$50,001 to $75,000......................	3,659	55	46	22	50	45
$75,001 to $100,000.....................	2,849	58	42	18	59	42
Over $100,000..........................	7,223	74	29	22	69	26
Assistance to pay for primary child care arrangement: [5]						
Parents received assistance.............	1,577	100	28	26	81	(X)
Parents did not receive assistance.....	7,013	100	25	27	71	(X)
No fee for care.........................	4,004	100	64	5	40	(X)

[1] Estimates represent about 12,594,000 children who have at least one weekly nonparental care arrangement. Eleven percent of children's parents reported having more than one type of regularly scheduled weekly nonparental care arrangement. [2] Includes day care centers, Head Start programs, preschools, prekindergartens, and other early childhood programs. [3] Includes children of all other races or multiple races, non-Hispanic. [4] GED, General Educational Development diploma. [5] Assistance could be from a state welfare or family assistance program, a relative, an employer, another social service, or someone else. [6] Interpret data with caution. The coefficient of variation (CV) for this estimate is between 30 and 50 percent.

Source: U.S. National Center for Education Statistics, National Household Education Surveys Program, *Early Childhood Program Participation: 2019, First Look,* May 2021, NCES 2020-075REV. See also <nces.ed.gov/nhes/>.

Table 605. Child Support—Award and Recipient Status of Custodial Parents: 2017

[In thousands (12,918 represents 12,918,000), except as noted. Income and support received in 2017 dollars. Based on the Child Support Supplement to the April 2018 Current Population Survey (CPS). Custodial parents are 15 years and older with own children under 21 years of age living with them who receive support from noncustodial parents living outside the household. Covers civilian noninstitutional population]

Award and recipient status	All custodial parents				Custodial parents below poverty level			
	Total		Mothers	Fathers	Total		Mothers	Fathers
	Number	Percent distri-bution			Number	Percent distri-bution		
Total............................	**12,918**	**(X)**	**10,319**	**2,598**	**3,110**	**(X)**	**2,817**	**292**
With child support agreement or award [1]........	6,376	(X)	5,301	1,075	1,452	(X)	1,328	124
Supposed to receive payments in 2017........	5,429	100.0	4,600	828	1,207	100.0	1,121	86
Actually received payments in 2017..........	3,792	69.8	3,282	510	829	68.7	781	48
Received full amount........................	2,491	45.9	2,133	357	483	40.0	456	27
Received partial payments..................	1,301	24.0	1,149	153	346	28.7	325	21
Did not receive payments in 2017.............	1,637	30.2	1,318	318	377	31.2	340	38
Child support not awarded.......................	6,542	(X)	5,018	1,524	1,658	(X)	1,489	169
MEAN INCOME AND CHILD SUPPORT								
Received child support payments in 2017: [2]								
Mean total money income (dol.).................	40,795	(X)	36,947	65,557	9,954	(X)	9,856	11,551
Mean child support received (dol.)..............	4,912	(X)	4,913	4,908	4,173	(X)	4,205	3,650
Received the full amount due:								
Mean total money income (dol.)...............	44,936	(X)	41,241	67,002	9,775	(X)	9,761	10,023
Mean child support received (dol.)...........	6,295	(X)	6,315	6,173	5,581	(X)	5,553	6,067
Received partial payments:								
Mean total money income (dol.)...............	32,870	(X)	28,972	62,178	10,203	(X)	9,989	13,469
Mean child support received (dol.)...........	2,266	(X)	2,309	1,948	2,210	(X)	2,315	615
Received no payments in 2017: [2]								
Mean total money income (dol.).................	35,189	(X)	31,908	48,777	9,024	(X)	9,600	3,842
Without child support agreement or award:								
Mean total money income (dol.).................	36,172	(X)	30,546	54,702	8,727	(X)	8,344	12,105

X Not applicable. [1] Child support award status as of April 2018. [2] For parents who were supposed to receive child support.

Source: U.S. Census Bureau, *Custodial Mothers and Fathers and Their Child Support: 2017*, Current Population Report P60-269, May 2020; and "2017 Child Support Detailed Tables," <www.census.gov/topics/families/child-support.Tables.html>, accessed June 2020. See also <www.census.gov/topics/families/child-support.html>.

Table 606. Child Support Enforcement Program—Caseload and Finances: 2010 to 2021

[In units as indicated (15,859 represents 15,859,000). For fiscal years ending September 30. Includes Puerto Rico, Guam, and the Virgin Islands. The Child Support Program is a federal/state/tribal/local partnership that operates under Title IV-D of the Social Security Act. The OCSE does not assist families directly but rather helps child support agencies in the states and tribes to develop, manage and operate their programs. Case types include IV-A cases in which children are eligible for Temporary Assistance for Needy Families (TANF); and IV-E cases in which children are entitled to foster care maintenance; case types reflect Social Security Act Titles IV-A and IV-E. Child support collected for families not receiving TANF goes to the family to help it remain self-sufficient. Most child support collected on behalf of TANF and foster care families goes to Federal and State governments to offset program payments. Some States pass-through a portion of their collections to help families become self-sufficient. Based on data reported by state agencies. Minus sign (-) indicates net outlay]

Item	Unit	2010	2015	2018	2019	2020 (P)	2021 (P)
Total cases....................................	**1,000**	**15,859**	**14,745**	**13,924**	**13,605**	**13,204**	**12,666**
Number of children.....................................	1,000	17,509	15,899	14,728	14,271	13,821	13,202
Paternities established or acknowledged, total....	1,000	1,734	1,484	1,413	1,401	1,224	1,473
Support orders established, total...................	1,000	1,297	1,016	872	838	620	611
FINANCES							
Total distributed collections......................	**Mil. dol.**	**26,556**	**28,559**	**28,584**	**28,767**	**31,423**	**29,522**
Total payments to families or foster care..........	Mil. dol.	24,474	26,592	26,703	26,890	28,660	27,250
Total medical support...............................	Mil. dol.	303	511	593	625	804	716
Total passed through................................	Mil. dol.	135	112	98	93	98	97
Total fees withheld by state.........................	Mil. dol.	37	53	53	59	77	77
Total assistance reimbursement [1].................	Mil. dol.	1,607	1,292	1,137	1,100	1,784	1,382
State share..	Mil. dol.	704	574	504	487	674	514
Federal share.......................................	Mil. dol.	903	717	633	613	1,110	868
Current Assistance Collections [2]...................	Mil. dol.	1,015	808	681	653	795	709
Former Assistance Collections [3]...................	Mil. dol.	8,971	8,959	8,445	8,322	9,591	8,776
Medicaid Never Assistance Collections [4]..........	Mil. dol.	4,729	7,368	8,724	9,080	9,950	9,654
Never Assistance Collections [5].....................	Mil. dol.	11,840	11,425	10,734	10,712	11,087	10,383
Total administrative expenditures..................	Mil. dol.	5,776	5,749	5,877	6,012	6,004	5,908
Federal share.......................................	Mil. dol.	3,811	3,474	3,551	3,618	3,622	3,529
State share..	Mil. dol.	1,964	2,275	2,326	2,394	2,383	2,379
Cost effectiveness ratio [6].........................	Dol.	4.88	5.26	5.14	5.06	5.51	5.27

P Preliminary. [1] Equals collections that will be divided between State and Federal governments to reimburse their respective shares of either Title IV-A (TANF) payments or Title IV-E (foster care) maintenance payments. [2] Made on behalf of families currently receiving Title IV-A (TANF) or Title IV-E (foster care) assistance. [3] Made on behalf of families formerly receiving Title IV-A (TANF) or Title IV-E (foster care) assistance. [4] Collections received and distributed on behalf of children who are receiving Child Support Enforcement services under Title IV-D of the Social Security Act, and who either currently receive or formerly received Medicaid payments, but who do not and never did receive assistance under either Title IV-A (TANF or AFDC) or Title IV-E (Foster Care) of the Social Security Act. [5] Made on behalf of families never receiving public assistance under Medicaid, TANF, or Foster Care. [6] Ratio of dollars collected to dollars expended.

Source: U.S. Department of Health and Human Services, Administration for Children & Families, Office of Child Support Enforcement, *Preliminary Report FY2021*, May 2022, and earlier editions. See also <www.acf.hhs.gov/css/data>.

Table 607. Children in Foster Care and Awaiting Adoption: 2020

[Data cover fiscal year ending September 30 of year shown, and are current as of October 2021. Data are preliminary. States may resubmit data, and therefore estimates may change. Due to missing data for some characteristics, data may not sum to totals]

Characteristic	In foster care [1]	Entered foster care	Exited foster care	Waiting to be adopted [1,2]	Adopted [3]
Total	**407,493**	**216,838**	**224,396**	**117,470**	**57,881**
SEX					
Male	209,063	(NA)	(NA)	61,297	29,714
Female	198,387	(NA)	(NA)	56,166	28,142
AGE					
Under 1 year	29,105	43,694	8,965	3,854	1,040
1 to 5 years	140,213	64,384	81,032	46,412	30,603
6 to 10 years	91,658	43,843	51,940	30,242	15,350
11 to 15 years	90,502	45,031	42,895	28,263	8,859
16 to 17 years	43,126	17,012	17,755	8,699	1,904
18 to 20 years	12,779	2,840	19,508	(X)	120
Mean age, years	8.4	7.1	8.7	7.9	6.5
Median age, years	7.7	6.0	7.8	7.3	5.3
RACE/ETHNICITY [4]					
American Indian/Alaska Native	9,851	4,983	4,997	2,311	936
Asian	2,061	1,325	1,336	472	206
Black	92,237	44,215	46,433	25,257	9,588
White	175,870	98,680	103,546	51,128	29,325
Hispanic origin [5]	88,111	45,983	46,475	26,520	11,631
Two or more races	31,669	16,245	17,303	10,079	5,304
TIME IN CARE					
Mean months	21.0	(X)	20.5	32.7	[6] 12.1
Median months	14.6	(X)	15.9	26.9	[6] 9.2

NA Not available. X Not applicable. [1] As of September 30. [2] Includes children whose goal is adoption and/or whose parents' parental rights have been terminated. Excludes children age 16 and older whose parents' parental rights have been terminated and whose goal is emancipation. [3] Children adopted with public agency involvement. Data are from the Adoption and Foster Care Analysis and Reporting System (AFCARS) Adoption file; the number of adoptions reported here may not equal the number reported as discharges to adoption from foster care. [4] Race groups exclude children of Hispanic origin. [5] Children of Hispanic origin may be of any race. [6] Time elapsed from termination of parental rights to adoption.

Source: U.S. Department of Health and Human Services, Administration for Children and Families, *The Adoption and Foster Care Analysis and Reporting System Report, Preliminary FY2020 Estimates as of October 4, 2021,* No. 28. See also <www.acf.hhs.gov/cb/data-research>.

Table 608. Child Care Mean Hourly Cost by Type of Child Care Arrangement and Child and Family Characteristics: 2019

[In dollars. Covers children from birth through age 5. Estimates represent 8,101,000 children who are not in kindergarten, and who have at least one regularly scheduled weekly nonparental care arrangement with an out-of-pocket expense. Excludes children for whom no fee was charged, or for whom another source paid the entire fee. Data cover the primary care arrangement where the child spends the most time. Some children have multiple primary care arrangements; a single child may be represented in multiple columns of this table. Based on the Early Childhood Program Participation Survey, a component of the National Household Education Surveys (NHES) Program. The NHES methodology changes over time and users should use caution when comparing results here to previous surveys. Detail may not sum to totals because of rounding]

Selected child and family characteristics	Relative care	Non-relative care	Center-based care [1]	Selected child and family characteristics	Relative care	Non-relative care	Center-based care [1]
Total children under 6 years old	**6.05**	**7.75**	**8.22**	Region:			
Age of child:				Northeast	7.90	10.55	10.20
Under 1 year old	6.63	8.85	7.91	South	5.80	7.35	6.71
1 to 2 years old	5.43	8.03	8.92	Midwest	4.09	5.29	7.05
3 to 5 years old	6.64	6.72	7.88	West	6.54	8.80	10.16
Non-Hispanic race of child:							
White	6.76	6.48	7.51	Household income:			
Black	4.29	6.66	6.97	$20,000 or less	7.85	(B)	[6] 8.26
Asian or Pacific Islander	6.45	[6] 16.45	11.87	$20,001 to $50,000	3.91	6.02	6.73
Other or multiple races	[6] 7.95	9.58	9.54	$50,001 to $75,000	5.87	5.27	5.60
Hispanic, any race	6.34	10.04	9.59	$75,001 to $100,000	7.10	5.40	7.85
Family type:				Over $100,000	6.85	9.07	9.16
Two parents or guardians	6.49	7.78	8.35				
One parent or guardian	5.10	7.60	7.55	Poverty status of household: [4]			
Parents' highest education: [2]				At or above poverty	6.07	7.50	8.26
Less than high school	6.79	[6] 7.91	3.47	Below poverty	5.97	[6] 10.00	7.71
High school/GED [3]	5.40	[6] 8.96	7.20				
Vocational/technical or				Assistance to pay for primary			
some college	5.53	5.51	6.23	child care arrangement: [5]			
Bachelor's degree	6.38	6.83	8.37	Received assistance	6.16	[6] 8.88	6.82
Graduate/professional degree	7.20	9.50	9.53	Did not receive assistance	6.02	7.58	8.43

B Reporting standards not met. There are too few cases for a reliable estimate. [1] Includes day care centers, Head Start programs, preschools, and prekindergartens. [2] Parents or guardians. [3] GED, General Educational Development diploma. [4] Children are considered poor if living in households with incomes below the poverty threshold, which is a dollar amount determined by the federal government, given household size and composition. Income is reported in categories rather than in exact amounts, and therefore the poverty measures are approximations. [5] Assistance to parents could be from a state welfare or family assistance program, a relative, an employer, another social service, or someone else. Parents were asked about assistance only for the primary arrangement within each type of care. [6] Interpret data with caution. The coefficient of variation for this estimate is 30 percent or greater.

Source: U.S. National Center for Education Statistics, *Early Childhood Program Participation: 2019, First Look,* May 2021, NCES 2020-075REV. See also <nces.ed.gov/nhes/>.

Table 609. Head Start—Summary: 2010 to 2021

[Funding data in millions of dollars (7,233.7 represents $7,233,700,000); all other data in thousands (904.1 represents 904,100). For fiscal years. The Head Start program serves children, families, and pregnant women in all 50 states, DC, and six territories. Data on cumulative enrollment, staff, and volunteers are submitted by Head Start grantees and delegates. Federal funding covers all Head Start programs, including Early Head Start, American Indian and Alaska Native programs, and Migrant and Seasonal Head Start Programs]

Item	2010	2015	2016	2017	2018	2019	2020 [4]	2021
Federal funding (million dollars)......	7,233.7	8,598.1	9,168.1	9,224.6	9,838.7	[5] 10,028.5	[5] 10,613.1	[5] 10,748.1
Funded enrollment slots [1]............	904.1	944.6	915.6	899.4	887.1	873.0	852.5	839.1
Cumulative enrollment [2]..........	**1,117.7**	**1,100.4**	**1,097.4**	**1,074.2**	**1,054.7**	**1,046.9**	**(NA)**	**755.8**
Children age 2 and under............	146.3	193.2	230.3	243.4	258.0	265.9	(NA)	231.3
Children age 3.........................	386.7	399.4	383.9	374.0	364.1	363.5	(NA)	224.5
Children age 4.........................	548.0	480.1	455.9	427.6	404.8	391.4	(NA)	280.0
Children age 5 and older.............	23.2	12.2	11.9	13.9	12.4	10.3	(NA)	8.3
Hispanic/Latino......................	405.4	414.0	411.4	400.4	385.7	387.7	(NA)	279.9
Non-Hispanic/non-Latino.............	712.3	686.3	686.0	673.7	669.0	659.1	(NA)	475.9
American Indian/Alaska Native.......	41.7	45.4	42.1	42.1	41.3	40.1	(NA)	26.5
Asian.................................	19.0	21.8	22.6	22.6	22.8	22.5	(NA)	17.1
Black/African American...............	326.5	318.3	319.9	313.5	312.7	310.7	(NA)	215.8
Native Hawaiian/Pacific Islander.....	6.9	9.8	7.4	7.7	7.1	7.1	(NA)	5.0
White.................................	450.3	473.5	477.8	469.6	461.2	462.1	(NA)	347.9
Biracial/multiracial...................	83.9	107.2	107.5	106.2	103.3	102.2	(NA)	78.6
Other/unspecified....................	189.4	124.3	120.1	112.5	106.2	102.2	(NA)	64.8
Total staff [3].........................	228.3	230.0	241.5	240.0	246.1	254.2	(NA)	243.6
Total volunteers......................	1,335.9	1,141.5	1,118.8	1,086.4	1,046.4	1,060.9	(NA)	378.0
Parent volunteers.................	881.1	782.2	783.6	769.6	738.7	749.5	(NA)	294.5

[1] Funded enrollment is the number of children and pregnant women supported by federal Head Start funds at any one time during the year. Data are derived from the annual Administration for Children and Families budget and congressional documents, and do not reflect changes made during the year. [2] Cumulative enrollment refers to actual number of children and pregnant women served, including enrollees who left during the year and enrollees who filled those empty slots. More children and families may receive Head Start services cumulatively throughout the year than indicated by funded enrollment numbers. [3] Excludes contracted staff. [4] Due to the coronavirus disease 2019 (COVID-19) pandemic, the Office of Head Start did not require program information reporting for FY2020. [5] Not included is supplemental funding for FY2019-FY2021 for expenses related to several natural disasters, including the COVID-2019 pandemic in FY2021. Amounts are: FY2019, $55 million; FY2020, $750 million; FY2021, $1,250 million.

Source: U.S. Department of Health and Human Services, Administration for Children and Families, Early Childhood Learning & Knowledge Center, "Head Start Program Facts Sheets," <eclkc.ohs.acf.hhs.gov/about-us/article/office-head-start-ohs>; "Program Information Report, Head Start Enterprise System," <eclkc.ohs.acf.hhs.gov/data-ongoing-monitoring/article/program-information-report-pir>, accessed March 2022; and *Justification of Estimates for Appropriations Committees, Fiscal Year 2023*.

Table 610. Social Assistance Services—Nonemployer Establishments and Receipts: 2010 to 2019

[Receipts in millions of dollars (12,753 represents $12,753,000,000). Includes only firms subject to federal income tax. Nonemployers are businesses with no paid employees. Nonemployer firm receipts may include commissions or earnings]

Kind of business	NAICS code [1]	2010	2014	2015	2016	2017	2018	2019
ESTABLISHMENTS								
Social assistance, total............................	**624**	**912,247**	**850,786**	**822,350**	**782,320**	**729,150**	**784,922**	**756,780**
Individual and family services...........................	6241	141,971	160,562	163,337	164,218	170,672	176,958	174,068
Community food and housing, and emergency and other relief services................	6242	6,080	6,399	6,355	6,384	6,512	6,296	6,123
Vocational rehabilitation services.......................	6243	11,984	12,938	12,916	12,700	12,510	12,355	11,889
Child day care services................................	6244	752,212	670,887	639,742	599,018	539,456	589,313	564,700
RECEIPTS (mil. dol)								
Social assistance, total............................	**624**	**12,753**	**13,114**	**13,238**	**13,099**	**12,992**	**14,100**	**14,328**
Individual and family services...........................	6241	2,599	3,275	3,492	3,641	3,881	4,176	4,403
Community food and housing, and emergency and other relief services................	6242	96	106	111	114	114	122	122
Vocational rehabilitation services.......................	6243	287	318	341	345	343	351	353
Child day care services................................	6244	9,772	9,415	9,294	8,999	8,653	9,451	9,449

[1] North American Industry Classification System; see text, Section 15. Data for 2010 based on NAICS 2007; data for 2013-2016 based on NAICS 2012; and beginning 2017, data based on 2017 NAICS.

Source: U.S. Census Bureau, Nonemployer Statistics, "All Sectors: Nonemployer Statistics by Legal Form of Organization and Receipts Size Class for the U.S., States, and Selected Geographies: 2019," <data.census.gov/>, accessed June 2022.

Table 611. Social Assistance Services—Revenue for Employer Firms: 2019 and 2020

[In millions of dollars (211,721 represents $211,721,000,000). Based on Census Bureau's Service Annual Survey and administrative data. Estimates have been adjusted using results of the 2017 Economic Census where applicable. In some instances, results from the 2017 Economic Census may reflect revisions based on additional analytical review following the release of the 2017 Geographic Area Statistics. See Appendix III]

Kind of business	NAICS code [1]	2019			2020		
		Total	Taxable firms	Tax-exempt firms	Total	Taxable firms	Tax-exempt firms
Social assistance, total..........................	**624**	**211,721**	**66,124**	**145,597**	**220,814**	**63,309**	**157,505**
Child and youth services.............................	62411	18,541	1,887	16,654	19,480	2,002	17,478
Services for elderly and disabled persons.........	62412	55,028	25,711	29,317	57,440	27,233	30,207
Other individual and family services................	62419	38,668	5,085	33,583	42,437	5,578	36,859
Community food services............................	62421	12,540	67	12,473	16,871	72	16,799
Community housing services.........................	62422	14,246	127	14,119	15,520	144	15,376
Emergency and other relief services...............	62423	10,579	122	10,457	12,184	(S)	12,074
Vocational rehabilitation services...................	6243	14,104	2,001	12,103	14,100	2,023	12,077
Child day care services.............................	6244	48,015	31,124	16,891	42,782	26,147	16,635

S Estimate does not meet publication standards. [1] 2012 North American Industry Classification System.

Source: U.S. Census Bureau, Service Annual Survey, "Service Annual Survey Latest Data (NAICS-basis): 2020," <www.census.gov/programs-surveys/sas/data.html>, accessed December 2021.

Table 612. Emergency and Transitional Beds in Homeless Assistance Systems: 2021

[Data cover all States, DC, Guam, Northern Marianas, Puerto Rico, and the Virgin Islands. Data were reported by approximately 400 Continuums of Care, and were collected during the last week of January 2021. Data represent inventory available during the entire year. Data are not independently verified by Department of Housing and Urban Development (HUD)]

Homeless program	Total year-round beds	Dedicated units/beds [1]				Other beds	
		Family units	Family beds	Adult-only beds	Child-only beds	Seasonal beds [2]	Overflow/voucher [3]
Total........................	**964,237**	**142,349**	**425,650**	**535,165**	**3,422**	**21,111**	**28,253**
Shelter for homeless people..............	396,466	57,359	178,740	214,593	3,133	21,111	28,253
Emergency shelters......................	307,908	44,174	139,345	165,961	2,602	21,111	28,253
Safe haven [4]............................	2,487	8	11	2,476	0	(X)	(X)
Transitional housing [5]....................	86,071	13,177	39,384	46,156	531	(X)	(X)
Permanent housing........................	567,771	84,990	246,910	320,572	289	(X)	(X)
Permanent supportive housing [6]........	376,709	43,997	124,471	252,172	66	(X)	(X)
Rapid re-housing..........................	137,206	31,158	92,984	44,051	171	(X)	(X)
Other permanent housing [7]..............	53,856	9,835	29,455	24,349	52	(X)	(X)

X Not applicable. [1] Dedicated beds are available for use throughout the year and are considered part of the stable inventory of beds for homeless persons. [2] Seasonal beds are typically available during particularly high-demand seasons of the year (e.g. winter months in the North or summer months in the South) to accommodate increased need for emergency shelters to prevent illness or death due to the weather. [3] Overflow beds are typically used during unanticipated emergencies (e.g., precipitous temperature drops or a natural disaster that displaces residents). Voucher beds are made available in a hotel or motel, and often function like overflow beds. [4] A safe haven provides temporary shelter and services for hard-to-reach homeless persons with severe mental illness who come primarily from the streets and have been unable or unwilling to participate in housing or supportive services. Accommodations are private or semi-private. [5] Provides a place to stay with supportive services for up to 24 months. [6] Provides long-term housing with supportive services for formerly homeless people with disabilities, and often also those with chronic homelessness. [7] May or may not include services, and does not require people to have a disability.

Source: U.S. Department of Housing and Urban Development, HUD Exchange, 2021 Annual Homeless Assessment Report (AHAR) to Congress: Part 1, PIT Estimates of Homelessness in the U.S., "2007-2021 Housing Inventory Count by State," <www.hudexchange.info/resource/6573/2021-ahar-part-1--pit-estimates-of-homelessness-in-the-us/>, accessed February 2022.

Table 613. Homeless Population by Type and Shelter Status: 2010 to 2021

[Data are point-in-time (PIT) counts made on a single night in January by Continuums of Care (CoCs) in all States, DC, and U.S. territories. Data are not independently verified by the Department of Housing and Urban Development (HUD). CoCs are required to provide an unduplicated count of homeless persons according to HUD standards. See HUD's Point-in-Time Count Methodology Guide at <www.hudexchange.info/programs/hdx/guides/pit-hic/#general-pit-guides-and-tools>. Sheltered homeless people may be staying in emergency shelters, hotels/motels paid for by charities or government programs, transitional housing programs, or safe havens (temporary shelter for hard-to-serve individuals). People staying in places not designed for use as regular accommodations, including cars, abandoned buildings, transit stations, and campgrounds, are considered unsheltered]

Homeless population by type	2010	2016	2017	2018	2019	2020	2021 [4]
Total	**637,077**	**549,928**	**550,996**	**552,830**	**567,715**	**580,466**	**[4] 326,126**
Male	(NA)	330,890	333,049	332,925	343,187	352,211	182,673
Female	(NA)	217,268	214,975	216,211	219,911	223,578	141,497
Transgender & gender nonconforming	(NA)	[3] 1,770	2,972	3,694	4,617	4,621	1,956
Sheltered	403,543	373,571	360,867	358,363	356,422	354,386	326,126
Unsheltered	233,534	176,357	190,129	194,467	211,293	226,080	(NA)
Individuals [1]	395,140	355,212	366,585	372,417	396,045	408,891	(NA)
Sheltered	212,218	198,008	193,144	194,340	199,531	199,478	194,749
Unsheltered	182,922	157,204	173,441	178,077	196,514	209,413	(NA)
Persons in families with children	241,937	194,716	184,411	180,413	171,670	171,575	(NA)
Sheltered	191,325	175,563	167,723	164,023	156,891	154,908	131,377
Unsheltered	50,612	19,153	16,688	16,390	14,779	16,667	(NA)
Children under age 18, total	(NA)	120,819	114,529	111,592	107,069	106,364	(NA)
Sheltered	(NA)	108,866	103,289	101,086	97,153	95,713	80,656
Unsheltered	(NA)	11,953	11,240	10,506	9,916	10,651	(NA)
Children under age 18, unaccompanied	8,153	3,824	4,635	4,093	3,976	3,389	(NA)
Sheltered	4,349	2,218	2,122	2,014	1,874	1,682	1,345
Unsheltered	3,804	1,606	2,513	2,079	2,102	1,707	(NA)
Chronically homeless individuals [2]	106,062	77,486	86,705	88,640	96,141	110,528	(NA)
Sheltered	43,329	24,596	26,629	30,754	35,200	37,111	44,346
Unsheltered	62,733	52,890	60,076	57,886	60,941	73,417	(NA)
Chronically homeless people in families [2]	(NA)	8,646	8,387	8,273	9,442	9,795	(NA)
Sheltered	(NA)	5,512	5,980	5,821	7,407	6,760	7,233
Unsheltered	(NA)	3,134	2,407	2,452	2,035	3,035	(NA)
Veterans	74,087	39,471	40,020	37,878	37,085	37,252	(NA)
Sheltered	43,437	26,404	24,690	23,312	22,740	22,048	19,750
Unsheltered	30,650	13,067	15,330	14,566	14,345	15,204	(NA)
Severely mentally ill	107,539	107,801	(NA)	111,122	116,179	120,642	(NA)
Sheltered	71,989	61,846	(NA)	58,942	63,936	62,023	64,131
Unsheltered	35,550	45,955	(NA)	52,180	52,243	58,619	(NA)
Chronic substance abuse	139,853	94,496	(NA)	86,647	88,873	98,646	(NA)
Sheltered	95,049	52,290	(NA)	45,372	45,804	43,216	39,428
Unsheltered	44,804	42,206	(NA)	41,275	43,069	55,430	(NA)
Persons with HIV/AIDS	14,498	9,240	(NA)	10,064	10,945	10,632	(NA)
Sheltered	10,590	6,860	(NA)	7,244	7,733	7,287	6,820
Unsheltered	3,908	2,380	(NA)	2,820	3,212	3,345	(NA)
Domestic violence victims	66,878	68,464	(NA)	48,666	44,752	48,532	(NA)
Sheltered	49,709	41,779	(NA)	30,607	31,509	32,695	30,545
Unsheltered	17,169	26,685	(NA)	18,059	13,243	15,837	(NA)

NA Not available. [1] People who are not part of a family with children. Includes homeless single adults, unaccompanied youth, or individuals in multiple-adult or multiple-child households. [2] An individual or household head of a family with a disability, and continuously homeless for a year or more, or with at least four episodes of homelessness in the last 3 years. [3] 2016 data only for persons identifying as transgender. [4] Data for 2021 cover sheltered homeless population only. In 2021, due to the coronavirus disease 2019 (COVID-19) pandemic, communities had the option to cancel or modify the unsheltered survey portion of their counts. See source, and *The 2021 Annual Homeless Assessment Report (AHAR) to Congress: Part 1, Point-in-Time Estimates of Sheltered Homelessness,*.

Source: U.S. Department of Housing and Urban Development, HUD Exchange, "PIT and HIC Data Since 2007: 2007-2020 PIT Counts by State," March 2021, <www.hudexchange.info/resource/3031/pit-and-hic-data-since-2007/>, accessed February 2022; and *2021 CoC (Continuum of Care) Homeless Populations and Subpopulations Report,* January 2022 and earlier reports.

Table 614. Volunteers by Selected Characteristics: 2017

[In percent. Covers adults age 16 and over who performed unpaid volunteer activities for an organization at any time during the 12-month period from September 1 to the week of the survey. Data were collected by the September 2017 Volunteering and Civic Life Supplement to the Current Population Survey (CPS)]

Volunteer characteristics	Percent volunteering	Percent of volunteers by main organization type [1]							
		Civic and political [2]	Educational or youth service	Environ-mental or animal care	Hospital or other health	Public safety	Religious	Sport, hobby, cultural, or arts	Other
Total [3]	**30.3**	**6.2**	**19.2**	**5.0**	**6.0**	**6.0**	**32.0**	**25.7**	**3.6**
Men	26.5	7.8	16.2	4.7	4.3	3.1	30.3	29.6	4.0
Women	33.8	5.1	21.4	5.1	7.2	1.7	33.3	22.8	3.3
Age 16 to 19	28.3	3.7	24.1	4.5	4.7	1.5	22.9	35.5	3.0
Age 20 to 24	22.7	8.7	19.9	9.5	10.1	2.4	25.6	20.6	3.2
Age 25 to 34	27.8	6.8	24.6	7.2	7.3	2.7	25.5	22.7	3.3
Age 35 to 44	36.9	5.1	27.1	3.7	4.3	2.7	24.2	29.7	3.2
Age 45 to 54	34.0	4.9	19.7	4.2	5.5	2.0	30.7	29.8	3.3
Age 55 to 64	30.2	7.3	12.7	5.3	6.0	2.5	40.0	22.1	4.2
Age 65 and older	28.0	7.5	9.4	3.5	6.2	1.9	45.7	21.5	4.4
Less than high school	10.1	4.0	25.3	2.8	3.2	1.7	32.6	26.7	3.7
High school [4]	18.8	4.6	19.4	4.6	5.4	2.4	39.1	19.8	4.5
Some college [5]	32.1	6.3	17.8	5.0	6.1	3.4	34.0	23.7	3.8
College graduate	45.7	7.0	19.1	5.4	6.5	1.7	28.6	28.6	3.2

[1] Main organization is the organization for which the volunteer worked the most hours. [2] Includes organizations involved in professional and/or international activities. [3] Data by education cover persons age 25 and over. [4] Includes high school diploma or equivalent. [5] Includes "some college, no degree" and "associate degree."

Source: Corporation for National and Community Service, "Volunteering in America," <www.americorps.gov/newsroom/news/via>, accessed April 2019.

Table 615. Charitable Giving by Source and Type of Recipient Organization: 1990 to 2019

[In billions of dollars (98.5 represents $98,500,000,000). Individual giving is estimated using Internal Revenue Service information from individual tax returns, and from a study of households participating in the Philanthropy Panel Study conducted by Indiana University Lilly Family School of Philanthropy. Data on foundation giving are provided by Candid (formerly the Foundation Center). Corporate giving data are based on itemized contributions claimed on federal tax returns, and also from Candid. Data on contributions by bequest are primarily based on data from the Council for Advancement and Support of Education, with additional calculations performed by Giving USA using IRS tax data on charitable bequest deductions. Giving to recipient organizations are from various research organizations, including the Evangelical Council for Financial Accountability and other nonprofit research organizations]

Source and allocation	1990	2000	2005	2010	2012	2013	2014	2015	2016	2017	2018	2019
Total charitable giving	**98.5**	**229.7**	**292.4**	**288.2**	**332.6**	**332.5**	**357.6**	**376.7**	**397.2**	**432.1**	**431.4**	**449.6**
Individuals	79.0	174.1	220.8	208.0	244.4	242.4	252.3	264.7	279.4	302.8	295.9	309.7
Foundations [1]	7.2	24.6	32.4	41.0	46.4	49.9	54.9	57.3	63.1	70.7	73.9	75.7
Corporations	5.5	10.7	15.2	15.8	17.2	15.9	18.3	19.1	20.0	19.3	18.6	21.1
Charitable bequests	6.8	20.3	24.0	23.4	24.6	24.4	32.2	35.6	34.6	39.3	43.1	43.2
Giving by recipient organization:												
Religion	49.8	77.0	90.9	97.5	105.8	110.4	116.0	119.2	123.8	125.0	125.3	128.2
Education	11.8	28.8	35.0	42.2	46.9	44.5	49.4	53.2	53.6	56.1	57.2	64.1
Human services	6.7	20.8	30.4	36.8	41.1	41.1	43.7	46.9	49.0	52.3	53.3	56.0
Health	7.8	15.3	20.3	27.7	26.2	32.3	33.1	34.3	38.1	38.3	38.8	41.5
Public/societal benefit	6.6	15.0	20.8	19.2	22.9	24.3	25.8	27.3	30.9	34.1	32.9	37.2
Arts, culture, and humanities	3.7	10.6	12.4	13.4	13.9	14.6	15.9	17.7	17.2	18.1	19.2	21.6
International affairs	2.1	6.3	12.7	13.9	16.0	19.4	20.2	23.5	21.6	25.5	29.0	28.9
Environment/animals	1.3	4.9	6.5	7.9	8.9	8.6	9.6	10.7	11.3	12.0	12.7	14.2
Gifts to foundations [1]	3.8	24.7	24.5	26.1	40.1	40.8	44.6	39.3	40.8	52.4	52.2	53.5
Gifts to individuals	(NA)	(NA)	3.1	4.9	5.8	7.2	6.7	6.7	9.5	10.9	9.9	10.1
Unallocated [2]	5.0	26.4	36.0	-1.4	5.0	-10.7	-7.5	-2.2	1.3	7.5	0.9	-5.5

NA Not available. [1] Data are from Candid, formerly the Foundation Center. [2] Money deducted as a charitable contribution by donors but not allocated to sources. May include gifts to governmental entities, in-kind giving, or gifts to new charities.

Source: Giving USA Foundation, Chicago, IL, *Giving USA 2020: The Annual Report on Philanthropy for the Year 2019* ©, researched and written at the Indiana University Lilly Family School of Philanthropy. See also <https://givingusa.org/>.

Table 616. Domestic Private Foundations—Financial Information: 2000 to 2018

[Financial data in billions of dollars (409.5 represents $409,500,000,000)]

Item	2000	2005	2010	2011	2012	2013	2014	2015	2016	2017	2018
Number of tax returns	66,738	79,535	93,436	92,990	93,542	95,121	97,484	99,683	100,488	101,194	102,078
Nonoperating foundations [1]	61,501	72,800	86,254	85,500	85,447	86,584	88,878	90,699	91,396	92,897	93,106
Operating foundations [2]	5,238	6,734	7,181	7,490	8,095	8,537	8,606	8,984	9,092	8,297	8,972
Total assets, book value [3]	409.5	481.8	584.2	594.3	633.1	693.3	738.4	754.3	796.5	883.3	895.0
Total assets, fair market value [3]	471.6	545.9	641.0	641.3	698.6	791.0	830.3	829.4	889.4	1,005.7	987.8
Investments in securities	361.4	373.1	353.3	344.8	373.3	430.9	459.3	451.7	476.7	551.2	525.8
Total revenue	72.8	76.4	72.5	79.4	95.3	106.1	119.5	107.0	114.1	139.0	144.7
Total expenses	37.4	42.8	60.1	64.3	64.8	73.7	79.2	81.0	88.1	93.4	98.1
Contributions, gifts, and grants paid	27.6	31.9	44.7	46.9	48.6	54.2	57.6	58.7	65.8	70.2	74.9
Excess of revenue over expenses (net)	35.3	33.5	12.3	15.1	30.5	32.4	40.3	26.0	26.0	45.7	46.6
Net investment income [4]	48.8	44.3	29.8	34.2	38.4	50.4	59.9	48.8	44.2	64.9	72.4

[1] Generally provide charitable support through grants and other financial means to charitable organizations; the majority of foundations are nonoperating. [2] Generally conduct their own charitable activities, e.g., museums. [3] Data for book and fair market value of assets were reduced to avoid overstating the joint assets of the Bill and Melinda Gates Foundation and the Bill and Melinda Gates Foundation Trust, by tax year as follows: 2009, $33.4 billion; 2010, $36.7 billion; 2011, $33.8 billion; 2012, $36.4 billion; 2013, $40.5 billion; 2014, $43.4 billion; 2015, $39.3 billion; 2016, $40.3 billion; 2017, $50.7 billion; and 2018, $46.8 billion. [4] This equals gross investment income less allowable deductions. Represents income not considered related to a foundation's charitable purpose, e.g., interest, dividends, and capital gains. Foundations could be subject to an excise tax on such income.

Source: Internal Revenue Service, *Statistics of Income Bulletin*, "SOI Tax Stats – Domestic Private Foundation and Charitable Trust Statistics," <www.irs.gov/statistics>, accessed March 2022.

Table 617. Foundations—Number and Finances by Foundation Type: 2000 to 2022

[In millions of dollars (24,563 represents $24,563,000,000), except number of foundations. Data are for fiscal years. Only grantmaking foundations are included. Covers nongovernmental nonprofit organizations with funds and programs managed by their own trustees or directors, whose goals are to maintain or aid social, educational, religious, or other activities to serve the common good]

Year and type	Number	Total giving [1] (million dollars)	Assets (million dollars)	Gifts received (million dollars)
2000	56,582	24,563	486,085	27,614
2010	76,610	45,858	643,974	37,961
2015	86,203	62,794	890,061	53,157
2018	86,310	80,664	1,017,899	72,526
2020 [2]	127,595	89,714	1,179,488	98,589
Total, 2022 [3]	**131,644**	**98,807**	**1,313,520**	**97,860**
Independent	119,052	67,558	1,069,566	56,057
Company-sponsored	2,836	10,060	41,325	9,639
Community	1,204	10,832	110,029	14,263
Operating	8,552	10,356	92,600	17,900

[1] Includes grants, scholarships, and employee matching gifts; excludes set-asides, loans, program-related investments (PRIs), and program and other administrative expenses. [2] Data are based on most recent IRS filing, 2016 or later, available for organizations appearing on any 2020 IRS Business Master File. Please note that the methodology has changed to include foundations that reported zero dollars or no value for total giving, resulting in a significant increase in the number of foundations included. [3] As of August 30, 2022.

Source: Candid, New York, NY ©, all rights reserved, *Key Facts on U.S. Nonprofits and Foundations*, <www.issuelab.org/resources/38265/38265.pdf>; and unpublished data. See also <candid.org/use-our-data/about-our-data>.

Table 618. Nonprofit Charitable Organizations—Financial Information: 2000 to 2018

[In billions of dollars (1,562.5 represents $1,562,500,000,000), except as indicated. Includes data reported by organizations described in Internal Revenue Code, Section 501(c)(3), excluding private foundations and most religious organizations. Prior to 2010, organizations with receipts under $25,000 were not required to file. Beginning with 2010, organizations with receipts under $50,000 were not required to file]

| Year | Number of tax returns (1,000) | Total assets | Net assets | Revenue | | | Total expenses | Excess of revenue over expenses (net) |
				Total [1]	Program service revenue [2]	Contributions, gifts, and grants		
2000	230.2	1,562.5	1,023.2	866.2	579.1	199.1	796.4	69.8
2001	240.6	1,631.7	1,020.3	897.0	630.8	212.4	862.7	34.3
2002	251.7	1,733.9	1,040.3	955.3	691.8	214.5	934.7	20.6
2003	263.4	1,899.9	1,164.3	1,072.2	754.6	230.0	1,009.7	62.5
2004	276.2	2,058.6	1,276.1	1,153.0	801.2	248.6	1,058.5	94.5
2005	286.6	2,241.9	1,411.3	1,252.9	852.6	276.3	1,137.9	115.0
2006	301.2	2,549.7	1,617.7	1,370.9	920.2	303.2	1,230.4	140.5
2007	313.1	2,683.4	1,674.4	1,445.9	980.3	324.5	1,317.2	128.7
2008	315.2	2,521.2	1,434.7	1,378.3	1,038.0	322.0	1,396.4	-18.1
2009	320.8	2,697.1	1,564.2	1,481.1	1,085.9	327.4	1,433.9	47.2
2010	269.5	2,946.5	1,772.4	1,593.0	1,147.3	344.9	1,497.2	95.8
2011	274.3	3,030.1	1,781.9	1,647.9	1,194.2	357.4	1,558.4	89.5
2012	279.4	3,274.0	1,970.4	1,734.2	1,248.2	371.1	1,624.1	110.1
2013	285.9	3,507.6	2,184.0	1,828.2	1,296.1	394.1	1,700.4	127.8
2014	293.0	3,711.1	2,288.0	1,949.9	1,384.1	422.5	1,801.3	148.6
2015	298.4	3,801.4	2,303.6	2,013.0	1,468.0	430.6	1,908.2	104.8
2016	302.1	4,027.9	2,519.0	2,124.4	1,530.5	465.3	2,013.3	111.2
2017	307.6	4,355.0	2,771.4	2,284.0	1,623.4	500.0	2,121.2	162.8
2018	300.4	4,239.8	2,664.4	2,299.0	1,664.9	485.9	2,186.3	112.7

[1] Includes other sources of revenue not shown separately. [2] Represents fees collected by organizations in support of their tax-exempt purposes, such as tuition and fees at educational institutions, hospital patient charges, and admission and activity fees collected by museums and other nonprofit organizations or institutions.

Source: U.S. Internal Revenue Service, Statistics of Income, "SOI Tax Stats – Charities & Other Tax-Exempt Organizations Statistics," August 2021, <www.irs.gov/statistics>, accessed March 2022.

Table 619. Individual Charitable Contributions by State: 2019

[In units, as indicated (188,691 represents $188,691,000,000). Covers returns primarily for 2019 tax year that were filed during 2020, but may also include a limited number of returns for earlier tax years that were also received during 2020. Also includes paper returns processed by mid-July 2021. Data reflect tax returns as initially processed and do not reflect amended returns or errors that were corrected after initial processing. Data will not agree with data in other tables due to differing survey methodology used to derive state data]

| State | Charitable contributions | | State | Charitable contributions | | State | Charitable contributions | | State | Charitable contributions | |
	Number of returns (1,000)	Amount (mil. dol.)		Number of returns (1,000)	Amount (mil. dol.)		Number of returns (1,000)	Amount (mil. dol.)		Number of returns (1,000)	Amount (mil. dol.)
Total [1]	14,273	188,691	ID	62	944	MO	174	2,730	PA	434	4,981
AL	151	2,533	IL	541	6,232	MT	37	507	RI	45	383
AK	18	222	IN	156	2,261	NE	57	964	SC	181	2,452
AZ	290	3,082	IA	86	1,098	NV	120	1,522	SD	18	508
AR	71	1,617	KS	88	1,567	NH	52	593	TN	174	3,414
CA	2,668	28,643	KY	103	1,370	NJ	613	5,357	TX	951	16,874
CO	306	3,512	LA	121	1,632	NM	53	756	UT	189	3,866
CT	211	2,823	ME	36	377	NY	976	15,553	VT	17	258
DE	45	421	MD	598	5,309	NC	390	5,144	VA	561	5,548
DC	63	913	MA	405	5,333	ND	15	373	WA	379	5,419
FL	740	13,651	MI	289	3,676	OH	291	3,929	WV	24	291
GA	535	8,385	MN	256	2,745	OK	105	1,873	WI	172	2,086
HI	74	517	MS	79	1,145	OR	224	1,844	WY	13	724

[1] Includes returns from Puerto Rico and Other areas. Other areas include returns filed from Army Post Office and Fleet Post Office addresses by members of the armed forces stationed overseas, and returns filed by other U.S. citizens abroad.

Source: U.S. Internal Revenue Service, Statistics of Income, Individual Income Tax Return (Form 1040) Statistics: State Data, "SOI Tax Stats - Historic Table 2," <www.irs.gov/uac/soi-tax-stats-individual-income-tax-return-form-1040-statistics>, accessed March 2022.

Labor Force, Employment, and Earnings

This section presents statistics on the labor force; its distribution by occupation and industry affiliation; and the supply of, demand for, and conditions of labor. The chief source of these data is the Current Population Survey (CPS) conducted by the U.S. Census Bureau for the Bureau of Labor Statistics (BLS). Comprehensive historical and current data are available from the BLS internet site at <www.bls.gov/cps>as well as the Current Employment Statistics (CES) Program. These data are published on a current basis in the BLS publication *Employment and Earnings*. Detailed data on the labor force are also available from the Local Area Unemployment Statistics (LAUS) program.

Types of data—Most statistics in this section are obtained by two methods: household interviews or questionnaires and reports of establishment payroll records. Each method provides data that the other cannot suitably supply. Population characteristics, for example, are readily obtainable only from the household survey, while detailed industrial classifications can be readily derived only from establishment records.

CPS data are obtained from a monthly sample survey of the population. The CPS is used to gather data for the calendar week, generally the week including the 12th of the month, and provides current comprehensive data on the labor force (see text, Section 1, Population). The CPS provides information on the work status of the population without duplication since each person is classified as employed, unemployed, or not in the labor force. Employed persons holding more than one job are counted only once, according to the job at which they worked the most hours during the survey week.

Employment and Earnings presents data including national totals of the number of persons in the civilian labor force by sex, disability status, race, Hispanic origin, and age; the number employed; hours of work; industry and occupational groups; usual weekly earnings; and the number unemployed, as well as reasons for and duration of unemployment. Annual data shown in this section are averages of monthly figures for each calendar year, unless otherwise specified.

The CPS also produces annual estimates of employment and unemployment for each state, 50 large metropolitan statistical areas, and selected cities. These estimates are published annually in *Geographic Profile of Employment and Unemployment* available at <www.bls.gov/opub/geographic-profile>.

Data based on establishment records are compiled by the BLS and cooperating state agencies as part of an ongoing Current Employment Statistics (CES) program. The BLS collects survey data monthly from a probability-based sample of nonfarm business establishments. Data collection centers perform initial enrollment of each firm via telephone, collect the data for several months via Computer Assisted Telephone Interviewing (CATI), and where possible transfer respondents to a self-reporting mode such as touch-tone data entry, fax, or web collection. Very large, multi-establishment firms' ongoing reporting is established via Electronic Data Interchange (EDI). CES data are adjusted annually to data from government unemployment insurance administrative records, which are supplemented by data from other government agencies. The estimates exclude self-employed persons, private household workers, unpaid family workers, agricultural workers, and members of the Armed Forces.

The CES counts workers each time they appear on a payroll during the reference period (the payroll period that includes the 12th of the month). Thus, unlike the CPS, a person with two jobs is counted twice. The establishment survey is designed to provide estimates of nonfarm wage and salary employment, average weekly hours, and average hourly and weekly earnings by detailed industry for the nation, states, and selected metropolitan areas. Establishment survey data also are published in *Employment and Earnings*. Historical national data are available at <www.bls.gov/ces/>.Historical data for states and metropolitan areas are available at <www.bls.gov/sae/>. CES estimates are currently classified by the 2017 North American Industry Classification System (NAICS). All published series for the nation have a NAICS-based history extending back to at least 1990. Employment series for total nonfarm and other high-level aggregates start in 1939.

For more information on data concepts, sample design, and estimating methods for the CES Survey, see the BLS Handbook of Methods, Chapter 2 <www.bls.gov/opub/hom/>.For information regarding revisions and collection rates, see <www.bls.gov/web/empsit/cesbmart.htm>.

Labor force—According to the CPS definitions, the civilian labor force comprises all civilians in the noninstitutionalized population aged 16 years and over classified as "employed" or "unemployed" according to specific criteria. *Employed* civilians comprise (a) all civilians, who, during the reference week, did any work for pay or profit (minimum of an hour's work) or worked 15 hours or more as unpaid workers in a family enterprise and (b) all civilians who were not working but who had jobs or businesses from which they were temporarily absent for noneconomic reasons (illness, weather conditions, vacation, labor-management dispute, etc.) whether they were paid for the time off or were seeking other jobs. *Unemployed* persons comprise all civilians who had no employment during the reference week, who made specific efforts to find a job within the previous 4 weeks (such as applying directly to an employer or to a public employment service or checking with friends) and who were available for work during that week, except for temporary illness. Persons on layoff from a job and expecting recall also are classified as unemployed. All other civilian persons, 16 years old and over, are classified as "not in the labor force."

Various breaks in the CPS data series have occurred over time due to the introduction of population adjustments and other changes. For details on these breaks in series and the effect that they had on the CPS data, see the BLS website at <www.bls.gov/cps/documentation.htm#concepts>.

Beginning in January of each year, the CPS data reflect the introduction of revised population controls. For additional information on the effects of revised population controls on estimates from the CPS, see <www.bls.gov/cps/documentation.htm#pop>.

Hours and earnings—Average hourly earnings, based on establishment data from the CES, are gross earnings (i.e., earnings before payroll deductions) and include overtime premiums; they exclude irregular bonuses and value of payments in kind. Hours are those for which pay was received. Annual wages and salaries, as presented by the CPS, consist of total monies received for work performed by an employee during the income year. It includes wages, salaries, commissions, tips, piece-rate payments, and cash bonuses earned before deductions were made for taxes, bonds, union dues, etc. Persons who worked 35 hours or more are classified as working full-time.

Industry and occupational groups—Industry data derived from the CPS for 1983-1991 utilize the 1980 census industrial classification developed from the 1972 Standard Industrial Classification (SIC). CPS data from 1971 to 1982 were based on the 1970 census classification system, which was developed from the 1967 SIC. Most of the industry categories were not affected by the change in classification.

The occupational classification system used in the 1980 census and in the CPS for 1983-1991, evolved from the 1980 Standard Occupational Classification (SOC) system, first introduced in 1977. Occupational categories used in the 1980 census classification system are so radically different from the 1970 census system used in the CPS through 1982 that their implementation represented a break in historical data series.

Beginning in January 1992, the occupational and industrial classification systems used in the 1990 census were introduced into the CPS. (These systems were largely based on the 1980 SOC and the 1987 SIC systems, respectively.)

Beginning in 2003, the 2002 occupational and industrial classification systems were introduced into the CPS. These systems were derived from the 2000 SOC and the 2002 NAICS. The composition of detailed occupational and industrial classifications in the new classification systems was substantially changed from the previous systems in use, as was the structure for aggregating them into broad groups. Consequently, the use of the new classification systems created breaks in existing data series at all levels of aggregation. CPS data using the new classification systems are available for data from 2000. Additional information on the occupational and industrial classifications systems used in the CPS, including changes over time, appear on the BLS website at <www.bls.gov/cps/documentation.htm#oi>. Establishments responding to the establishment survey are classified according to the 2017 NAICS. Previously they were classified according to the SIC manual. See text, Section 15, Business Enterprise, for information about the SIC manual and NAICS.

Productivity—BLS publishes data on output per hour (labor productivity), output per combined unit of labor and capital input (multifactor productivity), and, for industry groups and industries, output per combined unit of capital, labor, energy, materials, and purchased service inputs. Labor productivity and related indexes are published for the business sector as a whole and its major subsectors: nonfarm business, manufacturing, and nonfinancial corporations, and for over 200 detailed industries. Productivity indexes that take into account capital, labor, energy, materials, and service inputs are published for 18 major manufacturing industry groups, 86 detailed manufacturing industries, utility services, and air and railroad transportation. The major sector data are published in the BLS quarterly *Productivity and Costs* and in the annual *Total Factor Productivity* release. Industry productivity measures are updated and published annually in the *Productivity and Costs by Industry* and *Total Factor Productivity Trends for Detailed Industries*. The latest data are available at the Productivity website at <www.bls.gov/productivity/>. Detailed information on methods, limitations, and data sources appears in the BLS *Handbook of Methods*, Chapters 10 and 11 at <www.bls.gov/opub/hom/home.htm> and <www.bls.gov/productivity/handbook-of-methods.htm>.

Unions—As defined here, unions include traditional labor unions and employee associations similar to labor unions. Data on union membership status provided by BLS are for employed wage and salary workers and relate to their principal job. Earnings by union membership status are usual weekly earnings of full-time wage and salary workers. The information is collected through the Current Population Survey.

Work stoppages—Work stoppages include all strikes and lockouts known to BLS that last for at least 1 full day or shift and involve 1,000 or more workers. All stoppages, whether or not authorized by a union, legal or illegal, are counted. Excluded are work slowdowns and instances where employees report to work late or leave early to attend meetings or rallies.

Seasonal adjustment—Many economic statistics reflect a regularly recurring seasonal movement that can be estimated on the basis of past experience. By eliminating that part of the change which can be ascribed to usual seasonal variation (e.g., climate or school openings and closings), it is possible to observe the cyclical and other nonseasonal movements in the series. However, in evaluating deviations from the seasonal pattern—that is, changes in a seasonally adjusted series—it is important to note that seasonal adjustment is merely an approximation based on past experience. Seasonally adjusted estimates have a broader margin of possible error than the original data on which they are based, since they are subject not only to sampling and other errors, but also are affected by the uncertainties of the adjustment process itself. Consistent with BLS practices, annual estimates will be published only for not seasonally-adjusted data.

Statistical reliability—For discussion of statistical collection, estimation, sampling procedures, and measures of statistical reliability applicable to Census Bureau and BLS data, see Appendix III.

Table 620. Civilian Population—Employment Status: 1970 to 2021

[In thousands (137,085 represents 137,085,000), except as indicated. Annual averages of monthly figures. Civilian noninstitutionalized population 16 years old and over. Data not strictly comparable with data for earlier years; see BLS Handbook of Methods, <www.bls.gov/opub/hom>. Based on Current Population Survey; see text, Section 1 and Appendix III]

Year	Civilian noninsti-tutional population	Civilian labor force				Unemployed		Not in labor force	
		Total	Percent of population	Employed	Employ-ment/ population ratio [1]	Number	Percent of labor force	Number	Percent of population
1970	137,085	82,771	60.4	78,678	57.4	4,093	4.9	54,315	39.6
1980	167,745	106,940	63.8	99,303	59.2	7,637	7.1	60,806	36.2
1990	189,164	125,840	66.5	118,793	62.8	7,047	5.6	63,324	33.5
2000	212,577	142,583	67.1	136,891	64.4	5,692	4.0	69,994	32.9
2004	223,357	147,401	66.0	139,252	62.3	8,149	5.5	75,956	34.0
2005	226,082	149,320	66.0	141,730	62.7	7,591	5.1	76,762	34.0
2006	228,815	151,428	66.2	144,427	63.1	7,001	4.6	77,387	33.8
2007	231,867	153,124	66.0	146,047	63.0	7,078	4.6	78,743	34.0
2008	233,788	154,287	66.0	145,362	62.2	8,924	5.8	79,501	34.0
2009	235,801	154,142	65.4	139,877	59.3	14,265	9.3	81,659	34.6
2010	237,830	153,889	64.7	139,064	58.5	14,825	9.6	83,941	35.3
2011	239,618	153,617	64.1	139,869	58.4	13,747	8.9	86,001	35.9
2012	243,284	154,975	63.7	142,469	58.6	12,506	8.1	88,310	36.3
2013	245,679	155,389	63.2	143,929	58.6	11,460	7.4	90,290	36.8
2014	247,947	155,922	62.9	146,305	59.0	9,617	6.2	92,025	37.1
2015	250,801	157,130	62.7	148,834	59.3	8,296	5.3	93,671	37.3
2016	253,538	159,187	62.8	151,436	59.7	7,751	4.9	94,351	37.2
2017	255,079	160,320	62.9	153,337	60.1	6,982	4.4	94,759	37.1
2018	257,791	162,075	62.9	155,761	60.4	6,314	3.9	95,716	37.1
2019	259,175	163,539	63.1	157,538	60.8	6,001	3.7	95,636	36.9
2020	260,329	160,742	61.7	147,795	56.8	12,947	8.1	99,587	38.3
2021	261,445	161,204	61.7	152,581	58.4	8,623	5.3	100,241	38.3

[1] Civilian employed as a percent of the civilian noninstitutional population.

Source: U.S. Bureau of Labor Statistics, CPS Tables, "Employment status of the civilian noninstitutional population, 1950s to Date," February 2022, <www.bls.gov/cps/tables.htm#empstat>.

Table 621. Civilian Labor Force and Participation Rate Projections: 2021 to 2031

[161.2 represents 161,200,000. Civilian noninstitutionalized population 16 years old and over. Based on Current Population Survey; see text, Section 1 and Appendix III]

Race, Hispanic origin, sex, and age	Civilian labor force (mil.)						Participation rate (percent) [1]					
	2021 [2]	2027	2028	2029	2030	2031	2021 [2]	2027	2028	2029	2030	2031
Total [3]	**161.2**	**166.1**	**166.8**	**167.5**	**168.1**	**168.9**	**61.7**	**60.7**	**60.5**	**60.4**	**60.2**	**60.1**
Male	85.5	87.5	87.8	88.0	88.3	88.5	67.6	65.9	65.7	65.4	65.2	64.9
16 and 17 years	1.1	0.9	0.9	0.8	0.8	0.8	24.4	20.1	19.4	18.8	18.1	17.5
18 and 19 years	1.9	1.8	1.7	1.7	1.7	1.6	49.2	44.7	43.9	43.1	42.4	41.7
20 to 24 years	7.6	7.3	7.3	7.3	7.2	7.1	72.9	70.4	69.8	69.2	68.7	68.2
25 to 29 years	9.6	9.2	9.1	9.1	9.1	9.0	86.3	84.7	84.3	83.9	83.6	83.2
30 to 34 years	10.1	10.1	10.0	9.9	9.9	9.9	89.2	88.3	88.0	87.9	87.6	87.3
35 to 39 years	9.6	10.6	10.7	10.7	10.7	10.5	90.4	89.7	89.6	89.4	89.3	89.1
40 to 44 years	8.9	9.6	9.6	9.8	10.0	10.2	88.9	88.3	88.1	87.9	87.6	87.4
45 to 49 years	8.3	9.0	9.1	9.2	9.3	9.4	88.6	87.9	87.8	87.6	87.4	87.2
50 to 54 years	8.4	7.8	7.9	8.0	8.1	8.3	84.6	84.1	83.9	83.8	83.6	83.4
55 to 59 years	7.9	7.6	7.5	7.4	7.2	7.1	77.9	78.1	78.1	78.1	78.0	78.0
60 to 64 years	6.3	6.3	6.2	6.1	6.1	6.2	62.8	64.8	65.1	65.4	65.7	66.0
65 to 69 years	3.2	3.9	4.0	4.0	4.1	4.0	37.9	41.3	41.9	42.5	43.0	43.6
70 to 74 years	1.5	1.9	2.0	2.1	2.2	2.2	22.0	24.4	24.8	25.3	25.7	26.1
75 and over years	1.1	1.7	1.7	1.9	2.0	2.1	11.5	13.0	13.2	13.4	13.7	13.9
Female	75.7	78.6	79.0	79.4	79.9	80.4	56.1	55.7	55.6	55.6	55.6	55.5
16 and 17 years	1.2	1.0	0.9	0.9	0.9	0.9	26.8	22.8	22.2	21.6	21.0	20.4
18 and 19 years	1.8	1.7	1.7	1.7	1.6	1.6	47.6	44.4	43.9	43.3	42.8	42.2
20 to 24 years	7.1	7.2	7.2	7.1	7.1	7.1	68.6	68.1	67.9	67.8	67.7	67.5
25 to 29 years	8.5	8.5	8.5	8.5	8.5	8.5	76.8	77.6	77.6	77.7	77.8	77.8
30 to 34 years	8.6	8.6	8.6	8.6	8.6	8.7	75.6	76.1	76.1	76.2	76.3	76.3
35 to 39 years	8.0	8.8	8.8	8.8	8.8	8.7	73.9	74.1	74.0	74.0	73.9	73.9
40 to 44 years	7.8	8.3	8.3	8.4	8.6	8.8	75.3	75.1	75.0	74.9	74.9	74.7
45 to 49 years	7.5	8.1	8.3	8.4	8.4	8.5	76.2	76.7	76.7	76.7	76.7	76.8
50 to 54 years	7.7	7.3	7.4	7.5	7.7	7.9	73.9	75.5	75.7	75.9	76.1	76.3
55 to 59 years	7.2	7.1	7.1	7.0	7.0	6.8	66.8	69.7	70.1	70.5	71.0	71.4
60 to 64 years	5.6	5.8	5.8	5.7	5.8	5.9	51.7	55.8	56.5	57.2	57.8	58.4
65 to 69 years	2.7	3.3	3.4	3.5	3.5	3.5	27.7	31.7	32.3	33.0	33.7	34.4
70 to 74 years	1.2	1.6	1.6	1.7	1.8	1.9	14.3	16.9	17.4	17.8	18.3	18.8
75 and over years	0.8	1.3	1.4	1.5	1.6	1.7	6.4	7.9	8.1	8.4	8.7	8.9
White male	67.0	67.4	67.4	67.4	67.4	67.4	67.9	66.1	65.8	65.5	65.2	65.0
White female	57.1	58.2	58.3	58.4	58.6	58.8	55.4	54.8	54.7	54.6	54.6	54.5
Black male	9.8	10.2	10.3	10.3	10.4	10.4	63.5	61.9	61.6	61.3	61.0	60.8
Black female	10.7	11.3	11.4	11.5	11.6	11.7	58.8	58.5	58.5	58.5	58.4	58.4
All others male [4]	8.7	9.9	10.1	10.3	10.5	10.7	70.4	69.7	69.6	69.5	69.3	69.3
All others female [4]	7.9	9.1	9.3	9.5	9.7	9.9	58.0	58.2	58.3	58.3	58.4	58.4
Hispanic male [5]	16.8	19.1	19.4	19.8	20.1	20.5	75.4	74.1	73.9	73.6	73.4	73.2
Hispanic female [5]	12.6	14.6	14.9	15.2	15.6	15.9	55.8	56.3	56.4	56.5	56.5	56.6

[1] Civilian labor force as a percent of the civilian noninstitutional population projections. [2] Data for 2021 are actual. [3] Includes other races, not shown separately. [4] Includes those classified as being of multiple racial origin and also the racial categories of Asians, American Indian and Alaska Native, and Native Hawaiian and Other Pacific Islanders. [5] Persons of Hispanic origin may be of any race.

Source: U.S. Bureau of Labor Statistics, "Employment Projections Program," <www.bls.gov/emp/data/labor-force.htm>, accessed September 2022.

Table 622. Civilian Population—Employment Status by Sex, Race, and Ethnicity: 1980 to 2021

[In thousands (79,398 represents 79,398,000), except as indicated. Annual averages of monthly figures. Data not strictly comparable with data for earlier years; see BLS Handbook of Methods, <www.bls.gov/opub/hom/>. For U.S. totals see Table 620]

Year, sex, race, and Hispanic origin	Civilian noninstitutionalized population	Civilian labor force				Unemployed		Not in labor force	
		Total	Percent of population	Employed	Employment/ population ratio [1]	Number	Percent of labor force	Number	Percent of population
Male:									
1980	79,398	61,453	77.4	57,186	72.0	4,267	6.9	17,945	22.6
1990	90,377	69,011	76.4	65,104	72.0	3,906	5.7	21,367	23.6
2000	101,964	76,280	74.8	73,305	71.9	2,975	3.9	25,684	25.2
2010	115,174	81,985	71.2	73,359	63.7	8,626	10.5	33,189	28.8
2019	125,353	86,687	69.2	83,460	66.6	3,227	3.7	38,667	30.8
2020	125,922	85,204	67.7	78,560	62.4	6,644	7.8	40,718	32.3
2021	126,487	85,505	67.6	80,829	63.9	4,676	5.5	40,983	32.4
Female:									
1980	88,348	45,487	51.5	42,117	47.7	3,370	7.4	42,861	48.5
1990	98,787	56,829	57.5	53,689	54.3	3,140	5.5	41,957	42.5
2000	110,613	66,303	59.9	63,586	57.5	2,717	4.1	44,310	40.1
2010	122,656	71,904	58.6	65,705	53.6	6,199	8.6	50,752	41.4
2019	133,822	76,852	57.4	74,078	55.4	2,774	3.6	56,970	42.6
2020	134,407	75,538	56.2	69,234	51.5	6,304	8.3	58,869	43.8
2021	134,958	75,699	56.1	71,752	53.2	3,948	5.2	59,259	43.9
White: [2]									
1980	146,122	93,600	64.1	87,715	60.0	5,884	6.3	52,523	35.9
1990	160,625	107,447	66.9	102,261	63.7	5,186	4.8	53,178	33.1
2000	176,220	118,545	67.3	114,424	64.9	4,121	3.5	57,675	32.7
2010	192,075	125,084	65.1	114,168	59.4	10,916	8.7	66,991	34.9
2019	200,827	126,600	63.0	122,441	61.0	4,159	3.3	74,227	37.0
2020	201,306	124,431	61.8	115,341	57.3	9,090	7.3	76,875	38.2
2021	201,881	124,145	61.5	118,291	58.6	5,854	4.7	77,737	38.5
Black: [2]									
1980	17,824	10,865	61.0	9,313	52.2	1,553	14.3	6,959	39.0
1990	21,477	13,740	64.0	12,175	56.7	1,565	11.4	7,737	36.0
2000	24,902	16,397	65.8	15,156	60.9	1,241	7.6	8,505	34.2
2010	28,708	17,862	62.2	15,010	52.3	2,852	16.0	10,846	37.8
2019	33,036	20,632	62.5	19,381	58.7	1,251	6.1	12,404	37.5
2020	33,344	20,177	60.5	17,873	53.6	2,304	11.4	13,167	39.5
2021	33,613	20,482	60.9	18,726	55.7	1,756	8.6	13,131	39.1
Asian: [2,3]									
2000	9,330	6,270	67.2	6,043	64.8	227	3.6	3,060	32.8
2010	11,199	7,248	64.7	6,705	59.9	543	7.5	3,951	35.3
2019	16,351	10,460	64.0	10,179	62.3	280	2.7	5,891	36.0
2020	16,467	10,331	62.7	9,437	57.3	894	8.7	6,136	37.3
2021	16,521	10,545	63.8	10,016	60.6	529	5.0	5,976	36.2
Hispanic: [4]									
1980	9,598	6,146	64.0	5,527	57.6	620	10.1	3,451	36.0
1990	15,904	10,720	67.4	9,845	61.9	876	8.2	5,184	32.6
2000	23,938	16,689	69.7	15,735	65.7	954	5.7	7,249	30.3
2010	33,713	22,748	67.5	19,906	59.0	2,843	12.5	10,964	32.5
2019	43,507	29,053	66.8	27,805	63.9	1,248	4.3	14,454	33.2
2020	44,182	28,970	65.6	25,952	58.7	3,018	10.4	15,213	34.4
2021	44,902	29,424	65.5	27,429	61.1	1,995	6.8	15,479	34.5
Mexican:									
1990	9,752	6,707	68.8	6,146	63.0	561	8.4	3,045	31.2
2000	15,333	10,783	70.3	10,144	66.2	639	5.9	4,550	29.7
2010	21,267	14,403	67.7	12,622	59.4	1,781	12.4	6,864	32.3
2019	26,251	17,611	67.1	16,836	64.1	775	4.4	8,640	32.9
2020	26,393	17,278	65.5	15,568	59.0	1,710	9.9	9,116	34.5
2021	27,000	17,713	65.6	16,532	61.2	1,181	6.7	9,287	34.4
Puerto Rican:									
1990	1,718	960	55.9	870	50.6	91	9.5	758	44.1
2000	2,193	1,411	64.3	1,318	60.1	92	6.6	783	35.7
2010	3,110	1,906	61.3	1,612	51.8	293	15.4	1,204	38.7
2019	3,941	2,448	62.1	2,325	59.0	124	5.0	1,493	37.9
2020	4,019	2,491	62.0	2,200	54.7	291	11.7	1,527	38.0
2021	4,065	2,435	59.9	2,236	55.0	199	8.2	1,630	40.1
Cuban:									
1990	918	603	65.7	559	60.9	44	7.2	315	34.3
2000	1,174	740	63.1	707	60.3	33	4.5	434	37.0
2010	1,549	970	62.6	850	54.9	120	12.4	579	37.4
2019	2,043	1,304	63.8	1,265	62.0	39	3.0	738	36.1
2020	2,086	1,303	62.5	1,181	56.6	122	9.4	783	37.5
2021	2,115	1,289	60.9	1,217	57.6	72	5.6	826	39.1

[1] Civilian employed as a percent of the civilian noninstitutional population. [2] Beginning with the 2003 CPS, respondents could choose more than one race. Beginning in 2003, data represent persons who selected this race group only and exclude persons reporting more than one race. The CPS in prior years allowed respondents to report only one race group. See also comments on race in text for section 1. [3] Prior to 2003, Asian includes Pacific Islanders. [4] Persons of Hispanic origin may be of any race. Includes persons of other Hispanic or Latino ethnicity, not shown separately.

Source: U.S. Bureau of Labor Statistics, CPS Tables, "Employment status of the civilian noninstitutional population by age, sex, and race" and "Employment status of the Hispanic or Latino population by sex, age, and detailed ethnic group," January 2022, and earlier releases, <www.bls.gov/cps/tables.htm>.

Table 623. Foreign-Born and Native-Born Populations—Employment Status by Selected Characteristics: 2021

[261,445 represents 261,445,000. For civilian noninstitutional population 16 years old and over, except as indicated. The foreign born are persons who reside in the United States but who were born outside the country or in one of its outlying areas to parents who were not U.S. citizens. The foreign born include legally admitted immigrants, refugees, temporary residents such as students and temporary workers, and undocumented immigrants. Annual averages of monthly figures. Based on Current Population Survey; see text, Section 1 and Appendix III]

Characteristic	Civilian noninstitutionalized population (1,000)	Civilian labor force					Not in the labor force (1,000)
		Total (1,000)	Participation rate [1]	Employed (1,000)	Unemployed		
					Number (1,000)	Unemployment rate	
Total	**261,445**	**161,204**	**61.7**	**152,581**	**8,623**	**5.3**	**100,241**
Male	126,487	85,505	67.6	80,829	4,676	5.5	40,982
Female	134,958	75,699	56.1	71,752	3,948	5.2	59,259
FOREIGN BORN							
Total [2]	**43,226**	**27,987**	**64.7**	**26,431**	**1,556**	**5.6**	**15,239**
Male	20,922	16,069	76.8	15,245	823	5.1	4,853
Female	22,304	11,918	53.4	11,186	733	6.1	10,386
Age:							
16 to 24 years old	3,174	1,683	53.0	1,521	161	9.6	1,491
25 to 34 years old	6,987	5,397	77.2	5,099	298	5.5	1,590
35 to 44 years old	9,419	7,472	79.3	7,118	354	4.7	1,947
45 to 54 years old	8,949	7,125	79.6	6,762	363	5.1	1,824
55 to 64 years old	7,020	4,798	68.3	4,505	292	6.1	2,222
65 years old and over	7,678	1,512	19.7	1,425	87	5.8	6,166
Race and Hispanic ethnicity:							
White, non-Hispanic	7,555	4,545	60.2	4,310	234	5.2	3,010
Black, non-Hispanic	4,000	2,777	69.4	2,579	198	7.1	1,223
Asian, non-Hispanic	10,915	6,994	64.1	6,651	344	4.9	3,921
Hispanic [3]	20,170	13,308	66.0	12,545	763	5.7	6,862
Educational attainment:							
Total, 25 years old and over	40,052	26,304	65.7	24,909	1,395	5.3	13,748
Less than a high school diploma	8,972	5,037	56.1	4,708	330	6.5	3,935
High school graduates, no college [4]	10,497	6,530	62.2	6,115	414	6.3	3,967
Some college or associate's degree	6,129	4,071	66.4	3,849	222	5.4	2,058
Bachelor's degree and higher [5]	14,455	10,666	73.8	10,237	429	4.0	3,789
NATIVE BORN							
Total [2]	**218,219**	**133,217**	**61.0**	**126,150**	**7,067**	**5.3**	**85,002**
Male	105,565	69,436	65.8	65,584	3,852	5.5	36,129
Female	112,654	63,781	56.6	60,566	3,215	5.0	48,873
Age:							
16 to 24 years old	34,088	19,005	55.8	17,153	1,851	9.7	15,083
25 to 34 years old	37,764	31,273	82.8	29,479	1,794	5.7	6,491
35 to 44 years old	32,423	26,848	82.8	25,616	1,232	4.6	5,575
45 to 54 years old	30,566	24,752	81.0	23,792	960	3.9	5,814
55 to 64 years old	34,865	22,252	63.8	21,407	845	3.8	12,613
65 years old and over	48,513	9,088	18.7	8,703	385	4.2	39,425
Race and Hispanic ethnicity:							
White, non-Hispanic	154,513	93,561	60.6	89,674	3,886	4.2	60,952
Black, non-Hispanic	27,576	16,390	59.4	14,939	1,451	8.9	11,186
Asian, non-Hispanic	5,047	3,159	62.6	2,993	166	5.2	1,888
Hispanic [3]	24,733	16,115	65.2	14,884	1,232	7.6	8,618
Educational attainment:							
Total, 25 years and over	184,131	114,213	62.0	108,997	5,216	4.6	69,918
Less than a high school diploma	11,031	3,970	36.0	3,556	414	10.4	7,061
High school graduates, no college [4]	52,736	28,465	54.0	26,706	1,759	6.2	24,271
Some college or associate's degree	50,526	31,617	62.6	30,006	1,611	5.1	18,909
Bachelor's degree and higher [5]	69,838	50,162	71.8	48,729	1,432	2.9	19,676

[1] Civilian labor force as a percent of the civilian noninstitutionalized population. [2] Includes other races, not shown separately. [3] Persons of Hispanic origin may be of any race. [4] Includes persons with a high school diploma or equivalent. [5] Includes persons with bachelor's, master's, professional, and doctoral degrees.

Source: U.S. Bureau of Labor Statistics, *Foreign-Born Workers: Labor Force Characteristics—2021*, USDL 22-0902, May 2022. See also <www.bls.gov/news.release/forbrn.toc.htm>.

Table 624. Employment Status of Veterans by Period of Service and Sex: 2021

[In thousands (252,682 represents 252,682,000). For civilian noninstitutional population 18 years old and over. Veterans are defined as men and women who have previously served on active duty in the U.S. Armed Forces and who were civilians at the time of the survey. Veterans are counted in only one period of service, their most recent wartime period; veterans who served in both a wartime period and any other service period are classified in the wartime period. See text, Section 10. Annual averages of monthly figures. Based on Current Population Survey; see text, Section 1 and Appendix III]

| Veteran status, period of service, and sex | Civilian non-institu-tional popula-tion | Civilian labor force | | | | | | | Not in labor force |
| | | Total | Percent of popula-tion | Employed | | Unemployed | | | |
				Total	Percent of popula-tion	Total	Percent of labor force		
Total, 18 years and over..................	252,682	158,961	62.9	150,594	59.6	8,368	5.3		93,721
Veterans..................	**18,506**	**8,818**	**47.7**	**8,433**	**45.6**	**386**	**4.4**		**9,688**
Gulf War era, total..................	7,860	6,012	76.5	5,760	73.3	252	4.2		1,848
Gulf War era II [1]..................	4,670	3,673	78.7	3,502	75.0	171	4.6		997
Gulf War era I [2]..................	3,190	2,339	73.3	2,257	70.8	81	3.5		851
WWII, Korean War, and Vietnam era [3]......	6,587	1,080	16.4	1,033	15.7	48	4.4		5,506
Other service periods [4]..................	4,059	1,726	42.5	1,640	40.4	86	5.0		2,333
Nonveterans [5]..................	234,176	150,143	64.1	142,161	60.7	7,982	5.3		84,033
Male, 18 years and over..................	122,049	84,422	69.2	79,872	65.4	4,551	5.4		37,626
Veterans..................	**16,533**	**7,670**	**46.4**	**7,332**	**44.3**	**337**	**4.4**		**8,863**
Gulf War era, total..................	6,541	5,104	78.0	4,890	74.8	215	4.2		1,437
Gulf War era II [1]..................	3,858	3,113	80.7	2,970	77.0	144	4.6		745
Gulf War era I [2]..................	2,683	1,991	74.2	1,920	71.6	71	3.6		692
WWII, Korean War, and Vietnam era [3]......	6,341	1,037	16.4	992	15.6	46	4.4		5,304
Other service periods [4]..................	3,652	1,529	41.9	1,451	39.7	77	5.1		2,123
Nonveterans [5]..................	105,515	76,752	72.7	72,539	68.7	4,213	5.5		28,763
Female, 18 years and over..................	130,633	74,539	57.1	70,722	54.1	3,817	5.1		56,094
Veterans..................	**1,973**	**1,148**	**58.2**	**1,100**	**55.8**	**48**	**4.2**		**824**
Gulf War era, total..................	1,319	908	68.8	870	66.0	38	4.1		412
Gulf War era II [1]..................	812	560	69.0	533	65.6	27	4.9		252
Gulf War era I [2]..................	507	348	68.6	337	66.5	10	3.0		159
WWII, Korean War, and Vietnam era [3]......	246	43	17.7	41	16.7	2	5.2		202
Other service periods [4]..................	408	197	48.3	189	46.3	8	4.2		210
Nonveterans [5]..................	128,661	73,391	57.0	69,622	54.1	3,769	5.1		55,270

[1] Gulf War era II: September 2001–present. [2] Gulf War era I: August 1990–August 2001. [3] World War II: December 1941–December 1946. Korean War: July 1950–January 1955. Vietnam era: August 1964–April 1975. [4] Other service periods: all other time periods. [5] Nonveterans are men and women who never served on active duty in the U.S. Armed Forces.

Source: U.S. Bureau of Labor Statistics, *Employment Situation of Veterans—2021*, USDL 22-0675, April 2022. See also <www.bls.gov/news.release/vet.nr0.htm>.

Table 625. Labor Force Status of Persons With and Without a Disability: 2021

[31,084 represents 31,084,000. For civilian noninstitutional population 16 years old and over. Persons with a disability are those who have a physical, mental, or emotional condition that causes serious difficulty with their daily activities. Annual averages of monthly figures. Based on the Current Population Survey; see text, Section 1 and Appendix III]

| Characteristic | Civilian non-institutional popula-tion (1,000) | Civilian labor force | | | | | Not in the labor force (1,000) |
| | | Total (1,000) | Participation rate [1] | Employed (1,000) | Unemployed | | |
					Number (1,000)	Unemploy-ment rate	
WITH DISABILITY							
Total..................	**31,084**	**6,619**	**21.3**	**5,950**	**669**	**10.1**	**24,465**
Sex:							
Male..................	14,506	3,483	24.0	3,132	351	10.1	11,023
Female..................	16,578	3,136	18.9	2,818	318	10.1	13,442
Age:							
16 to 64 years..................	15,586	5,477	35.1	4,886	591	10.8	10,108
16 to 19 years..................	762	185	24.3	146	39	21.1	577
20 to 24 years..................	1,021	477	46.7	398	79	16.5	544
25 to 34 years..................	2,230	1,080	48.4	941	139	12.9	1,150
35 to 44 years..................	2,307	989	42.9	884	105	10.6	1,318
45 to 54 years..................	3,231	1,163	36.0	1,050	113	9.7	2,068
55 to 64 years..................	6,035	1,584	26.2	1,467	117	7.4	4,451
65 years and over..................	15,498	1,142	7.4	1,063	78	6.8	14,357
WITHOUT DISABILITY							
Total..................	**230,361**	**154,585**	**67.1**	**146,631**	**7,954**	**5.1**	**75,776**
Sex:							
Male..................	111,982	82,022	73.2	77,697	4,325	5.3	29,960
Female..................	118,380	72,563	61.3	68,934	3,629	5.0	45,816
Age:							
16 to 64 years..................	189,669	145,127	76.5	137,567	7,560	5.2	44,542
16 to 19 years..................	15,691	5,777	36.8	5,120	657	11.4	9,914
20 to 24 years..................	19,788	14,248	72.0	13,010	1,238	8.7	5,539
25 to 34 years..................	42,521	35,590	83.7	33,637	1,953	5.5	6,931
35 to 44 years..................	39,536	33,332	84.3	31,851	1,481	4.4	6,204
45 to 54 years..................	36,283	30,714	84.7	29,504	1,210	3.9	5,569
55 to 64 years..................	35,850	25,466	71.0	24,445	1,021	4.0	10,384
65 years and over..................	40,692	9,458	23.2	9,064	394	4.2	31,234

[1] Civilian labor force as a percent of the civilian noninstitutional population.

Source: U.S. Bureau of Labor Statistics, *Persons with A Disability: Labor Force Characteristics—2021*, USDL 22-0317, February 2022. See also <www.bls.gov/cps/demographics.htm#disability>.

Table 626. Civilian Labor Force—Percent Distribution by Sex and Age: 1990 to 2021

[125,840 represents 125,840,000. Civilian noninstitutionalized population 16 years old and over. Annual averages of monthly figures. Data not strictly comparable with data for earlier years; see BLS Handbook of Methods, <www.bls.gov/opub/hom/>. Based on Current Population Survey; see text, Section 1 and Appendix III]

Year and sex	Civilian labor force (1,000)	Percent distribution						
		16 to 19 years	20 to 24 years	25 to 34 years	35 to 44 years	45 to 54 years	55 to 64 years	65 years and over
Total:								
1990	125,840	6.2	11.7	28.6	25.5	16.1	9.2	2.7
2000	142,583	5.8	10.0	23.0	26.3	21.8	10.1	3.0
2010	153,889	3.8	9.8	21.8	21.7	23.4	15.1	4.4
2020	160,742	3.6	9.0	22.7	21.1	20.0	17.0	6.6
2021	161,204	3.7	9.1	22.7	21.3	19.8	16.8	6.6
Male:								
1990	69,011	5.9	11.4	28.8	25.3	16.1	9.6	2.9
2000	76,280	5.6	9.9	23.4	26.3	21.3	10.2	3.3
2010	81,985	3.6	9.6	22.4	22.1	23.0	14.8	4.5
2020	85,204	3.4	8.7	22.9	21.4	19.9	16.9	6.9
2021	85,505	3.5	8.9	22.9	21.6	19.5	16.6	6.9
Female:								
1990	56,829	6.5	12.0	28.3	25.8	16.1	8.7	2.6
2000	66,303	6.0	10.2	22.5	26.4	22.3	9.9	2.7
2010	71,904	4.1	10.0	21.2	21.2	23.8	15.6	4.2
2020	75,538	3.8	9.4	22.5	20.8	20.1	17.1	6.3
2021	75,699	3.9	9.4	22.5	20.9	20.0	17.0	6.2

Source: U.S. Bureau of Labor Statistics, CPS Tables, "Employment status of the civilian noninstitutional population by age, sex, and race," January 2022, and earlier releases, <www.bls.gov/cps/tables.htm>.

Table 627. Civilian Labor Force and Participation Rates by Educational Attainment, Sex, Race, and Hispanic Origin: 2010 to 2021

[132,955 represents 132,955,000. Civilian noninstitutional population 25 years old and over. Annual averages of monthly figures. Revisions to population controls and other changes can affect the comparability of data over time; see BLS Handbook of Methods, <www.bls.gov/opub/hom/>. See Table 662 for unemployment data. Rates are based on annual average civilian noninstitutional population of each specified group and represent proportion of each specified group in the civilian labor force]

Year, sex, and race/ethnicity	Civilian labor force					Participation rate [1] (percent)				
	Total (1,000)	Percent distribution				Total	Less than a high school diploma	High school graduate, no college	Less than a bachelor's degree	College graduate
		Less than a high school diploma	High school graduate, no college	Less than a bachelor's degree	College graduate					
Total: [2]										
2010	132,955	8.9	28.8	27.7	34.6	66.5	46.3	61.6	70.5	76.7
2015	135,907	8.1	26.0	27.6	38.4	64.0	45.4	57.2	66.6	74.4
2020	140,535	6.4	24.7	25.9	43.0	63.1	44.9	55.9	63.5	72.4
2021	140,516	6.4	24.9	25.4	43.3	62.7	45.0	55.3	63.0	72.2
Male:										
2010	71,129	10.6	30.4	25.6	33.4	74.1	59.1	71.4	76.7	81.3
2015	72,698	9.7	28.1	25.8	36.4	71.5	58.3	67.2	73.1	79.0
2020	74,929	7.7	27.6	24.9	39.9	70.0	56.7	65.9	70.0	76.7
2021	74,939	7.8	27.9	24.3	40.0	69.5	56.7	65.4	69.6	76.2
Female:										
2010	61,825	7.0	26.9	30.1	36.0	59.5	33.5	52.4	65.4	72.4
2015	63,209	6.2	23.6	29.6	40.7	57.2	32.3	47.6	61.1	70.2
2020	65,608	4.9	21.4	27.1	46.6	56.7	32.6	45.7	57.9	68.7
2021	65,577	4.8	21.4	26.7	47.1	56.3	32.6	45.1	57.3	68.6
White: [3]										
2010	108,274	8.9	28.7	27.5	34.9	66.5	47.7	61.2	70.1	76.5
2015	107,366	8.1	25.9	27.5	38.5	63.8	46.7	56.7	65.9	74.0
2020	109,013	6.5	24.7	26.0	42.8	62.7	46.8	55.7	62.8	71.6
2021	108,351	6.6	24.8	25.5	43.1	62.1	47.1	54.7	62.0	71.1
Black: [3]										
2010	15,114	9.4	33.3	32.8	24.5	65.8	38.8	63.8	73.5	79.5
2015	16,279	7.5	30.9	33.3	28.3	63.9	37.5	58.8	70.2	77.7
2020	17,453	6.0	29.4	30.5	34.1	62.7	35.7	56.3	66.4	76.6
2021	17,722	5.3	30.7	29.9	34.1	62.9	33.9	57.2	66.4	76.5
Asian: [3]										
2010	6,601	7.3	18.8	17.1	56.7	68.7	44.1	62.8	70.6	75.9
2015	8,200	6.1	17.1	16.0	60.9	66.7	40.8	58.8	68.1	73.7
2020	9,428	4.8	14.6	13.2	67.4	66.4	41.4	54.9	63.5	73.5
2021	9,642	4.4	14.7	13.5	67.4	67.2	40.0	54.1	65.2	75.0
Hispanic: [4]										
2010	18,987	31.4	30.8	21.7	16.0	71.4	61.9	73.9	77.8	81.7
2015	21,618	27.7	29.8	23.6	18.9	69.3	59.3	69.6	75.5	80.1
2020	24,249	21.1	30.8	24.2	24.0	68.5	57.0	67.9	73.3	78.5
2021	24,560	21.6	31.4	23.0	23.9	68.2	57.2	67.4	72.0	79.1

[1] Civilian labor force as a percent of the civilian noninstitutional population. [2] Includes other races, not shown separately. [3] For persons in this race group only. See footnote 2, Table 622. [4] Persons of Hispanic origin may be of any race.

Source: U.S. Bureau of Labor Statistics, CPS Tables, "Employment status of the civilian noninstitutional population 25 years and over by educational attainment, sex, race, and Hispanic or Latino ethnicity," January 2022, and earlier releases, <www.bls.gov/cps/tables.htm>.

Table 628. Civilian Labor Force by Employment Status and Sex by State: 2021

[In thousands (161,204 represents 161,204,000), except ratio and rate. Civilian noninstitutionalized population 16 years old and over. Annual averages of monthly figures. Data for states may not sum to national totals due to rounding]

State	Labor force Total	Labor force Female	Employed Total	Employed Female	Employment/ population ratio [1]	Unemployed Number Total	Unemployed Number Female	Unemployed Rate [2] Total	Unemployed Rate [2] Male	Unemployed Rate [2] Female	Participation rate [3] Male	Participation rate [3] Female
United States.....	**161,204**	**75,699**	**152,581**	**71,752**	**58.4**	**8,623**	**3,948**	**5.3**	**5.5**	**5.2**	**67.6**	**56.1**
Alabama.............	2,248	1,062	2,166	1,025	54.5	82	37	3.6	3.7	3.5	63.2	50.6
Alaska..............	353	166	329	156	60.3	24	10	6.8	7.4	6.1	67.0	62.2
Arizona.............	3,542	1,606	3,360	1,517	58.3	182	89	5.1	4.8	5.6	68.9	54.4
Arkansas............	1,345	636	1,289	611	54.7	55	25	4.1	4.2	3.9	62.6	51.9
California............	18,961	8,667	17,596	8,037	56.7	1,364	630	7.2	7.1	7.3	67.8	54.7
Colorado............	3,130	1,434	2,971	1,366	64.2	159	68	5.1	5.3	4.8	73.8	61.6
Connecticut.........	1,865	884	1,746	829	59.7	119	55	6.4	6.6	6.2	69.7	58.2
Delaware............	492	240	465	227	57.7	27	13	5.5	5.5	5.5	66.1	56.6
District of Columbia.........	378	193	355	180	65.0	23	13	6.1	5.6	6.6	73.3	65.8
Florida..............	10,320	4,841	9,852	4,617	55.7	467	224	4.5	4.4	4.6	64.5	52.6
Georgia.............	5,187	2,491	4,978	2,389	59.4	209	102	4.0	4.0	4.1	68.1	56.3
Hawaii..............	667	316	626	297	56.0	41	19	6.1	6.3	5.9	65.0	54.7
Idaho...............	923	411	889	396	60.6	35	15	3.7	3.9	3.6	70.7	55.4
Illinois..............	6,363	3,030	5,983	2,856	59.6	380	174	6.0	6.2	5.7	68.6	58.5
Indiana.............	3,318	1,521	3,193	1,468	60.1	125	54	3.8	4.0	3.5	69.7	55.6
Iowa................	1,683	792	1,619	763	64.6	64	29	3.8	3.9	3.7	71.9	62.5
Kansas.............	1,495	710	1,445	687	64.1	50	23	3.3	3.4	3.2	71.2	61.6
Kentucky...........	2,025	944	1,930	900	54.6	95	44	4.7	4.7	4.6	63.4	51.7
Louisiana...........	2,057	991	1,946	947	54.5	111	44	5.4	6.3	4.5	63.2	52.6
Maine...............	689	337	657	322	57.8	31	16	4.5	4.4	4.7	63.6	57.6
Maryland............	3,196	1,545	3,017	1,460	62.0	179	84	5.6	5.7	5.4	71.7	60.2
Massachusetts......	3,734	1,817	3,518	1,724	61.4	215	93	5.8	6.4	5.1	69.8	60.9
Michigan............	4,742	2,244	4,472	2,131	55.5	270	114	5.7	6.3	5.1	63.8	54.1
Minnesota...........	3,039	1,443	2,923	1,386	65.1	116	57	3.8	3.7	4.0	71.8	63.6
Mississippi..........	1,249	611	1,181	581	51.8	68	30	5.5	6.0	4.9	59.7	50.5
Missouri............	3,053	1,473	2,922	1,417	60.2	131	56	4.3	4.7	3.8	67.4	58.7
Montana............	556	266	537	258	60.9	18	8	3.3	3.7	2.8	65.9	60.1
Nebraska...........	1,051	495	1,022	480	67.7	29	15	2.8	2.5	3.1	74.7	64.8
Nevada.............	1,501	687	1,386	635	55.7	115	53	7.7	7.7	7.7	66.0	54.7
New Hampshire.....	743	350	716	340	62.2	28	11	3.7	4.3	3.1	69.4	59.9
New Jersey..........	4,649	2,163	4,356	2,019	59.0	293	144	6.3	6.0	6.7	69.8	56.5
New Mexico.........	936	438	873	412	52.5	63	26	6.7	7.4	5.9	61.8	51.1
New York............	9,480	4,514	8,816	4,207	55.1	665	307	7.0	7.2	6.8	65.0	54.1
North Carolina......	4,943	2,371	4,717	2,268	56.7	226	103	4.6	4.8	4.4	65.3	54.1
North Dakota........	406	183	393	178	66.2	13	5	3.3	3.6	2.9	73.8	62.9
Ohio................	5,719	2,727	5,434	2,592	58.3	285	135	5.0	5.0	5.0	66.3	56.6
Oklahoma...........	1,858	860	1,784	830	58.3	74	31	4.0	4.4	3.6	67.4	54.5
Oregon.............	2,146	1,015	2,034	964	59.0	112	51	5.2	5.4	5.0	67.1	57.5
Pennsylvania........	6,385	3,056	5,970	2,875	57.3	415	181	6.5	7.0	5.9	66.1	56.7
Rhode Island........	571	282	540	268	60.2	31	14	5.5	6.0	4.9	67.3	60.3
South Carolina......	2,350	1,142	2,254	1,094	54.7	95	48	4.1	3.9	4.2	62.1	52.5
South Dakota........	472	215	460	210	67.3	12	5	2.6	2.8	2.5	75.2	63.0
Tennessee..........	3,323	1,594	3,188	1,522	57.9	135	72	4.1	3.7	4.5	65.7	55.4
Texas...............	14,162	6,377	13,350	6,020	59.4	812	357	5.7	5.8	5.6	71.2	55.3
Utah................	1,685	763	1,636	741	66.1	50	22	2.9	3.0	2.9	74.7	61.5
Vermont............	334	163	322	157	59.9	12	6	3.6	3.6	3.6	64.9	59.4
Virginia.............	4,317	2,106	4,147	2,028	61.1	170	79	3.9	4.1	3.7	68.1	59.5
Washington.........	3,910	1,819	3,693	1,726	60.1	217	93	5.5	5.9	5.1	68.9	58.5
West Virginia.......	786	368	749	352	51.9	37	16	4.7	5.2	4.3	59.2	49.9
Wisconsin...........	3,131	1473	3,014	1,413	64.0	116	60	3.7	3.4	4.1	71.4	61.7
Wyoming............	291	134	278	129	61.3	13	5	4.5	5.2	3.7	68.4	59.9

[1] Civilian employment as a percent of civilian noninstitutionalized population. [2] Percent unemployed of the civilian labor force. [3] Percent of civilian noninstitutionalized population of each specified group in the civilian labor force.

Source: U.S. Bureau of Labor Statistics, Labor Force Statistics from the Current Population Survey, "Employment status of the civilian noninstitutional population by sex, age, and race," <www.bls.gov/cps/tables.htm>; and Local Area Unemployment Statistics, "Expanded State Employment Status Demographic Data," <www.bls.gov/lau/#tables>; accessed July 2022.

Table 629. Civilian Labor Force Status by Selected Metropolitan Area: 2021

[161,204 represents 161,204,000. Civilian noninstitutional population 16 years old and over. Annual averages of monthly figures. Data are derived from the Local Area Unemployment Statistics program, a Federal-State cooperative effort in which monthly estimates of total employment and unemployment are prepared for approximately 7,500 areas. For definitions of metropolitan areas, see Appendix II]

Metropolitan area ranked by 2020 population	Civilian labor force (1,000)	Unemployment rate [1]	Metropolitan area ranked by 2020 population	Civilian labor force (1,000)	Unemployment rate [1]
United States, total	**161,204**	**5.3**	Sacramento-Roseville-Folsom, CA	1,099	6.4
New York-Newark-Jersey City, NY-NJ-PA	10,016	7.3	Pittsburgh, PA	1,178	6.4
Los Angeles-Long Beach-Anaheim, CA	6,548	8.2	Austin-Round Rock-Georgetown, TX	1,306	4.1
Chicago-Naperville-Elgin, IL-IN-WI	4,804	6.2	Las Vegas-Henderson-Paradise, NV	1,100	8.3
Dallas-Fort Worth-Arlington, TX	4,095	5.1	Cincinnati, OH-KY-IN	1,125	4.4
Houston-The Woodlands-Sugar Land, TX	3,424	6.4	Kansas City, MO-KS	1,143	4.2
Washington-Arlington-Alexandria, DC-VA-MD-WV	3,356	4.9	Columbus, OH	1,118	4.6
Philadelphia-Camden-Wilmington, PA-NJ-DE-MD	3,155	6.3	Indianapolis-Carmel-Anderson, IN	1,082	3.5
Miami-Fort Lauderdale-West Palm Beach, FL	3,071	4.9	Cleveland-Elyria, OH	1,012	5.9
Atlanta-Sandy Springs-Alpharetta, GA	3,132	3.9	San Jose-Sunnyvale-Santa Clara, CA	1,046	4.8
Boston-Cambridge-Newton, MA-NH NECTA [2]	2,780	5.3	Nashville-Davidson-Murfreesboro-Franklin, TN	1,098	3.6
Phoenix-Mesa-Chandler, AZ	2,504	4.5	Virginia Beach-Norfolk-Newport News, VA-NC	830	4.5
San Francisco-Oakland-Berkeley, CA	2,458	5.6	Providence-Warwick, RI-MA NECTA [2]	705	5.8
Riverside-San Bernardino-Ontario, CA	2,118	7.4	Jacksonville, FL	797	4.0
Detroit-Warren-Dearborn, MI	2,114	6.2	Milwaukee-Waukesha-West Allis, WI	821	4.4
Seattle-Tacoma-Bellevue, WA	2,164	4.8	Oklahoma City, OK	698	3.7
Minneapolis-St. Paul-Bloomington, MN-WI	1,981	3.4	Raleigh-Cary, NC	729	4.0
San Diego-Chula Vista-Carlsbad, CA	1,544	6.5	Memphis, TN-MS-AR	642	6.2
Tampa-St. Petersburg-Clearwater, FL	1,575	4.2	Richmond, VA	666	4.2
Denver-Aurora-Lakewood, CO	1,683	5.5	Louisville-Jefferson County, KY-IN	665	4.3
Baltimore-Columbia-Towson, MD	1,483	5.5	New Orleans-Metairie, LA	585	6.3
St. Louis, MO-IL	1,457	4.6	Salt Lake City, UT	691	2.8
Orlando-Kissimmee-Sanford, FL	1,331	5.1	Hartford-East Hartford-Middletown, CT [2]	610	6.3
Charlotte-Concord-Gastonia, NC-SC	1,360	4.6	Buffalo-Cheektowaga-Niagara Falls, NY	532	5.5
San Antonio-New Braunfels, TX	1,209	5.2	Birmingham-Hoover, AL	555	3.2
Portland-Vancouver-Hillsboro, OR-WA	1,344	5.1	Rochester, NY	517	4.9

[1] Percent of the civilian labor force unemployed. [2] New England City and Town Areas. See Appendix II.

Source: U.S. Bureau of Labor Statistics, "Local Area Unemployment Statistics," <www.bls.gov/lau/>, accessed June 2022.

Table 630. School Enrollment and Labor Force Status of Teenagers and Young Adults: 2021

[In thousands (37,222 represents 37,222,000), except rate. As of October. Covers civilian noninstitutional population age 16 to 24. Based on Current Population Survey; see text, Section 1 and Appendix III]

Characteristic	Population	Civilian labor force	Employed	Unemployed Total	Unemployed Rate [1]	Not in labor force
Total, 16 to 24 years [2]	**37,222**	**20,785**	**19,121**	**1,663**	**8.0**	**16,437**
Enrolled in school [2]	**20,541**	**7,512**	**7,045**	**467**	**6.2**	**13,029**
Enrolled in high school	9,324	2,165	1,985	180	8.3	7,159
Male	4,729	1,015	934	81	8.0	3,714
Female	4,595	1,150	1,051	99	8.6	3,445
Enrolled in college	11,217	5,347	5,060	287	5.4	5,870
Male	4,930	2,194	2,071	123	5.6	2,736
Female	6,287	3,153	2,989	164	5.2	3,134
Enrolled in two-year college	2,479	1,445	1,360	84	5.8	1,034
Enrolled in four-year college	8,738	3,902	3,700	202	5.2	4,835
White:						
Enrolled in high school	6,750	1,742	1,592	150	8.6	5,007
Enrolled in college	7,996	3,936	3,769	167	4.2	4,060
Black or African American:						
Enrolled in high school	1,409	250	238	11	4.6	1,159
Enrolled in college	1,606	711	646	65	9.1	895
Asian:						
Enrolled in high school	459	41	39	2	(NA)	419
Enrolled in college	1,057	409	379	31	7.5	648
Hispanic: [3]						
Enrolled in high school	2,227	400	338	62	15.4	1,827
Enrolled in college	2,359	1,222	1,157	65	5.3	1,137
Not enrolled in school [2]	**16,681**	**13,273**	**12,077**	**1,196**	**9.0**	**3,408**
White	12,565	10,138	9,340	798	7.9	2,428
Black	2,428	1,873	1,617	256	13.7	555
Asian	658	515	455	61	11.8	143
Hispanic [3]	4,331	3,356	3,027	330	9.8	974

NA Not available. [1] Percent unemployed of civilian labor force in each category. [2] Includes other races, not shown separately. [3] Persons of Hispanic origin may be of any race.

Source: U.S. Bureau of Labor Statistics, *College Enrollment and Work Activity of Recent High School and College Graduates—2021*, USDL 22-0708, April 2022. See also <www.bls.gov/news.release/hsgec.toc.htm>.

Table 631. Labor Force Participation Rates by Marital Status, Sex, and Age: 1970 to 2021

[In percent. For the civilian noninstitutional population 16 years old and over. Annual averages of monthly figures. Participation rate is the civilian labor force as a percent of the civilian noninstitutional population. Based on Current Population Survey; see text, Section 1 and Appendix III]

Marital status and year	Male participation rate							Female participation rate						
	Total	16–19 years	20–24 years	25–34 years	35–44 years	45–64 years	65 years and over	Total	16–19 years	20–24 years	25–34 years	35–44 years	45–64 years	65 years and over
Single: [1]														
1970	65.5	54.6	73.8	87.9	86.2	75.7	25.2	56.8	44.7	73.0	81.4	78.6	73.0	19.7
1980	72.6	59.9	81.3	89.2	82.2	66.9	16.8	64.4	53.6	75.2	83.3	76.9	65.6	13.9
1990	74.8	55.1	81.6	89.9	84.5	67.3	15.7	66.7	51.7	74.5	80.9	80.8	66.2	12.1
2000	73.6	52.5	80.5	89.4	82.9	69.7	17.3	68.9	51.1	76.1	83.9	80.9	69.9	10.8
2010	67.3	34.6	73.1	85.8	83.7	67.6	25.0	63.3	34.9	69.8	81.3	78.2	69.4	20.1
2014	66.7	33.3	72.5	85.1	82.4	64.4	25.9	62.9	34.4	69.1	79.9	77.6	65.5	21.3
2015	66.8	33.9	71.7	85.6	81.2	64.6	26.6	62.9	34.1	69.3	79.7	77.6	65.8	20.9
2016	67.3	35.1	71.8	85.5	82.5	65.2	26.1	63.4	35.0	69.2	80.9	77.3	65.4	22.6
2017	67.4	34.4	72.9	85.6	82.8	64.2	26.3	64.3	35.7	69.8	81.7	78.9	66.0	23.7
2018	67.7	34.0	72.1	85.9	83.4	66.4	25.9	64.5	35.9	70.2	81.4	78.4	66.3	25.2
2019	68.1	34.7	72.9	86.0	82.6	67.0	26.5	65.0	35.7	71.5	81.9	77.9	67.0	24.4
2020	66.3	33.9	69.8	83.3	81.0	66.3	26.4	63.5	34.9	68.3	80.2	77.7	66.6	23.6
2021	67.6	35.7	71.9	84.2	81.6	65.8	26.7	64.3	36.5	69.2	80.7	77.3	66.7	21.7
Married: [2]														
1970	86.1	92.3	94.7	98.0	98.1	91.2	29.9	40.5	37.8	47.9	38.8	46.8	44.0	7.3
1980	80.9	91.3	96.9	97.5	97.2	84.3	20.5	49.8	49.3	61.4	58.8	61.8	46.9	7.3
1990	78.6	92.1	95.6	96.9	96.7	82.6	17.5	58.4	49.5	66.1	69.6	74.0	56.5	8.5
2000	77.3	79.5	94.1	96.7	95.8	83.0	19.2	61.1	53.2	63.8	70.3	74.8	65.4	10.1
2010	75.8	78.2	89.3	94.3	94.5	83.6	23.5	61.0	40.2	60.9	68.8	72.8	68.8	15.2
2014	73.5	76.8	92.0	93.4	94.0	82.9	24.9	58.4	45.1	58.9	67.7	71.3	66.6	16.8
2015	73.4	75.9	89.7	93.5	94.2	83.1	25.2	58.1	47.1	61.6	67.1	71.9	66.0	16.8
2016	73.1	71.5	89.3	93.7	94.2	83.2	25.5	57.9	43.8	59.9	67.9	71.8	66.3	16.6
2017	72.9	80.1	89.1	93.4	94.1	83.5	25.4	58.2	50.6	61.0	68.4	72.3	67.0	17.0
2018	73.1	89.5	88.9	94.4	94.4	83.9	25.7	58.2	48.7	61.7	69.4	72.4	67.2	17.1
2019	73.0	89.9	90.6	94.4	94.6	84.3	26.4	58.6	48.4	62.4	70.5	73.5	67.6	17.9
2020	71.4	77.3	89.0	93.5	93.7	83.2	25.3	57.4	36.6	61.4	70.4	72.7	66.6	17.0
2021	70.9	86.3	89.5	93.7	93.8	83.3	24.7	56.9	43.8	63.5	70.6	72.3	66.8	16.3
Other: [3]														
1970	60.7	(B)	90.4	93.7	91.1	78.5	19.3	40.3	48.6	60.3	64.6	68.8	61.9	10.0
1980	67.5	(B)	92.6	94.1	91.9	73.3	13.7	43.6	50.0	68.4	76.5	77.1	60.2	8.2
1990	68.9	(B)	93.1	93.0	90.7	74.9	12.0	47.2	53.9	65.4	77.0	82.1	65.0	8.4
2000	66.8	60.5	88.1	93.2	89.9	73.9	12.9	49.0	46.0	74.0	83.1	82.9	69.8	8.7
2010	63.0	37.6	78.8	89.0	88.5	71.8	17.2	48.8	35.2	66.3	77.7	80.7	68.8	12.1
2014	59.6	31.2	80.3	88.8	87.1	70.4	16.9	47.3	38.2	66.3	77.2	80.1	66.8	13.0
2015	58.8	36.6	73.0	87.0	86.8	70.3	17.7	46.7	42.9	67.0	75.4	79.0	66.4	13.4
2016	59.6	37.7	71.0	88.2	87.1	71.0	19.1	46.9	40.4	67.5	76.1	80.6	66.4	13.8
2017	59.0	34.7	77.5	88.7	87.9	71.1	19.0	46.0	31.8	63.5	79.0	79.7	66.0	13.5
2018	58.3	33.3	75.3	87.0	87.6	71.7	19.1	45.9	31.9	64.3	79.8	80.6	66.4	13.8
2019	58.2	39.0	71.3	86.9	88.0	72.0	19.6	45.9	31.7	66.9	79.3	81.0	67.2	14.2
2020	57.1	41.0	74.8	87.6	86.6	71.7	19.3	44.3	38.5	65.0	77.7	80.5	66.5	13.5
2021	56.0	40.4	76.6	88.7	86.5	71.0	18.7	43.9	34.8	66.9	76.8	79.7	67.0	13.2

B Percentage not shown where base is less than 50,000. [1] Never married. [2] Spouse present. [3] Widowed, divorced, and separated (married, spouse absent).

Source: U.S. Bureau of Labor Statistics, Current Population Survey, unpublished data. See also <www.bls.gov/cps/home.htm>.

Table 632. Marital Status of Women in the Civilian Labor Force: 1970 to 2021

[31,543 represents 31,543,000. For civilian noninstitutional population 16 years and over. Annual averages of monthly figures. Based on the Current Population Survey; see text, Section 1 and Appendix III]

Year	Female civilian labor force (1,000)				Female participation rate (percent) [3]			
	Total	Never married	Married [1]	Other [2]	Total	Never married	Married [1]	Other [2]
1970	31,543	7,265	18,475	5,804	43.3	56.8	40.5	40.3
1980	45,487	11,865	24,980	8,643	51.5	64.4	49.8	43.6
1990	56,829	14,612	30,901	11,315	57.5	66.7	58.4	47.2
2000	66,303	17,849	35,146	13,308	59.9	68.9	61.1	49.0
2010	71,904	20,592	36,742	14,570	58.6	63.3	61.0	48.8
2011	71,642	20,878	36,141	14,623	58.1	62.8	60.2	48.8
2012	72,648	21,506	36,436	14,706	57.7	62.8	59.5	48.3
2013	72,722	22,070	36,137	14,515	57.2	63.0	58.9	47.3
2014	73,039	22,320	36,082	14,637	57.0	62.9	58.4	47.3
2015	73,510	22,738	36,135	14,637	56.7	62.9	58.1	46.7
2016	74,433	23,321	36,387	14,725	56.8	63.4	57.9	46.9
2017	75,174	23,993	36,776	14,405	57.0	64.3	58.2	46.0
2018	75,979	24,556	36,885	14,538	57.1	64.5	58.2	45.9
2019	76,852	25,023	37,214	14,615	57.4	65.0	58.6	45.9
2020	75,539	24,749	37,157	13,633	56.2	63.5	57.4	44.3
2021	75,699	25,766	36,260	13,673	56.1	64.3	56.9	43.9

[1] Spouse present. [2] Widowed, divorced, and separated (married, spouse absent). [3] Civilian labor force as a percent of the civilian noninstitutional population.

Source: U.S. Bureau of Labor Statistics, Current Population Survey, unpublished data. See also <www.bls.gov/cps/home.htm>.

Table 633. Employment Status of Women by Marital Status and Presence and Age of Children: 1970 to 2018

[7.0 represents 7,000,000. As of March. Data are from the Current Population Survey, Annual Social and Economic Supplement (ASEC), which includes civilian noninstitutionalized population, age 16 years old and over. For more information; see text, Section 1 and Appendix III]

Item	Total			With any children under age 18								
				Total			Children 6 to 17 years			Children under 6 years		
	Single [1]	Married [2]	Other [3]	Single [1]	Married [2]	Other [3]	Single [1]	Married [2]	Other [3]	Single [1]	Married [2]	Other [3]
IN LABOR FORCE (millions)												
1970	7.0	18.4	5.9	(NA)	10.2	1.9	(NA)	6.3	1.3	(NA)	3.9	0.6
1980	11.2	24.9	8.8	0.6	13.7	3.6	0.2	8.4	2.6	0.3	5.2	1.0
1990	14.0	31.0	11.2	1.5	16.5	4.2	0.6	9.3	3.0	0.9	7.2	1.2
2000	17.8	35.0	13.2	3.1	18.2	4.5	1.2	10.8	3.4	1.8	7.3	1.1
2010	20.0	37.2	14.7	3.6	17.6	4.5	1.6	10.4	3.3	2.1	7.2	1.2
2016	23.2	36.9	14.7	4.1	16.9	4.1	1.9	10.2	3.0	2.2	6.7	1.1
2017	23.7	37.4	14.4	4.0	16.9	3.9	2.0	10.2	2.9	2.1	6.7	1.0
2018	24.4	37.1	14.5	4.0	16.9	3.9	2.0	10.1	3.0	2.1	6.8	0.9
PARTICIPATION RATE [4]												
1970	53.0	40.8	39.1	(NA)	39.7	60.7	(NA)	49.2	66.9	(NA)	30.3	52.2
1980	61.5	50.1	44.0	52.0	54.1	69.4	67.6	61.7	74.6	44.1	45.1	60.3
1990	66.4	58.2	46.8	55.2	66.3	74.2	69.7	73.6	79.7	48.7	58.9	63.6
2000	68.6	62.0	50.2	73.9	70.6	82.7	79.7	77.2	84.9	70.5	62.8	76.6
2010	62.3	61.7	49.2	70.1	69.7	79.2	77.0	75.9	81.8	65.6	62.5	73.1
2016	62.7	58.9	47.2	72.8	68.6	79.3	78.3	73.0	80.6	68.6	62.9	75.5
2017	63.9	59.1	46.4	73.4	69.3	79.0	78.9	74.3	80.8	68.9	62.9	74.1
2018	64.5	58.3	46.3	75.0	69.0	79.7	79.5	74.7	81.2	71.3	61.8	75.1
EMPLOYMENT (millions)												
1970	6.5	17.5	5.6	(NA)	9.6	1.8	(NA)	6.0	1.2	(NA)	3.6	0.6
1980	10.1	23.6	8.2	0.4	12.8	3.3	0.2	8.1	2.4	0.2	4.8	0.9
1990	12.9	29.9	10.5	1.2	15.8	3.8	0.5	8.9	2.7	0.7	6.9	1.1
2000	16.4	34.0	12.7	2.7	17.6	4.3	1.1	10.6	3.2	1.6	7.1	1.1
2010	17.5	35.0	13.3	3.0	16.5	4.0	1.3	9.8	2.9	1.6	6.7	1.1
2016	21.4	35.7	14.0	3.7	16.3	3.9	1.8	9.9	2.9	1.9	6.5	1.0
2017	22.3	36.4	13.6	3.7	16.4	3.7	1.8	9.9	2.8	1.9	6.5	0.9
2018	23.0	36.2	13.9	3.7	16.5	3.7	1.8	9.9	2.8	1.9	6.6	0.8
UNEMPLOYMENT RATE [5]												
1970	7.1	4.8	4.8	(NA)	6.0	7.2	(NA)	4.8	5.9	(NA)	7.9	9.8
1980	10.3	5.3	6.4	23.2	5.9	9.2	15.6	4.4	7.9	29.2	8.3	12.8
1990	8.2	3.5	5.7	18.4	4.2	8.5	14.5	3.8	7.7	20.8	4.8	10.2
2000	7.3	2.7	4.3	11.0	2.9	5.1	8.7	2.6	4.8	12.6	3.5	5.9
2010	12.3	6.0	9.7	18.1	6.3	11.1	14.4	6.0	10.3	20.9	6.7	13.4
2016	8.0	3.1	4.7	10.4	3.2	5.5	8.7	3.1	4.5	11.9	3.4	8.2
2017	6.3	2.8	5.1	9.4	3.1	5.4	7.3	3.1	4.8	11.3	3.1	7.3
2018	5.6	2.6	4.2	8.0	2.5	5.2	6.6	2.3	4.7	9.3	2.8	6.6

NA Not available. [1] Never married. [2] Spouse present. [3] Widowed, divorced, or separated (married, spouse absent). [4] Percent of women in each specific category in the labor force. [5] Unemployed as a percent of civilian labor force in specified group.

Source: U.S. Bureau of Labor Statistics, unpublished data. See also <www.bls.gov/cps/home.htm>.

Table 634. Labor Force Participation Rates for Wives, Spouse Present, by Age of Own Youngest Child: 1990 to 2018

[In percent. As of March. Based on Current Population Survey, Annual Social and Economic Supplement (ASEC), which includes civilian noninstitutionalized population, 16 years old and over, and military personnel who live in households with at least one other civilian adult. Armed Forces includes only those Armed Forces members living on or off post with their families; all other members of the Armed Forces are excluded. Data refer to persons in primary families. For more information; see text, Section 1 and Appendix III]

Presence and age of child	1990	2000	2010	2016	2017	2018				
						Total	White [1]	Black [1]	Asian [1, 2]	Hispanic [3]
Wives, total	**58.3**	**62.2**	**61.9**	**59.1**	**59.3**	**58.5**	**58.2**	**62.7**	**56.9**	**55.0**
No children under 18 years	51.1	54.8	56.0	52.7	52.8	51.8	51.3	54.6	52.9	52.1
With children under 18 years	66.5	70.9	70.1	68.9	69.5	69.2	69.9	75.0	60.4	57.2
Under 6 years, total	59.1	63.1	62.9	63.1	63.1	62.1	63.5	68.3	50.0	47.2
Under 3 years	55.9	59.4	59.5	62.3	62.1	60.0	61.7	62.1	46.6	43.3
Under 1 year	53.9	58.4	59.0	60.0	60.4	59.2	60.6	64.1	46.6	30.4
1 year	(NA)	(NA)	57.6	62.3	62.3	59.7	62.5	54.6	43.1	47.9
2 years	60.9	61.9	62.4	64.9	63.7	61.3	62.0	69.3	49.3	51.1
3 to 5 years	64.1	68.6	67.7	64.2	64.5	64.9	66.0	76.3	53.7	51.6
3 years	63.0	66.0	66.4	61.2	62.2	64.3	67.0	70.1	44.4	49.4
4 years	65.0	69.6	68.9	65.7	65.4	65.0	65.3	76.6	57.5	57.2
5 years	64.4	70.7	68.1	66.2	66.5	65.7	65.4	83.7	59.9	48.2
6 to 13 years	73.1	76.0	74.8	72.2	73.5	74.1	74.0	81.4	69.3	63.5
14 to 17 years	75.0	80.8	79.0	75.8	76.8	76.6	77.1	77.4	71.8	68.8

NA Not available. [1] Persons in this race group only. See footnote 2, Table 622. [2] Excludes Pacific Islanders. [3] Persons of Hispanic origin may be of any race.

Source: U.S. Bureau of Labor Statistics, unpublished data. See also <www.bls.gov/cps/home.htm>.

Table 635. Married Couples by Labor Force Status of Spouses: 1990 to 2021

[52,317 represents 52,317,000. As of March. For opposite-sex married family groups only. Based on the Annual Social and Economic Supplement (ASEC) to the Current Population Survey; for details see source and Appendix III]

Year	Number (1,000)					Percent distribution				
	All married couples	In labor force			Husband & wife not in labor force	All married couples	In labor force			Husband & wife not in labor force
		Husband & wife	Husband only	Wife only			Husband & wife	Husband only	Wife only	
TOTAL										
1990	52,317	28,056	13,013	2,453	8,794	100.0	53.6	24.9	4.7	16.8
2000	55,311	31,095	11,815	3,301	9,098	100.0	56.2	21.4	6.0	16.4
2010	60,384	32,731	13,074	4,526	10,053	100.0	54.2	21.7	7.5	16.6
2015	62,230	31,688	14,164	4,757	11,622	100.0	50.9	22.8	7.6	18.7
2016	62,628	32,120	13,885	4,790	11,833	100.0	51.3	22.2	7.6	18.9
2017	63,325	32,658	13,803	4,797	12,068	100.0	51.6	21.8	7.6	19.1
2018	63,739	32,373	14,202	4,826	12,339	100.0	50.8	22.3	7.6	19.4
2019	63,882	32,773	13,614	4,976	12,519	100.0	51.3	21.3	7.8	19.6
2020	64,248	32,598	13,626	4,804	13,222	100.0	50.7	21.2	7.5	20.6
2021	63,131	31,435	13,165	4,812	13,721	100.0	49.8	20.9	7.6	21.7
WITH CHILDREN UNDER AGE 18										
1990	24,537	15,768	7,667	558	544	100.0	64.3	31.2	2.3	2.2
2000	25,248	17,116	6,950	795	387	100.0	67.8	27.5	3.1	1.5
2010	25,317	16,710	7,220	962	425	100.0	66.0	28.5	3.8	1.7
2015	24,857	15,828	7,454	987	589	100.0	63.7	30.0	4.0	2.4
2016	24,638	15,873	7,176	1,042	546	100.0	64.4	29.1	4.2	2.2
2017	24,465	15,895	7,029	1,058	483	100.0	65.0	28.7	4.3	2.0
2018	24,555	15,903	7,132	1,043	476	100.0	64.8	29.0	4.2	1.9
2019	24,421	16,175	6,868	921	458	100.0	66.2	28.1	3.8	1.9
2020	24,378	16,196	6,720	957	506	100.0	66.4	27.6	3.9	2.1
2021	23,743	15,564	6,640	988	552	100.0	65.6	28.0	4.2	2.3
WITH CHILDREN UNDER AGE 6										
1990	12,051	6,932	4,692	192	235	100.0	57.5	38.9	1.6	2.0
2000	11,393	6,984	4,077	211	121	100.0	61.3	35.8	1.9	1.1
2010	11,599	6,924	4,181	335	159	100.0	59.7	36.0	2.9	1.4
2015	10,862	6,351	3,969	320	222	100.0	58.5	36.5	2.9	2.0
2016	10,688	6,349	3,759	383	197	100.0	59.4	35.2	3.6	1.8
2017	10,727	6,410	3,811	339	166	100.0	59.8	35.5	3.2	1.5
2018	11,001	6,464	4,025	356	157	100.0	58.8	36.6	3.2	1.4
2019	10,903	6,697	3,770	290	147	100.0	61.4	34.6	2.7	1.3
2020	10,979	6,846	3,605	326	202	100.0	62.4	32.8	3.0	1.8
2021	10,418	6,418	3,431	361	208	100.0	61.6	32.9	3.5	2.0

Source: U.S. Census Bureau, Families and Living Arrangements, Historical Families Tables, "Table MC-1. Opposite-Sex Married Couples by Labor Force Status of Spouses: 1986 to Present," <www.census.gov/data/tables/time-series/demo/families/families.html>, accessed January 2022.

Table 636. Employed Civilians and Weekly Hours: 1990 to 2021

[In thousands (118,793 represents 118,793,000), except as indicated. Annual averages of monthly figures. Civilian noninstitutionalized population 16 years old and over. Based on Current Population Survey; see text, Section 1 and Appendix III]

Item	1990	2000	2010	2015	2018	2019	2020	2021
Total employed	**118,793**	**136,891**	**139,064**	**148,834**	**155,761**	**157,538**	**147,795**	**152,581**
Age:								
16 to 19 years old	6,581	7,189	4,378	4,734	5,126	5,150	4,695	5,266
20 to 24 years old	13,401	13,229	12,699	14,022	14,051	14,172	12,497	13,409
25 to 34 years old	33,935	31,549	30,229	32,742	35,324	35,807	33,426	34,578
35 to 44 years old	30,817	36,433	30,663	31,252	32,616	33,127	31,807	32,734
45 to 54 years old	19,525	30,310	33,191	32,643	32,373	32,042	30,099	30,554
55 to 64 years old	11,189	14,002	21,636	24,975	26,565	26,893	25,454	25,912
65 years old and over	3,346	4,179	6,268	8,465	9,705	10,347	9,818	10,127
Sex:								
Male	65,104	73,305	73,359	79,131	82,698	83,460	78,560	80,829
Female	53,689	63,586	65,705	69,703	73,063	74,078	69,234	71,752
Marital status:								
Single (never married)	30,741	36,967	38,800	45,148	49,566	50,855	47,137	51,272
Married, spouse present	70,543	78,287	77,874	79,935	81,920	82,315	78,925	78,867
Widowed, divorced, separated	17,510	21,636	22,390	23,751	24,276	24,369	21,733	22,443
Class of worker:								
Nonagricultural industries	115,570	134,427	136,858	146,411	153,336	155,113	145,446	150,290
Wage and salary worker [1]	106,598	125,114	127,914	137,678	144,326	146,262	136,881	140,993
Self-employed	8,719	9,205	8,860	8,665	8,941	8,799	8,511	9,230
Unpaid family workers	253	108	84	68	69	53	55	67
Agriculture and related industries	3,223	2,464	2,206	2,422	2,425	2,425	2,349	2,291
Wage and salary worker [1]	1,740	1,421	1,353	1,547	1,632	1,658	1,578	1,524
Self-employed	1,378	1,010	821	844	766	741	742	727
Unpaid family workers	105	33	33	32	27	26	29	40
Weekly hours:								
Nonagricultural industries:								
Wage and salary workers [1]	39.2	39.6	38.3	38.7	39.0	39.1	38.4	38.9
Self-employed	40.8	39.7	35.6	36.1	36.4	36.1	34.3	35.0
Unpaid family workers	34.0	32.5	33.3	28.9	32.4	32.3	30.9	31.3

[1] Includes the incorporated self-employed.

Source: U.S. Bureau of Labor Statistics, "Labor Force Statistics from the Current Population Survey," <www.bls.gov/cps>, accessed June 2022.

Table 637. Persons at Work by Hours Worked: 2021

[In thousands (146,758 represents 146,758,000), except as indicated. Annual averages of monthly figures. Persons "at work" are a subgroup of employed persons. This subgroup excludes those absent from their jobs during reference period for reasons such as vacation, illness, or industrial dispute. Civilian noninstitutionalized population 16 years old and over. Based on Current Population Survey; see text, Section 1, and Appendix III]

Hours of work	Persons at work (1,000)			Percent distribution		
	Total	Agriculture and related industries	Non-agricultural industries	Total	Agriculture and related industries	Non-agricultural industries
Total..........................	**146,758**	**2,202**	**144,556**	**100.0**	**100.0**	**100.0**
1 to 34 hours........................	32,673	527	32,147	22.3	23.9	22.2
1 to 4 hours.........................	1,512	43	1,469	1.0	1.9	1.0
5 to 14 hours........................	5,002	129	4,874	3.4	5.9	3.4
15 to 29 hours.......................	16,242	239	16,003	11.1	10.8	11.1
30 to 34 hours.......................	9,917	116	9,801	6.8	5.3	6.8
35 hours and over....................	114,085	1,676	112,409	77.7	76.1	77.8
35 to 39 hours.......................	8,843	94	8,749	6.0	4.3	6.1
40 hours.............................	71,177	770	70,407	48.5	35.0	48.7
41 hours and over....................	34,065	812	33,254	23.2	36.8	23.0
41 to 48 hours.......................	11,737	126	11,612	8.0	5.7	8.0
49 to 59 hours.......................	13,456	262	13,194	9.2	11.9	9.1
60 hours and over....................	8,872	423	8,448	6.0	19.2	5.8
Average weekly hours of:						
Total persons at work................	38.7	42.1	38.7	(X)	(X)	(X)
Persons usually working full-time [1]...	42.1	47.6	42.1	(X)	(X)	(X)

X Not applicable. [1] Full-time workers are those who usually worked 35 hours or more (at all jobs).

Source: U.S. Bureau of Labor Statistics, CPS Tables, "Persons at work in agriculture and nonagricultural industries by hours of work," January 2022, <www.bls.gov/cps/tables.htm>.

Table 638. Persons With a Job, But Not at Work by Reason: 1990 to 2021

[In thousands (6,160 represents 6,160,000), except percent. For civilian noninstitutionalized population 16 years old and over. Annual averages of monthly figures. Based on Current Population Survey; see text, Section 1 and Appendix III]

Reason for not working	1990	2000	2010	2014	2015	2016	2017	2018	2019	2020	2021
Total not at work..................	**6,160**	**5,681**	**5,060**	**5,029**	**5,066**	**5,284**	**5,607**	**5,367**	**5,298**	**6,734**	**5,822**
Percent of employed...............	5.2	4.2	3.6	3.4	3.4	3.5	3.7	3.4	3.4	4.6	3.9
Reason for not working:											
Vacation.............................	3,529	3,109	2,487	2,512	2,563	2,671	2,893	2,724	2,702	1,903	2,201
Illness...............................	1,341	1,156	942	953	907	1,001	951	981	960	1,463	1,436
Child care problems..................	(NA)	(NA)	(NA)	28	32	29	30	33	33	66	56
Other family/personal obligations..	(NA)	(NA)	(NA)	258	259	284	266	269	271	266	318
Labor/industrial dispute.............	24	14	8	3	5	5	5	6	11	5	9
Bad weather.........................	90	89	172	138	119	130	241	179	125	92	149
Maternity or paternity leave........	(NA)	(NA)	(NA)	288	322	303	315	331	344	355	364
School/training......................	(NA)	(NA)	(NA)	120	134	125	135	131	140	99	125
Civic/military duty...................	(NA)	(NA)	(NA)	7	8	7	9	6	7	7	6
All other.............................	1,177	1,313	1,451	721	718	729	762	707	706	2,479	1,158

NA Not available.

Source: U.S. Bureau of Labor Statistics, Current Population Survey, unpublished data. See also <www.bls.gov/cps/>.

Table 639. Class of Worker by Sex and Selected Characteristics: 2016

[In percent, except as indicated (9,604 represents 9,604,000). Civilian noninstitutionalized population 16 years old and over. Annual averages of monthly figures. Based on Current Population Survey; see text, Section 1 and Appendix III]

Characteristic	Unincorporated self-employed			Incorporated self-employed			Wage and salary workers [1]		
	Total	Male	Female	Total	Male	Female	Total	Male	Female
Total (1,000)......................	**9,604**	**5,980**	**3,624**	**5,643**	**3,963**	**1,680**	**136,111**	**70,600**	**65,511**
PERCENT DISTRIBUTION........	100.0	100.0	100.0	100.0	100.0	100.0	100.0	100.0	100.0
Age:									
16 to 19 years old.................	0.8	0.8	0.9	0.2	0.1	0.3	3.6	3.4	3.7
20 to 24 years old.................	2.8	2.9	2.5	1.0	1.1	1.0	10.1	9.9	10.2
25 to 34 years old.................	14.2	14.1	14.4	10.6	10.3	11.1	23.3	24.0	22.6
35 to 44 years old.................	19.8	19.5	20.4	20.1	19.6	21.5	21.0	21.4	20.5
45 to 54 years old.................	23.6	23.1	24.3	29.0	28.5	30.1	21.2	20.9	21.4
55 to 64 years old.................	23.6	23.7	23.5	26.0	26.0	25.9	16.0	15.5	16.5
65 years old and over.............	15.2	16.0	14.0	13.2	14.5	10.2	4.9	4.8	5.0
Race/ethnicity:									
White [2].............................	85.4	85.4	85.3	85.1	86.4	82.0	78.1	79.4	76.6
Black [2].............................	6.8	6.8	6.7	5.5	5.3	6.1	12.5	11.1	14.0
Asian [2].............................	5.1	5.0	5.4	7.3	6.4	9.4	6.1	6.2	6.0
Hispanic [3].........................	16.3	17.7	14.0	9.5	9.6	9.3	17.0	18.6	15.3
Country of birth:									
U.S. born..........................	80.1	78.7	82.3	82.1	82.4	81.4	83.2	81.6	85.0
Foreign-born......................	19.9	21.3	17.7	17.9	17.6	18.6	16.8	18.4	15.0

[1] Excludes the incorporated self-employed. [2] For persons in this race group only. [3] Persons of Hispanic origin may be of any race.

Source: U.S. Bureau of Labor Statistics, Current Population Survey, unpublished data. See also <www.bls.gov/cps>.

Table 640. Self-Employed Workers by Industry and Occupation: 2000 to 2021

[In thousands (10,214 represents 10,214,000). Civilian noninstitutionalized population 16 years old and over. Annual averages of monthly figures. Data represent the unincorporated self-employed. Excludes the incorporated self-employed who are considered wage and salary workers. Based on the occupational and industrial classification derived from those used in the 2000 census. See text, this section. Based on the Current Population Survey (CPS); see text, Section 1 and Appendix III]

Item	2000	2010	2015	2017	2018	2019	2020	2021
Total self-employed............................	**10,214**	**9,681**	**9,509**	**9,526**	**9,707**	**9,539**	**9,253**	**9,956**
INDUSTRY								
Agriculture and related industries..............................	1,010	821	844	790	766	741	742	727
Mining...	12	20	21	11	10	14	10	13
Construction..	1,728	1,699	1,603	1,567	1,650	1,671	1,558	1,704
Manufacturing...	334	304	288	280	258	264	273	272
Wholesale and retail trade.............................	1,221	962	870	842	812	762	772	853
Transportation and utilities..........................	348	360	397	453	443	550	531	601
Information..	139	139	161	143	144	139	143	154
Financial activities.......................................	735	641	625	666	724	678	744	808
Professional and business services....................	1,927	1,999	1,944	2,102	2,054	1,982	1,922	2,065
Education and health services........................	1,107	1,100	1,069	985	1,072	1,034	1,000	1,057
Leisure and hospitality..................................	660	610	698	682	701	683	604	652
Other services..	993	1,028	988	1,005	1,075	1,022	954	1,052
OCCUPATION								
Management, professional, and related occupations........	4,169	3,928	3,958	3,985	4,109	4,051	3,964	4,187
Service occupations.....................................	1,775	1,885	1,948	1,984	2,023	1,904	1,772	1,993
Sales and office occupations..........................	1,982	1,586	1,470	1,448	1,432	1,432	1,441	1,584
Natural resources, construction, and maintenance occupations..	1,591	1,635	1,482	1,418	1,463	1,405	1,384	1,459
Production, transportation, and material moving occupations..	698	647	650	691	679	748	692	732

Source: U.S. Bureau of Labor Statistics, "Labor Force Statistics from the Current Population Survey," <www.bls.gov/cps/tables.htm>, accessed June 2022; and unpublished CPS data.

Table 641. Multiple Jobholders: 2021

[7,007 represents 7,007,000. Annual average of monthly figures. Civilian noninstitutionalized population 16 years old and over. Multiple jobholders are employed persons who either had jobs as wage or salary workers with two employers or more; were self-employed and also held a wage and salary job; or were unpaid family workers and also held a wage and salary job. Based on the Current Population Survey; see text, Section 1 and Appendix III]

Characteristic	Total		Male		Female	
	Number (1,000)	Percent of employed	Number (1,000)	Percent of employed	Number (1,000)	Percent of employed
Total [1,2]..........................	**7,007**	**4.6**	**3,445**	**4.3**	**3,562**	**5.0**
Age:						
16 to 19 years old.................................	181	3.4	64	2.5	116	4.4
20 to 24 years old.................................	618	4.6	256	3.7	362	5.5
25 to 54 years old.................................	4,722	4.8	2,368	4.5	2,353	5.1
55 to 64 years old.................................	1,122	4.3	538	4.0	584	4.7
65 years old and over.............................	364	3.6	218	3.9	146	3.3
Race and ethnicity:						
White..	5,363	4.5	2,693	4.2	2,670	4.9
Black...	1,008	5.4	472	5.3	537	5.4
Asian..	314	3.1	137	2.6	178	3.8
Hispanic [3]..	859	3.1	458	2.9	401	3.4
Marital status:						
Married, spouse present [4]........................	3,571	4.5	2,000	4.6	1,570	4.5
Widowed, divorced, or separated....................	1,157	5.2	431	4.5	726	5.6
Single, never married............................	2,280	4.4	1,014	3.7	1,265	5.3
Full- or part-time status: [5]						
Primary job full-time, secondary job part-time..............	3,935	(S)	2,095	(S)	1,840	(S)
Both jobs part-time..................................	1,652	(S)	565	(S)	1,088	(S)
Both jobs full-time..................................	358	(S)	210	(S)	148	(S)
Hours vary on primary or secondary job..................	1,010	(S)	548	(S)	462	(S)

S No data or data do not meet publication criteria. [1] Includes a small number of persons who work part-time on their primary job and full-time on their secondary job(s), not shown separately. [2] Includes other races, not shown separately. [3] Persons of Hispanic origin may be of any race. [4] Beginning with data for January 2020, refers to persons in both opposite-sex and same-sex married couples. [5] Full-time work is 35 or more hours per week; part-time work is less than 35 hours per week.

Source: U.S. Bureau of Labor Statistics, CPS Tables, "Multiple jobholders by selected characteristics," January 2022, <www.bls.gov/cps/tables.htm>.

Table 642. Working Poor and People and Families in the Labor Force by Poverty Status: 2010 to 2020

[In thousands (146,859 represents 146,859,000), except rate. The labor force includes people working or looking for work for at least 27 weeks during the year. The working poor rate is the number of individuals in the labor force (working or looking for work) whose incomes are below the official poverty level, as a percent of all people in the labor force. Based on the Current Population Survey, Annual Social and Economic Supplement]

Characteristic	2010	2012	2013	2014	2015	2016	2017	2018	2019	2020
Total in the labor force [1]	**146,859**	**148,735**	**149,483**	**150,319**	**152,230**	**153,364**	**154,762**	**156,454**	**157,769**	**153,201**
In poverty	10,512	10,612	10,450	9,487	8,560	7,572	6,946	6,964	6,318	6,306
Working poor rate	7.2	7.1	7.0	6.3	5.6	4.9	4.5	4.5	4.0	4.1
Unrelated individuals	34,099	34,810	35,061	35,018	35,953	35,789	36,959	37,082	36,805	37,080
In poverty	3,947	3,851	4,141	3,395	3,137	2,792	2,524	2,684	2,445	2,424
Working poor rate	11.6	11.1	11.8	9.7	8.7	7.8	6.8	7.2	6.6	6.5
Primary families [2]	64,931	66,541	66,462	66,732	67,193	67,628	67,588	68,099	68,318	66,781
In poverty	5,269	5,478	5,137	5,108	4,607	4,082	3,854	3,628	3,232	3,260
Working poor rate	8.1	8.2	7.7	7.7	6.9	6.0	5.7	5.3	4.7	4.9

[1] Includes individuals in families, not shown separately. [2] Primary families with at least one member in the labor force for more than half the year.

Source: U.S. Bureau of Labor Statistics, "A Profile of the Working Poor, 2020," <www.bls.gov/opub/reports/working-poor/2020/home.htm>, accessed September 2022.

Table 643. Average Number of Jobs Held From Ages 18 to 52 During 1978 to 2018

[For persons ages 53 to 62 in 2018-2019 (and who were ages 14 to 22 when first interviewed in 1979). A job is an uninterrupted period of work with a particular employer. Educational attainment as of 2018-2019 survey. Based on the National Longitudinal Survey of Youth 1979; see source for details]

Sex, race, ethnicity and educational attainment	Average jobs held [1]	Average number of jobs held by age			
		18 to 24 years	25 to 34 years	35 to 44 years	45 to 54 years
Total [2]	**12.4**	**5.6**	**4.5**	**2.9**	**2.1**
Less than a high school diploma	12.1	5.1	4.6	2.8	1.7
High school graduate, no college	12.1	5.2	4.4	2.9	2.0
Some college or associate's degree	13.1	5.8	4.7	3.1	2.3
Bachelor's degree or more	12.5	6.2	4.4	2.8	2.3
Male	12.6	5.8	4.7	2.9	2.1
Less than a high school diploma	13.8	6.1	5.4	3.1	1.7
High school graduate, no college	12.6	5.7	4.7	2.8	2.0
Some college or associate's degree	13.2	5.9	5.0	3.0	2.3
Bachelor's degree or more	11.9	5.9	4.3	2.9	2.2
Female	12.3	5.4	4.2	2.9	2.1
Less than a high school diploma	10.0	3.8	3.4	2.4	1.6
High school graduate, no college	11.5	4.6	4.0	2.9	2.0
Some college or associate's degree	13.0	5.6	4.5	3.1	2.4
Bachelor's degree or more	13.1	6.6	4.5	2.8	2.3
White, non-Hispanic	12.5	5.8	4.5	2.9	2.1
Less than a high school diploma	12.6	5.5	4.7	2.9	1.7
High school graduate, no college	12.1	5.4	4.3	2.8	2.0
Some college or associate's degree	13.4	6.0	4.8	3.0	2.4
Bachelor's degree or more	12.5	6.3	4.4	2.8	2.2
Black, non-Hispanic	12.1	4.8	4.6	3.1	2.1
Less than a high school diploma	10.7	3.7	4.3	2.5	1.5
High school graduate, no college	11.9	4.6	4.7	3.1	2.0
Some college or associate's degree	12.1	4.8	4.6	3.3	2.2
Bachelor's degree or more	13.2	5.7	4.7	3.2	2.7
Hispanic [3]	12.1	5.0	4.3	3.0	2.2
Less than a high school diploma	11.5	4.5	4.3	2.9	1.9
High school graduate, no college	12.0	4.9	4.2	3.0	2.1
Some college or associate's degree	12.8	5.4	4.5	3.2	2.4
Bachelor's degree or more	11.4	5.2	4.4	2.7	2.1

[1] Jobs held in more than one age category were counted in each category, but only once in the total. [2] Includes other races, not shown separately. [3] Persons of Hispanic origin may be of any race.

Source: U.S. Bureau of Labor Statistics, *Number of Jobs Held, Labor Market Experience, and Earnings Growth: Results from a National Longitudinal Survey,* USDL 21-1567, August 2021. See also <www.bls.gov/news.release/nlsoy.nr0.htm>.

Table 644. Distribution of Workers by Tenure With Current Employer by Selected Characteristics: 2020

[141,374 represents 141,374,000. As of January. From the 2020 Displaced Worker Supplement to the Current Population Survey. For employed wage and salary workers 16 years old and over. Data exclude the incorporated and unincorporated self-employed; see source and Appendix III]

Characteristic	Number employed (1,000)	Percent distribution by tenure with current employer								Median years [1]
		12 months or less	13-23 months	2 years	3-4 years	5-9 years	10-14 years	15-19 years	20 years or more	
Total [2]........	**141,374**	**22.2**	**7.0**	**5.7**	**17.8**	**19.3**	**10.6**	**6.6**	**10.8**	**4.1**
AGE AND SEX										
16 to 19 years old...........	4,792	74.9	11.3	7.7	5.8	0.3	–	–	–	(NA)
20 years old and over..........	136,581	20.4	6.8	5.6	18.3	19.9	11.0	6.8	11.2	(NA)
20 to 24 years old...........	13,514	50.8	13.5	10.8	20.2	4.6	–	–	–	1.3
25 to 34 years old...........	34,141	27.6	9.5	7.9	26.4	23.0	5.0	0.7	–	2.8
35 to 44 years old...........	30,001	16.9	5.9	4.9	18.6	24.7	16.2	8.8	4.0	4.9
45 to 54 years old...........	27,932	12.7	4.6	3.5	13.6	20.7	14.8	11.4	18.6	7.5
55 to 64 years old...........	23,027	9.7	4.0	3.3	12.7	18.1	13.5	10.6	28.2	9.9
65 years old and over..........	7,966	9.0	3.5	3.6	11.2	17.4	14.8	10.6	30.0	10.3
Male...........	**72,676**	**21.2**	**6.6**	**5.6**	**18.0**	**19.7**	**10.6**	**6.7**	**11.7**	**4.3**
16 to 19 years old...........	2,310	73.8	11.2	7.6	7.3	–	–	–	–	(NA)
20 years old and over..........	70,366	19.5	6.4	5.6	18.3	20.3	11.0	6.9	12.1	(NA)
20 to 24 years old...........	6,870	48.5	13.6	11.3	21.8	4.8	0.1	–	–	1.4
25 to 34 years old...........	17,795	25.9	9.0	7.8	27.0	23.9	5.5	0.8	–	2.9
35 to 44 years old...........	15,649	15.9	5.3	5.0	17.7	25.4	16.6	9.3	4.8	5.1
45 to 54 years old...........	14,321	12.0	4.3	3.5	13.1	20.3	14.6	11.3	20.8	8.2
55 to 64 years old...........	11,646	9.8	3.9	2.9	12.4	18.1	12.4	10.4	30.2	10.0
65 years old and over..........	4,085	9.7	3.0	3.1	11.9	17.6	14.2	10.1	30.4	10.3
Female..........	**68,697**	**23.3**	**7.4**	**5.7**	**17.7**	**18.8**	**10.6**	**6.6**	**9.9**	**3.9**
16 to 19 years old...........	2,482	76.0	11.5	7.7	4.3	0.5	–	–	–	(NA)
20 years old and over..........	66,215	21.4	7.2	5.6	18.2	19.5	11.0	6.8	10.3	(NA)
20 to 24 years old...........	6,644	53.2	13.5	10.3	18.6	4.4	–	–	–	1.2
25 to 34 years old...........	16,346	29.4	10.1	8.0	25.7	21.9	4.4	0.5	–	2.7
35 to 44 years old...........	14,352	17.9	6.7	4.7	19.5	24.0	15.7	8.4	3.1	4.6
45 to 54 years old...........	13,612	13.5	4.9	3.5	14.1	21.2	15.0	11.5	16.4	6.8
55 to 64 years old...........	11,381	9.5	4.1	3.7	13.0	18.2	14.7	10.7	26.1	9.8
65 years old and over..........	3,881	8.2	4.0	4.1	10.4	17.2	15.4	11.2	29.6	10.4
RACE AND HISPANIC ORIGIN										
White [3]...............	109,188	21.5	7.0	5.4	17.3	19.5	10.7	6.8	11.7	(NA)
Male...............	56,942	20.6	6.5	5.4	17.3	19.9	10.6	7.0	12.8	(NA)
Female..............	52,247	22.6	7.5	5.4	17.4	19.1	10.8	6.7	10.5	(NA)
Black [3]...............	17,353	25.8	6.4	6.4	20.1	17.9	9.2	5.6	8.5	(NA)
Male...............	8,039	25.3	6.5	6.4	21.5	17.3	9.3	5.3	8.4	(NA)
Female..............	9,315	26.3	6.4	6.4	18.9	18.4	9.1	5.9	8.6	(NA)
Asian [3]...............	9,321	19.5	7.4	6.8	19.4	20.8	12.1	7.0	7.0	(NA)
Male...............	4,886	18.5	7.6	5.8	19.9	22.1	12.3	7.0	6.9	(NA)
Female..............	4,435	20.7	7.2	8.0	18.7	19.5	12.0	7.0	7.0	(NA)
Hispanic [4]...............	25,806	25.5	6.2	6.8	20.0	19.3	9.8	5.4	7.0	(NA)
Male...............	14,242	24.6	5.1	6.7	19.6	20.6	10.4	5.6	7.4	(NA)
Female..............	11,564	26.6	7.4	7.0	20.5	17.8	9.2	5.0	6.5	(NA)

– Represents or rounds to zero. NA Not available. [1] Median definition, see Guide to Tabular Presentation. [2] Includes other races, not shown separately. [3] For persons in this race group only. See footnote 2, Table 622. [4] Persons of Hispanic origin may be of any race.

Source: U.S. Bureau of Labor Statistics, "Employee Tenure in 2020," USDL 20-1791, September 2020, <www.bls.gov/news.release/tenure.toc.htm>.

Table 645. Part-Time Workers by Reason: 2021

[32,673 represents 32,673,000, except hours. For persons working 1 to 34 hours during the reference week of the survey. For civilian noninstitutionalized population 16 years old and over. Annual average of monthly figures. Based on the Current Population Survey; see text, Section 1 and Appendix III]

Reason	All industries			Nonagricultural industries		
		Usually work—			Usually work—	
	Total	Full-time	Part-time	Total	Full-time	Part-time
Total working fewer than 35 hours.....................	**32,673**	**9,653**	**23,020**	**32,147**	**9,522**	**22,624**
Economic reasons.................................	4,914	1,621	3,292	4,844	1,582	3,262
Slack work or business conditions........................	3,623	1,417	2,206	3,575	1,389	2,186
Could find only part time work........................	1,030	(S)	1,030	1,023	(S)	1,023
Seasonal work.................................	169	112	57	156	102	53
Job started or ended during the week...................	92	92	(S)	91	91	(S)
Non-economic reasons...............................	27,760	8,032	19,728	27,303	7,940	19,362
Child-care problems...........................	1,035	82	953	1,026	81	945
Other family or personal obligations....................	4,342	624	3,718	4,264	616	3,648
Health or medical limitations.........................	922	(S)	922	906	(S)	906
In school or training............................	5,568	77	5,491	5,524	77	5,447
Retired or social security limit on earnings................	2,433	(S)	2,433	2,308	(S)	2,308
Vacation or personal day........................	3,634	3,634	(S)	3,603	3,603	(S)
Holiday, legal, or religious.......................	836	836	(S)	829	829	(S)
Weather-related curtailment........................	378	378	(S)	366	366	(S)
Other..	8,612	2,402	6,210	8,476	2,369	6,107
Average hours per week:						
Economic reasons...............................	22.4	23.0	22.1	22.4	23.1	22.1
Noneconomic reasons............................	21.4	24.4	20.1	21.4	24.4	20.2

S No data or data do not meet publication standards.

Source: U.S. Bureau of Labor Statistics, CPS Tables, "Persons at work 1 to 34 hours in all and in nonagricultural industries by reason for working less than 35 hours and usual full- or part-time status," January 2022, <www.bls.gov/cps/tables.htm>.

Table 646. Displaced Workers by Selected Characteristics: 2022

[In percent, except total (3,596 represents 3,596,000). As of January 2022. For persons 20 years old and over with job tenure of 3 years or more who lost or left a job between January 2019 and December 2021 because of plant closings or moves, insufficient work for workers to do, or the abolishment of their positions. Based on Current Population Survey; see source and Appendix III]

Characteristic	Total (1,000)	Employment status in January 2022			Reason for job loss, 2019-2021		
		Employed	Unemployed	Not in the labor force	Plant or company closed down or moved	Insufficient work	Position or shift abolished
Total [1]	**3,596**	**65.2**	**12.4**	**22.3**	**38.1**	**30.9**	**31.0**
20 to 24 years old	119	67.7	16.8	15.5	39.1	39.2	21.7
25 to 54 years old	2,227	72.2	12.3	15.6	37.9	31.2	30.8
55 to 64 years old	852	63.9	13.2	23.0	35.7	32.8	31.5
65 years old and over	398	28.7	10.4	60.9	43.5	23.0	33.5
Males	1,889	68.0	13.6	18.4	35.2	33.3	31.5
20 to 24 years old	65	(3)	(3)	(3)	(3)	(3)	(3)
25 to 54 years old	1,201	75.9	13.9	10.2	35.7	32.5	31.8
55 to 64 years old	426	65.4	14.3	20.3	35.9	35.0	29.1
65 years old and over	197	27.0	8.7	64.4	37.8	26.6	35.6
Females	1,708	62.2	11.2	26.7	41.3	28.3	30.4
20 to 24 years old	54	(3)	(3)	(3)	(3)	(3)	(3)
25 to 54 years old	1,027	67.8	10.3	21.9	40.5	29.7	29.8
55 to 64 years old	426	62.3	12.0	25.7	35.5	30.6	33.8
65 years old and over	201	30.4	12.2	57.5	49.1	19.5	31.4
White only	2,819	64.2	12.2	23.5	37.1	30.2	32.7
Male	1,428	68.2	13.1	18.7	34.1	33.4	32.5
Female	1,391	60.2	11.3	28.5	40.2	27.0	32.9
Black only	357	71.2	8.3	20.4	44.4	28.4	27.2
Male	203	68.5	8.0	23.6	39.3	30.1	30.7
Female	154	74.9	8.8	16.3	51.2	26.2	22.6
Asian only	278	66.0	17.2	16.8	29.7	42.0	28.3
Male	189	64.7	22.8	12.5	26.5	41.1	32.5
Female	89	68.7	5.4	25.9	36.4	44.1	19.5
Hispanic [2]	597	64.7	16.7	18.6	46.3	35.2	18.5
Male	312	73.8	14.2	12.0	40.6	42.8	16.6
Female	285	54.7	19.5	25.8	52.5	26.9	20.6

[1] Includes other races, not shown separately. [3] Persons of Hispanic or Latino origin may be of any race. [3] Data not shown where base is less than 75,000.

Source: U.S. Bureau of Labor Statistics, *Worker Displacement: 2019-2021,* USDL 22-1715, August 2022. See also <www.bls.gov/news.release/disp.toc.htm>.

Table 647. Persons Not in the Labor Force By Age, Sex, and Reason: 2021

[In thousands (100,241 represents 100,241,000). For civilian noninstitutional population 16 years old and over. Persons who are neither employed nor unemployed are not in the labor force. This includes retired persons, students, those taking care of children or other family members, and others who are neither working nor seeking work. Annual average of monthly figures. Based on the Current Population Survey; see text, Section 1, and Appendix III]

Status and reason	Total	Age			Sex	
		16 to 24 years old	25 to 54 years old	55 years old and over	Male	Female
Total not in the labor force	**100,241**	**16,574**	**23,241**	**60,426**	**40,983**	**59,259**
Do not want a job now [1]	93,912	14,919	20,272	58,722	37,999	55,913
Want a job now [1]	6,329	1,656	2,969	1,704	2,984	3,346
In the previous year:						
Did not search for a job	3,925	1,010	1,699	1,216	1,774	2,151
Did search for a job, but not in past 4 weeks [2]	2,404	646	1,270	488	1,209	1,194
Not available for work now	622	206	329	87	253	369
Available for work now, but not looking for work [3]	1,782	440	941	401	956	826
Reason for not currently looking for work:						
Discouraged over job prospects [4]	510	104	279	127	312	198
Family responsibilities	155	20	107	28	54	101
In school or training	154	108	41	4	76	78
Ill health or disability	142	18	70	54	79	63
Other [5]	820	190	444	187	435	385

[1] Includes some persons who are not asked if they want a job. [2] Persons who had a job in previous 12 months must have searched since the end of that job. [3] Persons who want a job, have searched for work during the previous 12 months, and were available to take a job during the reference week, but had not looked for work in the past 4 weeks; persons are referred to as "marginally attached to the labor force." [4] Includes such things as believes no work available, could not find work, lacks necessary schooling or training, employer thinks too young or old, and other types of discrimination. [5] Includes such things as child care and transportation problems.

Source: U.S. Bureau of Labor Statistics, CPS Tables, "Persons not in the labor force by desire and availability for work, age, and sex," January 2022, <www.bls.gov/cps/tables.htm>.

Table 648. Employment Status of Parents by Age of Youngest Child and Family Type: 2019 to 2021

[In thousands (33,460 represents 33,460,000), except percent distribution. Annual average of monthly figures. For families with own children under age 18 living in the household (biological children, step-children, and adopted children). Based on the Current Population Survey, see text, Section 1, and Appendix III]

Characteristic	Number			Percent distribution		
	2019	2020	2021	2019	2020	2021
WITH OWN CHILDREN UNDER 18 YEARS OLD						
Total families	**33,460**	**33,047**	**32,756**	**100.0**	**100.0**	**100.0**
Parent(s) employed	30,584	29,259	29,198	91.4	88.5	89.1
No parent employed	2,876	3,788	3,558	8.6	11.5	10.9
Total married-couple families [1]	23,005	22,921	22,156	100.0	100.0	100.0
Parent(s) employed	22,421	21,846	21,372	97.5	95.3	96.5
Both parents employed	14,810	13,705	13,794	64.4	59.8	62.3
Only one parent employed	7,611	8,141	7,577	33.1	35.5	34.2
Neither parent employed	583	1,075	784	2.5	4.7	3.5
Opposite-sex married couple families	22,923	22,826	22,050	100.0	100.0	100.0
Parent(s) employed	22,342	21,755	21,269	97.5	95.3	96.5
Mother employed	15,841	15,044	14,955	69.1	65.9	67.8
Both parents employed	14,754	13,642	13,720	64.4	59.8	62.2
Mother employed, not father	1,088	1,402	1,234	4.7	6.1	5.6
Father employed, not mother	6,501	6,711	6,315	28.4	29.4	28.6
Neither parent employed	581	1,071	780	2.5	4.7	3.5
Families maintained by mother [2]	7,850	7,526	7,904	100.0	100.0	100.0
Mother employed	5,934	5,344	5,624	75.6	71.0	71.2
Mother not employed	1,916	2,181	2,280	24.4	29.0	28.8
Families maintained by father [2]	2,605	2,601	2,696	100.0	100.0	100.0
Father employed	2,228	2,069	2,202	85.5	79.6	81.7
Father not employed	377	531	494	14.5	20.4	18.3
WITH OWN CHILDREN 6 to 17 YEARS OLD						
Total families	**19,351**	**19,246**	**19,029**	**100.0**	**100.0**	**100.0**
Parent(s) employed	17,700	17,109	17,058	91.5	88.9	89.6
No parent employed	1,651	2,137	1,971	8.5	11.1	10.4
Total married-couple families [1]	12,943	12,939	12,553	100.0	100.0	100.0
Parent(s) employed	12,555	12,315	12,085	97.0	95.2	96.3
Both parents employed	8,766	8,090	8,140	67.7	62.5	64.9
Only one parent employed	3,790	4,224	3,945	29.3	32.6	31.4
Neither parent employed	388	624	467	3.0	4.8	3.7
Opposite-sex married couple families	12,898	12,887	12,491	100.0	100.0	100.0
Parent(s) employed	12,512	12,266	12,026	97.0	95.2	96.3
Mother employed	9,469	8,944	8,908	73.4	69.4	71.3
Both parents employed	8,736	8,058	8,098	67.7	62.5	64.8
Mother employed, not father	733	886	810	5.7	6.9	6.5
Father employed, not mother	3,043	3,322	3,118	23.6	25.8	25.0
Neither parent employed	387	621	464	3.0	4.8	3.7
Families maintained by mother [2]	4,842	4,731	4,881	100.0	100.0	100.0
Mother employed	3,835	3,538	3,687	79.2	74.8	75.5
Mother not employed	1,007	1,193	1,194	20.8	25.2	24.5
Families maintained by father [2]	1,566	1,576	1,595	100.0	100.0	100.0
Father employed	1,311	1,256	1,286	83.7	79.7	80.6
Father not employed	255	320	309	16.3	20.3	19.4
WITH OWN CHILDREN UNDER 6 YEARS OLD						
Total families	**14,109**	**13,801**	**13,727**	**100.0**	**100.0**	**100.0**
Parent(s) employed	12,884	12,150	12,140	91.3	88.0	88.4
No parent employed	1,225	1,651	1,587	8.7	12.0	11.6
Total married-couple families [1]	10,061	9,983	9,603	100.0	100.0	100.0
Parent(s) employed	9,866	9,531	9,286	98.1	95.5	96.7
Both parents employed	6,045	5,614	5,654	60.1	56.2	58.9
Only one parent employed	3,821	3,917	3,632	38.0	39.2	37.8
Neither parent employed	195	451	317	1.9	4.5	3.3
Opposite-sex married couple families	10,025	9,939	9,559	100.0	100.0	100.0
Parent(s) employed	9,830	9,490	9,243	98.1	95.5	96.7
Mother employed	6,372	6,100	6,046	63.6	61.4	63.3
Both parents employed	6,017	5,584	5,622	60.0	56.2	58.8
Mother employed, not father	355	516	424	3.5	5.2	4.4
Father employed, not mother	3,458	3,390	3,197	34.5	34.1	33.4
Neither parent employed	194	450	316	1.9	4.5	3.3
Families maintained by mother [2]	3,008	2,795	3,023	100.0	100.0	100.0
Mother employed	2,099	1,807	1,937	69.8	64.6	64.1
Mother not employed	909	988	1,086	30.2	35.4	35.9
Families maintained by father [2]	1,040	1,024	1,101	100.0	100.0	100.0
Father employed	918	813	916	88.3	79.4	83.2
Father not employed	122	211	185	11.7	20.6	16.8

[1] Includes both opposite-sex and same-sex married-couple families. [2] Includes families with no spouse of either sex present.

Source: U.S. Bureau of Labor Statistics, *Employment Characteristics of Families—2021,* USDL 22-0673, April 2022. See also <www.bls.gov/news.release/famee.toc.htm>.

Table 649. Employed Civilians by Occupation, Sex, Race, and Hispanic Origin: 2021

[152,581 represents 152,581,000. Civilian noninstitutionalized population 16 years old and over. Annual average of monthly figures. Based on Current Population Survey; see text, Section 1 and Appendix III. Effective with January 2020 data, occupations reflect the 2018 Standard Occupational Classification]

Occupation	Total employed	Percent of total		
		Female	Black [1]	Asian [1]	His-panic [2]
Total, 16 years and over...................................	**152,581**	**47.0**	**12.3**	**6.6**	**18.0**
Management, professional and related occupations...............	**64,744**	**52.0**	**9.8**	**9.0**	**10.4**
Management, business, and financial operations occupations.........	27,864	45.3	9.2	7.1	10.8
Management occupations [3]..........................	18,986	40.9	8.6	6.5	11.1
Chief executives..........................	1,664	29.1	5.9	6.8	7.4
General and operations managers..........................	1,085	36.4	9.3	4.6	10.3
Marketing managers..........................	576	61.4	6.2	7.3	8.3
Sales managers..........................	537	30.6	5.9	5.0	10.6
Public relations and fundraising managers..........................	100	68.0	3.5	4.4	7.2
Facilities managers..........................	146	21.3	7.4	0.2	14.5
Computer and information systems managers..........................	715	26.7	7.2	17.8	7.3
Financial managers..........................	1,307	54.6	9.0	9.0	10.4
Human resources managers..........................	273	80.8	12.3	6.4	12.5
Industrial production managers..........................	256	24.1	5.7	9.3	10.9
Purchasing managers..........................	232	45.9	8.5	6.7	8.2
Transportation, storage, and distribution managers..........................	314	22.4	10.7	3.7	16.3
Farmers, ranchers, and other agricultural managers..........................	875	26.3	1.5	0.9	6.0
Construction managers..........................	999	8.6	5.1	1.7	16.3
Education and childcare administrators..........................	956	65.5	14.0	3.3	9.7
Architectural and engineering managers..........................	178	11.5	4.5	15.0	7.2
Food service managers..........................	1,133	48.5	11.0	10.4	19.5
Lodging managers..........................	116	47.6	10.3	12.5	14.1
Medical and health services managers..........................	791	75.0	14.1	7.0	10.5
Property, real estate, and community association managers..........................	780	50.7	10.3	4.0	11.4
Social and community service managers..........................	391	68.6	17.9	4.0	13.7
Business and financial operations occupations [3]..........................	8,878	54.8	10.5	8.6	10.3
Wholesale and retail buyers, except farm products..........................	159	55.1	9.4	4.2	15.9
Purchasing agents, except wholesale, retail, and farm products..........................	223	62.2	10.3	5.3	13.4
Claims adjusters, appraisers, examiners, and investigators..........................	330	58.2	16.7	4.3	14.6
Compliance officers..........................	291	53.2	14.4	4.2	13.2
Cost estimators..........................	127	15.5	3.8	4.8	10.8
Human resources workers..........................	871	75.2	13.8	6.2	12.4
Training and development specialists..........................	166	52.9	14.1	4.2	10.9
Logisticians..........................	132	39.3	13.4	4.9	10.2
Project management specialists..........................	769	42.9	8.0	9.6	8.0
Management analysts..........................	1,001	45.5	8.0	10.8	7.2
Meeting, convention, and event planners..........................	116	82.1	9.9	3.6	6.1
Market research analysts and marketing specialists..........................	400	63.6	4.4	9.7	10.7
Accountants and auditors..........................	1,630	62.0	9.8	11.8	9.8
Financial and investment analysts..........................	343	40.2	13.1	20.7	10.7
Personal financial advisors..........................	535	33.8	7.3	7.5	7.7
Insurance underwriters..........................	128	61.4	12.0	7.0	9.1
Credit counselors and loan officers..........................	440	52.2	12.8	3.7	12.0
Tax preparers..........................	101	54.2	14.2	6.2	17.7
Professional and related occupations..........................	36,880	56.9	10.3	10.4	10.0
Computer and mathematical occupations [3]..........................	5,688	26.2	8.5	23.3	8.3
Computer systems analysts..........................	464	37.5	11.3	16.0	11.0
Information security analysts..........................	152	18.2	11.8	9.0	7.4
Computer programmers..........................	444	19.5	6.0	22.0	6.4
Software developers..........................	1,932	19.7	5.4	37.1	5.8
Computer support specialists..........................	660	23.8	10.5	14.5	11.7
Database administrators and architects..........................	111	35.0	5.1	20.0	6.3
Network and computer systems administrators..........................	212	17.2	10.4	12.9	8.1
Computer network architects..........................	102	11.8	6.5	18.3	9.1
Operations research analysts..........................	141	51.0	14.9	10.7	10.1
Architecture and engineering occupations [3]..........................	3,235	17.4	5.8	14.6	9.9
Architects, except landscape and naval..........................	212	31.6	4.6	13.3	6.5
Aerospace engineers..........................	129	14.3	7.9	14.7	13.5
Civil engineers..........................	431	17.4	6.6	12.8	10.7
Electrical and electronics engineers..........................	299	7.1	4.4	19.1	10.2
Industrial engineers, including health and safety..........................	216	26.0	5.1	16.2	5.1
Mechanical engineers..........................	354	9.4	4.6	13.7	8.9
Other engineering technologists and technicians, except drafters..........................	293	21.3	9.6	5.3	14.9
Life, physical, and social science occupations [3]..........................	1,640	47.4	7.4	15.2	8.3
Medical scientists..........................	121	49.6	7.2	43.1	4.5
Physical scientists, all other..........................	370	41.2	6.9	27.3	6.5
Other psychologists..........................	149	74.9	5.6	5.4	6.4
Community and social service occupations [3]..........................	2,777	67.5	19.7	3.8	12.5
Substance abuse and behavioral disorder counselors..........................	121	69.1	25.9	1.3	11.6
Educational, guidance, and career counselors and advisors..........................	362	76.5	18.9	2.7	15.8
Mental health counselors..........................	212	75.6	17.6	2.0	10.0
Counselors, all other..........................	250	67.1	27.6	4.4	11.8
Social workers, all other..........................	681	83.6	25.8	4.6	15.2
Social and human service assistants..........................	194	81.2	15.1	5.5	13.2
Clergy..........................	404	16.2	8.7	4.7	8.0
Religious workers, all other..........................	96	70.9	6.6	7.3	2.9
Legal occupations..........................	1,805	53.5	8.1	4.8	10.4
Lawyers..........................	1,085	37.9	5.4	4.7	6.9
Paralegals and legal assistants..........................	431	84.8	11.2	5.1	20.6
Title examiners, abstractors, and searchers..........................	107	72.1	9.3	6.5	5.4
Education, training, and library occupations [3]..........................	8,946	73.7	9.9	5.6	10.8

See footnotes at end of table.

Table 649. Employed Civilians by Occupation, Sex, Race, and Hispanic Origin: 2021-Continued.

See headnote on page 417.

Occupation	Total employed	Percent of total			
		Female	Black [1]	Asian [1]	His-panic [2]
Postsecondary teachers	1,154	51.2	7.8	13.1	7.1
Preschool and kindergarten teachers	613	96.8	12.7	3.6	13.4
Elementary and middle school teachers	3,260	79.2	10.0	3.4	10.7
Secondary school teachers	940	59.5	7.2	3.6	8.3
Special education teachers	362	82.8	9.6	2.7	6.4
Tutors	168	70.5	6.0	15.6	11.7
Librarians and media collections specialists	158	79.9	7.1	3.7	3.7
Teaching assistants	1,309	81.0	12.0	7.4	16.6
Arts, design, entertainment, sports, and media occupations [3]	3,151	50.0	8.2	5.7	11.1
Artists and related workers	286	54.2	4.9	4.2	13.3
Graphic designers	271	59.9	6.4	5.3	10.7
Interior designers	123	83.8	3.0	6.6	4.1
Producers and directors	182	39.6	6.8	4.6	11.1
Coaches and scouts	235	44.3	10.9	3.5	11.7
Musicians and singers	127	24.0	14.2	2.8	11.2
Public relations specialists	122	59.1	8.9	4.5	12.1
Editors	105	66.7	4.0	4.8	3.2
Writers and authors	261	63.7	11.4	4.8	3.7
Photographers	192	49.3	6.7	5.1	14.4
Television, video, and film camera operators and editors	108	25.3	11.2	5.4	13.6
Healthcare practitioners and technical occupations [3]	9,639	74.3	12.0	9.5	9.4
Dentists	167	38.7	4.5	19.6	6.0
Dietitians and nutritionists	117	89.6	13.3	3.1	14.1
Pharmacists	352	57.8	7.9	19.8	6.0
Other physicians	921	39.7	8.1	22.9	5.8
Physician assistants	165	64.4	8.6	9.8	9.2
Occupational therapists	135	84.9	4.1	6.8	4.2
Physical therapists	273	66.9	5.4	12.6	5.3
Respiratory therapists	117	71.4	16.6	10.6	7.4
Speech-language pathologists	187	95.1	4.3	1.3	5.1
Therapists, all other	242	87.1	14.0	5.9	9.7
Veterinarians	104	64.2	1.2	5.6	4.7
Registered nurses	3,201	86.7	13.3	8.6	8.8
Nurse practitioners	237	87.4	7.0	3.9	5.5
Clinical laboratory technologists and technicians	369	68.8	17.4	9.2	15.6
Dental hygienists	207	95.1	3.3	5.3	10.7
Radiologic technologists and technicians	226	72.4	8.7	5.0	13.4
Emergency medical technicians	145	35.8	9.5	4.5	14.3
Paramedics	96	31.1	3.4	1.7	8.0
Pharmacy technicians	342	78.4	18.3	8.6	17.2
Surgical technologists	113	77.8	19.1	3.5	14.4
Veterinary technologists and technicians	129	89.8	3.6	2.3	15.3
Licensed practical and licensed vocational nurses	533	91.3	27.6	2.7	13.7
Medical records specialists	207	88.8	13.7	6.4	9.1
Miscellaneous health technologists and technicians	177	64.3	20.7	10.5	16.1
Service occupations	**24,403**	**57.7**	**16.5**	**5.9**	**25.7**
Healthcare support occupations [3]	4,887	85.1	24.5	6.8	20.9
Home health aides	570	87.0	32.0	8.9	25.9
Personal care aides	1,411	80.4	24.9	8.5	21.5
Nursing assistants	1,248	88.9	33.2	4.8	14.8
Massage therapists	166	83.5	11.7	10.8	12.4
Dental assistants	323	92.0	6.9	8.2	30.4
Medical assistants	561	91.1	18.0	5.0	29.8
Phlebotomists	114	90.6	22.3	5.3	25.1
Protective service occupations [3]	2,987	23.8	20.3	2.7	14.9
Firefighters	294	5.1	8.9	2.6	11.0
Correctional officers and jailers	297	30.4	26.7	2.2	14.2
Detectives and criminal investigators	130	27.3	18.1	3.6	12.3
Police officers	753	15.3	11.5	1.6	14.6
Private detectives and investigators	95	42.3	15.5	2.1	16.4
Security guards and gambling surveillance officers	844	26.8	33.3	3.8	18.4
Food preparation and serving related occupations	7,370	54.6	13.4	6.3	27.8
Chefs and head cooks	402	22.8	14.8	19.9	23.0
First-line supervisors of food preparation and serving workers	480	61.2	19.9	4.2	21.2
Cooks	1,905	40.2	15.8	6.0	35.9
Food preparation workers	872	58.3	14.0	5.6	29.3
Bartenders	362	57.4	4.9	2.0	19.9
Fast food and counter workers	775	65.7	13.0	5.7	23.3
Waiters and waitresses	1,631	68.2	8.9	6.6	24.7
Food servers, nonrestaurant	172	73.9	22.1	5.1	16.7
Dining room and cafeteria attendants and bartender helpers	243	46.8	14.0	4.1	33.0
Dishwashers	243	23.5	17.3	2.7	34.6
Hosts and hostesses, restaurant, lounge, and coffee shop	282	84.3	9.7	5.8	22.4
Building and grounds cleaning and maintenance occupations	5,482	41.7	14.2	3.4	38.3
First-line supervisors of housekeeping and janitorial workers	338	38.9	13.1	3.4	30.0
First-line supervisors of landscaping, lawn service, and groundskeeping workers	233	10.3	6.6	1.0	27.0
Janitors and building cleaners	2,113	39.7	18.1	3.5	31.5
Maids and housekeeping cleaners	1,357	88.7	15.2	5.2	48.2
Pest control workers	119	5.0	10.0	2.5	19.5
Landscaping and groundskeeping workers	1,211	6.2	9.2	1.8	47.1
Tree trimmers and pruners	98	2.2	9.0	1.3	19.9
Personal care and service occupations [3]	3,676	78.7	12.5	10.1	18.0
Supervisors of personal care and service workers	250	74.6	16.4	11.3	11.2

See footnotes at end of table.

Table 649. Employed Civilians by Occupation, Sex, Race, and Hispanic Origin: 2021-Continued.

See headnote on page 417.

Occupation	Total employed	Percent of total			
		Female	Black [1]	Asian [1]	His-panic [2]
Animal caretakers...	272	81.6	4.7	4.6	13.3
Other entertainment attendants and related workers.................	192	45.6	10.3	4.1	13.7
Barbers...	103	24.7	22.5	5.2	40.5
Hairdressers, hairstylists, and cosmetologists.....................	713	92.4	12.8	6.1	17.7
Manicurists and pedicurists.....................................	247	83.0	4.8	73.1	12.2
Childcare workers..	974	94.6	14.0	4.4	24.4
Exercise trainers and group fitness instructors...................	223	62.2	11.9	2.8	16.9
Recreation workers...	139	68.7	18.0	2.2	11.8
Sales and office occupations................................	**30,166**	**61.5**	**13.2**	**5.1**	**17.2**
Sales and related occupations [3]...............................	14,369	49.8	11.2	5.4	16.7
First-line supervisors of retail sales workers....................	3,058	47.0	10.3	6.2	15.1
First-line supervisors of non-retail sales workers................	1,184	32.9	7.2	5.5	12.2
Cashiers..	2,601	72.5	17.0	6.9	22.9
Parts salespersons..	124	19.1	6.8	0.7	17.2
Retail salespersons..	2,750	48.5	13.0	4.8	20.8
Advertising sales agents....................................	104	49.3	9.9	3.6	15.5
Insurance sales agents.....................................	600	50.0	11.8	4.1	16.5
Securities, commodities, and financial services sales agents.....	243	29.3	6.6	11.7	10.2
Sales representatives of services, except advertising, insurance, financial services, and travel....................	565	29.9	6.8	5.0	11.6
Sales representatives, wholesale and manufacturing..............	1,216	30.1	6.2	3.3	12.0
Real estate brokers and sales agents.........................	1,170	59.7	8.3	4.4	12.1
Door-to-door sales workers, news and street vendors, and related workers....	104	72.6	6.2	2.9	19.4
Office and administrative support occupations [3].................	15,797	72.2	15.0	4.8	17.7
First-line supervisors of office and administrative support workers...	1,217	71.3	12.0	3.9	14.0
Bill and account collectors.................................	97	72.1	21.6	2.8	17.2
Billing and posting clerks..................................	483	86.7	16.9	3.8	17.6
Bookkeeping, accounting, and auditing clerks..................	1,097	84.7	6.6	5.4	13.1
Payroll and timekeeping clerks..............................	153	86.7	14.8	6.9	18.7
Tellers...	215	76.1	16.6	3.5	20.7
Customer service representatives............................	2,512	64.8	18.5	5.4	19.7
File clerks..	161	80.1	14.4	4.1	17.2
Hotel, motel, and resort desk clerks.........................	119	70.3	16.1	7.2	24.0
Interviewers, except eligibility and loan.....................	203	75.9	23.9	1.7	18.6
Loan interviewers and clerks...............................	144	69.4	20.0	2.6	16.5
Order clerks..	112	56.5	10.7	9.7	15.3
Receptionists and information clerks.........................	1,215	90.0	15.2	4.5	21.0
Information and record clerks, all other......................	107	76.0	14.7	6.0	14.4
Couriers and messengers...................................	837	24.9	19.4	2.8	23.3
Dispatchers, except police, fire, and ambulance...............	189	47.5	12.6	2.6	29.2
Postal service clerks.......................................	105	58.8	40.0	10.3	6.3
Postal service mail carriers.................................	273	42.3	21.4	5.4	10.8
Production, planning, and expediting clerks...................	212	50.0	8.4	10.0	14.1
Shipping, receiving, and inventory clerks.....................	615	36.9	16.2	4.8	29.1
Executive secretaries and executive administrative assistants....	223	96.4	6.0	3.2	12.9
Secretaries and administrative assistants, except legal, medical, and executive..........	2,009	92.5	9.7	3.2	14.0
Data entry keyers...	220	76.2	14.9	7.0	19.2
Insurance claims and policy processing clerks.................	257	78.2	25.3	1.9	19.5
Office clerks, general......................................	1,249	83.6	14.3	6.4	19.0
Natural resources, construction, and maintenance occupations...	**13,959**	**5.6**	**7.4**	**2.3**	**33.4**
Farming, fishing, and forestry occupations [3]...................	1,061	24.2	4.4	2.3	43.9
Miscellaneous agricultural workers..........................	835	23.3	3.8	2.0	46.7
Construction and extraction occupations [3].....................	8,057	3.9	7.1	1.7	38.9
First-line supervisors of construction trades and extraction workers...	650	3.8	6.2	1.0	24.2
Brickmasons, blockmasons, and stonemasons.................	97	2.2	9.6	–	51.7
Carpenters...	1,230	3.1	6.3	1.6	39.3
Carpet, floor, and tile installers and finishers.................	156	7.7	6.2	0.2	48.2
Construction laborers......................................	2,165	4.5	8.1	2.6	48.9
Construction equipment operators...........................	360	3.0	8.0	0.1	21.8
Drywall installers, ceiling tile installers, and tapers...........	155	3.1	3.3	0.7	72.5
Electricians..	845	1.7	6.7	2.6	22.9
Painters and paperhangers.................................	556	8.9	7.0	1.0	59.3
Plumbers, pipefitters, and steamfitters......................	587	2.1	7.1	1.5	25.7
Roofers..	221	2.9	7.5	1.1	63.5
Sheet metal workers.......................................	125	3.9	4.6	0.8	19.8
Construction and building inspectors.........................	103	10.0	7.3	3.5	12.3
Highway maintenance workers...............................	99	3.6	10.1	0.7	17.3
Installation, maintenance, and repair occupations [3].............	4,840	4.3	8.3	3.3	22.0
First-line supervisors of mechanics, installers, and repairers.....	222	6.0	5.8	0.7	12.3
Computer, automated teller, and office machine repairers........	176	15.4	12.6	9.1	16.8
Radio and telecommunications equipment installers and repairers...	155	4.5	10.5	4.2	15.5
Aircraft mechanics and service technicians....................	150	3.2	5.7	4.2	15.3
Automotive body and related repairers.......................	123	2.4	5.6	1.9	29.0
Automotive service technicians and mechanics.................	864	2.3	8.0	4.6	28.2
Bus and truck mechanics and diesel engine specialists..........	362	1.2	7.1	3.2	19.2
Heavy vehicle and mobile equipment service technicians and mechanics....	248	1.2	5.4	2.4	19.1
Heating, air conditioning, and refrigeration mechanics and installers...	445	1.5	11.1	3.4	25.3
Industrial and refractory machinery mechanics.................	429	5.1	6.1	3.4	19.6
Maintenance and repair workers, general.....................	614	5.1	8.8	2.5	21.0
Electrical power-line installers and repairers..................	125	0.7	8.5	0.6	11.9
Telecommunications line installers and repairers...............	134	7.0	13.7	2.1	38.4
Production, transportation, and material moving occupations......	**19,309**	**24.3**	**17.3**	**4.7**	**23.7**

See footnotes at end of table.

Table 649. Employed Civilians by Occupation, Sex, Race, and Hispanic Origin: 2021-Continued.

See headnote on page 417.

Occupation	Total employed	Percent of total			
		Female	Black [1]	Asian [1]	His-panic [2]
Production occupations [3]..	7,950	28.3	13.3	5.5	24.0
First-line supervisors of production and operating workers....................	767	19.5	12.8	3.2	17.6
Electrical, electronics, and electromechanical assemblers.................	110	41.9	10.0	15.9	15.8
Other assemblers and fabricators..	957	34.1	18.5	7.6	21.9
Bakers...	229	64.8	11.1	3.5	32.7
Butchers and other meat, poultry, and fish processing workers..........................	246	19.4	15.4	4.6	39.7
Machinists...	323	3.4	5.8	3.3	17.9
Welding, soldering, and brazing workers.................................	555	3.5	9.8	2.4	22.5
Other metal workers and plastic workers.................................	335	22.0	15.8	5.9	27.7
Printing press operators...	143	15.2	14.5	5.8	22.2
Laundry and dry-cleaning workers.......................................	116	67.1	26.4	8.6	32.3
Sewing machine operators..	120	71.1	6.9	3.9	46.1
Water and wastewater treatment plant and system operators................	99	9.6	7.2	2.6	8.9
Inspectors, testers, sorters, samplers, and weighers.......................	829	39.3	11.6	7.1	21.7
Packaging and filling machine operators and tenders........................	253	51.5	21.0	7.3	43.9
Painting workers...	153	7.7	5.1	3.2	32.3
Transportation and material moving occupations [3]........................	11,359	21.6	20.1	4.2	23.6
Supervisors of transportation and material moving workers.................	355	24.3	14.4	4.4	21.2
Aircraft pilots and flight engineers.......................................	158	5.3	3.9	1.5	6.1
Flight attendants..	105	64.6	18.4	7.1	9.5
Bus drivers, school..	276	55.3	23.2	3.0	10.0
Bus drivers, transit and intercity.......................................	241	41.0	35.2	2.3	14.4
Driver/sales workers and truck drivers...................................	3,487	7.9	18.7	3.8	23.6
Taxi drivers...	337	12.0	25.1	15.3	28.2
Motor vehicle operators, all other.......................................	163	15.1	22.5	8.4	22.1
Industrial truck and tractor operators....................................	623	9.1	24.9	1.5	33.3
Cleaners of vehicles and equipment......................................	301	17.0	21.1	2.6	30.1
Laborers and freight, stock, and material movers, hand.....................	2,161	22.9	20.1	3.5	24.1
Packers and packagers, hand..	742	52.1	19.1	8.5	38.0
Stockers and order fillers...	1,652	37.1	21.3	3.8	20.4

– Represents or rounds to zero. [1] Data represent persons who selected this race group only and exclude persons reporting more than one race. See also comments on race in the text for Section 1. [2] Persons of Hispanic origin may be of any race. [3] Includes other occupations, not shown separately.

Source: U.S. Bureau of Labor Statistics, CPS Tables, "Employed persons by detailed occupation, sex, race, and Hispanic or Latino ethnicity," January 2022, <www.bls.gov/cps/tables.htm>.

Table 650. Employed Workers With Contract, On-Call, Temporary, and Traditional Work Arrangements: 2017

[In thousands (153,331 represents 153,331,000). As of February. For employed workers 16 years old and over. Based on the Current Population Survey; see text, Section 1 and Appendix III]

Characteristic	Total employed [1]	Workers with alternative arrangements				Workers with traditional arrangements
		Independent contractors	On-call workers	Temporary help agency workers	Workers provided by contract firms	
Total employed.......................	**153,331**	**10,614**	**2,579**	**1,356**	**933**	**137,853**
16 to 19 years old.....................	4,842	43	107	25	14	4,647
20 to 24 years old.....................	14,212	330	263	195	53	13,370
25 to 34 years old.....................	33,991	1,593	516	303	224	31,361
35 to 44 years old.....................	32,065	2,160	565	283	207	28,849
45 to 54 years old.....................	32,745	2,562	446	276	206	29,263
55 to 64 years old.....................	26,236	2,426	399	170	124	23,110
65 years old and over..................	9,240	1,500	283	105	106	7,253
Male...................................	81,545	6,820	1,355	709	625	72,035
16 to 19 years old.....................	2,365	42	53	20	9	2,235
20 to 24 years old.....................	7,412	187	169	100	28	6,931
25 to 34 years old.....................	18,169	1,016	271	170	157	16,554
35 to 44 years old.....................	17,585	1,430	329	122	144	15,557
45 to 54 years old.....................	17,099	1,611	208	166	146	14,971
55 to 64 years old.....................	13,840	1,547	209	81	81	11,914
65 years old and over..................	5,076	986	117	50	60	3,873
Female..................................	71,785	3,794	1,224	647	308	65,818
16 to 19 years old.....................	2,477	1	55	5	5	2,412
20 to 24 years old.....................	6,800	143	94	95	25	6,439
25 to 34 years old.....................	15,823	577	245	133	67	14,807
35 to 44 years old.....................	14,480	730	237	161	63	13,292
45 to 54 years old.....................	15,646	951	238	110	60	14,292
55 to 64 years old.....................	12,396	878	190	88	44	11,196
65 years old and over..................	4,164	514	166	55	45	3,380
Full-time workers......................	125,240	7,485	1,428	1,042	785	114,496
Part-time workers......................	28,091	3,129	1,151	314	148	23,357

[1] Includes day laborers (an alternative arrangement) and a small number of workers who were both "on call" and "provided by contract firms," not shown separately.

Source: U.S. Bureau of Labor Statistics, Contingent and Alternative Employment Arrangements, May 2017, USDL 18–0942, June 2018. See also <www.bls.gov/cps/lfcharacteristics.htm#contingent>.

Table 651. Employment and Annual and Hourly Wages by Occupation: 2021

[In dollars, except employment. As of May. Data from the Occupational Employment Statistics survey. For definition of mean and median, see Guide to Tabular Presentation]

Occupation	Employment (number)	Mean hourly wage	Annual wages [1]	Median hourly wage
All occupations [2]..................	**140,886,310**	**28.01**	**58,260**	**22.00**
Management occupations........................	8,909,910	59.31	123,370	49.25
Top executives............................	3,229,990	57.94	120,520	47.46
General and operations managers....................	2,984,920	55.41	115,250	47.10
Operations specialties managers....................	2,116,020	67.26	139,900	61.13
Other management occupations....................	2,725,860	51.55	107,230	46.94
Business and financial operations occupations....................	9,053,790	39.72	82,610	36.81
Business operations specialists....................	6,152,960	38.64	80,380	36.56
Financial specialists....................	2,900,840	41.99	87,350	37.16
Computer and mathematical occupations....................	4,654,750	48.01	99,860	46.90
Computer occupations....................	4,389,910	47.89	99,620	46.84
Software and web developers, programmers, and testers....................	1,874,100	54.68	113,720	49.49
Architecture and engineering occupations....................	2,436,520	44.10	91,740	38.39
Engineers....................	1,631,080	50.00	104,000	47.62
Life, physical, and social science occupations....................	1,273,640	38.81	80,730	34.97
Community and social service occupations....................	2,239,680	25.94	53,960	23.28
Counselors, social workers, and other community and social service specialists.......	2,157,410	25.94	53,950	23.27
Educational instruction and library occupations....................	8,191,930	29.88	62,140	27.51
Postsecondary teachers....................	1,340,560	([3])	95,200	([3])
Preschool, elementary, middle, secondary, and special education teachers.............	4,021,070	([3])	64,870	([3])
Elementary and middle school teachers....................	1,933,120	([3])	67,030	([3])
Arts, design, entertainment, sports, and media occupations....................	1,815,290	31.78	66,100	24.61
Healthcare practitioners and technical occupations....................	8,787,730	43.80	91,100	36.08
Healthcare diagnosing or treating practitioners....................	5,772,460	53.92	112,160	39.07
Registered nurses....................	3,047,530	39.78	82,750	37.31
Health technologists and technicians....................	2,887,210	24.18	50,300	22.55
Healthcare support occupations....................	6,603,620	16.02	33,330	14.37
Nursing, psychiatric, and home health aides....................	4,765,620	14.64	30,440	14.24
Protective service occupations....................	3,385,030	25.68	53,420	22.40
Food preparation and serving related occupations....................	11,201,480	14.16	29,450	13.65
Cooks and food preparation workers....................	3,281,610	14.13	29,380	13.99
Cooks....................	2,498,260	14.21	29,560	14.00
Food and beverage serving workers....................	5,627,500	13.23	27,520	12.50
Fast food and counter workers....................	3,095,120	12.53	26,060	12.07
Waiters and waitresses....................	1,804,030	13.95	29,010	12.50
Building and grounds cleaning and maintenance occupations....................	4,108,810	16.23	33,750	14.54
Building cleaning and pest control workers....................	2,862,840	15.19	31,590	14.25
Building cleaning workers....................	2,777,470	15.05	31,310	14.20
Janitors and cleaners, except maids and housekeeping cleaners....................	2,036,820	15.32	31,860	14.31
Personal care and service occupations....................	2,566,440	16.17	33,620	14.16
Sales and related occupations....................	13,256,290	22.15	46,080	14.71
Retail sales workers....................	7,665,410	14.45	30,060	13.79
Cashiers....................	3,335,170	12.88	26,780	13.12
Retail salespersons....................	3,693,490	15.35	31,920	14.00
Sales representatives, services....................	2,009,700	35.95	74,770	29.11
Sales representatives, wholesale and manufacturing....................	1,508,660	37.38	77,750	30.24
Office and administrative support occupations....................	18,299,380	20.88	43,430	18.29
Financial clerks....................	2,768,230	20.84	43,340	18.67
Bookkeeping, accounting, and auditing clerks....................	1,509,370	21.70	45,140	21.90
Information and record clerks....................	5,461,400	18.59	38,670	17.68
Customer service representatives....................	2,787,070	18.79	39,070	17.75
Material recording, scheduling, dispatching, and distributing workers....................	2,213,750	21.97	45,710	20.21
Secretaries and administrative assistants....................	3,104,790	21.76	45,250	19.08
Secretaries and administrative assistants, except legal, medical, and executive......	1,825,980	19.75	41,080	18.21
Other office and administrative support workers....................	3,254,180	18.98	39,480	17.88
Office clerks, general....................	2,578,180	18.75	38,990	17.81
Farming, fishing, and forestry occupations....................	452,490	16.70	34,730	14.36
Construction and extraction occupations....................	5,848,950	26.87	55,900	23.18
Construction trades workers....................	4,362,080	26.03	54,140	23.01
Installation, maintenance, and repair occupations....................	5,574,410	25.66	53,380	23.05
Vehicle and mobile equipment mechanics, installers, and repairers....................	1,570,020	24.23	50,400	22.79
Other installation, maintenance, and repair occupations....................	2,978,490	24.39	50,730	22.71
Production occupations....................	8,408,030	20.71	43,070	18.13
Assemblers and fabricators....................	1,769,890	18.75	39,000	17.87
Metal workers and plastic workers....................	1,633,980	21.56	44,840	20.65
Other production occupations....................	2,409,900	20.11	41,820	18.13
Transportation and material moving occupations....................	12,639,920	19.88	41,340	17.72
Motor vehicle operators....................	4,147,650	21.31	44,330	20.52
Driver/sales workers and truck drivers....................	3,390,490	21.85	45,460	21.91
Heavy and tractor-trailer truck drivers....................	1,903,420	24.20	50,340	23.23
Material moving workers....................	7,203,320	16.78	34,900	14.91
Laborers and material movers....................	6,178,560	16.14	33,570	14.58
Laborers and freight, stock, and material movers, hand....................	2,729,010	16.80	34,950	15.02

[1] Annual wages have been calculated by multiplying the hourly mean wage by a "year-round, full-time" hours figure of 2,080 hours; for those occupations where there is not an hourly mean wage published, the annual wage has been directly calculated from the reported survey data. [2] Includes occupations not shown separately. [3] Wages for some occupations that do not generally work year-round full-time are reported as either hourly wages or as annual salaries, depending on how they are typically paid.

Source: U.S. Bureau of Labor Statistics, Occupational Employment Statistics, *Occupational Employment and Wages—May 2021*, USDL 22-0556, March 2022. See also <www.bls.gov/oes/>.

Table 652. Employed Civilians by Occupation and State: 2020

[In thousands (147,795 represents 147,795,000). Excludes persons with no previous work experience. Based on the Current Population Survey see text, Section 1 and Appendix III]

State	Total employed	Management, business, and financial	Professional and related	Service occupations	Sales and related	Office and administrative	Farming, fishing, and forestry	Construction and extraction occupations	Installation, maintenance, and repair	Production	Transportation and material-moving
Total U.S....	147,795	27,143	36,502	22,853	14,168	15,558	1,045	7,710	4,602	7,590	10,625
AL..........	2,099	312	479	303	230	217	(S)	105	74	205	163
AK..........	317	53	78	53	28	40	(S)	21	11	(S)	22
AZ..........	3,307	616	735	510	345	417	(S)	202	91	138	232
AR..........	1,273	181	298	191	122	140	(S)	64	59	94	110
CA..........	16,887	3,061	4,265	2,750	1,547	1,753	220	903	495	693	1,200
CO..........	2,898	599	736	429	278	286	(S)	190	79	85	186
CT..........	1,723	326	500	272	173	164	(S)	83	43	76	85
DE..........	446	77	107	75	41	54	(S)	24	14	13	38
DC..........	374	127	146	34	17	28	(S)	(S)	(S)	(S)	11
FL..........	9,271	1,592	2,110	1,594	1,050	1,073	(S)	578	319	270	631
GA..........	4,716	812	1,100	703	525	463	(S)	239	151	276	417
HI..........	571	85	137	122	59	65	(S)	27	19	15	39
ID..........	849	164	172	132	91	84	(S)	49	27	48	61
IL..........	5,677	1,112	1,427	815	566	593	(S)	212	149	346	435
IN..........	3,100	521	720	438	285	328	(S)	148	108	276	258
IA..........	1,570	289	338	227	144	173	(S)	80	(S)	106	134
KS..........	1,417	230	332	206	133	160	(S)	68	47	116	109
KY..........	1,879	285	414	269	161	223	(S)	99	73	175	157
LA..........	1,906	285	425	348	201	198	(S)	139	72	97	136
ME..........	643	121	154	111	53	70	(S)	34	(S)	35	38
MD..........	2,966	619	886	446	250	297	(S)	132	(S)	79	191
MA..........	3,322	730	1,026	453	294	312	(S)	149	76	116	156
MI..........	4,377	799	1,113	649	382	445	(S)	184	139	351	297
MN..........	2,896	620	703	402	259	305	(S)	120	95	194	173
MS..........	1,153	157	231	175	113	124	(S)	71	55	94	119
MO..........	2,852	514	666	454	281	315	(S)	134	119	141	205
MT..........	508	97	117	86	48	52	(S)	30	19	17	32
NE..........	997	189	232	132	92	109	(S)	48	(S)	73	73
NV..........	1,336	229	255	261	146	145	(S)	98	50	40	110
NH..........	704	139	177	103	68	75	(S)	33	20	44	42
NJ..........	4,078	846	1,094	577	399	440	(S)	196	100	113	303
NM..........	849	129	222	146	73	103	(S)	52	28	30	57
NY..........	8,349	1,552	2,341	1,486	756	836	(S)	395	189	275	502
NC..........	4,623	784	1,100	717	475	451	(S)	256	153	303	351
ND..........	383	69	86	59	37	41	(S)	22	17	23	24
OH..........	5,246	970	1,282	778	419	581	(S)	209	152	390	438
OK..........	1,736	294	367	278	175	174	(S)	113	79	98	129
OR..........	1,952	399	515	284	171	188	(S)	81	56	96	142
PA..........	5,810	1,016	1,455	864	511	620	(S)	298	187	329	491
RI..........	496	93	134	79	46	48	(S)	24	12	28	31
SC..........	2,236	364	555	337	236	237	(S)	109	87	152	155
SD..........	447	83	89	70	40	53	(S)	(S)	(S)	36	30
TN..........	3,040	502	706	476	311	314	(S)	166	113	189	251
TX..........	12,945	2,450	2,952	1,942	1,332	1,396	(S)	846	446	563	985
UT..........	1,549	281	366	212	150	216	(S)	93	(S)	87	99
VT..........	312	58	88	45	27	29	(S)	19	9	16	17
VA..........	4,109	923	1,198	587	369	374	(S)	181	99	144	220
WA..........	3,595	740	936	560	302	318	81	165	107	161	225
WV..........	728	102	160	130	61	86	(S)	43	34	41	67
WI..........	2,878	477	689	423	260	305	(S)	123	85	277	215
WY..........	279	49	61	44	23	26	(S)	21	13	12	26

S Data are not shown when the labor force base does not meet publication standard of reliability for the particular area, as determined by the sample size.

Source: U.S. Bureau of Labor Statistics, "Geographic Profile of Employment and Unemployment, 2020," July 2021. See also <www.bls.gov/opub/geographic-profile>.

Table 653. Fastest Growing and Largest Growth Occupations—Projections by Occupation: 2020 to 2030

[1.7 represents 1,700. Estimates based on the Current Employment Statistics Program, the Occupational Employment Statistics Survey, and the Current Population Survey. See source(s) for methodological assumptions. Occupations based on the 2010 Standard Occupational Classification system. Additional information is available in the Occupational Outlook Handbook <www.bls.gov/ooh>]

Occupation	Employment (1,000)		Change, 2020–2030		Median annual wage (in dollars), 2020	Typical education needed for entry [1]
	2020	2030	Number (1,000)	Percent		
FASTEST GROWING						
Motion picture projectionists	1.7	2.9	1.2	70.5	27,490	No formal educational credential
Wind turbine service technicians	6.9	11.7	4.7	68.2	56,230	Postsecondary nondegree award
Ushers, lobby attendants, and ticket takers	81.5	131.9	50.4	61.8	25,110	No formal educational credential
Nurse practitioners	220.3	335.2	114.9	52.2	111,680	Master's degree
Solar photovoltaic installers	11.8	17.9	6.1	52.1	46,470	High school diploma or equivalent
Cooks, restaurant	1,153.2	1,716.7	563.5	48.9	28,800	No formal educational credential
Agents and business managers of artists, performers, and athletes	18.7	27.3	8.6	46.3	75,420	Bachelor's degree
Costume attendants	5.4	7.7	2.4	44.3	42,910	High school diploma or equivalent
Exercise trainers and group fitness instructors	309.8	431.4	121.7	39.3	40,510	High school diploma or equivalent
Model makers, wood	1.0	1.3	0.4	38.6	64,050	High school diploma or equivalent
Athletes and sports competitors	16.7	23.0	6.3	38.0	50,850	No formal educational credential
Makeup artists, theatrical and performance	3.1	4.2	1.1	37.0	106,920	Postsecondary nondegree award
Occupational therapy assistants	43.3	58.9	15.6	36.1	62,940	Associate's degree
Statisticians	42.0	56.9	14.9	35.4	92,270	Master's degree
Entertainment attendants and related workers, all other	3.9	5.3	1.4	35.4	27,230	High school diploma or equivalent
Physical therapist assistants	93.8	126.9	33.2	35.4	59,770	Associate's degree
Animal caretakers	272.4	366.1	93.6	34.4	26,080	High school diploma or equivalent
Miscellaneous entertainers and performers, sports and related workers	33.7	45.2	11.4	33.8	(NA)	No formal educational credential
Information security analysts	141.2	188.3	47.1	33.3	103,590	Bachelor's degree
Film and video editors	33.0	43.9	11.0	33.2	67,250	Bachelor's degree
Manicurists and pedicurists	123.0	163.1	40.1	32.6	27,870	Postsecondary nondegree award
Home health and personal care aides	3,470.7	4,600.6	1,129.9	32.6	27,080	High school diploma or equivalent
Bartenders	492.3	652.3	159.9	32.5	24,960	No formal educational credential
Medical and health services managers	429.8	569.4	139.6	32.5	104,280	Bachelor's degree
Actors	51.6	68.3	16.7	32.4	(NA)	Some college, no degree
Amusement and recreation attendants	264.4	349.8	85.4	32.3	24,760	No formal educational credential
Massage therapists	144.6	191.1	46.5	32.2	43,620	Postsecondary nondegree award
Choreographers	4.6	6.1	1.5	32.1	43,680	High school diploma or equivalent
Data scientists and mathematical science occupations, all other	63.2	83.0	19.8	31.4	98,230	Bachelor's degree
Physician assistants	129.4	169.5	40.1	31.0	115,390	Master's degree
LARGEST JOB GROWTH						
Home health and personal care aides	3,470.7	4,600.6	1,129.9	32.6	27,080	High school diploma or equivalent
Cooks, restaurant	1,153.2	1,716.7	563.5	48.9	28,800	No formal educational credential
Fast food and counter workers	3,455.5	3,973.0	517.5	15.0	23,860	No formal educational credential
Software developers and software quality assurance analysts and testers	1,847.9	2,257.4	409.5	22.2	110,140	Bachelor's degree
Waiters and waitresses	2,023.2	2,430.7	407.6	20.1	23,740	No formal educational credential
Registered nurses	3,080.1	3,356.8	276.8	9.0	75,330	Bachelor's degree
Laborers and freight, stock, and material movers, hand	2,821.7	3,077.5	255.8	9.1	31,120	No formal educational credential
General and operations managers	2,411.9	2,638.2	226.3	9.4	103,650	Bachelor's degree
First-line supervisors of food preparation and serving workers	915.4	1,106.1	190.8	20.8	34,570	High school diploma or equivalent
Passenger vehicle drivers, except bus drivers, transit and intercity	707.4	887.9	180.6	25.5	32,320	No formal educational credential
Market research analysts and marketing specialists	740.9	904.5	163.6	22.1	65,810	Bachelor's degree
Bartenders	492.3	652.3	159.9	32.5	24,960	No formal educational credential
Security guards	1,059.0	1,213.2	154.2	14.6	31,050	High school diploma or equivalent
Medical and health services managers	429.8	569.4	139.6	32.5	104,280	Bachelor's degree
Maids and housekeeping cleaners	1,212.8	1,350.3	137.5	11.3	26,220	No formal educational credential
Medical assistants	720.9	853.5	132.6	18.4	35,850	Postsecondary nondegree award
Janitors and cleaners, except maids and housekeeping cleaners	2,217.0	2,344.2	127.2	5.7	29,080	No formal educational credential
Management analysts	907.6	1,032.0	124.4	13.7	87,660	Bachelor's degree
Heavy and tractor-trailer truck drivers	1,951.6	2,073.6	122.1	6.3	47,130	Postsecondary nondegree award
Exercise trainers and group fitness instructors	309.8	431.4	121.7	39.3	40,510	High school diploma or equivalent
Financial managers	681.7	799.9	118.2	17.3	134,180	Bachelor's degree
Maintenance and repair workers, general	1,444.1	1,561.1	117.0	8.1	40,850	High school diploma or equivalent
Teaching assistants, except postsecondary	1306.3	1422.3	116	8.9	28,900	Some college, no degree
Nursing assistants	1,396.7	1,512.0	115.3	8.3	30,850	Postsecondary nondegree award
Nurse practitioners	220.3	335.2	114.9	52.2	111,680	Master's degree
Hairdressers, hairstylists, and cosmetologists	569.6	680.1	110.5	19.4	27,380	Postsecondary nondegree award
Dining room and cafeteria attendants and cafeteria attendants and bartender helpers	389.0	492.5	103.6	26.6	25,010	No formal educational credential
Construction laborers	1,285.2	1,388.3	103.2	8.0	37,890	No formal educational credential
Elementary school teachers, except special education	1,371.1	1,472.9	101.7	7.4	60,940	Bachelor's degree
Light truck drivers	1,035.8	1,136.8	101.1	9.8	37,050	High school diploma or equivalent

NA Not available. [1] An occupation is placed into 1 of 8 categories that best describes the typical education needed by most workers to enter that occupation. For more information, see "Measures of Education and Training" at <www.bls.gov/emp/documentation/education/tech.htm>.

Source: U.S. Bureau of Labor Statistics, Employment Projections, "EP Data Tables—Occupations," <www.bls.gov/emp/tables.htm>, accessed January 2022.

Table 654. Employment Projections by Industry: 2020 to 2030

[10,022.1 represents 10,022,100. Estimates based on the Current Employment Statistics program. See source for methodological assumptions. Minus sign (-) indicates decline]

Industry	2017 NAICS code [1]	Employment (1,000) 2020	Employment (1,000) 2030	Change, 2020–2030 (1,000)	Compound annual rate of change 2020–2030
LARGEST GROWTH					
Food services and drinking places	722	10,022.1	12,157.4	2,135.3	2.0
Individual and family services	6241	2,602.1	3,616.2	1,014.1	3.3
Computer systems design and related services	5415	2,188.0	2,706.0	518.0	2.1
Hospitals	622	5,143.2	5,622.4	479.2	0.9
Local government educational services compensation	(X)	7,574.1	8,016.8	442.7	0.6
Home health care services	6216	1,492.4	1,861.9	369.5	2.2
Accommodation	721	1,522.1	1,887.8	365.7	2.2
Other amusement and recreation industries	7139	1,063.5	1,415.6	352.1	2.9
Employment services	5613	3,062.6	3,399.4	336.8	1.0
Management, scientific, and technical consulting services	5416	1,527.0	1,856.7	329.7	2.0
Nursing and residential care facilities	623	3,209.6	3,533.0	323.4	1.0
Construction	23	7,269.4	7,584.4	315.0	0.4
Offices of physicians	6211	2,620.2	2,886.1	265.9	1.0
Local government, other compensation	(X)	4,135.3	4,392.8	257.5	0.6
Offices of other health practitioners	6213	917.7	1,170.0	252.3	2.5
Other educational services	6114-7	723.6	935.6	212.0	2.6
Outpatient care centers	6214	973.3	1,183.4	210.1	2.0
Junior colleges, colleges, universities, and professional schools	6112, 6113	1,700.7	1,896.0	195.3	1.1
Personal care services	8121	590.3	785.2	194.9	2.9
Investigation and security services	5616	904.2	1,083.6	179.4	1.8
FASTEST GROWTH					
Promoters of events, and agents and managers	7113, 7114	113.8	211.3	97.5	6.4
Independent artists, writers, and performers	7115	40.6	65.9	25.3	5.0
Motion picture, video, and sound recording industries	512	282.9	458.2	175.3	4.9
Amusement parks and arcades	7131	156.1	250.0	93.9	4.8
Performing arts companies	7111	76.8	118.1	41.3	4.4
Museums, historical sites, and similar institutions	712	138.4	199.6	61.2	3.7
Spectator sports	7112	112.8	161.8	49.0	3.7
Individual and family services	6241	2,602.1	3,616.2	1,014.1	3.3
Other personal services	8129	289.9	402.8	112.9	3.3
Support activities for agriculture and forestry	115	103.9	143.3	39.4	3.3
Support activities for mining	213	258.4	353.1	94.7	3.2
Transit and ground passenger transportation	485	374.9	509.9	135.0	3.1
Other amusement and recreation industries	7139	1,063.5	1,415.6	352.1	2.9
Personal care services	8121	590.3	785.2	194.9	2.9
Commercial and industrial machinery and equipment rental and leasing	5324	158.2	206.6	48.4	2.7
Other educational services	6114-7	723.6	935.6	212.0	2.6
Other information services	519	353.9	451.5	97.6	2.5
Offices of other health practitioners	6213	917.7	1,170.0	252.3	2.5
Motor vehicle manufacturing	3361	187.0	234.2	47.2	2.3
Home health care services	6216	1,492.4	1,861.9	369.5	2.2
MOST RAPIDLY DECLINING					
Tobacco manufacturing	3122	11.1	6.3	-4.8	-5.5
Apparel, leather and allied product manufacturing	315, 316	116.2	71.1	-45.1	-4.8
Consumer goods rental and general rental centers	5322, 5323	153.6	117.2	-36.4	-2.7
Printing and related support activities	323	377.8	301.3	-76.5	-2.2
Manufacturing and reproducing magnetic and optical media	3346	11.9	9.8	-2.1	-1.9
Wired telecommunications carriers	5171	500.1	411.4	-88.7	-1.9
Textile mills and textile product mills	313,314	199.4	170.5	-28.9	-1.6
Audio and video equipment manufacturing	3343	20.9	18.4	-2.5	-1.3
Ship and boat building	3366	138.7	122.3	-16.4	-1.3
Satellite, telecommunications resellers, and all other telecommunications	5174, 5179	91.6	81.4	-10.2	-1.2
Converted paper product manufacturing	3222	264.1	236.1	-28.0	-1.1
Cement and concrete product manufacturing	3273	192.4	173.0	-19.4	-1.1
Forestry	1131, 1132	11.8	10.6	-1.1	-1.0
Other chemical product and preparation manufacturing	3259	77.3	70.0	-7.3	-1.0
Other transportation equipment manufacturing	3369	35.0	31.7	-3.3	-1.0
Natural gas distribution	2212	109.2	99.2	-10.0	-1.0
Postal Service	491	602.1	549.9	-52.2	-0.9
Animal production	112	480.2	439.4	-40.7	-0.9
Food and beverage stores	445	3,101.6	2,844.1	-257.5	-0.9
Electric power generation, transmission and distribution	2211	380.7	349.5	-31.2	-0.9

X Not applicable. [1] Based on the North American Industry Classification System, 2017; see text, Section 15.

Source: U.S. Bureau of Labor Statistics, Employment Projections, "EP Data Tables—Industries," <www.bls.gov/emp/tables.htm>, accessed April 2022.

Table 655. Occupations of the Employed by Race/Ethnicity and Educational Attainment: 2021

[In thousands (133,906 represents 133,906,000). Annual averages of monthly figures. Civilian noninstitutional population 25 years old and over. Based on Current Population Survey; see text, Section 1 and Appendix III]

Race/ethnicity and educational attainment	Total employed	Managerial, professional, and related	Service	Sales and office	Natural resources, construction, and maintenance	Production, transportation, and material-moving
Total [1]	**133,906**	**61,057**	**18,870**	**25,229**	**12,353**	**16,397**
Less than a high school diploma	8,263	635	2,492	787	2,319	2,031
High school graduate, no college	32,821	5,795	6,928	7,247	5,287	7,564
Some college or associate degree	33,855	11,382	5,966	8,462	3,485	4,559
Bachelor's degree or higher	58,966	43,245	3,484	8,733	1,261	2,243
White	103,842	47,816	13,496	19,796	10,637	12,097
Less than a high school diploma	6,681	521	1,871	629	2,066	1,594
High school graduate, no college	25,408	4,749	4,763	5,771	4,547	5,579
Some college or associate degree	26,375	9,240	4,282	6,595	2,971	3,287
Bachelor's degree or higher	45,378	33,307	2,580	6,801	1,054	1,637
Black	16,374	6,034	3,340	3,194	930	2,876
Less than a high school diploma	799	54	319	84	105	238
High school graduate, no college	4,896	678	1,428	926	447	1,418
Some college or associate degree	4,899	1,381	1,114	1,243	273	889
Bachelor's degree or higher	5,779	3,922	479	942	105	331
Asian	9,201	5,502	1,235	1,344	295	825
Less than a high school diploma	395	28	167	39	44	116
High school graduate, no college	1,306	177	452	265	95	317
Some college or associate degree	1,223	361	295	282	91	193
Bachelor's degree or higher	6,277	4,936	321	757	64	199
Hispanic [2]	23,102	6,152	5,031	3,936	4,164	3,819
Less than a high school diploma	4,919	222	1,589	331	1,683	1,095
High school graduate, no college	7,222	958	1,762	1,338	1,559	1,605
Some college or associate degree	5,309	1,434	1,125	1,354	662	734
Bachelor's degree or higher	5,652	3,538	555	913	261	386

[1] Includes other races, not shown separately. [2] Persons of Hispanic origin may be of any race.

Source: U.S. Bureau of Labor Statistics, Current Population Survey, unpublished data. See also <www.bls.gov/cps/>.

Table 656. Employment by Industry, Sex, Race, and Hispanic Origin: 2000 to 2021

[In thousands (136,891 represents 136,891,000), except percent. Civilian noninstitutional population 16 years old and over. Annual average of monthly figures. Based on Current Population Survey; see text, Section 1, Population, and Appendix III]

Industry	Total				2021, percent of total			
	2000	2010	2020	2021	Female	Black [1]	Asian [1]	Hispanic [2]
Total employed	**136,891**	**139,064**	**147,795**	**152,581**	**47.0**	**12.3**	**6.6**	**18.0**
Agriculture and related industries	2,464	2,206	2,349	2,291	28.0	3.0	1.2	25.5
Mining and related industries	475	731	684	603	15.4	5.9	3.6	17.1
Construction	9,931	9,077	10,786	11,271	11.0	6.3	2.1	32.6
Manufacturing	19,644	14,081	14,550	14,718	29.2	10.3	7.1	17.4
Durable goods	12,519	8,789	9,129	9,349	25.2	9.8	7.4	15.4
Nondurable goods	7,125	5,293	5,421	5,369	36.2	11.2	6.5	20.7
Wholesale trade	4,216	3,805	3,380	3,451	29.8	9.1	5.4	19.1
Retail trade	15,763	15,934	15,609	16,172	48.6	13.3	5.8	18.5
Transportation and utilities	7,380	7,134	8,552	9,377	24.8	19.6	5.5	20.1
Transportation and warehousing	6,096	5,880	7,170	8,017	25.1	21.3	5.8	21.5
Utilities	1,284	1,253	1,382	1,360	23.1	9.7	3.6	11.8
Information	4,059	3,149	2,594	2,721	39.3	11.6	9.5	12.4
Financial activities	9,374	9,350	10,646	10,725	52.1	11.3	7.5	12.6
Finance and insurance	6,641	6,605	7,605	7,497	53.4	11.6	8.9	11.4
Real estate and rental and leasing	2,734	2,745	3,040	3,229	49.1	10.5	4.3	15.3
Professional and business services	13,649	15,253	18,816	19,295	42.6	9.8	9.8	16.6
Professional and technical services	8,266	9,115	12,643	12,877	43.1	7.1	13.1	9.9
Management, administrative, and waste services	5,383	6,138	6,173	6,418	41.6	15.3	3.2	30.2
Education and health services	26,188	32,062	34,105	34,725	74.3	14.8	6.7	13.3
Educational services	11,255	13,155	13,369	13,521	69.1	11.3	5.8	11.9
Health care and social assistance	14,933	18,907	20,736	21,204	77.6	17.1	7.3	14.2
Hospitals	5,202	6,249	7,305	7,364	75.0	15.9	8.9	11.5
Health services, except hospitals	7,009	9,406	10,284	10,696	77.4	17.5	7.0	14.5
Social assistance	2,722	3,252	3,147	3,144	84.0	18.6	4.8	19.5
Leisure and hospitality	11,186	12,530	11,480	12,635	50.9	11.9	6.7	24.2
Arts, entertainment, and recreation	2,539	2,966	2,601	2,896	45.6	9.7	4.6	13.9
Accommodation and food services	8,647	9,564	8,879	9,739	52.5	12.6	7.3	27.3
Other services	6,450	6,769	6,742	7,186	51.9	10.5	7.7	19.9
Other services, except private households	5,731	6,102	6,088	6,527	48.3	10.7	8.0	17.9
Private households	718	667	654	659	87.6	8.1	5.0	40.1
Public administration	6,113	6,983	7,501	7,410	46.3	16.9	4.9	13.0

[1] Persons in this race group only. See footnote 2, Table 622. [2] Persons of Hispanic origin may be of any race.

Source: U.S. Bureau of Labor Statistics, CPS Tables, "Employed persons by detailed industry, sex, race, and Hispanic or Latino ethnicity," January 2022, and earlier releases, <www.bls.gov/cps/tables.htm>.

Table 657. Unemployed Workers—Summary: 1990 to 2021

[In thousands (7,047 represents 7,047,000), except as indicated. For civilian noninstitutionalized population 16 years old and over. Annual averages of monthly figures. Revisions to population controls and other changes can affect the comparability of data over time. Based on the Current Population Survey; see text, Section 1 and Appendix III]

Item	1990	2000	2010	2015	2016	2017	2018	2019	2020	2021
UNEMPLOYED										
Total [1]	**7,047**	**5,692**	**14,825**	**8,296**	**7,751**	**6,982**	**6,314**	**6,001**	**12,947**	**8,623**
16 to 19 years old	1,212	1,081	1,528	966	925	827	759	746	1,025	696
20 to 24 years old	1,299	1,022	2,329	1,501	1,286	1,127	1,048	1,024	1,990	1,317
25 to 34 years old	1,995	1,207	3,386	1,905	1,797	1,647	1,450	1,384	3,080	2,092
35 to 44 years old	1,328	1,133	2,703	1,351	1,258	1,143	1,003	930	2,177	1,586
45 to 54 years old	723	762	2,769	1,259	1,189	1,060	938	890	2,042	1,323
55 to 64 years old	386	355	1,660	978	941	835	789	710	1,839	1,138
65 years and over	105	132	449	337	355	343	327	317	795	472
Male	3,906	2,975	8,626	4,490	4,187	3,743	3,398	3,227	6,644	4,676
16 to 19 years old	667	599	863	531	512	457	422	408	526	373
20 to 24 years old	715	547	1,398	865	742	667	596	602	1,016	739
25 to 34 years old	1,092	602	1,993	1,030	966	884	763	741	1,664	1,167
35 to 44 years old	711	557	1,534	695	644	575	515	475	1,126	852
45 to 54 years old	413	398	1,614	649	602	537	490	471	995	685
55 to 64 years old	249	189	962	536	528	445	435	361	916	603
65 years and over	59	83	262	184	193	179	177	170	401	257
Female	3,140	2,717	6,199	3,807	3,564	3,239	2,916	2,774	6,304	3,948
16 to 19 years old	544	483	665	435	413	371	338	339	500	323
20 to 24 years old	584	475	931	636	545	460	452	421	974	578
25 to 34 years old	902	604	1,392	874	832	763	687	643	1,416	925
35 to 44 years old	617	577	1,169	656	614	568	488	455	1,050	733
45 to 54 years old	310	364	1,156	610	586	523	448	419	1,047	638
55 to 64 years old	137	165	698	442	413	389	354	350	924	535
65 years and over	46	50	187	153	162	164	150	147	394	216
White [2]	5,186	4,121	10,916	5,662	5,345	4,765	4,354	4,159	9,090	5,854
Black [2]	1,565	1,241	2,852	1,846	1,655	1,501	1,322	1,251	2,304	1,756
Asian [2,3]	(NA)	227	543	347	349	333	304	280	894	529
Hispanic [4]	876	954	2,843	1,726	1,548	1,401	1,323	1,248	3,018	1,995
UNEMPLOYMENT RATE [5] (percent)										
Total [1]	**5.6**	**4.0**	**9.6**	**5.3**	**4.9**	**4.4**	**3.9**	**3.7**	**8.1**	**5.3**
16 to 19 years old	15.5	13.1	25.9	16.9	15.7	14.0	12.9	12.7	17.9	11.7
20 to 24 years old	8.8	7.2	15.5	9.7	8.4	7.4	6.9	6.7	13.7	8.9
25 to 34 years old	5.6	3.7	10.1	5.5	5.1	4.6	3.9	3.7	8.4	5.7
35 to 44 years old	4.1	3.0	8.1	4.1	3.8	3.5	3.0	2.7	6.4	4.6
45 to 54 years old	3.6	2.5	7.7	3.7	3.5	3.2	2.8	2.7	6.4	4.2
55 to 64 years old	3.3	2.5	7.1	3.8	3.6	3.1	2.9	2.6	6.7	4.2
65 years and over	3.0	3.1	6.7	3.8	3.8	3.6	3.3	3.0	7.5	4.5
Male	5.7	3.9	10.5	5.4	4.9	4.4	3.9	3.7	7.8	5.5
16 to 19 years old	16.3	14.0	28.8	18.4	17.1	15.5	14.5	13.8	18.4	12.5
20 to 24 years old	9.1	7.3	17.8	10.8	9.3	8.4	7.7	7.7	13.7	9.7
25 to 34 years old	5.5	3.4	10.9	5.5	5.0	4.6	3.9	3.7	8.5	5.9
35 to 44 years old	4.1	2.8	8.5	4.0	3.6	3.2	2.8	2.6	6.2	4.6
45 to 54 years old	3.7	2.4	8.6	3.6	3.4	3.0	2.8	2.7	5.9	4.1
55 to 64 years old	3.8	2.4	8.0	3.90	3.8	3.1	3.0	2.5	6.4	4.2
65 years and over	3.0	3.3	7.1	3.8	3.8	3.4	3.2	2.9	6.8	4.3
Female	5.5	4.1	8.6	5.2	4.8	4.3	3.8	3.6	8.3	5.2
16 to 19 years old	14.7	12.1	22.8	15.5	14.3	12.5	11.3	11.5	17.5	10.8
20 to 24 years old	8.5	7.1	13.0	8.5	7.4	6.3	6.2	5.7	13.8	8.1
25 to 34 years old	5.6	4.1	9.1	5.5	5.1	4.6	4.0	3.7	8.3	5.4
35 to 44 years old	4.2	3.3	7.7	4.4	4.1	3.7	3.2	2.9	6.7	4.6
45 to 54 years old	3.4	2.5	6.8	3.8	3.7	3.3	2.8	2.7	6.9	4.2
55 to 64 years old	2.8	2.5	6.2	3.6	3.3	3.1	2.7	2.7	7.2	4.2
65 years and over	3.1	2.7	6.2	3.9	3.9	3.8	3.3	3.1	8.3	4.6
White [2]	4.8	3.5	8.7	4.6	4.3	3.8	3.5	3.3	7.3	4.7
Black [2]	11.4	7.6	16.0	9.6	8.4	7.5	6.5	6.1	11.4	8.6
Asian [2,3]	(NA)	3.6	7.5	3.8	3.6	3.4	3.0	2.7	8.7	5.0
Hispanic [4]	8.2	5.7	12.5	6.6	5.8	5.1	4.7	4.3	10.4	6.8
PERCENT WITHOUT WORK FOR—										
Fewer than 5 weeks	46.3	44.9	18.7	28.9	30.5	32.5	34.4	34.8	28.6	24.8
5 to 14 weeks	32.0	31.9	22.0	27.7	28.7	28.8	29.7	29.8	36.5	23.0
15 weeks and over	21.6	23.2	59.3	43.3	40.8	38.7	35.9	35.4	34.8	52.2
15 to 26 weeks	11.7	11.8	16.0	15.3	14.9	14.6	14.5	14.3	19.4	13.5
27 weeks and over	10.0	11.4	43.3	28.1	25.9	24.2	21.4	21.1	15.4	38.7
Unemployment duration, average (weeks) [6]	12.0	12.6	33.0	29.2	27.5	25.0	22.7	21.6	16.5	28.7

NA Not available. [1] Includes other races not shown separately. [2] For persons reporting this race group only. [3] Prior to 2003, includes Pacific Islanders. [4] Persons of Hispanic or Latino origin may be of any race. [5] Unemployed as percent of civilian labor force in specified group. [6] Beginning 2011, the CPS increased the maximum duration of unemployment that respondents could report from 2 years to 5 years. For more information, see <www.bls.gov/cps/duration.htm>.

Source: U.S. Bureau of Labor Statistics, "Labor Force Statistics from the Current Population Survey," <www.bls.gov/cps>, accessed February 2022.

Table 658. Unemployed Jobseekers' Job Search Methods: 2021

[8,623 represents 8,623,000. For the civilian noninstitutionalized population 16 years old and over. Annual averages of monthly data. Based on the Current Population Survey; see text, Section 1 and Appendix III]

Characteristic	Population (1,000)		Jobseekers' job search methods (percent)							Average number of methods used
	Total unemployed	Total jobseekers [1]	Contact employer directly	Sent out a resume or filled out applications	Placed or answered ads	Friends or relatives	Public employment agency	Private employment agency	Other activities	
Total, 16 years and over [2]...	**8,623**	**7,041**	**50.3**	**53.3**	**14.0**	**24.8**	**12.9**	**7.3**	**14.5**	**1.8**
AGE										
16 to 19 years old..............	696	630	49.7	55.4	10.4	19.0	6.9	4.0	11.1	1.6
20 to 24 years old..............	1,317	1,171	49.5	55.7	12.1	22.5	10.8	6.1	13.2	1.7
25 to 34 years old..............	2,092	1,753	50.8	55.3	15.0	22.4	13.6	6.5	14.2	1.8
35 to 44 years old..............	1,586	1,266	49.8	52.9	14.1	26.9	14.5	8.3	15.8	1.8
45 to 54 years old..............	1,323	1,024	51.7	50.5	15.2	29.1	14.9	8.9	15.5	1.9
55 to 64 years old..............	1,138	855	51.1	51.5	15.0	28.8	14.8	9.4	14.8	1.9
65 years old and over..........	472	341	47.4	45.6	15.2	25.7	10.8	8.5	17.9	1.7
SEX										
Male, total......................	4,676	3,807	51.5	50.7	13.7	26.2	13.2	7.7	14.5	1.8
16 to 19 years old.............	373	342	50.5	51.5	10.3	20.3	7.7	4.8	10.0	1.6
20 to 24 years old.............	739	662	50.9	55.1	11.5	24.5	10.6	5.7	12.4	1.7
25 to 34 years old.............	1,167	965	52.8	50.7	14.1	22.5	13.9	6.9	14.2	1.8
35 to 44 years old.............	852	675	51.6	49.1	13.9	29.0	15.5	8.9	17.0	1.9
45 to 54 years old.............	685	523	50.6	49.7	15.3	30.3	15.6	8.9	15.4	1.9
55 to 64 years old.............	603	455	52.1	50.1	15.1	30.2	14.6	10.6	15.6	1.9
65 years old and over.........	257	186	48.9	43.2	16.3	31.2	11.2	9.4	17.4	1.8
Female, total....................	3,948	3,233	49.0	56.4	14.3	23.2	12.5	6.9	14.5	1.8
16 to 19 years old.............	323	288	48.8	60.0	10.5	17.5	6.1	3.0	12.4	1.6
20 to 24 years old.............	578	509	47.8	56.5	12.7	20.0	11.1	6.6	14.2	1.7
25 to 34 years old.............	925	788	48.4	60.9	16.1	22.3	13.1	6.1	14.1	1.8
35 to 44 years old.............	733	592	47.8	57.3	14.4	24.5	13.3	7.7	14.5	1.8
45 to 54 years old.............	638	501	52.7	51.3	15.0	27.9	14.1	9.0	15.6	1.9
55 to 64 years old.............	535	401	49.8	53.0	15.0	27.2	15.0	8.0	13.9	1.8
65 years old and over.........	216	155	45.7	48.6	13.9	19.1	10.2	7.4	18.6	1.6
RACE/ETHNICITY										
White [3]......................	5,854	4,678	50.7	53.4	14.3	25.4	12.1	7.0	14.5	1.8
Male......................	3,222	2,572	51.7	51.2	14.0	26.8	12.7	7.4	14.5	1.8
Female....................	2,632	2,107	49.5	56.1	14.7	23.7	11.4	6.5	14.5	1.8
Black [3]......................	1,756	1,534	50.2	52.8	12.8	22.4	15.5	7.3	13.7	1.8
Male......................	900	782	50.4	48.6	12.5	23.0	14.9	7.2	14.4	1.7
Female....................	857	753	49.9	57.3	13.1	21.8	16.1	7.4	13.1	1.8
Asian [3]......................	529	425	49.2	50.6	16.4	28.8	12.1	11.3	16.2	1.9
Male......................	275	223	52.1	47.6	16.2	30.1	13.3	12.7	15.7	1.9
Female....................	254	202	45.9	54.0	16.6	27.4	10.8	9.8	16.7	1.8
Hispanic [4]....................	1,995	1,584	50.6	50.4	11.1	30.8	12.7	7.0	11.6	1.7
Male......................	1,090	857	53.4	47.1	11.0	32.5	13.1	7.0	10.3	1.7
Female....................	904	727	47.2	54.2	11.2	28.9	12.3	7.1	13.0	1.7

[1] Excludes persons on temporary layoff. [2] Includes other races not shown separately. [3] Data for this race group only. [4] Persons of Hispanic or Latino origin may be of any race.

Source: U.S. Bureau of Labor Statistics, CPS Tables, "Unemployed jobseekers by sex, age, race, Hispanic or Latino ethnicity, and active jobsearch methods used," January 2022, <www.bls.gov/cps/tables.htm>.

Table 659. Unemployed Persons by Sex and Reason: 2000 to 2021

[In thousands (2,975 represents 2,975,000). For civilian noninstitutionalized population 16 years old and over. Annual averages of monthly figures. Revisions to population controls and other changes affect comparability of data over time. Based on Current Population Survey; see text, Section 1 and Appendix III]

Sex and reason	2000	2010	2012	2013	2014	2015	2016	2017	2018	2019	2020	2021
Male, total..............	**2,975**	**8,626**	**6,771**	**6,314**	**5,190**	**4,490**	**4,187**	**3,743**	**3,398**	**3,227**	**6,644**	**4,676**
Job losers [1]..............	1,516	5,919	4,103	3,690	2,926	2,441	2,232	2,038	1,772	1,611	5,045	2,901
Job leavers...............	387	457	487	465	416	397	414	382	413	444	367	407
Reentrants...............	854	1,608	1,481	1491	1,279	1,178	1,108	961	896	851	952	1,079
New entrants.............	217	641	699	668	569	474	433	362	317	321	280	288
Female, total.............	**2,717**	**6,199**	**5,734**	**5,146**	**4,426**	**3,807**	**3,564**	**3,239**	**2,916**	**2,774**	**6,304**	**3,948**
Job losers [1].............	1,001	3,331	2,774	2,383	1,952	1,622	1,508	1,397	1,218	1,175	4,725	2,198
Job leavers...............	393	432	480	467	408	423	444	396	381	370	316	396
Reentrants...............	1,107	1,858	1,864	1,716	1,550	1,357	1,222	1,118	1,032	959	1,017	1,124
New entrants.............	217	579	617	579	517	405	390	328	285	270	246	229

[1] Includes persons who completed temporary jobs.

Source: U.S. Bureau of Labor Statistics, CPS Tables, "Unemployed jobseekers by sex, reason for unemployment, and active jobsearch methods used," January 2022, and earlier releases, <www.bls.gov/cps/tables.htm>.

Table 660. Unemployment Rates by Industry and by Sex: 2010 to 2021

[In percent. Civilian noninstitutionalized population 16 years old and over. Annual averages of monthly figures. Rate represents unemployment as a percent of labor force in each specified group. Based on Current Population Survey; see text, Section 1 and Appendix III. See also headnote, Table 640, regarding industries]

Industry	Total				Male		Female	
	2010	2019	2020	2021	2020	2021	2020	2021
Total [1]	**9.6**	**3.7**	**8.1**	**5.3**	**7.8**	**5.5**	**8.3**	**5.2**
Wage and salary workers:								
Agriculture and related industries	13.9	7.4	8.1	7.6	6.8	7.2	11.5	8.5
Mining, quarrying, and oil and gas extraction	9.4	3.2	11.3	11.2	11.9	12.0	7.4	6.3
Construction	20.6	4.5	8.7	6.5	8.8	6.6	7.5	5.9
Manufacturing	10.6	3.0	6.8	4.3	6.4	4.2	7.5	4.6
Wholesale trade	7.3	2.8	5.6	4.3	5.5	3.8	5.8	5.7
Retail trade	10.0	4.4	8.9	6.2	8.0	5.9	9.9	6.5
Transportation and utilities	8.4	3.5	9.3	6.3	8.7	5.9	11.3	7.6
Transportation and warehousing	9.4	3.8	10.4	6.8	9.7	6.4	12.6	8.3
Utilities	3.4	1.8	2.4	3.0	2.5	3.2	2.4	2.3
Information	9.7	3.5	7.5	5.4	6.8	5.2	8.5	5.8
Telecommunications	9.2	2.1	4.4	3.4	4.1	2.9	5.2	4.5
Financial activities	6.9	2.1	3.8	2.9	3.7	3.1	4.0	2.7
Finance and insurance	6.6	2.0	2.9	2.5	2.8	2.9	3.0	2.2
Real estate and rental and leasing	7.6	2.5	6.4	3.9	5.9	3.8	7.0	4.1
Professional and business services	10.8	3.6	6.7	5.2	6.1	4.7	7.5	5.9
Professional and technical services	6.5	2.3	4.5	3.2	4.1	2.8	5.2	3.8
Management, administrative, and waste services	16.8	6.1	11.0	9.3	10.1	8.6	12.3	10.4
Education and health services	5.8	2.5	5.7	3.5	5.1	3.2	5.9	3.6
Educational services	6.4	3.5	8.1	4.3	8.1	4.2	8.0	4.3
Health care and social assistance	5.6	2.2	5.1	3.3	3.9	2.9	5.5	3.5
Leisure and hospitality	12.2	5.2	19.4	10.1	19.6	10.3	19.2	9.9
Arts, entertainment, and recreation	11.6	5.1	23.1	10.0	22.7	10.3	23.6	9.6
Accommodation and food services	12.3	5.3	18.5	10.1	18.8	10.3	18.3	10.0
Other services	8.5	3.2	9.8	5.4	7.9	5.2	11.5	5.5
Government workers	4.4	2.3	4.8	2.7	3.9	2.6	5.5	2.8

[1] Includes a small amount of persons whose last job was in the Armed Forces.

Source: U.S. Bureau of Labor Statistics, CPS Tables, "Unemployed persons by industry, class of worker, and sex," January 2022, and earlier releases, <www.bls.gov/cps/tables.htm>.

Table 661. Unemployment by Occupation: 2010 to 2021

[14,825 represents 14,825,000. Civilian noninstitutionalized population 16 years old and over. Annual averages of monthly data. Rate represents unemployment as a percent of the labor force for each specified group. Based on Current Population Survey; see text, Section 1 and Appendix III. See also headnote, Table 640, regarding occupations]

Occupation	Number unemployed (1,000)				Unemployment rate				
							2021		
	2010	2019	2020	2021	2010	2020	Total	Male	Female
Total [1]	**14,825**	**6,001**	**12,947**	**8,623**	**9.6**	**8.1**	**5.3**	**5.5**	**5.2**
Management, professional, and related occupations	2,566	1,310	3,029	1,889	4.7	4.5	2.8	2.8	2.9
Management, business, and financial operations	1,117	499	1,149	812	5.1	4.1	2.8	2.7	3.0
Management	762	314	752	529	4.8	3.9	2.7	2.4	3.1
Business and financial operations	355	185	397	283	5.6	4.4	3.1	3.4	2.8
Professional and related occupations	1,449	811	1,880	1,077	4.5	4.9	2.8	2.9	2.8
Computer and mathematical	195	107	199	124	5.2	3.4	2.1	2.0	2.4
Architecture and engineering	173	58	117	86	6.2	3.6	2.6	2.4	3.3
Life, physical, and social science	69	27	72	52	4.6	4.3	3.0	3.8	2.2
Community and social services	114	56	87	71	4.6	3.1	2.5	1.7	2.9
Legal	48	27	53	40	2.7	2.7	2.1	1.5	2.7
Education, training, and library	379	279	678	312	4.2	7.1	3.4	3.7	3.3
Arts, design, entertainment, sports, and media	269	121	372	237	8.9	10.9	7.0	7.4	6.6
Healthcare practitioner and technical	203	136	303	156	2.5	3.1	1.6	1.7	1.6
Service occupations	2,819	1,255	3,407	2,057	10.3	13.0	7.8	7.9	7.7
Healthcare support	276	122	380	304	7.6	7.3	5.9	5.3	6.0
Protective service	207	93	162	121	5.9	5.1	3.9	3.6	4.8
Food preparation and serving-related	1,079	491	1,595	850	12.4	19.6	10.3	11.1	9.7
Building and grounds cleaning and maintenance	780	310	623	446	12.8	10.9	7.5	6.6	8.8
Personal care and service	477	239	648	335	8.7	16.0	8.3	12.5	7.1
Sales and office occupations	3,315	1,274	2,591	1,685	9.0	8.0	5.3	4.9	5.5
Sales and related	1,596	614	1,367	853	9.4	8.8	5.6	4.6	6.6
Office and administrative support	1,719	659	1,224	832	8.7	7.3	5.0	5.5	4.8
Natural resources, construction, and maintenance	2,504	703	1,298	984	16.1	8.9	6.6	6.4	9.1
Farming, fishing, and forestry	193	123	120	104	16.3	10.3	8.9	8.3	10.9
Construction and extraction	1,809	452	862	681	20.1	10.1	7.8	7.7	11.0
Installation, maintenance, and repair	503	129	316	199	9.3	6.4	3.9	4.0	3.7
Production, transportation, and material moving	2,365	847	2,076	1,473	12.8	10.2	7.1	6.9	7.6
Production	1,206	350	747	485	13.1	9.0	5.8	5.5	6.3
Transportation and material moving	1,159	497	1,329	988	12.4	11.1	8.0	7.8	8.8

[1] Includes a small amount of persons whose last job was in the Armed Forces.

Source: U.S. Bureau of Labor Statistics, CPS Tables, "Unemployed persons by occupation and sex," January 2022, and earlier releases, <www.bls.gov/cps/tables.htm>.

Table 662. Unemployed and Unemployment Rates by Educational Attainment, Sex, Race, and Hispanic Origin: 2010 to 2021

[10,968 represents 10,968,000. Annual averages of monthly figures. Civilian noninstitutionalized population 25 years old and over. See Table 627 for civilian labor force and participation rate data. Revisions to population controls and other changes can affect the comparability of data over time. Based on Current Population Survey; see text, Section 1 and Appendix III]

Year, sex, and race/ethnicity	Unemployed (1,000)					Unemployment rate [1]				
	Total	Less than a high school diploma	High school graduate, no college	Some college or associate's degree	Bachelor's degree or higher	Total	Less than a high school diploma	High school graduate, no college	Some college or associate's degree	Bachelor's degree or higher
Total: [2]										
2010	10,968	1,765	3,943	3,093	2,167	8.2	14.9	10.3	8.4	4.7
2020	9,932	1,041	3,135	2,831	2,925	7.1	11.7	9.0	7.8	4.8
2021	6,611	744	2,173	1,833	1,861	4.7	8.3	6.2	5.1	3.1
Male:										
2010	6,365	1,137	2,452	1,646	1,130	8.9	15.0	11.3	9.0	4.8
2020	5,101	606	1,776	1,362	1,357	6.8	10.6	8.6	7.3	4.5
2021	3,564	444	1,287	931	902	4.8	7.6	6.1	5.1	3.0
Female:										
2010	4,603	628	1,492	1,447	1,037	7.4	14.6	9.0	7.8	4.7
2020	4,831	435	1,359	1,469	1,568	7.4	13.6	9.7	8.3	5.1
2021	3,047	300	886	902	959	4.6	9.5	6.3	5.2	3.1
White only:										
2010	8,174	1,337	2,937	2,278	1,622	7.5	13.9	9.5	7.6	4.3
2020	7,028	743	2,148	2,007	2,130	6.4	10.5	8.0	7.1	4.6
2021	4,508	522	1,423	1,260	1,303	4.2	7.3	5.3	4.6	2.8
Black only:										
2010	2,022	321	795	614	292	13.4	22.5	15.8	12.4	7.9
2020	1,726	169	666	540	351	9.9	16.1	13.0	10.2	5.9
2021	1,349	143	540	403	263	7.6	15.2	9.9	7.6	4.4
Asian only:										
2010	446	54	95	92	205	6.8	11.1	7.6	8.1	5.5
2020	746	75	189	129	353	7.9	16.6	13.7	10.3	5.6
2021	441	30	115	75	221	4.6	7.0	8.1	5.8	3.4
Hispanic: [3]										
2010	2,041	787	674	399	182	10.8	13.2	11.5	9.7	6.0
2020	2,229	572	753	523	381	9.2	11.2	10.1	8.9	6.6
2021	1,457	384	500	345	228	5.9	7.2	6.5	6.1	3.9

[1] Unemployed as percent of the civilian labor force. [2] Includes other races, not shown separately. [3] Persons of Hispanic origin may be of any race.

Source: U.S. Bureau of Labor Statistics, CPS Tables, "Employment status of the civilian noninstitutional population 25 years and over by educational attainment, sex, race, and Hispanic or Latino ethnicity," January 2022 and earlier releases, <www.bls.gov/cps/tables.htm>.

Table 663. Unemployed Persons by Reason for Unemployment and Duration: 2021

[8,623 represents 8,623,000. Annual averages of monthly data. Based on Current Population Survey; see text, Section 1 and Appendix III]

Age, sex, and reason	Total unemployed (1,000)	Percent distribution by duration				
		Less than 5 weeks	5 to 14 weeks	15 weeks and over		
				Total	15 to 26 weeks	27 weeks or longer
Total 16 years old and over	**8,623**	**24.8**	**23.0**	**52.2**	**13.5**	**38.7**
16 to 19 years old	696	46.3	29.3	24.4	10.3	14.0
Males, 20 years old and over	**4,302**	**22.1**	**22.1**	**55.9**	**14.2**	**41.7**
Job losers and persons who completed temporary jobs	2,827	21.3	20.6	58.0	13.6	44.4
On temporary layoff	837	33.4	22.3	44.2	12.0	32.2
Not on temporary layoff	1,990	16.2	19.9	63.8	14.3	49.6
Permanent job losers	1,554	13.9	18.4	67.6	14.2	53.4
Persons who completed temporary jobs	436	24.5	25.3	50.2	14.5	35.8
Job leavers	383	31.8	28.8	39.4	14.6	24.8
Reentrants	956	20.1	23.3	56.7	15.9	40.7
New entrants	136	23.4	23.7	52.8	14.5	38.4
Females, 20 years old and over	**3,625**	**24.0**	**22.9**	**53.2**	**13.2**	**39.9**
Job losers and persons who completed temporary jobs	2,130	21.6	20.9	57.6	13.1	44.4
On temporary layoff	680	31.7	22.1	46.2	9.1	37.1
Not on temporary layoff	1,450	16.9	20.3	62.9	15.0	47.9
Permanent job losers	1,190	14.4	19.0	66.5	14.8	51.7
Persons who completed temporary jobs	260	28.0	25.9	46.1	15.5	30.5
Job leavers	372	36.8	28.4	34.8	12.0	22.8
Reentrants	1,007	24.4	24.8	50.8	13.6	37.2
New entrants	116	22.4	25.4	52.2	16.5	35.7

Source: U.S. Bureau of Labor Statistics, CPS Tables, "Unemployed persons by reason for unemployment, sex, age, and duration of unemployment," January 2022, <www.bls.gov/cps/tables.htm>.

Table 664. Total Unemployed and Insured Unemployed by State: 2000 to 2021

[5,692 represents 5,692,000. Civilian noninstitutionalized population 16 years old and over. Annual averages of monthly figures, except as noted. State total unemployment estimates come from the Local Area Unemployment Statistics program, while U.S. totals come from the Current Population Survey; see text, Section 1 and Appendix III. U.S. totals derived by independent population controls; therefore, state data may not add to U.S. totals. Unemployment data are based on population controls updated annually]

| State | Total unemployed | | | | | | | | Insured unemployed [2, 4] | | | |
| | Number (1,000) | | | | Percent [1] | | | | Number (1,000) | | Percent [3] | |
	2000	2010	2020	2021	2000	2010	2020	2021	2020	2021	2020	2021
United States.........	5,692	14,825	12,947	8,623	4.0	9.6	8.1	5.3	10,093	3,192	7.4	2.3
Alabama................	99	228	147	77	4.6	10.4	6.5	3.4	74	15	4.0	0.8
Alaska.................	20	30	29	23	6.3	8.2	8.2	6.4	24	9	8.4	3.1
Arizona................	100	319	266	172	4.0	10.3	7.7	4.9	133	41	4.8	1.4
Arkansas..............	53	107	83	54	4.2	7.9	6.1	4.0	52	18	4.5	1.5
California.............	826	2,292	1,934	1,381	4.9	12.5	10.2	7.3	1,825	596	11.3	3.6
Colorado..............	64	249	212	169	2.7	9.2	6.9	5.4	136	54	5.3	2.0
Connecticut...........	37	183	148	116	2.1	9.6	7.8	6.3	146	50	9.6	3.2
Delaware..............	15	38	37	27	3.6	8.7	7.6	5.3	26	9	6.3	2.1
District of Columbia....	18	35	31	25	5.7	10.0	8.0	6.6	40	16	7.5	3.1
Florida................	297	992	828	470	3.8	10.8	8.2	4.6	351	98	4.2	1.1
Georgia...............	147	503	328	203	3.5	10.7	6.5	3.9	400	103	9.5	2.4
Hawaii................	26	44	80	38	4.2	6.8	12.0	5.7	72	16	13.8	2.9
Idaho.................	31	67	49	33	4.7	8.8	5.5	3.6	23	7	3.1	0.9
Illinois................	288	694	586	383	4.4	10.5	9.2	6.1	393	183	7.2	3.3
Indiana...............	94	321	240	118	3.0	10.1	7.2	3.6	150	45	5.2	1.5
Iowa..................	43	102	86	71	2.7	6.1	5.1	4.2	80	24	5.5	1.6
Kansas................	53	104	85	48	3.8	7.0	5.7	3.2	59	17	4.5	1.3
Kentucky..............	81	213	130	95	4.1	10.3	6.4	4.7	105	37	6.0	2.0
Louisiana.............	104	157	180	113	5.2	7.5	8.7	5.5	162	40	9.3	2.2
Maine.................	23	59	34	32	3.3	8.4	5.0	4.6	39	11	6.9	1.8
Maryland.............	99	241	215	183	3.5	7.8	6.7	5.8	135	42	5.7	1.7
Massachusetts.........	94	281	351	215	2.8	8.1	9.4	5.7	312	84	9.5	2.5
Michigan..............	188	581	484	280	3.6	12.2	10.0	5.9	381	100	9.7	2.4
Minnesota............	85	218	197	103	3.0	7.4	6.3	3.4	206	74	7.7	2.7
Mississippi...........	70	132	98	70	5.3	10.1	7.9	5.6	81	21	7.6	1.9
Missouri..............	101	289	184	134	3.4	9.5	6.1	4.4	109	39	4.2	1.4
Montana..............	23	36	31	19	4.8	7.2	5.8	3.4	26	8	5.8	1.7
Nebraska.............	26	47	43	26	2.8	4.7	4.1	2.5	27	7	2.9	0.8
Nevada...............	44	187	203	109	4.1	13.8	13.5	7.2	173	51	13.9	3.8
New Hampshire........	18	45	51	26	2.7	6.1	6.7	3.5	34	7	5.5	1.1
New Jersey............	157	441	440	296	3.7	9.7	9.5	6.3	315	122	8.5	3.1
New Mexico...........	42	72	76	64	5.0	7.8	8.1	6.8	57	21	7.6	2.8
New York..............	413	840	944	655	4.5	8.7	9.9	6.9	966	296	11.3	3.4
North Carolina.........	155	498	343	238	3.7	10.7	7.1	4.8	160	38	3.8	0.9
North Dakota..........	10	14	21	15	3.0	3.7	5.1	3.7	16	4	4.1	1.1
Ohio..................	237	604	471	295	4.1	10.3	8.2	5.1	286	87	5.7	1.7
Oklahoma.............	50	115	114	71	3.0	6.5	6.2	3.8	81	26	5.5	1.7
Oregon...............	94	214	160	112	5.2	10.7	7.6	5.2	134	49	7.4	2.7
Pennsylvania..........	258	522	589	407	4.2	8.2	9.1	6.3	502	179	9.3	3.2
Rhode Island..........	22	67	52	32	4.0	11.6	9.2	5.6	40	15	9.3	3.4
South Carolina........	73	246	140	95	3.7	11.3	6.0	4.0	108	31	5.4	1.5
South Dakota..........	10	22	20	15	2.5	4.9	4.3	3.1	9	2	2.3	0.5
Tennessee.............	110	304	244	143	3.9	9.8	7.4	4.3	139	38	4.9	1.3
Texas.................	455	1,005	1,062	807	4.4	8.2	7.7	5.7	711	209	6.0	1.7
Utah..................	38	107	78	45	3.3	7.9	4.7	2.7	43	12	2.9	0.8
Vermont..............	9	23	19	11	2.8	6.3	5.6	3.4	25	7	9.0	2.5
Virginia...............	82	305	271	167	2.3	7.3	6.2	3.9	190	47	5.3	1.3
Washington...........	158	316	333	205	5.1	9.1	8.5	5.2	244	75	7.7	2.3
West Virginia..........	45	70	64	40	5.6	8.7	8.2	5.0	45	14	7.4	2.1
Wisconsin.............	101	262	197	118	3.4	8.5	6.3	3.8	148	61	5.5	2.2
Wyoming..............	10	21	17	13	3.8	6.9	5.8	4.5	9	3	3.4	1.2

[1] Total unemployment as percent of civilian labor force. [2] Number of average weekly jobless workers who are receiving state unemployment benefits. Source: U.S. Employment and Training Administration, "Unemployment Insurance, Financial Data Handbook 394," <oui.doleta.gov/unemploy/hb394.asp>, accessed September 2022. [3] Those currently collecting unemployment insurance as a percent of the total number of eligible workers. [4] U.S. totals include Puerto Rico and the Virgin Islands.

Source: Except as noted, U.S. Bureau of Labor Statistics, "Local Area Unemployment Statistics," <www.bls.gov/lau/>, accessed September 2022.

Table 665. Nonfarm Establishments—Employees, Hours, and Earnings by Industry: 2000 to 2021

[132,011 represents 132,011,000. Annual averages of monthly data. Based on data from establishment reports. Includes all full- and part-time employees who worked during, or received pay for, any part of the pay period including the 12th of the month. Excludes proprietors, the self-employed, farm workers, unpaid family workers, private household workers, and Armed Forces. Establishment data shown here conform to industry definitions in the 2017 North American Industry Classification System (NAICS) and are adjusted to March employment benchmarks. Based on the Current Employment Statistics Program; see source and Appendix III]

Item and year	Total nonfarm	Private industry																Government
		Total [1]	Construction	Manufacturing	Wholesale trade	Retail trade	Transportation and warehousing	Utilities	Information	Finance and insurance	Real estate and rental and leasing	Professional and technical services	Administrative and waste services	Educational services	Health care and social assistance	Arts entertainment and recreation	Accommodations and food services	
EMPLOYEES (1,000)																		
2000	132,011	111,221	6,787	17,263	5,888	15,284	4,401	601	3,630	5,773	2,011	6,732	8,172	2,390	12,861	1,788	10,074	20,790
2010	130,345	107,855	5,518	11,528	5,387	14,446	4,179	553	2,707	5,761	1,934	7,486	7,419	3,155	16,820	1,913	11,135	22,490
2015	141,825	119,796	6,461	12,336	5,780	15,611	4,859	556	2,750	6,035	2,088	8,658	8,823	3,472	18,557	2,166	12,994	22,029
2016	144,336	122,112	6,728	12,354	5,787	15,846	5,004	556	2,794	6,148	2,139	8,881	8,881	3,570	19,069	2,252	13,408	22,224
2017	146,608	124,258	6,969	12,439	5,814	15,786	5,178	555	2,814	6,262	2,189	9,058	9,142	3,668	19,520	2,333	13,718	22,350
2018	148,908	126,454	7,288	12,688	5,841	15,620	5,426	553	2,839	6,337	2,253	9,282	9,294	3,715	19,923	2,383	13,913	22,455
2019	150,905	128,292	7,493	12,817	5,889	15,604	5,665	549	2,864	6,433	2,321	9,536	9,319	3,741	20,421	2,437	14,149	22,613
2020	142,186	120,200	7,257	12,167	5,633	14,871	5,640	543	2,720	6,489	2,215	9,435	8,529	3,478	19,796	1,773	11,375	21,986
2021	146,124	124,119	7,413	12,346	5,678	15,396	6,092	541	2,831	6,519	2,257	9,883	9,029	3,589	20,084	1,979	12,121	22,005
WEEKLY EARNINGS [2] (dollars)																		
2000	(NA)	480.90	685.78	590.92	630.09	333.48	559.63	955.09	700.92	(NA)	(NA)	746.12	387.72	(NA)	447.45	273.79	207.44	(NA)
2010	(NA)	636.02	891.83	765.18	814.04	400.38	707.93	1,262.89	939.85	(NA)	(NA)	1,073.43	536.08	(NA)	652.07	363.91	266.78	(NA)
2015	(NA)	708.70	998.02	832.22	907.72	446.01	800.14	1,444.03	1,038.10	(NA)	(NA)	1,201.23	569.06	(NA)	722.49	379.22	300.17	(NA)
2016	(NA)	723.20	1,031.88	855.77	929.09	447.69	807.25	1,502.09	1,068.23	(NA)	(NA)	1,223.94	585.46	(NA)	737.17	380.57	310.02	(NA)
2017	(NA)	742.48	1,061.98	876.10	957.95	463.10	813.69	1,540.27	1,100.03	(NA)	(NA)	1,254.18	605.86	(NA)	755.48	387.40	323.66	(NA)
2018	(NA)	766.99	1,108.59	908.01	979.82	483.03	835.39	1,569.38	1,139.52	(NA)	(NA)	1,294.63	622.68	(NA)	776.46	389.91	338.00	(NA)
2019	(NA)	790.44	1,135.73	921.87	1,007.42	503.06	847.97	1,566.91	1,198.97	(NA)	(NA)	1,321.57	655.82	(NA)	798.79	395.68	351.58	(NA)
2020	(NA)	837.39	1,145.52	928.94	1,023.97	542.14	870.19	1,639.19	1,288.27	(NA)	(NA)	1,367.24	707.62	(NA)	842.18	432.47	343.29	(NA)
2021	(NA)	886.06	1,203.77	985.92	1,078.17	571.02	920.68	1,699.88	1,342.87	(NA)	(NA)	1,430.48	771.72	(NA)	904.24	445.30	395.88	(NA)
WEEKLY HOURS [2]																		
2000	(NA)	34.3	39.2	41.3	38.8	30.7	37.3	42.0	36.8	(NA)	(NA)	36.2	33.1	(NA)	32.2	25.6	26.2	(NA)
2010	(NA)	33.4	38.4	41.1	37.9	30.2	37.1	42.0	36.3	(NA)	(NA)	35.9	33.9	(NA)	32.2	23.8	25.0	(NA)
2015	(NA)	33.7	39.6	41.8	38.6	30.1	38.7	42.4	35.7	(NA)	(NA)	36.4	34.0	(NA)	32.2	23.7	25.3	(NA)
2016	(NA)	33.6	39.7	41.9	38.6	29.7	38.8	42.4	35.5	(NA)	(NA)	36.3	33.9	(NA)	32.3	23.2	25.2	(NA)
2017	(NA)	33.7	39.7	41.9	39.0	30.2	38.4	42.5	35.8	(NA)	(NA)	36.5	34.0	(NA)	32.4	22.9	25.3	(NA)
2018	(NA)	33.8	40.0	42.2	38.9	30.4	38.4	42.7	35.6	(NA)	(NA)	36.6	34.0	(NA)	32.4	22.5	25.3	(NA)
2019	(NA)	33.6	39.8	41.6	38.7	30.3	37.9	42.4	35.3	(NA)	(NA)	36.4	34.1	(NA)	32.4	21.6	25.4	(NA)
2020	(NA)	33.9	39.2	40.7	38.2	30.8	38.3	42.6	36.0	(NA)	(NA)	36.5	34.7	(NA)	32.7	22.2	24.4	(NA)
2021	(NA)	34.2	39.5	41.4	38.8	30.8	38.5	42.5	36.5	(NA)	(NA)	36.7	35.4	(NA)	32.8	22.5	25.3	(NA)
HOURLY EARNINGS [2] (dollars)																		
2000	(NA)	14.01	17.48	14.32	16.24	10.87	15.00	22.75	19.07	(NA)	(NA)	20.62	11.70	(NA)	13.93	10.68	7.92	(NA)
2010	(NA)	19.04	23.22	18.61	21.46	13.25	19.10	30.04	25.87	(NA)	(NA)	29.93	15.81	(NA)	20.23	15.27	10.68	(NA)
2015	(NA)	21.03	25.20	19.91	23.52	14.83	20.66	34.02	29.05	(NA)	(NA)	32.96	16.73	(NA)	22.41	15.97	11.87	(NA)
2016	(NA)	21.53	25.97	20.44	24.07	15.05	20.83	35.33	30.05	(NA)	(NA)	33.72	17.26	(NA)	22.83	16.38	12.32	(NA)
2017	(NA)	22.05	26.74	20.90	24.58	15.33	21.22	36.22	30.74	(NA)	(NA)	34.41	17.82	(NA)	23.35	16.94	12.85	(NA)
2018	(NA)	22.71	27.75	21.54	25.17	15.91	21.75	36.76	31.97	(NA)	(NA)	35.42	18.32	(NA)	23.96	17.31	13.37	(NA)
2019	(NA)	23.51	28.52	22.15	26.06	16.62	22.36	36.91	33.93	(NA)	(NA)	36.27	19.24	(NA)	24.67	18.30	13.95	(NA)
2020	(NA)	24.68	29.21	22.80	26.81	17.60	22.71	38.46	35.74	(NA)	(NA)	37.41	20.39	(NA)	25.76	19.52	14.07	(NA)
2021	(NA)	25.89	30.48	23.80	27.76	18.54	23.90	39.97	36.82	(NA)	(NA)	39.02	21.79	(NA)	27.55	19.78	15.66	(NA)

NA Not available. [1] Includes other industries not shown separately. [2] Average hours and earnings of production and nonsupervisory employees.

Source: U.S. Bureau of Labor Statistics, Current Employment Statistics, "Employment, Hours, and Earnings—National," <www.bls.gov/ces/data/>, accessed April 2022.

Table 666. Employees in Nonfarm Establishments by State and Industry: 2021

[In thousands (146,060.4 represents 146,060,400). Includes all full- and part-time employees who worked during, or received pay for, any part of the pay period reported. Excludes proprietors, the self-employed, farm workers, unpaid family workers, private household workers, and Armed Forces. Compiled from data supplied by cooperating state agencies. Based on North American Industry Classification System, 2017; see text, section 15]

State	Total [1]	Con-struction	Manu-facturing	Trade, transpor-tation and utilities	Infor-mation	Fin-ancial activi-ties [2]	Profes-sional and business ser-vices [3]	Educa-tion and health ser-vices [4]	Leisure and hospi-tality [5]	Other ser-vices [6]	Govern-ment
U.S.......	146,060.4	7,425.4	12,299.9	27,713.6	2,848.0	8,676.7	21,266.9	23,606.5	14,135.9	5,399.0	22,130.2
AL.........	2,039.7	94.6	263.7	394.1	20.0	98.0	250.7	239.2	188.2	95.1	387.7
AK.........	309.9	16.0	12.3	60.8	4.8	10.8	26.4	50.5	30.3	10.5	77.1
AZ.........	2,957.6	177.6	180.8	582.6	47.5	245.8	445.0	464.4	304.3	91.2	406.6
AR.........	1,282.4	55.3	157.1	256.2	11.7	65.9	145.7	195.3	115.9	66.9	207.0
CA.........	16,708.1	880.3	1,273.2	3,031.7	566.5	823.1	2,702.7	2,809.1	1,632.6	500.7	2,469.2
CO.........	2,744.0	176.8	148.7	485.7	76.3	177.7	452.8	347.9	306.4	113.6	438.3
CT [7]......	1,613.0	59.5	153.4	289.6	29.8	117.6	213.2	333.4	133.9	58.2	224.1
DE [7]......	449.6	23.1	24.8	80.9	3.6	47.6	63.0	77.6	45.0	18.2	65.9
DC [7]......	743.1	15.0	1.1	29.2	19.6	28.1	167.2	120.3	49.9	71.2	241.4
FL.........	8,912.9	575.5	388.2	1,838.4	138.7	622.0	1,456.6	1,339.8	1,121.7	333.9	1,092.6
GA.........	4,570.2	205.3	394.6	961.9	123.3	258.4	733.7	604.9	451.5	157.4	669.7
HI [7]......	583.5	36.8	12.1	109.0	7.9	27.1	67.7	84.5	94.0	24.3	120.2
ID.........	795.0	60.1	70.5	158.4	8.0	39.1	103.5	116.7	83.6	26.2	125.0
IL.........	5,813.2	222.3	554.0	1,182.8	88.6	406.9	924.5	905.7	503.1	238.4	780.3
IN.........	3,088.5	150.1	525.2	608.8	26.0	144.4	347.1	465.0	283.2	121.1	412.8
IA.........	1,535.7	77.8	217.6	308.2	18.9	108.9	139.8	225.2	128.3	54.7	254.1
KS.........	1,373.3	64.1	160.4	264.9	16.8	75.8	169.7	197.6	120.1	47.3	250.6
KY.........	1,895.7	78.8	242.3	411.4	20.9	95.6	218.7	281.5	181.6	62.5	294.8
LA.........	1,869.4	127.8	129.0	364.2	21.0	89.3	212.3	315.5	199.1	69.1	312.3
ME.........	620.8	31.7	54.1	116.6	6.6	33.0	72.1	125.7	60.1	21.1	97.8
MD.........	2,646.8	160.2	109.1	466.0	33.7	137.5	458.6	440.9	229.7	105.8	504.1
MA.........	3,516.3	164.3	232.5	551.9	93.2	220.0	605.4	790.9	296.1	122.0	439.0
MI.........	4,193.5	176.3	583.7	777.3	51.7	232.7	630.4	650.3	357.6	153.3	573.5
MN.........	2,841.9	129.9	312.9	511.9	42.3	190.7	372.3	540.7	226.7	105.1	403.1
MS.........	1,136.6	44.8	143.8	235.7	9.5	42.4	114.5	140.3	126.3	39.0	234.4
MO.........	2,842.7	131.7	270.1	544.2	46.8	178.4	373.5	480.6	275.1	112.1	425.8
MT.........	492.1	33.1	21.4	96.7	5.6	27.0	46.9	80.0	66.1	18.5	90.1
NE.........	1,006.7	55.8	99.3	193.7	17.7	72.8	117.1	156.9	86.5	36.3	169.7
NV.........	1,365.9	96.9	60.7	276.0	15.0	70.1	190.1	149.5	294.4	39.2	159.1
NH.........	663.1	29.0	67.6	138.5	11.7	34.8	87.8	119.3	65.1	23.3	85.0
NJ.........	4,021.4	157.5	240.4	866.5	70.5	251.5	684.9	692.1	330.2	151.9	574.5
NM.........	812.9	47.9	27.7	135.8	10.1	33.5	111.2	138.9	85.9	26.6	177.0
NY.........	9,044.5	374.8	408.3	1,423.4	280.9	704.0	1,279.7	2,050.8	720.3	362.4	1,434.7
NC.........	4,585.7	237.8	462.9	890.1	77.1	272.5	674.8	630.4	458.2	161.8	714.4
ND.........	416.6	25.2	26.2	89.2	5.7	24.6	33.0	66.4	37.1	14.3	81.4
OH.........	5,373.2	223.5	665.1	1,032.3	64.9	308.1	717.6	896.5	504.9	200.7	750.9
OK.........	1,642.5	77.2	128.9	312.4	17.8	78.3	189.7	236.9	165.0	63.9	345.1
OR.........	1,874.3	111.1	187.3	362.2	35.1	103.5	250.3	298.9	175.5	59.0	284.9
PA.........	5,750.4	253.0	542.6	1,106.2	86.2	327.1	798.1	1,226.1	477.4	236.0	676.1
RI.........	479.9	20.1	39.0	75.0	5.5	34.5	68.6	102.0	51.3	20.7	63.0
SC.........	2,146.3	104.2	249.4	413.9	27.3	109.8	294.1	254.4	244.7	77.2	367.0
SD.........	439.5	25.1	43.8	86.6	5.0	28.2	34.3	74.2	45.3	17.0	78.9
TN.........	3,106.1	136.7	349.4	653.0	46.8	172.1	435.8	438.8	316.6	122.5	430.3
TX.........	12,705.5	736.8	873.5	2,566.7	207.9	833.0	1,895.5	1,732.6	1,295.6	418.3	1,965.2
UT.........	1,611.6	122.1	145.3	306.9	41.0	97.2	233.6	216.7	148.4	42.2	249.2
VT.........	293.6	15.1	28.7	51.3	4.0	11.9	30.0	60.6	29.6	9.5	52.2
VA.........	3,943.0	205.2	236.3	655.0	66.4	209.9	776.1	536.0	357.7	183.8	709.6
WA.........	3,356.5	223.0	259.1	652.7	157.1	160.6	446.8	495.6	282.2	113.1	560.5
WV.........	685.4	30.9	45.5	123.1	7.2	29.5	67.8	127.6	66.7	23.2	146.6
WI.........	2,882.5	126.6	466.6	532.9	44.9	154.3	316.4	453.2	251.0	143.0	390.0
WY.........	277.8	21.1	9.7	51.1	2.9	11.1	19.6	28.6	35.9	15.7	67.4

[1] Includes mining and logging, not shown separately. [2] Finance and insurance; and real estate and rental and leasing. [3] Professional, scientific, and technical services; management of companies and enterprises; and administrative and support, and waste management and remediation services. [4] Education services; and health care and social assistance. [5] Arts, entertainment, and recreation; and accommodations and food services. [6] Includes repair and maintenance; personal and laundry services; and membership associations and organizations. [7] Mining and logging is combined with construction.

Source: U.S. Bureau of Labor Statistics, State and Metro Area Employment, Hours, and Earnings, Annual Average Tables, "Employees on nonfarm payrolls in States and selected areas by major industry," <www.bls.gov/sae/tables/>, accessed April 2022.

Table 667. Nonfarm Industries—Employees and Earnings: 2000 to 2021

[Annual averages of monthly figures (132,011 represents 132,011,000). Covers all full- and part-time employees who worked during, or received pay for, any part of the pay period including the 12th of the month. See also headnote, Table 665]

Industry	2017 NAICS code [1]	All employees (1,000)				Average hourly earnings [2] (dol.)			
		2000	2010	2020	2021	2000	2010	2020	2021
Total nonfarm	(X)	**132,011**	**130,345**	**142,186**	**146,124**	**(NA)**	**(NA)**	**(NA)**	**(NA)**
Goods-producing [3]	(X)	24,649	17,751	20,023	20,325	15.27	20.28	25.41	26.49
Service-providing [4]	(X)	107,362	112,594	122,163	125,799	(NA)	(NA)	(NA)	(NA)
Total private	(X)	**111,221**	**107,855**	**120,200**	**124,119**	**14.01**	**19.04**	**24.68**	**25.89**
Mining and logging	(X)	**599**	**705**	**600**	**566**	**16.55**	**23.82**	**30.42**	**31.08**
Logging	1133	79	50	46	46	13.70	18.85	22.74	25.07
Mining	21	**520**	**655**	**553**	**520**	**16.94**	**24.24**	**31.09**	**31.61**
Oil and gas extraction	211	125	159	130	118	19.43	27.36	38.50	37.14
Mining, except oil and gas	212	225	205	176	175	18.07	24.63	28.33	29.42
Support activities for mining	213	171	292	247	227	14.55	22.95	30.29	31.19
Construction	23	**6,787**	**5,518**	**7,257**	**7,413**	**17.48**	**23.22**	**29.21**	**30.48**
Construction of buildings	236	1,633	1,230	1,606	1,648	16.74	22.73	28.99	30.47
Residential building	2361	823	572	809	860	15.18	19.80	26.38	27.97
Nonresidential building	2362	809	658	798	787	18.18	25.13	31.44	32.86
Heavy and civil engineering construction	237	937	825	1,046	1,041	16.80	23.76	30.74	31.55
Highway, street, and bridge construction	2373	340	287	346	341	18.17	23.76	29.92	31.66
Specialty trade contractors	238	4,217	3,463	4,605	4,725	17.91	23.22	28.88	30.21
Building foundation and exterior contractors	2381	919	680	905	923	16.93	21.20	27.38	28.56
Building equipment contractors	2382	1,897	1,634	2,209	2,278	19.52	24.89	31.00	32.48
Building finishing contractors	2383	857	634	799	812	16.44	22.06	26.62	27.62
Manufacturing	31-33	**17,263**	**11,528**	**12,167**	**12,346**	**14.32**	**18.61**	**22.80**	**23.80**
Durable goods	(X)	**10,877**	**7,064**	**7,573**	**7,676**	**14.93**	**19.81**	**23.76**	**24.83**
Wood products	321	615	342	396	410	11.63	14.85	19.18	19.97
Nonmetallic mineral products	327	554	371	399	402	14.53	17.48	22.67	23.90
Cement and concrete products	3273	234	170	194	195	14.64	17.84	24.15	25.90
Primary metals	331	622	362	354	350	16.64	20.13	23.96	24.86
Iron and steel mills and ferroalloy production	3311	135	87	82	79	(NA)	(NA)	(NA)	(NA)
Foundries	3315	217	112	103	104	14.72	18.22	22.63	24.65
Fabricated metal products	332	1,753	1,282	1,386	1,384	13.77	17.94	22.16	23.04
Architectural and structural metals	3323	428	321	383	387	13.43	17.47	22.20	22.99
Machine shops and threaded products	3327	365	313	335	328	14.53	18.68	23.38	23.69
Machinery	333	1,457	996	1,055	1,053	15.21	18.96	24.62	25.25
Agricultural, construction, and mining machinery	3331	222	208	201	198	14.21	18.95	23.69	24.76
HVAC and commercial refrigeration equipment	3334	194	125	133	136	(NA)	(NA)	(NA)	(NA)
Metalworking machinery	3335	274	155	164	159	16.66	20.00	24.49	24.71
Computer and electronic products	334	1,820	1,095	1,063	1,058	14.73	22.78	25.59	27.00
Computer and peripheral equipment	3341	302	158	160	158	(NA)	(NA)	(NA)	(NA)
Communications equipment	3342	239	117	86	85	14.39	23.88	21.92	23.54
Semiconductors and electronic components	3344	676	369	369	368	13.46	20.35	22.61	23.83
Electronic instruments	3345	488	406	418	417	15.80	24.82	30.39	32.15
Electrical equipment and appliances	335	591	360	384	394	13.23	16.87	20.59	22.14
Household appliances	3352	106	60	62	72	(NA)	(NA)	(NA)	(NA)
Electrical equipment	3353	210	136	136	139	13.28	16.51	21.15	23.22
Transportation equipment	336	2,057	1,333	1,591	1,640	18.89	25.23	28.03	29.36
Motor vehicles	3361	291	153	206	250	24.45	29.05	30.08	30.95
Motor vehicle parts	3363	840	419	530	545	17.95	20.66	22.08	23.71
Aerospace products and parts	3364	517	478	507	480	20.52	33.65	39.69	42.01
Ship and boat building	3366	154	125	140	147	(NA)	(NA)	(NA)	(NA)
Furniture and related products	337	680	357	359	375	11.73	15.06	19.01	19.67
Household and institutional furniture	3371	441	223	226	240	11.40	14.75	18.72	19.58
Miscellaneous durable goods manufacturing	339	728	567	586	610	11.93	16.56	20.77	21.61
Medical equipment and supplies	3391	305	303	317	327	12.70	17.56	22.10	22.67
Nondurable goods	(X)	**6,386**	**4,464**	**4,594**	**4,671**	**13.31**	**16.80**	**21.28**	**22.19**
Food manufacturing	311	1,553	1,451	1,615	1,638	11.77	14.41	18.90	19.96
Fruit and vegetable preserving	3114	197	173	170	173	11.90	14.56	19.01	19.67
Dairy products	3115	136	130	153	155	14.85	18.92	23.30	23.65
Animal slaughtering and processing	3116	507	489	537	528	10.27	12.69	16.64	18.35
Bakeries and tortilla manufacturing	3118	306	277	294	304	11.45	14.44	18.45	18.97
Textile mills	313	378	119	96	98	11.23	13.56	17.46	18.85
Textile product mills	314	230	119	103	103	10.31	11.79	16.03	16.94
Apparel	315	484	157	90	92	8.61	11.43	16.90	17.46
Paper and paper products	322	605	395	355	349	15.91	20.04	23.32	23.33
Pulp, paper, and paperboard mills	3221	191	112	92	88	(NA)	(NA)	(NA)	(NA)
Converted paper products	3222	413	282	263	261	(NA)	(NA)	(NA)	(NA)
Printing and related support activities	323	807	488	375	367	14.09	16.91	20.06	20.89
Petroleum and coal products	324	123	114	108	106	(NA)	(NA)	(NA)	(NA)
Chemicals	325	980	787	845	869	17.09	21.07	26.03	26.69
Basic chemicals	3251	188	142	149	148	21.06	24.93	30.66	32.57
Resin, rubber, and artificial fibers	3252	136	89	90	90	(NA)	(NA)	(NA)	(NA)
Pharmaceuticals and medicines	3254	274	277	315	332	17.27	21.95	24.86	25.45
Plastics and rubber products	326	951	625	707	724	12.70	15.71	20.20	21.62
Plastics products	3261	737	502	576	592	12.04	15.47	20.14	21.32
Rubber products	3262	214	123	131	132	14.83	16.64	20.43	23.01
Trade, transportation, and utilities	(X)	**26,174**	**24,565**	**26,687**	**27,707**	**13.28**	**16.78**	**21.41**	**22.41**
Wholesale trade	42	**5,888**	**5,387**	**5,633**	**5,678**	**16.24**	**21.46**	**26.81**	**27.76**
Durable goods	423	3,342	2,848	3,081	3,121	16.83	21.30	27.02	27.94
Motor vehicles and parts	4231	361	317	345	343	14.37	17.86	22.89	24.68
Lumber and construction supplies	4233	233	196	242	246	13.79	18.87	24.69	25.60
Commercial equipment	4234	758	657	678	686	20.35	25.29	32.27	33.23
Electric goods	4236	438	328	342	345	19.51	23.42	29.51	29.63
Hardware and plumbing	4237	253	227	278	287	15.21	20.14	25.31	25.42

See footnotes at end of table.

Industry	2017 NAICS code [1]	All employees (1,000)				Average hourly earnings [2] (dol.)			
		2000	2010	2020	2021	2000	2010	2020	2021
Machinery and supplies.........................	4238	739	629	687	686	16.57	21.27	27.60	28.91
Nondurable goods.................................	424	2,131	2,026	2,065	2,075	14.54	20.03	24.74	25.85
Paper and paper products......................	4241	184	135	121	117	15.87	22.96	24.93	25.79
Druggists' goods.................................	4242	212	219	235	240	19.22	24.08	32.62	34.14
Apparel and piece goods.......................	4243	166	141	131	137	14.70	21.54	23.91	24.56
Grocery and related products..................	4244	704	726	751	755	13.73	19.33	22.75	23.90
Alcoholic beverages.............................	4248	130	166	200	197	15.80	20.14	25.37	26.79
Electronic markets and agents and brokers...	425	415	513	487	482	20.38	28.21	34.53	35.14
Retail trade...................................	**44, 45**	**15,284**	**14,446**	**14,871**	**15,396**	**10.87**	**13.25**	**17.60**	**18.54**
Motor vehicle and parts dealers...............	441	1,847	1,629	1,897	1,940	14.94	17.06	22.52	24.25
Automobile dealers.............................	4411	1,217	1,012	1,203	1,223	16.95	18.22	24.52	26.27
Auto parts, accessories, and tire stores......	4413	499	489	544	549	11.04	14.54	17.96	19.32
Furniture and home furnishings stores........	442	544	438	404	442	12.33	15.25	19.86	21.17
Furniture stores.................................	4421	289	217	199	214	13.37	16.17	21.27	23.49
Home furnishings stores.......................	4422	254	221	205	228	11.06	14.03	18.22	18.58
Electronics and appliance stores...............	443	648	523	425	424	13.17	16.84	23.79	24.76
Building material and garden supply stores...	444	1,143	1,133	1,359	1,399	11.26	14.12	19.66	21.18
Building material and supplies dealers.......	4441	983	1,006	1,196	1,223	11.31	14.14	19.95	21.65
Food and beverage stores.......................	445	2,993	2,808	3,106	3,130	9.76	12.03	14.48	15.09
Grocery stores...................................	4451	2,582	2,461	2,744	2,750	9.71	12.12	14.40	15.02
Specialty food stores...........................	4452	270	211	204	215	9.97	11.13	15.15	15.80
Beer, wine, and liquor stores..................	4453	141	136	158	166	10.40	11.89	15.02	15.55
Health and personal care stores...............	446	928	981	964	1,029	11.68	16.99	20.56	21.46
Gasoline stations.................................	447	936	819	927	939	8.05	10.25	12.82	13.93
Clothing & clothing accessories stores........	448	1,322	1,353	950	1,033	9.96	11.59	16.79	17.83
Clothing stores..................................	4481	954	1,040	699	761	9.88	10.91	15.84	17.05
Shoe stores......................................	4482	193	182	151	161	8.96	11.80	16.88	16.73
Jewelry, luggage, and leather goods stores..	4483	175	131	101	111	11.48	15.56	22.00	23.53
Sporting goods, hobby, book, and music stores.............................	451	603	579	472	527	9.38	11.69	15.41	16.99
Sporting goods and musical instrument stores...................................	4511	437	459	418	466	9.55	11.82	15.49	17.30
Book stores and news dealers................	4512	166	120	54	61	8.91	11.10	14.51	14.08
General merchandise stores.....................	452	2,820	2,998	3,032	3,093	9.22	10.98	15.64	15.73
Department stores..............................	4522	1,740	1,485	931	937	(NA)	(NA)	(NA)	(NA)
Miscellaneous store retailers...................	453	1,007	762	747	805	10.20	12.50	15.19	16.47
Florists..	4531	130	69	50	55	8.95	11.05	14.29	14.72
Office supplies, stationery, and gift stores....	4532	471	303	192	197	10.46	13.06	14.82	15.35
Used merchandise stores.......................	4533	107	125	152	173	8.07	10.72	13.46	14.05
Nonstore retailers................................	454	495	425	588	635	13.27	17.83	22.18	23.22
Electronic shopping and mail-order houses..	4541	258	250	424	467	13.43	18.34	22.22	23.34
Transportation and warehousing...............	**48, 49**	**4,401**	**4,179**	**5,640**	**6,092**	**15.00**	**19.10**	**22.71**	**23.90**
Air transportation.................................	481	614	458	441	475	13.57	24.56	35.62	37.28
Scheduled air transportation..................	4811	570	417	396	426	(NA)	(NA)	(NA)	(NA)
Rail transportation................................	482	206	183	150	146	(NA)	(NA)	(NA)	(NA)
Water transportation.............................	483	56	62	60	56	(NA)	(NA)	(NA)	(NA)
Truck transportation.............................	484	1,406	1,251	1,471	1,514	15.86	18.62	24.40	25.33
General freight trucking........................	4841	1,013	868	1,022	1,058	16.37	18.51	24.35	25.64
Specialized freight trucking....................	4842	393	383	449	456	14.52	18.89	24.50	24.58
Transit and ground passenger transport.......	485	376	436	370	375	11.88	14.98	19.33	20.17
Taxi and limousine service.....................	4853	72	68	49	43	(NA)	(NA)	(NA)	(NA)
School and employee bus transportation....	4854	152	186	150	160	11.42	14.90	20.20	21.29
Urban, interurban, rural, and charter bus transportation.............................	4851, 2, 5	101	100	80	81	(NA)	(NA)	(NA)	(NA)
Pipeline transportation..........................	486	46	42	51	50	(NA)	(NA)	(NA)	(NA)
Scenic and sightseeing transportation.........	487	28	27	21	23	(NA)	(NA)	(NA)	(NA)
Support activities for transportation............	488	546	553	701	722	14.54	21.01	24.32	25.81
Support activities for air transportation......	4881	141	154	204	203	13.42	17.04	23.37	24.30
Support activities for water transportation....	4883	97	91	87	90	19.57	35.16	34.91	36.67
Support activities for road transportation.....	4884	66	80	103	110	13.98	15.68	21.11	21.89
Freight transportation arrangement..........	4885	178	169	233	242	13.46	21.24	23.73	26.00
Couriers and messengers.......................	492	605	528	967	1,082	13.51	17.67	18.62	20.03
Couriers and express delivery services......	4921	546	480	815	902	(NA)	(NA)	(NA)	(NA)
Warehousing and storage.......................	493	518	638	1,405	1,648	14.49	15.57	18.47	19.77
Utilities..	**22**	**601**	**553**	**543**	**541**	**22.75**	**30.04**	**38.46**	**39.97**
Power generation and supply....................	2211	434	398	381	378	23.13	31.25	38.97	40.33
Natural gas distribution..........................	2212	121	108	110	109	23.41	28.36	41.95	44.14
Water, sewage and other systems..............	2213	46	47	52	54	16.93	23.73	25.69	26.97
Information..	**51**	**3,630**	**2,707**	**2,720**	**2,831**	**19.07**	**25.87**	**35.74**	**36.82**
Publishing industries, except internet...........	511	1,035	759	768	791	(NA)	26.78	39.46	40.81
Newspaper, book, and directory publishers...	5111	774	498	264	247	(NA)	20.98	26.72	27.90
Software publishers.............................	5112	261	261	504	544	28.48	36.41	45.41	46.03
Motion picture and sound recording............	512	383	370	301	371	21.25	22.11	30.25	33.04
Broadcasting, except internet....................	515	344	290	247	236	16.74	24.01	30.22	32.65
Radio and television broadcasting.............	5151	253	210	199	191	(NA)	(NA)	(NA)	(NA)
Cable and other subscription programming...	5152	91	80	48	46	(NA)	(NA)	(NA)	(NA)
Telecommunications..............................	517	1,397	903	688	667	18.59	26.24	32.13	31.25
Wired telecommunications carriers............	517311	922	603	498	485	(NA)	(NA)	(NA)	(NA)
Wireless telecommunications carriers (except satellite)..............................	517312	186	170	99	92	(NA)	(NA)	(NA)	(NA)
Data processing, hosting and related services..	518	316	243	362	388	16.97	27.03	39.20	42.40
Financial activities.............................	**(X)**	**7,783**	**7,695**	**8,704**	**8,777**	**15.04**	**21.55**	**29.09**	**30.34**
Finance and insurance.........................	**52**	**5,773**	**5,761**	**6,489**	**6,519**	**(NA)**	**(NA)**	**(NA)**	**(NA)**
Monetary authorities—central bank...........	521	23	20	20	21	(NA)	(NA)	(NA)	(NA)

See footnotes at end of table.

Industry	2017 NAICS code [1]	All employees (1,000)				Average hourly earnings [2] (dol.)			
		2000	2010	2020	2021	2000	2010	2020	2021
Credit intermediation and related activities....	522	2,548	2,550	2,668	2,707	13.14	18.25	26.19	27.57
Depository credit intermediation...............	5221	1,723	1,763	1,772	1,742	12.01	17.65	24.76	26.08
Commercial banking..................	52211	1,325	1,366	1,388	1,359	11.92	17.70	25.24	26.61
Nondepository credit intermediation.........	5222	606	532	589	634	15.41	20.00	30.77	31.83
Activities related to credit intermediation.....	5223	219	255	308	332	15.42	18.27	24.94	26.54
Securities, commodity contracts, and investments, and funds and trusts...........	523, 5	851	850	965	990	20.04	31.21	42.99	45.52
Securities and commodity contracts brokerage and exchanges....................	5231, 2	569	471	447	449	20.05	31.72	42.68	47.45
Other financial investment activities, incl. funds trusts........................	5239, 525	282	379	518	541	20.03	30.51	43.28	43.74
Insurance carriers and related activities......	524	2,351	2,341	2,836	2,802	17.47	24.58	31.25	31.94
Insurance carriers..................	5241	1,544	1,445	1,627	1,567	18.03	25.95	32.65	33.44
Insurance agencies, brokerages, and related services..................	5242	807	896	1,209	1,235	16.32	22.18	29.23	29.90
Real estate and rental and leasing...........	**53**	**2,011**	**1,934**	**2,215**	**2,257**	(NA)	(NA)	(NA)	(NA)
Real estate........................	531	1,316	1,396	1,696	1,747	12.26	17.37	23.49	24.77
Lessors of real estate................	5311	610	565	599	600	11.19	16.52	22.34	23.38
Offices of real estate agents and brokers....	5312	281	286	360	388	12.57	17.10	22.98	24.31
Activities related to real estate.........	5313	424	544	738	759	13.60	18.37	24.71	26.12
Rental and leasing services................	532	667	514	496	490	11.69	15.96	22.07	22.93
Automotive equipment rental and leasing....	5321	208	161	189	189	(NA)	(NA)	(NA)	(NA)
Consumer goods rental................	5322	292	198	122	119	(NA)	(NA)	(NA)	(NA)
Machinery/equipment rental and leasing.....	5324	103	114	157	153	14.95	19.83	27.59	28.19
Lessors of nonfinancial intangible assets......	533	28	25	22	21	(NA)	(NA)	(NA)	(NA)
Professional and business services...........	**(X)**	**16,704**	**16,783**	**20,314**	**21,250**	**15.53**	**22.80**	**29.25**	**30.56**
Professional and technical services.........	**54**	**6,732**	**7,486**	**9,435**	**9,883**	**20.62**	**29.93**	**37.41**	**39.02**
Legal services........................	5411	1,066	1,114	1,129	1,155	21.38	31.04	37.28	39.43
Accounting and bookkeeping services.........	5412	867	887	994	1,049	14.42	21.03	27.77	28.80
Architectural and engineering services.........	5413	1,239	1,276	1,504	1,545	20.49	30.22	35.69	36.84
Specialized design services...............	5414	132	113	133	141	15.32	22.36	30.09	30.28
Computer systems design and related.........	5415	1,259	1,456	2,197	2,301	27.11	37.12	44.44	46.50
Management and technical consulting.........	5416	694	1,031	1,528	1,634	20.87	28.54	37.40	38.13
Scientific research and development...........	5417	517	623	764	823	21.39	35.63	45.13	47.61
Advertising and related services...............	5418	498	410	450	446	17.01	24.64	31.20	34.07
Management of companies and enterprises..	**55**	**1,800**	**1,878**	**2,350**	**2,338**	**15.30**	**23.81**	**31.69**	**32.62**
Administrative and waste services............	**56**	**8,172**	**7,419**	**8,529**	**9,029**	**11.70**	**15.81**	**20.39**	**21.79**
Administrative and support services............	561	7,859	7,062	8,082	8,573	11.53	15.60	20.11	21.54
Office administrative services............	5611	264	407	521	545	14.68	23.56	30.06	31.73
Facilities support services..................	5612	97	133	157	156	16.73	20.97	20.28	20.81
Employment services..................	5613	3,850	2,724	3,117	3,563	11.90	16.19	20.70	22.45
Temporary help services...............	56132	2,636	2,094	2,522	2,903	11.79	14.23	19.73	21.42
Business support services...............	5614	788	811	815	810	11.10	14.53	18.87	19.77
Travel arrangement and reservation...........	5615	299	186	165	138	12.72	17.10	24.46	25.20
Investigation and security services...........	5616	690	782	907	911	9.79	14.15	18.47	20.02
Services to buildings and dwellings...........	5617	1,571	1,745	2,101	2,153	10.02	12.97	17.41	18.50
Waste management and remediation services........................	562	313	357	447	456	15.29	19.32	24.80	26.05
Waste collection..................	5621	100	141	191	197	12.97	17.50	21.83	23.02
Waste treatment and disposal..............	5622	119	96	100	99	(NA)	(NA)	(NA)	(NA)
Education and health services.................	**(X)**	**15,252**	**19,975**	**23,275**	**23,673**	**13.91**	**19.95**	**25.40**	**27.12**
Educational services........................	**61**	**2,390**	**3,155**	**3,478**	**3,589**	(NA)	(NA)	(NA)	(NA)
Elementary and secondary schools............	6111	716	849	1,037	1,073	(NA)	(NA)	(NA)	(NA)
Junior colleges........................	6112	79	99	49	48	(NA)	(NA)	(NA)	(NA)
Colleges and universities....................	6113	1,196	1,591	1,674	1,709	(NA)	(NA)	(NA)	(NA)
Business, computer, and management training..................	6114	86	78	71	78	(NA)	(NA)	(NA)	(NA)
Technical and trade schools..................	6115	91	126	106	109	(NA)	(NA)	(NA)	(NA)
Other schools and instruction................	6116	184	309	386	406	(NA)	(NA)	(NA)	(NA)
Educational support services................	6117	39	103	154	167	(NA)	(NA)	(NA)	(NA)
Health care and social assistance...........	**62**	**12,861**	**16,820**	**19,796**	**20,084**	**13.93**	**20.23**	**25.76**	**27.55**
Health care........................	621,2,3	10,858	13,777	15,850	16,024	14.63	21.71	27.87	29.88
Ambulatory health care services...............	621	4,320	5,975	7,498	7,875	15.00	21.68	27.89	29.64
Offices of physicians..................	6211	1,801	2,264	2,632	2,739	15.65	24.03	33.51	35.90
Offices of dentists..................	6212	688	828	889	994	15.96	22.65	27.63	28.93
Offices of other health practitioners...........	6213	438	671	926	1,012	14.24	20.48	24.73	26.22
Outpatient care centers..................	6214	425	649	970	997	15.36	22.81	27.90	29.50
Medical and diagnostic laboratories..........	6215	162	228	282	306	15.74	23.48	26.82	28.15
Home health care services................	6216	633	1,085	1,495	1,514	12.86	16.64	20.10	21.04
Hospitals........................	622	3,954	4,679	5,137	5,126	16.71	26.11	33.25	35.65
General medical and surgical hospitals.......	6221	3,745	4,357	4,715	4,703	16.75	26.33	33.56	36.01
Psychiatric and substance abuse hospitals...	6222	86	109	153	150	(NA)	(NA)	(NA)	(NA)
Nursing and residential care facilities...........	623	2,583	3,124	3,214	3,023	10.67	14.21	18.05	19.16
Nursing care facilities....................	6231	1,514	1,657	1,499	1,375	11.08	15.26	19.21	20.47
Residential mental health facilities...........	6232	437	565	623	606	9.96	13.06	17.30	18.55
Community care facilities for the elderly......	6233	478	741	932	889	9.83	12.89	16.63	17.55
Social assistance..................	624	2,003	3,043	3,947	4,060	9.72	12.75	16.24	17.17
Individual and family services..................	6241	821	1,664	2,617	2,708	10.30	13.07	16.46	17.37
Emergency and other relief services...........	6242	117	143	186	193	10.95	14.41	19.47	21.25
Vocational rehabilitation services.............	6243	370	388	282	273	9.57	12.47	16.07	16.93
Child day care services....................	6244	696	848	861	886	8.88	11.99	14.97	15.85
Leisure and hospitality........................	**(X)**	**11,862**	**13,049**	**13,148**	**14,101**	**8.32**	**11.31**	**14.71**	**16.17**
Arts, entertainment, and recreation.........	**71**	**1,788**	**1,913**	**1,773**	**1,979**	**10.68**	**15.27**	**19.52**	**19.78**
Performing arts and spectator sports.........	711	382	406	336	381	13.11	21.01	29.56	28.87
Museums, historical sites, zoos, and parks....	712	110	128	138	139	12.20	15.60	20.09	19.88

See footnotes at end of table.

Table 667. Nonfarm Industries—Employees and Earnings: 2000 to 2021-Continued.

See headnote on page 433.

Industry	2017 NAICS code [1]	All employees (1,000)				Average hourly earnings [2] (dol.)			
		2000	2010	2020	2021	2000	2010	2020	2021
Amusements, gambling, and recreation.......	713	1,296	1,379	1,299	1,460	9.86	13.38	16.33	17.05
Accommodation and food services.........	**72**	**10,074**	**11,135**	**11,375**	**12,121**	**7.92**	**10.68**	**14.07**	**15.66**
Accommodation..................................	721	1,884	1,760	1,471	1,471	9.48	13.02	15.53	17.60
Traveler accommodation....................	7211	1,837	1,703	1,416	1,402	9.49	13.07	15.53	17.67
Food services and drinking places.............	722	8,189	9,376	9,904	10,651	7.49	10.15	13.83	15.36
Full-service restaurants....................	722511	3,845	4,482	4,212	4,598	7.78	10.93	15.18	16.92
Limited-service restaurants..................	722513	3,042	3,418	4,178	4,343	6.80	8.86	12.13	13.40
Special food services....................	7223	491	543	497	506	9.45	11.83	16.02	17.43
Drinking places, alcoholic beverages.........	7224	391	341	268	326	7.24	10.15	15.68	17.64
Other services..................................	**81**	**5,168**	**5,331**	**5,329**	**5,456**	**12.73**	**17.06**	**22.58**	**23.65**
Repair and maintenance.....................	811	1,242	1,139	1,281	1,350	13.28	16.82	22.22	22.98
Automotive repair and maintenance.............	8111	888	801	898	945	12.45	15.55	20.51	21.18
Electronic equipment repair and maintenance................................	8112	107	98	100	106	16.31	19.41	26.88	26.40
Commercial machinery repair and maintenance................................	8113	161	172	208	218	15.53	21.03	27.07	28.61
Personal and laundry services..................	812	1,243	1,265	1,239	1,355	10.18	13.42	16.99	18.95
Personal care services......................	8121	490	601	583	672	10.18	13.97	16.82	19.76
Death care services......................	8122	136	131	132	134	13.04	17.46	21.19	22.17
Dry-cleaning and laundry services..........	8123	388	302	239	235	9.17	11.80	15.26	16.82
Dry-cleaning and laundry services, except coin-operated......................	81232	211	146	93	85	(NA)	(NA)	(NA)	(NA)
Other personal services......................	8129	229	232	286	314	10.52	12.43	17.28	18.04
Pet care services, except veterinary..........	81291	31	63	122	139	12.12	12.83	15.88	17.13
Parking lots and garages....................	81293	93	111	95	97	8.81	11.18	15.14	15.52
Membership associations & organizations......	813	2,683	2,926	2,808	2,751	13.66	18.76	24.97	26.11
Grantmaking and giving services..............	8132	116	178	177	181	14.65	23.51	34.56	36.88
Social advocacy organizations...............	8133	143	202	232	244	12.08	17.36	24.16	25.09
Civic and social organizations..................	8134	404	392	271	279	9.85	12.16	18.43	18.26
Professional and similar organizations.........	8139	473	477	457	446	15.98	22.67	31.26	31.92
Government..................................	**(X)**	**20,790**	**22,490**	**21,986**	**22,005**	**(NA)**	**(NA)**	**(NA)**	**(NA)**
Federal......................................	(X)	2,865	2,977	2,930	2,886	(NA)	(NA)	(NA)	(NA)
Federal, except U.S. Postal Service.............	(X)	1,985	2,318	2,328	2,280	(NA)	(NA)	(NA)	(NA)
U.S. Postal Service..........................	(X)	880	659	602	606	(NA)	(NA)	(NA)	(NA)
State......................................	(X)	4,786	5,137	5,135	5,207	(NA)	(NA)	(NA)	(NA)
Local......................................	(X)	13,139	14,376	13,921	13,912	(NA)	(NA)	(NA)	(NA)

NA Not available. X Not applicable. [1] Based on the North American Industry Classification System, 2017. See text, Section 15. [2] Production employees in the goods-producing industries and nonsupervisory employees in service-providing industries. [3] Mining and logging, construction, and manufacturing. [4] Trade, transportation and utilities, information, financial activities, professional and business services, education and health services, leisure and hospitality, other services, and government.

Source: U.S. Bureau of Labor Statistics, Current Employment Statistics, "Employment, Hours, and Earnings—National," <www.bls.gov/ces/>, accessed June 2022.

Table 668. Women Employed by Nonfarm Industry: 2000 to 2021

[63,398 represents 63,398,000. Annual averages of monthly data. For coverage, see headnote, Table 665]

Industry	Women employees (1,000)				Percent of total employees			
	2000	2010	2020	2021	2000	2010	2020	2021
Total nonfarm..............................	**63,398**	**65,089**	**70,687**	**72,752**	**48.0**	**49.9**	**49.7**	**49.8**
Total private..............................	**51,627**	**52,260**	**58,033**	**60,050**	**46.4**	**48.5**	**48.3**	**48.4**
Construction...............................	846	723	961	1,012	12.5	13.1	13.2	13.7
Manufacturing..............................	5,359	3,268	3,472	3,539	31.0	28.3	28.5	28.7
Trade, transportation, and utilities..........	10,845	9,992	10,472	10,919	41.4	40.7	39.2	39.4
Wholesale trade..........................	1,812	1,619	1,685	1,712	30.8	30.1	29.9	30.2
Retail trade..............................	7,681	7,228	7,239	7,493	50.3	50.0	48.7	48.7
Transportation and warehousing..................	1,202	1,006	1,416	1,579	27.3	24.1	25.1	25.9
Utilities..................................	151	139	133	135	25.1	25.1	24.6	24.9
Information................................	1,697	1,104	1,085	1,124	46.7	40.8	39.9	39.7
Financial activities..........................	4,697	4,530	4,925	4,935	60.3	58.9	56.6	56.2
Professional and business services..............	7,693	7,472	9,293	9,816	46.1	44.5	45.7	46.2
Professional and technical services..........	3,156	3,537	4,432	4,674	46.9	47.2	47.0	47.3
Management of companies and enterprises......	925	940	1,170	1,175	51.4	50.1	49.8	50.3
Administrative and waste services..............	3,612	2,995	3,690	3,967	44.2	40.4	43.3	43.9
Education and health services.....................	11,703	15,435	17,962	18,254	76.7	77.3	77.2	77.1
Educational services......................	1,417	1,929	2,173	2,264	59.3	61.2	62.5	63.1
Health care and social assistance..................	10,286	13,505	15,788	15,990	80.0	80.3	79.8	79.6
Leisure and hospitality..........................	6,082	6,819	6,975	7,484	51.3	52.3	53.0	53.1
Arts, entertainment, and recreation.............	815	886	841	940	45.6	46.3	47.4	47.5
Accommodation and food services...............	5,267	5,933	6,135	6,544	52.3	53.3	53.9	54.0
Other services.............................	2,614	2,820	2,805	2,893	50.6	52.9	52.6	53.0
Government..............................	**11,771**	**12,829**	**12,654**	**12,701**	**56.6**	**57.0**	**57.6**	**57.7**
Federal....................................	1,231	1,326	1,324	1,309	43.0	44.5	45.2	45.4
State government...........................	2,464	2,639	2,781	2,821	51.5	51.4	54.2	54.2
Local government..........................	8,076	8,864	8,549	8,572	61.5	61.7	61.4	61.6

Source: U.S. Bureau of Labor Statistics, Current Employment Statistics, "Employment, Hours, and Earnings—National," <www.bls.gov/ces/data.htm>, accessed June 2022.

Table 669. Job Gains and Job Losses of Private Sector Establishments by Industry Sector: 2000 to 2021

[In thousands (16,145 represents 16,145,000). For year ending in March. Based on the Quarterly Census of Employment and Wages (QCEW). Excludes self-employed and certain nonprofit organizations. Minus sign (-) indicates a decrease in employment and comes from either closing establishments or contracting establishments. For more information, see source]

Year and industry	Gross job gains			Gross job losses			Net change [1]
	Total	Expanding establishments	Opening establishments	Total	Contracting establishments	Closing establishments	
2000..	16,145	10,620	5,525	13,160	8,291	4,869	2,985
2007..	13,517	9,243	4,274	12,002	8,249	3,753	1,515
2008..	12,786	8,718	4,068	12,674	8,776	3,898	112
2009..	10,149	6,668	3,481	15,969	11,706	4,263	-5,820
2010..	10,075	6,839	3,236	12,760	9,142	3,618	-2,685
2011..	11,629	8,295	3,334	9,721	6,623	3,098	1,908
2012..	12,216	8,662	3,554	9,546	6,508	3,038	2,670
2013..	12,045	8,553	3,492	9,924	6,829	3,095	2,121
2014..	12,282	8,700	3,582	10,008	6,945	3,063	2,274
2015..	12,834	9,143	3,691	10,115	6,940	3,175	2,719
2016..	13,168	9,394	3,774	10,656	7,426	3,230	2,512
2017..	12,953	9,156	3,797	10,921	7,638	3,283	2,032
2018..	13,116	9,359	3,757	10,948	7,635	3,313	2,168
2019..	13,134	9,377	3,757	11,289	7,855	3,434	1,845
2020..	12,780	8,963	3,817	12,413	8,669	3,744	367
2021, Total private...................	12,445	8,567	3,878	18,011	14,068	3,943	-5,566
Goods producing............................	1,954	1,478	476	2,709	2,228	481	-755
Natural resources and mining..........	185	133	52	314	250	64	-129
Construction...................................	1,014	715	299	1,166	904	262	-152
Manufacturing................................	755	630	125	1,229	1,074	155	-474
Service providing............................	10,491	7,089	3,402	15,303	11,841	3,462	-4,812
Wholesale trade..............................	495	358	137	687	526	161	-192
Retail trade....................................	1,437	1,089	348	1,715	1,285	430	-278
Transportation and warehousing......	903	670	233	720	579	141	183
Utilities...	26	20	6	28	24	4	-2
Information.....................................	319	231	88	450	347	103	-131
Financial activities..........................	826	586	240	926	684	242	-100
Professional and business services....	2,804	2,001	803	3,068	2,379	689	-264
Education and health services..........	1,697	1,133	564	2,553	2,002	551	-856
Leisure and hospitality....................	1,366	735	631	4,267	3,365	902	-2,901
Other services................................	440	253	187	854	642	212	-414

[1] Net change is the difference between total gross job gains and total gross job losses.

Source: U.S. Bureau of Labor Statistics, Business Employment Dynamics, "Annual Business Employment Dynamics Data," <www.bls.gov/bdm/bdmann.htm#TOTAL>, accessed February 2022.

Table 670. Private Sector Gross Job Gains and Job Losses by State: 2021

[In thousands (12,445 represents 12,445,000). For year ending in March. Based on the Quarterly Census of Employment and Wages (QCEW). Excludes self-employed and certain nonprofit organizations. Minus sign (-) indicates a decrease in employment and comes from either closing establishments or contracting establishments. For more information, see source]

State	Gross job gains			Gross job losses			Net change [1]	State	Gross job gains			Gross job losses			Net change [1]
	Total	Expanding establishments	Opening establishments	Total	Contracting establishments	Closing establishments			Total	Expanding establishments	Opening establishments	Total	Contracting establishments	Closing establishments	
U.S.....	12,445	8,567	3,878	18,011	14,068	3,943	-5,566	MO.....	230	159	71	299	231	68	-69
AL........	162	117	45	210	157	53	-48	MT.....	47	31	16	45	32	13	1
AK.......	22	16	6	37	30	6	-15	NE.....	77	56	21	101	73	28	-24
AZ.......	303	218	85	346	265	81	-43	NV.....	145	98	47	252	213	39	-107
AR.......	98	69	29	119	92	27	-21	NH.....	53	36	17	74	59	15	-21
CA.......	1,621	1,083	539	2,537	1,948	589	-916	NJ.....	362	242	120	550	431	119	-188
CO.......	261	175	86	339	261	78	-78	NM.....	63	43	20	110	82	28	-47
CT.......	123	84	39	197	155	42	-74	NY.....	659	433	226	1,392	1,077	315	-733
DE.......	37	24	13	53	40	13	-16	NC.....	432	295	137	475	369	106	-42
DC.......	41	27	15	113	91	22	-72	ND.....	28	19	9	51	38	13	-23
FL........	968	608	361	1,211	899	312	-243	OH.....	386	286	100	562	458	104	-176
GA.......	449	293	156	541	406	135	-92	OK.....	143	89	53	186	138	48	-43
HI........	42	27	14	126	101	24	-84	OR.....	166	114	51	246	185	61	-80
ID........	84	58	26	68	51	17	16	PA.....	394	281	112	682	562	120	-289
IL........	443	315	128	705	571	133	-262	RI.....	37	25	13	61	48	12	-24
IN........	246	179	67	301	245	56	-55	SC.....	188	131	57	228	177	51	-40
IA........	103	78	26	144	116	27	-40	SD.....	32	23	10	35	27	8	-2
KS.......	112	79	33	151	116	35	-39	TN.....	273	201	71	324	263	61	-51
KY.......	163	120	43	196	149	46	-33	TX.....	1,139	793	346	1,485	1,179	306	-346
LA........	151	105	47	244	192	53	-93	UT.....	180	129	51	157	122	35	23
ME.......	52	35	17	63	49	14	-11	VT.....	21	15	7	38	29	10	-17
MD.......	216	158	58	335	250	85	-119	VA.....	325	224	102	446	338	108	-121
MA.......	254	175	79	459	364	95	-204	WA.....	278	201	76	412	336	75	-134
MI........	287	204	83	502	407	94	-215	WV.....	55	36	20	75	56	19	-20
MN.......	188	140	48	307	250	57	-119	WI.....	193	143	50	279	230	49	-86
MS.......	92	66	26	112	85	26	-20	WY.....	22	15	7	32	24	8	-11

[1] Net change is the difference between total gross job gains and total gross job losses.

Source: U.S. Bureau of Labor Statistics, Business Employment Dynamics, "Annual Business Employment Dynamics Data," <www.bls.gov/bdm/bdmann.htm>, accessed February 2022.

Table 671. Hires and Separations Affecting Establishment Payrolls By Industry: 2018 to 2021

[68,556 represents 68,556,000. Hires represent any additions to payrolls, including new and rehired employees, full- and part-time workers, short-term and seasonal workers, and other hires. Separations represent terminations of employment, including quits, layoffs, and discharges, and other separations. Based on a monthly survey of private nonfarm establishments and governmental entities]

Industry	Annual hires (1,000)				Annual separations (1,000)			
	2018	2019	2020	2021	2018	2019	2020	2021
Total	**68,556**	**69,911**	**72,635**	**75,550**	**66,245**	**68,097**	**80,778**	**69,045**
Total private industry	64,255	65,505	68,451	71,164	62,096	63,852	75,642	65,055
Mining and logging	447	304	199	237	393	352	332	205
Construction	4,532	4,994	4,984	4,357	4,217	4,870	4,970	4,216
Manufacturing	4,394	4,052	4,810	5,271	4,121	4,046	5,378	4,923
Durable goods	2,511	2,271	2,750	2,937	2,287	2,296	3,158	2,713
Nondurable goods	1,879	1,780	2,061	2,335	1,829	1,748	2,219	2,209
Trade, transportation, and utilities	13,666	13,889	15,436	16,118	13,522	13,722	16,108	15,096
Wholesale trade	1,756	1,776	1,815	2,053	1,715	1,742	2,105	1,904
Retail trade	9,011	9,011	9,822	10,391	9,165	9,124	10,345	9,945
Transportation, warehousing, and utilities	2,901	3,099	3,799	3,673	2,642	2,854	3,654	3,249
Information	1,091	1,135	978	1,304	1,057	1,101	1,172	1,101
Financial activities	2,500	2,653	2,660	2,659	2,331	2,491	2,729	2,505
Finance and insurance	1,636	1,683	1,667	1,762	1,529	1,584	1,636	1,716
Real estate and rental and leasing	863	971	994	897	805	909	1,091	788
Professional and business services	13,746	13,785	13,419	14,771	13,301	13,512	13,931	13,644
Education and health services	8,503	8,650	9,365	9,374	8,032	8,068	10,364	8,823
Educational services	1,156	1,160	1,133	1,241	1,125	1,117	1,466	915
Health care and social assistance	7,344	7,494	8,232	8,132	6,905	6,951	8,897	7,908
Leisure and hospitality	12,782	13,432	13,565	14,227	12,562	13,146	17,071	11,968
Arts, entertainment, and recreation	2,215	1,998	1,640	1,960	2,116	1,960	2,262	1,510
Accommodation and food services	10,570	11,434	11,925	12,267	10,442	11,187	14,807	10,458
Other services	2,594	2,605	3,033	2,849	2,563	2,543	3,588	2,573
Government workers	4,301	4,403	4,185	4,385	4,150	4,245	5,138	3,991
Federal	420	503	887	522	403	469	825	544
State and local	3,879	3,904	3,297	3,860	3,748	3,774	4,312	3,444

Source: U.S. Bureau of Labor Statistics, *Job Openings and Labor Turnover—January 2022*, USDL 22-0413, March 2022. See also <www.bls.gov/jlt/news.htm>.

Table 672. Type of Separations Affecting Establishment Payrolls: 2021

[47,825 represents 47,825,000. Covers all private nonfarm establishments. Separations are the total number of terminations of employment occurring at any time during the year, and are reported by type of separation—quits, layoffs and discharges, and other separations. Annual rate estimates are computed by dividing annual levels by the Current Employment Statistics (CES) annual average employment level and multiplying that quotient by 100]

Industry	Number (1,000)			Rate (percent) [1]		
	Annual quits [2]	Annual layoffs and discharges [3]	Annual other separations [4]	Annual quits [2]	Annual layoffs and discharges [3]	Annual other separations [4]
Total	**47,825**	**17,019**	**4,199**	**32.7**	**11.6**	**2.9**
Total private industry	45,456	16,137	3,462	36.6	13.0	2.8
Mining and logging	117	73	16	20.6	12.9	2.8
Construction	2,198	1,863	158	29.7	25.1	2.1
Manufacturing	3,457	1,183	283	28.0	9.6	2.3
Durable goods	1,885	646	182	24.6	8.4	2.4
Nondurable goods	1,572	536	102	33.7	11.5	2.2
Trade, transportation, and utilities	11,204	3,238	657	40.4	11.7	2.4
Wholesale trade	1,334	472	98	23.5	8.3	1.7
Retail trade	7,792	1,781	374	50.6	11.6	2.4
Transportation, warehousing, and utilities	2,077	987	184	31.3	14.9	2.8
Information	626	367	110	22.1	13.0	3.9
Financial activities	1,565	537	400	17.8	6.1	4.6
Finance and insurance	1,045	328	346	16.0	5.0	5.3
Real estate and rental and leasing	522	211	55	23.1	9.3	2.4
Professional and business services	8,597	4,170	877	40.5	19.6	4.1
Education and health services	6,728	1,602	493	28.4	6.8	2.1
Educational services	613	246	59	17.1	6.9	1.6
Health care and social assistance	6,115	1,357	433	30.4	6.8	2.2
Leisure and hospitality	9,413	2,219	336	66.8	15.7	2.4
Arts, entertainment, and recreation	843	628	41	42.6	31.7	2.1
Accommodation and food services	8,574	1,590	298	70.7	13.1	2.5
Other services	1,552	885	136	28.4	16.2	2.5
Government workers	2,372	882	735	10.8	4.0	3.3
Federal	260	121	163	9.0	4.2	5.6
State and local	2,109	759	575	11.0	4.0	3.0

[1] As a percent of total employment. [2] Quits are voluntary separations by employees (except for retirements, which are reported as other separations). [3] Layoffs and discharges are involuntary separations initiated by the employer and include layoffs with no intent to rehire; formal layoffs lasting or expected to last more than seven days; discharges resulting from mergers, downsizing, or closings, firings or other discharges for cause; terminations of permanent or short term employees; and terminations of seasonal employees. [4] Other separations include retirements, transfers to other locations, deaths, and separations due to disability.

Source: U.S. Bureau of Labor Statistics, *Job Openings and Labor Turnover— January 2022*, USDL 22-0413, March 2022. See also <www.bls.gov/jlt/news.htm>.

Table 673. Private Nonprofit Establishments, Employees, and Average Annual Wages by Selected Industry: 2017

[In units, as indicated. 122,387 represents 122,387,000. Data from Bureau of Labor Statistics' Quarterly Census of Employment and Wages and IRS Exempt Organization Business Master File]

Industry	NAICS code	All establishments			501(c)(3) nonprofit establishments			501(c)(3) percent of total employment
		Establishments (number)	Annual average employment (1,000s)	Annual wages per employee (dollars)	Establishments (number)	Annual average employment (1,000s)	Annual wages per employee (dollars)	
Total private..........................	(X)	**9,536,831**	**122,387**	**55,338**	**299,457**	**12,489**	**53,667**	**10.2**
Agriculture, forestry, fishing and hunting..........	11	104,445	1,261	34,464	338	3	34,981	0.2
Construction............................	23	784,852	6,919	60,735	930	9	46,364	0.1
Manufacturing...........................	31-33	346,723	12,407	66,840	267	7	38,240	0.1
Wholesale trade.........................	42	612,359	5,899	75,904	732	4	57,227	0.1
Retail trade.............................	44-45	1,042,096	15,854	31,217	5,750	93	22,467	0.6
Transportation and warehousing..................	48-49	242,932	4,947	51,726	893	21	34,523	0.4
Information..............................	51	162,702	2,793	105,722	4,705	68	52,650	2.4
Finance and insurance....................	52	484,801	5,909	106,185	1,301	44	95,789	0.7
Real estate and rental and leasing..............	53	385,826	2,180	56,970	3,916	36	38,779	1.7
Professional, scientific, and technical services...	54	1,183,104	8,996	93,687	11,944	270	80,686	3.0
Management of companies and enterprises.....	55	64,772	2,278	119,885	4,633	281	69,142	12.3
Administrative and support and waste management and remediation services.........	56	534,038	9,065	39,621	5,098	101	53,689	1.1
Educational services.....................	61	117,479	2,824	50,053	32,832	2,004	55,389	70.9
Elementary and secondary schools..............	6111	17,969	811	41,234	12,879	684	41,766	84.3
Colleges, universities, and professional schools...........................	6113	8,934	1,242	64,605	5,331	1,138	66,097	91.6
Health care and social assistance..............	62	1,532,134	19,322	49,076	138,319	8,307	54,742	43.0
Hospitals...............................	622	10,024	5,018	62,595	5,171	4,207	63,923	83.8
Other residential care facilities..................	6239	6,585	165	31,853	3,680	112	33,615	67.8
Community food and housing, and emergency and other relief services..........	6242	11,389	169	37,870	9,871	154	37,301	91.2
Vocational rehabilitation services..........	6243	9,574	335	26,599	6,940	289	25,542	86.1
Arts, entertainment, and recreation..............	71	141,502	2,294	37,759	15,261	356	29,810	15.5
Performing arts companies.......................	7111	10,026	123	49,541	3,498	70	38,353	57.0
Museums, historical sites, and similar institutions............................	712	6,475	163	34,795	4,960	141	35,759	86.5
Accommodation and food services...............	72	697,728	13,607	20,731	1,909	38	20,838	0.3
Other services (except public administration)....	81	839,795	4,435	37,320	66,719	838	39,198	18.9
Religious, grantmaking, civic, professional, and similar organizations.......................	813	146,264	1,370	43,941	64,730	819	39,353	59.8
Religious organizations...........................	8131	23,174	192	28,976	18,324	163	29,495	84.9
Grantmaking and giving services..............	8132	16,042	143	66,667	14,118	131	66,139	91.5
Social advocacy organizations.................	8133	22,277	212	48,115	18,070	185	47,191	87.6
Civic and social organizations.................	8134	25,771	392	19,976	8,992	280	18,957	71.3

Source: U.S. Bureau of Labor Statistics, Business Employment Dynamics, "Research Data on the Nonprofit Sector," <www.bls.gov/bdm/nonprofits/nonprofits.htm>, accessed May 2019.

Table 674. Indexes of Total Factor Productivity and Related Measures: 1990 to 2021

[2012=100. Data shown for private nonfarm business. Total Factor Productivity is a measure of economic performance comparing the amount of goods and services produced (output) to the amount of combined inputs used to produce those goods and services. Measured using output and compensation data published by the Bureau of Economic Analysis (BEA), hours data published by other BLS programs, and capital data supplied by BEA and U.S. Department of Agriculture. See source for details]

Year	Productivity			Value added output [2]	Combined inputs			Capital intensity [5]
	Total factor productivity [1]	Labor productivity	Output per unit of capital input		Combined units of labor and capital input	Labor input [3]	Capital input [4]	
1990..................	80.9	60.5	117.1	53.4	66.0	79.6	45.6	51.7
2000..................	88.9	75.6	109.3	79.1	89.0	99.1	72.4	69.2
2005..................	96.7	88.5	105.8	90.7	93.8	98.8	85.7	83.7
2010..................	99.2	99.1	98.3	94.8	95.5	95.0	96.4	100.7
2015..................	101.2	102.4	100.3	109.0	107.8	107.2	108.7	102.0
2019..................	102.9	107.6	98.7	121.4	118.0	115.0	123.0	109.0
2020..................	100.9	110.3	91.9	116.1	115.1	108.9	126.3	120.0
2021..................	104.1	112.4	96.8	124.7	119.8	114.7	128.8	116.1
ANNUAL PERCENT CHANGE								
1990..................	0.1	1.7	-2.0	1.5	1.4	0.4	3.5	3.8
2000..................	1.2	2.9	-1.7	4.3	3.1	1.7	6.2	4.7
2005..................	1.5	2.2	0.5	4.0	2.4	1.9	3.4	1.7
2010..................	2.7	3.4	2.5	3.3	0.6	0.5	0.8	0.9
2015..................	0.7	1.2	0.3	3.5	2.7	2.4	3.1	0.9
2019..................	1.0	2.1	-0.4	2.8	1.9	1.0	3.3	2.6
2020..................	-2.0	2.5	-6.8	-4.3	-2.4	-5.3	2.7	10.1
2021..................	3.2	1.9	5.3	7.4	4.1	5.3	2.0	-3.2

[1] Derived by dividing an index of real output by an index of combined inputs of labor and capital. [2] Gross domestic product originating in the private nonfarm business sector. [3] Index of hours worked of all persons including employees, proprietors, and unpaid family workers, classified by age, education, and gender. [4] Services derived from the stock of physical assets and intellectual property assets. [5] Ratio of capital input growth to labor hours growth.

Source: U.S. Bureau of Labor Statistics, "Total Factor Productivity - 2021," March 2022. See also <www.bls.gov/productivity/home.htm>

Table 675. Productivity and Related Measures for Selected NAICS Industries: 1987 to 2021

[For a discussion of productivity measures and methodology, see text, this section and BLS Handbook of Methods, Chapter 11, <www.bls.gov/opub/hom/>. Minus sign (-) indicates decrease]

Industry	2017 NAICS code [1]	Average annual percent change [2] 1987-2021 [3]				Average annual percent change [2] 2020-2021			
		Labor produc-tivity	Unit labor costs	Output	Hours	Labor produc-tivity	Unit labor costs	Output	Hours
Mining...........................	21	2.0	1.4	1.4	-0.6	1.0	-10.6	0.6	-0.4
Oil and gas extraction....................	211	3.4	1.2	1.7	-1.6	8.8	-18.7	–	-8.1
Mining, except oil and gas.................	212	1.2	1.7	-0.2	-1.5	4.6	1.7	2.8	-1.7
Coal mining...........................	2121	1.9	0.7	-2.0	-3.9	18.3	-13.7	8.1	-8.6
Utilities...........................	22	2.0	1.6	1.3	-0.7	2.1	1.1	1.4	-0.7
Power generation and supply.............	2211	2.8	0.8	1.8	-0.9	2.7	-0.3	1.8	-0.9
Natural gas distribution.................	2212	1.0	3.1	0.1	-0.8	1.0	6.6	-0.3	-1.3
Water, sewage and other systems...........	2213	-1.7	4.7	0.6	2.3	1.6	-0.3	3.5	1.9
Manufacturing:									
Food...........................	311	0.6	2.1	1.1	0.5	-1.9	6.1	-0.6	1.3
Fruit and vegetable preserving and specialty...	3114	0.9	2.0	0.8	-0.1	-2.2	8.1	-1.6	0.6
Dairy products...........................	3115	1.0	2.1	1.2	0.2	-2.6	6.1	-0.6	2.1
Animal slaughtering and processing...........	3116	0.4	2.2	1.5	1.1	1.7	3.1	-0.1	-1.7
Bakeries and tortilla manufacturing..............	3118	0.1	1.9	0.3	0.2	-3.1	7.3	0.1	3.3
Beverages and tobacco products..............	312	-1.1	3.1	-0.4	0.7	-15.5	10.5	-1.4	16.6
Textile mills...........................	313	1.9	0.4	-2.6	-4.4	-1.6	5.0	3.8	5.4
Apparel...........................	315	–	1.6	-6.3	-6.2	1.2	2.3	4.6	3.3
Leather and allied products....................	316	0.5	2.4	-4.0	-4.4	0.7	7.5	1.3	0.5
Paper and paper products....................	322	1.3	1.7	-0.5	-1.7	-1.2	4.2	-1.4	-0.1
Converted paper products....................	3222	0.7	2.5	-0.5	-1.2	-2.7	6.9	-1.7	1.0
Printing and related support activities..............	323	1.2	1.1	-0.9	-2.0	0.6	-2.4	3.6	2.9
Petroleum and coal products..............	324	1.7	2.5	0.8	-0.9	-4.3	-10.1	6.3	11.1
Chemicals...........................	325	0.9	2.3	0.6	-0.3	-0.7	2.0	2.0	2.7
Pharmaceuticals and medicines..............	3254	-0.8	3.8	1.1	1.9	-1.9	-0.2	5.6	7.6
Plastics and rubber products..............	326	1.4	1.7	1.1	-0.3	-1.6	5.9	3.4	5.1
Plastics products...........................	3261	1.3	1.8	1.3	–	-1.9	6.6	2.7	4.7
Wood products...........................	321	0.9	2.2	–	-0.9	-1.2	8.4	4.0	5.3
Nonmetallic mineral products..............	327	0.7	2.0	–	-0.7	0.1	6.5	-0.4	-0.6
Primary metals...........................	331	2.0	0.7	0.1	-1.9	9.5	-3.0	9.3	-0.2
Fabricated metal products..............	332	0.9	1.8	0.5	-0.4	1.6	1.3	3.5	1.8
Forging and stamping....................	3321	1.9	0.6	0.8	-1.0	8.2	-10.1	15.2	6.5
Cutlery and hand tools....................	3322	0.9	1.7	-1.1	-2.0	-5.6	10.4	–	5.9
Architectural and structural metals..............	3323	0.5	2.3	0.8	0.3	-0.9	4.9	0.7	1.6
Machine shops and threaded products..............	3327	1.5	1.5	1.7	0.2	2.9	-2.3	3.9	0.9
Other fabricated metal products....................	3329	0.4	2.1	-0.2	-0.6	-1.1	7.3	1.7	2.8
Machinery...........................	333	1.6	1.3	0.8	-0.8	7.9	-4.0	8.2	0.3
Agriculture, construction, and mining machinery....................	3331	1.8	0.8	1.5	-0.3	12.3	-14.5	13.7	1.2
Industrial machinery....................	3332	1.5	1.2	1.1	-0.4	8.3	-1.3	13.9	5.1
Computer and electronic products....................	334	7.6	-4.2	5.6	-1.9	1.7	6.4	1.4	-0.3
Semiconductors and electronic components....	3344	11.1	-7.1	9.6	-1.4	2.4	7.6	1.5	-1.0
Electronic instruments....................	3345	2.5	0.6	1.1	-1.3	-1.5	0.9	1.2	2.7
Electrical equipment and appliances.............	335	1.5	1.5	–	-1.5	-0.5	3.1	4.1	4.6
Transportation equipment....................	336	2.1	0.3	1.3	-0.8	2.3	-3.4	7.6	5.2
Motor vehicles...........................	3361	2.1	0.3	1.5	-0.6	-11.1	8.1	4.5	17.5
Motor vehicle parts....................	3363	2.5	-0.6	2.1	-0.4	6.4	-1.9	9.9	3.3
Aerospace products and parts....................	3364	1.4	1.1	-0.1	-1.5	8.3	-12.9	9.5	1.1
Ship and boat building....................	3366	1.8	1.8	0.9	-0.9	-1.9	6.2	2.2	4.1
Furniture and related products....................	337	0.9	2.0	-0.5	-1.4	-3.2	7.4	0.4	3.8
Household and institutional furniture..............	3371	0.7	2.1	-0.8	-1.5	-3.4	10.9	0.4	3.9
Miscellaneous manufacturing....................	339	1.5	1.6	1.2	-0.3	-0.7	2.3	5.3	6.0
Medical equipment and supplies....................	3391	1.9	1.4	2.6	0.7	-0.2	2.5	3.8	4.0
Wholesale trade...........................	42	2.8	1.1	2.9	0.2	5.7	0.3	8.7	2.8
Durable goods...........................	423	4.1	-0.1	4.2	0.1	9.6	-1.8	11.8	2.0
Nondurable goods...........................	424	1.2	2.7	1.3	0.1	0.9	2.5	5.4	4.4
Electronic markets and agents and brokers.......	425	2.0	0.4	3.3	1.3	6.8	–	8.0	1.1
Retail trade...........................	44-45	3.1	0.1	3.5	0.4	6.6	2.2	10.4	3.6
Motor vehicle and parts dealers....................	441	2.4	1.1	3.0	0.6	7.6	12.1	10.4	2.6
Automobile dealers...........................	4411	2.5	1.1	3.0	0.5	5.7	15.8	9.9	3.9
Other motor vehicle dealers....................	4412	3.0	1.1	4.1	1.2	13.3	2.4	16.6	2.9
Auto parts, accessories, and tire stores..........	4413	1.4	1.3	2.0	0.5	10.7	2.0	10.2	-0.4
Furniture and home furnishings stores............	442	4.0	-0.8	3.8	-0.2	11.7	-3.2	18.3	5.9
Furniture stores...........................	4421	3.6	-0.5	3.3	-0.2	8.9	1.3	16.2	6.7
Home furnishings stores....................	4422	4.5	-1.2	4.3	-0.2	15.2	-8.3	21.0	5.1
Electronics and appliance stores....................	443	10.4	-6.5	10.2	-0.2	22.5	-9.5	22.8	0.3
Building material and garden supply stores.......	444	2.1	0.4	3.3	1.1	-1.7	5.7	2.1	3.9
Building material and supplies dealers...........	4441	2.0	0.4	3.3	1.3	-0.5	5.1	1.6	2.0
Lawn and garden equipment and supplies stores...........................	4442	2.9	-0.2	3.3	0.4	-10.2	10.3	5.6	17.7
Food and beverage stores....................	445	0.9	2.2	0.8	–	1.1	2.7	0.2	-0.9
Grocery stores...........................	4451	0.7	2.4	0.8	0.1	1.2	2.2	-0.3	-1.4
Specialty food stores....................	4452	0.7	1.8	–	-0.7	-2.3	7.1	6.7	9.3
Beer, wine and liquor stores....................	4453	2.5	0.7	1.8	-0.6	8.3	2.4	3.1	-4.8
Health and personal care stores....................	446	2.0	1.3	2.8	0.8	2.5	-3.1	11.0	8.4
Gasoline stations...........................	447	1.3	1.8	1.1	-0.2	6.8	-0.3	8.5	1.6
Clothing and clothing accessories stores....................	448	4.6	-1.4	3.7	-0.8	28.0	-16.3	41.9	10.9
Clothing stores...........................	4481	4.7	-1.7	4.0	-0.7	26.2	-20.7	41.1	11.7
Shoe stores...........................	4482	3.7	-0.7	2.5	-1.2	34.9	-12.9	32.2	-2.0
Jewelry, luggage, and leather goods stores.....	4483	4.5	-0.6	3.6	-0.9	26.9	-5.8	53.5	21.0
Sporting goods, hobby, book, and music stores..	451	4.2	-1.0	4.2	–	14.3	-6.5	23.5	8.1

See footnotes at end of table.

Table 675. Productivity and Related Measures for Selected NAICS Industries: 1987 to 2021-Continued.

See headnote on page 440.

Industry	2017 NAICS code [1]	Average annual percent change [2]							
		1987-2021 [3]				2020-2021			
		Labor produc- tivity	Unit labor costs	Output	Hours	Labor produc- tivity	Unit labor costs	Output	Hours
Sporting goods and musical instrument stores..	4511	4.9	-1.6	5.2	0.3	16.3	-6.0	23.2	6.0
Book, periodical, and music stores.............	4512	1.0	1.5	-0.7	-1.6	-1.5	-11.3	27.6	29.6
General merchandise stores......................	452	3.0	-0.5	4.2	1.1	4.4	2.6	7.2	2.7
Department stores.............................	4522	1.0	1.0	0.3	-0.8	14.3	-1.3	16.1	1.6
Other general merchandise stores..............	4523	4.7	-1.4	7.1	2.3	2.4	2.6	5.6	3.1
Miscellaneous store retailers.....................	453	3.5	-0.7	3.3	-0.2	10.8	-3.9	23.0	11.1
Florists..	4531	2.7	1.0	-0.1	-2.6	1.7	22.7	22.4	20.4
Office supplies, stationery and gift stores........	4532	5.7	-2.4	3.3	-2.3	17.6	-10.0	21.3	3.1
Used merchandise stores......................	4533	4.4	-1.7	5.8	1.3	1.7	0.5	25.3	23.3
Other miscellaneous store retailers............	4539	1.4	0.5	2.9	1.5	14.3	-5.8	23.1	7.7
Nonstore retailers................................	454	8.6	-3.9	9.7	1.0	9.0	1.8	15.2	5.6
Electronic shopping and mail-order houses.....	4541	9.9	-4.6	14.6	4.2	6.9	2.2	15.8	8.3
Vending machine operators.....................	4542	1.7	2.1	-1.8	-3.5	29.9	-10.5	15.5	-11.1
Direct selling establishments...................	4543	3.2	-0.2	1.6	-1.6	7.8	4.7	8.9	1.0
Transportation and warehousing:									
Air transportation................................	481	0.4	3.2	-0.1	-0.5	61.8	-37.2	71.3	5.9
Line-haul railroads...............................	482111	3.3	-0.2	1.0	-2.2	3.9	-3.2	2.6	-1.2
Truck transportation..............................	484	0.9	0.9	2.1	1.2	-0.2	2.5	7.4	7.7
General freight trucking.........................	4841	1.4	0.9	2.4	1.1	-1.1	4.0	7.4	8.6
Used household and office goods moving.......	48421	-0.6	2.7	-0.4	0.2	(NA)	(NA)	(NA)	(NA)
Postal service [4]................................	491	–	3.1	-0.6	-0.6	-3.6	-0.2	-2.3	1.4
Couriers and messengers.........................	492	-2.6	3.0	1.0	3.7	-0.1	15.8	10.4	10.5
Warehousing and storage.........................	493	0.8	1.2	5.6	4.7	-3.1	7.4	12.2	15.8
General warehousing and storage..............	49311	1.8	0.5	6.9	5.0	(NA)	(NA)	(NA)	(NA)
Refrigerated warehousing and storage.........	49312	0.5	1.4	3.3	2.8	(NA)	(NA)	(NA)	(NA)
Information:									
Publishing.......................................	511	4.2	1.4	4.0	-0.2	12.8	1.5	14.4	1.4
Newspaper, book, and directory publishers.....	5111	0.2	3.9	-2.9	-3.1	14.5	-10.8	5.3	-8.0
Software publishers.............................	5112	10.3	-4.9	17.2	6.3	9.9	4.3	16.8	6.3
Motion picture and video exhibition..............	51213	-0.1	3.9	-2.5	-2.4	(NA)	(NA)	(NA)	(NA)
Broadcasting, except internet....................	515	3.1	1.3	2.8	-0.3	18.4	-9.5	8.3	-8.5
Radio and television broadcasting..............	5151	2.6	1.0	2.0	-0.6	18.0	-8.2	8.3	-8.2
Cable and other subscription programming......	5152	4.8	2.9	5.7	0.8	20.4	-12.1	8.8	-9.7
Wired telecommunications carriers...............	517311	3.7	-0.4	2.2	-1.4	–	0.4	-0.2	-0.2
Wireless telecommunications carriers............	517312	11.8	-6.4	17.1	4.7	13.2	-5.6	7.7	-4.8
Finance and insurance:									
Commercial banking..............................	52211	2.6	2.4	2.5	-0.1	11.7	-2.6	9.1	-2.3
Real estate and rental and leasing:									
Passenger car rental.............................	532111	2.1	1.8	1.9	-0.2	(NA)	(NA)	(NA)	(NA)
Truck, trailer and RV rental and leasing..........	53212	2.4	1.0	3.0	0.6	3.8	–	9.3	5.3
Video tape and disc rental.......................	532282	5.3	0.1	-4.5	-9.3	(NA)	(NA)	(NA)	(NA)
Professional and technical services:									
Accounting and bookkeeping services............	5412	2.0	1.5	2.6	0.5	6.1	-0.1	9.0	2.7
Architectural services............................	54131	1.5	1.6	2.5	1.0	(NA)	(NA)	(NA)	(NA)
Engineering services.............................	54133	0.9	2.8	2.6	1.6	4.6	-3.3	7.8	3.1
Advertising agencies............................	54181	2.3	1.4	2.7	0.4	(NA)	(NA)	(NA)	(NA)
Photography studios, portrait....................	541921	1.5	0.6	0.9	-0.6	(NA)	(NA)	(NA)	(NA)
Administrative and waste services:									
Employment placement agencies.................	56131	4.5	-0.1	4.9	0.4	(NA)	(NA)	(NA)	(NA)
Travel arrangement and reservation services....	5615	5.5	-1.0	2.5	-2.8	136.8	-51.6	91.6	-19.1
Janitorial services...............................	56172	2.6	0.8	4.0	1.4	(NA)	(NA)	(NA)	(NA)
Health care and social assistance:									
Medical and diagnostic laboratories..............	6215	2.4	0.2	5.2	2.7	3.7	13.7	15.3	11.2
Arts, entertainment, and recreation:									
Amusement parks and arcades...................	7131	-1.9	7.9	-5.8	-3.9	87.4	-44.8	121.7	18.3
Fitness and recreational sports centers...........	71394	3.0	0.3	1.6	-1.4	(NA)	(NA)	(NA)	(NA)
Accommodation and food services:									
Food services and drinking places................	722	0.5	3.0	1.5	1.0	17.0	-6.2	29.3	10.5
Special food services...........................	7223	0.7	1.9	1.1	0.4	(NA)	(NA)	(NA)	(NA)
Drinking places, alcoholic beverages...........	7224	-0.7	3.6	-1.6	-1.0	(NA)	(NA)	(NA)	(NA)
Restaurants and other eating places............	72251	0.6	3.1	1.7	1.2	14.3	-4.0	27.0	11.1
Other services:									
Automotive repair and maintenance.............	8111	1.0	2.1	1.3	0.3	-2.8	9.4	4.8	7.8
Reupholstery and furniture repair.................	81142	-0.9	3.5	-3.0	-2.0	(NA)	(NA)	(NA)	(NA)
Personal care services..........................	8121	2.2	1.5	2.5	0.2	(NA)	(NA)	(NA)	(NA)
Funeral homes and funeral services.............	81221	-0.1	3.7	-0.3	-0.2	(NA)	(NA)	(NA)	(NA)
Dry cleaning and laundry services...............	8123	2.1	1.4	0.6	-1.5	5.2	-2.3	3.2	-1.9
Coin-operated laundries and drycleaners........	81231	2.1	2.3	-0.1	-2.2	(NA)	(NA)	(NA)	(NA)
Dry cleaning and laundry services...............	81232	0.5	2.2	-2.3	-2.8	(NA)	(NA)	(NA)	(NA)
Photofinishing...................................	81292	2.0	1.9	-5.2	-7.0	(NA)	(NA)	(NA)	(NA)

NA Not available. – Represents zero or rounds to less than half the unit of measurement shown. [1] North American Industry Classification System, 2017 (NAICS); see text, Section 15. [2] Average annual percent changes based on compound rate formula. Rates of change are calculated using index numbers to three decimal places. [3] For NAICS industries 484, 4841, 493, 49311, and 49312, annual percent changes are for 1992-2020. For NAICS industries 48421, 71391 and 71394, average annual percent changes are for 2002-2020. For NAICS industries 5412, and 5615, average annual percent changes are for 1997-2020. For NAICS industries 56131, and 6215, average annual percent changes are for 1994-2020. For NAICS industry 7131, average annual percent change is for 2007-2020. [4] For NAICS industry 491, average annual percent changes are for the fiscal year ending in September.

Source: U.S. Bureau of Labor Statistics, Labor Productivity and Costs, "Productivity and Costs by Industry," <www.bls.gov/lpc/data.htm>, accessed August 2022.

Table 676. Labor Productivity and Related Measures: 1980 to 2021

[See text, this section. Minus sign (-) indicates decrease]

Item	1980	1990	2000	2010	2017	2018	2019	2020	2021
INDEXES (2012=100)									
Output per hour, business sector	50.7	60.7	76.1	99.1	104.0	105.7	107.7	110.4	112.5
Nonfarm business	51.8	61.1	76.1	99.0	103.8	105.3	107.5	110.1	112.2
Manufacturing	(NA)	47.4	69.3	100.2	97.1	97.2	95.3	95.4	98.5
Output [1], business sector	38.1	54.0	79.8	95.0	114.1	118.1	121.2	116.0	124.4
Nonfarm business	38.2	53.9	79.7	94.8	113.8	117.8	121.0	115.7	124.2
Manufacturing	(NA)	68.0	98.8	96.0	101.4	103.4	101.2	94.5	100.6
Hours [2], business sector	75.2	88.9	104.9	95.9	109.7	111.7	112.5	105.1	110.6
Nonfarm business	73.7	88.3	104.7	95.8	109.7	111.8	112.6	105.1	110.7
Manufacturing	(NA)	143.4	142.7	95.8	104.5	106.4	106.2	99.0	102.1
Compensation per hour [3], business sector	27.3	46.5	69.1	95.3	112.0	115.9	120.3	128.6	135.8
Nonfarm business	27.6	46.6	69.3	95.3	112.1	116.0	120.5	128.9	136.0
Manufacturing	(NA)	48.2	69.9	96.6	109.8	112.3	115.4	123.5	128.4
Real hourly compensation [3], business sector	72.4	79.2	92.3	100.3	104.7	105.7	107.8	113.9	114.9
Nonfarm business	73.2	79.5	92.4	100.4	104.8	105.9	108.0	114.1	115.0
Manufacturing	(NA)	82.3	93.3	101.7	102.7	102.5	103.5	109.3	108.6
Unit labor costs [4], business sector	53.8	76.5	90.9	96.1	107.7	109.7	111.7	116.5	120.7
Nonfarm business	53.1	76.4	91.0	96.3	108.0	110.1	112.0	117.1	121.2
Manufacturing	(NA)	101.8	100.9	96.4	113.1	115.5	121.1	129.4	130.3
ANNUAL PERCENT CHANGE [5]									
Output per hour, business sector	–	2.0	3.1	3.4	1.1	1.6	2.0	2.5	1.9
Nonfarm business	–	1.7	3.0	3.4	1.1	1.5	2.1	2.4	1.9
Manufacturing	(NA)	3.3	3.5	7.0	-1.1	0.1	-1.9	0.2	3.2
Output [1], business sector	-0.9	1.6	4.5	3.2	2.7	3.5	2.6	-4.2	7.2
Nonfarm business	-0.9	1.5	4.4	3.3	2.7	3.5	2.7	-4.4	7.4
Manufacturing	(NA)	0.1	2.7	7.0	-0.2	2.0	-2.2	-6.7	6.5
Hours [2], business sector	-0.9	-0.4	1.4	-0.1	1.5	1.9	0.7	-6.6	5.2
Nonfarm business	-0.8	-0.2	1.4	-0.1	1.6	2.0	0.7	-6.7	5.4
Manufacturing	(NA)	-3.1	-0.8	–	1.0	1.9	-0.2	-6.8	3.2
Compensation per hour [3], business sector	10.7	6.3	6.9	1.8	3.5	3.5	3.8	6.9	5.6
Nonfarm business	10.8	6.0	7.0	1.9	3.5	3.4	3.9	7.0	5.4
Manufacturing	(NA)	5.5	6.5	1.3	3.2	2.2	2.8	7.0	4.0
Real hourly compensation [3], business sector	-0.4	1.3	3.4	0.2	1.3	1.0	2.0	5.6	0.9
Nonfarm business	-0.4	1.0	3.5	0.2	1.3	1.0	2.0	5.7	0.7
Manufacturing	(NA)	0.5	3.0	-0.4	1.0	-0.2	1.0	5.7	-0.7
Unit labor costs [4], business sector	10.8	4.2	3.7	-1.5	2.4	1.9	1.8	4.3	3.6
Nonfarm business	10.8	4.2	3.9	-1.5	2.3	1.9	1.8	4.5	3.5
Manufacturing	(NA)	2.1	2.9	-5.4	4.4	2.1	4.8	6.8	0.8

– Represents or rounds to zero. NA Not available. [1] Refers to gross sectoral product, a chain–type, current–weighted index. [2] Hours at work of all persons engaged in the business and nonfarm business sectors (employees, proprietors, and unpaid family workers), and employees' and proprietors' hours in manufacturing. [3] Wages and salaries of employees plus employers' contributions for social insurance and private benefit plans. Also includes an estimate of same for self-employed. Real compensation deflated by the Consumer Price Index research series; see text, Section 14. [4] Hourly compensation divided by output per hour. [5] All changes are from the immediate prior year.

Source: U.S. Bureau of Labor Statistics, Labor Productivity and Costs, "Major Sector Productivity and Costs," <www.bls.gov/data/#productivity>, accessed April 2022.

Table 677. Employed Persons and Average Hours Worked Per Day at Workplace and at Home: 2021

[162,328 represents 162,328,000. Civilian noninstitutionalized population 15 years old and over, except as indicated. Includes work at main job and any other jobs. Excludes travel related to work. Based on the American Time Use Survey]

Characteristic	Total em-ployed (1,000)	Employed persons who worked on an average day [1]					
		Total		Worked at workplace		Worked at home [2]	
		Percent of employed	Hours of work	Percent of those who worked	Hours of work	Percent of those who worked	Hours of work
Total	**162,328**	**67.8**	**7.75**	**68.4**	**7.84**	**38.1**	**5.61**
Work status: [3]							
Full-time workers [4]	129,809	71.4	8.18	67.9	8.24	39.6	5.88
Part-time workers [4]	32,519	53.3	5.45	70.7	5.77	30.1	3.69
Male [3]	85,746	71.0	8.07	71.2	8.06	35.3	5.77
Full-time workers [4]	73,134	72.9	8.44	70.9	8.43	36.7	5.94
Part-time workers [4]	12,612	60.3	5.42	73.2	5.56	25.5	4.01
Female [3]	76,582	64.1	7.36	64.9	7.53	41.5	5.45
Full-time workers [4]	56,675	69.5	7.82	63.9	7.95	43.5	5.82
Part-time workers [4]	19,907	48.9	5.48	68.8	5.95	33.8	3.50
Jobholding status:							
Single jobholders	148,358	66.8	7.72	68.6	7.84	36.8	5.72
Multiple jobholders	13,970	77.6	8.01	66.2	7.78	49.6	4.90
Educational attainment: [5]							
Less than high school	7,891	74.2	7.52	93.3	7.48	5.9	(S)
High school diploma [6]	35,075	63.6	8.08	86.1	8.05	18.8	4.76
Some college	30,133	66.5	7.93	75.0	8.03	30.6	5.38
Bachelor's degree or higher	68,024	71.4	7.72	49.8	7.92	59.8	5.88

S Data do not meet publication standards. [1] Individuals may have worked at more than one location. [2] "Working at home" includes any time persons did work at home and is not restricted to persons whose usual workplace is their home. [3] Includes workers whose hours vary. [4] Full-time workers usually worked 35 or more hours per week at all jobs combined; part-time workers worked fewer than 35 hours per week. [5] For persons 25 years old and over. [6] Includes persons with a high school diploma or equivalent.

Source: U.S. Bureau of Labor Statistics, American Time Use Survey—2021 Results, USDL 22-1261, June 2022. See also <www.bls.gov/tus>.

Table 678. Annual Total Compensation and Wages and Salary Accruals Per Full-Time Equivalent Employee by Industry: 2000 to 2020

[In dollars. Compensation averages are equal to the sum of wages and salaries and of supplements to wages and salaries; supplements are made on behalf of employees but are not included in regular wage payments to employees, such as contributions for employee pension and insurance funds, and employer contributions for government social insurance. Wages and salaries consist of cash remuneration of labor, including sick or vacation pay, severance pay, commissions, tips, and bonuses. Based on the 2012 North American Industry Classification System (NAICS); see text, Section 15]

Industry	Total annual compensation (average)				Annual salary and wages			
	2000	2010	2019	2020	2000	2010	2019	2020
Compensation of employees.................	**47,542**	**66,212**	**81,995**	**87,557**	**39,231**	**53,239**	**66,781**	**71,456**
Domestic industries....................	47,450	65,823	81,224	86,963	39,166	52,939	66,168	70,982
Private industries..................	46,136	62,441	77,900	83,598	38,862	51,913	65,459	70,369
Agriculture, forestry, fishing, and hunting........	25,814	37,634	45,985	49,595	22,146	30,610	37,562	38,338
Mining..........................	70,434	107,738	130,027	133,713	58,134	91,837	110,654	113,400
Utilities........................	84,821	123,905	161,636	173,344	64,772	89,603	117,200	120,925
Construction....................	46,201	63,648	80,397	83,313	38,551	52,757	67,530	70,420
Manufacturing..................	54,167	75,485	90,107	94,941	43,957	59,997	72,709	76,391
Wholesale trade................	59,068	78,065	97,574	102,817	50,896	67,167	84,121	88,244
Retail trade....................	31,224	38,464	47,516	51,441	26,589	32,028	39,490	42,908
Transportation and warehousing.................	48,462	62,458	75,620	75,818	39,055	49,744	60,647	61,666
Information...................	72,135	98,952	151,464	168,404	62,571	81,295	130,797	147,732
Finance and insurance..........	76,234	104,130	135,330	143,887	64,574	88,165	115,470	124,106
Real estate and rental and leasing......	43,235	58,043	77,595	82,154	37,150	49,209	67,621	71,591
Professional, scientific, and technical services..	71,592	95,391	122,386	129,084	62,472	82,570	105,958	113,114
Management of companies and enterprises [1]...	90,766	126,701	158,995	158,746	74,253	103,873	137,057	138,006
Administrative and waste management services.....	28,921	44,896	56,394	61,159	25,035	37,374	47,503	51,185
Educational services..............	34,164	50,711	63,312	67,438	29,244	41,367	51,116	54,420
Health care and social assistance...............	42,009	59,618	70,337	74,310	35,249	48,977	57,806	61,026
Arts, entertainment, and recreation..............	37,384	49,745	61,505	69,564	32,482	42,672	53,076	59,328
Accommodation and food services..............	20,819	27,965	36,518	36,448	18,045	24,138	31,939	31,121
Other services, except government.............	30,412	41,739	53,283	58,194	25,990	35,876	46,107	50,241
Government.........................	54,624	82,264	100,632	105,913	40,824	57,925	70,304	74,434
Federal.........................	61,449	104,416	128,462	141,435	46,749	74,664	89,077	97,817
State and local....................	52,718	76,234	93,720	97,339	39,169	53,369	65,642	68,791

[1] Consists of offices of bank and other holding companies and of corporate, subsidiary, and regional managing offices.

Source: U.S. Bureau of Economic Analysis, National Income and Product Accounts Tables, "Table 6.2D. Compensation of Employees by Industry," "Table 6.5D. Full-Time Equivalent Employees by Industry," and "Table 6.6D. Wages and Salaries Per Full-Time Equivalent Employee by Industry," <apps.bea.gov/itable/index.cfm>, accessed August 2021.

Table 679. Average Hourly and Weekly Earnings of Employees by Private Industry Group: 2000 to 2021

[In dollars. Average earnings include overtime. Data are for production and nonsupervisory employees. See headnote, Table 665]

Private industry group	Current dollars					Constant (1982–84) dollars [1]				
	2000	2010	2019	2020	2021	2000	2010	2019	2020	2021
AVERAGE HOURLY EARNINGS										
Total private.......................	**14.01**	**19.04**	**23.51**	**24.68**	**25.89**	**8.29**	**8.90**	**9.43**	**9.78**	**9.75**
Mining and logging...........................	16.55	23.82	29.92	30.42	31.08	9.80	11.13	12.01	12.06	11.71
Construction.......................	17.48	23.22	28.52	29.21	30.48	10.35	10.85	11.44	11.58	11.48
Manufacturing.......................	14.32	18.61	22.15	22.80	23.80	8.48	8.70	8.89	9.04	8.96
Trade, transportation, and utilities [2]........	13.28	16.78	20.63	21.41	22.41	7.86	7.84	8.28	8.49	8.44
Information.........................	19.07	25.87	33.93	35.74	36.82	11.29	12.09	13.61	14.17	13.87
Financial activities [2]...................	15.04	21.55	27.68	29.09	30.34	8.90	10.07	11.11	11.53	11.43
Professional and business services [2].....	15.53	22.80	27.79	29.25	30.56	9.19	10.66	11.15	11.60	11.51
Education and health services [2]..........	13.91	19.95	24.34	25.40	27.12	8.24	9.32	9.77	10.07	10.21
Leisure and hospitality [2].................	8.32	11.31	14.50	14.71	16.17	4.93	5.29	5.82	5.83	6.09
Other services......................	12.73	17.06	21.40	22.58	23.65	7.54	7.97	8.59	8.95	8.91
AVERAGE WEEKLY EARNINGS										
Total private.......................	**481**	**636**	**790**	**837**	**886**	**285**	**297**	**317**	**332**	**334**
Mining and logging...........................	735	1,063	1,402	1,365	1,444	435	497	563	541	544
Construction.......................	686	892	1,136	1,146	1,204	406	417	456	454	453
Manufacturing.......................	591	765	922	929	986	350	358	370	368	371
Trade, transportation, and utilities.........	449	558	698	731	769	266	261	280	290	290
Information.........................	701	940	1,199	1,288	1,343	415	439	481	511	506
Financial activities [2]...................	540	780	1,020	1,079	1,130	320	365	409	428	426
Professional and business services [2].....	536	799	984	1,047	1,106	317	374	395	415	416
Education and health services [2]..........	448	639	784	825	885	265	299	314	327	333
Leisure and hospitality [2].................	217	281	358	355	403	129	131	144	141	152
Other services......................	413	524	659	706	742	245	245	264	280	280

[1] Earnings in current dollars divided by the Consumer Price Index (CPI-W) on a 1982–84 base; see text, Section 14. [2] For composition of industries, see Table 667.

Source: U.S. Bureau of Labor Statistics, Current Employment Statistics, "Employment, Hours, and Earnings—National," <www.bls.gov/ces/data.htm>, accessed May 2022.

Table 680. Employment and Wages of Private Sector and Government Employees: 2000 to 2021

[7,879 represents 7,879,000. Based on federal-state cooperative program, The Quarterly Census of Employment and Wages (QCEW), also referenced as ES-202. Includes workers covered by state unemployment insurance laws and federal civilian workers covered by unemployment compensation for federal employees. Excludes most agricultural workers on small farms, all Armed Forces, elected officials in most states, railroad employees, most domestic workers, most student workers at school, value of meals and lodging, and tips and other gratuities]

Employment and wages	Unit	2000	2010	2015	2018	2019	2020	2021
Establishments:								
Total	1,000	**7,879**	**8,993**	**9,523**	**10,011**	**10,234**	**10,488**	**10,909**
Excluding federal	1,000	7,829	8,926	9,462	9,952	10,173	10,426	10,848
Private	1,000	7,622	8,696	9,224	9,712	9,932	10,185	10,606
State government	1,000	65	67	69	70	70	70	70
Local governments	1,000	141	164	169	170	171	171	171
Federal government	1,000	50	67	61	59	60	61	61
Average annual employment:								
Total	1,000	**129,877**	**127,820**	**139,492**	**146,132**	**148,105**	**139,104**	**143,780**
Excluding federal	1,000	127,006	124,840	136,735	143,337	145,281	136,176	140,897
Private	1,000	110,015	106,201	118,308	124,552	126,359	117,940	122,717
State government	1,000	4,370	4,606	4,567	4,625	4,666	4,593	4,540
Local governments	1,000	12,620	14,032	13,861	14,160	14,256	13,643	13,640
Federal government	1,000	2,871	2,981	2,756	2,795	2,824	2,928	2,883
Annual wages:								
Total	Bil. dol.	**4,588**	**5,976**	**7,385**	**8,368**	**8,769**	**8,906**	**9,721**
Excluding federal	Bil. dol.	4,455	5,769	7,170	8,135	8,531	8,655	9,464
Private	Bil. dol.	3,888	4,934	6,256	7,124	7,481	7,577	8,348
State government	Bil. dol.	159	226	255	281	293	302	312
Local governments	Bil. dol.	409	610	659	729	757	776	803
Federal government	Bil. dol.	133	206	215	234	238	250	257
Average annual wage per employee:								
Total	Dol.	**35,323**	**46,751**	**52,942**	**57,266**	**59,209**	**64,021**	**67,610**
Excluding federal	Dol.	35,077	46,215	52,439	56,752	58,721	63,560	67,168
Private	Dol.	35,337	46,455	52,876	57,198	59,202	64,247	68,029
State government	Dol.	36,296	48,960	55,878	60,751	62,830	65,762	68,835
Local governments	Dol.	32,387	43,493	47,573	51,515	53,112	56,884	58,870
Federal government	Dol.	46,228	69,198	77,900	83,657	84,310	85,467	89,205
Average weekly wage per employee:								
Total	Dol.	**679**	**899**	**1,018**	**1,101**	**1,139**	**1,231**	**1,300**
Excluding federal	Dol.	675	889	1,008	1,091	1,129	1,222	1,292
Private	Dol.	680	893	1,017	1,100	1,138	1,236	1,308
State government	Dol.	698	942	1,075	1,168	1,208	1,265	1,323
Local governments	Dol.	623	836	915	991	1,021	1,094	1,132
Federal government	Dol.	889	1,331	1,498	1,609	1,621	1,644	1,716

Source: U.S. Bureau of Labor Statistics, Quarterly Census of Employment and Wages, "QCEW Data Viewer," and earlier releases, <www.bls.gov/cew/>, accessed September 2022.

Table 681. Average Annual Wage by State: 2020 and 2021

[In dollars, except percent change. See headnote, Table 680]

State/area	Average wage per employee 2020	Average wage per employee 2021	Percent change, 2020-21	State/area	Average wage per employee 2020	Average wage per employee 2021	Percent change, 2020-21
United States	**64,021**	**67,610**	**5.6**	Montana	48,443	51,319	5.9
Alabama	52,210	54,358	4.1	Nebraska	51,488	53,853	4.6
Alaska	61,730	62,681	1.5	Nevada	55,996	59,463	6.2
Arizona	58,426	61,750	5.7	New Hampshire	64,888	72,063	11.1
Arkansas	48,672	51,519	5.8	New Jersey	73,974	76,340	3.2
California	79,480	85,741	7.9	New Mexico	50,369	52,522	4.3
Colorado	66,649	70,563	5.9	New York	83,122	88,035	5.9
Connecticut	75,317	77,840	3.3	North Carolina	56,214	59,594	6.0
Delaware	62,462	64,484	3.2	North Dakota	55,465	56,851	2.5
District of Columbia	107,075	112,148	4.7	Ohio	55,872	58,350	4.4
Florida	55,868	60,276	7.9	Oklahoma	49,566	51,317	3.5
Georgia	58,884	62,242	5.7	Oregon	59,938	63,989	6.8
Hawaii	57,934	59,644	3.0	Pennsylvania	62,049	64,697	4.3
Idaho	47,685	50,744	6.4	Rhode Island	60,508	62,280	2.9
Illinois	66,279	70,127	5.8	South Carolina	49,554	52,295	5.5
Indiana	51,957	54,968	5.8	South Dakota	49,167	51,254	4.2
Iowa	52,333	54,293	3.7	Tennessee	55,137	59,147	7.3
Kansas	51,490	53,422	3.8	Texas	62,872	65,970	4.9
Kentucky	50,794	52,862	4.1	Utah	54,890	57,837	5.4
Louisiana	51,964	53,838	3.6	Vermont	54,084	56,296	4.1
Maine	51,952	54,651	5.2	Virginia	65,159	67,990	4.3
Maryland	68,879	71,688	4.1	Washington	76,791	82,477	7.4
Massachusetts	83,738	87,752	4.8	West Virginia	48,741	50,498	3.6
Michigan	59,432	61,683	3.8	Wisconsin	53,809	56,350	4.7
Minnesota	64,191	67,009	4.4	Wyoming	50,986	53,022	4.0
Mississippi	43,222	44,958	4.0	Puerto Rico	29,570	30,525	3.2
Missouri	54,046	56,456	4.5	Virgin Islands	53,616	49,890	-6.9

Source: U.S. Bureau of Labor Statistics, Quarterly Census of Employment and Wages, "Employment and Wages Online Annual Averages, 2021," and earlier editions, <www.bls.gov/cew/home.htm>, accessed September 2022.

Table 682. Full-Time Wage and Salary Workers—Number and Earnings: 2010 to 2021

[99,531 represents 99,531,000. Earnings shown in current dollars; data represent annual averages of usual weekly earnings. Full time workers are those who usually worked 35 hours or more per week at all jobs combined. Based on the Current Population Survey; see text, Section 1 and Appendix III. For definition of median, see Guide to Tabular Presentation]

Characteristic	Number of workers (1,000)			Median weekly earnings (dollars)		
	2010	2020	2021	2010	2020	2021
All workers [1]	**99,531**	**110,387**	**114,316**	**747**	**984**	**998**
Male	55,059	60,911	62,928	824	1,082	1,097
Female	44,472	49,476	51,388	669	891	912
White [2]	80,656	85,142	87,738	765	1,003	1,018
Black [2]	11,658	14,044	14,740	611	794	801
Asian [2]	4,946	7,353	7,780	855	1,310	1,328
Hispanic [3]	14,837	19,558	20,841	535	758	777
OCCUPATION [4]						
Management, professional and related occupations	39,145	50,023	51,166	1,063	1,356	1,390
Management, business, and financial operations	15,648	20,811	21,529	1,155	1,461	1,482
Professional and related occupations	23,497	29,213	29,637	1,008	1,270	1,335
Computer and mathematical occupations	3,202	5,083	5,267	1,289	1,633	1,660
Architecture and engineering occupations	2,366	2,933	2,985	1,255	1,575	1,641
Life, physical, and social science occupations	1,127	1,401	1,391	1,062	1,336	1,407
Community and social services occupations	1,909	2,187	2,276	802	1,003	1,065
Legal occupations	1,248	1,410	1,401	1,213	1,540	1,586
Education, training, and library occupations	6,535	7,012	7,124	913	1,096	1,138
Arts, design, entertainment, sports, and media	1,431	1,681	1,707	920	1,179	1,229
Healthcare practitioner and technical occupations	5,678	7,504	7,485	986	1,227	1,273
Service occupations	14,424	13,771	14,630	479	621	644
Healthcare support occupations	2,219	3,210	3,269	471	606	637
Protective service occupations	2,872	2,690	2,608	747	982	998
Food preparation and serving-related occupations	3,823	3,353	3,863	406	530	573
Building and grounds cleaning and maintenance	3,310	3,138	3,347	446	603	623
Personal care and service occupations	2,199	1,380	1,543	455	616	618
Sales and office occupations	23,060	21,165	21,748	631	809	826
Sales and related occupations	9,121	8,958	9,281	666	880	887
Office and administrative support occupations	13,939	12,207	12,467	619	781	806
Natural resources, construction, and maintenance	9,869	10,690	11,182	719	905	919
Farming, fishing, and forestry occupations	729	787	800	416	589	623
Construction and extraction occupations	5,020	5,826	6,171	709	906	904
Installation, maintenance, and repair occupations	4,120	4,077	4,211	794	984	1,017
Production, transportation, and material-moving	13,034	14,738	15,590	599	746	774
Production occupations	6,861	6,820	7,107	599	775	809
Transportation and material-moving occupations	6,172	7,917	8,483	599	719	738

[1] Includes other races, not shown separately. [2] For persons in this race group only. [3] Persons of Hispanic origin may be of any race. [4] As of January 2020, occupations reflect the introduction of the 2018 Census occupational classification system, derived from the 2018 Standard Occupational Classification (SOC). No historical data have been revised. Data for 2020 and thereafter are not strictly comparable with earlier years.

Source: U.S. Bureau of Labor Statistics, CPS Tables, "Median weekly earnings of full-time wage and salary workers by selected characteristics," and "Median weekly earnings of full-time wage and salary workers by detailed occupation and sex," January 2022 and earlier releases, <www.bls.gov/cps/tables.htm>.

Table 683. Median Usual Weekly Earnings of Full-Time Wage and Salary Workers by Sex and Education: 1980 to 2021

[In current dollars. For wage and salary workers 25 years old and over. Based on Current Population Survey; see text, Section 1 and Appendix III. Wages and salaries are collected before taxes and other deductions and include overtime pay, commissions, or tips usually received at principal job. Earnings reported on basis other than weekly are converted to a weekly equivalent. Excludes all incorporated and unincorporated self employed. Data not strictly comparable to data for earlier years. See text this section and <www.bls.gov/cps/eetech_methods.pdf>]

Year and sex	Total	Less than a high school diploma	High school, no college [1]	Some college or associate's degree	Bachelor's degree and higher [2]
CURRENT DOLLARS					
Male:					
1980	339	267	327	358	427
1990	512	349	459	542	741
2000	693	406	591	691	1,020
2010	874	486	710	845	1,330
2020	1,144	674	881	1,027	1,644
2021	1,160	684	904	1,047	1,661
Female:					
1980	213	164	201	231	290
1990	369	240	315	395	535
2000	516	304	420	505	756
2010	704	388	543	638	986
2020	929	525	671	779	1,239
2021	954	550	698	803	1,272
WOMEN'S EARNINGS AS PERCENT OF MEN'S					
1980	62.8	61.4	61.5	64.5	67.9
1990	72.1	68.8	68.6	72.9	72.2
2000	74.5	74.9	71.1	73.1	74.1
2010	80.5	79.8	76.5	75.5	74.1
2020	81.2	77.9	76.2	75.9	75.4
2021	82.2	80.4	77.2	76.7	76.6

[1] Includes persons with a high school diploma or equivalent. [2] Includes bachelor's, master's, professional, or doctoral degree.

Source: U.S. Bureau of Labor Statistics, "Weekly & Hourly Earnings from the Current Population Survey," <www.bls.gov/cps/home.htm#data>, accessed April 2022.

Table 684. Workers With Earnings by Occupation of Longest Held Job and Sex: 2020

[79,248 represents 79,248,000. As of March. For definition of median, see Guide to Tabular Presentation. Based on the Current Population Survey, Annual Social and Economic Supplement (CPS ASEC); includes civilian noninstitutional population 15 years old and over, and military personnel who live in households with at least one other civilian adult. See text, Section 1, and Appendix III]

Major occupation group of longest job held in 2020	All workers				Full-time, year-round			
	Female		Male		Female		Male	
	Number (1,000)	Median earnings (dol.)	Number (1,000)	Median earnings (dol.)	Number (1,000)	Median earnings (dol.)	Number (1,000)	Median earnings (dol.)
Total	**79,248**	**35,838**	**87,599**	**49,389**	**45,859**	**50,982**	**59,634**	**61,417**
Management, business, and financial occupations	13,388	61,112	15,814	77,972	10,123	68,550	12,869	90,361
Professional and related occupations	22,427	51,706	16,587	75,509	14,768	61,744	12,764	85,460
Service occupations	16,084	19,094	11,803	25,893	6,128	30,588	5,757	41,376
Sales and office occupations	20,872	31,069	12,564	42,140	11,621	41,964	8,218	56,028
Natural resources, construction, and maintenance	924	25,769	14,172	41,046	434	40,338	9,396	50,062
Production, transportation, and material-moving occupations	5,440	25,645	15,799	36,223	2,683	32,527	9,844	46,421
Armed Forces	113	60,487	860	52,096	102	61,440	785	54,460

Source: U.S. Census Bureau, *Income and Poverty in the United States: 2020*, September 2021, Current Population Reports, P60-273; and "Current Population Survey Tables for Personal Income: Table PINC-06," <www.census.gov/data/tables/time-series/demo/income-poverty/cps-pinc.html>, accessed May 2022.

Table 685. Employment Cost Index (ECI) for Total Compensation by Occupation and Industry: 2010 to 2021

[As of December (2005 = 100). The ECI is a measure of the rate of change in compensation (wages, salaries, and employer costs for employee benefits). Data are not seasonally adjusted. Industry classifications based on North American Industry Classification System (NAICS); occupation classifications based on the 2010 Standard Occupational Classification (SOC)]

Occupational group and industry	Indexes (December 2005 = 100)				Annual percent change from immediate prior year			
	2010	2019	2020	2021	2010	2019	2020	2021
Civilian workers [1]	**113.2**	**138.7**	**142.2**	**147.9**	**2.0**	**2.7**	**2.5**	**4.0**
State and local government	**116.2**	**141.7**	**144.9**	**148.6**	**1.8**	**2.9**	**2.3**	**2.6**
Workers, by occupational group:								
Management, professional and related occupations	115.5	140.3	143.2	146.6	1.5	2.9	2.1	2.4
Sales and office occupations	116.6	144.0	148.0	151.4	1.9	2.9	2.8	2.3
Service occupations	118.0	145.1	149.1	154.1	2.3	3.1	2.8	3.4
Workers, by industry division:								
Service-providing industries: [2]								
Education and health services [2]	115.6	140.3	143.4	147.0	1.5	2.8	2.2	2.5
Schools	115.3	139.8	142.9	146.3	1.4	2.8	2.2	2.4
Health care and social assistance [2]	117.9	143.5	146.7	152.1	2.2	3.0	2.2	3.7
Hospitals	117.0	140.8	143.9	149.2	2.4	3.2	2.2	3.7
Public administration	116.8	143.4	146.8	150.6	1.9	3.0	2.4	2.6
Private industry workers [3]	**112.5**	**138.0**	**141.6**	**147.8**	**2.1**	**2.7**	**2.6**	**4.4**
Workers, by occupational group:								
Management, professional, and related occupations	113.0	136.8	139.5	144.4	2.1	2.2	2.0	3.5
Sales and office occupations	111.6	138.8	143.2	149.9	2.2	2.8	3.2	4.7
Natural resources, construction, and maintenance occupations	113.3	137.9	141.3	146.7	1.9	2.5	2.5	3.8
Production, transportation, and material moving occupations	111.5	139.2	143.8	150.9	2.4	3.3	3.3	4.9
Service occupations	113.5	140.6	145.6	155.9	1.5	3.7	3.6	7.1
Workers, by industry division:								
Goods-producing industries [2]	111.1	135.8	138.9	144.0	2.3	3.0	2.3	3.7
Construction	112.7	137.0	140.3	145.2	0.9	3.5	2.4	3.5
Manufacturing	110.0	135.3	138.5	143.5	2.8	2.8	2.4	3.6
Service-providing industries [2]	113.0	138.7	142.4	148.9	2.0	2.6	2.7	4.6
Trade, transportation, and utilities	111.4	140.7	145.1	152.6	2.4	2.9	3.1	5.2
Information	110.0	135.7	139.9	144.7	1.6	1.0	3.1	3.4
Financial activities	111.4	138.2	141.4	146.0	2.6	3.0	2.3	3.3
Professional and business services	114.6	138.7	142.4	147.9	2.0	2.6	2.7	3.9
Education and health services	114.7	137.2	140.2	146.1	1.7	2.3	2.2	4.2
Leisure and hospitality	114.1	140.0	144.7	156.3	1.2	3.2	3.4	8.0
Bargaining status:								
Union	114.8	142.3	146.3	151.2	3.3	2.5	2.8	3.3
Nonunion	112.1	137.3	140.9	147.2	1.8	2.7	2.6	4.5

[1] Includes workers in the private nonfarm economy except those in private households, and workers in the public sector except those in the federal government. [2] Includes all other items not shown separately. [3] Excludes farm and household workers.

Source: U.S. Bureau of Labor Statistics, Employment Cost Trends, "Employment Cost Index," <www.bls.gov/ncs/ect/home.htm#data>, accessed April 2022.

Table 686. Federal and State Minimum Wage Rates: 1940 to 2022

[In current dollars. Wage rates are as of January 1, except as noted. Where an employee is subject to both the state and federal minimum wage laws, the employee is entitled to the higher minimum wage rate]

Year	Federal minimum wage rates per hour	State	2022 minimum wage rates per hour	State	2022 minimum wage rates per hour	State	2022 minimum wage rates per hour
1940	0.30	AL	(X)	KY	7.25	ND	7.25
1945 (as of Oct. 24)	0.40	AK	10.34	LA	(X)	OH	[7] 7.25-9.30
1950 (as of Jan. 25)	0.75	AZ	12.80	ME	12.75	OK	[8] 2.00-7.25
1960	1.00	AR	[2] 11.00	MD	12.50	OR	12.75
1965 (as of Sept. 3)	1.25	CA	[9] 14.00-15.00	MA	14.25	PA	7.25
1970 (as of Feb. 1)	1.45	CO	12.56	MI	[1] 9.87	RI	12.25
1975	2.10	CT	13.00	MN	[4] 8.42-10.33	SC	(X)
1980	3.10	DE	10.50	MS	(X)	SD	9.95
1985	3.35	DC	15.20	MO	11.15	TN	(X)
1990 (as of Apr. 1)	3.80	FL	10.00	MT	[5] 4.00-9.20	TX	7.25
1995	4.25	GA	[3] 5.15	NE	[2] 9.00	UT	7.25
2000	5.15	HI	10.10	NV	[6] 8.75-9.75	VT	[1] 12.55
2005	5.15	ID	7.25	NH	7.25	VA	[2] 11.00
2007 (as of Jul. 24)	5.85	IL	[2] 12.00	NJ	13.00	WA	14.49
2008 (as of Jul. 24)	6.55	IN	[1] 7.25	NM	11.50	WV	[3] 8.75
2009 (as of Jul. 24)	7.25	IA	7.25	NY	[10] 13.20	WI	7.25
2022	**7.25**	KS	7.25	NC	7.25	WY	5.15

X Not applicable. [1] Employers of 2 or more. [2] Employers of 4 or more. [3] Employers of 6 or more. [4] Minnesota: $8.42 for small employer (annual revenues less than $500,000); $10.33 for large employer (annual revenues $500,000 or more). [5] Lower rate for businesses with gross annual sales of $110,000 or less. [6] Nevada: $9.75 with no health insurance benefits provided by employer; $8.75 with health insurance provided by employer and received by employee. [7] Ohio: $7.25 for those employers grossing $342,000 or less. [8] Oklahoma: employers of 10 or more full time employees at any one location, and employers with gross sales over $100,000 regardless of number of full-time employees. All other employers $2.00. [9] California: $14.00 minimum wage for employers with 25 or fewer employees, and $15.00 minimum wage for employers with 26 or more employees. [10] Basic minimum rate: $13.20; $15.00 (Long Island, Westchester, & NYC).

Source: U.S. Department of Labor, Wage and Hour Division, "Changes in Basic Minimum Wages in Non-Farm Employment Under State Law: Selected Years 1968 to 2021," and "State Minimum Wage Laws," <www.dol.gov/agencies/whd/minimum-wage/state>, accessed January 2022.

Table 687. Workers Paid Hourly Rates At or Below Federal Minimum Wage by Selected Characteristics: 2021

[76,125 represents 76,125,000. Data are annual averages. For employed wage and salary workers, excluding all self-employed. Based on the Current Population Survey; see text, Section 1 and Appendix III]

Characteristic	Number of workers paid hourly rates (1,000)				Percent of workers paid hourly rates at or below federal minimum wage		
		At or below federal minimum wage					
	Total	Total	At prevailing federal minimum wage	Below prevailing federal minimum wage	Total	At prevailing federal minimum wage	Below prevailing federal minimum wage
Total, 16 years and over [1]	**76,125**	**1,091**	**181**	**910**	**1.4**	**0.2**	**1.2**
16 to 24 years	15,153	484	111	373	3.2	0.7	2.5
25 years and over	60,973	607	70	538	1.0	0.1	0.9
Male, 16 years old and over	38,089	398	87	311	1.0	0.2	0.8
16 to 24 years	7,544	159	51	108	2.1	0.7	1.4
25 years and over	30,545	239	36	203	0.8	0.1	0.7
Female, 16 years old and over	38,036	693	94	599	1.8	0.2	1.6
16 to 24 years	7,608	325	61	264	4.3	0.8	3.5
25 years and over	30,428	368	34	335	1.2	0.1	1.1
White [2]	58,021	832	127	706	1.4	0.2	1.2
Men	29,656	293	64	229	1.0	0.2	0.8
Women	28,366	539	62	477	1.9	0.2	1.7
Black [2]	11,019	146	34	112	1.3	0.3	1.0
Men	5,009	62	13	49	1.2	0.3	1.0
Women	6,010	84	21	63	1.4	0.3	1.0
Asian [2]	3,809	44	9	34	1.1	0.2	0.9
Men	1,766	15	5	10	0.8	0.3	0.6
Women	2,044	29	4	24	1.4	0.2	1.2
Hispanic [3]	16,998	226	33	194	1.3	0.2	1.1
Men	9,464	90	21	69	0.9	0.2	0.7
Women	7,534	137	11	125	1.8	0.1	1.7
Full-time workers	58,259	520	47	473	0.9	0.1	0.8
Men	31,827	202	27	175	0.6	0.1	0.6
Women	26,432	318	20	297	1.2	0.1	1.1
Part-time workers [4]	17,757	567	134	433	3.2	0.8	2.4
Men	6,205	193	60	133	3.1	1.0	2.1
Women	11,552	374	74	300	3.2	0.6	2.6
Private sector industries	67,168	1,023	176	847	1.5	0.3	1.3
Public sector industries	8,957	68	5	63	0.8	0.1	0.7

[1] Includes other races, not shown separately. Also includes a small number of multiple jobholders whose full- or part-time status cannot be determined for their principal job. [2] For persons in this race group only. [3] Persons of Hispanic or Latino origin may be of any race. [4] Working fewer than 35 hours per week.

Source: U.S. Bureau of Labor Statistics, *Characteristics of Minimum Wage Workers: 2021*, April 2022. See also <www.bls.gov/cps/earnings.htm#minwage>.

Table 688. Earnings by Sex and Women's Earnings as a Percent of Men's Earnings by Occupation: 2017 and 2019

[Median earnings in inflation-adjusted dollars for the full-time, year round civilian employed population age 16 years and over. Estimates subject to sampling variability. Based on the American Community Survey]

Occupation	2017 Median earnings 2017 inflation-adjusted — Female	Male	Women's earnings as a percent of men's earnings	2018 Median earnings 2018 inflation-adjusted — Female	Male	Women's earnings as a percent of men's earnings	2019 Median earnings 2019 inflation-adjusted — Female	Male	Women's earnings as a percent of men's earnings
Total	41,512	51,421	80.7	42,295	52,144	81.1	43,394	53,544	81.0
Management, business, science, and arts	56,743	77,953	72.8	58,498	80,405	72.8	60,523	81,524	74.2
Management, business, and financial	61,683	81,395	75.8	62,477	82,285	75.9	65,379	85,162	76.8
Management	64,266	83,387	77.1	64,685	85,289	75.8	66,767	87,792	76.1
Business and financial operations	59,584	75,902	78.5	61,601	79,998	77.0	62,437	80,061	78.0
Computer, engineering, and science	71,502	84,802	84.3	72,103	85,843	84.0	75,030	88,755	84.5
Computer and mathematical	75,555	87,012	86.8	75,914	89,396	84.9	77,356	91,377	84.7
Architecture and engineering	72,047	83,593	86.2	73,701	85,119	86.6	76,547	87,639	87.3
Life, physical, and social science	62,345	71,799	86.8	63,226	71,923	87.9	66,846	75,732	88.3
Education, legal, community service, arts, and media	48,245	60,609	79.6	49,995	61,666	81.1	50,476	61,996	81.4
Community and social service	44,800	47,178	95.0	45,904	48,773	94.1	47,043	49,699	94.7
Legal	67,050	122,231	54.9	69,361	126,800	54.7	71,530	130,503	54.8
Education, training, and library	47,033	57,802	81.4	48,123	60,158	80.0	48,833	60,576	80.6
Arts, design, entertainment, sports, and media	50,300	57,128	88.0	51,939	60,227	86.2	52,040	60,198	86.4
Healthcare practitioners and technical	60,334	80,092	75.3	60,940	81,376	74.9	62,299	85,126	73.2
Health diagnosing and treating practitioners and other technical	70,039	102,039	68.6	71,232	106,777	66.7	72,382	111,696	64.8
Health technologists and technicians	41,031	46,933	87.4	41,030	50,212	81.7	42,088	50,138	83.9
Service	25,558	33,232	76.9	26,372	35,028	75.3	27,100	35,657	76.0
Healthcare support	29,262	32,119	91.1	29,172	32,025	91.1	30,163	32,452	92.9
Protective service	41,728	55,080	75.8	42,186	55,696	75.7	42,869	57,824	74.1
Fire fighting and prevention, and other protective service workers including supervisors	35,044	45,068	77.8	36,261	45,951	78.9	35,729	46,567	76.7
Law enforcement workers including supervisors	49,793	62,220	80.0	50,133	63,451	79.0	52,376	66,716	78.5
Food preparation and serving related	21,710	26,046	83.4	22,344	26,893	83.1	23,440	27,441	85.4
Building and grounds cleaning and maintenance	22,449	31,124	72.1	23,483	31,697	74.1	24,196	31,831	76.0
Personal care and service	24,682	31,141	79.3	26,103	34,453	75.8	27,066	33,951	79.7
Sales and office	36,103	47,360	76.2	37,068	50,679	73.1	37,229	50,536	73.7
Sales and related	35,512	52,335	67.9	36,519	54,754	66.7	36,458	54,461	66.9
Office and administrative support	36,261	40,709	89.1	37,220	44,296	84.0	37,457	43,475	86.2
Natural resources, construction, and maintenance	31,725	42,203	75.2	33,877	43,592	77.7	32,398	45,682	70.9
Farming, fishing, and forestry	21,200	30,115	70.4	22,783	31,411	72.5	23,252	31,640	73.5
Construction and extraction	35,760	41,422	86.3	37,272	42,023	88.7	35,282	43,525	81.1
Installation, maintenance, and repair	41,113	47,168	87.2	42,132	48,691	86.5	41,472	50,347	82.4
Production, transportation, and material moving	28,993	40,690	71.3	30,009	41,004	73.2	30,303	41,468	73.1
Production	29,317	41,565	70.5	30,617	42,766	71.6	30,856	43,346	71.2
Transportation	31,941	44,173	72.3	32,858	46,008	71.4	32,462	46,894	69.2
Material moving	25,935	31,790	81.6	26,535	31,792	83.5	26,999	32,305	83.6

Source: U.S. Census Bureau, 2018 and 2019 American Community Survey, B24022, "Sex by Occupation and Median Earnings in the Past 12 Months (in 2018 and 2019 Inflation-Adjusted Dollars) for the Full-time, Year-Round Civilian Employed Population 16 Years and Over," <data.census.gov>, accessed December 2020.

Table 689. Median Earnings of College Graduates by Age, Sex, and Occupation: 2019

[In dollars. Estimated annual earnings of the full-time, year-round civilian employed population aged 25 to 64 with a bachelor's degree or higher level of education. Data are from the 2019 American Community Survey. Based on a sample and subject to sampling variability; see text, Section 1 and Appendix III]

Occupation	Total	Sex		Age			
		Male	Female	25 to 34 years old	35 to 44 years old	45 to 54 years old	55 to 64 years old
Total...............	**74,010**	**86,370**	**63,860**	**58,330**	**78,740**	**86,240**	**87,060**
Management, business, science, and arts..............	80,670	95,950	69,630	62,100	83,500	92,470	96,920
Management, business, and financial.................	90,930	102,200	77,960	66,540	93,650	104,800	106,800
Management............................	100,200	112,300	82,400	68,330	100,600	113,700	117,400
Business and financial operations.................	80,290	90,160	72,140	65,440	84,430	92,320	94,060
Computer, engineering, and science..................	95,290	100,300	82,410	76,430	100,500	110,100	111,000
Computer and mathematical.....................	99,010	101,400	87,150	81,320	101,700	110,900	107,000
Architecture and engineering.................	98,620	100,500	87,540	78,930	101,400	112,700	120,300
Life, physical, and social science..................	76,670	81,810	71,710	55,830	82,420	96,270	101,200
Education, legal, community service, arts, and media.............	59,000	66,900	55,350	48,130	61,070	66,160	69,430
Community and social service........................	51,490	52,670	51,000	44,540	53,410	57,000	57,360
Legal............................	114,700	137,200	93,460	79,020	117,100	134,800	145,400
Educational instruction and library....................	55,780	61,690	53,620	45,600	57,170	62,410	66,140
Arts, design, entertainment, sports, and media......	62,890	66,800	60,790	52,350	71,170	76,110	71,170
Healthcare practitioners and technical.................	81,940	111,300	76,640	65,690	90,270	95,130	99,250
Service...................................	45,350	55,300	36,430	39,730	51,350	52,460	42,490
Healthcare support........................	36,070	38,760	35,550	32,910	37,850	39,070	37,070
Protective service........................	72,970	76,720	60,790	56,410	80,590	91,100	76,030
Food preparation and serving related................	31,920	35,870	30,420	31,090	35,700	31,450	33,550
Building and grounds cleaning and maintenance...	36,400	41,250	28,300	32,300	37,280	37,230	37,400
Personal care and service.......................	37,080	41,820	35,180	35,600	39,710	38,460	39,770
Sales and office............................	57,400	71,780	49,750	47,190	62,150	67,260	62,800
Sales and related..........................	75,290	82,660	61,330	57,540	82,090	90,120	81,620
Office and administrative support.................	47,200	53,170	45,120	41,410	50,280	52,010	51,640
Natural resources, construction, and maintenance....	52,200	52,440	47,930	46,060	55,950	60,400	57,030
Farming, fishing, and forestry..........................	40,480	41,710	33,340	33,010	42,390	50,510	40,960
Construction and extraction.......................	51,470	51,630	47,140	46,890	53,920	56,210	52,330
Installation, maintenance, and repair................	57,590	58,490	55,490	47,070	60,690	65,060	65,600
Production, transportation, and material moving.....	48,720	51,430	39,380	41,740	51,000	50,960	51,450
Production..........................	50,570	53,700	40,690	45,590	52,630	51,860	51,290
Transportation and material moving..................	46,630	50,240	36,900	38,720	49,490	50,120	51,610
Transportation.........................	53,620	56,470	42,470	47,350	53,380	57,180	60,980
Material moving.........................	35,350	36,800	31,460	31,040	37,260	38,480	37,540

Source: U.S. Census Bureau, Industry and Occupation, "Detailed Occupation by Sex Education Age Earnings: ACS 2019," <www.census.gov/data/tables/2022/demo/acs-2019.html>, accessed August 2022.

Table 690. Workers' Earnings by Certification and License Status and Selected Characteristics: 2021

[In dollars, unless otherwise noted (114,316 represents 114,316,000). Data shown for wage and salary workers aged 16 years old and over, unless otherwise noted. Excludes self-employed workers. Certifications are issued by a non-governmental certification body and convey that an individual has the knowledge or skill to perform a specific job. A license is awarded by a government agency and conveys a legal authority to work in an occupation. For definition of median, see Guide to Tabular Presentation]

Characteristic	Full-time wage and salary workers (1,000)	Median weekly earnings				
			With a certification or license [1]			Without a certification or license
		Total	Total	Certification only	With a license [2]	
Total workers, 16 years old and over....	**114,316**	**998**	**1,229**	**1,288**	**1,223**	**931**
AGE						
16 to 24 years old.............................	10,392	623	734	740	733	615
25 to 54 years old.............................	79,463	1,045	1,239	1,309	1,233	979
55 years old and over.........................	24,461	1,102	1,346	1,407	1,340	1,012
SEX						
Men............................	62,928	1,097	1,357	1,400	1,352	1,017
Women............................	51,388	912	1,135	1,150	1,134	829
RACE/ETHNICITY						
White............................	87,738	1,018	1,250	1,297	1,246	949
Black or African American.......................	14,740	801	1,009	1,075	1,003	764
Asian............................	7,780	1,328	1,483	1,736	1,470	1,253
Hispanic or Latino..........................	20,841	777	1,040	1,017	1,045	742
EDUCATIONAL ATTAINMENT						
Workers, 25 years old and over...............	103,924	1,057	1,257	1,332	1,251	987
Less than a high school diploma.............	6,033	626	765	756	768	621
High school graduates, no college [3].........	24,860	809	937	995	928	796
Some college or associate degree..........	25,824	925	1,002	1,018	999	900
Bachelor's degree and higher................	47,207	1,452	1,488	1,674	1,472	1,433

[1] A person may have more than one certification or license. [2] Persons with a license may also have a certification. [3] Includes persons with a high school diploma or equivalent.

Source: U.S. Bureau of Labor Statistics, "Labor Force Statistics from the Current Population Survey," <www.bls.gov/cps/certifications-and-licenses.htm>, accessed April 2022.

Table 691. Average Hours Spent Per Day on Primary Activities by Married Mothers and Fathers by Employment Status: 2015 to 2019

[Data are shown for households with own children under age 18. Data are averages for the 2015-2019 period and cover an individual's main activity. Does not include secondary activities done simultaneously]

Activity	Both spouses work full time		Mother employed part time and father employed full time		Mother not employed and father employed full time	
	Mothers	Fathers	Mothers	Fathers	Mothers	Fathers
Total, all activities...........................	24.00	24.00	24.00	24.00	24.00	24.00
Personal care activities.........................	9.20	8.63	9.21	8.60	9.59	8.90
Sleeping..	8.37	8.04	8.49	7.99	8.93	8.27
Household activities.............................	1.88	1.37	2.71	1.30	3.82	1.00
Housework.......................................	0.73	0.27	1.05	0.22	1.60	0.16
Food preparation and cleanup..................	0.83	0.42	1.22	0.41	1.75	0.30
Lawn and garden care..........................	0.05	0.24	0.08	0.23	0.11	0.19
Purchasing goods and services.................	0.49	0.34	0.56	0.29	0.64	0.35
Grocery shopping...............................	0.14	0.07	0.17	0.05	0.22	0.07
Consumer goods purchases, except grocery shopping........	0.27	0.21	0.30	0.20	0.34	0.22
Caring for and helping household members.................	1.43	0.94	1.97	0.89	2.73	0.88
Caring for and helping household children..................	1.41	0.91	1.95	0.88	2.71	0.86
Physical care...................................	0.61	0.31	0.71	0.29	1.01	0.23
Education-related activities....................	0.10	0.07	0.23	0.04	0.28	0.06
Reading to/with children.......................	0.05	0.03	0.08	0.04	0.09	0.03
Playing/doing hobbies with children...........	0.28	0.27	0.39	0.28	0.63	0.33
Working and work-related activities [1]	5.10	6.14	2.92	6.33	0.05	6.37
Working [1]	5.08	6.11	2.88	6.31	0.02	6.35
Leisure and sports...............................	2.86	3.60	3.19	3.45	3.71	3.31
Socializing and communicating.................	0.57	0.57	0.65	0.61	0.81	0.71
Watching television.............................	1.45	1.98	1.45	1.81	1.84	1.68
Participating in sports, exercise, and recreation.................	0.19	0.28	0.25	0.33	0.25	0.25
Travel..	1.40	1.41	1.40	1.45	1.17	1.45
Travel related to caring for/helping household children........	0.26	0.16	0.33	0.14	0.32	0.09
Other activities, not elsewhere classified..................	1.63	1.57	2.04	1.70	2.28	1.74

[1] Estimates include a small amount of work time done by persons who do not meet the American Time Use Survey definition of employed.

Source: U.S. Bureau of Labor Statistics, "American Time Use Survey," <www.bls.gov/tus/#tables>, accessed August 2020.

Table 692. Workers With Access to Unmarried Domestic Partner Benefits for Partners of Same and Opposite Sex by Selected Characteristics: 2011 to 2021

[In percent. All workers = 100 percent. As of March. For employees in private industry. Based on National Compensation Survey (NCS). See headnote, Table 695, and Appendix III. See Table 166 for data on health benefit program participation]

Characteristic	Defined benefit retirement survivor benefits for partners						Healthcare benefits for partners					
	Same sex			Opposite sex			Same sex			Opposite sex		
	2011	2020	2021	2011	2020	2021	2011	2020	2021	2011	2020	2021
Total........................	7	10	9	7	9	9	29	43	43	25	40	41
WORKER CHARACTERISTICS												
Management, professional, and related......................	11	16	15	10	16	15	46	61	62	38	56	59
Service.......................	3	4	3	3	3	3	17	24	23	14	24	23
Sales and office...............	8	9	9	7	9	9	30	44	43	26	42	41
Natural resources, construction, and maintenance.................	8	9	8	7	8	7	22	38	38	18	36	35
Production, transportation, and material moving................	8	10	9	7	9	8	25	39	41	21	35	38
Full-time [1]...................	9	11	11	8	11	10	36	51	52	31	47	49
Part-time [1]..................	4	5	5	4	5	5	9	18	16	8	18	16
Union [2]......................	25	37	34	22	31	30	46	65	66	31	57	58
Nonunion [2]..................	6	7	7	5	7	7	28	41	41	24	39	39
AVERAGE HOURLY WAGE [3]												
Lowest 25 percent (under $15.00)........	2	2	2	2	3	2	11	20	20	9	20	20
Lowest 10 percent (under $11.74)........	1	1	1	1	1	1	6	14	12	4	14	12
Second 25 percent ($15.00 to $20.00)....	5	7	7	5	7	7	26	41	42	23	39	41
Third 25 percent ($20.00 to $32.20).......	9	11	11	8	10	10	35	49	50	30	46	47
Highest 25 percent ($32.20 and over).......	15	21	19	14	20	19	50	67	66	41	60	61
Highest 10 percent ($50.78 and over)...	16	24	22	15	22	21	59	75	76	49	67	69
ESTABLISHMENT CHARACTERISTICS												
1 to 99 workers................	3	4	4	3	4	4	18	29	30	16	29	30
100 or more workers...........	12	16	17	12	15	16	42	58	60	34	53	55
Goods producing [4]...........	6	9	8	6	8	8	27	42	43	24	40	41
Service producing [4]..........	8	10	9	7	10	9	30	43	43	25	40	41

[1] Employees are classified as working either a full-time or part-time schedule based on the definition used by each establishment. [2] See footnote 6, Table 695. [3] The National Compensation Survey—Benefits program presents wage data in percentiles rather than dollar amounts; 2021 average wages shown here; for calculation detail, see "Technical Note" in source. [4] See Table 667 for composition of goods- and service-producing industries.

Source: U.S. Bureau of Labor Statistics, *National Compensation Survey: Employee Benefits in the United States, March 2021*, September 2021, and earlier reports. See also <www.bls.gov/ncs/ebs/benefits/2021/home.htm>.

Table 693. Employer Costs for Employee Compensation Per Hour Worked: 2021

[In dollars. As of December. Based on the National Compensation Survey (NCS). See Appendix III]

Compensation component	Total civilian workers	State and local government workers	Private industry workers						
			Total	Goods producing [1]	Service providing [2]	Union workers	Nonunion workers	1–99 workers	100 workers or more
Total compensation...............	**40.35**	**54.96**	**38.07**	**41.67**	**37.37**	**51.74**	**36.83**	**31.69**	**46.19**
Wages and salaries.................	27.83	34.09	26.86	28.21	26.59	31.09	26.47	23.53	31.09
Total benefits......................	12.52	20.87	11.22	13.47	10.78	20.65	10.36	8.17	15.10
Paid leave [3].......................	3.01	4.07	2.85	2.69	2.88	3.71	2.77	2.00	3.93
Vacation........................	1.47	1.55	1.46	1.36	1.48	1.89	1.42	1.00	2.04
Holiday.........................	0.89	1.15	0.84	0.92	0.83	1.09	0.82	0.63	1.12
Sick............................	0.48	1.05	0.39	0.30	0.41	0.57	0.38	0.28	0.54
Supplemental pay [3]...............	1.21	0.52	1.32	1.82	1.22	1.86	1.27	0.83	1.94
Overtime [4]......................	0.34	0.24	0.36	0.78	0.27	0.98	0.30	0.27	0.47
Insurance [3].......................	3.34	6.31	2.87	3.65	2.72	6.78	2.52	2.02	3.96
Health insurance................	3.17	6.15	2.70	3.41	2.56	6.36	2.37	1.91	3.70
Retirement and savings............	2.08	6.97	1.32	1.92	1.20	4.51	1.03	0.76	2.04
Defined benefit.................	1.26	6.48	0.45	0.87	0.36	3.00	0.21	0.21	0.74
Defined contributions............	0.82	0.49	0.88	1.05	0.84	1.51	0.82	0.55	1.30
Legally required..................	2.88	2.99	2.86	3.39	2.76	3.80	2.77	2.56	3.24
Social Security and Medicare.......	2.27	2.35	2.25	2.42	2.22	2.66	2.22	1.96	2.63
Social Security [5]..............	1.81	1.79	1.81	1.96	1.78	2.13	1.78	1.57	2.11
Medicare.......................	0.46	0.56	0.45	0.47	0.44	0.53	0.44	0.38	0.53
Federal unemployment...........	0.02	([6])	0.03	0.02	0.03	0.02	0.03	0.03	0.02
State unemployment.............	0.12	0.07	0.13	0.16	0.12	0.16	0.13	0.13	0.12
Workers' compensation..........	0.47	0.57	0.45	0.79	0.38	0.95	0.40	0.44	0.46

[1] Based on the 2012 North American Industry Classification System (NAICS). See text, this section. Includes mining, construction, and manufacturing. Excludes the agriculture, forestry, farming, and hunting sector. [2] Based on the 2012 NAICS. Includes utilities; wholesale and retail trade; transportation and warehousing; information; finance and insurance; real estate and rental and leasing; professional and technical services; management of companies and enterprises, administrative and waste services; education services; health care and social assistance; arts, entertainment, and recreation; accommodations and food services; and other services, except public administration. [3] Includes costs for other items not shown separately. [4] Includes premium pay for work in addition to regular work schedule, such as, overtime, weekends, and holidays. [5] Comprises the Old-Age, Survivors, and Disability Insurance Program (OASDI). [6] Cost per hour worked is $0.01 or less.

Source: U.S. Bureau of Labor Statistics, *Employer Costs for Employee Compensation—December 2021*, USDL 22-0469, March 2022. See also <www.bls.gov/ncs/ect/home.htm>.

Table 694. Workers With Access to Retirement and Health Care Benefits by Selected Characteristics: 2021

[In percent. All workers = 100 percent. As of March. For employees in private industry. Based on National Compensation Survey (NCS). See headnote, Table 695, and Appendix III. See Table 166 for data on health benefit program participation]

Characteristic	Retirement benefits			Healthcare benefits			
	All plans [1]	Defined benefit [2]	Defined contribution [2]	Medical care	Dental care	Vision care	Outpatient prescription drug coverage
Total......................	**68**	**15**	**65**	**70**	**40**	**26**	**69**
WORKER CHARACTERISTICS							
Management, professional, and related...............	86	22	84	88	59	35	87
Service................................	40	5	37	44	19	13	43
Sales and office........................	73	14	71	67	37	23	66
Natural resources, construction, and maintenance........................	65	19	58	76	38	26	74
Production, transportation, and material moving......	72	19	66	77	46	32	75
Full-time [3]...........................	78	18	74	86	50	32	84
Part-time [3]...........................	41	7	38	23	11	8	23
Union [4]..............................	93	64	61	95	69	55	92
Nonunion [4]..........................	66	11	66	68	38	23	67
AVERAGE HOURLY WAGE [5]							
Lowest 25 percent (under $15.00)......................	44	4	42	39	15	10	39
Lowest 10 percent (under $11.74).......	32	2	31	26	8	6	25
Second 25 percent ($15.00 to $20.00).............	68	13	64	71	39	25	69
Third 25 percent ($20.00 to $32.20)...................	79	18	75	85	50	31	83
Highest 25 percent ($32.20 and over).................	90	30	85	93	64	40	92
Highest 10 percent ($50.78 and over)...............	92	31	90	95	70	46	93
ESTABLISHMENT CHARACTERISTICS							
1 to 99 workers.......................	56	7	54	58	27	18	56
100 or more workers..................	85	27	79	86	57	36	85
Goods producing [6].................	76	20	73	85	50	35	82
Service producing [6].................	67	15	64	67	39	24	66

[1] Employees may have access to defined benefit and/or defined contribution plans. Total excludes duplication. [2] A defined benefit plan is a retirement plan that uses a specific, predetermined formula to calculate the amount of an employee's guaranteed future benefit. A defined contribution plan provides benefits based on employer and employee contributions to individual employee accounts and the rate of return on money invested; the retirement benefit depends on the account balance at retirement. [3] Employees are classified as working either a full-time or part-time schedule based on the definition used by each establishment. [4] See footnote 6, Table 695. [5] The National Compensation Survey—Benefits program presents wage data in percentiles rather than dollar amounts; for calculation detail, see "Technical Note" in source. [6] See Table 667 for composition of goods- and service-producing industries.

Source: U.S. Bureau of Labor Statistics, *National Compensation Survey: Employee Benefits in the United States, March 2021*, September 2021. See also <www.bls.gov/ncs/ebs/benefits/2021/home.htm>.

Table 695. Workers With Access to Selected Employee Benefits: 2021

[In percent. All workers = 100 percent. As of March. For employees in private industry. Based on National Compensation Survey (NCS). The NCS benefits survey obtained data from 6,007 private industry establishments of all sizes, representing approximately 114.5 million workers. Excludes agricultural establishments, private households, and the self-employed. An employee has access to a benefit plan if the plan is made available by the employer, regardless of whether the employee participates in the plan. See Appendix III. See also <www.bls.gov/ncs/ebs/national-compensation-survey-glossary-of-employee-benefit-terms.htm> for glossary of terms]

Characteristic	Leave benefits						Quality of life benefits			Nonproduction bonuses	
	Paid holidays	Paid sick leave	Paid vacation	Paid jury duty leave	Family leave [1] Paid	Family leave [1] Unpaid	Employer assistance for child care [2]	Flexible work-place [3]	Subsidized commuting	All non-production bonuses [4]	End of year bonus
Total	81	77	79	52	23	89	10	8	8	41	12
WORKER CHARACTERISTIC											
Management, professional, and related occupations	92	93	91	74	37	92	18	18	15	50	16
Service occupations	58	59	57	27	13	81	10	1	6	24	6
Sales and office occupations	84	78	80	52	25	90	7	8	7	43	10
Natural resources, construction, and maintenance occupations	85	73	86	42	15	88	5	2	4	43	16
Production, transportation, and material moving occupations	88	73	85	54	13	90	5	2	3	42	11
Full-time [5]	92	87	92	63	27	91	12	10	9	47	14
Part-time [5]	50	48	40	21	11	81	6	2	4	22	6
Union [6]	90	87	90	71	19	95	15	2	9	31	3
Nonunion [6]	81	76	78	50	23	88	10	8	8	41	12
AVERAGE HOURLY WAGE [7]											
Lowest 25 percent (under $15.00)	60	52	56	27	12	81	5	1	3	27	6
Lowest 10 percent (under $11.74)	46	33	43	18	6	78	5	1	3	18	4
Second 25 percent ($15.00 to $20.00)	85	81	83	53	21	90	8	4	6	40	12
Third 25 percent ($20.00 to $32.20)	91	88	91	59	25	91	11	9	9	45	13
Highest 25 percent ($32.20 and over)	94	94	94	75	37	94	19	19	16	53	17
Highest 10 percent ($50.78 and over)	95	95	95	81	43	96	25	25	21	58	19
ESTABLISHMENT CHARACTERISTICS											
1 to 99 workers	74	70	72	39	17	84	6	6	5	36	14
100 or more workers	91	86	89	69	31	95	17	10	12	47	9
Goods producing [8]	91	76	90	52	18	89	8	6	4	50	17
Service producing [8]	79	77	77	52	24	88	11	8	9	38	10
GEOGRAPHIC AREA [9]											
New England	80	85	76	57	23	87	12	5	14	40	13
Middle Atlantic	80	79	76	60	31	88	13	8	12	37	11
South Atlantic	83	73	81	52	21	85	12	8	8	42	13
East South Central	87	67	83	58	19	87	6	6	8	40	12
West South Central	79	69	79	53	22	90	8	8	6	46	16
East North Central	82	71	80	56	21	91	10	8	6	42	9
West North Central	77	71	79	48	20	89	9	8	4	41	9
Mountain	83	76	81	46	23	91	9	6	9	43	13
Pacific	82	95	79	42	24	90	10	8	12	36	10

[1] Some workers may have access to both types of plans. [2] A workplace program that provides for either the full or partial cost of caring for an employee's children in a nursery, day care center, or a babysitter in facilities either on or off the employer's premises. [3] Permits employees to work an agreed-upon portion of their work schedule at home or at some other approved location. [4] Includes cash profit-sharing, employee recognition, end-of-year, holiday, payment in lieu of benefits, longevity, referral, and all other bonuses. [5] Employees are classified as working either a full-time or part-time schedule based on the definition used by each establishment. [6] Union workers are those whose wages are determined through collective bargaining. [7] The National Compensation Survey—Benefits program presents wage data in percentiles rather than dollar amounts; see "Technical Note" in source. [8] See Table 667, for composition of goods- and service-producing industries. [9] For composition of census divisions, see inside front cover.

Source: U.S. Bureau of Labor Statistics, *National Compensation Survey: Employee Benefits in the United States, March 2021*, September 2021. See also <www.bls.gov/ncs/benefits/2021/home.htm>.

Table 696. Industries With the Highest Total Case Incidence Rates for Nonfatal Injuries and Illnesses: 2020

[Rates per 100 full-time employees. Private industry unless otherwise noted. Incidence rates refer to any Occupational Safety & Health Administration (OSHA)-recordable occupational injury or illness, whether or not it resulted in days away from work, job transfer, or restriction. Incidence rates were calculated as: number of injuries and illnesses divided by total hours worked by all employees during the year multiplied by 200,000 as base for 100 full-time equivalent workers (working 40 hours per week, 50 weeks per year)]

Industry	NAICS code [1]	Incidence rate	Industry	NAICS code [1]	Incidence rate
All industries, including state and local government [2]	(X)	2.9	Psychiatric and substance abuse hospitals	6222	7.9
Nursing care facilities (skilled)	6231	15.7	General medical and surgical hospitals	6221	7.7
Nursing and residential care facilities [3]	623	13.7	Travel trailer and camper manufacturing	336214	7.5
Nursing and residential care facilities [4]	623	10.5	Couriers and express delivery services	4921	7.5
Continuing care retirement communities & assisted living facilities for the elderly	6233	10.2	Animal (except poultry) slaughtering	311611	7.4
Skiing facilities	71392	10.0	Meat processed from carcasses	311612	7.3
Correctional institutions [3]	92214	9.2	Iron foundries	331511	7.3
Hospitals [3]	622	8.9	Ornamental & architectural metal work manufacturing	332323	7.3
Veterinary services	54194	8.8	Perishable prepared food manufacturing	311991	7.2
Ambulance services	62191	8.5	Noncurrent-carrying wiring device manufacturing	335932	7.1
Other animal production	1129	8.4	Pet and pet supplies stores	45391	7.1
Aluminum foundries (except die-casting)	331524	8.4	Rendering and meat byproduct processing	311613	7.0
Manufactured home (mobile home) manufacturing	321991	8.1	Armored car services	561613	6.9
			Hospitals [4]	622	6.9
			Other residential care facilities	6239	6.9

X Not applicable. [1] Based on the North American Industry Classification System, 2017 (NAICS). See text, this section. [2] Excludes farms with fewer than 11 employees. [3] State government. [4] Local government.

Source: U.S. Bureau of Labor Statistics, Injuries, Illnesses, and Fatalities, Survey of Occupational Injuries and Illnesses Data, "Supplemental News Release Tables," <www.bls.gov/iif/soii-data.htm>, accessed January 2022.

Table 697. Nonfatal Occupational Injuries and Illnesses by Industry: 2019 and 2020

[3,496.7 represents 3,496,700. Rates per 100 full-time employees. Except as noted, data refer to any Occupational Safety and Health Administration (OSHA) recordable occupational injury or illness, whether or not it resulted in days away from work, job transfer, or restriction. Incidence rates were calculated as: number of injuries and illnesses divided by total hours worked by all employees during the year multiplied by 200,000 as base for 100 full-time equivalent workers (working 40 hours per week, 50 weeks per year)]

Industry	2017 NAICS code [1]	Number of cases (1,000) 2019	Number of cases (1,000) 2020	Incidence rate of cases 2019	Incidence rate of cases 2020
Total	(X)	**3,496.7**	**3,229.2**	**3.0**	**2.9**
Private industry [2]	(X)	**2,814.0**	**2,654.7**	**2.8**	**2.7**
Agriculture, forestry, fishing, hunting [2]	11	50.9	45.9	5.2	4.6
Mining [3]	21	9.4	7.5	1.2	1.2
Construction	23	200.1	174.1	2.8	2.5
Manufacturing	31–33	421.4	373.3	3.3	3.1
Wholesale trade	42	153.6	132.2	2.7	2.4
Retail trade	44–45	395.7	341.1	3.4	3.1
Transportation and warehousing [4]	48–49	227.9	206.9	4.4	4.0
Utilities	22	12.0	8.4	2.2	1.5
Information	51	31.6	19.6	1.2	0.8
Finance and insurance	52	26.1	17.4	0.5	0.3
Real estate and rental and leasing	53	46.2	41.8	2.3	2.1
Professional, scientific, and technical services	54	72.8	59.5	0.8	0.7
Management of companies and enterprises	55	16.9	14.9	0.7	0.6
Administrative and support & waste management and remediation services	56	(NA)	103.4	(NA)	2.0
Educational services	61	38.6	22.5	2.0	1.1
Health care and social assistance	62	575.2	806.2	3.8	5.5
Arts, entertainment, and recreation	71	56.4	34.3	4.0	3.0
Accommodation and food services	72	288.7	191.0	3.2	2.6
Other services, except public administration	81	64.6	54.7	2.0	1.8
State and local government [2]	(X)	**682.7**	**574.5**	**4.6**	**3.9**
State government	(X)	138.7	131.1	3.5	3.3
Local government	(X)	544.0	443.4	5.0	4.2

X Not applicable. NA Not available. [1] North American Industry Classification System, 2017; see text, this section. [2] Excludes farms with fewer than 11 employees. [3] Data for Mining (2012 NAICS Sector 21) include establishments not governed by the Mine Safety and Health Administration rules and reporting, such as those in Oil and Gas Extraction and related support activities. Data for mining operators in coal, metal, and nonmetal mining are provided to BLS by the Mine Safety and Health Administration, U.S. Department of Labor. Independent mining contractors are excluded from the coal, metal, and nonmetal mining industries. These data do not reflect the changes the Occupational Safety and Health Administration made to its recordkeeping requirements effective January 1, 2002; therefore, estimates for these industries are not comparable to estimates in other industries. [4] Data for employers in railroad transportation are provided to BLS by the Federal Railroad Administration, U.S. Department of Transportation.

Source: U.S. Bureau of Labor Statistics, "Employer-Reported Workplace Injuries and Illnesses – 2020, Supplemental Files, Summary Tables," <www.bls.gov/news.release/osh.toc.htm>, accessed November 2021.

Table 698. Fatal Work Injuries by Event or Exposure: 2020

[For the 50 states and the District of Columbia. Based on the Census of Fatal Occupational Injuries. For details, see source]

Event or exposure	Number of fatalities	Percent distribution	Event or exposure	Number of fatalities	Percent distribution
Total [1]	**4,764**	**100.0**	Fires and explosions	71	1.5
Violence & other injuries [1]	705	14.8	Falls, slips, trips	805	16.9
Homicides [1]	392	8.2	Exposure to harmful substances or environments [1]	672	14.1
Shooting	304	6.4	Exposure to electricity	126	2.6
Stabbing, cutting, slashing, piercing	50	1.0	Exposure to caustic, noxious or allergenic substances	448	9.4
Self-inflicted injury, intentional (suicide)	259	5.4	Oxygen deficiency	36	0.8
Transportation incidents [1]	1,778	37.3	Contacts with objects and equipment [1]	716	15.0
Aircraft incidents	80	1.7	Struck by object or equipment [1]	468	9.8
Railway incidents	32	0.7	Struck by falling object or equipment	217	4.6
Pedestrians struck by vehicle [2]	330	6.9	Struck by flying object	37	0.8
Water vehicle incidents	74	1.6	Caught in or compressed by equipment or objects	142	3.0
Roadway incident with motor vehicle [1]	1,038	21.8			
Collision between vehicles	537	11.3			
Noncollision accidents	196	4.1			
Nonroadway accident involving motor vehicle	206	4.3	Caught in or crushed in collapsing materials	93	2.0

[1] Includes other causes, not shown separately. [2] Including mobile equipment.

Source: U.S. Bureau of Labor Statistics, "Census of Fatal Occupational Injuries—Current Data," <www.bls.gov/iif/oshcfoi1.htm>, accessed February 2022.

Table 699. Worker Fatalities on the Job by Industry and Occupation: 2020

[Excludes homicides and suicides]

Industry group	Deaths Number	Deaths Rate [1]	Occupations with highest fatal work injury rates	Deaths Number	Deaths Rate [1]
Total	**4,764**	**3.4**	Fishing and hunting workers	42	132.1
			Logging workers	42	91.7
			Roofers	88	47.0
Agriculture [2]	511	21.5	Helpers, construction trades	19	43.3
Mining [3]	78	10.5	Aircraft pilots and flight engineers	50	34.3
Construction	1,008	10.2	Refuse and recyclable material collectors	30	33.1
Manufacturing	340	2.3	Structural iron and steel workers	16	32.5
Wholesale trade	155	4.6	Driver/sales workers and truck drivers	887	25.8
Retail trade	275	2.0	Underground mining machine operators	10	21.6
Transportation & warehousing	805	13.4	Farmers, ranchers, and other agricultural managers	207	20.9
Utilities	19	1.8	Grounds maintenance workers	202	19.4
Information	31	1.3	Electrical power-line installers and repairers	26	18.6
Financial activities [4]	93	0.9	Construction laborers	308	18.1
Professional & technical services [4]	62	0.5	Construction equipment operators	65	17.6
Educational & health services	145	0.7	Miscellaneous agricultural workers	144	16.6
Leisure & hospitality [4]	219	2.5	First-line supervisors of landscaping, lawn service, & groundskeeping workers	37	15.3
Other services [5]	188	3.3			
Government	415	1.8	First-line supervisors of mechanics, installers, & repairers	35	14.4

[1] The rate represents the number of fatal occupational injuries per 100,000 full-time equivalent workers. [2] Includes forestry, fishing, and hunting. [3] Includes oil and gas extraction. [4] For composition of industry, see Table 667. [5] Excludes public service administration.

Source: U.S. Bureau of Labor Statistics, Census of Fatal Occupational Injuries, "Fatal Injury Rates," <stats.bls.gov/iif/oshcfoi1.htm>, accessed January 2022.

Table 700. Nonfatal Occupational Injury and Illness Cases in Private Industry by Type of Injury or Illness and Days Away from Work: 2020

[1,176.3 represents 1,176,300. Covers work-related injuries and illnesses involving one or more days of missed work]

Type of work-related injury or illness	All cases	1 day	2 days	3-5 days	6-10 days	11-20 days	21-30 days	31 days or more	Median number of days away from work
Total [1]	**1,176.3**	**100.2**	**80.8**	**152.0**	**215.7**	**265.7**	**89.4**	**272.6**	**12**
Traumatic injuries and disorders	767.3	95.8	75.8	131.4	89.3	86.3	51.8	236.9	10
Fractures	74.6	4.0	2.3	5.7	6.4	7.6	6.6	42.1	41
Sprains, strains, tears	266.5	25.6	23.3	43.9	32.9	31.5	19.5	89.8	13
Hernia	7.8	0.1	0.1	0.3	0.6	1.5	1.2	3.9	30
Concussions	13.5	1.2	1.8	3.2	2.2	1.7	0.9	2.6	6
Soreness, pain, hurt-nonspecified injury	150.5	17.8	14.2	28.2	17.0	16.3	9.4	47.6	10
Disease and disorders of body systems	10.3	0.8	0.7	1.4	1.2	1.2	0.9	4.0	20
Carpal tunnel syndrome	3.9	0.3	0.1	0.2	0.4	0.5	0.4	2.2	39
Disorders of the eye, adnexa, vision	0.6	0.1	0.2	0.2	0.1	0.1	–	(Z)	3
Infectious and parasitic diseases	390.5	2.4	3.6	18.0	124.2	176.3	36.1	30.0	13
Mental disorders or syndromes	2.0	0.1	0.1	0.2	0.2	0.2	0.3	1.0	30

– Represents zero. Z Less than 50 cases. [1] Total includes unclassified and ill-defined conditions.

Source: U.S. Bureau of Labor Statistics, Survey of Occupational Injuries and Illnesses, 2020 Resource Tables, "R.67. Detailed nature by number of days away from work," <stats.bls.gov/iif/oshcdnew2020.htm>, accessed April 2022.

Table 701. Labor Union Membership by Sector: 1990 to 2021

[16,740 represents 16,740,000. Annual averages of monthly figures. For wage and salary workers in agriculture and nonagricultural industries. Based on the Current Population Survey and subject to sampling error. For methodological details, see source]

Sector	1990	2000	2010	2015	2016	2017	2018	2019	2020	2021
TOTAL (1,000)										
Wage and salary workers:										
Union members..................	16,740	16,258	14,715	14,786	14,550	14,812	14,740	14,567	14,250	14,004
Covered by unions..............	19,058	17,944	16,290	16,433	16,265	16,436	16,374	16,375	15,936	15,795
Public sector workers:										
Union members.................	6,485	7,111	7,623	7,234	7,114	7,211	7,162	7,059	7,168	6,978
Covered by unions............	7,691	7,976	8,406	8,023	7,827	7,945	7,862	7,813	7,915	7,745
Private sector workers:										
Union members...............	10,255	9,148	7,092	7,552	7,436	7,600	7,578	7,508	7,082	7,026
Covered by unions............	11,366	9,969	7,884	8,410	8,438	8,491	8,512	8,562	8,021	8,050
PERCENT										
Wage and salary workers:										
Union members.................	16.1	13.5	11.9	11.1	10.7	10.7	10.5	10.3	10.8	10.3
Covered by unions..............	18.3	14.9	13.1	12.3	11.9	11.9	11.7	11.6	12.1	11.6
Public sector workers:										
Union members.................	36.5	37.5	36.2	35.2	34.4	34.4	33.9	33.6	34.8	33.9
Covered by unions............	43.3	42.0	40.0	39.0	37.9	37.9	37.2	37.2	38.4	37.6
Private sector workers:										
Union members...............	11.9	9.0	6.9	6.7	6.4	6.5	6.4	6.2	6.3	6.1
Covered by unions............	13.2	9.8	7.7	7.4	7.3	7.3	7.2	7.1	7.2	7.0

Source: *Union Membership and Coverage Database from the Current Population Survey*, accessed at <unionstats.com>, authored by Barry Hirsch of Georgia State University and David Macpherson of Trinity University. Copyright 2022.

Table 702. Labor Union Members by Selected Characteristics: 2021

[In units as indicated (136,393 represents 136,393,000). Annual averages of monthly data. Covers employed wage and salary workers 16 years old and over. Excludes self-employed workers whose businesses are incorporated and not incorporated. Based on Current Population Survey; see text, Section 1 and Appendix III]

Characteristic	Employed wage and salary workers			Median usual weekly earnings [3] (dollars)			
		Percent					
	Total (1,000)	Union members [1]	Repre- sented by union [2]	Total	Union members [1]	Repre- sented by union [2]	Not repre- sented by union
Total [4]...........................	**136,393**	**10.3**	**11.6**	**998**	**1,169**	**1,158**	**975**
SEX							
Men...........................	70,739	10.6	11.9	1,097	1,227	1,217	1,069
Women........................	65,654	9.9	11.3	912	1,104	1,086	884
AGE							
16 to 24 years old...............	18,083	4.2	5.3	623	757	744	617
25 to 34 years old...............	32,360	9.4	10.7	931	1,049	1,038	916
35 to 44 years old...............	29,260	11.4	12.8	1,131	1,264	1,252	1,107
45 to 54 years old...............	26,851	13.1	14.4	1,154	1,266	1,257	1,136
55 to 64 years old...............	22,210	12.1	13.6	1,132	1,224	1,224	1,111
65 years and over..............	7,629	8.7	9.8	994	1,083	1,093	980
RACE/ETHNICITY							
White [5]........................	104,921	10.3	11.6	1,018	1,199	1,182	996
Men...........................	55,408	10.6	11.9	1,125	1,257	1,248	1,097
Women........................	49,513	9.9	11.3	925	1,121	1,101	899
Black [5]........................	17,338	11.5	12.9	801	998	987	775
Men...........................	8,037	12.5	14.0	825	1,006	992	802
Women........................	9,300	10.6	11.9	776	988	980	752
Asian [5]........................	9,119	7.7	9.0	1,328	1,267	1,256	1,334
Men...........................	4,749	7.1	8.2	1,453	1,307	1,326	1,459
Women........................	4,369	8.4	9.8	1,141	1,248	1,218	1,132
Hispanic [6].....................	24,738	9.0	10.3	777	1,032	1,001	755
Men...........................	13,938	9.2	10.5	820	1,091	1,048	799
Women........................	10,799	8.7	10.0	718	949	924	699
INDUSTRY [7]							
Private sector....................	115,767	6.1	7.0	973	1,098	1,080	965
Mining.......................	561	5.7	6.0	1,317	(B)	(B)	1,315
Construction..................	8,157	12.6	13.6	966	1,344	1,322	922
Manufacturing................	14,134	7.7	8.5	1,033	1,016	1,015	1,036
Wholesale and retail trade.........	18,070	4.3	4.9	790	776	773	791
Transportation and utilities..........	7,057	15.4	16.8	973	1,199	1,170	934
Information...................	2,274	10.0	11.1	1,378	1,568	1,527	1,370
Financial activities.............	9,101	2.3	3.1	1,233	1,017	1,019	1,239
Professional and business services.......	15,374	2.2	2.9	1,241	1,023	1,017	1,249
Education and health services...........	22,891	7.9	9.2	982	1,140	1,134	966
Leisure and hospitality..................	11,208	2.2	2.7	650	752	756	645
Other services.....................	5,632	3.1	3.7	858	1,200	1,166	847
Public sector....................	20,626	33.9	37.6	1,133	1,237	1,229	1,055

B Base is less than 50,000. [1] Members of a labor union or an employee association similar to a labor union. [2] Members of a labor union or an employee association similar to a union as well as workers who report no union affiliation but whose jobs are covered by a union or an employee association contract. [3] For full-time employed wage and salary workers. [4] Includes other races not shown separately. Also includes a small number of multiple jobholders whose full- and part-time status cannot be determined for their principal job. [5] For persons in this race group only. [6] Persons of Hispanic origin may be of any race. [7] For composition of industries, see Table 667.

Source: U.S. Bureau of Labor Statistics, *Union Members—2021*, USDL 22-0079, January 2022. See also <www.bls.gov/news.release/union2.toc.htm>.

Table 703. Labor Union Membership by State: 2010 and 2021

[Annual averages of monthly figures (14,715.1 represents 14,715,100). For wage and salary workers in agriculture and nonagricultural industries. Data represent union members by place of residence. Based on the Current Population Survey and subject to sampling error. For methodological details, see source]

| State | Union members (1,000) | | Workers covered by unions (1,000) | | Percent of workers | | | | | |
| | | | | | Union members | | Covered by unions | | Private sector union members | |
	2010	2021	2010	2021	2010	2021	2010	2021	2010	2021
United States......	**14,715.1**	**14,003.6**	**16,289.5**	**15,795.4**	**11.9**	**10.3**	**13.1**	**11.6**	**6.9**	**6.1**
Alabama [1]............	183.3	114.5	202.8	133.2	10.1	5.9	11.2	6.9	5.7	4.0
Alaska................	67.6	46.0	73.0	50.3	22.9	15.7	24.8	17.2	11.2	7.5
Arizona [1]............	161.0	167.4	203.0	208.6	6.4	5.4	8.1	6.7	3.6	3.0
Arkansas [1]...........	43.6	45.5	58.6	51.4	4.0	3.9	5.4	4.4	2.7	3.3
California............	2,431.3	2,468.9	2,577.8	2,757.7	17.5	15.9	18.6	17.8	9.3	9.3
Colorado............	140.4	164.7	170.9	190.8	6.6	6.5	8.0	7.5	3.8	4.1
Connecticut.........	258.3	222.2	269.7	247.2	16.7	14.6	17.4	16.2	8.3	7.3
Delaware............	40.2	42.4	43.9	44.2	11.4	9.8	12.5	10.2	5.8	6.0
District of Columbia..	25.9	31.2	30.0	34.8	9.0	8.9	10.5	9.9	5.9	5.0
Florida [1]............	391.8	448.8	488.0	529.5	5.6	5.2	6.9	6.1	2.3	2.8
Georgia [1]............	153.3	210.8	191.3	255.4	4.0	4.8	5.0	5.8	2.5	2.8
Hawaii................	111.3	120.9	120.3	130.4	21.8	22.4	23.5	24.1	14.6	14.5
Idaho [1]................	41.5	35.7	50.1	42.2	7.1	4.7	8.6	5.5	3.6	3.0
Illinois................	843.8	752.1	891.2	818.3	15.5	13.9	16.4	15.2	9.5	8.6
Indiana [3]............	278.6	255.7	312.8	289.5	10.9	9.0	12.2	10.2	8.2	6.2
Iowa [1]................	158.2	92.8	191.8	117.7	11.4	6.5	13.8	8.3	7.1	4.1
Kansas [1]............	83.7	119.6	111.0	147.4	6.8	9.2	9.1	11.3	4.5	6.9
Kentucky [6]...........	146.5	124.9	166.1	169.3	8.9	7.2	10.1	9.7	7.2	6.3
Louisiana [1]...........	75.6	80.8	96.0	98.5	4.3	4.7	5.5	5.7	3.2	2.9
Maine................	62.9	69.6	70.7	82.8	11.6	12.4	13.0	14.7	5.1	5.9
Maryland............	296.1	294.0	328.8	331.4	11.6	10.9	12.9	12.3	6.1	5.5
Massachusetts.......	414.8	401.3	446.4	432.6	14.5	12.6	15.6	13.6	7.0	7.2
Michigan [3]............	627.3	538.7	658.7	619.0	16.5	13.3	17.3	15.3	11.1	9.1
Minnesota............	384.6	416.3	397.3	446.4	15.6	15.9	16.1	17.1	8.4	9.0
Mississippi [1].........	46.3	59.0	58.3	74.4	4.5	5.5	5.6	6.9	3.7	4.1
Missouri [7]............	244.3	235.2	274.4	266.6	9.9	9.0	11.1	10.2	8.5	6.6
Montana.............	46.1	49.0	52.2	56.3	12.7	11.2	14.4	12.9	5.6	6.3
Nebraska [1]...........	75.3	60.9	95.6	71.4	9.3	6.8	11.8	7.9	4.8	4.1
Nevada [1]............	151.3	152.2	169.9	175.3	15.0	12.2	16.8	14.0	10.8	8.3
New Hampshire......	63.2	64.6	72.6	72.9	10.2	10.0	11.7	11.3	4.4	4.3
New Jersey..........	636.9	608.8	660.0	672.9	17.1	16.2	17.7	17.9	9.0	9.0
New Mexico..........	54.8	57.9	72.4	69.7	7.3	7.5	9.7	9.1	2.6	4.2
New York............	1,958.7	1,727.7	2,098.6	1,868.4	24.2	22.2	26.0	24.0	13.7	13.1
North Carolina [1]......	116.7	108.1	179.6	142.1	3.2	2.6	4.9	3.4	1.8	1.5
North Dakota [1].......	23.0	18.8	28.4	24.2	7.4	5.4	9.1	6.9	4.6	3.0
Ohio................	654.9	595.8	701.9	647.6	13.7	12.0	14.7	13.0	8.4	6.5
Oklahoma [2]...........	77.4	86.6	98.5	105.7	5.5	5.6	6.9	6.8	3.5	2.7
Oregon...............	245.1	318.0	267.9	335.9	16.2	17.8	17.7	18.8	9.1	9.4
Pennsylvania.........	770.2	692.3	831.4	730.9	14.7	12.9	15.9	13.6	9.3	7.3
Rhode Island.........	74.9	74.8	79.4	83.0	16.4	15.8	17.4	17.5	8.4	8.7
South Carolina [1].....	79.6	34.8	106.8	42.5	4.6	1.7	6.2	2.0	2.7	1.1
South Dakota [1].......	20.0	15.6	23.5	19.6	5.6	4.0	6.6	5.0	3.0	2.5
Tennessee [1].........	115.5	144.8	142.5	165.1	4.7	5.1	5.8	5.9	2.2	3.0
Texas [1].............	545.4	452.9	676.7	570.2	5.4	3.8	6.7	4.7	3.2	2.2
Utah [1].............	74.6	51.0	95.6	95.4	6.5	3.5	8.4	6.5	3.9	1.7
Vermont.............	34.2	32.4	39.5	37.4	11.8	12.3	13.6	14.2	5.3	6.0
Virginia [1]............	160.6	175.5	196.4	239.9	4.6	4.8	5.7	6.5	2.9	2.4
Washington...........	551.8	627.6	605.2	659.4	19.4	19.0	21.3	19.9	10.7	10.9
West Virginia [5].......	99.9	66.6	111.4	72.9	14.8	9.6	16.5	10.5	11.2	6.1
Wisconsin [4]..........	354.9	214.5	379.8	251.2	14.2	7.9	15.1	9.3	8.4	5.7
Wyoming [1]...........	18.1	13.4	20.7	16.1	7.4	5.7	8.4	6.9	4.9	4.1

[1] Right to work state as of 2000. [2] Passed right to work law in 2001. [3] Passed right to work law in 2012. [4] Passed right to work law in 2015. [5] Passed right to work law in 2016. [6] Passed right to work law in 2017. [7] Passed right to work law in 2017; rejected by voters 2018.

Source: *Union Membership and Coverage Database from the Current Population Survey*, accessed at <unionstats.com>, authored by Barry Hirsch of Georgia State University and David Macpherson of Trinity University. Copyright 2022.

Table 704. Work Stoppages: 1960 to 2021

[896 represents 896,000. Excludes work stoppages involving fewer than 1,000 workers and lasting less than 1 day. The term "major work stoppage" includes both worker-initiated strikes and employer-initiated lockouts that involve 1,000 or more workers. Information is based on reports of labor disputes appearing in daily newspapers, trade journals, and other public sources]

Year	Number of work stop-pages [1]	Workers involved [2] (1,000)	Days idle total Number [3] (1,000)	Days idle total Percent estimated working time [4]	Year	Number of work stop-pages [1]	Workers involved [2] (1,000)	Days idle total Number [3] (1,000)	Days idle total Percent estimated working time [4]
1960.......	222	896	13,260	0.09	2001.......	29	99	1,151	(Z)
1970.......	381	2,468	52,761	0.29	2002.......	19	46	660	(Z)
1980.......	187	795	20,844	0.09	2003.......	14	129	4,091	0.01
1983.......	81	909	17,461	0.08	2004.......	17	171	3,344	0.01
1984.......	62	376	8,499	0.04	2005.......	22	100	1,736	0.01
1985.......	54	323.9	7,079	0.03	2006.......	20	70	2,688	0.01
1986.......	69	533.1	11,861	0.05	2007.......	21	189	1,265	(Z)
1987.......	46	174.4	4,481	0.02	2008.......	15	72	1,954	0.01
1988.......	40	118.3	4,381	0.02	2009.......	5	13	124	(Z)
1989.......	51	452.1	16,996	0.07	2010.......	11	45	302	(Z)
1990.......	44	184.9	5,926	0.02	2011.......	19	113	1,020	(Z)
1991.......	40	392	4,584	0.02	2012.......	19	148	1,131	(Z)
1992.......	35	363.8	3,989	0.01	2013.......	15	55	290	(Z)
1993.......	35	181.9	3,981	0.01	2014.......	11	34	200	(Z)
1994.......	45	322.2	5,021	0.02	2015.......	12	47	740	(Z)
1995.......	31	191.5	5,771	0.02	2016.......	15	99	1,543	(Z)
1996.......	37	272.7	4,889	0.02	2017.......	7	25	440	(Z)
1997.......	29	338.6	4,497	0.01	2018.......	20	485	2,815	0.01
1998.......	34	386.8	5,116	0.02	2019.......	25	426	3,244	0.01
1999.......	17	72.6	1,996	0.01	2020.......	8	27	966	(Z)
2000.......	39	394	20,419	0.06	2021.......	16	81	1,552	(Z)

Z Less than 0.005 percent. [1] Beginning in year indicated. [2] Workers counted more than once if involved in more than one stoppage during the year. [3] Resulting from all stoppages in effect in a year, including those that began in an earlier year. The number of total days of idleness is computed by multiplying the number of workers idled by the number of lost workdays during the reference period. [4] Agricultural and government employees are included in the total working time; private household and forestry and fishery employees are excluded.

Source: U.S. Bureau of Labor Statistics, *Major Work Stoppages in 2021*, USDL 22-0316, February 2022. See also <www.bls.gov/wsp>.

Income, Expenditures, Poverty, and Wealth

This section presents data on gross domestic product (GDP), gross national product (GNP), national and personal income, savings and investment, money income, poverty, and national and personal wealth. The data on income and expenditures measure two aspects of the U.S. economy. One aspect relates to the National Income and Product Accounts (NIPA), a summation reflecting the entire complex of the nation's economic income and output and the interaction of its major components; the other relates to personal and household income and wealth, and consumer expenditures.

The primary source for data on GDP, GNP, national and personal income, gross saving and investment, and fixed assets and consumer durables come from the Bureau of Economic Analysis (BEA), issued monthly in the *Survey of Current Business*, and available through an interactive tool on the BEA's website, <apps.bea.gov/itable/index.cfm>. Revisions occur annually. The BEA conducts a comprehensive revision about every 5 years using data from the Census Bureau's Economic Census. The most recent comprehensive revision to the NIPA occurred in 2018. Discussions are available on the BEA's website.

Sources of income distribution data are the Annual Social and Economic Supplement of the Current Population Survey (CPS), and the American Community Survey, both products of the U.S. Census Bureau (see text, Section 1). Annual data on income of families, individuals, and households are presented in *Current Population Reports, Income and Poverty in the United States*, in print and online. Detailed statistics and historical data are available on the Census Bureau's website at <www.census.gov/topics/income-poverty.html>.

Data on the household sector's savings and assets are published by the Board of Governors of the Federal Reserve System in the quarterly statistical release, *Financial Accounts of the United States*. The Federal Reserve Board also periodically conducts the *Survey of Consumer Finances*, which presents financial information on family assets and net worth. The most recent survey is available online at <www.federalreserve.gov/econres/scfindex.htm>. Detailed information on personal wealth is published periodically by the Internal Revenue Service (IRS) in the *SOI (Statistics of Income) Bulletin*.

National income and product—*GDP,* or value added, is the value of the goods and services produced by the nation's economy less the value of the goods and services used up in production. GDP is equal to the sum of personal consumption expenditures, gross private domestic investment, net exports of goods and services, and government consumption expenditures and gross investment. The goods and services included are largely those bought for final use (excluding illegal transactions) in the market economy. A number of inclusions, however, represent imputed values, the most important of which is the rental value of owner-occupied housing. GDP, in this broad context, measures the output attributable to factors of production located in the United States. GDP by state is the gross market value of the goods and

services attributable to labor and property located in a state. It is the state counterpart of the nation's GDP.

The BEA releases GDP and related data in current dollar estimates, which reflect the value when transactions occurred, and in real values that are inflation-adjusted estimates that exclude the effects of price changes. Quantities, or "real" volume measures, and prices are expressed as index numbers with a specified reference year equal to 100 (currently 2012). Quantity and price indexes are calculated using a Fisher-chained weighted formula that incorporates weights from two adjacent periods (years for annual data). Chained-dollar values are calculated by multiplying the quantity index by the current dollar value in the reference year (2012) and then dividing by 100. Percent changes calculated from real quantity indexes and chained-dollar levels are conceptually the same; any differences are due to rounding. Chained-dollar values are not additive because the relative weights for a given period differ from those of the reference year. In tables that display chained-dollar values, a "residual" line shows the difference between the sum of detailed chained-dollar series and its corresponding aggregate.

Gross national product measures the market value of the goods, services, and structures produced by labor and property supplied by U.S. residents regardless of where they are located. GNP is equal to GDP plus income receipts from the rest of the world less income payments to the rest of the world.

National income includes all net incomes, net of consumption of fixed capital (CFC), earned in production. National income is also the sum of compensation of employees, proprietors' income with inventory valuation adjustment (IVA) and capital consumption adjustment (CCAdj), rental income of persons with CCAdj, corporate profits with IVA and CCAdj, net interest and miscellaneous payments, taxes on production and imports less subsidies, business current transfer payments (net), and current surplus of government enterprises, less subsidies.

Capital consumption adjustment for corporations and for nonfarm sole proprietorships and partnerships is the difference between capital consumption based on income tax returns and capital consumption measured using empirical evidence on prices of used equipment and structures in resale markets, which have shown that depreciation for most types of assets approximates a geometric pattern. The tax return data are valued at historical costs and reflect changes over time in service lives and depreciation patterns as permitted by tax regulations. Inventory valuation adjustment represents the difference between the book value of inventories used up in production and the cost of replacing them.

Personal income is the current income that persons receive in return for their provision of labor, land, and capital used in current production, plus current transfer receipts less contributions for government social insurance (domestic). Classified as "persons" are households, nonprofit institutions that primarily serve households, private trust funds, and private noninsured welfare funds. Personal current transfer receipts from government and business include items such as social security benefits, public assistance, and payments for personal injury, and exclude transfers among persons. Also included are certain nonmonetary types of income—chiefly, estimated net rental value to owner-occupants of their homes and the value of services furnished without payment by financial intermediaries. Capital gains (and losses) are excluded.

Disposable personal income is personal income less personal current taxes. It is the income available to persons for spending or saving. Personal taxes are primarily income taxes and personal property taxes.

Gross domestic product by industry—The BEA also prepares estimates of value added by industry. *Value added* is a measure of the contribution of each private industry and of government to the nation's GDP. It is defined as an industry's gross output (which consists of sales or receipts and other operating income, commodity taxes, and inventory change) minus its intermediate inputs (which consist of energy, raw materials, semi-finished goods, and purchased services). Data are available by industry and for Federal and state and local government. Industries are classified according to the North American Industry Classification System.

The estimates by industry are available in current dollars and are derived from the estimates of gross domestic income, which consists of three components—the compensation of employees, gross operating surplus, and taxes on production and imports, less subsidies. Real, or inflation-adjusted, estimates are also available.

Regional Economic Accounts—These accounts consist of estimates of state and local area personal income and of gross domestic product by state and are consistent with estimates of personal income and gross domestic product in the BEA's national economic accounts. BEA's estimates of state and local area personal income provide a framework for analyzing individual state and local economies, and they show how the economies compare with each other. The *personal income* of a state and/or local area is the income received by, or on behalf of, the residents of that state or area. Estimates of labor and proprietors' earnings by place of work indicate the economic activity of business and government within that area, and estimates of personal income by place of residence indicate the income within the area that is available for spending. BEA prepares estimates for states, counties, and metropolitan statistical areas.

Gross domestic product by state estimates measure the value added to the nation's production by the labor and property in each state. GDP by state estimates enable analysis of the regional impacts of national economic trends. GDP by state is measured as the sum of the distributions by industry and state of the components of gross domestic income - that is, the sum of the costs incurred and incomes earned in the production of GDP by state. GDP estimates are available in current dollars and in real (chained dollars) by industry.

Consumer Expenditure Survey—The Consumer Expenditure Survey program began in 1980. The principal objective of the survey is to collect current consumer expenditure data, which provide a continuous flow of data on consumer spending habits. The data are necessary for revisions of the Consumer Price Index. The survey is conducted by the Census Bureau for the Bureau of Labor Statistics. See Appendix III for more information.

Money income of households, families, and individuals—Money income statistics are based on data collected in various field surveys of income conducted since 1936. Since 1947, the Census Bureau collects data annually and publishes results in *Current Population Reports*, P60 Series. See Appendix III for more information on Census Bureau surveys. *Money income* as defined by the Census Bureau differs from the BEA concept of "personal income." Data on consumer income collected in the CPS cover money income received (exclusive of certain money receipts such as capital gains) before payments for personal income taxes, social security, union dues, Medicare deductions, etc. Money income excludes tax credits, including the Earned Income Tax Credit, the Child Tax Credit, and the special COVID-19 related stimulus payments. Money income does not reflect the fact that some families receive part of their income in the form of noncash benefits (see Section 11) such as food stamps, health benefits, and subsidized housing; that some farm families receive noncash benefits from goods produced and consumed on the farm; or that some nonfarm residents receive noncash benefits such as the use of business transportation and facilities, and full or partial payments by business for retirement programs, medical and educational expenses, etc. These elements should be considered when comparing income levels. None of the aggregate income concepts (GDP, national income, or personal income) is exactly comparable with money income, although personal income is the closest. For a definition of families and households, see text, Section 1.

Poverty—Families and unrelated individuals are classified as being above or below poverty following the Office of Management and Budget's Statistical Policy Directive 14. The Census Bureau uses a set of thresholds that vary by family size and composition. Official poverty thresholds do not vary geographically, but they are updated every year to reflect changes in the consumer price index (CPI-U). The official poverty definition uses money income before taxes and does not include capital gains or noncash benefits (such as public housing, Medicaid, and food stamps). More information is available on the Census Bureau website at <www.census.gov/topics/income-poverty/poverty.html>, and on the U.S. Department of Health and Human Services website at <aspe.hhs.gov/topics/poverty-economic-mobility/poverty-guidelines>.

Statistical reliability—For discussions of statistical collections performed by the Census Bureau, see Appendix III.

Table 705. Gross Domestic Product in Current and Chained (2012) Dollars: 1990 to 2021

[In billions of dollars (5,963 represents $5,963,000,000,000). For explanation of gross domestic product and chained dollars, see text, this section. Minus sign (–) indicates decrease]

Item	1990	2000	2005	2009	2010	2011	2012	2013	2014	2015	2016	2017	2018	2019	2020	2021
CURRENT DOLLARS																
Gross domestic product	5,963	10,251	13,039	14,478	15,049	15,600	16,254	16,843	17,551	18,206	18,695	19,480	20,527	21,373	20,894	22,996
Personal consumption expenditures	3,809	6,767	8,769	9,891	10,260	10,699	11,047	11,364	11,848	12,263	12,693	13,239	13,914	14,429	14,048	15,742
Durable goods	497	913	1,129	1,012	1,049	1,093	1,144	1,189	1,242	1,308	1,345	1,397	1,469	1,513	1,616	2,026
Nondurable goods	994	1,541	1,954	2,168	2,269	2,425	2,494	2,541	2,621	2,615	2,647	2,762	2,885	2,966	3,037	3,455
Services	2,318	4,314	5,686	6,711	6,942	7,181	7,410	7,634	7,985	8,340	8,701	9,081	9,560	9,950	9,394	10,260
Gross private domestic investment	993	2,038	2,535	1,930	2,165	2,333	2,622	2,826	3,044	3,237	3,205	3,381	3,638	3,826	3,638	4,120
Fixed investment	979	1,984	2,477	2,080	2,112	2,286	2,551	2,721	2,960	3,100	3,169	3,352	3,579	3,753	3,697	4,140
Nonresidential	739	1,498	1,621	1,690	1,735	1,907	2,119	2,211	2,400	2,467	2,469	2,592	2,781	2,939	2,800	3,054
Residential	240	485	856	390	377	379	432	510	560	634	699	760	799	814	898	1,086
Change in private inventories	15	55	58	-151	54	46	71	105	84	137	36	29	59	74	-60	-20
Net exports of goods and services	-78	-381	-740	-419	-532	-580	-552	-479	-510	-526	-506	-540	-596	-596	-651	-918
Exports	552	1,096	1,302	1,583	1,857	2,116	2,218	2,287	2,377	2,269	2,232	2,384	2,534	2,520	2,123	2,478
Imports	630	1,477	2,041	2,002	2,390	2,695	2,769	2,766	2,887	2,795	2,738	2,924	3,130	3,116	2,775	3,396
Government consumption expenditures and gross investment	1,239	1,826	2,475	3,076	3,156	3,148	3,136	3,133	3,169	3,232	3,303	3,399	3,572	3,714	3,860	4,053
Federal	562	633	948	1,221	1,300	1,300	1,287	1,227	1,216	1,222	1,235	1,263	1,339	1,415	1,502	1,565
National defense	405	393	609	788	828	834	814	764	743	730	728	746	793	848	881	905
Nondefense	157	240	338	433	472	466	473	463	473	492	507	516	546	567	620	660
State and local	676	1,193	1,528	1,856	1,855	1,848	1,849	1,906	1,953	2,010	2,069	2,136	2,233	2,299	2,358	2,488
CHAINED (2012) DOLLARS [1]																
Gross domestic product	9,371	13,138	14,901	15,236	15,649	15,892	16,254	16,553	16,932	17,390	17,680	18,079	18,607	19,033	18,385	19,427
Personal consumption expenditures	6,024	8,666	10,094	10,516	10,716	10,898	11,047	11,212	11,515	11,893	12,188	12,484	12,845	13,126	12,630	13,625
Durable goods	(NA)	(NA)	1,005	973	1,027	1,080	1,144	1,214	1,302	1,401	1,476	1,568	1,678	1,750	1,884	2,225
Nondurable goods	(NA)	(NA)	2,383	2,423	2,461	2,483	2,494	2,538	2,605	2,694	2,761	2,834	2,904	2,988	3,080	3,359
Services	(NA)	(NA)	6,707	7,126	7,230	7,337	7,410	7,460	7,613	7,810	7,969	8,110	8,306	8,444	7,808	8,258
Gross private domestic investment	1,223	2,347	2,671	1,942	2,216	2,362	2,622	2,801	2,959	3,122	3,090	3,212	3,395	3,511	3,316	3,640
Fixed investment	(NA)	(NA)	2,619	2,100	2,164	2,318	2,551	2,692	2,869	2,979	3,041	3,164	3,316	3,421	3,329	3,588
Nonresidential	(NA)	(NA)	1,716	1,704	1,781	1,935	2,119	2,206	2,365	2,420	2,442	2,541	2,704	2,822	2,671	2,868
Residential	(NA)	(NA)	885	395	383	382	432	485	504	555	592	616	612	607	648	708
Change in private inventories	(NA)	(NA)	64	-177	57	47	71	109	86	138	36	34	66	75	-42	-33
Net exports of goods and services	(NA)	(NA)	-915	-516	-589	-571	-552	-519	-575	-722	-757	-799	-864	-905	-943	-1,284
Exports	692	1,377	1,526	1,762	1,990	2,132	2,218	2,284	2,372	2,379	2,388	2,486	2,556	2,554	2,208	2,308
Imports	797	1,943	2,441	2,279	2,579	2,703	2,769	2,803	2,948	3,100	3,145	3,285	3,420	3,459	3,150	3,592
Government consumption expenditures and gross investment	2,376	2,663	3,014	3,311	3,308	3,203	3,136	3,061	3,033	3,088	3,149	3,165	3,209	3,280	3,360	3,376
Federal	(NA)	(NA)	1,099	1,296	1,348	1,312	1,287	1,216	1,185	1,185	1,191	1,195	1,231	1,277	1,341	1,349
National defense	(NA)	(NA)	709	837	861	843	814	760	728	713	709	716	740	779	801	794
Nondefense	(NA)	(NA)	391	459	487	469	473	456	456	471	481	478	491	499	539	554
State and local	(NA)	(NA)	1,918	2,016	1,960	1,891	1,849	1,844	1,848	1,902	1,956	1,968	1,976	2,001	2,020	2,028
Residual	-168	-50	36	-15	-11	-4	—	(-Z)	1	11	15	12	-7	-32	-84	-74

– Represents zero. NA Not available. Z Less than $500 million. [1] Chained (2012) dollar series are calculated as the product of the chain-type quantity index and the 2012 current-dollar value of the corresponding series, divided by 100. Because the formula for the chain-type quantity indexes uses weights of more than one period, the corresponding chained-dollar estimates are usually not additive. The residual line is the difference between the first line and the sum of the most detailed lines.

Source: U.S. Bureau of Economic Analysis, National Income and Product Accounts Tables, "Table 1.1.5. Gross Domestic Product," and "Table 1.1.6. Real Gross Domestic Product, Chained Dollars," <apps.bea.gov/iTable/index_nipa.cfm>, accessed June 2022.

Table 706. Real Gross Domestic Product, Chained (2012) Dollars—Annual Percent Change: 1990 to 2021

[Percent change from immediate previous year; for example, 1990, change from 1989. Minus sign (-) indicates decrease]

Component	1990	2000	2010	2015	2016	2017	2018	2019	2020	2021
Gross domestic product (GDP)............	**1.9**	**4.1**	**2.7**	**2.7**	**1.7**	**2.3**	**2.9**	**2.3**	**-3.4**	**5.7**
Personal consumption expenditures...........	2.0	5.0	1.9	3.3	2.5	2.4	2.9	2.2	-3.8	7.9
Durable goods........................	-0.4	8.6	5.6	7.6	5.4	6.3	7.0	4.3	7.7	18.1
Nondurable goods....................	1.2	3.2	1.6	3.4	2.5	2.7	2.5	2.9	3.1	9.1
Services............................	2.9	5.0	1.5	2.6	2.0	1.8	2.4	1.7	-7.5	5.8
Gross private domestic investment...........	-2.6	6.7	14.1	5.5	-1.0	4.0	5.7	3.4	-5.5	9.8
Fixed investment.....................	-1.4	7.1	3.1	3.8	2.1	4.1	4.8	3.2	-2.7	7.8
Nonresidential....................	1.1	9.3	4.5	2.3	0.9	4.1	6.4	4.3	-5.3	7.4
Structures....................	1.5	8.1	-16.1	-0.9	-4.3	4.2	4.0	2.0	-12.5	-8.0
Equipment....................	-2.1	9.7	20.2	3.0	-1.8	2.8	6.4	3.3	-8.3	13.1
Intellectual property products..............	8.4	9.5	2.7	3.8	8.8	5.7	8.1	7.2	2.8	10.0
Residential........................	-8.5	0.7	-3.1	10.2	6.6	4.0	-0.6	-0.9	6.8	9.2
Exports...........................	8.8	8.3	12.9	0.3	0.4	4.1	2.8	-0.1	-13.6	4.5
Goods...........................	8.6	9.8	15.1	-0.4	0.6	4.1	4.2	-0.1	-10.2	7.6
Services..........................	9.5	4.5	8.3	1.5	–	4.0	0.2	-0.1	-19.8	-1.5
Imports............................	3.6	13.0	13.2	5.2	1.5	4.4	4.1	1.2	-8.9	14.0
Goods............................	2.9	13.1	15.4	5.8	1.1	4.5	5.1	0.5	-5.6	14.6
Services..........................	6.5	12.7	4.6	2.5	3.0	4.3	–	3.9	-22.6	11.5
Government consumption expenditures and gross investment........................	3.2	1.8	-0.1	1.8	2.0	0.5	1.4	2.2	2.5	0.5
Federal..........................	2.1	0.3	4.0	–	0.5	0.3	3.0	3.8	5.0	0.6
National defense.................	0.3	-0.9	2.9	-2.1	-0.6	0.9	3.4	5.2	2.9	-0.9
Nondefense....................	7.3	2.3	6.0	3.3	2.1	-0.5	2.5	1.6	8.1	2.8
State and local..................	4.1	2.7	-2.8	3.0	2.8	0.6	0.4	1.3	0.9	0.4

– Represents or rounds to zero.

Source: U.S. Bureau of Economic Analysis, National Income and Product Accounts Tables, "Table 1.1.1. Percent Change From Preceding Period in Real Gross Domestic Product," <apps.bea.gov/iTable/index_nipa.cfm>, accessed June 2022.

Table 707. Gross Domestic Product in Current and Chained (2012) Dollars by Type of Product and Sector: 1990 to 2021

[In billions of dollars (5,963 represents $5,963,000,000,000). For explanation of chained dollars, see text, this section]

Type of product and sector	1990	2000	2010	2016	2017	2018	2019	2020	2021
CURRENT DOLLARS									
Gross domestic product................	**5,963**	**10,251**	**15,049**	**18,695**	**19,480**	**20,527**	**21,373**	**20,894**	**22,996**
Product:									
Goods...........................	2,121	3,437	4,394	5,508	5,718	6,053	6,342	6,327	7,278
Durable goods..................	1,176	2,083	2,477	3,072	3,179	3,416	3,580	3,508	4,021
Nondurable goods...............	946	1,354	1,917	2,437	2,539	2,637	2,761	2,819	3,257
Services [1]......................	3,293	5,827	9,595	11,629	12,095	12,723	13,204	12,713	13,702
Structures......................	549	987	1,060	1,557	1,667	1,751	1,827	1,854	2,016
Sector:									
Business [2]......................	4,542	7,876	11,138	14,168	14,803	15,644	16,298	15,666	17,550
Nonfarm [3]...................	4,464	7,800	11,022	14,039	14,664	15,507	16,175	15,532	17,347
Farm.......................	78	76	116	130	139	137	123	135	203
Households and institutions................	636	1,191	1,965	2,344	2,436	2,551	2,669	2,755	2,885
General government [4]................	785	1,184	1,946	2,183	2,240	2,332	2,406	2,472	2,561
Federal........................	307	360	640	684	699	726	749	783	818
State and local..................	478	824	1,306	1,499	1,541	1,606	1,656	1,689	1,743
CHAINED (2012) DOLLARS									
Gross domestic product................	**9,371**	**13,138**	**15,649**	**17,680**	**18,079**	**18,607**	**19,033**	**18,385**	**19,427**
Product:									
Goods...........................	2,223	3,459	4,507	5,564	5,772	6,075	6,338	6,356	7,034
Durable goods..................	(NA)	(NA)	2,489	3,103	3,225	3,466	3,602	3,520	3,940
Nondurable goods...............	(NA)	(NA)	2,020	2,461	2,546	2,609	2,736	2,836	3,093
Services [1]......................	6,145	8,153	10,023	10,737	10,888	11,116	11,286	10,664	11,090
Structures......................	1,154	1,543	1,122	1,381	1,427	1,442	1,454	1,442	1,445
Sector:									
Business [2]......................	6,589	9,741	11,598	13,564	13,926	14,411	14,791	14,164	15,185
Nonfarm [3]...................	6,500	9,608	11,436	13,365	13,728	14,207	14,596	13,953	14,980
Farm.......................	91	137	163	203	198	204	186	221	207
Households and institutions................	1,233	1,634	2,035	2,126	2,152	2,185	2,212	2,183	2,207
General government [4]................	1,660	1,770	2,016	1,996	2,010	2,024	2,046	2,043	2,064
Federal........................	613	532	658	645	646	650	656	674	680
State and local..................	1,042	1,240	1,358	1,349	1,363	1,374	1,389	1,369	1,385

NA Not available. [1] Includes government consumption expenditures, which are for services (such as education and national defense) produced by government. In current dollars, these services are valued at their cost of production. [2] Equals gross domestic product excluding gross value added of households and institutions and of general government. [3] Equals gross domestic business value added excluding gross farm value added. [4] Equals compensation of general government employees plus general government consumption of fixed capital.

Source: U.S. Bureau of Economic Analysis, National Income and Product Accounts Tables, <apps.bea.gov/iTable/index_nipa.cfm>, accessed June 2022.

Table 708. Gross Domestic Product in Current and Chained (2012) Dollars by Industry: 2000 to 2021

[In billions of dollars (10,251 represents $10,251,000,000,000). Based on 2012 North American Industry Classification System (NAICS); see text, Section 15. GDP by industry is the contribution of each private industry and of government to the nation's output, or GDP. An industry's GDP, or its "value added," is equal to its gross output (sales or receipts and other operating income, commodity taxes, and inventory change) minus its intermediate inputs (energy, raw materials, semifinished goods, and services that are purchased from domestic industries or from foreign sources). Detail may not add to total due to rounding]

Industry	Current dollars				Chained (2012) dollars [1]			
	2000	2010	2020	2021	2000	2010	2020	2021
Gross domestic product	**10,251**	**15,049**	**20,894**	**22,996**	**13,138**	**15,649**	**18,385**	**19,427**
Private industries	8,928	12,941	18,223	20,224	11,368	13,514	16,142	17,155
Agriculture, forestry, fishing, and hunting	98	145	175	246	160	192	255	243
Farms	76	116	135	203	137	163	221	207
Forestry, fishing, and related activities	22	29	40	43	25	29	35	36
Mining	111	306	182	284	235	310	439	413
Oil and gas extraction	68	189	98	196	137	182	410	378
Mining, except oil and gas	29	70	57	64	92	75	60	62
Mining support activities	14	48	28	24	19	52	32	28
Utilities	180	279	342	381	258	266	299	282
Construction	461	526	896	959	782	548	650	671
Manufacturing	1,550	1,800	2,272	2,563	1,674	1,936	2,168	2,332
Durable goods	925	966	1,269	1,386	751	969	1,178	1,286
Wood products	28	23	42	58	25	23	28	28
Nonmetallic mineral products	43	38	67	71	49	39	49	51
Primary metals	47	51	58	82	61	51	91	89
Fabricated metal products	121	120	146	155	155	126	123	132
Machinery	113	127	158	167	130	132	128	141
Computer and electronic products	225	240	317	340	67	227	351	382
Electrical equipment, appliances, and components	46	51	64	69	54	53	58	64
Motor vehicles, bodies & trailers, & parts	137	89	155	169	99	87	138	175
Other transportation equipment	71	121	130	136	95	124	115	123
Furniture and related products	34	22	32	30	40	23	27	25
Miscellaneous manufacturing	59	83	101	107	61	84	89	98
Nondurable goods	625	834	1,003	1,178	964	975	990	1,045
Food & beverage & tobacco	163	224	290	311	225	234	245	268
Textile mills and textile product mills	28	16	15	17	31	17	15	16
Apparel and leather and allied products	22	10	10	12	20	11	9	11
Paper products	62	56	60	61	71	56	55	55
Printing and related support activities	44	39	40	41	38	38	35	37
Petroleum and coal products	53	124	114	209	184	213	246	270
Chemical products	188	303	395	439	289	348	328	330
Plastics and rubber products	66	62	81	89	77	68	75	81
Wholesale trade	623	890	1,243	1,383	803	945	1,084	1,114
Retail trade	685	852	1,202	1,386	820	901	1,090	1,113
Transportation and warehousing	308	434	572	643	424	461	490	504
Air transportation	58	84	58	67	76	92	60	77
Rail transportation	23	34	38	38	42	38	30	32
Water transportation	8	15	10	11	5	12	10	8
Truck transportation	98	114	165	184	129	122	131	127
Transit & ground passenger transport	18	31	37	42	31	33	36	39
Pipeline transportation	9	20	41	43	16	22	30	30
Other transportation & support	66	91	144	168	106	101	112	113
Warehousing and storage	27	45	80	90	27	41	81	87
Information	471	755	1,168	1,301	421	752	1,297	1,468
Publishing industries, except internet (includes software)	116	187	320	357	126	189	342	389
Motion picture and sound recording	54	91	70	91	45	92	74	98
Broadcasting and telecommunications	277	376	459	470	224	370	537	561
Data processing, internet publishing, & related services	24	101	318	383	24	100	342	414
Finance and insurance	744	1,006	1,788	1,950	916	1,071	1,260	1,377
Real estate and rental and leasing	1,230	1,984	2,804	2,935	1,536	2,033	2,307	2,374
Professional, scientific, and technical services	652	1,065	1,628	1,780	844	1,095	1,501	1,641
Legal services	129	205	282	302	236	223	206	211
Computer systems design, related services	114	203	367	393	86	199	407	448
Miscellaneous services	409	657	979	1,086	544	674	905	1,005
Management of companies & enterprises	171	265	410	434	278	270	440	479
Administrative and waste management services	282	438	652	759	338	445	550	633
Educational services	95	199	251	258	152	212	203	204
Health care and social assistance	600	1,112	1,547	1,675	835	1,150	1,359	1,438
Ambulatory health care services	288	532	739	816	374	546	706	765
Hospitals	190	370	513	548	279	385	427	444
Nursing and residential care facilities	69	121	155	158	108	125	123	122
Social assistance	53	90	141	154	76	94	107	112
Arts, entertainment, and recreation	99	152	163	196	138	159	132	158
Performing arts, spectator sports, museums, & related	49	88	91	107	72	90	74	88
Amusements, gambling, & recreation	50	65	72	89	66	69	58	70
Accommodation and food services	287	404	509	644	425	427	384	460
Accommodation	93	112	116	160	126	119	99	133
Food services and drinking places	194	292	393	483	298	308	284	329
Other services, except government	280	328	419	448	431	346	323	332
Government	1,323	2,108	2,671	2,773	1,977	2,183	2,195	2,228
Federal	424	697	848	881	624	716	734	737
State and local	899	1,411	1,822	1,891	1,354	1,466	1,462	1,492

[1] Chained (2012) dollar series are calculated as the product of the chain-type quantity index and the 2012 current-dollar value of the corresponding series, divided by 100. Because the formula for the chain-type quantity indexes uses weights of more than one period, the corresponding chained-dollar estimates are usually not additive.

Source: U.S. Bureau of Economic Analysis, Industry Economic Accounts, "GDP by Industry Data," <www.bea.gov/industry/index.htm>, accessed April 2022.

Table 709. Relation of GDP, GNP, Net National Product, National Income, Personal Income, Disposable Personal Income, and Personal Saving: 2000 to 2021

[In billions of dollars (10,251 represents $10,251,000,000,000). For definitions, see text, this section. Minus sign (-) indicates deficit or net disbursement]

Item	2000	2010	2016	2017	2018	2019	2020	2021
Gross domestic product (GDP)........	**10,251**	**15,049**	**18,695**	**19,480**	**20,527**	**21,373**	**20,894**	**22,996**
Plus: Income receipts from the rest of the world..	391	760	893	1,033	1,142	1,160	993	1,145
Less: Income payments to the rest of the world..	352	554	662	738	848	894	771	893
Equals: Gross national product (GNP).........	**10,289**	**15,255**	**18,927**	**19,774**	**20,821**	**21,639**	**21,116**	**23,249**
Less: Consumption of fixed capital.................	1,511	2,391	2,987	3,118	3,273	3,436	3,576	3,848
Equals: Net national product....................	**8,778**	**12,864**	**15,940**	**16,656**	**17,548**	**18,203**	**17,540**	**19,401**
Less: Statistical discrepancy........................	-94	83	-93	-119	-125	-70	-171	-537
Equals: National income.........................	**8,872**	**12,781**	**16,033**	**16,775**	**17,673**	**18,273**	**17,711**	**19,938**
Less:								
Corporate profits [1]..........................	787	1,729	2,038	2,129	2,305	2,368	2,244	2,806
Taxes on production and imports less subsidies......................................	663	1,007	1,250	1,306	1,398	1,459	773	1,148
Contributions for government social insurance..	706	984	1,239	1,299	1,360	1,421	1,459	1,593
Net interest and miscellaneous payments on assets....................................	542	471	567	612	599	558	619	686
Business current transfer payments (net).......	85	128	167	149	158	162	159	164
Current surplus of government enterprises......	11	-20	-4	-7	-9	-13	-17	-13
Plus: Personal income receipts on assets.........	1,490	1,787	2,543	2,708	2,868	2,968	2,912	2,941
Personal current transfer receipts..............	1,087	2,325	2,777	2,856	2,976	3,139	4,241	4,598
Equals: Personal income.........................	**8,656**	**12,595**	**16,097**	**16,850**	**17,706**	**18,424**	**19,628**	**21,093**
Less: Personal current taxes.......................	1,236	1,238	1,958	2,049	2,076	2,205	2,196	2,585
Equals: Disposable personal income.............	**7,420**	**11,357**	**14,139**	**14,801**	**15,630**	**16,219**	**17,432**	**18,508**
Less: Personal outlays.............................	7,068	10,648	13,151	13,725	14,439	14,981	14,544	16,226
Equals: Personal saving.........................	**351**	**709**	**988**	**1,076**	**1,191**	**1,238**	**2,888**	**2,281**

[1] Corporate profits with inventory valuation and capital consumption adjustments.

Source: U.S. Bureau of Economic Analysis, National Income and Product Accounts Tables, "Table 1.7.5. Relation of Gross Domestic Product, Gross National Product, Net National Product, National Income, and Personal Income," and "Table 2.1. Personal Income and Its Disposition," <apps.bea.gov/iTable/index_nipa.cfm>, accessed June 2022.

Table 710. Gross Saving and Investment: 2000 to 2021

[In billions of dollars (2,125 represents $2,125,000,000,000), except as noted. Minus (-) sign indicates deficit]

Item	2000	2010	2016	2017	2018	2019	2020	2021
Gross saving...........................	**2,125**	**2,288**	**3,535**	**3,796**	**4,026**	**4,156**	**4,003**	**4,628**
Net saving....................................	613	-103	548	678	752	721	427	781
Net private saving...........................	494	1,523	1,460	1,629	1,876	1,917	3,461	3,287
Domestic business...........................	143	813	472	552	685	679	573	1,006
Undistributed corporate profits....................	103	919	569	618	639	566	514	1,201
Inventory valuation adjustment, corporate.......	-17	-48	5	-47	-48	(-Z)	-18	-247
Capital consumption adjustment, corporate.....	57	-58	-101	-19	94	113	78	52
Households and institutions.....................	351	709	988	1,076	1,191	1,238	2,888	2,281
Personal saving................................	351	709	988	1,076	1,191	1,238	2,888	2,281
Net government saving.........................	119	-1,626	-912	-951	-1,124	-1,196	-3,034	-2,507
Federal....................................	160	-1,318	-668	-721	-928	-1,047	-3,110	-2,784
State and local..............................	-41	-307	-245	-231	-196	-149	76	277
Consumption of fixed capital.....................	1,511	2,391	2,987	3,118	3,273	3,436	3,576	3,848
Private......................................	1,232	1,934	2,460	2,576	2,708	2,849	2,970	3,202
Domestic business...........................	1,005	1,537	1,951	2,038	2,133	2,248	2,339	2,496
Households and institutions....................	227	397	509	538	575	600	631	706
Government..................................	280	457	527	542	565	587	606	646
Federal....................................	163	244	271	276	285	293	304	320
State and local..............................	117	213	256	266	280	294	303	325
Gross domestic investment, capital account transactions, and net lending.......	**2,030**	**2,370**	**3,441**	**3,677**	**3,900**	**4,086**	**3,832**	**4,091**
Gross domestic investment.......................	2,427	2,810	3,845	4,050	4,340	4,566	4,419	4,922
Gross private domestic investment...............	2,038	2,165	3,205	3,381	3,638	3,826	3,638	4,120
Gross government investment....................	389	645	640	668	703	740	782	802
Capital account transactions (net) [1].................	5	7	7	16	5	7	6	4
Net lending or net borrowing.....................	-401	-447	-411	-389	-445	-487	-593	-835
Statistical discrepancy.............................	-94	83	-93	-119	-125	-70	-171	-537
Addenda:								
Gross private saving.............................	1,726	3,456	3,920	4,205	4,584	4,766	6,430	6,490
Gross government saving........................	399	-1,169	-385	-409	-558	-610	-2,428	-1,861
Federal...................................	323	-1,075	-397	-445	-643	-754	-2,806	-2,464
State and local.............................	76	-94	12	36	85	145	379	602
Net domestic investment......................	916	419	858	932	1,067	1,131	843	1,074
Gross saving as a percent of gross national income...........................	20.5	15.1	18.6	19.1	19.2	19.1	18.8	19.5
Net saving as a percent of gross national income...........................	5.9	-0.7	2.9	3.4	3.6	3.3	2.0	3.3
Disaster losses [2]................................	–	–	–	104	51	–	–	62

– Represents zero. Z Less than $50 million. [1] Consists of capital transfers and the acquisition and disposal of nonproduced nonfinancial assets. [2] Consists of damages to fixed assets.

Source: U.S. Bureau of Economic Analysis, National Income and Product Accounts Tables, "Table 5.1 Saving and Investment by Sector," <apps.bea.gov/iTable/index_nipa.cfm>, accessed June 2022.

Table 711. Gross Domestic Product by State in Current and Chained (2012) Dollars: 2000 to 2021

[In billions of dollars (10,251.0 represents $10,251,000,000,000). For definition of gross domestic product by state or chained dollars, see text, this section]

State	Current dollars					Chained (2012) dollars [2]				
	2000	2010	2019	2020	2021 (P)	2000	2010	2019	2020	2021 (P)
United States [1]	**10,251.0**	**15,049.0**	**21,372.6**	**20,893.7**	**22,996.1**	**13,138.0**	**15,649.0**	**19,032.7**	**18,384.7**	**19,427.3**
Alabama	119.9	177.2	231.2	226.9	247.1	157.2	184.7	203.4	196.9	204.9
Alaska	26.8	53.3	54.5	49.8	55.0	39.4	54.6	53.3	50.2	50.3
Arizona	165.1	251.2	370.0	373.7	411.2	208.4	260.3	323.9	320.6	337.4
Arkansas	68.7	101.5	130.8	130.8	144.5	89.9	105.7	116.8	114.9	120.7
California	1,357.0	1,954.1	3,052.6	3,007.2	3,356.6	1,696.2	2,036.0	2,739.3	2,663.7	2,871.4
Colorado	180.1	258.3	392.2	382.6	421.9	231.6	267.9	356.8	346.0	365.9
Connecticut	165.6	234.7	288.1	276.4	296.5	216.2	244.4	251.5	235.9	245.8
Delaware	43.5	58.2	77.0	75.8	80.7	56.6	60.6	64.3	62.1	64.3
District of Columbia	61.1	106.1	144.4	144.6	152.0	85.4	110.0	125.0	122.3	125.8
Florida	490.4	746.9	1,116.4	1,106.0	1,226.3	642.7	775.0	971.6	944.0	1,008.7
Georgia	305.6	418.1	637.8	622.6	683.3	389.7	433.7	558.3	536.7	567.9
Hawaii	41.1	66.9	91.8	82.9	90.1	55.9	69.6	79.2	70.6	73.9
Idaho	38.1	55.6	82.4	83.8	94.3	47.3	58.3	73.9	73.7	77.9
Illinois	487.0	666.4	890.5	858.4	938.3	640.7	698.2	777.7	737.6	774.6
Indiana	203.8	282.6	381.0	375.3	420.3	264.1	297.5	338.4	329.9	352.6
Iowa	93.1	142.2	194.3	194.3	219.8	121.9	150.1	172.9	169.4	180.3
Kansas	86.1	128.6	176.7	175.1	192.3	114.0	135.7	160.2	156.8	162.7
Kentucky	114.2	166.4	216.1	212.5	234.5	151.5	173.8	191.4	185.5	194.3
Louisiana	132.6	225.3	254.6	235.4	255.3	205.7	246.8	235.9	222.3	227.7
Maine	36.9	52.3	68.5	69.3	76.1	48.5	54.3	59.4	58.8	61.8
Maryland	192.0	314.7	421.6	410.7	438.2	250.8	325.4	369.6	353.1	364.2
Massachusetts	288.8	411.1	593.3	582.5	636.5	358.1	425.8	517.7	498.6	530.5
Michigan	352.2	390.0	531.4	515.1	568.4	438.5	404.2	467.3	445.7	473.3
Minnesota	191.5	274.2	383.0	373.7	412.0	247.8	287.1	340.1	326.6	345.2
Mississippi	65.7	93.9	114.7	113.8	125.1	88.1	98.6	101.5	99.7	104.0
Missouri	186.7	259.8	332.3	329.4	360.0	244.7	270.7	290.8	282.7	295.7
Montana	21.9	38.3	51.8	51.5	59.3	31.2	40.8	46.8	46.2	49.3
Nebraska	56.5	91.6	131.4	133.4	150.4	76.4	97.5	118.3	117.7	123.9
Nevada	76.8	124.7	181.7	170.9	193.0	105.6	129.6	156.8	145.2	155.5
New Hampshire	45.3	64.8	87.5	87.6	98.2	56.8	67.1	77.1	75.5	81.9
New Jersey	361.0	492.8	639.4	618.6	672.1	471.4	513.9	561.8	535.8	561.8
New Mexico	55.1	84.6	102.0	98.5	108.9	71.7	87.6	94.9	92.7	95.0
New York	841.2	1,223.5	1,777.8	1,724.8	1,853.9	1,092.2	1,277.5	1,494.7	1,420.1	1,491.8
North Carolina	278.0	420.0	595.7	589.8	655.0	356.9	437.8	514.6	499.5	533.1
North Dakota	18.1	35.7	59.0	54.9	63.4	24.7	37.9	56.2	54.6	55.7
Ohio	392.3	500.5	693.2	677.6	736.4	509.9	524.0	611.1	589.9	615.4
Oklahoma	91.1	154.3	203.7	188.1	206.8	124.2	160.6	200.7	190.9	195.1
Oregon	117.2	164.1	246.6	243.8	266.9	137.4	169.2	219.5	212.8	224.4
Pennsylvania	409.2	604.7	799.7	771.9	839.4	538.8	627.7	716.2	683.8	713.7
Rhode Island	34.5	49.5	61.3	60.6	65.9	45.2	51.3	53.2	51.4	54.2
South Carolina	115.3	165.9	244.7	244.9	270.1	150.2	172.1	212.5	208.5	220.7
South Dakota	22.7	37.9	53.9	54.8	61.2	29.4	40.4	46.6	46.7	49.0
Tennessee	182.2	257.8	376.9	369.6	418.3	233.7	268.4	329.1	316.3	343.4
Texas	738.7	1,246.0	1,864.0	1,775.6	1,985.3	995.7	1,310.0	1,785.3	1,734.3	1,831.4
Utah	70.3	118.7	195.1	197.6	220.3	92.5	123.9	171.1	171.4	182.9
Vermont	18.3	27.4	34.1	33.4	36.2	23.0	28.4	29.9	28.6	29.7
Virginia	268.5	427.0	554.3	549.5	591.9	348.3	441.2	487.3	473.8	492.6
Washington	237.4	365.5	597.9	604.3	667.6	311.2	381.0	536.0	532.9	568.3
West Virginia	42.5	66.0	79.1	75.9	87.4	61.7	69.2	72.5	69.7	72.5
Wisconsin	180.4	256.4	344.7	337.7	365.9	232.4	266.8	303.9	291.7	302.8
Wyoming	17.2	37.7	39.6	36.3	41.6	27.4	40.1	38.6	36.3	36.7

P Preliminary. [1] The difference between the United States and sum-of-states reflects economic activity taking place outside the borders of the United States by the military and associated federal civilian support staff, as well as the differences in source data used to estimate GDP by industry and the expenditures measure of real GDP. [2] Chained (2012) dollar series are calculated as the product of the chain-type quantity index and the 2012 current-dollar value of the corresponding series, divided by 100. Because the formula for the chain-type quantity indexes uses weights of more than one period, the corresponding chained-dollar estimates are usually not additive.

Source: U.S. Bureau of Economic Analysis, Regional Economic Accounts, "Gross Domestic Product by State," <www.bea.gov/data/economic-accounts/regional>, accessed April 2022.

Table 712. Gross Domestic Product by Selected Industry and State: 2021

[In billions of current dollars (22,966.1 represents $22,996,100,000,000). Data are preliminary and subject to revision. For definition of gross domestic product by state, see text, this section. Industries based on 2012 North American Industry Classification System; see text, Section 15]

State	Total [1]	Manu-facturing	Whole-sale trade	Retail trade	Infor-mation	Finance and insur-ance	Real estate, rental, and leasing	Profes-sional and technical services	Health care and social assis-tance	Govern-ment [2]
United States [3]	22,996.1	2,563.3	1,383.0	1,385.5	1,300.7	1,949.5	2,935.5	1,779.9	1,675.3	2,772.6
Alabama	247.1	40.1	14.9	18.1	5.0	14.0	28.3	15.2	17.9	40.0
Alaska	55.0	(D)	1.5	2.7	1.1	1.5	5.7	1.8	4.6	12.1
Arizona	411.2	35.0	24.0	31.9	15.8	33.0	61.0	23.5	34.1	47.3
Arkansas	144.5	21.3	11.6	10.9	2.8	7.9	15.2	5.0	11.9	18.1
California	3,356.6	413.5	178.6	186.5	368.3	205.2	421.0	315.4	212.3	363.8
Colorado	421.9	27.8	25.9	24.5	25.9	26.5	61.8	43.9	26.1	50.8
Connecticut	296.5	32.2	16.5	16.4	16.9	45.7	39.7	20.4	24.4	28.5
Delaware	80.7	5.5	2.3	3.3	1.1	21.6	14.0	5.1	5.9	7.9
District of Columbia	152.0	(D)	1.8	1.7	9.8	8.1	11.9	32.1	6.9	51.0
Florida	1,226.3	64.3	86.7	93.9	47.4	84.0	227.1	90.9	99.7	120.4
Georgia	683.3	63.9	51.1	39.9	54.0	57.8	96.7	46.1	43.4	76.8
Hawaii	90.1	1.5	3.1	6.6	2.2	4.0	16.0	4.0	7.0	19.2
Idaho	94.3	10.3	6.4	8.4	2.0	4.7	12.4	5.6	7.6	11.4
Illinois	938.3	120.4	72.6	52.1	34.2	101.3	114.9	79.7	65.2	86.9
Indiana	420.3	111.6	24.2	24.1	6.3	23.6	42.7	18.7	34.0	39.3
Iowa	219.8	37.7	12.5	11.5	4.7	32.2	20.2	7.0	13.2	24.1
Kansas	192.3	28.9	12.8	11.8	4.7	11.7	27.4	9.7	13.8	23.6
Kentucky	234.5	40.8	17.1	14.7	5.0	14.8	24.9	9.5	20.8	30.0
Louisiana	255.3	43.0	14.1	18.2	4.7	13.7	30.2	12.0	21.0	30.4
Maine	76.1	7.6	4.1	6.4	1.3	5.8	12.3	4.1	8.4	9.5
Maryland	438.2	27.7	20.3	23.1	15.1	24.3	63.4	44.9	32.7	92.6
Massachusetts	636.5	61.9	31.9	27.3	39.3	66.4	80.7	90.1	55.7	58.2
Michigan	568.4	102.2	38.9	37.2	14.7	30.8	76.3	43.7	47.4	56.8
Minnesota	412.0	56.1	30.7	22.7	13.2	39.0	47.2	27.3	39.2	37.4
Mississippi	125.1	18.4	6.7	10.6	2.2	6.5	14.8	3.9	9.6	21.1
Missouri	360.0	43.4	24.6	22.7	12.2	30.9	41.1	25.1	31.7	40.6
Montana	59.3	3.3	3.4	4.2	1.3	3.1	8.0	3.2	5.7	8.4
Nebraska	150.4	17.8	8.8	7.6	4.3	17.7	13.7	5.9	10.5	17.5
Nevada	193.0	10.2	8.9	15.2	6.2	12.7	27.5	9.5	12.0	19.9
New Hampshire	98.2	9.8	7.3	6.9	4.0	7.7	14.5	8.0	8.6	10.0
New Jersey	672.1	63.6	56.4	42.4	31.1	47.3	103.4	63.3	54.4	66.3
New Mexico	108.9	4.6	3.5	7.1	2.5	4.1	12.9	8.3	8.0	25.6
New York	1,853.9	78.2	77.3	83.6	168.4	402.1	237.9	160.6	132.0	188.5
North Carolina	655.0	112.0	39.1	38.0	24.1	62.0	73.5	45.0	42.3	79.9
North Dakota	63.4	4.6	4.6	3.6	1.5	3.5	5.6	1.7	5.1	7.0
Ohio	736.4	117.9	45.6	46.1	18.2	80.3	80.1	38.1	62.7	78.3
Oklahoma	206.8	18.9	10.3	14.0	5.1	9.2	22.3	9.0	15.2	35.2
Oregon	266.9	36.7	15.3	15.2	11.0	12.4	38.4	16.0	23.0	35.0
Pennsylvania	839.4	106.3	48.3	46.5	49.1	57.7	102.0	63.8	81.3	78.1
Rhode Island	65.9	5.0	3.7	4.1	1.5	6.7	9.1	4.1	6.4	9.0
South Carolina	270.1	40.7	16.6	19.1	8.7	13.9	38.2	14.5	17.1	39.6
South Dakota	61.2	5.2	4.0	4.2	1.4	11.2	5.1	1.9	6.0	6.5
Tennessee	418.3	63.8	28.4	30.4	12.4	28.5	47.3	25.1	38.2	42.3
Texas	1,985.3	232.0	163.0	120.4	76.6	132.0	245.2	154.0	118.3	209.8
Utah	220.3	25.5	11.4	16.0	11.7	21.0	26.8	15.4	11.3	24.9
Vermont	36.2	3.6	1.9	2.8	0.9	2.0	5.0	2.6	3.8	5.2
Virginia	591.9	49.1	27.1	32.9	23.5	34.7	77.3	76.8	36.9	104.3
Washington	667.6	57.4	35.0	68.2	111.4	30.3	79.3	46.9	39.4	79.7
West Virginia	87.4	8.2	4.1	5.8	1.4	3.3	8.9	3.3	8.8	14.0
Wisconsin	365.9	69.3	22.7	21.8	13.5	29.5	42.0	16.9	32.0	38.5
Wyoming	41.6	2.7	1.4	2.4	0.6	1.4	4.4	1.4	1.8	6.8

D Figure withheld to avoid disclosure of confidential information; estimates are included in higher-level totals. [1] Includes industries not shown separately. [2] Includes federal civilian and military, and state and local government. [3] The difference between the United States and sum-of-states reflects overseas activity, economic activity taking place outside the borders of the United States by the military and associated federal civilian support staff.

Source: U.S. Bureau of Economic Analysis, Regional Economic Accounts, "Gross Domestic Product by State," <www.bea.gov/data/economic-accounts/regional>, accessed April 2022.

Table 713. Household Production Value: 1965 to 2020

[In billions of dollars (277.4 represents $277,400,000,000). Measures the value of time spent on the unpaid work of household production tasks. Household production hours are aggregated across seven categories: housework, cooking, odd jobs, gardening, shopping, child care, and domestic travel related to these tasks. The value of these nonmarket services is the product of the wage rate of general purpose domestic workers and the number of hours worked]

Year	Household production value (bil. dol.)	Year	Household production value (bil. dol.)	Year	Household production value (bil. dol.)	Year	Household production value (bil. dol.)
1965	277.4	2000	2,921.6	2007	3,631.5	2014	4,212.3
1970	428.0	2001	2,800.3	2008	3,828.5	2015	4,405.7
1975	707.4	2002	2,780.7	2009	3,691.9	2016	4,571.0
1980	1,106.9	2003	3,045.1	2010	3,643.5	2017	4,506.0
1985	1,467.0	2004	3,185.0	2011	3,704.6	2018	4,668.6
1990	1,902.6	2005	3,210.2	2012	3,780.4	2019	4,638.8
1995	2,395.9	2006	3,407.9	2013	4,096.5	2020	5,316.8

Source: U.S. Bureau of Economic Analysis, Special Topics, "Household Production Satellite Account," <www.bea.gov/data/special-topics/household-production>, accessed March 2022.

Table 714. Financial Accounts of the United States—Composition of Individuals' Savings: 1990 to 2021

[In billions of dollars (675.5 represents $675,500,000,000). Combined statement for households, nonprofit organizations, and nonfinancial noncorporate business. Minus sign (-) indicates decrease]

Composition of savings	1990	2000	2010	2017	2018	2019	2020	2021
Net acquisition of financial assets....................	**675.5**	**875.5**	**964.8**	**1,900.9**	**1,774.6**	**2,506.6**	**3,791.3**	**2,876.5**
Foreign deposits.............................	1.4	7.6	4.5	12.7	2.9	-1.0	7.8	-2.6
Checkable deposits and currency.....................	13.0	-91.6	-39.2	203.8	-145.9	22.5	1,799.0	1,289.8
Time and savings deposits.......................	43.8	342.5	175.8	266.3	477.5	607.9	611.7	862.7
Money market fund shares......................	43.1	184.1	-319.8	82.0	174.7	453.4	414.4	270.7
Debt securities............................	211.7	-48.1	194.4	-89.6	802.8	266.7	-544.5	-864.9
Treasury securities....................	97.0	-194.6	267.6	-42.0	581.9	172.8	-243.9	-499.4
Agency and GSE-backed securities [1]...........	36.5	30.9	42.2	18.5	167.7	87.0	-279.6	-105.4
Municipal securities.................	35.9	17.6	79.1	-34.1	0.2	-65.8	-40.0	-103.6
Corporate and foreign bonds..................	42.2	98.0	-194.4	-32.0	53.0	72.6	19.0	-156.6
Loans....................................	18.2	119.1	19.0	-54.7	-20.2	35.3	117.5	129.9
Corporate equities [2].....................	-67.4	-401.0	-152.2	130.1	-176.3	57.4	458.4	531.6
Mutual fund shares........................	29.8	82.1	260.0	308.0	18.7	312.6	-43.0	196.8
Trade receivables........................	5.9	10.1	6.3	16.0	3.5	7.6	7.6	6.9
Life insurance reserves....................	27.0	43.7	15.0	19.0	49.4	16.7	94.2	4.0
Pension entitlements......................	331.6	444.2	665.6	480.8	283.7	437.5	474.2	313.9
Miscellaneous and other assets............	17.5	182.7	135.4	526.6	303.8	289.9	393.9	137.9
Gross investment in nonfinancial assets.............	**829.7**	**1,592.6**	**1,675.2**	**2,517.1**	**2,643.4**	**2,722.4**	**2,877.4**	**3,485.4**
Minus: Consumption of fixed capital..................	617.7	1,010.5	1,568.4	1,929.6	2,018.7	2,106.5	2,203.6	2,407.7
Equals: Net investment in nonfinancial assets.......	**212.0**	**582.1**	**106.8**	**587.5**	**624.7**	**615.9**	**673.8**	**1,077.6**
Net increase in liabilities..............................	**240.5**	**931.3**	**-154.9**	**1,163.7**	**899.2**	**924.3**	**1,219.5**	**1,626.7**
Home mortgages..........................	206.9	423.0	-129.2	343.5	320.2	306.2	475.2	881.5
Other mortgages..........................	-4.4	106.3	-33.2	290.2	176.9	238.8	221.3	212.0
Consumer credit..........................	15.1	176.5	-28.2	194.3	172.7	185.2	-12.0	249.5
Other loans and advances.................	6.5	23.7	78.7	70.3	-21.7	32.5	264.6	154.6
Other liabilities..........................	16.4	201.6	-43.0	265.4	251.0	161.7	270.4	129.2
Personal saving, FOF concept (FOF) [3]........	662.7	562.0	1,198.4	1,300.3	1,506.7	2,213.5	3,248.1	2,280.5
Personal saving, NIPA concept (FOF) [3]........	585.8	318.7	1,142.3	1,073.0	1,251.3	1,962.0	2,953.2	1,698.7
Personal saving, NIPA concept (NIPA) [4]..........	361.1	351.4	709.3	1,076.4	1,190.9	1,237.8	2,887.5	2,264.2

[1] GSE = government-sponsored enterprises. [2] Only directly held and those in closed-end and exchange-traded funds. Other equities are included in mutual funds, life insurance reserves, and pension entitlements. [3] Flow of Funds measure. [4] National Income and Product Accounts measure.

Source: Board of Governors of the Federal Reserve System, "Z.1 Financial Accounts of the United States: Summary Table F.6 Derivation of Measures of Personal Saving," March 2022, <www.federalreserve.gov/releases/Z1/current/default.htm>, accessed March 2022.

Table 715. Government Consumption Expenditures and Gross Investment by Level of Government and Type: 2002 to 2021

[In billions of dollars (2,089 represents $2,089,000,000,000). Government consumption expenditures are services (such as education and national defense) produced by government that are valued at their cost of production; excludes government sales to other sectors and government own-account investment (construction, software, and research and development). Gross government investment consists of general government and government enterprise expenditures for fixed assets; inventory investment is included in government consumption expenditures. For explanation of national income and chained dollars, see text, Section 13]

Level of government and type	Current dollars				Chained (2012) dollars			
	2002	2010	2020	2021	2002	2010	2020	2021
Government consumption expenditures and gross investment, total..................	**2,089**	**3,156**	**3,860**	**4,053**	**2,887**	**3,308**	**3,360**	**3,376**
Consumption expenditures.......................	1,646	2,511	3,078	3,250	2,302	2,633	2,669	2,697
Gross investment.............................	444	645	782	802	585	675	692	679
Structures.................................	220	312	373	366	358	335	308	283
Equipment.................................	96	148	168	177	95	150	165	169
Intellectual property products............	127	184	240	258	147	190	220	231
Federal..	**743**	**1,300**	**1,502**	**1,565**	**969**	**1,348**	**1,341**	**1,349**
Consumption expenditures.......................	561	1,003	1,161	1,205	761	1,042	1,026	1,026
Gross investment.............................	182	297	340	360	210	306	315	324
Structures.................................	16	33	28	26	24	35	22	20
Equipment.................................	58	108	118	126	61	111	116	121
Intellectual property products............	108	156	195	208	127	161	177	183
National defense...............................	**459**	**828**	**881**	**905**	**606**	**861**	**801**	**794**
Consumption expenditures.......................	359	652	700	709	491	679	631	615
Gross investment.............................	100	176	181	196	116	182	170	180
Structures.................................	6	17	10	11	9	18	8	8
Equipment.................................	46	89	97	102	50	91	96	99
Intellectual property products............	48	70	74	84	57	73	66	73
Nondefense....................................	**284**	**472**	**620**	**660**	**363**	**487**	**539**	**554**
Consumption expenditures.......................	202	351	461	496	269	363	394	410
Gross investment.............................	82	121	159	164	94	124	145	144
Structures.................................	10	16	18	15	15	17	14	12
Equipment.................................	12	19	21	24	11	19	19	22
Intellectual property products............	60	86	121	125	70	88	111	111
State and local................................	**1,346**	**1,855**	**2,358**	**2,488**	**1,929**	**1,960**	**2,020**	**2,028**
Consumption expenditures.......................	1,085	1,508	1,917	2,045	1,547	1,591	1,643	1,670
Gross investment.............................	262	347	441	442	383	368	377	358
Structures.................................	204	280	345	340	334	301	285	263
Equipment.................................	38	40	50	52	34	40	49	49
Intellectual property products............	19	28	45	50	21	28	44	48

Source: U.S. Bureau of Economic Analysis, National Income and Product Accounts Tables, "Table 3.9.5. Government Consumption Expenditures and Gross Investment" and "Table 3.9.6. Real Government Consumption Expenditures and Gross Investment, Chained Dollars," <apps.bea.gov/iTable/index_nipa.cfm>, accessed June 2022.

Table 716. Personal Consumption Expenditures by Function: 2002 to 2020

[In billions of dollars (7,349 represents $7,349,000,000,000). In current and chained (2012) dollars. For definition of chained dollars, see text, this section. Minus sign (-) indicates decrease]

Function	Current dollars				Chained (2012) dollars			
	2002	2010	2019	2020	2002	2010	2019	2020
Personal consumption expenditures [1]	**7,349**	**10,260**	**14,429**	**14,048**	**9,106**	**10,716**	**13,126**	**12,630**
Food and nonalcoholic beverages purchased for off-premises consumption	490	679	884	979	645	728	849	907
Alcoholic beverages purchased for off-premises consumption	84	108	146	167	99	109	137	154
Clothing, footwear, and related services	295	332	415	377	298	349	420	401
Clothing (garments, cleaning, repair, and rental)	249	269	331	299	248	285	340	324
Footwear [2]	46	62	84	78	50	64	81	77
Housing [1]	1,129	1,648	2,223	2,316	1,413	1,706	1,794	1,816
Rental of tenant-occupied nonfarm housing [3]	248	361	537	559	324	377	423	426
Imputed rental of owner-occupied nonfarm housing [4]	867	1,268	1,661	1,732	1,069	1,308	1,351	1,370
Household utilities and fuels	215	324	370	371	334	336	336	337
Water supply and sanitation	55	78	109	112	92	87	84	84
Electricity, gas, and other fuels	160	246	261	258	243	249	251	252
Furnishings, household equipment, and routine household maintenance [1]	366	411	601	645	351	409	641	677
Furniture, furnishings, and floor coverings [5]	122	128	206	222	104	125	234	253
Household appliances [6]	42	50	65	71	45	52	73	77
Tools and equipment for house and garden	18	20	32	37	18	20	32	37
Medical products, appliances, and equipment [1]	234	379	616	646	305	401	538	561
Pharmaceutical and other medical products [7]	200	326	544	577	267	347	469	494
Outpatient services [8]	515	775	1,131	1,064	639	795	1,067	989
Physician services [8]	269	411	586	552	324	422	575	536
Dental services	76	104	140	110	112	109	118	90
Paramedical services [9]	170	260	405	402	205	264	376	367
Hospital and nursing home services	568	925	1,328	1,244	804	967	1,175	1,065
Transportation	807	962	1,327	1,133	1,162	1,085	1,417	1,249
Motor vehicles	360	288	437	461	359	300	449	465
New motor vehicles	244	182	286	293	250	191	278	283
Net purchases of used motor vehicles	116	106	151	168	109	109	174	186
Motor vehicle operation [1]	371	570	705	591	688	671	787	698
Motor vehicle fuels, lubricants, and fluids	154	312	317	229	411	406	420	356
Motor vehicle maintenance and repair	121	137	197	183	164	142	171	154
Public transportation	76	104	184	81	110	115	175	83
Telephone and related communication equipment	6	18	29	24	2	15	96	93
Postal and delivery services	9	15	13	15	14	16	11	12
Telecommunication services	131	148	160	160	130	145	222	226
Internet access	14	40	74	75	11	40	74	76
Recreation [1]	669	884	1,262	1,177	590	863	1,333	1,254
Video and audio equipment	86	83	92	100	28	66	177	208
Information processing equipment	44	95	157	178	16	81	231	284
Services related to video/audio goods and computers	61	97	140	144	78	103	119	118
Sports and recreational goods and related services	156	177	259	291	134	171	311	353
Magazines, newspapers, books, and stationery	81	75	99	113	89	76	90	98
Gambling	74	109	142	110	95	115	127	98
Pets, pet products, and related services	45	76	118	118	64	80	108	107
Education [1]	150	240	308	293	269	263	252	236
Higher education	87	155	190	186	164	171	155	149
Food services	383	537	851	723	514	567	716	589
Accommodations [10]	53	99	157	78	67	104	134	72
Financial services	324	479	741	756	418	516	493	494
Insurance [1]	215	289	431	440	294	304	364	365
Life insurance	59	78	92	94	74	80	78	77
Net health insurance	107	143	245	253	155	151	214	217
Net motor vehicle and other transportation insurance	46	60	83	82	60	65	65	63
Personal care [11]	143	207	301	240	169	211	280	219
Personal items [12]	63	85	107	105	73	90	111	110
Social services and religious activities [13]	93	139	214	205	120	145	179	164
Professional and other services [1]	127	159	205	198	181	167	170	162
Legal services	74	87	111	110	106	92	92	91
Accounting and other business services	20	28	41	39	29	30	32	29
Funeral and burial services	17	24	27	29	25	25	24	25
Tobacco	70	98	100	104	130	104	76	75
Net foreign travel and expenditures abroad by:								
U.S. residents [1]	-6	-12	-5	-10	6	-16	14	-3
Foreign travel by U.S. residents	71	112	186	54	111	119	188	56
Less: Expenditures in the United States by nonresidents	81	132	202	75	113	143	184	69
Final consumption expenditures of nonprofit institutions serving households (NPISHs) [14]	198	294	440	521	194	299	354	411

[1] Includes other expenditures not shown separately. [2] Also includes repair and hire of footwear. [3] Rent for space (see footnote 4), and for appliances, furnishings, and furniture. [4] Rent for space and for heating and plumbing facilities, water heaters, lighting fixtures, kitchen cabinets, linoleum, storm windows and doors, window screens, and screen doors; excludes rent for appliances and furniture and purchases of fuel and electricity. [5] Includes clocks, lamps, lighting fixtures, other household decorative items, and repair of furniture, furnishings, and floor coverings. [6] Includes appliance repair. [7] Excludes drug preparations and related products dispensed by physicians, hospitals, and other medical services. [8] Offices of physicians, HMO medical centers, and freestanding ambulatory surgical and emergency centers. [9] Includes home health care, medical laboratories, and other health professionals (except physicians) and services. [10] Hotels, motels, other traveler accommodations, clubs, and housing at schools. [11] Cosmetics, toiletries, and personal care appliances and services. [12] Jewelry, watches, luggage, and similar items. [13] Household purchases from business, government, and nonprofit institutions providing social services and religious activities. Purchases from nonprofit establishments exclude unrelated sales, secondary sales, and sales to businesses, government, and the rest of the world, but include membership dues and fees. [14] Net expenses of NPISHs, defined as their gross operating expenses less primary sales to households.

Source: U.S. Bureau of Economic Analysis, National Income and Product Accounts Tables, "2.5.5. Personal Consumption Expenditures by Function," and "2.5.6. Real Personal Consumption Expenditures by Function, Chained Dollars," <apps.bea.gov/iTable/index_nipa.cfm>, accessed July 2021.

Table 717. Personal Income By Source and Disposition: 2000 to 2021

[In billions of dollars (8,656 represents $8,656,000,000,000), except as indicated. For definition of personal income and chained dollars, see text, this section]

Item	2000	2010	2016	2017	2018	2019	2020	2021
Personal income	**8,656**	**12,595**	**16,097**	**16,850**	**17,706**	**18,424**	**19,628**	**21,093**
Compensation of employees, received	5,847	7,925	9,966	10,426	10,960	11,448	11,572	12,599
Wages and salaries	4,825	6,373	8,091	8,475	8,901	9,324	9,444	10,344
Supplements to wages and salaries	1,022	1,553	1,875	1,951	2,059	2,124	2,128	2,255
Proprietors' income [1]	754	1,107	1,423	1,506	1,580	1,599	1,650	1,822
Farm	31	38	34	39	39	38	70	98
Nonfarm	722	1,070	1,389	1,466	1,541	1,560	1,580	1,724
Rental income of persons [2]	183	434	627	653	682	692	712	726
Personal income receipts on assets	1,490	1,787	2,543	2,708	2,868	2,968	2,912	2,941
Personal interest income	1,106	1,243	1,465	1,553	1,615	1,652	1,614	1,641
Personal dividend income	384	544	1,077	1,155	1,253	1,316	1,298	1,301
Personal current transfer receipts	1,087	2,325	2,777	2,856	2,976	3,139	4,241	4,598
Government social benefits to persons [3]	1,045	2,281	2,717	2,808	2,926	3,083	4,181	4,531
Social security [4]	401	690	896	926	972	1,031	1,078	1,115
Unemployment insurance	21	139	32	30	28	28	537	339
Veterans' benefits	25	58	97	111	120	131	146	160
Other current transfer receipts, from business (net)	42	44	60	49	50	56	60	67
Less: Contributions for government social insurance	706	984	1,239	1,299	1,360	1,421	1,459	1,593
Less: Personal current taxes	1,236	1,238	1,958	2,049	2,076	2,205	2,196	2,585
Equals: Disposable personal income	**7,420**	**11,357**	**14,139**	**14,801**	**15,630**	**16,219**	**17,432**	**18,508**
Less: Personal outlays	7,068	10,648	13,151	13,725	14,439	14,981	14,544	16,226
Personal consumption expenditures	6,767	10,260	12,693	13,239	13,914	14,429	14,048	15,742
Personal interest payments [5]	218	242	273	292	321	340	285	266
Personal current transfer payments	83	145	185	194	204	212	212	218
Equals: Personal saving	**351**	**709**	**988**	**1,076**	**1,191**	**1,238**	**2,888**	**2,281**
Personal saving as a percentage of disposable personal income	4.7	6.2	7.0	7.3	7.6	7.6	16.6	12.3
Addenda:								
Disposable personal income:								
Total, billions of chained (2012) dollars [6]	9,501	11,861	13,576	13,957	14,429	14,755	15,673	16,019
Per capita:								
Current dollars	26,274	36,654	43,556	45,283	47,536	49,073	52,544	55,710
Chained (2012) dollars	33,645	38,282	41,821	42,699	43,886	44,644	47,241	48,219

[1] With inventory valuation and capital consumption adjustments. [2] Includes capital consumption adjustment. [3] Includes other benefits not shown separately. [4] Social security benefits include benefits distributed from the Old-Age and Survivors Insurance Trust Fund and the Disability Insurance Trust Fund. [5] Consists of nonmortgage interest paid by households. [6] The current-dollar measure is deflated by the implicit price deflator for personal consumption expenditures.

Source: U.S. Bureau of Economic Analysis, National Income and Product Accounts Tables, "Table 2.1. Personal Income and Its Disposition," <apps.bea.gov/iTable/index_nipa.cfm>, accessed June 2022.

Table 718. Selected Per Capita Income and Product Measures in Current and Chained (2012) Dollars: 1970 to 2021

[In dollars. Based on U.S. Census Bureau estimated population including Armed Forces abroad, and institutionalized population; based on monthly averages. For explanation of chained dollars, see text, this section]

Year	Current dollars					Chained (2012) dollars				
	Gross domestic product	Gross national product	Personal income	Disposable personal income	Personal consumption expenditures	Gross domestic product	Gross national product	Disposable personal income	Personal consumption expenditures	
1970	5,233	5,265	4,218	3,715	3,153	24,157	24,342	17,768	15,081	
1980	12,547	12,697	10,204	8,888	7,688	29,700	30,095	21,584	18,668	
1990	23,835	23,974	19,641	17,264	15,225	37,459	37,693	27,303	24,078	
2000	36,300	36,436	30,651	26,274	23,963	46,523	46,701	33,645	30,687	
2001	37,100	37,277	31,599	27,255	24,801	46,502	46,727	34,216	31,135	
2002	37,954	38,113	31,814	28,160	25,521	46,842	47,042	34,894	31,624	
2003	39,420	39,621	32,683	29,230	26,635	47,709	47,957	35,474	32,325	
2004	41,660	41,921	34,250	30,674	28,070	49,102	49,414	36,325	33,242	
2005	44,052	44,305	35,828	31,732	29,626	50,343	50,635	36,526	34,101	
2006	46,234	46,390	38,099	33,558	31,046	51,255	51,430	37,570	34,758	
2007	47,976	48,293	39,846	34,899	32,306	51,787	52,130	38,093	35,263	
2008	48,498	48,975	40,971	36,021	33,001	51,365	51,869	38,188	34,986	
2009	47,123	47,612	39,319	35,568	32,194	49,591	50,109	37,814	34,226	
2010	48,570	49,234	40,649	36,654	33,115	50,507	51,199	38,282	34,586	
2011	49,952	50,714	42,714	38,059	34,259	50,886	51,662	38,769	34,898	
2012	51,645	52,384	44,529	39,732	35,102	51,645	52,384	39,732	35,102	
2013	53,117	53,843	44,761	39,474	35,836	52,202	52,918	38,947	35,357	
2014	54,914	55,650	46,860	41,276	37,070	52,979	53,690	40,118	36,030	
2015	56,521	57,205	48,695	42,672	38,072	53,988	54,647	41,383	36,922	
2016	57,593	58,307	49,589	43,556	39,103	54,466	55,149	41,821	37,546	
2017	59,596	60,497	51,552	45,283	40,504	55,311	56,154	42,699	38,193	
2018	62,432	63,326	53,851	47,536	42,317	56,591	57,405	43,886	39,067	
2019	64,665	65,471	55,745	49,073	43,655	57,585	58,309	44,644	39,715	
2020	62,978	63,648	59,162	52,544	42,342	55,415	56,011	47,241	38,069	
2021	69,221	69,981	63,492	55,710	47,384	58,478	59,131	48,219	41,012	

Source: U.S. Bureau of Economic Analysis, National Income and Product Accounts Tables, "Table 7.1. Selected Per Capita Product and Income Series in Current and Chained Dollars," <apps.bea.gov/iTable/index_nipa.cfm>, accessed June 2022.

Table 719. Personal Income in Current and Constant (2012) Dollars by State: 2000 to 2021

[In billions of dollars (8,654.6 represents $8,654,600,000,000). Represents income that all persons who are state residents receive from all sources. Data exclude income of foreign nationals employed in the U.S. by their home governments, and income earned by U.S. citizens while living abroad. Data also exclude the earnings of federal civilian and military personnel stationed abroad. Totals may differ from those in Table 709, Table 717, and Table 718]

State	Current dollars					Constant (2012) dollars [1]				
	2000	2010	2019	2020	2021 (P)	2000	2010	2019	2020	2021 (P)
United States............	8,654.6	12,586.5	18,402.0	19,607.4	21,056.6	11,082.8	13,145.6	16,741.0	17,628.6	18,225.2
Alabama....................	108.2	162.5	215.9	228.7	245.0	138.6	169.8	196.4	205.7	212.0
Alaska.....................	20.1	35.5	45.3	46.4	49.2	25.8	37.0	41.2	41.7	42.6
Arizona....................	136.2	216.9	334.0	368.5	395.1	174.4	226.5	303.9	331.3	342.0
Arkansas..................	61.0	94.6	135.3	143.1	154.8	78.1	98.8	123.1	128.7	134.0
California..................	1,135.5	1,614.0	2,544.2	2,763.3	2,997.2	1,454.1	1,685.7	2,314.6	2,484.4	2,594.2
Colorado..................	147.2	205.9	350.4	370.4	401.1	188.6	215.0	318.8	333.0	347.2
Connecticut..............	146.9	221.1	270.3	279.6	296.0	188.2	230.9	245.9	251.4	256.2
Delaware..................	26.6	36.8	52.5	55.4	59.2	34.1	38.5	47.8	49.8	51.2
District of Columbia........	24.9	38.3	57.2	61.7	64.9	31.9	40.0	52.1	55.5	56.2
Florida....................	472.9	732.5	1,139.8	1,210.0	1,323.4	605.5	765.0	1,036.9	1,087.9	1,145.5
Georgia...................	237.4	338.3	518.3	554.6	597.1	304.0	353.3	471.5	498.6	516.8
Hawaii.....................	35.6	56.8	78.5	82.5	87.1	45.6	59.3	71.4	74.2	75.3
Idaho......................	32.7	50.4	81.8	89.1	97.7	41.9	52.7	74.4	80.1	84.5
Illinois....................	413.0	543.1	748.8	792.1	850.2	528.8	567.2	681.2	712.2	735.9
Indiana....................	171.5	231.7	329.7	350.8	382.2	219.6	242.0	299.9	315.4	330.8
Iowa.......................	80.2	116.9	159.7	169.2	181.9	102.7	122.1	145.3	152.1	157.5
Kansas....................	76.1	114.2	155.0	163.5	174.1	97.5	119.3	141.0	147.0	150.7
Kentucky..................	100.7	145.3	196.3	211.9	228.6	128.9	151.8	178.5	190.6	197.9
Louisiana.................	107.3	173.8	222.1	236.3	251.7	137.4	181.5	202.0	212.5	217.9
Maine.....................	35.1	50.6	67.9	73.2	78.4	45.0	52.9	61.7	65.8	67.9
Maryland..................	189.0	287.7	381.4	404.5	427.0	242.1	300.4	347.0	363.7	369.6
Massachusetts............	245.5	347.5	506.6	540.9	576.1	314.4	362.9	460.9	486.3	498.6
Michigan..................	302.0	353.3	492.0	530.8	558.3	386.7	369.0	447.6	477.2	483.3
Minnesota................	160.1	227.0	329.5	350.8	373.8	205.0	237.0	299.8	315.4	323.5
Mississippi...............	61.8	92.9	116.3	125.0	134.0	79.1	97.1	105.8	112.4	116.0
Missouri...................	156.7	222.6	300.5	318.0	340.2	200.6	232.5	273.4	285.9	294.5
Montana..................	20.9	36.1	53.6	57.7	62.6	26.7	37.7	48.8	51.8	54.2
Nebraska.................	49.8	75.5	104.4	111.5	121.9	63.7	78.8	95.0	100.3	105.5
Nevada...................	64.6	101.3	158.9	168.6	183.1	82.7	105.8	144.6	151.6	158.5
New Hampshire............	43.8	62.0	86.8	91.7	100.0	56.1	64.8	79.0	82.4	86.6
New Jersey...............	330.6	449.9	619.1	652.5	693.2	423.4	469.9	563.2	586.6	600.0
New Mexico..............	42.1	69.6	90.5	97.6	104.4	53.9	72.7	82.4	87.8	90.3
New York..................	685.8	947.1	1,361.5	1,440.0	1,515.8	878.2	989.1	1,238.6	1,294.7	1,311.9
North Carolina.............	222.3	343.3	500.5	533.3	580.8	284.7	358.6	455.3	479.5	502.7
North Dakota..............	16.6	29.9	44.4	47.1	50.8	21.3	31.2	40.4	42.3	44.0
Ohio.......................	325.0	425.4	587.2	627.2	665.4	416.2	444.3	534.2	563.9	575.9
Oklahoma.................	83.5	140.1	191.4	198.6	211.9	107.0	146.4	174.1	178.5	183.4
Oregon....................	97.4	138.3	221.2	238.8	257.6	124.7	144.4	201.2	214.7	223.0
Pennsylvania.............	374.0	537.3	737.2	788.7	830.4	478.9	561.1	670.6	709.1	718.7
Rhode Island..............	31.9	45.1	59.9	64.3	67.9	40.9	47.1	54.5	57.8	58.7
South Carolina............	101.1	152.2	234.4	250.6	270.3	129.5	159.0	213.3	225.3	234.0
South Dakota.............	20.3	33.8	48.5	52.9	57.9	26.0	35.3	44.2	47.6	50.2
Tennessee................	154.4	227.9	334.8	351.5	382.7	197.7	238.0	304.5	316.1	331.3
Texas.....................	594.5	985.2	1,544.0	1,618.6	1,762.1	761.3	1,028.9	1,404.7	1,455.3	1,525.1
Utah.......................	54.5	89.4	157.3	169.7	184.9	69.7	93.4	143.1	152.5	160.0
Vermont...................	17.7	26.1	34.6	36.9	38.5	22.7	27.3	31.4	33.2	33.4
Virginia....................	232.5	365.2	502.6	532.3	565.3	297.7	381.5	457.2	478.5	489.3
Washington...............	193.4	285.6	479.8	516.4	556.3	247.7	298.3	436.5	464.3	481.5
West Virginia.............	40.3	60.8	76.3	80.3	85.3	51.6	63.5	69.4	72.2	73.8
Wisconsin.................	158.8	223.0	308.2	324.3	345.3	203.4	232.9	280.4	291.5	298.9
Wyoming..................	14.6	26.3	35.4	36.0	38.0	18.7	27.5	32.2	32.4	32.9

P Preliminary. [1] Constant dollar estimates are calculated using the national implicit price deflator for personal consumption expenditures from the Bureau of Economic Analysis' National Income and Product Accounts Tables. Any regional differences in the rate of inflation are not reflected in these constant dollar estimates.

Source: Except as noted, U.S. Bureau of Economic Analysis, Regional Economic Accounts, Personal Income by State, "Table SAINC1 Personal Income Summary," <www.bea.gov/data/economic-accounts/regional>, accessed March 2022.

Table 720. Personal Income Per Capita in Current and Constant (2012) Dollars by State: 2000 to 2021

[In dollars, except as indicated. Represents income that all persons who are state residents receive from all sources. Data exclude income of foreign nationals employed in the U.S. by their home governments, and income earned by U.S. citizens while living abroad. Data also exclude the earnings of federal civilian and military personnel stationed abroad. Totals may differ from those in Table 709, Table 717, and Table 718]

State	Current dollars				Constant (2012) dollars [1]				Income rank [2]	
	2000	2010	2020	2021 (P)	2000	2010	2020	2021 (P)	2010	2021 (P)
United States.................	30,672	40,683	59,147	63,444	39,278	42,490	53,178	54,913	(X)	(X)
Alabama.........................	24,306	33,946	45,524	48,608	31,126	35,454	40,930	42,072	42	49
Alaska..........................	32,044	49,652	63,391	67,138	41,035	51,857	56,993	58,110	6	11
Arizona.........................	26,388	33,876	51,332	54,301	33,792	35,381	46,151	46,999	43	42
Arkansas........................	22,781	32,372	47,522	51,148	29,173	33,810	42,726	44,270	48	46
California.......................	33,410	43,246	69,958	76,386	42,784	45,167	62,898	66,114	12	5
Colorado........................	34,029	40,790	64,034	69,016	43,577	42,602	57,572	59,735	23	10
Connecticut.....................	43,070	61,743	77,664	82,082	55,154	64,486	69,826	71,045	2	3
Delaware........................	33,884	40,942	55,810	59,002	43,391	42,761	50,178	51,068	22	27
District of Columbia.............	43,524	63,368	89,417	96,873	55,736	66,183	80,393	83,847	1	1
Florida.........................	29,466	38,872	56,096	60,761	37,733	40,599	50,435	52,591	27	21
Georgia.........................	28,851	34,829	51,704	55,289	36,946	36,376	46,486	47,854	41	37
Hawaii..........................	29,319	41,574	56,840	60,389	37,545	43,421	51,104	52,269	19	23
Idaho...........................	25,183	32,097	48,208	51,379	32,249	33,523	43,343	44,470	50	45
Illinois.........................	33,212	42,278	61,957	67,095	42,530	44,156	55,704	58,073	16	12
Indiana.........................	28,153	35,695	51,691	56,153	36,052	37,281	46,474	48,602	40	34
Iowa............................	27,390	38,312	53,057	56,973	35,075	40,014	47,702	49,312	28	31
Kansas..........................	28,253	39,960	55,677	59,324	36,180	41,735	50,058	51,347	24	26
Kentucky........................	24,868	33,409	47,058	50,699	31,845	34,893	42,309	43,882	45	47
Louisiana.......................	23,997	38,242	50,810	54,435	30,730	39,941	45,682	47,115	29	41
Maine...........................	27,491	38,106	53,728	57,159	35,204	39,799	48,306	49,473	30	30
Maryland........................	35,591	49,668	65,534	69,266	45,577	51,874	58,920	59,952	5	9
Massachusetts...................	38,594	52,894	77,021	82,475	49,422	55,244	69,248	71,385	3	2
Michigan........................	30,344	35,760	52,724	55,551	38,858	37,348	47,403	48,081	39	35
Minnesota.......................	32,448	42,724	61,464	65,486	41,552	44,622	55,261	56,680	14	15
Mississippi......................	21,681	31,287	42,270	45,438	27,764	32,677	38,004	39,328	51	51
Missouri........................	27,941	37,118	51,673	55,159	35,781	38,767	46,458	47,742	33	38
Montana.........................	23,081	36,393	53,085	56,672	29,557	38,010	47,728	49,051	35	32
Nebraska........................	29,039	41,248	56,869	62,095	37,187	43,080	51,130	53,745	21	19
Nevada..........................	31,986	37,494	54,137	58,233	40,960	39,159	48,673	50,402	31	29
New Hampshire...................	35,335	47,098	66,534	72,003	45,249	49,190	59,819	62,321	8	7
New Jersey......................	39,216	51,076	70,314	74,805	50,219	53,345	63,218	64,746	4	6
New Mexico......................	23,102	33,710	46,092	49,320	29,584	35,207	41,440	42,688	44	48
New York........................	36,090	48,768	71,449	76,415	46,216	50,934	64,238	66,140	7	4
North Carolina..................	27,510	35,872	50,996	55,043	35,229	37,465	45,849	47,641	37	39
North Dakota....................	25,892	44,264	60,451	65,544	33,157	46,230	54,350	56,730	11	14
Ohio............................	28,598	36,854	53,198	56,483	36,622	38,491	47,829	48,888	34	33
Oklahoma........................	24,178	37,276	50,114	53,156	30,962	38,932	45,056	46,008	32	43
Oregon..........................	28,386	36,036	56,311	60,676	36,350	37,637	50,628	52,517	36	22
Pennsylvania....................	30,443	42,251	60,720	64,054	38,985	44,128	54,592	55,441	17	18
Rhode Island....................	30,417	42,766	58,656	61,942	38,951	44,666	52,736	53,613	13	20
South Carolina..................	25,133	32,852	48,838	52,074	32,185	34,311	43,909	45,072	46	44
South Dakota....................	26,825	41,423	59,656	64,720	34,351	43,263	53,635	56,017	20	17
Tennessee.......................	27,066	35,851	50,801	54,873	34,660	37,443	45,674	47,494	38	40
Texas...........................	28,383	39,034	55,399	59,674	36,347	40,768	49,808	51,650	26	25
Utah............................	24,260	32,218	51,698	55,392	31,067	33,649	46,481	47,943	49	36
Vermont.........................	29,014	41,733	57,423	59,704	37,155	43,587	51,628	51,676	18	24
Virginia........................	32,715	45,513	61,661	65,408	41,894	47,535	55,438	56,613	10	16
Washington......................	32,723	42,348	66,907	71,889	41,904	44,229	60,155	62,222	15	8
West Virginia...................	22,317	32,762	44,868	47,817	28,579	34,217	40,340	41,387	47	50
Wisconsin.......................	29,556	39,175	55,030	58,564	37,849	40,915	49,476	50,689	25	28
Wyoming.........................	29,607	46,649	62,397	65,627	37,914	48,721	56,100	56,802	9	13

P Preliminary. X Not applicable. [1] Constant dollar estimates are calculated using the national implicit price deflator for personal consumption expenditures from the Bureau of Economic Analysis' National Income and Product Accounts tables. Any regional differences in the rate of inflation are not reflected in these constant dollar estimates. [2] Ranking based on current dollar income.

Source: Except as noted, U.S. Bureau of Economic Analysis, Regional Economic Accounts, Personal Income by State, "Table SAINC1 Personal Income Summary," <www.bea.gov/data/economic-accounts/regional>, accessed March 2022.

Table 721. Disposable Personal Income Per Capita in Current and Constant (2012) Dollars by State: 2000 to 2021

[In dollars, except as indicated. Per capita disposable personal income is total disposable personal income divided by total midyear population. Disposable personal income is total personal income minus personal current taxes. It is the portion of personal income that is available for saving and spending. The estimate of personal income in the United States is derived as the sum of the state estimates and the estimate for the District of Columbia; it differs from the estimate of personal income in the national income and product accounts (NIPAs) because of differences in coverage, in the methodologies used to prepare the estimates, and in the timing of the availability of source data. See text, Section 13]

State	Current dollars				Constant (2012) dollars [1]				Index, compared to U.S. average [2]	
	2000	2010	2020	2021 (P)	2000	2010	2020	2021 (P)	2020	2021 (P)
United States...........	**26,294**	**36,688**	**52,531**	**55,671**	**33,671**	**38,318**	**47,229**	**48,185**	**100.0**	**100.0**
Alabama...................	21,574	31,187	41,521	44,003	27,627	32,572	37,331	38,086	79.0	79.0
Alaska....................	28,606	45,912	58,950	62,164	36,632	47,951	53,001	53,805	112.2	111.7
Arizona..................	23,048	31,157	46,552	48,732	29,515	32,541	41,854	42,179	88.6	87.5
Arkansas................	20,218	29,723	43,345	46,278	25,891	31,043	38,971	40,055	82.5	83.1
California................	27,660	38,472	60,593	64,994	35,421	40,181	54,478	56,254	115.3	116.7
Colorado.................	28,897	36,484	56,643	60,344	37,005	38,105	50,927	52,230	107.8	108.4
Connecticut..............	34,980	53,964	66,304	69,035	44,794	56,361	59,612	59,752	126.2	124.0
Delaware.................	29,292	36,987	49,549	51,916	37,511	38,630	44,548	44,935	94.3	93.3
District of Columbia......	36,488	55,622	75,991	81,193	46,726	58,093	68,322	70,275	144.7	145.8
Florida...................	25,759	35,766	50,575	54,099	32,986	37,355	45,471	46,824	96.3	97.2
Georgia..................	24,907	31,624	46,500	49,192	31,895	33,029	41,807	42,577	88.5	88.4
Hawaii...................	25,738	38,080	51,236	53,815	32,959	39,771	46,065	46,579	97.5	96.7
Idaho....................	22,059	29,552	43,639	46,026	28,248	30,865	39,235	39,837	83.1	82.7
Illinois..................	28,440	37,988	54,552	58,438	36,420	39,675	49,047	50,580	103.8	105.0
Indiana..................	24,664	32,532	46,660	50,264	31,584	33,977	41,951	43,505	88.8	90.3
Iowa.....................	24,223	34,933	47,831	51,031	31,019	36,485	43,004	44,169	91.1	91.7
Kansas..................	24,606	36,274	50,198	53,102	31,510	37,885	45,132	45,961	95.6	95.4
Kentucky................	21,792	30,430	42,467	45,357	27,906	31,782	38,181	39,258	80.8	81.5
Louisiana................	21,482	35,295	46,712	49,715	27,509	36,863	41,998	43,030	88.9	89.3
Maine....................	24,005	34,823	48,503	51,073	30,740	36,370	43,608	44,205	92.3	91.7
Maryland.................	30,130	43,985	56,734	59,105	38,584	45,939	51,008	51,157	108.0	106.2
Massachusetts...........	31,160	46,399	65,751	69,137	39,903	48,460	59,115	59,840	125.2	124.2
Michigan.................	26,225	32,623	47,500	49,427	33,583	34,072	42,706	42,781	90.4	88.8
Minnesota...............	27,620	38,071	53,928	56,794	35,369	39,762	48,486	49,157	102.7	102.0
Mississippi..............	19,594	28,975	39,214	41,916	25,092	30,262	35,256	36,280	74.6	75.3
Missouri.................	24,373	33,854	46,576	49,300	31,211	35,358	41,875	42,671	88.7	88.6
Montana.................	20,376	33,340	47,878	50,596	26,093	34,821	43,046	43,792	91.1	90.9
Nebraska................	25,500	37,682	51,429	55,892	32,655	39,356	46,239	48,376	97.9	100.4
Nevada..................	27,871	34,399	49,146	52,198	35,691	35,927	44,186	45,179	93.6	93.8
New Hampshire..........	30,508	43,254	60,205	64,229	39,068	45,175	54,129	55,592	114.6	115.4
New Jersey..............	32,872	45,207	61,290	64,258	42,095	47,215	55,105	55,617	116.7	115.4
New Mexico..............	20,618	31,185	42,576	45,293	26,403	32,570	38,279	39,202	81.0	81.4
New York................	30,065	42,053	60,225	63,161	38,500	43,921	54,147	54,668	114.6	113.5
North Carolina...........	23,834	32,634	45,679	48,792	30,521	34,084	41,069	42,231	87.0	87.6
North Dakota............	23,379	40,443	55,578	60,051	29,939	42,239	49,969	51,976	105.8	107.9
Ohio.....................	24,649	33,316	47,991	50,469	31,565	34,796	43,148	43,682	91.4	90.7
Oklahoma................	21,278	34,329	45,944	48,494	27,248	35,854	41,307	41,973	87.5	87.1
Oregon..................	24,189	32,347	49,576	52,748	30,976	33,784	44,573	45,655	94.4	94.7
Pennsylvania.............	26,321	38,068	54,393	56,715	33,706	39,759	48,904	49,089	103.5	101.9
Rhode Island.............	26,260	38,786	52,662	54,991	33,628	40,509	47,347	47,596	100.2	98.8
South Carolina...........	22,199	30,235	44,210	46,715	28,427	31,578	39,748	40,433	84.2	83.9
South Dakota............	24,265	38,681	55,333	59,792	31,073	40,399	49,749	51,752	105.3	107.4
Tennessee...............	24,367	33,498	46,965	50,292	31,204	34,986	42,225	43,529	89.4	90.3
Texas....................	25,024	35,953	50,771	54,280	32,045	37,550	45,647	46,981	96.6	97.5
Utah.....................	21,186	29,399	46,476	49,291	27,130	30,705	41,786	42,663	88.5	88.5
Vermont.................	25,338	38,284	52,034	53,506	32,447	39,985	46,783	46,311	99.1	96.1
Virginia..................	27,844	40,631	54,022	56,638	35,656	42,436	48,570	49,022	102.8	101.7
Washington..............	28,257	38,908	60,271	64,004	36,185	40,636	54,188	55,397	114.7	115.0
West Virginia.............	19,945	30,011	41,135	43,537	25,541	31,344	36,984	37,683	78.3	78.2
Wisconsin................	25,484	35,413	49,075	51,663	32,634	36,986	44,122	44,716	93.4	92.8
Wyoming................	25,645	42,508	56,913	59,434	32,840	44,396	51,169	51,442	108.3	106.8

P Preliminary. [1] Constant dollar estimates are calculated using the national implicit price deflator for personal consumption expenditures from the Bureau of Economic Analysis' National Income and Product Accounts Tables. Any regional differences in the rate of inflation are not reflected in these constant dollar estimates. [2] Indexes based on disposable personal income per capita in current dollars.

Source: Except as noted, U.S. Bureau of Economic Analysis, Regional Economic Accounts, Personal Income by State, "Table SAINC51 Disposable Personal Income Summary," <www.bea.gov/data/economic-accounts/regional>, accessed March 2022.

Table 722. Personal Income by Selected Large Metropolitan Area: 2000 to 2020

[7,655,312 represents $7,655,312,000,000. MSA=Metropolitan Statistical Area. The MSAs used by the Bureau of Economic Analysis are defined in the Office of Management and Budget Bulletin No. 20-01 issued March 6, 2020. Per capita personal income was computed using Census Bureau midyear population estimates. Estimates for 2010-2020 reflect county population estimates available as of March 2021]

Metropolitan statistical areas ranked by 2020 population	Personal income			Personal income per capita			Index (U.S.= 100), 2020
	2000 (mil. dol.)	2010 (mil. dol.)	2020 (mil. dol.)	2000 (dol.)	2010 (dol.)	2020 (dol.)	
United States, metropolitan portion.............	**7,655,312**	**11,108,179**	**17,521,595**	**32,172**	**42,130**	**61,674**	**100.0**
New York-Newark-Jersey City, NY-NJ-PA MSA.....	753,373	1,028,239	1,574,365	41,042	54,337	82,322	133.5
Los Angeles-Long Beach-Anaheim, CA MSA........	395,968	571,360	915,133	31,952	44,505	69,805	113.2
Chicago-Naperville-Elgin, IL-IN-WI MSA.............	329,264	421,552	636,555	36,130	44,511	67,671	109.7
Dallas-Fort Worth-Arlington, TX MSA...............	176,477	267,155	473,604	34,022	41,795	61,554	99.8
Houston-The Woodlands-Sugar Land, TX MSA.....	157,577	272,324	428,501	33,403	45,790	59,893	97.1
Washington-Arlington-Alexandria, DC-VA-MD-WV MSA........	207,730	331,887	485,551	42,603	58,444	76,771	124.5
Miami-Fort Lauderdale-Pompano Beach, FL MSA........	163,223	241,183	396,247	32,476	43,196	64,190	104.1
Philadelphia-Camden-Wilmington, PA-NJ-DE-MD MSA........	200,931	288,338	425,749	35,301	48,288	69,705	113.0
Atlanta-Sandy Springs-Alpharetta, GA MSA........	146,052	205,619	357,796	34,017	38,776	58,773	95.3
Phoenix-Mesa-Chandler, AZ MSA..............	95,078	147,897	262,363	29,045	35,178	51,851	84.1
Boston-Cambridge-Newton, MA-NH MSA...........	187,341	264,820	418,178	42,565	57,993	85,724	139.0
San Francisco-Oakland-Berkeley, CA MSA........	205,264	263,524	521,590	49,630	60,666	111,050	180.1
Riverside-San Bernardino-Ontario, CA MSA........	77,121	128,075	212,234	23,534	30,189	45,365	73.6
Detroit-Warren-Dearborn, MI MSA..............	154,532	164,671	251,173	34,683	38,373	58,356	94.6
Seattle-Tacoma-Bellevue, WA MSA..............	118,782	167,010	323,176	38,917	48,418	80,420	130.4
Minneapolis-St. Paul-Bloomington, MN-WI MSA....	112,425	155,080	245,833	37,115	46,430	67,214	109.0
San Diego-Chula Vista-Carlsbad, CA MSA.........	95,760	135,928	220,826	33,869	43,802	66,266	107.4
Tampa-St. Petersburg-Clearwater, FL MSA........	70,277	108,244	169,629	29,233	38,819	52,291	84.8
Denver-Aurora-Lakewood, CO MSA..............	82,670	111,611	208,853	38,080	43,690	69,822	113.2
St. Louis, MO-IL MSA..............	85,686	119,281	170,697	31,987	42,751	60,844	98.7
Baltimore-Columbia-Towson, MD MSA..........	88,401	131,152	186,760	34,559	48,292	66,695	108.1
Charlotte-Concord-Gastonia, NC-SC MSA........	53,706	87,639	152,149	30,620	38,947	56,682	91.9
Orlando-Kissimmee-Sanford, FL MSA..........	45,896	72,043	127,278	27,700	33,677	48,223	78.2
San Antonio-New Braunfels, TX MSA..........	46,510	78,870	129,593	27,041	36,632	50,022	81.1
Portland-Vancouver-Hillsboro, OR-WA MSA........	62,820	88,700	157,150	32,468	39,735	62,603	101.5
Sacramento-Roseville-Folsom, CA MSA............	56,989	88,002	146,882	31,521	40,863	61,852	100.3
Las Vegas-Henderson-Paradise, NV MSA..........	43,367	70,047	118,679	31,112	35,873	51,244	83.1
Pittsburgh, PA MSA..............	74,668	101,386	147,041	30,749	43,013	63,675	103.2
Austin-Round Rock-Georgetown, TX MSA..........	42,272	71,848	148,994	33,418	41,590	64,913	105.3
Cincinnati, OH-KY-IN MSA..............	62,734	87,233	133,098	31,029	40,745	59,607	96.6
Kansas City, MO-KS MSA..............	58,467	83,643	126,169	32,161	41,543	58,057	94.1
Columbus, OH MSA..............	52,108	74,023	120,321	30,979	38,829	56,252	91.2
Indianapolis-Carmel-Anderson, IN MSA..........	54,675	78,884	126,362	32,858	41,679	60,431	98.0
Cleveland-Elyria, OH MSA..............	68,563	82,867	120,270	31,926	39,927	58,846	95.4
San Jose-Sunnyvale-Santa Clara, CA MSA........	93,803	110,981	239,730	53,949	60,265	121,619	197.2
Nashville-Davidson--Murfreesboro--Franklin, TN MSA..............	43,808	69,432	121,745	32,095	42,057	62,076	100.7
Virginia Beach-Norfolk-Newport News, VA-NC MSA..............	45,236	69,244	94,883	27,966	40,326	53,310	86.4
Providence-Warwick, RI-MA MSA..............	47,374	67,423	98,890	29,869	42,056	60,897	98.7
Jacksonville, FL MSA..............	34,266	52,639	87,532	30,424	39,022	55,125	89.4
Milwaukee-Waukesha, WI MSA..............	50,670	67,982	95,448	33,726	43,671	60,499	98.1
Oklahoma City, OK MSA..............	29,293	49,678	75,100	26,675	39,496	52,688	85.4
Raleigh-Cary, NC MSA..............	27,668	49,038	86,479	34,406	43,115	60,884	98.7
Memphis, TN-MS-AR MSA..............	35,744	48,871	68,992	29,584	37,093	51,155	82.9
Richmond, VA MSA..............	33,740	50,951	79,704	32,335	42,872	61,148	99.1
New Orleans-Metairie, LA MSA..............	36,540	51,602	73,652	27,284	43,168	57,891	93.9
Louisville/Jefferson County, KY-IN MSA..........	33,195	45,959	70,652	30,376	38,151	55,676	90.3
Salt Lake City, UT MSA..............	26,038	39,310	71,932	27,626	36,015	58,008	94.1
Hartford-East Hartford-Middletown, CT MSA........	43,681	60,919	80,911	37,955	50,177	67,343	109.2
Buffalo-Cheektowaga, NY MSA..............	32,859	43,739	62,785	28,107	38,515	55,777	90.4
Birmingham-Hoover, AL MSA..............	29,087	41,979	60,136	29,599	39,532	55,074	89.3
Grand Rapids-Kentwood, MI MSA..............	27,790	36,362	58,434	29,597	36,571	54,037	87.6
Rochester, NY MSA..............	31,991	42,901	60,289	29,996	39,724	56,477	91.6
Tucson, AZ MSA..............	21,187	33,558	51,332	24,984	34,185	48,373	78.4
Tulsa, OK MSA..............	23,778	39,580	58,443	27,609	42,112	58,071	94.2
Fresno, CA MSA..............	18,468	29,074	48,539	23,048	31,195	48,495	78.6
Urban Honolulu, HI MSA..............	27,516	43,057	60,522	31,388	45,024	62,793	101.8
Omaha-Council Bluffs, NE-IA MSA..............	25,306	39,352	58,248	32,895	45,352	61,040	99.0
Worcester, MA-CT MSA..............	27,875	39,351	58,392	32,349	42,822	61,741	100.1
Bridgeport-Stamford-Norwalk, CT MSA..............	55,127	95,417	113,322	62,335	103,785	120,244	195.0
Greenville-Anderson, SC MSA..............	19,351	27,374	44,617	26,591	33,154	47,836	77.6
Albuquerque, NM MSA..............	19,570	30,782	43,819	26,727	34,603	47,442	76.9
Bakersfield, CA MSA..............	14,212	25,789	40,310	21,410	30,651	44,721	72.5
Albany-Schenectady-Troy, NY MSA..............	26,838	38,682	57,204	32,436	44,406	65,112	105.6
Knoxville, TN MSA..............	19,456	28,544	44,380	26,681	34,979	50,540	81.9
McAllen-Edinburg-Mission, TX MSA..............	8,166	17,355	27,265	14,246	22,276	31,153	50.5

Source: U.S. Bureau of Economic Analysis, Regional Economic Accounts, Personal Income by County, Metro, and Other Areas, "CAINC1 Personal Income Summary: Personal Income, Population, Per Capita Personal Income," <www.bea.gov/data/economic-accounts/regional>, accessed March 2022.

Table 723. Households by Income Level and Median Income by State: 2020

[In thousands (124,345 represents 124,345,000), except as indicated. Data are based on 2020 American Community Survey (ACS) 1-year experimental estimates. The coronavirus disease 2019 (COVID-19) pandemic impacted 2020 ACS data collection and quality, and standard estimates did not meet statistical quality standards. The Census Bureau does not recommend comparing experimental estimates to standard ACS estimates. For more information, see <www.census.gov/programs-surveys/acs/data/experimental-data.html>. The American Community Survey universe includes the household population and the population living in institutions, college dormitories, and other group quarters. Based on a sample and subject to sampling variability; see text, Section 1 and Appendix III. For definition of median, see Guide to Tabular Presentation]

State	Number of households (1,000)								Median income (dollars)
	Total	Less than $20,000	$20,000 to $39,999	$40,000 to $59,999	$60,000 to $99,999	$100,000 to $149,999	$150,000 to $199,999	$200,000 or more	
United States	**124,345**	**16,828**	**20,159**	**18,629**	**28,057**	**19,939**	**9,394**	**11,340**	**67,340**
Alabama	1,895	343	378	301	416	257	98	102	53,956
Alaska	255	25	31	34	66	50	26	23	80,197
Arizona	2,774	356	468	464	665	423	191	207	64,777
Arkansas	1,186	219	259	193	265	145	50	54	51,183
California	13,135	1,472	1,704	1,629	2,758	2,304	1,310	1,958	83,056
Colorado	2,202	225	290	322	517	403	203	242	77,673
Connecticut	1,406	172	177	183	302	244	140	188	79,719
Delaware	388	44	67	58	89	70	30	31	70,911
District of Columbia	292	37	28	31	52	47	30	66	96,762
Florida	8,134	1,154	1,469	1,318	1,848	1,204	517	624	61,736
Georgia	3,905	587	676	591	876	583	282	309	62,844
Hawaii	477	44	54	59	112	95	56	58	86,391
Idaho	679	80	117	122	178	105	38	39	62,774
Illinois	4,907	649	731	697	1,137	816	410	467	71,240
Indiana	2,642	368	482	450	641	420	139	142	60,813
Iowa	1,276	159	229	221	319	203	78	66	62,209
Kansas	1,152	148	202	195	288	176	73	70	63,321
Kentucky	1,759	300	349	303	402	242	83	78	54,191
Louisiana	1,763	357	348	272	353	236	103	95	51,730
Maine	584	90	112	96	134	86	36	31	58,782
Maryland	2,255	227	257	279	490	428	252	322	88,742
Massachusetts	2,687	334	319	308	527	484	288	427	87,328
Michigan	4,013	584	727	641	946	614	252	248	61,497
Minnesota	2,235	227	320	337	541	423	188	199	75,523
Mississippi	1,126	251	237	190	225	132	51	41	47,247
Missouri	2,463	364	467	419	565	372	137	139	58,838
Montana	447	64	91	78	102	65	23	23	57,211
Nebraska	774	91	139	127	198	125	50	44	64,591
Nevada	1,174	152	206	185	276	190	80	85	64,574
New Hampshire	539	50	68	74	132	106	53	55	80,972
New Jersey	3,346	355	429	399	695	601	349	518	87,016
New Mexico	817	160	160	132	172	112	46	34	52,059
New York	7,489	1,076	1,075	987	1,555	1,231	647	918	73,398
North Carolina	4,089	630	775	648	931	587	241	277	59,580
North Dakota	322	41	55	58	78	50	20	18	61,987
Ohio	4,742	714	869	772	1,134	703	277	272	60,338
Oklahoma	1,514	255	303	260	340	211	73	73	54,536
Oregon	1,689	212	270	262	393	287	127	139	67,927
Pennsylvania	5,179	705	893	807	1,199	817	359	400	64,910
Rhode Island	422	55	58	58	98	81	34	38	75,682
South Carolina	2,009	338	388	318	455	279	112	118	56,973
South Dakota	349	47	58	66	91	51	20	15	60,643
Tennessee	2,702	433	510	462	628	369	145	154	56,951
Texas	10,271	1,375	1,706	1,588	2,334	1,614	772	882	66,031
Utah	1,052	81	137	166	278	212	91	87	77,827
Vermont	263	35	43	40	66	45	17	18	67,428
Virginia	3,214	348	442	453	691	563	304	414	79,217
Washington	2,988	308	389	413	685	538	290	365	80,408
West Virginia	734	145	158	126	157	93	33	22	49,400
Wisconsin	2,393	311	401	392	601	406	151	131	64,868
Wyoming	237	30	37	42	58	41	16	14	66,432

Source: U.S. Census Bureau, 2020 ACS 1-Year Experimental Data Tables, "Table XK201901. Household Income in the Past 12 Months (in 2020 Inflation-Adjusted Dollars)," and "Table XK201902. Median Household Income in the Past 12 Months (in 2020 Inflation-Adjusted Dollars)," <www.census.gov/programs-surveys/acs/data/experimental-data.html>, accessed February 2022.

Table 724. Families by Income Level and Median Income by State: 2020

[In thousands (79,420 represents 79,420,000), except as indicated. Data are based on 2020 American Community Survey (ACS) 1-year experimental estimates. The coronavirus disease 2019 (COVID-19) pandemic impacted 2020 ACS data collection and quality, and standard estimates did not meet statistical quality standards. The Census Bureau does not recommend comparing experimental estimates to standard ACS estimates. For more information, see <www.census.gov/programs-surveys/acs/data/experimental-data.html>. The American Community Survey universe includes the household population and the population living in institutions, college dormitories, and other group quarters. Based on a sample and subject to sampling variability; see text, Section 1 and Appendix III. For definition of median, see Guide to Tabular Presentation]

State	Number of families (1,000)								Median income (dollars)
	Total	Less than $20,000	$20,000 to $39,999	$40,000 to $59,999	$60,000 to $99,999	$100,000 to $149,999	$150,000 to $199,999	$200,000 or more	
United States........	**79,420**	**5,797**	**10,001**	**11,155**	**19,487**	**15,619**	**7,774**	**9,588**	**84,394**
Alabama...............	1,198	107	190	193	304	224	88	93	71,781
Alaska.................	166	9	16	18	45	38	21	19	93,751
Arizona...............	1,764	136	232	278	455	332	161	170	79,260
Arkansas..............	767	79	138	129	202	126	45	48	66,166
California.............	8,873	588	1,013	1,071	1,882	1,705	1,027	1,587	96,821
Colorado..............	1,359	68	128	168	330	300	162	202	97,781
Connecticut...........	891	54	82	103	187	183	118	165	104,535
Delaware..............	241	14	28	34	59	55	25	26	89,996
District of Columbia. ..	110	7	11	9	12	13	13	44	160,212
Florida................	5,096	382	737	811	1,272	946	430	519	77,200
Georgia...............	2,528	206	370	363	613	468	237	270	78,530
Hawaii................	329	18	29	34	77	79	46	47	102,579
Idaho.................	464	28	63	78	137	91	31	35	75,634
Illinois................	3,069	209	340	398	742	641	342	398	90,509
Indiana...............	1,691	126	225	276	476	346	122	120	76,404
Iowa..................	800	49	98	126	232	167	69	58	80,513
Kansas................	745	50	91	117	223	143	61	61	78,929
Kentucky..............	1,125	112	178	188	303	200	73	71	69,485
Louisiana.............	1,082	127	182	159	250	192	90	81	70,245
Maine.................	345	23	47	58	95	65	30	26	76,453
Maryland.............	1,471	71	121	153	318	320	205	282	109,898
Massachusetts........	1,668	97	147	168	330	345	231	351	111,112
Michigan..............	2,490	188	330	371	666	504	217	214	79,736
Minnesota............	1,407	63	129	183	362	333	161	176	96,184
Mississippi............	725	103	131	121	175	113	46	36	60,955
Missouri..............	1,524	112	208	254	408	302	121	118	76,700
Montana..............	266	17	38	46	72	54	19	20	74,521
Nebraska.............	489	25	61	73	144	104	45	37	81,988
Nevada...............	743	52	113	112	199	139	62	67	76,779
New Hampshire.......	349	14	27	40	92	83	45	48	100,514
New Jersey............	2,258	140	220	228	469	460	286	454	105,788
New Mexico...........	488	54	80	77	120	88	39	29	67,774
New York..............	4,677	394	552	575	1,017	906	498	736	91,045
North Carolina........	2,570	206	380	396	662	478	203	245	76,279
North Dakota..........	193	12	24	28	54	42	17	15	82,225
Ohio..................	2,913	236	395	440	801	560	239	243	77,177
Oklahoma.............	973	87	163	163	256	177	64	63	69,656
Oregon...............	1,056	67	125	159	273	217	97	118	83,245
Pennsylvania..........	3,237	222	411	467	836	650	304	348	83,262
Rhode Island..........	262	16	26	34	64	62	29	31	93,564
South Carolina........	1,273	114	190	197	333	236	99	104	73,725
South Dakota.........	217	15	23	40	67	43	18	13	76,475
Tennessee............	1,713	147	251	276	473	307	124	135	72,728
Texas.................	6,848	559	921	987	1,652	1,299	660	770	80,872
Utah..................	777	32	75	113	220	179	82	77	88,591
Vermont..............	153	7	16	24	43	35	14	15	87,112
Virginia...............	2,076	110	216	255	457	426	251	360	99,927
Washington...........	1,903	107	173	235	455	400	232	299	97,980
West Virginia..........	445	47	73	80	118	79	29	19	65,900
Wisconsin.............	1,456	81	166	222	412	330	131	115	84,243
Wyoming..............	154	9	17	25	44	34	14	12	84,861

Source: U.S. Census Bureau, 2020 ACS 1-Year Experimental Data Tables, "Table XK201903. Family Income in the Past 12 Months (in 2020 Inflation-Adjusted Dollars)" and "Table XK201904. Median Family Income in the Past 12 Months (in 2020 Inflation-Adjusted Dollars)," <www.census.gov/programs-surveys/acs/data/experimental-data.html>, accessed February 2022.

Table 725. Personal Income by Source Including Federal COVID-19 Pandemic Response Programs: 2020 to 2022

[In billions of dollars (19,777.4 represents $19,774,400,000,000). Seasonally adjusted at annual rates. See source noted below for information on specific provisions of the Coronavirus Aid, Relief, and Economic Security Act and other federal programs. CCAdj=capital consumption adjustment. IVA=inventory valuation adjustment. NPISH=nonprofit institutions serving households. Data are subject to revision]

Income by source	2020 3rd quarter	2020 4th quarter	2021 1st quarter	2021 2nd quarter	2021 3rd quarter	2021 4th quarter	2022 1st quarter
Personal income	**19,777.4**	**19,542.0**	**21,867.3**	**20,669.9**	**20,823.8**	**20,947.7**	**21,215.6**
Compensation of employees	11,539.7	11,964.2	12,088.9	12,416.6	12,756.5	13,061.4	13,325.8
Wages and salaries	9,410.3	9,783.0	9,879.2	10,180.4	10,487.2	10,761.6	10,992.8
Supplements to wages and salaries	2,129.4	2,181.1	2,209.7	2,236.2	2,269.3	2,299.8	2,333.1
Proprietors' income with IVA and CCAdj	**1,760.7**	**1,730.0**	**1,714.0**	**1,848.2**	**1,867.0**	**1,858.5**	**1,880.9**
Farm income	69.2	108.5	73.0	119.4	110.6	88.0	110.4
Coronavirus Food Assistance Program	18.4	46.2	0.9	14.3	8.7	1.2	0.6
Paycheck Protection Program (PPP) loans to businesses	8.7	2.6	4.9	11.3	7.0	0.8	–
Nonfarm income	1,691.5	1,621.5	1,640.9	1,728.7	1,756.3	1,770.5	1,770.6
PPP loans to businesses	281.2	84.5	76.8	177.6	110.2	11.9	
Rental income of persons with CCAdj	**714.5**	**710.0**	**716.9**	**716.3**	**729.0**	**743.6**	**756.2**
Personal income receipts on assets	**2,851.7**	**2,909.6**	**2,898.8**	**2,932.1**	**2,945.2**	**2,989.2**	**3,015.0**
Personal interest income	1,597.6	1,610.3	1,630.2	1,639.4	1,636.3	1,656.8	1,684.9
Personal dividend income	1,254.2	1,299.2	1,268.7	1,292.8	1,308.8	1,332.4	1,330.1
Personal current transfer receipts	**4,369.4**	**3,729.5**	**5,982.5**	**4,329.0**	**4,137.5**	**3,942.2**	**3,924.4**
Government social benefits to persons	4,310.5	3,670.2	5,920.6	4,257.8	4,069.6	3,875.5	3,856.7
Social security	1,080.2	1,088.8	1,106.3	1,109.7	1,117.2	1,126.9	1,197.9
Medicare	825.8	821.0	814.1	815.3	826.5	847.9	875.0
Medicaid	690.4	678.3	695.9	730.5	775.0	782.9	810.4
Unemployment insurance	767.8	299.9	565.8	480.4	272.3	37.7	25.1
Pandemic emergency unemployment compensation	26.7	82.1	97.8	104.5	61.5	3.3	1.0
Pandemic unemployment assistance	138.3	106.8	95.3	82.1	50.0	2.4	0.9
Pandemic unemployment compensation	413.9	14.7	286.9	237.2	113.2	–	–
Veterans' benefits	147.4	149.5	152.4	156.5	162.3	169.2	177.5
Other transfer receipts	799.0	632.7	2,586.0	965.4	916.2	911.0	770.8
Economic impact payments	15.6	5.0	1,933.7	290.1	38.9	14.2	
Lost wages supplemental payments	106.2	35.9	1.6	0.6	0.1	–	–
Paycheck Protection Program loans to NPISH	81.2	24.4	10.8	24.7	14.0	2.0	–
Provider Relief Fund to NPISH	58.4	34.5	42.8	26.6	37.4	64.4	53.7
Other current transfer receipts, from business (net)	58.9	59.2	62.0	71.2	67.9	66.7	67.7
Less: Contributions for government social insurance	1,458.7	1,501.3	1,533.8	1,572.2	1,611.3	1,647.2	1,686.7
Less: Personal current taxes	2,181.8	2,259.8	2,412.1	2,532.5	2,641.1	2,744.9	2,796.2
Equals: Disposable personal income (DPI)	17,595.7	17,282.2	19,455.3	18,137.4	18,182.7	18,202.8	18,419.4
Less: Personal outlays	14,774.3	14,936.8	15,475.6	16,165.0	16,456.2	16,808.4	17,206.9
Equals: Personal saving	**2,821.3**	**2,345.5**	**3,979.7**	**1,972.4**	**1,726.4**	**1,394.4**	**1,212.5**

– Represents or rounds to zero.

Source: U.S. Bureau of Economic Analysis, Federal Recovery Programs and BEA Statistics, "The Effects of Selected Federal Pandemic Response Programs on: Personal Income," <www.bea.gov/recovery>, accessed April 2022.

Table 726. Consumer Spending Using Payment Card Transactions—Monthly Growth Rates by Type of Business: 2021 to August 2022

[Percent change for each monthly period. Data are based on the median estimates of the monthly level. Covers payments consumers make using credit cards, debit cards, or gift cards, primarily at brick-and-mortar merchants. Data are based on a panel of merchants that contribute data over a 13-month period. Numbers in parentheses are North American Industry Classification System codes]

Year and month	Total retail and food service [1]	Furniture, home furnishings (442)	Electronics, appliance (443)	Food and beverage (445)	Gasoline stations (447)	Clothing and accessories (448)	Amusement, gambling, recreation (713)	Accommodation (721)	Food services, drinking places (722)
2021									
December-January	7.5	13.0	4.5	9.0	15.8	3.7	17.3	2.9	13.1
January-February	-6.2	-13.9	-11.3	-3.0	-0.6	-7.7	0.8	12.0	-3.1
February-March	10.0	21.6	14.6	-0.5	11.3	29.7	19.0	16.5	16.7
March-April	1.5	3.4	0.1	0.6	-2.2	2.4	6.3	11.9	5.3
April-May	-1.9	-9.4	-3.8	0.7	1.3	-3.4	6.5	5.2	2.7
May-June	2.7	1.8	2.5	0.8	4.2	5.4	7.3	12.1	3.8
June-July	-1.1	-2.8	-0.6	-0.2	1.6	0.4	-1.4	9.0	0.7
July-August	0.1	-1.2	-3.9	0.1	-1.6	-2.2	-7.3	-7.3	-2.5
August-September	2.3	4.0	0.8	1.2	1.1	-0.4	4.0	-0.2	2.6
September-October	-1.9	-3.7	-1.7	-2.1	0.6	-0.6	1.5	-0.8	-1.1
October-November	-1.7	-5.2	-3.9	1.5	4.2	0.6	-9.2	7.6	-0.3
November-December	0.9	3.0	5.2	-1.3	2.9	-2.0	-5.7	7.2	-1.4
2022									
December-January	1.4	3.7	-2.5	7.3	3.7	-7.9	8.9	-13.3	-2.5
January-February	-3.0	-1.7	-7.2	-4.2	1.9	6.9	6.3	9.5	4.3
February-March	0.8	-2.3	-1.2	-0.6	10.7	2.5	1.8	4.2	1.0
March-April	2.2	5.2	-0.4	0.9	-4.2	2.4	1.8	4.2	2.6
April-May	-1.2	-7.6	-3.3	1.5	5.7	-5.8	-0.8	0.4	-0.1
May-June	-0.6	0.7	-6.0	-1.5	5.9	0.8	1.7	-0.6	-1.0
June-July	1.6	-1.4	5.7	1.6	-5.0	-0.1	-1.2	-0.4	-0.5
July-August	1.8	3.0	-0.2	1.0	-6.9	5.4	-0.3	-3.5	2.7

[1] Excludes merchants that do most of their business through e-commerce.

Source: U.S. Bureau of Economic Analysis, "COVID-19 and Recovery: Estimates From Payment Card Transactions," <www.bea.gov/recovery/estimates-from-payment-card-transactions>, accessed September 2022.

Table 727. Consumer Unit Expenditures—Annual Averages by Major Type of Expenditure: 1990 to 2020

[Consumer units in thousands (96,968 represents 96,968,000); expenditures in dollars. Based on Consumer Expenditure Survey. Data are averages for the noninstitutional population. Expenditures are direct out-of-pocket expenditures. Consumers units may be all members in a housing unit (families), a person living alone or sharing a household with others and financially independent, or 2 or more unrelated persons living together who share expenses. Information on the impact of the coronavirus disease 2019 (COVID-19) pandemic on the Consumer Expenditure Survey is available at <www.bls.gov/covid19/effects-of-covid-19-pandemic-and-response-on-the-consumer-expenditure-surveys. htm>]

Type of expenditure	1990	2000	2010	2016	2017	2018	2019	2020
Number of consumer units (1,000)............	96,968	109,367	121,107	129,549	130,001	131,439	132,242	131,234
Expenditures [1] (average dollars)..........	**28,381**	**38,045**	**48,109**	**57,311**	**60,060**	**61,224**	**63,036**	**61,334**
Food...	4,296	5,158	6,129	7,203	7,729	7,923	8,169	7,316
Food at home [1].............................	2,485	3,021	3,624	4,049	4,363	4,464	4,643	4,942
Cereals and bakery products...............	368	453	502	524	564	569	583	640
Meats, poultry, fish, and eggs............	668	795	784	890	944	961	980	1,075
Dairy products..........................	295	325	380	410	450	449	455	474
Fruits and vegetables....................	408	521	679	783	837	858	876	977
Other food at home.....................	746	927	1,278	1,442	1,568	1,627	1,749	1,776
Food away from home.....................	1,811	2,137	2,505	3,154	3,365	3,459	3,526	2,375
Alcoholic beverages...........................	293	372	412	484	558	583	579	478
Housing [1]...................................	8,703	12,319	16,557	18,886	19,884	20,091	20,679	21,409
Shelter....................................	4,836	7,114	9,812	11,128	11,895	11,747	12,190	12,604
Utilities, fuels, and public services...........	1,890	2,489	3,660	3,884	3,836	4,049	4,055	4,158
Apparel and services.........................	1,618	1,856	1,700	1,803	1,833	1,866	1,883	1,434
Transportation [1]...........................	5,120	7,417	7,677	9,049	9,576	9,761	10,742	9,826
Vehicle purchases.........................	2,129	3,418	2,588	3,634	4,054	3,975	4,394	4,523
Gasoline, other fuels, motor oil...........	1,047	1,291	2,132	1,909	1,968	2,109	2,094	1,568
Other vehicle expenses...................	1,642	2,281	2,464	2,884	2,842	2,859	3,474	3,471
Public transportation.....................	302	427	493	623	712	818	781	263
Health care [2]...............................	1,480	2,066	3,157	4,612	4,928	4,968	5,193	5,177
Entertainment...............................	1,422	1,863	2,504	2,913	3,203	3,226	3,090	2,912
Personal care products and services..........	364	564	582	707	762	768	786	646
Reading......................................	153	146	100	118	110	108	92	114
Education....................................	406	632	1,074	1,329	1,491	1,407	1,443	1,271
Tobacco products, smoking supplies...........	274	319	362	337	332	347	320	315
Personal insurance and pensions.............	2,592	3,365	5,373	6,831	6,771	7,296	7,165	7,246
Life and other personal insurance............	345	399	318	322	418	465	520	486
Pensions and Social Security.................	2,248	2,966	5,054	6,509	6,353	6,831	6,645	6,760

[1] Includes expenditures not shown separately. [2] Due to changes implemented with the 2014 questionnaire on health insurance, 2014 and subsequent data are not directly comparable to data from previous years.

Source: U.S. Bureau of Labor Statistics, Consumer Expenditure Surveys, CE Tables, "Calendar year means, shares across all items, and coefficients of variation by demographic characteristics, 2020," <www.bls.gov/cex/tables.htm>, accessed November 2021; and previous releases.

Table 728. Consumer Expenditures—Annual Averages by Metropolitan Statistical Area: 2019 to 2020

[In dollars. Annual averages for all consumer units, for 2-year period 2019-2020. See text, Section 1 and Appendix II. See headnote, Table 727. Information on the impact of the coronavirus disease 2019 (COVID-19) pandemic on the Consumer Expenditure Survey is available at <www.bls.gov/covid19/effects-of-covid-19-pandemic-and-response-on-the-consumer-expenditure-surveys.htm>]

Metropolitan statistical area	Total expenditures [1]	Food	Housing Total [1]	Housing Shelter	Housing Utility, fuels [2]	Transportation Total [1]	Transportation Vehicle purchases	Transportation Gasoline and motor oil	Health care
Anchorage, Alaska..........................	73,189	10,291	24,548	14,545	4,762	10,522	3,501	2,121	4,985
Atlanta, Georgia............................	62,746	9,430	22,379	12,676	4,359	8,711	2,559	1,915	5,071
Baltimore, Maryland........................	73,531	7,772	24,972	15,806	4,203	11,946	5,764	1,756	5,610
Boston, Massachusetts......................	91,578	10,860	30,997	20,368	4,652	11,176	5,215	1,609	6,962
Chicago, Illinois............................	63,251	8,750	23,757	14,849	3,985	8,852	3,547	1,638	5,628
Dallas-Fort Worth, Texas....................	62,306	6,208	23,277	14,513	4,794	9,696	3,570	1,981	5,515
Denver, Colorado...........................	75,760	7,838	25,965	16,262	4,065	12,749	5,861	1,684	5,645
Detroit, Michigan...........................	63,008	7,687	20,143	11,229	4,367	10,861	3,352	1,837	5,062
Honolulu, Hawaii...........................	60,884	9,953	23,572	16,007	4,455	8,213	2,975	1,670	3,909
Houston, Texas.............................	69,872	7,324	23,160	13,796	4,595	11,252	4,498	2,018	5,171
Los Angeles, California.....................	67,857	8,869	25,624	17,061	4,000	10,681	3,754	2,519	4,339
Miami, Florida..............................	53,147	6,178	20,399	13,968	3,620	9,730	3,143	1,981	4,348
Minneapolis-St. Paul, Minnesota...........	80,046	8,931	25,799	15,365	4,004	11,585	5,243	1,826	7,050
New York City..............................	75,275	9,693	29,425	19,342	4,144	9,350	3,081	1,322	4,683
Philadelphia, Pennsylvania.................	72,726	8,489	25,884	15,680	4,505	9,823	3,776	1,542	5,618
Phoenix, Arizona...........................	62,466	6,737	21,094	12,988	4,188	12,776	7,022	1,727	5,238
San Diego, California.......................	83,216	11,067	30,994	20,965	3,755	11,310	3,038	2,353	4,451
San Francisco, California...................	91,728	11,438	34,460	24,485	4,427	11,139	4,135	1,928	5,678
Seattle, Washington........................	81,728	9,928	30,007	19,469	4,092	10,766	3,946	1,949	4,994
St. Louis, Missouri..........................	64,389	7,429	20,493	11,322	4,183	9,314	3,706	1,705	6,408
Tampa, Florida.............................	60,720	8,545	20,648	12,163	4,181	11,178	4,641	1,883	5,254
Washington, DC............................	89,052	10,145	33,572	21,063	4,689	10,912	4,163	1,652	6,325

[1] Includes expenditures not shown separately. [2] Includes public services.

Source: U.S. Bureau of Labor Statistics, Consumer Expenditure Surveys, CE Tables, "Metropolitan Statistical Areas," <www.bls.gov/cex/tables.htm>, accessed November 2021.

Table 729. Personal Consumption Expenditures—Total and Per Capita by State: 2000 to 2020

[Total in millions of current dollars (6,767,179 represents $6,767,179,000,000); per capita amounts in current dollars. Per capita data reflect Census Bureau midyear population estimates for years 2010-2020 available as of December 2020; these population estimates are based on the 2010 census]

State	Total personal consumption expenditures (million dollars) 2000	2010	2018	2019	2020	Per capita personal consumption expenditures (dollars) 2000	2010	2018	2019	2020
United States......	**6,767,179**	**10,260,256**	**13,913,531**	**14,428,676**	**14,047,565**	**23,983**	**33,170**	**42,570**	**43,946**	**42,635**
Alabama............	89,929	132,956	170,857	177,751	176,480	20,199	27,783	34,928	36,217	35,859
Alaska...............	17,080	28,597	36,645	37,780	35,636	27,199	40,053	49,747	51,499	48,739
Arizona.............	121,307	196,466	273,434	287,660	287,090	23,507	30,663	38,167	39,450	38,684
Arkansas............	50,721	77,759	101,727	104,430	104,489	18,936	26,612	33,772	34,568	34,479
California............	838,174	1,290,347	1,835,635	1,921,463	1,835,981	24,661	34,576	46,545	48,722	46,636
Colorado............	116,595	175,698	259,864	273,403	270,883	26,946	34,809	45,613	47,478	46,642
Connecticut.........	100,843	145,877	181,568	185,316	179,406	29,557	40,757	50,795	51,967	50,437
Delaware............	21,270	33,778	44,250	45,865	44,835	27,049	37,546	45,761	46,960	45,434
Dist. of Columbia....	22,398	33,892	47,631	49,318	46,454	39,154	55,994	67,644	69,633	65,169
Florida.............	412,353	644,319	927,050	966,943	947,906	25,696	34,188	43,616	44,991	43,615
Georgia.............	188,692	283,500	400,690	416,543	408,753	22,935	29,190	38,091	39,193	38,165
Hawaii..............	30,439	47,969	64,439	66,977	63,428	25,083	35,168	45,281	47,313	45,080
Idaho...............	26,082	42,105	61,376	63,986	64,781	20,072	26,805	35,031	35,765	35,459
Illinois..............	311,284	438,798	559,565	574,300	553,612	25,035	34,173	43,975	45,338	43,981
Indiana.............	133,628	191,185	253,793	260,120	257,343	21,936	29,456	37,888	38,645	38,097
Iowa................	63,620	93,619	119,390	121,840	118,905	21,720	30,687	37,903	38,562	37,586
Kansas..............	61,411	89,314	111,458	114,771	113,185	22,798	31,248	38,266	39,404	38,845
Kentucky............	83,751	123,774	160,788	165,186	163,750	20,684	28,464	36,017	36,935	36,574
Louisiana...........	87,611	134,277	171,430	176,521	173,521	19,591	29,546	36,753	37,894	37,354
Maine...............	31,167	47,322	60,086	62,130	61,124	24,405	35,643	44,836	46,167	45,272
Maryland............	139,636	216,189	273,980	280,842	268,457	26,292	37,346	45,345	46,382	44,331
Massachusetts......	189,002	277,048	364,730	377,585	358,472	29,712	42,191	52,969	54,763	52,001
Michigan............	229,745	308,262	411,916	423,448	411,364	23,084	31,208	41,244	42,409	41,274
Minnesota..........	133,479	191,753	255,154	262,443	251,205	27,055	36,105	45,492	46,532	44,403
Mississippi..........	50,426	77,274	94,782	96,534	95,998	17,703	26,013	31,775	32,413	32,358
Missouri............	132,309	192,047	244,845	252,194	246,053	23,596	32,029	39,968	41,071	39,999
Montana............	19,466	32,497	43,990	45,545	45,720	21,539	32,801	41,429	42,560	42,310
Nebraska............	38,873	59,209	78,632	80,688	79,714	22,682	32,362	40,837	41,752	41,142
Nevada.............	50,610	85,190	120,132	125,927	123,054	25,070	31,523	39,638	40,743	39,211
New Hampshire.....	34,585	53,360	69,527	72,030	70,719	27,894	40,522	51,309	52,932	51,760
New Jersey.........	236,811	351,426	443,500	458,468	446,078	28,089	39,937	49,878	51,564	50,221
New Mexico.........	36,468	58,626	74,540	76,039	74,276	20,024	28,396	35,601	36,215	35,264
New York...........	467,342	714,029	976,857	1,015,020	961,707	24,595	36,806	49,982	52,151	49,735
North Carolina.......	181,767	281,630	388,543	407,916	405,954	22,491	29,414	37,391	38,844	38,295
North Dakota........	13,971	23,590	34,105	34,836	33,631	21,761	34,962	44,871	45,613	43,945
Ohio................	261,026	356,616	463,474	475,942	466,160	22,970	30,904	39,678	40,691	39,866
Oklahoma..........	67,648	105,508	135,983	138,946	137,469	19,583	28,060	34,483	35,081	34,533
Oregon.............	80,905	121,582	172,989	180,750	178,375	23,590	31,682	41,350	42,871	42,055
Pennsylvania........	306,159	455,820	577,036	594,861	570,772	24,923	35,859	45,049	46,478	44,650
Rhode Island........	25,345	36,684	45,923	47,198	45,397	24,132	34,804	43,351	44,604	42,944
South Carolina......	86,017	137,415	188,549	196,624	195,959	21,375	29,642	37,031	38,122	37,554
South Dakota........	15,553	26,007	36,219	37,599	37,338	20,577	31,864	41,187	42,383	41,825
Tennessee..........	126,206	186,743	250,646	260,814	258,252	22,127	29,383	36,978	38,185	37,499
Texas...............	472,006	772,105	1,128,352	1,173,809	1,164,466	22,536	30,588	39,419	40,495	39,661
Utah................	44,821	74,656	113,864	119,970	121,445	19,969	26,899	36,088	37,451	37,369
Vermont............	15,689	24,029	30,020	30,756	29,545	25,735	38,391	48,047	49,285	47,397
Virginia.............	175,778	287,429	366,753	377,556	367,303	24,737	35,821	43,092	44,124	42,757
Washington.........	151,834	236,110	347,411	363,100	354,219	25,689	35,016	46,157	47,688	46,041
West Virginia........	35,222	53,331	66,585	68,110	66,404	19,492	28,761	36,869	37,938	37,206
Wisconsin...........	125,129	184,972	238,008	244,555	238,923	23,284	32,505	40,970	41,987	40,963
Wyoming............	11,459	19,199	24,352	24,839	24,467	23,182	34,008	42,055	42,817	42,016

Source: U.S. Bureau of Economic Analysis, Regional Economic Accounts, "Personal Consumption Expenditures (PCE) by State," <www.bea.gov/data/consumer-spending/state>, accessed November 2021.

Table 730. Consumer Unit Expenditures—Averages by Income Level: 2020

[In dollars. See headnote, Table 727. See source for definitions, standard errors, and other information]

Income level	Total expenditures [1]	Food	Housing Total [1]	Shelter	Utilities, fuels [2]	Transportation Total [1]	Vehicle purchases	Gasoline and motor oil	Health care	Pensions and social security
All consumer units..........	**61,334**	**7,316**	**21,409**	**12,604**	**4,158**	**9,826**	**4,523**	**1,568**	**5,177**	**6,760**
BY INCOME										
Less than $15,000.............	28,235	4,226	12,163	7,581	2,638	4,388	1,996	816	2,267	282
$15,000 to $29,999...........	31,604	4,087	13,483	8,143	3,002	4,666	1,797	914	3,594	763
$30,000 to $39,999...........	40,689	5,756	15,404	9,001	3,446	6,491	2,376	1,284	4,180	1,863
$40,000 to $49,999...........	44,081	5,783	16,942	10,160	3,687	7,378	3,006	1,421	4,386	2,797
$50,000 to $69,999...........	51,285	6,026	18,511	10,786	4,035	9,225	4,044	1,658	4,958	4,300
$70,000 to $99,999...........	63,592	7,475	21,926	12,570	4,556	11,098	4,940	1,859	5,745	6,847
$100,000 to $149,999.........	83,050	9,901	26,257	15,508	5,050	14,888	7,785	2,054	6,508	11,202
$150,000 to $199,999.........	100,484	11,002	32,804	19,274	5,463	14,404	6,619	2,179	7,662	15,743
$200,000 and over............	145,402	14,066	46,591	27,432	6,568	19,397	9,804	2,258	8,997	25,906

[1] Includes expenditures not shown separately. [2] Includes public services.

Source: U.S. Bureau of Labor Statistics, Consumer Expenditure Surveys, CE Tables, "Calendar year means, shares across all items, and coefficients of variation by demographic characteristics, 2020," <www.bls.gov/cex/tables.htm>, accessed November 2021.

Table 731. Consumer Expenditures—Average for All Consumer Units by Race, Hispanic Origin, and Age of Householder: 2020

[In dollars. See headnote, Table 727. See source for definitions, standard errors, and other information]

Expenditure type	All consumer units [1]	White and other races [2]	Asian	Black or African American	His-panic [3]	Age of householder — Under 25 years	Age of householder — 65 years old and over
Expenditures, total	**61,334**	**63,227**	**67,306**	**47,389**	**52,540**	**38,070**	**47,579**
Food	7,316	7,458	8,521	5,923	6,893	4,526	5,698
Food at home	4,942	5,013	5,703	4,176	4,644	2,604	4,204
Cereals and bakery products	640	645	752	561	577	359	549
Cereals and cereal products	212	210	309	182	214	129	162
Bakery products	428	435	443	379	364	230	387
Meats, poultry, fish, and eggs [4]	1,075	1,065	1,310	1,047	1,131	570	899
Beef	296	301	299	260	312	137	246
Pork	214	219	224	180	224	113	195
Poultry	189	185	213	207	231	99	137
Fish and seafood	170	153	334	210	160	59	149
Eggs	64	62	101	58	76	50	53
Dairy products [4]	474	497	453	336	425	212	430
Fresh milk and cream	147	149	211	104	155	70	127
Fruits and vegetables [4]	977	976	1,351	827	1,005	514	866
Fresh fruits	349	348	518	281	364	185	303
Fresh vegetables	311	312	492	226	318	169	279
Processed vegetables	192	190	234	186	183	90	174
Other food at home [4]	1,776	1,830	1,836	1,406	1,505	949	1,460
Sugar and other sweets	166	171	148	140	124	110	143
Nonalcoholic beverages	455	475	402	348	436	255	384
Food away from home	2,375	2,446	2,818	1,746	2,249	1,923	1,494
Alcoholic beverages	478	527	326	226	251	225	363
Housing	21,409	21,697	25,482	18,177	19,693	14,745	17,435
Shelter	12,604	12,642	16,911	10,842	12,089	9,819	9,915
Owned dwellings	7,473	7,822	9,530	4,581	5,534	1,120	6,654
Mortgage interest and charges	2,962	3,050	4,144	1,993	2,526	488	1,488
Property taxes	2,353	2,479	3,424	1,196	1,590	347	2,464
Maintenance, repairs, insurance, other expenses	2,158	2,293	1,962	1,392	1,418	285	2,702
Rented dwellings	4,408	4,028	6,809	5,919	6,306	8,454	2,631
Other lodging	722	792	573	341	249	245	630
Utilities, fuels, and public services	4,158	4,195	3,921	4,009	4,135	2,315	3,783
Natural gas	414	406	492	437	333	186	424
Electricity	1,516	1,531	1,260	1,510	1,498	910	1,433
Fuel oil and other fuels	105	117	39	54	49	12	143
Telephone (includes mobile service)	1,441	1,440	1,348	1,479	1,558	917	1,120
Water and other public services	682	701	782	528	696	290	663
Household operations	1,465	1,522	1,730	1,012	979	638	1,240
Personal services	347	368	640	108	182	95	96
Other household expenses	1,118	1,154	1,090	905	797	543	1,144
Housekeeping supplies [4]	837	884	656	611	643	344	786
Laundry and cleaning supplies	170	168	133	199	196	74	154
Postage and stationery	130	140	122	67	87	44	137
Household furnishings and equipment [4]	2,346	2,454	2,264	1,702	1,847	1,628	1,711
Household textiles	116	126	50	78	107	119	74
Furniture	534	541	460	521	534	476	291
Major appliances	354	364	333	300	325	266	290
Miscellaneous household equipment	1,178	1,252	1,228	687	731	690	916
Apparel and services [4]	1,434	1,445	1,393	1,382	1,610	1,164	821
Men and boys	326	340	338	237	451	232	140
Women and girls	545	552	469	531	506	333	360
Footwear	314	308	316	350	409	446	150
Transportation	9,826	10,198	8,468	7,996	10,197	7,300	6,221
Vehicle purchases (net outlay) [4]	4,523	4,808	3,291	3,192	4,528	3,466	2,462
Cars and trucks, new	2,089	2,224	1,605	1,426	1,526	731	1,349
Cars and trucks, used	2,360	2,497	1,686	1,747	3,000	2,725	1,099
Gasoline, other fuels, and motor oil	1,568	1,600	1,469	1,404	1,879	1,370	989
Other vehicle expenses	3,471	3,526	3,287	3,192	3,525	2,293	2,603
Vehicle finance charges	258	272	223	184	246	184	125
Maintenance and repairs	879	901	718	804	783	518	710
Vehicle rental, leases, licenses, other charges	758	780	869	586	715	447	588
Vehicle insurance [5]	1,575	1,574	1,477	1,617	1,781	1,144	1,180
Public transportation	263	263	422	209	265	171	166
Health care	5,177	5,460	4,924	3,511	3,284	1,350	6,668
Entertainment	2,912	3,194	1,998	1,495	1,740	1,266	2,293
Personal care products and services	646	656	701	560	583	468	505
Reading	114	122	103	69	59	51	157
Education	1,271	1,256	2,936	779	540	2,264	450
Tobacco products and smoking supplies	315	335	176	237	171	237	207
Miscellaneous	907	950	874	651	732	317	921
Cash contributions	2,283	2,514	1,329	1,187	1,019	380	3,119
Personal insurance and pensions	7,246	7,415	10,074	5,195	5,769	3,776	2,721
Life and other personal insurance	486	490	520	446	251	75	513
Pensions and social security	6,760	6,925	9,554	4,749	5,518	3,701	2,208
Personal taxes	**9,402**	**10,002**	**14,793**	**3,773**	**2,440**	**1,764**	**2,158**

[1] Includes other races not shown separately. [2] Other races includes Native Hawaiian/Pacific Islander, Native American/Alaskan, and about 2 percent reporting more than one race. [3] People of Hispanic origin may be of any race. [4] Includes other types, not shown separately. [5] In 2019, the Consumer Expenditure survey program switched the data source used to estimate vehicle insurance spending from the Diary Survey to the Interview Survey. For more information, see <www.bls.gov/cex/2019-vehicle-insurance.htm>.

Source: U.S. Bureau of Labor Statistics, Consumer Expenditure Surveys, CE Tables, "Calendar year means, shares across all items, and coefficients of variation by demographic characteristics, 2020," <www.bls.gov/cex/tables.htm>, accessed November 2021.

Table 732. Consumer Expenditures—Averages for All Consumer Units by Region and Size of Unit: 2020

[In dollars. For composition of regions, see map, inside front cover. See headnote, Table 727. See source for definitions, standard errors, and other information]

Expenditure type	Region				Size of consumer unit				
	North-east	Mid-west	South	West	One person	Two persons	Three persons	Four persons	Five or more
Expenditures, total	**68,596**	**59,667**	**55,797**	**66,769**	**38,895**	**63,254**	**69,740**	**84,056**	**80,954**
Food	8,294	6,921	6,477	8,398	4,279	7,179	8,203	10,963	11,027
Food at home	5,803	4,664	4,310	5,639	2,831	4,791	5,520	7,407	7,848
Cereals and bakery products	793	619	555	688	349	614	709	988	1,060
Cereals and cereal products	258	200	174	253	104	197	238	331	400
Bakery products	535	418	381	435	245	417	471	657	661
Meats, poultry, fish, and eggs [1]	1,285	941	975	1,215	557	1,057	1,227	1,599	1,815
Beef	332	262	271	345	137	300	354	437	498
Pork	216	194	216	230	108	213	240	344	338
Poultry	244	158	168	213	102	179	206	263	368
Fish and seafood	229	139	143	200	92	178	182	250	261
Eggs	73	51	55	85	38	58	69	95	115
Dairy products [1]	587	454	395	541	280	451	528	729	733
Fresh milk and cream	181	136	123	171	85	134	171	223	244
Fruits and vegetables [1]	1,224	874	824	1,150	577	944	1,090	1,489	1,481
Fresh fruits	426	317	285	430	213	322	396	548	527
Fresh vegetables	399	272	249	388	176	324	334	468	442
Processed vegetables	229	174	184	195	113	182	218	284	311
Other food at home [1]	1,914	1,775	1,561	2,045	1,068	1,725	1,966	2,603	2,759
Sugar and other sweets	207	169	141	173	100	155	178	256	267
Nonalcoholic beverages	489	440	412	518	285	432	529	635	704
Food away from home	2,491	2,257	2,167	2,759	1,448	2,388	2,683	3,555	3,179
Alcoholic beverages	587	500	382	539	335	616	451	585	354
Housing	25,195	19,268	19,029	24,548	15,867	21,272	23,225	28,205	27,097
Shelter	15,342	10,674	10,755	15,439	9,995	12,374	13,664	15,921	15,361
Owned dwellings	8,786	6,949	6,516	8,577	4,296	7,870	8,413	10,976	9,811
Mortgage interest and charges	2,965	2,414	2,684	3,943	1,368	2,651	3,661	5,256	4,789
Property taxes	3,765	2,397	1,689	2,353	1,417	2,612	2,599	3,237	2,814
Maintenance, repair, insurance, other expenses	2,055	2,139	2,143	2,281	1,511	2,607	2,153	2,482	2,208
Rented dwellings	5,525	3,012	3,639	6,162	5,342	3,622	4,547	4,031	4,488
Other lodging	1,032	713	600	700	358	882	704	915	1,063
Utilities, fuels, and public services	4,364	4,002	4,176	4,114	2,655	4,237	4,823	5,370	5,857
Natural gas	608	600	246	378	285	430	433	548	551
Electricity	1,466	1,312	1,743	1,361	1,025	1,547	1,768	1,872	2,056
Fuel oil and other fuels	327	84	49	49	84	111	127	100	122
Telephone services (includes mobile)	1,489	1,381	1,446	1,449	839	1,450	1,744	1,935	2,128
Water and other public services	474	626	693	877	422	699	750	916	1,000
Household operations	1,523	1,380	1,401	1,605	904	1,300	1,696	2,662	1,823
Personal services	423	433	279	322	58	89	502	1,273	651
Other household expenses	1,100	947	1,123	1,283	846	1,211	1,194	1,389	1,171
Housekeeping supplies [1]	901	922	735	882	512	877	835	1,290	1,111
Laundry and cleaning supplies	167	185	157	181	113	171	186	222	251
Postage and stationery	151	146	110	133	84	162	130	149	137
Household furnishings and equipment [1]	3,064	2,290	1,962	2,508	1,800	2,484	2,207	2,962	2,946
Household textiles	93	137	103	138	89	121	133	129	138
Furniture	506	473	538	606	292	575	566	737	815
Major appliances	358	339	354	365	187	375	411	460	565
Miscellaneous household equipment	1,930	1,167	830	1,205	1,112	1,242	941	1,447	1,171
Apparel and services [1]	1,800	1,515	1,191	1,496	917	1,298	1,391	2,396	2,296
Men and boys	357	333	277	382	171	320	312	537	564
Women and girls	675	583	449	575	376	470	565	843	899
Footwear	458	327	250	302	201	281	242	646	455
Transportation	9,035	10,281	9,745	10,146	5,324	9,791	12,636	13,869	14,113
Vehicle purchases (net outlay)	3,684	4,998	4,699	4,427	2,228	4,525	6,332	6,534	6,171
Cars and trucks, new	1,780	2,346	2,123	2,029	1,058	2,432	3,119	2,625	1,865
Cars and trucks, used	1,870	2,477	2,530	2,338	1,021	2,039	3,194	3,883	4,243
Gasoline, other fuels, and motor oil	1,337	1,547	1,587	1,735	858	1,513	1,856	2,249	2,579
Other vehicle expenses	3,650	3,427	3,302	3,660	2,039	3,516	4,141	4,767	4,960
Vehicle finance charges	200	279	287	234	110	263	345	406	368
Maintenance and repair	780	945	816	1,004	566	886	977	1,183	1,262
Vehicle rental, leases, licenses, other charges	1,191	793	527	785	460	803	845	1,094	949
Vehicle insurance [2]	1,479	1,410	1,673	1,637	903	1,564	1,973	2,083	2,381
Public transportation	364	309	156	325	199	238	307	320	402
Health care	5,006	5,739	5,098	4,916	3,202	6,287	5,778	6,103	5,369
Entertainment	3,113	3,368	2,378	3,242	1,938	3,110	3,139	4,092	3,354
Personal care products and services	659	673	568	747	423	690	688	874	823
Reading	128	113	106	116	97	136	93	124	107
Education	2,368	937	1,069	1,082	570	936	1,936	2,530	1,902
Tobacco products/smoking supplies	313	347	339	246	231	322	394	339	392
Miscellaneous	1,098	808	816	1,007	661	1,083	763	1,039	1,105
Cash contributions	2,632	2,197	2,008	2,561	1,688	3,267	1,580	1,577	2,726
Personal insurance and pensions	8,367	7,000	6,591	7,724	3,363	7,266	9,464	11,360	10,287
Life and other personal insurance	564	499	491	404	237	552	616	684	567
Pensions and social security	7,803	6,502	6,099	7,320	3,126	6,714	8,849	10,676	9,720
Personal taxes	**12,324**	**7,321**	**8,523**	**10,592**	**5,108**	**10,007**	**14,514**	**13,471**	**7,672**

[1] Includes other types not shown separately. [2] In 2019, the Consumer Expenditure survey program switched the data source used to estimate vehicle insurance spending from the Diary Survey to the Interview Survey. For more information, see <www.bls.gov/cex/2019-vehicle-insurance.htm>.

Source: U.S. Bureau of Labor Statistics, Consumer Expenditure Surveys, CE Tables, "Calendar year means, shares across all items, and coefficients of variation by demographic characteristics, 2020," <www.bls.gov/cex/tables.htm>, accessed November 2021.

Table 733. Money Income of Households—Percent Distribution by Income Level, Race, and Hispanic Origin in Constant (2020) Dollars: 2000 to 2020

[In percent except as noted (108,209 represents 108,209,000). Households as of March of following year. Constant dollars based on CPI-U-RS deflator. Based on Current Population Survey, Annual Social and Economic Supplement (CPS ASEC); see text, this section and Section 1, and Appendix III. For definition of median, see Guide to Tabular Presentation. A household consists of all the persons who occupy a housing unit. Household count excludes persons living in group quarters and institutions. For 2001 data and earlier, the CPS allowed respondents to report only one race group. Beginning with the 2003 CPS covering data for 2002, refers to respondents reporting only one race. Two basic ways of defining a race group are possible: a group such as Asian may be defined as 1) those who reported Asian and no other race (the race-alone concept), or 2) those who reported Asian regardless of whether they also reported another race (the race-alone-or-in-combination concept). Data users should exercise caution when comparing trends over time due to changes in CPS ASEC methodology and data processing. Changes are noted below as appropriate. See source for more information]

Year and race/ethnicity	Number of house- holds (1,000)	Percent distribution							Median income (dollars)
		Under $15,000	$15,000 to $24,999	$25,000 to $34,999	$35,000 to $49,999	$50,000 to $74,999	$75,000 to $99,999	$100,000 and over	
ALL HOUSEHOLDS [1]									
2000 [4]	108,209	8.9	9.4	8.8	13.1	17.2	13.6	29.0	63,292
2010 [5]	119,927	11.1	10.6	9.4	13.1	16.8	12.2	26.7	58,627
2019 [6,7]	128,451	8.9	8.0	8.3	11.6	16.5	12.2	34.6	69,560
2020 [6,7]	129,931	9.4	8.7	8.1	11.6	16.5	12.2	33.6	67,521
WHITE [2]									
2000 [4]	90,030	7.7	9.1	8.5	13.0	17.2	13.9	30.4	66,195
2010 [5]	96,306	9.3	10.3	9.1	13.1	17.2	12.6	28.5	61,521
2019 [6,7]	100,568	7.6	7.5	7.9	11.4	16.7	12.6	36.3	73,105
2020 [6,7]	101,582	8.0	8.3	7.9	11.5	16.5	12.6	35.1	71,231
BLACK [2]									
2000 [4]	13,174	17.0	12.1	11.4	14.5	17.5	11.5	15.8	44,718
2010 [5]	15,265	21.9	13.5	11.2	14.6	15.4	9.9	13.4	38,220
2019 [6,7]	17,054	17.0	11.5	11.3	13.5	16.8	9.8	19.9	46,005
2020 [6,7]	17,358	18.0	11.7	10.3	13.3	17.1	9.9	19.6	45,870
ASIAN AND PACIFIC ISLANDER [2]									
2000 [4]	3,963	7.0	6.4	6.0	10.4	15.2	13.8	41.2	84,043
2010 [5]	5,212	9.7	7.5	6.8	9.4	15.7	12.1	38.7	76,453
2019 [6,7]	6,853	6.5	5.0	5.1	8.5	13.0	12.3	49.5	99,400
2020 [6,7]	6,987	7.6	6.1	4.9	8.4	13.5	11.3	48.2	94,903
HISPANIC [3]									
2000 [4]	10,034	10.7	12.2	11.5	15.9	19.3	12.9	17.5	49,995
2010 [5]	14,435	14.5	12.7	12.3	15.7	17.8	10.8	16.2	44,772
2019 [6,7]	17,667	10.5	8.8	10.6	14.0	19.5	12.0	24.7	56,814
2020 [6,7]	18,349	10.6	9.8	10.3	14.7	18.4	12.3	23.9	55,321

[1] Includes other races not shown separately. [2] Beginning 2002, data represent White alone, Black alone, or Asian alone. [3] People of Hispanic origin may be of any race. [4] Data reflect implementation of Census 2000-based population controls and a 28,000 household sample expansion to 78,000 households. [5] Beginning with 2009 income data, the Census Bureau expanded the upper income intervals used to calculate medians to $250,000 or more. Medians falling in the upper open-ended interval are plugged with "$250,000." Before 2009, the upper open-ended interval was $100,000 and a plug of "$100,000" was used. Data reflect implementation of Census 2010-based population controls. [6] Beginning 2013, data are based on redesigned questions on income. Beginning 2017, data reflect implementation of an updated processing system. [7] Please see source report for information on the impact of the coronavirus 2019 (COVID-19) pandemic on data collections for the 2020 and 2021 CPS ASEC.

Source: U.S. Census Bureau, *Income and Poverty in the United States: 2020,* Current Population Reports, P60-273, September 2021; and "Historical Income Tables: Households, Table H-17," <www.census.gov/topics/income-poverty/income/data/tables.html>, accessed November 2021.

Table 734. Money Income of Households—Median Income by Race and Hispanic Origin in Current and Constant (2020) Dollars: 1990 to 2020

[In dollars. See headnote, Table 733. Beginning 2013, data are based on redesigned questions on income]

Year	Median income in current dollars					Median income in constant (2020) dollars				
	All house- holds [1]	White [2]	Black [2]	Asian, Pacific Islander [2]	His- panic [3]	All house- holds [1]	White [2]	Black [2]	Asian, Pacific Islander [2]	His- panic [3]
1990	29,943	31,231	18,676	38,450	22,330	57,677	60,158	35,974	74,063	43,013
2000 [4,5]	41,990	43,916	29,667	55,757	33,168	63,292	66,195	44,718	84,043	49,995
2010 [6,7]	49,276	51,709	32,124	64,259	37,631	58,627	61,521	38,220	76,453	44,772
2013	53,585	56,745	35,324	72,383	39,687	59,640	63,157	39,315	80,562	44,171
2014	53,657	56,866	35,398	74,297	42,491	58,725	62,237	38,742	81,315	46,505
2015	56,516	60,109	36,898	77,166	45,148	61,748	65,674	40,314	84,310	49,328
2016	59,039	61,858	39,490	81,431	47,675	63,683	66,724	42,596	87,837	51,425
2017 [8]	61,136	64,833	39,365	81,392	50,167	64,557	68,461	41,568	85,946	52,974
2018 [8]	63,179	66,943	41,361	87,194	51,450	65,127	69,007	42,636	89,882	53,036
2019 [8,9]	68,703	72,204	45,438	98,174	56,113	69,560	73,105	46,005	99,400	56,814
2020 [8,9]	67,521	71,231	45,870	94,903	55,321	67,521	71,231	45,870	94,903	55,321

[1] Includes other races, not shown separately. [2] Beginning 2002, data represent White alone, Black alone, or Asian alone. [3] People of Hispanic origin may be of any race. [4] Implementation of Census 2000-based population controls. [5] Implementation of a 28,000 household sample expansion. [6] Median income is calculated using $2,500 income intervals. Beginning with 2009 income data, the Census Bureau expanded the upper income intervals used to calculate medians to $250,000 or more. Before 2009, the upper open-ended interval was $100,000 and a plug of "$100,000" was used. [7] Implementation of Census 2010-based population controls. [8] Implementation of an updated processing system. [9] Please see source report for information on the impact of the coronavirus 2019 (COVID-19) pandemic on data collection for the 2020 and 2021 CPS ASEC.

Source: U.S. Census Bureau, *Income and Poverty in the United States: 2020,* Current Population Reports, P60-273, September 2021; and "Historical Income Tables: Households, Table H-5," <www.census.gov/topics/income-poverty/income/data/tables.html>, accessed November 2021.

Table 735. Money Income of Households—Households by Income Level and Selected Characteristics: 2020

[129,931 represents 129,931,000. Households as of March of the following year. Based on Current Population Survey, Annual Social and Economic Supplement (CPS ASEC); see text, this section and Section 1, and Appendix III. For definition of median, see Guide to Tabular Presentation]

Characteristic	Total house-holds	Under $15,000	$15,000 to $24,999	$25,000 to $34,999	$35,000 to $49,999	$50,000 to $74,999	$75,000 to $99,999	$100,000 and over	Median house-hold income [1] (dollars)
Total.................	**129,931**	**12,246**	**11,276**	**10,515**	**15,069**	**21,417**	**15,807**	**43,601**	**67,521**
Region: [2]									
Northeast....................	22,082	1,932	1,778	1,560	2,293	3,442	2,614	8,464	75,211
Midwest....................	27,865	2,437	2,409	2,253	3,352	4,833	3,585	8,998	66,968
South....................	50,385	5,384	4,985	4,496	6,266	8,296	5,871	15,086	61,243
West....................	29,600	2,492	2,103	2,206	3,160	4,846	3,739	11,054	74,951
Type of household:									
Family household..............	83,907	4,139	4,253	5,425	8,580	13,843	11,386	36,279	86,372
Married-couple..............	61,454	1,671	2,067	3,124	5,310	9,321	8,560	31,404	101,517
Male householder, spouse absent..............	6,963	420	459	568	929	1,485	1,038	2,061	67,304
Female householder, spouse absent..............	15,490	2,048	1,725	1,733	2,340	3,037	1,789	2,820	49,214
Nonfamily household..........	46,024	8,107	7,024	5,090	6,489	7,573	4,421	7,319	40,464
Male householder........	21,781	3,352	2,697	2,239	3,043	3,893	2,340	4,218	47,259
Female householder........	24,244	4,755	4,326	2,852	3,447	3,681	2,081	3,104	35,574
Age of householder:									
15 to 24 years.................	5,485	739	571	679	910	1,149	665	773	46,886
25 to 34 years.................	20,654	1,428	1,278	1,484	2,563	4,081	3,110	6,709	71,566
35 to 44 years.................	22,105	1,445	1,044	1,360	2,189	3,544	3,051	9,475	85,694
45 to 54 years.................	21,663	1,560	1,202	1,148	1,911	3,340	2,634	9,867	90,359
55 to 64 years.................	24,336	2,543	1,879	1,725	2,396	3,710	2,852	9,232	74,270
65 years and over...........	35,688	4,531	5,303	4,119	5,103	5,592	3,496	7,547	46,360
Size of household:									
One person....................	36,972	7,661	6,596	4,535	5,507	5,860	2,955	3,859	34,018
Two people....................	45,515	2,580	2,654	3,488	5,400	8,271	6,385	16,737	76,069
Three people..................	19,523	956	990	1,200	1,808	3,125	2,761	8,681	89,660
Four people....................	16,098	573	588	657	1,268	2,326	2,059	8,627	107,091
Five people....................	7,577	281	296	390	702	1,162	992	3,754	98,843
Six people....................	2,635	120	91	174	226	414	421	1,191	91,773
Seven or more people.......	1,611	74	59	72	160	261	236	748	94,202
Number of earners:									
No earners....................	32,165	9,204	6,622	4,038	4,236	3,739	1,747	2,580	25,522
One earner....................	46,590	2,804	4,080	5,316	7,828	10,157	5,845	10,558	56,191
Two earners and more.......	51,176	239	574	1,163	3,007	7,520	8,214	30,460	114,964
Two earners.................	41,005	216	505	1,041	2,710	6,584	6,848	23,103	109,797
Three earners.............	7,580	22	53	107	271	785	1,101	5,241	130,913
Four earners or more.......	2,591	–	16	15	26	151	265	2,116	169,203
Work experience of householder:									
Total..........................	129,931	12,246	11,276	10,515	15,069	21,417	15,807	43,601	67,521
Worked....................	85,063	2,598	3,856	5,451	9,060	14,952	12,237	36,906	87,312
Worked at full-time jobs....	71,905	1,334	2,373	4,009	7,351	12,717	10,784	33,333	92,914
50 weeks or more..........	56,892	355	1,127	2,531	5,222	9,827	8,708	29,124	101,404
27 to 49 weeks.............	8,678	266	536	710	1,232	1,792	1,362	2,784	71,992
26 weeks or less..........	6,334	714	711	769	897	1,098	715	1,430	51,470
Worked at part-time jobs...	13,158	1,264	1,483	1,442	1,711	2,235	1,452	3,572	56,397
50 weeks or more..........	5,842	349	591	661	742	998	682	1,820	62,476
27 to 49 weeks.............	3,004	235	345	294	444	474	353	864	60,402
26 weeks or less...........	4,313	679	546	487	526	764	419	890	46,988
Did not work.................	44,869	9,648	7,420	5,065	6,009	6,465	3,570	6,693	35,599
Educational attainment of householder: [3]									
Total..........................	124,446	11,507	10,706	9,836	14,160	20,269	15,142	42,827	69,228
Less than 9th grade............	3,613	898	706	413	532	502	245	316	29,609
9th to 12th grade (no diploma)....................	6,439	1,573	1,190	907	903	837	467	561	29,520
High school graduate..........	31,647	4,347	3,932	3,620	4,553	5,705	3,584	5,907	47,405
Some college, no degree.....	20,097	1,783	1,993	1,858	2,712	3,801	2,624	5,326	60,392
Associate's degree..........	13,549	1,001	1,054	979	1,646	2,645	2,030	4,197	68,769
Bachelor's degree or more....	49,102	1,905	1,832	2,059	3,815	6,779	6,194	26,519	106,936
Bachelor's degree..............	29,791	1,234	1,269	1,370	2,662	4,438	3,894	14,925	100,128
Master's degree..............	14,409	516	449	544	907	1,897	1,767	8,327	114,900
Professional degree..........	2,046	69	57	42	105	207	188	1,378	151,560
Doctoral degree...............	2,856	86	56	102	141	237	342	1,893	142,493
Housing tenure:									
Owner occupied..............	85,480	5,116	5,721	5,681	8,849	13,633	10,995	35,483	82,311
Renter occupied..............	42,974	6,795	5,327	4,662	6,016	7,618	4,695	7,861	46,133
Occupier paid no cash rent..	1,477	335	228	174	205	168	116	250	35,197

– Represents or rounds to zero. [1] Median income calculated using $2,500 income intervals. Medians falling in the upper open-ended interval are plugged with "$250,000." [2] For composition of regions, see map, inside front cover. [3] Data shown for householders age 25 and over.

Source: U.S. Census Bureau, *Income and Poverty in the United States: 2020*, Current Population Reports, P60-273, September 2021; and "Current Population Survey Tables for Household Income: Table HINC-01," <www.census.gov/topics/income-poverty/income/data/tables.html>, accessed November 2021.

Table 736. Money Income of Households—Households by Income Level, Race, and Hispanic Origin: 2020

[129,931 represents 129,931,000. Households as of March of the following year. Based on Current Population Survey, Annual Social and Economic Supplement (ASEC); see text, this section and Section 1, and Appendix III]

Income level	Number of households (1,000)					Percent distribution				
	All races [1]	White alone	Black alone	Asian alone	His-panic [2]	All races [1]	White alone	Black alone	Asian alone	His-panic [2]
All households.............	**129,931**	**101,582**	**17,358**	**6,987**	**18,349**	**100.0**	**100.0**	**100.0**	**100.0**	**100.0**
Under $10,000.................	7,137	4,672	1,909	315	1,137	5.5	4.6	11.0	4.5	6.2
$10,000 to $14,999............	5,109	3,474	1,207	212	816	3.9	3.4	7.0	3.0	4.4
$15,000 to $19,999............	5,667	4,262	1,008	206	815	4.4	4.2	5.8	2.9	4.4
$20,000 to $24,999............	5,609	4,189	1,015	219	979	4.3	4.1	5.8	3.1	5.3
$25,000 to $29,999............	5,186	3,989	872	143	851	4.0	3.9	5.0	2.0	4.6
$30,000 to $34,999............	5,329	4,048	919	198	1,033	4.1	4.0	5.3	2.8	5.6
$35,000 to $39,999............	5,285	4,032	837	218	918	4.1	4.0	4.8	3.1	5.0
$40,000 to $44,999............	5,100	3,995	782	172	943	3.9	3.9	4.5	2.5	5.1
$45,000 to $49,999............	4,684	3,667	692	198	839	3.6	3.6	4.0	2.8	4.6
$50,000 to $59,999............	9,364	7,367	1,288	435	1,448	7.2	7.3	7.4	6.2	7.9
$60,000 to $74,999............	12,053	9,420	1,690	509	1,934	9.3	9.3	9.7	7.3	10.5
$75,000 to $84,999............	7,171	5,786	782	365	1,082	5.5	5.7	4.5	5.2	5.9
$85,000 to $99,999............	8,636	7,027	939	428	1,181	6.6	6.9	5.4	6.1	6.4
$100,000 to $149,999........	19,916	16,338	1,865	1,126	2,431	15.3	16.1	10.7	16.1	13.2
$150,000 to $199,999........	10,366	8,531	710	850	1,007	8.0	8.4	4.1	12.2	5.5
$200,000 to $249,999........	5,134	4,232	323	463	427	4.0	4.2	1.9	6.6	2.3
$250,000 and over............	8,185	6,554	518	929	511	6.3	6.5	3.0	13.3	2.8

[1] Includes other races, not shown separately. [2] Persons of Hispanic origin may be of any race.

Source: U.S. Census Bureau, *Income and Poverty in the United States: 2020*, Current Population Reports, P60-273, September 2021; and "Current Population Survey Tables for Household Income: Table HINC-06," <www.census.gov/topics/income-poverty/income/data/tables.html>, accessed November 2021.

Table 737. Share of Aggregate Income Received by Each Fifth and Top 5 Percent of Households: 1990 to 2020

[In units as indicated (94,312 represents 94,312,000). Households as of March of the following year. Income in constant 2020 CPI-U-RS-adjusted dollars. The shares method ranks households from highest to lowest on the basis of income and then divides them into groups of equal population size, typically quintiles. The aggregate income of each group is then divided by the overall aggregate income to derive shares. Based on the Current Population Survey, Annual Social and Economic Supplement (CPS ASEC); see text, this section and Section 1, and Appendix III. For data collection changes over time, see source. See also headnote, Table 733]

Year	Number of house-holds (1,000)	Income at selected positions in constant (2020) dollars					Percent distribution of aggregate income					
		Upper limit of each fifth				Top 5 percent, lower limit	Lowest 5th	Second 5th	Third 5th	Fourth 5th	Highest 5th	Top 5 percent
		Lowest	Second	Third	Fourth							
1990.....................	94,312	24,078	45,578	69,729	106,337	182,506	3.8	9.6	15.9	24.0	46.6	18.5
1995 [1].................	99,627	24,364	45,538	71,066	110,188	191,192	3.7	9.1	15.2	23.3	48.7	21.0
2000 [2,3].................	108,209	27,011	49,741	78,643	123,247	218,892	3.6	8.9	14.8	23.0	49.8	22.1
2005.....................	114,384	25,482	47,833	76,612	121,847	220,562	3.4	8.6	14.6	23.0	50.4	22.2
2006.....................	116,011	25,784	48,614	77,218	124,877	223,948	3.4	8.6	14.5	22.9	50.5	22.3
2007.....................	116,783	25,394	48,933	77,592	125,148	221,511	3.4	8.7	14.8	23.4	49.7	21.2
2008.....................	117,181	24,962	47,002	75,595	120,808	216,933	3.4	8.6	14.7	23.3	50.0	21.5
2009 [4].................	117,538	24,736	46,622	74,742	120,939	217,692	3.4	8.6	14.6	23.2	50.3	21.7
2010 [5].................	119,927	23,795	45,211	73,170	119,011	214,734	3.3	8.5	14.6	23.4	50.3	21.3
2011.....................	121,084	23,370	44,429	72,012	117,165	214,533	3.2	8.4	14.3	23.0	51.1	22.3
2012.....................	122,459	23,266	44,913	72,944	117,575	215,907	3.2	8.3	14.4	23.0	51.0	22.3
2013 [6].................	123,931	23,373	45,672	74,793	122,687	228,306	3.1	8.2	14.3	23.0	51.4	22.2
2014 [6].................	124,587	23,456	45,076	74,655	122,866	226,080	3.1	8.2	14.3	23.2	51.2	21.9
2015 [6].................	125,819	24,911	47,539	78,667	127,834	234,316	3.1	8.2	14.3	23.2	51.1	22.1
2016 [6].................	126,224	25,890	49,187	80,759	130,538	242,970	3.1	8.3	14.2	22.9	51.5	22.6
2017 [6].................	127,669	26,211	49,860	81,467	133,687	257,746	3.0	8.1	14.0	22.6	52.3	23.2
2018 [6].................	128,579	26,389	51,541	81,994	134,008	256,396	3.1	8.3	14.1	22.6	52.0	23.1
2019 [6,7].................	128,451	28,435	54,171	87,568	144,280	273,373	3.1	8.3	14.1	22.7	51.9	23.0
2020 [6,7].................	129,931	27,026	52,179	85,076	141,110	273,739	3.0	8.1	14.0	22.6	52.2	23.0

[1] Data reflect full implementation of the 1990 Census-based sample design and metropolitan definitions, 7,000 household sample reduction, and revised race edits. [2] Implementation of Census 2000-based population controls. [3] Implementation of a 28,000 household sample expansion. [4] Beginning with 2009 income data, the Census Bureau expanded the upper income interval used to calculate medians and Gini indexes to $250,000 or more. Medians falling in the upper open-ended interval are plugged with "$250,000." [5] Implementation of Census 2010-based population controls. [6] Beginning 2013, data are based on redesigned questions on income. Beginning 2017, data reflect implementation of an updated processing system. See source for more information. [7] See source for information on the impact of the coronavirus 2019 (COVID-19) pandemic on the 2020 and 2021 CPS ASEC.

Source: U.S. Census Bureau, *Income and Poverty in the United States: 2020,* Current Population Reports, P60-273, September 2021; and "Historical Income Tables: Households, Tables H1 and H2," <www.census.gov/topics/income-poverty/income/data/tables.html>, accessed November 2021.

Table 738. Money Income of Families—Families by Income Level, Race, and Hispanic Origin: 2020

[83,918 represents 83,918,000. Families as of March of the following year. Based on Current Population Survey Annual Social and Economic Supplement (CPS ASEC); see text, this section, Section 1, and Appendix III. A family is a group of persons residing together and related by birth, marriage, or adoption. See also headnote in Table 733 regarding changes in the CPS ASEC]

Income level	Number of families (1,000)					Percent distribution				
	All races	White alone	Black alone	Asian alone	His-panic[1]	All races	White alone	Black alone	Asian alone	His-panic[1]
All families............	**83,918**	**65,910**	**10,239**	**5,161**	**13,689**	**100.0**	**100.0**	**100.0**	**100.0**	**100.0**
Under $10,000..................	3,225	2,124	829	153	717	3.8	3.2	8.1	3.0	5.2
$10,000 to $14,999..........	1,556	1,032	378	66	386	1.9	1.6	3.7	1.3	2.8
$15,000 to $19,999..........	2,001	1,388	407	120	490	2.4	2.1	4.0	2.3	3.6
$20,000 to $24,999..........	2,493	1,708	555	125	678	3.0	2.6	5.4	2.4	5.0
$25,000 to $29,999..........	2,650	1,988	472	81	616	3.2	3.0	4.6	1.6	4.5
$30,000 to $34,999..........	2,952	2,234	485	131	756	3.5	3.4	4.7	2.5	5.5
$35,000 to $39,999..........	2,818	2,059	466	151	684	3.4	3.1	4.6	2.9	5.0
$40,000 to $44,999..........	3,067	2,370	487	116	756	3.7	3.6	4.8	2.2	5.5
$45,000 to $49,999..........	2,876	2,234	411	145	650	3.4	3.4	4.0	2.8	4.7
$50,000 to $59,999..........	5,829	4,527	812	306	1,116	6.9	6.9	7.9	5.9	8.2
$60,000 to $74,999..........	7,858	6,099	1,120	363	1,421	9.4	9.3	10.9	7.0	10.4
$75,000 to $84,999..........	5,038	4,087	514	275	873	6.0	6.2	5.0	5.3	6.4
$85,000 to $99,999..........	6,204	5,054	640	339	944	7.4	7.7	6.3	6.6	6.9
$100,000 to $149,999.......	15,476	12,775	1,402	860	1,991	18.4	19.4	13.7	16.7	14.5
$150,000 to $199,999.......	8,533	7,037	547	732	823	10.2	10.7	5.3	14.2	6.0
$200,000 to $249,999.......	4,278	3,535	268	381	346	5.1	5.4	2.6	7.4	2.5
$250,000 and over...........	7,065	5,657	446	815	444	8.4	8.6	4.4	15.8	3.2

[1] Persons of Hispanic origin may be of any race.

Source: U.S. Census Bureau, *Income and Poverty in the United States: 2020,* Current Population Reports, P60-273, September 2021; and "Current Population Survey Tables for Family Income: Table FINC-07," <www.census.gov/topics/income-poverty/income/data/tables.html>, accessed November 2021.

Table 739. Money Income of Families—Percent Distribution of Families by Income Level in Constant (2020) Dollars: 2000 to 2020

[73,778 represents 73,778,000. Income in 2020 Consumer Price Index Research Series Using Current Methods (CPI-U-RS) adjusted dollars. Families as of March of the following year. Based on Current Population Survey Annual Social and Economic Supplement (CPS ASEC); see text, this section and Section 1, and Appendix III. For definition of median, see Guide to Tabular Presentation. For comments on race, see headnote, Table 733, and also text for Section 1, Population. Data users should exercise caution when comparing trends over time due to changes in CPS ASEC methodology and data processing. See source for more information]

Year and race/ethnicity	Number of families (1,000)	Percent distribution							Median income (dollars)
		Under $15,000	$15,000 to $24,999	$25,000 to $34,999	$35,000 to $49,999	$50,000 to $74,999	$75,000 to $99,999	$100,000 and over	
ALL FAMILIES[1]									
2000[4].............................	73,778	5.1	6.4	7.5	12.3	17.8	15.2	35.7	76,469
2010[5].............................	79,559	7.4	7.2	8.2	12.4	17.4	13.7	33.7	71,667
2019[6].............................	83,698	5.0	4.7	6.7	10.4	16.4	13.3	43.4	87,085
2020[6].............................	83,918	5.7	5.4	6.7	10.4	16.3	13.4	42.1	84,008
WHITE[2]									
2000[4].............................	61,330	4.1	5.7	7.0	12.1	17.8	15.6	37.6	79,931
2010[5].............................	63,976	6.0	6.5	7.7	12.3	17.7	14.1	35.6	74,853
2019[6].............................	66,102	4.1	4.1	6.2	10.2	16.6	13.6	45.2	90,782
2020[6].............................	65,910	4.8	4.7	6.4	10.1	16.1	13.9	44.0	88,123
BLACK[2]									
2000[4].............................	8,731	12.3	11.1	11.3	14.8	18.3	12.9	19.3	50,760
2010[5].............................	9,571	16.2	11.6	11.6	14.8	16.8	11.5	17.4	45,918
2019[6].............................	9,954	10.4	8.9	11.3	12.6	17.4	12.2	27.3	59,248
2020[6].............................	10,239	11.8	9.4	9.3	13.3	18.9	11.3	26.0	57,476
ASIAN AND PACIFIC ISLANDER[2]									
2000[4].............................	2,982	4.0	5.5	5.2	9.5	14.8	14.5	46.5	94,384
2010[5].............................	3,879	5.9	6.1	5.7	9.3	15.0	13.0	44.8	89,490
2019[6].............................	5,137	4.0	3.5	4.3	7.6	12.6	12.4	55.7	113,627
2020[6].............................	5,161	4.2	4.8	4.1	8.0	12.9	11.9	54.1	109,448
HISPANIC ORIGIN[3]									
2000[4].............................	8,017	8.8	11.8	11.7	16.3	19.8	13.3	18.4	51,915
2010[5].............................	11,284	13.2	12.0	12.6	15.8	18.3	11.2	17.0	46,758
2019[6].............................	13,172	7.4	8.0	9.9	14.5	20.1	12.7	27.5	61,688
2020[6].............................	13,689	8.1	8.5	10.0	15.3	18.5	13.3	26.3	59,976

[1] Includes other races not shown separately. [2] Beginning with data for 2002, represents White alone, Black alone, or Asian alone. [3] People of Hispanic origin may be of any race. [4] Data reflect implementation of Census 2000-based population controls and a 28,000 household sample expansion to 78,000 households. [5] Median income is calculated using $2,500 income intervals. Beginning with 2009 income data, the Census Bureau expanded the upper income intervals used to calculate medians to $250,000 or more. Medians falling in the upper open-ended interval are plugged with "$250,000." Before 2009, the upper open-ended interval was $100,000 and a plug of "$100,000" was used. Implementation of Census 2010-based population controls. [6] Data are based on redesigned questions on income, and reflect an updated CPS ASEC processing system. See source for information on the impact of the coronavirus 2019 (COVID-19) pandemic on data collection for the 2020 and 2021 CPS ASEC.

Source: U.S. Census Bureau, *Income and Poverty in the United States: 2020,* Current Population Reports, P60-273, September 2021; and "Historical Income Tables: Families, Table F-23," <www.census.gov/topics/income-poverty/income/data/tables.html>, accessed November 2021.

Table 740. Money Income of Families—Median Income by Race and Hispanic Origin in Current and Constant (2020) Dollars: 1990 to 2020

[In dollars. For 2001 and earlier data, the CPS allowed respondents to report only one race group. Beginning with the 2003 CPS covering data for 2002, respondents could choose more than one race. The CPS uses two basic ways to define a race group. A group such as Asian may be defined as those who reported Asian and no other race (the race-alone or single-race concept), or as those who reported Asian regardless of whether they also reported another race (the race-alone-or-in-combination concept). See also comments on race in the text for Section 1, Population. See also headnote, Table 739]

Year	Median income in current dollars					Median income in constant (2020) dollars				
	All races [1]	White [2]	Black [2]	Asian, Pacific Islander [2]	His-panic [3]	All races [1]	White [2]	Black [2]	Asian, Pacific Islander [2]	His-panic [3]
1990.....	35,353	36,915	21,423	42,246	23,431	68,098	71,107	41,266	81,375	45,133
2000 [4].....	50,732	53,029	33,676	62,617	34,442	76,469	79,931	50,760	94,384	51,915
2010 [5].....	60,236	62,914	38,594	75,217	39,300	71,667	74,853	45,918	89,490	46,758
2015 [6].....	70,697	74,291	45,781	90,847	47,328	77,242	81,169	50,019	99,257	51,709
2016 [6].....	72,707	76,264	49,365	93,498	51,105	78,426	82,263	53,248	100,853	55,125
2017 [6].....	76,135	80,139	50,649	94,706	53,595	80,395	84,623	53,483	100,005	56,594
2018 [6].....	78,646	81,976	53,105	101,244	55,093	81,070	84,503	54,742	104,365	56,791
2019 [6, 7].....	86,011	89,663	58,518	112,226	60,927	87,085	90,782	59,248	113,627	61,688
2020 [6, 7].....	84,008	88,123	57,476	109,448	59,976	84,008	88,123	57,476	109,448	59,976

[1] Includes other races not shown separately. [2] Beginning 2002, data represent White alone, Black alone, or Asian alone. [3] Persons of Hispanic origin may be of any race. [4] Implementation of Census 2000-based population controls and 28,000 household sample expansion. [5] Beginning 2009, Census Bureau expanded upper income intervals used to calculate medians to $250,000 or more. Medians falling in the upper open-ended interval are plugged with "$250,000." Before 2009, the upper open-ended interval was $100,000 and a plug of "$100,000" was used. Implementation of Census 2010-based population controls. [6] Beginning 2013, based on redesigned questions on income. Beginning 2017, reflects updated processing system. [7] See source for information in the impact of the coronavirus disease 2019 (COVID-19) pandemic on data collection for the 2020 and 2021 CPS ASEC.

Source: U.S. Census Bureau, *Income and Poverty in the United States: 2020*, Current Population Reports, P60-273, September 2021; and "Historical Income Tables: Families, Table F-05," <www.census.gov/topics/income-poverty/income/data/tables.html>, accessed November 2021.

Table 741. Money Income of Families—Distribution of Families by Income Level and Selected Characteristics: 2020

[83,918 represents 83,918,000. See headnote, Table 739. Median income is calculated using $2,500 income intervals. Medians falling in the upper open-ended interval are plugged with "$250,000." For composition of regions, see map inside front cover]

Characteristic	Number of families (1,000)								Median income (dollars)
	Total	Under $15,000	$15,000 to $24,999	$25,000 to $34,999	$35,000 to $49,999	$50,000 to $74,999	$75,000 to $99,999	$100,000 and over	
All families......	**83,918**	**4,781**	**4,495**	**5,602**	**8,759**	**13,688**	**11,242**	**35,352**	**84,008**
Region:									
Northeast......	13,919	714	638	814	1,273	2,083	1,663	6,736	96,393
Midwest......	17,551	829	822	1,070	1,842	2,965	2,591	7,434	85,833
South......	32,856	2,224	2,152	2,481	3,726	5,512	4,301	12,459	76,481
West......	19,592	1,013	882	1,237	1,919	3,127	2,688	8,723	89,544
Type of family:									
Married-couple families......	61,463	1,687	2,083	3,139	5,342	9,356	8,578	31,276	101,240
Male householder, no spouse present......	6,964	531	564	634	1,051	1,484	991	1,706	60,216
Female householder, no spouse present......	15,491	2,562	1,848	1,829	2,367	2,847	1,673	2,368	43,895
Unrelated subfamilies......	431	117	53	52	70	70	32	37	33,794
Age of householder:									
15 to 24 years old......	2,537	365	233	276	433	450	352	429	48,439
25 to 34 years old......	12,795	1,152	841	927	1,438	2,345	1,792	4,299	71,785
35 to 44 years old......	17,293	993	810	1,007	1,619	2,551	2,339	7,972	92,242
45 to 54 years old......	16,287	658	652	695	1,274	2,264	2,092	8,656	105,393
55 to 64 years old......	15,628	698	689	801	1,258	2,302	2,114	7,765	99,279
65 years old and over......	19,378	916	1,269	1,895	2,740	3,776	2,553	6,229	68,067
Number of earners:									
No earners......	14,403	2,960	1,772	1,883	2,229	2,397	1,177	1,984	38,630
One earner......	26,829	1,626	2,256	2,855	4,182	5,422	3,361	7,127	59,931
Two earners or more......	42,686	194	467	864	2,350	5,867	6,703	26,240	119,197
Educational attainment of householder:									
All persons age 25 and over....	81,381	4,416	4,261	5,326	8,327	13,237	10,889	34,924	85,563
Less than 9th grade......	2,404	350	389	306	451	418	217	269	39,473
9th to 12th grade (no diploma)...	3,917	621	583	544	674	652	376	468	40,024
High school graduate (includes equivalency)......	19,975	1,497	1,604	2,065	2,823	4,146	2,870	4,971	60,583
Some college, no degree......	13,171	826	720	967	1,645	2,588	1,991	4,435	73,290
Associate's degree......	8,999	377	408	533	947	1,703	1,495	3,533	82,738
Bachelor's degree or more......	32,915	746	556	911	1,785	3,733	3,939	21,246	130,139
Bachelor's degree......	19,707	510	410	586	1,243	2,518	2,551	11,890	119,690
Master's degree......	9,729	182	101	256	405	942	1,114	6,728	139,640
Professional degree......	1,471	31	22	12	69	121	108	1,110	180,303
Doctoral degree......	2,007	24	23	56	67	153	166	1,517	171,210

Source: U.S. Census Bureau, *Income and Poverty in the United States: 2020*, Current Population Reports, P60-273, September 2021; and "Current Population Survey Tables for Family Income: Table FINC-01," <www.census.gov/topics/income-poverty/income/data/tables.html>, accessed November 2021.

Table 742. Median Income of Families by Type of Family in Current and Constant (2020) Dollars: 1990 to 2020

[In dollars. See headnote, Table 739. For definition of median, see Guide to Tabular Presentation]

Year	Current dollars						Constant (2020) dollars			
		Married-couple families			Male house-holder, no spouse present	Female house-holder, no spouse present			Male house-holder, no spouse present	Female house-holder, no spouse present
	All families	Total	Wife in paid labor force	Wife not in paid labor force			All families	Married-couple families		
1990.	35,353	39,895	46,777	30,265	29,046	16,932	68,098	76,847	55,949	32,615
1995 [1]	40,611	47,062	55,823	32,375	30,358	19,691	68,712	79,627	51,365	33,317
1996.	42,300	49,707	58,381	33,748	31,600	19,911	69,714	81,921	52,079	32,815
1997.	44,568	51,591	60,669	36,027	32,960	21,023	71,897	83,227	53,171	33,914
1998.	46,737	54,180	63,751	37,161	35,681	22,163	74,389	86,236	56,792	35,276
1999 [2]	48,831	56,501	66,478	38,480	37,339	23,762	76,101	88,055	58,191	37,032
2000 [3]	50,732	59,099	69,235	39,982	37,727	25,716	76,469	89,081	56,866	38,762
2001.	51,407	60,335	70,834	40,782	36,590	25,745	75,342	88,426	53,626	37,732
2002.	51,680	61,130	72,806	40,102	37,739	26,423	74,566	88,201	54,452	38,124
2003.	52,680	62,281	75,170	41,122	38,032	26,550	74,321	87,866	53,656	37,457
2004.	54,061	63,626	76,854	42,215	40,361	26,969	74,263	87,403	55,444	37,047
2005.	56,194	65,906	78,755	44,457	41,111	27,244	74,664	87,568	54,624	36,199
2006.	58,407	69,404	82,788	45,757	41,844	28,829	75,168	89,321	53,852	37,102
2007.	61,355	72,589	86,435	47,329	44,358	30,296	76,784	90,843	55,513	37,915
2008.	61,521	72,743	86,621	48,502	43,571	30,129	74,144	87,669	52,511	36,311
2009 [4]	60,088	71,627	85,948	47,649	41,501	29,770	72,670	86,625	50,191	36,004
2010 [5]	60,236	72,241	87,397	48,733	43,206	29,155	71,667	85,950	51,405	34,688
2011.	60,974	73,790	89,017	50,414	43,069	30,259	70,328	85,110	49,676	34,901
2012.	62,241	75,535	91,779	50,881	42,358	30,686	70,300	85,315	47,843	34,659
2013 [6]	63,815	76,339	94,299	51,839	44,475	31,408	71,026	84,965	49,500	34,957
2013 [7]	65,471	78,614	96,062	54,231	47,191	31,131	72,869	87,497	52,523	34,649
2014 [8]	66,632	80,814	99,983	54,779	47,597	31,770	72,926	88,448	52,093	34,771
2015.	70,697	84,324	103,699	56,010	49,772	34,126	77,242	92,130	54,380	37,285
2016.	72,707	86,811	106,082	58,694	51,568	36,658	78,426	93,640	55,625	39,542
2017.	75,938	90,148	110,893	61,901	52,950	37,098	80,187	95,192	55,913	39,174
2017 [9]	76,135	91,105	(NA)	(NA)	51,695	36,816	80,395	96,203	54,588	38,876
2018.	78,646	93,329	(NA)	(NA)	54,336	40,233	81,070	96,206	56,011	41,473
2019 [10]	86,011	102,032	(NA)	(NA)	61,705	43,359	87,085	103,306	62,475	43,900
2020 [10]	84,008	101,240	(NA)	(NA)	60,216	43,895	84,008	101,240	60,216	43,895

NA Not available. [1] Implementation of the 1990 census-based sample design and metropolitan definitions, 7,000 household sample reduction, and revised race edits. [2] Implementation of Census 2000-based population controls. [3] Implementation of 28,000 household sample expansion. [4] Median income is calculated using $2,500 income intervals. Beginning with 2009 data, the Census Bureau expanded the upper income intervals used to calculate medians to $250,000 or more. Medians falling in the upper open-ended interval are plugged with "$250,000." Before 2009, the upper open-ended interval was $100,000 and a plug of "$100,000" was used. [5] Implementation of Census 2010-based population controls. [6] The 2014 CPS ASEC included redesigned questions for income. The redesigned income questions were implemented to a subsample of the 98,000 addresses using a probability split panel design. Approximately 68,000 addresses received a set of income questions similar to those used in the 2013 CPS ASEC and the remaining 30,000 addresses received the redesigned income questions. The source of these 2013 estimates is the portion of the CPS ASEC sample that received the income questions consistent with the 2013 CPS ASEC, approximately 68,000 addresses. [7] The source of these 2013 estimates is the portion of the CPS ASEC sample which received the redesigned income questions, approximately 30,000 addresses. [8] Implementation of redesigned questionnaire for the full CPS ASEC survey sample. [9] Implementation of an updated CPS ASEC processing system. [10] See source for information in the impact of the coronavirus disease 2019 (COVID-19) pandemic on data collection for the 2020 and 2021 CPS ASEC.

Source: U.S. Census Bureau, *Income and Poverty in the United States: 2020*, Current Population Reports, P60-273, September 2021; and "Historical Income Tables: Families, Table F-7," <www.census.gov/topics/income-poverty/income/data/tables.html>, accessed November 2021.

Table 743. Median Income of People in Constant (2020) Dollars by Sex, Race, and Hispanic Origin: 2000 to 2020

[In dollars. People as of March of following year. People age 15 and over. Constant dollars based on CPI-U-RS deflator. Based on the Current Population Survey, Annual Social and Economic Supplement (CPS ASEC); see text, this section and Section 1 and Appendix III. For 2001 and earlier data, the CPS allowed respondents to report only one race group. Beginning with the 2003 CPS covering data for 2002, respondents could choose more than one race. The CPS uses two basic ways of defining a race group. A group such as Asian may be defined as 1) those who reported Asian and no other race (the race-alone or single-race concept), or 2) those who reported Asian regardless of whether they also reported another race (the race-alone-or-in-combination concept). See also headnote, Table 739]

Race and Hispanic origin	Male					Female				
	2000 [1]	2010 [2]	2015 [3]	2019 [3]	2020 [3]	2000 [1]	2010 [2]	2015 [3]	2019 [3]	2020 [3]
All races [4]	42,722	38,316	40,576	44,863	42,921	24,212	24,717	25,969	29,774	29,261
White [5]	44,913	40,897	43,147	47,051	45,645	24,236	24,861	26,526	30,252	29,759
Black [5]	32,171	27,717	29,941	31,651	31,316	23,938	23,374	23,614	27,358	26,650
Asian [5]	46,475	42,621	47,751	54,345	51,879	26,161	28,034	28,988	32,500	32,173
Hispanic [6]	29,390	26,674	30,712	32,688	32,115	18,462	19,384	20,655	23,712	22,856
White non-Hispanic	47,492	44,204	46,114	51,196	50,269	25,119	25,836	28,002	31,730	31,355

[1] Implementation of Census 2000-based population controls and sample expanded by 28,000 households. [2] See footnotes 4 and 5, Table 742. [3] Based on redesigned questions on income. As of 2017, data reflect an updated processing system. See source for information on the impact of the coronavirus disease 2019 (COVID-19) pandemic on data collection for the 2020 and 2021 CPS ASEC. [4] Includes other races not shown separately. [5] Data for 2002 and later refer to people reporting White alone, Black alone, or Asian alone. [6] People of Hispanic origin may be of any race.

Source: U.S. Census Bureau, *Income and Poverty in the United States: 2020*, Current Population Reports, P60-273, September 2021; and "Historical Income Tables: People, Tables P-2 and P-5," <www.census.gov/topics/income-poverty/income/data/tables.html>, accessed November 2021.

Table 744. Money Income of People—People by Income Level and by Sex and Selected Characteristics: 2020

[129,368 represents 129,368,000. People age 15 and over as of March of following year. Based on the Current Population Survey, Annual Social and Economic Supplement (CPS ASEC); see text, this section and Section 1, and Appendix III. Median income is calculated using $2,500 income intervals. Medians falling in the upper open-ended interval are plugged with "$250,000." For definition of median, see Guide to Tabular Presentation. Data reflect an updated CPS ASEC processing system]

Characteristic	All persons (1,000)	People with income (1,000)									Median income (current dollars)
		Total	Under $5,000 or loss	$5,000 to $9,999	$10,000 to $14,999	$15,000 to $24,999	$25,000 to $34,999	$35,000 to $49,999	$50,000 to $74,999	$75,000 and over	
MALE											
Total............	**129,368**	**116,965**	**7,067**	**5,555**	**6,648**	**14,769**	**13,796**	**16,854**	**20,685**	**31,591**	**42,921**
15 to 24 years old...........	21,041	13,438	3,415	1,936	1,348	2,350	1,879	1,238	891	383	15,087
25 to 34 years old...........	22,837	21,385	826	836	877	2,591	2,932	3,924	4,708	4,692	43,421
35 to 44 years old...........	20,814	19,849	593	549	679	1,612	1,901	2,925	4,280	7,312	57,105
45 to 54 years old...........	19,424	18,605	576	527	760	1,583	1,694	2,446	3,718	7,302	60,512
55 to 64 years old...........	20,033	19,120	754	709	963	2,013	1,893	2,635	3,683	6,473	52,072
65 years old and over........	25,219	24,568	903	998	2,023	4,621	3,497	3,689	3,409	5,428	35,808
Educational attainment:											
Total [1].................	108,327	103,527	3,653	3,619	5,301	12,418	11,917	15,618	19,792	31,210	48,917
Less than 9th grade.........	4,009	3,714	183	386	514	876	625	588	351	191	23,358
9th to 12th grade [2].........	6,274	5,578	292	517	780	1,185	953	867	645	336	25,102
High school graduate [3].......	31,855	29,803	1,304	1,395	2,126	4,881	4,488	5,490	5,747	4,370	36,271
Some college, no degree.....	16,299	15,672	661	486	719	2,086	2,092	2,772	3,359	3,496	42,920
Associate's degree...........	10,296	9,961	266	243	400	1,012	1,144	1,651	2,629	2,614	51,436
Bachelor's degree or more. . .	39,595	38,799	945	592	761	2,378	2,613	4,247	7,059	20,202	77,224
Bachelor's degree...........	24,773	24,164	624	404	507	1,665	1,788	3,021	4,786	11,368	70,653
Master's degree.............	10,265	10,115	202	122	180	539	590	947	1,712	5,825	87,172
Professional degree.........	1,968	1,952	36	34	41	82	118	106	246	1,288	110,937
Doctoral degree.............	2,589	2,567	83	32	33	92	118	172	318	1,720	112,912
Housing tenure:											
Owner-occupied..............	89,983	81,933	4,941	3,202	3,966	9,366	8,678	11,009	14,943	25,831	49,615
Renter-occupied.............	38,035	33,827	2,035	2,235	2,587	5,168	4,954	5,663	5,598	5,588	34,713
Occupier paid no cash rent..............	1,351	1,205	90	118	96	236	166	181	146	174	28,182
Region:											
Northeast....................	21,807	19,970	1,284	838	1,084	2,295	2,100	2,831	3,539	5,996	47,039
Midwest......................	26,954	24,953	1,577	1,249	1,334	2,927	2,882	3,711	4,709	6,564	43,811
South........................	49,095	43,883	2,494	2,193	2,701	6,164	5,423	6,350	7,713	10,849	41,051
West.........................	31,512	28,159	1,713	1,275	1,529	3,382	3,393	3,964	4,722	8,181	44,569
FEMALE											
Total............	**136,889**	**118,951**	**12,444**	**8,593**	**11,802**	**19,759**	**14,926**	**16,435**	**17,070**	**17,926**	**29,261**
15 to 24 years old...........	20,636	12,822	3,318	1,790	1,660	2,448	1,671	953	740	244	13,496
25 to 34 years old...........	22,447	20,040	1,819	1,095	1,140	2,752	2,881	3,726	3,803	2,825	35,917
35 to 44 years old...........	21,190	18,751	1,974	961	1,135	2,073	2,196	2,945	3,389	4,078	39,807
45 to 54 years old...........	20,256	18,315	1,549	802	1,103	2,261	2,136	2,848	3,381	4,236	40,994
55 to 64 years old...........	21,744	19,738	2,012	1,264	1,691	2,897	2,287	2,642	3,033	3,909	33,263
65 years old and over........	30,617	29,283	1,771	2,680	5,074	7,325	3,755	3,320	2,728	2,630	21,245
Educational attainment:											
Total [1].................	116,253	106,128	9,125	6,802	10,143	17,310	13,255	15,480	16,331	17,680	31,663
Less than 9th grade.........	3,927	2,877	400	527	698	696	279	203	49	24	13,468
9th to 12th grade [2].........	5,844	4,654	555	760	980	1,208	594	346	141	67	15,177
High school graduate [3].......	30,693	27,091	2,620	2,491	4,009	6,182	4,395	3,789	2,428	1,176	21,835
Some college, no degree.....	17,156	15,858	1,387	1,022	1,566	3,098	2,510	2,718	2,125	1,430	28,182
Associate's degree...........	13,191	12,360	943	689	1,014	2,112	1,869	2,337	2,047	1,350	31,858
Bachelor's degree or more. . .	45,442	43,288	3,220	1,312	1,875	4,012	3,608	6,087	9,541	13,633	52,212
Bachelor's degree...........	28,033	26,453	2,310	907	1,302	2,819	2,580	4,162	5,618	6,753	46,686
Master's degree.............	13,793	13,340	743	345	444	1,010	856	1,666	3,353	4,923	60,999
Professional degree.........	1,475	1,422	69	30	61	82	80	113	207	780	82,015
Doctoral degree.............	2,141	2,073	98	30	69	100	93	148	362	1,178	82,316
Housing tenure:											
Owner-occupied..............	94,251	83,140	8,740	5,381	7,746	13,107	9,672	11,299	12,717	14,480	31,288
Renter-occupied.............	41,262	34,656	3,563	3,083	3,868	6,452	5,088	4,988	4,252	3,361	25,550
Occupier paid no cash rent..............	1,376	1,155	140	129	188	199	166	148	102	84	19,937
Region:											
Northeast....................	23,713	21,218	2,073	1,382	1,930	3,225	2,445	2,936	3,356	3,871	32,525
Midwest......................	28,126	25,381	2,412	1,736	2,534	4,352	3,325	3,853	3,674	3,494	29,629
South........................	52,852	44,779	4,777	3,482	4,815	7,807	5,846	5,965	6,100	5,988	27,011
West.........................	32,199	27,572	3,181	1,992	2,523	4,374	3,310	3,681	3,940	4,571	29,792

[1] Population age 25 and over. [2] No diploma attained. [3] Includes high school equivalency.

Source: U.S. Census Bureau, *Income and Poverty in the United States: 2020*, Current Population Reports, P60-273, September 2021; and "Current Population Survey Tables for Personal Income: Table PINC-01," <www.census.gov/topics/income-poverty/income/data/tables.html>, accessed November 2021.

Table 745. Average Earnings of Year-Round, Full-Time Workers by Educational Attainment: 2020

[In dollars. For people 18 years old and over as of March of the following year. Based on the Current Population Survey, Annual Social and Economic Supplement (ASEC); see text, this section and Section 1, and Appendix III. See source for information on the impact of the coronavirus disease 2019 (COVID-19) pandemic on the CPS ASEC data collection]

| Sex and age | All workers | Less than 9th grade | High school | | College | | |
			9th to 12th grade (no diploma)	High school graduate [1]	Some college, no degree	Associate degree	Bachelor's degree or more
Male, total............	**84,190**	**46,962**	**42,751**	**55,561**	**65,589**	**70,073**	**118,750**
18 to 24 years old..........	39,665	(B)	29,011	35,476	36,457	43,740	58,364
25 to 34 years old..........	64,793	60,922	36,574	48,363	53,344	57,864	83,402
35 to 44 years old..........	90,827	52,373	43,058	58,353	73,199	71,276	123,845
45 to 54 years old..........	97,528	40,287	48,150	63,750	69,979	74,823	138,124
55 to 64 years old..........	94,132	42,914	51,479	60,139	75,861	78,960	137,547
65 years old and over......	102,732	44,779	39,939	70,422	87,937	87,780	134,766
Female, total.............	**63,899**	**28,658**	**33,951**	**41,851**	**48,548**	**50,997**	**81,805**
18 to 24 years old..........	33,626	(B)	32,372	27,371	30,069	28,651	45,588
25 to 34 years old..........	57,283	(B)	32,597	38,500	42,216	42,058	69,070
35 to 44 years old..........	70,285	31,543	35,424	43,183	47,570	54,005	88,549
45 to 54 years old..........	70,061	27,656	33,398	43,664	52,917	55,187	90,717
55 to 64 years old..........	67,078	25,068	33,344	48,097	57,435	55,688	87,642
65 years old and over......	64,147	(B)	(B)	42,291	60,758	58,379	84,676

B Base figure too small to meet statistical standards for reliability of derived figure. [1] Includes general educational development equivalency.

Source: U.S. Census Bureau, *Income and Poverty in the United States: 2020,* Current Population Reports, P60-273, September 2021; and "Current Population Survey Tables for Personal Income: Table PINC-04," <www.census.gov/topics/income-poverty/income/data/tables.html>, accessed November 2021.

Table 746. Per Capita Money Income in Current and Constant (2020) Dollars by Race and Hispanic Origin: 1990 to 2020

[In dollars. Constant dollars based on 2020 CPI-U-RS deflator. People as of March of following year. Based on the Current Population Survey, Annual Social and Economic Supplement (ASEC); see text, this section, Section 1, and Appendix III. See headnote, Table 739]

| Year | Current dollars | | | | | Constant (2020) dollars | | | | |
	All races [1]	White [2]	Black [2]	Asian [2]	His-panic [3]	All races [1]	White [2]	Black [2]	Asian [2]	His-panic [3]
1990.............	14,387	15,265	9,017	(NA)	8,424	27,713	29,404	17,369	(NA)	16,227
2000 [4].............	22,346	23,582	14,796	23,350	12,651	33,682	35,546	22,302	35,196	19,069
2005 [5].............	25,036	26,496	16,874	27,331	14,483	33,265	35,205	22,420	36,314	19,243
2010 [6].............	26,558	28,356	18,019	28,673	15,044	31,598	33,737	21,438	34,114	17,899
2015 [7].............	31,653	33,564	22,452	36,280	19,457	34,583	36,671	24,531	39,639	21,258
2016 [7].............	33,205	35,168	23,622	38,156	20,430	35,817	37,934	25,480	41,158	22,037
2017 [7].............	35,048	37,303	24,148	40,517	20,746	37,009	39,390	25,499	42,784	21,907
2018 [7].............	36,080	38,323	24,731	43,193	21,975	37,192	39,504	25,493	44,525	22,652
2019 [7, 8].............	39,156	41,374	27,593	47,525	23,289	39,644	41,890	27,937	48,118	23,580
2020 [7, 8].............	39,052	41,232	28,134	46,366	23,315	39,052	41,232	28,134	46,366	23,315

NA Not available. [1] Includes other races, not shown separately. [2] As of 2002, data refer to people reporting specified race alone. [3] People of Hispanic origin may be of any race. [4] Implementation of Census 2000-based population controls, and of a 28,000 household sample expansion. [5] Data have been revised to reflect a correction to the weights in the 2005 ASEC. [6] Implementation of Census 2010-based population controls. [7] As of 2013, data based on redesigned income questions. As of 2017, data reflect an updated processing system. [8] See source for information on the impact of the coronavirus disease 2019 (COVID-19) pandemic on CPS ASEC data collection.

Source: U.S. Census Bureau, *Income and Poverty in the United States: 2020,* Current Population Reports, P60-273, September 2021; and "Historical Income Tables: People, Table P-1," <www.census.gov/topics/income-poverty/income/data/tables.html>, accessed November 2021.

Table 747. Money Income of People—People by Income Level and by Sex, Race, and Hispanic Origin: 2020

[In thousands 129,368 represents 129,368,000). People age 15 years and over as of March of the following year. Based on Current Population Survey, Annual Social and Economic Supplement (ASEC); see text, this section, Section 1, and Appendix III. See source for information on the impact of the coronavirus disease 2019 (COVID-19) pandemic on the CPS ASEC data collection]

| Income level | Male | | | | | Female | | | | |
	All races [1]	White alone	Black alone	Asian alone	His-panic [2]	All races [1]	White alone	Black alone	Asian alone	His-panic [2]
Total........................	**129,368**	**101,204**	**15,752**	**7,807**	**22,867**	**136,889**	**104,581**	**18,507**	**8,872**	**22,965**
Under $10,000 [3].................	25,025	17,510	4,453	1,672	5,625	38,975	28,579	5,523	3,139	9,437
$10,000 to $19,999.............	13,826	10,380	2,210	687	2,944	22,098	16,990	3,280	1,069	3,703
$20,000 to $29,999.............	14,508	11,266	2,038	623	3,360	17,246	13,375	2,437	851	3,057
$30,000 to $39,999.............	13,089	10,438	1,543	660	2,907	13,352	10,278	1,989	618	2,197
$40,000 to $49,999.............	10,644	8,501	1,293	514	2,167	10,226	7,968	1,408	491	1,394
$50,000 to $59,999.............	9,734	8,003	1,005	450	1,568	8,334	6,444	1,111	491	886
$60,000 to $74,999.............	10,951	8,925	1,146	523	1,631	8,736	6,878	1,086	538	891
$75,000 to $84,999.............	5,464	4,516	454	341	569	4,069	3,218	407	321	375
$85,000 to $99,999.............	5,132	4,268	396	355	537	3,925	3,098	363	312	386
$100,000 to $149,999..........	10,947	9,179	661	886	938	5,916	4,612	531	616	404
$150,000 to $199,999..........	4,816	3,905	321	499	339	2,136	1,688	212	205	131
$200,000 to $249,999..........	2,038	1,645	92	268	119	806	611	69	108	34
$250,000 and above...........	3,195	2,667	141	329	162	1,075	841	91	116	67

[1] Includes other races not shown separately. [2] Persons of Hispanic origin may be of any race. [3] Includes persons without income.

Source: U.S. Census Bureau, *Income and Poverty in the United States: 2020,* Current Population Reports, P60-273, September 2021; and "Current Population Survey Tables for Personal Income: Table PINC-11," <www.census.gov/topics/income-poverty/income/data/tables.html>, accessed November 2021.

Table 748. Household, Family, and Per Capita Income, and Individuals and Families Below Poverty Level by City: 2019

[The American Community Survey universe includes the household population and the population living in institutions, college dormitories, and other group quarters. Based on a sample and subject to sampling variability; see text, Section 1 and Appendix III. For definition of median, see Guide to Tabular Presentation. CDP is Census designated place]

City	Median household income (dol.)	Median family income (dol.)	Per capita income (dol.)	Number below poverty level [1]		Percent below poverty level	
				Individuals [1]	Families	Individuals [1]	Families
Albuquerque, NM	55,567	66,550	32,216	88,953	16,889	16.0	13.0
Anaheim, CA	76,075	81,006	31,368	43,628	6,961	12.6	9.0
Anchorage, AK	82,716	104,660	41,422	28,365	4,007	10.1	6.2
Arlington, TX	61,716	73,488	29,207	47,421	8,291	12.0	8.9
Atlanta, GA	66,657	95,081	54,414	95,034	15,345	20.2	15.5
Aurora, CO	69,235	81,550	32,986	35,295	5,913	9.4	6.7
Austin, TX	75,413	98,238	46,217	116,046	17,745	12.2	8.5
Bakersfield, CA	62,402	72,247	28,428	55,566	9,776	14.6	11.2
Baltimore, MD	50,177	65,518	32,430	115,472	17,249	20.2	14.6
Boston, MA	79,018	95,885	48,978	111,442	14,932	17.1	11.7
Charlotte, NC	63,483	79,910	40,071	97,566	15,110	11.2	7.7
Chicago, IL	61,811	76,360	40,277	432,385	68,248	16.4	12.2
Cincinnati, OH	46,260	62,941	33,910	67,331	10,287	23.1	16.4
Cleveland, OH	32,053	40,905	21,782	114,309	21,543	30.8	26.0
Colorado Springs, CO	70,527	84,717	36,384	43,478	7,229	9.3	6.0
Columbus, OH	57,118	70,936	31,843	143,363	24,716	16.3	12.7
Corpus Christi, TX	55,564	71,505	26,979	54,926	10,209	17.2	12.6
Dallas, TX	55,332	63,180	36,288	232,209	40,385	17.5	14.2
Denver, CO	75,646	98,247	47,802	83,601	11,528	11.7	7.7
Detroit, MI	33,965	40,529	21,044	201,766	36,799	30.6	26.5
El Paso, TX	48,542	54,147	22,583	125,140	23,600	18.6	15.2
Fort Worth, TX	65,356	75,854	30,115	106,449	17,921	11.9	8.5
Fresno, CA	53,161	58,658	23,739	121,007	22,175	23.2	19.1
Greensboro, NC	49,748	63,841	30,112	55,327	9,487	19.7	13.7
Henderson, NV	81,505	101,522	44,274	23,015	3,736	7.2	4.7
Honolulu CDP, HI	72,943	89,777	39,928	31,475	4,410	9.4	5.8
Houston, TX	52,450	60,190	33,377	449,733	83,550	19.7	16.0
Indianapolis, IN	49,661	64,673	29,008	134,443	18,282	15.8	10.3
Jacksonville, FL	56,975	68,135	30,780	125,468	22,007	14.1	10.5
Kansas City, MO	55,259	72,775	32,517	74,648	12,133	15.3	11.1
Las Vegas, NV	58,713	72,368	31,292	95,279	16,965	14.9	11.7
Lexington-Fayette, KY	58,356	82,055	34,947	48,298	6,334	15.6	8.7
Lincoln, NE	59,228	78,437	33,249	32,564	3,745	11.8	5.5
Long Beach, CA	67,804	77,901	33,594	66,693	10,546	14.7	10.6
Los Angeles, CA	67,418	76,277	37,779	651,205	100,772	16.7	12.1
Louisville/Jefferson County, KY [2]	54,853	71,279	31,955	93,012	15,556	15.4	10.8
Memphis, TN	43,794	54,519	27,224	137,977	23,882	21.7	17.1
Mesa, AZ	63,836	74,359	32,448	59,387	10,379	11.6	8.6
Miami, FL	42,966	48,649	30,934	94,209	17,277	20.3	15.9
Milwaukee, WI	44,192	51,038	23,896	128,555	21,297	22.4	17.3
Minneapolis, MN	65,889	87,727	39,617	72,208	9,346	17.4	11.4
Nashville-Davidson, TN [2]	63,462	80,904	38,847	81,325	12,075	12.6	8.3
New Orleans, LA	45,615	67,322	34,034	88,044	11,003	23.2	15.9
New York, NY	69,407	78,113	43,046	1,312,028	234,431	16.0	12.4
Oakland, CA	82,018	99,659	47,763	59,426	9,698	13.9	11.0
Oklahoma City, OK	55,492	70,386	31,019	101,536	17,740	15.8	11.7
Omaha, NE	61,305	77,140	33,786	54,336	9,197	11.6	8.2
Philadelphia, PA	47,474	54,978	29,766	359,011	62,756	23.3	18.5
Phoenix, AZ	60,931	68,785	30,686	258,625	45,188	15.6	12.0
Pittsburgh, PA	53,799	74,938	37,278	53,373	6,778	19.1	11.6
Portland, OR	76,231	100,589	45,035	79,044	8,396	12.3	6.0
Raleigh, NC	69,333	90,081	38,494	49,601	6,100	10.9	5.8
Riverside, CA	71,967	82,148	25,953	36,325	5,257	11.5	8.2
Sacramento, CA	69,134	80,654	34,659	70,314	9,349	13.9	8.4
San Antonio, TX	53,751	63,605	26,826	255,532	42,654	16.8	13.3
San Diego, CA	85,507	100,470	43,249	153,361	21,399	11.0	6.9
San Francisco, CA	123,859	140,707	75,084	82,356	8,231	9.5	4.9
San Jose, CA	115,893	130,829	51,310	71,931	9,188	7.1	3.9
San Juan, Puerto Rico	23,045	30,086	19,887	121,799	27,366	40.0	36.1
Santa Ana, CA	70,084	70,231	22,566	41,488	6,895	12.6	10.5
Seattle, WA	102,486	152,242	65,205	71,810	6,880	9.8	4.5
St. Louis, MO	47,176	65,317	31,819	55,883	8,618	19.1	13.5
St. Paul, MN	63,174	80,676	32,477	47,726	6,773	15.9	11.2
Stockton, CA	59,504	66,861	26,417	47,377	8,381	15.4	12.4
Tampa, FL	57,709	71,151	36,747	65,968	10,259	17.0	12.4
Tucson, AZ	44,365	57,623	24,808	99,524	16,594	19.1	14.5
Tulsa, OK	49,158	64,820	32,746	73,586	13,230	18.6	14.2
Virginia Beach, VA	79,054	91,608	39,269	29,839	5,211	6.8	4.4
Washington, DC	92,266	130,291	59,808	90,534	11,036	13.5	8.8
Wichita, KS	55,056	73,745	30,315	54,498	8,010	14.2	8.8

[1] Poverty status was determined for all people except institutionalized people, people in military group quarters, people in college dormitories, and unrelated individuals under 15 years old. [2] Represents metropolitan government (balance) of locality.

Source: U.S. Census Bureau, 2019 American Community Survey, Tables DP03, B01003, B17001, and B17019, <data.census.gov>, accessed November 2020. See also <www.census.gov/topics/income-poverty/poverty.html>.

Table 749. Persons and Families Below Poverty Level—Number and Rate by State: 2020

[Represents number and percent below poverty in the past 12 months. Data are based on 2020 American Community Survey (ACS) 1-year experimental estimates. The coronavirus disease 2019 (COVID-19) pandemic impacted 2020 ACS data collection and quality, and standard estimates did not meet statistical quality standards. The Census Bureau does not recommend comparing experimental estimates to standard ACS estimates. For more information, see <www.census.gov/programs-surveys/acs/data/experimental-data.html>. Poverty status was determined for all people except institutionalized people, people in military group quarters, people in college dormitories, and unrelated individuals under 15 years old. These groups were excluded from the numerator and denominator when calculating poverty rates. Based on a sample and subject to sampling variability; see Appendix III]

State	Persons			Families		
	Population for whom poverty status is determined	Number in poverty	Percent in poverty	Population for whom poverty status is determined	Number in poverty	Percent in poverty
United States.................	**321,478,113**	**38,371,394**	**11.9**	**79,419,801**	**6,371,904**	**8.0**
Alabama..........	4,800,077	704,839	14.7	1,198,333	117,112	9.8
Alaska............	713,279	65,283	9.2	166,091	9,291	5.6
Arizona..........	7,259,758	928,590	12.8	1,764,216	155,363	8.8
Arkansas.........	2,944,607	451,459	15.3	767,021	84,534	11.0
California.........	38,585,594	4,409,704	11.4	8,872,651	686,797	7.7
Colorado........	5,685,737	509,201	9.0	1,359,005	73,003	5.4
Connecticut......	3,454,810	338,838	9.8	891,074	56,995	6.4
Delaware.........	961,223	108,373	11.3	241,372	17,311	7.2
District of Columbia...........	680,446	100,628	14.8	110,176	8,849	8.0
Florida...........	21,304,092	2,609,912	12.3	5,095,927	398,844	7.8
Georgia..........	10,432,307	1,446,416	13.9	2,527,784	235,523	9.3
Hawaii...........	1,366,378	121,806	8.9	329,059	19,723	6.0
Idaho............	1,793,934	180,578	10.1	463,868	31,250	6.7
Illinois...........	12,284,039	1,352,066	11.0	3,069,449	228,422	7.4
Indiana..........	6,554,325	768,531	11.7	1,690,829	135,038	8.0
Iowa.............	3,066,684	319,773	10.4	799,580	54,751	6.8
Kansas..........	2,827,832	306,273	10.8	744,723	55,024	7.4
Kentucky........	4,338,771	644,019	14.8	1,125,283	117,305	10.4
Louisiana........	4,511,381	801,788	17.8	1,081,585	134,455	12.4
Maine...........	1,313,171	139,865	10.7	345,390	22,065	6.4
Maryland.........	5,909,280	518,007	8.8	1,471,326	80,016	5.4
Massachusetts....	6,658,066	627,360	9.4	1,668,051	101,186	6.1
Michigan.........	9,758,279	1,239,010	12.7	2,490,382	205,184	8.2
Minnesota........	5,536,448	457,119	8.3	1,407,287	68,289	4.9
Mississippi.......	2,869,477	538,070	18.8	724,932	103,210	14.2
Missouri.........	5,979,135	724,601	12.1	1,523,719	121,780	8.0
Montana.........	1,057,045	137,215	13.0	266,352	19,762	7.4
Nebraska........	1,884,807	169,627	9.0	489,387	28,305	5.8
Nevada..........	3,096,860	382,345	12.3	743,006	59,557	8.0
New Hampshire....	1,325,234	92,684	7.0	349,356	14,524	4.2
New Jersey.......	8,708,059	831,476	9.5	2,258,155	158,325	7.0
New Mexico.......	2,061,628	366,971	17.8	487,667	60,726	12.5
New York.........	18,840,594	2,391,797	12.7	4,676,775	433,801	9.3
North Carolina....	10,308,746	1,341,095	13.0	2,569,953	219,155	8.5
North Dakota.....	742,278	81,889	11.0	192,738	14,189	7.4
Ohio.............	11,369,386	1,438,323	12.7	2,912,882	254,778	8.7
Oklahoma........	3,866,030	557,622	14.4	972,864	94,731	9.7
Oregon..........	4,162,955	455,894	11.0	1,055,566	69,394	6.6
Pennsylvania.....	12,382,199	1,344,659	10.9	3,237,255	237,627	7.3
Rhode Island.....	1,017,637	98,209	9.7	262,117	15,706	6.0
South Carolina....	5,085,300	710,672	14.0	1,273,262	117,500	9.2
South Dakota.....	864,272	100,807	11.7	217,216	15,945	7.3
Tennessee.......	6,715,312	919,090	13.7	1,713,362	155,083	9.1
Texas...........	28,725,851	3,866,560	13.5	6,848,234	658,064	9.6
Utah............	3,199,970	227,913	7.1	777,255	36,222	4.7
Vermont.........	598,899	57,292	9.6	153,354	6,650	4.3
Virginia..........	8,336,631	763,447	9.2	2,076,051	119,748	5.8
Washington......	7,547,553	718,201	9.5	1,902,731	115,840	6.1
West Virginia.....	1,734,108	280,336	16.2	444,679	48,616	10.9
Wisconsin........	5,689,330	572,491	10.1	1,456,179	88,097	6.0
Wyoming.........	568,299	52,670	9.3	154,292	8,239	5.3

Source: U.S. Census Bureau, 2020 ACS 1-Year Experimental Data Tables, "Table XK201701. Poverty Status in the Past 12 Months by Age" and "Table XK201703. Poverty Status in the Past 12 Months of Families by Household Type," <www.census.gov/programs-surveys/acs/data/experimental-data.html>, accessed February 2022.

Table 750. Poverty Thresholds by Size of Family Unit: 1980 to 2020

[In dollars per year. The official poverty definition uses money income before taxes and does not include capital gains and noncash benefits (such as public housing and food stamps). For information on the official poverty thresholds, see text, this section. For more on poverty, see <www.census.gov/topics/income-poverty/poverty.html>. See also headnote, Table 751]

Size of family unit	1980	1990	1995	2000 [2]	2005	2010 [3]	2015 [4]	2019 [4]	2020 [4]
One person (unrelated individual) [1]......	4,190	6,652	7,763	8,791	9,973	11,137	12,082	13,011	13,171
Under 65 years old.......................	4,290	6,800	7,929	8,959	10,160	11,344	12,331	13,300	13,465
65 years old and over....................	3,949	6,268	7,309	8,259	9,367	10,458	11,367	12,261	12,413
Two persons.............................	5,363	8,509	9,933	11,235	12,755	14,216	15,391	16,521	16,733
Householder under 65 years old........	5,537	8,794	10,259	11,589	13,145	14,676	15,952	17,196	17,413
Householder 65 years old and over.....	4,983	7,905	9,219	10,418	11,815	13,194	14,342	15,468	15,659
Three persons...........................	6,565	10,419	12,158	13,740	15,577	17,373	18,871	20,335	20,591
Four persons............................	8,414	13,359	15,569	17,604	19,971	22,315	24,257	26,172	26,496
Five persons............................	9,966	15,792	18,408	20,815	23,613	26,442	28,741	31,021	31,417
Six persons.............................	11,269	17,839	20,804	23,533	26,683	29,904	32,542	35,129	35,499
Seven persons...........................	12,761	20,241	23,552	26,750	30,249	34,019	36,998	40,016	40,406
Eight persons...........................	14,199	22,582	26,237	29,701	33,610	37,953	41,029	44,461	44,755
Nine or more persons....................	16,896	26,848	31,280	35,150	40,288	45,224	49,177	52,875	53,905

[1] A person living alone or with non-relatives. [2] Implementation of Census 2000-based population controls and sample expanded by 28,000 households. [3] Implementation of Census 2010-based population controls. [4] Based on redesigned questions on income. As of 2017, data reflect an updated processing system. See source for more information.

Source: U.S. Census Bureau, *Income and Poverty in the United States: 2020,* Current Population Reports, P60-273, September 2021; and "Poverty Thresholds," <www.census.gov/topics/income-poverty/poverty/data/tables.html>, accessed November 2021.

Table 751. People Below Poverty Level by Race and Hispanic Origin, and Below 125 Percent of Poverty Level: 1990 to 2020

[33,585 represents 33,585,000. People as of March of the following year. Based on Current Population Survey, Annual Social and Economic Supplement (ASEC); see text, this section, Section 1, and Appendix III. Beginning with 2003 CPS ASEC covering data for 2002, refers to persons of specified race only and who did not report any other race category; "Asian" replaced "Asian Pacific Islander." For information on measuring poverty, see <www.census.gov/topics/income-poverty/poverty/guidance/poverty-measures.html>. Data users should exercise caution when comparing trends over time due to changes in CPS ASEC methodology and data processing. Changes are noted below for the years as appropriate. See source for more information]

Year	Number of persons below poverty (1,000)					Percent of persons below poverty					Below 125 percent of poverty level [1]	
	All races [2]	White	Black	Asian	His-panic [3]	All races [2]	White	Black	Asian	His-panic [3]	Number (1,000)	Percent of total pop-ulation
1990.........	33,585	22,326	9,837	858	6,006	13.5	10.7	31.9	12.2	28.1	44,837	18.0
1991.........	35,708	23,747	10,242	996	6,339	14.2	11.3	32.7	13.8	28.7	47,527	18.9
1992 [4].......	38,014	25,259	10,827	985	7,592	14.8	11.9	33.4	12.7	29.6	50,592	19.7
1993 [5].......	39,265	26,226	10,877	1,134	8,126	15.1	12.2	33.1	15.3	30.6	51,801	20.0
1994.........	38,059	25,379	10,196	974	8,416	14.5	11.7	30.6	14.6	30.7	50,401	19.3
1995.........	36,425	24,423	9,872	1,411	8,574	13.8	11.2	29.3	14.6	30.3	48,761	18.5
1996.........	36,529	24,650	9,694	1,454	8,697	13.7	11.2	28.4	14.5	29.4	49,310	18.5
1997.........	35,574	24,396	9,116	1,468	8,308	13.3	11.0	26.5	14.0	27.1	47,853	17.8
1998.........	34,476	23,454	9,091	1,360	8,070	12.7	10.5	26.1	12.5	25.6	46,036	17.0
1999 [6].......	32,791	22,169	8,441	1,285	7,876	11.9	9.8	23.6	10.7	22.7	45,030	16.3
2000 [7].......	31,581	21,645	7,982	1,258	7,747	11.3	9.5	22.5	9.9	21.5	43,612	15.6
2001.........	32,907	22,739	8,136	1,275	7,997	11.7	9.9	22.7	10.2	21.4	45,320	16.1
2002.........	34,570	23,466	8,602	1,161	8,555	12.1	10.2	24.1	10.1	21.8	47,084	16.5
2003.........	35,861	24,272	8,781	1,401	9,051	12.5	10.5	24.4	11.8	22.5	48,687	16.9
2004 [8].......	37,040	25,327	9,014	1,201	9,122	12.7	10.8	24.7	9.8	21.9	49,693	17.1
2005.........	36,950	24,872	9,168	1,402	9,368	12.6	10.6	24.9	11.1	21.8	49,327	16.8
2006.........	36,460	24,416	9,048	1,353	9,243	12.3	10.3	24.3	10.3	20.6	49,688	16.8
2007.........	37,276	25,120	9,237	1,349	9,890	12.5	10.5	24.5	10.2	21.5	50,876	17.0
2008.........	39,829	26,990	9,379	1,576	10,987	13.2	11.2	24.7	11.8	23.2	53,805	17.9
2009.........	43,569	29,830	9,944	1,746	12,350	14.3	12.3	25.8	12.5	25.3	56,840	18.7
2010 [9].......	46,343	31,083	10,746	1,899	13,522	15.1	13.0	27.4	12.2	26.5	60,669	19.8
2011..........	46,247	30,849	10,929	1,973	13,244	15.0	12.8	27.6	12.3	25.3	60,949	19.8
2012.........	46,496	30,816	10,911	1,921	13,616	15.0	12.7	27.2	11.7	25.6	61,202	19.7
2013 [10]......	46,269	31,287	10,186	2,255	13,356	14.8	12.9	25.2	13.1	24.7	60,396	19.3
2014 [10]......	46,657	31,089	10,755	2,137	13,104	14.8	12.7	26.2	12.0	23.6	61,339	19.4
2015 [10]......	43,123	28,566	10,020	2,078	12,133	13.5	11.6	24.1	11.4	21.4	56,912	17.9
2016 [10]......	40,616	27,113	9,234	1,908	11,137	12.7	11.0	22.0	10.1	19.4	54,430	17.0
2017 [10]......	39,564	26,026	9,224	1,891	10,816	12.3	10.5	21.7	9.7	18.3	53,512	16.6
2018 [10]......	38,146	24,945	8,884	1,996	10,526	11.8	10.1	20.8	10.1	17.6	51,706	16.0
2019 [10, 11]...	33,984	22,512	8,073	1,464	9,545	10.5	9.1	18.8	7.3	15.7	46,538	14.3
2020 [10, 11]...	37,247	25,007	8,472	1,629	10,409	11.4	10.1	19.5	8.1	17.0	49,889	15.3

[1] People with incomes below 125 percent of poverty level. [2] Includes other races, not shown separately. [3] People of Hispanic origin may be of any race. [4] Implementation of 1990 Census population controls. [5] The 1994 CPS ASEC was revised to allow for the coding of different income amounts on selected questionnaire items. Limits changed as follows: earnings increased to $999,999; social security increased to $49,999; supplemental security income and public assistance increased to $24,999; veterans' benefits increased to $99,999; child support and alimony decreased to $49,999. [6] Implementation of Census-2000-based population controls. [7] Implementation of a 28,000 household expansion. [8] Data have been revised to reflect a correction to the weights in the 2005 CPS ASEC. [9] Implementation of Census 2010-based population controls. [10] Data based on redesigned income questions. Beginning 2017, data reflect an updated processing system. [11] See source for information on the impact of the coronavirus disease 2019 (COVID-19) pandemic on the 2020 and 2021 CPS ASEC.

Source: U.S. Census Bureau, *Income and Poverty in the United States: 2020,* Current Population Reports, P60-273, September 2021; and "Historical Poverty Tables: People and Families, Tables 2 and 6," <www.census.gov/topics/income-poverty/poverty/data/tables.html>, accessed November 2021.

Table 752. Children Below Poverty Level by Race and Hispanic Origin: 1990 to 2020

[12,715 represents 12,715,000. Persons as of March of the following year. Covers only children under age 18 related in families. Based on Current Population Survey, Annual Social and Economic Supplement (CPS ASEC); see text, this section, Section 1, and Appendix III. See headnote, Table 751]

Year	Number of children below poverty level (1,000)					Percent of children below poverty level				
	All races [1]	White	Black	Asian	His-panic [2]	All races [1]	White	Black	Asian	His-panic [2]
1990	12,715	7,696	4,412	356	2,750	19.9	15.1	44.2	17.0	37.7
1995 [3]	13,999	8,474	4,644	532	3,938	20.2	15.5	41.5	18.6	39.3
1999 [4]	11,678	7,194	3,698	367	3,561	16.6	13.1	32.8	11.5	29.9
2000 [5]	11,005	6,834	3,495	407	3,342	15.6	12.4	30.9	12.5	27.6
2001	11,175	7,086	3,423	353	3,433	15.8	12.8	30.0	11.1	27.4
2002	11,646	7,203	3,570	302	3,653	16.3	13.1	32.1	11.4	28.2
2003	12,340	7,624	3,750	331	3,982	17.2	13.9	33.6	12.1	29.5
2004 [6]	12,473	7,876	3,702	265	3,985	17.3	14.3	33.4	9.4	28.6
2005	12,335	7,652	3,743	312	3,977	17.1	13.9	34.2	11.0	27.7
2006	12,299	7,522	3,690	351	3,959	16.9	13.6	33.0	12.0	26.6
2007	12,802	8,002	3,838	345	4,348	17.6	14.4	34.3	11.8	28.3
2008	13,507	8,441	3,781	430	4,888	18.5	15.3	34.4	14.2	30.3
2009	14,774	9,440	3,919	444	5,419	20.1	17.0	35.3	13.6	32.5
2010 [7]	15,598	9,590	4,271	477	5,815	21.5	17.9	39.0	14.0	34.3
2011	15,539	9,643	4,247	466	5,820	21.4	18.1	38.6	13.0	33.7
2012	15,437	9,547	4,097	470	5,773	21.3	17.9	37.5	13.3	33.3
2013 [8]	15,116	9,702	3,678	538	5,638	20.9	18.4	33.8	14.4	32.2
2014 [8]	14,987	9,172	4,036	492	5,522	20.7	17.4	37.1	13.4	31.3
2015 [8]	13,962	8,838	3,571	420	5,139	19.2	16.7	32.7	11.4	28.6
2016 [8]	12,803	7,963	3,382	412	4,764	17.6	15.1	30.6	10.7	26.3
2017 [8]	12,358	7,520	3,280	405	4,525	17.0	14.3	30.2	10.1	24.7
2018 [8]	11,491	6,783	3,212	426	4,316	15.9	13.0	29.4	10.8	23.4
2019 [8,9]	10,165	6,209	2,831	272	3,796	14.1	12.0	26.3	7.0	20.6
2020 [8,9]	11,265	6,941	2,986	341	4,125	15.7	13.7	27.4	8.2	22.7

[1] Includes other races, not shown separately. [2] People of Hispanic origin may be of any race. [3] See Table 751, footnote 5. [4] Implementation of Census 2000-based population controls. [5] Sample expanded by 28,000 households. [6] Data have been revised to reflect a correction to the weights in the 2005 ASEC. [7] Implementation of Census 2010-based population controls. [8] Data based on redesigned income questions. As of 2017, data reflect an updated processing system. See source for more information. [9] See Table 751, footnote 11.

Source: U.S. Census Bureau, *Income and Poverty in the United States: 2020*, Current Population Reports, P60-273, September 2021; and "Historical Poverty Tables: People and Families, Table 3," <www.census.gov/topics/income-poverty/poverty/data/tables.html>, accessed November 2021.

Table 753. People Below Poverty Level by Selected Characteristics: 2020

[37,247 represents 37,247,000. People as of March of the following year. Based on the Current Population Survey, Annual Social and Economic and Supplement (CPS ASEC). Data by education cover people age 25 and over, based on the highest grade completed]

Characteristic	Number below poverty level (1,000)					Percent below poverty level				
	All races [1]	White alone	Black alone	Asian alone	His-panic [2]	All races [1]	White alone	Black alone	Asian alone	His-panic [2]
Total	**37,247**	**25,007**	**8,472**	**1,629**	**10,409**	**11.4**	**10.1**	**19.5**	**8.1**	**17.0**
Male	16,334	11,127	3,526	720	4,670	10.2	9.1	17.3	7.5	15.2
Female	20,912	13,880	4,946	909	5,739	12.6	11.1	21.5	8.6	18.8
AGE										
Under 18 years old	11,607	7,194	3,038	352	4,265	16.1	14.0	27.7	8.4	23.1
18 to 24 years old	4,197	2,887	817	256	1,052	14.6	13.6	19.3	15.0	15.3
25 to 34 years old	4,732	3,150	1,057	249	1,408	10.4	9.5	15.5	7.6	14.8
35 to 44 years old	4,145	2,866	933	147	1,376	9.9	9.1	16.5	4.6	15.8
45 to 54 years old	3,368	2,271	776	183	840	8.5	7.4	15.1	6.6	11.5
55 to 59 years old	1,961	1,423	398	60	330	9.5	8.6	15.9	5.2	11.0
60 to 64 years old	2,238	1,579	522	72	307	10.6	9.3	19.9	6.4	13.0
65 years old and over	5,000	3,637	933	310	831	9.0	7.8	17.2	11.5	16.6
65 to 74 years old	2,710	1,908	563	160	497	8.2	7.0	16.3	9.8	15.7
75 years old and over	2,290	1,729	370	150	334	10.0	8.9	18.6	14.0	18.1
EDUCATION [3]										
No high school diploma	7,489	5,169	1,626	268	3,060	20.4	18.7	32.0	14.3	22.8
High school, no college	9,800	6,690	2,386	320	2,063	13.6	12.0	21.5	11.4	14.8
Some college, less than 4-year degree	6,332	4,420	1,318	297	1,161	9.2	8.3	13.5	10.5	10.9
College, 4-year degree or higher	3,790	2,656	558	453	504	4.3	3.8	6.8	4.9	6.4
NATIVITY [4]										
Native	31,230	20,975	7,695	689	6,652	11.1	9.5	20.2	8.0	16.4
Foreign born	6,016	4,032	777	940	3,757	13.4	15.2	15.0	8.1	18.2
Naturalized citizen	2,078	1,209	323	492	929	9.2	9.8	11.2	7.3	11.6
Not a citizen	3,939	2,823	455	448	2,827	17.8	19.9	19.9	9.4	22.4
REGION										
Northeast	5,555	3,720	1,214	341	1,520	10.1	8.9	16.7	8.1	19.4
Midwest	6,812	4,557	1,600	215	700	10.1	8.2	22.1	9.0	12.6
South	16,619	10,491	4,978	384	4,649	13.3	11.6	20.0	7.8	19.3
West	8,261	6,238	680	689	3,540	10.6	10.4	16.9	8.0	14.9

[1] Includes other races, not shown separately. [2] Persons of Hispanic origin may be of any race. [3] Highest grade completed for persons age 25 and over. [4] For persons age 15 and over.

Source: U.S. Census Bureau, *Income and Poverty in the United States: 2020*, Current Population Reports, P60-273, September 2021; and "Current Population Survey Detailed Tables for Poverty: Tables POV01, POV29, and POV41," <www.census.gov/topics/income-poverty/poverty/data/tables.html>, accessed November 2021.

Table 754. Work Experience of People During Year by Poverty Status by Sex and Age: 2020

[105,478 represents 105,478,000. Covers persons age 16 and over. Based on the Current Population Survey, Annual Social and Economic Supplement (ASEC); see text, this section, Section 1, and Appendix III. Data reflect an updated processing system; see source for more information]

Sex and age	Worked full-time year-round			Did not work full-time year-round			Did not work		
	Number (1,000)	Below poverty level		Number (1,000)	Below poverty level		Number (1,000)	Below poverty level	
		Number (1,000)	Percent		Number (1,000)	Percent		Number (1,000)	Percent
BOTH SEXES									
Total	**105,478**	**1,640**	**1.6**	**61,211**	**6,289**	**10.3**	**95,395**	**18,862**	**19.8**
16 to 17 years old	143	5	3.5	1,811	109	6.0	6,713	1,037	15.5
18 to 64 years old	99,404	1,609	1.6	52,842	5,984	11.3	45,336	13,047	28.8
18 to 24 years old	6,587	229	3.5	12,163	1,515	12.5	10,087	2,453	24.3
25 to 34 years old	25,235	515	2.0	12,496	1,635	13.1	7,553	2,583	34.2
35 to 54 years old	48,151	717	1.5	19,085	2,176	11.4	14,448	4,619	32.0
55 to 64 years old	19,431	149	0.8	9,097	659	7.2	13,249	3,392	25.6
65 years old and over	5,931	26	0.4	6,559	196	3.0	43,346	4,778	11.0
MALE									
Total	**59,628**	**928**	**1.6**	**27,868**	**2,651**	**9.5**	**39,737**	**7,545**	**19.0**
16 to 17 years old	72	(B)	(B)	869	55	6.3	3,423	504	14.7
18 to 64 years old	55,918	917	1.6	23,801	2,485	10.4	17,932	5,239	29.2
18 to 24 years old	3,716	94	2.5	5,794	627	10.8	5,032	1,087	21.6
25 to 34 years old	14,262	278	1.9	5,742	592	10.3	2,833	834	29.4
35 to 54 years old	27,239	454	1.7	8,259	981	11.9	4,741	1,808	38.1
55 to 64 years old	10,701	91	0.9	4,006	285	7.1	5,326	1,511	28.4
65 years old and over	3,638	7	0.2	3,198	111	3.5	18,382	1,802	9.8
FEMALE									
Total	**45,850**	**712**	**1.6**	**33,343**	**3,638**	**10.9**	**55,658**	**11,317**	**20.3**
16 to 17 years old	71	(B)	(B)	942	54	5.7	3,290	533	16.2
18 to 64 years old	43,486	692	1.6	29,041	3,499	12.0	27,404	7,807	28.5
18 to 24 years old	2,872	135	4.7	6,369	888	13.9	5,055	1,366	27.0
25 to 34 years old	10,973	237	2.2	6,754	1,043	15.4	4,720	1,749	37.1
35 to 54 years old	20,912	262	1.3	10,826	1,195	11.0	9,707	2,811	29.0
55 to 64 years old	8,730	58	0.7	5,091	373	7.3	7,922	1,881	23.7
65 years old and over	2,293	19	0.8	3,360	85	2.5	24,964	2,976	11.9

B Estimates are not shown when the denominator is less than 75,000.

Source: U.S. Census Bureau, *Income and Poverty in the United States: 2020*, Current Population Reports, P60-273, September 2021; and "Current Population Survey Detailed Tables for Poverty: Table POV22," <www.census.gov/topics/income-poverty/poverty/data/tables.html>, accessed November 2021.

Table 755. Families Below Poverty Level by Race and Hispanic Origin, and Below 125 Percent of Poverty Level: 1990 to 2020

[7,098 represents 7,098,000. Families as of March of the following year. Based on Current Population Survey, Annual Social and Economic Supplement (ASEC); see text, this section and Section 1, and Appendix III. For data collection changes over time, see "Changes in Methodology for the March Current Population Survey" at <www.census.gov/topics/income-poverty/income/guidance/cps-methodology-changes.html>. Beginning with the 2003 CPS covering data for 2002, respondents could choose more than one race. Two basic ways of defining a race group are possible: a group such as Asian may be defined as those who reported Asian and no other race (the race-alone concept), or as those who reported Asian regardless of whether they also reported another race (the race-alone-or-in-combination concept). For 2001 data and earlier, the CPS allowed respondents to report only one race group. See also comments on race in the text for Section 1, Population]

Year	Number of families below poverty (1,000)					Percent of families below poverty					Below 125 percent of poverty level	
	All races [1]	White [2]	Black [2]	Asian [2]	His-panic [3]	All races [1]	White [2]	Black [2]	Asian [2]	His-panic [3]	Number (1,000)	Percent
1990	7,098	4,622	2,193	169	1,244	10.7	8.1	29.3	11.0	25.0	9,564	14.4
1995	7,532	4,994	2,127	264	1,695	10.8	8.5	26.4	12.4	27.0	10,223	14.7
2000 [4]	6,400	4,333	1,686	233	1,540	8.7	7.1	19.3	7.8	19.2	9,032	12.2
2005	7,657	5,068	1,997	289	1,948	9.9	8.0	22.1	9.0	19.7	10,442	13.5
2006	7,668	5,118	2,007	260	1,922	9.8	8.0	21.6	7.8	18.9	10,531	13.4
2007	7,623	5,046	2,045	261	2,045	9.8	7.9	22.1	7.9	19.7	10,551	13.5
2008	8,147	5,414	2,055	341	2,239	10.3	8.4	22.0	9.8	21.3	11,164	14.2
2009	8,792	5,994	2,125	337	2,369	11.1	9.3	22.7	9.4	22.7	11,620	14.7
2010 [5]	9,400	6,305	2,311	362	2,739	11.8	9.9	24.1	9.3	24.3	12,448	15.6
2011	9,497	6,334	2,334	401	2,651	11.8	9.8	24.2	9.7	22.9	12,500	15.5
2012	9,520	6,299	2,327	387	2,807	11.8	9.7	23.7	9.4	23.5	12,669	15.7
2013 [6]	9,645	6,526	2,204	448	2,865	11.7	9.9	22.4	10.2	23.1	12,605	15.3
2014 [6]	9,467	6,310	2,265	401	2,684	11.6	9.7	22.9	8.9	21.5	12,635	15.5
2015 [6]	8,589	5,743	2,082	374	2,502	10.4	8.8	21.1	8.0	19.6	11,603	14.1
2016 [6]	8,081	5,433	1,893	340	2,253	9.8	8.3	19.0	7.2	17.3	11,083	13.4
2017 [6]	7,790	5,135	1,898	367	2,178	9.3	7.8	18.9	7.4	16.4	10,696	12.8
2018 [6]	7,504	5,004	1,730	387	2,057	9.0	7.6	17.7	7.6	15.5	10,241	12.3
2019 [6,7]	6,554	4,323	1,618	291	1,833	7.8	6.5	16.3	5.7	13.9	9,104	10.9
2020 [6,7]	7,294	4,921	1,720	330	2,027	8.7	7.5	16.8	6.4	14.8	9,981	11.9

[1] Includes other races, not shown separately. [2] Beginning 2002, data refer to persons who reported specified race only and no other race; prior to 2002, Asian included Pacific Islander. [3] People of Hispanic origin may be of any race. [4] Implementation of Census 2000 based population controls and sample expanded by 28,000 households. [5] Implementation of Census 2010-based population controls. [6] Data are based on redesigned income questions. As of 2017, data reflect updated processing system. See source for more information. [7] See Table 751, footnote 11.

Source: U.S. Census Bureau, *Income and Poverty in the United States: 2020*, Current Population Reports, P60-273, September 2021; and "Historical Poverty Tables: People and Families, Table 4," and "Current Population Survey Detailed Tables for Poverty: Table POV04," <www.census.gov/topics/income-poverty/poverty/data/tables.html>, accessed November 2021.

Table 756. Families Below Poverty Level by Selected Characteristics: 2020

[In thousands (7,294 represents 7,294,000), except as noted. All families as of March of the following year. Based on the Current Population Survey, Annual Social and Economic Supplement (CPS ASEC); see text, this section and Section 1, and Appendix III. Data below represent persons who selected each race group only and exclude persons reporting more than one race. See also comments on race in the text for Section 1. For composition of regions, see map, inside front cover. See source report for information on the impact of the coronavirus disease 2019 (COVID-19) pandemic on the 2021 CPS ASEC collection of data for 2020]

Characteristic	Number below poverty level (1,000)					Percent below poverty level				
	All races [1]	White alone	Black alone	Asian alone	His-panic [2]	All races [1]	White alone	Black alone	Asian alone	His-panic [2]
Total families	**7,294**	**4,921**	**1,720**	**330**	**2,027**	**8.7**	**7.5**	**16.8**	**6.4**	**14.8**
Age of householder:										
18 to 24 years old	475	291	128	19	155	19.7	17.3	29.4	13.3	20.3
25 to 34 years old	1,860	1,170	530	59	568	14.5	12.4	27.1	7.3	19.8
35 to 44 years old	1,742	1,187	419	63	589	10.1	9.1	18.8	4.9	16.8
45 to 54 years old	1,092	738	254	66	318	6.7	5.9	12.4	5.4	11.0
55 to 64 years old	995	730	204	33	184	6.4	5.7	11.7	4.1	9.4
65 years old and over	1,094	793	175	86	200	5.6	4.9	9.7	10.0	12.2
Region:										
Northeast	1,081	700	267	68	279	7.8	6.4	15.8	6.5	16.4
Midwest	1,276	856	329	38	115	7.3	5.8	18.8	6.5	9.9
South	3,369	2,162	1,009	85	943	10.3	8.7	17.2	6.7	17.1
West	1,568	1,203	116	140	690	8.0	7.9	12.5	6.2	13.0
Type of family:										
Married couple	2,866	2,274	295	212	850	4.7	4.5	6.2	5.0	9.9
Male householder, no spouse present	796	481	231	29	203	11.4	9.6	18.8	8.1	12.1
Female householder, no spouse present	3,633	2,166	1,195	89	974	23.4	21.7	28.1	15.4	28.6
Families with children [3]	4,889	3,219	1,258	156	1,596	13.2	11.7	23.5	6.2	19.9

[1] Includes other races, not shown separately. [2] Hispanic persons may be of any race. [3] Children under age 18 related to the householder.

Source: U.S. Census Bureau, *Income and Poverty in the United States: 2020*, Current Population Reports, P60-273, September 2021; and "Current Population Survey Detailed Tables for Poverty: Tables POV04 and POV44," <www.census.gov/topics/income-poverty/poverty/data/tables.html>, accessed November 2021.

Table 757. Top Wealth Holders With Gross Assets of $5.45 Million or More—Debts, Mortgages, and Net Worth: 2016

[10,032,938 represents $10,032,938,000,000. Figures are estimates from the Personal Wealth Study, based on a sample of Federal estate tax returns (Form 706). Covers the segment of the population for whom personal wealth is at least equal to the estate tax filing threshold in effect for the estimation period; for 2016, the Federal estate tax filing threshold was $5.45 million or more in gross estate. Based on the estate multiplier technique to estimate the wealth of living individuals from Federal estate tax return data; for more information on this methodology, see source]

Sex and net worth	Total assets [1]		Debts and mortgages		Net worth [2]	
	Number of top wealth holders	Amount (mil. dol.)	Number of top wealth holders	Amount (mil. dol.)	Number of top wealth holders	Amount (mil. dol.)
Both sexes, total	**734,352**	**10,032,938**	**519,793**	**609,948**	**734,352**	**9,422,990**
Size of net worth:						
Under $5.45 million [3]	151,529	731,931	111,912	173,282	151,529	558,650
$5.45 million to under $10 million	373,730	2,784,741	254,071	118,794	373,730	2,665,947
$10 million to under $20 million	137,773	1,932,520	98,581	92,293	137,773	1,840,227
$20 million to under $50 million	52,325	1,627,627	40,723	78,392	52,325	1,549,235
$50 million or more	18,995	2,956,119	14,506	147,187	18,995	2,808,932
Males, total	**456,850**	**6,558,225**	**333,190**	**475,560**	**456,850**	**6,082,665**
Size of net worth:						
Under $5.45 million [3]	109,841	538,262	81,172	147,319	109,841	390,943
$5.45 million to under $10 million	222,781	1,673,434	154,980	84,559	222,781	1,588,875
$10 million to under $20 million	80,393	1,136,519	61,455	66,120	80,393	1,070,399
$20 million to under $50 million	31,373	995,835	25,509	57,733	31,373	938,102
$50 million or more	12,463	2,214,176	10,073	119,828	12,463	2,094,347
Females, total	**277,502**	**3,474,713**	**186,604**	**134,388**	**277,502**	**3,340,325**
Size of net worth:						
Under $5.45 million [3]	41,688	193,670	30,740	25,963	41,688	167,707
$5.45 million to under $10 million	150,949	1,111,307	99,092	34,235	150,949	1,077,072
$10 million to under $20 million	57,381	796,001	37,126	26,173	57,381	769,828
$20 million to under $50 million	20,952	631,792	15,214	20,659	20,952	611,133
$50 million or more	6,532	741,943	4,432	27,359	6,532	714,584

[1] Total assets is the sum of all assets owned by the individual before subtracting debts, mortgages, and liens owed to others. It differs from gross assets, which is a Federal estate tax concept of wealth, in that it includes the cash value of life insurance instead of the full face value of life insurance minus indebtedness. [2] Net worth is defined as total assets minus debts and mortgages. [3] Includes individuals with zero net worth.

Source: U.S. Internal Revenue Service, Statistics of Income Division, "SOI Tax Stats - Personal Wealth Statistics," May 2021, <www.irs.gov/statistics/soi-tax-stats-personal-wealth-statistics>.

Table 758. Top Wealth Holders With Gross Assets of $5.45 Million or More by Type of Property, Sex, and Size of Net Worth: 2016

[10,032,938 represents $10,032,938,000,000. Figures are estimates from the Personal Wealth Study, based on a sample of Federal estate tax returns (Form 706). Covers the segment of the population for whom personal wealth is at least equal to the estate tax filing threshold in effect for the estimation period; for 2016, the Federal estate tax filing threshold was $5.45 million or more in gross estate. Based on the estate multiplier technique to estimate the wealth of living individuals; for more information on this methodology, see source]

Sex and net worth	Number of top wealth holders	Assets (mil. dol.)					
		Total [1]	Personal residences	Other real estate	Closely held stock	Publicly traded stock	Retirement assets
Both sexes, total	**734,352**	**10,032,938**	**559,641**	**832,582**	**1,352,525**	**2,020,640**	**723,383**
Size of net worth:							
Under $5.45 million [2]	151,529	731,931	81,577	85,977	60,967	77,420	93,597
$5.45 million to under $10 million	373,730	2,784,741	217,332	267,102	270,007	562,743	324,620
$10 million to under $20 million	137,773	1,932,520	119,103	197,844	179,341	371,656	181,052
$20 million to under $50 million	52,325	1,627,627	91,508	172,853	216,344	348,512	70,566
$50 million or more	18,995	2,956,119	50,121	108,805	625,866	660,308	53,548
Males, total	**456,850**	**6,558,225**	**321,522**	**490,849**	**1,072,850**	**1,209,736**	**500,949**
Size of net worth:							
Under $5.45 million [2]	109,841	538,262	55,386	57,721	41,787	52,767	74,732
$5.45 million to under $10 million	222,781	1,673,434	118,736	141,515	218,740	299,604	216,985
$10 million to under $20 million	80,393	1,136,519	63,581	103,410	136,796	197,026	110,187
$20 million to under $50 million	31,373	995,835	50,591	116,876	134,353	208,360	52,387
$50 million or more	12,463	2,214,176	33,227	71,327	541,175	451,979	46,658
Females, total	**277,502**	**3,474,713**	**238,119**	**341,733**	**279,675**	**810,904**	**222,434**
Size of net worth:							
Under $5.45 million [2]	41,688	193,670	26,191	28,256	19,180	24,654	18,864
$5.45 million to under $10 million	150,949	1,111,307	98,596	125,587	51,268	263,139	107,635
$10 million to under $20 million	57,381	796,001	55,522	94,434	42,545	174,630	70,865
$20 million to under $50 million	20,952	631,792	40,917	55,977	81,991	140,152	18,179
$50 million or more	6,532	741,943	16,894	37,479	84,691	208,329	6,890

[1] Total assets is the sum of all assets owned by the individual before subtracting debts, mortgages, and liens owed to others. Includes other types of assets, not shown separately. [2] Includes individuals with zero or negative net worth.

Source: U.S. Internal Revenue Service, Statistics of Income Division, "SOI Tax Stats - Personal Wealth Statistics," May 2021, <www.irs.gov/statistics/soi-tax-stats-personal-wealth-statistics>.

Table 759. Top Wealth Holders With Net Worth of $5.45 Million or More—Number, Assets, and Net Worth by State: 2016

[9,301,007 represents $9,301,007,000,000. Estimates from the Personal Wealth Study, based on a sample of federal estate tax returns (Form 706). Covers the segment of the population for whom personal wealth is at least equal to the estate tax filing threshold in effect for the estimation period; for 2016, the Federal estate tax filing threshold was $5.45 million or more in gross estate. Estimates of wealth by State can be subject to significant year-to-year fluctuations. This is especially true for individuals at the extreme tail of the net worth distribution and for States with relatively small decedent populations. Based on the estate multiplier technique to estimate the wealth of living individuals; for more information on this methodology, see source. Detail may not sum to totals due to rounding]

State	Number of top wealth holders	Total assets [1] (mil. Dol.)	Net worth (mil. Dol.)	State	Number of top wealth holders	Total assets [1] (mil. Dol.)	Net worth (mil. Dol.)
Total [2]	**582,823**	**9,301,007**	**8,864,341**	Missouri	7,629	117,508	112,085
				Montana	1,486	21,032	19,240
Alabama	3,540	44,890	43,327	Nebraska	2,633	28,664	26,469
Alaska	1,541	11,196	11,076	Nevada	6,703	101,679	95,176
Arizona	8,291	146,718	142,041	New Hampshire	1,538	28,421	27,097
Arkansas	4,529	64,729	62,515	New Jersey	14,838	207,950	202,436
California	109,574	1,758,120	1,653,757	New Mexico	2,511	67,099	66,544
Colorado	13,421	150,608	140,346	New York	56,184	1,017,872	967,794
Connecticut	8,954	245,793	239,800	North Carolina	14,188	186,906	178,740
Delaware	544	10,411	9,980	North Dakota	2,393	22,867	22,347
District of Columbia	4,002	93,120	91,571	Ohio	16,011	172,249	167,872
Florida	56,016	1,428,879	1,345,761	Oklahoma	1,573	23,765	23,044
Georgia	11,887	147,788	138,124	Oregon	4,554	68,906	66,092
Hawaii	956	14,014	13,337	Pennsylvania	22,637	284,022	276,330
Idaho	1,854	50,727	49,492	Rhode Island	1,036	15,247	13,488
Illinois	29,626	393,062	375,005	South Carolina	5,861	64,726	63,368
Indiana	8,757	99,668	96,603	South Dakota	1,007	9,715	9,561
Iowa	3,668	42,428	38,739	Tennessee	6,268	116,237	108,462
Kansas	4,186	50,741	49,315	Texas	38,288	561,026	540,270
Kentucky	7,706	70,960	70,186	Utah	4,220	51,675	47,965
Louisiana	5,082	54,734	52,126	Vermont	1,237	18,586	17,700
Maine	1,049	13,145	12,742	Virginia	9,067	134,383	130,933
Maryland	9,725	117,664	113,053	Washington	11,180	173,547	167,698
Massachusetts	14,377	219,537	211,202	West Virginia	797	11,215	10,775
Michigan	9,189	132,204	121,952	Wisconsin	5,931	89,939	86,834
Minnesota	13,617	161,819	157,330	Wyoming	2,259	68,670	67,429
Mississippi	1,651	25,699	24,794	Other areas [1]	7,052	88,445	84,419

[1] Total assets is the sum of all assets owned by the individual before subtracting debts, mortgages, and liens owed to others. [2] Includes U.S. territories and possessions.

Source: U.S. Internal Revenue Service, Statistics of Income Division, "SOI Tax Stats - Personal Wealth Statistics," May 2021, <www.irs.gov/statistics/soi-tax-stats-personal-wealth-statistics>.

Table 760. Nonfinancial Assets Held by Families by Type of Asset: 2019

[Value of assets in thousands of constant (2019) dollars (227.6 represents $227,600). Families include one-person units and, as used in this table, are comparable to the U.S. Census Bureau's household concept. Based on internal data from the Survey of Consumer Finances; see Appendix III. All dollar amounts are adjusted to 2019 dollars using the "current methods" version of the consumer price index (CPI) for all urban consumers. For definition of median, see Guide to Tabular Presentation. For data on financial assets, see Table 1201]

Family characteristic	Any financial or non-financial asset	Any non-financial asset	Vehicles	Primary residence	Other resi-dential property	Equity in nonresi-dential property	Bus-iness equity	Other asset
PERCENT OF FAMILIES HOLDING ASSET								
All families, total	**99.6**	**91.4**	**85.4**	**64.9**	**13.1**	**6.7**	**13.4**	**7.9**
Age of family head:								
Under 35 years old	99.4	85.5	82.1	36.2	3.2	2.1	6.6	4.9
35 to 44 years old	99.5	92.1	85.3	61.4	10.3	5.0	15.6	6.4
45 to 54 years old	99.7	93.9	90.5	69.7	16.2	7.3	18.1	6.8
55 to 64 years old	99.7	92.3	86.8	74.1	18.2	10.0	17.1	7.3
65 to 74 years old	99.3	93.2	86.4	78.4	18.1	7.4	12.9	11.7
75 years old and over	100.0	93.3	80.1	82.4	16.0	10.7	10.1	13.2
Race or ethnicity of respondent:								
White, non-Hispanic	99.8	95.1	89.3	73.7	15.1	7.9	16.5	9.9
Black/African-American, non-Hispanic	98.9	79.4	71.5	45.0	8.2	2.6	4.8	1.7
Hispanic or Latino	99.0	88.0	84.5	47.6	8.6	3.9	7.0	3.5
Other or multiple race	99.7	87.7	81.1	54.2	12.0	7.9	12.0	8.1
Tenure:								
Owner occupied	100.0	100.0	92.6	100.0	17.9	9.2	17.3	9.3
Renter occupied or other	98.8	75.4	72.1	(B)	4.3	2.2	6.2	5.3
MEDIAN VALUE [1] ($1,000)								
All families, total	**227.6**	**194.3**	**17.2**	**225.0**	**160.0**	**72.0**	**89.1**	**15.0**
Age of family head:								
Under 35 years old	40.9	27.7	13.2	185.0	135.0	22.0	40.0	5.0
35 to 44 years old	242.3	207.2	19.7	250.0	170.0	60.0	51.0	8.6
45 to 54 years old	286.2	228.2	23.1	250.0	175.0	80.0	81.6	25.0
55 to 64 years old	299.1	230.4	18.5	230.0	187.5	90.0	150.0	32.0
65 to 74 years old	344.6	256.9	16.5	240.0	135.0	80.0	155.0	15.0
75 years old and over	310.7	211.6	13.5	200.0	137.0	85.0	80.0	15.0
Race or ethnicity of respondent:								
White, non-Hispanic	306.4	225.3	18.9	230.0	170.0	80.0	100.0	15.0
Black/African-American, non-Hispanic	53.0	69.0	12.3	150.0	72.0	40.0	70.0	10.0
Hispanic or Latino	71.9	82.0	16.0	200.0	130.0	65.0	52.3	10.0
Other or multiple race	168.4	192.2	15.6	310.0	185.0	64.4	92.2	6.0
Tenure:								
Owner occupied	393.8	288.2	22.2	225.0	170.0	80.0	100.0	16.0
Renter occupied or other	15.8	11.7	10.4	(B)	85.0	31.0	49.0	6.0

B Base too small to meet statistical standards for reliability of derived figure. [1] Median value of asset for families holding such assets.

Source: Board of Governors of the Federal Reserve System, 2019 Survey of Consumer Finances, *Changes in U.S. Family Finances From 2016 to 2019: Evidence from the Survey of Consumer Finances,* Federal Reserve Bulletin, September 2020, Vol. 106, No. 5; and "Historic Tables." See also <www.federalreserve.gov/econres/scfindex.htm>.

Table 761. Family Net Worth—Median and Mean Net Worth in Constant (2019) Dollars by Selected Family Characteristics: 2010 to 2019

[Net worth in thousands of constant (2019) dollars (91.1 represents $91,100). Constant dollar figures are based on Consumer Price Index for all urban consumers published by U.S. Bureau of Labor Statistics. Families include one-person units and, as used in this table, are comparable to the U.S. Census Bureau's household concept. Based on internal data from the Survey of Consumer Finances; see Appendix III. For definition of mean and median, see Guide to Tabular Presentation]

Family characteristic	2010		2013		2016		2019	
	Median	Mean	Median	Mean	Median	Mean	Median	Mean
All families	**91.1**	**587.7**	**89.2**	**587.1**	**103.5**	**736.0**	**121.7**	**748.8**
Age of family head:								
Under 35 years old	11.0	76.9	11.4	82.9	11.6	81.0	13.9	76.3
35 to 44 years old	49.6	256.2	51.3	381.3	63.6	306.9	91.3	436.2
45 to 54 years old	138.9	675.2	115.6	582.2	132.1	773.7	168.6	833.2
55 to 64 years old	211.4	1,037.4	182.2	876.8	199.2	1,241.6	212.5	1,175.9
65 to 74 years old	243.5	999.6	254.9	1,160.7	237.6	1,133.7	266.4	1,217.7
75 years old and over	255.4	798.7	213.9	708.5	281.6	1,134.8	254.8	977.6
Race or ethnicity of respondent:								
White, non-Hispanic	153.8	771.2	155.9	775.2	181.9	993.1	188.2	983.4
Black or African-American, non-Hispanic	18.8	117.0	14.5	108.7	18.2	146.8	24.1	142.5
Hispanic or Latino	19.1	136.2	15.1	118.3	21.9	203.3	36.2	165.5
Other or multiple race	50.2	395.2	45.3	408.6	68.8	486.8	74.5	657.2
Tenure:								
Owner occupied	205.6	840.6	214.6	859.8	246.2	1,099.9	255.0	1,102.1
Renter occupied or other	6.0	67.4	5.9	77.2	5.3	96.8	6.3	95.6

Source: Board of Governors of the Federal Reserve System, 2019 Survey of Consumer Finances, *Changes in U.S. Family Finances From 2016 to 2019: Evidence from the Survey of Consumer Finances,* Federal Reserve Bulletin, Vol. 106, No. 5, September 2020; and "Historic Tables." See also <www.federalreserve.gov/econres/scfindex.htm>.

Table 762. Household and Nonprofit Organization Sector Balance Sheet: 1990 to 2021

[In billions of dollars (26,369 represents $26,369,000,000,000), unless otherwise noted. As of December 31. Sector includes domestic hedge funds, private equity funds, and personal trusts. For details of financial assets and liabilities, see Table 1200 and Table 1202]

Item	1990	2000	2010	2017	2018	2019	2020	2021
Assets	**26,369**	**52,011**	**80,124**	**118,951**	**120,129**	**133,282**	**148,467**	**168,642**
Nonfinancial assets [1]	10,098	17,559	25,683	35,923	37,912	39,918	43,529	50,426
Real estate [2]	7,956	14,170	20,751	30,029	31,773	33,534	36,756	42,399
Households [3]	7,160	12,852	18,874	26,839	28,508	29,993	32,989	38,105
Consumer durable goods [4]	2,039	3,202	4,535	5,300	5,513	5,731	6,081	7,288
Financial assets [1]	16,271	34,452	54,442	83,028	82,218	93,364	104,938	118,216
Time and savings deposits	2,666	3,000	5,952	8,812	9,242	9,793	10,282	11,053
Money market fund shares	421	1,296	1,790	1,653	1,823	2,271	2,676	2,944
Debt securities [1]	1,531	2,035	4,638	3,677	4,367	4,714	4,417	3,146
Treasury securities	505	538	1,012	1,021	1,561	1,669	1,518	780
Municipal securities	660	476	1,903	1,923	1,904	1,928	1,941	1,815
Corporate and foreign bonds	249	443	1,583	336	351	507	651	458
Corporate equities [2]	1,702	7,068	8,546	17,943	16,279	21,052	26,107	32,503
Mutual fund shares	471	2,558	4,699	8,651	8,000	9,959	11,078	12,561
Life insurance reserves	391	839	1,273	1,627	1,659	1,731	1,867	1,929
Pension entitlements [5]	4,970	11,031	18,301	25,932	25,813	27,994	29,800	31,752
Equity in noncorporate business [6]	3,095	4,988	6,469	10,797	11,219	11,940	12,891	15,125
Liabilities [1]	**3,734**	**7,455**	**14,166**	**15,536**	**16,000**	**16,505**	**17,124**	**18,353**
Loans [1]	3,559	7,150	13,596	14,929	15,386	15,886	16,508	17,732
Home mortgages [7]	2,489	4,817	9,992	9,929	10,204	10,481	10,920	11,743
Consumer credit	824	1,741	2,647	3,831	4,007	4,192	4,185	4,434
Net worth	**22,635**	**44,556**	**65,959**	**103,415**	**104,130**	**116,777**	**131,343**	**150,290**
Replacement cost value of structures:								
Residential [1]	4,287	7,732	12,732	17,197	18,194	18,883	20,255	23,412
Households	4,184	7,596	12,529	16,917	17,897	18,579	19,936	23,045
Nonresidential (nonprofits)	469	808	1,415	1,802	1,916	2,011	2,055	2,308
Disposable personal income	4,319	7,420	11,357	14,801	15,630	16,219	17,432	18,494
Owners' equity in real estate	4,671	8,035	8,882	16,910	18,304	19,512	22,069	26,363
Owners' equity as percent of real estate	65.2	62.5	47.1	63.0	64.2	65.1	66.9	69.2

[1] Includes other types of assets and/or liabilities not shown separately. [2] At market value. [3] Includes all types of owner-occupied housing, including farm houses, mobile homes, second homes that are not rented, vacant homes for sale, and vacant land. [4] At replacement (current) cost. [5] Includes public and private defined benefit and defined contribution pension plans and annuities, including those in IRAs (individual retirement accounts) and at life insurance companies. Excludes social security. [6] Net worth of nonfinancial noncorporate business and owners' equity in unincorporated security brokers and dealers. [7] Includes loans made under home equity lines of credit and home equity loans secured by junior liens.

Source: Board of Governors of the Federal Reserve System, "Z.1 Financial Accounts of the United States: B.101 Balance Sheet of Households and Nonprofit Organizations," March 2022, <www.federalreserve.gov/releases/z1/default.htm>, accessed March 2022.

Table 763. Net Stock of Fixed Assets and Consumer Durable Goods in Current and Chained (2012) Dollars: 1990 to 2020

[In billions of dollars (18,896 represents $18,896,000,000,000)]

Item	1990	2000	2010	2016	2017	2018	2019	2020
CURRENT DOLLARS								
Net stock, total	**18,896**	**30,962**	**50,520**	**62,321**	**64,821**	**68,203**	**70,881**	**73,947**
Fixed assets	16,856	27,760	45,985	57,159	59,521	62,691	65,150	67,866
Private	12,774	21,419	34,468	43,342	45,155	47,600	49,541	51,720
Nonresidential	7,071	11,609	18,685	23,130	24,000	25,252	26,411	27,014
Equipment	2,424	3,805	5,224	6,460	6,651	6,956	7,197	7,336
Structures	4,055	6,468	11,286	13,765	14,250	14,982	15,683	15,866
Intellectual property products	592	1,335	2,174	2,905	3,100	3,314	3,530	3,813
Residential	5,702	9,810	15,783	20,212	21,155	22,347	23,130	24,705
Government	4,083	6,341	11,517	13,817	14,367	15,091	15,610	16,147
Nonresidential	3,941	6,111	11,185	13,401	13,939	14,644	15,149	15,657
Equipment	535	655	923	996	1,014	1,050	1,080	1,126
Structures	2,908	4,800	9,249	11,266	11,743	12,361	12,805	13,198
Intellectual property products	498	656	1,012	1,139	1,182	1,233	1,265	1,333
Residential	142	230	333	416	427	447	460	490
Consumer durable goods	2,039	3,202	4,535	5,163	5,300	5,513	5,731	6,081
Motor vehicles and parts	650	1,051	1,288	1,567	1,601	1,658	1,698	1,777
Furnishings and durable household equipment	649	977	1,396	1,533	1,576	1,692	1,779	1,934
Recreational goods and vehicles	419	724	1,061	1,128	1,167	1,213	1,272	1,394
Other	322	449	792	934	957	949	981	976
CHAINED (2012) DOLLARS								
Net stock, total	**(NA)**	**41,526**	**52,144**	**56,790**	**57,685**	**58,714**	**59,800**	**60,764**
Fixed assets	(NA)	39,055	47,611	51,288	51,959	52,740	53,584	54,276
Private	(NA)	29,088	35,481	38,506	39,058	39,720	40,432	40,976
Nonresidential	(NA)	15,959	19,461	21,883	22,292	22,797	23,329	23,646
Equipment	(NA)	3,970	5,311	6,607	6,791	7,023	7,259	7,363
Structures	(NA)	10,669	11,927	12,508	12,617	12,760	12,915	12,996
Intellectual property products	(NA)	1,478	2,227	2,803	2,931	3,080	3,244	3,387
Residential	(NA)	13,142	16,017	16,652	16,809	16,987	17,186	17,416
Government	(NA)	9,994	12,129	12,774	12,891	13,007	13,138	13,284
Nonresidential	(NA)	9,689	11,793	12,436	12,553	12,669	12,798	12,943
Equipment	(NA)	740	944	975	985	1,000	1,023	1,048
Structures	(NA)	8,159	9,819	10,364	10,458	10,542	10,636	10,737
Intellectual property products	(NA)	794	1,030	1,095	1,109	1,127	1,142	1,163
Residential	(NA)	300	336	340	340	340	341	343
Consumer durable goods	(NA)	2,757	4,535	5,557	5,812	6,103	6,390	6,730

NA Not available.

Source: U.S. Bureau of Economic Analysis, National Data, "Fixed Assets Accounts Tables," <apps.bea.gov/iTable/index_FA.cfm>, accessed September 2021.

The Prices section contains producer and consumer price indexes and actual prices for selected commodities. The primary sources of the data are monthly publications of the U.S. Department of Labor, Bureau of Labor Statistics (BLS), which include *Consumer Price Index Detailed Report*, *Producer Price Index Detailed Report*, and *U.S. Import and Export Price Indexes*. Additionally, BLS provides comprehensive databases for the respective price indexes at <www.bls.gov/data/>. The Bureau of Economic Analysis (BEA) is the source for gross domestic product measures. Table 768 on housing price indexes contains data from the Federal Housing Finance Agency's Housing Price Index. Other commodity, housing, and energy prices may be found in the Energy and Utilities; Forestry, Fishing and Mining; and Construction and Housing sections.

Most price data is measured by an index. An index is a tool that simplifies the measurement of movements in a numerical series. An index allows you to properly compare two or more values in different time periods or places by comparing both to a base year. An index of 110, for example, means there has been a 10-percent increase in price since the reference period; similarly, an index of 90 means a 10-percent decrease. Movements of the index from one date to another can be expressed as changes in index points (simply, the difference between index levels), but it is more useful to express the movements as percent changes. This is because index points are affected by the level of the index in relation to its reference period, while percent changes are not.

Consumer price indexes (CPI)—The CPI is a measure of the average change in prices over time in a "market basket" of goods and services purchased either by urban wage earners and clerical workers or by all urban consumers. The all urban consumer group represents approximately 93 percent of the total U.S. population and is based on the expenditures of residents of urban or metropolitan areas, including wage earners and clerical workers; professional, managerial, and technical workers; the self-employed; short-term workers; the unemployed; and retirees and others not in the labor force. Not included in the CPI are the spending patterns of people living in rural nonmetropolitan areas, farm families, people in the Armed Forces, and those in institutions, such as prisons and mental hospitals. Consumer inflation for all urban consumers is measured by two indexes, the Consumer Price Index for All Urban Consumers (CPI-U) and the Chained Consumer Price Index for All Urban Consumers (C-CPI-U). The broadest and most comprehensive CPI is called the All Items Consumer Price Index for All Urban Consumers (CPI-U) for the U.S. City Average. CPIs in this section generally have a base of 1982–84 = 100.

The CPI is a product of a series of interrelated samples. Data from the 2010 Decennial Census determines the urban areas from which data on prices are collected and the housing units within each area that are eligible for use in the shelter component of the CPI. The Census of Population also provides data on the number of consumers represented by each area selected as a CPI price collection area. Prices for the goods and services used to calculate the CPI are collected in 75 urban areas throughout the country and from about 23,000 retail and service establishments. Data on rents are collected from about 50,000 landlords or tenants. The CPI also uses data from the Consumer Expenditure (CE) survey which collects data on the out-of-pocket expenses spent to acquire all consumer products and services. There is a time lag between the expenditure survey and its use in the CPI. For example, CPI data in 2020 and 2021 was based on data collected from the Consumer Expenditure Surveys for 2017 and 2018. In each of those years, about 24,000 consumers from around the country provided information each quarter on their spending habits in the interview survey. To collect information on frequently purchased items, such as food and personal care products, another 12,000 consumers in each of these years kept diaries listing everything they bought during a 2-week period. Over that period, expenditure information came from approximately 24,000 weekly diaries and 48,000 quarterly interviews used to determine the importance, or weight, of the item categories in the CPI index structure.

The CPI represents all goods and services purchased for consumption by the reference population. BLS has classified all expenditure items into more than 200 categories, arranged into eight major groups which are food and beverages, housing, apparel, transportation, medical care, recreation, education and communication, and other goods and services. The CPI does not include investment items, such as stocks, bonds, real estate, and life insurance, as these items relate to savings and not to day-to-day consumption expenses.

Producer price index (PPI)—Dating from 1890, the PPI is the oldest continuous statistical series published by BLS. The PPI is a family of indexes that measures the average change over time in the selling prices received by domestic producers of goods and services. Imports are excluded. The target set of goods and services included in the PPI is the entire marketed output of U.S. producers. The set includes both goods and services purchased by other producers as inputs to their operations or as capital investment, as well as goods and services purchased by consumers either directly from the service producer or indirectly from a retailer. About 10,000 PPIs for individual products and groups of products are released each month.

PPIs are published for the output of almost all industries in the goods-producing sectors of the U.S. economy, and, while more indexes are gradually being introduced, are currently available for approximately 72 percent of the service sector. For any given industry, producers are usually selected for the PPI survey using a systematic sampling from a listing of all firms that file with the Unemployment Insurance System. Establishments are asked to report their prices as of Tuesday of the week containing the 13th of the month. Each month over 100,000 prices are solicited from roughly 25,000 reporters. Currently, some PPIs have an index base set at 1982 = 100, while the remainder have an index base that corresponds with the month prior to the month that the index was introduced. For further detail regarding the PPI, see the BLS*Handbook of Methods*, Chapter 14, <www.bls.gov/opub/hom/pdf/ppi-20111028.pdf>.

In January 2014, PPI transitioned from the Stage of Processing (SOP) system to the Final Demand–Intermediate Demand (FD-ID) system as its primary index aggregation structure. The transition to the FD-ID system is the culmination of a long-standing PPI objective to improve the SOP system (domestically produced goods for domestic, nongovernment consumption) by incorporating PPIs for services, construction, government purchases, and exports. The FD portion of the FD-ID system expands coverage relative to the finished goods stage of the SOP system by including indexes that examine inflation from the producer perspective for goods, services, and construction sold as personal consumption, capital investment, government purchase, and export. The ID portion of the system allows data users to examine inflation from the producer perspective for goods, services, and construction sold to businesses as inputs to production, excluding capital investment.

BEA price indexes—BEA chain-weighted price indexes are weighted averages of the detailed price indexes used in the deflation of the goods and services that make up the gross domestic product (GDP) and its major components. Growth rates are constructed for years and quarters using quantity weights for the current and preceding year or quarter; these growth rates are used to move the index for the preceding period forward a year or quarter at a time. All chain-weighted price indexes are expressed in terms of the reference year value 2012 = 100.

Personal consumption expenditures (PCE) price and quantity indexes are based on market transactions for which there are corresponding price measures. The price index provides a measure of the prices paid by persons for domestic purchases of goods and services. PCEs are defined as market value of spending by individuals and not-for-profit institutions on all goods and services. Personal consumption expenditures also include the value of certain imputed goods and services—such as the rental value of owner-occupied homes and compensation paid in kind—such as employer-paid health and life insurance premiums. The PCE price index is known for capturing inflation (or deflation) across a wide range of consumer expenses and for reflecting changes in consumer behavior. More information on this index may be found at <www.bea.gov/data/personal-consumption-expenditures-price-index>.

Measures of inflation—Inflation is a period of rising price levels for goods and factors of production. Inflation results in a decline in the purchasing power

of the dollar. It is suggested that changes in price levels be compared from the same month of the prior year and not as a change from the prior month. The BLS offers several indexes that measure different aspects of inflation, three of which are included in this section. The CPI measures inflation as experienced by consumers in their day-to-day living expenses. The PPI measures prices at the producer level only. The International Price Program measures change in the prices of imports and exports of nonmilitary goods between the United States and other countries.

Whereas the CPI and PPI measure a benchmark approach to price levels, the BEA's Personal Consumption Expenditures uses a chain-weight approach which links weighted averages from adjoining years.

Other measures of inflation include spot market price indexes from Barchart and the employment cost, hourly compensation, and unit labor cost indexes from the BLS. Found in Section 12, Labor Force, Employment, and Earnings, these BLS indexes are used as a measure of the change in cost of the labor factor of production and changes in long-term interest rates that are often used to measure changes in the cost of the capital factor of production.

International price indexes—The BLS International Price Program produces Import/Export Price Indexes (MXP) for nonmilitary goods traded between the United States and the rest of the world.

The U.S. Import and U.S. Export Price Indexes measure the change over time in the prices of goods or services purchased from abroad by U.S. residents (imports) or sold to foreign buyers by U.S. residents (exports). The reference period for the indexes is 2000 = 100, unless otherwise indicated. The product universe for both the import and export indexes includes raw materials, agricultural products, semifinished manufactures, and finished manufactures, including both capital and consumer goods. Price data for these items are collected primarily via a secure internet address.

To the extent possible, the data gathered refer to prices at the U.S. border for exports and at either the foreign border or the U.S. border for imports. For nearly all products, the prices refer to transactions completed during the first week of the month. Survey respondents are asked to indicate all discounts, allowances, and rebates applicable to the reported prices, so that the price used in the calculation of the indexes is the actual price for which the product was bought or sold.

Table 764. Purchasing Power of the Dollar: 1950 to 2021

[Indexes: PPI, 1982=$1.00; CPI, 1982-84=$1.00. Producer prices prior to 1961 and consumer prices prior to 1964 exclude Alaska and Hawaii. Producer prices based on final demand, finished goods index. Data is obtained by dividing the average price index for the 1982=100, PPI and the 1982-84=100, CPI base periods (100.0) by the price index for a given period and expressing the result in dollars and cents. Annual figures are based on average of monthly data]

Year	Annual average as measured by—		Year	Annual average as measured by—	
	Producer prices	Consumer prices		Producer prices	Consumer prices
1950	3.546	4.149	1991	0.822	0.734
1955	3.279	3.731	1992	0.812	0.713
1960	2.994	3.378	1993	0.802	0.692
1963	2.994	3.268	1994	0.797	0.675
1964	2.985	3.226	1995	0.782	0.656
1965	2.933	3.175	1996	0.762	0.637
1966	2.841	3.086	1997	0.759	0.623
1967	2.809	2.994	1998	0.765	0.613
1968	2.732	2.874	1999	0.752	0.600
1969	2.632	2.725	2000	0.725	0.581
1970	2.545	2.577	2001	0.711	0.565
1971	2.469	2.469	2002	0.720	0.556
1972	2.392	2.392	2003	0.698	0.543
1973	2.193	2.252	2004	0.673	0.529
1974	1.901	2.028	2005	0.642	0.512
1975	1.718	1.859	2006	0.623	0.496
1976	1.645	1.757	2007	0.600	0.482
1977	1.546	1.650	2008	0.565	0.464
1978	1.433	1.534	2009	0.580	0.466
1979	1.289	1.377	2010	0.556	0.459
1980	1.136	1.214	2011	0.524	0.445
1981	1.041	1.100	2012	0.515	0.436
1982	1.000	1.036	2013	0.508	0.429
1983	0.984	1.004	2014	0.499	0.422
1984	0.964	0.962	2015	0.516	0.422
1985	0.955	0.929	2016	0.521	0.417
1986	0.969	0.912	2017	0.505	0.408
1987	0.949	0.880	2018	0.490	0.398
1988	0.926	0.845	2019	0.486	0.391
1989	0.880	0.806	2020	0.493	0.386
1990	0.839	0.765	2021	0.452	0.369

Source: U.S. Bureau of Labor Statistics, "CPI Databases," <www.bls.gov/cpi/#data>; and "PPI Databases," <www.bls.gov/ppi/#data>; accessed June 2022.

Table 765. Consumer Price Indexes (CPI-U) by Major Group: 1990 to 2021

[1982-84=100, except as indicated. Represents annual averages of monthly figures. Reflects buying patterns of all urban consumers. Minus sign (-) indicates decrease. See text, this section]

Year	All items	Commodities	Services	Food	Food and beverages	Energy	All items less food and energy	Housing	Apparel	Transportation	Medical care	Education and communication [1]
1990	130.7	122.8	139.2	132.4	132.1	102.1	135.5	128.5	124.1	120.5	162.8	(NA)
1995	152.4	136.4	168.7	148.4	148.9	105.2	161.2	148.5	132.0	139.1	220.5	92.2
2000	172.2	149.2	195.3	167.8	168.4	124.6	181.3	169.6	129.6	153.3	260.8	102.5
2005	195.3	160.2	230.1	190.7	191.2	177.1	200.9	195.7	119.5	173.9	323.2	113.7
2010	218.1	174.6	261.3	219.6	220.0	211.4	221.3	216.3	119.5	193.4	388.4	129.9
2011	224.9	183.9	265.8	227.8	227.9	243.9	225.0	219.1	122.1	212.4	400.3	131.5
2012	229.6	187.6	271.4	233.8	233.7	246.1	229.8	222.7	126.3	217.3	414.9	133.8
2013	233.0	187.7	277.9	237.0	237.0	244.4	233.8	227.4	127.4	217.4	425.1	135.9
2014	236.7	187.9	285.1	242.7	242.4	243.6	237.9	233.2	127.5	215.9	435.3	137.5
2015	237.0	181.7	291.7	247.2	246.8	202.9	242.2	238.1	125.9	199.1	446.8	138.2
2016	240.0	179.2	299.9	247.9	247.7	189.5	247.6	244.0	126.0	194.9	463.7	139.1
2017	245.1	181.2	308.1	250.1	249.8	204.5	252.2	251.2	125.6	201.6	475.3	136.5
2018	251.1	184.6	316.6	253.6	253.3	219.9	257.6	258.5	125.7	210.7	484.7	136.8
2019	255.7	185.3	325.1	258.3	258.0	215.3	263.2	266.0	124.1	210.1	498.4	137.8
2020	258.8	184.8	332.0	267.2	266.6	196.9	267.7	271.8	118.1	201.3	518.9	140.3
2021	271.0	199.2	341.4	277.8	276.8	238.3	277.3	280.7	121.0	230.7	525.3	142.6
PERCENT CHANGE [2]												
1990	5.4	5.2	5.5	5.8	5.8	8.3	5.0	4.5	4.6	5.6	9.0	(NA)
1995	2.8	1.9	3.4	2.8	2.8	0.6	3.0	2.6	-1.0	3.6	4.5	3.8
2000	3.4	3.3	3.4	2.3	2.3	16.9	2.4	3.5	-1.3	6.2	4.1	1.3
2005	3.4	3.6	3.3	2.4	2.5	17.0	2.2	3.3	-0.7	6.6	4.2	1.9
2010	1.6	2.9	0.8	0.8	0.8	9.5	1.0	-0.4	-0.5	7.9	3.4	2.0
2011	3.2	5.3	1.7	3.7	3.6	15.4	1.7	1.3	2.2	9.8	3.0	1.2
2012	2.1	2.0	2.1	2.6	2.5	0.9	2.1	1.6	3.4	2.3	3.7	1.8
2013	1.5	–	2.4	1.4	1.4	-0.7	1.8	2.1	0.9	–	2.5	1.5
2014	1.6	0.1	2.6	2.4	2.3	-0.3	1.7	2.6	0.1	-0.7	2.4	1.2
2015	0.1	-3.3	2.3	1.9	1.8	-16.7	1.8	2.1	-1.3	-7.8	2.6	0.5
2016	1.3	-1.4	2.8	0.3	0.3	-6.6	2.2	2.5	0.1	-2.1	3.8	0.7
2017	2.1	1.1	2.7	0.9	0.9	7.9	1.8	3.0	-0.3	3.4	2.5	-1.9
2018	2.4	1.9	2.8	1.4	1.4	7.5	2.1	2.9	–	4.5	2.0	0.2
2019	1.8	0.4	2.7	1.9	1.8	-2.1	2.2	2.9	-1.3	-0.3	2.8	0.7
2020	1.2	-0.3	2.1	3.4	3.3	-8.5	1.7	2.2	-4.8	-4.2	4.1	1.8
2021	4.7	7.8	2.8	3.9	3.8	21.0	3.6	3.3	2.5	14.6	1.2	1.6

– Represents or rounds to zero. NA Not available. [1] Dec. 1997=100. [2] Change from immediate prior year. 1990 change from 1989.

Source: U.S. Bureau of Labor Statistics, "CPI Databases," <www.bls.gov/cpi/data.htm>, accessed April 2022.

Table 766. Consumer Price Indexes (CPI-U) and Annual Percent Change for Selected Urban Areas: 2021

[1982-84=100. Percent changes computed from annual averages of monthly figures published by source. In January 2018, BLS introduced a new geographic area sample for the Consumer Price Index (CPI) that utilizes the 2010 Decennial Census and incorporates an updated area sample design; see source for more information. Local area CPI indexes are by-products of the national CPI program. Each local index has a smaller sample size than the national index and is therefore subject to substantially more sampling and other measurement error. As a result, local area indexes show greater volatility than the national index, although their long-term trends are similar. Minus sign (-) indicates decrease. See also text, this section and Appendix III]

| Urban area | Consumer Price Index | | | | | | Medical care | Fuel and other utilities |
	All items	Food and beverage	Food	Housing	Apparel	Transportation		
U.S. city average	**271.0**	**276.8**	**277.8**	**280.7**	**121.0**	**230.7**	**525.3**	**260.5**
Atlanta-Sandy Springs-Roswell, GA	261.6	270.6	283.7	271.2	144.5	233.1	492.3	313.2
Baltimore-Columbia-Towson, MD	270.2	279.6	278.8	270.7	125.2	225.6	470.7	233.4
Boston-Cambridge-Newton, MA-NH	293.5	289.9	292.3	307.9	126.7	206.7	698.4	309.8
Chicago-Naperville-Elgin, IL-IN-WI	254.2	275.3	275.6	268.5	82.8	201.0	531.2	231.9
Dallas-Fort Worth-Arlington, TX	251.6	274.3	268.4	247.4	109.3	222.6	477.3	264.5
Denver-Aurora-Lakewood, CO	281.8	255.0	260.1	281.0	108.6	284.5	641.9	242.7
Detroit-Warren-Dearborn, MI	247.8	241.0	241.6	238.1	98.8	261.4	(NA)	279.8
Houston-The Woodlands-Sugar Land, TX	239.0	247.7	248.3	235.4	170.7	196.3	534.5	203.4
Los Angeles-Long Beach-Anaheim, CA	289.2	290.4	290.9	331.1	110.1	230.9	511.8	389.7
Miami-Fort Lauderdale-West Palm Beach, FL	284.0	283.6	288.9	299.0	140.8	242.0	584.8	184.7
Minneapolis-St. Paul-Bloomington, MN-WI	265.2	303.4	292.0	252.3	139.5	217.0	600.6	233.6
New York-Newark-Jersey City, NY-NJ-PA	292.3	291.3	291.8	314.6	126.1	237.0	537.3	207.8
Philadelphia-Camden-Wilmington, PA-NJ-DE-MD	269.4	251.5	252.3	278.6	108.4	230.4	569.8	215.8
Phoenix-Mesa-Scottsdale, AZ	153.0	158.6	160.2	161.3	134.1	138.7	(NA)	171.6
San Diego-Carlsbad, CA	319.8	285.0	283.3	375.3	166.1	256.3	523.2	390.1
San Francisco-Oakland-Hayward, CA	309.7	315.5	315.8	364.1	107.2	220.6	553.4	476.3
Seattle-Tacoma-Bellevue, WA	295.6	304.1	306.2	348.8	128.7	242.5	416.4	288.6
St. Louis, MO-IL	245.8	275.1	272.8	239.6	131.4	212.2	483.7	234.2
Tampa-St. Petersburg-Clearwater, FL	248.0	255.4	256.3	255.1	128.3	223.0	442.7	218.4
Urban Alaska	237.2	235.6	244.1	209.8	149.5	247.5	665.9	346.8
Urban Hawaii	296.8	312.6	313.0	323.6	109.1	237.3	438.2	377.2
Washington-Arlington-Alexandria, DC-VA-MD-WV	277.7	269.9	277.3	289.0	151.8	230.8	500.2	250.4
PERCENT CHANGE, 2020-2021								
U.S. city average	**4.7**	**3.8**	**3.9**	**3.3**	**2.5**	**14.6**	**1.2**	**6.8**
Atlanta-Sandy Springs-Roswell, GA	6.1	1.7	1.7	4.7	8.7	18.0	0.7	4.2
Baltimore-Columbia-Towson, MD	4.1	2.9	2.8	2.6	3.1	14.3	-0.6	3.5
Boston-Cambridge-Newton, MA-NH	3.3	3.2	3.2	3.0	-0.1	12.5	-0.2	10.5
Chicago-Naperville-Elgin, IL-IN-WI	4.2	5.3	5.4	3.9	1.1	12.9	-0.6	11.1
Dallas-Fort Worth-Arlington, TX	5.2	4.3	4.3	3.8	1.9	16.9	0.9	5.5
Denver-Aurora-Lakewood, CO	3.5	2.9	2.9	1.6	14.8	13.0	1.8	2.5
Detroit-Warren-Dearborn, MI	4.3	5.1	5.6	4.3	-7.2	8.3	(NA)	6.8
Houston-The Woodlands-Sugar Land, TX	4.3	3.6	3.7	2.9	-1.8	12.9	0.8	12.8
Los Angeles-Long Beach-Anaheim, CA	3.8	4.5	4.5	2.2	1.7	13.0	1.3	11.6
Miami-Fort Lauderdale-West Palm Beach, FL	4.4	1.8	2.8	3.5	2.5	14.4	1.1	5.3
Minneapolis-St. Paul-Bloomington, MN-WI	4.8	3.7	3.8	3.4	4.9	15.0	3.8	6.0
New York-Newark-Jersey City, NY-NJ-PA	3.3	3.8	3.9	2.1	6.2	10.4	0.7	6.8
Philadelphia-Camden-Wilmington, PA-NJ-DE-MD	4.0	2.2	2.1	2.9	3.3	12.9	2.3	5.3
Phoenix-Mesa-Scottsdale, AZ	5.0	3.1	3.4	5.1	5.5	11.7	(NA)	4.6
San Diego-Carlsbad, CA	5.2	5.3	5.2	3.3	5.9	16.2	2.2	12.1
San Francisco-Oakland-Hayward, CA	3.2	4.3	4.7	1.6	4.0	10.3	0.8	7.5
Seattle-Tacoma-Bellevue, WA	4.6	5.9	5.5	2.4	3.7	12.5	0.4	3.1
St. Louis, MO-IL	5.5	3.8	3.7	4.3	2.1	15.5	3.0	6.6
Tampa-St. Petersburg-Clearwater, FL	6.0	4.1	4.2	5.9	2.9	13.9	5.2	5.7
Urban Alaska	4.9	4.8	5.2	2.2	3.9	16.9	2.5	-1.5
Urban Hawaii	3.8	3.7	3.6	3.0	-3.7	11.6	(NA)	5.3
Washington-Arlington-Alexandria, DC-VA-MD-WV	4.0	3.7	3.9	2.4	0.3	10.4	3.0	5.7

NA Not available.

Source: U.S. Bureau of Labor Statistics, CPI Databases, "All Urban Consumers (Current Series)," <www.bls.gov/cpi/data.htm>, accessed April 2022.

Table 767. Consumer Price Indexes for All Urban Consumers (CPI-U) for Selected Items and Groups: 2000 to 2021

[1982-1984=100, unless otherwise noted. Annual averages of monthly figures. Reflects buying patterns of all urban consumers. For information about the CPI methodology, see the U.S. Bureau of Labor Statistics Handbook of Methods, Consumer Price Index at <www.bls.gov/opub/hom/cpi/home.htm>]

Item	2000	2010	2015	2017	2018	2019	2020	2021
All items........................	**172.2**	**218.1**	**237.0**	**245.1**	**251.1**	**255.7**	**258.8**	**271.0**
Food and beverages.................	**168.4**	**220.0**	**246.8**	**249.8**	**253.3**	**258.0**	**266.6**	**276.8**
Food........................	167.8	219.6	247.2	250.1	253.6	258.3	267.2	277.8
Food at home..................	167.9	215.8	242.3	238.6	239.7	241.8	250.2	258.9
Cereals and bakery products..........	188.3	250.4	274.1	271.7	272.8	276.6	282.6	289.1
Cereals and cereal products..........	175.9	217.6	234.1	227.7	226.6	227.6	231.8	235.8
Rice, pasta, and cornmeal..........	150.7	224.4	241.6	234.3	236.2	238.0	243.9	245.5
Rice [1, 2]........................	99.3	156.9	167.2	160.0	161.7	162.6	164.9	166.5
Bakery products..................	194.1	268.0	296.6	296.8	299.3	304.8	312.1	319.9
Bread [2]........................	107.4	159.8	178.7	178.3	179.4	184.1	190.7	194.5
Cakes, cupcakes, and cookies..........	187.9	251.7	278.8	282.7	287.5	291.2	294.9	302.7
Other bakery products..........	191.5	247.1	266.4	264.9	264.7	269.9	275.9	282.8
Meats, poultry, fish and eggs..........	154.5	207.7	260.3	245.8	248.9	249.8	265.2	282.8
Meats, poultry, and fish..........	155.5	208.6	258.5	249.0	250.7	253.3	269.3	287.5
Meats..................	150.7	206.2	264.2	251.0	252.1	255.3	274.2	295.2
Beef and veal..........	148.1	224.5	322.5	298.4	302.6	307.4	337.0	368.4
Uncooked ground beef..........	125.2	203.6	295.3	266.6	268.2	269.3	296.2	310.4
Uncooked beef steaks [2]..........	109.1	153.3	214.6	201.1	203.7	207.4	224.7	251.7
Pork..........	156.5	190.0	218.7	211.1	210.2	212.7	226.0	245.5
Poultry..........	159.8	204.0	237.3	231.3	232.1	231.5	244.4	256.9
Chicken [2]..........	102.5	131.8	152.1	148.6	150.3	149.9	157.3	165.7
Fish and seafood..........	190.4	243.2	286.3	287.7	293.8	298.5	308.2	324.9
Eggs..........	131.9	192.8	286.2	204.5	226.6	203.9	212.5	222.1
Dairy products [2]..........	160.7	199.2	222.4	217.5	216.5	218.7	228.3	231.4
Milk [2]..........	107.8	133.6	147.5	139.7	137.0	140.7	148.5	153.6
Cheese and related products..........	162.8	204.8	233.6	228.5	229.2	228.7	240.7	241.1
Ice cream and related products..........	164.4	195.0	219.2	219.9	220.6	221.8	230.4	232.2
Fruits and vegetables..........	204.6	273.5	293.8	295.7	297.8	300.9	304.9	314.8
Fresh fruits and vegetables..........	238.8	314.8	337.7	342.4	346.1	349.5	352.3	364.1
Fresh fruits..........	258.3	322.3	352.0	361.4	365.2	360.1	357.1	376.5
Fresh vegetables..........	219.4	305.5	321.4	321.1	324.7	337.1	345.8	349.7
Processed fruits and vegetables [2]..........	105.6	146.6	158.5	155.4	154.5	156.2	161.6	166.2
Nonalcoholic beverages and beverage materials...	137.8	161.6	167.9	167.6	167.6	170.8	176.9	181.8
Juices and nonalcoholic drinks [2]..........	105.6	124.5	128.5	129.0	129.7	133.4	139.5	143.6
Carbonated drinks..........	123.4	154.7	159.6	161.6	163.7	169.5	178.9	185.9
Nonfrozen noncarbonated juices and drinks [2]....	104.2	114.8	117.9	117.7	117.7	120.4	125.3	128.2
Beverage materials including coffee and tea [2].....	97.9	114.0	120.4	118.3	116.7	116.6	117.8	120.5
Coffee..........	154.0	186.4	205.5	199.2	194.9	193.2	194.2	199.3
Other food at home..........	155.6	191.1	209.3	209.9	210.2	211.1	217.3	222.9
Sugar and sweets..........	154.0	201.2	216.1	215.1	215.9	220.2	227.6	234.4
Candy and chewing gum [2]..........	103.8	132.5	145.4	144.3	145.7	150.0	154.9	159.2
Fats and oils..........	147.4	200.6	227.3	227.7	228.0	226.4	229.5	240.1
Frozen and freeze dried prepared food..........	148.5	165.3	170.9	167.9	166.8	166.7	172.1	176.3
Snacks..........	166.3	216.6	250.6	251.8	253.4	251.8	259.3	263.6
Spices, seasonings, condiments, sauces..........	175.6	214.4	235.6	239.6	241.7	242.9	249.4	254.5
Other miscellaneous food [2]..........	107.5	121.7	131.8	131.9	131.5	132.1	136.7	140.4
Food away from home..........	169.0	226.1	256.1	268.8	275.9	284.4	293.9	307.3
Full service meals and snacks [2]..........	106.8	141.1	159.4	167.1	171.0	176.4	181.5	189.7
Limited service meals and snacks [2]..........	106.3	143.9	163.3	171.8	176.6	182.1	189.9	202.7
At employee sites and schools [2]..........	104.4	141.0	161.7	172.1	178.1	181.2	176.9	113.8
From vending machines and mobile vendors [2]..........	102.4	133.1	146.3	154.8	159.5	166.5	170.2	178.0
Other food away from home [2]..........	109.0	159.3	179.6	184.5	191.8	196.4	200.6	206.4
Alcoholic beverages..........	174.7	223.3	239.5	245.4	249.1	252.5	257.2	262.8
Alcoholic beverages at home..........	158.1	191.0	197.3	200.3	202.5	205.5	209.0	212.5
Beer, ale, and other malt beverages at home..........	156.8	201.0	215.0	222.9	226.0	230.1	238.1	242.3
Distilled spirits at home..........	162.3	188.8	192.6	192.5	192.0	194.8	196.2	202.1
Wine at home..........	151.6	169.7	168.5	167.9	170.0	171.8	172.2	174.0
Alcoholic beverages away from home..........	207.1	291.9	330.5	343.5	350.9	355.2	363.1	373.4
Housing........................	**169.6**	**216.3**	**238.1**	**251.2**	**258.5**	**266.0**	**271.8**	**280.7**
Shelter..........	193.4	248.4	278.8	297.8	307.7	318.1	325.9	334.6
Rent of primary residence..........	183.9	249.4	286.0	308.1	319.3	331.1	341.5	349.1
Lodging away from home [2]..........	117.5	133.7	153.0	159.4	161.1	165.9	148.9	163.4
Other lodging away from home including hotels and motels..........	252.4	280.4	317.4	327.1	329.4	339.5	299.2	331.7
Owners' equivalent rent of primary residence [3]..........	198.7	256.6	285.9	305.1	315.2	325.7	334.8	343.4
Tenants' and household insurance [2]..........	103.7	125.7	146.4	148.8	150.7	151.8	151.1	150.7
Fuels and utilities..........	137.9	214.2	230.1	237.3	241.6	242.6	243.9	260.5
Household energy..........	122.8	189.3	194.7	198.3	200.8	200.0	199.5	215.2
Fuel oil and other fuels..........	129.7	275.1	256.2	254.4	293.0	280.8	237.6	302.6
Fuel oil..........	130.3	282.9	254.3	241.7	296.1	282.4	218.0	286.4
Propane, kerosene, and firewood [4]..........	155.5	320.6	305.9	322.1	340.9	329.1	319.8	390.0
Energy services..........	128.0	192.9	198.7	202.7	203.8	203.5	204.5	218.9
Electricity..........	128.5	193.1	209.2	211.4	212.9	213.4	214.6	223.9
Utility (piped) gas service..........	132.0	189.7	164.6	173.4	173.6	171.0	171.4	200.1
Water and sewer and trash collection services [2]..........	106.5	170.9	214.0	229.1	237.1	244.7	252.5	261.5
Water and sewerage maintenance..........	227.5	380.7	492.9	532.8	550.7	568.1	585.6	604.0
Garbage and trash collection [5]..........	269.8	384.4	432.0	449.1	466.9	481.9	498.7	522.3
Household furnishings and operations..........	**128.2**	**125.5**	**122.6**	**120.7**	**121.6**	**123.8**	**125.9**	**131.6**
Furniture and bedding..........	134.4	119.7	114.7	111.0	111.1	113.6	113.7	123.0
Living room, kitchen, and dining room furniture [2]..........	102.4	88.9	86.8	84.6	85.2	88.0	88.1	96.7
Appliances [2]..........	96.3	86.9	79.3	74.7	75.8	77.5	79.6	84.5
Other household equipment and furnishings [2]..........	98.0	70.8	59.1	54.4	51.5	50.7	50.3	51.7
Clocks, lamps, and decorator items..........	111.7	62.9	47.1	41.0	37.7	37.1	36.8	37.8

See footnotes at end of table.

Table 767. Consumer Price Indexes for All Urban Consumers (CPI-U) for Selected Items and Groups: 2000 to 2021-Continued.

See headnote on page 503.

Item	2000	2010	2015	2017	2018	2019	2020	2021
Nonelectric cookware and tableware [2]	98.4	96.6	90.4	86.3	83.9	81.2	78.6	81.0
Tools, hardware, outdoor equipment and supplies [2]	97.0	91.6	91.1	89.6	89.5	90.9	92.6	95.8
Tools, hardware, and supplies [2]	97.3	96.5	100.1	97.9	98.5	99.7	100.4	104.4
Outdoor equipment and supplies [2]	96.8	88.9	86.8	85.7	85.3	86.7	89.0	91.8
Housekeeping supplies	153.4	183.3	186.8	184.9	186.4	189.9	196.1	199.2
Household cleaning products [2]	105.1	120.6	118.9	118.2	118.7	120.8	124.4	127.6
Household paper products [2]	113.8	158.0	169.2	168.7	169.6	175.5	185.8	194.0
Miscellaneous household products [2]	104.3	116.9	119.0	116.4	118.3	119.2	121.0	119.3
Household operations [2]	110.5	150.3	166.9	176.3	186.0	194.5	200.6	213.5
Domestic services [2]	109.7	144.4	155.6	160.9	165.8	169.6	174.5	190.5
Gardening and lawncare services [2]	111.4	155.3	171.8	179.3	193.1	205.3	215.4	222.2
Apparel	**129.6**	**119.5**	**125.9**	**125.6**	**125.7**	**124.1**	**118.1**	**121.0**
Men's and boy's apparel	129.7	111.9	119.6	117.2	118.1	118.5	113.1	116.0
Men's apparel	133.1	117.5	124.0	121.5	120.7	120.2	115.7	118.2
Men's shirts and sweaters [2]	98.3	78.6	79.5	78.6	78.2	76.3	70.6	71.1
Boys' apparel	116.2	91.5	103.0	100.8	106.7	110.0	101.2	105.8
Women's and girl's apparel	121.5	107.1	111.2	111.0	110.4	106.7	99.7	100.9
Women's apparel	121.9	109.5	114.4	114.2	113.5	109.2	100.6	101.6
Women's suits and separates [2]	98.2	83.9	81.8	80.1	79.1	75.5	69.5	69.6
Women's underwear, nightwear, swimwear, and accessories [2]	101.8	96.0	105.2	107.1	105.6	104.2	100.5	101.6
Girls' apparel	119.7	95.4	96.0	95.8	95.0	94.3	95.0	97.3
Footwear	123.8	128.0	136.8	136.7	136.1	136.7	133.2	138.1
Men's footwear	129.5	127.6	137.9	138.6	139.7	140.2	137.7	144.2
Women's footwear	119.6	125.3	128.9	127.1	124.9	124.2	120.6	124.5
Jewelry and watches [4]	137.0	152.4	160.0	174.2	172.7	171.5	170.4	183.2
Jewelry [4]	141.2	161.2	165.5	179.4	175.0	172.5	167.0	181.2
Transportation	**153.3**	**193.4**	**199.1**	**201.6**	**210.7**	**210.1**	**201.3**	**230.7**
Private transportation	149.1	188.7	193.7	196.6	206.4	205.8	198.7	229.7
New and used motor vehicles [2]	100.8	97.1	100.8	98.9	99.1	99.5	100.7	114.5
New vehicles	142.8	138.0	147.1	147.0	146.3	146.8	147.6	156.2
Used cars and trucks	155.8	143.1	147.1	138.3	138.4	139.8	144.2	182.6
Leased cars and trucks [6]	(NA)	97.0	84.2	84.8	89.2	86.9	(NA)	(NA)
Motor fuel	129.3	239.2	213.1	212.7	241.9	233.2	195.2	265.1
Gasoline (all types)	128.6	238.6	212.0	211.8	240.6	232.0	194.1	264.0
Motor vehicle parts and equipment	101.5	137.0	144.2	143.0	143.7	146.4	148.1	155.1
Motor vehicle maintenance and repair	177.3	248.0	270.7	280.8	286.4	296.0	306.0	317.9
Motor vehicle insurance	256.7	375.2	460.6	526.9	566.0	571.0	544.6	565.3
Motor vehicle fees [2]	107.3	165.5	178.9	185.0	188.7	192.9	195.6	198.0
Public transportation	209.6	251.4	268.7	263.1	258.8	259.5	227.5	231.2
Airline fare	239.4	278.2	292.2	275.8	264.9	265.4	217.5	217.5
Medical care	**260.8**	**388.4**	**446.8**	**475.3**	**484.7**	**498.4**	**518.9**	**525.3**
Medical care commodities	238.1	314.7	354.6	377.0	381.4	381.3	383.2	377.1
Prescription drugs	285.4	407.8	479.3	519.6	528.0	526.8	532.1	522.4
Nonprescription drugs [10]	(NA)	100.0	97.8	97.4	96.9	97.3	96.4	95.9
Medical care services	266.0	411.2	476.2	506.8	517.8	536.1	562.7	573.1
Professional medical services	237.7	328.2	361.5	375.1	378.4	382.6	389.9	401.9
Physicians' services	244.7	331.3	366.1	380.1	380.5	383.2	389.9	406.5
Dental services	258.5	398.8	452.2	472.6	485.5	496.2	511.1	522.5
Eyeglasses and eye care [4]	149.7	176.7	184.0	187.3	189.6	191.4	192.9	194.0
Services by other medical professionals [4]	161.9	214.4	228.2	236.6	237.4	239.2	242.1	247.9
Hospital and related services	317.3	607.7	761.9	831.7	866.9	885.2	921.1	950.0
Hospital services [7]	115.9	227.2	290.1	318.2	332.2	338.8	353.0	363.5
Nursing homes and adult day services [7]	117.0	177.0	206.4	220.3	227.8	235.3	241.7	249.6
Health insurance [9]	(NA)	106.6	123.6	133.9	135.5	155.2	179.8	172.0
Recreation [2]	**103.3**	**113.3**	**115.9**	**118.5**	**119.1**	**120.6**	**122.2**	**125.2**
Video and audio [2]	101.0	99.1	99.6	104.2	104.2	104.7	107.1	110.4
Cable and satellite television and radio service [5]	266.8	372.4	422.8	462.0	470.5	479.4	500.1	520.6
Pets, pet products and services [2]	106.1	154.4	167.3	170.3	172.4	178.0	180.1	184.9
Sporting goods	119.0	118.8	114.6	111.0	111.0	112.3	113.7	121.2
Other recreational goods [2]	87.8	57.8	47.0	40.6	37.4	35.2	33.5	33.5
Other recreation services [2]	111.7	145.1	156.2	164.1	167.9	171.8	174.7	176.2
Club membership for shopping clubs, fraternal or other organizations & participant sports fees [2]	108.9	123.5	130.1	135.3	139.2	142.9	145.0	146.1
Admissions	230.5	322.8	354.1	374.8	381.6	389.2	396.6	395.6
Recreational reading materials	188.3	220.7	240.7	241.5	246.3	255.6	267.0	273.7
Education and communication [2]	**102.5**	**129.9**	**138.2**	**136.5**	**136.8**	**137.8**	**140.3**	**142.6**
Education [2]	112.5	199.3	240.5	253.2	258.8	265.8	270.7	274.6
Educational books and supplies	279.9	505.6	648.2	689.5	696.1	685.4	677.7	687.1
Tuition, other school fees, and childcare	324.0	573.2	688.8	724.7	741.3	762.7	777.7	788.7
College tuition and fees	331.9	638.2	785.9	823.1	841.3	865.4	877.3	884.9
Day care and preschool [11]	156.3	240.4	275.4	290.4	295.0	303.3	311.9	317.7
Communication [2]	93.6	84.7	80.2	75.0	73.9	73.2	74.5	75.9
Postage and delivery services [2]	103.2	145.9	174.6	180.3	184.9	194.8	202.7	211.2
Information and information processing [2]	92.8	81.5	76.4	71.1	70.0	69.2	70.4	71.6
Telephone services [2]	98.5	102.4	99.3	91.8	90.4	89.4	92.2	94.4
Wireless telephone services [2]	76.0	62.4	55.2	48.8	47.6	46.4	47.3	48.2
Residential telephone services [10]	(NA)	101.6	113.4	116.1	117.2	120.8	128.9	136.2
Information technology, hardware, and services [8]	25.9	9.4	8.1	7.6	7.5	7.4	7.3	7.4
Other goods and services	**271.1**	**381.3**	**414.9**	**432.6**	**442.3**	**451.3**	**462.4**	**476.8**
Tobacco and smoking products	394.9	807.3	930.8	1,022.8	1,063.5	1,115.9	1,171.6	1,256.4
Cigarettes [2]	159.9	329.0	380.0	418.3	434.9	457.0	481.6	518.1
Personal care	165.6	206.6	220.8	227.0	231.1	234.0	238.3	243.5
Personal care products	153.7	161.1	163.3	161.7	161.5	160.7	160.1	159.7
Hair, dental, shaving, and miscellaneous personal care products [2]	103.3	104.3	103.7	102.3	102.3	103.0	103.8	103.8

See footnotes at end of table.

Table 767. Consumer Price Indexes for All Urban Consumers (CPI-U) for Selected Items and Groups: 2000 to 2021-Continued.

See headnote on page 503.

Item	2000	2010	2015	2017	2018	2019	2020	2021
Cosmetics, perfume, bath, nail preparations and implements	166.8	182.2	188.2	187.0	186.3	182.8	179.5	178.5
Personal care services	178.1	229.6	247.2	257.4	264.2	271.4	283.2	297.5
Haircuts and other personal care services [2]	108.7	140.1	150.8	157.0	161.2	165.6	172.8	181.5
Miscellaneous personal services	252.3	354.1	399.3	424.0	439.8	448.9	456.7	465.4
Legal services [4]	189.3	288.1	323.6	346.4	361.2	364.8	368.7	374.4
Funeral expenses [4]	187.8	282.0	313.7	325.6	331.7	337.9	343.3	348.8
SPECIAL AGGREGATE INDEXES								
Commodities	149.2	174.6	181.7	181.2	184.6	185.3	184.8	199.2
Commodities less food and beverages	137.7	150.4	149.2	147.2	150.3	149.5	145.7	161.0
Nondurables less food and beverages	147.4	189.9	189.4	190.6	199.0	196.5	185.5	204.9
Nondurables less food, beverages, and apparel	162.5	238.1	233.3	235.3	249.0	245.9	231.5	261.5
Durables	125.4	111.3	109.1	105.3	104.4	104.8	105.7	116.9
Services	195.3	261.3	291.7	308.1	316.6	325.1	332.0	341.4
Rent of shelter [3]	201.3	258.8	290.4	310.3	320.7	331.6	339.9	349.1
Transportation services	196.1	259.8	291.0	309.9	321.8	325.0	312.8	324.2
Other services	229.9	309.6	339.4	347.8	352.7	358.9	367.8	375.8
All items less food	173.0	217.8	235.4	244.3	250.7	255.2	257.5	269.9
All items less shelter	165.7	208.6	223.3	227.2	231.8	234.2	235.7	249.1
All items less medical care	167.3	209.7	226.9	234.1	239.9	244.0	246.4	258.8
Commodities less food	139.2	153.0	152.2	150.5	153.6	152.9	149.3	164.4
Nondurables less food	149.1	191.9	192.3	193.8	201.9	199.7	189.7	208.2
Nondurables less food and apparel	162.9	235.6	232.7	235.0	247.8	245.3	232.8	260.3
Nondurables	158.2	205.3	217.6	219.6	225.8	226.6	225.0	240.0
Apparel less footwear	126.2	113.3	118.8	118.5	118.7	116.6	110.2	112.5
Services less rent of shelter [3]	202.9	284.4	315.8	329.3	336.4	342.8	348.6	359.1
Services less medical care services	188.9	249.6	277.7	293.0	301.3	309.1	314.5	323.9
Energy	124.6	211.4	202.9	204.5	219.9	215.3	196.9	238.3
All items less energy	178.6	220.5	242.3	251.2	256.3	261.8	266.9	276.6
All items less food and energy	181.3	221.3	242.2	252.2	257.6	263.2	267.7	277.3
Commodities less food and energy commodities	144.9	143.6	146.1	144.4	144.1	144.4	144.6	153.8
Energy commodities	129.5	242.6	216.7	216.3	246.2	237.4	198.8	269.1
Services less energy services	202.1	268.3	301.1	318.7	328.0	337.3	344.8	353.8
Domestically produced farm food	170.1	221.6	251.0	246.6	247.7	249.5	258.4	267.4
Utilities and public transportation	152.6	203.1	214.8	216.4	217.2	218.0	218.5	227.9

NA Not available. [1] Special indexes based on a substantially smaller sample. [2] December 1997=100. [3] December 1982=100. [4] December 1986=100. [5] December 1983=100. [6] December 2001=100. [7] December 1996=100. [8] December 1988=100. [9] December 2005=100. [10] December 2009=100. [11] December 1990=100.

Source: U.S. Bureau of Labor Statistics, CPI Databases, "All Urban Consumers (Current Series)," <www.bls.gov/cpi/data.htm>, accessed April 2022.

Table 768. Single-Family Housing Price Indexes by State: 2005 to 2021

[Data are for the fourth quarter of the year shown. Index 1991, 1st quarter = 100. Purchase only indexes. Data are seasonally adjusted. The index reflects average price changes in repeat sales or refinancings on the same properties. The information is obtained by reviewing repeat mortgage transactions on single-family properties whose mortgages have been purchased or securitized by either Fannie Mae or Freddie Mac; for more information on methodology, see source]

State	2005	2010	2015	2020	2021	State	2005	2010	2015	2020	2021
U.S.	**216.0**	**181.8**	**218.9**	**304.6**	**358.0**	MO	196.6	177.3	201.4	278.9	320.5
AL	182.7	175.5	190.9	260.3	306.0	MT	274.2	278.9	336.9	483.5	598.5
AK	208.1	219.4	246.4	286.5	318.9	NE	193.3	187.1	223.0	307.2	351.8
AZ	303.0	173.0	254.6	395.5	504.0	NV	268.9	124.7	193.9	303.4	373.3
AR	184.7	175.4	196.3	250.1	298.1	NH	237.8	193.6	212.9	305.7	362.2
CA	283.8	159.7	231.2	326.8	390.9	NJ	253.0	212.3	213.4	276.3	318.8
CO	267.9	254.7	353.0	536.7	634.4	NM	214.1	208.9	213.8	285.9	330.6
CT	193.9	165.2	162.6	200.3	227.6	NY	212.7	202.2	209.7	283.2	321.0
DE	208.4	187.1	187.5	236.8	272.6	NC	181.9	180.5	200.1	287.6	348.4
DC	316.0	314.4	450.9	585.4	624.1	ND	191.0	222.2	297.9	339.0	374.0
FL	299.1	171.8	241.8	362.6	455.6	OH	173.9	150.1	169.5	240.7	273.3
GA	190.4	152.0	194.8	284.6	344.0	OK	177.2	191.1	218.6	274.0	319.5
HI	204.8	177.5	221.9	284.1	341.4	OR	295.4	252.0	338.3	498.9	588.9
ID	228.1	189.7	249.5	456.8	580.2	PA	189.1	184.0	197.2	262.3	297.2
IL	202.8	172.1	181.2	222.6	250.5	RI	235.8	181.6	193.6	280.2	327.7
IN	164.9	155.3	175.5	252.7	289.6	SC	185.8	179.3	204.5	284.5	345.4
IA	190.2	193.4	218.2	273.8	305.6	SD	208.4	217.8	256.7	342.7	411.5
KS	188.4	189.1	209.2	285.8	322.8	TN	184.5	180.2	213.1	315.6	391.6
KY	184.4	186.8	206.3	278.6	317.2	TX	171.2	183.2	238.6	328.5	392.0
LA	213.7	225.6	255.5	303.2	334.1	UT	254.5	248.6	317.9	516.4	656.1
ME	220.3	200.5	212.2	308.0	370.1	VT	208.2	203.3	211.0	275.0	330.0
MD	253.8	204.8	220.9	281.9	312.2	VA	233.5	205.1	226.2	298.4	338.4
MA	251.5	212.0	241.6	335.6	385.3	WA	241.5	218.4	274.2	445.0	534.5
MI	199.4	142.4	185.3	267.2	308.4	WV	180.9	187.6	207.3	238.0	266.7
MN	251.2	204.0	240.8	330.8	373.1	WI	221.8	203.0	218.1	306.8	348.3
MS	179.0	173.7	190.1	230.7	271.2	WY	257.4	278.2	317.5	392.5	454.7

Source: Federal Housing Finance Agency, "House Price Index Datasets, Quarterly Data, Purchase-Only Indexes," <www.fhfa.gov/DataTools/Downloads/Pages/House-Price-Index-Datasets.aspx#qpo>, accessed March 2022.

Table 769. Average Prices of Selected Fuels and Electricity: 1990 to 2021

[Fuels in dollars per unit; electricity in cents per kWh. Represents price to end-users, except as noted]

Item	Unit	1990	2000	2010	2015	2017	2018	2019	2020	2021
Crude oil, composite [1]	Barrel	22.22	28.26	76.69	48.39	50.68	64.38	59.38	39.75	67.82
Motor gasoline: [2]										
Unleaded regular	Gallon	1.16	1.51	2.79	2.45	2.41	2.74	2.64	2.17	3.05
Unleaded premium	Gallon	1.35	1.69	3.05	2.87	2.91	3.27	3.21	2.79	3.69
No. 2 fuel oil (heating oil)	Gallon	0.73	0.93	2.46	2.02	2.01	2.38	2.27	1.66	2.41
No. 2 diesel fuel	Gallon	0.73	0.94	2.31	1.82	1.81	2.26	2.11	1.49	2.20
Propane, consumer grade	Gallon	0.75	0.60	1.48	0.48	0.77	0.93	0.60	0.50	1.09
Residual fuel oil	Gallon	0.44	0.60	1.71	1.29	1.29	1.66	1.58	1.25	1.86
Natural gas, residential	1,000 cu/ft	5.80	7.76	11.39	10.38	10.91	10.50	10.51	10.78	12.24
Electricity, residential	kWh	7.83	8.24	11.54	12.65	12.89	12.87	13.01	13.15	13.72

[1] Refiner acquisition cost. [2] Average, all service.

Source: U.S. Energy Information Administration, *Monthly Energy Review*, May 2022. See also <www.eia.gov/totalenergy/data/monthly/>.

Table 770. Retail Gasoline Prices—U.S. Total and Selected Cities: 2018 to 2021

[In dollars per gallon. Prices are annual averages. Gasoline is classified by octane rating: regular, 85 or less; midgrade, 88-90; and premium, greater than 90. Octane requirements may vary by altitude]

Area	Regular				Midgrade				Premium			
	2018	2019	2020	2021	2018	2019	2020	2021	2018	2019	2020	2021
U.S. total	**2.72**	**2.60**	**2.17**	**3.01**	**3.06**	**3.00**	**2.58**	**3.43**	**3.29**	**3.25**	**2.83**	**3.69**
Boston, MA	2.73	2.59	2.14	2.92	3.01	2.89	2.50	3.26	3.20	3.09	2.70	3.45
Chicago, IL	2.78	2.75	2.31	3.20	3.16	3.15	2.69	3.57	3.55	3.53	3.11	3.98
Cleveland, OH	2.56	2.51	2.07	2.90	2.88	2.85	2.42	3.22	3.20	3.20	2.78	3.59
Denver, CO	2.60	2.50	2.18	3.12	2.92	2.83	2.55	3.51	3.21	3.13	2.81	3.77
Houston, TX	2.42	2.29	1.82	2.62	2.78	2.68	2.24	3.03	3.02	2.90	2.47	3.27
Los Angeles, CA	3.51	3.59	3.04	3.99	3.68	3.81	3.30	4.27	3.78	3.88	3.34	4.31
Miami, FL	2.73	2.47	2.10	2.90	3.03	2.82	2.46	3.25	3.30	3.08	2.75	3.52
New York, NY	2.77	2.62	2.18	3.01	3.05	2.92	2.55	3.34	3.22	3.10	2.71	3.53
San Francisco, CA	3.54	3.65	3.14	4.13	3.72	3.86	3.38	4.36	3.85	4.02	3.53	4.53
Seattle, WA	3.27	3.29	2.84	3.61	3.53	3.63	3.19	3.93	3.61	3.66	3.24	4.01

Source: U.S. Energy Information Administration, "Weekly Retail Gasoline and Diesel Prices," <www.eia.gov/petroleum/data.php#prices>, accessed March 2022.

Table 771. Weekly Food Cost of a Nutritious Diet by Type of Family and Individual: 2010 to 2021

[In dollars. As of December. Suggested plans assume that food for all meals and snacks is purchased at the store and prepared at home. Food Plans are based on 2001-02 data and updated to current dollars by using the Consumer Price Index for specific food items. See source for details]

Family and individual type	2010			2020			2021		
	Low cost plan	Moderate cost plan	Liberal plan	Low cost plan	Moderate cost plan	Liberal plan	Low cost plan	Moderate cost plan	Liberal plan
FAMILIES									
Family of two (male & female):									
19 to 50 years old	103.40	128.40	160.80	118.50	147.10	183.90	(NA)	(NA)	(NA)
51 to 70 years old	99.20	122.60	148.00	113.70	141.70	171.30	(NA)	(NA)	(NA)
Family of four:									
Couple (male & female), 19 to 50 years old and children aged—									
2 to 3 and 4 to 5 years old	150.20	185.50	229.90	172.80	213.40	263.70	(NA)	(NA)	(NA)
6 to 8 and 9 to 11 years old	176.60	221.00	268.50	203.90	255.00	308.70	(NA)	(NA)	(NA)
INDIVIDUALS [1]									
Child:									
1 year old	26.80	30.60	37.10	30.60	34.80	42.10	32.30	36.60	44.60
2 to 3 years old	27.50	33.30	40.50	32.10	38.50	46.90	34.20	40.80	49.60
4 to 5 years old	28.70	35.50	43.30	32.90	41.20	49.60	35.00	43.70	52.90
6 to 8 years old	39.20	48.20	56.90	46.50	56.10	66.00	50.50	59.80	70.60
9 to 11 years old	43.40	56.10	65.50	49.70	65.10	75.60	53.00	69.10	80.40
Male:									
12 to 13 years old	49.50	61.70	72.70	57.40	71.80	84.40	61.30	76.70	90.10
14 to 18 years old	50.80	63.80	73.40	58.10	73.60	85.10	61.80	78.60	91.50
19 to 50 years old	50.30	62.90	77.10	57.70	72.30	88.60	61.60	77.00	94.70
51 to 70 years old	47.60	58.60	71.10	54.50	68.10	82.30	58.10	72.90	87.80
71 years old and over	47.00	58.50	71.90	53.50	66.70	82.30	57.20	71.00	87.60
Female:									
12 to 13 years old	42.90	51.90	63.00	49.20	59.90	73.10	52.40	63.40	78.10
14 to 18 years old	43.10	52.00	63.90	49.20	58.90	72.90	52.30	62.70	77.50
19 to 50 years old	43.70	53.80	69.00	50.00	61.40	78.60	53.50	65.50	83.70
51 to 70 years old	42.50	52.90	63.50	48.80	60.70	73.50	52.00	64.60	78.60
71 years old and over	42.10	52.50	63.40	48.10	60.10	72.40	51.50	63.90	77.00

NA Not available. [1] The costs given are for individuals in 4-person families. For individuals in other size families, the following adjustments are suggested: 1-person, add 20 percent; 2-person, add 10 percent; 3-person, add 5 percent; 5- or 6-person, subtract 5 percent; and 7-or-more person, subtract 10 percent.

Source: U.S. Department of Agriculture, Center for Nutrition Policy and Promotion, "USDA Food Plans: Cost of Food Reports," <www.fns.usda.gov/cnpp/usda-food-plans-cost-food-reports-monthly-reports>, accessed March 2022.

Table 772. Food—Retail Prices of Selected Items: 1990 to 2021

[In dollars per pound, except as indicated. As of December. See Appendix III]

Food	1990	2000	2005	2010	2015	2018	2019	2020	2021
Cereals and bakery products:									
Flour, white, all purpose............	0.24	0.28	0.30	0.44	0.50	0.44	0.43	0.45	0.39
Rice, white, long grain, raw.........	0.49	(NA)	0.52	0.73	0.71	0.71	0.71	0.79	0.82
Spaghetti and macaroni.............	0.85	0.88	0.87	1.19	1.29	1.16	1.19	1.31	1.09
Bread, white, pan...................	0.70	0.99	1.05	1.39	1.43	1.29	1.36	1.54	1.53
Bread, whole wheat.................	(NA)	1.36	1.29	1.88	1.95	1.92	1.96	2.20	2.10
Beef:									
Ground beef, 100% beef............	1.63	1.63	2.30	2.38	4.06	3.73	3.86	3.95	4.60
Ground chuck, 100% beef..........	2.02	1.98	2.61	2.93	4.03	3.71	4.07	4.20	4.79
Ground beef, lean and extra lean....	(NA)	2.33	2.91	3.49	5.89	5.26	5.52	5.72	6.32
Beef roasts (all, uncooked).........	(NA)	2.93	3.73	4.15	5.48	5.20	5.54	5.87	6.95
Beef steaks (all, uncooked)........	(NA)	4.09	5.03	5.60	7.51	7.58	7.71	8.09	9.93
Round steak, USDA Choice.........	3.42	3.28	4.12	4.30	5.93	5.69	5.98	6.34	7.34
Sirloin steak, boneless.............	4.24	4.81	5.93	6.07	8.29	8.31	8.48	8.98	11.06
Pork:									
Bacon, sliced.....................	2.28	3.03	3.33	4.16	5.73	5.50	5.47	5.83	7.21
Chops, center cut, bone-in........	3.32	3.46	3.28	3.58	4.09	3.95	3.77	4.25	4.36
Ham, boneless, excluding canned....	(NA)	2.75	3.09	3.47	4.03	3.88	4.07	4.47	4.83
Poultry, fish, and eggs:									
Chicken, fresh, whole..............	0.86	1.08	1.06	1.28	1.44	1.47	1.45	1.62	1.61
Chicken breast, boneless..........	(NA)	(NA)	(NA)	3.32	3.28	3.11	3.11	3.29	3.73
Chicken legs, bone-in.............	1.17	1.26	1.33	1.48	1.57	1.40	1.51	1.54	1.73
Turkey, frozen, whole.............	0.96	0.99	1.07	1.38	1.45	1.41	1.39	(NA)	(NA)
Tuna, light, chunk, canned.........	2.11	1.92	(NA)	(NA)	3.26	(NA)	(NA)	(NA)	(NA)
Eggs, grade A large (dozen)........	1.00	0.96	1.35	1.79	2.75	1.60	1.54	1.48	1.79
Dairy products:									
Milk, fresh, whole, fortified (per gal.)......	(NA)	2.79	3.24	3.32	3.31	2.85	3.19	3.54	3.74
Milk, low-fat, reduced fat, skim, per gallon...	(NA)	(NA)	(NA)	(NA)	(NA)	2.63	2.87	3.12	3.36
Yogurt, per 8 ounce...............	(NA)	(NA)	(NA)	(NA)	(NA)	1.08	1.15	1.25	1.27
Butter, in sticks..................	(NA)	(NA)	(NA)	(NA)	(NA)	3.93	3.62	3.53	3.47
American processed cheese.........	(NA)	3.69	3.92	3.80	4.35	3.94	3.91	4.20	3.89
Cheddar cheese, natural...........	(NA)	3.76	4.43	4.93	5.33	5.36	5.30	5.54	5.26
Ice cream, prepack., bulk, reg. (1/2 gal.).....	2.54	3.66	3.69	4.58	4.73	4.81	4.74	4.93	4.77
Fresh fruits and vegetables:									
Apples, Red Delicious.............	0.77	0.82	0.97	1.20	1.40	(NA)	(NA)	(NA)	(NA)
Bananas..........................	0.43	0.49	0.48	0.59	0.58	0.58	0.57	0.57	0.62
Oranges, navel....................	0.56	0.62	0.89	1.02	1.23	1.39	1.33	1.33	1.45
Grapefruit........................	0.56	0.58	1.10	0.99	1.09	1.35	1.25	(NA)	(NA)
Grapes, Thompson seedless........	(NA)	2.36	2.76	2.87	2.83	2.28	2.39	2.20	(NA)
Lemons...........................	0.97	1.11	1.51	1.60	1.98	2.39	2.00	1.90	2.01
Pears, Anjou......................	0.79	(NA)	1.00	1.42	(NA)	1.57	(NA)	(NA)	(NA)
Strawberries, dry pint, per 12 ounces........	(NA)	(NA)	2.67	3.07	3.50	3.17	3.10	3.29	(NA)
Lettuce, iceberg..................	0.58	0.85	0.85	0.99	1.48	1.25	1.30	(NA)	(NA)
Lettuce, romaine..................	(NA)	(NA)	(NA)	1.83	2.21	2.35	2.18	(NA)	3.27
Tomatoes, field grown.............	0.86	1.57	1.85	1.59	1.93	2.18	1.95	1.89	1.91
Peppers, sweet...................	(NA)	(NA)	(NA)	2.40	(NA)	2.65	2.50	(NA)	(NA)
Potatoes, white...................	0.32	0.35	0.50	0.58	0.64	0.72	0.78	0.75	0.78
Sugar and fats and oils:									
Sugar, white, all sizes.............	0.43	0.41	0.45	0.64	0.64	0.57	0.59	0.67	0.69
Margarine, tubs, soft..............	(NA)	0.84	0.91	1.62	1.86	1.57	(NA)	(NA)	(NA)
Peanut butter, creamy, all sizes.....	2.07	1.96	1.70	1.99	2.68	(NA)	(NA)	(NA)	(NA)
Nonalcoholic beverages:									
All soft drinks, 2 liter..............	(NA)	(NA)	(NA)	(NA)	(NA)	1.47	1.48	1.61	1.71
All soft drinks, per 12 oz can in 12-pack.....	(NA)	(NA)	(NA)	(NA)	(NA)	0.33	0.35	0.39	0.44
Coffee, 100% ground roast, all sizes.........	2.94	3.21	3.24	4.15	4.49	(NA)	4.05	4.52	4.97
Prepared foods:									
Potato chips, per 16 ounces........	2.97	3.44	3.46	4.74	4.41	4.45	4.53	5.08	5.15

NA Not available.

Source: U.S. Bureau of Labor Statistics, CPI Databases, "Average Price Data," <www.bls.gov/cpi/data.htm>, accessed March 2022.

Table 773. Employment Cost Index for Total Compensation, Wages and Salaries, and Benefits: 2011 to 2021

[As of December (2005=100). Data are not seasonally adjusted. For data by industry, see Table 685]

Compensation type and occupation	2011	2012	2013	2014	2015	2016	2017	2018	2019	2020	2021
Total compensation:											
All civilian workers [1]..............	115.5	117.7	120.0	122.7	125.1	127.9	131.2	135.0	138.7	142.2	147.9
Private industry workers............	115.0	117.1	119.4	122.2	124.5	127.2	130.5	134.4	138.0	141.6	147.8
State and local government workers..	117.7	119.9	122.2	124.7	127.8	130.9	134.2	137.7	141.7	144.9	148.6
Wages and salaries:											
All civilian workers [1]..............	114.6	116.5	118.7	121.2	123.7	126.6	129.8	133.8	137.7	141.3	147.7
Private industry workers............	114.6	116.6	119.0	121.6	124.2	127.1	130.6	134.7	138.7	142.6	149.7
State and local government workers..	114.9	116.2	117.5	119.4	121.6	124.1	126.7	129.7	133.0	135.4	139.0
Benefits:											
All civilian workers [1]..............	117.5	120.3	123.0	126.2	128.4	131.1	134.4	138.1	141.2	144.5	148.6
Private industry workers............	115.9	118.2	120.5	123.5	125.1	127.3	130.2	133.6	136.2	139.1	143.2
State and local government workers..	123.6	127.8	132.0	135.8	140.6	145.0	149.7	154.4	159.5	164.4	168.5

[1] Includes workers in the private nonfarm economy except those in private households and workers in the public sector except the federal government.

Source: U.S. Bureau of Labor Statistics, Employment Cost Trends, "Employment Cost Index," <www.bls.gov/ncs/ect/#data>, accessed March 2022.

Table 774. Indexes of Spot Primary Market Prices: 1990 to 2021

[1967=100. Represents unweighted geometric average of price quotations of 23 commodities. The indexes are computed daily and therefore much more sensitive to changes in market conditions than a monthly producer price index]

Items and number	1990	1995	2000	2005	2010	2015	2016	2017	2018	2019	2020	2021
All commodities (23)	**258.1**	**289.1**	**224.0**	**303.3**	**520.3**	**374.8**	**423.1**	**432.5**	**409.2**	**401.6**	**443.8**	**578.3**
Foodstuffs (10)	206.4	236.4	184.7	241.7	440.3	335.0	338.8	336.0	324.2	338.5	362.1	490.6
Raw industrials (13)	301.2	332.2	255.8	354.7	583.8	404.9	493.2	514.7	480.4	451.8	510.7	647.7
Livestock and products (5)	292.7	307.4	265.5	326.6	528.0	392.2	446.2	437.3	396.4	386.8	429.5	605.4
Metals (5)	283.2	300.6	214.0	440.9	1,006.2	556.0	803.9	911.6	829.9	752.1	903.5	1,277.6
Textiles and fibers (4)	257.6	274.3	245.7	252.5	342.1	271.9	287.3	304.5	286.9	280.9	304.8	357.4
Fats and oils (4)	188.7	226.7	163.6	223.4	478.3	315.2	393.3	380.8	357.4	366.5	423.6	691.4

Source: cmdty by Barchart, Chicago, IL, *Commodity Index Report*, weekly ©. See also <www.barchart.com/cmdty>.

Table 775. Producer Price Indexes—Final and Intermediate Demand: 2010 to 2021

[November 2009=100, except as noted. Minus sign (-) indicates decrease. For information on producer prices, see Bureau of Labor Statistics, <www.bls.gov/ppi/>]

Commodity type	2010	2015	2017	2018	2019	2020	2021
FINAL DEMAND PRICE INDEX							
Total	**101.8**	**109.9**	**113.0**	**116.2**	**118.2**	**118.4**	**126.7**
Final demand goods	102.8	109.1	111.2	115.0	115.5	113.8	125.8
Final demand foods	103.7	118.4	116.5	116.7	118.9	120.4	131.0
Final demand energy	107.2	98.6	99.8	110.0	105.0	91.5	119.5
Final demand goods less foods and energy	101.4	109.9	113.2	116.0	117.6	118.5	126.2
Final demand services	101.3	110.0	113.5	116.5	119.1	120.2	126.7
Final demand trade services	101.7	111.6	114.8	116.9	119.7	121.7	130.7
Final demand transportation and warehousing services	103.2	115.3	115.9	122.0	125.5	121.2	130.9
Final demand services less trade, transportation, and warehousing	100.9	108.7	112.8	115.8	118.2	119.5	124.5
INTERMEDIATE DEMAND PRICE INDEX							
Processed goods for intermediate demand [1]	183.4	188.0	190.7	200.9	198.1	192.5	230.0
Processed foods and feeds [1]	171.7	197.7	190.3	191.6	192.5	196.0	219.9
Processed energy goods [1]	187.8	168.9	171.0	190.8	179.2	157.9	211.0
Processed materials less foods and energy [1]	180.8	189.4	193.3	201.8	201.1	198.9	233.0
Unprocessed goods for intermediate demand [1]	212.2	189.1	190.8	200.1	185.9	167.6	242.3
Unprocessed foodstuffs and feedstuffs [1]	152.4	181.4	167.1	163.9	165.3	159.4	199.8
Unprocessed energy materials [1]	216.7	141.1	150.7	168.7	143.4	106.7	191.3
Unprocessed nonfood materials less energy [1]	329.1	296.0	324.1	340.7	323.4	346.0	462.6
Services for intermediate demand	101.1	110.2	115.0	118.6	121.4	121.9	130.7
Trade services for intermediate demand	100.8	113.1	115.3	120.0	125.0	131.0	150.6
Transportation and warehousing services for intermediate demand	103.3	119.1	120.6	125.4	129.0	128.3	139.5
Services less trade, transportation, and warehousing for intermediate demand	100.7	107.8	113.8	117.0	119.1	118.3	123.7
FINAL DEMAND PERCENT CHANGE [2]							
Total	**(NA)**	**-0.9**	**2.4**	**2.8**	**1.7**	**0.2**	**7.0**
Final demand goods	(NA)	-4.3	3.3	3.4	0.4	-1.5	10.6
Final demand foods	(NA)	-2.6	1.2	0.2	1.9	1.3	8.8
Final demand energy	(NA)	-20.6	10.4	10.2	-4.5	-12.9	30.6
Final demand goods less foods and energy	(NA)	0.4	2.3	2.5	1.4	0.8	6.5
Final demand services	(NA)	0.9	1.8	2.6	2.2	0.9	5.4
Final demand trade services	(NA)	1.3	1.5	1.8	2.4	1.7	7.4
Final demand transportation and warehousing services	(NA)	-2.0	2.1	5.3	2.9	-3.4	8.0
Final demand services less trade, transportation, and warehousing	(NA)	1.1	2.0	2.7	2.1	1.1	4.2
INTERMEDIATE DEMAND PERCENT CHANGE [2]							
Processed goods for intermediate demand	6.3	-6.9	4.7	5.3	-1.4	-2.8	19.5
Processed foods and feeds	3.4	-6.2	1.0	0.7	0.5	1.8	12.2
Processed energy goods	15.6	-20.1	12.1	11.6	-6.1	-11.9	33.6
Processed materials less foods and energy	4.3	-3.0	3.4	4.4	-0.3	-1.1	17.1
Unprocessed goods for intermediate demand	21.1	-24.1	10.0	4.9	-7.1	-9.8	44.5
Unprocessed foodstuffs and feedstuffs	13.3	-13.7	2.9	-1.9	0.9	-3.6	25.4
Unprocessed energy materials	22.6	-39.5	17.6	11.9	-15.0	-25.6	79.3
Unprocessed nonfood materials less energy	32.5	-14.4	12.5	5.1	-5.1	7.0	33.7
Services for intermediate demand	(NA)	1.2	2.6	3.1	2.4	0.4	7.2
Trade services for intermediate demand	(NA)	2.4	2.9	4.1	4.2	4.8	15.0
Transportation and warehousing services for intermediate demand	(NA)	-0.3	2.0	4.0	2.9	-0.5	8.8
Services less trade, transportation, and warehousing for intermediate demand	(NA)	1.2	2.6	2.8	1.8	-0.7	4.6

NA Not available. [1] 1982=100. [2] Change from immediate prior year. 2010, change from 2009.

Source: U.S. Bureau of Labor Statistics, PPI Databases, "Commodity Data including "headline" FD-ID Indexes," <www.bls.gov/ppi/data.htm>, accessed June 2022.

Table 776. Producer Price Indexes—Final and Intermediate Demand by Commodity: 2000 to 2021

[1982=100, unless otherwise noted. For information on producer prices, see Bureau of Labor Statistics, <www.bls.gov/ppi/>]

Commodity type	2000	2005	2010	2015	2019	2020	2021
Final demand (Nov. 2009=100)	**(NA)**	**(NA)**	**101.8**	**109.9**	**118.2**	**118.4**	**126.7**
Final demand goods (Nov. 2009=100)	**(NA)**	**(NA)**	**102.8**	**109.1**	**115.5**	**113.8**	**125.8**
Final demand foods (Nov. 2009=100)	**(NA)**	**(NA)**	**103.7**	**118.4**	**118.9**	**120.4**	**131.0**
Fresh fruits & melons	91.4	102.8	123.8	124.2	136.3	139.1	146.4
Fresh & dry vegetables	126.7	142.6	178.5	200.2	239.2	243.9	228.0
Grains	78.3	83.4	160.2	151.9	149.6	147.3	235.8
Eggs for fresh use (Dec. 1991=100)	84.9	79.6	123.4	219.3	116.1	132.6	144.4
Oilseeds	93.8	113.4	191.0	176.6	160.1	175.7	256.1
Bakery products	182.3	201.1	244.8	275.0	291.9	292.2	295.5
Milled rice	101.2	120.1	183.6	199.0	205.9	220.9	227.9
Dry macaroni, spaghetti, and egg noodle products (June 1985=100)	121.6	127.9	170.7	216.2	202.5	205.1	208.4
Beef & veal	113.7	147.4	157.1	243.6	209.0	213.4	268.5
Pork, except sausage	113.4	131.9	142.6	145.6	144.1	147.2	170.7
Processed young chickens	110.4	136.2	149.0	174.0	162.6	158.9	198.1
Processed turkeys	98.7	105.1	132.1	164.3	146.0	145.9	183.6
Unprocessed and prepared seafood	198.1	222.6	272.4	322.0	349.9	350.8	413.0
Dairy products	133.7	154.5	174.0	193.6	201.3	202.2	206.1
Processed fruits & vegetables	128.6	140.4	176.6	197.7	208.9	212.4	219.1
Confectionery end products	170.6	205.1	236.4	282.8	283.1	280.6	275.4
Soft drinks	144.1	159.1	183.9	196.7	213.5	218.1	227.8
Coffee (whole bean, ground, & instant)	133.5	151.1	190.2	204.7	194.2	194.9	198.0
Shortening, cooking oil, and margarine	132.4	176.7	233.6	243.3	239.0	243.0	325.9
Frozen specialty food	143.5	152.7	176.4	189.5	185.6	186.0	188.6
Final demand energy (Nov. 2009=100)	**(NA)**	**(NA)**	**107.2**	**98.6**	**105.0**	**91.5**	**119.5**
Liquefied petroleum gas	127.1	244.7	301.8	109.8	123.8	89.3	204.5
Residential electric power (Dec. 1990=100)	110.8	126.4	154.7	172.2	181.9	181.7	188.3
Residential natural gas (Dec. 1990=100)	135.5	216.8	201.7	184.4	200.8	202.3	236.1
Gasoline	94.6	168.6	225.3	177.2	183.3	129.2	218.8
Home heating oil & distillates	93.5	178.4	207.5	160.9	186.4	120.9	194.7
No. 2 diesel fuel	93.3	189.1	232.9	181.4	221.3	175.7	315.9
Other final demand goods (Nov. 2009=100)	**(NA)**	**(NA)**	**101.4**	**109.9**	**117.6**	**118.5**	**126.2**
Alcoholic beverages	140.6	158.5	175.1	192.6	199.8	202.4	201.3
Women's, girls', and infants' apparel (Dec. 2003=100)	(NA)	100.3	101.6	105.2	108.3	107.7	106.6
Men's and boys' apparel (Dec. 2003=100)	(NA)	98.7	101.5	113.0	117.4	118.4	120.2
Textile house furnishings	122.0	122.9	131.7	162.8	169.2	169.0	169.4
Footwear	144.9	148.1	162.4	196.0	208.8	210.0	216.2
Industrial chemicals	129.1	188.5	269.2	242.2	252.6	226.3	309.3
Pharmaceutical preparations (June 2001=100)	(NA)	117.9	155.1	212.8	268.4	273.9	277.0
Soaps and detergents	128.2	134.6	161.2	175.7	182.1	183.6	189.5
Cosmetics and other toilet preparations	137.4	143.0	149.9	161.4	167.0	167.9	168.8
Tires, tubes, tread, & repair materials	93.0	108.1	138.1	149.3	152.1	152.6	159.3
Agricultural machinery and equipment	153.7	174.7	203.5	222.2	237.3	242.8	258.0
Construction machinery and equipment	148.6	168.3	191.4	217.0	232.6	236.6	248.1
Industrial material handling equipment	134.7	150.6	183.1	207.0	225.4	228.8	244.4
Electronic computers (Dec. 2004=100)	261.6	85.5	30.3	20.4	16.6	15.4	15.6
Textile machinery and equipment	156.2	160.5	165.9	176.1	172.2	173.8	174.6
Paper industries machinery (June 1982=100)	164.7	178.1	197.2	216.2	227.8	229.2	235.1
Printing trades machinery and equipment	142.1	144.3	155.4	162.3	164.6	165.3	167.9
Transformers and power regulators	135.8	150.3	223.1	212.8	232.0	234.7	277.2
Oil field and gas field machinery	128.2	155.9	200.7	216.5	219.6	217.9	221.4
Mining machinery and equipment	146.1	175.9	221.5	260.6	298.0	307.4	326.0
Office and store machines and equipment	112.7	115.1	121.0	122.7	121.5	121.3	121.8
Household furniture	152.7	166.5	187.4	203.9	219.9	222.8	239.1
Household appliances	107.3	103.3	110.5	116.8	123.6	125.6	129.7
Home electronic equipment	71.8	62.6	52.9	51.3	52.0	53.0	55.0
Lawn and garden equipment	132.0	134.5	141.7	143.7	149.7	151.4	155.7
Passenger cars	132.8	131.8	129.0	133.4	134.9	134.6	137.8
Light motor trucks	157.6	148.4	153.3	171.4	177.8	176.8	182.8
Heavy motor trucks	148.0	162.4	195.7	218.1	232.3	234.6	236.5
Truck trailers	139.4	157.1	181.5	201.0	225.2	225.6	251.4
Aircraft	184.2	223.5	263.0	290.8	307.0	310.6	314.1
Ships (Dec. 1985=100)	146.9	176.6	215.1	225.2	227.7	230.6	234.0
Railroad equipment	135.7	160.4	184.4	201.9	203.7	204.4	206.5
Final demand services (Nov. 2009=100)	**(NA)**	**(NA)**	**101.3**	**110.0**	**119.1**	**120.2**	**126.7**
Final demand trade services (Nov. 2009=100)	**(NA)**	**(NA)**	**101.7**	**111.6**	**119.7**	**121.7**	**130.7**
Furnishings wholesaling (Mar. 2009=100)	(NA)	(NA)	78.5	89.1	98.5	101.8	113.3
Apparel wholesaling (Mar. 2009=100)	(NA)	(NA)	97.3	117.9	121.6	122.1	116.9
Food & alcohol wholesaling (June 2009=100)	(NA)	(NA)	105.7	105.2	114.6	116.2	119.6
Food & alcohol retailing (Mar. 2009=100)	(NA)	(NA)	98.9	126.4	134.7	136.7	139.0
Health, beauty, & optical goods retailing (Mar. 2009=100)	(NA)	(NA)	107.8	118.9	123.6	126.0	130.3
Apparel, jewelry, footwear, & accessories retailing (June 2009=100)	(NA)	(NA)	104.2	113.9	112.8	107.7	118.4
Automobiles & automobile parts retailing (June 2009=100)	(NA)	(NA)	105.9	101.2	95.4	105.2	158.1
Sporting goods, including boats, retailing (Mar. 2009=100)	(NA)	(NA)	96.6	108.9	114.2	116.5	124.4
Furniture retailing (Mar. 2009=100)	(NA)	(NA)	99.7	102.2	104.9	109.4	127.8
Major household appliances retailing (Mar. 2009=100)	(NA)	(NA)	97.3	80.5	96.8	105.6	117.3
Book retailing (Mar. 2009=100)	(NA)	(NA)	104.8	110.3	120.2	127.0	131.1
Final demand transportation & warehousing services (Nov. 2009=100)	**(NA)**	**(NA)**	**103.2**	**115.3**	**125.5**	**121.2**	**130.9**
Rail transportation of freight & mail (Dec. 2008=100)	(NA)	(NA)	101.6	116.5	128.4	128.3	134.7
Truck transportation of freight (June 2009=100)	(NA)	(NA)	102.0	113.4	125.4	124.7	140.3
Air transportation of freight (Dec. 2008=100)	(NA)	(NA)	100.1	112.5	111.8	113.3	117.7
Courier, messenger, & U.S. postal services (June 2009=100)	(NA)	(NA)	105.5	131.5	145.8	150.6	159.0

See footnotes at end of table.

Table 776. Producer Price Indexes—Final and Intermediate Demand by Commodity: 2000 to 2021-Continued.

See headnote on page 509.

Commodity type	2000	2005	2010	2015	2019	2020	2021
Rail transportation of passengers (Dec. 2008=100)...............	(NA)	(NA)	100.7	115.2	125.4	127.6	130.2
Airline passenger services (Dec. 2008=100)............................	(NA)	(NA)	102.8	112.3	117.7	103.6	104.2
Other final demand services (Nov. 2009=100)...............	**(NA)**	**(NA)**	**100.9**	**108.7**	**118.2**	**119.5**	**124.5**
Sales of books..	218.2	264.0	317.1	363.9	392.6	402.0	418.9
Cellphone & other wireless telecom services (Mar. 2009=100)........	(NA)	(NA)	94.4	77.6	63.7	63.3	63.3
Cable & satellite subscriber services (Dec. 2008=100)..............	(NA)	(NA)	103.7	112.7	135.3	137.9	144.1
Internet access services (Mar. 2009=100)...............................	(NA)	(NA)	98.3	98.2	93.4	92.5	91.9
Processed goods for intermediate demand............	**129.2**	**154.0**	**183.4**	**188.0**	**198.1**	**192.5**	**230.0**
Processed materials less foods & feeds........................	**130.1**	**155.1**	**184.4**	**187.2**	**198.8**	**192.2**	**231.0**
Synthetic fibers...	107.2	112.3	111.6	121.3	131.9	127.2	145.0
Processed yarns & threads..	107.9	111.7	130.0	135.6	141.2	136.9	158.5
Finished fabrics...	122.5	124.1	137.1	154.0	161.4	162.5	177.6
Commercial electric power..	131.5	149.8	182.5	195.8	199.6	200.4	210.3
Industrial electric power...	131.5	156.2	193.1	223.7	243.3	240.2	251.1
Commercial natural gas (Dec. 1990=100)..........................	134.7	232.5	208.0	176.6	191.5	187.3	230.3
Industrial natural gas (Dec. 1990=100).............................	139.0	249.4	202.0	158.6	149.2	138.3	187.4
Natural gas to electric power (Dec. 1990=100).................	120.7	204.0	174.8	159.6	152.2	149.8	208.4
Jet fuels...	88.5	169.6	225.5	171.3	202.4	124.6	197.7
Prepared paint...	160.8	187.9	237.1	273.0	299.1	305.2	329.9
Medicinal and botanical chemicals, drugs, and other products........	146.2	136.0	175.2	177.1	181.3	181.4	181.3
Biological products, including diagnostics...........................	172.2	195.1	223.7	256.4	275.6	281.1	296.6
Fats & oils, inedible..	70.1	146.9	244.3	204.9	193.4	201.8	339.2
Plastic resins & materials...	141.6	193.0	210.1	228.0	225.5	215.0	299.8
Synthetic rubber..	119.1	151.3	215.5	197.6	207.0	192.2	225.0
Plastic construction products...	135.8	158.8	190.9	213.1	229.4	233.5	285.5
Softwood lumber..	178.6	203.6	160.8	192.7	215.4	280.3	397.7
Hardwood lumber..	185.9	196.6	187.3	221.1	215.1	207.0	279.2
Millwork..	176.4	197.2	207.0	237.2	263.5	274.5	318.6
Plywood..	157.6	186.8	176.7	198.9	202.9	229.3	335.2
Paper..	149.8	159.6	182.1	189.8	200.6	195.4	214.3
Paperboard..	176.7	175.5	224.9	243.1	268.1	256.6	296.7
Paper boxes & containers..	172.6	183.7	219.4	247.3	269.5	268.1	289.6
Foundry & forge shop products...	136.5	156.2	191.2	209.2	211.9	214.0	230.7
Steel mill products...	108.4	159.7	191.7	177.1	204.0	184.4	350.9
Primary nonferrous metals...	113.6	158.2	210.3	170.7	184.3	191.4	245.2
Aluminum mill shapes..	149.0	161.1	171.9	172.4	197.5	180.6	225.7
Copper & brass mill shapes...	162.3	235.8	421.3	356.9	392.8	404.0	573.0
Nonferrous wire & cable..	143.7	169.4	258.1	238.2	247.4	247.8	314.6
Hardware..	151.2	168.0	194.0	209.7	223.8	227.6	245.9
Plumbing fixtures & fittings...	180.4	197.6	231.4	257.1	281.6	287.9	296.0
Heating equipment..	155.6	179.9	221.5	248.2	279.2	284.0	312.4
Fabricated structural metal products..................................	144.9	175.1	201.1	215.6	239.8	238.7	298.7
Air conditioning & refrigeration equipment.......................	135.3	146.2	163.8	179.2	200.2	204.0	221.9
Motors, generators, motor generator sets.........................	146.2	157.8	190.6	211.6	221.3	222.5	231.8
Electronic components & accessories.................................	97.1	87.0	73.5	68.2	65.3	64.7	64.7
Internal combustion engines..	143.8	147.7	161.7	168.4	169.5	171.1	172.9
Machine shop products..	138.0	151.0	174.7	184.0	194.3	195.6	198.7
Cement, hydraulic..	150.1	176.4	193.5	223.4	258.1	260.7	271.0
Concrete products..	147.8	177.2	210.6	239.4	271.7	279.1	292.9
Motor vehicle parts..	113.6	113.1	121.8	125.9	127.1	127.8	131.8
Aircraft engines & engine parts (Dec. 1985=100).............	141.0	165.9	197.4	221.2	229.7	231.8	235.2
Aircraft parts & auxiliary equipment (June 1985=100)......	145.7	155.3	167.7	183.3	188.5	191.8	193.8
Medical/surgical/personal aid devices...............................	146.0	159.2	169.0	176.2	182.8	185.4	187.2
Unprocessed goods for intermediate demand............	**120.6**	**182.2**	**212.2**	**189.1**	**185.9**	**167.6**	**242.3**
Unprocessed foodstuffs & feedstuffs.........................	**100.2**	**122.7**	**152.4**	**181.4**	**165.3**	**159.4**	**199.8**
Wheat...	80.3	102.7	157.2	153.3	138.3	148.7	214.8
Corn..	76.4	75.9	160.8	149.6	151.4	143.5	242.5
Slaughter cattle..	104.1	131.5	139.8	225.6	171.1	162.7	181.0
Slaughter hogs...	72.7	82.7	92.6	80.6	83.8	75.7	118.2
Broilers and other meat type chickens...............................	127.6	181.0	221.3	246.8	242.3	190.9	279.8
Slaughter turkeys...	120.7	131.1	173.0	234.3	186.3	220.0	253.8
Raw milk...	92.0	113.5	121.9	127.7	141.9	139.7	142.6
Hay and hayseeds..	156.3	190.1	214.3	309.2	338.2	322.9	377.9
Raw cane sugar & byproducts..	100.2	124.9	179.9	149.4	155.5	172.0	177.8
Unprocessed nonfood materials...................................	**130.4**	**223.4**	**249.3**	**183.7**	**192.0**	**165.3**	**261.3**
Raw cotton...	95.2	78.9	117.9	101.6	100.5	97.3	143.4
Hides & skins...	174.0	189.9	224.9	258.8	128.7	107.5	151.9
Coal...	87.9	116.8	189.5	194.0	199.9	189.0	189.5
Natural gas...	155.5	335.4	185.8	105.4	85.5	67.5	150.0
Crude petroleum..	85.2	150.1	218.6	129.5	157.7	102.1	185.0
Logs, bolts, timber, pulpwood and wood chips..................	196.4	197.4	213.4	241.9	239.9	239.0	262.3
Recyclable paper..	282.5	230.9	421.5	291.8	181.2	244.6	430.1
Iron ores...	94.8	116.9	147.1	132.0	145.5	148.7	175.5
Iron & steel scrap...	142.1	289.8	541.1	342.8	413.3	406.6	689.7
Nonferrous metal ores (Dec. 1983=100)..........................	68.0	150.0	298.6	272.6	360.1	439.9	514.2
Copper base scrap..	123.7	258.6	548.2	427.6	410.3	420.7	622.6
Aluminum base scrap...	177.0	210.1	241.6	208.7	178.0	155.9	261.1
Construction sand, gravel, & crushed stone.......................	163.1	195.8	262.2	299.9	348.7	364.3	378.8

NA Not available.

Source: U.S. Bureau of Labor Statistics, PPI Databases, "Commodity Data including "headline" FD-ID Indexes," <www.bls.gov/ppi/data.htm>, accessed June 2022.

Table 777. Chain-Type Price Indexes for Personal Consumption Expenditures by Type of Expenditure: 1990 to 2020

[2012=100. For explanation of "chain-type," see text, Section 13. See also Table 716]

Type of expenditure	1990	2000	2005	2010	2015	2018	2019	2020
Personal consumption expenditures	**63.2**	**78.1**	**86.9**	**95.7**	**103.1**	**108.3**	**109.9**	**111.2**
Household consumption expenditures [1]	62.5	77.6	86.5	95.7	102.9	108.0	109.5	110.8
Food and beverages purchased for off-premises consumption	61.1	73.9	82.6	93.9	104.1	103.4	104.4	108.0
Food and nonalcoholic beverages purchased for off-premises consumption	60.5	72.8	81.6	93.2	104.4	103.2	104.1	107.9
Alcoholic beverages purchased for off-premises consumption	64.6	81.7	89.3	98.7	102.1	104.7	106.3	108.3
Food produced and consumed on farms	76.5	64.1	75.6	81.7	101.9	92.0	90.0	89.2
Clothing, footwear, and related services	109.2	103.0	95.9	95.0	100.3	99.8	98.7	93.9
Clothing	111.8	105.0	96.6	94.5	99.5	99.0	97.5	92.2
Garments	117.3	108.0	97.7	94.4	99.1	98.3	96.4	90.7
Women's and girls' clothing	122.9	107.5	98.0	94.8	98.5	97.7	94.5	88.3
Men's and boys' clothing	109.9	108.5	97.1	93.6	100.1	98.8	99.2	94.5
Children's and infants' clothing	111.2	109.0	97.5	95.4	100.0	100.5	99.7	93.9
Footwear [2]	96.8	93.6	92.9	97.1	103.8	103.3	103.8	101.2
Housing, utilities, and fuels	54.4	71.8	85.1	96.6	107.7	118.2	121.7	124.7
Housing	55.3	74.0	86.2	96.6	108.4	119.8	123.9	127.5
Rental of tenant-occupied nonfarm housing [3]	53.5	70.8	83.5	95.8	109.9	122.6	127.2	131.1
Imputed rental of owner-occupied nonfarm housing [4]	56.1	75.0	86.9	96.9	108.0	119.0	123.0	126.4
Household utilities and fuels	49.9	61.9	80.5	96.6	103.9	109.6	110.1	110.0
Water supply and sanitation	37.1	56.2	68.9	90.5	112.8	124.9	128.9	133.0
Electricity, gas, and other fuels	54.3	63.9	84.7	98.8	100.8	104.4	103.8	102.3
Electricity	59.8	65.3	76.7	98.2	106.4	108.3	108.5	109.1
Natural gas	58.4	80.1	128.9	113.9	99.2	104.3	102.9	103.0
Fuel oil and other fuels	27.1	35.8	58.7	77.5	69.9	80.8	77.1	59.8
Furnishings, household equipment, & routine household maintenance	97.4	105.3	102.2	100.3	95.4	92.7	93.8	95.3
Furniture, furnishings, and floor coverings [5]	114.3	121.8	112.9	102.5	92.8	87.0	88.2	88.0
Household textiles	179.3	161.9	134.5	106.4	89.4	82.7	80.2	82.2
Household appliances [6]	95.8	93.2	91.4	96.3	90.2	87.1	89.3	92.8
Glassware, tableware, and household utensils [7]	126.5	126.6	113.1	106.3	92.8	83.6	81.7	80.0
Health	48.8	70.9	83.4	96.1	103.8	109.1	110.6	113.0
Medical products, appliances, and equipment	51.9	71.0	83.1	94.5	106.4	114.4	114.5	115.1
Pharmaceutical and other medical products [8]	49.1	68.5	81.5	93.9	107.2	116.2	116.0	116.8
Pharmaceutical products	48.8	68.2	81.3	93.8	107.3	116.4	116.2	117.1
Other medical products	76.4	95.2	96.6	98.5	99.2	99.6	101.6	98.6
Therapeutic appliances and equipment	70.0	88.2	93.4	98.3	100.9	102.8	104.3	103.3
Outpatient services	54.3	77.0	86.4	97.4	101.7	104.7	105.9	107.6
Physician services [9]	57.5	80.8	87.4	97.4	99.6	101.0	101.9	103.1
Dental services	37.5	61.9	77.6	95.5	108.3	116.3	118.9	122.4
Paramedical services	58.3	78.3	88.6	98.3	102.6	106.4	107.8	109.6
Hospital and nursing home services	43.8	65.9	81.1	95.7	104.4	110.5	113.0	116.8
Hospitals [10]	44.2	65.8	81.0	95.5	104.4	110.0	112.3	115.9
Nursing homes	42.5	66.2	81.5	96.3	104.1	113.2	117.4	122.2
Transportation	57.8	70.8	78.9	88.6	90.6	93.6	93.6	90.7
Motor vehicles	80.7	100.7	97.2	96.0	100.7	97.3	97.3	99.1
New motor vehicles	83.8	99.5	95.8	95.6	102.6	102.3	102.7	103.4
Net purchases of used motor vehicles	74.3	103.9	100.6	97.0	96.2	87.5	86.8	90.3
Motor vehicle operation	44.4	54.5	70.4	84.9	83.2	90.2	89.7	84.7
Motor vehicle parts and accessories	73.7	72.3	78.3	94.0	99.8	100.7	102.7	104.6
Motor vehicle fuels, lubricants, and fluids	32.3	41.3	62.3	76.9	68.7	78.0	75.3	64.2
Public transportation	67.5	77.5	76.1	90.4	101.9	103.2	105.6	97.9
Ground transportation [11]	49.7	63.3	77.2	93.7	104.9	110.2	110.6	107.8
Air transportation	75.8	82.9	74.5	88.5	100.5	99.7	103.1	92.9
Water transportation	130.4	145.3	115.3	103.2	100.4	105.3	104.6	100.9
Communication	111.9	111.8	105.2	102.6	88.6	76.7	73.7	71.5
Telecommunication services	106.4	102.9	97.9	101.9	89.7	76.0	72.1	70.6
Internet access	180.7	125.9	125.1	100.7	101.3	99.3	100.8	99.8
Recreation	120.6	116.7	109.4	102.4	97.1	95.0	94.6	93.8
Video and audio equipment, computers, and related services	398.7	216.5	156.1	110.7	89.6	81.9	78.7	75.5
Video and audio equipment	508.7	343.5	241.3	126.1	76.7	56.4	52.1	48.3
Sports and recreational goods and related services	124.4	120.8	110.5	104.1	92.9	85.0	83.3	82.3
Sports and recreational vehicles	78.0	90.4	92.4	96.3	100.3	103.0	105.9	108.2
Other sporting and recreational goods	145.1	133.3	117.0	106.4	90.7	79.7	76.9	75.1
Magazines, newspapers, books, and stationery	65.7	87.8	91.9	98.6	104.7	106.7	110.8	115.7
Education	27.8	49.4	69.3	91.3	110.9	119.3	122.3	124.3
Higher education	24.9	47.2	67.6	90.8	111.8	119.7	123.1	124.8
Net foreign travel and expenditures abroad by U.S. residents:								
Foreign travel by U.S. residents	48.3	59.5	77.5	93.9	98.2	98.7	99.0	96.1
Less: Expenditures in the United States by nonresidents	54.6	71.0	80.7	92.5	102.3	107.4	109.5	108.6

[1] Consists of household purchases of goods and services from business, government, nonprofit institutions, and the rest of the world. [2] Consists of shoes and other footwear, and of repair and hire of footwear. [3] Consists of rent for space (see footnote 4) and rent for appliances, furnishings, and furniture. [4] Consists of rent for space and for heating and plumbing facilities, water heaters, lighting fixtures, kitchen cabinets, linoleum, storm windows and doors, window screens, and screen doors, but excludes rent for appliances and furniture and purchases of fuel and electricity. [5] Includes clocks, lamps, lighting fixtures, and other household decorative items; also includes repair of furniture, furnishings, and floor coverings. [6] Consists of major household appliances, small electric household appliances, and repair of household appliances. [7] Consists of dishes, flatware, and non-electric cookware and tableware. [8] Excludes drug preparations and related products dispensed by physicians, hospitals, and other medical services. [9] Consists of offices of physicians, health maintenance organization medical centers, and freestanding ambulatory surgical and emergency centers. [10] Consists of nonprofit hospitals, proprietary hospitals, and government hospitals. Consists of primary sales of these hospitals for personal consumption. [11] Includes railway transportation, taxicab services, school and employee services, limousine services, and airport bus fares.

Source: U.S. Bureau of Economic Analysis, National Income and Product Accounts Tables, "Table 2.5.4. Price Indexes for Personal Consumption Expenditures by Function," <apps.bea.gov/iTable/index_nipa.cfm>, accessed July 2021.

Table 778. Chain-Type Price Indexes for Gross Domestic Product: 1990 to 2021

[2012=100. For explanation of "chain-type," see text, Section 13]

Component	1990	2000	2005	2010	2015	2017	2018	2019	2020	2021
Gross domestic product.............	**63.6**	**78.0**	**87.5**	**96.2**	**104.7**	**107.7**	**110.3**	**112.3**	**113.7**	**118.5**
Personal consumption expenditures...	**63.2**	**78.1**	**86.9**	**95.7**	**103.1**	**106.1**	**108.3**	**109.9**	**111.2**	**115.5**
Goods........................	81.9	89.1	91.1	95.2	95.9	94.6	95.3	94.8	94.2	98.9
Durable goods.................	131.9	125.7	112.3	102.1	93.4	89.1	87.5	86.5	85.8	91.2
Nondurable goods.............	63.1	74.0	82.0	92.2	97.1	97.5	99.3	99.2	98.6	102.8
Services......................	54.7	72.7	84.8	96.0	106.8	112.0	115.1	117.8	120.3	124.2
Gross private domestic investment.....	**81.3**	**86.8**	**94.8**	**97.7**	**103.5**	**105.2**	**107.2**	**108.9**	**110.2**	**113.8**
Fixed investment................	80.3	86.5	94.6	97.6	104.1	105.9	107.9	109.7	111.1	115.4
Nonresidential.................	92.5	92.7	94.4	97.4	101.9	102.0	102.8	104.1	104.8	106.4
Structures..................	40.9	55.3	75.7	92.0	109.4	112.5	114.4	119.1	120.9	127.7
Equipment.................	135.0	114.2	104.6	99.5	98.7	97.5	97.7	97.8	97.4	97.7
Intellectual property products...........	88.1	97.8	96.0	98.3	101.4	101.1	102.3	103.2	104.6	105.6
Residential.................	56.3	75.0	96.7	98.3	114.1	123.5	130.4	134.1	138.5	153.7
Net exports of goods and services:										
Exports.......................	79.8	79.6	85.3	93.4	95.4	95.9	99.1	98.7	96.2	107.5
Goods........................	85.7	80.0	84.9	93.0	91.3	90.1	93.3	91.8	88.2	100.9
Services......................	65.9	78.5	86.2	94.2	104.4	108.9	112.2	114.1	114.5	121.4
Imports.......................	79.0	76.0	83.6	92.7	90.1	89.0	91.5	90.1	88.1	94.6
Goods........................	82.7	76.4	83.0	92.0	87.6	85.9	88.3	86.4	84.0	90.5
Services......................	63.7	74.4	86.9	95.9	103.0	105.1	108.3	109.3	109.8	115.5
Government consumption expenditures and gross investment...	**52.1**	**68.6**	**82.1**	**95.4**	**104.6**	**107.4**	**111.3**	**113.2**	**114.9**	**120.0**
Federal.......................	57.3	72.9	86.2	96.4	103.1	105.7	108.8	110.8	112.0	116.0
National defense..............	57.2	71.9	86.0	96.1	102.3	104.3	107.2	108.9	110.0	114.1
Nondefense.................	57.1	74.6	86.6	97.0	104.5	107.9	111.3	113.8	115.1	119.1
State and local..............	49.2	66.0	79.6	94.7	105.7	108.5	113.0	114.9	116.7	122.7

Source: U.S. Bureau of Economic Analysis, National Income and Product Accounts Tables, "Table 1.1.4. Price Indexes for Gross Domestic Product," <apps.bea.gov/iTable/index_nipa.cfm>, accessed June 2022.

Table 779. Import and Export Price Indexes by End-Use Category: 1990 to 2022

[As of June. Import indexes are weighted by the 2000 Tariff Schedule of the United States Annotated, a scheme for describing and reporting product composition and value of U.S. imports. Import prices are based on U.S. dollar prices paid by importer. Export indexes are weighted by 2000 export values according to the Schedule B classification system of the U.S. Census Bureau. Prices used in these indexes were collected from a sample of U.S. manufacturers of exports and are factory transaction prices, except as noted. Minus sign (-) indicates decrease]

Year	Index (2000 = 100)						Percent change [1]					
	Imports			Exports			Imports			Exports		
	Total	Petroleum imports	Non–petroleum imports	Total	Agricultural exports	Non–agricultural exports	Total	Petroleum imports	Non–petroleum imports	Total	Agricultural exports	Non–agricultural exports
1990..........	90.8	55.4	96.4	95.1	107.7	93.5	-0.8	-13.4	0.5	-0.1	-4.0	0.5
1991..........	93.4	63.2	98.3	96.1	104.3	95.3	2.9	14.1	2.0	1.1	-3.2	1.9
1992..........	94.8	66.0	99.5	96.5	104.0	95.8	1.5	4.4	1.2	0.4	-0.3	0.5
1993..........	95.0	60.4	100.5	96.9	100.3	96.7	0.2	-8.5	1.0	0.4	-3.6	0.9
1994..........	96.3	57.6	102.6	98.5	109.3	97.5	1.4	-4.6	2.1	1.7	9.0	0.8
1995..........	101.4	62.9	107.6	104.5	117.0	103.3	5.3	9.2	4.9	6.1	7.0	5.9
1996..........	100.7	66.4	106.2	105.4	140.8	101.7	-0.7	5.6	-1.3	0.9	20.3	-1.5
1997..........	98.8	62.5	104.3	103.2	120.5	101.5	-1.9	-5.9	-1.8	-2.1	-14.4	-0.2
1998..........	93.1	44.3	100.5	99.9	110.8	98.8	-5.8	-29.1	-3.6	-3.2	-8.0	-2.7
1999..........	92.9	54.5	98.8	98.2	101.1	97.9	-0.2	23.0	-1.7	-1.7	-8.8	-0.9
2000 [2]........	100.2	101.9	99.9	100.1	100.5	100.0	7.9	87.0	1.1	1.9	-0.6	2.1
2001..........	97.6	89.4	98.9	99.4	100.9	99.3	-2.6	-12.3	-1.0	-0.7	0.4	-0.7
2002..........	94.1	85.3	96.2	98.0	100.7	97.8	-3.6	-4.6	-2.7	-1.4	-0.2	-1.5
2003..........	96.2	96.4	97.3	99.5	110.0	98.7	2.2	13.0	1.1	1.5	9.2	0.9
2004..........	101.7	129.7	99.7	103.4	127.4	101.5	5.7	34.5	2.5	3.9	15.8	2.8
2005..........	109.2	181.5	102.0	106.7	123.9	105.4	7.4	39.9	2.3	3.2	-2.7	3.8
2006..........	117.3	242.6	104.2	111.2	124.1	110.3	7.4	33.7	2.2	4.2	0.2	4.6
2007..........	120.0	245.6	107.1	116.0	146.7	113.8	2.3	1.2	2.8	4.3	18.2	3.2
2008..........	145.5	450.3	114.9	126.1	195.2	121.2	21.3	83.3	7.3	8.7	33.1	6.5
2009..........	120.0	241.5	107.4	117.8	169.7	114.1	-17.5	-46.4	-6.5	-6.6	-13.1	-5.9
2010..........	125.2	267.4	110.7	122.2	165.3	119.1	4.3	10.7	3.1	3.7	-2.6	4.4
2011..........	142.2	397.8	116.4	134.5	217.2	128.6	13.6	48.8	5.1	10.1	31.4	8.0
2012..........	138.7	357.2	116.3	131.7	204.5	126.5	-2.5	-10.2	-0.1	-2.1	-5.8	-1.6
2013..........	138.8	364.9	115.7	132.8	224.2	126.2	0.1	2.2	-0.5	0.8	9.6	-0.2
2014..........	140.5	387.9	115.8	133.0	221.4	126.6	1.2	6.3	0.1	0.2	-1.2	0.3
2015..........	126.6	229.7	112.8	125.3	184.3	120.9	-9.9	-40.8	-2.6	-5.8	-16.8	-4.5
2016..........	120.7	173.1	110.5	120.9	181.9	116.3	-4.7	-24.6	-2.0	-3.5	-1.3	-3.8
2017..........	122.4	178.7	112.0	121.6	174.9	117.5	1.4	3.2	1.4	0.6	-3.8	1.0
2018..........	128.2	255.4	113.5	128.0	184.2	123.7	4.7	42.9	1.3	5.3	5.3	5.3
2019..........	125.6	236.6	112.0	126.0	180.5	121.8	-2.0	-7.4	-1.3	-1.6	-2.0	-1.5
2020..........	120.6	142.6	111.9	120.3	172.4	116.3	-4.0	-39.7	-0.1	-4.5	-4.5	-4.5
2021..........	134.2	267.6	119.6	140.6	230.0	133.9	11.3	87.7	6.9	16.9	33.4	15.1
2022..........	148.5	456.5	126.1	166.2	264.0	158.9	10.7	70.6	5.4	18.2	14.8	18.7

[1] Percent change from immediate prior year. [2] June 2000 may not equal 100 because indexes were reweighted to an "average" trade value in 2000.

Source: U.S. Bureau of Labor Statistics, U.S. Import and Export Price Indexes, "History Tables: Complete Historical Index Information," <www.bls.gov/mxp/>, accessed July 2022.

Table 780. Export Price Indexes—Selected Commodities: 2000 to 2022

[2000=100, except as noted. As of June. Indexes are weighted by 2000 export values according to the Schedule B commodity classification system of the U.S. Census Bureau. Prices used in these indexes were collected from a sample of U.S. manufacturers of exports and are factory transaction prices; see source]

Commodity	2000 [1]	2005	2010	2015	2019	2020	2021	2022
All commodities	**100.1**	**106.7**	**122.2**	**125.3**	**126.0**	**120.3**	**140.6**	**166.2**
Live animals and animal products	102.2	130.9	172.2	193.5	217.8	208.9	258.9	290.9
Vegetable products	100.0	130.3	177.5	206.1	199.1	184.6	269.2	318.7
Fruit and nuts	94.8	126.5	131.0	175.1	139.9	122.9	140.6	146.7
Cereals	100.0	118.1	171.4	194.4	205.7	182.4	296.2	371.9
Wheat and meslin	99.4	130.0	151.6	198.3	197.0	196.6	250.7	391.4
Corn (maize)	101.0	111.8	174.3	181.1	204.7	164.3	326.0	352.3
Oilseeds	102.8	136.2	196.2	204.7	186.9	185.0	304.3	345.3
Prepared foodstuffs, beverages, and tobacco	100.0	110.3	139.3	153.2	153.5	151.2	174.5	182.5
Mineral products	97.8	182.3	247.9	211.3	217.0	147.5	251.6	458.5
Fuels	97.4	172.8	239.2	205.0	208.5	139.1	240.8	445.5
Petroleum oils	97.4	184.8	231.5	228.8	217.2	142.7	245.4	477.2
Chemicals and related products	100.3	115.3	144.5	143.9	138.6	134.2	153.1	166.5
Plastics and rubber products	101.5	118.4	136.8	143.0	143.9	136.1	176.3	177.0
Woodpulp and paper products	101.6	101.9	117.6	123.7	124.5	122.8	142.0	154.3
Textiles	100.2	100.8	115.7	122.2	121.4	116.6	128.4	152.7
Stone and glass products	100.7	103.5	115.9	122.4	127.5	126.3	133.4	147.2
Gems and precious metals	98.1	106.5	211.0	233.8	245.3	276.3	334.0	329.7
Base metals	100.5	131.8	160.4	153.1	158.5	151.1	196.9	219.3
Iron and steel (Dec. 2020=100)	(NA)	(NA)	(NA)	(NA)	(NA)	(NA)	143.5	173.4
Copper	98.7	143.1	217.0	191.3	178.6	165.7	284.8	291.9
Aluminum	98.4	113.2	117.8	115.5	104.1	91.1	137.7	154.5
Machinery	99.9	94.9	95.5	97.1	98.0	98.0	99.3	103.8
Nonelectrical machinery	100.0	100.5	106.8	113.5	116.3	115.7	118.4	124.4
Computer equipment	99.9	76.6	53.1	43.8	35.5	33.5	33.0	34.0
Electrical machinery	99.8	88.6	83.2	79.3	78.3	79.0	78.9	81.9
Transportation equipment	100.0	108.8	121.4	130.8	137.2	137.6	140.1	146.4
Motor vehicles and their parts	100.0	103.2	108.5	115.0	116.7	116.1	118.2	123.1
Instruments	100.0	101.3	106.2	107.8	110.0	110.3	111.3	113.8
Miscellaneous manufactured articles	100.4	100.6	108.1	111.3	112.9	114.1	118.3	129.1

NA Not available. [1] June 2000 may not equal 100 because indexes were reweighted to an "average" trade value in 2000.

Source: U.S. Bureau of Labor Statistics, U.S. Import and Export Price Indexes, "History Tables: Complete Historical Index Information," <www.bls.gov/mxp/>, accessed July 2022.

Table 781. Import Price Indexes—Selected Commodities: 2000 to 2022

[2000=100, unless otherwise noted. As of June. Indexes are weighted by the 2000 Tariff Schedule of the United States Annotated, a scheme for describing and reporting product composition and value of U.S. imports. Import prices are based on U.S. dollar prices paid by importer]

Commodity	2000 [1]	2005	2010	2015	2019	2020	2021	2022
All commodities	**100.2**	**109.2**	**125.2**	**126.6**	**125.6**	**120.6**	**134.2**	**148.5**
Live animals and animal products	99.9	112.7	143.0	185.2	195.7	193.0	229.0	237.9
Meat	100.5	138.7	183.2	234.5	265.8	293.2	368.2	341.2
Fish	100.2	88.3	107.1	127.3	139.6	128.8	153.9	165.6
Vegetable products	97.1	116.9	169.5	201.8	215.1	213.5	216.7	251.0
Vegetables	93.9	136.8	326.2	459.9	506.8	482.7	383.2	418.6
Fruit and nuts	96.9	89.7	106.8	95.5	124.5	114.2	114.1	127.6
Prepared foodstuffs, beverages and tobacco	100.0	114.0	141.2	160.7	165.3	168.0	174.8	187.1
Mineral products	101.3	178.1	248.5	210.9	215.4	138.0	250.9	440.2
Fuels	101.3	177.5	244.9	208.1	212.7	133.3	246.5	435.7
Chemicals and related products	99.8	111.3	139.3	148.3	156.1	153.6	166.4	180.4
Organic chemicals	100.6	109.6	133.8	123.7	127.5	120.1	140.3	155.2
Pharmaceutical products	99.8	111.0	117.9	136.7	152.3	154.4	152.5	148.7
Plastics and rubber products	99.9	113.5	136.7	142.1	140.9	138.2	153.1	162.4
Hides, skins, and leather products	100.2	104.0	114.5	128.1	124.6	(NA)	(NA)	(NA)
Wood products	100.5	124.2	134.3	138.6	143.5	152.3	376.7	266.4
Woodpulp and paper products	100.0	102.3	112.5	111.9	120.2	113.0	119.6	130.1
Textiles	99.7	100.4	103.1	114.5	114.2	114.4	115.7	120.4
Footwear	99.6	100.3	106.1	122.3	121.3	122.7	123.2	123.0
Stone and glass products	99.5	105.4	123.8	132.8	132.1	131.9	132.0	134.5
Gems and precious metals	99.3	98.3	161.5	170.8	177.6	200.0	248.8	235.2
Gold	98.3	150.7	430.5	424.4	476.6	613.4	677.0	660.9
Platinum (Dec. 2019=100)	(NA)	(NA)	(NA)	(NA)	(NA)	110.0	210.2	145.1
Base metals	101.5	132.1	180.2	168.1	174.3	164.3	213.2	253.7
Iron and steel	104.1	170.6	238.8	181.6	216.9	188.0	282.5	347.6
Articles of iron and steel	100.6	122.7	149.9	148.2	149.8	146.0	170.8	206.7
Copper	97.2	142.7	313.8	299.8	271.5	266.8	432.1	417.5
Aluminum	97.9	113.2	132.8	131.5	130.6	120.3	174.6	210.6
Machinery	100.2	89.7	86.5	82.5	79.3	79.1	80.1	82.8
Nonelectrical machinery	99.8	90.1	87.9	87.7	85.5	84.9	86.3	89.1
Electrical machinery	100.5	89.4	85.2	77.6	73.5	73.5	74.2	76.9
Transportation equipment	100.0	104.4	109.7	114.6	113.5	114.5	116.2	118.8
Motor vehicles and their parts	100.1	103.8	108.8	113.2	112.6	113.7	115.4	118.0
Instruments	99.8	100.1	100.8	103.7	101.6	102.0	102.5	105.5
Miscellaneous manufactured articles	99.7	99.4	106.5	112.8	112.2	110.9	112.6	117.6
Furniture	99.5	103.4	109.4	117.3	118.3	116.6	119.4	125.6

NA Not available. [1] June 2000 may not equal 100 because indexes were reweighted to an "average" trade value in 2000.

Source: U.S. Bureau of Labor Statistics, U.S. Import and Export Price Indexes, "History Tables: Complete Historical Index Information," <www.bls.gov/mxp/>, accessed July 2022.

Section 15
Business Enterprise

This section relates to the place and behavior of the business firm and to business initiative in the American economy. It includes data on the number, type, and size of businesses; financial data of domestic and multinational U.S. corporations; business investments, expenditures, and profits; and sales and inventories.

The principal sources of these data are the *Survey of Current Business*, published online by the Bureau of Economic Analysis (BEA); the web site of the Board of Governors of the Federal Reserve System at <federalreserve.gov/data.htm>; the annual *Statistics of Income (SOI)* reports of the Internal Revenue Service (IRS); and the U.S. Census Bureau's Economic Census, *County Business Patterns, Quarterly Financial Report for Manufacturing, Mining, Trade, and Selected Service Industries (QFR), the Annual Capital Expenditures Survey*, and beginning in 2019, the *Annual Business Survey*. See also BEA Interactive Tables <apps.bea.gov/itable/index.cfm>.

Business firms—A firm is generally defined as a business organization or entity consisting of one or more domestic establishment locations under common ownership or control. The terms firm, business, company, and enterprise are used interchangeably throughout this section. A firm doing business in more than one industry is classified by industry according to the major activity of the firm as a whole.

The IRS concept of a business firm relates primarily to the legal entity used for tax reporting purposes. A sole proprietorship is an unincorporated business owned by one person and may include large enterprises with many employees and hired managers and part-time operators. A partnership is an unincorporated business owned by two or more persons, each of whom has a financial interest in the business. A corporation is a business that is legally incorporated under state laws. While many corporations file consolidated tax returns, most corporate tax returns represent individual corporations, some of which are affiliated through common ownership or control with other corporations filing separate returns.

Economic Census—The Economic Census is the major source of facts about the structure and functioning of the nation's economy. It provides essential information for government, business, industry, and the general public. It establishes benchmarks for economic indicators such as the gross domestic product estimates, production and price indexes, business sales, and other statistical series that measure short-term changes in economic conditions. The Census Bureau takes the Economic Census every 5 years, covering years ending in "2" and "7."

The Economic Census is collected on an establishment basis. A company operating at more than one location is required to file a separate report for each store, factory, shop, or other location. Companies engaged in distinctly different lines of activity at one location are requested to submit separate reports, if the business records permit such a separation, and if the activities are substantial in size. Each establishment is assigned a separate industry classification based on

its primary activity and not that of its parent company. Establishments responding to the establishment survey are classified into industries on the basis of their principal product or activity (determined by self-reporting, annual sales volume, or products manufactured by a plant). The statistics issued by industry in the Economic Census are classified primarily on the North American Industry Classification System (NAICS).

Data from the Economic Census is released via the Census Bureau's dissemination platform at <data.census.gov>. The American FactFinder® service was discontinued in 2020. More detailed information about the scope, coverage, methodology, classification system, data items, and publications for the Economic Censuses and related surveys is available at <www.census.gov/programs-surveys/economic-census.html>.

Annual Business Survey—The Annual Business Survey replaces the five-year Survey of Business Owners (SBO) for employer businesses, the Annual Survey of Entrepreneurs (ASE), the Business R&D and Innovation for Microbusinesses survey (BRDI-M), and the innovation section of the Business R&D and Innovation Survey (BRDI-S). It is collected on an company or firm basis, not an establishment basis, and provides information on selected economic and demographic characteristics for businesses and business owners by sex, ethnicity, race, and veteran status. Data are published in a series of releases: *Characteristics of Businesses, Characteristics of Business Owners, Company Summary*, and a variable module designed to capture information on relevant business components.

North American Industry Classification System (NAICS)—NAICS is the standard used by federal statistical agencies in classifying business establishments for the purpose of collecting, analyzing, and publishing statistical data related to the U.S. business economy. NAICS was developed under the auspices of the Office of Management and Budget (OMB), and adopted in 1997 to replace the Standard Industrial Classification (SIC) system. The official *2017 NAICS Manual* includes definitions for each industry, background information, tables showing changes between the 2012 and 2017 revisions, and a comprehensive index. Noticeable changes were made to six of the twenty NAICS sectors during the 2012 revision of NAICS. Those sectors are 22 (utilities), 23 (construction), 31-33 (manufacturing), 42 (wholesale trade), 44-45 (retail trade) and 72 (accommodation and food services). The 2017 revision impacted 28 of the 2012 NAICS 6-digit industries. Noticeable changes were made to seven of the 20 NAICS sectors during the 2022 revision of NAICS. Those sectors were 21 (mining), 31-33 (manufacturing), 42 (wholesale trade), 44-45 (retail trade), 51 (information), 52 (finance and insurance), and 81 (other services). For more information, see <www.census.gov/naics/>.

Quarterly Financial Report—The Quarterly Financial Report (QFR) program publishes quarterly aggregate statistics on the financial conditions of U.S. corporations. The QFR requests companies to report estimates from their statements of income and retained earnings, and balance sheets. The statistical data are classified and aggregated by type of industry and asset size. The QFR sample includes corporations that have a plurality of business activity in manufacturing industries with domestic assets of $250,000 and above, and mining, wholesale, retail, and selected service industries with assets of $50 million and above. The data are available in the *Quarterly Financial Report for Manufacturing, Mining, Trade, and Selected Service Industries* at <www.census.gov/econ/qfr/>.

Multinational enterprises—BEA collects financial and operating data on U.S. multinational enterprises. These data provide a picture of the overall activities of foreign affiliates and U.S. parent enterprises, using a variety of indicators of their financial structure and operations. The data on foreign affiliates cover the entire operations of the affiliate, irrespective of the percentage of U.S. ownership. These data cover items such as sales, value added, employment and compensation of employees, capital expenditures, exports and imports, and research and development expenditures. Separate tabulations are available for all affiliates and for affiliates that are majority-owned by their U.S. parent(s). More information is available at <www.bea.gov/data/economic-accounts/international#omc>.

Statistical reliability—For a discussion of statistical collection, estimation, and sampling procedures and measures of reliability applicable to data from the Census Bureau and the Internal Revenue Service, see Appendix III.

Table 782. Number of Tax Returns, Receipts, and Net Income by Type of Business: 1990 to 2019

[14,783 represents 14,783,000. Covers active enterprises only. Nonfarm sole proprietorship and partnership data are for tax year shown, which covers returns processed by the IRS during the following calendar year. Corporation data are for tax year shown, which covers (a) corporate returns with accounting periods for the calendar year ending December of year shown and (b) those returns with accounting periods for the noncalendar year ending between July of year shown and June of the following year. Figures are estimates based on sample of unaudited tax returns; see Appendix III]

Year	Number of returns (1,000)			Business receipts [2] (bil. dol.)			Net income (less loss) [3] (bil. dol.)		
	Nonfarm proprietor- ships [1]	Partner- ships	Corpora- tions	Nonfarm proprietor- ships [1]	Partner- ships	Corpora- tions	Nonfarm proprietor- ships [1]	Partner- ships	Corpora- tions
1990	14,783	1,554	3,717	731	483	9,860	141	17	383
1991	15,181	1,515	3,803	713	483	9,966	142	21	361
1992	15,495	1,485	3,869	737	515	10,360	154	43	414
1993	15,848	1,468	3,965	757	561	10,866	156	67	510
1994	16,154	1,494	4,342	791	656	11,884	167	82	595
1995	16,424	1,581	4,474	807	761	12,786	169	107	736
1996	16,955	1,654	4,631	843	916	13,659	177	145	839
1997	17,176	1,759	4,710	870	1,142	14,461	187	168	957
1998	17,409	1,855	4,849	918	1,357	15,010	202	187	895
1999	17,576	1,937	4,936	969	1,616	16,314	208	228	985
2000	17,903	2,058	5,045	1,021	2,062	17,637	215	269	987
2001	18,338	2,132	5,136	1,017	2,278	17,504	217	276	649
2002	18,926	2,242	5,267	1,030	2,414	17,297	221	271	597
2003	19,710	2,375	5,401	1,050	2,546	18,264	230	301	822
2004	20,591	2,547	5,558	1,140	2,819	19,976	248	385	1,170
2005	21,468	2,764	5,671	1,223	3,280	21,800	270	546	2,027
2006	22,075	2,947	5,841	1,278	3,571	23,310	278	667	2,024
2007	23,123	3,096	5,869	1,324	3,847	24,217	281	683	1,950
2008	22,614	3,146	5,847	1,317	4,344	24,718	265	458	1,061
2009	22,660	3,169	5,825	1,178	3,562	21,585	245	410	971
2010	23,004	3,248	5,814	1,196	3,946	23,058	268	594	1,422
2011	23,427	3,285	5,823	1,266	4,455	25,198	283	581	1,406
2012	23,554	3,389	5,841	1,302	4,690	26,029	305	778	1,872
2013	24,075	3,461	5,888	1,342	5,069	26,850	302	769	1,994
2014	24,632	3,611	6,001	1,394	5,186	28,075	317	837	2,145
2015	25,226	3,715	6,120	1,444	4,877	27,492	332	781	2,034
2016	25,526	3,763	6,189	1,422	4,919	27,575	328	792	1,913
2017	26,426	3,905	6,325	1,531	5,460	29,180	346	810	1,656
2018	27,117	4,010	6,442	1,590	5,904	30,837	349	885	3,391
2019	27,817	3,821	6,474	1,640	5,397	31,367	355	761	2,869

[1] Number of returns represents returns with nonfarm business net income or deficit. [2] Excludes investment income for S corporations; for definition, see footnote 1, Table 790. [3] Net income (less loss) is defined differently by form of organization, basically as follows: (a) Proprietorships: Total taxable receipts less total business deductions, including cost of sales and operations, depletion, and certain capital expensing, excluding charitable contributions and owners' salaries; (b) Partnerships: Total taxable receipts (including investment income except capital gains) less deductions, including cost of sales and operations and certain payments to partners, excluding charitable contributions, oil and gas depletion, and certain capital expensing; and (c) Corporations: Includes "Total net income (less deficit)" from S Corporations; net income is before income tax.

Source: U.S. Internal Revenue Service, "Tax Statistics," <www.irs.gov/statistics>, accessed July 2022.

Table 783. Number of Business Tax Returns by Size of Receipts: 2000 to 2019

[In thousands (5,045 represents 5,045,000). Covers active enterprises only. Figures are estimates based on a sample of unaudited tax returns; see Appendix III]

Size-class of receipts	2000	2005	2010	2013	2014	2015	2016	2017	2018	2019
Corporations, total	**5,045**	**5,671**	**5,814**	**5,888**	**6,001**	**6,120**	**6,189**	**6,325**	**6,442**	**6,474**
Under $25,000 [1]	1,220	1,300	1,484	1,419	1,419	1,442	1,437	1,499	1,508	1,497
$25,000 to $100,000	783	884	977	922	953	974	969	968	992	996
$25,000 to $49,999	305	340	385	(NA)	(NA)	(NA)	(NA)	(NA)	(NA)	(NA)
$50,000 to $99,999	477	544	592	(NA)	(NA)	(NA)	(NA)	(NA)	(NA)	(NA)
$100,000 to $499,999	1,515	1,755	1,731	1,800	1,810	1,821	1,856	1,894	1,930	1,943
$500,000 to $999,999	582	644	618	644	670	707	719	713	730	748
$1,000,000 or more	946	1,088	1,005	1,103	1,151	1,176	1,207	1,251	1,282	1,290
Partnerships, total	**2,058**	**2,764**	**3,249**	**3,461**	**3,611**	**3,715**	**3,763**	**3,905**	**4,010**	**3,822**
Under $25,000 [1]	1,105	1,465	1,788	1,845	1,951	2,031	1,993	2,055	2,166	2,020
$25,000 to $49,999	183	218	238	297	267	275	345	347	306	302
$50,000 to $99,999	187	233	289	274	316	293	278	297	312	298
$100,000 to $499,999	353	489	531	580	590	621	645	670	661	645
$500,000 to $999,999	92	131	151	171	175	171	171	184	198	196
$1,000,000 or more	137	227	252	294	312	325	331	353	368	360
Nonfarm proprietorships, total	**17,903**	**21,468**	**23,004**	**24,075**	**24,632**	**25,226**	**25,526**	**26,426**	**27,117**	**27,817**
Under $25,000 [1]	11,997	14,456	16,258	16,843	17,181	17,528	17,718	18,066	18,372	18,764
$25,000 to $49,999	2,247	2,587	2,652	2,816	2,886	2,991	3,080	3,306	3,515	3,572
$50,000 to $99,999	1,645	1,981	1,892	1,969	2,034	2,107	2,215	2,333	2,424	2,562
$100,000 to $499,999	1,733	2,091	1,869	2,067	2,130	2,181	2,087	2,273	2,355	2,452
$500,000 to $999,999	190	235	219	239	251	265	271	279	278	289
$1,000,000 or more	92	117	114	140	150	154	155	170	172	178

NA Not available. [1] Includes firms with no receipts.

Source: U.S. Internal Revenue Service, Tax Statistics, "Corporation Complete Report, Table 3.1," <www.irs.gov/statistics/soi-tax-stats-corporation-tax-statistics>; "Partnerships, Historical and Projected Data, Historical Table 12," <www.irs.gov/statistics/soi-tax-stats-partnership-statistics>; and "SOI Tax Stats - Nonfarm Sole Proprietorship Statistics," <www.irs.gov/statistics/soi-tax-stats-nonfarm-sole-proprietorship-statistics>; accessed September 2022.

Table 784. Nonfarm Sole Proprietorships—Selected Income and Deduction Items: 2000 to 2018

[In billions of dollars (1,021 represents $1,021,000,000,000), except as indicated. Data are for tax year shown, which covers returns processed by the IRS during the following calendar year. All figures are estimates based on samples. Tax law changes have affected the comparability of the data over time; see Statistics of Income reports for a description]

Item	2000	2005	2010	2013	2014	2015	2016	2017	2018
Number of returns (1,000)	17,905	21,468	23,004	24,075	24,632	25,226	25,526	26,426	27,117
Returns with net income (1,000)	13,308	15,750	17,007	17,972	18,294	18,785	18,959	19,434	19,635
Business receipts	1,021	1,223	1,196	1,342	1,394	1,444	1,422	1,531	1,590
Income from sales and operations	1,008	1,205	1,176	1,323	1,375	1,423	1,404	1,511	1,570
Business deductions [1]	806	953	929	1,040	1,078	1,113	1,095	1,187	1,242
Cost of sales and operations [1]	387	397	367	406	417	432	411	432	442
Labor costs	29	32	27	33	33	37	36	42	41
Purchases	269	253	240	260	256	265	239	255	254
Materials and supplies	43	56	45	52	57	61	64	65	70
Advertising	10	14	13	15	15	16	16	17	18
Car and truck expenses	46	71	73	89	92	90	89	97	106
Commissions	12	15	12	14	14	17	16	19	19
Contract labor	(NA)	28	34	48	54	54	57	65	69
Depreciation	32	39	35	35	37	38	38	42	51
Insurance	14	19	16	18	19	20	20	21	22
Interest paid [2]	12	12	11	9	9	9	9	10	11
Legal and professional services	7	10	10	12	12	13	13	15	15
Office expenses	10	13	12	12	13	13	13	15	15
Rent paid [3]	33	39	42	45	47	48	48	51	54
Repairs	12	15	15	18	18	19	18	21	22
Salaries and wages (net)	63	75	74	83	87	89	91	97	98
Supplies	22	29	30	35	37	38	39	44	47
Taxes paid	14	17	18	19	19	20	20	21	21
Travel	8	11	12	14	15	17	17	18	19
Utilities	19	23	24	31	32	31	32	33	34
Net income (less loss) [4]	215	270	268	302	317	332	328	346	349
Net income [4]	245	315	323	357	375	392	389	416	430
Constant (2012) Dollars [5]									
Business receipts	1,308	1,399	1,244	1,318	1,345	1,380	1,345	1,422	1,441
Business deductions	1,033	1,091	967	1,022	1,041	1,064	1,036	1,102	1,126
Net income (less loss)	275	309	279	297	306	317	310	322	316
Net income	314	360	336	351	361	375	368	386	390

NA Not available. [1] Includes other amounts not shown separately. [2] Interest paid includes "mortgage interest" and "other interest paid on business indebtedness." [3] Rent paid includes "Rent on machinery and equipment" and "Rent on other business property." [4] After adjustment for the passive loss carryover from prior years. Therefore, "business receipts" minus "total deductions" do not equal "net income." [5] Based on the overall implicit price deflator for gross domestic product.

Source: U.S. Internal Revenue Service, "SOI Tax Stats - Nonfarm Sole Proprietorship Statistics," <www.irs.gov/uac/SOI-Tax-Stats-Nonfarm-Sole-Proprietorship-Statistics>, accessed July 2021.

Table 785. Partnerships—Selected Income and Balance Sheet Items: 2000 to 2019

[In billions of dollars (6,694 represents $6,694,000,000,000), except as indicated. Covers active partnerships only. Data are for tax year shown, which covers returns processed by the IRS during the following calendar year. All figures are estimates based on samples]

Item	2000	2005	2010	2014	2015	2016	2017	2018	2019
Number of returns (1,000)	2,058	2,764	3,248	3,611	3,715	3,763	3,905	4,010	3,821
Returns with net income (1,000)	1,261	1,580	1,635	2,019	2,152	2,196	2,200	2,205	2,111
Number of partners (1,000)	13,660	16,212	22,428	27,714	27,093	28,164	27,501	27,448	25,269
Assets [1,2]	6,694	13,734	19,820	26,129	27,366	28,950	32,404	34,348	36,048
Depreciable assets (net)	1,487	2,176	3,263	4,093	4,423	4,751	5,185	5,380	5,315
Inventories, end of year	150	315	277	331	343	367	378	364	391
Land	359	607	913	1,069	1,143	1,200	1,307	1,359	1,339
Liabilities [1,2]	3,696	7,483	8,994	10,625	11,019	12,022	13,125	14,346	14,942
Accounts payable	230	400	492	537	529	583	618	621	566
Short-term debt [3]	252	373	481	328	351	407	433	452	450
Long-term debt [4]	1,132	1,772	2,693	2,993	3,222	3,477	3,844	4,064	4,136
Nonrecourse loans	639	914	1,225	1,254	1,270	1,318	1,378	1,462	1,489
Partners' capital accounts [2]	2,999	6,251	10,826	15,504	16,347	16,928	19,279	20,002	21,107
Total receipts [1]	2,405	3,863	4,721	6,100	5,798	5,886	(NA)	(NA)	(NA)
Business receipts	2,062	3,280	3,946	5,186	4,877	4,919	5,460	5,904	5,397
Deductions from a trade or business [1]	2,136	3,317	4,128	5,263	5,018	5,094	(NA)	(NA)	(NA)
Cost of goods sold/operations	1,226	1,976	2,336	3,066	2,696	2,660	3,012	3,343	2,878
Salaries and wages	201	293	405	541	578	607	657	700	712
Taxes paid	31	47	63	83	87	89	95	99	92
Interest paid	93	103	86	83	85	97	111	107	114
Depreciation [5]	116	140	247	304	325	352	227	261	276
Net income (less loss)	269	546	594	837	781	792	810	885	761
Net income	410	724	904	1,156	1,137	1,173	1,278	1,382	1,342

NA Not available. [1] Includes items not shown separately. [2] Assets, liabilities, and partners' capital accounts are understated because not all partnerships file complete balance sheets. [3] Mortgages, notes, and bonds payable in less than 1 year. [4] Mortgages, notes, and bonds payable in 1 year or more. [5] Represents the more complete amounts reported in depreciation computation schedules, rather than the amounts reported as the depreciation deduction.

Source: U.S. Internal Revenue Service, "SOI Tax Stats - Partnership Statistics," <www.irs.gov/uac/SOI-Tax-Stats-Partnership-Statistics>, accessed February 2022.

Table 786. Partnerships—Selected Items by Industry: 2019

[In billions of dollars (36,048 represents $36,048,000,000,000), except as indicated. Covers active partnerships only. Data are for tax year shown, which covers returns processed by the IRS during 2020. Figures are estimates based on samples. Based on the North American Industry Classification System (NAICS), 2012; see text, this section. Minus sign (-) indicates net loss]

Industry	NAICS code	Partnerships (1,000) Total	With net income	With net loss	Total assets [1]	Business receipts	Total deductions	Net income (less loss)	Net income	Net loss
Total [2]	(X)	**3,821**	**2,111**	**1,710**	**36,048**	**5,397**	**5,611**	**761**	**1,342**	**581**
Agriculture, forestry, fishing, and hunting	11	136	61	75	249	37	51	-1	12	13
Mining	21	38	23	15	817	183	176	44	62	19
Utilities	22	8	4	4	537	211	234	-19	11	30
Construction	23	138	87	51	260	393	382	17	27	9
Manufacturing	31–33	67	27	40	728	676	680	16	51	35
Wholesale trade	42	71	30	41	372	709	710	8	24	16
Retail trade	44–45	161	77	84	262	581	589	10	20	10
Transportation and warehousing	48–49	64	38	25	683	246	266	-3	24	27
Information	51	42	21	21	1,120	370	361	34	65	31
Finance and insurance	52	344	218	126	20,670	254	417	440	533	93
Real estate and rental and leasing	53	1,939	1,094	845	7,864	219	269	42	240	198
Professional, scientific, and technical services	54	255	145	110	465	596	509	115	136	21
Management of companies and enterprises	55	35	16	19	1,038	37	63	20	42	22
Administrative and support & waste management and remediation services	56	89	45	44	137	135	143	7	13	6
Educational and other services [3]	61/81	136	69	66	61	60	60	2	6	5
Health care and social assistance	62	90	55	35	261	334	320	36	49	12
Arts, entertainment, and recreation	71	53	27	25	168	89	103	-2	10	12
Accommodation and food services	72	157	73	85	358	266	279	-6	18	23

X Not applicable. [1] Total assets are understated because not all partnerships file complete balance sheets. [2] Includes businesses not allocable to individual industries. [3] The educational and other services sectors were combined due to disclosure concerns.

Source: U.S. Internal Revenue Service, "SOI Tax Stats - Partnership Statistics," <www.irs.gov/uac/SOI-Tax-Stats-Partnership-Statistics-by-Sector-or-Industry>, accessed February 2022.

Table 787. Nonfinancial Noncorporate Business Sector Balance Sheet: 2000 to 2021

[In billions of dollars (7,798 represents $7,798,000,000,000), except as noted. Represents year-end (4th quarter) outstandings]

Item	2000	2005	2010	2015	2017	2018	2019	2020	2021
Assets	**7,798**	**11,828**	**12,147**	**16,320**	**18,722**	**19,605**	**20,749**	**22,305**	**24,944**
Nonfinancial assets	6,326	9,597	8,940	11,779	13,185	13,759	14,569	15,577	17,930
Real estate [1]	5,580	8,663	7,822	10,485	11,835	12,357	13,130	14,106	16,293
Residential	3,265	5,283	4,436	5,729	6,550	6,977	7,403	8,068	9,681
Nonresidential	2,316	3,380	3,385	4,756	5,284	5,380	5,727	6,038	6,611
Equipment [2]	447	562	682	800	829	864	886	910	1,048
Residential [3]	35	42	43	48	50	56	57	66	75
Nonresidential	412	521	639	752	778	807	829	844	972
Intellectual property products [2]	114	154	192	233	261	277	295	317	319
Inventories [2]	185	218	244	261	260	261	258	245	270
Financial assets	1,473	2,231	3,207	4,541	5,538	5,846	6,180	6,728	7,015
Checkable deposits and currency	181	224	182	254	306	317	338	437	527
Time and savings deposits	248	474	706	861	1,000	1,048	1,107	1,229	1,348
Money market fund shares	49	69	77	88	100	105	110	119	122
Debt securities	43	61	54	66	75	76	80	87	85
U.S. government securities	40	56	48	62	69	70	74	80	78
Municipal securities	2	4	6	4	6	6	6	6	7
Loans	23	36	42	42	48	49	52	56	60
Mortgages	23	36	42	42	48	49	52	56	60
Consumer credit	–	–	–	–	–	–	–	–	–
Trade receivables	342	431	533	671	803	853	900	947	994
Miscellaneous assets	587	936	1,613	2,559	3,206	3,398	3,593	3,852	3,879
Insurance receivables	77	99	132	119	120	119	129	136	153
Equity in Farm Credit System	3	4	7	9	12	12	13	13	14
Paycheck Protection Program receivables	(X)	(X)	(X)	(X)	(X)	(X)	(X)	118	3
Other	506	832	1,475	2,430	3,073	3,267	3,452	3,586	3,709
Liabilities	**2,820**	**4,207**	**5,702**	**6,724**	**7,970**	**8,384**	**8,787**	**9,383**	**9,772**
Loans	1,939	2,927	3,987	4,720	5,571	5,864	6,137	6,653	6,891
Depository institution loans n.e.c. [4]	402	671	928	1,139	1,387	1,465	1,481	1,655	1,569
Other loans and advances	155	164	206	233	239	248	256	352	410
Mortgages	1,381	2,093	2,853	3,348	3,945	4,151	4,399	4,646	4,911
Trade payables	267	335	426	520	593	599	642	615	675
Taxes payable	65	87	99	123	137	156	164	177	182
Foreign direct investment, intercompany debt	1	1	1	2	2	7	7	7	6
Miscellaneous liabilities	549	858	1,189	1,360	1,666	1,759	1,838	1,931	2,019
Net worth	**4,978**	**7,621**	**6,446**	**9,595**	**10,752**	**11,220**	**11,962**	**12,922**	**15,172**
Debt as percent of net worth	38.9	38.4	61.9	49.2	51.8	52.3	51.3	51.5	45.4

– Represents zero. X Not applicable. [1] At market value. [2] At replacement (current) cost. [3] Durable goods in rental properties. [4] Not elsewhere classified.

Source: Board of Governors of the Federal Reserve System, "Z.1, Financial Accounts of the United States," March 2022, <www.federalreserve.gov/releases/z1>, accessed March 2022.

Table 788. Nonfinancial Corporate Business Sector Balance Sheet: 2000 to 2021

[In billions of dollars (20,568 represents $20,568,000,000,000), except percent. Represents year-end outstandings]

Item	2000	2005	2010	2015	2017	2018	2019	2020	2021
Assets	**20,568**	**26,249**	**27,007**	**36,205**	**40,408**	**42,295**	**47,240**	**50,214**	**55,017**
Nonfinancial assets	10,776	14,296	14,851	20,227	22,418	23,183	24,758	25,898	28,635
Real estate [1]	5,463	8,054	7,414	11,205	12,674	12,911	14,070	14,863	16,682
Equipment [2]	2,889	3,258	3,835	4,595	4,841	5,074	5,255	5,356	5,634
Intellectual property products [2]	1,085	1,365	1,742	2,173	2,456	2,626	2,790	3,013	3,220
Inventories [2]	1,340	1,619	1,860	2,254	2,447	2,571	2,643	2,666	3,099
Financial assets [3]	9,792	11,953	12,155	15,979	17,989	19,113	22,482	24,316	26,381
Checkable deposits and currency	224	327	470	814	952	1,190	1,340	2,005	2,014
Money market fund shares	214	359	555	576	499	466	558	678	694
Debt securities	123	213	211	212	236	253	327	381	394
Corporate equities	1,718	1,059	917	1,500	1,949	1,790	2,318	2,543	3,077
Mutual fund shares	118	134	186	248	301	270	326	376	434
Trade receivables	1,939	2,108	2,203	2,754	3,116	3,513	4,053	4,088	4,767
U.S. direct investment abroad [4]	2,382	3,064	3,855	5,181	6,719	5,412	6,365	6,885	8,000
Liabilities [3]	**9,611**	**11,145**	**13,162**	**17,794**	**19,143**	**20,372**	**22,974**	**24,336**	**25,573**
Debt securities	2,700	2,993	3,971	5,554	6,175	6,327	6,597	7,213	7,390
Commercial paper	278	90	83	179	207	196	195	132	138
Municipal securities [5]	154	243	503	539	574	571	586	590	600
Corporate bonds [4]	2,268	2,660	3,385	4,837	5,394	5,559	5,816	6,491	6,652
Loans	1,958	2,261	2,102	2,657	2,801	3,339	3,550	3,862	4,260
Depository institution loans n.e.c. [6]	901	591	482	957	900	1,003	1,034	1,112	1,067
Other loans and advances	701	904	946	1,131	1,365	1,710	1,838	2,026	2,334
Mortgages	356	766	673	568	536	626	679	724	859
Trade payables	1,541	1,699	1,739	2,104	2,370	2,690	2,920	3,055	3,599
Taxes payable	78	86	78	74	277	267	260	274	204
Foreign direct investment in U.S.	281	276	406	508	472	408	411	367	330
Net worth (market value)	**10,957**	**15,103**	**13,844**	**18,411**	**21,265**	**21,923**	**24,265**	**25,878**	**29,443**
Debt as percent of net worth	42.5	34.8	43.9	44.6	42.2	44.1	41.8	42.8	39.6

[1] At market value. [2] At replacement (current) cost. [3] Includes items not shown separately. [4] Through 1992, corporate bonds include net issues by Netherlands Antillean financial subsidiaries, and U.S. direct investment abroad excludes net inflows from those bond issues. [5] Industrial revenue bonds. Issued by state and local governments to finance private investment and secured in interest and principal by the industrial user of the funds. [6] Not elsewhere classified.

Source: Board of Governors of the Federal Reserve System, "Z.1, Financial Accounts of the United States," March 2022, <federalreserve.gov/releases/z1>, accessed March 2022.

Table 789. Corporate Funds—Sources and Uses: 2000 to 2021

[In billions of dollars (451 represents $451,000,000,000)]

Item	2000	2005	2010	2015	2017	2018	2019	2020	2021
Profits before tax	451	1,030	1,042	1,286	1,260	1,287	1,208	1,227	1,936
- Taxes on corporate income	165	263	204	283	225	201	204	190	287
- Net dividends	251	171	375	641	721	226	696	796	814
+ Inventory valuation adjustment (IVA)	-17	-36	-48	56	-47	-48	0	-18	-260
+ Capital consumption allowance [1]	786	805	1,087	1,317	1,490	1,652	1,781	1,818	1,904
+ Foreign earnings retained abroad	103	-29	212	195	246	-322	40	122	137
- Net capital transfers	–	-16	21	-3	191	-6	-12	14	-10
=Gross saving less net capital transfers paid	907	1,352	1,694	1,934	1,813	2,149	2,142	2,149	2,625
Gross investment	1,352	1,511	1,568	1,841	2,139	2,084	2,620	2,017	2,570
Capital expenditures [2]	1,147	1,206	1,300	1,936	1,898	2,065	2,185	1,961	2,189
Fixed investment [3]	1,098	1,154	1,247	1,790	1,870	2,012	2,111	2,009	2,202
Inventory change + IVA	50	51	54	117	28	55	73	-48	-19
Net lending (+) or net borrowing (-)	205	305	268	-95	241	19	436	56	381
Net acquisition of financial assets [2]	1,483	928	555	1,140	542	866	2,396	1,430	1,351
Foreign deposits	-7	10	13	-19	119	-110	25	12	14
Checkable deposits and currency	35	100	130	49	-16	238	150	665	9
Time and savings deposits	35	10	6	11	-8	6	14	107	23
Money market fund shares	17	53	-170	19	36	-33	92	120	16
Debt securities	19	40	-6	4	29	19	69	53	18
Loans	8	2	-4	23	(Z)	2	2	2	3
Mortgages	2	2	-2	24	2	2	2	2	3
Mutual fund shares	(Z)	1	7	12	8	-9	5	11	11
Trade receivables	282	278	142	33	163	396	541	35	679
U.S. direct investment abroad	136	15	299	259	311	-134	20	226	331
Miscellaneous assets	1,119	596	189	776	41	557	1,469	309	388
Paycheck Protection Program receivables	(X)	(X)	(X)	(X)	(X)	(X)	(X)	210	-190
Net increase in liabilities and equity [2]	1,278	622	288	1,235	302	847	1,961	1,374	970
Debt securities [2]	189	-2	245	410	326	152	270	617	177
Commercial paper	48	-8	25	-3	26	-10	-2	-62	6
Corporate bonds	139	-37	188	400	285	165	257	675	161
Loans	157	269	-300	187	32	212	209	311	388
Depository institution loans n.e.c. [4]	55	-27	-85	103	-52	103	31	78	-45
Other loans and advances [5]	78	110	-109	-8	118	11	128	188	308
Mortgages	24	185	-106	92	-34	98	50	45	125
Trade payables	313	199	157	24	81	321	230	135	544
Foreign direct investment: intercompany debt	56	(Z)	-8	40	-9	-73	-5	-42	-15
Miscellaneous liabilities [2]	482	331	181	672	-313	628	1,505	326	213
Claims of pension fund on sponsor	118	93	-21	59	-67	76	74	46	32
Corporate equities	-118	-276	-201	-453	-326	-618	-458	-168	-625

– Represents zero. X Not applicable. Z Less than $500 million. [1] Consumption of fixed capital plus capital consumption adjustment. [2] Includes other items not shown separately. [3] Nonresidential fixed investment plus residential fixed investment. [4] Not elsewhere classified. [5] Loans from rest of the world, U.S. government, and nonbank financial institutions.

Source: Board of Governors of the Federal Reserve System, "Z.1, Financial Accounts of the United States," March 2022, <federalreserve.gov/releases/z1>, accessed March 2022.

Table 790. Corporations—Selected Financial Items: 2000 to 2019

[In billions of dollars (47,027 represents $47,027,000,000,000), except as noted. Covers active corporations only. Corporation data are for tax year shown, which covers (a) corporate returns with accounting periods for the calendar year ending December of year shown and (b) those returns with accounting periods for the noncalendar year ending between July of year shown and June of the following year. All corporations are required to file returns except those specifically exempt. See source for changes in law affecting comparability of historical data]

Item	2000	2005	2010	2015	2016	2017	2018	2019
Number of returns (1,000)	5,045	5,671	5,814	6,120	6,189	6,325	6,442	6,474
Number with net income (1,000)	2,819	3,324	3,265	3,801	3,881	3,936	4,018	4,007
S Corporation returns [1] (1,000)	2,860	3,684	4,128	4,487	4,592	4,726	4,875	4,940
Assets [2]	47,027	66,445	79,905	97,048	101,991	107,889	108,505	114,840
Cash	1,820	2,823	3,893	5,305	5,374	5,611	5,284	5,896
Notes and accounts receivable	8,754	11,962	12,718	13,753	15,102	16,359	15,738	14,980
Inventories	1,272	1,505	1,544	1,991	2,000	2,080	2,225	2,257
Investments in government obligations	1,236	1,613	2,730	3,450	4,107	4,328	4,519	4,537
Mortgage and real estate	2,822	4,777	7,914	8,151	8,192	8,447	8,767	11,134
Depreciable assets	7,292	8,416	9,875	12,350	12,680	13,121	13,790	14,591
Depletable assets	191	310	661	1,038	923	917	945	923
Land	303	407	548	669	691	715	747	808
Liabilities [2]	47,027	66,445	79,905	97,048	101,991	107,889	108,505	114,840
Accounts payable	3,758	6,029	5,768	6,111	6,433	7,000	6,295	6,691
Short-term debt [3]	4,020	4,192	3,752	3,643	3,404	3,568	3,621	4,108
Long-term debt [4]	6,184	8,332	14,680	14,998	15,753	16,436	16,732	17,830
Net worth [5]	17,349	23,525	28,938	38,072	40,834	44,753	45,133	46,453
Capital stock	3,966	2,482	3,064	3,472	3,588	3,619	3,758	3,784
Paid-in or capital surplus	12,265	17,828	24,283	31,327	33,175	34,692	35,055	35,411
Retained earnings [6]	3,627	4,331	3,534	6,341	7,364	9,981	10,142	11,366
Receipts [2, 7]	20,606	25,505	26,199	31,030	31,208	32,962	35,180	35,910
Business receipts [7, 8]	17,637	21,800	23,058	27,492	27,575	29,180	30,837	31,367
Interest [9]	1,628	1,773	1,366	1,107	1,190	1,344	1,587	1,710
Rents and royalties	254	290	307	376	402	397	423	453
Deductions [2, 7]	19,692	23,613	24,944	29,102	29,395	31,384	32,850	33,608
Cost of goods sold [8]	11,135	13,816	14,502	17,044	16,948	18,117	19,193	19,245
Compensation of officers	401	445	435	501	498	513	493	500
Rent paid on business property	380	439	467	529	540	549	566	593
Taxes paid	390	473	493	580	590	602	632	650
Interest paid	1,272	1,287	888	728	793	910	982	1,120
Depreciation	614	531	728	822	857	976	1,138	1,177
Advertising	234	253	256	316	325	336	354	379
Net income (less loss) [7, 10]	928	1,949	1,356	2,034	1,913	1,656	3,391	2,869
Net income	1,337	2,235	1,836	2,531	2,458	2,281	3,954	3,527
Deficit	409	286	480	498	545	625	563	659
Income subject to tax	760	1,201	1,022	1,375	1,271	1,002	1,957	1,733
Income tax before credits [11]	266	419	358	481	446	359	404	383
Income tax after credits [12]	204	312	223	330	316	265	245	257

[1] Represents certain small corporations with a limit on the number of shareholders, mostly individuals, electing to be taxed at the shareholder level. [2] Includes items not shown separately. [3] Payable in less than 1 year. [4] Payable in 1 year or more. [5] Net worth is the sum of capital stock, additional paid-in capital, retained earnings appropriated, retained earnings unappropriated, and adjustments to shareholders' equity, minus cost of treasury stock. [6] Appropriated and unappropriated and adjustments to shareholders' equity. [7] Receipts, deductions, and net income of S corporations are limited to those from trade or business. Those from investments are excluded. [8] Includes gross sales and cost of sales of securities, commodities, and real estate by exchanges, brokers, or dealers selling on their own accounts. Excludes investment income. [9] Includes tax-exempt interest in state and local government obligations. [10] Excludes regulated investment companies. [11] Consists of regular (and alternative tax) only. [12] Includes minimum tax, alternative minimum tax, adjustments for prior year credits, and other income-related taxes.

Source: U.S. Internal Revenue Service, "SOI Tax Stats - Corporation Complete Report," <www.irs.gov/statistics/soi-tax-stats-corporation-complete-report>, accessed July 2022.

Table 791. IRS Audits—Corporate and Partnership Income Tax Returns Filed and Examined: 2010 to 2018

[In units as indicated (13,922,416 represents $13,922,416,000). An IRS audit is a review/examination of an organization's or individual's tax return to determine if income, expenses, and credits are being reported accurately. Includes tax returns selected for examination based on an earned income tax credit claim, and the resulting recommended additional taxes]

Year	Returns filed [1] (number)	Returns examined				Returns examined with no change (number)	Average recommended additional tax ($1,000)
		Total (number)	Closed [2] (number)	In process [3] (number)	Percent coverage		
CORPORATIONS							
2010	1,684,341	26,168	25,939	229	1.6	7,802	13,922,416
2015	1,626,220	15,008	13,529	1,479	0.9	4,800	2,834,300
2017 [4]	1,593,379	9,307	5,224	4,083	0.6	2,319	340,955
2018 [4]	1,553,954	4,442	1,116	3,326	0.3	492	49,212
PARTNERSHIPS							
2010	3,248,481	15,730	15,385	345	0.5	7,598	(X)
2015	3,715,187	8,302	7,234	1,068	0.2	3,057	(X)
2017 [4]	3,905,335	4,384	1,590	2,794	0.1	762	(X)
2018 [4]	4,010,200	1,335	84	1,251	(Z)	37	(X)
S CORPORATIONS							
2010	4,127,554	17,623	17,517	106	0.4	5,725	(X)
2015	4,487,336	9,791	8,750	1,041	0.2	2,600	(X)
2017 [4]	4,725,684	7,209	3,566	3,643	0.2	1,420	(X)
2018 [4]	4,874,996	3,182	503	2,679	0.1	165	(X)

X Not applicable. Z Less than 0.05%. [1] Includes all returns filed for the specified tax year as of December 31, 2020. [2] Includes examinations closed as of September 30, 2020. Represents a distinct count of taxpayers by tax year and form type. During the course of an examination, additional related returns within the statute of limitations may require examination; these related return closures are counted by the appropriate tax year and form type. [3] Includes examinations that are in an open examination status. [4] Years inside the statute of limitations may have rapid data changes; use data with caution.

Source: U.S. Internal Revenue Service, IRS Data Book 2020, June 2021. See also <www.irs.gov/statistics/soi-tax-stats-irs-data-book>.

Table 792. Economic Census Summary (NAICS 2012 Basis): 2012 and 2017

[25 represents 25,000. Covers establishments with payroll. Data are based on the 2007 and 2012 Economic Censuses, which are subject to nonsampling error. Data for the construction sector are also subject to sampling errors. For details on survey methodology and nonsampling and sampling errors, see Appendix III]

Kind of business	2012 NAICS code [1]	Establish- ments (1,000)		Sales, receipts, or shipments (bil. dol.)		Annual payroll (bil. dol.)		Paid employees [2] (1,000)	
		2012	2017	2012	2017	2012	2017	2012	2017
Mining, quarrying, and oil and gas extraction....	21	25	25	529	400	59	48	848	599
Oil & gas extraction............................	211	7	6	311	230	15	13	176	125
Mining (except oil & gas)...................	212	6	6	98	84	14	12	212	170
Support activities for mining...............	213	13	13	120	87	30	23	460	303
Utilities..	22	18	19	532	577	59	68	651	658
Construction.....................................	23	598	715	1,366	1,994	273	399	5,670	6,647
Construction of buildings....................	236	164	214	508	800	55	85	1,085	1,346
Heavy and civil engineering construction......	237	33	38	256	318	55	72	961	1,008
Specialty trade contractors..................	238	401	463	603	876	163	241	3,623	4,293
Manufacturing..................................	31-33	297	292	5,697	5,549	593	671	11,214	11,522
Wholesale trade................................	42	419	408	7,900	8,735	362	427	5,882	6,242
Merchant wholesalers, durable goods..........	423	245	241	3,152	3,688	217	252	3,355	3,547
Merchant wholesalers, nondurable goods.....	424	131	130	4,108	4,344	132	160	2,244	2,397
Wholesale electronic markets and agents and brokers...................	425	43	38	639	703	14	14	283	298
Retail trade.......................................	44–45	1,062	1,064	4,220	4,950	369	442	14,704	15,939
Motor vehicle & parts dealers...............	441	116	119	869	1,168	70	91	1,710	2,003
Furniture & home furnishings stores.............	442	52	51	89	113	11	14	425	466
Electronics & appliance stores..............	443	49	30	103	91	10	10	432	332
Building material & garden equipment & supplies dealers.........................	444	78	75	279	347	34	39	1144.72	1,285
Food & beverage stores......................	445	148	150	620	721	61	72	2,865	3,176
Health & personal care stores..............	446	91	95	270	319	31	34	1,002	1,039
Gasoline stations..............................	447	114	115	554	475	16	19	857	943
Clothing & clothing accessories stores......	448	148	144	234	255	28	32	1,664	1,791
Sporting goods, hobby, musical instrument, and book stores............	451	46	45	78	81	9	10	519	539
General merchandise stores..................	452	49	54	641	690	58	68	2,773	2,793
Miscellaneous store retailers................	453	107	109	98	110	14	17	713	774
Nonstore retailers.............................	454	64	77	386	579	27	35	600	797
Transportation & warehousing [3,4]...............	48-49	214	237	731	895	184	242	4,305	4,955
Truck transportation..........................	484	112	127	238	291	58	71	1,363	1,480
Information......................................	51	138	154	1,238	1,582	269	361	3,321	3,565
Publishing industries (except internet)..........	511	28	30	272	368	80	125	876	1,016
Motion picture & sound recording industries....	512	25	26	92	102	16	18	304	341
Broadcasting (except internet)..............	515	10	8	127	166	20	23	278	262
Telecommunications..........................	517	51	60	546	617	76	82	1,134	1,085
Data processing, hosting, and related services........................	518	15	18	108	157	41	54	497	553
Other information services....................	519	11	12	94	172	35	58	231	309
Finance & insurance [5]........................	52	468	476	3,636	4,340	524	639	6,041	6,500
Credit intermediation & related activities........	522	196	193	1,095	1,287	184	231	2,815	2,944
Insurance carriers & related activities..........	524	176	180	1,925	2,340	169	211	2,304	2,583
Real estate & rental & leasing [5].................	53	354	411	488	674	85	113	1,924	2,195
Professional, scientific, & technical services.....	54	856	914	1,480	1,845	581	729	8,204	9,015
Management of companies & enterprises........	55	54	59	116	122	309	368	3,082	3,571
Admin & support and waste management & remediation services.............	56	386	417	673	951	329	470	9,774	11,889
Administrative & support services...............	561	363	392	594	851	311	447	9,406	11,461
Waste management & remediation services....	562	23	25	79	100	18	23	368	428
Educational services...........................	61	68	77	53	66	17	22	642	723
Health care and social assistance................	62	831	892	2,040	2,528	801	990	18,415	20,507
Ambulatory health care services.................	621	583	624	814	1,031	340	431	6,475	7,563
Hospitals.......................................	622	6	7	877	1,071	317	383	5,751	6,174
Nursing & residential care facilities..............	623	81	89	203	236	87	101	3,364	3,502
Social assistance..............................	624	161	172	146	191	58	76	2,824	3,267
Arts, entertainment, & recreation...............	71	125	143	201	266	64	82	2,082	2,390
Performing arts, spectator sports, & related industries.....................	711	46	54	86	120	32	41	434	489
Museums, historical sites, & like institutions....	712	7	8	14	20	4	5	135	158
Amusement, gambling, & recreation industries.....................................	713	72	82	101	126	28	36	1,513	1,743
Accommodation & food services.................	72	662	726	708	938	196	265	12,008	14,003
Accommodation..............................	721	64	68	196	260	50	62	1,950	2,121
Food services & drinking places..............	722	599	658	512	678	146	203	10,058	11,881
Other services (except public administration)....	81	530	561	427	544	108	134	3,431	3,697
Repair & maintenance.........................	811	210	218	144	181	41	51	1,194	1,286
Personal and laundry services.................	812	213	236	87	111	29	36	1,349	1,474
Religious, grantmaking, civic, professional, and similar organizations........................	813	107	107	196	252	38	47	887	937

[1] Based on North American Industry Classification System, 2012; see text, this section. [2] For pay period including March 12. [3] Railroad transportation and U.S. Postal Service are out of scope for the 2012 and 2017 Economic Censuses. [4] For detailed industries, see Table 1093. [5] For detailed industries, see Table 1193.

Source: U.S. Census Bureau, 2017 Economic Census of the United States, Table EC1700COMP, "All Sectors: Comparative Statistics for the U.S., States, and Selected Geographies (2012 NAICS Basis): 2017 and 2012," <data.census.gov>, accessed December 2021.

Table 793. Nonemployer Establishments and Receipts by Industry: 2010 to 2019

[22,111 represents 22,111,000. Includes only firms subject to federal income tax. Nonemployers are businesses with no paid employees. Data originate chiefly from administrative records of the Internal Revenue Service; see Appendix III. Data for 2010 based on the North American Industry Classification System (NAICS), 2007; data for 2015 based on NAICS 2012; and data for 2019 based on NAICS 2017]

Industry	NAICS code	Establishments (1,000)			Receipts (mil. dol.)		
		2010	2015	2019	2010	2015	2019
All industries.........	(X)	**22,111**	**24,331**	**27,104**	**950,814**	**1,148,716**	**1,341,362**
Agriculture, forestry, fishing and hunting................	11	237	236	255	10,115	11,014	12,191
Mining, quarrying, and oil and gas extraction............	21	106	98	79	6,923	6,111	5,437
Utilities.........	22	17	20	14	698	981	982
Construction.........	23	2,424	2,430	2,754	120,151	146,341	179,131
Manufacturing.........	31–33	318	355	354	14,572	17,473	19,156
Wholesale trade.........	42	393	417	392	34,082	37,946	38,260
Retail trade.........	44–45	1,822	1,986	2,100	75,720	87,352	94,135
Transportation & warehousing.........	48–49	1,021	1,528	2,856	60,746	83,890	124,742
Information.........	51	311	329	364	10,739	12,762	14,607
Finance & insurance.........	52	717	718	755	50,626	55,329	63,949
Real estate & rental & leasing.........	53	2,343	2,636	2,942	209,549	259,768	300,227
Professional, scientific, & technical services............	54	3,121	3,411	3,773	130,613	157,584	185,148
Administrative and support & waste management and remediation services...............	56	1,937	2,069	2,596	39,111	46,393	62,643
Educational services.........	61	567	710	895	7,703	9,893	13,519
Health care & social assistance.........	62	1,935	1,979	2,063	57,686	64,702	73,823
Arts, entertainment, & recreation.........	71	1,154	1,342	1,563	26,756	34,549	42,999
Accommodation & food services.........	72	329	371	497	14,355	17,658	19,481
Other services (except public administration)...........	81	3,358	3,695	2,852	80,669	98,971	90,930

X Not applicable.

Source: U.S. Census Bureau, Nonemployer Statistics, "All Sectors: Nonemployer Statistics by Legal Form of Organization and Receipts Size Class for the U.S., States, and Selected Geographies: 2019," <data.census.gov>, accessed June 2022. See also <www.census.gov/programs-surveys/nonemployer-statistics.html>.

Table 794. Establishments, Employees, and Payroll by Employment-Size Class: 1990 to 2020

[In units as noted (6,176 represents 6,176,000). Excludes self-employed individuals, employees of private households, railroad employees, agricultural production employees, and most government employees. Employees are for the pay period including March 12. Covers establishments with payroll. An establishment is a single physical location where business is conducted or where services or industrial operations are performed. For statement on methodology, see Appendix III]

Employment-size class	Unit	1990	2000	2005	2010	2015	2018	2019	2020
Establishments, total............	1,000	**6,176**	**7,070**	**7,500**	**7,397**	**7,664**	**7,912**	**7,959**	**8,000**
Under 20 employees................	1,000	5,354	6,069	6,468	6,408	6,559	6,746	6,781	6,819
20 to 99 employees................	1,000	684	826	856	824	919	971	979	981
100 to 499 employees.............	1,000	122	157	157	148	166	174	177	177
500 to 999 employees.............	1,000	10	12	12	11	13	13	14	14
1,000 or more employees..........	1,000	6	7	7	7	7	8	8	9
Employees, total................	1,000	**93,476**	**114,065**	**116,317**	**111,970**	**124,086**	**130,881**	**132,989**	**134,163**
Under 20 employees................	1,000	24,373	27,569	28,874	28,958	29,406	30,277	30,309	30,143
20 to 99 employees................	1,000	27,414	33,147	34,302	32,730	36,640	38,544	38,928	38,981
100 to 499 employees.............	1,000	22,926	29,736	29,591	27,718	31,416	32,933	33,553	33,758
500 to 999 employees.............	1,000	6,551	8,291	8,053	7,331	8,550	9,128	9,369	9,448
1,000 or more employees..........	1,000	12,212	15,322	15,497	15,233	18,074	19,999	20,831	21,834
Annual payroll, total.............	Bil. dol.	**2,104**	**3,879**	**4,483**	**4,941**	**6,253**	**7,097**	**7,429**	**7,565**
Under 20 employees................	Bil. dol.	485	818	970	1,057	1,235	1,350	1,388	1,384
20 to 99 employees................	Bil. dol.	547	1,006	1,177	1,281	1,584	1,764	1,834	1,822
100 to 499 employees.............	Bil. dol.	518	1,031	1,176	1,280	1,651	1,874	1,960	1,979
500 to 999 employees.............	Bil. dol.	174	336	376	410	550	637	672	683
1,000 or more employees..........	Bil. dol.	381	690	784	913	1,235	1,472	1,574	1,696

Source: U.S. Census Bureau, County Business Patterns, "County Business Patterns by Legal Form of Organization and Employment Size Class for U.S., States, and Selected Geographies," <data.census.gov>, accessed April 2022. See also <www.census.gov/programs-surveys/cbp.html>.

Table 795. Establishments, Employees, and Payroll by Employment-Size Class and Industry: 2000 to 2020

[Establishments and employees in thousands (7,070.0 represents 7,070,000); payroll in billions of dollars (3,879.4 represents $3,879,400,000,000). See headnote, Table 794. Data for 2000 based on the North American Industry Classification System (NAICS) 1997; 2010 data based on NAICS 2007; and 2020 data based on NAICS 2017. See text, this section]

Industry	NAICS code	2000, total	2010, total	2020 Total	Under 20 employees	20 to 99 employees	100 to 499 employees	500 to 999 employees	1,000 or more employees
ESTABLISHMENTS (1,000s)									
Total [1]	(X)	7,070.0	7,396.6	8,000.2	6,819.2	981.4	177.1	13.8	8.7
Agriculture, forestry, fishing & hunting	113–115	26.1	21.7	22.7	21.2	1.3	0.2	(Z)	(Z)
Mining, quarrying, & oil and gas extraction	21	23.7	27.1	23.9	18.7	4.2	0.9	0.1	(Z)
Utilities	22	17.3	17.6	19.5	14.0	4.2	1.1	0.1	(Z)
Construction	23	709.6	682.7	753.3	683.4	60.6	8.6	0.5	0.2
Manufacturing	31–33	354.5	300.0	283.5	194.7	63.1	22.5	2.3	1.0
Wholesale trade	42	446.2	414.6	391.1	328.3	53.2	8.8	0.6	0.2
Retail trade	44–45	1,113.6	1,068.0	1,036.8	870.2	137.1	29.0	0.4	0.1
Transportation and warehousing	48–49	190.0	208.5	257.8	215.6	32.2	8.5	0.9	0.5
Information	51	133.6	135.4	160.9	135.4	19.4	5.2	0.7	0.3
Finance and insurance	52	423.7	473.5	476.8	437.3	30.5	7.2	1.0	0.7
Real estate and rental and leasing	53	300.2	347.3	437.7	419.9	15.7	1.9	0.1	(Z)
Professional, scientific, & technical services	54	722.7	851.5	943.2	866.8	63.1	11.7	1.0	0.6
Management of companies and enterprises	55	47.4	50.9	52.4	33.6	12.2	5.3	0.8	0.6
Administrative/support waste management/ remediation services	56	351.5	381.8	431.1	363.8	49.1	15.2	1.8	1.3
Educational services	61	68.0	90.1	110.1	85.8	19.4	3.9	0.4	0.5
Health care and social assistance	62	658.6	812.9	928.2	767.2	129.0	27.6	2.1	2.2
Arts, entertainment, and recreation	71	103.8	123.2	151.9	127.8	19.6	4.0	0.2	0.1
Accommodation and food services	72	542.4	644.0	733.9	501.1	220.5	11.5	0.5	0.2
Other services [2]	81	723.3	725.5	771.3	720.5	46.7	3.9	0.2	0.1
Unclassified establishments	99	99.0	20.5	14.0	13.9	(Z)	(NA)	(NA)	(NA)
EMPLOYEES (1,000s)									
Total [1]	(X)	114,065	111,970	134,163	30,143	38,981	33,758	9,448	21,834
Agriculture, forestry, fishing & hunting	113–115	184	156	167	71	52	30	8	7
Mining, quarrying, & oil and gas extraction	21	456	582	578	91	174	175	55	83
Utilities	22	655	638	637	72	182	220	92	71
Construction	23	6,573	5,389	7,182	2,497	2,385	1,587	354	360
Manufacturing	31–33	16,474	10,863	12,000	1,105	2,787	4,549	1,540	2,019
Wholesale trade	42	6,112	5,599	6,145	1,584	2,118	1,676	383	384
Retail trade	44–45	14,841	14,497	15,808	4,784	5,260	5,267	243	255
Transportation and warehousing	48–49	3,790	4,012	5,712	790	1,354	1,682	656	1,229
Information	51	3,546	3,124	3,577	570	827	1,054	463	664
Finance and insurance	52	5,963	5,929	6,682	1,817	1,213	1,506	717	1,430
Real estate and rental and leasing	53	1,942	1,946	2,281	1,186	592	365	83	56
Professional, scientific, & technical services	54	6,816	7,822	9,554	2,771	2,522	2,284	695	1,282
Management of companies and enterprises	55	2,874	2,833	3,571	175	554	1,118	535	1,189
Administrative/support waste management/ remediation services	56	9,138	8,977	12,718	1,378	2,103	3,085	1,218	4,933
Educational services	61	2,532	3,274	3,832	416	819	761	315	1,521
Health care and social assistance	62	14,109	17,788	21,217	3,968	5,216	5,131	1,480	5,422
Arts, entertainment, and recreation	71	1,741	2,004	2,505	474	825	759	152	295
Accommodation and food services	72	9,881	11,312	14,377	3,425	8,306	1,838	344	464
Other services [2]	81	5,293	5,204	5,602	2,952	1,691	672	117	170
Unclassified establishments	99	144	([3])	17	16	1	(NA)	(NA)	(NA)
ANNUAL PAYROLL (BIL. DOLLARS)									
Total [1]	(X)	3,879.4	4,941.0	7,564.8	1,384.4	1,822.2	1,979.1	682.6	1,696.4
Agriculture, forestry, fishing & hunting	113–115	4.7	5.3	8.0	3.5	2.7	1.3	0.3	0.2
Mining, quarrying, & oil and gas extraction	21	22.1	46.1	49.3	6.5	13.5	16.0	5.0	8.4
Utilities	22	40.7	55.4	73.6	6.8	19.3	25.7	12.1	9.8
Construction	23	239.9	261.0	458.9	129.7	158.3	118.8	27.2	24.9
Manufacturing	31–33	644.0	550.4	738.2	51.3	150.6	272.4	98.6	165.4
Wholesale trade	42	270.1	339.1	464.6	100.5	145.5	127.6	38.2	52.7
Retail trade	44–45	302.6	359.4	484.9	136.9	159.5	167.3	8.8	12.5
Transportation and warehousing	48–49	125.6	166.8	292.4	40.2	67.8	79.9	32.1	72.4
Information	51	209.4	224.0	439.8	39.7	69.0	124.6	67.5	139.0
Finance and insurance	52	346.8	472.4	753.5	145.5	152.3	187.4	86.8	181.5
Real estate and rental and leasing	53	59.2	80.5	131.7	61.7	36.3	24.5	4.9	4.3
Professional, scientific, & technical services	54	362.0	543.1	893.8	194.2	229.5	244.5	80.3	145.3
Management of companies and enterprises	55	211.4	281.8	410.0	21.9	56.7	122.0	60.5	148.9
Administrative/support waste management/ remediation services	56	210.3	304.1	571.0	63.5	93.2	115.0	43.1	256.3
Educational services	61	61.9	110.4	159.2	11.3	27.1	33.3	11.5	76.0
Health care and social assistance	62	431.4	752.9	1,116.5	200.6	234.0	228.5	83.4	370.0
Arts, entertainment, and recreation	71	43.2	62.3	78.6	19.1	16.6	25.3	8.5	9.1
Accommodation and food services	72	125.6	185.6	249.5	62.1	132.6	33.9	7.8	13.1
Other services [2]	81	109.9	140.3	190.7	89.2	57.6	31.1	6.1	6.7
Unclassified establishments	99	3.9	0.3	0.6	0.5	(Z)	(NA)	(NA)	(NA)

NA Not available. X Not applicable. Z Less than 50 establishments, 500 employees, or $500 million. [1] Totals for 2000 include auxiliaries. Beginning 2003, cases previously classified under NAICS code 95 (auxiliaries) are coded in the operating NAICS sector of the establishment. [2] Except public administration. [3] 10,000 to 24,999 employees.

Source: U.S. Census Bureau, County Business Patterns, "County Business Patterns by Legal Form of Organization and Employment Size Class for U.S., States, and Selected Geographies," <data.census.gov>, accessed April 2022. See also <www.census.gov/programs-surveys/cbp.html>.

Table 796. Employer Firms by Industry and Owner's Education and Age: 2019

[In thousands (3,939 represents 3,939,000). Includes all U.S. firms with paid employees operating during the survey reference year with receipts of $1,000 or more and classified in the 2017 North American Industry Classification System (NAICS). Based on the 2020 Annual Business Survey that collected data for 2019; see <www.census.gov/programs-surveys/abs/technical-documentation/methodology.html>]

Industry	NAICS code	Highest education level of owner						Age of owner			
		Total [1]	High school or less	Some college, no degree	Associate's or technical degree	Bachelor's degree	Advanced degree [2]	Total [1]	Under 35	35 to 64	65 or over
All industries [3]	(X)	**3,939**	**848**	**557**	**445**	**1,188**	**902**	**3,942**	**224**	**2,895**	**823**
Forestry, fishing & hunting, and agricultural support services	113-115	19	7	3	3	5	1	19	1	13	5
Mining, quarrying, and oil & gas extraction	21	12	4	2	1	4	1	12	1	8	4
Utilities	22	1	(Z)	(Z)	(Z)	(Z)	(Z)	1	(Z)	1	(Z)
Construction	23	529	199	99	102	106	23	530	31	411	88
Manufacturing	31-33	168	45	28	24	52	20	168	8	113	47
Wholesale trade	42	226	47	35	21	96	27	226	9	155	62
Retail trade	44-45	428	122	75	51	135	46	429	27	305	97
Transportation & warehousing [4]	48-49	114	46	20	15	25	7	114	9	86	20
Information	51	46	4	6	3	23	10	46	4	33	9
Finance & insurance [5]	52	174	19	25	11	89	31	174	8	125	42
Real estate & rental & leasing	53	231	35	36	19	102	39	231	10	152	69
Professional, scientific, & technical services	54	621	31	50	33	227	280	621	28	460	133
Management of companies & enterprises	55	12	2	1	1	6	2	12	(D)	7	4
Administrative & support and waste management & remediation services	56	231	64	45	30	68	25	232	16	174	41
Educational services	61	46	4	7	4	19	13	46	4	34	8
Health care & social assistance	62	404	14	16	16	46	312	404	18	308	78
Arts, entertainment & recreation	71	76	12	10	5	34	13	76	7	55	14
Accommodation & food services	72	355	112	58	38	109	37	355	28	265	62
Other services (except public administration) [6]	81	262	83	42	68	52	17	263	16	202	45

X Not applicable. Z Less than 500. D Data withheld to avoid disclosure. [1] Total firms that reported either education or age of owner in survey response. [2] Master's, doctorate, or professional degree. [3] Firms with more than one domestic establishment are counted in each industry in which they operate, but only once in the total. [4] Excludes rail transportation (NAICS 482) and the postal service (NAICS 491). [5] Excludes monetary authorities-central banks (NAICS 521) and funds, trusts, and other financial vehicles (NAICS 525). [6] Excludes religious, grantmaking, civic, professional, and similar organizations (NAICS 813) and private households (NAICS 814).

Source: U.S. Census Bureau, Annual Business Survey, Table AB1900CSCBO, "Owner Characteristics of Respondent Employer Firms by Sector, Sex, Ethnicity, Race, and Veteran Status for the U.S., States, and Metro Areas: 2019," <data.census.gov>, accessed January 2022.

Table 797. Employer Firms by Industry and Source of Start Up Capital: 2017

[Includes all U.S. firms with paid employees operating during the survey reference year with receipts of $1,000 or more and classified in the 2017 North American Industry Classification System (NAICS). Based on the 2018 Annual Business Survey that collected data for 2017; see <www.census.gov/programs-surveys/abs/technical-documentation/methodology.html>]

Industry	NAICS code	Source of capital to start or acquire business [1]						
		Total firms [2]	Personal savings or assets	Personal home equity loan	Credit cards [3]	Business loans [4]	Grants	Investment by venture capitalists
All industries	(X)	**5,744,643**	**2,307,708**	**171,550**	**449,402**	**706,551**	**6,403**	**17,337**
Forestry, fishing & hunting, and agricultural support services	113-115	28,556	11,796	870	1,729	5,589	3	35
Mining, quarrying, and oil & gas extraction	21	19,382	6,387	226	667	2,737	(S)	264
Utilities	22	6,088	877	71	137	367	34	(S)
Construction	23	706,354	299,437	20,903	68,953	61,020	S	969
Manufacturing	31-33	251,707	104,533	10,921	21,586	43,553	709	1,920
Wholesale trade	42	303,607	115,804	9,035	19,502	33,422	172	1,285
Retail trade	44-45	648,335	265,314	26,796	53,277	103,288	588	1,325
Transportation & warehousing	48-49	188,227	63,238	5,193	14,326	25,236	71	360
Information	51	79,322	29,134	1,739	6,154	6,492	193	1,445
Finance & insurance	52	239,154	106,292	6,879	18,769	(S)	87	790
Real estate & rental & leasing	53	311,301	122,836	6,510	15,650	30,140	212	1,061
Professional, scientific, & technical services	54	817,377	397,237	18,495	71,853	66,204	1,578	3,568
Management of companies and enterprises	55	29,783	6,154	363	(S)	3,493	40	487
Administrative & support and waste management remediation services	56	350,537	143,478	9,110	32,043	31,608	201	806
Educational services	61	92,814	29,460	2,062	5,925	6,097	362	270
Health care & social assistance	62	659,399	229,269	15,452	43,705	122,101	1,276	1,095
Arts, entertainment, & recreation	71	129,066	40,742	2,556	7,106	12,743	124	449
Accommodation & food services	72	533,176	187,666	19,944	35,330	81,009	500	1,755
Other services (except public administration)	81	395,072	154,165	14,880	32,619	53,402	198	451

X Not applicable. S Data does not meet publication standards. [1] Not all sources of capital are shown separately. [2] Includes firms that did not respond to survey questions regarding source of capital. [3] Includes personal and business credit cards carrying balances. [4] Includes loans from federal/state/local government, banks/financial institutions, and loans/investments from family and friends.

Source: U.S. Census Bureau, Annual Business Survey, "Business Characteristics of Respondent Employer Firms by Sector, Sex, Ethnicity, Race, and Veteran Status for the U.S., States, Metro Areas, Counties, and Places: 2017," <data.census.gov>, accessed June 2020.

Table 798. Franchised Businesses by Type of Business: 2017

[172,396 represents $172,396,000,000. Data shown for franchisor- and franchisee-owned establishments with paid employees]

Kind of business	NAICS code [1]	Establishments (number)	Revenue (mil. dol.)	Annual payroll (mil. dol.)	Paid employees (number)
Limited-service restaurants	722513	144,941	172,396	44,141	3,214,717
Full-service restaurants	722511	31,418	45,542	15,664	975,055
Hotels (except casino hotels) and motels	721110	31,244	125,148	28,340	1,039,949
New car dealers	441110	21,637	906,487	62,676	1,166,388
Offices of real estate agents and brokers	531210	21,529	33,180	3,181	63,132
Beauty salons	812112	21,462	6,586	2,759	134,598
Snack and nonalcoholic beverage bars	722515	21,011	13,388	3,437	252,050
Gasoline stations with convenience stores	447110	17,782	65,570	2,813	139,236
Electronics stores	443142	10,992	32,564	2,421	125,385
Fitness and recreational sports centers	713940	9,757	6,021	1,626	127,609
Tax preparation services	541213	8,022	2,226	597	80,086
Janitorial services	561720	7,484	6,092	2,184	103,885
Convenience stores	445120	5,282	9,052	792	40,781

[1] Based on the 2017 North American Industry Classification System (NAICS); see text, this section.

Source: U.S. Census Bureau, 2017 Economic Census, Table "EC1700FRAN: Selected Sectors: Franchise Status for the U.S. and States: 2017," <data.census.gov>, accessed November 2021.

Table 799. Employer Firms, Employment, and Payroll by Employment Size of Firm and State: 2018 and 2019

[6,076 represents 6,076,000. A firm is an aggregation of all establishments owned by a parent company (within a state) with some annual payroll. A firm may have an establishment in a single location or multiple establishments in more than one location]

State	Employer firms (1,000) 2018			Employer firms (1,000) 2019			Employment (1,000), 2019			Annual payroll (bil. dol.), 2019		
	Total	Less than 20 employ-ees	Less than 500 employ-ees	Total	Less than 20 employ-ees	Less than 500 employ-ees	Total	Less than 20 employ-ees	Less than 500 employ-ees	Total	Less than 20 employ-ees	Less than 500 employ-ees
U.S.	6,076	5,411	6,055	6,102	5,432	6,082	132,989	21,318	61,694	7,429	921	2,925
AL	75	62	72	75	62	72	1,759	274	823	80	10	34
AK	17	15	17	17	15	17	265	58	139	17	3	8
AZ	112	95	109	114	97	110	2,615	364	1,111	130	15	48
AR	51	43	49	51	43	49	1,053	176	498	46	6	18
CA	780	692	773	791	702	784	15,517	2,674	7,433	1,077	136	415
CO	143	125	139	144	126	141	2,473	444	1,176	142	20	58
CT	71	60	69	70	59	68	1,538	252	742	100	12	40
DE	21	17	19	21	17	20	413	67	196	24	3	10
DC	19	14	17	19	14	17	529	60	257	45	4	19
FL	465	421	460	471	426	465	8,860	1,411	3,590	427	58	155
GA	184	159	180	186	161	182	4,041	596	1,719	213	25	76
HI	26	22	25	26	21	25	553	90	272	26	4	12
ID	41	36	40	43	37	41	617	138	347	27	5	13
IL	257	223	252	256	222	251	5,530	816	2,475	325	37	127
IN	110	92	107	110	92	107	2,834	396	1,242	133	15	51
IA	64	54	62	63	54	61	1,381	215	644	64	8	26
KS	58	48	56	57	48	55	1,209	196	601	57	7	25
KY	68	56	65	67	56	65	1,667	242	722	75	8	28
LA	82	69	79	81	68	79	1,720	295	906	82	11	39
ME	34	30	33	34	30	33	522	112	294	24	4	12
MD	110	93	107	110	93	107	2,381	381	1,176	137	18	61
MA	145	124	142	145	124	142	3,386	505	1,537	239	26	91
MI	175	150	171	174	148	170	3,979	628	1,908	204	26	85
MN	120	102	117	119	101	116	2,729	391	1,255	154	17	58
MS	45	37	43	44	37	42	958	160	441	38	5	16
MO	119	101	116	117	99	113	2,547	386	1,154	125	14	47
MT	33	30	32	34	30	33	375	108	251	16	4	10
NE	44	37	42	44	37	42	856	144	414	39	5	17
NV	54	45	52	55	45	52	1,262	177	540	58	8	23
NH	31	26	29	31	26	30	620	112	308	33	5	15
NJ	195	170	192	195	169	191	3,805	671	1,871	240	30	97
NM	35	28	33	34	28	33	645	119	346	28	4	14
NY	467	418	462	466	417	461	8,597	1,513	4,134	603	71	230
NC	180	155	176	182	157	178	3,933	623	1,748	195	24	72
ND	20	16	19	20	16	19	353	67	197	18	3	9
OH	184	154	180	183	153	179	4,917	684	2,197	244	26	94
OK	73	62	71	73	62	71	1,405	246	718	65	9	29
OR	97	84	94	97	84	95	1,643	343	893	88	13	39
PA	231	197	226	231	197	227	5,558	839	2,565	295	33	116
RI	24	20	23	24	20	23	445	82	228	23	4	10
SC	85	72	82	86	72	83	1,949	296	838	84	11	32
SD	22	19	22	22	19	21	359	75	208	16	3	8
TN	100	83	97	101	83	97	2,725	369	1,150	130	15	49
TX	452	390	446	459	396	452	11,104	1,616	4,937	611	71	233
UT	69	59	67	71	61	68	1,374	215	626	68	9	27
VT	18	15	17	18	15	17	261	61	157	12	2	7
VA	155	132	151	155	132	151	3,456	537	1,590	197	23	79
WA	159	139	156	160	140	157	2,898	544	1,444	192	25	74
WV	26	22	25	26	21	25	554	95	269	24	3	10
WI	109	91	106	109	91	106	2,611	395	1,273	131	15	53
WY	18	16	18	19	16	18	207	59	133	10	2	6

Source: U.S. Census Bureau, Statistics of U.S. Businesses (SUSB), "2019 SUSB Annual Data Tables by Establishment Industry," and earlier releases, <www.census.gov/programs-surveys/susb/data/tables.html>, accessed March 2022.

Table 800. Employer Firms, Employment, and Annual Payroll by Employment Size of Firm and Industry: 2019

[6,102 represents 6,102,000. A firm is an aggregation of all establishments owned by a parent company (within a geographic location and/or industry) with some annual payroll. A firm may have an establishment in a single location or multiple establishments in more than one location. Employment is measured in March and payroll is annual; some firms may have zero employment in March but with paid employees at some time during the year. Numbers in parentheses represent 2017 North American Industry Classification System codes; see text, this section]

Industry and data type	Unit	Total	All industries—employment size of firm						
			0 to 4	5 to 9	10 to 19	20 to 99	100 to 499	Less than 500	500 or more
Total, all industries [1]:									
Firms............	1,000	6,102	3,777	1,014	641	555	95	6,082	21
Employment........	1,000	132,989	6,004	6,682	8,633	21,763	18,613	61,694	71,296
Annual payroll........	Bil. dol.	7,429	295	268	359	996	1,008	2,925	4,503
Construction (23):									
Firms........	1,000	731	488	115	67	53	7	729	1
Employment........	1,000	7,044	760	751	893	2,032	1,259	5,694	1,350
Annual payroll........	Bil. dol.	457	37	36	49	132	93	347	111
Manufacturing (31–33):									
Firms........	1,000	244	99	45	37	46	13	240	4
Employment........	1,000	12,110	183	299	502	1,879	2,230	5,094	7,016
Annual payroll........	Bil. dol.	740	9	12	23	96	123	263	477
Wholesale trade (42):									
Firms........	1,000	287	165	47	33	32	8	284	3
Employment........	1,000	6,181	274	307	438	1,212	1,132	3,362	2,819
Annual payroll........	Bil. dol.	464	16	18	26	78	78	216	248
Retail trade (44–45):									
Firms........	1,000	637	381	130	68	47	8	634	2
Employment........	1,000	15,693	702	854	901	1,794	1,189	5,439	10,254
Annual payroll........	Bil. dol.	471	21	24	28	68	52	193	278
Transportation & warehousing (48–49):									
Firms........	1,000	197	133	24	18	16	4	195	2
Employment........	1,000	5,408	184	159	237	616	575	1,772	3,637
Annual payroll........	Bil. dol.	283	8	7	10	29	28	82	201
Information (51):									
Firms........	1,000	83	53	11	8	8	2	82	1
Employment........	1,000	3,572	73	73	102	311	419	979	2,593
Annual payroll........	Bil. dol.	402	6	4	6	23	40	80	321
Finance & insurance (52):									
Firms........	1,000	238	173	35	13	12	4	237	2
Employment........	1,000	6,553	295	220	174	485	716	1,890	4,663
Annual payroll........	Bil. dol.	699	17	14	15	46	75	168	531
Professional, scientific and technical services (54):									
Firms........	1,000	826	612	102	57	43	8	822	3
Employment........	1,000	9,284	869	666	763	1,637	1,405	5,340	3,945
Annual payroll........	Bil. dol.	845	57	41	53	137	134	423	422
Management of companies and enterprises (55):									
Firms........	1,000	26	3	1	1	5	8	18	8
Employment........	1,000	3,523	3	3	7	69	297	380	3,144
Annual payroll........	Bil. dol.	403	1	(Z)	1	5	25	32	372
Administrative & support and waste management & remediation services (56):									
Firms........	1,000	355	228	52	32	31	9	351	4
Employment........	1,000	12,642	336	341	429	1,204	1,495	3,805	8,837
Annual payroll........	Bil. dol.	551	16	14	18	51	58	157	393
Educational services (61):									
Firms........	1,000	97	48	15	13	16	4	96	1
Employment........	1,000	3,809	73	103	176	659	708	1,719	2,090
Annual payroll........	Bil. dol.	157	3	2	4	22	30	61	96
Health care and social assistance (62):									
Firms........	1,000	665	346	136	88	73	19	661	4
Employment........	1,000	20,865	582	907	1,175	2,916	3,572	9,153	11,712
Annual payroll........	Bil. dol.	1,090	34	40	52	122	144	392	697
Accommodation and food services (72):									
Firms........	1,000	554	203	109	111	118	10	551	2
Employment........	1,000	14,492	328	733	1,525	4,331	1,872	8,789	5,703
Annual payroll........	Bil. dol.	305	12	13	28	86	39	177	129
Other services (except public administration) (81):									
Firms........	1,000	704	453	138	66	41	5	703	1
Employment........	1,000	5,619	820	896	874	1,488	672	4,750	869
Annual payroll........	Bil. dol.	197	25	26	28	50	29	157	40

Z Less than $500 million. [1] Includes other industries, not shown separately.

Source: U.S. Census Bureau, Statistics of U.S. Businesses (SUSB), "2019 SUSB Annual Data Tables by Establishment Industry," <www.census.gov/programs-surveys/susb/data/tables.html>, accessed March 2022.

Table 801. Employer Firms, Establishments, Employment, and Annual Payroll by Firm Size: 1990 to 2019

[5,074 represents 5,074,000. Firms are an aggregation of all establishments owned by a parent company with some annual payroll. Establishments are locations with active payroll in any quarter. This table illustrates the importance of changes in employment size over time, not job growth, as enterprises can grow or decline and change employment size cells over time]

Item	Total	Employment size of firm						
		0 to 4 [1]	5 to 9	10 to 19	20 to 99	100 to 499	Less than 500	500 or more
Firms (1,000):								
1990	5,074	3,021	952	563	454	70	5,060	14
2000	5,653	3,397	1,021	617	516	84	5,635	17
2010	5,735	3,575	968	617	475	82	5,717	17
2015	5,901	3,644	1,005	617	526	89	5,881	19
2018	6,076	3,752	1,013	646	551	93	6,055	21
2019	6,102	3,777	1,014	641	555	95	6,082	21
Establishments (1,000):								
1990	6,176	3,032	971	600	590	255	5,448	728
2000	7,070	3,406	1,035	652	674	312	6,080	990
2010	7,397	3,583	982	653	648	354	6,220	1,176
2015	7,664	3,650	1,016	649	698	367	6,380	1,284
2018	7,912	3,758	1,026	680	730	371	6,565	1,347
2019	7,959	3,784	1,027	674	728	375	6,588	1,371
Employment (1,000):								
1990	93,469	5,117	6,252	7,543	17,710	13,545	50,167	43,302
2000	114,065	5,593	6,709	8,286	20,277	16,260	57,124	56,941
2010	111,970	5,926	6,359	8,288	18,554	15,869	54,997	56,973
2015	124,086	5,877	6,614	8,298	20,645	17,503	58,938	65,148
2018	130,881	5,968	6,676	8,693	21,582	18,325	61,244	69,637
2019	132,989	6,004	6,682	8,633	21,763	18,613	61,694	71,296
Annual payroll (bil. dol.):								
1990	2,104	117	114	144	352	279	1,007	1,097
2000	3,879	186	174	231	608	528	1,727	2,152
2010	4,941	227	212	283	719	666	2,107	2,834
2015	6,253	263	244	322	876	846	2,551	3,702
2018	7,097	287	261	351	961	960	2,819	4,278
2019	7,429	295	268	359	996	1,008	2,925	4,503

[1] Employment is measured in March, thus some firms (start-ups after March, closures before March, and seasonal firms) will have zero employment and some annual payroll.

Source: U.S. Census Bureau, Statistics of U.S. Businesses (SUSB), "SUSB Historical Data," <www.census.gov/programs-surveys/susb/data/tables.html>, accessed April 2022.

Table 802. Job Creation and Job Destruction of Active Establishments by Firm Age: 2019

[7,152 represents 7,152,000. An establishment is a single physical location where business is conducted or where services or industrial operations are performed. A firm is a business organization consisting of one or more domestic establishments that are under common ownership or control. Firms may have one or more establishments. The firm and the establishment are the same for single-establishment firms. Data cover nonfarm private establishments with paid employees; exclusions include self–employed individuals, employees of private households, and railroad, agricultural production, and most government employees. Data are from the Business Dynamics Statistics (BDS) program and compiled from the Longitudinal Business Database. The BDS program is based on the same basic source data as the Census Bureau's County Business Patterns and Statistics of U.S. Business programs, but differences in how the source data are processed lead to differences in published statistics. For more information about concepts and methodology, see <www.census.gov/programs-surveys/bds/documentation/methodology.html>]

Firm age [1]	Establish-ments (1,000)	Employees (1,000)	Percent of employ-ment	Job creation [2]		Job destruction [3]		Net job creation		
				Total (1,000)	Rate	Total (1,000)	Rate	Total (1,000)	Rate	Percent of net job creation
Total	**7,152**	**131,789**	**100.0**	**15,514**	**11.9**	**13,284**	**10.2**	**2,229**	**1.7**	**100.0**
Startups	440	2,416	1.8	2,416	200.0	–	–	2,416	200.0	108.4
1 year	340	2,382	1.8	623	26.2	611	25.7	12	0.5	0.5
2 years	302	2,281	1.7	453	19.8	460	20.1	-7	-0.3	-0.3
3 years	275	2,232	1.7	394	17.6	406	18.1	-12	-0.5	-0.5
4 years	243	2,227	1.7	356	15.9	376	16.8	-19	-0.9	-0.9
5 years	223	2,196	1.7	314	14.2	355	16.0	-40	-1.8	-1.8
6 to 10 years	868	10,030	7.6	1,331	13.2	1,403	13.9	-72	-1	-3
11 to 15 years	760	9,301	7.1	1,081	11.5	1,203	12.9	-122	-1.3	-5.5
16 to 20 years	584	9,113	6.9	943	10.3	997	10.9	-53	-0.6	-2.4
21 to 25 years	523	9,811	7.4	885	9.0	985	10.0	-100	-1.0	-4.5
26 years and older	1,242	28,803	21.9	2,665	9.3	2,542	8.8	123	0.4	5.5
Unknown\left censored [4]	1,353	50,997	38.7	4,068	8.0	3,953	7.8	116	0.2	5.2

– Represents or rounds to zero. [1] Establishment age is computed by taking the difference between the current year of operation and the birth year. Firm age is computed from the age of the establishments belonging to that particular firm. [2] Job creation is employment gains from either establishments opening or establishments expanding. [3] Job destruction is all employment losses from either establishments contracting or establishments closing (shutting down). [4] Within the BDS, all firms/establishments born prior to 1976 have an unknown birth year and are therefore of an unknown age and are grouped into the age category "left censored."

Source: U.S. Census Bureau, Center for Economic Studies, "Business Dynamics Statistics (BDS)," <www.census.gov/programs-surveys/bds.html>, accessed February 2022.

Table 803. Firms with Employees Who Worked from Home by Industry: 2019

[2,686.0 represents 2,686,000. Based on the 2020 Annual Business Survey, see headnote Table 796]

Industry	2017 NAICS Code	Total reporting firms [1] (1,000)	Firms with employees who worked from home		Firms with no employees who worked from home	
			Number (1,000)	Percent	Number (1,000)	Percent
Total............................	**(X)**	**2,686.0**	**754.0**	**28.1**	**1,932.0**	**71.9**
Forestry, fishing & hunting, and agricultural support services.........................	113-115	12.2	1.6	13.3	10.6	86.7
Mining, quarrying, and oil and gas extraction..........	21	7.9	2.0	25.8	5.9	74.2
Utilities...........................	22	1.1	0.4	35.6	0.7	64.4
Construction.......................	23	356.8	60.4	16.9	296.4	83.1
Manufacturing.....................	31-33	104.5	20.4	19.6	84.0	80.4
Wholesale trade...................	42	144.8	56.8	39.2	88.0	60.8
Retail trade........................	44-45	276.4	36.0	13.0	240.4	87.0
Transportation and warehousing [2]............	48-49	78.7	16.4	20.8	62.4	79.2
Information.......................	51	30.6	20.7	67.6	9.9	32.4
Finance and insurance [3].....................	52	129.1	53.5	41.4	75.7	58.6
Real estate and rental and leasing................	53	155.0	73.7	47.5	81.3	52.5
Professional, scientific, and technical services.....	54	448.6	257.4	57.4	191.2	42.6
Management of companies and enterprises..........	55	10.5	4.1	39.0	6.4	61.0
Administrative & support and waste management & remediation services..........................	56	163.6	40.4	24.7	123.2	75.3
Educational services...............	61	31.6	11.6	36.7	20.0	63.3
Healthcare and social assistance.......................	62	312.2	63.4	20.3	248.8	79.7
Arts, entertainment, and recreation....................	71	51.4	18.3	35.6	33.1	64.4
Accommodation and food services....................	72	209.2	9.6	4.6	199.7	95.4
Other services, except public administration [4].........	81	182.5	17.1	9.4	165.4	90.6

X Not applicable. [1] Firms reporting whether they had employees who worked from home. [2] Excludes rail transportation (NAICS 482) and the postal service (NAICS 491). [3] Excludes central banks (NAICS 521) and funds, trusts, and other financial vehicles (NAICS 525). [4] Excludes religious, grantmaking, civic, professional, and similar organizations (NAICS 813) and private households (NAICS 814).

Source: U.S. Census Bureau, Annual Business Survey, "Business Characteristics of Respondent Employer Firms by Sector, Sex, Ethnicity, Race, and Veteran Status for the U.S., States, and Metro Areas: 2019," <data.census.gov>, accessed May 2022.

Table 804. Establishments Born, Exited, and Jobs Created and Lost, 1980 to 2019, and by Employment Size of Establishment, 2019

[In thousands (4,491 represents 4,491,000), except rate. An establishment is a single physical location at which business is conducted or where services or industrial operations are performed]

Item	Establish-ments	Employees	Establishments born			Establishments exited		
			Number	Rate	Jobs created	Number	Rate	Jobs lost
1980............................	4,491	73,753	581	13.1	4,637	498	11.2	3,746
1990............................	5,575	93,776	704	12.8	5,713	545	9.9	4,217
2000............................	6,294	113,244	686	11.0	6,431	621	9.9	5,822
2010............................	6,671	111,189	632	9.4	4,683	683	10.2	4,559
2015............................	6,910	123,137	682	9.9	5,317	584	8.5	4,110
2019, total......................	**7,152**	**131,789**	**658**	**9.2**	**4,840**	**605**	**8.5**	**4,225**
Establishment size:								
1 to 4 employees...............	3,677	8,173	568	15.6	1,356	524	14.3	1,242
5 to 9 employees...............	1,376	9,732	46	3.4	618	43	3.1	570
10 to 19 employees.............	961	13,602	25	2.6	670	22	2.3	585
20 to 99 employees.............	945	38,636	17	1.8	1,260	15	1.6	1,124
100 to 499 employees.........	171	33,154	2	1.1	679	1	0.9	518
500 to 999 employees.........	13	9,240	(Z)	0.8	142	(Z)	0.5	90
1,000 employees or more.....	8	19,251	(Z)	0.5	114	(Z)	0.3	96

Z Less than 500 establishments.

Source: U.S. Census Bureau, "Business Dynamics Statistics (BDS)," <www.census.gov/programs-surveys/bds.html>, accessed February 2022.

Table 805. Small Business Administration Loans to Minority-Owned Small Businesses: 1980 to 2021

[381 represents $381,000,000. For year ending September 30. A small business must be independently owned and operated, must not be dominant in its particular industry, and must meet standards set by the Small Business Administration as to its annual receipts or number of employees. Includes 7(a) loans, 504 loans, and, beginning 2015, Community Advantage loans]

Year	Number of loans					Amount (mil. dol.)				
	Total minority loans [1]	Black	Asian or Pacific Islander	Hispanic	Amer-ican Indian	Total minority loans [1]	Black	Asian or Pacific Islander	Hispanic	Amer-ican Indian
1980...........	4,276	1,732	659	1,715	170	381	146	70	149	15
1990...........	2,368	515	1,074	694	85	576	97	316	149	14
2000...........	12,041	2,183	5,827	3,491	540	3,675	415	2,390	767	102
2005...........	30,226	7,302	13,353	8,748	823	6,294	756	4,072	1,341	125
2010...........	11,235	1,707	5,942	3,192	387	3,982	345	2,743	806	86
2015...........	17,240	2,409	8,752	5,617	462	7,953	652	5,527	1,625	149
2019...........	15,685	2,643	7,236	5,405	400	8,437	818	5,594	1,858	167
2020...........	11,712	1,811	5,321	3,919	317	7,391	605	4,791	1,633	129
2021...........	16,344	2,828	7,810	5,268	436	12,893	1,078	8,713	2,827	274

[1] Beginning 2009, includes other minority loans not shown separately.

Source: U.S. Small Business Administration, "SBA Lending Statistics for Major Programs (as of 9/30/2021)" and earlier reports, <www.sba.gov/about-sba/sba-newsroom/weekly-lending-report/archive>, accessed February 2022.

Table 806. Employer Firm Ownership by Industry and Sex, Race/Ethnicity, and Veteran Status: 2019

[In thousands (3,508.3 represents 3,508,300). Includes all U.S. firms with paid employees operating during the survey reference year with receipts of $1,000 or more and classified in the 2017 North American Industry Classification System (NAICS). Each owner had the option of selecting more than one race and is therefore included in each race selected. Race groups include persons of Hispanic and non-Hispanic ethnicity. Based on the 2020 Annual Business Survey that collected data for 2019; see <www.census.gov/programs-surveys/abs/technical-documentation/methodology.html>]

Industry	NAICS code	Sex		Race/ethnicity						Veteran owned
		Male	Female	White	Black	American Indian and Alaska Native	Asian	Native Hawaiian and other Pacific Islander	Hispanic [1]	
All industries [2]	(X)	3,508.3	1,208.4	4,819.1	134.6	26.1	581.2	7.3	346.8	331.2
Agriculture, forestry, fishing and hunting [3]	11	16.7	(S)	25.7	(S)	(S)	(S)	(Z)	(S)	(S)
Mining, quarrying, and oil & gas extraction	21	13.1	1.9	17.3	(Z)	0.2	0.1	(D)	0.7	1.5
Utilities	22	2.3	0.4	3.0	(Z)	(Z)	0.1	(D)	(S)	0.3
Construction	23	557.1	65.8	697.0	10.6	4.6	16.7	1.1	56.8	47.1
Manufacturing	31-33	160.1	38.6	220.6	1.6	1.0	11.0	0.2	11.4	16.5
Wholesale trade	42	202.7	41.6	243.8	2.2	1.1	34.1	(S)	15.7	18.6
Retail trade	44-45	368.7	134.7	507.5	8.8	2.4	105.4	(S)	30.4	29.7
Transportation & warehousing [4]	48-49	134.3	26.1	171.1	8.8	1.5	11.8	0.4	22.0	12.6
Information	51	53.3	11.8	67.4	1.3	0.2	5.9	(S)	3.0	3.4
Finance & insurance [5]	52	164.4	40.0	213.6	5.0	1.0	10.7	(S)	11.1	17.9
Real estate & rental & leasing	53	174.7	80.8	292.0	4.9	0.7	18.6	(S)	13.2	19.2
Professional, scientific, & technical services	54	523.3	198.8	720.5	17.9	3.9	65.1	1.3	40.3	58.2
Management of companies and enterprises	55	12.7	2.5	15.9	0.2	(Z)	(S)	(S)	(S)	1.3
Administrative & support and waste management & remediation services	56	210.6	75.9	311.5	10.4	1.8	12.8	(S)	31.6	22.4
Educational services	61	26.3	29.9	57.2	2.6	0.4	7.6	(S)	3.1	2.5
Health care & social assistance	62	325.1	202.4	464.1	39.7	3.1	79.5	0.6	33.1	36.1
Arts, entertainment, & recreation	71	68.8	23.6	103.3	4.0	0.3	3.8	0.1	4.0	5.3
Accommodation & food services	72	305.0	118.7	382.2	8.3	2.2	138.0	0.7	44.9	18.4
Other services (except public administration) [6]	81	207.8	112.5	321.0	8.1	(S)	59.9	0.9	24.2	20.1
Industries not classified	99	9.1	2.5	18.3	0.3	(S)	0.5	(Z)	0.5	1.4

X Not applicable. D Data withheld. S Data does not meet publication standards. Z Less than 50. [1] A Hispanic firm may be of any race and therefore may be included in more than one race group. [2] Firms with more than one domestic establishment are counted in each industry in which they operate but only once in the total. [3] Excludes crop production (NAICS 111) and animal production and aquaculture (NAICS 112). [4] Excludes rail transportation (NAICS 482) and the postal service (NAICS 491). [5] Excludes monetary authorities-central banks (NAICS 521) and funds, trusts, and other financial vehicles (NAICS 525). [6] Excludes religious, grantmaking, civic, professional, and similar organizations (NAICS 813) and private households (NAICS 814).

Source: U.S. Census Bureau, Annual Business Survey, Table AB1900CSA01, "Statistics for Employer Firms by Industry, Sex, Ethnicity, Race, and Veteran Status for the U.S., States, and Metro Areas: 2019," <data.census.gov>, accessed March 2022.

Table 807. Women-Owned Employer Firms by Kind of Business: 2019

[1,808,254,793 represents $1,808,254,793,000. Data are shown for U.S. firms with paid employees, operating during the survey reference year, and with receipts of $1,000 or more. Based on the 2020 Annual Business Survey that collected data for 2019; see <www.census.gov/programs-surveys/abs/technical-documentation/methodology.html>]

Kind of business	NAICS code [1]	Firms (number)	Sales, value of shipments, or revenue ($1,000)	Employees [2] (number)	Annual payroll ($1,000)
Total [3]	(X)	1,208,407	1,808,254,793	10,791,948	418,552,132
Forestry, fishing & hunting, and agricultural support services	113–115	(S)	(S)	([10])	(S)
Mining, quarrying, and oil & gas extraction	21	1,879	([8])	21,631	1,607,648
Utilities	22	374	([7])	3,738	301,471
Construction	23	65,849	([8])	565,339	35,090,237
Manufacturing	31–33	38,613	([8])	659,887	31,315,321
Wholesale trade	42	41,598	([8])	394,046	23,714,462
Retail trade	44–45	134,655	([8])	885,411	25,760,865
Transportation and warehousing [4]	48–49	26,056	([8])	270,531	12,370,043
Information	51	11,847	([8])	112,445	8,314,806
Finance and insurance [5]	52	40,001	([8])	233,956	14,000,958
Real estate and rental and leasing	53	80,766	([8])	251,461	11,776,618
Professional, scientific, and technical services	54	198,815	([8])	1,018,245	65,037,103
Management of companies and enterprises	55	2,455	(S)	63,403	4,740,044
Administrative & support and waste management & remediation services	56	75,876	([8])	1,418,249	51,762,722
Educational services	61	29,928	([8])	317,412	7,846,383
Health care and social assistance	62	202,401	([8])	2,144,012	69,565,989
Arts, entertainment, and recreation	71	23,618	([8])	179,946	5,876,345
Accommodation and food services	72	118,686	([8])	1,637,145	32,851,271
Other services (except public administration) [6]	81	112,480	([8])	557,490	14,693,896
Industries not classified	99	2,502	([9])	4,555	125,492

X Not applicable. S Estimate does not meet publication standards. [1] Based on the 2017 North American Industry Classification System (NAICS); see text, this section. [2] Paid employees for pay period including March 12. [3] Firms with more than one domestic establishment are counted in each industry in which they operate, but only once in the total. [4] Excludes rail transportation (NAICS 482) and the postal service (NAICS 491). [5] Excludes monetary authorities-central banks (NAICS 521) and funds, trusts, and other financial vehicles (NAICS 525). [6] Excludes religious, grantmaking, civic, professional, and similar organizations (NAICS 813) and private households (NAICS 814). [7] $1 billion to less than $5 billion dollars. [8] $5 billion dollars or more. [9] $500 million to less than $1 billion dollars. [10] 50,000 to 99,999 employees.

Source: U.S. Census Bureau, Annual Business Survey, Table AB1900CSA01, "Statistics for Employer Firms by Industry, Sex, Ethnicity, Race, and Veteran Status for the U.S., States, and Metro Areas: 2019," <data.census.gov>, accessed January 2022.

Table 808. Minority-Owned Employer Firms by Kind of Business: 2019

[1,508,782,783 represents $1,508,782,783,000. Data are shown for U.S. firms with paid employees, operating during the survey reference year, and with receipts of $1,000 or more. Based on the 2020 Annual Business Survey that collected data for 2019; see <www.census.gov/programs-surveys/abs/technical-documentation/methodology.html>]

Kind of business	NAICS code [1]	Firms (number)	Sales, value of shipments, or revenue ($1,000)	Employees [2] (number)	Annual payroll ($1,000)
Total [3]....................	**(X)**	**1,077,319**	**1,508,782,783**	**9,348,384**	**344,460,624**
Forestry, fishing & hunting, and agricultural support services.............	113–115	(S)	(S)	([11])	(S)
Mining, quarrying, and oil & gas extraction....................	21	968	([9])	12,272	768,246
Utilities........................	22	209	([8])	1,447	101,472
Construction.....................	23	86,955	([10])	548,042	27,999,467
Manufacturing.....................	31–33	24,726	([10])	372,116	16,987,519
Wholesale trade...................	42	52,835	([10])	351,457	18,865,548
Retail trade......................	44–45	145,733	([10])	811,252	21,558,060
Transportation and warehousing [4]...............	48–49	43,301	([10])	276,317	11,017,982
Information......................	51	10,342	([10])	118,482	9,872,912
Finance and insurance [5]...............	52	27,413	([10])	133,905	7,999,883
Real estate and rental and leasing.................	53	37,034	([10])	106,517	4,445,603
Professional, scientific, and technical services...............	54	126,007	([10])	803,591	60,228,810
Management of companies and enterprises.................	55	1,425	(S)	37,181	2,224,331
Administrative & support and waste management & remediation services.................	56	55,225	([10])	891,819	31,765,612
Educational services................	61	13,583	([10])	130,015	3,451,253
Health care and social assistance................	62	152,996	([10])	1,642,310	59,661,746
Arts, entertainment, and recreation................	71	11,970	([10])	65,506	3,292,481
Accommodation and food services................	72	192,946	([10])	2,557,181	51,362,856
Other services (except public administration) [6]...............	81	92,978	([10])	406,565	10,179,010
Industries not classified................	99	1,391	([7])	2,609	72,441

X Not applicable. S Data does not meet publishing standards. [1] Based on the 2017 North American Industry Classification System (NAICS); see text, this section. [2] Paid employees for pay period including March 12. [3] Firms with more than one domestic establishment are counted in each industry in which they operate, but only once in the total. [4] Excludes rail transportation (NAICS 482) and the postal service (NAICS 491). [5] Excludes monetary authorities-central banks (NAICS 521) and funds, trusts, and other financial vehicles (NAICS 525). [6] Excludes religious, grantmaking, civic, professional, and similar organizations (NAICS 813) and private households (NAICS 814). [7] $150 million to under $500 million. [8] $500 million to under $1 billion. [9] $1 billion to less than $5 billion. [10] $5 billion or more. [11] 50,000 to 99,000 employees.

Source: U.S. Census Bureau, Annual Business Survey (ABS), Table AB1900CSA01, "Statistics for Employer Firms by Industry, Sex, Ethnicity, Race, and Veteran Status for the U.S., States, and Metro Areas: 2019," <data.census.gov>, accessed January 2022.

Table 809. Hispanic-Owned Employer Firms by Kind of Business: 2019

[463,280,122 represents $463,280,122,000. Data are shown for U.S. firms with paid employees, operating during the survey reference year, and with receipts of $1,000 or more. Based on the 2020 Annual Business Survey that collected data for 2019; see <www.census.gov/programs-surveys/abs/technical-documentation/methodology.html>]

Kind of business	NAICS code [1]	Firms (number)	Sales, value of shipments, or revenue ($1,000)	Employees [2] (number)	Annual payroll ($1,000)
Total [3]....................	**(X)**	**346,836**	**463,280,122**	**2,930,548**	**108,355,725**
Forestry, fishing & hunting, and agricultural support services.............	113–115	(S)	(S)	([10])	(S)
Mining, quarrying, and oil & gas extraction....................	21	671	([8])	9,355	539,402
Utilities........................	22	(S)	(S)	([11])	(S)
Construction.....................	23	56,832	([9])	376,070	18,538,166
Manufacturing.....................	31–33	11,356	([9])	150,977	6,478,079
Wholesale trade...................	42	15,692	([9])	98,351	4,944,955
Retail trade......................	44–45	30,382	([9])	189,016	5,540,825
Transportation and warehousing [4]...............	48–49	22,043	([9])	124,042	5,319,848
Information......................	51	2,970	([9])	20,707	1,490,272
Finance and insurance [5]...............	52	11,124	([9])	71,625	3,940,138
Real estate and rental and leasing.................	53	13,184	([9])	40,015	1,651,435
Professional, scientific, and technical services...............	54	40,252	([9])	206,757	12,480,841
Management of companies and enterprises.................	55	(S)	(S)	([12])	(S)
Administrative & support and waste management & remediation services.................	56	31,627	([9])	420,901	14,974,904
Educational services................	61	3,142	([8])	25,935	867,546
Health care and social assistance................	62	33,125	([9])	345,260	11,529,402
Arts, entertainment, and recreation................	71	3,995	([8])	21,708	624,627
Accommodation and food services................	72	44,893	([9])	654,995	13,677,596
Other services (except public administration) [6]...............	81	24,198	([9])	98,837	2,991,773
Industries not classified................	99	516	([7])	892	27,286

X Not applicable. S Data does not meet publication standards. [1] Based on the 2017 North American Industry Classification System (NAICS); see text, this section. [2] Paid employees for pay period including March 12. [3] Firms with more than one domestic establishment are counted in each industry in which they operate, but only once in the total. [4] Excludes rail transportation (NAICS 482) and the postal service (NAICS 491). [5] Excludes monetary authorities-central banks (NAICS 521) and funds, trusts, and other financial vehicles (NAICS 525). [6] Excludes religious, grantmaking, civic, professional, and similar organizations (NAICS 813) and private households (NAICS 814). [7] $150 million to less than $500 million. [8] $1 billion to less than $5 billion. [9] $5 billion or more. [10] 50,000 to 99,999 employees. [11] 500 to 999 employees. [12] 5,000 to 9,999 employees.

Source: U.S. Census Bureau, Annual Business Survey, Table AB1900CSA01, "Statistics for Employer Firms by Industry, Sex, Ethnicity, Race, and Veteran Status for the U.S., States, and Metro Areas: 2019," <data.census.gov>, accessed January 2022.

Table 810. Black-Owned Employer Firms by Kind of Business: 2019

[133,653,091 represents $133,653,091,000. Data are shown for U.S. firms with paid employees, operating during the survey reference year, and with receipts of $1,000 or more. Based on the 2020 Annual Business Survey that collected data for 2019; see <www.census.gov/programs-surveys/abs/technical-documentation/methodology.html>]

Kind of business	NAICS code [1]	Firms (number)	Sales, value of shipments, or revenue ($1,000)	Employees [2] (number)	Annual payroll ($1,000)
Total [3].....	(X)	**134,567**	**133,653,091**	**1,273,002**	**40,492,389**
Forestry, fishing & hunting, and agricultural support services.....	113–115	(S)	(S)	([11])	(S)
Mining, quarrying, and oil & gas extraction.....	21	26	([7])	84	6,083
Utilities.....	22	26	([7])	88	3,532
Construction.....	23	10,616	([8])	50,263	2,478,263
Manufacturing.....	31–33	1,622	([8])	21,184	939,356
Wholesale trade.....	42	2,161	([8])	12,965	626,031
Retail trade.....	44–45	8,798	([8])	43,288	1,320,899
Transportation and warehousing [4].....	48–49	8,792	([8])	53,343	1,751,482
Information.....	51	1,250	([9])	11,661	822,016
Finance and insurance [5].....	52	4,969	([9])	16,149	988,179
Real estate and rental and leasing.....	53	4,921	([9])	14,451	604,324
Professional, scientific, and technical services.....	54	17,898	([8])	104,600	6,500,629
Management of companies and enterprises.....	55	172	(S)	3,438	175,694
Administrative & support and waste management & remediation services.....	56	10,352	([8])	180,914	4,913,472
Educational services.....	61	2,556	([9])	23,053	640,252
Health care and social assistance.....	62	39,705	([8])	508,545	13,234,805
Arts, entertainment, and recreation.....	71	3,977	([9])	16,561	1,491,025
Accommodation and food services.....	72	8,337	([8])	169,899	2,917,206
Other services (except public administration) [6].....	81	8,052	([9])	40,601	1,014,479
Industries not classified.....	99	312	([10])	517	12,782

X Not applicable. S Data does not meet publication standards. [1] Based on the 2017 North American Industry Classification System (NAICS); see text, this section. [2] Paid employees for pay period including March 12. [3] Firms with more than one domestic establishment are counted in each industry in which they operate, but only once in the total. [4] Excludes rail transportation (NAICS 482) and the postal service (NAICS 491). [5] Excludes monetary authorities-central banks (NAICS 521) and funds, trusts, and other financial vehicles (NAICS 525). [6] Excludes religious, grantmaking, civic, professional, and similar organizations (NAICS 813) and private households (NAICS 814). [7] $15 million to less than $50 million. [8] $5 billion or more. [9] $1 billion to less than $5 billion. [10] $50 million to less than $75 million. [11] 1,000 to 2,499 employees.

Source: U.S. Census Bureau, Annual Business Survey, Table AB1900CSA01, "Statistics for Employer Firms by Industry, Sex, Ethnicity, Race, and Veteran Status for the U.S., States, and Metro Area: 2019," <data.census.gov>, accessed January 2022.

Table 811. Asian-Owned Employer Firms by Kind of Business: 2019

[874,618,317 represents $874,618,317,000. Data are shown for U.S. firms with paid employees, operating during the survey reference year, and with receipts of $1,000 or more. Based on the 2020 Annual Business Survey that collected data for 2019; see <www.census.gov/programs-surveys/abs/technical-documentation/methodology.html>]

Kind of business	NAICS code [1]	Firms (number)	Sales, value of shipments, or revenue ($1,000)	Employees [2] (number)	Annual payroll ($1,000)
Total [3].....	(X)	**581,200**	**874,618,317**	**4,946,547**	**185,813,228**
Forestry, fishing & hunting, and agricultural support services.....	113–115	(S)	(S)	([11])	(S)
Mining, quarrying, and oil & gas extraction.....	21	108	([7])	1,250	101,532
Utilities.....	22	61	([8])	466	36,750
Construction.....	23	16,712	([9])	95,680	5,373,114
Manufacturing.....	31–33	10,969	([9])	189,006	9,064,770
Wholesale trade.....	42	34,073	([9])	233,856	12,920,623
Retail trade.....	44–45	105,388	([9])	568,157	14,370,419
Transportation and warehousing [4].....	48–49	11,781	([9])	92,977	3,652,748
Information.....	51	5,946	([9])	83,438	7,328,934
Finance and insurance [5].....	52	10,689	([9])	43,601	2,982,591
Real estate and rental and leasing.....	53	18,622	([9])	49,585	2,070,997
Professional, scientific, and technical services.....	54	65,132	([9])	470,625	39,575,884
Management of companies and enterprises.....	55	(S)	(S)	([12])	(S)
Administrative & support and waste management & remediation services.....	56	12,767	([9])	248,346	10,233,309
Educational services.....	61	7,573	([9])	79,757	1,918,629
Health care and social assistance.....	62	79,545	([9])	762,677	33,206,975
Arts, entertainment, and recreation.....	71	3,794	([10])	25,193	916,463
Accommodation and food services.....	72	138,043	([9])	1,707,139	34,350,044
Other services (except public administration) [6].....	81	59,947	([9])	258,394	5,881,394
Industries not classified.....	99	539	([8])	1,038	29,677

X Not applicable. S Data does not meet publication standards. [1] Based on the 2017 North American Industry Classification System (NAICS); see text, this section. [2] Paid employees for pay period including March 12. [3] Firms with more than one domestic establishment are counted in each industry in which they operate, but only once in the total. [4] Excludes rail transportation (NAICS 482) and the postal service (NAICS 491). [5] Excludes monetary authorities-central banks (NAICS 521) and funds, trusts, and other financial vehicles (NAICS 525). [6] Excludes religious, grantmaking, civic, professional, and similar organizations (NAICS 813) and private households (NAICS 814). [7] $500 million to less than $1 billion. [8] $150 million to less than $500 million. [9] $5 billion or more. [10] $1 billion to less than $5 billion. [11] 5,000 to 9,999 employees. [12] 25,000 to 49,999 employees.

Source: U.S. Census Bureau, Annual Business Survey, Table AB1900CSA01, "Statistics for Employer Firms by Industry, Sex, Ethnicity, Race, and Veteran Status for the U.S., States, and Metro Areas: 2019," <data.census.gov/>, accessed January 2022.

Table 812. American Indian and Alaska Native-Owned Employer Firms by Kind of Business: 2019

[35,776,597 represents $35,776,597,000. Data are shown for U.S. firms with paid employees, operating during the survey reference year, and with receipts of $1,000 or more. Based on the 2020 Annual Business Survey that collected data for 2019; see <www.census.gov/programs-surveys/abs/technical-documentation/methodology.html>]

Kind of business	NAICS code [1]	Firms (number)	Sales, value of shipments, or revenue ($1,000)	Employees [2] (number)	Annual payroll ($1,000)
Total [3]......	(X)	26,064	35,776,597	215,049	8,660,699
Forestry, fishing & hunting, and agricultural support services......	113–115	(S)	(S)	([12])	(S)
Mining, quarrying, and oil & gas extraction......	21	162	([7])	1,513	116,987
Utilities......	22	7	([8])	73	7,079
Construction......	23	4,573	([9])	33,762	1,970,778
Manufacturing......	31–33	956	([10])	11,603	513,127
Wholesale trade......	42	1,129	([10])	7,982	399,965
Retail trade......	44–45	2,447	([10])	15,445	412,693
Transportation and warehousing [4]......	48–49	1,540	([10])	10,652	476,380
Information......	51	189	([7])	1,827	65,149
Finance and insurance [5]......	52	1,007	([11])	2,876	166,873
Real estate and rental and leasing......	53	739	([7])	3,014	116,431
Professional, scientific, and technical services......	54	3,927	([10])	18,509	1,143,107
Management of companies and enterprises......	55	20	(S)	758	34,736
Administrative & support and waste management & remediation services......	56	1,783	([10])	36,685	1,255,493
Educational services......	61	352	([8])	1,595	35,619
Health care and social assistance......	62	3,148	([10])	29,497	796,908
Arts, entertainment, and recreation......	71	337	([11])	1,856	263,966
Accommodation and food services......	72	2,167	([10])	27,427	572,533
Other services (except public administration) [6]......	81	(S)	(S)	([13])	(S)
Industries not classified......	99	(S)	(S)	([14])	(S)

X Not applicable. S Data does not meet publication standards. [1] Based on the 2017 North American Industry Classification System (NAICS); see text, this section. [2] Paid employees for pay period including March 12. [3] Firms with more than one domestic establishment are counted in each industry in which they operate, but only once in the total. [4] Excludes rail transportation (NAICS 482) and the postal service (NAICS 491). [5] Excludes monetary authorities-central banks (NAICS 521) and funds, trusts, and other financial vehicles (NAICS 525). [6] Excludes religious, grantmaking, civic, professional, and similar organizations (NAICS 813) and private households (NAICS 814). [7] $150 million to less than $500 million. [8] $75 million to less than $150 million. [9] $5 billion or more. [10] $1 billion to less than $5 billion. [11] $500 million to less than $1 billion. [12] 1,000 to 2,499 employees. [13] 5,000 to 9,999 employees. [14] 100 to 249 employees.

Source: U.S. Census Bureau, Annual Business Survey, Table AB1900CSA01, "Statistics for Employer Firms by Industry, Sex, Ethnicity, Race, and Veteran Status for the U.S., States, and Metro Areas: 2019," <data.census.gov>, accessed January 2022.

Table 813. Bankruptcy Petitions by Type and Chapter: 2000 to 2021

[For years ending June 30. Covers only bankruptcy cases filed under the Bankruptcy Reform Act of 1978. Bankruptcy: legal recognition that a company or individual is insolvent and must restructure or liquidate assets. Section 101 of the U.S. Bankruptcy Code defines consumer (nonbusiness) debt as that incurred by an individual primarily for a personal, family, or household purpose. If the debtor is a corporation or partnership, or if debt related to operation of a business predominates, the nature of the debt is business]

Item	2000	2005	2010	2015	2017	2018	2019	2020	2021
Total filed......	1,276,922	1,637,254	1,572,597	879,736	796,037	775,578	773,361	682,363	462,309
Chapter 7 [1]......	885,447	1,196,212	1,133,320	568,679	489,011	479,151	479,043	440,593	335,886
Chapter 9 [2]......	8	6	12	7	9	6	3	6	4
Chapter 11 [3]......	9,947	6,703	14,272	6,672	6,999	7,141	7,007	7,355	6,871
Chapter 12 [4]......	732	290	660	357	482	475	535	580	438
Chapter 13 [5]......	380,770	433,945	424,242	303,945	299,398	288,741	286,635	233,644	118,864
Section 304 [6]......	18	98	(X)	(X)	(X)	(X)	(X)	(X)	(X)
Chapter 15 [7]......	(X)	(X)	91	76	138	64	138	185	246
Business [8]......	36,910	32,406	59,608	25,046	23,443	22,245	22,483	22,482	18,511
Nonbusiness [9]......	1,240,012	1,604,848	1,512,989	854,690	772,594	753,333	750,878	659,881	443,798
Chapter 7 [1]......	864,183	1,174,681	1,091,322	551,808	474,258	465,472	464,978	426,876	325,420
Chapter 11 [3]......	722	847	1,827	1,078	1,099	1,071	1,039	777	496
Chapter 13 [5]......	375,107	429,315	419,836	301,802	297,237	286,790	284,861	232,228	117,882
Total pending......	1,400,416	1,750,562	1,659,399	1,316,672	1,100,309	1,050,476	1,032,572	954,786	807,243

X Not applicable. [1] Chapter 7, liquidation of nonexempt assets of businesses or individuals. [2] Chapter 9, adjustment of debts of a municipality. [3] Chapter 11, individual or business reorganization. [4] Chapter 12, adjustment of debts of a family farmer with regular income, effective November 26, 1986. [5] Chapter 13, adjustment of debts of an individual with regular income. [6] Chapter 11, U.S.C., Section 304, cases ancillary to foreign proceedings. [7] Chapter 15 was added and Section 304 was terminated by changes in Bankruptcy Laws effective October 2005. [8] Business bankruptcies include those filed under Chapters 7, 9, 11, 12, 13, or 15. [9] Includes other petitions, not shown separately.

Source: Administrative Office of the United States Courts, "Caseload Statistics Data Tables," <www.uscourts.gov/statistics-reports/caseload-statistics-data-tables>, accessed January 2022.

Table 814. Bankruptcy Cases Filed by State: 2000 to 2021

[In thousands (1,276.9 represents 1,276,900). For years ending June 30. Covers only bankruptcy cases filed under the Bankruptcy Reform Act of 1978. Bankruptcy: legal recognition that a company or individual is insolvent and must restructure or liquidate. Petitions "filed" means the commencement of a proceeding through the presentation of a petition to the clerk of the court]

State	2000	2005	2010	2014	2015	2016	2017	2018	2019	2020	2021
Total [1]	**1,276.9**	**1,637.3**	**1,572.6**	**1,000.1**	**879.7**	**819.2**	**796.0**	**775.6**	**773.4**	**682.4**	**462.3**
Alabama...........	31.4	42.6	34.9	26.1	25.2	26.1	27.2	26.7	26.6	24.2	15.3
Alaska..............	1.4	1.6	1.1	0.5	0.4	0.5	0.5	0.4	0.5	0.4	0.3
Arizona............	21.7	32.4	40.7	21.9	18.0	16.5	15.4	16.1	16.7	15.6	11.7
Arkansas..........	16.3	25.5	16.9	11.8	10.4	10.4	10.7	10.5	10.6	9.7	5.9
California..........	160.6	122.6	242.0	116.7	91.9	77.8	73.4	69.5	69.0	61.7	46.5
Colorado...........	15.6	30.2	31.9	20.3	16.0	13.8	12.5	11.8	11.4	10.1	7.5
Connecticut.......	11.4	11.8	11.3	7.1	6.6	6.1	5.7	5.9	6.2	5.4	3.4
Delaware...........	4.9	3.6	4.5	3.4	2.7	2.9	2.8	3.2	2.9	3.1	2.5
District of Columbia. ..	2.6	1.9	1.3	0.8	0.8	0.7	0.7	0.8	0.8	0.7	0.4
Florida..............	74.0	85.8	107.4	73.3	62.4	50.3	44.7	41.3	45.8	42.7	34.5
Georgia............	57.9	77.3	77.8	55.2	51.1	49.4	48.1	45.7	44.5	38.4	22.4
Hawaii..............	5.0	3.2	3.7	1.9	1.6	1.5	1.4	1.5	1.6	1.6	1.5
Idaho...............	7.3	9.7	8.3	5.1	4.4	3.9	3.8	3.7	3.7	3.3	2.4
Illinois..............	62.3	83.6	80.8	62.9	58.8	55.8	52.3	49.7	47.9	42.1	24.3
Indiana.............	37.5	55.9	49.3	31.2	28.0	25.1	24.0	23.0	23.0	20.7	15.8
Iowa................	8.2	14.3	10.4	5.5	4.7	4.4	4.2	4.6	4.7	4.6	3.2
Kansas.............	11.4	17.3	11.4	8.0	7.2	6.5	6.8	6.8	6.8	5.7	3.9
Kentucky...........	20.8	29.2	26.0	17.9	15.8	15.4	15.5	15.4	15.1	13.9	9.9
Louisiana..........	23.1	31.1	19.5	15.6	14.3	14.0	13.4	13.5	13.3	10.7	6.5
Maine..............	4.1	4.7	4.1	2.2	2.0	1.7	1.4	1.5	1.4	1.3	0.8
Maryland...........	31.1	28.5	29.1	21.9	19.0	17.9	17.5	17.5	17.4	15.0	9.2
Massachusetts.........	16.7	19.6	22.9	11.4	9.6	8.9	8.6	8.5	8.1	6.2	3.6
Michigan...........	36.4	68.5	71.0	38.6	33.6	32.1	30.6	30.2	30.0	26.8	18.7
Minnesota.........	15.4	19.4	22.6	13.4	11.3	10.1	9.6	9.9	9.8	9.1	5.8
Mississippi.........	17.9	21.8	14.8	12.4	10.9	11.1	11.9	12.6	12.6	11.5	6.6
Missouri............	26.3	39.2	32.9	22.3	19.9	18.8	18.4	17.8	17.0	15.3	10.7
Montana............	3.3	4.4	3.1	1.7	1.4	1.4	1.3	1.3	1.3	1.1	0.7
Nebraska...........	5.6	9.6	7.9	4.9	4.3	4.2	4.0	4.0	4.1	3.8	3.0
Nevada.............	14.3	16.3	31.0	12.3	10.2	9.2	8.9	9.0	9.8	8.8	8.0
New Hampshire.......	3.9	4.9	5.7	2.9	2.3	2.0	1.8	1.8	1.8	1.5	0.8
New Jersey.........	38.7	40.7	39.7	28.4	26.1	25.7	26.5	26.7	25.9	20.0	11.9
New Mexico.........	7.1	10.1	6.6	4.0	3.6	3.3	3.4	3.3	3.2	2.8	1.9
New York...........	61.7	81.7	58.2	34.6	30.9	30.2	31.6	34.2	35.5	28.4	17.3
North Carolina........	25.8	37.5	27.7	17.6	16.2	15.4	14.7	14.3	13.4	11.9	7.1
North Dakota..........	2.0	2.5	1.6	0.7	0.6	0.6	0.8	0.8	0.8	0.7	0.6
Ohio................	53.6	95.8	72.9	43.6	39.9	37.7	37.4	37.9	37.2	33.3	22.7
Oklahoma..........	19.3	28.2	15.1	10.2	9.4	9.1	9.5	9.6	9.5	8.7	6.5
Oregon.............	18.1	25.3	20.1	13.1	11.5	9.9	9.1	9.0	8.9	8.2	5.5
Pennsylvania.........	43.8	62.3	38.8	25.9	22.7	22.2	22.4	21.7	21.4	17.9	12.0
Rhode Island...........	4.8	4.4	5.4	3.3	2.7	2.4	2.2	2.3	2.0	1.7	1.2
South Carolina........	11.7	15.2	9.7	7.6	7.1	6.7	6.6	6.6	6.8	6.1	3.7
South Dakota.........	2.1	2.9	2.0	1.3	1.2	1.1	1.0	1.1	1.0	0.9	0.7
Tennessee...........	47.1	60.8	52.5	40.7	37.3	36.5	35.8	34.5	34.0	29.0	17.4
Texas...............	62.9	97.5	57.8	38.9	34.7	33.7	35.6	33.5	35.2	32.3	22.1
Utah................	14.4	20.5	17.0	14.0	13.0	11.8	11.7	10.3	9.6	8.8	6.6
Vermont............	1.6	1.7	1.7	0.8	0.7	0.6	0.5	0.6	0.6	0.5	0.3
Virginia.............	37.1	38.8	37.8	25.1	23.2	23.3	22.8	22.8	22.9	20.6	14.1
Washington...........	31.2	37.7	33.5	22.9	19.7	17.4	15.5	13.9	13.0	10.9	7.1
West Virginia.........	8.2	12.6	6.6	3.5	3.3	3.3	3.4	3.1	2.9	2.7	1.9
Wisconsin..........	18.0	29.0	30.0	22.0	19.9	17.7	17.1	16.9	16.4	14.2	10.5
Wyoming............	2.0	2.5	1.5	1.1	0.9	0.9	1.0	1.0	0.9	0.7	0.7

[1] Includes Island Areas, not shown separately.

Source: Administrative Office of the United States Courts, "Caseload Statistics Data Tables," <www.uscourts.gov/statistics-reports/caseload-statistics-data-tables>, accessed January 2022.

Table 815. Patents and Trademarks: 2000 to 2020

[In thousands (176.0 represents 176,000), unless otherwise noted. Calendar year data. Covers U.S. patents issued to citizens of the United States and residents of foreign countries. For data on foreign countries, see Table 1402]

Type	2000	2005	2010	2015	2016	2017	2018	2019	2020
Patents issued	**176.0**	**157.7**	**244.3**	**326.0**	**333.6**	**351.4**	**340.0**	**391.1**	**388.9**
Inventions	157.5	143.8	219.6	298.4	303.0	318.8	307.8	354.4	352.0
Individuals	22.4	14.7	16.6	18.9	18.7	19.3	18.7	20.9	20.3
Corporations:									
United States	70.9	65.2	97.8	133.4	136.8	145.3	140.0	162.8	161.5
Foreign [1]	63.3	63.2	104.3	145.1	146.7	153.3	148.1	169.7	169.3
U.S. government	0.9	0.7	0.9	1.0	0.9	1.0	0.9	1.1	0.9
Designs	17.4	13.0	22.8	26.0	28.9	30.9	30.5	34.8	34.9
Botanical plants	0.5	0.7	1.0	1.1	1.2	1.3	1.2	1.3	1.4
Reissues	0.5	0.2	0.9	0.5	0.4	0.4	0.5	0.6	0.6
U.S. residents	96.9	82.6	121.2	156.0	160.5	169.2	161.8	186.1	183.1
Foreign country residents	79.1	75.2	123.2	170.0	173.0	182.2	178.2	205.0	205.7
Percent of total	44.9	47.6	50.4	52.1	51.9	51.8	52.4	52.4	52.9
Trademarks:									
Applications filed	361.8	334.7	368.9	503.9	530.3	594.1	638.8	673.2	738.1

[1] Includes patents to foreign governments.

Source: U.S. Patent and Trademark Office, "General Patent Statistics Reports Available for Viewing," <www.uspto.gov/web/offices/ac/ido/oeip/taf/reports.htm>, accessed January 2022.

Table 816. Patents by State and Island Areas: 2020

[Includes only U.S. patents granted to residents of the United States and U.S. territories]

State	Total	Inventions	Designs	Botanical plants	Reissues	State	Total	Inventions	Designs	Botanical plants	Reissues
Total [1]	**183,147**	**164,572**	**17,701**	**597**	**277**	Missouri	1,657	1,510	143	1	3
						Montana	180	148	27	4	1
Alabama	607	537	69	1	0	Nebraska	427	365	62	0	0
Alaska	67	59	8	0	0	Nevada	1,045	895	150	0	0
Arizona	3,140	2,870	264	2	4	New Hampshire	1,103	990	110	0	3
Arkansas	535	453	79	2	1	New Jersey	5,027	4,479	530	4	14
California	50,496	46,040	4,168	208	80	New Mexico	509	479	30	0	0
Colorado	3,740	3,357	380	0	3	New York	10,540	9,361	1,155	3	21
Connecticut	3,478	3,259	213	3	3	North Carolina	3,917	3,603	294	11	9
Delaware	358	333	25	0	0	North Dakota	138	128	10	0	0
District of Columbia	339	318	21	0	0	Ohio	5,386	4,583	790	8	5
Florida	5,513	4,659	801	37	16	Oklahoma	689	626	56	6	1
Georgia	3,365	2,942	398	21	4	Oregon	4,093	3,192	877	18	6
Hawaii	161	141	19	1	0	Pennsylvania	4,737	4,271	448	13	5
Idaho	1,213	1,161	51	0	1	Rhode Island	503	407	95	0	1
Illinois	6,175	5,379	781	11	4	South Carolina	1,382	1,206	173	3	0
Indiana	2,529	2,242	284	0	3	South Dakota	165	145	19	0	1
Iowa	1,202	1,130	72	0	0	Tennessee	1,494	1,227	257	3	7
Kansas	905	788	115	2	0	Texas	13,192	12,201	953	23	15
Kentucky	869	776	92	1	0	Utah	2,036	1,699	336	0	1
Louisiana	512	454	47	11	0	Vermont	359	325	34	0	0
Maine	228	204	24	0	0	Virginia	3,002	2,827	165	1	9
Maryland	2,482	2,309	167	2	0	Washington	9,112	8,553	530	22	7
Massachusetts	8,790	8,176	587	9	18	West Virginia	134	118	15	1	0
Michigan	7,478	6,493	829	147	9	Wisconsin	2,939	2,416	506	9	8
Minnesota	4,734	4,350	372	2	10	Wyoming	159	147	12	0	0
Mississippi	205	165	34	6	0	Island areas	81	57	23	1	0

[1] Includes unspecified areas.

Source: U.S. Patent and Trademark Office, "General Patent Statistics Reports Available for Viewing," <www.uspto.gov/web/offices/ac/ido/oeip/taf/reports_stco.htm>, accessed January 2022.

Table 817. Copyright Registration by Subject Matter: 1990 to 2020

[In thousands (590.7 represents 590,700). For years ending September 30. Comprises claims to copyrights registered for both U.S. and foreign works. Semiconductor chips and renewals are not considered copyright registration claims]

Subject matter	1990	2000	2005	2010	2015	2016	2017	2018	2019	2020
Total copyright basic registrations	590.7	497.6	515.2	636.0	443.0	414.1	451.7	559.5	547.7	443.9
Monographs [1]	179.7	169.7	191.4	245.8	175.5	168.8	153.0	197.3	185.9	152.0
Serials	111.5	69.0	57.7	90.5	55.1	41.9	49.5	54.9	41.9	26.1
Sound recordings	37.5	34.2	49.9	77.9	43.0	42.4	59.2	77.2	83.7	(NA)
Performing arts [2]	185.3	138.9	133.7	124.5	80.1	75.3	103.5	136.4	147.5	183.1
Works of the visual arts [3]	76.7	85.8	82.5	97.2	89.2	85.6	86.5	93.7	88.8	82.7
Renewals	51.8	16.8	15.8	0.1	0.8	0.2	0.4	0.4	0.1	–
Mask work (semiconductor chip products)	1.0	0.7	0.5	0.3	0.1	(Z)	(Z)	0.2	(Z)	–

NA Not available. Z Less than 50. – Represents zero. [1] Includes computer software and machine readable works. [2] Includes musical works, dramatic works, choreography, pantomimes, motion pictures, and filmstrips. Beginning 2020, includes sound recordings. [3] Two-dimensional works of fine and graphic art, including prints and art reproductions; sculptural works; technical drawings and models; photographs; commercial prints and labels; and works of applied arts, cartographic works, and multimedia works.

Source: The Library of Congress, *Annual Report of the Librarian of Congress, For the Fiscal Year Ending September 30, 2020*, 2021. See also <www.loc.gov/about/reports-and-budgets/annual-reports/>.

Table 818. Net Stock of Private Fixed Assets by Industry: 2010 to 2020

[In billions of dollars (34,468 represents $34,468,000,000,000). Estimates as of Dec. 31. Fixed assets are assets that are used repeatedly, or continuously, in processes of production for more than a year. Net stock estimates are presented in terms of current-cost, and cover equipment, structures, and intellectual property products. (pt) = part]

Industry	NAICS code [1]	2010	2015	2018	2019	2020
Private fixed assets.............	(X)	**34,468**	**41,444**	**47,600**	**49,541**	**51,720**
Agriculture, forestry, fishing, and hunting.............	11	487	640	703	722	735
Farms [2].............	111, 112	438	579	627	643	654
Forestry, fishing, and related activities.............	113-115	49	61	76	79	82
Mining.............	21	1,574	2,228	2,083	2,109	1,943
Oil and gas extraction.............	211	1,328	1,881	1,726	1,746	1,581
Mining, except oil and gas.............	212	137	196	216	227	234
Support activities for mining.............	213	109	151	141	136	128
Utilities.............	22	1,859	2,268	2,623	2,769	2,882
Construction.............	23	263	309	357	385	396
Manufacturing.............	31-33	3,137	3,643	4,047	4,185	4,324
Durable goods.............	(X)	1,630	1,868	2,045	2,094	2,131
Wood products.............	321	38	42	47	49	49
Nonmetallic mineral products.............	327	89	93	102	104	105
Primary metals.............	331	161	173	188	194	198
Fabricated metal products.............	332	161	187	206	210	213
Machinery.............	333	199	231	250	256	260
Computer and electronic products.............	334	467	535	567	578	594
Electrical equipment, appliances, and components.............	335	66	74	81	84	87
Motor vehicles, bodies and trailers, and parts.............	3361-3363	186	240	271	278	280
Other transportation equipment.............	3364, 3365, 3369	153	169	200	204	206
Furniture and related products.............	337	21	22	25	25	26
Miscellaneous manufacturing.............	339	89	101	109	112	115
Nondurable goods.............	(X)	1,507	1,776	2,002	2,092	2,193
Food and beverage and tobacco products.............	311, 312	285	328	367	382	391
Textile mills and textile product mills.............	313, 314	42	41	41	41	41
Apparel and leather and allied products.............	315, 316	18	18	18	18	18
Paper products.............	322	110	118	122	126	129
Printing and related support activities.............	323	49	47	48	48	47
Petroleum and coal products.............	324	195	236	259	266	271
Chemical products.............	325	717	887	1,033	1,091	1,174
Plastics and rubber products.............	326	91	102	115	119	121
Wholesale trade.............	42	490	587	687	720	737
Retail trade.............	44-45	1,131	1,293	1,434	1,501	1,513
Transportation and warehousing [3].............	48-49	1,095	1,320	1,510	1,591	1,643
Air transportation.............	481	219	250	292	303	307
Railroad transportation.............	482	359	413	433	441	448
Water transportation.............	483	43	55	63	64	66
Truck transportation.............	484	106	142	168	178	179
Transit and ground passenger transportation.............	485	42	44	48	49	49
Pipeline transportation.............	486	161	232	296	325	354
Warehousing and storage.............	493	40	49	61	68	73
Information.............	51	1,817	2,109	2,462	2,577	2,687
Publishing industries (includes software).............	511	249	315	356	365	380
Motion picture and sound recording industries.............	512	258	275	302	314	318
Broadcasting and telecommunications.............	515, 517	1,213	1,322	1,451	1,495	1,533
Information and data processing services.............	516 (pt), 518, 519	97	197	353	404	457
Finance and insurance.............	52	1,152	1,339	1,513	1,596	1,636
Federal Reserve banks.............	521	10	10	11	11	11
Credit intermediation and related activities.............	522	716	861	970	1,021	1,038
Securities, commodity contracts, and investments.............	523	152	164	199	216	229
Insurance carriers and related activities.............	524	235	264	293	307	317
Funds, trusts, and other financial vehicles.............	525	40	40	41	41	41
Real estate and rental and leasing.............	53	17,227	20,697	24,391	25,286	26,901
Real estate.............	531	16,880	20,214	23,827	24,684	26,292
Rental and leasing services and lessors of intangible assets [4].............	532, 533	347	483	563	602	609
Professional, scientific, and technical services [3].............	54	562	651	774	835	897
Legal services.............	5411	43	45	48	50	50
Computer systems design and related services.............	5415	93	94	104	113	122
Management of companies and enterprises [5].............	55	355	384	414	425	427
Administrative and support and waste management.............	56	245	299	344	364	377
Administrative and support services.............	561	153	198	233	248	259
Waste management and remediation services.............	562	92	101	111	116	118
Educational services.............	61	469	570	656	690	702
Health care and social assistance.............	62	1,219	1,461	1,658	1,738	1,808
Ambulatory health care services.............	621	317	368	421	441	461
Hospitals.............	622	773	931	1,051	1,097	1,135
Nursing and residential care facilities.............	623	76	96	113	119	124
Social assistance.............	624	53	66	74	82	87
Arts, entertainment, and recreation.............	71	289	360	460	494	517
Performing arts, spectator sports, museums, and related activities....	711, 712	142	174	206	218	225
Amusements, gambling, and recreation industries.............	713	147	186	253	276	293
Accommodation and food services.............	72	542	648	768	814	841
Accommodation.............	721	327	401	498	531	554
Food services and drinking places.............	722	215	247	270	284	287
Other services, except government.............	81	556	638	715	740	753

X Not applicable. [1] Based on North American Industry Classification System; see text this section. [2] NAICS crop and animal production. [3] Includes other activities, not shown separately. [4] Intangible assets include patents, trademarks, and franchise agreements, but not copyrights. [5] Consists of bank and other holding companies.

Source: U.S. Bureau of Economic Analysis, National Economic Accounts, "Table 3.1ESI. Current-Cost Net Stock of Private Fixed Assets by Industry," <apps.bea.gov/itable/>, accessed January 2022.

Table 819. Capital Expenditures: 2000 to 2020

[In billions of dollars (1,161 represents $1,161,000,000,000). Based on the Annual Capital Expenditure Survey, which is a sample survey and subject to sampling error; see source for details]

Item	All companies				Companies with employees				Companies without employees			
	2000	2010	2019	2020	2000	2010	2019	2020	2000	2010	2019	2020
Capital expenditures, total...........	**1,161**	**1,106**	**1,917**	**1,706**	**1,090**	**1,036**	**1,806**	**1,597**	**71**	**70**	**111**	**109**
Structures.....................................	364	430	770	675	338	396	711	616	26	33	59	59
New..	329	395	704	624	309	368	658	578	20	28	45	46
Used..	35	34	67	51	29	29	53	38	6	6	14	13
Equipment...................................	797	676	1,147	1,031	752	640	1,095	981	45	36	52	50
New..	751	638	1,074	968	718	612	1,037	927	32	27	37	41
Used..	46	38	73	63	34	28	58	55	12	10	15	8
Capitalized computer software [1]..........	(NA)	(NA)	(NA)	(NA)	(NA)	(NA)	120	118	(NA)	(NA)	(NA)	(NA)
Capital leases [1]...............................	20	16	53	51	19	15	52	51	(Z)	1	1	1

NA Not available. Z Less than $500 million. [1] Included in structures and equipment data shown above.

Source: U.S. Census Bureau, "Annual Capital Expenditures: 2020," and earlier reports, <www.census.gov/programs-surveys/aces.html>, accessed January 2022.

Table 820. Capital Expenditures by Industry: 2000 to 2020

[In billions of dollars (1,090 represents $1,090,000,000,000). Covers only companies with employees. Data from 2000 based on the North American Industry Classification System (NAICS), 1997; 2005 data based on NAICS 2002; 2010 through 2013 based on NAICS 2007; 2014 through 2017 data based on NAICS 2012; and, beginning 2018, data based on NAICS 2017, see text this section. Based on the Annual Capital Expenditure Survey, which is a sample survey and subject to sampling error; see source for details]

Industry	NAICS code	2000	2005	2010	2015	2017	2018	2019	2020
Total expenditures............................	**(X)**	**1,090**	**1,063**	**1,036**	**1,548**	**1,578**	**1,699**	**1,806**	**1,597**
Forestry, fishing, and agricultural services......	113–115	1	3	3	3	4	5	4	3
Mining...	21	43	67	116	174	134	153	161	97
Utilities..	22	61	58	94	131	134	151	173	182
Construction....................................	23	25	30	18	33	35	39	51	53
Manufacturing..................................	31–33	215	166	161	245	247	258	273	258
Durable goods...............................	321, 327, 33	134	92	87	128	129	138	142	130
Nondurable goods...........................	31, 322–326	81	73	74	117	118	120	131	128
Wholesale trade................................	42	34	41	31	42	44	43	40	36
Retail trade......................................	44–45	70	74	65	86	90	89	99	106
Transportation and warehousing................	48–49	60	57	59	117	109	122	131	98
Information......................................	51	160	91	97	133	159	175	177	170
Finance and insurance.........................	52	134	161	103	165	163	182	195	174
Real estate and rental and leasing.............	53	92	103	81	152	161	174	180	134
Professional, scientific, & technical services...	54	34	33	28	33	37	42	44	40
Management of companies and enterprises...	55	5	3	5	5	7	7	7	7
Administrative & support and waste management & remediation services..........	56	18	18	17	26	27	29	31	29
Educational services............................	61	18	17	23	33	37	35	32	33
Health care and social assistance...............	62	52	74	78	94	105	109	114	105
Arts, entertainment, and recreation.............	71	19	14	12	16	22	25	25	18
Accommodation and food services.............	72	26	31	20	33	36	35	41	30
Other services (except public administration)...	81	21	20	21	23	22	22	25	23
Structure and equipment expenditures serving multiple industry categories............	(X)	2	2	2	4	5	3	3	2

X Not applicable.

Source: U.S. Census Bureau, "Annual Capital Expenditures: 2020," and earlier reports, <www.census.gov/programs-surveys/aces.html>, accessed January 2022.

Table 821. Private Domestic Investment in Current and Chained (2012) Dollars: 2000 to 2020

[In billions of dollars (2,038 represents $2,038,000,000,000). Covers equipment, structures, and intellectual property products. For explanation of chained dollars; see text, Section 13]

Item	2000	2005	2010	2015	2017	2018	2019	2020
CURRENT DOLLARS								
Gross private domestic investment............	**2,038**	**2,535**	**2,165**	**3,237**	**3,381**	**3,638**	**3,826**	**3,638**
Less: Consumption of fixed capital................	1,232	1,623	1,934	2,388	2,576	2,708	2,849	2,970
Equals: Net private domestic investment........	807	912	232	849	805	930	978	668
Fixed investment................................	1,984	2,477	2,112	3,100	3,352	3,579	3,753	3,697
Less: Consumption of fixed capital..............	1,232	1,623	1,934	2,388	2,576	2,708	2,849	2,970
Equals: Net fixed investment....................	752	855	178	712	776	871	904	728
Nonresidential................................	1,498	1,621	1,735	2,467	2,592	2,781	2,939	2,800
Residential....................................	485	856	377	634	760	799	814	898
Change in private inventories....................	55	58	54	137	29	59	74	-60
CHAINED (2012) DOLLARS								
Gross private domestic investment...........	**2,347**	**2,671**	**2,216**	**3,122**	**3,212**	**3,395**	**3,511**	**3,316**
Less: Consumption of fixed capital................	1,413	1,732	1,986	2,296	2,440	2,521	2,610	2,688
Equals: Net private domestic investment........	933	938	230	826	772	874	900	629
Fixed investment................................	2,294	2,619	2,164	2,979	3,164	3,316	3,421	3,329
Nonresidential................................	1,616	1,716	1,781	2,420	2,541	2,704	2,822	2,671
Residential....................................	647	885	383	555	616	612	607	648
Change in private inventories....................	79	64	57	138	34	66	75	-42

Source: U.S. Bureau of Economic Analysis, National Economic Accounts, "Table 5.2.5. Gross and Net Domestic Investment by Major Type" and "Table 5.2.6. Real Gross and Net Domestic Investment by Major Type, Chained Dollars," <apps.bea.gov/itable/index.cfm>, accessed July 2021.

Table 822. Firms Utilizing Selected Digital Technology by Industry: 2018

[In percent. Data cover U.S. nonfarm businesses with paid employees, with receipts of $1,000 or more, and which are classified in the 2017 North American Industry Classification System (NAICS). Data are based on estimates from the 2019 Annual Business Survey (ABS) collection of data for 2018. For methodology, see <www.census.gov/programs-surveys/abs/technical-documentation/methodology.html> and <www2.census.gov/programs-surveys/abs/tables/2019/2019-A-B-S-Technology-Tables-Methodology_final.pdf>]

Kind of business	NAICS code	Any use of technology by type				
		Artificial intelligence [1]	Cloud-based computing [2]	Specialized software [3]	Robotics	Specialized equipment [4]
Total	**(X)**	**3.0**	**32.4**	**38.3**	**1.9**	**17.9**
Forestry, fishing & hunting, and agricultural support services	113-115	1.5	14.8	19.7	1.3	19.9
Mining, quarrying, and oil and gas extraction	21	1.9	20.2	27.8	1.8	17.2
Utilities	22	2.8	33.8	41.2	1.7	26.9
Construction	23	1.7	22.9	25.5	1.2	17.3
Manufacturing	31-33	3.0	29.1	41.9	9.6	39.3
Wholesale trade	42	2.2	30.7	32.5	2.8	15.6
Retail trade	44-45	2.4	23.7	30.7	1.9	14.8
Transportation and warehousing [5]	48-49	2.5	24.1	29.0	0.9	14.5
Information	51	6.7	58.4	59.9	2.6	22.7
Finance and insurance [6]	52	4.5	48.8	55.2	0.8	6.4
Real estate and rental and leasing	53	3.4	38.0	40.1	0.6	6.6
Professional, scientific, and technical services	54	5.6	52.7	58.3	2.3	15.4
Management of companies and enterprises	55	4.5	47.0	50.4	8.4	25.1
Administrative & support and waste management & remediation services	56	2.7	30.1	32.9	1.0	16.3
Educational services	61	2.9	43.3	44.3	1.1	12.0
Health care and social assistance	62	3.3	39.3	50.6	2.2	31.5
Arts, entertainment, and recreation	71	1.6	32.3	37.2	0.9	15.7
Accommodation and food services	72	2.0	21.0	25.4	0.8	11.3
Other services (except public administration) [7]	81	1.8	20.6	31.6	1.2	25.0
Industries not classified	99	3.9	11.1	18.1	1.6	16.2

X Not applicable. [1] Artificial intelligence is a branch of computer science and engineering devoted to making machines intelligent. Intelligence is that quality that enables an entity to perceive, analyze, determine response and act appropriately in its environment. [2] Cloud based computing systems and applications are computing resources available on-demand via the internet. [3] Excludes artificial intelligence. [4] Excludes robotics. [5] Excludes rail transportation (NAICS 482) and the postal service (NAICS 491). [6] Excludes monetary authorities-central banks (NAICS 521) and funds, trusts, and other financial vehicles (NAICS 525). [7] Excludes religious, grantmaking, civic, professional, and similar organizations (NAICS 813) and private households (NAICS 814).

Source: U.S. Census Bureau, Annual Business Survey, Technology Characteristics of Businesses 2019 Tables, Table AB1800TCB01A, "Extent of Technology Use of Employer Firms by 2-digit NAICS for the United States and States: 2018," <www.census.gov/data/tables/2019/econ/abs/2019-abs-automation-technology-module.html>, accessed March 2021.

Table 823. Paycheck Protection Program Loans by Industry: 2020 and 2021

[In units as indicated (525.0 represents $525,000,000,000). The Coronavirus Aid, Relief, and Economic Security Act (CARES) temporarily added the Paycheck Protection Program (PPP) to the U.S. Small Business Administration's (SBA's) 7(a) Loan Program to assist small businesses and nonprofit institutions in covering payroll and other operational expenses during the COVID-19 pandemic. Lending was available in three rounds from April 3 to April 16, 2020, April 27 to August 8, 2020, and December 27, 2020 to May 31, 2021. Data for 2020 are for Round 1 and 2 of PPP approved lending through August 8, 2020; data for 2021 are for Round 3 approvals through May 31, 2021]

Industry	2020			2021		
	Number of loans	Net loans (bil. dol.)	Percent of total value	Number of loans	Net loans (bil. dol.)	Percent of total value
Total	**5,212,128**	**525.0**	**100**	**6,681,929**	**277.70**	**100**
Accommodation and food services	383,561	42.5	8	462,478	41.51	15
Construction	496,551	65.1	12	558,180	33.44	12
Health care and social assistance	532,775	67.8	13	485,698	28.82	10
Professional, scientific, and technical services	681,111	66.8	13	657,326	28.56	10
Other services, except public administration	583,385	31.7	6	1,107,768	27.35	10
Manufacturing	238,494	54.1	10	221,216	22.15	8
Transportation and warehousing	229,565	17.5	3	763,810	15.77	6
Retail trade	472,418	40.6	8	468,043	15.26	5
Administrative and support & waste management and remediation services	258,907	26.6	5	393,563	12.96	5
Wholesale trade	174,707	27.7	5	187,490	10.38	4
Agriculture, forestry, fishing, and hunting	149,535	8.1	2	532,884	10.02	4
Arts, entertainment, and recreation	130,760	8.2	2	223,882	7.45	3
Real estate and rental and leasing	262,921	15.7	3	262,928	7.34	3
Educational services	88,022	12.1	2	101,773	5.12	2
Information	73,824	9.3	2	75,128	4.12	1
Finance and insurance	181,493	12.2	2	127,088	3.42	1
Mining	22,503	4.5	1	21,676	2.84	1
Public administration	14291	1.8	(Z)	18,359	0.78	(Z)
Management of companies and enterprises	9,472	1.6	(Z)	6,812	0.46	(Z)
Utilities	8,331	1.5	(Z)	5,827	0.39	(Z)
Unclassified establishments	219,502	9.7	2	(X)	(X)	(X)

X Not applicable. Z Less than 0.5%.

Source: U.S. Small Business Administration, "Paycheck Protection Program (PPP) Report Approvals through 05/31/2021" and earlier reports, <www.sba.gov/funding-programs/loans/covid-19-relief-options/paycheck-protection-program/ppp-data>, accessed April 2022.

Table 824. Business Cycle Expansions and Contractions—Months of Duration: 1945 to 2020

[A trough is the low point of a business cycle; a peak is the high point. Contraction, or recession, is the period from peak to subsequent trough; expansion is the period from trough to subsequent peak. Business cycle reference dates are determined by the National Bureau of Economic Research, Inc]

Business cycle reference date				Contraction (peak to trough)	Expansion (previous trough to peak)	Length of cycle	
Peak		Trough				Trough from previous trough	Peak from previous peak
Month	Year	Month	Year				
February....................	1945	October	1945	8	[1] 80	[1] 88	[2] 93
November..................	1948	October	1949	11	37	48	45
July.........................	1953	May	1954	10	45	55	56
August.....................	1957	April	1958	8	39	47	49
April.......................	1960	February	1961	10	24	34	32
December.................	1969	November	1970	11	106	117	116
November..................	1973	March	1975	16	36	52	47
January....................	1980	July	1980	6	58	64	74
July.........................	1981	November	1982	16	12	28	18
July.........................	1990	March	1991	8	92	100	108
March......................	2001	November	2001	8	120	128	128
December.................	2007	June	2009	18	73	91	81
February...................	2020	April	2020	2	128	130	146
Average, all cycles: 1945 to 2020 (12 cycles)...	(X)	(X)	(X)	10.3	64.2	74.5	75.0

X Not applicable. [1] Previous trough: June 1938. [2] Previous peak: May 1937.

Source: National Bureau of Economic Research, Inc., Cambridge, MA, "US Business Cycle Expansions and Contractions," <www.nber.org/research/data/us-business-cycle-expansions-and-contractions>, accessed July 2021 ©.

Table 825. The Conference Board Leading, Coincident, and Lagging Economic Indexes®: 2000 to 2021

[299.4 represents 299,400]

Item	Unit	2000	2010	2015	2020	2021
The Conference Board Leading Economic Index® (LEI) for the U.S., composite....................	2016=100	91.0	82.7	99.6	108.0	115.6
Average weekly hours, manufacturing....................	Hours	41.2	41.1	41.8	40.7	41.5
Average weekly initial claims for unemployment insurance....................	1,000	299.4	458.5	277.1	1,376.5	462.6
Manufacturers' new orders, consumer goods and materials (1982 dollars)....................	Mil. dol.	152,070	122,219	134,706	120,165	116,008
Building permits, new private housing units....................	1,000	1,598	604	1,177	1,476	1,737
Manufacturers' new orders, nondefense capital goods excluding aircraft (1982 dollars)....................	Mil. dol.	45,991	36,339	37,585	33,809	36,642
Leading Credit Index™ (standard deviation from the mean)..	Std. dev.	1.1	-0.8	0.0	0.8	-1.7
Interest rate spread, 10-year Treasury bonds less federal funds....................	Percent	-0.21	3.04	2.00	0.52	1.36
The Conference Board Coincident Economic Index® (CEI) for the U.S., composite....................	2016=100	84.7	87.8	99.1	102.0	106.0
Employees on nonagricultural payrolls....................	1,000	132,018	130,337	141,804	142,146	146,102
Index of industrial production....................	2012=100	92.9	91.7	100.9	95.3	100.0
Personal income less transfer payments (2012 dollars)........	Bil. dol.	9,691	10,725	12,607	13,832	14,275
Manufacturing and trade sales (2012 dollars)....................	Mil. dol.	1,127,075	1,198,692	1,389,536	1,473,241	1,565,177
Composite index of 7 lagging indicators	2016=100	76.0	83.1	97.3	109.0	109.0
Inventories to sales ratio, manufacturing and trade............	Ratio	1.4	1.4	1.4	1.4	1.4
Average duration of unemployment....................	Weeks	12.7	33.1	29.1	18.2	18.2
Consumer installment credit to personal income ratio.........	Percent	18.7	20.2	21.7	21.2	21.2
Commercial and industrial loans outstanding (2012 dollars)....................	Mil. dol.	1,252,937	806,770	1,268,815	1,491,997	1,491,997
Change in labor cost per unit of output, manufacturing........	Percent	2.4	-2.4	4.1	4.5	4.5
Change in consumer price index for services..................	Percent	3.8	0.9	2.4	1.9	1.9
Average prime rate....................	Percent	9.2	3.3	3.3	3.5	3.5

Source: The Conference Board, New York, NY 10022-6601, *Business Cycle Indicators* (BCI), monthly. Reproduced with permission from The Conference Board, Inc. © 2022, The Conference Board, Inc. For more information, see <www.conference-board.org/data>.

Table 826. Manufacturing and Trade—Sales and Inventories: 1995 to 2021

[In billions of dollars (655 represents $655,000,000,000), except ratios. Based on North American Industry Classification System (NAICS); see text, this section]

Year	Sales, average monthly [1]				Inventories [2]				Inventory-sales ratio [3]			
	Total	Manufac-turing	Retail trade	Merchant whole-salers	Total	Manufac-turing	Retail trade	Merchant whole-salers	Total	Manufac-turing	Retail trade	Merchant whole-salers
1995......	655	290	185	180	985	425	322	238	1.48	1.44	1.72	1.29
1996......	687	300	197	190	1,005	430	333	241	1.45	1.44	1.67	1.27
1997......	723	320	206	198	1,045	443	344	258	1.42	1.37	1.64	1.26
1998......	742	325	215	202	1,077	448	357	272	1.44	1.39	1.62	1.32
1999......	786	336	234	217	1,137	463	384	290	1.40	1.35	1.59	1.30
2000......	834	351	249	235	1,196	481	406	309	1.41	1.35	1.59	1.29
2001......	818	331	255	232	1,119	427	394	298	1.42	1.38	1.58	1.32
2002......	823	326	261	236	1,140	423	415	301	1.36	1.29	1.55	1.26
2003......	855	335	272	248	1,148	408	431	308	1.34	1.25	1.56	1.22
2004......	926	359	289	278	1,242	441	460	340	1.30	1.19	1.56	1.17
2005......	1,006	395	307	303	1,314	475	472	368	1.27	1.17	1.51	1.17
2006......	1,069	418	323	328	1,409	523	486	399	1.28	1.20	1.49	1.17
2007......	1,128	443	333	352	1,488	563	501	425	1.28	1.22	1.49	1.17
2008......	1,161	456	328	377	1,466	543	477	446	1.31	1.26	1.52	1.20
2009......	989	369	301	319	1,332	505	429	398	1.38	1.39	1.47	1.29
2010......	1,089	409	318	362	1,451	554	454	443	1.27	1.28	1.39	1.15
2011......	1,207	458	342	407	1,567	607	471	489	1.26	1.29	1.35	1.15
2012......	1,268	475	359	434	1,658	625	507	526	1.28	1.30	1.38	1.18
2013......	1,306	485	372	450	1,727	632	545	551	1.29	1.30	1.41	1.19
2014......	1,347	491	387	469	1,790	643	562	586	1.32	1.31	1.43	1.22
2015......	1,304	461	394	449	1,824	638	588	598	1.39	1.40	1.46	1.33
2016......	1,296	447	404	445	1,859	636	611	612	1.42	1.42	1.50	1.36
2017......	1,357	462	420	475	1,918	659	625	633	1.39	1.39	1.48	1.31
2018......	1,437	491	438	508	2,002	677	653	672	1.36	1.37	1.46	1.28
2019......	1,434	478	450	506	2,043	709	654	680	1.42	1.46	1.47	1.35
2020......	1,382	435	464	483	1,987	697	622	668	1.44	1.61	1.34	1.38
2021......	1,622	483	547	592	2,198	759	649	789	1.28	1.51	1.13	1.23

[1] Averages of monthly not-seasonally-adjusted figures. [2] Seasonally adjusted end-of-year data. [3] Averages of seasonally adjusted monthly ratios.

Source: U.S. Census Bureau, "Manufacturing & Trade Inventories & Sales," <www.census.gov/mtis/index.html>, accessed June 2022.

Table 827. Industrial Production Indexes by Industry: 2000 to 2021

[2017 = 100]

Industry	NAICS code [1]	2000	2005	2010	2015	2018	2019	2020	2021
Total index..................................	([2])	**92.7**	**96.8**	**91.6**	**100.8**	**103.2**	**102.5**	**95.3**	**100.0**
Manufacturing (SIC) [3].........................	([4])	**97.0**	**102.0**	**93.5**	**100.2**	**101.3**	**99.4**	**93.1**	**98.4**
Manufacturing (NAICS).......................	31–33	93.4	99.3	92.5	100.1	101.5	99.6	93.3	98.8
Durable goods..............................	([5])	82.2	90.1	86.2	100.5	103.1	100.2	91.5	98.7
Wood products..........................	321	116.9	124.8	79.6	95.3	100.4	95.7	96.0	101.2
Nonmetallic mineral products...........	327	119.9	125.2	86.6	99.2	100.4	100.8	97.1	97.5
Primary metals.........................	331	114.6	108.2	103.8	105.7	103.2	97.3	86.2	96.6
Fabricated metal products...............	332	113.4	106.9	92.9	102.6	104.5	102.4	93.2	95.8
Machinery...............................	333	110.5	103.6	95.7	103.7	104.6	101.5	90.2	98.7
Computers and electronic products......	334	31.9	49.9	72.2	91.2	104.9	106.3	106.1	112.2
Electrical equipment, appliances, and components.........................	335	134.2	112.4	92.6	100.8	101.6	101.3	96.9	103.3
Motor vehicles and parts.................	3361–3363	83.6	88.0	66.9	99.7	104.1	102.3	88.4	96.4
Aerospace and other misc. transportation equipment.................	3364–3369	70.2	74.0	86.8	102.3	99.8	91.3	77.0	90.7
Furniture and related products...........	337	139.2	141.7	86.9	100.6	101.1	94.5	85.4	88.1
Miscellaneous products....................	339	96.0	110.3	108.3	105.2	103.5	100.1	93.7	103.5
Nondurable goods...........................	([6])	107.8	110.6	99.8	99.7	99.7	98.8	95.2	98.8
Food, beverage, and tobacco products..	311–312	93.2	97.5	94.8	98.5	99.8	99.9	100.3	101.5
Textile and product mills.................	313–314	220.4	190.8	113.8	109.0	98.6	95.6	88.5	94.2
Apparel and leather.......................	315–316	516.8	285.8	136.5	107.3	96.4	96.7	82.4	90.6
Paper....................................	322	124.1	116.2	100.6	101.9	99.1	99.1	94.0	95.5
Printing and related support..............	323	145.7	132.4	104.6	98.6	100.4	96.5	88.2	89.1
Petroleum and coal products.............	324	82.5	92.6	90.5	90.6	99.9	99.9	80.3	92.0
Chemical.................................	325	103.0	117.0	108.6	102.0	98.6	97.2	95.4	99.8
Plastics and rubber products.............	326	110.3	110.2	89.0	99.9	103.0	101.1	95.5	99.7
Other manufacturing (non-NAICS) [7]........	1133, 5111	224.0	196.9	129.5	103.9	96.7	92.6	85.2	85.0
Mining..	21	**83.9**	**79.3**	**82.4**	**104.6**	**113.3**	**120.8**	**102.7**	**105.9**
Electric and gas utilities....................	2211–2212	**90.6**	**98.0**	**101.2**	**101.2**	**104.9**	**104.0**	**101.0**	**102.9**
Electric power generation, transmission, and distribution.............	2211	89.6	98.3	101.5	101.0	103.7	102.5	100.0	102.1
Natural gas distribution......................	2212	97.0	95.6	99.5	102.7	112.2	113.6	106.8	106.9

[1] Except as noted, based on North American Industry Classification System, 2012; see text, this section. [2] Includes NAICS codes 31–33, 1133, 5111, 21, 2211, and 2212. [3] Standard Industrial Classification (SIC); see text, this section. [4] Includes NAICS codes 31–33, 1133, and 5111. [5] Includes NAICS codes 321, 327, and 331–339. [6] Includes NAICS codes 311–316, and 322–326. [7] Industries that have traditionally been considered to be manufacturing (logging and newspaper, periodical, book, and directory publishing).

Source: Board of Governors of the Federal Reserve System, "Industrial Production and Capacity Utilization, G.17," <www.federalreserve.gov/econres.htm>, accessed July 2022.

Table 828. Index of Industrial Capacity and Utilization Rate: 1990 to 2021

[2017 output = 100. Annual figures are averages of monthly data. The capacity index is an indicator of the maximum sustainable output a plant can maintain under realistic circumstances; capacity here is expressed as a proportion of 2017 actual output. Capacity utilization rate is a measure of output as a proportion of capacity; this is the output index divided by the capacity index]

| Year | Index of capacity | | Utilization rate | | | | | |
| | | | | Stage of process | | | | |
	Total industry	Manufacturing [1]	Total industry	Crude [2]	Primary and semifinished [3]	Finished [4]	Manufacturing [1]
1990	75.8	76.4	82.4	88.0	82.6	80.6	81.6
1995	85.9	87.9	83.9	89.0	86.3	79.8	83.1
2000	113.7	121.6	81.5	88.6	83.8	77.1	79.8
2005	120.7	129.8	80.2	86.7	81.9	75.8	78.6
2010	125.0	133.1	73.3	83.6	71.3	70.9	70.3
2014	130.0	133.0	78.7	87.6	77.2	75.0	75.8
2015	130.9	131.6	77.1	79.7	77.1	75.9	76.1
2016	131.0	131.9	75.3	74.2	76.3	74.6	75.4
2017	130.7	131.2	76.5	78.6	77.0	75.1	76.2
2018	129.8	129.8	79.5	86.1	79.8	76.2	78.1
2019	130.8	129.3	78.3	86.0	78.4	75.2	76.9
2020	131.2	128.6	72.6	73.6	72.9	71.9	72.4
2021	129.2	127.5	77.4	81.0	76.6	76.7	77.1

[1] Manufacturing consists of those industries included in the North American Industry Classification System (NAICS) definition of manufacturing plus those industries—logging and newspaper, periodical, book, and directory publishing—that have traditionally been considered to be a part of manufacturing and are included in the industrial sector under the Standard Industrial Classification (SIC) system. [2] Crude processing covers a relatively small portion of total industrial capacity and consists of logging (NAICS 1133), much of mining (excluding stone, sand, and gravel mining, and oil and gas drilling, NAICS 21231, 21221–2, and 213111) and some basic manufacturing industries, including basic chemicals (NAICS 3251); fertilizers, pesticides, and other agricultural chemicals (NAICS 32531, 2); pulp, paper, and paperboard mills (NAICS 3221); and alumina, aluminum, and other nonferrous production and processing mills (NAICS 3313, 4). [3] Primary and semifinished processing loosely corresponds to the previously published aggregate, primary processing. Includes utilities and portions of several 2-digit SIC industries included in the former advanced processing group. These include printing and related support activities (NAICS 3231); paints and adhesives (NAICS 3255); and newspaper, periodical, book, and directory publishers (NAICS 5111). [4] Finished processing generally corresponds to the previously published aggregate, advanced processing. Includes oil and gas well drilling and carpet and rug mills.

Source: Board of Governors of the Federal Reserve System, "Industrial Production and Capacity Utilization, G.17," <www.federalreserve.gov/data.htm>, accessed July 2022.

Table 829. Corporate Profits, Taxes, and Dividends: 2000 to 2021

[In billions of dollars (786.6 represents $786,600,000,000). Covers corporations organized for profit and other entities treated as corporations. Represents profits to U.S. residents, without deduction of depletion charges and exclusive of capital gains and losses; intercorporate dividends from profits of domestic corporations are eliminated; and net receipts of dividends, reinvested earnings of incorporated foreign affiliates, and earnings of unincorporated foreign affiliates are added. Minus (-) sign indicates loss]

Item	2000	2010	2015	2016	2017	2018	2019	2020	2021
Corporate profits with IVA and CCAdj [1]	786.6	1,728.7	2,060.5	2,037.7	2,128.9	2,305.0	2,367.8	2,243.8	2,805.8
Taxes on corporate income	233.4	272.3	396.3	376.2	312.3	281.5	302.2	275.6	381.2
Profits after tax with IVA and CCAdj [1]	553.1	1,456.5	1,664.2	1,661.5	1,816.6	2,023.4	2,065.6	1,968.1	2,424.6
Net dividends	410.2	643.2	1,164.9	1,189.4	1,264.1	1,338.4	1,386.4	1,394.9	1,418.6
Undistributed profits with IVA and CCAdj [1]	142.9	813.3	499.3	472.1	552.5	685.0	679.2	573.3	1,006.0
Addenda for corporate cash flow:									
Net cash flow with IVA and CCAdj [1]	981.5	2,105.0	2,090.7	2,095.1	1,959.1	2,454.9	2,571.8	2,516.6	3,074.5
Undistributed profits with IVA and CCAdj [1]	142.9	813.3	499.3	472.1	552.5	685.0	679.2	573.3	1,006.0
Consumption of fixed capital	838.6	1,271.2	1,588.2	1,627.4	1,700.8	1,780.5	1,880.2	1,957.0	2,081.4
Less: Capital transfers paid (net)	–	-20.6	-3.2	4.4	294.2	10.7	-12.4	13.6	12.8

– Represents or rounds to zero. [1] Inventory valuation adjustment (IVA) and capital consumption adjustment (CCAdj).

Source: U.S. Bureau of Economic Analysis, National Income and Product Accounts Tables, "Table 1.12. National Income by Type of Income," <apps.bea.gov/itable/index.cfm>, accessed June 2022.

Table 830. Corporate Profits With Inventory Valuation and Capital Consumption Adjustments—Financial and Nonfinancial Industries: 2000 to 2021

[In billions of dollars (787 represents $787,000,000,000). Based on the North American Industry Classification System, 2012; see text, this section. Minus sign (-) indicates loss. See headnote, Table 829]

Industry group	2000	2010	2015	2016	2017	2018	2019	2020	2021
Corporate profits with IVA/CCAdj [1]	**787**	**1,729**	**2,060**	**2,038**	**2,129**	**2,305**	**2,368**	**2,244**	**2,806**
Domestic industries	641	1,343	1,665	1,618	1,630	1,783	1,854	1,789	2,314
Rest of the world	146	386	395	420	499	522	513	455	491
Corporate profits with IVA [1]	**730**	**1,786**	**2,185**	**2,139**	**2,148**	**2,211**	**2,255**	**2,166**	**2,754**
Domestic industries	584	1,401	1,789	1,719	1,649	1,690	1,741	1,711	2,262
Financial [2]	150	406	447	457	436	450	533	503	574
Nonfinancial	434	995	1,342	1,261	1,213	1,239	1,208	1,209	1,688
Utilities	24	31	20	9	14	22	8	10	18
Manufacturing	176	282	427	337	317	347	356	329	477
Wholesale trade	59	99	152	128	123	114	118	124	141
Retail trade	51	116	169	175	150	148	159	219	282
Transportation and warehousing	10	45	61	65	59	49	38	19	48
Information	-12	102	136	158	139	140	128	135	171
Other nonfinancial [3]	126	320	376	390	411	419	402	373	550
Rest of the world	146	386	395	420	499	522	513	455	491

[1] Inventory valuation adjustment (IVA) and capital consumption adjustment (CCAdj). [2] Consists of finance and insurance and bank and other holding companies. [3] Consists of agriculture, forestry, fishing, and hunting; mining; construction; real estate and rental and leasing; professional, scientific, and technical services; administrative and waste management services; educational services; health care and social assistance; arts, entertainment, and recreation; accommodation and food services; and other services, except government.

Source: U.S. Bureau of Economic Analysis, National Income and Product Accounts Tables, "Table 6.16D. Corporate Profits by Industry," <apps.bea.gov/itable/index.cfm>, accessed June 2022.

Table 831. Corporate Profits Before Taxes by Industry: 2000 to 2020

[In billions of dollars (747 represents $747,000,000,000). Profits are without inventory valuation and capital consumption adjustments. Covers corporations organized for profit and other entities treated as corporations. Represents profits to U.S. residents, without deduction of depletion charges and exclusive of capital gains and losses; intercorporate dividends from profits of domestic corporations are eliminated; net receipts of dividends, reinvested earnings of incorporated foreign affiliates, and earnings of unincorporated foreign affiliates are added]

Industry	NAICS code [1]	2000	2010	2015	2017	2018	2019	2020
Corporate profits before tax	**(X)**	**747**	**1,834**	**2,128**	**2,195**	**2,259**	**2,255**	**2,184**
Domestic industries	(X)	601	1,448	1,733	1,696	1,737	1,741	1,729
Agriculture, forestry, fishing, and hunting	11	1	8	12	8	5	4	3
Mining	21	15	33	-9	-4	6	-27	-105
Utilities	221	25	31	19	14	22	7	10
Construction	23	36	27	76	101	103	106	139
Manufacturing	31-33	186	299	393	343	371	350	332
Wholesale trade	42	63	117	136	137	126	119	131
Retail trade	44-45	53	126	167	153	154	163	224
Transportation and warehousing	48-49	10	45	60	60	49	38	19
Information	51	-12	102	136	140	141	129	136
Finance and insurance	52	46	220	289	312	322	371	345
Real estate and rental and leasing	53	9	14	20	20	-7	-6	-9
Professional, scientific, and technical services	54	9	82	75	69	92	87	85
Management of companies and enterprises [2]	551111, 2	103	186	158	124	129	162	157
Administrative and waste management services	56	9	28	34	40	44	48	51
Educational services	61	2	11	5	5	7	6	6
Health care and social assistance	62	23	78	86	99	95	101	141
Arts, entertainment, and recreation	71	3	8	11	16	17	17	6
Accommodation and food services	72	14	18	44	40	39	43	33
Other services, except public administration	81	6	15	21	21	25	24	24
Rest of the world [3]	(X)	146	386	395	499	522	513	455

X Not applicable. [1] Based on North American Industry Classification System, 2012; see text, this section. [2] Consists of bank and other holding companies. [3] Consists of receipts by all U.S. residents, including both corporations and persons, of dividends from foreign corporations, and, for U.S. corporations, their share of reinvested earnings of their incorporated foreign affiliates, and earnings of unincorporated foreign affiliates, net of corresponding payments.

Source: U.S. Bureau of Economic Analysis, National Income and Product Accounts Tables, "Table 6.17D. Corporate Profits Before Tax by Industry," <apps.bea.gov/itable/index.cfm>, accessed July 2021.

Table 832. U.S. Majority-Owned Foreign Affiliates—Value Added by Industry of Affiliate and Country: 2019

[In millions of dollars (1,436,986 represents $1,436,986,000,000). Data are preliminary. A foreign affiliate is a foreign business enterprise owned or controlled by a U.S. parent enterprise. A majority-owned foreign affiliate (MOFA) is a foreign business enterprise in which a U.S. parent enterprise owns or controls more than 50% of the voting securities. Numbers in parentheses represent North American Industry Classification System codes; see text, this section]]

Country	All industries [1]	Mining (21)	Manufacturing (31-33) Total [1]	Manufacturing (31-33) Chemicals (325)	Wholesale trade (42)	Information (51)	Finance and insurance (52)	Professional, scientific, and technical services (54)
All countries [2]	**1,436,986**	**104,170**	**578,085**	**116,723**	**182,885**	**111,349**	**108,014**	**136,744**
United Kingdom	163,802	3,441	53,058	7,047	14,574	15,637	26,189	22,603
Canada	130,731	10,290	50,214	7,062	13,996	4,291	5,697	7,889
Ireland	101,637	(D)	46,627	20,968	8,601	32,200	-724	6,194
Germany	80,935	609	37,263	6,724	13,643	2,826	2,505	9,539
China	80,622	810	46,555	8,676	10,974	1,896	2,677	4,762
Singapore	63,444	529	30,622	4,720	7,431	4,728	9,624	3,497
Switzerland	61,132	(D)	19,769	7,428	20,278	3,282	950	1,869
Netherlands	55,069	412	19,923	6,745	7,430	11,097	11,680	3,930
France	54,805	(D)	24,778	4,601	6,378	2,749	2,387	6,466
Mexico	53,959	2,765	27,429	3,391	4,267	787	1,707	1,836
Japan	52,169	–	20,029	6,022	7,485	3,938	6,353	6,825
Australia	45,849	6,510	13,764	1,787	7,497	3,108	2,243	6,708
India	37,857	4	7,185	2,377	3,785	4,060	4,120	16,899
Italy	35,029	139	12,896	3,982	3,657	1,481	794	3,086
Brazil	34,921	466	20,070	4,613	3,380	1,555	3,648	3,444
Belgium	26,134	26	10,060	3,054	6,789	1,439	3,985	1,804
Hong Kong	20,601	1	3,164	270	5,655	967	5,743	3,217
Spain	18,022	20	10,082	2,921	2,618	602	153	2,080
Korea, South	17,289	(D)	9,910	1,336	1,897	585	2,019	1,023
Thailand	15,405	(D)	8,532	855	1,790	176	622	313
Israel	14,260	(D)	7,959	384	1,458	1,325	298	2,476

– Represents or rounds to zero. D Data withheld to avoid disclosure. [1] Includes other industries, not shown separately. [2] Includes other countries, not shown separately.

Source: U.S. Bureau of Economic Analysis, International Economic Accounts, "Activities of U.S. Multinational Enterprises, Majority-owned Foreign Affiliates, Value Added by Country and Industry 2009-2019," <www.bea.gov/international/di1usdop.htm>, accessed January 2022.

Table 833. U.S. Multinational Enterprises—Value Added, Employment, and Capital Expenditures: 1989 to 2019

[Value added and capital expenditures in billions of dollars (1,401 represents $1,401,000,000,000); employees in thousands. Consists of U.S. parent enterprises and their foreign affiliates. U.S. parent comprises the domestic operations of a multinational and is a U.S. person that owns or controls directly or indirectly, 10 percent or more of the voting securities of an incorporated foreign business enterprise, or an equivalent interest in an unincorporated foreign business enterprise. A U.S. person can be an incorporated business enterprise. A foreign affiliate is a foreign business enterprise owned or controlled by a U.S. parent enterprise. A majority-owned foreign affiliate (MOFA) is a foreign business enterprise in which a U.S. parent enterprise owns or controls more than 50% of the voting securities. For the years shown prior to 2007, the data items needed to calculate value added and capital expenditures for individual U.S. parents and foreign affiliates were collected for nonbank businesses only. The value added and capital expenditures statistics for bank parents and affiliates for those years are estimates. MOFA = Majority-owned foreign affiliate]

Item	1989	1994	1999	2004	2007	2009	2014	2017	2018	2019 (P)
VALUE ADDED (bil. dol.)										
Parents and MOFAs.................	1,401	1,773	2,645	3,221	3,866	3,741	5,380	5,308	5,671	5,672
Parents..............................	1,077	1,362	2,064	2,366	2,705	2,596	3,889	3,949	4,212	4,235
MOFAs...............................	324	411	580	854	1,161	1,145	1,490	1,359	1,458	1,437
EMPLOYEES (1,000s)										
Parents and MOFAs.................	24,826	25,142	31,913	31,466	33,203	33,727	41,640	42,127	42,884	43,908
Parents..............................	19,617	19,330	23,985	22,446	22,832	22,933	27,587	28,046	28,532	29,297
MOFAs...............................	5,209	5,812	7,928	9,020	10,372	10,794	14,052	14,081	14,352	14,611
CAPITAL EXPENDITURES (bil. dol.)										
Parents and MOFAs.................	263	306	531	476	670	599	968	927	913	944
Parents..............................	204	235	417	351	495	432	722	713	723	739
MOFAs...............................	59	72	115	125	174	167	245	215	190	205

P Preliminary.

Source: U.S. Bureau of Economic Analysis, International Economic Accounts, "Activities of U.S. Multinational Enterprises in 2019," <www.bea.gov/data/intl-trade-investment/activities-us-multinational-enterprises-mnes>, accessed January 2022, and earlier reports.

Table 834. U.S. Multinational Enterprises—Selected Characteristics: 2019

[In billions of dollars (46,970 represents $46,970,000,000,000), except as indicated. Data are preliminary. Consists of U.S. parent enterprises and their foreign affiliates. U.S. parent comprises the domestic operations of a multinational and is a U.S. person that owns or controls, directly or indirectly, 10 percent or more of the voting securities of an incorporated foreign business enterprise, or an equivalent interest in an unincorporated foreign business enterprise. A U.S. person can be an incorporated business enterprise. A majority-owned foreign affiliate (MOFA) is a foreign business enterprise in which a U.S. parent enterprise owns or controls more than 50 percent of the voting securities]

Industry	NAICS code [1]	U.S. parents [2] Total assets	U.S. parents [2] Capital expenditures	U.S. parents [2] Value added	U.S. parents [2] Employment (1,000)	Majority-owned foreign affiliates [3] Capital expenditures	Majority-owned foreign affiliates [3] Value added	Majority-owned foreign affiliates [3] Employment (1,000)
All industries.....................	(X)	**46,970**	**739**	**4,235**	**29,297**	**205**	**1,437**	**14,611**
Mining [4].............................	21	627	39	81	257	35	104	229
Oil and gas extraction.............................	211	339	27	43	53	28	75	41
Manufacturing [4].........................	31-33	9,008	227	1,433	7,445	76	578	5,369
Food..................................	311	734	15	135	927	6	33	455
Beverages and tobacco products...................	312	362	5	54	124	3	52	242
Petroleum and coal products.................	324	1,145	42	115	263	3	(D)	14
Chemicals [4].........................	325	2,109	32	247	925	14	117	624
Pharmaceuticals and medicines.................	3254	1,389	14	152	414	4	61	275
Machinery........................	333	540	11	99	613	3	49	560
Computers and electronic products [4].............	334	1,253	27	260	963	20	116	906
Computers and peripheral equipment...........	3341	384	7	88	223	2	44	238
Transportation equipment [4].........................	336	1,473	59	238	1,411	9	58	1,085
Motor vehicles, bodies and trailers, & parts.....	3361-3363	801	47	125	599	8	46	971
Wholesale trade.........................	42	2,080	59	273	1,775	12	183	1,015
Retail trade [4].............................	44, 45	1,190	45	382	5,877	7	76	1,497
General merchandise stores......................	452	311	15	137	2,502	3	29	868
Information [4].............................	51	3,297	117	508	2,197	16	111	615
Publishing industries....................	511	636	11	106	501	5	56	197
Broadcasting (except internet)....................	515	422	7	59	276	1	4	22
Telecommunications....................	517	1,422	62	194	777	6	13	82
Finance and insurance [4].....................	52	26,571	71	564	2,991	12	108	716
Insurance carriers and related activities...........	524	8,039	16	152	1,211	2	27	235
Professional, scientific, & technical services [4].........	54	981	12	278	1,753	9	137	1,615
Computer systems design & related services....	5415	444	5	73	447	6	68	826
Other industries [4].....................	(X)	3,218	168	715	7,002	37	140	3,554
Utilities.................................	22	820	57	94	169	5	11	42
Transportation and warehousing..................	48-49	626	39	201	1,469	5	28	385
Real estate & rental and leasing..................	53	486	36	77	394	15	48	224
Administration, support, and waste management...................	56	233	6	80	1,357	2	49	1,235

X Not applicable. D Data withheld to avoid disclosure. [1] Based on North American Industry Classification System; see text, this section. [2] Data are by industry of U.S. parent. [3] Data are by industry of foreign affiliate. [4] Includes other industries, not shown separately.

Source: U.S. Bureau of Economic Analysis, International Economic Accounts, "Direct Investment and Multinational Enterprises," <apps.bea.gov/iTable/index_MNC.cfm>, accessed January 2022.

Table 835. U.S. Multinational Enterprises—Value Added: 2010 and 2019

[In billions of dollars (4,191 represents $4,191,000,000,000). Data for 2019 are preliminary. A U.S. parent comprises the domestic operations of a multinational and is a U.S. person that owns or controls 10 percent or more of the voting securities, or the equivalent, of a foreign business enterprise. A U.S. person can be an incorporated business enterprise. A majority-owned foreign affiliate is a foreign business enterprise in which a U.S. parent enterprise owns or controls more than 50% of the voting securities. Data are by industry of U.S. parent. Based on the North American Industry Classification System (NAICS). See text this section]

Industry	NAICS [1] code	U.S. multinationals		U.S. parents		Majority-owned foreign affiliates	
		2010	2019 (P)	2010	2019 (P)	2010	2019 (P)
All industries...	(X)	**4,191**	**5,672**	**2,949**	**4,235**	**1,242**	**1,437**
Mining [2]...	21	118	108	75	81	43	27
Oil and gas extraction..................................	211	58	59	41	43	18	16
Manufacturing [2]..	31-33	1,900	2,134	1,147	1,433	753	701
Food...	311	145	171	96	135	49	36
Beverages and tobacco products.................	312	67	73	49	54	18	19
Petroleum and coal products.......................	324	383	249	135	115	248	134
Chemicals [2]..	325	337	375	197	247	140	128
Pharmaceuticals and medicines..................	3254	187	211	113	152	74	58
Machinery..	333	104	149	69	99	35	51
Computers and electronic products [2]...........	334	235	416	155	260	80	155
Computers and peripheral equipment..........	3341	68	159	38	88	31	71
Semiconductors and other electronic components.....	3344	79	121	51	76	28	45
Transportation equipment [2].......................	336	314	312	229	238	85	74
Motor vehicles, bodies and trailers, and parts..........	3361-3363	133	173	83	125	49	48
Wholesale trade..	42	174	335	143	273	32	61
Retail trade [2]..	44, 45	303	441	257	382	46	59
General merchandise stores......................	452	(NA)	(NA)	122	137	(D)	(D)
Information [2]...	51	392	636	333	508	58	127
Publishing industries.................................	511	100	170	72	106	27	64
Broadcasting (except internet)...................	515	49	67	41	59	8	8
Telecommunications..................................	517	172	205	162	194	10	10
Finance and insurance [2]............................	52	480	748	357	564	123	184
Depository credit intermediation (banking)............	5221	157	241	139	218	18	23
Insurance carriers and related activities.......	524	101	177	84	152	17	25
Professional, scientific, and technical services [2]..........	54	275	384	196	278	79	106
Computer systems design and related services..........	5415	133	134	80	73	53	61
Other industries [2].....................................	(X)	548	887	440	715	108	172
Utilities..	22	66	100	61	94	5	6
Transportation and warehousing.................	48-49	132	222	116	201	17	21
Real estate and rental and leasing..............	53	44	98	35	77	9	21
Administration, support, and waste management........	56	99	113	73	80	26	33
Accommodation and food services..............	72	75	90	54	65	22	25

P Preliminary. X Not applicable. NA Not available. D Data withheld to avoid disclosure. [1] Based on North American Industry Classification System; see text, this section. [2] Includes other industries, not shown separately.

Source: U.S. Bureau of Economic Analysis, International Economic Accounts, "Direct Investment and Multinational Enterprises," <apps.bea.gov/iTable/index_MNC.cfm>, accessed January 2022.

Science and Technology

This section presents statistics on scientific, engineering, and technological resources, with emphasis on patterns of research and development (R&D) funding and education and employment in science and engineering fields.

The National Science Foundation (NSF) gathers data chiefly through recurring surveys and reports the data via detailed statistical tables, information briefs, and annual, biennial, and special reports; see <nsf.gov/statistics>. Areas of coverage include R&D expenditures; Federal R&D funding; scientific employment; graduate enrollment and support in academic science and engineering; characteristics of doctoral scientists and engineers; and of recent graduates in the United States. Report titles include: *Science and Engineering Indicators; National Patterns of R&D Resources; Federal Funds for Research and Development; Federal R&D Funding by Budget Function; Federal Support for S&E to Universities, Colleges, and Nonprofit Institutions*; and *Business Research and Development*. Statistical surveys in these areas pose problems of concept and definition and the data should therefore be regarded as broad estimates rather than precise, quantitative statements. See sources for methodological and technical details.

The National Science Board's biennial *Science and Engineering Indicators* at <nsf.gov/statistics/seind/> contains data and analysis of international and domestic science and technology, including education and workforce statistics.

Research and development outlays—NSF defines *research* as "systematic study directed toward fuller scientific knowledge of the subject studied" and *development* as "the systematic use of scientific knowledge directed toward the production of useful materials, devices, systems, or methods, including design and development of prototypes and processes." *Basic research* is generally defined as research activities aimed at acquiring new knowledge or understanding without specific immediate commercial applications or uses. *Applied research* is generally defined as activities aimed at solving a specific problem or meeting a specific commercial objective.

National coverage of R&D expenditures is developed primarily from periodic surveys in four principal economic sectors: (1) *government*, made up primarily of federal executive agencies; (2) *industry*, consisting of manufacturing and nonmanufacturing firms and the federally funded research and development centers (FFRDCs) they administer; (3) *universities and colleges*, composed of universities, colleges, and their affiliated institutions, agricultural experiment stations, and associated schools of agriculture and of medicine, and FFRDCs administered by educational institutions; and (4) *other nonprofit institutions*, consisting of organizations such as private philanthropic foundations, nonprofit research institutes, voluntary health agencies, and FFRDCs administered by nonprofit organizations.

The R&D funds reported consist of current operating costs, including planning and administration costs, except as otherwise noted. They exclude funds for routine testing, mapping and surveying, collection of general purpose data, dissemination of scientific information, and training of scientific personnel.

Scientists, engineers, and technicians—*Scientists and engineers* are defined as persons engaged in scientific and engineering work at a level requiring a knowledge of sciences equivalent at least to that acquired through completion of a 4-year college course. *Technicians* are defined as persons engaged in technical work at a level requiring knowledge acquired through a technical institute, junior college, or other type of training less extensive than 4-year college training. Craftsmen and skilled workers are excluded.

Table 836. Research and Development (R&D) Expenditures by Source of Funding: 1960 to 2020

[In millions of dollars (13,711 represents $13,711,000,000), except percent]

Year	Total	Sources of funds					Percent of total				
		Federal govern-ment	Industry	Univer-sities & colleges [1]	Non-profit	Non-federal govern-ment [2]	Federal govern-ment	Industry	Univer-sities & colleges [1]	Non-profit	Non-federal govern-ment [2]
1960......	13,711	8,915	4,516	67	123	90	65.0	32.9	0.5	0.9	0.7
1970......	26,271	14,984	10,449	259	343	237	57.0	39.8	1.0	1.3	0.9
1980......	63,224	29,986	30,929	920	871	519	47.4	48.9	1.5	1.4	0.8
1985......	114,671	52,641	57,962	1,743	1,491	834	45.9	50.5	1.5	1.3	0.7
1988......	133,881	60,131	67,977	2,527	2,081	1,165	44.9	50.8	1.9	1.6	0.9
1989......	141,891	60,465	74,966	2,852	2,333	1,274	42.6	52.8	2.0	1.6	0.9
1990......	151,993	61,610	83,208	3,187	2,589	1,399	40.5	54.7	2.1	1.7	0.9
1991......	160,876	60,783	92,300	3,458	2,852	1,483	37.8	57.4	2.1	1.8	0.9
1992......	165,350	60,915	96,229	3,569	3,113	1,525	36.8	58.2	2.2	1.9	0.9
1993......	165,730	60,528	96,549	3,709	3,388	1,557	36.5	58.3	2.2	2.0	0.9
1994......	169,207	60,777	99,204	3,938	3,665	1,623	35.9	58.6	2.3	2.2	1.0
1995......	183,625	62,969	110,871	4,110	3,925	1,751	34.3	60.4	2.2	2.1	1.0
1996......	197,346	63,394	123,417	4,436	4,239	1,861	32.1	62.5	2.2	2.1	0.9
1997......	211,894	64,362	136,208	4,852	4,571	1,902	30.4	64.3	2.3	2.2	0.9
1998......	225,759	65,908	147,774	5,193	4,963	1,920	29.2	65.5	2.3	2.2	0.9
1999......	244,451	66,817	164,545	5,654	5,399	2,036	27.3	67.3	2.3	2.2	0.8
2000......	267,950	67,238	185,975	6,270	6,285	2,182	25.1	69.4	2.3	2.3	0.8
2001......	278,539	73,793	188,408	6,874	7,122	2,341	26.5	67.6	2.5	2.6	0.8
2002......	277,911	78,873	180,704	7,673	8,109	2,553	28.4	65.0	2.8	2.9	0.9
2003......	291,365	85,133	186,171	8,286	8,988	2,788	29.2	63.9	2.8	3.1	1.0
2004......	302,731	90,795	191,346	8,637	9,028	2,926	30.0	63.2	2.9	3.0	1.0
2005......	325,288	95,413	207,775	9,353	9,771	2,977	29.3	63.9	2.9	3.0	0.9
2006......	350,908	99,938	227,182	10,176	10,320	3,293	28.5	64.7	2.9	2.9	0.9
2007......	377,890	105,128	246,815	10,933	11,420	3,594	27.8	65.3	2.9	3.0	1.0
2008......	404,777	117,615	258,020	11,738	13,184	4,221	29.1	63.7	2.9	3.3	1.0
2009......	402,932	125,765	246,609	12,057	14,205	4,296	31.2	61.2	3.0	3.5	1.1
2010......	406,600	126,617	248,126	12,262	15,292	4,303	31.1	61.0	3.0	3.8	1.1
2011......	426,215	127,014	266,427	13,103	15,284	4,387	29.8	62.5	3.1	3.6	1.0
2012......	433,716	123,837	275,728	14,300	15,694	4,158	28.6	63.6	3.3	3.6	1.0
2013......	454,271	120,132	297,188	15,378	17,330	4,243	26.4	65.4	3.4	3.8	0.9
2014......	475,969	118,367	318,410	16,210	18,768	4,213	24.9	66.9	3.4	3.9	0.9
2015......	494,499	119,532	333,243	17,292	20,156	4,277	24.2	67.4	3.5	4.1	0.9
2016......	521,700	118,174	360,291	18,415	20,300	4,520	22.7	69.1	3.5	3.9	0.9
2017......	554,012	121,632	386,385	19,554	21,862	4,578	22.0	69.7	3.5	3.9	0.8
2018......	604,837	129,625	426,193	20,679	23,607	4,731	21.4	70.5	3.4	3.9	0.8
2019......	666,875	133,807	481,799	21,559	24,778	4,929	20.1	72.2	3.2	3.7	0.7
2020 [3]....	707,967	137,818	517,431	22,604	25,073	5,038	19.5	73.1	3.2	3.5	0.7

[1] Figures for university and college R&D prior to 2003 cover only science and engineering (S&E) fields; in 2003 and later years, R&D in non-S&E fields is also included. Also, adjustments have been made to university and college R&D for 1998 and later years to eliminate double counting of funds passed through from one academic institution to another. [2] Nonfederal R&D expenditures to university and college performers. [3] Estimated.

Source: U.S. National Science Foundation, National Center for Science and Engineering Statistics, *National Patterns of R&D Resources, 2019-20 Data Update*, NSF 22-320, February 2022. See also <www.nsf.gov/statistics/natlpatterns/>.

Table 837. National Research and Development (R&D) Expenditures as a Percent of Gross Domestic Product by Country: 1990 to 2020

Year	United States [1]	Japan [2]	Ger-many [3]	France	United Kingdom	Italy	Canada	South Korea	OECD total [4]	Russia	China
1990....	[5] 2.56	[6] 2.66	[6] 2.61	2.27	1.95	[9] 1.20	1.48	(NA)	(NA)	1.89	(NA)
1995....	[5] 2.41	[6] 2.56	2.14	2.24	1.64	0.93	1.65	[10] 2.16	1.92	0.79	[11] 0.57
2000....	[5] 2.63	2.86	2.41	[7] 2.09	1.61	1.00	1.86	[10] 2.13	2.08	0.98	[7] 0.89
2005....	[5] 2.52	3.13	2.44	2.05	1.55	1.04	1.97	[10] 2.52	2.10	0.99	1.31
2009....	[5] 2.81	3.20	2.74	2.21	[6] 1.66	1.22	1.92	3.15	2.29	1.17	[7] 1.66
2010....	[5] 2.73	3.10	2.73	[7] 2.18	[6] 1.64	1.22	1.83	3.32	2.25	1.05	1.71
2011....	[5] 2.76	3.21	2.81	2.19	1.64	1.20	1.79	3.59	2.27	1.02	1.78
2012....	[5] 2.67	3.17	2.88	2.23	[6] 1.57	1.26	[7] 1.77	3.85	2.27	1.03	1.91
2013....	[5] 2.70	[7] 3.28	2.84	2.24	1.61	1.30	1.71	3.95	2.29	1.03	2.00
2014....	[5] 2.72	3.37	2.88	[7] 2.28	[6] 1.63	[6] 1.34	[7] 1.71	4.08	2.32	1.07	2.02
2015....	[5] 2.79	3.24	2.93	2.23	1.63	1.34	1.69	3.98	2.33	1.10	2.06
2016....	[5] 2.85	3.11	2.94	2.22	[6] 1.64	[7] 1.37	1.73	3.99	2.33	1.10	2.10
2017....	[5] 2.91	3.17	3.05	2.20	1.66	1.37	1.69	4.29	2.37	1.11	2.12
2018....	[5] 3.01	[7] 3.22	3.11	2.20	1.70	1.42	1.68	4.52	2.44	0.99	2.14
2019....	[5] 3.18	3.21	3.17	2.20	[8] 1.71	1.46	[8] 1.59	4.63	2.51	1.04	2.23
2020....	[5] 3.45	3.27	[8] 3.14	[6,8] 2.35	(NA)	1.53	[8] 1.70	4.81	2.68	1.10	2.40

NA Not available. [1] Excludes most or all capital expenditure. [2] Data on Japanese research and development after 1996 may not be consistent with data in earlier years because of changes in methodology. [3] Data for 1990 are for West Germany only. [4] Organisation for Economic Cooperation and Development. Values for the OECD are estimated for all years. [5] Excludes R&D expenditures by state and local governments. [6] Estimated value. [7] Time series break. [8] Provisional. [9] Excluding extramural R&D expenditure. [10] Excluding R&D in the social sciences and humanities. [11] Underestimated or based on underestimated data.

Source: Organisation for Economic Co-operation and Development (OECD), 2022, "Main Science and Technology Indicators," OECD Science, Technology and R&D Statistics (database) ©, <dx.doi.org/10.1787/data-00182-en>, accessed August 2022.

Table 838. Research and Development (R&D) Expenditures By Performing Sector and Source of Funds: 1990 to 2020

[In millions of dollars (151,993 represents $151,993,000,000). For calendar year. FFRDCs are federally funded research and development centers]

Column groups: Federal (All federal research; Federal intramural[1]; FFRDCs[2]). Industry — Total[3]; Funded by: Industry[4], Federal government, Non-federal government. Universities and colleges — Total; Funded by: Federal government, Non-federal government, Industry, Universities & colleges, Non-profits. Other nonprofit institutions — Total; Funded by: Federal government, Industry, Non-profits.

Year	Total	All federal research	Federal intra-mural[1]	FFRDCs[2]	Non-federal govern-ment	Industry Total[3]	Industry: Indus-try[4]	Industry: Federal govern-ment	Univ. Total	Univ. Federal govern-ment	Univ. Non-federal govern-ment	Univ. Indus-try	Universi-ties & colleges	Univ. Non-profits	Other Total	Other Federal govern-ment	Other Indus-try	Other Non-profits
R&D TOTAL																		
1990	151,993	23,524	15,671	7,853	(NA)	107,404	81,602	25,802	16,939	9,939	1,399	1,166	3,187	1,249	4,126	2,346	440	1,340
2000	267,950	28,516	19,247	9,269	(NA)	199,961	182,844	17,117	29,916	17,095	2,182	2,112	6,270	2,258	9,557	4,510	1,020	4,027
2010	406,600	50,798	31,970	18,828	691	278,977	218,187	34,199	58,084	34,682	3,674	2,953	12,262	4,515	18,050	7,093	1,266	9,691
2015	494,499	52,847	34,199	18,649	595	355,821	289,892	26,990	64,635	33,564	3,782	3,844	17,292	6,154	20,601	6,247	1,605	12,749
2016	521,700	51,187	31,762	19,424	620	379,529	310,391	24,154	67,792	34,688	3,937	4,049	18,415	6,704	22,573	8,257	1,993	12,323
2017	554,012	52,553	32,231	20,322	632	405,792	324,177	24,974	71,115	36,008	4,057	4,284	19,554	7,214	23,921	8,218	2,071	13,632
2018	604,837	58,356	36,793	21,563	643	445,563	357,862	25,192	74,914	37,758	4,224	4,586	20,679	7,668	25,361	8,451	2,189	14,721
2019[5]	666,875	62,802	39,870	22,932	675	498,175	405,960	22,653	78,176	39,556	4,364	4,808	21,559	7,889	27,048	8,900	2,347	15,800
2020[5]	707,967	65,685	41,936	23,749	696	531,941	436,135	20,996	81,111	40,919	4,458	5,002	22,604	8,128	28,533	10,304	2,444	15,786
BASIC RESEARCH																		
1990	23,029	5,352	2,319	3,033	(NA)	4,629	3,760	869	11,126	6,889	847	705	1,929	756	1,922	947	245	730
2000	42,033	7,801	3,765	4,037	(NA)	7,040	6,115	925	22,290	13,469	1,501	1,453	4,314	1,553	4,902	2,099	566	2,236
2010	76,388	11,748	5,111	6,637	103	16,371	13,239	1,406	38,669	23,618	2,277	1,783	8,010	2,983	9,498	3,414	703	5,381
2015	84,273	10,017	5,890	4,127	100	21,792	15,933	2,038	41,360	22,084	2,297	2,205	10,577	3,798	11,004	3,034	891	7,079
2016	85,689	10,315	6,119	4,196	93	25,053	18,792	2,037	42,679	22,450	2,355	2,286	11,577	4,012	7,548	2,401	716	4,431
2017	88,696	10,388	6,259	4,128	100	25,617	18,299	1,853	44,556	23,197	2,387	2,407	12,228	4,337	8,036	2,390	745	4,901
2018	96,043	11,096	6,827	4,269	107	29,204	21,100	2,535	47,099	24,361	2,449	2,599	12,971	4,720	8,538	2,457	787	5,293
2019[5]	102,874	11,932	7,352	4,580	120	32,582	24,558	2,349	49,126	25,358	2,531	2,729	13,594	4,916	9,113	2,588	844	5,681
2020[5]	107,895	12,598	7,839	4,759	131	34,682	26,381	2,174	50,933	26,051	2,610	2,843	14,333	5,096	9,551	2,996	879	5,676
APPLIED RESEARCH																		
1990	34,897	4,808	3,652	1,156	(NA)	24,399	18,432	5,967	4,406	2,140	453	377	1,031	404	1,284	780	120	384
2000	56,503	7,856	6,105	1,750	(NA)	39,176	36,494	2,682	6,361	3,081	558	540	1,604	578	3,110	1,831	258	1,021
2010	79,017	13,203	8,016	5,187	572	44,906	34,912	4,705	14,518	8,645	1,002	763	3,074	1,034	5,818	3,041	321	2,456
2015	97,249	16,698	9,347	7,351	481	56,472	43,330	6,102	17,170	8,964	1,085	1,086	4,457	1,579	6,429	2,791	407	3,231
2016	110,484	17,433	9,805	7,628	509	62,871	48,543	5,327	18,731	9,665	1,162	1,202	4,877	1,826	10,940	4,541	891	5,508
2017	114,069	18,170	10,124	8,046	510	64,040	47,727	5,386	19,811	10,146	1,223	1,270	5,230	1,943	11,538	4,520	926	6,093
2018	119,837	19,704	11,111	8,593	514	66,587	50,898	5,355	20,826	10,616	1,290	1,363	5,523	2,034	12,206	4,648	979	6,579
2019[5]	132,021	20,523	11,264	9,258	524	76,176	57,549	5,246	21,793	11,144	1,341	1,449	5,763	2,097	13,006	4,895	1,049	7,062
2020[5]	139,527	21,560	12,032	9,527	526	81,007	61,748	4,877	22,620	11,565	1,366	1,504	6,033	2,151	13,815	5,667	1,092	7,055
DEVELOPMENT																		
1990	94,067	13,363	9,700	3,663	(NA)	78,376	59,410	18,966	1,407	910	99	83	226	89	920	619	75	226
2000	169,414	12,859	9,377	3,482	(NA)	153,745	140,235	13,510	1,265	545	123	119	352	127	1,545	580	195	771
2010	251,195	25,847	18,841	7,004	16	217,700	170,036	28,089	4,898	2,419	396	407	1,178	498	2,734	638	242	1,854
2015	312,977	26,132	18,961	7,171	14	277,557	230,629	18,850	6,106	2,517	401	554	1,857	778	3,168	422	307	2,439
2016	325,528	23,439	15,838	7,601	18	291,605	243,056	16,790	6,382	2,573	420	561	1,962	866	4,084	1,314	386	2,384
2017	351,248	23,995	15,848	8,147	22	316,136	285,151	17,736	6,749	2,665	448	607	2,096	934	4,347	1,308	401	2,638
2018	388,957	27,556	18,856	8,701	23	349,771	285,863	17,301	6,990	2,782	486	624	2,185	914	4,617	1,345	424	2,848
2019[5]	431,981	30,347	21,253	9,094	31	389,418	323,854	15,058	7,257	3,055	492	631	2,202	877	4,928	1,417	454	3,057
2020[5]	460,545	31,527	22,064	9,463	40	416,253	348,007	13,945	7,558	3,303	482	654	2,239	881	5,167	1,640	473	3,054

NA Not available. [1] Federal intramural performers are agencies of the federal government, with work carried on directly by agency personnel. Intramural expenditures include those for federal intramural R&D as well as cost associated with administering extramural R&D. Extramural R&D is performed outside the federal sector with federal funds under contract, grant, or cooperative agreement. [2] R&D expenditures of FFRDC's are chiefly federally funded; the remainder reflects funding from state or local government, businesses, other nonprofit organizations, and other sources. [3] Beginning 2008, total funding for industry R&D includes other sources of funding not shown separately, including funding from other nonfederal U.S. sources and sources outside the U.S. [4] Through 2007, includes all other nonfederal sources. Beginning 2008, excludes funding from parent or unaffiliated businesses outside the U.S. and foreign subsidiaries of U.S. businesses. [5] Estimates.

Source: U.S. National Science Foundation, National Center for Science and Engineering Statistics, *National Patterns of R&D Resources: 2019-20 Data Update*, NSF 22-320, February 2022. See also <www.nsf.gov/statistics/natlpatterns/>.

Table 839. Federal Obligations for Research by Field of Science: 2010 to 2021

[In millions of dollars (63,728 represents $63,728,000,000). For years ending September 30. Excludes development, and research and development (R&D) plant (facilities and fixed equipment)]

Field of science	2010	2015	2016	2017	2018	2019	2020	2021 (P)
Research, total............................	**63,728**	**63,825**	**67,105**	**69,871**	**74,588**	**81,118**	**85,305**	**85,155**
Basic..	31,795	31,527	32,293	33,271	36,195	40,017	41,547	41,231
Applied.......................................	31,933	32,298	34,812	36,600	38,392	41,101	43,758	43,924
Computer sciences and mathematics.......	3,412	3,863	4,223	3,894	4,207	4,330	5,912	6,063
Engineering.................................	11,081	11,984	12,972	13,207	13,759	15,279	13,222	14,238
Environmental sciences....................	3,339	4,414	4,450	4,470	4,568	5,075	5,040	4,632
Life sciences...............................	33,909	30,625	32,045	34,090	36,994	38,304	42,525	42,014
Physical sciences..........................	5,871	6,510	6,706	6,582	7,881	9,816	8,420	8,775
Psychology.................................	2,156	1,995	2,021	2,081	2,327	2,754	3,276	3,265
Social sciences............................	1,197	1,136	1,227	1,027	1,039	1,156	1,137	1,266
Other sciences, n.e.c. [1]..................	2,763	3,299	3,461	4,521	3,812	4,405	5,773	4,902

P Data are preliminary. [1] Not elsewhere classified.

Source: U.S. National Science Foundation, *Federal Funds for Research and Development, Fiscal Years 2020-21; Data Tables*, NSF 22-323, April 2022, and earlier reports. See also <www.nsf.gov/statistics/fedfunds/>.

Table 840. Federal Budget Authority for Research and Development (R&D) by Selected Budget Function: 2000 to 2021

[In millions of current dollars (78,664 represents $78,664,000,000). For year ending September 30. Excludes R&D plant]

Function	2000	2010	2015	2017	2018	2019	2020	2021 (P)
Total [1].....................................	**78,664**	**146,596**	**136,090**	**124,710**	**140,701**	**145,615**	**163,875**	**161,412**
National defense.........................	42,580	86,517	72,560	57,055	68,325	71,396	79,389	78,609
Health.......................................	17,869	31,488	30,331	34,255	37,151	38,755	43,936	43,199
General science and basic research.....	4,977	9,280	10,068	9,947	10,692	10,961	11,620	11,683
Space flight, research, and supporting activities....................	5,363	8,232	10,875	10,134	10,455	10,016	14,158	12,542
Energy.......................................	996	2,455	3,153	3,519	4,212	4,433	4,391	4,433
Natural resources and environment......	1,999	2,237	2,161	2,378	2,383	2,486	2,653	2,654
Agriculture..................................	1,426	2,043	1,989	2,090	2,074	2,205	2,332	2,469
Transportation.............................	1,636	1,496	1,363	1,444	1,551	1,582	1,674	1,672
Veterans benefits and services..........	645	1,034	1,178	1,346	1,286	1,370	1,366	1,420

P Preliminary. [1] Includes other functions, not shown separately.

Source: U.S. National Science Foundation, "Federal R&D Funding by Budget Function: Fiscal Years 2020-22, Data Tables," <www.nsf.gov/statistics/fedbudget/>, accessed January 2022, and earlier releases.

Table 841. Federal Research and Development (R&D) Budget by Federal Agency: 2021 to 2023

[In millions of dollars (160,724 represents $160,724,000,000). Table shows funding levels for departments or independent agencies with more than $200 million in R&D activities in 2022. For fiscal years ending September 30. R&D refers to actual research and development activities as well as R&D facilities. R&D facilities (also known as R&D plants) includes construction, repair, or alteration of physical plant used in the conduct of R&D]

Federal agency	2021	2022, estimated	2023, proposed
Total research and development [1, 2]............................	**160,724**	**159,613**	**204,936**
Defense.......................................	70,079	65,691	83,769
Health and Human Services..............	42,226	42,023	61,816
Energy..	17,788	21,027	23,731
National Aeronautics and Space Administration.................	12,176	12,279	13,547
National Science Foundation.............	7,515	7,065	8,448
Agriculture...................................	3,031	3,193	3,579
Commerce....................................	2,099	1,994	2,918
Veterans Affairs............................	1,445	1,436	1,655
Interior.......................................	1,009	1,123	1,443
Transportation..............................	1,070	1,281	1,498
Basic research [2]........................	**42,784**	**42,592**	**56,544**
Defense.......................................	2,540	2,296	2,416
Health and Human Services..............	21,051	20,951	31,911
Energy..	5,526	5,623	6,373
National Aeronautics and Space Administration.................	5,162	5,490	6,086
National Science Foundation.............	5,974	5,664	6,787
Agriculture...................................	1,195	1,218	1,381
Applied research [2]......................	**43,283**	**42,557**	**54,311**
Defense.......................................	6,438	5,625	6,028
Health and Human Services..............	20,876	20,744	29,480
Energy..	6,360	6,130	7,129
National Aeronautics and Space Administration.................	2,654	2,684	3,030
National Science Foundation.............	968	879	1,115
Agriculture...................................	1,347	1,432	1,582
Commerce....................................	1,163	1,167	1,508

[1] Total includes experimental development and facilities and equipment, not shown separately. [2] Incudes other agencies not shown separately.

Source: U.S. Office of Management and Budget, *Budget of the U.S. Government, Fiscal Year 2023: Analytical Perspectives*, March 2022. See also <www.whitehouse.gov/omb/budget>.

Table 842. Funds for Domestic Business Research and Development (R&D) Performed by Companies by Industry: 2019

[In millions of dollars (492,956 represents $492,956,000,000), except percent. For the calendar year. The data represent for-profit companies that have ten or more paid employees in the United States, have at least one establishment that is in business during the survey year, and is located in the United States. Beginning in survey year 2018, statistics represent companies that performed or funded $50,000 or more of R&D. This change affects the comparability of these estimates with estimates published for years prior to 2018. Covers basic research, applied research, and development performed by the company and others. Based on the Business Enterprise R&D Survey]

Industry	NAICS [1] code	Domestic R&D paid for by the company and others		Domestic R&D paid for by the company	
		Value (million dollars)	As a percent of domestic sales [2]	Value (million dollars)	As a percent of domestic sales [2]
All industries, total [3]	(X)	**492,956**	**4.4**	**428,968**	**3.8**
All manufacturing industries, total [3]	31–33	**285,674**	**5.0**	**248,109**	**4.4**
Chemicals	325	97,063	8.4	87,288	7.5
Pharmaceuticals and medicines	3254	87,619	16.3	78,652	14.7
Machinery	333	15,184	4.2	13,930	3.8
Semiconductor machinery	333242	4,459	18.1	3,854	15.6
Computer and electronic products	334	86,729	12.8	75,570	11.1
Electrical equipment, appliances, and components	335	5,263	3.7	4,886	3.4
Transportation equipment	336	45,375	3.9	31,505	2.7
Aerospace products and parts	3364	18,358	6.5	8,900	3.2
All nonmanufacturing industries, total [3]	(X)	**207,283**	**3.8**	**180,858**	**3.3**
Mining, extraction, and support activities	21	2,717	1.5	2,535	1.4
Information	51	110,227	7.7	109,062	7.6
Software publishers	5112	32,958	17.7	32,386	17.4
Professional, scientific, and technical services	54	53,233	10.9	29,131	6.0
Computer systems design and related services	5415	21,046	10.7	18,395	9.3
Scientific research and development services	5417	21,669	26.7	3,265	4.0

X Not applicable. [1] 2012 North American Industry Classification System (NAICS); see text, Section 15. [2] Includes companies located in the United States that performed or funded R&D. [3] Includes industries not shown separately.

Source: U.S. National Science Foundation, *Business Research and Development: 2019*, NSF 22-329, April 2022, <ncses.nsf.gov/pubs/nsf22329>. See also <www.nsf.gov/statistics/srvyberd/>.

Table 843. Academic and Industrial Research and Development (R&D) Expenditures by State: 2019

[In millions of dollars (78,176 represents $78,176,000,000). Industry R&D data refer to calendar years; other R&D data refer to fiscal years but are used here as approximations to calendar year data]

State	Academic R&D [2] (mil. dol.)	Academic R&D per $1,000 of state GDP	Industry-performed R&D (mil. dol.)	Industry R&D per $1,000 of state GDP	State	Academic R&D [2] (mil. dol.)	Academic R&D per $1,000 of state GDP	Industry-performed R&D (mil. dol.)	Industry R&D per $1,000 of state GDP
U.S. [1]	**78,176**	**3.66**	**498,175**	**23.31**	MO	1,325	3.99	6,344	19.09
AL	1,123	4.86	2,423	10.48	MT	273	5.27	205	3.96
AK	169	3.10	49	0.90	NE	572	4.35	795	6.05
AZ	1,434	3.88	6,403	17.31	NV	282	1.55	1,045	5.75
AR	365	2.79	461	3.52	NH	492	5.62	2,541	29.04
CA	10,490	3.44	171,961	56.33	NJ	1,331	2.08	20,390	31.89
CO	1,622	4.14	6,070	15.48	NM	366	3.59	637	6.25
CT	1,387	4.81	7,421	25.76	NY	7,076	3.98	20,180	11.35
DE	229	2.97	2,156	27.98	NC	3,388	5.69	13,249	22.24
DC	665	4.61	412	2.85	ND	263	4.46	349	5.91
FL	2,686	2.41	7,259	6.50	OH	2,499	3.61	10,642	15.35
GA	2,668	4.18	4,844	7.59	OK	534	2.62	1,067	5.24
HI	301	3.28	159	1.73	OR	864	3.50	7,890	31.99
ID	168	2.04	2,697	32.72	PA	4,647	5.81	15,245	19.06
IL	2,710	3.04	14,112	15.85	RI	391	6.38	715	11.66
IN	1,661	4.36	7,952	20.87	SC	743	3.04	1,784	7.29
IA	880	4.53	3,087	15.89	SD	118	2.19	194	3.60
KS	704	3.98	2,748	15.55	TN	1,337	3.55	1,663	4.41
KY	611	2.83	1,481	6.85	TX	5,967	3.20	23,906	12.83
LA	778	3.06	703	2.76	UT	925	4.74	2,857	14.64
ME	151	2.21	417	6.09	VT	139	4.07	244	7.15
MD	4,629	10.98	5,852	13.88	VA	1,814	3.27	6,061	10.93
MA	4,306	7.26	30,843	51.99	WA	1,830	3.06	37,330	62.44
MI	2,891	5.44	21,283	40.05	WV	213	2.69	246	3.11
MN	1,061	2.77	8,026	20.95	WI	1,652	4.79	6,517	18.90
MS	536	4.67	324	2.82	WY	80	2.02	686	17.32

[1] States will not sum to U.S. totals because the U.S. totals include data for outlying areas (Puerto Rico, Guam, American Samoa, and Virgin Islands), R&D expenditures that cannot be allocated to specific states, and double counting of universities and colleges data. [2] State level university R&D data have not been adjusted to eliminate double counting of funds passed through from one academic institution to another. See source for more information.

Source: U.S. National Science Foundation, National Center for Science and Engineering Statistics, *National Patterns of R&D Resources: 2019-20 Data Update*, NSF 22-320, February 2022. See also <www.nsf.gov/statistics/natlpatterns/>.

Table 844. Higher Education Research and Development (R&D) Expenditures, Total and in Science and Engineering: 2010 to 2020

[In millions of dollars (61,287 represents $61,287,000,000). Data include R&D expenditures for both science and engineering (S&E) as well as non S&E fields, except for data by field. Beginning with FY2012, includes institutions reporting $1 million or more in total R&D expenditures; prior to FY2012 includes all institutions. Totals may not add due to rounding. Reference period is the fiscal year of the surveyed institutions. Data are based on the Higher Education R&D (HERD) Survey, which in 2010 succeeded the Survey of Research and Development Expenditures at Colleges and Universities; see source for details]

Characteristic	2010	2015	2016	2017	2018	2019	2020
Expenditures, total	**61,287**	**68,550**	**71,768**	**75,147**	**79,026**	**83,534**	**86,296**
Basic research	40,880	44,230	45,510	46,912	49,618	52,504	54,133
Applied & experimental R&D	20,407	24,320	26,258	28,235	29,408	31,030	32,163
SOURCE OF FUNDS							
Federal government	37,478	37,847	38,789	40,249	41,863	44,483	46,144
State and local government	3,887	3,855	4,043	4,175	4,313	4,511	4,597
Institutions' own funds	11,943	16,592	17,904	18,850	20,179	21,094	21,947
Industry	3,202	4,003	4,214	4,434	4,721	5,062	5,185
Nonprofit organizations	3,730	4,220	4,618	5,141	5,442	5,689	5,745
Other	1,048	2,033	2,200	2,299	2,508	2,696	2,679
FIELD							
Science and engineering, total	58,388	64,936	67,635	70,847	74,385	78,669	81,261
Computer and information sciences	1,638	1,963	2,080	2,192	2,398	2,639	2,923
Geosciences	2,992	3,247	3,084	3,148	3,160	3,186	3,281
Life sciences	34,984	38,774	40,869	43,099	45,611	48,257	49,641
Mathematics and statistics	592	641	679	700	750	770	799
Physical sciences	4,622	4,659	4,888	5,050	5,232	5,551	5,667
Psychology	1,078	1,184	1,221	1,245	1,259	1,326	1,357
Social sciences	2,000	2,319	2,365	2,555	2,722	2,808	2,947
Other sciences	1,156	1,078	1,075	946	890	915	952
Engineering	9,326	11,070	11,373	11,911	12,364	13,216	13,693

Source: U.S. National Science Foundation, "Higher Education Research and Development: Fiscal Year 2020, Data Tables," and earlier reports, <ncses.nsf.gov/pubs/nsf22311>, accessed January 2022.

Table 845. Federal Research and Development (R&D) Obligations to Selected Universities and Colleges: 1990 to 2019

[In millions of dollars (9,031.4 represents $9,031,400,000). Year ending September 30. Top 40 institutions receiving Federal Research & Development (R&D) funds in FY2019. From the Survey of Federal Science and Engineering Support to Universities, Colleges, and Nonprofit Institutions. Included are colleges of liberal arts; schools of arts and sciences; professional schools, as in engineering and medicine, including affiliate hospitals and associated research institutes; and agricultural experiment stations. Does not cover academic Federally Funded Research and Development Centers (FFRDC) administered by higher education institutions. Includes administrative expenses for R&D and excludes investments in physical assets, routine testing, quality control, and monitoring, and training of scientific and technical personnel]

Major institution ranked by 2019 obligations	1990	2000	2010 [2]	2015	2018	2019
Total, all institutions [1]	**9,031.4**	**17,271.7**	**30,748.2**	**26,772.3**	**31,883.0**	**34,825.8**
Johns Hopkins University	469.5	795.5	1,515.8	1,340.7	1,753.5	1,856.1
University of Michigan, all campuses	176.4	346.7	686.6	606.1	703.8	745.8
University of Washington, all campuses	217.2	396.1	736.6	611.9	665.7	726.6
University of California—San Diego	164.8	314.4	613.2	536.6	636.4	679.6
University of California—San Francisco	167.3	289.2	531.3	528.5	617.0	675.4
Columbia University in the City of New York	154.1	284.6	497.6	476.1	601.8	653.4
Duke University	116.1	232.2	496.8	428.5	543.7	629.1
University of Pennsylvania	142.5	348.5	609.0	494.6	540.9	625.5
Georgia Institute of Technology—Atlanta	54.3	58.4	234.9	295.2	485.3	620.1
Stanford University	248.0	355.0	516.8	504.0	576.3	612.5
University of Pittsburgh, all campuses	116.6	246.2	497.1	450.0	558.2	581.8
University of California—Los Angeles	176.7	372.4	548.8	481.8	509.9	555.1
University of North Carolina at Chapel Hill	100.2	232.7	429.7	416.8	475.6	535.6
Washington University, Saint Louis	117.9	287.3	445.5	391.6	484.6	535.1
Yale University	142.5	260.0	470.5	370.8	466.9	530.7
Pennsylvania State University, all campuses	136.4	230.1	413.1	362.9	459.0	520.0
University of Colorado—Boulder	116.4	272.3	427.0	416.7	517.2	511.5
Harvard University	148.1	299.9	548.7	425.5	463.8	486.2
Northwestern University	61.1	151.5	282.0	337.0	421.5	470.8
University of Wisconsin—Madison	155.2	263.4	461.9	386.6	451.4	435.6
New York University	80.0	130.0	257.1	263.8	356.2	430.2
University of Minnesota, all campuses	137.5	276.8	420.3	359.5	397.6	426.9
Cornell University, all campuses	144.7	240.1	359.8	296.4	378.1	423.7
Vanderbilt University	70.6	138.4	399.1	329.3	405.4	422.5
University of Southern California	122.7	203.9	378.9	289.2	411.1	408.7
Emory University	49.6	145.6	303.1	324.2	366.5	398.0
Mount Sinai School of Medicine	44.0	119.5	216.5	262.4	331.1	395.7
University of Utah	65.3	125.0	230.2	201.4	261.3	376.0
University of Alabama at Birmingham	74.5	182.9	236.0	254.2	306.7	348.8
University of California—Davis	68.9	148.5	313.2	315.4	331.2	328.5
Massachusetts Institute of Technology	218.3	248.9	340.2	350.5	332.2	320.6
University of Florida	55.5	129.2	228.2	239.0	275.4	314.9
Ohio State University, all campuses	80.1	140.8	313.6	232.5	272.2	311.6
Case Western Reserve University	71.3	179.4	287.0	273.3	299.1	308.9
Baylor College of Medicine	72.3	172.3	251.3	227.5	266.0	302.9
University of Texas at Austin	91.8	135.0	192.9	203.4	284.1	301.6
Boston University	59.4	139.4	226.0	188.2	229.9	292.7
Carnegie Mellon University	50.0	88.3	132.1	104.3	259.9	292.3
Oregon Health & Science University	25.3	113.2	225.3	198.9	243.5	280.9
University of Chicago	88.5	144.5	252.8	224.2	235.0	274.1

[1] Includes other institutions, not shown separately. [2] Includes American Recovery and Reinvestment Act of 2009 expenditures.

Source: U.S. National Science Foundation, National Center for Science and Engineering Statistics, "NCES Survey Data," <ncsesdata.nsf.gov/home>, accessed October 2021. See also <www.nsf.gov/statistics/fedsupport/>.

Table 846. Research and Development (R&D) Spending and Employment by Company Size: 2019

[Expenditures in millions of dollars (492,956 represents $492,956,000,000); employment in thousands (21,213 represents 21,213,000). Data are from the Business Enterprise Research and Development Survey. Data represent all for-profit, nonfarm companies that are publicly or privately held, have ten or more employees in the United States, and that performed or funded $50,000 or more in R&D]

Company size	Domestic R&D expenditures [1] (mil. dollars)	R&D as a percent of domestic sales of R&D performers or funders	R&D as a percent of domestic sales of R&D performers	Domestic employment of R&D performing companies		
				Total employment (1,000s)	R&D employment [2] (1,000s)	R&D employment as a percent of total employment
All companies..................	**492,956**	**4.4**	**4.6**	**21,213**	**1,832**	**8.6**
Small companies:						
10–19 employees.................	5,501	24.7	25.2	79	35	44.3
20–49 employees.................	12,418	11.4	11.6	257	83	32.3
Medium companies:						
50–99 employees.................	14,021	11.6	11.9	356	85	23.9
100–249 employees...............	19,793	7.4	7.5	719	127	17.7
Large companies:						
250–499 employees..............	18,883	6.3	6.4	760	105	13.8
500–999 employees..............	23,969	6.5	6.5	859	100	11.6
1,000–4,999 employees.........	75,671	5.1	5.2	2,854	305	10.7
5,000–9,999 employees.........	50,811	4.4	4.6	1,677	182	10.9
10,000–24,999 employees......	88,263	4.2	4.3	3,518	267	7.6
25,000 or more employees......	183,626	3.5	3.8	10,135	542	5.3

[1] Domestic R&D paid for by the company and others and performed by the company. [2] Includes researchers, R&D technicians, and other supporting staff.

Source: U.S. National Science Foundation, *Business Research and Development: 2019*, Data Tables, NSF 22-329, April 2022, <ncses.nsf.gov/pubs/nsf22329>. See also <www.nsf.gov/statistics/srvyberd/>.

Table 847. Graduate Science and Engineering Students in Doctorate-Granting Colleges by Characteristic and Field: 2018 to 2020

[In thousands (602.3 represents 602,300). As of Fall. Includes outlying areas. Based on the Survey of Graduate Students and Postdoctorates in Science and Engineering (GSS). In 2017, the GSS underwent a redesign, which included a reorganization of the taxonomy of academic disciplines; therefore, data from 2017 and after are not fully comparable to earlier data. See source for more information]

Field of science or engineering	Total			Characteristic								
				Female			Foreign [1]			Part-time		
	2018	2019	2020	2018	2019	2020	2018	2019	2020	2018	2019	2020
Total, all surveyed fields....	**602.3**	**627.1**	**628.2**	**270.9**	**287.7**	**295.6**	**219.7**	**224.6**	**202.5**	**144.8**	**157.4**	**171.8**
Science/engineering..........	541.4	565.0	564.8	225.5	240.8	247.6	211.9	216.8	195.1	126.1	137.5	149.9
Engineering, total............	156.5	157.9	151.1	39.6	41.5	40.8	83.5	81.6	71.1	39.4	39.8	42.9
Sciences, total................	384.9	407.1	413.7	185.9	199.3	206.9	128.3	135.2	124.0	86.7	97.7	107.0
Agricultural sciences.......	9.1	9.1	10.3	4.9	5.0	6.1	2.9	2.8	2.9	2.4	2.5	3.2
Biological sciences.........	81.6	85.4	87.7	46.9	50.0	52.3	17.6	18.6	17.7	11.1	12.7	14.0
Computer & information. ..	80.3	89.1	87.2	24.0	27.1	26.5	46.5	50.0	43.4	27.8	32.1	36.1
Geosciences [2].............	11.6	11.2	11.0	5.2	5.3	5.4	2.7	2.5	2.3	2.2	2.0	1.9
Math & statistics,..........	29.0	30.9	29.6	10.7	11.3	10.5	15.6	16.5	14.5	5.0	6.0	6.4
Multidisciplinary and interdisciplinary studies...	9.0	9.8	12.8	4.8	5.2	6.8	2.5	2.9	3.8	2.9	3.4	4.4
Natural resources and conservation...............	10.1	10.5	11.2	5.5	6.0	6.6	1.6	1.6	1.5	2.8	3.0	3.4
Physical sciences..........	41.1	42.0	41.6	13.8	14.5	14.6	16.3	16.6	15.7	3.9	4.3	4.5
Psychology..................	41.7	46.0	50.6	31.6	35.6	39.8	3.0	3.3	3.4	11.3	13.2	14.5
Social sciences.............	71.3	73.2	71.6	38.4	39.4	38.4	19.7	20.4	18.7	17.3	18.5	18.5
Health fields, total.............	60.9	62.1	63.4	45.4	46.9	48.0	7.8	7.9	7.3	18.7	19.9	21.9

[1] Temporary residents. [2] Earth or geosciences, atmospheric, and ocean sciences.

Source: U.S. National Science Foundation, National Center for Science and Engineering Statistics, Data Explorer, "Survey of Graduate Students and Postdoctorates in Science and Engineering," <ncsesdata.nsf.gov/explorer>, accessed August 2022. See also <www.nsf.gov/statistics/srvygradpostdoc>.

Table 848. Temporary Visa Holders Awarded Doctorates in Science and Engineering For Top 10 Countries of Origin: 2010 to 2020

[Based on the Survey of Earned Doctorates; for information, see <www.nsf.gov/statistics/srvydoctorates/>]

Country of origin	2010	2011	2012	2013	2014	2015	2016	2017	2018	2019	2020
All temporary visa holders [1]	**13,636**	**14,235**	**14,784**	**15,674**	**15,839**	**16,129**	**16,477**	**16,288**	**17,586**	**18,324**	**18,482**
Science	7,809	8,021	8,374	8,676	8,764	8,902	9,471	9,085	9,631	10,098	10,048
Engineering	3,866	4,164	4,355	4,759	4,961	5,108	4,842	5,037	5,576	5,680	5,955
COUNTRY											
China [2]	3,457	3,652	3,906	4,443	4,650	4,970	5,141	5,147	5,692	5,755	5,730
India	1,994	2,036	2,142	2,074	2,208	2,119	2,085	1,884	1,922	1,910	2,116
Iran	(D)	193	278	380	463	608	664	728	871	882	895
South Korea	1,076	1,085	1,132	1,012	928	920	891	815	729	824	756
Saudi Arabia	26	34	41	53	76	98	175	232	295	432	472
Taiwan	501	570	581	571	558	514	499	435	445	426	417
Turkey	405	422	352	391	360	386	380	392	364	324	303
Canada	339	307	299	332	321	318	272	288	307	313	281
Mexico	169	159	185	146	161	155	191	145	156	162	196
Thailand	182	235	240	227	200	193	168	153	155	139	117

D Data is suppressed to avoid disclosure of confidential information. [1] Total includes doctorates awarded in fields other than science and engineering and to temporary visa holders from other countries, not shown separately. [2] Includes Hong Kong.

Source: U.S. National Science Foundation, National Center for Science and Engineering Statistics, "Doctorate Recipients from U.S. Colleges and Universities: 2020, Data Tables," <ncses.nsf.gov/pubs/nsf22300/data-tables>, accessed January 2022.

Table 849. Science and Engineering (S&E) Degrees Awarded by Degree Level and Sex of Recipient: 1970 to 2019

[Aggregated for degrees in the following science and engineering (S&E) fields: astronomy, chemistry, physics, atmospheric sciences, earth sciences, ocean sciences, mathematics and statistics, computer sciences, agricultural sciences, biological sciences, psychology, social sciences, and engineering. For doctoral degrees, medical and health sciences are included under S&E because these data correspond to the doctor's research/scholarship degree level which are research focused degrees]

Academic year ending	Bachelor's degree				Master's degree				Doctoral degree [1]			
	Total S&E	Men	Women	Percent women	Total S&E	Men	Women	Percent women	Total S&E	Men	Women	Percent women [2]
1970	284,230	204,528	79,702	28.0	53,695	43,973	9,722	18.1	18,052	16,404	1,648	9.1
1975	313,555	210,741	102,814	32.8	63,198	49,410	13,788	21.8	18,799	15,870	2,929	15.6
1980	304,695	191,215	113,480	37.2	64,089	46,004	18,085	28.2	17,775	13,814	3,961	22.3
1985	332,273	203,402	128,871	38.8	70,578	48,247	22,331	31.6	18,934	14,043	4,891	25.8
1990	329,094	189,082	140,012	42.5	77,788	51,230	26,558	34.1	22,868	16,498	6,370	27.9
1995	378,148	202,217	175,931	46.5	94,309	58,518	35,791	38.0	26,535	18,119	8,286	31.4
1996	384,674	203,341	181,333	47.1	95,313	57,860	37,453	39.3	27,240	18,461	8,649	31.9
1997	388,482	201,471	187,011	48.1	93,485	55,223	38,262	40.9	27,228	18,084	8,934	33.1
1998	390,618	200,221	190,397	48.7	93,918	55,335	38,583	41.1	27,274	17,810	9,349	34.4
1999	(NA)	(NA)	(NA)	(NA)	(NA)	(NA)	(NA)	(NA)	25,930	16,735	9,083	35.2
2000	398,602	197,650	200,952	50.4	96,230	54,560	41,670	43.3	27,862	17,024	10,838	38.9
2001	400,435	197,771	202,664	50.6	99,528	55,884	43,644	43.9	28,096	16,873	11,223	39.9
2002	415,983	204,675	211,308	50.8	99,650	55,939	43,711	43.9	27,588	16,164	11,424	41.4
2003	442,755	219,815	222,940	50.4	108,355	61,183	47,172	43.5	28,746	16,569	12,177	42.4
2004	458,658	227,861	230,797	50.3	119,296	67,215	52,081	43.7	30,979	17,532	13,447	43.4
2005	470,214	233,924	236,290	50.3	120,870	67,244	53,626	44.4	34,468	18,970	15,498	45.0
2006	478,858	238,029	240,829	50.3	120,999	66,249	54,750	45.2	37,541	20,254	17,287	46.0
2007	485,772	241,697	244,075	50.2	120,278	65,353	54,925	45.7	40,980	21,653	19,327	47.2
2008	496,168	246,719	249,449	50.3	126,404	68,810	57,594	45.6	41,480	21,995	19,485	47.0
2009	505,435	250,742	254,693	50.4	134,517	73,489	61,028	45.4	41,111	21,743	19,368	47.1
2010	525,374	261,091	264,283	50.3	139,926	76,266	63,660	45.5	36,711	20,361	16,350	44.5
2011	554,365	275,258	279,107	50.3	150,653	82,451	68,202	45.3	38,470	21,377	17,093	44.4
2012	589,567	291,890	297,677	50.5	161,372	87,859	73,513	45.6	39,864	22,107	17,757	44.5
2013	615,475	305,777	309,698	50.3	166,397	90,046	76,351	45.9	41,563	23,021	18,542	44.6
2014	635,915	318,015	317,900	50.0	171,228	92,457	78,771	46.0	43,995	24,072	19,923	45.3
2015	650,057	327,122	322,935	49.7	180,955	99,282	81,673	45.1	44,521	24,371	20,150	45.3
2016	666,157	335,274	330,883	49.7	198,292	110,442	87,850	44.3	44,845	24,699	20,146	44.9
2017	684,557	346,087	338,470	49.4	206,172	116,326	89,846	43.6	45,729	25,048	20,681	45.2
2018	707,158	356,484	350,674	49.6	208,427	115,295	93,132	44.7	46,798	25,379	21,419	45.8
2019	724,947	364,648	360,299	49.7	209,566	113,535	96,031	45.8	47,753	25,905	21,848	45.8

[1] Prior to 2008, the National Center for Education Statistics (NCES) used two doctoral degree categories (doctor's and first professional). Data in this table for those years include only the doctor's category. In 2008 and 2009, NCES allowed optional reporting in three new doctoral degree categories (doctor's research/scholarship, doctor's professional practice, and doctor's other) in addition to the doctor's category. For those 2 years, data in this table include only doctorates reported in the doctor's category plus those reported in doctor's research/scholarship. In 2010, NCES required institutions to use only the three new doctoral degree categories, and data in this table for 2010 and later include only doctorates reported in the category doctor's research/scholarship. [2] After 1988 a number of doctoral degree holders did not report sex. From 1988 on, percentages of women are calculated based on the total of men plus women, not on the total number of degrees reported in the total column.

Source: U.S. National Science Foundation, Science and Engineering Indicators 2022, *Higher Education in Science and Engineering, Supplemental Tables*, NSB-2022-3, February 2022. See also <www.nsf.gov/statistics/seind/>.

Table 850. Science and Engineering (S&E) Degrees as Percent of Higher Education Degrees Conferred by State: 2019

[Includes bachelor's, master's, and doctorate degrees. S&E degrees include degrees in physical, life, earth, ocean, atmospheric, computer, and social sciences; mathematics; engineering; and psychology. They do not include medical fields or technologies]

State	S&E degrees conferred	All higher education degrees	S&E higher education degrees (percent)	State	S&E degrees conferred	All higher education degrees	S&E higher education degrees (percent)	State	S&E degrees conferred	All higher education degrees	S&E higher education degrees (percent)
U.S.[1]	975,183	2,947,649	33.1	KS	7,615	28,587	26.6	ND	2,447	8,673	28.2
				KY	11,026	37,486	29.4	OH	30,172	98,640	30.6
AL	12,476	47,280	26.4	LA	9,310	32,458	28.7	OK	8,613	28,804	29.9
AK	893	2,570	34.7	ME	3,268	9,703	33.7	OR	12,420	33,074	37.6
AZ	23,261	91,982	25.3	MD	25,258	58,178	43.4	PA	45,194	133,734	33.8
AR	5,756	22,833	25.2	MA	41,730	107,198	38.9	RI	5,296	16,035	33.0
CA	126,953	311,641	40.7	MI	28,600	82,841	34.5	SC	10,747	34,147	31.5
CO	20,580	54,627	37.7	MN	19,366	66,942	28.9	SD	2,617	8,357	31.3
CT	12,545	36,212	34.6	MS	5,746	22,578	25.4	TN	12,604	48,589	25.9
DE	3,877	11,158	34.7	MO	16,690	62,081	26.9	TX	62,681	200,791	31.2
DC	9,799	24,116	40.6	MT	3,075	7,679	40.0	UT	14,412	66,065	21.8
FL	44,595	146,029	30.5	NE	5,681	20,314	28.0	VT	3,476	8,922	39.0
GA	25,805	76,049	33.9	NV	3,869	12,281	31.5	VA	28,430	87,110	32.6
HI	2,866	7,884	36.4	NH	8,029	28,688	28.0	WA	19,743	47,077	41.9
ID	4,175	15,112	27.6	NJ	23,288	63,563	36.6	WV	6,733	22,998	29.3
IL	35,953	118,838	30.3	NM	4,037	12,246	33.0	WI	16,565	47,286	35.0
IN	21,501	71,880	29.9	NY	78,806	226,049	34.9	WY	1,285	2,818	45.6
IA	10,320	30,863	33.4	NC	27,513	79,088	34.8	PR	7,229	26,540	27.2

[1] Total higher education degrees and S&E degrees include U.S. territories.

Source: National Science Foundation, Science and Engineering Indicators 2022, "State Indicators," <ncses.nsf.gov/indicators/states>, accessed March 2022.

Table 851. Doctorates Conferred in Science and Engineering by Field, Sex, Citizenship Status, Race, and Hispanic Origin: 2020

[In percent, except as indicated. Based on the Survey of Earned Doctorates. For description of methodology, see <www.nsf.gov/statistics/srvydoctorates/>]

Characteristic	Total	Life sciences		Physical sciences			Mathematics and computer science		Social sciences		Engineering
		Total [1]	Biological	Total [1]	Chemistry	Physics [2]	Total [1]	Mathematics	Total [1]	Psychology	
Total conferred (number)	42,622	12,561	8,418	6,247	2,763	2,241	4,392	2,031	8,946	3,879	10,476
SEX											
Male	57.5	44.2	46.2	66.9	60.4	79.0	75.1	70.8	40.1	27.9	75.2
Female	42.5	55.8	53.8	33.1	39.5	21.0	24.9	29.2	59.9	72.1	24.8
CITIZENSHIP											
U.S. citizen or permanent resident	58.5	69.3	71.4	59.9	61.4	55.1	39.5	45.7	73.8	85.5	39.7
Temporary visa holders	37.5	27.3	25.8	37.0	36.0	41.3	56.4	50.4	20.5	6.6	56.8
RACE/ETHNICITY [3]											
Total conferred (number)	24,943	8,707	6,008	3,741	1,696	1,234	1,736	928	6,605	3,317	4,154
Non-Hispanic:											
White	69.9	68.8	69.0	77.3	74.6	79.5	68.9	71.2	68.9	69.3	67.5
Asian [4]	10.6	11.0	12.5	8.4	9.3	9.0	15.2	12.7	6.7	5.8	16.0
Black	5.6	6.4	4.4	2.1	2.7	1.7	3.2	3.2	8.1	7.9	4.3
American Indian/Alaska Native	0.2	0.3	0.1	0.1	0.1	0.2	0.1	–	0.3	0.1	0.1
Two or more races	3.6	3.6	3.9	3.7	4.2	2.6	4.4	4.7	3.6	3.7	3.1
Hispanic [5]	8.0	8.2	8.7	6.6	7.0	5.5	5.8	6.0	9.9	10.7	6.9
Other/unknown [6]	2.1	1.8	1.4	1.8	2.2	1.5	2.4	2.0	2.4	2.5	2.1

– Represents or rounds to zero. [1] Includes other fields, not shown separately. [2] Includes astronomy. [3] Covers U.S. citizens and permanent residents only. [4] Excludes Native Hawaiians or Other Pacific Islanders. [5] Persons reporting Hispanic ethnicity may be of any race or combination of races. [6] Includes other non-Hispanic race, and individuals who did not report race nor ethnicity.

Source: U.S. National Science Foundation, National Center for Science and Engineering Statistics, "Doctorate Recipients from U.S. Colleges and Universities: 2020, Data Tables," <ncses.nsf.gov/pubs/nsf22300/data-tables>, accessed January 2022.

Table 852. Doctorates Awarded by Field of Study and Year of Doctorate: 2010 to 2020

[Based on the Survey of Earned Doctorates. For description of methodology, see <www.nsf.gov/statistics/srvydoctorates/>]

Field of study	2010	2014	2015	2016	2017	2018	2019	2020
Total, all fields	**48,028**	**53,986**	**54,886**	**54,809**	**54,552**	**55,085**	**55,614**	**55,283**
Science and engineering, total	**34,997**	**40,630**	**41,175**	**41,240**	**41,288**	**42,150**	**42,904**	**42,622**
Science, total	27,419	31,004	31,300	31,781	31,512	31,985	32,606	32,146
Life sciences	11,319	12,484	12,493	12,539	12,554	12,755	12,753	12,561
Agricultural sciences and natural resources	1,100	1,338	1,434	1,379	1,493	1,442	1,488	1,472
Biological/biomedical sciences	8,046	8,868	8,783	8,863	8,566	8,782	8,681	8,418
Health sciences	2,173	2,278	2,276	2,297	2,495	2,531	2,584	2,671
Physical and earth sciences	4,995	5,910	5,916	6,251	6,082	6,331	6,579	6,247
Chemistry	2,304	2,673	2,666	2,703	2,699	2,808	2,939	2,763
Geosciences, atmospheric and ocean sciences	862	1,098	1,057	1,227	1,169	1,185	1,272	1,243
Physics and astronomy	1,829	2,139	2,193	2,321	2,214	2,338	2,368	2,241
Mathematics and computer sciences	3,223	3,862	3,818	3,954	3,842	4,022	4,231	4,392
Computer and information sciences	1,633	1,988	2,003	2,082	1,998	2,000	2,221	2,361
Mathematics and statistics	1,590	1,874	1,815	1,872	1,844	2,022	2,010	2,031
Psychology and social sciences	7,882	8,748	9,073	9,037	9,034	8,877	9,043	8,946
Psychology	3,420	3,724	3,776	3,910	3,925	3,821	3,909	3,879
Anthropology	507	523	492	460	446	424	445	448
Economics	1,073	1,196	1,255	1,236	1,239	1,245	1,247	1,216
Political science and government	728	775	859	745	743	734	707	637
Sociology	639	678	741	613	683	668	632	607
Other social sciences	1,515	1,852	1,950	2,073	1,998	1,985	2,103	2,159
Engineering, total	7,578	9,626	9,875	9,459	9,776	10,165	10,298	10,476
Aerospace, aeronautical and astronautical	252	386	361	370	379	383	379	399
Bioengineering and biomedical	824	1,046	1,125	1,089	1,032	1,133	1,163	1083
Chemical	822	973	1,002	921	931	981	980	994
Civil	643	617	632	564	713	675	700	796
Electrical, electronics and communications	1,778	1,952	1,997	1,823	1,879	1,943	1,799	1,973
Industrial and manufacturing	215	298	243	256	249	272	234	304
Materials science	670	832	871	984	937	992	992	880
Mechanical	983	1,331	1,466	1,297	1,398	1,503	1,532	1,634
Other	1,391	2,191	2,178	2,155	2,258	2,283	2,519	2,413
Non-science and engineering, total	**13,031**	**13,356**	**13,711**	**13,569**	**13,264**	**12,935**	**12,710**	**12,661**
Education	5,287	4,789	5,098	5,146	4,826	4,818	4,633	4,716
Humanities	5,015	5,524	5,594	5,482	5,286	5,139	5,051	4,939
Professional/other/unknown	2,729	3,043	3,019	2,941	3,152	2,978	3,026	3,006

Source: U.S. National Science Foundation, National Center for Science and Engineering Statistics, "Doctorate Recipients from U.S. Colleges and Universities: 2020, Data Tables," <ncses.nsf.gov/pubs/nsf22300/data-tables>, accessed January 2022.

Table 853. Employed Scientists and Engineers by Sex, Race/Ethnicity, and Selected Characteristics: 2019

[In thousands (28,627 represents 28,627,000). Scientists and engineers are individuals who have a bachelor's or higher degree, and have an S&E (Science and Engineering) or S&E-related degree or occupation. Data based on various NSF (National Science Foundation) and non-NSF surveys; see <ncses.nsf.gov/pubs/nsf19304/technical-notes> for details]

Characteristic	Total [1]	Female	Male	Hispanic or Latino [2]	Asian [3]	Black or African American [3]	White [3]	More than one race [3]
All employed scientists and engineers	**28,627**	**13,720**	**14,907**	**2,646**	**3,869**	**2,065**	**19,225**	**650**
Age:								
Under 30 years	4,507	2,480	2,028	511	736	309	2,778	153
30-39 years	7,848	3,911	3,937	801	1,146	559	5,068	227
40-49 years	6,611	3,177	3,433	627	1,064	526	4,195	142
50-75 years	9,661	4,153	5,508	706	924	672	7,183	128
Employment status:								
Employed, full-time	23,961	10,673	13,288	2,176	3,296	1,786	16,000	550
Employed, part-time	4,666	3,047	1,618	470	574	280	3,225	100
Highest degree attained:								
Bachelor's	16,042	7,460	8,581	1,668	1,829	1,153	10,888	388
Master's	8,624	4,537	4,087	661	1,325	691	5,724	186
Doctorate	1,761	742	1,019	115	399	110	1,104	29
Professional	2,200	981	1,220	202	316	111	1,509	47
By occupation:								
S&E occupations	7,466	2,193	5,274	564	1,543	379	4,784	158
Science occupations	5,545	1,883	3,662	405	1,212	302	3,479	121
Engineering occupations	1,921	310	1,612	159	331	77	1,305	37
S&E related occupations	8,893	5,109	3,785	821	1,151	613	6,053	198
Non-S&E related occupations	12,267	6,419	5,848	1,261	1,176	1,074	8,388	295
By employment sector:								
Business or industry	15,580	5,972	9,608	1,380	2,461	933	10,399	333
Federal government	1,262	492	770	126	127	156	792	43
Nonprofit	3,354	2,272	1,083	275	382	289	2,281	95
Self-employed	1,658	828	830	110	165	97	1,240	43
State or local government	1,640	850	790	227	155	227	987	31
Universities and 4-year colleges	2,290	1,275	1,015	215	419	132	1,464	42
Other educational institutions	2,843	2,031	811	314	160	231	2,062	64

[1] Total includes other races, not shown separately. [2] Persons of Hispanic origin may be of any race. [3] Non-Hispanic.

Source: U.S. National Science Foundation, National Center for Science and Engineering Statistics, "Women, Minorities, and Persons with Disabilities in Science and Engineering - Data Tables," <ncses.nsf.gov/pubs/nsf21321/data-tables>, accessed June 2021.

Table 854. Science and Engineering (S&E) Degree Holders by Occupation: 2019

[In thousands (22,791 represents 22,791,000). Data represents all workers who attained their highest degree (bachelor's or higher) in an S&E or S&E-related field. Detail may not add to total due to rounding]

Occupation	Total S&E and S&E-related degree holders	Employees by field of highest degree [1]						S&E related fields [5]
		Total S&E fields	Computer and mathematical sciences	Biological, agricultural, and environmental life sciences [2]	Physical and related sciences [3]	Social and related sciences [4]	Engineering	
All occupations	**22,791**	**15,362**	**2,837**	**2,437**	**889**	**5,474**	**3,725**	**7,429**
S&E occupations	**6,137**	**5,709**	**1,670**	**705**	**422**	**754**	**2,159**	**428**
Computer & mathematical scientists	2,828	2,642	1,584	94	79	258	628	186
Computer & information scientists [6]	2,546	2,393	1,429	80	66	218	600	153
Computer support specialists	183	168	95	(S)	(S)	22	31	15
Computer system analysts	268	246	155	13	5	26	47	22
Network/computer systems administrators	129	125	80	2	4	17	21	4
Software developers	568	536	345	15	16	23	137	32
Computer engineers—software	816	776	441	3	18	39	276	40
Mathematical scientists	184	164	76	13	12	39	24	20
Biological, agricultural, & environmental life scientists [6]	656	579	4	488	47	18	22	77
Biological & medical scientists [6]	471	404	4	328	42	11	19	67
Biological scientists [7]	134	128	(S)	118	3	3	1	6
Medical scientists (excluding practitioners)	151	107	(S)	89	8	3	6	44
Physical & related scientists [6]	(NA)	374	4	87	246	8	28	(S)
Chemists, except biochemists	(NA)	117	(S)	31	78	(S)	7	(S)
Physicists & astronomers	46	45	(S)	(S)	38	(S)	6	1
Social & related scientists [6]	521	477	6	17	1	448	5	44
Psychologists, including clinical	196	188	(S)	(S)	(S)	182	(S)	8
Postsecondary teachers—social sciences	142	139	1	4	(S)	134	(S)	3
Engineers [6]	1,740	1,637	71	19	49	22	1,477	103
Aerospace, aeronautical, or astronautical engineers	116	112	3	(S)	5	(S)	104	4
Civil, architectural, or sanitary engineers	280	271	1	2	(S)	1	262	9
Electrical or computer hardware engineers	389	371	33	(S)	9	(S)	327	18
Mechanical engineers	350	325	4	2	1	1	316	25
S&E-related occupations	**7,440**	**2,131**	**366**	**660**	**176**	**367**	**562**	**5,309**
Health-related occupations [6]	5,175	696	27	389	52	211	17	4,479
Diagnosing/treating practitioners [8]	1,252	98	(S)	60	(S)	11	2	1,154
Registered nurses, pharmacists, dieticians, therapists, physician assistants, & nurse practitioners	2,732	148	(S)	88	2	51	(S)	2,584
S&E managers	777	517	106	68	37	57	249	260
Computer & information systems managers	150	140	82	(S)	(S)	11	32	10
Engineering managers	289	258	23	3	12	(S)	213	31
Medical & health services managers	273	60	(S)	20	(S)	32	(S)	213
S&E precollege teachers [9]	477	237	74	72	30	48	13	240
S&E technicians & technologists [6]	768	635	132	129	54	48	272	133
Computer programmers	96	88	49	2	(S)	10	22	8
Electrical, electronic, industrial, & mechanical technicians	240	200	29	19	7	15	130	40
Other S&E-related occupations [6]	242	46	27	2	3	4	10	196
Architects	203	22	(S)	2	(S)	(S)	10	181
Non-S&E occupations	**9,214**	**7,522**	**801**	**1,072**	**291**	**4,352**	**1,004**	**1,692**
Non-S&E managers	1,476	1,205	161	162	56	509	317	271
Management-related occupations [6]	1,997	1,717	265	236	64	916	236	280
Accountants, auditors, & other financial specialists	578	516	93	31	7	344	41	62
Personnel, training, & labor relations specialists	231	187	16	13	(S)	128	20	44
Non-S&E precollege teachers [6]	563	405	22	67	11	289	14	158
Prekindergarten and kindergarten	105	84	(S)	12	(S)	68	(S)	21
Elementary	215	169	13	18	(S)	127	6	46
Secondary—other subjects	108	69	(S)	16	(S)	43	6	39
Special education—primary & secondary	90	50	2	9	(S)	37	(S)	40
Non-S&E postsecondary teachers	108	78	4	(S)	5	61	2	30
Social services & related occupations [6]	724	605	(S)	29	9	541	7	119
Counselors [10]	340	280	(S)	6	(S)	270	(S)	60
Social workers	319	264	(S)	16	(S)	239	(S)	55
Sales & marketing occupations	1,229	996	87	131	41	602	134	233
Arts, humanities, & related occupations	222	183	9	(S)	(S)	123	8	39
Other non-S&E occupations [6]	2,892	2,332	234	404	99	1,309	285	560

NA Not available. S Data suppressed for reasons of confidentiality and/or reliability. [1] Includes bachelor's, master's, and doctorate degrees. [2] Biological sciences include biology, ecology, nutritional sciences, pharmacology, zoology, and related fields. [3] Physical sciences include chemistry; earth, atmospheric, and ocean sciences; physics and astronomy; and related fields. [4] Social sciences include economics, political science, psychology, sociology and anthropology, linguistics, geography, history and philosophy of science, and related fields. [5] S&E-related fields include health fields, science and math teacher education, technology and technical fields, architecture, and actuarial science. [6] Includes other occupations not shown separately. [7] Includes botanists, ecologists, zoologists, etc. [8] Includes dentists, optometrists, physicians, psychiatrists, podiatrists, surgeons, and veterinarians. [9] Secondary teachers in computer, mathematics, sciences, and social sciences. [10] Includes educational, vocational, mental health, substance abuse, etc.

Source: U.S. National Science Foundation, Science & Engineering Indicators, *The STEM Labor Force of Today: Scientists, Engineers, and Skilled Technical Workers, Supplemental Tables,* NSB-2021-2, August 2021. See also <www.nsf.gov/statistics/seind/>.

Table 855. Civilian Employment of Scientists, Engineers, and Related Occupations by Occupation and Industry: 2020

[In thousands (482.0 represents 482,000). As of 2018, the Standard Occupational Classification (SOC) system classifies workers into over 860 detailed occupations. Industry classifications correspond to 2017 North American Industry Classification (NAICS) industrial groups]

Occupation	Total employ-ment, all workers [1]	Wage and salary workers						Self em-ployed [3]
		Mining (NAICS 21) [2]	Con-struction (NAICS 23)	Manu-facturing (NAICS 31–33)	Informa-tion (NAICS 51)	Profes-sional, scientific, technical services (NAICS 54)	Govern-ment	
Computer and information systems............	482.0	1.1	2.6	30.5	54.7	159.4	26.9	10.5
Architectural and engineering managers.......	197.8	2.4	4.0	67.8	3.6	73.3	17.5	(NA)
Natural science managers....................	79.0	0.3	(NA)	12.7	(NA)	33.6	17.2	(NA)
Computer and mathematical scientists [4]......	5,225.0	12.7	18.6	312.0	614.0	1,667.4	293.0	506.9
Computer occupations...................	4,985.3	12.0	18.4	300.8	602.5	1,604.0	268.4	503.3
Mathematical science occupations...........	239.8	11.2	0.2	11.2	11.5	63.4	24.6	3.6
Surveyors, cartographers, and photogrammetrists............................	59.2	0.1	3.4	0.1	(NA)	37.9	10.0	2.5
Engineers [4]................................	1,719.4	23.6	56.6	603.2	37.2	528.6	210.1	23.1
Aerospace engineers......................	61.4	(NA)	(NA)	26.3	(NA)	18.5	10.6	(NA)
Civil engineers...........................	309.8	0.9	34.8	3.4	0.2	171.1	78.8	4.3
Computer hardware engineers..............	66.2	(NA)	0.1	20.7	6.7	25.6	5.7	0.8
Electrical and electronics engineers........	313.2	0.7	8.3	107.8	25.7	84.2	29.1	2.3
Industrial engineers [5].....................	316.1	2.3	5.5	214.7	2.4	39.5	5.6	0.5
Mechanical engineers.....................	299.2	1.1	4.9	143.5	0.3	88.3	17.2	2.3
Drafters, engineering, and mapping technicians [4]	674.0	5.8	29.1	196.2	4.2	263.8	86.0	5.7
Engineering technicians, except drafters.....	332.7	2.7	7.8	127.4	2.6	95.8	52.1	1.0
Surveying and mapping technicians...........	54.8	0.7	1.8	0.3	0.2	36.1	8.1	1.2
Life, physical, and social science occupations.............................	1,444.0	15.6	15.8	148.1	3.2	369.2	348.9	75.6
Life scientists.............................	346.1	(NA)	(NA)	30.9	0.2	114.8	72.3	10.7
Physical scientists........................	269.1	6.0	0.4	41.7	1.3	93.2	75.9	3.5
Social scientists and related occupations.....	312.3	(NA)	(NA)	0.2	0.7	35.2	91.3	54.4
Life, physical, & social science technicians...	397.2	5.9	0.5	53.6	0.3	111.8	84.6	6.7

NA Not available. [1] Includes other industries not shown separately. [2] Includes oil and gas extraction. [3] Includes unpaid family workers. [4] Includes other occupations not shown separately. [5] Includes health and safety engineers.

Source: U.S. Bureau of Labor Statistics, National Employment Matrix, "Employment Projections," <www.bls.gov/emp/tables.htm>, accessed September 2022.

Table 856. Top Metropolitan Areas with the Largest Number of Workers in Science and Engineering Occupations: 2019

[In thousands, except as indicated (146,875 represents 146,875,000). As of May. Ranked for top 19 metro areas with highest number of S&E (science and engineering) workers. Data are from U.S. Bureau of Labor Statistics' Occupational Employment Statistics Survey. Excludes metropolitan statistical areas where S&E proportions were suppressed. Differences among employment estimates may not be statistically significant; see source for details]

Metropolitan area	Workers employed		Metropolitan workers in S&E occupations as percentage of national total in S&E occupations
	All occupations	S&E occupations	
U.S. total................................	**146,875**	**7,317**	**100.0**
Top 19 total.............................	**56,041**	**3,668**	**50.1**
New York-Newark-Jersey City, NY-NJ-PA.......	9,655	440	6.0
Washington-Arlington-Alexandria, DC-VA-MD-WV....	3,179	345	4.7
Los Angeles-Long Beach-Anaheim, CA..........	6,240	291	4.0
Boston-Cambridge-Nashua, MA-NH.............	2,798	233	3.2
San Francisco-Oakland-Hayward, CA...........	2,472	229	3.1
Chicago-Naperville-Elgin, IL-IN-WI.............	4,676	214	2.9
Dallas-Fort Worth-Arlington, TX...............	3,657	210	2.9
Seattle-Tacoma-Bellevue, WA.................	2,021	202	2.8
San Jose-Sunnyvale-Santa Clara, CA...........	1,141	194	2.6
Atlanta-Sandy Springs-Roswell, GA............	2,744	171	2.3
Houston-The Woodlands-Sugar Land, TX........	3,052	162	2.2
Philadelphia-Camden-Wilmington, PA-NJ-DE-MD....	2,876	160	2.2
Detroit-Warren-Dearborn, MI.................	1,981	153	2.1
Minneapolis-St. Paul-Bloomington, MN-WI.......	1,971	130	1.8
Denver-Aurora-Lakewood, CO.................	1,513	119	1.6
Phoenix-Mesa-Scottsdale, AZ.................	2,121	111	1.5
San Diego-Carlsbad, CA.....................	1,495	109	1.5
Baltimore-Columbia-Towson, MD..............	1,376	100	1.4
Austin-Round Rock, TX......................	1,073	95	1.3

Source: U.S. National Science Foundation, Science & Engineering Indicators, *The STEM Labor Force of Today: Scientists, Engineers, and Skilled Technical Workers, Supplemental Tables*, NSB-2021-2, August 2021. See also <www.nsf.gov/statistics/seind/>.

Table 857. High Science, Engineering, and Technology Establishments, Business Formations, and Employment by State: 2016

[Employment in thousands (126,753 represents 126,753,000). High science, engineering, and technology (SET) industries are those industries for which employment in technology-oriented occupations accounts for a proportion of that industry's total employment that is at least twice the average for all industries. Includes only private-sector businesses. For a complete list of included industries, see source. Minus sign (-) indicates loss]

State	All establishments		High science, engineering, and technology establishments					
			Establishments		Net business formations		Employment	
	Total	Employment (1,000)	Total	Percent of all establishments	Total	Percent of all establishments	Total (1,000)	Percent of total employment
United States.......	**7,743,176**	**126,753**	**714,591**	**9.2**	**9,367**	**0.1**	**15,317**	**12.1**
Alabama...............	99,422	1,673	7,212	7.3	51	0.1	165	9.9
Alaska.................	21,032	266	1,772	8.4	41	0.2	39	14.7
Arizona...............	138,945	2,378	13,065	9.4	327	0.2	256	10.8
Arkansas.............	65,549	1,024	5,149	7.9	21	(Z)	103	10.1
California.............	920,062	14,606	98,176	10.7	1,536	0.2	2,032	13.9
Colorado.............	164,978	2,317	20,726	12.6	137	0.1	342	14.7
Connecticut...........	89,234	1,534	7,525	8.4	-69	-0.1	202	13.2
Delaware.............	25,334	400	3,268	12.9	105	0.4	42	10.6
District of Columbia...	23,143	527	4,147	17.9	139	0.6	92	17.4
Florida................	545,367	8,168	52,807	9.7	1,299	0.2	692	8.5
Georgia...............	228,064	3,804	23,250	10.2	349	0.2	512	13.5
Hawaii................	32,330	528	2,374	7.3	61	0.2	31	5.8
Idaho.................	45,742	562	3,302	7.2	49	0.1	59	10.5
Illinois................	319,063	5,513	29,923	9.4	52	(Z)	702	12.7
Indiana...............	145,839	2,720	10,722	7.4	131	0.1	254	9.3
Iowa..................	81,395	1,355	5,043	6.2	64	0.1	122	9.0
Kansas...............	74,737	1,186	6,462	8.6	79	0.1	156	13.2
Kentucky..............	91,870	1,603	6,403	7.0	19	(Z)	135	8.4
Louisiana.............	105,650	1,709	8,644	8.2	-223	-0.2	160	9.4
Maine.................	41,114	511	2,788	6.8	59	0.1	42	8.1
Maryland..............	138,265	2,282	17,496	12.7	456	0.3	371	16.2
Massachusetts........	177,230	3,255	18,349	10.4	243	0.1	504	15.5
Michigan..............	220,048	3,805	17,063	7.8	258	0.1	467	12.3
Minnesota............	149,878	2,661	13,926	9.3	143	0.1	402	15.1
Mississippi...........	58,744	939	3,663	6.2	-13	(Z)	67	7.2
Missouri..............	160,609	2,495	10,810	6.7	378	0.2	298	12.0
Montana..............	37,527	379	2,830	7.5	9	(Z)	27	7.2
Nebraska.............	54,193	884	3,689	6.8	25	(Z)	74	8.4
Nevada...............	64,719	1,165	6,860	10.6	130	0.2	75	6.5
New Hampshire.......	37,787	594	3,472	9.2	14	(Z)	70	11.8
New Jersey...........	231,666	3,637	23,699	10.2	12	(Z)	520	14.3
New Mexico...........	43,678	628	3,571	8.2	-7	(Z)	77	12.2
New York..............	542,316	8,179	41,983	7.7	611	0.1	827	10.1
North Carolina........	226,937	3,795	20,248	8.9	293	0.1	422	11.1
North Dakota.........	24,554	347	1,548	6.3	-27	-0.1	31	9.0
Ohio..................	251,781	4,789	20,873	8.3	151	0.1	522	10.9
Oklahoma.............	93,115	1,361	7,992	8.6	-161	-0.2	157	11.5
Oregon...............	114,252	1,550	9,371	8.2	217	0.2	179	11.5
Pennsylvania..........	301,057	5,355	25,359	8.4	175	0.1	617	11.5
Rhode Island.........	28,632	435	2,241	7.8	–	–	41	9.3
South Carolina........	105,808	1,715	7,729	7.3	134	0.1	181	10.6
South Dakota.........	26,689	358	1,596	6.0	16	0.1	28	7.9
Tennessee............	135,123	2,592	9,593	7.1	207	0.2	249	9.6
Texas.................	578,168	10,431	59,036	10.2	374	0.1	1,385	13.3
Utah..................	77,389	1,240	8,582	11.1	280	0.4	149	12.0
Vermont...............	21,145	262	1,627	7.7	17	0.1	23	8.9
Virginia...............	199,302	3,254	26,415	13.3	519	0.3	575	17.7
Washington...........	185,624	2,686	17,300	9.3	423	0.2	485	18.1
West Virginia.........	36,533	559	2,483	6.8	23	0.1	46	8.2
Wisconsin.............	140,602	2,526	10,445	7.4	230	0.2	289	11.4
Wyoming..............	20,935	208	1,984	9.5	10	(Z)	19	9.1

– Represents zero. Z Less than .05 percent.

Source: National Science Foundation, Science and Engineering Indicators 2020, "State Indicators," <ncses.nsf.gov/indicators/states>, accessed February 2020.

Table 858. Employment and Median Salary of Worker With Highest Degree in Science and Engineering (S&E) Field by Sex and Occupation: 2019

[Rounded to the nearest 1,000. Data are for full-time workers who typically work 35 or more hours weekly in their principal job. Data are from National Science Foundation, National Survey of College Graduates]

Occupation	Total		Female			Male		
	Number	Median salary (dollars)	Number	Percent	Median salary (dollars)	Number	Percent	Median salary (dollars)
All occupations............................	**13,130,000**	**80,000**	**4,822,000**	**36.7**	**63,000**	**8,308,000**	**63.3**	**94,000**
S&E..	5,211,000	96,000	1,357,000	26.0	82,000	3,854,000	74.0	100,000
Engineers....................................	1,550,000	100,000	234,000	15.1	90,000	1,316,000	84.9	100,000
Computer and mathematical scientists..	2,465,000	105,000	557,000	22.6	94,000	1,908,000	77.4	108,000
Biological, agricultural, and environmental life scientists............	510,000	64,000	234,000	45.9	65,000	277,000	54.3	64,000
Physical scientists..........................	330,000	72,000	110,000	33.3	59,000	220,000	66.7	80,000
Social scientists............................	356,000	75,000	223,000	62.6	70,000	133,000	37.4	84,000
S&E related occupations....................	1,864,000	76,000	648,000	34.8	62,000	1,216,000	65.2	89,000
Health-related occupations................	537,000	52,000	328,000	61.1	55,000	210,000	39.1	48,000
Non-S&E related occupations..............	6,055,000	67,000	2,817,000	46.5	55,000	3,238,000	53.5	80,000

Source: U.S. National Science Foundation, Science & Engineering Indicators, *The STEM Labor Force of Today: Scientists, Engineers, and Skilled Technical Workers, Supplemental Tables*, NSB-2021-2, August 2021. See also <www.nsf.gov/statistics/seind/>.

Table 859. Federal Discretionary Outlays for General Science and Space and Other Technology: 1970 to 2021, and Estimates for 2022 and 2023

[In billions of dollars (4.5 represents $4,500,000,000). For fiscal years ending in year shown; see text, Section 8]

Year	Current dollars			Constant (2012) dollars		
	Total	General science and research	Space/other technologies	Total	General science and research	Space/other technologies
1970.....................	4.5	0.9	3.6	26.0	5.5	20.6
1980.....................	5.8	1.4	4.5	16.9	4.0	12.9
1990 [1].................	14.4	2.8	11.6	29.8	5.8	24.0
2000.....................	18.6	6.2	12.4	26.3	8.7	17.5
2010.....................	30.0	11.6	18.4	31.1	12.1	19.1
2020.....................	33.9	13.2	20.7	28.8	11.2	17.6
2021.....................	35.4	13.9	21.5	29.3	11.5	17.8
2022, estimate........	38.7	16.1	22.6	31.0	12.9	18.1
2023, estimate........	40.9	16.9	24.0	32.2	13.3	18.9

[1] Due to the effects of the Credit Reform Act of 1990 on the measurement and classification of Federal credit activities, the discretionary outlays for years prior to 1992 are not strictly comparable to those for 1992 and beyond.

Source: U.S. Office of Management and Budget, *Budget of the U.S. Government, Fiscal Year 2023: Historical Tables*, March 2022. See also <www.whitehouse.gov/omb/budget>.

Table 860. Space-Related Industries Gross Output and Value Added by Industry: 2015 to 2019

[In millions of current dollars (190,493 represents $190,493,000,000). The space economy consists of space-related goods and services, both public and private. This includes goods and services that are used in space, or directly support those used in space; require direct input from space to function, or directly support those that do; and are associated with studying space]

Industry	Gross output (mil. dol.)				Value added (mil. dol.)			
	2015	2017	2018	2019	2015	2017	2018	2019
Space-related industries, total [1].................	**190,493**	**190,481**	**192,498**	**194,596**	**118,750**	**116,818**	**119,115**	**120,339**
Construction................................	606	893	566	980	423	618	387	691
Manufacturing [1]............................	52,084	49,728	50,568	51,158	36,813	34,854	37,306	37,459
Computer and electronic products [2]................	29,859	30,170	30,631	30,030	24,186	25,062	26,280	25,419
Other transportation equipment [3]...........	19,788	16,981	16,970	18,224	10,742	7,891	8,942	9,966
Wholesale trade............................	29,335	31,676	33,577	31,587	16,533	17,699	18,199	17,468
Retail trade.................................	826	1,569	1,743	2,280	569	1,050	1,146	1,496
Transportation and warehousing................	1,331	1,359	1,675	1,329	731	755	883	686
Information [1]..............................	65,500	63,577	60,681	59,704	35,165	32,837	30,762	29,482
Wired telecommunications carriers [4]................	46,258	43,428	39,858	38,284	26,866	24,495	22,567	20,882
Satellite telecommunications................	6,817	6,343	6,453	6,461	2,870	2,523	2,439	2,621
Professional and business services..................	6,864	6,720	6,677	6,370	4,131	3,748	3,749	3,559
Educational services........................	2,133	2,110	2,465	2,701	1,644	1,570	1,872	2,038
Health care and social assistance..................	101	98	109	87	79	75	84	67
Government [5].............................	31,420	32,268	34,023	37,894	22,473	23,330	24,487	27,119
Federal......................................	28,928	29,838	31,226	34,771	20,527	21,498	22,345	24,743
State and local.............................	2,492	2,430	2,797	3,124	1,946	1,833	2,142	2,376
Addenda:								
Private industries..........................	159,073	158,213	158,475	156,701	96,277	93,487	94,628	93,220
Space Economy excluding satellite television, satellite radio, and educational services [6]..........	138,759	140,174	145,494	148,683	89,726	89,696	94,150	96,798

[1] Includes other industries, not shown separately. [2] Includes manufacturing of satellites; ground equipment; search, detection, navigation, and guidance systems (GPS/PNT equipment). [3] Includes manufacturing of space vehicles and space weapons systems (intercontinental ballistic missiles). [4] Includes direct-to-home satellite television services. [5] Includes spending on personnel, operations, and maintenance. Government spending on private sector investment (structures, equipment, intellectual property) is included within the individual industries. [6] Represents a narrower interpretation of the "Space Economy" definition. These commodities are primarily produced by the information and educational services industries.

Source: U.S. Bureau of Economic Analysis, Special Topics: Space Economy, "U.S. Space Economy Data, 2012-2019," <www.bea.gov/data/special-topics/space-economy>, accessed February 2022.

Table 861. Space-Related Industries Employment and Compensation by Industry: 2015 to 2019

[Employment in thousands (359 represents 359,000); compensation in millions of current dollars (43,215 represents $43,215,000,000). Excludes government employees. The space economy consists of space-related goods and services, both public and private. This includes goods and services that are used in space, or directly support those used in space; require direct input from space to function, or directly support those that do; and are associated with studying space]

Industry	Employment [1] (1,000)				Compensation [2] (mil. dol.)			
	2015	2017	2018	2019	2015	2017	2018	2019
Space-related industries, private, total........	**359**	**360**	**352**	**354**	**43,215**	**41,680**	**41,609**	**42,442**
Manufacturing..	115	116	115	124	18,921	17,244	17,576	18,749
Wholesale trade...	65	71	70	67	7,351	8,392	8,517	8,172
Information...	120	111	103	97	11,401	10,470	9,788	9,550
Professional and business services..................	27	23	22	21	3,396	3,033	2,989	2,851
Educational services...................................	16	15	17	19	1,172	1,157	1,379	1,551
All other private industries............................	16	24	24	27	975	1,384	1,361	1,568

[1] Includes full time and part time employees. [2] Compensation consists of wages and salaries and employer contributions to pensions and insurance.

Source: U.S. Bureau of Economic Analysis, Special Topics: Space Economy, "U.S. Space Economy Data, 2012-2019," <www.bea.gov/data/special-topics/space-economy>, accessed February 2022.

This section presents statistics on farms and farm operators; farm income, expenditures, and debt; farm output, productivity, and marketings; foreign trade in agricultural products; specific crops; livestock, poultry, and their products; and direct marketing to consumers.

The principal sources are the data collected by the National Agricultural Statistics Service (NASS), the Economic Research Service (ERS), and the Foreign Agricultural Service (FAS) of the U.S. Department of Agriculture (USDA) and published in reports or databases. The ERS publishes data on farm assets, debt, and income on the internet at <ers.usda.gov/data-products/farm-income-and-wealth-statistics>. The ERS also provides data on commodity supply and disappearance via commodity outlook reports, yearbooks, and databases, available on the ERS site at <ers.usda.gov/data-products>. Sources of current data on agricultural exports and imports include the Global Agricultural Trade System database provided by the FAS at <apps.fas.usda.gov/gats/> and the "Foreign Agricultural Trade of the United States (FATUS)" data, published by the ERS, available on the ERS site at <ers.usda.gov/data-products/foreign-agricultural-trade-of-the-united-states-fatus>.

The field offices of the NASS collect data on crops, livestock and products, agricultural prices, farm employment, and other related subjects mainly through sample surveys. Information is obtained on crops, livestock, and products pertaining to agricultural production and marketing. State estimates and supporting information are sent to the Agricultural Statistics Board of NASS, which reviews the estimates and issues reports containing state and national data. Among these reports are annual summaries such as *Crop Production, Crop Values, Agricultural Prices,* and *Meat Animals Production, Disposition, and Income.* The NASS also provides data through the QuickStats database at <quickstats.nass.usda.gov>.

With the release of the January 2021 data, the USDA adopted the World Trade Organization (WTO) definitions of agricultural products and revised historical data to reflect the new definitions, both adding and removing some products from the definitions. The change was made in order to harmonize U.S. trade reporting practices with those of the international community and ensure that USDA numbers are aligned with those of the Office of the U.S. Trade Representative, which already uses the WTO definition when negotiating WTO binding trade agreements. For additional information, please see <www.fas.usda.gov/updated-agricultural-products-definition-trade-reporting>. For general information on foreign trade, see text, Section 28, Foreign Commerce and Aid.

The USDA conducts the Census of Agriculture every 5 years and collects information concerning all areas of farming and ranching operations, including production expenses, market value of products, and operator characteristics. The information from the 2017 Census of Agriculture is available in print form in the Volume 1, Geographic Area Series; and on the internet at <nass.usda.gov/Publications/AgCensus/

2017/>. An evaluation of coverage has been conducted for each census of agriculture since 1945 to provide estimates of the completeness of census farm counts. Beginning with the 1997 Census of Agriculture, census farm counts and totals were statistically adjusted for coverage and reported at the county level. The size of the adjustments varies considerably by state. In general, farms not on the census mail list tended to be small in acreage, production, and sales of farm products.

For more explanation about census mail list compilation, collection methods, coverage measurement, and adjustments, see Appendix A, *2017 Census of Agriculture,* Volume 1, <nass.usda.gov/Publications/AgCensus/2017/>.

Farms and farmland—The definitions of a farm have varied through time. Since 1850, when minimum criteria defining a farm for census purposes first were established, the farm definition has changed nine times. The current definition, first used for the 1974 census, is any place from which $1,000 or more of agricultural products were produced and sold, or normally would have been sold, during the census year.

Acreage designated as "land in farms" consists primarily of agricultural land used for crops, pasture, or grazing. It also includes woodland and wasteland not actually under cultivation or used for pasture or grazing, provided it was part of the farm operator's total operation. Land in farms includes acres set aside under annual commodity acreage programs as well as acres idled by federal conservation programs for places meeting the farm definition. Land in farms is an operating unit concept and includes land owned and operated as well as land rented from others. All grazing land, except land used under government permits on a per-head basis, was included as "land in farms" provided it was part of a farm or ranch.

Farm income—The final agricultural sector output comprises cash receipts from farm marketings of crops and livestock, federal government payments made directly to farmers for farm-related activities, rental value of farm homes, value of farm products consumed in farm homes, and other farm-related income such as machine hire and custom work. Farm marketings represent quantities of agricultural products sold by farmers multiplied by prices received per unit of production at the local market. Information on prices received for farm products is generally obtained by the NASS Agricultural Statistics Board from surveys of firms (such as grain elevators, packers, and processors) purchasing agricultural commodities directly from producers. In some cases, the price information is obtained directly from the producers.

Crops—Estimates of crop acreage and production by the NASS are based on current sample survey data obtained from individual producers and objective yield counts, reports of carlot shipments, market records, personal field observations by field statisticians, and reports from other sources.

Prices received by farmers are marketing year average prices and do not include allowances for outstanding loans, government purchases, deficiency payments or disaster payments. These averages are based on monthly prices weighted by monthly sales during specific periods. All state marketing year average prices are based on individual state marketing years, while U.S. marketing year average prices are based on standard U.S. marketing years for each crop. For a description of how U.S. prices are computed as well as a listing of the crop marketing years, see *Crop Values Annual Summary*.

Value of production is computed by multiplying state prices by each state's production. The U.S. value of production is the sum of state values for all states. Value of production figures should not be confused with cash receipts from farm marketings which relate to sales during a calendar year, irrespective of the year of production.

Livestock—Annual inventory numbers of livestock and estimates of livestock, dairy, and poultry production prepared by the Department of Agriculture are based on information from farmers and ranchers obtained by probability survey sampling methods.

Statistical reliability—For a discussion of statistical collection and estimation, sampling procedures, and measures of statistical reliability pertaining to Department of Agriculture data, see Appendix III.

Table 862. Selected Characteristics of Farms by North American Industry Classification System (NAICS): 2017

[388,522,695 represents $388,522,695,000. See text this section and Appendix III]

Industry	2012 NAICS code [1]	Farms	Land in farms (acres)	Harvested cropland (acres)	Market value of agricultural products sold ($1,000) Total	Crops	Livestock [2]
Total.............................	(X)	**2,042,220**	**900,217,576**	**320,041,858**	**388,522,695**	**193,546,699**	**194,975,996**
Crop production.................	111	967,090	421,544,023	262,718,038	189,264,224	181,697,779	7,566,445
Oilseed and grain farming......	1111	325,033	275,696,715	209,754,358	102,018,657	96,275,715	5,742,943
Soybean farming..............	11111	105,832	53,532,004	44,561,866	20,411,246	20,077,387	333,859
Oilseed (except soybean) farming..........	11112	849	1,488,090	1,073,701	251,972	248,984	2,988
Dry pea and bean farming.................	11113	1,296	1,782,380	1,173,169	321,225	316,886	4,339
Wheat farming.................	11114	18,312	29,720,570	15,595,523	3,125,617	2,993,054	132,563
Corn farming.................	11115	133,981	97,079,475	81,479,149	46,437,032	45,435,179	1,001,853
Rice farming.................	11116	2,680	3,323,806	2,451,234	1,893,094	1,860,141	32,953
Other grain farming.............	11119	62,083	88,770,390	63,419,716	29,578,471	25,344,085	4,234,387
Vegetable and melon farming...............	11121	45,165	9,310,059	6,008,800	19,731,533	19,627,511	104,022
Potato farming.................	111211	2,568	3,189,793	2,516,571	4,605,952	4,587,516	18,435
Other vegetable (except potato) and melon farming..........	111219	42,597	6,120,266	3,492,229	15,125,582	15,039,994	85,587
Fruit and tree nut farming.............	1113	95,441	13,357,346	6,173,016	28,336,564	28,211,310	125,254
Orange groves.................	11131	4,500	1,093,218	562,704	1,589,218	1,563,214	26,004
Citrus (except orange) groves..............	11132	3,451	513,909	277,376	1,621,780	1,613,949	7,831
Noncitrus fruit and tree nut farming..........	11133	87,490	11,750,219	5,332,936	25,125,566	25,034,147	91,419
Apple orchards..............	111331	10,087	2,226,789	472,433	3,518,947	3,512,021	6,926
Grape vineyards.............	111332	17,949	2,254,802	1,143,044	6,073,378	6,059,901	13,477
Strawberry farming.............	111333	1,391	137,455	60,565	2,018,159	2,017,404	755
Berry (except strawberry) farming..........	111334	11,005	1,073,431	254,450	1,359,836	1,355,865	3,971
Tree nut farming..............	111335	24,174	4,493,273	2,620,517	8,391,403	8,344,887	46,516
Fruit and tree nut combination farming..........	111336	1,477	250,421	140,631	516,724	510,459	6,265
Other noncitrus fruit farming..............	111339	21,407	1,314,048	641,296	3,247,118	3,233,609	13,509
Greenhouse, nursery, and floriculture production..............	1114	45,477	3,934,004	1,364,516	16,496,154	16,460,012	36,142
Food crops grown under cover..............	11141	4,199	155,700	22,701	2,081,839	2,076,997	4,841
Nursery and floriculture production..........	11142	41,278	3,778,304	1,341,815	14,414,316	14,383,015	31,301
Nursery and tree production..........	111421	26,174	3,294,378	1,202,706	8,175,668	8,150,549	25,119
Floriculture production.................	111422	15,104	483,926	139,109	6,238,648	6,232,466	6,182
Other crop farming.............	1119	455,974	119,245,899	39,417,348	22,681,315	21,123,231	1,558,084
Tobacco farming.................	11191	3,757	1,586,381	938,702	1,413,240	1,365,986	47,253
Cotton farming.................	11192	8,815	15,874,682	11,237,600	6,011,120	5,908,080	103,040
Sugarcane farming.................	11193	467	1,351,038	940,656	967,695	965,173	2,522
Hay farming.................	11194	244,035	46,273,222	16,001,743	5,585,232	5,124,522	460,710
All other crop farming.............	11199	198,900	54,160,576	10,298,647	8,704,028	7,759,469	944,559
Animal production.............	112	1,075,130	478,673,553	57,323,820	199,258,471	11,848,920	187,409,551
Cattle ranching and farming.............	1121	692,625	394,097,473	48,045,215	114,809,219	7,935,980	106,873,239
Beef cattle ranching and farming including feedlots.............	11211	654,875	376,699,018	36,258,728	72,426,397	5,259,911	67,166,486
Beef cattle ranching and farming..........	112111	641,496	362,543,006	31,777,036	33,370,653	3,454,114	29,916,539
Cattle feedlots..............	112112	13,379	14,156,012	4,481,692	39,055,744	1,805,797	37,249,947
Dairy cattle and milk production...........	11212	37,750	17,398,455	11,786,487	42,382,822	2,676,069	39,706,753
Hog and pig farming.............	1122	23,048	5,793,498	4,308,268	27,143,555	2,386,171	24,757,384
Poultry and egg production.................	1123	44,260	5,916,544	2,087,155	50,155,733	875,539	49,280,194
Chicken egg production.................	11231	19,785	1,295,219	371,262	8,905,165	161,201	8,743,964
Broilers and other meat-type chicken production.................	11232	15,609	3,394,774	1,223,669	31,068,699	482,203	30,586,497
Turkey production.................	11233	2,517	763,815	410,201	5,972,474	197,628	5,774,846
Poultry hatcheries.................	11234	264	12,237	878	3,402,867	188	3,402,679
Other poultry production.................	11239	6,085	450,499	81,145	806,527	34,319	772,208
Sheep and goat farming.................	1124	92,974	13,975,994	383,580	877,791	49,649	828,143
Sheep farming.................	11241	46,799	9,952,322	275,661	638,150	37,251	600,899
Goat farming.................	11242	46,175	4,023,672	107,919	239,641	12,398	227,244
Animal aquaculture.................	1125	3,981	1,008,935	53,195	1,778,231	26,807	1,751,425
Other animal production.................	1129	218,242	57,881,109	2,446,407	4,493,942	574,774	3,919,168
Apiculture.................	11291	10,517	439,719	15,109	357,124	3,590	353,534
Horse and other equine production........	11292	157,237	22,695,698	829,208	1,444,757	30,969	1,413,788
Fur-bearing animal and rabbit production.................	11293	773	30,476	5,662	140,297	2,235	138,062
All other animal production.................	11299	49,715	34,715,216	1,596,428	2,551,764	537,981	2,013,784

X Not applicable. [1] Based on the North American Industry Classification System (NAICS) 2012; see text, Section 15. [2] Includes poultry and poultry products sold.

Source: U.S. Department of Agriculture, National Agricultural Statistics Service, *2017 Census of Agriculture*, Vol. 1, April 2019. See also <www.nass.usda.gov/AgCensus/>.

Table 863. Farms—Number and Acreage: 2000 to 2021

[2,167 represents 2,167,000. As of June. Based on 1974 census definition; for definition of farms and farmland, see text, this section. Data for census years have been adjusted for underenumeration]

Item	Unit	2000	2005	2010	2015	2017	2018	2019	2020	2021
Number of farms..........	1,000	2,167	2,099	2,150	2,064	2,042	2,029	2,023	2,019	2,012
Land in farms.............	Million acres	945	928	916	906	900	900	897	897	895
Average per farm........	Acres	436	442	426	439	441	443	444	444	445

Source: U.S. Department of Agriculture, National Agricultural Statistics Service, *Farm Numbers and Land in Farms, Final Estimates, 2013–2017* and earlier reports; and *Farms and Land in Farms 2021 Summary*, February 2022. See also <www.nass.usda.gov/Publications/>.

Table 864. Farms—Number and Acreage by State: 2020 and 2021

[2,019 represents 2,019,000. See headnote, Table 863]

State	Farms (1,000) 2020	Farms (1,000) 2021	Land in farms (mil. acres) 2020	Land in farms (mil. acres) 2021	Acreage per farm 2020	Acreage per farm 2021	State	Farms (1,000) 2020	Farms (1,000) 2021	Land in farms (mil. acres) 2020	Land in farms (mil. acres) 2021	Acreage per farm 2020	Acreage per farm 2021
United States.....	**2,019**	**2,012**	**896.6**	**895.3**	**444**	**445**	Missouri.............	95	95	27.5	27.5	289	289
Alabama...........	39	39	8.3	8.2	213	213	Montana.............	27	27	58.0	57.9	2,156	2,137
Alaska..............	1	1	0.9	0.9	810	810	Nebraska............	46	45	44.9	44.8	987	1,000
Arizona............	19	19	26.2	26.2	1,379	1,379	Nevada.............	3	3	6.1	6.1	1,821	1,794
Arkansas...........	42	42	14.0	14.0	332	333	New Hampshire....	4	4	0.4	0.4	105	105
California..........	70	69	24.3	24.2	349	351	New Jersey.........	10	10	0.8	0.8	76	76
Colorado..........	39	39	31.8	31.8	820	815	New Mexico........	25	25	40.0	40.0	1,613	1,619
Connecticut.......	6	6	0.4	0.4	69	69	New York...........	33	33	6.9	6.9	207	207
Delaware..........	2	2	0.5	0.5	230	230	North Carolina.....	46	45	8.4	8.3	183	184
Florida............	48	48	9.7	9.7	204	204	North Dakota.......	26	26	39.3	39.3	1,512	1,512
Georgia............	41	41	10.2	10.2	246	247	Ohio...............	78	77	13.6	13.5	175	176
Hawaii.............	7	7	1.1	1.1	151	151	Oklahoma..........	77	77	34.4	34.4	445	446
Idaho..............	25	25	11.5	11.5	467	467	Oregon.............	37	37	15.8	15.7	425	423
Illinois............	71	71	27.0	27.0	380	381	Pennsylvania.......	53	53	7.3	7.3	139	139
Indiana............	56	55	14.8	14.8	267	269	Rhode Island.......	1	1	0.1	0.1	55	55
Iowa...............	85	85	30.6	30.5	360	359	South Carolina.....	25	25	4.8	4.8	195	195
Kansas............	58	59	45.7	45.7	784	780	South Dakota.......	30	29	43.2	43.2	1,459	1,469
Kentucky..........	75	74	12.9	12.9	173	174	Tennessee..........	70	70	10.8	10.7	155	154
Louisiana..........	27	27	8.0	8.0	292	292	Texas..............	247	247	126.0	126.0	510	510
Maine.............	8	8	1.3	1.3	171	171	Utah...............	18	18	10.7	10.7	601	598
Maryland..........	12	12	2.0	2.0	161	161	Vermont...........	7	7	1.2	1.2	176	176
Massachusetts.....	7	7	0.5	0.5	69	69	Virginia............	42	42	7.8	7.7	184	186
Michigan..........	47	46	9.8	9.7	211	211	Washington.........	36	35	14.6	14.5	411	411
Minnesota.........	68	67	25.4	25.4	376	377	West Virginia......	23	22	3.5	3.5	154	157
Mississippi.........	34	34	10.4	10.4	302	303	Wisconsin..........	64	64	14.3	14.2	222	222
							Wyoming...........	12	12	29.0	29.0	2,417	2,377

Source: U.S. Department of Agriculture, National Agricultural Statistics Service, "Quick Stats," <quickstats.nass.usda.gov/>, accessed February 2022. See also <www.nass.usda.gov/Publications/>.

Table 865. Farms by Size and Type of Organization: 1982 to 2017

[2,241 represents 2,241,000. For comments on adjustment, see text, this section]

Size and type of organization	Unit	Not adjusted for coverage 1982	Not adjusted for coverage 1987	Not adjusted for coverage 1992	Adjusted for coverage [1] 1997	Adjusted for coverage [1] 2002	Adjusted for coverage [1] 2007	Adjusted for coverage [1] 2012	Adjusted for coverage [1] 2017
Farms..................	1,000	2,241	2,088	1,925	2,216	2,129	2,205	2,109	2,042
Land in farms.................	Mil. acres	987	964	946	955	938	922	915	900
Average size of farm................	Acres	440	462	491	431	441	418	434	441
Farms by size:									
1 to 9 acres....................	1,000	188	183	166	205	179	233	224	273
10 to 49 acres...................	1,000	449	412	388	531	564	620	590	583
50 to 179 acres.................	1,000	712	645	584	694	659	661	634	565
180 to 499 acres................	1,000	527	478	428	428	389	368	346	315
500 to 999 acres................	1,000	204	200	186	179	162	150	143	133
1,000 to 1,999 acres............	1,000	97	102	102	103	99	93	91	88
2,000 acres or more.............	1,000	65	67	71	74	78	80	82	85
Farms by type of organization:									
Family or individual..............	1,000	1,946	1,809	1,653	1,923	1,910	1,906	1,829	1,751
Partnership....................	1,000	223	200	187	186	130	174	138	130
Corporation...................	1,000	60	67	73	90	74	96	107	117
Other [2]	1,000	12	12	12	17	16	28	36	44

[1] Data have been adjusted for coverage; see text, this section. [2] Cooperative, estate or trust, institutional, etc.

Source: U.S. Department of Agriculture, National Agricultural Statistics Service, *2017 Census of Agriculture*, Vol. 1, April 2019, and earlier reports. See also <www.nass.usda.gov/AgCensus/>.

Table 866. Farms—Number and Acreage by Size of Farm: 2012 and 2017

[2,109 represents 2,109,000. Data have been adjusted for coverage; see text, this section]

Size of farm	Number of farms (1,000)		Land in farms (mil. acres)		Cropland harvested (mil. acres)		Percent distribution, 2017		
	2012	2017	2012	2017	2012	2017	Number of farms	All land in farms	Cropland harvested
Total..........................	2,109	2,042	914.5	900.2	315.0	320.0	100.0	100.0	100.0
Under 10 acres.................	224	273	1.0	1.3	0.3	0.4	13.4	0.1	0.1
10 to 49 acres.................	590	583	15.1	14.8	4.1	4.1	28.5	1.6	1.3
50 to 69 acres.................	154	135	8.9	7.8	2.5	2.2	6.6	0.9	0.7
70 to 99 acres.................	185	163	15.2	13.4	4.4	3.9	8.0	1.5	1.2
100 to 139 acres...............	166	149	19.3	17.3	5.7	5.2	7.3	1.9	1.6
140 to 179 acres...............	129	117	20.3	18.4	6.3	5.8	5.7	2.0	1.8
180 to 219 acres...............	84	74	16.7	14.6	5.6	5.0	3.6	1.6	1.6
220 to 259 acres...............	64	57	15.1	13.6	5.5	5.0	2.8	1.5	1.6
260 to 499 acres...............	198	184	70.6	65.8	28.8	27.0	9.0	7.3	8.4
500 to 999 acres...............	143	133	99.0	92.9	49.5	45.9	6.5	10.3	14.3
1,000 to 1,999 acres...........	91	88	125.1	120.7	68.7	66.2	4.3	13.4	20.7
2,000 acres or more...........	82	85	508.2	519.6	133.6	149.4	4.2	57.7	46.7

Source: U.S. Department of Agriculture, National Agricultural Statistics Service, *2017 Census of Agriculture*, Vol. 1, April 2019. See also <www.nass.usda.gov/AgCensus/>.

Table 867. Farms—Number, Acreage, and Value by Tenure of Principal Operator and Type of Organization: 2012 and 2017

[2,109 represents 2,109,000. Full owners own all the land they operate. Part owners own a part and rent from others the rest of the land they operate. A principal operator is the person primarily responsible for the on-site, day-to-day operation of the farm or ranch business. Data have been adjusted for coverage; see text, this section]

Item and year	Unit	Total [1]	Tenure of operator			Type of organization		
			Full owner	Part owner	Tenant	Family or individual	Partner-ship	Corpora-tion
NUMBER OF FARMS								
2012..	1,000	2,109	1,428	533	148	1,829	138	107
2017..	1,000	2,042	1,409	493	140	1,751	130	117
Under 50 acres..................................	1,000	856	740	62	54	779	29	33
50 to 179 acres.................................	1,000	565	419	113	33	499	29	24
180 to 499 acres................................	1,000	315	167	126	23	262	25	19
500 to 999 acres................................	1,000	133	45	76	12	101	15	14
1,000 acres or more............................	1,000	173	37	117	19	110	31	27
LAND IN FARMS								
2012..	Mil. acres	915	336	491	87	562	156	131
2017..	Mil. acres	900	310	503	87	541	158	140
Value of land and buildings, 2017.............	Bil. dol.	2,679	907	1,538	234	1,732	451	418
Value of farm products sold, 2017.............	Bil. dol.	389	142	207	40	182	89	111

[1] Includes other types, not shown separately.

Source: U.S. Department of Agriculture, National Agricultural Statistics Service, *2017 Census of Agriculture*, Vol. 1, April 2019, and earlier reports. See also <www.nass.usda.gov/AgCensus/>.

Table 868. Corporate Farms—Characteristics by Type: 2002 to 2017

[139.6 represents 139,600,000. Data have been adjusted for coverage; see text, this section and Appendix III]

Item	Unit	All corpora-tions	Family held corporations			Other corporations		
			Total	1 to 10 stock-holders	11 or more stock-holders	Total	1 to 10 stock-holders	11 or more stock-holders
Farms:								
2002..	Number	73,752	66,667	65,017	1,650	7,085	6,010	1,075
2007..	Number	96,074	85,837	83,796	2,041	10,237	9,330	907
2012..	Number	106,716	95,142	92,834	2,308	11,574	10,438	1,136
2017								
Farms...	Number	116,840	104,155	101,851	2,304	12,685	11,541	1,144
Percent distribution.......................	Percent	100.0	89.1	87.2	2.0	10.9	9.9	1.0
Land in farms.............................	Mil. acres	139.6	126.7	119.6	7.1	12.9	10.5	2.4
Average per farm..........................	Acres	1,194	1,216	1,174	3,084	1,016	910	2,090
Value of—								
Land and buildings........................	Bil. dol.	417.6	378.7	360.8	18.0	38.8	30.0	8.8
Average per farm........................	$1,000	3,574	3,636	3,542	7,798	3,062	2,601	7,712
Farm products sold.......................	Bil. dol.	111.0	89.1	83.2	5.9	22.0	13.8	8.2
Average per farm........................	$1,000	950	855	817	2,547	1,733	1,197	7,133

Source: U.S. Department of Agriculture, National Agricultural Statistics Service, *2017 Census of Agriculture*, Vol. 1, April 2019, and earlier reports. See also <www.nass.usda.gov/AgCensus/>.

Table 869. Farms—Number, Acreage, and Value by State: 2012 and 2017

[2,109 represents 2,109,000. Data have been adjusted for coverage; see text, this section and Appendix III]

State	Number of farms (1,000) 2012	2017	Land in farms (mil. acres) 2012	2017	Average size of farm (acres) 2012	2017	Total value of land and buildings (bil. dol.) 2012	2017	Market value of agricultural products sold and government payments (mil. dol.) 2012	2017
U.S.	**2,109**	**2,042**	**914.5**	**900.2**	**434**	**441**	**2,268.5**	**2,679.0**	**402,698**	**397,466**
AL.	43	41	8.9	8.6	206	211	23.7	25.6	5,659	6,115
AK.	1	1	0.8	0.8	1,094	858	0.5	0.6	61	73
AZ.	20	19	26.2	26.1	1,312	1,369	16.9	21.2	3,763	3,874
AR.	45	43	13.8	13.9	306	326	36.4	43.9	10,039	9,973
CA.	78	71	25.6	24.5	328	348	160.5	229.4	42,774	45,282
CO.	36	39	31.9	31.8	881	818	40.8	51.2	7,946	7,690
CT.	6	6	0.4	0.4	73	69	4.8	4.8	555	582
DE.	2	2	0.5	0.5	208	228	4.2	4.4	1,284	1,481
FL.	48	48	9.5	9.7	200	204	49.7	57.4	7,742	7,416
GA.	42	42	9.6	10.0	228	235	29.7	34.9	9,397	9,821
HI.	7	7	1.1	1.1	161	155	10.2	10.6	667	572
ID.	25	25	11.8	11.7	474	468	26.1	33.5	7,901	7,697
IL.	75	73	26.9	27.0	359	372	169.8	196.5	17,740	17,531
IN.	59	57	14.7	15.0	251	264	78.8	98.4	11,478	11,450
IA.	89	86	30.6	30.6	345	355	195.6	215.8	31,604	29,639
KS.	62	59	46.1	45.8	747	781	75.3	84.6	18,903	19,292
KY.	77	76	13.0	13.0	169	171	39.5	48.8	5,237	5,865
LA.	28	27	7.9	8.0	281	292	20.2	24.4	3,948	3,350
ME.	8	8	1.5	1.3	178	172	3.4	3.4	773	676
MD.	12	12	2.0	2.0	166	160	14.1	15.6	2,307	2,517
MA.	8	7	0.5	0.5	68	68	5.5	5.4	500	479
MI.	52	48	9.9	9.8	191	205	40.0	48.4	8,834	8,388
MN.	75	69	26.0	25.5	349	371	109.9	123.8	21,748	18,790
MS.	38	35	10.9	10.4	287	298	24.8	28.6	6,622	6,410
MO.	99	95	28.3	27.8	285	291	78.9	94.0	9,489	10,850
MT.	28	27	59.8	58.1	2,134	2,149	46.9	53.2	4,440	3,805
NE.	50	46	45.3	45.0	907	971	107.9	123.9	23,461	22,623
NV.	4	3	5.9	6.1	1,429	1,790	5.5	5.6	767	671
NH.	4	4	0.5	0.4	108	103	2.0	2.2	194	191
NJ.	9	10	0.7	0.7	79	74	9.1	9.9	1,015	1,105
NM.	25	25	43.2	40.7	1,748	1,624	18.7	21.2	2,621	2,646
NY.	36	33	7.2	6.9	202	205	18.7	22.2	5,490	5,428
NC.	50	46	8.4	8.4	168	182	36.5	39.1	12,708	13,008
ND.	31	26	39.3	39.3	1,268	1,492	56.0	67.1	11,332	8,701
OH.	75	78	14.0	14.0	185	179	67.5	86.6	10,293	9,692
OK.	80	79	34.4	34.2	428	435	46.0	59.2	7,386	7,698
OR.	35	38	16.3	16.0	460	424	30.7	38.8	4,970	5,099
PA.	59	53	7.7	7.3	130	137	41.8	47.7	7,487	7,833
RI.	1	1	0.1	0.1	56	55	1.0	0.9	62	59
SC.	25	25	5.0	4.7	197	191	14.8	17.0	3,087	3,064
SD.	32	30	43.3	43.2	1,352	1,443	73.0	89.4	10,454	10,141
TN.	68	70	10.9	10.9	160	155	38.7	42.6	3,679	3,915
TX.	249	248	130.2	127.0	523	511	218.1	243.5	26,020	25,673
UT.	18	18	11.0	10.8	609	587	16.0	19.6	1,840	1,866
VT.	7	7	1.3	1.2	171	175	4.0	4.2	790	787
VA.	46	43	8.3	7.8	180	180	35.8	36.1	3,836	4,021
WA.	37	36	14.7	14.7	396	410	33.9	40.9	9,280	9,803
WV.	21	24	3.6	3.7	168	155	8.9	9.7	814	763
WI.	70	65	14.6	14.3	209	221	57.2	70.2	11,982	11,554
WY.	12	12	30.4	29.0	2,587	2,430	20.6	22.6	1,718	1,502

Source: U.S. Department of Agriculture, National Agricultural Statistics Service, *2017 Census of Agriculture*, Vol. 1, April 2019.

Table 870. Farms—Number, Value of Sales, and Government Payments by Economic Class of Farm: 2012 and 2017

[2,109 represents 2,109,000. Economic class of farm is a combination of market value of agricultural products sold and federal farm program payments. Data have been adjusted for coverage; see text, this section and Appendix III]

Economic class	Number of farms (1,000) 2012, total	2017 Total	2017 Receiving government payments	Market value of agricultural products sold and government payments (mil. dol.) 2012, total	2017 Total	2017 Agricultural products sold	2017 Government payments
Total	**2,109**	**2,042**	**643**	**402,698**	**397,466**	**388,523**	**8,944**
Less than $1,000	429	472	17	80	97	88	8
$1,000 to $2,499	237	217	44	393	360	295	65
$2,500 to $4,999	231	211	47	832	757	629	128
$5,000 to $9,999	249	234	59	1,769	1,666	1,415	251
$10,000 to $24,999	272	253	83	4,323	4,041	3,505	536
$25,000 to $49,999	162	155	67	5,736	5,494	4,915	578
$50,000 to $99,999	134	126	68	9,575	8,934	8,255	679
$100,000 to $249,999	142	134	86	23,196	21,730	20,614	1,116
$250,000 to $499,999	96	89	64	34,463	31,718	30,478	1,241
$500,000 to $999,999	78	72	54	55,663	50,677	49,011	1,666
$1,000,000 to $2,499,999	58	56	39	90,534	86,284	84,438	1,846
$2,500,000 to $4,999,999	15	15	9	50,511	50,087	49,521	567
$5 million or more	9	9	4	125,624	135,622	135,359	263

Source: U.S. Department of Agriculture, National Agricultural Statistics Service, *2017 Census of Agriculture*, Vol. 1, April 2019.

Table 871. Farms—Number, Acreage, and Value of Sales by Size of Sales: 2012 and 2017

[2,109 represents 2,109,000. Data have been adjusted for coverage; see text, this section and Appendix III]

Market value of agricultural products sold	Farms (1,000)	Acreage		Value of sales		Percent distribution		
		Total (mil.)	Average per farm	Total (mil. dol.)	Average per farm (dol.)	Farms	Acreage	Value of sales
2012								
Total..........................	2,109	914.5	434	394,644	187,097	100.0	100.0	100.0
Less than $2,500...................	788	118.4	150	380	483	37.4	12.9	0.1
$2,500 to $4,999.................	191	19.6	102	688	3,592	9.1	2.1	0.2
$5,000 to $9,999.................	214	25.4	119	1,522	7,104	10.2	2.8	0.4
$10,000 to $24,999...............	245	59.4	243	3,908	15,954	11.6	6.5	1.0
$25,000 to $49,999...............	153	48.4	316	5,418	35,440	7.2	5.3	1.4
$50,000 to $99,999...............	129	64.0	495	9,251	71,507	6.1	7.0	2.3
$100,000 to $249,999.............	139	115.9	835	22,822	164,328	6.6	12.7	5.8
$250,000 to $499,999.............	94	121.1	1,288	33,964	361,045	4.5	13.2	8.6
$500,000 to $999,999.............	76	129.4	1,704	54,686	719,996	3.6	14.2	13.9
$1,000,000 or more................	79	212.9	2,687	262,006	3,307,109	3.8	23.3	66.4
2017								
Total..........................	2,042	900.2	441	388,523	190,245	100.0	100.0	100.0
Less than $2,500...................	792	103.6	131	404	510	38.8	11.5	0.1
$2,500 to $4,999.................	185	16.1	87	663	3,577	9.1	1.8	0.2
$5,000 to $9,999.................	208	24.7	119	1,478	7,101	10.2	2.7	0.4
$10,000 to $24,999...............	228	50.0	219	3,650	15,994	11.2	5.6	0.9
$25,000 to $49,999...............	144	50.0	347	5,100	35,389	7.1	5.6	1.3
$50,000 to $99,999...............	119	66.3	555	8,478	70,982	5.8	7.4	2.2
$100,000 to $249,999.............	131	119.6	914	21,171	161,697	6.4	13.3	5.4
$250,000 to $499,999.............	88	126.6	1,441	31,319	356,545	4.3	14.1	8.1
$500,000 to $999,999.............	70	131.7	1,889	49,339	707,846	3.4	14.6	12.7
$1,000,000 or more................	77	211.6	2,752	266,922	3,472,604	3.8	23.5	68.7

Source: U.S. Department of Agriculture, National Agricultural Statistics Service, *2017 Census of Agriculture*, Vol. 1, April 2019, and earlier reports. See also <www.nass.usda.gov/AgCensus/>.

Table 872. Farmers by Selected Producer Characteristics: 2017

[A producer is a person who is involved in making decisions for the farm operation including decisions about planting, harvesting, livestock management, and marketing. A producer may be the owner, a household member of the owner, hired manager, tenant, renter, or sharecropper. Demographic information was collected for up to four producers per farm. The primary producer is the producer designated as the person who made the most decisions for the farm; if equal decisions were made, the primary was designated as the person who worked off the farm the least. See source for more details]

Characteristics	All producers	Primary producers	Characteristics	All producers	Primary producers
Total............................	3,399,834	2,042,220	Primary occupation:		
By sex:			Farming.............................	1,416,848	964,477
Male............................	2,172,373	1,553,220	Other...............................	1,982,986	1,077,743
Female...........................	1,227,461	489,000	By place of residence:		
			On farm operated....................	2,530,442	1,562,320
By age:			Not on farm operated...............	869,392	479,900
Under 25 years......................	50,943	10,518	Days of work off farm:		
25 to 34 years.......................	234,496	111,236	None................................	1,311,334	859,347
35 to 44 years.......................	390,345	207,348	Any.................................	2,088,500	1,182,873
45 to 54 years.......................	614,654	351,677	1 to 49 days......................	285,477	172,209
55 to 64 years.......................	955,354	580,769	50 to 99 days.....................	151,972	92,576
65 to 74 years.......................	757,936	498,595	100 to 199 days...................	282,056	168,777
75 years and older...................	396,106	282,077	200 days or more..................	1,368,995	749,311
Average age..........................	57.5	59.4	Years on present farm:		
			2 years or less......................	201,061	100,947
By race/ethnicity:			3 or 4 years........................	268,316	140,359
American Indian/Alaska Native....	58,199	35,494	5 to 9 years........................	495,022	269,230
Asian...............................	22,016	11,955	10 years or more....................	2,435,435	1,531,684
Black or African American..........	45,508	31,071	Years operating any farm:		
Native Hawaiian or other			5 years or less......................	474,198	237,838
Pacific Islander.....................	3,018	1,662	6 to 10 years.......................	434,076	234,522
White...............................	3,244,344	1,945,696	11 years or more....................	2,491,560	1,569,860
More than one race reported.......	26,749	16,342	Military service:		
			Never served........................	3,029,215	1,768,912
Hispanic or Latino [1]................	112,451	66,727	Served [2]............................	370,619	273,308

[1] Persons of Hispanic origin may be of any race. [2] Includes producers who currently or previously served on active duty in the U.S. Armed Forces.

Source: U.S. Department of Agriculture, National Agricultural Statistics Service, *2017 Census of Agriculture*, Vol. 1, April 2019. See also <www.nass.usda.gov/AgCensus/>.

Table 873. Family Farm Household Income and Wealth: 2015 to 2020, and by Farm Type, 2020

[In dollars, except for number of farms. Based on Agricultural Resource Management Survey (ARMS) Phase III. A family farm is defined as one in which the majority of the ownership of the farm business is held by related individuals. Nearly all farms (98 percent in 2020) are family farms. The farm operator is the person who runs the farm, making the day-to-day management decisions. The operator could be an owner, hired manager, cash tenant, share tenant, and/or a partner. If land is rented or worked on shares, the tenant or renter is the operator. For multiple-operator farms, a principal operator is identified as the individual making most of the day-to-day decisions about the operation. If secondary operators are the spouses of principal operators, both operators are considered part of the principal operator household. Minus sign (-) indicates loss]

Item	2015	2017	2018	2019	2020 Total	Rural residence farms [1]	Intermediate farms [2]	Commercial farms [3]
Number of family farms...............	2,032,300	1,989,574	1,979,368	1,967,617	1,963,389	999,055	794,379	169,955
INCOME PER FAMILY FARM HOUSEHOLD								
Net earnings from farming activities......	24,740	21,842	18,425	21,730	25,603	-703	6,085	271,466
Off-farm income of the household.........	95,140	89,747	93,786	101,638	96,688	126,765	63,753	73,829
Earned income.............................	65,814	61,359	65,596	73,320	63,530	94,180	29,105	44,264
Unearned income.........................	29,326	28,387	28,190	28,318	33,158	32,585	34,648	29,565
Total household income, mean [4].........	119,880	111,589	112,210	123,368	122,291	126,062	69,838	345,294
WEALTH PER FAMILY FARM HOUSEHOLD								
Assets, mean [4].............................	1,599,151	1,761,623	1,707,669	1,946,001	1,915,447	1,470,009	1,719,009	5,452,061
Farm assets..............................	1,012,486	1,077,709	1,166,122	1,178,070	1,227,474	714,072	1,123,937	4,729,372
Non-farm assets.........................	586,666	683,914	541,547	767,931	687,974	755,938	595,072	722,688
Debt, mean [4].............................	190,885	213,561	160,871	214,796	200,889	144,899	133,317	845,851
Farm debt...............................	101,430	106,514	100,805	99,248	97,252	29,689	56,795	683,506
Non-farm debt...........................	89,454	107,047	60,066	115,548	103,637	115,209	76,522	162,345
Net worth, mean [4].........................	1,408,267	1,548,062	1,546,799	1,731,205	1,714,559	1,325,111	1,585,692	4,606,209
Farm net worth..........................	911,055	971,195	1,065,317	1,078,822	1,130,222	684,383	1,067,142	4,045,866
Non-farm net worth......................	497,211	576,867	481,481	652,383	584,337	640,729	518,550	560,343

[1] Farms in which the principal operator is retired or has a major occupation other than farming. [2] Farms with farming as the operator's major occupation, but with less than $350,000 in gross sales. [3] Farms with more than $350,000 in gross sales. [4] For definition of mean see Guide to Tabular Presentation.

Source: U.S. Department of Agriculture, Economic Research Service, "Farm Household Income and Characteristics," <www.ers.usda.gov/data-products/farm-household-income-and-characteristics.aspx>, accessed February 2022.

Table 874. Farm Type, Acreage, and Production: 2000 to 2020

[2,166 represents 2,166,000. Based on Agricultural Resource Management Survey (ARMS). The farm typology used by the Economic Research Service was revised in 2013, and has been applied to data beginning in 2011. For more information, see <www.ers.usda.gov/publications/pub-details/?pubid=43744>]

Type of farm	Unit	2000	2005	2010	2015	2016	2017	2018	2019	2020
Total farms:										
Number of farms..................	1,000	2,166	2,095	2,193	2,059	2,052	2,034	2,021	2,015	2,011
Total value of production..........	Mil. dol.	177,286	214,010	286,758	368,144	353,164	361,648	347,884	338,972	368,890
Total acres operated..............	Mil.	995	916	912	850	897	844	812	797	832
Acres operated per farm..........	Acres	459	437	416	413	437	415	402	395	414
Commercial farms: [1]										
Number of farms..................	1,000	178	216	264	212	208	214	208	209	217
Total value of production..........	Mil. dol.	121,202	165,267	240,769	279,081	273,505	275,649	273,770	266,034	293,784
Total acres operated..............	Mil.	392	418	482	439	443	407	424	408	430
Acres operated per farm..........	Acres	2,205	1,939	1,829	2,066	2,129	1,899	2,036	1,952	1,981
Intermediate farms: [2]										
Number of farms..................	1,000	668	550	618	632	617	752	743	757	794
Total value of production..........	Mil. dol.	41,813	33,887	30,270	61,283	56,277	64,433	54,652	51,342	55,331
Total acres operated..............	Mil.	392	307	242	232	255	255	248	233	269
Acres operated per farm..........	Acres	587	558	392	367	414	339	333	307	338
Residence farms: [3]										
Number of farms..................	1,000	1,320	1,329	1,311	1,215	1,228	1,067	1,069	1,049	999
Total value of production..........	Mil. dol.	14,272	14,856	15,719	27,780	23,382	21,565	19,462	21,597	19,775
Total acres operated..............	Mil.	211	191	187	179	198	181	140	156	133
Acres operated per farm..........	Acres	160	144	143	147	161	170	131	149	133

[1] Data for 2010 and earlier include farms with sales of $250,000 or more. Beginning in 2011, data are for farms with $350,000 or more gross cash farm income and nonfamily farms. [2] Data for 2010 and earlier include small family farms whose operators report farming as their major occupation. Beginning in 2011, data are for farms with less than $350,000 in gross cash farm income and a principal operator whose primary occupation is farming. [3] Data for 2010 and earlier include retirement and residential farms. Beginning in 2011, data are for farms with less than $350,000 in gross cash farm income and where the principal operator is either retired or has a primary occupation other than farming.

Source: U.S. Department of Agriculture, Economic Research Service, "ARMS Farm Financial and Crop Production Practices," <www.ers.usda.gov/data-products/arms-farm-financial-and-crop-production-practices.aspx>, accessed March 2022.

Table 875. Farms with Renewable Energy Systems by Type of Farm: 2017

[Farms reporting renewable energy systems on their operation. Based on the 1974 definition of farms and farmland, see text, this section. Farm types are based on the USDA's Economic Research Service typology. Family farms, farms in which the majority of the business is owned by the operator and individuals related to the operator, are classified based on the gross cash farm income (GCFI). GCFI includes sales of crops and livestock, fees for delivering commodities under production contracts, government payments, and farm-related income]

Energy system	All farms	Family farms							Non-family farms [1]
		Small			Mid-sized	Large-scale			
		Total	GCFI less than $150,000	GCFI $150,000 to $349,999	GCFI $350,000 to $999,999	Total	GCFI $1,000,000 to $4,999,999	GCFI $5,000,000 and more	
Number of farms, total............	2,042,220	1,798,439	1,668,776	129,663	108,304	52,592	47,056	5,536	82,885
Number of farms with any renewable energy system....	**133,176**	**111,486**	**100,653**	**10,833**	**9,934**	**5,543**	**4,767**	**776**	**6,213**
Percent of all farms..............	6.5	6.2	6.0	8.4	9.2	10.5	10.1	14.0	7.5
By type of system:									
Solar panels......................	90,142	77,944	71,347	6,597	4,994	2,984	2,450	534	4,220
Wind turbines....................	14,136	9,950	8,138	1,812	2,120	1,113	1,017	96	953
Methane digesters...............	686	406	357	49	62	142	66	76	76
Geothermal/geoexchange systems.........................	30,343	24,803	22,351	2,452	3,026	1,466	1,380	86	1,048
Small hydro systems.............	1,710	1,465	1,331	134	81	47	42	5	117
Biodiesel.........................	2,034	1,580	1,345	235	206	116	107	9	132
Ethanol..........................	1,759	1,340	1,141	199	195	118	113	5	106
Other............................	3171	2855	2637	218	119	60	47	13	137
Wind rights leased to others.......	20,072	14,426	11,634	2,792	3,093	1,364	1,255	109	1,189

[1] Any farm where the operator and persons related to the operator do not own a majority of the business.

Source: U.S. Department of Agriculture, National Agricultural Statistics Service, *2017 Census of Agriculture, Farm Typology*, Volume 2, January 2021. See also <www.nass.usda.gov/AgCensus/>.

Table 876. Sales of Agricultural Products Direct to Consumers: 2007 to 2017

[1,211,270 represents $1,211,270,000. Farm operations who sell directly to consumers for human consumption at roadside stands, farmers' markets, pick-your-own, on-farm stores, and community support agricultural arrangements. Excludes non-edible products such as nursery crops, cut flowers, and wool, but includes livestock sales. Sales of agricultural products by vertically integrated operations through their own processing and marketing operations are also excluded]

Item	Number of farms with direct sales		Number of farms with direct and value added sales	Value of direct sales ($1,000)		Value of direct and value added sales ($1,000)
	2007	2012	2017 [4]	2007	2012	2017 [4]
Total, all farms with direct sales................	**136,817**	**144,530**	**130,056**	**1,211,270**	**1,309,827**	**2,805,310**
Percent of all farms................................	6.2	6.9	6.4	0.4	0.3	0.7
BY VALUE OF SALES						
$1 to $499..	35,440	37,398	30,695	7,217	7,770	6,559
$500 to $999..	20,547	20,170	17,318	14,013	13,685	11,615
$1,000 to $4,999....................................	49,957	52,750	43,934	113,960	121,750	101,770
$5,000 to $9,999....................................	13,060	14,452	13,707	88,174	97,308	92,663
$10,000 to $24,999..................................	10,032	11,045	11,669	151,063	164,774	176,745
$25,000 to $49,999..................................	3,903	4,244	5,068	133,328	143,722	172,716
$50,000 or more.....................................	3,878	4,471	7,665	703,515	760,819	2,243,242
BY PRIMARY ACTIVITY OF FARM [1,2]						
Oilseed and grains...................................	7,052	8,715	5,143	37,930	63,321	64,610
Vegetables and melons..............................	17,961	23,218	20,013	335,311	420,466	632,095
Fruit and tree nuts..................................	17,161	18,399	19,724	343,878	319,523	1,267,029
Greenhouse and nursery [3].........................	3,834	6,031	6,105	50,169	59,845	107,661
Beef cattle ranching and farming....................	35,984	35,980	28,156	141,427	147,315	179,653
Dairy cattle and milk production....................	3,221	2,982	2,264	52,594	43,546	152,584
Hog and pig farming.................................	5,227	3,897	3,552	18,970	15,970	20,662
Poultry and egg production..........................	8,833	9,999	8,107	54,898	36,782	88,818
Sheep and goat farming.............................	9,127	10,198	9,538	16,613	19,647	32,240

[1] Based on the farms' North American Industry Classification (NAICS) codes, indicating main commodity type produced. [2] Includes other types, not shown separately. [3] Includes floriculture. [4] 2017 data includes value added sales and is not directly comparable to prior data.

Source: U.S. Department of Agriculture, National Agricultural Statistics Service, *2017 Census of Agriculture*, Vol. 1, April 2019, and earlier reports. See also <www.nass.usda.gov/AgCensus/>.

Table 877. Farm to School Program Participation by State: 2019

[Percent, except total. For school year ending in 2019. Farm to School programs support a range of farm to school activities in which schools serve locally produced foods in their cafeteria and expose students to food and agricultural education experiences. The 2019 Farm to School Census collected data on farm to school activities from School Food Authorities (SFA) that participated in the National School Lunch Program (NSLP) in the 2018-2019 school year. The SFA is the entity responsible for school food service operations. Respondents included public, private and charter school SFAs, as well as residential child care institutions participating in NSLP]

State	Total SFAs (number)	Percent of SFAs	Served local foods [1]	Had an edible school garden	Served products from school based gardens or farms [2]	Organized field trips to farms	Had farmers visit cafeteria or classroom	Promoted local foods at school in general [3]	Spending on local food costs as a percent of total food costs [4]
United States....	**18,832**	**65.4**	**76.8**	**34.3**	**48.4**	**30.7**	**15.3**	**42.3**	**19.9**
Alabama............	140	65.7	73.9	46.7	41.9	32.6	19.6	55.4	12.2
Alaska..............	48	60.4	62.1	51.7	53.3	13.8	10.3	41.4	12.7
Arizona.............	341	52.2	74.7	25.3	24.4	26.4	9.6	33.1	26.8
Arkansas...........	259	68.0	68.8	34.1	58.3	25.6	16.5	30.7	22.8
California..........	843	70.7	76.7	47.8	34.4	29.9	18.1	40.1	27.5
Colorado...........	127	59.1	68.0	49.3	56.8	32.0	21.3	50.7	18.1
Connecticut........	129	80.6	85.6	36.5	47.4	17.3	13.5	60.6	19.5
Delaware...........	38	86.8	90.9	42.4	64.3	27.3	9.1	66.7	18.9
District of Columbia.........	41	82.9	91.2	55.9	21.1	38.2	8.8	38.2	23.9
Florida.............	201	63.7	77.3	39.8	27.5	30.5	21.1	46.1	18.2
Georgia............	215	84.7	89.6	62.1	50.4	49.5	46.7	65.9	23.3
Hawaii..............	23	87.0	85.0	70.0	28.6	70.0	35.0	55.0	28.8
Idaho...............	140	67.9	68.4	35.8	44.1	21.1	11.6	34.7	20.8
Illinois.............	516	54.7	63.1	22.7	43.8	38.7	15.6	26.2	20.3
Indiana.............	299	56.9	80.6	28.2	37.5	43.5	13.5	28.8	17.1
Iowa................	268	60.4	66.0	36.4	54.2	30.9	11.1	31.5	16.8
Kansas.............	276	59.8	77.6	27.9	63.0	44.2	22.4	31.5	16.7
Kentucky...........	170	69.4	67.8	35.6	42.9	35.6	29.7	37.3	12.1
Louisiana..........	153	55.6	69.4	36.5	22.6	20.0	8.2	29.4	14.9
Maine..............	143	83.2	80.7	58.0	69.6	31.9	24.4	57.1	17.1
Maryland...........	50	82.0	80.5	41.5	23.5	24.4	17.1	58.5	15.5
Massachusetts.....	317	72.2	81.2	48.5	65.8	23.1	15.7	63.3	16.3
Michigan...........	576	77.1	84.5	25.9	42.6	25.9	11.7	48.0	20.8
Minnesota..........	398	65.8	79.0	38.5	69.3	29.0	14.5	44.3	15.8
Mississippi.........	153	71.9	66.4	32.7	27.8	20.0	14.5	46.4	20.0
Missouri............	507	51.5	69.7	25.7	50.7	28.4	12.6	30.3	22.8
Montana............	153	68.6	83.8	37.1	53.8	30.5	14.3	50.5	21.8
Nebraska...........	251	66.1	75.3	31.9	67.9	25.3	15.1	39.8	15.8
Nevada.............	28	46.4	38.5	46.2	16.7	46.2	23.1	7.7	37.8
New Hampshire....	41	82.9	76.5	55.9	68.4	47.1	11.8	55.9	11.2
New Jersey........	421	72.7	78.4	32.0	27.6	34.6	8.8	57.2	17.4
New Mexico........	180	52.8	80.0	27.4	42.3	24.2	18.9	40.0	20.7
New York...........	661	77.3	83.6	36.8	58.0	28.6	13.7	54.4	20.4
North Carolina.....	174	62.6	81.7	25.7	10.7	42.2	27.5	56.9	17.7
North Dakota.......	143	65.7	73.4	24.5	78.3	34.0	24.5	35.1	12.7
Ohio................	674	58.3	76.3	25.2	54.5	30.5	8.7	34.1	18.7
Oklahoma..........	315	45.1	55.6	21.1	50.0	23.2	11.3	22.5	19.2
Oregon.............	182	85.2	89.0	45.8	57.7	40.0	13.5	58.7	20.9
Pennsylvania.......	522	75.3	80.9	27.7	45.9	34.4	11.2	38.2	21.5
Rhode Island.......	57	78.9	88.9	28.9	46.2	37.8	20.0	66.7	16.5
South Carolina.....	119	60.5	76.4	44.4	21.9	36.1	26.4	37.5	17.7
South Dakota......	133	44.4	72.9	28.8	41.2	28.8	13.6	30.5	14.6
Tennessee..........	177	72.9	80.6	41.1	37.7	34.9	20.9	41.1	13.0
Texas..............	850	62.9	75.7	19.8	30.2	12.3	8.6	41.9	22.7
Utah................	130	59.2	84.4	35.1	40.7	32.5	14.3	28.6	18.9
Vermont............	44	88.6	82.1	84.6	63.6	51.3	33.3	59.0	17.5
Virginia............	151	82.8	84.0	41.6	46.2	33.6	32.8	51.2	9.5
Washington.........	224	67.9	76.3	36.8	39.3	21.1	14.5	46.7	24.8
West Virginia.......	64	78.1	80.0	50.0	60.0	40.0	22.0	48.0	16.3
Wisconsin..........	477	70.2	75.2	41.2	68.1	41.8	18.5	46.0	18.2
Wyoming...........	59	67.8	72.5	40.0	68.8	35.0	20.0	32.5	9.5
American Samoa...	1	100.0	–	–	(NA)	(NA)	(NA)	(NA)	8.5
Guam...............	3	33.3	100.0	100.0	(NA)	100.0	(NA)	100.0	4.8
Northern Mariana Islands..........	1	100.0	100.0	–	(NA)	(NA)	(NA)	(NA)	1.3
Puerto Rico........	27	92.6	88.0	24.0	16.7	12.0	12.0	48.0	58.3
Virgin Islands.......	1	100.0	100.0	–	(NA)	(NA)	(NA)	100.0	10.0

– Represents or rounds to zero. NA Not available. [1] The definition of "local" is determined by individual respondents. The Census questionnaire asked respondents how they defined "local" as it relates to their food procurement. Respondents could choose from one of seven options or specify a different definition: (a) produced within a 20 mile radius, (b) produced within a 50 mile radius, (c) produced within a 100 mile radius, (d) produced within a 200 mile radius, (e) produced within the county, (f) produced within the state, and (g) produced within the region. [2] Responses only include SFAs that had edible school gardens during the 2018-2019 school year. [3] Promotion activities include promoting local foods via cafeteria signs, posters, and newsletters, and through themed or branded events such as "Harvest of the Month"; and implementing strategies to encourage student selection and consumption of local foods. [4] For SFAs participating in farm to school programs. Costs include milk.

Source: U.S. Department of Agriculture, Food and Nutrition Service, "2019 Farm to School Census Data Explorer," <farmtoschoolcensus.fns.usda.gov/census-results/census-data-explorer >, accessed June 2022. See also <www.fns.usda.gov/f2s/farm-to-school>.

Table 878. Organic Agriculture—Number of Farms, Acreage, and Value of Sales, 2008 to 2019, and for Leading States, 2019

[3,164,995 represents $3,164,995,000. Includes all known organic producers that are either certified organic or exempt from certification in the United States (those grossing less than $5,000 annually from organic sales). Organic food must be produced without the use of conventional pesticides, petroleum-based or sewage sludge-based fertilizers, herbicides, pesticides, genetic engineering (biotechnology), antibiotics, growth hormones, or irradiation. Animals raised on an organic operation must not be fed antibiotics or growth hormones, be fed 100 percent organic feed, and given access to the outdoors. Land must have no prohibited substances applied to it for at least 3 years before the harvest of an organic crop]

Year and leading states	Organic farms (number)	Organic land (acres)	Value of sales ($1,000) [1]			
			Total product sales	Crops [2]	Livestock and poultry	Livestock and poultry products
2008	14,540	4,077,337	3,164,995	1,942,317	316,470	906,207
2014	14,093	3,670,560	5,454,979	3,290,188	660,340	1,504,452
2015	12,818	4,361,849	6,163,472	3,509,632	743,227	1,910,613
2019, U.S. total [3]	**16,585**	**5,495,274**	**9,925,911**	**5,786,759**	**1,663,077**	**2,476,075**
California	3,012	965,257	3,596,923	2,874,463	386,057	336,403
Washington	745	111,930	885,970	717,331	76,461	92,178
Pennsylvania	1,048	107,550	741,764	123,656	449,208	168,900
Oregon	456	196,045	454,406	323,295	19,947	111,164
Texas	233	246,307	424,303	111,631	35,540	277,132
North Carolina	347	42,740	369,768	65,429	221,328	83,012
New York	1,321	323,081	298,420	105,014	30,370	163,035
Wisconsin	1,364	250,940	268,921	65,749	34,750	168,422
Michigan	541	122,253	230,955	75,153	26,577	129,224
Idaho	240	180,732	205,968	66,906	14,483	124,579

[1] Value of sales of commodities; excludes value-added organic products. [2] Includes nursery and greenhouse. [3] Includes other states not shown separately.

Source: U.S. Department of Agriculture, National Agricultural Statistics Service, *2019 Organic Survey*, October 2020. See also <www.nass.usda.gov/Surveys/Guide_to_NASS_Surveys/Organic_Production/>.

Table 879. Adoption of Genetically Engineered Crops: 2000 to 2020

[As percent of all crops planted. As of June. Based on June Agricultural Survey conducted by National Agricultural Statistical Services (NASS). Excludes conventionally bred herbicide tolerant varieties. Insect resistant varieties include only those containing bacillus thuringiensis (Bt). The Bt varieties include those that contain more than one gene that can resist different types of insects. Stacked gene varieties include only those varieties containing biotech traits for both herbicide tolerance and insect resistance]

Genetically engineered crop	2000	2005	2010	2013	2014	2015	2016	2017	2018	2019	2020
Corn	**25**	**52**	**86**	**90**	**93**	**92**	**92**	**92**	**92**	**92**	**92**
Insect resistant	18	26	16	5	4	4	3	3	2	3	3
Herbicide tolerant	6	17	23	14	13	12	13	12	10	9	10
Stacked gene	1	9	47	71	76	77	76	77	80	80	79
Cotton	**61**	**79**	**93**	**90**	**96**	**94**	**93**	**96**	**94**	**98**	**96**
Insect resistant	15	18	15	8	5	5	4	5	3	3	5
Herbicide tolerant	26	27	20	15	12	10	9	11	9	6	8
Stacked gene	20	34	58	67	79	79	80	80	82	89	83
Soybean	**54**	**87**	**93**	**93**	**94**	**94**	**94**	**94**	**94**	**94**	**94**
Insect resistant	(X)	(X)	(X)	(X)	(X)	(X)	(X)	(X)	(X)	(X)	(X)
Herbicide tolerant	54	87	93	93	94	94	94	94	94	94	94
Stacked gene	(X)	(X)	(X)	(X)	(X)	(X)	(X)	(X)	(X)	(X)	(X)

X Not applicable.

Source: U.S. Department of Agriculture, Economic Research Service, "Adoption of Genetically Engineered Crops in the U.S.," <www.ers.usda.gov/data-products/adoption-of-genetically-engineered-crops-in-the-us.aspx>, accessed July 2020.

Table 880. Farm Production Expenses: 2012 and 2017

[2,109 represents 2,109,000. Data have been adjusted for coverage; see text, this section and Appendix III]

Production expenses	2012			2017		
	Farms (1,000)	Expenses (mil. dol.)	Percent of total	Farms (1,000)	Expenses (mil. dol.)	Percent of total
Total	**2,109**	**328,939**	**100.0**	**2,042**	**326,391**	**100.0**
Fertilizer	1,012	28,533	8.7	1,025	23,543	7.2
Chemicals	1,000	16,460	5.0	894	17,585	5.4
Seeds, plants, vines, and trees	829	19,493	5.9	703	20,970	6.4
Livestock and poultry	545	41,586	12.6	556	44,934	13.8
Feed	1,256	75,706	23.0	1,262	62,625	19.2
Gasoline and fuel	1,988	16,573	5.0	1,922	13,474	4.1
Utilities	1,353	8,262	2.5	1,339	9,009	2.8
Supplies, repairs, and maintenance	1,663	18,868	5.7	1,665	19,671	6.0
Farm labor [1]	784	33,461	10.2	709	39,231	12.0
Customwork and custom hauling	462	6,611	2.0	428	7,555	2.3
Cash rent for land, buildings and grazing fees	560	21,001	6.4	482	21,060	6.5
Rent and lease for machinery, equipment, and farm share	133	2,332	0.7	138	2,424	0.7
Interest expense	784	12,124	3.7	669	12,396	3.8
Property taxes	1,980	7,429	2.3	1,920	9,415	2.9
Medical supplies, veterinary, custom services for livestock	(NA)	(NA)	(NA)	944	4,446	1.4
Other production expenses [2]	1,135	20,501	6.2	849	18,052	5.5

NA Not available. [1] Includes hired and contract labor. [2] Data for 2012 include expenses for medical supplies, veterinary, and custom services for animals. Starting 2017, these data are reported separately.

Source: U.S. Department of Agriculture, National Agricultural Statistics Service, *2017 Census of Agriculture*, Vol. 1, April 2019. See also <www.nass.usda.gov/AgCensus/>.

Table 881. Balance Sheet of the Farming Sector: 1990 to 2021

[In billions of dollars, except as indicated (841 represents $841,000,000,000). As of December 31. Balance sheet estimates exclude the personal portion of farm households' assets and debts]

Item	1990	2000	2010	2014	2015	2016	2017	2018	2019	2020	2021
Assets.	841	1,203	2,171	2,931	2,880	2,914	3,006	3,027	3,075	3,175	3,498
Investments and other financial assets.	38	57	135	111	88	78	81	73	87	92	113
Investment in cooperatives.	(NA)	(NA)	6	8	7	7	8	7	6	5	7
Financial assets and net accounts receivable.	(NA)	(NA)	130	103	80	71	73	65	81	87	106
Inventories.	97	110	168	210	187	180	180	173	163	163	181
Crops.	23	28	57	62	53	56	57	60	50	51	58
Livestock and poultry.	71	77	91	128	118	109	107	97	99	98	104
Purchased inputs [1].	3	5	20	20	16	15	16	16	14	14	18
Real estate [2].	619	946	1,660	2,365	2,366	2,401	2,473	2,510	2,546	2,641	2,896
Value of machinery and motor vehicles [3].	86	90	208	246	240	255	272	271	279	279	308
Debt [4].	131	164	279	345	357	374	390	403	420	441	474
Real estate.	68	85	154	197	209	226	236	246	268	289	324
Commercial banks [5].	15	30	51	73	79	84	88	93	98	97	101
Farm Credit System.	23	30	72	89	97	104	107	113	125	141	158
Farm Service Agency.	7	3	3	4	5	6	6	7	8	9	11
Farmer Mac [6].	(NA)	(NA)	4	5	5	5	6	7	8	9	10
Individuals and others [5].	14	11	10	13	10	12	13	10	11	13	23
Storage facility loans.	(Z)	(NA)	1	1	1	1	1	1	1	1	1
Life insurance companies.	9	11	12	12	13	13	15	16	18	19	21
Nonreal estate.	63	79	125	148	148	148	154	157	153	153	150
Commercial banks [5].	31	45	56	71	73	73	73	75	71	63	65
Farm Credit System.	10	17	39	48	48	49	51	53	53	55	57
Farm Service Agency.	10	4	4	4	4	4	4	4	4	4	3
Individuals and others [5].	12	13	26	26	23	22	26	24	25	31	25
Equity.	709	1,039	1,892	2,585	2,523	2,540	2,616	2,624	2,655	2,733	3,024
FINANCIAL RATIOS (percent)											
Farm debt/asset ratio.	15.60	13.62	12.85	11.78	12.39	12.84	12.99	13.30	13.67	13.90	13.56
Farm debt/equity ratio.	18.48	15.77	14.74	13.35	14.14	14.73	14.93	15.34	15.84	16.14	15.68

Z Less than $500 million. NA Not available. [1] Purchased inputs represent value of prepaid expenses on supplies such as fertilizer and lime applied, seed, feed and other inputs purchased for next year's production. It also includes the seed, fertilizer, fuel, and other expenses already invested in crops. [2] Includes farmland, buildings and other service structures. Includes farm real estate assets leased from non-operator landlords. [3] Includes automobiles, trucks and farm machinery leased to farm operators. [4] Reflects outstanding agricultural sector debt where it is held rather than where it originated. Excludes debt on operator dwellings and for nonfarm purposes. Sector-level estimates of farm debt report aggregate data by lender type and therefore does not identify who owes the debt. [5] Beginning with 2012, farm sector debt held by savings associations is reported with the commercial bank lender group instead of the individuals and others grouping. [6] The Federal Agricultural Mortgage Corporation (known as Farmer Mac) operates as a federally sponsored enterprise providing a secondary market for agricultural real estate mortgage loans, rural housing mortgage loans, and rural utility cooperative loans.

Source: U.S. Department of Agriculture, Economic Research Service, "U.S. and State Farm Income and Wealth Statistics," <www.ers.usda.gov/data-products/farm-income-and-wealth-statistics.aspx>, accessed September 2022.

Table 882. Farm Sector Output and Value Added: 2000 to 2020

[In millions of dollars (204,316 represents $204,316,000,000). For definition of value added and explanation of chained dollars, see text, Section 13. Minus sign (-) indicates decrease]

Item	2000	2005	2010	2014	2015	2016	2017	2018	2019	2020
CURRENT DOLLARS										
Farm output.	204,316	253,551	320,921	441,666	402,907	379,678	395,379	395,103	392,289	402,077
Cash receipts from farm marketings.	197,589	241,431	321,651	424,869	381,878	366,623	381,913	386,358	388,388	391,194
Farm products consumed on farms.	318	384	386	588	622	498	433	436	487	508
Other farm income.	8,426	11,840	12,139	20,527	19,987	16,958	19,094	16,543	16,526	16,264
Change in farm finished goods inventories.	-2,016	-104	-13,255	-4,319	420	-4,402	-6,061	-8,235	-13,112	-5,888
Less: Intermediate goods and services consumed.	128,272	147,975	204,691	275,668	257,679	249,785	255,983	257,990	269,294	267,415
Equals: Gross farm value added.	76,043	105,576	116,229	165,998	145,229	129,892	139,396	137,114	122,995	134,661
Less: Consumption of fixed capital.	22,807	27,483	33,062	44,418	47,182	47,731	48,188	48,970	49,963	50,662
Equals: Net farm value added.	53,237	78,093	83,167	121,580	98,047	82,161	91,208	88,143	73,031	83,999
Compensation of employees.	19,645	22,033	24,281	29,109	27,205	29,030	30,857	28,423	28,627	29,062
Taxes on production and imports.	4,626	5,345	7,516	9,931	9,345	8,768	9,408	9,342	9,771	10,574
Less: Subsidies to operators.	19,960	20,914	10,516	7,463	8,556	10,781	9,476	11,798	20,461	45,292
Net operating surplus.	48,837	71,629	61,903	90,004	70,052	55,144	60,419	62,176	55,095	89,655
CHAINED (2012) DOLLARS										
Farm output, total.	(NA)	403,675	413,022	438,568	449,015	476,171	482,790	482,611	480,809	504,964
Cash receipts from farm marketings.	(NA)	384,387	415,513	417,197	421,753	456,254	462,497	467,530	472,082	488,198
Farm products consumed on farms.	(NA)	507	472	510	611	557	466	475	541	569
Other farm income.	(NA)	20,463	15,499	23,474	24,697	22,000	24,461	20,999	20,653	20,090
Change in farm finished goods inventories.	(NA)	-170	-19,512	-4,256	208	-5,254	-7,290	-9,364	-15,172	-7,603
Less: Intermediate goods and services consumed.	(NA)	234,227	250,331	259,784	259,949	274,553	284,018	279,777	290,776	288,072
Equals: Gross farm value added.	(NA)	168,642	162,710	178,294	189,972	203,030	198,199	203,624	186,188	221,018
Less: Consumption of fixed capital.	(NA)	31,982	34,392	42,994	45,214	45,288	45,042	44,961	44,937	44,985
Equals: Net farm value added.	(NA)	139,098	129,056	135,022	144,733	160,244	154,805	161,556	139,844	185,627

NA Not available.

Source: U.S. Bureau of Economic Analysis, National Income and Product Accounts, "Table 7.3.5. Farm Sector Output, Gross Value Added, and Net Value Added," and "Table 7.3.6. Real Farm Sector Output, Real Gross Value Added, and Real Net Value Added, Chained Dollars," <apps.bea.gov/iTable/index_nipa.cfm>, accessed July 2021.

Table 883. Value Added to Economy by Agricultural Sector: 1990 to 2021

[In billions of dollars (188.5 represents $188,500,000,000). Value of agricultural sector production is the gross value of the commodities and services produced within a year. Net value-added is the sector's contribution to the national economy and is the value of farm sector production minus the value of intermediate goods used. Net farm income is the farm operators' share of income from the sector's production activities. Minus sign (-) indicates decrease]

Item	1990	2000	2010	2014	2015	2016	2017	2018	2019	2020	2021
Value of agricultural production	**188.5**	**218.4**	**344.1**	**473.5**	**430.0**	**399.3**	**413.9**	**411.2**	**405.2**	**406.7**	**485.7**
Value of crop production	83.2	95.0	168.1	206.3	184.3	189.3	187.9	186.0	177.5	189.6	239.4
Crop cash receipts	80.2	92.5	180.3	211.7	187.9	195.8	194.9	194.9	191.7	199.1	237.8
Cotton	5.5	2.9	7.5	7.1	4.8	5.5	7.6	7.5	6.8	6.8	7.6
Feed crops	18.7	20.5	55.1	65.9	56.9	55.4	53.9	57.3	58.6	57.7	82.6
Food grains	7.5	6.5	14.3	16.1	12.3	11.3	11.2	12.1	11.5	11.8	15.1
Fruits and tree nuts	9.4	12.3	21.6	32.2	28.4	29.7	30.6	29.2	29.0	27.9	30.1
Oil crops	12.3	13.5	36.5	42.6	35.5	44.0	41.1	39.5	36.2	43.8	51.6
Tobacco	2.7	2.3	1.3	1.7	1.6	1.3	1.4	1.2	1.0	0.9	0.9
Vegetables and melons	11.3	15.8	17.4	19.0	20.4	19.5	20.5	18.5	18.3	19.4	17.8
All other crops	12.9	18.6	26.5	27.1	28.0	28.9	28.6	29.5	30.2	30.8	32.1
Home consumption	0.1	0.2	0.1	0.2	0.3	0.2	0.2	0.1	0.2	0.2	0.2
Value of inventory adjustment [1]	2.8	2.2	-12.3	-5.6	-3.8	-6.6	-7.1	-9.0	-14.3	-9.6	1.5
Value of livestock production	90.0	99.1	140.2	214.3	194.1	165.4	176.9	177.4	175.1	164.8	193.9
Animals and products cash receipts	89.1	99.6	140.9	212.3	189.5	162.7	175.6	176.3	175.6	164.4	195.8
Milk and dairy products	20.2	20.6	31.4	49.4	35.7	34.5	37.9	35.2	40.5	40.4	41.8
Meat animals	51.1	53.0	69.1	107.6	98.8	82.7	88.0	87.9	88.1	82.3	100.9
Miscellaneous livestock	2.5	4.1	5.7	6.9	6.7	6.7	6.9	6.9	6.9	6.7	7.0
Poultry and eggs	15.3	21.9	34.7	48.5	48.3	38.8	42.8	46.2	40.0	35.1	46.1
Home consumption	0.5	0.1	0.3	0.3	0.4	0.3	0.3	0.3	0.3	0.4	0.5
Value of inventory adjustment [1]	0.4	-0.6	-0.9	1.7	4.3	2.4	1.1	0.8	-0.8	(Z)	-2.4
Farm-related income	15.3	24.4	35.8	52.9	51.5	44.5	49.1	47.8	52.6	52.2	52.4
Forest products sold	1.8	0.8	0.5	0.6	0.7	0.7	0.7	0.7	0.6	0.6	0.7
Gross imputed rental value of farm dwellings	7.2	12.7	15.8	16.3	17.1	16.6	17.9	18.7	17.9	18.0	20.1
Machine hire and custom work	1.8	2.2	3.8	4.4	4.7	3.6	4.6	3.9	4.1	3.8	4.6
Other farm income	4.5	8.7	15.7	31.5	29.0	23.6	25.8	24.5	30.0	29.8	27.0
Less: Intermediate product expenses [2]	90.7	119.1	189.1	255.5	235.7	221.6	228.0	230.1	233.1	239.2	257.3
Farm origin	39.5	47.9	82.2	117.0	110.1	99.5	104.5	104.9	109.2	108.9	118.3
Feed purchased	20.4	24.5	45.4	63.7	58.5	55.6	54.5	53.8	59.4	56.8	65.2
Livestock and poultry purchased	14.6	15.9	20.4	31.2	30.3	22.1	27.4	29.2	28.5	29.0	30.7
Seed purchased	4.5	7.5	16.3	22.1	21.3	21.8	22.5	21.9	21.2	23.0	22.3
Manufactured inputs	22.0	28.7	50.1	67.5	59.1	56.5	56.3	57.9	56.8	58.9	67.7
Electricity	2.6	3.0	4.6	5.9	5.7	5.6	5.8	6.1	5.7	6.0	6.4
Fertilizers, lime, and soil conditioners	8.2	10.0	21.0	28.1	25.5	23.5	22.0	23.2	22.3	24.4	29.5
Pesticides	5.4	8.5	10.7	15.8	14.6	15.2	15.7	15.4	15.5	16.5	17.8
Petroleum fuel and oils	5.8	7.2	13.8	17.7	13.2	12.2	12.8	13.2	13.2	12.0	13.9
Other intermediate expenses [2]	29.2	42.5	56.8	70.9	66.5	65.6	67.2	67.3	67.1	71.4	71.4
Machine hire and custom work	3.0	4.1	4.3	5.9	4.8	4.4	4.6	4.3	5.2	5.1	4.9
Marketing, storage, and transportation	4.2	7.5	9.0	10.8	9.2	9.7	9.8	11.9	10.1	11.1	10.5
Repair and maintenance of capital items [2]	8.6	10.9	14.6	17.8	16.6	15.9	16.6	15.3	15.7	17.4	18.2
Miscellaneous expenses [2]	13.4	19.9	29.0	36.5	35.9	35.5	36.3	35.7	36.2	37.8	37.9
Total insurance premiums [3]	3.4	4.8	7.5	10.6	10.0	9.6	10.3	9.9	9.9	10.2	12.3
Irrigation	(NA)	(NA)	0.8	1.6	1.4	1.3	1.6	1.5	1.7	1.6	1.6
Less: Contract labor	1.6	2.7	3.9	6.4	5.7	6.0	5.9	6.0	6.6	6.5	6.7
Plus: Net government transactions [4]	3.1	15.8	0.9	-4.6	-2.7	0.3	-1.9	0.1	8.3	30.6	10.3
Direct government payments [5]	9.3	23.2	12.4	9.8	10.8	13.0	11.5	13.7	22.4	45.5	25.8
Property taxes [2]	6.2	7.4	11.5	14.3	13.5	12.6	13.5	13.6	14.1	14.9	15.5
Motor vehicle registration and licensing fees	0.4	0.5	0.6	0.7	0.7	0.7	0.7	0.7	0.7	0.8	0.8
Equals: Gross value added	**99.3**	**112.5**	**152.1**	**207.0**	**185.8**	**171.9**	**178.0**	**175.2**	**173.9**	**191.7**	**232.1**
Less: Capital consumption [2]	18.1	20.1	17.6	50.3	41.3	44.4	36.3	29.9	28.7	29.4	23.7
Equals: Net value added	**81.2**	**92.4**	**134.5**	**156.7**	**144.5**	**127.5**	**141.7**	**145.3**	**145.1**	**162.3**	**208.4**
Less: Factor payments to stakeholders [6]	35.0	41.7	57.4	64.5	62.8	65.2	66.6	64.2	65.9	67.8	68.0
Employee compensation [7]	12.4	17.9	23.6	28.1	26.4	28.4	30.4	28.1	28.5	30.5	30.4
Net rent paid to operator landlords	(NA)	(NA)	2.1	4.7	4.7	4.5	4.1	3.7	3.9	4.1	4.3
Net rent paid to nonoperator landlords	9.0	9.2	14.8	15.9	15.4	14.9	13.6	11.7	12.8	13.8	14.3
Total interest expenses	13.5	14.6	16.9	15.7	16.4	17.3	18.6	20.7	20.7	19.4	18.9
Equals: Net farm income	**46.3**	**50.7**	**77.1**	**92.2**	**81.7**	**62.3**	**75.1**	**81.1**	**79.2**	**94.5**	**140.4**

NA Not available. Z Less than $500 million. [1] A positive value of inventory change represents current-year production not sold by December 31. A negative value is an offset to production from prior years included in current-year sales. [2] Including expenses associated with operator dwellings. [3] Includes federal and private crop and livestock insurance premiums as well as casualty, hail, motor vehicle and all other insurance premiums. [4] Direct government payments minus motor vehicle registration and licensing fees and property taxes. [5] Government payments reflect payments made directly to all recipients in the farm sector, including landlords. The nonoperator landlords share is offset by its inclusion in rental expenses paid to these landlords and thus is not reflected in net farm income or net cash income. [6] Prior to 2008, factor payments to stakeholders only includes net rent paid to nonoperator landlords. [7] Includes hired labor and non-cash employee compensation.

Source: U.S. Department of Agriculture, Economic Research Service, "U.S. and State Farm Income and Wealth Statistics," <www.ers.usda.gov/data-products/farm-income-and-wealth-statistics.aspx>, accessed September 2022.

Table 884. Value of Agricultural Production, Income, and Government Payments by State: 2019 and 2020

[In millions of dollars (405,159 represents $405,159,000,000). See headnote, Table 883. Minus sign (-) indicates loss]

State	Value of agricultural production 2019	Value of agricultural production 2020	Net farm income 2019	Net farm income 2020	Govern-ment payments, 2020	State	Value of agricultural production 2019	Value of agricultural production 2020	Net farm income 2019	Net farm income 2020	Govern-ment payments, 2020
U.S.	**405,159**	**406,938**	**79,098**	**94,847**	**45,688**	MO	10,486	11,398	2,050	3,204	1,505
						MT	4,489	4,621	1,403	1,470	771
AL	5,942	5,443	1,159	721	426	NE	22,224	21,897	3,930	5,290	2,461
AK	52	49	-6	-11	12	NV	829	822	223	209	90
AZ	4,797	4,402	1,361	584	313	NH	275	247	71	44	28
AR	9,152	8,980	877	1,165	1,025	NJ	1,569	1,455	647	552	126
CA	53,801	52,273	11,575	14,127	3,354	NM	3,403	3,345	1,051	965	388
CO	8,307	8,390	1,730	1,184	739	NY	6,068	5,777	1,904	1,830	713
CT	747	676	241	177	57	NC	12,570	11,906	2,161	1,560	755
DE	1,525	1,293	587	266	48	ND	8,455	9,259	1,587	2,976	1,760
FL	8,328	8,320	2,424	1,343	773	OH	9,483	10,603	1,278	2,787	1,074
GA	9,791	8,826	2,552	1,932	999	OK	7,366	6,936	1,673	1,475	1,101
HI	710	658	123	107	83	OR	5,474	5,856	1,211	1,117	554
ID	8,567	9,010	2,529	2,602	823	PA	8,139	7,702	2,203	1,585	589
IL	16,015	18,344	2,597	4,535	2,610	RI	81	74	25	22	12
IN	11,080	12,141	1,837	3,228	1,324	SC	2,700	2,631	308	321	271
IA	29,079	27,134	2,795	3,537	3,613	SD	9,941	10,784	2,205	3,680	1,782
KS	17,952	17,928	2,177	4,429	2,223	TN	4,235	4,144	826	609	550
KY	6,870	6,552	2,172	1,690	682	TX	23,553	23,096	4,753	5,590	3,115
LA	3,304	3,654	889	1,316	588	UT	2,063	2,099	606	611	229
ME	815	751	262	229	94	VT	902	812	278	224	114
MD	2,763	2,452	817	363	174	VA	4,417	4,127	975	566	390
MA	659	586	207	162	84	WA	10,110	10,969	2,932	2,535	963
MI	8,163	8,851	738	2,082	951	WV	896	834	128	39	64
MN	17,211	18,874	968	4,606	2,737	WI	12,361	12,741	2,288	3,718	1,570
MS	5,601	5,337	1,347	1,054	766	WY	1,838	1,880	427	440	212

Source: U.S. Department of Agriculture, Economic Research Service, "U.S. and State Farm Income and Wealth Statistics," <www.ers.usda.gov/data-products/farm-income-and-wealth-statistics.aspx>, accessed January 2022.

Table 885. Farm Income—Cash Receipts From Farm Marketings: 2010 to 2021

[In millions of dollars (321,196 represents $321,196,000,000). Represents gross receipts from commercial market sales as well as net Commodity Credit Corporation loans. The source estimates and publishes individual cash receipt values only for major commodities and major producing states. The U.S. receipts for individual commodities, computed as the sum of the reported states, may understate the value of sales for some commodities, with the balance included in the appropriate category labeled "other" or "miscellaneous." The degree of underestimation in some of the minor commodities can be substantial]

Commodity	2010	2015	2020	2021	Commodity	2010	2015	2020	2021
Total [1]	**321,196**	**377,432**	**363,464**	**433,569**	Broccoli	727	1,059	875	719
Animals and products	**140,871**	**189,516**	**164,401**	**195,792**	Carrots	647	820	827	831
Meat animals	69,144	98,806	82,259	100,894	Corn, sweet	952	1,043	743	775
Cattle and calves	51,246	78,253	63,090	72,874	Lettuce	2,213	3,150	3,789	2,680
Hogs	17,898	20,553	19,169	28,020	Lettuce, head	1,058	1,253	1,216	965
Dairy products, milk	31,372	35,717	40,362	41,756	Onions	1,050	1,039	958	1,037
Poultry/eggs [1]	34,690	48,292	35,121	46,104	Peppers, bell	592	733	599	462
Broilers	23,692	28,716	21,267	31,520	Tomatoes	2,281	2,603	1,616	1,506
Chicken eggs	6,553	13,763	8,665	8,677	Tomatoes, fresh	1,355	1,221	756	600
Turkeys	4,372	5,708	5,171	5,891	Cantaloupes	305	264	292	278
Miscellaneous animals [1]	5,664	6,701	6,659	7,037	Watermelons	499	488	577	534
Aquaculture	474	468	473	518	Fruits/nuts [1]	21,613	28,447	27,892	30,118
Honey	282	329	308	321	Grapefruit	291	216	199	220
Crops	**180,325**	**187,916**	**199,063**	**237,777**	Lemons	395	697	665	661
Food grains [1]	14,314	12,296	11,802	15,092	Oranges	1,997	1,963	1,712	1,593
Rice	3,263	2,803	2,872	3,264	Apples	2,311	3,366	2,937	3,033
Wheat	11,021	9,427	8,848	11,741	Cherries	756	838	959	950
Feed crops [1]	55,143	56,930	57,715	82,584	Grapes	4,024	5,914	4,791	5,531
Corn	47,540	47,023	47,658	71,101	Peaches	617	602	580	624
Hay	5,217	6,961	7,341	8,480	Pears	387	494	333	373
Sorghum grain	1,487	1,837	1,775	2,095	Blueberries	644	867	932	1,100
Cotton	7,465	4,756	6,808	7,610	Cranberries	299	262	287	272
Tobacco	1,336	1,607	849	925	Raspberries	259	721	453	531
Oil crops [1]	36,544	35,519	43,842	51,582	Strawberries	2,261	2,239	2,609	3,422
Peanuts	824	1,275	1,211	1,420	Almonds	2,903	5,869	5,251	5,028
Soybeans	34,665	33,118	41,482	48,609	Pistachios	1,159	888	2,623	2,911
Sunflower	507	568	498	631	Walnuts	1,028	1,012	948	1,022
Vegetables and melons [1]	17,405	20,359	19,392	17,795	All other crops [1]	26,506	28,002	30,762	32,071
Beans, dry	780	915	1,205	1,165	Sugarcane	1,075	1,017	1,265	1,085
Potatoes	3,336	3,708	3,720	3,666	Sugar beets	1,734	1,503	1,298	1,131
Sweet potatoes	472	676	668	680	Floriculture	4,149	4,374	4,796	6,430
Beans, snap	434	414	261	276	Mushrooms	884	1,124	980	904

[1] Includes other commodities not shown separately.

Source: U.S. Department of Agriculture, Economic Research Service, "U.S. and State Farm Income and Wealth Statistics," <www.ers.usda.gov/data-products/farm-income-and-wealth-statistics.aspx>, accessed September 2022.

Table 886. Cash Receipts for Cattle, Corn, Soybeans, and Milk—Total and for Leading States: 2021

[In millions of dollars (72,874 represents $72,874,000,000). See headnote Table 885]

State	Value	State	Value	State	Value	State	Value
Cattle and calves...	**72,874**	**Corn.................**	**71,101**	**Milk.................**	**41,756**	**Soybeans............**	**48,609**
Nebraska..............	11,354	Iowa......................	11,784	California..............	7,572	Illinois...................	7,211
Texas..................	10,054	Illinois..................	10,443	Wisconsin..............	5,913	Iowa.....................	6,516
Kansas................	9,855	Nebraska.............	8,933	Idaho..................	3,062	Minnesota..............	4,193
Colorado..............	4,220	Minnesota.............	6,810	New York...............	2,925	Indiana..................	3,832
Iowa..................	4,096	Indiana.................	5,050	Texas...................	2,834	Nebraska...............	3,382

Source: U.S. Department of Agriculture, Economic Research Service, "U.S. and State Farm Income and Wealth Statistics," <www.ers.usda.gov/data-products/farm-income-and-wealth-statistics.aspx>, accessed September 2022.

Table 887. Farm Marketings: 2020 and 2021; and Principal Commodities, 2021, by State

[In millions of dollars (363,464 represents 363,464,000,000). See headnote Table 885]

State	2020 Total	2020 Animals and products	2020 Crops	2021 Total	2021 Animals and products	2021 Crops	2021 State rank for total farm marketings and three principal commodities in order of marketing receipts
U.S.........	**363,464**	**164,401**	**199,063**	**433,569**	**195,792**	**237,777**	**Cattle and calves, corn, soybeans**
AL...........	4,658	3,390	1,268	5,960	4,570	1,390	25—Broilers, chicken eggs, cattle and calves
AK...........	38	8	30	44	7	37	50—Floriculture, hay, cattle and calves
AZ...........	3,864	1,572	2,292	3,967	1,718	2,249	31—Milk, cattle and calves, lettuce
AR...........	8,183	4,195	3,988	10,346	5,808	4,538	14—Broilers, soybeans, rice
CA...........	49,354	11,895	37,459	51,110	12,821	38,288	1—Milk, grapes, almonds
CO...........	7,284	5,071	2,213	8,219	5,694	2,525	20—Cattle and calves, milk, corn
CT...........	571	166	404	589	169	420	46—Floriculture, milk, chicken eggs
DE...........	1,068	741	327	1,310	957	353	40—Broilers, corn, soybeans
FL...........	7,741	1,458	6,283	7,506	1,574	5,931	22—Floriculture, oranges, sugarcane
GA...........	7,707	4,361	3,346	9,454	5,794	3,660	16—Broilers, cotton lint, peanuts
HI...........	523	137	386	593	147	446	45—Macadamia nuts, coffee, floriculture
ID...........	8,074	4,744	3,330	8,346	4,939	3,407	19—Milk, cattle and calves, potatoes
IL...........	16,097	2,490	13,607	21,720	3,097	18,623	5—Corn, soybeans, hogs
IN...........	10,753	3,644	7,108	14,063	4,504	9,559	8—Corn, soybeans, hogs
IA...........	26,269	12,478	13,791	34,627	15,990	18,636	2—Corn, hogs, soybeans
KS...........	17,594	9,590	8,004	21,391	11,483	9,907	6—Cattle and calves, corn, wheat
KY...........	5,217	2,764	2,453	6,864	3,530	3,333	24—Corn, soybeans, broilers
LA...........	3,176	928	2,248	3,431	1,108	2,323	33—Soybeans, broilers, sugarcane
ME...........	694	295	399	762	293	468	42—Potatoes, milk, blueberries
MD...........	2,055	1,047	1,008	2,450	1,318	1,132	36—Broilers, corn, soybeans
MA...........	466	104	363	495	109	386	47—Floriculture, cranberries, milk
MI...........	7,627	3,260	4,367	9,359	3,692	5,667	17—Milk, corn, soybeans
MN...........	16,467	7,215	9,252	21,264	8,361	12,904	7—Corn, soybeans, hogs
MS...........	4,827	2,418	2,409	5,856	3,206	2,650	27—Broilers, soybeans, corn
MO...........	9,562	3,806	5,755	12,389	5,052	7,336	11—Soybeans, corn, cattle and calves
MT...........	3,768	1,515	2,253	4,102	1,845	2,257	30—Cattle and calves, wheat, hay
NE...........	21,209	10,884	10,325	26,345	12,922	13,423	3—Cattle and calves, corn, soybeans
NV...........	677	484	194	754	547	207	43—Cattle and calves, milk, hay
NH...........	200	101	98	189	102	87	48—Milk, floriculture, chicken eggs
NJ...........	1,273	120	1,153	1,367	117	1,250	39—Floriculture, blueberries, corn
NM...........	3,026	2,370	656	3,168	2,411	756	34—Milk, cattle and calves, pecans
NY...........	5,345	3,254	2,091	5,897	3,511	2,386	26—Milk, corn, apples
NC...........	10,028	6,590	3,439	13,284	9,234	4,050	9—Broilers, hogs, turkeys
ND...........	7,369	1,117	6,252	8,548	1,389	7,159	18—Soybeans, wheat, corn
OH...........	8,697	3,418	5,279	11,138	3,859	7,279	13—Soybeans, corn, milk
OK...........	6,185	4,654	1,531	7,652	5,808	1,844	21—Cattle and calves, hogs, broilers
OR...........	4,905	1,505	3,400	5,532	1,631	3,901	28—Cattle and calves, milk, wheat
PA...........	6,606	3,980	2,626	7,445	4,470	2,975	23—Milk, corn, broilers
RI...........	59	22	37	65	21	44	49—Floriculture, chicken eggs, turkeys
SC...........	2,079	1,023	1,055	2,697	1,404	1,293	35—Broilers, corn, soybeans
SD...........	8,806	4,002	4,803	11,923	4,952	6,971	12—Corn, cattle and calves, soybeans
TN...........	3,641	1,231	2,410	4,367	1,558	2,808	29—Soybeans, corn, broilers
TX...........	20,391	14,387	6,004	24,899	16,776	8,122	4—Cattle and calves, milk, broilers
UT...........	1,788	1,248	539	1,988	1,361	628	37—Cattle and calves, milk, hay
VT...........	728	562	166	788	588	201	41—Milk, cattle and calves, maple products
VA...........	3,348	1,997	1,351	3,785	2,393	1,392	32—Broilers, cattle and calves, turkeys
WA...........	9,943	2,822	7,121	10,179	3,022	7,156	15—Apples, cattle and calves, milk
WV...........	641	482	158	693	531	162	44—Cattle and calves, broilers, turkeys
WI...........	11,362	7,755	3,607	12,938	8,108	4,830	10—Milk, corn, cattle and calves
WY...........	1,522	1,100	423	1,715	1,289	426	38—Cattle and calves, hay, hogs

Source: U.S. Department of Agriculture, Economic Research Service, "U.S. and State Farm Income and Wealth Statistics," <www.ers.usda.gov/data-products/farm-income-and-wealth-statistics.aspx>, accessed September 2022.

Table 888. Indexes of Prices Received and Paid by Farmers: 2010 to 2021

[2011=100]

Item	2010	2015	2020	2021	Item	2010	2015	2020	2021
Prices received, all products....	**87**	**99**	**95**	**105**	Livestock and poultry............	86	147	98	109
Crops.........................	87	87	101	105	Seed and plants.................	93	125	113	118
Food grains.....................	74	76	80	104	Fertilizer [2].....................	77	87	68	91
Feed grains.....................	66	63	81	89	Agricultural chemicals..........	100	107	95	103
Cotton.......................	81	(NA)	(NA)	(NA)	Fuels........................	78	64	58	77
Tobacco.....................	99	(NA)	(NA)	(NA)	Supplies and repairs..........	96	106	117	125
Oil-bearing crops................	81	76	98	98	Trucks and autos................	97	106	107	113
Fruits and nuts.................	89	139	139	136	Farm machinery.............	94	115	125	146
Commercial vegetables........	104	109	126	118	Building materials...............	97	107	121	141
Potatoes and dry beans........	82	(NA)	(NA)	(NA)	Agricultural services...........	98	114	117	121
Animals and products............	86	113	89	105	Rent........................	93	130	118	116
Livestock....................	82	120	90	105					
Dairy products.................	81	85	90	92	Interest......................	92	98	111	111
Poultry and eggs...............	102	128	85	117	Taxes.......................	96	110	127	130
Prices paid, total [1]................	**90**	**111**	**110**	**119**	Wage rates..................	99	112	138	146
Production...................	88	112	106	116					
Feed.........................	80	106	106	121	Parity ratio [3].....................	96	90	80	87

NA Not available. [1] Includes production items, interest, taxes, wage rates, and a family living component. The family living component is the Consumer Price Index for all urban consumers from the Bureau of Labor Statistics. See text, Section 14 and Table 764. [2] Includes lime and soil conditioners. [3] Ratio of prices received by farmers to prices paid.

Source: U.S. Department of Agriculture, National Agricultural Statistics Service, "Quick Stats," <quickstats.nass.usda.gov/>, accessed August 2022.

Table 889. Farm and Marketing Bill Share of the U.S. Food Dollar (Nominal) by Selected Characteristics: 2000 to 2020

[In percent. The food dollar series measures annual expenditures by U.S. consumers on domestically produced food; a food dollar represents the average $1 expenditure. Farm share is measured as the average payment from each food dollar expenditure that farmers receive for their raw food dollar commodities. The food marketing bill is measured as the average value added to the raw food dollar from each consumer food dollar expenditure. Based on input-output data from the Bureau of Labor Statistics and Bureau of Economic Analysis]

Item	2000	2005	2010	2015	2016	2017	2018	2019	2020
SHARE OF FOOD DOLLAR									
Food dollar, total:									
Farm share............	15.8	15.8	16.9	16.6	15.9	15.5	15.3	15.0	16.0
Marketing bill share...............	84.2	84.2	83.1	83.4	84.1	84.5	84.7	85.0	84.0
Food at home dollar:									
Farm share............	22.5	23.6	25.0	25.2	24.6	24.0	24.0	23.6	23.3
Marketing bill share...............	77.5	76.4	75.0	74.8	75.4	76.0	76.0	76.4	76.7
Food away from home dollar:									
Farm share............	6.2	5.1	5.0	4.2	3.9	4.0	3.8	3.7	3.8
Marketing bill share...............	93.8	94.9	95.0	95.8	96.1	96.0	96.2	96.3	96.2
Food and beverage dollar: [1]									
Farm share............	13.1	13.2	14.0	13.5	13.0	12.6	12.4	12.2	12.8
Marketing bill share...............	86.9	86.8	86.0	86.5	87.0	87.4	87.6	87.8	87.2
Home food and beverage dollar: [1]									
Farm share............	18.0	18.9	20.4	20.7	20.1	19.6	19.4	19.2	18.8
Marketing bill share...............	82.0	81.1	79.6	79.3	79.9	80.4	80.6	80.8	81.2
Away food and beverage dollar: [1]									
Farm share............	5.4	4.5	4.1	3.4	3.1	3.2	3.1	3.0	3.0
Marketing bill share...............	94.6	95.5	95.9	96.6	96.9	96.8	96.9	97.0	97.0
MARKETING BILL COST COMPONENTS									
Primary factors:									
Salary and benefits [2]...............	52.9	50.4	49.0	50.1	50.8	51.2	51.2	51.5	51.6
Output taxes [3]................	7.3	8.0	9.3	9.2	9.1	9.2	9.2	9.0	4.3
Property income [4]..............	34.6	35.6	36.1	35.7	35.2	34.5	34.3	34.7	39.4
Imports [5].....................	5.1	6.0	5.6	5.1	5.0	5.2	5.2	4.9	4.7
Industry groups: [6]									
Farm and agribusiness [7].................	10.6	10.9	11.2	10.9	10.3	10.1	9.9	9.7	10.5
Food processing..................	18.2	15.8	16.2	15.6	15.7	15.8	15.2	15.2	16.7
Packaging.....................	4.2	3.6	3.1	2.7	2.8	2.8	2.9	2.9	3.1
Transportation..................	3.8	3.6	3.5	3.7	3.7	3.6	3.8	3.9	4.1
Wholesale trade..................	9.4	9.2	10.3	11.3	11.2	11.2	10.9	10.9	11.9
Retail trade.....................	13.0	13.7	14.2	13.4	13.3	13.2	12.9	12.9	14.2
Food services..................	28.4	30.6	29.0	30.7	31.8	32.0	32.5	33.1	27.9
Energy.......................	4.7	5.5	5.6	4.0	3.5	3.8	4.0	3.6	3.6
Finance and insurance..............	3.8	3.3	2.9	3.4	3.4	3.2	3.3	3.2	3.3
Advertising.....................	2.5	2.5	2.4	2.5	2.6	2.6	2.8	2.9	2.9
Legal and accounting...............	1.5	1.5	1.6	1.8	1.8	1.7	1.8	1.8	1.8

[1] Includes alcoholic beverages and soft drinks. [2] Pre-tax employee wages plus employer and employee costs for employee benefits. [3] Value of excise, sales, property, and severance taxes (less subsidies), customs duties, and other non-tax government fees levied on establishments. [4] Allocated compensation to various owners for services on behalf of a domestic establishment that directs sales to the U.S. food supply. Includes machinery, equipment, structures, natural resources, product inventory, and other tangible or intangible assets. [5] Food and non-food commodities imported from international sources and used by U.S. food supply chain industries producing for the U.S. market. [6] For each industry group, the amount shown excludes value-added contributions to the food dollar that trace back to other supply chain industry groups. For example, the value of energy used by the transportation and packaging industries is deducted from those groups and included with the energy group. [7] Farm and agribusiness value-added contributions from non-farm supply chain industry groups, such as energy, transportation, and financial services, are deducted from the farm share and therefore the industry group series value for farms and agribusiness is smaller than the farm share value of the marketing bill series.

Source: U.S. Department of Agriculture, Economic Research Service, "Food Dollar Series," <www.ers.usda.gov/data-products/food-dollar-series.aspx>, accessed June 2022.

Table 890. Federal Government Subsidies for Agriculture by Farm and Payment Characteristics: 2000 to 2020

[932 represents 932,000. Based on Agricultural Resource Management Survey (ARMS)]

Payment and farm characteristic	Unit	2000	2005	2010	2015	2017	2018	2019	2020
Farms receiving government payments	**1,000**	**932**	**900**	**772**	**574**	**600**	**583**	**628**	**809**
Farms not receiving government payments	1,000	1,234	1,195	1,421	1,485	1,434	1,438	1,387	1,202
All government payments	**Mil. dol.**	**16,093**	**16,283**	**9,205**	**8,577**	**8,649**	**10,396**	**16,003**	**28,833**
Countercyclical-type payments [1]	Mil. dol.	–	2,967	659	4,319	4,007	1,977	1,928	3,716
Direct payments [2]	Mil. dol.	4,720	4,800	4,102	(X)	(X)	(X)	(X)	(X)
Conservation payments [3]	Mil. dol.	1,287	1,971	2,530	2,688	2,973	2,841	3,090	3,155
Marketing loan benefits payments [4]	Mil. dol.	5,519	4,087	158	112	486	519	874	1,491
Other government program payments [5]	Mil. dol.	4,567	2,458	1,756	1,458	1,182	5,058	10,111	20,472
Average payments per participating farm	Dollars	17,260	18,095	11,924	14,946	14,416	17,822	25,481	35,646
Commercial farms [6]	Dollars	61,997	62,567	32,054	41,092	39,832	51,374	78,050	135,352
Intermediate farms [7]	Dollars	16,411	13,857	7,210	9,092	8,325	9,924	11,731	14,180
Residence farms [8]	Dollars	4,870	5,680	4,713	6,749	5,878	6,288	8,147	7,474
Average payment by select production specialty: [9]									
Corn	Dollars	33,182	37,936	15,690	24,941	18,081	28,118	39,730	52,777
General cash grains [10]	Dollars	36,300	40,551	21,959	30,432	30,805	39,385	64,810	70,214
Soybeans	Dollars	17,046	19,472	12,810	12,913	16,982	22,098	31,907	35,064
Wheat	Dollars	34,973	25,303	38,163	30,315	36,547	30,196	38,152	70,077
Cattle	Dollars	7,197	8,539	8,244	12,970	9,995	9,206	12,105	19,267
Dairy	Dollars	16,705	14,249	10,190	15,609	10,895	19,269	33,233	141,675
Hogs	Dollars	25,594	38,358	19,547	21,410	16,737	40,753	61,083	107,995
Poultry	Dollars	8,279	21,642	9,749	7,013	15,386	13,795	14,255	35,052

– Represents or rounds to zero. X Not applicable. [1] Countercyclical-type program payments are made to producers of eligible crops based on historical production of program crops, but the payment rates depend on market prices. [2] Direct payments are payments made to producers based on historical acreage of program crops and historical yields. [3] Conservation program payments are payments made to producers that include land-retirement programs, as well as working-land programs that provide payments for maintaining or adopting resource conservation practices on land in production. [4] Marketing loan benefits are payments made to farmers based on market prices for eligible commodities falling below program target prices. Marketing assistance loan programs are based on current production and tend to provide payments when market prices fall below target levels. [5] Other government program payments include payments from disaster relief programs and emergency payments which tend to be temporary, as-needed government responses to natural disasters. Also includes milk income support programs, the tobacco transition program, peanut quota buyouts, and/or all other programs not specified in ARMS questionnaires. [6] Data for 2010 and earlier include farms with sales of $250,000 or more. Beginning in 2011, data are for farms with $350,000 or more gross cash farm income and nonfamily farms. [7] Data for 2010 and earlier include small family farms whose operators report farming as their major occupation. Beginning in 2011, data are for farms with less than $350,000 in gross cash farm income and a principal operator whose primary occupation is farming. [8] Data for 2010 and earlier include retirement and residential farms. Beginning in 2011, data are for farms with less than $350,000 in gross cash farm income and where the principal operator is either retired or has a primary occupation other than farming. [9] Production specialty is where that commodity is the majority of value of production for the farm. [10] Sorghum and rice.

Source: U.S. Department of Agriculture, Economic Research Service, "ARMS Farm Financial and Crop Production Practices," <www.ers.usda.gov/data-products/arms-farm-financial-and-crop-production-practices.aspx>, accessed May 2022.

Table 891. Percent of U.S. Agricultural Consumption Imported: 2010 to 2020

[In percent. Import value share of consumption. The import share of food available for consumption based on value is the ratio of imported food value to domestic consumption value. Value of food consumption is estimated as production value excluding stocks, plus imports, then minus exports. See source for more information]

Commodity group	2010	2013	2014	2015	2016	2017	2018	2019	2020
Total food and beverages	**13.1**	**14.4**	**14.7**	**15.6**	**16.0**	**16.7**	**17.4**	**17.7**	**18.3**
Animal foods [1]	5.8	6.2	6.8	7.3	7.1	7.0	7.2	7.4	7.8
Plant foods [2]	18.7	20.3	22.4	23.3	23.6	25.4	26.0	25.9	27.2
Non-manufactured products	**10.9**	**10.7**	**11.5**	**12.6**	**13.8**	**14.2**	**14.5**	**15.1**	**16.2**
Crops	16.0	16.0	18.5	20.7	21.2	22.5	22.9	23.7	25.2
Food grains	18.4	29.0	22.4	22.1	22.1	29.3	25.9	30.9	32.3
Feed grains	1.1	2.4	1.7	1.9	1.7	1.7	1.4	1.3	1.4
Oilseeds	3.4	5.3	9.8	6.4	4.2	4.7	4.0	4.5	4.8
Vegetables and melons	29.1	31.7	32.7	31.5	35.6	34.1	37.9	39.9	42.7
Fruits and tree nuts	37.1	36.2	36.7	44.4	44.0	46.5	49.6	51.3	51.1
Sweeteners	45.0	38.9	45.7	46.9	44.8	47.1	45.0	45.3	48.3
Livestock	3.1	2.6	3.0	3.0	3.0	2.9	2.8	3.1	3.2
Manufactured products	**19.8**	**24.4**	**25.1**	**24.5**	**23.6**	**25.3**	**26.1**	**25.9**	**26.3**
Grain & oilseed milling products	31.2	48.9	51.2	47.2	45.2	58.1	57.0	49.9	57.4
Sugar & confections	33.7	36.2	37.7	35.9	36.1	36.6	36.7	36.2	37.0
Preserved fruit & vegetables	22.3	25.0	26.1	25.8	26.5	27.4	28.2	28.2	27.9
Dairy products	6.7	9.8	10.7	9.9	9.0	8.4	8.3	8.4	8.2
Meat products	13.8	18.4	22.5	21.8	18.0	18.7	18.6	19.1	18.6
Bakery products	8.5	10.4	10.6	10.7	11.4	12.6	13.7	13.8	14.2
Other foods	13.6	19.1	17.4	17.3	16.0	16.1	20.2	20.3	21.1
Beverages	31.9	34.5	34.5	34.3	34.2	40.2	38.7	39.2	40.8

[1] Animal products include red meats, poultry meat and eggs, and dairy products. [2] Plant or crop food products include food grains, vegetable oils, fruits, nuts, vegetables, sweeteners (sugarcane, sugar beets, honey), tropical products (coffee, cocoa, spices), grain and oilseed milling products, sugar and confections, and bakery products.

Source: U.S. Department of Agriculture, Economic Research Service, "U.S. Agricultural Trade," <www.ers.usda.gov/topics/international-markets-trade/us-agricultural-trade/>, accessed May 2022.

Table 892. Agricultural Exports and Import Volume, Selected Commodities: 2000 to 2021

[In thousands (2,380 represents 2,380,000). 1 kiloliter equals 264.17 gallons. Includes Puerto Rico, U.S. territories, and shipments under foreign aid programs. Imports are imports for consumption; see text, Section 28 for definition. Commodity and commodity grouping definitions used are Foreign Agricultural Trade of the United States (FATUS) groupings. In January 2021, the U.S. Department of Agriculture adopted the World Trade Organization (WTO) definitions of agricultural products and revised historical data to reflect the new definitions. Therefore, data here may not be comparable to data presented in previous editions. See source for details]

Commodity	Unit	2000	2005	2010	2015	2019	2020	2021
EXPORTS								
Red meat and products [1]	Metric tons	2,380	1,909	3,355	3,577	4,973	5,289	5,441
Poultry meat	Metric tons	2,555	2,711	3,401	3,271	3,574	3,654	3,623
Wheat, unmilled	Metric tons	27,568	27,040	27,608	21,258	26,949	26,114	23,913
Wheat flour	Metric tons	743	192	332	309	279	278	244
Rice, paddy, milled	Metric tons	3,241	4,388	4,464	3,880	3,631	3,280	3,366
Feed grains	Metric tons	54,946	50,865	54,504	54,604	44,473	58,598	75,953
Feed grain products	Metric tons	657	3,442	1,081	851	922	918	976
Feeds and fodders [2]	Metric tons	13,065	11,422	19,024	22,725	21,193	21,173	22,266
Fruits and preparations	Metric tons	3,273	3,312	3,750	3,740	3,240	3,110	3,030
Fruit juices	Kiloliters	1,162	1,048	1,112	869	548	515	510
Vegetables, fresh	Metric tons	2,100	2,077	2,140	2,236	2,437	2,336	2,496
Oilcake and meal	Metric tons	6,760	6,905	10,004	11,689	12,348	13,025	12,431
Oilseeds	Metric tons	27,715	26,462	43,282	48,914	53,248	64,747	53,719
Vegetable oils	Metric tons	2,075	1,989	3,644	2,759	2,434	2,810	2,395
Tobacco, unmanufactured	Metric tons	180	154	179	156	101	94	103
Cotton, excluding linters	Metric tons	1,485	3,405	2,956	2,396	3,560	3,814	2,964
IMPORTS								
Red meat and products [1]	Metric tons	1,562	1,759	1,291	1,817	1,683	1,764	1,940
Wheat, excluding seed	Metric tons	1,859	1,298	2,490	2,448	1,822	1,878	1,450
Oats, unmilled	Metric tons	1,696	1,684	1,567	1,672	1,477	1,577	1,425
Biscuits and wafers	Metric tons	427	696	796	1,066	1,624	1,699	1,913
Feeds and fodders [2]	Metric tons	1,224	963	1,423	2,221	1,839	1,948	2,156
Fruits and preparations	Metric tons	8,093	9,242	10,580	13,362	14,482	14,768	15,368
Fruit juices	Kiloliters	3,114	4,149	4,274	4,477	4,640	4,031	4,730
Vegetables, fresh	Metric tons	2,905	3,857	5,472	6,570	8,071	8,327	8,941
Sugar, cane and beet	Metric tons	1,474	2,140	2,982	3,254	2,891	3,576	2,945
Coffee, including products	Metric tons	1,370	1,307	1,390	1,584	1,753	1,593	1,643
Wine	Kiloliters	458	726	959	1,157	1,269	1,298	1,495
Malt beverages	Kiloliters	2,346	2,995	3,161	3,675	4,259	4,312	4,669
Oilseeds and oilnuts	Metric tons	951	818	1,223	1,643	1,169	1,273	1,313
Vegetable oils and waxes	Metric tons	1,893	2,518	3,925	5,174	6,044	5,983	6,498
Oilcake and meal	Metric tons	1,254	1,541	1,504	4,020	3,989	4,170	4,108
Tobacco, unmanufactured	Metric tons	216	233	164	155	131	108	133

[1] Includes variety meats. [2] Excluding oilcake and meal.

Source: U.S. Department of Agriculture, Foreign Agricultural Service, "Global Agricultural Trade System," <apps.fas.usda.gov/gats/>, accessed August 2022.

Table 893. Agricultural Chemical and Fertilizer Exports and General Imports by Type: 2005 to 2021

[In thousands of metric tons (30,397 represents 30,397,000). Metric ton = 1.102 short tons or .984 long tons. Includes Puerto Rico, U.S. territories, and shipments under foreign aid programs. Commodity and commodity grouping definitions used are Foreign Agricultural Trade of the United States (FATUS) commodity code groupings. See source for details]

Commodity	2005	2010	2015	2016	2017	2018	2019	2020	2021
GENERAL IMPORTS [1]									
Fertilizers, total	30,397	43,657	35,676	31,894	33,437	34,477	31,852	31,616	36,210
Potassium	10,215	10,230	10,275	8,878	12,288	12,903	11,632	11,975	13,585
Nitrogen	17,901	17,171	18,304	16,134	14,004	12,779	12,048	11,291	13,518
Phosphate	2,243	16,200	6,975	6,798	7,028	8,694	8,099	8,264	9,004
Mixed/organic fertilizer	37	56	122	83	117	101	73	85	104
Agricultural chemicals, total	80	90	115	125	141	142	114	138	175
Fungicides	21	25	33	35	38	40	35	38	42
Herbicides	23	15	19	27	34	33	20	18	24
Insecticides	7	1	1	1	2	2	1	1	2
Other pesticides	29	49	61	60	68	68	58	80	106
EXPORTS									
Fertilizers, total	32	10,310	9,916	10,569	11,835	10,565	10,165	9,604	8,287
Potassium	–	333	54	56	83	61	103	103	69
Nitrogen	26	1,741	2,346	2,842	4,001	3,557	3,055	2,934	2,158
Phosphate	6	7,820	6,467	6,660	6,619	6,180	6,389	6,124	5,122
Mixed/organic fertilizer	–	416	1,048	1,011	1,133	767	618	443	937
Agricultural chemicals, total	127	146	150	156	1,170	1,153	1,159	1,203	1,245
Fungicides	18	15	19	18	19	20	19	20	23
Herbicides	56	83	81	91	117	94	86	88	86
Insecticides	23	27	24	20	–	–	–	–	–
Other pesticides	29	22	26	27	1,035	1,039	1,054	1,095	1,136

– Represents or rounds to zero. [1] Total shipments arriving in the U.S., including both merchandise that enters consumption channels immediately and merchandise entered into bonded warehouses or Foreign Trade Zones under Customs custody.

Source: U.S. Department of Agriculture, Foreign Agricultural Service, "Global Agricultural Trade System," <apps.fas.usda.gov/gats/>, accessed August 2022.

Table 894. Agricultural Exports and Imports—Value: 2005 to 2021

[In billions of dollars, except percent (2.3 represents $2,300,000,000). Includes Puerto Rico, U.S. territories, and shipments under foreign aid programs. Excludes fish, forest products, distilled liquors, manufactured tobacco, and products made from cotton; but includes raw tobacco, raw cotton, rubber, beer and wine, and processed agricultural products]

Year	Trade balance	Exports, domestic products	Percent of all exports	Imports for con- sumption	Percent of all imports	Year	Trade balance	Exports, domestic products	Percent of all exports	Imports for con- sumption	Percent of all imports
2005.........	2.3	65.6	8.2	63.3	3.8	2015.........	16.1	137.2	10.7	121.1	5.4
2009.........	24.0	100.8	10.8	76.7	4.9	2016.........	16.3	138.9	11.3	122.6	5.6
2010.........	33.1	118.7	10.6	85.6	4.5	2017.........	13.7	142.9	10.9	129.2	5.6
2011.........	40.1	142.1	10.9	102.0	4.7	2018.........	6.7	144.7	10.2	138.0	5.4
2012.........	37.2	145.9	10.8	108.8	4.8	2019.........	-0.5	141.1	10.1	141.6	5.7
2013.........	37.5	148.5	10.8	111.0	5.0	2020.........	3.5	149.7	12.5	146.3	6.3
2014.........	35.8	154.5	11.0	118.7	5.1	2021.........	6.5	177.0	12.0	170.6	6.0

Source: U.S. Department of Agriculture, Economic Research Service, "Foreign Agricultural Trade of the United States (FATUS)," <www.ers.usda.gov/data-products/foreign-agricultural-trade-of-the-united-states-fatus/>, accessed July 2022.

Table 895. Agricultural Imports—Value by Selected Commodity: 2010 to 2021

[In millions of dollars (85,582 represents $85,582,000,000). For calendar year. Data are imports for consumption; for definition, see text, Section 28. Includes Puerto Rico, U.S. territories, and shipments under foreign aid programs. In January 2021, the U.S. Department of Agriculture adopted the World Trade Organization (WTO) definitions of agricultural products and revised historical data to reflect the new definitions. Therefore, data here may not be comparable to data presented in previous editions. See source for details]

Commodity [1]	Value (mil. dol.)							Percent distribution		
	2010	2015	2017	2018	2019	2020	2021	2010	2020	2021
Total [2].....................	85,582	121,122	129,210	137,991	141,567	146,282	170,553	100.0	100.0	100.0
Cattle, live........................	1,575	2,195	1,533	1,586	1,799	1,756	1,566	1.8	1.2	0.9
Beef and veal.....................	2,830	6,655	5,257	5,616	5,997	6,822	8,186	3.3	4.7	4.8
Pork..............................	1,185	1,622	1,734	1,601	1,478	1,464	2,104	1.4	1.0	1.2
Dairy products....................	2,619	3,493	2,826	2,938	3,108	3,236	3,942	3.1	2.2	2.3
Grains and feeds.................	7,788	11,085	12,197	13,648	14,096	15,087	16,829	9.1	10.3	9.9
Fruits and preparations...........	9,168	14,047	16,323	17,232	18,132	18,573	21,305	10.7	12.7	12.5
Vegetables and preparations [3]..........	9,318	12,063	13,578	14,485	15,082	16,852	18,229	10.9	11.5	10.7
Sugar and related products..............	4,047	4,600	4,660	4,645	4,651	5,163	5,644	4.7	3.5	3.3
Cocoa and products.....................	4,295	4,860	5,012	4,712	4,977	5,052	5,633	5.0	3.5	3.3
Coffee and products....................	4,943	6,303	6,617	6,052	6,100	6,018	7,241	5.8	4.1	4.2
Wine.................................	4,279	5,478	6,023	6,317	6,337	5,830	7,416	5.0	4.0	4.3
Malt beverages.......................	3,506	4,547	5,084	5,339	5,633	5,816	6,441	4.1	4.0	3.8
Oilseeds and products.................	5,681	8,706	9,709	9,847	9,123	9,692	13,525	6.6	6.6	7.9

[1] Commodity and commodity grouping definitions used are the Foreign Agricultural Trade of the United States (FATUS) commodity code groupings. See source for more details. [2] Includes other commodities not shown separately. [3] Includes pulses.

Source: U.S. Department of Agriculture, Foreign Agricultural Service, "Global Agricultural Trade System," <apps.fas.usda.gov/gats/>, accessed April 2022.

Table 896. Agricultural Imports—Value by Selected Country of Origin: 2010 to 2021

[In millions of dollars (85,582 represents $85,582,000,000). Data are imports for consumption; for definition, see text, Section 28. In January 2021, the U.S. Department of Agriculture adopted the World Trade Organization (WTO) definitions of agricultural products and revised historical data to reflect the new definitions. Therefore, data here may not be comparable to data presented in previous editions. See source for details]

Country	Value (mil. dol.)							Percent distribution		
	2010	2015	2017	2018	2019	2020	2021	2010	2020	2021
Total........................	85,582	121,122	129,210	137,991	141,567	146,282	170,553	100.0	100.0	100.0
Argentina......................	1,164	1,533	1,384	1,399	1,358	1,379	1,656	1.4	0.9	1.0
Australia [1].....................	2,314	4,277	3,250	3,211	3,522	3,382	3,535	2.7	2.3	2.1
Brazil..........................	3,141	3,974	3,900	3,939	4,061	4,054	4,736	3.7	2.8	2.8
Canada........................	16,773	22,443	22,945	23,714	24,363	25,318	31,161	19.6	17.3	18.3
Chile...........................	2,298	2,863	2,894	3,080	2,806	2,769	3,133	2.7	1.9	1.8
China..........................	3,309	4,302	4,481	4,933	3,731	3,811	4,038	3.9	2.6	2.4
Colombia.......................	1,983	2,434	2,614	2,614	2,673	2,722	3,354	2.3	1.9	2.0
Costa Rica.....................	1,297	1,486	1,619	1,592	1,548	1,606	1,725	1.5	1.1	1.0
Ecuador........................	870	1,227	1,003	1,077	1,105	1,271	1,438	1.0	0.9	0.8
European Union [2]..............	16,615	22,776	25,092	27,148	28,380	27,453	32,065	19.4	18.8	18.8
Guatemala......................	1,361	1,951	2,084	2,200	2,148	2,196	2,490	1.6	1.5	1.5
India...........................	1,599	2,679	2,599	2,678	2,655	2,724	3,047	1.9	1.9	1.8
Indonesia......................	1,260	2,009	2,766	2,622	2,355	2,370	3,646	1.5	1.6	2.1
Malaysia.......................	1,650	1,197	1,047	1,093	1,045	1,089	967	1.9	0.7	0.6
Mexico.........................	14,291	22,188	25,915	27,504	30,216	32,919	37,951	16.7	22.5	22.3
New Zealand [1].................	1,686	2,899	2,610	2,588	2,374	2,623	3,055	2.0	1.8	1.8
Peru...........................	976	1,681	1,988	2,233	2,582	2,849	3,055	1.1	1.9	1.8
Philippines.....................	904	1,162	1,260	1,150	949	972	1,266	1.1	0.7	0.7
Thailand........................	1,435	2,035	2,131	2,390	2,532	2,754	2,843	1.7	1.9	1.7
Vietnam........................	915	1,801	2,346	2,280	1,970	2,108	2,423	1.1	1.4	1.4
Rest of world...................	9,742	14,205	15,284	18,546	19,195	19,910	22,968	11.4	13.6	13.5

[1] Data is a summarization of component countries. [2] For consistency, data for all years are shown on the basis of 27 countries in the European Union; see footnote 3, Table 1387.

Source: U.S. Department of Agriculture, Foreign Agricultural Service, "Global Agricultural Trade System," <apps.fas.usda.gov/gats/>, accessed April 2022.

Table 897. Selected Farm Products—U.S. and World Production and Exports: 2010 to 2021

[315.6 represents 315,600,000. Metric ton = 1.102 short tons or .984 long tons]

Commodity	Unit	Quantity						United States as percent of world		
		United States			World					
		2010	2020	2021	2010	2020	2021	2010	2020	2021
PRODUCTION [1]										
Corn for grain............	Mil. metric tons	315.6	358.4	383.9	849.4	1,129.4	1,218.8	37.2	31.7	31.5
Cotton....................	Million bales [2]	18.1	14.6	17.5	117.2	111.4	116.0	15.4	13.1	15.1
Soybeans.................	Mil. metric tons	90.7	114.7	120.7	264.8	368.4	352.7	34.2	31.1	34.2
Rice, milled..............	Mil. metric tons	7.6	7.2	6.1	451.4	509.3	513.7	1.7	1.4	1.2
Wheat...................	Mil. metric tons	58.9	49.8	44.8	650.6	774.3	779.2	9.0	6.4	5.7
EXPORTS [3]										
Corn.....................	Mil. metric tons	46.5	69.8	62.2	91.6	182.6	200.4	50.8	38.2	31.0
Cotton...................	Million bales [2]	14.4	16.4	14.7	34.9	48.5	43.3	41.2	33.7	33.8
Soybeans.................	Mil. metric tons	41.0	61.7	58.8	91.6	164.7	153.3	44.7	37.4	38.4
Rice, milled basis.........	Mil. metric tons	3.5	3.0	2.7	35.2	50.9	54.6	10.0	5.8	4.9
Wheat [4].................	Mil. metric tons	35.1	27.0	21.8	133.0	203.4	202.7	26.4	13.3	10.7

[1] Production years vary by commodity. In most cases, includes harvests from July 1 of the year shown through June 30 of the following year. [2] Bales of 480 lb. net weight. [3] Data are for local marketing year beginning in year shown. See source for more information. [4] Includes wheat flour on a grain equivalent.

Source: U.S. Department of Agriculture, Foreign Agricultural Service, "Production, Supply and Distribution Online," <apps.fas.usda.gov/psdonline>, accessed August 2022.

Table 898. Percent of U.S. Agricultural Commodity Output Exported: 2010 to 2020

[In percent. All export shares are estimated from export and production values]

Commodity group	2010	2013	2014	2015	2016	2017	2018	2019	2020
Total agriculture......................	**19.5**	**21.1**	**21.1**	**19.7**	**20.2**	**20.7**	**20.5**	**19.8**	**21.0**
Total food and beverages...........	**18.7**	**20.2**	**20.3**	**19.0**	**19.4**	**19.7**	**19.4**	**18.8**	**20.1**
Animal foods [1].....................	9.6	11.2	10.5	9.1	9.6	10.2	10.2	10.3	10.7
Plant foods [2].......................	28.3	28.8	31.5	29.8	29.7	30.3	29.6	28.4	30.9
Non-manufactured products........	**23.3**	**21.1**	**22.2**	**21.5**	**23.8**	**23.2**	**22.4**	**21.9**	**25.5**
Crops.............................	34.5	31.6	36.0	35.5	36.4	36.4	35.2	34.7	38.9
Food grains......................	63.6	73.3	60.3	62.1	63.3	69.5	58.4	70.4	69.5
Feed grains......................	20.8	11.7	20.5	20.9	22.7	21.6	25.6	16.7	21.5
Oilseeds.........................	52.5	47.6	57.9	55.2	54.0	54.0	45.1	53.7	60.0
Vegetables and melons...........	16.4	16.8	17.5	15.8	17.2	16.6	17.4	18.3	18.8
Fruits and tree nuts..............	38.2	41.5	39.6	45.1	41.4	42.7	44.6	45.9	44.7
Sweeteners......................	6.5	5.9	6.5	5.2	3.9	4.6	4.8	3.7	4.4
Livestock...........................	0.8	0.8	0.6	0.5	0.6	0.7	0.8	0.7	0.8
Manufactured products..............	**19.4**	**25.1**	**25.0**	**22.2**	**20.4**	**21.9**	**21.8**	**20.9**	**20.7**
Grain & oilseed milling products.....	45.4	59.0	59.6	54.7	49.8	60.5	60.1	52.4	59.4
Sugar & confections...............	14.0	19.6	20.7	18.7	17.9	18.2	18.4	17.0	14.9
Preserved fruit & vegetables........	17.1	19.4	20.4	19.1	18.8	18.7	17.5	17.7	15.6
Dairy products....................	12.3	22.7	23.1	17.0	14.3	15.5	14.9	15.2	15.8
Meat products....................	31.9	40.0	40.6	33.1	30.8	33.3	32.6	32.7	30.8
Bakery products..................	4.3	5.8	5.7	5.3	4.9	5.1	5.4	5.4	5.2
Other foods......................	14.9	20.0	18.5	18.7	18.2	17.0	17.8	17.4	16.7
Beverages.......................	13.7	18.0	17.7	17.3	15.1	18.4	17.9	16.1	16.8

[1] Animal products include red meats, poultry meat and eggs, and dairy products. [2] Plant or crop food products include food grains, vegetable oils, fruits, nuts, vegetables, sweeteners (sugarcane, sugar beets, honey), tropical products (coffee, cocoa, spices), grain and oilseed milling products, sugar and confections, and bakery products.

Source: U.S. Department of Agriculture, Economic Research Service, "U.S. Agricultural Trade," <www.ers.usda.gov/topics/international-markets-trade/us-agricultural-trade/>, accessed May 2022.

Table 899. Top 10 U.S. Export Markets for Soybeans, Corn, Wheat, and Poultry: 2021

[In thousands of metric tons (52,875 represents 52,875,000). Commodity and commodity grouping definitions used are the Foreign Agricultural Trade of the United States (FATUS) commodity code groupings. In January 2021, the U.S. Department of Agriculture adopted the World Trade Organization (WTO) definitions of agricultural products; data reflect the new definitions. See source for details]

Country	Soybeans	Country	Corn	Country	Wheat [1]	Country	Poultry meat
World, total.......	**52,875**	**World, total**.......	**69,198**	**World, total**.......	**23,913**	**World, total**.......	**3,623**
China............	27,372	China..............	18,681	Mexico.............	4,153	Mexico.............	900
Mexico.............	4,856	Mexico.............	16,840	Philippines.........	2,868	Cuba..............	311
Egypt.............	2,837	Japan.............	11,578	China.............	2,692	China.............	179
Japan.............	2,386	Colombia..........	4,188	Japan.............	2,231	Taiwan............	163
Indonesia..........	2,038	Korea, South........	3,229	Korea, South........	1,733	Canada............	158
Germany...........	1,733	Canada............	2,908	Nigeria............	1,671	Philippines........	154
Taiwan............	1,405	Taiwan............	1,515	Taiwan............	955	Angola............	141
Spain.............	1,064	Guatemala..........	1,310	Colombia..........	657	Guatemala..........	140
Thailand...........	914	Honduras...........	785	Thailand...........	627	Haiti..............	98
Bangladesh........	904	Costa Rica.........	782	Yemen............	521	Vietnam...........	97
Rest of world.......	7,366	Rest of world........	7,381	Rest of world.......	5,804	Rest of world.......	1,281

[1] Unmilled.

Source: U.S. Department of Agriculture, Foreign Agricultural Service, "Global Agricultural Trade System," <apps.fas.usda.gov/gats/>, accessed August 2022.

Table 900. Agricultural Exports—Value by Principal Commodity: 2000 to 2021

[In millions of dollars (55,916 represents $55,916,000,000). Includes Puerto Rico, U.S. territories, and shipments under foreign aid programs. Commodity and commodity grouping definitions used are the Foreign Agricultural Trade of the United States (FATUS) commodity code groupings. In January 2021, the U.S. Department of Agriculture adopted the World Trade Organization (WTO) definitions of agricultural products and revised historical data to reflect the new definitions. See source for details]

Commodity	Value (mil. dol.)							Percent distribution		
	2000	2005	2010	2015	2019	2020	2021	2010	2020	2021
Total agricultural exports......	55,916	65,550	118,719	137,216	141,082	149,675	176,542	100.0	100.0	100.0
Animals and animal products [1]....	11,679	12,268	22,501	26,901	30,309	30,949	37,709	19.0	20.7	21.4
Red meat and meat products.....	5,276	4,299	9,336	12,407	15,739	16,098	19,615	7.9	10.8	11.1
Poultry and poultry products......	2,235	3,139	4,806	4,915	5,172	5,109	6,287	4.0	3.4	3.6
Grains and feeds [1]..................	13,620	16,364	29,224	31,277	28,974	31,733	44,369	24.6	21.2	25.1
Wheat and products..............	3,578	4,520	7,061	5,977	6,527	6,612	7,556	5.9	4.4	4.3
Corn.............................	4,469	4,789	9,792	8,271	7,671	9,246	18,629	8.2	6.2	10.6
Fruits and preparations...........	2,743	3,468	5,262	6,285	5,970	5,832	6,135	4.4	3.9	3.5
Nuts and preparations.............	1,322	2,992	4,795	9,058	9,699	8,983	9,455	4.0	6.0	5.4
Vegetables and preparations [2].....	3,112	3,571	5,375	6,995	7,189	6,853	7,310	4.5	4.6	4.1
Oilseeds and products [1]...........	8,675	10,366	27,511	28,694	27,810	35,498	38,892	23.2	23.7	22.0
Soybeans.......................	5,258	6,274	18,611	18,862	18,694	25,516	27,395	15.7	17.0	15.5
Vegetable oils and waxes........	1,324	1,754	4,039	3,341	2,978	3,283	3,830	3.4	2.2	2.2
Tobacco, unmanufactured.........	1,204	990	1,168	1,109	732	666	827	1.0	0.4	0.5
Cotton, excluding linters...........	1,873	3,921	5,734	3,889	6,140	5,949	5,684	4.8	4.0	3.2
Other.............................	11,688	11,610	17,149	23,009	24,258	23,213	26,161	14.4	15.5	14.8

[1] Includes commodities not shown separately. [2] Includes pulses (legumes).

Source: U.S. Department of Agriculture, Foreign Agricultural Service, "Global Agricultural Trade System," <apps.fas.usda.gov/gats/>, accessed August 2022.

Table 901. Agricultural Exports—Value by World Region and Selected Country of Destination: 2000 to 2021

[55,916 represents $55,916,000,000. Includes Puerto Rico, U.S. territories, and shipments under foreign aid programs. In January 2021, the U.S. Department of Agriculture adopted the World Trade Organization (WTO) definitions of agricultural products and revised historical data to reflect the new definitions. Therefore, data here may not be comparable to data presented in previous editions. See source for details]

Country	Value (mil. dol.)							Percent distribution		
	2000	2005	2010	2015	2019	2020	2021	2010	2020	2021
Total agricultural exports [1]....	55,916	65,550	118,719	137,216	141,082	149,675	176,542	100.0	100.0	100.0
Canada.............................	7,822	10,884	17,687	22,153	21,944	22,278	25,314	14.9	14.9	14.3
Mexico..............................	6,468	9,486	14,700	17,899	19,399	18,343	25,451	12.4	12.3	14.4
Caribbean..........................	1,442	1,964	3,248	3,451	3,817	3,644	4,407	2.7	2.4	2.5
Central America....................	1,133	1,635	2,949	3,805	4,362	4,334	5,921	2.5	2.9	3.4
South America.....................	1,747	1,958	4,292	6,672	7,042	7,106	7,972	3.6	4.7	4.5
Asia, excluding Middle East [2]......	22,398	23,666	50,383	57,474	58,377	68,920	80,387	42.4	46.0	45.5
China [3]............................	1,726	5,244	17,555	20,362	13,853	26,406	32,777	14.8	17.6	18.6
Indonesia..........................	667	953	2,243	2,190	2,859	2,821	2,908	1.9	1.9	1.6
Japan..............................	11,471	8,975	12,238	11,553	12,000	11,729	14,199	10.3	7.8	8.0
Korea, South......................	2,661	2,242	5,333	6,185	7,742	7,593	9,320	4.5	5.1	5.3
Taiwan.............................	2,067	2,326	3,211	3,169	3,573	3,260	3,831	2.7	2.2	2.2
Europe [2]...........................	8,573	8,752	12,218	14,981	14,370	13,792	14,673	10.3	9.2	8.3
European Union [4].................	6,221	6,142	8,208	10,999	10,788	10,383	10,967	6.9	6.9	6.2
Russia.............................	633	982	1,141	433	201	208	241	1.0	0.1	0.1
Middle East........................	3,060	3,120	6,124	5,714	5,935	5,149	5,693	5.2	3.4	3.2
Africa [2]............................	2,374	2,805	5,766	3,604	4,289	4,592	5,477	4.9	3.1	3.1
Egypt..............................	1,066	819	2,097	1,052	1,556	1,936	2,073	1.8	1.3	1.2
Oceania............................	580	851	1,563	2,162	2,285	2,201	2,099	1.3	1.5	1.2

[1] Totals include transshipments through Canada, but transshipments are not distributed by country after 2000. [2] Includes areas not shown separately. [3] China includes Macao; however, Hong Kong remains separate economically until 2050 and is not included. [4] For consistency, data for all years are shown on the basis of the 27 countries currently in the European Union.

Source: U.S. Department of Agriculture, Foreign Agricultural Service, "Global Agricultural Trade System," <apps.fas.usda.gov/gats/>, accessed August 2022.

Table 902. Cropland Used for Crops and Acres Harvested: 2000 to 2020

[In millions of acres, except as indicated (341 represents 341,000,000)]

Item	2000	2010	2014	2015	2016	2017	2018	2019	2020 (P)
Cropland used for crops..................	345	335	341	337	336	334	338	323	329
Cropland harvested [1]...........................	314	315	318	316	317	313	311	297	304
Crop failure.....................................	11	5	10	7	7	9	11	10	10
Cultivated summer fallow.....................	20	14	14	13	12	12	16	15	15
Cropland idled by all federal programs [2,3]	31	31	25	24	24	23	23	22	(NA)
Acres of crops harvested [4].................	325	322	325	323	323	319	317	303	309

P Preliminary. [1] Land supporting one or more harvested crops. [2] Includes only the Conservation Reserve Program; all other federal acreage reduction programs were eliminated by the Federal Agricultural Improvement Act of 1996. [3] Data are for fiscal years. [4] Area in principal crops harvested plus acreages in fruits, vegetables for sale, tree nuts, and other minor crops. Acres are counted twice for land that is double cropped.

Source: U.S. Department of Agriculture, Economic Research Service, *Agricultural Resources and Environmental Indicators*, 2006, and earlier reports; "Major Land Uses," <ers.usda.gov/data-products/major-land-uses.aspx>, accessed September 2022; and Farm Service Agency, "CRP Enrollment and Rental Payments by State, 1986-2019," <fsa.usda.gov/programs-and-services/conservation-programs/reports-and-statistics/index>, accessed September 2022.

Table 903. Cotton, Hay, and Potatoes—Acreage and Production: 2000 to 2021

[13.1 represents 13,100,000. Calendar year except as indicated. Marketing year begins January 1 for potatoes, May 1 for hay, and August 1 for cotton. Acreage, production, and yield of all crops are periodically revised on basis of census data]

Item	Unit	2000	2005	2010	2015	2019	2020	2021
COTTON								
Acreage harvested...............	Million	13.1	13.8	10.7	8.1	11.5	8.2	10.3
Yield per acre......................	Pounds	632	831	812	766	831	853	819
Production.........................	Mil. bales [2]	17.2	23.9	18.1	12.9	19.9	14.6	17.5
Price per unit [1]...................	Cents/lb.	51.6	49.7	84.6	64.5	62.3	68.9	88.2
Value of production..............	Mil. dol.	4,260	5,695	7,347	3,989	5,865	4,829	7,460
HAY								
Acreage harvested...............	Million	60.4	61.6	59.6	54.5	52.4	52.2	50.7
Yield per acre......................	Tons	2.5	2.4	2.4	2.5	2.5	2.4	2.4
Production.........................	Mil. tons	154	150	145	135	129	127	120
Price per unit [3, 4]................	Dol./ton	84.6	98.2	114.0	145.0	163.0	156.0	193.0
Value of production..............	Mil. dol.	11,557	12,534	14,607	16,568	18,040	17,552	19,277
POTATOES								
Acreage harvested...............	Million [5]	1.3	1.1	1.0	1.1	0.9	0.9	0.9
Yield per acre......................	Cwt. [5]	381	390	401	419	453	461	438
Production.........................	Mil. cwt. [5]	514	424	405	449	424	420	410
Price per unit [1]...................	Dol./cwt. [5]	5.08	7.04	9.20	8.79	9.94	9.3	9.92
Value of production..............	Mil. dol.	2,590	2,982	3,725	3,942	4,217	3,907	4,065

[1] Marketing year average price. U.S. prices are computed by weighting U.S. monthly prices by estimated monthly marketings and do not include an allowance for outstanding loans and government purchases and payments. [2] Bales of 480 pounds, net weight. [3] Prices are for hay sold baled. [4] Season average prices received by farmers. U.S. prices are computed by weighting state prices by estimated sales. [5] Cwt = hundredweight (100 pounds).

Source: U.S. Department of Agriculture, National Agricultural Statistics Service, "Quick Stats," <quickstats.nass.usda.gov>, accessed August 2022.

Table 904. Horticultural Specialty Crop Operations, Value of Sales, and Total Land Area Used to Grow Horticultural Crops: 2019

[In units as indicated (13,778,944 represents $13,778,944,000). Horticultural specialty operation is defined as any place that produced and sold $10,000 or more of horticultural specialty products. Excludes mushrooms as well as grass seeds, vegetables, and fruits grown in the open. See source for more information]

Item	Operations	Value of sales ($1,000)	Greenhouses (1,000 square feet)	Shade structures (1,000 square feet)	Natural shade (acres)	Area in open (acres) [2]
			Total land area [1]			
Horticultural specialty crops, total.....................	**20,655**	**13,778,944**	**884,816**	**391,987**	**6,729**	**549,063**
Annual bedding/garden plants.............................	6,687	2,244,460	251,202	18,304	425	13,822
Herbaceous perennial plants, potted.....................	5,108	922,616	33,699	6,461	255	5,177
Potted flowering plants for indoor or patio use...........	3,977	1,200,387	65,746	23,107	148	2,102
Foliage plants for indoor or patio use....................	2,336	691,472	43,171	85,422	67	2,261
Cut flowers..	2,035	385,668	37,529	8,414	178	20,798
Cut cultivated greens.....................................	644	99,984	3,411	151,479	1,564	4,008
Nursery stock sold..	6,458	4,545,276	247,458	82,982	3,552	367,290
Propagative material......................................	1,038	720,448	29,307	3,760	135	20,858
Sod, sprigs, or plugs......................................	1,068	1,271,561	(D)	(D)	(D)	(D)
Dried bulbs, corms, rhizomes, and tubers.................	263	60,072	791	(D)	9	6,446
Food crops grown under protection.......................	2,994	703,469	79,046	2,997	56	10,247
Transplants for commercial vegetable production [3].....	491	369,864	26,117	(D)	0	5,011
Vegetable seeds..	335	127,198	1,461	(D)	(D)	42,523
Flower seeds..	166	43,927	(D)	21	0	6,409
Aquatic plants..	238	25,034	976	94	12	(D)
Cultivated Christmas trees................................	2,857	357,190	414	163	(D)	13,141
Short rotation woody crops................................	18	5,090	(NA)	(NA)	(NA)	(NA)
Tobacco transplants [4]...................................	99	5,228	(NA)	(NA)	(NA)	(NA)

D Withheld to avoid disclosure. NA Not available. [1] Total land area represents the land utilized on the operation for horticultural production. [2] Excludes acres in production for Christmas trees or sod, sprigs, or plugs. [3] Includes strawberries. [4] Includes transplants grown for sale; excludes transplants for the farmer's own use.

Source: U.S. Department of Agriculture, National Agricultural Statistics Service, *2019 Census of Horticultural Specialties,* Vol. 3, December 2020. See also <www.agcensus.usda.gov/Publications/Census_of_Horticulture_Specialties/>.

Table 905. Corn—Acreage, Production, and Value by Leading State: 2019 to 2021

[81,337 represents 81,337,000. One bushel of corn (bu.) = 56 pounds. State value of production is computed by multiplying the state price by its production; acreage harvested and production value for the United States is the sum of state values]

State	Acreage harvested (1,000 acres)			Yield per acre (bu.)			Production (mil. bu.)			Price per unit ($/bu.)			Value of production (mil. dol.)		
	2019	2020	2021	2019	2020	2021	2019	2020	2021	2019	2020	2021	2019	2020	2021
U.S. [1]....	81,337	82,313	85,388	168	171	177	13,620	14,111	15,115	3.56	4.53	5.45	48,941	64,314	82,579
IA.........	13,050	12,900	12,450	198	177	205	2,584	2,283	2,552	3.50	4.64	5.45	9,044	10,595	13,910
IL.........	10,200	11,100	10,850	181	191	202	1,846	2,120	2,192	3.55	4.46	5.40	6,554	9,456	11,835
NE.........	9,810	9,890	9,560	182	180	194	1,785	1,780	1,855	3.52	4.47	5.40	6,285	7,957	10,015
MN.........	7,250	7,510	7,840	173	191	178	1,254	1,434	1,396	3.26	4.52	5.35	4,089	6,484	7,466
IN.........	4,820	5,250	5,270	169	187	195	815	982	1,028	3.84	4.65	5.45	3,128	4,565	5,601
KS.........	6,020	5,720	5,400	133	134	139	801	766	751	3.56	4.35	5.55	2,850	3,334	4,166
SD.........	3,870	4,450	5,480	144	162	135	557	721	740	3.32	4.37	5.60	1,850	3,150	4,143
OH.........	2,570	3,300	3,340	164	171	193	421	564	645	3.91	4.69	5.45	1,648	2,647	3,513
MO.........	2,990	3,280	3,430	155	171	160	463	561	549	3.67	4.59	5.50	1,701	2,574	3,018
WI.........	2,670	2,930	3,040	166	173	180	443	507	547	3.43	4.44	5.20	1,520	2,251	2,845
ND.........	3,130	1,780	3,630	131	139	105	410	247	381	3.07	4.44	5.30	1,259	1,099	2,020
MI.........	1,610	1,990	1,990	147	153	174	237	304	346	3.73	4.72	5.35	883	1,437	1,852
KY.........	1,450	1,360	1,440	169	184	192	245	250	276	3.92	4.52	5.35	961	1,131	1,479
TX.........	2,150	1,810	1,850	133	128	128	286	232	237	4.20	4.52	6.00	1,201	1,047	1,421
PA.........	1,060	1,000	990	153	138	169	162	138	167	4.13	5.51	6.05	670	760	1,012
TN.........	910	815	960	177	170	170	161	139	163	3.78	4.70	5.45	609	651	889
CO.........	1,300	1,060	1,150	123	116	129	160	123	148	3.68	4.62	5.70	588	568	846
AR.........	735	605	830	175	184	184	129	111	153	3.86	4.49	5.40	496	500	825
NC.........	930	940	905	111	113	149	103	106	135	4.41	4.70	5.95	455	499	802
MS.........	620	490	700	174	180	181	108	88	127	3.86	4.03	5.25	416	355	665

[1] Includes other states, not shown separately.

Source: U.S. Department of Agriculture, National Agricultural Statistics Service, "Quick Stats," <quickstats.nass.usda.gov/>, accessed March 2022.

Table 906. Soybeans—Acreage, Production, and Value by Leading State: 2019 to 2021

[74,939 represents 74,939,000. One bushel of soybeans (bu.) = 60 pounds. State value of production is computed by multiplying the state price by its production; value for the United States is the sum of state values]

State	Acreage harvested (1,000 acres)			Yield per acre (bu.)			Production (mil. bu.)			Price per unit ($/bu.)			Value of production (mil. dol.)		
	2019	2020	2021	2019	2020	2021	2019	2020	2021	2019	2020	2021	2019	2020	2021
U.S. [1]...	74,939	82,603	86,332	47	51	51	3,552	4,216	4,435	8.57	10.80	13.00	30,526	45,732	57,479
IL.........	9,860	10,250	10,510	54	60	64	532	615	673	8.84	10.90	13.20	4,707	6,704	8,879
IA.........	9,120	9,370	10,030	55	54	62	502	506	622	8.48	11.10	13.00	4,254	5,616	8,084
MN.........	6,770	7,380	7,580	44	50	47	298	369	356	8.29	11.00	13.10	2,469	4,059	4,667
NE.........	4,840	5,160	5,570	59	58	63	283	299	351	8.27	10.20	12.60	2,342	3,053	4,421
IN.........	5,360	5,730	5,640	51	59	60	273	338	336	8.92	11.10	13.10	2,438	3,753	4,396
MO.........	5,010	5,810	5,650	46	51	49	230	296	277	8.75	11.10	13.30	2,017	3,289	3,682
OH.........	4,270	4,920	4,880	49	55	57	209	271	276	9.04	11.30	13.10	1,891	3,058	3,612
SD.........	3,440	4,920	5,390	43	46	40	146	226	216	8.22	10.30	12.90	1,202	2,331	2,781
KS.........	4,490	4,750	4,800	42	41	40	186	195	190	8.28	10.70	12.60	1,543	2,084	2,389
ND.........	5,400	5,700	7,120	32	34	26	170	194	182	7.93	10.20	12.80	1,349	1,977	2,324
AR.........	2,610	2,800	3,010	49	52	51	128	144	154	8.87	10.50	12.70	1,134	1,514	1,950
MS.........	1,630	2,060	2,180	50	54	54	82	111	118	8.80	10.20	12.70	717	1,135	1,495
MI.........	1,720	2,190	2,140	41	48	51	70	105	109	8.81	11.70	13.40	614	1,230	1,462
WI.........	1,690	1,990	2,070	47	52	55	79	103	114	8.42	10.40	12.60	669	1,076	1,435
KY.........	1,690	1,840	1,840	46	55	56	78	101	103	8.98	10.80	13.00	698	1,093	1,340

[1] Includes other states, not shown separately.

Source: U.S. Department of Agriculture, National Agricultural Statistics Service, "Quick Stats," <quickstats.nass.usda.gov/>, accessed March 2022.

Table 907. Wheat—Acreage, Production, and Value by Leading State: 2019 to 2021

[37,394 represents 37,394,000. One bushel of wheat (bu.) = 60 pounds. State value of production is computed by multiplying the price per unit by total production, for each state; value for the United States is the sum of production values for all states]

State	Acreage harvested (1,000 acres)			Yield per acre (bu.)			Production (mil. bu.)			Price per unit ($/bu.)			Value of production (mil. dol.)		
	2019	2020	2021	2019	2020	2021	2019	2020	2021	2019	2020	2021	2019	2020	2021
U.S. [1]......	37,394	36,789	37,163	52	50	44	1,932	1,828	1,646	4.58	5.05	7.30	8,923	9,386	11,915
KS.........	6,700	6,250	7,000	52	45	52	348	281	364	4.08	4.53	6.55	1,421	1,274	2,384
ND.........	6,630	6,563	6,090	48	48	32	321	313	196	4.47	5.22	9.15	1,436	1,632	1,795
MT.........	5,135	5,490	4,545	42	42	22	218	229	101	4.69	5.24	8.40	1,021	1,198	847
WA.........	2,215	2,295	2,230	65	72	39	143	166	87	5.53	5.70	8.50	792	948	741
OK.........	2,750	2,600	2,950	40	40	39	110	104	115	4.31	4.55	6.40	474	473	736
ID.........	1,125	1,164	1,132	88	97	68	99	113	77	5.03	5.11	6.85	497	575	524
MN.........	1,400	1,360	1,160	57	53	48	80	72	56	4.57	5.20	8.65	365	375	482
TX.........	2,100	2,050	2,000	34	30	37	71	62	74	4.44	5.12	6.50	317	315	481
CO.........	2,000	1,520	1,880	49	27	37	98	41	70	4.01	4.62	6.70	393	190	466
SD.........	1,360	1,355	1,310	48	52	34	65	70	44	4.53	5.04	7.95	296	354	354

[1] Includes other states, not shown separately.

Source: U.S. Department of Agriculture, National Agricultural Statistics Service, "Quick Stats," <quickstats.nass.usda.gov/>, accessed March 2022.

Table 908. Commercial Vegetable and Other Specified Crops—Area, Production, and Value: 2019 to 2021

[7 represents 7,000. Except as noted, relates to commercial production for fresh market and processing combined. Includes market garden areas but excludes minor producing acreage in minor producing states. Value is for season or crop year and should not be confused with calendar-year income. Hundredweight (cwt.) is the unit used for fresh market yield and production and is equal to one hundred pounds]

Crop	Area harvested (1,000 acres)			Utilized production [1] (1,000 cwt.)			Value of production [2] (mil. dol.)		
	2019	2020	2021	2019	2020	2021	2019	2020	2021
Artichokes	7	5	5	956	759	833	75	64	57
Asparagus	20	18	17	725	618	599	98	78	70
Beans, snap	184	175	173	16,103	14,283	15,088	298	261	276
Broccoli	105	100	106	16,594	15,760	13,785	851	875	719
Cabbage	60	58	57	22,152	23,512	21,088	511	452	457
Cantaloupes	48	37	37	11,295	11,218	10,562	238	292	278
Carrots	72	69	71	33,297	30,730	31,555	767	827	831
Cauliflower	45	43	45	10,067	9,000	8,205	460	351	343
Celery	28	29	28	15,720	16,112	15,275	475	359	375
Corn, sweet	391	373	357	62,498	60,267	57,406	652	743	775
Fresh market	(NA)	(NA)	(NA)	16,773	13,850	14,218	479	572	582
Processed	(NA)	(NA)	(NA)	45,726	46,417	43,188	173	171	193
Cucumbers	101	92	91	14,738	12,294	14,342	278	225	261
Lettuce, head	116	106	104	42,008	38,388	35,117	1,427	1,216	965
Lettuce, leaf	57	62	61	12,467	15,636	12,474	650	1,092	655
Lettuce, Romaine	88	94	94	27,212	30,287	27,232	881	1,480	1,059
Onions	129	131	137	68,646	72,228	67,747	1,002	958	1,037
Peas, green	128	127	130	5,033	5,241	4,534	68	74	71
Peppers, bell	37	34	31	11,550	10,540	9,970	540	599	462
Pumpkins	61	63	70	13,221	13,026	16,469	180	183	233
Spinach	65	58	54	9,466	7,164	6,936	614	553	496
Squash	44	44	42	6,954	6,579	6,848	222	242	216
Tomatoes	274	273	270	237,940	239,327	228,663	1,600	1,616	1,506
Fresh market	(NA)	(NA)	(NA)	14,215	13,081	13,165	705	756	600
Processed	(NA)	(NA)	(NA)	223,725	226,245	215,498	895	860	905
Watermelons	99	95	99	35,792	34,393	33,703	545	578	534

NA Not available. [1] Utilized production is the amount of a crop sold plus the quantities used at home or held in storage. It is equal to the difference between the total production and what was harvested but not sold. [2] Fresh market vegetables valued at f.o.b. (free on board) shipping point. Processing vegetables are equivalent returns at packinghouse door.

Source: U.S. Department of Agriculture, National Agricultural Statistics Service, "Quick Stats," <quickstats.nass.usda.gov/>, accessed April 2022.

Table 909. Fruits and Nuts: Utilized Production and Value, 2010 to 2021; and Leading Producing States, 2021

[4,603 represents 4,603,000]

Fruits and nuts	Utilized production [1] (1,000 tons)				Value of utilized production (mil. dol.)				Leading states in order of production, 2021
	2010	2015	2020	2021	2010	2015	2020	2021	
NONCITRUS FRUITS									
Apples [2]	4,603	4,983	4,966	4,779	2,311	3,366	2,937	3,033	WA, NY, MI
Avocados	174	229	206	150	479	433	427	342	CA, FL, HI
Blueberries	247	330	342	383	644	873	932	1,100	WA, OR, ME
Cherries, sweet	308	334	319	372	716	751	906	866	WA, CA, OR
Cranberries	340	423	389	349	299	262	287	272	WI, MA, NJ
Dates	29	39	62	59	37	61	190	229	CA, AZ
Grapes	7,430	7,621	6,040	6,050	4,024	5,914	4,791	5,531	CA, WA
Kiwifruit (CA)	33	21	40	40	25	31	76	96	CA
Nectarines	233	173	120	116	129	158	121	135	CA
Olives (CA)	206	179	67	100	137	160	58	85	CA
Peaches	1,130	825	637	662	617	606	580	624	CA, SC, GA
Pears	813	803	654	698	387	494	333	373	WA, OR, CA
Plums (CA)	142	105	97	81	79	105	115	92	CA
Prunes (dried basis) (CA)	390	319	171	213	176	226	110	142	CA
Raspberries	75	145	111	89	259	670	453	531	CA, WA
Strawberries	1,426	1,533	1,331	1,333	2,261	2,239	2,609	3,422	CA, FL
CITRUS FRUITS									
Grapefruit	1,238	910	570	426	291	216	199	220	FL, CA, TX
Lemons	882	904	1,084	884	395	697	665	661	CA, AZ
Oranges	8,243	6,353	5,254	4,426	1,997	1,963	1,712	1,593	FL, CA, TX
Tangerines and mandarins	596	863	944	1,166	275	468	821	837	CA, FL
NUTS [3]									
Almonds (CA)	1,414	1,630	2,585	2,413	2,903	5,869	5,251	5,028	CA
Hazelnuts (OR)	28	31	62	78	67	87	130	167	OR
Macadamia nuts (HI)	20	24	20	26	30	46	50	63	HI
Pecans	147	127	152	128	675	560	433	551	GA, NM, AZ
Pistachios (CA)	261	135	523	578	1,159	888	2,623	2,911	CA
Walnuts (CA)	504	606	790	725	1,028	1,012	948	1,022	CA

[1] Excludes quantities not harvested or not marketed. Utilized production is the amount sold plus the quantities used at home or held in storage. [2] Production in commercial orchards with 100 or more bearing-age trees. [3] In-shell equivalent.

Source: U.S. Department of Agriculture, National Agricultural Statistics Service, *Noncitrus Fruits and Nuts Final Estimates 2007-2012*, October 2014; *Citrus Fruits Final Estimates, 2008-2012*, August 2014; *Citrus Fruits 2021 Summary*, September 2021; and *Noncitrus Fruits and Nuts 2021 Summary*, May 2022. See also <www.nass.usda.gov/Publications/>.

Table 910. Tree Nuts—Supply and Use: 2000 to 2020

[In thousands of pounds (shelled) (331,466 represents 331,466,000). Season begins in July for hazelnuts, August for almonds, September for pistachios, and October for pecans. For walnuts, season began in August through 2007; as of 2008, season begins September 1]

Year	Beginning stocks	Marketable production [1]	Imports	Supply, total	Consumption	Exports	Ending stocks
Total nuts:							
2000	331,466	1,127,940	293,047	1,752,452	733,765	780,988	237,699
2010	422,055	2,482,242	485,098	3,389,395	1,195,946	1,786,058	407,391
2018	536,089	3,472,403	720,218	4,728,709	1,704,930	2,487,232	536,547
2019	536,547	3,617,415	755,918	4,909,880	1,786,119	2,440,270	683,490
2020, total [2,3]	**683,490**	**4,473,985**	**705,203**	**5,862,679**	**1,875,345**	**3,057,595**	**929,740**
Almonds	450,122	3,044,813	21,625	3,516,560	815,834	2,092,588	608,137
Pecans	103,045	(NA)	137,505	393,230	192,895	116,143	84,192
Pistachios	72,078	524,822	3,097	599,997	197,543	259,817	142,637
Hazelnuts	3,724	49,218	10,539	63,482	29,284	27,032	7,166
Walnuts	54,521	684,508	2,089	741,117	177,693	475,816	87,608

NA Not available. [1] Utilized production minus inedibles and noncommercial usage. [2] Includes macadamia nuts, Brazil nuts, cashew nuts, pine nuts, chestnuts, and mixed nuts, not shown separately. [3] Data are preliminary.

Source: U.S. Department of Agriculture, Economic Research Service, "Fruit and Tree Nut Yearbook Tables," <www.ers.usda.gov/data-products/fruit-and-tree-nut-data/fruit-and-tree-nut-yearbook-tables/>, accessed November 2021.

Table 911. Honey—Bee Colonies, Yield, and Production: 2000 to 2021

[2,622 represents 2,622,000. Includes only beekeepers with five or more colonies. Colonies were not included if honey was not harvested]

Year	Honey-producing colonies [1] (1,000)	Yield per colony (pounds)	Production (1,000 pounds)	Average price per pound (cents)	Value of production (1,000 dollars)
2000	2,622	84.0	220,286	60	132,865
2005	2,409	72.5	174,614	92	160,994
2010	2,692	65.6	176,462	162	285,692
2015	2,661	58.9	156,705	208	325,946
2016	2,780	58.4	162,246	212	343,962
2017	2,684	55.5	149,025	220	327,855
2018	2,828	54.5	154,008	221	340,358
2019	2,812	55.8	156,922	199	312,275
2020	2,706	54.5	147,594	210	309,947
2021	2,696	46.9	126,466	254	321,224

[1] Honey producing colonies are the maximum number of colonies from which honey was taken during the year. It is possible to take honey from colonies which did not survive the entire year.

Source: U.S. Department of Agriculture, National Agricultural Statistics Service, *Honey–Final Estimates 2013-2017*, June 2019, and earlier editions; and *Honey*, March 2022. See also <www.nass.usda.gov/Surveys/Guide_to_NASS_Surveys/Bee_and_Honey>.

Table 912. Vegetables and Dry Edible Beans—Supply and Utilization: 2000 to 2021

[40,556 represents 40,556,000,000. Data for calendar year except where noted. Food availability is a proxy for food consumption. Vegetable data excludes melons]

Item	Unit	2000	2005	2010	2015	2019	2020	2021 (P)
VEGETABLES, FRESH MARKET								
Production	Mil. lbs.	40,556	40,332	38,028	35,983	34,091	33,519	32,262
Imports	Mil. lbs.	5,499	7,783	10,931	13,183	16,006	16,318	17,551
Total supply	Mil. lbs.	47,400	49,606	50,529	50,913	51,800	51,465	51,170
Exports	Mil. lbs.	3,718	3,721	3,388	3,069	3,119	3,010	3,102
Ending stocks [1]	Mil. lbs.	1,266	1,280	1,488	1,685	1,627	1,357	1,509
Domestic availability	Mil. lbs.	41,460	43,864	44,819	45,509	46,680	46,685	46,198
Per capita availability	Lbs.	146.8	148.1	144.9	141.9	142.1	141.4	139.3
VEGETABLES, PROCESSED MARKET [2]								
Production	Mil. lbs.	35,369	33,265	36,570	40,142	33,000	33,019	31,616
Imports	Mil. lbs.	3,581	5,555	6,354	7,192	10,471	11,583	12,405
Total supply	Mil. lbs.	62,174	62,646	71,282	73,264	71,363	69,986	64,881
Exports	Mil. lbs.	4,479	4,889	6,627	10,220	8,748	8,475	8,567
Ending stocks	Mil. lbs.	23,291	20,838	27,999	30,642	25,550	20,860	19,079
Domestic availability	Mil. lbs.	34,404	36,919	36,656	32,402	37,065	40,651	37,235
Per capita availability	Lbs.	121.8	124.6	118.5	101.0	112.8	123.1	112.2
POTATOES, FRESH MARKET								
Utilized production [3]	Mil. lbs.	13,185	12,075	11,342	10,982	10,173	9,991	9,992
Imports	Mil. lbs.	805	788	916	882	909	1,105	1,031
Total supply	Mil. lbs.	13,990	12,863	12,258	11,864	11,083	11,096	11,022
Exports	Mil. lbs.	677	639	856	905	1,204	1,108	1,316
Domestic availability	Mil. lbs.	13,314	12,224	11,402	10,960	9,879	9,988	9,706
Per capita availability	Lbs.	47.1	41.3	36.9	34.2	30.1	30.3	29.3
DRY EDIBLE BEANS								
Production	Mil. lbs.	2,654	2,658	3,180	3,006	2,701	3,675	2,558
Imports	Mil. lbs.	129	225	289	350	314	439	421
Exports	Mil. lbs.	788	564	1,001	947	1,128	1,144	1,031
Domestic availability	Mil. lbs.	2,170	1,813	2,221	2,283	1,972	2,663	2,397
Per capita availability	Lbs.	7.7	6.1	7.2	7.1	6.0	8.1	7.2

P Preliminary. [1] Applies only to brussel sprouts, onions, and okra. [2] Includes vegetables for canning and freezing. Excludes potatoes. [3] Crop year utilization for the past season and the current season distributed on a calendar year basis using National Agricultural Statistics Service potato marketing distributions.

Source: U.S. Department of Agriculture, Economic Research Service, "Vegetable and Pulses Yearbook Datasets," accessed September 2022. See also <www.ers.usda.gov/data-products/vegetables-and-pulses-data.aspx>.

Table 913. Organic Vegetable, Fruit, and Field Crops—Farms, Production, and Value of Sales: 2019

[Unit column indicates quantity harvested and sales. Includes certified organic producers who have been certified by state or private agencies accredited by the USDA. Organic food must be produced without the use of conventional pesticides, petroleum-based or sewage sludge-based fertilizers, herbicides, pesticides, genetic engineering (biotechnology), antibiotics, growth hormones, or irradiation. Land must have no prohibited substances applied to it for at least 3 years before the harvest of an organic crop. Cwt = hundredweight (100 pounds)]

Commodity	Unit	Farms (number)	Acres harvested (number)	Quantity harvested	Sales Quantity	Sales Value of sales (1,000 dollars)
Vegetables, potatoes, and melons [1,2]	(X)	3,300	224,122	(X)	(X)	2,084,302
Beans, snap	Cwt	782	6,513	371,773	371,234	23,930
Broccoli	Cwt	821	11,945	1,608,589	1,602,615	109,438
Cabbage, all	Cwt	970	3,568	762,766	762,467	29,838
Cantaloupes and muskmelons	Cwt	411	427	67,326	67,314	5,567
Carrots	Cwt	961	11,959	3,503,842	3,492,605	131,807
Cauliflower	Cwt	450	7,583	1,118,299	1,117,759	68,289
Celery	Cwt	328	3,786	1,540,323	1,540,323	64,630
Garlic	Cwt	1,047	2,419	152,711	152,711	21,777
Herbs	Pounds	853	2,047	10,469,760	10,468,101	28,933
Lettuce	Cwt	1,129	38,525	6,086,142	6,086,142	400,117
Onions, all	Cwt	964	7,520	3,300,290	3,300,290	112,710
Peas, green	Tons	524	9,397	284,100	283,261	14,719
Peppers, bell	Cwt	926	1,779	376,611	376,474	23,125
Potatoes	Cwt	886	23,612	3,948,714	3,948,684	154,936
Spinach	Cwt	603	23,018	2,015,494	2,015,489	179,498
Squash	Cwt	1,540	7,848	1,178,666	1,178,646	56,557
Sweet corn	Cwt	497	11,059	1,332,976	1,332,976	27,837
Sweet potatoes	Cwt	401	9,130	1,669,935	1,668,563	77,187
Tomatoes	Cwt	1,238	10,751	5,869,683	5,869,677	132,332
Watermelon	Cwt	451	2,159	502,436	502,436	16,108
Apples, all	Pounds	728	27,311	947,894,900	947,498,821	474,703
Grapes, all	Tons	742	37,400	236,644	255,451	332,487
Citrus fruits, all [1]	Tons	622	13,344	127,609	127,521	115,872
Lemons	Tons	299	4,132	46,694	46,694	40,396
Oranges, all	Tons	282	5,931	51,312	51,241	37,426
Other fruits and berries [1]	(X)	2,325	53,279	(X)	(X)	989,638
Avocado	Tons	289	4,047	8,419	8,407	27,587
Peaches	Tons	238	3,237	20,208	20,200	36,411
Pears	Tons	267	3,506	35,367	35,333	26,169
Plums	Tons	177	1,008	4,854	4,854	11,161
Blueberries, cultivated, all	Pounds	539	10,313	77,492,046	77,491,590	205,227
Strawberries	Cwt	580	5,158	1,461,988	1,461,266	320,794
Tree nuts [1]	(X)	430	24,994	(X)	(X)	109,754
Almonds	Pounds	73	5,915	7,146,088	7,144,888	32,976
Walnuts, English	Tons	262	9,210	10,044	10,044	34,893
Field crops [1]	(X)	9,024	2,268,646	(X)	(X)	1,180,235
Barley for grain or seed	Bushels	487	63,839	3,792,565	3,405,339	27,794
Corn for grain or seed	Bushels	3,985	319,953	37,856,835	32,269,911	278,157
Corn for silage or greenchop	Tons	1,466	54,683	930,899	284,421	18,532
Hay, all dry	Tons	5,040	613,124	1,787,757	1,210,531	191,994
Oats for grain or seed	Bushels	1,200	54,147	2,981,264	2,555,539	13,523
Soybeans for beans	Bushels	2,135	170,074	5,757,938	5,404,343	108,999
Wheat, all	Bushels	1,268	450,854	14,192,924	13,969,610	149,113

X Not applicable. [1] Includes commodities not shown separately. [2] Vegetables grown in the open.

Source: U.S. Department of Agriculture, National Agricultural Statistics Service, *2019 Organic Survey*, October 2020. See also <www.nass.usda.gov/Surveys/Guide_to_NASS_Surveys/Organic_Production/index.php>.

Table 914. Organic Livestock and Poultry—Farms, Inventory, and Value of Sales: 2016 and 2019

[Includes all known organic producers that are certified organic. Animals raised on an organic operation must meet animal health and welfare standards, not be fed antibiotics or growth hormones, be fed 100 percent organic feed, and must be provided access to the outdoors]

Type of livestock and poultry	2016 Farms (number)	2016 Inventory [1] (number)	2016 Value of sales (dollars)	2019 Farms (number)	2019 Inventory [1] (number)	2019 Value of sales (dollars)
Milk cows	2,559	267,523	57,801,387	3,134	337,540	71,731,366
Beef cows	490	42,554	10,531,380	533	39,412	9,111,635
Other cattle [2]	3,048	218,268	164,407,528	3,667	280,797	211,796,720
Hogs and pigs	151	14,707	6,891,039	166	15,041	8,105,916
Sheep and lambs	102	9,446	1,199,815	109	8,281	1,175,158
Goats and kids	70	3,609	227,551	59	4,075	113,131
Other livestock [3]	42	(X)	659,340	52	(X)	192,060
Chickens, layers	818	15,475,570	2,462,123	1,057	18,450,112	11,316,343
Chickens, broilers	215	19,437,579	749,929,661	369	23,020,265	1,115,102,146
Turkeys	103	410,711	83,129,395	129	903,160	139,301,405
Other poultry [4]	130	(X)	79,265,683	162	(X)	95,131,213

X Not applicable. [1] As of December 31. [2] Includes organic bulls, beef calves, replacement milk heifers, etc. [3] Includes organic livestock not listed separately on the report form, such as farm raised bison, deer, rabbits, and fish. [4] Includes organic poultry not listed separately on the report form, including ducks, quail, etc.

Source: U.S. Department of Agriculture, National Agricultural Statistics Service, *2019 Organic Survey*, October 2020, and earlier reports. See also <www.nass.usda.gov/Surveys/Guide_to_NASS_Surveys/Organic_Production/index.php>.

Table 915. Meat Supply and Consumption: 2000 to 2021

[In millions of pounds, carcass weight equivalent (82,372 represents 82,372,000,000). Carcass weight equivalent is the weight of the animal minus entrails, head, hide, and internal organs; includes fat and bone. Covers federal and state inspected, and farm slaughtered]

Year and type of meat	Production	Imports	Supply [1]	Exports	Consumption [2]	Ending stocks
RED MEAT AND POULTRY [3]						
2000	82,372	4,144	88,460	9,343	77,073	2,044
2010	91,744	3,459	97,197	13,960	81,123	2,113
2015	94,289	4,875	101,230	14,275	84,593	2,361
2018	102,068	4,473	108,957	16,805	89,733	2,419
2019	104,889	4,421	111,729	17,176	92,048	2,504
2020	106,172	4,713	113,389	18,248	92,866	2,274
2021, preliminary	106,420	5,070	113,765	18,418	93,327	2,021
RED MEATS, TOTAL						
2000	46,299	4,127	51,313	3,760	46,556	996
2010	49,155	3,323	53,592	6,538	45,908	1,145
2015	48,520	4,698	54,408	7,282	45,806	1,320
2018	53,507	4,313	59,065	9,042	48,758	1,266
2019	55,108	4,276	60,650	9,353	49,968	1,330
2020	55,774	4,545	61,648	10,233	50,198	1,217
2021, preliminary	55,906	4,890	62,014	10,470	50,397	1,147
Beef: [4]						
2000	26,888	3,032	30,332	2,468	27,338	525
2010	26,389	2,298	29,251	2,300	26,367	585
2015	23,760	3,368	27,719	2,267	24,769	683
2018	26,938	2,998	30,585	3,160	26,763	662
2019	27,224	3,058	30,944	3,026	27,276	642
2020	27,244	3,339	31,225	2,951	27,559	716
2021, preliminary	28,016	3,346	32,078	3,441	27,962	676
Pork:						
2000	18,952	965	20,378	1,287	18,639	453
2010	22,456	859	23,840	4,223	19,077	541
2015	24,517	1,116	26,191	5,010	20,592	590
2018	26,329	1,042	27,926	5,877	21,490	559
2019	27,652	945	29,156	6,321	22,189	646
2020	28,318	904	29,869	7,279	22,122	467
2021, preliminary	27,690	1,180	29,337	7,026	21,865	446
Veal:						
2000	225	([4])	230	([4])	225	5
2010	143	([4])	152	([4])	148	4
2015	88	([4])	94	([4])	88	6
2018	81	([4])	97	([4])	89	8
2019	79	([4])	87	([4])	81	6
2020	69	([4])	75	([4])	66	9
2021, preliminary	58	([4])	68	([4])	64	4
Lamb and mutton:						
2000	234	130	372	5	354	13
2010	168	166	348	16	317	15
2015	155	214	403	4	357	41
2018	158	273	458	6	415	36
2019	153	272	462	6	422	35
2020	143	302	479	3	451	25
2021, preliminary	143	364	532	3	506	22
POULTRY, TOTAL [3]						
2000	36,073	16	37,147	5,583	30,516	1,048
2010	42,589	136	43,605	7,422	35,215	968
2015	45,768	177	46,822	6,994	38,787	1,041
2018	48,562	160	49,892	7,763	40,976	1,153
2019	49,781	146	51,080	7,824	42,081	1,175
2020	50,398	167	51,740	8,015	42,669	1,057
2021, preliminary	50,514	180	51,751	7,947	42,930	874
Broiler chickens:						
2000	30,209	13	31,017	4,918	25,302	798
2010	36,515	107	37,238	6,762	29,703	773
2015	39,620	131	40,430	6,321	33,278	832
2018	42,145	139	43,140	7,069	35,226	845
2019	43,435	131	44,411	7,103	36,371	937
2020	44,106	145	45,188	7,368	36,989	830
2021, preliminary	44,419	155	45,403	7,355	37,343	705
Other chicken:						
2000	531	2	541	220	312	9
2010	504	4	510	78	428	4
2015	522	2	527	144	375	8
2018	539	2	546	84	456	6
2019	528	2	536	81	449	5
2020	549	2	556	75	477	4
2021, preliminary	537	3	544	44	497	3
Turkeys:						
2000	5,333	1	5,589	445	4,902	241
2010	5,570	25	5,857	581	5,084	192
2015	5,627	45	5,865	529	5,135	201
2018	5,878	19	6,206	611	5,293	303
2019	5,818	12	6,133	639	5,261	233
2020	5,743	21	5,997	571	5,203	223
2021, preliminary	5,558	22	5,804	548	5,090	166

[1] Total supply equals production plus imports plus ending stocks of previous year. [2] Includes shipments to territories. [3] Poultry production is ready-to-cook production; prior to 2001, includes other production (not federally inspected). [4] Veal exports and imports included with beef.

Source: U.S. Department of Agriculture, Economic Research Service, "Livestock and Meat Domestic Data," <ers.usda.gov/data-products/livestock-meat-domestic-data.aspx>, accessed August 2022.

Table 916. Livestock Inventory and Production: 2000 to 2021

[98.2 represents 98,200,000. Production in live weight; includes animals-for-slaughter market, younger animals shipped to other states for feeding or breeding purposes, farm slaughter and custom slaughter consumed on farms where produced, minus livestock shipped into states for feeding or breeding with an adjustment for changes in inventory. Prices are for the marketing year, which for cattle and sheep and lambs starts January 1; for hogs the marketing year starts December 1]

Type of livestock	Unit	2000	2010	2014	2015	2016	2017	2018	2019	2020	2021
ALL CATTLE [1]											
Inventory (number on farms): [2]	Mil.	98.2	94.1	88.2	89.2	91.9	93.6	94.3	94.8	93.8	93.8
Total value	Bil. dol.	67.1	78.3	107.9	141.3	129.6	103.8	108.1	97.7	96.2	97.5
Value per head	Dol.	683	833	1,223	1,584	1,410	1,109	1,146	1,031	1,026	1,039
Production: Quantity	Bil. lb.	43.0	41.4	40.3	41.5	42.7	44.2	45.7	44.6	45.6	45.9
Cattle, price per 100 pounds [3]	Dol.	(NA)	92	152	147	119	120	115	116	109	121
Calves, price per 100 pounds	Dol.	(NA)	117	261	247	158	168	170	159	161	171
Value of production	Bil. dol.	28.5	36.9	60.1	60.1	48.6	50.4	49.1	48.2	45.9	51.9
HOGS AND PIGS											
Inventory (number on farms): [4]	Mil.	59.3	64.7	64.8	67.6	69.0	71.3	73.1	75.1	76.8	77.3
Total value	Bil. dol.	4.3	5.4	8.9	9.7	6.6	6.6	7.2	7.4	8.0	7.7
Value per head	Dol.	72	83	138	144	96	92	99	98	102	100
Production: Quantity	Bil. lb.	25.7	30.3	32.1	34.7	35.9	37.0	38.5	42.2	40.5	40.0
Price per 100 pounds	Dol.	(NA)	54.1	76.5	55.3	49.3	53.1	50.2	51.4	46.9	67.3
Value of production	Bil. dol.	10.8	16.0	24.2	18.8	17.4	19.2	18.8	21.4	18.0	28.9
SHEEP AND LAMBS											
Inventory (number on farms): [2]	Mil.	7.0	5.6	5.2	5.3	5.3	5.3	5.3	5.2	5.2	5.2
Total value	Mil. dol.	669.9	761.1	982.3	1,127.2	1,071.5	1,067.9	1,071.4	1,061.5	1,066.3	1,071.4
Value per head	Dol.	95	135	188	214	202	203	204	203	205	207
Production: Quantity	Mil. lb.	512	405	(NA)	(NA)	(NA)	(NA)	(NA)	(NA)	(NA)	(NA)
Value of production	Mil. dol.	365.2	442.9	(NA)	(NA)	(NA)	(NA)	(NA)	(NA)	(NA)	(NA)

NA Not available. [1] Includes milk cows. [2] As of January 1. [3] Cattle weighing 500 pounds or more. [4] As of December 1 of preceding year.

Source: U.S. Department of Agriculture, National Agricultural Statistics Service, "Quick Stats," <quickstats.nass.usda.gov/>, accessed May 2022. See also *Meat Animals Production, Disposition, and Income Annual Summary*, <www.nass.usda.gov/Publications>.

Table 917. Livestock Operations by Size of Herd: 2000 to 2017

[In thousands (1,076 represents 1,076,000). Prior to 2007, an operation is any place having one or more head on hand at any time during the year. Beginning 2007, operations are any place having one or more head on hand on December 31]

Size of herd	2000	2010	2012	2017	Size of herd	2000	2010	2012	2017
CATTLE [1]					**MILK COWS [2]**				
Total operations	**1,076**	**935**	**913**	**883**	**Total operations**	**105**	**63**	**64**	**55**
1 to 49 head	671	635	637	599	1 to 49 head	53	31	34	28
50 to 99 head	186	129	118	119	50 to 99 head	31	16	15	12
100 to 499 head	192	142	130	136	100 head or more	21	16	14	14
500 to 999 head	19	19	17	18					
1,000 head or more	10	11	11	11	**HOGS AND PIGS**				
					Total operations	**87**	**69**	**63**	**66**
BEEF COWS [2]					1 to 99 head	50	49	47	52
Total operations	**831**	**742**	**728**	**729**	100 to 499 head	17	5	4	3
1 to 49 head	655	588	594	577	500 to 999 head	8	3	2	1
50 to 99 head	100	82	71	80	1,000 to 1,999 head	6	4	3	2
100 to 499 head	71	66	57	66	2,000 to 4,999 head	5	5	5	5
500 head or more	6	6	5	6	5,000 or more	2	3	3	4

[1] Includes calves. [2] Included in operations with cattle.

Source: U.S. Department of Agriculture, National Agricultural Statistics Service, *Livestock Operations Final Estimates 2003–2007*, March 2009; and *Farms, Land in Farms, and Livestock Operations 2012 Summary*, February 2013. Beginning with 2012 data, *Census of Agriculture*, Vol. 1, April 2019, and earlier reports. See also <www.nass.usda.gov/Publications/>.

Table 918. Hogs and Pigs—Number, Production, and Slaughter by Leading State: 2019 to 2021

[76,833 represents 76,833,000. Production in live weight. See headnote, Table 916]

State	Number on farms [1] (1,000)			Quantity produced (mil. lb.)			Value of production (mil. dol.)			Commercial slaughter [2] (mil. lb.)	
	2019	2020	2021	2019	2020	2021	2019	2020	2021	2020	2021
U.S. [3]	**76,833**	**77,312**	**74,446**	**42,197**	**40,500**	**39,973**	**21,354**	**18,048**	**28,873**	**37,962**	**37,117**
IA	24,600	24,600	23,900	14,584	12,928	13,239	7,548	5,926	9,513	11,553	11,262
MN	9,100	9,400	8,900	4,999	4,640	4,600	2,588	2,126	3,315	3,325	3,461
NC	9,300	8,800	8,000	4,502	4,597	4,242	2,101	1,840	3,086	(D)	(D)
IL	5,350	5,450	5,400	2,362	2,887	2,780	1,225	1,323	2,012	3,681	3,374
IN	4,250	4,450	4,350	2,358	2,106	2,207	1,221	962	1,603	2,416	2,452
NE	3,700	3,800	3,650	1,590	1,546	1,549	825	702	1,142	2,287	2,221
MO	3,200	3,750	3,450	1,804	1,626	1,376	842	648	1,030	2,541	2,526

D Data withheld to limit disclosure. [1] As of December 1. [2] Includes slaughter in federally inspected and other slaughter plants; excludes animals slaughtered on farms. [3] Includes other states, not shown separately.

Source: U.S. Department of Agriculture, National Agricultural Statistics Service, "Quick Stats," <quickstats.nass.usda.gov/>, accessed September 2022. See also *Meat Animals Production, Disposition, and Income Annual Summary* and *Livestock Slaughter Annual Summary*, <www.nass.usda.gov/Publications>.

Table 919. Cattle and Calves—Number, Production, and Value by Leading State: 2019 to 2021

[94,805 represents 94,805,000. Includes milk cows. See headnote, Table 916]

State	Number on farms [1] (1,000)			Production (mil. lb.)			Value of production (mil. dol.)			Commercial slaughter [2] (mil. lb.)	
	2019	2020	2021	2019	2020	2021	2019	2020	2021	2020	2021
U.S. [3]..........	**94,805**	**93,793**	**93,790**	**44,629**	**45,595**	**45,935**	**48,212**	**45,947**	**51,888**	**44,916**	**46,294**
TX............	13,000	12,900	13,100	6,135	6,857	6,685	7,189	7,529	8,182	7,435	7,756
NE............	6,800	6,750	6,850	5,578	5,626	5,819	5,416	5,072	6,088	10,078	10,228
KS............	6,400	6,400	6,550	4,431	4,825	4,937	4,655	4,611	5,302	9,282	9,516
OK............	5,300	5,150	5,300	2,107	2,109	2,095	2,559	2,405	2,660	53	64
CA............	5,150	5,150	5,150	2,318	2,277	2,355	2,432	2,206	2,552	2,162	2,185
MO............	4,250	4,300	4,310	1,452	1,248	1,361	1,879	1,510	1,853	100	189
SD............	4,050	3,900	4,000	1,704	1,691	1,706	2,103	1,984	2,193	730	747
IA............	3,950	3,850	3,700	2,115	2,103	2,160	2,581	2,316	2,747	(D)	(D)
WI............	3,450	3,450	3,450	1,472	1,399	1,438	1,562	1,429	1,614	1,869	1,947
CO............	2,850	2,750	2,700	1,894	2,029	2,024	2,072	2,025	2,347	3,259	3,213
ID............	2,500	2,470	2,500	1,250	1,236	1,251	1,395	1,250	1,415	691	708

D Data withheld to limit disclosure. [1] As of January 1. [2] Data cover cattle only. Includes slaughter in federally inspected and other slaughter plants; excludes animals slaughtered on farms. [3] Includes other states, not shown separately.

Source: U.S. Department of Agriculture, National Agricultural Statistics Service, "Quick Stats," <quickstats.nass.usda.gov>, accessed May 2022. See also *Meat Animals Production, Disposition, and Income Annual Summary* and *Livestock Slaughter Annual Summary*, <www.nass.usda.gov/Publications>.

Table 920. Milk Cows—Number, Production, and Value by Leading State: 2019 to 2021

[9,337 represents 9,337,000]

State	Number on farms [1] (1,000)			Milk produced on farms [2] (mil. lb.)			Milk produced per milk cow [2] (pounds)			Value of production [3] (mil. dol.)		
	2019	2020	2021	2019	2020	2021	2019	2020	2021	2019	2020	2021
U.S. [4]..........	**9,337**	**9,392**	**9,448**	**218,441**	**223,309**	**226,258**	**23,395**	**23,777**	**23,948**	**40,738**	**40,560**	**41,951**
CA............	1,725	1,722	1,719	40,595	41,311	41,864	23,533	23,990	24,354	7,388	7,271	7,577
WI............	1,268	1,259	1,274	30,588	30,749	31,702	24,123	24,423	24,884	5,751	5,812	5,960
ID............	625	645	652	15,632	16,237	16,412	25,011	25,174	25,172	2,861	2,988	3,069
NY............	627	626	627	15,122	15,296	15,540	24,118	24,435	24,785	2,858	2,707	2,937
TX............	565	595	622	13,850	14,855	15,599	24,513	24,966	25,079	2,645	2,763	2,839
PA............	490	482	474	10,108	10,279	10,114	20,629	21,326	21,338	1,951	1,871	1,932
MN............	448	448	461	9,922	10,167	10,548	22,147	22,694	22,881	1,915	2,044	2,004
MI............	426	430	441	11,385	11,685	11,952	26,725	27,174	27,102	1,970	1,916	2,104
NM............	326	330	318	8,187	8,169	7,804	25,113	24,755	24,541	1,392	1,332	1,272

[1] Average number during year. Represents cows and heifers that have calved, kept for milk; excluding heifers not yet fresh. [2] Excludes milk sucked by calves. [3] Valued at average returns per 100 pounds of milk in combined marketings of milk and cream. Includes value of milk fed to calves. [4] Includes other states, not shown separately.

Source: U.S. Department of Agriculture, National Agricultural Statistics Service, "Quick Stats," <quickstats.nass.usda.gov/>, accessed June 2022. See also *Milk: Production, Disposition, and Income Annual Summary*, <www.nass.usda.gov/Publications>.

Table 921. Milk Production and Manufactured Dairy Products: 2010 to 2021

[63 represents 63,000]

Item	Unit	2010	2014	2015	2016	2017	2018	2019	2020	2021
Number of farms with milk cows..............	**1,000**	**63**	**(NA)**	**(NA)**	**(NA)**	**55**	**(NA)**	**(NA)**	**(NA)**	**(NA)**
Cows and heifers that have calved, kept for milk [1].....................	Mil. head	9.1	9.3	9.3	9.3	9.4	9.4	9.3	9.4	9.4
Milk produced on farms.......................	Bil. lb.	193	206	209	212	216	218	218	223	226
Production per cow.......................	1,000 lb.	21.1	22.2	22.4	22.8	22.9	23.2	23.4	23.8	23.9
Milk marketed by producers [2].......	Bil. lb.	192	205	208	211	215	217	217	222	225
Value of milk produced...................	Bil. dol.	31.5	49.6	35.9	34.7	38.1	35.4	40.7	40.6	42.0
Cash receipts from marketing of milk and cream [2]........................	Bil. dol.	31.4	49.4	35.7	34.5	37.9	35.2	40.5	40.4	41.8
Number of dairy manufacturing plants.......	**Number**	**1,250**	**1,269**	**1,273**	**1,298**	**1,305**	**1,275**	**1,270**	**1,231**	**1,196**
Manufactured dairy products:										
Butter (including whey butter)..................	Mil. lb.	1,564	1,855	1,850	1,839	1,847	1,968	1,994	2,146	2,072
Cheese, total [3].........................	Mil. lb.	10,443	11,512	11,831	12,182	12,640	13,037	13,137	13,240	13,707
American (excl. full-skim American)...........	Mil. lb.	4,289	4,588	4,694	4,769	5,072	5,254	5,232	5,338	5,568
Cream and Neufchatel.................	Mil. lb.	745	852	876	909	918	915	935	1,012	1,036
All Italian varieties....................	Mil. lb.	4,416	4,950	5,082	5,304	5,395	5,570	5,671	5,612	5,752
Cottage cheese—creamed and lowfat........	Mil. lb.	719	668	681	697	675	695	686	671	642
Nonfat dry milk [4]................................	Mil. lb.	1,563	1,765	1,822	1,753	1,835	1,778	1,851	1,952	2,024
Dry whey [5]................................	Mil. lb.	1,013	870	978	955	1,035	999	978	959	934
Yogurt, plain and flavored......................	Mil. lb.	4,181	4,757	4,646	4,458	4,478	4,453	4,378	4,510	4,743
Ice cream, regular........................	Mil. gal.	929	866	897	907	871	852	879	916	872
Ice cream, lowfat [6].....................	Mil. gal.	415	412	439	436	461	460	474	463	461

NA Not available. [1] Average number during year, excluding heifers not yet fresh. [2] Comprises sales to plants and dealers, and retail sales by farmers direct to consumers. [3] Includes varieties not shown separately. [4] Data for 2000 includes dry skim milk for animal feed. [5] Includes animal but excludes modified whey production. [6] Includes freezer-made milkshake in most states.

Source: U.S. Department of Agriculture, National Agricultural Statistics Service, "Quick Stats," <quickstats.nass.usda.gov/>, accessed June 2022. See also *Dairy Products Annual Summary*; *Milk Production, Disposition, and Income Annual*; and *Farms, Land in Farms, And Livestock Operations, Summary*; <www.nass.usda.gov/Publications/index>.

Table 922. Milk Production and Commercial Use in All Products: 2011 to 2021

[In billions of pounds milkfat basis (10.1 represents 10,100,000,000) except as noted. Beginning in 2011, commercial uses and stocks from Government uses and stocks are not separated, and there are no longer Government-subsidized exports. Therefore the data in this table are not comparable to data previously presented. See <www.ers.usda.gov/data-products/dairy-data/documentation/>]

Year	Begin-ning stocks	Farm milk supply use — Produc-tion	Farm milk supply use — Farm use	Farm milk supply use — Farm market-ings	Imports	Total supply	Utilization — Exports	Utilization — Ending stocks	Utilization — Disap-pear-ance [1]	Apparent domestic human use [2]	Milk price per 100 pounds (dollars)
2011.....	10.1	196.3	1.0	195.3	3.5	208.8	9.1	10.2	189.6	188.1	20.10
2012.....	10.2	200.6	1.0	199.7	4.1	214.0	8.5	11.4	194.1	192.8	18.50
2013.....	11.4	201.3	1.0	200.3	3.8	215.4	12.1	10.3	193.0	191.8	20.10
2014.....	10.3	206.0	1.0	205.1	4.4	219.8	12.2	10.4	197.1	195.8	24.00
2015.....	10.4	208.5	1.0	207.5	5.8	223.7	8.5	12.3	203.0	201.5	17.10
2016.....	12.3	212.5	1.0	211.5	6.9	230.7	8.4	12.7	209.6	208.2	16.30
2017.....	12.7	215.5	1.0	214.5	6.0	233.2	9.2	13.4	210.6	209.2	17.70
2018.....	13.4	217.6	1.0	216.6	6.3	236.2	10.4	13.8	212.1	210.6	16.30
2019.....	13.8	218.4	1.0	217.4	6.9	238.2	9.1	13.6	215.4	214.0	18.60
2020.....	13.6	223.3	1.1	222.2	6.8	242.6	9.3	15.6	217.7	215.9	18.30
2021.....	15.6	226.3	1.0	225.2	6.5	247.4	11.6	14.3	221.4	(NA)	18.30

NA Not available. [1] Disappearance is domestic disappearance equals total commercial supply minus exports and ending stocks. [2] Apparent human use is domestic disappearance and household farm use minus net shipments to U.S. territories; use as animal food; and milk and products pooled on Federal Milk Marketing Orders (FMMOs) that is dumped, used for animal feed, destroyed, or lost by a handler in a vehicular accident, flood, fire, or similar occurrence beyond the handler's control.

Source: U.S. Department of Agriculture, Economic Research Service, "Dairy Data," <www.ers.usda.gov/data-products/dairy-data.aspx>, accessed June 2022.

Table 923. Chicken, Turkey, and Egg Production: 2000 to 2021

[437 represents 437,000,000. For years ending November 30, except as noted]

Item	Unit	2000	2005	2010	2015	2016	2017	2018	2019	2020	2021
Chickens: [1]											
Number [2]................	Million	437	456	457	484	501	515	534	532	520	523
Value per head [2]........	Dollars	2.44	2.52	3.58	4.38	4.23	4.20	4.32	4.43	4.99	5.75
Value, total [2]............	Mil. dol.	1,064	1,150	1,637	2,116	2,115	2,163	2,308	2,360	2,593	3,004
Number sold............	Million	218	194	173	199	208	190	191	187	185	180
Value of sales...........	Mil. dol.	64	65	73	105	88	47	49	38	19	15
PRODUCTION Broiler chickens: [3]											
Number...............	Million	8,284	8,872	8,624	8,689	8,777	8,914	9,038	9,177	9,222	9,131
Weight..................	Bil. lb.	41.6	47.9	49.2	53.4	54.3	55.6	56.8	58.3	59.4	59.2
Production value........	Mil. dol.	13,989	20,878	23,692	28,716	25,936	30,232	31,750	28,314	21,267	31,520
Turkeys: [4]											
Number.................	Million	270	250	244	233	244	245	238	229	223	217
Weight..................	Bil. lb.	7.0	7.0	7.1	7.0	7.5	7.5	7.4	7.5	7.3	7.2
Production value........	Mil. dol.	2,828	3,108	4,372	5,708	6,184	4,874	3,786	4,324	5,171	5,891
Eggs: Average number of layers...................	Thousand	329,067	345,027	341,505	356,370	369,949	381,175	394,361	399,500	391,772	389,044
Eggs per layer..........	Number	257	262	269	276	279	281	279	283	285	285
Total production........	Billion	84.7	90.3	91.8	98.3	103.2	107.2	110.1	113.2	111.7	110.7
Production value........	Mil. dol.	4,359	4,067	6,553	13,763	6,591	7,635	10,653	7,335	8,665	8,677

NA Not available. [1] Excludes commercial broilers. [2] As of December 1. [3] Young chickens of the heavy breeds and other meat-type birds, to be marketed at 2-5 lbs. live weight and from which no pullets are kept for egg production. Not included in sales of chickens. [4] Data for turkeys are for year ending August 31.

Source: U.S. Department of Agriculture, National Agricultural Statistics Service, "Quick Stats," <quickstats.nass.usda.gov/>, accessed June 2022. See also *Poultry—Production and Value* and *Chickens and Eggs*, <www.nass.usda.gov/Publications>.

Table 924. Broiler Chicken and Turkey Production by Leading State: 2019 to 2021

[In millions of pounds, live weight production (58,259 represents 58,259,000,000)]

State	Broiler chickens 2019	Broiler chickens 2020	Broiler chickens 2021	Turkeys 2019	Turkeys 2020	Turkeys 2021	State	Broiler chickens 2019	Broiler chickens 2020	Broiler chickens 2021	Turkeys 2019	Turkeys 2020	Turkeys 2021
U.S. [1].....	58,259	59,406	59,248	7,468	7,293	7,176	MS......	4,845	4,613	4,454	(NA)	(NA)	(NA)
AL.........	6,240	6,605	6,561	(NA)	(NA)	(NA)	MO......	1,455	1,490	1,566	607	581	553
AR.........	7,429	7,348	7,464	576	595	540	NC......	7,420	7,883	8,063	1,203	1,134	1,167
CA.........	(NA)	(NA)	(NA)	254	232	191	OH......	570	552	555	290	271	268
DE.........	1,935	1,929	1,713	(NA)	(NA)	(NA)	OK......	1,500	1,494	1,399	(NA)	(NA)	(NA)
FL.........	358	391	396	(NA)	(NA)	(NA)	PA......	1,127	1,260	1,387	170	191	198
GA.........	8,298	8,083	7,923	(NA)	(NA)	(NA)	SC......	1,838	1,875	1,895	(NA)	(NA)	(NA)
IN.........	(NA)	(NA)	(NA)	804	814	836	SD......	(NA)	(NA)	(NA)	200	206	184
IA.........	(NA)	(NA)	(NA)	498	505	512	TN......	942	1,031	1,133	(NA)	(NA)	(NA)
KY.........	1,915	1,944	1,933	(NA)	(NA)	(NA)	TX......	4,455	4,637	4,734	(NA)	(NA)	(NA)
MD.........	1,833	1,868	1,715	(NA)	(NA)	(NA)	VA......	1,744	1,712	1,798	446	446	421
MI.........	(NA)	(NA)	(NA)	237	232	217	WV......	287	274	258	109	126	116
MN.........	390	358	352	1,104	1,065	1,045	WI......	228	226	224	(NA)	(NA)	(NA)

NA Not available. [1] Includes other states, not shown separately.

Source: U.S. Department of Agriculture, National Agricultural Statistics Service, "Quick Stats," <quickstats.nass.usda.gov/>, accessed June 2022. See also *Poultry—Production and Value*, <www.nass.usda.gov/Publications>.

Section 18
Forestry, Fishing, and Mining

This section presents data on the area, ownership, production, trade, reserves, and disposition of natural resources, defined here as including forestry, fisheries, and mining and mineral products.

Forestry—This section presents data on the area, ownership, and timber resource of commercial timberland; forestry statistics covering the National Forests and Forest Service cooperative programs; product data for lumber, pulpwood, woodpulp, paper and paperboard; and similar data.

The principal sources of data relating to forests and forest products are *Forest Resources of the United States, 2017; U.S. Timber Production, Trade, Consumption, and Price Statistics, 1965 to 2017; Land Areas of the National Forest System*, issued annually by the Forest Service of the U.S. Department of Agriculture; *Agricultural Statistics*, issued by the Department of Agriculture; and reports of the Annual Survey of Manufactures issued by the U.S. Census Bureau, see <www.census.gov/programs-surveys/asm.html>. Further sources used in this section and issued by the U.S. Census Bureau include the annual *County Business Patterns* reports, and the 2012 and 2017 Economic Census. Additional information is published in the *Paper Industry Annual Statistical Summary* of the American Forest and Paper Association, Washington, DC.

The completeness and reliability of statistics on forests and forest products vary considerably. The data for forest land area and stand volumes are much more reliable for areas that have been recently surveyed than for those for which only estimates are available. In general, more data are available for lumber and other manufactured products such as particle board and softwood panels, etc., than for the primary forest products such as poles and piling and fuelwood.

Fisheries—The principal source of data relating to fisheries is data issued annually by the National Marine Fisheries Service (NMFS), National Oceanic and Atmospheric Administration (NOAA). The NMFS collects and disseminates data on commercial landings of fish and shellfish. Annual reports include quantity and value of commercial landings of fish and shellfish, disposition of landings, and number and kinds of fishing vessels and fishing gear. Reports for the fish-processing industry include annual output for wholesaling, and fish processing establishments and annual and seasonal employment. The principal source for these data is the annual *Fisheries of the United States*. Additional government sources include *Agricultural Statistics*, issued annually by the Department of Agriculture; and *Trout Production* and *Catfish Production*, issued by the National Agricultural Statistics service of the U.S. Department of Agriculture.

Mining and mineral products—This section presents data relating to mineral industries and their products, summary measures of production and employment, and more detailed data on production, prices, imports and exports, consumption, and distribution for specific industries and products. Data on mining and mineral products may also be found in Sections 19,

21, 28, and 30 of this *Abstract*; data on mining employment may be found in Section 12.

Mining comprises the extraction of minerals occurring naturally (coal, ores, crude petroleum, natural gas) and quarrying, well operation, milling, refining and processing, and other preparation customarily done at the mine or well site or as a part of extraction activity. (Mineral preparation plants are usually operated together with mines or quarries.) Exploration for minerals is included as is the development of mineral properties.

The principal governmental sources of these data are the *Minerals Yearbook* and *Mineral Commodity Summaries*, published by the U.S. Geological Survey, U.S. Department of the Interior, and various monthly and annual publications of the Energy Information Administration, U.S. Department of Energy. See text, Section 19, for a list of Department of Energy publications.

Mineral statistics, with principal emphasis on commodity detail, have been collected by the U.S. Geological Survey and the former Bureau of Mines since 1880. Current data in U.S. Geological Survey publications cover quantity and value of nonfuel minerals produced, sold, or used by producers, or shipped; quantity of minerals stocked; crude materials treated and prepared minerals recovered; and consumption of mineral raw materials.

The Economic Census, conducted by the Census Bureau at various intervals since 1840, collects data on mineral industries. Beginning with the 1967 census, legislation provides for a census to be conducted every 5 years for years ending in "2" and "7." Economic Census data are based on the North American Industry Classification System (NAICS). The Census provides, for the various types of mineral establishments, information on operating costs, capital expenditures, labor, equipment, and energy requirements in relation to their value of shipments and other receipts.

Table 925. Natural Resource–Related Industries—Establishments, Employees, and Annual Payroll by Industry: 2019 and 2020

[In units as indicated (1,554.5 represents 1,554,500; 108,489 represents $108,489,000,000). Excludes most government employees, railroad employees, and self-employed persons. See source for definitions and statement on reliability of data. An establishment is a single physical location where business is conducted or where services or industrial operations are performed. See Appendix III]

Industry	NAICS code [1]	Establishments (number)		Number of employees [2] (1,000)		Annual payroll (mil. dol.)	
		2019	2020	2019	2020	2019	2020
Natural resource–related industries, total..........	(X)	**66,055**	**64,272**	**1,554.5**	**1,499.5**	**108,489**	**99,131**
Percent of all industries....................................	(X)	0.8	0.8	1.2	1.1	1.5	1.3
Forestry, fishing, hunting, and agriculture support...	**11**	**22,817**	**22,747**	**164.6**	**167.2**	**7,609**	**8,003**
Forestry and logging..................................	113	8,366	8,212	51.9	50.7	2,579	2,611
Timber tract operations.............................	1131	475	465	3.6	3.6	213	230
Forest nurseries and gathering forest products........	1132	169	188	1.0	1.0	43	42
Logging..	1133	7,722	7,559	47.3	46.1	2,323	2,340
Fishing, hunting and trapping............................	114	2,944	2,927	7.3	7.1	498	465
Fishing..	1141	2,569	2,559	5.6	5.3	431	394
Hunting and trapping..................................	1142	375	368	1.7	1.8	66	70
Agriculture and forestry support activities................	115	11,507	11,608	105.3	109.4	4,532	4,927
Crop production support activities......................	1151	5,034	5,086	70.9	74.0	3,108	3,341
Animal production support activities....................	1152	4,702	4,675	21.4	21.7	788	852
Forestry support activities............................	1153	1,771	1,847	13.0	13.7	635	734
Mining, quarrying and oil, and gas extraction........	**21**	**25,077**	**23,908**	**626.7**	**577.9**	**59,454**	**49,312**
Oil and gas extraction.......................................	211	6,139	5,779	108.1	100.2	15,912	14,281
Mining (except oil and gas)...............................	212	5,857	5,812	177.7	170.8	14,194	13,331
Coal mining...	2121	656	576	50.3	43.3	4,278	3,349
Metal ore mining......................................	2122	293	303	37.7	39.3	3,477	3,600
Nonmetallic mineral mining and quarrying..............	2123	4,908	4,933	89.7	88.2	6,439	6,382
Mining support activities...................................	213	13,081	12,317	341.0	306.9	29,348	21,700
Timber–related manufacturing...........................	(X)	**18,161**	**17,617**	**763.1**	**754.4**	**41,426**	**41,816**
Wood product manufacturing............................	321	14,223	13,747	415.8	412.7	18,554	18,904
Sawmills and wood preservation.......................	3211	3,146	3,038	91.1	87.7	4,348	4,389
Veneer, plywood and engineered wood product manufacturing..	3212	1,425	1,427	78.1	79.0	3,855	3,990
Other wood product manufacturing.....................	3219	9,652	9,282	246.6	246.0	10,350	10,525
Paper manufacturing.....................................	322	3,938	3,870	347.4	341.7	22,873	22,912
Pulp, paper and paperboard mills........................	3221	440	430	99.4	92.5	8,164	7,969
Converted paper product manufacturing................	3222	3,498	3,440	247.9	249.2	14,708	14,943

X Not applicable. [1] Data based on North American Industry Classification System (NAICS), 2017. [2] Covers full- and part-time employees who are on the payroll in the pay period including March 12.

Source: U.S. Census Bureau, County Business Patterns, "County Business Patterns by Legal Form of Organization and Employment Size Class for U.S., States, and Selected Geographies," <data.census.gov>, accessed April 2022. See also <census.gov/programs-surveys/cbp.html>.

Table 926. Natural Resource–Related Industries—Establishments, Sales, Payroll, and Employees by Industry: 2012 and 2017

[529 represents $529,000,000,000. Includes only establishments with payroll. Data are based on the 2012 and 2017 economic censuses, which are subject to nonsampling error. For details on methodology and nonsampling and sampling errors, see Appendix III]

Industry	2012 NAICS code [1]	Establishments (number)		Value of shipments (bil. dol.)		Annual payroll (bil. dol.)		Paid employees [2] (1,000)	
		2012	2017	2012	2017	2012	2017	2012	2017
Mining..	21	25,417	25,273	529	400	59	48	848	599
Oil & gas extraction...........................	211	6,735	6,409	311	230	15	13	176	125
Mining (except oil & gas).....................	212	6,091	5,618	98	84	14	12	212	170
Mining support activities.......................	213	12,591	13,246	120	87	30	23	460	303
Manufacturing [3]..............................	31–33	297,191	291,586	5,697	5,549	593	671	11,214	11,522
Wood product manufacturing.................	321	13,741	14,645	78	107	13	17	339	393
Paper manufacturing.........................	322	4,425	4,046	181	186	20	21	350	334
Petroleum & coal products manufacturing...	324	2,193	2,116	851	543	9	11	101	108

[1] Data based on North American Industry Classification System (NAICS), 2012. [2] For pay period including March 12. [3] Includes other industries, not shown separately.

Source: U.S. Census Bureau, 2017 Economic Census of the United States, Table EC1700COMP, "All Sectors: Comparative Statistics for the U.S., States, and Selected Geographies (2012 NAICS Basis): 2017 and 2012," <data.census.gov>, accessed December 2021.

Table 927. Gross Domestic Product of Natural Resource-Related Industries in Current and Chained (2012) Dollars by Industry: 2010 to 2021

[In billions of dollars (15,049.0 represents $15,049,000,000,000). Data are based on the North American Industry Classification System (NAICS); see text, Section 15. Data include nonfactor charges (capital consumption allowances, indirect business taxes, etc.) as well as factor charges against gross product; corporate profits and capital consumption allowances have been shifted from a company to an establishment basis]

Industry	Current dollars				Chained (2012) dollars			
	2010	2015	2020	2021	2010	2015	2020	2021
All industries, total [1]	**15,049.0**	**18,206.0**	**20,893.7**	**22,996.1**	**15,649.0**	**17,390.3**	**18,384.7**	**19,427.3**
Private industries	12,941.0	15,866.6	18,223.1	20,223.5	13,514.2	15,197.8	16,142.3	17,154.5
Natural resource-related industries [2]	**531.0**	**534.0**	**458.5**	**649.4**	**580.2**	**754.2**	**776.9**	**739.6**
Percent of all industries	3.5	2.9	2.2	2.8	3.7	4.3	4.2	3.8
Agriculture, forestry, fishing, and hunting	144.9	180.1	174.5	246.4	191.6	221.9	254.7	242.7
Farms	116.2	145.2	134.7	203.0	162.7	190.0	221.0	207.5
Forestry, fishing, and related activities	28.7	34.9	39.9	43.5	29.1	32.0	35.2	36.3
Mining	306.4	261.7	182.1	283.7	309.9	451.2	438.6	413.4
Oil and gas extraction	189.1	158.1	97.7	196.2	182.1	363.3	410.2	378.4
Mining, except oil and gas	69.7	50.0	56.7	63.6	75.5	62.1	59.9	62.2
Support activities for mining	47.6	53.6	27.7	23.9	52.4	51.5	32.0	28.4
Timber-related manufacturing	79.7	92.2	101.9	119.3	78.7	81.1	83.6	83.5
Wood products	23.3	32.5	42.2	58.2	22.9	26.5	28.4	28.2
Paper products	56.4	59.7	59.7	61.1	55.8	54.6	55.2	55.3

[1] Includes industries not shown separately. [2] Sum of agriculture/forestry/fishing/hunting, mining, and timber-related manufacturing.

Source: U.S. Bureau of Economic Analysis, Industry Economic Data, GDP-by-Industry, "Value Added by Industry" and "Real Value Added by Industry," <apps.bea.gov/itable/>, accessed April 2022.

Table 928. Timber–Based Manufacturing Industries—Establishments, Shipments, Payroll, and Employees: 2017

[107,214,630 represents $107,214,630,000. Includes only establishments or firms with payroll. See Appendix III]

Industry	NAICS code [1]	Establish-ments (number)	Value of shipments ($1,000)	Annual payroll ($1,000)	Paid employees [2]
Wood product manufacturing	**321**	**14,645**	**107,214,630**	**16,814,046**	**393,459**
Saw mills	321113	2,891	26,076,004	3,491,826	72,958
Wood preservation	321114	415	6,598,491	508,251	10,268
Hardwood veneer and plywood manufacturing	321211	236	3,129,223	508,967	12,069
Softwood veneer and plywood manufacturing	321212	86	4,240,227	709,411	13,965
Engineered wood member (except truss) manufacturing	321213	112	2,067,452	251,214	4,982
Truss manufacturing	321214	800	6,492,236	1,264,406	30,994
Reconstituted wood product manufacturing	321219	203	8,615,109	819,591	13,719
Wood window and door manufacturing	321911	1,117	12,212,352	2,338,538	52,071
Cut stock, resawing lumber, and planing	321912	833	5,878,591	841,300	21,555
Other millwork (including flooring)	321918	1,568	7,282,366	1,256,121	32,983
Wood container and pallet manufacturing	321920	2,729	9,551,288	1,956,953	55,389
Manufactured home (mobile home) manufacturing	321991	236	4,271,307	845,405	21,182
Prefabricated wood building manufacturing	321992	644	4,207,937	765,697	17,777
All other miscellaneous wood product manufacturing	321999	2,775	6,592,047	1,256,366	33,547
Paper manufacturing	**322**	**4,046**	**186,385,471**	**21,277,301**	**333,712**
Pulp mills	322110	35	6,862,408	823,592	9,349
Paper (except newsprint) mills	322121	167	36,968,156	3,522,358	48,615
Newsprint mills	322122	9	880,301	103,890	1,248
Paperboard mills	322130	156	32,734,398	3,215,993	36,586
Corrugated and solid fiber box manufacturing	322211	1,236	44,943,191	5,255,689	84,975
Folding paperboard box manufacturing	322212	448	12,486,722	1,946,488	35,462
Other paperboard container manufacturing	322219	289	8,401,957	1,042,956	21,698
Paper bag and coated and treated paper manufacturing	322220	751	21,521,926	2,841,491	47,945
Stationery product manufacturing	322230	378	5,769,014	763,851	16,048
Sanitary paper product manufacturing	322291	132	11,449,543	1,047,846	17,566
All other converted paper product manufacturing	322299	445	4,367,855	713,147	14,220

[1] North American Industry Classification System, 2017. [2] For pay period including March 12.

Source: U.S. Census Bureau, 2017 Economic Census, "EC1700BASIC: All sectors: Summary Statistics for the U.S., States, and Selected Geographies: 2017," <data.census.gov>, accessed November 2021.

Table 929. Timber-Based Manufacturing Industries—Employees, Payroll, and Shipments: 2020

[In units, as indicated (11,353 represents 11,353,000). Based on the Annual Survey of Manufactures, see Appendix III]

Selected industry	NAICS code [1]	All employees — Number (1,000)	All employees — Payroll — Total (mil. dol.)	All employees — Payroll — Per employee (dol.)	Production workers, total (1,000)	Value added by manufactures — Total (mil. dol.)	Value added by manufactures — Per production worker (dol.)	Value of shipments (mil. dol.)
Manufacturing, all industries [2]............	31–33	**11,353**	**693,181**	**61,059**	**8,098**	**2,377,065**	**293,528**	**5,221,325**
Timber-based manufacturing, total.....	321–322	**725**	**40,219**	**55,481**	**579**	**136,445**	**235,745**	**298,059**
Percent of total manufacturing..........	(X)	6.4	5.8	(X)	7.1	5.7	(X)	5.7
Wood product manufacturing.................	321	400	18,050	45,124	328	54,662	166,752	117,715
Sawmills and wood preservation...........	3211	83	4,246	51,278	72	16,656	231,096	37,281
Veneer, plywood, and engineered wood product................................	3212	73	3,612	49,209	57	11,553	200,942	25,334
Other wood product.......................	3219	244	10,192	41,803	198	26,453	133,443	55,100
Millwork.................................	32191	111	4,754	42,906	88	13,700	154,996	28,104
Wood container and pallet.................	32192	57	2,242	39,449	49	4,822	99,389	9,982
All other wood products..................	32199	76	3,197	41,956	61	7,931	129,322	17,014
Manufactured (mobile) home...........	321991	24	949	39,260	20	2,185	111,252	4,873
Prefabricated wood building...........	321992	18	865	47,725	14	2,267	162,518	4,718
All other misc. wood product.............	321999	34	1,382	40,795	28	3,478	125,422	7,423
Paper manufacturing.......................	322	325	22,168	68,232	251	81,783	325,855	180,344
Pulp, paper, and paperboard mills..........	3221	91	7,698	84,131	73	37,749	520,242	68,532
Pulp mills...............................	32211	9	880	96,198	7	2,905	404,063	5,989
Paper mills..............................	32212	46	3,458	75,657	36	19,117	530,771	33,049
Paperboard mills.........................	32213	37	3,360	91,686	29	15,727	535,781	29,493
Converted paper product...................	3222	233	14,471	61,999	178	44,034	246,802	111,812
Paperboard container....................	32221	141	8,790	62,446	109	23,848	218,640	67,139
Paper bag and coated and treated paper.............................	32222	48	3,091	64,669	34	9,013	261,287	21,823
Stationery product......................	32223	14	707	49,367	12	1,708	147,117	5,071
Other converted paper products...........	32229	31	1,882	61,680	23	9,465	407,233	17,779

X Not applicable. [1] North American Industry Classification System, 2017; see text, Section 15. [2] Includes other industries, not shown separately.

Source: U.S. Census Bureau, Annual Survey of Manufactures, "Summary Statistics for Industry Groups and Industries in the U.S.: 2018-2020," <data.census.gov>, accessed April 2022.

Table 930. Forest Land and Timberland by Type of Owner and Region: 2017

[In thousands of acres (765,493 represents 765,493,000). As of January 1. Data are from the U.S. Forest Service's Forest Inventory and Analysis National Program. Forest land is land at least 10 percent stocked by forest trees of any size, including land that formerly had such tree cover and that will be naturally or artificially regenerated. The minimum area for classification of forest land is 1 acre and a crown width of at least 120 feet wide. Timberland is forest land that is producing or is capable of producing crops of industrial wood and that is not withdrawn from timber utilization by statute or administrative regulation]

Region	Forest land, total	Timberland — Total	Timberland — Federal — Total	Timberland — Federal — National forest	Timberland — Federal — Bureau of Land Management lands	Timberland — Federal — Other	Timberland — State, county, and municipal	Timberland — Private [1]
Total.......................	**765,493**	**514,425**	**108,178**	**96,138**	**6,109**	**5,931**	**47,095**	**359,152**
North............................	175,789	164,894	11,348	10,146	12	1,190	25,650	127,896
Northeast.....................	84,727	78,539	2,852	2,355	–	498	10,102	65,586
North Central.................	91,062	86,355	8,495	7,792	12	692	15,549	62,310
South...........................	245,513	208,092	16,397	12,258	–	4,138	9,561	182,135
Southeast.....................	89,692	85,754	7,016	5,061	–	1,955	5,618	73,119
South Central.................	155,821	122,338	9,380	7,197	–	2,183	3,942	109,016
Rocky Mountains..............	130,641	69,654	47,111	44,206	2,688	217	3,193	19,350
Great Plains..................	6,797	6,084	1,217	1,051	18	148	265	4,602
Intermountain.................	123,844	63,569	45,894	43,154	2,670	70	2,927	14,748
Pacific Coast...................	213,549	71,784	33,323	29,527	3,409	386	8,691	29,771
Alaska........................	128,735	12,996	4,874	3,848	812	213	4,810	3,313
Pacific Northwest.............	51,827	41,462	19,200	16,802	2,299	98	3,637	18,625
Pacific Southwest [2].........	32,986	17,326	9,249	8,877	297	75	245	7,833

– Represents or rounds to zero. [1] Includes Indian lands. [2] Includes Hawaii.

Source: U.S. Forest Service, National Assessment - Resources Planning Act (RPA), *Forest Resources of the United States, 2017: A Technical Document Supporting the Forest Service 2020 Update of the RPA Assessment,* May 2018. See also <www.fia.fs.fed.us/program-features/rpa/>.

Table 931. National Forest System Lands by State: 2021

[In thousands of acres (232,414 represents 232,414,000). As of September 30, 2021. Data do not include Delaware, District of Columbia, Hawaii, Iowa, Maryland, Massachusetts, New Jersey, or Rhode Island]

State	Total lands	National Forest System lands [1]	Other lands [2]	State	Total lands	National Forest System lands [1]	Other lands [2]
United States	**232,414**	**193,084**	**39,330**	Nevada	6,287	5,760	527
Alabama	1,290	673	618	New Hampshire	851	754	97
Alaska	23,935	22,143	1,792	New Mexico	10,249	9,225	1,024
Arizona	11,813	11,180	633	New York	17	16	(Z)
Arkansas	3,549	2,593	955	North Carolina	3,027	1,257	1,769
California	24,289	20,828	3,461	North Dakota	1,106	1,103	3
Colorado	15,960	14,489	1,471	Ohio	856	244	612
Connecticut	(Z)	(Z)	–	Oklahoma	778	400	378
Florida	1,423	1,203	220	Oregon	17,655	15,697	1,958
Georgia	1,796	868	929	Pennsylvania	741	514	227
Idaho	21,714	20,450	1,265	South Carolina	1,381	637	744
Illinois	958	305	653	South Dakota	2,436	2,007	429
Indiana	647	204	443	Tennessee	1,291	724	567
Kansas	109	109	(Z)	Texas	2,002	757	1,245
Kentucky	2,205	818	1,387	Utah	9,205	8,193	1,012
Louisiana	1,032	608	424	Vermont	837	411	426
Maine	94	54	41	Virginia	3,217	1,674	1,543
Michigan	4,888	2,878	2,011	Washington	11,990	9,343	2,647
Minnesota	5,488	2,845	2,642	West Virginia	1,893	1,047	846
Mississippi	2,374	1,191	1,183	Wisconsin	2,003	1,525	478
Missouri	3,093	1,508	1,584	Wyoming	9,725	9,226	499
Montana	19,195	17,240	1,955	Puerto Rico	56	29	27
Nebraska	562	351	211	Virgin Islands	(Z)	(Z)	–

– Represents zero. Z Less than 500 acres. [1] National Forest System is a nationally significant system of federally owned units of forest, range, and related land consisting of national forests, purchase units, national grasslands, land utilization project areas, experimental forest areas, experimental range areas, designated experimental areas, and other land areas; water areas; and interests in lands that are administered by USDA Forest Service or designated for administration through the Forest Service. [2] Other lands are lands within the unit boundaries in private, state, county, and municipal ownership and the federal lands over which the Forest Service has no jurisdiction. Also includes lands offered to the United States and approved for acquisition and subsequent Forest Service administration, but to which title has not yet been accepted by the United States.

Source: U.S. Forest Service, *Land Areas of the National Forest System as of September 30, 2021*, October 2021. See also <www.fs.fed.us/land/staff/lar/LAR2021/lar2021index.html>.

Table 932. Timber Volume, Growth, and Removal on Timberland by Species Group and Region: 2016 and 2017

[In millions of cubic feet (1,116,012 represents 1,116,012,000,000). Data are from the U.S. Forest Service's Forest Inventory and Analysis National Program]

Region	2017 Net volume [1]						2016 Net growth and removals of growing stock					
	All timber [2]			Growing stock [3]			Timber growth [4]			Timber removals [5]		
	All species	Soft-woods	Hard-woods	All species	Soft-woods	Hard-woods	All spe-cies	Soft-woods	Hard-woods	All spe-cies	Soft-woods	Hard-woods
Total	1,116,012	598,873	517,139	985,238	560,526	424,712	25,009	15,468	9,542	13,041	8,901	4,140
North	314,204	68,278	245,926	270,041	60,601	209,440	5,932	1,546	4,386	2,491	654	1,837
Northeast	172,556	41,465	131,091	152,780	37,108	115,672	3,264	917	2,347	1,176	377	799
North Central	141,647	26,813	114,834	117,261	23,494	93,768	2,668	629	2,039	1,315	277	1,038
South	377,781	149,800	227,981	319,088	141,307	177,781	13,764	9,268	4,496	7,859	5,647	2,212
Southeast	167,894	71,539	96,355	142,603	67,540	75,063	6,393	4,285	2,108	3,527	2,736	790
South Central	209,887	78,261	131,626	176,485	73,767	102,717	7,371	4,983	2,388	4,333	2,911	1,422
Rocky Mountains	144,222	128,750	15,472	130,005	119,102	10,903	299	189	109	405	396	8,626
Great Plains	8,476	2,537	5,938	4,487	1,885	2,601	57	-2	59	34	29	6
Intermountain	135,747	126,213	9,534	125,518	117,217	8,301	242	192	50	370	367	3
Pacific Coast	279,805	252,044	27,760	266,104	239,515	26,589	5,015	4,465	550	2,286	2,204	82
Alaska	39,229	35,639	3,590	37,140	33,761	3,379	254	133	121	39	39	(Z)
Pacific Northwest	166,844	153,680	13,163	159,238	146,480	12,758	3,707	3,423	284	1,892	1,811	81
Pacific Southwest [6]	73,732	62,725	11,007	69,726	59,273	10,452	1,054	909	145	355	355	(Z)

Z Less than 500,000. [1] As of January 1. [2] Includes growing stock, live cull and sound dead. [3] Live trees of commercial species meeting specified standards of quality or vigor. Cull trees are excluded. Includes only trees 5.0-inches in diameter or larger at 4 1/2 feet above ground. [4] The net increase in the volume of trees during a specified year. Components include the increment in net volume of trees at the beginning of the specific year surviving to its end, plus the net volume of trees reaching the minimum size class during the year, minus the volume of trees that died during the year, and minus the net volume of trees that became cull trees during the year. [5] The net volume of trees removed from the inventory during a specified year by harvesting, cultural operations such as timber stand improvement, or land clearing. [6] Includes Hawaii.

Source: U.S. Forest Service, National Assessment - Resources Planning Act (RPA), *Forest Resources of the United States, 2017: A Technical Document Supporting the Forest Service 2020 Update of the RPA Assessment*, May 2018. See also <www.fia.fs.fed.us/program-features/rpa/>.

Table 933. Timber Removals—Roundwood Product Output by Source and Species Group: 2016

[In millions of cubic feet (13,972 represents 13,972,000,000). Data are from U.S. Forest Service's Forest Inventory and Analysis National Program]

Source and species group	Total	Sawlogs	Pulpwood	Veneer logs	Other products [1]	Fuelwood [2]
Total	**13,972**	**5,521**	**5,368**	**660**	**728**	**1,695**
Softwoods	9,480	4,075	3,640	590	576	599
Hardwoods	4,493	1,446	1,728	69	153	1,096
Growing stock [3]	11,650	5,334	4,773	648	563	332
Softwoods	8,393	3,959	3,280	582	423	149
Hardwoods	3,257	1,374	1,493	65	141	183
Other sources [4]	2,323	187	596	12	165	1,363
Softwoods	1,086	115	360	8	153	450
Hardwoods	1,236	72	235	4	12	913

[1] Includes poles, pilings, posts, cooperage and miscellaneous products. [2] Downed and dead wood volume left on the ground after trees have been cut on timberland and used for conversion to some form of energy, primarily in residential use. [3] Includes live trees of commercial species meeting specified standards of quality or vigor. Cull trees are excluded. Includes only trees 5.0 inches in diameter or larger at 4.5 feet above the ground. [4] Includes salvable dead trees, rough and rotten trees, trees of noncommercial species, trees less than 5.0 inches in diameter at 4.5 feet above the ground, tops, and roundwood harvested from nonforest land (for example, fence rows).

Source: U.S. Forest Service, National Assessment - Resources Planning Act (RPA), *Forest Resources of the United States, 2017: A Technical Document Supporting the Forest Service 2020 Update of the RPA Assessment,* May 2018. See also <www.fia.fs.fed.us/program-features/rpa/>.

Table 934. Timber Products—Production, Foreign Trade, and Consumption by Type of Product: 1990 to 2017

[In millions of cubic feet, roundwood equivalent (15,577 represents 15,577,000,000)]

Type of product	1990	2000	2010	2011	2012	2013	2014	2015	2016	2017
Industrial roundwood:										
Domestic production	15,577	15,528	11,006	11,587	12,046	12,547	12,954	13,124	13,329	13,643
Softwoods	10,968	10,327	8,235	8,672	9,079	9,399	9,630	9,715	9,925	10,181
Hardwoods	4,609	5,201	2,771	2,914	2,967	3,148	3,324	3,409	3,403	3,463
Imports	3,044	4,626	2,488	2,469	2,564	2,838	3,119	3,257	3,615	3,522
Exports	2,413	2,039	1,888	2,118	2,073	2,320	2,304	2,214	2,216	2,315
Consumption	16,208	18,115	11,607	11,938	12,537	13,065	13,769	14,167	14,727	14,851
Softwoods	11,620	12,830	8,912	9,120	9,681	10,073	10,585	10,931	11,495	11,624
Hardwoods	4,588	5,285	2,695	2,818	2,856	2,992	3,184	3,235	3,233	3,227
Lumber:										
Domestic production	7,317	7,384	4,569	5,005	5,219	5,607	5,995	6,065	6,143	6,338
Imports	1,905	2,943	1,422	1,403	1,480	1,703	1,915	2,097	2,426	2,328
Exports	697	435	389	454	464	519	545	492	527	580
Consumption	8,526	9,892	5,602	5,955	6,234	6,791	7,366	7,670	8,042	8,086
Plywood and veneer:										
Domestic production	1,423	1,187	655	651	679	703	693	688	703	729
Imports	97	154	161	166	176	205	209	244	263	285
Exports	109	51	55	52	57	55	46	39	43	47
Consumption	1,410	1,290	760	765	798	853	856	893	923	967
Pulp products:										
Domestic production	5,313	5,881	4,863	4,922	5,088	5,068	5,016	5,056	5,099	5,081
Imports	1,038	1,448	880	875	874	902	969	882	896	875
Exports	645	776	802	887	864	1,040	1,016	1,009	995	1,013
Consumption	5,705	6,553	4,941	4,911	5,099	4,929	4,969	4,929	5,000	4,943
Logs: [1]										
Imports	4	72	20	19	28	26	22	29	24	32
Exports	674	422	407	485	432	463	444	363	390	393
Pulpwood chips, exports	288	355	235	241	256	242	253	311	262	280
Other industrial timber products: [2]										
Production and consumption	562	300	277	283	373	463	552	642	732	822
Fuelwood:										
Production and consumption	2,900	1,622	1,725	1,804	1,882	1,960	2,039	2,117	2,195	2,273

[1] Prior to 2010, pulpwood logs are not included in logs. [2] Includes cooperage logs, poles and piling, fence posts, hewn ties, round mine timbers, box bolts, etc.

Source: U.S. Forest Service, *U.S. Timber Production, Trade, Consumption, and Price Statistics, 1965-2017,* July 2019. See also <www.fs.usda.gov/treesearch/pubs/58506>.

Table 935. Selected Timber Products—Imports and Exports: 1990 to 2017

[In million board feet (13,107 represents 13,107,000,000), except as indicated]

Product	Unit	1990	2000	2010	2012	2013	2014	2015	2016	2017
IMPORTS										
Lumber, total.................	Mil. bd. ft.	13,107	20,243	9,769	10,172	11,713	13,170	14,429	16,730	16,058
Softwood....................	Mil. bd. ft.	12,875	19,449	9,468	9,864	11,358	12,729	13,947	16,323	15,704
Hardwood..................	Mil. bd. ft.	232	795	301	308	355	441	482	407	354
From Canada..............	Mil. bd. ft.	11,918	18,616	9,151	9,633	11,044	12,311	13,413	15,555	14,479
Logs, total [1]...............	Mil. bd. ft. [2]	23	450	126	176	164	139	139	116	153
Softwood....................	Mil. bd. ft.	13	390	99	136	120	99	97	79	69
Hardwood..................	Mil. bd. ft.	10	59	28	41	44	40	42	37	83
From Canada..............	Mil. bd. ft.	19	426	120	133	161	137	136	114	147
Paper and board [3]............	1,000 tons	12,195	17,356	11,144	10,441	10,967	11,301	10,746	10,512	10,454
Woodpulp.....................	1,000 tons	4,893	7,227	6,163	5,599	6,112	6,126	5,872	6,161	6,026
Plywood......................	Mil. sq. ft. [4]	1,687	2,902	3,046	3,339	3,873	3,955	4,609	4,926	5,314
EXPORTS										
Lumber, total.................	Mil. bd. ft.	4,566	2,700	2,425	2,900	3,250	3,387	3,056	3,261	3,585
To: Canada..................	Mil. bd. ft.	658	701	621	634	636	600	533	553	549
Japan.......................	Mil. bd. ft.	1,270	325	179	189	207	162	153	130	122
European Union...........	Mil. bd. ft.	686	507	209	166	164	196	174	189	173
Softwood....................	Mil. bd. ft.	3,753	1,400	1,347	1,582	1,788	1,734	1,563	1,602	1,700
Hardwood..................	Mil. bd. ft.	813	1,300	1,078	1,318	1,462	1,653	1,493	1,659	1,885
Logs, total [1]...............	Mil. bd. ft. [2]	4,213	2,638	2,542	2,698	2,897	2,778	1,742	1,872	1,888
To: Canada..................	Mil. bd. ft. [2]	396	1,350	835	754	641	593	507	464	386
Japan.......................	Mil. bd. ft. [2]	2,626	934	425	469	531	478	324	314	303
China.......................	Mil. bd. ft. [2]	362	22	780	1,052	1,399	1,385	741	942	1,028
Softwood....................	Mil. bd. ft.	3,994	2,066	2,074	2,280	2,550	2,336	1,411	1,515	1,522
Hardwood..................	Mil. bd. ft.	220	573	468	418	348	442	330	357	366
Paper and board [3]............	1,000 tons	5,163	8,701	8,781	9,036	12,842	12,743	12,326	11,679	12,274
Woodpulp.....................	1,000 tons	5,905	6,409	8,265	8,125	8,147	7,901	8,096	8,315	8,367
Plywood......................	Mil. sq. ft. [4]	1,766	916	1,004	1,039	990	832	710	774	859

[1] Prior to 2000, pulpwood logs are not included. [2] Log scale. [3] Includes paper and board products. Excludes hardboard. [4] 3/8 inch basis.

Source: U.S. Forest Service. *U.S. Timber Production, Trade, Consumption, and Price Statistics, 1965-2017*, July 2019. See also <www.fs.usda.gov/treesearch/pubs/58506>.

Table 936. Lumber Production and Consumption by Species Group: 1990 to 2017

[In billion board feet (48.1 represents 48,100,000,000), except per capita in board feet. Per capita consumption based on estimated resident population as of July 1]

Item	1990	1995	2000	2005	2010	2011	2012	2013	2014	2015	2016	2017
Production, total.................	**48.1**	**44.9**	**48.6**	**50.9**	**30.5**	**33.3**	**34.8**	**37.3**	**39.8**	**40.3**	**40.8**	**42.2**
By species:												
Softwoods.......................	35.8	32.2	36.0	39.8	24.8	26.8	28.3	30.0	31.5	32.0	32.5	33.9
Hardwoods......................	12.3	12.6	12.6	11.2	5.7	6.6	6.5	7.3	8.3	8.3	8.3	8.3
Consumption, total..............	**55.3**	**60.3**	**66.6**	**72.3**	**37.7**	**40.6**	**43.6**	**47.2**	**50.9**	**54.0**	**53.6**	**38.6**
Per capita......................	221	229	236	244	122	130	139	149	159	168	166	118
By species:												
Softwoods.......................	43.6	48.4	54.6	61.6	32.7	35.0	38.0	40.9	43.7	46.8	46.6	32.2
Hardwoods......................	11.7	12.0	11.9	10.6	4.9	5.7	5.6	6.3	7.1	7.2	7.0	6.4

Source: U.S. Forest Service, *U.S. Timber Production, Trade, Consumption, and Price Statistics, 1965-2017*, July 2019. See also <www.fs.usda.gov/treesearch/pubs/58506>.

Table 937. Pulpwood Consumption, Woodpulp Production, and Paper and Board Production and Consumption: 1990 to 2017

[In thousands (99,361 represents 99,361,000) except where otherwise indicated]

Item	Unit	1990	2000	2010	2012	2013	2014	2015	2016	2017
Pulpwood consumption.......	1,000 cords [1]	99,361	95,904	89,306	90,744	87,319	86,714	84,979	85,798	84,152
Woodpulp production [2].......	1,000 tons	63,048	62,758	55,343	55,475	54,466	53,367	52,646	52,701	52,701
Paper and board: [3]										
Production.....................	1,000 tons	78,679	94,491	82,968	80,916	80,478	79,488	79,024	78,342	78,445
Consumption [4]..............	1,000 tons	85,711	103,147	85,331	82,321	78,603	78,046	77,444	77,175	76,625
Per capita...................	Pounds	686	731	551	524	497	489	482	477	470

[1] One cord equals 128 cubic feet. [2] Includes dissolving and special alpha pulps; excludes defibrated/exploded pulps and screenings. [3] Excludes wet machine board and construction grades. [4] Production plus imports, minus exports.

Source: U.S. Forest Service, *U.S. Timber Production, Trade, Consumption, and Price Statistics, 1965-2017*, July 2019. See also <www.fs.usda.gov/treesearch/pubs/58506>.

Table 938. Selected Timber Products—Producer Price Indexes: 1990 to 2021

[1982=100, unless otherwise noted. For information about producer prices, see text, Section 14]

Product	1990	2000	2010	2015	2017	2018	2019	2020	2021
Lumber and wood products............................	**129.7**	**178.2**	**192.7**	**221.9**	**230.4**	**243.9**	**236.7**	**254.5**	**315.5**
Lumber...	124.6	178.8	167.3	199.3	217.2	232.3	210.4	248.2	347.0
Softwood lumber..........................	123.8	178.6	160.8	192.7	223.7	241.9	215.4	280.3	397.7
Softwood cut stock and dimension....	129.7	195.3	206.0	199.7	214.2	228.1	204.1	235.6	363.9
Softwood lumber, not edge worked [1]	(NA)	(NA)	85.8	104.9	121.9	131.0	114.4	154.1	217.7
Softwood lumber, MFPL [1, 2].........	(NA)	(NA)	111.5	128.3	152.3	171.4	169.2	188.3	267.0
Hardwood lumber.........................	131.0	185.9	187.3	221.1	219.6	230.1	215.1	207.0	279.2
Millwork..	130.4	176.4	207.0	237.2	247.6	259.5	263.5	274.5	318.6
General millwork...........................	132.0	178.0	211.2	238.0	245.7	251.4	256.9	261.7	283.6
Prefabricated structural members......	122.3	175.1	185.6	232.6	255.5	299.2	295.6	338.4	498.3
Plywood..	114.2	157.6	176.7	198.9	204.2	230.2	202.9	229.3	335.2
Softwood veneer and plywood..........	119.6	173.3	197.1	234.5	234.8	274.5	222.8	270.6	449.6
Hardwood veneer and plywood [3].....	(NA)	(NA)	103.6	108.6	115.3	123.5	123.9	125.2	140.4
Other wood products...........................	114.7	130.5	142.5	161.4	160.5	169.3	176.6	177.8	206.6
Wood pallets and pallet containers....	127.6	178.5	206.6	242.1	242.2	262.8	281.1	283.0	361.3
Wood boxes.................................	119.1	155.2	183.0	199.4	201.3	205.4	211.5	220.2	242.9
Pulp, paper, and allied products...............	**141.2**	**183.7**	**236.9**	**248.8**	**254.6**	**260.0**	**259.4**	**259.9**	**288.6**
Pulp, paper, and products, excl. building paper......	132.9	161.4	206.8	218.4	223.9	229.7	227.3	224.7	250.7
Woodpulp...................................	151.3	145.3	186.0	181.6	179.3	216.0	174.0	141.7	193.1
Recyclable paper............................	138.9	282.5	421.5	291.8	399.9	276.9	181.2	244.6	430.1
Paper..	128.8	149.8	182.1	189.8	186.4	197.6	200.6	195.4	214.3
Writing and printing papers..............	129.1	146.6	179.5	183.6	176.7	188.5	197.2	191.0	200.7
Newsprint....................................	119.6	127.5	125.6	113.6	118.5	138.5	138.8	115.6	127.1
Paperboard..................................	135.7	176.7	224.9	243.1	257.5	273.5	268.1	256.6	296.7
Converted paper and paperboard products..........	135.2	162.7	209.0	228.2	233.8	237.4	241.4	241.3	256.5
Sanitary paper products, including stock...........	135.3	146.7	181.8	182.2	181.4	179.5	182.7	184.1	187.0
Paper, plastic, and foil bags.............	156.6	173.7	246.0	280.5	279.1	287.0	285.7	285.3	318.4
Paper boxes and containers..............	129.9	172.6	219.4	247.3	259.5	264.8	269.5	268.1	289.6
Paperboard fiber drums................	130.6	180.6	293.4	354.7	391.7	414.9	433.5	447.4	506.3
Office supplies and accessories.......	121.4	133.8	159.9	174.0	177.2	186.6	193.7	192.0	199.0
Die-cut paper & paperboard office supplies [1].....	(NA)	(NA)	125.2	143.8	147.0	150.3	174.0	176.1	184.4
Fiber cans, tubes, and similar fiber products......	147.8	205.5	268.6	283.0	307.6	323.8	331.6	340.8	370.5
Building paper & building board mill products........	112.2	138.8	168.4	186.3	221.3	222.9	200.1	260.5	411.3
Hardboard, particleboard & fiberboard products.....	107.5	132.8	158.5	175.2	209.1	210.5	188.8	245.8	388.0

NA Not available. [1] December 2003=100. [2] Made from purchased lumber. [3] December 2005=100.

Source: U.S. Bureau of Labor Statistics, "Producer Price Indexes," <www.bls.gov/ppi>, accessed July 2022.

Table 939. Paper and Paperboard—Production and New Supply: 1990 to 2021

[In millions of short tons (80.55 represents 80,550,000). 1 short ton = 2,000 lbs]

Item	1990	2000	2010	2015	2017	2018	2019	2020	2021
Production, total............................	**80.55**	**96.05**	**83.70**	**79.80**	**79.17**	**78.87**	**75.38**	**73.60**	**75.15**
Paper, total...................................	39.36	45.52	35.51	29.60	27.34	26.25	24.35	21.60	21.02
Paperboard, total............................	39.42	48.97	47.46	49.40	51.07	51.86	50.28	51.23	53.36
Recycled & unbleached Kraft board.....	29.39	37.59	36.41	39.30	41.17	41.86	40.44	41.58	43.61
Recycled..................................	9.03	15.79	15.05	16.89	17.86	(NA)	(NA)	(NA)	(NA)
Unbleached kraft........................	20.36	21.80	21.36	22.41	23.31	(NA)	(NA)	(NA)	(NA)
Semichemical..............................	5.64	5.95	5.44	4.75	4.61	4.61	4.48	4.53	4.62
Bleached kraft.............................	4.26	5.30	5.62	5.35	5.29	5.40	5.36	5.12	5.13
Wet machine board and construction grades.........................	1.82	1.56	0.73	0.80	0.76	0.76	0.76	0.77	0.77
New supply, all grades, excluding products............	**87.68**	**105.02**	**84.16**	**79.99**	**78.94**	**79.41**	**76.13**	**73.25**	**75.78**
Paper, total...................................	49.49	57.13	40.34	34.43	31.86	31.38	28.98	25.44	25.10
Newsprint.................................	13.41	12.92	5.00	3.51	2.91	2.54	2.11	1.57	1.46
Printing/writing papers.................	25.46	32.99	23.73	19.08	16.79	16.53	14.56	11.29	11.36
Packaging and industrial converting papers.........................	4.72	4.27	4.18	4.17	4.36	4.41	4.42	4.34	4.52
Tissue....................................	5.90	6.95	7.43	7.68	7.80	7.90	7.88	8.23	7.76
Paperboard, total..........................	36.30	46.02	43.06	44.77	46.33	47.29	46.42	47.07	49.93

NA Not available.

Source: American Forest and Paper Association, Washington, DC, *Paper Industry Annual Statistical Summary* ©.

Table 940. Fishery Products—Domestic Catch, Imports, and Disposition: 1990 to 2020

[Live weight, in millions of pounds (11,713 represents 11,713,000,000)]

Item	1990	2000	2010	2015	2016	2017	2018	2019	2020
Total supply	**11,713**	**10,212**	**12,033**	**13,227**	**13,446**	**13,639**	**13,893**	**13,384**	**14,238**
Edible, for human food	(NA)	(NA)	10,788	12,463	12,569	13,100	13,053	13,067	13,568
Finfish	(NA)	(NA)	7,884	7,931	7,872	8,023	7,806	7,957	8,282
Shellfish [1]	(NA)	(NA)	2,904	4,531	4,697	5,077	5,247	5,110	5,287
For industrial use [2]	(NA)	(NA)	1,245	764	877	539	840	316	670
Domestic catch	**9,806**	**8,854**	**8,314**	**9,757**	**9,659**	**9,962**	**9,426**	**9,363**	**8,388**
Edible, for human food	(NA)	(NA)	6,593	7,776	7,553	8,259	7,532	7,584	6,711
Finfish	(NA)	(NA)	5,271	6,644	6,452	7,143	6,438	6,620	5,788
Shellfish [1]	(NA)	(NA)	1,322	1,132	1,101	1,116	1,093	964	923
For industrial use [2]	(NA)	(NA)	1,721	1,981	2,106	1,704	1,895	1,779	1,678
Imports [3]	**6,064**	**7,081**	**9,843**	**12,077**	**12,298**	**12,653**	**12,990**	**12,458**	**13,063**
Edible, for human food	4,723	6,639	9,360	11,460	11,624	11,880	12,251	11,818	12,312
Finfish	4,228	5,195	7,093	7,408	7,465	7,396	7,587	7,229	7,566
Shellfish [1]	495	1,444	2,267	4,052	4,159	4,484	4,663	4,588	4,746
For industrial use [2]	1,341	442	483	617	675	773	739	641	751
Exports	**4,157**	**5,723**	**6,124**	**8,607**	**8,512**	**8,976**	**8,523**	**8,438**	**7,213**
Edible, for human food	3,362	4,552	5,165	6,773	6,608	7,039	6,730	6,335	5,454
Finfish	2,905	3,957	4,480	6,121	6,045	6,516	6,220	5,892	5,073
Shellfish [1]	457	595	685	652	563	523	510	442	382
For industrial use [1]	795	1,171	959	1,834	1,903	1,938	1,794	2,104	1,759
Disposition of domestic catch	**9,806**	**8,854**	**8,314**	**9,757**	**9,659**	**9,962**	**9,426**	**9,363**	**8,388**
Fresh and frozen [4]	(NA)	(NA)	6,585	7,649	7,582	8,129	7,475	7,453	6,593
Canned [4]	(NA)	(NA)	374	361	184	289	179	169	185
Cured	(NA)	(NA)	100	68	58	139	141	150	117
Reduced to meal, oil, etc.	(NA)	(NA)	1,255	1,678	1,835	1,405	1,631	1,592	1,493

NA Not available. [1] For univalve and bivalve mollusks (conchs, clams, oysters, scallops, etc.), the weight of meats, excluding the shell, is reported. [2] Processed into meal, oil, solubles, and shell products, or used as bait and animal food. [3] Includes landings of tuna caught by foreign vessels in American Samoa. [4] Includes for human food, and bait and animal food.

Source: U.S. National Oceanic and Atmospheric Administration, National Marine Fisheries Service, "Fisheries One Stop Shop," <www.fisheries.noaa.gov/foss/>, accessed June 2022.

Table 941. Supply of Selected Shellfish and Fish Products: 1990 to 2020

[In millions of pounds (248 represents 248,000,000). Totals available for U.S. consumption are supply minus exports plus imports. Round weight is the complete or full weight as caught]

Species	Unit	1990	2000	2010	2015	2016	2017	2018	2019	2020
Shrimp	Heads-off weight	248	513	712	1,764	1,836	2,049	2,155	2,111	2,317
Tuna, canned	Canned weight	856	980	833	704	671	641	689	731	846
Snow crab	Round weight	210	122	197	216	205	194	174	187	218
Clams	Meat weight	152	133	100	95	84	74	76	80	49
Salmon, canned [1]	Canned weight	116	95	73	101	-11	92	33	96	61
American lobster	Round weight	103	186	254	324	341	201	196	204	187
Spiny lobster	Round weight	94	99	59	14	28	46	46	43	43
Scallops	Meat weight	74	78	85	62	68	71	87	80	73
Oysters	Meat weight	59	71	58	64	62	66	71	54	56
King crab	Round weight	38	39	44	52	50	46	49	55	54
Crab meat, canned	Canned weight	9	29	66	64	61	64	71	64	58

[1] The method of calculating canned salmon supply does not incorporate annual beginning and ending warehouse stock. Due to the biennial nature of the pink salmon fishery, some salmon canned in one year may be exported in the following year.

Source: U.S. National Oceanic and Atmospheric Administration, "Fisheries One Stop Shop," <www.fisheries.noaa.gov/foss/>, accessed June 2022. See also <www.fisheries.noaa.gov/national/sustainable-fisheries/fisheries-united-states>.

Table 942. U.S. Private Aquaculture—Trout and Catfish Production and Value: 1990 to 2021

[67.8 represents 67,800,000. Data are for calendar year and foodsize fish (trout at least 12 inches long; catfish weighing at least three quarters of a pound). Data are based on surveys of trout and catfish farms. For descriptions of surveys, see under "Catfish Production" and "Trout Production" at <www.nass.usda.gov/Surveys/Guide_to_NASS_Surveys/index.php>]

Item	Unit	1990	1995	2000	2005	2010	2015	2017	2018	2019	2020	2021
TROUT FOODSIZE												
Number sold.............	Mil.	67.8	60.2	58.4	55.6	38.7	45.4	41.0	35.9	31.9	25.9	26.3
Total weight..........	Mil. lb.	56.8	55.6	59.0	59.9	45.3	57.9	53.9	47.5	51.0	44.5	44.8
Total value of sales.......	Mil. dol.	64.6	60.8	63.3	63.5	63.2	96.4	102.7	91.8	98.5	88.6	90.0
Avg. price received by processors............	Dol./lb.	1.14	1.09	1.07	1.06	1.40	1.66	1.91	1.93	1.93	1.99	2.01
Percent sold to processors..............	Percent	58.0	68.0	69.7	66.0	63.4	57.6	59.4	57.2	60.5	66.3	67.3
CATFISH FOODSIZE												
Number sold.............	Mil.	272.9	321.8	420.1	395.6	263.4	195.5	199.8	208.6	196.4	204.4	191.4
Total weight..........	Mil. lb.	392.4	481.5	633.8	605.5	478.9	317.4	330.4	343.6	348.0	324.1	323.4
Total value of sales.......	Mil. dol.	305.1	378.1	468.8	427.8	375.1	346.4	355.4	335.0	362.0	352.1	398.2
Avg. price received by processors............	Dol./lb.	0.78	0.79	0.74	0.71	0.78	1.09	1.08	0.97	1.04	1.09	1.23

Source: U.S. Department of Agriculture, National Agricultural Statistics Service, *Trout Production*, February 2022, and *Catfish Production*, February 2022. See also <www.nass.usda.gov/Publications/Reports_by_Release_Day/index.php>.

Table 943. Fisheries—Quantity and Value of Domestic Catch: 1980 to 2020

[In millions of pounds (6,607 represents 6,607,000,000), except as noted. Data shown for commercial landings]

Year	Quantity [1] (mil. lbs.) Total	For human food	For industrial products [2]	Value (mil. dol.)	Average price per lb. (cents)	Year	Quantity [1] (mil. lbs.) Total	For human food	For industrial products [2]	Value (mil. dol.)	Average price per lb. (cents)
1980......	6,607	(NA)	(NA)	2,248	34.0	2001......	9,272	(NA)	(NA)	3,233	34.9
1982......	6,487	(NA)	(NA)	2,389	36.8	2002......	9,227	7,077	2,150	3,093	33.5
1983......	6,456	(NA)	(NA)	2,338	36.2	2003......	9,309	7,364	1,946	3,319	35.7
1984......	6,464	(NA)	(NA)	2,356	36.4	2004......	9,619	7,743	1,876	3,755	39.0
1985......	6,382	(NA)	(NA)	2,360	37.0	2005......	9,597	7,965	1,631	3,989	41.6
1986......	6,132	(NA)	(NA)	2,840	46.3	2006......	9,630	7,964	1,666	4,221	43.8
1987......	7,013	(NA)	(NA)	3,238	46.1	2007......	9,368	7,569	1,799	4,307	46.0
1988......	7,385	(NA)	(NA)	3,590	48.6	2008......	8,419	6,710	1,709	4,543	54.0
1989......	8,751	(NA)	(NA)	3,419	39.1	2009......	8,116	6,225	1,891	3,958	48.8
1990......	9,806	(NA)	(NA)	3,659	37.3	2010......	8,314	6,593	1,721	4,665	56.1
1991......	9,632	(NA)	(NA)	3,416	35.4	2011......	9,917	7,963	1,954	5,540	55.9
1992......	9,948	(NA)	(NA)	3,777	37.9	2012......	9,727	7,558	2,169	5,570	57.3
1993......	9,967	(NA)	(NA)	3,344	33.5	2013......	9,794	7,982	1,812	5,562	56.8
1994......	10,088	(NA)	(NA)	3,699	36.6	2014......	9,561	7,888	1,673	5,609	58.7
1995......	9,661	(NA)	(NA)	3,806	39.4	2015......	9,757	7,776	1,981	5,391	55.3
1996......	9,370	(NA)	(NA)	3,542	37.8	2016......	9,659	7,553	2,106	5,521	57.2
1997......	9,613	(NA)	(NA)	3,572	37.2	2017......	9,962	8,259	1,704	5,835	58.6
1998......	8,987	(NA)	(NA)	3,205	35.7	2018......	9,426	7,532	1,895	5,692	60.4
1999......	9,087	(NA)	(NA)	3,570	39.3	2019......	9,363	7,584	1,779	5,598	59.8
2000......	8,854	(NA)	(NA)	3,657	41.3	2020......	8,388	6,711	1,678	4,781	57.0

NA Not available. [1] Live weight. [2] Processed into meal, oil, solubles, and shell products, or used as bait and animal food.

Source: U.S. National Oceanic and Atmospheric Administration, "Fisheries One Stop Shop," <www.fisheries.noaa.gov/foss/>, accessed June 2022. See also <www.fisheries.noaa.gov/national/sustainable-fisheries/fisheries-united-states>.

Table 944. Mineral and Mining Industries—Employment, Hours, and Earnings: 2010 to 2021

[In units, as indicated. 654.8 represents 654,800. Industries based on North American Classification System (NAICS) 2017. Based on the Current Employment Statistics Program, see Appendix III]

Industry and item	Unit	2010	2015	2016	2017	2018	2019	2020	2021 [2]
All mining: [1]									
All employees..................	1,000	654.8	760.4	616.8	626.1	677.8	678.0	552.9	519.6
Avg. weekly hours..............	Number	43.6	44.2	43.6	45.7	46.4	46.5	44.8	45.5
Avg. weekly earnings...........	Dollars	1,222	1,407	1,427	1,499	1,541	1,599	1,589	1,623
Production workers...............	1,000	482.6	550.1	430.0	449.7	499.4	492.8	385.4	378.1
Oil and gas extraction:									
All employees..................	1,000	158.7	193.4	169.8	143.9	142.3	143.6	129.8	117.7
Avg. weekly hours..............	Number	40.6	41.2	40.3	42.0	42.4	42.8	41.8	41.2
Avg. weekly earnings...........	Dollars	1,461	1,744	1,787	1,873	1,952	2,030	2,017	1,914
Production workers...............	1,000	89.0	107.6	89.5	74.4	78.5	81.0	74.2	71.8
Coal mining:									
All employees..................	1,000	80.8	64.2	50.8	51.5	51.6	50.5	39.8	36.6
Avg. weekly hours..............	Number	47.5	45.6	45.0	45.8	47.0	48.3	44.6	45.3
Avg. weekly earnings...........	Dollars	1,335	1,487	1,444	1,486	1,545	1,617	1,520	1,613
Metal ore mining:									
All employees..................	1,000	36.7	41.8	39.0	39.5	41.7	42.2	41.4	41.4
Avg. weekly hours..............	Number	38.9	43.3	44.0	44.1	43.5	44.1	43.8	41.6
Avg. weekly earnings...........	Dollars	1,123	1,370	1,440	1,410	1,406	1,469	1,504	1,572
Nonmetallic minerals mining, and quarrying:									
All employees..................	1,000	87.0	91.8	91.1	94.8	98.0	97.8	95.1	96.8
Avg. weekly hours..............	Number	42.4	45.2	45.3	44.4	45.0	46.7	46.0	45.3
Avg. weekly earnings...........	Dollars	935	1,139	1,165	1,185	1,239	1,352	1,346	1,334

[1] Includes other industries not shown separately. [2] Data are preliminary.

Source: U.S. Bureau of Labor Statistics, Current Employment Statistics, "Employment, Hours, and Earnings—National," <www.bls.gov/ces/data.htm>, accessed February 2022.

Table 945. Mine Safety: 2010 to 2021

[In units, as indicated. Calendar year data]

Item	Total 2010	Total 2020	Total 2021	Coal 2010	Coal 2020	Coal 2021	Metal and non-metal 2010	Metal and non-metal 2020	Metal and non-metal 2021
Number of mines..........................	14,283	12,749	12,563	1,939	1,006	970	12,344	11,733	11,593
Number of miners........................	362,028	297,522	301,068	136,057	63,762	61,315	225,971	233,760	239,753
Fatalities (number).........................	72	29	37	48	5	10	24	24	27
Fatal injury rate [1].........................	0.024	0.012	0.015	0.038	0.009	0.019	0.013	0.012	0.014
All injury rate [1]............................	2.83	1.84	1.89	3.47	2.69	2.80	2.38	1.59	1.65
Mining area inspection hours per mine [2]................................	63	43	42	259	200	205	23	21	21
Citations and orders [3]....................	170,031	77,839	77,993	96,327	28,668	29,722	73,704	49,171	48,271
S&S citations and orders [4] (percent). ..	32	18	20	32	17	19	31	18	20
Amount assessed [5] (mil. dol.)..........	162.3	40.6	41.7	110.2	17.9	17.1	52.1	22.7	24.5
Coal production (mil. tons)...............	1,086	536	578	1,086	535	578	(X)	(X)	(X)

X Not applicable. [1] Reported injury rates per 200,000 hours worked. [2] Includes on-site Inspection Time (metal/non-metal), MMU Pit Time (Coal), Outby Area Time (Coal), Surface Area Time (Coal), Citation/Order writing On-Site. On-site inspection hours represent hours entered by Authorized Representatives of the Secretary (AR) for certain inspection activities and task codes. [3] Citations and orders are those not vacated. [4] A violation that "significantly and substantially" contributes to the cause and effect of a coal or other mine safety or health hazard. [5] Government penalties or fines.

Source: U.S. Mine Safety and Health Administration, Office of Program Education and Outreach Services, "Mine Safety and Health At a Glance," <www.msha.gov/msha-glance>, accessed April 2022.

Table 946. Mining and Primary Metal Production Indexes: 1990 to 2021

[Index 2017=100]

Industry group	2017 NAICS code	1990	2000	2010	2015	2017	2018	2019	2020	2021
Mining [1]..........................	**21**	**87.1**	**83.9**	**82.4**	**104.6**	**100.0**	**113.3**	**120.8**	**102.7**	**105.9**
Oil and gas extraction [1]...............	211	64.4	60.9	62.8	99.2	100.0	116.1	129.9	122.1	122.3
Crude oil............................	21112	78.6	62.2	58.6	100.9	100.0	116.9	131.3	120.7	119.5
Natural gas.........................	211130	63.6	68.9	76.6	98.4	100.0	112.9	124.7	123.5	126.5
Coal mining.........................	2121	144.7	146.0	142.6	115.9	100.0	98.2	92.3	68.7	74.9
Metal ore mining.....................	2122	112.7	119.8	99.3	102.2	100.0	98.0	95.8	92.3	91.0
Iron ore.............................	21221	121.9	135.6	106.9	96.2	100.0	103.3	97.9	79.5	100.8
Gold ore and silver ore..............	21222	126.8	151.4	99.0	91.2	100.0	95.1	84.9	81.0	79.8
Copper, nickel, lead, and zinc.......	21223	114.7	114.8	89.9	109.4	100.0	97.8	99.4	94.3	97.5
Oil and gas drilling..................	213111	105.6	97.9	114.2	121.2	100.0	128.8	128.1	75.7	89.2
Primary metal manufacturing [1]......	**331**	**99.6**	**114.6**	**103.8**	**105.7**	**100.0**	**103.2**	**97.3**	**86.2**	**96.6**
Iron and steel........................	3311, 3312	95.2	110.5	101.7	101.5	100.0	103.4	95.2	86.5	101.8
Aluminum...........................	3313	100.0	102.1	89.8	108.0	100.0	106.1	101.5	90.3	104.1
Nonferrous metals [1].................	3314	103.0	105.1	125.5	113.9	100.0	102.2	101.6	93.9	95.5

[1] Includes other industries not shown separately.

Source: Board of Governors of the Federal Reserve System, "Industrial Production and Capacity Utilization, Statistical Release G.17," <www.federalreserve.gov/datadownload/default.htm>, accessed July 2022.

Table 947. Mineral Production: 2000 to 2021

[In units as indicated (1,073.6 represents 1,073,600,000). Data represent production as measured by mine shipments, mine sales, or marketable production. See Appendix IV for information on weights and measures]

Minerals and metals	Unit	2000	2010	2015	2020	2021 [6]
FUEL MINERALS						
Coal, total.................................	Mil. short tons	1,073.6	1,084.4	896.9	535.4	(NA)
Bituminous................................	Mil. short tons	574.3	489.5	404.4	237.9	(NA)
Subbituminous...........................	Mil. short tons	409.2	514.8	419.5	245.8	(NA)
Lignite.....................................	Mil. short tons	85.6	78.2	70.9	49.4	(NA)
Anthracite.................................	Mil. short tons	4.6	1.8	2.1	2.4	(NA)
Natural gas (marketed production)........	Tril. cu. ft.	20.2	22.4	28.8	36.2	37.0
Petroleum (crude)........................	Mil. barrels [1]	2,131	2,002	3,446	4,142	4,108
Uranium concentrate (recoverable content).........	Mil. lb.	4.0	4.2	3.3	(D)	–
NONFUEL MINERALS						
Asbestos (sales).........................	1,000 metric tons	5	–	–	–	–
Barite, primary, sold/used by producers.............	1,000 metric tons	392	662	433	–	–
Boron minerals, sold or used by producers........	1,000 metric tons	1,070	(D)	(D)	(D)	(D)
Bromine, sold or used by producers................	1,000 metric tons	228	(D)	(D)	(D)	(D)
Cement [2]...................................	Mil. metric tons	(NA)	66	84.4	[7] 89.0	92.0
Clays......................................	1,000 metric tons	40,800	25,600	25,500	25,100	25,000
Diatomite.................................	1,000 metric tons	677	595	832	822	830
Feldspar...................................	1,000 metric tons	790	500	520	430	400
Fluorspar, finished shipments..............	1,000 metric tons	–	(NA)	(NA)	(NA)	(NA)
Garnet (industrial)........................	1,000 metric tons	60	53	77	101	75
Gypsum, crude............................	Mil. metric tons	20	10	19	21	23
Helium [3]...................................	Mil. cu. meters	98	75	71	76	71
Lime, sold or used by producers [4]...........	Mil. metric tons	20	18	18	16	17
Mica, scrap/flake, sold or used by producers.......	1,000 metric tons	101	56	33	35	43
Peat, sales by producers...................	1,000 metric tons	847	628	455	444	420
Perlite, processed, sold or used............	1,000 metric tons	672	414	444	493	500
Phosphate rock, marketable................	Mil. metric tons	39	26	27	24	22
Potash (K2O equivalent), marketable............	1,000 metric tons	1,300	930	740	460	480
Pumice & pumicite, sold and used..............	1,000 metric tons	1,050	241	310	578	580
Salt [2].....................................	Mil. metric tons	46	43	45	[7] 41	40
Sand & gravel:						
Construction..............................	Mil. metric tons	1,120	807	880	942	1,000
Industrial.................................	Mil. metric tons	28	32	102	70	72
Soda ash (sodium carbonate)..............	1,000 metric tons	10,200	10,600	11,600	9,990	12,000
Stone:						
Crushed and broken......................	Mil. metric tons	1,560	1,160	1,340	1,470	1,500
Dimension [4].............................	1,000 metric tons	1,250	1,670	2,700	2,350	2,300
Sulfur: total shipments....................	1,000 metric tons	10,700	9,170	9,560	7,900	8,200
Talc.......................................	1,000 metric tons	851	604	615	[7] 490	490
Vermiculite concentrate....................	1,000 metric tons	150	100	100	100	100
METALS						
Aluminum.................................	1,000 metric tons	3,668	1,726	1,587	1,012	880
Copper (recoverable content)...............	1,000 metric tons	1,450	1,110	1,380	1,200	1,200
Gold (recoverable content).................	Metric tons	353	231	214	193	180
Iron ore, usable (gross weight).............	Mil. metric tons	61	50	46	38	46
Lead (recoverable content).................	1,000 metric tons	449	369	370	306	300
Magnesium metal..........................	1,000 metric tons	(D)	(D)	(D)	(D)	(D)
Molybdenum, mine.........................	1,000 metric tons	41	59	47	51	48
Nickel ore, refinery byproduct..............	1,000 metric tons	(D)	(D)	(D)	(D)	(D)
Palladium metal...........................	Kilograms	10,300	11,600	12,500	14,600	14,000
Platinum metal............................	Kilograms	3,110	3,450	3,670	4,200	4,200
Silicon (Si content) [5].....................	1,000 metric tons	367	176	411	277	310
Silver (recoverable content)................	Metric tons	1,860	1,280	1,090	1,030	1,000
Titanium concentrate, (TiO2 content).............	1,000 metric tons	300	200	200	[7] 100	100
Vanadium (recoverable content)............	Metric tons	–	1060	–	17	–
Zinc, ore and concentrate.................	1,000 metric tons	796	748	825	718	740

NA Not available. D Withheld to avoid disclosing individual company data. – Represents or rounds to zero. [1] 42-gallon barrels. [2] Excludes Puerto Rico. [3] Extracted from natural gas. Both grade A and crude helium. [4] Includes Puerto Rico. [5] For 2006-2010, ferrosilicon only; silicon metal withheld to avoid disclosing proprietary data. Beginning in 2011, silicon alloys and metal. Beginning 2012, includes statistics for ferrosilicon and silicon metal containing less than 99.9% silicon. [6] Nonfuel minerals and metals estimated. [7] Estimated.

Source: Nonfuels, through 1994, U.S. Bureau of Mines; thereafter, U.S. Geological Survey, *Mineral Commodity Summaries 2022*, January 2022, and earlier reports; see also <www.usgs.gov/centers/nmic/publications>. Fuels, U.S. Energy Information Administration, *Annual Energy Review 2011*, September 2012, and earlier reports; *Annual Coal Report, 2020*, October 2021; and "Natural Gas Gross Withdrawals and Production," <www.eia.gov/naturalgas/data.php>, "Uranium & Nuclear Fuel Summary Production Statistics," <www.eia.gov/nuclear/data.php>, and "Crude Oil Production," <www.eia.gov/petroleum/data.php>, accessed September 2022.

Table 948. Nonfuel Mineral Commodities—Summary: 2020

[1,340 represents 1,340,000. Except as noted, data are for mine or crude production, and average price or value are in dollars per metric ton]

Mineral	Unit	Mineral disposition				Average price per unit (dollars)	Employ-ment (number)
		Produc-tion	Exports	Net import reliance [1,2] (percent)	Con-sumption, apparent		
Alumina (metal equivalent)	1,000 metric tons	1,340	162	48	2,560	[3] 412	[21] 30,100
Aluminum	1,000 metric tons	1,012	2,755	39	3,980	[4] 0.89	[21] 30,100
Antimony (contained)	Metric tons	–	[5] 1,634	81	23,400	[4] 2.67	(NA)
Asbestos	Metric tons	–	–	100	450	[7] 2,110	–
Barite	1,000 metric tons	(D)	48	>75	(D)	[6] 183	330
Bauxite (metal equiv.)	1,000 metric tons	(D)	15	>75	(D)	[3] 26	(NA)
Beryllium (contained)	Metric tons	165	25	16	196	[8] 620	(NA)
Bismuth (contained)	Metric tons	–	749	93	1,150	[4] 2.72	(NA)
Boron (B2O3 content)	1,000 metric tons	(D)	[9] 257	([10])	(D)	[7,11] 380	1,330
Bromine (contained)	Metric tons	(D)	[12] 36,800	([10])	(D)	[8,11] 2.73	1,050
Cadmium (contained)	Metric tons	(D)	[13] 4	<50	(D)	[8,14] 2.29	(NA)
Cement	1,000 metric tons	[15] 89,000	888	15	103,000	[7] 124	12,200
Chromium	1,000 metric tons	[16] 116	111	75	465	[17] 179	(NA)
Clays	1,000 metric tons	[18] 25,100	[18] 3,360	([10])	22,100	(NA)	5,320
Cobalt (contained)	Metric tons	[19] 2,000	3,440	76	8,500	[4] 15.70	(NA)
Copper (mine, recoverable)	1,000 metric tons	1,200	383	38	1,650	[4] 2.87	11,000
Diamond, stones (industrial)	Million carats	–	(Z)	83	0.6	[20] 8.4	(NA)
Diatomite	1,000 metric tons	822	66	([10])	770	[7] 330	370
Feldspar	1,000 metric tons	430	3	8	470	[7] 108	240
Fluorspar	1,000 metric tons	(NA)	9	100	470	[7,11] 149	14
Garnet (industrial)	Metric tons	101,000	13,600	50	202,000	[7] 250	130
Gemstones	Million dollars	[22] 75.8	[23] 1,320	99	15,100	(NA)	1,100
Germanium (contained)	Kilograms	(D)	7,100	>50	30,000	[8] 1,046	(NA)
Gold (contained)	Metric tons	193	297	47	185	[24] 1,774	12,500
Graphite (natural)	Metric tons	–	5,930	100	30,000	[25] 1,540	(NA)
Gypsum (crude)	1,000 metric tons	21,200	32	15	40,200	8.6	4,500
Iodine	Metric tons	(D)	1,130	>50	(D)	[27] 31.57	60
Iron ore (usable)	1,000 metric tons	38,100	10,400	([10])	31,100	[7] 91.27	4,300
Iron and steel scrap (metal)	Million metric tons	[28] 57.8	17	([10])	45	[7,43] 228	24,000
Iron and steel slag (metal)	Million metric tons	13	(Z)	14	13	[7] 25.50	1,500
Lead (contained)	1,000 metric tons	306	265	26	1,400	[4] 0.91	1,810
Lime [30]	1,000 metric tons	15,800	266	<1	15,900	[7] 132.1	(NA)
Lithium	Metric tons	(D)	1,170	>50	2,000	8,000	70
Magnesium compounds	1,000 metric tons	[26] 363	66	53	777	(NA)	260
Magnesium metal	1,000 metric tons	(D)	15	<50	(D)	[4] 2.49	400
Manganese (gross weight)	1,000 metric tons	–	1	100	378	[31] 4.59	(NA)
Mercury [32]	Metric tons	(NA)	–	(NA)	(NA)	(NA)	(NA)
Mica, scrap and flake	Metric tons	34,600	4,000	31	50,000	111	(NA)
Molybdenum (contained)	Metric tons	51,100	62,400	([10])	13,300	[8] 19.90	950
Nickel (contained) [34]	Metric tons	16,700	58,800	49	190,000	13,772	(NA)
Niobium (columbium)	Metric tons	–	785	100	6,330	[8] 21	(NA)
Nitrogen (fixed)-ammonia	1,000 metric tons	14,000	369	11	15,700	[35] 223	1,600
Peat	1,000 metric tons	444	46	75	1,780	[7] 24.74	530
Perlite	1,000 metric tons	845	25	21	626	[7] 61	140
Phosphate rock	1,000 metric tons	23,500	(NA)	5	25,100	[7] 75.86	1,800
Platinum-group metals	Kilograms	[36] 18,800	[36] 77,500	[37] 77	[37] 47,200	[24,37] 886.02	1,881
Potash (K2O equivalent)	1,000 metric tons	[44] 460	147	92	[44] 5,700	[38] 850	900
Pumice and pumicite	1,000 metric tons	578	8	12	660	[7] 31	140
Salt	1,000 metric tons	41,000	1,250	27	54,000	[7,39] 215.00	4,000
Silicon, metal	1,000 metric tons	[40] 277	31	<50	[40] 481	[4] 0.97	(NA)
Silver (contained)	Metric tons	1,030	140	80	8,260	[24] 20.58	1,180
Soda ash (sodium carbonate)	1,000 metric tons	9,990	5,590	([10])	4,480	145.67	2,400
Stone (crushed)	Million metric tons	1,470	(Z)	1	1,530	12.22	67,000
Sulfur (all forms)	1,000 metric tons	7,890	1,374	21	9,960	[7,41] 24.4	2,400
Talc	1,000 metric tons	490	188	<1	460	265	187
Thallium (contained)	Kilograms	–	1,239	(NA)	57	[8] 8,200	(NA)
Tin (contained)	Metric tons	[19] 17,550	2,849	77	41,300	[4] 7.99	(NA)
Titanium dioxide	Metric tons	890,000	386,000	([10])	770,000	2,710	3,100
Tungsten (contained)	Metric tons	(D)	2,940	>50	(D)	[42] 270	(NA)
Vermiculite	1,000 metric tons	100	8	[44] 20	130	(NA)	73
Zinc (contained)	1,000 metric tons	718	546	([10])	[33] 878	[4] 1.11	2,580
Zirconium (ZrO2)	Metric tons	[44] 20,000	13,694	<25	[44] 30,000	[29] 1,380	(NA)

– Represents or rounds to zero. < Less than. > Greater than. D Withheld to avoid disclosing company proprietary data. NA Not available. Z Less than .05 million metric tons or less than half a unit shown. [1] Net imports calculated as imports minus exports and may include adjustments for industry stock changes. [2] Calculated as percent of apparent consumption. [3] Alumina, average value, U.S. imports (f.a.s.). [4] Dollars per pound. [5] Ore and concentrates not included. [6] Estimated price, ground, average value, dollars per ton, ex-works. [7] Dollars per ton. [8] Dollars per kilogram. [9] Boric acid, gross weight. [10] Net exporter. [11] Average value of imports (cost, insurance, and freight, c.i.f.). [12] Elemental bromine and compounds. [13] Unwrought cadmium and powders. [14] Average free market price for 99.95% purity in 10-ton lots; cost, insurance, and freight; global ports. Source: Metal Bulletin. [15] Production for Portland and masonry cement includes cement made from imported clinker; excludes Puerto Rico. [16] Recycling production. [17] Unit value of imported chromite ore; dollars per metric ton gross weight. [18] Excludes attapulgite. [19] Secondary production. [20] Value of imports, dollars per carat. [21] Alumina and aluminum production workers. Source: U.S. Department of Labor, Bureau of Labor Statistics. [22] Natural gemstone production, 9.8 million dollars; laboratory-created (synthetic) gemstone production, 66 million dollars. [23] Includes reexports. [24] Dollars per troy ounce. [25] Price of flake imports (average at foreign ports). Graphite lump/chip (Sri Lankan) price, $2,940 per ton. [26] Magnesium compound shipments. [27] Average value of imports (c.i.f.), dollars per kilogram. [28] Iron and steel scrap production includes receipts for purchased scrap. Exports excludes rails for rerolling and other uses, and ships, boats, and other vessels for scrapping. [29] Unit value based on annual imports for consumption from Australia, Senegal, and South Africa. [30] Lime production data are sold or used by producers. Price data are for quicklime only. [31] 44% Mn metallurgical ore, per metric ton unit, contained Mn; cost, insurance, and freight (c.i.f.) value, U.S. ports. [32] Mercury not produced as principal commodity in U.S. since 1992; secondary production (recycled) not reported. [33] Value for refined zinc. [34] Primary and secondary materials. [35] Dollars per short ton, average, f.o.b. Gulf Coast. [36] Platinum and palladium. [37] Platinum. [38] Dollars per ton of K2O, all products. [39] Vacuum and open pan, bulk, pellets and packaged, f.o.b. mine and plant. [40] Combined for ferrosilicon and silicon metal. [41] Elemental sulfur, f.o.b., mine or plant. [42] A metric ton unit of tungsten trioxide (WO3) contains 7.93 kilograms of tungsten. Platts Metals Week. [43] No 1. Heavy Melting composite price. [44] Data are rounded to avoid disclosing company proprietary data.

Source: U.S. Geological Survey, *Mineral Commodity Summaries 2022*, January 2022. See also <www.usgs.gov/centers/national-minerals-information-center/mineral-commodity-summaries>.

| Year | Nonfuel minerals | | | | | | | | | Fuels | | |
	Copper, cath-ode (cents/ lb.)	Plati-num [1] (dol./troy oz.)	Gold (dol./troy oz.) [2]	Silver (dol./troy oz.) [2]	Lead [3] (cents/ lb.)	Nickel [4] (cents/ lb.)	Tin (New York) [4] (cents/ lb.)	Zinc [5] (cents/ lb.)	Sulfur, crude [6] (dol./ metric ton)	Bitumi-nous coal [7] (dol./ short ton)	Crude oil [7] (dol./ bbl.)	Natural gas [8] (dol./ 1,000 cu. ft.)
1990	123	467	385	4.82	46	402	386	75	80	27.43	20.03	3.03
1995	138	425	386	5.15	42	373	416	56	44	25.56	14.62	2.78
2000	88	549	280	5.00	44	392	370	56	25	24.15	26.72	4.62
2001	77	533	272	4.39	44	270	315	44	10	25.36	21.84	5.72
2002	76	543	311	4.62	44	307	292	39	12	26.57	22.51	4.12
2003	85	694	365	4.91	44	437	340	41	29	26.57	27.56	5.85
2004	134	849	411	6.69	55	627	547	52	33	30.56	36.77	6.65
2005	174	900	446	7.34	61	669	483	67	31	36.80	50.28	8.67
2006	315	1,144	606	11.61	77	1,100	565	159	33	39.32	59.69	8.61
2007	328	1,308	699	13.43	124	1,688	899	154	36	40.80	66.52	8.16
2008	319	1,578	874	15.00	120	957	1,129	89	264	51.39	94.04	9.18
2009	241	1,208	975	14.69	87	665	837	78	2	55.44	56.35	6.48
2010	348	1,616	1,228	20.20	109	989	1,240	102	70	60.88	74.71	6.18
2011	406	1,725	1,572	35.28	122	1,038	1,575	106	160	68.50	95.73	5.63
2012	367	1,555	1,673	31.22	114	795	1,283	96	124	66.04	94.52	4.73
2013	340	1,490	1,415	23.89	110	681	1,352	96	69	60.61	95.99	4.88
2014	318	1,388	1,269	19.09	106	765	1,023	107	80	55.99	87.39	5.71
2015	256	1,056	1,163	15.72	91	537	756	96	88	51.57	44.39	4.26
2016	225	990	1,252	17.20	94	435	839	101	38	48.40	38.29	3.71
2017	285	951	1,261	17.08	115	472	937	139	46	55.6	48.05	4.16
2018	299	883	1,272	15.73	111	595	936	141	81	59.43	61.40	4.23
2019	280	867	1,395	16.24	100	631	868	124	51	58.93	55.59	3.81
2020	287	886	1,774	20.58	91	625	799	111	24	50.05	36.86	3.43
2021 [9]	430	1,200	1,800	25.00	110	830	1,600	145	90	(NA)	65.73	5.73

NA Not available. [1] Average annual dealer prices. [2] 99.95 percent purity. [3] North American delivered basis. 1990-2012, North American producer price. Beginning 2013, North American market price. [4] Nickel: London Metal Exchange. Tin: Metals Week composite. [5] Platt's Metals Week price for North American special high grade zinc. Average prices for 1990 are for U.S. high grade zinc. [6] F.o.b. (Free on Board). [7] Average value at the point of production or domestic first purchase price. [8] Citygate price. Citygate is a point or measuring station at which a distributing gas utility receives gas from a natural gas pipeline company or transmission system. [9] Estimated.

Source: Nonfuels, through 1994, U.S. Bureau of Mines; thereafter, U.S. Geological Survey, *Mineral Commodity Summaries 2022*, January 2022 and earlier reports. Fuels, U.S. Energy Information Administration, *Monthly Energy Review*, March 2022 and earlier reports; and *Annual Coal Report, 2020*, October 2021 and earlier reports. See also <www.usgs.gov/centers/nmic/mineral-commodity-summaries>, <www.eia.gov/coal/annual/>, and <www.eia.gov/totalenergy/data/monthly>.

Table 950. **Value of Domestic Nonfuel Mineral Production by State: 2000 to 2021**

[In millions of dollars (39,400 represents $39,400,000,000)]

State	2000	2010	2020 [1]	2021 [1]	State	2000	2010	2020 [1]	2021 [1]
United States [2]	**39,400**	**66,400**	**82,300**	**90,400**	Missouri	1,370	2,010	3,030	3,300
					Montana	596	1,140	1,680	2,010
Alabama	930	969	1,580	1,860	Nebraska	[3] 84	234	[3] 215	[3] 220
Alaska	1,140	3,400	3,160	3,890	Nevada	2,980	7,700	9,140	9,350
Arizona	2,510	6,790	7,030	9,960	New Hampshire	[3] 57	[3] 94	110	95
Arkansas	484	709	869	1,000	New Jersey	[3] 291	[3] 258	345	396
California	3,270	2,890	4,680	5,270	New Mexico	786	1,020	864	1,290
Colorado	592	1,850	1,620	1,610	New York	1,020	1,310	[3] 1,690	[3] 1,570
Connecticut	[3] 112	[3] 148	[3] 190	183	North Carolina	744	880	[3] 1,150	[3] 1,460
Delaware	[3] 14	[3] 12	[3] 23	[3] 22	North Dakota	35	[3] 70	[3] 74	[3] 65
Florida	1,820	2,680	3,520	[3] 2,400	Ohio	999	1,170	[3] 1,340	[3] 1,380
Georgia	1,620	1,430	2,020	[3] 2,040	Oklahoma	473	702	1,040	916
Hawaii	[3] 92	106	128	134	Oregon	299	312	513	595
Idaho	358	1,180	[3] 247	722	Pennsylvania	[3] 1,250	[3] 1,670	[3] 1,750	[3] 1,950
Illinois	913	924	[3] 1,100	[3] 992	Rhode Island	[3] 20	[3] 33	[3] 48	[3] 66
Indiana	695	782	[3] 695	1,160	South Carolina	[3] 551	[3] 468	[3] 895	[3] 953
Iowa	503	583	[3] 727	959	South Dakota	233	258	449	495
Kansas	629	1,090	[3] 1,250	[3] 1,210	Tennessee	737	831	1,330	1,550
Kentucky	501	762	[3] 566	[3] 586	Texas	1,950	2,780	6,090	5,760
Louisiana	325	549	[3] 656	661	Utah	1,430	4,380	3,150	3,750
Maine	96	110	[3] 148	[3] 127	Vermont	[3] 67	[3] 121	[3] 119	[3] 112
Maryland	[3] 358	[3] 305	[3] 429	[3] 461	Virginia	710	1,040	1,370	1,550
Massachusetts	[3] 200	[3] 233	[3] 267	[3] 209	Washington	607	712	630	732
Michigan	1,640	2,190	2,630	3,000	West Virginia	172	272	[3] 164	360
Minnesota	1,460	[3] 4,180	[3] 4,090	[3] 402	Wisconsin	[3] 372	509	[3] 1,020	[3] 997
Mississippi	149	198	[3] 286	[3] 200	Wyoming	978	1,860	2,440	2,750

[1] Preliminary. [2] Includes data not distributed to States, not shown separately. [3] Partial data only; excludes values withheld to avoid disclosing individual company data.

Source: U.S. Geological Survey, "Minerals Yearbook," <www.usgs.gov/centers/national-minerals-information-center/minerals-yearbook-metals-and-minerals>, accessed May 2022; and *Mineral Commodities Summaries 2022*, January 2022, and earlier reports. See also <www.usgs.gov/centers/national-minerals-information-center/commodity-statistics-and-information>.

Table 951. Net U.S. Imports of Selected Minerals and Metals as Percent of Apparent Consumption: 1980 to 2021

[In percent. Net imports are the difference between imports and exports plus or minus government stockpile and industry stock changes]

Minerals and metals	1980	1990	2000	2010	2015	2018	2019	2020	2021 [1]
Fluorspar	87	91	100	100	100	100	100	100	100
Manganese	98	100	100	100	100	100	100	100	100
Mica (sheet)	100	100	100	100	100	100	100	100	100
Niobium	100	100	100	100	100	100	100	100	100
Strontium	100	100	100	100	100	100	100	100	100
Tantalum	90	86	80	100	100	100	100	100	100
Vanadium	35	(D)	100	82	100	100	95	99	100
Potash	65	68	80	83	89	92	91	92	93
Titanium	(NA)	(NA)	79	65	85	91	92	88	90
Chromium	67	80	77	63	64	76	73	75	80
Silver	7	(NA)	43	65	67	73	74	80	79
Tin	79	71	88	73	76	77	76	77	78
Zinc	60	64	72	73	81	87	88	79	76
Cobalt	93	84	78	81	73	64	78	76	76
Barite	44	71	84	75	78	87	86	>75	>75
Bauxite	(NA)	98	100	100	>75	>75	>75	>75	>75
Platinum	(NA)	(NA)	78	91	66	74	67	77	70
Tungsten	53	81	66	63	>25	>50	>50	>50	>50
Nickel	76	64	54	41	50	52	49	49	48
Copper	16	15	37	32	32	33	37	38	45
Aluminum	([2])	([2])	33	14	41	50	47	39	44
Palladium	(NA)	(NA)	84	49	53	42	34	35	37
Sulfur	14	15	18	19	14	7	6	21	18
Gypsum	21	27	27	12	10	12	15	15	16
Iron and steel	13	13	18	6	29	15	12	8	10

D Withheld to avoid disclosure. NA Not available. > Greater than. [1] Preliminary. [2] Net exporter.

Source: Through 1990, U.S. Bureau of Mines; thereafter, U.S. Geological Survey, *Mineral Commodity Summaries 2022*, January 2022, and earlier reports. See also <www.usgs.gov/centers/nmic>.

Table 952. Crude Petroleum and Natural Gas Extraction Industry—Establishments, Employees, and Payroll by State: 2020

[10,313,099 represents $10,313,099,000. Based on the North American Classification System (NAICS) 2017. Excludes self-employed individuals, employees of private households, railroad employees, agricultural production employees, and most government employees. See source for definitions and statement on reliability of data. An establishment is a single physical location where business is conducted or where services or industrial operations are performed. See Appendix III]

State	Crude petroleum extraction (NAICS 211120)			Natural gas extraction (NAICS 211130)		
	Establish-ments	Number of employees [1]	Annual payroll ($1,000)	Establish-ments	Number of employees [1]	Annual payroll ($1,000)
United States	**4,446**	**70,407**	**10,313,099**	**1,333**	**29,838**	**3,967,581**
Alabama	15	86	9,930	7	[2] 177	[2] 23,106
Alaska	13	[2] 1,819	427,143	5	[2] 111	[2] 21,060
Arizona	3	3	[2] 176	4	[2] 11	[2] 698
Arkansas	54	451	37,542	23	245	29,363
California	117	4,173	597,881	25	300	40,322
Colorado	245	4,637	863,923	61	1,988	291,767
Florida	11	[2] 34	2,848	3	[2] 30	[2] 6,600
Idaho	3	3	183	(NA)	(NA)	(NA)
Illinois	123	546	25,342	6	[2] 61	[2] 5,016
Indiana	24	[2] 155	8,483	4	6	304
Kansas	271	1,238	71,481	29	274	21,571
Kentucky	41	207	11,349	18	456	29,270
Louisiana	242	3,393	406,406	103	2,366	280,593
Massachusetts	3	[2] 12	1,037	(NA)	(NA)	(NA)
Michigan	42	550	34,521	20	264	19,912
Minnesota	3	[2] 3	[2] 156	(NA)	(NA)	(NA)
Mississippi	51	509	72,333	11	86	7,265
Missouri	5	[2] 4	475	(NA)	(NA)	(NA)
Montana	70	474	50,923	6	[2] 182	[2] 21,838
Nebraska	11	[2] 40	[2] 2,616	(NA)	(NA)	(NA)
Nevada	11	50	4,116	(NA)	(NA)	(NA)
New Jersey	4	[2] 23	[2] 3,986	41	1,156	139,324
New Mexico	101	2,401	291,857	4	27	1,381
New York	19	82	8,555	3	4	473
North Dakota	59	2,250	302,219	14	[2] 791	[2] 114,415
Ohio	104	635	34,265	57	1,056	87,084
Oklahoma	755	6,863	818,257	149	3,059	318,395
Pennsylvania	75	916	114,651	84	2,957	397,697
Tennessee	4	[2] 20	[2] 1,096	(NA)	(NA)	(NA)
Texas	1,731	36,575	5,889,597	539	11,810	1,831,237
Utah	31	647	71,266	10	249	37,764
Virginia	4	2	71	10	[2] 205	[2] 24,335
Washington	6	[2] 11	578	(NA)	(NA)	(NA)
West Virginia	80	654	46,704	62	1,102	96,839
Wyoming	99	845	92,012	24	827	115,479

NA Not available. [1] Covers full- and part-time employees who are on the payroll in the pay period including March 12. [2] Data is flagged for high noise; the value was changed by 5 percent or more to avoid disclosure of data for individual businesses.

Source: U.S. Census Bureau, County Business Patterns, "County Business Patterns by Legal Form of Organization and Employment Size Class for U.S., States, and Selected Geographies," <data.census.gov>, accessed April 2022.

Table 953. Petroleum Industry—Production, Foreign Trade, Reserves, and Refineries: 1990 to 2021

[In units as indicated (2,685 represents 2,685,000,000); mil. bbl.= millions of barrels. For definitions, see source below]

Item	Unit	1990	2000	2010	2015	2018	2019	2020	2021
Crude oil production, total [1]	Mil. bbl.	2,685	2,125	2,002	3,446	3,993	4,486	4,131	4,108
Average price per barrel	Dollars	20	27	75	44	61	56	37	66
Lower 48 states [2]	Mil. bbl.	2,037	1,771	1,783	3,270	3,818	4,316	3,968	3,948
Alaska	Mil. bbl.	647	354	219	176	175	170	163	160
Imports: Crude oil [1, 3]	Mil. bbl.	2,151	3,320	3,363	2,687	2,835	2,482	2,150	2,232
Refined petroleum products	Mil. bbl.	775	874	942	761	794	854	728	861
Exports: Crude oil [1]	Mil. bbl.	40	18	15	170	748	1,088	1,173	1,081
Proved reserves	Bil. bbl.	26	22	23	32	44	44	36	(NA)
Operable refineries	Number	205	158	148	140	135	135	135	129
Daily capacity (Jan. 1)	1,000 bbl.	15,572	16,512	17,584	17,967	18,598	18,802	18,976	18,128
Refinery input, total	Mil. bbl.	5,325	5,964	6,345	6,871	7,137	7,070	6,063	6,463
Crude oil [1]	Mil. bbl.	4,894	5,514	5,374	5,909	6,194	6,045	5,202	5,528
Hydrocarbon gas liquids	Mil. bbl.	171	139	161	189	210	209	186	200
Other liquids [4]	Mil. bbl.	260	311	810	773	734	816	676	734
Refinery output, total [5]	Mil. bbl.	5,574	6,311	6,735	7,258	7,553	7,460	6,401	6,812
Hydrocarbon gas liquids	Mil. bbl.	182	258	240	224	232	221	200	225
Motor gasoline [6]	Mil. bbl.	2,540	2,910	3,306	3,560	3,672	3,685	3,200	3,478
Jet fuel (kerosene type)	Mil. bbl.	478	588	517	580	659	656	373	478
Distillate fuel oil	Mil. bbl.	1,067	1,310	1,542	1,819	1,886	1,875	1,734	1,704
Residual fuel oil	Mil. bbl.	347	255	213	152	155	132	69	78
Petroleum coke	Mil. bbl.	202	266	296	319	329	308	281	279
Asphalt and road oil	Mil. bbl.	164	192	138	124	120	117	117	124
Still gas	Mil. bbl.	246	241	245	249	256	244	223	235
Utilization rate	Percent	87	93	86	91	93	90	79	87

NA Not available. [1] Includes lease condensate. [2] Excluding Alaska and Hawaii. [3] Includes imports for the Strategic Petroleum Reserve. [4] Unfinished oils (net), other hydrocarbons, hydrogen, aviation and motor gasoline blending components (net). Beginning 1995, also includes oxygenates (net). [5] Includes other products not shown separately. [6] Finished motor gasoline. Beginning 1995, also includes ethanol blended into motor gasoline.

Source: U.S. Energy Information Administration, "Petroleum & Other Liquids Data," <www.eia.gov/naturalgas/data.cfm>; and "Monthly Energy Review, Petroleum," <www.eia.gov/totalenergy/data/monthly/#petroleum>; accessed August 2022.

Table 954. Crude Oil and Petroleum Products Supply, Disposition, and Ending Stocks: 2021

[In millions of barrels (4,107.6 represents 4,107,600,000). Minus sign (-) indicates decrease]

Commodity	Supply				Disposition				
	Field production [1]	Refinery and blender net production	Imports	Adjustments [2]	Stock change	Refinery and blender net inputs	Exports	Products supplied [3]	Ending stocks [4]
Crude oil	4,107.6	(X)	2,231.6	162.0	-108.7	5,528.5	1,081.4	–	1,014.9
Hydrocarbon gas liquids	1,980.1	225.2	63.2	(X)	-38.2	200.3	842.8	1,255.6	193.1
Natural gasoline	222.4	(NA)	0.1	(X)	-11.9	60.7	71.7	94.0	20.7
Ethane	784.5	1.5	(NA)	(X)	-8.3	(NA)	134.8	659.5	63.2
Propane	636.7	101.3	41.6	(X)	-7.1	(NA)	484.3	302.5	63.8
Normal butane	184.9	21.1	13.2	(X)	-8.0	67.9	150.9	8.3	33.6
Isobutane	151.6	-3.1	2.4	(X)	-2.6	71.7	1.1	80.8	9.7
Finished motor gasoline	(X)	3,478.0	39.4	-11.1	-7.6	(X)	298.0	3,217.7	17.8
Kerosene-type jet fuel	(X)	478.5	57.8	(X)	-2.8	(X)	39.2	500.0	35.8
Distillate fuel oil [4]	(X)	1,703.7	105.3	(X)	-31.1	(X)	390.3	1,449.8	130.0

– Represents or rounds to zero. NA Not available. X Not applicable. [1] Represents crude oil production on leases, natural gas liquids production at natural gas processing plants, new supply of other hydrocarbons/oxygenates and motor gasoline blending components, and fuel ethanol blended into finished motor gasoline. [2] Includes an adjustment for crude oil, previously referred to as "Unaccounted For Crude Oil." Also included is an adjustment for motor gasoline blending components, fuel ethanol, and distillate fuel oil. [3] Products supplied is equal to field production, plus refinery and blender net production, plus import, plus adjustments, minus stock change, minus refinery and blender net inputs, minus export. [4] Total stocks do not include distillate fuel oil stocks located in the Northeast Heating Oil Reserve.

Source: U.S. Energy Information Administration, Petroleum & Other Liquids, "Supply and Disposition," <www.eia.gov/petroleum>, accessed August 2022.

Table 955. Natural Gas Plant Liquids—Production and Value: 1990 to 2021

[In units as indicated (569 represents 569,000,000). Barrels of 42 gallons]

Item	Unit	1990	2000	2005	2010	2015	2018	2019	2020	2021
Field production [1]	Mil. bbl.	569	699	627	757	1,220	1,595	1,761	1,894	1,980
Pentanes plus	Mil. bbl.	113	112	97	101	158	184	203	214	222
Liquefied petroleum gases	Mil. bbl.	456	587	529	656	1,062	1,411	1,558	1,680	1,758
Natural gas processed	Tril. cu. ft.	14.6	17.0	14.9	16.3	20.7	22.1	24.6	24.7	(NA)

NA Not available. [1] Includes other finished petroleum products, not shown separately.

Source: U.S. Energy Information Administration, "Natural Gas Plant Processing," <www.eia.gov/naturalgas/data.php>; and "Natural Gas Plant Field Production," <www.eia.gov/petroleum/data.php>; accessed August 2022.

Table 956. Crude Petroleum and Natural Gas—Production and Value for Major Producing States: 2010 to 2021

[In units as indicated (2,002 represents 2,002,000,000 barrels)]

State	Crude petroleum								Natural gas marketed production [1]			
	Quantity (mil. bbl.)				Value (mil. dol.) [2]				Quantity (bil. cu. ft.)			
	2010	2015	2020	2021	2010	2015	2020	2021	2010	2015	2020	2021
Total [3]	2,002	3,446	4,142	4,108	149,555	152,968	152,684	270,443	22,382	28,772	36,202	37,011
Alabama	7	10	4	4	540	432	155	277	(NA)	(NA)	(NA)	(NA)
Alaska [4]	215	170	159	156	15,561	6,970	5,418	9,713	374	344	338	355
Arkansas	6	6	6	4	407	268	146	261	927	1,010	481	449
California	200	201	142	135	14,930	9,185	5,719	9,198	287	237	171	140
Colorado	33	122	172	153	2,406	4,951	5,389	10,117	1,578	1,689	1,990	1,876
Florida	2	2	1	1	(NA)	(NA)	(NA)	(NA)	(NA)	(NA)	(NA)	(NA)
Illinois	9	10	7	7	664	419	272	456	(NA)	(NA)	(NA)	(NA)
Indiana	2	2	1	2	134	99	54	99	(NA)	(NA)	(NA)	(NA)
Kansas	40	45	28	28	2,931	1,963	1,026	1,786	325	284	163	148
Kentucky	3	3	2	2	178	130	84	153	(NA)	(NA)	(NA)	(NA)
Louisiana	68	64	37	35	5,289	3,087	1,428	2,308	2,210	1,805	3,206	3,384
Michigan	7	7	4	4	523	298	163	292	(NA)	(NA)	(NA)	(NA)
Mississippi	24	25	14	13	1,832	1,167	535	875	(NA)	(NA)	(NA)	(NA)
Montana	25	29	19	19	1,779	1,153	634	1,185	88	51	38	37
Nebraska	2	3	2	2	162	108	58	106	(NA)	(NA)	(NA)	(NA)
New Mexico	66	148	375	457	4,960	6,575	13,838	30,596	1,292	1,245	1,948	2,328
New York	(Z)	(Z)	(Z)	(Z)	(NA)	(NA)	(NA)	(NA)	(NA)	(NA)	(NA)	(NA)
North Dakota	113	430	434	405	7,908	17,795	15,448	25,572	82	471	882	945
Ohio	5	27	24	19	352	1,025	796	1,147	78	1,007	2,379	2,267
Oklahoma	70	166	173	143	5,277	7,466	6,418	9,444	1,827	2,500	2,786	2,572
Pennsylvania	3	7	6	6	226	276	179	376	573	4,813	7,148	7,693
Texas	427	1,262	1,773	1,740	32,532	56,712	65,904	116,314	6,715	7,890	9,336	9,417
Utah	25	37	31	35	1,679	1,511	1,082	2,151	432	417	242	239
West Virginia	2	12	19	18	130	390	568	1,077	265	1,315	2,592	2,760
Wyoming	54	86	89	85	3,670	3,514	3,058	5,483	2,306	1,809	1,306	1,238
Federal offshore	588	564	614	627	(NA)	(NA)	(NA)	(NA)	2,245	1,292	789	770
Lower 48 states	1,783	3,270	3,978	3,948	133,789	145,766	147,401	260,881	22,008	28,428	35,864	36,657

Z Less than 500,000. NA Not available. [1] Excludes nonhydrocarbon gases. [2] Crude petroleum production value calculated using production quantity and domestic crude oil first purchase price. [3] Includes other states, not shown separately. State production includes state offshore production, as well as extractions from the Gulf not distributed to states. U.S. level totals shown in Table 953 and Table 958 may contain revisions not carried to state level. [4] Alaska crude oil production and value for North Slope only.

Source: U.S. Energy Information Administration, "Petroleum & Other Liquids Data," <www.eia.gov/petroleum/data.cfm>, and "Natural Gas Data," <www.eia.gov/naturalgas/data.cfm>, accessed August 2022.

Table 957. Crude Oil and Natural Gas—Reserves by State: 2010 to 2020

[23,267 mil. bbl. represents 23,267,000,000 barrels. As of December 31. Proved reserves are estimated quantities of the mineral that geological and engineering data demonstrate with reasonable certainty to be recoverable in future years from known reservoirs under existing economic and operating conditions. Based on a sample of operators of oil and gas wells]

Area	2010		2015		2019		2020	
	Crude oil proved reserves (mil. bbl.)	Natural gas (bil. cu. ft.)	Crude oil proved reserves (mil. bbl.)	Natural gas (bil. cu. ft.)	Crude oil proved reserves (mil. bbl.)	Natural gas (bil. cu. ft.)	Crude oil proved reserves (mil. bbl.)	Natural gas (bil. cu. ft.)
United States [1]	23,267	304,625	32,318	307,730	44,191	465,405	35,835	445,299
Alabama	42	2,629	64	2,182	39	1,387	34	1,493
Alaska	3,722	8,838	2,034	4,566	2,680	9,297	2,423	36,176
Arkansas	40	14,178	51	8,339	33	5,834	29	4,981
California	2,938	2,647	2,333	1,832	2,213	1,280	1,496	1,065
Colorado	386	24,119	1,212	17,139	1,414	22,332	1,061	18,653
Florida	18	56	16	–	(NA)	(NA)	(NA)	(NA)
Illinois	64	(NA)	31	(NA)	(NA)	(NA)	(NA)	(NA)
Indiana	8	(NA)	8	(NA)	(NA)	(NA)	(NA)	(NA)
Kansas	295	3,673	337	3,183	313	2,125	277	1,989
Kentucky	15	2,613	10	1,362	8	1,275	4	1,158
Louisiana	424	29,277	424	16,097	389	36,497	317	37,397
Michigan	40	2,919	43	1,386	48	1,245	39	881
Mississippi	247	853	158	480	114	227	90	167
Montana	369	944	326	692	298	613	256	555
Nebraska	10	(NA)	17	(NA)	12	(NA)	12	(NA)
New Mexico	823	15,412	1,486	14,364	3,456	21,509	3,365	23,698
New York	(NA)	281	(NA)	104	(NA)	81	(NA)	115
North Dakota	1,814	1,667	5,193	6,203	5,897	11,104	3,669	7,133
Ohio	42	832	62	12,104	88	34,056	74	27,514
Oklahoma	710	26,345	1,262	28,486	2,047	32,527	1,483	27,227
Pennsylvania	22	13,960	13	55,894	16	105,917	11	96,463
Texas	5,674	88,997	11,759	78,866	18,622	113,736	15,612	102,370
Utah	449	6,981	389	3,547	275	2,279	378	2,296
Virginia	(NA)	3,215	(NA)	2,496	(NA)	2,297	(NA)	1,950
West Virginia	17	7,000	12	20,553	13	36,600	8	35,247
Wyoming	567	35,074	725	20,436	1,013	17,569	703	12,484
Federal offshore	4,496	11,765	4,335	7,296	5,103	5,568	4,410	4,245
Lower 48 states	19,545	295,787	30,284	303,164	41,511	456,108	33,412	409,123

– Represents zero. NA Not available. [1] Includes other states, not shown separately.

Source: U.S. Energy Information Administration, "Petroleum & Other Liquids Data," <www.eia.gov/petroleum/data.php>; and "Natural Gas Data," <www.eia.gov/naturalgas/data.php>; accessed January 2022.

Table 958. Dry Natural Gas—Supply, Consumption, Reserves, and Marketed Production: 1990 to 2021

[270 represents 270,000. Data are for dry natural gas, plus a small amount of supplemental gaseous fuels. Minus sign (-) indicates debit]

Item	Unit	1990	2000	2005	2010	2015	2019	2020	2021 (P)
Producing wells (year-end)............	1,000	270	342	426	488	575	498	483	(NA)
Proved reserves [1]......................	Bil. cu. ft.	169,346	177,427	204,385	304,625	307,730	465,405	445,299	(NA)
Marketed production [2]..................	Bil. cu. ft.	18,593.8	20,197.5	18,927.1	22,381.9	28,772.0	36,446.9	36,202.4	37,011.5
Minus: Natural gas plant liquids production [3].............................	Bil. cu. ft.	784.1	1,015.5	876.5	1,066.4	1,706.6	2,547.9	2,717.2	2,865.8
Equals: Dry production................	Bil. cu. ft.	17,809.7	19,182.0	18,050.6	21,315.5	27,065.5	33,899.0	33,485.3	34,145.7
Plus: Supplemental gas supplies.....	Bil. cu. ft.	122.8	90.2	63.7	64.6	58.6	60.8	63.1	59.1
Equals: Dry production with supplemental gas......................	Bil. cu. ft.	17,932.5	19,272.2	18,114.3	21,380.1	27,124.1	33,959.8	33,548.4	34,204.8
Plus: Withdrawals from storage [4].....	Bil. cu. ft.	1,933.8	3,498.2	3,056.6	3,274.4	3,099.7	3,652.8	3,411.9	3,760.5
Plus: Imports............................	Bil. cu. ft.	1,532.3	3,781.6	4,341.0	3,740.8	2,718.1	2,741.7	2,551.3	2,808.0
Plus: Balancing item [5].................	Bil. cu. ft.	307.3	-305.7	236.1	115.5	-267.9	-408.4	-158.9	-156.7
Equals: Total supply....................	Bil. cu. ft.	21,705.8	26,246.3	25,748.0	28,510.7	32,674.0	39,945.9	39,352.7	40,616.5
Minus: Exports.........................	Bil. cu. ft.	85.6	243.7	728.6	1,136.8	1,783.5	4,657.7	5,283.6	6,652.6
Minus: Additions to storage [4].........	Bil. cu. ft.	2,433.5	2,684.3	3,001.6	3,291.4	3,638.3	4,152.5	3,589.8	3,677.4
Equals: Consumption, total............	Bil. cu. ft.	19,173.6	23,333.1	22,014.4	24,086.8	27,243.9	31,132.0	30,477.5	30,286.5
Lease and plant fuel..................	Bil. cu. ft.	1,236.4	1,150.9	1,111.5	1,285.6	1,576.4	1,822.9	1,804.7	1,845.1
Pipeline fuel [6].........................	Bil. cu. ft.	(NA)	642.2	584.0	674.1	678.2	1,018.1	1,007.1	1,001.0
Residential.............................	Bil. cu. ft.	4,391.3	4,996.2	4,826.8	4,782.4	4,612.9	5,018.5	4,674.3	4,654.3
Commercial [7]..........................	Bil. cu. ft.	2,622.7	3,182.5	2,998.9	3,102.6	3,201.7	3,514.6	3,170.2	3,264.2
Industrial..............................	Bil. cu. ft.	(NA)	8,142.2	6,601.2	6,826.2	7,521.9	8,416.7	8,150.7	8,198.2
Vehicle fuel............................	Bil. cu. ft.	(NA)	12.8	22.9	28.7	39.4	53.2	49.1	53.2
Electric power sector..................	Bil. cu. ft.	(NA)	5,206.3	5,869.1	7,387.2	9,613.4	11,288.1	11,616.0	11,270.6
World production (dry).................	Tril. cu. ft.	73.4	86.8	98.6	113.8	125.7	142.6	(NA)	(NA)
U.S. production (dry).................	Tril. cu. ft.	17.8	19.2	18.1	21.3	27.1	33.9	33.5	34.2
U.S. percent of world...............	Percent	24.3	22.1	18.3	18.7	21.5	23.8	(NA)	(NA)

P Preliminary. NA Not available. [1] Estimated, end of year. [2] Gross withdrawals less gas used for repressuring, quantities vented and flared, and nonhydrocarbon gases removed in treating or processing operations. Includes all quantities of gas used in field and processing plant operations. [3] Volumetric reduction in natural gas resulting from the removal of natural gas plant liquids, which are transferred to petroleum supply. [4] Underground storage. [5] Quantities lost and imbalances in data due to differences among data sources. Since 1980, excludes in-transit shipments that cross U.S.-Canada border (i.e., natural gas delivered to its destination via the other country). [6] Natural gas consumed in the operation of pipelines, primarily in compressors. [7] Includes gas used by local, State, and Federal agencies engaged in nonmanufacturing activities.

Source: U.S. Energy Information Administration, "Natural Gas Data," <www.eia.gov/naturalgas/data.php>; "Monthly Energy Review, Natural Gas," <www.eia.gov/totalenergy/data/monthly/#naturalgas>; and "International Energy Statistics," <www.eia.gov/international/overview/world>; accessed June 2022.

Table 959. Shale Natural Gas Production and Proved Reserves: 2016 to 2020

[In billions of cubic feet (17,032 represents 17,032,000,000,000). For states not listed, no production or reserves were reported. Natural gas produced from organic (black) shale formations]

State	Production					Proved reserves [1]				
	2016	2017	2018	2019	2020	2016	2017	2018	2019	2020
United States.......	**17,032**	**18,589**	**22,054**	**25,556**	**26,139**	**209,809**	**307,903**	**342,135**	**353,086**	**317,756**
Alabama...............	(NA)	(NA)	–	–	–	(NA)	(NA)	–	–	–
Alaska.................	–	–	–	–	–	–	–	–	–	–
Arkansas..............	733	618	521	471	419	6,262	7,090	5,970	5,093	4,210
California..............	6	6	4	(NA)	(NA)	41	62	41	(NA)	(NA)
Colorado..............	164	97	126	149	116	2,032	1,885	2,727	2,500	1,331
Kansas................	–	–	–	–	–	–	–	–	–	–
Kentucky..............	–	(NA)	–	–	–	12	(NA)	–	–	–
Louisiana.............	1,111	1,450	2,044	2,518	2,555	9,637	26,484	25,598	29,553	28,533
Michigan..............	84	63	77	72	57	1,128	942	1,457	1,138	823
Mississippi............	2	2	–	–	–	7	8	–	–	–
Montana..............	19	18	18	21	16	213	258	221	268	227
New Mexico...........	497	592	785	1,101	1,337	5,581	9,451	13,082	13,827	14,667
North Dakota..........	582	664	840	1,043	970	8,259	9,984	11,737	12,542	8,376
Ohio..................	1,386	1,747	2,337	2,558	2,320	15,472	26,468	23,956	34,376	27,775
Oklahoma.............	1,082	1,290	1,325	1,490	1,195	20,327	22,675	21,396	20,897	15,483
Pennsylvania.........	5,049	5,365	6,079	6,782	7,040	60,979	89,478	103,388	105,394	96,699
Texas.................	5,029	5,171	6,392	7,440	7,844	56,577	78,666	100,789	93,477	87,296
Virginia...............	4	4	–	–	–	45	66	–	–	–
West Virginia.........	1,270	1,486	1,504	1,911	2,270	23,146	34,296	31,748	34,020	32,335
Wyoming..............	5	6	–	–	–	17	28	–	–	–

– Represents or rounds to zero. NA Not available. [1] Proved reserves of natural gas as of December 31 of the report year are the estimated quantities which analysis of geological and engineering data demonstrate with reasonable certainty to be recoverable in future years from known reservoirs under existing economic and operating conditions.

Source: U.S. Energy Information Administration, "Natural Gas Data," <www.eia.gov/naturalgas/data.cfm>, accessed January 2022.

Table 960. Coal Production, Supply, Disposition, and Prices: 2000 to 2021

[In millions of short tons (1,073.6 represents 1,073,600,000). 1 short ton = 2,000 lbs]

Item	2000	2005	2010	2015	2019	2020	2021
United States, total production..............	**1,073.6**	**1,131.5**	**1,084.4**	**896.9**	**706.3**	**535.4**	**(NA)**
Consumption by sector:							
Total..	1,084.1	1,126.0	1,048.5	798.1	586.5	476.7	545.9
Residential [1]...............................	0.5	0.4	(NA)	(NA)	(NA)	(NA)	(NA)
Commercial.................................	3.7	4.3	3.1	1.5	0.9	0.8	0.8
Industrial...................................	94.1	83.8	70.4	58.2	47.1	40.1	43.7
Coke plants.............................	28.9	23.4	21.1	19.7	18.0	14.4	17.8
Other industrial plants...............	65.2	60.3	49.3	38.5	29.1	25.7	25.8
Combined heat and power (CHP).....	28.0	25.9	24.6	17.0	10.9	9.5	10.0
Noncombined heat and power.........	37.2	34.5	24.7	21.5	18.2	16.2	15.9
Electric power.............................	985.8	1,037.5	975.1	738.4	538.6	435.8	501.4
Year-end coal stocks:							
Total..	140.3	144.3	231.7	238.4	165.3	161.7	125.5
Residential and commercial..............	(NA)	(NA)	0.6	0.4	0.2	0.3	0.2
Industrial...................................	6.1	8.2	6.5	6.6	5.6	4.5	5.4
Coke plants.............................	1.5	2.6	1.9	2.2	2.3	1.7	2.0
Other industrial plants...............	4.6	5.6	4.5	4.4	3.3	2.8	3.4
Electric power.............................	102.3	101.1	174.9	195.5	128.2	133.3	94.7
Producers/distributors....................	31.9	35.0	49.8	35.9	31.3	23.6	25.3
U.S. coal trade:							
Net exports [2]...............................	46.0	19.5	62.4	62.6	87.1	63.9	79.8
Exports......................................	58.5	49.9	81.7	74.0	93.8	69.1	85.2
Steam coal.............................	25.7	21.3	25.6	28.0	40.8	27.1	39.9
Metallurgical coal.....................	32.8	28.7	56.1	46.0	52.9	42.0	45.3
Coke......................................	1.3	1.7	1.5	0.9	1.0	0.7	2.1
Imports......................................	12.5	30.5	19.4	11.3	6.7	5.1	5.4
Average delivered price (dollars per short ton) to:							
Electric power sector.....................	24.28	31.22	44.27	42.60	38.64	36.36	37.69

NA Not available. [1] Beginning in 2008, residential coal consumption data are not collected by Energy Information Administration. [2] Exports minus imports.

Source: U.S. Energy Information Administration, *Annual Coal Report 2020*, October 2021, and earlier reports; and "Coal Data," <www.eia.gov/coal/data.cfm> and "Monthly Energy Review, Coal," <www.eia.gov/totalenergy/data/monthly/#coal>, accessed April 2022.

Table 961. Coal and Coke—Summary: 1990 to 2020

[In millions of short tons (1,029 represents 1,029,000,000), except as indicated. Includes coal consumed at mines. Recoverability varies between 40 and 90 percent for individual deposits; 50 percent or more of overall U.S. coal reserve base is believed to be recoverable]

Item	Unit	1990	2000	2010	2015	2017	2018	2019	2020
COAL									
Production, total [1, 2]....................	Mil. sh. tons	**1,029**	**1,074**	**1,084**	**897**	**775**	**756**	**706**	**535**
Average price per short ton..............	Dollars	21.76	16.78	35.61	31.81	33.72	35.99	36.07	31.41
Anthracite production [2]....................	Mil. sh. tons	3.5	4.6	1.8	2.1	1.9	1.9	2.6	2.4
Bituminous coal and lignite [3]...........	Mil. sh. tons	1,026	1,069	1,083	895	773	754	704	533
Underground...............................	Mil. sh. tons	425	374	337	307	273	275	267	196
Surface [2]...................................	Mil. sh. tons	605	700	747	590	501	481	439	340
Exports......................................	Mil. sh. tons	106	58	82	73	96	115	94	69
Imports......................................	Mil. sh. tons	3	13	17	9	6	4	7	5
Consumption [4].............................	Mil. sh. tons	904	1,084	1,049	798	717	688	587	477
Electric power sector [5]..................	Mil. sh. tons	783	986	975	738	665	637	539	436
Industrial...................................	Mil. sh. tons	115	94	70	58	51	50	47	40
Number of mines..........................	Number	3,243	1,453	1,285	853	680	679	669	552
Daily employment.........................	1,000	135	85	86	66	53	54	53	42
Production, by state:									
Alabama....................................	Mil. sh. tons	29	19	20	13	13	15	14	12
Illinois......................................	Mil. sh. tons	60	33	33	56	48	50	46	32
Indiana.....................................	Mil. sh. tons	36	28	35	34	31	35	32	(NA)
Kentucky...................................	Mil. sh. tons	173	131	105	61	42	40	36	24
Montana....................................	Mil. sh. tons	38	38	45	42	35	39	34	26
Ohio..	Mil. sh. tons	35	22	27	17	9	9	8	4
Pennsylvania..............................	Mil. sh. tons	71	75	59	50	49	50	50	36
Virginia.....................................	Mil. sh. tons	47	33	22	14	13	13	12	10
West Virginia..............................	Mil. sh. tons	169	158	135	96	93	95	93	67
Wyoming...................................	Mil. sh. tons	184	339	443	376	316	304	277	219
Other states...............................	Mil. sh. tons	187	197	161	138	124	108	104	106
World production...........................	Mil. sh. tons	5,184	5,125	8,197	8,668	8,382	8,711	8,846	8,377
U.S. percent of world.....................	Percent	19.8	20.9	13.2	10.3	9.2	8.7	8.0	6.4
COKE									
Production....................................	Mil. sh. tons	27.6	20.8	15.0	13.8	12.9	13.8	12.9	10.4
Imports..	Mil. sh. tons	0.8	3.8	1.2	0.1	0.1	0.1	0.1	0.2
Exports [6]...................................	Mil. sh. tons	0.6	1.1	1.5	0.9	1.2	1.2	1.0	0.7
Consumption [6].............................	Mil. sh. tons	27.8	23.2	14.8	13.1	11.8	13.0	11.9	9.8

NA Not available. [1] Includes bituminous coal, subbituminous coal, lignite, and anthracite. [2] Beginning 2005, includes a small amount of refuse recovery. [3] Includes subbituminous. [4] Includes other categories not shown separately. [5] Electricity-only and combined-heat-and-power (CHP) plants whose primary business is to sell electricity and/or heat to the public. [6] Consumption is calculated as the sum of production and imports minus exports and stock change.

Source: U.S. Energy Information Administration, *Annual Energy Review 2011*, September 2012; *Annual Coal Report 2020*, October 2021; *Quarterly Coal Report*, July 2022; *Monthly Energy Review*, March 2022; and "International Energy Statistics," <www.eia.gov/international/data/world>, accessed March 2022. See also <www.eia.gov/totalenergy> and <www.eia.gov/coal/annual>.

Table 962. Demonstrated Coal Reserves by Major Producing State: 2019 and 2020

[Reserves in millions of short tons (472,623 represents 472,623,000,000). As of January 1 the following year. The demonstrated reserve base represents the sum of coal in both measured and indicated resource categories of reliability. Measured resources of coal are estimates that have a high degree of geologic assurance from sample analyses and measurements from closely spaced and geologically well-known sample sites. Indicated resources are estimates based partly from sample and analyses and measurements and partly from reasonable geologic projections]

	2019				2020			
	Reserves (mil. short tons)				Reserves (mil. short tons)			
			Method of mining				Method of mining	
State	Number of mines	Total reserves	Under-ground	Surface	Number of mines	Total reserves	Under-ground	Surface
United States [1]	**669**	**472,623**	**325,637**	**146,986**	**552**	**471,811**	**325,241**	**146,570**
Alabama	29	3,791	687	3,103	26	3,768	667	3,101
Alaska	1	6,084	5,423	661	1	6,083	5,423	660
Arkansas	(NA)	415	271	144	(NA)	415	271	144
Colorado	6	15,612	10,858	4,754	7	15,595	10,840	4,754
Illinois	21	103,309	86,841	16,468	14	103,247	86,782	16,466
Indiana	17	8,718	8,333	385	18	8,686	8,315	371
Iowa	(NA)	2,189	1,732	457	(NA)	2,189	1,732	457
Kansas	(NA)	970	(NA)	970	(NA)	970	(NA)	970
Kentucky	136	28,032	15,581	12,452	97	27,987	15,541	12,446
Kentucky, Eastern	124	9,373	468	8,905	90	9,359	459	8,900
Kentucky, Western	12	18,660	15,113	3,547	7	18,628	15,082	3,546
Maryland	12	594	555	39	11	592	554	38
Missouri	1	5,984	1,479	4,504	1	5,983	1,479	4,504
Montana	6	118,478	70,826	47,651	6	118,440	70,814	47,626
New Mexico	3	11,719	6,000	5,719	3	11,705	5,997	5,708
North Dakota	5	8,548	(NA)	8,548	5	8,515	(NA)	8,515
Ohio	15	22,800	17,158	5,642	10	22,794	17,153	5,641
Oklahoma	3	1,533	1,221	312	2	1,533	1,221	312
Pennsylvania	149	25,991	21,890	4,101	134	25,921	21,826	4,095
Anthracite [2]	52	7,165	3,840	3,325	46	7,162	3,840	3,322
Bituminous	97	18,826	18,050	776	88	18,759	17,986	773
Tennessee	3	745	494	251	2	744	494	251
Texas	8	11,719	(NA)	11,719	7	11,695	(NA)	11,695
Utah	8	4,883	4,621	262	7	4,857	4,596	261
Virginia	53	1,235	780	454	41	1,217	766	451
Washington	(NA)	1,340	1,332	8	(NA)	1,340	1,332	8
West Virginia	162	30,042	26,981	3,062	135	29,917	26,869	3,048
Wyoming	16	56,995	42,420	14,575	16	56,720	42,415	14,304

NA Not available. [1] Includes other states not shown separately. [2] All of the anthracite mines in the United States are located in northeastern Pennsylvania.

Source: U.S. Energy Information Administration, *Annual Coal Report 2020*, October 2021, and earlier reports. See also <www.eia.gov/coal/annual/>.

Table 963. Uranium Concentrate Industry—Summary: 1990 to 2021

[In units as indicated (1.7 represents 1,700,000). See also Section 19, Table 983]

Item	Unit	1990	2000	2010	2015	2017	2018	2019	2020	2021
Exploration and development, surface drilling	Mil. ft.	1.7	1.0	4.9	0.9	0.2	(D)	(D)	(D)	0.1
Expenditures	Mil. dol.	(NA)	5.6	44.6	28.7	4.0	(D)	(D)	(D)	(D)
Mines operated	Number	39	10	9	9	7	7	6	6	3
Underground	Number	27	1	4	1	–	–	1	1	–
Open pit	Number	2	–	–	–	–	–	–	–	–
In situ leaching	Number	7	4	4	7	6	6	5	5	3
Other sources [1]	Number	3	5	1	1	1	1	–	–	–
Mine production	1,000 pounds	5,876	3,123	4,237	3,711	1,150	721	174	(D)	21
Underground	1,000 pounds	(D)	(D)	(D)	(D)	(D)	(D)	(D)	(D)	(D)
Open pit	1,000 pounds	1,881	–	–	–	–	–	–	–	–
In situ leaching	1,000 pounds	(D)	2,995	(D)	(D)	(D)	(D)	(D)	(D)	(D)
Other sources [1]	1,000 pounds	3,995	128	(D)	(D)	(D)	(D)	(D)	(D)	(D)
Uranium concentrate production	1,000 pounds	8,886	3,958	4,228	3,343	2,443	1,647	174	(D)	21
Concentrate shipments from mills and plants	1,000 pounds	12,957	3,187	5,137	4,023	2,277	1,489	190	(D)	(D)
Employment	Person-years [2]	1,335	627	1,073	625	424	372	265	225	207

– Represents zero. D Data withheld to avoid disclosing figures for individual companies. NA Not available. [1] Includes mine water, mill site cleanup and mill tailings, and well field restoration as sources of uranium. [2] A person-year is defined as one whole year, or fraction thereof, worked by an employee, including contracted man power. 12 months worked is 1 person year.

Source: U.S. Energy Information Administration, through 2002, *Uranium Industry*, annual. Thereafter, *Domestic Uranium Production Report*, May 2022, and earlier reports. See also <www.eia.gov/uranium/production/annual>.

Section 19
Energy and Utilities

This section presents statistics on fuel resources, energy production and consumption, electric energy, renewable energy, and the electric and gas utility industries. The principal sources are the U.S. Department of Energy's Energy Information Administration (EIA), the Edison Electric Institute, Washington, DC, and the American Gas Association, Arlington, VA. The Department of Energy was created in October 1977 and assumed and centralized the responsibilities of all or part of several agencies including the Federal Power Commission (FPC), the U.S. Bureau of Mines, the Federal Energy Administration, and the U.S. Energy Research and Development Administration. For additional data on transportation, see Section 23; on fuels, see Section 18; and on energy-related housing characteristics, see Section 20.

The EIA, in its *Annual Energy Review*, provides statistics and trend data on energy supply, demand, and prices. Information is included on petroleum and natural gas, coal, electricity, hydroelectric power, nuclear power, solar, wind, wood, and geothermal energy. Due to budget constraints the EIA suspended publication of the *Annual Energy Review* in 2013. Data previously found in the *Annual Energy Review* can now be found in the *Monthly Energy Review*, which presents data on current supply, disposition, and price data for energy resources and monthly publications on petroleum, coal, natural gas, and electric power. Additional EIA reports include the *Electric Power Annual*; *Natural Gas Annual*; *Petroleum Supply Annual*; *U.S. Crude Oil and Natural Gas*; *Electric Sales, Revenue, and Price*; *State Energy Data System (SEDS)*; *Annual Energy Outlook*; *Uranium Marketing Annual Report*; *Domestic Uranium Production Report—Quarterly*; and *International Energy Statistics*. These various reports contain state, national, and international data on the production of electricity, net summer capability of generating plants, fuels used in energy production, energy sales and consumption, and hydroelectric power. The EIA also provides access to regular data updates through its Open Data program. For more information, please refer to the EIA's Open Data program's web site <www.eia.gov/opendata/>.

Data on residential energy consumption, expenditures, and conservation activities are available from EIA's Residential Energy Consumption Survey (RECS) and are published every 4 years. The Commercial Buildings Energy Consumption Survey (CBECS), collects information on the stock of U.S. commercial buildings, their energy-related characteristics, and their energy consumption and expenditures. Data on manufacturing energy consumption, use, and expenditures are also collected every 4 years from EIA's Manufacturing Energy Consumption Survey (MECS). Due to the long gaps between the RECS, CBECS, and MECS, tables are rotated in and out of Section 19 in an effort to keep the data as current as possible. The results from these surveys are published at <www.eia.gov/consumption>.

The Edison Electric Institute's annual *Statistical Yearbook of the Electric Power Industry* contains data on the distribution of electric energy by public utilities. The American Gas Association, in its annual yearbook, *Gas Facts*, presents data on gas utilities and financial and operating statistics.

Btu conversion factors—Various energy sources are converted from original units to the thermal equivalent using British thermal units (Btu). A Btu is the amount of energy required to raise the temperature of 1 pound of water 1 degree Fahrenheit (F) at or near 39.2 degrees F. Factors are calculated annually from the latest final annual data available; some are revised as a result.

Electric power industry—In recent years, EIA has restructured the industry categories it once used to gather and report electricity statistics. The electric power industry, previously divided into electric utilities and non-utilities, now consists of the Electric Power Sector, the Commercial Sector, and the Industrial Sector.

The Electric Power Sector is composed of electricity-only and combined-heat-and-power plants (CHPs) whose primary business is to sell electricity, or electricity and heat, to the public.

Electricity-only plants are composed of traditional electric utilities, and nontraditional participants, including energy service providers, power marketers, independent power producers (IPPs), and the portion of CHPs that produce only electricity.

A utility is defined as a corporation, person, agency, authority, or other legal entity or instrumentality aligned with distribution facilities for delivery of electric energy for use primarily by the public. Electric utilities include investor-owned electric utilities, municipal and state utilities, federal electric utilities, and rural electric cooperatives.

An independent power producer is an entity defined as a corporation, person, agency, authority, or other legal entity or instrumentality that owns or operates facilities whose primary business is to produce electricity for use by the public. They are not generally aligned with distribution facilities and are not considered electric utilities.

Combined-heat-and-power producers are plants designed to produce both heat and electricity from a single heat source. These types of electricity producers can be independent power producers or industrial or commercial establishments. As some independent power producers are CHPs, their information is included in the data for the combined-heat-and-power sector.

The Commercial Sector consists of commercial CHPs and commercial electricity-only plants. Industrial CHPs and industrial electricity-only plants make up the Industrial Sector. For more information, please refer to the *Electric Power Annual* web site at <www.eia.gov/electricity/annual/>.

Table 964. Utilities—Establishments, Revenue, Payroll, and Employees by Kind of Business: 2017

[577,100 represents $577,100,000,000. Includes only establishments or firms with payroll. Data based on the 2017 Economic Census. See Appendix III]

Kind of business	NAICS code [1]	Establish-ments (number)	Revenue		Annual payroll		Paid employees for pay period including March 12 (number)
			Total (mil. dol.)	Per paid employee (dol.)	Total (mil. dol.)	Per paid employee (dol.)	
Utilities..............................	22	**18,913**	**577,100**	**876,541**	**67,667**	**102,777**	**658,384**
Electric power generation, transmission, & distribution...........	2211	11,496	461,919	888,903	56,541	108,806	519,651
Electric power generation....................	22111	3,280	119,266	860,216	15,610	112,590	138,647
Hydroelectric power generation..................	221111	523	3,334	915,503	328	90,185	3,642
Fossil fuel electric power generation............	221112	1,711	75,455	992,072	8,193	107,715	76,058
Nuclear electric power generation..............	221113	176	29,014	597,959	6,063	124,959	48,521
Solar electric power generation..................	221114	205	1,801	832,698	222	102,581	2,163
Wind electric power generation..................	221115	454	7,762	1,556,811	511	102,400	4,986
Geothermal electric power generation..........	221116	34	974	801,967	121	99,859	1,214
Biomass electric power generation..............	221117	141	906	460,174	163	82,940	1,968
Other electric power generation..................	221118	36	21	219,832	9	96,179	95
Electric power transmission, control & distribution.......................	22112	8,216	342,653	899,342	40,931	107,429	381,004
Electric bulk power transmission & control..........................	221121	273	13,772	893,328	1,828	118,571	15,416
Electric power distribution......................	221122	7,943	328,881	899,596	39,103	106,960	365,588
Natural gas distribution.............................	2212	2,550	100,586	1,096,344	8,155	88,890	91,747
Water, sewage, & other systems...................	2213	4,867	14,595	310,623	2,970	63,215	46,986
Water supply & irrigation systems.................	22131	4,108	11,759	307,997	2,411	63,152	38,180
Sewage treatment facilities.......................	22132	634	1,524	239,375	337	52,977	6,367
Steam & air-conditioning supply...................	22133	125	1,312	537,732	222	90,919	2,439

[1] North American Industry Classification System, 2017; see text, Section 15.

Source: U.S. Census Bureau, 2017 Economic Census, EC1700BASIC, "All Sectors: Summary Statistics for the U.S., States, and Selected Geographies: 2017," <data.census.gov>, accessed November 2021.

Table 965. Utilities—Employees, Annual Payroll, and Establishments by Industry: 2019 and 2020

[71,813 represents $71,813,000,000. Excludes most government employees, railroad employees, and self-employed persons. An establishment is a single physical location where business is conducted or where services or industrial operations are performed. See Appendix III]

Industry	NAICS code [1]	2019				2020			
		Estab-lish-ments	Number of employ-ees [2]	Annual payroll (mil. dol.)	Average payroll per em-ployee (dol.)	Estab-lish-ments	Number of employ-ees [2]	Annual payroll (mil. dol.)	Average payroll per em-ployee (dol.)
Utilities, total................	22	**19,146**	**641,700**	**71,813**	**111,910**	**19,484**	**637,058**	**73,610**	**115,547**
Electric power generation, transmission and distribution..........	2211	11,663	502,660	59,048	117,470	12,121	500,563	60,914	121,690
Electric power generation................	22111	3,491	130,597	15,900	121,747	3,664	127,456	15,863	124,455
Hydroelectric power................	221111	542	4,615	463	100,273	550	5,184	521	100,497
Fossil fuel electric power...............	221112	1,741	68,890	8,139	118,146	1,822	66,770	8,123	121,663
Nuclear electric power...............	221113	183	44,480	5,929	133,301	169	41,909	5,587	133,304
Solar electric power.................	221114	270	2,953	344	116,402	333	3,169	391	123,520
Wind electric power.................	221115	510	6,104	696	114,071	534	6,940	890	128,192
Geothermal electric power.............	221116	31	1,138	125	109,417	35	1,222	135	110,878
Biomass electric power.................	221117	124	2,180	181	83,013	121	1,923	175	90,952
Other electric power generation.......	221118	90	237	23	98,051	100	339	40	118,147
Electric power transmission, control & distribution................	22112	8,172	372,063	43,148	115,969	8,457	373,107	45,051	120,746
Electric bulk power transmission & control........................	221121	319	15,867	2,062	129,941	332	16,065	2,204	137,174
Electric power distribution..............	221122	7,853	356,196	41,086	115,347	8,125	357,042	42,847	120,006
Natural gas distribution...................	2212	2,542	92,694	9,625	103,839	2,473	90,000	9,402	104,461
Water, sewage, & other systems........	2213	4,941	46,346	3,140	67,749	4,890	46,487	3,294	70,859
Water supply & irrigation systems......	22131	4,237	38,741	2,599	67,075	4,228	38,888	2,734	70,304
Sewage treatment facilities..............	22132	579	5,597	326	58,255	536	5,703	349	61,240
Steam & air-conditioning supply........	22133	125	2,008	215	107,219	126	1,896	211	111,178

[1] North American Industry Classification System, 2017; see text, Section 15. [2] Covers full- and part-time employees who are on the payroll in the pay period including March 12.

Source: U.S. Census Bureau, County Business Patterns, "County Business Patterns by Legal Form of Organization and Employment Size Class for U.S., States, and Selected Geographies," <data.census.gov>, accessed April 2022. See also <www.census.gov/programs-surveys/cbp.html>.

Table 966. Energy Supply and Disposition by Type of Fuel: 1973 to 2021

[In quadrillion British thermal units (Btu) (63.53 represents 63,530,000,000,000,000). For definition of Btu, see source and text, this section]

Year	Production Total[1]	Crude oil[2]	Dry natural gas	Coal[3]	Nuclear electric power	Renewable energy[4] Total[1]	Hydroelectric power[5]	Biomass[6]	Solar/photovoltaic	Wind	Net imports, total[7]	Consumption Total[1,8]	Petroleum[9]	Natural gas[10]	Coal	Nuclear electric power	Renewable energy, total[4]
1973	63.53	19.49	22.19	13.99	0.91	4.41	2.86	1.53	(NA)	(NA)	12.58	75.65	34.81	22.51	12.97	0.91	4.41
1975	61.28	17.73	19.64	14.99	1.90	4.69	3.15	1.50	(NA)	(NA)	11.71	71.93	32.70	19.95	12.66	1.90	4.69
1980	67.15	18.25	19.91	18.60	2.74	5.43	2.90	2.48	(NA)	(NA)	12.10	78.02	34.16	20.24	15.42	2.74	5.43
1985	67.66	18.99	16.98	19.33	4.08	6.08	2.97	3.02	(Z)	(Z)	7.58	76.33	30.87	17.70	17.48	4.08	6.08
1990	70.67	15.57	18.33	22.49	6.10	6.04	3.05	2.74	0.06	0.03	14.06	84.43	33.50	19.60	19.17	6.10	6.04
1995	71.13	13.89	19.08	22.13	7.08	6.56	3.21	3.10	0.07	0.03	17.68	90.93	34.34	22.67	20.09	7.08	6.56
1996	72.44	13.72	19.34	22.79	7.09	7.01	3.59	3.16	0.07	0.03	19.02	93.93	35.59	23.08	21.00	7.09	7.01
1997	72.42	13.66	19.39	23.31	6.60	7.02	3.64	3.11	0.07	0.03	20.63	94.51	36.07	23.22	21.45	6.60	7.01
1998	72.83	13.24	19.61	24.05	7.07	6.49	3.30	2.93	0.07	0.03	22.24	94.92	36.72	22.83	21.66	7.07	6.49
1999	71.69	12.45	19.34	23.30	7.61	6.52	3.27	2.97	0.07	0.05	23.48	96.54	37.73	22.91	21.62	7.61	6.51
2000	71.27	12.36	19.66	22.74	7.86	6.10	2.81	3.01	0.06	0.06	24.90	98.70	38.15	23.82	22.58	7.86	6.10
2001	71.68	12.28	20.17	23.55	8.03	5.16	2.24	2.62	0.06	0.07	26.32	96.06	38.08	22.77	21.91	8.03	5.16
2002	70.65	12.16	19.38	22.73	8.15	5.73	2.69	2.71	0.06	0.11	25.72	97.54	38.12	23.51	21.90	8.15	5.73
2003	69.88	11.96	19.63	22.09	7.96	5.94	2.79	2.80	0.06	0.11	26.99	97.83	38.71	22.83	22.32	7.96	5.94
2004	70.17	11.55	19.07	22.85	8.22	6.06	2.69	3.00	0.06	0.14	29.14	100.00	40.14	22.92	22.47	8.22	6.07
2005	69.38	10.77	18.56	23.19	8.16	6.22	2.70	3.10	0.06	0.18	30.20	100.10	40.22	22.57	22.80	8.16	6.23
2006	70.68	10.77	19.02	23.79	8.21	6.59	2.87	3.21	0.06	0.26	29.92	99.39	39.73	22.24	22.45	8.21	6.64
2007	71.34	10.74	19.79	23.49	8.46	6.51	2.45	3.47	0.07	0.34	29.34	100.89	39.37	23.66	22.75	8.46	6.52
2008	73.15	10.61	20.70	23.85	8.43	7.19	2.51	3.87	0.07	0.55	26.02	98.75	36.77	23.84	22.39	8.43	7.18
2009	72.59	11.34	21.14	21.62	8.36	7.63	2.67	3.96	0.08	0.72	22.77	93.94	34.78	23.42	19.69	8.36	7.61
2010	74.91	11.61	21.81	22.04	8.43	8.32	2.54	4.55	0.09	0.92	21.69	97.51	35.32	24.57	20.83	8.43	8.27
2011	78.11	12.01	23.41	22.22	8.27	9.31	3.10	4.71	0.11	1.17	18.38	96.87	34.64	24.95	19.66	8.27	9.21
2012	79.25	13.85	24.61	20.68	8.06	8.90	2.63	4.55	0.16	1.34	15.80	94.39	33.83	26.09	17.38	8.06	8.86
2013	81.87	15.87	24.86	20.00	8.24	9.44	2.56	4.83	0.22	1.60	12.84	97.13	34.40	26.81	18.04	8.24	9.46
2014	87.76	18.61	26.72	20.29	8.34	9.80	2.47	5.05	0.34	1.73	10.97	98.30	34.66	27.38	18.00	8.34	9.76
2015	88.29	19.70	28.07	17.95	8.34	9.77	2.32	5.03	0.43	1.78	10.89	97.41	35.37	28.19	15.55	8.34	9.75
2016	84.34	18.52	27.58	14.67	8.43	10.48	2.47	5.13	0.57	2.10	11.26	97.38	35.71	28.40	14.23	8.43	10.41
2017	88.13	19.55	28.29	15.63	8.42	11.26	2.77	5.17	0.78	2.34	7.51	97.66	36.04	28.06	13.84	8.42	11.14
2018	95.78	22.79	31.88	15.36	8.44	11.58	2.66	5.31	0.92	2.48	3.61	101.23	36.89	31.15	13.25	8.44	11.37
2019	101.44	25.56	35.19	14.26	8.45	11.63	2.56	5.22	1.02	2.63	-0.61	100.47	36.87	32.25	11.32	8.45	11.47
2020	95.67	23.50	34.72	10.70	8.25	11.69	2.50	4.80	1.21	2.96	-3.47	92.97	32.33	31.54	9.18	8.25	11.52
2021	97.71	23.23	35.41	11.56	8.13	12.32	2.28	5.00	1.50	3.33	-3.87	97.30	35.07	31.34	10.51	8.13	12.16

NA Not available. Z Less than 5 trillion. [1] Includes other types of fuel not shown separately. [2] Includes lease condensate. [3] Beginning 1989, includes waste coal supplied. Beginning 2001, also includes a small amount of refuse recovery. [4] Electricity net generation from conventional hydroelectric power, geothermal, solar, and wind. Consumption of electricity from wood, biomass waste, and alcohol fuels; geothermal heat pump and direct use energy; and solar thermal direct use energy. [5] Conventional hydroelectricity net generation. [6] Organic nonfossil material of biological origin constituting a renewable energy source. [7] Imports minus exports. [8] Includes coal coke net imports and electricity net imports, not shown separately. [9] Petroleum products supplied, including natural gas plant liquids and crude oil burned as fuel. Does not include biofuels that have been blended with petroleum. [10] Excludes supplemental gaseous fuels.

Source: U.S. Energy Information Administration, *Monthly Energy Review*, March 2022. See also <www.eia.gov/totalenergy/data/monthly>.

Table 967. Energy Supply and Disposition by Type of Fuel—Estimates, 2021, and Projections, 2025 to 2050

[Quadrillion Btu (101.02 represents 101,020,000,000,000,000) per year. Btu = British thermal unit. For definition of Btu, see source and text, this section. Projections are "reference" or mid-level forecasts. See report for methodology and assumptions used in generating projections]

Type of fuel	2021, estimate	Projections 2025	2030	2035	2040	2045	2050
Production, total	**101.02**	**108.42**	**110.53**	**111.19**	**112.63**	**115.47**	**118.59**
Crude oil and lease condensate	23.17	27.06	27.58	26.60	26.19	26.34	26.86
Natural gas plant liquids	7.01	8.23	8.28	8.43	8.60	8.90	9.00
Natural gas, dry	35.68	37.83	39.01	40.02	41.11	42.85	44.16
Coal [1]	13.08	11.25	10.71	9.99	9.46	9.08	9.01
Nuclear power	8.12	8.16	7.38	7.00	6.95	7.00	6.92
Renewable energy [2]	11.83	15.09	16.76	18.47	19.65	20.63	21.99
Other [3]	2.13	0.79	0.80	0.67	0.67	0.66	0.65
Imports, total	**21.67**	**22.45**	**21.43**	**22.31**	**22.56**	**21.77**	**21.19**
Crude oil	13.85	15.99	15.53	16.67	16.97	16.42	15.91
Petroleum and other liquids [4]	4.72	4.03	3.72	3.57	3.58	3.61	3.67
Natural gas	2.81	2.32	2.04	1.93	1.87	1.60	1.47
Other imports [5]	0.30	0.11	0.15	0.14	0.14	0.14	0.14
Exports, total	**25.80**	**30.68**	**31.61**	**32.31**	**32.09**	**31.52**	**30.77**
Petroleum and other liquids [6]	16.73	19.84	19.82	19.77	19.51	18.91	18.19
Natural gas	6.81	8.09	9.01	9.75	9.84	9.89	9.84
Coal	2.25	2.75	2.78	2.79	2.74	2.71	2.74
Consumption, total	**97.00**	**99.84**	**99.96**	**100.76**	**102.71**	**105.38**	**108.68**
Petroleum and other liquids [7]	36.04	37.95	37.83	37.93	38.36	39.07	40.12
Natural gas	31.36	31.61	31.54	31.70	32.63	34.07	35.27
Coal [8]	10.88	8.47	7.86	7.12	6.65	6.31	6.21
Nuclear power	8.12	8.16	7.38	7.00	6.95	7.00	6.92
Renewable energy [9]	10.25	13.40	15.05	16.72	17.82	18.66	19.88
Other [10]	0.34	0.26	0.29	0.28	0.29	0.28	0.28
Net imports of petroleum	**1.83**	**0.18**	**-0.57**	**0.47**	**1.04**	**1.12**	**1.39**
Prices (2021 dollars per unit):							
Crude oil spot prices (dol. per barrel):							
Brent spot price	71.59	66.97	73.93	78.83	83.92	88.60	89.91
West Texas Intermediate spot price	69.02	64.73	71.33	75.90	80.80	85.73	87.07
Natural gas at Henry Hub (dol. per mil. Btu)	4.11	3.00	3.46	3.64	3.72	3.61	3.59
Coal minemouth price (dol. per ton) [11]	35.11	32.93	30.93	31.42	33.10	34.22	34.89
Electricity price (cents per kWh)	11.1	10.5	10.6	10.6	10.5	10.3	10.2

[1] Includes waste coal. [2] Includes grid-connected electricity from conventional hydroelectric power; biomass (including wood and wood waste, and other biomass); landfill gas; biogenic municipal waste; wind; photovoltaic and solar thermal sources; and nonelectric energy from renewable sources, such as active and passive solar systems, and wood. Excludes electricity imports using renewable sources and nonmarketed renewable energy. [3] Includes nonbiogenic municipal waste, hydrogen, methanol, and some domestic inputs to refineries. [4] Includes imports of finished petroleum products, unfinished oils, alcohols, ethers, blending components, and renewable fuels such as ethanol. [5] Includes coal, coal coke (net), and electricity (net). Excludes imports of fuel used in nuclear power plants. [6] Includes crude oil, petroleum products, ethanol, and biodiesel. [7] Includes petroleum-derived fuels and non-petroleum-derived fuels, such as ethanol, biodiesel, and coal-based synthetic liquids. Petroleum coke, which is a solid, is included. Also included are hydrocarbon gas liquids and crude oil consumed as a fuel. [8] Excludes coal converted to coal-based synthetic liquids and natural gas. [9] Includes grid-connected electricity from wood and wood waste, non-electric energy from wood, and biofuels heat and coproducts used in the production of liquid fuels, but excludes the energy content of the liquid fuels. See also footnote 2. [10] Includes non-biogenic municipal waste, hydrogen, and net electricity imports. [11] Includes reported prices for both open market and captive mines.

Source: U.S. Energy Information Administration, *Annual Energy Outlook 2022*, March 2022. See also <www.eia.gov/outlooks/aeo>.

Table 968. Energy Consumption by End-Use Sector: 1980 to 2021

[Trillion Btu (15,753.8 represents 15,753,800,000,000,000). Btu=British thermal unit. Represents consumption of fossil fuels and renewable energy, plus electricity retail sales and electrical system energy losses. For definition of Btu, see source and text, this section]

Year	Residential	Commercial [1]	Industrial [2]	Transportation	Year	Residential	Commercial [1]	Industrial [2]	Transportation
1980	15,753.8	10,578.4	31,993.3	19,696.7	2001	20,038.3	17,137.0	32,652.5	26,242.1
1981	15,261.9	10,616.0	30,662.4	19,514.1	2002	20,786.5	17,345.9	32,590.1	26,807.8
1982	15,531.3	10,860.4	27,561.0	19,089.3	2003	21,120.0	17,346.4	32,488.6	26,881.0
1983	15,425.5	10,938.5	27,372.0	19,176.7	2004	21,082.1	17,655.8	33,443.7	27,826.5
1984	15,959.9	11,444.0	29,508.4	19,655.6	2005	21,613.3	17,853.8	32,374.2	28,260.7
1985	16,041.7	11,451.4	28,757.0	20,088.0	2006	20,670.9	17,707.6	32,316.9	28,696.8
1986	15,975.5	11,606.2	28,224.9	20,788.8	2007	21,519.6	18,253.4	32,306.4	28,815.1
1987	16,263.7	11,946.1	29,332.0	21,468.9	2008	21,668.3	18,403.0	31,261.1	27,421.4
1988	17,133.1	12,578.2	30,626.8	22,317.8	2009	21,082.1	17,888.4	28,380.4	26,592.2
1989	17,790.2	13,196.5	31,282.6	22,478.6	2010	21,894.8	18,059.8	30,574.5	26,978.2
1990	16,940.5	13,317.5	31,750.3	22,419.0	2011	21,381.9	17,983.2	30,893.3	26,606.2
1991	17,419.8	13,500.1	31,342.9	22,118.0	2012	19,870.1	17,424.2	30,955.1	26,135.0
1992	17,355.3	13,441.3	32,514.2	22,415.1	2013	21,051.8	17,930.0	31,529.2	26,620.3
1993	18,212.1	13,817.0	32,560.5	22,670.8	2014	21,445.6	18,264.7	31,700.7	26,880.9
1994	18,110.8	14,097.4	33,463.4	23,318.7	2015	20,617.5	18,156.9	31,375.1	27,255.8
1995	18,517.2	14,690.1	33,909.8	23,811.9	2016	20,178.7	18,030.4	31,367.0	27,812.0
1996	19,502.4	15,172.1	34,837.8	24,419.3	2017	19,886.8	17,899.9	31,823.4	28,049.4
1997	18,962.8	15,681.3	35,135.4	24,722.6	2018	21,509.6	18,439.8	32,787.4	28,505.0
1998	18,952.5	15,967.6	34,780.1	25,224.5	2019	21,073.4	18,013.2	32,707.3	28,670.9
1999	19,554.2	16,376.5	34,693.1	25,916.0	2020	20,594.3	16,721.5	31,218.3	24,443.7
2000	20,421.8	17,175.5	34,588.5	26,515.5	2021	20,915.1	17,373.3	32,088.0	26,935.3

[1] Commercial sector fuel use, including use at commercial combined-heat-and-power (CHP) and commercial electricity-only plants. [2] Industrial sector fuel use, including use at industrial combined-heat-and-power (CHP) and industrial electricity-only plants.

Source: U.S. Energy Information Administration, *Monthly Energy Review*, March 2022. See also <www.eia.gov/totalenergy/data/monthly>.

Table 969. Energy Consumption by Mode of Transportation: 2010 to 2019

[27 represents 27,000,000,000,000. Btu = British thermal unit. For conversion rates for each fuel type, see source]

Mode	Trillion Btu				Physical units		
	2010	2015	2019	Unit	2010	2015	2019
AIR [1]							
Aviation gasoline	27	24	28	Mil. gal.	221	196	200
Jet fuel	1,686	1,637	1,899	Mil. gal.	12,492	12,124	13,694
HIGHWAY							
Light duty vehicle, short wheel base & motorcycle [2]	10,491	10,883	11,291	Mil. gal.	87,215	90,479	93,874
Light duty vehicle, long wheel base [2]	4,360	4,383	4,574	Mil. gal.	36,251	36,437	38,030
Single-unit 2-axle 6-tire or more truck	1,816	1,786	2,004	Mil. gal.	15,097	14,851	16,657
Combination truck [3]	3,600	3,475	3,487	Mil. gal.	29,927	28,886	28,987
Bus	231	268	295	Mil. gal.	1,921	2,228	2,451
TRANSIT [4]							
Electricity	22	23	23	Mil. kWh	6,414	6,668	6,877
Diesel (includes bio-diesel)	87	79	77	Mil. gal.	633	576	561
Gasoline and other nondiesel fuels [5]	12	14	14	Mil. gal.	98	114	116
Compressed natural gas	18	22	26	Mil. gal.	126	156	188
RAIL [6]							
Distillate/diesel fuel	489	516	478	Mil. gal.	3,557	3,754	3,482
Electricity	2	2	2	Mil. kWh	559	504	484
WATER							
Residual fuel oil	770	503	328	Mil. gal.	5,143	3,358	2,189
Distillate/diesel fuel oil	275	332	281	Mil. gal.	2,003	2,417	2,042
Gasoline	140	248	256	Mil. gal.	1,167	2,066	2,128
PIPELINE							
Natural gas	699	703	979	Mil. cu. ft.	674,124	678,183	1,018,095

[1] Includes general aviation and certified carriers, domestic operations only; and fuel used in air taxi operations, but not commuter operations. [2] "Light duty vehicle, short wheel base" includes passenger cars, light trucks, vans and sport utility vehicles with a wheelbase (WB) equal to or less than 121 inches. "Light duty vehicle, long wheel base" includes large passenger cars, vans, pickup trucks, and sport/utility vehicles with wheelbases (WB) larger than 121 inches. [3] A power unit (truck tractor) and one or more trailing units (a semitrailer or trailer). [4] Includes light, heavy, and commuter rail; motor bus; trolley bus; van pools; automated guideway; and demand-responsive vehicles. [5] Includes gasoline, liquefied petroleum gas, liquefied natural gas, methane, ethanol, bunker fuel, kerosene, grain additive, and other fuel. [6] Includes Amtrak and freight service carriers that have an annual operating revenue of $250 million or more.

Source: U.S. Department of Transportation, Bureau of Transportation Statistics, "National Transportation Statistics," <www.bts.gov/topics/national-transportation-statistics>, accessed January 2022.

Table 970. Renewable Energy Consumption by Source and Sector: 1990 to 2021

[In trillion Btu (6,040.0 represents 6,040,000,000,000,000). For definition of Btu, see source and text, this section. Renewable energy is obtained from sources that are essentially inexhaustible, unlike fossil fuels of which there is a finite supply]

Source and sector	1990	2000	2010	2015	2019	2020	2021
Consumption, total	**6,040.0**	**6,104.3**	**8,268.1**	**9,751.9**	**11,472.7**	**11,522.7**	**12,156.7**
Conventional hydroelectric power [1]	3,046.4	2,811.1	2,538.5	2,321.2	2,563.5	2,502.7	2,283.0
Geothermal energy [2]	170.7	164.4	208.0	211.8	201.3	202.9	206.0
Biomass energy [3]	2,735.1	3,008.2	4,505.6	5,014.9	5,056.0	4,640.2	4,834.9
Solar energy [4]	58.8	63.5	92.5	426.7	1,017.1	1,212.2	1,501.2
Wind energy [5]	29.0	57.1	923.4	1,777.3	2,634.8	2,964.7	3,331.7
Residential [6]	**640.2**	**486.3**	**642.0**	**680.5**	**836.5**	**766.7**	**832.1**
Wood [7]	580.0	420.0	540.5	512.7	545.5	440.8	463.8
Geothermal [2]	5.5	8.6	36.8	39.6	39.6	39.6	39.6
Solar [4]	54.7	57.7	64.7	128.2	251.4	286.3	328.7
Commercial [8]	**98.4**	**128.4**	**143.5**	**229.9**	**279.4**	**291.9**	**313.0**
Biomass [3]	94.0	119.1	110.9	151.9	149.3	147.0	146.8
Geothermal [2]	2.8	7.6	18.5	19.7	23.6	23.6	24.1
Hydroelectric [1]	1.4	1.0	0.8	0.3	1.7	1.9	2.2
Solar energy [4]	0.2	0.6	13.1	56.9	103.2	118.0	138.4
Wind energy [5]	(NA)	(NA)	0.2	1.1	1.6	1.5	1.5
Industrial [9]	**1,717.1**	**1,928.2**	**2,343.7**	**2,505.9**	**2,458.6**	**2,319.2**	**2,368.9**
Biomass [3]	1,684.2	1,881.5	2,320.3	2,474.3	2,416.5	2,269.4	2,312.7
Geothermal [2]	1.9	4.4	4.2	4.2	4.2	4.2	4.2
Hydroelectric [1]	30.9	42.2	16.3	13.1	9.2	8.8	8.4
Solar energy [4]	(Z)	0.1	2.9	13.7	27.8	31.5	35.1
Wind energy [5]	(NA)	(NA)	(NA)	0.5	0.9	5.4	8.5
Transportation [10]	**60.4**	**134.9**	**1,074.5**	**1,401.5**	**1,600.3**	**1,467.2**	**1,476.9**
Fuel ethanol	60.4	134.9	1,041.4	1,109.9	1,161.6	1,004.4	1,104.6
Biodiesel [11]	(NA)	(NA)	33.2	190.6	231.3	239.4	210.1
Electric power [12]	**3,523.9**	**3,426.5**	**4,064.4**	**4,984.5**	**6,401.6**	**6,789.4**	**7,165.8**
Biomass [3]	316.5	452.8	459.4	524.9	448.1	427.6	434.7
Geothermal [2]	160.5	143.8	148.5	148.3	133.9	135.5	138.1
Hydroelectric [1]	3,014.0	2,767.9	2,521.5	2,307.7	2,552.6	2,492.1	2,272.3
Solar [4]	3.8	5.0	11.8	227.9	634.6	776.5	999.0
Wind [5]	29.0	57.1	923.3	1,775.7	2,632.4	2,957.8	3,321.7

NA Not available. Z Less than 50 billion. [1] Power produced from the kinetic energy of falling water. [2] As used at electric power plants, hot water or steam extracted from geothermal reservoirs supplied to steam turbines at electric power plants that drive generators to produce electricity. [3] Wood and wood-derived fuels, municipal solid waste, fuel ethanol, and biodiesel. [4] The radiant energy of the sun, which can be converted into other forms of energy. Solar thermal and photovoltaic electricity net generation and solar thermal direct use energy. [5] Energy present in wind motion that can be converted to mechanical energy for driving pumps, mills, and electric power generators. [6] Living quarters for private households; excludes institutional living quarters. [7] Wood and wood-derived fuels. [8] Service-providing facilities and equipment of businesses, governments, and other private and public organizations. Includes commercial combined-heat-and-power and commercial electricity-only plants. [9] All facilities and equipment used for producing, processing, or assembling goods. Includes industrial combined-heat-and-power and industrial electricity-only plants. [10] Beginning in 2009, includes other renewable diesel fuel and other renewable fuels consumption, not shown separately. [11] Any liquid biofuel suitable as a diesel fuel substitute, additive, or extender. [12] Electricity-only and combined-heat-and-power plants whose primary business is to sell electricity and/or heat to the public. Includes sources not shown separately.

Source: U.S. Energy Information Administration, *Monthly Energy Review*, March 2022. See also <www.eia.gov/totalenergy/data/monthly>.

Table 971. Energy Consumption—End-Use Sector and Selected Source by State: 2020

[In trillions of British thermal units (92,862 represents 92,862,000,000,000,000 Btu), except as indicated. For definition of Btu, see source and text, this section. U.S. totals may not equal sum of states due to independent rounding and/or interstate flows of electricity that are not allocated to the states. For technical notes and documentation, see source <www.eia.gov/state/seds/seds-technical-notes-complete. php?sid=US>]

State	Total [1,2]	Per capita [3] (mil. Btu)	End-use sector [4]				Source				
			Resi-dential	Com-mercial	Indus-trial [2]	Trans-portation	Petro-leum [5]	Natural gas (dry) [6]	Coal	Hydro-electric power [7]	Nuclear electric power
U.S.	**92,862**	**280**	**20,521**	**16,733**	**31,260**	**24,349**	**33,638**	**31,590**	**9,183**	**2,503**	**8,248**
AL	1,839	366	332	236	773	498	552	713	257	117	455
AK	640	874	54	58	363	165	223	374	19	15	–
AZ	1,508	210	442	334	224	508	573	514	157	56	329
AR	1,035	344	216	170	377	271	330	335	162	40	157
CA	6,923	175	1,508	1,358	1,701	2,355	2,814	2,144	28	188	170
CO	1,451	251	377	281	415	378	459	557	217	15	–
CT	667	185	230	170	71	196	275	298	(Z)	3	164
DE	277	279	63	56	85	73	109	94	2	–	–
DC	144	208	37	85	5	17	16	28	–	–	–
FL	4,003	186	1,216	908	462	1,417	1,561	1,619	180	2	307
GA	2,728	254	689	498	717	824	921	780	153	41	343
HI	233	160	37	39	47	109	192	2	13	1	–
ID	550	298	134	90	169	158	185	129	3	83	–
IL	3,613	283	940	740	1,131	803	1,098	1,167	391	1	1,047
IN	2,564	378	515	337	1,187	526	683	875	669	2	–
IA	1,526	479	233	181	834	278	421	431	183	9	30
KS	1,070	364	218	203	390	258	348	301	194	(Z)	111
KY	1,595	354	331	234	565	465	572	344	482	44	–
LA	4,200	903	301	234	3,059	606	1,795	1,924	49	11	177
ME	365	268	103	64	100	98	163	47	2	28	–
MD	1,213	197	381	358	87	387	419	297	50	15	157
MA	1,278	182	412	369	138	360	471	401	–	7	–
MI	2,611	259	770	571	620	650	793	1,003	334	15	317
MN	1,731	303	411	339	577	405	573	496	163	9	153
MS	1,037	351	180	139	386	332	386	610	54	–	68
MO	1,702	277	507	379	305	511	606	304	551	16	81
MT	429	395	100	82	130	116	180	87	99	94	–
NE	864	440	160	137	376	191	238	193	214	12	65
NV	710	228	184	145	155	226	257	311	28	17	–
NH	296	215	101	65	40	89	143	54	2	11	103
NJ	1,894	204	559	521	238	576	718	679	12	(Z)	279
NM	700	330	126	116	239	218	249	292	139	2	–
NY	3,354	166	1,076	1,013	356	909	1,113	1,305	6	259	401
NC	2,471	236	671	537	527	736	849	558	224	70	442
ND	626	804	66	85	347	128	169	156	363	21	–
OH	3,404	289	849	633	1,107	815	1,028	1,234	557	3	190
OK	1,579	399	282	223	648	426	494	836	71	25	–
OR	983	232	249	185	270	279	316	282	18	280	–
PA	3,413	263	850	525	1,254	784	993	1,783	374	23	799
RI	176	160	58	45	22	50	71	101	–	(Z)	–
SC	1,533	299	359	254	487	433	491	343	137	34	572
SD	397	447	70	62	168	97	125	91	22	51	–
TN	2,039	295	500	412	513	615	690	399	176	118	383
TX	13,481	461	1,744	1,631	7,266	2,840	6,331	4,710	873	9	433
UT	829	253	192	169	215	253	298	267	244	7	–
VT	126	196	44	25	18	39	73	14	–	10	–
VA	2,273	263	550	610	420	693	777	748	75	18	315
WA	1,779	231	465	331	479	505	646	355	59	670	98
WV	804	449	151	102	381	170	187	265	540	14	–
WI	1,708	290	428	338	538	404	518	572	249	24	102
WY	504	874	52	53	292	107	143	169	388	10	–

– Represents zero. Z Less than 500 billion Btu. [1] Includes other sources, not shown separately. [2] U.S. total energy and U.S. industrial sector include net imports of coal coke that are not allocated to the states. [3] Based on estimated resident population as of July 1. [4] End-use sector data include electricity sales and associated electrical system energy losses. [5] Includes fuel ethanol blended into motor gasoline. [6] Includes supplemental gaseous fuels. [7] Conventional hydroelectric power. Does not include pumped-storage hydroelectricity.

Source: U.S. Energy Information Administration, "State Energy Data System," <www.eia.gov/state/seds>, accessed June 2022.

Table 972. Energy-related Carbon Dioxide Emissions by Sector and State: 2019

[5,158.8 represents 5,158,800,000. Total state CO2 emissions include those from direct fuel use across all sectors as well as primary fuels consumed for electricity generation. Covers emissions released at the location where fossil fuels are consumed. Regarding fuels that are used in one state to generate electricity consumed in another state, emissions are attributed to the state in which the electricity is generated and fuels are combusted. Data are derived from EIA's State Energy Data System]

State	Total carbon dioxide emissions (mil. metric tons)	Percent of carbon dioxide emissions by sector					Metric tons per capita
		Commercial	Electric Power	Residential	Industrial	Transportation	
Total [1]...............	**5,158.8**	**5.0**	**31.2**	**6.7**	**19.5**	**37.6**	**15.7**
Alabama........................	106.3	2.1	45.6	1.9	18.5	31.8	21.6
Alaska..........................	34.3	5.9	7.9	4.2	47.4	34.6	46.7
Arizona.........................	92.5	3.3	47.0	2.9	5.0	41.8	12.7
Arkansas.......................	65.1	5.4	48.0	3.2	13.1	30.3	21.5
California.......................	358.2	5.6	8.7	7.6	19.8	58.3	9.1
Colorado........................	91.7	5.2	36.5	9.8	14.6	34.0	15.9
Connecticut....................	36.6	11.5	21.6	20.0	4.7	42.3	10.3
Delaware........................	13.6	8.0	13.0	7.3	28.8	42.9	13.9
District of Columbia..........	2.8	33.6	–	23.7	0.8	42.0	4.0
Florida..........................	233.6	3.0	40.4	0.6	5.1	51.0	10.9
Georgia.........................	136.5	3.3	35.6	5.3	9.0	46.8	12.8
Hawaii..........................	20.5	2.8	30.7	0.3	6.4	59.8	14.5
Idaho...........................	20.1	7.9	8.4	10.2	16.1	57.4	11.2
Illinois..........................	203.4	7.6	28.6	12.6	17.8	33.3	16.1
Indiana.........................	176.1	3.5	43.0	5.1	26.2	22.2	26.2
Iowa............................	77.3	5.8	31.0	7.3	29.3	26.6	24.5
Kansas.........................	60.5	4.5	33.6	7.2	22.4	32.3	20.8
Kentucky.......................	115.4	2.5	51.6	2.8	13.5	29.6	25.8
Louisiana.......................	194.9	1.2	15.7	1.1	61.2	20.7	41.8
Maine...........................	14.4	12.4	4.9	21.0	11.5	50.2	10.7
Maryland.......................	56.9	10.0	20.7	10.1	5.2	54.0	9.4
Massachusetts................	63.3	12.7	9.8	21.6	5.3	50.6	9.2
Michigan........................	159.2	7.4	34.3	13.5	11.9	32.9	15.9
Minnesota......................	92.1	8.0	24.8	11.1	19.5	36.6	16.3
Mississippi.....................	62.5	2.6	39.2	2.6	18.1	37.5	21.0
Missouri........................	117.0	4.0	49.5	6.2	7.2	33.1	19.1
Montana........................	32.3	5.4	49.4	6.1	14.5	24.7	30.2
Nebraska.......................	50.5	4.7	43.6	5.7	17.5	28.5	26.1
Nevada.........................	41.7	6.1	32.6	6.7	8.9	45.8	13.5
New Hampshire................	13.9	10.6	13.0	21.3	5.6	49.4	10.2
New Jersey.....................	100.8	10.0	17.2	15.1	9.4	48.2	11.3
New Mexico.....................	48.9	4.1	41.4	5.3	16.6	32.6	23.3
New York........................	169.0	13.6	12.7	21.1	5.3	47.3	8.7
North Carolina.................	122.6	4.2	37.6	4.2	8.1	45.9	11.7
North Dakota...................	57.2	2.2	49.6	2.4	29.0	16.9	74.8
Ohio............................	196.7	6.3	34.3	9.3	19.2	30.9	16.8
Oklahoma......................	90.8	3.8	29.7	4.7	26.6	35.2	22.9
Oregon.........................	41.8	6.1	25.2	7.1	10.8	50.8	9.9
Pennsylvania...................	218.7	5.5	34.3	8.9	23.1	28.2	17.1
Rhode Island...................	10.4	9.0	27.1	19.9	6.1	37.9	9.8
South Carolina.................	69.4	3.3	35.9	2.8	10.8	47.3	13.5
South Dakota..................	16.0	5.8	20.0	7.9	23.9	42.4	18.0
Tennessee.....................	92.2	4.6	26.1	4.7	15.3	49.4	13.5
Texas...........................	683.2	2.1	27.9	2.0	34.6	33.4	23.6
Utah............................	61.5	5.0	46.3	7.2	11.5	30.0	19.2
Vermont........................	6.0	14.8	(Z)	25.8	7.5	51.9	9.6
Virginia.........................	106.8	5.7	25.2	5.7	10.8	52.5	12.5
Washington....................	84.2	5.6	16.3	7.3	15.5	55.4	11.1
West Virginia...................	85.4	2.1	67.6	2.0	13.9	14.4	47.6
Wisconsin......................	94.8	7.1	35.1	11.4	14.1	32.3	16.3
Wyoming.......................	59.1	1.7	61.7	1.7	21.4	13.5	101.9

– Represents zero. Z represents less than 0.05%. [1] For the United States as a whole, see, EIA's *Monthly Energy Review,* Section 11: Environment. The total for all states is different from the national-level estimate because of differing methodologies. These values are unadjusted. See source for details on the data series differences.

Source: U.S. Energy Information Agency, "Energy-Related CO2 Emission Data Tables," <www.eia.gov/environment/emissions/state/>, accessed April 2022.

Table 973. Energy Expenditures and Average Fuel Prices by Source and Sector: 1990 to 2020

[In millions of dollars (474,652 represents $474,652,000,000), except as indicated. Btu = British thermal units. For definition of Btu, see text, this section. End-use sector and electric utilities exclude expenditures and prices on energy sources such as hydropower, solar, wind, and geothermal. Also excludes expenditures for reported amounts of energy consumed by the energy industry for production, transportation, and processing operations]

Source and sector	1990	2000	2010	2015	2016	2017	2018	2019	2020
EXPENDITURES (mil. dol.)									
Total [1,2,3]	**474,652**	**687,711**	**1,214,277**	**1,128,437**	**1,038,871**	**1,136,365**	**1,271,812**	**1,223,862**	**1,007,433**
Natural gas [3]	65,278	119,094	161,303	140,294	127,618	142,072	157,747	150,267	134,780
Petroleum products	237,677	359,403	717,097	623,501	549,912	631,892	742,591	700,447	504,521
Motor gasoline [4]	126,558	192,153	376,492	342,578	310,961	348,456	387,586	370,930	268,098
Coal	28,419	27,959	50,245	36,578	31,694	30,326	29,227	25,387	19,550
Retail electricity	176,691	231,578	365,913	388,344	383,567	387,222	403,349	398,774	390,934
Residential sector [5]	110,910	155,299	249,772	248,045	238,550	246,110	267,013	264,333	261,258
Commercial sector [2,3]	79,602	113,421	177,662	185,971	178,885	184,766	193,092	189,355	173,893
Industrial sector [2,3]	103,351	140,963	221,659	186,849	169,733	190,594	213,492	197,773	166,828
Transportation sector [2]	180,790	278,028	565,184	507,573	451,703	514,895	598,216	572,400	405,453
Motor gasoline [4]	123,845	189,836	369,433	329,609	299,361	335,666	373,095	356,962	256,276
Electric utilities [2]	40,627	60,053	94,791	76,352	68,514	69,714	75,624	64,855	54,067
AVERAGE FUEL PRICES (dol. per mil. Btu)									
All sectors	**8.29**	**10.33**	**18.92**	**17.31**	**15.95**	**17.32**	**18.61**	**17.96**	**16.25**
Residential sector [5]	11.87	14.21	22.37	22.93	22.92	23.77	23.29	23.13	23.80
Commercial sector [2]	11.87	13.90	20.92	20.72	20.17	20.86	20.66	20.40	20.13
Industrial sector [2]	5.30	6.50	12.14	9.88	9.01	9.95	10.67	9.92	8.73
Transportation sector	8.33	10.77	21.54	19.16	16.71	18.91	21.74	20.83	17.43
Electric utilities [2]	1.48	1.71	2.63	2.28	2.09	2.21	2.33	2.08	1.84

[1] Includes other sources not shown separately. [2] There are no direct fuel costs for hydroelectric, geothermal, wind, photovoltaic, or solar thermal energy. [3] Natural gas as it is consumed; includes supplemental gaseous fuels that are commingled with natural gas. [4] Beginning 1993, includes fuel ethanol blended into motor gasoline. [5] There are no direct fuel costs for geothermal, photovoltaic, or solar thermal energy.

Source: U.S. Energy Information Administration, "State Energy Data System (SEDS)," <www.eia.gov/state/seds>, accessed July 2022.

Table 974. Fuel Ethanol and Biodiesel—Summary: 2000 to 2021

[233.1 represents 233,100,000,000,000. Btu=British thermal units. For definition of Btu, see source and text, this section. Minus sign (-) indicates an excess of exports over imports, except where noted]

Fuel	2000	2010	2015	2016	2017	2018	2019	2020	2021
FUEL ETHANOL									
Feedstock [1] (tril. Btu)	233.1	1,823.5	2,012.5	2,092.3	2,163.6	2,187.3	2,139.9	1,885.8	2,030.1
Production:									
1,000 barrels	38,627	316,617	352,553	366,981	379,435	383,127	375,678	331,928	357,502
Tril. Btu	137.7	1,127.8	1,254.4	1,305.7	1,349.3	1,361.3	1,335.5	1,180.7	1,270.9
Net imports [2] (1,000 barrels)	116	-9,115	-17,632	-27,002	-31,268	-39,410	-30,276	-27,692	-28,356
Stocks [3] (1,000 barrels)	3,400	17,941	21,596	19,758	23,043	23,418	22,352	24,663	22,011
Stock change [4] (1,000 barrels)	-624	1,347	2,857	-1,838	3,285	375	-1,066	2,311	-2,676
Consumption:									
1,000 barrels	39,367	306,155	332,064	341,817	344,882	343,342	346,468	301,925	331,823
Tril. Btu	140.3	1,090.5	1,181.5	1,216.2	1,226.4	1,219.9	1,231.7	1,073.9	1,179.6
BIODIESEL									
Feedstock [5] (tril. Btu)	(NA)	44.4	163.4	202.8	206.4	240.3	223.1	234.7	212.0
Production:									
1,000 barrels	(NA)	8,177	30,080	37,327	37,993	44,222	41,060	43,207	39,019
Tril. Btu	(NA)	43.8	161.2	200.04	203.61	236.99	220.04	231.55	209.10
Net imports (1,000 barrels)	(NA)	-2,024	6,308	14,781	7,146	1,499	1,348	1,226	490
Stocks [6] (1,000 barrels)	(NA)	672	3,943	6,398	4,268	4,662	3,907	3,665	4,184
Stock change [4] (1,000 barrels)	(NA)	-39.0	813	2,454	-2,130	394	-756	-241	301
Consumption:									
1,000 barrels	(NA)	6,192	35,575	49,653	47,269	45,326	43,163	44,675	39,208
Tril. Btu	(NA)	33.2	190.6	266.1	253.3	242.9	231.3	239.4	210.1

NA Not available. [1] Total corn and other biomass inputs to the production of undenatured ethanol used for fuel ethanol. [2] Through 2009, data are for fuel ethanol imports only; data for fuel ethanol exports are not available. Beginning in 2010, data are for fuel ethanol imports minus fuel ethanol exports. [3] Stocks are at end of year. [4] A negative number indicates a decrease in stocks. [5] Total vegetable oil and other biomass inputs to the production of biodiesel. [6] Stocks are at end of period. Includes biodiesel stocks at (or in) refineries, pipelines, and bulk terminals. Beginning in 2011, also includes stocks at biodiesel production plants.

Source: U.S. Energy Information Administration, *Monthly Energy Review*, March 2022. See also <www.eia.gov/totalenergy/data/monthly>.

Table 975. Energy Expenditures—End-Use Sector and Selected Source by State: 2020

[In millions of dollars (1,007,433 represents $1,007,433,000,000). End-use sector and electric utilities exclude expenditures on energy sources such as hydroelectric, photovoltaic, solar thermal, wind, and geothermal. Also excludes expenditures for reported amounts of energy consumed by the energy industry for production, transportation, and processing operations. For technical notes and documentation, see source, <www.eia.gov/state/seds/seds-technical-notes-complete.php>]

State	Total [1,2]	End-use sector				Source			
		Residential	Commercial	Industrial [2]	Transportation	Petroleum products [3]	Natural gas [4]	Coal	Electricity sales
U.S.	1,007,433	261,258	173,893	166,828	405,453	504,521	134,780	19,550	390,934
AL	18,570	4,518	2,886	3,629	7,537	8,528	2,430	605	8,186
AK	4,709	860	825	575	2,449	3,111	594	125	1,162
AZ	20,340	5,432	3,459	1,875	9,574	10,901	1,818	342	8,553
AR	10,368	2,342	1,451	2,265	4,311	5,084	1,696	309	3,802
CA	114,485	26,556	22,760	14,148	51,020	56,453	15,128	99	44,682
CO	15,449	3,782	2,655	2,433	6,579	7,917	2,181	371	5,729
CT	11,540	4,618	2,549	808	3,565	4,981	1,739	(Z)	5,188
DE	3,153	855	575	431	1,292	1,507	581	5	1,117
DC	1,763	445	979	53	286	303	295	–	1,164
FL	51,441	15,613	9,548	3,430	22,851	25,161	6,198	459	24,394
GA	31,018	9,073	5,179	3,745	13,021	14,561	3,876	419	13,247
HI	4,696	904	912	886	1,993	2,791	70	46	2,413
ID	5,949	1,241	711	1,054	2,942	3,437	541	6	1,953
IL	34,115	9,583	5,985	5,477	13,070	15,615	6,095	740	12,703
IN	24,287	5,644	3,226	6,634	8,784	10,421	4,143	1,747	9,537
IA	12,694	2,631	1,629	3,832	4,602	6,343	1,811	294	4,543
KS	10,263	2,463	1,937	1,810	4,054	4,976	1,332	303	4,016
KY	15,508	3,483	2,299	2,732	6,994	8,113	1,482	929	6,117
LA	24,234	3,380	2,354	11,928	6,572	14,587	4,048	236	6,280
ME	4,885	1,579	813	659	1,833	2,886	358	6	1,537
MD	15,952	4,976	3,600	838	6,537	7,593	2,140	118	6,426
MA	20,902	7,589	5,218	1,814	6,281	8,349	3,794	–	9,098
MI	29,070	9,090	5,590	3,958	10,433	12,504	5,133	768	11,816
MN	17,647	4,579	3,095	3,281	6,692	8,662	2,430	326	6,668
MS	10,581	2,362	1,628	1,735	4,856	5,470	1,738	143	4,186
MO	18,888	5,232	3,153	2,157	8,346	9,663	2,008	870	7,297
MT	4,402	955	724	561	2,162	2,638	439	225	1,279
NE	7,637	1,523	1,055	1,810	3,250	3,975	877	267	2,797
NV	8,778	2,169	1,227	1,193	4,189	4,779	1,346	70	3,187
NH	4,621	1,672	890	448	1,611	2,511	375	5	1,779
NJ	24,827	7,437	5,875	1,816	9,699	11,413	4,073	34	9,745
NM	6,791	1,338	1,053	927	3,472	4,036	577	355	2,297
NY	47,968	17,226	12,862	2,812	15,068	18,767	9,116	18	20,872
NC	28,737	8,035	4,864	3,478	12,362	14,317	3,021	583	12,294
ND	4,848	686	747	1,627	1,788	2,658	273	561	1,845
OH	34,994	9,598	5,506	6,565	13,325	16,118	5,789	1,251	13,345
OK	13,106	3,041	1,907	2,026	6,133	7,074	2,080	125	4,676
OR	12,066	2,854	1,866	1,667	5,679	6,401	1,273	40	4,502
PA	37,545	11,641	4,915	6,927	14,061	17,894	6,912	903	13,517
RI	3,140	1,193	746	306	896	1,286	661	–	1,363
SC	16,657	4,465	2,534	2,581	7,077	7,942	1,480	433	7,597
SD	3,714	762	551	792	1,609	2,068	380	42	1,277
TN	21,401	5,147	4,138	2,608	9,507	10,628	1,823	381	9,017
TX	108,196	21,054	12,865	34,347	39,930	66,034	10,636	1,792	35,055
UT	8,709	1,755	1,330	1,151	4,473	5,029	1,237	500	2,593
VT	2,325	856	442	288	739	1,310	96	–	871
VA	25,577	7,062	5,013	2,411	11,091	12,676	3,029	235	10,740
WA	19,932	4,946	3,277	2,193	9,515	10,805	2,027	135	7,143
WV	6,729	1,666	901	1,620	2,541	3,317	527	1,140	2,803
WI	18,496	4,841	3,146	3,405	7,104	8,782	2,649	513	7,301
WY	3,869	506	443	1,221	1,699	2,154	427	677	1,230

– Represents zero. Z Less than $500,000. [1] Total expenditures are the sum of purchases for each source (including electricity sales) less electric power sector purchases of fuel. There are no direct fuel costs for hydroelectric, geothermal, wind, photovoltaic, or solar thermal energy. [2] U.S. total includes sources not shown separately, such as electricity imports and exports and coal coke net imports, which are not allocated to the states. [3] Includes fuel ethanol blended into motor gasoline. [4] Includes supplemental gaseous fuels.

Source: U.S. Energy Information Administration, "State Energy Data System," <www.eia.gov/state/seds>, accessed July 2022.

Table 976. Energy Imports and Exports by Type of Fuel: 1980 to 2021

[In quadrillion Btu (12.10 represents 12,100,000,000,000,000 Btu). Btu=British thermal units; for definition, see text, this section]

Type of fuel	1980	1990	2000	2010	2015	2016	2017	2018	2019	2020	2021
Net imports, total [1]	**12.10**	**14.06**	**24.90**	**21.69**	**10.89**	**11.26**	**7.51**	**3.61**	**-0.61**	**-3.47**	**-3.87**
Coal	-2.39	-2.70	-1.21	-1.62	-1.60	-1.33	-2.22	-2.70	-2.17	-1.62	-2.02
Natural gas (dry)	0.96	1.46	3.62	2.69	0.99	0.73	-0.07	-0.68	-1.89	-2.72	-3.84
Petroleum [2]	13.50	15.29	22.31	20.58	11.29	11.71	9.77	7.07	3.50	0.87	2.06
Other [3]	0.04	0.01	0.18	0.04	0.21	0.15	0.04	-0.07	-0.06	-0.01	-0.08
Imports, total	15.80	18.82	28.87	29.87	23.79	25.38	25.46	24.83	22.87	19.99	21.43
Coal	0.03	0.07	0.31	0.48	0.26	0.22	0.17	0.12	0.14	0.10	0.11
Natural gas (dry)	1.01	1.55	3.87	3.83	2.79	3.08	3.11	2.96	2.81	2.62	2.88
Petroleum [2]	14.66	17.12	24.42	25.36	20.41	21.70	21.87	21.50	19.64	16.98	18.18
Other [3]	0.10	0.08	0.26	0.19	0.34	0.38	0.31	0.25	0.28	0.29	0.27
Exports, total	3.69	4.75	3.96	8.18	12.90	14.12	17.95	21.22	23.48	23.46	25.31
Coal	2.42	2.77	1.53	2.10	1.85	1.55	2.39	2.82	2.31	1.72	2.13
Natural gas (dry)	0.05	0.09	0.25	1.15	1.80	2.36	3.18	3.64	4.70	5.33	6.71
Petroleum	1.16	1.82	2.11	4.78	9.12	9.99	12.11	14.43	16.14	16.11	16.12
Other [3]	0.07	0.07	0.08	0.15	0.13	0.23	0.27	0.32	0.33	0.30	0.34

[1] Imports minus exports. Minus sign (-) indicates exports are greater than imports. [2] Includes imports into the Strategic Petroleum Reserve. [3] Coal coke, small amounts of electricity transmitted to Canada and Mexico, and small amounts of biomass fuel.

Source: U.S. Energy Information Administration, *Monthly Energy Review*, March 2022. See also <www.eia.gov/totalenergy/data/monthly/>.

Table 977. U.S. Foreign Trade in Natural Gas, Crude Oil, Petroleum Products, and Coal: 1980 to 2021

[985 represents 985,000,000,000 cubic feet. Minus sign (-) indicates trade deficit]

Mineral fuel	Unit	1980	1990	2000	2010	2015	2018	2019	2020	2021 (P)
Natural gas:										
Imports	Bil. cu. ft.	985	1,532	3,782	3,741	2,718	2,889	2,742	2,551	2,808
Exports	Bil. cu. ft.	49	86	244	1,137	1,784	3,608	4,658	5,284	6,653
Net trade [1]	Bil. cu. ft.	-936	-1,447	-3,538	-2,604	-935	719	1,916	2,732	3,845
Crude oil: [2]										
Imports [3]	Mil. barrels	1,926	2,151	3,320	3,363	2,687	2,835	2,482	2,150	2,230
Exports	Mil. barrels	105	40	18	15	170	748	1,088	1,173	1,088
Net trade [1]	Mil. barrels	-1,821	-2,112	-3,301	-3,348	-2,518	-2,088	-1,394	-977	-1,142
Petroleum products:										
Imports	Mil. barrels	(NA)	775	874	942	761	794	854	728	861
Exports	Mil. barrels	(NA)	273	362	843	1,560	2,027	2,004	1,937	2,063
Net trade [1]	Mil. barrels	(NA)	-502	-512	-98	798	1,233	1,149	1,209	1,202
Coal:										
Imports	Mil. sh. tons	1	3	13	19	11	6	7	5	5
Exports	Mil. sh. tons	92	106	58	82	74	116	94	69	85
Net trade [1]	Mil. sh. tons	91	103	46	62	63	110	87	64	80

P Preliminary. NA Not available. [1] Exports minus imports. [2] Includes lease condensate. [3] Includes Strategic Petroleum Reserve imports.

Source: U.S. Energy Information Administration, *Monthly Energy Review*, March 2022; and "Petroleum and Other Liquids, Imports/Exports," <www.eia.gov/petroleum/data.cfm>, accessed March 2022.

Table 978. Crude Oil Imports Into the U.S. by Country of Origin: 1995 to 2021

[In millions of barrels (2,639 represents 2,639,000,000). A barrel contains 42 gallons. Crude oil imports are reported by the Petroleum Administration for Defense (PAD) District in which they are to be processed. A PAD District is a geographic aggregation of the 50 states and D.C. into 5 districts. Includes crude oil imported for storage in the Strategic Petroleum Reserve (SPR). Total Organization of Petroleum Exporting Countries (OPEC) excludes, and non-OPEC includes, petroleum imported into the United States indirectly from members of OPEC, primarily from Caribbean and West European areas, as petroleum products that were refined from crude oil produced by OPEC]

Country of origin	1995	2000	2005	2010	2015	2016	2017	2018	2019	2020	2021
Total imports	**2,639**	**3,320**	**3,696**	**3,363**	**2,687**	**2,873**	**2,909**	**2,835**	**2,482**	**2,150**	**2,230**
OPEC, total [1, 2]	**1,303**	**1,663**	**1,758**	**1,662**	**976**	**1,164**	**1,138**	**943**	**541**	**298**	**290**
Algeria	10	(Z)	83	120	1	19	24	29	7	2	7
Angola	131	108	166	140	45	58	47	33	12	10	12
Iran	(NA)	(NA)	(NA)	(NA)	(NA)	(NA)	(NA)	(NA)	(NA)	(NA)	1
Iraq	(NA)	227	193	152	84	154	219	189	121	64	55
Kuwait	78	96	83	71	74	76	53	28	16	8	8
Libya	(NA)	(NA)	16	16	1	4	21	20	22	3	33
Nigeria	227	320	393	359	20	76	113	64	68	24	39
Saudi Arabia	460	558	527	395	384	402	347	318	182	182	130
United Arab Emirates	2	1	3	1	1	4	7	2	1	2	6
Non-OPEC, total [2]	**1,336**	**1,657**	**1,938**	**1,701**	**1,712**	**1,709**	**1,771**	**1,893**	**1,942**	**1,852**	**1,940**
Brazil	(NA)	2	34	93	69	53	72	46	44	28	38
Canada	380	493	596	719	1,157	1,181	1,258	1,353	1,392	1,316	1,372
Colombia	75	116	57	124	136	162	121	108	116	91	66
Ecuador	35	46	101	76	82	87	75	64	73	62	54
Ghana	(NA)	(NA)	(NA)	(NA)	(NA)	(NA)	6	4	9	9	19
Guyana	(NA)	(NA)	(NA)	(NA)	(NA)	(NA)	(NA)	(NA)	(NA)	10	28
Mexico	375	480	568	421	251	213	222	243	219	240	213
Norway	94	111	43	9	3	13	14	20	17	5	18
Russia	5	3	73	98	14	14	18	27	49	28	73

NA Not available. Z represents less than 500,000. [1] Countries listed under OPEC and non-OPEC are based on current affiliations. OPEC and non-OPEC totals are based on affiliations for the stated period of time which may differ from current affiliations. Indonesia withdrew from OPEC in January 2009, rejoined in 2016 and withdrew again in December 2016; Angola joined OPEC in January 2007; Ecuador withdrew from OPEC in January 1993, rejoined in November 2007 and withdrew again in January 2020; Gabon terminated its membership in 1995 and rejoined in July 2016; Equatorial Guinea joined OPEC in May 2017; Congo (Republic of) joined OPEC in June 2018; and Qatar withdrew from OPEC in January 2019. [2] Includes countries not shown separately.

Source: U.S. Energy Information Administration, Petroleum & Other Liquids, "U.S. Imports by Country of Origin," <www.eia.gov/petroleum/data.php#imports>, accessed March 2022.

Table 979. Crude Oil and Refined Products—Summary: 1980 to 2021

[13,481 represents 13,481,000 bbl. One barrel (bbl.) contains 42 gallons. Data are averages]

Year	Crude oil [1] (1,000 bbl. per day)					Refined oil products (1,000 bbl. per day)			Total oil imports [5] (1,000 bbl. per day)	Crude oil stocks [1,2] (mil. bbl.)	
	Refinery and blender input	Domestic production	Imports Total [3]	Imports Strategic reserve [4]	Exports	Domestic demand	Imports	Exports		Total [6]	Strategic reserve [7]
1980....	13,481	8,597	5,263	44	287	17,056	1,646	258	6,909	466	108
1981....	12,470	8,572	4,396	256	228	16,058	1,599	367	5,996	594	230
1982....	11,774	8,649	3,488	165	236	15,296	1,625	579	5,113	644	294
1983....	11,685	8,688	3,329	234	164	15,231	1,722	575	5,051	723	379
1984....	12,044	8,879	3,426	197	181	15,726	2,011	541	5,437	796	451
1985....	12,002	8,971	3,201	118	204	15,726	1,866	577	5,067	814	493
1986....	12,716	8,680	4,178	48	154	16,281	2,045	631	6,224	843	512
1987....	12,854	8,349	4,674	73	151	16,665	2,004	613	6,678	890	541
1988....	13,246	8,140	5,107	51	155	17,283	2,295	661	7,402	890	560
1989....	13,401	7,613	5,843	56	142	17,325	2,217	717	8,061	921	580
1990....	13,409	7,355	5,894	27	109	16,988	2,123	748	8,018	908	586
1991....	13,301	7,417	5,782	(NA)	116	16,714	1,844	885	7,627	893	569
1992....	13,411	7,171	6,083	10	89	17,033	1,805	861	7,888	893	575
1993....	13,613	6,847	6,787	15	98	17,237	1,833	904	8,620	922	587
1994....	13,866	6,662	7,063	12	99	17,718	1,933	843	8,996	929	592
1995....	13,973	6,560	7,230	(NA)	95	17,725	1,605	855	8,835	895	592
1996....	14,195	6,465	7,508	(NA)	110	18,309	1,971	871	9,478	850	566
1997....	14,662	6,452	8,225	(NA)	108	18,620	1,936	896	10,162	868	563
1998....	14,889	6,252	8,706	(NA)	110	18,917	2,002	835	10,708	895	571
1999....	14,804	5,881	8,731	8	118	19,519	2,122	822	10,852	852	567
2000....	15,067	5,822	9,071	8	50	19,701	2,389	990	11,459	826	541
2001....	15,128	5,801	9,328	11	20	19,649	2,543	951	11,871	862	550
2002....	14,947	5,744	9,140	16	9	19,761	2,390	975	11,530	877	599
2003....	15,304	5,649	9,665	(NA)	12	20,034	2,599	1,014	12,264	907	638
2004....	15,475	5,441	10,088	77	27	20,731	3,057	1,021	13,145	961	676
2005....	15,220	5,184	10,126	52	32	20,802	3,588	1,133	13,714	992	685
2006....	15,242	5,086	10,118	8	25	20,687	3,589	1,292	13,707	984	689
2007....	15,156	5,074	10,031	7	27	20,680	3,437	1,405	13,468	965	697
2008....	14,648	5,000	9,783	19	29	19,498	3,132	1,773	12,915	1,010	702
2009....	14,336	5,357	9,013	56	44	18,771	2,678	1,980	11,691	1,034	727
2010....	14,724	5,484	9,213	(NA)	42	19,178	2,580	2,311	11,793	1,039	727
2011....	14,806	5,674	8,935	(NA)	47	18,896	2,501	2,939	11,436	1,004	696
2012....	14,999	6,523	8,527	(NA)	67	18,482	2,071	3,137	10,598	1,033	695
2013....	15,312	7,498	7,730	(NA)	134	18,967	2,129	3,487	9,859	1,023	696
2014....	15,848	8,792	7,344	(NA)	351	19,100	1,897	3,824	9,241	1,052	691
2015....	16,188	9,441	7,363	(NA)	465	19,532	2,086	4,273	9,449	1,144	695
2016....	16,187	8,844	7,850	(NA)	591	19,692	2,205	4,670	10,055	1,180	695
2017....	16,590	9,357	7,969	(NA)	1,158	19,952	2,175	5,218	10,144	1,084	663
2018....	16,969	10,941	7,768	(NA)	2,048	20,512	2,174	5,553	9,943	1,092	649
2019....	16,563	12,289	6,801	(NA)	2,982	20,543	2,340	5,490	9,141	1,068	635
2020....	14,212	11,283	5,875	(NA)	3206	18,186	1,988	5,292	7,863	1,124	638
2021....	15,148	11,185	6,110	(NA)	2,980	19,782	2,359	5,653	8,468	1,015	594

NA Not available. [1] Includes lease condensate. [2] Crude oil at end of period. Includes commercial and Strategic Petroleum Reserve (SPR) stocks. [3] Includes Strategic Petroleum Reserve. [4] Through 2000, includes imports by SPR only; beginning in 2004, includes imports by SPR, and imports into SPR by others. [5] Crude oil (including Strategic Petroleum Reserve imports) plus refined products. [6] Beginning in 1981, includes stocks of Alaskan crude oil in transit. [7] Crude oil stocks in the Strategic Petroleum Reserve include non-U.S. stocks held under foreign or commercial storage agreements.

Source: U.S. Energy Information Administration, *Monthly Energy Review*, March 2022. See also <www.eia.gov/totalenergy/data/monthly>.

Table 980. Petroleum and Coal Products Corporations—Sales, Net Profit, and Profit Per Dollar of Sales: 2005 to 2021

[956.0 represents $956,000,000,000. Covers North American Industry Classification System (NAICS) 324. Profit rates are averages of quarterly figures at annual rates]

Item	Unit	2005	2010	2014	2015	2016	2017	2018	2019	2020	2021
Sales.....................	Bil. dol.	956.0	1,077.1	1,283.8	834.3	681.9	850.1	1,029.3	985.3	636.5	971.4
Net profit:											
Before income taxes..............	Bil. dol.	120.2	56.0	82.3	21.0	1.2	34.0	70.9	30.9	-68.2	84.7
After income taxes................	Bil. dol.	96.3	54.2	74.2	24.0	11.2	48.0	63.3	29.7	-52.1	72.3
Depreciation [1]................	Bil. dol.	18.6	30.8	32.0	33.6	34.6	35.2	34.7	38.4	39.2	38.3
Profits per dollar of sales:											
Before income taxes..............	Cents	12.6	5.2	6.4	2.5	0.2	4.0	6.9	3.1	-10.7	8.7
After income taxes................	Cents	10.1	5.0	5.8	2.9	1.6	5.7	6.2	3.0	-8.2	7.4
Stockholders' equity................	Bil. dol.	1,263.1	1,826.5	2,286.8	2,160.2	2,102.7	2,183.5	2,328.7	2,427.6	2,165.1	2,129.0

[1] Includes depletion and accelerated amortization of emergency facilities.

Source: U.S. Census Bureau, Quarterly Financial Report (QFR), Manufacturing, Mining, Trade, and Selected Service Industries, "Time Series/Trend Charts," <www.census.gov/econ/qfr>, accessed March 2022.

Table 981. Nuclear Power Plants—Number, Capacity, and Generation: 1980 to 2021

[51.8 represents 51,800,000 kilowatts (kW)]

Item	1980	1990	2000	2010	2015	2017	2018	2019	2020	2021
Operable generating units [1,2]	71	112	104	104	99	99	98	96	94	93
Net summer capacity [2,3] (mil. kW)	51.8	99.6	97.9	101.2	98.7	99.6	99.4	98.1	96.5	95.5
Net generation (bil. kWh)	251.1	576.9	753.9	807.0	797.2	805.0	807.1	809.4	789.9	778.2
Percent of total electricity net generation	11.0	19.0	19.8	19.6	19.6	20.0	19.3	19.6	19.7	18.9
Capacity factor [4] (percent)	56.3	66.0	88.1	91.1	92.3	92.3	92.5	93.4	92.4	92.7

[1] Total of nuclear generating units holding full-power licenses, or equivalent permission to operate, at the end of the year. Includes units retaining full-power licenses during long, non-routine shutdowns that for a time rendered them unable to generate electricity. [2] As of year-end. [3] Net summer capacity is the peak steady hourly output that generating equipment is expected to supply to system load, exclusive of auxiliary and other power plant, as demonstrated by a test at the time of summer peak demand. [4] Weighted average of monthly capacity factors. Monthly factors are derived by dividing actual monthly generation by the maximum possible generation for the month (number of hours in the month multiplied by the net summer capacity at the end of the month). Please note that as of 2008, the methodology changed; see U.S. Energy Information Administration, *Electric Power Monthly*, Appendix C, under "Average Capacity Factors."

Source: U.S. Energy Information Administration, *Monthly Energy Review*, March 2022. See also <www.eia.gov/totalenergy/data/monthly>.

Table 982. Nuclear Power Plants—Number of Reactors, Net Generation, and Net Summer Capacity by State: 2020

[789,879 represents 789,879,000,000 kilowatt hours (kWh)]

State	Number of reactors	Nuclear net generation Total (mil. kWh)	Nuclear net generation Percent of total [1]	Nuclear net summer capacity Total (mil. kWh)	Nuclear net summer capacity Percent of total [2]	State	Number of reactors	Nuclear net generation Total (mil. kWh)	Nuclear net generation Percent of total [1]	Nuclear net summer capacity Total (mil. kWh)	Nuclear net summer capacity Percent of total [2]
US	96	789,879	19.7	96.5	8.6	MS	1	6,471	9.7	1.4	9.6
AL	5	43,551	31.7	5.5	19.3	MO	1	7,742	10.7	1.2	5.7
AZ	3	31,552	28.9	3.9	14.5	NE	1	6,189	16.8	0.8	7.8
AR	2	15,063	27.6	1.8	12.3	NH	1	9,865	60.3	1.2	27.9
CA	2	16,259	8.4	2.2	2.9	NJ	3	26,738	43.8	3.5	19.8
CT	2	15,715	38.2	2.1	20.2	NY	6	38,430	29.7	4.2	10.5
FL	4	29,419	11.7	3.7	5.9	NC	5	42,329	34.0	5.2	14.7
GA	4	32,826	27.3	4.1	10.9	OH	2	18,219	15.1	2.1	7.9
IL	11	100,246	57.8	11.6	26.1	PA	8	76,521	33.2	9.1	18.6
IA	1	2,905	4.9	(3)	(3)	SC	7	54,751	55.6	6.6	27.3
KS	1	10,582	19.4	1.2	7.2	TN	4	36,688	45.5	4.5	21.1
LA	2	16,950	16.8	2.1	8.3	TX	4	41,439	8.8	5.0	3.9
MD	2	15,081	41.9	1.7	12.5	VA	4	30,140	29.2	3.6	12.8
MI	4	30,333	28.4	4.1	13.8	WA	1	9,427	8.1	1.2	3.8
MN	3	14,677	26.0	1.7	9.2	WI	2	9,771	15.9	1.2	7.2

[1] Percent of total electric power generation. See also Table 989. [2] Percent of total net summer capacity. See also Table 989. [3] Plant was damaged and ceased operations in August 2020.

Source: U.S. Energy Information Administration, *Electric Power Annual*, and "Electricity: Detailed State Data," <www.eia.gov/electricity/data/state/>, accessed March 2022.

Table 983. Uranium Concentrate—Supply, Inventories, and Average Prices: 1990 to 2021

[8.89 represents 8,890,000 pounds (lbs.). Years ending December 31. For additional data on uranium, see Table 947 and Table 963]

Item	Unit	1990	2000	2005	2010	2015	2018	2019	2020	2021
Production [1]	Mil. lbs.	8.89	3.98	2.69	4.23	3.34	1.65	0.17	(D)	0.02
Imports [2]	Mil. lbs.	23.7	44.9	65.5	55.3	64.2	41.5	42.9	39.6	41.3
Exports [2]	Mil. lbs.	2.0	13.6	20.5	23.1	25.7	13.9	11.7	9.9	7.5
Electric plant purchases from domestic suppliers	Mil. lbs.	20.5	24.3	27.3	16.2	19.6	11.1	(D)	10.5	8.2
Loaded into U.S. nuclear reactors [3]	Mil. lbs.	(NA)	51.5	58.3	44.3	47.4	50.4	43.2	48.6	[5] 44.4
Inventories, total	Mil. lbs.	129.1	111.3	93.8	111.3	135.5	130.5	130.7	131.0	[5] 141.7
At domestic suppliers	Mil. lbs.	26.4	56.5	29.1	24.7	14.3	19.3	17.5	24.2	[5] 33.2
At electric plants	Mil. lbs.	102.7	54.8	64.7	86.5	121.1	111.2	113.1	106.9	[5] 108.5
Average price per pound: Purchased imports [4]	Dollars	12.55	9.84	14.83	47.01	42.95	35.73	34.77	33.79	33.26
Domestic purchases	Dollars	15.70	11.45	13.98	44.88	43.03	42.98	(D)	35.92	35.18

D Data withheld. NA Not available. [1] Data are for uranium concentrate, a yellow or brown powder obtained by the milling of uranium ore, processing of in situ leach mining solutions, or as a by-product of phosphoric acid production. [2] Includes transactions by uranium buyers (consumers). Buyer imports and exports prior to 1990 are believed to be small. [3] Does not include any fuel rods removed from reactors and later reloaded into the reactor. [4] For purchases made by U.S. suppliers and by U.S. owners and operators of civilian nuclear power plants. [5] Preliminary.

Source: U.S. Energy Information Administration, *Monthly Energy Review*, <www.eia.gov/totalenergy/data/monthly/>, June 2022. See also <www.eia.gov/nuclear/data.php>.

Table 984. Renewable Energy Generating Capacity and Generation Projections: Estimates, 2021, and Projections, 2025 to 2050

[In gigawatts, unless otherwise noted. Reference case projections are business-as-usual trend estimates, given known technology, as well as market, demographic, and technological trends. Based on results from EIA's National Energy Modeling System]

Net summer capacity and generation	2021, estimate	Projections						Annual growth 2021-2050 (percent)
		2025	2030	2035	2040	2045	2050	
ELECTRIC POWER SECTOR [1]								
Total net summer capacity	**286.25**	**411.52**	**489.37**	**567.72**	**618.35**	**660.19**	**720.67**	**3.2**
Conventional hydroelectric power	79.24	79.35	79.34	79.38	79.38	79.38	79.40	(Z)
Geothermal [2]	2.50	2.65	3.47	4.47	5.42	6.11	6.47	3.3
Municipal waste [3]	3.45	3.93	4.55	5.24	5.91	6.47	6.90	2.4
Wood and other biomass [4]	2.81	2.81	2.66	2.66	2.66	2.66	2.66	-0.2
Solar thermal	1.48	1.48	1.48	1.48	1.48	1.48	1.48	—
Solar photovoltaic [5]	61.39	150.93	210.68	271.38	313.45	345.23	394.90	6.6
Wind	135.34	169.50	177.24	179.74	186.69	195.50	205.50	1.5
Offshore wind	0.04	0.86	9.96	23.36	23.36	23.36	23.36	24.4
Total generation (bil. kWh)	**788.13**	**1,179.95**	**1,415.90**	**1,641.50**	**1,795.55**	**1,911.54**	**2,060.40**	**3.4**
Conventional hydroelectric power	258.55	299.77	299.02	297.69	296.03	294.56	288.27	0.4
Geothermal [2]	15.86	16.99	23.55	31.48	39.03	44.47	47.38	3.8
Biogenic municipal waste [6]	17.41	21.56	26.98	33.26	39.14	44.25	48.57	3.6
Wood and other biomass	12.72	11.70	10.66	10.91	10.85	10.82	10.81	-0.6
Dedicated plants	12.52	11.10	10.53	10.81	10.77	10.69	10.68	-0.5
Co-firing	0.20	0.60	0.13	0.10	0.08	0.13	0.13	-1.5
Solar thermal	3.28	2.95	2.86	2.87	2.77	2.60	2.85	-0.5
Solar photovoltaic [5]	103.41	308.75	460.11	617.38	730.59	811.48	926.29	7.9
Wind	376.76	514.87	557.69	564.94	583.13	609.42	642.38	1.9
Offshore wind	0.13	3.36	35.04	82.97	94.01	93.95	93.85	25.5
END-USE SECTORS [7]								
Total net summer capacity	**47.05**	**64.76**	**81.74**	**99.84**	**124.04**	**153.71**	**190.30**	**4.9**
Conventional hydropower	0.23	0.23	0.23	0.23	0.23	0.23	0.23	—
Geothermal	—	—	—	—	—	—	—	(X)
Municipal waste [3]	0.44	0.44	0.44	0.44	0.44	0.44	0.44	—
Biomass	5.43	5.68	5.79	5.85	5.92	6.11	6.26	0.5
Solar photovoltaic [5]	40.38	57.83	74.69	92.74	116.86	146.33	182.76	5.3
Wind	0.57	0.57	0.58	0.58	0.58	0.59	0.59	0.1
Total generation (bil. kWh)	**90.66**	**118.91**	**146.98**	**177.23**	**216.50**	**264.89**	**324.22**	**4.5**
Conventional hydropower	1.18	1.18	1.18	1.18	1.18	1.18	1.18	—
Geothermal	—	—	—	—	—	—	—	(X)
Municipal waste [3]	3.39	3.38	3.38	3.38	3.38	3.38	3.38	-(Z)
Biomass	27.73	29.03	29.62	29.88	30.25	31.23	32.04	0.5
Solar photovoltaic [5]	57.59	84.55	112.02	142.00	180.90	228.30	286.81	5.7
Wind	0.77	0.78	0.79	0.80	0.80	0.81	0.81	0.2
ALL SECTORS								
Total net summer capacity	**333.31**	**476.28**	**571.11**	**667.56**	**742.39**	**813.90**	**910.97**	**3.5**
Conventional hydropower	79.48	79.59	79.57	79.62	79.62	79.62	79.64	(Z)
Geothermal	2.50	2.65	3.47	4.47	5.42	6.11	6.47	3.3
Municipal waste	3.90	4.38	4.99	5.69	6.35	6.91	7.35	2.2
Wood and other biomass [4]	8.23	8.49	8.45	8.50	8.57	8.76	8.92	0.3
Solar [5]	103.25	210.24	286.85	365.60	431.79	493.05	579.14	6.1
Wind	135.95	170.94	187.78	203.68	210.63	219.45	229.45	1.8
Total generation (bil. kWh)	**878.79**	**1,298.86**	**1,562.88**	**1,818.72**	**2,012.05**	**2,176.43**	**2,384.62**	**3.5**
Conventional hydropower	259.73	300.95	300.19	298.86	297.21	295.74	289.45	0.4
Geothermal	15.86	16.99	23.55	31.48	39.03	44.47	47.38	3.8
Municipal waste	20.80	24.93	30.36	36.64	42.52	47.62	51.95	3.2
Wood and other biomass	40.46	40.73	40.28	40.78	41.10	42.05	42.85	0.2
Solar [5]	164.28	396.24	574.99	762.26	914.26	1,042.39	1,215.96	7.1
Wind	377.67	519.02	593.52	648.71	677.93	704.17	737.03	2.3

– Represents zero. Z Less than .05%. X Not applicable. [1] Includes electricity-only and combined heat and power plants that have a regulatory status. [2] Includes both hydrothermal resources and near-field enhanced geothermal systems (EGS). [3] Includes municipal waste, landfill gas, and municipal sewage sludge. [4] Facilities co-firing biomass and coal are classified as coal. [5] Does not include off-grid photovoltaics (PV). [6] Includes biogenic municipal waste, landfill gas, and municipal sludge. [7] Includes combined heat and power plants and electricity-only plants in the commercial and industrial sectors with nonregulatory status, and small on-site generating systems in the residential, commercial, and industrial sectors used primarily for own-use generation, but which many also sell some power to the grid.

Source: U.S. Energy Information Administration, *Annual Energy Outlook 2022*, March 2022. See also <www.eia.gov/forecasts/aeo>.

Table 985. Energy Distribution System Reliability—Number and Duration of Electric Interruption Events: 2013 to 2020

[The average number and length in minutes of non-momentary electric interruptions the average customer in the United States experienced annually. Data includes only utilities that use the IEEE 1366-2003 or the IEEE 1366-2012 standard set by the Institute of Electrical and Electronics Engineers (IEEE)]

Year	All events (with major event days) [1]			Without major event days			Loss of supply removed [2]		
	Minutes per year (SAIDI) [3]	Interruptions per year (SAIFI) [4]	Average minutes per interruption (CAIDI) [5]	Minutes per year (SAIDI) [3]	Interruptions per year (SAIFI) [4]	Average minutes per interruption (CAIDI) [5]	Minutes per year (SAIDI) [3]	Interruptions per year (SAIFI) [4]	Average minutes per interruption (CAIDI) [5]
2013	227.2	1.2	191.5	111.9	1.0	112.6	225.5	1.1	202.6
2014	236.2	1.3	188.0	114.2	1.0	110.0	244.8	1.2	203.7
2015	209.0	1.3	163.9	117.0	1.1	109.1	198.2	1.2	170.4
2016	268.4	1.3	202.2	119.8	1.1	110.7	257.0	1.2	209.0
2017	505.9	1.4	356.2	117.0	1.0	114.3	489.6	1.3	390.6
2018	349.2	1.3	260.5	121.4	1.1	115.5	338.5	1.2	283.8
2019	295.5	1.3	221.8	122.2	1.0	117.5	289.1	1.2	243.0
2020	456.1	1.4	329.3	116.0	1.0	114.5	460.5	1.2	371.9

[1] A major event day is any day that exceeds a daily threshold called Tmed, a duration statistic calculated from daily interruption values from the past five years. [2] Excludes outages due to loss of supply from the high-voltage/bulk power system. [3] SAIDI = System Average Interruption Duration Index, the minutes of non-momentary electric interruptions the average customer experienced per year. [4] SAIFI = System Average Interruption Frequency Index, the number of non-momentary electric interruptions the average customer experienced per year. [5] CAIDI = Customer Average Interruption Duration Index, the average number of minutes it took to restore non-momentary electric interruptions.

Source: U.S. Energy Information Administration, *Electric Power Annual 2020*, March 2022. See also <www.eia.gov/electricity/annual/>.

Table 986. Electricity Net Generation by Sector and Source: 1990 to 2021

[3,037.8 represents 3,037,800,000,000 kilowatt hours (kWh). Data are for fuels consumed to produce electricity. Also includes fuels consumed to produce useful thermal output at a small number of electric utility combined-heat-and-power (CHP) plants]

Sector and source	Unit	1990	2000	2010	2015	2019	2020	2021
Net generation, total	Bil. kWh.	**3,037.8**	**3,802.1**	**4,125.1**	**4,077.6**	**4,127.9**	**4,007.1**	**4,115.5**
Electric power sector, total	Bil. kWh.	2,901.3	3,637.5	3,972.4	3,919.3	3,965.6	3,851.0	3,962.8
Commercial sector [1]	Bil. kWh.	5.8	7.9	8.6	12.6	13.7	13.0	13.1
Industrial sector [2]	Bil. kWh.	130.8	156.7	144.1	145.7	148.5	143.1	139.6
Net generation by source, all sectors:								
Fossil fuels, total	Bil. kWh.	2,103.6	2,692.5	2,883.4	2,727.2	2,581.7	2,426.7	2,504.0
Coal [3]	Bil. kWh.	1,594.0	1,966.3	1,847.3	1,352.4	965.0	773.4	898.7
Petroleum [4]	Bil. kWh.	126.5	111.2	37.1	28.2	18.3	17.3	18.8
Natural gas [5]	Bil. kWh.	372.8	601.0	987.7	1,333.5	1,585.8	1,624.2	1,575.2
Other gases [6]	Bil. kWh.	10.4	14.0	11.3	13.1	12.6	11.8	11.3
Nuclear electric power	Bil. kWh.	576.9	753.9	807.0	797.2	809.4	789.9	778.2
Hydroelectric pumped storage [7]	Bil. kWh.	-3.5	-5.5	-5.5	-5.1	-5.3	-5.3	-5.1
Renewable energy, total	Bil. kWh.	357.2	356.5	427.4	544.2	728.7	783.0	826.4
Conventional hydroelectric power	Bil. kWh.	292.9	275.6	260.2	249.1	287.9	285.3	260.2
Biomass, total	Bil. kWh.	45.8	60.7	56.1	63.6	57.5	54.7	55.5
Wood [8]	Bil. kWh.	32.5	37.6	37.2	41.9	38.5	36.2	37.2
Waste [9]	Bil. kWh.	13.3	23.1	18.9	21.7	19.0	18.5	18.3
Geothermal	Bil. kWh.	15.4	14.1	15.2	15.9	15.5	15.9	16.2
Solar [10]	Bil. kWh.	0.4	0.5	1.2	24.9	71.9	89.2	114.7
Wind	Bil. kWh.	2.8	5.6	94.7	190.7	295.9	337.9	379.8
Other [11]	Bil. kWh.	3.6	4.8	12.9	14.0	13.3	12.9	12.1
Consumption of fuels for electricity generation:								
Coal [3]	Mil. short tons	792.5	994.9	979.7	739.6	537.6	435.4	500.6
Petroleum, total	Mil. bbl.	218.8	195.2	65.1	49.1	34.5	33.4	35.4
Distillate fuel oil [12]	Mil. bbl.	18.1	31.7	14.1	12.4	9.6	8.0	9.5
Residual fuel oil [13]	Mil. bbl.	190.7	143.4	24.0	14.1	9.3	8.3	9.1
Other liquids [14]	Mil. bbl.	0.4	1.4	2.1	2.4	2.0	1.7	2.1
Petroleum coke	Mil. short tons	1.9	3.7	5.0	4.0	2.7	3.1	2.9
Natural gas [5]	Bil. cu. ft.	3,691.6	5,691.5	7,680.2	10,016.5	11,601.6	11,917.6	11,550.8
Other gases [6]	Tril. Btu.	111.8	126.0	90.1	106.0	71.9	69.6	66.5
Biomass	Tril. Btu.	653.5	825.9	630.3	719.6	604.9	580.0	582.6
Wood [8]	Tril. Btu.	442.3	495.8	349.5	406.7	338.3	318.3	330.7
Waste [9]	Tril. Btu.	211.2	330.1	280.8	313.0	266.6	261.7	251.9
Other [11]	Tril. Btu.	36.0	46.2	184.4	203.6	198.6	192.9	180.8

[1] Commercial combined-heat-and-power (CHP) and commercial electricity-only plants. [2] Industrial CHP and industrial electricity-only plants. [3] Anthracite, bituminous coal, subbituminous coal, lignite, waste coal, and coal synfuel. [4] Distillate fuel oil, residual fuel oil, petroleum coke, jet fuel, kerosene, other petroleum, waste oil, and beginning in 2011, propane. [5] Includes a small amount of supplemental gaseous fuels that cannot be identified separately. [6] Blast furnace gas and other manufactured and waste gases derived from fossil fuels. [7] Pumped storage facility production minus energy used for pumping. [8] Wood and wood-derived fuels. [9] Municipal solid waste from biogenic sources, landfill gas, sludge waste, agricultural byproducts, and other biomass. Through 2000, also includes nonrenewable waste (municipal solid waste from non-biogenic sources and tire-derived fuels). [10] Solar thermal and photovoltaic energy. Does not include estimated distributed solar photovoltaic generation. [11] Batteries, chemicals, hydrogen, pitch, purchased steam, sulfur, miscellaneous technologies, and beginning 2001, nonrenewable waste (municipal solid waste from nonbiogenic sources, and tire-derived fuels). [12] Fuel oil numbers 1, 2, and 4. For 1990 through 2000, electric utility data also include small amounts of kerosene and jet fuel. [13] Fuel oil numbers 5 and 6. For 1990 through 2000, electric utility data also include a small amount of fuel oil number 4. [14] Jet fuel, kerosene, other petroleum liquids, waste oil, and beginning in 2011, propane.

Source: U.S. Energy Information Administration, *Monthly Energy Review*, March 2022. See also <www.eia.gov/totalenergy/data/monthly>.

Table 987. Total Electric Net Summer Capacity for All Sectors by Energy Source: 1990 to 2020

[In million kilowatts (734.1 represents 734,100,000). Data are shown for utility scale capacity at year end. For plants that use multiple sources of energy, capacity is assigned to the predominant energy source]

Source	1990	2000	2010	2015	2016	2017	2018	2019	2020
Net summer capacity, total............	**734.1**	**811.7**	**1,039.1**	**1,064.1**	**1,074.3**	**1,084.4**	**1,094.7**	**1,099.1**	**1,115.7**
Fossil fuels, total............................	527.8	598.9	782.2	758.5	750.3	748.2	747.8	739.1	731.2
Coal [1]............................	307.4	315.1	316.8	279.7	266.6	256.5	242.8	228.7	215.6
Petroleum [2].........................	77.9	61.8	55.6	36.8	34.4	33.3	32.2	31.4	27.6
Natural gas [3].......................	140.8	219.6	407.0	439.4	446.8	456.0	470.2	476.6	485.8
Other gases [4].......................	1.6	2.3	2.7	2.5	2.5	2.4	2.5	2.5	2.3
Nuclear electric power....................	99.6	97.9	101.2	98.7	99.6	99.6	99.4	98.1	96.5
Hydroelectric pumped storage..............	19.5	19.5	22.2	22.6	22.8	22.8	22.8	22.8	23.0
Renewable energy, total...................	86.8	94.9	132.6	192.3	212.5	227.0	241.9	259.7	289.5
Conventional hydroelectric power..........	73.9	79.4	78.8	79.7	79.9	79.8	79.9	79.8	79.9
Biomass, total................................	8.1	10.0	11.4	14.1	14.0	14.0	13.7	13.1	12.9
Wood [5]............................	5.5	6.1	7.0	9.0	8.9	8.8	8.7	8.4	8.3
Waste [6]............................	2.5	3.9	4.4	5.1	5.1	5.1	5.0	4.7	4.6
Geothermal..............................	2.7	2.8	2.4	2.5	2.5	2.5	2.4	2.6	2.6
Solar [7]...............................	0.3	0.4	0.9	23.4	34.7	43.1	51.4	60.7	75.6
Wind...................................	1.8	2.4	39.1	72.6	81.3	87.6	94.4	103.6	118.4
Other [8]................................	0.5	0.5	0.9	1.8	2.0	2.9	2.3	2.6	3.1

[1] Coal includes anthracite, bituminous, subbituminous, lignite, and waste coal; coal synfuel and refined coal; and, beginning in 2011, coal-derived synthesis gas. Prior to 2011, coal-derived synthesis gas was included in other gases. [2] Distillate fuel oil, residual fuel oil, petroleum coke, jet fuel, kerosene, other petroleum, waste oil, and, beginning in 2011, synthetic gas and propane. Prior to 2011, synthetic gas and propane were included in other gases. [3] Includes a small amount of supplemental gaseous fuels that cannot be identified separately. [4] Blast furnace gas, propane gas, and other manufactured and waste gases derived from fossil fuels. [5] Wood and wood-derived fuels. [6] Municipal solid waste, landfill gas, sludge waste, agricultural byproducts, other biomass solids, other biomass liquids, and other biomass gases (including digester gases, methane, and other biomass gases). [7] Solar thermal and photovoltaic energy. [8] Batteries, hydrogen, purchased steam, sulfur, tire-derived fuels and other miscellaneous energy sources.

Source: U.S. Energy Information Administration, *Electric Power Annual 2020*, October 2021, and earlier reports. See also <www.eia.gov/electricity/annual/>.

Table 988. Electricity—End Use and Average Retail Prices: 1990 to 2020

[2,837.1 represents 2,837,100,000,000. Beginning 2003, the category "other" has been replaced by "transportation," and the categories "commercial" and "industrial" have been redefined. Data represent revenue from electricity retail sales divided by the amount of retail electricity sold (in kilowatt-hours). Prices include state and local taxes, energy or demand charges, customer service charges, environmental surcharges, franchise fees, fuel adjustments, and other miscellaneous charges applied to end-use customers during normal billing operations. Prices do not include deferred charges, credits, or other adjustments, such as fuel or revenue from purchased power, from previous reporting periods. Data are for a census of electric utilities. Beginning in 2000, data also include energy service providers selling to retail customers]

Item	1990	2000	2010	2015	2016	2017	2018	2019	2020
END USE (Billion kilowatt-hours)									
Total end use [1]........................	**2,837.1**	**3,592.4**	**3,886.8**	**3,900.2**	**3,902.3**	**3,864.3**	**4,003.1**	**3,954.4**	**3,856.4**
Direct use [2]............................	124.5	170.9	131.9	141.2	139.8	141.0	143.9	143.3	138.7
Retail sales, total [3]...................	**2,712.6**	**3,421.4**	**3,754.8**	**3,759.0**	**3,762.5**	**3,723.4**	**3,859.2**	**3,811.2**	**3,717.7**
Residential...........................	924.0	1,192.4	1,445.7	1,404.1	1,411.1	1,378.6	1,469.1	1,440.3	1,464.6
Commercial [4].......................	838.3	1,159.3	1,330.2	1,360.8	1,367.2	1,352.9	1,381.8	1,360.9	1,287.4
Industrial [5].........................	945.5	1,064.2	971.2	986.5	976.7	984.3	1,000.7	1,002.4	959.1
Transportation [6]....................	4.8	5.4	7.7	7.6	7.5	7.5	7.7	7.6	6.5
AVERAGE RETAIL PRICES (Cents per kilowatt-hour)									
Total....................................	**6.57**	**6.81**	**9.83**	**10.41**	**10.27**	**10.48**	**10.53**	**10.54**	**10.59**
Residential...........................	7.83	8.24	11.54	12.65	12.55	12.89	12.87	13.01	13.15
Commercial [7].......................	7.34	7.43	10.19	10.64	10.43	10.66	10.67	10.68	10.59
Industrial [5].........................	4.74	4.64	6.77	6.91	6.76	6.88	6.92	6.81	6.67
Transportation [6]....................	(NA)	(NA)	10.56	10.09	9.63	9.68	9.70	9.66	9.90
Other [8]..............................	6.40	6.56	(NA)	(NA)	(NA)	(NA)	(NA)	(NA)	(NA)

NA Not available. [1] The sum of "total retail sales" and "direct use." [2] Use of electricity that is 1) self-generated, 2) produced by either the same entity that consumes the power or an affiliate, and 3) used in direct support of a service or industrial process located within the same facility or group of facilities that house the generating equipment. Direct use is exclusive of station use. [3] Electricity retail sales to ultimate customers reported by electric utilities and, beginning in 2000, other energy service providers. [4] Includes public street and highway lighting, interdepartmental sales, and other sales to public authorities. [5] Beginning 2003, includes agriculture and irrigation. [6] Includes sales to railroads and railways. [7] Beginning 2003, includes public street and highway lighting, interdepartmental sales, and other sales to public authorities. [8] Public street and highway lighting, interdepartmental sales, other sales to public authorities, agriculture and irrigation, and transportation including railroads and railways.

Source: U.S. Energy Information Administration, *Electric Power Annual 2020*, October 2021, and earlier reports. See also <www.eia.gov/electricity/>.

Table 989. Electric Power Industry—Net Generation and Net Summer Capacity by State: 2010 to 2020

[4,125.1 represents 4,125,100,000,000. Capacity as of December 31. Covers utilities for public use]

| State | Net generation (billion kilowatt-hours) | | | | | | | | Net summer capacity (million kilowatts) | |
	2010	2019	2020 Total [1] (bil. kWh)	Percent from— Petro-leum	Natural gas	Hydro-electric	Nuclear	Coal	2019	2020
United States	**4,125.1**	**4,127.9**	**4,007.1**	**0.4**	**40.5**	**7.1**	**19.7**	**19.3**	**1,099.1**	**1,115.7**
Alabama	152.2	142.7	137.5	(Z)	40.2	9.7	31.7	15.8	29.3	28.7
Alaska	6.8	6.1	6.3	15.7	42.1	28.1	–	11.5	2.8	2.8
Arizona	111.8	113.6	109.3	(Z)	46.5	5.9	28.9	12.6	26.8	27.1
Arkansas	61.0	64.4	54.6	0.1	33.5	8.3	27.6	28.2	14.8	14.8
California	204.1	201.8	193.1	(Z)	47.7	11.1	8.4	0.2	75.5	78.1
Colorado	50.7	56.3	54.1	-0.3	33.6	3.1	–	36.0	16.6	17.6
Connecticut	33.3	40.1	41.2	0.1	57.1	0.8	38.2	(-Z)	10.5	10.3
Delaware	5.6	5.3	5.2	0.2	92.6	–	–	2.0	3.4	3.4
District of Columbia	0.2	0.2	0.2	(Z)	66.4	–	–	–	(Z)	(Z)
Florida	229.1	245.6	250.8	0.7	75.5	0.1	11.7	6.6	60.5	61.8
Georgia	137.6	128.7	120.1	0.2	49.3	3.9	27.3	11.6	36.6	37.3
Hawaii	10.8	9.7	9.1	67.7	–	1.1	–	12.8	3.0	3.0
Idaho	12.0	18.4	17.7	(Z)	23.5	53.8	–	0.1	5.2	5.2
Illinois	201.4	184.5	173.4	(Z)	14.1	0.1	57.8	18.0	44.2	44.4
Indiana	125.2	102.5	90.1	0.1	35.6	0.3	–	53.0	26.7	27.3
Iowa	57.5	62.6	59.6	0.2	11.8	1.7	4.9	23.7	20.4	21.3
Kansas	47.9	50.9	54.5	0.1	5.1	0.1	19.4	31.1	16.2	17.0
Kentucky	98.2	71.8	63.5	0.1	22.6	7.9	–	68.7	19.5	17.6
Louisiana	102.9	100.2	100.8	3.4	70.2	1.2	16.8	3.9	24.3	25.6
Maine	17.0	10.5	10.0	0.4	19.0	31.6	–	0.6	4.8	4.9
Maryland	43.6	39.3	36.0	0.2	39.1	4.7	41.9	9.3	14.6	13.8
Massachusetts	42.8	21.5	18.2	0.2	77.8	4.6	–	–	12.9	13.0
Michigan	111.6	116.7	106.6	0.9	34.2	1.6	28.4	26.2	29.5	29.6
Minnesota	53.7	59.4	56.5	0.1	20.9	1.8	26.0	24.8	17.4	17.9
Mississippi	54.5	66.0	66.6	(Z)	80.6	–	9.7	6.9	14.5	14.6
Missouri	92.3	78.3	72.6	0.1	10.4	2.6	10.7	71.3	21.1	22.0
Montana	29.8	27.8	23.4	2.0	1.2	46.0	–	36.4	6.4	5.9
Nebraska	36.6	37.3	36.8	(Z)	3.3	3.8	16.8	51.0	9.5	9.8
Nevada	35.1	39.9	40.4	(Z)	66.3	4.8	–	4.8	11.9	12.1
New Hampshire	22.2	18.0	16.4	0.3	22.3	7.5	60.3	0.8	4.5	4.5
New Jersey	65.7	71.0	61.1	0.1	50.1	(Z)	43.8	1.5	17.3	17.4
New Mexico	36.3	35.2	34.1	0.1	35.2	0.6	–	37.5	8.8	9.1
New York	137.0	131.6	129.4	0.3	40.9	22.8	29.7	0.1	41.1	40.2
North Carolina	128.7	131.2	124.4	0.1	33.3	6.4	34.0	16.7	34.9	35.1
North Dakota	34.7	41.1	42.2	0.1	3.5	5.8	–	58.1	8.7	9.2
Ohio	143.6	120.0	121.0	1.0	43.3	0.3	15.1	37.2	28.5	27.0
Oklahoma	72.3	85.2	82.3	(Z)	53.2	3.5	–	7.2	27.4	28.7
Oregon	55.1	62.3	63.6	(Z)	29.9	50.2	–	2.6	16.8	16.7
Pennsylvania	229.8	229.0	230.1	(Z)	52.5	1.2	33.2	10.2	47.8	48.9
Rhode Island	7.7	7.6	8.9	0.1	93.0	(Z)	–	–	2.0	2.1
South Carolina	104.2	100.1	98.5	0.1	24.6	3.9	55.6	12.6	24.0	24.1
South Dakota	10.0	14.5	14.1	0.1	7.8	41.2	–	11.7	4.7	5.4
Tennessee	82.3	82.3	80.6	0.1	19.4	16.7	45.5	17.7	21.4	21.4
Texas	411.7	483.2	473.5	(Z)	52.1	0.2	8.8	16.6	125.1	128.9
Utah	42.2	39.1	37.1	0.1	25.5	2.2	–	61.5	9.0	9.3
Vermont	6.6	2.3	2.2	0.1	0.1	52.4	–	–	0.8	0.8
Virginia	73.0	96.8	103.1	0.2	60.8	2.0	29.2	3.7	28.0	27.9
Washington	103.5	106.5	116.1	(Z)	12.1	65.8	8.1	4.5	30.9	30.7
West Virginia	80.8	63.9	56.7	0.3	4.9	2.8	–	88.6	14.9	14.9
Wisconsin	64.3	62.8	61.4	0.2	35.8	4.5	15.9	38.7	15.3	16.5
Wyoming	48.1	42.1	42.0	0.1	3.3	2.6	–	79.4	8.7	9.6

– Represents zero. Z Represents less than .05 percent of net electricity generation, or less than .05 million kilowatts summer capacity. [1] Includes other sources not shown separately.

Source: U.S. Energy Information Administration, *Electric Power Annual*, "Data Tables" and "Detailed State Data," <www.eia.gov/electricity/annual/>, accessed March 2022.

Table 990. Electricity Generation Existing Summer and Winter Capacity by Energy Source and Producer Type: 2020

[Capacity in megawatts. Data shown are for utility scale power plants that have at least 1 megawatt of generation capacity. For plants that use multiple sources of energy, capacity is assigned to the predominant energy source]

Source and producer type	Number of generators	Generator nameplate capacity	Net summer capacity	Net winter capacity
Total................	**23,417**	**1,212,239**	**1,115,681**	**1,155,453**
ENERGY SOURCE				
Fossil fuels, total...........	10,470	820,497	731,206	769,480
Coal [1]........	599	234,126	215,554	217,108
Petroleum [2]............	3,705	32,071	27,569	30,521
Natural gas...............	6,075	551,681	485,807	519,554
Other gases [3]............	91	2,618	2,275	2,297
Nuclear electric power............	94	100,899	96,501	98,719
Hydroelectric pumped storage............	153	21,969	23,016	22,836
Renewable energy, total............	12,389	265,579	261,879	261,280
Conventional hydroelectric power............	4,009	79,896	79,924	79,370
Wind............	1,422	118,728	118,379	118,381
Solar [4]............	4,617	48,339	48,054	47,414
Biomass, total............	2,171	14,752	12,950	13,128
Wood [5]............	332	9,491	8,327	8,446
Waste [6]............	1,839	5,261	4,623	4,682
Geothermal............	170	3,865	2,572	2,987
Other energy sources [7]............	311	3,296	3,079	3,138
PRODUCER TYPE				
Electric power sector, total............	20,303	1,176,216	1,084,234	1,122,114
Electric utilities............	9,582	661,542	607,398	627,395
Independent power producers				
Non-combined heat and power plants............	10,261	482,701	448,340	464,187
Combined heat and power plants............	460	31,972	28,496	30,532
Commercial and industrial sectors, total............	3,114	36,024	31,447	33,339
Commercial............	1,601	5,099	4,642	4,734
Industrial............	1,513	30,925	26,805	28,605

[1] Coal includes anthracite, bituminous, subbituminous, lignite, and waste coal; coal synfuel and refined coal; and coal-derived synthesis gas. [2] Distillate fuel oil, residual fuel oil, jet fuel, kerosene, petroleum coke, waste oil, and synthetic gas and propane. [3] Includes blast furnace gas. [4] Solar thermal and photovoltaic energy. [5] Wood and wood-derived fuels. [6] Municipal solid waste, landfill gas, sludge waste, agricultural byproducts, and other biomass solids, liquids, and gases (including digester gases, methane, and other biomass gases). [7] Includes batteries, hydrogen, purchased steam, sulfur, tire-derived fuels and other miscellaneous energy sources.

Source: U.S. Energy Information Administration, *Electric Power Annual 2020*, October 2021. See also <www.eia.gov/electricity/annual>.

Table 991. Electric Energy Retail Sales by Class of Service and State: 2020

[In billions of kilowatt-hours (3,717.7 represents 3,717,700,000,000). Data include both bundled and unbundled consumers]

State	Total [1]	Resi-dential	Com-mercial	Indus-trial	State	Total [1]	Resi-dential	Com-mercial	Indus-trial
United States..........	**3,717.7**	**1,464.6**	**1,287.4**	**959.1**	Missouri....................	75.7	35.0	27.9	12.8
Alabama.................	83.4	31.3	21.3	30.8	Montana....................	14.6	5.4	4.7	4.5
Alaska....................	5.9	2.1	2.5	1.3	Nebraska....................	31.2	10.5	9.1	11.6
Arizona.................	82.0	38.7	29.1	14.1	Nevada....................	38.2	14.3	12.0	11.9
Arkansas.................	45.9	18.0	11.1	16.8	New Hampshire.........	10.7	4.8	4.0	1.9
California.................	250.2	94.9	107.0	47.6	New Jersey....................	72.0	29.7	35.3	6.7
Colorado.................	56.1	20.5	20.0	15.4	New Mexico....................	24.8	7.3	8.4	9.1
Connecticut.............	27.1	13.0	11.1	2.9	New York....................	140.4	52.3	69.0	16.6
Delaware.................	11.1	5.0	4.1	2.1	North Carolina....................	130.4	58.6	45.9	25.8
District of Columbia.....	9.8	2.5	6.8	0.2	North Dakota....................	21.8	5.0	6.6	10.1
Florida....................	242.4	133.3	92.5	16.6	Ohio....................	142.6	52.6	43.2	46.8
Georgia....................	133.5	58.2	44.3	30.8	Oklahoma....................	62.3	23.2	18.7	20.4
Hawaii....................	8.8	2.8	2.7	3.3	Oregon....................	51.0	19.6	15.7	15.6
Idaho....................	24.5	9.0	6.3	9.2	Pennsylvania....................	139.7	55.3	35.4	48.6
Illinois....................	132.5	46.2	45.5	40.4	Rhode Island....................	7.4	3.1	3.6	0.6
Indiana....................	97.2	32.9	22.0	42.3	South Carolina....................	76.7	30.8	20.8	25.1
Iowa....................	50.6	14.6	11.6	24.5	South Dakota....................	12.7	5.1	4.7	2.9
Kansas....................	39.5	13.6	14.8	11.0	Tennessee....................	95.0	41.1	33.5	20.4
Kentucky....................	71.8	25.9	18.1	27.8	Texas....................	426.9	156.4	145.2	125.1
Louisiana....................	89.1	30.4	22.4	36.3	Utah....................	31.7	10.5	11.4	9.7
Maine....................	11.3	4.9	3.8	2.6	Vermont....................	5.3	2.2	1.8	1.4
Maryland....................	57.6	27.3	26.5	3.4	Virginia....................	117.3	46.1	53.5	17.5
Massachusetts...........	50.0	20.3	23.1	6.2	Washington....................	86.7	36.9	27.3	22.4
Michigan....................	97.0	35.9	35.5	25.7	West Virginia....................	32.1	10.9	7.0	14.2
Minnesota....................	64.1	22.9	21.5	19.6	Wisconsin....................	67.4	22.8	22.4	22.2
Mississippi....................	46.5	18.0	13.2	15.3	Wyoming....................	15.3	2.9	3.3	9.1

[1] Includes transportation, not shown separately.

Source: U.S. Energy Information Administration, "Electric Sales, Revenue, and Average Price," <www.eia.gov/electricity/sales_revenue_price/index.cfm>, accessed January 2022.

Table 992. Electric Energy Average Retail Price by Class of Service and State: 2020

[In cents per kilowatt-hour (kWh). Data include both bundled and unbundled consumers]

State	Total [1]	Residential	Commercial	Industrial	State	Total [1]	Residential	Commercial	Industrial
United States........	**10.59**	**13.15**	**10.59**	**6.67**	Missouri..........	9.64	11.22	8.93	6.84
Alabama.................	9.84	12.58	11.55	5.87	Montana...........	9.13	11.24	10.51	5.18
Alaska..................	19.82	22.57	19.58	15.88	Nebraska...........	8.97	10.80	8.89	7.38
Arizona.................	10.44	12.27	10.11	6.07	Nevada............	8.33	11.34	7.45	5.61
Arkansas..............	8.32	10.41	8.61	5.89	New Hampshire...	16.63	19.04	15.41	13.11
California..............	18.00	20.45	17.53	14.27	New Jersey........	13.63	16.03	12.35	10.01
Colorado...............	10.27	12.36	10.29	7.48	New Mexico.......	9.33	12.94	10.28	5.58
Connecticut...........	19.13	22.71	16.58	13.07	New York..........	14.87	18.36	14.56	5.54
Delaware..............	10.24	12.56	9.18	6.70	North Carolina. ...	9.43	11.38	8.69	6.31
District of Columbia. ...	11.90	12.63	11.85	7.99	North Dakota......	8.53	10.44	9.02	7.26
Florida.................	10.06	11.27	8.85	7.15	Ohio..............	9.44	12.29	9.53	6.16
Georgia.................	9.93	12.02	10.08	5.77	Oklahoma.........	7.63	10.12	7.82	4.61
Hawaii..................	27.55	30.28	28.41	24.45	Oregon............	8.82	11.17	9.00	5.70
Idaho..................	7.99	9.95	7.75	6.23	Pennsylvania......	9.70	13.58	8.50	6.16
Illinois.................	9.75	13.04	9.15	6.70	Rhode Island......	18.54	22.01	15.94	15.76
Indiana.................	9.92	12.83	11.21	6.98	South Carolina....	9.90	12.78	10.35	5.98
Iowa...................	8.97	12.46	9.96	6.43	South Dakota.....	10.06	11.75	9.65	7.79
Kansas.................	10.38	12.85	10.40	7.30	Tennessee.........	9.52	10.76	10.56	5.33
Kentucky...............	8.58	10.87	10.34	5.31	Texas.............	8.36	11.71	7.60	5.07
Louisiana..............	7.51	9.67	8.85	4.88	Utah..............	8.27	10.44	8.27	5.90
Maine..................	13.54	16.81	12.56	8.86	Vermont...........	16.33	19.54	16.39	11.20
Maryland...............	11.15	13.01	9.72	7.81	Virginia...........	9.16	12.03	7.63	6.28
Massachusetts.........	18.19	21.97	16.03	14.51	Washington........	8.33	9.87	8.92	5.08
Michigan...............	12.21	16.26	11.71	7.24	West Virginia......	8.75	11.80	9.40	6.09
Minnesota..............	10.57	13.17	10.43	7.67	Wisconsin.........	10.82	14.32	10.75	7.29
Mississippi.............	9.13	11.17	10.38	5.63	Wyoming..........	8.27	11.11	9.65	6.88

[1] Includes transportation, not shown separately.

Source: U.S. Energy Information Administration, "Electric Sales, Revenue, and Average Price," <www.eia.gov/electricity/sales_revenue_price/index.cfm>, accessed January 2022.

Table 993. Electric Power Industry—Generation, Sales, Revenue, and Customers: 2005 to 2021

[4,055 represents 4,055,000,000,000 kilowatt-hours (kWh). Sales and revenue are to and from ultimate customers]

Item	Unit	2005	2010	2014	2015	2016	2017	2018	2019	2020	2021
Generation [1].............	Bil. kWh	4,055	4,125	4,094	4,078	4,077	4,034	4,178	4,128	4,007	4,116
Sales.....................	Bil. kWh	3,661	3,755	3,765	3,759	3,762	3,723	3,859	3,811	3,718	3,795
Residential..............	Bil. kWh	1,359	1,446	1,407	1,404	1,411	1,379	1,469	1,440	1,465	1,477
Percent of total........	Percent	37.1	38.5	37.4	37.4	37.5	37.0	38.1	37.8	39.4	38.9
Commercial..............	Bil. kWh	1,275	1,330	1,352	1,361	1,367	1,353	1,382	1,361	1,287	1,325
Industrial................	Bil. kWh	1,019	971	998	987	977	984	1,001	1,002	959	987
Transportation..........	Bil. kWh	8	8	8	8	7	8	8	8	7	6
Revenue..................	Mil. dol.	298,003	368,918	393,096	391,341	386,509	390,322	406,420	401,738	393,639	424,295
Residential..............	Mil. dol.	128,393	166,778	176,178	177,624	177,077	177,661	189,033	187,436	192,663	202,632
Percent of total........	Percent	43.1	45.2	44.8	45.4	45.8	45.5	46.5	46.7	48.9	47.8
Commercial..............	Mil. dol.	110,522	135,554	145,253	144,781	142,643	144,242	147,425	145,280	136,372	149,328
Industrial................	Mil. dol.	58,445	65,772	70,855	68,166	66,068	67,691	69,218	68,285	63,956	71,682
Transportation..........	Mil. dol.	643	814	810	771	722	728	744	737	648	653
Ultimate customers......	1,000	(NA)	144,140	147,374	148,633	150,055	151,780	153,339	154,898	156,523	(NA)
Residential..............	1,000	(NA)	125,718	128,680	129,812	131,069	132,580	133,893	135,250	136,682	(NA)
Commercial..............	1,000	(NA)	17,674	17,854	17,986	18,148	18,359	18,605	18,694	18,849	(NA)
Industrial................	1,000	(NA)	748	839	836	838	840	840	954	992	(NA)
Transportation..........	1,000	(NA)	(Z)	(Z)	(Z)	(Z)	(Z)	(Z)	(Z)	(Z)	(NA)
Average retail price of electricity.............	Cents/kWh	8.1	9.8	10.4	10.4	10.3	10.5	10.5	10.5	10.6	11.2
Residential..............	Cents/kWh	9.5	11.5	12.5	12.7	12.6	12.9	12.9	13.0	13.2	13.7
Commercial..............	Cents/kWh	8.7	10.2	10.7	10.6	10.4	10.7	10.7	10.7	10.6	11.3
Industrial................	Cents/kWh	5.7	6.8	7.1	6.9	6.8	6.9	6.9	6.8	6.7	7.3
Transportation..........	Cents/kWh	8.6	10.6	10.5	10.1	9.6	9.7	9.7	9.7	9.9	10.2

NA Data not available. Z less than 500. [1] Generation at utility scale facilities.

Source: Energy Information Administration, *Electric Power Annual*, October 2021; and "Electricity Data Browser," <www.eia.gov/electricity/data/browser>, accessed March 2022.

Table 994. Revenue and Expense Statistics for Major U.S. Investor-Owned Electric Utilities: 2000 to 2020

[In millions of dollars (233,915 represents $233,915,000,000). Covers investor-owned electric utilities that met any one or more of the following conditions, during each of the last 3 years: 1 million megawatt-hours of total sales, 100 megawatt-hours of annual sales for resale, 500 megawatt-hours of annual power exchange delivered, or 500 megawatt-hours of annual wheeling for others. Missing or erroneous respondent data may result in slight imbalances in some of the expense account subtotals]

Item	2000	2005	2010	2015	2017	2018	2019	2020
Utility operating revenues	**233,915**	**265,652**	**285,512**	**282,695**	**286,501**	**293,868**	**293,000**	**294,756**
Electric utility	213,634	234,909	260,119	260,121	263,265	268,421	266,876	269,869
Other utility	20,281	30,743	25,393	22,574	23,235	25,447	26,124	24,888
Utility operating expenses	**210,250**	**236,786**	**253,022**	**242,728**	**240,041**	**253,944**	**250,136**	**240,802**
Electric utility	191,564	207,830	234,173	228,366	226,110	238,526	234,892	227,084
Operation	132,607	150,645	166,922	149,939	142,000	163,479	157,265	144,335
Production	107,554	120,586	128,831	107,201	98,859	104,185	99,518	93,505
Cost of fuel	32,407	36,106	44,138	34,711	32,165	33,592	29,614	25,856
Purchased power	62,608	77,902	67,284	52,970	49,030	53,060	50,378	50,407
Other	12,561	6,599	17,409	19,521	17,664	17,533	19,526	17,242
Transmission	2,713	5,664	6,948	9,624	10,804	11,387	11,941	12,949
Distribution	3,092	3,502	4,007	4,406	4,358	4,806	5,218	5,480
Customer accounts	4,239	4,229	5,091	5,184	4,789	4,969	4,978	5,775
Customer service	1,826	2,291	4,741	6,445	5,961	6,019	6,156	5,868
Sales	405	219	185	201	213	203	204	211
Administrative and general	12,768	14,130	17,120	16,878	17,016	31,911	29,248	20,546
Maintenance	12,064	12,033	14,957	16,392	17,996	17,786	19,898	20,030
Depreciation	20,636	17,123	20,951	26,847	30,323	32,125	34,883	38,208
Taxes and other	24,479	26,805	31,343	35,188	35,791	25,136	22,846	24,510
Other utility	18,686	28,956	18,849	14,362	13,931	15,418	15,245	13,718
Net utility operating income	**23,665**	**28,866**	**32,490**	**39,968**	**46,460**	**39,924**	**42,864**	**53,954**

Source: U.S. Energy Information Administration, *Electric Power Annual 2020*, October 2021, and earlier reports. See also <www.eia.gov/electricity/annual/>.

Table 995. Renewable Energy Net Generation of Electricity by Source and State: 2021

[In millions of kilowatt-hours (260,225 represents 260,225,000,000). Data based on results from the Energy Information Agency's annual survey form EIA-923. For more on net generation, see Table 989]

State	Hydro-electric	Other renewable Total [1]	Wind	Bio-mass [2]	Solar [3]	State	Hydro-electric	Other renewable Total [1]	Wind	Bio-mass [2]	Solar [3]
U.S.	**260,225**	**615,187**	**379,767**	**55,479**	**163,703**	MO	1,850	7,275	6,607	121	547
AL	12,518	3,697	(NA)	3,185	512	MT	9,774	2,930	2,822	32	76
AK	1,645	177	127	38	12	NE	1,277	9,891	9,720	90	81
AZ	5,817	11,903	1,600	261	10,042	NV	1,952	12,047	340	61	7,718
AR	4,318	1,585	(NA)	992	593	NH	1,167	1,727	504	1,026	197
CA	14,559	86,959	15,626	5,799	54,087	NJ	18	4,956	20	722	4,214
CO	1,650	17,994	15,029	175	2,790	NM	187	12,952	10,648	28	2,225
CT	324	1,987	13	824	1,150	NY	27,973	10,234	4,387	1,921	3,926
DE	(NA)	278	5	71	202	NC	7,596	13,012	505	2,134	10,373
DC	(NA)	230	(NA)	56	174	ND	2,218	14,543	14,541	1	1
FL	221	14,931	(NA)	4,206	10,725	OH	357	4,174	2,597	642	935
GA	4,168	10,861	(NA)	5,680	5,181	OK	2,709	33,841	33,388	319	134
HI	109	2,919	674	287	1,792	OR	28,361	12,632	9,593	1,022	1,812
ID	8,650	3,924	2,657	502	684	PA	2,580	6,338	3,535	1,838	965
IL	129	20,535	18,690	397	1,448	RI	4	1,098	174	204	720
IN	257	9,244	7,903	452	889	SC	3,721	5,016	(NA)	2,311	2,705
IA	955	37,253	36,578	200	475	SD	5,295	9,338	9,322	12	4
KS	30	25,813	25,625	64	124	TN	12,850	1,117	41	652	424
KY	5,268	471	(NA)	362	109	TX	1,117	117,813	100,049	1,400	16,364
LA	1,159	2,544	(NA)	2,114	430	UT	758	5,393	826	79	4,127
ME	2,969	5,039	2,550	2,175	314	VT	1,075	1,251	338	538	375
MD	2,120	2,596	517	380	1,699	VA	1,816	7,177	50	3,452	3,675
MA	819	5,588	217	1,066	4,305	WA	70,442	11,306	9,508	1,436	362
MI	1,533	10,735	7,809	2,270	656	WV	1,516	1,652	1,624	6	22
MN	898	16,361	12,941	1,318	2,102	WI	2,504	3,324	1,615	1,128	581
MS	(NA)	1,879	(NA)	1,429	450	WY	990	8,646	8,449	(NA)	197

NA Not available. [1] Includes generation from geothermal energy, not shown separately. [2] Includes wood and wood derived fuels, landfill gas, biogenic municipal solid waste, and other biomass waste. [3] Includes generation from all utility-scale solar and small-scale solar photovoltaic sources.

Source: Energy Information Administration, "Electricity Data Browser," <www.eia.gov/electricity/data/browser>, accessed March 2022.

Table 996. Major Power Outages by Type of Disturbance and Duration: 2021

[Data shown for power outages lasting longer than 70 hours]

Type of disturbance	Month	Counties and/or states affected	Duration	Number of customers affected [1]
Severe Weather	February	Texas	312 hours, 0 minutes	2,000,000
Fuel Supply Deficiency	February	Illinois: Scott County	264 hours, 30 minutes	(NA)
Fuel Supply Deficiency	February	Texas	232 hours, 0 minutes	(NA)
Severe Weather	February	Oregon: Clackamas, Marion, Polk, Multnomah, Washington, and Yamhill Counties	188 hours, 15 minutes	300,187
Severe Weather	February	Texas	162 hours, 30 minutes	(NA)
Severe Weather	February	West Virginia; Virginia	151 hours, 30 minutes	55,097
Severe Weather	February	Texas	129 hours, 30 minutes	(NA)
Severe Weather	February	Texas	129 hours, 30 minutes	(NA)
Severe Weather	February	Texas	117 hours, 0 minutes	175,000
Severe Weather	August	Louisiana	115 hours, 41 minutes	91,315
Severe Weather	September	Texas: Harris County	114 hours, 45 minutes	705,415
Severe Weather	February	Kansas; Missouri	110 hours, 57 minutes	222,000
Severe Weather	December	Tennessee: Davidson and Sumner Counties	108 hours, 17 minutes	107,344
Severe Weather	August	Louisiana	105 hours, 59 minutes	50,000
Severe Weather	February	Texas	103 hours, 40 minutes	(NA)
Severe Weather	February	Texas: Travis County	103 hours, 6 minutes	(NA)
System Operations	June	Texas	102 hours, 45 minutes	(NA)
Severe Weather	February	Texas: Travis County	102 hours, 9 minutes	219,306
System Operations	June	Texas	102 hours, 5 minutes	(NA)
Severe Weather	February	Oklahoma	100 hours, 30 minutes	(NA)
Severe Weather	February	Texas	100 hours, 7 minutes	(NA)
Severe Weather	February	Louisiana	91 hours, 0 minutes	(NA)
Severe Weather	February	North Dakota; South Dakota; Nebraska; Kansas; Oklahoma; Texas	85 hours, 28 minutes	(NA)
Severe Weather	February	Arkansas; Louisiana; Texas; Oklahoma	85 hours, 9 minutes	125,484
Severe Weather	February	Missouri	79 hours, 20 minutes	(NA)
Severe Weather	February	Texas	74 hours, 51 minutes	(NA)
Fuel Supply Deficiency	February	Oklahoma	74 hours, 0 minutes	0
Severe Weather	February	Kansas	72 hours, 40 minutes	(NA)
Severe Weather	February	Texas: Lubbock County	71 hours, 28 minutes	29,942
Severe Weather	February	Texas: Hidalgo and Cameron Counties	71 hours, 22 minutes	(NA)
Severe Weather	February	Texas: Harris County	70 hours, 42 minutes	1,390,000
Severe Weather	February	Texas	70 hours, 2 minutes	(NA)

NA Not available. [1] Number of customers affected are preliminary estimates.

Source, U.S. Energy Information Administration, *Electric Power Monthly*, March 2022. See also <www.eia.gov/electricity/monthly>.

Table 997. Gas Utility Industry—Summary: 1990 to 2020

[54,261 represents 54,261,000. Covers natural, manufactured, mixed, and liquid petroleum gas. Based on a questionnaire mailed to all privately and municipally owned gas utilities in the United States, except those with annual revenues less than $25,000]

Item	Unit	1990	2000	2005	2010	2015	2018	2019	2020
End users [1]	**1,000**	54,261	61,262	64,395	64,960	65,612	67,597	68,311	69,349
Residential	1,000	49,802	56,494	59,569	60,246	60,922	62,837	63,520	64,500
Commercial	1,000	4,246	4,610	4,678	4,582	4,559	4,630	4,665	4,721
Industrial	1,000	166	157	145	129	120	119	118	118
Other	1,000	48	2	2	3	10	10	9	10
Sales [2]	**Tril. Btu** [3]	**9,842**	**9,232**	**8,848**	**7,980**	**7,602**	**8,324**	**8,276**	**7,357**
Residential	Tril. Btu	4,468	4,741	4,516	4,371	4,080	4,459	4,520	3,971
Percent of total	Percent	45.4	51.4	51.0	54.8	53.7	53.6	54.6	54.0
Commercial	Tril. Btu	2,192	2,077	2,056	1,842	1,766	1,965	1,967	1,616
Industrial	Tril. Btu	3,010	1,698	1,654	1,209	1,172	1,240	1,126	1,062
Other	Tril. Btu	171	715	622	558	584	659	663	713
Revenues [2]	**Mil. dol.**	**45,153**	**59,243**	**96,909**	**72,886**	**60,923**	**67,843**	**66,618**	**61,972**
Residential	Mil. dol.	25,000	35,828	55,680	47,231	40,451	44,923	45,229	43,239
Percent of total	Percent	55.4	60.5	57.5	64.8	66.4	66.2	67.9	69.8
Commercial	Mil. dol.	10,604	13,339	22,653	16,578	14,057	15,386	14,980	13,170
Industrial	Mil. dol.	8,996	7,432	13,751	6,437	4,434	5,034	4,236	3,561
Other	Mil. dol.	553	2,645	4,825	2,640	1,982	2,500	2,173	2,002
Prices per mil. Btu [3]	**Dollars**	**4.59**	**6.42**	**10.95**	**9.13**	**7.99**	**8.15**	**8.05**	**8.42**
Residential	Dollars	5.60	7.56	12.33	10.81	9.91	10.07	10.01	10.89
Commercial	Dollars	4.84	6.42	11.02	9.00	7.96	7.83	7.62	8.15
Industrial	Dollars	2.99	4.38	8.31	5.32	3.78	4.06	3.76	3.35
Gas mains mileage	**1,000**	**1,189**	**1,369**	**1,438**	**1,531**	**1,594**	**1,627**	**1,638**	**1,648**
Field and gathering	1,000	32	27	23	19	18	18	17	17
Transmission	1,000	292	297	297	308	301	302	302	300
Distribution	1,000	865	1,046	1,118	1,204	1,276	1,308	1,319	1,329
Construction expenditures	**Mil. dol.**	**7,899**	**8,624**	**10,089**	**11,042**	**21,074**	**34,186**	**35,791**	**29,854**
Transmission	Mil. dol.	2,886	1,590	3,368	3,524	6,578	12,222	8,961	7,268
Distribution	Mil. dol.	3,714	5,437	5,129	5,674	11,614	17,090	21,625	18,765
Production and storage	Mil. dol.	309	138	179	151	135	1,070	884	614
General	Mil. dol.	770	1,273	1,070	1,185	1,928	2,624	2,590	2,494
Underground storage	Mil. dol.	219	185	343	509	819	1,180	1,732	714

[1] Annual average. [2] Excludes sales for resale. [3] For definition of Btu (British thermal unit), see text, this section.

Source: American Gas Association, Washington, DC, *Annual Statistics* ©. See also <www.aga.org>.

Table 998. Gas Utility Industry—Customers, Sales, and Revenues by State: 2020

[69,349 represents 69,349,000. See headnote, Table 997. For definition of Btu, see text, this section]

State	Customers [1] (1,000) Total	Resi-dential	Sales [2] (tril. Btu) Total	Resi-dential	Revenues [2] (mil. dol.) Total	Resi-dential	State	Customers [1] (1,000) Total	Resi-dential	Sales [2] (tril. Btu) Total	Resi-dential	Revenues [2] (mil. dol.) Total	Resi-dential
U.S.	69,349	64,500	7,785	4,217	61,972	43,239	MO	1,554	1,438	160	104	1,410	1,039
AL	850	777	99	29	838	451	MT	321	283	35	22	241	157
AK	151	137	62	22	539	234	NE	518	475	58	34	381	261
AZ	1,364	1,306	79	43	760	544	NV	952	906	71	48	631	477
AR	634	565	53	31	531	372	NH	128	112	14	8	175	108
CA	11,183	10,748	627	454	7,706	6,189	NJ	2,979	2,772	292	224	2,703	2,144
CO	1,994	1,840	226	142	1,401	986	NM	656	606	57	38	342	256
CT	638	576	102	49	1,135	688	NY	4,393	4,081	468	345	5,102	4,150
DE	199	185	18	11	199	140	NC	1,463	1,332	128	66	1,325	847
DC	145	138	11	9	128	99	ND	174	150	42	12	184	82
FL	835	795	52	17	594	341	OH	612	578	63	46	510	395
GA	365	331	64	16	438	200	OK	1,056	962	99	63	719	553
HI	32	29	3	1	70	23	OR	862	777	85	47	762	496
ID	472	428	49	32	297	206	PA	2,652	2,472	253	197	2,669	2,186
IL	3,936	3,686	459	362	3,361	2,772	RI	269	247	25	19	347	275
IN	1,881	1,731	194	134	1,501	1,108	SC	798	735	183	30	986	393
IA	1,045	945	143	66	816	499	SD	224	198	26	14	152	94
KS	964	881	99	65	771	584	TN	1,333	1,194	149	68	1,079	589
KY	853	767	94	47	797	500	TX	5,221	4,889	1,331	211	5,351	2,371
LA	960	902	88	33	651	390	UT	1,073	1,002	108	77	805	605
ME	50	38	11	3	121	44	VT	54	48	14	4	96	50
MD	1,031	976	81	62	978	783	VA	1,279	1,186	119	70	1,183	855
MA	1,668	1,537	193	122	2,410	1,734	WA	1,343	1,233	145	90	1,416	957
MI	3,456	3,197	406	298	3,074	2,375	WV	371	336	37	24	327	231
MN	1,727	1,582	258	135	1,733	1,046	WI	1,989	1,811	287	144	1,689	1,041
MS	514	464	48	21	410	237	WY	131	116	17	9	128	80

[1] Averages for the year. [2] Excludes sales for resale.

Source: American Gas Association, Washington, DC, *Annual Statistics* ©. See also <www.aga.org>.

Table 999. Privately Owned Gas Utility Industry—Balance Sheet and Income Account: 1990 to 2020

[In millions of dollars (121,686 represents $121,686,000,000). The gas utility industry consists of pipeline and distribution companies. Excludes operations of companies distributing gas in bottles or tanks]

Item	1990	1995	2000	2005	2010	2015	2018	2019	2020
COMPOSITE BALANCE SHEET									
Assets, total	121,686	141,965	165,709	196,215	220,860	262,805	324,955	350,563	367,210
Total utility plant	112,863	143,636	162,206	207,976	239,718	292,252	364,856	389,111	402,887
Depreciation and amortization	49,483	62,723	69,366	91,794	92,012	104,615	120,067	120,103	122,185
Utility plant (net)	63,380	80,912	92,839	116,183	147,707	187,637	244,789	269,008	280,703
Investment and fund accounts	23,872	26,489	10,846	16,331	7,132	12,202	9,202	7,924	8,647
Current and accrued assets	23,268	18,564	35,691	32,325	27,288	21,309	24,648	23,230	25,136
Deferred debits [1]	9,576	13,923	24,279	29,574	37,307	40,253	44,895	48,803	51,178
Liabilities, total	121,686	141,965	165,709	196,215	220,860	262,805	324,955	350,563	367,210
Capitalization, total	74,958	90,581	96,079	120,949	133,414	157,916	215,880	237,063	249,821
Capital stock	43,810	54,402	47,051	62,470	74,157	87,760	119,549	133,832	137,434
Long-term debts	31,148	35,548	48,267	58,264	59,223	70,194	96,242	103,231	112,387
Current and accrued liabilities	29,550	28,272	42,312	34,936	28,564	26,408	39,006	36,301	36,997
Deferred income taxes [2]	11,360	14,393	17,157	24,937	34,401	43,688	44,729	47,779	48,721
Other liabilities and credits	5,818	8,715	10,161	15,393	24,515	34,793	25,340	29,420	31,671
COMPOSITE INCOME ACCOUNT									
Operating revenues, total	66,027	58,390	72,042	102,018	82,315	72,298	81,351	80,037	76,793
Minus: Operating expenses [3]	60,137	50,760	64,988	89,385	71,761	61,229	46,531	43,437	38,730
Operation and maintenance	51,627	37,966	54,602	77,673	57,758	45,746	50,938	46,548	41,865
Federal, state, and local taxes	4,957	6,182	6,163	7,513	7,569	7,872	7,803	7,258	8,200
Equals: Operating income	5,890	7,630	7,053	12,632	10,554	11,069	13,519	16,681	16,660
Utility operating income	6,077	7,848	7,166	12,812	11,045	11,620	14,173	17,263	16,895
Income before interest charges	8,081	9,484	7,589	13,972	12,368	12,049	14,603	18,602	17,484
Net income	4,410	5,139	4,245	9,777	8,619	8,719	10,311	14,117	13,041
Dividends	3,191	4,037	3,239	2,419	2,080	1,487	1,214	1,547	1,879

[1] Includes capital stock discount and expense and reacquired securities. [2] Includes reserves for deferred income taxes. [3] Includes expenses not shown separately.

Source: American Gas Association, Washington, DC, *Annual Statistics* ©. See also <www.aga.org>.

Table 1000. Sewage Treatment Facilities and Employees: 2019 and 2020

[Data are based on the North American Industry Classification System (NAICS) 2017; see text, Section 15]

State	Sewage treatment facilities (NAICS 22132)				State	Sewage treatment facilities (NAICS 22132)			
	2019		2020			2019		2020	
	Number of establishments	Paid employees	Number of establishments	Paid employees		Number of establishments	Paid employees	Number of establishments	Paid employees
U.S.............	579	5,597	536	5,703	MO.............	17	76	17	78
AL.............	13	348	13	351	MT.............	7	26	7	23
AK.............	(NA)	(NA)	(NA)	(NA)	NE.............	(NA)	(NA)	(NA)	(NA)
AZ.............	19	148	18	162	NV.............	(NA)	(NA)	(NA)	(NA)
AR.............	7	68	7	72	NH.............	5	20	4	23
CA.............	35	277	33	254	NJ.............	11	161	10	150
CO.............	5	101	7	97	NM.............	11	195	6	199
CT.............	6	105	6	103	NY.............	26	431	25	450
DE.............	3	63	4	64	NC.............	17	94	16	102
DC.............	(NA)	(NA)	(NA)	(NA)	ND.............	(NA)	(NA)	(NA)	(NA)
FL.............	42	616	31	577	OH.............	9	54	7	49
GA.............	21	253	11	250	OK.............	17	197	17	204
HI.............	19	101	16	91	OR.............	4	6	3	4
ID.............	7	42	7	42	PA.............	44	406	45	402
IL.............	17	182	17	180	RI.............	(NA)	(NA)	(NA)	(NA)
IN.............	21	94	21	90	SC.............	11	57	9	60
IA.............	5	101	5	101	SD.............	(NA)	(NA)	(NA)	(NA)
KS.............	(NA)	(NA)	(NA)	(NA)	TN.............	5	30	5	28
KY.............	8	42	6	40	TX.............	58	305	60	464
LA.............	22	200	23	216	UT.............	(NA)	(NA)	(NA)	(NA)
ME.............	(NA)	(NA)	(NA)	(NA)	VT.............	(NA)	(NA)	(NA)	(NA)
MD.............	7	48	5	37	VA.............	7	41	5	19
MA.............	7	83	7	90	WA.............	7	58	5	63
MI.............	16	193	15	177	WV.............	6	43	5	42
MN.............	12	86	14	99	WI.............	5	13	4	13
MS.............	12	152	12	154	WY.............	(NA)	(NA)	(NA)	(NA)

NA Not available.

Source: U.S. Census Bureau, County Business Patterns, "County Business Patterns by Legal Form of Organization and Employment Size Class for U.S., States, and Selected Geographies," <data.census.gov>, accessed April 2022.

Section 20
Construction and Housing

This section presents data on the construction industry and on various indicators of its activity and costs; on housing units and their characteristics and occupants; and on the characteristics of commercial buildings.

The principal source of these data is the U.S. Census Bureau, which issues a variety of current publications, as well as data from the decennial census. Current construction statistics compiled by the Census Bureau appear in its *New Residential Construction* and *New Residential Sales* press releases and web sites at <census.gov/construction/nrc/> and <census.gov/construction/nrs/>. *Construction Spending*, available at <census.gov/construction/c30/c30index.html>, presents data on all types of construction. Reports of the censuses of construction industries (see below) are also issued on various topics.

Other Census Bureau publications include the quarterly *Housing Vacancies and Homeownership*, the quarterly *Survey of Market Absorption*, the biennial *American Housing Survey* (formerly *Annual Housing Survey*), and other reports of the censuses of housing and of construction industries.

Other sources include the Bureau of Economic Analysis, which presents data on residential fixed assets; the U.S. Energy Information Administration, which provides data on commercial and residential buildings through its periodic sample surveys; and the Federal Financial Institutions Examination Council, which provides data on home purchase loans.

Censuses and surveys—Censuses of the construction industry were first conducted by the Census Bureau for 1929, 1935, and 1939; beginning in 1967, a census has been taken every 5 years for years ending in "2" and "7". The construction sector of the Economic Census covers all employer establishments primarily engaged in (1) building construction by general contractors or operative builders; (2) heavy (nonbuilding) construction by general contractors; and (3) construction by special trade contractors. This sector includes construction management and land subdividers and developers. The census is conducted in accordance with the North American Industrial Classification System (NAICS). See text, Section 15, Business Enterprise.

The *American Housing Survey* (*Current Housing Reports* Series H-150 and H-170), which began in 1973, provided an annual and ongoing series of data on selected housing and demographic characteristics until 1983. In 1984, the name of the survey was changed from the *Annual Housing Survey*. Currently, national data are collected every other year, and data for selected metropolitan areas are collected on a rotating basis. The supplemental sample of housing units is selected for no more than 30 metropolitan units and combined with the national sample in order to produce metropolitan estimates using the national survey. All samples represent a cross section of the housing stock in their respective areas. Estimates are subject to both sampling and nonsampling errors; caution should therefore be used in making comparisons between years. More information about the survey can be found at <census.gov/programs-surveys/ahs.html>

Data on residential mortgages were collected continuously from 1890 to 1970, except 1930, as part of the decennial census by the Census Bureau. Since 1973, mortgage status data have been presented in the *American Housing Survey*. Data on mortgage activity are covered in Section 25, Banking and Finance.

Housing units—In general, a housing unit is a house, an apartment, a group of rooms or a single room occupied or intended for occupancy as separate living quarters; that is, the occupants live separately from any other individual in the building, and there is direct access from the outside or through a common hall. Transient accommodations, barracks for workers, and institutional-type quarters are not counted as housing units.

Statistical reliability—For a discussion of statistical collection and estimation, sampling procedures, and measures of statistical reliability applicable to Census Bureau data, see Appendix III.

Table 1001. Construction—Establishments, Employees, and Payroll by Kind of Business (NAICS Basis): 2019 and 2020

[7,044 represents 7,044,000. Covers establishments with payroll. Excludes most government employees, railroad employees, and self-employed persons. For statement on methodology, see Appendix III]

Kind of business	NAICS code [1]	Establishments 2019	Establishments 2020	Paid employees [2] (1,000) 2019	Paid employees [2] (1,000) 2020	Annual payroll (mil. dol.) 2019	Annual payroll (mil. dol.) 2020
Construction.................................	**23**	**745,207**	**753,341**	**7,044**	**7,182**	**457,268**	**458,934**
Construction of buildings............................	236	228,282	233,058	1,452	1,495	99,565	102,018
Residential building construction...................	2361	185,624	190,430	753	781	43,581	46,322
New single-family housing construction (except for-sale builders).........................	236115	54,735	55,868	199	210	10,712	11,592
New multifamily housing construction (except for-sale builders).........................	236116	3,372	3,545	47	49	4,141	4,388
New housing for-sale builders....................	236117	12,643	12,381	119	120	10,685	11,438
Residential remodelers............................	236118	114,874	118,636	388	401	18,044	18,904
Nonresidential building construction..............	2362	42,658	42,628	699	715	55,984	55,696
Industrial building construction...................	23621	3,290	3,293	75	75	5,558	5,132
Commercial and institutional building construction..	23622	39,368	39,335	624	639	50,425	50,564
Heavy and civil engineering construction...........	237	38,137	37,991	1,039	1,047	81,728	80,417
Utility system construction........................	2371	19,338	19,358	640	633	48,598	46,109
Water and sewer line and related structures....	23711	10,773	10,656	155	160	10,756	11,148
Oil and gas pipeline and related structures......	23712	2,194	2,153	238	217	18,548	14,811
Power and communication line and related structures..............................	23713	6,371	6,549	247	256	19,294	20,150
Land subdivision..................................	2372	4,682	4,606	22	22	1,758	1,769
Highway, street, and bridge construction.........	2373	9,702	9,577	304	313	25,555	26,226
Other heavy and civil engineering construction...	2379	4,415	4,450	73	79	5,817	6,313
Specialty trade contractors......................	238	478,788	482,292	4,553	4,640	275,974	276,498
Foundation, structure, and building exterior contractors.......................................	2381	96,703	97,516	896	915	51,061	52,147
Poured concrete foundation and structures contractors.....................................	23811	21,104	21,193	241	250	14,460	14,958
Structural steel and precast concrete contractors.....................................	23812	3,671	3,648	81	80	5,258	5,235
Framing contractors...............................	23813	11,976	11,736	86	86	4,105	4,159
Masonry contractors..............................	23814	18,507	18,207	143	145	7,552	7,538
Glass and glazing contractors....................	23815	6,145	6,275	66	67	4,018	4,025
Roofing contractors...............................	23816	21,197	22,147	193	198	10,869	11,409
Siding contractors................................	23817	8,126	8,220	36	38	1,752	1,871
Other foundation, structure, and building exterior contractors............................	23819	5,977	6,090	50	50	3,046	2,952
Building equipment contractors....................	2382	187,388	189,342	2,151	2,191	139,406	139,439
Electrical contractors.............................	23821	76,328	77,079	904	930	59,294	58,947
Plumbing, heating, and air-conditioning contractors.....................................	23822	103,359	104,367	1,099	1,116	68,668	69,625
Other building equipment contractors...........	23829	7,701	7,896	147	145	11,445	10,867
Building finishing contractors......................	2383	121,472	121,151	844	843	43,689	42,504
Drywall and insulation contractors...............	23831	19,457	19,504	270	266	15,254	14,595
Painting and wall covering contractors...........	23832	36,214	35,747	199	198	9,383	9,040
Flooring contractors..............................	23833	17,034	17,068	83	83	4,307	4,171
Tile and terrazzo contractors.....................	23834	10,201	10,113	60	59	2,951	2,881
Finish carpentry contractors......................	23835	31,191	31,177	158	160	7,792	7,877
Other building finishing contractors..............	23839	7,375	7,542	75	77	4,002	3,941
Other specialty trade contractors..................	2389	73,225	74,283	662	690	41,819	42,409
Site preparation contractors......................	23891	37,491	37,751	407	421	26,544	26,757
All other specialty trade contractors..............	23899	35,734	36,532	254	269	15,275	15,651

[1] Data are based on the North American Industry Classification System (NAICS) 2017; see text, Section 15. [2] Employees on the payroll for the pay period including March 12.

Source: U.S. Census Bureau, County Business Patterns, "County Business Patterns by Legal Form of Organization and Employment Size Class for U.S., States, and Selected Geographies," <data.census.gov>, accessed April 2022. See also <www.census.gov/programs-surveys/cbp.html>.

Table 1002. Construction Industries—Establishments, Shipments, Payroll, and Employees: 2017

[1,994,166,047 represents $1,994,166,047,000. Includes only establishments with payroll]

Industry	2017 NAICS code [1]	Establishments (number)	Value of shipments ($1,000)	Annual payroll ($1,000)	Paid employees [2] Total	Paid employees [2] Construction workers
Construction.....	**23**	**715,364**	**1,994,166,047**	**398,815,537**	**6,647,047**	**4,989,303**
Construction of buildings.....	236	214,085	800,474,908	85,499,623	1,345,938	857,765
Residential buildings.....	2361	171,814	342,010,528	37,276,291	694,023	453,287
New single-family housing (except for-sale builders).....	236115	48,673	68,574,751	8,530,682	176,059	119,553
New multifamily housing (except for-sale builders)...	236116	3,200	46,910,655	3,595,548	44,444	24,062
New housing for-sale builders.....	236117	17,123	148,898,346	10,298,600	132,191	50,793
Residential remodelers.....	236118	102,818	77,626,776	14,851,461	341,329	258,879
Nonresidential buildings.....	2362	42,271	458,464,380	48,223,332	651,915	404,478
Industrial buildings.....	23621	3,164	25,454,943	4,479,129	71,562	49,219
Commercial and institutional buildings.....	23622	39,107	433,009,437	43,744,203	580,353	355,259
Heavy and civil engineering construction.....	237	38,016	318,079,667	72,037,723	1,007,942	785,314
Utility system.....	2371	19,142	158,659,104	42,300,448	594,859	480,820
Water and sewer line and related structures.....	23711	10,838	44,333,746	9,613,699	150,664	116,563
Oil and gas pipeline and related structures.....	23712	2,226	49,691,899	15,491,081	211,334	178,222
Power and communication line and related structures.....	23713	6,078	64,633,459	17,195,668	232,861	186,035
Land subdivision.....	2372	4,893	9,376,544	1,586,225	23,692	9,862
Highway, street, and bridge.....	2373	9,721	126,575,188	23,248,153	322,243	245,658
Other heavy and civil engineering.....	2379	4,260	23,468,831	4,902,897	67,148	48,974
Specialty trade contractors.....	238	463,263	875,611,472	241,278,191	4,293,167	3,346,224
Foundation, structure, and building exterior.....	2381	92,711	178,670,037	45,019,907	866,527	695,994
Poured concrete foundation and structure.....	23811	20,707	52,694,411	13,122,241	239,062	205,652
Structural steel and precast concrete.....	23812	3,577	15,476,984	4,663,204	77,366	64,447
Framing.....	23813	11,516	16,165,452	3,630,233	85,674	72,421
Masonry.....	23814	18,329	23,560,290	6,852,561	141,977	121,823
Glass and glazing.....	23815	5,816	14,124,308	3,498,088	61,758	39,977
Roofing.....	23816	19,366	40,770,160	9,145,104	178,559	130,909
Siding.....	23817	7,812	6,574,724	1,466,580	35,070	24,079
Other foundation, structure, and building exterior.....	23819	5,588	9,303,708	2,641,896	47,061	36,686
Building equipment.....	2382	184,566	411,178,579	121,531,110	1,999,953	1,532,225
Electrical and other wiring installation.....	23821	73,907	171,416,144	51,456,683	845,813	677,055
Plumbing, heating, and air-conditioning.....	23822	103,275	206,208,216	60,218,491	1,020,861	754,717
Other building equipment.....	23829	7,384	33,554,219	9,855,936	133,279	100,453
Building finishing.....	2383	116,026	136,104,427	38,592,728	800,677	635,737
Drywall and insulation.....	23831	18,359	45,083,613	13,522,558	258,608	224,797
Painting and wall covering.....	23832	35,484	25,388,981	8,438,133	190,200	161,916
Flooring.....	23833	15,925	18,039,180	3,800,490	78,494	52,036
Tile and terrazzo.....	23834	9,787	9,264,998	2,687,228	57,235	45,376
Finish carpentry.....	23835	29,697	27,561,178	6,807,059	145,852	102,006
Other building finishing.....	23839	6,774	10,766,477	3,337,260	70,288	49,606
Other specialty trade.....	2389	69,960	149,658,429	36,134,446	626,010	482,268
Site preparation.....	23891	35,417	97,460,244	22,894,974	385,177	307,808
All other specialty trade.....	23899	34,543	52,198,185	13,239,472	240,833	174,460

[1] North American Industry Classification System, 2017. [2] For pay period including March 12.

Source: U.S. Census Bureau, 2017 Economic Census, "EC1723BASIC: Construction: Summary Statistics for the U.S., States, and Selected Geographies: 2017," <data.census.gov>, accessed November 2021.

Table 1003. Value of New Construction Put in Place: 1990 to 2021

[In millions of dollars (476,778 represents $476,778,000,000). Represents value of construction put in place during year; differs from building permit and construction contract data in timing and coverage. Includes installed cost of normal building service equipment and selected types of industrial production equipment (largely site fabricated). Excludes cost of shipbuilding, land, and most types of machinery and equipment. For methodology, see Appendix III]

Year	Total	Private Total	Private Residential buildings	Private Non-residential	Public Total	Public Federal	Public State and local
1990.....	476,778	369,300	191,103	178,197	107,478	12,099	95,379
1995.....	548,666	408,655	228,121	180,534	140,011	15,751	124,260
2000.....	802,756	621,431	346,138	275,293	181,325	14,168	167,157
2005.....	1,116,811	882,651	624,574	258,077	234,160	17,300	216,860
2007.....	1,147,951	858,878	488,846	370,032	289,073	20,580	268,494
2008.....	1,077,350	768,612	359,171	409,440	308,738	23,731	285,007
2009.....	911,767	596,872	252,751	344,121	314,895	28,439	286,456
2010.....	812,964	508,998	245,743	263,255	303,966	31,133	272,833
2011.....	791,237	504,830	247,028	257,803	286,407	31,654	254,753
2012.....	854,401	575,091	273,730	301,360	279,311	26,933	252,378
2013.....	914,582	643,900	329,640	314,260	270,682	23,727	246,955
2014.....	1,015,292	739,164	377,461	361,704	276,128	22,416	253,712
2015.....	1,140,162	846,394	431,769	414,625	293,768	22,548	271,220
2016.....	1,223,671	926,698	479,415	447,283	296,972	22,242	274,731
2017.....	1,279,841	983,302	539,013	444,289	296,539	21,267	275,272
2018.....	1,333,183	1,023,016	557,558	465,457	310,167	21,979	288,188
2019.....	1,391,039	1,046,693	546,554	500,139	344,346	26,277	318,069
2020.....	1,499,570	1,130,370	634,726	495,644	369,200	28,958	340,241
2021.....	1,626,444	1,279,464	793,660	485,805	346,980	24,837	322,143

Source: U.S. Census Bureau, "Construction Spending," <www.census.gov/construction/c30/historical_data.html>, accessed August 2022.

Table 1004. New Privately Owned Housing Units Authorized by State: 2020 and 2021

[1,471.1 represents 1,471,100. Based on the 2014 Universe, which includes approximately 20,100 places in the United States that have building permit systems in 2014]

State	Housing units (1,000) 2020	Total 2021	1-unit [1] 2021	Valuation (mil. dol.) 2020	Total 2021	1-unit [1] 2021
U.S.	1,471.1	1,737.0	1,115.4	307,210	380,036	295,965
AL	20.0	22.1	17.9	4,359	4,816	4,324
AK	1.4	1.6	1.2	381	413	354
AZ	60.3	65.3	46.6	13,798	15,323	12,666
AR	12.5	14.2	10.6	2,354	2,858	2,510
CA	106.1	119.4	65.9	25,423	28,725	18,780
CO	40.5	56.5	30.2	10,267	13,744	9,850
CT	5.5	4.7	2.9	1,062	1,225	1,043
DE	8.5	8.5	7.3	1,099	1,176	1,048
DC	7.4	4.7	0.4	887	626	89
FL	164.1	213.5	148.7	36,884	49,326	39,939
GA	55.8	67.2	53.4	11,593	14,437	12,604
HI	3.2	3.5	2.4	1,170	1,396	1,071
ID	19.1	21.7	16.2	3,949	4,949	4,214
IL	18.1	19.7	10.9	3,646	4,273	3,209
IN	24.9	29.9	22.2	5,872	7,583	6,693
IA	12.6	13.7	9.2	2,702	3,182	2,553
KS	8.2	9.5	6.6	1,991	2,593	2,209
KY	11.3	14.8	10.1	2,143	2,912	2,430
LA	17.3	19.1	16.9	3,428	4,054	3,784
ME	5.3	6.5	5.2	1,194	1,594	1,405
MD	18.0	18.5	12.5	3,854	4,012	3,201
MA	17.0	19.9	7.2	4,761	4,942	2,840
MI	19.7	21.7	16.8	4,580	5,684	4,767
MN	28.1	33.7	16.7	6,179	7,726	5,146
MS	7.8	8.0	7.4	1,429	1,542	1,502
MO	19.8	21.4	13.9	4,022	4,748	3,921
MT	6.0	7.3	3.2	1,052	1,411	868
NE	9.5	10.7	6.3	1,644	2,016	1,542
NV	19.7	23.4	16.3	4,057	5,293	4,476
NH	4.3	4.9	3.4	1,059	1,261	1,041
NJ	36.1	37.1	13.9	4,796	5,234	2,906
NM	5.2	7.8	5.5	1,226	1,622	1,413
NY	37.3	40.1	11.1	6,406	7,652	3,936
NC	80.5	94.9	68.6	16,112	20,486	17,263
ND	3.5	3.6	2.3	727	866	667
OH	29.7	30.4	20.5	6,418	7,339	6,325
OK	13.7	14.7	13.3	2,853	3,454	3,314
OR	18.7	21.9	13.2	4,067	5,128	3,748
PA	25.7	47.9	18.8	5,077	9,311	4,887
RI	1.4	1.4	1.0	299	328	287
SC	42.3	50.7	43.3	9,505	11,652	10,770
SD	6.7	7.9	4.3	1,167	1,565	1,127
TN	49.7	57.5	37.0	9,207	11,478	9,597
TX	230.5	266.0	179.6	42,986	52,319	42,407
UT	31.8	39.1	24.4	7,287	9,188	7,045
VT	2.1	2.3	1.4	396	500	386
VA	33.8	39.4	25.1	6,342	7,750	6,210
WA	43.9	56.9	25.1	9,488	12,501	7,542
WV	3.2	3.7	3.1	574	778	702
WI	21.2	25.4	13.2	4,733	5,986	4,368
WY	2.1	2.7	2.2	704	1,058	989

[1] The 1-unit structure category is a single-family home. It includes fully detached, semi-detached (semi-attached, side-by-side), row houses, and townhouses.

Source: U.S. Census Bureau, Construction Reports, "Building Permits Survey," <www.census.gov/construction/bps/>, accessed June 2022.

Table 1005. New Residential Building Permits—Total and for Single-Family Homes by Region: 2014 to 2021

[1,052.1 represents 1,052,100. Based on the 2014 Universe, which includes approximately 20,100 places in the United States that have building permit systems in 2014]

Year	Total	1-unit [1]	Northeast Total	Northeast 1-unit [1]	Midwest Total	Midwest 1-unit [1]	South Total	South 1-unit [1]	West Total	West 1-unit [1]
HOUSING UNITS (1,000)										
2014	1,052.1	640.3	118.5	54.6	165.2	101.0	524.1	347.7	244.3	137.1
2015	1,182.6	696.0	162.0	52.4	170.6	104.7	572.8	378.2	277.2	160.7
2016	1,206.6	750.8	116.4	54.3	186.1	112.4	594.5	406.0	309.6	178.1
2017	1,282.0	820.0	123.6	54.2	195.1	121.5	626.9	447.6	336.4	196.7
2018	1,328.8	855.3	123.4	53.9	185.5	117.9	677.1	474.9	342.8	208.7
2019	1,386.0	862.1	141.2	52.7	184.8	114.2	710.3	486.2	349.8	209.0
2020	1,471.1	979.4	134.8	56.3	202.1	128.0	776.3	568.5	358.0	226.7
2021	1,737.0	1,115.4	164.8	65.0	227.6	142.9	917.5	655.2	427.1	252.2
VALUATION (mil. dol.)										
2014	194,350	149,633	20,568	13,369	30,467	23,588	92,009	75,576	51,306	37,100
2015	223,611	166,277	26,513	13,131	32,968	25,148	102,723	83,584	61,408	44,414
2016	237,102	182,207	21,821	13,921	36,069	27,684	111,212	91,251	68,000	49,352
2017	258,505	200,600	22,969	13,954	38,525	30,102	122,214	102,896	74,798	53,647
2018	271,120	210,850	23,328	13,916	38,481	30,313	131,120	108,674	78,192	57,948
2019	280,534	213,271	24,608	13,854	39,104	30,383	137,328	110,864	79,494	58,169
2020	307,210	243,424	25,052	14,549	43,681	34,735	155,607	131,373	82,869	62,767
2021	380,036	295,965	32,047	18,730	53,561	42,526	193,675	161,693	100,753	73,016

[1] The 1-unit structure category is a single-family home. It includes fully detached, semi-detached (semi-attached, side-by-side), row houses, and townhouses.

Source: U.S. Census Bureau, Construction Reports, "Building Permits Survey," <www.census.gov/construction/bps/>, accessed June 2022.

Table 1006. Value of Private Construction Put in Place: 2010 to 2021

[In millions of dollars (508,998 represents $508,998,000,000). Represents value of construction put in place during year; differs from building permit and construction contract data in timing and coverage. See Appendix III]

Type of construction	2010	2014	2015	2016	2017	2018	2019	2020	2021
Total private construction [1]	**508,998**	**739,164**	**846,394**	**926,698**	**983,302**	**1,023,016**	**1,046,693**	**1,130,370**	**1,279,464**
Residential	245,743	377,461	431,769	479,415	539,013	557,558	546,554	634,726	793,660
New single family	112,569	193,600	221,128	242,476	270,163	289,582	279,962	309,388	423,869
New multifamily	18,395	49,221	62,157	73,339	74,011	77,544	82,215	91,737	100,635
Improvements [2]	114,780	134,639	148,484	163,600	194,840	190,432	184,377	233,601	269,156
Nonresidential	263,255	361,704	414,625	447,283	444,289	465,457	500,139	495,644	485,805
Lodging	11,201	16,306	21,436	26,632	28,065	30,453	32,318	27,418	17,579
Office [1]	24,368	38,864	47,864	59,758	59,918	66,835	77,536	80,523	74,871
General	22,203	36,958	46,051	57,524	57,259	64,628	75,232	77,950	72,950
Financial	2,122	1,867	1,669	1,857	2,392	2,049	2,137	2,482	1,852
Commercial	37,154	60,890	64,493	75,514	84,479	82,808	80,269	85,573	90,885
Automotive [1]	3,546	4,830	5,830	7,472	8,127	7,638	6,191	7,323	6,450
Sales	1,355	2,117	2,164	3,113	3,128	3,202	2,072	1,965	1,605
Service/parts	1,679	2,047	2,885	3,367	3,928	3,289	2,867	4,025	3,611
Parking	511	666	780	992	1,071	1,148	1,253	1,333	1,235
Food/beverage	4,605	7,230	7,273	8,252	8,155	8,678	9,310	8,756	7,905
Food	2,027	3,447	3,109	3,554	3,231	2,748	3,667	4,082	3,272
Dining/drinking	1,911	2,170	2,589	2,913	3,416	4,027	4,226	3,519	3,678
Fast food	667	1,613	1,575	1,784	1,508	1,904	1,416	1,155	956
Multi-retail [1]	12,486	19,543	20,036	22,404	24,048	20,818	14,615	10,922	10,049
General merchandise	3,794	2,792	2,362	2,659	1,864	2,581	2,361	2,237	2,702
Shopping center	6,725	12,946	13,752	15,713	17,558	14,676	9,355	6,865	5,973
Shopping mall	1,332	2,868	3,035	3,292	3,921	2,861	2,072	975	545
Other commercial [1]	4,220	4,586	5,225	6,451	5,219	5,494	7,374	7,775	7,388
Drug store	1,077	943	535	505	358	255	325	389	456
Building supply store	772	495	586	529	650	593	742	804	892
Other stores	1,741	2,409	2,881	4,212	3,129	2,777	4,197	4,402	4,185
Warehouse [1]	5,661	13,698	16,850	22,634	29,053	33,056	34,758	42,376	49,357
General commercial	5,229	12,894	15,699	20,323	24,745	27,921	29,852	37,512	45,247
Ministorage	401	589	963	2,116	3,932	4,893	4,646	4,642	3,986
Farm	6,637	11,005	9,280	8,303	9,877	7,123	8,023	8,421	9,735
Health care	29,552	28,885	30,939	31,756	33,517	33,962	36,751	39,051	38,545
Hospital	21,528	17,680	19,665	19,773	20,210	20,747	20,996	20,246	19,841
Medical building	5,276	7,167	7,056	8,025	9,229	9,653	11,170	13,348	13,690
Special care	2,748	4,039	4,219	3,958	4,078	3,562	4,585	5,457	5,013
Educational [1]	13,418	16,583	17,688	20,036	21,232	22,346	21,627	18,801	16,107
Preschool	492	462	355	515	554	598	708	667	583
Primary/secondary	2,585	3,599	3,676	3,910	4,574	5,111	5,068	5,249	4,385
Higher education [1]	8,322	10,501	11,932	13,340	12,934	13,657	13,083	10,325	8,726
Instructional	4,993	4,944	5,472	6,101	5,775	5,759	5,628	4,184	4,427
Dormitory	1,654	3,559	3,931	4,604	4,528	4,532	4,559	4,254	3,057
Sports/recreation	790	974	1,055	1,146	1,300	1,487	1,363	861	730
Other educational [1]	1,687	1,656	1,471	1,840	2,393	2,116	1,915	1,937	1,859
Gallery/museum	1,522	1,224	1,038	1,414	1,628	1,573	1,422	1,520	1,521
Religious	5,237	3,380	3,589	3,752	3,586	3,499	3,730	3,469	2,920
House of worship	4,214	2,853	3,029	3,279	3,028	2,956	3,100	2,781	2,295
Other religious	1,023	527	561	473	558	543	631	689	625
Auxiliary building	795	391	491	384	508	434	413	431	308
Public safety	241	227	225	105	107	204	240	92	96
Amusement and recreation [1]	6,483	7,719	10,032	12,588	14,518	15,712	15,785	13,548	12,423
Theme/amusement park	353	943	1,213	2,072	2,125	2,054	1,810	1,417	896
Sports	1,596	1,889	3,452	4,495	6,071	5,652	4,492	4,674	4,512
Fitness	1,150	1,182	1,192	1,306	1,289	1,835	2,073	1,843	1,173
Performance/meeting center	565	657	724	928	1,204	1,950	2,541	1,730	1,578
Social center	914	757	869	969	899	1,249	1,588	1,529	1,778
Movie theater/studio	426	717	832	1,043	835	976	985	678	344
Transportation [1]	9,894	12,151	13,563	13,081	14,796	17,880	17,183	16,311	15,414
Air	259	729	886	2,058	3,458	4,144	4,421	4,232	4,013
Land	9,503	11,035	12,412	10,907	11,041	13,154	12,075	11,468	10,719
Railroad	8,973	10,225	11,653	9,900	10,089	11,204	10,621	10,423	9,812
Communication	17,689	17,105	21,505	22,014	23,571	24,320	22,111	23,770	24,474
Power	66,117	98,206	99,549	102,263	89,774	94,390	110,427	110,593	112,402
Electricity	48,972	69,970	75,169	81,883	65,136	70,422	78,741	88,478	88,531
Gas	8,297	11,033	12,546	14,474	15,745	18,787	19,316	15,787	17,520
Oil	8,848	17,203	11,834	5,906	8,893	5,181	12,370	6,328	6,351
Sewage and waste disposal	439	241	375	403	240	408	683	419	451
Water supply	717	573	542	221	277	287	409	574	641
Manufacturing	40,607	60,139	82,382	78,873	69,970	72,005	80,537	75,069	78,461
Food/beverage/tobacco	4,000	6,607	7,216	7,851	8,447	9,661	7,050	7,444	9,715
Textile/apparel/leather/furniture	591	826	639	992	865	528	161	260	483
Wood	438	640	347	469	1,320	1,759	2,197	1,055	806
Paper/printing/publishing	634	654	1,035	1,207	1,522	2,444	2,298	1,792	1,482
Petroleum/coal	11,612	5,222	4,428	4,103	3,938	3,557	3,933	3,017	2,579
Chemical	7,580	23,525	37,818	35,841	32,245	30,698	34,717	30,118	28,949
Plastic/rubber	728	2,248	3,317	3,600	3,157	4,257	3,026	1,334	1,250
Nonmetallic mineral	1,150	976	1,153	1,434	1,038	660	790	979	1,274
Primary metal	4,738	3,968	6,142	4,204	2,823	2,088	3,670	3,772	4,157
Fabricated metal	1,104	847	1,212	2,242	1,972	1,653	1,547	1,302	1,897
Machinery	1,030	1,203	1,938	1,503	903	1,252	2,175	2,179	1,636
Computer/electronic/electrical	4,614	5,133	3,510	1,998	2,141	5,487	8,308	9,167	11,613
Transportation equipment	1,962	7,227	12,639	12,500	8,818	6,765	8,196	9,630	9,461

[1] Includes other types of construction, not shown separately. [2] Private residential improvement does not include expenditures on rental, vacant, or seasonal properties.

Source: U.S. Census Bureau, "Construction Spending," <www.census.gov/construction/c30/c30index.html>, accessed August 2022.

Table 1007. Value of State and Local Government Construction Put in Place: 2010 to 2021

[In millions of dollars (272,833 represents $272,833,000,000)]

Type of construction	2010	2014	2015	2016	2017	2018	2019	2020	2021
Total construction [1]	272,833	253,712	271,220	274,731	275,272	288,188	318,069	340,241	322,143
Residential	7,576	4,128	6,032	5,851	6,233	5,782	6,143	8,437	8,256
Multifamily	6,536	3,444	5,224	5,158	5,911	5,368	5,517	7,393	7,309
Nonresidential	265,256	249,585	265,188	268,879	269,039	282,406	311,925	331,804	313,887
Office	8,317	5,424	5,924	5,693	6,049	6,905	8,052	9,761	8,781
Commercial [1]	1,456	898	1,396	1,710	1,505	1,936	2,334	2,738	2,070
Automotive	769	499	852	699	618	982	1,485	1,790	1,159
Parking	675	443	807	568	602	899	1,051	1,199	839
Warehouse	286	184	245	423	403	324	290	287	336
Health care	6,193	6,174	5,537	5,731	6,372	6,508	6,498	6,912	7,320
Hospital	4,789	4,762	4,276	4,172	4,409	4,726	4,019	4,210	4,825
Medical building	747	990	816	919	1,167	1,095	1,703	1,529	1,363
Special care	657	422	446	639	795	687	777	1,174	1,132
Educational [1]	71,948	61,176	65,782	69,907	73,992	77,168	85,154	90,359	80,924
Primary/secondary [1]	44,559	35,936	38,221	42,343	46,488	50,226	56,212	62,696	57,319
Elementary	13,171	11,887	10,538	12,820	14,362	15,850	16,126	18,164	17,369
Middle/junior high	7,029	6,781	7,520	8,867	9,557	10,138	10,706	11,813	10,066
High	24,055	16,475	19,765	19,917	21,429	22,772	27,828	31,396	28,669
Higher education [1]	24,384	22,722	25,116	25,004	24,882	24,375	25,971	24,483	20,304
Instructional	14,138	11,948	13,390	13,847	13,815	14,499	14,582	14,476	12,490
Parking	593	391	552	534	414	406	773	491	330
Administration	357	528	590	669	540	436	331	344	280
Dormitory	3,371	3,468	4,130	4,221	3,219	2,779	3,900	3,454	2,556
Library	662	279	684	464	511	562	469	401	357
Student union/cafeteria	1147	1412	1,306	1,306	1,590	1,505	1,619	1,247	913
Sports/recreation	2398	2,901	2,885	2,658	3,325	2,750	2,625	2,405	2,282
Infrastructure	1381	1,683	1,570	1,268	1,296	1,407	1,624	1,458	1,018
Other educational [1]	2,223	2,062	1,902	1,887	1,643	1,616	2,049	2,171	2,468
Library/archive	1386	1,079	1,144	1,325	990	1,004	1,392	1,596	1,922
Public safety [1]	7,586	6,414	5,859	5,842	6,216	7,090	8,065	9,366	8,334
Correctional	4,624	4,249	3,619	3,480	3,698	4,222	5,034	5,732	4,905
Detention	2,789	2,171	1,981	1,985	2,071	2,493	2,932	3,462	3,249
Police/sheriff	1836	2,079	1,638	1,496	1,626	1,730	2,102	2,270	1,656
Other public safety	2,962	2,165	2,240	2,362	2,518	2,868	3,031	3,634	3,429
Fire/rescue	1747	1,496	1,561	1,733	2,092	2,358	2,450	2,942	2,909
Amusement and recreation [1]	9,668	8,713	10,048	10,686	11,570	11,909	14,201	14,202	12,220
Sports	1,819	1,856	1,759	1,686	1,614	2,242	3,335	3,499	2,954
Performance/meeting center	1,841	1,780	1,587	1,741	1,926	2,580	3,489	3,203	2,311
Convention center	1,119	1,154	850	862	1,032	1,562	2,358	2,255	1,525
Social center	1,561	887	1,120	1,223	1,568	1,509	1,767	1,745	1,635
Neighborhood center	1395	774	1,055	1,040	1,338	1,219	1,516	1,478	1,323
Park/camp	4,259	4,070	5,441	5,795	6,348	5,412	5,115	5,453	5,130
Transportation	26,493	27,757	29,365	27,858	29,286	32,811	37,598	41,398	37,901
Air [1]	11,897	10,821	10,762	10,494	12,297	16,094	18,140	21,386	19,177
Passenger terminal	6,503	4,922	4,969	5,901	7,751	11,172	12,256	14,034	12,179
Runway	4,710	4,980	5,213	3,881	3,819	4,336	4,795	6,388	6,010
Land [1]	12,954	15,106	16,940	15,767	15,444	14,920	16,690	17,255	16,567
Passenger terminal	3,380	3666	4,584	4,494	3,744	3,154	2,180	1,216	1,050
Mass transit	6,447	7,161	7,842	7,067	7,726	7,824	10,399	11,435	10,967
Railroad	751	1695	1,666	1,175	1,169	1,486	1,844	2,576	2,471
Water	1,642	1,829	1,663	1,598	1,545	1,796	2,769	2,756	2,158
Dock/marina	1115	1360	1,233	1,261	1,215	1,405	2,498	2,572	2,013
Dry dock/marine terminal	527	469	430	337	331	392	271	184	145
Power [1]	10,770	10,732	10,307	8,511	5,401	4,612	7,115	7,121	7,963
Electrical	9,972	8,946	9,019	7,324	4,599	3,684	5,933	6,017	5,767
Distribution	3,253	3,120	2,623	2,912	2,586	2,253	4,382	4,700	4,999
Highway and street	81,309	84,014	90,810	92,126	88,290	90,405	97,520	100,809	98,837
Pavement	51,433	50,509	54,073	55,279	54,404	57,224	66,245	73,317	71,630
Lighting	1975	1,221	1,520	1,842	1,936	2,301	2,463	2,529	2,700
Retaining wall	1,250	878	1,071	873	819	1,451	1,273	1,515	1,468
Tunnel	810	1038	830	1,182	1,119	674	550	486	1,065
Bridge	24,222	29,234	31,765	31,031	28,935	27,412	25,794	21,253	20,712
Toll/weigh	214	137	210	310	292	312	273	246	219
Maintenance building	275	282	429	510	344	333	318	637	499
Rest facility/streetscape	1130	715	910	1,099	441	698	603	826	545
Sewage and waste disposal	24,555	21,870	23,403	23,169	22,415	23,219	25,044	26,437	27,152
Sewage/dry waste [1]	13,234	12,517	14,009	13,936	13,277	12,994	13,331	12,537	12,336
Plant	3,755	2,565	2,839	2,524	2,660	2,612	2,629	1,908	1,328
Line/pump station	9,375	9,815	10,986	11,174	10,427	10,220	10,551	10,475	10,717
Waste water	11,321	9,353	9,394	9,234	9,138	10,226	11,713	13,901	14,816
Plant	9,428	7,354	7,001	6,935	6,984	7,027	8,461	9,780	10,056
Line/drain	1,893	1,999	2,393	2,298	2,154	3,199	3,252	4,120	4,760
Water supply	14,420	12,731	12,760	13,623	13,701	14,855	15,613	18,010	18,249
Plant	5,683	4,221	4,432	4,373	5,077	5,105	5,206	5,665	5,470
Well	383	513	295	355	415	501	752	715	868
Line	6,246	5,816	6,098	6,264	5,865	6,654	7,189	8,096	8,913
Pump station	970	817	642	972	1,015	1,150	1,071	1,688	1,563
Reservoir	393	618	401	738	883	857	720	879	649
Tank/tower	744	747	892	922	446	587	676	968	786
Conservation and development [1]	2035	3,071	3,133	3,270	3,393	3,719	3,256	3,426	3,199
Dam/levee	783	1096	958	976	1,105	1,250	1,136	1,364	1,289
Breakwater/jetty	675	1098	1,405	1,479	1,171	1,255	1,181	1,249	1,257
Dredging	173	259	301	330	300	272	238	244	316

[1] Includes other types of construction, not shown separately.

Source: U.S. Census Bureau, "Construction Spending," <www.census.gov/construction/c30/c30index.html>, accessed August 2022.

Table 1008. Construction of New Privately Owned Housing Units Started: 1960 to 2021

[In thousands of units (1,252 represents 1,252,000). For composition of regions, see map inside front cover]

Year	Total	1 unit structures	Northeast	Midwest	South	West
1960	1,252	995	221	292	429	309
1970	1,434	813	218	294	612	311
1980	1,292	852	125	218	643	306
1990	1,193	895	131	253	479	329
1995	1,354	1,076	118	290	615	331
1996	1,477	1,161	132	322	662	361
1997	1,474	1,134	137	304	670	363
1998	1,617	1,271	149	331	743	395
1999	1,641	1,302	156	347	746	392
2000	1,569	1,231	155	318	714	383
2001	1,603	1,273	149	330	732	391
2002	1,705	1,359	158	350	782	416
2003	1,848	1,499	163	374	839	472
2004	1,956	1,611	175	356	909	516
2005	2,068	1,716	190	357	996	525
2006	1,801	1,465	167	280	910	444
2007	1,355	1,046	143	210	681	321
2008	906	622	121	135	453	196
2009	554	445	62	97	278	117
2010	587	471	72	98	298	120
2011	609	431	68	101	308	133
2012	781	535	80	128	398	175
2013	925	618	97	150	464	215
2014	1,003	648	110	163	496	235
2015	1,112	715	138	153	556	266
2016	1,174	782	116	182	585	291
2017	1,203	849	111	180	599	313
2018	1,250	876	111	173	630	336
2019	1,290	888	115	169	685	321
2020	1,380	991	112	192	736	341
2021	1,601	1,127	137	216	848	401

Source: U.S. Census Bureau, "New Residential Construction, Historical Data," <www.census.gov/construction/nrc/historical_data/>, accessed June 2022.

Table 1009. Characteristics of New Privately Owned Single-Family Houses Completed: 2000 to 2021

[Percent distribution, except as noted (1,242 represents 1,242,000). Data are shown as percent distribution of houses by each set of characteristics, for all houses completed (includes new houses completed, houses built for sale completed, contractor-built and owner-built houses completed, and houses completed for rent). Excludes houses for which the type of characteristic was not reported. Percents are computed using unrounded data]

Characteristic	2000	2010	2020	2021	Characteristic	2000	2010	2020	2021
Total houses (1,000)	1,242	496	912	970	Bedrooms	100	100	100	100
Construction type	100	100	100	100	2 or less	11	13	10	10
Site built	94	95	97	98	3	54	52	46	45
Modular	3	2	1	1	4 or more	35	35	44	46
Other	3	2	2	1	Bathrooms	100	100	100	100
Exterior wall material	100	100	100	100	1-1/2 or less	7	8	3	3
Brick	20	23	19	19	2	39	36	35	35
Wood	14	8	5	4	2-1/2 or more	34	32	28	30
Stucco	17	17	27	27	3 baths or more	20	25	34	33
Vinyl siding	39	36	25	26	Heating fuel	100	100	100	100
Fiber cement	(NA)	13	22	22	Gas	70	54	55	54
Other	8	2	2	2	Electricity	27	43	45	45
Floor area	100	100	100	100	Oil [3]	3	1	(NA)	(NA)
Under 1,400 sq. ft.	14	13	7	7	Other or none [3]	1	2	1	(Z)
1,400 to 1,799 sq. ft.	22	19	18	17	Heating system	100	100	100	100
1,800 to 2,399 sq. ft.	29	27	32	32	Forced air furnace	71	56	59	60
2,400 to 2,999 sq. ft.	17	18	21	21	Electric heat pump	23	38	39	38
3,000 to 3,999 sq. ft.	13	15	15	16	Other or none	6	5	2	2
4,000 or more	5	7	8	7	Central air-conditioning	100	100	100	100
Average (sq. ft.)	2,266	2,392	2,480	2,480	With	85	88	95	96
Median (sq. ft.)	2,057	2,169	2,261	2,273	Without	15	12	5	4
Number of stories	100	100	100	100	Fireplaces	100	100	100	100
1	47	47	50	49	No fireplace	40	51	63	64
2 or more [1]	52	53	50	51	1 or more	59	49	36	36
Foundation	100	100	100	100	Parking facilities	100	100	100	100
Full or partial basement	37	30	22	21	Garage	89	85	91	92
Slab and other [2]	46	52	65	66	Carport	1	1	1	1
Crawl space	17	18	12	12	No garage or carport	11	13	7	7

NA Not available. Z Less than .5%. [1] Includes houses with 1-1/2 and 2-1/2 stories and split-level houses. [2] Includes raised supports such as pilings and piers, and other types. [3] Beginning in 2014, heating oil and kerosene are included in Other heating fuel.

Source: U.S. Census Bureau, "Annual Characteristics of New Housing," <www.census.gov/construction/chars>, accessed August 2022.

Table 1010. Construction Materials—Producer Price Indexes: 2010 to 2021

[1982=100, except as noted. This index, more formally known as the special commodity grouping index for construction materials, covers materials incorporated as integral parts of a building or normally installed during construction and not readily removable. Excludes consumer durables such as kitchen ranges, refrigerators, etc. For discussion of producer price indexes, see text, Section 14]

Commodity	2010	2015	2016	2017	2018	2019	2020	2021
Construction materials	**194.5**	**213.6**	**213.9**	**221.6**	**235.7**	**235.7**	**239.2**	**303.4**
Architectural coatings	264.1	302.3	303.0	306.1	320.7	343.5	352.6	382.0
Plastic construction products	190.9	213.1	211.9	217.3	226.1	229.4	233.5	285.5
Softwood cut stock and dimension	206.0	199.7	200.0	214.2	228.1	204.1	235.6	363.9
Softwood lumber, not edge worked [1]	85.8	104.9	108.6	121.9	131.0	114.4	154.1	217.7
Softwood lumber, made from purchased lumber [1]	111.5	128.3	130.5	152.3	171.4	169.2	188.3	267.0
Hardwood cut stock and dimension	186.2	246.6	239.8	250.9	262.9	256.0	255.6	342.2
Hardwood flooring [2]	161.2	195.8	188.5	179.1	184.7	193.8	188.7	218.7
Millwork	207.0	237.2	240.6	247.6	259.5	263.5	274.5	318.6
Softwood veneer and plywood	197.1	234.5	214.5	234.8	274.5	222.8	270.6	449.6
Hardwood veneer and plywood [3]	103.6	108.6	112.9	115.3	123.5	123.9	125.2	140.4
Prefabricated wood buildings and components [4]	215.6	240.4	243.3	251.6	263.7	270.2	277.7	328.5
Building paper and building board mill products	168.4	186.3	201.0	221.3	222.9	200.1	260.5	411.3
Pressure and soil pipe and fittings, cast iron	348.4	392.9	396.4	384.4	398.5	403.5	410.8	466.4
Hot rolled steel sheet and strip, incl. tin mill products [5]	150.7	115.9	107.2	126.9	149.6	136.0	113.8	287.4
Hot rolled steel bars, plates, and structural shapes [5]	192.9	185.2	164.5	178.7	205.9	205.2	187.0	257.8
Aluminum extruded and drawn pipe and tube [6]	98.1	95.6	90.2	102.2	111.2	107.3	105.0	118.9
Builders' hardware [7]	219.4	244.5	246.8	251.0	256.7	264.0	269.3	291.6
Plumbing fixtures and fittings	231.4	257.1	257.8	262.4	270.2	281.6	287.9	296.0
Heating equipment	221.5	248.2	253.1	255.9	266.5	279.2	284.0	312.4
Metal doors, sash, and trim	208.1	233.6	235.5	243.1	260.1	269.8	276.4	322.2
Sheet metal products	191.0	199.3	197.6	202.3	212.7	218.2	217.0	259.5
Fabricated structural metal bar joists and concrete reinforcing bars	176.1	190.5	194.0	199.5	216.4	214.9	215.4	289.1
Fabricated metal pipe, tube, and fittings [8]	(NA)	101.5	100.3	100.9	104.9	106.0	105.9	125.4
Residential electric lighting fixtures, except portable [9]	121.1	130.4	131.5	130.2	133.9	145.2	149.8	157.7
Elevators, escalators, and other lifts	133.8	145.4	147.1	151.2	155.0	161.7	164.2	171.5
Air purification equipment/industrial and commercial fans and blowers	192.2	217.3	218.4	220.9	228.6	238.4	241.3	254.1
Plumbing and heating valves (low pressure) [10]	249.5	292.6	296.9	310.8	(NA)	(NA)	(NA)	(NA)
Electric switches [11]	124.4	153.4	151.0	150.8	149.9	150.4	152.9	162.1
Wire connectors for electrical circuitry [11]	132.1	138.8	132.8	134.6	137.7	139.4	141.0	151.6
Current-carrying wiring devices not elsewhere classified [12]	105.2	111.3	108.8	109.3	111.3	112.7	111.8	117.6
Noncurrent-carrying electrical conduit and fittings [6,13]	119.2	134.1	134.1	136.1	141.8	141.5	148.5	236.0
Other noncurrent-carrying wiring devices [6,14]	126.4	135.6	136.1	138.1	141.7	147.9	151.1	167.0
Carpets and rugs	167.5	184.1	183.9	184.5	193.1	196.0	194.8	201.9
Resilient (hard surface) floor coverings	203.2	(NA)	(NA)	232.8	236.8	242.5	243.4	248.6
Flat glass (float, sheet, and plate process)	88.2	91.0	97.3	98.5	105.3	107.1	107.2	115.9
Construction sand, gravel, and crushed stone	262.2	299.9	312.6	323.2	334.7	348.7	364.3	378.8
Cement, hydraulic	193.5	223.4	235.2	246.0	252.1	258.1	260.7	271.0
Concrete products	210.6	239.4	247.0	254.1	263.7	271.7	279.1	292.9
Clay construction products excluding refractories	179.4	182.4	184.7	184.5	187.7	189.6	192.7	199.4
Prepared asphalt and tar roofing and siding products	218.9	223.2	221.6	220.5	233.8	243.9	249.2	277.7
Roofing asphalts, pitches, coatings, and cement	227.5	234.3	201.3	210.5	221.4	224.7	222.8	230.7
Gypsum products	206.6	293.1	297.1	322.9	342.6	320.9	322.0	374.3
Insulation materials	146.6	182.6	187.8	189.1	194.7	193.3	195.4	217.3
Paving mixtures and blocks	279.4	313.0	294.6	293.4	313.4	322.6	312.9	324.2
Cut stone and stone products [4]	147.8	156.8	161.6	163.3	168.1	174.9	179.8	191.7

NA Not available. [1] December 2003=100. [2] June 1984=100. [3] December 2005=100. [4] June 1984=100. [5] June 1982=100. [6] December 2004=100. [7] Includes lock units, key blanks, door and window hardware, cabinet hardware, etc. [8] December 2011=100. [9] June 1998=100. [10] December 1982=100. [11] December 1999=100. [12] June 2006=100. [13] Includes plastic conduit and fittings. [14] Includes boxes, covers, bar hangers, etc.

Source: U.S. Bureau of Labor Statistics, "Producer Price Indexes," <www.bls.gov/ppi/data.htm>, accessed June 2022.

Table 1011. Subsidized Apartments Completed by Type of Subsidy: 2015 to 2020

[Data shown for rental apartments in buildings with five units or more. Detail may not sum to totals because of rounding and because more than one subsidy could be selected per unit. Based on a sample and subject to sampling variability; see source for details]

Completions and type of subsidy	2015	2016	2017	2018	2019	2020
Total apartments completed	310,000	310,100	346,800	335,600	342,900	364,700
Subsidized apartments completed	**29,160**	**20,160**	**35,200**	**31,910**	**36,840**	**40,990**
Percent subsidized	9.4	6.5	10.1	9.5	10.7	11.2
Subsidized by type: [1]						
Section 8	10,680	6,010	12,080	16,570	10,090	17,260
Housing for Elderly Direct Loan Program	1,163	1,298	(S)	1,790	1,536	(S)
Low Income Housing Tax Credit (LHITC)	19,190	13,310	21,630	15,020	24,930	22,680
Federal tax exempt multifamily bond financing	(S)	1,003	2,223	(S)	2,870	(S)
Other subsidized programs	6,881	6,442	10,080	9,871	10,500	11,420

S Data estimates do not meet publication standards. [1] Respondents were instructed to select all subsidies that applied to the building.

Source: U.S. Census Bureau, "Survey of Market Absorption of New Multifamily Units, Table Creator," <www.census.gov/programs-surveys/soma/data/tools.html>, accessed April 2022.

Table 1012. Housing Starts and Average Length of Time to Completion of New Privately Owned Single-Family Homes: 1990 to 2021

[895 represents 895,000. For buildings started in permit-issuing places]

Year	Total [1]	Purpose of construction			Region [2]			
		Built for sale	Contractor built	Owner built	North-east	Mid-west	South	West
STARTS (1,000)								
1990	895	529	196	147	104	193	371	226
1995	1,076	712	199	133	102	234	485	256
1999	1,302	912	208	142	126	289	580	308
2000	1,231	871	195	128	118	260	556	297
2001	1,273	919	186	129	111	269	590	303
2002	1,359	999	198	125	118	277	628	336
2003	1,499	1,120	205	127	116	309	686	388
2004	1,611	1,240	198	130	128	306	743	433
2005	1,716	1,358	197	129	138	306	831	441
2006	1,465	1,121	189	119	118	235	757	356
2007	1,046	760	151	104	93	171	540	242
2008	622	408	107	74	63	102	324	133
2009	445	297	83	51	44	76	232	93
2010	471	306	83	55	52	79	247	93
2011	431	287	74	47	41	74	229	86
2012	535	373	82	47	46	92	283	114
2013	618	457	91	45	55	102	326	134
2014	648	460	110	50	51	106	346	145
2015	715	526	109	50	55	107	387	165
2016	782	579	116	49	60	121	421	179
2017	849	635	116	55	62	130	453	204
2018	876	660	119	51	64	123	466	222
2019	888	669	124	55	57	120	497	214
2020	990	764	123	53	60	136	553	241
2021	1,126	868	140	59	67	148	643	267
COMPLETION (months)								
1990	6.4	5.9	5.3	10.3	9.3	5.6	5.7	6.9
1995	5.9	5.2	5.8	9.5	7.4	6.0	5.4	6.0
1999	6.1	5.5	6.4	9.2	7.0	6.4	5.7	6.3
2000	6.2	5.6	6.5	9.2	7.5	6.4	5.9	6.0
2001	6.2	5.6	7.0	9.2	7.6	6.5	5.8	6.3
2002	6.1	5.5	6.6	9.6	7.3	6.4	5.6	6.2
2003	6.2	5.5	6.8	9.9	7.5	6.7	5.7	6.2
2004	6.2	5.7	7.0	9.1	7.3	6.7	5.8	6.3
2005	6.4	5.9	7.6	9.8	7.7	6.6	6.0	6.8
2006	6.9	6.3	7.8	10.7	8.3	7.1	6.3	7.4
2007	7.1	6.5	7.9	10.2	8.5	7.4	6.5	8.0
2008	7.7	6.8	8.5	11.1	8.9	8.2	6.7	9.0
2009	7.9	6.6	8.7	11.9	10.7	8.2	6.7	9.0
2010	6.9	5.8	7.6	11.0	10.1	7.3	5.9	7.3
2011	6.6	5.4	7.7	10.8	8.9	6.9	5.9	6.8
2012	6.0	4.9	7.3	10.5	8.5	6.5	5.2	6.1
2013	6.0	5.0	7.5	11.0	8.4	6.7	5.5	5.6
2014	6.2	5.4	7.5	10.8	8.6	6.9	5.7	6.2
2015	6.3	5.5	7.6	11.1	8.9	7.0	5.8	6.1
2016	6.6	5.8	7.8	11.5	9.6	6.9	6.0	6.7
2017	6.5	5.7	8.1	11.2	9.5	7.2	5.9	6.7
2018	6.7	5.9	8.4	11.4	9.3	7.5	6.0	7.1
2019	7.0	6.1	8.9	12.3	11.1	7.7	6.1	7.7
2020	6.8	5.9	8.8	11.8	10.7	7.4	5.9	7.5
2021	7.2	6.5	9.4	12.1	10.7	8.0	6.5	7.6

[1] Includes units built for rent not shown separately. [2] For composition of regions, see map, inside front cover.

Source: U.S. Census Bureau, "New Residential Construction," <www.census.gov/construction/nrc/index.html>, accessed June 2022.

Table 1013. Price Indexes of New Single-Family Houses Sold by Region: 1970 to 2021

[2005=100. Based on kinds of homes sold in 2005. Includes value of the lot. For composition of regions, see map, inside front cover]

Year	Total	North-east	Midwest	South	West	Year	Total	North-east	Midwest	South	West
1970	14.9	13.4	17.9	18.2	10.2	2007	104.9	101.5	102.8	107.4	102.6
1980	38.9	30.2	41.2	44.4	31.9	2008	99.5	100.8	98.9	103.7	92.7
1990	55.7	58.0	58.6	60.6	46.2	2009	95.1	97.1	96.0	101.1	84.8
1995	64.3	62.3	70.9	70.1	52.7	2010	95.0	101.1	96.9	99.5	85.4
1996	66.0	63.2	72.5	71.2	55.3	2011	94.3	100.0	97.8	99.6	83.1
1997	67.5	65.9	74.3	72.7	56.5	2012	97.6	102.1	101.5	102.7	86.3
1998	69.2	66.1	76.0	74.4	58.4	2013	104.7	108.2	105.3	110.1	94.7
1999	72.8	69.1	79.5	78.1	62.0	2014	110.2	115.2	112.6	115.4	99.5
2000	75.6	73.0	83.5	80.6	64.4	2015	112.9	115.7	116.4	118.3	101.9
2001	77.9	76.7	84.4	82.8	67.1	2016	120.4	121.0	118.7	125.1	113.3
2002	81.4	80.2	86.1	86.3	71.5	2017	126.8	130.5	126.5	131.9	117.9
2003	86.0	84.3	90.6	89.4	78.2	2018	132.4	127.6	128.9	136.2	128.9
2004	92.8	91.6	96.7	94.4	88.2	2019	135.5	127.7	134.1	141.9	127.5
2005	100.0	100.0	100.0	100.0	100.0	2020	140.0	133.1	140.7	145.3	132.2
2006	104.7	102.6	102.9	105.4	105.2	2021	161.3	152.0	159.2	169.1	151.7

Source: U.S. Census Bureau, "Construction Price Indexes," <www.census.gov/construction/cpi/>, accessed July 2022.

Table 1014. New Privately Owned Single-Family Houses Sold by Region and Type of Financing, 2005 to 2021, and by Sales-Price Group, 2021

[In thousands (1,283 represents 1,283,000). Based on a national probability sample of monthly interviews with builders or owners of single-family houses for which building permits have been issued or, for nonpermit areas, on which construction has started. Components may not add to total due to rounding. For details, see source and Appendix III. For composition of regions, see map inside front cover]

Year and sales-price group	Total sold	Region				Financing type			
		Northeast	Midwest	South	West	Conventional[1]	FHA insured[2]	VA guaranteed[3]	Cash
2005	1,283	81	205	638	358	1,150	51	28	52
2010	323	31	45	173	74	189	81	35	19
2015	501	24	61	286	130	348	81	42	30
2016	561	32	69	318	142	396	88	48	29
2017	613	40	72	339	163	442	86	49	36
2018	617	32	76	348	160	461	74	43	39
2019	683	30	72	399	182	469	119	52	42
2020	822	37	93	474	218	570	153	63	37
2021	**771**	**36**	**86**	**453**	**197**	**571**	**106**	**45**	**48**
Under $125,000	1	(Z)	–	1	–	(Z)	(Z)	(Z)	1
$125,000 to $149,999	2	–	(Z)	1	–	1	(Z)	(Z)	(Z)
$150,000 to $199,999	13	(Z)	2	10	(Z)	8	3	1	2
$200,000 to $249,999	58	1	9	45	3	27	22	2	6
$250,000 to $299,999	107	1	20	81	4	60	35	6	5
$300,000 to $399,999	210	5	24	144	37	152	33	13	12
$400,000 to $499,999	154	7	17	81	49	125	9	12	8
$500,000 to $749,999	158	11	10	64	73	136	3	11	9
$750,000 and over	69	12	3	24	30	62	(Z)	1	6

– Represents zero. Z Less than 500 units. [1] Includes houses reporting other types of financing, not shown separately. [2] Federal Housing Administration. [3] U.S. Department of Veterans Affairs.

Source: U.S. Census Bureau, "Annual Characteristics of New Housing," <www.census.gov/construction/chars>, accessed August 2022.

Table 1015. Median Sales Price of New Privately Owned Single-Family Houses Sold by Region: 1980 to 2021

[In dollars. For definition of median, see Guide to Tabular Presentation. For composition of regions, see map inside front cover. Based on a national probability sample of monthly interviews with builders or owners of single-family houses selected from building permits and a canvassing of areas not requiring permits. For more details, see source]

Year	U.S.	Northeast	Midwest	South	West	Year	U.S.	Northeast	Midwest	South	West
1980	64,600	69,500	63,400	59,600	72,300	2015	294,200	442,800	276,700	271,500	348,500
1985	84,300	103,300	80,300	75,000	92,600	2016	307,800	428,300	277,100	281,400	367,700
1990	122,900	159,000	107,900	99,000	147,500	2017	323,100	490,400	284,400	291,200	390,000
1995	133,900	180,000	134,000	124,500	141,000	2018	326,400	484,600	290,900	294,600	410,600
2000	169,000	227,400	169,700	148,000	196,400	2019	321,500	482,500	289,200	289,000	408,000
2005	240,900	343,800	216,900	197,300	332,600	2020	336,900	470,700	298,100	299,000	412,600
2010	221,800	329,900	197,700	196,800	259,300	2021	397,100	560,900	339,900	355,900	510,400

Source: U.S. Census Bureau, "Annual Characteristics of New Housing," <www.census.gov/construction/chars/>, accessed August 2022.

Table 1016. New Manufactured (Mobile) Homes Placed for Residential Use and Average Sales Price by Region: 1990 to 2021

[195.4 represents 195,400. A mobile home is a moveable dwelling, 8 feet or more wide and 40 feet or more long, designed to be towed on its own chassis, with transportation gear integral to the unit when it leaves the factory, and without need of permanent foundation. Excluded are travel trailers, motor homes, and modular housing. Data are based on a probability sample and subject to sampling variability; see source. For composition of regions, see map inside front cover]

Year	Units placed (1,000)					Average sales price (dollars)				
	Total	Northeast	Midwest	South	West	U.S.	Northeast	Midwest	South	West
1990	195.4	18.8	37.7	108.4	30.6	27,800	30,000	27,000	24,500	39,300
1995	319.4	15.0	57.5	203.2	43.7	35,300	35,800	35,700	33,300	44,100
2000	280.9	14.9	48.7	178.7	38.6	46,400	47,000	47,900	44,300	54,100
2005	122.9	9.2	17.1	68.1	28.5	62,600	67,000	60,600	55,700	79,900
2008	80.5	5.0	8.2	54.0	13.3	64,700	68,400	65,700	59,600	84,900
2009	54.5	3.5	5.3	37.8	7.9	63,100	61,600	65,400	59,300	81,500
2010	50.7	3.8	5.8	34.6	6.6	62,800	65,200	60,700	60,000	79,000
2011	47.6	3.3	6.3	31.5	6.5	60,500	62,700	60,800	58,400	70,600
2012	52.8	3.9	7.9	34.4	6.6	62,200	63,400	60,900	60,100	75,300
2013	56.3	4.0	7.5	37.4	7.5	64,000	66,500	62,900	61,200	79,100
2014[1]	44.1	3.0	6.8	27.5	6.8	65,300	67,900	60,600	63,000	80,700
2015[1]	45.6	3.1	6.6	28.5	7.5	68,000	72,100	60,800	65,100	88,200
2016[1]	51.5	3.1	8.2	32.3	7.8	70,600	77,600	61,500	68,500	88,500
2017[1]	53.9	3.6	7.7	34.9	7.8	71,900	78,400	65,400	68,200	97,600
2018[1]	55.1	4.0	8.6	33.8	8.7	78,500	80,100	72,100	75,700	99,000
2019[1]	62.2	4.0	9.0	40.1	9.0	81,900	81,300	72,100	80,600	99,400
2020[1]	60.5	3.5	8.1	41.0	7.9	87,000	85,200	76,700	85,800	106,000
2021[1,2]	66.8	4.4	11.4	41.4	9.5	108,100	100,300	96,400	108,100	123,700

[1] Beginning 2014, data not comparable to prior years due to a change in methodology. See source for details. [2] Beginning in 2021, placements include homes that are leased or sold and homes placed on site but not yet sold or leased. Prior to 2021, placements represented units that were sold and placed.

Source: U.S. Census Bureau, "Manufactured Housing Survey (MHS) Tables," <www.census.gov/data/tables/time-series/econ/mhs/annual-data.html>, accessed August 2022.

Table 1017. Existing Single-Family Homes Sold and Price by Region: 1990 to 2021

[2,914 represents 2,914,000. Includes existing detached single-family homes and townhomes. Based on data (adjusted and aggregated to regional and national totals) reported by participating real estate multiple listing services. For definition of median, see Guide to Tabular Presentation. See Table 1019 for data on condominiums and cooperatives. For composition of regions, see map inside front cover]

Year	Homes sold (1,000)					Median sales price (dollars)				
	U.S.	Northeast	Midwest	South	West	U.S.	Northeast	Midwest	South	West
1990	2,914	513	804	1,008	589	97,300	146,200	76,700	86,300	141,200
1995	3,519	615	940	1,212	752	117,000	146,500	96,500	99,200	153,600
1996	3,797	656	986	1,283	872	122,600	147,800	102,800	105,000	160,200
1997	3,964	683	1,004	1,356	921	129,000	152,400	108,900	111,300	169,000
1998	4,495	745	1,129	1,592	1,029	136,000	157,100	116,300	118,000	179,500
1999	4,649	728	1,145	1,704	1,072	141,200	160,700	121,600	122,100	189,400
2000	4,603	715	1,116	1,707	1,065	147,300	161,200	125,600	130,300	199,200
2001	4,735	710	1,154	1,795	1,076	156,600	169,400	132,300	139,600	211,700
2002	4,974	730	1,217	1,872	1,155	167,600	190,100	138,300	149,700	234,300
2003	5,446	770	1,323	2,073	1,280	180,200	220,300	143,700	159,700	254,700
2004	5,958	821	1,389	2,310	1,438	195,200	254,400	151,500	171,800	289,100
2005	6,180	838	1,411	2,457	1,474	219,000	281,600	168,300	181,100	340,300
2006	5,677	787	1,314	2,352	1,224	221,900	280,300	164,800	183,700	350,500
2007	4,398	587	1,091	1,819	901	217,900	288,100	161,400	178,800	342,500
2008	3,665	471	882	1,439	873	196,600	271,500	150,500	169,400	276,100
2009	3,870	480	918	1,460	1,012	172,100	243,200	142,900	155,000	215,400
2010	3,708	465	859	1,426	958	173,100	243,900	140,800	153,700	220,700
2011	3,787	449	863	1,471	1,004	166,200	237,500	135,800	149,300	204,500
2012	4,128	492	1,002	1,605	1,029	177,200	237,200	143,700	158,400	234,300
2013	4,484	540	1,122	1,775	1,047	197,400	248,900	155,700	174,200	276,400
2014	4,344	533	1,060	1,789	962	208,900	252,200	164,200	182,900	294,400
2015	4,646	576	1,162	1,885	1,023	223,900	262,500	175,500	196,400	319,100
2016	4,838	617	1,222	1,955	1,044	235,500	265,400	184,400	209,200	342,900
2017	4,892	615	1,222	1,989	1,066	248,800	275,700	196,200	222,700	369,400
2018	4,742	581	1,192	1,972	997	261,600	289,200	201,700	231,600	388,600
2019	4,765	581	1,183	2,016	985	274,600	301,900	214,500	241,900	405,200
2020	5,066	604	1,264	2,175	1,023	300,200	341,700	235,400	265,100	451,500
2021	5,413	633	1,313	2,358	1,109	357,100	394,100	263,300	317,500	558,800

Source: NATIONAL ASSOCIATION OF REALTORS ®. See also <www.nar.realtor/research-and-statistics>.

Table 1018. Median Sales Price of Existing Single-Family Homes by Selected Metropolitan Area: 2020 and 2021

[In thousands of dollars (300.2 represents $300,200). Covers existing detached single-family homes and townhouses. Areas are metropolitan statistical areas defined by Office of Management and Budget, though in some areas an exact match is not possible from available data]

Metropolitan area	2020	2021	Metropolitan area	2020	2021
United States, total	**300.2**	**353.6**	New Orleans-Metairie, LA	240.5	268.1
Allentown-Bethlehem-Easton, PA-NJ	234.9	266.4	New York-Jersey City-White Plains, NY-NJ	442.4	535.8
Anaheim-Santa Ana-Irvine, CA	900.0	1,099.0	New York-Newark-Jersey City, NY-NJ-PA	469.1	561.0
Atlanta-Sandy Springs-Marietta, GA	260.8	317.2	Oklahoma City, OK	174.9	194.2
Atlantic City-Hammonton, NJ	247.2	293.3	Omaha-Council Bluffs, NE-IA	220.6	242.0
Baltimore-Columbia-Towson, MD	328.5	358.1	Orlando-Kissimmee-Sanford, FL	301.6	356.9
Boston-Cambridge-Newton, MA-NH	563.7	642.2	Philadelphia-Camden-		
Boulder, CO	645.9	782.7	Wilmington, PA-NJ-DE-MD	272.9	305.0
Bridgeport-Stamford-Norwalk, CT	544.0	630.0	Phoenix-Mesa-Scottsdale, AZ	333.0	415.4
Charleston-North Charleston, SC	324.4	375.2	Portland-South Portland, ME	356.2	418.1
Chicago-Naperville-Elgin, IL-IN-WI	287.6	330.4	Portland-Vancouver-Hillsboro, OR-WA	451.0	536.4
Cincinnati, OH-KY-IN	208.9	243.4	Providence-Warwick, RI-MA	347.3	396.1
Cleveland-Elyria, OH	179.5	198.8	Raleigh, NC	325.2	392.8
Colorado Springs, CO	361.7	432.9	Reno, NV	440.8	531.8
Dallas-Fort Worth-Arlington, TX	287.2	336.7	Richmond, VA	303.4	342.8
Deltona-Daytona Beach-Ormond Beach, FL	244.9	290.0	Riverside-San Bernardino-Ontario, CA	422.6	510.0
Denver-Aurora-Lakewood, CO	492.7	607.1	Sacramento-Roseville-Arden-Arcade, CA	421.0	500.0
Des Moines-West Des Moines, IA	229.6	258.2	Saint Louis, MO-IL	205.8	226.1
Eugene-Springfield, OR	354.9	417.1	Salem, OR	353.6	411.1
Hartford-West Hartford-East Hartford, CT	264.5	297.8	Salt Lake City, UT	391.0	486.1
Houston-The Woodlands-Sugar Land, TX	263.8	304.1	San Diego-Carlsbad, CA	710.0	830.0
Indianapolis-Carmel-Anderson, IN	227.6	260.5	San Francisco-Oakland-Hayward, CA	1,100.0	1,320.0
Las Vegas-Henderson-Paradise, NV	331.0	397.0	San Jose-Sunnyvale-Santa Clara, CA	1,385.0	1,640.0
Little Rock-North Little Rock-Conway, AR	166.9	184.6	Seattle-Tacoma-Bellevue, WA	596.9	698.6
Los Angeles-Long Beach-Glendale, CA	673.1	801.3	Tampa-St. Petersburg-Clearwater, FL	272.0	330.0
Louisville/Jefferson County, KY-IN	212.1	235.6	Trenton, NJ	300.0	353.7
Madison, WI	326.4	361.5	Tucson, AZ	265.1	331.2
Memphis, TN-MS-AR	221.2	248.7	Urban Honolulu, HI	851.5	996.2
Miami-Fort Lauderdale-West Palm Beach, FL	398.0	480.0	Virginia Beach-Norfolk-		
Milwaukee-Waukesha-West Allis, WI	291.3	319.0	Newport News, VA-NC	275.0	285.0
Minneapolis-St. Paul-Bloomington, MN-WI	315.2	354.8	Washington-Arlington-		
New Haven-Milford, CT	265.9	300.0	Alexandria, DC-VA-MD-WV	475.4	544.3

Source: NATIONAL ASSOCIATION OF REALTORS ®. See also <www.nar.realtor/research-and-statistics>.

Table 1019. Existing Apartment Condominiums and Cooperatives—Units Sold and Median Sales Price by Region: 1990 to 2021

[272 represents 272,000. Data shown here reflect revisions from prior estimates. For definition of median, see Guide to Tabular Presentation. For composition of regions, see map inside front cover]

Year	Units sold (1,000)					Median sales price (dollars)				
	U.S.	Northeast	Midwest	South	West	U.S.	Northeast	Midwest	South	West
1990	272	73	55	80	64	86,900	107,500	70,200	64,200	114,600
1991	261	76	55	75	55	87,500	104,600	73,900	65,600	114,500
1992	282	88	61	77	56	87,700	100,600	79,000	66,600	117,400
1993	312	98	66	89	59	86,000	96,800	78,900	66,500	112,000
1994	343	108	68	101	66	88,800	97,100	86,200	66,700	118,600
1995	333	108	66	96	63	89,000	92,500	90,700	67,800	114,800
1996	370	120	72	105	73	92,600	95,100	95,200	70,600	119,800
1997	407	134	79	111	83	97,300	98,600	99,100	73,300	128,900
1998	470	157	92	126	95	102,500	100,900	106,400	76,800	137,700
1999	534	182	102	145	105	110,100	109,800	114,600	80,700	143,900
2000	571	197	106	160	108	114,000	108,500	121,700	84,200	149,100
2001	601	203	116	174	108	125,600	121,200	134,800	93,200	160,400
2002	657	221	129	193	114	144,900	143,500	148,600	109,900	187,000
2003	732	250	146	211	125	168,500	178,100	162,600	126,900	222,400
2004	820	292	161	230	137	197,100	214,100	181,000	156,600	258,000
2005	896	331	177	245	143	223,900	245,100	189,100	187,300	283,800
2006	801	299	169	211	122	221,900	249,700	190,900	184,000	264,700
2007	624	126	100	236	162	226,300	256,100	195,200	185,100	263,300
2008	459	103	71	164	121	209,800	252,500	188,200	166,800	218,500
2009	464	105	58	180	121	175,600	232,800	157,100	132,700	162,100
2010	474	95	53	202	124	171,700	242,200	150,500	118,500	154,700
2011	477	89	52	210	126	165,100	237,700	129,000	107,800	176,000
2012	528	104	66	229	129	173,700	240,100	127,800	123,900	196,700
2013	603	118	79	265	141	194,900	250,200	138,300	147,900	249,200
2014	591	112	76	262	141	204,300	254,900	149,300	154,700	273,300
2015	608	115	78	266	149	210,700	249,300	157,900	162,900	294,500
2016	614	116	82	263	153	220,700	256,600	166,200	172,600	321,300
2017	619	116	80	271	152	234,300	271,700	175,200	183,800	345,600
2018	601	110	77	273	141	241,000	284,600	177,600	184,500	361,500
2019	579	106	72	270	131	249,500	294,900	184,400	193,500	369,900
2020	578	103	74	275	126	266,300	313,700	192,300	210,900	390,200
2021	707	124	86	347	150	302,200	344,900	216,700	253,400	448,000

Source: NATIONAL ASSOCIATION OF REALTORS ®. See also <www.nar.realtor/research-and-statistics>.

Table 1020. New Unfurnished Apartments Completed and Rented in 3 Months by Region: 2015 to 2020

[268.3 represents 268,300. Structures with five or more units, privately financed, nonsubsidized, unfurnished rental apartments. Based on sample and subject to sampling variability; see source for details. For composition of regions, see map, inside front cover]

Year and rent	Number (1,000)					Percent rented in 3 months				
	U.S.	North-east	Midwest	South	West	U.S.	North-east	Midwest	South	West
2015	268.3	32.0	47.4	117.8	71.1	60	63	67	53	66
2016	266.3	30.5	41.0	128.1	66.7	55	49	56	51	64
2017	294.8	42.2	43.9	138.9	69.9	54	55	56	51	61
2018	277.8	36.3	39.0	125.5	77.1	54	49	55	53	59
2019	279.8	35.6	39.7	120.4	84.1	56	65	55	53	56
2020	**301.4**	**23.0**	**48.5**	**149.1**	**80.8**	**51**	**78**	**47**	**50**	**49**
Less than $850	11.2	(S)	(S)	8.9	(S)	81	(S)	68	80	100
$850 to $1,049	21.8	(S)	7.5	9.9	4.2	66	95	74	54	80
$1,050 to $1,249	34.8	(S)	7.6	21.8	5.2	54	90	52	52	65
$1,250 to $1,449	49.5	1.2	9.0	29.7	9.6	51	76	52	49	56
$1,450 to $1,649	41.4	1.2	5.4	25.3	9.4	50	73	40	49	56
$1,650 to $1,849	34.0	1.9	3.9	19.8	8.4	51	77	36	50	53
$1,850 to $2,409	22.3	2.4	3.2	10.8	5.9	49	80	41	43	52
$2,050 to $2,249	17.2	3.0	2.8	5.8	5.6	47	74	28	43	46
$2,250 to $2,449	14.3	2.1	2.1	5.5	4.6	43	71	25	42	40
$2,450 to $2,699	11.5	2.1	1.5	3.5	4.4	46	81	27	31	47
$2,700 to $2,999	10.9	2.5	1.3	2.6	4.5	47	73	24	42	42
$3,000 or more	32.5	5.7	3.1	5.5	18.2	39	81	28	31	29
Median asking rent (dol.)	1,611	2,332	1,428	1,483	1,946	(X)	(X)	(X)	(X)	(X)

X Not applicable. S Data withheld because they did not meet publication standards.

Source: U.S. Census Bureau, "Survey of Market Absorption of New Multifamily Units, Table Creator," <www.census.gov/programs-surveys/soma/data/tools.html>, accessed April 2022.

Table 1021. Total Housing Inventory for the United States: 2000 to 2021

[In thousands (116,264 represents 116,264,000), except percent. Based on the Current Population Survey/Housing Vacancy Survey and subject to sampling error; see source and Appendix III for details]

Item	2000	2005	2010	2015	2016	2017	2018	2019	2020	2021
All housing units.................	**116,264**	**125,363**	**131,810**	**135,201**	**136,170**	**137,221**	**138,347**	**139,511**	**140,725**	**141,947**
Vacant..........................	13,680	15,880	18,908	17,420	17,379	17,381	16,980	16,749	14,879	15,347
Year-round vacant..................	10,315	12,060	14,422	13,025	13,017	13,209	12,989	12,895	11,298	11,627
For rent.......................	2,980	3,763	4,322	3,292	3,242	3,398	3,231	3,181	2,854	2,865
For sale only...................	1,088	1,468	2,000	1,421	1,349	1,257	1,191	1,114	838	726
Rented or sold..................	935	1,073	915	1,083	1,059	1,163	1,107	1,091	922	1,055
Held off market.................	5,313	5,755	7,182	7,228	7,367	7,393	7,459	7,508	6,683	6,981
Occasional use..................	1,901	1,909	2,264	2,019	2,104	2,182	2,114	2,158	1,984	2,006
Usual residence elsewhere......	1,050	1,142	1,266	1,355	1,452	1,354	1,365	1,344	1,116	1,198
Other.........................	2,363	2,703	3,654	3,853	3,812	3,856	3,979	4,006	3,583	3,777
Seasonal [1].......................	3,364	3,820	4,485	4,396	4,361	4,170	3,990	3,854	3,581	3,720
Total occupied........................	102,584	109,484	112,902	117,781	118,790	119,842	121,367	122,762	125,846	126,600
Owner...........................	69,223	75,411	75,462	74,983	75,343	76,533	78,157	79,252	83,842	82,874
Renter...........................	33,362	34,073	37,441	42,797	43,447	43,309	43,210	43,510	42,004	43,727
PERCENT DISTRIBUTION										
All housing units....................	100.0	100.0	100.0	100.0	100.0	100.0	100.0	100.0	100.0	100.0
Vacant.............................	11.8	12.7	14.3	12.9	12.8	12.7	12.3	12.0	10.6	10.8
Total occupied......................	88.2	87.3	85.7	87.1	87.2	87.3	87.7	88.0	89.4	89.2
Owner.............................	59.5	60.2	57.3	55.5	55.3	55.8	56.5	56.8	59.6	58.4
Renter.............................	28.7	27.2	28.4	31.7	31.9	31.6	31.2	31.2	29.8	30.8

[1] Includes vacant seasonal mobile homes.

Source: U.S. Census Bureau, "Housing Vacancies and Home Ownership, Historical Tables," <www.census.gov/housing/hvs/index.html>, accessed March 2022.

Table 1022. Occupied Housing Inventory by Age of Householder: 2000 to 2021

[In thousands (102,584 represents 102,584,000). Based on the Current Population Survey/Housing Vacancy Survey; see source for details]

Age of householder	2000	2005	2010	2015	2016	2017	2018	2019	2020	2021
Total......................	**102,584**	**109,484**	**112,902**	**117,782**	**118,790**	**119,842**	**121,367**	**122,762**	**125,846**	**126,600**
Under 25 years old.......	5,966	6,614	6,116	6,144	6,183	5,959	6,023	5,970	5,282	5,735
25 to 29 years old.........	8,199	8,893	9,125	9,041	9,115	9,303	9,531	9,570	9,447	9,322
30 to 34 years old.........	9,941	9,696	9,569	10,127	10,180	10,187	10,232	10,476	10,764	10,992
35 to 39 years old.........	11,576	10,648	9,888	9,858	10,124	10,384	10,573	10,593	11,048	10,978
40 to 44 years old.........	12,016	11,858	10,624	10,123	9,904	9,762	9,667	9,975	10,460	10,688
45 to 49 years old.........	10,837	11,916	11,798	10,603	10,552	10,569	10,490	10,228	10,402	10,169
50 to 54 years old.........	9,416	10,716	11,829	11,490	11,264	10,921	10,841	10,708	10,801	10,876
55 to 59 years old.........	7,457	9,614	10,534	11,608	11,725	11,637	11,533	11,592	11,867	11,470
60 to 64 years old.........	6,013	7,422	9,432	10,533	10,679	11,023	11,305	11,446	11,915	12,031
65 to 69 years old.........	5,680	5,968	7,104	9,333	9,663	9,799	10,001	10,136	10,541	10,784
70 to 74 years old.........	5,421	5,073	5,499	6,715	6,969	7,587	8,017	8,375	8,997	9,080
75 years old and over....	10,061	11,066	11,388	12,205	12,433	12,712	13,154	13,692	14,323	14,477

Source: U.S. Census Bureau, "Housing Vacancies and Home Ownership, Historical Tables," <www.census.gov/housing/hvs/index.html>, accessed March 2022.

Table 1023. Vacancy Rates for Housing Units—Characteristics: 2000 to 2021

[In percent. Rate is the proportion of vacant housing for rent or for sale to the total rental and homeowner supply, which comprises occupied units, units rented or sold and awaiting occupancy, and vacant units available for rent or sale. Based on the Current Population Survey/Housing Vacancy Survey; see source for details. For composition of regions, see map inside front cover]

Characteristic	Rental units					Homeowner units				
	2000	2010	2015	2020	2021	2000	2010	2015	2020	2021
Total units.............	**8.0**	**10.2**	**7.1**	**6.3**	**6.1**	**1.6**	**2.6**	**1.8**	**1.0**	**0.9**
Northeast.................	5.6	7.6	5.5	5.2	5.2	1.2	1.7	1.9	1.0	0.8
Midwest..................	8.8	10.8	7.6	7.1	7.0	1.3	2.6	1.7	0.9	0.8
South.....................	10.5	12.7	8.9	7.8	7.1	1.9	2.8	2.1	1.1	1.0
West......................	5.8	8.2	5.1	4.4	4.5	1.5	2.7	1.4	0.8	0.8
Units in structure:										
1 unit....................	7.0	9.2	7.1	5.5	5.1	1.5	2.2	1.7	0.9	0.8
2 units or more..........	8.7	11.1	7.2	6.8	6.8	4.7	9.2	5.1	2.9	2.9
5 units or more..........	9.2	11.7	7.4	7.5	7.3	5.8	9.2	4.5	2.9	2.9
Units with:										
3 rooms or fewer........	10.3	13.8	9.9	10.0	10.5	10.4	14.8	13.6	6.9	7.3
4 rooms.................	8.2	10.5	7.0	5.8	5.5	2.9	5.7	4.4	2.1	2.0
5 rooms.................	6.9	8.9	6.1	4.7	4.0	2.0	3.0	2.2	1.1	1.0
6 rooms or more........	5.2	7.1	5.6	4.9	4.6	1.1	1.7	1.2	0.7	0.5

Source: U.S. Census Bureau, "Housing Vacancies and Home Ownership: Annual Statistics: 2021," <www.census.gov/housing/hvs/index.html>, accessed March 2022.

Table 1024. Housing Units and Tenure—States: 2019

[139,686 represents 139,686,000. The American Community Survey universe includes the household population and the population living in institutions, college dormitories, and other group quarters. Based on a sample and subject to sampling variability; see Appendix III]

State	Housing units (1,000) Total	Occu-pied	Vacant Total [1]	For rent only	For sale only	For sea-sonal use [2]	Owner-occupied units Total (1,000)	Average house-hold size (persons)	Renter-occupied units Total (1,000)	Average house-hold size (persons)
United States............	139,686	122,803	16,883	2,837	1,202	5,387	78,725	2.70	44,078	2.44
Alabama..................	2,285	1,898	387	65	19	73	1,305	2.60	592	2.35
Alaska....................	320	252	68	9	3	31	163	2.90	89	2.60
Arizona...................	3,076	2,670	406	53	27	196	1,743	2.71	928	2.59
Arkansas.................	1,389	1,164	226	32	15	51	762	2.59	402	2.39
California.................	14,367	13,158	1,209	254	90	397	7,219	3.02	5,939	2.85
Colorado.................	2,464	2,235	229	37	15	112	1,472	2.63	763	2.32
Connecticut..............	1,525	1,377	148	33	14	30	896	2.65	482	2.24
Delaware.................	444	376	68	8	5	38	265	2.57	112	2.40
District of Columbia.......	323	292	31	13	2	3	121	2.54	171	2.11
Florida....................	9,674	7,906	1,768	258	124	948	5,238	2.67	2,668	2.66
Georgia...................	4,378	3,853	526	110	48	84	2,471	2.77	1,382	2.54
Hawaii....................	550	465	85	18	4	36	280	3.10	185	2.73
Idaho.....................	751	656	95	8	6	52	469	2.76	186	2.48
Illinois....................	5,388	4,866	522	100	55	46	3,212	2.70	1,654	2.25
Indiana...................	2,921	2,598	323	60	24	46	1,800	2.63	797	2.26
Iowa......................	1,419	1,287	131	26	13	26	908	2.48	379	2.13
Kansas...................	1,288	1,138	150	33	14	15	757	2.63	382	2.21
Kentucky.................	2,006	1,749	258	40	19	36	1,172	2.56	577	2.32
Louisiana.................	2,090	1,741	349	54	23	65	1,158	2.67	583	2.45
Maine....................	751	574	177	8	7	129	414	2.38	159	2.02
Maryland.................	2,470	2,227	244	50	22	58	1,488	2.74	739	2.46
Massachusetts...........	2,929	2,651	278	32	18	121	1,648	2.68	1,003	2.22
Michigan.................	4,630	3,970	660	68	41	289	2,841	2.56	1,129	2.21
Minnesota................	2,478	2,223	255	32	14	133	1,598	2.62	624	2.12
Mississippi...............	1,339	1,100	239	44	17	35	741	2.67	360	2.52
Missouri..................	2,819	2,458	361	44	24	86	1,650	2.55	808	2.18
Montana..................	520	438	82	11	5	42	301	2.49	136	2.12
Nebraska.................	851	771	80	17	4	17	511	2.60	260	2.13
Nevada...................	1,286	1,144	142	41	10	42	648	2.75	496	2.55
New Hampshire...........	642	541	101	7	3	70	384	2.60	157	2.04
New Jersey...............	3,642	3,286	356	54	30	137	2,082	2.77	1,204	2.43
New Mexico..............	948	793	155	23	11	46	540	2.64	253	2.48
New York.................	8,404	7,447	957	146	66	351	3,986	2.71	3,461	2.34
North Carolina............	4,748	4,046	702	101	42	211	2,643	2.59	1,404	2.40
North Dakota.............	380	324	56	11	5	13	198	2.49	125	1.94
Ohio......................	5,233	4,730	503	80	37	60	3,124	2.52	1,607	2.17
Oklahoma................	1,750	1,495	254	45	19	37	980	2.64	515	2.44
Oregon...................	1,808	1,649	159	26	14	64	1,037	2.63	612	2.29
Pennsylvania.............	5,733	5,119	613	84	52	168	3,502	2.54	1,617	2.16
Rhode Island.............	470	407	63	12	3	19	251	2.69	156	2.20
South Carolina...........	2,351	1,976	375	60	27	127	1,388	2.58	587	2.45
South Dakota.............	402	354	48	9	3	15	240	2.54	114	2.12
Tennessee................	3,028	2,655	374	71	24	71	1,766	2.59	889	2.36
Texas....................	11,284	9,985	1,299	343	93	229	6,179	2.99	3,806	2.60
Utah......................	1,134	1,024	110	25	6	52	723	3.26	301	2.66
Vermont..................	339	263	77	4	3	58	186	2.41	77	1.95
Virginia...................	3,562	3,192	370	64	28	82	2,111	2.69	1,081	2.42
Washington...............	3,195	2,932	263	49	21	92	1,850	2.66	1,083	2.35
West Virginia.............	895	728	167	15	10	40	535	2.45	194	2.24
Wisconsin................	2,725	2,387	339	41	18	194	1,604	2.51	783	2.10
Wyoming.................	280	233	47	10	2	14	168	2.50	66	2.22

[1] Includes other reasons not shown separately. [2] For seasonal, recreational, or occasional use.

Source: U.S. Census Bureau, 2019 American Community Survey, B25002, "Occupancy Status"; B25003, "Tenure"; B25004, "Vacancy Status"; and B25010, "Average Household Size of Units by Tenure"; <data.census.gov/>, accessed November 2020.

Table 1025. Net Stock of Residential Fixed Assets: 1990 to 2020

[In billions of dollars (5,844 represents $5,844,000,000,000). End of year estimates]

Item	1990	2000	2005	2010	2015	2016	2017	2018	2019	2020
Total residential fixed assets........	**5,844**	**10,040**	**15,482**	**16,116**	**19,348**	**20,627**	**21,582**	**22,794**	**23,590**	**25,195**
By type of owner and legal form of organization:										
Private......................	5,702	9,810	15,150	15,783	18,957	20,212	21,155	22,347	23,130	24,705
Corporate....................	63	100	151	169	207	218	233	247	253	264
Noncorporate..............	5,640	9,710	14,999	15,614	18,750	19,994	20,922	22,101	22,877	24,441
Government.................	142	230	332	333	391	416	427	447	460	490
Federal....................	52	75	103	98	107	114	117	121	123	128
State and local.............	90	154	229	234	284	302	311	326	337	362
By tenure group: [1]										
Owner-occupied............	4,184	7,596	12,053	12,529	15,118	16,171	16,917	17,897	18,579	19,936
Tenant-occupied............	1,634	2,408	3,377	3,531	4,154	4,374	4,576	4,801	4,911	5,151

[1] Excludes stocks of other nonfarm residential assets, which consists primarily of dormitories and of fraternity and sorority houses.

Source: U.S. Bureau of Economic Analysis, Fixed Assets Accounts Tables, "Table 5.1 Current-Cost Net Stock of Residential Fixed Assets by Type of Owner, Legal Form of Organization, and Tenure Group," <apps.bea.gov/iTable/index_FA.cfm>, accessed September 2021.

Table 1026. Homeowner and Rental Vacancy Rates by State: 2021

[In percent. From the Current Population Survey/Housing Vacancy Survey, and includes the civilian noninstitutionalized population, people in noninstitutional group quarters, and military households off post or with families on post (must include 1 household member who is a civilian adult). Based on a sample and subject to sampling variability, see Appendix III]

State	Home-owner vacancy rate	Rental vacancy rate	State	Home-owner vacancy rate	Rental vacancy rate	State	Home-owner vacancy rate	Rental vacancy rate
United States......	**0.9**	**6.1**	Iowa..............	0.9	7.3	North Carolina....	0.7	5.3
			Kansas............	0.9	8.8	North Dakota.....	1.2	13.3
			Kentucky..........	0.9	6.2	Ohio..............	0.6	5.8
Alabama..............	1.0	11.7	Louisiana........	1.2	7.7	Oklahoma.........	1.0	7.7
Alaska..............	1.2	4.2	Maine............	0.6	4.1	Oregon...........	0.8	4.5
Arizona............	0.8	4.8	Maryland..........	0.8	5.0	Pennsylvania......	0.5	6.3
Arkansas...........	1.2	7.5	Massachusetts. ..	0.7	4.2	Rhode Island.....	0.7	2.8
California..........	0.7	4.3	Michigan..........	0.6	5.7	South Carolina. ..	0.8	8.0
Colorado...........	1.2	4.5	Minnesota........	0.7	6.6	South Dakota.....	0.8	8.7
Connecticut........	0.6	5.1	Mississippi.......	1.5	9.2	Tennessee........	0.9	7.3
Delaware...........	0.6	3.8	Missouri..........	0.8	8.6	Texas............	1.0	8.4
Dist. of Columbia....	1.5	9.8	Montana..........	0.8	4.1	Utah.............	0.6	4.4
Florida.............	1.1	6.5	Nebraska.........	0.9	5.7	Vermont..........	0.4	2.5
Georgia............	1.0	6.0	Nevada...........	0.7	4.6	Virginia..........	0.8	5.4
Hawaii.............	0.7	7.3	New Hampshire..	0.6	3.5	Washington.......	0.7	4.5
Idaho..............	0.7	4.4	New Jersey.......	0.8	3.6	West Virginia.	0.9	6.5
Illinois.............	1.2	8.2	New Mexico......	0.9	6.9	Wisconsin.........	0.2	4.7
Indiana............	0.9	8.4	New York..........	1.3	5.9	Wyoming..........	1.2	8.0

Source: U.S. Census Bureau, "Housing Vacancies and Home Ownership: Annual Statistics: 2021," <www.census.gov/housing/hvs/index.html>, accessed March 2022.

Table 1027. Homeowner and Rental Vacancy Rates by Metropolitan Area: 2021

[In percent. From the Current Population Survey/Housing Vacancy Survey, and includes the civilian noninstitutionalized population, people in noninstitutional group quarters, and military households off post or with families on post (must include 1 household member who is a civilian adult). Data are based on 2010 metropolitan/nonmetropolitan definitions. Subject to sampling error; see source and Appendix III for details]

Metropolitan area	Home-owner vacancy rate	Rental vacancy rate	Metropolitan area	Home-owner vacancy rate	Rental vacancy rate
Inside metropolitan areas..................	**0.9**	**6.0**	Memphis, TN-AR-MS................	0.8	6.9
Akron, OH..................................	(Z)	0.7	Miami-Fort Lauderdale-West Palm Beach, FL..........	1.0	5.5
Albany-Schenectady-Troy, NY................	2.2	10.6	Milwaukee-Waukesha-West Allis, WI........	0.5	2.2
Albuquerque, NM............................	0.5	6.4	Minneapolis-St. Paul-Bloomington, MN-WI....	0.6	4.9
Allentown-Bethlehem-Easton, PA-NJ.........	0.1	4.0	Nashville-Davidson-Murfreesboro-Franklin, TN........	1.0	7.9
Atlanta-Sandy Springs-Roswell, GA...........	1.0	5.2	New Haven-Milford, CT...................	0.5	5.4
Austin-Round Rock, TX......................	1.3	8.5	New Orleans-Metairie, LA.................	1.0	7.2
Baltimore-Columbia-Towson, MD.............	1.0	6.1	New York-Newark-Jersey City, NY-NJ-PA.....	1.2	5.2
Baton Rouge, LA............................	0.7	8.1	North Port-Bradenton-Sarasota, FL...........	0.8	6.8
Birmingham-Hoover, AL......................	0.7	14.4	Oklahoma City, OK........................	0.8	5.7
Boston-Cambridge-Newton, MA-NH..........	0.5	4.5	Omaha-Council Bluffs, NE-IA...............	0.7	5.1
Bridgeport-Stamford-Norwalk, CT............	0.3	4.7	Orlando-Kissimmee-Sanford, FL............	0.5	7.5
Buffalo-Cheektowaga-Niagara Falls, NY......	0.2	6.0	Philadelphia-Camden-Wilmington, PA-NJ-DE-MD.....	0.5	4.8
Cape Coral-Fort Myers, FL...................	2.4	10.7	Phoenix-Mesa-Scottsdale, AZ..............	0.6	4.9
Charleston-N. Charleston-Summerville, SC...	1.3	15.4	Pittsburgh, PA...........................	0.4	9.4
Charlotte-Concord-Gastonia, NC-SC.........	1.3	6.8	Portland-Vancouver-Hillsboro, OR-WA......	0.9	5.2
Chicago-Naperville-Elgin, IL.................	1.3	8.0	Providence-Warwick, RI-MA................	0.7	2.7
Cincinnati, OH-KY-IN........................	0.5	7.2	Raleigh, NC..............................	1.1	2.9
Cleveland-Elyria, OH........................	0.4	3.6	Richmond, VA............................	1.0	1.8
Columbia, SC..............................	1.1	4.7	Riverside-San Bernardino-Ontario, CA.......	0.8	3.1
Columbus, OH.............................	0.8	6.5	Rochester, NY............................	0.5	3.1
Dallas-Ft. Worth-Arlington, TX...............	0.7	7.0	Sacramento-Roseville-Arden-Arcade, CA.....	0.7	3.6
Dayton, OH................................	0.5	7.2	St. Louis, MO-IL..........................	0.5	6.5
Denver-Aurora-Lakewood, CO................	1.0	4.6	Salt Lake City, UT........................	0.8	4.1
Detroit-Warren-Dearborn, MI.................	0.5	6.4	San Antonio-New Braunfels, TX.............	1.1	8.4
Fresno, CA................................	0.9	2.6	San Diego-Carlsbad, CA...................	0.7	3.1
Grand Rapids-Wyoming, MI..................	0.7	3.4	San Francisco-Oakland-Hayward, CA........	1.1	6.5
Greensboro-High Point, NC..................	0.5	2.7	San Jose-Sunnyvale-Santa Clara, CA........	0.4	6.6
Hartford-West Hartford-East Hartford, CT....	0.8	6.7	Seattle-Tacoma-Bellevue, WA..............	0.7	5.3
Houston-The Woodlands-Sugar Land, TX....	0.8	8.8	Syracuse, NY............................	1.6	9.2
Indianapolis-Carmel-Anderson, IN............	0.7	8.2	Tampa-St. Petersburg-Clearwater, FL........	1.0	7.3
Jacksonville, FL............................	0.4	5.6	Toledo, OH..............................	1.7	3.5
Kansas City, MO-KS........................	1.2	8.9	Tucson, AZ..............................	0.6	5.0
Knoxville, TN..............................	0.8	5.8	Tulsa, OK...............................	1.5	5.3
Las Vegas-Henderson-Paradise, NV..........	0.9	3.7	Urban Honolulu, HI.......................	0.6	5.1
Little Rock-North Little Rock-Conway, AR.....	1.2	10.0	Virginia Beach-Norfolk-Newport News, VA....	0.6	5.5
Los Angeles-Long Beach-Anaheim, CA.......	0.7	4.6	Washington-Arlington-Alexandria, DC-VA-MD-WV. ...	0.5	5.9
Louisville/Jefferson County, KY-IN...........	0.7	8.5	Worcester, MA...........................	0.7	2.2

Z Represents a value less than .05.

Source: U.S. Census Bureau, "Housing Vacancies and Home Ownership: Annual Statistics: 2021," <www.census.gov/housing/hvs/index.html>, accessed March 2022.

Table 1028. Housing Units—Characteristics by Occupancy and Tenure: 2017 and 2019

[In thousands of units (137,403 represents 137,403,000), except as indicated. As of Fall. Based on the American Housing Survey; see Appendix III]

Characteristic	2017 Total housing units [1]	2017 Occupied Total	2017 Occupied Owner	2017 Occupied Renter	2017 Vacant	2019 Total housing units [1]	2019 Occupied Total	2019 Occupied Owner	2019 Occupied Renter	2019 Vacant
Total units............	**137,403**	**121,560**	**77,567**	**43,993**	**13,050**	**139,684**	**124,135**	**79,475**	**44,660**	**12,968**
Percent distribution................	100.0	88.5	56.5	32.0	9.5	100.0	88.9	56.9	32.0	9.3
Units in structure:										
Single family detached...............	84,827	76,833	64,385	12,448	6,310	87,379	79,335	66,781	12,554	6,407
Single family attached...............	10,040	8958	4,735	4,223	928	7,179	6,482	3,962	2,520	589
2 to 4 units..................	9,744	8363	1,120	7,243	1,248	10,659	9,118	1,304	7,814	1,431
5 to 9 units.................	6,645	5780	528	5253	805	6,825	6,008	543	5,465	772
10 to 19 units..............	6,180	5282	413	4869	826	6080	5164	434	4,730	830
20 to 49 units..............	4,903	4116	459	3657	719	5537	4706	474	4,231	769
50 or more units..............	6,593	5427	887	4,539	1,021	7,667	6,472	839	5,632	1,073
Manufactured/mobile home [2].........	8,397	6727	4,969	1,758	1,192	8262	6,756	5,061	1,694	1,097
Year structure built:										
Median year (est.).................	1977	1977	1978	1974	1975	1977	1978	1979	1975	1975
2018 to 2019..................	(X)	(X)	(X)	(X)	(X)	1,171	986	742	244	171
2016 to 2017..................	1,007	841	621	220	145	2,755	2,474	1,537	937	254
2010 to 2015..................	5,772	5,113	3,105	2,007	557	6,018	5,459	3,225	2,233	483
2005 to 2009..................	9,046	7,936	5,449	2,487	877	8,871	7,939	5,680	2,259	751
2000 to 2004..................	10,522	9,448	6,325	3,123	827	10,392	9,409	6,365	3,044	778
1995 to 1999..................	10,004	9,132	6,537	2,596	718	10,372	9,429	6,651	2,778	799
1990 to 1994..................	7,271	6,564	4,825	1,739	554	7,236	6,550	4,707	1,843	536
1985 to 1989..................	10,125	8,952	5,749	3,203	934	10,031	8,906	5,653	3,254	916
1980 to 1984..................	8,851	7,736	4,843	2,893	922	8,600	7,529	4,624	2,905	853
1970 to 1979..................	20,456	17,953	11,106	6,846	2,038	20,391	17,967	11,244	6,723	2,022
1960 to 1969..................	14,289	12,685	8,167	4,518	1,350	14,777	13,190	8,106	5,084	1,308
1950 to 1959..................	14,254	12,818	8,436	4,382	1,182	14,252	12,835	8,640	4,195	1,197
1940 to 1949..................	6,617	5740	3,490	2,250	735	6,511	5,566	3,326	2,240	761
1930 to 1939..................	4,205	3620	2,012	1,608	461	3,989	3,437	1,920	1,517	464
1920 to 1929..................	5,409	4682	2,417	2,265	662	5,444	4,770	2,566	2,203	614
1919 or earlier. [3]	9,575	8,340	4,483	3,857	1,088	8,875	7,690	4,490	3,200	1,061
Stories in structure: [3]										
1 story...................	42,835	37,751	26,101	11,650	4,038	43,219	38,293	26,739	11,554	3,891
2 stories..................	46,568	41,635	26,125	15,510	4,208	47,788	42,749	27,232	15,517	4,368
3 stories..................	29,214	26471	16,940	9,532	2,395	29,533	26,819	17,022	9,797	2,412
4 to 6 stories..............	7,267	6458	2,745	3,713	721	7,567	6,798	2,767	4031	706
7 or more stories...............	3,048	2443	615	1,828	496	3,219	2,626	578	2048	494
Foundation: [4]										
Full basement.................	29,135	26954	23,216	3,738	1,830	28,934	26,832	23,332	3,500	1,784
Partial building..............	9,895	9139	7,991	1,149	629	9,666	8,934	7,896	1,038	623
Crawlspace.................	20,392	18135	14,146	3,988	1,796	20373	18,080	14,517	3,563	1,744
Concrete slab.................	33,463	29,941	22,610	7,331	2,766	33,575	30,359	23,804	6,555	2,583
Equipment:										
With complete kitchen facilities [5]......	132,968	120,144	77,216	42,929	10,379	135,293	122,697	79,127	43,570	10,365
Lacking complete kitchen facilities [5]..	4,436	1416	351	1,064	2,671	4392	1438	349	1090	2,604
Kitchen sink.................	136,262	121,260	77,505	43,755	12,359	139,008	123,891	79,420	44,471	12,605
Refrigerator.................	134,282	121,073	77,351	43,722	10,716	136,503	123,550	79,230	44,320	10,686
Cooking stove or range..............	133,547	120,096	76,963	43,132	10,965	135,711	122,432	78,719	43,713	10,997
Microwave oven only.................	863	703	271	431	136	905	773	349	424	99
Dishwasher.........................	95,689	87,084	62,164	24,920	7,117	100,337	91,727	65,011	26,716	7,227
Washing machine..................	110,547	102,901	75,207	27,694	5,966	114,171	106,448	77,313	29,134	6,163
Clothes dryer.....................	108,659	101,110	74,337	26,773	5,894	112,503	104,891	76,585	28,306	6,078
Main heating equipment:										
Warm-air furnace......................	88,919	79,382	53,312	26,070	8,063	91,470	82,186	55,309	26,877	7,943
Steam or hot water system...........	12,250	11095	6,335	4,761	1,011	11,909	10,912	6323	4589	903
Electric heat pump..................	16,255	14128	9,751	4,377	1,744	16404	14294	9,887	4,407	1,699
Built-in electric units.................	5,667	4925	1,898	3,026	557	5,825	4,995	1870	3,125	662
Floor, wall, or pipeless furnace........	6,324	5616	2,481	3,135	579	6474	5624	2,384	3,239	731
Room heaters with flue..............	884	740	398	342	112	938	821	454	367	100
Room heaters without flue..............	903	749	476	273	117	813	711	449	262	85
Portable electric heaters..............	2,268	2018	950	1068	150	2364	2103	1118	986	168
Stoves..........................	1,527	1348	1,081	267	100	1418	1195	938	257	142
Fireplaces with inserts................	232	212	176	37	(S)	226	204	158	46	(S)
Fireplaces without inserts.............	119	83	69	(S)	(S)	85	74	68	S	(S)
Cooking stove.................	66	58	(S)	(S)	(S)	75	72	36	36	(S)
None...........................	1,459	848	453	395	451	1129	594	316	279	372
Main cooling equipment:										
Central air conditioning................	93,841	84,481	58,684	25,797	7,794	97,947	88,632	61,297	27,335	7,871
Room air conditioning.................	27,356	25404	12,741	12,663	1,568	26,332	24,628	12,441	12,188	1,422
None...........................	16,206	11674	6,141	5,533	3,688	15,406	10,875	5,738	5,137	3,675
Source of water:										
Public system or private company....	(NA)	107,764	65,817	41,948	(NA)	(NA)	110,171	67,391	42,780	(NA)
Individual well.................	(NA)	13,525	11,545	1,981	(NA)	(NA)	13,755	11,927	1,828	(NA)
Means of sewage disposal:										
Public sewer.................	(NA)	99,571	58,522	41,049	(NA)	(NA)	103,565	61,395	42,170	(NA)
Septic tank or cesspool...............	(NA)	21,718	18,860	2,858	(NA)	(NA)	20,293	17,931	2,362	(NA)

X Not applicable. NA Not available. S Estimate did not meet publication standards or withheld to avoid disclosure. [1] Includes seasonal units, not shown separately. [2] Includes trailers. Includes width not reported, not shown separately. [3] Excludes mobile homes; includes basements and finished attics. [4] Includes only single family homes (1 unit, attached or detached). [5] A complete kitchen includes sink, refrigerator, oven or burners.

Source: U.S. Census Bureau, "American Housing Survey: AHS Table Creator," <www.census.gov/programs-surveys/ahs/data.html>, accessed January 2021.

Table 1029. Housing Units by Units in Structure and State: 2020

[In percent, except total units. Data are based on 2020 American Community Survey (ACS) 1-year experimental estimates. The coronavirus disease 2019 (COVID-19) pandemic impacted 2020 ACS data collection and quality, and standard estimates did not meet statistical quality standards. The Census Bureau does not recommend comparing experimental estimates to standard ACS estimates. For more information, see <www.census.gov/programs-surveys/acs/data/experimental-data.html>. The American Community Survey universe includes the household population and the population living in institutions, college dormitories, and other group quarters. Based on a sample and subject to sampling variability; see Appendix III]

| State | Total housing units | Percent of units by units in structures— | | | | | |
		1-unit, detached and attached	2 units	3 or 4 units	5 or 9 units	10 or more units	Mobile home, boat, RV, van, etc.
United States.......	**140,766,987**	**67.7**	**3.5**	**4.3**	**4.4**	**14.1**	**6.0**
Alabama...............	2,302,582	71.1	1.9	2.9	3.9	7.2	12.9
Alaska.................	321,385	70.8	5.4	7.2	4.4	8.0	4.3
Arizona...............	3,120,061	68.7	1.4	3.3	3.8	12.4	10.4
Arkansas..............	1,401,087	72.5	3.5	3.3	3.0	6.0	11.8
California.............	14,383,549	64.7	2.4	5.4	5.6	18.1	3.8
Colorado..............	2,432,832	69.3	1.7	3.1	4.2	18.0	3.7
Connecticut...........	1,530,056	65.0	8.4	7.9	5.0	13.0	0.7
Delaware..............	449,537	73.3	1.8	2.7	3.6	10.4	8.2
District of Columbia...	327,525	31.9	3.4	7.5	5.5	51.6	0.1
Florida................	9,814,540	60.9	2.1	3.9	4.6	19.9	8.6
Georgia...............	4,426,892	71.1	2.0	3.1	4.1	11.4	8.3
Hawaii................	554,102	63.6	2.3	4.3	6.0	23.5	0.3
Idaho.................	768,816	77.8	2.1	4.0	2.6	5.6	7.9
Illinois................	5,399,497	64.5	5.8	6.6	6.5	14.2	2.4
Indiana...............	2,940,473	77.2	2.5	3.6	4.4	7.7	4.7
Iowa..................	1,428,906	76.8	2.2	3.7	3.2	10.4	3.7
Kansas................	1,294,032	77.0	2.2	3.8	3.9	8.6	4.5
Kentucky..............	2,016,609	70.6	2.7	4.4	4.5	7.0	10.9
Louisiana.............	2,103,943	68.7	3.7	3.8	3.1	7.9	12.7
Maine.................	755,380	72.7	4.7	5.5	3.1	5.1	8.9
Maryland..............	2,482,043	72.1	1.8	2.4	5.0	17.4	1.3
Massachusetts........	2,944,398	57.6	9.4	10.4	6.0	15.7	0.9
Michigan..............	4,643,918	76.8	2.4	2.7	3.9	8.9	5.3
Minnesota.............	2,503,010	74.8	2.2	1.8	2.1	15.9	3.1
Mississippi............	1,345,251	71.0	2.6	3.3	3.6	5.2	14.3
Missouri...............	2,833,623	73.7	3.3	4.8	3.9	8.8	5.5
Montana...............	524,644	73.8	2.6	4.1	2.7	6.0	10.8
Nebraska..............	857,908	75.9	2.0	1.9	3.7	13.0	3.4
Nevada................	1,305,950	64.9	1.5	6.3	7.4	14.5	5.5
New Hampshire.......	646,849	69.4	5.6	4.8	3.8	10.5	5.8
New Jersey............	3,654,920	62.9	9.1	6.5	4.5	15.9	1.0
New Mexico...........	955,942	67.8	1.7	4.0	2.7	7.2	16.6
New York..............	8,444,156	47.7	10.2	6.9	5.0	27.8	2.4
North Carolina........	4,813,617	69.9	2.1	2.6	4.1	9.6	11.6
North Dakota..........	382,115	64.1	2.4	3.0	4.5	17.9	8.1
Ohio..................	5,247,933	74.0	3.9	4.2	4.1	10.1	3.7
Oklahoma.............	1,759,576	75.4	1.8	2.6	3.2	8.1	9.0
Oregon................	1,830,846	67.4	2.6	4.2	4.4	13.2	8.2
Pennsylvania..........	5,753,228	75.5	4.2	3.9	3.1	9.5	3.8
Rhode Island..........	471,340	59.9	10.9	12.0	4.5	11.7	1.1
South Carolina........	2,386,402	67.4	1.8	2.6	4.1	8.9	15.2
South Dakota.........	404,906	71.0	2.2	4.2	3.7	9.7	9.2
Tennessee.............	3,065,835	72.1	2.6	3.1	4.4	9.2	8.6
Texas.................	11,487,050	67.4	1.9	3.4	4.1	16.3	6.8
Utah..................	1,161,907	76.8	1.9	3.7	3.3	11.5	2.8
Vermont...............	341,405	71.7	5.6	7.0	4.5	4.9	6.2
Virginia...............	3,586,869	72.5	1.6	3.2	4.5	13.7	4.4
Washington............	3,242,721	67.1	2.3	3.6	4.0	17.1	5.9
West Virginia.........	896,570	73.2	2.2	2.8	3.1	4.7	14.0
Wisconsin.............	2,738,305	71.5	6.0	3.4	4.5	11.3	3.3
Wyoming..............	281,946	72.1	1.3	5.6	3.4	4.7	12.8

Source: U.S. Census Bureau, 2020 ACS 1-Year Experimental Data Tables, "Table XK202504. Units in Structure," <www.census.gov/programs-surveys/acs/data/experimental-data.html>, accessed June 2022.

Table 1030. Housing Units—Size of Units and Lot: 2017 and 2019

[In thousands (137,403 represents 137,403,000), except as indicated. As of Fall. Based on the American Housing Survey; see Appendix III]

Characteristic	2017 Total housing units [1]	2017 Occupied Total	2017 Occupied Owner	2017 Occupied Renter	2017 Vacant	2019 Total housing units [1]	2019 Occupied Total	2019 Occupied Owner	2019 Occupied Renter	2019 Vacant
Total units	**137,403**	**121,560**	**77,567**	**43,993**	**13,050**	**139,684**	**124,135**	**79,475**	**44,660**	**12,968**
Rooms:										
1 room	732	530	(S)	511	149	633	505	(S)	476	100
2 rooms	1,474	1,181	98	1,083	231	1,686	1,333	117	1,216	250
3 rooms	11,649	9,597	1,145	8,452	1,692	11,841	9,850	1,151	8,699	1,718
4 rooms	23,959	19,459	6,109	13,350	3,621	23,631	19,541	6,253	13,288	3,336
5 rooms	31,316	27,563	16,644	10,919	3,125	32,034	28,018	16,751	11,267	3,336
6 rooms	28,510	25,826	20,072	5,753	2,227	29,407	26,736	20,816	5,920	2,283
7 rooms	18,724	17,438	15,078	2,359	1,092	19,289	17,955	15,678	2,276	1,128
8 rooms	11,386	10,766	9,773	994	523	11,577	11,067	10,073	994	408
9 rooms	5,358	5,129	4,757	372	200	5,299	5,071	4,761	310	211
10 rooms or more	4,296	4,071	3,873	199	191	4,287	4,060	3,847	214	198
Bathrooms:										
No complete bathroom	339	149	(S)	117	90	291	127	35	92	93
1 bathroom	46,499	39,080	13,235	25,845	6,291	46,181	39,218	13,298	25,920	5,950
1 and one-half bathrooms	16,067	14,432	9,989	4,444	1,384	16,072	14,212	9,658	4,554	1,515
2 bathrooms	41,634	37,462	27,106	10,356	3,357	42,636	38,501	27,897	10,604	3,441
2 and one-half bathrooms	17,316	16,211	14,032	2,179	933	17,898	16,704	14,408	2,296	1,007
3 bathrooms	12,774	11,807	10,920	887	747	13,483	12,594	11,606	988	708
4 or more bathrooms	2,773	2,419	2,253	166	248	3,125	2,779	2,574	205	252
Square footage of unit:										
Less than 500	3,409	2,765	490	2,275	484	3,675	2,954	530	2,425	570
500 to 749	9,527	7,702	1,246	6,457	1,533	9,759	8,080	1,213	6,867	1,389
750 to 999	16,506	13,808	4,257	9,551	2,277	17,427	14,695	4,482	10,213	2,332
1,000 to 1,499	31,569	27,730	17,024	10,706	3,170	33,086	29,272	17,898	11,374	3,179
1,500 to 1,999	24,342	22,203	18,352	3,851	1,734	25,227	23,016	18,881	4,135	1,851
2,000 to 2,499	15,667	14,554	12,933	1,621	883	16,480	15,293	13,484	1,809	959
2,500 to 2,999	8,352	7,828	7,299	529	400	8,779	8,237	7,654	583	467
3,000 to 3,999	7,875	7,333	6,919	414	417	8,275	7,684	7,209	475	466
4,000 or more	3,926	3,555	3,260	294	298	4,285	3,932	3,607	325	278
Not reported	16,231	14,081	5,784	8,297	1,855	12,691	10,972	4,518	6,453	1,478
Median square footage	1,473	1,500	1,800	974	1,144	1,473	1,500	1,800	980	1,200
Lot size:										
Single detached and attached units and mobile homes [2]	99,751	89,493	71,877	17,617	8,094	99,671	89,786	73,742	16,045	7,842
Less than one-eighth acre	14,697	12,864	8,811	4,053	1,476	14,239	12,516	8,988	3,528	1,426
One-eighth to one-quarter acre	33,401	30,638	23,674	6,964	2,311	32,124	29,588	23,377	6,211	2,134
One-quarter to one-half acre	19,934	18,225	15,507	2,718	1,314	19,134	17,430	15,152	2,279	1,390
One-half up to one acre	9,455	8,369	7,229	1,140	787	9,621	8,624	7,540	1,084	743
1 up to 5 acres	15,157	13,332	11,375	1,958	1,439	15,752	14,043	12,202	1,841	1,259
5 up to 10 acres	3,079	2,696	2,412	285	308	3,312	2,942	2,556	386	285
10 or more acres	4,028	3,368	2,869	499	459	5,488	4,642	3,927	715	604

S Estimate did not meet publication standards or withheld to avoid disclosure. [1] Includes seasonal units, not shown separately. [2] Does not include cooperatives or condominiums.

Source: U.S. Census Bureau, "American Housing Survey: AHS Table Creator," <www.census.gov/programs-surveys/ahs/data.html>, accessed January 2021.

Table 1031. Occupied Housing Units—Tenure by Race of Householder: 2005 to 2019

[In thousands (108,871 represents 108,871,000), except percent. As of Fall. Based on the American Housing Survey; see Appendix III]

Race of householder and tenure	2005	2007	2009	2011	2013	2015	2017	2019
ALL RACES [1]								
Occupied units, total	**108,871**	**110,692**	**111,806**	**114,907**	**115,852**	**118,290**	**121,560**	**124,135**
Owner-occupied	74,931	75,647	76,428	76,091	75,650	74,299	77,567	79,475
Percent of occupied	68.8	68.3	68.4	66.2	65.3	62.8	63.8	64.0
Renter-occupied	33,940	35,045	35,378	38,816	40,201	43,991	43,993	44,660
WHITE [2]								
Occupied units, total	**89,449**	**90,413**	**91,137**	**92,820**	**93,284**	**93,748**	**95,324**	**96,999**
Owner-occupied	65,023	65,554	65,935	65,357	65,088	63,049	65,234	66,433
Percent of occupied	72.7	72.5	72.3	70.4	69.8	67.3	68.4	68.5
Renter-occupied	24,426	24,859	25,202	27,463	28,196	30,699	30,089	30,566
BLACK [2]								
Occupied units, total	**13,447**	**13,856**	**13,993**	**14,694**	**15,015**	**16,002**	**16,552**	**17,114**
Owner-occupied	6,471	6,464	6,547	6,662	6,480	6,665	7,131	7,397
Percent of occupied	48.1	46.7	46.8	45.3	43.2	41.7	43.1	43.2
Renter-occupied	6,975	7,392	7,446	8,033	8,535	9,337	9,421	9,717
HISPANIC ORIGIN [3]								
Occupied units, total	**11,651**	**12,609**	**12,739**	**13,841**	**14,675**	**15,620**	**16,496**	**17,299**
Owner-occupied	5,752	6,364	6,439	6,530	6,897	7,109	7,763	8,355
Percent of occupied	49.4	50.5	50.5	47.2	47.0	45.5	47.1	48.3
Renter-occupied	5,899	6,244	6,300	7,311	7,778	8,511	8,733	8,945

[1] Includes other races not shown separately. [2] The 2003 American Housing Survey (AHS) allowed respondents to choose more than one race. Beginning in 2003, data represent householders who selected this race group only and exclude householders reporting more than one race. See also comments on race in the text for Section 1 and the below cited source. [3] Persons of Hispanic origin may be of any race.

Source: U.S. Census Bureau, "American Housing Survey: AHS Table Creator," <www.census.gov/programs-surveys/ahs/data.html>, accessed December 2020.

Table 1032. Homeownership Rates by Age of Householder and Household Type: 2000 to 2021

[In percent. Represents the proportion of owner households to the total number of occupied households. Based on the Current Population Survey/Housing Vacancy Survey, and includes the civilian noninstitutionalized population, people in noninstitutional group quarters, and military in households off post or with their families on post (must have 1 household member who is a civilian adult). See source and Appendix III for details]

Age of householder and household type	2000	2005	2010	2015	2016	2017	2018	2019	2020	2021
Total.............................	**67.4**	**68.9**	**66.9**	**63.7**	**63.4**	**63.9**	**64.4**	**64.6**	**66.6**	**65.5**
AGE OF HOUSEHOLDER										
Less than 25 years old........................	21.7	25.7	22.8	21.8	21.9	22.6	22.7	23.2	25.7	24.3
25 to 29 years old............................	38.1	40.9	36.8	31.7	30.9	32.1	32.5	32.9	35.3	34.6
30 to 34 years old............................	54.6	56.8	51.6	45.9	45.4	45.7	47.7	48.0	49.1	48.4
35 to 39 years old............................	65.0	66.6	61.9	55.3	55.3	56.4	57.6	57.2	60.0	58.5
40 to 44 years old............................	70.6	71.7	67.9	61.6	62.0	61.8	62.9	63.2	65.5	64.6
45 to 49 years old............................	74.7	75.0	72.0	68.0	66.7	67.5	68.4	68.2	68.8	67.3
50 to 54 years old............................	78.5	78.3	75.0	71.8	71.6	71.1	71.7	71.9	73.2	72.0
55 to 59 years old............................	80.4	80.6	77.7	74.7	74.0	73.8	74.0	73.9	74.9	73.2
60 to 64 years old............................	80.3	81.9	80.4	76.2	76.1	76.9	76.8	76.6	78.2	76.8
65 to 69 years old............................	83.0	82.8	81.6	79.3	79.0	79.1	79.3	78.8	79.6	78.9
70 to 74 years old............................	82.6	82.9	82.4	81.3	81.7	81.4	80.6	80.6	82.1	81.4
75 years old and over........................	77.7	78.4	78.9	77.2	77.0	76.8	76.6	77.3	79.0	78.7
Less than 35 years old........................	40.8	43.0	39.1	35.0	34.5	35.3	36.2	36.7	39.1	38.2
35 to 44 years old............................	67.9	69.3	65.0	58.5	58.6	59.0	60.1	60.1	62.7	61.5
45 to 54 years old............................	76.5	76.6	73.5	70.0	69.3	69.3	70.1	70.1	71.1	69.7
55 to 64 years old............................	80.3	81.2	79.0	75.4	75.0	75.3	75.4	75.2	76.6	75.1
65 years and over............................	80.4	80.6	80.5	78.9	78.8	78.7	78.5	78.6	80.0	79.5
TYPE OF HOUSEHOLD										
Family households:										
Married-couple families....................	82.4	84.2	82.1	79.6	80.0	80.1	80.8	81.0	82.2	82.1
Male householder, no spouse present......	57.5	59.1	56.9	53.8	53.7	55.6	56.3	56.1	57.5	56.7
Female householder, no spouse present...	49.1	51.0	48.6	45.9	45.7	46.7	47.9	48.6	50.8	49.3
Nonfamily households:										
One-person..............................	53.6	55.6	55.3	52.2	51.3	51.5	51.8	51.8	54.1	53.0
Male householder........................	47.4	50.3	51.3	48.5	47.2	47.3	47.4	48.5	50.7	49.3
Female householder......................	58.1	59.6	58.6	55.3	54.6	54.9	55.4	54.6	57.0	56.1
Two-or-more-persons:.....................	39.1	43.0	41.9	38.3	37.0	38.1	39.8	40.2	42.0	40.9
Male householder........................	38.0	41.7	40.7	36.6	36.1	37.2	38.6	39.7	41.6	40.0
Female householder......................	40.6	44.7	41.9	40.7	38.4	39.4	41.5	40.8	42.6	42.1

Source: U.S. Census Bureau, "Housing Vacancies and Home Ownership: Annual Statistics: 2021," <www.census.gov/housing/hvs/index.html>, accessed March 2022.

Table 1033. Homeownership Rates by State: 2000 to 2021

[In percent. Represents the proportion of owner households to the total number of occupied households. Based on the Current Population Survey/Housing Vacancy Survey, and includes the civilian noninstitutionalized population, people in noninstitutional group quarters, and military in households off post or with their families on post (must have 1 household member who is a civilian adult). See source and Appendix III for details]

State	2000	2010	2015	2019	2020	2021	State	2000	2010	2015	2019	2020	2021
United States.....	**67.4**	**66.9**	**63.7**	**64.6**	**66.6**	**65.5**	Missouri.............	74.2	71.2	68.5	69.1	71.1	72.8
Alabama.............	73.2	73.2	70.0	70.7	74.8	73.4	Montana.............	70.2	68.1	66.4	68.7	68.4	68.1
Alaska.............	66.4	65.7	62.3	62.6	64.1	64.0	Nebraska.............	70.2	70.4	68.1	68.2	69.8	68.4
Arizona.............	68.0	66.6	61.7	65.8	68.7	65.2	Nevada.............	64.0	59.7	54.8	58.2	61.2	60.5
Arkansas.............	68.9	67.9	67.1	65.3	68.8	66.1	New Hampshire....	69.2	74.9	71.6	75.0	74.5	74.0
California.............	57.1	56.1	54.3	54.8	55.9	54.2	New Jersey.........	66.2	66.5	64.0	65.0	64.3	62.7
Colorado.............	68.3	68.5	63.6	64.7	64.9	65.9	New Mexico.........	73.7	68.6	66.5	67.4	70.3	69.0
Connecticut.........	70.0	70.8	66.5	64.3	66.9	66.1	New York.........	53.4	54.5	51.5	52.0	53.6	53.6
Delaware.............	72.0	74.7	73.3	73.1	77.9	73.5	North Carolina......	71.1	69.5	65.2	65.1	68.7	65.8
Dist. of Columbia. ..	41.9	45.6	40.4	40.2	42.5	42.3	North Dakota........	70.7	67.1	61.8	61.4	64.2	63.5
Florida.............	68.4	69.3	64.8	66.0	68.7	67.2	Ohio.............	71.3	69.7	66.4	68.2	69.4	67.4
Georgia.............	69.8	67.1	62.9	64.4	67.3	64.0	Oklahoma.............	72.7	69.2	67.4	68.8	71.0	67.0
Hawaii.............	55.2	56.1	59.3	60.0	58.8	58.1	Oregon.............	65.3	66.3	61.1	62.4	65.2	65.8
Idaho.............	70.5	72.4	70.0	70.6	71.5	71.0	Pennsylvania.........	74.7	72.2	69.6	69.2	69.9	70.2
Illinois.............	67.9	68.8	65.4	65.1	67.3	68.3	Rhode Island.........	61.5	62.8	58.9	63.8	64.5	62.8
Indiana.............	74.9	71.2	69.4	69.5	72.7	73.0	South Carolina......	76.5	74.8	67.1	72.6	73.6	73.2
Iowa.............	75.2	71.1	68.8	69.5	72.1	72.1	South Dakota.......	71.2	70.6	70.1	69.5	71.4	71.1
Kansas.............	69.3	67.4	64.9	69.2	69.5	69.3	Tennessee..........	70.9	71.0	66.5	68.8	70.0	66.7
Kentucky.............	73.4	70.3	67.9	69.5	72.5	72.1	Texas.............	63.8	65.3	61.9	62.4	66.5	64.1
Louisiana.............	68.1	70.4	63.3	65.6	69.1	68.9	Utah.............	72.7	72.5	69.9	71.9	71.7	68.8
Maine.............	76.5	73.8	69.9	73.8	77.1	75.9	Vermont.............	68.7	73.6	71.8	70.9	73.1	73.9
Maryland.............	69.9	68.9	67.1	68.8	72.0	69.7	Virginia.............	73.9	68.7	67.1	67.6	70.4	68.0
Massachusetts......	59.9	65.3	60.5	61.3	62.7	62.0	Washington........	63.6	64.4	62.6	63.8	64.1	63.4
Michigan.............	77.2	74.5	74.6	73.0	74.3	73.0	West Virginia........	75.9	79.0	74.9	75.6	78.2	79.0
Minnesota.............	76.1	72.6	70.1	71.4	74.5	75.6	Wisconsin.............	71.8	71.0	66.6	66.1	67.9	68.3
Mississippi.............	75.2	74.8	70.7	72.7	74.2	71.3	Wyoming.............	71.0	73.4	69.9	71.3	73.9	72.1

Source: U.S. Census Bureau, "Housing Vacancies and Home Ownership: Annual Statistics: 2021," <www.census.gov/housing/hvs/index.html>, accessed March 2022.

Table 1034. Occupied Housing Units—Costs by Census Division: 2019

[In thousands of units (79,475 represents 79,475,000), except as indicated. As of Fall. See headnote, Table 1035, for an explanation of housing costs. Based on the American Housing Survey; see Appendix III. For composition of census divisions, see map inside front cover]

Category	Total units	New England Division	Middle Atlantic Division	East North Central Division	West North Central Division	South Atlantic Division	East South Central Division	West South Central Division	Moun- tain Division	Pacific Division
OWNER-OCCUPIED UNITS										
Total	79,475	3,786	9,699	12,726	6,058	16,047	5,137	9,194	6,168	10,660
Monthly housing costs:										
Less than $100	170	(S)	(S)	(S)	(S)	(S)	(S)	(S)	37	(S)
$100 to $199	1,145	–	39	80	(S)	366	185	214	101	74
$200 to $249	1,222	(S)	(S)	123	117	359	190	284	64	54
$250 to $299	1,621	(S)	(S)	209	99	509	262	257	147	101
$300 to $349	2,297	(S)	127	422	146	647	288	312	191	131
$350 to $399	2,460	(S)	118	459	196	658	295	380	169	163
$400 to $449	2,619	(S)	195	489	244	672	248	321	251	180
$450 to $499	2,543	(S)	219	586	220	565	231	299	183	199
$500 to $599	4,823	114	488	964	409	1,012	349	658	377	452
$600 to $699	4,654	150	495	1,019	413	924	268	571	328	485
$700 to $799	3,954	202	458	758	330	742	312	394	255	502
$800 to $999	7,567	384	1,006	1,512	577	1,501	473	847	458	810
$1,000 to $1,249	8,234	412	1,043	1,498	570	1,621	651	993	566	880
$1,250 to $1,499	7,496	406	1,044	1,158	716	1,361	426	872	684	829
$1,500 to $1,999	10,292	596	1,366	1,505	926	1,921	504	1,157	948	1,371
$2,000 to $2,499	6,835	564	944	861	541	1,306	204	629	633	1,152
$2,500 or more	11,545	821	2,099	1,082	450	1,850	220	990	776	3,257
Median amount (dollars)	1,137	1,576	1,385	966	1,083	1,003	766	1,012	1,230	1,649
RENTER-OCCUPIED UNITS										
Total	44,660	2,158	6,419	5,917	2,645	8,355	2,620	5,384	3,245	7,917
Monthly housing costs:										
Less than $100	169	(S)	(S)	36	(S)	(S)	(S)	14	(S)	20
$100 to $199	617	(S)	115	106	45	109	34	103	20	75
$200 to $249	847	58	164	123	59	143	70	102	44	84
$250 to $299	740	66	140	98	50	130	60	56	107	107
$300 to $349	664	52	107	114	49	126	(S)	71	22	88
$350 to $399	638	28	122	98	55	94	80	48	(S)	85
$400 to $449	729	34	95	116	56	143	61	83	(S)	88
$450 to $499	837	30	127	110	84	168	101	91	(S)	86
$500 to $599	2,191	97	289	404	202	386	244	279	128	163
$600 to $699	2,609	59	272	471	251	484	311	390	192	178
$700 to $799	2,988	97	350	612	225	495	279	522	188	219
$800 to $999	6,097	232	656	1,214	524	1,030	458	913	405	664
$1,000 to $1,249	6,574	304	881	995	377	1,279	344	956	554	885
$1,250 to $1,499	4,912	254	746	486	197	1,191	134	569	482	852
$1,500 to $1,999	6,205	371	1,019	413	212	1,323	92	559	584	1,634
$2,000 to $2,499	2,786	182	515	121	(S)	454	49	159	206	1,054
$2,500 or more	3,141	206	604	162	59	345	51	161	105	1,448
No cash rent [1]	1,916	75	191	237	127	428	216	309	146	187
Median amount (dollars) [1]	1,071	1,200	1,175	891	862	1,115	780	962	1,159	1,574

– Represents or rounds to zero. S Estimate does not meet publication standards or has been withheld to avoid disclosure. [1] Excludes no cash rent.

Source: U.S. Census Bureau, "American Housing Survey: AHS Table Creator," <www.census.gov/programs-surveys/ahs/data.html>, accessed January 2021.

Table 1035. Occupied Housing Units—Financial Summary by Selected Characteristics of the Householder: 2019

[In thousands of units (124,135,000), except as indicated. As of Fall. Housing costs include real estate taxes, property insurance, utilities, fuel, water, garbage collection, homeowner association fees, cooperative or condominium fees, mobile home fees, routine maintenance, mortgages, other charges in mortgages, and mortgage insurance. Based on the American Housing Survey; see Appendix III]

Characteristic	Total occupied units [3]	Tenure		Black [1]		Hispanic origin [2]		Elderly			
								65 to 74 years old		75 years old and over	
		Owner	Renter	Owner	Renter	Owner	Renter	Owner	Renter	Owner	Renter
Total units [3]	**124,135**	**79,475**	**44,660**	**7,397**	**9,717**	**8,355**	**8,945**	**14,696**	**3,924**	**10,791**	**3,291**
Monthly housing costs:											
Less than $100	339	170	169	(S)	46	(S)	32	(S)	(S)	36	(S)
$100 to $199	1,762	1,145	617	194	187	118	118	260	84	317	71
$200 to $249	2,069	1,222	847	150	313	160	125	208	175	362	97
$250 to $299	2,360	1,621	740	200	238	155	128	403	142	424	145
$300 to $349	2,961	2,297	664	316	184	211	126	550	110	643	122
$350 to $399	3,098	2,460	638	302	169	241	102	628	77	610	138
$400 to $449	3,348	2,619	729	267	207	275	123	706	142	735	101
$450 to $499	3,380	2,543	837	213	255	234	111	586	130	692	85
$500 to $599	7,014	4,823	2,191	506	520	482	337	1,219	291	1,104	217
$600 to $699	7,263	4,654	2,609	400	689	397	434	1,259	264	942	136
$700 to $799	6,942	3,954	2,988	326	802	407	492	987	278	704	186
$800 to $999	13,664	7,567	6,097	685	1,569	755	1,166	1,690	515	1,270	341
$1,000 to $1,249	14,808	8,234	6,574	843	1,521	908	1,461	1,543	472	934	351
$1,250 to $1,499	12,408	7,496	4,912	651	1,039	799	1,232	1,226	244	785	187
$1,500 to $1,999	16,497	10,292	6,205	841	991	1,199	1,581	1,467	359	525	216
$2,000 to $2,499	9,621	6,835	2,786	637	388	827	594	788	188	306	131
$2,500 or more	14,686	11,545	3,141	848	299	1,167	517	1,138	197	402	440
Median amount (dol.) [4]	1,106	1,137	1,071	1,038	941	1,178	1,178	859	847	647	912
Monthly housing costs as percent of income: [5]											
Less than 5 percent	3,280	2,798	482	234	106	265	92	427	39	299	32
5 to 9 percent	12,949	11,428	1,521	882	255	989	302	2,172	91	1,372	33
10 to 14 percent	17,240	13,784	3,457	1,046	627	1,230	514	2,484	156	1,748	78
15 to 19 percent	17,852	12,920	4,932	1,078	968	1,154	846	1,942	193	1,444	124
20 to 24 percent	15,040	9,912	5,128	874	1,124	961	841	1,586	300	1,081	180
25 to 29 percent	11,307	6,649	4,658	624	1,051	732	913	1,149	390	868	243
30 to 34 percent	8,572	4,708	3,863	485	837	630	807	902	413	642	256
35 to 39 percent	6,082	3,141	2,941	366	618	376	691	652	258	474	197
40 to 49 percent	7,803	3,991	3,812	463	835	520	943	912	417	599	269
50 to 59 percent	4,525	2,143	2,382	283	591	359	574	525	242	375	256
60 to 69 percent	2,772	1,321	1,450	157	340	212	387	260	170	326	142
70 to 99 percent	4,151	1,932	2,219	223	525	304	524	508	229	353	276
Median amount (percent) [4, 6]	22	19	30	21	32	22	34	20	39	22	51
Median monthly costs (dol.): [4]											
Electricity	109	122	86	124	85	129	88	112	76	103	74
Piped gas	53	58	41	58	42	48	37	55	39	56	37
Fuel oil	125	125	83	133	(S)	(S)	(S)	125	100	125	(S)

S Estimate did not meet publication standards or was withheld to avoid disclosure. [1] For persons who selected this race group only. [2] Persons of Hispanic origin may be of any race. [3] Include units with no cash rents, not shown separately. [4] For explanation of median, see Guide to Tabular Presentation. [5] Money income before taxes. [6] Excludes households with zero or negative income and those with no cash rent.

Source: U.S. Census Bureau, "American Housing Survey: AHS Table Creator," <www.census.gov/programs-surveys/ahs/data.html>, accessed January 2021.

Table 1036. Owner-Occupied Housing Units—Value and Costs by State: 2019

[In percent, except as indicated (78,725 represents 78,725,000). The American Community Survey universe includes the household population and excludes the population living in institutions, college dormitories, and other group quarters. Based on a sample and subject to sampling variability; see Appendix III. For definition of median, see Guide to Tabular Presentation]

State	Total (1,000)	Percent of units with value of—			Median value (dol.)	Median selected monthly owner costs [1] (dol.)	Selected monthly owner costs as a percent income in the past 12 months [1]			
		$99,999 or less	$100,000 to $199,999	$200,000 or more			Less than 15.0 percent	15.0 to 24.9 percent	25.0 to 29.9 percent	30.0 percent or more
U.S..........	78,725	16.4	24.7	58.9	240,500	1,609	26.8	36.0	10.2	26.5
AL............	1,305	30.9	34.6	34.5	154,000	1,172	33.8	34.1	8.9	22.6
AK............	163	10.6	16.6	72.8	281,200	1,882	24.2	37.0	11.5	27.1
AZ............	1,743	12.6	20.3	67.1	255,900	1,457	27.6	35.6	10.7	25.5
AR............	762	35.4	36.4	28.2	136,200	1,094	34.4	35.2	8.6	21.5
CA............	7,219	4.3	4.6	91.1	568,500	2,421	18.2	32.4	12.0	36.9
CO............	1,472	5.5	7.3	87.2	394,600	1,845	24.7	36.2	10.8	27.9
CT............	896	4.8	22.2	72.9	280,700	2,087	23.0	35.0	11.0	30.6
DE............	265	8.4	22.5	69.1	261,700	1,557	29.7	34.7	10.3	25.1
DC............	121	1.1	2.1	96.8	646,500	2,684	27.2	36.3	10.7	25.2
FL............	5,238	13.8	23.7	62.5	245,100	1,530	23.2	33.5	10.5	32.2
GA............	2,471	18.5	30.9	50.6	202,500	1,450	29.1	37.0	9.1	24.2
HI............	280	1.5	3.3	95.2	669,200	2,472	18.0	28.5	12.4	40.9
ID............	469	10.3	23.5	66.2	255,200	1,306	27.5	39.1	9.5	23.5
IL............	3,212	18.6	29.1	52.3	209,100	1,688	26.8	37.2	10.1	25.5
IN............	1,800	26.5	39.7	33.8	156,000	1,146	36.5	35.9	8.5	18.7
IA............	908	26.2	37.8	36.0	158,900	1,266	32.5	39.4	9.2	18.8
KS............	757	29.4	31.8	38.9	163,200	1,387	30.9	40.1	9.5	19.3
KY............	1,172	29.9	37.1	33.0	151,700	1,179	32.7	36.6	9.2	21.2
LA............	1,158	24.8	34.6	40.6	172,100	1,279	32.7	33.8	8.1	24.6
ME............	414	18.2	31.7	50.1	200,500	1,387	26.4	37.8	9.8	25.8
MD............	1,488	5.6	14.0	80.5	332,500	2,015	25.0	37.9	10.6	26.0
MA............	1,648	2.7	8.0	89.3	418,600	2,276	23.2	35.9	11.7	29.0
MI............	2,841	25.2	34.2	40.6	169,600	1,285	32.0	36.5	9.1	22.1
MN............	1,598	10.6	24.6	64.9	246,700	1,595	29.4	39.8	10.0	20.7
MS............	741	39.2	34.2	26.5	128,200	1,149	30.9	33.3	9.5	25.6
MO............	1,650	24.7	35.8	39.5	168,000	1,271	31.9	38.2	9.2	20.4
MT............	301	14.8	21.0	64.3	253,600	1,466	23.0	37.5	10.2	28.9
NE............	511	21.3	38.5	40.2	172,700	1,427	29.1	41.1	10.0	19.6
NV............	648	6.1	11.7	82.2	317,800	1,589	24.1	35.5	11.4	28.3
NH............	384	8.2	18.3	73.5	281,400	1,963	21.2	38.5	10.9	29.1
NJ............	2,082	4.6	13.8	81.6	348,800	2,413	19.3	36.3	11.6	32.5
NM............	540	23.0	33.2	43.8	180,900	1,269	27.6	34.0	10.2	27.5
NY............	3,986	13.0	19.7	67.3	338,700	2,156	25.6	32.6	10.1	31.3
NC............	2,643	20.3	31.6	48.1	193,200	1,318	31.1	36.2	9.0	23.2
ND............	198	19.9	28.4	51.6	205,400	1,430	33.5	40.1	9.8	16.3
OH............	3,124	26.8	38.0	35.2	157,200	1,250	33.9	37.1	8.9	19.7
OK............	980	31.5	37.6	31.0	147,000	1,231	32.4	37.6	9.2	20.5
OR............	1,037	7.2	9.7	83.1	354,600	1,750	21.7	37.0	12.2	28.8
PA............	3,502	20.2	31.9	47.8	192,600	1,477	30.1	36.5	9.6	23.4
RI............	251	3.5	15.7	80.8	283,000	1,837	20.5	38.5	11.6	29.1
SC............	1,388	24.2	31.8	44.0	179,800	1,250	31.7	35.6	8.7	23.4
SD............	240	22.3	32.7	45.0	185,000	1,371	27.7	40.3	9.4	22.5
TN............	1,766	21.1	31.1	47.8	191,900	1,264	30.4	37.4	9.1	22.8
TX............	6,179	21.1	28.8	50.1	200,400	1,675	25.4	37.5	10.2	26.5
UT............	723	4.9	10.7	84.4	330,300	1,605	25.5	38.8	11.1	24.3
VT............	186	10.9	29.5	59.6	233,200	1,606	21.3	39.0	13.4	25.9
VA............	2,111	10.0	21.0	69.0	288,800	1,792	27.0	37.9	10.3	24.5
WA............	1,850	5.4	9.1	85.5	387,600	1,951	21.9	36.9	12.2	28.6
WV............	535	40.1	34.1	25.8	124,600	1,052	38.0	33.5	8.0	20.0
WI............	1,604	14.9	36.0	49.1	197,200	1,412	28.9	39.9	9.8	21.3
WY............	168	13.2	26.0	60.9	235,200	1,417	26.6	40.9	9.5	22.4

[1] For homes with a mortgage. Selected monthly owner costs are the sum of payments for mortgages, deeds of trust, contracts to purchase, or similar debts on the property (including payments for the first mortgage, second mortgages, home equity loans, and other junior mortgages); real estate taxes; fire, hazard, and flood insurance on the property; utilities; and fuels. It also includes, where appropriate, the monthly condominium fee for condominiums and mobile home costs.

Source: U.S. Census Bureau, 2019 American Community Survey, B25075, "Value"; B25077, "Median Value"; B25088, "Median Selected Monthly Owner Costs by Mortgage Status"; and B25091, "Mortgage Status by Selected Monthly Owner Cost as a Percentage of Household Income in the Past 12 Months"; <data.census.gov/>, accessed November 2020. See also <census.gov/programs-surveys/acs/>.

Table 1037. Renter-Occupied Housing Units—Gross Rent by State: 2019

[In percent, except as indicated (44,078 represents 44,078,000). The American Community Survey universe includes the household population, and excludes the population living in institutions, college dormitories, and other group quarters. For definition of median, see Guide to Tabular Presentation. Based on a sample and subject to sampling variability; see Appendix III]

State	Total [1] (1,000)	Percent of units with gross rent of—					Median gross rent (dol.)	Gross rent as a percent of household income in the past 12 months [3]			
		$299 or less [2]	$300 to $499	$500 to $749	$750 to $999	$1,000 or more		Less than 15.0 percent	15.0 to 24.9 percent	25.0 to 29.9 percent	30.0 percent or more
U.S..............	44,078	4.0	5.2	14.0	20.1	56.7	1,097	12.8	24.3	10.8	45.1
AL..............	592	5.7	11.0	27.3	28.4	27.6	807	14.5	21.9	9.6	40.9
AK..............	89	2.3	4.8	7.3	20.3	65.3	1,201	12.2	28.4	9.7	41.0
AZ..............	928	2.7	3.6	13.4	21.4	58.9	1,101	13.0	25.3	11.7	43.4
AR..............	402	6.2	11.4	33.7	28.4	20.4	742	15.8	23.9	10.1	38.6
CA..............	5,939	2.3	2.6	4.8	9.1	81.2	1,614	10.8	22.7	11.1	50.7
CO..............	763	2.8	2.9	6.7	11.5	76.2	1,369	11.1	25.2	11.6	47.7
CT..............	482	5.0	5.4	7.4	17.0	65.3	1,177	12.6	23.4	11.9	46.3
DE..............	112	4.2	4.1	8.7	20.5	62.4	1,116	13.8	24.2	9.8	46.6
DC..............	171	5.9	4.3	4.5	8.1	77.1	1,603	16.6	26.1	11.8	40.6
FL..............	2,668	2.4	2.7	8.2	16.8	69.9	1,238	8.5	21.9	11.0	52.4
GA..............	1,382	3.3	5.5	15.1	22.0	54.2	1,049	12.6	24.5	10.7	44.8
HI..............	185	4.4	2.6	4.6	7.3	81.0	1,651	10.1	21.3	11.9	49.7
ID..............	186	3.5	8.6	22.2	27.8	38.0	880	14.2	26.3	10.2	42.7
IL..............	1,654	5.0	6.0	15.2	22.3	51.5	1,020	14.5	25.5	10.5	42.4
IN..............	797	4.4	7.1	25.8	33.1	29.6	840	14.5	24.5	11.2	41.7
IA..............	379	4.1	10.9	27.5	29.7	27.8	808	15.7	27.3	10.8	38.6
KS..............	382	3.8	8.3	23.8	28.8	35.3	862	15.6	28.2	10.0	39.5
KY..............	577	6.5	10.1	30.5	28.2	24.8	773	16.9	23.5	9.8	38.3
LA..............	583	5.9	8.0	20.6	32.1	33.3	866	12.5	20.0	8.3	44.4
ME..............	159	7.5	9.6	19.9	25.7	37.4	870	11.2	25.0	14.8	39.8
MD..............	739	3.8	3.4	5.5	10.1	77.2	1,401	11.2	25.3	11.2	47.4
MA..............	1,003	6.6	7.1	7.1	11.0	68.3	1,360	12.6	24.0	11.8	46.3
MI..............	1,129	4.9	6.7	21.3	29.5	37.5	888	13.8	24.0	10.4	44.3
MN..............	624	5.3	6.6	13.8	23.1	51.2	1,016	13.7	27.4	12.0	41.8
MS..............	360	7.3	11.7	27.3	29.8	23.9	777	12.7	21.1	9.5	40.2
MO..............	808	4.6	7.3	27.1	29.5	31.5	834	14.6	26.1	10.4	40.7
MT..............	136	4.8	9.4	26.5	25.4	33.9	831	17.1	22.4	11.2	41.1
NE..............	260	3.9	7.3	24.9	31.2	32.7	859	16.1	27.7	11.0	38.4
NV..............	496	1.3	2.2	9.5	21.6	65.4	1,168	11.6	24.0	10.5	48.2
NH..............	157	4.4	4.4	8.8	20.9	61.5	1,147	10.6	26.0	13.5	44.3
NJ..............	1,204	4.3	3.5	4.5	10.2	77.4	1,376	11.6	25.7	11.3	46.6
NM..............	253	6.0	7.8	25.5	26.2	34.5	847	15.2	23.1	9.1	41.7
NY..............	3,461	5.2	5.3	9.7	13.4	66.4	1,309	14.6	22.3	10.2	47.3
NC..............	1,404	4.1	6.6	20.3	26.3	42.8	931	13.5	25.2	10.4	42.6
ND..............	125	5.9	8.3	28.1	28.2	29.4	804	21.1	27.9	8.7	35.5
OH..............	1,607	5.3	7.7	28.2	30.0	28.7	813	15.0	26.6	11.0	40.4
OK..............	515	4.7	7.9	28.5	29.6	29.2	814	15.7	24.9	9.5	39.5
OR..............	612	3.3	3.2	10.4	17.5	65.7	1,185	11.7	24.1	12.5	45.5
PA..............	1,617	5.2	6.6	18.4	24.5	45.3	951	14.6	24.6	10.2	43.6
RI..............	156	8.5	7.8	7.4	22.5	53.8	1,043	12.0	25.5	10.5	45.9
SC..............	587	3.4	6.8	19.8	28.3	41.6	922	12.1	23.3	11.1	42.0
SD..............	114	6.6	10.9	30.3	26.6	25.6	769	17.1	27.9	9.7	35.9
TN..............	889	4.9	6.7	21.8	27.0	39.7	904	13.1	24.6	10.9	42.1
TX..............	3,806	2.6	3.8	11.3	24.2	58.2	1,091	11.9	25.6	11.0	44.8
UT..............	301	2.0	3.9	11.5	23.7	58.8	1,098	14.4	26.7	12.1	41.8
VT..............	77	5.7	5.5	14.9	25.8	48.0	980	8.5	22.0	11.9	50.6
VA..............	1,081	3.2	4.2	10.9	15.6	66.1	1,254	12.2	27.0	11.0	42.9
WA..............	1,083	3.5	2.9	7.8	13.9	71.9	1,359	12.4	25.6	11.8	45.3
WV..............	194	9.0	11.8	32.6	27.7	18.9	727	14.1	19.6	9.6	36.3
WI..............	783	3.3	6.4	23.3	33.1	33.9	867	16.5	26.8	11.1	40.0
WY..............	66	3.8	9.0	26.3	28.2	32.7	822	17.2	22.9	9.4	39.5

[1] Includes units with no cash rent. [2] Includes only units with cash rent. [3] Percent distribution of rental units by gross rent as a percent of household income. Percentage calculated from totals which include units "not computed"; therefore, rows will not total 100 percent.

Source: U.S. Census Bureau, 2019 American Community Survey, B25063, "Gross Rent"; B25064, "Median Gross Rent"; and B25070, "Gross Rent as a Percentage of Household Income in Past 12 Months"; <data.census.gov/>, accessed November 2020.

Table 1038. Occupied Housing Units—Characteristics by Poverty Status: 2019

[124,135 represents 124,135,000. As of Fall. Based on the American Housing Survey (AHS); see Appendix III. The AHS uses a poverty definition based on household income received during the 12 months just before the survey. This differs from other poverty estimates so data will not be comparable to data in other tables. The poverty thresholds consider only money income, not assets of benefits in kind, and are updated every year to reflect changes in the Consumer Price Index; see <www2.census.gov/programs-surveys/ahs/2019/2019%20AHS%20Definitions.pdf> for details]

Characteristic	Total (1,000)	Poverty level (percent)				
		Less than 50 percent	50 to 99 percent	100 to 149 percent	150 to 199 percent	200 percent or more
Total units	**124,135**	**100.0**	**100.0**	**100.0**	**100.0**	**100.0**
Tenure:						
Owner	79,475	42.3	38.5	47.4	54.5	71.8
Renter	44,660	57.7	61.5	52.6	45.5	28.2
Units in structure:						
1, detached	79,335	43.6	43.1	50.3	56.5	70.5
1, attached	6,482	5.1	3.8	4.0	4.6	5.6
2 to 4	9,118	12.2	13.0	11.8	8.7	5.6
5 to 9	6,008	8.3	8.2	6.7	7.3	3.7
10 to 19	5,164	6.6	5.5	5.0	4.7	3.6
20 to 49	4,706	5.3	5.7	5.0	3.8	3.3
50 or more	6,472	10.9	9.5	6.8	5.0	4.1
Manufactured/mobile home or trailer	6,756	7.7	11.0	10.4	9.1	3.7
Square footage of unit:						
Less than 500	2,954	6.2	6.2	4.1	2.5	1.4
500 to 749	8,080	11.5	12.6	10.3	9.2	4.6
750 to 999	14,695	16.9	17.2	16.5	14.5	9.9
1,000 to 1,499	29,272	24.0	24.2	26.1	27.2	22.7
1,500 to 1,999	23,016	12.4	10.2	15.0	17.3	20.5
2,000 to 2,499	15,293	6.7	5.8	6.9	10.1	14.4
2,500 to 2,999	8,237	2.5	2.2	2.4	3.7	8.3
3,000 to 3,999	7,684	2.3	1.6	2.6	2.8	7.9
4,000 or more	3,932	1.3	1.2	1.7	1.5	3.9
Not reported	10,972	16.2	18.6	14.3	11.1	6.2
Monthly total housing costs as a percent of household income:						
Less than 5 percent	3,280	(NA)	(NA)	(NA)	0.6	3.7
5 to 9 percent	12,949	(NA)	0.7	1.7	3.4	14.3
10 to 14 percent	17,240	(NA)	1.8	4.3	7.0	18.4
15 to 19 percent	17,852	(NA)	2.8	5.4	9.7	18.6
20 to 24 percent	15,040	0.4	4.3	7.7	10.3	14.8
25 to 29 percent	11,307	0.4	7.8	9.6	10.7	9.8
30 to 34 percent	8,572	0.8	7.8	10.0	10.5	6.6
35 to 39 percent	6,082	0.4	7.1	9.1	10.0	4.0
40 to 49 percent	7,803	1.1	10.1	14.8	14.3	4.5
50 to 59 percent	4,525	1.2	9.4	10.7	8.6	1.9
60 to 69 percent	2,772	2.0	7.9	7.4	4.1	0.9
70 to 99 percent	4,151	4.4	16.8	9.6	5.0	1.0
100 percent or more [1]	8,476	59.4	20.4	6.7	3.5	0.7
Description of area within 1/2 block: [2]						
Single-family detached houses	89,883	60.4	64.3	66.7	68.5	75.5
Single-family attached houses	16,753	14.8	13.9	13.6	12.4	13.4
Multiunit residential buildings	31,200	38.2	37.3	32.0	28.3	21.4
Manufactured/mobile homes	8,606	9.1	11.4	11.2	10.5	5.3
Commercial or institutional [3]	34,399	38.1	36.3	33.9	30.8	24.7
Industrial structures or factories	5,861	7.2	7.6	6.3	5.5	3.9
Primary air conditioning:						
With primary air conditioning	113,260	88.2	88.2	91.2	90.0	92.0
Central air conditioning	88,632	64.6	57.2	63.7	66.4	75.0
Room air conditioning	24,628	23.6	31.0	27.5	23.6	17.0
Unit does not have air conditioning	10,875	11.8	11.8	8.8	10.0	8.0
Equipment:						
With complete kitchen [4]	122,697	97.1	97.6	98.0	99.0	99.2
Lacking complete kitchen facilities	1,438	2.9	2.4	2.0	1.0	0.8
Kitchen sink	123,891	99.2	99.6	99.5	99.7	99.9
Refrigerator	123,550	98.7	99.1	99.2	99.5	99.7
Cooking stove or range	122,432	96.9	97.1	97.9	98.2	99.1
Dishwasher	91,727	56.3	46.0	54.1	63.2	82.0
Washing machine	106,448	71.1	68.5	76.7	81.8	90.5
Clothes dryer	104,891	68.5	64.7	74.7	79.8	89.8
Selected deficiencies: [2]						
Signs of mice or rats inside home in last 12 months	14,787	12.4	15.9	13.6	14.0	11.0
Signs of cockroaches in last 12 months	13,994	15.4	18.8	15.6	13.2	9.4
Holes in floors	1,518	2.1	3.3	1.8	1.6	0.8
Open cracks or holes (interior)	6,761	7.0	9.5	7.9	7.0	4.4
Broken plaster or peeling paint (interior)	2,627	2.9	4.5	3.4	2.9	1.5
Exposed wiring	3,378	3.7	4.4	3.0	2.9	2.4
Rooms without electric outlets	2,376	3.3	2.7	2.7	2.1	1.6

NA Not available. [1] May reflect a temporary situation, living off savings, or response error. [2] More than one category may apply to a unit. [3] Examples include stores, restaurants, schools, or hospitals. [4] Includes a sink, refrigerator, and oven or burners.

Source: U.S. Census Bureau, "American Housing Survey: AHS Table Creator," <www.census.gov/programs-surveys/ahs/data.html>, accessed February 2021.

Table 1039. Occupied Housing Units—Characteristics by Census Division: 2019

[In thousands (124,135 represents 124,135,000), except as indicated. As of Fall. Based on the American Housing Survey; see Appendix III]

Characteristic	Total units	New England	Middle Atlantic	East North Central	West North Central	South Atlantic	East South Central	West South Central	Mountain	Pacific
Total units	**124,135**	**5,944**	**16,118**	**18,643**	**8,703**	**24,402**	**7,757**	**14,578**	**9,414**	**18,576**
Units in structure:										
Single family detached	79,335	3,573	8,423	12,836	6,312	15,269	5,399	10,130	6,158	11,234
Single family attached	6,482	190	1,561	792	368	1,687	142	332	503	907
2 to 4 units	9,118	983	1,718	1,416	477	1,239	426	788	507	1,565
5 to 9 units	6,008	322	749	961	290	1,161	411	668	383	1,065
10 to 19 units	5,164	208	593	672	293	1,145	255	720	385	892
20 to 49 units	4,706	254	869	579	308	855	170	471	295	905
50 or more units	6,472	305	1,792	788	315	1,101	130	450	366	1,226
Manufactured/mobile home [1]	6,756	110	409	599	338	1,929	821	1,016	780	753
Year structure built:										
Median year (estimated date)	1978	1964	1960	1970	1976	1986	1983	1985	1987	1976
2018 to 2019	986	50	67	76	(S)	210	59	241	86	154
2016 to 2017	2,474	64	135	222	161	744	143	485	236	284
2010 to 2015	5,459	146	456	503	432	1,319	370	1,080	567	586
2005 to 2009	7,939	224	582	860	494	1,998	566	1,231	966	1,019
2000 to 2004	9,409	267	568	1,310	567	2,345	751	1,321	1,025	1,255
1995 to 1999	9,429	197	589	1,280	729	2,551	757	1,316	924	1,086
1990 to 1994	6,550	215	603	958	449	1,577	493	643	574	1,038
1985 to 1989	8,906	411	808	970	463	2,260	632	1,094	728	1,539
1980 to 1984	7,529	290	683	788	489	1,651	482	1,224	730	1,192
1970 to 1979	17,967	756	1,627	2,517	1,358	3,381	1,253	2,368	1,567	3,138
1960 to 1969	13,190	597	1,955	2,093	934	2,299	818	1,369	756	2,371
1950 to 1959	12,835	708	2,264	2,483	871	1,935	661	1,114	564	2,238
1940 to 1949	5,566	278	1,136	1,108	281	823	314	468	212	946
1930 to 1939	3,437	235	1,034	518	236	425	161	205	146	478
1920 to 1929	4,770	377	1,479	1,080	367	429	110	207	95	625
1919 or earlier	7,690	1,129	2,133	1,878	830	457	188	210	238	628
Stories in structure: [2]										
1 story	38,293	341	1,249	2,979	1,544	9,353	3,560	8,330	3,444	7,492
2 stories	42,749	2,074	5,166	7,145	3,879	7,215	2,508	4,044	3,391	7,327
3 stories	26,819	2,554	5,820	6,583	2,463	4,276	700	889	1,467	2,067
4 to 6 stories	6,798	736	2,431	917	406	1,053	117	223	243	671
7 or more stories	2,626	129	1,039	418	73	560	47	71	53	237
Foundation: [3]										
Full basement	26,832	2,753	6,197	7,831	4,038	2,920	761	44	1,622	667
Partial building	8,934	632	2,020	2,332	1,117	1,101	466	79	651	537
Crawlspace	18,080	148	643	1,830	838	4,934	2,289	1,906	1,150	4,342
Concrete slab	30,359	165	1,039	1,453	618	7,707	1,848	7,990	3,211	6,329
Equipment:										
With complete kitchen facilities [4]	122,697	5,895	15,839	18,474	8,626	24,135	7,648	14,452	9,317	18,311
Lacking complete kitchen facilities [5]	1,438	50	280	169	77	266	109	126	97	265
Kitchen sink	123,891	5,942	16,063	18,617	8,691	24,347	7,741	14,553	9,395	18,540
Refrigerator	123,550	5,937	16,008	18,560	8,683	24,272	7,717	14,516	9,369	18,486
Cooking stove or range	122,432	5,907	15,874	18,438	8,625	24,043	7,633	14,362	9,285	18,266
Microwave oven only	773	(S)	82	104	49	153	60	109	56	135
Dishwasher	91,727	4,223	10,424	12,715	6,710	19,175	5,595	11,040	7,745	14,099
Washing machine	106,448	4,816	11,950	15,910	7,725	22,099	7,102	13,066	8,482	15,298
Clothes dryer	104,891	4,761	11,522	15,820	7,690	21,725	7,024	12,912	8,392	15,045
Main heating equipment:										
Warm-air furnace	82,186	2,430	8,121	15,445	7,184	13,477	4,833	11,536	7,023	12,136
Steam or hot water system	10,912	2,566	5,501	1,259	486	458	(S)	(S)	278	346
Electric heat pump	14,294	101	409	409	365	8,291	1,834	1,241	915	727
Built-in electric units	4,995	404	1,047	829	296	504	178	92	255	1,390
Floor, wall, or pipeless furnace	5,624	226	607	389	175	639	265	543	460	2,320
Room heaters with flue	821	103	98	(S)	(S)	109	89	112	(S)	132
Room heaters without flue	711	(S)	45	(S)	(S)	152	182	218	(S)	61
Portable electric heaters	2,103	(S)	34	60	(S)	429	198	685	92	552
Stoves	1,195	(S)	190	120	71	126	(S)	42	214	276
Fireplaces with inserts	204	(S)	(S)	35	(S)	54	(S)	(S)	(S)	39
Fireplaces without inserts	74	–	–	(S)	(S)	(S)	10	(S)	(S)	(S)
Cooking stove	72	(S)	(S)	–	–	(S)	(S)	(S)	(S)	(S)
None	594	–	(S)	(S)	–	52	(S)	(S)	(S)	479
Main cooling equipment:										
Central air conditioning	88,632	1,894	7,339	13,768	7,327	21,853	6,640	12,843	7,181	9,786
Room air conditioning	24,628	3,279	7,284	3,827	1,173	2,117	998	1,532	1,036	3,382
None	10,875	771	1,496	1,047	203	432	119	203	1,196	5,408
Source of water:										
Public system or private company	110,171	4,763	13,790	15,487	7,714	21,202	7,390	13,771	8,591	17,464
Individual well	13,755	1,177	2,289	3,135	989	3,177	359	802	793	1,034
Means of sewage disposal:										
Public sewer	103,565	4,388	13,610	15,332	7,376	19,599	5,578	12,570	8,243	16,868
Septic tank or cesspool	20,293	1,542	2,443	3,271	1,315	4,765	2,158	1,966	1,162	1,672

– Represents or rounds to zero. S Estimate did not meet publication standards or withheld to avoid disclosure. [1] Includes trailers. [2] Excludes mobile homes; includes basements and finished attics. [3] Covers only single family homes (1 unit, attached or detached). [4] A complete kitchen includes sink, refrigerator, oven or burners.

Source: U.S. Census Bureau, "American Housing Survey: AHS Table Creator," <www.census.gov/programs-surveys/ahs/data.html>, accessed March 2021.

Table 1040. Heating Equipment and Fuels for Occupied Housing Units: 2011 to 2019

[114,833 represents 114,833,000. As of Fall. Data beginning 2011 based on Census 2010 controls. Based on American Housing Survey]

Type of equipment or fuel	Number (1,000)					Percent distribution				
	2011	2013	2015	2017	2019	2011	2013	2015	2017	2019
Occupied units, total	**114,833**	**115,852**	**118,290**	**121,560**	**124,135**	**100.0**	**100.0**	**100.0**	**100.0**	**100.0**
MAIN HEATING EQUIPMENT										
Warm air furnace	73,559	74,712	76,207	79,382	82,186	64.1	64.5	64.4	65.3	66.2
Steam or hot water	12,684	12,448	10,919	11,095	10,912	11.0	10.7	9.2	9.1	8.8
Electric heat pumps	13,395	13,526	13,980	14,128	14,294	11.7	11.7	11.8	11.6	11.5
Built-in electric units	4,886	5,064	4,616	4,925	4,995	4.3	4.4	3.9	4.1	4.0
Floor, wall, or pipeless furnace	4,570	4,571	5,963	5,616	5,624	4.0	3.9	5.0	4.6	4.5
Room heaters with flue	949	851	776	740	821	0.8	0.7	0.7	0.6	0.7
Room heaters without flue	1,095	1,034	647	749	711	1.0	0.9	0.5	0.6	0.6
Portable electric heaters	1,412	1,589	1,879	2,018	2,103	1.2	1.4	1.6	1.7	1.7
Stoves	1,094	1,050	1,197	1,348	1,195	1.0	0.9	1.0	1.1	1.0
Fireplaces with inserts	180	183	212	212	204	0.2	0.2	0.2	0.2	0.2
Fireplaces without inserts	70	61	87	83	74	0.1	0.1	0.1	0.1	0.1
Cooking stove	88	68	68	58	72	0.1	0.1	0.1	(Z)	0.1
Other	369	309	919	357	349	0.3	0.3	0.8	0.3	0.3
None	481	386	818	848	594	0.4	0.3	0.7	0.7	0.5
MAIN HEATING FUEL										
Housing units with heating fuel	114,352	115,465	117,472	120,712	123,541	100.0	100.0	100.0	100.0	100.0
Electricity	40,029	42,041	48,323	52,329	53,605	35.0	36.4	41.1	43.4	43.4
Utility gas	57,889	58,225	54,791	54,091	56,025	50.6	50.4	46.6	44.8	45.3
Bottled, tank, or liquid propane gas	5,474	5,198	4,703	5,074	5,279	4.8	4.5	4.0	4.2	4.3
Fuel oil	8,060	7,173	6,111	5,865	5,722	7.0	6.2	5.2	4.9	4.6
Kerosene or other liquid fuel	533	450	543	556	431	0.5	0.4	0.5	0.5	0.3
Coal or coke	79	98	80	89	84	0.1	0.1	0.1	0.1	0.1
Wood	2,004	1,992	2,197	2,305	2,118	1.8	1.7	1.9	1.9	1.7
Solar energy	20	31	40	(S)	(S)	(Z)	(Z)	(Z)	(S)	(S)
Other	263	257	684	372	247	0.2	0.2	0.6	0.3	0.2
COOKING FUEL										
Housing units with cooking fuel	114,640	115,694	117,849	121,183	123,672	100.0	100.0	100.0	100.0	100.0
Electricity	68,710	69,330	71,262	72,874	74,452	59.9	59.9	60.5	60.1	60.2
Piped gas	40,828	41,503	41,400	42,609	43,469	35.6	35.9	35.1	35.2	35.1
Bottled gas	5,015	4,791	4,986	5,607	5,648	4.4	4.1	4.2	4.6	4.6
Other	86	71	200	92	103	0.1	0.1	0.2	0.1	0.1

S Estimate does not meet publication standards or has been withheld to avoid disclosure. Z represents less than 0.05%.

Source: U.S. Census Bureau, "American Housing Survey: AHS Table Creator," <www.census.gov/programs-surveys/ahs/data.html>, accessed January 2021.

Table 1041. Occupied Housing Units—Housing Amenities and Deficiencies by Selected Characteristics of the Householder: 2019

[In thousands of units (79,475 represents 79,475,000). As of Fall. Based on the American Housing Survey; see Appendix III]

Characteristic	Total occupied units		Black [1]		Hispanic origin [2]		Elderly			
							65 to 74 years old		75 years old and over	
	Owner	Renter	Owner	Renter	Owner	Renter	Owner	Renter	Owner	Renter
Total units	**79,475**	**44,660**	**7,397**	**9,717**	**8,355**	**8,945**	**14,696**	**3,924**	**10,791**	**3,291**
Selected amenities:										
Porch, deck, balcony or patio	74,673	32,521	6,621	6,612	7,563	6,157	13,901	2,578	10,086	2,110
Usable fireplace	37,428	6,154	2,833	1,045	2,898	1,016	7,099	473	4,686	280
Separate dining room	46,291	15,347	4,804	3,797	4,792	3,411	8,685	1,215	6,179	831
With 2 or more living rooms or recreation rooms	35,061	4,176	2,773	672	2,484	582	6,721	390	4,733	263
Garage or carport with home	64,933	17,870	5,261	2,683	6,450	3,639	12,067	1,523	9,088	1,147
Selected deficiencies:										
Signs of mice or rats in last 12 months	9,929	4,858	856	1,231	737	1,024	1,948	389	1,259	231
Signs of cockroaches in last 12 months	6,907	7,087	934	1,869	1,224	1,990	1,236	559	885	293
Holes in floors	711	808	93	188	103	176	142	57	66	(S)
Open cracks or holes (interior)	3,685	3,076	511	807	463	625	643	221	360	108
Broken/peeling paint or plaster (interior)	1,279	1,347	207	290	156	261	251	103	132	43
Exposed wiring	1,960	1,418	190	301	292	357	320	111	283	87
Rooms without electric outlet	1,290	1,085	148	266	137	230	245	88	168	71
Water leakage from inside structure [3]	5,159	4,283	607	981	504	801	823	349	545	160
Water leakage from outside structure [3]	7,904	3,832	789	813	676	667	1,522	263	928	107
Sagging roof [4]	1,163	510	167	97	179	96	172	26	112	(S)
Missing roof material [4]	2,569	748	405	142	368	124	463	64	322	(S)
Hole in roof [4]	872	440	154	113	168	83	147	49	118	(S)
Missing bricks, siding, or other outside wall material [4]	1,890	687	239	116	261	105	254	67	173	(S)
Boarded up windows [4]	677	298	98	62	136	62	120	(S)	61	(S)
Broken windows [4]	2,591	992	295	181	397	216	445	64	210	(S)
Foundation crumbling or has open crack or hole [4]	3,555	1,220	431	267	458	209	632	93	368	47
Units with mold in the last 12 months	1,700	1,964	258	507	204	470	282	151	216	55

S Does not meet publication standards. [1] For persons who selected this race group only. [2] Persons of Hispanic origin may be of any race. [3] During the 12 months prior to the survey. [4] Excludes multiunit structures.

Source: U.S. Census Bureau, "American Housing Survey: AHS Table Creator," <www.census.gov/programs-surveys/ahs/data.html>, accessed January 2021.

Table 1042. Household Energy Consumption and Expenditures by Selected Characteristics: 2015

[118.2 represents 118,200,000. Btu=British thermal units; for definition, see text, Section 19. Includes all primary occupied housing units in the 50 states and the District of Columbia. Vacant housing units, seasonal units, second homes, military houses, and group quarters are excluded. Consumption and expenditures for biomass (wood), coal, district steam, and solar thermal are excluded. Electricity consumption from on-site solar photovoltaic generation (i.e., solar panels) is included. Data from the Residential Energy Consumption Survey (RECS). Data were collected between August 2015 and April 2016]

Characteristic	Total housing units (millions)	Energy consumption				Energy expenditures			
		Total (trillion Btu)	Per household (million Btu)	Per household member (million Btu)	Per square foot (thousand Btu)	Total (billion dollars)	Per household (dollars)	Per household member (dollars)	Per square foot (dollars)
All homes	**118.2**	**9,114**	**77.1**	**30.3**	**38.4**	**219.3**	**1,856**	**728**	**0.92**
Region:									
Northeast	21.0	1,984	94.4	38.1	45.2	47.7	2,269	915	1.09
Midwest	26.4	2,486	94.3	37.8	41.4	46.4	1,760	706	0.77
South	44.4	3,064	68.9	27.3	35.6	85.2	1,917	758	0.99
West	26.4	1,581	59.9	22.3	33.4	40.1	1,518	565	0.85
Housing unit type:									
Single-family detached	73.9	6,991	94.6	34.6	37.1	161.7	2,188	801	0.86
Single-family attached	7.0	491	70.0	28.6	39.5	11.2	1,602	655	0.90
Apartment buildings with 2-4 units	9.4	503	53.5	22.3	52.5	12.5	1,329	555	1.30
Apartment buildings with 5 or more units	21.1	724	34.2	17.3	38.8	22.1	1,045	529	1.18
Mobile homes	6.8	406	59.8	22.8	50.0	11.9	1,750	666	1.46
Housing tenure:									
Owned	74.5	6,825	91.6	35.4	37.1	159.9	2,146	829	0.87
Single-family	66.2	6,347	95.9	36.5	36.5	146.2	2,208	840	0.84
Apartments	3.3	175	52.4	26.6	45.5	4.9	1,476	748	1.28
Mobile homes	5.0	304	61.1	24.6	49.9	8.8	1,768	712	1.44
Rented [1]	43.7	2,289	52.4	21.2	42.7	59.4	1,360	550	1.11
Single-family	14.7	1,135	77.4	25.3	41.8	26.7	1,818	594	0.98
Apartments	27.2	1,052	38.7	18.2	43.1	29.7	1,090	514	1.22
Mobile homes	1.8	103	56.3	18.7	50.2	3.1	1,702	565	1.52
Year of construction:									
Before 1950	20.8	1,842	88.7	35.5	44.1	39.5	1,901	762	0.94
1950 to 1959	12.6	1,067	84.4	34.5	45.2	23.5	1,861	760	1.00
1960 to 1969	12.8	961	75.0	32.0	40.0	22.5	1,756	750	0.94
1970 to 1979	18.3	1,290	70.3	27.9	39.8	32.4	1,765	700	1.00
1980 to 1989	16.0	1,053	65.7	27.3	35.9	28.0	1,747	725	0.95
1990 to 1999	16.8	1,317	78.3	29.1	35.9	32.6	1,937	719	0.89
2000 to 2009	17.0	1,328	78.2	28.0	32.7	34.2	2,013	721	0.84
2010 to 2015	3.8	257	67.0	23.9	28.5	6.7	1,755	626	0.75
Total square footage: [2]									
Fewer than 1,000	26.6	1,072	40.3	19.9	53.8	29.9	1,126	554	1.50
1,000 to 1,499	26.1	1,542	59.0	23.2	48.2	41.0	1,569	618	1.28
1,500 to 1,999	17.5	1,359	77.8	30.4	44.6	33.5	1,919	750	1.10
2,000 to 2,499	14.1	1,268	89.8	32.7	40.3	29.5	2,088	759	0.94
2,500 to 2,999	10.8	1,111	102.9	38.5	37.7	24.7	2,282	854	0.84
3,000 or greater	23.1	2,762	119.6	40.4	29.4	60.8	2,631	888	0.65
Number of household members:									
1 member	28.7	1,591	55.3	55.3	36.6	37.9	1,319	1,319	0.87
2 members	42.7	3,229	75.6	37.8	36.6	79.0	1,849	924	0.90
3 members	19.4	1,643	84.6	28.2	39.9	39.0	2,009	670	0.95
4 members	15.5	1,472	94.9	23.7	40.2	35.3	2,274	569	0.96
5 members	7.2	698	97.1	19.4	42.2	16.8	2,338	468	1.02
6 or more members	4.6	481	103.8	15.7	42.0	11.4	2,457	371	0.99
Annual household income:									
Less than $20,000	22.9	1,303	57.0	25.9	43.1	32.5	1,421	645	1.08
$20,000 to $39,999	27.3	1,882	68.9	29.3	40.7	44.5	1,629	692	0.96
$40,000 to $59,999	18.4	1,354	73.6	29.9	38.7	32.7	1,778	723	0.93
$60,000 to $79,999	15.2	1,218	80.0	29.9	37.0	29.6	1,940	725	0.90
$80,000 to $99,999	9.7	827	85.4	31.5	37.4	19.5	2,014	741	0.88
$100,000 to $119,999	8.1	733	90.4	30.6	34.2	17.7	2,187	739	0.83
$120,000 to $139,999	5.4	552	101.7	33.7	37.1	13.0	2,396	794	0.87
$140,000 or more	11.2	1,244	111.2	36.8	36.0	29.9	2,669	884	0.86
Main heating fuel									
Natural gas	57.7	5,517	95.7	37.0	43.1	108.1	1,875	726	0.84
Electricity	40.9	2,096	51.2	20.6	30.5	68.4	1,672	672	1.00
Fuel oil/kerosene	5.8	645	111.2	43.6	47.9	16.9	2,919	1,144	1.26
Propane	5.0	468	93.4	37.6	37.4	13.3	2,645	1,066	1.06

[1] Rented includes households that occupy their primary housing units without paying rent. [2] Total square footage includes all basements, finished or conditioned (heated or cooled) areas of attics, and conditioned garage space that is attached to the home. Unconditioned and unfinished areas in attics and attached garages are excluded.

Source: U.S. Energy Information Administration, 2015 RECS Survey Data, "Consumption & Energy Expenditures (C&E) Tables," <eia.gov/consumption/residential/index.php>, accessed May 2019.

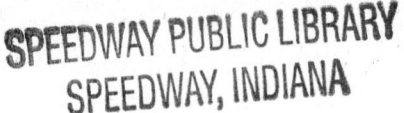

Table 1043. Household Energy Insecurity By Selected Characteristics: 2020

[In percent, except total units (123.5 represents 123,500,000). Data are from the Residential Energy Consumption Survey (RECS). Energy insecurity defined in this table includes only those issues collected as part of the RECS questionnaire. Other factors, such as energy costs as a percentage of household income, could be considered as household energy insecurity, but are not included here. Respondents may report more than one energy insecurity issue. Data were collected in late 2020 and early 2021. Includes all primary occupied housing units in the 50 states and the District of Columbia. Vacant housing units, seasonal units, and group quarters are excluded. Housing units located on military installations are included]

Characteristic	Total housing units (millions)	Percent of households reporting:					
		Any household energy insecurity	Reducing or forgoing food or medicine to pay energy costs	Leaving home at unhealthy temperature	Receiving disconnect or delivery stop notice	Unable to use heating equipment [1]	Unable to use cooling equipment [1]
All homes..........................	**123.5**	**27.2**	**19.9**	**9.9**	**10.0**	**4.1**	**5.1**
Region:							
Northeast.......................	21.9	25.3	17.4	10.9	8.4	3.7	3.8
Midwest.........................	27.0	24.3	18.0	7.4	10.4	3.5	3.8
South............................	46.8	29.9	22.8	9.9	12.1	4.7	6.6
West.............................	27.7	26.9	18.9	11.4	7.3	4.1	4.9
Housing unit type:							
Single-family detached..............	77.1	22.2	15.5	7.6	8.2	3.7	4.9
Single-family attached..............	7.5	28.2	21.1	10.7	10.2	3.4	4.6
Apartment buildings with 2-4 units..............................	9.3	44.9	35.5	17.2	16.6	5.7	6.3
Apartment buildings with 5 or more units.............................	22.8	30.6	23.1	12.0	9.9	2.8	3.9
Mobile homes....................	6.8	47.0	36.7	16.8	21.2	11.7	11.6
Number of household members:							
1 member........................	33.6	25.4	18.1	10.9	7.8	3.2	3.6
2 members.......................	45.3	21.1	14.8	8.0	7.0	2.9	4.1
3 members.......................	18.3	32.1	24.2	10.1	11.9	5.3	5.6
4 members.......................	15.6	32.6	25.1	10.3	13.5	4.7	7.0
5 members.......................	6.4	38.0	30.0	11.6	18.9	8.1	9.6
6 or more members..................	4.4	47.6	36.4	15.6	24.9	10.3	12.8
Annual household income:							
Less than $5,000................	4.5	58.0	46.9	24.8	26.6	11.4	12.1
$5,000 to $9,999................	4.0	56.1	46.6	21.2	19.5	9.7	8.0
$10,000 to $19,999...............	10.3	46.8	37.7	20.7	18.1	8.1	8.6
$20,000 to $39,999...............	24.1	39.7	31.3	15.0	14.4	6.5	8.2
$40,000 to $59,999...............	19.6	29.3	21.5	8.9	11.5	4.4	5.8
$60,000 to $99,999...............	27.7	20.1	12.8	5.7	7.0	2.1	3.3
$100,000 to $149,999...............	16.5	11.1	6.1	4.1	3.7	1.3	2.1
$150,000 or more..................	16.9	7.2	2.6	3.1	1.5	0.8	1.4
Householder age 60 or older: [2]							
Yes..............................	52.1	19.2	13.3	8.4	5.3	2.7	3.6
No...............................	71.4	33.0	24.7	10.9	13.4	5.1	6.2
Children under age 18 in household:							
Yes..............................	34.6	37.2	29.0	11.5	17.1	6.7	8.1
No...............................	89.0	23.3	16.4	9.2	7.3	3.1	4.0
Ethnicity of householder: [2]							
Hispanic or Latino...................	14.0	47.0	36.7	17.2	16.0	6.8	8.5
Not Hispanic or Latino..............	109.5	24.7	17.8	8.9	9.2	3.8	4.7
Race of householder: [2, 3]							
White............................	100.0	23.2	16.8	8.5	8.0	3.3	4.3
Hispanic or Latino..................	12.0	45.8	36.8	16.8	15.5	6.5	8.3
Not Hispanic or Latino..............	87.9	20.1	14.0	7.3	7.0	2.9	3.7
Black or African American...........	13.0	52.0	40.2	17.5	26.0	10.0	11.0
Hispanic or Latino..................	0.6	55.6	41.3	17.5	22.2	(S)	(S)
Not Hispanic or Latino..............	12.3	51.9	40.2	17.5	26.2	9.8	10.9
Asian............................	6.1	25.2	17.0	12.4	3.5	3.3	4.3
American Indian or Alaska Native...	1.1	51.9	38.0	15.7	17.6	10.2	6.5
Native Hawaiian or Other Pacific Islander..........................	0.4	42.9	34.3	(S)	(S)	(S)	(S)
More than one race.................	3.1	46.1	34.2	16.5	17.1	6.1	10.0
Housing tenure: [4]							
Owned...........................	82.9	20.4	14.2	7.2	6.6	3.5	4.6
Rented...........................	40.6	41.0	31.6	15.3	16.9	5.3	6.2

S Data withheld because either the relative standard error was greater than 50% or fewer than 10 cases responded. [1] Includes inability to use equipment at any time during the previous 12 months because equipment was broken and household could not have it repaired, or because of an electricity, natural gas, or bulk fuel disruption due to lack of payment. [2] A householder is a person in whose name the home is owned or rented. These characteristics refer to the householder that completed the RECS questionnaire. [3] Householders were permitted to select more than one racial category to describe themselves. These householders are only included as "more than one race." [4] Rented includes households that occupy their primary housing units without paying rent.

Source: U.S. Energy Information Administration, 2020 RECS Survey Data, "Housing Characteristics Tables," <www.eia.gov/consumption/residential/>, accessed June 2022.

Table 1044. Home Remodeling—Number of Households With Work Done by Amount Spent: 2022

[In thousands (3,689 represents 3,689,000), except percent. As of Winter 2022. For work done in the prior 12 months. Based on a household survey and subject to sampling error; see source]

Remodeling project	Total households with work done [1]		Households with work done by outside contractor	Number of households by amount spent		
	Number	Percent of households		Under $1,000	$1,000 to $2,999	Over $3,000
Conversion of garage/attic/basement into living space..........	3,689	1.5	1,107	590	640	1,604
Remodel bathroom...................	18,146	7.2	7,114	6,230	4,137	5,884
Remodel kitchen.....................	10,875	4.3	4,783	2,294	2,114	5,242
Remodel bedroom....................	8,851	3.5	1,884	4,125	1,795	1,264
Convert room to home office...........	7,848	3.1	502	5,567	956	237
Remodel other rooms.................	7,803	3.1	1,775	3,549	1,383	1,587
Add bathroom.......................	1,942	0.8	884	327	512	675
Add other rooms - exterior addition........	1,403	0.6	662	18	112	905
Add deck/porch/patio.................	7,710	3.0	3,932	1,396	2,081	3,656
Roofing............................	11,844	4.7	9,319	1,794	2,001	7,231
Siding - vinyl/metal..................	3,035	1.2	1,740	573	564	1,449
Aluminum windows..................	1,390	0.6	787	281	431	464
Clad-wood/wood windows.............	1,222	0.5	711	225	110	613
Vinyl windows......................	5,142	2.0	3,539	813	1,086	2,708
Ceramic tile floors..................	4,563	1.8	2,301	1,935	1,010	1,005
Hardwood floors....................	6,497	2.6	3,195	1,547	2,114	1,917
Laminate flooring...................	8,222	3.2	3,148	2,920	2,598	1,525
Vinyl flooring......................	6,402	2.5	2,315	2,408	1,542	1,532
Carpeting.........................	6,871	2.7	5,162	1,803	2,546	1,841
Kitchen cabinets....................	6,268	2.5	2,755	1,500	1,229	2,625
Kitchen counter tops.................	7,021	2.8	4,152	1,659	1,867	2,663
Skylights..........................	1,385	0.6	851	447	259	227
Exterior doors......................	7,503	3.0	3,780	4,028	1,456	976
Interior doors......................	4,403	1.7	1,384	2,489	715	410
Garage doors......................	3,695	1.5	2,358	1,317	1,366	417
Concrete or masonry work.............	8,081	3.2	4,854	2,468	1,801	3,017
Landscaping.......................	21,897	8.6	5,697	12,270	3,590	2,995
Swimming pool - in ground............	1,314	0.5	775	126	120	730
Ceramic wall tile....................	3,211	1.3	1,189	1,681	635	371

[1] Includes no response and amount unknown.

Source: © MRI-Simmons Winter 2022 USA Study. Courtesy of MRI-Simmons. See also <www.mrisimmons.com/>.

Table 1045. Residential Mortgage Home Purchase Loans by Borrower Race/Ethnicity and Income Level: 2005 to 2020

[In percent, except as noted. Includes conventional and nonconventional first-lien home-purchase loans for 1- to 4-family owner-occupied, site-built homes. Based on data collected under the Home Mortgage Disclosure Act (HDMA). In 2018 significant changes were made to HMDA data collection. Therefore, beginning in 2018, data are not strictly comparable to prior years. See source for more information]

Race/ethnicity and income	2005	2010	2014	2015	2016	2017	2018	2019	2020
Home purchase loans (1,000)............	**4,836**	**2,157**	**2,747**	**3,134**	**3,463**	**3,606**	**3,594**	**3,736**	**4,101**
PERCENT DISTRIBUTION OF HOME PURCHASE LOANS									
Borrower race and ethnicity: [1]									
All borrowers........................	100.0	100.0	100.0	100.0	100.0	100.0	100.0	100.0	100.0
Asian.............................	5.0	5.5	5.4	5.3	5.5	5.8	5.9	5.7	5.5
Black or African American.............	7.7	6.0	5.2	5.5	6.0	6.4	6.8	7.0	7.3
Hispanic white.....................	10.5	8.1	7.9	8.3	8.8	8.8	8.9	9.2	9.1
Non-Hispanic white..................	61.7	67.6	69.1	68.1	66.4	64.9	62.0	60.3	59.1
Other minority [2]....................	1.3	0.9	0.8	0.8	0.8	0.9	0.8	0.8	0.9
Joint.............................	2.3	2.7	3.4	3.5	3.6	3.7	3.6	3.7	3.9
Missing...........................	11.5	9.1	8.3	8.5	8.9	9.6	12.0	13.3	14.1
Borrower income: [3]									
Low or moderate....................	24.6	35.4	27.0	27.9	26.2	26.3	28.0	28.6	30.4
Middle............................	25.7	25.6	25.6	26.1	26.4	26.7	26.7	27.2	27.4
High..............................	45.5	37.3	46.1	44.9	46.4	46.0	43.9	43.1	41.2
DENIAL RATES FOR HOME PURCHASE LOANS									
Applicant race and ethnicity: [1]									
All applicants [4]....................	16.0	15.6	13.3	12.1	11.5	10.7	9.8	8.9	9.3
Asian.............................	15.9	15.9	14.1	12.7	11.6	10.6	10.2	9.1	9.7
Black or African American.............	26.5	24.9	23.0	20.8	19.8	18.4	17.4	15.9	18.1
Hispanic white.....................	21.1	21.8	18.4	16.2	15.0	13.4	13.1	11.6	12.5
Non-Hispanic white..................	12.2	13.0	11.1	10.0	9.5	8.8	7.9	7.0	6.9
Other minority [2]....................	20.8	22.0	19.0	17.2	16.6	14.7	14.3	13.0	13.7

[1] Applications are placed in one category for race and ethnicity. The application is designated as joint if one applicant was reported as white and the other was reported as one or more minority races, or if the application is designated as white with one Hispanic applicant and one non-Hispanic applicant. If there are two applicants and each reports a different minority race, the application is designated as two or more minority races. If an applicant reports two races and one is white, that applicant is categorized under the minority race. Otherwise, the applicant is categorized under the first race reported. [2] Consists of applications by American Indians or Alaska Natives, Native Hawaiians or other Pacific Islanders, and borrowers reporting two or more minority races. [3] Not shown are borrowers whose income was not used or not applicable. The categories for the borrower-income group are as follows: low- or moderate-income is less than 80 percent of estimated current area median family income (AMFI), middle-income is at least 80 percent and less than 120 percent of AMFI, and high-income is at least 120 percent of AMFI. [4] Includes other race/ethnic groups not shown separately.

Source: Consumer Financial Protection Bureau, Federal Financial Institutions Examination Council, *Data Point: 2020 Mortgage Market Activity and Trends*, August 2021. See also <www.consumerfinance.gov/data-research/research-reports/>.

Table 1046. Median Loan Amount for Home Purchase and Refinance Loans by Borrower Race/Ethnicity and Income Level: 2018 to 2020

[In thousands of dollars (225 represents $225,000). Includes conventional and nonconventional first-lien home-purchase loans for 1- to 4-family owner-occupied, site-built homes. Based on data collected under the Home Mortgage Disclosure Act (HDMA); see source for more information]

Race/ethnicity and income	Home purchase loans			Refinance loans		
	2018	2019	2020	2018	2019	2020
HOME PURCHASE LOANS						
All home purchase loans.......................	**225**	**237**	**256**	**196**	**250**	**259**
Borrower race and ethnicity: [1]						
Asian..	333	340	362	317	387	359
Black or African American..................	204	217	236	177	222	235
Hispanic white..............................	209	221	241	196	244	250
Non-Hispanic white.........................	216	227	247	187	239	246
Other minority [2]...........................	224	234	254	202	250	261
Joint..	278	291	315	246	304	303
Borrower income: [3]						
Low or moderate............................	150	161	180	136	170	180
Middle......................................	212	225	248	186	224	235
High..	309	321	350	271	328	319

[1] Applications are placed in one category for race and ethnicity. The application is designated as joint if one applicant was reported as white and the other was reported as one or more minority races or if the application is designated as white with one Hispanic applicant and one non-Hispanic applicant. If there are two applicants and each reports a different minority race, the application is designated as two or more minority races. If an applicant reports two races and one is white, that applicant is categorized under the minority race. Otherwise, the applicant is categorized under the first race reported. [2] Consists of applications by American Indians or Alaska Natives, Native Hawaiians or other Pacific Islanders, and borrowers reporting two or more minority races. [3] The categories for the borrower-income group are as follows: Low- or moderate-income is less than 80 percent of estimated current area median family income (AMFI), middle-income is at least 80 percent and less than 120 percent of AMFI, and high-income is at least 120 percent of AMFI.

Source: Bureau of Consumer Financial Protection, Federal Financial Institutions Examination Council, *Data Point: 2020 Mortgage Market Activity and Trends*, August 2021. See also <www.consumerfinance.gov/data-research/research-reports/>.

Table 1047. Commercial Buildings—Summary: 2018

[5,918 represents 5,918,000. Covers roofed and walled structures whose principal activities are nonresidential, nonagricultural, and nonindustrial and that are larger than 1,000 square feet. Building type based on predominant activity in which the occupants were engaged. Based on the Commercial Buildings Energy Consumption Survey (CBECS), a sample survey of building representatives conducted in 2018; subject to sampling variability]

Characteristic	All buildings (1,000)	Total floor-space (mil. sq. ft.)	Total workers in all buildings (1,000)	Mean square foot per building [1] (1,000)	Mean square foot per worker [1]	Mean operating hours per week [1]
All buildings..........................	**5,918**	**96,758**	**85,927**	**16.3**	**1,074**	**62**
Building floorspace (sq. ft.):						
1,001 to 5,000............................	2,837	8,031	9,715	2.8	677	57
5,001 to 10,000...........................	1,358	10,206	9,185	7.5	971	61
10,001 to 25,000..........................	966	15,623	12,066	16.2	1,225	64
25,001 to 50,000..........................	397	14,430	10,930	36.4	1,300	77
50,001 to 100,000.........................	218	15,387	12,873	70.4	1,169	78
100,001 to 200,000........................	93	13,042	11,412	140.1	1,128	84
200,001 to 500,000........................	40	11,723	10,523	294.1	1,103	95
Over 500,000.............................	9	8,317	9,224	947.6	897	114
Principal activity within building:						
Education.................................	438	13,686	10,375	31.2	1,319	48
Food sales................................	163	1,032	916	6.3	1,127	110
Food service..............................	284	1,372	2,866	4.8	479	81
Health care...............................	137	4,011	6,656	29.3	603	59
Inpatient.................................	9	2,259	3,597	264.8	628	168
Outpatient................................	129	1,753	3,059	13.6	573	52
Lodging...................................	214	6,997	2,941	32.7	2,291	166
Mercantile................................	518	10,781	8,900	20.8	1,211	64
Retail (other than mall)...................	352	5,193	3,269	14.8	1,589	66
Enclosed and strip malls..................	167	5,588	5,631	33.5	992	61
Office....................................	970	16,682	32,856	17.2	508	54
Public assembly...........................	488	7,157	3,333	14.7	2,075	51
Public order and safety...................	74	1,563	1,542	21.0	998	128
Religious worship.........................	439	5,686	1,948	13.0	2,767	28
Service...................................	867	6,343	4,736	7.3	1,265	53
Warehouse and storage....................	1,004	17,429	7,081	17.4	2,214	71
Other.....................................	113	2,403	1,585	21.2	1,351	82
Vacant....................................	209	1,616	(S)	7.7	(S)	5

– Represents zero. S Data withheld because either the relative standard error was greater than 50 percent or fewer than 20 buildings were sampled. [1] For explanation of mean, see Guide to Tabular Presentation.

Source: U.S. Energy Information Administration, Commercial Buildings Energy Consumption Survey (CBECS), "2018 CBECS Survey Data," <www.eia.gov/consumption/commercial/>, accessed November 2021.

Section 21
Manufactures

This section presents summary data for manufacturing as a whole and more detailed information for major industry groups and selected products. The types of measures shown at the different levels include data for establishments, employment and payroll, value and quantity of production and shipments, value added by manufacture, inventories, and various indicators of financial status.

The principal source of these data is the U.S. Census Bureau's Annual Survey of Manufactures. Reports on current activities of industries or current movements of individual commodities are also compiled by such government agencies as the Bureau of Economic Analysis; Bureau of Labor Statistics; the Department of Commerce, International Trade Administration; and by private research or trade associations.

The Census Bureau's *Quarterly Financial Report* publishes up-to-date aggregate statistics on the financial results and position of U.S. corporations. Based upon a sample survey, the QFR presents estimated statements of income and retained earnings, balance sheets, and related financial and operating ratios for manufacturing corporations with assets of $250,000 or over, and mining, wholesale trade and retail trade corporations with assets of $50 million and over or above industry-specific receipt cut-off values. These statistical data are classified by industry and by asset size.

Several private trade associations provide industry coverage for certain sections of the economy.

Censuses and annual surveys—The first census of manufactures covered the year 1809. Between 1809 and 1963, a census was conducted at periodic intervals. Since 1967, it has been conducted every 5 years for years ending in "2" and "7". Results from the census are presented in this section utilizing the North American Industry Classification System (NAICS). Census data, either directly reported or estimated from administrative records, are obtained for every manufacturing plant with one or more paid employees. For additional information see text, Section 15, Business Enterprise, and the Census Bureau website at <census.gov/programs-surveys/economic-census.html>.

The Annual Survey of Manufactures (ASM), conducted for the first time in 1949, collects data for the years between censuses for the more general measure of manufacturing activity covered in detail by the censuses. The annual survey data are estimates derived from a scientifically selected sample of establishments. The ASM is a sample survey of approximately 50,000 establishments conducted annually, except for years ending in 2 and 7, at which time ASM statistics are included in the manufacturing sector of the Economic Census. In 2017, there were approximately 291,000 active manufacturing establishments. For sample efficiency and cost considerations, the manufacturing population is partitioned into two groups: (1) establishments

eligible to be mailed a questionnaire, defined as the mail stratum, which is comprised of larger single-location manufacturing companies and all manufacturing establishments of multi-location companies, supplemented annually with new large single-location companies from IRS data and new multi-location companies from The Report of Organization; and (2) establishments not eligible to be mailed a questionnaire, defined as the nonmail stratum, which includes small- and medium-sized single establishment companies.

Establishments and classification—Each of the establishments covered in the 2017 Economic Census—Manufacturing was classified in accordance with the industry definitions in the 2017 NAICS manual. In NAICS, an industry is generally defined as a group of establishments that have similar production processes. To the extent practical, the system uses supply-based or production-oriented concepts in defining industries. The resulting group of establishments must be significant in terms of number, value added by manufacture, value of shipments, and number of employees. Establishments frequently make products classified both in their industry (primary products) and other industries (secondary products). Industry statistics (employment, payroll, value added by manufacture, value of shipments, etc.) reflect the activities of the establishments, which may make both primary and secondary products. Product statistics, however, represent the output of all establishments without regard for the classification of the producing establishment. For this reason, when relating the industry statistics, especially the value of shipments, to the product statistics, the composition of the industry's output should be considered.

Establishment—An establishment is a single physical location where business is conducted or where services or industrial operations are performed. Data in this sector includes those establishments where manufacturing is performed. A separate report is required for each manufacturing establishment (plant) with one employee or more that is in operation at any time during the year. An establishment not in operation for any portion of the year is requested to return the report form with the proper notation in the "Operational Status" section of the form. In addition, the establishment is requested to report data on any employees, capital expenditures, inventories, or shipment from inventories during the year.

Durable goods—Items with a normal life expectancy of 3 years or more. Automobiles, furniture, household appliances, and mobile homes are common examples.

Nondurable goods—Items which generally last for only a short time (3 years or less). Food, beverages, clothing, shoes, and gasoline are common examples.

Statistical reliability—For a discussion of statistical collection and estimation, sampling procedures, and measures of statistical reliability applicable to Census Bureau data, see Appendix III.

Table 1048. Manufacturing—Contribution to Gross Domestic Product in Current and Real (2012) Dollars by Industry: 2000 to 2021

[In billions of dollars (10,251.0 represents $10,251,000,000,000). Value added GDP is the contribution of each industry's labor and capital to its gross output and to the overall gross domestic product (GDP) of the United States. Value added is equal to an industry's gross output (sales or receipts and other operating income, commodity taxes, and inventory change) minus its intermediate inputs (consumption of goods and services purchased from other industries or imported). Current-dollar value added is calculated as the sum of distributions by an industry to its labor and capital which are derived from the components of gross domestic income]

Industry	NAICS [1]	2000	2010	2015	2019	2020	2021
CURRENT DOLLARS							
Gross domestic product, total [2]	(X)	10,251.0	15,049.0	18,206.0	21,372.6	20,893.7	22,996.1
Private industries	(X)	8,927.9	12,941.0	15,866.6	18,750.8	18,223.1	20,223.5
Manufacturing	31–33	1,549.8	1,799.8	2,131.0	2,370.9	2,272.0	2,563.3
Durable goods	33, 321, 327	924.6	965.5	1,184.4	1,327.9	1,268.8	1,385.7
Wood products	321	28.3	23.3	32.5	39.9	42.2	58.2
Nonmetallic mineral products	327	42.6	38.4	54.7	65.1	66.8	71.0
Primary metals	331	47.0	50.9	60.1	66.2	58.3	82.4
Fabricated metal products	332	121.3	120.0	147.4	162.9	145.8	155.5
Machinery	333	113.1	127.3	152.5	167.5	157.6	167.1
Computer & electronic products	334	225.3	240.2	267.5	307.7	317.3	340.4
Electrical equipment, appliances, & components	335	45.7	50.8	63.7	65.0	63.6	69.4
Motor vehicles, bodies & trailers, & parts	3361–63	137.5	88.8	146.3	158.7	154.6	169.4
Other transportation equipment	3364–66, 69	71.1	120.8	149.2	165.7	130.5	135.6
Furniture & related products	337	33.5	21.8	29.2	32.3	31.5	29.8
Nondurable goods	31, 32 [3]	625.2	834.3	946.6	1,043.0	1,003.1	1,177.6
Food & beverage & tobacco products	311, 312	163.2	223.5	261.9	277.8	289.8	310.5
Textile mills & textile product mills	313, 314	28.0	15.6	17.9	16.8	15.3	16.6
Apparel & leather & allied products	315, 316	22.2	10.4	9.7	9.3	9.8	11.6
Paper products	322	62.2	56.4	59.7	59.7	59.7	61.1
Printing & related support activities	323	43.7	39.5	40.2	41.3	39.6	41.1
Petroleum & coal products	324	52.7	123.8	145.6	163.6	113.7	208.8
Chemical products	325	187.8	303.3	333.3	391.0	394.6	438.9
Plastics & rubber products	326	65.5	61.8	78.3	83.7	80.6	89.1
CHAINED (2012) DOLLARS							
Gross domestic product, total [2]	(X)	13,138.0	15,649.0	17,390.3	19,032.7	18,384.7	19,427.3
Private industries	(X)	11,367.6	13,514.2	15,197.8	16,773.6	16,142.3	17,154.5
Manufacturing	31–33	1,673.7	1,936.2	2,046.3	2,233.9	2,167.8	2,332.1
Durable goods	33, 321, 327	750.7	968.8	1,124.0	1,239.2	1,178.3	1,285.6
Wood products	321	25.3	22.9	26.5	29.5	28.4	28.2
Nonmetallic mineral products	327	49.1	38.7	46.4	49.7	49.4	50.9
Primary metals	331	60.7	50.9	74.7	79.7	91.1	88.6
Fabricated metal products	332	155.4	125.6	134.7	141.5	123.3	131.8
Machinery	333	129.8	132.3	134.9	140.5	128.2	140.6
Computer & electronic products	334	67.5	227.1	282.3	340.7	351.0	382.1
Electrical equipment, appliances, & components	335	54.3	52.8	61.4	59.1	57.8	63.7
Motor vehicles, bodies & trailers, & parts	3361–63	99.5	87.1	123.3	141.3	138.2	175.5
Other transportation equipment	3364–66, 69	95.2	124.4	139.2	149.0	114.9	122.6
Furniture & related products	337	40.0	22.6	27.3	28.3	26.6	25.0
Nondurable goods	31, 32 [3]	964.0	974.8	922.2	994.1	989.9	1,045.4
Food & beverage & tobacco products	311, 312	224.6	234.0	234.7	251.6	245.2	268.1
Textile mills & textile product mills	313, 314	30.8	16.6	17.3	16.1	14.7	15.8
Apparel & leather & allied products	315, 316	20.0	10.6	9.0	8.1	8.6	10.5
Paper products	322	70.8	55.8	54.6	52.1	55.2	55.3
Printing & related support activities	323	37.7	37.6	37.6	37.7	35.4	37.4
Petroleum & coal products	324	183.8	213.0	198.5	244.3	246.1	270.5
Chemical products	325	288.7	347.5	301.7	322.6	327.6	330.1
Plastics & rubber products	326	76.9	67.7	74.0	78.5	75.5	80.9

X Not applicable. [1] North American Industry Classification System (NAICS) code; see text, Section 15. [2] Includes industries, not shown separately. For additional industries, see Table 708. [3] Except NAICS 321 and 327.

Source: U.S. Bureau of Economic Analysis, Industry Data, Gross Domestic Product by Industry, "Value Added by Industry," <apps.bea.gov/itable>, accessed April 2022.

Table 1049. Manufacturing Plants Using Industrial Robotic Equipment and Employees Exposed to Robots by Industry: 2019

[In percent. Industrial robotic equipment (or industrial robots) are automatically controlled, reprogrammable, and multipurpose machines used in industrial automated operations. Data shown for establishments that have either active robots at the plant, capital expenditures on robotic equipment, or purchases of robots. Data are experimental and based on the 2018 and 2019 Annual Survey of Manufactures]

Industry	2017 NAICS code [1]	Plants with robots	Employees exposed to robots	Industry	2017 NAICS code [1]	Plants with robots	Employees exposed to robots
Manufacturing	31-33	11.1	25.7	Chemical	325	6.7	14.3
Food	311	13.7	25.4	Plastics & rubber products	326	23.2	34.6
Beverage & tobacco products	312	4.7	11.3	Nonmetallic mineral products	327	6.3	18.5
Textile mills	313	6.2	11.1	Primary metal	331	18.9	31.2
Textile product mills	314	2.9	7.7	Fabricated metal products	332	13.4	23.7
Apparel	315	0.8	1.4	Machinery	333	14.7	29.4
Leather & allied products	316	4.6	17.0	Computer & electronic products	334	9.9	18.2
Wood products	321	4.1	6.2	Electrical equipment & appliances [2]	335	18.9	34.1
Paper	322	9.9	16.9	Transportation equipment	336	28.6	47.6
Printing & related activities	323	3.1	[3] 8.7	Furniture & related products	337	7.4	18.6
Petroleum & coal products	324	4.1	8.7	Miscellaneous	339	7.5	20.2

[1] Based on the North American Industry Classification System, 2017 (NAICS). [2] Includes component manufacturing. [3] Standard error exceeds 40% of the estimate.

Source: U.S. Census Bureau, "Annual Survey of Manufactures Industrial Robotic Equipment: 2018 and 2019," <www.census.gov/library/publications/2022/econ/2019-asm-robotic-equipment.html>, accessed August 2022.

Table 1050. Manufacturing—Establishments, Employees, and Annual Payroll by Industry: 2019 and 2020

[132,989 represents 132,989,000. Excludes most government employees, railroad employees, and self-employed persons. See Appendix III]

Industry	NAICS code [1]	Establishments		Employees (1,000) [2]		Payroll (mil. dol.)	
		2019	2020	2019	2020	2019	2020
All industries, total..........................	(X)	7,959,103	8,000,178	132,989	134,163	7,428,554	7,564,810
Manufacturing, total.....................	31–33	287,626	283,524	12,110	12,000	740,234	738,225
Percent of all industries.................	(X)	3.61	3.54	9.11	8.94	9.96	9.76
Food..	311	28,090	28,652	1,594	1,614	73,564	78,475
Beverage and tobacco products............	312	10,875	11,134	256	268	13,146	13,305
Textile mills.................................	313	1,926	1,898	93	86	4,157	3,818
Textile product mills........................	314	5,605	5,340	106	108	4,226	4,242
Apparel manufacturing......................	315	5,462	4,961	81	74	2,596	2,256
Leather and allied products................	316	1,171	1,108	26	25	991	928
Wood products..............................	321	14,223	13,747	416	413	18,554	18,904
Paper..	322	3,938	3,870	347	342	22,873	22,912
Printing and related support activities......	323	24,194	23,393	429	415	20,650	19,047
Petroleum and coal products..............	324	2,108	2,133	108	112	11,483	11,831
Chemical....................................	325	13,832	13,987	817	835	69,513	73,721
Plastics and rubber products..............	326	11,951	11,804	797	795	40,749	41,107
Nonmetallic mineral products..............	327	15,008	14,930	402	397	22,535	22,495
Primary metal...............................	331	4,021	3,858	386	371	25,816	23,487
Fabricated metal products.................	332	54,430	53,565	1,467	1,432	80,985	78,284
Machinery...................................	333	22,768	22,274	1,079	1,051	70,789	68,022
Computer and electronic products..........	334	11,870	11,690	795	797	71,573	72,901
Electrical equipment, appliance and components...............................	335	5,402	5,312	349	343	21,872	22,081
Transportation equipment..................	336	11,509	11,284	1,641	1,618	113,355	111,018
Furniture and related products.............	337	14,397	14,359	367	360	16,361	15,856
Miscellaneous...............................	339	24,846	24,225	553	545	34,447	33,535

X Not applicable. [1] Data based on North American Industry Classification System (NAICS) 2017. See text, Section 15. [2] Covers full- and part-time employees who are on the payroll in the pay period including March 12.

Source: U.S. Census Bureau, County Business Patterns, "All Sectors: County Business Patterns, including ZIP Code Business Patterns, by Legal Form of Organization and Employment Size Class for the U.S., States, and Selected Geographies: 2020," <data.census.gov>, accessed May 2022. See also <www.census.gov/programs-surveys/cbp.html>.

Table 1051. Manufacturing—Establishments, Employees, and Annual Payroll by State: 2020

[12,000 represents 12,000,000. Excludes most government employees, railroad employees, and self-employed persons. Data are for North American Industry Classification System (NAICS) 2017, codes 31–33. See Appendix III]

State	Establishments	Employees (1,000) [1]	Payroll (mil. dol.)	State	Establishments	Employees (1,000) [1]	Payroll (mil. dol.)
United States.......	283,524	12,000	738,225	Missouri.............	5,551	276	15,893
Alabama.............	4,102	265	14,263	Montana.............	1,351	21	1,078
Alaska...............	549	13	756	Nebraska............	1,739	100	5,380
Arizona..............	4,269	156	10,383	Nevada.............	1,900	50	2,972
Arkansas............	2,525	163	7,982	New Hampshire.....	1,754	66	4,121
California............	36,052	1,162	88,863	New Jersey..........	7,065	222	14,478
Colorado............	5,121	130	8,370	New Mexico.........	1,314	28	1,463
Connecticut.........	3,809	160	12,267	New York............	14,257	407	25,133
Delaware............	580	30	1,936	North Carolina......	8,543	446	23,642
District of Columbia..	106	1	46	North Dakota........	695	28	1,536
Florida..............	13,298	325	18,500	Ohio................	13,493	674	38,993
Georgia.............	7,544	392	20,745	Oklahoma...........	3,304	131	7,136
Hawaii...............	760	13	523	Oregon.............	5,330	178	11,537
Idaho...............	1,930	64	3,897	Pennsylvania........	13,239	551	32,514
Illinois..............	12,634	542	34,757	Rhode Island.......	1,228	39	2,315
Indiana.............	7,849	511	28,360	South Carolina.......	3,880	249	14,395
Iowa...............	3,427	216	12,865	South Dakota.......	1,036	46	2,286
Kansas.............	2,673	167	9,745	Tennessee..........	5,695	333	18,471
Kentucky............	3,645	248	13,674	Texas..............	20,179	830	54,524
Louisiana............	3,067	119	8,741	Utah...............	3,450	132	8,005
Maine...............	1,677	51	2,873	Vermont............	1,015	31	1,756
Maryland............	2,892	99	6,919	Virginia..............	4,906	241	14,232
Massachusetts.......	6,111	235	18,990	Washington..........	6,787	269	18,918
Michigan............	12,143	598	34,456	West Virginia........	1,071	47	2,696
Minnesota...........	6,853	316	19,730	Wisconsin..........	8,525	471	27,019
Mississippi...........	2,005	147	7,324	Wyoming............	596	10	766

[1] Covers full- and part-time employees who are on the payroll in the pay period including March 12.

Source: U.S. Census Bureau, County Business Patterns, CB2000CBP, "All Sectors: County Business Patterns, including ZIP Code Business Patterns, by Legal Form of Organization and Employment Size Class for the U.S., States, and Selected Geographies: 2020," <data.census.gov>, accessed May 2022. See also <www.census.gov/programs-surveys/cbp.html>.

Table 1052. Manufactures—Summary by Selected Industry: 2020

[Employee data in thousands (11,352.6 represents 11,352,600); financial data in millions of dollars (693,181 represents $693,181,000,000), except as noted. Based on data from the Annual Survey of Manufactures]

Industry based on shipments	2017 NAICS code [1]	All employees			Production workers [2] (1,000)	Value added by manufactures [3] (mil. dol.)	Value of shipments [4] (mil. dol.)
		Number [2] (1,000)	Payroll				
			Total (mil. dol.)	Per employee (dol.)			
Manufacturing, total [5]	**31–33**	**11,352.6**	**693,181**	**61,059**	**8,098.2**	**2,377,065**	**5,221,325**
Food [5]	311	1,516.4	75,342	49,685	1,222.6	324,514	827,132
Animal food	3111	58.4	3,338	57,165	43.3	23,246	59,883
Grain and oil seed milling	3112	52.1	3,756	72,076	39.5	22,190	88,595
Sugar and confectionery products	3113	82.2	4,057	49,372	63.2	17,121	38,984
Fruit and vegetable preserving and specialty food	3114	154.8	8,097	52,293	126.0	36,108	76,583
Dairy products	3115	152.8	8,956	58,620	113.3	42,369	129,288
Animal slaughtering and processing	3116	527.7	23,543	44,613	464.0	73,829	227,896
Seafood product preparation and packaging	3117	33.1	1,513	45,764	26.8	5,185	13,186
Bakeries and tortilla	3118	254.8	11,329	44,464	192.4	43,117	72,739
Beverage and tobacco products	312	216.1	12,420	57,467	123.2	98,019	156,041
Beverage	3121	205.4	11,483	55,896	115.2	54,962	105,997
Textile mills	313	80.6	3,623	44,932	64.6	10,620	24,531
Textile product mills	314	99.2	3,935	39,675	76.3	10,447	21,286
Apparel [5]	315	67.6	2,096	30,984	54.9	4,753	8,428
Cut and sew apparel	3152	51.6	1,618	31,386	41.9	3,794	6,594
Leather and allied products	316	25.3	961	38,029	19.6	2,004	4,009
Wood products [5]	321	400.0	18,050	45,124	327.8	54,662	117,715
Sawmills and wood preservation	3211	82.8	4,246	51,278	72.1	16,656	37,281
Paper	322	324.9	22,168	68,232	251.0	81,783	180,344
Pulp, paper, and paperboard mills	3221	91.5	7,698	84,131	72.6	37,749	68,532
Converted paper products	3222	233.4	14,471	61,999	178.4	44,034	111,812
Printing and related support activities	323	373.8	18,739	50,139	271.2	43,783	74,428
Petroleum and coal products	324	106.1	11,465	108,023	69.9	65,915	361,888
Chemical [5]	325	760.6	63,565	83,569	477.5	398,425	696,046
Basic chemical	3251	144.1	13,745	95,398	91.0	83,235	178,466
Pharmaceutical and medicine	3254	254.6	24,068	94,542	145.6	171,328	231,284
Soap, cleaning compound, and toilet preparation	3256	100.6	6,350	63,136	67.0	51,277	83,345
Plastics and rubber products	326	770.6	39,552	51,325	601.7	117,246	235,404
Plastics products	3261	638.3	32,408	50,771	497.2	96,946	196,458
Rubber product	3262	132.3	7,144	53,997	104.5	20,299	38,946
Nonmetallic mineral products	327	386.5	21,938	56,759	301.2	74,967	132,981
Glass and glass product	3272	90.5	4,730	52,269	71.7	15,408	26,439
Cement and concrete products	3273	174.1	10,071	57,846	138.9	34,647	63,836
Primary metal [5]	331	347.0	21,880	63,053	272.3	73,077	200,919
Iron and steel mills and ferroalloy	3311	81.1	6,488	79,981	66.1	23,914	74,883
Foundries	3315	107.2	5,664	52,851	85.2	13,439	24,509
Fabricated metal products [5]	332	1,343.5	75,469	56,174	1,011.0	190,416	347,336
Forging and stamping	3321	97.1	5,281	54,369	73.9	12,473	27,219
Cutlery and hand tool manufacturing	3322	32.0	1,750	54,668	23.5	6,071	9,724
Architectural and structural metals	3323	355.8	19,966	56,123	259.5	51,100	96,326
Boiler, tank, and shipping container	3324	84.0	5,515	65,615	63.7	14,947	35,519
Machine shops, turned product and screw, nut, and bolt	3327	358.6	19,576	54,597	280.5	39,155	62,287
Coating, engraving, heat treating, and allied activities	3328	115.7	5,904	51,016	92.8	14,837	24,710
Machinery [5]	333	1,019.7	65,562	64,292	663.0	173,557	355,335
Agriculture, construction, and mining machinery	3331	177.4	10,614	59,827	123.6	34,796	83,587
Industrial machinery	3332	107.0	8,631	80,639	60.3	19,196	36,069
HVAC and commercial refrigeration equipment	3334	146.7	7,341	50,042	107.4	24,235	45,787
Metalworking machinery	3335	136.7	8,342	61,029	97.9	17,290	28,192
Engine, turbine, and power transmission equipment	3336	89.1	5,963	66,905	56.6	16,316	36,500
Computer and electronic products [5]	334	784.2	67,530	86,113	368.6	176,386	312,277
Computer and peripheral equipment	3341	38.2	3,195	83,722	14.7	8,852	19,270
Communications equipment	3342	83.7	8,041	96,066	32.1	17,085	34,753
Semiconductor and other electronic component	3344	262.6	21,186	80,692	157.3	51,922	100,158
Navigational, measuring, medical, and control instruments	3345	384.1	34,194	89,020	155.2	96,043	153,838
Electrical equipment, appliance, and component [5]	335	337.8	21,268	62,954	225.7	63,718	128,342
Electrical equipment	3353	111.3	7,138	64,127	71.3	19,605	40,154
Other electrical equipment and component	3359	138.0	9,175	66,473	88.0	25,451	50,922
Transportation equipment [5]	336	1,528.0	102,380	67,004	1,092.5	284,082	821,412
Motor vehicle	3361	216.0	15,477	71,663	174.9	68,898	301,958
Motor vehicle parts	3363	559.0	29,220	52,268	426.2	73,836	223,171
Aerospace product and parts	3364	406.6	37,282	91,686	237.9	94,362	182,291
Ship and boat building	3366	131.6	8,454	64,251	89.0	19,856	38,419
Furniture and related products [5]	337	349.9	15,349	43,864	269.8	37,692	68,999
Miscellaneous [5]	339	514.6	29,889	58,080	333.7	90,999	146,475
Medical equipment and supplies	3391	267.6	17,586	65,730	169.8	57,419	87,692

[1] North American Industrial Classification System, 2017; see text, Section 15. [2] Includes all full-time and part-time employees on payrolls of operating manufacturing establishments. All employees represents the average of production workers plus all other employees for the payroll period ended nearest the 12th of March. [3] Adjusted value added; takes into account (a) value added by merchandising operations (difference between sales value and cost of merchandise sold without further manufacture, processing, or assembly), plus (b) net change in finished goods and work-in-process inventories between beginning and end of year. [4] Received or receivable net selling values, "free on board" (FOB) plant (exclusive of freight and taxes), of all products shipped as well as all miscellaneous receipts. In the case of multiunit companies, the manufacturer was requested to report the value of products transferred to other establishments of the same company at full economic or commercial value. [5] Includes industries not shown separately.

Source: U.S. Census Bureau, Annual Survey of Manufactures, "Annual Survey of Manufactures: Summary Statistics for Industry Groups and Industries in the U.S.: 2018-2020," December 2021, <data.census.gov/>, accessed May 2022. See also <www.census.gov/programs-surveys/asm.html>.

Table 1053. Manufactures—Summary by State: 2020

[Employment data in thousands (11,352.6 represents 11,352,600); financial data in millions of dollars (693,181 represents $693,181,000,000). Based on data from the Annual Survey of Manufactures. Data are for North American Industry Classification System (NAICS) 2017 codes 31–33. Sum of state totals may not add to U.S. total due to independent rounding. See Appendix III]

| State | All employees [1] | | | Production workers [1] | | Value added by manufactures [2] | | Value of shipments [3] (mil. dol.) |
| | Number (1,000) | Payroll | | | | | | |
		Total (mil. dol.)	Per employee (dol.)	Number (1,000)	Wages (mil. dol.)	Total (mil. dol.)	Per production worker (dol.)	
United States.............	**11,352.6**	**693,181**	**61,059**	**8,098.2**	**400,410**	**2,377,065**	**293,528**	**5,221,325**
Alabama......................	254.7	14,098	55,342	194.5	9,137	48,144	247,466	128,151
Alaska.......................	11.6	629	54,197	9.7	456	1,700	175,041	5,142
Arizona......................	146.8	9,788	66,656	93.8	4,560	32,537	346,697	61,909
Arkansas....................	154.6	7,692	49,759	125.4	5,435	26,921	214,716	61,968
California....................	1,097.4	77,111	70,265	703.1	36,384	265,516	377,644	507,503
Colorado....................	122.4	7,881	64,410	84.7	4,392	23,580	278,552	50,533
Connecticut.................	152.6	11,442	74,987	94.2	5,632	34,225	363,431	58,840
Delaware....................	26.9	1,615	59,920	20.1	971	6,852	341,123	16,736
District of Columbia........	1.2	65	52,902	0.9	48	226	240,442	381
Florida......................	297.4	17,650	59,351	203.8	9,394	56,220	275,883	109,607
Georgia.....................	360.7	19,596	54,330	274.1	12,338	74,689	272,499	169,850
Hawaii.......................	10.4	496	47,894	7.0	299	1,585	227,996	4,853
Idaho........................	58.5	3,719	63,551	44.2	2,386	10,666	241,272	24,474
Illinois......................	513.2	30,333	59,104	374.6	18,080	100,763	269,023	233,451
Indiana......................	484.7	27,715	57,175	373.1	18,415	96,245	257,982	234,514
Iowa.........................	208.4	12,219	58,619	155.4	7,605	46,739	300,808	111,259
Kansas......................	156.3	9,362	59,888	115.0	5,774	28,158	244,919	77,506
Kentucky....................	226.6	12,716	56,107	176.6	8,789	45,883	259,756	123,341
Louisiana....................	114.4	8,428	73,639	82.9	5,267	38,336	462,487	130,792
Maine........................	49.5	2,747	55,532	36.9	1,788	8,571	232,372	15,663
Maryland....................	95.6	6,507	68,057	61.7	3,256	23,240	376,717	41,309
Massachusetts.............	240.7	17,727	73,651	141.3	7,513	47,940	339,394	86,701
Michigan....................	564.1	31,917	56,578	413.3	19,743	95,673	231,471	234,622
Minnesota...................	301.7	18,933	62,747	207.9	10,500	56,250	270,628	119,457
Mississippi.................	136.2	6,884	50,541	107.6	4,634	24,054	223,461	58,409
Missouri.....................	263.0	15,498	58,925	193.3	9,574	56,574	292,625	119,907
Montana.....................	17.5	986	56,271	12.5	619	4,612	368,746	11,171
Nebraska....................	95.8	5,145	53,738	75.1	3,555	21,444	285,427	57,033
Nevada......................	45.8	2,868	62,672	32.6	1,790	9,561	293,195	18,336
New Hampshire..............	63.6	4,073	64,057	41.6	2,032	10,564	254,243	20,462
New Jersey..................	212.8	13,987	65,719	145.1	7,389	46,856	322,977	93,071
New Mexico.................	23.3	1,351	57,933	16.6	806	5,236	316,035	13,491
New York....................	382.6	24,420	63,821	259.8	13,409	79,326	305,368	150,351
North Carolina..............	414.4	22,661	54,681	309.4	13,777	100,271	324,084	193,810
North Dakota...............	25.4	1,415	55,636	19.3	903	5,739	296,712	13,634
Ohio.........................	644.3	37,487	58,184	471.5	23,072	119,459	253,372	286,256
Oklahoma...................	121.6	6,813	56,017	90.7	4,387	22,684	250,220	54,759
Oregon......................	182.8	11,810	64,620	129.5	6,543	32,902	254,086	66,618
Pennsylvania...............	521.3	30,332	58,182	369.2	18,018	104,164	282,123	205,148
Rhode Island................	36.3	2,263	62,398	25.1	1,228	6,568	262,046	12,066
South Carolina..............	228.8	13,372	58,446	170.8	8,265	52,315	306,232	118,327
South Dakota...............	44.0	2,315	52,598	33.3	1,528	6,661	199,790	17,533
Tennessee..................	323.5	18,014	55,685	242.6	11,323	69,740	287,419	148,607
Texas.......................	768.5	50,436	65,628	536.7	27,752	209,239	389,865	493,558
Utah.........................	125.9	7,610	60,466	87.7	4,300	26,064	297,136	54,467
Vermont.....................	29.7	1,805	60,713	19.9	937	4,593	230,449	9,057
Virginia......................	228.5	13,475	58,983	165.1	8,230	58,178	352,412	101,035
Washington.................	257.0	18,047	70,216	175.6	9,843	36,857	209,921	92,328
West Virginia................	46.0	2,738	59,572	34.3	1,873	10,570	307,802	22,553
Wisconsin...................	453.8	26,269	57,887	332.4	15,994	79,010	237,725	173,096
Wyoming....................	9.4	718	75,983	6.9	469	3,165	455,914	7,678

[1] Includes all full-time and part-time employees on the payrolls of operating manufacturing establishments during the pay period that included March 12. Included are employees on paid sick leave, paid holidays, and paid vacations; not included are proprietors and partners of unincorporated businesses. [2] Value added is derived by subtracting the cost of materials, supplies, containers, fuel, purchased electricity, and contract work from the value of shipments (products manufactured plus receipts for services rendered). The result of this calculation is adjusted by the addition of value added by merchandising operations (i.e., the difference between the sales value and the cost of merchandise sold without further manufacture, processing, or assembly) plus the net change in finished goods and work-in-process between the beginning and end of year inventories. [3] Includes extensive and unmeasurable duplication from shipments between establishments in the same industry classification.

Source: U.S. Census Bureau, Annual Survey of Manufactures, "Annual Survey of Manufactures: Summary Statistics for Industry Groups and Industries in the U.S.: 2018-2020," December 2021, <data.census.gov/>, accessed May 2022. See also <www.census.gov/programs-surveys/asm.html>

Table 1054. Manufacturing Industries—Employees by Industry: 2000 to 2021

[Annual averages of monthly figures (132,011 represents 132,011,000). Covers all full- and part-time employees who worked during, or received pay for, any part of the pay period including the 12th of the month. Minus sign (-) indicates decrease. See also headnote, Table 665]

Industry	2017 NAICS code [1]	All employees (1,000)					Percent change		
		2000	2010	2019	2020	2021	2000-2010	2010-2020	2020-2021
All industries...............................	(X)	**132,011**	**130,345**	**150,905**	**142,186**	**146,124**	**-1.3**	**9.1**	**2.8**
Manufacturing...........................	**31–33**	**17,263**	**11,528**	**12,817**	**12,167**	**12,346**	**-33.2**	**5.5**	**1.5**
Percent of all industries..........................	(X)	13.1	8.8	8.5	8.6	8.4	-32.4	-3.2	-1.3
Durable goods................................	(X)	10,877	7,064	8,039	7,573	7,676	-35.1	7.2	1.4
Wood products [2].............................	321	615	342	409	396	410	-44.4	15.8	3.5
Sawmills & wood preservation..................	3211	134	82	91	88	90	-38.5	6.6	2.1
Nonmetallic mineral products [2]...............	327	554	371	419	399	402	-33.1	7.7	0.7
Cement & concrete products....................	3273	234	170	198	194	195	-27.4	14.4	0.1
Primary metals [2]............................	331	622	362	387	354	350	-41.7	-2.4	-0.9
Iron & steel mills & ferroalloy production........	3311	135	87	87	82	79	-35.9	-5.5	-3.4
Steel products from purchased steel............	3312	73	52	59	54	53	-28.7	4.0	-3.3
Other nonferrous metal, including alumina and aluminum...............	3313,4	197	112	122	114	115	-43.1	2.2	0.4
Foundries...................................	3315	217	112	119	103	104	-48.4	-7.8	1.1
Fabricated metal products [2].................	332	1,753	1,282	1,486	1,386	1,384	-26.9	8.1	-0.2
Architectural & structural metals..............	3323	428	321	398	383	387	-25.0	19.2	1.2
Machine shops & threaded products...........	3327	365	313	365	335	328	-14.4	7.0	-1.9
Coating, engraving, & heat treating metals.....	3328	175	122	142	129	123	-30.0	5.4	-4.3
Machinery [2]................................	333	1,457	996	1,127	1,055	1,053	-31.6	5.9	-0.2
Agricultural, construction, & mining machinery..........................	3331	222	208	221	201	198	-6.4	-3.2	-1.7
HVAC & commercial refrigeration equipment...	3334	194	125	138	133	136	-35.9	6.7	2.5
Metalworking machinery......................	3335	274	155	179	164	159	-43.3	5.5	-2.5
Turbine & power transmission equipment.......	3336	111	92	100	91	87	-17.6	-1.3	-4.0
Other general purpose machinery..............	3339	344	226	276	262	265	-34.4	16.0	1.2
Computer & electronic products [2]............	334	1,820	1,095	1,075	1,063	1,058	-39.9	-2.9	-0.5
Computer & peripheral equipment..............	3341	302	158	161	160	158	-47.8	1.3	-1.3
Communications equipment....................	3342	239	117	84	86	85	-50.8	-27.1	-0.4
Semiconductors & electronic components......	3344	676	369	376	369	368	-45.4	-0.2	-0.1
Electronic instruments.......................	3345	488	406	422	418	417	-16.7	2.8	-0.2
Electrical equipment & appliances [2]............	335	591	360	403	384	394	-39.2	6.9	2.5
Household appliances........................	3352	106	60	62	62	72	-43.3	2.7	16.3
Electrical equipment.........................	3353	210	136	146	136	139	-35.1	0.3	1.5
Transportation equipment [2]..................	336	2,057	1,333	1,729	1,591	1,640	-35.2	19.3	3.1
Motor vehicles..............................	3361	291	153	237	206	250	-47.6	35.2	21.2
Motor vehicle bodies & trailers................	3362	183	107	162	151	163	-41.4	40.9	8.0
Motor vehicle parts..........................	3363	840	419	594	530	545	-50.1	26.6	2.7
Aerospace products & parts...................	3364	517	478	535	507	480	-7.5	6.1	-5.4
Ship & boat building.........................	3366	154	125	143	140	147	-19.1	12.2	5.2
Furniture & related products [2]..............	337	680	357	388	359	375	-47.5	0.6	4.4
Household & institutional furniture.............	3371	441	223	243	226	240	-49.3	1.3	6.0
Miscellaneous manufacturing.................	339	728	567	618	586	610	-22.1	3.4	4.1
Medical equipment & supplies.................	3391	305	303	325	317	327	-0.7	4.8	3.0
Other miscellaneous manufacturing............	3399	423	264	293	269	283	-37.6	1.7	5.4
Nondurable goods.............................	(X)	6,386	4,464	4,778	4,594	4,671	-30.1	2.9	1.7
Food manufacturing [2]......................	311	1,553	1,451	1,645	1,615	1,638	-6.6	11.3	1.4
Fruit & vegetable preserving & specialty........	3114	197	173	174	170	173	-12.6	-1.7	2.0
Dairy products..............................	3115	136	130	156	153	155	-4.2	17.2	1.3
Animal slaughtering & processing..............	3116	507	489	532	537	528	-3.5	9.7	-1.6
Bakeries & tortilla manufacturing..............	3118	306	277	316	294	304	-9.7	6.3	3.4
Textile mills [2].............................	313	378	119	108	96	98	-68.5	-19.6	2.5
Fabric mills.................................	3132	192	53	51	45	45	-72.2	-15.2	-0.2
Textile product mills [2]......................	314	230	119	113	103	103	-48.2	-13.9	0.9
Textile furnishings mills......................	3141	129	57	50	45	45	-55.7	-21.8	1.6
Apparel [2].................................	315	484	157	110	90	92	-67.6	-42.5	2.0
Cut & sew apparel, ex. contractors.............	31522,4,8	234	78	56	47	49	-66.7	-39.1	3.6
Paper & paper products......................	322	605	395	365	355	349	-34.7	-10.1	-1.7
Pulp, paper, & paperboard mills...............	3221	191	112	96	92	88	-41.3	-17.7	-4.5
Converted paper products....................	3222	413	282	269	263	261	-31.7	-7.0	-0.8
Printing & related support activities..............	323	807	488	425	375	367	-39.6	-23.0	-2.1
Petroleum & coal products....................	324	123	114	114	108	106	-7.5	-5.5	-1.9
Chemicals [2]...............................	325	980	787	851	845	869	-19.8	7.5	2.8
Basic chemicals............................	3251	188	142	152	149	148	-24.5	4.8	-0.8
Pharmaceuticals & medicines.................	3254	274	277	307	315	332	0.9	13.8	5.5
Soaps, cleaning compounds, & toiletries........	3256	129	102	110	112	116	-20.6	9.3	4.4
Plastics & rubber products [2].................	326	951	625	732	707	724	-34.3	13.1	2.4
Plastics products...........................	3261	737	502	594	576	592	-31.9	14.8	2.9
Rubber products............................	3262	214	123	137	131	132	-42.5	6.6	0.2
Miscellaneous nondurable goods manufacturing [2].................................	312,6	276	211	313	300	325	-23.5	42.2	8.3
Beverages..................................	3121	175	167	274	264	289	-4.5	58.1	9.7

X Not applicable. [1] Based on the North American Industry Classification System, 2017 (NAICS); see text, this section and Section 15. [2] Includes other industries, not shown separately.

Source: U.S. Bureau of Labor Statistics, Current Employment Statistics, "Employment, Hours, and Earnings—National," <www.bls.gov/ces/data.htm>, accessed March 2022.

Table 1055. Manufacturing—Value of Imports and Exports by Commodity: 2016

[In thousands of dollars (22,933,334 represents $22,933,334,000). Values are based on manufacturing data from the Annual Survey of Manufacturers and administrative records from official U.S. import and export merchandise trade statistics]

Commodity description	Product code [1]	Value of product shipments [2]	Total export value of goods [3]	General import value of goods [4]
Food manufacturing:				
Dog and cat food...	311111	22,933,334	1,315,436	750,587
Other animal food..	311119	32,310,895	1,633,277	552,029
Soybean and other oilseed products......................	311224	31,282,491	6,470,490	6,770,328
Fruit and vegetable canning products.....................	311421	25,481,320	2,992,732	5,659,242
Fluid milk products..	311511	33,320,569	259,924	59,719
Cheese products...	311513	40,139,943	1,209,024	1,259,170
Animal (except poultry) slaughtering products...........	311611	87,629,077	14,721,102	8,533,537
Meat processed from carcasses...........................	311612	50,661,463	(NA)	75,688
Poultry processing products................................	311615	61,740,224	3,892,349	519,487
Commercial bakery products................................	311812	30,589,439	(NA)	(NA)
Beverage and tobacco product manufacturing:				
Soft drinks..	312111	35,464,262	1,042,512	2,817,168
Brewery products..	312120	30,518,887	2,779,377	4,940,274
Tobacco products..	312230	41,360,631	1,155,877	1,413,967
Wood product manufacturing:				
Sawmill products..	321113	22,332,560	3,594,972	6,821,382
Paper manufacturing:				
Paper (except newsprint) mill products..................	322121	38,387,992	2,387,662	3,523,186
Paperboard mill products....................................	322130	28,456,285	4,749,078	1,974,937
Corrugated and solid fiber boxes..........................	322211	37,137,108	1,541,479	456,034
Paper bags and coated and treated paper...............	322220	20,496,725	5,066,946	3,499,012
Printing and related support activities manufacturing:				
Commercial printing products (except screen and books)...................	323111	63,006,196	2,975,117	3,448,871
Petroleum and coal products manufacturing:				
Petroleum refinery products................................	324110	367,379,559	66,138,901	41,757,855
Chemical manufacturing:				
Petrochemicals..	325110	49,724,229	1,962,962	1,161,965
Other basic inorganic chemicals..........................	325180	27,160,725	12,087,142	9,063,331
Ethyl alcohol...	325193	25,171,720	2,052,938	474,199
All other basic organic chemical manufacturing.........	325199	71,734,847	30,009,159	32,781,551
Plastics materials and resins..............................	325211	75,842,384	27,410,887	12,529,935
Pharmaceutical preparations...............................	325412	151,058,524	28,369,122	76,867,073
Biological products (except diagnostic)..................	325414	27,776,154	19,053,878	20,053,806
Paints and coatings..	325510	27,445,132	2,688,799	1,043,696
Soaps and other detergents...............................	325611	22,433,822	1,474,230	1,005,264
Toilet preparations...	325620	36,599,913	9,059,348	8,408,216
Plastics and rubber products manufacturing:				
All other plastics products..................................	326199	91,168,720	11,139,675	19,174,669
Nonmetallic mineral product manufacturing:				
Ready-mix concrete..	327320	28,910,513	4,133	1,188
Primary metal manufacturing:				
Iron and steel mill products and ferroalloys.............	331110	75,671,972	11,693,601	24,284,212
Fabricated metal product manufacturing:				
Fabricated structural metal products.....................	332312	27,415,851	1,022,136	3,990,190
Machine shops...	332710	35,017,553	(NA)	(NA)
Machinery manufacturing:				
Farm machinery and equipment...........................	333111	22,568,333	6,607,460	7,145,733
Construction machinery......................................	333120	24,010,377	10,958,135	16,189,841
Air-conditioning and warm air heating equipment and commercial and industrial refrigeration equipment......................	333415	31,113,498	5,513,311	10,004,731
Other engine equipment.....................................	333618	23,203,303	10,431,523	11,859,221
Computer and electronic product manufacturing:				
Semiconductors and related devices......................	334413	45,729,550	42,932,709	45,535,817
Electromedical and electrotherapeutic apparatus......	334510	26,291,936	10,217,928	10,747,574
Search, detection, navigation, guidance, aeronautical, and nautical systems and instruments..................	334511	40,690,878	3,958,648	7,571,485
Transportation equipment manufacturing:				
Automobiles..	336111	123,557,447	47,654,237	168,796,384
Light truck and utility vehicles.............................	336112	190,316,687	9,834,772	18,359,171
Heavy duty trucks..	336120	26,779,308	5,259,339	10,645,150
Motor vehicle gasoline engines and engine parts.......	336310	31,209,958	9,731,596	18,415,781
Motor vehicle electrical and electronic equipment......	336320	23,457,092	7,035,692	20,087,287
Motor vehicle transmission and power train parts......	336350	39,919,280	2,901,242	8,637,523
Motor vehicle seating and interior trim...................	336360	31,773,837	2,451,721	7,802,656
Motor vehicle metal stampings............................	336370	35,529,192	1,587,182	665,764
Other motor vehicle parts...................................	336390	65,150,150	16,318,203	36,476,598
Aircraft..	336411	120,974,701	4,546,595	13,844,272
Aircraft engines and engine parts.........................	336412	39,652,987	2,267,804	19,039,796
Other aircraft parts and auxiliary equipment............	336413	40,570,416	5,983,217	16,508,498
Guided missiles and space vehicles......................	336414	23,130,420	1,509,744	2,264
Ships and ship repair..	336611	23,417,674	1,366,634	493,378
Miscellaneous manufacturing:				
Surgical and medical instruments.........................	339112	41,039,499	16,998,378	13,476,651
Surgical appliances and supplies..........................	339113	30,630,740	11,014,731	14,101,341

NA Not available. [1] Based on North American Industry Classification (NAICS) product codes. [2] Includes total value of all products produced and shipped by all producers. For selected products, this can represent value of receipts, value of production, or value of work done. [3] Exports measure total physical movement of merchandise out of the U.S. to foreign countries whether such merchandise is exported from within the U.S. Customs territory, from a U.S. Customs bonded warehouse, or a U.S. Foreign Trade Zone. [4] Imports include commodities of foreign origin as well as goods of domestic origin returned to the U.S. with no change in condition or after having been processed and/or assembled in other countries.

Source: U.S. Census Bureau, *Manufacturing and International Trade Report: 2016*, February 2018. See also <www.census.gov/foreign-trade/index.html>.

Table 1056. Manufacturing Industries—Average Weekly Hours and Average Weekly Overtime Hours of Production Workers: 2000 to 2021

[Covers all full- and part-time employees who worked during, or received pay for, any part of the pay period including the 12th of the month]

Industry	2017 NAICS code [1]	Average weekly hours of production workers					Average weekly overtime hours of production workers				
		2000	2010	2019	2020	2021	2000	2010	2019	2020	2021
Total...............	31–33	**41.3**	**41.1**	**41.6**	**40.7**	**41.4**	**4.7**	**3.8**	**4.3**	**3.7**	**4.1**
Durable goods....................	(X)	**41.8**	**41.4**	**42.0**	**40.9**	**41.5**	**4.8**	**3.8**	**4.3**	**3.7**	**4.1**
Wood products......................	321	41.0	39.1	41.5	41.7	42.1	4.1	3.0	5.1	4.3	4.7
Nonmetallic mineral products.....	327	41.6	41.7	43.8	43.4	42.6	6.1	4.7	5.7	5.5	5.4
Primary metals......................	331	44.2	43.7	43.8	42.1	43.2	6.5	5.7	6.2	4.9	5.6
Fabricated metal products.........	332	41.9	41.4	41.7	40.7	41.4	4.9	3.8	4.1	3.5	3.9
Machinery...........................	333	42.3	42.1	42.4	41.0	41.6	5.1	3.9	4.0	3.1	3.9
Computer and electronic products...................	334	41.4	40.9	40.5	40.0	40.3	4.6	2.9	2.5	2.7	3.2
Electrical equipment and appliances......................	335	41.6	41.1	41.4	40.7	42.2	3.7	3.6	3.8	3.4	4.0
Transportation equipment........	336	43.3	42.9	43.4	41.6	42.2	5.6	4.7	5.5	4.6	4.8
Furniture and related products....	337	39.2	38.5	39.4	39.6	39.5	3.5	2.3	2.7	2.9	3.3
Miscellaneous manufacturing.....	339	39.0	38.7	39.7	38.4	39.6	3.1	2.7	2.8	2.0	2.6
Nondurable goods.................	(X)	**40.3**	**40.8**	**41.1**	**40.5**	**41.3**	**4.5**	**3.8**	**4.2**	**3.8**	**4.1**
Food manufacturing................	311	40.1	40.7	41.5	41.3	41.5	4.9	4.5	4.7	4.2	4.4
Textile mills........................	313	41.4	41.2	43.5	43.7	46.2	4.8	3.3	4.7	4.6	5.0
Textile product mills...............	314	38.7	39.0	37.8	38.5	39.5	3.4	2.4	2.2	3.0	4.1
Apparel.............................	315	35.7	36.6	37.0	36.6	38.7	2.1	1.1	2.0	2.0	2.2
Paper and paper products.........	322	42.8	42.9	42.1	42.4	43.5	5.7	4.9	4.8	4.8	4.8
Printing and related support activities........................	323	39.2	38.2	38.8	38.1	39.1	3.7	2.2	2.8	2.4	3.0
Petroleum and coal products......	324	42.7	43.0	48.3	43.8	(NA)	6.5	6.4	12.3	8.8	(NA)
Chemicals...........................	325	42.2	42.2	41.8	40.9	41.3	5.0	3.6	3.8	3.8	3.8
Plastics and rubber products......	326	40.8	41.9	41.0	39.5	40.6	3.9	4.0	4.0	3.1	3.5
Misc. nondurable manufacturing..	329	40.5	37.8	36.1	37.1	(NA)	5.4	2.3	2.3	2.5	(NA)

X Not applicable. NA Not available. [1] Based on the North American Industry Classification System (NAICS), 2017; see text, this section and Section 15.

Source: U.S. Bureau of Labor Statistics, Current Employment Statistics, "Employment, Hours, and Earnings — National," <www.bls.gov/ces/data/home.htm>, accessed June 2022.

Table 1057. Indexes of Employment and Hours Worked of All Persons in Manufacturing: 2010 to 2021

[2012=100. Based on Current Employment Statistics and supplemented with Current Population Survey. Employment and hours of all persons include those of paid employees, the self employed (partners and proprietors), and unpaid family workers. See text, Section 12]

Industry	NAICS code [1]	Employment					Hours worked				
		2010	2015	2019	2020	2021	2010	2015	2019	2020	2021
Food manufacturing..............	311	97.6	102.7	111.3	109.9	111.1	97.3	102.8	112.1	111.0	112.5
Beverage and tobacco products.........................	312	95.5	118.4	147.3	143.5	156.7	92.0	115.5	136.5	135.0	157.4
Textile mills......................	313	101.2	97.6	88.9	79.4	79.5	98.9	97.5	92.6	83.8	88.4
Textile product mills.............	314	101.7	103.8	98.0	91.6	89.8	103.9	96.9	92.6	87.7	88.0
Apparel manufacturing...........	315	105.5	93.1	72.9	61.9	59.3	107.9	96.8	70.9	59.9	61.9
Leather and allied products.....	316	92.0	93.1	93.1	86.2	84.5	82.7	86.1	83.2	80.1	80.5
Wood product manufacturing. ..	321	101.4	111.1	122.6	114.0	120.4	97.6	109.7	123.3	114.4	120.4
Paper and paper products.......	322	103.8	97.8	95.8	93.0	91.4	105.5	99.1	95.0	93.1	93.0
Printing and related support activities........................	323	109.2	98.3	92.6	82.0	81.0	107.9	99.1	92.9	80.6	83.0
Petroleum and coal products....	324	100.9	100.0	101.5	95.1	93.5	89.9	94.2	101.5	86.2	95.7
Chemical manufacturing.........	325	99.8	102.8	108.5	108.4	110.7	100.1	102.2	107.6	104.8	107.6
Plastics and rubber products....	326	96.4	106.3	113.2	109.5	112.8	96.5	108.5	112.3	104.2	109.5
Nonmetallic mineral products. ..	327	99.2	105.6	110.7	105.4	106.6	100.3	105.4	114.3	108.4	107.8
Primary metal products..........	331	89.9	97.5	95.2	87.6	86.6	90.2	97.5	96.1	84.8	84.6
Fabricated metal products.......	332	92.0	103.7	105.2	98.4	98.4	90.1	104.3	103.6	94.7	96.5
Machinery manufacturing........	333	90.4	101.8	101.9	95.4	95.0	89.7	99.3	100.2	91.0	91.2
Computer and electronic products.........................	334	100.7	96.2	98.7	98.0	97.4	101.9	97.7	98.4	95.8	95.5
Electrical equipment and appliances......................	335	96.5	102.4	108.5	103.3	106.5	96.0	104.2	106.9	102.9	107.5
Transportation equipment.......	336	91.6	109.6	118.1	108.9	112.3	89.1	108.8	115.4	102.5	107.8
Furniture and related products..	337	101.9	108.8	108.6	101.8	105.5	96.7	106.9	107.8	101.6	105.4
Miscellaneous manufacturing. ..	339	98.3	103.6	107.1	100.4	102.9	97.7	106.1	107.2	97.0	102.8

[1] North American Industry Classification System; see text, Section 15.

Source: U.S. Bureau of Labor Statistics, Labor Productivity and Costs, "LPC Tables and Charts," <www.bls.gov/lpc/tables.htm>, accessed July 2022.

Table 1058. Average Hourly Earnings of Production Workers in Manufacturing Industries by State: 2018 to 2021

[In dollars. Data are based on the North American Industry Classification System (NAICS), 2017. Based on the Current Employment Statistics Program. Covers full- and part-time employees who received pay for any part of the pay period including the 12th of the month. Excludes proprietors, self-employed, unpaid family or volunteer workers, farm workers, and domestic workers. See source, and Appendix III]

State	2018	2019	2020	2021	State	2018	2019	2020	2021
United States	**21.54**	**22.15**	**22.80**	**23.80**	Montana	20.94	20.60	20.55	21.04
Alabama	20.10	19.93	20.37	21.41	Nebraska	19.12	19.99	20.68	21.58
Alaska	20.21	21.31	25.64	26.87	Nevada	19.75	20.61	20.10	20.53
Arizona	19.49	20.36	20.77	21.99	New Hampshire	21.64	22.48	22.98	23.77
Arkansas	17.40	18.49	18.77	19.74	New Jersey	22.10	23.67	24.16	24.86
California	23.15	23.95	24.06	25.26	New Mexico	18.09	19.59	20.28	19.46
Colorado	26.91	27.70	26.53	25.40	New York	22.04	22.82	23.06	24.30
Connecticut	26.85	27.20	29.00	28.07	North Carolina	18.27	18.40	19.02	19.92
Delaware	19.14	20.13	21.24	22.22	North Dakota	19.77	20.99	21.33	23.19
Florida	21.76	23.28	24.02	24.82	Ohio	21.52	21.72	21.67	22.65
Georgia	18.92	19.59	21.00	22.27	Oklahoma	19.00	18.94	20.08	21.49
Hawaii	20.63	22.19	23.48	22.93	Oregon	21.70	22.66	23.04	23.61
Idaho	18.37	18.80	19.60	20.40	Pennsylvania	20.78	21.60	22.56	23.57
Illinois	21.30	21.89	22.11	22.53	Rhode Island	19.15	19.59	20.29	22.01
Indiana	20.19	20.96	20.98	21.40	South Carolina	19.31	20.53	21.87	23.63
Iowa	19.68	20.61	20.94	22.51	South Dakota	18.80	19.48	19.58	20.31
Kansas	19.97	20.73	20.76	20.96	Tennessee	19.51	19.76	20.33	21.57
Kentucky	20.45	20.78	22.48	23.88	Texas	21.87	21.89	23.40	25.80
Louisiana	22.01	22.57	22.41	21.61	Utah	20.82	21.21	20.92	22.32
Maine	22.48	22.49	22.43	22.76	Vermont	21.17	21.00	20.65	21.61
Maryland	20.32	20.34	22.15	21.97	Virginia	19.10	19.47	20.19	21.06
Massachusetts	24.58	25.03	24.96	25.33	Washington	28.43	29.16	28.32	28.03
Michigan	21.32	22.22	22.51	23.41	West Virginia	21.38	21.51	21.79	21.20
Minnesota	21.71	22.77	23.69	24.75	Wisconsin	20.56	21.49	21.90	22.15
Mississippi	20.54	20.77	21.27	20.46	Wyoming	23.94	25.76	26.82	27.60
Missouri	21.10	21.55	22.04	22.93	Puerto Rico	12.37	12.51	12.13	12.03

Source: U.S. Bureau of Labor Statistics, Current Employment Statistics, "Employment, Hours, and Earnings – National," <www.bls.gov/ces/data.htm>; and "Employment, Hours, and Earnings – State and Metro Area," <www.bls.gov/sae/data.htm>; accessed March 2022.

Table 1059. Manufacturing Full–Time Equivalent (FTE) Employees and Wages by Industry: 2000 to 2020

[123,384 represents 123,384,000. Based on National Income and Product Account tables. Full-time equivalent employees equals the number of employees on full-time schedules plus the number of employees for part-time schedules converted to full-time basis]

Industry	2012 NAICS code [1]	Full-time equivalent (FTE) employees (1,000)				Wage and salary accruals per FTE worker (dol.)			
		2000	2010	2019	2020	2000	2010	2019	2020
Domestic industries, total	(X)	**123,384**	**120,519**	**141,085**	**133,161**	**39,166**	**52,939**	**66,168**	**70,982**
Manufacturing	31–33	**16,948**	**11,223**	**12,524**	**11,840**	**43,957**	**59,997**	**72,709**	**76,391**
Percent of all industries	(X)	13.7	9.3	8.9	8.9	112.2	113.3	109.9	107.6
Durable goods	(X)	10,713	6,900	7,891	7,416	46,573	63,311	77,022	80,486
Wood products	321	602	333	398	389	30,351	38,149	49,892	52,546
Nonmetallic mineral products	327	549	357	413	389	39,021	50,628	62,558	65,893
Primary metals	331	611	353	379	344	45,836	61,058	73,638	74,068
Fabricated metal products	332	1,735	1,249	1,453	1,348	37,766	51,445	61,066	63,016
Machinery	333	1,427	975	1,105	1,030	46,612	62,656	74,962	76,685
Computer and electronic products	334	1,779	1,079	1,059	1,047	70,449	96,001	129,276	138,914
Electrical equipment, appliances, and components	335	583	351	393	375	40,241	59,438	72,491	75,139
Motor vehicles, bodies and trailers, and parts	3361–3363	1,301	666	987	881	48,754	57,922	65,747	67,249
Other transportation equipment	3364–3365	740	645	726	694	53,294	79,421	97,914	99,431
Furniture and related products	337	671	345	375	351	29,571	39,980	49,711	52,112
Miscellaneous manufacturing	339	715	547	603	569	38,744	56,903	70,674	72,575
Nondurable goods	(X)	6,235	4,322	4,633	4,423	39,464	54,706	65,364	69,526
Food and beverage and tobacco products	311–312	1,728	1,561	1,843	1,789	33,956	44,711	52,919	57,549
Textile mills and textile product mills	313–314	588	230	212	190	29,013	39,110	48,765	51,019
Apparel and leather and allied products	315	539	179	131	109	24,198	38,244	47,615	50,588
Paper products	322	598	382	359	346	45,834	61,586	72,521	74,749
Printing and related support activities	323	757	472	412	367	39,142	45,783	53,624	55,003
Petroleum and coal products	324	120	109	112	108	62,998	97,162	123,861	124,047
Chemical products	325	967	775	838	832	61,314	84,813	101,794	106,654
Plastics and rubber products	326	938	615	725	682	35,624	47,778	56,969	60,349

X Not applicable. [1] North American Industry Classification System, 2012; see text, Section 15.

Source: U.S. Bureau of Economic Analysis, National Income and Product Accounts, "Table 6.5D. Full-Time Equivalent Employees by Industry," and "Table 6.6D. Wages and Salaries Per Full-Time Equivalent Employee by Industry," <apps.bea.gov/iTable/index_nipa.cfm>, accessed August 2021.

Table 1060. Manufacturers' Shipments, Inventories, and New Orders: 1995 to 2021

[In billions of dollars (3,480 represents $3,480,000,000,000), except ratio. Data are not seasonally adjusted, except ratios as noted. Based on the Manufacturers' Shipments, Inventories, and Orders (M3) survey. See source for details]

Year	Shipments	Inventories (December 31) [1]	Ratio of inventories to shipments [2]	New orders	Unfilled orders (December 31)
1995	3,480	415	1.41	3,427	443
1996	3,597	421	1.40	3,567	485
1997	3,835	433	1.36	3,780	508
1998	3,900	439	1.37	3,808	492
1999	4,032	453	1.34	3,957	501
2000	4,209	470	1.37	4,161	545
2001	3,970	417	1.33	3,869	506
2002	3,915	412	1.30	3,823	476
2003	4,015	398	1.20	3,976	503
2004	4,309	429	1.17	4,289	555
2005	4,742	461	1.14	4,764	652
2006	5,016	509	1.22	5,090	796
2007	5,319	547	1.22	5,397	946
2008	5,469	529	1.42	5,452	995
2009	4,424	491	1.29	4,206	825
2010	4,911	538	1.28	4,896	870
2011	5,492	589	1.30	5,512	953
2012	5,697	607	1.30	5,710	1,015
2013	5,814	614	1.29	5,899	1,146
2014	5,889	626	1.35	5,953	1,256
2015	5,533	622	1.44	5,433	1,206
2016	5,364	620	1.39	5,296	1,188
2017	5,549	643	1.38	5,492	1,184
2018	5,891	662	1.39	5,822	1,168
2019	5,734	692	1.52	5,538	1,023
2020	5,221	681	1.52	5,141	997
2021	5,798	741	1.49	5,818	1,075

[1] Inventories are stated at current cost. [2] Ratio based on December seasonally adjusted inventory data.

Source: U.S. Census Bureau, Manufacturers' Shipments, Inventories, and Orders, "Historical Data," <www.census.gov/manufacturing/m3/historical_data/index.html>, accessed June 2022.

Table 1061. Ratios of Manufacturers' Inventories to Shipments and Unfilled Orders to Shipments by Industry Group: 2000 to 2021

[Based on the Manufacturers' Shipments, Inventories, and Orders (M3) survey. Ratio based on December seasonally adjusted inventory and unfilled orders data. See source for details]

Industry	2017 NAICS code [1]	2000	2010	2017	2018	2019	2020	2021
INVENTORIES-TO-SHIPMENTS RATIO								
All manufacturing industries	(X)	**1.37**	**1.28**	**1.38**	**1.39**	**1.52**	**1.52**	**1.49**
Durable goods	(X)	1.56	1.63	1.65	1.66	1.88	1.82	1.82
Wood products	321	1.41	1.39	1.25	1.40	1.38	1.15	1.11
Nonmetallic mineral products	327	1.26	1.52	1.24	1.34	1.40	1.22	1.23
Primary metals	331	1.77	1.56	1.74	1.85	1.99	1.86	1.88
Fabricated metals	332	1.56	1.57	1.67	1.70	1.76	1.68	1.69
Machinery	333	2.05	1.86	2.08	2.16	2.29	2.24	2.15
Computers and electronic products	334	1.47	1.58	1.71	1.79	1.83	1.84	1.85
Electrical equipment, appliances, and components	335	1.41	1.47	1.74	1.75	1.79	1.72	1.67
Transportation equipment	336	1.42	1.68	1.54	1.42	1.91	1.90	1.94
Furniture and related products	337	1.36	1.17	1.17	1.17	1.25	1.35	1.59
Miscellaneous products	339	1.83	1.72	1.71	1.83	2.04	1.91	1.93
Nondurable goods	(X)	1.13	0.98	1.12	1.12	1.17	1.20	1.16
Food products	311	0.86	0.79	0.85	0.84	0.85	0.84	0.83
Beverages and tobacco products	312	1.50	1.65	1.96	1.93	2.07	1.97	1.82
Textile mills	313	1.54	1.25	1.35	1.42	1.44	1.39	1.43
Textile product mills	314	1.87	1.67	2.08	2.15	2.25	2.05	2.11
Apparel	315	1.91	1.62	2.27	2.15	2.20	2.59	2.69
Leather and allied products	316	1.88	1.78	2.12	2.54	2.71	2.45	2.21
Paper products	322	1.11	0.98	0.94	0.99	1.01	0.99	0.98
Printing	323	0.78	0.77	0.82	0.89	0.88	0.95	0.96
Petroleum and coal products	324	0.68	0.73	0.75	0.77	0.81	0.92	0.84
Chemical products	325	1.35	1.23	1.48	1.45	1.57	1.59	1.55
Plastics and rubber products	326	1.24	1.20	1.31	1.32	1.33	1.36	1.38
UNFILLED ORDERS-TO-SHIPMENTS RATIO								
All manufacturing industries	(X)	**4.02**	**6.14**	**7.08**	**6.71**	**6.33**	**6.32**	**6.13**
Durable goods	(X)	4.02	6.14	7.08	6.71	6.33	6.32	6.13
Primary metals	331	1.52	1.87	1.43	1.41	1.52	1.48	1.53
Fabricated metals	332	2.13	2.79	2.36	2.67	3.09	3.28	3.35
Machinery	333	2.66	3.82	3.20	3.41	3.60	4.03	3.92
Computers and electronic products	334	4.24	5.92	5.61	5.68	6.11	6.39	6.54
Electrical equipment, appliances, and components	335	1.83	1.96	2.27	2.31	2.52	3.00	3.14
Transportation equipment	336	8.06	14.33	16.09	14.65	13.42	12.85	12.43
Furniture and related products	337	1.29	1.39	1.43	1.53	1.57	1.74	2.12

X Not applicable. [1] Based on the North American Industry Classification System, 2017; see text, this section and Section 15.

Source: U.S. Census Bureau, Manufacturers' Shipments, Inventories, and Orders, "Historical Data," <www.census.gov/manufacturing/m3/historical_data/index.html>, accessed June 2022.

Table 1062. Value of Manufacturers' Shipments, Inventories, and New Orders by Industry: 2000 to 2021

[In billions of dollars (4,209 represents $4,209,000,000,000). Data are not seasonally adjusted. Based on the Manufacturers' Shipments, Inventories, and Orders (M3) survey. See source for details]

Industry	2017 NAICS code [1]	2000	2010	2015	2019	2020	2021
SHIPMENTS							
All manufacturing industries	(X)	**4,209**	**4,911**	**5,533**	**5,734**	**5,221**	**5,798**
Durable goods	(X)	2,374	2,281	2,782	2,861	2,632	2,923
Wood products	321	94	69	97	107	118	148
Nonmetallic mineral products	327	97	90	118	134	133	140
Primary metals	331	157	231	229	236	201	225
Fabricated metals	332	268	295	349	376	347	400
Machinery	333	292	316	381	393	355	404
Computers and electronic products	334	511	328	302	317	312	325
Electrical equipment, appliances, and components	335	125	110	127	132	128	145
Transportation equipment	336	640	636	952	938	821	908
Furniture and related products	337	75	60	74	75	69	69
Miscellaneous products	339	115	145	154	153	146	159
Nondurable goods	(X)	1,835	2,631	2,751	2,874	2,590	2,875
Food products	311	435	654	778	800	827	866
Beverages and tobacco products	312	112	130	155	157	156	169
Textile mills	313	52	30	29	27	25	27
Textile product mills	314	34	21	24	23	21	23
Apparel	315	60	13	11	10	8	9
Leather and allied products	316	10	5	5	5	4	5
Paper products	322	165	172	185	192	180	190
Printing	323	104	83	82	81	74	75
Petroleum and coal products	324	235	628	510	600	362	516
Chemical products	325	449	705	737	732	696	747
Plastics and rubber products	326	178	189	234	249	235	249
INVENTORIES (as of December 31)							
All manufacturing industries	(X)	**470**	**538**	**622**	**692**	**681**	**741**
Durable goods	(X)	298	313	383	422	417	455
Wood products	321	10	8	11	13	13	14
Nonmetallic mineral products	327	10	11	13	15	14	15
Primary metals	331	22	31	32	36	33	37
Fabricated metals	332	34	40	47	53	50	59
Machinery	333	49	52	65	70	67	76
Computers and electronic products	334	63	42	42	47	48	50
Electrical equipment, appliances, and components	335	15	14	16	19	18	20
Transportation equipment	336	69	90	129	138	143	149
Furniture and related products	337	8	6	7	7	8	9
Miscellaneous products	339	18	20	21	24	24	26
Nondurable goods	(X)	172	225	239	270	263	287
Food products	311	32	44	53	57	59	61
Beverages and tobacco products	312	14	18	23	27	27	27
Textile mills	313	6	3	3	3	3	3
Textile product mills	314	5	3	4	4	4	4
Apparel	315	9	2	2	2	2	2
Leather and allied products	316	2	1	1	1	1	1
Paper products	322	15	14	16	16	15	16
Printing	323	6	5	5	6	6	6
Petroleum and coal products	324	13	43	28	36	29	38
Chemical products	325	52	73	81	92	93	99
Plastics and rubber products	326	18	19	24	27	26	30
NEW ORDERS							
All manufacturing industries	(X)	**4,161**	**4,896**	**5,433**	**5,538**	**5,141**	**5,818**
Durable goods	(X)	2,327	2,265	2,682	2,664	2,552	2,944
Wood products	321	94	(NA)	(NA)	(NA)	(NA)	(NA)
Nonmetallic mineral products	327	97	(NA)	(NA)	(NA)	(NA)	(NA)
Primary metals	331	154	244	225	235	200	229
Fabricated metals	332	270	304	338	385	352	419
Machinery	333	295	334	372	394	362	420
Computers and electronic products	334	436	270	245	272	265	275
Electrical equipment, appliances, and components	335	126	110	127	135	133	151
Transportation equipment	336	663	638	932	775	772	931
Furniture and related products	337	75	60	75	74	70	71
Miscellaneous products	339	117	(NA)	(NA)	(NA)	(NA)	(NA)
Nondurable goods	(X)	1,835	2,631	2,751	2,874	2,590	2,875

NA Not available. X Not applicable. [1] Based on the North American Industry Classification System, 2017; see text, this section and Section 15.

Source: U.S. Census Bureau, Manufacturers' Shipments, Inventories, and Orders, "Annual Benchmark Data and Benchmark Procedures," <www.census.gov/manufacturing/m3/index.html>, and "Historical Data," <www.census.gov /manufacturing/m3/historical_data/index.html>; accessed June 2022.

Table 1063. Value of Manufacturers' Shipments, Inventories, and New Orders by Market Grouping: 2000 to 2021

[In billions of dollars (4,209 represents $4,209,000,000,000). Data are not seasonally adjusted. Based on the Manufacturers' Shipments, Inventories, and Orders (M3) survey. See source for details]

Market grouping	2000	2010	2015	2017	2018	2019	2020	2021
SHIPMENTS								
All manufacturing industries............	**4,209**	**4,911**	**5,533**	**5,549**	**5,891**	**5,734**	**5,221**	**5,798**
Consumer goods................	1,501	2,059	2,257	2,273	2,434	2,384	2,133	2,392
Consumer durable goods............	391	323	458	453	475	470	436	478
Consumer nondurable goods.........	1,109	1,735	1,799	1,820	1,959	1,914	1,697	1,914
Aircraft and parts..................	112	147	210	224	224	180	150	177
Defense aircraft and parts...........	25	63	55	56	56	53	61	64
Nondefense aircraft and parts.........	87	84	155	168	168	127	89	113
Construction materials and supplies.........	445	444	554	574	608	606	593	678
Motor vehicles and parts............	471	401	639	632	669	656	573	623
Computers and related products............	110	42	27	20	21	20	19	21
Information technology industries............	400	270	258	256	263	266	260	276
Nondefense capital goods..................	808	728	884	855	903	859	770	867
Excluding aircraft................	758	675	779	737	784	786	718	793
Defense capital goods................	67	130	112	124	126	131	145	159
INVENTORIES (as of December 31)								
All manufacturing industries............	**470**	**538**	**622**	**643**	**662**	**692**	**681**	**741**
Consumer goods................	128	169	179	197	195	207	201	221
Consumer durable goods............	26	21	27	28	30	32	31	38
Consumer nondurable goods.........	102	148	151	169	165	174	170	183
Aircraft and parts..................	36	55	79	71	66	84	90	86
Defense aircraft and parts...........	9	12	11	12	11	12	12	13
Nondefense aircraft and parts.........	27	43	68	58	55	72	77	74
Construction materials and supplies.........	49	52	63	67	73	74	70	81
Motor vehicles and parts............	22	22	34	34	37	40	39	47
Computers and related products............	8	4	4	3	3	3	3	4
Information technology industries............	51	36	36	35	37	38	38	41
Nondefense capital goods..................	127	135	173	162	167	186	188	198
Excluding aircraft................	107	100	116	115	123	126	122	135
Defense capital goods................	17	21	22	21	19	20	21	22
NEW ORDERS								
All manufacturing industries............	**4,161**	**4,896**	**5,433**	**5,492**	**5,822**	**5,538**	**5,141**	**5,818**
Consumer goods................	1,502	2,059	2,257	2,273	2,434	2,384	2,138	2,394
Consumer durable goods............	393	323	458	454	476	470	441	480
Consumer nondurable goods.........	1,109	1,735	1,799	1,820	1,959	1,914	1,697	1,914
Aircraft and parts..................	131	155	184	203	165	19	91	196
Defense aircraft and parts...........	31	63	50	49	57	46	58	62
Nondefense aircraft and parts.........	99	91	134	154	108	(28)	33	134
Construction materials and supplies.........	447	451	555	575	617	610	597	699
Motor vehicles and parts............	468	403	641	636	669	655	576	627
Computers and related products............	108	40	27	20	21	20	19	21
Information technology industries............	410	273	251	261	267	274	268	286
Nondefense capital goods..................	831	748	845	874	852	706	727	912
Excluding aircraft................	768	685	761	743	795	790	728	819
Defense capital goods................	80	137	106	125	137	132	159	158

Source: U.S. Census Bureau, Manufacturers' Shipments, Inventories, and Orders, "Historical Data," <www.census.gov/manufacturing/m3/historical_data/index.html>, accessed June 2022.

Table 1064. Finances and Profits of Manufacturing Corporations: 2005 to 2021

[In billions of dollars (5,411 represents $5,411,000,000,000). Data exclude estimates for corporations with less than $250,000 in assets at time of sample selection]

Item	2005 [1]	2010 [2]	2014 [3]	2015 [3]	2016 [3]	2017 [4]	2018 [4]	2019 [4]	2020 [4]	2021 [4]
Net sales..........................	5,411	5,756	6,903	6,433	6,249	6,552	6,971	6,836	6,068	7,231
Net operating profit....................	359	420	538	516	502	530	572	528	434	719
Net profit:										
Before taxes.......................	524	584	745	612	649	681	720	645	456	1,104
After taxes.......................	401	478	609	506	541	549	636	584	419	980
Cash dividends.....................	179	180	259	275	276	290	312	313	310	328
Net income retained in business.............	222	298	350	231	265	259	324	271	109	652

[1] Based on the North American Industry Classification System, 2002. [2] Based on the North American Industry Classification System, 2007. [3] Based on the North American Industry Classification System, 2012. [4] Based on the North American Industry Classification System, 2017.

Source: U.S. Census Bureau, Quarterly Financial Report (QFR) Manufacturing, Mining, Trade, and Selected Service Industries, "Time Series/Trend Charts," <www.census.gov/econ/qfr>, accessed June 2022.

Table 1065. Manufacturing Corporations—Selected Finances: 2000 to 2021

[In billions of dollars (4,548 represents $4,548,000,000,000). Data are not necessarily comparable from year to year due to changes in accounting procedures, industry classifications, sampling procedures, etc.; for details, see source. Through 2000, based on Standard Industrial Classification code; beginning 2001, based on North American Industry Classification System; see text, Section 15. Minus sign (-) indicates loss]

Year	All manufacturing corporations [a]			Durable goods			Nondurable goods		
		Profits [1]			Profits [1]			Profits [1]	
	Sales	Before taxes	After taxes	Sales	Before taxes	After taxes	Sales	Before taxes	After taxes
2000	4,548	381	275	2,457	191	132	2,091	190	144
2001 [2]	4,295	83	36	2,321	-69	-76	1,974	152	112
2002	4,216	195	135	2,261	46	22	1,956	150	113
2003	4,397	306	237	2,283	118	88	2,114	188	149
2004	4,934	447	348	2,537	200	157	2,397	248	192
2005	5,411	524	401	2,731	211	161	2,681	313	240
2006	5,783	605	470	2,910	249	193	2,873	356	278
2007	6,060	603	443	3,016	247	159	3,044	356	283
2008	6,374	388	266	2,970	98	43	3,405	290	223
2009	5,110	361	286	2,427	84	55	2,683	276	232
2010	5,756	584	478	2,708	287	232	3,048	297	245
2011	6,486	722	594	2,927	335	284	3,558	387	310
2012	6,668	676	564	3,102	303	260	3,567	373	304
2013	6,743	722	601	3,178	358	294	3,566	365	308
2014	6,903	745	609	3,342	378	308	3,561	367	301
2015	6,433	612	506	3,367	324	265	3,065	289	241
2016	6,249	649	541	3,320	333	273	2,929	316	268
2017	6,552	681	549	3,403	373	273	3,149	308	276
2018	6,971	720	636	3,611	399	356	3,359	321	280
2019	6,836	645	584	3,556	359	330	3,280	286	255
2020	6,068	456	419	3,219	322	296	2,849	134	123
2021	7,231	1,104	980	3,679	627	562	3,552	477	418

[1] Beginning 1998, profits before and after income taxes reflect inclusion of minority stockholders' interest in net income before and after income taxes. [2] Beginning 2001, data reported based on the North American Industry Classification System.

Source: U.S. Census Bureau, Quarterly Financial Report (QFR) Manufacturing, Mining, Trade, and Selected Service Industries, "Time Series/Trend Charts," <www.census.gov/econ/qfr/>, accessed July 2022.

Table 1066. Motor Vehicle Manufactures—Summary by Selected Industry: 2020

[52,709 represents $52,709,000,000. Based on the Annual Survey of Manufactures; see Appendix III]

Industry	2017 NAICS code [1]	All employees [2]			Production workers [2]	Value of product shipments [3] (mil. dol.)
			Payroll			
		Number	Total (mil. dol.)	Payroll per employee (dol.)		
Motor vehicle manufacturing, total	**3361-3363**	**926,840**	**52,709**	**56,870**	**723,655**	**572,619**
Motor vehicle, total	3361	215,977	15,477	71,663	174,913	301,958
Automobile and light duty motor vehicle	33611	186,492	13,849	74,261	151,480	280,524
Automobile	336111	69,076	5,523	79,949	49,270	87,118
Light truck and utility vehicle	336112	117,416	8,327	70,915	102,210	193,405
Heavy duty truck	33612	29,485	1,628	55,227	23,433	21,434
Motor vehicle body and trailer	3362	151,824	8,012	52,772	122,543	47,490
Motor vehicle body	336211	47,086	2,492	52,921	36,247	14,532
Truck trailer	336212	35,382	1,655	46,776	29,485	9,900
Motor home	336213	9,770	521	53,356	6,819	3,947
Travel trailer and camper	336214	59,587	3,344	56,117	49,992	19,111
Motor vehicle parts	3363	559,039	29,220	52,268	426,199	223,171
Motor vehicle gasoline engine and engine parts	33631	67,280	3,920	58,270	52,024	34,118
Motor vehicle electrical and electronic equipment	33632	55,630	2,869	51,566	40,825	20,710
Motor vehicle steering and suspension	33633	33,477	1,757	52,494	23,137	13,003
Motor vehicle brake system	33634	19,960	1,045	52,345	14,671	8,697
Motor vehicle transmission and power train parts	33635	73,438	4,427	60,275	56,510	36,752
Motor vehicle seating and interior trim	33636	68,594	3,126	45,569	53,088	25,038
Motor vehicle metal stamping	33637	100,362	5,110	50,915	78,810	30,075
Other motor vehicle parts	33639	140,297	6,966	49,655	107,135	54,778

[1] North American Industry Classification System, 2017; see text, Section 15. [2] Includes all full-time and part-time employees on the payrolls of operating manufacturing establishments during any part of the pay period that included the 12th of the month specified on the report form. Included are employees on paid sick leave, paid holidays, and paid vacations; not included are proprietors and partners of unincorporated businesses. [3] Includes extensive and unmeasurable duplication from shipments between establishments in the same industry classification.

Source: U.S. Census Bureau, Annual Survey of Manufactures, "Annual Survey of Manufactures: Summary Statistics for Industry Groups and Industries in the U.S.: 2018-2020," <data.census.gov/>, accessed July 2022.

Table 1067. Motor Vehicle Manufactures—Employees, Payroll, and Shipments by Major Producing State: 2020

[15,477,497 represents $15,477,497,000. Industry based on the 2017 North American Industry Classification System (NAICS); see text, Section 15. See footnote 3, Table 1066 for information regarding shipments. Based on the Annual Survey of Manufactures; see Appendix III]

State	Motor vehicle manufacturing (NAICS 3361)			Motor vehicle parts manufacturing (NAICS 3363)		
	Employees	Payroll ($1,000)	Value of shipments ($1,000)	Employees	Payroll ($1,000)	Value of shipments ($1,000)
United States [1]	215,977	15,477,497	301,957,889	559,039	29,219,765	223,171,289
Alabama	12,126	904,058	24,480,645	27,583	1,300,955	13,762,647
Alaska	([2])	(D)	(D)	([2])	(D)	(D)
Arizona	46	3,556	34,114	3,079	146,582	1,097,429
Arkansas	([3])	(D)	3,337	5,214	231,310	1,582,379
California	22,384	2,236,002	(D)	13,878	782,309	5,023,885
Colorado	6	318	1,019	1,011	58,941	375,540
Connecticut	([2])	(D)	(D)	([8])	(D)	(D)
Delaware	([2])	(D)	(D)	([4])	(D)	(D)
Florida	1,263	85,955	414,130	2,778	153,282	1,004,876
Georgia	([9])	(D)	(D)	15,461	726,572	7,622,883
Hawaii	(NA)	(NA)	(NA)	([2])	(D)	(D)
Idaho	([4])	(D)	(D)	266	17,726	(D)
Illinois	([9])	(D)	(D)	27,092	1,290,741	8,320,524
Indiana	16,900	1,243,129	35,280,766	57,372	3,142,259	22,236,959
Iowa	67	4,351	(D)	4,809	194,255	1,154,787
Kansas	([7])	(D)	(D)	2,515	120,751	(D)
Kentucky	22,388	1,597,992	30,513,266	34,037	1,706,144	14,356,116
Louisiana	(NA)	(NA)	(NA)	309	(D)	(D)
Maine	([2])	(D)	(D)	([4])	(D)	(D)
Maryland	([2])	(D)	(D)	724	41,810	(D)
Massachusetts	([3])	(D)	(D)	720	39,113	153,477
Michigan	35,032	2,427,521	50,807,906	116,450	6,339,000	45,325,971
Minnesota	1,708	89,943	(D)	2,277	130,194	712,557
Mississippi	([9])	(D)	5,060,930	4,443	221,841	1,842,170
Missouri	11,909	920,632	(D)	11,785	562,838	4,269,640
Montana	([3])	(D)	(D)	([3])	(D)	(D)
Nebraska	([3])	(D)	(D)	4,066	189,016	1,113,639
Nevada	74	(D)	32,561	249	(D)	(D)
New Hampshire	([2])	(D)	(D)	1,595	82,365	348,499
New Jersey	([2])	(D)	686	884	55,800	258,565
New Mexico	(NA)	(NA)	(NA)	([3])	(D)	(D)
New York	32	2,507	31,798	10,255	608,488	3,724,497
North Carolina	([8])	(D)	(D)	17,988	942,430	8,438,954
North Dakota	([5])	(D)	(D)	849	32,925	(D)
Ohio	22,489	1,407,775	27,830,418	70,476	3,865,874	30,874,349
Oklahoma	([7])	(D)	(D)	970	53,570	397,965
Oregon	([6])	(D)	(D)	1,079	65,004	282,054
Pennsylvania	([7])	(D)	(D)	7,992	341,210	2,262,949
Rhode Island	(NA)	(NA)	(NA)	([4])	(D)	(D)
South Carolina	13,552	882,072	18,248,339	18,913	1,041,160	9,197,004
South Dakota	([5])	(D)	(D)	867	39,595	184,504
Tennessee	9,618	758,185	14,009,799	47,249	2,426,409	19,051,835
Texas	8,622	744,229	22,114,256	15,800	770,867	5,805,527
Utah	([3])	(D)	(D)	4,043	211,727	1,772,752
Vermont	([2])	(D)	(D)	([5])	(D)	(D)
Virginia	([8])	(D)	(D)	3,679	166,359	(D)
Washington	([6])	(D)	(D)	2,484	124,649	572,477
West Virginia	([5])	(D)	(D)	3,333	190,641	2,613,490
Wisconsin	([7])	(D)	(D)	10,706	544,259	4,252,011
Wyoming	([2])	(D)	(D)	([3])	(D)	(D)

D Withheld to avoid disclosing data on individual companies. NA Not available. [1] Includes states not shown separately. [2] Employee class size of 0 to 19. [3] Employee class size of 20 to 99. [4] Employee class size of 100 to 249. [5] Employee class size of 250 to 499. [6] Employee class size of 500 to 999. [7] Employee class size of 1,000 to 2,499. [8] Employee class size of 2,500 to 4,999. [9] Employee class size of 5,000 to 9,999.

Source: U.S. Census Bureau, Annual Survey of Manufactures, "Annual Survey of Manufactures: Summary Statistics for Industry Groups and Industries in the U.S.: 2018-2020," <data.census.gov/>, accessed July 2022.

Table 1068. General Aviation Airplane Shipments and Billings: 1990 to 2019

[2,008 represents $2,008,000,000. Data are for U.S. manufactured airplanes. Totals may not add up due to rounding]

Type of airplane	1990	2000	2010	2015	2016	2017	2018	2019
Airplane units shipped (number)	1,144	2,816	1,334	1,592	1,531	1,599	1,746	1,771
Total piston	695	1,913	746	783	718	786	829	883
Single-engine	608	1,810	679	740	685	745	771	825
Multi-engine	87	103	67	43	33	41	58	58
Total turbine	449	903	588	809	813	813	917	888
Turboprop	281	315	224	420	411	409	444	385
Business jet	168	588	364	389	402	404	473	503
Factory net billings (mil. dol.)	2,008	8,558	7,875	11,982	11,560	10,641	11,598	13,972
Total piston	92	446	368	477	505	434	466	513
Single-engine	68	(NA)	(NA)	(NA)	(NA)	(NA)	(NA)	(NA)
Multi-engine	24	(NA)	(NA)	(NA)	(NA)	(NA)	(NA)	(NA)
Total turbine	1,916	8,112	7,506	11,506	11,055	10,207	11,132	13,459
Turboprop	644	934	724	1,282	1,180	1,032	1,151	1,006
Business jet	1,272	7,178	6,782	10,224	9,875	9,175	9,981	12,453

NA Not available.

Source: General Aviation Manufacturers Association, *2019 Databook* ©, 2020, and earlier reports. See also <www.gama.aero>.

Table 1069. Beverage Manufacturing Industry—Brewery, Distillery, and Winery Establishments and Employment: 2010 to 2020

[Beverage manufacturer data are from the Quarterly Census of Employment and Wages (QCEW). Covers North American Industry Classification System (NAICS) 31212, 31213, 31214, and 31211]

Industry characteristic	2010	2012	2013	2014	2015	2016	2017	2018	2019	2020
Establishments (number):										
Breweries	527	843	1,167	1,616	2,190	2,843	3,509	4,156	4,733	5,093
Wineries	2,616	2,978	3,201	3,560	3,848	4,083	4,343	4,643	4,845	5,014
Distilleries	145	243	306	424	558	675	805	964	1,115	1,248
Soft drink and ice manufacturing	1,845	1,802	1,830	1,864	1,858	1,969	2,053	2,065	2,079	2,119
Employment (number):										
Breweries	24,864	29,309	34,519	40,101	48,401	58,580	68,148	77,911	86,668	79,457
Wineries	40,830	45,351	48,386	52,879	57,003	60,436	64,212	67,832	70,596	63,817
Distilleries	7,252	8,001	8,872	10,579	11,075	12,207	13,759	15,839	17,699	18,148
Soft drink and ice manufacturing	94,225	94,576	93,854	93,333	94,334	102,793	104,743	103,124	101,550	101,533
Average weekly wages (in dollars):										
Breweries	1,321	1,226	1,140	1,129	1,163	969	906	866	857	924
Wineries	773	808	789	803	833	846	861	871	889	981
Distilleries	1,352	1,550	1,430	1,415	1,462	1,362	1,300	1,279	1,230	1,298
Soft drink and ice manufacturing	938	955	952	980	1,020	1,028	1,044	1,079	1,101	1,168

Source: U.S. Bureau of Labor Statistics, Quarterly Census of Employment and Wages, QCEW Databases, "State and County Wages," <www.bls.gov/cew/home.htm>, accessed October 2021.

Section 22
Wholesale and Retail Trade

This section presents statistics relating to the distributive trades, specifically wholesale trade and retail trade. Data shown for the trades are classified by kind of business and cover sales, establishments, employees, payrolls, and other items. The principal sources of these data are from the U.S. Census Bureau and include the 2012 and 2017 Economic Censuses, annual and monthly surveys, and the County Business Patterns program. These data are supplemented by several tables from trade associations, such as the National Automobile Dealers Association.

Data on wholesale and retail trade also appear in several other sections. For instance, labor force employment and earnings data appear in Section 12, Labor Force, Employment, and Earnings; gross domestic product of the industry (Table 708) appears in Section 13, Income, Expenditures, Poverty, and Wealth; and financial data (several tables) from the quarterly *Statistics of Income Bulletin*, published by the Internal Revenue Service, appear in Section 15, Business Enterprise.

Censuses—Censuses of wholesale trade and retail trade have been taken at various intervals since 1929. Beginning with the 1967 Economic Census, legislation provides for a census to be conducted every 5 years (for years ending in "2" and "7"). The industries covered in the censuses and surveys of business are defined in the North American Industry Classification System (NAICS). Retail trade refers to places of business primarily engaged in retailing merchandise to the general public; and wholesale trade, to establishments primarily engaged in selling goods to other businesses and normally operating from a warehouse or office that have little or no display of merchandise. Census Bureau tables in this section primarily utilize the 2012 or 2017 NAICS codes. NAICS codes are reviewed every 5 years to identify areas for revision, so that the classification system can keep pace with the changing economy. For information on this system and how it affects the comparability of wholesale and retail statistics historically, see text, Section 15, Business Enterprise, and especially the Census Bureau Web site at <www.census.gov/naics/>.

The 2012 and 2017 Economic Censuses have three series of publications for these two sectors: 1) subject series with reports such as product lines and establishment and firm sizes, 2) geographic reports with individual reports for each state, and 3) industry series with individual reports for industry groups. For information on these series, see the Census Bureau Web site at <www.census.gov/programs-surveys/economic-census.html>.

Current surveys—Current sample surveys conducted by the Census Bureau cover various aspects of wholesale and retail trade. Its *Monthly Retail Trade and Food Services* release at <www.census.gov/retail/index.html> contains monthly estimates of sales, inventories, and inventory/sales ratios for the United States, by kind of business. Annual figures on retail sales, year-end inventories, purchases, accounts receivable, and gross margins by kind of business are located on the Census Bureau Web site at <www.census.gov/programs-surveys/arts.html>.

Statistics from the Census Bureau's monthly wholesale trade survey include national estimates of sales, inventories, and inventory/sales ratios for merchant wholesalers excluding manufacturers' sales branches and offices. Data are presented by major summary groups "durable and nondurable," and 4-digit NAICS industry groups. Merchant wholesalers excluding manufacturers' sales branches and offices are those wholesalers who take title to the goods they sell (e.g., jobbers, exporters, importers, industrial distributors). These data, based on reports submitted by a sample of firms, appear in the *Monthly Wholesale Trade Report*. This report includes monthly sales, inventories, and inventories/sales ratios and data on annual sales, inventories, and year-end inventories/sales ratios. The *Annual Wholesale Trade Report* provides data on merchant wholesalers excluding manufacturer sales branches and offices as well as summary data for all merchant wholesalers. This report also provides separate data for manufacturer sales branches and offices, and electronic markets, agents, brokers, and commission merchants. Included in the *Annual Wholesale Trade Report* are data on annual sales, year-end inventories, inventories/sales ratios, operating expenses, purchases, and gross margins. Data are presented by major summary groups "durable and nondurable" and 4-digit NAICS industry groups. These reports are available on the Census Bureau Web site at <www.census.gov/wholesale/index.html>.

E-commerce—Electronic commerce (or e-commerce) is the sale of goods and services over the internet and extranet, electronic data interchange (EDI) network, electronic mail, or other online systems. Payment may or may not be made online. E-commerce data are collected in four separate Census Bureau surveys. These surveys use different measures of economic activity such as shipments for manufacturing, sales for wholesale and retail trade, and revenues for service industries. Data can be found at <www.census.gov/programs-surveys/e-stats.html>. Consequently, measures of total economic and e-commerce activity vary by economic sector, are conceptually and definitionally different, and therefore, are not additive. This edition has several tables on e-commerce sales, such as Tables 1073, 1083, and 1084 in this section; and Table 1296 in Section 27, Accommodation, Food Services, and Other Services.

Statistical reliability—For a discussion of statistical collection and estimation, sampling procedures, and measures of statistical reliability applicable to Census Bureau data, see Appendix III.

Table 1070. Wholesale and Retail Trade—Establishments, Sales, Payroll, and Employees: 2012 and 2017

[In units as indicated (7,900 represents $7,900,000,000,000). Covers establishments with payroll. Based on data from the Economic Census; see Appendix III]

Kind of business	2012 NAICS code [1]	Establishments		Sales (bil. dollars)		Annual payroll (bil. dollars)		Paid employees (1,000)	
		2012	2017	2012	2017	2012	2017	2012	2017
Wholesale trade..................	**42**	**419,464**	**408,333**	**7,900**	**8,735**	**362**	**427**	**5,882**	**6,242**
Wholesale trade, durable goods...............	423	245,362	240,906	3,152	3,688	217	252	3,355	3,547
Wholesale trade, nondurable goods...........	424	130,669	129,714	4,108	4,344	132	160	2,244	2,397
Wholesale electronic markets and agents and brokers.............	425	43,433	37,713	639	703	14	14	283	298
Retail trade..........	**44–45**	**1,062,083**	**1,064,087**	**4,220**	**4,950**	**369**	**442**	**14,704**	**15,939**
Motor vehicle and parts dealers...............	441	116,482	118,882	869	1,168	70	91	1,710	2,003
Furniture and home furnishings stores.........	442	51,635	50,664	89	113	11	14	425	466
Electronics and appliance stores...............	443	48,826	30,440	103	91	10	10	432	332
Building material and garden equipment and supplies dealers................	444	78,282	75,054	279	347	34	39	1,145	1,285
Food and beverage stores................	445	147,579	150,238	620	721	61	72	2,865	3,176
Health and personal care stores...............	446	90,959	94,666	270	319	31	34	1,002	1,039
Gasoline stations................	447	114,474	115,369	554	475	16	19	857	943
Clothing and clothing accessories stores......	448	147,709	143,534	234	255	28	32	1,664	1,791
Sporting goods, hobby, musical instrument, and book stores.........	451	46,353	45,054	78	81	9	10	519	539
General merchandise stores.....................	452	49,147	53,777	641	690	58	68	2,773	2,793
Miscellaneous store retailers..................	453	107,040	109,019	98	110	14	17	713	774
Nonstore retailers.................	454	63,597	77,390	386	579	27	35	600	797

[1] North American Industrial Classification System, 2012; see text, Section 15.

Source: U.S. Census Bureau, "EC1700COMP: All Sectors: Comparative Statistics for the U.S., States, and Selected Geographies (2012 NAICS Basis): 2017 and 2012," <data.census.gov>, accessed December 2021.

Table 1071. Wholesale Trade—Nonemployer Firms and Receipts by Industry Type: 2019

[38,260,241 represents $38,260,241,000. Includes only firms subject to federal income tax. Nonemployers are businesses with no paid employees. Each distinct business income tax return filed by a nonemployer business is counted as a firm]

Industry type	2017 NAICS code [1]	Firms				Receipts ($1,000)
		Total	Corpora- tions [2]	Individual proprietor- ships [3]	Partner- ships [4]	
Wholesale trade, total................	**42**	**391,670**	**70,341**	**292,561**	**28,768**	**38,260,241**
Durable goods merchant wholesalers...............	**423**	**185,263**	**37,424**	**133,149**	**14,690**	**19,418,078**
Motor vehicle and motor vehicle parts and supplies merchant wholesalers............	4231	16,764	3,402	12,221	1,141	2,399,697
Furniture and home furnishing merchant wholesalers..............	4232	11,893	1,892	9,211	790	1,105,401
Lumber and other construction materials merchant wholesalers................	4233	6,846	1,420	4,760	666	852,590
Professional and commercial equipment and supplies merchant wholesalers............	4234	11,204	2,309	7,809	1,086	1,225,422
Metal and mineral (except petroleum) merchant wholesalers......	4235	2,512	626	1,677	209	364,440
Household appliance and electrical and electronic goods merchant wholesalers................	4236	8,661	2,678	5,150	833	1,093,541
Hardware and plumbing and heating equipment and supplies merchant wholesalers................	4237	4,004	980	2,674	350	451,338
Machinery, equipment, and supplies merchant wholesalers................	4238	17,251	4,762	10,821	1,668	2,436,657
Miscellaneous durable goods merchant wholesalers..............	4239	106,128	19,355	78,826	7,947	9,488,992
Nondurable goods merchant wholesalers........................	**424**	**140,851**	**24,879**	**104,756**	**11,216**	**13,844,941**
Paper and paper product merchant wholesalers.............	4241	4,365	878	3,200	287	431,560
Drugs and druggists' sundries merchant wholesalers.............	4242	2,731	633	1,793	305	261,083
Apparel, piece goods, and notions merchant wholesalers..........	4243	25,176	3,912	19,617	1,647	1,844,439
Grocery and related products merchant wholesalers..............	4244	26,880	5,516	19,113	2,251	3,978,007
Farm product raw material merchant wholesalers.............	4245	5,873	624	4,858	391	641,727
Chemical and allied products merchant wholesalers.............	4246	3,122	923	1,850	349	437,855
Petroleum and petroleum products merchant wholesalers.........	4247	2,217	481	1,509	227	275,414
Beer, wine, and distilled alcoholic beverage merchant wholesalers................	4248	6,389	961	4,411	1,017	587,899
Miscellaneous nondurable goods merchant wholesalers...........	4249	64,098	10,951	48,405	4,742	5,386,957
Wholesale electronic markets and agents and brokers..........	**425**	**65,556**	**8,038**	**54,656**	**2,862**	**4,997,222**
Business to business electronics markets...........................	42511	9,067	1,320	7,186	561	834,354
Wholesale trade agents and brokers.................	42512	56,489	6,718	47,470	2,301	4,162,868

[1] North American Industry Classification System, 2017; see text, Section 15. [2] A legally incorporated business under state laws. [3] Also referred to as "sole proprietorship," an unincorporated business with a sole owner. Includes self-employed persons. [4] An unincorporated business where two or more persons join to carry on a trade or business with each having a shared financial interest in the business.

Source: U.S. Census Bureau, Nonemployer Statistics, "All Sectors: Nonemployer Statistics by Legal Form of Organization and Receipts Size Class for the U.S., States, and Selected Geographies: 2019," <data.census.gov>, accessed June 2022.

Table 1072. Wholesale Trade—Establishments, Employees, and Payroll: 2019 and 2020

[397.4 represents 397,400. Covers establishments with payroll. Excludes self-employed individuals, employees of private households, railroad employees, agricultural production employees, and most government employees. For statement on methodology, see Appendix III]

Kind of business	NAICS code [1]	Establishments (1,000)		Employees [2] (1,000)		Payroll (bil. dol.)	
		2019	2020	2019	2020	2019	2020
Wholesale trade, total............................	**42**	**397.4**	**391.1**	**6,181**	**6,145**	**464.3**	**464.6**
Merchant wholesalers, durable goods..........................	423	233.3	230.1	3,540	3,551	279.7	280.8
Motor vehicle and motor vehicle parts and supply merchant wholesalers................................	4231	23.2	22.8	419	418	25.4	24.8
Furniture and home furnishing merchant wholesalers......	4232	12.6	12.2	168	165	10.9	10.5
Lumber and other construction materials merchant wholesalers..	4233	17.9	17.8	263	266	16.9	17.5
Professional and commercial equipment and supplies merchant wholesalers................................	4234	34.8	34.5	644	666	64.8	67.7
Metal and mineral (except petroleum) merchant wholesalers..	4235	9.4	9.2	154	152	10.5	10.1
Household appliances and electrical and electronic goods merchant wholesalers................	4236	27.9	27.2	520	517	55.9	55.9
Hardware, plumbing and heating equipment and supplies merchant wholesalers.......................	4237	19.6	19.7	261	262	18.2	18.4
Machinery, equipment, and supplies merchant wholesalers..	4238	56.4	55.5	787	783	57.2	55.9
Miscellaneous durable goods merchant wholesalers.......	4239	31.5	31.1	326	321	19.8	19.8
Merchant wholesalers, nondurable goods....................	424	126.0	124.2	2,368	2,329	169.1	168.8
Paper and paper product merchant wholesalers............	4241	8.9	8.6	147	144	9.0	8.8
Drugs and druggists' sundries merchant wholesalers......	4242	10.5	10.4	301	302	38.8	42.0
Apparel, piece goods and notions merchant wholesalers..	4243	14.5	14.0	193	183	12.5	10.9
Grocery and related product merchant wholesalers........	4244	35.1	34.8	859	829	49.1	47.7
Farm product raw material merchant wholesalers..........	4245	6.2	6.1	63	61	3.9	3.9
Chemical and allied products merchant wholesalers.......	4246	12.1	12.0	161	161	13.4	13.3
Petroleum and petroleum products merchant wholesalers..	4247	6.2	6.2	102	102	8.6	8.3
Beer, wine, and distilled alcoholic beverages................	4248	4.6	4.6	206	208	14.0	13.9
Miscellaneous nondurable goods merchant wholesalers...	4249	28.0	27.7	335	340	19.7	20.0
Wholesale electronic markets and agents and brokers......	425	38.0	36.8	273	266	15.5	15.0

[1] Data based on North American Industry Classification System (NAICS) 2017. See text, Section 15. [2] Covers full- and part-time employees who are on the payroll in the pay period including March 12.

Source: U.S. Census Bureau, County Business Patterns, CB2000CBP, "County Business Patterns, including ZIP Code Business Patterns, by Legal Form of Organization and Employment Size Class for the U.S., States, and Selected Geographies: 2020," <data.census.gov>, accessed May 2022. See also <www.census.gov/programs-surveys/cbp.html>.

Table 1073. Merchant Wholesale Trade Sales—Total and E-Commerce: 2020

[5,795,028 represents $5,795,028,000,000. Covers only businesses with paid employees. Excludes manufacturers' sales branches and offices. Based on the Annual Wholesale Trade Survey; see Appendix III]

Kind of business	NAICS code [1]	Value of sales (mil. dol.)		E-commerce as percent of total sales	Percent distribution of E-commerce sales
		Total	E-commerce		
Total merchant wholesale trade...............................	**42**	**5,795,028**	**1,820,300**	**31.4**	**100.0**
Durable goods..	**423**	**2,847,389**	**756,858**	**26.6**	**41.6**
Motor vehicles, parts and supplies.........................	4231	439,713	176,030	40.0	9.7
Furniture and home furnishings............................	4232	96,872	(S)	(S)	(S)
Lumber and other construction materials...................	4233	169,719	(S)	(S)	(S)
Professional and commercial equipment and supplies.........	4234	508,580	152,909	30.1	8.4
Computers and peripheral equipment and software...........	42343	268,715	83,474	31.1	4.6
Medical, dental, and hospital equipment and supplies.......	42345	151,798	(S)	(S)	(S)
Metals and minerals (except petroleum).....................	4235	146,202	19,984	13.7	1.1
Household appliances and electrical and electronic goods.....	4236	600,060	214,026	35.7	11.8
Hardware, plumbing and heating equipment.................	4237	173,362	31,791	18.3	1.7
Machinery, equipment and supplies........................	4238	451,011	66,586	14.8	3.7
Miscellaneous durable goods..............................	4239	261,870	54,878	21.0	3.0
Nondurable goods..	**424**	**2,947,639**	**1,063,442**	**36.1**	**58.4**
Paper and paper products.................................	4241	82,872	(S)	(S)	(S)
Drugs and druggists' sundries.............................	4242	763,898	608,259	79.6	33.4
Apparel, piece goods and notions.........................	4243	129,536	37,588	29.0	2.1
Groceries and related products............................	4244	675,770	220,115	32.6	12.1
Farm product raw materials...............................	4245	200,710	17,543	8.7	1.0
Chemical and allied products..............................	4246	114,873	(S)	(S)	(S)
Petroleum and petroleum products........................	4247	505,676	62,064	12.3	3.4
Beer, wine, and distilled alcoholic beverages..............	4248	171,495	25,845	15.1	1.4
Miscellaneous nondurable goods..........................	4249	302,809	(S)	(S)	(S)

S Figure does not meet publication standards. [1] North American Industry Classification System, 2012. See text, Section 15.

Source: U.S. Census Bureau, "Annual Report for Wholesale Trade: 2020," <www.census.gov/programs-surveys/awts/data/tables.html>, accessed March 2022.

Table 1074. Merchant Wholesalers' Sales and Inventories by Kind of Business: 2010 to 2020

[In billions of dollars (4,339.2 represents $4,339,200,000,000), except ratios. Inventories and inventories/sales ratios as of December, not seasonally adjusted. Excludes manufacturers' sales branches and offices. Data adjusted using final results of the 2017 Economic Census. Based on data from the Annual Wholesale Trade Survey and the Monthly Wholesale Trade Survey; see Appendix III]

Kind of business	NAICS code [1]	2010	2015	2016	2017	2018	2019	2020
SALES								
Merchant wholesalers........	42	**4,339.2**	**5,387.2**	**5,339.7**	**5,701.0**	**6,098.7**	**6,071.4**	**5,795.0**
Durable goods........	423	**2,001.1**	**2,553.5**	**2,548.2**	**2,732.5**	**2,922.6**	**2,906.3**	**2,847.4**
Motor vehicles, parts, and supplies........	4231	304.8	433.0	428.9	450.0	469.3	483.0	439.7
Furniture and home furnishings........	4232	57.4	81.1	85.9	91.8	94.8	97.2	96.9
Lumber and other construction materials........	4233	86.5	122.9	135.8	148.2	160.8	161.4	169.7
Professional, commercial equipment and supplies........	4234	397.8	446.3	456.1	472.8	503.2	515.9	508.6
Computer, peripheral equipment and software........	42343	220.1	232.9	234.1	244.2	264.4	265.7	268.7
Medical, dental, and hospital equipment and supplies....	42345	(NA)	121.2	127.0	129.8	137.0	145.7	151.8
Metals and minerals (except petroleum)........	4235	138.4	162.9	145.6	168.7	193.8	181.8	146.2
Household appliances and electrical and electronic goods........	4236	391.2	546.1	539.2	585.2	615.5	590.4	600.1
Hardware, plumbing, heating equipment and supplies.....	4237	96.1	134.0	141.1	149.9	160.5	168.6	173.4
Machinery, equipment, and supplies........	4238	305.3	408.9	396.6	424.8	463.6	464.4	451.0
Miscellaneous durable goods........	4239	223.7	218.2	219.0	241.1	261.0	243.6	261.9
Nondurable goods........	424	**2,338.1**	**2,833.7**	**2,791.5**	**2,968.4**	**3,176.1**	**3,165.0**	**2,947.6**
Paper and paper products........	4241	86.0	92.8	92.2	92.0	92.3	89.5	82.9
Drugs and druggists' sundries........	4242	415.9	605.3	644.6	662.5	693.6	721.8	763.9
Apparel, piece goods, and notions........	4243	137.0	169.4	167.0	167.0	165.2	164.1	129.5
Grocery and related products........	4244	491.3	633.3	635.4	660.6	676.4	685.1	675.8
Farm product raw materials........	4245	188.3	230.1	216.9	212.4	212.2	200.2	200.7
Chemical and allied products........	4246	102.7	117.4	111.4	120.8	131.6	126.1	114.9
Petroleum and petroleum products........	4247	591.0	584.1	511.4	627.0	758.5	718.7	505.7
Beer, wine, and distilled alcoholic beverages........	4248	111.3	134.8	141.3	145.4	151.6	159.6	171.5
Miscellaneous nondurable goods........	4249	214.5	266.6	271.4	280.9	294.9	299.8	302.8
INVENTORIES								
Merchant wholesalers........	42	**445.6**	**599.5**	**614.9**	**637.0**	**675.1**	**684.2**	**674.9**
Durable goods........	423	**256.0**	**351.7**	**353.7**	**370.4**	**403.3**	**405.7**	**394.9**
Motor vehicles, parts, and supplies........	4231	40.7	61.5	61.4	60.9	64.7	66.2	61.1
Furniture and home furnishings........	4232	8.6	12.0	12.4	12.8	13.8	13.6	13.4
Lumber and other construction materials........	4233	10.2	14.5	16.3	17.8	20.5	20.8	22.0
Professional, commercial equipment and supplies........	4234	32.8	41.3	42.9	45.0	48.6	49.5	48.5
Computer, peripheral equipment and software........	42343	13.1	15.2	15.4	16.9	18.6	18.1	17.5
Medical, dental, and hospital equipment and supplies....	42345	(NA)	15.3	15.7	16.2	17.7	18.5	20.0
Metals and minerals (except petroleum)........	4235	22.6	27.3	26.2	30.3	35.3	32.5	28.8
Household appliances and electrical and electronic goods........	4236	35.7	51.0	50.4	53.0	56.1	55.5	56.0
Hardware, plumbing, heating equipment and supplies.....	4237	16.8	23.1	23.8	25.5	28.2	29.2	30.9
Machinery, equipment, and supplies........	4238	63.8	93.1	90.8	94.4	103.4	106.2	102.0
Miscellaneous durable goods........	4239	24.8	28.0	29.5	30.8	32.8	32.3	32.2
Nondurable goods........	424	**189.6**	**247.9**	**261.1**	**266.6**	**271.8**	**278.5**	**280.0**
Paper and paper products........	4241	7.6	8.6	8.6	8.8	8.8	8.2	8.2
Drugs and druggists' sundries........	4242	38.9	64.5	66.7	66.8	67.4	68.6	75.1
Apparel, piece goods, and notions........	4243	20.1	28.1	27.1	26.9	27.5	28.6	23.6
Grocery and related products........	4244	27.3	37.3	38.4	39.2	40.5	41.6	41.6
Farm product raw materials........	4245	28.5	26.3	29.1	31.0	31.9	32.3	37.4
Chemical and allied products........	4246	9.5	12.2	12.5	13.1	13.3	12.7	11.9
Petroleum and petroleum products........	4247	23.2	19.8	26.3	25.2	22.3	24.0	21.0
Beer, wine, and distilled alcoholic beverages........	4248	10.7	14.2	14.9	15.7	15.9	16.9	16.7
Miscellaneous nondurable goods........	4249	23.8	36.8	37.5	40.1	44.2	45.8	44.5
INVENTORIES/SALES RATIO								
Merchant wholesalers........	42	**1.03**	**1.11**	**1.15**	**1.12**	**1.11**	**1.13**	**1.16**
Durable goods........	423	**1.28**	**1.38**	**1.39**	**1.36**	**1.38**	**1.40**	**1.39**
Motor vehicles, parts, and supplies........	4231	1.33	1.42	1.43	1.35	1.38	1.37	1.39
Furniture and home furnishings........	4232	1.49	1.47	1.44	1.39	1.46	1.40	1.39
Lumber and other construction materials........	4233	1.18	1.18	1.20	1.20	1.27	1.29	1.30
Professional, commercial equipment and supplies........	4234	0.83	0.92	0.94	0.95	0.97	0.96	0.95
Computer, peripheral equipment and software........	42343	0.59	0.65	0.66	0.69	0.70	0.68	0.65
Medical, dental, and hospital equipment and supplies....	42345	(NA)	1.26	1.24	1.25	1.29	1.27	1.32
Metals and minerals (except petroleum)........	4235	1.63	1.67	1.80	1.80	1.82	1.79	1.97
Household appliances and electrical and electronic goods........	4236	0.91	0.93	0.93	0.91	0.91	0.94	0.93
Hardware, plumbing, heating equipment and supplies.....	4237	1.75	1.72	1.68	1.70	1.76	1.73	1.78
Machinery, equipment, and supplies........	4238	2.09	2.28	2.29	2.22	2.23	2.29	2.26
Miscellaneous durable goods........	4239	1.11	1.28	1.35	1.28	1.25	1.32	1.23
Nondurable goods........	424	**0.81**	**0.87**	**0.94**	**0.90**	**0.86**	**0.88**	**0.95**
Paper and paper products........	4241	0.88	0.93	0.94	0.96	0.95	0.92	1.00
Drugs and druggists' sundries........	4242	0.94	1.07	1.03	1.01	0.97	0.95	0.98
Apparel, piece goods, and notions........	4243	1.47	1.66	1.62	1.61	1.67	1.74	1.82
Grocery and related products........	4244	0.56	0.59	0.60	0.59	0.60	0.61	0.62
Farm product raw materials........	4245	1.51	1.14	1.34	1.46	1.50	1.62	1.86
Chemical and allied products........	4246	0.92	1.04	1.12	1.08	1.01	1.00	1.03
Petroleum and petroleum products........	4247	0.39	0.34	0.51	0.40	0.29	0.33	0.42
Beer, wine, and distilled alcoholic beverages........	4248	0.97	1.06	1.05	1.08	1.05	1.06	0.98
Miscellaneous nondurable goods........	4249	1.11	1.38	1.38	1.43	1.50	1.53	1.47

NA Not available. [1] North American Industry Classification System, 2012. See text, Section 15.

Source: U.S. Census Bureau, "Annual Report for Wholesale Trade: 2020," <www.census.gov/programs-surveys/awts.html>, accessed March 2022.

Table 1075. Wholesale and Retail Trade—Establishments, Employees, and Payroll by State: 2019 and 2020

[6,181 represents 6,181,000. Covers establishments with payroll. Excludes self-employed individuals, employees of private households, railroad employees, agricultural production employees, and most government employees. Data based on North American Industry Classification System (NAICS), 2017. See text, Section 15. For statement on methodology, see Appendix III]

State	Wholesale trade (NAICS 42)						Retail trade (NAICS 44, 45)					
	Establishments		Employees [1] (1,000)		Annual payroll (mil. dol.)		Establishments		Employees [1] (1,000)		Annual payroll (mil. dol.)	
	2019	2020	2019	2020	2019	2020	2019	2020	2019	2020	2019	2020
U.S.	397,365	391,114	6,181	6,145	464,319	464,554	1,044,957	1,036,821	15,693	15,808	470,532	484,898
AL	5,096	5,047	75	75	4,447	4,552	17,725	17,565	228	227	6,270	6,499
AK	737	707	9	9	583	558	2,456	2,369	33	33	1,150	1,169
AZ	6,497	6,390	100	100	7,083	7,188	17,585	17,602	328	335	10,499	11,344
AR	3,284	3,241	49	49	2,709	2,761	10,709	10,606	138	137	3,804	4,043
CA	57,394	56,484	828	822	73,707	74,934	105,624	105,548	1,677	1,682	58,018	59,240
CO	7,170	7,069	104	103	8,383	8,321	18,622	18,462	281	284	9,091	9,386
CT	3,930	3,820	73	69	6,410	5,886	11,928	11,737	180	182	5,831	5,853
DE	1,207	1,209	17	18	1,720	1,977	3,608	3,674	57	55	1,619	1,598
DC	376	383	4	3	307	307	1,694	1,670	22	23	727	708
FL	30,444	30,390	333	335	21,448	21,628	73,481	74,226	1,090	1,118	31,892	33,397
GA	12,678	12,518	207	206	14,465	14,420	34,132	34,637	478	488	13,321	13,942
HI	1,560	1,503	19	18	1,050	924	4,559	4,486	72	70	2,271	2,094
ID	2,134	2,113	33	33	2,087	2,283	6,099	6,185	84	86	2,556	2,750
IL	17,264	16,874	323	321	26,376	26,228	36,948	36,418	582	584	16,949	17,209
IN	7,397	7,290	127	126	8,312	8,364	20,935	20,784	328	328	9,151	9,466
IA	4,899	4,819	69	70	4,044	4,139	11,355	11,147	187	184	4,787	4,920
KS	4,291	4,191	63	63	4,026	4,225	9,762	9,591	147	146	3,909	3,984
KY	4,073	4,019	71	70	4,372	4,330	14,841	14,817	218	216	6,019	6,073
LA	5,212	5,114	74	73	4,525	4,359	16,248	15,995	224	221	6,165	6,282
ME	1,517	1,479	19	18	1,122	1,144	6,088	5,983	84	82	2,473	2,575
MD	5,300	5,171	90	90	6,693	6,714	17,381	17,082	288	294	8,677	8,930
MA	7,284	7,049	151	149	14,957	14,926	23,323	22,773	363	365	12,603	12,486
MI	10,486	10,260	183	185	12,922	12,722	33,678	33,088	460	467	13,183	13,659
MN	7,607	7,415	145	144	11,975	12,148	18,247	17,921	299	303	8,461	8,610
MS	2,652	2,568	38	38	2,084	2,109	11,324	11,290	137	136	3,496	3,620
MO	7,232	7,130	130	133	7,814	7,917	20,210	19,926	308	310	8,426	8,940
MT	1,560	1,540	15	15	827	820	4,631	4,602	58	58	1,757	1,844
NE	3,117	3,073	40	41	2,505	2,532	7,032	6,919	110	108	3,003	3,097
NV	3,104	3,137	42	40	2,631	2,496	8,591	8,660	149	155	4,622	4,933
NH	1,791	1,733	25	24	2,092	2,044	5,833	5,739	98	97	2,981	3,086
NJ	13,464	13,229	278	271	27,365	26,598	30,548	30,165	451	464	14,194	14,698
NM	1,697	1,660	20	20	1,125	1,121	6,207	6,021	93	91	2,659	2,687
NY	29,050	27,989	348	341	26,741	26,358	75,882	73,794	914	917	29,502	29,425
NC	11,309	11,198	192	195	14,353	14,889	34,594	34,506	506	500	13,610	14,157
ND	1,704	1,698	22	22	1,407	1,437	3,154	3,138	48	48	1,444	1,478
OH	13,215	12,974	236	232	15,741	15,523	34,752	34,372	556	561	15,563	16,319
OK	4,439	4,401	59	60	3,476	3,443	13,027	13,055	179	183	5,004	5,350
OR	5,117	5,013	78	77	5,631	5,670	14,167	13,965	210	215	6,553	6,917
PA	13,723	13,471	251	251	18,952	19,031	41,641	41,045	648	658	18,169	18,484
RI	1,293	1,273	20	21	1,476	1,480	3,647	3,620	48	50	1,511	1,542
SC	4,914	4,856	76	76	4,699	4,724	17,717	17,673	252	255	6,640	7,014
SD	1,529	1,528	18	19	1,046	1,124	3,802	3,725	53	52	1,451	1,524
TN	6,673	6,620	123	123	8,072	8,196	22,653	22,650	319	320	9,137	9,566
TX	32,826	32,669	537	532	40,281	39,071	80,878	80,932	1,322	1,334	39,621	40,883
UT	3,658	3,671	61	61	3,888	4,082	10,152	10,392	156	160	4,801	5,228
VT	752	720	11	11	668	662	3,062	3,033	38	37	1,176	1,202
VA	6,732	6,695	107	105	7,655	7,800	26,384	26,064	431	429	12,177	12,394
WA	9,003	8,852	138	137	10,178	10,404	21,324	20,897	340	345	11,786	12,196
WV	1,370	1,343	18	18	982	945	5,779	5,658	80	79	2,120	2,128
WI	6,802	6,704	125	127	8,422	8,584	18,379	18,064	311	309	8,770	9,014
WY	802	814	8	8	484	456	2,559	2,550	30	30	932	957

[1] Covers full- and part-time employees who are on the payroll in the pay period including March 12.

Source: U.S. Census Bureau, County Business Patterns, CB2000CBP, "County Business Patterns, including ZIP Code Business Patterns, by Legal Form of Organization and Employment Size Class for the U.S., States, and Selected Geographies: 2020," <data.census.gov>, accessed May 2022.

Table 1076. Retail Trade—Establishments, Employees, and Payroll: 2019 and 2020

[1,045.0 represents 1,045,000. Covers establishments with payroll. Excludes self-employed individuals, employees of private households, railroad employees, agricultural production employees, and most government employees. For statement on methodology, see Appendix III]

Kind of business	NAICS code [1]	Establishments (1,000)		Employees (1,000) [2]		Payroll (bil. dol.)	
		2019	2020	2019	2020	2019	2020
Retail trade, total.................	44–45	1,045.0	1,036.8	15,693	15,808	470.5	484.9
Motor vehicle and parts dealers.................	441	117.8	117.2	2,023	2,043	98.5	100.0
Automobile dealers.................	4411	46.5	46.6	1,334	1,344	74.1	74.8
New car dealers.................	44111	21.4	21.4	1,178	1,182	67.0	67.4
Used car dealers.................	44112	25.1	25.2	156	162	7.2	7.4
Other motor vehicle dealers.................	4412	13.5	13.5	153	156	7.1	8.0
Recreational vehicle dealers.................	44121	2.7	2.8	49	53	2.6	3.0
Motorcycle and boat and other motor vehicle dealers [3]......	44122	10.8	10.7	104	104	4.6	5.0
Motorcycle, ATV, and all other motor vehicle dealers.........	441228	6.7	6.5	70	69	2.9	3.1
Automotive parts, accessories, and tire stores.................	4413	57.7	57.2	536	543	17.2	17.2
Automotive parts and accessories stores.................	44131	37.4	36.9	359	368	10.1	10.1
Tire dealers.................	44132	20.3	20.2	177	176	7.2	7.1
Furniture and home furnishing stores.................	442	48.8	47.5	473	461	15.3	14.9
Furniture stores.................	4421	22.9	22.5	205	204	8.2	8.1
Home furnishings stores.................	4422	25.9	25.1	268	257	7.1	6.7
Floor covering stores.................	44221	10.7	10.4	71	71	3.3	3.4
Other home furnishings stores [3]	44229	15.2	14.7	197	186	3.7	3.4
Window treatment stores.................	442291	1.9	2.0	7	8	0.3	0.3
Electronics and appliance stores.................	443	25.8	24.0	293	269	9.5	8.7
Household appliance stores.................	443141	6.6	6.3	54	52	2.2	2.3
Electronics stores.................	443142	19.2	17.7	239	217	7.3	6.4
Building material & garden equipment & supplies dealers.......	444	73.8	72.5	1,340	1,345	42.9	46.9
Building material & supplies dealers [3].................	4441	56.6	55.6	1,184	1,188	37.7	41.3
Home centers.................	44411	6.0	5.9	[5] 719	[5] 717	[5] 18.0	[5] 20.0
Hardware stores.................	44413	15.3	15.1	145	143	4.1	4.4
Lawn & garden equipment & supplies stores [3].................	4442	17.2	16.9	155	157	5.1	5.6
Nursery, garden center, and farm supply stores.................	44422	13.3	13.1	126	129	4.0	4.4
Food & beverage stores.................	445	150.1	150.3	3,117	3,183	75.5	83.3
Grocery stores.................	4451	93.3	93.5	2,780	2,840	67.9	75.2
Supermarkets & grocery (except convenience) stores.......	44511	62.9	62.3	2,648	2,696	65.2	72.3
Convenience stores.................	44512	30.3	31.2	131	144	2.7	2.9
Specialty food stores.................	4452	22.3	22.1	163	165	3.5	3.6
Beer, wine, & liquor stores [4].................	4453	34.6	34.7	174	178	4.1	4.4
Health & personal care stores [3].................	446	94.3	93.9	1,022	1,021	37.1	37.3
Pharmacies & drug stores.................	44611	44.9	44.4	676	667	27.3	27.7
Cosmetics, beauty supplies, & perfume stores.................	44612	17.5	17.5	160	159	3.5	3.3
Optical goods stores.................	44613	11.9	12.2	82	88	2.4	2.3
Gasoline stations.................	447	112.6	111.8	994	994	21.3	22.7
Gasoline stations with convenience stores.................	44711	99.3	98.9	848	846	17.7	18.6
Other gasoline stations.................	44719	13.3	12.8	146	148	3.6	4.0
Clothing & clothing accessories stores.................	448	137.0	133.0	1,666	1,614	33.2	28.5
Clothing stores [3].................	4481	93.0	90.2	1,325	1,287	24.6	20.9
Men's clothing stores.................	44811	6.6	6.5	51	50	1.5	1.1
Women's clothing stores.................	44812	31.6	30.1	303	279	5.2	3.9
Children's & infants' clothing stores.................	44813	6.0	5.2	60	[5] 52	0.9	0.7
Family clothing stores.................	44814	28.8	28.6	730	727	13.2	11.7
Shoe stores.................	4482	22.6	22.0	223	211	4.1	3.6
Jewelry, luggage, & leather goods stores [3].................	4483	21.4	20.8	119	116	4.5	4.0
Jewelry stores.................	44831	20.5	19.9	112	109	4.2	3.7
Sporting goods, hobby, musical instrument, & book stores......	451	42.5	41.2	477	465	9.9	9.8
Sporting goods/hobby/musical instrument stores [3].............	4511	35.6	34.7	413	403	8.7	8.9
Sporting goods stores.................	45111	20.4	19.8	239	232	5.5	5.7
Hobby, toy, and game stores.................	45112	7.9	7.8	108	106	2.0	2.0
Book stores and news dealers [3].................	4512	6.9	6.6	[5] 64	[5] 63	1.1	0.9
Book stores.................	451211	6.0	5.7	[5] 61	[5] 60	1.1	0.8
General merchandise stores.................	452	55.8	56.1	2,734	2,764	69.6	68.8
Department stores.................	4522	3.9	3.7	426	450	9.0	6.7
General merchandise stores.................	4523	51.9	52.4	2,308	2,314	60.6	62.1
Warehouse clubs and supercenters.................	452311	8.3	8.1	1,782	1,797	52.5	53.6
All other general merchandise stores.................	452319	43.6	44.3	526	518	8.1	8.5
Miscellaneous store retailers [3].................	453	108.0	106.4	769	767	18.8	18.7
Florists.................	4531	12.0	11.7	55	52	1.1	1.0
Office supplies, stationery, and gift stores.................	4532	25.4	24.0	204	185	4.3	3.5
Office supplies and stationery stores.................	45321	5.1	4.8	60	54	1.4	1.2
Gift, novelty, and souvenir stores.................	45322	20.3	19.1	144	131	2.9	2.3
Used merchandise stores.................	4533	19.3	18.9	201	206	4.2	3.7
Other miscellaneous store retailers [3].................	4539	51.2	51.8	309	323	9.3	10.5
Pet and pet supplies stores.................	45391	10.1	10.0	122	125	2.8	3.3
Nonstore retailers [3].................	454	78.4	82.9	785	879	39.0	45.5
Electronic shopping & mail-order houses.................	4541	43.5	47.9	561	662	29.1	35.7
Direct selling establishments.................	4543	31.4	31.5	181	176	8.3	8.4
Fuel dealers.................	45431	8.1	8.0	74	74	3.8	3.9

[1] Data based on North American Industry Classification System (NAICS), 2017. See text, Section 15. [2] Covers full- and part-time employees who are on the payroll in the pay period including March 12. [3] Includes other kinds of business, not shown separately. [4] Includes government employees. [5] Data is flagged for high noise; the value was changed by 5 percent or more to avoid disclosure of data for individual businesses.

Source: U.S. Census Bureau, County Business Patterns, CB2000CBP "County Business Patterns, including ZIP Code Business Patterns, by Legal Form of Organization and Employment Size Class for the U.S., States, and Selected Geographies: 2020," <data.census.gov>, accessed May 2022.

Table 1077. Retail Trade—Nonemployer Firms and Receipts by Industry Type: 2019

[94,135,224 represents $94,135,224,000. See headnote, Table 1071]

Industry type	2017 NAICS code [1]	Firms				Receipts ($1,000)
		Total	Corpora-tions [2]	Individual proprietor-ships [3]	Partner-ships [4]	
Retail trade, total........................	**44–45**	**2,100,019**	**123,178**	**1,897,141**	**79,700**	**94,135,224**
Motor vehicle & parts dealers............................	441	167,147	15,922	143,920	7,305	18,446,173
Furniture & home furnishings stores....................	442	37,040	4,696	29,711	2,633	2,473,063
Electronics and appliance stores.......................	443	22,438	3,053	18,275	1,110	1,327,219
Building material & garden equipment & supplies dealers......	444	34,392	3,600	29,011	1,781	2,383,218
Building material & supplies dealers.....................	4441	22,314	2,891	18,077	1,346	1,817,934
Food & beverage stores................................	445	95,801	11,452	77,350	6,999	7,255,875
Grocery stores.......................................	4451	36,825	4,774	29,951	2,100	3,117,968
Specialty food stores.................................	4452	49,493	4,971	40,653	3,869	2,733,685
Health & personal care stores..........................	446	165,207	8,223	152,014	4,970	4,611,048
Gasoline stations....................................	447	7,304	1,642	5,049	613	1,021,577
Clothing & clothing accessories stores.................	448	173,878	10,616	154,141	9,121	6,755,282
Clothing stores.....................................	4481	128,418	7,729	113,012	7,677	4,767,065
Jewelry, luggage, and leather goods stores.............	4483	40,329	2,417	36,731	1,181	1,682,695
Sporting goods, hobby, musical instrument, & book stores.....	451	75,107	4,977	65,830	4,300	3,338,081
Book stores and news dealer..........................	4512	11,619	617	10,507	495	427,742
General merchandise stores............................	452	32,920	2,094	29,447	1,379	1,594,621
Miscellaneous store retailers..........................	453	269,376	20,820	232,934	15,622	13,284,328
Office supplies, stationery, and gift stores..............	4532	43,929	3,396	37,931	2,602	1,737,470
Nonstore retailers....................................	454	1,019,409	36,083	959,459	23,867	31,644,739
Electronic shopping & mail-order houses...............	4541	187,947	13,724	164,942	9,281	10,019,801
Direct selling establishments.........................	4543	815,082	20,806	781,051	13,225	20,935,833

[1] North American Industry Classification System, 2017; see text, Section 15. [2] A legally incorporated business under state laws. [3] Also referred to as "sole proprietorship," an unincorporated business with a sole owner. Includes self-employed persons. [4] An unincorporated business where two or more persons join to carry on a trade or business with each having a shared financial interest in the business.

Source: U.S. Census Bureau, Nonemployer Statistics, "All Sectors: Nonemployer Statistics by Legal Form of Organization and Receipts Size Class for the U.S., States, and Selected Geographies: 2019," <data.census.gov>, accessed June 2022.

Table 1078. Retail Industries—Employees, Average Weekly Hours, and Average Hourly Earnings: 2010 to 2021

[Annual averages of monthly figures (14,446 represents 14,446,000). Covers all full- and part-time employees who worked during, or received pay for, any part of the pay period including the 12th of the month]

Industry	NAICS code [1]	Employees (1,000)			Average weekly hours [2]			Average hourly earnings [2] (dol.)		
		2010	2020	2021	2010	2020	2021	2010	2020	2021
Retail trade, total [3]........................	**44,45**	**14,446**	**14,871**	**15,396**	**30.2**	**30.8**	**30.8**	**13.25**	**17.60**	**18.54**
Motor vehicle and parts dealers [3]...............	441	1,629	1,897	1,940	36.5	36.5	36.8	17.06	22.52	24.25
Automobile dealers................................	4411	1,012	1,203	1,223	36.7	36.4	36.8	18.22	24.52	26.27
Auto parts, accessories, and tire stores...........	4413	489	544	549	36.9	37.1	37.2	14.54	17.96	19.32
Furniture and home furnishings stores..............	442	438	404	442	29.1	31.8	31.5	15.25	19.86	21.17
Electronics and appliance stores [3]...............	443	523	425	424	31.6	34.3	34.1	16.84	23.79	24.76
Building material and garden supply stores [3].......	444	1,133	1,359	1,399	33.9	34.9	35.3	14.12	19.66	21.18
Building material and supplies dealers.............	4441	1,006	1,196	1,223	34.2	35.2	35.5	14.14	19.95	21.65
Lawn and garden equip. and supplies stores.....	4442	127	163	176	31.6	33.3	33.2	13.98	17.35	17.74
Food and beverage stores [3].....................	445	2,808	3,106	3,130	29.0	28.5	28.1	12.03	14.48	15.09
Grocery stores...................................	4451	2,461	2,744	2,750	29.0	28.6	28.1	12.12	14.40	15.02
Supermarkets and other grocery stores...........	44511	2,323	2,589	2,589	28.9	28.6	28.0	12.27	14.55	15.12
Convenience stores.............................	44512	138	155	161	31.3	28.8	29.2	9.43	11.75	13.38
Specialty food stores.............................	4452	211	204	215	29.7	27.1	27.3	11.13	15.15	15.80
Beer, wine, and liquor stores.....................	4453	136	158	166	27.2	28.7	28.0	11.89	15.02	15.55
Health and personal care stores [3]...............	446	981	964	1,029	29.4	29.2	29.4	16.99	20.56	21.46
Pharmacies and drug stores......................	44611	715	670	701	29.3	29.2	29.6	17.59	21.46	22.55
Gasoline stations [3].............................	447	819	927	939	30.7	30.6	30.8	10.25	12.82	13.93
Gasoline stations with convenience stores........	44711	719	833	843	30.4	30.4	30.8	9.99	12.58	13.68
Clothing and clothing accessories stores [3].........	448	1,353	950	1,033	21.2	23.3	23.5	11.59	16.79	17.83
Clothing stores..................................	4481	1,040	699	761	20.1	22.1	22.6	10.91	15.84	17.05
Shoe stores.....................................	4482	182	151	161	23.3	25.1	24.3	11.80	16.88	16.73
Jewelry, luggage, and leather goods stores.......	4483	131	101	111	28.1	29.5	29.7	15.56	22.00	23.53
Sporting goods, hobby, book, and music stores [3]..	451	579	472	527	23.4	26.7	25.7	11.69	15.41	16.99
Sporting goods and musical instrument stores....	4511	459	418	466	23.8	27.2	26.0	11.82	15.49	17.30
Book stores and news dealers...................	4512	120	54	61	22.0	22.2	22.8	11.10	14.51	14.08
General merchandise stores.......................	452	2,998	3,032	3,093	31.7	30.3	30.7	10.98	15.64	15.73
Miscellaneous store retailers [3]..................	453	762	747	805	28.0	28.2	28.8	12.50	15.19	16.47
Florists...	4531	69	50	55	22.4	25.9	23.3	11.05	14.29	14.72
Office supplies, stationary, and gift stores........	4532	303	192	197	27.1	25.2	25.6	13.06	14.82	15.35
Used merchandise stores.........................	4533	125	152	173	29.5	28.9	28.9	10.72	13.46	14.05
Other miscellaneous store retailers...............	4539	264	353	381	29.8	29.8	31.1	13.07	16.22	18.20
Pet and pet supplies stores......................	45391	99	115	117	27.4	28.0	28.0	12.83	15.28	16.18
Nonstore retailers [3]............................	454	425	588	635	36.3	36.1	35.7	17.83	22.18	23.22
Electronic shopping and mail-order houses.......	4541	250	424	467	35.9	36.0	35.5	18.34	22.22	23.34

[1] Based on the North American Industry Classification System (NAICS), 2017; see text, this section and Section 15. [2] Data shown for production and nonsupervisory employees. [3] Includes other kind of businesses, not shown separately.

Source: U.S. Bureau of Labor Statistics, Current Employment Statistics, "Employment, Hours, and Earnings—National," <www.bls.gov/ces/data.htm>, accessed March 2022.

Table 1079. Retail Trade—Sales by Kind of Business: 2000 to 2020

[In billions of dollars (2,983.3 represents $2,983,300,000,000). Data have been adjusted using final results of the 2017 Economic Census]

Kind of business	NAICS code [1]	2000	2010	2015	2017	2018	2019	2020
Retail sales, total................................	**44, 45**	**2,983.3**	**3,818.0**	**4,726.1**	**5,040.2**	**5,255.4**	**5,402.3**	**5,570.4**
GAFO, total [2]................................	(X)	862.7	1,114.4	1,262.8	1,275.0	1,298.2	1,306.3	1,229.2
Motor vehicle and parts dealers....................	441	796.2	742.9	1,103.5	1,185.7	1,204.9	1,237.7	1,208.3
Automobile dealers..............................	4411	687.8	621.2	949.2	1,020.6	1,035.7	1,065.5	1,023.2
New car dealers..............................	44111	630.1	549.5	848.2	906.5	918.3	942.8	905.5
Used car dealers.............................	44112	57.7	71.7	101.1	114.1	117.4	122.7	117.7
Other motor vehicle dealers.......................	4412	45.0	43.8	63.4	71.7	74.3	75.4	87.1
Auto parts, accessories, and tire stores..........	4413	63.4	77.9	90.9	93.4	94.9	96.8	98.0
Furniture and home furnishings stores.............	442	91.2	85.2	107.9	115.3	119.0	120.7	113.0
Furniture stores................................	4421	50.6	46.7	58.3	61.3	63.3	64.2	62.2
Home furnishings stores........................	4422	40.6	38.5	49.6	54.0	55.7	56.5	50.8
Electronics and appliance stores [3]................	443	90.4	99.6	100.2	92.4	94.1	90.9	76.0
Electronics stores..............................	443142	77.8	84.1	82.9	75.6	77.2	74.0	57.8
Building materials, garden equipment, and supplies dealers................................	444	229.0	260.6	324.0	349.4	367.7	373.3	422.2
Food and beverage stores [3]......................	445	444.8	580.5	687.4	728.8	749.9	775.0	850.2
Grocery stores..................................	4451	402.5	520.8	616.1	653.2	671.3	694.4	759.7
Supermarkets and other grocery (except convenience) stores........................	44511	381.4	498.0	590.7	625.0	640.2	661.9	728.9
Beer, wine and liquor stores....................	4453	28.5	41.4	49.2	52.6	55.1	57.0	66.3
Health and personal care stores [3]................	446	155.2	260.4	307.9	323.9	337.8	344.0	351.3
Pharmacies and drug stores.....................	44611	130.9	222.2	257.4	269.1	279.6	284.6	298.8
Gasoline stations................................	447	249.8	448.3	455.6	476.2	522.9	513.5	428.1
Clothing and clothing accessory stores [3]..........	448	167.7	213.3	257.3	261.4	267.5	269.5	201.4
Clothing stores [3]...............................	4481	118.1	158.3	187.8	191.1	195.2	196.1	138.3
Shoe stores....................................	4482	22.9	27.2	35.3	36.3	37.1	37.4	29.3
Jewelry, luggage, and leather goods stores......	4483	26.7	27.8	34.2	34.0	35.3	36.1	33.9
Sporting goods, hobby, musical instrument, and book stores [3]............................	451	67.6	78.2	85.4	83.9	80.2	79.8	84.4
Sporting goods stores...........................	45111	25.3	37.4	46.9	46.0	44.1	45.1	52.9
Hobby, toy, and game stores....................	45112	16.9	15.8	18.0	18.1	16.9	16.4	17.0
Book stores and news dealers....................	4512	16.1	16.3	11.6	10.9	10.0	9.4	6.6
General merchandise stores [3]....................	452	404.2	603.8	680.1	691.9	707.1	716.5	730.6
Department stores..............................	4521	232.5	184.8	165.1	146.7	142.1	134.7	112.3
Discount department stores....................	452112	136.2	119.9	107.8	98.2	97.5	95.1	91.0
Other general merchandise stores...............	4529	171.8	419.0	515.1	545.2	565.0	581.8	618.2
Warehouse clubs and supercenters............	45291	139.6	368.0	447.1	470.2	486.7	501.3	527.1
Miscellaneous store retailers [3]...................	453	106.7	104.2	118.5	123.2	128.5	130.6	126.7
Office supplies, stationery, and gift stores........	4532	41.7	34.3	32.0	30.1	30.3	28.9	23.9
Office supplies and stationery stores............	45321	22.7	18.8	14.5	12.3	11.4	10.7	10.3
Gift, novelty, and souvenir stores.................	45322	18.9	15.5	17.5	17.8	19.0	18.2	13.6
Used merchandise stores........................	4533	9.8	11.8	16.2	16.7	17.0	18.0	16.4
Nonstore retailers [3].............................	454	180.5	341.0	498.3	608.2	675.8	750.6	978.3
Electronic shopping and mail-order houses......	4541	113.8	263.5	419.0	524.6	583.8	657.1	888.5
Direct selling establishments.......................	4543	58.1	71.0	72.2	75.6	83.6	84.5	82.8
Fuel dealers....................................	45431	26.7	35.5	32.9	31.4	36.6	35.0	29.2

X Not applicable. [1] North American Industry Classification System, 2012; see text, Section 15. [2] GAFO (General Merchandise, Apparel, Furniture, and Office Supplies) represents stores classified in the following NAICS codes: 442, 443, 448, 451, 452, and 4532. [3] Includes other kinds of businesses, not shown separately.

Source: U.S. Census Bureau, "Annual Retail Trade Survey (ARTS) Tables," <www.census.gov/programs-surveys/arts/data/tables.html>, accessed March 2022.

Table 1080. Retail Trade Corporations—Sales, Net Profit, and Profit Per Dollar of Sales: 2020 and 2021

[3,351.3 represents $3,351,300,000,000. Represents 2017 North American Industry Classification System (NAICS) groups 44 and 45. Profit rates are averages of quarterly figures at annual rates. Covers corporations with assets of $50,000,000 or more]

Item	Unit	Total retail trade		Food and beverage stores (NAICS 445)		Clothing & general merchandise stores (NAICS 448, 452)		All other retail stores	
		2020	2021	2020	2021	2020	2021	2020	2021
Sales....................................	Bil. dol.	3,351.3	3,799.9	540.4	545.2	1,042.6	1,176.1	1,768.2	2,078.6
Net profit:									
Before income taxes.................	Bil. dol.	158.9	265.7	18.4	20.4	28.1	72.6	112.4	172.7
After income taxes...................	Bil. dol.	130.2	224.8	14.6	16.7	20.8	58.4	94.8	149.7
Profits per dollar of sales:									
Before income taxes.................	Cents	4.7	7.0	3.4	3.7	2.7	6.2	6.4	8.3
After income taxes...................	Cents	3.9	5.9	2.7	3.1	2.0	5.0	5.4	7.2
Stockholders' equity...................	Bil. dol.	2,602.9	3,075.0	307.5	322.9	690.5	746.0	1,604.9	2,006.1

Source: U.S. Census Bureau, Quarterly Financial Report (QFR) Manufacturing, Mining, Trade, and Selected Service Industries, "Time Series/Trend Charts," <www.census.gov/econ/qfr/>, accessed May 2022.

Table 1081. Retail Trade—Estimated Per Capita Sales by Selected Kind of Business: 2000 to 2020

[Estimates are shown in dollars and are based on data from the Annual Retail Trade Survey and the Census Bureau's Population Estimates Program. Based on estimated resident population estimates as of July 1. Data have been adjusted using final results of the 2017 Economic Census. For additional information, see source and Appendix III]

Kind of business	NAICS code [1]	2000	2010	2015	2017	2018	2019	2020
Retail, total.............................	**44–45**	**10,573**	**12,343**	**14,735**	**15,503**	**16,080**	**16,454**	**16,906**
Total excluding motor vehicle and parts dealers.......	*44–45, ex 441*	7,751	9,941	11,295	11,856	12,393	12,684	13,239
Motor vehicle and parts dealers..........................	441	2,822	2,402	3,441	3,647	3,687	3,770	3,667
Furniture and home furnishings stores.....................	442	323	275	336	355	364	367	343
Electronics and appliance stores..........................	443	320	322	312	284	288	277	231
Building material and garden equipment and supplies dealers.................................	444	812	842	1,010	1,075	1,125	1,137	1,281
Food and beverage stores..............................	445	1,576	1,877	2,143	2,242	2,294	2,360	2,580
Health and personal care stores.........................	446	550	842	960	996	1,034	1,048	1,066
Gasoline stations..	447	885	1,449	1,420	1,465	1,600	1,564	1,299
Clothing and clothing accessories stores..................	448	594	690	802	804	818	821	611
Sporting goods, hobby, musical instrument, and book stores..................................	451	240	253	266	258	245	243	256
General merchandise stores..............................	452	1,433	1,952	2,120	2,128	2,163	2,182	2,217
Miscellaneous store retailers............................	453	378	337	370	379	393	398	384
Nonstore retailers.......................................	454	640	1,102	1,554	1,871	2,068	2,286	2,969

[1] North American Industry Classification System, 2012; see text, Section 15.

Source: U.S. Census Bureau, "Annual Retail Trade Survey (ARTS) Tables," <www.census.gov/programs-surveys/arts/data/tables.html>, accessed March 2022.

Table 1082. Retail Trade—Merchandise Inventories and Inventory/Sales Ratios by Kind of Business: 2018 to 2021

[Inventories in billions of dollars (652.7 represents $652,700,000,000). As of Dec. 31. Estimates exclude food services. Includes warehouses. Adjusted for seasonal variations. Sales data also adjusted for holiday and trading-day differences. Based on data from the Monthly Retail Trade Survey, Annual Retail Trade Survey, and administrative records; see Appendix III]

Kind of business	2012 NAICS code [1]	Inventories				Inventory/sales ratio			
		2018	2019	2020	2021	2018	2019	2020	2021
Retail inventories, total [2]............................	**44–45**	**652.7**	**653.7**	**622.2**	**649.2**	**1.49**	**1.42**	**1.27**	**1.17**
Total excluding motor vehicle and parts dealers...	44–45, ex 441	417.5	422.9	428.8	487.2	1.25	1.19	1.13	1.12
Motor vehicle and parts dealers..........................	441	235.2	230.8	193.4	162.0	2.31	2.22	1.74	1.34
Furniture, home furnishings, electronics, and appliance stores......................................	442, 443	27.9	26.9	23.4	28.7	1.59	1.53	1.38	1.55
Building material and garden equipment and supplies dealers.................................	444	55.7	57.8	62.9	74.2	1.79	1.82	1.72	1.80
Food and beverage stores..............................	445	50.5	51.7	53.3	55.3	0.80	0.79	0.76	0.73
Clothing and clothing accessories stores..............	448	54.6	53.3	45.1	48.4	2.46	2.29	2.26	1.93
General merchandise stores..............................	452	82.3	80.2	80.4	92.4	1.38	1.32	1.33	1.37
Department stores.....................................	4521	24.4	21.8	18.3	21.5	2.12	1.99	2.06	2.10

[1] North American Industry Classification System, 2012; see text, Section 15. [2] Includes other kind of businesses, not shown separately.

Source: U.S. Census Bureau, Monthly Retail Trade Report, "Retail Inventories and Inventories/Sales Ratios," <www.census.gov/retail/index.html>, accessed May 2022.

Table 1083. Retail Trade Sales—Total and E-Commerce by Kind of Business: 2020

[5,570,393 represents $5,570,393,000,000. Covers retailers with and without payroll. Based on the Annual Retail Trade Survey; see Appendix III]

Kind of business	NAICS code [1]	Value of sales (mil. dol.)		E-commerce as percent of total sales	Percent distribution of E-commerce sales
		Total	E-commerce		
Retail trade, total............................	**44-45**	**5,570,393**	**815,447**	**14.6**	**100.0**
Motor vehicle and parts dealers.........................	441	1,208,304	(D)	(D)	(D)
Furniture and home furnishings stores....................	442	113,023	3,572	3.2	0.4
Electronics and appliance stores........................	443	75,978	2,320	3.1	0.3
Building material and garden equipment and supplies stores.......	444	422,211	2,180	0.5	0.3
Food and beverage stores..............................	445	850,215	23,286	2.7	2.9
Health and personal care stores........................	446	351,257	(D)	(D)	(D)
Gasoline stations......................................	447	428,076	(S)	(S)	(S)
Clothing and clothing accessories stores................	448	201,422	16,044	8.0	2.0
Sporting goods, hobby, book, and music stores..........	451	84,363	5,421	6.4	0.7
General merchandise stores............................	452	730,570	(D)	(D)	(D)
Miscellaneous store retailers...........................	453	126,668	6,263	4.9	0.8
Nonstore retailers.....................................	454	978,306	705,657	72.1	86.5
Electronic shopping and mail-order houses..............	4541	888,502	703,017	79.1	86.2

S Data do not meet publication standards because of high sampling variability or poor response quality. D Withheld to avoid disclosing individual company data. [1] North American Industry Classification System, 2012; see text, Section 15.

Source: U.S. Census Bureau, "Annual Retail Trade Survey (ARTS) Tables," <www.census.gov/programs-surveys/arts/data/tables.html>, accessed March 2022.

Table 1084. Electronic Shopping and Mail-Order Houses—Total and E-Commerce Sales by Merchandise Line: 2019 and 2020

[657,089 represents $657,089,000,000. Represents 2012 North American Industry Classification System code 4541, which comprises establishments primarily engaged in retailing all types of merchandise using nonstore means, including catalogs, toll-free telephone numbers, and electronic media, such as interactive television or computer. Covers businesses with and without paid employees. Based on the Annual Retail Trade Survey; see Appendix III]

Merchandise lines	2019			2020		
	Value of sales (million dollars)		E-commerce as percent of total sales	Value of sales (million dollars)		E-commerce as percent of total sales
	Total	E-commerce		Total	E-commerce	
Total............................	**657,089**	**489,094**	**74.4**	**888,502**	**703,017**	**79.1**
Books (includes audio books and e-books)........	16,749	14,696	87.7	20,681	18,586	89.9
Clothing and clothing accessories (includes footwear).......................	90,204	82,162	91.1	114,384	105,459	92.2
Computer software (including video game)........	14,218	12,856	90.4	20,396	18,900	92.7
Drugs, health aids, beauty aids.....................	164,206	51,709	31.5	198,569	75,463	38.0
Electronics and appliances.........................	56,647	51,285	90.5	(S)	(S)	(S)
Food, beer, and wine..............................	18,980	16,973	89.4	28,626	26,309	91.9
Furniture and home furnishings.....................	73,758	68,345	92.7	115,717	109,888	95.0
Jewelry...	9,146	7,555	82.6	11,491	10,425	90.7
Audio and video recordings [1].....................	11,981	11,041	92.2	16,375	15,292	93.4
Office equipment and supplies......................	(S)	(S)	(S)	11,045	9,442	85.5
Sporting goods....................................	22,213	19,970	89.9	35,153	32,306	91.9
Toys, hobby goods, and games...................	17,777	16,209	91.2	25,119	23,413	93.2
Other merchandise [2].............................	82,926	67,243	81.1	124,977	106,769	85.4
Nonmerchandise receipts [3]......................	34,294	30,446	88.8	46,867	42,408	90.5

S Figure does not meet publication standards. [1] Includes purchased downloads. [2] Includes other merchandise such as collectibles, souvenirs, auto parts and accessories, hardware, and lawn and garden equipment and supplies. [3] Includes auction commissions, shipping and handling, customer training, customer support, and advertising.

Source: U.S. Census Bureau, "Annual Retail Trade Survey (ARTS) Tables," <www.census.gov/programs-surveys/arts/data/tables.html>, accessed March 2022.

Table 1085. Franchised New Car Dealerships—Summary: 2000 to 2021

[In units as indicated (8.8 represents 8,800,000)]

Item	Unit	2000	2005	2010	2015	2016	2017	2018	2019	2020	2021
Dealerships [1]......................	Number	20,490	19,898	16,181	16,545	16,708	16,802	16,753	16,682	16,623	16,676
Sales............................	Bil. dol.	(NA)	(NA)	(NA)	938	996	1,003	1,026	1,027	980	1,184
New light duty vehicle sales.......	Millions	(NA)	16.9	11.6	17.4	17.5	17.1	17.2	17.1	14.5	14.9
New cars sold................	Millions	8.8	7.7	5.6	7.5	6.9	6.1	5.3	4.8	3.4	3.3
New light trucks sold.............	Millions	(NA)	9.3	5.9	9.9	10.6	11.1	11.9	12.3	11.1	11.6
Average retail new vehicle selling price................	Dollars	(NA)	(NA)	30,079	33,456	34,449	34,670	35,608	36,824	38,961	42,379
Used vehicles sold................	Millions	20.5	19.7	15.3	14.1	14.2	14.4	14.4	14.9	13.7	14.7
Employment.......................	1,000	1,114	1,138	892	1,085	1,118	1,130	1,132	1,134	1,078	1,055
Annual payroll.....................	Bil. dol.	46.1	51.5	42.4	61.8	64.9	65.3	66.5	68.8	68.1	83.2
Average dealer pretax profits as percent of sales.................	Percent	(NA)	(NA)	(NA)	2.7	2.5	2.3	2.2	2.3	(NA)	(NA)
Inventory: [2] Domestic: [3]											
Total........................	Millions	3.2	3.0	1.7	1.9	2.1	1.9	2.1	1.9	2.1	0.9
Days' supply....................	Days	68	70	60	72	74	70	76	67	47	26
Imported: [3]											
Total........................	Millions	0.5	0.6	0.5	1.7	1.9	1.9	1.8	1.7	0.7	0.2
Days' supply....................	Days	50	52	55	53	54	56	54	50	52	22

NA Not available. [1] Light-duty new vehicle dealerships, as of December 31. [2] Annual average. [3] Classification based on location of automobile production (i.e., automobiles manufactured by foreign companies but produced in the U.S., Canada, and Mexico are classified as domestic).

Source: National Automobile Dealers Association, <www.nada.org>. *NADA Data 2021: Annual Financial Profile of America's Franchised New-Car Dealerships*, annual ©.

Table 1086. New Motor Vehicle Sales and Car Production: 1990 to 2021

[In thousands (14,137 represents 14,137,000). Data are primarily from "Ward's Automotive Reports" published by Ward's Communications, Southfield, MI]

Type of vehicle	1990	2000	2010	2015	2016	2017	2018	2019	2020	2021
New motor vehicle sales..	**14,137**	**17,812**	**11,773**	**17,857**	**17,878**	**17,565**	**17,713**	**17,488**	**14,881**	**15,409**
New car sales...................	9,300	8,778	5,636	7,529	6,883	6,089	5,310	4,720	3,402	3,350
Domestic.......................	6,897	6,762	3,791	5,595	5,146	4,593	4,087	3,544	2,560	2,376
Import..........................	2,403	2,016	1,844	1,933	1,738	1,496	1,223	1,176	842	974
New truck sales.................	4,837	9,034	6,137	10,329	10,995	11,476	12,403	12,768	11,480	12,059
Light..........................	4,560	8,572	5,919	9,879	10,594	11,061	11,915	12,241	11,070	11,597
Domestic....................	3,957	7,720	5,020	8,097	8,436	8,652	9,153	9,622	8,615	9,006
Import......................	603	852	899	1,782	2,158	2,409	2,761	2,620	2,455	2,590
Heavy.........................	278	462	218	449	401	415	488	527	410	462
Domestic car production....	**6,231**	**5,471**	**2,731**	**4,163**	**3,917**	**3,033**	**2,785**	**2,512**	**1,924**	**1,563**

Source: U.S. Bureau of Economic Analysis, National Economic Accounts, "Supplemental Information & Additional Data: Motor Vehicles," <www.bea.gov/data/gdp/gross-domestic-product#supp>, accessed April 2022.

Table 1087. Retail Sales and Leases of New and Used Vehicles: 2010 to 2021

[In thousands, except as noted (48,500 represents 48,500,000). Data are primarily from Edmunds, except as noted]

Item	2010	2013	2014	2015	2016	2017	2018	2019	2020	2021
Vehicle sales and leases, total.........	**48,500**	**51,368**	**52,758**	**54,727**	**56,162**	**56,435**	**57,545**	**57,865**	**(NA)**	**(NA)**
New vehicle sales and leases..............	11,589	15,592	16,516	17,472	17,559	17,231	17,312	17,059	14,555	15,016
Passenger cars............................	5,724	7,583	7,695	7,532	6,882	6,104	5,326	4,733	3,426	3,326
Light trucks..............................	5,865	8,010	8,821	9,940	10,677	11,127	11,986	12,326	11,129	11,690
New vehicle sales......................	9,610	12,364	12,944	13,473	13,251	13,048	13,077	12,817	11,014	11,741
Passenger cars.......................	4,515	5,712	5,751	5,559	4,981	4,479	4,005	3,506	2,511	2,533
Light trucks..........................	5,095	6,653	7,193	7,914	8,270	8,568	9,072	9,311	8,502	9,208
New vehicle leases......................	1,979	3,228	3,572	3,999	4,308	4,183	4,234	4,242	3,541	3,275
Passenger cars.......................	1,209	1,871	1,944	1,973	1,901	1,624	1,320	1,227	915	793
Light trucks..........................	770	1,357	1,628	2,026	2,407	2,559	2,914	3,015	2,626	2,482
Used vehicle sales [1].................	36,911	35,776	36,242	37,255	38,602	39,204	40,233	40,807	(NA)	(NA)
Electric vehicle sales: [2]										
Hybrid electric.........................	275	496	452	384	347	363	338	381	455	(NA)
Plug-in hybrid electric.................	(Z)	49	55	43	73	91	124	86	66	(NA)
Electric................................	–	48	64	71	87	104	207	234	240	(NA)
New and used vehicle sales, total value [3] (billion dollars).............	**945**	**1,103**	**1,176**	**1,273**	**1,340**	**1,371**	**1,435**	**1,477**	**(NA)**	**(NA)**
New vehicle sales.........................	347	495	535	580	599	606	626	636	571	683
Used vehicle sales........................	598	608	641	693	741	764	809	841	(NA)	(NA)
Average price [3] (current dollars):										
New and used vehicle sales.................	25,809	26,184	26,600	27,506	28,044	28,329	28,757	29,302	(NA)	(NA)
New vehicle sales.........................	35,417	35,368	35,500	36,412	36,888	37,158	37,414	38,003	39,251	45,458
Used vehicle sales........................	16,200	17,000	17,700	18,600	19,200	19,500	20,100	20,600	(NA)	(NA)

– Represents zero or value too small to report. Z Less than 500. NA Not available. [1] Used car sales include sales from franchised dealers, independent dealers, and casual sales. [2] Data from U.S. Department of Energy, Energy Vehicle Technologies Office. Includes new sales of light duty vehicles certified for highway use. [3] Includes leased vehicles.

Source: U.S. Bureau of Transportation Statistics, "National Transportation Statistics," <www.bts.gov/topics/national-transportation-statistics>, accessed May 2022.

Table 1088. Food and Alcoholic Beverage Expenditures by Sales Outlet: 2000 to 2021

[In millions of dollars (294,292 represents $294,292,000,000). In constant dollars (1988=100). Includes taxes and tips. Data are shown for final purchasers, including individuals and households, government (food assistance programs, Medicare/Medicaid inpatient meals, expensed meals), and businesses (expensed meals) for final use by individuals and households (including food assistance programs)]

Sales outlet	2000	2005	2010	2015	2018	2019	2020	2021
Food at home................................	294,292	323,175	329,764	352,897	389,147	398,220	413,856	430,363
Grocery stores..........................	199,081	198,339	195,127	198,580	214,339	219,717	233,861	232,139
Convenience stores......................	7,167	5,625	5,588	5,498	6,273	6,492	5,972	6,608
Other food stores.......................	7,825	8,448	8,016	8,328	8,644	8,648	8,534	9,205
Warehouse clubs and supercenters........	35,858	62,999	74,881	87,542	91,833	93,099	93,487	99,015
Other stores and foodservice.............	30,758	34,029	33,873	33,424	38,229	37,923	34,358	40,580
Mail order and home delivery.............	10,648	10,891	9,355	15,254	25,256	27,674	33,017	37,688
Direct selling by farmers, manufacturers, and wholesalers......................	2,187	1,800	1,905	3,229	3,614	3,637	3,556	3,859
Home production and donations...........	767	1,044	1,019	1,042	958	1,029	1,071	1,270
Food away from home (FAFH)..............	287,324	325,941	331,167	404,170	446,021	453,765	382,108	462,676
Full-service restaurants.................	100,586	115,925	114,118	140,215	150,771	153,561	112,215	162,201
Limited-service restaurants..................	93,964	110,908	114,508	134,667	149,529	153,970	143,988	164,136
Drinking places.........................	1,461	1,828	1,999	2,098	2,631	2,697	1,569	2,241
Hotels and motels.......................	15,568	13,383	12,172	15,648	16,411	16,546	9,457	14,534
Retail stores and vending...............	13,396	15,324	16,151	37,714	52,572	52,281	52,475	54,895
Recreational places.....................	12,245	12,412	11,224	13,057	13,876	14,051	8,031	10,881
Schools and colleges....................	23,019	27,457	32,221	30,976	29,488	29,779	27,560	17,888
Other FAFH sales, not elsewhere classified.............................	9,117	10,169	9,670	9,962	10,280	10,561	7,803	10,976
Food furnished and donated...............	17,968	18,536	19,104	19,833	20,464	20,320	19,011	24,925
Alcohol at home.............................	41,684	44,949	49,608	62,628	72,911	74,376	80,536	87,479
Liquor stores...........................	18,093	20,008	22,743	26,047	28,358	28,916	33,096	34,451
Food stores.............................	11,546	12,187	13,396	17,069	18,945	19,331	20,560	21,031
All other...............................	12,044	12,754	13,469	19,512	25,607	26,128	26,880	31,997
Alcohol away from home.....................	32,755	34,070	32,889	38,902	42,860	44,488	30,952	44,840
Eating and drinking places..................	26,059	27,689	26,834	31,760	35,278	36,666	25,939	37,651
Hotels and motels.......................	3,500	3,066	2,917	3,731	3,934	4,040	2,332	3,639
All other...............................	3,195	3,316	3,138	3,412	3,648	3,782	2,681	3,551

Source: U.S. Department of Agriculture, Economic Research Service, "Food Expenditure Series," <www.ers.usda.gov/data-products/food-expenditure-series/>, accessed June 2022.

Section 23
Transportation

This section presents data on civil air transportation, both passenger and cargo, and on water transportation, including inland waterways, oceanborne commerce, the merchant marine, cargo, and vessel tonnages.

This section also presents statistics on revenues, passenger and freight traffic volume, and employment in various revenue-producing modes of the transportation industry, including motor vehicles, trains, and pipelines. Data are also presented on highway mileage and finances, motor vehicle travel, accidents, and registrations; and characteristics of public transit, railroads, and pipelines.

The principal source of transportation data is the annual *National Transportation Statistics* publication of the U.S. Bureau of Transportation Statistics. Principal sources of water transportation data is provided by the Corps of Engineers of the Department of Army. In addition, the U.S. Census Bureau in its Commodity Flow Survey (part of the Economic Census, taken every 5 years, for years ending in "2" and "7") provides data on the type, weight, and value of commodities shipped by manufacturing establishments in the United States, by means of transportation, origin, and destination. This census is conducted in accordance with the North American Industry Classification System (NAICS). See text, Section 15, Business Enterprise, for a discussion of the Economic Census and NAICS.

The Bureau of Transportation Statistics (BTS) was established within the U.S. Department of Transportation (DOT) in 1992 to collect, report, and analyze transportation data. BTS products include reports to Congress, the Secretary of Transportation, and stakeholders in the nation's transportation community. These stakeholders include: federal agencies, state and local governments, metropolitan planning organizations, universities, the private sector, and the general public. Congress requires, by congressional mandate laid out in 49 U.S.C. 111 (1), the BTS to report on transportation statistics to the President and Congress. *The Transportation Statistics Annual Report* (TSAR) provides a data overview of U.S. transportation issues; it can be found online at <www.bts.gov/tsar>. The BTS publication *National Transportation Statistics* (NTS), a companion report to the TSAR, has more comprehensive and longer time-series data. NTS presents information on the U.S. transportation system, including its physical components, safety record, economic performance, energy use, and environmental impacts. The BTS publication *State Transportation Statistics* presents a statistical profile of transportation in the 50 states and the District of Columbia. This profile includes infrastructure, freight movement and passenger travel, system safety, vehicles, transportation-related economy and finance, energy usage, and the environment.

The principal compiler of data on public roads and on operation of motor vehicles is the U.S. Department of Transportation's (DOT) Federal Highway Administration (FHWA). These data appear in FHWA's annual *Highway Statistics* and other publications.

The U.S. National Highway Traffic Safety Administration (NHTSA), through its *Traffic Safety Facts Annual Report Tables*, <cdan.nhtsa.gov/tsftables /tsfar.htm#>, and Fatality and Injury Reporting System Tool (FIRST), <cdan.dot.gov/query>, presents descriptive statistics about traffic crashes of all severities, from those that result in property damage to those that result in the loss of life. The tool compiles motor vehicle crash data from the Fatality Analysis Reporting System (FARS), the General Estimates System (GES), and Crash Report Sampling System (CRSS). Other publications and reports can be found at the National Center for Statistics and Analysis (NCSA), NCSA Tools, Publications, and Data, located on the internet at <cdan.nhtsa.gov>. DOT's Federal Railroad Administration (FRA), Office of Safety Analysis presents railroad safety information, including accidents and incidents, inspections, and highway-rail crossing data at its "Safety Data," located at <safetydata.fra.dot.gov/officeofsafety>.

Civil aviation—Federal promotion and regulation of civil aviation have been carried out by the Federal Aviation Administration (FAA) and the Civil Aeronautics Board (CAB). The CAB promoted and regulated the civil air transportation industry within the United States and between the United States and foreign countries. The Board granted licenses to provide air transportation service, approved or disapproved proposed rates and fares, and approved or disapproved proposed agreements and corporate relationships involving air carriers. In December 1984, the CAB ceased to exist as an agency. Some of its functions were transferred to the DOT, as outlined below. The responsibility for investigation of aviation accidents resides with the National Transportation Safety Board.

The Office of the Secretary, DOT aviation activities include: negotiation of international air transportation rights, selection of U.S. air carriers to serve capacity controlled international markets, oversight of international rates and fares, maintenance of essential air service to small communities, and consumer affairs. DOT's Bureau of Transportation Statistics (BTS) handles aviation information functions formerly assigned to CAB. Prior to BTS, the Research and Special Programs Administration handled these functions.

The principal activities of the FAA include: the promotion of air safety; controlling the use of navigable airspace; prescribing regulations dealing with the competency of airmen, airworthiness of aircraft, and air traffic control; operation of air route traffic control centers, airport traffic control towers, and flight service stations; the design, construction, maintenance, and inspection of navigation, traffic control, and communications equipment; and the development of general aviation.

The CAB published monthly and quarterly financial and traffic statistical data for the certificated route air carriers. BTS continues these publications, including both certificated and noncertificated (commuter) air carriers. The FAA annually publishes data on the use of airway facilities; data related to the location of airmen, aircraft, and airports; the volume of activity in the field of nonair carrier (general aviation) flying; and aircraft production and registration.

General aviation comprises all civil flying (including such commercial operations as small demand air taxis, agriculture application, powerline patrol, etc.) but excludes certificated route air carriers, supplemental operators, large-aircraft commercial operators, and commuter airlines.

Air carriers and service—The CAB previously issued "certificates of public convenience and necessity" under Section 401 of the Federal Aviation Act of 1958 for scheduled and nonscheduled (charter) passenger services and cargo services. It also issued certificates under Section 418 of the Act to cargo air carriers for domestic all-cargo service only. The DOT Office of the Secretary now issues the certificates under a "fit, willing, and able" test of air carrier operations. Carriers operating only a 60-seat-or-less aircraft are given exemption authority to carry passengers, cargo, and mail in scheduled and nonscheduled service under Part 298 of the DOT (formerly CAB) regulations. Exemption authority carriers who offer scheduled passenger service to an essential air service point must meet the "fit, willing, and able" test.

Vessel shipments, entrances, and clearances—Shipments by dry cargo vessels comprise shipments on all types of watercraft, except tanker vessels; shipments by tanker vessels comprise all types of cargo, liquid and dry, carried by tanker vessels. A vessel is reported as entered only at the first port which it enters in the United States, whether or not cargo is unloaded at that port.

A vessel is reported as cleared only at the last port at which clearance is made to a foreign port, whether or not it takes on cargo. Army and Navy vessels entering or clearing without commercial cargo are not included in the figures.

Units of measurement—Cargo (or freight) tonnage and shipping weight both represent the gross weight of the cargo including the weight of containers, wrappings, crates, etc.; however, shipping weight excludes lift and cargo vans and similar substantial outer containers. Other tonnage figures generally refer to stowing capacity of vessels, 100 cubic feet being called 1 ton. *Gross tonnage* comprises the space within the frames and the ceiling of the hull, together with those closed-in spaces above deck available for cargo, stores, passengers, or crew, with certain minor exceptions. Net or registered tonnage is the gross tonnage less the spaces occupied by the propelling machinery, fuel, crew quarters, master's cabin, and navigation spaces. Net tonnage represents space available for cargo and passengers. The net tonnage capacity of a ship may bear little relation to weight of cargo. Deadweight tonnage is the weight in long tons required to depress a vessel from light water line (that is, with only the machinery and equipment on board) to load line. It is, therefore, the weight of the cargo, fuel, etc., which a vessel is designed to carry with safety.

Federal-aid highway systems—The Intermodal Surface Transportation Efficiency Act (ISTEA) of 1991 eliminated the historical Federal-Aid Highway Systems and created the National Highway System (NHS) and other federal-aid highway categories. The final NHS was approved by Congress in December of 1995 under the National Highway System Designation Act.

Functional systems—Roads and streets are assigned to groups according to the character of service intended. The functional systems are (1) arterial highways that generally handle the long trips, (2) collector facilities that collect and disperse traffic between the arterials and the lower systems, and (3) local roads and streets that primarily serve direct access to residential areas, farms, and other local areas.

Regulatory bodies—The Federal Energy Regulatory Commission (FERC) is an independent agency that regulates the interstate transmission of electricity, natural gas, and oil. FERC also reviews proposals to build liquefied natural gas (LNG) terminals and interstate natural gas pipelines, and licenses hydropower projects. The Energy Policy Act of 2005 gave FERC additional responsibilities such as regulating the transmission and wholesale sales of electricity in interstate commerce.

The Surface Transportation Board (STB) was created in the Interstate Commerce Commission Termination Act of 1995, Pub. L. No.104-88, 109 Stat. 803 (1995) (ICCTA), and is the successor agency to the Interstate Commerce Commission. The STB is an economic regulatory agency that Congress charged with the fundamental missions of resolving railroad rate and service disputes and reviewing proposed railroad mergers. The STB makes decisions independently, although it is administratively affiliated with the Department of Transportation.

The STB serves as both an adjudicatory and a regulatory body. The agency has jurisdiction over railroad rate and service issues and rail restructuring transactions (mergers, line sales, line construction, and line abandonment); certain trucking company, moving van, and noncontiguous ocean shipping company rate matters; certain intercity passenger bus company structure, financial, and operational matters; and rates and services of certain pipelines not regulated by the Federal Energy Regulatory Commission. Other ICC regulatory functions were either eliminated or transferred to the Federal Highway Administration or the Bureau of Transportation Statistics within DOT.

Rail carriers are regulated by the STB and subject to the Uniform System of Accounts and required to file annual and periodic reports. Railroads are classified based on their annual operating revenues. The class to which a carrier belongs is determined by comparing its adjusted operating revenues for 3 consecutive years to the following scale: Class I, $943 million or more; Class II, $42.4 million to $943 million; and Class III, $0 to $42.4 million. Operating revenue dollar ranges are indexed for inflation.

Postal Service—The U.S. Postal Service provides mail processing and delivery services within the United States. The Postal Accountability and Enhancement Act of 2006 was the first major legislative change to the Postal Service since 1971 when the Postal Reorganization Act of 1970 created the Postal Service as an independent establishment of the Federal Executive Branch. The Act of 2006 changed the way the U.S. Postal Service operates and conducts business. Now annual rate increases for market dominant products are linked to the Consumer Price Index and the Postal Service has more flexibility for pricing competitive products, enabling it to respond to dynamic market conditions and changing customer needs.

Revenue and cost analysis describes the Postal Service's system of attributing revenues and costs to classes of mail and service. This system draws primarily upon probability sampling techniques to develop estimates of revenues, volumes, and weights, as well as costs by class of mail and special service. The costs attributed to classes of mail and special services are primarily incremental costs that vary in response to changes in volume; they account for roughly 60 percent of the total costs of the Postal Service. The balance represents "institutional costs." Statistics on revenues, volume of mail, and distribution of expenditures are presented in the Postal Service's annual reports *Public Cost and Revenue Analysis* and *Annual Report to Congress*.

Statistical reliability—For a discussion of statistical collection and estimation, sampling procedures, and measures of statistical reliability applicable to Census Bureau data, see Appendix III.

Table 1089. Transportation-Related Components of U.S. Gross Domestic Product: 2010 to 2020

[In billions of dollars (1,335.4 represents $1,335,400,000,000), except percent. For explanation of chained dollars, see text, Section 13]

Item	2010	2015	2017	2018	2019	2020
CURRENT DOLLARS						
Total transportation-related final demand [1]	**1,335.4**	**1,667.1**	**1,751.1**	**1,859.4**	**1,859.9**	**1,525.6**
Total gross domestic product (GDP)	15,049.0	18,206.0	19,479.6	20,527.2	21,372.6	20,893.7
Transportation as a percent of GDP	8.9	9.2	9.0	9.1	8.7	7.3
Personal consumption of transportation	961.8	1,163.7	1,233.2	1,317.3	1,326.5	1,133.4
Motor vehicles and parts	344.5	475.3	501.3	519.5	514.5	541.3
Motor vehicle fuels, lubricants, and fluids	312.1	289.7	291.0	328.4	316.7	228.7
Transportation services	305.2	398.7	440.9	469.4	495.3	363.4
Gross private domestic investment	145.7	319.8	308.8	327.4	337.5	221.9
Transportation structures	9.9	13.6	14.8	17.9	17.2	15.9
Transportation equipment	135.8	306.3	294.0	309.5	320.3	206.0
Net exports of transportation-related goods and service [2]	-85.0	-149.0	-141.8	-155.1	-171.9	-172.2
Exports (+)	260.3	355.8	365.2	382.7	379.7	256.6
Civilian aircraft, engines, and parts	71.9	119.5	121.0	130.8	126.0	71.9
Automotive vehicles, engines, and parts	112.0	151.9	157.9	158.8	162.8	127.9
Transport	76.4	84.4	86.3	93.1	91.0	56.7
Imports (-)	345.3	504.9	507.0	537.8	551.6	428.7
Civilian aircraft, engines, and parts	31.3	55.2	51.4	55.4	62.8	45.0
Automotive vehicles, engines, and parts	225.6	350.0	359.1	372.0	376.0	311.3
Transport	88.4	99.6	96.5	110.4	112.8	72.4
Government transportation-related purchases	301.2	322.7	338.9	350.9	361.3	364.6
Federal purchases [3]	38.5	40.4	42.0	43.7	45.1	45.7
State and local purchases [3]	238.1	268.6	282.4	291.9	300.1	306.3
Defense-related purchases [4]	24.6	13.6	14.5	15.3	16.1	12.6
CHAINED (2012) DOLLARS						
Total transportation-related final demand [1]	**1,486.2**	**1,751.8**	**1,810.5**	**1,854.5**	**1,840.3**	**1,552.0**
Total gross domestic product (GDP)	15,649.0	17,390.3	18,079.1	18,606.8	19,032.7	18,384.7
Transportation as a percent of GDP	9.5	10.1	10.0	10.0	9.7	8.4
Personal consumption of transportation	1,086.9	1,282.6	1,354.3	1,391.5	1,399.7	1,235.4
Motor vehicles and parts	360.0	472.8	510.4	531.2	524.9	542.0
Motor vehicle fuels, lubricants, and fluids	406.0	421.7	422.4	421.0	420.4	356.3
Transportation services	320.8	388.1	421.4	439.2	454.4	337.1
Gross private domestic investment	151.8	305.6	286.8	302.7	309.6	204.4
Transportation structures	10.2	12.8	13.3	15.6	14.6	13.1
Transportation equipment	141.5	292.8	273.5	287.0	295.0	191.3
Net exports of transportation-related goods and service [2]	-91.8	-160.3	-163.5	-176.7	-196.9	-188.6
Exports (+)	277.4	349.2	354.7	366.4	360.4	245.5
Civilian aircraft, engines, and parts	76.6	110.7	106.2	112.1	105.0	59.1
Automotive vehicles, engines, and parts	115.9	150.4	157.1	156.9	160.2	126.2
Transport	84.9	88.2	91.4	97.4	95.2	60.2
Imports (-)	369.2	509.5	518.3	543.0	557.3	434.0
Civilian aircraft, engines, and parts	36.1	52.8	48.2	51.3	56.2	40.2
Automotive vehicles, engines, and parts	237.0	360.7	374.5	387.9	394.8	324.4
Transport	96.1	95.9	95.5	103.8	106.2	69.5
Government transportation-related purchases	327.1	314.0	320.8	317.8	321.5	323.3
Federal purchases [3]	39.9	38.7	38.9	39.2	39.6	39.9
State and local purchases [3]	260.3	261.7	267.2	263.8	266.8	270.9
Defense-related purchases [4]	26.9	13.5	14.7	14.9	15.1	12.5

[1] Sum of total personal consumption of transportation, total gross private domestic investment, net exports of transportation-related goods and services, and total government transportation-related purchases. [2] Exports minus imports. [3] Federal purchases and state and local purchases are the sum of consumption expenditures and gross investment. [4] Defense-related purchases are the sum of transportation of material and travel.

Source: U.S. Bureau of Transportation Statistics, "National Transportation Statistics," <www.bts.gov/product/national-transportation-statistics>, accessed December 2021.

Table 1090. Employment in Transportation and Warehousing: 2000 to 2021

[In thousands (4,401 represents 4,401,000). Annual average of monthly figures. Based on Current Employment Statistics program; see Appendix III]

Industry	NAICS code [1]	2000	2010	2015	2016	2017	2018	2019	2020	2021
Transportation and warehousing	**48–49**	**4,401**	**4,179**	**4,859**	**5,004**	**5,178**	**5,426**	**5,665**	**5,640**	**6,092**
Air transportation	481	614	458	459	478	492	497	505	441	475
Rail transportation	482	206	183	204	184	182	182	174	150	146
Water transportation	483	56	62	66	66	65	65	67	60	56
Truck transportation	484	1,406	1,251	1,453	1,448	1,457	1,496	1,529	1,471	1,514
Transit and ground passenger	485	376	436	485	490	495	495	494	370	375
Pipeline transportation	486	46	42	50	50	49	50	52	51	50
Scenic and sightseeing	487	28	27	33	35	35	35	36	21	23
Support activities	488	546	553	663	678	701	729	754	701	722
Couriers and messengers	492	605	528	613	645	676	740	827	967	1,082
Warehousing and storage	493	518	638	834	932	1,027	1,139	1,229	1,405	1,648

[1] North American Industry Classification System 2017, see text, Sections 12 and 15.

Source: U.S. Bureau of Labor Statistics, Current Employment Statistics, "Employment, Hours, and Earnings—National," <www.bls.gov/ces/data.htm/>, accessed March 2022.

Table 1091. Transportation and Warehousing—Establishments, Employees, and Payroll by Industry: 2019 and 2020

[Employment in thousands (5,408.4 represents 5,408,400); payroll in millions of dollars (283,230.7 represents $283,230,700,000). Covers establishments with payroll. Excludes self-employed individuals, railroad employees, and most government employees. For statement on methodology, see Appendix III. County Business Patterns excludes rail transportation (NAICS 482) and the Postal Service (NAICS 491)]

Industry	NAICS code [1]	Establishments		Paid employees (1,000) [2]		Annual payroll (mil. dol.)	
		2019	2020	2019	2020	2019	2020
Transportation & warehousing.....................	**48–49**	**250,080**	**257,785**	**5,408.4**	**5,711.9**	**283,230.7**	**292,377.4**
Air transportation.............................	481	4,442	4,464	501.3	525.4	43,998.9	42,669.1
Scheduled air transportation.....................	4811	2,224	2,185	457.1	479.2	39,516.2	38,038.0
Scheduled passenger air transportation..............	481111	1,870	1,825	448.9	470.6	38,825.6	37,299.6
Scheduled freight air transportation.............	481112	354	360	8.1	8.6	690.6	738.4
Nonscheduled air transportation......................	4812	2,218	2,279	44.3	46.2	4,482.7	4,631.1
Water transportation............................	483	1,653	1,715	62.2	64.7	5,518.7	5,392.5
Deep sea, coastal, & Great Lakes water transportation............................	4831	1,054	1,084	42.0	44.6	3,917.8	3,803.5
Inland water transportation.......................	4832	599	631	20.2	20.0	1,600.9	1,589.0
Inland water freight transportation..............	483211	318	333	16.9	16.6	1,414.6	1,426.4
Inland water passenger transportation..............	483212	281	298	3.3	3.4	186.3	162.6
Truck transportation.............................	484	138,591	144,774	1,581.9	1,624.2	81,694.5	84,483.9
General freight trucking........................	4841	87,718	94,362	1,078.1	1,121.0	55,403.0	58,575.9
General freight trucking, local................	48411	34,541	36,624	224.2	259.2	10,358.5	11,992.4
General freight trucking, long distance..............	48412	53,177	57,738	853.9	861.8	45,044.5	46,583.5
Specialized freight trucking.....................	4842	50,873	50,412	503.8	503.2	26,291.5	25,908.0
Used household & office goods moving.............	48421	8,375	8,630	97.1	97.5	3,763.8	3,773.6
Specialized freight (except used goods) trucking, local.......	48422	31,127	30,522	228.2	231.5	12,347.1	12,353.2
Specialized freight (except used goods) trucking, long-distance.......	48423	11,371	11,260	178.6	174.1	10,180.6	9,781.2
Transit & ground passenger transportation..............	485	20,397	19,857	511.8	512.2	19,182.7	16,515.5
Urban transit systems...........................	4851	714	674	55.9	53.9	2,898.0	2,623.2
Mixed mode systems.......................	485111	41	38	0.9	[3] 0.9	37.0	[3] 38.3
Commuter rail...........................	485112	19	21	3.8	4.0	349.7	393.4
Bus and other motor vehicle mode systems..........	485113	596	559	49.8	47.6	2,424.2	2,111.5
Other................................	485119	58	56	1.4	1.5	87.1	80.0
Interurban & rural bus transportation....................	4852	611	593	18.5	18.2	661.3	511.8
Taxi & limousine service.........................	4853	7,892	7,537	71.7	68.7	5,613.3	[3] 5,448.0
Taxi service..............................	48531	3,256	3,221	35.3	34.8	4,481.2	[3] 4,835.7
Limousine service..........................	48532	4,636	4,316	36.4	33.8	1,132.1	612.3
School & employee bus transportation................	4854	4,354	4,089	235.4	240.0	5,969.5	4,732.5
Charter bus industry...........................	4855	1,205	1,155	30.9	29.9	1,096.3	630.9
Other transit & ground passenger transportation......	4859	5,621	5,809	99.5	101.5	2,944.2	2,569.0
Special needs transportation......................	485991	3,699	3,891	75.6	78.1	2,226.5	1,972.0
Pipeline transportation............................	486	3,409	3,411	47.2	[3] 45.9	5,847.9	5,812.4
Pipeline transportation of crude oil......................	4861	735	610	11.3	10.1	1,406.2	1,395.8
Pipeline transportation of natural gas...................	4862	1,984	2,080	27.3	[3] 26.5	3,319.3	3,247.4
Other pipeline transportation.......................	4869	690	721	8.6	9.3	1,122.4	1,169.2
Scenic & sightseeing transportation....................	487	2,990	2,965	29.7	28.2	1,270.9	828.9
Scenic & sightseeing transportation, land...............	4871	779	747	11.1	10.6	410.8	220.6
Scenic & sightseeing transportation, water...........	4872	1,936	1,956	15.0	14.2	686.3	489.7
Scenic & sightseeing transportation, other.............	4879	275	262	3.6	3.4	173.8	118.7
Support activities for transportation................	488	46,393	47,511	797.6	808.7	43,329.7	42,518.8
Support activities for air transportation..............	4881	6,237	6,068	224.3	219.9	10,273.1	9,101.6
Airport operations..............................	48811	2,229	2,202	130.1	127.3	4,155.2	3,420.3
Air traffic control.............................	488111	204	210	1.4	[3] 1.8	111.7	115.5
Other support activities for air transportation.........	48819	4,008	3,866	94.2	92.6	6,117.9	5,681.4
Support activities for rail transportation...............	4882	1,526	1,673	42.2	45.4	2,338.0	2,476.9
Support activities for water transportation..............	4883	2,623	2,627	102.5	102.1	7,474.5	7,402.4
Port and harbor operations.........................	48831	350	352	12.5	12.4	810.7	812.9
Marine cargo handling............................	48832	471	467	67.7	67.0	4,946.9	4,834.5
Navigational services to shipping..................	48833	1,026	1,046	14.6	15.0	1,219.0	1,241.6
Other support activities for water transportation.....	48839	776	762	7.6	7.7	497.9	513.5
Support activities for road transportation.............	4884	12,926	13,904	113.9	115.3	4,149.0	4,238.4
Motor vehicle towing............................	48841	9,502	9,609	66.1	65.6	2,656.6	2,620.2
Freight transportation arrangement....................	4885	21,249	21,341	295.7	305.5	18,142.3	18,231.8
Other support activities for transportation.............	4889	1,832	1,898	19.0	20.5	952.8	1,067.6
Couriers & messengers.............................	492	14,860	15,611	855.2	961.4	34,565.2	41,398.8
Couriers.................................	4921	10,245	10,538	779.6	856.8	31,828.2	36,975.1
Local messengers & local delivery....................	4922	4,615	5,073	75.6	104.6	2,737.0	4,423.7
Warehousing & storage.............................	493	17,345	17,477	1,021.4	1,141.4	47,822.2	52,757.6

[1] Data based on 2017 North American Industry Classification System (NAICS). See text, Section 15. [2] Covers full- and part-time employees who are on the payroll in the pay period including March 12. [3] Data is flagged for high noise; the value was changed by 5 percent or more to avoid disclosure of data for individual businesses.

Source: U.S. Census Bureau, County Business Patterns, "All Sectors: County Business Patterns, including ZIP Code Business Patterns, by Legal Form of Organization and Employment Size Class for the U.S., States, and Selected Geographies: 2020," <data.census.gov>, accessed May 2022. See also <www.census.gov/programs-surveys/cbp.html>.

Table 1092. Transportation Sector—Estimated Revenue by Kind of Business: 2010 to 2020

[In millions of dollars (660,440 represents $660,440,000,000). For taxable employer firms. Estimates for 2010 have been adjusted to the results of the 2012 Economic Census. Beginning 2013, estimates have been adjusted to results of the 2017 Economic Census. Based on the Service Annual Survey; see Appendix III]

Kind of business	NAICS code [1]	2010	2015	2018	2019	2020
Transportation and warehousing (excl. 482 and 491)	**4849y**	**660,440**	**891,657**	**1,026,502**	**1,070,520**	**919,668**
Air transportation [2]	481	148,419	199,733	224,690	236,830	110,158
Scheduled passenger air transportation	481111	126,902	174,667	195,170	206,768	81,198
Nonscheduled chartered passenger air transportation	481211	10,499	14,004	15,393	16,569	15,235
Water transportation [2]	483	37,392	44,373	46,042	48,902	29,653
Deep sea freight transportation	483111	9,281	8,656	5,921	6,388	6,316
Deep sea passenger transportation	483112	14,393	18,917	24,746	26,502	9,497
Coastal and great lakes freight transportation	483113	6,254	8,166	7,901	8,102	7,103
Inland water freight transportation	483211	6,879	7,758	6,245	6,588	5,829
Truck transportation	484	197,963	273,250	313,814	320,817	316,982
General freight trucking, local	48411	19,902	29,068	35,865	37,891	38,762
General freight trucking, long-distance, truckload	484121	77,474	104,855	124,361	124,589	126,607
General freight trucking, long-distance, less than truckload	484122	31,698	42,899	49,982	51,897	50,515
Used household and office goods moving	48421	12,361	15,508	16,389	16,492	15,967
Specialized freight (except used goods) trucking, local	48422	28,465	40,538	44,634	46,741	44,026
Specialized freight (except used goods) trucking, long-distance	48423	28,063	40,382	42,583	43,207	41,105
Transit and ground passenger transportation [2]	485	26,900	35,572	50,319	55,964	39,382
Urban transit systems	4851	4,460	5,596	6,340	6,584	6,192
Interurban and rural bus transportation	4852	1,037	1,463	1,718	1,708	992
Taxi service	48531	2,225	4,213	14,030	17,287	10,438
Limousine service	48532	3,554	4,625	4,406	4,543	2,279
School and employee bus transportation	4854	8,628	10,235	11,723	12,641	9,642
Charter bus industry	4855	2,888	3,420	3,843	4,101	1,925
Pipeline transportation [2]	486	33,069	43,891	54,125	59,522	56,319
Pipeline transportation of crude oil	4861	5,004	9,793	13,330	14,882	13,692
Pipeline transportation of natural gas	4862	21,831	25,296	30,774	34,057	32,834
Pipeline transportation of refined petroleum products	48691	5,993	8,439	9,652	10,204	9,451
Scenic and sightseeing transportation [2]	487	2,545	4,064	4,318	4,426	1,934
Scenic and sightseeing transportation, land	4871	903	1,136	1,362	1,415	523
Scenic and sightseeing transportation, water	4872	1,236	2,229	2,294	2,465	1,183
Support activities for transportation [2]	488	125,423	178,269	196,246	201,150	206,055
Airport operations	48811	5,699	8,277	9,126	9,548	9,338
Other support activities for air transportation	48819	15,072	17,334	18,054	19,697	18,850
Support activities for rail transportation	4882	3,945	5,517	6,178	6,481	6,399
Port and harbor operations	48831	1,856	3,013	3,497	3,745	3,923
Marine cargo handling	48832	7,572	10,370	10,655	10,962	10,605
Navigational services to shipping	48833	2,886	3,963	4,427	4,043	3,859
Motor vehicle towing	48841	5,040	6,326	7,607	8,339	8,993
Freight transportation arrangement	4885	77,359	116,044	128,850	129,921	135,177
Couriers and messengers	492	63,855	79,326	97,111	101,664	117,016
Couriers and express delivery services	4921	60,917	75,167	90,784	94,941	108,540
Local messengers and local delivery	4922	2,938	4,159	6,327	6,723	8,476
Warehousing and storage	493	24,874	33,179	39,837	41,245	42,169
General warehousing and storage	49311	15,966	20,717	25,360	26,168	27,369
Refrigerated warehousing and storage	49312	4,083	(S)	6,123	6,523	6,287
Farm product warehousing and storage	49313	698	777	832	876	834
Other warehousing and storage	49319	4,127	6,804	7,522	7,678	7,679

S Estimate does not meet publication standards. [1] 2010 data are based on 2007 North American Industry Classification System (NAICS). Beginning 2013, data are based on 2012 NAICS; see text, this section and Section 15. [2] Includes other kinds of business not shown separately.

Source: U.S. Census Bureau, Service Annual Survey, "Service Annual Survey Latest Data (NAICS-basis): 2020," <www.census.gov/programs-surveys/sas/data.html>, accessed November 2021.

Table 1093. Transportation and Warehousing—Establishments, Revenue, Payroll, and Employees by Industry: 2017

[895,225 represents $895,225,000,000. For establishments with payroll. Based on the 2017 Economic Censuses. Paid employees for pay period including March 12. See Appendix III]

Industry type	NAICS code [1]	Number of establishments	Revenue (mil. dol.)	Annual payroll (mil. dol.)	Paid employees (1,000)
Transportation and warehousing total	**48–49**	**237,095**	**895,225**	**242,145**	**4,954.9**
Air transportation	481	4,450	208,830	39,652	508.3
Water transportation	483	1,643	43,009	5,083	62.7
Truck transportation	484	126,803	290,531	71,121	1,480.1
Transit and ground passenger transportation	485	20,267	44,040	15,320	535.2
Pipeline transportation	486	3,688	47,193	5,980	52.6
Scenic and sightseeing transportation	487	2,865	4,162	1,157	32.0
Support activities for transportation	488	45,956	128,966	35,943	729.5
Couriers and messengers	492	14,467	90,408	28,164	633.1
Warehousing and storage	493	16,956	38,086	39,726	921.3

[1] Data based on the 2017 North American Industry Classification System (NAICS); see text, Section 15.

Source: U.S. Census Bureau, 2017 Economic Census, EC1748BASIC, "Transportation and Warehousing: Summary Statistics for the U.S., States, and Selected Geographies: 2017," <data.census.gov/>, accessed July 2020.

Table 1094. Transportation and Warehousing—Nonemployer Establishments and Receipts by Kind of Business: 2010 to 2019

[1,021.2 represents 1,021,200. Includes only firms subject to federal income tax. Nonemployers are businesses with no paid employees. Data originate chiefly from administrative records of the Internal Revenue Service; see Appendix III]

Kind of business	NAICS code [1]	Establishments (1,000)			Receipts (mil. dol.)		
		2010	2018	2019	2010	2018	2019
Transportation and warehousing............	**48–49**	**1,021.2**	**2,572.4**	**2,856.4**	**60,746**	**117,316**	**124,742**
Air transportation.....................................	481	19.1	24.0	24.2	1,219	1,586	1,602
Water transportation.................................	483	6.6	7.7	7.6	490	620	633
Truck transportation.................................	484	490.3	682.6	721.5	42,485	71,325	72,264
General freight trucking........................	4841	445.1	626.5	661.8	39,277	67,062	67,807
General freight trucking, local.................	48411	168.7	210.7	219.4	12,144	19,578	20,236
General freight trucking, long-distance.........	48412	276.4	415.9	442.4	27,133	47,484	47,571
Specialized freight trucking......................	4842	45.2	56.1	59.7	3,207	4,263	4,457
Transit and ground passenger transportation....	485	218.4	1,327.5	1,446.8	7,463	29,257	34,590
Urban transit system............................	4851	1.1	2.4	2.1	39	77	72
Interurban and rural bus transportation..........	4852	1.5	2.5	2.6	67	86	90
Taxi and limousine service......................	4853	176.4	1,196.3	1,330.3	6,107	25,892	31,178
School and employee bus transportation........	4854	6.9	7.1	7.2	191	219	231
Charter bus industry............................	4855	3.8	4.4	4.2	172	219	230
Other transit and ground passenger transportation.....................................	4859	28.7	114.9	100.4	887	2,763	2,789
Pipeline transportation.............................	486	0.9	1.5	1.5	76	107	98
Scenic and sightseeing transportation...........	487	4.9	6.6	7.0	163	252	275
Support activities for transportation...............	488	105.2	143.6	131.5	4,624	7,378	7,264
Couriers and messengers.........................	492	166.6	361.7	496.8	3,772	6,121	7,282
Warehousing and storage.........................	493	9.2	17.2	19.5	455	671	735

[1] 2010 data based on the 2007 North American Industry Classification System (NAICS); and beginning 2017 data based on 2017 NAICS.

Source: U.S. Census Bureau, Nonemployer Statistics, "All Sectors: Nonemployer Statistics by Legal Form of Organization and Receipts Size Class for the U.S., States, and Selected Geographies: 2019," <data.census.gov>, accessed June 2022.

Table 1095. Transportation System Mileage Within the United States: 1985 to 2020

[3,864 represents 3,864,000. Numbers, except where indicated]

System	Unit	1985	1990	1995	2000	2005	2010	2015	2019	2020
Highway [1]........................	1,000	3,864	3,867	3,912	3,936	3,996	4,067	4,155	4,171	4,173
Class 1 rail [2]....................	Number	145,764	119,758	108,264	99,250	95,830	95,700	93,628	92,282	91,773
Amtrak [2].........................	Number	24,000	24,000	24,000	23,000	22,007	21,178	21,358	21,407	20,787
Transit: [3]										
Commuter rail [4]...............	Number	3,574	4,132	4,160	5,209	7,118	7,630	7,697	7,901	7,930
Heavy rail [5]....................	Number	1,293	1,351	1,458	1,558	1,622	1,617	1,643	1,661	1,663
Light rail [6].....................	Number	384	483	568	834	1,188	1,497	1,893	2,088	2,096
Navigable channels [7]..........	Number	25,000	25,000	25,000	25,000	25,000	25,000	25,000	25,000	25,000
Oil pipeline [8]..................	Number	(NA)	(NA)	(NA)	(NA)	166,760	181,986	208,622	225,015	229,264
Gas pipeline [9].................	1,000	1,641	1,871	2,028	2,115	2,287	2,427	2,509	2,583	2,604

NA Not available. [1] All public road and street mileage in the 50 states and the District of Columbia. Beginning in 1998, approximately 43,000 miles of Bureau of Land Management Roads are excluded. [2] Data represent miles of road owned (aggregate length of road, excluding yard tracks, sidings, and parallel lines). Portions of class I freight railroads, Amtrak, and commuter rail networks share common trackage. Amtrak data represent miles of road operated. [3] Transit system length is measured in directional route-miles; see source. [4] Urban passenger train service for short-distance travel between a central city and adjacent suburb. Does not include rapid rail transit or light rail service. [5] Also known as subway, elevated (railway), or metropolitan railway (metro). [6] A streetcar-type vehicle operated on city streets. Beginning in 2011, "Light rail" includes light rail, street car rail, and hybrid rail. [7] Estimated sums of domestic waterways which include rivers, bays, channels, and the inner route of the Southeast Alaskan Islands, but does not include the Great Lakes or deep ocean traffic. Beginning in 2007, includes waterways connecting the Great Lakes and the St. Lawrence Seaway inside the U.S. [8] Includes trunk and gathering lines for crude-oil pipeline and highly volatile liquid (HVL), carbon dioxide, and other hazardous liquid systems. Oil pipeline data has been discontinued for years prior to 2001. [9] Data includes gathering, transmission, service, and distribution mains.

Source: U.S. Bureau of Transportation Statistics, "National Transportation Statistics," <www.bts.gov/content/system-mileage-within-united-states>, accessed March 2022.

Table 1096. U.S. Aircraft, Vehicles, and Other Conveyances: 2000 to 2020

[Number, or in thousands (225,821 represents 225,821,000), as indicated]

Mode	2000	2010	2014	2015	2016	2017	2018	2019	2020
AIR									
Air carrier [1]	7,826	7,185	6,761	6,876	7,077	7,196	7,475	7,628	5,882
General aviation [2] (active fleet)	217,533	223,370	204,408	210,031	211,794	211,757	211,749	210,981	204,980
HIGHWAY, REGISTERED VEHICLES (1,000s)									
Total registered vehicles	225,821	250,070	260,351	263,610	268,799	272,481	273,602	276,491	275,924
Light duty vehicle, short wheel base [3]	133,621	190,203	187,555	189,618	192,775	193,672	192,856	194,349	193,922
Motorcycle	4,346	8,010	8,418	8,601	8,679	8,715	8,666	8,596	8,317
Light duty vehicle, long wheel base [4]	79,085	40,242	52,600	53,299	54,870	56,881	57,854	59,465	59,199
Trucks [5]	5,926	8,217	8,329	8,456	8,747	9,337	10,328	10,160	10,500
Truck, combination	2,097	2,553	2,577	2,747	2,752	2,892	2,906	2,925	2,979
Bus	746	846	872	889	976	983	992	995	1,006
TRANSIT									
Motor bus	58,578	63,108	62,449	63,573	63,270	63,759	63,284	64,000	63,830
Light rail cars [6]	1,306	2,096	2,444	2,478	2,553	2,557	2,729	2,811	2,799
Heavy rail cars [7]	10,311	11,510	10,551	10,737	10,775	10,705	10,763	11,198	11,064
Trolley bus	652	571	537	611	601	539	571	572	633
Commuter rail cars and locomotives	5,497	6,768	7,177	7,151	7,190	7,129	7,023	7,144	7,524
Demand responsive	22,087	32,696	31,359	32,490	33,225	33,012	33,253	34,613	34,561
Other [8]	7,705	18,066	17,994	18,601	17,042	18,104	17,803	17,491	17,503
RAIL									
Class I, freight cars	560,154	397,730	371,642	330,996	315,227	306,268	293,742	270,378	252,400
Class I, locomotive	20,028	23,893	25,916	26,574	26,716	26,547	26,086	24,597	23,544
Nonclass I freight cars	132,448	101,755	(NA)	(NA)	(NA)	(NA)	(NA)	(NA)	(NA)
Car companies' and shippers' freight cars	688,194	809,544	(NA)	(NA)	(NA)	(NA)	(NA)	(NA)	(NA)
Amtrak, passenger train car	1,894	1,274	1,419	1,428	1,402	1,405	1,403	1,415	1,313
Amtrak, locomotive	378	282	428	423	434	419	431	403	384
WATER									
Non-self-propelled vessels [9]	35,008	31,906	32,275	32,819	33,212	32,808	33,266	33,600	34,168
Self-propelled vessels [10]	10,410	10,775	10,187	10,108	9,462	9,344	9,904	10,152	10,333
Ocean-going self-propelled vessels (1,000 gross tons and over) [11]	282	221	179	170	169	176	182	182	180
Recreational boats (1,000s)	12,782	12,439	11,804	11,867	11,862	11,962	11,853	11,879	11,838

NA Not available. [1] Air carrier aircraft are those carrying passengers or cargo for hire under 14 CFR 121 and 14 CFR 135. Number of aircraft is the monthly average number of aircraft reported in use for the last three months of the year. [2] Includes air taxi aircraft. [3] Data for 2000-06 are for passenger cars. Beginning 2007, data are for Light Duty Vehicles Short Wheel Base—passenger cars, light trucks, vans and sport utility vehicles with a wheelbase of 121 inches or less. [4] Data for 2000-06 are for 2-axle, 4-tire vehicles other than passenger cars, motorcycles, and buses. Beginning 2007, data are for Light Duty Vehicles Long Wheel Base—large passenger cars, vans, pickup trucks, and sport/utility vehicles with wheelbases larger than 121 inches. [5] Includes trucks on a single frame with at least 2 axles and 6 tires. [6] Fixed rail streetcar or trolley, for example. [7] Metro, subway, or rapid transit, for example. [8] Includes Alaska railroad, automated guideway transit, cable car, ferry boat, inclined plane, monorail, and vanpool. [9] Includes dry-cargo barges, tank barges, and railroad-car floats. [10] Includes dry-cargo and/or passenger, offshore supply vessels, railroad-car ferries, tankers, and towboats. [11] 2000-06 data include private and government owned vessels of 1,000 gross tons or more. Beginning 2007, data are reported only for privately owned vessels of 1,000 gross tons or more.

Source: U.S. Bureau of Transportation Statistics, "National Transportation Statistics," <www.bts.gov/topics/national-transportation-statistics>, accessed March 2022.

Table 1097. Transportation Shipments by Mode: 2012 to 2045

[16,952 represents 16,952,000,000. All truck, rail, water, and pipeline movements that involve more than one mode, including exports and imports that change mode at international gateways, are included in multiple modes & mail to avoid double counting. Data do not include imports and exports that pass through the United States from a foreign origin to a foreign destination by any mode]

Mode	2012 Total	2012 Domestic	2012 Exports	2012 Imports	2018 [1] Total	2018 [1] Domestic	2018 [1] Exports	2018 [1] Imports	2045 [2] Total	2045 [2] Domestic	2045 [2] Exports	2045 [2] Imports
WEIGHT (millions of tons)												
Total	**16,952**	**14,895**	**889**	**1,169**	**18,616**	**16,474**	**1,037**	**1,104**	**25,472**	**20,932**	**2,282**	**2,259**
Truck	10,098	9,893	115	90	11,320	11,108	101	111	14,836	14,226	304	306
Rail	1,625	1,481	57	87	1,580	1,404	67	108	1,926	1,588	112	226
Water	959	502	76	380	1,020	542	218	261	1,183	609	201	373
Air, air and truck	11	2	5	4	12	2	5	5	41	4	19	18
Multiple modes and mail [3]	1,317	309	584	425	1,368	328	601	440	2,895	431	1,435	1,028
Pipeline	2,901	2,672	50	179	3,277	3,061	39	177	4,559	4,058	205	296
Other and unknown	42	37	2	3	39	30	7	2	32	16	5	11
VALUE (billions of 2012 dollars)												
Total	**17,729**	**13,965**	**1,545**	**2,219**	**18,907**	**14,838**	**1,658**	**2,412**	**37,064**	**22,469**	**6,511**	**8,084**
Truck	10,929	10,251	366	311	11,520	10,784	361	375	18,682	16,219	1,244	1,219
Rail	582	411	63	109	613	434	64	115	1,080	646	157	278
Water	631	270	73	288	664	300	154	210	1,031	340	281	411
Air, air and truck	1,067	135	461	472	1,184	140	482	562	5,221	324	2,544	2,354
Multiple modes and mail [3]	3,246	1,746	552	947	3,342	1,794	501	1,047	8,981	3,393	2,123	3,465
Pipeline	1,233	1,150	13	70	1,489	1,387	22	80	1,744	1,546	88	110
Other and unknown	40	1	17	22	96	1	74	22	325	–	76	248

– Represents zero. [1] Data are provisional estimates that are based on selected modal and economic trend data. [2] Freight Analysis Framework forecasts. [3] Multiple modes and mail also includes some air movements.

Source: U.S. Department of Transportation, Bureau of Transportation Statistics, *Transportation Statistics Annual Report 2020*, January 2021. See also <www.bts.gov/TSAR>.

Table 1098. Shipment Characteristics by Mode of Transportation: 2012 and 2017

[13,852,143 represents $13,852,143,000,000. For business establishments in mining, manufacturing, wholesale trade, and selected retail and services industries. 2017 industries classified by the 2012 North American Industry Classification System (NAICS). 2012 industries classified by 2007 NAICS. Selected auxiliary establishments are also included. Based on the Commodity Flow Survey, conducted as part of the Economic Census; see Appendix III]

Mode of transportation	Value (mil. dol.)		Tons (1,000)		Ton-miles (mil.)		Average miles per shipment	
	2012	2017	2012	2017	2012	2017	2012	2017
All modes.....................	**13,852,143**	**14,517,812**	**11,299,409**	**12,468,902**	**2,969,506**	**3,116,876**	**630**	**679**
Single modes..................	**11,900,364**	**11,737,969**	**10,905,518**	**11,604,764**	**2,697,418**	**2,479,593**	**262**	**243**
Truck [1]............................	10,132,229	10,398,910	8,060,166	8,843,334	1,247,717	1,327,094	227	206
For-hire truck......................	6,504,636	6,968,184	4,298,693	5,232,034	1,050,942	1,162,179	508	369
Private truck......................	3,627,592	3,430,726	3,761,472	3,611,300	196,775	164,915	58	45
Rail.................................	473,070	254,209	1,628,537	1,251,240	1,211,481	824,763	805	579
Water...............................	301,554	243,855	575,996	804,392	192,866	259,610	908	259
Inland water......................	218,927	117,321	424,542	471,854	118,742	177,494	275	188
Great Lakes.......................	424	614	31,403	41,947	10,959	15,638	347	304
Deep sea...........................	59,878	120,651	72,987	268,634	22,130	50,866	1,157	359
Multiple waterways.............	22,325	5,268	47,064	21,958	41,035	15,612	1,034	525
Air (includes truck and air)......	450,575	496,637	4,845	8,019	5,810	9,822	1,295	1,403
Pipeline [2].........................	542,936	344,357	635,975	697,778	(S)	(S)	(S)	(S)
Multiple modes................	**1,950,753**	**2,777,749**	**357,047**	**770,504**	**271,832**	**637,155**	**922**	**953**
Parcel, U.S. Postal Service or courier.........................	1,688,242	2,117,135	28,490	38,008	22,716	29,838	922	953
Truck and rail......................	224,833	348,047	213,814	471,398	169,524	443,188	988	1,177
Truck and water...................	29,035	251,439	56,720	109,861	48,568	51,853	1,562	784
Rail and water.....................	7,976	43,638	55,570	143,013	29,170	102,715	1,073	1,075
Other multiple modes............	668	17,490	2,452	8,224	1,853	9,562	(S)	1,425
Other and unknown modes..	**1,026**	**2,095**	**36,844**	**93,634**	**256**	**128**	**(S)**	**1**

S Data do not meet publication standards due to high sampling variability or other reasons. [1] Truck as a single mode includes shipments that went by private truck only, for-hire truck only, or a combination of private truck and for-hire truck. [2] Commodity Flow Survey data exclude shipments of crude oil.

Source: U.S. Department of Transportation, Bureau of Transportation Statistics, and U.S. Census Bureau, Commodity Flow Survey, "Geographic Area Series: Shipment Characteristics by Origin Geography by Mode: 2017 and 2012," <data.census.gov>, accessed July 2021. See also <www.census.gov/programs-surveys/cfs.html>.

Table 1099. Hazardous Shipments—Value, Tons, and Ton-Miles: 2012 and 2017

[2,334,425 represents $2,334,425,000,000. For business establishments in mining, manufacturing, wholesale trade, and selected retail industries. Data cover industries classified by the 2012 North American Industry Classification System (NAICS). Also includes auxiliary establishments of multi-establishment companies. Due to definitional and processing changes made each survey year, any data comparisons between one CFS survey and another should be made with caution, see Methodology. Based on the Commodity Flow Survey, conducted as part of the Economic Census; see Appendix III]

Mode of transportation and class of material	Value (mil. dol.)		Tons (1,000)		Ton-miles (mil.)		Average miles per shipment	
	2012	2017	2012	2017	2012	2017	2012	2017
All modes.................................	**2,334,425**	**1,680,231**	**2,580,153**	**2,967,965**	**307,524**	**382,472**	**114**	**189**
Single modes...............................	2,304,743	1,612,129	2,552,868	2,889,521	275,628	307,204	68	72
Truck [1]....................................	1,466,021	1,091,250	1,531,405	1,814,848	96,559	126,800	56	63
For-hire truck.............................	870,893	567,599	882,288	932,658	62,018	92,146	150	153
Private truck, company-owned.............	595,128	523,651	649,117	882,190	34,541	34,655	33	28
Rail..	79,222	39,040	110,988	90,387	84,850	61,669	808	640
Water......................................	217,816	137,109	283,561	304,189	54,902	60,934	212	72
Air (includes truck and air).................	4,380	4,817	261	251	271	201	1,120	1,333
Pipeline [2].................................	537,304	339,912	626,652	679,846	(S)	(S)	(S)	(S)
Multiple modes [3].........................	29,682	68,101	27,285	78,444	31,896	75,268	654	947
Parcel, U.S. Postal Service or courier.......	10,294	13,475	305	345	178	236	650	949
Class of Material.........................	**2,334,425**	**1,680,231**	**2,580,153**	**2,967,965**	**307,524**	**382,472**	**114**	**189**
Class 1, Explosives..........................	18,397	14,936	4,045	3,290	1,012	1,011	840	1,046
Class 2, Gases..............................	125,054	114,845	164,794	227,616	33,157	28,880	57	210
Class 3, Flammable and combustible liquid.......................................	2,016,681	1,373,803	2,203,490	2,466,634	204,573	269,803	93	100
Class 4, Flammable solid; spontaneously combustible material; dangerous when wet material...........................	5,415	5,308	11,321	28,210	5,804	7,614	565	478
Class 5, Oxidizers and organic peroxides...	7,562	9,753	12,025	14,978	5,479	5,827	437	204
Class 6, Toxic materials and infectious substances..................................	15,196	13,298	7,612	6,358	3,607	3,838	513	828
Class 7, Radioactive materials..............	12,288	6,945	(S)	427	39	42	34	63
Class 8, Corrosive materials.................	75,850	79,322	125,287	151,007	37,784	45,704	264	273
Class 9, Miscellaneous hazardous material....................................	57,981	62,020	51,006	69,444	16,068	19,753	530	944

S Data do not meet publication standards. [1] Truck as a single mode includes shipments that went by private truck only, for-hire truck only, or a combination of private truck and for-hire truck. [2] Commodity Flow Survey Data exclude shipments of crude oil. [3] Includes other modes not shown.

Source: U.S. Department of Transportation, Bureau of Transportation Statistics, and U.S. Census Bureau, 2017 Commodity Flow Survey, CF1700H01, "Hazardous Materials Series: HazMat Shipment Characteristics by Mode for the United States: 2017 and 2012," and CF1700H02, "Hazardous Materials Series: HazMat Shipment Characteristics by Hazardous Class or Division for the United States: 2017 and 2012," <data.census.gov>, accessed July 2020. See also <census.gov/programs-surveys/cfs.html>.

Table 1100. Transportation Accidents, Deaths, and Injuries: 2010 to 2020

[5,419 represents 5,419,000]

Mode	Unit	Accidents			Deaths			Injuries		
		2010	2019	2020	2010	2019	2020	2010	2019	2020
Air, total..................................	Number	1,507	1,302	1,144	477	452	349	278	260	202
Air carrier [1]............................	Number	30	40	14	2	4	–	17	17	8
Commuter [2]...........................	Number	6	9	5	–	2	5	2	–	–
On-demand [3].........................	Number	30	33	40	17	32	21	3	14	9
General aviation......................	Number	1,441	1,220	1,085	458	414	332	256	229	187
Land:										
Highway crashes [4].................	1,000	5,419	6,756	(NA)	33.0	36.1	38.7	2,248	2,740	(NA)
Passenger car occupants..........	1,000	5,350	6,561	(NA)	12.5	12.2	(NA)	1,256	1,498	(NA)
Motorcyclists............................	1,000	96	111	(NA)	4.5	5.0	5.5	82	84	(NA)
Light truck occupants................	1,000	3,775	4,847	(NA)	9.8	10.0	(NA)	737	950	(NA)
Large truck occupants...............	1,000	276	538	(NA)	0.5	0.9	(NA)	20	46	(NA)
Bus occupants..........................	1,000	54	74	(NA)	–	–	(NA)	18	15	(NA)
Pedestrians..............................	1,000	(NA)	(NA)	(NA)	4.3	6.2	6.2	70	76	(NA)
Pedalcyclists............................	1,000	(NA)	(NA)	(NA)	0.6	0.8	0.9	52	49	(NA)
Other.....................................	1,000	(NA)	(NA)	(NA)	0.7	0.9	(NA)	13	23	(NA)
Railroad [5]...............................	Number	10,032	10,078	7,322	735	863	752	8,379	7,997	5,503
Highway-rail grade crossing [6]......	Number	453	554	522	261	294	197	888	837	688
Transit [7]................................	Number	3,492	7,232	(NA)	222	268	289	25,376	23,363	15,418
Waterborne [8]..........................	Number	9,889	7,299	7,818	821	707	851	3,770	3,002	3,536
Recreational boating [9]...............	Number	4,604	4,168	5,265	672	613	767	3,153	2,559	3,191
Pipeline..................................	Number	586	657	578	22	11	15	108	36	42
Hazard liquid............................	Number	350	384	333	1	–	5	3	–	12
Gas.......................................	Number	236	273	245	21	11	10	105	36	30

– Represents or rounds to zero. NA Not available. [1] See footnote 1, Table 1106. Injuries classified as serious. [2] See footnote 2, Table 1106. Injuries classified as serious. [3] See footnote 3, Table 1106. Injuries classified as serious. [4] Highway crashes often involve more than one motor vehicle, and hence "total highway crashes" is smaller than the sum of the components. Data on deaths are from U.S. National Highway Traffic Safety Administration and are based on deaths within 30 days of the accident. Includes only police reported crashes. [5] Accidents and incidents resulting from freight and passenger rail operations including commuter rail. Grade crossing accidents are also included when classified as a train accident. Deaths and injuries exclude those in highway-rail grade crossing accidents involving motor vehicles. Injury figures also include occupational illness. [6] Accidents and incidents occurring at highway-rail crossings resulting from freight and passenger rail operations including commuter rail. Public highway-rail grade crossing incidents, fatalities, and injuries involving motor vehicles are excluded and counted under Highway. Highway-rail grade crossing injuries, except train occupants, are also counted under Highway. [7] Includes motor bus, commuter rail, heavy rail, light rail, demand response, van pool, and automated guideway. Starting with 2002, only injuries requiring immediate medical treatment are included. [8] To include vessel-related deaths and injuries include those involving damage to vessels, such as collisions or groundings. Totals include deaths and injuries not related to vessel casualties, not shown separately. [9] Covers occurrences involving a vessel or its equipment that results in 1) a death; 2) an injury that requires medical treatment beyond first aid; 3) damage to a vessel and other property, totaling to more than $2,000 or complete loss of a vessel; or 4) the disappearance of the vessel under circumstances that indicate death or injury.

Source: U.S. Bureau of Transportation Statistics, "National Transportation Statistics," <www.bts.gov/topics/national-transportation-statistics>, accessed November 2021.

Table 1101. On-Time Flight Arrivals and Departures at Major U.S. Airports: 2021

[In percent. All U.S. airlines with 1 percent or more of total U.S. domestic scheduled airline passenger revenues are required to report on-time data. Based on gate arrival and departure times for operations of U.S. major airlines. A flight is considered on time if it operated within 15 minutes of the scheduled time shown in the carrier's computerized reservation system. See source for data on individual airlines]

Airport	Code	On-time destination arrivals				On-time origin departures			
		1st quarter	2nd quarter	3rd quarter	4th quarter	1st quarter	2nd quarter	3rd quarter	4th quarter
Total, all airports [1]................	(X)	**86.4**	**82.7**	**77.5**	**80.1**	**87.7**	**82.6**	**77.5**	**79.3**
Atlanta, Hartsfield-Jackson Intl................	ATL	90.7	89.2	85.5	87.0	90.4	85.3	81.4	84.4
Baltimore/Washington Intl....................	BWI	86.9	80.0	74.4	80.4	81.1	69.6	62.1	67.4
Boston, Logan Intl............................	BOS	86.1	83.3	77.7	84.3	89.4	85.8	81.6	85.9
Charlotte, Douglas............................	CLT	88.1	87.7	82.9	87.5	90.4	87.1	80.3	86.2
Chicago, Midway Intl..........................	MDW	86.2	78.9	75.1	77.8	80.3	68.2	59.7	66.8
Chicago, O'Hare...............................	ORD	84.3	84.2	78.2	82.1	85.9	83.8	76.6	80.2
Dallas-Fort Worth Intl........................	DFW	77.3	75.6	76.4	81.5	81.2	74.2	71.3	78.5
Denver Intl....................................	DEN	83.7	79.6	74.9	79.6	83.1	76.2	68.7	71.6
Detroit, Metro Wayne County..................	DTW	90.6	87.7	84.2	84.5	91.7	88.6	85.3	83.6
Fort Lauderdale-Hollywood Intl...............	FLL	83.7	79.0	68.5	77.6	86.3	76.7	66.7	76.9
Houston, George Bush Intercontinental.....	IAH	85.6	81.0	76.0	82.8	87.0	82.1	75.4	79.6
Las Vegas, McCarran Intl.....................	LAS	88.8	80.8	74.4	74.9	89.4	77.4	69.3	70.2
Los Angeles Intl..............................	LAX	89.0	84.7	80.5	77.3	90.8	84.4	78.9	76.4
Miami Intl....................................	MIA	88.4	82.2	74.8	77.7	88.2	78.5	73.1	75.3
Minneapolis-St. Paul Intl.....................	MSP	90.5	90.2	86.2	84.1	91.6	90.4	86.7	83.9
New York, JFK Intl............................	JFK	86.1	82.5	73.7	80.9	88.0	83.5	72.9	82.4
New York, LaGuardia..........................	LGA	87.7	85.2	79.7	84.7	87.6	85.3	80.6	84.3
Newark Intl..................................	EWR	86.5	80.7	65.5	74.6	86.7	83.3	66.4	71.8
Orlando Intl..................................	MCO	84.2	77.1	69.7	76.9	86.6	76.3	68.5	75.7
Philadelphia Intl.............................	PHL	87.0	82.8	76.2	84.2	90.0	86.1	79.2	85.3
Phoenix, Sky Harbor Intl......................	PHX	89.0	85.3	78.5	78.4	89.4	81.1	74.3	73.2
Portland Intl.................................	PDX	86.1	85.1	80.7	77.3	90.1	88.3	84.0	82.3
Salt Lake City Intl............................	SLC	89.7	88.6	83.8	81.4	89.4	88.2	84.1	80.8
San Diego Intl................................	SAN	89.6	83.6	80.5	76.9	92.5	85.3	82.0	78.9
San Francisco Intl............................	SFO	90.4	85.5	81.8	78.6	92.5	88.6	84.9	79.3
Seattle-Tacoma Intl...........................	SEA	86.2	87.4	84.0	79.0	89.2	86.9	83.6	78.7
Tampa, Tampa Intl............................	TPA	85.0	80.7	72.9	78.4	87.5	80.7	76.5	81.6
Washington, Reagan National.................	DCA	89.3	85.9	80.5	82.4	90.9	87.0	81.2	83.3
Washington Dulles Intl........................	IAD	87.2	85.7	76.3	83.6	87.3	87.2	77.6	82.8

X Not applicable. [1] Includes other airports not shown separately.

Source: U.S. Department of Transportation, Bureau of Transportation Statistics, "TranStats," <transtats.bts.gov>, accessed July 2022.

Table 1102. Airline Fuel Consumption and Fuel Costs: 2000 to 2021

[20,373 represents 20,373,000,000. Data shown are aggregated for scheduled and unscheduled service on U.S. carriers with over $20 million in revenue per year]

Year	Total fuel consumption (million gallons)	Total fuel cost (million dollars)	Cost per gallon (dollars)	Domestic service Con-sumption (million gallons)	Domestic service Cost (million dollars)	Domestic service Cost per gallon (dollars)	International service Con-sumption (million gallons)	International service Cost (million dollars)	International service Cost per gallon (dollars)
2000........	20,373	16,448	0.81	14,865	11,708	0.79	5,508	4,739	0.86
2010........	17,298	39,350	2.27	11,257	25,571	2.27	6,042	13,779	2.28
2015........	17,349	32,196	1.86	10,929	20,006	1.83	6,421	12,190	1.90
2016........	17,668	25,742	1.46	11,374	16,636	1.46	6,295	9,106	1.45
2017........	18,029	30,630	1.70	11,588	19,728	1.70	6,441	10,902	1.69
2018........	18,750	40,490	2.16	12,151	26,108	2.15	6,599	14,382	2.18
2019........	19,205	38,534	2.01	12,541	25,133	2.00	6,663	13,401	2.01
2020........	11,481	16,463	1.43	7,643	10,955	1.43	3,838	5,509	1.44
2021........	15,126	29,943	1.98	10,380	20,677	1.99	4,746	9,266	1.95

Source: U.S. Bureau of Transportation Statistics, "Airline Fuel Cost and Consumption," <transtats.bts.gov/fuel.asp>, accessed April 2022.

Table 1103. Top 50 Airports in 2020—Passengers Enplaned: 2019 and 2020

[In thousands (935,281 represents 935,281,000), except rank. For calendar year. Intl = international. Airports ranked by total passengers enplaned on U.S. carrier scheduled domestic and international service and foreign carrier scheduled international service from the U.S.]

Airport city and code	2019 Rank	2019 Total	2020 Rank	2020 Total	Airport city and code	2019 Rank	2019 Total	2020 Rank	2020 Total
All U.S. airports................	(X)	**935,281**	(X)	**368,712**	Chicago, IL (MDW).................	28	10,081	25	4,237
Total, top 50 [1].....................	(X)	**786,861**	(X)	**306,184**	New York, NY (LGA)...............	21	15,393	26	4,147
Atlanta, GA (ATL)................	1	53,505	1	20,560	Nashville, TN (BNA)...............	31	8,935	27	4,014
Dallas/Fort Worth, TX (DFW)...	4	35,785	2	18,595	Washington Dulles, DC (IAD).....	25	11,894	28	3,897
Denver, CO (DEN)................	5	33,593	3	16,243	Dallas, TX (DAL).................	33	8,079	29	3,670
Chicago, IL (ORD)................	3	40,888	4	14,613	Washington, DC (DCA).............	26	11,595	30	3,573
Los Angeles, CA (LAX)...........	2	42,966	5	14,058	Portland, OR (PDX)...............	30	9,797	31	3,456
Charlotte-Douglas, NC (CLT).......	11	24,199	6	12,955	Austin, TX (AUS).................	32	8,507	32	3,141
Las Vegas, NV (LAS).............	10	24,578	7	10,564	Houston, TX (HOU))...............	36	7,069	33	3,127
Phoenix, AZ (PHX)...............	13	22,453	8	10,531	Honolulu, HI (HNL)...............	29	9,984	34	3,123
Orlando, FL (MCO)...............	9	24,583	9	10,468	St. Louis, MO (STL)...............	34	7,760	35	3,035
Seattle-Tacoma, WA (SEA).........	8	25,002	10	9,462	Fort Myers, FL (RSW).............	43	5,044	36	2,947
Miami, FL (MIA).................	15	21,456	11	8,786	Sacramento, CA (SMF).............	40	6,455	37	2,710
Houston, TX (IAH)...............	14	21,908	12	8,683	New Orleans, LA (MSY)............	38	6,874	38	2,633
New York, NY (JFK)...............	6	31,123	13	8,286	San Juan, PR (SJU)...............	48	4,562	39	2,357
Fort Lauderdale, FL (FLL)............	19	17,958	14	8,016	Raleigh, NC (RDU)...............	37	6,919	40	2,338
Newark, NJ (EWR)...............	12	23,172	15	7,992	San Jose, CA (SJC)...............	35	7,687	41	2,283
San Francisco, CA (SFO)...........	7	27,715	16	7,746	Oakland, CA (OAK)...............	39	6,666	42	2,271
Minneapolis-St. Paul, MN (MSP)....	17	19,195	17	7,070	Kansas City, MO (MCI)............	41	5,759	43	2,168
Detroit, MI (DTW)...............	18	18,143	18	6,823	Cleveland, OH (CLE)...............	45	4,894	44	1,992
Boston, MA (BOS)...............	16	20,706	19	6,036	Indianapolis, IN (IND).............	47	4,709	45	1,989
Salt Lake City, UT (SLC)............	23	12,840	20	5,981	San Antonio, TX (SAT)............	44	5,037	46	1,920
Philadelphia, PA (PHL)...........	20	16,013	21	5,755	Santa Ana, CA (SNA).............	42	5,198	47	1,825
Baltimore, MD (BWI).............	22	13,292	22	5,451	Pittsburgh, PA (PIT)...............	46	4,715	48	1,743
Tampa, FL (TPA).................	27	10,941	23	4,967	Cincinnati, OH (CVG)..............	49	4,413	49	1,730
San Diego, CA (SAN)................	24	12,648	24	4,638	Columbus, OH (CMH)..............	50	4,171	50	1,578

X Not applicable. [1] The 2019 totals for the top 50 airports will not sum to total top 50 because some top 50 airports in 2020 were not in the top 50 in 2019.

Source: U.S. Bureau of Transportation Statistics, "National Transportation Statistics," <www.bts.gov/topics/national-transportation-statistics>, accessed November 2021.

Table 1104. Consumer Complaints Filed Against U.S. Airlines: 2000 to 2021

[Calendar year data. Represents complaints filed by consumers to the U.S. Department of Transportation (DOT), Aviation Consumer Protection Division, regarding service problems with air carriers. See source for data on individual airlines]

Complaint category	2000	2010	2015	2016	2017	2018	2019	2020	2021
Total...................	**20,564**	**10,988**	**20,175**	**17,908**	**18,156**	**15,544**	**15,342**	**102,560**	**49,958**
Flight problems [1].................	8,698	3,337	6,434	6,179	6,078	4,517	4,757	1,498	6,311
Baggage.........................	2,753	1,938	3,133	2,770	2,745	2,728	2,565	1,047	1,994
Ticketing/boarding [2].............	1,405	1,510	2,695	2,115	2,194	1,908	1,824	4,449	4,028
Customer service [3]..............	4,074	1,345	2,276	1,934	1,781	1,618	1,705	1,484	1,902
Refunds........................	803	730	1,573	1,361	1,359	1,329	1,574	89,511	29,507
Fares [4]........................	708	465	1,813	1,363	2,022	1,542	1,033	3,303	4,077
Disability [5].....................	612	572	944	865	850	827	905	541	1,394
Oversales [6].....................	759	544	648	597	511	409	376	132	286
Discrimination [7].................	(NA)	143	65	95	98	97	107	49	132
Advertising......................	42	77	163	124	80	57	61	25	45
Animals.........................	1	8	3	1	1	2	2	1	1
Other [8]........................	709	319	428	504	437	510	433	520	281

NA Not available. [1] Cancellations, delays, and other deviations from schedule. [2] Errors in reservations and ticketing; and problems in making reservations, obtaining tickets, and boarding (except oversales). Prior to 1998, includes disability complaints. [3] Unhelpful employees, inadequate meals or cabin service, treatment of delayed passengers. [4] Incorrect or incomplete information about fares, discount fare conditions, and availability, etc. [5] Civil rights complaints by air travelers with disabilities. Prior to 2000, included in ticketing/boarding. [6] All bumping problems, whether or not airline complied with DOT regulations. [7] Civil rights complaints by air travelers (other than disability) based on factors such as race, religion, national origin or sex. [8] Frequent flyer, smoking, tours credit, cargo problems, security, airport facilities, claims for bodily injury, and others not classified above.

Source: U.S. Department of Transportation, Aviation Consumer Protection Division, *Air Travel Consumer Report*, February 2022, and earlier reports. See also <www.transportation.gov/airconsumer>.

Table 1105. U.S. Airline Carrier Delays, Cancellations, and Diversions: 2000 to 2021

[In thousands (5,683.0 represents 5,683,000), except percent. For calendar year. See headnote, Table 1101]

Item	2000	2010	2014	2015	2016	2017	2018	2019	2020	2021
Total operations	**5,683.0**	**6,450.1**	**5,819.8**	**5,819.1**	**5,617.7**	**5,674.6**	**7,213.4**	**7,422.0**	**4,688.4**	**5,995.4**
NUMBER										
Delayed departures [1]	1,131.7	1,111.9	1,193.2	1,055.5	952.2	1,012.5	1,304.2	1,359.6	400.8	1,023.5
Delayed arrivals [2]	1,356.0	1,174.9	1,240.5	1,063.4	964.2	1,029.5	1,352.7	1,389.3	431.9	1,010.3
Cancellations [3]	187.5	113.3	127.0	89.9	65.9	82.7	116.6	134.9	281.0	103.1
Diversions [4]	14.3	15.5	14.4	15.2	13.7	12.5	17.9	18.9	7.7	14.1
PERCENT										
Delayed departures [1]	19.9	17.2	20.5	18.1	17.0	17.8	18.1	18.3	8.5	17.1
Delayed arrivals [2]	23.9	18.2	21.3	18.3	17.2	18.1	18.8	18.7	9.2	16.9
Cancellations [3]	3.3	1.8	2.2	1.5	1.2	1.5	1.6	1.8	6.0	1.7
Diversions [4]	0.3	0.2	0.2	0.3	0.2	0.2	0.2	0.3	0.2	0.2

[1] Late departures departed 15 minutes or more after the scheduled departure time. [2] Late arrivals arrived 15 minutes or more after the scheduled arrival time. [3] A cancelled flight is one that was not operated, but was listed in a carrier's computer reservation system within seven days of the scheduled departure. [4] A diverted flight is one that left from the scheduled departure airport but flew to a destination point other than the scheduled destination point.

Source: U.S. Bureau of Transportation Statistics, "National Transportation Statistics," <www.bts.gov/topics/national-transportation-statistics>, accessed March 2022.

Table 1106. U.S. Air Carrier Aircraft Accidents: 2000 to 2020

[For years ending December 31. See source for more details]

Item	Unit	2000	2010	2015	2016	2017	2018	2019	2020 (P)
Air carrier accidents, all services [1]	Number	56	30	28	30	33	31	40	14
Fatal accidents	Number	3	1	–	–	–	1	2	–
Fatalities	Number	92	2	–	–	–	1	4	–
Aboard	Number	92	2	–	–	–	1	4	–
Rates per 100,000 flight hours:									
Accidents	Rate	0.31	0.17	0.16	0.16	0.18	0.16	0.20	0.16
Fatal accidents	Rate	0.02	0.01	–	–	–	0.01	0.01	–
Commuter air carrier accidents [2]	Number	12	6	4	9	6	2	9	5
Fatal accidents	Number	1	–	1	2	–	–	1	1
Fatalities	Number	5	–	1	8	–	–	2	5
Aboard	Number	5	–	1	6	–	–	2	5
Rates per 100,000 flight hours:									
Accidents	Rate	3.25	1.91	1.11	2.39	1.53	0.48	2.16	2.22
Fatal accidents	Rate	0.27	–	0.28	0.53	–	–	0.24	0.45
On-demand air taxi accidents [3]	Number	80	30	39	29	44	40	33	40
Fatal accidents	Number	22	6	7	7	8	7	12	6
Fatalities	Number	71	17	27	19	16	16	32	21
Aboard	Number	68	17	27	19	16	16	32	20
Rates per 100,000 flight hours:									
Accidents	Rate	2.04	0.96	1.09	0.83	1.25	1.04	0.88	1.32
Fatal accidents	Rate	0.56	0.19	0.20	0.20	0.23	0.18	0.32	0.20
General aviation accidents [4]	Number	1,837	1,441	1,211	1,269	1,234	1,275	1,220	1,085
Fatal accidents	Number	345	271	230	213	203	224	233	205
Fatalities	Number	596	458	378	386	331	379	414	332
Aboard	Number	585	455	375	379	331	376	406	323
Rates per 100,000 flight hours:									
Accidents	Rate	6.57	6.63	5.85	5.93	5.68	5.87	5.58	5.57
Fatal accidents	Rate	1.21	1.24	1.10	0.98	0.94	1.03	1.06	1.05

– Represents or rounds to zero. P Preliminary. [1] U.S. air carriers operating aircraft with 10 or more seats, under 14 CFR 121. [2] All scheduled service of U.S. air carriers operating aircraft with fewer than 10 seats, under 14 CFR 135. [3] All nonscheduled service of U.S. air carriers operating aircraft with fewer than 10 seats, under 14 CFR 135. [4] U.S. civil registered aircraft not operated under 14 CFR 121 or 135.

Source: U.S. National Transportation Safety Board, Safety Research-Statistical Reviews, "US Civil Aviation Accident Rates," <www.ntsb.gov/safety/Pages/research.aspx>, accessed November 2021.

Table 1107. Worldwide Airline Accidents and Fatalities by World Region: 2020

[Regions are Regional Aviation Safety Group (RASG) regions]

Region	Departures	Accidents	Accident rates [1]	Fatal accidents	Fatalities
World	**22,470,582**	**48**	**2.1**	**4**	**298**
Africa-Indian Ocean (AFI)	659,502	4	6.1	–	–
Asia and Pacific (APAC)	8,590,721	10	1.2	2	119
Europe (EUR) [2]	4,504,203	10	2.2	1	3
Middle East (MID)	694,941	4	5.8	1	176
Americas (PA)	8,021,215	20	2.5	–	–

– Represents zero. [1] Number of accidents per million departures of scheduled commercial operations that involve the transportation of passengers, cargo and mail for remuneration or hire. [2] RASG EUR includes Algeria, Morocco, and Tunisia.

Source: International Civil Aviation Organization, Montreal, Canada, *ICAO Safety Report 2021 Edition* ©, <www.icao.int/safety/Pages/Safety-Report.aspx>.

Table 1108. Airports, Aircraft, and Airmen: 1990 to 2021

[As of December 31 or for years ending December 31]

Item	1990	2000	2010	2017	2018	2019	2020	2021
AIRPORTS								
Airports, total [1]...............	**17,490**	**19,281**	**19,802**	**19,655**	**19,627**	**19,636**	**19,919**	**20,061**
Public use [1]........................	5,589	5,317	5,175	5,104	5,099	5,080	5,217	5,211
Percent with lighted runways.............	71.4	75.9	(NA)	(NA)	(NA)	(NA)	(NA)	(NA)
Percent with paved runways.............	70.7	74.3	(NA)	(NA)	(NA)	(NA)	(NA)	(NA)
Private use........................	11,901	13,964	14,353	14,263	14,528	14,556	14,702	14,850
Percent with lighted runways.............	7.0	7.2	(NA)	(NA)	(NA)	(NA)	(NA)	(NA)
Percent with paved runways.............	31.5	32.0	(NA)	(NA)	(NA)	(NA)	(NA)	(NA)
Military owned........................	(NA)	(NA)	274	288	305	308	312	313
Certificated [2]........................	680	651	551	526	523	522	519	519
General aviation........................	16,810	18,630	19,251	19,129	19,116	19,114	19,400	19,542
AIRCRAFT								
Active air carrier fleet [3]...............	**6,083**	**7,826**	**7,185**	**7,196**	**7,475**	**7,628**	**5,882**	**(NA)**
Fixed wing........................	6,072	8,010	(NA)	(NA)	(NA)	(NA)	(NA)	(NA)
Helicopter [4]........................	11	39	(NA)	(NA)	(NA)	(NA)	(NA)	(NA)
General aviation fleet [5]...............	**198,000**	**217,533**	**223,370**	**211,757**	**211,749**	**210,981**	**204,980**	**(NA)**
Fixed-wing........................	184,500	183,276	176,272	167,082	167,561	166,526	165,765	(NA)
Turbojet........................	4,100	7,001	11,484	14,217	14,596	14,888	15,245	(NA)
Turboprop........................	5,300	5,762	9,369	9,949	9,925	10,242	10,205	(NA)
Piston........................	175,200	170,513	155,419	142,916	143,040	141,396	140,315	(NA)
Rotorcraft........................	6,900	7,150	10,102	10,511	9,990	10,199	10,155	(NA)
Other........................	6,600	6,700	5,684	4,692	4,114	4,133	2,460	(NA)
Gliders........................	(X)	2,041	1,899	1,747	1,772	1,517	(NA)	(NA)
Lighter than air........................	(X)	4,660	3,785	2,945	2,343	2,617	(NA)	(NA)
Experimental........................	(X)	20,407	29,662	26,921	27,531	27,449	24,455	(NA)
AIRMAN CERTIFICATES HELD								
Pilot, total........................	**702,659**	**625,581**	**627,588**	**609,306**	**633,317**	**664,565**	**691,691**	**720,605**
Female........................	40,515	36,757	42,218	42,694	46,463	52,740	58,541	64,979
Student [6]........................	128,663	93,064	119,119	149,121	167,804	197,665	222,629	250,197
Recreational........................	87	340	212	153	144	127	105	85
Sport........................	(X)	(X)	3,682	6,097	6,246	6,467	6,643	6,801
Airplane:								
Private........................	299,111	251,561	202,020	162,455	163,695	161,105	160,860	161,459
Commercial........................	149,666	121,858	123,705	98,161	99,880	100,863	103,879	104,610
Air transport........................	107,732	141,596	142,198	159,825	162,145	164,947	164,193	163,934
Rotorcraft only........................	9,567	7,775	15,377	15,355	15,033	14,248	13,629	13,191
Glider only........................	7,833	9,387	21,275	18,139	18,370	19,143	19,753	20,328
Flight instructor certificates........................	63,775	80,931	96,473	106,692	108,564	113,445	117,558	121,270
Instrument ratings........................	297,073	311,944	318,001	306,652	311,017	314,168	316,651	317,169
Remote pilots [7]........................	(X)	(X)	(X)	69,166	106,321	160,302	206,322	254,587
Nonpilot [8]........................	**492,237**	**547,453**	**686,717**	**671,222**	**688,002**	**714,201**	**724,307**	**733,127**
Mechanic........................	344,282	344,434	331,989	286,268	292,002	301,087	306,301	313,093
Repairmen........................	(X)	38,208	41,267	35,040	35,382	36,294	36,741	37,261
Parachute rigger........................	10,094	10,477	8,407	6,192	6,430	6,800	7,014	7,230
Ground instructor........................	66,882	72,326	75,205	66,423	67,784	69,991	71,991	74,105
Dispatcher........................	11,002	16,340	20,691	20,664	21,465	22,598	23,286	23,835
Flight navigator........................	1,290	570	174	64	58	40	36	30
Flight attendant........................	(NA)	(NA)	159,946	222,037	231,355	245,699	248,742	249,043
Flight engineer........................	58,687	65,098	49,038	34,534	33,526	31,692	30,196	28,530

NA Not available. X Not applicable. [1] Includes civil and joint-use civil-military airports, heliports, STOL (short takeoff and landing) ports, and seaplane bases in the U.S. and its territories. Sole-use military airports are included beginning in 2007. [2] Certificated airports serve scheduled air carrier operations in aircraft designed for more than 9 passenger seats but less than 31 passenger seats. As of 2005, the Federal Aviation Administration (FAA) no longer certificates military airports. [3] Air-carrier aircraft carry passengers or cargo for hire under 14 CFR 121 (large aircraft—more than 30 seats) and 14 CFR 135 (small aircraft—30 seats or fewer). Beginning in 1990, the number of aircraft is the monthly average reported in use for the last three months of the year. Prior to 1990, it was the number of aircraft reported in use during December of a given year. [4] 2000 change in helicopters due to estimating methods. [5] Beginning 1995, excludes commuters. [6] Beginning 2010, duration of validity for student pilot certificates for pilots under age 40 increased from 36 to 60 months. Starting with April 2016, there is no expiration date on the new student pilot certificates, which generates a cumulative increase in the numbers. [7] Remote pilot certification started in August 2016. These numbers are not included in the pilot totals. [8] All certificates on record. No medical examination required.

Source: Prior to 2000: *FAA Statistical Handbook of Aviation*, annual. Thereafter: U.S. Bureau of Transportation Statistics, "National Transportation Statistics," <www.bts.gov/topics/national-transportation-statistics>, accessed June 2022. U.S. Federal Aviation Administration, "U.S. Civil Airmen Statistics," <www.faa.gov/data_research/aviation_data_statistics/>, accessed June 2022.

Table 1109. Passenger Airline Revenues from Fares, Fees, and Services; and Expenses and Profits: 2015 to 2021

[In millions of dollars (169,057 represents $169,057,000,000). Data shown for U.S. scheduled passenger airlines. Data for 2015 and 2021 are compiled from 25 airlines; data for 2016, 2017, and 2020 are compiled from 23 reporting airlines; 2018 and 2019 data are compiled from 21 airlines]

Item	2015	2016	2017	2018	2019	2020	2021 (P)
Total operating revenue [1]	169,057	169,158	175,337	187,474	196,478	77,297	129,994
Passenger fares, scheduled/charter	127,061	125,916	130,491	138,982	145,437	49,887	86,671
Cargo	2,890	2,629	2,985	3,522	3,196	3,412	5,203
Baggage fees	3,814	4,321	4,576	5,072	5,801	2,842	5,310
Reservation change fees	3,012	2,906	2,856	2,858	2,886	898	698
Transport-related [2]	27,385	28,095	28,694	28,474	29,382	13,897	23,194
Other [3]	4,895	5,291	5,735	8,566	9,776	6,361	8,919
Total operating expenses	141,070	143,792	153,893	169,828	175,733	123,786	147,328
Fuel	26,979	22,549	26,241	34,460	32,814	12,149	22,978
Labor	45,487	49,948	53,556	56,104	60,460	49,106	52,577
Rentals	8,632	8,777	8,887	9,098	9,786	9,733	11,313
Depreciation and amortization	7,513	8,773	9,051	9,495	10,058	10,251	9,842
Landing fees	2,853	2,977	3,056	3,211	3,340	2,107	3,600
Maintenance materials	2,521	2,500	2,438	2,208	2,487	1,829	2,475
Transport-related [2]	18,173	17,995	19,009	21,493	22,463	14,527	17,226
Other [4]	28,913	30,272	31,656	33,760	34,325	24,084	27,318
Operating profit	27,987	25,366	21,444	17,646	20,746	-46,488	-17,335
Operating margin (percent) [5]	17	15	12	9	11	-60	-13
Nonoperating income/expense [6]	-4,109	-3,331	-2,298	-2,483	-1,549	1,258	13,991
Pre-tax income	23,877	22,035	19,146	15,163	19,196	-45,231	-3,344
Income tax benefit/expense	911	-7,989	-3,851	-3,388	-4,458	10,185	573
Other income/expense	–	–	–	–	–	–	3
Net income	24,788	14,047	15,295	11,775	14,738	-35,045	-2,768
Net margin (percent) [7]	15	8	9	6	8	-45	-2

P Preliminary. – Represents or rounds to zero. [1] Based on U.S. Department of Transportation accounting standards. Total operating revenues are overstated by code share revenues, which are included in both mainline transport-related revenues and code share passenger revenues. Code share revenues are expensed out in the mainline transport-related expense to allow a true operating profit (loss). Reporting may understate all components of operating revenue, including passenger revenue, as a percent of total operating revenue. [2] Includes in-flight onboard sales, code share revenues, and revenues and expenses from associated businesses (aircraft maintenance, fuel sales, restaurants, vending machines). [3] Includes pet transportation, sale of frequent flyer award miles to airline business partners, standby passenger fees, and public service revenues subsidy. [4] Includes purchase of materials such as passenger food and services such as advertising, communication, insurance, outside flight equipment maintenance, and traffic commissions. [5] Operating profit or loss as a percent of operating revenue. [6] Interest on long-term debt and capital leases, other interest expense, foreign exchange gains and losses, capital gains and losses, and other income and expenses. [7] Net income or loss as a percent of operating revenue.

Source: U.S. Department of Transportation, Bureau of Transportation Statistics, "Airline Financials Tables 4Q 2021," and earlier releases, <www.bts.gov/statistical-releases>, accessed May 2022.

Table 1110. Water Transportation System Summary: 2000 to 2018

[12.8 represents 12,800,000. Data compiled from U.S. Army Corps of Engineers, Department of Homeland Security/Coast Guard, and Bureau of Transportation Statistics publications; see source for details]

Item or characteristic	Unit	2000	2010	2013	2014	2016	2017	2018
U.S.-flag privately owned merchant fleet [1]	Number	282	221	187	179	(NA)	(NA)	(NA)
Recreational boats	Millions	12.8	12.4	12.0	11.8	11.9	12.0	11.9
Lock chambers	Number	276	239	239	239	239	239	239
Lock sites	Number	230	193	193	193	193	193	193
Average age of locks	Years	50.2	59.5	62.5	63.5	(NA)	(NA)	(NA)
Waterway facilities (incl. cargo handling docks)	Number	9,309	8,060	8,231	8,229	8,227	8,239	8,238
Ports (handling over 250,000 tons)	Number	197	178	182	183	181	186	181
Miles of navigable waterways	Number	25,000	25,000	25,000	25,000	25,000	25,000	25,000
Total U.S. flag vessels [2]	Number	41,354	39,883	39,999	40,082	41,328	42,152	42,138
Barge/non-self-propelled vessels	Number	33,152	30,265	31,081	31,043	32,354	32,808	32,828
Self-propelled vessels	Number	8,202	9,618	8,918	9,039	8,974	9,344	9,310

NA Not available. [1] Includes only oceangoing self-propelled, cargo-carrying vessels of 1,000 gross tons and above. [2] Includes unclassified.

Source: U.S. Department of Transportation, Bureau of Transportation Statistics, *Transportation Statistics Annual Report 2020*, December 2020. See also <www.bts.dot.gov/tsar>.

Table 1111. Freight Carried on Major U.S. Waterways: 2000 to 2020

[In millions of short tons (3.1 represents 3,100,000). One short ton equals 2,000 pounds]

Waterway	2000	2005	2010	2015	2016	2017	2018	2019	2020
Atlantic Intracoastal Waterway	3.1	2.7	2.9	2.6	2.3	2.3	2.4	2.1	1.7
Great Lakes	187.5	169.4	129.5	123.7	118.2	125.4	122.2	122.0	101.8
Gulf Intracoastal Waterway	113.8	116.1	116.2	118.9	111.7	111.2	110.4	110.5	101.2
Mississippi River system [1]	715.5	678.0	663.2	684.4	680.9	702.1	692.3	631.6	588.5
Mississippi River main stem [2]	515.6	464.6	483.2	521.1	526.3	552.3	557.6	495.9	473.7
Ohio River system [3]	274.4	280.1	245.2	223.1	204.7	202.1	198.0	194.0	165.7
Columbia River	55.2	51.5	54.7	54.7	61.3	63.4	67.1	60.0	62.5
Snake River	6.7	5.3	3.4	3.6	3.4	3.5	3.9	3.9	4.2

[1] Main channels and all tributaries of the Mississippi, Illinois, Missouri, and Ohio Rivers. [2] Minneapolis, MN to Mouth of Passes. [3] Main channels and all navigable tributaries and embayments of the Ohio, Tennessee, and Cumberland Rivers.

Source: U.S. Army Corps of Engineers, Institute for Water Resources: *Waterborne Commerce of the United States, 2017*, December 2018, and earlier reports; and Commerce Data, "Ports and Waterways Webtool," <ndc.ops.usace.army.mil/wcsc>, accessed April 2022.

Table 1112. Top 30 U.S. Ports by Tons of Traffic: 2020

[In thousands of short tons (275,940 represents 275,940,000). One short ton equals 2,000 lbs. For calendar year. Represents tons of cargo shipped from or received by the specified port. Excludes cargo carried on general ferries; coal and petroleum products loaded from shore facilities directly onto bunkers of vessels for fuel; and amounts of less than 100 tons of government-owned equipment in support of Corps of Engineers projects]

Port name	Total	Domestic	Foreign Total	Foreign Inbound	Foreign Outbound
Houston Port Authority, TX	275,940	79,178	196,762	56,971	139,792
South Louisiana, LA, Port of	225,087	112,372	112,715	30,424	82,291
Corpus Christi, TX	150,755	25,056	125,699	17,606	108,093
New York, NY & NJ	123,697	40,088	83,610	68,357	15,253
New Orleans, LA	81,067	43,220	37,847	15,324	22,523
Port of Long Beach, CA	79,178	13,490	65,688	46,552	19,136
Port of Greater Baton Rouge, LA	71,687	43,420	28,266	5,663	22,604
Beaumont, TX	70,567	24,786	45,782	16,171	29,611
Port of Los Angeles, CA	59,452	4,501	54,951	38,658	16,292
Virginia, VA, Port of	58,049	4,956	53,092	12,363	40,730
Mobile, AL	53,207	18,794	34,412	17,860	16,552
Plaquemines Port District, LA	46,751	25,880	20,871	4,556	16,315
Port of Savannah, GA	43,453	1,136	42,317	24,505	17,812
Lake Charles Harbor District, LA	43,054	20,334	22,720	5,026	17,694
Port Arthur, TX	41,222	17,297	23,925	7,317	16,608
Port Freeport, TX	38,749	4,172	34,577	6,560	28,016
Mid-Ohio Valley Port, OH and WV	35,939	35,939	–	–	–
Baltimore, MD	35,202	4,212	30,990	12,937	18,053
Cincinnati-Northern KY, Ports of	34,476	34,476	–	–	–
Texas City, TX	33,721	12,541	21,180	7,601	13,579
St. Louis Metro Port, IL and MO	30,488	30,488	–	–	–
Huntington-Tristate, KY, OH, WV	29,700	29,700	–	–	–
Philadelphia Regional Port, PA	28,518	11,590	16,928	9,834	7,094
Tampa Port Authority, FL	28,512	15,913	12,599	8,251	4,348
Valdez, AK	25,113	23,020	2,093	–	2,093
Duluth-Superior, MN and WI	25,071	19,363	5,708	693	5,015
Port of Charleston, SC	24,947	1,823	23,125	14,996	8,128
Indiana (Northern District), IN	24,684	24,129	555	513	43
Jackson County Port, MS	23,097	8,312	14,785	7,451	7,334
Seattle, WA	22,965	4,815	18,150	9,098	9,052

– Represents or rounds to zero. [1] The Port of Huntington is the largest inland shipping port in the United States. Port operations occur in Ashland, KY; Ironton, OH; and Huntington, WV.

Source: U.S. Army Corps of Engineers, Waterborne Commerce Statistics Center, Ports & State Data, "Tonnage for Selected U.S. Ports in 2020," <iwr.usace.army.mil/About/Technical-Centers/WCSC-Waterborne-Commerce-Statistics-Center-2/WCSC-Waterborne-Commerce/>, accessed March 2022.

Table 1113. Top 30 U.S. Ports/Waterways Ranked by Container Traffic: 2020

[In thousands of twenty-foot equivalent units (TEUs) (41,193.7 represents 41,193,700). For calendar year. For the 30 leading ports/waterways in total TEUs. A TEU is a measure of containerized cargo capacity equal to one standard 20-foot length by 8-foot width by 8-foot, 6 inch height container. Does not include empty foreign containers]

Port/waterway name	Rank	Total loaded	Domestic loaded Total [1]	Domestic loaded Inbound	Domestic loaded Outbound	Foreign loaded Total	Foreign loaded Inbound	Foreign loaded Outbound
Total U.S. [2]	(X)	41,193.7	5,739.2	2,108.3	2,108.3	36,977.1	25,520.7	11,456.4
Anchorage, AK	19	382.1	504.8	289.9	92.1	0.1	0.1	–
Baltimore, MD	15	730.0	0.5	0.3	0.2	729.5	524.2	205.3
Boston, MA	23	213.0	–	–	–	213.0	143.5	69.5
Charleston, SC	8	1,821.1	–	–	–	1,821.1	1,084.5	736.7
Gulfport, MS	25	137.5	–	–	–	137.5	79.1	58.5
Honolulu, HI	14	785.0	1,031.6	471.5	280.1	33.3	19.3	14.1
Houston, TX	5	2,527.5	–	–	–	2,527.5	1,343.0	1,184.5
Jacksonville, FL	12	882.1	704.1	109.4	446.8	325.9	224.9	100.9
Juneau, AK	29	85.1	113.7	65.1	20.0	–	–	–
Ketchikan, AK	30	82.1	131.2	21.2	60.9	–	–	–
Long Beach, CA	2	5,691.8	347.1	43.9	264.5	5,383.4	4,228.0	1,155.4
Los Angeles, CA	1	6,450.6	46.6	3.4	43.2	6,404.0	5,027.9	1,376.1
Miami, FL	13	799.6	–	–	–	799.6	504.2	295.4
Mobile, AL	20	354.0	–	–	–	354.0	221.3	132.7
New Orleans, LA	18	420.3	–	–	–	420.3	142.9	277.4
New York (NJ-NY), NY	3	5,439.1	–	–	–	5,439.1	4,185.7	1,253.4
Oakland, CA	7	1,916.0	165.7	20.2	85.1	1,810.6	1,014.9	795.8
Palm Beach, FL	26	119.7	–	–	–	119.7	21.5	98.1
Philadelphia, PA	17	530.9	0.3	0.2	0.2	530.6	435.4	95.3
Port Everglades, FL	16	623.7	–	–	–	623.7	302.3	321.4
Port Hueneme, CA	27	100.3	–	–	–	100.3	88.1	12.1
Port of Virginia, VA	6	2,172.3	0.5	0.2	0.3	2,171.8	1,319.5	852.3
San Juan, PR	11	902.3	823.8	495.7	157.4	249.2	206.3	42.8
Savannah, GA	4	3,701.3	–	–	–	3,701.3	2,364.8	1,336.5
Seattle, WA	10	1,151.1	317.3	53.0	122.0	976.2	618.3	357.8
South Jersey Port District, NJ	24	161.1	119.7	48.0	48.9	64.1	62.6	1.5
Tacoma, WA	9	1,526.7	538.7	95.3	307.9	1,123.4	709.6	413.8
Tampa, FL	28	87.0	–	–	–	87.0	76.7	10.3
Wilmington, NC	21	231.5	–	–	–	231.5	126.6	104.9
Wilmington, DE	22	214.5	–	–	–	214.5	196.3	18.2

– Represents or rounds to zero. X Not applicable. [1] Includes empty TEUs, not shown separately. [2] Includes other ports/waterways not shown separately.

Source: U.S. Army Corps of Engineers, Waterborne Commerce Statistics Center, "Annual U.S. Waterborne Container Traffic by Port/Waterway," <www.iwr.usace.army.mil/About/Technical-Centers/WCSC-Waterborne-Commerce-Statistics-Center-2/WCSC-Waterborne-Commerce/>, accessed March 2022.

Table 1114. Highway Mileage—Urban and Rural by Ownership: 1990 to 2020

[In thousands (3,880 represents 3,880,000). As of December 31. Includes Puerto Rico beginning 2000]

Type and control of roadways	1990	2000	2010	2015	2016	2017	2018	2019	2020
Total mileage [1]	**3,880**	**3,951**	**4,084**	**4,171**	**4,157**	**4,184**	**4,195**	**4,189**	**4,192**
Urban mileage	757	859	1,103	1,223	1,226	1,235	1,241	1,254	1,254
Under state control	96	112	(NA)	174	173	172	173	173	174
Under local control [1]	661	746	(NA)	1,042	1,044	1,054	1,060	1,073	1,072
Under federal control [2]	(NA)	(NA)	(NA)	7	8	8	8	8	8
Rural mileage	3,123	3,092	2,980	2,949	2,931	2,949	2,955	2,936	2,939
Under state control	703	664	(NA)	612	612	613	612	612	613
Under local control [1]	2,242	2,311	(NA)	2,198	2,186	2,180	2,184	2,175	2,190
Under federal control [2]	178	117	(NA)	139	133	156	159	149	136

NA Not available. [1] Includes state park, state toll, other state agency, other local agency, and other roadways not identified by ownership. [2] Includes roadways in federal parks, forest, and reservations that are not part of the state and local highway system.

Source: U.S. Federal Highway Administration, "Highway Statistics 2020," and earlier reports, <www.fhwa.dot.gov/policyinformation/statistics.cfm>, accessed March 2022.

Table 1115. Highway Mileage—Functional Systems and Urban/Rural Status by State: 2020

[As of December 31. For definition of functional systems, see text, this section]

State	Total	Functional systems					Urban	Rural
		Interstate	Other freeways and expressways	Arterial	Collector	Local		
United States	**4,192,479**	**48,756**	**18,709**	**405,337**	**820,688**	**2,898,988**	**1,253,815**	**2,938,663**
Alabama	100,171	1,004	33	9,687	21,985	67,462	30,032	70,139
Alaska	17,681	1,080	–	1,571	3,285	11,745	3,165	14,516
Arizona	66,968	1,169	271	6,843	11,783	46,903	26,578	40,390
Arkansas	99,246	749	174	7,411	20,978	69,934	17,227	82,019
California	175,562	2,456	1,894	26,829	32,986	111,397	102,593	72,969
Colorado	89,207	952	353	8,919	16,192	62,791	20,996	68,211
Connecticut	21,575	346	279	2,724	3,410	14,815	15,882	5,693
Delaware	6,526	41	68	628	1,132	4,657	3,663	2,862
District of Columbia	1,516	12	15	270	156	1,063	1,516	–
Florida	123,488	1,495	776	12,998	15,575	92,643	87,030	36,457
Georgia	128,572	1,247	174	14,340	22,759	90,052	52,344	76,228
Hawaii	4,501	55	34	794	753	2,866	2,843	1,658
Idaho	53,281	615	59	4,287	9,676	38,645	7,064	46,217
Illinois	145,993	2,185	166	14,168	22,774	106,700	49,799	96,194
Indiana	97,110	1,261	312	8,915	22,751	63,872	30,330	66,780
Iowa	114,838	788	–	9,931	31,604	72,515	12,840	101,999
Kansas	140,112	875	594	8,562	34,054	96,027	14,133	125,979
Kentucky	80,006	944	462	5,581	16,991	56,028	14,937	65,069
Louisiana	63,746	954	151	5,812	11,785	45,045	22,225	41,521
Maine	22,851	366	19	2,111	5,949	14,406	3,237	19,614
Maryland	32,430	478	380	3,637	5,404	22,532	18,835	13,596
Massachusetts	36,815	568	334	6,423	4,554	24,936	30,627	6,188
Michigan	122,040	1,238	697	14,324	24,669	81,112	38,037	84,003
Minnesota	141,957	913	254	13,318	30,671	96,800	23,477	118,479
Mississippi	77,512	832	64	7,582	15,836	53,198	13,091	64,421
Missouri	132,519	1,380	1,619	8,913	25,220	95,387	24,727	107,792
Montana	73,490	1,193	–	6,170	16,132	49,995	4,271	69,218
Nebraska	95,331	483	462	7,712	20,842	65,832	8,070	87,261
Nevada	47,793	618	55	3,517	6,042	37,561	10,430	37,364
New Hampshire	16,193	225	83	1,662	2,647	11,575	5,077	11,116
New Jersey	38,991	432	488	5,896	4,436	27,738	33,535	5,456
New Mexico	72,092	999	12	5,637	8,812	56,632	11,294	60,798
New York	114,205	1,738	996	13,628	20,723	77,120	49,951	64,254
North Carolina	107,954	1,358	877	10,130	17,349	78,240	41,965	65,989
North Dakota	88,429	571	–	5,998	12,468	69,392	2,918	85,511
Ohio	122,992	1,576	917	10,599	23,300	86,600	47,517	75,475
Oklahoma	115,079	933	211	8,364	25,728	79,844	18,979	96,099
Oregon	78,991	730	69	7,027	18,769	52,397	15,134	63,857
Pennsylvania	120,845	1,863	917	12,959	19,979	85,127	48,510	72,336
Rhode Island	6,025	70	92	853	901	4,109	4,661	1,363
South Carolina	79,190	851	128	7,369	14,925	55,917	24,425	54,765
South Dakota	81,697	679	309	6,137	18,983	55,589	3,261	78,437
Tennessee	96,182	1,201	205	9,263	18,186	67,326	31,855	64,327
Texas	316,567	3,463	1,525	33,177	67,092	211,312	110,552	206,016
Utah	48,812	938	58	3,831	8,400	35,585	12,405	36,407
Vermont	14,248	320	16	1,340	3,155	9,418	1,498	12,750
Virginia	75,527	1,119	459	8,873	15,742	49,334	26,940	48,587
Washington	81,022	764	1,035	7,585	17,309	54,330	24,519	56,503
West Virginia	38,879	556	15	3,494	8,642	26,172	6,673	32,206
Wisconsin	115,751	878	545	12,273	23,486	78,569	24,039	91,712
Wyoming	30,051	913	3	3,679	12,041	13,415	2,871	27,180
Puerto Rico	19,916	284	53	1,588	1,663	16,328	15,235	4,682

– Represents zero.

Source: U.S. Federal Highway Administration, "Highway Statistics 2020," <www.fhwa.dot.gov/policyinformation/statistics.cfm>, accessed March 2022.

Table 1116. Bridge Inventory—Total, Area, and Condition: 2012 to 2021, and by State, 2021

[Based on the National Bridge Inventory program; for details, see source]

State and year	Number of bridges	Bridge deck area (square meters)	Bridge condition [1]					
			Number			Percent		
			Good	Fair	Poor	Good	Fair	Poor
2012.........................	607,380	358,547,072	287,194	262,878	57,049	47.3	43.3	9.4
2013.........................	607,751	362,428,004	287,581	265,456	54,492	47.3	43.7	9.0
2014.........................	610,749	365,542,771	287,701	269,734	52,905	47.1	44.2	8.7
2015.........................	611,845	369,109,088	289,158	271,690	50,917	47.3	44.4	8.3
2016.........................	614,387	371,463,919	291,412	274,306	48,559	47.4	44.6	7.9
2017.........................	615,002	374,362,285	288,030	279,270	47,619	46.8	45.4	7.7
2018.........................	616,096	390,438,601	283,316	285,676	47,054	46.0	46.4	7.6
2019.........................	617,084	393,265,002	279,582	291,339	46,163	45.3	47.2	7.5
2020.........................	618,456	396,244,439	278,433	294,992	45,031	45.0	47.7	7.3
U.S. total, 2021........	**619,622**	**398,580,883**	**278,128**	**297,908**	**43,586**	**44.9**	**48.1**	**7.0**
Alabama.....................	16,164	9,979,973	6,550	9,028	586	40.5	55.9	3.6
Alaska.......................	1,632	757,896	716	782	134	43.9	47.9	8.2
Arizona......................	8,467	6,069,459	5,275	3,075	117	62.3	36.3	1.4
Arkansas....................	12,941	6,837,378	6,234	6,028	679	48.2	46.6	5.2
California....................	25,737	30,124,854	12,224	12,020	1,493	47.5	46.7	5.8
Colorado.....................	8,869	5,155,162	3,063	5,337	469	34.5	60.2	5.3
Connecticut.................	4,361	3,448,066	1,249	2,881	231	28.6	66.1	5.3
Delaware....................	875	1,026,306	291	567	17	33.3	64.8	1.9
District of Columbia......	246	572,196	74	165	7	30.1	67.1	2.8
Florida......................	12,680	18,229,935	8,052	4,169	459	63.5	32.9	3.6
Georgia.....................	14,987	10,453,854	11,054	3,614	319	73.8	24.1	2.1
Hawaii.......................	1,162	1,375,035	265	810	87	22.8	69.7	7.5
Idaho........................	4,561	1,787,321	1,322	3,001	238	29.0	65.8	5.2
Illinois......................	26,846	13,560,234	12,848	11,593	2,405	47.9	43.2	9.0
Indiana......................	19,337	8,346,936	7,866	10,389	1,082	40.7	53.7	5.6
Iowa.........................	23,870	8,981,008	9,354	10,012	4,504	39.2	41.9	18.9
Kansas......................	24,925	8,992,619	13,335	10,313	1,277	53.5	41.4	5.1
Kentucky....................	14,410	6,639,366	4,089	9,331	990	28.4	64.8	6.9
Louisiana...................	12,782	16,707,128	5,931	5,220	1,631	46.4	40.8	12.8
Maine........................	2,485	1,274,099	728	1,443	314	29.3	58.1	12.6
Maryland....................	5,446	5,478,185	1,789	3,404	253	32.8	62.5	4.6
Massachusetts.............	5,245	4,148,482	1,321	3,468	456	25.2	66.1	8.7
Michigan....................	11,284	6,486,938	4,091	5,953	1,240	36.3	52.8	11.0
Minnesota...................	13,496	7,135,710	7,857	5,021	618	58.2	37.2	4.6
Mississippi..................	16,788	9,884,290	9,921	5,693	1,174	59.1	33.9	7.0
Missouri.....................	24,590	10,795,966	9,654	12,718	2,218	39.3	51.7	9.0
Montana.....................	5,266	2,070,501	1,600	3,301	365	30.4	62.7	6.9
Nebraska....................	15,348	4,382,788	7,966	6,102	1,280	51.9	39.8	8.3
Nevada......................	2,067	1,911,947	1,070	968	29	51.8	46.8	1.4
New Hampshire............	2,527	1,157,396	1,344	989	194	53.2	39.1	7.7
New Jersey.................	6,798	7,501,410	1,809	4,507	482	26.6	66.3	7.1
New Mexico.................	4,025	2,094,826	1,466	2,351	208	36.4	58.4	5.2
New York....................	17,555	13,379,835	6,355	9,528	1,672	36.2	54.3	9.5
North Carolina.............	18,877	10,672,362	7,840	9,712	1,325	41.5	51.4	7.0
North Dakota...............	4,285	1,326,782	2,046	1,758	481	47.7	41.0	11.2
Ohio.........................	27,151	14,189,311	16,493	9,324	1,334	60.7	34.3	4.9
Oklahoma...................	23,220	9,015,245	9,898	11,026	2,296	42.6	47.5	9.9
Oregon......................	8,235	5,096,809	2,800	5,053	382	34.0	61.4	4.6
Pennsylvania...............	23,166	13,315,383	7,705	12,263	3,198	33.3	52.9	13.8
Rhode Island...............	779	766,405	168	475	136	21.6	61.0	17.5
South Carolina.............	9,395	7,129,031	4,142	4,754	499	44.1	50.6	5.3
South Dakota...............	5,886	1,859,316	1,943	2,925	1,018	33.0	49.7	17.3
Tennessee..................	20,331	10,395,496	8,689	10,801	841	42.7	53.1	4.1
Texas........................	55,175	53,243,079	27,807	26,579	789	50.4	48.2	1.4
Utah.........................	3,056	1,973,115	1,005	1,988	63	32.9	65.1	2.1
Vermont.....................	2,836	944,777	1,494	1,274	68	52.7	44.9	2.4
Virginia.....................	13,997	10,264,213	4,644	8,823	530	33.2	63.0	3.8
Washington.................	8,358	7,166,874	4,331	3,626	401	51.8	43.4	4.8
West Virginia...............	7,314	3,828,355	1,719	4,105	1,490	23.5	56.1	20.4
Wisconsin...................	14,307	7,098,826	7,289	6,031	987	50.9	42.2	6.9
Wyoming....................	3,114	1,329,562	920	1,964	230	29.5	63.1	7.4
Guam........................	10	769	2	6	2	20.0	60.0	20.0
Puerto Rico.................	2,334	2,213,107	426	1,626	282	18.3	69.7	12.1
Virgin Islands..............	24	4,969	4	14	6	16.7	58.3	25.0

[1] Good: pavement and bridge infrastructure that is free of significant defects, and has a condition that does not adversely affect its performance. Fair: pavement and bridge infrastructure that has isolated surface defects or functional deficiencies on pavements; or minor deterioration of bridge elements. Poor: pavement and bridge infrastructure that is exhibiting advanced deterioration and conditions that impact structural capacity.

Source: U.S. Federal Highway Administration, Office of Bridges and Structures, "Bridge Condition by Highway System," <www.fhwa.dot.gov/bridge/britab.cfm>, accessed January 2022.

Table 1117. Funding for Highways and Disposition of Highway–User Revenue: 1990 to 2020

[In millions of dollars (75,444 represents $75,444,000,000). Data compiled from reports of state and local authorities]

Type	1990	2000	2010	2015	2016	2017	2018	2019	2020
Total receipts	**75,444**	**131,115**	**220,977**	**241,063**	**267,941**	**(NA)**	**237,833**	**260,822**	**257,016**
Current income	69,880	119,815	187,960	218,812	248,789	(NA)	216,154	238,027	231,258
Highway-user revenues	44,346	81,335	93,830	113,454	111,296	(NA)	121,325	135,293	127,545
Other taxes and fees	19,827	31,137	80,220	85,434	118,366	(NA)	72,859	80,313	82,099
Investment income, other receipts	5,707	7,342	13,910	19,924	19,126	(NA)	21,970	22,420	21,615
Bond issue proceeds [1]	5,564	11,301	33,017	22,251	19,152	(NA)	21,679	22,795	25,758
Funds drawn from or placed in reserves [2,3]	-36	-8,418	-15,664	-5,868	-48,940	(NA)	6,666	-2,767	4,464
Total funds available	75,408	122,697	205,313	235,195	219,001	(NA)	244,498	258,055	261,480
Total disbursements	**75,408**	**122,697**	**205,313**	**235,195**	**219,001**	**(NA)**	**244,498**	**258,055**	**261,480**
Current disbursements	72,457	117,592	193,034	207,537	204,617	(NA)	228,609	236,932	244,193
Capital outlay	35,151	61,323	100,175	106,539	106,780	(NA)	117,025	120,934	127,716
Maintenance and traffic services	20,365	30,636	48,773	51,817	49,749	(NA)	59,139	61,503	61,346
Administration and research	6,501	10,020	16,165	16,930	19,706	(NA)	19,437	20,605	20,238
Highway law enforcement and safety	7,235	11,031	18,080	20,165	17,850	(NA)	21,205	21,918	22,118
Interest on debt	3,205	4,583	9,842	12,087	10,532	(NA)	11,802	11,972	12,776
Bond retirement [1]	2,951	5,105	12,279	27,658	14,384	(NA)	15,890	21,123	17,287

NA Not available. [1] Amounts shown represent Federal payments to territories, and Federal expenditures in territories for highways and mass transit. [2] Proceeds and redemptions of short-term notes and refunding issues are excluded. [3] Negative numbers indicate that funds were placed in reserves.

Source: U.S. Federal Highway Administration, "Highway Statistics 2020," and earlier reports, <www.fhwa.dot.gov/policyinformation/statistics.cfm>, accessed April 2022.

Table 1118. State Motor Fuel Tax and Related Receipts, 2017 to 2020; and Gasoline Tax Rates, 2020

[672 represents $672,000,000. Federal tax rate is 18.4 cents a gallon. This table includes revenues from state taxes on all motor-vehicle fuels and related receipts due to motor-fuel taxation and administration. In many states, however, the tax on special fuels (fuels other than gasoline and gasohol) is applicable only to the amount used on the highways. For the states that apply the tax to all fuel sold, the revenue and refunds covering the nonhighway portion of these special fuels have been excluded]

State	Adjusted total receipts (million dollars)				Tax rate, [1] 2020	State	Adjusted total receipts (million dollars)				Tax rate, [1] 2020
	2017	2018	2019	2020	2020		2017	2018	2019	2020	2020
AL	672	644	654	814	26.00	MO	700	706	707	693	17.00
AK	29	31	30	29	8.00	MT	193	244	242	240	32.75
AZ	718	719	742	725	18.00	NE	357	374	391	398	34.10
AR	473	482	486	532	24.80	NV	665	701	731	698	23.81
CA	4,587	6,153	7,285	7,383	50.50	NH	185	187	190	178	23.83
CO	670	682	673	629	22.00	NJ	545	535	529	469	37.10
CT	719	799	787	644	25.00	NM	290	305	313	152	17.00
DE	129	131	143	136	23.00	NY	1,653	1,604	1,705	1,686	25.45
DC	26	135	81	22	23.50	NC	1,914	1,963	2,091	1,934	36.35
FL	2,685	2,750	2,858	2,809	37.78	ND	190	194	198	191	23.00
GA [2]	1,740	1,801	1,838	1,873	27.90	OH	1,871	1,861	1,861	2,488	38.50
HI	82	82	82	76	16.00	OK	161	163	564	569	20.00
ID	324	335	345	344	33.00	OR	629	620	620	567	36.00
IL	1,251	1,268	1,237	2,269	39.80	PA	3,533	3,872	3,841	3,575	57.60
IN	848	826	1,834	1,527	32.00	RI	150	152	166	146	35.00
IA	705	637	651	694	31.00	SC	606	677	742	787	24.00
KS	448	465	470	437	24.00	SD	187	185	186	183	30.00
KY	759	763	771	740	24.60	TN	914	1,100	1,171	1,216	26.00
LA	629	598	604	549	20.00	TX	3,560	3,682	3,738	3,389	20.00
ME	252	250	250	237	30.00	UT	482	496	514	504	30.00
MD	1,063	1,068	1,117	1,062	36.30	VT	119	120	120	109	30.46
MA	764	769	775	707	24.00	VA	927	923	932	887	16.20
MI	1,342	1,444	1,436	1,297	26.30	WA	1,632	1,701	1,655	1,585	49.40
MN	923	942	922	854	28.50	WV	358	403	424	392	35.70
MS	425	413	423	412	18.40	WI	1,034	1,054	1,054	1,019	30.90
						WY	168	166	175	163	24.00

[1] Effective dates vary by state. Data shown are latest rates in effect during 2020. Includes other miscellaneous tax (environmental, etc.). [2] Beginning 2014, Georgia receipts includes special fuel and use tax.

Source: U.S. Federal Highway Administration, "Highway Statistics 2020," and earlier reports, <www.fhwa.dot.gov/policyinformation/statistics.cfm>, accessed March 2022.

Table 1119. Public Obligations for Highways—Changes in Indebtedness During the Year: 2000 to 2020

[In millions of dollars (56,264 represents $56,264,000,000). Table summarizes state indebtedness from all state bond issues, including the toll facility issues and the state issues for local roads. This table is compiled from reports of state authorities. Table also summarizes the change in status of the highway obligations of local governments, including toll authorities]

Item	2000	2010	2015	2016	2017	2018	2019	2020
STATE GOVERNMENT								
Obligations outstanding, beginning of year.........	56,264	138,798	211,692	216,516	217,090	139,481	224,515	227,820
Obligations issued.................................	9,067	26,895	29,155	20,103	34,186	26,394	23,268	29,963
Obligations retired...............................	3,897	11,143	22,909	16,991	23,355	11,334	25,170	24,488
Obligations outstanding, end of year..............	61,434	154,550	217,938	219,628	227,921	154,541	222,613	233,296
LOCAL GOVERNMENT [1,2]								
Obligations outstanding, beginning of year.........	34,904	65,679	51,377	78,923	79,109	80,313	156,261	(NA)
Bonds outstanding, beginning of year.............	34,229	63,891	48,262	75,524	75,506	76,584	150,973	(NA)
Bonds outstanding, end of year....................	34,949	67,707	49,189	75,867	76,419	71,380	153,505	(NA)
Obligations outstanding, end of year..............	35,557	69,794	52,579	79,552	80,148	77,037	161,015	(NA)

NA Not available. [1] Short-term notes data not shown. The data are included in beginning and ending year obligations. [2] Local government reporting is on a biennial basis with even-numbered years optional; therefore, data for some states is estimated in non-reporting years.

Source: U.S. Federal Highway Administration, "Highway Statistics 2020," and earlier reports, <www.fhwa.dot.gov/policyinformation/statistics.cfm>, accessed March 2022.

Table 1120. State Disbursements for Highways by State: 2000 to 2020

[In millions of dollars (89,832 represents $89,832,000,000). Comprises disbursements from current revenues or loans for construction, maintenance, interest and principal payments on highway bonds, transfers to local units, and miscellaneous. Includes transactions by state toll authorities. Data exclude amounts allocated for collection expenses, nonhighway purposes, and mass transit]

State	2000	2005	2010	2015	2017	2018	2019	2020
United States............	**89,832**	**116,517**	**145,944**	**168,242**	**168,666**	**177,582**	**184,543**	**189,346**
Alabama.....................	1,246	1,519	1,781	2,281	1,963	2,273	2,285	2,167
Alaska......................	501	643	756	1,185	(NA)	1,122	1,159	1,031
Arizona.....................	2,040	2,458	2,663	3,388	3,158	2,765	3,047	3,250
Arkansas....................	817	1,078	1,376	1,473	1,901	1,860	1,591	1,725
California..................	6,750	8,308	19,961	12,162	11,001	15,837	16,502	17,356
Colorado....................	1,392	1,652	2,249	2,632	2,081	2,225	2,333	2,650
Connecticut.................	1,304	1,434	1,761	2,097	1,975	1,947	2,117	2,117
Delaware....................	595	1,104	1,353	984	1,717	1,702	1,780	1,660
District of Columbia........	244	327	582	413	607	571	597	724
Florida.....................	4,208	7,369	7,867	9,635	10,390	11,356	11,517	11,214
Georgia.....................	1,567	2,070	2,926	3,017	4,796	4,450	3,781	3,650
Hawaii......................	272	506	460	568	702	385	415	474
Idaho.......................	492	608	959	853	790	1,025	1,097	1,037
Illinois....................	3,447	4,201	(NA)	6,783	6,350	6,317	5,761	6,830
Indiana.....................	1,932	2,235	2,839	2,636	3,360	3,072	3,495	3,245
Iowa........................	1,494	1,392	1,888	2,183	2,341	2,404	2,337	2,545
Kansas......................	1,206	1,394	1,571	1,806	1,200	1,333	1,481	1,559
Kentucky....................	1,651	1,723	2,528	3,013	2,525	2,565	2,594	2,645
Louisiana...................	1,301	1,387	2,457	2,698	2,177	2,293	1,725	1,847
Maine.......................	488	616	684	988	1,159	1,164	1,190	1,278
Maryland....................	1,599	2,049	2,255	3,395	3,673	4,380	3,441	3,316
Massachusetts...............	3,524	3,196	2,923	(NA)	4,364	(NA)	3,730	(NA)
Michigan....................	2,748	3,561	3,484	3,111	3,659	3,794	4,225	4,384
Minnesota...................	1,692	2,131	2,625	3,486	3,071	3,316	3,506	3,657
Mississippi.................	1,039	1,081	1,345	1,200	1,365	1,245	1,328	1,325
Missouri....................	1,818	2,069	2,814	2,364	2,422	2,446	2,542	2,497
Montana.....................	474	664	778	783	698	712	814	883
Nebraska....................	745	876	1,409	1,595	1,721	1,793	1,803	1,388
Nevada......................	651	865	1,007	867	1,250	1,273	1,216	1,078
New Hampshire...............	387	389	793	858	642	658	650	708
New Jersey..................	4,503	7,119	5,201	7,146	8,545	6,834	10,008	9,147
New Mexico..................	1,162	911	1,163	1,142	956	1,442	1,038	1,139
New York....................	5,307	9,638	7,711	9,821	9,735	9,597	15,290	10,103
North Carolina..............	2,621	3,698	3,646	4,324	5,334	6,128	7,289	6,330
North Dakota................	385	456	559	950	838	493	629	619
Ohio........................	3,351	4,040	4,520	5,838	5,343	5,345	5,496	6,367
Oklahoma....................	1,417	1,163	2,040	2,669	3,018	2,783	2,787	3,122
Oregon......................	1,010	1,628	1,522	2,265	2,571	(NA)	(NA)	2,567
Pennsylvania................	4,517	4,567	8,835	8,592	10,091	11,529	9,641	10,285
Rhode Island................	256	407	540	(NA)	473	488	645	824
South Carolina..............	970	1,360	1,899	1,555	1,709	2,082	2,632	2,864
South Dakota................	466	466	532	625	541	509	565	780
Tennessee...................	1,440	1,718	2,076	1,879	1,959	2,235	2,323	2,512
Texas.......................	5,665	8,918	9,365	21,222	15,372	13,866	15,541	20,921
Utah........................	1,072	986	2,303	1,622	1,571	2,006	2,007	2,415
Vermont.....................	287	310	436	568	552	568	565	598
Virginia....................	2,678	3,384	3,334	5,235	5,691	7,449	5,569	5,639
Washington..................	1,871	2,625	4,149	5,489	5,159	4,981	4,562	5,019
West Virginia...............	1,170	1,425	1,327	1,227	1,295	2,315	1,489	2,219
Wisconsin...................	1,663	2,363	2,702	3,547	3,071	3,200	3,275	3,295
Wyoming.....................	396	429	605	635	506	513	564	612

NA Not available.

Source: U.S. Federal Highway Administration, "Highway Statistics 2020," and earlier reports, <www.fhwa.dot.gov/policyinformation/statistics.cfm>, accessed March 2022.

Table 1121. Federal Highway Trust Fund—Receipts, Expenditures, and Balance: 1960 to 2020

[In millions of dollars (2,535.8 represents $2,535,800,000). For fiscal year ending September 30. Established as part of the Federal Aid Highway Act of 1956]

Year	Receipts	Expend-itures	Balance	Year	Receipts	Expend-itures	Balance
1960	2,535.8	2,940.3	119.2	2011	32,009.9	37,324.7	14,322.5
1970	5,469.0	4,378.3	2,611.6	2012	37,641.1	41,149.8	9,730.7
1980	7,647.3	9,212.3	10,999.5	2013	37,704.2	42,917.2	3,771.1
1990	13,453.1	14,375.2	9,629.0	2014	52,503.5	43,791.1	11,375.6
2000	30,347.1	26,999.8	22,553.5	2015	41,833.8	42,951.5	9,040.4
2005	32,908.6	33,121.4	10,592.3	2016	88,273.9	44,787.4	51,435.3
2007	34,309.9	34,979.2	8,110.4	2017	36,107.9	44,977.3	41,443.0
2008	39,361.3	37,011.9	10,032.2	2018	37,928.4	45,132.3	32,605.4
2009	37,317.5	37,571.3	8,881.3	2019	38,985.1	45,607.4	24,651.6
2010	44,892.5	32,006.7	20,743.3	2020	37,710.5	48,265.1	12,540.9

Source: U.S. Federal Highway Administration, "Highway Statistics 2020," <www.fhwa.dot.gov/policyinformation/statistics.cfm>, accessed February 2022.

Table 1122. Federal Highway Trust Fund Receipts from Highway Users by State: 2020

[In thousands of dollars (42,763,973 represents $42,763,973,000). For fiscal year ending September 30. Federal Highway Trust Fund receipts are reported by the U.S. Department of the Treasury. Payments into the Fund attributable to highway users in each state are estimated by the Federal Highway Administration]

State	Total	Highway account Motor fuel — Motor fuel, total	Gasoline	Special fuels	Other — Federal use tax	Trucks and trailers	Tires	Mass transit account — Gasoline	Special fuels
Total	42,763,973	30,644,666	21,424,262	9,220,404	1,462,859	4,951,354	507,042	3,971,727	1,226,325
Alabama	840,137	600,806	417,564	183,242	29,072	98,401	10,077	77,410	24,371
Alaska	95,154	64,633	38,082	26,551	4,212	14,258	1,460	7,060	3,531
Arizona	900,732	642,984	444,564	198,420	31,480	106,552	10,911	82,415	26,390
Arkansas	535,013	367,341	224,740	142,601	22,624	76,577	7,842	41,663	18,966
California	4,068,792	3,000,026	2,265,906	734,120	116,471	394,222	40,370	420,064	97,639
Colorado	691,813	499,423	356,490	142,933	22,677	76,755	7,860	66,088	19,010
Connecticut	380,634	285,731	225,678	60,053	9,528	32,249	3,302	41,837	7,987
Delaware	130,460	99,671	82,040	17,631	2,797	9,468	970	15,209	2,345
Dist. of Columbia	27,608	21,248	17,781	3,467	550	1,862	191	3,296	461
Florida	2,301,246	1,721,434	1,348,101	373,333	59,231	200,480	20,530	249,917	49,654
Georgia	1,412,805	1,026,098	744,707	281,391	44,644	151,107	15,474	138,057	37,425
Hawaii	100,602	78,824	68,563	10,261	1,628	5,510	564	12,711	1,365
Idaho	265,722	183,789	115,245	68,544	10,875	36,808	3,769	21,365	9,116
Illinois	1,429,787	1,018,329	699,430	318,899	50,595	171,248	17,537	129,664	42,414
Indiana	1,041,586	723,757	460,741	263,016	41,729	141,240	14,464	85,414	34,982
Iowa	567,012	387,555	233,444	154,111	24,450	82,758	8,475	43,277	20,497
Kansas	437,474	306,990	201,626	105,364	16,717	56,581	5,794	37,378	14,014
Kentucky	719,904	507,094	336,953	170,141	26,994	91,365	9,356	62,466	22,629
Louisiana	687,810	486,734	327,992	158,742	25,185	85,244	8,729	60,805	21,113
Maine	196,963	144,169	106,838	37,331	5,923	20,047	2,053	19,806	4,965
Maryland	701,749	524,000	408,560	115,440	18,315	61,991	6,348	75,741	15,354
Massachusetts	673,505	512,282	417,398	94,884	15,054	50,952	5,218	77,379	12,620
Michigan	1,198,213	891,115	687,897	203,218	32,241	109,128	11,175	127,526	27,028
Minnesota	794,098	561,902	378,549	183,353	29,090	98,460	10,083	70,177	24,386
Mississippi	590,856	410,788	261,970	148,818	23,611	79,915	8,184	48,565	19,793
Missouri	991,591	700,657	470,023	230,634	36,591	123,850	12,683	87,135	30,675
Montana	200,343	134,586	76,147	58,439	9,272	31,382	3,214	14,116	7,773
Nebraska	353,533	237,931	135,543	102,388	16,244	54,982	5,630	25,128	13,618
Nevada	368,107	262,781	181,706	81,075	12,863	43,537	4,458	33,685	10,783
New Hampshire	166,600	127,859	106,323	21,536	3,417	11,565	1,184	19,711	2,864
New Jersey	1,017,875	759,828	592,002	167,826	26,626	90,123	9,229	109,748	22,321
New Mexico	418,488	278,007	150,630	127,377	20,209	68,402	7,005	27,924	16,941
New York	1,597,105	1,162,217	847,963	314,254	49,858	168,754	17,281	157,199	41,796
North Carolina	1,339,190	980,598	727,392	253,206	40,172	135,972	13,924	134,847	33,677
North Dakota	203,359	131,912	64,612	67,300	10,677	36,140	3,701	11,978	8,951
Ohio	1,545,167	1,098,969	751,726	347,243	55,092	186,469	19,095	139,358	46,184
Oklahoma	706,068	480,525	285,095	195,430	31,006	104,946	10,747	52,852	25,992
Oregon	507,057	356,882	236,563	120,319	19,089	64,611	6,617	43,855	16,003
Pennsylvania	1,488,697	1,062,679	734,703	327,976	52,035	176,123	18,036	136,203	43,621
Rhode Island	96,075	72,332	57,533	14,799	2,348	7,947	814	10,666	1,968
South Carolina	845,212	604,087	419,146	184,941	29,342	99,313	10,170	77,703	24,597
South Dakota	175,845	118,704	68,386	50,318	7,983	27,021	2,767	12,678	6,692
Tennessee	1,056,630	751,749	514,705	237,044	37,608	127,293	13,035	95,418	31,527
Texas	5,018,055	3,494,624	2,240,681	1,253,943	198,944	673,367	68,956	415,388	166,776
Utah	412,374	288,206	186,899	101,307	16,073	54,402	5,571	34,648	13,474
Vermont	82,043	60,372	45,364	15,008	2,381	8,059	825	8,410	1,996
Virginia	1,270,137	924,093	673,856	250,237	39,701	134,377	13,761	124,923	33,282
Washington	813,825	595,671	441,393	154,278	24,477	82,847	8,484	81,827	20,519
West Virginia	301,611	201,838	112,538	89,300	14,168	47,954	4,911	20,863	11,877
Wisconsin	799,054	567,435	386,379	181,056	28,725	97,227	9,957	71,629	24,081
Wyoming	200,257	123,401	46,095	77,306	12,265	41,513	4,251	8,545	10,282

Source: U.S. Federal Highway Administration, "Highway Statistics 2020," <www.fhwa.dot.gov/policyinformation/>, accessed March 2022.

Table 1123. Motor Vehicle Distance Traveled by Type of Vehicle: 1970 to 2020

[1,110 represents 1,110,000,000,000. The travel data by vehicle type and stratification of trucks are estimated by the Federal Highway Administration (FHWA)]

Year	Vehicle miles of travel (bil.) [1]					Average miles traveled per vehicle (1,000) [1]				
	Total [2]	Light duty vehicle short WB [3]	Buses [4]	Light duty vehicle long WB [3]	Trucks [5,6]	Total [2]	Light duty vehicle short WB [3]	Buses [4]	Light duty vehicle long WB [3]	Trucks [5,6]
1970........	1,110	920	4.5	123	62	10.0	10.0	12.0	8.7	13.6
1975........	1,328	1,040	6.1	201	81	9.6	9.3	13.1	9.8	15.2
1980........	1,527	1,122	6.1	291	108	9.5	8.8	11.5	10.4	18.7
1985........	1,775	1,256	4.5	391	124	10.0	9.4	7.5	10.5	20.6
1990........	2,144	1,418	5.7	575	146	11.1	10.3	9.1	11.9	23.6
1995........	2,423	1,438	6.4	790	178	11.8	11.2	9.4	12.0	26.5
2000........	2,747	1,967	14.8	491	262	12.2	11.0	19.8	14.6	29.1
2001........	2,796	1,987	13.0	512	272	11.9	10.7	17.3	14.7	28.9
2002........	2,856	2,036	13.3	520	276	12.2	11.1	17.5	14.3	29.4
2003........	2,890	2,051	13.4	528	286	12.2	11.1	17.2	14.8	30.3
2004........	2,965	2,083	13.5	569	284	12.2	11.0	17.0	15.2	29.7
2005........	2,989	2,096	13.2	581	285	12.1	11.0	16.3	14.8	28.8
2006........	3,014	2,048	14.0	633	301	12.0	10.5	17.1	16.3	29.1
2007........	3,031	2,104	14.5	587	304	11.9	10.7	17.4	15.0	28.3
2008........	2,977	2,025	14.8	605	311	11.6	10.3	17.6	15.3	28.6
2009........	2,957	2,016	14.4	617	288	11.6	10.4	17.1	15.3	26.3
2010........	2,967	2,026	13.8	623	287	11.9	10.7	16.3	15.5	26.6
2011........	2,950	2,046	13.8	604	268	11.7	11.2	20.7	12.0	26.1
2012........	2,969	2,063	14.8	601	269	11.7	11.3	19.3	11.9	25.3
2013........	2,988	2,074	15.2	603	275	11.7	11.2	17.5	11.7	26.0
2014........	3,026	2,072	16.0	638	279	11.6	11.0	18.3	12.1	25.6
2015........	3,095	2,148	16.2	632	280	11.7	11.3	18.3	11.9	25.0
2016........	3,174	2,192	16.3	658	288	11.8	11.4	16.7	12.0	25.0
2017........	3,212	2,221	17.2	657	298	11.8	11.5	17.5	11.5	24.3
2018........	3,240	2,233	18.3	664	305	11.8	11.6	18.4	11.5	23.0
2019........	3,262	2,254	18.0	670	300	11.8	11.6	18.1	11.3	22.9
2020........	2,904	1,897	15.1	672	302	10.5	9.8	15.0	11.4	22.4

[1] Beginning with 2000 data, FHWA updated data using an enhanced methodology implemented in March 2011. Prior to 2000, "Light Duty Vehicles Short WB" were categorized as "Cars"; and "Light Duty Vehicles Long WB" were categorized as "Vans, pickups, sport utility vehicles." [2] Motorcycles included with "Cars" through 1994; thereafter in total, not shown separately. [3] Light Duty Vehicles Short WB—passenger cars, light trucks, vans and sport utility vehicles with a wheelbase (WB) equal to or less than 121 inches. Light Duty Vehicles Long WB—large passenger cars, vans, pickup trucks, and sport/utility vehicles with WB larger than 121 inches. [4] Includes school buses. [5] Includes combination trucks. [6] Beginning in 2000: Single-Unit—single frame trucks that have 2-axles and at least 6 tires or a gross vehicle weight rating exceeding 10,000 lbs.

Source: U.S. Federal Highway Administration, "Highway Statistics 2020," and earlier reports, <www.fhwa.dot.gov/policyinformation/statistics.cfm>, accessed March 2022.

Table 1124. Licensed Drivers, Total and as a Percent of Age Group, by Age: 2000 to 2020

[Licensed drivers in thousands (190,625 represents 190,625,000). Percentages are computed using Census Bureau data]

Age or range	Licensed drivers (1,000)							Licensed drivers as percent of age group [1]		
	2000	2010	2016	2017	2018	2019	2020	2010	2019	2020
Total.................	190,625	210,115	221,712	225,346	227,558	228,680	228,196	83.5	84.1	83.9
Under 16 years old [2].....	27	398	63	77	43	44	62	4.7	0.5	0.7
16 years old............	1,470	1,213	1,121	1,100	1,066	1,088	1,042	28.1	26.2	25.1
17 years old............	2,331	2,028	1,973	1,990	1,976	1,957	1,852	46.1	47.2	44.7
18 years old............	2,839	2,731	2,619	2,629	2,630	2,621	2,467	60.7	61.6	58.0
19 years old............	3,077	3,187	3,040	3,049	3,040	3,072	2,930	69.5	70.9	67.7
20 to 24 years old.......	15,966	17,468	17,710	17,611	17,519	17,478	17,278	80.9	80.8	79.9
20 years old............	3,140	3,426	3,250	3,253	3,249	3,254	3,237	75.8	76.2	75.8
21 years old............	3,172	3,474	3,390	3,365	3,355	3,360	3,346	79.8	78.5	78.2
22 years old............	3,182	3,483	3,547	3,528	3,506	3,508	3,444	81.7	81.6	80.1
23 years old............	3,247	3,515	3,691	3,667	3,645	3,624	3,558	83.7	83.5	81.9
24 years old............	3,225	3,571	3,832	3,797	3,764	3,733	3,694	84.0	84.0	83.1
25 to 29 years old.......	17,586	18,431	19,723	20,076	20,186	20,117	19,714	87.3	85.6	83.9
30 to 34 years old.......	19,155	17,849	19,472	19,755	19,979	20,182	20,186	89.4	90.0	90.0
35 to 39 years old.......	21,059	18,161	18,649	19,194	19,603	19,743	19,743	90.0	90.8	90.8
40 to 44 years old.......	21,093	19,178	17,852	17,897	18,043	18,247	18,465	91.8	91.6	92.7
45 to 49 years old.......	19,154	20,814	19,221	19,345	19,198	18,919	18,355	91.7	92.7	90.0
50 to 54 years old.......	16,868	20,628	20,186	19,831	19,445	19,174	19,018	92.5	93.6	92.9
55 to 59 years old.......	12,760	18,440	20,304	20,502	20,539	20,497	20,123	93.8	93.7	92.0
60 to 64 years old.......	9,915	15,858	18,076	18,677	19,042	19,243	19,294	94.3	93.5	93.8
65 to 69 years old.......	8,386	11,468	15,417	15,626	15,942	16,242	16,575	92.2	93.1	95.0
70 to 74 years old.......	7,468	8,231	10,653	11,705	12,252	12,763	13,297	88.7	91.0	94.8
75 to 79 years old.......	5,911	6,158	7,151	7,581	8,054	8,346	8,635	84.1	86.5	89.5
80 to 84 years old.......	3,511	4,464	4,606	4,723	4,936	4,880	5,169	77.7	77.3	81.8
85 and over.............	2,050	3,411	3,877	3,980	4,065	4,067	3,992	62.1	60.1	59.0

[1] Calculated based on Census Bureau population estimates for the population aged 14 and over. [2] Percent of age group data based on Census Bureau population estimates for 14- and 15-year olds.

Source: U.S. Federal Highway Administration, "Highway Statistics 2020," and earlier reports, <www.fhwa.dot.gov/policyinformation/statistics.cfm>, accessed May 2022.

Table 1125. State Motor Vehicle Registrations, 1990 to 2020; and Motorcycle Registrations and Licensed Drivers, 2020

[In thousands (188,798 represents 188,798,000). Motor vehicle registrations cover publicly, privately, and commercially owned vehicles. Some states did not provide complete current registration data. Table displays estimates by FHWA, transaction data, or previous year data; see source and earlier editions for more information. For uniformity, data have been adjusted to a calendar-year basis as registration years in states differ; figures represent net numbers where possible. See also Table 1126]

| State | Motor vehicle registrations [1] | | | | | | 2020 | | Motor-cycle registra-tions [2], in 2020 | Licensed drivers in 2020 |
	1990	2000	2010	2015	2018	2019	Total	Auto-mobile		
U.S.	188,798	221,475	242,061	255,009	264,936	267,895	267,607	105,144	8,288	228,196
AL	3,744	3,960	4,654	5,285	5,190	5,180	5,205	2,035	115	4,043
AK	477	594	710	783	772	767	766	171	27	519
AZ	2,825	3,795	4,320	5,470	5,636	5,822	5,933	2,410	121	5,681
AR	1,448	1,840	2,073	2,680	2,726	2,732	2,744	872	170	2,154
CA	21,926	27,698	31,014	28,595	30,199	30,439	29,613	14,201	772	27,005
CO	3,155	3,626	4,180	4,814	5,165	5,227	5,172	1,639	179	4,299
CT	2,623	2,853	3,082	2,755	2,792	2,793	2,787	1,211	81	2,509
DE	526	630	799	936	980	989	1,002	416	4	829
DC	262	242	212	319	348	346	353	210	3	521
FL	10,950	11,781	14,373	15,532	16,909	17,242	17,844	7,842	617	15,715
GA	5,489	7,155	7,702	7,937	8,309	8,391	8,622	3,495	208	7,522
HI	771	738	904	1,209	1,236	1,233	1,230	484	26	922
ID	1,054	1,178	1,325	1,788	1,813	1,888	1,858	588	59	1,285
IL	7,873	8,973	10,079	10,249	10,269	10,377	10,307	4,162	280	8,225
IN	4,366	5,571	5,698	5,822	5,940	5,971	5,990	2,124	210	4,533
IA	2,632	3,106	3,313	3,447	3,497	3,594	3,595	1,164	191	2,269
KS	2,012	2,296	2,436	2,539	2,589	2,590	2,513	889	91	2,004
KY	2,909	2,826	3,589	4,041	4,267	4,271	4,363	1,644	97	2,906
LA	2,995	3,557	4,086	3,787	3,771	3,762	3,760	1,316	101	3,417
ME	977	1,024	1,054	1,049	1,074	1,078	1,083	356	38	1,048
MD	3,607	3,848	4,557	4,009	4,087	4,091	4,099	1,824	113	4,454
MA	3,726	5,265	5,334	4,902	4,893	4,898	4,899	2,003	137	4,940
MI	7,209	8,436	9,286	8,037	8,128	8,187	8,216	2,692	236	7,027
MN	3,508	4,630	4,848	5,033	5,163	5,191	5,447	1,842	244	4,090
MS	1,875	2,289	2,016	2,041	2,039	2,035	2,028	788	31	2,017
MO	3,905	4,580	5,153	5,406	5,345	5,398	5,460	1,991	127	4,260
MT	783	1,026	926	1,448	1,552	1,562	1,597	459	355	827
NE	1,384	1,619	1,802	1,925	1,906	1,915	1,885	625	50	1,439
NV	853	1,220	1,362	2,242	2,440	2,472	2,480	1,028	69	2,056
NH	946	1,052	1,203	1,222	1,267	1,284	1,279	461	79	1,060
NJ	5,652	6,390	6,628	5,786	5,905	5,885	5,885	2,541	121	6,231
NM	1,301	1,529	1,612	1,760	1,764	1,765	1,728	624	55	1,473
NY	10,196	10,235	10,255	10,284	11,093	11,005	10,940	4,233	385	12,194
NC	5,162	6,223	5,743	7,740	8,022	8,340	8,550	3,398	189	7,637
ND	630	694	736	852	861	865	863	216	36	539
OH	8,410	10,467	9,801	10,152	10,504	10,495	10,212	4,248	381	8,100
OK	2,649	3,014	3,357	2,859	3,570	3,577	3,596	1,224	134	2,551
OR	2,445	3,022	3,050	3,479	3,809	3,784	3,972	1,441	123	2,945
PA	7,971	9,260	9,991	10,205	10,355	10,434	10,330	4,044	360	8,931
RI	672	760	782	843	844	845	843	382	24	732
SC	2,521	3,095	3,661	4,046	4,341	4,400	4,447	1,767	114	3,906
SD	704	793	926	986	1,149	1,157	1,165	325	129	658
TN	4,444	4,820	5,114	5,446	5,590	5,633	5,678	2,116	176	4,877
TX	12,800	14,070	17,194	21,478	21,837	22,656	22,091	8,088	326	17,667
UT	1,206	1,628	2,655	2,150	2,288	2,324	2,356	903	123	2,150
VT	462	515	567	624	589	590	579	193	29	461
VA	4,938	6,046	6,149	7,046	7,409	7,454	7,422	3,057	184	5,910
WA	4,257	5,116	4,683	6,489	6,917	7,145	7,036	2,800	221	5,813
WV	1,225	1,442	1,436	1,555	1,633	1,621	1,614	509	43	1,102
WI	3,815	4,366	4,968	5,142	5,347	5,383	5,340	1,901	276	4,316
WY	528	586	663	784	808	815	833	191	28	427

[1] Automobiles, trucks, and buses (excludes motorcycles). Excludes vehicles owned by military services. [2] Private and commercial, excluding publicly-owned.

Source: U.S. Federal Highway Administration, "Highway Statistics 2020," and earlier reports, <www.fhwa.dot.gov/policyinformation/statistics.cfm>, accessed May 2022.

Table 1126. State Motor Vehicle Registrations: 2000 to 2020

[In thousands (221,475 represents 221,475,000). Information obtained from state authorities; see source. For motorcycles; see Table 1125]

Type	2000	2010	2015	2016	2017	2018	2019	2020
All motor vehicles	221,475	242,061	255,009	260,120	263,766	264,936	267,895	267,607
Private and commercial	217,567	237,784	250,967	255,972	259,623	260,788	263,836	263,535
Publicly owned	3,908	4,277	4,042	4,148	4,142	4,148	4,059	4,072
Automobiles	133,621	130,892	112,864	112,961	111,177	111,242	108,548	105,144
Private and commercial	132,247	129,434	111,412	111,491	109,750	109,814	107,181	103,805
Publicly owned	1,374	1,458	1,453	1,471	1,427	1,429	1,367	1,339
Buses	746	846	889	976	983	992	995	1,006
Private and commercial	314	347	466	568	572	576	575	569
Publicly owned	432	499	423	409	411	417	420	438
Trucks [1]	87,108	110,322	141,256	146,182	151,605	152,702	158,352	161,457
Private and commercial	85,005	108,003	139,090	143,913	149,301	150,398	156,080	159,161
Publicly owned	2,103	2,319	2,166	2,269	2,304	2,303	2,272	2,296

[1] Includes panel, delivery, personal, passenger vans, minivans, pickups, and utility vehicles.

Source: U.S. Federal Highway Administration, "Highway Statistics 2020," and earlier reports, <www.fhwa.dot.gov/policyinformation/statistics.cfm>, accessed March 2022.

Table 1127. Domestic Motor Fuel Consumption by Type of Vehicle: 1970 to 2020

[Consumption in billions (92.3 represents 92,300,000,000 gallons). See Table 1123. Comprises all fuel types used for propulsion of vehicles under state motor fuels laws. Excludes federal purchases for military use. Minus sign (-) indicates decrease]

Year	Annual fuel consumption (bil. gal.) [1]						Average miles per gallon [1]				
	All vehicles [2]	Annual percent change [3]	Light duty vehicle short WB [4]	Buses [5]	Light duty vehicle long WB [4]	Trucks [6,7]	All vehicles [2]	Light duty vehicle short WB [4]	Buses [5]	Light duty vehicle long WB [4]	Trucks [6,7]
1970......	92.3	4.8	67.8	0.8	12.3	11.3	12.0	13.5	5.5	10.0	5.5
1980......	115.0	-5.9	70.2	1.0	23.8	20.0	13.3	16.0	6.0	12.2	5.4
1990......	130.8	-0.8	69.8	0.9	35.6	24.5	16.4	20.3	6.4	16.1	6.0
2000......	162.5	0.7	88.9	2.2	28.9	42.0	16.9	22.1	6.7	17.0	6.2
2001......	163.5	0.6	87.8	1.9	30.1	43.0	17.1	22.6	6.8	17.0	6.3
2002......	168.7	3.2	91.5	1.9	30.8	43.3	17.0	22.3	6.9	16.9	6.4
2003......	170.0	0.8	91.6	1.9	31.3	44.8	17.0	22.4	7.1	16.9	6.4
2004......	173.5	2.1	93.4	1.9	33.8	44.4	17.1	22.3	7.1	16.9	6.4
2005......	174.8	0.7	93.2	1.9	34.4	44.5	17.2	22.5	7.1	16.9	6.4
2006......	175.0	0.1	88.6	2.0	37.0	46.4	17.2	23.1	7.1	17.1	6.5
2007......	176.2	0.7	89.6	2.0	36.9	47.2	17.2	22.9	7.2	17.1	6.4
2008......	170.8	-3.1	85.6	2.1	34.9	47.7	17.4	23.7	7.2	17.3	6.5
2009......	168.1	-1.6	85.7	2.0	35.7	44.3	17.6	23.5	7.2	17.3	6.5
2010......	170.4	1.4	86.8	1.9	36.3	45.0	17.4	23.3	7.2	17.2	6.4
2011......	168.5	-1.1	88.4	1.9	35.3	42.4	17.5	23.2	7.1	17.1	6.3
2012......	168.6	0.1	88.6	2.1	35.1	42.4	17.6	23.3	7.2	17.1	6.4
2013......	169.7	0.6	88.6	2.1	35.2	46.8	17.6	23.4	7.2	17.2	6.4
2014......	173.3	2.2	89.3	2.2	37.3	44.0	17.5	23.2	7.2	17.1	6.3
2015......	172.9	-0.2	90.0	2.2	36.4	43.7	17.9	23.9	7.3	17.3	6.4
2016......	176.9	2.3	91.5	2.2	37.8	44.9	17.9	24.0	7.3	17.4	6.4
2017......	178.0	0.6	91.7	2.4	37.5	46.0	18.1	24.2	7.3	17.5	6.5
2018......	178.1	0.1	91.6	2.5	37.2	46.4	18.2	24.4	7.3	17.9	6.6
2019......	180.0	1.0	93.4	2.5	38.0	45.6	18.1	24.1	7.3	17.6	6.6
2020......	159.2	-11.6	74.9	2.1	37.0	44.8	18.2	25.3	7.4	18.2	6.7

[1] See footnote 1, Table 1123. [2] Motorcycles included with Light Duty Vehicles Short WB through 1994; thereafter in total, not shown separately. [3] Change from immediate prior year. [4] Light Duty Vehicles Short WB—passenger cars, light trucks, vans and sport utility vehicles with a wheelbase (WB) equal to or less than 121 inches. Light Duty Vehicles Long WB—large passenger cars, vans, pickup trucks, and sport/utility vehicles with WB larger than 121 inches. [5] Includes school buses. [6] Includes combination trucks. [7] Beginning 2000: Single-Unit—single frame trucks that have 2-axles and at least 6 tires or a gross vehicle weight rating over 10,000 lbs.

Source: U.S. Federal Highway Administration, "Highway Statistics 2020," and earlier reports, <www.fhwa.dot.gov/policyinformation/statistics.cfm>, accessed March 2022.

Table 1128. Alternative Fuel Vehicles—Models Available and Refueling Stations by Vehicle Fuel Type: 1995 to 2021

[Data gathered as close to September 30 as possible. The Energy Policy Act of 1992 defines alternative fuels and allows the U.S. Department of Energy (DOE) to add to the list of alternative fuels if the fuel is substantially nonpetroleum, yields substantial energy security benefits, and offers substantial environmental benefits]

Fuel type	1995	2000	2005	2010	2015	2019	2020	2021
MODELS AVAILABLE								
Total..........................	**13**	**37**	**29**	**36**	**141**	**130**	**130**	**(NA)**
Propane [1].....................	–	2	–	–	10	7	8	(NA)
Compressed natural gas (CNG) [1]..............	10	15	5	1	17	7	10	(NA)
Ethanol (E85)...................	–	8	24	34	84	40	25	(NA)
Methanol (M85).................	2	–	–	–	–	–	–	(NA)
Electric vehicle [2].............	1	12	–	1	27	72	83	(NA)
Hydrogen......................	–	–	–	–	3	4	4	(NA)
REFUELING STATIONS								
Total..........................	**4,677**	**5,205**	**5,164**	**7,111**	**22,929**	**36,290**	**41,070**	**56,528**
Propane.......................	3,299	3,268	2,995	2,604	3,749	3,176	2,956	2,869
Compressed Natural Gas (CNG)...............	1,065	1,217	787	869	1,607	1,576	1,549	1,532
LNG (Liquid Natural Gas).......................	(NA)	44	40	43	117	118	106	102
Biodiesel [3]....................	–	2	304	615	713	611	712	722
Ethanol (E85)..................	37	113	436	2,296	3,012	3,786	3,946	4,196
Methanol (M85).................	88	3	–	–	–	–	–	–
Electric vehicle [4].............	188	558	588	626	13,696	26,959	31,738	47,040
Hydrogen......................	(NA)	(NA)	14	58	35	64	63	67

– Represents zero. NA Not available. [1] Dedicated and bi-fuel vehicles. [2] Electric vehicles include plug-in hybrid-electric vehicles but do not include neighborhood electric vehicles, low-speed electric vehicles, or two-wheeled electric vehicles. [3] Stations selling biodiesel blends less than B20 are only included in the 2005-2007 station counts. [4] Electric vehicle station is one geographic location where electric vehicles can charge.

Source: U.S. Department of Energy, Office of Energy Efficiency and Renewable Energy, *Transportation Energy Data Book*, Edition 40, February 2022. See also <tedb.ornl.gov>.

Table 1129. Traffic Fatalities—Number and Rate by State: 2000 to 2020

[For deaths within 30 days of the accident]

State	2000	2010	2019	2020	Fatality rate [1] 2010	Fatality rate [1] 2020	State	2000	2010	2019	2020	Fatality rate [1] 2010	Fatality rate [1] 2020
U.S.	41,945	32,999	36,096	38,824	1.11	1.34	MO	1,157	821	880	987	1.16	1.36
AL	996	862	930	934	1.34	1.38	MT	237	189	184	213	1.69	1.76
AK	106	56	67	64	1.17	1.21	NE	276	190	248	233	0.98	1.20
AZ	1,036	759	981	1,054	1.27	1.60	NV	323	257	304	317	1.16	1.26
AR	652	571	505	638	1.70	1.88	NH	126	128	101	104	0.98	0.87
CA	3,753	2,720	3,606	3,847	0.84	1.28	NJ	731	556	559	584	0.76	0.88
CO	681	450	596	622	0.96	1.28	NM	432	349	424	398	1.38	1.68
CT	341	320	249	295	1.02	0.99	NY	1,460	1,201	931	1,046	0.92	1.02
DE	123	101	132	116	1.13	1.39	NC	1,557	1,320	1,373	1,538	1.29	1.45
DC	48	24	23	36	0.67	1.19	ND	86	105	100	100	1.27	1.14
FL	2,999	2,444	3,183	3,331	1.25	1.60	OH	1,366	1,080	1,153	1,230	0.97	1.19
GA	1,541	1,247	1,491	1,664	1.12	1.43	OK	650	668	640	652	1.40	1.55
HI	132	113	108	85	1.13	0.97	OR	451	317	489	508	0.94	1.57
ID	276	209	224	214	1.32	1.23	PA	1,520	1,324	1,059	1,129	1.32	1.28
IL	1,418	927	1,009	1,194	0.88	1.27	RI	80	67	57	67	0.81	0.98
IN	886	754	809	897	1.00	1.17	SC	1,065	809	1,001	1,064	1.65	1.97
IA	445	390	336	337	1.24	1.13	SD	173	140	102	141	1.58	1.45
KS	461	431	411	426	1.44	1.53	TN	1,307	1,032	1,135	1,217	1.47	1.59
KY	820	760	732	780	1.58	1.68	TX	3,779	3,023	3,615	3,874	1.29	1.49
LA	938	721	727	828	1.59	1.71	UT	373	253	248	276	0.95	0.91
ME	169	161	157	164	1.11	1.25	VT	76	71	47	62	0.98	1.03
MD	588	496	521	567	0.88	1.11	VA	929	740	831	850	0.90	1.12
MA	433	347	334	343	0.64	0.63	WA	631	460	519	560	0.80	1.04
MI	1,382	942	985	1,084	0.97	1.25	WV	411	315	260	267	1.64	1.66
MN	625	411	364	394	0.73	0.76	WI	799	572	566	614	0.96	1.07
MS	949	641	643	752	1.61	1.90	WY	152	155	147	127	1.66	1.30

[1] Deaths per 100 million vehicle miles traveled.

Source: U.S. National Highway Traffic Safety Administration, "Traffic Safety Facts Annual Report Tables," <cdan.nhtsa.gov/tsftables/tsfar.htm>, and "Fatality Analysis Reporting System," <www.nhtsa.gov/research-data/fatality-analysis-reporting-system-fars>; accessed June 2022.

Table 1130. Motor Vehicle Occupants and Nonoccupants Killed and Injured: 1990 to 2020

[Injuries in thousands (3,206 represents 3,206,000). For deaths within 30 days of the accident. Beginning 2016, data for persons injured are not comparable to previous years due to a new data collection system. The National Automotive Sampling System (NASS) GES (General Estimates System) was replaced with the Crash Report Sampling System (CRSS). See <crashstats.nhtsa.dot.gov/Api/Public/ViewPublication/812509> for details]

Year	Total	Occupants Total	Occupants Passenger cars	Occupants Light trucks [1]	Occupants Large trucks [1]	Occupants Buses	Occupants Other/unknown [2]	Motorcycle occupants [3]	Nonoccupants Total	Nonoccupants Pedestrian	Nonoccupants Pedalcyclist	Nonoccupants Other/unknown [2]
KILLED												
1990	44,599	33,890	24,092	8,601	705	32	460	3,244	7,465	6,482	859	124
2000	41,945	33,451	20,699	11,526	754	22	450	2,897	5,597	4,763	693	141
2005	43,510	33,070	18,512	13,037	804	58	659	4,576	5,864	4,892	786	186
2008	37,423	26,791	14,646	10,816	682	67	580	5,312	5,320	4,414	718	188
2009	33,883	24,526	13,135	10,312	499	26	554	4,469	4,888	4,109	628	151
2010	32,999	23,371	12,491	9,782	530	44	524	4,518	5,110	4,302	623	185
2011	32,479	22,510	12,014	9,302	640	55	499	4,630	5,339	4,457	682	200
2012	33,782	23,017	12,361	9,418	697	39	502	4,986	5,779	4,818	734	227
2013	32,893	22,483	12,037	9,186	695	54	511	4,692	5,718	4,779	749	190
2014	32,744	22,307	11,947	9,103	656	44	557	4,594	5,843	4,910	729	204
2015	35,484	23,899	12,763	9,878	665	49	544	5,029	6,556	5,494	829	233
2016	37,806	25,276	13,508	10,279	815	64	610	5,337	7,193	6,080	853	260
2017	37,473	25,130	13,477	10,186	878	43	546	5,226	7,117	6,075	806	236
2018	36,835	24,332	12,888	9,957	890	44	553	5,038	7,465	6,374	871	220
2019	36,355	23,891	12,355	10,017	893	35	591	5,044	7,420	6,272	859	289
2020	38,824	25,536	13,472	10,352	831	16	865	5,579	7,709	6,516	938	255
INJURED (1,000)												
1990	3,206	2,935	2,360	499	40	33	4	84	186	105	75	7
2000	3,194	3,001	2,057	886	31	17	10	58	135	78	51	6
2005	2,709	2,504	1,580	874	28	12	10	88	118	65	45	8
2008	2,356	2,130	1,308	773	24	16	9	96	130	69	52	9
2009	2,224	2,017	1,219	762	16	13	7	89	117	59	51	7
2010	2,248	2,036	1,256	737	20	18	5	82	130	70	52	8
2011	2,227	2,019	1,244	733	23	14	6	82	126	69	48	9
2012	2,369	2,140	1,330	766	25	12	6	93	136	76	49	10
2013	2,319	2,105	1,299	753	25	24	5	89	125	66	48	11
2014	2,343	2,125	1,294	784	27	14	6	92	125	65	50	10
2015	2,455	2,241	1,382	809	30	12	8	89	125	70	45	10
2016 [4]	3,062	2,791	1,690	1,035	36	25	5	104	166	86	64	16
2017 [4]	2,745	2,523	1,529	937	40	12	5	89	133	71	50	12
2018 [4]	2,710	2,492	1,511	921	39	15	5	82	137	75	47	15
2019 [4]	2,740	2,516	1,498	950	46	15	7	84	140	76	49	16
2020 [4]	2,282	2,093	1,221	814	45	7	7	83	106	55	39	13

[1] See footnotes 2 and 3, Table 1132. [2] Includes combination trucks. [3] Includes mopeds, three wheel motorcycles, off-road motorcycles, etc. [4] Beginning 2016, data are not comparable to previous years due to a new data collection system. Numbers are not actual counts but estimates of actual counts.

Source: U.S. National Highway Traffic Safety Administration, "Traffic Safety Facts Annual Report Tables," <cdan.nhtsa.gov/tsftables/tsfar.htm>, accessed June 2022. See also <www.nhtsa.gov/research>.

Table 1131. Fatal Motor Vehicle Accidents—National Summary: 2000 to 2020

[Based on data from the Fatality Analysis Reporting System (FARS). FARS gathers data on accidents that result in loss of human life. FARS is operated and maintained by National Highway Traffic Safety Administration's (NHTSA), National Center for Statistics and Analysis (NCSA). FARS data are gathered on motor vehicle accidents that occurred on a roadway customarily open to the public, resulting in the death of a person within 30 days of the accident. Collection of these data depend on the use of police, hospital, medical examiner/coroner, and Emergency Medical Services reports; state vehicle registration, driver licensing, and highway department files; and vital statistics documents and death certificates. See source for further detail]

Item	2000	2010	2015	2016	2017	2018	2019	2020
Fatal crashes, total	**37,526**	**30,296**	**32,538**	**34,748**	**34,560**	**33,919**	**33,487**	**35,766**
One vehicle involved	21,117	18,221	18,902	20,264	19,714	19,263	19,041	20,753
Two or more vehicles involved	16,409	12,075	13,636	14,484	14,846	14,656	14,446	15,013
Occupants involved	94,325	69,418	74,624	78,850	78,281	76,479	75,061	77,759
Drivers involved	57,280	44,599	49,163	52,399	52,752	51,905	51,302	53,890
Persons killed in fatal crashes [1]	**41,945**	**32,999**	**35,484**	**37,806**	**37,473**	**36,835**	**36,355**	**38,824**
Occupants	33,451	23,371	23,899	25,276	25,130	24,332	23,891	25,536
Drivers	22,914	16,864	17,615	18,717	18,819	18,321	17,984	19,519
Passengers	10,451	6,451	6,213	6,485	6,237	5,962	5,846	5,966
Other	86	56	71	74	74	49	61	51
Motorcyclists	2,897	4,518	5,029	5,337	5,226	5,038	5,044	5,579
Nonoccupants	5,597	5,110	6,556	7,193	7,117	7,465	7,420	7,709
Pedestrians	4,763	4,302	5,494	6,080	6,075	6,374	6,272	6,516
Pedalcyclists	693	623	829	853	806	871	859	938
Other	141	185	233	260	236	220	289	255
Occupants killed by vehicle type:								
Passenger cars	20,699	12,491	12,763	13,508	13,477	12,888	12,355	13,472
Mini-compact (95 inches)	1,113	171	135	140	145	178	(NA)	(NA)
Subcompact (95 to 99 inches)	3,660	1,259	1,018	943	949	867	(NA)	(NA)
Compact (100 to 104 inches)	7,022	3,977	3,532	3,669	3,475	3,291	(NA)	(NA)
Intermediate (105 to 109 inches)	5,204	4,244	4,621	4,966	5,145	4,850	(NA)	(NA)
Full-size (110 to 114 inches)	2,287	1,993	2,353	2,549	2,478	2,507	(NA)	(NA)
Largest (115 inches and over)	897	685	796	875	915	801	(NA)	(NA)
Unknown	516	162	308	366	370	394	(NA)	(NA)
Motorcycles and other motorized cycles	2,897	4,518	5,029	5,337	5,226	5,038	5,044	5,579
Motorcycles	2,783	4,281	4,696	4,971	4,765	4,589	4,589	5,006
Other motorized cycles	114	237	333	366	461	449	455	573
Light trucks [2]	11,526	9,782	9,878	10,279	10,186	9,957	10,017	10,352
Pickup	6,003	4,486	4,471	4,470	4,335	4,267	4,213	4,330
Utility	3,358	3,942	4,213	4,462	4,610	4,554	4,727	5,075
Van	2,129	1,346	1,128	1,240	1,175	1,081	1,025	933
Other	36	8	66	107	66	55	52	14
Large trucks [3]	754	530	665	815	878	890	893	831
Buses	22	44	49	64	43	44	35	16
Other/unknown vehicles	450	524	544	610	546	553	591	865
Persons killed, and % distribution by highest driver BAC in the crash [6]	41,945	32,999	35,484	37,806	37,473	36,835	36,355	38,824
0.00 percent	62	64	65	65	66	66	67	64
0.01 to 0.07 percent	6	5	5	5	5	5	5	5
0.08 percent and over	32	31	29	29	29	29	28	30
Drivers in fatal crashes by BAC [6]	57,280	44,599	49,163	52,399	52,752	51,905	51,302	53,890
0.00 percent	42,643	33,190	37,529	40,005	40,497	39,735	39,762	40,785
0.01 to 0.07 percent	2,376	1,812	1,964	2,041	1,937	1,911	1,911	2,083
0.08 percent and over	12,261	9,598	9,670	10,353	10,318	10,259	9,629	11,022
Fatalities per 100,000 resident population:								
Under 5 years old	3.70	2.00	1.90	2.01	2.03	1.78	1.64	1.62
5 to 9 years old	3.55	1.74	1.73	1.88	1.58	1.65	1.61	1.52
10 to 15 years old	5.65	2.71	2.46	2.65	2.50	2.09	2.37	2.70
16 to 20 years old	29.38	15.44	14.85	15.20	14.72	13.70	12.71	14.77
21 to 24 years old	27.02	19.49	18.89	20.07	18.80	18.39	17.18	19.21
25 to 34 years old	17.29	13.47	14.39	15.50	15.05	14.90	14.34	16.74
35 to 44 years old	15.08	11.09	11.64	12.41	12.50	12.17	12.37	13.85
45 to 54 years old	13.79	11.32	12.33	12.55	12.72	12.48	12.21	12.94
55 to 64 years old	13.61	10.94	11.92	12.62	12.86	12.87	12.69	13.22
65 to 74 years old	15.29	10.96	11.42	12.07	11.13	11.64	11.67	10.85
75 years old and over	23.29	16.80	15.36	16.47	16.83	15.64	15.90	13.05
Fatalities per 100 million VMT [4]	1.53	1.11	1.15	1.19	1.17	1.14	1.11	1.34
Fatalities per 100,000 licensed drivers	22.00	15.71	16.27	17.05	16.63	16.19	15.88	17.01
VMT per registered vehicle [4]	12,657	11,531	10,984	11,020	11,056	10,908	10,900	9,757
Fatalities per 100,000 registered vehicles	19.33	12.82	12.61	13.13	12.91	12.40	12.15	13.04
Fatal crashes per 100 million VMT [4]	1.37	1.02	1.05	1.09	1.08	1.05	1.03	1.23
Fatalities per 100,000 resident population	14.87	10.67	11.06	11.70	11.53	11.27	11.07	11.78
Vehicle miles traveled (VMT) (bil.)	2,747	2,967	3,090	3,174	3,210	3,240	3,262	2,904
Licensed drivers (1,000)	190,625	210,115	218,084	221,712	225,346	227,558	228,916	228,196
Registered vehicles (1,000) [5]	217,028	257,312	281,312	288,034	290,336	297,036	299,267	297,644

NA Not available. [1] Deaths within 30 days of the crash. [2] Trucks with a gross vehicle weight rating of 10,000 pounds or less, including pickups, vans, truck-based station wagons, and utility vehicles. [3] Trucks with a gross vehicle weight rating of over 10,000 pounds. [4] VMT = vehicle miles of travel. [5] Data on motor vehicle registrations for 2011 and beyond are not strictly comparable to data for prior years due to methodology changes. See source for details. [6] BAC = blood alcohol concentration. NHTSA estimates alcohol involvement when test results are unknown. Includes crashes in which there was no driver present.

Source: National Highway Traffic Safety Administration, *Traffic Safety Facts, 2017*, and earlier reports; and "Traffic Safety Facts Annual Report Tables," <cdan.nhtsa.gov/tsftables/tsfar.htm> and "Fatality Analysis Reporting System," <www-fars.nhtsa.dot.gov/Main/index.aspx>, accessed August 2022. See also <www.nhtsa.gov/research>.

Table 1132. Vehicles Involved in Crashes by Vehicle Type, Rollover Occurrence, and Crash Severity: 2020

[Excludes motorcycles. Beginning 2016, data for injury and property damage only crashes are not comparable to previous years due to a new data collection system. The National Automotive Sampling System (NASS) General Estimates System (GES) was replaced with the Crash Report Sampling System (CRSS). See <crashstats.nhtsa.dot.gov/Api/Public/ViewPublication/812509> for details]

Crash severity by vehicle type	Total	Rollover occurrence			
		Yes		No	
	Number	Number	Percent	Number	Percent
Vehicles involved in all crashes [1]	**9,038,212**	**216,246**	**2.4**	**8,821,966**	**97.6**
Passenger cars	4,747,597	81,984	1.7	4,665,613	98.3
Light trucks: [2]					
Pickup	1,333,440	46,499	3.5	1,286,940	96.5
Utility	2,051,929	58,965	2.9	1,992,964	97.1
Van	406,500	5,496	1.4	401,004	98.6
Other	9,310	8	0.1	9,302	99.9
Large truck [3]	439,206	19,507	4.4	419,699	95.6
Bus	31,161	121	0.4	31,041	99.6
Other/unknown	19,069	3,667	19.2	15,402	80.8
Fatal crashes	**48,557**	**8,246**	**17.0**	**40,311**	**83.0**
Passenger cars	20,868	2,895	13.9	17,973	86.1
Light trucks: [2]					
Pickup	8,789	1,953	22.2	6,836	77.8
Utility	9,913	2,165	21.8	7,748	78.2
Van	1,800	220	12.2	1,580	87.8
Other	64	8	12.5	56	87.5
Large truck [3]	4,842	584	12.1	4,258	87.9
Bus	156	8	5.1	148	94.9
Other/unknown	2,125	413	19.4	1,712	80.6
Injury crashes	**2,765,636**	**127,195**	**4.6**	**2,638,441**	**95.4**
Passenger cars	1,514,640	50,735	3.3	1,463,905	96.7
Light trucks: [2]					
Pickup	375,726	24,982	6.6	350,743	93.4
Utility	627,045	35,684	5.7	591,361	94.3
Van	123,328	3,796	3.1	119,531	96.9
Other	3,136	(Z)	(Z)	3,136	100.0
Large truck [3]	106,902	9,403	8.8	97,499	91.2
Bus	7,481	113	1.5	7,369	98.5
Other/unknown	7,379	2,481	33.6	4,898	66.4

Z less than 500 or 0.05 percent. [1] Includes property-only crashes, not shown separately. [2] Light trucks of 10,000 pounds gross vehicle weight rating or less, including pickups, vans, truck-based station wagons and utility vehicles. [3] Large trucks over 10,000 pounds gross vehicle weight rating.

Source: U.S. National Highway Traffic Safety Administration, "Traffic Safety Facts Annual Report Tables," <cdan.nhtsa.gov/tsftables/tsfar.htm>, accessed June 2022. See also <www.nhtsa.gov/research>.

Table 1133. Distracted Drivers—Crashes, Road Fatalities, and Injuries: 2010 to 2020

["Distraction" is defined as a specific type of inattention that occurs when drivers divert their attention from the driving task to focus on some other activity instead. "Distraction" is a subset of "inattention" (which also includes fatigue and physical and emotional conditions of the driver). For more information, including revision in coding of "distracted driving," see appendix in source report]

Description	2010	2015	2016	2017	2018	2019	2020
FATAL CRASHES [1]							
Total	30,296	32,538	34,748	34,560	33,919	33,487	35,766
Drivers involved	44,599	49,163	52,399	52,752	51,905	51,302	53,890
Fatalities	32,999	35,484	37,806	37,473	36,835	36,355	38,824
Crashes involving driver distraction [2]	**2,993**	**3,242**	**3,197**	**3,003**	**2,645**	**2,872**	**2,880**
Percent	10	10	9	9	8	9	8
Involving cell phone use	366	453	453	418	356	395	354
Percent	12	14	14	14	13	14	12
Drivers involved	3,064	3,313	3,252	3,065	2,704	2,979	2,968
Percent	7	7	6	6	5	6	6
Fatalities	3,267	3,526	3,490	3,242	2,858	3,119	3,142
Percent	10	10	9	9	8	9	8
INJURY CRASHES [3] (ESTIMATED)							
Total	1,542,000	1,715,000	2,116,308	1,888,525	1,893,704	1,916,344	1,593,390
People injured	2,248,000	2,455,000	3,061,885	2,745,268	2,710,059	2,740,141	2,282,015
In crashes involving driver distraction	416,000	393,000	444,623	434,733	400,303	423,847	324,652
Percent of total	19	16	15	16	15	15	14
In crashes involving cell phone use	24,000	30,000	33,864	31,076	32,632	28,300	29,999
Percent of total distracted	6	8	8	7	8	7	9

[1] Data from NHTSA's Fatality Analysis Reporting System (FARS). [2] For multiple-vehicle crashes, the crash was reported as a distracted-driving crash if at least one driver was reported as distracted. In some of these multiple-vehicle crashes, multiple drivers were reported as distracted. [3] Data for 2010 to 2015 are from the National Automotive Sampling System (NASS) General Estimates System (GES). Beginning 2016, data are from the Crash Report Sampling System (CRSS). CRSS estimates and NASS GES estimates are not comparable due to different sample designs. See <www.nhtsa.gov/crash-data-systems/crash-report-sampling-system-crss> for details.

Source: U.S. National Highway Traffic Safety Administration, *Distracted Driving, 2020*, May 2022, and earlier reports. See also <www-fars.nhtsa.dot.gov/> and <nhtsa.gov/risky-driving/distracted-driving>.

Table 1134. Traffic Fatalities by State and Highest Driver Blood Alcohol Concentration (BAC) in the Crash: 2020

[A crash is a police-reported event that produces injury and/or property damage, involves a vehicle in transport, and occurs on a trafficway or while the vehicle is in motion after running off the trafficway. A positive blood alcohol concentration (BAC level of .01 grams per deciliter and higher) indicates that alcohol was consumed by the person tested, and the incident is alcohol related or alcohol involved; a BAC level of .08 g/dL or more indicates that the person was alcohol impaired]

State	Traffic fatalities, total [1]	Traffic fatalities not involving alcohol (BAC=.00)		Alcohol involved driving fatalities (BAC=.01–.07)		Alcohol impaired driving fatalities (BAC=.08 or more)		Total fatalities involving alcohol (BAC=.01 or more)	
		Number	Percent	Number	Percent	Number	Percent	Number	Percent
United States [2]	**38,824**	**25,038**	**64**	**2,041**	**5**	**11,654**	**30**	**13,695**	**35**
Alabama	934	641	69	54	6	236	25	290	31
Alaska	64	45	70	5	8	14	22	19	30
Arizona	1,054	711	67	48	5	293	28	341	32
Arkansas	638	432	68	40	6	166	26	206	32
California	3,847	2,474	64	209	5	1,159	30	1,367	36
Colorado	622	406	65	28	5	186	30	214	34
Connecticut	295	161	54	17	6	118	40	135	46
Delaware	116	81	70	3	3	27	23	30	26
District of Columbia	36	25	69	4	11	7	21	11	31
Florida	3,331	2,291	69	166	5	871	26	1,037	31
Georgia	1,664	1,178	71	78	5	402	24	481	29
Hawaii	85	51	60	8	9	27	31	34	40
Idaho	214	138	64	15	7	61	29	76	36
Illinois	1,194	752	63	61	5	379	32	441	37
Indiana	897	612	68	36	4	249	28	285	32
Iowa	337	203	60	21	6	113	34	134	40
Kansas	426	317	74	12	3	96	23	108	25
Kentucky	780	546	70	34	4	199	26	233	30
Louisiana	828	536	65	53	6	233	28	286	35
Maine	164	93	56	8	5	64	39	72	44
Maryland	567	356	63	28	5	183	32	211	37
Massachusetts	343	226	66	17	5	98	29	115	34
Michigan	1,084	719	66	58	5	306	28	364	34
Minnesota	394	260	66	25	6	107	27	132	34
Mississippi	752	566	75	25	3	162	21	186	25
Missouri	987	616	62	51	5	312	32	362	37
Montana	213	105	49	13	6	96	45	108	51
Nebraska	233	147	63	13	6	73	31	86	37
Nevada	317	214	68	17	5	83	26	101	32
New Hampshire	104	62	59	5	5	37	36	43	41
New Jersey	584	402	69	32	5	151	26	182	31
New Mexico	398	253	64	14	4	130	33	144	36
New York	1,046	695	66	63	6	286	27	349	33
North Carolina	1,538	1,001	65	81	5	454	30	536	35
North Dakota	100	59	59	5	5	35	35	40	40
Ohio	1,230	706	57	70	6	448	36	518	42
Oklahoma	652	438	67	30	5	179	27	209	32
Oregon	508	287	56	30	6	191	38	221	44
Pennsylvania	1,129	750	66	50	4	322	29	371	33
Rhode Island	67	34	51	5	7	28	42	33	49
South Carolina	1,064	680	64	69	6	315	30	384	36
South Dakota	141	84	60	7	5	49	35	56	40
Tennessee	1,217	838	69	53	4	326	27	379	31
Texas	3,874	2,138	55	232	6	1,495	39	1,727	45
Utah	276	206	75	12	4	58	21	70	25
Vermont	62	40	64	4	6	18	28	21	34
Virginia	850	520	61	42	5	286	34	328	39
Washington	560	321	57	39	7	199	35	238	43
West Virginia	267	177	66	14	5	76	29	90	34
Wisconsin	614	372	61	32	5	210	34	242	39
Wyoming	127	76	60	7	5	44	34	50	39
Puerto Rico	242	148	61	15	6	77	32	92	38

[1] Total fatalities include those in which there was no driver or motorcycle rider present. [2] U.S. total excludes Puerto Rico.

Source: U.S. National Highway Traffic Safety Administration, "Traffic Safety Facts Annual Report Tables," <cdan.nhtsa.gov/tsftables/tsfar.htm>, accessed July 2022. See also <www.nhtsa.gov/research>.

Table 1135. Alcohol Involvement for Drivers in Fatal Crashes: 2000 to 2020

[BAC = blood alcohol concentration. See headnote, Table 1134. NHTSA estimates alcohol involvement when alcohol test results are unknown; see source for more information]

Age, sex, and vehicle type	2000 Total drivers in fatal crashes	2000 Percent with .08% BAC or greater	2010 Total drivers in fatal crashes	2010 Percent with .08% BAC or greater	2015 Total drivers in fatal crashes	2015 Percent with .08% BAC or greater	2019 Total drivers in fatal crashes	2019 Percent with .08% BAC or greater	2020 Total drivers in fatal crashes	2020 Percent with .08% BAC or greater
Total drivers involved in fatal crashes [1]	57,280	21	44,599	22	49,163	20	51,302	19	53,890	20
Drivers by age group:										
Under 16 years old	320	10	159	6	155	9	139	10	209	12
16 to 20 years old	8,024	18	4,505	18	4,258	16	3,921	15	4,440	17
21 to 24 years old	5,950	32	4,608	34	5,014	28	4,636	27	4,884	26
25 to 34 years old	11,739	28	8,567	30	9,994	27	10,592	25	11,933	26
35 to 44 years old	11,132	26	7,333	25	7,768	23	8,382	22	8,896	23
45 to 54 years old	8,234	18	7,517	21	7,915	19	7,581	18	7,731	19
55 to 64 years old	4,766	12	5,577	14	6,525	14	7,216	15	7,294	16
65 to 74 years old	3,134	8	2,902	8	3,794	9	4,425	10	4,116	12
75 years old and over	3,147	4	2,688	4	2,762	6	3,252	6	2,810	7
Drivers by sex:										
Male	41,795	24	32,079	24	35,850	22	37,196	20	39,393	22
Female	14,790	13	11,859	15	12,382	14	13,000	14	13,033	16
Drivers by vehicle type:										
Passenger cars	27,661	24	17,710	24	19,689	21	19,689	20	20,742	23
Light trucks [2]	20,393	22	17,385	22	18,762	21	19,817	19	20,402	19
Large trucks [3]	4,948	1	3,456	1	4,020	2	4,977	2	4,778	3
Motorcycles	2,971	32	4,647	28	5,126	26	5,143	28	5,711	27

[1] Includes age and sex unknown, and other and unknown types of vehicles. [2] See footnote 2, Table 1132. [3] See footnote 3, Table 1132.

Source: U.S. National Highway Traffic Safety Administration, "Traffic Safety Facts Annual Report Tables," <cdan.nhtsa.gov/tsftables/tsfar.htm>, accessed June 2022. See also <www.nhtsa.gov/research>.

Table 1136. Fatalities by Highest Driver Blood Alcohol Concentration (BAC) in the Crash: 1990 to 2020

[A motor vehicle crash is alcohol impaired if at least one driver involved in the crash is determined to have a BAC of .08 gram per deciliter (g/dl) or higher. Thus, any fatality that occurs in an alcohol impaired crash is considered an alcohol impaired driving fatality. A person is considered to be legally impaired with a BAC of .08 g/dl or more. See source for more information]

Item	1990	2000	2005	2010	2015	2017	2018	2019	2020
Total fatalities [1]	44,599	41,945	43,510	32,999	35,484	37,473	36,835	36,355	38,824
BAC=.00									
Number	23,823	26,082	27,423	21,005	23,165	24,589	24,186	24,251	25,038
Percent	53.4	62.2	63.0	63.7	65.3	65.6	65.7	66.7	64.5
BAC=.01–.07									
Number	2,901	2,422	2,404	1,771	1,930	1,895	1,850	1,834	2,041
Percent	6.5	5.8	5.5	5.4	5.4	5.1	5.0	5.0	5.3
Alcohol impaired driving fatalities: BAC=.08 or more									
Number	17,705	13,324	13,582	10,136	10,280	10,880	10,710	10,196	11,654
Percent	39.7	31.8	31.2	30.7	29.0	29.0	29.1	28.0	30.0

[1] Total fatalities include those in which there was no driver or motorcycle rider present.

Source: U.S. National Highway Traffic Safety Administration, "Traffic Safety Facts Annual Report Tables," <cdan.nhtsa.gov/tsftables/tsfar.htm>, accessed June 2022. See also <www.nhtsa.gov/research>.

Table 1137. Motor Vehicle Crashes by Crash Severity: 2000 to 2020

[6,394 represents 6,394,000. A crash is a police-reported event that produces injury and/or property damage, involves a vehicle in transport, and occurs on a trafficway or while the vehicle is in motion after running off the trafficway. A fatal crash involves at least 1 person dying within 30 days of the crash. Beginning 2016, data for injury and property damage crashes are not comparable to previous years due to a new data collection system. The National Automotive Sampling System (NASS) General Estimates System (GES) was replaced with the Crash Report Sampling System (CRSS). See <crashstats.nhtsa.dot.gov/Api/Public/ViewPublication/812509> for details]

Item	2000	2010	2014	2015	2016 [1]	2017 [1]	2018 [1]	2019 [1]	2020 [1]
Crashes (1,000)	6,394	5,419	6,064	6,296	6,821	6,453	6,735	6,756	5,251
Fatal	37.5	30.3	30.1	32.5	34.7	34.6	33.9	33.5	35.8
Nonfatal injury	2,070	1,542	1,648	1,715	2,116	1,889	1,894	1,916	1,593
Property damage only	4,286	3,847	4,387	4,548	4,670	4,530	4,807	4,806	3,622
Percent of total crashes:									
Fatal	0.6	0.6	0.5	0.5	0.5	0.5	0.5	0.5	0.7
Nonfatal injury	32.4	28.5	27.2	27.2	31.0	29.3	28.1	28.4	30.3
Property damage only	67.0	71.0	72.3	72.2	68.5	70.2	71.4	71.1	69.0

[1] Beginning 2016, injury and property damage only data are not comparable to previous years due to a new data collection system. Numbers are not actual counts but estimates of actual counts.

Source: U.S. National Highway Traffic Safety Administration, "Traffic Safety Facts Annual Report Tables," <cdan.nhtsa.gov/tsftables/tsfar.htm>, accessed June 2022. See also <www.nhtsa.gov/research>.

Table 1138. Motor Vehicle Crashes—Number and Deaths: 2000 to 2020

[6,394 represents 6,394,000. Beginning 2016, data for injury and property damage crashes are not comparable to previous years due to a new data collection system. The National Automotive Sampling System (NASS) General Estimates System (GES) was replaced with the Crash Report Sampling System (CRSS). See <crashstats.nhtsa.dot.gov/Api/Public/ViewPublication/812509> for details]

Item	Unit	2000	2010	2015	2016	2017	2018	2019	2020
CRASHES									
Total [1,2]	1,000	**6,394**	**5,419**	**6,296**	**6,821**	**6,453**	**6,735**	**6,756**	**5,251**
Fatal	1,000	38	30	33	35	35	34	33	36
Injury [2]	1,000	2,070	1,542	1,715	2,116	1,889	1,894	1,916	1,593
Property damage only [2]	1,000	4,286	3,847	4,548	4,670	4,530	4,807	4,806	3,622
DEATHS									
Deaths within 30 days of crash	Number	**41,945**	**32,999**	**35,484**	**37,806**	**37,473**	**36,835**	**36,355**	**38,824**
Occupants	Number	33,451	23,371	23,899	25,276	25,130	24,332	23,891	25,536
Passenger cars	Number	20,699	12,491	12,763	13,508	13,477	12,888	12,355	13,472
Light trucks [3]	Number	11,526	9,782	9,878	10,279	10,186	9,957	10,017	10,352
Large trucks [3]	Number	754	530	665	815	878	890	893	831
Buses	Number	22	44	49	64	43	44	35	16
Other/unknown	Number	450	524	544	610	546	553	591	865
Motorcycle riders [4]	Number	2,897	4,518	5,029	5,337	5,226	5,038	5,044	5,579
Nonoccupants	Number	5,597	5,110	6,556	7,193	7,117	7,465	7,420	7,709
Pedestrians	Number	4,763	4,302	5,494	6,080	6,075	6,374	6,272	6,516
Pedalcyclist	Number	693	623	829	853	806	871	859	938
Other/unknown	Number	141	185	233	260	236	220	289	255
TRAFFIC DEATH RATES [5]									
Per 100 million vehicle miles	Rate	1.5	1.1	1.2	1.2	1.2	1.1	1.1	1.3
Per 100,000 licensed drivers	Rate	22.0	15.7	16.3	17.1	16.6	16.2	15.9	17.0
Per 100,000 registered vehicles	Rate	19.3	12.8	12.6	13.1	12.9	12.4	12.2	13.0
Per 100,000 resident population	Rate	14.9	10.7	11.1	11.7	11.5	11.3	11.1	11.8

[1] Covers police-reported accidents in which at least one person dies within 30 days of the crash; or no one dies but at least one person is injured; or no one is injured but property damage has occurred. [2] Beginning 2016, injury and property damage only data are not comparable to previous years due to a new data collection system. Numbers are not actual counts but estimates of actual counts. [3] See footnotes 2 and 3 in Table 1132. [4] Includes motor scooters, minibikes, and mopeds. [5] Based on 30-day definition of traffic deaths.

Source: U.S. National Highway Traffic Safety Administration, "Traffic Safety Facts Annual Report Tables," <cdan.nhtsa.gov/tsftables/tsfar.htm>, accessed June 2022. See also <www.nhtsa.gov/research>.

Table 1139. Licensed Drivers and Number in Fatal Accidents by Age and Sex: 2020

[228,196 represents 228,196,000]

Age group	Licensed drivers (1,000)			Drivers in fatal accidents			Accident rates per number of drivers [1]	
	Total	Male	Female	Total [2]	Male	Female	Male	Female
Total	**228,196**	**112,595**	**115,601**	**53,890**	**39,393**	**13,033**	**35.0**	**11.3**
19 years old and under	8,351	4,221	4,130	3,413	2,468	941	58.5	22.8
Under 16 years old	62	30	31	209	146	62	479.0	199.0
16 years old	1,042	511	531	414	286	128	56.0	24.1
17 years old	1,852	925	927	653	474	178	51.2	19.2
18 years old	2,467	1,253	1,214	1,007	738	268	58.9	22.1
19 years old	2,930	1,502	1,427	1,130	824	305	54.8	21.4
20 to 24 years old	17,278	8,780	8,498	6,120	4,530	1,585	51.6	18.7
20 years old	3,237	1,656	1,581	1,236	924	311	55.8	19.7
21 years old	3,346	1,707	1,638	1,248	923	323	54.1	19.7
22 years old	3,444	1,751	1,693	1,220	906	314	51.7	18.5
23 years old	3,558	1,803	1,755	1,213	885	327	49.1	18.6
24 years old	3,694	1,862	1,831	1,203	892	310	47.9	16.9
25 to 29 years old	19,714	9,877	9,837	6,398	4,760	1,628	48.2	16.5
30 to 34 years old	20,186	10,041	10,146	5,535	4,170	1,360	41.5	13.4
35 to 39 years old	19,743	9,791	9,952	4,780	3,565	1,207	36.4	12.1
40 to 44 years old	18,465	9,135	9,331	4,116	3,137	977	34.3	10.5
45 to 49 years old	18,355	9,094	9,261	3,841	2,954	883	32.5	9.5
50 to 54 years old	19,018	9,429	9,589	3,890	2,983	902	31.6	9.4
55 to 59 years old	20,123	9,910	10,213	3,915	3,013	898	30.4	8.8
60 to 64 years old	19,294	9,421	9,872	3,379	2,601	776	27.6	7.9
65 to 69 years old	16,575	8,022	8,553	2,350	1,780	569	22.2	6.7
70 to 74 years old	13,297	6,415	6,882	1,766	1,269	495	19.8	7.2
75 to 79 years old	8,635	4,136	4,498	1,246	908	337	22.0	7.5
80 to 84 years old	5,169	2,459	2,710	824	592	231	24.1	8.5
85 and over	3,992	1,863	2,129	740	528	211	28.3	9.9

[1] Per 100,000 male or female licensed drivers. Rates for drivers 19 years old and under are likely overstated because of a higher proportion of unlicensed drivers. [2] Total includes unknown/unreported instances.

Source: U.S. Federal Highway Administration, "Highway Statistics 2020," <fhwa.dot.gov/policyinformation/>; and National Highway Traffic Safety Administration, "Fatality and Injury Reporting System Tool," <cdan.dot.gov/query>; accessed August 2022.

Table 1140. Speeding-Related Traffic Fatalities by Road Type and State: 2020

[Speeding consists of exceeding the posted speed limit or driving too fast for the road conditions or any speed-related violation charged (racing, driving above speed limit, speed greater than reasonable, exceeding special speed limit)]

State	Traffic fatalities, total	Speeding-related fatalities by roadway function class							
		Total [2]	Interstate		Non-interstate				
			Rural	Urban	Freeway and expressway	Other principal arterial	Minor arterial	Collector	Local
United States [1]	38,824	11,258	503	935	501	2,836	2,404	2,189	1,704
Alabama	934	265	15	19	1	53	54	95	28
Alaska	64	23	1	3	–	3	5	6	5
Arizona	1,054	353	32	16	21	97	71	68	16
Arkansas	638	164	12	6	1	10	7	4	52
California	3,847	1,228	44	146	121	352	301	164	100
Colorado	622	287	10	32	17	105	47	48	27
Connecticut	295	96	3	13	4	17	36	14	9
Delaware	116	33	–	8	1	11	1	10	2
District of Columbia	36	16	–	–	–	7	5	2	2
Florida	3,331	285	9	11	7	75	65	44	40
Georgia	1,664	380	11	29	13	70	91	83	82
Hawaii	85	37	–	2	1	21	13	–	–
Idaho	214	62	3	–	3	19	16	15	6
Illinois	1,194	460	22	64	–	122	94	84	65
Indiana	897	238	21	10	1	66	51	46	43
Iowa	337	61	4	2	–	20	4	18	13
Kansas	426	102	2	4	2	7	34	29	24
Kentucky	780	162	5	11	1	32	40	45	27
Louisiana	828	189	8	21	4	40	32	40	42
Maine	164	47	2	1	–	7	5	21	11
Maryland	567	163	–	19	11	54	36	26	16
Massachusetts	343	97	–	19	7	24	26	14	7
Michigan	1,084	292	5	33	17	64	58	52	61
Minnesota	394	122	4	9	5	19	29	33	21
Mississippi	752	126	9	7	1	25	18	60	6
Missouri	987	421	13	38	24	95	104	83	64
Montana	213	83	16	2	–	24	9	13	19
Nebraska	233	39	4	1	1	11	12	5	5
Nevada	317	93	4	7	2	42	9	1	28
New Hampshire	104	37	–	–	–	6	10	17	4
New Jersey	584	142	2	13	18	42	36	21	9
New Mexico	398	160	16	11	–	44	35	34	19
New York	1,046	378	6	27	49	118	41	32	105
North Carolina	1,538	489	6	40	17	80	92	137	116
North Dakota	100	26	3	–	–	9	7	3	4
Ohio	1,230	340	6	25	12	49	79	93	63
Oklahoma	652	156	11	12	–	32	27	32	42
Oregon	508	124	4	7	–	48	24	32	9
Pennsylvania	1,129	459	29	33	25	100	86	86	99
Rhode Island	67	20	1	2	1	7	6	1	2
South Carolina	1,064	494	37	22	5	153	205	26	46
South Dakota	141	42	7	2	–	14	10	3	6
Tennessee	1,217	187	6	20	2	51	42	40	26
Texas	3,874	1,446	68	128	89	381	295	310	171
Utah	276	72	6	5	1	31	10	13	6
Vermont	62	17	2	–	–	3	5	4	3
Virginia	850	260	18	26	4	71	47	64	29
Washington	560	167	3	19	10	18	17	40	58
West Virginia	267	60	1	5	–	14	11	14	11
Wisconsin	614	216	5	5	2	60	42	48	53
Wyoming	127	42	7	–	–	13	4	16	2
Puerto Rico	242	73	4	5	–	24	21	19	–

– Represents zero. [1] U.S. totals do not include Puerto Rico. [2] Includes fatalities that occurred on roads for which the type was unknown.

Source: U.S. National Highway Traffic Safety Administration, "Traffic Safety Facts Annual Report Tables," <cdan.nhtsa.gov/tsftables/tsfar.htm>, accessed June 2022. See also <www.nhtsa.gov/research>.

Table 1141. Roadway Traffic Congestion by Urbanized Area: 2020

[13,822 represents 13,822,000. Various federal, state, and local information sources were used to develop the database with the primary source being the Federal Highway Administration's Highway Performance Monitoring System]

Urbanized area	Daily vehicle miles of travel (1,000)		Annual person hours of delay		Annual congestion cost [1]		
	Freeway	Arterial streets	Total hours (1,000)	Per auto commuter [2]	Delay and fuel cost (million dollars)	Per person (dollars) [2]	Fuel wasted (gal. per person) [2]
101 urban areas, average [3]...............	**13,822**	**12,757**	**37,249**	**33**	**841**	**742**	**13**
Akron, OH..........	5,093	3,894	11,120	27	253	552	12
Albany-Schenectady, NY....................	5,288	4,381	10,518	33	241	555	15
Albuquerque, NM...........	5,101	6,739	10,229	22	231	516	9
Allentown, PA-NJ..........	4,430	4,250	7,535	19	169	360	8
Atlanta, GA.........	49,227	52,545	109,475	37	2,477	869	15
Austin, TX..........	13,877	12,845	48,435	41	1,077	945	15
Baltimore, MD..........	24,319	15,036	44,292	27	993	549	10
Birmingham, AL..........	11,126	8,123	12,935	23	291	521	9
Boston, MA-NH-RI..........	34,625	35,016	122,348	50	2,732	1,103	20
Bridgeport-Stamford, CT-NY..........	8,312	4,699	27,235	40	633	782	16
Buffalo, NY..........	5,233	7,529	16,005	29	362	649	14
Charleston-North, Charleston, SC..........	4,079	6,783	10,973	26	242	521	10
Charlotte, NC-SC..........	14,411	12,922	23,138	24	516	585	10
Chicago, IL-IN..........	45,636	60,709	172,876	39	3,969	852	16
Cincinnati, OH-KY-IN..........	16,355	12,023	28,436	26	637	608	12
Cleveland, OH..........	15,715	11,312	33,300	29	760	686	15
Colorado Springs, CO..........	5,189	5,095	12,116	29	268	582	12
Columbus OH..........	13,983	10,748	26,055	27	589	645	12
Dallas-Fort, Worth-Arlington, TX..........	63,448	39,764	136,953	40	3,051	848	16
Dayton, OH..........	6,976	5,351	9,187	21	210	435	9
Denver-Aurora, CO..........	23,863	20,162	46,181	26	1,034	545	10
Detroit, MI..........	24,560	34,573	92,996	35	2,082	710	13
El Paso, TX-NM..........	5,905	5,672	17,490	32	394	688	14
Fresno, CA..........	3,926	4,551	13,890	29	320	626	14
Grand Rapids, MI..........	4,603	6,102	9,472	22	213	435	9
Hartford, CT..........	9,047	6,095	16,928	31	385	606	13
Honolulu, HI..........	4,670	2,360	13,365	24	308	562	10
Houston, TX..........	53,242	44,249	169,765	49	3,795	1,097	21
Indianapolis, IN..........	13,131	15,038	23,362	26	540	487	12
Jackson, MS..........	4,791	5,862	8,409	29	189	533	10
Jacksonville, FL..........	13,503	9,209	16,143	21	355	448	7
Kansas City, MO-KS..........	20,759	11,889	35,061	34	812	694	11
Las Vegas -Henderson, NV..........	11,245	14,452	21,702	18	487	363	7
Los Angeles-Long Beach-Anaheim, CA....	107,548	86,678	365,543	46	8,230	1,142	14
Louisville-Jefferson Co., KY-IN..........	8,846	6,425	13,886	22	319	386	9
Memphis, TN-MS-AR..........	8,840	13,677	16,285	28	387	427	11
Miami, FL..........	39,716	43,472	112,879	27	2,491	608	13
Milwaukee, WI..........	10,134	12,918	24,340	29	557	602	14
Minneapolis-St Paul, MN-WI..........	25,979	20,987	59,835	32	1,322	620	12
Nashville-Davidson, TN..........	19,404	13,047	25,770	28	595	659	13
New Haven, CT..........	6,175	3,275	10,778	31	243	583	13
New Orleans, LA..........	4,735	6,167	24,668	26	571	597	13
New York-Newark, NY-NJ-CT..........	92,383	79,482	494,268	56	11,177	1,322	23
Oklahoma City, OK..........	10,151	8,024	30,057	35	685	656	15
Omaha, NE-IA..........	5,604	5,459	9,777	19	216	377	8
Orlando, FL..........	14,383	15,473	25,458	22	570	471	9
Oxnard, CA..........	1,748	2,355	3,379	18	78	416	6
Philadelphia, PA-NJ-DE-MD..........	31,077	35,720	100,726	37	2,274	789	15
Phoenix-Mesa, AZ..........	29,884	36,602	68,645	25	1,545	489	10
Pittsburgh, PA..........	10,841	12,304	24,743	25	561	552	12
Portland, OR-WA..........	12,190	11,996	36,065	31	836	690	14
Providence, RI-MA..........	8,194	7,887	26,373	33	584	630	13
Raleigh, NC..........	9,287	10,979	11,144	17	246	361	7
Richmond, VA..........	11,426	9,175	15,862	24	353	482	12
Riverside-San Bernardino, CA..........	23,038	10,478	38,687	25	872	511	7
Sacramento, CA..........	15,331	11,456	47,492	38	1,057	800	15
Salt Lake City-West Valley City, UT........	8,865	9,022	17,124	26	392	544	14
San Antonio, TX..........	21,522	15,222	44,999	32	1,010	682	15
San Diego, CA..........	33,333	16,433	55,433	24	1,219	665	9
San Francisco-Oakland, CA..........	27,433	14,912	112,507	46	2,604	1,301	17
San Jose, CA..........	13,046	9,927	46,377	31	1,066	712	13
Seattle, WA..........	24,062	21,698	69,016	31	1,556	685	13
St Louis, MO-IL..........	26,906	15,892	51,115	33	1,175	719	14
Tampa-St Petersburg, FL..........	15,741	28,097	34,479	18	767	401	7
Toledo, OH-MI..........	3,668	3,872	5,328	19	120	393	10
Tucson, AZ..........	3,676	8,584	13,189	21	306	381	8
Tulsa, OK..........	6,766	7,466	14,440	27	325	479	10
Virginia Beach, VA..........	11,085	12,632	19,220	22	423	399	8
Washington, DC-VA-MD..........	34,873	33,496	101,775	42	2,263	905	16
Worcester, MA..........	5,482	4,445	8,922	28	201	603	12

[1] Value of extra time (delay) and the extra fuel consumed by vehicles traveling at slower speeds. Fuel cost per gallon is the average price for each state. [2] Per auto commuter data are based on estimated commuters in the urban area. [3] Includes additional areas not shown below.

Source: Texas A&M Transportation Institute, College Station, Texas, *Urban Mobility Report 2021*, June 2021 ©. See also <mobility.tamu.edu>.

Table 1142. Commuting to Work by Transportation Method and State: 2019

[In percent, except as indicated. Workers in thousands (156,941 represents 154,941,000). For workers 16 years old and over. The American Community Survey universe includes the household population and the population living in institutions, college dormitories, and other group quarters. Based on a sample and subject to sampling variability; see Appendix III]

State	Total workers (1,000)	Percent of workers who commuted to work by—						Mean travel time to work (minutes)
		Car, truck, or van		Public transpor- tation [1]	Walking	Taxi, motorcycle, bicycle or other means	Working at home	
		Drove alone	Car- pooled					
U.S.............	156,941	75.9	8.9	5.0	2.6	1.9	5.7	27.6
AL................	2,134	85.2	8.7	0.4	1.2	1.1	3.4	25.4
AK................	350	70.0	12.0	1.0	7.1	5.7	4.3	20.2
AZ................	3,276	75.6	10.6	1.7	1.9	2.5	7.6	26.6
AR................	1,314	82.4	10.7	0.4	1.9	1.0	3.5	21.9
CA................	18,730	73.5	9.8	5.2	2.6	2.6	6.3	30.7
CO................	3,012	74.2	8.6	3.2	2.7	2.2	9.1	26.5
CT................	1,796	78.3	7.5	4.5	2.8	1.2	5.6	27.0
DE................	464	80.7	8.5	2.4	2.3	1.0	5.2	26.7
DC................	386	33.0	5.5	34.2	13.4	6.6	7.4	31.7
FL................	9,858	78.1	9.1	1.6	1.6	2.6	7.0	28.4
GA................	4,958	78.4	9.3	2.0	1.5	2.0	6.9	29.3
HI................	702	69.3	13.3	5.4	4.6	2.8	4.8	28.1
ID................	839	78.3	9.2	0.8	2.7	1.7	7.4	21.5
IL................	6,205	72.4	7.6	9.6	3.0	1.9	5.4	29.6
IN................	3,227	81.6	9.5	0.9	2.3	1.4	4.3	24.2
IA................	1,589	80.2	8.6	1.1	3.2	1.2	5.8	19.8
KS................	1,448	82.7	8.5	0.5	2.2	1.0	5.1	20.0
KY................	1,974	82.0	9.0	1.0	2.3	1.4	4.3	24.2
LA................	2,024	82.1	8.8	1.2	2.1	1.9	3.9	26.6
ME................	668	78.5	9.5	0.6	3.8	1.3	6.3	24.6
MD................	3,074	73.9	8.7	8.0	2.2	1.7	5.5	33.7
MA................	3,637	69.6	7.3	10.4	5.0	2.2	5.4	31.0
MI................	4,662	81.8	8.9	1.4	2.2	1.3	4.5	25.1
MN................	2,959	77.6	8.2	3.4	2.6	1.7	6.4	24.4
MS................	1,235	84.8	8.9	0.2	1.1	1.8	3.1	25.1
MO................	2,915	82.1	8.4	1.1	2.1	1.2	5.1	24.3
MT................	515	76.2	9.9	0.9	4.2	2.3	6.5	19.5
NE................	1,001	81.8	9.0	0.8	2.8	1.0	4.6	19.5
NV................	1,461	77.0	10.6	3.1	1.6	2.9	4.9	25.6
NH................	723	80.4	7.8	0.9	2.4	1.2	7.3	28.0
NJ................	4,421	71.0	7.9	11.6	2.7	2.0	4.9	33.1
NM................	908	80.7	9.4	1.1	2.0	1.8	5.1	22.6
NY................	9,435	52.8	6.3	27.7	6.2	2.3	4.8	34.0
NC................	4,938	80.2	8.7	1.1	1.8	1.5	6.7	25.7
ND................	405	82.5	8.5	0.7	3.2	1.5	3.6	17.9
OH................	5,589	82.4	8.0	1.5	2.3	1.2	4.6	24.3
OK................	1,787	82.7	9.5	0.4	1.5	1.6	4.4	22.7
OR................	2,011	71.5	9.5	4.7	3.8	3.3	7.3	24.2
PA................	6,179	75.2	8.4	5.7	3.6	1.6	5.4	27.8
RI................	537	79.6	8.2	3.1	3.3	1.4	4.5	25.7
SC................	2,358	82.1	8.6	0.6	2.0	1.6	5.1	26.0
SD................	448	79.8	9.0	0.4	3.2	1.6	6.1	17.9
TN................	3,178	82.0	8.9	0.6	1.4	1.4	5.6	25.9
TX................	13,716	80.1	9.7	1.3	1.5	1.6	5.7	27.2
UT................	1,584	76.1	10.4	2.5	2.0	1.6	7.4	22.5
VT................	324	76.2	8.6	1.6	5.3	1.3	7.0	24.0
VA................	4,292	76.6	9.0	4.4	2.3	1.9	5.8	29.1
WA................	3,724	70.9	10.0	7.1	3.5	2.0	6.5	28.8
WV................	731	82.0	9.0	0.8	2.9	1.4	3.9	26.4
WI................	2,959	80.8	8.0	1.7	3.0	1.5	5.1	22.7
WY................	280	76.9	11.5	1.2	3.0	1.7	5.7	19.1
PR................	1,023	84.3	7.7	1.2	2.8	1.6	2.4	29.8

[1] Excluding taxicabs.

Source: U.S. Census Bureau, 2019 American Community Survey, B08006, "Sex of Workers by Means of Transportation to Work," and DP03, "Selected Economic Characteristics," <data.census.gov>, accessed December 2020.

Table 1143. Use of Ride Hailing Services by Age Group: 2017

[Data from the 2017 National Household Travel Survey. Approximately 8% of the U.S. population used a ride-hailing service (services such as Uber and Lyft) at least once in the last 30 days. Age groups are based on Pew Research Center definitions]

Item	Millennials, aged 21 to 36	Generation X, aged 37 to 52	Baby Boomers, aged 53 to 71	Matures, aged 72 and over
Used ride-hailing service (percent)....................	19	10	5	2
Total respondents (millions) [2]........................	8.6	6.3	6.9	1.4
Used public transit and ride hailing...................	4.8	2.1	1.1	0.1
Used public transit but not ride hailing..............	3.8	4.2	5.8	1.3

[1] Data shown for metropolitan statistical areas with populations of 3 million or more people.

Source: U.S. Department of Transportation, Federal Highway Administration, Changing Attitudes and Transportation Choices, 2017 National Household Travel Survey, February 2019. See also <nhts.ornl.gov/>.

Table 1144. Passenger Transit Industry—Summary: 1990 to 2019

[16,053 represents $16,053,000,000. Includes Puerto Rico. Includes aggregate information for all transit systems in the United States. Excludes nontransit services such as taxicab, school bus, unregulated jitney (a small bus or automobile that transports passengers on a route for a small fare), sightseeing bus, intercity bus, and special application mass transportation systems (e.g., amusement parks, airports, island, and urban park ferries). Includes active vehicles only]

Item	Unit	1990	2000	2010	2015	2017	2018	2019
Operating systems	Number	5,078	6,000	7,088	6,752	6,770	6,704	6,782
Motor bus systems	Number	2,688	2,262	1,206	1,163	1,226	1,241	1,240
Revenue vehicles, active	Number	93,430	131,089	174,425	183,601	181,652	181,541	185,732
Motor bus	Number	58,714	75,013	66,239	72,075	72,338	71,743	72,665
Commuter rail	Number	4,982	5,498	6,927	7,216	7,290	7,184	7,209
Demand response [1]	Number	16,471	33,080	68,621	71,299	69,316	70,093	73,155
Heavy rail	Number	10,567	10,311	11,510	10,737	10,705	10,763	11,198
Surface rail (light rail, street car)	Number	910	1,327	2,104	2,423	2,502	2,663	2,716
Trolley bus	Number	610	652	571	611	539	571	572
Other	Number	1,176	5,208	18,453	19,240	18,962	18,524	18,215
Operating funding, total	Mil. dol.	16,053	24,243	39,117	48,367	50,807	52,278	55,099
Agency funds	Mil. dol.	6,786	11,004	14,675	18,105	18,457	18,845	18,740
Passenger funding	Mil. dol.	5,891	8,746	12,556	15,727	15,929	16,031	16,271
Other	Mil. dol.	895	2,258	2,119	2,378	2,528	2,814	2,470
Government funds [2]	Mil. dol.	9,267	13,239	24,442	30,262	32,350	33,433	36,358
Directly generated [3]	Mil. dol.	([4])	1,959	2,549	3,242	3,484	3,196	4,502
Local	Mil. dol.	5,327	5,319	8,458	11,812	12,866	13,857	14,851
State	Mil. dol.	2,971	4,967	9,761	11,197	11,673	11,867	12,639
Federal	Mil. dol.	970	994	3,675	4,011	4,327	4,513	4,366
Operating expense	Mil. dol.	15,742	22,646	37,755	45,353	47,544	49,482	51,786
Vehicle operations	Mil. dol.	6,653	10,111	17,009	19,388	19,902	20,760	21,526
Maintenance	Mil. dol.	4,631	6,445	9,797	12,237	13,327	13,404	13,919
General administration	Mil. dol.	3,450	3,329	5,731	7,300	7,543	8,154	8,582
Purchased transportation	Mil. dol.	1,008	2,761	5,218	6,427	6,772	7,165	7,759
Capital expenditures	Mil. dol.	(NA)	9,587	17,824	19,696	20,185	21,772	24,286
Vehicle-miles operated	Million	3,242	4,081	5,455	5,509	5,696	5,719	5,692
Motor bus	Million	2,130	2,315	2,413	2,428	2,502	2,532	2,555
Trolley bus	Million	14	15	12	11	11	11	10
Heavy rail	Million	537	595	666	695	704	705	719
Surface rail (light rail, street car)	Million	24	53	94	114	127	128	131
Commuter rail	Million	213	271	345	374	378	377	382
Demand response [1]	Million	306	759	1,694	1,617	1,705	1,702	1,629
Other	Million	18	74	232	271	270	264	266
Trips taken	Million	8,799	9,363	10,218	10,599	10,152	9,953	9,969
Motor bus	Million	5,677	5,678	5,256	5,199	4,793	4,707	4,660
Trolley bus	Million	126	122	99	90	83	77	76
Heavy rail	Million	2,346	2,632	3,550	3,860	3,816	3,724	3,790
Surface rail (light rail, street car)	Million	175	320	457	529	555	543	532
Commuter rail	Million	328	413	464	495	503	505	511
Demand response [1]	Million	68	105	190	223	207	204	201
Other	Million	79	93	202	204	195	192	199
Avg. fare per trip	Dollars	(NA)	0.93	1.23	1.50	1.56	1.62	1.63
Employees, number (avg.) [5]	1,000	273	360	394	433	432	436	448
Salaries and wages, employee	Mil. dol.	7,226	10,400	14,286	15,913	16,688	16,947	17,512
Fringe benefits, employee	Mil. dol.	3,986	5,413	10,342	11,992	12,729	13,477	14,042

NA Not available. [1] This operation (also called paratransit or dial-a-ride) is comprised of passenger cars, vans or small buses operating in response to calls from passengers or their agents to the transit operator, who then dispatches a vehicle to pick up the passengers and transport them to their destinations. [2] Represents the sum of federal, state, and local assistance, and that portion of directly generated funds that accrue from tax collections, toll transfers from other sectors of operations, and bond proceeds. [3] These are any funds generated from taxes controlled by the transit agency. [4] Funds data are included in local government data through 1993. [5] Through 1990, represents employee equivalents of 2,080 hours = one employee; beginning 1995, equals actual employees.

Source: American Public Transportation Association, Washington, DC, *Public Transportation Fact Book*, annual ©. See also <www.apta.com/research-technical-resources/research-reports>.

Table 1145. Top Twenty Cities—Public Transit Savings for Daily Commuters: 2020

[Individuals who use public transportation for their daily commute can save on average $9,848 annually based on the February 28, 2020 national average gas price and the national unreserved monthly parking rate. On a per month basis, transit riders can save on average $821 per month versus driving. See source report and other monthly "Transit Savings" releases for information and methodology on how savings are calculated. The cities with the highest transit ridership are ranked in order of their transit savings based on the purchase of a monthly public transit pass and factoring in local gas prices and the local monthly unreserved parking rate]

City	Savings (dollars)		City	Savings (dollars)	
	Monthly	Annual		Monthly	Annual
New York	1,218	14,618	Minneapolis	859	10,306
San Francisco	1,113	13,356	Denver	846	10,152
Boston	1,068	12,810	Baltimore	842	10,105
Seattle	998	11,979	Washington, DC	823	9,837
Philadelphia	989	11,866	Pittsburgh	810	9,716
Chicago	979	11,753	Cleveland	801	9,613
Honolulu	972	11,669	Miami	773	9,279
Los Angeles	958	11,497	Las Vegas	773	9,278
San Diego	911	10,936	Atlanta	767	9,200
Portland	891	10,691	Dallas	752	9,029

Source: American Public Transportation Association, Media Center, Press Releases ©. See also <www.apta.com/news-publications/public-transportation-facts/>.

Table 1146. Characteristics of Rail Transit by Transit Authority: 2020

[4,942.8 represents $4,942,800,000. Due to the impacts of the COVID-19 pandemic, use caution when comparing data to previous years]

Mode and transit agency	Metro area served	Directional route–miles [1]	Grade cross-ings	Number of stations	Fare revenues earned (mil. dol.)	Total operating expenses (mil. dol.)	Unlinked passenger trips (million)
Total [2]	(X)	**12,648.3**	**8,505**	**3,663**	**4,942.8**	**18,368.2**	**2,413.6**
Heavy rail	(X)	**1,662.7**	**88**	**1,057**	**2,904.0**	**9,098.9**	**1,777.9**
Chicago Transit Authority	Chicago	207.8	33	145	102.5	632.5	76.0
Greater Cleveland Regional Transit Authority	Cleveland	38.1	–	18	3.7	36.0	2.6
Los Angeles County Metropolitan Transportation Authority, Metro	Los Angeles	31.9	–	16	19.9	152.3	33.7
Maryland Transit Administration	Baltimore	29.4	1	14	8.0	70.8	5.9
Massachusetts Bay Transportation Authority	Boston	76.3	–	54	177.9	323.9	115.7
Metropolitan Atlanta Rapid Transit Authority	Atlanta	96.1	–	38	64.1	206.7	45.3
Miami-Dade Transit	Miami	49.8	47	23	8.4	101.8	11.9
MTA New York City Transit	New York	493.7	–	472	1,610.0	4,937.0	1,112.7
Port Authority Trans-Hudson Corporation	New York	28.6	2	13	71.2	447.0	29.7
Port Authority Transit Corporation	Philadelphia	31.5	5	13	9.3	55.5	3.9
San Francisco Bay Area Rapid Transit District	San Francisco	221.2	–	48	332.4	658.2	88.7
Southeastern Pennsylvania Transportation Authority	Philadelphia	74.9	–	75	86.2	200.6	71.1
Staten Island Rapid Transit Operating Authority, MTA Staten Island Railway	New York	28.6	–	21	2.9	56.7	2.7
Washington Metropolitan Area Transit Authority	Washington	234.2	–	91	402.8	1,153.8	174.5
Alternativa de Transporte Integrado ATI	San Juan, PR	20.6	–	16	4.9	66.2	3.5
Light rail	(X)	**1,599.1**	**2,389**	**982**	**337.2**	**2,467.5**	**331.5**
Missouri-Illinois Metropolitan District Metro	St. Louis	91.1	25	38	11.4	88.7	10.5
Central Puget Sound Regional Transit Authority	Seattle	40.4	37	16	11.4	151.4	7.9
Charlotte Area Transit System	Charlotte	37.3	39	26	6.3	37.9	7.3
Greater Cleveland Regional Transit Authority	Cleveland	30.4	25	34	1.1	11.7	0.6
Dallas Area Rapid Transit	Dallas	182.4	136	64	15.0	191.4	20.1
Denver Regional Transportation District	Denver	119.8	40	57	16.0	120.8	10.5
Los Angeles County Metropolitan Transportation Authority, Metro	Los Angeles	171.9	197	79	26.6	433.5	42.1
Maryland Transit Administration (MTA)	Baltimore	57.6	44	33	4.7	46.1	4.7
Massachusetts Bay Transportation Authority	Boston	51.0	53	74	64.3	186.0	41.5
Metro Transit	Minneapolis	44.3	154	37	11.5	80.2	10.3
Harris County, Texas (Metro)	Houston	43.6	165	63	2.5	87.0	12.9
New Jersey Transit Corporation	Newark	46.5	48	41	15.8	118.5	16.4
Niagara Frontier Transportation Authority	Buffalo	12.4	8	14	4.8	26.5	4.2
Port Authority of Allegheny County	Pittsburgh	49.6	51	30	6.2	69.5	5.6
Sacramento Regional Transit District	Sacramento	84.9	137	43	10.9	77.6	9.0
San Diego Metropolitan Transit System	San Diego	108.4	96	54	36.5	95.7	32.0
San Francisco Municipal Railway	San Francisco	64.4	335	9	30.7	209.4	37.4
Santa Clara Valley Transportation Authority	San Jose	81.0	168	64	6.1	121.2	6.3
Hampton Roads Transit	Hampton	14.8	40	11	1.1	11.4	1.0
Metropolitan Transportation District of Oregon	Portland	118.9	212	96	35.4	169.8	30.3
Utah Transit Authority	Salt Lake City	93.9	187	56	10.6	82.2	8.2
Valley Metro Rail, Inc.	Phoenix	54.5	192	43	8.3	50.9	12.8
Commuter rail [2]	(X)	**8,889.6**	**3,888**	**1,319**	**1,661.4**	**6,454.1**	**259.4**
Alaska Railroad Corporation	Anchorage	959.9	137	8	2.7	38.2	(Z)
Altamont Corridor Express	San Jose	166.5	175	10	8.3	22.5	1.1
Central Florida Commuter Rail	Orlando	97.9	117	16	2.7	49.0	1.2
Central Puget Sound Regional Transit Authority	Seattle	163.8	63	12	5.7	54.3	1.3
Connecticut Department of Transportation	Hartford	101.2	66	9	1.4	31.9	0.5
Dallas Area Rapid Transit	Dallas	72.3	45	10	5.6	35.7	1.3
Denver Regional Transportation District	Denver	79.4	38	23	16.1	110.1	5.0
Fort Worth Transportation Authority	Ft. Worth	50.6	38	12	0.3	21.2	0.3
Maryland Transit Administration	Baltimore	400.4	1	42	37.2	161.2	6.7
Massachusetts Bay Transportation Authority	Boston	776.1	304	140	202.9	384.2	24.8
Metro Transit	Minneapolis	77.9	30	7	0.5	15.5	0.2
MTA Metro-North Railroad	New York	545.7	178	112	243.4	1,202.8	29.4
MTA Long Island Rail Road	New York	638.2	361	125	272.5	1,464.4	43.5
New Jersey Transit Corporation	New York	920.4	337	165	426.5	1,083.5	66.3
North County Transit District	San Diego	82.2	36	8	4.1	21.3	0.9
Northeast Illinois Regional Commuter Railroad Corporation	Chicago	975.0	565	243	102.4	710.2	16.7
Northern Indiana Commuter Transport District	Chicago	151.2	138	19	6.3	52.7	1.0
Northern New England Passenger Rail Authority	Boston	224.6	103	12	7.8	20.0	0.4
Peninsula Corridor Joint Powers Board: Caltrain	San Francisco	153.7	80	31	76.1	131.0	13.7
Pennsylvania Department of Transportation	Philadelphia	144.4	–	12	15.5	26.0	0.6
Regional Transportation Authority	Nashville	62.8	48	7	0.8	4.4	0.2
Rio Metro Regional Transit District	Albuquerque	193.1	98	15	1.3	29.5	0.5
Sonoma-Marin Area Rail Transit District	Bay Area, CA	88.3	78	12	3.1	28.6	0.6
South Florida Regional Transportation Authority	Miami	142.2	72	18	9.5	92.5	3.5
Southeastern Pennsylvania Transportation Authority	Philadelphia	446.9	287	155	107.2	307.5	25.2
Southern California Regional Rail Authority	Los Angeles	826.8	387	62	63.1	234.6	9.4
Utah Transit Authority	Salt Lake City	174.5	87	15	3.4	43.1	2.0
Virginia Railway Express	Washington	173.6	19	19	34.7	78.0	3.2

– Represents zero. X Not applicable. Z Less than 500,000. [1] The mileage in each direction over which public transportation vehicles travel while in revenue service. The mileage is computed without regard to the number of traffic lanes or rail tracks existing in the right-of-way. [2] Includes hybrid and streetcar rail, not shown separately. Excludes commuter-type services operated independently by Amtrak.

Source: U.S. Department of Transportation, Federal Transit Administration, National Transit Database, Annual Data Tables and Annual Database, "Transit Way Mileage," "Federal Funding Allocation," "Metrics," and "Transit Stations," <transit.dot.gov/ntd/ntd-data>, accessed July 2022.

Table 1147. Commuters by Commuting Time to Work for Top Metropolitan Statistical Areas: 2019

[147,971 represents 147,971,000, except percent. For workers 16 years and over who did not work at home. Covers any mode of travel. Based on a sample, subject to sampling variability]

Metropolitan Statistical Area	Total com-muters (1,000)	Per-cent over 35 min-utes	Commuters by commuting time								
			Less than 10 min-utes	10 to 14 min-utes	15 to 19 min-utes	20 to 24 min-utes	25 to 29 min-utes	30 to 34 min-utes	35 to 44 min-utes	45 to 59 min-utes	60 or more min-utes
United States...............	**147,971**	**25.7**	**17,648**	**19,078**	**22,114**	**20,817**	**9,774**	**20,512**	**10,819**	**12,642**	**14,564**
Atlanta-Sandy Springs-Alpharetta, GA...	2,715	36.1	185	241	339	356	185	430	256	338	385
Baltimore-Columbia-Towson, MD.	1,335	34.2	104	120	175	172	99	209	124	154	178
Boston-Cambridge-Newton, MA-NH. ...	2,500	37.1	216	253	289	294	148	372	231	308	389
Charlotte-Concord-Gastonia, NC-SC....	1,222	25.7	109	152	186	182	97	183	102	112	100
Chicago-Naperville-Elgin, IL-IN-WI......	4,459	37.0	353	424	524	530	284	697	439	566	643
Dallas-Fort Worth-Arlington, TX.........	3,555	28.0	288	401	482	521	255	610	300	367	330
Denver-Aurora-Lakewood, CO..........	1,473	28.9	106	155	200	218	113	255	152	153	121
Detroit-Warren-Dearborn, MI..........	1,952	26.1	176	219	280	298	162	308	176	184	150
Houston-The Woodlands-Sugar Land, TX..................................	3,199	33.0	237	303	416	423	194	572	305	386	364
Los Angeles-Long Beach-Anaheim, CA....................................	6,114	32.9	398	639	832	835	353	1,048	498	628	883
Miami-Fort Lauderdale-Pompano Beach, FL...............................	2,844	30.2	187	265	353	437	190	554	258	284	316
Minneapolis-St. Paul-Bloomington, MN-WI................................	1,836	23.3	180	222	274	290	166	275	164	153	111
New York-Newark-Jersey City, NY-NJ-PA..............................	9,034	45.2	580	723	881	945	481	1,337	834	1,199	2,055
Orlando-Kissimmee-Sanford, FL........	1,200	31.0	80	114	156	163	88	227	123	136	114
Philadelphia-Camden-Wilmington, PA-NJ-DE-MD..........................	2,836	33.0	258	303	359	357	203	421	264	323	349
Phoenix-Mesa-Chandler, AZ.............	2,157	26.6	206	231	296	333	178	337	180	208	187
Portland-Vancouver-Hillsboro, OR-WA..	1,168	24.5	125	147	169	176	93	171	91	106	91
Riverside-San Bernardino-Ontario, CA..	1,883	34.3	166	220	252	253	94	251	133	167	347
San Antonio-New Braunfels, TX........	1,159	23.5	110	133	179	186	87	192	79	101	92
San Diego-Chula Vista-Carlsbad, CA. ..	1,546	24.4	117	184	254	255	110	249	127	126	123
San Francisco-Oakland-Berkeley, CA. ..	2,264	40.7	148	215	268	267	119	327	205	275	440
Seattle-Tacoma-Bellevue, WA...........	1,964	34.9	149	171	240	267	137	313	204	238	245
St. Louis, MO-IL.........................	1,323	22.5	135	154	202	215	109	209	116	107	75
Tampa-St. Petersburg-Clearwater, FL...	1,361	28.3	126	163	191	205	88	202	113	144	128
Washington-Arlington-Alexandria, DC-VA-MD-WV..........................	3,161	43.1	186	245	334	359	189	485	331	455	578

Source: U.S. Census Bureau, 2019 American Community Survey, B08134, "Means of Transportation to Work by Travel Time to Work," <data.census.gov>, accessed December 2020.

Table 1148. Commuters Who Ride Bicycles or Walk to Work—Selected Large Cities: 2016

[Covers cities with the highest percent of commuters who walk or bike to work, based on the American Community Survey. Data are weighted 5-year averages for 2012-2016]

Leading cities	Walking			Leading cities	Bicycling		
	Percent of commuters who walk to work	Percent male	Percent female		Percent of commuters who bike to work	Percent male	Percent female
Boston.........................	14.8	47.3	52.7	Portland, OR..................	6.5	64.0	36.0
Washington, DC..............	13.3	50.1	49.9	Minneapolis..................	4.3	65.3	34.7
San Francisco.................	10.6	52.2	47.8	Washington, DC.............	4.3	61.0	39.0
Seattle........................	10.1	56.9	43.1	San Francisco.............	4.1	68.7	31.3
New York City.................	10.0	48.5	51.5	Seattle.......................	3.8	70.2	29.8
Philadelphia...................	8.2	46.4	53.6	Oakland......................	3.1	62.3	37.7
Minneapolis...................	7.2	52.7	47.3	Tucson.......................	2.9	67.5	32.5
Baltimore.....................	6.7	47.2	52.8	Denver.......................	2.3	70.7	29.3
Chicago.......................	6.7	49.8	50.2	Boston.......................	2.1	71.5	28.5
Portland, OR..................	6.0	52.8	47.2	Philadelphia..................	2.1	62.9	37.1
Cleveland.....................	5.3	55.8	44.2	Sacramento..................	2.1	64.8	35.2
Milwaukee....................	5.0	47.7	52.3	Chicago......................	1.6	71.5	28.5
Atlanta........................	4.6	59.0	41.0	Albuquerque.................	1.5	73.4	26.6
Denver........................	4.5	55.8	44.2	Austin........................	1.4	70.7	29.3
Miami.........................	4.2	52.9	47.1	Los Angeles..................	1.2	80.1	19.9
Oakland.......................	4.0	45.8	54.2	Fresno.......................	1.1	75.0	25.0
Detroit........................	3.7	53.5	46.5	New York City................	1.1	73.5	26.5
Los Angeles..................	3.5	51.2	48.8	Long Beach..................	1.0	71.3	28.7
Tucson........................	3.3	56.2	43.8	Miami........................	1.0	77.0	23.0
Sacramento...................	3.1	51.7	48.3	Milwaukee...................	1.0	70.0	30.0
San Diego.....................	3.1	60.4	39.6	San Diego...................	1.0	75.4	24.6
Columbus, OH................	3.0	55.7	44.3	Mesa.........................	0.9	70.7	29.3
Virginia Beach................	2.6	66.4	33.6	San Jose.....................	0.9	76.0	24.0
Long Beach...................	2.5	49.1	50.9	Atlanta.......................	0.8	80.2	19.8
Austin.........................	2.3	53.7	46.3	Baltimore....................	0.8	72.2	27.8

Source: League of American Bicyclists, *Bicycling and Walking in the United States: 2018 Benchmarking Report* ©. See also <http://bikeleague.org/benchmarking-report/>.

Table 1149. Federal Transit Administration (FTA) Funding Allocations by State: 2018 and 2022

[In millions of dollars (12,958.0 represents $12,985,000,000). For fiscal years ending September 30. Data shown are apportionments and allocations for formula and discretionary programs]

State	2018	2019	2020	2021	2022	State	2018	2019	2020	2021	2022
Total [1]...	12,958.0	11,417.7	13,459.2	12,852.7	13,737.0	MO.......	114.0	110.1	175.4	206.7	146.5
AL........	64.1	62.2	78.0	65.8	81.2	MT.......	29.2	24.3	30.2	28.5	34.2
AK........	65.6	60.5	81.2	60.8	80.1	NE.......	34.8	31.6	50.3	32.2	37.0
AZ........	158.0	232.1	314.9	283.8	177.7	NV.......	109.8	71.7	86.2	77.3	94.6
AR........	38.4	36.6	37.3	43.3	47.4	NH.......	21.2	19.7	20.9	19.5	24.3
CA........	2,798.5	2,070.4	2,112.9	2,870.7	2,056.9	NJ.......	664.6	664.2	950.2	657.7	840.6
CO........	211.4	134.7	169.4	143.8	205.0	NM.......	92.1	58.2	70.3	62.5	75.8
CT........	196.6	189.8	198.3	212.2	261.8	NY.......	1,656.8	1,597.4	1,641.4	1,544.0	2,180.7
DE........	31.6	31.6	32.1	38.3	40.6	NC.......	219.0	135.2	175.8	176.7	194.7
DC........	222.8	213.2	219.9	214.2	311.8	ND.......	20.7	18.0	32.9	17.3	21.6
FL........	435.1	410.2	589.8	411.3	565.3	OH.......	207.3	203.1	223.5	198.6	294.7
GA........	215.3	214.9	234.4	216.2	298.5	OK.......	58.7	56.5	80.0	55.4	69.1
HI........	47.0	47.2	69.9	53.0	65.8	OR.......	309.4	186.8	234.7	123.0	170.7
ID........	29.3	32.3	34.5	32.5	39.1	PA.......	469.4	458.6	570.9	452.1	628.0
IL........	851.6	633.6	765.2	728.7	858.2	RI.......	45.9	42.7	68.2	48.0	56.0
IN........	126.9	98.2	335.8	256.7	135.6	SC.......	67.1	57.1	74.9	59.7	74.1
IO........	52.6	46.9	83.1	50.1	63.5	SD.......	19.7	19.1	23.0	20.3	24.2
KS........	41.0	41.1	64.0	43.0	49.4	TN.......	104.1	98.7	115.1	101.4	124.2
KY........	66.5	61.5	84.2	62.7	79.5	TX.......	595.1	579.9	562.5	528.9	677.8
LA........	76.4	72.6	107.0	77.6	99.0	UT.......	98.1	92.2	176.9	112.1	129.2
ME.......	42.4	39.1	54.4	37.7	53.1	VT.......	13.7	14.9	13.7	13.8	15.1
MD........	396.1	393.1	402.6	400.3	352.1	VA.......	177.9	181.7	192.7	190.5	235.5
MA........	558.4	557.5	565.0	503.9	546.7	WA......	444.5	484.7	555.3	577.0	403.3
MI........	174.3	152.0	201.0	161.2	213.1	WV......	28.3	29.0	35.5	29.4	38.7
MN........	211.4	127.3	141.4	328.7	176.7	WI.......	104.6	92.3	152.4	90.9	122.3
MS........	35.2	33.9	52.5	36.9	42.1	WY......	16.6	14.5	19.0	15.8	18.0

[1] Includes data for Island Areas of the U.S. and unallocated funds, not shown separately. Does not include oversight funds.

Source: U.S. Department of Transportation, Federal Transit Administration, "FTA Allocations for Formula and Discretionary Programs by State FY1998-2022," <transit.dot.gov/funding/apportionments/funding-state>, accessed September 2022.

Table 1150. Truck Transportation—Revenue and Equipment Inventory: 2015 to 2020

[In millions of dollars (273,250 represents $273,250,000,000), except where noted. For all employer firms regardless of tax status. Covers NAICS 484. Estimates have been adjusted to the results of the 2017 Economic Census. Data are based on the 2012 North American Industry Classification System (NAICS); see text, this section and Section 15]

Item	2015	2016	2017	2018	2019	2020
Total operating revenue..............................	**273,250**	**273,083**	**290,532**	**313,814**	**320,817**	**316,982**
Total motor carrier revenue..............................	253,689	253,170	270,159	293,799	300,114	295,072
Revenue by commodities handled:						
Agricultural products..............................	28,911	30,433	30,200	32,968	34,316	34,100
Grains, alcohol, and tobacco products..........................	9,909	10,151	10,667	10,910	11,175	10,603
Stone, nonmetallic minerals, and metallic ores.................	18,680	18,502	20,941	23,209	24,540	22,707
Coal and petroleum products..............................	16,383	15,409	14,848	15,233	16,216	14,426
Pharmaceutical and chemical products..........................	13,192	12,776	13,579	13,548	13,929	13,729
Wood products, textiles, and leathers..........................	16,689	16,885	19,623	21,517	21,709	21,394
Base metal and machinery..............................	25,052	23,620	25,257	27,405	28,228	25,515
Electronic and precision instruments, motorized vehicles....	12,273	11,989	14,073	15,579	15,932	15,915
Used household and office goods..............................	12,649	12,993	13,599	14,572	14,806	14,525
New furniture and miscellaneous manufactured products....	18,258	18,206	19,735	22,128	22,001	22,812
Other goods..............................	81,693	82,206	87,637	96,730	97,262	99,346
Hazardous materials..............................	17,117	16,408	17,070	18,138	19,141	18,666
Inventory of revenue-generating equipment (1,000):						
Trucks..............................	171	180	201	212	216	209
Owned and/or leased with drivers..............................	155	163	183	191	191	185
Leased without drivers..............................	16	17	18	21	25	24
Truck-tractors..............................	591	610	666	682	713	684
Owned and/or leased with drivers..............................	512	530	579	583	615	587
Leased without drivers..............................	79	80	87	99	98	97
Trailers..............................	1,478	1,545	1,595	1,697	1,736	1,635
Owned and/or leased with drivers..............................	1,314	1,367	1,450	1,544	1,578	1,476
Leased without drivers..............................	164	178	145	153	158	159

Source: U.S. Census Bureau, Service Annual Survey, "Service Annual Survey Latest Data (NAICS-basis): 2020," <www.census.gov/programs-surveys/sas/data.html>, accessed November 2021.

Table 1151. Crude Oil, Fuel Ethanol and Biodiesel Movements by Rail: 2010 to 2021

[In thousands of barrels (23,788 represents 23,788,000). Crude oil movements on railroads to and from Canada, within the 50 States and the District of Columbia (including interstate and intrastate). Estimates based on data from the Surface Transportation Board and other information]

Item	2010	2013	2014	2015	2016	2017	2018	2019	2020	2021
Crude oil.....................	23,788	296,064	382,034	317,446	175,701	139,389	201,208	251,224	156,817	117,638
Intra-U.S. movements....	23,712	259,194	316,276	275,218	142,587	87,053	114,004	141,015	94,844	61,638
U.S. exports to Canada...	55	7,391	12,605	4,414	–	102	180	–	369	–
U.S. imports from Canada.....................	21	29,479	53,153	37,814	33,114	52,234	87,023	110,209	61,605	56,000
Fuel ethanol.................	208,061	202,412	211,692	220,877	237,259	253,874	258,954	247,752	224,196	240,511
Biodiesel....................	2,606	7,950	9,473	8,332	12,226	11,706	13,668	13,099	18,578	16,242

– Represents zero.

Source: U.S. Energy Information Administration, Petroleum & Other Liquids, "Movements of Crude Oil and Selected Products by Rail," <www.eia.gov/petroleum/data.php>, accessed August 2022.

Table 1152. Petroleum Pipeline Companies—Characteristics: 1980 to 2019

[173 represents 173,000. Covers pipeline companies operating in interstate commerce and subject to the jurisdiction of the Federal Energy Regulatory Commission]

Item	Unit	1980	1990	2000	2010	2015	2016	2017	2018	2019
Miles of pipeline, total.........	1,000	173	168	152	148	165	166	168	172	174
Gathering lines...............	1,000	36	32	18	10	16	15	15	16	18
Trunk lines....................	1,000	136	136	134	138	149	152	154	156	156
Total deliveries.................	Mil. barrel	10,600	11,378	14,450	13,518	18,148	18,504	19,331	21,779	22,532
Crude oil......................	Mil. barrel	6,405	6,563	6,923	7,204	10,865	10,730	11,421	13,216	13,889
Products......................	Mil. barrel	4,195	4,816	7,527	6,314	7,283	7,785	7,911	8,562	8,657
Total trunk line traffic.........	Bil. barrel miles	3,405	3,500	3,508	3,565	4,589	4,771	5,135	5,556	6,110
Crude oil......................	Bil. barrel miles	1,948	1,891	1,602	1,634	2,339	2,499	2,775	3,126	3,587
Products......................	Bil. barrel miles	1,458	1,609	1,906	1,931	2,250	2,272	2,359	2,430	2,553
Carrier property value........	Mil. dol.	19,752	25,828	29,648	45,380	93,485	99,565	111,862	122,370	138,289
Operating revenues...........	Mil. dol.	6,356	7,149	7,483	11,219	22,019	23,100	25,427	29,035	32,895
Net income...................	Mil. dol.	1,912	2,340	2,705	4,582	6,689	10,542	13,856	16,522	19,780

Source: Endeavor Business Media, *Oil & Gas Journal*, annual ©. See also <www.ogj.com>.

Table 1153. Pipelines—Mileage and Incident Summary: 2005 to 2020

[In miles except where indicated (1,245,463 represents $1,245,463,000)]

Year	Pipeline mileage								Pipeline incidents [2]	
	Natural gas systems			Hazardous liquid or carbon dioxide systems						
	Distri-bution [1]	Trans-mission	Gathering	Total [3]	Petro-leum/ refined products	Highly volatile liquids	Crude oil	CO2 or other	Number of incidents	Total cost as reported ($1,000)
2005........	1,962,351	300,468	23,754	166,760	62,899	51,284	48,732	3,846	719	1,245,463
2006........	2,022,474	300,324	20,898	166,719	61,905	52,533	48,453	3,827	639	151,984
2007........	2,025,731	301,066	20,042	169,846	62,091	54,382	49,488	3,884	610	153,772
2008........	2,075,191	303,181	20,663	173,789	61,599	57,024	50,963	4,203	659	564,831
2009........	2,086,689	304,560	20,376	175,965	61,803	57,233	52,737	4,192	627	179,070
2010........	2,102,483	304,811	19,621	181,986	64,800	57,980	54,631	4,560	586	1,692,502
2011........	2,121,355	305,070	19,277	183,575	64,124	58,599	56,100	4,735	588	426,330
2012........	2,138,000	303,394	16,532	186,221	64,042	59,861	57,463	4,840	571	229,853
2013........	2,149,819	302,880	17,377	192,412	63,351	62,768	61,087	5,190	617	368,994
2014........	2,169,375	301,824	17,530	199,795	61,768	65,792	66,943	5,276	706	368,066
2015........	2,190,257	301,166	17,783	208,622	62,634	67,676	73,057	5,241	712	351,450
2016........	2,211,522	300,353	17,865	212,164	62,461	68,729	75,764	5,195	632	376,498
2017........	2,226,053	300,735	18,097	216,052	62,370	69,163	79,268	5,237	646	340,276
2018........	2,238,709	301,626	17,916	219,137	62,721	70,306	80,889	5,206	634	2,262,345
2019........	2,262,919	302,338	17,763	225,024	63,117	72,632	84,111	5,147	657	351,035
2020........	2,284,372	301,693	17,522	229,252	64,123	74,762	85,201	5,150	578	339,659

[1] Includes main and estimated service mileage. [2] Includes serious and significant incidents. Serious incidents include a fatality or injury requiring in-patient hospitalization. Significant incidents include serious incidents; those with $50,000 or more in total costs; highly volatile liquid releases of 5 barrels or more, or other liquid releases of 50 barrels or more; and liquid releases resulting in an unintentional fire or explosion. [3] Beginning 2010, includes fuel grade ethanol, not shown separately.

Source: U.S. Department of Transportation, Pipeline and Hazardous Materials Safety Administration, "Pipeline Mileage and Facilities" and "Pipeline Incidents: 20 Year Trends," <www.phmsa.dot.gov/data-and-statistics/pipeline/data-and-statistics-overview>, accessed March 2022.

Table 1154. U.S. Postal Service—Summary: 1990 to 2021

[[In units as indicated (166,301 represents 166,301,000,000). For years ending September 30. Includes Puerto Rico and all Island Areas]

Item	1990	2000	2010	2015	2019	2020	2021
Offices, stations, and branches (number)...	**40,067**	**38,060**	**36,222**	**35,520**	**34,613**	**34,451**	**34,223**
Post offices..........	28,959	27,876	27,077	26,615	26,362	26,362	26,362
Stations and branches................	11,108	10,184	9,145	8,905	8,251	8,089	7,861
Delivery points (mil.)..............	**(NA)**	**135.9**	**150.9**	**155.0**	**159.9**	**161.4**	**163.1**
Residential...............	(NA)	123.9	137.5	142.1	147.2	148.6	150.4
City................	(NA)	76.1	80.5	82.0	83.7	84.2	84.8
P.O. Box...............	(NA)	15.9	15.7	15.9	16.0	16.0	16.0
Rural/highway contract...............	(NA)	31.9	41.2	44.2	47.4	48.4	49.6
Business...................	(NA)	12.1	13.3	12.8	12.8	12.8	12.8
Pieces of mail handled (mil.)................	**166,301**	**207,882**	**170,859**	**154,321**	**142,562**	**129,171**	**128,861**
First-class mail [1,2]............	89,270	103,526	77,592	62,599	54,936	52,628	50,695
Periodicals (formerly 2nd class)..............	10,680	10,365	7,269	5,838	4,635	4,006	3,679
Marketing Mail (formerly Standard A) [2]...........	63,725	90,057	81,841	80,030	75,653	64,004	66,200
U.S. Postal Service..................	538	363	438	356	284	441	280
Free for the blind................	35	47	68	46	34	25	20
Shipping and package services [2,3,6].............	(X)	(X)	3,057	4,539	6,165	7,325	7,578
Express mail [2,3,5]...............	59	71	43	36	26	24	29
Package services (formerly Standard B).........	663	1,128	657	566	622	571	517
Priority mail [2,3,4]...............	518	1,223	779	1,007	1,097	1,274	1,405
International economy mail (surface) [3].............	166	79	(3)	(3)	(3)	(3)	(3)
International, airmail or total [3,7]..................	632	1,021	594	913	855	742	409
Employees, total (1,000)..............	**843**	**901**	**672**	**622**	**633**	**644**	**653**
Career......	**761**	**788**	**584**	**492**	**497**	**496**	**517**
Headquarters..............	2	2	3	3	3	3	6
Headquarters support..............	6	6	5	4	3	3	3
Inspection Service..............	4	4	2	2	2	2	2
Inspector General..............	(X)	1	1	1	1	1	1
Field Career.................	749	775	573	482	487	486	504
Postmasters..............	27	26	23	15	14	14	13
Supervisors/managers..............	43	39	28	24	26	25	23
Professional, administrative, and technical.......	10	10	6	4	5	5	2
Clerks.................	290	282	157	126	122	119	129
Mail handlers..............	51	61	49	38	37	37	47
City carriers..................	236	241	192	164	166	168	173
Motor vehicle operators..............	7	9	7	7	9	9	9
Rural carriers..................	42	57	67	67	73	74	75
Special delivery messengers.................	2	(X)	(X)	(X)	(X)	(X)	(X)
Building and equipment maintenance.............	33	42	37	31	30	29	28
Vehicle maintenance.................	5	6	5	5	5	5	5
Other [8].................	1	2	(X)	(X)	(X)	(X)	(X)
Pre-career..............	**83**	**114**	**88**	**130**	**136**	**148**	**137**
Casuals.................	27	30	7	2	1	10	(Z)
Transitional..............	(X)	13	16	–	–	–	–
Rural part-time.................	43	58	52	51	58	59	54
Relief/leave replacements..............	12	12	11	5	2	2	2
Non-bargaining temporary......................	(Z)	1	2	(Z)	(Z)	(Z)	(Z)
Compensation and employee benefits (mil. dol.)..	34,214	49,532	48,909	47,278	47,519	48,730	50,085
Avg. salary per employee (dol.) [9]...............	37,570	50,103	72,099	(NA)	(NA)	(NA)	(NA)
Pieces of mail per employee (1,000)................	197	231	254	248	225	201	197
Operating postal revenue (million dollars)...	**39,201**	**64,476**	**67,052**	**68,928**	**71,136**	**73,123**	**77,009**
Mail revenue........	**37,891**	**62,285**	**63,262**	**65,548**	**67,241**	**69,651**	**73,049**
First-class mail [1,2].................	24,023	35,516	32,111	28,412	24,431	23,781	23,281
Periodicals (formerly 2nd class)................	1,509	2,171	1,879	1,589	1,194	1,024	942
Marketing Mail (formerly Standard A) [2].............	8,082	15,193	16,728	17,646	16,359	13,909	14,590
Shipping and Package Services [2,3,6]..............	(X)	(X)	10,156	15,061	22,783	28,529	32,013
Express mail [2,3,5]................	630	996	829	779	716	697	820
Package Services (formerly Standard B).........	919	1,912	1,531	810	821	832	835
Priority mail [2,3,4]...............	1,555	4,837	5,455	7,664	9,728	11,831	13,514
International economy mail (surface) [3].............	222	180	(3)	(3)	(3)	(3)	(3)
International, airmail or total [3,7]..................	941	1,477	2,388	2,702	2,474	2,408	2,223
Service revenue..................	**1,310**	**2,191**	**3,790**	**3,380**	**3,895**	**3,472**	**3,960**
Certified [10].................	310	385	791	669	653	598	567
Insurance [10].................	47	109	128	90	78	93	105
Money orders.................	155	235	182	159	148	146	147
Other [10]................	592	1,342	2,635	2,462	3,016	2,635	3,141
Operating expenses (million dollars) [11]......	**40,490**	**62,992**	**75,426**	**73,641**	**80,119**	**82,401**	**81,999**

– Represents zero. NA Not available. X Not applicable. Z Fewer than 500. [1] Items mailed at 1st class rates and weighing 11 ounces or less. [2] Beginning 2010, Express Mail, Priority Mail, First-Class Parcels, and Standard Parcels are not included in Mail categories but are reclassified under Shipping and Package Services. [3] "Volume" and "Mailing & Shipping Revenue" restructured for the "Postal Accountability and Enhancement Act (PAEA) of 2006." Some categories eliminated. [4] Provides 2 to 3 day delivery service. [5] Overnight delivery of packages weighing up to 70 pounds. [6] Beginning 2010, also includes Package Services. [7] Airmail only, for 2005 and earlier. Beginning 2010, total international, including all international revenues and pieces formerly included in First-Class Mail, Standard Mail, and Package Services. [8] Includes discontinued operations, area offices, and nurses. Beginning 2010, nurses are included with clerks. [9] For career bargaining unit employees. Includes fringe benefits. [10] Beginning 2000, return receipt revenue broken out from registry, certified, and insurance and included in "other." [11] Shown in year in which obligation was incurred.

Source: U.S. Postal Service, *FY2021 Annual Report to Congress*, 2022, and earlier reports, and unpublished data. See also <about.usps.com/strategic-planning/future-postal-service/publications.htm>.

Table 1155. U.S. Postal Service Rates for Letters and Postcards: 1991 to 2022

[In dollars. For 1st class retail mail. Prior to 2013, international rates exclude Canada and Mexico]

Domestic mail date of rate change	Letters		Post-cards	Express mail— first 1/2 pound [1]	International air mail date of rate change	Letters	Post-cards
	First ounce	Each added ounce					
1991 (Feb. 3)............	0.29	0.23	0.19	9.95	**First 1/2 ounce**		
1995 (Jan. 1)............	0.32	0.23	0.20	10.75	1991 (Feb. 3)........................	0.50	0.40
1999 (Jan. 10)..........	0.33	0.22	0.20	11.75	1995 (July 9).........................	0.60	0.40
2001 (Jan. 7)............	0.34	0.21	0.20	12.25	1999 (Jan. 10)......................	0.60	0.50
2001 (July 1)............	0.34	0.23	0.21	12.45	**First ounce** [2]		
2002 (June 30).........	0.37	0.23	0.23	13.65	2001 (Jan. 7)........................	0.80	0.70
2006 (Jan. 8)............	0.39	0.24	0.24	14.40	2006 (Jan. 8)........................	0.84	0.75
2007 (May 14)..........	0.41	0.17	0.26	16.25	2007 (May 14)......................	0.90	0.90
2008 (May 12)..........	0.42	0.17	0.27	12.60 to 19.50	2008 (May 12)......................	0.94	0.94
2009 (May 11)..........	0.44	0.17	0.28	13.05 to 21.20	2009 (May 11)......................	0.98	0.98
2010 (Jan. 4)............	0.44	0.17	0.28	13.65 to 22.20	2010 (no change)..................	0.98	0.98
2011 (Apr. 17)..........	0.44	0.20	0.29	13.25 to 26.65	2011 (no change)..................	0.98	0.98
2012 (Jan. 22)..........	0.45	0.20	0.32	12.95 to 28.00	2012 (Jan. 22)......................	1.05	1.05
2013 (Jan. 27)..........	0.46	0.20	0.33	14.10 to 30.60	2013 (Jan. 27)......................	1.10	1.10
2014 (Jan. 26)..........	0.49	0.21	0.34	16.95 to 38.05	2014 (Jan. 26)......................	1.15	1.15
2015 (May 31)..........	0.49	0.22	0.35	16.95 to 38.05	2015 (May 31)......................	1.20	1.20
2016 (Apr. 10)..........	0.47	0.21	0.34	22.95 to 38.05	2016 (Apr. 10)......................	1.15	1.15
2017 (Jan. 22)..........	0.49	0.21	0.34	23.75 to 39.40	2017 (no change)..................	1.15	1.15
2018 (Jan. 21)..........	0.50	0.21	0.35	24.70 to 40.95	2018 (no change)..................	1.15	1.15
2019 (Jan. 27)..........	0.55	0.15	0.35	25.50 to 47.70	2019 (no change)..................	1.15	1.15
2020 (Jan. 26)..........	0.55	0.15	0.35	26.35 to 50.60	2020 (Jan. 26)......................	1.20	1.20
2021 (Jan. 24)..........	0.55	0.20	0.36	26.35 to 53.10	2021 (Jan. 24)......................	1.20	1.20
2021 (Aug. 29).........	0.58	0.20	0.40	26.35 to 53.10	2021 (Aug. 29).....................	1.30	1.30
2022 (Jan. 9)............	0.58	0.20	0.40	26.95 to 56.00	2022 (Jan. 9)........................	1.30	1.30

[1] On May 12, 2008, the Postal Service initiated a zoned pricing structure for Express Mail. Price range reflects starting retail price from Zones 1 and 2 to Zone 8 and, beginning 2014, to Zone 9. [2] International letter prices after the first ounce vary according to the price group that is applicable to each destination country.

Source: U.S. Postal Service, *Domestic Rate History*, July 2009; and "Price List Notice 123," <pe.usps.com/text/dmm300/Notice123.htm>, accessed January 2022.

Information and Communications

This section presents statistics on the various information and communications media: publishing, including newspapers, periodicals, books, and software; motion pictures, sound recordings, and broadcasting; telecommunications; computers, and internet access and use; and information services, such as libraries.

Information industry—The U.S. Census Bureau's *Service Annual Survey* provides estimates of revenues and expenses of firms in the information sector. Data are based on the North American Industry Classification System (NAICS). The information sector comprises establishments engaged in the following: (1) producing and distributing information and cultural products, (2) providing the means to transmit or distribute these products as well as data or communications, and (3) processing data.

The main components of the information sector include the publishing industries, including software publishing, and both traditional publishing and publishing exclusively on the internet; the motion picture and sound recording industries; the broadcasting industries, including traditional broadcasting and broadcasting over the internet (streaming); the telecommunications industries; and web search portals, data processing industries, and information services.

Telecommunications encompasses wired (including broadband internet service), wireless (including mobile), and satellite telecommunications. Broadcasting covers radio, television, and cable and other subscription programming. Internet publishing and broadcasting and web search portals are grouped together.

The NAICS is periodically updated. The information sector in particular has been subject to changes to reflect developments in communications and other technology. Major revisions in many communications industries affect the comparability of these data over time. For detailed information about NAICS, see <www.census.gov/naics/>.See also the text in Section 15, Business Enterprise.

The 1997 Economic Census was the first to cover the new information sector of the economy. The Economic Census is conducted every 5 years for the years ending in "2" and "7," and provides information on the number of establishments, receipts, payroll, and paid employees for the United States and various geographic levels in the U.S., including the U.S. territories.

In 2018, the Bureau of Economic Analysis began producing statistics to measure the digital economy. The BEA is developing a digital economy satellite account to provide economic measures on the infrastructure that enables a digital economy, electronic commerce transactions, and priced digital services (the computing and communication services performed for a fee charged to the consumer). Currently, the BEA covers goods and services that are primarily digital, and the digital portion of goods and services categories that include a mix of both digital and nondigital goods and services. The BEA is working on expanding coverage of the digital economy.

The Federal Communications Commission (FCC), established in 1934, regulates interstate and international communications by radio, television, wire, satellite, and cable across the entire U.S. Large carriers and holding companies file annual financial reports that are publicly available. The FCC has jurisdiction over interstate and foreign communication services but not over intrastate or local services. The gross operating revenues of the telephone carriers reporting publicly available data annually to the FCC are estimated to cover about 90 percent of the revenues of all U.S. telephone companies. Data are not comparable with Census Bureau's *Service Annual Survey* because of coverage and different accounting practices for those telephone companies which report to the FCC.

Reports filed by the broadcasting industry cover all radio and television stations operating in the United States. Private radio services represent the largest and most diverse group of licensees regulated by the FCC. These services provide voice, data communications, point-to-point, and point-to-multipoint radio communications for fixed and mobile communicators. Major users of these services are small businesses, the aviation industry, the maritime trades, the land transportation industry, the manufacturing industry, state and local public safety and governmental authorities, emergency medical service providers, amateur radio operators, and personal radio operations (CB and the General Mobile Radio Service). The FCC also licenses entities as private and common carriers. Private and common carriers provide fixed and land mobile communications service on a for-profit basis.

Statistics on publishing are available from the Census Bureau and various private agencies. Data on public libraries are from the Institute of Museums and Library Services. The Pew Research Center in Washington D.C. collects data on media use, including the internet and social media, and of mobile electronic devices, among the general public. MRI-Simmons (launched as a joint venture under GfK in 2019) also collects data on internet use, and use of other traditional media.

Statistical reliability—For a discussion of statistical collection and estimation, sampling procedures, and measures of statistical reliability applicable to Census Bureau data, see Appendix III.

Table 1156. Information Industries—Type of Establishment, Employees, and Payroll: 2020

[Employees in thousands (3,577 represents 3,577,000); payroll in millions of dollars (439,777 represents $439,777,000,000). Excludes self-employed individuals, employees of private households, railroad employees, agricultural production employees, and most government employees. For more information, see source and Appendix III]

| Industry | NAICS code [1] | Establishments | | | | Employ-ees [6] (1,000) | Annual payroll (mil. dol.) |
		Total [2]	Corpora-tions [3]	Partner-ships [4]	Non-profits [5]		
Information industries.............	**51**	**160,930**	**131,320**	**18,088**	**5,624**	**3,577**	**439,777**
Publishing industries (except internet)...............	511	29,900	24,545	3,092	709	1,045	157,034
Newspaper, periodical, book, and directory.........	5111	14,701	11,469	1,523	678	308	20,308
Newspaper publishers................................	51111	6,567	5,277	642	157	134	6,595
Periodical publishers................................	51112	4,519	3,414	555	295	74	6,472
Book publishers.....................................	51113	2,357	1,765	184	199	68	5,470
Directory and mailing list publishers...............	51114	594	502	67	6	12	1,009
Other publishers....................................	51119	664	511	75	21	20	762
Greeting card publishers.........................	511191	107	92	9	(NA)	15	500
All other publishers..............................	511199	557	419	66	21	4	262
Software publishers..................................	5112	15,199	13,076	1,569	31	737	136,726
Motion picture and sound recording industries.......	512	28,478	23,079	3,321	634	319	18,538
Motion picture and video industries.................	5121	24,506	20,028	2,821	556	295	15,978
Motion picture and video production...............	51211	16,432	13,891	1,565	261	120	12,234
Motion picture and video distribution.............	51212	424	322	58	17	3	293
Motion picture and video exhibition...............	51213	4,532	3,059	967	264	140	1,016
Motion picture theaters (except drive-ins)........	512131	4,329	2,949	916	263	139	995
Drive-in motion picture theaters..................	512132	203	110	51	(NA)	1	21
Postproduction and other motion picture and video industries...........................	51219	3,118	2,756	231	14	32	2,436
Teleproduction and other post-production services...........................	512191	2,889	2,565	210	10	31	2,356
Other motion picture and video industries........	512199	229	191	21	4	1	80
Sound recording industries..........................	5122	3,972	3,051	500	78	24	2,559
Music publishers....................................	51223	758	566	113	8	6	561
Sound recording studios............................	51224	1,955	1,547	204	12	5	323
Record production and distribution.................	51225	766	580	126	12	11	1,560
Other sound recording industries..................	51229	493	358	57	46	2	115
Broadcasting (except internet)........................	515	8,266	5,706	1,108	1,129	274	26,294
Radio and television broadcasting...................	5151	7,122	4,813	1,034	971	220	18,365
Radio broadcasting..................................	51511	5,013	3,300	797	699	83	5,044
Radio networks....................................	515111	688	424	76	155	11	1,045
Radio stations....................................	515112	4,325	2,876	721	544	72	3,999
Television broadcasting............................	51512	2,109	1,513	237	272	137	13,321
Cable and other subscription programming.........	5152	1,144	893	74	158	54	7,929
Telecommunications....................................	517	64,043	54,991	7,531	255	1,020	85,081
Wired and wireless telecommunications carriers....	5173	58,783	51,337	6,192	247	954	78,503
Wired telecommunications carriers..................	517311	32,552	31,293	764	237	666	58,862
Wireless telecommunications carriers (except satellite)................................	517312	26,231	20,044	5,428	10	287	19,640
Satellite telecommunications.........................	5174	429	342	48	4	8	1,000
Other telecommunications...........................	5179	4,831	3,312	1,291	4	58	5,578
Telecommunications resellers......................	517911	3,005	1,858	1,052	(NA)	29	1,818
All other telecommunications.....................	517919	1,826	1,454	239	3	29	3,760
Data processing, hosting, and related services.....	518	17,273	14,276	1,830	516	557	67,047
Other information services............................	519	12,970	8,723	1,206	2,381	363	85,783
News syndicates.....................................	51911	439	363	26	38	6	612
Libraries and archives...............................	51912	2,257	138	19	2,058	26	879
Internet publishing and broadcasting and web search portals.............................	51913	8,947	7,207	1,014	235	320	83,342
All other information services........................	51919	1,327	1,015	147	50	10	951

NA Not available. [1] 2017 North American Industry Classification System; see text, this section and Section 15. [2] Includes other types of establishments, not shown separately. [3] Includes C- and S-Corporations. [4] An unincorporated business where two or more persons join to carry on a trade or business with each having a shared financial interest in the business. [5] An organization that does not distribute surplus funds to its owners or shareholders, but instead uses surplus funds to help pursue its goals. Most non-profit organizations are exempt from income taxes. [6] For employees on the payroll for the pay period including March 12.

Source: U.S. Census Bureau, County Business Patterns, "County Business Patterns by Legal Form of Organization and Employment Size Class for U.S., States, and Selected Geographies: 2020," <data.census.gov/>, accessed April 2022. See also <www.census.gov/programs-surveys/cbp.html>.

Table 1157. Information Industries—Establishments, Revenue, Payroll, and Employees by Kind of Business: 2017

[1,582,098 represents $1,582,098,000,000. For establishments with payroll. Based on the 2017 Economic Census; see Appendix III]

Kind of business	2017 NAICS code [1]	Establishments	Receipts [2] (mil. dol.)	Annual payroll (mil. dol.)	Paid employees (1,000)
Information............	**51**	**153,928**	**1,582,098**	**360,580**	**3,565**
Publishing industries (except internet) [3]............	511	29,755	368,107	124,857	1,016
Newspaper publishers............	51111	7,230	26,012	7,799	174
Periodical publishers............	51112	5,283	26,733	6,803	87
Book publishers............	51113	2,462	29,116	5,647	75
Software publishers............	5112	13,371	276,234	102,415	647
Motion picture & sound recording industries............	512	25,818	102,088	18,134	341
Motion picture & video industries............	5121	22,118	88,587	15,795	317
Sound recording industries [3]............	5122	3,700	13,501	2,339	24
Music publishers............	51223	709	4,653	535	6
Sound recording studios............	51224	1,863	922	294	5
Record production and distribution............	51225	690	7,344	1,323	9
Broadcasting (except internet)............	515	8,269	165,970	23,339	262
Radio broadcasting............	51511	5,440	20,627	5,479	91
Television broadcasting............	51512	2,123	56,242	10,597	118
Cable & other subscription programming............	5152	706	89,101	7,262	52
Telecommunications............	517	60,474	616,800	82,025	1,085
Wired telecommunications carriers............	517311	30,332	320,758	56,657	707
Wireless telecommunications carriers (except satellite)............	517312	25,736	254,082	19,776	312
Satellite telecommunications............	5174	441	5,742	900	9
Other telecommunications............	5179	3,965	36,218	4,692	57
Data processing, hosting, and related services............	518	17,693	157,477	53,787	553
Other information services [3]............	519	11,919	171,655	58,437	309
Internet publishing & broadcasting and web search portals........	51913	8,136	165,430	56,351	267

[1] North American Industry Classification System, 2017; see text, this section and Section 15. [2] Includes value of sales, shipments, receipts, or revenue. [3] Includes other kinds of businesses not shown separately.

Source: U.S. Census Bureau, 2017 Economic Census, "EC1751BASIC: Information: Summary Statistics for the U.S., States, and Selected Geographies: 2017," <data.census.gov/>, accessed February 2021.

Table 1158. Information Industries—Establishments, Payroll, and Employees by State and Island Area: 2020

[Annual payroll in millions of dollars (439,777 represents $439,777,000,000). Based on Census Bureau's County Business Patterns program. Data based on 2017 North American Industry Classification System (NAICS) code 51]

State and Island area	Establishments	Annual payroll (mil. dol.)	Paid employees [1]	State and Island area	Establishments	Annual payroll (mil. dol.)	Paid employees [1]
United States.......	**160,930**	**439,777**	**3,577,460**	Montana...............	695	445	7,832
Alabama...............	1,829	1,988	30,662	Nebraska...............	956	1,447	20,346
Alaska................	415	479	6,366	Nevada...............	1,571	1,382	19,698
Arizona................	2,662	4,259	56,460	New Hampshire.......	784	1,488	16,249
Arkansas...............	1,178	1,541	20,589	New Jersey...........	3,854	9,114	85,372
California...............	27,894	147,702	731,391	New Mexico...........	850	563	10,366
Colorado...............	3,952	10,505	96,186	New York...........	12,352	41,505	314,340
Connecticut...........	1,818	4,242	38,543	North Carolina........	4,114	8,513	93,020
Delaware...............	718	567	7,225	North Dakota..........	347	512	7,048
District of Columbia...	853	3,547	28,831	Ohio.................	4,285	6,921	97,517
Florida...............	10,058	15,838	175,499	Oklahoma...............	1,515	1,522	26,003
Georgia...............	5,167	12,030	117,449	Oregon...............	2,412	3,225	36,903
Hawaii................	602	506	8,037	Pennsylvania..........	5,674	10,722	108,115
Idaho................	873	1,008	15,777	Rhode Island..........	443	573	7,139
Illinois...............	5,917	12,180	124,872	South Carolina........	1,762	2,419	35,773
Indiana...............	2,483	3,192	41,589	South Dakota..........	449	318	6,330
Iowa................	1,610	1,830	31,568	Tennessee...............	2,951	3,282	46,708
Kansas................	1,424	2,245	25,944	Texas...................	11,165	24,580	264,355
Kentucky...............	1,809	1,509	28,772	Utah.................	1,880	5,661	58,421
Louisiana...............	1,558	1,208	20,795	Vermont...............	491	517	7,207
Maine................	805	588	10,311	Virginia...............	3,964	10,930	97,012
Maryland...............	2,475	4,734	50,597	Washington............	4,186	34,712	158,998
Massachusetts........	3,806	17,328	126,134	West Virginia.........	654	403	7,725
Michigan...............	4,207	5,462	66,418	Wisconsin...............	2,527	4,297	54,591
Minnesota...............	2,717	5,413	59,382	Wyoming...............	444	207	3,816
Mississippi............	1,043	618	12,880	Guam.................	52	69	1,699
Missouri...............	2,732	4,003	54,299	Puerto Rico...........	766	751	16,881

[1] Number of paid employees for pay period including March 12.

Source: U.S. Census Bureau, County Business Patterns, "County Business Patterns, including ZIP Code Business Patterns, by Legal Form of Organization and Employment Size Class for the U.S., States, and Selected Geographies: 2020," <data.census.gov/>, accessed April 2022.

Table 1159. Digital Economy—Value Added, Gross Output, Employment, and Compensation by Industry: 2010 to 2020

[In billions of dollars (1,303.3 represents $1,303,300,000,000), except as noted. Estimates are based on goods and services that are primarily digital and partially digital (mix of digital and nondigital components—only the digital portion is covered). BEA includes in its definition of the digital economy: (1) infrastructure, or the basic physical materials and organizational arrangements that support the existence and use of computer networks and the digital economy—primarily information and communications technology (ICT) goods and services; (2) electronic commerce (e-commerce), the remote sale of goods and services over computer networks; and (3) priced digital services, the computing and communication services performed for a fee charged to the consumer. Industries are based on 2012 North American Classification System (NAICS). For more information, see <www.bea.gov/data/special-topics/digital-economy>. All estimates are revised and are not directly comparable to previously published estimates]

Industry	Value added (bil. dol.) [1]		Gross output (bil. dol.) [1]		Employees (1,000)		Employee compensation (bil. dol.)	
	2010	2020	2010	2020	2010	2020	2010	2020
All industries	**1,303.3**	**2,139.9**	**2,025.5**	**3,305.9**	**6,073.4**	**7,809.8**	**602.6**	**1,089.5**
Private industries	**1,289.6**	**2,127.9**	**2,011.6**	**3,293.6**	**5,975.5**	**7,747.1**	**595.8**	**1,083.8**
Mining	0.4	0.5	0.4	0.5	0.8	0.9	0.1	0.1
Utilities	0.4	0.4	0.4	0.4	0.5	0.4	0.1	0.1
Construction	0.2	0.5	0.2	0.5	0.8	0.7	(Z)	0.2
Manufacturing	195.7	225.0	277.6	280.0	810.5	809.1	89.6	124.5
Wholesale trade	251.8	407.4	399.5	711.7	1,454.6	1,840.3	128.3	207.9
Retail trade	52.7	174.1	70.8	261.2	259.5	608.7	18.2	63.1
Transportation and warehousing	5.3	9.6	10.0	19.0	48.9	75.8	2.8	5.7
Information	533.6	872.2	888.4	1,441.0	1,546.6	1,735.5	172.5	314.9
Publishing, except internet (includes software)	110.6	258.6	154.8	336.0	287.9	601.7	49.6	146.7
Motion picture and sound recording	31.7	20.2	44.7	41.0	100.5	82.0	9.6	10.5
Broadcasting and telecommunications	315.2	385.2	569.3	717.7	930.9	712.3	89.5	94.2
Data processing, internet publishing, and other information services	76.1	208.2	119.5	346.3	227.2	339.6	23.8	63.6
Finance, insurance, real estate, rental, and leasing	6.3	8.9	6.3	8.9	20.5	20.1	1.8	2.5
Professional and business services [2]	225.0	408.2	332.9	539.8	1,607.3	2,402.9	169.0	349.6
Computer systems design & related svcs.	193.2	349.7	290.7	462.7	1,383.8	2,105.3	148.8	311.5
Educational services	9.5	9.4	13.7	15.8	135.1	131.0	7.1	7.3
Health care and social assistance	2.4	4.4	2.4	4.5	18.2	30.5	1.2	2.2
Arts, entertainment, recreation, accommodation, and food services	0.4	0.6	0.4	0.7	4.1	7.0	0.1	0.3
Other services, except government	5.8	6.6	8.8	9.6	68.2	84.1	5.0	5.3
Government	**13.6**	**12.0**	**13.9**	**12.3**	**97.9**	**62.8**	**6.8**	**5.8**
Federal	6.2	6.0	6.2	6.0	27.5	21.9	2.4	2.5
State and local	7.4	6.0	7.7	6.3	70.4	40.9	4.4	3.3

Z Less than $50 million. [1] Estimates are based on data valued in purchasers' prices (instead of producers' prices), which include wholesale and retail trade margins and transportation costs, and sales and excise taxes collected and remitted by producers. [2] Includes other industries not shown separately.

Source: U.S. Bureau of Economic Analysis, Special Topics: Digital Economy, "Data: 2005-2020," May 2022, <www.bea.gov/data/special-topics/digital-economy>.

Table 1160. Digital Economy—Value Added and Gross Output by Commodity: 2010 to 2020

[In billions of dollars (1,303.3 represents $1,303,300,000,000). Estimates cover goods and services that are primarily digital, and the digital portion of partially digital goods and services. See headnote, Table 1159]

Commodity	Value added (GDP) [1,2]				Gross output [2]			
	2010	2015	2019	2020	2010	2015	2019	2020
Digital economy, total	**1,303.3**	**1,665.9**	**2,052.3**	**2,139.9**	**2,025.5**	**2,602.2**	**3,168.9**	**3,305.9**
Digital-enabling infrastructure	482.3	575.5	727.6	770.9	686.3	777.8	962.0	1,022.2
Hardware	235.4	242.6	257.5	277.6	355.6	354.6	369.2	394.4
Software	247.0	333.0	470.1	493.3	330.7	423.1	592.8	627.8
E-commerce	242.8	376.2	457.3	500.0	368.5	614.0	771.9	831.5
Business-to-business	192.5	287.7	326.3	334.0	302.5	489.3	573.1	581.3
Business-to-consumer	50.4	88.5	131.0	166.0	66.1	124.7	198.8	250.2
Priced digital services	578.1	714.1	867.4	869.0	970.7	1,210.5	1,435.0	1,452.2
Cloud services	42.4	50.2	88.6	104.1	62.8	87.6	133.3	161.8
Telecommunications services	343.2	384.7	416.0	401.1	610.0	717.2	774.9	754.6
Internet and data services	49.3	74.0	112.2	117.0	77.2	127.5	189.5	202.5
All other priced digital services	143.1	205.1	250.5	246.8	220.7	278.2	337.3	333.4

[1] Value added by commodity is prepared by (1) calculating ratios of commodity output to total industry output for each industry and digital commodity, (2) applying these ratios to each industry's value added, and (3) aggregating the result by digital commodity. [2] These estimates are based on data valued in purchasers' prices (instead of producers' prices), which include wholesale and retail trade margins and transportation costs, and sales and excise taxes collected and remitted by producers.

Source: U.S. Bureau of Economic Analysis, Special Topics: Digital Economy, "Data: 2005-2020," May 2022, <www.bea.gov/data/special-topics/digital-economy>.

Table 1161. Information Sector Services—Estimated Revenue and Expenses: 2018 to 2020

[In millions of dollars (1,680,739 represents $1,680,739,000,000). For all employer firms regardless of tax status. Data are based on the 2012 North American Industry Classification System (NAICS). Estimates have been adjusted using results of the 2017 Economic Census where applicable. Based on the Service Annual Survey and administrative data; see Appendix III]

Industry	NAICS code	Operating revenue			Operating expenses		
		2018	2019	2020	2018	2019	2020
Information industries...................	**51**	**1,680,739**	**1,755,214**	**1,791,438**	**1,227,008**	**1,282,663**	**1,300,054**
Publishing industries (except internet)................	511	392,801	417,324	440,921	281,273	300,717	299,801
Newspaper publishers...................	51111	25,436	23,689	22,149	24,002	22,398	21,465
Periodical publishers...................	51112	25,795	26,409	23,919	20,106	21,430	18,899
Book publishers...................	51113	27,978	27,056	25,552	17,378	17,926	16,076
Directory and mailing list publishers................	51114	5,090	4,623	4,409	4,214	3,786	3,704
Greeting card publishers................	511191	3,552	3,004	2,931	(S)	1,860	1,772
All other publishers...................	511199	1,338	1,384	1,356	826	841	778
Software publishers...................	5112	303,612	331,159	360,605	212,421	232,476	237,107
Motion picture and sound recording industries.............	512	111,452	113,475	91,711	76,915	77,360	72,098
Motion picture and video production and distribution [1]....	5121x	74,000	74,972	65,854	48,683	48,519	47,411
Motion picture and video exhibition.................	51213	17,579	17,375	4,729	13,150	13,338	8,445
Teleproduction and other postproduction services......	512191	4,868	4,671	4,153	3,764	3,538	3,322
Other motion picture and video industries.............	512199	256	305	277	171	215	159
Record production...................	51221	312	344	319	247	252	237
Integrated record production/distribution.................	51222	7,715	8,467	8,987	7,276	7,683	8,702
Music publishers...................	51223	5,079	5,525	5,765	2,433	2,563	2,679
Sound recording studios...................	51224	1,019	1,198	1,118	779	851	800
Other sound recording industries...................	51229	624	618	509	412	401	343
Broadcasting (except internet)...................	515	173,894	168,752	171,889	121,299	121,121	122,915
Radio networks...................	515111	8,361	8,910	9,773	6,194	7,908	9,691
Radio stations...................	515112	12,787	12,681	10,955	11,323	11,421	9,975
Television broadcasting...................	51512	61,322	62,421	64,912	48,776	50,827	51,901
Cable and other subscription programming.............	5152	91,424	84,740	86,249	55,006	50,965	51,348
Telecommunications...................	517	629,550	639,253	635,454	464,098	483,063	473,766
Wired telecommunications carriers...................	5171	316,766	319,252	312,008	254,235	267,133	259,555
Wireless telecommunications carriers (except satellite)...	5172	270,220	276,114	278,868	178,599	182,268	181,153
Satellite telecommunications...................	5174	5,844	5,635	5,630	4,555	4,518	4,494
Telecommunications resellers...................	517911	19,037	18,825	19,129	11,773	12,331	11,945
All other telecommunications...................	517919	17,683	19,427	19,819	14,936	16,813	16,619
Data processing, hosting, and related services.............	518	175,092	193,228	205,869	142,548	148,256	155,026
Other information services...................	519	197,950	223,182	245,594	140,875	152,146	176,448
News syndicates...................	51911	1,400	1,454	1,466	1,126	1,120	1,135
Libraries and archives...................	51912	2,258	2,299	2,289	2,058	2,107	2,059
Internet publishing and broadcasting, and Web search portals...................	51913	191,581	216,851	239,073	135,543	146,996	171,312
Other information services...................	51919	2,711	2,578	2,766	2,148	1,923	1,942

S Estimate does not meet publication standards. [1] Includes NAICS 51211 (Motion Picture and Video Production) and NAICS 51212 (Motion Picture and Video Distribution).

Source: U.S. Census Bureau, Service Annual Survey, "Service Annual Survey Latest Data (NAICS-basis): 2020," <www.census.gov/programs-surveys/sas/data.html>, accessed December 2021.

Table 1162. Audience Use of Media by Type: 2022

[In percent, except total population (253,853 represents 253,853,000). As of Winter 2022. For persons age 18 and over. Represents the percent of persons using each media type during an average week, except as noted. Based on a sample and subject to sampling error]

Audience characteristic	Total population (1,000)	Magazine reading [1]	Newspaper reading [2]	Radio/ audio listening	TV prime time viewing [3]	Spanish language TV network viewing	Internet use	Social media use
Total...................	**253,853**	**76.3**	**34.3**	**79.5**	**81.1**	**7.7**	**94.4**	**79.4**
18 to 24 years old.........	29,257	73.1	32.0	73.6	63.9	10.5	95.0	91.3
25 to 34 years old.........	45,574	72.1	28.5	79.6	74.5	8.7	94.8	88.7
35 to 44 years old.........	41,691	72.1	27.0	82.7	78.7	10.5	95.7	85.5
45 to 54 years old.........	39,866	74.7	31.0	84.8	85.0	10.3	95.6	82.1
55 to 64 years old.........	42,467	78.0	36.8	81.9	87.5	5.1	94.8	74.3
65 years old and over......	54,998	84.6	46.3	74.6	89.7	3.6	91.7	62.7
Male...................	122,706	72.8	34.0	80.8	79.2	7.8	93.9	75.4
Female...................	131,147	79.7	34.6	78.4	82.8	7.7	95.0	83.2
White only...................	182,943	76.6	34.0	79.5	82.7	5.3	95.2	78.7
Black only...................	31,069	76.6	38.9	82.2	82.3	1.7	90.9	79.8
Other/multiple categories...	39,841	74.9	31.9	77.8	72.7	23.6	93.6	82.4
Employed:								
Full time...................	118,312	74.0	30.4	82.8	80.9	7.3	96.1	83.9
Part time...................	32,206	76.5	34.5	80.8	78.0	9.8	95.0	83.4
Not employed...................	103,334	79.0	38.6	75.4	82.3	7.7	92.3	73.0
Household income:								
Less than $50,000........	74,027	74.4	36.7	78.3	78.0	13.6	90.3	75.3
$50,000 to $74,999.......	41,454	75.0	33.9	79.9	81.3	9.2	94.9	79.6
$75,000 to $149,999......	79,775	77.0	32.9	80.4	82.8	5.1	95.9	80.7
$150,000 or more........	58,597	78.8	33.4	79.6	82.6	2.9	97.3	82.6

[1] One or more issues in a month. [2] One or more issues over a 28-day period. [3] Includes broadcast and cable TV.

Source: © MRI-Simmons Winter 2022 USA Study. Courtesy of MRI-Simmons. See also <www.mrisimmons.com/>.

Table 1163. Utilization and Number of Selected Media: 2000 to 2020

[100.2 represents 100,200,000]

Media	Unit	2000	2005	2010	2014	2015	2016	2017	2018	2019	2020
Households with—											
Telephones [1]	Millions	100.2	107.0	114.0	119.9	122.2	122.6	122.1	124.2	125.2	127.2
Telephone service [1]	Percent	94.1	92.9	95.5	96.1	96.3	96.3	95.8	96.0	95.8	97.2
Landline households with											
wireless telephone [2]	Percent	(X)	42.4	58.1	44.7	41.6	40.2	37.8	36.3	37.2	34.3
Wireless-only [2]	Percent	(X)	7.3	26.6	44.0	47.4	49.3	52.5	54.9	59.2	62.5
Total broadcast stations [3,4]	Number	(NA)	27,354	30,630	30,592	31,032	32,397	33,006	33,342	33,513	33,564
Radio stations	Number	(NA)	13,660	14,619	15,432	15,480	15,516	15,503	15,508	15,500	15,445
AM stations	Number	4,685	4,757	4,782	4,705	4,684	4,669	4,639	4,619	4,593	4,551
FM commercial	Number	5,892	6,231	6,526	6,652	6,701	6,746	6,744	6,754	6,772	6,699
FM educational	Number	(NA)	2,672	3,311	4,075	4,095	4,101	4,120	4,135	4,135	4,195
Television stations [3]	Number	1,663	1,750	1,781	1,785	1,782	1,778	1,767	1,761	1,762	1,758
Commercial	Number	1,288	1,370	1,390	1,390	1,387	1,384	1,377	1,373	1,374	1,371
UHF TV band	Number	721	782	1,022	1,032	1,031	1,033	1,013	1,006	1,004	994
VHF TV band	Number	567	588	368	358	356	351	364	367	370	377
Educational	Number	(NA)	380	391	395	395	394	390	388	388	387
UHF TV band	Number	(NA)	254	284	289	289	289	276	270	270	267
VHF TV band	Number	(NA)	126	107	106	106	105	114	118	118	120
Broadband subscribers: [5,9]											
Total fixed broadband [6]	Millions	6.8	47.8	84.5	98.2	102.1	105.6	108.1	110.8	112.7	(NA)
25 Mbps/3 Mbps [7]	Millions	(NA)	(NA)	(NA)	42.7	54.3	62.9	73.9	82.9	86.7	(NA)
Mobile wireless [8]	Millions	(NA)	(NA)	97.5	240.0	273.7	299.3	312.8	330.5	336.2	(NA)
Residential fixed broadband [6]	Millions	5.2	44.0	76.9	89.5	93.4	96.6	98.8	101.3	103.0	(NA)
25 Mbps/3 Mbps [7]	Millions	(NA)	(NA)	(NA)	40.9	51.8	59.5	69.4	76.9	80.2	(NA)
Residential mobile wireless	Millions	(NA)	(NA)	72.5	201.2	229.1	241.4	253.1	267.2	270.1	(NA)

NA Not available. X Not applicable. [1] As of November. Based on Current Population Survey. Source: Federal Communications Commission, prior to 2011, *Telephone Subscribership in the United States,* December 2011, and earlier reports. Beginning 2012, *Universal Service Monitoring Report, 2021,* and earlier reports. See also <www.fcc.gov/general/federal-state-joint-board-monitoring-reports>. [2] For January to June. Based on National Health Interview Survey. For families living in the same housing unit. Source: U.S. National Center for Health Statistics, *Wireless Substitution: Early Release of Estimates From the National Health Interview Survey, January–June 2021,* November 2021, and earlier reports. [3] As of December 31. Source: Federal Communications Commission, "Broadcast Station Totals," <www.fcc.gov/media/broadcast-station-totals>, accessed July 2022. [4] Includes Class A UHF and VHF, UHF and VHF Low Power TV, UHF and VHF Translators, FM Translators and Boosters, and Low Power FM stations. [5] As of December. Internet access over 200 kilobits per second in at least one direction. Based on FCC Form 477. Source: Federal Communications Commission, Wireline Competition Bureau, *Internet Access Services: Status as of June 30, 2019,* March 2022 and previous reports. [6] Includes aDSL, sDSL, cable modem, fiber-to-the-premises, satellite, fixed wireless, and power line/other. [7] Internet download and upload speeds, measured in megabits per second (Mbps). [8] Data prior to 2008 not shown due to reporting instruction changes on FCC Form 477. [9] For 2019, data under broadband internet subscribers are as of June 30, 2019.

Source: Compiled from sources mentioned in footnotes.

Table 1164. Publishing Industries—Estimated Revenue by Source and Media Type: 2016 to 2020

[In millions of dollars (342,059 represents $342,059,000,000). Data are based on the 2012 North American Industry Classification System (NAICS). Estimates have been adjusted using results of the 2017 Economic Census where applicable. Based on the Service Annual Survey; see text, this section and Section 15, and Appendix III]

Source of revenue and media type	2016	2017	2018	2019	2020
Publishing industries (except internet), NAICS 511 [1]	**342,059**	**368,107**	**392,801**	**417,324**	**440,921**
Newspaper publishers, NAICS 51111	25,564	26,012	25,436	23,689	22,149
Subscription and sales	8,960	9,158	9,258	8,850	8,795
Advertising space	13,799	13,788	12,788	11,648	10,221
Printing services	1,090	1,153	1,163	1,188	(S)
Distribution services	553	544	455	(S)	(S)
All other operating revenue	1,162	1,369	1,772	(S)	(S)
Print newspapers	17,936	17,679	16,985	14,717	13,642
Online newspapers	4,780	5,207	5,011	5,730	5,332
Other media newspapers	(S)	60	(S)	(S)	(S)
Periodical publishers, NAICS 51112 [1]	27,008	26,733	25,795	26,409	23,919
Subscription and sales	9,432	(S)	8,513	9,766	9,168
Advertising space	13,797	(S)	(S)	9,949	8,958
Print periodicals	15,829	(S)	(S)	12,477	10,914
Online periodicals	6,296	6,238	6,673	7,087	7,079
Book publishers, NAICS 51113 [1]	28,608	29,116	27,978	27,056	25,552
Textbooks	10,482	10,240	9,135	8,389	7,849
Children's books	2,942	3,085	3,067	2,840	(S)
General reference books	(S)	(S)	265	287	250
Professional, technical, and scholarly books	7,217	(S)	(S)	(S)	(S)
Adult trade books	5,589	5,578	5,379	5,242	5,253
Print books	17,068	16,752	14,390	13,594	(S)
Online books	7,994	(S)	(S)	(S)	(S)
Other media books	1,473	(S)	(S)	(S)	1,034
Directory and mailing list publishers, NAICS 51114 [1]	6,365	4,968	5,090	4,623	4,409
Subscription and sales	2,435	1,653	2,432	2,480	2,038
Advertising space	3,079	2,770	2,066	1,618	1,781
Print directories, databases, and other information collections	2,135	(S)	1,582	1,238	1,717
Online directories, databases, and other information collections	2,946	2,332	2,716	2,791	1,979
Greeting card publishers operating revenue, NAICS 511191	3,371	3,732	3,552	3,004	2,931

S Figure does not meet publication standards. [1] Includes other industries or revenue sources not shown separately.

Source: U.S. Census Bureau, Service Annual Survey, "Service Annual Survey Latest Data (NAICS-basis): 2020," <www.census.gov/programs-surveys/sas/data.html>, accessed December 2021.

Table 1165. Daily and Sunday Newspapers—Number and Circulation: 1970 to 2018

[Circulation in millions (62.1 represents 62,100,000). Number of newspapers as of February 1 the following year, except as noted. Circulation figures as of 6-month period ended primarily September 30 of year shown. Covers all 50 States and D.C. For English language newspapers only]

Type	1970	1980	1990	2000	2005	2010	2013[3]	2014[3]	2015[3]	2016[3]	2017[3]	2018[3]
NUMBER												
Total daily newspapers [1]	**1,748**	**1,745**	**1,611**	**1,480**	**1,452**	(NA)	**1,395**	**1,331**	**1,338**	**1,286**	**1,277**	**1,279**
Morning	334	387	559	766	817	(NA)	980	953	972	939	947	925
Evening	1,429	1,388	1,084	727	645	(NA)	444	402	389	369	356	354
Sunday newspapers	586	736	863	917	914	(NA)	934	923	904	866	857	840
NET PAID CIRCULATION (mil.)												
Total daily newspapers [1]	62.1	62.2	62.3	55.8	53.3	(NA)	40.7	40.4	34.9	33.4	29.2	25.7
Morning	25.9	29.4	41.3	46.8	46.1	(NA)	37.0	36.8	31.6	30.4	26.2	23.0
Evening	36.2	32.8	21.0	9.0	7.2	(NA)	3.7	3.7	3.3	3.1	3.0	2.7
Sunday newspapers	49.2	54.7	62.6	59.4	55.3	(NA)	43.3	42.8	40.0	37.8	33.2	29.3
PER CAPITA CIRCULATION [2]												
Total daily newspapers [1]	0.30	0.27	0.25	0.20	0.18	(NA)	0.13	0.13	0.11	0.10	0.09	0.08
Morning	0.13	0.13	0.17	0.17	0.16	(NA)	0.12	0.12	0.10	0.09	0.08	0.07
Evening	0.18	0.14	0.08	0.03	0.02	(NA)	0.01	0.01	0.01	0.01	0.01	0.01
Sunday newspapers	0.24	0.24	0.25	0.21	0.19	(NA)	0.14	0.13	0.12	0.12	0.10	0.09

NA Not available. [1] All-day newspapers are counted in both morning and evening rows but only once in total. Circulation is divided equally between morning and evening. [2] Based on U.S. Census Bureau estimated resident population as of July 1 of year shown. [3] Number of newspapers as of January 1 of following year.

Source: Editor & Publisher, *Editor & Publisher Newspaper DataBook* ©, annual. See also <www.editorandpublisher.com/>.

Table 1166. Daily and Sunday Newspapers—Number and Circulation: Total, 1997 to 2018, and by State, 2018

[Circulation in thousands (56,728 represents 56,728,000). Number of newspapers as of February 1 the following year, except as noted. Circulation as of 6-month period ended primarily September 30 of year shown. Covers the 50 states and D.C. For English language newspapers only]

State	Daily Number	Daily Circulation[1] Net paid (1,000)	Daily Circulation[1] Per capita[2]	Sunday Number	Sunday Net paid circulation[1] (1,000)	State	Daily Number	Daily Circulation[1] Net paid (1,000)	Daily Circulation[1] Per capita[2]	Sunday Number	Sunday Net paid circulation[1] (1,000)
1997	1,509	56,728	0.21	903	60,484	IN	67	719	0.11	29	777
1998	1,489	56,182	0.20	898	60,066	IA	33	321	0.10	13	305
1999	1,483	55,979	0.20	905	59,894	KS	30	219	0.08	11	170
2000	1,480	55,773	0.20	917	59,421	KY	21	284	0.06	14	307
2001	1,468	55,578	0.19	913	59,090	LA	18	232	0.05	13	254
2002	1,457	55,186	0.19	913	58,780	ME	7	108	0.08	5	95
2003	1,456	55,185	0.19	917	58,495	MD	9	213	0.04	8	340
2004	1,457	54,626	0.19	915	57,753	MA	30	633	0.09	16	651
2005	1,452	53,345	0.18	914	55,270	MI	47	670	0.07	24	744
2006	1,437	52,329	0.18	907	53,175	MN	22	586	0.10	14	787
2007	1,422	50,742	0.17	907	51,246	MS	17	161	0.05	15	163
2008	1,408	48,598	0.16	902	49,115	MO	36	388	0.06	16	388
2009	1,397	46,278	0.15	919	46,895	MT	11	133	0.13	8	153
2010	(NA)	(NA)	(NA)	(NA)	(NA)	NE	15	218	0.11	6	196
2011	1,381	44,243	0.14	899	48,301	NV	5	241	0.08	5	276
2012	1,425	43,154	0.14	980	44,612	NH	10	105	0.08	7	108
2013[3]	1,395	40,712	0.13	934	43,292	NJ	17	460	0.05	16	652
2014[3]	1,331	40,420	0.13	923	42,751	NM	14	157	0.07	10	161
2015[3]	1,338	34,901	0.11	904	40,014	NY	55	3,366	0.17	39	3,936
2016[3]	1,286	33,419	0.10	866	37,771	ND	44	579	0.06	36	651
2017[3]	1,277	29,185	0.09	857	33,160	ND	10	103	0.14	7	102
						OH	81	1,113	0.10	46	1,231
Total, 2018[3]	**1,279**	**25,705**	**0.08**	**840**	**29,273**	OK	33	309	0.08	26	330
AL	22	186	0.04	16	214	OR	16	293	0.07	11	310
AK	8	98	0.13	4	89	PA	70	1,167	0.09	41	1,386
AZ	12	285	0.04	10	403	RI	5	77	0.07	2	79
AR	25	253	0.08	14	256	SC	16	268	0.05	14	315
CA	69	2,178	0.06	49	2,846	SD	11	84	0.10	4	55
CO	28	418	0.07	14	503	TN	25	424	0.06	18	466
CT	18	279	0.08	14	357	TX	66	1,100	0.04	64	1,562
DE	2	73	0.08	2	89	UT	6	174	0.05	6	274
DC	3	473	0.67	2	483	VT	8	52	0.08	4	37
FL	37	1,159	0.05	33	1,598	VA	20	2,174	0.26	17	1,415
GA	29	435	0.04	23	494	WA	20	534	0.07	16	657
HI	6	183	0.13	5	198	WV	17	175	0.10	11	174
ID	12	130	0.07	9	213	WI	32	470	0.08	20	525
IL	56	1,183	0.09	27	1,437	WY	8	62	0.11	6	61

NA Not available. [1] Circulation figures based on the principal community served by a newspaper, which is not necessarily the same location as the publisher's office. [2] Per capita based on estimated resident population as of July 1 of year shown. [3] Number of newspapers as of January 1 of following year.

Source: Editor & Publisher, *Editor & Publisher Newspaper DataBook* ©, annual. See also <www.editorandpublisher.com/>.

Table 1167. Software Publishers—Estimated Revenue, Expenses, and Inventories by Type: 2015 to 2020

[In millions of dollars (222,564 represents $222,564,000,000). For all employer firms regardless of tax status. Data are based on the 2012 North American Industry Classification System (NAICS), and cover NAICS 5112. Estimates have been adjusted using results of the 2017 Economic Census where applicable. Based on the Service Annual Survey; see text, this section, and Section 15, Business Enterprise. See also Appendix III]

Item	2015	2016	2017	2018	2019	2020
Operating revenue	**222,564**	**249,823**	**276,234**	**303,612**	**331,159**	**360,605**
System software publishing [1]	61,971	66,749	74,698	86,417	85,420	98,513
Operating system software	21,294	23,006	25,472	28,047	27,654	36,493
Network software	14,456	16,471	18,039	23,788	22,951	27,340
Database management software	15,517	16,089	17,136	17,557	18,272	19,548
Development tools and programming languages software	2,653	2,653	2,618	2,675	2,483	3,171
Application software publishing [1]	99,860	111,530	122,079	136,690	157,946	172,291
General business productivity and home use applications	46,534	52,340	60,051	66,725	86,134	91,842
Cross-industry application software	28,258	31,285	31,863	35,248	32,863	(S)
Vertical market application software	12,544	14,229	16,504	17,752	16,235	22,166
Utilities application software	2,610	3,021	3,037	4,172	4,553	5,274
Other services: [1]						
Custom application design and development	3,906	4,232	4,587	6,218	(S)	8,792
Information technology technical consulting services	6,918	8,986	11,621	11,829	12,272	(S)
Resale of computer hardware and software	9,133	10,167	10,063	11,227	15,366	(S)
Information technology-related training services	3,316	4,118	4,110	4,049	4,022	4,078
By software sales type:						
System software	61,971	66,749	74,698	86,417	85,420	98,513
Personal computer software	16,525	18,038	19,138	18,535	18,845	27,511
Enterprise or network software	26,933	30,369	35,289	45,802	43,335	46,974
Mainframe computer software	11,081	11,391	13,756	14,710	15,384	14,774
Other system software	7,432	6,951	6,515	7,370	7,856	9,254
Application software	99,860	111,530	122,079	136,690	157,946	172,291
Personal computer software	25,038	28,873	31,449	37,306	45,023	43,465
Enterprise or network software	49,712	54,015	59,663	67,392	80,273	89,495
Mainframe computer software	5,630	5,963	5,459	(S)	(S)	(S)
Other application software	19,480	22,679	25,508	(S)	30,910	(S)
Operating expenses, total	**148,408**	**168,104**	**185,131**	**212,421**	**232,476**	**237,107**
Inventories at end of year, total	**4,149**	**4,131**	**4,101**	**4,738**	**5,834**	**9,846**
Finished goods	2,680	2,679	2,563	3,554	4,965	8,570
Works-in-process	1,046	999	1,123	939	(S)	(S)
Materials, supplies, fuel, etc	423	453	(S)	245	671	1,067

S Data do not meet publication standards. [1] Includes other sources of revenue not shown separately.

Source: U.S. Census Bureau, Service Annual Survey, "Service Annual Survey Latest Data (NAICS-basis): 2020," <www.census.gov/programs-surveys/sas/data.html>, accessed December 2021.

Table 1168. Internet Publishing and Broadcasting, and Web Search Portals—Estimated Revenue and Expenses: 2015 to 2020

[In millions of dollars (122,279 represents $122,279,000,000). For all employer firms regardless of tax status. Data are based on the 2012 North American Industry Classification System (NAICS). Covers NAICS 51913. See headnote, Table 1167. See text, Section 15, and Appendix III]

Item	2015	2016	2017	2018	2019	2020
Operating revenue	**122,279**	**145,759**	**165,430**	**191,581**	**216,851**	**239,073**
Source of revenue:						
Publishing and broadcasting of content on the internet	34,830	39,659	43,847	50,474	50,894	56,875
Licensing of rights to use intellectual property	(S)	2,958	(S)	(S)	(S)	(S)
Online advertising space	74,600	92,729	106,982	125,032	144,803	160,393
All other operating revenue	10,119	10,413	11,290	(S)	16,358	17,449
Revenue by type of customer:						
Household consumers and individual users	38,297	44,891	49,399	(S)	(S)	(S)
Business firms, nonprofit organizations, and government	83,982	100,868	116,031	(S)	(S)	(S)
Operating expenses	**97,514**	**108,010**	**125,882**	**135,543**	**146,996**	**171,312**

S Data do not meet publication standards.

Source: U.S. Census Bureau, Service Annual Survey, "Service Annual Survey Latest Data (NAICS-basis): 2020," <www.census.gov/programs-surveys/sas/data.html>, accessed December 2021.

Table 1169. Motion Picture and Sound Recording Industries—Estimated Revenue and Sources of Revenue: 2015 to 2020

[In millions of dollars (99,230 represents $99,230,000,000). For all employer firms regardless of tax status. Data are based on the 2012 North American Industry Classification System (NAICS). Covers NAICS 512. See headnote, Table 1167. See text, this section, and Section 15, Business Enterprise. See also Appendix III]

Kind of business and revenue source	2015	2016	2017	2018	2019	2020
Total revenue, NAICS 512....	**99,230**	**103,599**	**102,088**	**111,452**	**113,475**	**91,711**
Motion picture and video production and distribution, NAICS 5121X [1,2]...	66,137	69,201	67,300	74,000	74,972	65,854
Domestic licensing of rights to motion picture films........	14,966	14,247	13,549	12,950	12,493	(S)
Domestic licensing of rights to television programs........	13,671	14,726	14,134	16,178	17,082	15,317
International licensing of rights to motion picture films........	7,961	7,869	6,618	6,650	(S)	(S)
International licensing of rights to television programs........	3,788	3,976	3,604	3,577	(S)	(S)
Contract production of audiovisual works........	5,893	5,819	6,039	6,091	7,059	6,085
Sale of audiovisual works for wholesale, retail, and rental markets.......	7,806	7,353	6,161	6,014	4,806	(S)
Motion picture and video exhibition, NAICS 51213 [1]........	15,785	16,539	15,967	17,579	17,375	4,729
Admissions to feature film exhibitions........	9,592	10,024	9,676	10,329	9,914	2,445
Food and beverage sales........	4,937	5,303	5,091	5,632	5,696	1,436
Postproduction services and other motion picture and video industries, NAICS 51219 [1]........	5,238	5,381	5,319	5,124	4,976	4,430
Audiovisual postproduction services........	3,033	3,178	3,070	3,210	3,091	2,733
Motion picture film laboratory services........	(S)	(S)	69	(S)	(S)	59
Duplication and copying services........	205	209	(S)	(S)	(S)	(S)
Integrated record production and distribution, NAICS 51222 [1]........	5,663	6,116	7,048	7,715	8,467	8,987
Licensing revenue........	463	491	550	601	548	604
Sales of recordings........	4,526	4,859	5,607	6,165	6,879	7,295
Music publishers, NAICS 51223 [1]........	4,532	4,527	4,653	5,079	5,525	5,765
Licensing of rights to use musical compositions........	3,732	3,717	3,751	4,041	4,484	4,698
Print music........	239	223	242	208	194	157
Sound recording studios, NAICS 51224 [1]........	982	954	922	1,019	1,198	1,118
Studio recording........	699	651	566	546	625	580

S Data do not meet publication standards. [1] Includes other sources of revenue not shown separately. [2] Includes NAICS 51211 (Motion Picture and Video Production) and NAICS 51212 (Motion Picture and Video Distribution).

Source: U.S. Census Bureau, Service Annual Survey, "Service Annual Survey Latest Data (NAICS-basis): 2020," and "Service Annual Survey Historical Tables," <www.census.gov/programs-surveys/sas/data.html>, accessed December 2021.

Table 1170. Recorded Music Industry—Estimated Retail Volume and Value: 2000 to 2021

[1,079.2 represents 1,079,200,000. Data are net after returns. Formats with no retail value equivalent included at wholesale value. Based on reports of Recording Industry Association of America member companies who distribute about 85 percent of the music sold in the U.S.]

Medium	2000	2005	2010	2015	2017	2018	2019	2020	2021
VOLUME (million units)									
Total [1]........	**1,079.2**	**1,301.9**	**1,739.5**	**1,255.5**	**730.9**	**531.2**	**445.0**	**348.9**	**334.2**
Physical [2]........	**1,079.2**	**748.8**	**267.7**	**135.1**	**104.5**	**70.3**	**67.7**	**56.8**	**88.4**
Compact disk, album [3]........	942.5	705.4	253.0	117.1	86.7	51.8	47.5	31.6	46.6
Compact disk, single........	34.2	2.8	1.0	0.4	(Z)	(Z)	(Z)	(Z)	(Z)
Vinyl LP/EP (long play/extended play)........	2.2	1.0	4.2	13.7	15.6	16.7	18.5	23.7	39.7
Music video [4]........	18.2	33.8	9.1	3.1	1.8	1.4	1.3	1.0	1.3
Digital [2]........	**(NA)**	**554.4**	**1,473.3**	**1,131.2**	**661.6**	**507.8**	**437.6**	**367.6**	**329.8**
Download single........	(NA)	366.9	1,177.4	986.4	544.8	399.3	329.7	249.3	209.3
Download album........	(NA)	13.6	85.8	106.8	64.5	49.3	37.5	33.1	29.1
Mobile [5]........	(NA)	170.0	188.5	21.9	14.3	10.0	8.3	8.1	6.0
Paid subscription [6]........	(NA)	1.3	1.5	10.8	35.3	46.9	60.4	75.5	84.0
VALUE (million dollars) [12]									
Total........	**14,323.7**	**12,289.9**	**7,013.8**	**6,710.8**	**8,503.2**	**9,738.2**	**11,130.6**	**12,144.7**	**14,988.6**
Physical [2]........	**14,323.7**	**11,195.0**	**3,663.7**	**1,862.2**	**1,477.3**	**1,150.4**	**1,144.6**	**1,163.3**	**1,655.8**
Compact disk, album [3]........	13,214.5	10,520.2	3,389.4	1,445.0	1,043.9	695.8	630.7	483.2	584.2
Compact disk, single........	142.7	10.9	2.9	1.2	0.2	(Z)	0.1	0.4	0.1
Vinyl LP/EP (long play/extended play)........	27.7	14.2	88.9	333.4	388.5	419.2	479.5	643.9	1,037.7
Music video [4]........	281.9	602.2	177.6	70.4	37.5	28.4	25.8	27.4	19.9
Digital [2]........	**(NA)**	**1,094.9**	**3,161.4**	**4,645.7**	**6,793.8**	**8,302.3**	**9,704.9**	**10,716.1**	**13,030.0**
Permanent download........	(NA)	925.3	2,699.8	2,314.4	1,375.1	1,034.1	822.7	664.7	586.8
Download single........	(NA)	363.2	1,336.4	1,185.2	667.9	489.9	408.4	303.3	256.0
Download album........	(NA)	135.7	872.4	1,064.4	649.7	495.3	368.8	319.3	282.2
Mobile [5]........	(NA)	421.6	448.0	54.6	35.5	25.0	20.6	20.2	15.0
Subscription and streaming........	(NA)	169.6	461.6	2,331.3	5,418.7	7,268.2	8,882.2	10,051.5	12,443.2
Paid subscription [6]........	(NA)	149.2	212.4	1,156.7	3,359.8	4,614.0	6,115.2	6,972.7	8,573.6
Limited tier paid subscription [7]........	(NA)	(NA)	(NA)	–	568.8	740.5	638.2	719.9	907.3
SoundExchange distributions [8]........	(NA)	20.4	249.2	802.6	652.0	952.8	908.2	947.4	992.5
On-demand streaming [9]........	(NA)	(NA)	(NA)	372.0	614.3	752.7	1,013.3	1,200.1	1,760.7
Other ad-supported streaming [10]........	(NA)	(NA)	(NA)	(NA)	223.9	208.2	207.3	211.2	209.0
Synchronization royalties [11]........	**(NA)**	**(NA)**	**188.7**	**202.9**	**232.1**	**285.5**	**281.1**	**265.2**	**302.9**

– Represents zero. Z Represents less than 50,000. NA Not available. [1] Total volume excludes paid digital subscriptions. [2] Includes other media or digital formats not shown separately. [3] Prior to 2006, includes DualDisc. [4] Includes DVD video. [5] Master ringtones and ringbacks; prior to 2013, also included music videos, full length downloads, and other mobile. [6] Streaming, tethered, and other paid subscription services not operating under statutory licenses. Volume is annual average number of subscribers. [7] Includes streaming services with interactivity limitations by availability, device restriction, catalog limitations, on demand access, or other factors. [8] SoundExchange is a nonprofit organization that collects and distributes digital performance royalties on behalf of recording artists and master rights owners. [9] Advertising supported audio and music video services not operating under statutory licenses. [10] Includes revenues from services paid directly that are not distributed by SoundExchange and not included in other streaming categories. [11] Include fees and royalties from synchronization of sound recordings with other media. [12] In 2016, accounting standards updated.

Source: Recording Industry Association of America, Washington, D.C., Facts & Research, *Year-End 2021 RIAA Revenue Statistics* ©, March 2022, <www.riaa.com/reports/>.

Table 1171. Radio and Television Broadcasting—Estimated Revenue and Expenses: 2015 to 2020

[In millions of dollars (6,661 represents $6,661,000,000). For all employer firms regardless of tax status. Based on the 2012 North American Industry Classification System (NAICS). Estimates have been adjusted using results of the 2017 Economic Census where applicable. Based on the Service Annual Survey; see text, this section, and Section 15, Business Enterprise]

Item	2015	2016	2017	2018	2019	2020
RADIO AND TELEVISION BROADCASTING (NAICS 5151)						
Operating expenses, total.	57,686	63,007	61,695	66,293	70,156	71,567
RADIO NETWORKS (NAICS 515111)						
Total operating revenue.	6,661	7,293	7,922	8,361	8,910	9,773
National/regional/local air time.	1,497	1,625	1,851	1,991	2,347	2,933
Public and non-commercial programming services.	377	407	431	465	458	503
All other operating revenue.	4,787	5,261	5,640	5,905	6,105	6,337
Operating expenses, total.	5,131	5,439	5,822	6,194	7,908	9,691
RADIO STATIONS (NAICS 515112)						
Total operating revenue.	12,657	13,113	12,705	12,787	12,681	10,955
National/regional/local air time.	10,801	11,257	10,832	10,804	10,708	8,636
Public and non-commercial programming services.	745	694	795	805	785	792
All other operating revenue.	1,111	1,162	1,078	1,178	1,188	1,527
Operating expenses, total.	10,514	11,103	10,903	11,323	11,421	9,975
TELEVISION BROADCASTING (NAICS 51512)						
Total operating revenue.	50,067	56,978	56,242	61,322	62,421	64,912
National/regional/local air time.	35,274	38,709	36,064	39,816	40,426	41,054
Public and non-commercial programming services.	2,111	2,164	1,980	2,225	2,240	3,587
All other operating revenue.	12,682	16,105	18,198	19,281	19,755	20,271
Operating expenses, total.	42,041	46,465	44,970	48,776	50,827	51,901

Source: U.S. Census Bureau, Service Annual Survey, "Service Annual Survey Latest Data (NAICS-basis): 2020," <www.census.gov/programs-surveys/sas/data.html>, accessed December 2021.

Table 1172. Cable and Other Subscription Programming—Estimated Revenue and Expenses: 2015 to 2020

[In millions of dollars (82,061 represents $82,061,000,000). For all employer firms regardless of tax status. Based on the 2012 North American Industry Classification System. Covers NAICS 5152. See headnote, Table 1171. See text, this section and Section 15, and Appendix III]

Item	2015	2016	2017	2018	2019	2020
Operating revenue, total [1]	82,061	85,929	89,101	91,424	84,740	86,249
Advertising and program revenue [1]	50,747	53,465	55,775	58,248	53,253	54,925
Air time.	27,305	28,196	28,771	27,379	26,057	25,260
All other operating services revenue.	4,009	4,268	4,555	5,797	5,430	6,064
Operating expenses, total [2]	48,227	50,986	53,111	55,006	50,965	51,348

[1] Licensing of rights to broadcast specialty programming protected by copyright.

Source: U.S. Census Bureau, Service Annual Survey, "Service Annual Survey Latest Data (NAICS-basis): 2020," <www.census.gov/programs-surveys/sas/data.html>, accessed December 2021.

Table 1173. Telecommunications Industry Revenue by Service Type: 2010 to 2020

[Revenue in millions of dollars (446,386 represents $446,386,000,000). Data are based on carrier Form 499-A filings to the Federal Communications Commission, and are the basis for establishing Universal Service Fund (USF) program collections]

Category	Revenue (mil. dol.)						
	2010	2015	2016	2017	2018	2019	2020
Total reported revenue.	446,386	515,598	509,679	504,516	507,474	511,692	512,497
Non-telecommunications revenue.	173,228	301,121	311,404	321,597	337,212	361,245	379,509
Total telecommunications revenue.	273,158	214,477	198,276	182,918	170,262	150,447	132,989
Local service and payphone revenue.	102,847	90,495	87,162	83,572	77,048	72,964	65,576
Local exchange.	43,878	28,410	25,900	23,208	20,771	18,806	16,115
Pay telephone.	197	286	271	269	265	280	286
Local private line.	26,809	32,191	30,472	30,272	26,906	25,560	21,608
Voice over internet protocol (VoIP) local.	8,234	11,968	14,398	14,428	14,503	14,355	14,317
Other local.	3,032	1,493	1,510	1,749	1,710	1,265	1,164
Federal and State USF support.	4,880	6,137	6,016	5,904	5,994	6,422	6,484
Subscriber line charges.	7,481	5,175	4,787	4,431	4,049	3,700	3,345
Access.	8,336	4,836	3,809	3,312	2,850	2,575	2,257
Mobile service revenue.	111,643	75,262	65,636	56,952	52,890	39,631	33,379
Toll service revenue.	50,006	39,678	36,342	34,075	31,885	29,405	25,975
Operator.	3,585	2,351	1,876	1,844	1,810	1,711	1,464
VoIP toll.	1,943	5,238	3,447	3,768	3,925	3,518	2,491
Non-operator switched toll.	25,189	16,261	14,850	11,841	11,068	9,913	9,054
Long distance private line.	14,344	12,778	13,353	13,316	12,850	11,991	10,698
Other long distance.	4,945	3,050	2,816	3,306	2,233	2,273	2,268
Universal service surcharges.	8,662	9,041	9,135	8,319	8,438	8,447	8,059

Source: U.S. Federal Communications Commission, Universal Service Monitoring Report, 2021, January 2022. See also <www.fcc.gov/general/federal-state-joint-board-monitoring-reports>.

Table 1174. Wired and Wireless Telecommunications Carriers—Estimated Revenue: 2013 to 2020

[In millions of dollars (289,645 represents $289,645,000,000). For all employer firms regardless of tax status. Covers NAICS 5171 Wired Telecommunications Carriers and NAICS 5172 Wireless Telecommunications Carriers (except satellite). Data are based on the 2012 North American Industry Classification System. Estimates have been adjusted using results of the 2017 Economic Census where applicable. Based on the Service Annual Survey; see text, this section and Section 15, and Appendix III]

Revenue source	2013	2014	2015	2016	2017	2018	2019	2020
Wired telecommunications carriers operating revenue	**289,645**	**298,811**	**309,485**	**330,437**	**320,758**	**316,766**	**319,252**	**312,008**
Fixed local telephony	31,309	30,602	18,980	19,651	17,378	15,423	13,762	12,843
Fixed long-distance telephony	16,504	15,583	(S)	19,061	(S)	20,748	19,965	17,562
Fixed all distance	1,253	1,139	2,023	1,977	1,614	2,808	3,544	(S)
Carrier services	16,443	18,714	21,706	(S)	13,480	14,522	14,352	14,459
Private network services	19,998	19,561	17,640	17,840	10,596	7,727	8,023	6,976
Internet access services	70,387	73,546	79,148	88,408	93,272	97,418	100,043	103,256
Internet telephony	13,021	13,102	11,828	11,438	10,418	9,746	10,030	9,495
Telecommunications network installation services	506	658	906	829	856	1,315	(S)	1,686
Reselling services for telecommunications equipment, retail	1,310	1,151	1,644	1,497	1,491	816	1,866	1,838
Rental of telecommunications equipment	486	596	569	1,724	4,534	7,041	7,314	8,496
Repair and maintenance services for telecommunications equipment	568	910	984	(S)	873	(S)	(S)	(S)
Subscriber line charges	3,567	3,453	3,263	3,266	2,945	2,831	2,292	2,123
Basic programming package	58,772	60,442	61,709	64,502	61,766	61,348	61,599	60,721
Premium programming package	21,254	21,268	23,493	24,717	23,369	22,557	22,842	20,047
Pay-per-view	(S)	3,107	2,922	2,936	2,829	2,020	1,629	1,399
Air time	(S)	5,055	5,780	6,428	5,702	6,561	5,884	5,838
Rental and reselling services for program distribution equipment	11,598	12,215	14,364	14,045	12,254	11,188	10,600	10,771
Installation services for connections to program distribution networks	1,365	1,669	(S)	(S)	(S)	(S)	(S)	(S)
Website hosting services	134	179	574	(S)	(S)	(S)	(S)	(S)
All other operating revenue	13,391	15,861	20,974	31,685	35,131	29,423	30,608	28,600
Wireless telecommunications carrier operating revenue [1]	**232,458**	**250,391**	**252,264**	**256,298**	**254,082**	**270,220**	**276,114**	**278,868**
Messaging (paging) services	(S)	(S)	3,691	2,928	(S)	2,185	(S)	(S)
Mobile telephony	61,838	59,563	46,089	(S)	(S)	(S)	5,755	(S)
Mobile long distance	(D)	4,161	2,891	2,418	2,494	2,448	2,585	1,971
Mobile all distance	59,496	53,798	46,696	(S)	(S)	81,992	82,536	86,778
Internet access services	66,084	76,950	90,177	96,397	94,877	89,647	92,179	96,949
Telecommunications network installation services	195	206	205	239	189	(S)	195	267
Reselling services for telecommunications equipment, retail	24,620	35,289	41,022	43,956	46,096	56,902	58,217	56,276
Rental of telecommunications equipment	432	486	(S)	(S)	4,646	6,671	6,643	6,954
Repair and maintenance services for telecommunications equipment	(D)	2,220	2,289	2,316	1,834	1,660	1,694	1,656
All other operating revenue	13,684	17,183	15,691	16,700	17,833	22,195	24,052	19,364

S Data do not meet publication standards. D Estimate withheld to avoid disclosing data of individual companies; data are included in higher level totals. [1] Excludes satellite telecommunications.

Source: U.S. Census Bureau, Service Annual Survey, "Service Annual Survey Latest Data (NAICS-basis): 2020," <www.census.gov/programs-surveys/sas/data.html>, accessed December 2021.

Table 1175. Data Processing, Hosting, and Related Services—Estimated Revenue and Expenses: 2015 to 2020

[In millions of dollars (132,249 represents $132,249,000,000). For all employer firms regardless of tax status. Data are based on the 2012 North American Industry Classification System (NAICS), and cover NAICS 518. Estimates have been adjusted using results of the 2017 Economic Census where applicable. Based on the Service Annual Survey; see text, Section 15, and Appendix III]

Item	2015	2016	2017	2018	2019	2020
Total operating revenue	**132,249**	**139,462**	**157,477**	**175,092**	**193,228**	**205,869**
Data processing, information technology infrastructure provisioning, and hosting services	(S)	97,054	110,107	125,064	134,969	146,405
Information technology design and development services	6,686	6,453	(S)	(S)	(S)	(S)
Information technology technical support services	5,631	5,422	5,660	5,589	6,207	6,289
Information technology technical consulting services	4,092	4,142	(S)	(S)	(S)	(S)
Information and document transformation services	2,457	(S)	2,701	(S)	(S)	(S)
Software publishing	3,406	3,432	3,586	4,422	6,350	5,589
Resale of computer hardware and software	2,539	2,540	3,227	(S)	(S)	(S)
All other operating revenue	18,758	(S)	(S)	(S)	28,301	31,046
Total operating expenses	**126,827**	**120,800**	**133,147**	**142,548**	**148,256**	**155,026**

S Data do not meet publication standards.

Source: U.S. Census Bureau, Service Annual Survey, "Service Annual Survey Latest Data (NAICS-basis): 2020," <www.census.gov/programs-surveys/sas/data.html>, accessed December 2021.

Table 1176. Mobile Wireless Cellular Telecommunications Industry: 2000 to 2021

[In units as indicated (109.5 represents 109,500,000). Calendar year data, except as noted. Based on a survey sent to facilities-based commercial mobile radio service providers, including cellular, personal communications services, advanced wireless service, mobile WiMAX, and enhanced special mobile radio (ESMR) systems. Beginning 2000, the number of operational systems differs from that reported for previous periods as a result of the consolidated operation of ESMR systems in a broader service area instead of by a city-to-city basis]

Item	Unit	2000	2005	2010	2015	2018	2019	2020	2021
Wireless subscriber connections [1]	Millions	109.5	207.9	296.3	377.9	421.8	442.5	468.9	498.9
Wireless penetration [2]	Percent	38.0	69.0	94.2	115.7	126.6	132.7	139.7	148.5
Cell sites [3]	Number	104,288	183,689	253,086	307,626	349,344	395,562	417,215	418,887
Employees	Number	184,449	233,067	250,393	235,818	205,855	188,639	179,460	171,955
Service revenue	Mil. dol.	52,466	113,538	159,930	191,949	182,779	187,362	189,912	204,214
Capital investment [4]	Mil. dol.	89,624	199,025	310,015	462,605	542,033	571,125	601,018	635,759
Average monthly revenue per unit [5]	Dollars	48.55	50.65	47.53	44.65	37.85	36.86	35.31	35.74
Voice minutes, annual reported	Billions	258.9	1,495.5	2,241.3	2,881.0	2,389.3	3,078.3	2,928.0	2,361.3
Voice minutes, monthly [6]	Minutes	248.0	716.0	683.0	670.0	495.0	606.0	544.0	413.0
Wireless data usage (megabytes), annual	Billions	(NA)	(NA)	388.0	9,649.9	28,584.7	37,059.6	42,205.0	53,356.0
Number of text messages [7]	Billions	(Z)	9.8	187.7	156.7	141.0	138.4	140.0	137.2
Number of MMS [7, 8]	Billions	(NA)	0.2	4.3	19.8	31.0	36.5	45.4	43.8

NA Not available. Z Entry less than half the unit of measurement shown. [1] Number of active wireless devices. Does not represent individual subscribers. [2] Number of active wireless devices divided by total U.S. population (including U.S. territories). [3] The basic geographic unit for wireless telecommunications coverage. [4] Beginning 2005, cumulative capital investment figure reached by summing the incremental capital investment in year shown with cumulative capital investment of prior year. [5] As of December 31. [6] Derived, based on minutes divided by reported devices. [7] Number of messages in final month of survey (December). [8] Multimedia Messaging Service.

Source: CTIA-The Wireless Association, Washington, DC, *Annual Wireless Industry Survey* ©.

Table 1177. Landline and Wireless Telephone Status of Adults by Selected Characteristics: 2010 to 2021

[In percent. Data cover 6-month period from January to June. Estimates are preliminary. Based on interviews of a sample of the civilian noninstitutionalized population conducted for the National Health Interview Survey (NHIS). The 2016 NHIS implemented a new sample design. The 2019 NHIS implemented a redesigned questionnaire and changes in weighting methodology, both of which may impact comparisons between estimates for 2019 and earlier years. See source for details]

Telephone status and characteristics	2010	2014	2015	2016	2017	2018	2019	2020 [5]	2021 [6]
Adults by household telephone status:									
Wireless only	24.9	43.1	46.7	49.0	52.0	55.2	59.2	62.5	68.0
Landline with wireless	62.2	47.3	43.9	42.1	39.6	37.4	37.2	34.3	29.3
Landline only (no wireless)	10.9	7.0	6.2	5.8	4.8	4.1	2.5	2.3	1.9
Without any telephone	1.7	2.4	3.1	2.9	3.4	3.2	1.0	0.7	0.5
Other [1]	0.3	0.2	0.1	0.1	0.1	0.1	0.1	0.2	0.1
Children in wireless telephone only households	29.0	52.1	55.3	59.4	62.3	64.9	70.5	73.6	79.1
ADULTS IN WIRELESS ONLY HOUSEHOLDS [2]									
Total	(NA)	(NA)	(NA)	(NA)	(NA)	(NA)	58.4	61.8	67.2
Sex:									
Male	26.2	44.3	48.2	50.3	53.2	56.4	59.6	62.7	69.3
Female	23.7	41.9	45.3	47.8	51.0	54.1	57.4	61.0	65.1
Age:									
18 to 24 years	39.9	57.8	59.4	62.7	64.2	65.0	66.5	72.6	75.9
25 to 29 years	51.3	69.3	71.3	72.1	73.3	77.3	80.2	80.4	85.0
30 to 34 years	40.4	64.9	67.8	69.8	74.4	77.3	78.3	83.0	86.1
35 to 44 years	27.0	52.5	56.6	60.0	63.9	65.7	70.9	74.5	79.1
45 to 64 years	16.9	35.7	40.8	43.3	47.1	50.7	55.6	58.5	65.9
65 and over years	5.4	15.7	19.3	21.1	23.9	29.2	30.9	35.0	40.8
Race/ethnicity:									
White only, non-Hispanic	22.7	39.6	43.2	45.0	48.0	51.6	56.0	58.7	64.5
Black only, non-Hispanic	28.5	44.9	48.1	49.2	52.5	55.6	54.3	58.6	64.3
Asian only, non-Hispanic	18.8	41.3	47.9	51.4	53.1	53.8	55.5	62.5	68.7
Other race or multiple race, non-Hispanic	(NA)	(NA)	(NA)	(NA)	(NA)	(NA)	64.3	69.4	74.3
Hispanic or Latino, any race	34.7	56.1	59.2	63.7	66.3	69.1	71.2	74.8	77.4
Education:									
Some high school or less	28.6	46.6	49.0	52.1	54.8	58.7	58.1	63.4	67.1
High school graduate or GED [3]	23.6	43.3	46.7	48.4	51.5	56.5	57.2	58.4	66.3
Some post-high school, no degree	26.5	45.6	49.0	50.8	55.1	56.0	60.1	63.4	67.3
4-year college degree or higher	22.7	39.0	43.5	46.5	48.6	51.9	58.1	62.6	68.0
Family poverty status: [4]									
Poor	39.3	59.1	59.3	63.1	67.5	67.1	67.1	69.7	73.9
Near poor	32.9	50.8	54.4	54.0	61.6	62.8	62.2	66.8	68.3
Not poor	21.7	40.8	45.7	48.2	50.3	53.4	57.4	61.1	67.1
Home ownership status:									
Owned or home being bought	15.5	32.9	37.2	39.0	42.9	46.8	50.2	54.4	60.7
Renting	47.1	64.6	67.0	69.7	70.7	74.4	75.1	78.7	81.9
Other arrangement	34.9	52.2	52.8	52.0	64.8	60.0	61.6	57.8	66.6

NA Not available. [1] Other includes unknown cellular telephone or unknown landline status. [2] Through 2018, data are for adults who live in households without a landline telephone. Beginning 2019, data are for "wireless only adults" who have their own wireless cellular telephone and who live in a household without a landline telephone. [3] GED is General Educational Development high school equivalency diploma. [4] Based on the U.S. Census Bureau's poverty thresholds by household income and size. "Poor" persons have incomes below the poverty threshold. "Near poor" persons have incomes of 100% to less than 200% of the poverty threshold. "Not poor" persons have incomes at or above 200% of the poverty threshold. [5] Due to the coronavirus disease 2019 (COVID-19) pandemic, on March 19, 2020, the NHIS switched to a telephone-only survey mode. This resulted in lower response rates and differences in respondent characteristics during 2nd quarter 2020. Differences observed in estimates between 1st half 2020 and earlier years, particularly estimates of persons living in households without any telephone, may be partially or fully attributable to the change in survey mode. See source for more information. [6] The majority of interviews for the January-June 2021 period were conducted by telephone. See source for more information.

Source: U.S. National Center for Health Statistics, *Wireless Substitution: Early Release of Estimates From the National Health Interview Survey, January–June 2021*, November 2021, and earlier reports. See also <www.cdc.gov/nchs/nhis/erwirelesssubs.htm>.

Table 1178. Average Annual Telephone Service Expenditures by All Consumer Units: 2001 to 2020

[In dollars except percent distribution. Based on the Consumer Expenditure Survey. Expenditures reported are direct out-of-pocket expenditures. A consumer unit is defined as members of a household related by blood, marriage, adoption, or some other legal arrangement; a single person living alone, or sharing a household with others but who is financially independent; or two or more persons living together who share responsibility for at least two out of the three major types of expenses: food, housing, and other expenses]

Year	Average annual expenditures (dollars)				Percent distribution			
	Total telephone services	Residential and other telephone services [1]	Cellular phone service	Other services [2]	Total telephone services	Residential and other telephone services [1]	Cellular phone service	Other services [2]
2001	914	686	210	19	100.0	75.1	23.0	2.1
2002	957	641	294	22	100.0	67.0	30.7	2.3
2003	956	620	316	20	100.0	64.9	33.1	2.1
2004	990	592	378	20	100.0	59.8	38.2	2.0
2005	1,048	570	455	23	100.0	54.4	43.4	2.2
2006	1,087	542	524	21	100.0	49.9	48.2	1.9
2007	1,110	482	608	20	100.0	43.4	54.8	1.8
2008	1,127	467	643	17	100.0	41.4	57.0	1.5
2009	1,162	434	712	17	100.0	37.3	61.2	1.4
2010	1,178	401	760	17	100.0	34.1	64.5	1.4
2011	1,226	381	826	20	100.0	31.1	67.3	1.6
2012	1,239	359	862	19	100.0	28.9	69.6	1.5
2013	1,271	358	913	(NA)	100.0	28.2	71.8	(NA)
2014	1,315	353	963	(NA)	100.0	26.8	73.2	(NA)
2015	1,347	324	1,023	(NA)	100.0	24.1	75.9	(NA)
2016	1,431	307	1,124	(NA)	100.0	21.5	78.5	(NA)
2017	1,356	238	1,118	(NA)	100.0	17.6	82.4	(NA)
2018	1,407	220	1,188	(NA)	100.0	15.6	84.4	(NA)
2019	1,409	191	1,218	(NA)	100.0	13.6	86.4	(NA)
2020	1,441	188	1,253	(NA)	100.0	13.0	87.0	(NA)

NA Not available. [1] Beginning 2013, data are shown for residential telephone, phone cards, VoIP (Voice over Internet Protocol), and pay phone services combined. Prior to 2013, data are shown for residential and pay telephone services only. [2] Phone cards, pager services, and for 2007-2012, VoIP.

Source: U.S. Bureau of Labor Statistics, Consumer Expenditure Surveys, CE Tables, "Calendar year means, shares across all items, and coefficients of variation by demographic characteristics," <www.bls.gov/cex/home.htm>, accessed November 2021; prior to 2013, unpublished data.

Table 1179. Electronic Device Ownership by Device Type and Owner Characteristics: 2021

[In percent. Based on a January 25 to February 8, 2021 survey of adults age 18 and older. Surveys are conducted in English and Spanish, on landline and cellular telephones]

Owner characteristic	Any cellular telephone	Smart-phone	Cellphone, not smart-phone	Tablet computer	Computer [1]
Total	**97**	**85**	**11**	**53**	**77**
SEX					
Men	97	85	11	50	78
Women	98	85	12	56	77
RACE/ETHNICITY					
White, non-Hispanic	97	85	11	53	80
Black, non-Hispanic	99	83	15	54	69
Hispanic	100	85	14	53	67
AGE					
18 to 29 years	100	96	4	46	78
30 to 49 years	100	95	5	61	84
50 to 64 years	97	83	12	53	76
65 years and older	92	61	29	44	66
EDUCATION					
High school or less	96	75	19	39	60
Some college	98	89	9	59	81
College graduate or higher	98	93	5	63	95
HOUSEHOLD INCOME					
Less than $30,000	97	76	19	41	59
$30,000 to $49,999	97	83	14	44	76
$50,000 to $74,999	97	85	12	54	83
$75,000 and over	100	96	3	67	93
METRO STATUS					
Urban	98	89	9	55	80
Suburban	97	84	12	54	78
Rural	94	80	14	44	72

[1] Desktop or laptop computer.

Source: Pew Research Center ©, "Mobile Fact Sheet," <www.pewresearch.org/internet/fact-sheet/mobile/>, accessed June 2021; and unpublished data.

Table 1180. Computer and Internet Use by Selected Characteristics: 2019

[In thousands (286,322 represents 286,322,000), except percent. Based on the American Community Survey. Data are based on a sample and are subject to sampling variability. Due to changes in the ACS questionnaire, use caution when comparing data on computer and internet use before and after 2016. For more information, see <www.census.gov/programs-surveys/acs/methodology/content-test.html>]

| Characteristic | Population with computer in household [1] | | | | No computer in household | |
| | With broadband internet subscription [2] | | No internet subscription [3] | | | |
	Number	Percent	Number	Percent	Number	Percent
Total population in households.............	**286,322**	**89.4**	**19,277**	**6.0**	**14,076**	**4.4**
AGE						
Under 18 years.....................................	67,374	92.6	3,920	5.4	1,440	2.0
18 to 64 years.......................................	177,958	91.3	11,255	5.8	5,427	2.8
65 years and over..................................	40,990	78.0	4,102	7.8	7,209	13.7
RACE AND ETHNICITY						
White alone...	208,319	90.1	12,599	5.4	9,917	4.3
Black or African American alone...................	33,724	83.9	3,759	9.4	2,671	6.6
American Indian and Alaska Native alone........	2,142	77.9	328	11.9	274	10.0
Asian alone...	17,342	94.9	583	3.2	325	1.8
Native Hawaiian/Other Pacific Islander alone....	528	86.8	48	7.8	32	5.3
Some other race alone.............................	13,984	87.0	1,450	9.0	627	3.9
Two or more races..................................	10,284	93.2	510	4.6	229	2.1
Hispanic or Latino origin [4]........................	52,017	87.6	4,902	8.3	2,404	4.0
White alone, not Hispanic or Latino..............	174,226	90.6	9,389	4.9	8,265	4.3
EDUCATIONAL ATTAINMENT						
Household population age 25 and over..........	194,100	88.1	13,616	6.2	12,176	5.5
Less than high school graduate...................	17,710	72.6	2,925	12.0	3,729	15.3
High school graduate/some college [5]............	105,684	86.7	8,572	7.0	7,317	6.0
Bachelor's degree or higher.......................	70,706	95.5	2,120	2.9	1,130	1.5
EMPLOYMENT STATUS						
Civilian population age 16 and over.............	225,718	88.6	15,722	6.2	12,757	5.0
In labor force..	152,459	92.5	8,592	5.2	3,605	2.2
Employed...	145,970	92.7	8,040	5.1	3,334	2.1
Unemployed..	6,490	88.7	552	7.5	271	3.7
Not in labor force...................................	73,258	81.6	7,129	7.9	9,152	10.2

[1] Includes desktop or laptop; smartphone; tablet or other portable wireless computer; or some other type of computer. [2] Paid internet access services via cable, fiber optic, or DSL; a cellular data plan (smartphone or mobile phone); satellite; or a fixed wireless subscription. [3] Includes those who accessed the internet without a subscription and also those with no internet access at all. [4] Persons of Hispanic or Latino origin may be of any race. [5] Includes persons with high school equivalency, and with associate's degree.

Source: U.S. Census Bureau, 2019 American Community Survey, S2802 "Types of Internet Subscriptions by Selected Characteristics," <data.census.gov>, accessed December 2020.

Table 1181. Percent of Households with a Computer and Paid Internet Subscription by State: 2020

[In percent. Data are based on 2020 American Community Survey (ACS) 1-year experimental estimates. The coronavirus disease 2019 (COVID-19) pandemic impacted 2020 ACS data collection and quality, and standard estimates did not meet statistical quality standards. The Census Bureau does not recommend comparing experimental estimates to standard ACS estimates. For more information, see <www.census.gov/programs-surveys/acs/data/experimental-data.html>. Survey respondents could select more than one type of computer and more than one type of internet subscription. Household computer can include desktop or laptop; smartphone; tablet or other portable wireless computer; or some other type of computer. Please note that although the ACS includes people living in group quarters, computer and internet use data were not collected from group quarters. See also headnote Table 1180]

| State | Total households with computer | Type of internet subscription | | | State | Total households with computer | Type of internet subscription | | |
		Dial-up internet service	Broadband internet service [1]	No paid internet service [2]			Dial-up internet service	Broadband internet service [1]	No paid internet service [2]
U.S.......	**94.0**	**0.2**	**93.4**	**6.4**	MO........	92.9	0.3	92.2	7.5
AL.........	91.4	0.4	91.1	8.5	MT.........	93.1	0.6	91.9	7.5
AK.........	96.6	0.2	94.2	5.6	NE.........	94.0	0.3	93.6	6.0
AZ.........	95.2	0.2	92.7	7.1	NV.........	95.4	0.2	93.2	6.6
AR.........	91.6	0.3	89.1	10.7	NH.........	94.9	0.2	94.7	5.1
CA.........	96.0	0.1	95.1	4.8	NJ.........	94.7	0.2	95.1	4.8
CO.........	96.6	0.2	94.8	5.1	NM........	91.0	0.1	89.8	10.0
CT.........	94.2	0.2	95.5	4.3	NY.........	93.0	0.2	93.9	5.9
DE.........	94.7	0.4	94.3	5.3	NC.........	92.6	0.1	92.9	7.0
DC.........	94.5	0.1	93.4	6.5	ND.........	93.6	0.1	93.5	6.3
FL.........	95.1	0.2	92.8	7.0	OH.........	93.2	0.2	93.7	6.1
GA.........	94.3	0.1	92.4	7.5	OK.........	93.0	0.2	90.8	9.0
HI.........	95.2	0.2	95.4	4.4	OR.........	95.8	0.3	94.3	5.4
ID.........	95.5	0.2	94.5	5.3	PA.........	91.7	0.3	93.9	5.9
IL.........	93.7	0.2	93.8	6.0	RI.........	93.2	0.2	95.6	4.3
IN.........	93.1	0.2	93.6	6.2	SC.........	92.0	0.1	90.6	9.3
IA.........	93.1	0.4	92.2	7.4	SD.........	93.3	0.2	92.2	7.6
KS.........	94.4	0.1	93.1	6.7	TN.........	92.4	0.1	91.7	8.2
KY.........	92.3	0.2	92.3	7.5	TX.........	94.9	0.1	93.0	6.9
LA.........	91.6	0.2	90.9	8.9	UT.........	97.0	0.2	94.4	5.4
ME.........	92.1	0.5	92.8	6.7	VT.........	92.3	1.1	90.7	8.2
MD........	95.4	0.2	94.4	5.4	VA.........	94.2	0.1	93.8	6.0
MA........	94.7	0.1	95.4	4.5	WA........	96.2	0.2	95.0	4.8
MI.........	93.5	0.3	93.1	6.7	WV........	88.9	0.3	91.5	8.3
MN........	94.4	0.3	94.0	5.7	WI.........	92.6	0.4	93.4	6.2
MS........	90.4	0.3	87.9	11.8	WY........	94.5	0.2	92.4	7.4

[1] Broadband internet service includes access via cable, fiber optic, or DSL; a cellular data plan; satellite; or a fixed wireless subscription. [2] Includes households accessing the internet without a subscription and also households with no internet access.

Source: U.S. Census Bureau, 2020 ACS 1-Year Experimental Data Tables, "Table XK202801. Presence of a Computer and Type of Internet Subscription in Household," <www.census.gov/programs-surveys/acs/data/experimental-data.html>, accessed February 2022.

Table 1182. Internet Access by Location and Selected User Characteristics: 2022

[In percent, except as noted (253,853 represents 253,853,000). For persons aged 18 and over. As of Winter 2022. Based on a sample and subject to sampling error]

Characteristic	Total adults (1,000)	Accessed the internet (percent)					Wireless internet connection from home [1] (percent)
		At home	At work	At school or library	At another place	Using a cellphone or smart-phone	
Total adults [2]................	**253,853**	**93.4**	**38.1**	**6.5**	**35.6**	**85.7**	**87.5**
Age:							
18 to 34 years old....................	74,831	92.4	46.5	13.8	43.2	90.1	86.8
35 to 54 years old....................	81,557	93.8	50.2	4.7	37.6	91.2	88.7
55 years old and over...................	97,465	93.9	21.6	2.5	28.1	77.8	87.0
Sex:							
Male.............................	122,706	93.3	41.5	5.9	35.2	85.6	87.6
Female...........................	131,147	93.6	35.0	7.1	36.0	85.8	87.4
Census region: [3]							
Northeast........................	44,147	93.8	38.4	6.7	35.1	84.1	88.2
South............................	97,498	92.6	37.3	6.5	34.8	86.0	86.4
Midwest..........................	52,802	93.3	40.9	7.1	36.2	85.0	88.0
West.............................	59,406	94.6	36.9	6.0	36.7	87.2	88.3
Household size:							
1 to 2 persons.....................	121,851	93.4	33.0	3.7	33.6	81.5	86.4
3 to 4 persons.....................	89,954	93.9	44.4	8.0	37.8	89.6	89.4
5 or more persons..................	42,048	92.7	39.7	11.5	36.8	89.5	86.5
Presence of child in household.............	88,847	93.1	44.6	8.8	36.6	90.4	87.7
Marital status:							
Never married.....................	74,819	92.0	42.5	13.5	40.3	87.9	85.5
Married...........................	134,106	95.0	39.1	3.7	35.3	87.1	90.0
Other [4].........................	52,922	91.3	31.5	4.0	30.4	80.0	84.0
Education:							
Graduated college..................	88,346	97.3	48.2	5.3	45.3	91.1	93.5
Attended college...................	70,018	94.5	37.9	7.2	36.5	88.1	88.7
Did not attend college..............	95,489	89.1	28.9	7.2	26.0	79.0	81.1
Employment status:							
Employed full-time.................	118,312	94.2	67.5	4.4	38.6	91.1	90.4
Employed part-time.................	32,206	93.3	45.9	13.7	40.1	87.6	86.9
Occupation of employed:							
Professional.......................	36,867	96.6	71.7	8.5	47.4	93.2	92.7
Management/business/financial..................	27,824	96.9	67.9	3.5	44.4	92.6	94.3
Sales/office.......................	29,417	93.6	68.0	6.3	35.9	89.1	89.4
Natural resources/construction/maintenance. ..	13,815	92.1	52.3	3.5	30.6	88.2	85.4
Other.............................	42,595	90.9	52.0	7.6	32.8	88.0	85.6
Sector of employment:							
Business..........................	45,951	95.9	65.1	4.5	42.2	92.5	92.3
Government.......................	21,229	94.1	72.9	7.3	36.4	90.8	90.7
Other.............................	67,916	92.8	55.8	6.6	36.6	88.4	87.2
Household income:							
Less than $50,000..................	74,027	88.7	21.0	7.4	25.5	76.8	77.8
$50,000 to $74,999.................	41,454	93.4	34.5	5.9	32.1	84.5	88.1
$75,000 to $149,999................	79,775	95.5	45.0	6.2	39.9	89.5	91.2
$150,000 or more..................	58,597	96.7	53.0	6.3	45.1	92.6	94.3

[1] Excludes cellphone access. [2] Includes other labor force status and employment categories not shown separately. [3] For composition of regions, see map inside front cover. [4] Includes separated, divorced, and widowed, and persons engaged to be married.

Source: © MRI-Simmons Winter 2022 USA Study. Courtesy of MRI-Simmons. See also <www.mrisimmons.com/>.

Table 1183. Internet Activities by Sex and Age: 2021

[In percent. Covers population age 15 and over. Based on the November 2021 Computer and Internet Use supplement to the Current Population Survey, for the National Telecommunications and Information Administration's Digital Nation research project]

Activity conducted online or via the internet	Total	By sex		By age			
		Male	Female	15 to 24 years old	25 to 44 years old	45 to 64 years old	65 years and over
Uses the internet, any location....................	**82.1**	**82.2**	**82.0**	**85.6**	**85.7**	**83.1**	**72.6**
Interact with household equipment.....................	22.3	23.5	21.2	17.4	28.9	22.4	14.5
Offer services for sale........................	8.8	8.9	8.7	8.6	11.6	8.4	4.5
Video or voice calls, or conferencing....................	65.6	63.1	68.0	73.5	74.1	62.5	48.5
Post or upload blog posts, videos, or other original content.........................	17.0	16.2	17.7	27.4	21.6	12.8	6.6
Request services provided by other people............	43.0	42.5	43.5	47.6	56.1	38.2	23.6
Search for a job............................	21.3	21.0	21.6	36.3	28.0	15.7	5.5
Shop, make travel reservations, or use other consumer services......................	74.1	72.0	76.1	70.7	81.8	73.9	63.6
Stream or download music, radio, podcasts, etc......	60.0	61.2	58.9	77.7	72.9	53.0	33.1
Take class or participate in job training...............	25.7	24.5	26.9	43.4	29.7	22.1	9.4
Telecommute..............................	27.7	28.8	26.6	15.2	39.3	33.0	8.8
Use email................................	91.8	91.1	92.5	93.4	95.2	91.1	85.5
Use financial services such as banking, investing, paying bills...........................	74.3	73.7	74.9	64.8	84.6	75.4	62.0
Use social networks........................	74.6	70.4	78.5	88.5	84.0	69.4	54.1
Use text messaging or instant messaging............	93.3	93.3	93.3	97.3	97.1	93.9	82.0
Use internet to sell goods....................	10.5	10.4	10.6	9.5	13.6	10.2	6.2
Watch videos.............................	70.1	71.4	68.9	84.0	81.2	64.7	47.1

Source: U.S. Department of Commerce, National Telecommunications and Information Administration, Data Central, "NTIA Data Explorer," <www.ntia.doc.gov/category/data-central>, accessed May 2022.

Table 1184. Home Internet Access—Broadband and Smartphone Only Service by Selected Characteristics: 2016 to 2021

[In percent. Based on a survey of 4,535 adults conducted in April and November 2016 (sampling error plus or minus 1.7 percentage points); a survey of 2,002 adults conducted in January 2018; a survey of 1,502 adults conducted January 8-February 7, 2019 (sampling error plus or minus 2.8 percentage points); and a survey of 1,502 adults conducted January 25-February 8, 2021 (sampling error plus or minus 2.9 percentage points). Surveys were conducted in English and Spanish on landline and cellular telephones]

Characteristic	Internet broadband service in the home				Internet via smartphone only [1]			
	2016	2018	2019	2021	2016	2018	2019	2021
Total adults	**72**	**65**	**73**	**77**	**12**	**20**	**17**	**15**
SEX								
Male	74	66	73	77	12	20	17	14
Female	70	64	73	77	12	19	16	15
RACE/ETHNICITY								
White, non-Hispanic	77	72	79	80	9	14	12	12
Black, non-Hispanic	65	57	66	71	15	24	23	17
Hispanic	55	47	61	65	23	35	25	25
AGE								
18 to 29 years	78	67	77	70	17	28	22	28
30 to 49 years	80	70	77	86	13	24	18	11
50 to 64 years	72	68	79	79	11	16	14	13
65 years and older	51	50	59	64	7	10	12	12
EDUCATION								
Less than high school graduate	30	24	46	(NA)	27	39	32	(NA)
High school graduate	61	56	59	(NA)	15	22	24	(NA)
High school graduate or less	(NA)	(NA)	(NA)	59	(NA)	(NA)	(NA)	23
Some college	80	68	77	80	12	21	16	15
College graduate	90	85	93	94	5	10	4	4
HOUSEHOLD INCOME								
Less than $30,000	52	45	56	57	21	31	26	27
$30,000 to $49,999	72	67	72	74	12	22	20	19
$50,000 to $74,999	82	79	87	87	10	14	10	6
$75,0000 and over	92	87	92	92	5	9	6	6
METRO STATUS								
Urban	73	67	75	77	12	22	17	16
Suburban	74	70	79	79	12	17	13	12
Rural	62	58	63	72	14	17	20	17

NA Not available. [1] Persons without traditional home broadband internet service who own a smartphone that can access the internet.

Source: Pew Research Center ©, Internet & Technology, "Internet/Broadband Fact Sheet," <www.pewresearch.org/internet/fact-sheet/internet-broadband/>, accessed May 2021; and unpublished data.

Table 1185. Adult Internet Users and Home Internet Connection by Selected Characteristics: 2000 to 2021

[In percent. Covers persons age 18 and over who use the internet at a workplace, school, home, or anywhere else, on at least an occasional basis. Based on telephone surveys of persons with landline telephones unless otherwise noted. Beginning 2011, surveys include interviews conducted in English and Spanish. Data for 2021 are from February 2021 interviews of 1,502 persons, including 1,202 cellphone interviews. Data for 2019 are from January-February 2019 interviews of 1,502 persons, including 1,200 cellphone users. Data for 2018 are from January 2018 interviews of 2,002 persons, including 1,502 cellphone users. Data for 2015 are from July 2015 interviews with 2,001 persons, including 1,300 cellphone users. Data for 2010 are from interviews with 2,252 persons, including 744 cellphone users]

Characteristic	Adult internet users							All adults, by type of home connection, 2021	
	2000	2005	2010	2015	2018	2019	2021	Broadband	Dial-up
Total adults	**53**	**69**	**79**	**87**	**89**	**90**	**93**	**77**	**1**
Sex:									
Male	56	70	79	87	89	90	94	77	2
Female	51	67	79	87	88	91	93	77	1
Race/ethnicity:									
White, non-Hispanic	55	70	80	87	89	92	93	80	1
Black, non-Hispanic	42	54	71	84	87	85	91	71	3
Hispanic	48	73	82	84	88	86	95	65	4
Age:									
18 to 29 years old	72	82	95	97	98	100	99	70	2
30 to 49 years old	62	80	87	97	97	97	98	86	1
50 to 64 years old	48	68	78	80	87	88	96	79	2
65 years old and over	15	28	42	65	66	73	75	64	1
Education:									
Less than high school	19	35	52	68	65	71	(NA)	(NA)	(NA)
High school or less [1]	(NA)	(NA)	(NA)	(NA)	(NA)	(NA)	86	59	3
High school graduate [1]	41	59	67	77	84	84	(NA)	(NA)	(NA)
Some college	69	80	90	93	93	95	97	80	(Z)
College graduate or higher	79	88	96	97	97	98	98	94	1
Annual household income:									
Less than $30,000	35	50	63	78	81	82	86	57	2
$30,000 to $49,999	61	74	84	87	93	93	91	74	1
$50,000 to $74,999	74	86	89	94	97	97	98	87	2
$75,000 or more	81	91	95	97	98	98	99	92	1

NA Not available. Z Less than 0.5 percent. [1] Includes those with a GED certificate.

Source: Pew Research Center, Internet & Technology Surveys © conducted September-December 2000, September and December of 2005, May 2010, July 2015, January 2018, January-February 2019, and February 2021. See also <www.pewresearch.org/topic/internet-technology/>.

Table 1186. Teen Electronic Device Ownership and Social Media Use by Selected Characteristics: 2022

[In percent. Based on responses from 1,316 teenagers age 13 to 17 participating in a survey conducted by Ipsos, April 14 to May 4, 2022. The margin of sampling error is plus or minus 3.2 percentage points. Research was reviewed and approved by an external institutional review board. Teenage respondents were recruited via their parents who were part of Ipsos's KnowledgePanel. Direct comparisons cannot be made with a similar 2018 Pew Research Center survey due to differences in the ways the surveys were conducted]

Characteristic	Device ownership [1]			Social media platform use						
	Smart-phone	Desktop or laptop computer	Gaming console	YouTube	TikTok	Insta-gram	Snap-chat	Face-book	Twitter	Twitch
Total [2].....................	**95**	**90**	**80**	**95**	**67**	**62**	**59**	**32**	**23**	**20**
Sex:										
Male.........................	95	90	91	97	60	55	54	31	24	26
Female.......................	95	90	70	92	73	69	64	34	22	13
Race and ethnicity:										
White, non-Hispanic......	96	90	82	94	62	58	59	32	20	20
Black, non-Hispanic.......	91	90	81	94	81	69	59	34	31	18
Hispanic [3].................	96	89	73	95	71	68	62	32	28	22
Age:										
13 to 14 years.............	91	86	79	94	61	45	51	23	15	17
15 to 17 years.............	98	92	81	95	71	73	65	39	29	22
Household income:										
Less than $30,000........	93	79	70	93	72	64	60	44	26	17
$30,000 to $74,999.......	94	85	80	94	68	62	57	39	24	19
$75,000 and over..........	96	94	82	95	65	62	60	27	22	21

[1] Percent of U.S. teens who say they have or have access at home to the listed device. [2] Includes teenagers of other races, such as Asian American, not shown separately. [3] Persons of Hispanic origin may be of any race.

Source: Pew Research Center, *Teens, Social Media and Technology 2022,* August 2022 ©. See also <www.pewresearch.org/topic/internet-technology/>.

Table 1187. Households Using Electronics, Internet Devices, and Cell Phones by Type and Household Income: 2020

[In millions (123.5 represents 123,500,000). Based on the Residential Energy Consumption Survey. Includes single-family homes, units in multifamily buildings, and mobile homes. Excludes secondary homes, vacant, seasonal and vacation homes, group quarters, and common areas of apartment buildings. Data may not sum to totals due to rounding]

Item	Total	Households by income (millions)							
		Less than $5,000	$5,000 to $9,999	$10,000 to $19,999	$20,000 to $39,999	$40,000 to $59,999	$60,000 to $99,999	$100,000 to $149,999	$150,000 or more
Total households..................	**123.5**	**4.5**	**4.0**	**10.3**	**24.1**	**19.6**	**27.7**	**16.5**	**16.9**
TELEVISION AND VIDEO									
Number of televisions:									
0..	3.8	0.3	0.3	0.6	0.7	0.6	0.7	0.4	0.3
1..	33.8	1.6	1.5	4.0	7.5	5.4	7.1	3.6	3.2
2..	41.1	1.5	1.3	3.7	8.9	6.9	8.9	5.2	4.9
3 or more.................................	44.8	1.2	0.9	2.1	7.1	6.7	11.0	7.4	8.5
Hours TV used per weekday: [1]									
Less than 1 hour.......................	4.5	0.3	0.2	0.4	0.8	0.7	0.9	0.6	0.7
1 to 3 hours.............................	29.6	0.6	0.7	1.4	4.0	4.2	7.1	5.0	6.5
4 to 6 hours.............................	41.7	1.3	0.9	2.3	7.7	6.6	10.4	6.4	6.0
7 to 10 hours...........................	24.8	1.0	0.8	2.9	5.8	4.2	5.3	2.6	2.2
More than 10 hours....................	19.2	1.0	1.0	2.7	5.1	3.4	3.3	1.6	1.1
Hours TV used per weekend day: [1]									
Less than 1 hour.......................	4.1	0.3	0.3	0.5	0.8	0.6	0.8	0.4	0.5
1 to 3 hours.............................	20.6	0.5	0.6	1.3	3.1	3.1	4.8	3.0	4.2
4 to 6 hours.............................	39.6	1.2	0.8	2.2	6.9	5.8	9.7	6.5	6.5
7 to 10 hours...........................	32.2	1.1	1.0	3.0	6.7	5.5	7.3	3.9	3.6
More than 10 hours....................	23.3	1.0	1.0	2.8	5.9	4.1	4.4	2.4	1.7
Cable or satellite TV boxes: [2]									
1..	25.6	0.6	0.4	1.6	4.5	4.2	6.2	3.7	4.3
2 or more.................................	16.4	0.2	0.3	0.6	2.5	2.4	4.1	2.8	3.5
Internet streaming devices:									
1..	34.7	1.3	1.0	2.3	6.8	5.6	8.2	5.0	4.6
2 or more.................................	34.6	0.7	0.7	1.6	4.9	5.2	8.5	5.9	7.2
COMPUTERS AND PHONES									
Desktop computers:									
1..	39.9	0.7	0.6	2.0	7.2	6.6	10.3	6.3	6.3
2 or more.................................	10.5	0.2	(NA)	0.4	1.3	1.3	2.7	1.9	2.5
Laptop computers:									
1..	44.7	1.3	1.2	3.2	9.5	8.7	11.4	5.6	4.0
2..	28.2	0.6	0.5	1.3	3.6	4.0	7.3	5.4	5.5
3 or more.................................	19.3	0.4	0.4	0.6	1.6	1.8	4.2	3.9	6.3
Tablets and e-readers:									
1..	39.9	1.0	1.1	2.5	7.5	6.5	10.3	5.8	5.1
2..	22.3	0.3	0.3	0.8	3.0	3.1	5.9	4.0	4.9
3 or more.................................	11.4	0.3	0.2	0.3	1.1	1.2	2.5	2.3	3.5
Smartphones:									
1..	31.0	1.3	1.2	3.6	8.1	6.3	6.6	2.3	1.5
2..	46.1	1.1	0.9	2.1	6.8	7.1	12.4	7.9	7.9
3 or more.................................	31.7	1.0	0.8	1.5	4.5	4.1	7.1	5.7	7.1

[1] Data shown for primary television. [2] Cable and satellite boxes with digital video recorder (DVR).

Source: U.S. Energy Information Administration, Residential Energy Consumption Survey—2020 Data, "Housing characteristics tables: Table HC4.5 Electronics in U.S. homes, by household income, 2020," <www.eia.gov/consumption/residential/index.php>, accessed May 2022.

Table 1188. Social Media—Use of Social Networking Sites Among Adult Internet Users: 2021

[In percent. Based on a survey of 1,502 adults age 18 and older living in all 50 states and DC, conducted January 25 to February 8, 2021, in English and Spanish on landline and cellular telephones. Margin of error for results for the total sample that would be expected at 95% level of confidence is plus or minus 2.9 percentage points]

Characteristic	Social media platform								
	Facebook	Instagram	LinkedIn	Twitter	Pinterest	Snapchat	YouTube	WhatsApp	TikTok
Total...............	**69**	**40**	**28**	**23**	**31**	**25**	**81**	**23**	**21**
SEX									
Male........................	61	36	31	25	16	22	82	26	17
Female.....................	77	44	26	22	46	28	80	21	24
RACE/ETHNICITY									
White, non-Hispanic............	67	35	29	22	34	23	79	16	18
Black, non-Hispanic............	74	49	27	29	35	26	84	23	30
Hispanic origin [1]...............	72	52	19	23	18	31	85	46	31
AGE									
18 to 29 years..................	70	71	30	42	32	65	95	24	48
30 to 49 years..................	77	48	36	27	34	24	91	30	22
50 to 64 years..................	73	29	33	18	38	12	83	23	14
65 years and over...............	50	13	11	7	18	2	49	10	4
EDUCATION									
High school graduate or less...	64	30	10	14	22	21	70	20	21
Some college....................	71	44	28	26	36	32	86	16	24
College graduate or higher.....	73	49	51	33	37	23	89	33	19
INCOME									
Under $30,000...................	70	35	12	12	21	25	75	23	22
$30,000 to $49,999.............	76	45	21	29	33	27	83	20	29
$50,000 to 74,999..............	61	39	21	22	29	29	79	19	20
$75,000 and over...............	70	47	50	34	40	28	90	29	20
METRO STATUS									
Urban...........................	70	45	30	27	30	28	84	28	24
Suburban.......................	70	41	33	23	32	25	81	23	20
Rural..........................	67	25	15	18	34	18	74	9	16

[1] Persons of Hispanic origin may be of any race.

Source: Pew Research Center ©, Internet & Technology, "Social Media Fact Sheet," <www.pewresearch.org/internet/fact-sheet/social-media/>, accessed May 2021. See also <www.pewresearch.org/internet/2021/04/07/social-media-use-in-2021/>.

Table 1189. Public Libraries—Selected Characteristics: 2019

[Total operating income in thousands of dollars (14,200,729 represents $14,200,729,000). Data are generally for the fiscal year ending in June; see source for reporting periods. Based on a census of all public libraries in the 50 states and the District of Columbia. See source for details]

Population of service area	Number of—		Operating income			Paid staff [4]		Avg. number of public use internet computers per stationary outlet [6]
				Source (percent)				
	Public libraries [1]	Stationary outlets [2]	Total [3] ($1,000)	State government	Local government	Total FTE	Librarians with ALA-MLS [5]	
Total...................	**9,057**	**16,607**	**14,200,729**	**6.7**	**85.9**	**143,883**	**34,007**	**18.0**
Less than 1,000........	930	932	39,460	7.7	75.4	714	36	4.6
1,000 to 2,499.........	1,467	1,480	134,277	4.9	77.3	2,149	166	6.2
2,500 to 4,999.........	1,266	1,302	219,242	5.6	80.7	3,255	384	8.1
5,000 to 9,999.........	1,488	1,637	521,005	6.8	83.1	6,906	1,277	11.1
10,000 to 24,999.......	1,761	2,253	1,410,092	6.1	86.2	16,711	4,093	15.4
25,000 to 49,999.......	996	1,754	1,674,718	6.6	86.8	18,096	4,652	19.0
50,000 to 99,999.......	577	1,580	1,730,588	7.5	86.4	18,115	4,594	22.0
100,000 to 249,999....	367	2,003	2,175,835	7.4	86.5	22,839	5,287	23.1
250,000 to 499,999....	113	1,201	1,670,043	7.1	87.7	16,631	3,850	26.4
500,000 to 999,999....	57	1,104	2,132,449	6.8	86.4	18,803	4,325	29.9
1,000,000 or more.....	35	1,361	2,493,021	5.6	84.3	19,663	5,342	32.0

[1] A public library is the administrative entity, the agency, that provides public library services. Of the 9,057 public libraries in the 50 States and DC, 7,330 were single-outlet libraries and 1,727 were multiple-outlet libraries. There are 8,884 central library outlets, 7,723 branch library outlets, and 671 bookmobiles. [2] The sum of central and branch libraries. [3] Total includes income from the federal government (0.3%) and other sources (7.2%), not shown separately. [4] Full-time equivalents. Forty hours per week equals 1 FTE. [5] Librarians with master's degrees from a graduate library education program accredited by the American Library Association (ALA). Total librarians, including those without ALA-MLS, is 50,926. [6] The average per stationary outlet was calculated by dividing the total number of public use internet computers in central and branch outlets by the total number of such outlets.

Source: Institute of Museum and Library Services, Public Libraries Survey, "Public Libraries Survey, Fiscal Year 2019, Supplementary Tables," August 2021. See also <www.imls.gov/research-evaluation/data-collection/public-libraries-survey>.

Table 1190. Number of Public Libraries and Library Services by State: 2019

[1,243,130 represents 1,243,130,000. Data are generally for the fiscal year ending in June; see source documentation for reporting periods. Based on a census of all public libraries that meet the definition of a Federal State Cooperative System (FSCS) Public Library, which can have one or more outlets (central, branch, bookmobile, or books-by-mail-only) that provide direct service to the public]

| State | Number of public libraries [1] | Visits | | Circulation [3] | | | | Average number of public use internet computers [4] |
		Library visits (1,000s)	Per capita visits [2]	Total circulation (1,000s)	Per capita circulation of materials [2]	Children's circulation (1,000s)	Children's circulation as percent of total circulation	
United States	**9,057**	**1,243,130**	**3.9**	**2,171,880**	**6.9**	**776,063**	**35.7**	**18.0**
Alabama	220	14,450	3.0	20,606	4.3	7,060	34.3	16.3
Alaska	64	3,062	4.8	5,036	7.8	1,503	29.8	11.4
Arizona	89	23,446	3.3	49,272	6.9	13,862	28.1	24.4
Arkansas	60	9,236	3.4	14,013	5.1	4,120	29.4	12.7
California	185	139,011	3.5	215,768	5.4	88,669	41.1	21.2
Colorado	112	29,582	5.3	64,123	11.4	24,103	37.6	26.7
Connecticut	180	19,014	5.8	24,927	7.6	8,913	35.8	18.5
Delaware	21	4,056	4.2	5,593	5.8	1,829	32.7	31.7
District of Columbia	1	3,820	5.4	4,865	6.9	1,654	34.0	38.5
Florida	81	63,289	3.0	103,314	4.9	31,864	30.8	32.1
Georgia	62	26,003	2.4	35,986	3.3	15,885	44.1	23.9
Hawaii	1	3,436	2.4	5,625	4.0	2,290	40.7	11.4
Idaho	103	8,290	5.5	16,379	10.9	7,002	42.8	14.4
Illinois	623	60,853	5.2	105,752	9.0	40,492	38.3	21.2
Indiana	236	30,247	5.0	65,173	10.7	21,379	32.8	19.3
Iowa	535	16,434	5.4	24,515	8.0	8,903	36.3	9.0
Kansas	318	13,459	5.4	25,225	10.1	9,867	39.1	10.4
Kentucky	120	16,157	3.6	28,888	6.5	9,077	31.4	24.4
Louisiana	67	15,934	3.5	21,990	4.8	5,376	24.4	17.5
Maine	228	6,602	5.4	7,993	6.6	3,028	37.9	7.8
Maryland	24	24,905	4.1	56,180	9.3	22,233	39.6	28.5
Massachusetts	367	39,202	5.8	54,839	8.0	20,413	37.2	15.3
Michigan	396	43,741	4.4	75,915	7.7	25,175	33.2	19.4
Minnesota	136	21,902	3.9	51,248	9.1	20,747	40.5	16.0
Mississippi	53	6,983	2.3	6,690	2.2	2,107	31.5	11.8
Missouri	149	24,159	4.4	51,838	9.5	16,923	32.6	13.1
Montana	82	4,053	4.1	6,121	6.2	2,049	33.5	9.9
Nebraska	236	7,158	4.5	13,682	8.6	6,470	47.3	11.0
Nevada	22	9,391	3.1	17,397	5.7	5,549	31.9	17.2
New Hampshire	220	6,836	5.1	10,037	7.5	3,380	33.7	6.9
New Jersey	296	42,036	4.8	51,097	5.9	20,146	39.4	19.4
New Mexico	88	6,811	4.6	9,350	6.2	2,425	25.9	15.3
New York	756	95,175	4.9	110,536	5.7	34,726	31.4	18.2
North Carolina	82	30,188	2.9	51,051	4.9	22,919	44.9	19.4
North Dakota	73	2,064	3.0	3,542	5.2	1,309	37.0	9.0
Ohio	251	67,938	5.9	178,937	15.6	55,555	31.0	19.8
Oklahoma	119	13,169	4.1	25,524	7.9	9,590	37.6	14.8
Oregon	132	19,623	5.6	54,174	15.4	12,084	22.3	13.9
Pennsylvania	452	40,276	3.2	64,084	5.2	21,681	33.8	12.8
Rhode Island	48	5,171	4.9	6,675	6.3	2,212	33.1	20.5
South Carolina	42	13,592	2.9	24,546	5.3	8,831	36.0	21.4
South Dakota	111	3,693	4.8	5,822	7.5	2,434	41.8	8.0
Tennessee	186	18,036	2.7	28,621	4.3	10,246	35.8	20.8
Texas	544	65,948	2.5	116,451	4.4	48,061	41.3	24.0
Utah	70	14,822	4.8	35,488	11.5	15,791	44.5	20.2
Vermont	162	3,416	5.9	4,201	7.2	1,367	32.5	6.3
Virginia	93	33,548	4.0	60,979	7.3	24,003	39.4	22.2
Washington	60	36,055	4.8	86,800	11.7	27,630	31.8	19.3
West Virginia	97	4,667	2.5	6,413	3.5	1,963	30.6	8.1
Wisconsin	381	29,071	5.0	54,093	9.3	19,432	35.9	13.9
Wyoming	23	3,124	5.4	4,506	7.8	1,733	38.5	11.8

[1] A public library is the administrative entity, the agency, that provides public library services. Of the 9,057 public libraries in the 50 States and DC, 7,330 were single-outlet libraries and 1,727 were multiple-outlet libraries. There are 8,884 central library outlets, 7,723 branch library outlets, and 671 bookmobiles. Excludes 184 libraries that do not meet the criteria in the FSCS public library definition but that qualify as public libraries under state law. [2] Per capita rate based on total unduplicated population of legal service area determined by the state library agency of each state. [3] Total circulation includes physical and electronic materials. Children's circulation includes materials in all formats, including renewals. [4] The average per stationary outlet was calculated by dividing the total number of public use Internet computers in central and branch outlets by the total number of such outlets.

Source: Institute of Museum and Library Services, Public Libraries Survey, "Public Libraries Survey, Fiscal Year 2019, Supplementary Tables," August 2021. See also <www.imls.gov/research-evaluation/data-collection/public-libraries-survey>.

Table 1191. Public Library Holdings by Type by State: 2019

[In thousands (686,878 represents 686,878,000). Data are generally for the fiscal year ending in June; see source for reporting periods. Based on a census of all public libraries conducted by Institute of Museum and Library Services. Covers only libraries that meet the definition of a Federal State Cooperative System (FSCS) public library. State data comparisons should be made with caution because of differences in reporting periods and adherence to survey definitions. Data are not subject to sampling error; census results may contain nonsampling error]

State	Print		Electronic materials		Audio		Video	
	Print materials [1]	Current print serial subscriptions	Electronic books [2]	Electronic collections [3]	Physical units	Download-able units [4]	Physical units	Download-able units [4]
United States..........	**686,878**	**1,492.2**	**615,709**	**493.2**	**40,866**	**326,075**	**68,462**	**27,533**
Alabama.................	8,668	7.4	8,886	14.1	434	4,381	715	478
Alaska...................	2,077	4.2	1,343	3.5	113	660	278	44
Arizona.................	7,632	11.1	9,211	3.2	573	7,123	1,179	494
Arkansas...............	5,897	5.9	3,910	5.2	239	2,416	583	198
California...............	55,979	80.7	21,847	4.8	3,034	10,268	5,173	2,300
Colorado...............	9,485	19.3	4,548	19.7	898	3,932	1,364	651
Connecticut............	12,429	17.0	2,531	8.3	750	1,076	1,257	25
Delaware...............	1,453	3.4	539	0.2	122	181	168	21
District of Columbia......	971	1.9	32	0.1	26	14	76	1
Florida..................	26,035	36.3	10,572	6.3	1,640	46,415	3,434	900
Georgia................	15,817	13.3	1,175	4.1	504	1,169	1,222	148
Hawaii..................	2,896	2.3	105	0.1	113	31	174	–
Idaho...................	4,229	4.7	832	5.4	220	408	375	1
Illinois..................	38,460	89.2	33,600	14.7	2,798	15,903	3,798	1,248
Indiana.................	21,183	34.8	12,359	35.9	1,223	3,821	2,319	459
Iowa....................	11,540	23.7	22,093	20.2	640	10,077	1,193	32
Kansas.................	8,623	11.6	41,521	24.1	451	11,689	989	120
Kentucky...............	9,144	13.4	17,178	8.1	542	4,220	1,032	350
Louisiana...............	11,417	19.9	8,437	4.6	463	5,406	1,355	664
Maine...................	5,897	8.8	2,759	18.2	243	1,546	437	164
Maryland...............	10,077	15.9	3,022	1.2	912	1,841	1,073	227
Massachusetts..........	28,923	45.5	16,981	21.0	1,514	6,396	2,194	450
Michigan...............	25,928	42.2	16,144	2.3	1,814	8,399	2,736	1,347
Minnesota..............	13,475	22.0	6,134	7.6	787	1,211	1,081	34
Mississippi.............	5,464	3.6	1,245	2.8	186	492	410	32
Missouri................	15,456	27.7	9,558	2.6	932	2,515	1,357	294
Montana................	2,412	3.0	2,137	0.2	119	1,651	228	72
Nebraska...............	5,552	8.9	4,974	6.2	240	3,112	413	15
Nevada.................	3,688	4.7	834	1.3	248	310	572	87
New Hampshire..........	5,524	9.3	6,443	4.9	275	5,796	521	516
New Jersey.............	25,058	338.6	13,327	10.3	1,858	9,101	2,374	1,941
New Mexico.............	4,008	5.4	808	4.7	197	481	381	65
New York...............	64,494	150.1	38,647	25.2	2,880	10,106	5,496	637
North Carolina..........	15,426	18.1	9,483	7.8	643	1,815	925	184
North Dakota...........	2,079	3.5	1,146	2.3	89	1,091	142	70
Ohio....................	37,947	92.5	110,550	18.0	3,046	48,385	5,615	5,917
Oklahoma..............	6,152	29.3	5,814	4.9	334	1,844	593	189
Oregon.................	8,702	12.6	8,250	4.3	625	4,609	1,000	710
Pennsylvania...........	23,930	42.4	12,507	61.0	1,666	5,565	2,125	1,765
Rhode Island...........	3,144	4.1	3,565	2.0	152	1,154	282	42
South Carolina.........	8,483	36.0	3,792	2.5	413	3,129	803	422
South Dakota...........	2,767	3.9	2,113	6.5	131	826	180	1
Tennessee..............	10,884	9.6	25,324	13.1	520	11,685	817	676
Texas..................	36,348	38.5	12,865	32.8	1,905	5,384	3,447	523
Utah...................	6,359	8.3	3,911	4.2	584	3,131	697	158
Vermont................	2,747	4.7	1,448	8.6	127	1,243	233	(Z)
Virginia................	15,400	21.6	15,225	6.1	866	8,873	1,333	1,338
Washington............	11,857	41.7	5,304	2.6	938	2,023	1,399	252
West Virginia...........	4,736	5.1	9,085	2.0	204	19,438	362	664
Wisconsin..............	17,777	31.6	60,199	21.5	1,477	22,776	2,296	533
Wyoming...............	2,247	3.0	1,396	1.9	158	957	255	75

– Represents zero. Z Less than 500. [1] Includes books, and non-serial government documents. [2] E-books include digital documents digitized by the library, licensed or not; and non-serial government documents. [3] An electronic collection is a collection of electronically stored data or unit records (facts, bibliographic data, abstracts, texts, photographs, music, video, etc.) with a common user interface and software for the retrieval and use of the data. Electronic collections do not have a circulation period. [4] Downloadable units are items for which permanent or temporary access rights have been acquired. For items with a finite number of simultaneous users, the number of units equals the number of simultaneous users (equivalent to purchasing multiple copies of a single title). For items with unlimited simultaneous users, the number of units equals the number of titles acquired.

Source: Institute of Museum and Library Services, Public Libraries Survey, "Public Libraries Survey, Fiscal Year 2019, Supplementary Tables," August 2021. See also <www.imls.gov/research-evaluation/data-collection/public-libraries-survey>.

Section 25
Banking, Finance, and Insurance

This section presents data on the nation's finances, various types of financial institutions, money and credit, securities, insurance, and real estate. The primary sources of these data are publications of several departments of the federal government, especially the U.S. Treasury Department, and independent agencies such as the Federal Deposit Insurance Corporation, the Board of Governors of the Federal Reserve System, and the Securities and Exchange Commission. National data on insurance are available primarily from private organizations, such as the American Council of Life Insurers.

Financial Accounts of the United States—The Federal Reserve Board brings together statistics on all of the major forms of financial instruments to present an economy-wide view of asset and liability relationships in the Financial Accounts of the United States. The accounts relate borrowing and lending to one another and to the nonfinancial activities that generate income and production. Each claim outstanding is included simultaneously as an asset of the lender and as a liability of the debtor. The accounts also indicate the balance between asset totals and liability totals over the economy as a whole. Several publications of the Federal Reserve Board contain information on these financial accounts: Summary data on flows and outstandings in the statistical release *Financial Accounts of the United States* (quarterly); and concepts and organization of the accounts in *Financial Accounts Guide* <federalreserve.gov/apps/fof/>. Data are also available on the Federal Reserve Board's website at <federalreserve.gov/releases/z1/>.

Survey of Consumer Finances (SCF)—The Federal Reserve Board, in cooperation with the Treasury Department, sponsors this survey, which is conducted every 3 years to provide detailed information on the finances of U.S. families. Among the topics covered are the balance sheet, pension, income, and other demographic characteristics of U.S. families. The survey also gathers information on the use of financial institutions. Since 1992, data for the SCF have been collected by NORC at the University of Chicago. Information on the survey is available on the Federal Reserve Board's website at <federalreserve.gov/econres/scfindex.htm>.

Banking system—Banks in this country are organized under the laws of both the states and the federal government and are regulated by several bank supervisory agencies. National banks are supervised by the Comptroller of the Currency. *Reports of Condition and Income*, commonly known as call reports, have been collected from national banks since 1863. Summaries of these reports are published in the Comptroller's *Annual Report*, which also presents data on the structure of the national banking system.

The Federal Reserve System was established in 1913 to exercise central banking functions, some of which are shared with the U.S. Treasury. It includes national banks and state banks that voluntarily join the system. Statements of state bank members are consolidated by the Federal Reserve Board with data for national banks collected by the Comptroller of the Currency into totals for all member banks of the system.

Balance sheet data for member banks and other commercial banks are available on the Federal Reserve Board's website at <federalreserve.gov/data.htm>.

The Federal Deposit Insurance Corporation (FDIC), established in 1933, insures each depositor up to $250,000. Major item balance sheet and income data for all insured financial institutions are published in the *FDIC Quarterly Banking Profile*. This publication is also available on the internet at <fdic.gov/analysis/quarterly-banking-profile/>. Quarterly financial information for individual institutions is available through the FDIC and Federal Financial Institutions Examination Council websites at <fdic.gov> and <ffiec.gov>.

Credit unions—Federally chartered credit unions are under the supervision of the National Credit Union Administration (NCUA). State-chartered credit unions are supervised by the respective state supervisory authorities. The NCUA publishes comprehensive program and statistical information on all federal and federally insured state credit unions in the *Annual Report of the National Credit Union Administration*.

Other credit agencies—Insurance companies, finance companies dealing primarily in installment sales financing, and personal loan companies represent important sources of funds for the credit market. Statistics on loans, investments, cash, etc., of life insurance companies are published principally by the American Council of Life Insurers in its *Life Insurers Fact Book*. Consumer credit data are available on the Federal Reserve Board's website at <federalreserve.gov/data.htm>. Government corporations and credit agencies make available credit of specified types or to specified groups of private borrowers, either by lending directly or by insuring or guaranteeing loans made by private lending institutions. Data on operations of government credit agencies, along with other government corporations, are available in reports of individual agencies.

Securities—The Securities and Exchange Commission (SEC) was established in 1934 to protect the interests of the public and investors against malpractices in the securities and financial markets and to provide the fullest possible disclosure of information regarding securities to the investing public.

Data on the securities industry and securities transactions are also available from a number of private sources. The Securities Industry and Financial Markets Association (SIFMA), New York, NY, <sifma.org/>, publishes the *SIFMA Fact Book*. The Investment Company Institute, Washington, DC, <ici.org/>, publishes a reference book, research newsletters, and a variety of research reports that examine the industry, its shareholders, or industry issues. The annual *Investment Company Fact Book* is a guide to trends and statistics observed in the investment company industry. Institute research reports provide a detailed examination of shareholder demographics and other aspects of fund ownership.

Among the many sources of data on stock and bond prices and sales are the New York Stock Exchange, New York, NY, <nyse.com/>; NASDAQ, Washington,

DC, <nasdaq.com/>; and Global Financial Data, Los Angeles, CA, <globalfinancialdata.com/>.

Insurance—Insuring companies, which are regulated by the various states or the District of Columbia, are classified as either life or property. Both life and property insurance companies may underwrite health insurance. Insuring companies, other than those classified as life, are permitted to underwrite one or more property lines provided they are so licensed and have the necessary capital or surplus. There are a number of published sources for statistics on the various classes of insurance—life, health, fire, marine,

and casualty. Organizations representing certain classes of insurers publish reports for these classes. The American Council of Life Insurers publishes statistics on life insurance purchases, ownership, benefit payments, and assets in its *Life Insurers Fact Book*.

Statistical reliability—For a discussion of statistical collection, estimation, and sampling procedures and measures of reliability applicable to data from the Census Bureau and the Federal Reserve Board's Survey of Consumer Finances, see Appendix III.

Table 1192. Gross Domestic Product in Finance, Insurance, Real Estate, Rental and Leasing Industries in Current and Chained (2012) Dollars: 2010 to 2021

[In billions of dollars, except percent (1,006 represents $1,006,000,000,000). Represents value added by industry. For definition of gross domestic product and explanation of chained dollars, see text, Section 13, Income]

Industry	2012 NAICS code [1]	Current dollars				Chained (2012) dollars			
		2010	2015	2020	2021	2010	2015	2020	2021
Finance & insurance, total.............	52	**1,006**	**1,384**	**1,788**	**1,950**	**1,071**	**1,206**	**1,260**	**1,377**
Percent of gross domestic product......	(X)	6.7	7.6	8.6	8.5	6.8	6.9	6.9	7.1
Federal Reserve banks, credit inter- mediation, and related activities..........	521, 522	420	582	781	854	436	487	465	521
Securities, commodity contracts, & investments..................	523	197	231	341	394	234	182	221	228
Insurance carriers & related activities......	524	373	555	640	674	386	531	574	621
Funds, trusts, & other financial vehicles. ..	525	17	17	25	27	19	21	20	28
Real estate & rental & leasing, total.....	53	**1,984**	**2,329**	**2,804**	**2,935**	**2,033**	**2,172**	**2,307**	**2,374**
Percent of gross domestic product......	(X)	13.2	12.8	13.4	12.8	13.0	12.5	12.5	12.2
Real estate..............	531	1,824	2,123	2,563	2,650	1,868	1,964	2,065	2,109
Rental & leasing services and lessors of intangible assets................	532, 533	160	206	241	286	165	209	245	272

X Not applicable. [1] Data based on the 2012 North American Industry Classification System (NAICS). See text, Section 15.

Source: U.S. Bureau of Economic Analysis, "Value Added by Industry" and "Real Value Added by Industry," <www.bea.gov/data/gdp/gdp-industry>, accessed August 2022.

Table 1193. Finance, Insurance, Real Estate, and Rental and Leasing—Establishments, Revenue, Payroll, and Employees by Kind of Business: 2012 and 2017

[3,636 represents $3,636,000,000,000. For establishments with payroll. Based on the 2017 Economic Censuses; see Appendix III]

Industry	2012 NAICS code [1]	Establishments (number)		Value of shipments (bil. dol.)		Annual payroll (bil. dol.)		Paid employees [2] (1,000)	
		2012	2017	2012	2017	2012	2017	2012	2017
Finance & insurance [2]....................	52	**468,183**	**475,780**	**3,636**	**4,340**	**524**	**639**	**6,041**	**6,500**
Monetary authorities—central bank............	521	56	57	100	117	2	2	17	19
Credit intermediation & related activities.......	522	196,147	192,924	1,095	1,287	184	231	2,815	2,944
Security, commodity contracts, & like activity...	523	95,906	102,555	515	596	168	195	904	954
Insurance carriers & related activities...........	524	176,074	180,244	1,925	2,340	169	211	2,304	2,583
Real estate & rental & leasing.............	53	**354,106**	**410,820**	**488**	**674**	**85**	**113**	**1,924**	**2,195**
Real estate...........................	531	295,780	350,913	325	469	61	85	1,403	1,644
Rental & leasing services......................	532	55,795	57,147	129	158	21	25	485	515
Lessors of other nonfinancial intangible assets.............................	533	2,531	2,760	33	47	3	4	36	37

[1] Based on the North American Industry Classification System (NAICS); see text, Section 15. [2] Total does not include NAICS 525, Funds, trusts, and other financial vehicles.

Source: U.S. Census Bureau, 2017 Economic Census, EC1700COMP, "All Sectors: Comparative Statistics for the U.S., States, and Selected Geographies (2012 NAICS Basis): 2017 and 2012," <data.census.gov/>, accessed December 2021.

Table 1194. Finance and Insurance—Nonemployer Establishments and Receipts by Kind of Business: 2010 to 2019

[716.8 represents 716,800. Includes only firms subject to federal income tax. Nonemployers are businesses with no paid employees. Data originate chiefly from administrative records of the Internal Revenue Service; see Appendix III]

Kind of business	NAICS code [1]	Establishments (1,000)			Receipts (mil. dol.)		
		2010	2015	2019	2010	2015	2019
Finance and insurance...........................	52	**716.8**	**718.5**	**755.3**	**50,626**	**55,329**	**63,949**
Credit intermediation & related activities..........................	522	53.3	45.8	47.0	2,790	3,134	3,577
Depository credit intermediation....................	5221	6.2	5.9	6.1	181	214	249
Nondepository credit intermediation..............................	5222	21.8	22.1	22.5	1,554	1,864	2,052
Activities related to credit intermediation..................	5223	25.3	17.8	18.4	1,056	1,056	1,276
Securities, commodity contracts, & related activities...........	523	273.4	272.2	301.0	29,202	30,204	36,239
Securities & commodity contracts intermediation and brokerage..............................	5231	29.8	27.6	26.9	4,969	4,812	5,437
Investment banking and securities dealing..................	52311	7.2	7.4	7.9	1,748	1,389	1,661
Securities brokerage..............................	52312	18.6	17.0	15.5	2,589	2,914	3,286
Commodity contracts dealing.......................	52313	1.1	1.0	1.5	236	175	198
Commodity contracts brokerage.....................	52314	2.9	2.2	1.9	397	334	293
Securities & commodity exchanges....................	5232	1.9	1.8	1.1	660	354	248
Other financial investment activities................	5239	241.7	242.7	273.0	23,573	25,038	30,554
Insurance carriers & related activities.....................	524	390.1	400.5	407.3	18,634	21,991	24,132
Insurance carriers..................	5241	2.7	1.8	1.9	185	172	191
Agencies & other insurance-related activities.................	5242	387.4	398.7	405.4	18,449	21,819	23,942
Insurance agencies & brokerages..................	52421	270.5	279.0	292.0	13,854	16,340	17,988
Other insurance related activities.................	52429	116.9	119.8	113.4	4,595	5,479	5,954

[1] Data for 2010 are based on 2007 North American Industry Classification System (NAICS); data for 2015 are based on 2012 NAICS; and beginning 2017, data based on 2017 NAICS. For more information, see text, Section 15.

Source: U.S. Census Bureau, Nonemployer Statistics, "All Sectors: Nonemployer Statistics by Legal Form of Organization and Receipts Size Class for the U.S., States, and Selected Geographies: 2019," <data.census.gov>, accessed July 2022.

Table 1195. Finance and Insurance—Establishments, Employees, and Payroll: 2019 and 2020

[476.7 represents 476,700. Covers establishments with payroll. Employees are for the week including March 12. Excludes most government employees, railroad employees, and self-employed persons. For statement on methodology, see Appendix III]

Kind of business	NAICS code [1]	Establishments (1,000)		Employees (1,000)		Payroll (bil. dol.)	
		2019	2020	2019	2020	2019	2020
Finance & insurance, total [2]	**52**	**476.7**	**476.8**	**6,553**	**6,682**	**698.7**	**753.5**
Monetary authorities—central bank	521	0.1	0.1	20	20	2.5	2.7
Credit intermediation & related activities	522	190.4	188.8	2,869	2,926	254.2	283.6
Depository credit intermediation [2]	5221	115.6	113.9	1,954	1,967	164.1	174.5
Commercial banking	52211	89.2	87.6	1,537	1,540	137.6	145.2
Savings institutions	52212	7.2	7.0	104	105	8.0	8.8
Credit unions	52213	19.2	19.2	310	320	18.2	20.1
Nondepository credit intermediation [2]	5222	46.3	46.0	604	640	59.0	73.7
Real estate credit	522292	15.6	15.8	259	287	28.0	41.8
Activities related to credit intermediation	5223	28.4	29.0	311	320	31.2	35.4
Security, commodity contracts & like activity [2]	523	103.6	104.9	927	930	205.7	217.8
Security & commodity contracts intermediation & brokerage [2]	5231	28.5	27.4	351	350	84.2	88.3
Securities brokerage	52312	23.1	22.0	246	247	47.4	50.6
Other financial investment activities [2]	5239	75.0	77.5	571	574	120.0	128.1
Portfolio management	52392	40.9	41.7	360	361	89.0	95.0
Insurance carriers & related activities	524	181.2	181.3	2,730	2,798	235.2	248.3
Insurance carriers [2]	5241	30.9	30.9	1,552	1,569	150.3	156.4
Direct life insurance carriers	524113	7.9	8.1	330	332	37.9	38.7
Direct health & medical insurance carriers	524114	6.5	6.0	561	540	49.9	50.5
Direct property & casualty insurance carriers	524126	11.7	11.9	578	607	53.5	57.5
Agencies & other insurance-related activities [2]	5242	150.3	150.4	1,177	1,230	84.9	91.9
Insurance agencies & brokerages	52421	135.1	134.9	740	753	53.9	57.1

[1] North American Industry Classification System (NAICS). Data based on NAICS 2017. See text, Section 15. [2] Includes other kinds of businesses, not shown separately.

Source: U.S. Census Bureau, County Business Patterns, "All Sectors: County Business Patterns, including ZIP Code Business Patterns, by Legal Form of Organization and Employment Size Class for the U.S., States, and Selected Geographies: 2020," <data.census.gov>, accessed May 2022. See also <www.census.gov/programs-surveys/cbp.html>.

Table 1196. Revenues of Finance and Insurance Industries: 2010 to 2020

[In billions of dollars (3,495.7 represents $3,495,700,000,000). Covers taxable employer firms only. Based on Service Annual Survey. Estimates have been adjusted to the results of the 2017 Economic Census. See Appendix III]

Kind of business	NAICS code [1]	2010	2016	2017	2018	2019	2020
Finance & insurance, total	**52**	**3,495.7**	**4,146.7**	**4,340.0**	**4,610.6**	**4,854.3**	**4,959.9**
Monetary authorities—central bank	521	88.2	112.3	116.9	113.2	104.0	105.1
Credit intermediation & related activities	522	1,161.3	1,207.1	1,286.8	1,402.4	1,487.1	1,444.3
Commercial banking	52211	407.9	432.4	465.2	518.0	540.7	518.1
Savings institutions	52212	48.2	36.8	(D)	42.5	45.9	45.6
Credit unions	52213	47.7	59.2	65.1	73.2	81.9	84.0
Other depository credit intermediation	52219	0.9	1.0	(D)	1.1	1.1	1.0
Credit card issuing	52221	81.5	114.5	128.4	139.9	150.2	135.3
Sales financing	52222	89.5	109.5	114.9	123.8	131.0	127.5
Other nondepository credit intermediation	52229	416.6	352.0	365.6	391.6	420.8	410.7
Mortgage & nonmortgage loan brokers	52231	6.3	10.1	10.2	10.3	12.1	16.4
Financial transactions processing, reserve, and clearinghouse activities	52232	52.7	73.2	78.5	82.2	83.5	86.4
Other activities related to credit intermediation	52239	9.8	18.3	19.2	19.8	19.8	19.2
Securities, commodity contracts, and other financial investment activities	523	497.6	573.7	595.9	618.3	653.6	692.6
Investment banking and securities dealing	52311	119.6	101.7	104.9	108.1	112.4	119.8
Securities brokerage	52312	114.8	126.7	126.5	123.8	132.0	135.7
Commodity contracts dealing	52313	6.9	7.4	7.1	7.8	8.3	9.2
Commodity contracts brokerage	52314	6.2	5.4	5.5	5.5	5.7	6.2
Securities and commodity exchanges	5232	10.1	11.8	11.8	12.8	13.4	15.2
Miscellaneous intermediation	52391	17.2	25.3	30.0	36.8	41.0	46.2
Portfolio management	52392	172.3	229.9	245.5	254.6	267.3	282.3
Investment advice	52393	25.7	40.2	40.1	43.2	46.6	49.8
All other financial investment activities	52399	24.9	25.3	24.4	25.7	26.9	28.2
Insurance carriers & related activities	524	1,748.6	2,253.6	2,340.4	2,476.7	2,609.6	2,718.0
Direct life, health, medical insurance carriers	52411	1,060.7	1,319.0	1,357.7	1,441.8	1,516.9	1,580.7
Other direct insurance carriers	52412	441.6	559.9	585.4	616.7	649.4	666.7
Reinsurance carriers	52413	45.7	61.6	66.6	71.1	77.1	83.8
Insurance agencies & brokerages	52421	98.4	132.3	137.7	144.8	153.2	159.5
Other insurance-related activities	52429	102.1	180.9	192.9	202.3	213.1	227.4

D Estimate in table is withheld to avoid disclosing data of individual companies; data are included in higher level totals. [1] Data for 2010 are based on the 2007 North American Industry Classification System (NAICS); beginning 2013, data are based on 2012 NAICS. See text, this section and Section 15 for more information.

Source: U.S. Census Bureau, Service Annual Survey, "Service Annual Survey Latest Data (NAICS-basis): 2020" and "Service Annual Survey Historical Survey Tables," <www.census.gov/programs-surveys/sas/data.html>, accessed November 2021.

Table 1197. Financial Accounts of the United States—Financial Assets of Nonfinancial and Financial Institutions by Holder Sector: 2000 to 2021

[In billions of dollars (96,384 represents $96,384,000,000,000). As of Dec. 31]

Sector	2000	2005	2010	2015	2016	2017	2018	2019	2020	2021
All sectors	96,384	134,898	163,981	212,529	222,771	242,230	241,918	271,625	307,302	341,428
DOMESTIC NONFINANCIAL										
Households [1]	34,452	46,153	54,442	72,605	76,020	83,028	82,218	93,364	104,938	118,216
Nonfinancial business	11,264	14,183	15,362	20,520	22,007	23,527	24,958	28,662	31,044	33,396
Nonfinancial corporations	9,792	11,953	12,155	15,979	17,083	17,989	19,113	22,482	24,316	26,381
Nonfinancial noncorporate	1,473	2,231	3,207	4,541	4,924	5,538	5,846	6,180	6,728	7,015
Federal government	565	655	1,675	2,155	2,353	2,550	2,860	2,884	4,665	3,620
State and local government	1,673	2,359	2,798	2,933	3,114	3,246	3,271	3,435	3,893	4,429
DOMESTIC FINANCIAL										
Monetary authority	636	879	2,452	4,632	4,561	4,572	4,096	4,379	7,656	8,887
Private depository institutions	7,496	11,092	13,644	17,265	17,963	18,834	19,195	20,056	23,446	25,606
U.S.-chartered depository institutions	6,323	9,435	11,443	14,114	14,820	15,318	15,633	16,333	19,410	21,116
Foreign banking offices in U.S.	691	889	1,244	1,900	1,798	2,085	2,051	2,094	2,103	2,339
Banks in U.S.-affiliated areas	62	107	82	85	92	88	91	96	109	113
Credit unions	421	661	876	1,166	1,254	1,342	1,419	1,534	1,823	2,037
Property-casualty insurance companies	1,059	1,718	1,868	2,142	2,224	2,388	2,412	2,688	2,879	3,111
Life insurance companies	3,250	4,631	5,635	6,895	7,248	7,747	7,566	8,515	9,420	9,785
Private pension funds	4,283	5,391	6,604	8,649	9,073	10,020	9,696	11,043	12,026	13,152
Defined benefit plans	1,785	2,251	2,836	3,400	3,433	3,479	3,496	3,624	3,666	3,706
Defined contribution plans	2,497	3,140	3,768	5,250	5,641	6,541	6,200	7,419	8,360	9,447
Federal government retirement funds	2,028	2,504	3,144	3,770	3,808	3,941	4,036	4,223	4,434	4,634
State and local government employee retirement funds	3,301	4,667	6,169	8,054	8,358	8,704	8,930	9,202	9,539	9,826
Money market mutual funds [2]	1,845	2,027	3,034	3,078	2,955	3,121	3,290	4,002	4,766	5,205
Mutual funds [2]	5,119	6,865	9,030	12,897	13,616	15,899	14,670	17,660	19,563	22,209
Closed-end funds	143	276	238	263	265	277	252	279	282	309
Exchange-traded funds	66	301	992	2,101	2,525	3,401	3,371	4,396	5,449	7,191
Government-sponsored enterprises (GSE) [3]	1,965	2,822	6,687	6,503	6,694	6,820	6,927	7,130	7,730	8,278
Agency- and GSE-backed mortgage pools [4]	2,493	3,548	1,147	1,775	1,933	2,126	2,292	2,406	2,428	2,502
Asset-backed securities issuers [5]	1,509	3,499	2,346	1,319	1,183	1,122	1,120	1,180	1,226	1,370
Finance companies [5]	1,241	1,880	1,814	1,604	1,531	1,524	1,490	1,537	1,607	1,682
Real estate investment trusts	65	306	302	659	675	754	821	898	757	797
Security brokers and dealers	2,522	4,709	4,133	3,599	3,471	3,573	3,811	3,945	4,199	4,504
Holding companies [6]	841	1,500	2,894	3,608	3,853	3,858	3,841	3,999	4,263	4,413
Other financial business [7]	1,002	1,305	630	448	700	736	814	822	1,260	1,321
Rest of the world	7,565	11,630	16,940	25,117	26,642	30,464	29,981	34,921	39,843	46,984

[1] Includes nonprofit organizations. [2] Open-end investment companies including variable annuity money market funds or mutual funds. [3] Federal Home Loan Banks, Federal National Mortgage Association (Fannie Mae), Federal Home Loan Mortgage Corporation (Freddie Mac), Federal Agriculture Mortgage Corporation, Farm Credit System, the Financing Corporation, and the Resolution Funding Corporation. The Student Loan Marketing Association (Sallie Mae), was included until it was fully privatized in 2004. [4] Government National Mortgage Association, Federal National Mortgage Association, Federal Home Loan Mortgage Corporation, Federal Agriculture Mortgage Corporation, and Farmers Home Administration pools. Also includes agency- and GSE-backed mortgage pool securities that are used as collateral for agency- and GSE-backed collateralized mortgage obligations (CMOs) and privately issued CMOs. Excludes Federal Financing Bank holdings of pool securities, which are included with federal government mortgages and other loans and advances. [5] Includes retail captive finance companies and mortgage companies. [6] Parent-only bank holding companies, savings and loan holding companies and security holding companies that file Federal Reserve Board form FR Y-9LP, FR Y-9SP, or FR 2320. [7] Includes funding subsidiaries, custodial accounts for reinvested collateral of securities lending operations, Federal Reserve funding, credit, and liquidity special purpose vehicles created in response to the 2008 Financial Crisis and COVID-19 pandemic, and U.S. central clearing parties.

Source: Board of Governors of the Federal Reserve System, "Financial Accounts of the United States, Z.1," <www.federalreserve.gov/data.htm>, accessed March 2022.

Table 1198. Financial Accounts of the United States—Debt Securities and Debt Loans Outstanding By Sector: 2000 to 2021

[In billions of dollars (28,696 represents $28,696,000,000,000). As of December 31. Represents credit market debt owed by sectors shown. Some sectors only borrow/lend through debt securities or loans, but not both]

Item	2000	2005	2010	2015	2016	2017	2018	2019	2020	2021
Total debt outstanding	**28,696**	**43,611**	**55,044**	**63,345**	**65,765**	**68,773**	**71,843**	**75,077**	**83,031**	**88,308**
Total debt securities [1]	**16,397**	**24,775**	**33,523**	**39,438**	**40,967**	**42,609**	**44,499**	**46,724**	**53,109**	**56,188**
Domestic nonfinancial	8,117	11,440	17,976	24,051	25,215	25,989	27,508	28,947	34,225	36,145
Nonprofit and household sector	138	217	270	220	217	218	216	213	202	201
Nonfinancial corporate business	2,700	2,993	3,971	5,554	5,849	6,175	6,327	6,597	7,213	7,390
Federal government	4,090	5,585	10,529	15,166	16,008	16,455	17,865	19,040	23,621	25,304
State and local governments [2]	1,189	2,646	3,206	3,110	3,141	3,140	3,100	3,098	3,188	3,249
Financial sectors	7,577	12,126	13,471	12,634	12,950	13,276	13,585	13,977	14,874	15,689
U.S.-chartered depository institutions	99	134	585	301	277	223	247	210	271	230
Foreign banking offices in U.S.	2	1	88	43	49	38	41	39	36	36
Government-sponsored enterprises (GSE)	1,826	2,592	6,435	6,369	6,563	6,716	6,797	7,002	7,638	8,145
Agency- and GSE-backed mortgage pools	2,493	3,548	1,147	1,775	1,933	2,126	2,292	2,406	2,428	2,502
Asset-backed securities issuers	1,515	3,503	2,346	1,319	1,183	1,122	1,120	1,180	1,226	1,370
Finance companies	743	966	1,188	953	886	835	879	835	815	770
Real estate investment trusts	65	217	145	396	417	439	470	539	580	633
Securities brokers and dealers	41	62	130	131	129	186	184	174	184	225
Holding companies	290	482	1,241	1,213	1,376	1,449	1,402	1,446	1,577	1,638
Other financial business	503	620	167	134	136	142	151	146	118	140
Rest of the world	703	1,209	2,076	2,753	2,801	3,344	3,406	3,800	4,010	4,354
Total loans [3]	**12,300**	**18,836**	**21,520**	**23,907**	**24,798**	**26,164**	**27,344**	**28,353**	**29,922**	**32,121**
Domestic nonfinancial	11,056	17,098	19,707	21,366	22,142	23,471	24,609	25,594	27,045	28,915
Financial sectors	1,110	1,621	1,642	2,063	2,145	2,149	2,139	2,068	2,123	2,294
Rest of the world	134	117	171	478	511	544	596	690	754	911

[1] Includes open market paper, Treasury securities, agency- and GSE-backed securities, municipal securities, and corporate and foreign bonds. [2] Excludes employee retirement funds. [3] Includes depository loans not elsewhere classified, other loans and advances, mortgages, and consumer credit.

Source: Board of Governors of the Federal Reserve System, "Financial Accounts of the United States, Z.1," <www.federalreserve.gov/data.htm>, accessed March 2022.

Table 1199. Financial Accounts of the United States—Financial Assets and Liabilities of Foreign Sector: 2000 to 2021

[In billions of dollars (7,565 represents $7,565,000,000,000). As of December 31. Minus sign (-) indicates loss]

Type of instrument	2000	2005	2010	2015	2016	2017	2018	2019	2020	2021
Total financial assets	**7,565**	**11,630**	**16,940**	**25,117**	**26,642**	**30,464**	**29,981**	**34,921**	**39,843**	**46,984**
Special Drawing Rights allocations	6	7	54	49	47	50	49	49	51	161
Net interbank assets	49	-42	-68	198	54	158	207	124	153	198
U.S. checkable deposits and currency	236	300	390	707	767	848	928	987	1,143	1,204
U.S. time deposits	226	223	308	480	551	565	602	600	699	705
Money market fund shares	11	23	70	108	93	93	111	125	127	139
Security repurchase agreements	91	736	641	903	972	1,003	972	1,065	1,075	1,359
Debt securities, excluding negotiable certificates of deposit	2,335	4,980	8,252	10,337	10,661	11,342	11,186	12,246	12,906	13,576
Open market (commercial) paper	114	157	102	104	141	135	125	130	85	108
Treasury securities	1,021	1,984	4,459	6,146	6,003	6,211	6,270	6,844	7,071	7,718
Agency- and GSE-backed securities [1]	348	1,006	1,096	916	992	1,012	1,087	1,204	1,196	1,255
Municipal securities	8	29	72	87	94	101	100	104	108	109
U.S. corporate bonds	843	1,804	2,523	3,083	3,432	3,882	3,604	3,964	4,446	4,386
Nonfinancial business loans	117	163	162	208	203	376	733	831	904	1,030
U.S. corporate equities	1,483	2,118	3,213	5,501	5,783	7,019	6,630	8,199	10,449	13,145
Mutual fund shares	149	163	263	601	694	829	799	896	1,029	1,387
Trade receivables	70	122	203	247	254	300	333	349	430	459
Life insurance reserves	(Z)	1	6	6	17	20	10	11	2	2
Pension entitlements	(Z)	(Z)	1	3	4	4	15	16	2	2
Foreign direct investment in U.S. [2]	2,783	2,818	3,422	5,731	6,503	7,806	7,347	9,363	10,814	13,552
Miscellaneous assets (insurance receivables)	7	19	22	39	40	50	59	61	59	65
Total liabilities	**2,016**	**3,440**	**5,009**	**5,399**	**5,417**	**6,257**	**6,656**	**7,239**	**7,673**	**8,126**
U.S. official reserve assets [3]	57	54	121	106	106	112	115	118	134	240
U.S. private deposits	803	1,165	1,304	591	501	758	824	767	868	829
Security repurchase agreements	(Z)	381	664	789	905	872	990	1,226	1,287	1,172
Debt securities	703	1,209	2,076	2,753	2,801	3,344	3,406	3,800	4,010	4,354
Commercial paper	121	87	173	329	270	362	368	453	464	485
Bonds	582	1,122	1,903	2,424	2,531	2,982	3,038	3,348	3,546	3,869
Loans	134	117	171	478	511	544	596	690	754	911
Depository institution loans n.e.c. [4,5]	84	85	149	441	475	487	546	633	699	859
Other loans and advances	50	32	22	37	36	56	51	58	55	53
Trade credit and advances	47	46	65	66	69	77	79	82	82	85
Life insurance reserves	22	49	68	51	75	98	67	68	84	86
Pension entitlements	6	16	33	21	15	19	78	81	128	133
U.S. direct investment abroad [2]	148	189	189	247	210	181	232	130	64	41
Miscellaneous liabilities	96	214	318	296	224	251	270	276	263	273

Z Less than $500,000. [1] GSE = Government-sponsored enterprises. [2] Direct investment is valued on a market value basis. [3] Excludes monetary gold. [4] N.e.c. = not elsewhere classified. [5] Beginning with 2010, includes loans to foreign non-depository financial institutions.

Source: Board of Governors of the Federal Reserve System, "Financial Accounts of the United States, Z.1," <www.federalreserve.gov/data.htm>, accessed March 2022.

Table 1200. Financial Accounts of the United States—Assets of Households and Nonprofit Organizations: 2000 to 2021

[In billions of dollars (34,452 represents $34,452,000,000,000). As of December 31. See also Table 762]

Type of instrument	Total (billion dollars)							Percent distribution		
	2000	2005	2010	2015	2019	2020	2021	2010	2020	2021
Total financial assets...................	34,452	46,153	54,442	72,605	93,364	104,938	118,216	100.0	100.0	100.0
Foreign deposits............................	48	64	67	32	41	49	46	0.1	–	–
Checkable deposits and currency.........	397	355	527	1,200	1,163	2,863	4,064	1.0	2.7	3.4
Time and savings deposits................	3,000	4,758	5,952	7,947	9,793	10,282	11,053	10.9	9.8	9.3
Money market fund shares................	1,296	1,262	1,790	1,724	2,271	2,676	2,944	3.3	2.5	2.5
Debt securities.............................	2,035	3,186	4,638	3,906	4,714	4,417	3,146	8.5	4.2	2.7
Treasury securities.......................	538	239	1,012	911	1,669	1,518	780	1.9	1.4	0.7
Agency and GSE-backed securities [1]....	579	369	140	428	610	307	93	0.3	0.3	0.1
Municipal securities......................	476	1,709	1,903	1,927	1,928	1,941	1,815	3.5	1.8	1.5
Corporate and foreign bonds.............	443	870	1,583	639	507	651	458	2.9	0.6	0.4
Loans [2].....................................	633	872	1,090	1,206	1,148	1,261	1,387	2.0	1.2	1.2
Mortgages................................	96	127	132	99	82	80	76	0.2	0.1	0.1
Consumer credit (student loans).........	–	–	71	45	27	24	23	0.1	–	–
Corporate equities [3].......................	7,068	8,065	8,546	13,739	21,052	26,107	32,503	15.7	24.9	27.5
Mutual fund shares........................	2,558	3,405	4,699	6,956	9,959	11,078	12,561	8.6	10.6	10.6
Trade receivables.........................	124	153	184	241	271	279	286	0.3	0.3	0.2
Life insurance reserves...................	839	1,136	1,273	1,511	1,731	1,867	1,929	2.3	1.8	1.6
Pension entitlements [4].....................	11,031	14,516	18,301	23,431	27,994	29,800	31,752	33.6	28.4	26.9
Equity in noncorporate business...........	4,988	7,636	6,469	9,630	11,940	12,891	15,125	11.9	12.3	12.8
Miscellaneous assets......................	437	744	905	1,082	1,287	1,368	1,420	1.7	1.3	1.2

– Represents or rounds to zero. [1] GSE = government-sponsored enterprises. [2] Includes other instruments not shown separately. [3] Directly held corporate equities, including closed-end fund, exchange-traded fund, and real estate investment trust shares. [4] Includes public and private defined benefit and defined contribution plans and annuities, including those in IRAs and at life insurance companies. Excludes social security.

Source: Board of Governors of the Federal Reserve System, "Financial Accounts of the United States, Z.1," <www.federalreserve.gov/data. htm>, accessed March 2022.

Table 1201. Financial Assets Held by Families by Type of Asset: 2016 and 2019

[Median value in thousands of constant 2019 dollars (25.0 represents $25,000). All dollar figures are adjusted to 2019 dollars using the "current methods" version of the consumer price index for all urban consumers published by U.S. Bureau of Labor Statistics. Families include one-person units; for definition of family, see text, Section 1. Based on Survey of Consumer Finances; see Appendix III]

Age of family head and family income	Any financial asset [1]	Trans-action accounts [2]	Certifi-cates of deposit	Savings bonds	Stocks [3]	Pooled invest-ment funds [4]	Retire-ment accounts [5]	Life insur-ance [6]	Other man-aged [7]
PERCENT OF FAMILIES OWNING ASSET									
2016, total..................	98.5	98.0	6.5	8.6	13.9	10.0	52.1	19.4	5.5
2019, total.................	**98.7**	**98.2**	**7.7**	**7.5**	**15.2**	**9.0**	**50.5**	**19.0**	**5.9**
Under 35 years old..........	98.0	97.6	3.4	6.3	13.8	4.8	45.3	9.9	1.1
35 to 44 years old...........	98.9	98.6	4.5	8.9	14.3	7.0	55.8	12.7	2.1
45 to 54 years old...........	98.7	98.4	4.4	7.9	14.5	9.6	57.9	16.8	2.4
55 to 64 years old...........	98.6	97.9	8.5	7.4	15.6	10.6	54.5	22.4	7.1
65 to 74 years old...........	98.7	98.4	11.8	7.2	15.3	13.3	48.1	27.8	12.5
75 years old and over........	99.5	98.8	18.4	7.6	19.2	10.8	37.7	30.7	14.6
Percentiles of income: [8]									
Less than 20................	95.7	94.3	2.8	2.3	5.3	2.1	10.7	9.6	2.7
20 to 39.9...................	97.9	97.4	5.7	5.8	7.9	3.5	33.0	16.3	3.3
40 to 59.9...................	99.8	99.4	7.9	7.4	11.5	6.5	53.8	18.2	5.2
60 to 79.9...................	100.0	100.0	8.8	8.2	17.0	8.8	69.5	22.8	7.0
80 to 89.9...................	100.0	100.0	12.0	12.9	24.8	14.2	80.4	26.6	9.2
90 to 100...................	100.0	100.0	14.4	14.6	43.8	34.7	90.6	29.1	13.1
MEDIAN VALUE [9]									
2016, total..................	25.0	4.8	21.3	1.1	26.6	121.2	63.8	9.0	117.0
2019, total.................	**25.7**	**5.3**	**25.0**	**0.8**	**25.0**	**110.0**	**65.0**	**9.0**	**115.0**
Under 35 years old..........	8.4	3.2	5.0	0.8	2.6	11.0	13.0	2.8	12.0
35 to 44 years old...........	22.7	4.7	5.0	0.6	20.0	49.5	60.0	6.0	75.0
45 to 54 years old...........	36.2	6.3	10.8	0.5	28.0	150.0	100.0	11.0	100.0
55 to 64 years old...........	46.3	5.7	35.0	1.5	53.4	273.0	133.5	13.5	140.0
65 to 74 years old...........	53.7	8.0	40.3	1.0	55.0	190.8	164.0	10.0	128.0
75 years old and over.......	51.5	9.3	35.0	0.9	50.0	120.0	83.0	10.0	125.0

[1] Includes other types of financial assets, not shown separately. [2] Checking, savings, and money market deposit accounts, money market mutual funds, call or cash accounts at brokerages, and prepaid debit cards. [3] Covers only publicly traded stocks that are directly held by families—that is, corporate equities not held as part of a managed investment account or mutual fund. [4] Excludes money market mutual funds and indirectly held mutual funds and includes all other types of directly held pooled investment funds, such as traditional open-ended and closed-end mutual funds, real estate investment trusts, and hedge funds. [5] The tax-deferred retirement accounts consist of IRAs, Keogh accounts, and certain employer-sponsored accounts. Employer-sponsored accounts include 401(k), 403(b), and thrift saving accounts from current or past jobs; other current job plans from which loans or withdrawals can be made; and accounts from past jobs from which the family expects to receive the account balance in the future. [6] The value of such policies according to their current cash value, not their death benefit. [7] Includes personal annuities and trusts with an equity interest and managed investment accounts. [8] Percentiles of income distribution in 2019 dollars: 20th: $28,400; 40th: $47,900; 60th: $75,300; 80th: $127,300; 90th: $188,400. Percentile: A value on a scale of zero to 100 that indicates the percent of a distribution that is equal to or below it. [9] Median value of financial asset for families holding such assets.

Source: Board of Governors of the Federal Reserve System, 2019 Survey of Consumer Finances, *Changes in U.S. Family Finances From 2016 to 2019: Evidence from the Survey of Consumer Finances*, Federal Reserve Bulletin, Vol. 106, No. 5, September 2020. See also <www.federalreserve.gov/econres/scfindex.htm>.

Table 1202. Financial Accounts of the United States—Liabilities of Households and Nonprofit Organizations: 2000 to 2021

[In billions of dollars (7,455 represents $7,455,000,000,000). As of December 31. Minus sign (-) indicates decrease. See also Table 762]

Type of instrument	Total (billion dollars)							Percent distribution		
	2000	2005	2010	2015	2019	2020	2021	2010	2020	2021
Total liabilities.............................	7,455	12,342	14,166	14,564	16,505	17,124	18,353	100.0	100.0	100.0
Debt securities (municipal securities).......	138	217	270	220	213	202	201	1.9	1.2	1.1
Loans..	7,150	11,900	13,596	13,971	15,886	16,508	17,732	96.0	96.4	96.6
Home mortgages [1]........................	4,817	8,940	9,992	9,493	10,481	10,920	11,743	70.5	63.8	64.0
Consumer credit...........................	1,741	2,321	2,647	3,400	4,192	4,185	4,434	18.7	24.4	24.2
Depository institution loans, not elsewhere classified [2]................	61	36	214	281	350	371	424	1.5	2.2	2.3
Other loans and advances.................	402	435	545	559	604	772	870	3.8	4.5	4.7
Commercial mortgages....................	129	168	198	239	259	260	262	1.4	1.5	1.4
Trade payables..............................	148	203	274	341	370	376	383	1.9	2.2	2.1
Deferred and unpaid life insurance premiums..................................	20	23	25	32	36	37	37	0.2	0.2	0.2

[1] Includes loans made under home equity lines of credit and home equity loans secured by junior liens. [2] Includes loans extended by the Federal Reserve to financial institutions such as domestic hedge funds through the Term Asset-Backed Securities Loan Facility (TALF).

Source: Board of Governors of the Federal Reserve System, "Financial Accounts of the United States, Z.1," <www.federalreserve.gov/data.htm>, accessed March 2022.

Table 1203. Financial Debt Held by Families by Type of Debt: 2016 and 2019

[Median debt in thousands of constant 2019 dollars (63.6 represents $63,600). See headnote, Table 1201]

Age and race of family head and family income	Any debt	Secured by residential property		Installment loans [2]	Credit card balances [3]	Lines of credit not secured by residential property	Other [4]
		Primary residence [1]	Other				
PERCENT OF FAMILIES HOLDING DEBT							
2016, total..............................	77.1	41.9	5.6	50.2	43.9	1.8	5.4
2019, total.............................	**76.6**	**42.1**	**4.7**	**51.5**	**45.4**	**1.5**	**5.2**
Under 35 years old......................	78.7	30.3	1.9	64.5	47.6	2.2	4.2
35 to 44 years old.......................	87.2	53.7	5.4	63.6	50.5	1.6	6.0
45 to 54 years old.......................	85.6	54.0	6.4	61.4	51.7	1.5	8.4
55 to 64 years old.......................	77.3	46.2	6.8	47.4	46.6	1.5	5.0
65 to 74 years old.......................	70.0	37.6	4.5	34.2	41.1	1.0	4.4
75 years old and over...................	51.4	27.7	2.6	24.4	28.0	(B)	2.5
White, non-Hispanic.....................	77.7	47.4	5.4	50.8	44.5	1.5	4.9
Black, non-Hispanic.....................	74.0	27.7	2.9	53.7	47.7	(B)	5.4
Hispanic or Latino.......................	72.2	32.3	2.9	52.4	49.9	(B)	4.5
Other or multiple race..................	77.6	38.1	4.1	51.7	43.7	2.4	7.8
Percentiles of income: [5]							
Less than 20...........................	53.1	11.5	0.5	32.0	30.4	1.3	3.0
20 to 39.9..............................	72.5	27.1	(B)	48.2	45.5	1.6	4.2
40 to 59.9..............................	82.9	40.6	2.3	58.7	55.1	1.5	5.2
60 to 79.9..............................	88.5	61.0	5.6	62.9	56.9	1.5	5.8
80 to 89.9..............................	88.3	69.7	10.1	63.4	45.9	(B)	9.3
90 to 100..............................	84.3	70.8	17.6	47.6	32.1	1.4	6.7
MEDIAN DEBT [6]							
2016, total..............................	63.6	118.1	106.4	18.2	2.4	3.2	5.3
2019, total.............................	**64.8**	**134.8**	**122.0**	**17.9**	**2.7**	**2.0**	**5.0**
Under 35 years old......................	44.1	140.0	94.7	20.4	1.9	0.9	2.5
35 to 44 years old.......................	128.0	176.6	110.0	22.4	2.6	2.0	7.0
45 to 54 years old.......................	108.0	142.0	130.0	20.5	3.2	2.6	5.0
55 to 64 years old.......................	61.1	110.0	165.0	14.4	3.0	1.7	6.0
65 to 74 years old.......................	39.4	89.0	119.5	14.3	2.9	3.5	6.0
75 years old and over...................	29.3	82.0	78.0	9.8	2.7	(B)	8.7
White, non-Hispanic.....................	78.6	130.0	112.0	18.1	3.2	2.0	7.4
Black, non-Hispanic.....................	27.5	116.0	60.0	17.2	1.3	(B)	2.3
Hispanic or Latino.......................	40.0	130.0	215.0	16.9	1.9	(B)	4.2
Other or multiple race..................	71.0	180.0	140.0	17.8	2.4	1.0	3.0

B Base figure too small to meet statistical standards for reliability. [1] Debt secured by residential property consists of first-lien and junior-lien mortgages and home equity lines of credit secured by the primary residence. [2] Consumer loans that typically have fixed payments and a fixed term. Examples are automobile loans, student loans, and loans for furniture, appliances, and other durable consumer goods. [3] Balances exclude purchases made after the most recent bill was paid. [4] Includes loans on insurance policies, loans against pension accounts, borrowing on margin accounts, and unclassified loans. [5] See footnote 8, Table 1201. [6] Median amount of financial debt for families holding such debts.

Source: Board of Governors of the Federal Reserve System, 2019 Survey of Consumer Finances, *Changes in U.S. Family Finances From 2016 to 2019: Evidence from the Survey of Consumer Finances*, Federal Reserve Bulletin, Vol. 106, No. 5, September 2020. See also <www.federalreserve.gov/econres/scfindex.htm>.

Table 1204. Debt Held by Families—Percent Distribution by Type and Purpose of Debt: 2010 to 2019

[See headnote, Table 1201]

Type and purpose of debt	2010	2016	2019	Type and purpose of debt	2010	2016	2019
TYPE OF DEBT				**PURPOSE OF DEBT**			
Total...................................	**100.0**	**100.0**	**100.0**	**Total**.................................	**100.0**	**100.0**	**100.0**
Secured by residential property:				Primary residence:			
Primary residence....................	74.1	69.4	70.6	Purchase..............................	69.5	66.7	68.8
Other..................................	9.8	9.4	8.9	Improvement.........................	1.9	1.5	1.2
Lines of credit not secured				Other residential property............	10.5	10.3	9.2
by residential property..............	1.0	1.1	0.6	Investments, except real estate.....	2.0	1.5	1.5
Installment loans......................	11.1	16.0	16.1	Vehicles..............................	4.7	6.3	6.1
Credit card balances..................	2.9	2.6	2.6	Goods and services..................	5.7	4.9	4.6
Other..................................	1.1	1.5	1.2	Education............................	5.2	8.2	8.2
				Other................................	0.4	0.5	0.5

Source: Board of Governors of the Federal Reserve System, 2019 Survey of Consumer Finances, *Changes in U.S. Family Finances From 2016 to 2019: Evidence from the Survey of Consumer Finances*, Federal Reserve Bulletin, Vol. 106, No. 5, September 2020. See also <www.federalreserve.gov/econres/scfindex.htm>.

Table 1205. Ratios of Debt Payments to Family Income: 2010 to 2019

[In percent. See headnote, Table 1201]

Family characteristic	Ratio of debt payments to family income						Percent of debtors with—					
	Aggregate [1]			Median for debtors [2]			Ratios above 40 percent			Any payment 60 days or more past due		
	2010	2016	2019	2010	2016	2019	2010	2016	2019	2010	2016	2019
All families.................	**14.7**	**10.8**	**11.8**	**18.1**	**14.7**	**15.3**	**13.8**	**9.1**	**9.7**	**10.8**	**7.5**	**6.0**
Under 35 years old..........	17.0	14.1	14.3	16.4	13.1	14.7	11.6	8.5	8.6	10.4	10.6	8.6
35 to 44 years old...........	18.4	15.2	15.9	20.9	16.0	16.5	16.4	8.7	10.3	15.7	10.5	8.0
45 to 54 years old...........	16.2	11.7	12.5	19.2	16.2	16.2	15.5	8.5	10.4	12.6	6.9	7.2
55 to 64 years old...........	12.5	9.1	10.3	17.6	15.1	15.5	13.0	10.9	9.6	8.4	5.7	3.9
65 to 74 years old...........	11.3	7.9	8.6	17.0	13.7	13.6	12.1	8.5	9.6	6.1	4.5	2.5
75 years old and over.......	6.8	6.0	7.3	14.1	12.5	13.9	11.9	9.9	9.9	3.2	2.8	2.6
Percentiles of income: [3]												
Less than 20.................	23.5	16.2	16.2	16.3	11.8	13.9	26.1	21.6	20.9	21.2	13.9	11.1
20 to 39.9..................	16.9	14.6	15.9	17.5	15.6	15.6	18.7	13.3	15.6	15.2	11.1	9.4
40 to 59.9..................	19.5	15.3	16.3	20.0	14.4	16.0	15.3	8.3	11.0	10.2	9.1	6.7
60 to 79.9..................	19.3	15.7	16.4	20.4	16.1	17.3	11.0	4.2	4.9	8.8	4.4	3.8
80 to 89.9..................	18.0	15.4	15.1	19.3	16.3	16.6	5.3	4.2	1.9	5.4	2.9	3.0
90 to 100..................	9.4	6.2	7.0	13.1	11.3	11.0	2.9	1.5	1.2	2.1	0.8	0.2
Percentiles of net worth: [3]												
Less than 25.................	19.2	13.2	14.0	13.6	9.9	11.8	14.9	8.2	10.4	22.2	16.7	13.8
25 to 49.9..................	19.3	16.1	16.5	21.2	17.2	18.2	15.3	10.7	11.2	13.3	8.9	7.3
50 to 74.9..................	19.2	16.9	17.5	20.8	17.7	18.7	14.0	9.9	11.2	6.8	3.9	2.8
75 to 89.9..................	15.9	13.3	13.0	16.7	14.9	14.8	11.0	7.8	6.6	2.0	1.9	1.6
90 to 100..................	8.8	5.5	6.5	13.4	11.2	10.0	11.0	6.3	4.5	1.2	0.4	0.4
Owner occupied.............	16.1	11.7	12.8	22.2	18.9	19.2	17.1	11.5	11.9	8.7	5.0	3.3
Renter occupied or other. .,	7.0	6.7	6.9	6.8	6.5	7.4	5.0	3.9	4.7	16.6	13.1	12.3

[1] The aggregate measure is the ratio of total debt payments to total income for all families. [2] The median is the median of the distribution of ratios calculated for individual families with debt. [3] Percentiles of income distribution in 2019 dollars: 20th: $28,400; 40th: $47,900; 60th: $75,300; 80th: $127,300; 90th: $188,400. Percentiles of distribution of net worth in 2019 dollars: 25th: $12,400; 50th: $121,700; 75th: $403,800; 90th: $1,220,200.

Source: Board of Governors of the Federal Reserve System, 2019 Survey of Consumer Finances, *Changes in U.S. Family Finances From 2016 to 2019: Evidence from the Survey of Consumer Finances*, Federal Reserve Bulletin, Vol. 106, No. 5, September 2020. See also <www.federalreserve.gov/econres/scfindex.htm>.

Table 1206. Household Debt-Service Payments and Financial Obligations as a Percent of Disposable Personal Income: 2000 to 2021

[As of end of year (4th quarter), seasonally adjusted. Mortgage debt service ratio (DSR) is defined as the total quarterly required mortgage payments divided by total quarterly disposable personal income. The consumer DSR is defined as the total quarterly required consumer debt payments divided by total quarterly disposable personal income. The financial obligations ratio adds automobile lease payments, rental payments on tenant-occupied property, homeowners' insurance, and property tax payments to the debt service ratio]

Year	Financial obligations ratio	Household debt service ratio			Year	Financial obligations ratio	Household debt service ratio		
		Total	Mortgage	Consumer			Total	Mortgage	Consumer
2000...........	17.00	12.02	5.70	6.32	2015...........	15.02	9.88	4.45	5.43
2005...........	17.41	12.61	6.50	6.11	2016...........	15.13	9.99	4.35	5.64
2010...........	15.90	10.95	5.93	5.02	2017...........	14.92	9.91	4.22	5.69
2011...........	15.39	10.45	5.44	5.01	2018...........	14.74	9.81	4.14	5.67
2012...........	14.75	9.81	4.93	4.87	2019...........	14.87	9.94	4.13	5.81
2013...........	15.25	10.05	4.84	5.21	2020...........	14.19	9.40	3.96	5.45
2014...........	14.91	9.83	4.53	5.30	2021...........	13.97	9.32	3.84	5.48

Source: Board of Governors of the Federal Reserve System, "Household Debt Service and Financial Obligations Ratios," <www.federalreserve.gov/data.htm>, accessed August 2022.

Table 1207. FDIC-Insured Financial Institutions—Number and Assets by State and Island Area: 2021

[In billions of dollars, except as indicated (23,839.2 represents $23,839,200,000,000). As of December 31. Includes data from U.S. banks and U.S. branches of foreign banks that have insured deposits. Information is obtained primarily from the Federal Financial Institutions Examination Council (FFIEC) Call Reports and the Office of Thrift Supervision's Thrift Financial Reports. Data are based on the location of each reporting institution's main office. Reported data may include assets located outside of the reporting institution's home state]

State or Island Area	Number of institu-tions	Assets by asset size of bank				State or Island Area	Number of institu-tions	Assets by asset size of bank			
		Total	Less than $100 mil.	$100 mil. to $1 bil.	Greater than $1 bil.			Total	Less than $100 mil.	$100 mil. to $1 bil.	Greater than $1 bil.
Total......	4,848	23,839.2	50.0	1,125.0	22,664.2	NE..........	154	92.5	2.6	32.6	57.3
AL..........	102	222.4	0.7	25.9	195.8	NV..........	17	52.4	–	4.3	48.2
AK..........	5	10.2	–	1.9	8.3	NH..........	17	15.1	–	5.2	9.9
AZ..........	13	62.1	–	3.1	59.0	NJ..........	59	195.2	–	14.4	180.9
AR..........	84	145.4	0.8	21.4	123.2	NM..........	34	17.1	0.1	11.6	5.4
CA..........	137	1,238.4	0.4	27.5	1,210.5	NY..........	133	1,718.8	0.4	28.0	1,690.4
CO..........	73	84.0	0.5	17.1	66.4	NC..........	44	3,152.7	0.4	10.3	3,142.0
CT..........	32	137.5	0.1	7.0	130.4	ND..........	67	47.3	1.3	11.7	34.3
DE..........	20	1,292.8	0.1	2.5	1,290.3	OH..........	175	4,569.3	2.9	32.1	4,534.2
DC..........	4	2.6	–	1.5	1.1	OK..........	181	173.5	3.4	40.9	129.2
FL..........	96	266.2	0.6	29.4	236.2	OR..........	15	39.4	–	7.7	31.7
GA..........	150	151.5	1.2	36.6	113.7	PA..........	134	304.0	0.5	36.9	266.6
HI..........	7	67.9	–	1.5	66.5	RI..........	7	201.8	0.1	0.3	201.4
ID..........	11	10.0	–	2.9	7.1	SC..........	47	49.4	0.3	13.9	35.2
IL..........	391	656.4	5.4	80.3	570.8	SD..........	59	3,502.8	1.0	8.2	3,493.6
IN..........	93	137.5	0.4	23.8	113.3	TN..........	124	218.4	0.6	34.9	182.8
IA..........	259	116.2	3.3	53.5	59.4	TX..........	399	1,173.2	3.7	99.7	1,069.8
KS..........	214	90.8	4.0	37.7	49.1	UT..........	42	900.0	0.2	7.5	892.3
KY..........	127	73.8	1.2	28.2	44.4	VT..........	11	7.4	0.1	3.6	3.6
LA..........	112	68.4	1.1	29.4	37.9	VA..........	66	904.1	0.3	14.7	889.0
ME..........	23	37.5	0.2	3.6	33.8	WA..........	40	114.2	0.3	8.6	105.2
MD..........	35	56.2	0.1	11.4	44.6	WV..........	46	41.6	0.3	12.2	29.2
MA..........	105	504.5	0.2	28.0	476.3	WI..........	174	143.6	1.2	47.4	94.9
MI..........	81	87.9	0.6	23.1	64.2	WY..........	29	12.0	0.3	8.7	2.9
MN..........	263	110.4	5.5	49.5	55.4	GU..........	3	3.4	–	0.6	2.8
MS..........	68	161.6	0.5	18.6	142.4	FM..........	1	0.2	–	0.2	–
MO..........	221	238.7	2.2	55.2	181.3	PR..........	3	94.8	–	–	94.8
MT..........	40	63.5	0.7	7.6	55.2	VI..........	1	0.4	–	0.4	–

– Represents or round zero. GU—Guam, FM—Federated States of Micronesia, PR—Puerto Rico, VI—Virgin Islands.

Source: U.S. Federal Deposit Insurance Corporation, "Statistics on Depository Institutions (SDI)," <www.fdic.gov/bank/statistical/index.html>, accessed July 2022.

Table 1208. FDIC-Insured Financial Institutions—Income and Selected Measures of Financial Condition: 2000 to 2021

[In billions of dollars, except as indicated (511.9 represents $511,900,000,000). Includes Island Areas. Includes foreign branches of U.S. banks. Minus sign (-) indicates decrease]

Item	2000	2005	2010	2015	2017	2018	2019	2020	2021
INCOME									
Interest income......................................	511.9	522.2	536.9	478.5	572.3	661.1	705.4	603.8	563.5
Interest expense.....................................	276.6	205.1	106.9	46.9	73.3	119.8	158.7	77.1	36.1
Net interest income..............................	235.3	317.0	430.0	431.6	499.0	541.3	546.7	526.7	527.4
Provisions for loan losses.........................	32.1	29.8	158.0	37.1	51.1	50.0	55.1	132.3	-31.0
Noninterest income.................................	165.6	223.4	235.7	253.3	255.2	266.1	264.4	280.2	300.4
Noninterest expense................................	242.3	317.4	391.8	416.9	442.9	459.3	466.1	499.0	510.2
Income taxes...	43.6	64.6	38.4	70.6	97.8	61.0	60.9	36.3	72.4
Net income attributable to bank.................	81.5	133.8	85.5	163.4	164.1	236.8	232.8	147.1	279.1
PERFORMANCE RATIOS									
Return on assets (percent) [1].....................	1.14	1.28	0.65	1.04	0.97	1.35	1.29	0.72	1.23
Return on equity (percent) [2].....................	13.53	12.43	5.85	9.29	8.60	11.98	11.38	6.85	12.21
Net interest margin (percent) [3]..................	3.77	3.47	3.76	3.08	3.25	3.40	3.36	2.82	2.54
Net charge-offs (bil. dol.) [4].....................	26.32	31.59	187.64	37.28	46.81	47.50	52.16	54.11	27.36
Net charge-offs to loans and leases, total (percent)...	0.59	0.49	2.55	0.44	0.50	0.48	0.52	0.50	0.25
Net charge-off rate, credit card loans (percent)...	4.36	4.74	10.08	2.92	3.61	3.75	3.82	3.48	2.17
CONDITION RATIOS									
Equity capital to assets (percent).................	8.49	10.28	11.15	11.24	11.22	11.25	11.32	10.17	9.94
Noncurrent assets plus other real estate owned to assets (percent) [5]	0.71	0.50	3.11	0.97	0.73	0.60	0.55	0.61	0.44

[1] Net income (including securities transactions and nonrecurring items) as a percentage of average total assets. [2] Net income as a percentage of average total equity capital. [3] Interest income less interest expense as a percentage of average earning assets (i.e. the profit margin a bank earns on its loans and investments). [4] Total loans and leases charged off (removed from balance sheet because of uncollectibility), less amounts recovered on loans and leases previously charged off. [5] Noncurrent assets: the sum of loans, leases, debt securities and other assets that are 90 days or more past due, or in nonaccrual status, plus other real estate owned, primarily foreclosed property.

Source: U.S. Federal Deposit Insurance Corporation, *Quarterly Banking Profile*, Fourth Quarter 2021, and earlier reports; and "QBP Time Series Spreadsheets, Annual Income," <www.fdic.gov/analysis/quarterly-banking-profile/>, accessed September 2022.

Table 1209. FDIC-Insured Financial Institutions—Assets, and Liabilities: 2000 to 2021

[In billions of dollars, except as indicated (7,463 represents $7,463,000,000,000). As of December 31. Includes Island Areas. Excludes insured branches of foreign banks. Includes foreign branches of U.S. banks]

Item	2000	2010	2015	2016	2017	2018	2019	2020	2021
Number of financial institutions									
reporting.................................	**9,904**	**7,658**	**6,182**	**5,913**	**5,670**	**5,406**	**5,177**	**5,002**	**4,839**
Assets, total [1]..................	**7,463**	**13,319**	**15,968**	**16,780**	**17,415**	**17,943**	**18,646**	**21,869**	**23,720**
Net loans and leases [1].....................	4,572	7,144	8,721	9,183	9,597	10,027	10,394	10,627	11,069
Real estate loans [1].....................	2,396	4,267	4,375	4,603	4,774	4,887	5,049	5,118	5,258
1-4 family residential mortgages............	1,340	1,900	1,904	1,995	2,064	2,119	2,202	2,211	2,259
Nonfarm nonresidential.....................	525	1,071	1,232	1,324	1,391	1,444	1,516	1,569	1,646
Construction and development.............	197	321	275	313	338	350	362	386	401
Home equity loans.........................	151	637	465	434	411	376	342	300	265
Multifamily residential real estate.........	117	213	344	383	404	431	459	479	513
Commercial and industrial loans.............	1,086	1,184	1,837	1,932	2,009	2,164	2,208	2,441	2,314
Loans to individuals [1].....................	672	1,316	1,498	1,589	1,678	1,743	1,838	1,744	1,882
Credit cards and related plans.............	266	702	756	800	865	903	942	822	871
Other loans to individuals..................	406	614	741	790	813	839	896	922	1,011
Auto loans............................	(NA)	(NA)	415	442	450	455	484	492	538
Loans to depository institutions [2]...........	118	109	98	88	87	84	75	60	85
Lease financing receivables.................	167	102	116	127	130	133	132	124	118
Less: Reserve for losses....................	71	231	119	122	124	125	124	237	178
Securities....................................	1,361	2,668	3,354	3,560	3,632	3,723	3,982	5,112	6,246
Domestic office assets........................	6,702	11,693	14,408	15,177	15,714	16,150	16,840	19,709	21,485
Foreign office assets [2]......................	760	1,626	1,560	1,603	1,702	1,793	1,806	2,160	2,234
Liabilities and capital, total [1]............	**7,463**	**13,319**	**15,968**	**16,780**	**17,415**	**17,943**	**18,646**	**21,869**	**23,720**
Deposits.....................................	4,915	9,423	12,190	12,895	13,399	13,866	14,536	17,824	19,702
Foreign office deposits [2]...................	707	1,550	1,282	1,246	1,318	1,253	1,315	1,534	1,512
Domestic office deposits....................	4,208	7,873	10,908	11,649	12,081	12,613	13,221	16,290	18,189
Interest-bearing deposits..................	3,437	6,184	7,908	8,497	8,832	9,478	10,060	11,683	12,746
Noninterest-bearing deposits..............	771	1,689	3,000	3,152	3,250	3,135	3,161	4,607	5,444
Equity capital................................	633	1,511	1,801	1,869	1,958	2,023	2,114	2,227	2,360

NA Not available. [1] Includes other items not shown separately. [2] Prior to 2012, data do not include insured savings institutions that file Thrift Financial Reports (TFRs). Beginning 3/31/2012, all insured institutions file Call reports.

Source: U.S. Federal Deposit Insurance Corporation, "QBP Time Series Spreadsheets, Balance Sheet," <www.fdic.gov/analysis/quarterly-banking-profile/>, accessed September 2022.

Table 1210. FDIC-Insured Financial Institutions by Asset Size: 2021

[22,195.3 represents $22,195,300,000,000. Includes Island Areas. Includes foreign branches of U.S. banks]

Item	Unit	Total	Less than $100 mil.	$100 mil. to $1 bil.	$1 bil. to $10 bil.	Greater than $10 bil.
COMMERCIAL BANKS						
Institutions reporting.............................	Number	4,231	712	2,702	675	142
Assets, total.....................................	Billion dollars	22,195.3	44.0	988.0	1,866.0	19,297.2
Deposits..	Billion dollars	18,410.4	37.5	854.1	1,584.8	15,934.0
Net income.......................................	Billion dollars	263.1	0.4	11.9	25.9	225.0
Percentage of banks losing money................	Percent	2.60	8.57	1.70	0.44	(NA)
Return on assets.................................	Percent	1.24	1.00	1.26	1.46	1.21
Return on equity.................................	Percent	12.27	7.61	11.79	13.59	12.18
Net charge-offs to loans and leases..............	Percent	0.24	0.07	0.06	0.14	0.27
Noncurrent assets plus other real estate owned to assets...................................	Percent	0.40	0.57	0.42	0.44	0.40
Equity capital to assets...........................	Percent	9.96	12.83	10.51	10.71	9.85
SAVINGS INSTITUTIONS						
Institutions reporting.............................	Number	608	105	347	138	18
Assets, total.....................................	Billion dollars	1,524.1	5.9	136.9	355.8	1,025.5
Deposits..	Billion dollars	1,291.3	4.6	112.8	293.4	880.5
Net income.......................................	Billion dollars	16.0	0.1	2.0	3.8	10.1
Percentage of banks losing money................	Percent	6.41	20.95	4.32	0.72	5.56
Return on assets.................................	Percent	1.11	1.35	1.53	1.12	1.05
Return on equity.................................	Percent	11.29	7.13	11.63	9.65	12.06
Net charge-offs to loans and leases..............	Percent	0.39	0.02	0.01	0.06	0.70
Noncurrent assets plus other real estate owned to assets...................................	Percent	0.94	0.60	0.42	0.44	1.18
Equity capital to assets...........................	Percent	9.66	18.35	13.16	11.63	8.45

NA Not available.

Source: U.S. Federal Deposit Insurance Corporation, "Statistics on Depository Institutions," <www7.fdic.gov/sdi/main.asp>, accessed August 2022.

Table 1211. FDIC-Insured Financial Institutions—Deposit Insurance Fund (DIF) Indicators: 2010 to 2021

[In billions of dollars, except as indicated (7,888 represents $7,888,000,000,000). As of December 31. Includes Island Areas. Includes insured branches of foreign banks. Minus sign (-) indicates decrease]

Item	2010	2013	2014	2015	2016	2017	2018	2019	2020	2021
Number of institutions reporting..........	7,667	6,821	6,518	6,191	5,922	5,679	5,415	5,186	5,011	4,848
Domestic deposits, total [1].............	7,888	9,825	10,408	10,953	11,693	12,130	12,659	13,263	16,339	18,237
Estimated insured deposits [2].........	6,302	5,998	6,196	6,519	6,917	7,154	7,523	7,825	9,123	9,729
DIF balance...	-7	47	63	73	83	93	103	110	118	123
Reserve ratio [3].............................	-0.12	0.79	1.01	1.11	1.20	1.3	1.36	1.41	1.29	1.27
Number of problem institutions..........	884	467	291	183	123	95	60	51	56	44
Assets of problem institutions............	390.0	152.7	86.7	46.8	27.6	13.9	48.5	46.2	55.8	170.2
Number of failed institutions..............	157	24	18	8	5	8	–	4	4	–
Assets of failed institutions................	92.1	6.0	2.9	6.7	0.3	5.1	–	0.2	0.5	–

– Represents zero. [1] Excludes foreign office deposits, which are uninsured. [2] In general, insured deposits are total domestic deposits minus estimated uninsured deposits. Prior to September 30, 2009, insured deposits included deposits in accounts of $100,000 or less. Beginning September 30, 2009, insured deposits include deposits in accounts of $100,000 to $250,000 that are covered by a temporary increase in the FDIC's standard maximum deposit insurance amount. The Dodd-Frank Wall Street Reform and Consumer Protection Act of July 21, 2010 (Dodd-Frank) made permanent the standard maximum deposit insurance amount of $250,000. The Dodd-Frank Act also provided unlimited coverage for noninterest bearing transaction accounts for two years beginning December 31, 2010, and ending December 31, 2012. [3] DIF balance as percent of DIF-insured deposits.

Source: U.S. Federal Deposit Insurance Corporation, *Quarterly Banking Profile*, Fourth Quarter 2021, and earlier reports. See also <www.fdic.gov/analysis/quarterly-banking-profile/>.

Table 1212. FDIC-Insured Financial Institutions—Number of Offices and Deposits by State: 2021

[17,235 represents $17,235,000,000,000. As of June 30. Includes insured U.S. branches of foreign banks. The term "offices" includes both main offices and branches. "Banking office" is defined to include all offices and facilities that actually hold deposits, and does not include loan production offices, computer centers, and other nondeposit installations, such as automated teller machines (ATMs). Several institutions have designated home offices that do not accept deposits; these have been included to provide a more complete listing of all offices. The figures for each geographical area only include deposits of offices located within that area. Based on the Summary of Deposits survey]

State	Number of offices	Total deposits (bil. dol.)	State	Number of offices	Total deposits (bil. dol.)	State	Number of offices	Total deposits (bil. dol.)
Total [1].....	81,791	17,235	IA.............	1,462	113	NC............	2,144	503
			KS.............	1,393	97	ND............	415	38
U.S..........	81,439	17,118	KY.............	1,541	111	OH............	3,276	479
AL............	1,423	141	LA.............	1,357	138	OK............	1,301	129
AK............	115	17	ME............	443	42	OR............	816	113
AZ............	1,062	204	MD............	1,346	201	PA............	3,730	564
AR............	1,294	91	MA............	2,048	579	RI.............	236	42
CA............	6,267	2,094	MI.............	2,241	312	SC............	1,171	118
CO............	1,402	197	MN............	1,621	283	SD............	445	675
CT............	1,059	179	MS............	1,090	71	TN............	1,971	213
DE............	260	479	MO............	2,171	230	TX............	6,333	1,572
DC............	210	68	MT............	375	34	UT............	502	768
FL............	4,540	808	NE............	1,045	79	VT............	228	19
GA............	2,160	336	NV............	449	125	VA............	2,069	427
HI............	238	57	NH............	397	49	WA............	1,546	224
ID............	443	40	NJ.............	2,598	444	WV............	583	44
IL............	3,917	661	NM............	425	43	WI............	1,799	201
IN.............	1,827	180	NY............	4,436	2,464	WY............	219	22

[1] Includes outlying areas not shown separately.

Source: U.S. Federal Deposit Insurance Corporation, "Summary of Deposits, Reference Tables," <www7.fdic.gov/sod/sodSummary.asp?barItem=3>, accessed September 2022.

Table 1213. U.S. Banking Offices of Foreign Banks—Summary: 2000 to 2021

[In billions of dollars (1,358 represents $1,358,000,000,000), except as indicated. As of December. The U.S. offices of foreign banking organizations consist of U.S. branches and agencies of foreign banks and bank subsidiaries of foreign banking organizations. Foreign-owned institutions are those owned by a bank located outside of the United States and its affiliated insular areas. Bank subsidiaries of foreign banking organizations are U.S. commercial banks of which more than 25 percent are owned by a foreign banking organization or where the relationship is reported as being a controlling relationship by the filer of the FR Y-10 (Report of Changes in Organizational Structure) report form. Covers the U.S. offices of foreign banking organizations that are located in the 50 states and the District of Columbia; excludes offices located in Puerto Rico, American Samoa, Guam, the Virgin Islands and other U.S.-affiliated insular areas]

Item	2000	2005	2010	2015	2018	2019	2020	2021	Share [1] 2010	Share [1] 2020	Share [1] 2021
Assets......................	1,358	2,123	2,838	3,539	3,739	3,849	4,036	4,255	20.4	17.3	16.8
Loans, total.................	557	802	960	1,416	1,560	1,589	1,614	1,644	13.7	14.6	14.4
Business loans............	308	276	326	580	600	601	619	606	25.1	23.6	23.6
Deposits.....................	770	1,162	1,752	2,029	2,036	2,174	2,406	2,453	18.3	13.3	12.3

[1] Foreign owned banks plus U.S. branches and offices of foreign banks as percent of all banks in the United States.

Source: Board of Governors of the Federal Reserve System, "Structure and Share Data for U.S. Banking Offices of Foreign Entities," <www.federalreserve.gov/releases/iba/default.htm>, accessed September 2022.

Table 1214. Federal and State-Chartered Credit Unions—Summary: 2000 to 2021

[43,883 represents 43,883,000. As of December 31. Federal data include District of Columbia, Puerto Rico, Guam, and Virgin Islands. Excludes state-insured, privately insured, and noninsured state-chartered credit unions and corporate central credit unions, which have mainly other credit unions as members]

Year	Operating credit unions		Number of failed institutions [1]	Members (1,000)		Assets (mil. dol.)		Loans outstanding (mil. dol.)		Savings (mil. dol.)	
	Federal	State		Federal	State	Federal	State	Federal	State	Federal	State
2000......	6,336	3,980	29	43,883	33,705	242,881	195,363	163,851	137,485	210,188	169,053
2010......	4,589	2,750	29	50,081	40,447	500,075	414,395	306,276	258,555	427,603	358,877
2011......	4,447	2,647	16	50,743	41,093	525,633	436,121	308,845	262,640	449,316	378,093
2012......	4,272	2,547	22	51,797	42,043	557,119	464,612	322,675	275,066	474,903	402,948
2013......	4,105	2,449	17	52,499	43,762	571,326	490,588	343,780	301,440	485,500	424,587
2014......	3,927	2,346	15	53,355	45,870	596,145	525,942	373,387	338,938	499,683	451,107
2015......	3,764	2,257	16	54,284	48,369	628,012	576,266	404,729	382,288	522,109	493,892
2016......	3,608	2,177	14	56,598	50,205	670,124	622,354	444,516	424,591	559,825	532,759
2017......	3,499	2,074	10	59,036	52,261	718,287	660,530	490,115	467,175	594,662	564,807
2018......	3,376	1,999	8	61,272	54,891	753,546	699,853	532,693	510,860	625,464	594,269
2019......	3,283	1,953	2	63,080	57,283	802,993	763,706	561,192	546,766	670,912	648,837
2020......	3,185	1,914	1	64,861	59,452	931,190	913,333	583,311	579,326	794,937	792,664
2021......	3,100	184	7	68,223	61,358	1,039,739	1,020,615	632,114	623,189	893,609	895,010

[1] A failed institution is defined as a credit union which has ceased operation because it was involuntarily liquidated or merged with assistance from the National Credit Union Share Insurance Fund.

Source: National Credit Union Administration, *National Credit Union Administration 2021 Annual Report,* February 2022, and earlier reports; and "5300 Call Report Aggregate Financial Performance Report," December 2021, <www.ncua.gov/analysis/credit-union-corporate-call-report-data>. See also <www.ncua.gov/news/annual-reports>.

Table 1215. Noncash Payments by Method of Payment: 2012 to 2018

[123.8 represents 123,800,000,000. Estimates are based on survey data from the Federal Reserve Payments Survey, which is conducted every three years and updated with a smaller supplemental annual data collection between the triennial studies. The Study combines information gathered in three related survey efforts. Some estimates are based on data collected in the Depository and Financial Institutions Payments Survey (DFIPS), which is sent to a nationally representative, stratified random sample of depository and financial institutions. Other estimates are based on data collected in the Networks, Processors, and Issuers Payments Surveys (NPIPS) of payment organizations such as card networks, issuers and processors of card and alternative payment methods and services. Finally, some estimates are from data collected in the Check Sample Survey (CSS), which are based on the information from a random sample of checks processed by a selected number of large commercial banks. ATM withdrawals are excluded here]

Method of payment [1]	Transactions (billions)			Value (trillion dollars)			Average value per transaction (dollars)		
	2012	2015	2018	2012	2015	2018	2012	2015	2018
Total noncash payments.............	123.8	143.6	173.7	78.0	86.8	98.0	630	604	564
Total card payments....................	83.3	101.5	131.2	4.6	5.5	7.1	56	54	54
Debit cards.............................	56.5	67.8	86.4	2.1	2.5	3.1	37	36	36
Non-prepaid...........................	47.2	56.6	72.7	1.9	2.2	2.7	40	38	38
Prepaid................................	9.3	11.2	13.8	0.2	0.3	0.3	25	26	25
General purpose [2].................	3.1	4.3	6.0	0.1	0.1	0.2	35	35	32
Private label [3]....................	3.7	4.4	5.5	(Z)	0.1	0.1	13	16	18
Electronic benefits transfer (EBT)...	2.5	2.6	2.2	0.1	0.1	0.1	30	29	26
Credit cards.........................	26.8	33.7	44.7	2.5	3.1	4.0	95	91	89
General purpose [2].................	24.4	31.0	40.9	2.3	2.8	3.6	93	90	89
Private label [3]....................	2.5	2.7	3.8	0.3	0.2	0.3	112	93	89
Automated clearinghouse (ACH) [4]....	20.7	23.9	28.5	46.2	52.1	64.2	2,225	2,177	2,250
Network [5].............................	16.7	19.3	22.9	36.9	41.6	51.3	2,205	2,159	2,234
Credit transfers......................	6.9	8.0	9.5	22.6	26.8	33.4	3,259	3,333	3,512
Debit transfers.......................	9.8	11.3	13.4	14.2	14.9	17.8	1,456	1,321	1,328
On-us [6]..............................	4.0	4.6	5.6	9.3	10.4	12.9	2,311	2,249	2,315
Credit transfers......................	1.7	2.0	2.4	4.9	5.7	7.5	2,920	2,922	3,154
Debit transfers.......................	2.3	2.7	3.2	4.4	4.7	5.5	1,880	1,761	1,697
Checks.................................	19.7	18.1	14.0	27.2	29.2	26.8	1,378	1,609	1,908
Interbank..............................	14.0	13.6	10.9	17.3	21.3	20.3	1,236	1,564	1,865
On-us [6]..............................	5.7	4.5	3.1	9.9	7.9	6.5	1,725	1,746	2,058

Z Less than $500 billion. [1] ATM withdrawals are not included in the data. [2] Cards issued by depository institutions and processed over card networks. They carry a network brand from one of the four major card networks or from smaller or regional networks and can be used wherever that network card is accepted, regardless of merchant or merchant type. [3] Cards issued by merchants and processed over proprietary networks. They are accepted only by the sponsoring merchant. [4] The Automated Clearing House (ACH) is an electronic funds transfer system that processes financial transactions for consumers, businesses, and governments. The ACH provides many payment services, including payroll, direct deposit, tax payments and refunds, and consumer bills. [5] Network ACH payments are mainly passed between two depository institutions (interbank payments). Some depository institutions send all ACH transfers to ACH operators; ACH network payments also include a small portion of payments that are received by the same depository institution that sent them. [6] On-us payments are those payment processed by a depository institution between their own customers internally.

Source: Board of Governors of the Federal Reserve System, "The 2019 Federal Reserve Payments Study: Detailed Data Release," <www.federalreserve.gov/paymentsystems/fr-payments-study.htm>, accessed August 2021.

Table 1216. Debit Cards: Holders, Number, Transactions, and Volume: 2000 and 2010, and Projections, 2018

[160 represents 160,000,000]

Type of debit card	Cardholders (mil.)			Number of cards (mil.)			Number of point-of-sale transactions (mil.)			Purchase volume (bil. dol.)		
	2000	2010	2018 (P)	2000	2010	2018 (P)	2000	2010	2018 (P)	2000	2010	2018 (P)
Total [1]	160	185	209	235	4,008	5,357	9,571	49,281	84,585	342	1,825	3,321
Bank [2]	137	164	192	137	516	752	5,290	36,879	62,717	210	1,387	2,452
EFT networks [3]	159	184	206	223	281	321	2,979	7,239	14,313	100	262	569
Private label prepaid [4]	(NA)	(NA)	(NA)	(NA)	3,447	5,004	1,280	5,125	7,284	31	172	283
ACH network [5]	11	13	31	11	13	32	22	39	270	1	3	17

NA Not available. P Projected. [1] Cardholders may hold more than one type of card. Bank cards and electronic funds transfer (EFT) cards are the same pieces of plastic that carry multiple brands. The total card figure shown does not include any duplication. [2] Visa and MasterCard debit cards, including prepaid cards. Beginning 2006, includes Interlink & MasterCard PIN debit. [3] Cards issued by financial institution members of regional and national switches such as Star, Interlink (for 2000), Pulse, Nyce, etc. EFT = Electronic funds transfer. [4] Prepaid cards without the Visa, MasterCard, American Express, or Discover logos. [5] ACH = Automated clearing house. Retail cards such as those issued by Target, Nordstrom, etc.

Source: The Nilson Report, Carpinteria, CA, twice-monthly newsletter. © Used by permission.

Table 1217. Credit Cards: Holders, Number, Purchase Volume, and Debt: 2000 and 2010, and Projections, 2018

[159 represents 159,000,000]

Type of credit card	Cardholders (mil.)			Number of cards (mil.)			Credit card purchase volume (bil. dol.)			Credit card debt outstanding (bil. dol.)		
	2000	2010	2018 (P)	2000	2010	2018 (P)	2000	2010	2018 (P)	2000	2010	2018 (P)
Total [1]	159	152	180	1,425	877	1,123	1,242	2,061	3,936	680	811	1,125
Visa	93	100	124	255	240	338	487	809	1,956	268	332	471
MasterCard	86	75	97	200	171	231	281	479	811	212	240	310
Store	114	95	110	597	318	392	120	138	182	92	92	131
Oil company	76	38	27	98	35	32	45	47	56	5	6	6
Discover	36	41	44	50	55	57	69	106	139	48	50	73
American Express	23	34	36	33	49	54	221	476	772	50	90	120
The rest [2]	7	6	16	192	9	19	18	5	20	5	1	15

P Projected. [1] Cardholders may hold more than one type of card. [2] Includes Universal Air Travel Plan (UATP), medical cards, automobile rental, and miscellaneous cards.

Source: The Nilson Report, Carpinteria, CA, twice-monthly newsletter. © Used by permission.

Table 1218. Consumer Credit by Type of Holder: 2000 to 2021

[In billions of dollars (1,741 represents $1,741,000,000,000). As of December 31. Not seasonally adjusted]

Type of holder	2000	2005	2010	2014	2015	2016	2017	2018	2019	2020	2021
Total	1,741	2,321	2,647	3,310	3,400	3,636	3,831	4,007	4,192	4,185	4,434
Nonprofit organizations [1]	–	–	71	48	45	41	35	31	27	24	23
Nonfinancial corporate business	81	60	44	38	37	38	36	36	36	36	36
Federal government [2]	60	90	364	846	950	1,049	1,146	1,236	1,319	1,381	1,437
U.S.-chartered depository institutions	616	816	1,186	1,343	1,428	1,532	1,612	1,682	1,771	1,686	1,826
Credit unions	184	229	226	301	353	397	439	481	498	505	534
Government-sponsored enterprises	37	–	–	–	–	–	–	–	–	–	–
Asset-backed securities issuers	528	610	50	50	26	30	21	5	3	2	1
Finance companies	234	517	705	684	561	548	541	534	538	551	577
Memo:											
Credit card loans [3]	702	857	839	887	898	960	1,017	1,054	1,092	975	1,043
Auto loans	581	823	713	955	990	1,062	1,102	1,140	1,184	1,224	1,314
Student loans [4]	–	–	855	1,236	1,320	1,405	1,489	1,571	1,646	1,703	1,749
Other consumer credit [5]	458	641	239	231	192	209	223	243	270	283	328

– Represents or rounds to zero. [1] Student loans originated under the Federal Family Education Loan Program. Asset of the households and nonprofit organizations sector. [2] Includes loans originated by the Department of Education under the Federal Direct Loan Program and Perkins Loans, as well as Federal Family Education Loan Program loans that the government purchased from depository institutions, finance companies, and nonprofit and educational institutions, and loans in default. [3] Revolving credit that also includes overdraft plans on checking accounts and other loans without a fixed repayment schedule. [4] Includes student loans held by nonprofit organizations, the federal government, depository institutions, and finance companies. Data begin in 2006. [5] Prior to 2006, includes student loans.

Source: Board of Governors of the Federal Reserve System, "Financial Accounts of the United States, Z.1," <www.federalreserve.gov/data.htm>, accessed March 2022.

Table 1219. Consumer Credit Outstanding and Finance Rates: 2000 to 2021

[In billions of dollars (1,717 represents $1,717,000,000,000), except percent. Covers most short- and intermediate-term credit extended to individuals, excluding loans secured by real estate. Estimated amounts of seasonally adjusted credit outstanding as of end of year; finance rates are annual averages]

Type of credit	2000	2005	2010	2015	2016	2017	2018	2019	2020	2021
Total	1,717	2,291	2,647	3,400	3,636	3,831	4,007	4,192	4,185	4,431
Revolving	683	830	839	898	960	1,017	1,054	1,092	975	1,042
Nonrevolving [1]	1,034	1,461	1,808	2,502	2,676	2,814	2,953	3,100	3,210	3,389
FINANCE RATES (percent)										
Commercial banks:										
New automobiles (48 months)	9.34	7.07	6.21	4.19	4.30	4.61	5.03	5.39	5.09	5.05
Personal loans (24 months)	13.90	12.06	10.87	9.75	9.69	10.13	10.32	10.32	9.51	9.38
Credit card plans, all accounts	15.78	12.51	13.78	12.09	12.35	12.89	14.22	15.05	14.71	14.60
Credit card plans, accounts assessed interest	14.92	14.55	14.26	13.66	13.56	14.44	16.05	16.98	16.28	16.45
Finance companies:										
New automobiles [2]	(NA)	(NA)	4.70	5.13	5.05	5.36	6.13	6.41	5.25	4.64

NA Not available. [1] Includes motor vehicle loans and all other loans not included in revolving credit, such as loans for mobile homes, education, boats, trailers, or vacations. These loans may be secured or unsecured. [2] Covers most of the captive and non-captive finance companies. Amount of finance weighted.

Source: Board of Governors of the Federal Reserve System, Data Releases, Household Finances, "Consumer Credit-G.19," <www.federalreserve.gov/econresdata/statisticsdata.htm>, accessed August 2022.

Table 1220. Mortgage Debt Outstanding by Type and Holder: 2000 to 2021

[In billions of dollars (6,767 represents $6,767,000,000,000). As of December 31]

Type of property and holder	2000	2005	2010	2015	2016	2017	2018	2019	2020	2021
MORTGAGES BY TYPE										
Total	6,767	12,113	13,893	13,883	14,334	14,912	15,463	16,042	16,777	17,980
Home [1]	5,125	9,449	10,523	10,076	10,279	10,596	10,897	11,187	11,653	12,532
Multifamily residential	404	674	863	1,119	1,236	1,363	1,488	1,622	1,755	1,882
Commercial	1,152	1,885	2,352	2,479	2,592	2,716	2,832	2,965	3,081	3,265
Farm	85	105	154	209	226	236	246	268	289	302
Total liabilities	6,767	12,113	13,893	13,883	14,334	14,912	15,463	16,042	16,777	17,980
Household sector	4,946	9,108	10,191	9,732	9,912	10,188	10,460	10,740	11,180	12,004
Nonfinancial business	1,737	2,859	3,526	3,916	4,185	4,481	4,777	5,078	5,370	5,771
Nonfinancial corporate business	356	766	673	568	570	536	626	679	724	859
Nonfinancial noncorporate business	1,381	2,093	2,853	3,348	3,615	3,945	4,151	4,399	4,646	4,911
Real estate investment trusts	84	145	176	235	236	242	226	224	226	206
Total assets	6,767	12,113	13,893	13,883	14,334	14,912	15,463	16,042	16,777	17,980
Household sector	96	127	132	99	93	90	85	82	80	76
Nonfinancial corporate business	44	68	28	53	30	32	34	36	39	41
Nonfinancial noncorporate business	23	36	42	42	40	48	49	52	56	60
Federal government	76	77	107	116	120	120	123	124	127	133
State and local governments	136	171	222	231	243	257	259	257	262	265
Private depository institutions	2,503	4,337	4,583	4,778	5,071	5,283	5,442	5,655	5,741	5,953
Property-casualty insurance companies	2	3	4	13	15	18	20	23	24	28
Life insurance companies	236	286	319	431	465	507	568	619	645	679
Private pension funds	12	10	26	22	22	27	24	23	18	15
State and local government retirement funds	22	11	11	8	15	7	12	8	7	8
Government-sponsored enterprises (GSE)	264	589	5,021	4,920	5,027	5,194	5,334	5,511	6,142	6,924
Agency- and GSE-backed mortgage pools	2,493	3,548	1,147	1,775	1,933	2,126	2,292	2,406	2,428	2,502
Asset-backed securities issuers	604	2,161	1,962	1,018	894	845	851	855	838	877
Finance companies	238	541	244	159	138	124	115	117	110	105
Real estate investment trusts	18	147	45	218	228	235	255	274	259	314
HOME MORTGAGES [1]										
Total liabilities	5,125	9,449	10,523	10,076	10,279	10,596	10,897	11,187	11,653	12,532
Household sector	4,817	8,940	9,992	9,493	9,659	9,929	10,204	10,481	10,920	11,743
Nonfinancial corporate business	14	31	14	13	15	16	17	17	17	19
Nonfinancial noncorporate business	294	477	518	570	605	651	676	689	716	770
Total assets	5,125	9,449	10,523	10,076	10,279	10,596	10,897	11,187	11,653	12,532
Household sector	87	118	124	91	82	79	75	72	68	65
Nonfinancial corporate business	21	41	17	32	18	19	21	22	23	25
Nonfinancial noncorporate business	9	13	15	15	14	17	18	19	20	22
Federal government	16	13	24	28	30	29	29	29	30	33
State and local governments	69	88	115	119	125	132	133	132	134	135
U.S.-chartered depository institutions	1,556	2,730	2,616	2,434	2,510	2,557	2,586	2,638	2,581	2,606
Foreign banking offices in U.S.	–	–	1	2	1	1	2	1	1	1
Banks in U.S.-affiliated areas	9	16	20	16	15	15	14	13	13	12
Credit unions	120	226	317	405	439	481	523	565	610	670
Life insurance companies	7	7	9	19	23	25	32	38	39	41
Private pension funds	8	1	2	1	1	1	1	1	1	(Z)
State and local government retirement funds	7	4	4	3	5	2	4	3	2	3
Government-sponsored enterprises (GSE)	210	454	4,691	4,571	4,645	4,776	4,884	5,016	5,575	6,324
Agency- and GSE-backed mortgage pools	2,426	3,446	1,075	1,569	1,685	1,826	1,949	2,025	2,009	2,044
Asset-backed securities issuers	385	1,671	1,315	603	518	474	467	452	415	403
Finance companies	187	490	170	123	107	95	87	85	77	74
Real estate investment trusts	8	128	9	46	60	65	73	76	52	75
Memo:										
Home equity loans included above [2]	408	918	929	642	601	570	533	501	442	396

– Represents zero. Z less than $500 million. [1] Mortgages on one- to four-family properties, including mortgages on farm houses. [2] Loans made under home equity lines of credit and home equity loans secured by junior liens. Excludes home equity loans held by individuals.

Source: Board of Governors of the Federal Reserve System, "Financial Accounts of the United States, Z.1," <www.federalreserve.gov/data.htm>, accessed March 2022.

Table 1221. Mortgage Originations and Delinquency and Foreclosure Rates: 2000 to 2021

[In percent, except as indicated (1,139 represents $1,139,000,000,000). Covers one- to four-family residential nonfarm mortgage loans. Mortgage origination is the making of a new mortgage, including all steps taken by a lender to attract and qualify a borrower, process the mortgage loan, and place it on the lender's books. Based on the National Delinquency Survey, which covers 45 million loans on one- to four-unit properties, representing between 80 to 85 percent of all 'first-lien' residential mortgage loans outstanding. Loans surveyed were reported by approximately 120 lenders, including mortgage bankers, commercial banks, and thrifts]

Item	2000	2005	2010	2015	2016	2017	2018	2019	2020	2021
MORTGAGE ORIGINATIONS										
Total (bil. dol.)	**1,139**	**2,908**	**1,698**	**1,679**	**2,051**	**1,710**	**1,250**	**2,173**	**3,828**	**3,991**
Purchase (bil. dol.)	905	1,512	530	903	1,052	1,110	873	1,272	1,433	1,646
Refinance (bil. dol.)	234	1,397	1,168	776	999	600	377	901	2,395	2,345
DELINQUENCY RATES [1]										
Total	**4.4**	**4.5**	**9.3**	**5.1**	**4.7**	**4.8**	**4.4**	**4.2**	**6.7**	**5.3**
Conventional loans [2]	(NA)	3.6	8.8	4.4	3.9	3.9	3.5	3.2	5.2	3.9
Prime conventional loans	2.3	2.3	6.5	3.0	2.8	(NA)	(NA)	(NA)	(NA)	(NA)
Subprime conventional loans	11.9	10.8	25.9	16.5	14.9	(NA)	(NA)	(NA)	(NA)	(NA)
Federal Housing Administration loans	9.1	12.5	12.8	9.0	8.6	9.0	8.8	8.7	13.8	12.3
Veterans Administration loans	6.8	7.0	7.5	4.5	4.1	4.1	4.0	4.0	7.0	6.2
FORECLOSURE RATES										
Total loans in foreclosure process [3]	**1.2**	**1.0**	**4.6**	**2.0**	**1.6**	**1.3**	**1.0**	**0.9**	**0.6**	**0.5**
Conventional loans [2]	(NA)	0.9	4.8	1.9	1.5	1.2	0.9	0.7	0.5	0.4
Prime conventional loans	0.4	0.4	3.5	1.2	0.9	(NA)	(NA)	(NA)	(NA)	(NA)
Subprime conventional loans	9.4	3.3	14.5	8.3	7.2	(NA)	(NA)	(NA)	(NA)	(NA)
Federal Housing Administration loans	1.7	2.3	3.5	2.6	2.2	1.8	1.7	1.6	1.1	0.8
Veterans Administration loans	1.2	1.1	2.4	1.4	1.2	1.0	0.9	0.9	0.6	0.4
Loans entering foreclosure process [4]	**1.5**	**1.6**	**5.0**	**1.6**	**1.3**	**1.1**	**1.0**	**0.9**	**0.3**	**0.2**
Conventional loans [2]	(NA)	1.5	5.1	1.4	1.1	0.9	0.8	0.7	0.2	0.1
Prime conventional loans	0.6	0.7	4.0	1.0	0.7	(NA)	(NA)	(NA)	(NA)	(NA)
Subprime conventional loans	9.2	5.6	12.9	5.2	4.7	(NA)	(NA)	(NA)	(NA)	(NA)
Federal Housing Administration loans	2.3	3.4	4.7	2.5	2.2	1.9	2.0	1.8	0.5	0.2
Veterans Administration loans	1.5	1.5	3.3	1.4	1.3	1.1	1.1	1.0	0.3	0.1

NA Not available. [1] Number of loans delinquent 30 days or more as a percent of mortgage loans serviced in survey. Annual average of quarterly figures, not seasonally adjusted. Delinquency rate does not include loans in the process of foreclosure. [2] Conventional loans include any non-government (FHA or VA) loans. The prime and subprime criteria used in the National Delinquency Survey are based on survey participants' reporting of what they consider to be their prime or subprime servicing portfolio, since internal servicing guidelines vary. Participants who service both prime and subprime loans report the results of each separately for maximum precision in the classification. [3] Percent of loans in the foreclosure process at year-end, not seasonally adjusted. [4] Percent of loans entering foreclosure process at year-end, not seasonally adjusted.

Source: Mortgage Bankers Association of America, Washington, DC, "MBA Mortgage Originations Estimates," and National Delinquency Survey, <mba.org/>, and unpublished data ©.

Table 1222. Delinquency Rates and Charge-Off Rates on Loans at Insured Commercial Banks: 2000 to 2021

[In percent. Annual averages of quarterly figures, not seasonally adjusted. Delinquent loans are those past due 30 days or more and still accruing interest as well as those in nonaccrual status. They are measured as a percentage of end-of-period loans. Charge-offs, which are the value of loans removed from the books and charged against loss reserves, are measured, net of recoveries, as a percentage of average loans and annualized. Includes only U.S.-chartered commercial banks]

Type of loan	2000	2005	2010	2015	2017	2018	2019	2020	2021
DELINQUENCY RATES									
Total loans	**2.20**	**1.57**	**6.96**	**2.34**	**1.85**	**1.62**	**1.48**	**1.56**	**1.35**
Real estate	1.87	1.37	9.69	3.62	2.31	1.97	1.63	1.82	1.65
Residential [1, 2]	2.08	1.55	10.81	5.64	3.71	3.12	2.51	2.63	2.43
Commercial [2, 3]	1.48	1.07	8.53	1.23	0.77	0.72	0.68	0.97	0.90
Consumer	3.55	2.81	4.15	2.00	2.23	2.29	2.34	2.05	1.57
Credit cards	4.51	3.70	4.90	2.14	2.48	2.52	2.58	2.31	1.64
Other	2.98	2.23	3.32	1.88	2.00	2.07	2.10	1.83	1.51
Leases	1.62	1.28	1.89	0.77	1.00	1.01	1.18	1.42	1.26
Business	2.30	1.51	3.46	0.87	1.34	1.03	1.11	1.24	1.08
Agricultural production	2.54	1.30	3.04	0.84	1.53	1.70	1.87	2.01	1.44
Farmland [2]	2.30	1.59	3.57	1.55	2.01	2.15	2.29	2.46	1.78
CHARGE-OFF RATES									
Total loans	**0.66**	**0.54**	**2.66**	**0.42**	**0.47**	**0.46**	**0.49**	**0.49**	**0.25**
Real estate	0.09	0.06	2.15	0.13	0.03	0.01	0.01	0.04	(Z)
Residential [1, 2]	0.12	0.08	2.11	0.21	0.04	(-Z)	-0.01	-0.02	-0.04
Commercial [2, 3]	0.05	0.05	2.34	0.04	0.02	0.01	0.03	0.09	0.04
Consumer	2.32	2.74	5.90	1.75	2.18	2.24	2.28	2.00	1.16
Credit cards	4.30	4.83	9.43	2.93	3.56	3.64	3.70	3.46	2.18
Other	1.13	1.38	2.05	0.68	0.90	0.88	0.91	0.73	0.38
Leases	0.31	0.58	0.72	0.18	0.17	0.17	0.21	0.52	0.15
Business	0.76	0.26	1.71	0.24	0.36	0.28	0.36	0.52	0.19
Agricultural production	0.27	0.07	0.77	0.05	0.21	0.24	0.23	0.25	0.05
Farmland [2]	0.04	0.04	0.43	0.01	0.05	0.04	0.08	0.06	0.02

Z Represents less than .005%. [1] Residential real estate loans include loans secured by one- to four-family properties, including home equity lines of credit. [2] Booked in domestic offices only. [3] Commercial real estate loans include construction and land development loans, loans secured by multifamily residences, and loans secured by nonfarm, nonresidential real estate, only.

Source: Board of Governors of the Federal Reserve, Data Releases, Bank Assets and Liabilities, "Charge-Off and Delinquency Rates on Loans and Leases at Commercial Banks," <www.federalreserve.gov/releases/chargeoff/>, accessed March 2022.

Table 1223. Banked Households by Primary Method of Accessing Bank Account and Selected Characteristics: 2015 to 2019

[In percent, except as indicated (127,538 represents 127,538,000). Data cover banked households that have accessed their accounts in the past 12 months. A "banked" household is one in which at least one member of the household has a checking or savings account. Data collected through a Federal Deposit Insurance Corporation (FDIC)-sponsored supplement to the Current Population Survey; see source for more information]

Characteristic	Total households (1,000)	Banked households						
		Total (1,000)	Primary method used to access bank account (percent)					
			Bank teller	ATM/ Kiosk	Telephone banking	Online banking	Mobile banking	Other/ unknown
2015................	127,538	113,315	28.2	21.0	3.0	36.9	9.5	1.5
2017................	129,276	115,040	24.3	19.9	2.9	36.0	15.6	1.3
2019, total......	**131,248**	**120,847**	**21.0**	**19.5**	**2.4**	**22.8**	**34.0**	**0.3**
AGE								
15 to 24 years..................	6,307	5,643	10.2	17.3	2.2	7.2	62.9	0.1
25 to 34 years..................	21,412	19,714	8.0	15.1	0.6	14.4	61.7	0.2
35 to 44 years..................	22,349	20,699	10.6	18.2	1.1	20.1	49.8	0.2
45 to 54 years..................	22,334	20,900	15.5	19.9	1.6	26.6	36.3	0.1
55 to 64 years..................	24,450	22,599	24.3	21.9	2.9	29.3	21.3	0.3
65 years or more..................	34,397	31,292	39.2	21.6	4.5	25.7	8.3	0.7
EDUCATION								
No high school diploma...........	11,392	8,223	39.6	29.5	5.1	5.8	19.2	0.8
High school diploma...............	32,659	28,607	30.3	24.0	3.5	14.6	27.3	0.5
Some college....................	37,165	34,894	20.3	19.8	2.5	20.6	36.5	0.4
College degree..................	50,032	49,123	12.9	15.1	1.2	32.1	38.6	0.2
FAMILY INCOME								
Less than $15,000..............	14,048	9,761	35.9	23.6	5.8	9.9	23.5	1.3
$15,000 to $30,000..............	18,848	16,027	31.7	24.7	4.7	12.7	25.9	0.4
$30,000 to $50,000..............	24,694	22,822	24.7	21.7	2.8	17.1	33.2	0.5
$50,000 to $75,000..............	23,857	23,065	20.3	20.4	2.1	21.2	35.9	0.2
At least $75,000................	49,801	49,172	13.1	15.6	0.9	32.1	38.1	0.2
EMPLOYMENT STATUS								
Employed........................	81,542	77,759	14.3	18.0	1.2	23.0	43.3	0.1
Unemployed.....................	2,887	2,469	18.6	21.1	3.1	19.6	37.4	0.3
Not in labor force..............	46,820	40,619	33.8	22.3	4.6	22.7	15.9	0.7

Source: Federal Deposit Insurance Corporation, *How America Banks: Household Use of Banking and Financial Services, 2019 FDIC Survey*, October 2020. See also <www.economicinclusion.gov/surveys/>.

Table 1224. Households Using Nonbank Financial Transaction Services by Type of Service and Household Characteristics: 2019

[Percent, except households (131,248 represents 131,248,000). Percent of households using nonbank financial services during the last 12 months. These services can also be used to receive payments, including income. Data collected through a Federal Deposit Insurance Corporation (FDIC)-sponsored supplement to the Current Population Survey; see source for more information]

Characteristic	Total households (1,000)	Nonbank financial transaction service use (percent)				
		Money order	Check cashing	International remittance	Bill payment service	P2P payment service [1]
Total households...............	**131,248**	**11.9**	**5.5**	**5.5**	**4.9**	**31.1**
BANK ACCOUNT OWNERSHIP [2]						
Unbanked........................	7,056	42.3	31.9	9.4	14.4	8.8
Banked..........................	124,192	10.2	4.0	5.3	4.4	32.3
FAMILY INCOME						
Less than $15,000..............	14,048	23.0	11.0	4.8	6.6	14.6
$15,000 to $30,000..............	18,848	18.2	9.0	6.3	6.6	17.1
$30,000 to $50,000..............	24,694	15.2	7.4	7.0	6.6	24.5
$50,000 to $75,000..............	23,857	9.6	4.3	6.2	5.1	31.3
At least $75,000................	49,801	6.0	2.4	4.4	2.8	44.2
EDUCATION						
No high school diploma..............	11,392	23.3	14.6	14.7	9.8	10.2
High school diploma....................	32,659	14.6	7.1	5.5	5.6	18.4
Some college.......................	37,165	12.9	5.8	4.1	5.2	30.1
College degree.....................	50,032	6.8	2.3	4.5	3.1	44.8
EMPLOYMENT STATUS						
Employed.........................	81,542	11.9	5.2	6.8	5.5	39.8
Unemployed.......................	2,887	18.5	9.6	8.3	6.5	30.1
Not in labor force.................	46,820	11.5	5.8	3.2	3.7	16.0
HOUSING TENURE						
Homeowner........................	84,688	6.8	3.4	3.9	3.1	30.2
Non-homeowner....................	46,561	21.2	9.5	8.4	8.2	32.6

[1] Peer-to-peer or person-to-person (P2P) payment service is use of a website or app to send or receive money inside the United States. Examples are Paypal, Venmo, and CashApp. To conduct P2P payments, households typically must have a bank account, a prepaid card, or a credit card, with requirements varying across P2P payment service providers. [2] A household is 'unbanked' if no one in the household has a checking or savings account at an insured bank. A 'banked' household is one that at least one member of the household has a checking or savings account.

Source: Federal Deposit Insurance Corporation, *How American Banks: Household Use of Banking and Financial Services, 2019 FDIC Survey*, October 2020. See also <www.economicinclusion.gov/surveys/>.

Table 1225. Money Stock: 2000 to 2021

[In billions of dollars (1,089 represents $1,089,000,000,000). As of December. Seasonally adjusted averages of daily figures]

Item	2000	2005	2010	2015	2016	2017	2018	2019	2020	2021
M1, total [1]	**1,089**	**1,374**	**1,837**	**3,096**	**3,345**	**3,619**	**3,771**	**4,011**	**17,812**	**20,553**
Currency [2]	531	725	919	1,339	1,421	1,525	1,624	1,710	1,969	2,125
Travelers' checks [3]	8.3	7.2	4.7	2.5	2.2	1.9	1.7	(NA)	(NA)	(NA)
Demand deposits [4]	311	324	517	1,240	1,375	1,498	1,516	1,627	3,318	4,827
Other checkable deposits [5]	239	318	397	515	547	594	629	674	(NA)	(NA)
Other liquid deposits [6]	(NA)	(NA)	(NA)	(NA)	(NA)	(NA)	(NA)	(NA)	12,525	13,602
M2, total	**4,925**	**6,680**	**8,799**	**12,340**	**13,214**	**13,855**	**14,374**	**15,326**	**19,130**	**21,638**
M1	1,089	1,374	1,837	3,096	3,345	3,619	3,771	4,011	17,812	20,553
Non-M1 components of M2	3,836	5,306	6,963	9,244	9,869	10,236	10,603	11,315	1,317	(NA)
Retail money funds	911	710	698	662	698	712	819	988	1,066	1,000
Savings deposits (including money market deposit accounts) [6]	1,879	3,602	5,331	8,156	8,802	9,091	9,229	9,721	(NA)	(NA)
Commercial banks	1,425	2,777	4,412	7,013	7,543	7,794	7,898	8,389	(NA)	(NA)
Thrift institutions	454	825	919	1,143	1,259	1,297	1,331	1,332	(NA)	(NA)
Small-denomination time deposits [7]	1,046	994	934	426	369	434	555	606	252	85
Commercial banks	701	647	664	315	267	322	448	483	200	(NA)
Thrift institutions	345	346	270	111	102	112	108	122	51	(NA)

NA Not available. [1] As of May 2020, M1 consists of currency outside the U.S. Treasury, Federal Reserve Banks, and vaults of depository institutions; demand deposits at commercial banks; and other liquid deposits, consisting of other checkable deposits (OCDs), and savings deposits (including money market deposit accounts). Prior to May 2020, savings deposits were not included as a type of transaction account and not included in M1. See source for more information. [2] Currency outside U.S. Treasury, Federal Reserve Banks and the vaults of depository institutions. [3] Outstanding amount of U.S. dollar-denominated travelers' checks of nonbank issuers. Travelers' checks issued by depository institutions are included in demand deposits. [4] Demand deposits at domestically chartered commercial banks, U.S. branches and agencies of foreign banks, and Edge Act corporations (excluding those amounts held by depository institutions, the U.S. government, and foreign banks and official institutions) less cash items in the process of collection and Federal Reserve float. [5] Other checkable deposits consist of negotiable order of withdrawal (NOW) and automatic transfer service (ATS) balances at depository institutions, share draft accounts at credit unions, and demand deposits at thrift institutions. Beginning 2020, data are included in other liquid deposits. [6] Beginning May 2020, savings deposits were reclassified as transaction accounts and were combined with other checkable deposits, with the sum being reported as "other liquid assets." [7] Small-denomination time deposits are those issued in amounts of less than $100,000. All Individual Retirement Account (IRA) and Keogh account balances at commercial banks and thrift institutions are subtracted from small-denomination time deposits.

Source: Board of Governors of the Federal Reserve System, Data Releases, Money Stock and Reserve Balances, "Money Stock Measures – H.6," weekly releases, <www.federalreserve.gov/releases/h6/>, accessed January 2022.

Table 1226. Volume of Debt Markets by Type of Security: 2000 to 2021

[In billions of dollars (2,604 represents $2,604,000,000,000). Covers fixed income securities as represented by the source]

Type of security	2000	2005	2010	2015	2018	2019	2020	2021
NEW ISSUE VOLUME [1]								
Total	**2,604**	**5,810**	**7,342**	**6,821**	**7,454**	**8,447**	**12,483**	**13,441**
Municipal	198	407	433	405	347	426	485	482
U.S. Treasury securities [2]	313	746	2,320	2,122	2,685	2,935	3,896	5,139
Federal agency debt [3]	447	635	1,362	645	654	989	1,251	693
Mortgage-backed securities [4]	780	2,765	2,013	1,801	1,875	2,243	4,271	4,584
Asset-backed securities [5]	240	474	126	333	517	435	304	582
Corporate debt [6]	626	784	1,089	1,514	1,378	1,418	2,275	1,961
AVERAGE DAILY TRADING VOLUME								
Total	**284.8**	**834.9**	**889.6**	**728.6**	**816.4**	**895.4**	**954.3**	**955.2**
Municipal	8.8	16.9	13.3	8.6	11.6	11.5	12.0	8.8
U.S. Treasury securities [7]	206.5	549.7	523.8	490.0	547.8	593.6	603.2	624.1
Federal agency debt [3]	(NA)	(NA)	11.5	5.2	3.5	4.2	5.3	3.2
Mortgage-backed securities [4, 8]	69.5	251.8	320.6	192.3	219.0	249.0	291.1	279.3
Non-agency mortgaged-back securities [5, 9]	(NA)	(NA)	(NA)	3.1	1.6	1.4	1.9	1.4
Corporate [10]	(NA)	16.6	20.5	27.9	31.5	34.3	38.9	37.0
Asset-backed securities [11]	(NA)	(NA)	(NA)	1.4	1.4	1.5	1.9	1.4
VOLUME OF SECURITIES OUTSTANDING								
Total	**16,123**	**24,642**	**33,388**	**37,911**	**42,168**	**44,025**	**50,071**	**52,828**
Municipal [12]	1,481	3,109	3,982	3,874	3,894	3,904	3,988	4,064
U.S. Treasury securities [2]	2,952	4,170	8,853	13,192	15,608	16,673	20,973	22,584
Federal agency debt [3]	1,854	2,616	2,538	1,995	1,842	1,726	1,689	1,433
Mortgage-backed securities [4]	4,119	7,218	9,258	8,895	9,732	10,229	11,214	12,202
Asset-backed securities [5]	702	1,281	1,508	1,377	1,616	1,663	1,535	1,585
Money market instruments [13]	1,614	1,644	1,058	941	996	1,045	987	1,014
Corporate debt [6]	3,401	4,604	6,193	7,637	8,481	8,783	9,685	9,945

NA Not available. [1] Covers only long-term issuance. [2] Long-term only, interest bearing marketable coupon public debt. Includes floating rate notes. [3] Agency debt of Fannie Mae, Freddie Mac, Farmer Mac, FHLB, the Farm Credit System, and federal budget agencies (e.g., TVA); beginning with 2004, Sallie Mae excluded due to privatization. [4] Includes Government National Mortgage Association (GNMA), Federal National Mortgage Association (FNMA), and Federal Home Loan Mortgage Corporation (FHLMC) mortgage-backed securities (MBS), and collateralized mortgage obligations (CMOs) and private-label MBS/CMOs. [5] Excludes mortgage-backed assets. Includes auto, credit card, home equity loans, manufacturing, student loan and other. Collateralized debt obligations are also included. [6] Debt obligations of U.S. financial and nonfinancial corporations including bonds, notes, debentures, mandatory convertible securities, long-term debt, private mortgage-backed securities, and unsecured debt. Includes nonconvertible corporate debt, Yankee bonds, and MTNs (Medium-Term Notes). Excludes federal agency debt, certificates of deposit and bonds issued in foreign countries by foreign subsidiaries of U.S. corporations. Recorded at book value. [7] Primary dealer reporting, includes double counting of some trades. [8] Primary dealer trading volume through May 2011. After that date, data from FINRA (Financial Industry Regulatory Authority). [9] Includes mortgage securities issued by private institutions, such as subsidiaries of investment banks, banks, financial institutions, non-bank mortgage lenders, and home builders. After October 2017, incudes Commercial mortgages backed securities. [10] Includes nonconvertible bonds only. [11] Includes collateralized debt obligations and other trading volumes. Prior to October 2017, includes Commercial mortgage backed securities figures. [12] Due to the change in underlying source data, municipal securities outstanding has been restated from 2004 onward and revised. [13] Commercial paper, bankers acceptances, and large time deposits.

Source: The Securities Industry and Financial Markets Association, New York, NY. © Based on data supplied by Bloomberg, Dealogic, Refinitiv, U.S. Treasury, Fannie Mae, Freddie Mac, Ginnie Mae, Farmer Mac, Farm Credit, FHLB, Federal Reserve Bank of New York, Municipal Securities Rulemaking Board, and FINRA Trace (Financial Industry Regulatory Authority Trade Reporting and Compliance Engine). See also <www.sifma.org/>.

Table 1227. New Security Issues of Corporations by Type of Offering: 2010 to 2021

[In billions of dollars (1,025 represents $1,025,000,000,000). Represents gross proceeds of issues maturing in more than one year. Figures are the principal amount or the number of units multiplied by the offering price. Excludes secondary offerings, employee stock plans, investment companies other than closed-end, intracorporate transactions, Yankee bonds, and private placements listed. Stock data include ownership securities issued by limited partnerships]

Type of offering	2010	2015	2020	2021	Type of offering	2010	2015	2020	2021
Total [1]..................	**1,025**	**1,664**	**2,476**	**2,323**	Nonfinancial..........	498	888	1,444	1,012
					Financial..............	396	723	954	1,239
Bonds, total.....................	894	1,611	2,398	2,251	Stocks, total [2]..........	131	174	335	419
Sold in the U.S...............	880	1,511	2,280	2,150	Nonfinancial..........	61	111	187	170
Sold abroad..................	14	100	118	101	Financial..............	70	63	148	249

[1] Total reflects the sum of the gross issuance of bonds and the gross proceeds of stocks in the domestic market. [2] Gross proceeds of stocks in all markets.

Source: Board of Governors of the Federal Reserve System, "New Security Issues, U.S. Corporations," <www.federalreserve.gov/data/corpsecure/current.htm>, June 2022.

Table 1228. Equities, Corporate Bonds, and Municipal and Treasury Securities—Holdings and Net Purchases by Type of Investor: 2010 to 2021

[In billions of dollars (24,077 represents $24,077,000,000,000). Holdings as of December 31. Minus sign (-) indicates net sales]

Type of investor	Holdings					Net purchases				
	2010	2015	2019	2020	2021	2010	2015	2019	2020	2021
EQUITIES [1]										
Total [2]........	**24,077**	**37,211**	**54,644**	**65,523**	**80,058**	**90.9**	**-28.5**	**-272.6**	**724.2**	**378.8**
Household sector [3]...........	8,546	13,739	20,972	26,006	31,798	-152.3	-26.8	140.3	566.3	448.5
State and local governments............	105	148	214	250	306	-3.4	-3.4	-3.4	-3.4	-3.4
Property-casualty insurance companies...........	224	334	494	519	643	-5.2	-1.5	-1.8	-21.8	2.6
Life insurance companies................	410	547	645	731	763	44.1	26.9	1.2	1.1	-79.6
Private pension funds....................	1,778	2,220	2,962	3,396	4,093	38.7	-29.3	-168.8	-98.6	-109.3
Federal government retirement funds. ..	145	240	371	419	524	6.1	(Z)	-5.0	-23.9	10.2
State and local government retirement funds.............	1,723	2,250	2,523	2,844	3,392	-67.4	22.6	76.0	-27.6	-124.4
Mutual funds.................	5,873	8,625	11,935	13,391	15,534	68.5	57.9	-219.2	-481.5	-317.1
Exchange-traded funds..................	753	1,709	3,476	4,230	5,804	79.8	173.6	166.1	260.2	732.4
Brokers and dealers....................	117	167	167	214	234	-23.0	-18.4	-22.4	6.8	-33.7
Rest of the world [4].....................	3,213	5,501	8,279	10,673	13,486	129.6	-191.4	-249.2	669.0	-45.2
CORPORATE & FOREIGN BONDS										
Total [2]........	**10,452**	**11,151**	**13,403**	**15,231**	**15,412**	**-6.5**	**290.0**	**368.2**	**1,038.2**	**875.4**
Household sector [3]...........	1,482	643	285	377	215	-188.6	-262.6	36.3	48.4	-108.4
U.S.-chartered depository institutions....	551	507	499	511	711	-98.2	-12.0	44.1	8.3	204.9
Foreign banking offices in U.S...........	238	173	135	153	146	-9.4	-10.8	-29.1	6.8	0.8
Property-casualty insurance companies...........	348	452	595	661	702	24.3	19.2	34.7	47.1	55.1
Life insurance companies................	2,074	2,425	3,175	3,556	3,632	85.8	91.4	134.9	196.0	208.0
Private pension funds....................	446	691	867	980	950	27.6	5.8	-13.8	60.1	22.9
State and local government retirement funds.............	427	558	446	529	572	12.0	37.2	-130.4	53.2	71.6
Mutual funds.................	1,264	1,692	2,242	2,608	2,734	211.1	80.2	54.0	266.3	270.6
Exchange-traded funds..................	78.0	242	533	708	800	21.0	36.8	89.9	149.3	115.4
Rest of the world [4].....................	2,523	3,083	3,986	4,491	4,360	-36.8	334.9	156.0	213.4	74.5
MUNICIPAL SECURITIES [5]										
Total [2]........	**3,807**	**4,090**	**4,198**	**4,389**	**4,423**	**117.5**	**20.1**	**9.7**	**84.5**	**76.4**
Household sector [3]...........	1,900	1,928	1,903	1,925	1,799	78.5	-36.6	-64.1	-31.0	-103.9
U.S.-chartered depository institutions....	255	508	508	584	630	30.3	45.4	-29.5	69.0	52.1
Property-casualty insurance companies...........	370	358	285	298	289	-24.0	10.2	-4.7	3.0	-1.1
Money market funds..................	410	247	139	125	111	-53.1	-28.1	-8.2	-14.0	-14.6
Mutual funds.................	490	604	831	891	991	33.0	16.2	105.8	49.7	109.4
TREASURY SECURITIES										
Total [2]........	**10,493**	**15,215**	**19,339**	**24,651**	**25,639**	**1,645.3**	**724.4**	**1,176.6**	**4,582.2**	**1,683.8**
Household sector [3]...........	1,012	911	1,621	1,368	593	265.6	319.2	123.8	-347.8	-677.3
State and local governments............	631	654	793	1,112	1,437	16.3	16.8	51.4	291.3	383.9
Monetary authority.................	1,021	2,676	2,541	5,255	6,052	244.9	-15.6	99.1	2,554.3	961.6
U.S.-chartered depository institutions....	218	435	704	1,044	1,472	93.0	14.8	125.6	327.8	449.0
Life insurance companies................	161	206	215	241	231	20.7	7.2	-6.4	6.9	-2.6
Private pension funds....................	202	287	440	463	469	46.0	-13.1	52.1	2.9	30.8
Federal government retirement funds. ..	1,277	1,715	2,151	2,297	2,457	77.2	91.6	111.2	145.5	160.2
State and local governments retirement funds...........	154	175	329	347	431	3.4	-22.2	-36.6	1.0	103.0
Money market funds..................	381	530	1,123	2,466	1,815	-72.4	45.6	177.5	1,343.3	-651.3
Mutual funds.................	417	827	1,287	1,316	1,589	129.8	155.3	96.1	1.5	340.8
Rest of the world [4].....................	4,459	6,146	6,918	7,292	7,748	740.4	42.7	297.7	67.0	639.6

Z Less than $500 million. [1] Includes shares of exchange-traded funds, closed-end funds, and real estate investment trusts. Excludes mutual fund shares of open-end investment companies; see Table 1235. [2] Includes other types not shown separately. [3] Includes nonprofit organizations. [4] Holdings and net purchases of U.S. issues by foreign residents. [5] Includes loans.

Source: Board of Governors of the Federal Reserve System, "Financial Accounts of the United States, Z.1," <www.federalreserve.gov/data.htm>, accessed September 2022.

Table 1229. Foreign Securities Held by U.S. Residents: 2010 to 2020

[In billions of dollars (6,763 represents $6,763,000,000,000). Estimates for end of calendar year]

Country	Total			Equities			Long-term and short-term debt		
	2010	2019	2020	2010	2019	2020	2010	2019	2020
Total holdings [1]	6,763	13,087	14,387	4,647	9,478	10,615	2,116	3,609	3,772
Australia	323	366	378	150	202	227	174	164	151
Belgium	35	65	64	29	54	54	7	11	11
Bermuda	160	275	283	134	239	240	25	35	44
Brazil	235	198	168	194	169	144	41	29	24
Canada	695	1,098	1,168	409	593	683	287	505	484
Cayman Islands	366	2,001	2,565	166	1,501	2,027	200	499	539
China [2]	102	222	287	101	204	251	2	18	35
Curacao [3]	(NA)	41	23	(NA)	40	21	(NA)	1	2
France	366	662	698	244	468	479	122	193	220
Germany	299	467	535	207	381	422	92	86	113
Hong Kong	135	181	166	133	171	158	2	10	8
India	91	201	234	86	185	223	5	16	11
Ireland	132	648	698	101	561	608	31	87	90
Israel	64	70	94	45	51	71	19	19	23
Italy	66	143	148	51	99	96	14	44	52
Japan	519	1,147	1,296	450	927	1,013	69	220	283
Jersey	42	106	138	21	96	126	21	10	11
Korea, South	148	231	300	122	212	277	26	20	23
Luxembourg	100	157	198	33	81	131	68	75	67
Mexico	109	151	153	77	66	64	32	84	89
Netherlands	233	573	628	120	371	423	112	202	205
Norway	56	67	72	23	36	37	33	31	34
Russia	62	83	74	56	67	57	7	17	17
Singapore	64	99	92	56	64	58	8	35	34
South Africa	78	85	79	70	71	65	8	14	14
Spain	87	162	163	66	115	113	22	47	49
Sweden	122	155	196	63	110	155	59	45	42
Switzerland	327	597	632	319	552	590	8	45	42
Taiwan	95	215	304	94	215	304	(Z)	(Z)	(Z)
United Kingdom	1,001	1,517	1,395	626	1,014	919	375	504	476

NA Not available. Z Less than $500 million. [1] Includes other countries, not shown separately. [2] Excludes Hong Kong, Macau, and Taiwan. [3] Separate reporting for Curacao began with the 2013 survey. In previous years, data were reported as part of Netherlands Antilles.

Source: U.S. Department of Treasury, "U.S. Residents' Portfolio Holdings of Foreign Securities," <www.treasury.gov/resource-center/data-chart-center/tic/Pages/shcreports.aspx>, accessed November 2021.

Table 1230. U.S. Securities Held by Foreign Residents: 2020 and 2021

[In billions of dollars (21,954 represents $21,954,000,000,000). Estimates as of June. Long-term securities include all forms of equity and all debt securities with an original term-to-maturity of over one year]

Region and country	U.S. securities, total [1]		U.S. equities [2]		U.S Treasury long-term securities		Long-term corporate debt	
	2020	2021	2020	2021	2020	2021	2020	2021
Total [3]	21,954	27,190	9,168	13,705	6,005	6,574	4,331	4,589
Australia	352	467	267	374	33	37	37	42
Belgium	852	925	59	104	175	195	565	583
Bermuda	367	383	111	138	39	35	157	153
Brazil	276	266	8	16	248	248	1	1
British Virgin Islands	170	206	106	149	31	30	24	20
Canada	1,335	1,977	971	1,495	102	150	210	231
Cayman Islands	1,903	2,465	1,059	1,538	114	141	567	623
China, mainland [4]	1,569	1,575	233	273	1,040	1,058	23	23
Denmark	157	254	115	215	14	17	25	21
France	399	682	192	359	119	206	61	83
Germany	421	562	210	332	67	76	127	141
Hong Kong	455	471	126	170	236	198	51	73
India	189	230	6	9	151	210	(Z)	1
Ireland	1,182	1,499	517	821	201	192	241	293
Israel	138	205	80	130	41	53	7	7
Italy	107	132	45	71	39	38	18	21
Japan	2,553	2,765	667	866	1,194	1,213	312	308
Korea, South	414	570	187	329	118	117	63	66
Kuwait	304	371	211	285	35	35	24	23
Luxembourg	1,777	2,301	731	1,195	182	200	694	724
Netherlands	425	530	264	354	67	71	78	85
Norway	467	614	325	446	88	114	52	53
Saudi Arabia	279	323	133	182	89	103	19	12
Singapore	377	565	169	327	139	178	42	45
Sweden	238	356	194	307	38	42	6	6
Switzerland	854	1,184	496	759	214	270	99	98
Taiwan	699	757	79	110	200	234	147	165
Thailand	111	95	16	27	74	52	3	2
United Arab Emirates	162	204	127	134	15	34	8	9
United Kingdom	1,988	2,617	1,019	1,540	370	464	478	499

Z Less than $500 million. [1] Includes short-term debt and other long-term debt. [2] Includes common and preferred stock, all types of investment company shares (open-end funds, closed-end funds, money market mutual funds, and hedge funds), interests in limited partnerships, and other equity interests that may not involve stocks or shares. [3] Includes other countries not shown separately. [4] Excludes Hong Kong, Macau, and Taiwan.

Source: U.S. Department of Treasury, "U.S. International Portfolio Investment: Foreign Residents' Portfolio Holdings of U.S. Securities," <www.treasury.gov/resource-center/data-chart-center/tic/Pages/fpis.aspx>, accessed August 2022.

Table 1231. Stock Prices and Yields: 2000 to 2021

[Closing values as of end of December, except as noted]

Index	2000	2005	2010	2015	2018	2019	2020	2021
STOCK PRICES								
Standard & Poor's indices: [1]								
S&P 500 Composite Return Index (Jan. 4, 1988 = 255.94)	1,837	1,888	2,114	3,822	4,984	6,554	7,759	9,987
S&P 500 composite (1941–43 = 10)	1,320	1,248	1,257	2,044	2,507	3,231	3,756	4,766
S&P 400 MidCap Index (1982 = 100)	517	738	907	1,399	1,663	2,063	2,307	2,842
S&P 600 SmallCap Index (Dec. 31, 1993 = 100)	220	351	416	672	845	1,021	1,119	1,402
S&P 500 Citigroup Value Index (Dec. 31, 1974 = 35)	636	648	590	876	1,000	1,286	1,267	1,548
S&P 500 Citigroup Growth Index (Dec. 31, 1974 = 35)	688	597	659	1,164	1,512	1,953	2,577	3,377
Russell indices: [2]								
Russell 1000 (Dec. 31, 1986 = 130)	700	679	697	1,132	1,384	1,784	2,121	2,646
Russell 2000 (Dec. 31, 1986 = 135)	484	673	784	1,136	1,349	1,668	1,975	2,245
Russell 3000 (Dec. 31, 1986 = 140)	726	723	749	1,206	1,472	1,892	2,248	2,788
N.Y. Stock Exchange (NYSE) common stock index:								
Composite (Dec. 31, 2002 = 5000)	6,946	7,754	7,964	10,143	11,374	13,913	14,525	17,164
Yearly high	7,165	7,868	7,983	11,255	11,378	13,944	14,533	17,443
Yearly low	6,095	6,903	6,356	9,510	11,272	11,190	8,665	13,989
NYSE American Stock Exchange Composite Index (Dec. 29, 1995 = 550)	898	1,759	2,208	2,149	2,292	2,553	2,361	3,134
NASDAQ Composite Index (Feb. 5, 1971 = 100)	2,471	2,205	2,653	5,007	6,635	8,973	12,888	15,645
Nasdaq-100 (Jan. 31, 1985 = 125)	2,342	1,645	2,218	4,593	6,330	8,733	12,888	16,320
Industrial (Feb. 5, 1971 = 100)	1,483	1,860	2,184	4,101	5,401	6,808	10,397	11,313
Banks (Feb. 5, 1971 = 100)	1,939	3,078	1,847	2,853	3,274	3,969	3,547	4,955
Computers (Oct. 29, 1993 = 200)	1,295	992	1,372	2,606	3,911	5,879	8,818	12,156
Transportation (Feb. 5, 1971 = 100)	1,160	2,438	2,562	3,334	4,605	5,292	5,526	6,692
Telecommunications (Oct. 29, 1993 = 200)	463	184	226	251	349	389	474	497
Biotech (Oct. 29, 1993 = 200)	1,085	790	970	3,540	3,044	3,787	4,759	4,729
Dow Jones Averages:								
Composite (65 stocks)	3,317	3,638	4,033	5,978	7,710	9,386	10,109	12,267
Industrial (30 stocks)	10,787	10,718	11,578	17,425	23,327	28,538	30,606	36,338
Transportation (20 stocks)	2,947	4,196	5,107	7,509	9,170	10,901	12,507	16,478
Utility (15 stocks)	412	405	405	578	713	879	865	981
COMMON STOCK YIELDS (percent)								
Standard & Poor's Composite Index (500 stocks): [3]								
Dividend-price ratio [4]	1.15	1.83	1.98	2.2	2.2	1.87	1.52	1.31
Earnings-price ratio [5]	3.63	5.36	6.04	4.64	4.60	4.19	2.64	3.36

[1] Standard & Poor's Indices are market-value weighted and are chosen for market size, liquidity, and industry group representation. The S&P 500 index represents 500 large publicly-traded companies. The S&P MidCap Index tracks mid-cap companies. The S&P SmallCap Index consists of 600 domestic small-cap stocks. [2] The Russell 1000 and 3000 indices show respectively the 1000 and 3000 largest capitalization stocks in the United States. The Russell 2000 index shows the 2000 largest capitalization stocks in the United States after the first 1000. [3] Source: U.S. Council of Economic Advisors, *Economic Indicators*, monthly. [4] Aggregate cash dividends (based on latest known annual rate) divided by aggregate market value based on Wednesday closing prices. Averages of monthly figures. [5] Averages of quarterly ratios which are ratio of earnings (after taxes) for 4 quarters ending with particular quarter- to-price index for last day of that quarter.

Source: Except as noted, Global Financial Data, Los Angeles, CA, <www.globalfinancialdata.com/> ©.

Table 1232. Stock Ownership by Age of Head of Family and Family Income: 2010 to 2019

[Median value in thousands of constant (2019) dollars (34.2 represents $34,200). All dollar figures are adjusted to 2019 dollars using the "current methods" version of the consumer price index for all urban consumers published by U.S. Bureau of Labor Statistics. Families include one-person units; for definition of family, see text, Section 1. Based on Survey of Consumer Finance; see Appendix III. For definition of median, see Guide to Tabular Presentation]

Age of family head and family income (constant (2019) dollars)	Families having direct or indirect stock holdings [1] (percent)			Median value among families with holdings			Stock holdings share of group's financial assets (percent)		
	2010	2016	2019	2010	2016	2019	2010	2016	2019
All families	**49.9**	**51.9**	**52.6**	**34.2**	**42.5**	**40.0**	**47.0**	**53.4**	**54.7**
Under 35 years old	39.8	41.1	47.8	8.2	8.2	7.3	39.3	40.2	38.1
35 to 44 years old	50.1	55.7	56.1	23.3	23.3	31.6	50.5	50.0	58.1
45 to 54 years old	58.0	57.4	57.5	44.5	54.1	51.2	48.6	55.0	56.4
55 to 64 years old	59.7	57.5	54.9	66.0	85.1	72.3	48.3	56.0	53.8
65 to 74 years old	45.6	50.4	51.5	90.6	100.5	110.0	44.2	50.2	54.6
75 years old and over	42.0	48.9	47.0	64.8	106.4	84.0	44.6	54.2	55.5
Percentiles of income: [2]									
Less than 20	12.5	11.6	14.5	6.3	6.4	6.9	40.5	39.8	35.2
20 to 39.9	30.5	32.5	34.2	8.4	10.6	8.7	31.3	33.1	35.2
40 to 59.9	51.7	51.8	55.8	14.1	16.0	15.0	37.5	38.3	43.5
60 to 79.9	68.1	73.6	71.0	26.2	34.5	33.8	41.6	45.3	46.4
80 to 89.9	82.6	85.3	83.3	68.2	86.4	87.2	44.4	49.3	53.5
90 to 100	90.6	94.7	92.3	315.2	386.5	425.2	50.9	57.9	59.0

[1] Indirect holdings are those in pooled investment trusts, retirement accounts and other managed assets. [2] See footnote 8, Table 1201.

Source: Board of Governors of the Federal Reserve System, 2019 Survey of Consumer Finances, *Changes in U.S. Family Finances From 2016 to 2019: Evidence from the Survey of Consumer Finances*, Federal Reserve Bulletin, Vol. 106, No. 5, September 2020. See also <www.federalreserve.gov/econres/scfindex.htm>.

Table 1233. Bond Yields: 2000 to 2021

[Percent per year. Annual averages of daily figures]

Type	2000	2005	2010	2015	2016	2017	2018	2019	2020	2021
U.S. Treasury, constant maturities: [1]										
1-year	6.11	3.62	0.32	0.32	0.61	1.20	2.33	2.05	0.37	0.10
2-year	6.26	3.85	0.70	0.69	0.83	1.40	2.53	1.97	0.39	0.27
3-year	6.22	3.93	1.11	1.02	1.00	1.58	2.63	1.94	0.42	0.46
5-year	6.16	4.05	1.93	1.53	1.33	1.91	2.75	1.95	0.53	0.86
7-year	6.20	4.15	2.62	1.89	1.63	2.16	2.85	2.05	0.72	1.20
10-year	6.03	4.29	3.22	2.14	1.84	2.33	2.91	2.14	0.89	1.45
20-year	6.23	4.64	4.03	2.55	2.22	2.65	3.02	2.40	1.35	1.98
High-grade municipal bonds (Standard & Poor's) [2]	5.77	4.29	4.16	3.48	3.07	3.36	3.53	3.38	2.41	2.00

[1] Yields on actively traded non-inflation-indexed issues adjusted to constant maturities. Yields are based on closing indicative prices quoted by secondary market participants. [2] Source: U.S. Council of Economic Advisors, *Economic Indicators*, monthly, <www.govinfo.gov/app/collection/econi>, accessed April 2022.

Source: Except as noted, Board of Governors of the Federal Reserve System, "H15, Selected Interest Rates," <www.federalreserve.gov/releases/h15/>, accessed April 2022.

Table 1234. Total Returns of Stocks, Bonds, and Treasury Bills: 1980 to 2021

[Average annual percent change. Stock return data are based on the Standard & Poor's 500 index. Minus sign (-) indicates loss]

Period	Stocks				Treasury bills, total return	Bonds (10-year), total return
	Total return before inflation	Capital gains	Dividends and reinvestment	Total return after inflation		
1980 to 1989	17.55	12.59	4.40	11.85	9.13	13.01
1990 to 1999	18.21	15.31	2.51	14.85	4.95	8.02
2000 to 2009	-0.45	-2.73	2.27	-3.39	2.74	6.63
2001	-11.89	-13.04	1.32	-13.68	3.32	5.53
2002	-22.10	-23.37	1.65	-23.91	1.61	15.37
2003	28.68	26.38	1.82	26.31	1.03	0.46
2004	10.88	8.99	1.73	7.38	1.43	4.61
2005	4.91	3.00	1.85	1.45	3.30	3.09
2006	15.80	13.62	1.91	11.97	4.97	2.21
2007	5.49	3.53	1.89	1.35	4.52	10.54
2008	-37.00	-38.49	1.88	-37.10	1.24	20.23
2009	26.25	23.45	2.44	23.11	0.15	-9.50
2010	15.06	12.78	2.02	13.36	0.03	7.26
2011	2.96	–	2.96	0.83	0.06	16.89
2012	16.00	13.41	2.29	14.02	0.08	2.77
2013	32.39	29.60	2.15	30.43	0.05	-8.56
2014	13.69	11.39	2.06	12.83	0.03	10.74
2015	1.32	-0.73	2.05	0.58	0.06	11.27
2016	11.96	9.53	2.22	9.68	0.33	-5.40
2017	21.83	19.41	2.03	19.30	0.95	2.81
2018	-4.38	-6.24	1.98	-6.37	2.00	0.34
2019	31.49	28.88	2.02	28.55	2.09	9.28
2020	18.40	16.26	1.02	16.81	0.32	10.35
2021	28.71	26.89	1.43	20.24	0.04	-3.97

– Represents or rounds to zero.

Source: Global Financial Data, Los Angeles, CA, "GFD Guide to Total Returns," <www.globalfinancialdata.com>, and unpublished data ©.

Table 1235. Mutual Fund Shares—Holdings and Net Purchases by Type of Investor: 2000 to 2021

[In billions of dollars (5,119.4 represents $5,119,400,000,000). Holdings as of Dec. 31. A mutual fund is an open-end investment company that continuously issues and redeems shares that represent an interest in a pool of financial assets. Excludes money market funds and exchange-traded funds. Minus sign (-) indicates net sales]

Type of investor	Holdings					Net purchases				
	2000	2010	2015	2020	2021	2000	2010	2015	2020	2021
Total	**5,119.4**	**9,029.8**	**12,897.2**	**19,562.6**	**22,208.7**	**295.2**	**395.2**	**98.7**	**-224.8**	**228.5**
Households, nonprofit organizations	2,557.9	4,699.2	6,955.8	11,078.2	12,560.5	82.1	260.0	97.3	-43.0	196.8
Nonfinancial corporate business	118.0	185.7	248.2	376.4	433.8	0.3	7.5	12.2	10.6	10.6
State and local governments	32.2	50.4	70.4	112.8	127.9	1.1	1.2	1.2	1.2	1.2
U.S.-chartered depository institutions	15.0	45.0	53.0	63.4	74.9	2.5	-5.8	-0.9	-0.8	–
Credit unions	2.3	1.5	1.9	4.8	7.6	-0.7	-0.3	-0.1	0.9	2.1
Property-casualty insurance companies	3.0	11.4	19.1	29.7	33.1	0.5	-0.7	0.7	0.8	-2.5
Life insurance companies	632.8	1,115.5	1,396.6	1,701.3	1,843.0	57.6	27.5	-30.7	-99.2	-135.9
Private pension funds	1,246.1	2,220.2	3,127.9	4,728.9	5,272.3	106.9	55.4	16.9	-112.4	-46.3
State and local government retirement funds	362.5	438.4	423.8	437.9	469.2	51.5	-6.1	0.3	8.7	-22.4
Rest of the world	149.5	262.5	600.6	1,029.1	1,386.5	-6.7	56.5	1.8	8.4	225.0

– Represents zero.

Source: Board of Governors of the Federal Reserve System, "Financial Accounts of the United States, Z.1," <www.federalreserve.gov/data.htm>, accessed March 2022.

Table 1236. Household Ownership of Mutual Funds by Age and Income: 2011 and 2021

[In percent. Ownership includes money market, stock, bond, and hybrid mutual funds, variable annuities, and mutual funds owned through Individual Retirement Accounts (IRAs), Keoghs, and employer-sponsored retirement plans. In 2021, an estimated 59,000,000 households own mutual funds. A mutual fund is an open-end investment company that continuously issues and redeems shares that represent an interest in a pool of financial assets]

Age of household head [1]	Percent distribution of all households owning mutual funds, 2021 [3]	As a percent of all households within each group		Household income [2]	Percent distribution of all households owning mutual funds, 2021 [3]	As a percent of all households within each group	
		2011	2021 [3]			2011	2021 [3]
Total............................	**100**	**44**	**45**	Less than $25,000......	3	12	7
Less than 35 years old......	18	32	41	$25,000 to $34,999....	3	29	19
35 to 44 years old............	19	52	51	$35,000 to $49,999....	7	32	26
45 to 54 years old............	19	52	51	$50,000 to $74,999....	16	52	45
55 to 64 years old............	21	50	51	$75,000 to $99,999....	15	67	58
65 years old and over........	23	37	38	$100,000 and over.....	56	81	75

[1] Age is based on the sole or co-decision maker for household saving and investing. [2] Total reported is household income before taxes in prior year. [3] Starting in 2014, the survey was revised to include a dual frame random digit dial (RDD) sample design of landline and cellular telephone numbers. See source for details.

Source: Investment Company Institute. Holden, Sarah, Daniel Schrass, and Michael Bogdan. 2021. "Ownership of Mutual Funds, Shareholder Sentiment, and Use of the Internet, 2021." ICI Research Perspective 27, no. 11 (October) ©. See also <www.ici.org/system/files/2021-10/per27-11.pdf>.

Table 1237. Characteristics of Mutual Fund Owners: 2021

[In percent, except as indicated. The 2021 data are based on responses from 1,362 households owning mutual funds. Interviews were conducted with the person most knowledgeable about the household's investments and savings. Prior to 2014, the annual mutual fund shareholder survey was conducted via landline telephones only; starting in 2014, the survey was expanded and is based on a dual frame sample of landline and cellular telephone numbers. Mutual fund ownership includes holdings of money market, stock, bond, and hybrid mutual funds; and funds owned through variable annuities, Individual Retirement Accounts (IRAs), Keoghs, and employer-sponsored retirement plans. A mutual fund is an open-end investment company that continuously issues and redeems shares that represent an interest in a pool of financial assets. For definition of median, see Guide to Tabular Presentation]

Characteristic	Total	Age [1]				Household income [2]			
		Under 35 years	35 to 54 years	55 to 64 years	65 years and over	Less than $50,000	$50,000 to $99,000	$100,000 to $149,000	$150,000 or more
Median age [1] (years).........................	51	29	44	60	73	56	51	50	50
Median household income [2] (dol.)........	104,900	87,500	125,000	125,000	81,500	35,000	72,000	120,000	200,000
Median household financial assets [3] (dol.)..	320,000	100,000	300,000	500,000	500,000	65,000	128,000	357,000	500,000
Own an IRA.......................................	66	59	61	72	74	59	61	65	74
Household with defined contribution retirement plan(s) [4]..........................	84	87	93	83	65	65	83	87	89
401(k) plan.....................................	73	78	85	75	47	49	70	79	81
403(b), state, local, or federal government plan...............................	35	34	37	30	36	29	32	35	39
Median mutual fund assets (dol.)...............	200,000	50,000	150,000	400,000	350,000	50,000	75,000	250,000	400,000
Own:									
Equity funds....................................	89	91	93	90	82	77	88	91	93
Bond funds......................................	44	40	45	45	45	35	36	45	54

[1] See Table 1236, footnote 1. [2] See Table 1236, footnote 2. [3] Includes assets in employer-sponsored retirement plans but excludes value of primary residence. [4] For definition of defined contribution plan, see headnote, Table 586.

Source: Investment Company Institute. Schrass, Daniel, and Michael Bogdan. 2021. "Profile of Mutual Fund Shareholders, 2021." ICI Research Report (December) ©. See also <www.ici.org/system/files/2021-12/21_rpt_profiles.pdf>.

Table 1238. Mutual Funds—Summary: 2000 to 2021

[6,956 represents $6,956,000,000,000. Number of funds and assets as of December 31. A mutual fund is an open-end investment company that continuously issues and redeems shares that represent an interest in a pool of financial assets. Excludes data for funds that invest in other mutual funds. Minus sign (-) indicates net redemptions]

Type of fund	Unit	2000	2005	2010	2015	2017	2018	2019	2020	2021
Number of funds, total......................	**Number**	**8,134**	**7,967**	**7,539**	**8,115**	**7,959**	**8,087**	**7,937**	**7,629**	**7,481**
Equity funds.....................................	Number	4,359	4,566	4,507	4,762	4,704	4,765	4,648	4,456	4,380
Hybrid funds.....................................	Number	506	480	489	721	735	779	770	718	699
Bond funds.......................................	Number	2,232	2,052	1,891	2,151	2,138	2,175	2,155	2,115	2,097
Money market funds, taxable [1].............	Number	703	592	442	336	299	287	284	265	245
Money market funds, tax-exempt [2]..........	Number	334	277	210	145	83	81	80	75	60
Net assets, total.............................	**Bil. dol.**	**6,956**	**8,889**	**11,825**	**15,648**	**18,750**	**17,698**	**21,277**	**23,883**	**26,964**
Equity funds.....................................	Bil. dol.	3,933	4,885	5,590	8,140	10,291	9,216	11,362	12,717	14,715
Hybrid funds.....................................	Bil. dol.	361	621	842	1,341	1,546	1,383	1,578	1,619	1,869
Bond funds.......................................	Bil. dol.	817	1,356	2,589	3,412	4,065	4,061	4,704	5,214	5,625
Money market funds, taxable [1].............	Bil. dol.	1,611	1,690	2,474	2,500	2,716	2,892	3,494	4,228	4,669
Money market funds, tax-exempt [2]..........	Bil. dol.	234	336	330	255	131	145	138	105	87
Net new cash flow:...........................	**Bil. dol.**	**390**	**254**	**-282**	**-98**	**178**	**-187**	**454**	**207**	**363**
Equity funds.....................................	Bil. dol.	315	124	-25	-76	-160	-257	-362	-644	-435
Hybrid funds.....................................	Bil. dol.	-37	43	35	-19	-28	-91	-49	-84	-13
Bond funds.......................................	Bil. dol.	-48	25	232	-25	260	2	312	244	389
Money market funds...........................	Bil. dol.	159	62	-525	21	107	159	553	691	422

[1] Funds invest in short-term, high-grade securities sold in the money market. [2] Funds invest in municipal securities with relatively short maturities.

Source: Investment Company Institute. 2022. *Investment Company Fact Book: A Review of Trends and Activities in the U.S. Investment Company Industry.* © Washington, DC: Investment Company Institute. See also <www.icifactbook.org>.

Table 1239. Retirement Assets by Type of Asset: 2000 to 2021

[In billions of dollars, except as indicated (11,556 represents $11,556,000,000,000). As of December 31]

Item	2000	2005	2010	2015	2017	2018	2019	2020	2021
Retirement assets, total	**11,556**	**14,384**	**17,945**	**23,986**	**28,824**	**27,586**	**32,054**	**35,243**	**39,277**
IRA assets [1]	2,629	3,425	5,029	7,477	9,439	9,135	10,949	12,333	13,913
Bank and thrift deposits [2]	250	278	461	523	548	568	558	685	676
Life insurance companies [3]	202	301	313	383	417	429	468	523	557
Mutual funds	1,262	1,780	2,418	3,493	4,279	3,994	4,820	5,455	6,210
Other assets [1,4]	916	1,067	1,837	3,078	4,196	4,143	5,103	5,669	6,470
Traditional [1]	2,407	3,034	4,340	6,387	8,018	7,745	9,297	10,478	11,798
Roth [1]	78	156	355	625	842	846	1,014	1,150	1,325
SEP and SAR-SEP [1,5]	134	193	265	364	453	423	491	540	605
SIMPLE [1,6]	10	42	69	101	127	122	146	165	185
Defined contribution plans	2,958	3,739	4,770	6,456	7,905	7,554	8,925	9,784	10,970
401(k) plans	1,738	2,393	3,119	4,377	5,486	5,207	6,256	6,840	7,725
Other private-sector defined contribution plans [7]	500	413	464	483	550	510	588	620	685
403(b) plans	519	622	726	875	991	969	1,091	1,206	1,288
Thrift Savings Plan [8]	92	168	272	458	557	559	639	735	827
457 plans	110	143	189	263	321	309	351	384	445
Private-sector defined benefit plans	2,020	2,262	2,481	2,861	3,238	2,934	3,313	3,544	3,794
State and local government defined benefit plans	2,340	2,761	2,946	3,679	4,306	4,093	4,661	5,138	5,903
Federal defined benefit plans [9]	705	912	1,168	1,519	1,695	1,796	1,910	2,011	2,182
Annuities [10]	904	1,285	1,550	1,994	2,241	2,074	2,296	2,433	2,515
Memo:									
Mutual fund retirement assets	2,545	3,656	4,920	7,121	8,812	8,170	9,933	11,123	12,577
Percent of total retirement assets	22	25	27	30	31	30	31	32	32
Percent of all mutual funds	37	41	42	46	47	46	47	47	47

[1] Data for 2020 and 2021 are estimated. [2] Includes Keogh deposits. [3] Annuities held by IRAs, excluding variable annuity mutual fund IRA assets, which are included in mutual funds. [4] Excludes mutual fund assets held through brokerage accounts, which are included in mutual funds. [5] Simplified Employee Pension (SEP) IRAs and salary reduction (SAR) IRAs. [6] Savings Incentive Match Plan for Employees (SIMPLE) IRAs. [7] Includes Keoghs and other defined contribution plans (profit-sharing, thrift-savings, stock bonus, and money purchase) without 401(k) features. [8] Federal Employees Retirement System (FERS) Thrift Savings Plan (TSP) as reported by the Federal Reserve Board. [9] Federal pension plans include U.S. Treasury security holdings of the civil service retirement and disability fund, the military retirement fund, the judicial retirement funds, the Railroad Retirement Board, and the foreign service retirement and disability fund. These plans also include securities held in the National Railroad Retirement Investment Trust. [10] Annuities include all fixed and variable annuities held outside of retirement plans and IRAs.

Source: Investment Company Institute. 2022. "The US Retirement Market, First Quarter 2022" (June) ©. For the most up-to-date figures about the fund industry, please visit <www.ici.org/research/stats>.

Table 1240. Pension Funds—Summary: 2000 to 2021

[In billions of dollars (9,612 represents $9,612,000,000,000). As of end of year. Covers private pension funds, state and local government employee retirement funds, and federal government retirement funds in defined benefit plans and defined contribution plans (including 401(k) type plans). Excludes social security trust funds; see Table 581]

Item	2000	2005	2010	2015	2016	2017	2018	2019	2020	2021
Total financial assets [1]	**9,612**	**12,562**	**15,917**	**20,413**	**21,239**	**22,665**	**22,661**	**24,467**	**25,989**	**27,612**
Money market fund shares	104	143	195	208	223	221	218	203	244	270
Debt securities [1]	2,058	2,371	2,927	3,792	3,961	4,100	4,453	4,698	5,097	5,334
Treasury securities [2]	1,029	1,225	1,633	2,176	2,337	2,371	2,779	2,921	3,194	3,480
Agency- and GSE (government-sponsored enterprises)-backed securities	374	514	334	268	277	312	356	401	423	409
Corporate and foreign bonds	578	583	881	1,262	1,249	1,317	1,225	1,328	1,436	1,394
Corporate equities	3,178	3,931	3,646	4,711	4,912	5,744	5,219	5,856	6,644	7,848
Mutual fund shares	1,609	2,213	2,659	3,552	3,770	4,368	4,041	4,691	5,167	5,741
Miscellaneous assets [1]	2,443	3,766	6,377	8,020	8,236	7,949	8,608	8,900	8,715	8,258
Unallocated insurance contracts [3]	462	533	626	723	768	805	789	846	881	914
Contributions receivable	73	45	91	91	100	119	85	85	70	57
Claims of pension fund on sponsor [4]	1,755	2,991	4,995	6,417	6,514	6,053	6,772	6,284	5,917	5,228
Pension entitlements (liabilities) [5]	**9,700**	**12,655**	**16,060**	**20,590**	**21,387**	**22,787**	**22,767**	**24,646**	**26,161**	**27,827**
Memo:										
Defined benefit plan funded status:										
Pension entitlements, total	**6,820**	**8,985**	**11,545**	**14,442**	**14,824**	**15,222**	**15,591**	**16,111**	**16,550**	**16,992**
Funded by assets [6]	5,065	5,994	6,549	8,025	8,310	9,168	8,820	9,827	10,633	11,764
Unfunded	1,755	2,991	4,995	6,417	6,514	6,053	6,772	6,284	5,917	5,228
Household retirement assets, total [7]	**13,435**	**17,596**	**22,931**	**30,398**	**31,802**	**34,800**	**34,452**	**38,295**	**41,429**	**(NA)**
Defined benefit plans	6,820	8,985	11,545	14,442	14,824	15,222	15,591	16,111	16,550	16,992
Defined contribution plans	2,880	3,671	4,515	6,149	6,562	7,565	7,176	8,535	9,611	10,835
Individual retirement plans (IRAs) [8]	2,629	3,425	5,029	7,477	8,015	9,439	9,135	10,850	12,210	(NA)
Annuities at life insurance companies [9]	1,106	1,516	1,843	2,331	2,400	2,575	2,550	2,799	3,058	(NA)

NA Not available. [1] Includes other types of assets not shown separately. [2] Includes both marketable and nonmarketable government securities. [3] Assets of pension plans held at life insurance companies. [4] Unfunded defined benefit pension entitlements. [5] Actuarial value of accrued pension entitlements in defined benefit plans and assets of defined contribution plans. These liabilities are assets of the household sector. [6] Total defined benefit financial assets plus nonfinancial assets less claims of pension fund on sponsor. [7] Households' retirement assets in tax-deferred accounts, including employer sponsored pension plans, individual retirement accounts (IRAs), Roth IRAs, and annuities. [8] IRA assets are not included in above assets or entitlements. [9] Excludes annuities held in IRAs at life insurance companies.

Source: Board of Governors of the Federal Reserve System, "Financial Accounts of the United States, Z.1," <www.federalreserve.gov/data.htm>, accessed March 2022.

Table 1241. Private Pension Fund Assets by Type, and Liabilities: 2000 to 2021

[In billions of dollars (4,283 represents $4,283,000,000,000). As of December 31. Covers private defined benefit plans and defined contribution plans (including 401(k) type plans). Minus sign (-) indicates overfunding]

Type of instrument	2000	2005	2010	2015	2017	2018	2019	2020	2021
Total financial assets [1]	**4,283**	**5,391**	**6,604**	**8,649**	**10,020**	**9,696**	**11,043**	**12,026**	**13,152**
Money market fund shares	84	90	142	154	159	158	180	220	238
Debt securities [1]	596	665	867	1,176	1,391	1,416	1,566	1,696	1,637
Treasury securities	111	111	202	287	351	372	440	550	574
Agency and GSE-backed securities [2]	194	245	181	158	194	205	224	222	194
Corporate and foreign bonds	263	286	446	691	804	802	867	889	836
Corporate equities	1,823	2,288	1,778	2,220	2,713	2,448	2,962	3,382	4,120
Mutual fund shares	1,246	1,727	2,220	3,128	3,887	3,595	4,308	4,729	5,272
Miscellaneous assets [1]	387	518	1,524	1,895	1,784	2,006	1,950	1,922	1,803
Unallocated insurance contracts [3]	362	405	466	527	565	556	592	614	639
Pension entitlements (liabilities) [4]	**4,323**	**5,430**	**6,641**	**8,686**	**10,057**	**9,732**	**11,079**	**12,062**	**13,189**
Funded status of defined benefit plans:									
Pension entitlements	1,826	2,290	2,872	3,436	3,516	3,532	3,661	3,702	3,742
Funded by assets [5]	2,020	2,321	2,435	2,827	3,189	2,931	3,256	3,484	3,735
Unfunded	-193	-30	437	609	327	602	405	218	7
Defined benefit plan assets	1,785	2,251	2,836	3,400	3,479	3,496	3,624	3,666	3,706
Defined contribution plan assets	2,497	3,140	3,768	5,250	6,541	6,200	7,419	8,360	9,447

[1] Includes other types of assets not shown separately. [2] GSE=Government-sponsored enterprises. [3] Assets of private pension plans held at life insurance companies (e.g., GICs, variable annuities). [4] Actuarial value of accrued pension entitlements in defined benefit plans and assets of defined contribution plans. [5] Total defined benefit financial assets plus nonfinancial assets less claims of pension fund on sponsor.

Source: Board of Governors of the Federal Reserve System, "Financial Accounts of the United States, Z.1," <www.federalreserve.gov/data.htm>, accessed March 2022.

Table 1242. Public Employee Retirement Systems—Assets and Liabilities: 2000 to 2021

[In billions of dollars (3,301 represents $3,301,000,000,000). As of December 31. Includes claims of sponsor (unfunded pension entitlements). Minus sign (-) indicates overfunding]

Type of instrument	2000	2005	2010	2015	2017	2018	2019	2020	2021
STATE AND LOCAL GOVERNMENT EMPLOYEE RETIREMENT PLANS									
Total financial assets [1]	**3,301**	**4,667**	**6,169**	**8,054**	**8,704**	**8,930**	**9,202**	**9,539**	**9,826**
Debt securities [1]	721	740	765	881	955	976	955	1,075	1,214
Treasury securities	179	163	154	175	289	368	329	347	450
Agency and GSE-backed securities [2]	179	261	144	101	109	142	167	190	204
Corporate and foreign bonds	314	289	427	558	499	410	446	529	541
Corporate equities	1,299	1,530	1,723	2,250	2,707	2,479	2,523	2,844	3,207
Mutual fund shares	363	486	438	424	481	447	383	438	469
Miscellaneous assets [1]	825	1,823	3,150	4,393	4,454	4,922	5,276	5,114	4,836
Claims of pension fund on sponsor [3]	717	1,596	2,855	4,075	4,016	4,489	4,205	4,020	3,602
Pension entitlements (liabilities) [4]	**3,348**	**4,721**	**6,275**	**8,195**	**8,789**	**8,999**	**9,343**	**9,674**	**10,004**
Funded status of defined benefit plans:									
Pension entitlements	3,058	4,358	5,801	7,754	8,321	8,582	8,866	9,158	9,451
Funded by assets [5]	2,340	2,761	2,946	3,679	4,306	4,093	4,661	5,138	5,849
Unfunded [3]	717	1,596	2,855	4,075	4,016	4,489	4,205	4,020	3,602
Defined benefit plan assets	3,011	4,304	5,695	7,614	8,237	8,513	8,725	9,023	9,273
Defined contribution plan assets	291	363	474	441	467	417	477	516	553
FEDERAL GOVERNMENT EMPLOYEE RETIREMENT FUNDS									
Total financial assets [1]	**2,028**	**2,504**	**3,144**	**3,709**	**3,941**	**4,036**	**4,223**	**4,424**	**4,634**
Debt securities [1]	740	966	1,295	1,736	1,754	2,062	2,177	2,326	2,484
Treasury securities [6]	739	951	1,277	1,715	1,730	2,040	2,151	2,297	2,456
Corporate equities	57	113	145	240	324	292	371	418	521
Claims of pension fund on sponsor [7]	1,231	1,425	1,703	1,732	1,711	1,681	1,674	1,679	1,619
Pension entitlements (liabilities) [8]	**2,028**	**2,504**	**3,144**	**3,709**	**3,941**	**4,036**	**4,223**	**4,424**	**4,634**
Funded status of defined benefit plans:									
Pension entitlements	1,936	2,336	2,871	3,251	3,384	3,477	3,583	3,690	3,799
Funded by assets [9]	705	912	1,168	1,519	1,673	1,796	1,910	2,011	2,181
Unfunded [7]	1,231	1,425	1,703	1,732	1,711	1,681	1,674	1,679	1,619
Defined benefit plan assets [10]	1,936	2,336	2,871	3,251	3,384	3,477	3,583	3,690	3,799
Defined contribution plan assets [11]	92	168	272	458	557	559	639	735	835

[1] Includes other types of instruments not shown separately. [2] GSE=Government sponsored enterprises. [3] Unfunded defined benefit pension entitlements. [4] Actuarial value of projected pension entitlements. These liabilities are assets of the household sector. [5] Total defined benefit financial assets plus nonfinancial assets less claims of pension fund on sponsor. [6] Comprised primarily of nonmarketable Treasury securities. [7] Unfunded defined benefit pension entitlements. [8] Actuarial value of projected pension entitlements in defined benefit plans and assets of defined contribution plans. These liabilities are assets of the household sector. [9] Total defined benefit financial assets less defined benefit claims of pension fund on sponsor. [10] Includes the Civil Service Retirement and Disability Fund, Railroad Retirement Board, judicial retirement fund, Military Retirement Fund, Foreign Service Retirement and Disability Fund, and National Railroad Retirement Investment Trust. [11] Thrift Savings Plan.

Source: Board of Governors of the Federal Reserve System, "Financial Accounts of the United States, Z.1," <www.federalreserve.gov/data.htm>, accessed March 2022.

Table 1243. Life Insurance in Force and Purchases in the United States—Summary: 2000 to 2021

[369 represents 369,000,000. As of December 31 or calendar year, as applicable. Covers life insurance with life insurance companies, and beginning in 2003, also with fraternal benefit societies. Data represents all life insurance in force on lives of U.S. residents whether issued by U.S. or foreign companies]

Year	Number of policies, total (millions)	Life insurance in force			Life insurance purchases [1]					
		Value (bil. dol.)			Number (1,000)			Amount (bil. dol.)		
		Total [2]	Individual	Group	Total	Individual	Group	Total	Individual	Group
2000.......	369	15,953	9,376	6,376	34,882	13,345	21,537	2,515	1,594	921
2010.......	284	18,426	10,484	7,831	28,621	10,123	18,498	2,809	1,673	1,135
2011.......	286	19,219	10,994	8,120	27,177	10,309	16,867	2,832	1,673	1,160
2012.......	272	19,321	11,215	8,012	27,063	10,306	16,757	2,800	1,679	1,121
2013.......	275	19,662	11,365	8,215	25,264	9,929	15,336	2,779	1,640	1,139
2014.......	278	20,115	11,826	8,209	27,147	9,440	17,707	2,759	1,590	1,168
2015.......	281	20,779	12,342	8,361	28,315	10,305	18,010	2,877	1,647	1,229
2016.......	291	20,316	11,992	8,246	27,523	11,005	16,518	2,874	1,685	1,190
2017.......	289	20,416	11,927	8,411	28,035	10,478	17,557	3,027	1,712	1,316
2018.......	267	19,571	12,120	7,367	27,748	10,289	17,459	2,972	1,728	1,244
2019.......	259	19,834	12,388	7,358	31,356	10,118	21,238	3,042	1,803	1,239
2020.......	255	20,426	12,850	7,478	35,433	10,088	25,345	3,293	1,854	1,440
2021.......	261	21,188	13,569	7,524	34,428	10,401	24,027	3,243	1,974	1,268

[1] Excludes revivals, increases, dividend additions, and reinsurance acquired. Includes long-term credit insurance (life insurance on loans of more than 10 years' duration). [2] Includes other types of policies not shown separately such as credit.

Source: American Council of Life Insurers, Washington, DC, *Life Insurers Fact Book*, annual ©.

Table 1244. U.S. Life Insurance Companies—Summary: 2000 to 2021

[811.5 represents $811,500,000,000. As of December 31 or calendar year, as applicable. Covers domestic and foreign business of U.S. companies. Includes annual statement data for companies that primarily are health insurance companies. Beginning in 2005, includes also fraternal benefit societies]

Item	Unit	2000	2010	2015	2016	2017	2018	2019	2020	2021
U.S. companies [1]	**Number**	**1,269**	**917**	**814**	**797**	**781**	**773**	**761**	**747**	**737**
Income [2]	Bil. dol.	**811.5**	**862.6**	**1,064.7**	**985.8**	**973.4**	**1,008.2**	**1,094.4**	**1,020.2**	**1,086.5**
Life insurance premiums...................	Bil. dol.	130.6	104.6	155.9	119.3	141.8	150.2	156.6	148.0	164.6
Annuity considerations [3].................	Bil. dol.	306.7	293.6	333.0	326.8	294.9	279.3	347.5	301.3	290.6
Health insurance premiums...............	Bil. dol.	105.6	172.7	159.9	164.0	170.5	185.4	188.1	186.3	192.0
Investment and other [4]....................	Bil. dol.	268.5	291.6	416.0	375.7	366.3	393.3	402.2	384.6	439.2
Payments under life insurance and annuity contracts....................	Bil. dol.	375.2	365.6	447.7	443.0	490.1	536.9	530.3	529.1	584.3
Payments to life insurance beneficiaries................................	Bil. dol.	44.1	58.4	74.3	76.0	77.1	79.7	78.4	90.4	100.2
Surrender values under life insurance [5].................................	Bil. dol.	27.2	35.8	28.8	30.2	33.2	35.3	34.1	30.4	28.3
Surrender values under annuity contracts [5, 6].............................	Bil. dol.	214.0	184.1	247.2	238.0	279.4	319.1	310.4	297.5	339.1
Policyholder dividends....................	Bil. dol.	20.0	15.9	18.5	18.4	17.7	18.4	18.2	18.1	17.8
Annuity payments [6]......................	Bil. dol.	68.7	70.1	77.8	79.1	81.6	83.4	88.1	91.6	97.7
Matured endowments......................	Bil. dol.	0.6	0.6	0.4	0.4	0.5	0.4	0.4	0.5	0.5
Other payments............................	Bil. dol.	0.6	0.7	0.7	0.7	0.6	0.7	0.7	0.7	0.7
Health insurance benefit payments................................	Bil. dol.	78.8	122.5	115.3	119.8	126.7	132.2	141.6	137.7	147.2
BALANCE SHEET										
Assets................................	**Bil. dol.**	**3,182**	**5,311**	**6,478**	**6,772**	**7,183**	**6,993**	**7,567**	**8,150**	**8,671**
Mortgage-backed securities...............	Bil. dol.	(NA)	631.0	556	568	568	576	564	549	520
Government bonds.........................	Bil. dol.	364	413	496	522	547	475	485	501	524
Corporate securities.......................	Bil. dol.	2,238	3,271	4,150	4,313	4,627	4,441	4,887	5,291	5,697
Bonds....................................	Bil. dol.	1,241	1,700	2,150	2,257	2,365	2,441	2,589	2,820	3,008
Stocks...................................	Bil. dol.	997	1,570	2,001	2,056	2,262	2,000	2,298	2,471	2,689
Mortgages.................................	Bil. dol.	237	327	437	472	514	565	615	641	691
Real estate................................	Bil. dol.	36	28	44	47	43	39	42	41	39
Policy loans...............................	Bil. dol.	102	127	135	135	137	137	134	133	131
Other......................................	Bil. dol.	204	515	659	715	749	760	841	994	1,069
Interest earned on assets [7]................	Percent	7.05	4.33	4.81	4.50	4.28	4.72	4.57	3.93	4.28
Obligations and surplus funds [8]...........	Bil. dol.	3,182	5,311	6,478	6,772	7,183	6,993	7,567	8,150	8,671
Policy reserves..........................	**Bil. dol.**	**2,712**	**4,098**	**5,025**	**5,232**	**5,542**	**5,375**	**5,788**	**6,104**	**6,388**
Annuities [9].............................	Bil. dol.	1,875	2,660	3,320	3,467	3,701	3,554	3,880	4,103	4,286
Group...............................	Bil. dol.	960	863	1,022	1,053	1,129	1,079	1,179	1,274	1,324
Individual...........................	Bil. dol.	881	1,780	2,276	2,391	2,548	2,449	2,675	2,802	2,935
Supplementary contracts [10]...........	Bil. dol.	34	17	23	23	24	25	26	27	28
Life insurance.......................	Bil. dol.	742	1,224	1,463	1,500	1,563	1,574	1,650	1,738	1,831
Health insurance....................	Bil. dol.	96	214	242	264	279	247	257	264	271
Liabilities for deposit-type contracts [11]................................	Bil. dol.	21	420	470	495	530	524	572	626	702
Capital and surplus.......................	Bil. dol.	188	319	383	398	413	419	441	454	497

NA Not available. [1] Includes life insurance companies that sell accident and health insurance. [2] Premiums are net of reinsurance business and fluctuate with reinsurance activities as well as sale changes. [3] Beginning 2005, excludes certain deposit-type funds from income due to codification. [4] Investment represents gross investment income. [5] "Surrender values" include annuity withdrawals of funds. [6] Beginning 2005, excludes payments under deposit-type contracts. [7] Net rate. [8] Includes other obligations not shown separately. [9] Beginning 2005, excludes reserves for guaranteed interest contracts (GICs). [10] Data for 2000 include reserves for contracts with and without life contingencies; beginning 2005, includes only reserves for contracts with life contingencies. [11] Policyholder dividend accumulations for all years. Beginning 2005, also includes liabilities for guaranteed interest contracts, supplementary contracts without life contingencies, and premium and other deposits.

Source: American Council of Life Insurers, Washington, DC, *Life Insurers Fact Book*, annual ©.

Table 1245. Real Estate and Rental and Leasing—Nonemployer Establishments and Receipts by Kind of Business: 2010 to 2019

[2,343.1 represents 2,343,100. Includes only firms subject to federal income tax. Nonemployers are businesses with no paid employees. Data originate chiefly from administrative records of the Internal Revenue Service; see Appendix III]

Kind of business	NAICS code [1]	Establishments (1,000)			Receipts (mil. dol.)		
		2010	2015	2019	2010	2015	2019
Real estate & rental & leasing, total..........................	**53**	**2,343.1**	**2,635.8**	**2,942.2**	**209,549**	**259,768**	**300,227**
Real estate...	531	2,262.2	2,552.5	2,855.1	203,065	252,450	292,095
Lessors of real estate..	5311	989.3	1,156.2	1,243.1	135,015	158,624	177,565
Offices of real estate agents & brokers..........................	5312	641.6	694.7	819.1	25,502	38,904	47,122
Activities related to real estate..........................	5313	631.3	701.6	793.0	42,549	54,922	67,409
Rental & leasing services.......................................	532	78.9	80.2	84.2	6,288	7,024	7,821
Automotive equipment rental & leasing..........................	5321	18.3	18.6	21.7	990	1,171	1,365
Consumer goods rental..........................	5322	18.3	19.1	19.4	779	887	905
General rental centers..........................	5323	4.8	6.5	7.4	409	519	638
Commercial/industrial equipment rental & leasing..............	5324	37.5	36.0	35.7	4,109	4,448	4,913
Lessors of other nonfinancial intangible assets.................	533	2.0	3.1	2.9	197	293	311

[1] Data for 2010 based on 2007 North American Industry Classification System (NAICS); data for 2015 based on 2012 NAICS; data for 2019 based on 2017 NAICS. For more information, see text, Section 15.

Source: U.S. Census Bureau, Nonemployer Statistics, "All Sectors: Nonemployer Statistics by Legal Form of Organization and Receipts Size Class for the U.S., States, and Selected Geographies: 2019," <data.census.gov>, accessed July 2022.

Table 1246. Real Estate and Rental and Leasing—Establishments, Employees, and Payroll: 2019 and 2020

[425.3 represents 425,300. Covers establishments with payroll. Data based on the North American Industry Classification System (NAICS) 2017; see text, section 15, Business Enterprise. Employees are for the week including March 12. Most government employees are excluded]

Kind of business	NAICS code	Establishments (1,000)		Employees (1,000)		Payroll (bil. dol.)	
		2019	2020	2019	2020	2019	2020
Real estate & rental & leasing, total..........................	**53**	**425.3**	**437.7**	**2,240.1**	**2,280.6**	**130.6**	**131.7**
Real estate...	531	370.0	383.9	1,676.9	1,720.1	97.5	101.6
Lessors of real estate..	5311	131.5	132.4	604.2	608.0	31.6	31.5
Offices of real estate agents & brokers..........................	5312	136.5	146.6	349.2	362.2	24.1	25.7
Activities related to real estate [1]................................	5313	102.0	104.8	723.5	749.9	41.8	44.4
Residential property managers..........................	531311	52.9	54.2	470.3	486.8	22.4	23.7
Rental & leasing services.......................................	532	52.6	51.2	527.5	521.8	28.7	25.3
Automotive equipment rental & leasing..........................	5321	16.2	16.0	177.6	175.8	8.3	7.3
Passenger car rental & leasing..........................	53211	10.3	10.1	105.6	103.7	4.6	3.7
Truck, utility trailer & RV rental & leasing..........................	53212	6.0	5.9	72.0	72.1	3.7	3.6
Consumer goods rental [1]..........................	5322	17.5	16.8	131.2	123.2	5.1	4.3
Consumer electronics and appliances rental.................	53221	5.9	5.6	29.8	26.8	1.1	1.0
Other consumer goods rental..........................	53228	11.5	11.2	101.4	96.4	4.0	3.3
Video tape & disc rental..........................	532282	1.3	1.3	10.1	7.5	0.2	0.2
Home health equipment rental..........................	532283	2.3	2.2	26.7	26.3	1.3	1.2
Recreational goods rental..........................	532284	2.4	2.4	13.2	13.1	0.5	0.5
General rental centers..........................	5323	3.0	2.8	19.6	19.6	0.9	0.9
Commercial/industrial equipment rental & leasing [1]...........	5324	15.9	15.6	199.2	203.2	14.4	12.8
Construction, transportation, mining & forestry equipment..	53241	5.5	5.4	70.1	71.5	6.0	5.4
Lessors of other nonfinancial intangible assets.................	533	2.7	2.6	35.7	38.8	4.4	4.8

[1] Includes industries not shown separately.

Source: U.S. Census Bureau, County Business Patterns, "All Sectors: County Business Patterns, including ZIP Code Business Patterns, by Legal Form of Organization and Employment Size Class for the U.S., States, and Selected Geographies: 2020," <data.census.gov>, accessed May 2022.

Table 1247. Real Estate and Rental and Leasing Services—Revenue by Kind of Business: 2010 to 2020

[In millions of dollars (427,687 represents $427,687,000,000). Covers taxable and tax-exempt employer firms. Estimates for 2010 are based on the 2007 North American Industry Classification System (NAICS); beginning 2013, estimates are based on the 2012 NAICS. See text, this section and Section 15. Estimates have been adjusted using the results of the 2017 Economic Census. Based on Service Annual Survey; see Appendix III]

Kind of business	NAICS code	2010	2016	2017	2018	2019	2020
Real estate and rental and leasing, total....................	**53**	**427,687**	**635,119**	**670,304**	**712,099**	**756,268**	**730,742**
Real estate [1]...	531	289,294	442,677	468,995	492,475	524,185	524,018
Lessors of residential buildings and dwellings.................	53111	73,899	112,383	118,350	122,072	131,519	130,347
Lessors of nonresidential buildings (excl. miniwarehouses)...	53112	86,933	115,601	120,412	126,234	132,113	122,668
Offices of real estate agents and brokers..........................	5312	55,966	105,235	112,934	121,236	129,797	135,250
Real estate property managers..........................	53131	43,659	68,285	73,113	76,792	80,934	84,328
Offices of real estate appraisers..........................	53132	5,225	6,690	6,584	6,219	6,570	7,459
Rental and leasing services [1]..........................	532	108,491	149,361	154,108	168,077	177,846	156,312
Passenger car rental..........................	532111	22,534	29,840	29,838	30,843	33,465	24,390
Passenger car leasing..........................	532112	6,063	9,911	10,819	11,995	12,990	12,356
Truck, trailer, and recreational vehicle rental and leasing.....	53212	13,941	21,215	22,486	25,306	26,326	26,210
Consumer electronics and appliances rental.................	53221	5,253	7,148	6,924	7,263	7,496	7,927
Construction/transportation/mining/forestry equipment rental and leasing..........................	53241	19,483	30,403	33,691	38,495	40,431	37,291
Lessors of other nonfinancial intangible assets.................	533	29,902	43,081	47,201	51,547	54,237	50,412

[1] Includes other kinds of business, not shown separately.

Source: U.S. Census Bureau, Service Annual Survey, "Service Annual Survey Latest Data (NAICS-basis): 2020" and "Service Annual Survey Historical Survey Tables," <www.census.gov/programs-surveys/sas/data.html>, accessed November 2021.

Arts, Recreation, and Travel

This section presents data on the arts, entertainment, and recreation economic sector of the economy, and personal recreational activities, the arts and humanities, and domestic and foreign travel.

Arts, entertainment, and recreation industry—The U.S. Census Bureau surveys—County Business Patterns, Economic Census, Nonemployer Statistics, and Service Annual Survey—provide data on the arts, entertainment, and recreation sector. The County Business Patterns' annual data include number of establishments, number of employees, first quarter and annual payrolls, and number of establishments by employment size class. The Economic Census, conducted every five years for the years ending in '2' and '7', provides information on the number of establishments, receipts, payroll, and paid employees for the United States and various geographic levels. Nonemployer Statistics is an annual tabulation of economic data by industry for active businesses that are subject to federal income tax and that do not have paid employees. The Service Annual Survey provides estimates of operating revenue of taxable firms and revenues and expenses of firms exempt from federal taxes for industries in this sector of the economy. See Appendix III for more details.

Recreation and leisure activities—Data on the participation in various recreation and leisure time activities are based on several sample surveys. Data on the public's involvement with arts events and activities are published by the National Endowment for Arts (NEA). The NEA's Survey of Public Participation in the Arts remains the largest periodic study of arts participation in the United States. The most recent data are from the 2017 survey. Data on participation in fishing, hunting, and other forms of wildlife associated recreation are published periodically by the U.S. Department of Interior, Fish and Wildlife Service and the U.S. Census Bureau in *The National Survey of Fishing, Hunting, and Wildlife-Associated Recreation*. The most recent data are from the 2016 survey. MRI-Simmons (launched as joint venture under GfK in 2019) also conducts periodic surveys on sports and leisure activities, as well as other topics.

Parks and recreation—The Department of the Interior has responsibility for administering the national parks. The National Park Service publishes information on visits to national park areas in its annual report, *National Park Statistical Abstract*. Additional data regarding acreage and visits for each area administered by the service can be found at <irma.nps.gov/STATS>. Statistics for state parks are compiled by the National Association of State Park Directors in its annual *Statistical Report of State Park Operations*.

Travel—Statistics on arrivals and departures to the United States, cities and states visited by overseas travelers, and tourism sales and employment are reported by the International Trade Administration (ITA), Office of Travel & Tourism Industries (OTTI). Data on domestic travel and travel expenditures are published by the research department of the U.S. Travel Association. Other data on household transportation characteristics are in Section 23, Transportation.

Statistical reliability—For a discussion of statistical collection and estimation, sampling procedures, and measures of statistical reliability applicable to Census Bureau data, see Appendix III.

Table 1248. Arts, Entertainment, and Recreation Services—Estimated Revenue: 2010 to 2020

[In millions of dollars (188,117 represents $188,117,000,000). For taxable and tax-exempt employer firms. Data for 2010 are based on the 2007 North American Industry Classification System (NAICS); beginning 2013, data are based on 2012 NAICS. Selected estimates have been adjusted using the results of the 2017 Economic Census. Based on the Service Annual Survey, see Appendix III]

Kind of business	NAICS Code	2010	2015	2017	2018	2019	2020
Arts, entertainment, and recreation............	**71**	**188,117**	**236,296**	**265,621**	**280,100**	**296,444**	**210,185**
Performing arts, spectator sports, and related industries.....................................	711	80,461	104,735	119,508	127,864	134,855	89,500
Performing arts companies.........................	7111	13,814	14,759	16,157	16,788	17,622	9,912
Sports teams and clubs.............................	711211	21,442	28,576	34,249	35,741	37,083	26,170
Racetracks...	711212	6,951	7,470	8,285	8,618	8,827	5,974
Other spectator sports..............................	711219	3,344	3,556	3,668	3,731	3,948	3,662
Promoters of performing arts, sports, and similar events.......................................	7113	16,312	25,473	29,367	32,105	33,760	17,858
Agents and managers for artists, athletes, entertainers and other public figures..............	7114	5,358	7,223	7,868	8,674	9,298	6,729
Independent artists, writers, and performers.......	7115	13,240	17,678	19,914	22,207	24,317	19,195
Museums, historical sites, and similar institutions. ..	712	14,241	16,536	19,632	19,551	21,553	17,561
Amusement, gambling, and recreation industries. ..	713	93,415	115,025	126,481	132,685	140,036	103,124
Amusement and theme parks.......................	71311	10,205	16,184	17,816	19,011	20,090	(S)
Amusement arcades.................................	71312	1,627	2,345	3,576	4,093	4,362	2,695
Casinos (except casino hotels).....................	71321	15,367	16,279	15,951	16,536	17,575	13,866
Other gambling industries...........................	71329	8,065	8,395	9,633	10,381	11,184	8,850
Golf courses and country clubs.....................	71391	19,788	21,993	23,090	23,744	24,096	23,583
Skiing facilities......................................	71392	2,265	2,382	2,989	3,160	3,357	3,149
Marinas..	71393	3,604	4,253	4,539	4,926	5,174	5,239
Fitness and recreational sports centers.............	71394	22,311	28,838	33,042	33,971	35,889	24,361
Bowling centers.....................................	71395	3,007	3,386	3,480	3,708	4,109	2,334
All other amusement and recreation industries.....	71399	7,176	10,970	12,365	13,155	14,200	10,955

S Estimate does not meet publication standards.

Source: U.S. Census Bureau, Service Annual Survey, "Service Annual Survey Latest Data (NAICS-basis): 2020," <www.census.gov/programs-surveys/sas/data.html>, accessed January 2022.

Table 1249. Arts, Entertainment, and Recreation—Establishments, Revenue, Payroll, and Employees by Kind of Business: 2012 and 2017

[201,193 represents $201,193,000,000. For establishments with payroll only. Definition of paid employees varies among NAICS sectors. Data are based on the 2012 and 2017 Economic Censuses which are subject to nonsampling error. For details on survey methodology, sampling and nonsampling errors, see Appendix III]

Kind of business	2012 NAICS code [1]	Number of establishments		Revenue (mil. dol.)		Annual payroll (mil. dol.)		Paid employees (1,000)	
		2012	2017	2012	2017	2012	2017	2012	2017
Arts, entertainment, and recreation, total..	**71**	**124,591**	**142,938**	**201,193**	**265,620**	**64,052**	**82,256**	**2,082**	**2,390**
Performing arts, spectator sports, and related industries [2]........................	711	45,612	53,613	86,421	119,507	31,545	41,237	434	489
Performing arts companies.........................	7111	8,508	8,836	13,857	16,157	3,950	4,552	119	121
Spectator sports....................................	7112	4,164	3,900	33,298	46,201	16,653	21,624	118	130
Promoters of performing arts, sports and similar events.......................................	7113	6,846	8,072	18,474	29,367	3,211	4,984	137	167
Agents and managers for artists, athletes, entertainers and other public figures............	7114	3,716	4,111	5,832	7,868	1,886	2,408	18	22
Independent artists, writers, and performers.....	7115	22,378	28,694	14,960	19,914	5,844	7,669	41	49
Museums, historical sites, and similar institutions [2]......................................	712	7,319	7,557	13,726	19,631	4,197	5,414	135	158
Amusement, gambling, and recreation industries [2]......................................	713	71,660	81,768	101,046	126,481	28,310	35,605	1,513	1,743
Amusement parks and arcades....................	7131	3,299	4,317	14,302	21,392	3,386	5,140	155	226
Gambling industries.................................	7132	2,886	3,038	24,385	25,584	4,272	4,469	149	135
Other amusement and recreation services.......	7139	65,475	74,413	62,359	79,505	20,652	25,996	1,208	1,383

[1] Based on 2012 North American Industry Classification System (NAICS); see text, this section and section 15. [2] Includes other industries not shown separately.

Source: U.S. Census Bureau, 2017 Economic Census, EC1700COMP, "All Sectors: Comparative Statistics for the U.S., States, and Selected Geographies (2012 NAICS Basis): 2017 and 2012," <data.census.gov/>, accessed December 2021.

Table 1250. Arts, Entertainment, and Recreation—Nonemployer Establishments and Receipts by Kind of Business (NAICS Basis): 2010 to 2019

[Firms in thousands (1,154.0 represents 1,154,000); receipts in millions of dollars (26,756 represents $26,756,000,000). Includes only firms subject to federal income tax. Nonemployers are businesses with no paid employees but with annual receipts of $1,000 or more]

Kind of business	NAICS code [1]	Firms (1,000)			Receipts (mil. dol.)		
		2010	2015	2019	2010	2015	2019
Arts, entertainment, and recreation.............	71	**1,154.0**	**1,341.7**	**1,563.3**	**26,756**	**34,549**	**42,999**
Performing arts, spectator sports, and related industries............	711	1,004.9	1,177.3	1,400.5	21,053	27,590	35,213
Performing arts companies............	7111	61.2	93.8	95.8	1,249	1,832	2,221
Spectator sports............	7112	151.9	169.8	225.4	2,515	3,242	4,244
Promoters of performing arts, sports, and similar events..........	7113	45.0	55.9	72.2	1,699	2,467	3,127
Agents/managers for artists, athletes, and other public figures. ..	7114	36.3	38.5	37.1	1,300	1,678	2,026
Independent artists, writers, and performers............	7115	710.3	819.2	970.0	14,290	18,371	23,596
Museums, historical sites, and similar institutions............	712	5.8	6.5	5.7	95	122	138
Amusement, gambling, and recreation industries............	713	143.4	158.0	157.1	5,607	6,837	7,647
Amusement parks and arcades............	7131	4.7	4.3	4.1	251	248	251
Gambling industries............	7132	10.2	10.5	12.4	1,185	1,325	1,626
Other amusement and recreation services............	7139	128.5	143.2	140.5	4,171	5,265	5,770

[1] Data for 2010 are based on 2007 North American Industry Classification System; 2015 data are based on the 2012 NAICS; 2019 data are based on the 2017 NAICS. See text, Section 15.

Source: U.S. Census Bureau, Nonemployer Statistics, "All Sectors: Nonemployer Statistics by Legal Form of Organization and Receipts Size Class for the U.S., States, and Selected Geographies: 2019," <data.census.gov>, accessed June 2022.

Table 1251. Arts, Entertainment, and Recreation—Establishments, Employees, and Payroll by Kind of Business (NAICS Basis): 2019 and 2020

[Employees in thousands (2,504.4 represents 2,504,400); payroll in millions of dollars (94,162 represents $94,162,000,000). Covers establishments with paid employees. Excludes self-employed individuals, employees of private households, railroad employees, agricultural production employees, and most government employees. For statement on methodology, see Appendix III]

Kind of business	NAICS code [1]	Establishments		Employees [2] (1,000)		Payroll (mil. dol.)	
		2019	2020	2019	2020	2019	2020
Arts, entertainment, & recreation.............	71	**151,241**	**151,881**	**2,504.4**	**2,505.0**	**94,162**	**78,615**
Performing arts, spectator sports............	711	58,627	59,909	543.3	539.5	48,298	40,141
Performing arts companies............	7111	9,417	9,341	126.8	124.6	5,085	3,206
Theater companies & dinner theaters............	71111	3,385	3,239	71.0	69.4	2,464	1,420
Dance companies............	71112	710	751	11.1	11.1	333	268
Musical groups & artists............	71113	5,066	5,061	38.1	37.1	1,971	1,363
Other performing arts companies............	71119	256	290	6.6	6.9	317	156
Spectator sports............	7112	4,293	4,401	138.5	138.0	24,968	21,194
Sports teams & clubs............	711211	963	1,041	85.8	83.8	22,679	19,161
Racetracks............	711212	594	525	36.8	37.4	1,290	1,055
Other spectator sports............	711219	2,736	2,835	15.8	16.8	1,000	977
Promoters of performing arts, sports, & similar events............	7113	8,320	8,175	197.9	195.2	5,854	4,720
Promoters of performing arts, sports, & similar events with facilities............	71131	3,768	3,757	159.6	159.0	4,016	3,258
Promoters of performing arts, sports, & similar events without facilities............	71132	4,552	4,418	38.3	36.2	1,838	1,462
Agents/managers for artists, athletes, and other public figures............	7114	4,346	4,523	23.1	25.2	2,931	2,539
Independent artists, writers, & performers............	7115	32,251	33,469	57.0	56.6	9,460	8,483
Museums, historical sites, & similar institutions............	712	7,759	7,710	159.8	160.6	5,787	5,268
Museums............	71211	5,266	5,210	97.8	97.7	3,642	3,327
Historical sites............	71212	1,116	1,112	13.0	12.7	395	333
Zoos & botanical gardens............	71213	687	681	41.2	42.1	1,451	1,323
Nature parks & other similar institutions............	71219	690	707	7.9	8.1	298	284
Amusement, gambling, & recreation industries............	713	84,855	84,262	1,801.3	1,804.9	40,077	33,206
Amusement parks & arcades............	7131	3,922	3,917	240.0	229.3	5,924	4,354
Amusement & theme parks............	71311	516	567	172.5	162.6	4,766	3,604
Amusement arcades............	71312	3,406	3,350	67.4	66.7	1,157	750
Gambling industries............	7132	3,105	3,130	137.2	138.5	5,096	4,545
Casinos (except casino hotels)............	71321	287	311	86.0	87.4	3,273	2,861
Other gambling industries............	71329	2,818	2,819	51.2	51.1	1,823	1,685
Other amusement & recreation services............	7139	77,828	77,215	1,424.2	1,437.1	29,058	24,307
Golf courses & country clubs............	71391	10,544	10,261	295.1	299.8	9,808	9,291
Skiing facilities............	71392	330	346	73.2	69.4	949	961
Marinas............	71393	3,760	3,714	29.3	28.7	1,202	1,203
Fitness & recreational sports centers............	71394	39,297	39,562	777.6	786.9	12,014	8,941
Bowling centers............	71395	3,489	3,370	71.6	69.6	1,190	776
All other amusement & recreation industries............	71399	20,408	19,962	177.4	182.8	3,894	3,135

[1] Data based on 2017 North American Industry Classification System (NAICS) see text, this section and Section 15. [2] For employees on the payroll for the period including March 12.

Source: U.S. Census Bureau, County Business Patterns, "All Sectors: County Business Patterns by Legal Form of Organization and Employment Size Class for U.S., States, and Selected Geographies," <data.census.gov>, accessed April 2022.

Table 1252. Arts and Culture Production—Real Value Added In Chained (2012) Dollars and Employment by Industry: 2010 to 2020

[Value in millions of dollars (677,897 represents $677,897,000,000); employment in thousands (4,721 represents 4,721,000)]

Industry	2010	2015	2017	2018	2019	2020
REAL VALUE ADDED, CHAINED (2012) DOLLARS (Million dollars)						
Total	677,897	767,370	819,551	846,864	875,452	819,815
Core arts and cultural production	136,959	161,778	171,363	183,193	190,434	151,252
Performing arts	52,820	62,761	66,777	70,901	73,135	45,450
Performing arts companies	12,486	12,216	13,137	13,343	13,473	6,615
Promoters of performing arts and similar events	9,643	11,927	13,273	14,041	14,331	3,895
Agents/managers for artists	3,046	3,995	4,207	4,500	4,801	3,176
Independent artists, writers, and performers	27,635	34,653	36,167	39,031	40,539	32,195
Museums	5,704	6,346	6,954	7,425	7,160	5,584
Design services [1]	69,836	84,186	88,847	95,768	100,668	94,239
Advertising	27,019	28,876	32,256	35,168	36,590	34,833
Architectural services	14,129	18,496	19,436	20,861	22,706	22,582
Landscape architectural services	2,175	2,531	2,729	2,933	3,134	3,153
Interior design services	7,224	10,418	10,015	11,065	11,469	9,042
Industrial design services	1,285	1,855	1,820	1,812	1,944	1,568
Graphic design services	6,931	8,725	8,305	8,151	8,722	7,280
Computer systems design	2,086	3,399	4,289	4,850	5,143	5,125
Photography and photofinishing services	8,353	8,782	9,020	10,003	9,916	10,032
Fine arts education	2,789	2,144	2,326	2,561	2,906	1,821
Education services	5,856	6,437	6,552	6,704	6,855	6,564
Supporting arts and cultural production	520,553	586,107	628,999	643,928	665,198	652,440
Art support services [1]	101,725	97,810	99,556	100,145	100,483	97,801
Rental and leasing	5,367	4,656	4,707	4,863	4,974	4,097
Grant-making and giving services	776	899	905	883	905	778
Unions	1,059	1,104	1,136	1,160	1,216	982
Government	94,237	90,878	92,473	92,877	93,077	91,761
Information services [1]	322,350	391,550	426,179	439,481	461,417	462,568
Publishing	77,369	84,350	94,720	102,066	106,265	107,003
Motion pictures	77,669	75,096	77,204	69,771	69,243	56,879
Sound recording	12,598	11,746	13,370	12,984	14,796	11,809
Broadcasting	121,386	139,516	143,650	141,307	140,455	138,410
Manufacturing [1]	15,166	15,341	15,481	16,135	15,129	13,485
Jewelry and silverware manufacturing	3,252	2,688	2,917	3,288	2,741	2,585
Printed goods manufacturing	7,042	6,395	6,318	6,245	6,063	5,309
Musical instruments manufacturing	719	610	759	791	727	574
Custom architectural woodwork & metalwork manufacturing	2,142	2,693	2,795	2,837	2,740	2,174
Construction	15,391	11,643	13,371	13,045	13,148	9,947
Wholesale and transportation industries	20,413	19,572	19,365	19,635	19,702	17,396
Retail industries	31,036	33,178	35,175	34,897	34,450	31,487
All other industries	34,966	37,451	40,751	42,287	43,832	42,330
EMPLOYMENT (1,000s)						
Total	4,721	4,982	5,121	5,149	5,195	4,591
Core arts and cultural production	1,012	1,178	1,238	1,270	1,297	1,066
Performing arts	241	280	300	313	322	204
Performing arts companies	108	116	122	125	128	78
Promoters of performing arts and similar events	78	99	113	120	124	68
Agents/managers for artists	10	13	15	16	16	13
Independent artists, writers, and performers	45	53	51	52	54	44
Museums	118	138	147	152	155	120
Design services [1]	483	554	569	573	578	525
Advertising	131	172	175	175	175	157
Architectural services	117	131	141	144	147	141
Landscape architectural services	30	33	32	32	33	33
Interior design services	28	38	42	44	46	43
Industrial design services	12	17	19	19	19	18
Graphic design services	58	60	61	60	58	53
Computer systems design	17	22	24	25	26	26
Photography and photofinishing services	84	72	66	64	64	46
Fine arts education	88	113	125	134	143	118
Education services	81	93	96	98	99	98
Supporting arts and cultural production	3,546	3,647	3,728	3,723	3,742	3,392
Art support services [1]	1,281	1,250	1,271	1,270	1,276	1,219
Rental and leasing	38	20	20	19	19	15
Grant-making and giving services	7	9	9	9	9	9
Unions	17	23	23	21	23	16
Government	1,216	1,195	1,216	1,217	1,221	1,177
Information services [1]	1,198	1,307	1,332	1,329	1,341	1,173
Publishing	338	322	316	314	318	299
Motion pictures	347	378	392	384	394	258
Sound recording	17	15	16	17	18	16
Broadcasting	405	441	436	429	414	392
Manufacturing [1]	172	177	174	171	167	145
Jewelry and silverware manufacturing	21	26	24	23	21	17
Printed goods manufacturing	91	77	74	69	68	56
Musical instruments manufacturing	9	10	10	10	10	9
Custom architectural woodwork & metalwork manufacturing	29	36	39	41	41	38
Construction	127	112	122	126	131	82
Wholesale and transportation industries	201	203	216	211	211	194
Retail industries	567	597	614	616	615	579
All other industries	163	157	155	156	155	133

[1] Includes other services or goods manufacturing, not shown separately.

Source: U.S. Bureau of Economic Analysis, "Arts and Cultural Production Satellite Account," <www.bea.gov/data/special-topics/arts-and-culture>, accessed March 2022.

Table 1253. Arts and Cultural Production—Summary by State: 2020

[In millions of dollars (876,665 represents $876,665,000,000); except employment (4,591 represents 4,591,000). Arts and cultural production is defined narrowly to include creative artistic activity; the goods and services produced by it; the goods and services produced in the support of it; and the construction of buildings in which it is taking place]

State	Total arts and cultural production industries [1]			Core arts and cultural production industries			Supporting arts and cultural production industries		
	Value added (mil. dol.) [2]	Employment (1,000)	Compensation (mil. dol.)	Value added (mil. dol.) [2]	Employment (1,000)	Compensation (mil. dol.)	Value added (mil. dol.) [2]	Employment (1,000)	Compensation (mil. dol.)
Total..............	876,665	4,591	445,975	167,764	1,066	94,039	689,043	3,392	341,423
Alabama...........	4,845	42	2,562	705	7	409	3,901	33	2,034
Alaska.............	1,281	11	974	105	1	68	1,137	9	885
Arizona............	9,646	79	5,590	1,913	17	1,061	7,369	59	4,329
Arkansas..........	2,815	31	1,683	523	5	287	2,141	25	1,324
California..........	225,046	681	108,684	48,238	164	26,523	174,423	502	80,749
Colorado...........	14,420	97	8,737	2,965	(D)	(D)	11,081	72	6,831
Connecticut.......	8,936	49	5,057	1,719	(D)	(D)	6,943	35	3,927
Delaware..........	860	7	487	172	2	106	616	5	346
Dist. of Columbia...	11,890	53	8,212	2,812	14	1,614	8,985	39	6,537
Florida.............	32,468	233	17,515	7,991	60	4,114	23,343	165	12,824
Georgia............	23,780	134	11,438	4,570	29	2,265	18,602	101	8,867
Hawaii.............	2,569	18	1,440	563	5	339	1,940	12	1,067
Idaho..............	1,857	19	1,138	323	4	186	1,448	15	908
Illinois............	26,556	190	15,380	6,752	(D)	(D)	18,931	134	11,148
Indiana............	7,634	78	4,618	1,313	(D)	(D)	5,927	61	3,678
Iowa...............	4,166	38	2,374	632	8	372	3,325	29	1,906
Kansas............	4,184	41	2,657	587	7	342	3,408	33	2,229
Kentucky..........	5,623	47	2,796	715	8	388	4,675	37	2,291
Louisiana..........	5,458	46	2,805	909	(D)	(D)	4,296	35	2,194
Maine..............	1,607	15	902	393	4	214	1,144	11	651
Maryland...........	10,167	68	6,104	1,896	16	1,161	7,910	50	4,761
Massachusetts.....	23,749	125	13,643	4,649	38	3,119	18,549	84	10,193
Michigan...........	13,429	106	7,798	2,965	27	1,880	9,856	75	5,613
Minnesota.........	10,882	82	6,415	2,431	20	1,372	8,042	59	4,824
Mississippi........	2,074	23	1,197	239	3	139	1,708	19	1,001
Missouri...........	9,501	84	5,450	2,098	(D)	(D)	7,035	62	4,057
Montana...........	1,773	15	995	316	3	181	1,405	12	788
Nebraska..........	3,001	27	1,792	579	6	351	2,293	20	1,382
Nevada............	8,053	37	3,008	1,377	8	658	6,530	28	2,265
New Hampshire. ..	2,899	20	1,657	447	4	278	2,360	15	1,329
New Jersey........	20,826	120	11,659	3,407	26	1,919	16,788	90	9,396
New Mexico........	2,589	22	1,404	329	4	209	2,170	17	1,151
New York..........	126,720	436	53,376	27,420	133	14,675	97,932	295	37,894
North Carolina.....	16,549	116	8,827	2,894	25	1,711	13,110	87	6,825
North Dakota......	1,325	12	798	153	2	92	1,117	10	679
Ohio...............	21,179	153	9,878	3,447	35	2,127	17,003	113	7,390
Oklahoma..........	4,146	39	2,364	798	7	409	3,129	31	1,865
Oregon............	7,984	61	4,753	1,640	14	986	6,105	45	3,635
Pennsylvania......	25,749	157	13,045	4,454	42	2,724	20,472	110	9,893
Rhode Island......	1,945	16	1,064	366	4	234	1,516	11	797
South Carolina.....	5,949	50	3,236	1,086	10	585	4,624	38	2,530
South Dakota......	1,128	13	739	174	2	101	901	10	612
Tennessee.........	11,881	81	5,884	2,695	21	1,519	8,796	58	4,162
Texas..............	49,185	351	26,226	9,035	72	5,173	38,323	267	20,134
Utah...............	6,824	61	4,016	1,216	(D)	(D)	5,437	45	3,219
Vermont...........	985	10	637	230	3	152	721	7	467
Virginia............	16,207	110	8,688	2,860	23	1,662	12,820	84	6,749
Washington........	62,393	180	28,929	2,753	(D)	(D)	59,215	155	27,037
West Virginia......	1,279	14	819	100	2	62	1,101	12	720
Wisconsin.........	9,607	83	5,730	1,657	16	912	7,576	64	4,631
Wyoming...........	1,046	11	795	150	1	81	864	9	700

D Withheld to avoid disclosing data on individual companies. [1] Total arts and cultural production industries includes core industries, supporting industries, and, not shown separately, industries with secondary production that is designated as artistic and cultural. [2] Nominal, not adjusted for inflation.

Source: U.S. Bureau of Economic Analysis, "Arts and Cultural Production Satellite Account," <www.bea.gov/data/special-topics/arts-and-culture>, accessed March 2022.

Table 1254. Broadway Shows and Tours—Selected Data: 2000 to 2022

[In units, as indicated (603 represents $603,000,000). For season ending in year shown. Due to the coronavirus disease 2019 (COVID-19) pandemic, the Broadway theatre seasons for 2019-2020, 2020-2021, and 2021-2022 were either shortened or cancelled altogether; see source for details]

Item	Unit	2000	2010	2015	2016	2017	2018	2019	2020	2021	2022
Broadway shows:											
New productions....................	Number	36	39	37	39	45	33	38	33	([4])	39
Attendance.........................	Millions	11.4	11.9	13.1	13.3	13.3	13.8	14.8	11.1	([4])	6.7
Playing weeks [1, 2]...................	Number	1,464	1,464	1,626	1,648	1,580	1,624	1,737	1,282	([4])	946
Gross ticket sales..................	Mil. dol.	603	1,020	1,365	1,373	1,449	1,697	1,829	1,358	([4])	845
Broadway road tours: [3]											
Attendance.........................	Millions	11.4	15.9	13.7	14.0	13.9	17.0	18.5	(NA)	([4])	(NA)
Playing weeks......................	Number	854	1,250	953	1,014	983	1,125	1,188	(NA)	([4])	(NA)
Gross ticket sales..................	Mil. dol.	553	947	957	981	1,007	1,416	1,633	(NA)	([4])	(NA)

[1] All shows (new productions and holdovers from previous seasons). [2] Eight performances constitute one playing week. [3] North American Tours include U.S. and Canadian companies. [4] Broadway was dark for the 2020-2021 season.

Source: The Broadway League, New York, NY ©. See also <www.broadwayleague.com>.

Table 1255. Arts and Humanities—Selected Federal Aid Programs: 1990 to 2021

[In millions of dollars (170.8 represents $170,800,000), except as indicated. For fiscal year ending September 30. FY2010 includes funds from the American Recovery and Reinvestment Act. FY2020 includes funding provided under the Coronavirus Aid, Relief, and Economic Security (CARES) Act of 2020. FY2021 includes funds provided under the American Rescue Plan (ARP) Act of 2021]

Type of fund and program	1990	2000	2010	2015	2017	2018	2019	2020	2021
National Endowment for the Arts:									
Funds available [1]	170.8	85.2	153.1	127.1	129.5	124.3	128.1	210.6	269.5
Program appropriation [2]	152.3	79.6	138.7	116.6	119.2	120.7	122.9	203.9	264.2
Grants awarded (number) [3]	4,252.0	1,906.0	2,731.0	2,346.0	2,509.0	2,306.0	2,381.0	3,335.0	2,551.0
Funds obligated [4,5]	157.6	83.5	141.1	118.4	128.0	121.7	122.9	207.4	186.1
National Endowment for the Humanities:									
Funds available [1]	140.6	102.6	146.6	129.8	128.7	134.4	145.0	225.4	292.6
Program appropriation	114.2	82.7	125.7	108.1	111.2	113.4	115.0	195.5	255.8
Matching funds [6]	26.3	15.1	14.3	10.9	10.7	11.3	11.3	12.5	15.0
Grants awarded (number)	2,195.0	1,230.0	1,204.0	822.0	813.0	836.0	849.0	1,207.0	1,020.0
Funds obligated [4]	141.0	100.0	142.7	121.5	120.7	116.1	126.1	197.6	202.0
Education programs	16.3	13.0	16.0	13.8	13.3	10.3	11.7	25.9	12.8
State partnership	29.6	30.6	49.1	42.6	46.5	47.2	48.7	81.4	105.0
Research grants	22.5	6.9	12.5	10.1	10.1	9.4	10.3	8.9	29.8
Fellowships	15.3	6.1	6.8	7.0	5.8	5.9	6.2	7.1	7.5
Challenge [7]	14.6	10.8	10.5	7.8	6.9	4.8	12.1	8.8	7.2
Public programs	25.4	11.8	19.4	17.6	14.4	13.4	12.8	29.5	15.0
Digital Humanities	(X)	(X)	4.9	4.7	4.7	4.8	4.9	8.4	5.0
A More Perfect Union initiative	(X)	(X)	(X)	(X)	(X)	(X)	(X)	2.7	6.0
Preservation and access	17.5	20.7	22.6	17.1	15.4	20.3	19.4	24.9	19.7

X Not applicable. [1] Includes other program funds not shown separately. Excludes administrative funds. [2] FY1990–FY1996 include Regular Program Funds, Treasury Funds, Challenge Grant Funds, and Policy, Planning, and Research Funds. FY1997 includes Regular Program Funds, Matching Grant Funds, and Policy, Research and Technology Funds. FY1998–FY2000 includes Regular Program Funds and Matching Grant Funds. [3] Excludes cooperative agreements and interagency agreements. FY2021 includes grants amended with funding provided under the CARES Act and the ARP Act. [4] Includes obligations for new grants, supplemental awards on previous years' grants, cooperative agreements, and interagency agreements. Excludes obligations funded with administrative funds. [5] Beginning with 1997 data, the grantmaking structure changed from discipline-based categories to thematic ones. [6] Represents federal funds obligated only upon receipt or certification by endowment of matching nonfederal gifts. Funds for matching grants are not allocated by program area because they are awarded on a grant-by-grant basis. [7] Program designed to stimulate new sources and higher levels of giving to institutions for the purpose of guaranteeing long-term stability and financial independence. Program currently requires a match of at least 3 private dollars to each federal dollar.

Source: U.S. National Endowment for the Arts, unpublished data; and U.S. National Endowment for the Humanities, unpublished data.

Table 1256. State Arts Agency Legislative Appropriations: 2021 and 2022

[In thousands of dollars (402,761 represents $402,761,000). For fiscal year ending June 30 in most states. The National Assembly of State Arts Agencies (NASAA) is the membership organization of the nations' state and jurisdictional arts agencies. Legislative appropriations include funds designated to the state arts agency by state legislatures. These include line items, which are not controlled by the agency but passed through to designated entities. State arts agencies also receive monies from other sources including other state funds, the federal government (primarily the National Endowment for the Arts), private funds, and legislative earmarks. Minus sign (-) indicates decrease in spending]

State	Legislative appropriations including line items 2021, revised	Legislative appropriations including line items 2022, enacted	Percent change, 2021 to 2022	State	Legislative appropriations including line items 2021, revised	Legislative appropriations including line items 2022, enacted	Percent change, 2021 to 2022	State	Legislative appropriations including line items 2021, revised	Legislative appropriations including line items 2022, enacted	Percent change, 2021 to 2022
U.S.	**402,761**	**820,846**	**103.8**	LA	2,181	2,171	-0.4	OR	3,085	4,078	32.2
AL	6,421	7,048	9.8	ME	966	1,020	5.5	PA	10,457	10,542	0.8
AK [1]	734	744	1.3	MD	23,410	26,334	12.5	RI	2,488	2,241	-9.9
AZ [1]	–	–	(NA)	MA	18,180	21,375	17.6	SC [10]	4,366	45,281	937.1
AR	1,452	1,356	-6.6	MI	8,350	9,850	18.0	SD	898	1,057	17.7
CA [2]	32,781	169,525	417.1	MN	40,691	41,913	3.0	TN [11]	8,431	9,540	13.2
CO [3]	1,300	2,023	55.6	MS	1,508	1,659	10.0	TX	10,215	10,165	-0.5
CT [4,14]	5,425	34,289	532.1	MO	6,630	7,079	6.8	UT [12]	5,377	9,356	74.0
DE	3,867	3,880	0.3	MT [14]	528	558	5.7	VT	719	786	9.4
DC	33,250	37,523	12.8	NE [6,14]	1,530	2,542	66.1	VA [14]	3,981	3,992	0.3
FL	17,212	30,741	78.6	NV	1,189	1,954	64.3	WA	2,574	2,634	2.3
GA	1,502	1,502	–	NH	817	822	0.7	WV	934	927	-0.7
HI	6,530	7,757	18.8	NJ [7]	20,263	61,455	203.3	WI [13]	813	807	-0.7
ID [5]	875	883	1.0	NM	1,483	1,418	-4.4	WY	929	929	–
IL [5]	13,272	63,880	381.3	NY [8]	45,174	106,622	136.0	AS	114	154	34.6
IN	3,920	3,632	-7.3	NC [9]	8,278	23,278	181.2	GU	234	494	111.2
IA [14]	1,467	1,467	–	ND [14]	814	831	2.1	MP	125	233	86.4
KS	500	500	–	OH	16,816	20,000	18.9	PR	12,997	14,873	14.4
KY	1,538	1,740	13.1	OK	2,796	3,004	7.4	VI	375	382	1.9

– Represents zero. NA Not available. [1] AZ: The Arizona Commission on the Arts did not receive an appropriation in FY22, but did receive $1.2 million (mil.) in other state funds. [2] CA: In FY22, the California Arts Council received one-time funding that includes $100 mil. in general fund investments for creative workforce and youth development programs to be spent over three years. [3] CO: Figures do not include $15.5 mil. in state funds for the Colorado Artist Relief Program and $65 mil. in funding for the Community Revitalization Grant Program. [4] CT: State allocated $32.8 mil. in line items in FY22. [5] IL: The Illinois Arts Council Agency was allocated more than $50 mil. in one-time appropriations for capital projects in FY22. [6] NE: Increase of $1 mil. to the Nebraska Arts Council appropriation to fund the agency's new Creative Districts Certification and Grants program. [7] NJ: For FY22, the New Jersey State Council on the Arts received $24 mil. for the City of Jersey City. [8] NY: The FY22 appropriation includes $40 mil. in recovery funds and $20 mil. in capital projects funds. [9] NC: The state budget includes an additional $15 mil. in ARP Act funding for the North Carolina Arts Council in FY22 and another $1 mil. in year two of the budget. [10] SC: In addition to the increased line items, the South Carolina Arts Commission's general appropriation received an additional $1.5 mil. and $2 mil. in nonrecurring funding in FY22. [11] TN: The Tennessee Arts Commission received a three year, $1 mil. grant from the Department of Health Nursing Home Civil Monetary Penalty Fund. The general assembly authorized expenditures of the total amount in FY21 and $750,000 in FY22. [12] UT: The Utah Division of Arts & Museums received multiyear grants from the National Endowment for the Humanities and the Institute of Museum and Library Services. [13] WI: Appropriation figures are contingent upon the legislature's Joint Committee on Finance to supply matching funds for the agency's NEA Partnership Agreement. [14] Figure reflects state arts agency appropriation only and does not include appropriation to the state's cultural endowment.

Source: National Assembly of State Arts Agencies, *State Arts Agency Revenues, Fiscal Year 2022* ©, February 2022. See also <www.nasaa-arts.org>.

Table 1257. Attendance/Participation Rates for Various Arts Activities by Selected Characteristics: 2017

[In percent. For persons 18 years old and over. Represents attendance at least once in the prior twelve months. Excludes elementary and high school performances]

Characteristic	Adult population	Jazz concert	Classical music concert	Musicals	Non-musical plays	Art museums/galleries	Craft/visual art festivals	Parks/historic buildings [1]
Total	**100.0**	**8.6**	**8.6**	**16.5**	**9.4**	**23.7**	**23.8**	**28.3**
Sex:								
Male	48.2	8.7	6.8	12.8	8.2	21.1	19.5	26.6
Female	51.8	8.5	10.3	19.9	10.5	26.2	27.8	29.9
Race and ethnicity:								
White alone	63.9	9.2	10.4	20.2	11.6	26.7	29.6	33.2
African American alone	11.8	12.1	3.9	10.1	7.7	17.1	12.7	18.6
Hispanic	16.0	5.8	5.5	9.7	4.0	16.2	12.8	17.1
Asian	5.9	3.9	8.5	9.4	4.8	26.2	13.2	24.9
Other alone	2.4	[2] 6.3	[2] 5.5	11.5	[2] 7.0	22.1	20.8	27.4
Age:								
18 to 24 years old	12.0	8.6	8.0	16.0	8.9	24.0	18.9	24.6
25 to 34 years old	17.8	8.8	7.5	15.1	8.0	25.3	24.4	29.2
35 to 44 years old	16.2	8.2	7.5	17.0	8.8	27.3	22.3	32.0
45 to 54 years old	16.9	8.6	8.2	15.1	10.0	23.4	24.2	31.1
55 to 64 years old	16.9	9.7	9.0	17.9	9.7	21.6	26.4	27.8
65 to 74 years old	11.9	9.2	11.5	20.2	11.4	23.6	29.1	28.9
75 years old and older	8.1	5.8	10.1	13.6	9.8	17.3	18.2	18.0
Education:								
Grade school	3.7	(S)	(S)	[2] 1.8	(S)	[2] 3.1	[2] 4.5	6.2
Some high school	6.7	[2] 2.6	(S)	[2] 4.0	[2] 2.2	6.7	8.1	8.8
High school graduate	29.4	4.6	3.7	8.2	4.2	10.4	14.8	17.1
Some college	28.0	8.0	7.2	16.2	8.2	23.0	25.1	27.1
College graduate	20.7	13.7	14.7	26.1	16.0	39.5	34.3	42.7
Graduate school	11.5	17.5	21.9	34.0	21.6	49.0	40.9	53.9

[1] Visiting historic parks or monuments or touring buildings or neighborhoods for the historic or design value. [2] Interpret data with caution.

Source: U.S. National Endowment for the Arts, *US Patterns of Arts Participation: A Full Report from the 2017 Survey of Public Participation in the Arts*, December 2019. See also <www.arts.gov/publications/state-level-estimates-arts-participation-patterns-2017-2018>.

Table 1258. Personal Participation in Various Arts or Creative Activities and Reading by Selected Characteristics: 2017

[In percent. Represents creating or performing or reading at least once in the prior 12 months. Based on the 2017 household survey of Public Participation in the Arts. Data are subject to sampling error; see source]

Characteristic	Art-making activities				Took art lessons or classes	Reading				
	Any art-making [1]	Performing art [1]	Visual art [2]	Creative art [3]		Any books	Novels or short stories	Poetry	Listen to audio-books	Read any books using electronic devices
Total	**53.7**	**40.0**	**32.7**	**6.5**	**9.5**	**52.7**	**41.8**	**11.7**	**16.5**	**23.5**
Sex:										
Male	49.8	35.5	26.3	5.8	7.4	44.3	33.0	8.7	14.2	19.2
Female	57.3	44.2	38.8	7.3	11.5	60.5	50.0	14.5	18.6	27.5
Race and ethnicity:										
White alone	58.2	41.2	37.6	7.6	9.9	59.6	48.1	11.4	17.8	25.9
African American alone	49.3	43.4	21.7	5.6	11.2	46.5	30.8	15.3	13.4	21.3
Hispanic	44.6	36.1	24.6	3.9	5.6	32.2	26.8	9.7	11.5	15.4
Asian alone	37.8	29.4	23.1	3.2	10.5	44.8	36.1	12.6	19.7	25.8
Other alone	62.6	44.9	38.0	9.2	15.7	53.7	39.6	14.2	21.2	19.0
Age:										
18 to 24 years old	64.7	46.1	37.2	11.7	19.2	47.3	38.7	17.5	17.1	25.7
25 to 34 years old	64.7	45.8	36.5	9.2	10.5	52.6	42.6	12.3	20.3	25.9
35 to 44 years old	50.4	38.5	31.9	7.1	9.8	53.6	42.4	11.4	18.5	26.3
45 to 54 years old	51.4	38.7	29.8	4.3	8.1	50.5	38.3	9.9	16.8	25.1
55 to 64 years old	49.4	37.2	31.0	5.0	7.7	53.6	41.8	10.6	15.3	22.0
65 to 74 years old	55.2	38.9	34.2	4.4	6.4	57.2	46.8	10.3	13.2	19.4
75 years old and older	37.0	33.5	27.1	3.1	4.7	55.4	42.9	11.0	9.1	14.2

[1] Includes singing, dancing, playing a musical instrument, or acting. [2] Includes painting, drawing, sculpting, or making prints; photography; videography; animation, digital art, computer graphics, or video games; pottery, ceramics, or jewelry; doing leatherwork, metalwork, or woodwork; weaving, crocheting, quilting, needleworking, knitting, or sewing; and scrapbooking, origami, or other paper-based art. [3] Includes through email, websites, or social media.

Source: U.S. National Endowment for the Arts, *U.S. Patterns of Arts Participation: A Full Report from the 2017 Survey of Public Participation in the Arts*, December 2019. See also <www.arts.gov/publications/state-level-estimates-arts-participation-patterns-2017-2018>.

Table 1259. Outdoor Recreation Sector Gross Output by Activity: 2015 to 2020

[In millions of current dollars (733,925 represents $733,925,000,000)]

Activity	2015	2016	2017	2018	2019	2020
Total outdoor recreation	**733,925**	**742,697**	**781,958**	**825,406**	**844,968**	**688,573**
Total core outdoor recreation	**383,172**	**391,541**	**412,474**	**429,354**	**436,627**	**385,665**
Conventional outdoor recreation	243,426	250,266	261,055	268,248	271,581	263,232
Bicycling	3,427	3,584	3,671	3,651	4,156	4,694
Boating/fishing	35,803	39,185	41,632	43,407	44,730	56,698
Canoeing	118	129	136	136	159	165
Kayaking	691	710	773	830	866	1,018
Fishing (excludes boating)	5,903	8,076	9,218	9,711	9,815	9,651
Sailing	2,101	2,273	2,289	2,318	2,512	1,841
Other boating	26,990	27,995	29,216	30,412	31,378	44,023
Climbing/hiking/tent camping	5,834	5,692	6,664	6,782	7,240	7,186
Equestrian	8,054	8,836	9,677	11,474	10,330	9,179
Hunting/shooting/trapping	13,331	15,651	15,841	15,287	15,311	14,888
Motorcycling/ATVing	18,381	18,277	18,880	19,421	18,547	18,181
Recreational flying	2,636	2,489	2,591	2,290	2,373	2,746
RVing	31,911	33,624	35,587	36,553	36,463	36,133
Snow activities	10,754	10,667	10,971	11,811	12,384	9,209
Skiing	3,439	3,438	3,403	3,569	3,849	2,547
Snowboarding	2,977	3,064	3,146	3,302	3,568	2,305
Other snow activities [1]	4,339	4,165	4,422	4,940	4,966	4,357
Other conventional outdoor recreation activities	17,419	16,446	16,819	17,439	18,591	19,105
Multi-use apparel and accessories (conventional) [2]	95,877	95,817	98,722	100,131	101,455	85,213
Other outdoor recreation	139,746	141,275	151,419	161,106	165,046	122,434
Amusement parks/water parks	14,464	15,702	18,823	21,280	22,401	10,792
Festivals/sporting events/concerts	24,084	24,845	27,138	28,322	29,561	16,874
Field sports	5,928	6,006	6,197	6,502	6,868	6,385
Game areas (includes golfing and tennis)	33,380	33,699	35,177	36,516	38,521	30,079
Guided tours/outfitted travel	26,654	25,565	27,577	31,616	29,849	23,911
Productive activities (includes gardening)	10,932	11,392	11,614	11,469	11,895	12,081
Other outdoor recreation activities [3]	17,313	17,017	17,647	18,186	18,676	15,254
Multi-use apparel and accessories (other) [2]	6,989	7,049	7,246	7,215	7,274	7,059
Supporting outdoor recreation	**350,753**	**351,156**	**369,484**	**396,052**	**408,341**	**302,908**
Construction	10,358	10,274	9,591	10,537	11,590	11,821
Local trips [4]	64,207	61,435	66,009	71,560	71,556	61,503
Travel and tourism [5]	239,339	241,061	254,223	272,288	283,772	186,983
Food and beverages	36,280	38,106	40,073	42,256	44,609	37,866
Lodging	54,797	57,100	58,470	60,986	63,207	36,677
Shopping and souvenirs	43,097	43,081	45,087	46,821	47,498	49,404
Transportation	105,165	102,775	110,594	122,225	128,459	63,035
Government expenditures	36,849	38,386	39,660	41,666	41,423	42,600
Federal Government	3,799	3,976	4,029	4,364	3,171	3,023
State and local government	33,050	34,410	35,631	37,303	38,251	39,578

[1] Dog mushing, sleighing, snowmobiling, snow shoeing, and snow tubing. [2] Backpacks, bug spray, coolers, general outdoor clothing, GPS equipment, hydration equipment, lighting, sports racks, sunscreen, watches, and other miscellaneous gear and equipment. [3] Agritourism, augmented reality games, beachgoing, disc golf, hot springs soaking, kite flying, model airplane/rocket/UAV, paintball, photography, stargazing/astronomy, swimming, therapeutic programs, water polo, and yard sports. [4] Trip expenses less than 50 miles away from home, including food and beverages, lodging, shopping and souvenirs, and transportation. [5] Expenses for travel at least 50 miles away from home.

Source: U.S. Bureau of Economic Analysis, Satellite Accounts, *Outdoor Recreation Satellite Account, U.S. and States, 2020*, November 2021. See also <www.bea.gov/data/special-topics/outdoor-recreation>.

Table 1260. Personal Consumption Expenditures for Recreation: 1990 to 2020

[In billions of dollars (314.7 represents $314,700,000,000), except percent. Represents market value of purchases of goods and services by individuals and nonprofit institutions]

Type of product or service	1990	2000	2005	2010	2015	2019	2020
Total recreation expenditures	**314.7**	**633.7**	**805.2**	**884.4**	**1,045.6**	**1,261.5**	**1,176.9**
Percent of total personal consumption [1]	8.3	9.4	9.2	8.6	8.5	8.7	8.4
Video and audio equipment, computers, and related services	81.1	181.2	240.0	275.5	313.9	388.9	421.8
Video and audio equipment	43.7	79.9	101.4	83.2	77.5	92.2	100.4
Information processing equipment	9.6	44.1	68.4	95.0	111.6	156.9	177.6
Services related to video and audio goods and computers	27.8	57.2	70.2	97.3	124.8	139.8	143.8
Sports and recreational goods and related services	74.2	146.0	184.1	177.4	226.3	259.4	290.7
Sports and recreational vehicles	16.6	34.9	49.1	35.8	52.0	63.5	75.1
Other sporting and recreational goods	55.4	106.8	130.0	137.2	168.6	189.6	211.4
Maintenance and repair of recreational vehicles and sports equipment	2.1	4.2	4.9	4.4	5.6	6.3	4.1
Membership clubs, sports centers, parks, theaters, and museums	49.7	91.9	117.9	146.1	177.7	220.3	104.0
Membership clubs and participant sports centers	14.3	26.4	34.3	40.9	49.6	59.0	41.6
Amusement parks, campgrounds, and related services	19.2	31.1	33.6	40.1	54.2	70.2	29.9
Admissions to specified spectator amusements	14.4	30.6	43.7	58.7	65.4	81.3	24.1
Motion picture theaters	5.1	8.6	9.7	12.3	13.3	13.7	2.9
Live entertainment, excluding sports	4.5	10.4	18.3	26.7	28.9	38.4	11.2
Spectator sports	4.8	11.6	15.7	19.7	23.1	29.2	10.0
Museums and libraries	1.9	3.8	6.4	6.5	8.4	9.9	8.3
Magazines, newspapers, books, and stationery	47.3	81.0	85.0	74.8	77.0	99.2	113.5
Gambling	23.7	67.6	96.1	109.4	125.7	141.7	110.1
Pets, pet products, and related services	18.8	39.7	57.2	76.2	98.4	118.2	118.2
Photographic goods and services	16.7	19.7	17.7	15.2	15.9	17.1	12.0
Package tours [2]	3.2	6.7	7.2	9.8	10.9	16.8	6.7

[1] See Table 716. [2] Consists of tour operators' and travel agents' margins. Purchases of travel and accommodations included in tours are accounted for separately in other personal consumption expenditures categories.

Source: U.S. Bureau of Economic Analysis, National Income and Product Accounts Tables, "Table 2.5.5. Personal Consumption Expenditures by Function," <www.bea.gov/iTable/index_nipa.cfm>, accessed July 2021.

Table 1261. Expenditures Per Consumer Unit for Entertainment and Reading: 1985 to 2020

[Data are annual averages. In dollars, except as indicated. Based on the Consumer Expenditure Survey (CES). For description of survey, see text, Section 13; also see headnote, Table 727. For composition of regions, see map, inside front cover]

| Year and characteristic | Entertainment and reading | | Entertainment | | | | Reading |
	Total	Percent of total expenditures	Total	Fees and admissions	Audio and visual equipment and services	Other supplies, equipment & services [1]	
1985	1,311	5.6	1,170	320	371	479	141
1990	1,575	5.6	1,422	371	454	597	153
1995	1,775	5.5	1,612	433	542	637	163
2000	2,009	5.3	1,863	515	622	727	146
2005	2,514	5.4	2,388	588	888	912	126
2006	2,493	5.2	2,376	606	906	863	117
2007	2,816	5.7	2,698	658	987	1,053	118
2008	2,951	5.8	2,835	616	1,036	1,183	116
2009	2,803	5.7	2,693	628	975	1,090	110
2010	2,604	5.4	2,504	581	954	970	100
2011	2,687	5.4	2,572	594	977	1,001	115
2012	2,714	5.3	2,605	614	979	1,011	109
2013	2,584	5.1	2,482	569	964	949	102
2014	2,831	5.3	2,728	636	1,051	1,041	103
2015	2,956	5.3	2,842	652	1,084	1,106	114
2016	3,031	5.3	2,913	681	1,085	1,146	118
2017	3,313	5.5	3,203	750	985	1,468	110
2018	3,334	5.4	3,226	766	1,030	1,430	108
2019	3,182	5.0	3,090	880	1,000	1,210	92
2020, total	**3,026**	**4.9**	**2,912**	**425**	**1,049**	**1,438**	**114**
Age of reference person:							
Under 25 years old	1,317	3.5	1,266	113	522	632	51
25 to 34 years old	2,655	4.6	2,570	298	885	1,388	85
35 to 44 years old	3,729	5.0	3,628	703	1,086	1,839	101
45 to 54 years old	3,291	4.4	3,175	597	1,147	1,431	116
55 to 64 years old	3,622	5.6	3,521	363	1,192	1,967	101
65 years old and older	2,450	5.1	2,293	302	1,034	957	157
65 to 74 years old	2,854	5.5	2,723	327	1,083	1,313	131
75 years old and over	1,878	4.6	1,682	267	965	450	196
Hispanic or Latino origin of reference person:							
Hispanic	1,799	3.4	1,740	182	810	748	59
Non-Hispanic	3,228	5.1	3,105	465	1,089	1,552	123
Race of reference person: [2]							
White, and all other races [2]	3,316	5.2	3,194	466	1,072	1,656	122
Asian	2,101	3.1	1,998	479	824	696	103
Black	1,564	3.3	1,495	148	983	364	69
Region of residence:							
Northeast	3,241	4.7	3,113	421	1,077	1,614	128
Midwest	3,481	5.8	3,368	392	1,126	1,850	113
South	2,484	4.5	2,378	377	1,005	995	106
West	3,358	5.0	3,242	539	1,031	1,672	116
Size of consumer unit:							
One person	2,035	5.2	1,938	170	733	1,035	97
Two or more persons	3,447	4.9	3,326	533	1,184	1,610	121
Two persons	3,246	5.1	3,110	417	1,260	1,433	136
Three persons	3,232	4.6	3,139	536	1,071	1,532	93
Four persons	4,216	5.0	4,092	757	1,126	2,210	124
Five persons or more	3,461	4.3	3,354	626	1,172	1,556	107
Income before taxes: Quintiles of income:							
Lowest 20 percent	1,260	4.4	1,192	99	643	450	68
Second 20 percent	1,980	5.0	1,894	161	816	917	86
Third 20 percent	2,133	4.1	2,034	240	972	822	99
Fourth 20 percent	3,625	5.0	3,513	424	1,101	1,987	112
Highest 20 percent	6,144	5.4	5,940	1,202	1,717	3,021	204
Education:							
Less than a high school graduate	2,447	7.3	2,391	24	582	1,785	56
High school graduate	1,821	4.7	1,774	77	845	852	47
High school graduate with some college	2,186	4.4	2,118	199	903	1,016	68
Associate's degree	2,872	5.1	2,758	248	983	1,526	114
Bachelor's degree	3,322	4.7	3,200	539	1,172	1,488	122
Master's, professional, or doctoral degree	4,730	5.2	4,512	1,004	1,357	2,151	218

[1] Includes pets, toys, hobbies, and playground equipment, and other entertainment supplies, equipment, and services. [2] All other races includes Native Hawaiian or other Pacific Islander, American Indian or Alaska Native, and approximately 2 percent reporting more than one race.

Source: U.S. Bureau of Labor Statistics, Consumer Expenditure Survey, "Calendar year and midyear means tables by demographic characteristics," <www.bls.gov/cex/tables.htm>, accessed January 2022.

Table 1262. Adult Participation in Selected Leisure Activities by Frequency: 2022

[In thousands (28,425 represents 28,425,000), except percent. For Winter 2022. Percent is based on total projected population of 253,853,000. Based on sample and subject to sampling error; see source]

Activity	Participated in the last 12 months [1] Number (1,000)	Percent	Two or more times a week Number (1,000)	Percent	Once a week Number (1,000)	Percent	Two to three times a month Number (1,000)	Percent	Once a month Number (1,000)	Percent
Adult education courses	28,425	11.2	5,947	2.3	2,905	1.1	2,433	1.0	2,911	1.2
Antique shopping	23,568	9.3	587	0.2	646	0.3	1,562	0.6	3,223	1.3
Aquarium attendance	14,998	5.9	238	0.1	102	(Z)	163	0.1	357	0.1
Attend a food/beverage festival	19,995	7.9	70	(Z)	200	0.1	225	0.1	1,664	0.7
Attend a state or county fair	16,793	6.6	166	0.1	212	0.1	216	0.1	674	0.3
Attend a virtual/online event	37,885	14.9	3,072	1.2	2,385	0.9	3,749	1.5	5,605	2.2
Attend art galleries or shows	18,327	7.2	113	(Z)	85	(Z)	529	0.2	1,646	0.7
Attend auto shows	11,018	4.3	41	(Z)	142	0.1	374	0.2	839	0.3
Attend rock music performances	12,976	5.1	46	(Z)	182	0.1	300	0.1	1,450	0.6
Attend/coach youth sports event	19,743	7.8	5,026	2.0	3,601	1.4	2,932	1.2	1,676	0.7
Baking	78,203	30.8	10,118	4.0	11,135	4.4	19,070	7.5	15,733	6.2
Barbecuing	81,886	32.3	8,458	3.3	12,853	5.1	19,685	7.8	13,857	5.5
Billiards/pool	10,923	4.3	786	0.3	617	0.2	725	0.3	1,099	0.4
Birdwatching	20,119	7.9	9,278	3.7	1,956	0.8	1,787	0.7	1,483	0.6
Board games	54,826	21.6	3,811	1.5	5,375	2.1	9,590	3.8	11,867	4.7
Book clubs	10,245	4.0	244	0.1	1,017	0.3	817	0.3	3,903	1.5
Chess	10,190	4.0	1,401	0.6	703	0.3	768	0.3	1,192	0.5
Cooking for fun	71,293	28.1	28,233	11.1	12,021	4.7	11,778	4.6	6,917	2.7
Creating social media content (memes, videos, etc.)	17,669	7.0	4,411	1.7	2,611	1.0	2,538	1.0	1,939	0.8
Crossword puzzles	33,131	13.1	14,578	5.7	3,685	1.5	3,952	1.6	2,528	1.0
Dance/go dancing	14,420	5.7	2,205	0.9	1,239	0.5	2,004	0.8	1,617	0.6
Dining out	134,539	53.0	19,446	7.7	27,995	11.0	34,003	13.4	21,265	8.4
Entertain friends or relatives at home	88,731	35.0	4,840	1.9	9,152	3.6	17,787	7.0	20,637	8.1
Fantasy sports league	11,884	4.7	3,331	1.3	2,306	0.9	769	0.3	773	0.3
Furniture refinishing	12,316	4.9	357	0.1	329	0.1	635	0.3	1,264	0.5
Genealogy	12,571	5.0	1,421	0.6	939	0.4	1,220	0.5	2,089	0.8
Go to bars/night clubs	39,984	15.8	2,032	0.8	3,796	1.5	6,996	2.8	7,669	3.0
Go to beach	67,802	26.7	2,663	1.1	2,671	1.1	5,608	2.2	6,804	2.7
Go to live theater	13,438	5.3	83	(Z)	160	0.1	259	0.1	1,583	0.6
Go to museums	24,235	9.6	1,092	0.6	2,355	0.9	559	0.2	2,654	1.1
Home decoration and furnishing	38,105	15.0	1,620	0.6	10,500	4.1	4,434	1.8	7,937	3.1
Indoor gardening & plants	42,262	16.7	11,468	4.5	7,739	3.1	5,209	2.1	4,028	1.6
Listening to music	133,600	52.6	109,668	43.2	3,007	1.2	4,245	1.7	1,224	0.5
Painting, drawing, sculpting	26,616	10.5	4,773	1.9	2,194	0.9	4,047	1.6	3,227	1.3
PC/computer games (play offline with software)	21,310	8.4	11,712	4.6	3,823	1.5	1,709	0.7	1,192	0.5
PC/computer games (play online)	37,238	14.7	23,028	9.1	565	0.2	2,288	0.9	1,724	0.7
Photo album/scrapbooking	10,892	4.3	783	0.3	4,179	1.7	1,090	0.4	1,868	0.7
Photography	28,964	11.4	9,126	3.6	839	0.3	4,719	1.9	3,523	1.4
Picnic	20,966	8.3	237	0.1	4,705	1.9	1,830	0.7	3,427	1.4
Play cards	44,702	17.6	5,278	2.1	3,018	1.2	6,650	2.6	8,016	3.2
Play musical instrument	20,679	8.2	7,533	3.0	10,667	4.2	2,184	0.9	1,849	0.7
Reading books	99,368	39.1	56,819	22.4	1,691	0.7	8,321	3.3	7,722	3.0
Stargazing	17,056	6.7	2,675	1.1	2,652	1.0	2,095	0.8	2,426	1.0
Sudoku puzzles	24,141	9.5	11,079	4.4	1,972	0.8	2,320	0.9	1,937	0.8
Trivia games	17,777	7.0	3,329	1.3	3,369	1.3	1,980	0.8	2,182	0.9
Video/electronic games (console)	31,500	12.4	14,236	5.6	1,699	0.7	3,553	1.4	2,409	1.0
Video/electronic games (portable)	16,617	6.6	8,832	3.5	913	0.4	1,441	0.6	749	0.3
Wine tasting	18,698	7.4			1,370	0.5	1,346	0.5	2,387	0.9
Woodworking	13,784	5.4	2,346	0.9	215	0.1	2,147	0.9	1,967	0.8
Zoo attendance	27,412	10.8	187	0.1			683	0.3	2,247	0.9

Z Represents less than 0.05. [1] Includes those participating less than once a month, not shown separately.

Source: © MRI-Simmons Winter 2022 USA Study. Courtesy of MRI-Simmons. See also <www.mrisimmons.com/>.

Table 1263. Selected Recreational Activities: 1990 to 2021

[18,719 represents 18,719,000]

Activity	Unit	1990	2000	2005	2010	2015	2018	2019	2020	2021
Golf facilities [1]	Number	12,846	15,489	16,052	15,890	15,204	14,613	14,300	14,145 [5]	14,000
Tennis players: [2]	1,000	(NA)	(NA)	(NA)	18,719	17,963	17,841	17,681	21,642	22,617
Skiing: [3]										
Skier & snowboarder visits [4]	Million	50.0	52.2	56.9	59.8	53.6	53.3	59.3	51.1	59.0
Operating resorts	Number	591	503	492	471	470	472	476	470	462

NA Not available. [1] Source: National Golf Foundation, Jupiter, FL. [2] Source: Tennis Industry Association, Hilton Head Island, SC. Based on a nationwide telephone survey of households, in which all household members ages 6 and up are enumerated, with data on tennis participation collected for each person. Data prior to 2007 are not available due to new methodology being implemented after 2007. [3] Source: National Ski Areas Association, Lakewood, CO. ©. [4] Represents one person visiting a ski area for all or any part of a day or night, and includes full-and half-day, night, complimentary, adult, child, season, and other types of tickets. Data are estimated and are for the season ending in the year shown. [5] Rounded estimate.

Source: Compiled from sources listed in footnotes.

Table 1264. Amusement Park Attendance at Top 15 U.S. Facilities: 2010 to 2020

[In thousands (16,972 represents 16,972,000). Covers gated (entry ticket required) commercial theme and amusement parks with annual attendance of one million or more. 2020 attendance declines were largely due to agency restrictions limiting operating days and capacities during the COVID-19 pandemic. Due to 2020 declines, rankings are for top 15 parks in 2019. Excludes water parks]

Park name	Location	Attendance				
		2010	2015	2018	2019	2020
Magic Kingdom, Walt Disney World	Lake Buena Vista, FL	16,972	20,492	20,859	20,963	6,941
Disneyland Park	Anaheim, CA	15,980	18,278	18,666	18,666	3,674
Disney's Animal Kingdom	Lake Buena Vista, FL	9,886	10,922	13,750	13,888	4,166
EPCOT, Walt Disney World	Lake Buena Vista, FL	10,825	11,798	12,444	12,444	4,044
Disney's Hollywood Studios	Lake Buena Vista, FL	9,603	10,828	11,258	11,483	3,675
Universal Studios at Universal Orlando	Orlando, FL	5,925	9,585	10,708	10,922	4,096
Universal's Islands of Adventure	Orlando, FL	5,949	8,792	9,788	10,375	4,005
Disney's California Adventure	Anaheim, CA	6,278	9,383	9,861	9,861	1,919
Universal Studios Hollywood	Universal City, CA	5,040	7,097	9,147	9,147	1,299
SeaWorld Orlando	Orlando, FL	5,100	4,777	4,594	4,640	1,598
Knott's Berry Farm	Buena Park, CA	3,600	3,867	4,115	4,238	811
Busch Gardens	Tampa, FL	4,200	4,252	4,139	4,180	1,288
SeaWorld San Diego	San Diego, CA	3,800	3,528	3,723	3,731	1,139
Cedar Point	Sandusky, OH	3,051	3,507	3,676	3,610	1,020
Six Flags Magic Mountain	Valencia, CA	2,600	3,104	3,592	3,521	686

Source: Themed Entertainment Association and AECOM, *2020 Theme Index and Museum Index: The Global Attractions Attendance Report* ©, and previous reports. See also <aecom.com/theme-index/> and <teaconnect.org/Resources/Theme-Index/index.cfm>.

Table 1265. Reading in Print, Electronic, and Audio Formats Among Adults: 2019 and 2021

[In percent. Data shown for adults aged 18 years and older who read at least one book in the formats shown during the previous 12 months. Based on telephone surveys conducted January 8-February 7, 2019 among a nationally representative sample of 1,502 adults, and January 25-February 8, 2021 among a nationally representative sample of 1,502 adults]

Characteristic	2019				2021			
	Total	Print	E-book	Audio-book	Total	Print	E-book	Audio-book
Total	**72**	**65**	**25**	**20**	**75**	**65**	**30**	**23**
GENDER								
Male	67	60	24	17	73	62	29	22
Female	76	70	27	22	78	67	31	25
RACE/ETHNICITY								
White, non-Hispanic	76	70	27	22	78	69	31	25
Black, non-Hispanic	65	58	19	13	74	62	34	26
Hispanic	59	54	20	15	60	48	18	19
AGE								
18 to 29 years	81	73	34	23	83	68	42	30
30 to 49 years	72	76	28	27	77	67	32	27
50 to 64 years	67	74	22	16	72	62	28	22
65 years and older	68	65	17	8	68	61	18	12
EDUCATION								
High school or less [1]	(NA)	(NA)	(NA)	(NA)	59	51	17	13
Some college	75	70	26	17	81	66	36	28
College graduate	90	82	41	34	88	80	39	32
HOUSEHOLD INCOME								
Less than $30,000	62	56	18	14	67	53	23	22
$30,000 to $49,000	67	63	19	13	71	65	23	15
$50,000 to $74,999	78	71	28	27	77	68	32	23
$75,000 and higher	86	78	38	30	85	74	36	33
METRO STATUS								
Urban	75	68	27	23	81	67	33	28
Suburban	74	68	27	19	74	65	28	23
Rural	66	58	20	18	69	62	26	16

NA Not available. [1] Includes both "Less than high school" and "High school graduate."

Source: Pew Research Center, *Three-in-ten Americans now read e-books*, January 2022 ©; and unpublished data. See also <www.pewinternet.org/>.

Table 1266. Leisure Time Use on Weekends and Holidays by Type of Activity and Selected Demographic Characteristics: 2021

[Data are based on interviews of approximately 9,000 individuals age 15 years and over who reported their activities for a single 24-hour period. Respondents engaging in more than one activity at a time reported only their primary activity; except for child care, secondary activities were not reported]

Selected characteristics	Average hours per day spent on all leisure and sports activities			Percent distribution of leisure time on weekends and holidays						
	All days (hours)	Weekdays (hours)	Weekends and holidays (hours)	Sports, exercise, recreation	Socializing, communicating	Watching TV	Reading	Relaxing, thinking	Playing games, using computers for leisure	Other [1]
Total, 15 years old and over	**5.27**	**4.72**	**6.57**	**5.2**	**13.5**	**54.0**	**4.7**	**5.3**	**9.3**	**7.9**
Sex:										
Men	5.61	5.01	7.04	6.1	12.5	54.4	3.3	4.8	10.9	8.1
Women	4.94	4.44	6.13	4.2	14.7	53.7	6.2	6.0	7.7	7.7
Age:										
15 to 19 years	5.74	5.28	6.79	8.5	13.1	34.9	2.5	4.3	26.5	10.3
20 to 24 years	4.91	4.25	6.43	5.8	14.8	43.4	3.6	2.2	14.9	15.4
25 to 34 years	4.50	3.89	5.88	6.8	15.3	48.1	2.4	4.1	14.6	8.5
35 to 44 years	3.93	3.21	5.67	5.1	17.5	54.3	3.0	5.5	6.7	7.9
45 to 54 years	4.53	3.80	6.28	5.6	15.0	56.5	4.8	6.4	4.6	7.3
55 to 64 years	5.43	4.93	6.66	4.1	13.8	61.4	4.7	6.0	4.7	5.4
65 to 74 years	6.89	6.60	7.58	4.1	9.9	60.6	6.7	6.2	6.2	6.3
75 years and over	7.73	7.43	8.46	3.0	7.8	61.5	9.6	7.1	5.0	6.3
Race/ethnicity:										
White	5.29	4.72	6.64	5.1	14.0	53.2	5.0	5.0	9.3	8.3
Black	5.58	5.08	6.74	3.6	10.5	63.2	1.9	7.3	6.8	6.7
Asian	4.32	3.81	5.52	10.3	12.3	48.0	(S)	6.2	10.0	5.8
Hispanic origin [2]	4.82	4.25	6.15	3.9	16.9	52.0	2.0	6.3	8.1	10.6
Employment status:										
Employed	4.21	3.49	5.92	6.1	15.7	52.5	3.5	4.9	9.1	8.3
Full-time workers	4.01	3.20	5.91	5.9	15.7	53.3	3.2	4.7	8.6	8.3
Part-time workers	5.01	4.63	5.94	6.4	15.5	49.5	4.7	5.2	10.6	8.1
Not employed	6.93	6.64	7.60	4.2	10.9	55.9	5.9	6.1	9.7	7.5
Weekly earnings: [3]										
$0 to $690	4.10	3.40	5.75	3.8	16.7	54.6	2.3	4.7	11.7	6.4
$691 to $1,080	4.19	3.21	6.14	4.7	12.5	59.6	2.0	3.7	9.0	8.6
$1,081 to $1,730	4.05	3.19	6.27	6.2	16.6	51.2	3.5	4.9	8.1	9.4
$1,731 and higher	3.81	3.02	5.82	8.1	17.4	48.3	5.5	5.5	7.4	8.1
Presence and age of children:										
No household children under age 18	5.84	5.32	7.08	4.5	11.7	56.4	5.2	5.4	9.3	7.5
Household children under age 18	4.16	3.54	5.60	7.0	17.7	48.6	3.2	5.4	9.3	8.8
Children age 13 to 17, none younger	4.88	4.30	6.16	5.8	14.0	50.5	3.9	6.3	11.7	7.8
Children age 6 to 12, none younger	4.32	3.66	5.85	8.0	16.4	47.5	3.4	4.4	9.7	10.4
Youngest child under age 6	3.56	2.96	5.00	7.0	22.0	48.2	2.4	5.6	6.8	8.0
Educational attainment, age 25 and over:										
Less than a high school diploma	5.76	5.29	6.90	2.5	14.6	62.8	1.0	12.2	2.3	4.6
High school graduates, no college	5.82	5.29	7.07	3.7	11.3	63.5	2.8	6.6	5.8	6.1
Some college or associate degree	5.40	4.88	6.65	4.5	14.3	56.1	5.1	4.8	8.0	7.1
Bachelor's degree and higher	4.68	4.08	6.10	6.4	14.4	50.5	7.4	4.3	8.9	8.0

S Estimate does not meet publication standards. [1] Includes other leisure and sports activities, not elsewhere classified, and travel related to leisure and sports activities. The earnings data are limited to wage and salary workers (both incorporated and unincorporated self-employed workers are excluded). [2] People of Hispanic origin may be of any race. [3] These values are based on usual weekly earnings. The earnings data are limited to wage and salary workers who held only one job. Each earnings range represents approximately 25 percent of full-time wage and salary workers who held only one job.

Source: U.S. Bureau of Labor Statistics, *American Time Use Survey—2021 Results*, USDL 22-1261, June 2022. See also <www.bls.gov/tus/>.

Table 1267. Characteristics of Selected Spectator Sports: 1990 to 2021

[54,824 represents 54,824,000]

Sport	Unit	1990	2000	2010	2015	2017	2018	2019	2020 [8]	2021 [8]
Baseball, major leagues: [1]										
Regular season attendance	1,000	54,824	72,749	73,054	73,760	72,670	69,625	68,495	([9])	45,305
National League	1,000	24,492	39,851	40,890	38,903	38,307	37,251	37,902	([9])	25,364
American League	1,000	30,332	32,898	32,164	34,857	34,364	32,375	30,593	([9])	19,940
Playoffs attendance [2]	1,000	479	1,314	1,210	1,420	1,399	1,258	1,345	[9] 76	1,268
World Series attendance	1,000	209	277	244	215	347	239	305	[9] 69	258
Basketball: [3, 4]										
NCAA—Men's college:										
Teams	Number	768	937	1,027	1,067	1,071	1,074	1,080	1,091	1,079
Attendance	1,000	28,741	28,949	32,632	32,382	31,277	31,401	30,268	(NA)	26,999
NCAA—Women's college:										
Teams	Number	782	958	1,048	1,084	1,092	1,093	1,097	1,092	1,078
Attendance [5]	1,000	2,777	8,825	11,160	11,367	11,496	11,514	11,058	(NA)	8,902
NCAA—Men's college football: [4]										
Teams	Number	534	624	644	666	666	669	669	669	(NA)
Attendance	1,000	35,330	39,059	49,671	49,058	47,622	46,985	47,538	(NA)	(NA)
National Hockey League: [6]										
Regular season attendance	1,000	12,580	18,800	20,996	21,533	21,545	22,174	22,187	18,835	1,005
Playoffs attendance	1,000	1,356	1,525	1,702	1,701	1,606	1,518	1,575	–	769
Professional rodeo: [7]										
Rodeos	Number	754	688	570	624	650	644	(NA)	(NA)	(NA)
Performances	Number	2,159	2,081	1,671	1,663	1,711	1,682	(NA)	(NA)	(NA)
Members	Number	5,693	6,255	5,323	4,782	4,885	4,618	(NA)	(NA)	(NA)
Permit-holders	Number	3,290	3,249	1,881	1,784	1,734	1,694	(NA)	(NA)	(NA)
Total prize money	Mil. dol.	18.2	32.3	39.9	46.3	48.2	49.0	(NA)	(NA)	(NA)

– Represents zero. NA Not available. [1] Source: Major League Baseball, New York, NY, National League Green Book ©; and The American League of Professional Baseball Clubs, New York, NY, American League Red Book ©. [2] Beginning 1995, two rounds of playoffs were played. Prior years had one round. [3] Season beginning in year shown. [4] Source: National Collegiate Athletic Association, Indianapolis, IN ©. [5] Attendance for women's basketball includes doubleheaders with men's teams beginning with the 1997 season, if attendance was taken by halftime of the women's game. [6] For season ending in year shown. Source: National Hockey League, Montreal, Quebec ©. In September 2004, franchise owners locked out their players upon the expiration of the collective bargaining agreement. The entire season was cancelled in February 2005. [7] Source: Professional Rodeo Cowboys Association, Colorado Springs, CO, Official Professional Rodeo Media Guide, annual ©. [8] Due to the COVID-19 pandemic, sports attendance was drastically impacted. Numbers not comparable to prior years. [9] Due to the COVID-19 pandemic, fans were not hosted during the regular season. Fans were hosted in limited capacities during the National League Championship Series and the World Series.

Source: Compiled from sources listed in footnotes.

Table 1268. Adult Attendance at Sports Events by Frequency: 2022

[In thousands (136 represents 136,000), except percent. For Winter 2022. Percent is based on total projected population of 253,853,000. Based on a survey and subject to sampling error; see source]

Event	Attend regularly Number (1,000)	Attend regularly Per-cent	Attend on occasion [1] Number (1,000)	Attend on occasion [1] Per-cent	Event	Attend regularly Number (1,000)	Attend regularly Per-cent	Attend on occasion [1] Number (1,000)	Attend on occasion [1] Per-cent
Alpine skiing and ski jumping	136	0.05	290	0.11	Gymnastics	287	0.11	562	0.22
Auto racing – NASCAR	335	0.13	702	0.28	High school sports	4,010	1.58	7,062	2.78
Auto racing – other	266	0.10	913	0.36	Horse racing (track or OTB)	261	0.10	945	0.37
Baseball:					Ice hockey:				
College	339	0.13	1,070	0.42	NHL regular season	545	0.21	1,844	0.73
Pro (MLB) regular season	1,257	0.50	7,081	2.79	NHL playoffs and Stanley				
Pro (MLB) playoffs/					Cup finals	139	0.05	392	0.15
World Series	333	0.13	1,025	0.40	Lacrosse (MLL)	393	0.15	724	0.29
Basketball:					Marathon, triathlon & other				
College	816	0.32	1,880	0.74	obstacle events	112	0.04	417	0.16
Pro (NBA) regular season	346	0.14	1,764	0.69	Mixed martial arts (other)	70	0.03	200	0.08
Pro (NBA) playoffs	115	0.05	465	0.18	Motorcycle racing	158	0.06	409	0.16
NCAA tournament	228	0.09	450	0.18	Olympics – Summer	94	0.04	203	0.08
Pro (WNBA)	92	0.04	259	0.10	Olympics – Winter	90	0.04	143	0.06
Bicycle racing	69	0.03	201	0.08	Poker	157	0.06	282	0.11
Bowling	232	0.09	835	0.33	Rodeo	295	0.12	1,023	0.40
Boxing	103	0.04	270	0.11	Soccer:				
Bull riding (Pro)	72	0.03	545	0.21	MLS	363	0.14	1,131	0.45
Esports	46	0.02	182	0.07	World Cup	88	0.03	172	0.07
Extreme sports – Summer	112	0.04	162	0.06	Men's national team	92	0.04	254	0.10
Extreme sports – Winter	121	0.05	181	0.07	Women's national team	89	0.04	250	0.10
Figure skating	109	0.04	258	0.10	International	111	0.04	300	0.12
Fishing	262	0.10	869	0.34	Tennis:				
Football:					Men's	107	0.04	399	0.16
College regular season	1,610	0.63	4,211	1.66	Women's	123	0.05	394	0.16
College playoffs/National					Track & field	211	0.08	545	0.21
Championship	177	0.07	417	0.16	Truck and tractor				
Pro (NFL) Monday, Thursday					pull/mud racing	77	0.03	331	0.13
or Sunday night games	393	0.15	1,558	0.61	Ultimate Fighting				
NFL weekend games	609	0.24	1,827	0.72	Championship (UFC)	59	0.02	189	0.07
NFL playoffs/Super Bowl	181	0.07	385	0.15	Volleyball (Pro beach)	80	0.03	162	0.06
Golf:					Wrestling:				
PGA	185	0.07	566	0.22	WWE	81	0.03	365	0.14
LPGA	56	0.02	197	0.08	Other Pro	66	0.03	184	0.07
Other golf	107	0.04	254	0.10					

[1] Attended at least once during last 12 months.

Source: © MRI-Simmons Winter 2022 USA Study. Courtesy of MRI-Simmons. See also <www.mrisimmons.com>.

Table 1269. Participation in NCAA Sports by Sex: 2020 to 2021

[For the academic year ending in 2021. Due to the COVID-19 pandemic some seasons were disrupted or cancelled]

Sport	Males			Females		
	Teams	Athletes	Average squad	Teams	Athletes	Average squad
Total................................	**9,222**	**278,988**	**(X)**	**10,733**	**219,177**	**(X)**
Acrobat and tumbling [3]........................	(X)	(X)	(X)	27	698	25.9
Baseball................................	940	38,431	40.9	(X)	(X)	(X)
Basketball................................	1,071	18,179	17.0	1,085	16,090	14.8
Bowling [2]................................	3	27	9.0	92	797	8.7
Cross country [1]........................	968	13,489	13.9	1,045	14,122	13.5
Equestrian [1,2,3]........................	8	18	2.3	46	1,303	28.3
Esport [2,3]................................	8	137	17.1	6	71	11.8
Fencing [1]................................	33	573	17.4	44	668	15.2
Field hockey................................	(X)	(X)	(X)	279	6,024	21.6
Football................................	657	70,711	107.6	(X)	(X)	(X)
Golf [1]................................	805	8,075	10.0	695	5,473	7.9
Gymnastics................................	15	307	20.5	81	1,586	19.6
Ice hockey................................	149	4,266	28.6	108	2,513	23.3
Lacrosse................................	391	15,180	38.8	521	12,921	24.8
Rifle [1]................................	22	117	5.3	27	180	6.7
Rowing [2]................................	57	2,033	35.7	146	6,196	42.4
Rugby [2,3]................................	4	161	40.3	18	552	30.7
Sailing [1,2]................................	24	414	17.3	(X)	(X)	(X)
Beach volleyball................................	(X)	(X)	(X)	82	1,485	18.1
Skiing [1]................................	32	386	12.1	32	374	11.7
Soccer................................	821	24,362	29.7	1,026	27,986	27.3
Softball................................	(X)	(X)	(X)	983	21,478	21.8
Squash [2,3]................................	33	429	13.0	31	385	12.4
Swimming/diving................................	447	9,321	20.9	560	12,889	23.0
Synchronized swimming [3]........................	(X)	(X)	(X)	3	37	12.3
Tennis................................	709	7,122	10.0	865	8,130	9.4
Track, indoor................................	724	25,202	34.8	818	27,304	33.4
Track, outdoor [1]........................	841	29,167	34.7	936	30,425	32.5
Triathlon [3]................................	(X)	(X)	(X)	29	220	7.6
Volleyball................................	158	2,412	15.3	1,053	17,610	16.7
Water polo................................	49	1,033	21.1	65	1,235	19.0
Wrestling [3]................................	253	7,436	29.4	30	425	14.2

X Not applicable. [1] Co-ed sport. [2] Sport recognized by the NCAA but does not have an NCAA men's championship. [3] Sport recognized by the NCAA as an emerging or other sport for women.

Source: The National Collegiate Athletic Association (NCAA), Indianapolis, IN, *NCAA Sports Sponsorship and Participation Rates Report* ©, January 2022. See also <www.ncaapublications.com>.

Table 1270. Participation in High School Athletic Programs by Sex: 1980 to 2019

[For academic years. Data based on number of state associations reporting and may underrepresent the number of schools with and participants in athletic programs]

Year	Participants [1]		Sex and sport	Most popular sports, 2018–2019 [2]	
	Males	Females		Schools	Participants
1980 to 1981....................	3,503,124	1,853,789	MALE		
1985 to 1986....................	3,344,275	1,807,121	Football (11-player)...............	14,247	1,006,013
1990 to 1991....................	3,406,355	1,892,316	Track & field (outdoor)............	17,052	605,354
1995 to 1996....................	3,634,052	2,367,936	Basketball..........................	18,617	540,769
2000 to 2001....................	3,921,069	2,784,154	Baseball.............................	16,170	482,740
2002 to 2003....................	3,988,738	2,856,358	Soccer................................	12,552	459,077
2003 to 2004....................	4,038,253	2,865,299	Cross country.....................	15,632	269,295
2004 to 2005....................	4,110,319	2,908,390	Wrestling............................	10,843	247,441
2005 to 2006....................	4,206,549	2,953,355	Tennis................................	9,809	159,314
2006 to 2007....................	4,321,103	3,021,807	Golf...................................	13,590	143,200
2007 to 2008....................	4,372,115	3,057,266	Swimming & diving..............	7,704	136,638
2008 to 2009....................	4,422,662	3,114,091	FEMALE		
2009 to 2010....................	4,455,740	3,172,637	Track & field (outdoor)............	17,012	488,267
2010 to 2011....................	4,494,406	3,173,549	Volleyball...........................	16,572	452,808
2011 to 2012....................	4,484,987	3,207,533	Basketball..........................	18,210	399,067
2012 to 2013....................	4,490,854	3,222,723	Soccer................................	12,107	394,105
2013 to 2014....................	4,527,994	3,267,664	Softball (fast pitch)..............	15,877	362,038
2014 to 2015....................	4,519,312	3,287,735	Cross country.....................	15,435	219,345
2015 to 2016....................	4,541,959	3,324,306	Tennis................................	10,290	189,436
2016 to 2017....................	4,563,238	3,400,297	Swimming & diving..............	8,007	173,088
2017 to 2018....................	4,565,580	3,415,306	Competitive spirit squads........	7,214	161,358
2018 to 2019....................	4,534,758	3,402,733	Lacrosse............................	2,877	99,750

[1] Participants are counted in each sport in which they participate. [2] Ten most popular sports for each gender, ranked by number of participants.

Source: National Federation of State High School Associations, Indianapolis, IN, *The 2018–19 High School Athletics Participation Survey* ©. Reprinted with permission of the National Federation of State High School Associations. See also <www.nfhs.org/>.

Table 1271. National Park Service—Summary: 1990 to 2021

[In units as indicated (986 represents $986,000,000). For year ending September 30, except as noted. Covers all States, the District of Columbia, and the U.S. territories of American Samoa, Guam, Puerto Rico, and the U.S. Virgin Islands]

Item	1990	2000	2010	2015	2018	2019	2020	2021
FINANCES (mil. dol.): [1]								
Expenditures reported...	986	1,833	3,239	2,949	3,245	(NA)	(NA)	(NA)
Salaries and wages...	459	799	1,237	1,167	1,195	(NA)	(NA)	(NA)
Improvements, maintenance...	160	299	531	532	606	(NA)	(NA)	(NA)
Construction...	109	215	443	184	228	(NA)	(NA)	(NA)
Other...	259	520	1,028	1,066	1,227	(NA)	(NA)	(NA)
Funds available...	1,506	3,316	5,402	5,161	6,366	(NA)	(NA)	(NA)
Appropriations...	1,053	1,881	2,848	2,967	3,804	(NA)	(NA)	(NA)
Other [2]...	453	1,435	2,554	2,194	2,515	(NA)	(NA)	(NA)
Revenue from operations...	79	234	387	589	551	(NA)	(NA)	(NA)
RECREATION VISITS (millions): [3]								
All areas...	**258.7**	**285.9**	**281.3**	**307.2**	**318.2**	**327.5**	**237.1**	**297.1**
National parks [4]...	57.7	66.1	64.6	75.3	85.9	89.8	67.9	92.3
National monuments...	23.9	23.8	23.0	24.9	22.2	22.4	9.1	13.8
National historical, commemorative, archaeological [5]...	57.5	72.2	80.0	93.9	93.2	95.4	52.4	73.2
National parkways...	29.1	34.0	28.6	29.6	29.8	30.2	27.8	30.8
National recreation areas [4]...	47.2	50.0	49.0	46.2	51.0	52.1	48.2	50.4
National seashores and lakeshores...	23.3	22.5	22.2	22.8	21.0	22.9	21.2	25.1
National Capital Parks [6]...	7.5	4.1	2.5	3.1	3.2	3.0	1.6	1.9
Recreation overnight stays [7]...	17.6	15.4	14.4	14.9	14.0	13.8	8.0	12.7
In commercial lodgings...	4.7	4.7	4.7	4.8	4.5	4.5	2.3	3.7
In Park Service campgrounds...	7.9	5.9	5.5	5.9	6.0	6.0	3.3	5.7
In backcountry...	1.7	1.9	1.8	2.0	1.9	1.9	1.4	2.0
Miscellaneous overnight stays...	3.4	2.9	2.4	2.2	1.5	1.4	0.9	1.4
LAND (1,000 acres): [8]								
Total...	76,362	78,153	80,527	80,603	81,041	81,090	81,098	81,104
National Parks...	46,089	49,785	50,662	50,737	50,752	50,678	50,947	50,947
Recreation areas...	3,344	3,388	3,418	3,421	3,425	3,155	3,425	3,425
Other...	26,929	24,980	26,447	26,445	26,864	26,194	26,726	26,732
Acquisition, net...	21	186	23	127	33	49	8	7

[1] Financial data are those associated with the National Park System. Certain other functions of the National Park Service (principally the activities absorbed from the former Heritage Conservation and Recreation Service in 1981) are excluded. [2] Includes funds carried over from prior years. [3] For calendar year. Includes other types of areas, not shown separately. [4] For 1990, combined data for North Cascades National Park and two adjacent National Recreation Areas are included in National Parks total. [5] Includes National Battlefields, National Battlefield Parks, National Historic Sites, National Historical Parks, National Memorials, National Military Parks, National Preserves, and National Reserves. [6] For 1990 to 1996, data are for National Capital Parks combined. Beginning 1997, data are summed for National Capital Parks East and National Capital Parks Central (also known as National Mall and Memorial Park). [7] Data may not sum due to rounding. [8] Federal land only, as of December 31. Federal land acreages, in addition to National Park Service administered lands, also include lands within national park system area boundaries but under the administration of other agencies. Year-to-year changes in the federal lands figures includes changes in the acreages of these other lands and hence often differ from "net acquisition."

Source: U.S. National Park Service, *National Park Statistical Abstract 2021*, May 2022, and earlier reports; unpublished data; and "National Park Service Visitor Use Statistics, National Reports" <irma.nps.gov/STATS/Reports/National>, and National Park Service Acreage Reports, <www.nps.gov/subjects/lwcf/acreagereports.htm>, accessed March 2022.

Table 1272. National Park Service (NPS) Visits and Acreage by Type of Area: 2021

[Includes data for four areas in Virgin Islands, and one area in each Puerto Rico, American Samoa, and Guam]

Type of area	Recreation visits [1]	Gross area acres	Federal land			Non-federal land	
			NPS fee acres [2]	NPS less than fee acres [3]	Other federal fee acres [4]	Other public acres [5]	Private acres
Total...	**297,115,406**	**85,116,467**	**80,041,622**	**352,150**	**710,568**	**1,394,920**	**2,617,207**
International historic site...	10,299	7	7	–	–	–	–
National battlefield parks...	2,733,207	16,173	11,370	45	1	21	4,735
National battlefield sites...	(NA)	1	1	–	–	–	–
National battlefields...	1,893,551	21,485	12,195	956	226	169	7,940
National historic sites...	5,909,000	31,663	20,001	833	40	374	10,414
National historical parks...	23,733,266	199,509	143,732	4,338	300	29,819	21,321
National lakeshores...	3,327,095	213,924	135,010	673	46	53,172	25,022
National memorials...	29,483,249	10,500	9,597	3	48	60	792
National military parks...	3,751,741	46,347	39,987	690	(Z)	1,025	4,646
National monuments...	13,786,614	1,993,525	1,827,232	14,703	23,474	8,575	119,540
National parks...	92,251,857	52,410,601	50,679,187	222,571	45,583	572,952	890,309
National parkways...	30,774,635	183,193	162,155	9,191	125	483	11,239
National preserves...	5,647,048	24,656,432	22,969,116	10,760	273,502	350,745	1,052,310
National recreation areas...	50,366,960	3,714,642	3,154,873	24,831	245,749	113,625	175,563
National reserves...	97,376	33,741	10,709	2,089	–	708	20,235
National rivers...	3,907,831	352,551	258,520	12,485	–	17,015	64,531
National scenic trails...	(NA)	252,194	109,857	14,651	58,599	48,960	20,127
National seashores...	21,776,435	596,931	404,612	14,947	61,226	106,820	9,326
National wild & scenic rivers...	1,508,467	344,160	59,105	15,578	1,649	90,199	177,628
Parks (other)...	6,156,775	38,889	34,356	2,807	–	196	1,530

– Represents zero. Z Less than .05 acres. NA Not available. [1] Recreation visit represents the entry of a person onto lands or waters administered by the NPS for recreational purposes, excluding government personnel, through traffic, tradespeople, and persons residing within park boundaries. [2] Complete Federal ownership of all rights in the land. [3] Federal ownership of some rights in the land. [4] Tracts under the administration of another federal agency (e.g., U.S. Forest Service, Department of the Army, etc.). Bureau of Land Management tracts are also identified as Other Fee (Federal) until they are withdrawn for NPS use; then status changes to Fee (Federal). [5] Non-federal tracts owned by the state, county, and/or other municipalities, including quasi-public entities.

Source: U.S. National Park Service, Public Use Statistics Office, "National Park Service Visitor Use Statistics, National Reports," <irma.nps.gov/STATS/Reports/National>; and Land and Water Conservation Fund, "National Park Service Acreage Reports," <www.nps.gov/subjects/lwcf/acreagereports.htm>; accessed March 2022.

Table 1273. National Park Service (NPS) Visits and Acreage by State: 2021

State	Recreation visits [1]	Gross area acres	Federal land			Nonfederal land	
			NPS fee acres [2]	NPS less than fee acres [3]	Other federal fee acres [4]	Other public acres [5]	Private acres
Total [6].............	[7] 29,7115,401	85,116,467	80,041,622	352,150	710,568	1,394,920	2,617,207
Alabama.............	1,405,064	22,747	17,540	203	13	3,288	1,702
Alaska...............	1,001,956	54,653,962	52,456,215	103,094	8	372,384	1,722,262
Arizona.............	10,683,594	2,948,372	2,658,341	94	75,949	57,093	156,894
Arkansas...........	3,979,627	104,982	100,609	3,449	20	470	434
California............	35,099,250	8,215,978	7,654,660	22,427	12,445	352,604	173,841
Colorado............	7,819,152	738,672	665,538	4,276	42,456	303	26,099
Connecticut.........	31,512	7,782	5,846	1,055	–	874	6
Delaware............	(NA)	904	890	6	–	2	6
District of Columbia.....	28,599,636	8,628	8,477	8	8	134	2
Florida..............	13,442,112	2,638,605	2,477,396	1,350	44,486	101,784	13,589
Georgia.............	6,335,804	68,770	40,051	167	1,461	18,607	8,483
Hawaii..............	3,864,447	371,494	360,111	1	22	11,228	132
Idaho...............	691,800	806,298	511,986	1,226	273,488	9,058	10,539
Illinois..............	89,964	115	12	(Z)	–	17	85
Indiana.............	3,407,651	15,575	10,781	538	–	3,419	836
Iowa................	136,577	2,713	2,670	–	–	42	1
Kansas..............	101,079	11,627	462	271	–	56	10,838
Kentucky............	1,909,423	99,059	95,056	137	–	838	3,028
Louisiana...........	288,483	27,000	21,145	(Z)	–	2,779	3,075
Maine...............	4,118,882	182,002	157,740	11,204	22	10,646	2,390
Maryland............	6,675,116	74,064	41,395	5,874	395	23,936	2,465
Massachusetts........	6,694,799	58,526	33,334	1,030	44	21,922	2,196
Michigan............	3,337,907	718,249	632,309	673	46	58,515	26,705
Minnesota...........	1,003,605	301,352	139,825	3,193	143	98,659	59,532
Mississippi..........	6,642,885	119,391	105,091	5,229	–	151	8,920
Missouri............	2,810,908	83,576	54,740	9,029	–	14,072	5,735
Montana............	5,946,417	1,274,134	1,214,193	1,850	6,137	1,464	50,489
Nebraska............	357,074	66,557	6,462	485	845	435	58,330
Nevada.............	5,880,514	801,172	797,613	–	2,508	44	1,008
New Hampshire........	26,058	21,190	13,696	1,556	5,772	162	5
New Jersey...........	5,561,120	99,598	35,812	140	3,208	59,050	1,388
New Mexico..........	2,449,307	483,504	472,679	5	25	4,675	6,119
New York............	11,952,676	97,448	34,111	3,921	148	19,988	39,280
North Carolina........	20,983,351	411,338	367,147	12,272	20,782	3,289	7,848
North Dakota.........	818,787	72,570	71,359	242	–	122	847
Ohio................	2,809,563	34,555	20,293	1,462	84	8,480	4,236
Oklahoma...........	1,532,339	10,241	10,011	9	189	5	27
Oregon.............	1,104,459	203,385	196,197	1,404	4,976	295	513
Pennsylvania.........	6,252,092	116,961	53,818	3,043	387	19,586	40,127
Rhode Island.........	20,719	1,494	8	85	–	–	1,401
South Carolina........	1,152,980	32,778	32,555	60	16	51	96
South Dakota.........	4,848,398	296,584	148,007	122,326	–	78	26,173
Tennessee...........	11,030,447	389,206	359,438	1,714	9,665	4,162	14,226
Texas...............	5,887,579	1,260,178	1,204,918	1,133	1,932	11,161	41,033
Utah................	14,796,738	2,117,689	2,097,901	833	1,142	12,819	4,994
Vermont.............	47,997	23,866	10,465	3,927	8,809	544	120
Virginia.............	22,233,319	372,828	307,220	7,126	25,198	6,815	26,469
Washington..........	8,176,244	1,967,552	1,834,644	2,165	100,222	12,798	17,723
West Virginia.........	2,187,125	92,857	66,316	371	118	6,893	19,159
Wisconsin...........	657,012	133,757	62,032	11,302	802	47,473	12,148
Wyoming............	8,586,450	2,396,431	2,345,655	177	48,462	497	1,639

– Represents zero. Z Less than 0.5 acres. NA Not available. [1] Represents the entry of a person onto lands or waters administered by the National Park Service (NPS) for recreational purposes, excluding government personnel, through traffic (commuters), tradespeople, and persons residing within park boundaries. [2] Fee represents complete Federal ownership of all rights in the land. [3] Represents Federal ownership of some rights in the land. [4] Tracts under the administration of another federal agency (e.g., U.S. Forest Service, Department of the Army, Coast Guard, etc.). Bureau of Land Management tracts are also identified as Other Fee (Federal) until they are withdrawn for NPS use; then status changes to Fee (Federal). [5] Non-federal tracts owned by the state, county, and/or other municipalities, including quasi-public entities. [6] Includes Island Areas of the U.S., not shown separately. [7] Differs slightly from data shown in other tables due to rounding.

Source: U.S. National Park Service, Public Use Statistics Office, "National Park Service Visitor Use Statistics, National Reports," <irma.nps.gov/STATS/Reports/National>; and Land and Water Conservation Fund, "National Park Service Acreage Reports," <www.nps.gov/subjects/lwcf/acreagereports.htm>; accessed March 2022.

Table 1274. State Parks and Recreation Areas by State: 2020

[In units as indicated (19,041 represents 19,041,000). For year ending June 30. Data are shown as reported by state park directors. In some states, the park agency has forests, fish and wildlife areas, and/or other areas under its control. In other states, the park agency is responsible for state parks only]

State	Acreage (1,000)	Visitors (1,000) [1]	Total revenue generated ($1,000)	Operating expenditures ($1,000)	Revenue share of operating expenditures
United States........................	19,041	786,136	1,128,374	3,412,038	33.1
Alabama............................	48	6,412	38,012	41,049	92.6
Alaska..............................	3,387	40	4,749	13,667	34.7
Arizona.............................	62	2,972	15,763	26,708	59.0
Arkansas...........................	55	6,549	21,719	70,160	31.0
California...........................	1,649	68,166	126,202	782,312	16.1
Colorado...........................	1,468	17,066	(NA)	76,216	(NA)
Connecticut........................	212	12,968	14,896	17,896	83.2
Delaware...........................	29	6,238	19,513	29,993	65.1
Florida.............................	723	24,838	54,251	144,654	37.5
Georgia............................	83	10,294	40,962	55,016	74.5
Hawaii..............................	33	8,354	6,515	14,280	45.6
Idaho...............................	59	6,519	8,438	18,841	44.8
Illinois..............................	265	34,392	14,300	157,300	9.1
Indiana.............................	172	15,046	56,611	68,214	83.0
Iowa................................	116	16,069	5,025	19,768	25.4
Kansas.............................	165	7,313	11,505	18,904	60.9
Kentucky...........................	48	1,277	37,971	86,083	44.1
Louisiana..........................	32	1,292	715	31,539	2.3
Maine..............................	99	3,647	(NA)	9,254	(NA)
Maryland...........................	141	17,490	10,445	45,492	23.0
Massachusetts.....................	354	26,786	14,660	101,020	14.5
Michigan...........................	304	38,183	52,981	65,618	80.7
Minnesota..........................	289	11,128	25,742	113,508	22.7
Mississippi.........................	24	1,281	6,543	10,428	62.7
Missouri............................	160	19,321	6,844	58,165	11.8
Montana............................	44	3,317	4,537	10,621	42.7
Nebraska...........................	169	8,114	21,210	29,064	73.0
Nevada.............................	151	3,698	5,462	21,046	26.0
New Hampshire.....................	232	1,091	23,210	23,210	100.0
New Jersey.........................	812	14,084	6,486	45,754	14.2
New Mexico........................	192	4,030	6,585	16,317	40.4
New York...........................	4,349	79,152	89,450	227,454	39.3
North Carolina......................	249	17,413	10,580	49,753	21.3
North Dakota.......................	35	1,329	4,739	14,596	32.5
Ohio................................	175	40,604	28,943	73,901	39.2
Oklahoma..........................	62	11,525	25,250	38,525	65.5
Oregon.............................	123	44,236	21,601	70,433	30.7
Pennsylvania.......................	304	40,715	26,000	114,393	22.7
Rhode Island.......................	9	8,386	(NA)	14,015	(NA)
South Carolina.....................	82	8,219	30,860	34,772	88.7
South Dakota.......................	102	8,381	18,611	26,588	70.0
Tennessee..........................	217	36,121	38,765	90,872	42.7
Texas..............................	637	7,317	16,204	82,492	19.6
Utah................................	154	12,080	19,780	139,780	14.2
Vermont............................	74	863	6,168	10,777	57.2
Virginia.............................	80	7,066	22,699	42,934	52.9
Washington.........................	111	34,718	54,950	76,824	71.5
West Virginia.......................	151	6,354	26,844	46,248	58.0
Wisconsin..........................	447	18,674	21,936	22,439	97.8
Wyoming...........................	102	5,007	3,143	13,144	23.9

NA Not available. [1] Includes day and overnight visitors.

Source: National Association of State Park Directors, Raleigh NC, *Statistical Report of State Park Operations: 2019-2020, Annual Information Exchange for the Period of July 1, 2019 through June 30, 2020* ©, May 2022. See also <www.stateparks.org>.

Table 1275. Participants in Wildlife-Related Recreation Activities: 2016

[In thousands (39,553 represents 39,553,000). For persons 16 years old and over engaging in activity at least once in 2016. Based on survey and subject to sampling error; see source for details]

Participant	Number	Days of participation	Trips	Participant	Number	Days of participation
Total sportspersons [1]	**39,553**	**643,362**	**530,167**	**Wildlife watchers** [1]	**86,042**	**(X)**
Total anglers	35,754	459,341	383,296	Away from home [2]	23,720	386,045
Freshwater	30,137	383,192	322,266	Observe wildlife	19,583	308,769
Excluding Great Lakes	29,490	372,660	311,237	Photograph wildlife	13,721	151,559
Great Lakes	1,824	13,440	11,029	Feed wildlife	4,869	70,846
Saltwater	8,320	75,392	61,030	Around the home [3]	81,128	(X)
				Observe wildlife	43,829	(X)
Total hunters	11,453	184,021	146,871	Photograph wildlife	30,473	(X)
Big game	9,208	132,665	88,561	Feed wildlife	59,083	(X)
Small game	3,505	38,306	31,772	Visit public parks	11,359	(X)
Migratory birds	2,353	15,621	14,548	Maintain plantings or		
Other animals	1,315	13,275	11,989	natural areas	11,024	(X)

X Not applicable. [1] Detail does not add to total due to multiple responses and nonresponse. [2] Persons taking a trip of at least 1 mile from home for activity. [3] Activity within 1 mile of home.

Source: U.S. Fish and Wildlife Service, *2016 National Survey of Fishing, Hunting, and Wildlife Associated Recreation*, April 2018. See also <www.fws.gov/wsfrprograms/Subpages/NationalSurvey/2016_Survey.html>.

Table 1276. Expenditures for Wildlife-Related Recreation Activities: 2016

[46,115 represents $46,115,000,000. For persons 16 years old and over. Based on survey and subject to sampling error; see source]

Expenditure item	Fishing			Hunting			Wildlife watching		
		Spenders			Spenders			Spenders	
	Expenditures (mil. dol.)	Number (1,000)	Percent of anglers	Expenditures (mil. dol.)	Number (1,000)	Percent of hunters	Expenditures [1] (mil. dol.)	Number (1,000)	Percent [2]
Total, all items [3]	**46,115**	**32,511**	**91**	**26,190**	**10,992**	**96**	**75,867**	**63,578**	**74**
Total trip-related	21,730	31,260	87	9,196	9,984	87	11,588	20,235	85
Food and lodging	7,849	27,127	76	3,114	9,065	79	6,068	17,058	72
Food	4,759	26,867	75	2,507	9,053	79	3,810	16,955	71
Lodging	3,090	8,625	24	607	1,775	16	2,258	6,331	27
Transportation	5,049	26,337	74	3,184	9,047	79	4,229	19,018	80
Public	543	2,852	8	193	912	8	1,233	3,052	13
Private	4,506	25,622	72	2,991	8,937	78	2,996	17,766	75
Other trip costs	8,832	26,212	73	2,898	3,664	32	1,291	8,609	36
Equipment expenditures:									
Equipment	7,431	22,393	63	7,384	8,413	73	64,279	57,496	67
Auxiliary equipment	3,164	4,522	13	2,019	4,436	39	1,044	6,669	8
Special equipment [4]	10,483	2,291	6	[5] 3,353	[5] 396	[5] 3	41,934	3,037	4
Other expenditures:									
Magazines and books	147	3,142	9	166	1,130	10	237	7,022	8
Land leasing and ownership	2,359	1,019	3	2,899	1,845	16	4,196	1,195	1
Membership dues and contributions	214	1,741	5	182	1,403	12	3,817	10,076	12
Plantings	(X)	(X)	(X)	[5] 165	[5] 1,020	[5] 9	946	7,289	8
Licenses, stamps, tags, and permits	587	15,647	44	826	8,668	76	(X)	(X)	(X)

X Not applicable. [1] Information on trip-related expenditures for wildlife watching was collected for away-from-home participants only. Equipment and other expenditures for wildlife watching are base on information collected from both away-from-home and around-the-home participants. [2] Based on away-from-home participants for trip-related expenditures. For equipment and other expenditures the percent of wildlife-watching participants is based on total participants. [3] Total not adjusted for multiple responses or nonresponse. [4] Special equipment includes boats, campers, cabins, trail bikes, etc. [5] Estimate based on a sample size of 10 to 29.

Source: U.S. Fish and Wildlife Service, *2016 National Survey of Fishing, Hunting, and Wildlife Associated Recreation*, April 2018. See also <www.fws.gov/wsfrprograms/Subpages/NationalSurvey/2016_Survey.html>.

Table 1277. Tribal Gaming Operations and Revenues: 2010 to 2020

[Revenue in millions of dollars (26,503 represents $26,503,000,000). For year ending September 30]

Region	2010		2015		2018		2019		2020	
	Operations (number)	Revenue	Operations (number)	Revenue	Operations (number)	Revenue	Operations (number)	Revenue	Operations (number)	Revenue
Total [1]	**422**	**26,503**	**474**	**29,882**	**501**	**33,720**	**522**	**34,579**	**524**	**27,832**
Portland	50	2,655	52	3,022	55	3,663	57	3,811	57	3,116
Sacramento	62	6,794	71	7,881	73	9,279	76	9,680	77	8,399
Phoenix	48	2,539	53	2,808	59	3,141	57	3,276	52	2,358
St. Paul [2]	119	4,452	134	4,829	95	4,796	100	4,922	103	3,730
Rapid City [3]	(X)	(X)	(X)	(X)	36	369	42	376	42	239
Tulsa	65	1,769	68	2,207	73	2,466	75	2,468	76	2,104
Oklahoma City	51	1,583	65	2,142	72	2,480	73	2,670	74	2,064
Washington DC	27	6,711	31	6,994	38	7,525	42	7,374	43	5,823

X Not applicable. [1] Regions formerly were numbered I to VI, as follows: Portland (Region I): Alaska, Idaho, Oregon, and Washington. Sacramento (Region II): California, and Northern Nevada. Phoenix (Region III): Arizona, Colorado, New Mexico, and Southern Nevada. St. Paul (Region IV): Iowa, Michigan, Minnesota, Montana, North Dakota, Nebraska, South Dakota, Wisconsin, and Wyoming. Tulsa (Eastern part of Region V): Kansas, and Eastern Oklahoma. Oklahoma City (Western part of Region V): Western Oklahoma and Texas. Washington (Region VI): Alabama, Connecticut, Florida, Louisiana, Mississippi, North Carolina, and New York. See footnote 2 regarding St. Paul region and footnote 3 regarding Rapid City region. [2] Through FY2015, St. Paul region covers Iowa, Michigan, Minnesota, Montana, North Dakota, Nebraska, South Dakota, Wisconsin, and Wyoming. Beginning FY2016, St. Paul region covers Indiana, Iowa, Michigan, Minnesota, Nebraska, and Wisconsin. Also known as Region IV. [3] Rapid City region data begins with data for FY2016, and covers North Dakota, South Dakota, Montana, and Wyoming.

Source: National Indian Gaming Commission, *Gross Gaming Revenues 2016-2020*, December 2021, and earlier reports; and *Gross Gaming Revenues by Region 2019 and 2020*, December 2021, and earlier reports.

Table 1278. Real Tourism Output by Tourism Commodity: 2010 to 2020

[In millions of dollars (721,672 represents $721,672,000,000)]

Tourism commodity	Direct output (current dollars)			Real output (chained 2012 dollars)		
	2010	2015	2020	2010	2015	2020
Total............................	**721,672**	**960,270**	**564,767**	**785,048**	**975,601**	**568,380**
Traveler accommodations..........................	138,442	193,451	146,275	145,855	177,549	134,283
Food and beverage services......................	91,775	133,448	78,262	96,595	123,996	63,126
Domestic passenger air transportation services..........	107,275	142,893	85,548	121,253	142,157	92,124
International passenger air transportation services.......	38,359	50,026	26,685	43,442	51,005	29,410
Passenger rail transportation services....................	1,843	2,181	741	1,853	2,224	726
Passenger water transportation services................	12,394	14,684	10,714	12,015	14,619	10,620
Intercity bus transportation services.................	1,248	1,326	986	1,312	1,321	984
Intercity charter bus transportation services.............	1,827	2,398	1,423	1,919	2,387	1,415
Local bus and other transportation services.............	3,781	4,983	5,090	4,080	4,621	4,519
Taxicab services..................................	4,058	5,584	2,165	4,379	5,176	1,908
Scenic and sightseeing transportation services..........	2,380	3,346	1,226	2,433	3,179	1,043
Automotive rental and leasing........................	23,528	29,888	28,657	22,240	30,196	32,621
Other vehicle rental and leasing......................	620	638	593	620	619	572
Automotive repair services...........................	10,596	11,052	9,385	10,994	10,546	7,945
Parking...	2,227	2,529	1,511	2,477	2,324	1,245
Highway tolls......................................	688	872	733	766	801	604
Travel arrangement and reservation services.............	33,356	41,439	23,408	33,683	40,791	24,308
Motion pictures and performing arts...................	13,814	16,058	9,494	14,226	15,255	8,054
Spectator sports..................................	4,259	4,518	5,071	4,390	3,991	3,964
Participant sports.................................	10,006	13,170	9,605	10,171	12,701	8,325
Gambling...	43,769	50,019	18,160	46,078	48,453	16,084
All other recreation and entertainment.................	15,538	14,098	4,114	16,663	13,749	3,808
Gasoline..	64,037	92,110	16,865	83,489	135,454	26,636
Shopping...	95,852	129,559	78,056	103,982	133,439	79,163

Source: U.S. Bureau of Economic Analysis, "Travel Satellite Accounts Data Sheets," <www.bea.gov/data/special-topics/travel-and-tourism>, accessed May 2022.

Table 1279. Chain–Type Price Indexes for Real Tourism Output by Tourism Commodity: 2000 to 2020

[Index numbers, 2012=100. For explanation of chain-type price indexes, see text, Section 13]

Tourism commodity	2000	2010	2015	2016	2017	2018	2019	2020
All tourism goods and services..........................	**73.1**	**91.9**	**98.6**	**97.6**	**99.9**	**102.9**	**104.4**	**99.4**
Traveler accommodations..........................	78.0	94.9	109.0	111.8	113.0	114.1	117.4	108.9
Food and beverage services......................	71.1	95.0	107.6	110.3	113.0	115.9	119.5	123.0
Domestic passenger air transportation services.............	82.9	88.5	100.5	97.3	97.9	99.7	103.1	92.9
International passenger air transportation services.........	56.8	88.3	98.1	94.0	93.8	98.2	98.4	90.7
Passenger rail transportation services......................	74.4	99.4	98.1	100.2	103.5	105.2	100.0	102.1
Passenger water transportation services....................	145.3	103.2	100.4	104.0	104.9	105.2	104.6	100.9
Intercity bus transportation services......................	64.0	95.2	100.4	104.1	105.0	105.3	104.7	100.2
Intercity charter bus transportation services.............	64.0	95.2	100.5	104.1	105.0	105.3	104.6	100.6
Local bus and other transportation services.............	62.1	92.7	107.8	109.6	111.6	113.5	114.8	112.6
Taxicab services..................................	62.1	92.7	107.9	109.7	111.6	113.5	114.8	113.4
Scenic and sightseeing transportation services.............	75.2	97.8	105.3	107.8	110.6	113.2	115.8	117.6
Automotive rental and leasing........................	76.6	105.8	99.0	91.6	91.9	94.0	93.5	87.8
Other vehicle rental and leasing......................	87.1	100.0	103.0	105.7	103.2	102.3	102.9	103.7
Automotive repair services...........................	69.5	96.4	104.8	106.5	108.5	110.5	114.2	118.1
Parking...	57.0	89.9	108.8	111.8	114.6	117.2	120.5	121.4
Highway tolls......................................	57.0	89.9	108.8	111.8	114.6	117.3	120.5	121.3
Travel arrangement and reservation services...............	107.4	99.0	101.6	101.5	101.3	101.9	104.0	96.3
Motion pictures and performing arts...................	71.4	97.1	105.3	109.0	111.8	114.2	116.3	117.9
Spectator sports..................................	64.0	97.0	113.2	117.0	119.6	121.7	124.2	127.9
Participant sports.................................	86.8	98.4	103.7	105.4	107.8	110.9	113.8	115.4
Gambling...	75.0	95.0	103.2	104.5	106.8	109.4	111.4	112.9
All other recreation and entertainment.................	78.5	93.2	102.5	104.2	106.6	107.2	108.2	108.0
Gasoline..	41.3	76.7	68.0	60.3	68.2	77.3	74.6	63.3
Shopping...	74.0	92.2	97.1	95.9	97.5	99.3	99.2	98.6

Source: U.S. Bureau of Economic Analysis, "Travel Satellite Accounts Data Sheets," <www.bea.gov/data/special-topics/travel-and-tourism>, accessed May 2022.

Table 1280. Travel Forecast Summary: 2020 to 2026

[In units as indicated (722 represents $722,000,000,000). Data for 2022 to 2026 are forecast]

Indicator	Unit	2020	2021	2022	2023	2024	2025	2026
Consumer price index (CPI) [1].............	Percent	259	271	291	297	302	308	314
Travel price index (TPI) [1].............	Percent	275	300	332	332	337	343	350
Total travel expenditures in U.S............	Bil. dol.	722	886	1,050	1,150	1,210	1,240	1,260
U.S. residents................................	Bil. dol.	682	846	941	1,010	1,040	1,050	1,060
International visitors [2]........................	Bil. dol.	41	40	109	141	167	186	198
Total international visitors to the U.S.......	Millions	19	22	53	56	77	85	90
Total domestic person trips [3]................	Millions	1,580	2,020	2,260	2,380	2,470	2,520	2,550
Business.....................................	Millions	181	250	377	446	476	483	487
Leisure.......................................	Millions	1,400	1,770	1,880	1,940	2,000	2,030	2,060

[1] 1982-1984=100. [2] Excludes international traveler spending on medical, educational, and cross-border/seasonal work-related activities or international passenger fares on U.S. airlines. [3] One person on one trip 50 miles or more, one way, away from home or including one or more nights away from home.

Source: U.S. Travel Association, *Travel Forecast Summary Table*, June 2022 ©. See also <www.ustravel.org/research>.

Table 1281. Tourism Sales and Employment by Tourism Commodity: 2000 to 2020

[Sales in millions of dollars (602,548 represents $602,548,000,000); employment in thousands (6,213 represents 6,213,000). Direct tourism-related sales comprise all output purchased directly by visitors (e.g., traveler accommodations, passenger air transportation, souvenirs). Direct tourism-related employment comprises all jobs where the workers are engaged in the production of direct tourism-related sales (output), such as hotel staff, airline pilots, and souvenir sellers]

Tourism commodity	2000	2005	2010	2015	2018	2019	2020
DIRECT TOURISM SALES (OUTPUT) (mil. dol.)							
All tourism goods and services [1]	**602,548**	**709,209**	**721,672**	**960,270**	**1,114,493**	**1,141,491**	**564,767**
Traveler accommodations	108,664	125,132	138,442	193,451	218,878	225,094	146,275
Food and beverage services	90,181	107,356	91,775	133,448	151,543	149,973	78,262
Domestic passenger air transportation services	91,900	97,016	107,275	142,893	162,847	177,968	85,548
Gasoline	36,993	56,381	64,037	92,110	125,669	121,640	16,865
Shopping	96,640	110,137	95,852	129,559	135,170	138,326	78,056
DIRECT TOURISM EMPLOYMENT (1,000)							
All tourism goods and services [1]	**6,213**	**5,933**	**4,939**	**5,734**	**6,103**	**6,070**	**3,887**
Traveler accommodations	1,421	1,372	1,310	1,462	1,537	1,565	1,083
Vacation home rentals	16	15	17	15	15	16	15
Food services and drinking places	1,676	1,741	1,321	1,697	1,776	1,701	878
Air transportation services	641	540	484	535	594	618	484
Rail transportation services	11	9	9	10	9	9	4
Water transportation services	28	31	32	36	38	44	28
Interurban bus transportation	23	20	18	18	18	18	13
Interurban charter bus transportation	32	23	19	20	20	19	11
Urban transit systems and other transportation	82	79	55	55	78	70	50
Taxi service	14	10	9	9	6	7	3
Scenic and sightseeing transportation services	30	26	25	30	32	33	18
Automotive equipment rental and leasing	136	122	96	97	113	128	103
Automotive repair services	97	86	69	73	75	74	53
Parking lots and garages	21	30	30	36	38	42	18
Toll highways	3	5	3	4	5	5	3
Travel arrangement and reservation services	283	213	175	188	204	203	156
Motion pictures and performing arts	80	76	54	50	48	43	38
Spectator sports	36	46	35	38	43	44	35
Participant sports	239	255	193	223	290	291	154
Gambling	140	155	154	127	136	120	42
All other recreation and entertainment	103	101	76	69	62	50	13
Petroleum refineries	8	7	6	9	9	10	6
Wholesale trade and transportation services	167	156	121	160	163	167	121
Gasoline service stations	140	121	107	167	194	198	47
Retail trade services, excluding gasoline service stations	460	427	330	390	382	383	321
All other industries	111	98	77	80	81	77	60

[1] Includes other goods and services not shown separately.

Source: U.S. Bureau of Economic Analysis, "Tourism Satellite Accounts Data Sheets," <www.bea.gov/data/special-topics/travel-and-tourism>, accessed May 2022.

Table 1282. Top States and Cities Visited by Overseas Travelers: 2000 to 2019

[25,975 represents 25,975,000. Excludes visitors from Canada and Mexico. Includes travelers for business and pleasure, international travelers in transit through the United States, and students. Excludes travel by international personnel and international businessmen employed in the United States. Beginning 2006, the statistical policy for visitation estimates of international visitation requires a minimum sample of 400 respondents. States and cities are ranked by the latest overseas visitors data and may not reflect revisions for previous years]

State and other area	Overseas visitors (1,000)				City/MSA	Overseas visitors (1,000)			
	2000	2010	2015	2019		2000	2010	2015	2019
Total [1, 2]	**25,975**	**26,363**	**38,700**	**40,393**	New York-White Plains-Wayne, NY-NJ	5,714	8,462	10,132	10,288
New York	5,922	8,647	10,385	10,518	Miami-Miami Beach-Kendall, FL	2,935	3,111	5,509	5,211
Florida	6,026	5,826	9,667	9,610	Los Angeles-Long Beach-Glendale, CA	3,533	3,348	4,857	4,645
California	6,364	5,615	8,139	8,050	Orlando-Kissimmee-Sanford, FL	3,013	2,715	4,718	4,415
Hawaii	2,727	2,135	3,021	3,296	San Francisco-San Mateo-Redwood City, CA	2,831	2,636	3,632	3,308
Nevada	2,364	2,504	3,505	3,058	Las Vegas-Paradise, NV	2,260	2,425	3,409	2,989
Guam	1,325	1,318	1,505	1,842	Honolulu, HI	2,234	1,634	2,380	2,751
Massachusetts	1,429	1,292	1,789	1,745	Washington (DC Metro Area), DC-MD-VA	1,481	1,740	2,135	1,907
Texas	1,169	1,028	1,789	1,745	Boston-Quincy, MA	1,325	1,186	1,609	1,567
Illinois	1,377	1,186	1,708	1,555	Chicago-Joliet-Naperville, IL	1,351	1,134	1,620	1,491
Arizona	883	765	1,044	1,196	Fort Lauderdale, FL [3]	(X)	(X)	902	982
New Jersey	909	975	994	1,159	San Diego-Carlsbad-San Marcos, CA	701	765	1,159	881
Pennsylvania	649	923	1,029	1,054	Seattle-Bellevue-Everett, WA	416	475	783	844
Washington	468	501	852	925	Houston-Sugar Land-Baytown, TX	442	448	864	828
Georgia	805	817	998	868	Flagstaff, AZ	(B)	501	672	731
Utah	(B)	475	595	739	Atlanta-Sandy Springs-Marietta, GA	701	712	837	727
Virginia	364	369	453	529	Philadelphia, PA	390	633	680	703
Colorado	519	343	461	509	Santa Ana-Anaheim-Irvine, CA	494	369	610	630
Louisiana	(X)	(X)	518	501	Dallas-Plano-Irving, TX	494	343	545	610

B Figure too small to meet statistical standards for reliability of a derived figure. X Not applicable (not ranked). [1] Total overseas travelers; includes other states and cities, not shown separately. [2] A person is counted in each area visited, but only once in the total. [3] Fort Lauderdale-Pompano Beach-Deerfield Beach, FL.

Source: U.S. Department of Commerce, International Trade Administration, National Travel and Tourism Office, "2019 U.S. Travel and Tourism Statistics (Inbound), Overseas Visitation Estimates," <travel.trade.gov/outreachpages/inbound.general_information.inbound_overview.asp>, accessed February 2021.

Table 1283. International Travel: 2010 to 2021

[In thousands (60,271 represents 60,271,000), except percent. U.S. travelers cover residents of the United States, its territories and possessions. International travelers to the U.S. include travelers for business and pleasure, and excludes travel by international personnel and international businessmen employed in the United States. Some traveler data revised since originally issued]

Item and world region	2010	2014	2015	2016	2017	2018	2019	2020	2021
U.S. TRAVELERS TO FOREIGN COUNTRIES BY WORLD REGION OF DESTINATION [1]									
Total	60,271	68,176	74,191	80,226	87,555	92,587	99,270	33,160	49,097
Canada	11,749	11,515	12,669	13,895	14,280	14,440	15,005	1,929	2,093
Mexico	20,015	25,882	28,733	31,194	34,947	36,373	39,458	21,390	28,789
Total overseas [2]	28,507	30,780	32,789	35,137	38,327	41,774	44,808	9,841	18,214
Europe	11,104	11,892	12,599	13,614	15,793	17,742	19,049	2,582	5,238
Caribbean	5,716	7,172	7,648	7,879	8,321	8,702	9,368	3,098	6,399
Asia	4,861	4,509	4,843	5,383	5,771	6,253	6,546	1,114	626
South America	2,129	1,772	1,869	2,010	1,925	2,104	2,338	772	1,401
Central America	2,263	2,697	2,791	2,984	3,032	3,237	3,451	1,104	2,585
Oceania	687	601	643	725	776	861	958	247	63
Middle East	1,339	1,780	2,045	2,176	2,306	2,443	2,545	737	1,516
Africa	408	358	351	365	403	432	552	187	385
INTERNATIONAL TRAVELERS TO U.S. BY VISITOR REGION OF RESIDENCE									
Total	60,010	75,379	77,774	76,407	77,187	79,746	79,442	19,212	22,100
Canada	20,176	23,014	20,699	19,287	20,493	21,475	20,720	4,809	2,529
Mexico	13,472	17,070	18,374	18,991	17,788	18,387	18,328	6,809	10,397
Total overseas [2]	26,363	35,296	38,700	38,129	38,906	39,883	40,393	7,594	9,175
Europe	11,985	14,269	15,790	14,831	14,974	15,424	15,706	2,469	1,962
Asia	7,020	9,833	10,946	11,538	12,137	11,874	12,250	2,165	1,289
South America	3,250	5,533	5,699	5,407	5,556	6,027	5,733	1,433	3,019
Caribbean	1,201	1,339	1,479	1,587	1,671	1,793	1,921	511	990
Oceania	1,095	1,592	1,768	1,661	1,632	1,687	1,641	257	67
Central America	760	943	1,077	1,187	1,168	1,283	1,360	391	1,181
Middle East	736	1,254	1,369	1,342	1,182	1,197	1,216	262	513
Africa	316	533	573	576	586	598	567	107	154

[1] A person is counted in each area visited but only once in the total. [2] "Overseas" excludes Canada and Mexico.

Source: U.S. Department of Commerce, International Trade Administration, National Travel and Tourism Office, "Annual Arrivals 2000 to Present - Country of Residence (COR)," <www.trade.gov/i-94-arrivals-program>, and "US Outbound Travel by World Regions," <www.trade.gov/us-international-air-travel-statistics-i-92-data>; accessed September 2022.

Table 1284. International Travel Payments, Receipts, and Balance of Trade: 2000 to 2021

[In millions of dollars (85,490 represents $85,490,000,000)]

Year	Travel and passenger fare (mil. dol.)						U.S. net travel and passenger receipts (mil. dol.)
	Payments by U.S. travelers abroad			Receipts from international visitors			
	Total	Travel payments [1, 2]	Air transport [3]	Total	Travel receipts [1, 2]	Air transport [3]	
2000	85,490	64,174	21,316	118,317	96,872	21,445	32,827
2001	82,185	60,525	21,660	105,453	86,408	19,045	23,268
2002	79,362	59,017	20,345	97,416	79,625	17,791	18,054
2003	81,708	61,244	20,464	94,817	76,983	17,834	13,109
2004	93,342	70,332	23,010	107,210	85,648	21,562	13,868
2005	98,695	74,112	24,583	116,682	93,423	23,259	17,987
2006	105,404	78,375	27,029	121,029	96,148	24,881	15,625
2007	112,930	82,606	30,324	134,800	106,918	27,882	21,870
2008	119,133	84,317	34,816	149,095	117,030	32,065	29,962
2009	115,126	82,512	32,614	137,114	110,757	26,357	21,988
2010	123,833	85,166	38,667	161,821	130,315	31,506	37,988
2011	130,607	86,623	43,984	178,935	142,197	36,738	48,328
2012	138,167	90,340	47,827	195,114	153,921	41,193	56,947
2013	132,324	91,119	41,205	213,103	170,979	42,124	80,779
2014	140,228	96,248	43,980	222,747	180,265	42,482	82,519
2015	144,667	102,664	42,003	230,574	192,602	37,972	85,907
2016	147,639	109,155	38,484	228,551	192,868	35,683	80,912
2017	158,290	117,931	40,359	233,759	196,469	37,290	75,469
2018	176,817	126,139	50,678	241,985	200,724	41,261	65,168
2019	186,080	133,285	52,795	239,446	199,364	40,082	53,366
2020	48,840	35,808	13,032	84,206	72,813	11,393	35,366
2021, preliminary	74,121	57,940	16,181	80,956	68,759	12,197	6,835

[1] Covers purchases of goods and services by U.S. persons traveling abroad and by foreign travelers in the United States for business or personal reasons. These goods and services include food, lodging, recreation, gifts, entertainment, local transportation in the country of travel, and other items incidental to a foreign visit. [2] Covers business travel, including expenditures by border, seasonal, and other short-term workers; and personal travel, including health-related and education-related travel, along with spending on day-trips (less than one night). [3] Fares received for the transport of nonresidents by U.S. air carriers between the United States and foreign countries and between two foreign points, and the transport of U.S. residents by foreign air carriers between the United States and foreign countries.

Source: U.S. Department of Commerce, International Trade Administration, National Travel and Tourism Office, "Annual Visitor Spending 1960-2021," <www.trade.gov/travel-and-tourism-research>, accessed May 2022.

Table 1285. Inbound Crossings for Top 5 U.S.-Canadian and U.S.-Mexican Border Land Passenger Gateways: 2021

[4,431 represents 4,431,000. Data reflect all personal vehicles and buses, passengers, and pedestrians entering the U.S.-Canadian border and U.S.-Mexican border, regardless of nationality]

Item and gateway	Entering the U.S. (1,000)	Item and gateway	Entering the U.S. (1,000)
All U.S.-Canadian land gateways:		**All U.S.-Mexican land gateways:**	
Personal vehicles...................	4,431	Personal vehicles...................	58,548
Personal vehicle passengers............	6,389	Personal vehicle passengers............	96,562
Buses........................	4	Buses........................	96
Bus passengers....................	35	Bus passengers....................	1,350
Train passengers..................	47	Train passengers..................	17
Pedestrians......................	37	Pedestrians......................	27,935
Top five gateways:		**Top five gateways:**	
Personal vehicles:		Personal vehicles:	
Detroit, MI......................	1,211	San Ysidro, CA...................	13,881
Buffalo-Niagara Falls, NY...........	692	El Paso, TX.....................	6,330
Massena, NY....................	545	Otay Mesa, CA..................	4,714
Blaine, WA.....................	439	Calexico, CA....................	4,652
Port Huron, MI...................	188	Brownsville, TX.................	3,564
Personal vehicle passengers:		Personal vehicle passengers:	
Detroit, MI......................	1,422	San Ysidro, CA...................	21,989
Buffalo-Niagara Falls, NY...........	1,093	El Paso, TX.....................	10,150
Massena, NY....................	831	Otay Mesa, CA..................	7,185
Blaine, WA.....................	673	Calexico, CA....................	7,123
Champlain Rouses Point, NY........	301	Laredo, TX.....................	6,001
Pedestrians:		Pedestrians:	
Buffalo-Niagara Falls, NY...........	23	San Ysidro, CA...................	5,278
Sweetgrass, MT..................	3	El Paso, TX.....................	2,982
International Falls, MN.............	2	Otay Mesa, CA..................	2,270
Champlain Rouses Point, NY........	2	Calexico, CA....................	2,224
Sumas, WA.....................	2	San Luis, AZ....................	1,876

Source: U.S. Department of Transportation, Bureau of Transportation Statistics, "Border Crossing / Entry Data," <www.bts.gov/browse-statistical-products-and-data/border-crossing-data/border-crossingentry-data>, accessed February 2022.

Table 1286. Foreign Tourists Admitted by Country of Citizenship: 2000 to 2020

[In thousands (30,511 represents 30,511,000). For years ending September 30. Represents non-U.S. citizens admitted to the country for a temporary period of time, for pleasure (tourists). Includes nonimmigrant admission classes B2 (temporary visitors for pleasure), GMT (Commonwealth of the Northern Marianas Islands visa waiver program–temporary visitors for pleasure, Guam or Northern Mariana Islands), and WT (visa waiver program–temporary visitors for pleasure)]

Country and region	2000 [1]	2010	2015	2020	Country and region	2000 [1]	2010	2015	2020
All countries [2, 3]...........	**30,511**	**35,131**	**61,017**	**28,732**	Thailand....................	76	48	72	30
Europe [3].................	**11,806**	**11,741**	**13,552**	**5,795**	Turkey......................	93	74	143	60
Austria......................	182	166	181	67	United Arab Emirates......	36	8	28	10
Belgium.....................	254	227	244	86	**Africa [3]**....................	**327**	**274**	**540**	**212**
Czechia.....................	44	58	87	45	Egypt......................	44	34	73	34
Denmark....................	150	244	281	103	Nigeria.....................	27	62	170	48
Finland.....................	95	106	128	59	South Africa...............	114	63	99	43
France [4]....................	1,113	1,371	1,658	765	**Oceania [3]**..................	**748**	**1,047**	**1,545**	**593**
Germany....................	1,925	1,599	1,786	689	Australia...................	535	843	1,245	475
Greece......................	60	54	57	35	New Zealand [3, 6]...........	170	191	281	111
Hungary.....................	58	49	68	43	**North America [3, 6]**...........	**6,501**	**12,754**	**30,038**	**15,464**
Iceland......................	27	35	48	25	Canada [7]..................	277	87	9,977	5,011
Ireland......................	325	406	402	208	Mexico.....................	3,972	11,010	17,904	9,148
Italy........................	626	924	1,052	426	**Caribbean**.................	**1,404**	**999**	**1,226**	**703**
Netherlands [4]..............	559	598	596	261	Bahamas, The..........	24	250	229	129
Norway.....................	144	197	273	85	Dominican Republic......	195	219	295	239
Poland......................	116	103	146	88	Haiti......................	72	90	126	61
Portugal....................	86	120	151	75	Jamaica...................	240	180	249	130
Russia......................	74	134	242	105	Trinidad and Tobago......	133	129	163	75
Spain.......................	370	692	846	401	**Central America**...........	**792**	**657**	**930**	**602**
Sweden.....................	321	330	505	177	Costa Rica................	172	143	202	164
Switzerland..................	400	315	409	131	El Salvador...............	175	105	150	95
United Kingdom [4]..........	4,671	3,768	3,991	1,702	Guatemala................	177	159	209	131
Asia [3]....................	**7,853**	**6,254**	**9,826**	**4,240**	Honduras..................	87	101	156	100
China [5].....................	656	482	1,950	619	Nicaragua.................	47	38	56	31
India........................	253	490	921	393	Panama....................	106	94	136	72
Indonesia...................	62	44	84	41	**South America [3]**...........	**2,867**	**2,785**	**5,484**	**2,402**
Israel.......................	319	253	340	146	Argentina..................	515	375	713	316
Japan.......................	4,946	3,252	3,350	1,445	Bolivia.....................	48	31	55	29
Korea, South................	606	896	1,564	941	Brazil......................	706	976	2,222	918
Malaysia....................	64	37	59	24	Chile.......................	194	119	298	177
Pakistan....................	47	39	87	37	Colombia...................	411	455	854	391
Philippines..................	163	179	255	132	Ecuador....................	122	169	351	202
Saudi Arabia................	67	36	138	24	Peru.......................	190	162	269	150
Singapore...................	131	72	97	47	Uruguay....................	66	35	70	24
Taiwan......................	(NA)	183	344	146	Venezuela..................	570	423	560	161

[1] Due to the expiration of the Visa Waiver Program during May-October 2000, data for business and pleasure not available separately. [2] Total includes visitors of unknown country of citizenship. [3] Total includes other countries, not shown separately. [4] As of 2005, includes overseas territories; see source for details. [5] Prior to 2005, data for China includes Taiwan. As of 2005, data for China includes Hong Kong and Macau. [6] The majority of short-term admissions from Canada and Mexico are excluded. [7] Beginning in 2014, the number of admissions greatly exceeds totals reported in previous years due to a more complete count of Canadian air and sea admissions.

Source: U.S. Department of Homeland Security, Office of Immigration Statistics, "2020 Yearbook of Immigration Statistics," and earlier reports, <www.dhs.gov/immigration-statistics/yearbook>, accessed February 2022.

Table 1287. Top 20 U.S. Gateway Airports for Nonstop International Air Travel Passengers: 2021

[94,943 represents 94,943,000. International passengers are residents of any country traveling nonstop to and from the United States on U.S. and foreign carriers. The data cover all passengers arriving and departing from U.S. airports on nonstop commercial international flights with 60 seats or more]

Gateway airport	Airport code	Passengers (1,000)	Gateway airport	Airport code	Passengers (1,000)
Total, all airports	**(X)**	**94,943**	Fort Lauderdale, FL	FLL	4,035
Total, top 20 airports	(X)	86,417	Washington, DC (Dulles)	IAD	3,299
Top 20, percentage of total	(X)	91.0	San Francisco, CA	SFO	3,291
			Boston, MA	BOS	2,088
New York, NY	JFK	12,812	Charlotte, NC	CLT	2,043
Miami, FL	MIA	11,954	Orlando, FL	MCO	1,913
Los Angeles, CA	LAX	7,887	Denver, CO	DEN	1,866
Houston, TX	IAH	6,502	Seattle, WA	SEA	1,542
Newark, NJ	EWR	6,464	Phoenix, AZ	PHX	1,230
Dallas/Fort Worth, TX	DFW	5,894	Philadelphia, PA	PHL	1,020
Atlanta, GA	ATL	5,566	Detroit, MI	DTW	968
Chicago, IL	ORD	5,278	Las Vegas, NV	LAS	765

X Not applicable.

Source: U.S. Department of Transportation, Research and Innovative Technology Administration, Bureau of Transportation Statistics, Office of Airline Information, "T-100 International Segment data," <www.transtats.bts.gov/Fields.asp?gnoyr_VQ=FJE>, accessed June 2022.

Table 1288. Average Cost of Airfare for Domestic Routes: 1995 to 2021

[In dollars, except percent. Fares based on domestic itinerary fares. Itinerary fares consist of round-trip fares unless the customer does not purchase a return trip. In that case, the one-way fare is included. Fares are based on the total ticket value, which consists of the price charged by the airlines plus any additional taxes and fees levied by an outside entity at the time of purchase. Fares include only the price paid at the time of the ticket purchase and do not include other fees paid at the airport or onboard the aircraft. Averages do not include frequent-flyer or "zero fares."]

Year	Current dollars			Constant (2021) dollars [1]		
		Percent change			Percent change	
	Average fare	From previous year	Cumulative from 1995	Average fare	From previous year	Cumulative from 1995
1995	292	(NA)	(NA)	520	(NA)	(NA)
2000	339	4.7	16.0	533	1.3	2.7
2005	307	0.6	5.2	426	-2.7	-17.9
2010	336	8.3	15.0	418	6.5	-19.6
2014	392	2.5	34.1	448	0.9	-13.7
2015	377	-3.8	29.0	431	-3.9	-17.0
2016	349	-7.4	19.5	394	-8.5	-24.1
2017	348	-0.4	19.0	384	-2.7	-26.2
2018	350	0.6	19.7	377	-1.7	-27.4
2019	355	1.5	21.4	373	-1.0	-28.1
2020	292	-17.6	0.1	306	-18.0	-41.1
2021	307	5.0	5.1	307	0.3	-40.9

NA Not available. [1] Rate calculated using Bureau of Labor Statistics Consumer Price Index.

Source: U.S. Department of Transportation, Bureau of Transportation Statistics, Air Fares, "National Level Fares since 1995—Annual," <www.bts.gov/air-fares>, accessed April 2022.

Section 27
Accommodation, Food Services, and Other Services

This section presents statistics relating to services other than those covered in the previous sections on wholesale and retail trade, transportation, communications, financial services, and recreation services. Data shown for services are classified by kind of business and cover sales or receipts, establishments, employees, payrolls, and other items.

The principal sources of these data are from the U.S. Census Bureau and include the 2012 and 2017 Economic Censuses, Service Annual Survey, and the County Business Patterns program.

Data on these services also appear in several other sections. For instance, labor force employment and earnings data appear in Section 12, Labor Force, Employment, and Earnings; gross domestic product of the industry (Table 708) appears in Section 13, Income, Expenditures, Poverty, and Wealth; and financial data (several tables) from the quarterly *Statistics of Income Bulletin*, published by the Internal Revenue Service, appear in Section 15, Business Enterprise.

Censuses—Limited coverage of the service industries started in 1933. Beginning with the 1967 Economic Census, legislation provides for a census to be conducted every 5 years (for years ending in "2" and "7"). For more information on the most current census, see the Census Bureau's Economic Census website at <www.census.gov/programs-surveys/economic-census.html>. The industries covered in the censuses and surveys of business are defined in the North American Industry Classification System (NAICS). For information on NAICS, see the Census website at <www.census.gov/naics/>.

In general, the 2012 and 2017 Economic Censuses have three series of publications for these sectors: 1) subject series with reports such as product lines, and

establishment and firm sizes, 2) geographic reports with individual reports for each state, and 3) industry series with individual reports for industry groups.

Current surveys—The Service Annual Survey provides annual estimates of nationwide receipts for selected personal, business, leasing and repair, amusement and entertainment, social and health, and other professional service industries in the United States. For selected social, health, and other professional service industries, separate estimates are developed for receipts of taxable firms and revenue and expenses for firms and organizations exempt from federal income taxes. Several service sectors from this survey are covered in other sections of this publication. The estimates for tax exempt firms in these industries are derived from a sample of employer firms only. Estimates obtained from annual and monthly surveys are based on sample data and are not expected to agree exactly with results that would be obtained from a complete census of all establishments. Data include estimates for sampling units not reporting. Data are released in the *Annual Services Report* at <www.census.gov/programs-surveys/sas.html>. The *Quarterly Services Report* is a principal economic indicator that produces, for selected service industries, quarterly estimates of total operating revenue and the percentage of revenue by class of customer (government, business, household consumers/individual users). Data can be found at <www.census.gov/services/index.html>.

Statistical reliability—For a discussion of statistical collection and estimation, sampling procedures, and measures of statistical reliability applicable to Census Bureau data, see Appendix III.

Table 1289. Selected Service-Related Industries—Establishments, Sales, Payroll, and Employees by Kind of Business: 2017

[1,884,780,952 represents $1,884,780,952,000. Covers only establishments with payroll. Based on the 2017 Economic Census; for statement on methodology, see Appendix III]

Kind of business	NAICS code [1]	Establish-ments, (number)	Sales or receipts ($1,000)	Annual payroll ($1,000)	Paid employees [2] (number)
Professional, scientific, and technical services..................	54	913,624	1,844,780,952	729,370,858	9,015,366
Professional, scientific, and technical services...............	541	913,624	1,844,780,952	729,370,858	9,015,366
Management of companies and enterprises.....................	55	59,224	121,526,125	367,702,894	3,571,409
Administrative and support and waste management and remediation services............................	56	417,259	950,894,923	470,191,457	11,889,169
Administrative and support services.....................	561	391,982	851,306,186	446,899,503	11,461,331
Waste management and remediation services...............	562	25,277	99,588,737	23,291,954	427,838
Accommodation and food services.........................	72	726,081	938,237,077	264,603,598	14,002,624
Accommodation...............................	721	68,196	260,088,830	62,064,428	2,121,450
Food services and drinking places............................	722	657,885	678,148,247	202,539,170	11,881,174
Other services (except public administration)...................	81	560,845	544,127,699	133,751,085	3,696,831
Repair and maintenance............................	811	217,722	180,982,087	51,111,339	1,285,621
Personal and laundry services............................	812	236,300	111,390,006	35,571,229	1,473,881
Religious, grantmaking, civic, professional, and similar organizations...	813	106,823	251,755,606	47,068,517	937,329

[1] North American Industrial Classification System, 2017; see text, Section 15. [2] For employees on the payroll during the pay period including March 12.

Source: U.S. Census Bureau, 2017 Economic Census, "EC1700BASIC: All Sectors: Summary Statistics for the U.S., States, and Selected Geographies: 2017," <data.census.gov>, accessed December 2021.

Table 1290. Selected Service-Related Industries—Nonemployer Establishments and Receipts by Kind of Business: 2017 to 2019

[3,535 represents 3,535,000. Includes only firms subject to federal income tax. Nonemployers are businesses with no paid employees. Data originate chiefly from administrative records of the Internal Revenue Service; see Appendix III]

Kind of business	NAICS code [1]	Firms (1,000) 2017	2018	2019	Receipts (mil. dol.) 2017	2018	2019
Professional, scientific, and technical services..............	**54**	**3,535**	**3,727**	**3,773**	**166,944**	**178,373**	**185,148**
Professional, scientific, and technical services [2]...............	541	3,535	3,727	3,773	166,944	178,373	185,148
Legal services..	5411	290	293	290	20,432	21,060	21,791
Accounting, tax preparation, bookkeeping, and payroll services..	5412	373	382	385	10,428	10,984	11,437
Architectural, engineering, and related services...............	5413	230	237	232	11,924	12,570	12,790
Specialized design services.................................	5414	238	254	254	9,171	10,106	10,339
Computer systems design and related services...............	5415	309	316	339	15,306	16,098	16,931
Management, scientific and technical consulting...............	5416	800	889	920	39,543	43,792	46,161
Scientific research and development services.................	5417	48	51	53	1,575	1,706	1,804
Advertising, public relations, and related services.............	5418	158	169	172	8,700	9,230	9,649
Administrative and support and waste management and remediation services................................	**56**	**2,143**	**2,522**	**2,596**	**50,102**	**59,169**	**62,643**
Administrative and support services [2]........................	561	2,124	2,502	2,577	48,497	57,460	60,883
Office administrative services.............................	5611	266	295	302	4,748	5,343	5,673
Business support services.................................	5614	215	233	233	6,334	6,791	6,995
Services to buildings and dwellings.........................	5617	1,301	1,582	1,633	27,540	34,114	36,288
Waste management and remediation services................	562	19	20	19	1,605	1,709	1,760
Accommodation and food services...........................	**72**	**403**	**460**	**497**	**18,580**	**18,744**	**19,481**
Accommodation..	721	79	112	113	4,077	4,554	4,533
Food services and drinking places...........................	722	323	348	384	14,503	14,190	14,948
Special food services.....................................	7223	200	221	248	5,555	5,952	6,567
Drinking places (alcoholic beverages).......................	7224	25	25	27	1,600	1,592	1,650
Restaurants and other eating places.........................	7225	98	101	109	7,348	6,645	6,730
Full-service restaurants.................................	722511	43	45	49	3,603	3,134	3,185
Limited-service eating places.............................	722513	34	34	36	3,053	2,784	2,720
Other services (except public administration)................	**81**	**3,740**	**2,978**	**2,852**	**104,780**	**90,820**	**90,930**
Repair and maintenance [2]................................	811	753	559	551	29,895	25,241	25,625
Automotive repair and maintenance...........................	8111	331	313	323	15,269	14,893	15,522
Personal and household goods repair and maintenance.....	8114	331	176	161	10,319	6,704	6,520
Personal and laundry services [2]...........................	812	2,776	2,221	2,111	71,490	62,312	62,047
Personal care services.................................	8121	1,335	1,299	1,307	33,487	35,236	37,103
Hair, nail, and skin care services.........................	81211	1,098	1,123	1,140	28,270	30,647	32,267
Beauty salons...	812112	733	750	758	17,214	18,752	19,640
Death care services......................................	8122	17	16	15	900	881	885
Drycleaning and laundry services...........................	8123	29	25	24	1,739	1,661	1,651
Other personal services...................................	8129	1,395	882	764	35,365	24,534	22,408
Religious, grantmaking, civic, professional, and similar organizations..	813	211	198	190	3,395	3,268	3,258

[1] Data for 2016, based on North American Industry Classification System (NAICS), 2012; beginning 2017, based on NAICS 2017. See text, Section 15. [2] Includes other kinds of business not shown separately.

Source: U.S. Census Bureau, Nonemployer Statistics, "All Sectors: Nonemployer Statistics by Legal Form of Organization and Receipts Size Class for the U.S., States, and Selected Geographies: 2019," and previous releases, <data.census.gov>, accessed June 2022.

Table 1291. Selected Service-Related Industries—Establishments, Employees, and Payroll by Industry: 2019 and 2020

[In thousands (927.2 represents 927,200); payroll in billions of dollars (845.0 represents $845,000,000,000). Covers establishments with paid employees. Excludes self-employed individuals, employees of private households, railroad employees, agricultural production employees, and most government employees; see source for NAICS and other exclusions. For statement on methodology, see Appendix III]

Industry	NAICS code [1]	Establishments (1,000)		Employees [2] (1,000)		Annual payroll (bil. dol.)	
		2019	2020	2019	2020	2019	2020
Professional, scientific, & technical services...............	**54**	**927.2**	**943.2**	**9,284.5**	**9,554.5**	**845.0**	**893.8**
Professional, scientific, & technical services..................	541	927.2	943.2	9,284.5	9,554.5	845.0	893.8
Legal services..	5411	183.9	183.4	1,149.1	1,161.7	115.4	119.6
Offices of lawyers.................................	54111	170.3	169.6	1,063.0	1,071.1	110.0	113.5
Accounting, tax preparation, bookkeeping, and payroll services..................................	5412	134.5	137.8	1,159.2	1,188.6	73.8	76.2
Offices of certified public accountants..............	541211	55.6	55.6	520.1	533.2	44.2	45.2
Tax preparation services..........................	541213	30.9	32.3	158.1	156.7	2.3	2.5
Architectural, engineering, & related services [3]	5413	114.4	114.2	1,568.9	1,603.5	141.6	144.8
Architectural services............................	54131	21.9	21.9	179.3	181.3	15.5	15.2
Engineering services.............................	54133	62.0	61.6	1,125.9	1,157.3	108.7	112.3
Specialized design services [3]....................	5414	33.8	34.3	122.5	122.7	7.7	7.4
Graphic design services..........................	54143	15.6	15.5	52.6	51.7	3.1	3.0
Computer systems design & related services [3].....	5415	140.6	143.1	1,924.2	2,018.8	201.7	222.6
Custom computer programming services..........	541511	65.4	66.0	913.7	951.1	96.0	106.7
Computer systems design services...............	541512	58.7	60.0	786.9	813.9	83.5	90.4
Management, scientific, & technical consulting services [3]...............................	5416	187.9	196.3	1,384.8	1,456.5	125.6	132.9
Management consulting services.................	54161	151.6	160.2	1,145.6	1,211.0	105.9	112.6
Environmental consulting services...............	54162	10.1	10.2	91.9	95.2	6.7	7.0
Scientific research & development services...........	5417	19.6	20.1	804.6	835.4	107.7	118.1
Research & development in the physical engineering & life sciences.....................	54171	17.6	18.1	762.9	792.7	104.6	114.8
Advertising & related services [3]...................	5418	37.5	37.7	469.6	465.0	35.8	34.9
Advertising agencies............................	54181	13.8	14.3	183.9	181.7	17.5	16.9
Public relations agencies........................	54182	8.5	8.6	56.3	57.1	5.9	6.1
Other professional, scientific, & technical services..........	5419	75.0	76.3	701.5	702.3	35.5	37.3
Veterinary services...............................	54194	32.1	32.1	401.0	397.4	16.4	17.5
Management of companies and enterprises...............	**55**	**52.7**	**52.4**	**3,523.3**	**3,571.1**	**403.3**	**410.0**
Administrative and support and waste management and remediation services.................	**56**	**424.9**	**431.1**	**12,642.0**	**12,718.0**	**550.6**	**571.0**
Administrative & support services [3]................	561	399.2	404.7	12,203.5	12,267.4	524.2	543.5
Employment services..............................	5613	53.7	53.3	7,012.5	7,050.5	319.8	334.8
Temporary help services..........................	56132	37.5	37.3	3,506.6	3,390.2	122.1	116.5
Business support services [3]......................	5614	31.0	33.5	797.8	781.7	31.4	32.5
Telephone call centers...........................	56142	5.1	4.9	444.0	427.6	13.4	14.2
Collection agencies..............................	56144	3.5	3.4	126.2	125.7	5.4	5.3
Travel arrangement & reservation services..........	5615	18.0	17.2	225.8	221.8	15.4	13.2
Travel agencies................................	56151	11.3	10.7	102.2	101.4	7.7	6.5
Investigation & security services...................	5616	25.8	26.1	1,014.5	1,002.5	31.4	32.2
Investigation, guard, & armored car services......	56161	14.7	14.7	867.9	862.9	23.7	23.9
Security systems services........................	56162	11.1	11.4	146.6	139.6	7.7	8.2
Services to buildings & dwellings [3]...............	5617	207.7	210.8	2,026.6	2,067.9	64.3	68.1
Landscaping services............................	56173	108.0	109.2	697.5	719.2	29.8	32.0
Waste management & remediation services...........	562	25.7	26.3	438.6	450.6	26.4	27.5
Waste collection.................................	5621	11.7	11.9	229.4	234.8	13.6	14.1
Waste treatment & disposal......................	5622	2.7	2.7	59.4	61.1	4.1	4.3
Remediation & other waste management services........	5629	11.4	11.7	149.7	154.7	8.8	9.1
Accommodation & food services......................	**72**	**741.8**	**733.9**	**14,492.4**	**14,377.0**	**305.5**	**249.5**
Accommodation...................................	721	69.2	69.2	2,161.4	2,161.8	68.8	51.3
Traveler accommodation [3].......................	7211	59.7	59.9	2,102.4	2,103.5	66.7	49.6
Hotels (except casino hotels) & motels...........	72111	55.0	55.2	1,648.1	1,647.5	50.1	35.9
RV (recreational vehicle) parks & recreational camps......	7212	7.6	7.5	48.3	48.1	1.8	1.5
Rooming & boarding houses.....................	7213	1.9	1.8	10.7	10.2	0.3	0.2
Food services & drinking places....................	722	672.6	664.7	12,331.0	12,215.2	236.6	198.2
Drinking places (alcoholic beverages).............	7224	39.9	39.1	382.7	375.9	7.5	5.0
Restaurants and other eating places...............	7225	583.4	576.0	11,099.2	11,041.5	208.0	177.7
Full-service restaurants........................	722511	254.9	250.0	5,598.8	5,456.1	119.3	90.1
Limited-service restaurants.....................	722513	254.6	251.5	4,660.1	4,661.6	74.6	73.8
Cafeterias, grill buffets, and buffets.............	722514	5.5	5.4	101.7	92.3	1.7	1.0
Snack and nonalcoholic beverage bars...........	722515	68.5	69.1	738.6	831.5	12.4	12.8
Other services (except public administration).........	**81**	**769.6**	**771.3**	**5,619.2**	**5,601.7**	**197.1**	**190.7**
Repair & maintenance [3]...........................	811	216.9	216.1	1,306.5	1,304.6	57.7	56.8
Automotive repair & maintenance.................	8111	162.1	161.7	929.6	923.2	36.5	35.9
Personal & household goods repair & maintenance........	8114	21.2	21.1	72.3	72.2	2.6	2.6
Personal & laundry services [3].....................	812	244.4	248.6	1,540.2	1,546.4	41.5	35.8
Personal care services..........................	8121	140.9	143.6	762.2	748.3	18.0	14.3
Death care services.............................	8122	20.5	20.3	134.1	134.2	5.2	5.4
Drycleaning & laundry services....................	8123	32.4	31.3	281.7	280.3	8.6	7.2
Religious/grantmaking/civic/professional [4]...........	813	308.2	306.6	2,772.5	2,750.7	97.9	98.1
Religious organizations..........................	8131	185.1	183.3	1,682.9	1,649.4	39.3	38.6
Grantmaking & giving services...................	8132	20.8	21.5	198.1	204.4	13.3	14.0
Social advocacy organizations...................	8133	19.1	19.7	183.6	191.0	9.8	10.3
Civic & social organizations.....................	8134	25.7	25.4	221.4	218.3	5.5	4.8
Business/professional/labor/political [4]............	8139	57.5	56.8	486.6	487.6	29.9	30.4
Labor unions [4]................................	81393	13.3	13.0	143.3	138.1	6.1	6.1

[1] Data based on North American Industry Classification System (NAICS) 2017. See text, section 15. [2] Includes employees on the payroll for the pay period including March 12. [3] Includes other kinds of business, not shown separately. [4] Also includes other similar organizations.

Source: U.S. Census Bureau, County Business Patterns, "County Business Patterns, including ZIP Code Business Patterns, by Legal Form of Organization and Employment Size Class for the U.S., States, and Selected Geographies: 2020," <data.census.gov>, accessed May 2022.

Table 1292. Employed Persons in Service Industries by Sex, Race, and Hispanic Origin and by Industry: 2021

[19,295 represents 19,295,000. Civilian noninstitutionalized population 16 years and older. Based on the Current Population Survey (CPS); see text, Section 1, and Appendix III. For information on employees in other sectors, see Table 649 and Table 667]

Industry	NAICS code [1]	Total employed (1,000)	Percent of total				
			Female	White	Black [2]	Asian [2]	Hispanic or Latino [3]
Professional and business services.........	**54-56**	**19,295**	**42.6**	**77.2**	**9.8**	**9.8**	**16.6**
Professional and technical services.........	**54**	**12,877**	**43.1**	**77.1**	**7.1**	**13.1**	**9.9**
Legal services.........	5411	1,578	56.9	84.8	7.5	4.8	12.8
Accounting, tax preparation, bookkeeping, and payroll services.........	5412	1,124	63.7	78.1	8.2	10.4	12.4
Architectural, engineering, and related services.........	5413	1,723	27.1	85.3	4.7	8.0	10.2
Specialized design services.........	5414	437	62.8	83.8	7.8	5.5	10.0
Computer systems design and related services.........	5415	4,026	29.1	66.4	7.0	23.7	8.1
Management, scientific, and technical consulting services.........	5416	1,651	43.9	80.6	8.8	9.1	7.8
Scientific research and development services.........	5417	728	44.7	72.8	4.9	19.3	8.8
Advertising, public relations, and related services.........	5418	554	49.6	81.6	9.4	7.4	10.2
Veterinary services.........	54194	407	81.9	89.8	3.3	2.8	11.1
Other professional, scientific, and technical services [4].........	5419	649	55.1	80.7	9.1	6.2	14.0
Management, administrative, and waste services.........	**55-56**	**6,418**	**41.6**	**77.4**	**15.3**	**3.2**	**30.2**
Management of companies and enterprises.........	55	64	51.2	77.9	10.9	6.9	10.2
Administrative and support services.........	561	5,906	43.2	77.2	15.4	3.3	31.1
Employment services.........	5613	850	60.2	71.7	19.3	5.2	17.2
Business support services.........	5614	539	67.0	70.5	20.5	3.2	16.6
Travel arrangement and reservation services.........	5615	240	55.1	81.3	7.5	9.7	13.5
Investigations and security services.........	5616	820	29.7	65.0	28.2	3.1	17.3
Services to buildings and dwellings [5].........	5617	1,755	57.6	79.5	14.1	2.8	41.2
Landscaping services.........	56173	1,395	9.9	86.6	7.5	1.3	45.7
Other administrative and support services.........	5611,2,9	307	49.5	78.2	10.7	6.2	21.0
Waste management and remediation services.........	562	448	19.5	80.0	14.5	1.6	21.5
Accommodation and food services.........	**72**	**9,739**	**52.5**	**74.6**	**12.6**	**7.3**	**27.3**
Accommodation.........	721	1,075	57.0	72.5	12.9	9.3	25.8
Traveler accommodation.........	7211	988	57.7	71.1	13.6	9.8	27.4
Recreational vehicle parks and camps, and rooming and board houses.........	7212,3	87	49.1	88.2	4.6	4.3	7.9
Food services and drinking places.........	722	8,664	51.9	74.9	12.6	7.0	27.5
Restaurants and other food services [6].........	722, excl. 7224	8,500	51.8	74.7	12.7	7.1	27.8
Drinking places, alcoholic beverages.........	7224	164	58.5	84.1	4.9	2.2	10.1
Other services.........	**81**	**7,186**	**51.9**	**78.2**	**10.5**	**7.7**	**19.9**
Other services (except private households).........	81	6,527	48.3	77.8	10.7	8.0	17.9
Repair and maintenance.........	811	2,125	11.6	85.2	7.8	3.9	25.0
Automotive repair and maintenance [7].........	8111	1,306	9.5	86.8	7.1	2.9	24.8
Car washes.........	811192	195	11.9	77.5	14.6	2.8	37.6
Electronic and precision equipment repair and maintenance.........	8112	120	19.4	77.6	6.9	13.9	23.1
Commercial and industrial machinery and equipment repair and maintenance.........	8113	322	8.5	87.2	7.3	3.2	22.1
Personal and household goods repair and maintenance.........	8114	183	26.2	82.7	7.3	6.4	19.7
Personal and laundry services.........	812	2,440	74.7	69.4	12.3	14.2	18.3
Barber shops.........	812111	130	34.0	70.0	17.0	7.7	39.4
Beauty salons.........	812112	943	91.4	75.9	13.5	7.4	17.3
Nail salons and other personal care services.........	812113, 81219	543	78.9	46.5	7.7	40.0	12.1
Drycleaning and laundry services.........	8123	231	46.8	68.7	14.0	12.9	28.9
Funeral homes, cemeteries, and crematories.........	8122	126	42.1	80.3	14.3	1.6	16.2
Other personal services.........	8129	467	69.9	80.2	12.4	3.5	16.8
Membership associations and organizations.........	813	1,962	55.3	80.4	11.9	4.7	9.6
Religious organizations.........	8131	979	45.4	84.0	9.5	4.2	9.3
Civic, social, advocacy organizations, grantmaking and giving services.........	8132,3,4	754	67.3	74.0	16.8	5.9	9.9
Labor unions.........	81393	75	45.6	82.2	7.3	3.1	16.9
Business, professional, political, and similar organizations [8].........	8139	154	63.7	87.6	5.6	2.4	6.6
Other services, private households.........	814	659	87.6	81.5	8.1	5.0	40.1

[1] Based on the North American Industry Classification System, 2017; see Section 15. [2] The Current Population Survey (CPS) allows respondents to choose more than one race. Data represent persons who selected this race group only and exclude persons reporting more than one race. See also comments on race in text for Section 1. [3] Persons of Hispanic origin may be of any race. [4] Excludes NAICS 54194 (veterinary services). [5] Excludes NAICS 56173 (landscaping services). [6] Excludes NAICS 7224 (drinking places, alcoholic beverages). [7] Excludes NAICS 811192 (car washes). [8] Excludes NAICS 81393 (labor unions).

Source: U.S. Bureau of Labor Statistics, CPS Tables, "Employed persons by detailed industry, sex, race, and Hispanic or Latino ethnicity," <www.bls.gov/cps/tables.htm>, accessed March 2022.

Table 1293. Selected Service-Related Industries—Establishments, Employees, and Annual Payroll by State: 2020

[Employees in thousands (9,554 represents 9,554,000); payroll in millions of dollars (893,792 represents $893,792,000,000). Covers establishments with paid employees. Excludes most government employees, railroad employees, and self-employed persons. Data are from Census Bureau's County Business Patterns program. For statement on methodology, see Appendix III]

State	Professional, scientific, and technical services (NAICS 54) [1]			Administrative and support and waste management and remediation services (NAICS 56) [1]			Accommodation and food services (NAICS 72) [1]		
	Establish-ments	Employ-ees [2] (1,000)	Annual payroll (mil. dol.)	Establish-ments	Employ-ees [2] (1,000)	Annual payroll (mil. dol.)	Establish-ments	Employ-ees [2] (1,000)	Annual payroll (mil. dol.)
United States......	**943,222**	**9,554**	**893,792**	**431,073**	**12,718**	**571,012**	**733,872**	**14,377**	**249,536**
Alabama...............	9,485	114	9,201	4,720	170	5,278	9,322	192	2,857
Alaska.................	1,977	20	1,579	1,153	22	1,139	2,098	27	606
Arizona...............	19,366	169	13,490	8,932	282	10,836	13,521	315	5,884
Arkansas..............	6,067	40	2,440	2,928	66	1,826	6,079	110	1,698
California.............	137,424	1,318	154,959	47,139	1,654	94,102	90,445	1,778	35,048
Colorado..............	27,585	219	20,609	9,620	276	14,015	14,358	301	5,788
Connecticut...........	8,891	113	11,116	5,397	88	4,169	8,777	146	2,812
Delaware..............	3,473	33	3,610	1,591	30	1,301	2,268	43	720
District of Columbia.....	6,030	108	15,210	1,117	32	1,551	2,742	74	1,511
Florida................	85,614	565	42,940	39,635	2,009	96,097	44,110	1,014	18,383
Georgia...............	31,130	304	25,776	13,437	417	16,529	22,348	459	7,139
Hawaii................	3,387	24	1,727	1,869	68	2,448	3,842	110	2,268
Idaho.................	5,159	39	2,665	2,824	46	1,592	4,021	72	1,140
Illinois................	38,239	413	41,871	16,933	490	19,850	28,899	536	8,878
Indiana...............	13,072	133	10,310	7,813	216	7,175	13,737	282	4,244
Iowa..................	6,480	60	4,064	3,904	96	3,535	7,186	122	1,835
Kansas................	7,117	67	4,928	3,807	86	3,250	6,206	119	1,745
Kentucky..............	8,224	77	4,683	4,299	123	3,565	8,201	178	2,596
Louisiana..............	12,402	101	6,843	4,986	109	4,144	10,105	214	3,460
Maine.................	3,534	24	1,757	2,327	23	831	4,121	56	1,127
Maryland..............	21,223	296	29,008	8,579	213	9,393	12,147	242	4,228
Massachusetts.........	21,704	327	42,241	11,259	206	10,952	17,476	307	6,080
Michigan..............	21,641	294	24,528	11,612	383	12,432	20,506	394	6,002
Minnesota.............	16,353	186	15,889	7,903	169	7,099	11,760	244	3,907
Mississippi............	4,651	31	1,717	2,409	57	1,613	5,767	133	2,087
Missouri..............	13,856	167	13,279	7,550	185	7,101	12,981	268	4,292
Montana...............	4,013	20	1,264	2,034	20	647	3,575	53	904
Nebraska..............	4,656	40	2,769	2,822	73	2,949	4,536	78	1,144
Nevada................	9,669	62	4,330	4,680	128	4,233	7,079	325	7,820
New Hampshire........	3,664	36	3,232	2,461	60	3,046	3,816	62	1,189
New Jersey............	28,334	339	34,640	14,199	355	15,274	21,505	333	6,004
New Mexico...........	4,628	60	4,737	1,967	37	1,453	4,427	97	1,554
New York..............	61,739	677	70,576	27,374	733	49,524	53,198	793	15,718
North Carolina.........	25,714	241	19,788	13,938	289	10,768	22,226	454	6,930
North Dakota..........	1,903	18	1,185	1128	13	477	2,072	35	567
Ohio..................	23,745	262	19,637	13,803	467	16,415	24,322	480	6,989
Oklahoma.............	9,848	79	5,273	4,707	122	5,093	8,542	164	2,559
Oregon................	12,885	99	8,330	6,193	108	4,328	11,709	189	3,385
Pennsylvania..........	29,921	337	29,586	16,265	336	13,623	28,471	488	7,171
Rhode Island..........	3,025	23	1,749	1,846	26	1,090	3,128	52	976
South Carolina........	11,392	101	7,169	6,469	306	11,126	11,108	241	3,797
South Dakota..........	2,009	14	749	1,211	11	398	2,490	40	655
Tennessee.............	11,784	126	9,213	7,550	271	9,361	14,139	308	5,027
Texas.................	74,903	783	71,116	30,705	1,049	44,300	60,264	1,277	21,106
Utah..................	12,007	100	7,079	4,995	160	6,918	6,093	128	2,105
Vermont...............	2,046	12	911	1,186	9	301	1,885	33	567
Virginia...............	31,659	509	50,901	11,235	281	12,629	18,419	373	5,909
Washington............	22,796	224	22,362	10,360	164	8,532	17,769	300	6,008
West Virginia..........	2,688	24	1,375	1,517	34	1,078	3,544	68	994
Wisconsin.............	11,392	115	8,692	7,572	146	5,346	14,763	245	3,554
Wyoming..............	2,718	11	688	1,113	7	281	1,769	28	567

[1] North American Industry Classification System, 2017. See text, section 15. [2] For employees on the payroll for the pay period including March 12.

Source: U.S. Census Bureau, County Business Patterns, CB2000CBP, "County Business Patterns, including ZIP Code Business Patterns, by Legal Form of Organization and Employment Size Class for the U.S., States, and Selected Geographies: 2020," <data.census.gov>, accessed May 2022.

Table 1294. Professional, Scientific, and Technical Services—Estimated Revenue by Kind of Business: 2015 to 2020

[In millions of dollars (1,611,725 represents $1,611,725,000,000). For taxable employer firms. Estimates have been adjusted to the results of the 2017 Economic Census. Based on the Service Annual Survey and administrative data; see Appendix III]

Kind of business	NAICS code [1]	2015	2016	2017	2018	2019	2020
Professional, scientific, and technical services (except notaries) [2]	**54**	**1,611,725**	**1,696,157**	**1,806,506**	**1,912,989**	**2,021,019**	**2,084,448**
Offices of lawyers	54111	256,528	261,794	279,613	280,229	288,889	290,435
Other legal services	54119	13,789	14,117	14,269	15,134	16,525	18,874
Offices of certified public accountants	541211	92,443	99,183	103,314	108,169	113,381	116,187
Tax preparation services	541213	7,069	6,970	7,053	7,375	7,704	7,480
Payroll services	541214	24,006	20,823	21,946	21,794	23,920	23,721
Other accounting services	541219	18,842	19,238	20,067	20,281	22,080	23,479
Architectural services	54131	33,907	36,180	37,805	40,516	43,237	42,182
Landscape architectural services	54132	3,540	3,821	4,144	4,427	4,574	4,738
Engineering services	54133	223,530	228,014	237,304	249,085	264,653	263,164
Drafting services	54134	1,171	1,095	1,140	1,232	1,276	1,325
Building inspection services	54135	2,533	2,599	2,741	3,014	3,395	3,652
Surveying and mapping services [3]	5413z	9,116	8,389	8,809	9,694	10,547	9,770
Testing laboratories	54138	18,454	18,930	20,551	21,426	23,115	24,106
Drafting, building inspection, and mapping services [4]	5413x	12,820	12,083	12,690	13,940	15,218	14,747
Interior design services	54141	11,154	11,710	12,203	12,753	13,591	14,067
Industrial design services	54142	1,978	1,888	2,162	2,217	2,448	2,785
Graphic design services	54143	8,127	8,464	8,551	8,597	9,342	9,521
Other specialized design services	54149	1,796	1,878	1,966	1,949	2,098	1,872
All other design services [5]	5414y	3,774	3,766	4,128	4,166	4,546	4,657
Computer systems design and related services	5415	370,302	404,970	442,827	485,553	497,222	519,068
Management consulting services	54161	197,854	208,339	214,126	224,169	236,012	241,078
Environmental consulting services	54162	14,465	15,152	15,590	17,084	17,189	17,081
Other scientific and technical consulting services	54169	28,456	28,508	29,116	30,575	34,300	34,074
Research and development in physical, engineering and life sciences	54171	91,774	99,150	112,693	123,478	143,722	159,776
Research and development in social sciences and humanities	54172	2,224	2,307	2,294	2,603	2,756	2,938
Advertising agencies	54181	40,699	43,592	46,241	50,220	51,186	54,457
Public relations agencies	54182	11,795	13,514	12,505	13,813	14,066	14,536
Media buying agencies	54183	8,320	8,898	8,780	9,316	10,063	9,659
Media representatives	54184	7,214	9,309	14,137	19,330	25,214	35,088
Outdoor advertising	54185	7,070	7,056	7,979	7,820	8,231	6,554
Direct mail advertising	54186	9,699	10,032	9,598	9,511	9,818	9,470
Advertising material distribution services	54187	3,945	3,878	3,611	3,516	3,499	3,504
Other services related to advertising	54189	13,339	14,174	14,767	15,433	15,878	15,537
All other advertising [6]	5418y	17,284	18,052	18,378	18,949	19,377	19,041
Marketing research and public opinion polling	54191	18,719	20,201	19,830	20,928	23,174	22,645
Photography studios, portrait	541921	4,132	4,073	4,153	4,246	4,465	3,284
Commercial photography	541922	1,914	2,036	2,131	2,310	2,250	1,867
Translation and interpretation services	54193	3,767	4,133	4,449	4,973	5,307	5,748
Veterinary services	54194	35,363	38,638	41,693	42,272	45,947	50,998
All other professional, scientific, and technical services	54199	12,691	13,104	16,348	17,947	19,945	19,728

[1] Data are based on the 2012 North American Industry Classification System (NAICS). See text Section 15 for more information. [2] Excludes NAICS 54112 (Offices of Notaries). [3] Includes NAICS 54136 (Geophysical Surveying and Mapping Services) and NAICS 54137 (Surveying and Mapping Services, except Geophysical Services). [4] Includes NAICS 54134 (Drafting Services), NAICS 54135 (Building Inspection Services), NAICS 54136 (Geophysical Surveying and Mapping Services), and NAICS 54137 (Surveying and Mapping (except Geophysical) Services). [5] Includes NAICS 54142 (Industrial Design Services) and NAICS 54149 (Other Specialized Design Services). [6] Includes NAICS 54187 (Advertising Material Distribution Services) and NAICS 54189 (Other Services Related to Advertising).

Source: U.S. Census Bureau, Service Annual Survey, "Service Annual Survey Latest Data (NAICS-basis): 2020," <www.census.gov/programs-surveys/sas/data.html>, accessed January 2022.

Table 1295. Administrative and Support and Waste Management and Remediation Services—Estimated Revenue by Kind of Business: 2015 to 2020

[In millions of dollars (818,683 represents $818,683,000,000). For taxable and tax-exempt employer firms. Estimates have been adjusted to results of the 2017 Economic Census. Based on the Service Annual Survey and administrative data; see Appendix III]

Kind of business	NAICS code [1]	2015	2016	2017	2018	2019	2020
Administrative and support and waste management and remediation services	**56**	**818,683**	**886,391**	**950,896**	**1,023,171**	**1,090,944**	**1,042,582**
Administrative and support services	**561**	**730,251**	**792,443**	**851,306**	**916,022**	**977,831**	**930,369**
Office administrative services	5611	55,734	57,746	58,930	60,942	63,162	62,809
Facilities support services	5612	26,795	26,955	28,571	32,073	33,514	33,504
Employment placement agencies & executive search services	56131	17,517	18,672	19,313	22,338	23,782	23,954
Temporary help services	56132	155,930	173,338	180,118	188,702	195,153	182,364
Professional employer organizations	56133	141,020	156,135	177,827	191,324	209,821	209,795
Document preparation services	56141	3,025	3,187	3,285	3,320	3,403	3,542
Telephone answering services	561421	2,041	2,189	2,226	2,333	2,368	2,196
Telemarketing bureaus and other contact centers	561422	18,252	20,188	19,486	21,736	20,118	20,509
Private mail centers	561431	2,533	2,625	2,829	2,981	3,018	3,270
Other business service centers (including copy shops)	561439	5,883	6,494	6,243	5,947	7,718	8,074
Collection agencies	56144	13,502	14,198	15,171	15,325	16,280	15,380
Credit bureaus	56145	8,828	9,455	10,152	10,613	11,082	11,831
Repossession services	561491	780	896	998	1,015	1,080	881
Court reporting and stenotype services	561492	2,192	2,312	2,426	2,530	2,799	2,374
All other business support services	561499	7,605	8,282	8,939	9,431	10,142	9,696
Travel agencies	56151	19,050	22,979	27,512	31,089	32,959	17,525
Tour operators	56152	6,748	7,051	8,425	9,652	9,892	3,669
Convention and visitors bureaus	561591	1,946	2,099	2,239	2,396	2,513	1,908
All other travel arrangement and reservation services	561599	16,435	16,620	16,996	18,005	20,441	11,361
Investigation services	561611	5,316	5,608	5,893	6,316	6,240	6,091
Security guards and patrol services	561612	22,369	23,527	29,617	28,724	31,874	30,167
Armored car services	561613	2,663	2,972	3,110	3,260	3,464	3,667
Security systems services (except locksmiths)	561621	19,216	20,973	22,268	24,123	26,813	25,982
Locksmiths	561622	1,745	1,882	2,016	2,131	2,380	2,290
Exterminating and pest control services	56171	11,298	11,829	13,089	14,872	16,368	17,374
Janitorial services	56172	44,178	47,978	49,680	55,210	58,911	60,770
Landscaping services	56173	65,451	71,993	77,034	86,870	95,314	98,282
Carpet and upholstery cleaning services	56174	3,295	3,457	3,426	3,529	3,756	4,011
Other services to buildings and dwellings	56179	7,008	7,555	7,891	8,817	9,734	9,845
Packaging and labeling services	56191	7,032	7,132	7,299	7,954	8,303	9,003
Convention and trade show organizers	56192	13,966	15,407	16,361	17,262	18,612	11,360
All other support services	56199	20,898	20,709	21,936	25,202	26,817	26,885
Waste management and remediation services	**562**	**88,432**	**93,948**	**99,590**	**107,149**	**113,113**	**112,213**
Solid waste collection	562111	42,287	45,712	49,228	53,436	56,477	55,152
Hazardous waste collection	562112	2,427	2,352	2,100	2,215	2,245	(S)
Other waste collection	562119	1,646	1,729	1,926	2,287	2,579	2,950
Hazardous waste treatment and disposal	562211	7,700	8,251	8,712	8,426	8,573	8,313
Solid waste landfill	562212	6,419	7,181	7,535	7,876	8,531	8,606
Solid waste combustors and incinerators	562213	(S)	(S)	(S)	(S)	(S)	(S)
Other nonhazardous waste treatment and disposal	562219	718	642	815	878	961	926
Remediation services	56291	14,622	15,645	16,076	17,615	18,525	18,759
Materials recovery facilities	56292	5,363	5,399	5,940	6,587	6,927	7,177
Septic tank and related services	562991	3,418	3,763	3,920	4,415	4,723	4,781
All other miscellaneous waste management services	562998	2,060	1,856	2,063	2,081	2,218	2,133

S Figure does not meet publication standards. [1] Data are based on the 2012 North American Industry Classification System (NAICS). See text Section 15 for more information.

Source: U.S. Census Bureau, Service Annual Survey, "Service Annual Survey Latest Data (NAICS-basis): 2020," <www.census.gov/programs-surveys/sas/data.html>, accessed December 2021.

Table 1296. Selected Service Industries Revenue—Total and from Electronic Sources: 2019 and 2020

[16,999,369 represents $16,999,369,000,000. Data shown for service businesses with paid employees. Revenues from electronic sources include revenues from customers entering orders directly on a firm's website or mobile application, entering orders directly on third party websites or mobile applications, and entering orders via any other electronic system (such as private networks, dedicated lines, kiosks, etc.). Based on the Service Annual Survey, see Appendix III]

Kind of business	NAICS code [1]	Total revenue (million dollars)		Electronic sources revenue (million dollars)		Electronic sources revenue as a percent of total revenue	
		2019	2020	2019	2020	2019	2020
Selected service industries, total..........................	(X)	**16,999,369**	**16,668,151**	**1,350,529**	**1,362,639**	**7.9**	**8.2**
Utilities [2]..	22	599,220	580,647	(S)	(S)	(S)	(S)
Selected transportation and warehousing [3]..................	4849y	1,070,520	919,668	192,627	120,181	18.0	13.1
Air transportation...	481	236,830	110,158	98,897	38,118	41.8	34.6
Water transportation...	483	48,902	29,653	12,153	(S)	24.9	(S)
Truck transportation..	484	320,817	316,982	31,939	33,422	10.0	10.5
Transit and ground passenger transportation.............	485	55,964	39,382	(S)	(S)	(S)	(S)
Pipeline transportation.......................................	486	59,522	56,319	(S)	(S)	(S)	(S)
Scenic and sightseeing transportation....................	487	4,426	1,934	1,465	531	33.1	27.5
Support activities for transportation......................	488	201,150	206,055	15,338	16,733	7.6	8.1
Information..	51	1,755,214	1,791,438	479,850	525,031	27.3	29.3
Publishing industries (except internet)...................	511	417,324	440,921	140,306	160,597	33.6	36.4
Motion picture and sound recording industries............	512	113,475	91,711	13,481	9,523	11.9	10.4
Broadcasting (except internet).............................	515	168,752	171,889	3,236	2,756	1.9	1.6
Telecommunications..	517	639,253	635,454	(S)	153,223	(S)	24.1
Data processing, hosting, and related services............	518	193,228	205,869	21,943	23,665	11.4	11.5
Other information services..................................	519	223,182	245,594	155,175	175,267	69.5	71.4
Finance and insurance [4]..	52	4,854,315	4,959,947	247,297	(S)	5.1	(S)
Activities related to credit intermediation.................	5223	115,478	122,104	27,128	35,456	23.5	29.0
Securities and commodity contracts intermediation and brokerage.............................	5231	258,381	270,869	15,978	(S)	6.2	(S)
Real estate and rental and leasing............................	53	756,268	730,742	54,127	57,700	7.2	7.9
Rental and leasing services..................................	532	177,846	156,312	27,586	27,973	15.5	17.9
Selected professional, scientific, and technical services [5]..	54	2,077,668	2,143,768	80,929	116,797	3.9	5.4
Computer systems design and related services............	5415	497,222	519,068	21,610	34,280	4.3	6.6
Administrative and support and waste management and remediation services..............	56	1,090,944	1,042,582	70,668	51,463	6.5	4.9
Travel arrangement and reservation services.............	5615	65,805	34,463	29,547	16,116	44.9	46.8
Educational services [6]...	61	72,812	67,793	(S)	14,731	(S)	21.7
Health care and social assistance.............................	62	2,786,127	2,828,912	(S)	(S)	(S)	(S)
Arts, entertainment, and recreation..........................	71	296,444	210,185	42,413	23,646	14.3	11.3
Accommodation and food services [7].........................	72	1,040,970	807,086	124,621	126,063	12.0	15.6
Other services (except public administration) [8]..............	81	598,867	585,383	37,047	36,822	6.2	6.3
Repair and maintenance......................................	811	199,754	190,074	4,980	3,196	2.5	1.7
Personal and laundry services..............................	812	123,060	107,216	7,686	9,612	6.2	9.0
Religious, grantmaking, civic, professional, and similar organizations...	813	276,053	288,093	24,381	24,014	8.8	8.3

X Not applicable. S Data do not meet publication standards. [1] North American Industry Classification System (NAICS), 2012; see text Section 15. [2] Excludes government owned utilities. [3] Excludes NAICS 482 (Rail Transportation) and NAICS 491 (Postal Service). [4] Excludes NAICS 525 (Funds, Trusts, and Other Financial Vehicles). [5] Excludes NAICS 54112 (Offices of Notaries). [6] Excludes NAICS 6111 (Elementary and Secondary Schools), NAICS 6112 (Junior Colleges), and NAICS 6113 (Colleges, Universities, and Professional Schools). [7] Prior to 2016, NAICS sector 72 was collected and published by the Annual Retail Trade Report. [8] Excludes NAICS 81311 (Religious Organizations), NAICS 81393 (Labor Unions and Similar Labor Organizations), NAICS 81394 (Political Organizations), and NAICS 814 (Private Households).

Source: U.S. Census Bureau, Service Annual Survey, "Service Annual Survey Latest Data (NAICS-basis): 2020," <www.census.gov/programs-surveys/sas/data.html>, accessed December 2021.

Table 1297. Accommodation and Food Services Revenue by Kind of Business: 2015 to 2020

[In millions of dollars (847,078 represents $847,078,000,000). Based on data from the Service Annual Survey, see headnote Table 1295. Prior to 2016, data were collected and published by the Annual Retail Trade Report]

Kind of business	NAICS code [1]	2015	2016	2017	2018	2019	2020
Accommodation and food services, total.....	72	**847,078**	**895,080**	**938,236**	**989,813**	**1,040,970**	**807,086**
Accommodation..	721	236,734	250,965	260,089	271,984	283,002	168,736
Hotels (except casino hotels) and motels..........	72111	168,118	179,429	184,411	193,160	200,890	116,127
Casino hotels...	72112	59,656	62,173	65,659	68,048	70,819	43,589
Other traveler accommodations.....................	72119	1,951	1,943	1,937	2,115	2,013	1,603
RV (recreation vehicle) parks and recreational camps.....................................	7212	5,448	5,834	6,337	6,731	7,125	5,496
Rooming and boarding houses.......................	7213	1,561	1,586	1,745	1,930	2,155	1,921
Food services and drinking places....................	722	610,344	644,115	678,147	717,829	757,968	638,350
Food services contractors............................	72231	41,896	44,467	45,317	46,868	49,624	35,723
Caterers...	72232	8,826	9,563	10,934	11,535	11,994	6,892
Mobile food services...................................	72233	947	1,104	1,179	1,394	1,673	1,723
Drinking places (alcoholic beverages)..............	7224	20,343	22,457	23,936	25,547	27,001	16,254
Full-service restaurants...............................	722511	273,225	284,572	298,164	314,740	330,389	251,456
Limited-service restaurants..........................	722513	222,613	237,949	253,349	269,097	284,024	279,371
Cafeterias, grill buffets, and buffets................	722514	6,271	6,249	6,457	6,893	7,275	3,687
Snack and nonalcoholic beverage bars............	722515	36,223	37,754	38,811	41,755	45,988	43,244

[1] North American Industry Classification System (NAICS), 2012; see text, Section 15.

Source: U.S. Census Bureau, Service Annual Survey, "Service Annual Survey Latest Data (NAICS-basis): 2020," <www.census.gov/programs-surveys/sas/data.html>, accessed December 2021.

Table 1298. Other Services—Estimated Revenue for Employer Firms by Kind of Business: 2016 to 2020

[In millions of dollars (507,802 represents $507,802,000,000). For taxable and tax exempt employer firms. Estimates have been adjusted to results of the 2017 Economic Census. Based on the Service Annual Survey; see Appendix III]

Kind of business	NAICS code [1]	2016	2017	2018	2019	2020
Other services (except public administration) [2]	**81**	**507,802**	**544,131**	**570,655**	**598,867**	**585,383**
Repair and maintenance	811	174,174	180,985	191,038	199,754	190,074
General automotive repair	811111	49,326	50,121	53,032	55,494	51,225
Automotive exhaust system repair	811112	633	614	625	665	660
Automotive transmission repair	811113	2,190	2,209	2,345	2,449	2,609
Other automotive mechanical and electrical repair and maintenance	811118	2,056	1,944	1,989	2,008	1,939
Automotive body, paint, interior repair and maintenance	811121	36,143	38,670	39,847	41,868	40,069
Automotive glass replacement shops	811122	4,430	4,312	4,590	5,110	5,340
Automotive oil change and lubrication shops	811191	5,000	5,609	5,940	6,621	7,035
Car washes	811192	8,872	9,724	10,953	11,496	11,435
All other automotive repair and maintenance	811198	1,929	2,100	2,386	2,501	2,522
Consumer electronics repair and maintenance	811211	1,586	1,416	1,449	1,502	1,483
Computer and office machine repair and maintenance	811212	4,623	4,612	4,474	4,510	4,432
Communication equipment repair and maintenance	811213	3,002	2,909	2,988	3,210	2,984
Other electronic and precision equipment repair and maintenance	811219	8,511	8,127	8,742	8,954	7,918
Commercial and industrial machinery and equipment (except automotive and electronic) repair and maintenance	8113	36,978	39,258	42,075	43,583	40,643
Home and garden equipment and appliance repair and maintenance	81141	3,911	4,142	3,938	3,616	3,791
Reupholstery and furniture repair	81142	1,146	1,106	1,172	1,170	1,146
Footwear and leather goods repair	81143	212	200	207	206	132
Other personal and household goods repair and maintenance	81149	3,626	3,912	4,286	4,791	4,711
Personal and laundry services	812	105,839	111,390	117,765	123,060	107,216
Barber shops	812111	860	1,048	1,207	1,452	1,132
Beauty shops	812112	22,237	22,636	23,967	24,831	18,186
Nail salons	812113	5,474	6,239	7,257	8,200	6,272
Diet and weight reducing centers	812191	1,717	1,780	2,002	1,898	1,809
Other personal care services	812199	7,084	8,071	9,006	9,710	8,329
Funeral homes and funeral services	81221	14,453	14,677	14,331	14,393	15,633
Cemeteries and crematories	81222	4,123	4,183	4,319	4,279	4,579
Coin-operated laundries and drycleaners	81231	4,196	4,340	4,560	4,508	4,191
Dry-cleaning and laundry services (except coin-operated)	81232	7,788	7,972	8,139	8,251	5,771
Linen supply	812331	4,907	4,649	4,573	5,002	4,156
Industrial launders	812332	8,837	9,088	9,989	10,983	11,664
Pet care (except veterinary) services	81291	4,764	5,354	6,143	6,666	5,961
Photofinishing	81292	1,550	1,566	1,568	1,499	1,177
Parking lots and garages	81293	9,165	9,644	9,893	9,861	6,975
All other personal services	81299	8,684	10,143	10,811	11,527	11,381
Religious, grantmaking, civic, professional, and similar organizations [3]	813	227,789	251,756	261,852	276,053	288,093
Grantmaking and giving services	8132	105,324	119,877	125,632	134,019	149,825
Social advocacy organizations	8133	32,764	35,087	36,985	38,929	41,929
Civic and social organizations	8134	16,725	17,834	18,360	19,358	17,039
Business, professional, labor, political, and similar organizations [4]	8139	72,976	78,958	80,875	83,747	79,300

[1] Data based on 2012 NAICS. See section 15, Business Enterprise. [2] Excludes NAICS 8131 (Religious Organizations), NAICS 81393 (Labor Unions and Similar Labor Organizations), NAICS 81394 (Political Organizations), and NAICS 814 (Private Households). [3] Excludes NAICS 8131 (Religious Organizations), NAICS 81393 (Labor Unions and Similar Labor Organizations), and NAICS 81394 (Political Organizations). [4] Excludes NAICS 81393 (Labor Unions and Similar Labor Organizations) and NAICS 81394 (Political Organizations).

Source: U.S. Census Bureau, Service Annual Survey, "Service Annual Survey Latest Data (NAICS-basis): 2020," <www.census.gov/programs-surveys/sas/data.html>, accessed December 2021.

Table 1299. National Nonprofit Associations—Number by Type: 1980 to 2022

[Data compiled during last few months of year previous to year shown and the beginning months of year shown]

Type	1980	1990	2000	2005	2010 [1]	2015	2020	2021	2022
Total	**14,726**	**22,289**	**21,840**	**22,720**	**23,983**	**23,891**	**24,414**	**24,684**	**25,225**
Trade, business, commercial	3,118	3,918	3,880	3,789	3,761	3,487	3,670	3,671	3,780
Agriculture and environment	677	940	1,103	1,170	1,442	1,421	1,484	1,492	1,501
Legal, governmental, public admin., military	529	792	790	868	913	894	977	985	1,044
Scientific, engineering, technical	1,039	1,417	1,302	1,354	1,563	1,507	1,564	1,551	1,592
Educational	[2] 2,376	1,291	1,297	1,318	1,444	1,344	1,438	1,441	1,447
Cultural	([2])	1,886	1,786	1,733	1,717	1,610	1,657	1,653	1,708
Social welfare	994	1,705	1,829	2,072	2,673	3,166	2,979	3,231	3,243
Health, medical	1,413	2,227	2,495	2,982	3,481	4,069	4,293	4,280	4,271
Public affairs	1,068	2,249	1,776	1,854	1,734	1,601	1,463	1,475	1,655
Fraternal, nationality, ethnic	435	573	525	550	461	398	398	394	393
Religious	797	1,172	1,123	1,147	1,056	964	1,000	1,008	1,003
Veteran, hereditary, patriotic	208	462	835	774	585	545	566	559	562
Hobby, avocational	910	1,475	1,330	1,433	1,374	1,287	1,341	1,350	1,347
Athletic sports	504	840	717	762	946	899	904	913	965
Labor unions	235	253	232	208	188	162	168	171	206
Chambers of Commerce [3]	105	168	143	135	142	125	105	102	101
Greek and non-Greek letter societies	318	340	296	349	305	294	313	314	313
Fan clubs	(NA)	581	381	314	198	118	94	94	94

NA Not available. [1] Beginning in 2007, there was an increase in the number of associations due to an increase in newly discovered and established associations. [2] Data for cultural associations included with educational associations. [3] National and binational. Includes trade and tourism organizations.

Source: Gale, Cengage Learning. *Encyclopedia of Associations: National Organizations* © 2022 Gale, a part of Cengage, Inc. Reproduced by permission. See <www.cengage.com/permissions>.

Section 28
Foreign Commerce and Aid

This section presents data on the flow of goods, services, and capital between the United States and other countries; changes in official reserve assets of the United States; international investments; and foreign assistance programs.

The Bureau of Economic Analysis publishes current figures on U.S. international transactions and the U.S. international investment position in its monthly *Survey of Current Business* and in an interactive database on the internet at <apps.bea.gov/iTable/>. Statistics for the foreign aid programs are presented by the Agency for International Development (USAID) in its annual *U.S. Overseas Loans and Grants*.

The principal source of merchandise import and export data is the U.S. Census Bureau. Current data are presented monthly in *U.S. International Trade in Goods and Services Report* Series FT 900, as well as in the "USA Trade Online" database at <usatrade.census.gov/>. The *Guide to Foreign Trade Statistics*, found on the Census Bureau website at <census.gov/foreign-trade/guide/index.html>, lists the Census Bureau's monthly and annual products and services in this field. In addition, the International Trade Administration and the Bureau of Economic Analysis present summary as well as selected commodity and country data for U.S. foreign trade on their websites: <trade.gov/trade-data-analysis> and <bea.gov/data/economic-accounts/international>, respectively. The merchandise trade data published by the Bureau of Economic Analysis in the *Survey of Current Business* and on the web include balance of payments adjustments to the Census Bureau data. The U.S. Treasury Department's *Monthly Treasury Statement of Receipts and Outlays of the United States Government* contains information on import duties. The International Trade Commission, U.S. Department of Agriculture (agricultural products), U.S. Department of Energy (mineral fuels, like petroleum and coal), and the U.S. Geological Survey (minerals) release various reports and specialized products on U.S. trade.

International accounts—The international transactions tables (Tables 1300, 1303, and 1304) show, for given time periods, the transfer of goods, services, grants, and financial assets and liabilities between the United States and the rest of the world. The international investment position table (Table 1302) presents, for specific dates, the value of U.S. investments abroad and of foreign investments in the United States. The movement of foreign and U.S. capital as presented in the balance of payments is not the only factor affecting the total value of foreign investments. Among the other factors are changes in the valuation of assets or liabilities, including changes in prices of securities, defaults, expropriations, and write-offs.

Direct investment abroad means the ownership or control, directly or indirectly, by one person of 10 percent or more of the voting securities of an incorporated business enterprise or an equivalent interest in an unincorporated business enterprise. Direct investment position is the value of U.S. parents' claims on the equity of and receivables due from foreign affiliates, less foreign affiliates' receivables due from their U.S. parents. Income consists of

parents' shares in the earnings of their affiliates plus net interest received by parents on intercompany accounts, less withholding taxes on dividends and interest.

Foreign aid—Foreign assistance is divided into three major categories—grants (military supplies and services and other grants), credits, and other assistance (through net accumulation of foreign currency claims from the sale of agricultural commodities). *Grants* are transfers for which no payment is expected (other than a limited percentage of the foreign currency "counterpart" funds generated by the grant), or which at most involve an obligation on the part of the receiver to extend aid to the United States or other countries to achieve a common objective. *Credits* are loan disbursements or transfers under other agreements which give rise to specific obligations to repay, over a period of years, usually with interest. All known returns to the U.S. government stemming from grants and credits (reverse grants, returns of grants, and payments of principal) are taken into account in net grants and net credits, but no allowance is made for interest or commissions. *Other assistance* represents the transfer of U.S. farm products in exchange for foreign currencies (plus, since enactment of Public Law 87-128, currency claims from principal and interest collected on credits extended under the farm products program), less the government's disbursements of the currencies as grants, credits, or for purchases. The net acquisition of currencies represents net transfers of resources to foreign countries under the agricultural programs, in addition to those classified as grants or credits.

Exports—Export statistics consist of goods valued at more than $2,500 per commodity shipped by individuals and organizations (including exporters, freight forwarders, and carriers) from the U.S. to other countries. The Census Bureau compiles export data primarily from three sources: Shipper's Export Declaration documents filed with Customs and Border Protection and sent to the Census Bureau; data in electronic form submitted directly by exporters and their agents; and special computer tapes from Canada for U.S. exports to Canada. Estimates are made for low-value exports by country of destination, and based on bilateral trade patterns. They include U.S. exports under mutual security programs and exclude shipments to U.S. Armed Forces for their own use.

The value reported in the export statistics is generally equivalent to a free alongside ship (f.a.s.) value at the U.S. port of export, based on the transaction price, including inland freight, insurance, and other charges incurred in placing the merchandise alongside the carrier at the U.S. port of exportation. This value, as defined, excludes the cost of loading merchandise aboard the exporting carrier and also excludes freight, insurance, and any other charges or transportation and other costs beyond the U.S. port of exportation. The country of destination is defined as the country of ultimate destination or country where the merchandise is to be consumed, further processed, or manufactured, as known to the shipper at the time of exportation. When ultimate destination is not known, the shipment is statistically credited to the last country to which the shipper knows the merchandise will be shipped in the same form as exported.

Statistics for U.S. exports to Canada are based on import documents filed with Canadian agencies and forwarded to the U.S. Census Bureau under a 1987 data exchange agreement. Under this agreement, each country eliminated most cross-border export documents; maintains detailed statistics on cross-border imports; exchanges monthly files of cross-border import statistics; and publishes exchanged statistics in place of previously compiled export statistics.

Prior to 1989, exports were based on Schedule B, Statistical Classification of Domestic and Foreign Commodities Exported from the United States. Beginning in 1989, Schedule B classifications are based on the Harmonized System and coincide with the Standard International Trade Classification, Revision 3.

Imports—Import statistics consist of goods valued at more than $2,000 per commodity shipped by individuals and organizations (including importers and customs brokers) into the U.S. from other countries. The Census Bureau compiles import data from records filed with Customs and Border Protection, usually within 10 days after the merchandise enters the United States. Estimates are made for low-value shipments by country of origin, based on previous bilateral trade patterns and periodically updated. Country of origin is defined as country where the merchandise was grown, mined, or manufactured. If country of origin is unknown, country of shipment is reported. Statistics for over 95 percent of all commodity transactions are compiled from records filed electronically with Customs and forwarded as computer tape files to the U.S. Census Bureau. Statistics for other transactions are compiled from hard-copy documents filed with Customs and forwarded on a flow basis for U.S. Census Bureau processing.

Data on import values are presented on two valuations bases in this section: the c.i.f. (cost, insurance, and freight) and the customs import value (as appraised by the U.S. Customs Service in accordance with legal requirements of the Tariff Act of 1930, as amended). This latter valuation, primarily used for collection of import duties, frequently does not reflect the actual transaction value.

Imports are classified either as "General imports" or "Imports for consumption." *General imports* are a combination of entries for immediate consumption, entries into customs bonded warehouses, and entries into U.S. Foreign Trade Zones, thus generally reflecting total arrivals of merchandise. *Imports for consumption* are a combination of entries for immediate consumption, withdrawals from warehouses for consumption, and entries of merchandise into U.S. customs territory from U.S. Foreign Trade Zones, thus generally reflecting the total of the commodities entered into U.S. consumption channels.

Beginning in 1989, import statistics are based on the Harmonized Tariff Schedule of the United States, which coincides with import Standard International Trade Classification, Revision 3.

Area coverage—Except as noted, the geographic area covered by the export and import trade statistics is the United States Customs area (includes the 50 states, the District of Columbia, and Puerto Rico), the U.S. Virgin Islands (effective January 1981), and U.S. Foreign Trade Zones (effective July 1982).

Statistical reliability—For a discussion of statistical collection and estimation, sampling procedures, and measures of statistical reliability applicable to Census Bureau data, see Appendix III.

Table 1300. U.S. International Transactions by Type of Transaction: 2000 to 2021

[In millions of dollars (1,486,120 represents $1,486,120,000,000). Minus sign (-) indicates debits. N.i.e. is not indicated elsewhere]

Type of transaction	2000	2005	2010	2015	2016	2017	2018	2019	2020	2021
Exports of goods and services and income receipts.	**1,486,120**	**1,893,153**	**2,687,457**	**3,238,571**	**3,239,190**	**3,550,432**	**3,794,005**	**3,839,725**	**3,260,095**	**3,780,154**
Exports of goods and services.	1,082,963	1,291,503	1,872,320	2,280,778	2,240,824	2,394,476	2,542,462	2,546,276	2,158,651	2,556,638
Goods.	784,940	913,016	1,290,279	1,511,381	1,457,393	1,557,003	1,676,913	1,655,098	1,432,218	1,761,364
General merchandise.	778,718	906,104	1,271,972	1,489,795	1,436,552	1,535,249	1,654,629	1,635,273	1,407,355	1,729,061
Foods, feeds, and beverages.	47,871	58,955	107,719	127,721	130,515	132,761	133,144	130,988	139,280	164,749
Industrial supplies and materials.	171,108	236,812	388,561	418,141	387,600	459,380	536,866	526,431	450,606	616,784
Capital goods except automotive.	357,000	358,426	447,839	539,805	520,001	533,696	563,438	550,749	462,894	520,769
Automotive vehicles, parts, and engines.	80,356	98,406	112,008	151,894	150,398	157,867	158,833	163,075	128,834	144,066
Consumer goods except food and automotive.	89,305	115,228	164,909	197,318	193,258	197,190	205,513	204,982	174,009	221,720
Other general merchandise.	33,078	38,276	50,938	54,917	54,781	54,357	56,835	59,048	51,731	60,974
Net exports of goods under merchanting.	159	1,330	411	261	300	210	338	474	835	832
Nonmonetary gold.	6,063	5,582	17,896	21,325	20,542	21,544	21,947	19,351	24,028	31,472
Services.	298,023	378,487	582,041	769,397	783,431	837,474	865,549	891,177	726,433	795,273
Manufacturing services on physical inputs owned by others.	(NA)	(NA)	(NA)	(NA)	(NA)	(NA)	(NA)	(NA)	(NA)	(NA)
Maintenance and repair services n.i.e.	4,423	6,652	13,111	19,847	21,587	23,239	28,036	27,671	13,196	12,526
Transport [1]	49,462	58,377	76,357	84,434	81,779	86,342	93,107	91,058	57,168	65,777
Travel (for all purposes including education) [2]	96,872	93,423	130,315	192,602	192,868	196,469	200,724	198,982	72,481	70,214
Construction.	1,993	1,489	2,951	2,759	1,690	2,053	2,842	3,161	2,395	3,129
Insurance services.	3,631	7,566	14,854	15,763	16,663	18,976	19,118	18,579	20,277	22,741
Financial services.	29,192	47,405	86,512	115,688	117,249	131,733	136,273	142,546	151,033	171,740
Charges for the use of intellectual property n.i.e.	43,476	64,466	94,968	115,151	112,981	118,147	114,819	122,533	115,558	124,613
Telecommunications, computer, and information services.	12,250	15,568	26,556	41,427	43,122	47,657	49,245	55,742	56,456	59,797
Other business services. [3]	38,217	56,846	99,595	141,421	153,089	167,270	176,540	186,178	195,046	217,426
Personal, cultural, and recreational services [4,5]	9,351	11,114	17,612	24,220	23,626	25,664	22,715	22,192	20,820	23,915
Government goods and services n.i.e.	9,156	15,582	19,210	20,087	18,777	19,924	22,131	22,535	22,003	23,394
Primary income receipts.	365,612	536,294	723,223	824,929	857,240	995,442	1,102,964	1,136,799	936,236	1,052,080
Investment income.	361,217	531,498	717,292	818,351	850,911	989,095	1,096,023	1,129,749	929,608	1,045,181
Compensation of employees.	4,395	4,796	5,931	6,578	6,329	6,347	6,941	7,050	6,628	6,899
Secondary income (current transfer) receipts [6]	37,545	65,356	91,915	132,864	141,126	160,514	148,579	156,651	165,209	171,436
Imports of goods and services and income payments.	**1,888,038**	**2,642,385**	**3,119,466**	**3,647,025**	**3,635,406**	**3,911,453**	**4,233,855**	**4,285,683**	**3,879,793**	**4,626,508**
Imports of goods and services.	1,452,650	2,008,045	2,375,407	2,771,554	2,720,282	2,904,863	3,121,057	3,105,952	2,812,640	3,401,685
Goods.	1,231,722	1,695,820	1,938,950	2,273,249	2,207,195	2,356,345	2,555,662	2,512,358	2,346,103	2,851,660
General merchandise.	1,225,780	1,691,201	1,924,446	2,260,659	2,189,041	2,343,660	2,544,465	2,500,408	2,284,441	2,825,919
Foods, feeds, and beverages.	46,489	69,072	92,492	128,762	131,010	138,825	148,257	151,555	155,445	183,323
Industrial supplies and materials.	303,768	533,686	610,268	492,483	441,793	508,645	580,206	525,275	429,307	641,595
Capital goods except automotive.	347,706	382,833	450,406	607,160	593,614	642,864	694,229	679,133	647,208	764,758
Automotive vehicles, parts, and engines.	194,954	238,715	225,641	350,049	350,847	359,118	372,009	375,320	309,865	347,898
Consumer goods except food and automotive.	284,634	412,734	485,121	596,417	584,900	603,470	647,659	655,293	639,900	767,137
Other general merchandise.	48,229	54,161	60,519	85,789	86,876	90,739	102,104	113,833	102,717	121,207
Nonmonetary gold.	5,942	4,618	14,504	12,590	18,154	12,685	11,197	11,950	61,662	25,741
Services.	220,927	312,225	436,456	498,305	513,088	548,475	565,395	593,594	466,537	550,025
Manufacturing services on physical inputs owned by others.	(NA)	(NA)	(NA)	(NA)	(NA)	(NA)	(NA)	(NA)	(NA)	(NA)
Maintenance and repair services n.i.e.	2,316	2,730	5,857	8,084	7,595	6,796	7,354	8,716	6,203	7,982
Transport [1]	58,526	78,796	88,394	99,557	92,391	96,515	110,441	112,813	72,763	105,255
Travel (for all purposes including education) [2]	64,174	74,112	85,166	102,664	109,155	117,931	125,717	132,271	34,159	56,851
Construction.	1,447	1,295	2,578	3,012	1,768	1,950	3,077	1,361	1,131	1,495
Insurance services.	11,284	28,710	63,452	50,300	52,790	53,267	43,797	51,219	57,673	59,377
Financial services.	16,445	21,971	27,215	32,686	33,142	37,952	41,336	44,360	45,314	49,529
Charges for the use of intellectual property n.i.e.	16,139	24,127	31,116	35,178	41,974	44,405	42,736	42,273	47,708	43,342
Telecommunications, computer, and information services.	14,128	18,404	29,421	38,815	39,720	43,091	41,701	42,768	39,728	43,142
Other business services. [3]	20,306	32,076	65,903	95,119	100,505	106,991	107,435	112,496	112,979	129,601
Personal, cultural, and recreational services n.i.e. [4,7]	1,645	2,550	5,393	11,358	12,544	17,530	18,825	21,316	24,325	28,304
Government goods and services n.i.e.	14,516	27,454	31,960	21,531	21,503	22,047	22,975	24,000	24,553	25,147
Primary income payments.	350,980	492,108	553,311	639,724	660,798	737,501	847,589	893,244	773,146	912,587
Investment income.	339,107	475,701	539,783	623,031	643,482	720,549	830,466	874,336	758,716	895,030
Compensation of employees.	11,873	16,407	13,528	16,693	17,316	16,952	17,223	18,908	14,430	17,557
Secondary income (current transfer) payments [6]	84,408	142,232	190,749	235,747	254,325	269,132	265,109	286,487	294,008	312,236
Capital transfer receipts and other credits.	**42**	**15,473**	**9**	**67**	**76**	**19,200**	**3,281**	**71**	**372**	**3,864**

See footnotes at end of table.

Table 1300. U.S. International Transactions by Type of Transaction: 2000 to 2021-Continued.

See headnote on page 815.

Type of transaction	2000	2005	2010	2015	2016	2017	2018	2019	2020	2021
Capital transfer payments and other debits.	4,259	14,523	6,900	8,006	6,682	6,805	7,541	6,527	5,903	6,338
Net U.S. acquisition of financial assets [8]	587,682	562,996	958,737	144,104	336,438	1,161,984	429,710	307,192	943,091	1,278,599
Direct investment assets	186,371	52,591	349,829	302,072	299,814	409,413	-130,720	105,677	271,798	421,749
Equity	170,011	42,287	338,294	292,455	325,722	392,467	-219,334	157,122	291,207	426,081
Debt instruments	16,360	10,304	11,535	9,618	-25,908	16,947	88,613	-51,445	-19,409	-4,332
Portfolio investment assets	159,713	267,290	199,620	107,154	37,489	540,728	381,863	-11,453	406,364	719,095
Equity and investment fund shares	106,714	186,684	79,150	196,922	21,743	139,940	171,300	-25,304	395,995	154,795
Debt securities [9]	52,999	80,606	120,469	-89,767	15,746	400,788	210,562	13,851	10,369	564,299
Other investment assets	241,308	257,210	407,454	-258,831	-2,955	213,533	173,578	208,310	255,956	23,763
Other equity	1,438	1,138	1,907	2,098	1,746	1,506	1,329	1,367	1,847	1,206
Currency and deposits	(NA)	82,879	150,249	-191,472	-91,039	170,890	106,125	130,517	92,767	-47,977
Loans	(NA)	171,906	249,255	-67,754	85,434	35,715	64,945	75,263	169,652	68,611
Insurance technical reserves	(NA)	(NA)	(NA)	(NA)	(NA)	(NA)	(NA)	(NA)	(NA)	(NA)
Trade credit and advances	680	1,286	6,043	-1,702	903	5,422	1,179	1,163	-8,311	1,922
Reserve assets	290	-14,094	1,835	-6,292	2,090	-1,690	4,989	4,659	8,974	113,993
Special drawing rights	722	-4,511	31	9	684	78	156	237	81	113,685
Reserve position in the International Monetary Fund	-2,308	-10,200	1,293	-6,485	1,348	-1,812	4,824	4,271	8,814	460
Other reserve assets	1,876	617	511	185	58	44	10	150	78	-153
Net U.S. incurrence of liabilities [8]	1,066,074	1,277,056	1,391,042	503,468	706,693	1,559,219	712,178	831,045	1,634,965	1,977,294
Direct investment liabilities	349,124	142,345	264,039	511,434	474,388	380,823	214,716	314,743	148,914	448,325
Equity	258,438	116,476	207,842	426,321	374,243	333,318	318,946	277,005	167,803	380,786
Debt instruments	90,686	25,869	56,197	85,114	100,145	47,505	-104,230	37,738	-18,889	67,539
Portfolio investment liabilities	441,966	832,037	820,434	213,910	231,265	790,810	303,075	233,469	946,560	676,112
Equity and investment fund shares	193,600	89,258	178,952	-187,306	-139,700	149,633	156,916	-291,427	687,417	-19,562
Debt securities [9]	248,366	742,779	641,481	401,216	370,965	641,177	146,159	524,896	259,144	695,674
Other investment liabilities	274,984	302,673	306,569	-221,876	1,040	387,586	194,387	282,834	539,490	852,857
Financial derivatives, net [10]	(NA)	(NA)	-14,076	-27,035	7,827	23,998	-20,404	-41,670	-5,107	-41,902
Statistical discrepancy [11]	-72,257	34,223	-7,481	29,993	40,394	-24,610	141,238	-113,111	-71,751	108,231
Balance on current account (exports less imports)	-401,918	-749,232	-432,009	-408,453	-396,216	-361,021	-439,850	-445,957	-619,698	-846,354
Balance on goods and services	-369,686	-716,542	-503,087	-490,776	-479,458	-510,344	-578,594	-559,676	-653,989	-845,047
Balance on goods	-446,783	-782,804	-648,671	-761,868	-749,801	-799,343	-878,749	-857,260	-913,885	-1,090,296
Balance on services	77,096	66,262	145,584	271,092	270,343	288,999	300,155	297,584	259,896	245,248
Balance on primary income	14,632	44,186	169,911	185,205	196,442	257,942	255,275	243,555	163,090	139,493
Balance on secondary income	-46,863	-76,876	-98,834	-102,882	-113,199	-108,618	-116,530	-129,836	-128,799	-140,800
Balance on capital account	-4,217	950	-6,891	-7,940	-6,606	12,394	-4,261	-6,456	-5,532	-2,474
Net lending/borrowing from current- and capital-account transactions [12]	-406,135	-748,283	-438,900	-416,393	-402,821	-348,627	-444,110	-452,413	-625,229	-848,828
Net lending/borrowing from financial-account transactions [12]	-478,392	-714,059	-446,381	-386,400	-362,427	-373,237	-302,872	-565,524	-696,980	-740,597

NA Not available. [1] Includes passenger fares. [2] All travel purposes include 1) business travel, including expenditures by border, seasonal, and other short-term workers and 2) personal travel, including health-related and education-related travel. [3] Includes audiovisual services, artistic-related services, educational services delivered online, remotely provided telemedicine services, and services associated with museums and other cultural, sporting, gambling, and recreational activities, except those acquired by customers traveling outside their country of residence. [4] Includes goods and services supplied by and to embassies, consulates, and military bases; goods and services acquired from the host economy by diplomatic and military personnel; and services supplied by and to governments that are not included in other service categories. [5] Includes transfers under U.S. military sales contracts. [6] Secondary income (current transfer) receipts and payments include U.S. government and private transfers, such as U.S. government grants and pensions, fines and penalties, withholding taxes, personal transfers (remittances), insurance-related transfers, and other current transfers. [7] Includes direct defense expenditures. [8] Excluding financial derivatives. [9] Includes transactions in U.S. Treasury and other U.S. securities. [10] Transactions for financial derivatives are only available as a net value equal to transactions for assets less transactions for liabilities. A positive value represents net U.S. cash payments arising from derivatives contracts, and a negative value represents net U.S. cash receipts. [11] The statistical discrepancy is the difference between total debits and total credits recorded in the current, capital, and financial accounts; credits and debits are labeled in the table. In the financial account, an acquisition of an asset or a repayment of a liability is a debit, and an incurrence of a liability or a disposal of an asset is a credit. [12] Net lending means that U.S. residents are net suppliers of funds to foreign residents, and net borrowing means the opposite. Net lending or net borrowing can be computed from current- and capital-account transactions or from financial-account transactions. The two amounts differ by the statistical discrepancy.

Source: U.S. Bureau of Economic Analysis, International Economic Accounts, "Table 1.2. U.S. International Transactions, Expanded Detail," <www.bea.gov/data/economic-accounts/international>, accessed July 2022.

Table 1301. U.S. Government Reserve Assets: 1990 to 2021

[In billions of dollars (83.3 represents $83,300,000,000). As of end of year]

Type	1990	2000	2010	2013	2014	2015	2016	2017	2018	2019	2020	2021
Total	**83.3**	**67.6**	**132.4**	**144.6**	**130.1**	**117.6**	**117.3**	**123.3**	**125.8**	**129.5**	**144.9**	**251.2**
Gold stock	11.1	11.0	11.0	11.0	11.0	11.0	11.0	11.0	11.0	11.0	11.0	11.0
Special drawing rights	11.0	10.5	56.8	55.2	51.9	49.7	48.9	51.9	50.8	50.7	52.9	163.6
Reserve position in IMF [1]	52.2	14.8	12.5	30.8	25.2	17.6	18.4	17.6	22.0	26.2	36.4	35.8
Foreign currencies	9.1	31.2	52.1	47.6	41.9	39.2	39.0	42.8	41.9	41.5	44.5	40.7

[1] International Monetary Fund.

Source: Data prior to 2005, U.S. Department of the Treasury, *Treasury Bulletin*. Beginning in 2005, Board of Governors of the Federal Reserve System, "International Summary Statistics," August 2022 and earlier releases, <www.federalreserve.gov/data.htm>.

Table 1302. U.S. International Investment Position by Type of Investment: 2010 to 2021

[In billions of dollars (-2,511 represents -$2,511,000,000,000). Estimates as of end of 4th quarter. Minus sign (-) indicates loss or deficit]

Type of investment	2010	2015	2017	2018	2019	2020	2021
U.S. net international investment position	**-2,511**	**-7,590**	**-7,831**	**-9,796**	**-11,653**	**-14,707**	**-18,124**
Net international investment position excluding financial derivatives	-2,621	-7,645	-7,868	-9,838	-11,673	-14,701	-18,144
Financial derivatives other than reserves, net	110	54	38	42	20	-7	20
U.S. assets	**21,769**	**23,302**	**27,582**	**25,107**	**28,869**	**32,042**	**35,065**
Assets excluding financial derivatives	18,116	20,858	26,021	23,657	27,079	29,496	33,078
Financial derivatives other than reserves, gross positive fair value	3,652	2,443	1,561	1,450	1,790	2,546	1,987
By functional category:							
Direct investment at market value	5,486	7,057	8,894	7,417	8,692	9,367	10,971
Equity	4,621	5,812	7,684	6,139	7,464	8,162	9,750
Debt instruments	866	1,245	1,210	1,278	1,228	1,204	1,221
Portfolio investment	7,160	9,440	12,414	11,322	13,124	14,399	16,309
Equity and investment fund shares	4,900	6,756	9,118	7,900	9,478	10,615	12,022
Debt securities	2,260	2,684	3,296	3,423	3,646	3,784	4,287
Financial derivatives other than reserves, gross positive fair value	3,652	2,443	1,561	1,450	1,790	2,546	1,987
Over-the-counter contracts	3,622	2,400	1,497	1,409	1,755	2,492	1,927
Exchange-traded contracts	31	44	64	41	35	54	60
Other investment [1]	4,981	3,978	4,264	4,468	4,748	5,102	5,086
Currency and deposits	2,767	1,633	1,774	1,854	2,059	2,192	2,128
Loans	2,110	2,238	2,373	2,495	2,567	2,795	2,839
Trade credit and advances	51	45	51	52	54	46	47
Reserve assets	489	384	450	449	514	627	712
Monetary gold	368	277	338	334	396	494	472
Special drawing rights	57	50	52	51	51	53	164
Reserve position in the International Monetary Fund	12	18	18	22	26	36	36
Other reserve assets	52	39	43	42	41	44	41
U.S. liabilities	**24,280**	**30,892**	**35,413**	**34,903**	**40,522**	**46,749**	**53,190**
Liabilities excluding financial derivatives	20,738	28,503	33,890	33,495	38,752	44,196	51,222
Financial derivatives other than reserves, gross negative fair value	3,542	2,389	1,523	1,408	1,770	2,553	1,968
By functional category:							
Direct investment at market value	4,099	6,729	8,835	8,394	10,466	11,897	14,813
Equity	2,928	5,110	7,116	6,746	8,791	10,252	13,102
Debt instruments	1,171	1,619	1,719	1,648	1,675	1,645	1,711
Portfolio investment	11,869	16,646	19,398	18,844	21,764	25,172	28,480
Equity and investment fund shares	3,546	6,209	7,942	7,539	9,296	11,835	14,804
Debt securities	8,323	10,437	11,457	11,305	12,467	13,337	13,676
Financial derivatives other than reserves, gross negative fair value	3,542	2,389	1,523	1,408	1,770	2,553	1,968
Over-the-counter contracts	3,512	2,346	1,461	1,366	1,738	2,501	1,903
Exchange-traded contracts	30	43	62	41	32	51	65
Other investment	4,769	5,128	5,656	6,257	6,523	7,127	7,929
Currency and deposits	2,365	2,947	3,228	3,257	3,475	3,820	4,129
Loans	2,238	1,970	2,194	2,752	2,793	3,041	3,403
Trade credit and advances	112	162	183	199	206	216	236
Special drawing rights allocations	54	49	50	49	49	51	161

[1] Includes value of other equity, not shown separately.

Source: U.S. Bureau of Economic Analysis, International Economic Accounts, International Investment Position, "Table 1.2 U.S. Net International Investment Position at the End of the Period, Expanded Detail," <www.bea.gov/data/economic-accounts/international>, accessed July 2022.

Table 1303. International Service Transactions by Selected Type of Service and Selected Country: 2000 to 2021

[In millions of dollars (298,023 represents $298,023,000,000). Country data are based on information available from U.S. reporting sources. In some instances, the statistics may not necessarily reflect the ultimate foreign transactor. With the June 2020 data release, the Bureau of Economic Analysis has revised all International Transactions data to incorporate a number of changes including new services categories, new classifications, and improved methodologies. For details, see <apps.bea.gov/scb/2020/04-april/0420-international-annual-revision-preview. htm>. N.i.e. is not included elsewhere]

Type of service and country	Exports				Imports			
	2000	2010	2020	2021	2000	2010	2020	2021
Services, total........................	298,023	582,041	726,433	795,273	220,927	436,456	466,537	550,025
TYPE OF SERVICE								
Maintenance and repair services n.i.e. [1]...............	4,423	13,111	13,196	12,526	2,316	5,857	6,203	7,982
Transport [2]................................	49,462	76,357	57,168	65,777	58,526	88,394	72,763	105,255
Sea transport............................	11,554	16,308	17,782	19,558	21,787	28,022	34,159	55,904
Air transport [2]...........................	34,971	55,877	34,704	41,405	33,598	56,617	35,062	45,304
Passenger............................	21,445	31,506	11,817	12,759	21,316	38,667	13,371	16,635
Travel [2].................................	96,872	130,315	72,481	70,214	64,174	85,166	34,159	56,851
Business...............................	38,023	38,171	11,964	13,689	18,940	19,115	4,852	6,410
Personal...............................	58,849	92,145	60,517	56,525	45,235	66,051	29,307	50,440
Health related.......................	1,033	879	267	184	240	366	235	312
Education related....................	9,695	18,365	38,710	32,104	2,117	5,957	5,030	4,590
Construction............................	1,993	2,951	2,395	3,129	1,447	2,578	1,131	1,495
Insurance services......................	3,631	14,854	20,277	22,741	11,284	63,452	57,673	59,377
Direct insurance........................	628	4,348	1,735	1,970	1,683	4,470	5,395	6,520
Reinsurance............................	3,002	9,046	16,146	17,978	9,601	57,511	50,066	50,364
Financial services [2].....................	29,192	86,512	151,033	171,740	16,445	27,215	45,314	49,529
Explicitly charged and other financial services [2]......	23,385	79,295	132,010	152,977	11,326	17,067	37,945	42,392
Credit card and credit-related services..............	(NA)	10,569	23,983	28,908	(NA)	3,862	8,701	10,442
Financial management services...........	(NA)	23,889	61,348	68,715	(NA)	3,112	13,950	15,625
Charges for the use of intellectual property n.i.e. [2]....	43,476	94,968	115,558	124,613	16,139	31,116	47,708	43,342
Franchises and trademarks licensing fees............	(NA)	19,349	23,575	27,267	(NA)	4,757	4,798	5,915
License to use outcomes of research & development [3]	(NA)	37,561	52,459	56,396	(NA)	19,422	29,870	22,313
License to reproduce/distribute computer software...	(NA)	35,906	34,388	36,628	(NA)	5,192	11,537	11,984
License to reproduce/distribute audiovisual products....	(NA)	2,152	5,136	4,322	(NA)	1,745	1,503	3,130
Telecommunications, computer, and information services....	12,250	26,556	56,456	59,797	14,128	29,421	39,728	43,142
Telecommunications services....................	5,266	10,921	7,837	7,563	6,167	8,077	5,193	5,607
Computer services...........................	4,393	10,124	42,102	45,254	7,666	19,665	31,627	33,594
Information services.........................	2,591	5,510	6,518	6,980	295	1,680	2,908	3,941
Other business services.........................	38,217	99,595	195,046	217,426	20,306	65,903	112,979	129,601
Research and development services.................	7,123	22,165	44,684	47,185	3,370	22,593	29,718	32,913
Professional and management consulting services...	17,640	48,657	112,772	132,452	10,763	29,380	56,727	63,586
Technical, trade-related, and other business services [4]	13,455	28,774	37,590	37,789	6,173	13,930	26,534	33,103
Personal, cultural, and recreational services [5].........	9,351	17,612	20,820	23,915	1,645	5,393	24,325	28,304
Government goods and services n.i.e. [6]...............	9,156	19,210	22,003	23,394	14,516	31,960	24,553	25,147
AREA AND COUNTRY								
Canada.................................	25,184	57,288	52,771	56,136	19,802	28,518	30,574	33,094
Europe [7]................................	109,786	221,283	300,363	331,525	97,268	178,884	197,614	230,149
European Union [7, 8]........................	94,671	184,990	182,306	201,712	84,323	150,251	110,144	130,339
Euro Area [7, 9]...........................	57,578	114,783	164,276	180,071	52,102	95,907	95,853	112,608
France...............................	10,413	17,926	15,636	17,189	11,357	17,746	13,430	18,396
Germany..............................	15,974	26,541	29,858	32,037	16,676	31,356	31,501	34,749
Italy..................................	5,611	8,394	5,879	6,430	6,529	8,982	4,514	5,969
Netherlands...........................	6,963	13,569	21,162	23,834	5,884	8,846	11,097	12,177
United Kingdom........................	32,562	55,811	61,741	67,761	26,801	44,481	54,617	61,072
Latin America, other Western Hemisphere [7]..........	57,711	113,715	135,101	158,108	44,959	102,534	89,840	114,417
Brazil.................................	6,748	18,418	14,991	15,287	1,486	5,895	4,784	5,211
Mexico................................	16,285	23,730	23,486	30,488	11,435	15,891	17,226	27,801
Africa...................................	6,209	11,875	11,087	12,146	3,395	7,745	5,324	7,167
Middle East..............................	9,476	21,531	28,344	29,639	5,438	18,011	13,117	17,077
Asia and Pacific [7].........................	85,649	153,674	196,215	204,738	48,811	99,659	130,010	146,646
Australia..............................	6,396	16,096	15,075	16,489	2,731	6,073	6,038	6,265
China.................................	5,497	20,518	41,183	39,498	3,109	11,493	16,162	21,469
Hong Kong............................	3,977	5,836	12,544	14,031	3,878	7,381	9,857	11,901
India.................................	3,047	9,898	16,339	18,516	1,777	15,257	26,172	28,831
Japan.................................	37,169	43,519	38,009	36,892	17,085	25,064	32,563	31,121
Korea, South...........................	7,023	16,618	17,809	19,238	5,222	9,530	9,719	12,343
Singapore.............................	6,515	10,664	25,813	30,149	2,472	5,214	11,158	11,614
Taiwan................................	5,581	9,921	9,271	9,986	3,181	5,724	6,278	9,816
International organizations and unallocated............	4,008	2,674	2,552	2,982	1,254	1,105	58	1,473

NA Not available. [1] Covers maintenance and repair services by residents of country on goods owned by residents of another country. Excludes transportation equipment, construction, and computer maintenance and repair. [2] Includes types not shown separately. [3] Includes patents, industrial processes, and trade secrets. [4] Includes construction, architectural and engineering services, waste treatment, operational leasing, trade-related, and other business services. [5] Includes audiovisual services, artistic-related services, educational services delivered online, remotely provided telemedicine services, and services associated with museums and other cultural, sporting, gambling, and recreational activities, except those acquired by customers traveling outside their country of residence. [6] See footnote 4, Table 1300. Exports include transfers under U.S. military sales contracts; imports include direct defense expenditures. [7] Includes countries not shown separately. [8] Only those countries that are members of the European Union in a given year are included in the data for that year. [9] Euro area refers to European Union member countries that have adopted the Euro as the common currency. Data for each year cover only member countries in that year.

Source: U.S. Bureau of Economic Analysis, International Economic Accounts, International Services, "Table 2.1. U.S. Trade in Services, by Type of Service," and "Table 2.2. U.S. Trade in Services by Type of Service and by Country or Affiliation," <www.bea.gov/data/economic-accounts/international>, accessed July 2022.

Table 1304. U.S. Balances on International Transactions by Area and Selected Country: 2020 and 2021

[In millions of dollars (-616,698 represents -$616,698,000,000). Country data are based on information available from U.S. reporting sources. In some instances, the statistics may not necessarily reflect the ultimate foreign transactor. With the June 2020 data release, the Bureau of Economic Analysis has revised all International Transactions data to incorporate a number of changes including new services categories, new classification of certain services and transactions, and improved methodologies. For more information and details, see <apps.bea.gov/scb/2020/04-april/0420-international-annual-revision-preview.htm>. Minus sign (-) indicates debits]

Area or country	2020, balance on—				2021, balance on—			
	Current account	Goods	Services	Primary income [1]	Current account	Goods	Services	Primary income [1]
All areas............................	**-619,698**	**-913,885**	**259,896**	**163,090**	**-846,354**	**-1,090,296**	**245,248**	**139,493**
Canada................................	932	-18,665	22,197	-318	-35,992	-56,811	23,042	582
Europe................................	-57,450	-245,722	102,750	93,860	-109,841	-284,324	101,375	85,075
European Union [2]................	-51,860	-183,782	72,162	58,610	-71,318	-219,856	71,373	76,798
Euro Area [3].....................	-25,498	-156,669	68,422	60,807	-38,097	-189,004	67,462	82,351
Germany........................	-67,152	-57,378	-1,643	-9,866	-88,727	-70,504	-2,712	-16,458
Italy...............................	-28,123	-29,562	1,364	868	-37,660	-39,363	461	2,231
Netherlands....................	84,133	17,160	10,065	57,028	96,884	17,854	11,657	67,526
United Kingdom................	42,162	8,079	7,125	26,730	23,725	4,703	6,689	12,425
Latin America, other Western Hemisphere...	12,552	-79,842	45,261	86,053	19,964	-61,382	43,691	81,067
Brazil................................	20,089	11,258	10,207	-229	24,696	15,513	10,076	586
Mexico..............................	-130,157	-117,404	6,260	-3,505	-130,796	-114,208	2,687	-2,868
Africa...............................	-15,084	-1,817	5,763	2,979	-23,645	-10,918	4,978	6,528
Middle East.........................	9,449	11,422	15,226	-9,529	-1,645	1,070	12,562	-6,670
Asia and Pacific.....................	-577,506	-580,096	66,205	-28,031	-698,558	-678,763	58,091	-44,589
Australia...........................	23,167	8,892	9,038	6,241	30,193	13,860	10,224	6,134
China...............................	-307,067	-307,627	25,021	-18,598	-365,940	-352,798	18,029	-24,964
Hong Kong..........................	25,247	15,975	2,687	6,373	35,289	25,906	2,130	6,781
India...............................	-38,231	-24,221	-9,833	3,581	-45,855	-33,409	-10,294	6,202
Japan...............................	-75,941	-55,860	5,446	-28,504	-96,562	-60,689	5,771	-44,974
Singapore..........................	30,273	-4,050	14,655	19,210	45,283	5,733	18,534	20,634
Korea, South........................	-21,833	-25,300	8,090	-3,615	-30,906	-29,252	6,895	-7,834
Taiwan..............................	-41,542	-29,923	2,993	-13,684	-53,945	-39,820	170	-12,500
International organizations and unallocated...........................	7,409	835	2,494	18,076	3,363	832	1,509	17,501

[1] Primary income consists of investment income and compensation of employees. [2] Data for the European Union (EU) reflect the EU membership during the reference period. In 2020 and 2021, the EU was composed of Austria, Belgium, Bulgaria, Croatia, Cyprus, Czechia, Denmark, Estonia, Finland, France, Germany, Greece, Hungary, Ireland, Italy, Latvia, Lithuania, Luxembourg, Malta, Netherlands, Poland, Portugal, Romania, Slovakia, Slovenia, Spain, and Sweden. Beginning with first quarter 2020, the United Kingdom was no longer part of the EU. [3] Euro area refers to European Union member countries that have adopted the Euro as the common currency. Data here cover Austria, Belgium, Cyprus, Estonia, Finland, France, Germany, Greece, Ireland, Italy, Latvia, Lithuania, Luxembourg, Malta, Netherlands, Portugal, Slovakia, Slovenia, and Spain.

Source: U.S. Bureau of Economic Analysis, International Transactions, "Table 1.3. U.S. International Transactions, Expanded Detail by Area and Country," <www.bea.gov/data/economic-accounts/international>, accessed July 2022.

Table 1305. Employment of Majority-Owned U.S. Affiliates of Foreign Companies by State: 2010 to 2019

[In thousands (5,435.4 represents 5,435,400). Covers full-time and part-time employees on the payroll, generally at the end of the fiscal year. A U.S. majority-owned affiliate is a U.S. business enterprise in which a foreign entity has a direct or indirect voting interest greater than 50 percent]

State and other area	2010	2015	2018	2019	State and other area	2010	2015	2018	2019
Total......................	**5,435.4**	**6,822.8**	**7,862.2**	**7,947.0**	Montana.................	6.3	6.8	8.8	9.5
					Nebraska................	23.9	31.4	35.8	36.5
Alabama....................	81.9	104.6	122.0	120.1	Nevada.................	39.0	47.8	56.2	57.5
Alaska.....................	14.1	16.3	17.8	17.4	New Hampshire.........	39.3	41.2	48.0	49.8
Arizona....................	77.0	104.4	120.2	122.9	New Jersey.............	222.9	270.7	292.5	294.7
Arkansas...................	35.9	46.1	47.8	47.4	New Mexico.............	15.3	16.9	18.1	18.8
California..................	584.0	734.2	846.4	843.9	New York...............	398.9	477.9	527.1	531.3
Colorado...................	80.9	105.0	121.0	119.1	North Carolina.........	194.7	252.6	290.3	292.5
Connecticut................	100.9	102.6	115.1	114.8	North Dakota...........	11.5	13.0	14.0	15.0
Delaware...................	26.7	25.2	24.5	24.6	Ohio....................	210.2	257.7	307.4	310.7
District of Columbia......	22.4	23.5	24.1	24.5	Oklahoma...............	38.6	49.6	57.2	59.3
Florida....................	232.9	331.2	364.0	366.0	Oregon.................	43.0	60.6	68.7	72.0
Georgia....................	189.5	228.9	285.3	287.4	Pennsylvania...........	261.3	291.4	319.4	329.5
Hawaii.....................	26.8	36.7	41.8	41.6	Rhode Island...........	26.1	25.5	27.2	28.2
Idaho......................	13.4	15.6	18.7	19.3	South Carolina.........	108.4	134.6	161.3	162.9
Illinois...................	252.7	321.7	380.6	381.1	South Dakota...........	7.2	11.9	14.2	14.3
Indiana....................	136.0	189.7	215.1	214.0	Tennessee..............	117.2	164.2	199.2	203.4
Iowa.......................	44.9	59.9	59.2	61.4	Texas..................	451.4	588.5	668.2	678.1
Kansas.....................	54.5	56.1	71.9	76.1	Utah...................	31.4	42.6	50.4	54.4
Kentucky...................	89.2	120.2	136.1	136.8	Vermont................	11.1	11.0	11.6	15.1
Louisiana..................	56.1	67.5	77.3	75.8	Virginia...............	147.8	180.6	212.1	210.9
Maine......................	30.3	34.3	35.6	35.6	Washington.............	94.4	113.3	139.9	143.1
Maryland...................	101.6	116.9	113.9	116.7	West Virginia..........	28.7	29.4	27.7	29.1
Massachusetts..............	187.3	203.0	233.6	234.1	Wisconsin..............	77.5	97.3	121.7	127.9
Michigan...................	145.4	243.3	316.4	317.0	Wyoming................	7.8	7.2	8.2	7.7
Minnesota..................	90.7	113.9	147.8	157.7	Puerto Rico............	21.9	24.0	22.6	23.9
Mississippi................	26.8	37.4	43.9	45.5	Other U.S. areas.......	13.9	24.2	28.1	27.1
Missouri...................	81.7	109.8	139.2	135.7	Foreign................	2.3	([1])	6.9	7.2

[1] 2,500 to 4,999 employees.

Source: U.S. Bureau of Economic Analysis, International Economic Accounts, "Direct Investment and Multinational Enterprises (MNEs)," <www.bea.gov/data/economic-accounts/international>, accessed December 2021.

Table 1306. New Foreign Direct Investment in the U.S. by Industry of U.S. Business Enterprise and Country of Ultimate Beneficial Owner: 2020 and 2021

[In millions of dollars (141,372 represents $141,372,000,000). Data shown are first year expenditures by foreign direct investors to acquire, establish, or expand U.S. businesses. First year expenditures include those expenditures in the calendar year in which the transaction occurred. A U.S. business enterprise is categorized as "acquired" if a foreign entity acquired a 10 percent or more voting interest in an incorporated U.S. business, or an equivalent interest of an unincorporated U.S. business, either directly or indirectly through an existing U.S. affiliate. A U.S. business enterprise is categorized as "established" if a foreign entity or existing U.S. affiliate of a foreign entity establishes a new legal entity in the U.S. in which the foreign entity owns 10 percent or more of the new business enterprise's voting interest, or an equivalent interest if unincorporated. An existing U.S. affiliate is categorized as "expanded" if it expands its operations to include a new facility where business is conducted and the expansion has a projected total cost of more than $3 million]

Industry and country	2020 Total	U.S. businesses acquired	U.S. businesses established	U.S. businesses expanded	2021 Total	U.S. businesses acquired	U.S. businesses established	U.S. businesses expanded
Total [1]	**141,372**	**135,919**	**2,623**	**2,829**	**333,567**	**330,165**	**1,640**	**1,761**
INDUSTRY [2]								
Manufacturing	71,130	69,178	555	1,397	121,327	120,772	246	308
Wholesale trade	5,602	5,529	67	5	4,421	(D)	45	(D)
Retail trade	1,792	1,401	56	335	(D)	(D)	60	62
Information	21,029	20,883	133	13	25,338	25,150	(D)	(D)
Finance and insurance	6,966	6,912	48	6	13,739	13,621	118	(D)
Real estate and rental and leasing	4,128	2,853	1,069	206	43,756	43,501	255	–
Professional, scientific, and technical services	15,741	15,520	215	7	37,938	37,749	178	11
Other industries	14,984	13,642	481	860	(D)	(D)	(D)	(D)
COUNTRY [3]								
Canada	16,799	16,599	(D)	(D)	29,692	29,186	234	272
Europe [1]	93,095	90,440	722	1,932	233,492	231,350	777	1,365
France	11,080	10,943	(D)	(D)	35,319	35,316	3	–
Germany	23,762	23,282	30	449	26,754	26,667	(D)	(D)
Ireland	4,160	4,140	(D)	(D)	18,306	(D)	12	(D)
Netherlands	3,940	3,908	92	(D)	43,071	43,053	(D)	(D)
Switzerland	14,136	13,510	258	534	18,764	18,752	10	2
United Kingdom	10,609	10,332	(D)	19	59,731	59,400	301	30
Latin America/other Western Hemisphere	7,675	7,252	(D)	(D)	8,434	8,337	96	(D)
South and Central America	1,703	(D)	(D)	–	829	756	72	–
Other Western Hemisphere [1]	5,971	(D)	(D)	(D)	7,605	7,581	24	(D)
Bermuda	3,554	(D)	(D)	–	6,012	5,989	(D)	–
Caribbean Islands (British)	(D)	(D)	9	(D)	(D)	(D)	23	(D)
Africa	6	5	1	–	3	(D)	3	–
Middle East	1,423	1,388	35	–	2,583	2,553	30	(D)
Asia and Pacific [1]	22,222	20,102	1,250	870	55,535	54,934	481	120
Australia	2,779	2,266	(D)	(D)	(D)	(D)	40	(D)
China	597	551	(D)	(D)	294	254	(D)	(D)
Hong Kong	375	169	(D)	(D)	(D)	(D)	2	1
Japan	9,282	8,592	589	100	29,248	28,895	(D)	(D)
Singapore	832	(D)	(D)	–	(D)	(D)	(D)	(D)
South Korea	925	(D)	(D)	(D)	11,001	(D)	89	(D)

– Represents or rounds to zero. D Suppressed to avoid disclosure of data of individual companies. [1] Includes other countries not shown separately. [2] Based on 2012 North American Industry Classification System (NAICS); see text, Section 15. [3] Country of ultimate beneficial owner (UBO). The UBO is the entity proceeding up a U.S. affiliate's ownership chain, beginning with the foreign parents, which is not owned more than 50 percent by another entity.

Source: U.S. Bureau of Economic Analysis, International Economic Accounts, New Foreign Direct Investment in the United States, "Direct Investment and Multinational Enterprises," <www.bea.gov/data/economic-accounts/international>, accessed August 2022.

Table 1307. Foreign Direct Investment Position in the United States on a Historical-Cost Basis: by Selected Country, 2010 to 2021, and by Industry, 2021

[In millions of dollars (2,280,044 represents $2,280,044,000,000). Foreign direct investment is defined as the ownership or control, directly or indirectly, by one foreign entity of 10 percent or more of the voting interest of a U.S. business enterprise. As used here, "entity" is synonymous with "person," used in a broad legal sense that includes any individual, branch, partnership, association, trust, corporation, or government. Data are based on surveys of U.S. affiliates of foreign companies]

| Country | All industries total | | | | 2021 | | | |
	2010	2015	2019	2020	Total [1]	Manufac-turing	Wholesale trade	Finance and insurance [2]
All countries................	**2,280,044**	**3,354,907**	**4,398,763**	**4,471,403**	**4,977,492**	**2,108,607**	**483,308**	**620,552**
Canada..........................	192,463	323,207	481,722	495,327	527,896	79,543	65,923	93,754
Europe [3].......................	1,659,774	2,306,254	2,791,464	2,807,583	3,186,004	1,551,535	199,200	364,450
Austria.........................	4,532	7,159	14,454	15,419	16,202	7,586	(D)	(D)
Belgium........................	69,565	88,121	68,133	65,495	71,571	61,397	3,253	(D)
Denmark........................	7,772	14,509	22,658	30,179	34,625	13,649	11,933	(D)
Finland.........................	4,943	6,471	8,141	7,828	10,086	6,172	2,146	(Z)
France..........................	189,763	233,547	266,448	284,194	276,146	144,674	26,051	33,524
Germany........................	203,077	281,295	319,615	347,965	403,646	175,939	55,016	52,070
Ireland.........................	24,097	55,861	235,786	235,448	269,429	73,148	9,625	23,190
Italy...........................	20,142	27,709	29,788	31,999	34,373	17,650	2,450	249
Luxembourg.....................	170,309	350,772	322,291	334,680	382,914	303,860	5,875	10,230
Netherlands....................	234,408	298,782	496,672	506,276	629,523	316,955	27,124	62,813
Norway.........................	10,478	20,641	34,391	30,360	32,498	2,003	(D)	(D)
Spain..........................	43,095	67,349	86,370	85,090	79,253	13,200	718	(D)
Sweden.........................	38,780	44,961	55,295	60,155	71,453	46,592	10,484	1,800
Switzerland....................	180,642	241,008	254,975	275,208	282,279	141,239	889	(D)
United Kingdom................	400,435	522,954	500,921	421,766	512,431	193,557	26,157	47,435
Latin America and other Western Hemisphere......................	62,130	123,846	203,097	211,186	239,855	58,817	11,685	30,613
South and Central America [3].....	17,943	25,261	44,186	46,413	59,120	12,987	3,069	849
Brazil.........................	1,357	142	5,740	7,041	8,017	3,571	-195	423
Mexico.........................	10,970	15,262	19,583	20,645	28,012	6,477	3,195	280
Venezuela......................	3,122	4,186	1,671	1,381	1,075	(D)	24	(D)
Other Western Hemisphere [3]....	44,187	98,585	158,911	164,773	180,735	45,830	8,616	29,765
Bermuda........................	365	-7,323	44,752	48,506	49,488	17,885	-888	-9,776
Curacao........................	(X)	1,630	1,191	1,193	1,116	(D)	(D)	(D)
U.K. Islands, Caribbean........	38,477	101,725	101,538	101,906	116,392	18,477	8,470	38,554
Africa..........................	2,265	4,310	9,007	9,861	10,333	6,562	137	-8
Middle East [3]...................	16,808	17,582	41,454	41,238	42,356	22,750	5,296	536
Israel..........................	8,714	6,865	13,429	10,608	11,253	2,438	(D)	(D)
Asia and Pacific [3]..............	346,605	579,708	872,020	906,208	971,048	389,398	201,067	131,207
Australia.......................	35,632	65,259	76,477	85,802	97,745	25,325	2,446	6,934
China..........................	3300	14,714	38,792	36,785	38,249	5,954	6,577	(D)
Hong Kong.......................	4,440	10,981	14,049	14,069	14,429	2,395	3,142	(D)
India..........................	4102	9,639	4,036	1,679	2,947	2,827	55	(D)
Japan..........................	255,012	401,835	633,882	651,075	690,022	326,327	124,172	110,385
Singapore......................	21,517	21,585	27,134	28,427	30,167	8,430	2,954	(D)
South Korea....................	15,746	39,784	55,606	63,137	72,521	9,749	55,611	639
Taiwan.........................	4,642	6,889	14,558	17,972	17,336	5,448	4,973	(D)

D Suppressed to avoid disclosure of data of individual companies. X Not applicable. Z Between -$500,000 and +$500,000. [1] Includes other industries, not shown separately. [2] Excludes depository institutions. [3] Includes other countries, not shown separately.

Source: U.S. Bureau of Economic Analysis, International Economic Accounts, New Foreign Direct Investment in the United States, "Direct Investment and Multinational Enterprises," <www.bea.gov/data/economic-accounts/international>, accessed September 2022.

Table 1308. U.S. Majority-Owned Affiliates of Foreign Companies—Assets, Sales, Employment, Value, Exports, and Imports by Industry of Affiliate: 2018

[In billions of dollars (14,847 represents $14,847,000,000,000), except number of employees, shown in thousands (7,862 represents 7,862,000). A majority-owned U.S. affiliate is a U.S. business enterprise in which a foreign entity ("entity" is used here in a broad legal sense including any individual, branch, partnership, association, trust, corporation, or government) has a direct or indirect voting interest greater than 50 percent]

Industry	NAICS code [2]	Total assets	Sales	Employ-ment (1,000)	Employee compen-sation	Gross property, plant, and equipment	Mer-chandise exports	Mer-chandise imports
All industries....................	**(X)**	**14,847**	**4,958**	**7,862**	**649**	**2,741**	**397**	**751**
Manufacturing [1]...................	31-33	3,095	2,136	2,827	261	1,156	241	350
Petroleum and coal products..................	324	258	331	39	9	257	24	46
Chemicals.........................	325	1,059	425	414	58	250	50	59
Machinery.........................	333	144	116	255	21	35	20	17
Transportation equipment......................	336	467	537	619	52	235	67	144
Wholesale trade....................	42	1,005	1,187	677	61	411	140	372
Retail trade.......................	44-45	165	258	881	36	88	3	22
Information.......................	51	433	193	354	34	151	1	1
Finance and insurance..............	52	8,297	494	419	81	131	(D)	(Z)
Real estate and rental and leasing..............	53	303	43	72	7	178	(Z)	(D)
Professional, scientific, and technical services.......................	54	269	161	429	51	27	1	1
Other industries...................	(X)	1,280	485	2,203	118	600	(D)	(D)

X Not applicable. D Suppressed to avoid disclosure of data of individual companies. Z Less than $500,000,000. [1] Includes other industries not shown separately. [2] Based on the North American Industry Classification System (NAICS); see text, Section 15.

Source: U.S. Bureau of Economic Analysis, International Economic Accounts, "Foreign Direct Investment in the United States: Activities of U.S. Affiliates of Foreign Multinational Enterprises," <www.bea.gov/international/di1fdiop.htm>, accessed December 2021.

Table 1309. U.S. Direct Investment Position Abroad, Capital Outflows, and Income by Industry of Foreign Affiliates: 2000 to 2021

[In millions of dollars (1,316,247 represents $1,316,247,000,000). U.S. investment abroad is the ownership or control by one U.S. person (in the broad legal sense to include any individual, partnership, corporation, or other form of organization) of 10 percent or more of the voting securities of an incorporated foreign business enterprise or an equivalent interest in an unincorporated foreign business enterprise]

Industry	2000	2005	2010	2015	2019	2020	2021
DIRECT INVESTMENT POSITION ON A HISTORICAL-COST BASIS							
All industries, total [1]	**1,316,247**	**2,241,656**	**3,741,910**	**5,289,071**	**5,834,566**	**6,085,708**	**6,489,012**
Mining	72,111	109,280	172,819	180,418	154,428	130,220	137,196
Manufacturing [1]	343,899	430,737	518,321	693,847	786,581	864,386	912,625
Food	23,497	27,638	47,704	81,914	76,404	98,150	97,159
Chemicals	75,807	106,975	111,327	151,369	205,205	239,736	260,669
Primary and fabricated metals	21,644	23,013	18,674	34,506	46,157	42,015	46,642
Machinery	22,229	26,433	41,285	45,932	41,648	42,316	44,239
Computer and electronic products	59,909	50,773	72,935	97,641	126,672	137,040	150,041
Electrical equipment, appliances, and components	10,005	15,449	19,941	17,591	14,598	21,000	22,452
Transportation equipment	49,887	50,739	49,636	62,087	84,616	83,343	84,781
Wholesale trade	93,936	132,915	168,722	225,217	229,581	245,924	257,516
Information	52,345	102,848	126,063	198,689	306,199	317,448	350,853
Depository institutions (banking)	40,152	66,707	118,585	118,271	144,849	122,338	137,123
Finance and insurance	217,086	463,981	734,859	719,608	900,433	939,238	1,011,076
Professional, scientific, and technical services	32,868	57,164	81,874	117,646	158,941	147,396	157,621
Holding companies (nonbank)	(NA)	710,386	1,584,903	2,686,477	2,737,171	2,892,662	3,071,480
FINANCIAL OUTFLOWS [INFLOWS(-)] WITHOUT CURRENT-COST ADJUSTMENT							
All industries, total [1]	**142,627**	**15,369**	**277,779**	**264,359**	**20,342**	**204,461**	**349,957**
Mining	2,174	12,015	11,884	416	-8,478	-2,556	8,292
Manufacturing [1]	43,002	28,121	33,320	43,502	64,399	85,264	56,497
Food	2,014	1,171	5,341	4,449	1,005	3,056	1,126
Chemicals	3,812	3,911	7,614	6,470	32,787	61,205	22,120
Primary and fabricated metals	1,233	-703	546	503	3,019	1,623	2,509
Machinery	2,659	2,077	4,229	3,110	3,002	-98	1,943
Computer and electronic products	17,303	3,607	6,772	6,440	13,257	11,210	16,072
Electrical equipment, appliances, and components	2,100	1,662	1,743	1,545	1,142	7,454	1,569
Transportation equipment	7,814	-250	-380	11,282	5,620	-2,539	2,345
Wholesale trade	11,938	12,517	15,487	9,495	17,852	14,122	22,050
Information	16,531	2,831	8,777	13,488	11,364	-2,219	32,181
Depository institutions	-1,274	-4,751	-4,811	-6,448	722	-5,967	1,038
Finance and insurance	21,659	13,079	21,887	15,632	-30,138	-26,770	54,805
Professional, scientific, and technical services	5,441	-2,055	2,774	5,121	6,772	12,240	11,789
Holding companies (nonbank)	(NA)	-66,351	169,743	161,310	-77,799	120,623	115,703
INCOME WITHOUT CURRENT-COST ADJUSTMENT [2]							
All industries, total [1]	**133,692**	**271,877**	**417,605**	**433,333**	**536,336**	**433,691**	**542,313**
Mining	13,164	24,559	29,138	3,541	10,973	5,509	17,755
Manufacturing [1]	42,230	46,896	61,240	67,102	72,751	59,350	77,459
Food	2,681	3,558	4,322	4,149	3,820	2,455	3,369
Chemicals	11,552	13,056	14,088	18,114	24,725	19,264	21,557
Primary and fabricated metals	1,536	1,815	1,349	1,721	2,203	2,320	2,614
Machinery	2,257	2,253	4,465	3,495	3,313	3,045	4,692
Computer and electronic products	8,860	7,714	11,440	10,868	14,603	15,588	21,853
Electrical equipment, appliances, and components	1,079	1,703	1,653	1,461	1,398	1,073	1,748
Transportation equipment	4,107	1,936	6,471	10,632	6,820	4,878	5,923
Wholesale trade	14,198	24,494	24,538	19,129	22,569	16,479	28,368
Information	-964	10,832	12,229	14,756	21,088	15,175	14,200
Depository institutions	2,191	164	1,328	3,521	4,262	844	3,178
Finance and insurance	15,210	27,911	35,143	45,760	52,333	48,595	62,914
Professional, scientific, and technical services	3,548	9,272	8,856	11,145	16,468	12,810	18,759
Holding companies (nonbank)	(NA)	109,566	220,101	233,272	288,253	242,977	271,247

NA Not available. [1] Includes other industries, not shown separately. [2] Prior to 2006, income is shown net of withholding taxes. Beginning 2006, income is shown gross of withholding taxes.

Source: U.S. Bureau of Economic Analysis, International Economic Accounts, Direct Investment by Country and Industry, "Direct Investment and Multinational Enterprises," <www.bea.gov/data/economic-accounts/international>, accessed September 2022.

Table 1310. U.S. Direct Investment Position Abroad on a Historical-Cost Basis by Selected Country: 2000 to 2021

[In millions of dollars (1,316,247 represents $1,316,247,000,000). U.S. investment abroad is the ownership or control by one U.S. person (in the broad legal sense to include any individual, partnership, corporation, or other form of organization) of 10 percent or more of the voting securities of an incorporated foreign business enterprise or an equivalent interest in an unincorporated foreign business enterprise. Negative position can occur when a U.S. parent company's liabilities to the foreign affiliate are greater than its equity in and loans to the foreign affiliate]

Country	2000	2005	2010	2015	2018	2019	2020	2021
All countries	1,316,247	2,241,656	3,741,910	5,289,071	5,792,290	5,834,566	6,085,708	6,489,012
Canada	132,472	231,836	295,206	361,954	373,604	370,633	373,823	406,356
Europe [1]	687,320	1,210,679	2,034,559	3,075,567	3,413,031	3,453,820	3,628,811	3,981,383
Austria	2,872	11,236	11,485	6,508	6,848	5,948	4,585	4,632
Belgium	17,973	49,306	43,975	48,096	59,397	61,782	66,901	61,934
Czechia	1,228	2,729	5,268	6,343	5,253	5,234	5,086	5,253
Denmark	5,270	6,914	11,802	15,794	10,692	12,770	15,793	16,414
Finland	1,342	1,950	1,597	1,258	4,063	2,685	3,454	6,487
France	42,628	60,526	78,320	81,274	67,548	87,692	104,635	106,167
Germany	55,508	100,473	103,319	120,519	134,794	141,516	151,475	170,218
Greece	795	1,884	1,775	1,007	431	134	157	303
Hungary	1,920	2,795	4,237	7,625	5,283	12,144	12,800	11,436
Ireland	35,903	55,173	158,851	337,831	444,037	377,158	373,443	556,599
Italy	23,484	24,528	27,137	30,869	32,842	25,573	27,441	28,096
Luxembourg	27,849	79,937	272,206	599,001	720,628	723,760	713,615	715,591
Netherlands	115,429	240,205	514,689	829,693	809,663	825,002	829,352	885,305
Norway	4,379	8,533	28,541	31,697	25,905	24,934	21,325	30,554
Poland	3,884	5,575	13,152	11,872	11,870	10,632	12,920	13,372
Portugal	2,664	2,138	2,612	1,971	2,504	2,280	2,151	2,154
Russia	1,147	9,363	10,040	10,259	12,779	14,381	13,243	12,298
Spain	21,236	50,197	52,390	36,075	31,916	35,446	37,712	38,956
Sweden	25,959	30,153	23,275	32,593	43,521	42,140	57,561	57,698
Switzerland	55,377	100,692	119,891	171,342	210,800	192,950	225,230	216,116
Turkey	1,826	2,563	4,155	3,798	4,193	4,006	6,221	6,190
United Kingdom	230,762	351,513	501,247	632,327	754,139	833,850	918,147	1,005,470
Latin America and other Western Hemisphere	266,576	379,582	752,788	902,642	1,000,673	961,480	1,028,615	1,017,716
South America [1]	84,220	73,311	136,598	129,303	134,707	135,121	139,099	141,099
Argentina	17,488	10,103	11,747	14,624	8,907	10,693	12,073	12,543
Brazil	36,717	30,882	66,963	56,847	78,963	76,024	66,476	67,547
Chile	10,052	11,127	30,747	28,134	25,660	25,425	23,426	22,582
Colombia	3,693	4,292	6,181	7,750	7,236	7,035	6,844	6,802
Ecuador	832	941	1,283	913	781	751	193	70
Peru	3,130	5,542	7,196	7,573	5,455	6,448	7,260	7,544
Venezuela	10,531	8,934	10,255	9,825	2,338	2,940	2,595	2,630
Central America [1]	73,841	82,496	97,752	112,690	107,381	108,714	115,961	122,685
Costa Rica	1,716	1,598	1,827	1,642	1,589	2,537	2,569	2,807
Honduras	399	821	936	1,274	1,202	1,488	1,107	1,251
Mexico	39,352	73,687	85,751	101,326	95,543	95,659	104,351	110,684
Panama	30,758	4,826	5,156	4,447	5,206	4,554	3,900	3,460
Other Western Hemisphere [1]	108,515	223,775	518,438	660,650	758,586	717,645	773,555	753,933
Barbados	2,141	3,881	7,524	14,084	40,015	35,968	48,996	36,419
Bermuda	60,114	113,222	265,524	303,244	339,399	309,240	324,592	278,842
Dominican Republic	1,143	815	1,432	1,079	2,101	2,554	2,411	2,722
U.K. Islands, Caribbean	33,451	83,164	191,680	303,438	304,716	301,989	333,792	371,601
Africa [1]	11,891	22,756	54,816	52,004	48,069	45,811	44,562	44,808
Egypt	1,998	5,475	12,599	14,068	11,028	10,968	11,001	11,697
Nigeria	470	1,105	5,058	5,872	4,504	6,510	6,686	5,920
South Africa	3,562	3,969	6,017	6,926	9,088	7,943	7,242	7,553
Middle East [1]	10,863	21,115	34,431	49,802	76,945	79,949	79,431	81,280
Israel	3,735	7,978	9,464	10,251	28,997	32,925	39,461	41,302
Saudi Arabia	3,661	3,830	7,436	10,025	10,807	10,595	10,793	11,875
United Arab Emirates	683	2,285	4,935	16,205	18,055	15,992	15,892	16,241
Asia and Pacific [1]	207,125	375,689	570,111	847,102	879,968	922,874	930,464	957,469
Australia	34,838	75,669	125,421	160,061	166,269	163,465	169,669	167,193
China	11,140	19,016	58,996	92,150	107,557	105,613	115,026	118,186
Hong Kong	27,447	36,415	41,264	69,367	81,215	97,535	86,303	86,836
India	2,379	7,162	24,666	35,361	42,197	42,000	42,257	45,448
Indonesia	8,904	8,603	10,558	15,717	19,886	19,981	13,164	15,737
Japan	57,091	81,175	113,523	106,932	108,933	120,907	121,809	118,746
Malaysia	7,910	11,097	11,791	15,765	10,385	11,326	12,114	12,537
New Zealand	4,271	5,191	6,724	11,427	11,379	11,779	11,715	12,129
Philippines	3,638	6,522	5,399	5,992	5,562	5,427	4,548	4,724
Singapore	24,133	76,390	102,778	253,277	232,940	253,805	273,137	294,540
South Korea	8,968	19,760	26,233	38,608	37,282	36,277	34,300	38,115
Taiwan	7,836	14,356	22,188	15,295	27,479	25,123	17,939	16,768
Thailand	5,824	10,252	12,999	17,942	16,415	17,484	16,693	15,474

[1] Includes other countries, not shown separately.

Source: U.S. Bureau of Economic Analysis, International Economic Accounts, Direct Investment by Country and Industry, "Direct Investment and Multinational Enterprises," <www.bea.gov/data/economic-accounts/international>, accessed August 2022.

Table 1311. U.S. Foreign Economic and Military Aid by Major Recipient Country: 2000 to 2020

[In millions of dollars (17,111.9 represents $17,111,900,000). For years ending September 30. Annual figures are for obligations. Total aid may not add due to rounding]

Region/country	2000	2010	2015	2019	2020 Total	2020 Economic aid	2020 Military aid
Total [1]	17,111.9	48,356.8	49,946.2	48,176.4	51,058.0	39,417.2	11,640.8
Middle East & North Africa [1]	6,799.2	8,827.9	10,697.8	11,993.9	12,151.7	5,428.5	6,723.2
Egypt	2,076.1	1,602.8	1,568.3	1,467.0	1,471.1	169.1	1,302.0
Iraq	1.2	2,091.8	1,550.6	959.3	1,180.5	632.4	548.1
Israel	3,863.4	2,837.6	3,293.6	3,308.5	3,310.9	10.9	3,300.0
Jordan	448.3	765.7	1,512.5	1,723.3	2,594.0	2,090.0	504.0
Lebanon	35.0	158.7	507.7	791.0	830.6	586.1	244.5
Morocco	51.1	56.1	116.5	67.0	64.0	39.8	24.3
Syria	-	22.4	913.5	653.7	837.1	837.1	(Z)
Tunisia	7.1	21.2	122.9	202.2	277.3	175.2	102.1
West Bank/Gaza [2]	122.0	686.9	556.8	28.0	18.3	18.3	–
Yemen	57.2	122.4	176.8	809.8	556.5	555.4	1.2
Sub-Saharan Africa [1]	2,025.1	8,422.2	11,417.0	13,129.6	13,810.3	13,394.9	415.4
Angola	105.4	99.9	58.3	50.4	62.6	62.3	0.4
Botswana	0.9	51.1	42.5	63.0	75.1	74.8	0.4
Burkina Faso	18.1	33.3	33.0	100.8	212.8	211.9	1.0
Chad	4.1	184.4	108.7	154.9	139.6	137.2	2.4
Congo, Democratic Republic of	32.6	366.2	469.7	790.7	964.6	959.5	5.1
Ethiopia	277.6	831.2	809.7	966.9	1,213.2	1,209.4	3.8
Ghana	66.8	109.4	290.3	140.6	-63.8	-68.1	4.3
Kenya	93.5	569.0	939.6	823.2	830.5	826.4	4.1
Lesotho	2.1	33.0	29.2	92.6	104.5	104.5	(Z)
Liberia	22.4	179.9	771.8	159.7	146.2	145.3	0.9
Madagascar	27.4	58.2	156.5	108.6	129.6	128.6	0.9
Malawi	44.4	172.9	244.2	344.2	367.4	366.8	0.5
Mali	43.7	125.1	206.5	220.7	213.2	211.9	1.4
Mozambique	82.1	298.6	338.3	579.6	567.7	566.5	1.2
Namibia	15.5	88.7	43.7	71.0	81.8	81.7	0.1
Nigeria	112.6	408.5	591.5	863.6	1,114.8	1,104.9	9.9
Rwanda	39.0	173.1	246.0	202.7	234.4	232.9	1.5
Senegal	37.4	656.6	121.1	217.4	160.3	158.5	1.7
Somalia	13.9	156.2	252.7	665.4	689.6	551.2	138.4
South Africa	56.8	466.6	354.6	624.1	1,114.2	1,114.0	0.2
South Sudan [3]	—	—	848.9	685.7	759.7	739.2	20.5
Sudan	51.0	894.2	233.5	373.3	375.1	374.1	1.0
Tanzania	44.5	421.9	592.9	574.5	622.3	620.8	1.5
Uganda	76.2	422.8	591.7	913.7	800.4	797.6	2.8
Zambia	35.4	263.6	244.5	405.4	451.3	450.9	0.3
Zimbabwe	20.9	217.4	188.4	316.7	340.2	340.2	–
Latin America & Caribbean [1]	2,301.2	4,347.3	3,942.7	3,093.5	3,122.3	2,950.3	171.9
Bolivia	241.1	91.7	56.0	3.2	13.2	13.2	–
Colombia	1,168.6	794.5	839.6	800.7	812.6	745.0	67.5
El Salvador	34.9	62.1	332.1	85.4	92.1	89.4	2.7
Guatemala	71.8	154.8	138.2	157.2	125.0	115.3	9.7
Haiti	84.5	1,366.5	493.4	293.0	265.6	265.5	0.2
Honduras	41.8	39.7	133.6	70.8	125.4	121.4	4.0
Mexico	43.9	718.1	583.6	444.7	270.7	250.8	19.9
Peru	204.2	203.4	304.7	182.5	223.8	219.5	4.3
Asia [1]	1,163.2	15,170.6	11,462.1	8,358.7	6,917.9	3,765.7	3,152.2
Afghanistan	54.1	10,873.6	8,263.3	4,888.8	3,946.3	1,184.8	2,761.5
Bangladesh	78.3	184.8	228.3	448.3	559.1	542.2	16.9
Cambodia	27.5	72.3	96.0	105.3	128.0	127.5	0.5
India	188.0	115.2	117.7	100.8	160.1	158.4	1.7
Indonesia	242.3	309.4	220.5	263.0	177.8	153.7	24.2
Mongolia	25.8	38.0	12.3	26.8	36.9	25.9	11.0
Nepal	22.6	67.6	264.9	174.2	124.5	123.2	1.2
Pakistan	23.8	2,681.1	1,141.5	684.8	197.0	158.9	38.1
Philippines	82.2	200.3	265.2	428.3	387.4	222.4	165.1
Sri Lanka	10.5	81.5	30.7	61.5	78.0	72.3	5.7
Oceania [1]	164.7	209.7	231.3	289.0	336.2	317.3	18.9
Micronesia, Federated States of	81.0	90.1	112.8	135.8	146.6	138.9	7.8
Central Asia [1]	1,461.9	2,141.1	1,141.1	1,111.0	1,289.7	870.7	419.0
Armenia	104.2	53.4	50.3	41.1	66.7	64.0	2.7
Georgia	112.4	229.2	109.1	124.8	169.8	89.0	80.8
Kazakhstan	53.4	331.2	106.3	49.8	60.8	32.8	28.1
Kyrgyzstan	47.3	128.2	61.4	43.1	45.9	45.8	(Z)
Moldova	48.6	294.0	47.1	66.8	49.3	44.9	4.5
Russia	708.6	505.1	314.9	6.8	10.3	10.3	–
Ukraine	199.5	314.3	269.1	592.8	677.9	393.9	284.0
Eastern Europe [1]	1,045.3	706.8	316.5	643.8	793.3	263.0	530.4
Kosovo	–	35.0	52.2	72.9	57.4	46.6	10.8
Poland	84.8	220.8	11.1	14.9	12.1	(Z)	12.1
Western Europe	24.0	77.5	202.6	201.3	263.6	233.2	30.4

– Represents zero. Z Less than $50,000. [1] Includes other countries, not shown separately, and aid not assigned to specific countries within their parent regions. [2] See footnote 3, Table 1353. [3] South Sudan seceded from Sudan in July 2011.

Source: U.S. Agency for International Development, *U.S. Overseas Loans and Grants: Obligations and Loan Authorizations, July 1, 1945–September 30, 2020*, and earlier reports. See also <foreignassistance.gov/reports>.

Table 1312. U.S. Foreign Economic and Military Aid Programs: 1990 to 2020

[In millions of dollars (16,003 represents $16,003,000,000). For years ending September 30. Total foreign aid programs are the sum of economic and military assistance. Major components in recent years include U.S. Agency for International Development (USAID), U.S. Department of Agriculture (USDA), U.S. Department of State, and U.S. Department of Treasury. Annual figures are in obligations]

Year and world region	Total foreign assistance	Military assistance	Economic assistance, by funding agency					
			Total	USAID	USDA	State Department	Treasury Department	Other U.S. agencies
1990............................	16,003	4,959	11,044	6,964	1,643	590	1,469	377
2000............................	17,112	5,149	11,963	5,907	1,936	2,278	1,110	731
2005............................	35,461	9,071	26,390	14,160	2,208	4,674	1,240	4,108
2007............................	39,726	13,973	25,754	10,371	1,806	5,594	1,476	6,507
2008............................	46,745	16,457	30,288	9,800	2,755	8,967	1,217	7,550
2009............................	46,641	14,801	31,840	11,810	2,614	11,261	1,638	4,518
2010............................	48,357	14,853	33,504	12,053	2,562	11,538	2,245	5,106
2011............................	49,145	18,668	30,476	10,553	1,999	10,577	2,034	5,313
2012............................	50,502	17,861	32,641	11,282	2,028	13,085	2,829	3,418
2013............................	46,065	13,808	32,257	11,779	1,675	11,548	2,672	4,582
2014............................	43,949	11,073	32,876	10,871	1,728	14,232	2,735	3,310
2015............................	49,946	15,097	34,849	13,398	1,679	13,423	2,642	3,708
2016............................	49,473	14,814	34,659	12,577	1,981	14,071	2,286	3,744
2017............................	48,120	12,753	35,368	14,469	2,072	13,627	1,846	3,353
2018............................	47,973	14,662	33,311	13,537	2,206	13,200	1,558	2,810
2019............................	48,176	14,082	34,095	14,525	2,024	13,687	1,552	2,306
2020, total...............	**51,058**	**11,641**	**39,417**	**16,166**	**1,235**	**18,479**	**1,874**	**1,662**
Asia..........................	6,918	3,152	3,766	2,235	15	1,260	51	204
Eurasia......................	1,290	419	871	514	1	273	1	82
Eastern Europe..............	793	530	263	159	(Z)	84	(Z)	20
Latin America and Caribbean...	3,122	172	2,950	1,314	17	1,473	8	137
Middle East and North Africa...	12,152	6,723	5,429	3,814	226	1,308	–	81
Oceania......................	336	19	317	62	(Z)	19	(Z)	235
Sub-Saharan Africa...........	13,810	415	13,395	4,746	893	7,407	178	171
Western Europe...............	264	30	233	37	(Z)	185	–	12
Canada.......................	35	(Z)	35	(Z)	–	–	–	35
World, not specified [1]......	12,338	179	12,158	3,286	83	6,470	1,635	685

– Represents zero. Z indicates a value less than $50,000. [1] Includes U.S. Government loan and grant assistance not assigned to a specific country nor region, including assistance to international financial institutions, international organizations and global programs.

Source: U.S. Agency for International Development, *U.S. Overseas Loans and Grants: Obligations and Loan Authorizations, July 1, 1945–September 30, 2020*, and earlier reports. See also <foreignassistance.gov/reports>.

Table 1313. U.S. International Trade in Goods by Related Parties: 2010 to 2021

[In millions of dollars (1,900,587 represents $1,900,587,000,000). "Related party trade" is trade by U.S. companies with their subsidiaries abroad as well as trade by U.S. subsidiaries of foreign companies with their parent companies]

Country and commodity	NAICS code [2]	2010	2015	2019	2020	2021
IMPORTS FOR CONSUMPTION						
Total imports................	(X)	1,900,587	2,227,237	2,495,687	2,330,836	2,822,516
Related party trade, imports, total [1]........	**(X)**	**922,340**	**1,113,211**	**1,226,777**	**1,115,694**	**1,307,662**
Mexico.......................	(X)	135,989	207,923	245,221	214,054	250,694
Canada.......................	(X)	138,210	148,471	164,497	130,318	169,405
Japan........................	(X)	94,001	101,753	111,312	94,005	105,651
Germany......................	(X)	54,005	83,616	88,313	78,829	92,382
China........................	(X)	107,007	131,390	86,114	79,131	91,087
Ireland......................	(X)	27,980	35,350	52,285	53,104	58,946
Transportation equipment......	336	179,675	276,328	305,619	246,170	266,589
Computer & electronic products..	334	203,829	221,761	187,069	187,085	224,021
Chemicals....................	325	134,018	152,484	191,617	195,074	214,836
Machinery, except electrical...	333	53,722	81,871	99,724	85,818	105,204
Oil & gas....................	211	80,046	53,351	67,645	44,459	74,961
Electrical equipment, appliances & components.........	335	33,496	50,007	57,688	57,500	67,782
Primary metal manufacturing....	331	26,738	29,629	30,075	48,213	45,090
EXPORTS						
Total exports................	(X)	1,122,567	1,286,172	1,395,308	1,204,149	1,478,269
Related party trade, domestic exports, total [1].......	**(X)**	**311,693**	**382,910**	**460,188**	**396,679**	**474,595**
Canada.......................	(X)	85,861	91,863	98,294	81,457	97,979
Mexico.......................	(X)	49,612	78,123	77,715	63,566	79,517
China........................	(X)	13,396	22,196	27,747	32,455	33,597
Japan........................	(X)	16,690	17,702	23,164	20,176	24,934
Netherlands..................	(X)	15,032	17,309	24,391	21,521	23,933
Germany......................	(X)	12,571	15,557	19,367	19,279	21,382
Chemicals....................	325	64,361	79,695	85,522	82,432	102,034
Transportation equipment......	336	55,466	86,973	102,416	76,983	83,232
Oil & gas....................	211	4,316	5,362	44,919	32,173	46,797
Computer & electronic products..	334	42,795	38,524	42,198	40,647	42,569
Machinery, except electrical...	333	32,318	34,338	39,462	35,076	42,227
Petroleum & coal products....	324	23,367	24,271	26,275	19,520	29,432

X Not applicable. [1] Includes other countries and other commodities, not shown separately. [2] Based on the North American Industry Classification System (NAICS); see text, Section 15.

Source: U.S. Census Bureau, "Imports and Exports by Related Parties," <www.census.gov/foreign-trade/Press-Release/related_party/index.html>, accessed September 2022.

Table 1314. U.S. International Trade in Goods and Services: 2000 to 2021

[In millions of dollars (-369,686 represents -$369,686,000,000). Data are presented on a balance of payments basis and will not agree with the following merchandise trade tables in this section. Additionally, all data were revised due to updates to classifications and change in methodology and will not necessarily be comparable with data previously presented. See source for more information. Minus sign (-) indicates deficit]

Category	2000	2010	2015	2018	2019	2020	2021
TRADE BALANCE							
Total	**-369,686**	**-503,087**	**-490,776**	**-578,594**	**-559,676**	**-653,989**	**-845,047**
Goods	-446,783	-648,671	-761,868	-878,749	-857,260	-913,885	-1,090,296
Services	77,096	145,584	271,092	300,155	297,584	259,896	245,248
Maintenance and repair services, n.i.e. [1]	2,107	7,254	11,763	20,682	18,955	6,993	4,544
Transport [2]	-9,064	-12,037	-15,123	-17,334	-21,755	-15,595	-39,478
Travel for all purposes [3]	32,698	45,149	89,938	75,007	66,711	38,322	13,363
Construction [4]	546	373	-253	-235	1,800	1,264	1,634
Insurance services	-7,653	-48,598	-34,537	-24,679	-32,640	-37,396	-36,636
Financial services	12,747	59,297	83,002	94,937	98,186	105,719	122,211
Charges for the use of intellectual property, n.i.e. [1,5]	27,337	63,852	75,973	72,083	80,260	67,850	81,271
Telecommunications, computer, and information services	-1,878	-2,865	2,612	7,544	12,974	16,728	16,655
Other business services [6]	17,911	33,692	46,302	69,105	73,682	82,067	87,825
Personal, cultural, recreational services [7]	7,706	12,219	12,862	3,890	876	-3,505	-4,389
Government goods and services, n.i.e. [1,8]	-5,360	-12,750	-1,444	-844	-1,465	-2,550	-1,753
EXPORTS							
Total	**1,082,963**	**1,872,320**	**2,280,778**	**2,542,462**	**2,546,276**	**2,158,651**	**2,556,638**
Goods	784,940	1,290,279	1,511,381	1,676,913	1,655,098	1,432,218	1,761,364
Services	298,023	582,041	769,397	865,549	891,177	726,433	795,273
Maintenance and repair services, n.i.e. [1]	4,423	13,111	19,847	28,036	27,671	13,196	12,526
Transport [2]	49,462	76,357	84,434	93,107	91,058	57,168	65,777
Travel for all purposes [3]	96,872	130,315	192,602	200,724	198,982	72,481	70,214
Construction [4]	1,993	2,951	2,759	2,842	3,161	2,395	3,129
Insurance services	3,631	14,854	15,763	19,118	18,579	20,277	22,741
Financial services	29,192	86,512	115,688	136,273	142,546	151,033	171,740
Charges for the use of intellectual property, n.i.e. [1,5]	43,476	94,968	111,151	114,819	122,533	115,558	124,613
Telecommunications, computer, and information services	12,250	26,556	41,427	49,245	55,742	56,456	59,797
Other business services [6]	38,217	99,595	141,421	176,540	186,178	195,046	217,426
Personal, cultural, recreational services [7]	9,351	17,612	24,220	22,715	22,192	20,820	23,915
Government goods and services, n.i.e. [1,8]	9,156	19,210	20,087	22,131	22,535	22,003	23,394
IMPORTS							
Total	**1,452,650**	**2,375,407**	**2,771,554**	**3,121,057**	**3,105,952**	**2,812,640**	**3,401,685**
Goods	1,231,722	1,938,950	2,273,249	2,555,662	2,512,358	2,346,103	2,851,660
Services	220,927	436,456	498,305	565,395	593,594	466,537	550,025
Maintenance and repair services, n.i.e. [1]	2,316	5,857	8,084	7,354	8,716	6,203	7,982
Transport [2]	58,526	88,394	99,557	110,441	112,813	72,763	105,255
Travel for all purposes [3]	64,174	85,166	102,664	125,717	132,271	34,159	56,851
Construction [4]	1,447	2,578	3,012	3,077	1,361	1,131	1,495
Insurance services	11,284	63,452	50,300	43,797	51,219	57,673	59,377
Financial services	16,445	27,215	32,686	41,336	44,360	45,314	49,529
Charges for the use of intellectual property, n.i.e. [1,5]	16,139	31,116	35,178	42,736	42,273	47,708	43,342
Telecommunications, computer, and information services	14,128	29,421	38,815	41,701	42,768	39,728	43,142
Other business services [6]	20,306	65,903	95,119	107,435	112,496	112,979	129,601
Personal, cultural, recreational services [7]	1,645	5,393	11,358	18,825	21,316	24,325	28,304
Government goods and services, n.i.e. [1,8]	14,516	31,960	21,531	22,975	24,000	24,553	25,147

[1] N.i.e. means not included elsewhere. [2] Covers transactions associated with moving people and freight, and related supporting and auxiliary services. [3] All travel purposes include 1) business travel, including expenditures by border, seasonal, and other short-term workers and 2) personal travel, including health-related and education-related travel. Excludes air passenger services for travel between countries, which are included in transport. [4] Construction covers the services provided to create, renovate, repair, or extend buildings, land improvements, and civil engineering constructions, such as roads and bridges. Construction exports exclude inputs purchased by foreign contractors for projects in the U.S. Construction imports include inputs purchased abroad by U.S. contractors. See source for more detail. [5] Includes charges for the use of proprietary rights, such as patents, trademarks, and copyrights, and charges for licenses to use, reproduce and/or distribute intellectual property. [6] Consists of research and development services, professional and management consulting services (including advertising and market research), and technical, trade-related, and other business services. [7] Covers three subcategories: 1) Audiovisual services, which covers production of audiovisual content, end-user rights to use audiovisual content, and outright sales and purchases of audiovisual originals; 2) artistic-related services, which includes the services provided by performing artists, authors, composers, and other visual artists; set, costume, and lighting design; presentation and promotion of performing arts and other live entertainment events; and fees to artists and athletes for performances, sporting events, and similar events; and 3) other personal, cultural, and recreational services, which includes services such as education services delivered online, telemedicine, and services associated with museum and other cultural, sporting gambling, and recreational activities, except those acquired by customers traveling outside their country of residence. See source for more information. [8] Includes goods and services supplied by and to embassies, military bases, and international organizations; goods and services acquired by diplomatic and military personnel in the host economy; and services supplied by and to governments not included in other categories of services.

Source: U.S. Bureau of Economic Analysis, "International Economic Accounts: Trade in Goods and Services," <www.bea.gov/data/economic-accounts/international#trade>, accessed June 2022.

Table 1315. U.S. Freight Gateways—Value of Shipments: 2021

[In billions of dollars (4,585.4 represents $4,585,400,000,000), except as indicated. For the top 40 gateways ranked by value of total shipments]

Port	Rank	Total trade	Exports	Imports	Exports as a percent of total
Total U.S. merchandise trade [1]	(X)	4,585.4	1,754.3	2,831.1	38.3
Top 40 gateways	(X)	3,673.1	1,343.0	2,330.1	36.6
As a percent of total	(X)	80.1	76.6	82.3	(X)
Chicago, IL	1	304.8	64.6	240.2	21.2
Los Angeles, CA	2	296.1	26.9	269.2	9.1
Laredo, TX	3	248.3	99.0	149.3	39.9
JFK International Airport, NY	4	236.4	105.1	131.3	44.5
Newark, NJ	5	228.2	19.4	208.8	8.5
Houston, TX	6	170.9	95.1	75.8	55.6
Detroit, MI	7	144.3	76.7	67.6	53.2
New Orleans, LA	8	141.0	80.3	60.7	56.9
Los Angeles International Airport, CA	9	139.2	56.8	82.4	40.8
Savannah, GA	10	127.6	30.2	97.4	23.6
Port Huron, MI	11	109.4	49.2	60.3	44.9
Long Beach, CA	12	103.7	26.8	76.9	25.9
Norfolk-Newport News, VA	13	90.8	30.6	60.2	33.7
Charleston, SC	14	90.0	29.8	60.1	33.2
Buffalo-Niagara Falls, NY	15	83.5	42.6	40.9	51.0
Cleveland, OH	16	82.0	43.6	38.3	53.3
Anchorage, AK	17	72.1	25.1	47.0	34.8
San Francisco International Airport, CA	18	70.5	38.4	32.1	54.4
Miami International Airport, FL	19	69.3	39.7	29.6	57.3
Ysleta, TX	20	64.5	21.1	43.4	32.7
Atlanta, GA	21	63.7	21.6	42.1	34.0
Dallas-Fort Worth, TX	22	61.4	25.9	35.5	42.2
Baltimore, MD	23	61.4	17.0	44.3	27.8
Corpus Christi, TX	24	56.7	51.5	5.2	90.7
Otay Mesa, CA	25	55.4	18.7	36.7	33.8
Oakland, CA	26	50.0	20.8	29.3	41.5
New York, NY	27	44.9	31.1	13.9	69.2
Tacoma, WA	28	44.4	7.9	36.5	17.7
Hidalgo, TX	29	41.7	16.4	25.2	39.4
Philadelphia, PA	30	34.1	5.4	28.7	15.9
Eagle Pass, TX	31	33.8	10.5	23.3	31.0
Seattle, WA	32	31.5	8.9	22.6	28.3
Pembina, ND	33	30.1	16.0	14.0	53.3
Blaine, WA	34	30.0	14.3	15.8	47.4
Champlain-Rouses Point, NY	35	29.5	10.1	19.4	34.3
Miami, FL	36	28.6	10.2	18.4	35.7
Santa Teresa, NM	37	27.4	11.6	15.8	42.3
Seattle-Tacoma International Airport, WA	38	26.5	18.6	7.9	70.1
Nogales, AZ	39	25.1	9.9	15.2	39.4
El Paso, TX	40	24.5	15.8	8.7	64.4

X Not applicable. [1] Includes ports not shown separately, as well as low value and mail shipments.

Source: U.S. Census Bureau, Foreign Trade Division, "USA Trade Online," <usatrade.census.gov/>, accessed June 2022.

Table 1316. U.S. Agricultural Exports by State: 2000 to 2020

[In millions of dollars (51,258 represents $51,258,000,000). Calendar year. Export estimates based on U.S. farm cash receipts. Export values are calibrated such that the sum of state export estimates for a commodity equals the total U.S. export value for the commodity]

State	2000	2010	2015	2019	2020	State	2000	2010	2015	2019	2020
U.S.	51,258	115,806	133,016	135,950	144,749	MO	1,348	3,485	3,611	3,759	4,503
						MT	503	1,077	1,182	1,391	1,514
AL	576	1,135	1,217	1,359	1,376	NE	2,299	5,335	6,479	6,294	7,141
AK	6	11	15	18	17	NV	66	111	135	144	141
AZ	486	1,070	1,283	1,737	1,315	NH	33	65	86	75	71
AR	1,308	3,190	3,135	3,106	3,562	NJ	247	399	546	597	628
CA	6,855	15,355	22,844	23,463	22,332	NM	322	682	750	784	728
CO	893	1,511	1,650	1,865	1,766	NY	501	1,225	1,453	1,502	1,576
CT	132	214	297	280	259	NC	1,844	3,391	3,573	3,377	3,670
DE	131	241	260	262	280	ND	1,228	3,691	3,817	4,088	4,316
FL	1,883	2,963	3,494	3,414	3,238	OH	1,461	3,407	3,708	3,509	4,096
GA	1,303	2,588	2,846	2,781	3,014	OK	817	1,541	1,511	1,829	1,867
HI	151	308	367	321	295	OR	800	1,353	1,870	2,106	2,075
ID	718	1,488	1,860	2,255	2,316	PA	700	1,615	2,038	2,025	2,118
IL	3,109	7,464	8,034	7,838	8,810	RI	13	32	33	32	28
IN	1,710	4,299	4,706	4,472	5,224	SC	398	809	808	800	812
IA	3,471	9,368	9,987	10,009	11,425	SD	1,209	2,964	3,702	3,286	3,748
KS	1,953	4,667	4,163	4,938	5,659	TN	552	1,241	1,522	1,510	1,796
KY	1,276	1,515	2,100	2,119	2,363	TX	2,697	6,325	5,739	6,300	5,814
LA	614	1,510	1,566	1,484	1,723	UT	163	330	432	455	475
ME	144	237	248	262	274	VT	49	140	188	193	176
MD	338	565	670	682	727	VA	541	875	1,052	1,087	1,172
MA	106	198	210	212	221	WA	1,313	2,801	3,477	3,601	3,863
MI	910	2,355	2,855	2,700	3,054	WV	60	115	144	158	159
MN	2,206	6,113	6,339	6,367	7,216	WI	922	2,412	2,869	2,841	3,232
MS	750	1,784	1,840	1,932	2,228	WY	147	235	304	330	339

Source: U.S. Department of Agriculture, Economic Research Service, "State Agricultural Trade Data," <www.ers.usda.gov/data-products/state-agricultural-trade-data/>, accessed November 2021.

Table 1317. U.S. Exports and General Imports of Merchandise by Customs District: 2010 to 2021

[In billions of dollars (1,278.5 represents $1,278,500,000,000). Exports are f.a.s. (free alongside ship) value basis; imports are on customs-value basis. General imports are a combination of entries for immediate consumption, entries into customs bonded warehouses, and entries into U.S. Foreign Trade Zones. These data may differ from those in Table 1313, Table 1320, and Table 1321. For methodology, see Foreign Trade Statistics in Appendix III]

Customs district	Exports					General imports				
	2010	2015	2019	2020	2021	2010	2015	2019	2020	2021
Total [1]	1,278.5	1,503.3	1,645.9	1,428.5	1,754.3	1,913.9	2,248.8	2,491.7	2,330.8	2,831.1
Anchorage, AK	14.5	18.7	20.9	19.6	25.8	16.2	16.9	17.0	15.2	20.2
Baltimore, MD	14.7	15.6	15.4	12.9	17.4	28.8	36.8	44.4	37.5	45.4
Boston, MA	8.2	7.4	8.7	6.1	8.7	19.2	25.2	25.6	18.9	22.1
Buffalo, NY	40.6	47.3	41.2	36.8	42.6	39.2	41.6	39.4	34.2	41.8
Charleston, SC	19.5	31.7	40.3	30.6	30.4	29.4	47.2	49.8	47.1	59.5
Chicago, IL	35.8	46.6	50.7	53.7	65.6	125.6	155.2	204.6	214.9	277.8
Cleveland, OH	25.4	34.1	51.4	48.4	52.0	69.2	95.8	99.8	100.9	116.1
Columbia-Snake, OR	12.3	12.1	13.8	13.2	19.3	12.2	12.3	13.5	11.9	13.7
Dallas-Fort Worth, TX	18.1	21.9	25.4	23.1	26.8	38.4	52.0	54.1	45.4	57.1
Detroit, MI	113.2	120.5	129.8	110.8	128.0	106.0	124.7	133.3	116.3	138.8
Duluth, MN	2.6	5.0	4.3	3.6	4.8	6.8	8.9	9.8	8.1	11.5
El Paso, TX	29.3	41.9	46.1	39.1	48.9	44.1	56.9	68.8	62.8	75.2
Great Falls, MT	17.4	14.3	16.1	16.5	19.0	26.9	24.2	29.0	24.3	34.6
Honolulu, HI	7.4	13.9	3.5	1.4	2.2	4.6	4.1	4.4	6.1	10.8
Houston-Galveston, TX	94.5	109.2	150.1	126.9	177.2	116.9	86.2	85.3	67.3	96.1
Laredo, TX	81.4	121.7	127.8	109.7	141.2	104.2	163.5	196.3	180.8	213.2
Los Angeles, CA	105.1	114.1	121.5	107.5	113.6	242.7	279.5	305.9	297.0	365.0
Miami, FL	58.9	58.6	60.7	51.0	64.8	36.6	48.2	49.2	45.7	55.4
Milwaukee, WI	0.1	0.3	0.3	0.2	0.3	0.9	1.0	1.0	0.9	1.8
Minneapolis, MN	2.6	2.6	2.0	1.2	1.7	13.6	12.6	14.7	12.7	15.8
Mobile, AL	8.7	10.6	9.4	7.5	10.7	20.8	22.8	24.8	20.3	27.7
New Orleans, LA	69.1	84.1	105.6	95.9	117.9	125.3	115.2	113.6	98.3	110.3
New York, NY	136.3	143.8	135.8	124.7	155.9	190.6	226.5	245.5	269.6	308.6
Nogales, AZ	8.9	14.9	14.2	11.1	13.3	17.4	21.7	22.4	21.5	22.7
Norfolk, VA	21.1	28.8	24.8	24.5	30.7	23.9	34.4	36.0	32.4	42.3
Ogdensburg, NY	16.2	17.2	18.6	16.7	19.6	27.8	29.3	28.4	28.0	36.5
Pembina, ND	21.3	25.7	27.8	23.5	28.8	14.7	17.3	20.0	17.5	22.8
Philadelphia, PA	14.3	15.8	19.7	14.6	18.1	56.9	56.0	61.1	54.0	60.2
Port Arthur, TX	6.5	12.2	30.5	19.7	36.6	26.4	14.3	10.6	6.7	11.9
Portland, ME	4.4	4.3	5.1	3.9	5.7	9.8	14.0	13.7	11.7	16.0
Providence, RI	0.3	0.2	0.4	0.2	0.3	5.8	8.6	10.3	7.3	7.3
San Diego, CA	16.2	22.7	25.2	22.2	28.3	32.4	47.4	49.8	45.8	55.5
San Francisco, CA	47.1	47.8	61.2	61.9	65.7	60.6	70.0	79.9	71.0	79.0
San Juan, PR	19.7	17.3	16.3	12.5	13.9	19.4	20.1	24.7	20.9	22.3
Savannah, GA	41.0	47.6	57.4	50.6	60.9	68.0	101.1	122.9	119.8	140.0
Seattle, WA	58.5	87.9	68.8	48.3	58.5	52.6	66.9	74.3	62.9	82.0
St. Albans, VT	3.3	2.1	2.4	1.8	2.0	6.9	9.3	8.3	7.6	7.9
St. Louis, MO	1.0	1.6	0.7	0.3	0.5	11.5	17.3	18.4	15.4	17.7
Tampa, FL	14.4	14.7	11.4	8.4	10.1	16.4	25.6	32.1	29.9	33.9
Virgin Islands, U.S.	1.9	0.1	1.0	0.7	2.1	10.5	0.1	0.9	0.8	1.4
Washington, DC	6.0	5.1	7.6	4.5	7.3	8.2	7.1	10.1	8.4	10.2
Wilmington, NC	5.3	5.1	7.5	4.6	5.6	12.8	13.6	19.3	15.6	23.0

[1] Totals include the following special districts, not shown separately: vessels under their own power or afloat, low valued imports and exports, and mail shipments. Totals may also include data for two or more Customs Districts that have been combined and published under an arbitrary designation, as a solution to disclosure situations.

Source: U.S. Census Bureau, U.S. Foreign Trade Division, "USA Trade Online," <usatrade.census.gov/>, accessed June 2022.

Table 1318. U.S. Exports of Goods by State of Origin: 2010 to 2021

[In millions of dollars (1,278,495 represents $1,278,495,000,000), except as indicated. Data are on a Census Basis. Exports are on a f.a.s. (free alongside ship) value basis and are based on origin of movement]

State [1]	2010	2012	2013	2014	2015	2016	2017	2018	2019	2020	2021 Total	2021 Rank
Total [1]	1,278,495	1,545,821	1,578,517	1,621,874	1,503,328	1,451,460	1,547,195	1,665,787	1,645,940	1,428,518	1,754,300	(X)
United States	1,208,081	1,478,314	1,509,865	1,551,164	1,436,224	1,385,513	1,481,701	1,595,168	1,572,598	1,365,350	1,679,539	(X)
Alabama	15,495	19,577	19,301	19,450	19,322	20,471	21,798	21,416	20,796	17,392	20,932	23
Alaska	4,155	4,543	4,528	5,111	4,620	4,350	4,941	4,834	4,989	4,611	5,989	38
Arizona	15,721	18,405	19,478	21,247	22,654	22,004	20,104	22,516	24,966	20,201	24,168	21
Arkansas	5,219	7,615	7,161	6,866	5,871	5,722	6,234	6,449	6,231	5,193	5,604	39
California	143,208	161,757	168,192	173,869	165,360	163,261	171,920	178,175	173,755	155,925	174,927	2
Colorado	6,726	8,170	8,545	8,364	7,950	7,569	8,054	8,332	8,097	8,174	9,073	33
Connecticut	16,029	15,871	16,427	15,963	15,242	14,394	14,792	17,403	16,231	13,827	14,542	29
Delaware	4,945	5,114	5,327	5,267	5,408	4,517	4,565	4,704	4,406	3,912	4,745	42
District of Columbia	1,483	2,014	2,708	940	1,088	1,331	1,483	2,724	3,689	2,770	1,535	49
Florida	55,399	66,223	60,482	58,439	53,903	52,036	54,897	57,252	55,989	45,746	55,749	7
Georgia	28,899	36,039	37,578	39,413	38,596	35,673	37,222	40,619	41,260	38,585	42,416	12
Hawaii	684	732	599	1,447	1,896	795	952	659	460	320	340	51
Idaho	5,157	6,120	5,789	5,138	4,302	4,877	3,863	4,028	3,433	3,407	3,752	43
Illinois	50,061	68,158	66,213	68,394	63,369	59,862	65,288	65,468	59,767	53,252	66,027	5
Indiana	28,764	34,399	34,216	35,589	33,819	34,653	37,747	39,320	39,422	35,496	41,156	13
Iowa	10,880	14,622	13,903	15,112	13,238	12,330	13,422	14,370	13,225	12,640	15,756	27
Kansas	9,900	11,684	12,459	12,022	10,689	10,155	11,244	11,582	11,681	10,405	12,541	31
Kentucky	19,346	22,132	25,412	27,757	27,637	29,192	30,919	31,808	33,007	24,602	29,563	19
Louisiana	41,371	62,869	63,247	64,770	48,679	48,367	56,865	67,233	63,878	58,590	76,364	4
Maine	3,162	3,048	2,687	2,811	2,762	2,863	2,712	2,836	2,724	2,339	3,105	44
Maryland	10,167	11,745	11,747	12,228	10,052	9,656	9,317	12,105	13,051	12,676	16,418	26
Massachusetts	26,305	25,614	26,812	27,384	25,289	25,893	27,561	27,160	26,132	24,900	32,417	16
Michigan	44,851	57,051	59,400	57,573	53,945	54,752	59,921	58,007	55,988	44,710	55,966	6
Minnesota	18,904	20,827	20,760	21,398	20,013	19,201	20,692	22,681	22,188	20,175	23,463	22
Mississippi	8,224	11,794	12,415	11,485	10,849	10,505	10,985	11,586	11,833	10,289	12,888	30
Missouri	12,925	13,903	12,958	14,190	13,647	13,935	14,289	14,512	13,490	12,868	15,487	28
Montana	1,393	1,576	1,506	1,545	1,404	1,360	1,616	1,666	1,697	1,468	1,975	47
Nebraska	5,821	7,455	7,393	7,890	6,644	6,381	7,210	7,947	7,440	6,998	7,966	34
Nevada	5,913	10,261	8,701	7,692	8,667	9,766	12,162	11,138	9,101	10,359	10,546	32
New Hampshire	4,368	3,488	3,511	4,233	4,061	4,143	5,148	5,306	5,827	5,456	6,366	35
New Jersey	32,131	37,286	36,612	36,587	32,063	31,164	34,258	35,305	35,699	37,999	49,398	10
New Mexico	1,543	2,958	2,726	3,802	3,782	3,616	3,696	3,899	4,679	3,688	5,461	40
New York	69,685	81,338	86,407	88,834	83,125	76,691	78,190	84,734	75,607	65,611	90,142	3
North Carolina	24,918	28,839	29,347	31,420	30,202	30,183	32,620	32,765	34,333	28,465	33,462	15
North Dakota	2,532	4,310	4,402	5,513	4,027	5,294	6,148	7,800	6,971	5,171	5,196	41
Ohio	41,505	48,819	51,048	52,641	51,262	49,330	50,071	54,393	53,225	45,183	50,702	9
Oklahoma	5,354	6,579	6,920	6,308	5,251	5,046	5,363	6,112	6,151	5,396	6,228	37
Oregon	17,684	18,388	18,634	20,889	20,557	21,772	21,894	22,332	25,880	26,588	29,923	17
Pennsylvania	34,943	38,852	41,181	40,411	39,439	36,453	38,640	41,150	42,731	37,408	44,707	11
Rhode Island	1,949	2,366	2,164	2,388	2,133	2,278	2,391	2,405	2,675	2,358	2,950	45
South Carolina	20,336	25,115	26,341	29,773	31,021	31,324	32,202	34,627	41,461	30,291	29,656	18
South Dakota	1,259	1,557	1,582	1,578	1,421	1,218	1,356	1,430	1,356	1,389	1,858	48
Tennessee	25,948	31,143	32,474	33,251	32,617	31,476	33,233	32,717	31,116	28,167	34,695	14
Texas	206,992	264,665	277,716	285,559	248,780	231,527	265,068	315,843	328,585	276,590	376,331	1
Utah	13,808	19,260	16,111	12,224	13,308	12,078	11,583	14,390	17,367	17,688	18,106	25
Vermont	4,278	4,139	4,027	3,670	3,176	2,993	2,776	2,920	2,842	2,358	2,585	46
Virginia	17,169	18,277	17,896	19,391	17,801	16,311	16,508	18,336	17,826	16,373	20,035	24
Washington	53,345	75,654	81,630	90,558	86,375	79,562	76,351	77,868	60,336	41,153	53,749	8
West Virginia	6,443	11,407	8,732	7,597	5,833	5,045	7,110	8,233	5,949	4,562	6,341	36
Wisconsin	19,800	23,119	23,110	23,426	22,442	21,036	22,305	22,716	21,668	20,487	24,811	20
Wyoming	983	1,439	1,351	1,757	1,175	1,099	1,196	1,357	1,367	1,164	1,428	50

X Not applicable. [1] Includes other areas, not shown separately, and exports with an unknown state or area of origin.

Source: U.S. Census Bureau, Foreign Trade Division, "USA Trade Online," <usatrade.census.gov/>, accessed June 2022. See also <www.census.gov/foreign-trade/data/index.html>.

Table 1319. Value of State Exports to Top Trading Countries by State: 2021

[In millions of dollars (1,754,300 represents $1,754,300,000,000). Data are on a f.a.s. (free alongside ship) value basis. Exports are based on origin of movement]

	Total	Canada	Mexico	China	Japan	Korea, South	Germany	Nether-lands	Brazil
United States [1]	**1,754,300**	**307,758**	**276,491**	**151,442**	**74,565**	**65,942**	**65,333**	**53,080**	**46,935**
Alabama	20,932	3,485	2,472	3,153	729	923	3,707	133	334
Alaska	5,989	744	26	1,381	915	786	230	209	17
Arizona	24,168	2,313	8,165	1,492	636	455	555	805	377
Arkansas	5,604	1,269	983	263	343	112	129	133	79
California	174,927	18,044	27,211	16,636	11,797	11,615	7,598	6,104	1,900
Colorado	9,073	1,591	1,420	921	448	606	289	246	134
Connecticut	14,542	1,733	979	1,257	401	455	2,333	974	321
Delaware	4,745	593	262	556	246	484	434	97	84
District of Columbia	1,535	8	7	1	3	3	13	2	22
Florida	55,749	4,175	3,318	1,473	874	773	1,454	1,143	4,705
Georgia	42,416	6,305	3,700	4,189	1,214	859	2,451	1,239	741
Hawaii	340	20	2	11	58	23	3	1	(Z)
Idaho	3,752	1,461	234	153	208	69	22	104	54
Illinois	66,027	18,577	8,926	3,500	1,723	1,340	3,759	1,545	2,480
Indiana	41,156	13,401	5,288	3,237	2,082	671	2,415	1,263	719
Iowa	15,756	4,128	2,952	925	1,245	363	681	400	573
Kansas	12,541	2,046	2,759	1,124	1,072	578	479	131	274
Kentucky	29,563	8,225	2,781	2,376	820	423	786	1,240	1,667
Louisiana	76,364	3,528	7,116	12,399	4,437	5,031	1,152	2,214	3,643
Maine	3,105	1,590	56	103	55	60	78	84	20
Maryland	16,418	1,964	365	1,271	725	380	680	1,182	299
Massachusetts	32,417	3,669	2,794	3,516	1,627	1,584	1,939	1,674	392
Michigan	55,966	22,172	10,617	2,748	1,385	1,278	1,713	486	2,424
Minnesota	23,463	6,607	2,449	2,406	1,308	583	820	538	239
Mississippi	12,888	2,269	1,685	715	306	147	251	503	453
Missouri	15,487	5,224	3,308	700	471	403	677	223	390
Montana	1,975	911	88	109	102	223	23	27	6
Nebraska	7,966	1,611	1,797	696	782	632	113	143	112
Nevada	10,546	1,522	1,641	1,243	152	318	369	267	61
New Hampshire	6,366	909	400	396	269	76	915	201	50
New Jersey	49,398	9,947	3,236	4,142	3,251	1,667	2,100	1,569	701
New Mexico	5,461	158	2,474	1,467	49	115	62	21	36
New York	90,142	21,727	2,940	3,613	2,027	1,649	3,588	1,553	547
North Carolina	33,462	6,584	4,567	4,075	939	611	873	946	455
North Dakota	5,196	3,999	457	65	39	15	82	13	48
Ohio	50,702	18,375	6,290	3,748	1,666	1,019	1,248	1,384	1,867
Oklahoma	6,228	1,589	742	221	303	118	650	290	76
Oregon	29,923	3,263	562	10,626	1,567	1,643	394	399	381
Pennsylvania	44,707	12,127	4,845	3,254	1,643	1,036	1,872	1,526	794
Rhode Island	2,950	460	165	148	121	53	158	25	18
South Carolina	29,656	3,844	2,117	4,602	1,025	1,396	4,588	263	624
South Dakota	1,858	726	425	130	120	60	41	24	14
Tennessee	34,695	7,431	4,057	2,948	2,007	802	1,349	1,668	684
Texas	376,331	29,033	123,104	21,636	13,532	18,810	5,888	13,071	14,453
Utah	18,106	1,524	1,143	963	713	433	346	561	117
Vermont	2,585	828	48	285	29	187	111	79	12
Virginia	20,035	3,228	913	3,180	528	389	766	655	669
Washington	53,749	7,742	2,850	12,063	5,218	2,872	1,266	1,201	712
West Virginia	6,341	1,449	193	1,234	228	272	168	307	318
Wisconsin	24,811	7,538	3,103	1,798	687	570	875	474	792
Wyoming	1,428	316	49	48	52	83	7	3	108

Z Less than $500,000. [1] Total includes data for Puerto Rico and the Virgin Islands, not shown separately. Total also includes exports to unknown partners and to countries not shown separately.

Source: U.S. Census Bureau, Foreign Trade Division, "USA Trade Online," <usatrade.census.gov/>, accessed September 2022. See also <www.census.gov/foreign-trade/statistics/state/index.html>.

Table 1320. U.S. Exports, Imports, and Trade Balance by Country: 2005 to 2021

[In millions of dollars (901,082 represents $901,082,000,000). Data reflect trade between foreign countries and the U.S., Puerto Rico, the U.S. Virgin Islands, and U.S. Foreign Trade Zones. Data are shown on a Census Basis. Country totals include exports of special category commodities, if any. Minus sign (-) denotes an excess of imports over exports]

Country	Exports, domestic and foreign					General imports					Merchandise trade balance				
	2005	2010	2015	2020	2021	2005	2010	2015	2020	2021	2005	2010	2015	2020	2021
Total [1]	901,082	1,278,495	1,503,328	1,428,518	1,754,300	1,673,455	1,913,857	2,248,811	2,330,836	2,831,111	-772,373	-635,362	-745,483	-902,318	-1,076,810
Afghanistan	262	2,151	479	671	236	67	85	24	18	22	195	2,066	455	653	214
Algeria	1,106	1,194	1,876	735	784	10,446	14,518	3,372	488	1,888	-9,340	-13,324	-1,496	247	-1,104
Angola	929	1,293	1,166	470	445	8,484	11,940	2,806	472	1,044	-7,555	-10,646	-1,640	-2	-598
Antigua and Barbuda	190	158	678	291	570	4	5	5	5	29	186	153	671	286	541
Argentina	4,122	7,392	9,362	5,909	7,762	4,584	3,803	3,951	4,195	5,123	-462	3,589	5,411	1,714	2,639
Armenia	65	113	50	28	45	46	75	62	68	88	19	38	-12	-40	-43
Aruba	559	540	1,168	309	543	2,920	19	55	34	28	-2,361	521	1,113	274	515
Australia	15,589	21,805	25,032	23,365	26,454	7,342	8,583	10,886	14,416	12,466	8,246	13,222	14,147	8,949	13,987
Austria	2,544	2,429	4,024	3,430	3,935	6,103	6,835	11,312	11,618	15,145	-3,558	-4,407	-7,288	-8,188	-11,210
Azerbaijan	132	253	478	162	132	45	1,989	507	38	103	87	-1,736	-29	124	29
Bahamas, The	1,787	3,178	2,387	2,805	2,899	700	815	453	276	449	1,087	2,363	1,934	2,529	2,450
Bahrain	351	1,235	1,271	885	934	432	420	902	634	1,231	-81	815	368	251	-297
Bangladesh	320	576	943	1,852	2,351	2,693	4,294	5,990	6,062	8,299	-2,373	-3,718	-5,048	-4,210	-5,949
Barbados	395	397	595	505	754	32	43	68	48	44	363	355	527	457	710
Belarus	35	133	59	122	218	345	175	158	333	479	-310	-41	-99	-211	-261
Belgium	18,691	25,458	34,174	27,581	33,721	13,023	15,552	19,487	20,786	20,996	5,668	9,906	14,687	6,794	12,725
Belize	218	289	285	395	412	98	120	75	51	67	119	169	210	344	345
Benin	72	463	631	197	292	1	(Z)	5	6	8	72	462	626	191	284
Bermuda	490	637	601	459	551	87	22	109	24	10	403	614	492	435	541
Bolivia	219	508	932	447	552	293	680	1,006	380	495	-74	-172	-75	67	57
Botswana	67	48	39	49	53	178	170	212	175	252	-111	-121	-173	-126	-199
Brazil	15,372	35,418	31,641	34,580	46,935	24,436	23,958	27,474	23,364	31,264	-9,064	11,460	4,167	11,216	15,671
British Virgin Islands	125	146	260	284	273	34	19	16	8	5	91	127	243	275	268
Brunei	50	124	133	146	100	563	12	19	83	17	-513	112	114	64	83
Bulgaria	268	171	289	375	339	454	260	598	847	1,154	-186	-89	-308	-472	-815
Cambodia	70	154	391	344	416	1,767	2,301	3,026	6,551	8,742	-1,697	-2,147	-2,635	-6,207	-8,326
Cameroon	117	132	225	187	149	158	297	132	470	249	-41	-165	93	-283	-100
Canada	211,899	249,256	280,855	256,212	307,758	290,384	277,637	296,305	270,025	357,788	-78,486	-28,380	-15,450	-13,813	-50,029
Chad	54	90	57	46	42	1,498	2,044	1,303	3	4	-1,444	-1,954	-1,247	43	38
Chile	5,134	10,907	15,449	12,463	17,338	6,664	7,017	8,777	10,102	15,063	-1,531	3,889	6,672	2,361	2,275
China	41,192	91,911	115,873	124,544	151,442	243,470	364,953	483,202	432,683	504,935	-202,278	-273,042	-367,329	-308,140	-353,493
Colombia	5,462	12,068	16,302	11,930	16,687	8,849	15,659	14,079	10,780	13,178	-3,387	-3,592	2,223	1,150	3,509
Congo, Rep. of	104	254	249	99	114	1,623	3,316	304	132	52	-1,519	-3,062	-55	-33	62
Congo, Dem. Rep. of	65	93	136	152	213	264	528	154	30	269	-199	-434	-18	122	-56
Costa Rica	3,599	5,178	6,045	5,673	7,345	3,415	8,697	4,489	5,349	6,536	183	-3,519	1,556	324	809
Cote d'Ivoire	124	163	266	219	359	1,198	1,177	1,028	881	1,226	-1,074	-1,014	-761	-662	-867
Croatia	159	312	332	316	751	364	336	577	601	818	-206	-24	-245	-285	-67
Cuba	369	363	186	177	327	(X)	(Z)	(Z)	15	3	369	363	186	162	324
Curacao [2]	(X)	(X)	521	350	342	(X)	(X)	335	28	41	(X)	(X)	186	322	301
Cyprus	84	134	102	103	247	31	11	32	59	65	54	123	70	44	181
Czechia	1,054	1,411	1,977	2,973	3,661	2,193	2,450	4,489	5,533	6,366	-1,139	-1,039	-2,512	-2,560	-2,705
Denmark	1,918	2,132	2,203	2,942	3,544	5,144	6,012	7,760	11,626	12,108	-3,226	-3,879	-5,557	-8,684	-8,565
Djibouti	48	123	145	184	187	1	3	35	41	32	46	120	109	144	154
Dominican Republic	4,719	6,579	7,115	7,500	10,673	4,604	3,672	4,668	5,166	6,331	115	2,908	2,447	2,334	4,342
Ecuador	1,964	5,409	5,818	4,134	5,009	5,759	7,451	7,467	5,939	8,159	-3,795	-2,042	-1,649	-1,805	-3,150
Egypt	3,159	6,833	4,759	4,705	5,849	2,091	2,238	1,406	2,180	3,304	1,068	4,594	3,353	2,526	2,545
El Salvador	1,854	2,434	3,249	2,584	4,116	1,989	2,206	2,532	1,922	2,516	-134	228	717	663	1,599
Equatorial Guinea	281	272	162	94	51	1,561	2,214	163	135	265	-1,280	-1,942	-1	-41	-214
Ethiopia	456	773	1,555	911	575	62	128	310	524	601	394	645	1,245	386	-26
Fiji	28	44	57	40	180	169	179	203	224	238	-141	-135	-146	-184	-57
Finland	2,254	2,180	1,560	1,595	1,727	4,342	3,884	4,510	4,926	6,774	-2,088	-1,704	-2,951	-3,331	-5,047
France	22,259	26,970	30,026	27,273	29,893	33,842	38,355	47,809	42,935	50,104	-11,583	-11,386	-17,782	-15,662	-20,210
French Polynesia	112	122	120	126	129	60	53	43	20	82	52	69	77	106	47
Gabon	99	243	204	92	129	2,816	2,212	337	76	115	-2,716	-1,969	-133	16	14

See footnotes at end of table.

Table 1320. U.S. Exports, Imports, and Trade Balance by Country: 2005 to 2021—Continued.

See headnote on page 831.

Country	Exports, domestic and foreign 2005	2010	2015	2020	2021	General imports 2005	2010	2015	2020	2021	Merchandise trade balance 2005	2010	2015	2020	2021
Georgia	214	301	340	436	657	194	198	181	149	190	20	103	159	287	466
Germany	34,184	48,155	49,979	58,002	65,333	84,751	82,450	124,888	114,905	135,216	-50,567	-34,295	-74,909	-56,903	-69,883
Ghana	337	989	950	829	957	158	273	309	717	1,720	179	716	641	112	-762
Gibraltar	163	1,494	1,979	828	775	5	1	2	22	4	159	1,493	1,978	806	771
Greece	1,192	1,106	726	1,403	1,556	884	798	1,357	1,301	1,681	309	309	-631	102	-125
Grenada	82	71	90	99	125	6	8	9	13	15	77	64	81	86	109
Guatemala	2,835	4,477	5,821	5,844	8,070	3,137	3,523	4,121	3,843	4,667	-302	954	1,700	2,001	3,403
Guyana	177	291	368	655	1,012	120	299	431	748	2,243	57	-8	-63	-94	-1,231
Haiti	710	1,209	1,141	1,398	1,322	447	551	950	827	1,107	262	658	190	571	216
Honduras	3,254	4,606	5,216	4,192	6,393	3,749	3,933	4,760	3,841	5,214	-495	673	457	350	1,179
Hong Kong	16,351	26,570	37,183	23,833	29,894	8,892	4,296	6,802	7,873	4,116	7,459	22,274	30,381	15,959	25,778
Hungary	1,023	1,290	1,715	2,111	2,908	2,561	2,491	5,719	5,278	7,086	-1,538	-1,201	-4,004	-3,166	-4,178
Iceland	512	325	415	292	629	269	201	317	424	580	243	124	99	-132	49
India	7,919	19,249	21,453	27,078	40,052	18,804	29,533	44,783	51,200	73,173	-10,886	-10,284	-23,330	-24,122	-33,120
Indonesia	3,054	6,948	7,118	7,379	9,379	12,014	16,478	19,605	20,201	27,053	-8,960	-9,530	-12,487	-12,822	-17,674
Iran	96	211	282	36	39	174	95	11	4	1	-79	117	271	32	38
Iraq	1,374	1,643	1,973	770	803	9,054	12,143	4,353	3,100	3,790	-7,680	-10,500	-2,380	-2,330	-2,988
Ireland	8,447	7,276	8,931	10,668	13,785	28,733	33,848	39,351	66,038	73,697	-20,286	-26,572	-30,421	-55,370	-59,913
Israel	9,737	11,295	13,539	11,223	12,862	16,830	20,985	24,495	15,246	18,646	-7,093	-9,690	-10,956	-4,023	-5,784
Italy	11,524	14,220	16,212	19,918	21,661	31,009	28,514	44,221	49,406	60,951	-19,485	-14,294	-28,008	-29,488	-39,290
Jamaica	1,701	1,661	1,716	1,662	1,975	376	328	306	384	506	1,325	1,334	1,410	1,278	1,470
Japan	54,681	60,472	62,388	64,018	74,565	138,004	120,552	131,445	119,505	134,860	-83,323	-60,080	-69,058	-55,487	-60,296
Jordan	644	1,172	1,360	1,318	1,203	1,267	974	1,492	1,869	2,744	-623	198	-132	-551	-1,541
Kazakhstan	538	730	510	509	808	1,101	1,872	816	904	1,715	-563	-1,142	-306	-395	-907
Kenya	573	375	943	372	562	348	311	573	568	685	225	64	370	-196	-123
Korea, South	27,572	38,821	43,484	50,975	65,942	43,781	48,875	71,775	76,018	94,919	-16,210	-10,055	-28,291	-25,043	-28,976
Kuwait	1,975	2,775	2,741	2,206	3,038	4,335	5,382	4,685	714	1,070	-2,360	-2,607	-1,944	1,492	1,967
Kyrgyzstan	31	79	32	32	34	4	3	16	5	6	27	76	16	27	28
Laos	10	13	25	25	33	4	59	45	107	219	6	-46	-21	-82	-185
Latvia	178	345	267	306	413	362	193	303	520	686	-185	152	-36	-214	-273
Lebanon	466	2,009	1,286	677	665	86	84	93	194	191	379	1,925	1,193	483	474
Liberia	69	191	136	93	140	91	180	45	45	73	-22	11	91	48	67
Libya	84	666	231	290	295	1,590	2,117	155	215	2,169	-1,506	-1,451	76	75	-1,874
Liechtenstein	20	29	35	40	45	296	213	310	287	274	-276	-183	-274	-247	-229
Lithuania	390	628	528	1,021	1,237	634	637	1,060	1,341	2,062	-244	-9	-532	-320	-825
Luxembourg	711	1,440	1,394	1,352	1,531	389	451	639	493	593	323	989	755	859	939
Macau	102	225	542	183	220	1,249	141	122	101	148	-1,147	84	420	82	72
Madagascar	28	116	55	36	56	324	151	320	614	673	-295	-35	-265	-578	-617
Malawi	28	37	37	13	23	116	29	61	43	48	-87	8	-24	-30	-25
Malaysia	10,461	14,079	12,278	12,296	15,174	33,685	25,901	33,972	44,105	56,117	-23,224	-11,821	-21,694	-31,809	-40,943
Malta	194	457	491	138	130	283	261	241	172	249	-89	196	249	-33	-119
Marshall Islands	75	91	54	120	238	17	12	29	28	15	58	79	25	92	222
Martinique	35	297	133	118	163	22	23	37	2	6	13	274	95	116	157
Mauritania	86	84	126	128	132	1	53	1	6	5	85	31	125	122	127
Mexico	120,248	163,665	236,460	211,441	276,491	170,109	229,986	296,433	323,520	384,649	-49,861	-66,321	-59,973	-112,078	-108,158
Mongolia	22	116	69	118	148	144	12	17	12	20	-122	104	52	106	129
Morocco	481	1,948	1,625	2,301	2,794	446	686	1,012	1,048	1,270	35	1,262	613	1,253	1,524
Mozambique	63	224	264	127	191	12	65	96	108	156	51	159	168	19	35
Namibia	112	110	128	60	93	130	195	85	90	151	-17	-85	42	-30	-57
Nepal	25	28	36	94	197	111	60	87	86	108	-87	-32	-51	7	89
Netherlands	26,468	34,740	40,212	44,741	53,080	14,862	19,055	16,844	27,381	35,105	11,606	15,685	23,368	17,359	17,975
New Zealand	2,592	2,820	3,631	3,196	3,724	3,155	2,764	4,293	4,207	4,949	-563	57	-662	-1,011	-1,225
Nicaragua	625	981	1,267	1,426	2,153	1,181	2,008	3,189	3,543	4,656	-555	-1,026	-1,921	-2,117	-2,503
Niger	79	49	72	145	137	66	27	4	79	95	13	22	67	66	43
Nigeria	1,620	4,061	3,431	2,801	3,887	24,239	30,516	1,916	1,485	3,444	-22,620	-26,455	1,516	1,316	443
North Macedonia [3]	32	33	31	44	45	48	37	203	159	168	-17	-4	-173	-116	-122
Norway	1,942	3,100	3,570	2,763	3,956	6,776	6,950	4,763	3,943	6,732	-4,834	-3,850	-1,192	-1,180	-2,776

See footnotes at end of table.

Table 1320. U.S. Exports, Imports, and Trade Balance by Country: 2005 to 2021-Continued.

See headnote on page 831.

Country	Exports, domestic and foreign 2005	2010	2015	2020	2021	General imports 2005	2010	2015	2020	2021	Merchandise trade balance 2005	2010	2015	2020	2021
Oman	571	1,105	2,355	1,130	1,397	555	773	907	815	1,848	16	332	1,448	315	-451
Pakistan	1,252	1,901	1,838	2,912	3,614	3,253	3,509	3,701	3,899	5,279	-2,002	-1,608	-1,863	-987	-1,665
Panama	2,162	6,066	7,669	5,657	8,133	327	381	408	707	756	1,835	5,685	7,261	4,950	7,378
Papua New Guinea	55	186	208	63	44	58	97	91	86	78	-3	89	117	-24	-34
Paraguay	896	1,810	1,492	1,267	2,055	52	62	163	150	188	844	1,748	1,329	1,118	1,868
Peru	2,309	6,750	8,724	7,570	10,323	5,119	5,243	5,056	5,520	6,885	-2,810	1,506	3,668	2,050	3,439
Philippines	6,895	7,377	7,903	7,721	9,290	9,250	7,982	10,232	11,122	14,006	-2,355	-605	-2,329	-3,402	-4,716
Poland	1,268	2,983	3,715	5,046	5,843	1,949	2,964	5,611	8,601	9,741	-681	19	-1,896	-3,555	-3,897
Portugal	1,132	1,058	942	1,663	2,369	2,329	2,142	3,271	3,777	4,946	-1,197	-1,084	-2,328	-2,114	-2,577
Qatar	987	3,160	4,222	3,410	2,581	448	466	1,354	1,181	1,912	-539	2,693	2,868	2,230	669
Romania	609	730	754	923	1,412	1,208	1,000	2,150	2,126	2,916	-599	-278	-1,396	-1,203	-1,505
Russia	3,962	5,994	7,087	4,889	6,387	15,307	25,691	16,372	16,900	29,635	-11,344	-19,697	-9,286	-12,011	-23,248
Rwanda	11	31	14	27	50	6	21	46	33	31	4	9	-31	-5	18
Saudi Arabia	6,805	11,506	19,792	11,130	11,133	27,193	31,413	22,083	8,994	13,714	-20,387	-19,907	-2,292	2,136	-2,581
Senegal	141	219	199	281	382	4	5	72	101	148	138	214	127	180	234
Serbia	(X)	104	126	142	181	(X)	164	273	441	537	(X)	-60	-146	-299	-356
Sierra Leone	38	61	77	74	115	9	29	40	32	17	29	32	38	42	98
Singapore	20,466	29,009	28,481	26,929	35,285	15,110	17,428	18,272	30,784	29,505	5,356	11,581	10,209	-3,855	5,780
Sint Maarten [2]	(X)	(X)	741	335	386	(X)	(X)	52	47	49	(X)	(X)	690	288	336
Slovakia	150	256	380	333	336	961	1,073	2,300	5,000	5,090	-811	-817	-1,920	-4,666	-4,754
Slovenia	234	328	346	298	243	413	465	678	1,192	1,567	-179	-137	-332	-893	-1,324
South Africa	3,907	5,632	5,457	4,375	5,479	5,886	8,220	7,323	11,361	15,726	-1,979	-2,589	-1,866	-6,986	-10,247
Spain	6,839	10,355	10,310	13,058	16,332	8,615	8,554	14,133	15,298	18,586	-1,776	1,802	-3,823	-2,240	-2,254
Sri Lanka	198	179	362	359	389	2,083	1,748	2,891	2,443	2,851	-1,885	-1,569	-2,529	-2,084	-2,462
Suriname	246	362	444	267	301	165	191	146	180	67	80	171	297	87	234
Sweden	3,715	4,740	3,939	4,772	5,263	13,821	10,497	9,910	12,282	14,831	-10,106	-5,757	-5,971	-7,510	-9,568
Switzerland	10,718	20,704	22,154	18,063	23,638	13,000	19,137	31,431	74,656	63,181	-2,282	1,567	-9,277	-56,593	-39,543
Syria	155	503	3			324	429	7	10	9	-169	74	-8	-8	-8
Taiwan	21,614	26,050	25,826	30,213	36,838	34,826	35,847	40,911	60,432	77,064	-13,211	-9,797	-15,085	-30,218	-40,226
Tajikistan	29	57	19	8	15	241	2	31	1	1	-212	56	-12	7	14
Tanzania	96	163	173	243	283	34	43	105	121	98	63	121	68	122	185
Thailand	7,257	8,976	11,229	11,266	12,652	19,890	22,694	28,622	37,545	47,351	-12,633	-13,717	-17,393	-26,279	-34,698
Togo	28	158	312	310	235	6	9	14	20	18	21	149	298	291	218
Trinidad and Tobago	1,417	1,925	2,512	2,401	2,676	7,891	6,613	4,320	2,478	4,297	-6,474	-4,688	-1,808	-78	-1,621
Tunisia	261	573	602	429	466	264	405	546	569	718	-3	167	56	-139	-251
Turkey	4,239	10,538	9,520	9,987	11,905	5,182	4,207	7,886	10,971	15,870	-943	6,331	1,633	-984	-3,965
Turkmenistan	215	40	81	33	79	135	48	56	14	22	80	-8	25	19	57
Uganda	63	94	88	95	167	26	58	64	83	92	37	36	24	12	75
Ukraine	533	1,349	862	1,908	2,525	1,098	1,078	852	1,305	1,889	-565	271	11	603	636
United Arab Emirates	8,120	11,662	23,001	14,743	17,064	1,468	1,145	2,474	3,052	5,954	6,651	10,517	20,527	11,691	11,110
United Kingdom	38,568	48,410	56,095	58,474	61,425	51,033	49,805	58,057	50,261	56,364	-12,465	-1,395	-1,962	8,213	5,061
Uruguay	357	975	1,295	1,217	1,799	732	235	605	550	634	-376	740	-690	667	1,165
Uzbekistan	74	101	138	181	401	96	68	10	81	187	-22	33	128	100	214
Venezuela	6,421	10,645	8,344	1,130	1,614	33,978	32,707	15,564	167	295	-27,557	-22,063	-7,221	963	1,319
Vietnam	1,193	3,706	7,101	9,915	11,011	6,631	14,868	38,015	79,540	101,896	-5,438	-11,162	-30,914	-69,625	-90,885
Yemen	219	398	158	329	271	279	181	48	4	10	-60	216	110	325	261
Zambia	29	56	84	72	94	32	30	47	40	175	-3	27	37	31	-81
Zimbabwe	46	68	38	46	45	94	59	67	37	43	-49	9	-29	9	2

X Not applicable. Z Less than $500,000. [1] Includes additional countries, not shown separately. [2] The Netherlands Antilles dissolved on October 10, 2010. Curacao and Sint Maarten became autonomous territories of the Kingdom of the Netherlands. [3] In June 2018, The Republic of Macedonia agreed to change its name to the Republic of North Macedonia. The agreement became effective February 2019.

Source: U.S. Census Bureau, "USA Trade Online," <usatrade.census.gov/>, accessed June 2022. See also U.S. International Trade in Goods and Services, Series FT-900, <www.census.gov/foreign-trade/Press-Release/ft900_index.html>.

Table 1321. U.S. Exports and General Imports by Selected Commodity Groups: 2019 to 2021

[In millions of dollars (1,645,940 represents $1,645,940,000,000). All data are presented on a Census basis. For methodology, see Foreign Trade Statistics in Appendix III]

Selected commodity	Exports			General imports		
	2019	2020	2021	2019	2020	2021
Total [1]	**1,645,940**	**1,428,518**	**1,754,300**	**2,491,700**	**2,330,836**	**2,831,111**
Manufactured goods [2]	1,128,677	956,041	1,134,970	2,152,925	2,063,291	2,460,410
Agricultural commodities [2]	141,050	149,648	176,542	142,393	146,759	171,096
Food and live animals [3]	100,335	101,701	124,538	115,935	120,060	140,742
Live animals other than fish	977	910	1,220	3,009	2,915	3,299
Meat and preparations	19,226	19,601	23,940	9,682	10,387	13,199
Cereals and preparations	20,977	23,414	34,586	11,001	11,720	12,717
Vegetables and fruits	22,490	21,397	22,524	37,642	39,025	43,819
Coffee, tea, cocoa, and spices	2,994	2,697	3,018	13,429	13,416	15,472
Feeding stuff for animals	11,898	12,454	14,830	3,321	3,663	4,536
Crude materials except fuels [3]	73,931	77,854	96,310	34,198	33,875	49,110
Hides, skins, and furskins, raw	1,048	817	1,169	46	47	51
Oil seeds and oleaginous fruits	20,735	27,701	29,541	976	1,057	1,235
Crude rubber	2,215	1,884	2,490	3,120	2,372	3,448
Cork and wood	6,131	5,690	7,171	7,323	9,643	15,949
Pulp and waste paper	8,318	7,417	9,352	3,418	2,958	4,021
Textile fibers including waste	7,965	7,585	7,633	1,315	1,136	1,438
Crude fertilizers	2,687	2,267	2,863	3,005	2,637	3,285
Metalliferous ores and metal scrap	21,480	21,432	32,724	9,016	8,158	12,321
Mineral fuels and lubricants [3]	197,740	149,832	235,781	200,829	122,486	216,013
Coal, coke, and briquettes	10,160	6,258	10,307	918	828	1,069
Petroleum products and preparations	156,390	110,149	157,139	189,040	113,077	198,665
Gas, natural and manufactured	30,754	33,244	67,830	8,976	6,661	13,642
Animal and vegetable oils [3]	2,498	2,944	3,446	6,088	6,423	9,676
Animal oil and fat	813	906	1,092	339	394	703
Fixed vegetable fats and oil, crude	1,455	1,686	1,768	5,494	5,779	8,632
Chemicals and related products [3]	209,060	196,675	249,328	267,697	278,534	322,179
Organic chemicals	35,890	32,276	42,536	49,268	49,984	56,470
Inorganic chemicals	10,729	10,318	12,569	11,388	9,395	12,492
Dyeing, tanning, and coloring materials	7,197	6,452	7,628	4,302	4,217	5,028
Medicinal and pharmaceutical products	52,426	50,056	69,604	134,161	146,281	157,657
Fertilizers	3,101	2,744	3,303	6,555	5,269	9,545
Plastics in primary forms	35,510	32,300	41,218	15,623	13,701	21,784
Plastics in nonprimary forms	13,373	12,367	14,760	11,553	11,641	14,454
Manufactured goods by material	103,832	90,885	107,766	256,511	246,843	324,784
Leather and leather manufactures	776	539	772	1,270	1,128	1,543
Rubber manufactures	9,365	7,821	8,785	22,606	20,051	24,188
Cork and wood manufactures	1,937	1,720	2,241	10,965	11,901	17,922
Paper and paperboard	14,725	13,518	14,915	17,020	15,432	17,320
Textile yarn, fabric	11,945	9,867	11,388	29,761	43,056	36,813
Nonmetallic mineral manufactures	11,739	10,448	11,751	43,275	33,233	47,072
Iron and steel	12,125	10,022	13,928	31,749	22,339	43,163
Nonferrous metals	15,115	15,054	18,509	42,268	43,868	66,828
Manufactures of metals	26,106	21,896	25,477	57,598	55,834	69,935
Machinery and transport equipment	510,756	410,498	459,991	1,055,178	961,626	1,121,536
Power generating machinery	36,448	31,228	34,036	78,214	62,194	68,656
Specialized industrial machinery	45,220	42,763	52,084	56,813	48,807	61,488
Metalworking machinery	4,815	3,687	4,407	11,123	9,301	10,562
General industrial machinery	60,790	52,889	58,435	107,102	98,289	119,829
Office machinery	17,720	16,345	18,486	125,551	140,342	162,567
Telecommunications equipment	19,609	16,504	17,412	152,630	144,197	170,576
Electrical machinery	81,771	76,183	83,121	185,183	182,631	226,681
Road vehicles	120,633	96,777	111,529	299,613	244,821	271,708
Transport equipment	123,750	74,122	80,481	38,949	31,044	29,471
Miscellaneous manufactured articles [3]	126,665	106,953	120,018	403,993	395,095	477,364
Prefabricated buildings	2,399	1,977	2,208	13,151	12,377	14,982
Furniture	5,969	4,671	5,092	50,423	49,216	60,095
Travel goods	668	499	589	10,639	8,019	10,774
Apparel and clothing accessories	3,217	2,485	3,296	92,232	79,356	101,095
Footwear	1,133	798	818	26,865	20,195	26,925
Scientific and controlling equipment	51,202	46,801	50,493	64,293	61,711	70,877
Photographic equipment	6,550	5,812	6,479	15,053	12,603	17,248
Miscellaneous commodities [4]	64,677	61,418	74,985	123,634	138,887	138,102
Re-exports	**250,632**	**224,369**	**276,031**	**(X)**	**(X)**	**(X)**

X Not applicable. [1] Total exports including re-exports (exports of foreign merchandise). [2] Manufactured goods is based on the North American Industry Classification System (NAICS) and Agricultural commodities is based on the Harmonized System commodities specified by the U.S. Department of Agriculture definition. All other commodity detail is based on Standard International Trade Classification (SITC). [3] Includes other commodities, not shown separately. [4] Includes special transactions, coin, nonmonetary gold, and the low value estimate.

Source: U.S. Census Bureau, *U.S. International Trade in Goods and Services, Annual Revision for 2021*, Series FT-900, June 2022. See also <www.census.gov/foreign-trade/Press-Release/ft900_index.html>.

Table 1322. Domestic Exports and Imports for Consumption of Merchandise by Selected NAICS Product Category: 2005 to 2021

[In millions of dollars (799,957 represents $799,957,000,000). Includes nonmonetary gold. For methodology, see Foreign Trade Statistics in Appendix III. NAICS = North American Industry Classification System; see text, Section 15. N.e.c. = Not elsewhere classified]

Product category	2005	2010	2015	2019	2020	2021
Domestic exports, total.................................	**799,957**	**1,122,567**	**1,286,172**	**1,395,308**	**1,204,149**	**1,478,269**
Agricultural, forestry, and fishery products.................	37,109	65,753	69,766	70,483	77,751	93,055
Agricultural products, total.............................	30,683	58,023	60,200	61,617	69,945	83,518
Livestock and livestock products.......................	1,118	1,539	2,032	1,916	1,842	2,315
Forestry products, n.e.c...............................	1,686	2,181	2,354	1,978	1,895	2,391
Fish, fresh or chilled, and other marine products.........	3,622	4,011	5,180	4,972	4,069	4,831
Mining, total..	12,629	26,394	34,188	113,371	96,359	154,606
Oil and gas...	4,547	9,248	19,802	94,393	82,267	134,357
Minerals and ores.....................................	8,082	17,146	14,386	18,978	14,091	20,248
Manufacturing, total....................................	708,205	952,360	1,110,979	1,128,677	956,041	1,134,970
Food and kindred products............................	28,937	50,902	61,982	64,936	65,575	76,058
Beverages and tobacco products.......................	3,423	5,339	8,476	7,182	6,955	8,133
Textiles and fabrics...................................	8,483	7,833	9,001	8,389	6,699	7,819
Textile mill products..................................	2,344	2,583	2,793	2,649	2,517	2,781
Apparel and accessories..............................	4,075	3,070	3,104	3,042	2,263	3,002
Leather and allied products............................	2,300	2,421	3,041	2,873	2,073	2,439
Wood products.......................................	4,463	5,075	6,812	6,708	6,030	7,731
Paper products.......................................	16,640	22,962	23,321	22,849	20,851	23,985
Printed, publishing, & similar products.................	5,526	6,021	5,088	4,540	3,983	4,681
Petroleum and coal products..........................	17,979	61,010	78,168	93,133	61,399	91,176
Chemicals..	114,821	171,365	182,411	195,766	183,840	233,740
Plastics and rubber products [1].......................	18,784	24,262	29,970	30,507	27,702	32,247
Nonmetallic mineral products [1].......................	6,663	9,226	10,699	10,758	9,439	11,119
Primary metal products...............................	27,455	49,725	51,694	47,023	45,712	59,474
Fabricated metal products.............................	23,370	32,690	41,602	42,208	35,254	39,523
Machinery, except electrical...........................	97,001	126,023	123,736	119,109	106,605	125,314
Computers and electronic products [1]..................	122,744	121,121	119,879	114,780	107,005	116,223
Electrical equipment, appliances, and components [1]....	26,457	31,035	46,671	45,845	39,920	43,454
Transportation equipment [1]..........................	144,985	176,337	252,299	255,225	178,861	197,724
Furniture and fixtures.................................	2,844	3,979	4,960	4,679	3,813	4,218
Miscellaneous manufactured commodities..............	28,909	39,381	45,271	46,480	39,544	44,128
Newspapers, books, & other published matter, n.e.c......	960	851	(NA)	(NA)	(NA)	(NA)
Special classification provisions.......................	41,055	77,210	71,239	82,777	73,998	95,639
Waste and scrap......................................	10,389	29,420	17,548	19,491	20,983	31,444
Used or second-hand merchandise.....................	2,570	4,711	12,432	16,225	11,626	14,332
Goods returned or reimported.........................	65	30	32	43	64	20
Special classification provision, n.e.c..................	28,030	43,049	41,228	47,019	41,325	49,842
Imports for consumption, total.......................	**1,664,625**	**1,900,587**	**2,227,237**	**2,495,687**	**2,330,836**	**2,822,516**
Agricultural, forestry, and fishery products.................	30,761	42,686	56,308	63,768	63,549	76,285
Agricultural products, total.............................	15,818	24,017	33,435	38,485	39,115	44,180
Livestock and livestock products.......................	3,277	4,116	6,124	6,599	6,253	11,187
Forestry products, n.e.c...............................	2,250	3,356	2,380	2,633	2,467	3,298
Fish, fresh or chilled, and other marine products.........	9,416	11,198	14,369	16,051	15,714	17,620
Mining, total..	192,115	235,401	115,949	129,795	82,717	143,955
Oil and gas...	185,621	228,066	109,006	123,718	78,300	138,046
Minerals and ores.....................................	6,494	7,335	6,943	6,077	4,417	5,908
Manufacturing, total....................................	1,372,004	1,550,204	1,948,837	2,166,932	2,067,337	2,459,431
Food and kindred products............................	29,779	41,039	58,434	68,541	72,928	86,870
Beverages and tobacco products.......................	12,849	15,515	21,201	26,394	26,128	30,565
Textiles and fabrics...................................	7,450	6,525	8,570	8,150	8,248	9,795
Textile mill products..................................	13,508	15,825	20,752	23,375	36,916	30,023
Apparel and accessories..............................	74,478	75,411	89,281	89,453	72,536	87,340
Leather and allied products............................	26,559	30,859	40,163	39,191	30,224	39,797
Wood products.......................................	23,654	11,364	17,107	18,277	21,503	33,982
Paper products.......................................	22,094	21,029	20,324	21,135	19,320	22,631
Printed, publishing, & similar products.................	5,599	5,324	5,532	5,891	4,906	5,945
Petroleum and coal products..........................	81,359	102,169	67,950	73,499	42,468	72,697
Chemicals..	131,936	187,576	217,099	262,810	269,436	310,597
Plastics and rubber products..........................	28,072	34,364	49,836	59,037	59,640	72,782
Nonmetallic mineral products.........................	18,445	16,075	21,799	23,961	21,788	27,876
Primary metal products...............................	64,666	79,617	85,118	85,904	128,155	135,085
Fabricated metal products.............................	41,026	46,712	67,397	75,355	69,622	87,370
Machinery, except electrical...........................	109,619	104,832	156,908	187,999	168,870	206,457
Computers and electronic products....................	269,921	324,379	372,260	389,698	390,840	459,798
Electrical equipment, appliances, and components......	55,179	68,465	101,912	121,909	124,226	152,168
Transportation equipment.............................	251,386	239,870	375,354	414,559	335,835	366,970
Furniture and fixtures.................................	25,096	25,702	36,874	42,205	42,585	52,205
Miscellaneous manufactured commodities..............	79,329	97,554	114,987	129,589	121,163	168,475
Newspapers, books, & other published matter, n.e.c......	128	35	(NA)	(NA)	(NA)	(NA)
Special classification provisions.......................	69,617	72,261	106,143	135,192	117,233	142,847
Waste and scrap......................................	3,207	5,261	5,089	6,545	6,869	10,279
Used or second-hand merchandise.....................	6,026	6,403	13,159	13,128	6,524	10,375
Goods returned or reimported.........................	37,024	40,992	66,960	92,510	82,249	96,945
Special classification provision, n.e.c..................	23,359	19,605	20,935	23,008	21,591	25,248

NA Not available. [1] Beginning 2009, export statistics for certain commodity classifications related to the aircraft industry are subject to suppression and have been aggregated in a manner that prevents the disclosure of confidential information.

Source: U.S. Census Bureau, Foreign Trade Division, USA Trade Online, <usatrade.census.gov/>, accessed July 2022. See also U.S. International Trade in Goods and Services, Series FT-900, <www.census.gov/foreign-trade/data/index.html>.

Table 1323. Knowledge- and Technology-Intensive Products Exports and Imports by World Region and Country: 2005 to 2018

[In billions of dollars (4,759.9 represents $4,759,900,000,000). Knowledge- and technology-intensive products include high research and development (R&D) intensive and medium-high R&D intensive products classified by the Organisation for Economic Co-operation and Development. High R&D intensive products include aircraft; pharmaceuticals; and computer, electronic, and optical products. Medium-high R&D intensive products include weapons and ammunition; motor vehicles; medical and dental instruments; machinery and equipment; chemicals and chemical products; electrical equipment; and railroad, military vehicles, and transport. World exports do not equal imports due to statistical errors in reporting of trade data and lack of trade data for sub-Sahara African countries. Data are primarily from Oxford Economics, special tabulations (2019) of Global Trade Databank]

Region and country	2005	2010	2011	2012	2013	2014	2015	2016	2017	2018
EXPORTS										
World [1]	**4,759.9**	**6,582.7**	**7,491.7**	**7,499.6**	**7,707.6**	**7,955.3**	**7,377.7**	**7,318.8**	**8,058.9**	**8,587.8**
North America	791.9	995.1	1,103.3	1,161.3	1,173.9	1,219.9	1,190.2	1,154.2	1,208.1	1,271.8
Canada	146.0	136.9	151.9	159.4	155.6	159.7	156.4	154.2	153.6	159.9
Mexico	125.4	182.8	203.4	222.7	234.6	254.5	257.9	252.9	276.3	302.7
United States	**520.4**	**675.4**	**748.0**	**779.1**	**783.7**	**805.7**	**775.9**	**747.0**	**778.2**	**809.3**
Central & South America [2]	59.8	81.7	97.9	97.6	102.3	88.3	78.4	78.1	84.6	87.0
Brazil	38.1	46.3	54.4	53.8	58.9	46.8	43.3	46.3	49.8	53.3
Europe	2,351.3	2,922.9	3,391.3	3,247.5	3,396.8	3,499.0	3,142.6	3,183.2	3,475.0	3,670.6
European Union [2, 3]	2,198.4	2,694.0	3,116.9	2,966.2	3,110.9	3,209.3	2,877.7	2,920.5	3,186.3	3,359.2
France	254.3	296.6	327.5	317.8	323.9	323.9	287.5	288.8	310.4	336.4
Germany	640.9	793.0	933.5	900.4	927.1	961.6	865.8	872.8	955.5	1,023.8
United Kingdom	212.1	206.5	233.9	228.6	232.2	257.7	245.5	234.4	244.7	252.8
Other Europe	152.9	228.9	274.3	281.3	285.9	289.7	264.9	262.8	288.7	311.4
Middle East	50.4	106.0	125.1	172.7	185.1	191.2	135.1	124.1	168.8	119.0
Asia [2]	1,486.9	2,453.1	2,746.9	2,791.8	2,822.8	2,930.7	2,807.7	2,755.4	3,098.5	3,414.1
China [4]	394.0	832.7	966.7	1,006.3	1,046.1	1,131.1	1,112.8	1,062.6	1,196.2	1,344.7
India	22.4	56.2	74.0	75.0	86.5	86.7	80.3	81.1	91.1	108.3
Indonesia	18.2	27.9	33.5	33.6	33.3	33.2	28.5	29.6	31.5	34.1
Japan	443.2	550.0	580.9	570.6	504.1	487.1	442.6	461.9	495.7	525.1
Malaysia	85.1	100.9	104.2	102.5	103.5	108.5	99.9	97.9	112.4	132.3
Philippines	31.3	24.5	22.0	33.3	34.3	38.3	40.2	38.2	47.2	47.5
Singapore	93.5	222.0	242.2	243.3	245.4	245.7	229.4	221.8	238.5	258.7
South Korea	210.6	344.5	390.2	378.8	399.5	410.3	393.6	369.1	428.1	444.0
Taiwan	123.1	174.0	193.6	187.1	193.3	203.4	190.1	191.0	219.5	230.6
Thailand	58.5	100.0	109.4	117.0	120.7	123.8	117.1	118.6	130.9	140.0
Vietnam	3.7	13.5	22.0	34.8	47.2	53.3	65.1	75.1	98.4	139.1
Oceania [2]	19.5	23.9	27.2	28.6	26.8	26.2	23.7	23.7	23.9	25.3
Australia	15.6	19.8	22.3	23.6	21.9	21.2	18.9	19.1	19.3	20.7
IMPORTS										
World [1]	**4,880.0**	**6,677.7**	**7,621.8**	**7,652.6**	**7,864.3**	**8,093.1**	**7,580.8**	**7,669.4**	**8,416.0**	**9,046.2**
North America	1,127.7	1,322.3	1,479.9	1,580.6	1,608.8	1,686.7	1,719.7	1,693.5	1,798.8	1,936.5
Canada	178.0	207.3	231.7	242.2	243.5	244.7	231.9	225.7	241.8	254.8
Mexico	134.0	181.9	204.5	219.7	230.1	240.1	242.7	238.0	250.3	271.6
United States	**815.6**	**933.1**	**1,043.7**	**1,118.7**	**1,135.2**	**1,201.9**	**1,245.1**	**1,229.7**	**1,306.7**	**1,410.1**
Central & South America [2]	132.8	269.0	333.8	342.9	348.2	326.0	284.0	245.7	263.6	290.4
Brazil	43.6	107.2	130.8	130.1	138.7	130.8	103.9	87.0	90.5	111.9
Europe	2,200.4	2,759.1	3,177.3	2,970.2	3,074.2	3,172.1	2,850.2	2,918.9	3,217.4	3,388.5
European Union [2, 3]	1,961.4	2,379.4	2,696.9	2,474.9	2,570.1	2,694.7	2,465.4	2,524.0	2,762.4	2,923.9
France	237.5	295.2	341.6	316.4	318.9	318.9	288.1	297.4	318.3	333.1
Germany	389.8	507.1	586.5	542.1	552.2	580.2	529.4	537.7	603.0	660.1
United Kingdom	256.7	267.8	295.4	270.7	283.0	328.0	313.5	305.6	312.0	319.8
Other Europe [2]	239.0	379.6	480.4	495.3	504.1	477.4	384.9	394.9	455.0	464.6
Middle East	130.2	222.4	253.4	309.2	334.7	360.3	307.6	286.1	408.7	367.3
Asia [2]	1,204.2	1,987.7	2,246.1	2,304.6	2,365.0	2,416.0	2,297.5	2,405.0	2,586.4	2,921.6
China [4]	461.8	812.6	924.6	931.1	989.1	1,025.7	950.9	1,045.2	1,061.2	1,207.5
India	42.6	100.1	121.1	125.9	122.9	125.4	129.7	127.7	148.8	209.8
Indonesia	23.5	64.1	78.8	87.8	80.9	75.9	67.4	65.3	72.8	87.2
Japan	178.4	232.0	264.3	275.2	264.5	268.8	249.3	253.4	269.9	294.8
Malaysia	75.3	97.9	103.2	105.6	108.2	109.3	95.8	95.1	108.0	119.3
Philippines	32.3	33.3	25.0	34.5	35.0	35.4	41.8	51.2	57.8	64.4
Singapore	71.1	166.9	177.7	183.5	183.7	180.3	166.7	165.6	180.3	203.7
South Korea	110.2	170.0	187.4	181.2	187.1	195.2	195.2	191.5	219.7	229.6
Taiwan	102.1	130.1	139.9	128.9	131.9	135.2	126.6	132.7	146.1	158.3
Thailand	57.4	85.0	99.5	116.0	111.4	104.4	99.4	99.3	107.9	115.3
Vietnam	14.7	37.7	47.2	55.6	68.2	75.3	91.1	97.0	120.9	133.0
Oceania [2]	84.8	117.2	131.3	145.1	133.3	132.1	121.7	120.2	141.2	141.8
Australia	70.8	103.2	114.8	127.5	114.6	111.0	102.7	101.2	120.0	119.6

[1] World total does not include all countries and economies due to limitations in data availability. [2] Includes other countries not shown separately. [3] Data are not available for EU member Luxembourg. [4] Includes Hong Kong but, excludes bilateral flows between mainland China and Hong Kong.

Source: National Science Foundation, *Science and Engineering Indicators 2020, Production and Trade of Knowledge- and Technology-Intensive Industries, Supplemental Tables*, NSB-2020-5, January 2020. See also <ncses.nsf.gov/pubs/nsb20205/data#supplemental-tables>.

Table 1324. Exporting Firms and Revenue, Employees, and Payroll by Country and Area of Export Destination: 2017

[36,579,576 represents $36,579,576,000,000. Covers nonfarm employer firms. A company or firm is a business consisting of one or more domestic establishments that the reporting firm specified under its ownership or control. Data were compiled from two Census Bureau data products, the 2017-2018 Profile of U.S. Importing and Exporting Companies and the 2018 Annual Business Survey. Excludes firms without reported sales, payroll, and employment; non-employer firms; firms operating primarily in out of scope industries, such as crop and animal production; and firms located in the U.S. Island Areas]

Export destination	Firms (number)	Receipts (mil. dol.)	Value of exports (mil. dol.)	Paid employees (1,000)	Annual payroll (mil. dol.)
All firms with and without exports	5,745,000	36,579,576	1,227,479	127,738	6,534,271
Firms with exports [1]	**179,000**	**21,565,993**	**1,227,479**	**47,702**	**3,089,731**
Australia	24,500	10,421,670	19,288	17,210	1,332,637
Belgium	8,700	8,102,603	26,493	11,876	980,526
Brazil	12,000	9,856,676	31,221	15,023	1,151,087
Canada	72,500	16,780,333	194,864	34,099	2,236,103
Chile	11,500	10,441,920	10,410	16,641	1,178,387
China	28,000	11,705,141	107,988	19,864	1,392,907
Colombia	10,000	9,293,115	10,094	13,230	1,057,882
France	16,000	9,695,725	29,126	14,985	1,208,645
Germany	26,000	11,762,305	47,188	21,173	1,555,167
Hong Kong	19,500	10,275,614	31,632	18,267	1,364,187
India	15,000	10,500,157	19,270	18,939	1,358,323
Ireland	6,000	6,155,986	9,311	10,137	856,866
Israel	11,500	8,943,635	10,360	14,368	1,075,842
Italy	15,000	9,494,551	17,489	14,649	1,145,456
Japan	21,000	11,502,155	53,854	19,334	1,431,432
Korea, South	18,500	10,460,394	40,330	15,734	1,249,229
Malaysia	9,800	8,275,088	11,295	11,585	953,732
Mexico	41,500	13,726,667	189,396	24,865	1,702,073
Netherlands	15,500	10,490,912	35,555	18,342	1,347,463
Saudi Arabia	8,100	7,416,827	12,083	11,355	867,536
Singapore	16,500	9,737,183	24,885	15,231	1,245,465
Switzerland	9,000	7,088,783	23,078	11,070	935,129
Taiwan	14,500	9,461,292	27,621	14,331	1,135,878
United Arab Emirates	13,000	8,727,016	17,544	13,668	1,023,641
United Kingdom	33,000	12,678,591	47,989	22,846	1,763,150
APEC (Asia-Pacific Economic Cooperation)	136,000	19,922,443	755,594	42,553	2,763,975
ASEAN (Association of Southeast Asian Nations)	30,500	12,331,525	63,940	20,506	1,543,722
European Union	68,500	16,019,433	243,810	31,959	2,257,898
LAFTA (Latin American Free Trade Area)	58,000	15,217,709	265,550	28,636	1,935,878
OECD [2]	142,000	20,563,780	798,686	44,282	2,913,425
OPEC [3]	26,000	11,856,925	46,507	19,687	1,443,469

[1] Includes other countries, not shown separately. [2] Organisation for Economic Cooperation and Development. [3] Organization of Petroleum Exporting Countries.

Source: U.S. Census Bureau, Annual Business Survey, "U.S. Exporting Firms by Demographics 2018 Tables," accessed July 2021. See also <www.census.gov/data/tables/2017/econ/abs/2017-abs-exporting-firms.html>.

Table 1325. U.S. Exporting and Importing Companies by Employment-Size Class: 2010 and 2020

[Value in millions of dollars (1,140,406 represents $1,140,406,000,000). Data include all companies that can be linked to import and/or export transactions. Trade values are taken from the transactions used to compile the official U.S. Trade statistics; company information is taken from the Census Bureau Business Register. For information on data limitations, see Technical Documentation in source]

Employment-size class and company type	Number		Known value [1] (mil. dol.)		Percent of—			
					Number		Known value	
	2010	2020	2010	2020	2010	2020	2010	2020
EXPORTERS								
All companies, total	293,988	271,705	1,140,406	1,265,900	100.0	100.0	100.0	100.0
By employment-size:								
1 to 19 employees	112,572	93,041	82,739	67,552	38.3	34.2	7.3	5.3
20 to 49 employees	30,984	27,114	45,037	38,940	10.5	10.0	3.9	3.1
50 to 99 employees	15,179	14,054	43,710	37,963	5.2	5.2	3.8	3.0
100 to 249 employees	11,581	11,649	59,349	95,649	3.9	4.3	5.2	7.6
250 to 499 employees	4,336	4,759	46,254	53,822	1.5	1.8	4.1	4.3
500 or more employees	6,490	7,339	755,466	852,612	2.2	2.7	66.2	67.4
Unknown [2]	112,846	113,749	107,851	119,362	38.4	41.9	9.5	9.4
IMPORTERS								
All companies, total	181,648	221,580	1,679,522	2,024,454	100.0	100.0	100.0	100.0
By employment-size:								
1 to 19 employees	77,796	88,095	112,664	126,744	42.8	39.8	6.7	6.3
20 to 49 employees	18,487	20,857	71,093	76,640	10.2	9.4	4.2	3.8
50 to 99 employees	9,472	10,683	58,075	69,192	5.2	4.8	3.5	3.4
100 to 249 employees	7,820	9,205	96,080	109,104	4.3	4.2	5.7	5.4
250 to 499 employees	3,174	3,857	69,812	86,919	1.7	1.7	4.2	4.3
500 or more employees	5,013	6,077	1,148,183	1,373,661	2.8	2.7	68.4	67.9
Unknown [2]	59,886	82,806	123,616	182,194	33.0	37.4	7.4	9.0

[1] Known value is defined as the portion of U.S. total exports and general imports that could be matched to specific companies. Export values are on f.a.s. or "free alongside ship" basis. [2] Includes missing employment data, nonemployers, and companies that reported annual payroll but did not report any employees on their payroll.

Source: U.S. Census Bureau, Profile of U.S. Importing and Exporting Companies 2019-2020, April 2022, and earlier reports. See also <www.census.gov/foreign-trade/statistics/press-release/>.

Table 1326. Export and Import Value Indexes—Selected Countries: 2016 to 2020

[Indexes in U.S. dollars, 2000=100. Values are the current value of exports/imports converted to U.S. dollars and expressed as a percentage of the average for the base period]

Country	Export value index					Import value index				
	2016	2017	2018	2019	2020	2016	2017	2018	2019	2020
United States	**185.6**	**197.8**	**212.8**	**210.1**	**183.1**	**178.7**	**191.3**	**207.6**	**203.9**	**191.2**
Australia	301.4	361.9	402.5	424.3	392.3	274.4	319.8	329.1	309.8	295.1
Belgium	211.9	228.6	249.4	237.9	223.5	214.3	231.1	256.9	241.5	223.7
Canada	141.0	152.1	162.9	161.4	141.2	168.7	181.2	192.2	189.5	169.2
France	153.4	163.8	178.2	174.7	149.4	167.9	183.2	200.1	193.6	172.3
Germany	242.4	263.1	283.5	270.6	250.8	212.8	234.5	259.0	248.8	236.0
Greece	240.2	278.3	337.0	323.4	300.0	140.2	160.2	191.3	187.2	166.8
Ireland	169.5	177.9	213.4	219.7	232.8	159.5	183.0	211.5	198.6	193.9
Italy	192.0	211.0	228.5	223.6	206.3	170.4	189.8	210.8	198.9	177.1
Japan	134.6	145.7	154.0	147.2	133.8	160.1	177.1	197.2	190.0	167.4
Korea, South	287.6	333.0	351.1	314.8	297.5	253.1	298.2	333.5	313.6	291.4
Netherlands	245.4	280.4	312.5	304.7	290.2	230.0	263.9	296.5	292.0	273.7
Norway	147.2	168.3	202.8	171.2	140.6	209.7	236.3	251.8	248.1	233.9
Spain	252.2	277.9	301.6	290.5	267.0	199.6	226.0	250.8	239.3	208.7
Sweden	160.3	175.9	190.9	184.7	179.0	194.0	212.1	234.7	218.7	206.2
Switzerland	376.3	372.2	386.0	390.0	(NA)	327.3	327.0	338.7	336.7	(NA)
United Kingdom	144.3	154.9	170.8	165.0	142.1	183.4	184.6	193.6	200.4	182.8

NA Not available.

Source: World Bank, "World Development Indicators" database ©, <data.worldbank.org/>, accessed August 2022.

Table 1327. U.S. Trade with China—Leading Commodity Imports and Exports: 2010 to 2021

[In billions of dollars (365.0 represents $365,000,000,000), except as noted]

Commodity	NAICS code [1]	2010	2015	2019	2020	2021	2020-2021- percent change
IMPORTS FROM CHINA [2]							
Total imports [3]	(X)	**365.0**	**483.2**	**449.1**	**432.7**	**504.9**	**16.7**
Computer equipment	3341	57.2	57.8	52.8	59.2	69.6	17.5
Communications equipment	3342	33.0	67.4	63.9	55.5	63.0	13.6
Plastics products	3261	7.2	12.1	15.7	17.8	21.1	18.6
Apparel	3152	26.6	27.9	22.2	13.2	17.8	34.7
Household and institutional furniture and kitchen cabinets	3371	11.6	15.9	14.9	13.1	15.8	21.1
Motor vehicle parts	3363	6.7	13.3	12.5	10.2	12.7	23.7
Audio and video equipment	3343	19.5	15.0	12.1	10.8	12.2	13.3
Semiconductors and other electronic components	3344	18.3	19.6	10.5	11.0	11.8	7.2
Footwear	3162	15.7	17.1	13.1	8.2	11.1	36.0
Basic chemicals	3251	5.2	7.4	8.0	7.7	10.1	30.6
EXPORTS TO CHINA							
Total exports [3]	(X)	**85.8**	**107.2**	**94.1**	**110.5**	**132.4**	**19.9**
Oilseeds and grains	1111	11.3	13.0	8.3	17.1	21.8	27.4
Oil and gas	2111	(Z)	1.0	2.7	9.0	11.2	25.0
Semiconductors and other electronic components	3344	6.1	5.3	7.8	9.5	11.2	17.4
Industrial machinery	3332	2.0	2.2	4.3	5.3	6.9	31.0
Motor vehicles	3361	3.2	8.3	6.7	5.9	6.3	6.4
Basic chemicals	3251	4.1	4.4	3.9	4.4	5.8	31.0
Navigational, measuring, electromedical, and control instruments	3345	3.5	4.8	5.0	5.1	5.4	6.9
Meat products and meat packaging products	3116	1.3	1.7	2.0	3.9	4.9	26.2
Pharmaceuticals and medicines	3254	0.8	2.1	3.8	4.4	4.8	9.5
Aerospace products and parts	3364	5.7	15.1	9.9	4.0	4.2	6.2

X Not applicable. Z Less than $500 million. [1] Based on the North American Industry Classification System (NAICS); see text, Section 15. [2] Imports classified as general imports. For definition of General Imports, see Text, this section. [3] Includes items not shown separately.

Source: U.S. International Trade Commission, "Interactive Tariff and Trade DataWeb," <dataweb.usitc.gov/>, accessed September 2022.

Table 1328. U.S. Trade with Canada and Mexico—Leading Commodity Imports and Exports: 2010 to 2021

[In billions of dollars (277.6 represents $277,600,000,000), except as noted]

Commodity	NAICS code [1]	2010	2015	2019	2020	2021	2020-2021 percent change
IMPORTS FROM CANADA [2]							
Total imports [3]	(X)	**277.6**	**296.3**	**318.6**	**270.0**	**357.8**	**32.5**
Oil & gas	2111	66.3	55.0	70.2	48.3	87.9	82.0
Motor vehicles	3361	36.5	43.4	41.5	30.3	26.1	-14.0
Motor vehicle parts	3363	12.1	14.4	13.6	11.4	13.2	15.9
Petroleum & coal products	3241	14.5	12.0	12.7	7.9	12.2	54.3
Nonferrous metal (except aluminum) production and processing	3314	10.3	9.4	10.1	11.0	12.2	10.7
Sawmill and wood products	3211	3.0	4.9	4.5	6.4	11.3	77.3
Alumina and aluminum and processing	3313	6.2	5.9	5.6	5.6	9.2	63.9
Aerospace products & parts	3364	6.4	10.7	10.3	8.5	8.7	2.5
Iron and steel and ferroalloy	3311	5.4	4.7	4.6	4.0	8.3	107.2
Basic chemicals	3251	7.4	6.4	6.4	5.7	8.0	39.6
EXPORTS TO CANADA							
Total exports [3]	(X)	**206.8**	**234.1**	**242.1**	**210.1**	**252.0**	**20.0**
Motor vehicles	3361	20.7	25.0	29.0	22.4	26.6	18.6
Motor vehicle parts	3363	19.5	17.1	17.2	12.6	12.1	-4.5
Petroleum & coal products	3241	5.9	10.1	10.8	7.4	11.3	51.5
Oil & gas	2111	5.2	10.5	12.7	8.1	10.1	25.0
Basic chemicals	3251	6.1	6.3	6.5	6.4	8.4	31.4
Pharmaceuticals and medicines	3254	4.0	4.2	3.7	4.1	7.8	89.6
Resin, synthetic rubber, artificial and synthetic fibers and filaments	3252	5.8	5.9	5.7	5.1	7.4	44.8
Plastics products	3261	4.9	5.9	6.2	6.1	7.1	16.8
Agriculture, construction, and mining machinery	3331	7.4	6.9	7.0	5.5	7.0	29.1
Aerospace products & parts	3364	4.7	7.2	8.4	6.0	5.8	-2.8
IMPORTS FROM MEXICO [2]							
Total imports [3]	(X)	**230.0**	**296.4**	**356.1**	**323.5**	**384.6**	**18.9**
Motor vehicles	3361	27.5	50.0	70.7	56.2	62.1	10.5
Motor vehicle parts	3363	23.6	43.9	50.1	43.3	50.5	16.7
Computer & peripheral equipment	3341	13.2	17.1	27.9	27.0	29.1	7.9
Audio & video equipment	3343	16.5	14.5	12.4	12.7	15.6	23.1
Electrical equipment	3353	6.8	10.5	12.4	11.6	13.6	17.0
Oil and gas	2111	29.7	12.5	12.1	8.7	13.1	50.5
Communications equipment	3342	14.1	13.3	9.1	8.8	9.6	9.3
Beverages	3121	2.6	4.2	6.3	7.6	9.5	24.7
Navigational, measuring, electromedical, and control instruments	3345	5.0	8.4	9.6	8.1	9.0	11.6
Fruits and tree nuts	1113	2.4	4.7	7.6	7.4	8.9	19.6
EXPORTS TO MEXICO							
Total exports [3]	(X)	**131.8**	**186.0**	**195.8**	**158.9**	**216.7**	**36.4**
Petroleum & coal products	3241	12.0	15.4	28.1	17.1	27.8	62.1
Motor vehicle parts	3363	12.6	17.6	16.5	12.9	14.5	12.8
Oil & gas	2111	2.0	3.0	6.1	5.9	13.9	135.0
Basic chemicals	3251	7.0	8.3	9.6	8.7	11.9	36.9
Resin, synthetic rubber, artificial and synthetic fibers and filaments	3252	6.2	7.9	7.8	6.8	10.4	52.4
Oilseeds & grains	1111	4.5	4.9	6.0	5.8	9.2	58.6
Engines, turbines, & power transmission equipment	3336	3.3	5.2	7.2	5.6	7.3	30.3
Plastics products	3261	4.2	6.5	6.3	5.6	6.4	14.5
Iron and steel and ferroalloy	3311	2.8	4.2	4.0	3.1	5.0	63.1
Meat products and meat packaging products	3116	3.1	3.9	4.0	3.5	4.9	40.2

X Not applicable. [1] Based on the North American Industry Classification System (NAICS); see text, Section 15. [2] Imports classified as general imports. For definition of general imports, see Text, this section. [3] Includes items not shown separately.

Source: U.S. International Trade Commission, "Interactive Tariff and Trade DataWeb," <dataweb.usitc.gov/>, accessed September 2022.

Table 1329. U.S. Trade in Processed Foods By Commodity: 2000 to 2021

[Units as indicated. Includes Puerto Rico, U.S. territories, and shipments under foreign aid programs. Metric ton = 1.102 short tons or .984 long tons. In January 2021, the U.S. Department of Agriculture adopted the World Trade Organization (WTO) definitions of agricultural products and revised historical data to reflect the new definitions; therefore, data here may not be comparable to data presented in previous editions. See source for details]

Product category	Units	2000	2010	2019	2020	2021
Processed foods imports, total [1, 2]	**Metric tons**	**11,107,438**	**16,896,934**	**24,626,229**	**25,282,610**	**27,605,727**
Chocolate and confectionery [2]	Metric tons	858,136	1,362,569	1,719,559	1,715,887	1,858,626
Chocolate	Metric tons	525,437	820,017	1,018,298	1,014,814	1,060,940
Sugar confectionery	Metric tons	293,105	499,236	666,894	673,395	765,343
Condiments and sauces	Metric tons	351,000	569,652	863,046	1,003,855	1,078,028
Fats and oils [2]	Metric tons	1,686,891	3,497,902	5,223,694	5,151,701	5,693,301
Olive oil	Metric tons	203,960	275,435	347,306	408,032	377,175
Soybean oil	1,000 kilograms	35,949	53,697	169,444	134,498	152,415
Vegetable oils (excl. soybean)	Metric tons	1,427,711	3,075,082	4,478,524	4,382,119	4,877,789
Food preparations [2]	Metric tons	1,111,342	2,052,605	2,983,330	3,052,905	3,289,723
Baking inputs, mixes, and types of dough [3]	Metric tons	682,340	1,097,081	1,748,649	1,835,702	1,887,253
Non-alcoholic beverages [2]	Kiloliters	3,689,991	5,552,744	6,720,272	6,382,103	7,378,494
Bottled drinks [4]	Kiloliters	555,954	1,222,531	2,152,077	2,400,813	2,698,511
Juices	Kiloliters	3,134,037	4,330,213	4,568,195	3,981,290	4,679,983
Alcoholic beverages	Kiloliters	2,818,882	4,115,172	5,581,129	5,775,864	6,363,730
Beer	Kiloliters	2,331,185	3,146,395	4,225,392	4,262,148	4,623,437
Wine	Kiloliters	439,989	932,137	1,207,147	1,219,966	1,388,085
Pasta and processed cereals [2]	Metric tons	517,471	881,572	1,518,070	1,681,166	1,647,592
Breakfast cereals and other breakfast products	Metric tons	113,024	277,763	735,632	684,757	788,009
Pasta	Metric tons	316,886	367,974	494,398	658,825	553,590
Prepared/preserved meats	Metric tons	197,083	143,248	208,734	219,758	252,638
Prepared/preserved seafood	Metric tons	889,804	1,306,813	1,457,907	1,559,695	1,745,504
Processed fruit	Metric tons	865,350	1,422,793	1,929,467	2,012,182	2,167,470
Processed vegetables and pulses [2]	Metric tons	1,695,961	2,455,785	3,271,623	3,567,249	3,870,951
Frozen potato products [5]	Metric tons	527,642	725,033	1,030,034	1,134,344	1,293,145
Processed/prepared dairy products [2]	Metric tons	245,530	230,269	370,654	366,450	397,903
Cheese	Metric tons	188,707	138,539	179,796	165,970	187,663
Cream & powdered/condensed milk	Metric tons	18,897	33,250	44,663	49,441	35,645
Ice cream	Metric tons	9,151	30,263	29,283	41,015	67,617
Yogurt and dairy drinks	Liters	23,060	11,197	1,814,124	693,032	715,589
Snack foods	Metric tons	627,030	1,126,307	2,033,482	2,156,191	2,450,349
Baked snack foods [6]	Metric tons	480,515	899,781	1,832,893	1,938,978	2,182,112
Mixes of nuts and fruit [7]	Metric tons	92,782	156,182	97,882	107,843	144,830
Potato chips	Metric tons	23,758	40,569	56,859	64,723	70,497
Prepared peanuts and peanut butter	Metric tons	29,976	29,774	45,848	44,647	52,910
Spices	Metric tons	243,766	360,962	492,558	538,747	570,719
Syrups and sweeteners [2]	Metric tons	1,106,543	866,613	1,281,877	1,107,885	1,208,306
Fructose and fructose syrup	Metric tons	66,513	92,496	107,188	99,489	112,927
Glucose and glucose syrup	Metric tons	113,647	217,058	308,857	268,731	306,583
Processed foods exports, total [2]	**Metric tons**	**10,910,343**	**17,721,588**	**19,565,459**	**19,870,918**	**20,127,550**
Chocolate and confectionery [2]	Metric tons	302,600	420,212	494,698	442,862	499,613
Chocolate	Metric tons	192,742	303,757	353,122	321,128	357,341
Sugar confectionery	Metric tons	98,043	108,527	134,430	117,682	136,872
Condiments and sauces	Metric tons	363,963	638,943	969,178	914,600	997,570
Fats and oils [2]	Metric tons	1,931,660	3,280,825	2,055,132	2,458,702	2,033,904
Soybean oil	1,000 kilograms	586,786	1,656,926	956,519	1,237,220	715,602
Vegetable oils (excl. soybean)	Metric tons	1,044,199	1,066,611	662,599	590,546	560,905
Food preparations [2]	Metric tons	2,492,061	3,397,278	4,846,460	5,068,850	4,915,312
Baking inputs, mixes, and types of dough [3]	Metric tons	1,904,460	2,280,017	3,605,751	3,981,800	3,638,490
Non-alcoholic beverages [2]	Kiloliters	1,661,547	1,617,263	1,099,593	1,090,148	1,144,460
Bottled drinks [4]	Kiloliters	487,448	636,964	628,298	639,022	689,001
Juices	Kiloliters	1,174,098	980,299	471,295	451,126	455,460
Alcoholic beverages	Kiloliters	550,712	727,964	891,283	740,376	744,425
Beer	Kiloliters	262,305	320,694	517,901	366,148	405,783
Wine	Kiloliters	264,523	383,301	350,093	353,694	318,360
Pasta and processed cereals [2]	Metric tons	683,017	983,674	758,696	819,216	769,634
Breakfast cereals and other breakfast products	Metric tons	265,399	568,666	414,320	458,120	423,202
Pasta	Metric tons	102,295	181,765	176,190	194,595	199,274
Prepared/preserved meats	Metric tons	313,841	643,614	656,582	614,689	719,193
Prepared/preserved seafood	Metric tons	501,314	533,726	501,327	426,845	458,565
Processed fruit	Metric tons	388,844	571,165	488,670	456,946	484,100
Processed vegetables and pulses [2]	Metric tons	1,272,076	1,679,157	2,393,542	2,152,779	2,297,058
Frozen potato products [5]	Metric tons	568,709	790,607	1,164,372	970,716	1,106,306
Processed/prepared dairy products [2]	Metric tons	398,655	1,179,545	1,628,056	1,826,253	2,039,973
Cheese	Metric tons	47,760	173,327	356,515	355,508	402,457
Cream & powdered/condensed milk	Metric tons	114,847	466,853	757,215	859,542	936,896
Ice cream	Metric tons	41,652	35,680	72,303	72,195	73,833
Snack foods	Metric tons	490,079	784,168	1,001,648	960,954	1,018,798
Baked snack foods [6]	Metric tons	274,577	476,137	684,028	653,549	677,350
Mixes of nuts and fruit [7]	Metric tons	72,748	160,303	141,288	141,189	168,494
Potato chips	Metric tons	106,040	86,510	97,358	93,168	96,094
Prepared peanuts and peanut butter	Metric tons	36,713	61,218	78,974	73,049	76,860
Soups	1,000 kilograms	97,212	140,420	255,917	310,469	264,130
Syrups and sweeteners [2]	Metric tons	726,427	2,525,583	2,197,628	2,050,169	2,047,203
Fructose and fructose syrup	Metric tons	322,904	1,395,278	1,292,452	1,178,210	1,073,201
Glucose and glucose syrup	Metric tons	209,686	738,966	423,632	382,595	454,584
Molasses	Kiloliters	199,070	203,841	39,275	61,582	11,631

[1] Imports for consumption. Excludes merchandise entered into bonded warehouses of Foreign Trade Zones under Customs custody; see source for details. [2] Includes commodities not shown separately. [3] Includes pudding. [4] Includes soda, juice mixes, beer, milk-based drinks, etc. [5] Includes French fries. [6] Pastries, pretzels, corn chips, etc. [7] Includes packaged and microwaveable popcorn.

Source: U.S. Department of Agriculture, Foreign Agricultural Service, "Global Agricultural Trade System," <apps.fas.usda.gov/gats/default.aspx>, accessed August 2022.

Section 29
Puerto Rico and the Island Areas

This section presents summary economic and social statistics for Puerto Rico, the U.S. Virgin Islands, Guam, American Samoa, and the Northern Mariana Islands. Primary sources include the decennial censuses of population and housing and the annual Puerto Rico Community Survey conducted by the U.S. Census Bureau; County Business Patterns and other Census Bureau publications and databases; and the *National Vital Statistics Reports* (NSVR) series, issued by the National Center for Health Statistics; and the *Informe Económico al Gobernadora/Economic Report to the Governor issued by the Gobierno De Puerto Rico, Junta de Planificación [Puerto Rico Planning Board]*.

Jurisdiction—The United States gained jurisdiction over these areas as follows: the islands of Puerto Rico and Guam, surrendered by Spain in December 1898, were ceded to the United States by the Treaty of Paris, ratified in 1899. Puerto Rico became a commonwealth on July 25, 1952, thereby achieving a high degree of local autonomy under its own constitution. The U.S. Virgin Islands, comprising approximately 50 islands and cays, was purchased by the United States from Denmark in 1917. American Samoa, a group of seven islands, was acquired in accordance with a convention among the United States, Great Britain, and Germany, ratified in 1900 (Swains Island was annexed in 1925). By an agreement approved by the United Nations Security Council and the United States, the Northern Mariana Islands, previously under Japanese mandate, was administered by the United States between 1947 and 1986 under the United Nations trusteeship system. The Northern Mariana Islands became a U.S. commonwealth in 1986.

Censuses—Because characteristics of Puerto Rico and the Island Areas differ, the presentation of census data for them is not uniform. The 1960 Census of Population covered all the territories listed above except the Northern Mariana Islands (their census was conducted in April 1958 by the Office of the High Commissioner of the Trust Territory of the Pacific Islands), while the 1960 Census of Housing excluded American Samoa. The 1970, 1980, 1990, 2000, and 2010 censuses of population and housing covered all five areas. Beginning in 1967, Congress authorized the Economic Censuses, to be taken at 5-year intervals, for years ending in "2" and "7." Prior economic censuses were conducted in Puerto Rico for 1949, 1954, 1958, and 1963 and in Guam and the U.S. Virgin Islands for 1958 and 1963. In 1967, the census of construction industries was added for the first time in Puerto Rico; in 1972, the U.S. Virgin Islands and Guam were covered; and in 1982, the Economic Census was taken for the first time for the Northern Mariana Islands. Agricultural censuses have been conducted with increasing regularity in Puerto Rico since 1910, in the U.S. Virgin Islands since 1917, and in Guam and American Samoa since 1920; the first agricultural census in the Northern Mariana Islands was conducted in 1970.

Puerto Rico Community Survey—The Puerto Rico Community Survey (PRCS) began in 2005 and was an important element in the Census Bureau's re-engineered 2010 census plan. The American Community Survey (ACS) is the equivalent of the PRCS for the United States (50 states and District of Columbia). The PRCS collects and produces population and housing information every year instead of every 10 years. About 36,000 households are surveyed each year from across every municipio in Puerto Rico.

Information in other sections—In addition to the statistics presented in this section, other data on Puerto Rico and the island areas are included in many tables showing distribution by states in various sections of the *Abstract*. See "Puerto Rico" and "Island Areas of the U.S." in the Index.

Selected Island Areas of the United States

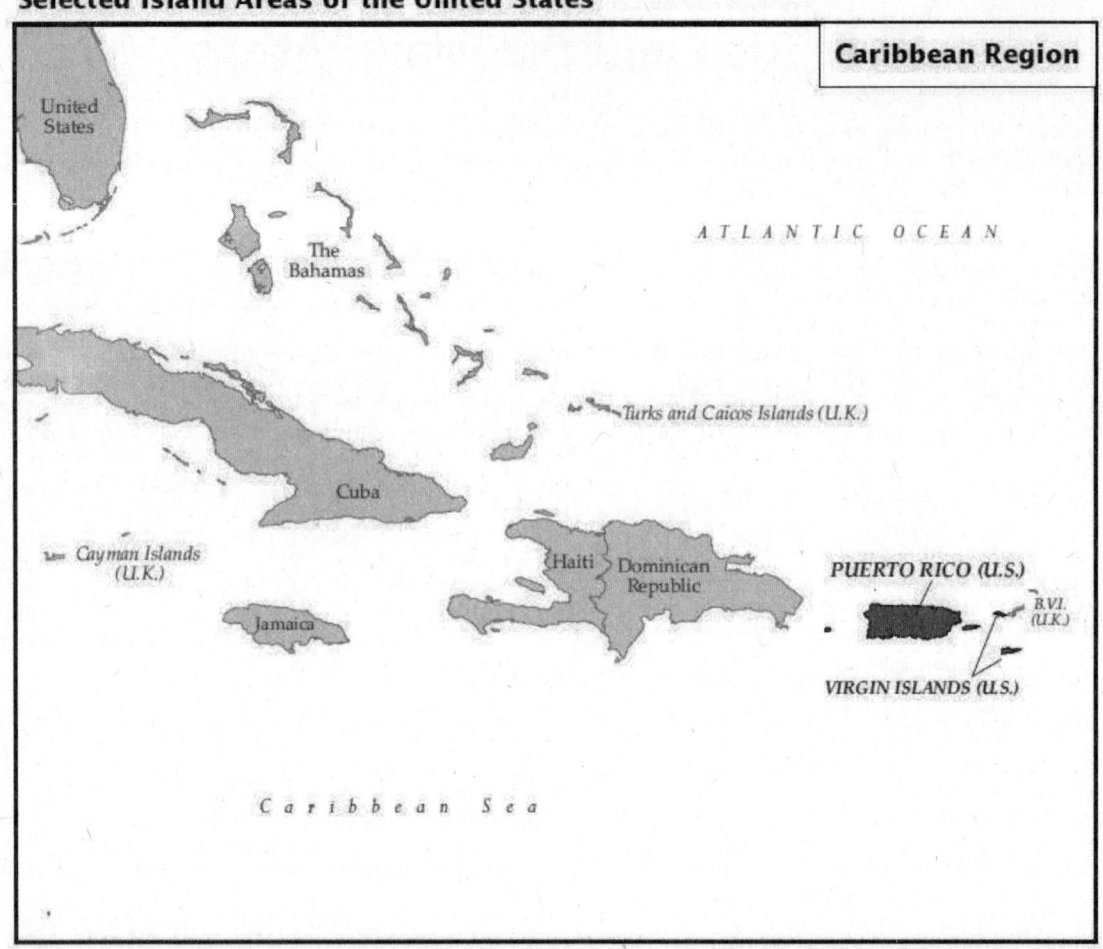

Caribbean Region

United States

ATLANTIC OCEAN

The Bahamas

Turks and Caicos Islands (U.K.)

Cuba

Cayman Islands (U.K.)

Haiti

Dominican Republic

Jamaica

PUERTO RICO (U.S.)

B.V.I. (U.K.)

VIRGIN ISLANDS (U.S.)

Caribbean Sea

Pacific Region

NORTHERN MARIANA ISLANDS (U.S.)

• *Wake Island (U.S.)*

Johnston Atoll (U.S.)•

GUAM (U.S.)

PACIFIC OCEAN

Federated States of Micronesia

Marshall Islands

Kingman Reef (U.S.)

Palmyra Atoll (U.S.) •

Kiribati

Nauru

Howland Island (U.S.)

Baker Island (U.S.)

Papua New Guinea

Solomon Islands

Tuvalu

Vanuatu

Coral Sea

Samoa

AMERICAN SAMOA (U.S.)

Australia

Fiji

Table 1330. Estimated and Projected Resident Population of Puerto Rico and Island Areas: 2000 to 2040

[In thousands (58 represents 58,000). Population as of July 1. Population data generally are de facto figures for the present territory. For details of methodology, coverage, and reliability, see source]

Area	2000	2010	2015	2018	2019	2020	2021	Projected		
								2030	2035	2040
American Samoa...............	58	56	52	49	48	47	46	40	38	35
Guam.........................	155	163	166	168	168	168	169	170	169	167
Northern Mariana Islands......	70	55	53	52	52	52	52	50	49	48
Puerto Rico....................	3,811	3,722	3,473	3,295	3,241	3,190	3,143	2,818	2,646	2,469
Virgin Islands..................	109	108	108	107	107	106	106	100	96	92

Source: U.S. Census Bureau, "International Data Base (IDB)," <www.census.gov/data-tools/demo/idb/>, accessed June 2022.

Table 1331. Births, Deaths, and Infant Deaths for Puerto Rico and the Island Areas: 2000 to 2020

[Births, deaths, and infant deaths by place of residence. Rates for 2000 and 2010 based on population enumerated as of April 1; for other years, on population estimated as of July 1]

Area and year	Births		Deaths		Infant deaths	
	Number	Rate [1]	Number	Rate [2]	Number	Rate [3]
Puerto Rico:						
2000.............................	59,333	15.6	28,365	7.4	574	9.7
2010.............................	42,153	11.3	29,153	7.8	341	8.1
2015.............................	31,157	9.0	28,085	8.1	218	7.0
2019.............................	20,353	6.4	29,362	9.2	133	6.5
2020.............................	18,933	6.0	(NA)	(NA)	(NA)	(NA)
Guam:						
2000.............................	3,766	24.2	648	4.2	22	5.8
2010.............................	3,416	21.4	857	5.4	48	14.1
2015.............................	3,366	20.8	985	6.1	47	14.0
2019.............................	3,041	18.1	1,002	6.0	30	9.9
2020.............................	2,935	17.4	(NA)	(NA)	(NA)	(NA)
Virgin Islands:						
2000.............................	1,564	14.4	641	5.9	21	13.4
2010.............................	1,600	15.1	715	6.7	13	(B)
2015.............................	1,325	12.8	673	6.5	4	(B)
2019.............................	(NA)	(NA)	(NA)	(NA)	(NA)	(NA)
2020.............................	876	8.2	(NA)	(NA)	(NA)	(NA)
American Samoa:						
2000.............................	1,731	30.0	219	3.8	11	(B)
2010.............................	1,234	22.2	224	4.0	14	(B)
2015.............................	1,078	19.8	303	5.6	10	(B)
2019.............................	(NA)	(NA)	(NA)	(NA)	(NA)	(NA)
2020.............................	(NA)	(NA)	(NA)	(NA)	(NA)	(NA)
Northern Marianas:						
2000.............................	1,431	20.5	136	2.0	11	(B)
2010.............................	1,072	20.0	174	3.3	4	(B)
2015.............................	427	8.2	223	4.3	5	(B)
2019.............................	686	13.3	209	4.0	4	(B)
2020.............................	628	12.1	(NA)	(NA)	(NA)	(NA)

NA Not available. B Base figure too small to meet statistical standards of reliability. [1] Birth rates are births per 1,000 women of child-bearing age. [2] Death rates are deaths per 1,000 population. [3] Infant death rates are infant deaths (under 1 year old) per 1,000 live births.

Source: U.S. National Center for Health Statistics, National Vital Statistics Reports (NVSR), *Births: Final Data for 2020*, Vol. 70, No. 17, February 2022, and earlier reports; and *Deaths: Final Data for 2019*, Vol. 70, No. 8, July 2021, and earlier reports. See also <www.cdc.gov/nchs/nvss/index.htm>.

Table 1332. Public Elementary and Secondary Education by Island Area: 2019

[Enrollment and staff are for Fall of year shown. Revenues and expenditures are for school year ending in year shown]

Item	Puerto Rico	Guam	U.S. Virgin Islands	American Samoa	Northern Marianas
Enrollment......	292,518	28,812	10,907	10,448	[3] 10,638
Elementary (pre-kindergarten to grade 8 and ungraded).......	198,918	19,611	7,457	6,760	[3] 7,340
Secondary (grades 9 to 12 and ungraded)......................	93,600	9,201	3,450	3,688	[3] 3,298
Total staff........	34,644	3,755	2,079	(NA)	[3] 876
School district staff.....................	1,421	329	143	(NA)	[3] 98
School staff........	27,975	3,144	1,466	(NA)	[3] 679
Teachers........	24,840	2,119	976	(NA)	[3] 417
Student support staff.................	1,386	132	35	(NA)	[3] 22
Other support services staff................	3,862	150	435	(NA)	[3] 77
Revenues, total [1] ($1,000)...........	2,580,472	314,990	216,965	77,018	89,071
Current expenditures [2] ($1,000).................	2,420,595	293,766	178,471	65,702	89,470
Per pupil [2] (dollars)............	7,877	9,885	16,651	5,427	[4] 5,875

NA Not available. [1] Includes federal, territorial, local, and private revenues. [2] Includes current expenditures only, and excludes capital expenditures, interest on school debt, community services, private school programs, adult education, and other expenditures not directly allocable to public school operations. [3] 2013 data. [4] 2014 data.

Source: U.S. National Center for Education Statistics, *Digest of Education Statistics*, "Latest version of all Digest tables," <nces.ed.gov/programs/digest>, accessed July 2022.

Table 1333. Puerto Rico—Selected Social, Demographic, and Housing Characteristics: 2010 and 2019

[The Puerto Rico Community Survey universe includes the household population and the population living in institutions, college dormitories, and other group quarters. Based on a sample and subject to sampling variability; see text, this section and Appendix III]

Characteristic	2010 Number	2010 Percent	2019 Number	2019 Percent
Total population	**3,722,133**	**100.0**	**3,193,694**	**100.0**
SEX				
Male	1,785,266	48.0	1,515,994	47.5
Female	1,936,867	52.0	1,677,700	52.5
AGE				
Under 5 years	223,247	6.0	115,403	3.6
5 to 9 years	236,531	6.4	153,900	4.8
10 to 14 years	268,378	7.2	189,662	5.9
15 to 19 years	284,254	7.6	208,460	6.5
20 to 24 years	264,790	7.1	224,534	7.0
25 to 34 years	482,756	13.0	385,530	12.1
35 to 44 years	487,539	13.1	395,192	12.4
45 to 54 years	486,273	13.1	412,923	12.9
55 to 59 years	219,460	5.9	215,519	6.7
60 to 64 years	223,184	6.0	212,906	6.7
65 to 74 years	313,604	8.4	366,492	11.5
75 to 84 years	170,712	4.6	226,345	7.1
85 years and over	61,405	1.6	86,828	2.7
MARITAL STATUS				
Males 15 years and over	**1,410,023**	**100.0**	**1,283,894**	**100.0**
Never married	566,489	40.2	581,268	45.3
Married, not separated	610,584	43.3	480,526	37.4
Separated	39,169	2.8	25,911	2.0
Widowed	39,752	2.8	47,508	3.7
Divorced	154,029	10.9	148,681	11.6
Females 15 years and over	**1,583,954**	**100.0**	**1,450,835**	**100.0**
Never married	523,558	33.1	553,498	38.2
Married, not separated	601,632	38.0	473,972	32.7
Separated	50,458	3.2	39,387	2.7
Widowed	171,416	10.8	168,033	11.6
Divorced	236,890	15.0	215,945	14.9
HOUSEHOLDS				
Total households	**1,319,448**	**100.0**	**1,170,982**	**100.0**
Family households (families)	966,123	73.2	(NA)	(NA)
With own children under 18 years	405,933	30.8	(NA)	(NA)
Married-couple families	557,851	42.3	431,179	36.8
With own children under 18 years	200,406	15.2	108,308	9.2
Cohabiting couple household	(NA)	(NA)	112,764	9.6
With own children under 18 years	(NA)	(NA)	50,043	4.3
Male householder, no spouse/partner present	82,129	6.2	196,518	16.8
With own children under 18 years	39,285	3.0	7,902	0.7
Female householder, no spouse/partner present	326,143	24.7	430,521	36.8
With own children under 18 years	166,242	12.6	96,207	8.2
Nonfamily households	353,325	26.8	(NA)	(NA)
Householder living alone	306,036	23.2	343,642	29.4
65 years and over	125,754	9.5	175,773	15.0
Average household size	2.79	(X)	2.70	(X)
Average family size	3.28	(X)	3.38	(X)
DISABILITY STATUS				
Total civilian noninstitutionalized population	**3,695,636**	**100.0**	**3,169,528**	**100.0**
With a disability	726,334	19.7	684,955	21.6

X Not applicable. NA Not available.

Source: U.S. Census Bureau, 2019 Puerto Rico Community Survey, DP02PR, "Selected Social Characteristics in Puerto Rico," and DP05, "Demographic and Housing Estimates," <data.census.gov>, accessed May 2021. See also <www.census.gov/programs-surveys/acs/about/puerto-rico-community-survey.html>.

Table 1334. Puerto Rico—Owner and Renter Occupied Housing by Household Type: 2019

[The Puerto Rico Community Survey universe includes the household population and the population living in institutions, college dormitories, and other group quarters. Based on a sample and subject to sampling variability; see text, this section and Appendix III]

Household type	Owner occupied	Renter occupied	Household type	Owner occupied	Renter occupied
Total households	**803,460**	**367,522**			
Family households	**557,007**	**216,791**	Householder 15 to 34 years	9,381	39,626
Married-couple family	359,067	72,112	Householder 35 to 64 years	93,273	63,170
Householder 15 to 34 years	14,002	14,697	Householder 65 years and over	50,048	12,157
Householder 35 to 64 years	204,068	44,647	**Nonfamily households**	**246,453**	**150,731**
Householder 65 years and over	140,997	12,768	Householder living alone	215,629	128,013
Other family	197,940	144,679	Householder 15 to 34 years	5,429	16,978
Male householder, no wife present	45,238	29,726	Householder 35 to 64 years	83,616	61,846
Householder 15 to 34 years	4,944	10,576	Householder 65 years and over	126,584	49,189
Householder 35 to 64 years	27,379	15,964	Householder not living alone	30,824	22,718
Householder 65 years and over	12,915	3,186	Householder 15 to 34 years	2,008	9,427
Female householder,			Householder 35 to 64 years	17,950	11,374
no husband present	152,702	114,953	Householder 65 years and over	10,866	1,917

Source: U.S. Census Bureau, 2019 Puerto Rico Community Survey, B25011, "Tenure by Household Type and Age of Householder," <data.census.gov/>, accessed June 2021. See also <www.census.gov/programs-surveys/acs/about/puerto-rico-community-survey.html>.

Table 1335. Puerto Rico—Socioeconomic Summary: 2000 to 2020

[3,805 represents 3,805,000. Data are for fiscal years]

Item	Unit	2000	2010	2015	2016	2017	2018	2019	2020 (P)
POPULATION									
Total [1]	1,000	3,805	3,731	3,504	3,440	3,366	3,259	3,194	3,240
Persons per family	Number	3.4	3.0	2.9	2.8	2.8	2.7	2.7	2.8
LABOR FORCE									
Total [2]	1,000	1,292	1,284	1,121	1,122	1,111	1,080	1,087	1,077
Employed [3]	1,000	1,150	1,075	977	989	982	968	995	986
Agriculture [4]	1,000	24	18	16	16	18	16	14	16
Manufacturing	1,000	158	101	81	84	79	88	100	100
Trade	1,000	237	238	237	235	228	237	244	232
Services	1,000	304	319	330	347	348	324	333	347
Government	1,000	247	249	197	188	197	191	175	167
Unemployed	1,000	142	209	144	132	128	111	92	91
Unemployment rate [5]	Rate	11.0	16.3	12.8	11.8	11.5	10.3	8.4	8.4
Compensation of employees	Mil. dol.	23,504	29,870	28,874	28,572	28,484	27,859	27,524	27,948
Average compensation	Dollar	20,438	27,786	29,554	28,890	29,006	28,780	27,662	28,345
Salary and wages	Mil. dol.	20,489	25,793	24,768	24,347	24,287	23,979	23,902	24,358
INCOME									
Personal income:									
Current dollars	Mil. dol.	38,856	59,983	63,756	63,601	64,863	70,148	68,163	71,080
Constant (1954) dollars	Mil. dol.	8,491	9,958	9,726	9,530	9,411	9,970	9,532	9,252
Disposable personal income:									
Current dollars	Mil. dol.	36,239	57,111	61,238	61,359	62,656	67,944	65,557	68,912
Constant (1954) dollars	Mil. dol.	7,919	9,481	9,342	9,194	9,091	9,657	9,168	8,970
Average family income:									
Current dollars	Dollar	34,717	48,231	52,766	51,769	53,956	58,116	57,621	61,427
Constant (1954) dollars	Dollar	7,587	8,007	8,050	7,756	7,829	8,260	8,058	7,995
TOURISM									
Number of visitors	1,000	4,566	4,379	5,051	5,002	4,927	4,260	4,930	3,882
Visitor expenditures	Mil. dol.	2,388	3,211	3,825	3,974	3,868	3,303	3,612	2,921
Average per visitor	Dollar	523	733	757	794	785	775	733	752

P Preliminary. [1] Average of population estimates at the beginning and end of the fiscal year. Intercensal data released July 2019 and Decennial Census 2020 (U.S. Bureau of the Census, Population Division, Population Estimates, Vintage 2019 and 2020-apportionment-data). Data gathered from <www.census.gov>. [2] For population 16 years old and over. [3] Includes employment in other industries, not shown separately. [4] Includes forestry and fisheries. [5] Unemployed as percent of the labor force.

Source: Puerto Rico Planning Board, San Juan, PR, *Informe Económico al Gobernador Puerto Rico 2020/Economic Report for the Governor 2020*, April 2021, and earlier reports. See also <jp.gobierno.pr/Econom%C3%ADa>.

Table 1336. Puerto Rico—School Enrollment and Educational Attainment by Level: 2005 to 2019

[The Puerto Rico Community Survey universe includes the household population and the population living in institutions, college dormitories, and other group quarters. Based on a sample and subject to sampling variability; see text, this section and Appendix III]

Item	2005	2010	2015	2016	2017	2018	2019
EDUCATIONAL ENROLLMENT							
Population 3 years and over enrolled in school	1,138,768	995,743	892,872	846,874	804,711	742,847	747,920
Nursery school, preschool	69,731	55,298	52,792	48,916	45,061	35,928	34,961
Kindergarten	52,261	45,366	37,989	36,227	33,751	27,389	26,301
Elementary school (grades 1-8)	486,546	414,233	340,580	320,223	307,128	289,314	279,078
High school (grades 9-12)	242,548	213,581	189,446	179,748	168,446	153,451	154,094
College or graduate school	287,682	267,265	272,065	261,760	250,325	236,765	253,486
EDUCATIONAL ATTAINMENT							
Population 25 years and over	2,431,653	2,444,933	2,382,526	2,372,197	2,343,675	2,288,030	2,301,735
Less than 9th grade	547,055	484,138	391,558	370,922	370,702	336,242	320,083
9th to 12th grade, no diploma	269,039	262,682	210,220	207,689	188,871	178,663	168,325
High school graduate (includes equivalency)	588,130	623,709	647,581	657,523	653,789	644,702	648,146
Some college, no degree	290,283	317,797	314,431	298,426	285,018	276,042	279,696
Associate's degree	231,848	212,186	228,508	237,746	242,776	241,678	258,905
Bachelor's degree	377,437	389,954	424,255	433,120	428,558	430,692	443,589
Graduate or professional degree	127,861	154,467	165,973	166,771	173,961	180,011	182,991
Percent high school graduate or higher	66.4	69.5	74.7	75.6	76.1	77.5	78.8
Percent bachelor's degree or higher	20.8	22.3	24.8	25.3	25.7	26.7	27.2

Source: U.S. Census Bureau, 2019 Puerto Rico Community Survey, DP02PR, "Selected Social Characteristics in Puerto Rico," <data.census.gov>, accessed May 2021. See also <census.gov/programs-surveys/acs/about/puerto-rico-community-survey.html>.

Table 1337. Puerto Rico—Gross Product and Net Income: 2010 to 2020

[In millions of dollars (64,295 represents $64,295,000,000). For fiscal years ending June 30. Minus sign (-) indicates decrease]

Item	2010	2015	2016	2017	2018	2019	2020 (P)
Gross product [1]	**64,295**	**69,602**	**69,985**	**69,050**	**67,740**	**70,765**	**70,187**
Manufacturing	46,577	49,520	50,544	48,966	48,192	49,581	49,757
Wholesale trade	2,993	2,794	2,781	2,665	2,691	2,771	2,769
Retail trade	4,473	4,908	5,074	5,452	5,594	6,054	5,839
Information	2,646	2,699	2,959	1,985	1,486	1,511	1,573
Finance and insurance	5,241	4,617	4,495	4,371	4,034	4,023	4,759
Real estate and rental	13,785	15,301	15,757	15,987	16,555	17,154	17,100
Health care and social services	3,294	3,828	3,836	3,894	3,752	3,936	3,948
Government	8,350	7,264	7,236	7,175	6,343	5,861	5,318
Commonwealth	6,862	5,741	5,686	5,626	4,946	4,597	4,048
Municipalities	1,488	1,523	1,550	1,549	1,397	1,264	1,271
Rest of the world	-34,087	-33,774	-34,352	-34,396	-33,186	-34,150	-32,951
Statistical discrepancy	-294	371	-318	529	-306	549	-609
Net income [1]	**50,246**	**55,995**	**56,192**	**54,284**	**54,090**	**55,807**	**57,323**
Manufacturing	43,292	45,893	46,640	45,119	44,460	45,801	46,296
Wholesale trade	2,352	2,238	2,315	2,316	2,313	2,376	2,398
Retail trade	3,803	4,260	4,373	4,697	4,836	5,247	5,102
Information	1,244	1,340	1,371	503	300	308	417
Finance and insurance	2,410	3,074	3,008	3,008	2,739	2,729	3,492
Real estate and rental	10,689	12,251	12,360	12,343	12,774	13,144	13,313
Health care and social services	2,775	3,320	3,305	3,352	3,225	3,380	3,438
Government	8,350	7,264	7,236	7,175	6,343	5,861	5,318
Commonwealth	6,862	5,741	5,686	5,626	4,946	4,597	4,048
Municipalities	1,488	1,523	1,550	1,549	1,397	1,264	1,271
Rest of the world	-34,087	-33,774	-34,352	-34,396	-33,186	-34,150	-32,951

P Preliminary. [1] Includes all other industries not elsewhere classified.

Source: Puerto Rico Planning Board, San Juan, PR, *Informe Económico al Gobernador 2020/Economic Report to the Governor 2020*, April 2021, and earlier reports. See also <jp.gobierno.pr/Econom%C3%ADa>.

Table 1338. Puerto Rico—Transfer Payments: 2000 to 2020

[8,659 represents $8,659,000,000. Data represent transfer payments between federal and state governments and other nonresidents]

Item	2000	2005	2010	2015	2018	2019	2020 (P)
Total receipts	**8,659**	**10,551**	**16,504**	**18,017**	**23,383**	**23,154**	**25,501**
Federal government	7,966	9,673	15,585	17,091	22,640	22,036	25,030
Transfers to individuals [1]	7,868	9,547	15,352	16,863	22,389	21,751	24,744
Veterans benefits	491	491	733	1,416	1,170	1,222	2,636
Medicare	1,196	1,825	2,529	4,467	6,526	5,221	5,939
Social security	3,863	5,118	7,074	7,718	7,202	6,784	5,679
Nutritional assistance	1,193	1,306	1,605	1,846	2,282	2,728	2,324
Industry subsidies	98	127	233	228	251	285	286
U.S. state governments	15	15	29	34	30	22	17
Other nonresidents	679	863	890	892	713	1,095	453
Total payments	**2,763**	**3,583**	**3,804**	**3,961**	**4,218**	**4,484**	**4,285**
Federal government	2,693	3,516	3,586	3,844	4,073	4,348	4,123
Transfers from individuals [1]	1,326	1,792	1,862	1,984	2,098	2,145	2,067
Contribution to Medicare	191	303	392	464	560	535	624
Employee contributions to social security systems	1,133	1,483	1,467	1,516	1,534	1,607	1,441
Transfers from industries	51	74	93	133	114	216	223
Unemployment insurance	234	221	207	248	364	419	470
Employer contributions to social security systems	1,081	1,429	1,424	1,479	1,497	1,568	1,363
Other nonresidents [2]	70	67	215	114	142	134	161
Net balance	**5,897**	**6,968**	**12,700**	**14,056**	**19,165**	**18,670**	**21,216**
Federal government	5,273	6,157	11,999	13,247	18,567	17,688	20,907
U.S. state governments	10	10	26	31	27	21	16
Other nonresidents	614	801	675	778	571	961	293

P Preliminary. [1] Includes other receipts and payments not shown separately. [2] Includes U.S. state governments.

Source: Puerto Rico Planning Board, San Juan, PR, *Informe Económico al Gobernador 2020/Economic Report to the Governor 2020*, April 2021, and earlier reports. See also <jp.gobierno.pr/Econom%C3%ADa>.

Table 1339. Puerto Rico—Merchandise Imports and Exports: 1990 to 2021

[In millions of dollars (16,200 represents $16,200,000,000). Data shown is trade for the San Juan, Puerto Rico Customs District. Imports are imports for consumption; see text, Section 28]

Item	1990	2000	2010	2013	2014	2015	2016	2017	2018	2019	2020	2021
Imports	16,200	27,006	39,766	43,811	42,768	42,288	45,833	41,950	52,887	46,550	42,540	47,244
From U.S.	10,792	15,172	20,641	20,314	20,848	22,882	25,151	23,160	26,994	23,560	23,135	26,522
From other	5,408	11,834	19,125	23,497	21,920	19,406	20,682	18,789	25,893	22,990	19,405	20,722
Exports	20,402	43,191	67,347	61,632	66,746	70,621	71,976	64,278	62,525	64,343	59,586	57,667
To U.S.	17,915	38,335	47,630	44,229	49,194	53,281	56,136	51,287	48,508	48,052	47,054	43,757
To other	2,487	4,856	19,717	17,404	17,552	17,339	15,840	12,991	14,018	16,292	12,532	13,910

Source: U.S. Census Bureau, Foreign Trade Division, *U.S. Trade with Puerto Rico and U.S. Possessions* (FT 895), 2021 and earlier reports; *U.S. Merchandise Trade: Selected Highlights* (FT 920), December 2011 and earlier reports; and "USA Trade Online," <usatrade.census.gov/>, accessed July 2022.

Table 1340. Puerto Rico—Exports and Imports of Goods and Services by Type of Product: 2012 to 2019

[In millions of current dollars (70,888 represents $70,888,000,000). Detail may not add to total because of rounding]

Type of product	2012	2013	2014	2015	2016	2017 (P)	2018 (P)	2019 (P)
Exports of goods and services........	**70,888**	**74,374**	**80,189**	**84,477**	**86,612**	**78,577**	**77,025**	**78,799**
Exports of goods....................	58,696	61,832	66,945	70,826	72,273	64,266	62,644	64,498
Foods, feeds, and beverages.........	3,708	4,095	4,224	4,565	4,654	4,028	1,055	1,085
Pharmaceuticals and organic chemicals [1].................	43,571	46,045	48,797	52,453	53,921	47,801	46,961	49,679
Consumer goods, except food, automotive, and pharmaceuticals. ..	3,562	3,868	5,935	6,284	5,507	4,918	5,690	5,445
Capital goods, including parts.........	5,172	5,334	5,452	5,411	5,811	5,400	6,486	6,251
All other..................................	2,685	2,489	2,537	2,113	2,379	2,118	2,451	2,038
Exports of services......................	12,192	12,542	13,244	13,651	14,339	14,311	14,381	14,301
Travel [2]................................	3,055	3,191	3,439	3,662	3,709	3,288	3,287	3,758
All other [3]...........................	9,137	9,351	9,805	9,990	10,630	11,023	11,094	10,543
Imports of goods and services........	**51,604**	**49,812**	**49,663**	**47,956**	**51,818**	**47,537**	**59,360**	**54,326**
Imports of goods......................	46,281	44,341	44,060	42,212	45,989	41,523	52,640	47,266
Foods, feeds, and beverages.........	4,457	4,527	4,563	4,636	4,412	4,471	4,571	4,400
Pharmaceuticals and organic chemicals [1].................	18,421	17,248	17,835	18,321	23,887	18,355	25,120	22,289
Petroleum and other energy products...............	7,339	6,529	6,238	4,066	3,237	3,884	4,468	4,198
Transportation equipment.............	2,519	2,570	2,098	2,148	2,389	2,755	3,556	3,151
Capital goods, except transportation equipment, including parts..........	4,566	4,313	4,693	4,808	4,125	4,296	5,170	4,634
All other..................................	8,980	9,154	8,632	8,233	7,939	7,763	9,755	8,594
Imports of services......................	5,323	5,471	5,603	5,744	5,829	6,014	6,720	7,060
Travel [2]................................	1,118	1,078	1,053	1,039	1,037	1,059	1,126	1,145
All other..................................	4,205	4,393	4,550	4,705	4,792	4,955	5,595	5,915
Addendum: Exports of medical and scientific equipment and appliances [4]..........	4,742	5,120	7,262	7,737	7,164	6,638	7,804	7,465

P Preliminary. [1] Includes medicinal and dental products. [2] For all purposes including education, business, and medical. Includes spending by nonresidents on travel and tourism, including passenger transportation services provided by domestic establishments. Other transportation services, such as freight charges on goods, are included in "all other" exports of services. [3] Includes computer services, such as software. [4] Includes consumer medical appliances embedded in "Consumer goods, except food, automotive, and pharmaceuticals;" and lab testing and control instruments and other scientific, medical, and hospital equipment embedded in "Capital goods, including parts."

Source: U.S. Bureau of Economic Analysis, "Gross Domestic Product for Puerto Rico, 2019," accessed February 2022. See also <www.bea.gov/data/gdp/gdp-puerto-rico>.

Table 1341. Puerto Rico—Gross Domestic Product: 2012 to 2019

[In millions of current dollars (103,481 represents $103,481,000,000). For definition of gross domestic product, see text, Section 13. Detail may not add to total because of rounding]

Item	2012	2013	2014	2015	2016	2017 (P)	2018 (P)	2019 (P)
Gross domestic product..............	**103,481**	**107,858**	**113,103**	**117,752**	**116,268**	**111,734**	**110,261**	**111,702**
Personal consumption expenditures......	55,367	56,227	56,013	55,700	55,755	55,458	58,131	57,742
Goods.....................................	23,463	23,777	23,328	23,395	23,706	24,013	26,019	25,182
Durable goods..........................	6,819	6,806	6,342	6,227	6,378	6,379	7,854	7,491
Nondurable goods.......................	16,644	16,971	16,986	17,168	17,327	17,635	18,166	17,691
Services...................................	33,964	34,682	35,187	35,044	34,837	33,789	34,399	35,302
Net foreign travel.......................	-2,060	-2,232	-2,502	-2,739	-2,787	-2,344	-2,287	-2,742
Gross private domestic investment.......	10,748	10,077	10,567	10,390	10,919	9,953	16,579	13,434
Fixed investment........................	10,409	10,361	10,403	10,378	10,380	11,137	13,335	13,585
Structures................................	2,110	1,975	1,944	1,912	1,786	1,697	2,518	2,665
Nonresidential..........................	768	680	650	664	605	559	743	695
Residential..............................	1,341	1,295	1,295	1,248	1,180	1,139	1,775	1,971
Equipment..............................	5,200	5,086	4,952	4,836	4,779	5,295	6,227	5,815
Intellectual property products..........	3,099	3,301	3,506	3,630	3,816	4,145	4,590	5,105
Change in private inventories...........	340	-285	164	12	539	-1,184	3,244	-151
Net exports of goods and services.......	19,285	24,562	30,526	36,522	34,794	31,040	17,665	24,472
Exports.....................................	70,888	74,374	80,189	84,477	86,612	78,577	77,025	78,799
Goods...................................	58,696	61,832	66,945	70,826	72,273	64,266	62,644	64,498
Services..................................	12,192	12,542	13,244	13,651	14,339	14,311	14,381	14,301
Imports.....................................	51,604	49,812	49,663	47,956	51,818	47,537	59,360	54,326
Goods...................................	46,281	44,341	44,060	42,212	45,989	41,523	52,640	47,266
Services..................................	5,323	5,471	5,603	5,744	5,829	6,014	6,720	7,060
Government consumption expenditures and gross investment....................	18,081	16,992	15,997	15,140	14,800	15,283	17,886	16,055
Federal [1]................................	2,653	2,336	2,353	2,399	2,486	3,235	4,036	3,474
Central [2]................................	12,321	11,655	10,763	9,869	9,455	9,370	11,213	10,015
Municipal.................................	3,107	3,002	2,881	2,872	2,860	2,678	2,637	2,566

P Preliminary. [1] U.S. federal government spending in Puerto Rico. [2] Spending by the Commonwealth Government of Puerto Rico and its components.

Source: U.S. Bureau of Economic Analysis, "Gross Domestic Product for Puerto Rico, 2019," accessed February 2022. See also <www.bea.gov/data/gdp/gdp-puerto-rico>.

Table 1342. Puerto Rico—Agricultural Summary: 1993 to 2018

[1 cuerda = 0.97 acre]

All farms	Unit	1993	1998	2002	2007	2012	2018
Farms.........................	Number	22,350	19,951	17,659	15,745	13,159	8,230
Farm land.........................	Cuerdas	826,893	865,478	690,687	557,530	584,988	487,775
Average size of farm.............	Cuerdas	37.0	43.4	39.1	35.4	44.5	59.3
Approximate land area............	Cuerdas	2,254,365	2,254,365	2,254,365	2,254,365	2,254,365	2,254,365
Proportion in farms...............	Percent	36.7	38.4	30.6	24.7	25.9	21.6
Farms by size:							
Less than 10 cuerdas...........	Number	10,413	7,759	7,943	7,502	5,129	2,213
10 to 19 cuerdas.................	Number	4,475	4,473	3,847	3,545	2,859	1,853
20 to 49 cuerdas.................	Number	3,966	4,023	3,228	2,680	2,872	1,950
50 to 99 cuerdas.................	Number	1,723	1,792	1,282	865	940	952
100 to 174 cuerdas...............	Number	820	809	590	524	563	579
175 to 259 cuerdas..............	Number	366	421	281	207	401	330
260 cuerdas or more............	Number	587	674	488	422	395	353
Tenure of operator:							
Operators.........................	Number	22,350	19,951	17,659	15,745	13,159	8,230
Full owners.....................	Number	17,759	15,620	13,693	11,402	9,362	5,474
Part owners.....................	Number	2,218	2,207	2,330	1,918	1,069	948
Tenants.........................	Number	2,373	2,124	1,636	2,425	2,728	1,808
Average size of farm by operator:							
Full owners........................	Cuerdas	27	29	27	25	29	41
Part owners.......................	Cuerdas	92	112	96	83	134	115
Tenants...........................	Cuerdas	63	76	61	46	61	87
Farms by type of organization:							
Individual or family...............	Number	19,911	17,887	15,843	13,958	11,938	6,886
Partnership.......................	Number	288	211	162	49	117	77
Corporation.......................	Number	382	437	595	575	738	1,147
Other..............................	Number	1,769	1,416	1,059	1,163	366	120
Farms by value of sales:							
Less than $1,000.................	Number	4,456	3,307	3,977	4,442	2,973	2,885
$1,000 to $2,499.................	Number	4,591	3,633	3,471	2,771	2,015	814
$2,500 to $4,499.................	Number	4,593	3,900	3,044	2,428	1,986	778
$5,000 to $7,499.................	Number	2,566	2,408	1,575	1,206	1,209	621
$7,500 to $9,999.................	Number	1,248	1,233	1,087	882	771	403
$10,000 to $19,999..............	Number	2,115	2,366	1,781	1,497	1,521	781
$20,000 to $39,999..............	Number	1,071	1,247	1,062	1,030	968	648
$40,000 to $59,999..............	Number	348	405	375	281	394	303
$60,000 or more.................	Number	1,362	1,452	1,287	1,208	1,322	997

Source: U.S. Department of Agriculture, National Agricultural Statistics Service (NASS), *2017 Census of Agriculture: Puerto Rico (2018), Island and Regional Data*, Geographic Area Series, Volume 1: Part 52, June 2020. See also <nass.usda.gov/Publications/AgCensus/2017>.

Table 1343. Puerto Rico—Farms and Market Value of Agricultural Products Sold: 2018

[For market value, 485,053 represents $485,053,000]

Type of product	Number of farms	Market value ($1,000)	Average value per farm (dol.)	Type of product	Number of farms	Market value ($1,000)	Average value per farm (dol.)
Total.............................	**8,230**	**485,053**	**58,937**	Horticultural specialties.........	303	34,853	115,027
Crops.................................	3,877	242,419	(NA)	Grasses and other crops.......	282	11,482	40,716
Coffee............................	1,363	4,773	3,502	Livestock, poultry, and their			
Pineapples.......................	90	2,977	33,077	products...........................	3,074	242,634	78,931
Plantains.........................	1,353	42,272	31,243	Cattle and calves...............	2,305	37,689	16,351
Bananas..........................	801	10,830	13,521	Poultry and poultry products. ..	409	20,095	49,131
Grains.............................	317	74,399	234,698	Dairy products...................	281	172,208	612,840
Root crops or tubers.............	770	8,706	11,306	Hogs and pigs...................	423	6,215	14,694
Fruits and coconuts..............	858	18,594	21,672	Aquaculture.....................	37	136	3,686
Vegetables and melons [1]........	750	33,533	44,711	Other.............................	490	6,290	12,837

NA Not available. [1] Includes hydroponic crops.

Source: U.S. Department of Agriculture, National Agricultural Statistics Service (NASS), *2017 Census of Agriculture: Puerto Rico (2018), Island and Regional Data*, Geographic Area Series, Volume 1: Part 52, June 2020. See also <nass.usda.gov/Publications/AgCensus/2017>.

Table 1344. Puerto Rico—Business Summary by Industry: 2019 and 2020

[Payroll in millions of dollars (18,589.4 represents $18,589,400,000). Covers establishments with payroll. Excludes self-employed individuals, employees of private households, railroad employees, agricultural production employees, and most government employees. For statement on methodology, see Appendix III]

Industry	NAICS code [1]	Establishments		Paid employees [2]		Annual payroll (mil. dol.)	
		2019	2020	2019	2020	2019	2020
Total, all industries	(X)	**44,748**	**45,451**	**680,204**	**680,586**	**18,589.4**	**17,904.0**
Agriculture, forestry, fishing and hunting	11	6	10	36	53	0.6	0.7
Mining, quarrying, and oil and gas extraction	21	38	39	504	556	12.3	13.9
Utilities	22	31	31	319	397	21.6	23.5
Construction	23	2,089	2,205	25,176	26,135	620.5	601.4
Manufacturing	31–33	1,819	1,814	75,007	74,065	2,980.6	2,888.6
Wholesale trade	42	1,961	1,997	29,870	30,680	1,186.9	1,208.7
Retail trade	44–45	9,193	9,248	129,569	123,171	2,552.9	2,445.1
Transportation and warehousing	48–49	1,029	999	16,906	16,363	504.5	462.7
Information	51	748	766	17,406	16,881	791.1	751.0
Finance and insurance	52	1,778	1,804	32,329	30,750	1,541.3	1,532.4
Real estate and rental and leasing	53	1,649	1,656	11,767	12,331	318.6	305.0
Professional, scientific, and technical services	54	4,682	4,973	35,094	38,681	1,446.5	1,482.7
Management of companies and enterprises	55	105	104	5,063	5,994	289.1	309.3
Administrative, support, waste management and remediation services	56	2,081	2,070	81,008	80,290	1,669.4	1,568.4
Educational services	61	829	837	35,724	35,807	790.0	735.2
Health care and social assistance	62	7,582	7,597	83,642	85,839	2,225.8	2,199.7
Arts, entertainment, and recreation	71	464	458	3,868	4,074	87.3	70.8
Accommodation and food services	72	4,991	5,115	78,980	80,470	1,185.6	969.6
Other services (except public administration)	81	3,275	3,307	17,392	17,490	344.1	319.2
Industries not classified	99	398	421	544	559	20.7	15.9

X Not applicable. [1] Data based on the North American Industry Classification System (NAICS) 2017. See text, Section 15. [2] Covers full- and part-time employees who are on the payroll in the pay period including March 12.

Source: U.S. Census Bureau, County Business Patterns, "All Sectors: County Business Patterns, including ZIP Code Business Patterns, by Legal Form of Organization and Employment Size Class for the U.S., States, and Selected Geographies: 2020," <data.census.gov>, accessed May 2022. See also <www.census.gov/programs-surveys/cbp.html>.

Table 1345. Guam, Virgin Islands, Northern Mariana Islands, and American Samoa—Economic Summary by Sector: 2017

[Sales and payroll in millions of dollars (1,080 represents $1,080,000,000). Data for establishments with annual payroll. Based on the 2017 Economic Census of Island Areas; see Appendix III]

Kind of business	American Samoa	Guam	Northern Mariana Islands	Virgin Islands	Kind of business	American Samoa	Guam	Northern Mariana Islands	Virgin Islands
Total: [1]					Paid employees [2]	293	3,074	797	872
Establishments	511	3,508	1,742	2,419	Retail trade:				
Sales	1,080	8,465	3,616	5,836	Establishments	190	680	332	489
Annual payroll	144	1,630	420	1,018	Sales	292	2,064	460	1,205
Paid employees [2]	8,767	60,539	22,652	30,506	Annual payroll	23	223	45	128
Construction:					Paid employees [2]	1,759	10,073	2,910	6,118
Establishments	33	358	108	137	Professional, scientific, & technical services:				
Sales	34	662	146	146	Establishments	25	256	112	254
Annual payroll	9	168	34	47	Sales	18	336	53	240
Paid employees [2]	562	5,501	2,803	1,298	Annual payroll	5	116	14	59
Manufacturing:					Paid employees [2]	231	2,723	899	1,134
Establishments	46	58	46	52	Accommodation & food services:				
Sales	390	96	49	175	Establishments	52	557	206	304
Annual payroll	36	25	10	26	Sales	35	1,083	341	520
Paid employees [2]	2,506	942	523	601	Annual payroll	7	267	72	150
Wholesale trade:					Paid employees [2]	800	15,121	4,710	6,737
Establishments	23	228	88	62					
Sales	125	1,016	350	527					
Annual payroll	5	88	14	47					

[1] Includes other industries, not shown separately. [2] For pay period including March 12.

Source: U.S. Census Bureau, Economic Census of the Island Areas, Table IA1700BASIC01, "Geographic Area Series: Summary Statistics for American Samoa, Commonwealth of the Northern Mariana Islands, Guam, Puerto Rico, and U.S. Virgin Islands: 2017," <data.census.gov/>, accessed November 2021.

Table 1346. Virgin Islands—Business Summary by Industry: 2019 and 2020

[Payroll in thousands of dollars (1,285,804 represents $1,285,804,000). Covers establishments with payroll. Excludes self-employed individuals, employees of private households, railroad employees, agricultural production employees, and most government employees. For statement on methodology, see Appendix III]

Industry	NAICS code [1]	Establishments		Paid employees [2]		Annual payroll ($1,000)	
		2019	2020	2019	2020	2019	2020
Total, all industries..................	(X)	2,405	2,352	29,222	30,541	1,285,804	1,216,549
Agriculture, forestry, fishing and hunting...............	11	(NA)	(NA)	(NA)	(NA)	(NA)	(NA)
Mining, quarrying, and oil and gas extraction..........	21	(NA)	3	(NA)	39	(NA)	1,961
Utilities...............................	22	4	5	36	40	2,559	3,262
Construction.........................	23	168	168	3,875	4,126	298,023	252,935
Manufacturing........................	31-33	48	47	721	658	40,249	39,488
Wholesale trade......................	42	58	57	667	913	39,519	64,879
Retail trade..........................	44-45	449	434	5,511	5,683	140,674	132,891
Transportation and warehousing.........................	48-49	107	114	1,805	1,832	60,887	51,468
Information..........................	51	38	37	574	546	29,446	25,982
Finance and insurance.................	52	111	107	1,117	957	77,756	74,128
Real estate and rental and leasing.........	53	189	172	921	955	36,070	35,245
Professional, scientific, and technical services........	54	248	245	1,160	1,124	83,409	75,790
Management of companies and enterprises...........	55	7	5	52	20	3,354	1,269
Administrative, support, waste management and remediation services................	56	150	141	2,179	2,045	90,760	72,324
Educational services....................	61	32	32	629	621	19,805	18,692
Health care and social assistance..........	62	206	206	2,635	2,938	136,699	148,254
Arts, entertainment, and recreation....................	71	45	50	615	725	17,195	17,495
Accommodation and food services.....................	72	303	306	5,499	5,882	155,675	122,865
Other services (except public administration)..........	81	211	202	1,111	1,391	45,971	75,729
Industries not classified.................	99	28	20	60	45	2,766	1,839

X Not applicable. NA Not available. [1] Data based on the North American Industry Classification System (NAICS) 2017. See text, Section 15. [2] Covers full- and part-time employees who are on the payroll in the pay period including March 12.

Source: U.S. Census Bureau, County Business Patterns, "All Sectors: County Business Patterns, including ZIP Code Business Patterns, by Legal Form of Organization and Employment Size Class for the U.S., States, and Selected Geographies: 2020," <data.census.gov>, accessed May 2022. See also <www.census.gov/programs-surveys/cbp.html>.

Table 1347. Guam—Business Summary by Industry: 2019 and 2020

[Payroll in thousands of dollars (1,702,232 represents $1,702,232,000). Covers establishments with payroll. Excludes self-employed individuals, employees of private households, railroad employees, agricultural production employees, and most government employees. For statement on methodology, see Appendix III]

Industry	NAICS code [1]	Establishments		Paid employees [2]		Annual payroll ($1,000)	
		2019	2020	2019	2020	2019	2020
Total, all industries..................	(X)	3,472	3,425	59,683	61,114	1,702,232	1,554,327
Agriculture, forestry, fishing and hunting............	11	(NA)	(NA)	(NA)	(NA)	(NA)	(NA)
Mining, quarrying, and oil and gas extraction......	21	(NA)	(NA)	(NA)	(NA)	(NA)	(NA)
Utilities...............................	22	3	3	53	62	4,503	3,059
Construction.........................	23	364	364	5,735	7,158	192,987	218,587
Manufacturing........................	31-33	56	53	822	795	19,910	18,045
Wholesale trade......................	42	213	216	3,128	3,123	98,246	92,076
Retail trade..........................	44-45	649	607	10,345	9,920	235,000	200,873
Transportation and warehousing....................	48-49	96	87	2,193	2,317	119,390	113,835
Information..........................	51	56	52	1,747	1,699	67,662	68,744
Finance and insurance.................	52	124	123	2,506	2,182	102,375	98,333
Real estate and rental and leasing............	53	286	284	2,137	2,248	55,520	49,753
Professional, scientific, and technical services....	54	253	247	2,863	2,857	133,063	130,293
Management of companies and enterprises.......	55	8	10	88	117	4,399	5,455
Administrative, support, waste management and remediation services................	56	159	166	3,550	4,109	78,200	82,941
Educational services....................	61	60	62	1,159	1,232	26,449	24,387
Health care and social assistance..............	62	221	214	4,564	4,664	206,890	209,166
Arts, entertainment, and recreation................	71	75	70	1,118	1,118	23,050	13,651
Accommodation and food services.................	72	547	526	15,416	15,077	279,414	172,317
Other services (except public administration)......	81	231	244	2,042	2,061	49,837	46,108
Industries not classified.................	99	69	95	213	370	5,119	6,504

X Not applicable. NA Not available. [1] Data based on NAICS 2017. See text, Section 15. [2] Covers full- and part-time employees who are on the payroll in the pay period including March 12.

Source: U.S. Census Bureau, County Business Patterns, "All Sectors: County Business Patterns, including ZIP Code Business Patterns, by Legal Form of Organization and Employment Size Class for the U.S., States, and Selected Geographies: 2020," <data.census.gov>, accessed May 2022. See also <www.census.gov/programs-surveys/cbp.html>.

Table 1348. Northern Marianas—Business Summary by Industry: 2019 and 2020

[Payroll in thousands of dollars (431,286 represents $431,286,000). Covers establishments with payroll. Excludes self-employed individuals, employees of private households, railroad employees, agricultural production employees, and most government employees. For statement on methodology, see Appendix III]

Industry	NAICS code [1]	Establishments		Paid employees [2]		Annual payroll ($1,000)	
		2019	2020	2019	2020	2019	2020
Total, all industries...............................	(X)	1,719	1,614	18,462	17,248	431,286	325,124
Agriculture, forestry, fishing and hunting............	11	4	4	12	14	240	108
Mining, quarrying, and oil and gas extraction......	21	(NA)	(NA)	(NA)	(NA)	(NA)	(NA)
Utilities..	22	4	4	431	411	17,487	14,366
Construction...	23	105	94	1,063	1,258	22,853	22,314
Manufacturing...	31-33	45	42	559	543	11,890	12,925
Wholesale trade......................................	42	91	83	841	802	17,202	15,271
Retail trade..	44-45	323	315	2,442	2,452	47,865	37,675
Transportation and warehousing....................	48-49	50	46	1,039	1,027	25,588	18,681
Information...	51	23	21	454	378	13,239	11,629
Finance and insurance...............................	52	50	48	287	271	9,038	8,149
Real estate and rental and leasing.................	53	165	160	640	637	12,188	9,418
Professional, scientific, and technical services....	54	99	95	474	459	13,791	13,694
Management of companies and enterprises.......	55	6	6	85	72	1,546	1,202
Administrative, support, waste management and remediation services...........................	56	169	150	1,688	1,439	27,018	17,043
Educational services.................................	61	54	48	420	326	9,860	7,189
Health care and social assistance.................	62	45	46	1,173	1,170	53,483	57,419
Arts, entertainment, and recreation.................	71	48	44	2,172	1,488	69,419	20,293
Accommodation and food services.................	72	201	187	3,812	3,709	63,880	45,402
Other services (except public administration)......	81	150	141	593	528	10,495	8,939
Industries not classified.............................	99	85	78	231	221	3,168	2,528

X Not applicable. NA Not available. [1] Data based on North American Industry Classification System (NAICS) 2017. See text, Section 15. [2] Covers full- and part-time employees who are on the payroll in the pay period including March 12.

Source: U.S. Census Bureau, County Business Patterns, "All Sectors: County Business Patterns, including ZIP Code Business Patterns, by Legal Form of Organization and Employment Size Class for the U.S., States, and Selected Geographies: 2020," <data.census.gov>, accessed May 2022. See also <www.census.gov/programs-surveys/cbp.html>.

Table 1349. American Samoa—Business Summary by Industry: 2019 and 2020

[Payroll in thousands of dollars (138,780 represents $138,780,000). Covers establishments with payroll. Excludes self-employed individuals, employees of private households, railroad employees, agricultural production employees, and most government employees. For statement on methodology, see Appendix III]

Industry	NAICS code [1]	Establishments		Paid employees [2]		Annual payroll ($1,000)	
		2019	2020	2019	2020	2019	2020
Total, all industries...............................	(X)	510	546	7,602	7,335	138,780	140,441
Agriculture, forestry, fishing and hunting..........	11	(NA)	(NA)	(NA)	(NA)	(NA)	(NA)
Construction...	23	33	38	480	435	8,598	10,053
Manufacturing...	31-33	39	40	2,496	2,152	44,820	41,973
Wholesale trade......................................	42	28	27	293	273	5,343	5,401
Retail trade..	44-45	173	169	1,494	1,483	21,690	21,444
Transportation and warehousing....................	48-49	21	21	278	273	4,790	4,806
Information...	51	4	4	130	131	3,716	3,771
Finance and insurance...............................	52	14	13	92	105	2,629	2,846
Real estate and rental and leasing...............	53	18	24	76	104	1,199	1,792
Professional, scientific, and technical services...	54	26	27	183	164	5,229	3,394
Management of companies and enterprises.....	55	(NA)	(NA)	(NA)	(NA)	(NA)	(NA)
Administrative, support, waste management and remediation services.........................	56	24	23	187	212	2,687	3,245
Educational services.................................	61	7	7	148	163	2,253	2,288
Health care and social assistance.................	62	17	22	800	846	23,174	26,738
Arts, entertainment, and recreation...............	71	(NA)	(NA)	(NA)	(NA)	(NA)	(NA)
Accommodation and food services...............	72	49	61	614	673	8,007	7,712
Other services (except public administration).....	81	37	45	277	244	3,539	3,663
Industries not classified.............................	99	14	21	22	63	630	1,023

X Not applicable. NA Not available. [1] Data based on the North American Industry Classification System (NAICS) 2017. See text, Section 15. [2] Covers full- and part-time employees who are on the payroll in the pay period including March 12.

Source U.S. Census Bureau, County Business Patterns, "All Sectors: County Business Patterns, including ZIP Code Business Patterns, by Legal Form of Organization and Employment Size Class for the U.S., States, and Selected Geographies: 2020," <data.census.gov>, accessed May 2022. See also <www.census.gov/programs-surveys/cbp.html>.

Table 1350. Occupational Employment and Average Annual Wages in Guam, Puerto Rico, and Virgin Islands: 2021

[Wages in dollars. The Occupational Employment Survey (OES) program conducts a semiannual survey designed to produce estimates of employment and wages for specific occupations. Excludes self-employed persons. For more details on the survey, see <www.bls.gov/oes/oes_emp.htm>]

Selected occupation	SOC code [1]	Guam		Puerto Rico		Virgin Islands	
		Employ-ment	Average annual wages [2]	Employ-ment	Average annual wages [2]	Employ-ment	Average annual wages [2]
Total, all occupations [3]........................	**(X)**	**58,390**	**39,720**	**843,810**	**30,480**	**33,260**	**47,980**
Management occupations...........................	11	4,890	74,990	38,950	76,480	2,830	85,680
Business and financial operations...................	13	2,920	56,060	45,720	41,790	1,800	63,030
Computer and mathematical occupations...........	15	740	51,920	10,790	44,890	340	62,460
Architecture and engineering.......................	17	950	65,120	13,250	57,130	220	82,630
Life, physical, and social sciences..................	19	580	60,570	7,140	50,430	290	60,110
Community and social services......................	21	800	45,970	16,130	30,110	430	48,630
Legal occupations...................................	23	320	79,560	4,620	64,810	320	126,610
Educational instruction and library occupations.....	25	4,500	46,680	54,190	34,090	2,130	49,950
Arts, design, entertainment, sports, and media.....	27	450	36,410	7,240	36,350	150	48,280
Healthcare practitioner and technical occupations..	29	2,060	67,600	51,470	38,480	1,610	73,040
Healthcare support...................................	31	1,130	27,670	15,920	19,820	560	34,260
Protective service occupations......................	33	2,450	39,900	51,500	28,690	2,130	44,730
Food preparation and serving related occupations..	35	5,580	22,000	62,950	19,940	3,360	29,250
Buildings and grounds cleaning and maintenance.....................................	37	2,170	22,850	37,100	20,360	1,860	29,940
Personal care and service occupations..............	39	770	22,310	6,370	21,680	480	30,990
Sales and related occupations.......................	41	4,750	25,830	100,540	23,880	3,130	34,920
Office and administrative support....................	43	8,030	32,320	139,270	26,010	4,410	40,350
Farming, fishing, and forestry.......................	45	60	35,740	2,060	21,940	30	35,190
Construction and extraction..........................	47	5,790	35,460	30,560	23,730	2,300	50,470
Installation, maintenance, and repair................	49	3,180	37,170	31,850	27,590	1,580	46,730
Production occupations..............................	51	1,510	33,980	55,330	24,230	830	45,360
Transportation and material moving.................	53	4,780	31,120	60,840	22,920	2,470	36,920

X Not applicable. [1] Office of Management and Budget's Standard Occupational Classification (SOC) is used to define occupations. SOC categorizes workers into one of approximately 800 detailed occupations, which are classified into 23 major occupational groups. [2] Annual wages have been calculated by multiplying the hourly mean wage by a "year-round, full-time" hours figure of 2,080 hours; for those occupations where there is not an hourly mean wage published, the annual wage has been directly calculated from the reported survey data. [3] Estimates do not sum to the total because the total may include data for occupations not shown separately. See source for more information.

Source: U.S. Bureau of Labor Statistics, "Occupational Employment Statistics," <www.bls.gov/oes/current/oessrcst.htm>, accessed June 2022.

This section presents statistics for the world as a whole and for many countries on a comparative basis with the United States. Data are shown for population, births and deaths, social and economic indicators, finances, agriculture, energy, climate, science and technology, communications, and military affairs.

Statistics for individual countries may be found primarily in official national publications, generally in the form of yearbooks, issued by most countries in their own national languages and expressed in their own customary units of measure. For a listing of selected publications, see Appendix I table under international statistical abstracts from a foreign agency.

For international comparisons, the United Nations Statistics Division compiles data as submitted by member countries and issues a number of summary publications, generally in English and French. Among these are the annual *Statistical Yearbook, Demographic Yearbook, Population and Vital Statistics Report, International Trade Statistics Yearbook, Energy Statistics Yearbook, Industrial Commodity Statistics Yearbook, National Accounts Statistics,* and the *Monthly Bulletin of Statistics.* Specialized agencies of the United Nations also issue international summary publications on various topics, including agricultural, labor, health, and trade statistics. Among these are *Food Outlook* and the *Statistical Pocketbook* issued by the Food and Agriculture Organization (FAO); *World Employment and Social Outlook* issued by the International Labor Organization (ILO); *World Health Statistics* issued by the World Health Organization (WHO); and the *Handbook of Statistics* issued by the Conference on Trade and Development (UNCTAD).

The U.S. Census Bureau publishes estimates and projections of key demographic measures for countries and regions of the world in its International Data Base at <www.census.gov/programs-surveys/international-programs.html>.

The International Monetary Fund (IMF), the World Bank, and the Organisation for Economic Co-operation and Development (OECD) also compile international statistics. The IMF publishes a series of reports related to financial data. These include *World Economic Outlook, Global Financial Stability Report,* and *Fiscal Monitor.* The World Bank publishes many reports on a wide range of topics related to international development. Three of their flagship statistical publications are *World Development Report, World Development Indicators,* and *Global Economic Prospects.* The OECD also produces numerous statistical publications in fields including economics, health, and education. Among these are the *Economic Outlook; National Accounts of OECD Countries; Science, Technology and Innovation Outlook; International Migration Outlook; Employment Outlook;* and *Education at a Glance.*

Statistical coverage and country classifications— Problems of space and availability of data limit the number of countries and the extent of statistical coverage shown. The lists of countries and territories included in individual tables are generally based on source publications and databases, as cited.

In the last four decades several important changes took place in the status of the world's nations. In 1991, the Soviet Union broke up into 15 independent countries: Armenia, Azerbaijan, Belarus, Estonia, Georgia, Kazakhstan, Kyrgyzstan, Latvia, Lithuania, Moldova, Russia, Tajikistan, Turkmenistan, Ukraine, and Uzbekistan.

Germany was reunified in 1990, when the German Democratic Republic (former East Germany) joined the Federal Republic of Germany (former West Germany) to form a single country. On January 1, 1993, Czechoslovakia was succeeded by two independent countries: the Czech Republic, now known as Czechia, and Slovakia.

Following the breakup of the Socialist Federal Republic of Yugoslavia in 1992, the United States recognized Bosnia and Herzegovina, Croatia, Slovenia, and Macedonia as independent countries. Serbia and Montenegro, both former republics of Yugoslavia, became independent of one another on May 31, 2006. This separation is reflected in the population estimates of Table 1353. On February 17, 2008, Kosovo declared its independence from Serbia. In 2019, Macedonia formally adopted the name Republic of North Macedonia.

The Treaty of Maastricht created the European Union (EU) in 1992 with 12 member countries. The EU is not a state intended to replace existing states, but it is more than just an international organization. Its member states have set up common institutions to which they delegate some of their sovereignty so that decisions on specific matters of joint interest can be made democratically at a European level. This pooling of sovereignty is also called "European integration." The EU has grown in size with successive waves of accessions in 1995, 2004, 2007, and 2013. The 27 current members of the EU are: Austria, Belgium, Bulgaria, Croatia, Cyprus, Czechia, Denmark, Estonia, Finland, France, Germany, Greece, Hungary, Ireland, Italy, Latvia, Lithuania, Luxembourg, Malta, the Netherlands, Poland, Portugal, Romania, Slovakia, Slovenia, Spain, and Sweden. In June 2016, the electorate of the United Kingdom voted to withdraw from the EU. The withdrawal became official in January of 2020.

In 1992, the EU decided to establish an economic and monetary union (EMU), with the introduction of a single European currency managed by a European Central Bank. The single currency—the euro—became a reality on January 1, 2002, when euro notes and coins replaced national currencies in 12 of the then 15 countries of the European Union (Austria, Belgium, Finland, France, Germany, Greece, Ireland, Italy, Luxembourg, the Netherlands, Portugal, and Spain). Since then, 13 additional countries have acceded to EU membership, but Cyprus, Estonia, Latvia, Lithuania, Malta, Slovakia, and Slovenia have been the only new members of the EU to adopt the euro as the national currency. In total, the euro is the official currency of 19 of the 27 EU member countries.

Elsewhere in the world, Eritrea announced its independence from Ethiopia in April 1993 and was subsequently recognized as an independent nation by the United States. In the South Pacific, the Marshall Islands, Micronesia, and Palau gained independence from the United States in 1991. In May of 2002, Timor-Leste won independence from Indonesia. The Netherlands Antilles dissolved on October 10, 2010. As a result, Curaçao and Sint Maarten became autonomous territories of the Netherlands. As of July 2011, Sudan and South Sudan became separate countries. And, in 2018, Swaziland was officially renamed Eswatini.

The population estimates and projections used in Tables 1351 through 1354, 1356, and 1357 were prepared by the U.S. Census Bureau. For each country, available data on population by age and sex, fertility, mortality, and international migration were evaluated and, where necessary, adjusted for inconsistencies and errors in the data. Comprehensive population projections were made by the cohort-component method based on an assessment of probable future trends.

Economic associations—The Organisation for European Economic Co–operation (OEEC) was originally a regional grouping of Western European countries established in 1948 for the purpose of harmonizing national economic policies and conditions. It was succeeded on September 30, 1961 by the Organisation for Economic Co-operation and Development (OECD). As of 2022, the 38 member nations of the OECD are Australia, Austria, Belgium, Canada, Chile, Colombia, Costa Rica, Czechia, Denmark, Estonia, Finland, France, Germany, Greece, Hungary, Iceland, Ireland, Israel, Italy, Japan, Latvia, Lithuania, Luxembourg, Mexico, the Netherlands, New Zealand, Norway, Poland, Portugal, Slovakia, Slovenia, South Korea, Spain, Sweden, Switzerland, Turkey, the United Kingdom, and the United States.

Quality and comparability of the data—The quality and comparability of the data presented here are affected by a number of factors:

1 The year for which data are presented may not be the same for all subjects for a particular country or for a given subject for different countries, though the data shown are the most recent available. All such variations have been noted. The data shown are for calendar years except as otherwise specified.

2 The statistical bases, methods of estimating, methods of data collection, extent of coverage, precision of definition, scope of territory, and margins of error may vary for different items within a particular country, and for like items for different countries. Footnotes and headnotes to the tables describe some of the major coverage qualifications attached to the figures; considerably more detail is presented in the source publications. Many of the measures shown are merely rough indicators of magnitude.

3 Figures shown in this section for the United States may not always agree with figures shown in the preceding sections. Discrepancies may be attributable to the use of differing original sources, differences in the definition of geographic limits (the 50 states, continental U.S. only, or the U.S. including certain outlying areas and possessions), or to possible adjustments made to the U.S. figures in order to make them more comparable with figures from other countries.

International comparisons of national accounts data—To compare national accounts data for different countries, it is necessary to convert each country's data into a common unit of currency, usually the U.S. dollar. The market exchange rates, which often are used in converting national currencies, do not necessarily reflect the relative purchasing power in the various countries. It is necessary that the goods and services produced in different countries be valued consistently if the differences observed are meant to reflect real differences in the volumes of goods and services produced. The use of purchasing power parities (see Tables 1365, 1366, and 1372) instead of exchange rates is intended to achieve this objective.

The method used to present the data shown in Table 1372 is to construct volume measures directly by revaluing the goods and services sold in different countries at a common set of international prices. By dividing the ratio of the gross domestic products of two countries expressed in their own national currencies by the corresponding ratio calculated at constant international prices, it is possible to derive the implied purchasing power parity (PPP) between the two currencies concerned. PPPs show how many units of currency are needed in one country to buy the same amount of goods and services that one unit of currency will buy in the other country. For further information, see *National Accounts of OECD Countries, Main Aggregates*, issued annually by the Organisation for Economic Co-operation and Development (OECD), Paris, France.

International Standard Industrial Classification—The original version of the International Standard Industrial Classification of All Economic Activities (ISIC) was adopted in 1948. A number of countries have utilized ISIC as the basis for devising their industrial classification schemes. Substantial comparability has been attained among the industrial classification schemes of many countries, including the United States, by ensuring that national classification categories correspond to ISIC categories. The United Nations, the International Labour Organization, the Food and Agriculture Organization, and other international bodies use ISIC in publishing and analyzing statistical data. Revisions of ISIC were issued in 1958, 1968, 1989, 2002, and 2008.

Table 1351. Total World Population and Population Projections: 1950 to 2050

[2,557.62 represents 2,557,620,000. As of midyear]

Year	Population (mil.)	Population change [1] Percent	Population change [1] Number (mil.)	Year	Population (mil.)	Population change [1] Percent	Population change [1] Number (mil.)
1950	2,557.62	(NA)	(NA)	2016	7,435.15	1.11	81.68
1955	2,782.11	1.90	51.87	2017	7,516.77	1.10	81.62
1960	3,043.03	1.41	42.29	2018	7,597.07	1.07	80.30
1965	3,350.77	2.11	69.30	2019	7,676.69	1.05	79.62
1970	3,713.46	2.08	75.64	2020	7,756.87	1.04	80.19
1975	4,089.39	1.78	71.61	2021	7,831.72	0.96	74.85
1980	4,445.98	1.62	71.04	**2022**	**7,905.34**	**0.94**	**73.62**
1985	4,862.32	1.78	85.26	2023	7,979.26	0.94	73.92
1989	5,222.66	1.78	91.09	2024	8,053.47	0.93	74.21
1990	5,315.51	1.78	92.85	2025	8,127.11	0.91	73.64
1991	5,403.25	1.65	87.74	2026	8,200.03	0.90	72.92
1992	5,490.48	1.61	87.23	2027	8,272.67	0.89	72.64
1993	5,568.23	1.42	77.75	2028	8,344.95	0.87	72.28
1994	5,650.18	1.47	81.95	2029	8,416.77	0.86	71.82
1995	5,733.21	1.47	83.03	2030	8,488.00	0.85	71.23
1996	5,815.33	1.43	82.12	2031	8,558.75	0.83	70.75
1997	5,895.84	1.38	80.50	2032	8,628.99	0.82	70.24
1998	5,975.19	1.35	79.35	2033	8,698.46	0.81	69.47
1999	6,053.96	1.32	78.77	2034	8,767.11	0.79	68.64
2000	6,132.46	1.30	78.50	2035	8,834.87	0.77	67.76
2001	6,211.33	1.29	78.87	2036	8,901.84	0.76	66.97
2002	6,290.28	1.27	78.95	2037	8,968.11	0.74	66.28
2003	6,369.19	1.25	78.90	2038	9,033.57	0.73	65.45
2004	6,448.26	1.24	79.08	2039	9,098.09	0.71	64.52
2005	6,527.06	1.22	78.79	2040	9,161.63	0.70	63.54
2006	6,607.40	1.23	80.34	2041	9,224.28	0.68	62.65
2007	6,689.44	1.24	82.05	2042	9,286.12	0.67	61.84
2008	6,773.32	1.25	83.88	2043	9,346.93	0.65	60.82
2009	6,857.16	1.24	83.84	2044	9,406.60	0.64	59.67
2010	6,939.76	1.20	82.60	2045	9,465.11	0.62	58.51
2011	7,022.08	1.19	82.32	2046	9,522.53	0.61	57.42
2012	7,105.00	1.18	82.92	2047	9,578.90	0.59	56.37
2013	7,188.53	1.18	83.53	2048	9,634.06	0.58	55.16
2014	7,271.60	1.16	83.07	2049	9,687.92	0.56	53.86
2015	7,353.48	1.13	81.88	2050	9,740.51	0.54	52.60

NA Not available. [1] Represents change from year shown to immediate preceding year.

Source: U.S. Census Bureau, "International Data Base (IDB)," <www.census.gov/programs-surveys/international-programs/about/idb.html>, accessed May 2022.

Table 1352. World Population by World Region: 1950 to 2050

[In millions, except percent (2,557.6 represents 2,557,600,000). As of midyear. For geographic classification of individual countries, see source]

Year	World	Africa	North America [1]	Latin America and the Caribbean [2]	Asia	Europe	Oceania
1950	2,557.6	229.0	165.9	165.4	1,437.6	547.1	12.5
1960	3,043.0	285.8	198.3	217.2	1,720.5	605.6	15.6
1970	3,713.5	366.8	225.8	284.5	2,159.2	657.9	19.2
1980	4,446.0	479.1	251.9	359.4	2,637.8	695.2	22.6
1990	5,315.5	631.7	277.5	447.6	3,209.0	723.1	26.5
2000	6,132.5	807.6	313.4	521.6	3,727.5	731.6	30.8
2010	6,939.8	1,043.8	343.7	589.8	4,186.1	740.1	36.3
2020	7,756.9	1,345.5	370.4	646.7	4,601.9	749.4	43.0
2022	**7,905.3**	**1,412.3**	**375.7**	**656.0**	**4,668.1**	**748.9**	**44.3**
2030	8,488.0	1,697.3	395.6	693.5	4,907.0	745.6	49.0
2040	9,161.6	2,093.2	416.0	729.6	5,129.0	739.3	54.5
2050	9,740.5	2,518.0	433.1	750.8	5,250.9	728.3	59.4
PERCENT DISTRIBUTION							
1950	100.0	9.0	6.5	6.5	56.2	21.4	0.5
1960	100.0	9.4	6.5	7.1	56.5	19.9	0.5
1970	100.0	9.9	6.1	7.7	58.1	17.7	0.5
1980	100.0	10.8	5.7	8.1	59.3	15.6	0.5
1990	100.0	11.9	5.2	8.4	60.4	13.6	0.5
2000	100.0	13.2	5.1	8.5	60.8	11.9	0.5
2010	100.0	15.0	5.0	8.5	60.3	10.7	0.5
2020	100.0	17.3	4.8	8.3	59.3	9.7	0.6
2022	**100.0**	**17.9**	**4.8**	**8.3**	**59.1**	**9.5**	**0.6**
2030	100.0	20.0	4.7	8.2	57.8	8.8	0.6
2040	100.0	22.8	4.5	8.0	56.0	8.1	0.6
2050	100.0	25.9	4.4	7.7	53.9	7.5	0.6

[1] Data for North America include Bermuda, Canada, Greenland, Saint Pierre and Miquelon, and the United States. [2] Latin American includes Mexico and Central and South America.

Source: U.S. Census Bureau, "International Data Base (IDB)," <www.census.gov/programs-surveys/international-programs/about/idb.html>, accessed May 2022.

Table 1353. Population and Land Area by Country or Territory: 2010 to 2022 and Projected 2030

[6,939,762 represents 6,939,762,000. Covers 227 countries or territories with populations of 5,000 or more in 2022. Population estimates were derived from information available as of December 2021. See text of this section for general comments concerning the data. For details of methodology, coverage, and reliability, see source. Minus sign (-) indicates decrease]

Country or territory	Mid-year population (1,000)				Population rank, 2022	Population percent change, 2010 to 2020	Population per sq. km, 2022	Land area, (sq. km)
	2010	2020	2022	2030 (P)				
World	6,939,762	7,756,873	7,905,337	8,488,001	(X)	11.8	60	131,821,061
Afghanistan	29,117	36,595	38,347	45,503	37	25.7	59	652,230
Albania	2,989	3,081	3,095	3,116	136	3.1	113	27,398
Algeria	35,950	42,952	44,179	48,245	34	19.5	19	2,381,740
Andorra	85	86	86	85	199	1.4	183	468
Angola	22,641	32,522	34,795	45,369	42	43.6	28	1,246,700
Antigua and Barbuda	87	98	100	109	196	13.1	227	443
Argentina	41,358	45,480	46,246	49,142	32	10.0	17	2,736,690
Armenia	3,072	3,021	3,001	2,892	138	-1.6	106	28,203
Australia	21,840	25,468	26,141	28,467	54	16.6	3	7,682,300
Austria	8,448	8,856	8,913	9,111	99	4.8	108	82,445
Azerbaijan	9,302	10,207	10,353	10,814	90	9.7	125	82,629
Bahamas, The	319	350	356	377	178	9.6	36	10,010
Bahrain	1,180	1,505	1,541	1,639	155	27.5	2,027	760
Bangladesh	146,554	162,533	165,650	177,171	8	10.9	1,273	130,170
Barbados	290	301	303	307	180	3.9	704	430
Belarus	9,680	9,469	9,414	9,154	96	-2.2	46	202,900
Belgium	10,866	11,708	11,847	12,310	81	7.8	391	30,278
Belize	327	399	412	466	175	22.1	18	22,806
Benin	9,178	12,861	13,755	17,818	74	40.1	124	110,622
Bhutan	759	851	868	933	165	12.0	23	38,394
Bolivia	10,024	11,775	12,054	13,011	79	17.5	11	1,083,301
Bosnia and Herzegovina	3,885	3,833	3,816	3,730	130	-1.3	75	51,187
Botswana	1,978	2,317	2,384	2,643	145	17.2	4	566,730
Brazil	197,855	214,752	217,240	227,310	7	8.5	26	8,358,140
Brunei	395	464	478	532	173	17.6	91	5,265
Bulgaria	7,391	6,965	6,873	6,521	107	-5.8	63	108,489
Burkina Faso	15,634	20,833	21,935	26,350	59	33.3	80	273,800
Burma	51,415	56,599	57,526	60,691	25	10.1	88	653,508
Burundi	9,140	11,846	12,696	16,039	77	29.6	494	25,680
Cabo Verde	508	582	597	651	172	14.5	148	4,033
Cambodia	14,327	16,337	16,713	17,987	72	14.0	95	176,515
Cameroon	20,900	27,744	29,322	36,269	51	32.7	62	472,710
Canada	34,201	37,650	38,233	40,326	38	10.1	4	9,093,507
Central African Republic	4,683	5,263	5,455	6,257	119	12.4	9	622,984
Chad	11,989	16,876	17,963	22,767	67	40.8	14	1,259,200
Chile	16,760	18,182	18,430	19,263	66	8.5	25	743,812
China	1,340,789	1,404,032	1,410,540	1,424,439	1	4.7	151	9,326,410
Colombia	43,821	48,420	49,059	50,908	29	10.5	47	1,038,700
Comoros	710	852	876	969	164	20.0	392	2,235
Congo, Republic of (Brazzaville)	4,238	5,293	5,546	6,673	118	24.9	16	341,500
Congo, Democratic Republic of (Kinshasa)	72,742	101,769	108,408	138,708	14	39.9	48	2,267,048
Costa Rica	4,516	5,097	5,204	5,588	124	12.9	102	51,060
Cote d'Ivoire	21,718	27,470	28,713	33,889	52	26.5	90	318,003
Croatia	4,417	4,230	4,189	4,037	128	-4.3	75	55,974
Cuba	11,262	11,059	11,008	10,843	84	-1.8	100	109,820
Cyprus	1,103	1,267	1,295	1,381	159	14.9	140	9,241
Czechia	10,551	10,698	10,705	10,660	86	1.4	139	77,247
Denmark	5,547	5,869	5,921	6,119	114	5.8	140	42,434
Djibouti	739	920	957	1,105	162	24.4	41	23,180
Dominica	73	75	75	74	201	1.8	99	751
Dominican Republic	9,433	10,499	10,695	11,416	87	11.3	221	48,320
Ecuador	14,786	16,894	17,290	18,756	71	14.3	63	276,841
Egypt	81,571	103,995	107,771	120,413	15	27.5	108	995,450
El Salvador	5,967	6,481	6,569	6,697	109	8.6	317	20,721
Equatorial Guinea	986	1,561	1,679	2,135	154	58.4	60	28,051
Eritrea	5,369	6,089	6,209	6,837	111	13.4	62	101,000
Estonia	1,303	1,228	1,212	1,138	160	-5.7	29	42,388
Eswatini	1,019	1,105	1,122	1,182	161	8.4	65	17,204
Ethiopia	82,066	108,108	113,657	136,593	13	31.7	104	1,096,570
Fiji	876	935	944	972	163	6.8	52	18,274
Finland	5,355	5,572	5,602	5,669	116	4.1	18	303,815
France	64,934	67,859	68,305	69,922	21	4.5	107	640,427
Gabon	1,628	2,230	2,341	2,818	146	37.0	9	257,667
Gambia, The	1,750	2,302	2,413	2,844	144	31.6	239	10,120
Georgia	4,903	4,931	4,936	4,923	126	0.6	71	69,700
Germany	81,751	84,498	84,317	83,392	18	3.4	242	348,672
Ghana	24,609	31,643	33,107	39,139	44	28.6	146	227,533
Greece	11,040	10,605	10,534	10,243	88	-3.9	81	130,647
Grenada	108	113	114	116	190	4.9	331	344
Guatemala	14,212	17,140	17,703	19,842	69	20.6	165	107,159
Guinea	9,571	12,527	13,238	16,465	75	30.9	54	245,717
Guinea-Bissau	1,516	1,927	2,027	2,484	150	27.1	72	28,120
Guyana	787	787	790	814	166	(-Z)	4	196,849
Haiti	9,553	11,061	11,335	12,388	83	15.8	411	27,560
Honduras	7,991	9,232	9,459	10,321	95	15.5	85	111,890
Hungary	9,989	9,756	9,700	9,439	93	-2.3	108	89,608
Iceland	318	351	358	381	177	10.3	4	100,250
India	1,220,719	1,369,541	1,389,637	1,472,251	2	12.2	467	2,973,193

See footnotes at end of table.

Country or territory	Mid-year population (1,000)				Population rank, 2022	Population percent change, 2010 to 2020	Population per sq. km, 2022	Land area, (sq. km)
	2010	2020	2022	2030 (P)				
Indonesia	246,257	272,856	277,329	293,085	4	10.8	153	1,811,569
Iran	75,035	84,983	86,758	92,448	17	13.3	57	1,531,595
Iraq	29,073	38,829	40,463	47,088	36	33.6	93	437,367
Ireland	4,623	5,173	5,275	5,649	123	11.9	77	68,883
Israel	7,353	8,660	8,915	9,962	98	17.8	415	21,497
Italy	60,786	61,338	61,096	60,840	24	0.9	208	294,140
Jamaica	2,839	2,815	2,819	2,846	140	-0.8	260	10,831
Japan	127,646	125,136	124,215	119,732	11	-2.0	341	364,485
Jordan	6,800	10,820	10,999	12,264	85	59.1	124	88,802
Kazakhstan	17,080	19,085	19,398	20,415	64	11.7	7	2,699,700
Kenya	41,761	53,514	55,865	65,582	27	28.1	98	569,140
Kiribati	100	112	114	123	189	12.2	141	811
Korea, North	24,372	25,702	25,955	26,704	55	5.5	216	120,408
Korea, South	49,258	51,577	51,845	52,579	28	4.7	535	96,920
Kosovo	1,815	1,932	1,953	2,060	152	6.5	179	10,887
Kuwait	2,543	2,995	3,068	3,337	137	17.8	172	17,818
Kyrgyzstan	5,410	5,964	6,072	6,438	112	10.2	32	191,801
Laos	6,393	7,540	7,750	8,520	103	17.9	34	230,800
Latvia	2,115	1,883	1,842	1,680	153	-11.0	30	62,249
Lebanon	4,489	5,464	5,297	5,540	122	21.7	518	10,230
Lesotho	1,994	2,162	2,194	2,333	147	8.4	72	30,355
Liberia	3,817	5,073	5,358	6,627	121	32.9	56	96,320
Libya	6,367	6,891	7,138	7,922	106	8.2	4	1,759,540
Liechtenstein	36	39	40	42	212	8.3	248	160
Lithuania	3,089	2,740	2,684	2,468	142	-11.3	43	62,680
Luxembourg	509	629	650	728	168	23.4	252	2,586
Madagascar	20,808	26,899	28,172	33,282	53	29.3	48	581,540
Malawi	15,016	19,823	20,794	24,645	61	32.0	221	94,080
Malaysia	29,063	33,164	33,871	36,520	43	14.1	103	328,657
Maldives	396	391	390	401	176	-1.1	1,309	298
Mali	14,514	19,553	20,742	26,038	62	34.7	17	1,220,190
Malta	417	457	464	480	174	9.6	1,469	316
Marshall Islands	66	78	80	88	200	18.2	442	181
Mauritania	3,203	3,997	4,162	4,830	129	24.8	4	1,030,700
Mauritius	1,282	1,305	1,308	1,312	158	1.8	644	2,030
Mexico	114,222	128,093	129,151	137,038	10	12.1	66	1,943,945
Micronesia, Federated States of	107	102	101	95	194	-4.4	144	702
Moldova	3,731	3,360	3,287	2,989	133	-9.9	100	32,891
Monaco	31	31	31	33	216	1.6	15,700	2
Mongolia	2,783	3,169	3,228	3,411	134	13.8	2	1,553,556
Montenegro	623	610	605	582	171	-2.1	45	13,452
Morocco	32,267	36,055	36,738	39,141	40	11.7	51	716,550
Mozambique	23,012	30,098	31,693	38,879	46	30.8	40	786,380
Namibia	2,183	2,630	2,727	3,137	141	20.5	3	823,290
Nauru	9	10	10	10	222	5.3	467	21
Nepal	26,663	30,175	30,667	32,341	49	13.2	214	143,351
Netherlands	16,574	17,274	17,401	17,872	70	4.2	513	33,893
New Zealand	4,269	4,925	5,053	5,412	125	15.4	19	264,537
Nicaragua	5,595	6,186	6,302	6,739	110	10.6	53	119,990
Niger	15,613	22,760	24,485	32,731	56	45.8	19	1,266,700
Nigeria	165,891	213,986	225,082	275,155	6	29.0	247	910,768
North Macedonia	2,080	2,125	2,131	2,142	148	2.2	84	25,433
Norway	4,891	5,465	5,554	5,889	117	11.7	18	304,282
Oman	2,963	3,625	3,764	4,294	131	22.3	12	309,500
Pakistan	188,341	233,431	242,924	280,266	5	23.9	315	770,875
Palau	21	22	22	22	218	3.3	47	459
Panama	3,481	4,210	4,338	4,846	127	20.9	58	74,340
Papua New Guinea	7,064	9,146	9,593	11,422	94	29.5	21	452,860
Paraguay	6,372	7,189	7,356	7,985	104	12.8	19	397,302
Peru	29,348	31,867	32,276	33,867	45	8.6	25	1,279,996
Philippines	93,746	110,462	114,597	129,001	12	17.8	384	298,170
Poland	38,616	38,270	38,093	37,074	39	-0.9	125	304,255
Portugal	10,650	10,288	10,242	10,140	91	-3.4	112	91,470
Qatar	1,720	2,447	2,508	2,605	143	42.3	217	11,586
Romania	20,533	18,986	18,520	17,338	65	-7.5	81	229,891
Russia	143,493	142,588	142,022	139,143	9	-0.6	9	16,377,742
Rwanda	9,923	12,709	13,174	14,973	76	28.1	534	24,668
Saint Kitts and Nevis	50	54	54	57	207	7.8	209	261
Saint Lucia	161	166	167	170	186	3.4	276	606
Saint Vincent and the Grenadines	104	101	101	100	195	-2.7	260	389
Samoa	192	204	206	217	184	6.1	73	2,821
San Marino	31	34	35	36	214	8.8	569	61
Sao Tome and Principe	176	211	217	243	183	19.9	225	964
Saudi Arabia	27,963	34,224	35,354	40,070	41	22.4	16	2,149,690
Senegal	12,667	17,005	17,923	21,631	68	34.2	93	192,530
Serbia	7,233	6,857	6,739	6,424	108	-5.2	87	77,474
Seychelles	88	96	97	101	197	8.7	213	455
Sierra Leone	6,122	8,256	8,693	10,372	100	34.9	121	71,620
Singapore	5,190	5,810	5,921	6,325	113	12.0	8,352	709
Slovakia	5,426	5,440	5,431	5,354	120	0.3	113	48,105
Slovenia	2,084	2,102	2,101	2,079	149	0.9	104	20,151
Solomon Islands	555	678	703	798	167	22.2	25	27,986

See footnotes at end of table.

Country or territory	Mid-year population (1,000)				Population rank, 2022	Population percent change, 2010 to 2020	Population per sq. km, 2022	Land area, (sq. km)
	2010	2020	2022	2030 (P)				
Somalia	9,787	11,819	12,386	15,139	78	20.8	20	627,337
South Africa	51,122	56,435	57,517	61,486	26	10.4	47	1,214,470
South Sudan [1]	9,765	10,561	11,545	15,309	82	8.2	18	644,329
Spain	46,412	47,041	47,163	47,592	31	1.4	95	498,980
Sri Lanka	21,083	22,896	23,188	24,187	58	8.6	359	64,630
Sudan [1]	34,984	45,544	47,959	58,882	30	30.2	26	1,861,484
Suriname	535	618	633	686	170	15.5	4	156,000
Sweden	9,432	10,383	10,484	10,893	89	10.1	26	410,335
Switzerland	7,770	8,398	8,509	8,934	101	8.1	213	39,997
Syria	22,223	19,392	21,564	26,206	60	-12.7	116	185,887
Taiwan	23,111	23,563	23,581	23,602	57	2.0	731	32,260
Tajikistan	7,486	8,860	9,119	10,085	97	18.4	64	141,510
Tanzania	44,521	60,363	63,853	79,023	23	35.6	72	885,800
Thailand	66,271	69,292	69,648	70,281	20	4.6	136	510,890
Timor-Leste	1,088	1,383	1,445	1,686	156	27.1	97	14,874
Togo	6,178	8,077	8,492	10,255	102	30.7	156	54,385
Tonga	106	106	106	102	191	0.4	147	717
Trinidad and Tobago	1,321	1,401	1,406	1,412	157	6.0	274	5,128
Tunisia	10,526	11,719	11,897	12,372	80	11.3	77	155,360
Turkey	74,647	82,009	83,048	86,893	19	9.9	108	769,632
Turkmenistan	4,940	5,523	5,636	6,028	115	11.8	12	469,930
Tuvalu	10	11	12	12	221	8.3	444	26
Uganda	31,002	43,250	46,206	59,136	33	39.5	234	197,100
Ukraine	45,768	43,904	43,528	41,679	35	-4.1	75	579,330
United Arab Emirates	8,021	9,792	9,916	10,479	92	22.1	119	83,600
United Kingdom	62,502	67,023	67,791	70,089	22	7.2	280	241,930
United States	**309,322**	**332,639**	**337,342**	**355,101**	**3**	**7.5**	**37**	**9,150,541**
Uruguay	3,302	3,389	3,407	3,475	132	2.6	20	175,015
Uzbekistan	27,869	30,576	31,105	32,917	47	9.7	73	425,400
Vanuatu	245	298	308	347	179	21.6	25	12,189
Venezuela	28,663	28,612	29,790	33,060	50	-0.2	34	882,050
Vietnam	90,459	101,745	103,808	110,901	16	12.5	335	310,070
Yemen	23,195	29,811	30,985	35,493	48	28.5	59	527,968
Zambia	13,647	18,523	19,642	24,494	63	35.7	26	743,398
Zimbabwe	12,722	14,546	15,121	17,628	73	14.3	39	386,847
TERRITORIES AND DEPENDENCIES								
American Samoa	56	47	45	40	210	-14.7	230	198
Anguilla	15	18	19	21	219	22.5	206	91
Aruba	105	119	122	133	188	14.3	680	180
Bermuda	68	72	72	74	202	5.1	1,340	54
Cayman Islands	50	62	64	73	204	23.6	244	264
Cook Islands	11	9	8	7	223	-25.5	34	236
Curacao [2]	143	151	152	155	187	5.5	343	444
Faroe Islands	49	52	52	55	208	5.2	38	1,393
French Polynesia	269	295	299	314	181	9.7	78	3,827
Gaza Strip [3]	1,503	1,917	1,997	2,321	151	27.6	5,548	360
Gibraltar	29	29	30	30	217	2.4	4,225	7
Greenland	58	58	58	57	206	0.3	(Z)	2,166,086
Guam	163	168	169	170	185	3.2	311	544
Guernsey	65	67	67	68	203	3.7	865	78
Hong Kong	7,029	7,248	7,277	7,315	105	3.1	6,782	1,073
Isle of Man	84	90	91	94	198	7.8	160	572
Jersey	93	101	102	106	193	8.0	881	116
Macau	569	625	635	667	169	9.9	22,689	28
Montserrat	5	5	5	6	226	4.7	53	102
New Caledonia	252	290	297	324	182	14.9	16	18,275
Northern Mariana Islands	55	52	51	50	209	-5.9	109	472
Puerto Rico	3,722	3,190	3,098	2,818	135	-14.3	349	8,869
Saint Barthelemy	7	7	7	7	225	-3.7	284	25
Saint Helena, Ascension, and Tristan da Cunha	8	8	8	8	224	2.9	20	394
Saint Martin	30	33	33	34	215	7.8	607	54
Saint Pierre and Miquelon	6	5	5	5	227	-9.9	22	242
Sint Maarten [2]	38	44	45	49	211	16.1	1,327	34
Turks and Caicos Islands	43	56	58	67	205	29.8	62	948
Virgin Islands, British	30	37	39	44	213	25.4	256	151
Virgin Islands, U.S.	108	106	105	100	192	-1.9	303	348
Wallis and Futuna	15	16	16	16	220	3.1	112	142
West Bank [3]	2,403	2,899	3,000	3,397	139	20.6	532	5,640

P Projected. X Not applicable. Z Less than 0.05 percent or less than 1 person per square kilometer. [1] Sudan and South Sudan became separate countries in July 2011. [2] The Netherlands Antilles dissolved on October 10, 2010. Curacao and Sint Maarten became autonomous territories of the Kingdom of the Netherlands. [3] The Gaza Strip and West Bank are Israeli occupied with interim status subject to Israeli/Palestinian negotiations. The final status is yet to be determined.

Source: U.S. Census Bureau, "International Data Base (IDB)," <www.census.gov/programs-surveys/international-programs/about/idb.html>, accessed May 2022.

Table 1354. Net Migration Rate by Country: 1990 to 2021

[Net migration is the difference between the number of migrants entering and those leaving a country in a year, per 1,000 midyear population. A positive figure is known as net immigration and a negative figure as net emigration]

Country	1990	2000	2005	2010	2014	2015	2016	2017	2018	2019	2020	2021
Afghanistan	-51.23	-45.30	9.43	-3.25	-1.83	-1.51	-1.20	-0.90	-0.62	-0.35	-0.10	-0.10
Algeria	-0.22	-0.62	-3.38	-0.92	-0.93	-0.92	-0.90	-0.89	-0.87	-0.86	-0.85	-0.84
Angola	-0.31	-5.05	1.89	1.52	0.92	0.53	0.32	0.22	0.13	0.04	-0.21	-0.20
Argentina	0.60	-0.44	-0.64	-0.12	-0.11	-0.10	-0.10	-0.10	-0.09	-0.09	-0.09	-0.08
Australia	7.45	5.70	6.18	7.88	7.67	7.66	10.17	9.92	9.28	8.66	8.07	7.49
Bangladesh	-2.19	-4.79	-4.87	-4.14	-3.94	-3.89	-3.08	-3.05	-3.02	-2.99	-2.96	-2.93
Belgium	(NA)	2.45	4.38	6.37	6.10	5.87	5.64	5.42	5.21	4.99	4.79	4.58
Benin	0.81	0.50	3.89	0.43	0.35	0.31	0.34	0.32	0.28	0.27	0.26	0.25
Bolivia	(NA)	-1.47	-1.27	-1.15	-1.08	-1.06	-1.05	-1.03	-1.02	-0.52	-1.00	-0.99
Brazil	0.16	0.03	-0.04	0.03	0.09	0.10	-0.13	-0.11	-0.02	0.14	-0.05	-0.12
Burkina Faso	(NA)	-6.42	-5.40	-3.18	-1.37	-1.03	-0.88	-0.69	-0.67	-0.66	-0.64	-0.62
Burma	-0.25	-1.46	-2.49	-2.98	-1.65	-1.14	-1.58	-1.54	-1.49	-1.44	-1.40	-1.38
Burundi	-8.82	-6.88	2.39	0.83	-1.00	-22.45	-11.01	-6.61	-4.60	-2.67	-0.84	7.35
Cambodia	3.91	-3.61	-4.10	-8.83	-8.45	-2.11	-2.07	-2.04	-2.01	-2.39	-2.76	-2.73
Cameroon	-0.69	-1.34	-1.53	-0.18	6.13	2.54	0.72	-2.31	-0.35	-0.34	-0.33	-0.32
Canada	(NA)	5.31	4.83	7.41	5.22	5.87	6.22	5.87	5.85	5.75	5.65	5.55
Chad	(NA)	-0.76	1.71	0.68	1.33	-3.57	1.30	-0.15	-0.14	-0.14	-0.14	-0.13
Chile	1.38	0.40	0.38	0.36	0.35	0.34	0.34	0.34	0.33	0.33	0.33	0.33
China	-0.14	-0.26	-0.21	-0.17	-0.15	-0.15	-0.14	-0.14	-0.13	-0.13	–	–
Colombia	-0.80	-9.58	-3.10	-5.67	-4.73	-5.43	-4.80	-2.64	21.52	6.83	-1.58	-1.31
Congo, Dem. Rep	1.73	-1.24	0.76	-0.60	-0.03	0.33	0.75	-0.58	-1.04	-0.95	-0.87	-0.78
Cote d'Ivoire	56.15	–	-0.93	0.17	1.84	1.42	2.30	1.32	1.29	1.26	1.24	1.21
Ecuador	-13.32	-6.38	3.89	-0.67	-0.13	–						
Egypt	(NA)	-0.36	-0.46	-0.44	-0.37	-0.56	-0.29	-0.16	-0.16	-0.28	-0.34	-0.32
Ethiopia	3.90	-1.30	-0.64	0.05	2.11	0.59	0.37	0.72	-0.12	-0.21	-0.20	-0.20
France	1.37	1.17	1.46	1.11	1.09	1.09	1.08	1.08	1.07	1.07	1.07	1.06
Germany	(NA)	2.03	0.96	1.85	6.81	14.83	5.92	4.24	4.19	3.67	1.78	1.78
Ghana	0.11	0.11	1.76	1.02	0.47	0.24	0.33	0.30	0.12	-0.06	-0.17	-0.17
Guatemala	-4.36	-11.47	-0.14	-1.49	-2.43	-2.75	-3.18	-2.79	-2.42	-2.06	-1.71	-1.69
Guinea	55.97	-9.55	-8.93	-0.13	0.02	0.01	-0.34					
Haiti	-4.10	-3.58	-2.45	-4.82	-3.37	11.86	1.52	-2.00	-1.98	-1.95	-1.93	-1.90
India	(NA)	-0.12	-0.27	-0.42	-0.22	-0.20	-0.19	-0.20	-0.20	-0.20	0.39	0.20
Indonesia	-0.47	-1.58	-1.32	-1.20	-1.15	-1.13	-1.05	-0.97	-0.88	-0.80	-0.72	-0.72
Iran	22.04	-1.87	-1.48	-0.27	1.56	-0.13	-0.13	-0.16	-0.21	-0.26	-0.31	-0.30
Iraq	-58.60	–	1.90	3.19	-0.09	-0.60	-2.95	-0.64	-0.37	-0.35	-0.52	-0.68
Italy	(NA)	2.95	4.41	6.25	2.30	2.16	2.34	3.06	2.85	2.49	2.67	2.85
Japan	0.02	0.30	-0.41	–	0.29	0.75	0.75	0.75	0.75	0.75	0.75	0.75
Kazakhstan	-7.80	-3.23	1.41	0.44	0.42	0.41	0.41	0.41	0.40	0.40	0.39	0.39
Kenya	0.24	-0.77	0.32	1.05	0.35	0.05	-2.10	-0.38	-0.21	-0.20	-0.20	-0.20
Korea, North	(NA)	1.63	0.14	-0.04	-0.04	-0.04	-0.04	-0.04	-0.04	-0.04	-0.04	-0.04
Korea, South	0.77	0.17	-1.97	1.67	2.81	2.78	2.76	2.73	2.71	2.69	2.67	2.65
Malawi	7.96	-3.29	-2.11	-1.20	-0.64	-0.52	-0.40	-0.29	-0.19	-0.09	–	–
Malaysia	2.46	10.92	7.82	7.06	1.62	1.60	1.58	1.56	1.54	1.52	1.51	1.49
Mali	-7.88	-7.75	-4.93	-3.76	-3.29	-4.57	-4.09	-3.86	-3.86	-3.86	-3.86	-3.17
Mexico	-4.82	-5.19	-4.31	-0.36	-0.86	-0.82	-0.79	-0.75	-0.72	-0.73	-0.74	-0.75
Morocco	-0.90	-3.95	-2.49	-2.34	-2.25	-1.88	-1.87	-1.83	-1.81	-1.77	-1.77	-1.76
Mozambique	-9.04	-5.00	-4.60	-4.02	-1.85	-1.84	-2.09	-1.84	-1.55	-1.61	-1.66	-1.62
Nepal	-0.20	-6.56	-10.94	-2.44	-2.12	-2.43	-2.49	-2.88	-3.27	-3.66	-4.04	-4.12
Netherlands	(NA)	3.38	-1.68	2.07	1.97	1.95	1.94	1.93	1.92	1.92	1.91	1.90
Niger	-1.83	-1.39	-1.28	-1.05	0.21	1.59	1.30	-0.87	-0.18	-0.72	-0.69	-0.66
Nigeria	-0.10	-0.02	-0.19	-0.32	-0.86	-1.36	-1.73	-0.21	-0.21	-0.21	-0.21	-0.21
Pakistan	0.91	8.41	-3.63	-0.49	-2.40	-2.09	-3.49	-0.95	-0.77	-0.82	-0.87	-0.92
Peru	-1.18	-1.80	-3.94	-11.12	-10.70	-10.59	-10.36	-9.33	14.73	3.53	3.23	-0.62
Philippines	-1.10	-1.33	-1.71	-2.55	-0.99	-1.14	-3.61	-1.07	-0.43	0.15	3.60	0.31
Poland	-0.41	-0.51	-0.28	-0.05	-0.49	-0.46	-0.44	-0.41	-0.38	-0.36	-0.33	-0.33
Romania	(NA)	-5.66	-5.89	-4.45	-4.10	-4.80	-5.06	-6.71	-6.35	-6.70	-5.32	-4.85
Russia	3.92	2.20	1.14	1.68	1.68	1.68	1.68	1.69	1.69	1.69	1.69	1.70
Rwanda	-4.68	-21.77	-11.59	-2.35	0.50	-12.29	0.89	0.17	-0.51	-1.16	-3.33	-3.27
Saudi Arabia	(NA)	0.59	-1.84	16.26	5.65	4.97	4.39	3.93	4.07	4.30	4.63	5.04
Senegal	-5.62	-3.93	-2.40	-1.74	-0.63	-0.81	-0.71	-0.08	-1.93	-0.90	-0.80	-0.73
Somalia	-38.47	6.59	-0.70	-11.97	-9.48	-8.46	-7.47	-6.51	-5.58	-4.68	-3.81	-2.98
South Africa	-0.47	0.76	3.82	-3.45	1.17	2.42	-0.94	-0.93	-0.92	-0.58	-0.24	-0.12
South Sudan	(NA)	(NA)	(NA)	30.66	-41.87	-14.35	-59.89	-64.21	-29.19	0.20	0.20	22.04
Spain	(NA)	9.60	14.55	-0.92	-2.06	-0.04	1.89	3.53	7.19	9.70	4.60	4.47
Sri Lanka	-7.14	0.31	-2.12	-2.37	-1.54	-1.35	-1.33	-1.31	-1.29	-1.27	-1.26	-1.24
Sudan	(NA)	(NA)	(NA)	-9.94	1.90	1.18	1.67	4.20	1.86	-0.45	-0.44	-1.71
Syria	(NA)	(NA)	0.72	-2.45	-77.36	-69.67	-32.77	-42.46	36.62	18.83	27.07	34.34
Taiwan	0.29	0.25	0.68	0.95	0.59	0.37	0.50	0.37	0.38	0.54	0.65	0.75
Tanzania	-1.57	1.75	-1.38	-0.21	-0.23	2.38	1.30	0.49	-0.53	-0.50	-0.47	-0.44
Thailand	-1.82	1.37	1.65	1.06	0.62	0.53	0.22	0.27	0.20	0.13	0.06	-0.03
Tunisia	(NA)	-1.00	-2.14	-2.04	-2.10	-1.97	-1.84	-1.71	-1.59	-1.47	-1.35	-1.34
Turkey	-0.50	-1.34	-1.82	-1.72	2.19	2.17	-1.15	-4.53	-4.45	-4.38	-4.30	-1.55
Uganda	-0.75	-2.28	-9.97	-8.47	-3.22	-4.74	5.58	4.05	-10.37	-4.07	-3.48	-3.37
Ukraine	1.54	-2.36	0.10	0.35	-13.35	-2.25	–	4.55	4.55	2.28	-0.26	
United Kingdom	(NA)	2.69	3.39	4.03	4.86	5.12	3.80	4.33	3.92	4.69	4.32	3.95
United States	**(NA)**	**(NA)**	**(NA)**	**(NA)**	**3.10**	**3.10**	**3.10**	**2.50**	**2.00**	**1.90**	**3.04**	**3.03**
Uzbekistan	-3.58	-2.66	-3.36	-2.84	-2.46	-2.37	-2.28	-2.19	-2.11	-2.02	-1.94	-1.86
Venezuela	-0.99	-1.71	-1.68	-1.35	-6.98	-2.80	-6.24	-26.29	-66.09	-21.29	-3.44	14.22
Vietnam	-1.14	-0.38	-0.42	-0.36	-0.31	-0.30	-0.29	-0.27	-0.26	-0.25	-0.24	-0.23
Yemen	(NA)	-1.73	-0.48	0.97	2.61	1.01	0.67	0.35	0.05	-0.20	-0.20	-0.19
Zambia	0.11	4.38	-1.56	-0.64	0.12	0.06	0.25	0.79	0.41	0.52	0.42	0.33
Zimbabwe	0.76	-7.76	-17.59	-13.74	-12.09	-10.86	-9.65	-8.45	-7.28	-6.14	-5.02	-4.93

– Represents or rounds to zero. NA Not available.

Source: U.S. Census Bureau, "International Data Base (IDB)," <www.census.gov/programs-surveys/international-programs/about/idb.html>, accessed May 2022.

Table 1355. Foreign or Foreign-Born Population in Selected OECD Countries: 2000 to 2020

[30,273 represents 30,273,000. In Australia, Chile, Israel, and the United States, the data refer to residents who are foreign born. In the European countries, Japan, and South Korea, data represent the legal nationality or citizenship status of residents. Data are based on censuses, population registers, and residence permits. For details about data methodology for individual countries, see source]

Country	2000	2005	2010	2015	2016	2017	2018	2019	2020
United States	**30,273**	**34,258**	**38,453**	**42,391**	**43,290**	**43,739**	**44,525**	**44,933**	**(NA)**
Australia	4,412	4,877	5,881	6,730	6,912	7,139	7,333	7,533	7,653
Austria	694	774	884	1,146	1,268	1,342	1,396	1,439	1,486
Belgium	897	871	1,058	1,277	1,333	1,367	1,389	1,414	1,479
Chile	(NA)	236	352	465	(NA)	746	(NA)	1,252	1,493
Czechia	229	254	433	449	465	493	524	564	593
Denmark	259	268	330	423	463	485	506	526	537
France	3,259	(NA)	3,821	4,335	4,542	4,704	4,617	4,763	(NA)
Germany	7,344	6,717	6,695	8,153	9,108	10,039	10,624	10,915	11,228
Ireland	(NA)	(NA)	575	606	607	567	594	623	644
Israel [1]	1,944	1,961	1,878	1,817	1,818	1,812	1,811	1,809	1,812
Italy	1,341	2,402	3,648	5,014	5,027	5,047	5,144	4,996	5,040
Japan	1,556	1,974	2,185	2,122	2,232	2,383	2,562	2,731	2,933
Korea, South	169	491	921	1,092	1,143	1,162	1,172	1,951	2,025
Netherlands	652	699	735	847	901	972	1,041	1,111	1,192
Norway	179	213	334	512	538	559	568	584	605
Portugal	191	449	454	395	389	398	422	480	590
Spain	924	3,731	5,403	4,454	4,418	4,419	4,563	4,840	5,227
Sweden	482	481	603	739	783	852	897	932	941
Switzerland	1,369	1,495	1,680	1,947	1,994	2,030	2,054	2,081	2,111
Turkey	(NA)	(NA)	167	518	650	816	919	1,211	1,531
United Kingdom	2,208	2,857	4,524	5,592	5,951	6,137	5,991	6,227	(NA)

NA Not available. [1] See footnote 1, Table 1358.

Source: Organisation for Economic Co-operation and Development (OECD), 2022, "International Migration Database," OECD International Migration Statistics (database) ©, <dx.doi.org/10.1787/data-00342-en>, accessed August 2022.

Table 1356. Youth and Elderly Population Distribution by Country: 2022 and Projected 2030

[Percent of total population, as of mid-year. Covers countries with 12 million or more population in 2022]

Country	2022 Under 15 years old	2022 65 years old and over	2030 (P) Under 15 years old	2030 (P) 65 years old and over	Country	2022 Under 15 years old	2022 65 years old and over	2030 (P) Under 15 years old	2030 (P) 65 years old and over
Afghanistan	40.0	2.8	37.7	3.2	Malawi	39.3	3.8	33.5	4.4
Algeria	29.1	6.7	24.6	9.2	Malaysia	22.7	7.8	20.6	10.3
Angola	47.4	2.3	45.1	2.6	Mali	47.3	3.0	44.7	3.2
Argentina	23.7	12.5	21.8	13.8	Mexico	24.3	7.9	20.7	9.8
Australia	18.6	16.4	17.5	18.6	Morocco	26.3	7.7	23.6	10.5
Bangladesh	25.7	7.3	23.7	9.4	Mozambique	45.2	2.9	42.3	2.9
Benin	45.4	2.4	44.3	2.5	Nepal	26.8	6.0	23.2	7.6
Bolivia	29.7	6.7	24.8	8.2	Netherlands	16.1	20.5	16.1	23.8
Brazil	20.0	10.2	18.7	13.3	Niger	50.0	2.7	48.4	2.7
Burkina Faso	42.7	3.2	37.9	3.4	Nigeria	41.0	3.3	39.1	3.6
Burma	25.3	6.5	22.2	9.0	Pakistan	35.2	4.7	31.8	5.7
Burundi	43.0	3.2	40.4	3.7	Peru	26.2	8.1	23.7	8.9
Cambodia	30.0	5.0	25.2	7.2	Philippines	30.8	5.3	29.0	6.3
Cameroon	41.9	3.2	40.2	3.4	Poland	14.7	20.0	13.0	23.4
Canada	15.8	20.0	15.0	23.9	Romania	15.8	21.9	14.4	23.0
Chad	46.7	2.5	43.4	2.6	Russia	17.1	16.6	14.7	20.4
Chile	19.5	12.6	18.0	17.0	Rwanda	38.6	2.8	32.8	3.7
China	16.7	13.6	14.8	17.8	Saudi Arabia	24.0	4.0	20.0	5.9
Colombia	22.7	10.6	21.1	13.6	Senegal	41.7	3.3	37.2	4.0
Congo, Dem. Rep.	46.2	2.5	43.8	2.6	Somalia	41.7	2.6	40.1	3.6
Cote d'Ivoire	37.3	2.9	33.7	3.1	South Africa	27.5	6.4	25.1	7.6
Ecuador	24.9	8.8	22.2	11.2	Spain	13.7	20.2	11.6	23.8
Egypt	34.8	5.1	28.6	6.9	Sri Lanka	22.4	11.4	19.6	14.7
Ethiopia	39.2	3.5	36.3	4.0	Sudan	40.9	3.1	38.5	3.8
France	18.2	21.1	17.2	23.7	Syria	33.3	4.3	29.7	5.3
Germany	13.7	22.9	13.9	27.0	Taiwan	12.3	17.3	11.4	23.5
Ghana	38.0	4.3	34.6	4.9	Tanzania	41.8	3.3	39.0	3.8
Guatemala	32.5	5.1	28.3	6.3	Thailand	16.2	13.8	14.9	19.4
Guinea	41.0	4.0	40.5	4.2	Tunisia	25.0	9.6	20.7	13.1
India	25.1	6.8	22.6	7.8	Turkey	22.5	9.0	19.8	12.0
Indonesia	24.7	7.4	21.3	9.7	Uganda	47.6	2.4	45.2	2.6
Iran	23.7	6.4	20.9	8.9	Ukraine	16.1	17.7	14.1	20.9
Iraq	35.8	3.5	31.1	4.4	United Kingdom	17.1	18.8	15.9	21.4
Italy	12.3	23.0	11.1	26.3	**United States**	**18.3**	**17.7**	**17.8**	**20.6**
Japan	12.5	29.0	11.3	30.8	Uzbekistan	22.7	6.5	20.7	9.8
Kazakhstan	25.7	9.1	21.5	12.2	Venezuela	25.3	8.6	23.1	11.0
Kenya	37.2	3.2	32.6	4.0	Vietnam	23.7	7.5	21.3	11.0
Korea, North	20.3	10.2	19.7	12.9	Yemen	35.9	3.2	30.3	4.1
Korea, South	11.8	17.5	10.2	24.5	Zambia	42.9	2.7	40.1	3.1
Madagascar	37.9	3.7	34.2	4.6	Zimbabwe	38.2	4.5	37.7	4.5

P Projected.

Source: U.S. Census Bureau, "International Data Base (IDB)," <www.census.gov/programs-surveys/international-programs/about/idb.html>, accessed May 2022.

Table 1357. Births, Deaths, and Life Expectancy by Country or Territory: 2022 and 2030

[Covers countries with 13 million or more population in 2022]

Country or territory	Crude birth rate [1]		Crude death rate [2]		Expectation of life at birth (years)		Infant mortality rate [3]		Total fertility rate per woman [4]	
	2022	2030 (P)	2022	2030 (P)	2022	2030 (P)	2022	2030 (P)	2022	2030 (P)
Afghanistan............	35.5	30.3	12.3	10.6	53.7	56.8	104.9	90.8	4.62	3.90
Algeria.................	18.5	14.4	4.3	4.6	78.0	79.9	19.7	16.0	2.51	2.19
Angola.................	41.8	39.2	8.0	6.5	62.1	65.3	58.9	46.5	5.83	5.29
Argentina..............	15.6	14.3	7.3	7.2	78.3	80.2	9.4	7.9	2.18	2.07
Australia...............	12.3	11.5	6.8	7.0	83.1	84.6	3.0	2.7	1.73	1.72
Bangladesh............	17.7	15.9	5.5	5.8	74.7	76.8	30.4	24.6	2.09	2.04
Benin..................	41.2	37.8	8.0	6.6	62.2	65.2	55.8	45.1	5.43	5.09
Brazil..................	14.0	12.4	6.8	7.4	75.9	77.7	13.3	11.4	1.80	1.73
Burkina Faso..........	33.6	27.7	7.7	6.4	63.4	66.4	49.4	40.0	4.27	3.38
Burma.................	16.3	14.3	7.1	7.4	69.9	72.2	32.9	27.4	2.02	1.87
Cambodia..............	19.3	15.9	5.8	5.6	70.7	73.6	29.6	23.5	2.24	2.01
Cameroon..............	35.5	32.2	7.7	6.4	63.3	66.7	48.7	38.9	4.55	4.12
Canada................	10.2	9.5	8.1	8.7	83.8	85.3	4.4	3.9	1.57	1.61
Chad...................	40.5	36.5	9.5	7.8	59.2	62.4	65.5	54.1	5.46	4.71
Chile..................	12.8	11.3	6.5	7.1	79.8	81.6	6.6	5.6	1.76	1.73
China..................	9.9	8.5	7.9	8.4	77.7	80.3	6.8	5.4	1.45	1.52
Colombia...............	15.2	13.8	7.7	7.1	74.9	78.2	11.7	11.5	1.95	1.92
Congo, Dem. Rep......	40.1	37.0	7.9	6.6	61.8	64.9	60.9	48.0	5.63	5.07
Cote d'Ivoire..........	28.3	25.1	7.6	6.7	62.3	65.7	55.7	43.6	3.53	3.04
Ecuador...............	16.5	14.5	5.2	5.4	78.0	79.9	18.1	15.1	2.04	1.89
Egypt..................	21.5	16.7	4.3	4.5	74.5	76.5	17.7	14.5	2.88	2.22
Ethiopia...............	30.5	26.7	5.7	5.1	68.3	70.8	33.5	25.7	3.99	3.43
France.................	11.7	11.0	9.5	9.5	82.6	84.1	3.2	2.8	2.03	1.93
Germany...............	9.1	8.5	12.0	12.0	81.5	83.1	3.2	2.8	1.57	1.61
Ghana.................	28.6	25.2	6.1	5.3	69.4	72.0	32.6	27.2	3.66	3.27
Guatemala.............	22.3	19.3	4.9	4.9	72.9	75.1	26.2	21.6	2.62	2.30
Guinea................	35.7	34.0	8.1	7.0	63.9	66.7	49.6	39.8	4.85	4.59
India..................	16.8	14.7	10.3	7.4	67.2	71.3	30.3	30.7	2.10	1.91
Indonesia..............	15.3	13.8	6.8	7.0	73.1	75.2	19.7	16.4	2.01	1.84
Iran...................	15.3	12.3	5.2	5.6	75.3	77.1	14.8	12.4	1.93	1.86
Iraq...................	24.7	21.6	3.9	3.9	73.2	75.3	19.6	16.3	3.25	2.74
Italy..................	7.0	7.6	11.3	11.2	82.6	84.1	3.2	2.8	1.22	1.36
Japan..................	7.0	6.9	11.6	12.8	84.8	86.2	1.9	1.7	1.38	1.45
Kazakhstan............	15.4	13.0	8.1	8.0	72.5	74.7	19.2	16.1	2.11	1.92
Kenya.................	26.4	23.8	5.0	4.7	69.7	72.3	27.9	21.4	3.29	2.82
Korea, North..........	14.2	12.4	9.5	9.8	71.8	73.7	22.2	18.9	1.90	1.82
Korea, South..........	6.9	6.8	7.1	8.5	83.0	84.5	2.9	2.6	1.10	1.19
Madagascar............	28.7	24.5	6.0	5.5	68.2	70.5	39.0	33.3	3.62	3.04
Malawi................	27.9	23.4	4.6	4.1	72.4	74.7	33.4	28.0	3.40	2.69
Malaysia...............	14.6	13.1	5.7	6.1	76.1	78.1	6.6	5.8	1.75	1.71
Mali...................	41.1	36.7	8.5	7.0	62.4	65.5	60.6	48.4	5.54	4.78
Mexico................	13.6	13.9	7.7	6.1	72.3	76.9	11.9	11.1	1.68	1.80
Morocco...............	17.4	15.4	6.6	6.9	73.7	75.8	19.2	15.8	2.29	2.17
Mozambique...........	37.5	35.1	10.3	8.1	57.1	61.7	61.4	49.5	4.81	4.35
Nepal..................	17.5	15.4	5.6	5.7	72.4	74.6	25.1	20.8	1.90	1.75
Netherlands............	11.0	10.7	9.2	9.7	82.2	83.7	3.4	3.0	1.78	1.75
Niger..................	47.1	44.3	9.9	8.2	60.1	63.1	66.8	57.1	6.82	6.10
Nigeria................	34.2	32.4	8.7	7.4	61.3	64.7	56.7	45.5	4.62	4.22
Pakistan...............	26.5	22.9	6.0	5.6	69.7	71.9	54.0	44.7	3.46	2.94
Peru..................	17.2	15.2	11.3	6.2	68.9	75.8	10.8	10.4	2.20	2.01
Philippines.............	22.3	21.1	6.4	6.7	70.1	70.9	22.2	22.0	2.78	2.67
Poland.................	8.5	7.6	10.7	11.3	78.8	80.6	4.2	3.7	1.40	1.49
Romania...............	8.8	8.4	15.3	14.3	75.8	78.6	5.8	4.9	1.63	1.63
Russia.................	9.5	8.7	13.4	13.2	72.4	74.6	6.4	5.7	1.60	1.60
Rwanda................	26.4	22.0	5.9	5.4	65.9	68.6	26.4	20.9	3.33	2.67
Saudi Arabia...........	14.2	12.7	3.4	3.7	76.7	78.6	12.3	10.1	1.92	1.78
Senegal................	31.5	26.5	5.1	4.6	70.0	72.3	32.4	27.3	4.27	3.45
South Africa...........	18.6	16.2	9.3	9.3	65.3	67.4	25.9	19.7	2.18	2.05
Spain..................	7.1	7.5	10.2	9.9	82.6	84.1	2.5	2.2	1.27	1.40
Sri Lanka..............	13.8	12.8	6.5	7.0	78.0	79.9	8.2	7.0	1.98	1.88
Sudan.................	33.5	30.9	6.3	5.6	67.1	69.7	42.3	35.8	4.60	4.01
Syria..................	22.7	19.5	4.2	4.0	74.3	76.4	15.9	13.0	2.80	2.44
Taiwan................	7.4	6.9	7.9	8.9	81.2	82.8	4.0	3.5	1.08	1.17
Tanzania...............	33.3	30.4	5.1	4.6	70.2	72.5	30.9	26.1	4.39	3.93
Thailand...............	10.1	9.2	7.8	8.7	77.7	79.6	6.5	5.7	1.54	1.56
Turkey................	14.3	12.7	6.1	6.6	76.2	78.2	19.4	15.7	1.93	1.83
Uganda................	40.9	35.5	5.0	4.1	69.0	71.8	30.5	23.3	5.36	4.62
Ukraine................	9.0	8.4	13.8	13.6	73.5	75.6	7.3	6.4	1.56	1.60
United Kingdom........	10.8	10.5	9.1	9.3	81.9	83.3	3.8	3.5	1.63	1.65
United States.........	**12.3**	**11.7**	**8.4**	**8.9**	**80.6**	**81.8**	**5.2**	**4.8**	**1.84**	**1.84**
Uzbekistan.............	15.5	12.7	5.4	5.7	75.3	77.3	19.0	15.8	1.73	1.71
Venezuela..............	17.3	15.2	6.8	6.8	73.3	76.1	17.7	12.4	2.22	2.07
Vietnam...............	15.7	13.2	5.8	6.1	75.5	77.6	14.8	12.3	2.05	1.95
Yemen.................	24.6	20.8	5.6	5.3	67.5	70.0	46.5	39.1	3.01	2.41
Zambia................	34.9	31.6	6.1	5.4	66.3	68.9	37.1	31.4	4.56	4.02
Zimbabwe.............	33.1	29.8	8.8	7.1	63.3	66.9	28.5	22.4	3.89	3.70

P Projection. [1] Number of births per 1,000 persons, based on midyear population. [2] Number of deaths per 1,000 persons, based on midyear population. [3] Number of deaths of children under 1 year of age per 1,000 live births in a calendar year. [4] Average number of children that would be born if all women lived to the end of childbearing age, based on birth rates for each specified year.

Source: U.S. Census Bureau, "International Data Base (IDB)," <www.census.gov/programs-surveys/international-programs/about/idb.html>, accessed May 2022.

Table 1358. Life Expectancy at Birth and at Age 65 by Sex—Selected Countries: 2010 and 2020

Country	Life expectancy at birth (years)				Life expectancy at age 65 (years)			
	Females		Males		Females		Males	
	2010	2020	2010	2020	2010	2020	2010	2020
United States............	**81.0**	**79.9**	**76.2**	**74.2**	**20.3**	**19.8**	**17.7**	**17.0**
Australia................	84.0	85.3	79.5	81.2	21.8	23.0	18.9	20.3
Austria..................	83.5	83.6	77.8	78.9	21.4	21.0	17.9	17.9
Belgium.................	83.0	83.0	77.5	78.6	21.3	20.8	17.6	17.6
Canada.................	83.3	84.0	78.8	79.5	21.5	22.1	18.4	19.4
Colombia...............	77.9	80.0	70.8	73.6	18.9	20.0	16.6	17.4
Costa Rica..............	81.6	83.2	76.6	78.1	20.7	21.4	18.2	18.8
Czechia.................	80.9	81.3	74.5	75.3	19.0	19.1	15.5	15.2
Denmark................	81.4	83.6	77.2	79.7	19.7	21.2	17.0	18.4
Finland.................	83.5	84.8	76.9	79.2	21.5	22.2	17.5	18.8
France..................	85.3	85.3	78.3	79.2	23.4	23.1	18.9	19.0
Germany................	83.0	83.5	78.0	78.7	20.9	21.2	17.8	18.0
Greece.................	83.3	83.9	78.0	78.8	21.0	21.4	18.2	18.5
Hungary................	78.6	79.0	70.7	72.3	18.2	17.9	14.1	14.0
Iceland.................	84.1	84.6	79.8	81.6	21.5	22.0	18.3	20.3
Ireland.................	83.1	84.4	78.5	80.8	20.8	21.9	17.7	19.4
Israel [1]................	83.6	84.8	79.7	80.7	21.2	22.0	18.9	19.3
Italy....................	84.7	84.5	79.5	80.0	22.1	21.7	18.3	18.3
Japan...................	86.3	87.7	79.6	81.6	23.8	24.9	18.7	20.1
Korea, South............	83.6	86.5	76.8	80.5	21.2	23.6	16.8	19.2
Mexico.................	77.9	78.1	71.6	72.4	18.8	18.7	16.6	16.7
Netherlands.............	83.0	83.1	78.9	79.7	21.0	20.7	17.7	18.2
New Zealand............	82.7	84.1	78.9	80.5	21.0	22.1	18.5	19.8
Norway.................	83.3	84.9	79.0	81.6	21.2	22.1	18.0	19.8
Poland..................	80.7	80.7	72.2	72.5	19.5	19.2	15.1	14.6
Portugal................	83.2	84.1	76.8	78.0	21.0	21.6	17.2	17.8
Slovenia................	83.1	83.4	76.4	77.8	21.0	20.6	16.8	16.9
Spain...................	85.5	85.2	79.2	79.6	22.9	22.4	18.6	18.4
Sweden.................	83.6	84.2	79.6	80.6	21.2	21.4	18.3	18.9
Switzerland.............	84.9	85.1	80.3	81.0	22.5	22.2	19.0	19.3
United Kingdom.........	82.6	82.4	78.6	78.4	20.8	20.6	18.2	18.0

[1] The statistical data for Israel are supplied by and under the responsibility of the relevant Israeli authorities. The use of such data by the OECD is without prejudice to the status of the Golan Heights, East Jerusalem and Israeli settlements in the West Bank under the terms of international law.

Source: Organisation for Economic Co-operation and Development (OECD), 2022, "OECD Health Data: Health Status," OECD Health Statistics (database) ©, <dx.doi.org/10.1787/data-00540-en>, accessed July 2022.

Table 1359. Percent of the Adult Population Considered to Be Obese: 2000 to 2020

[Obesity rates are defined as the percentage of the population with a Body Mass Index (BMI) over 30 kg/m^2. The BMI is a single number that evaluates an individual's weight status in relation to height (weight/height^2). Obesity estimates derived from health examinations are generally higher and more reliable than those coming from self-reports because they preclude any misreporting of people's height and weight; however, health examinations are only conducted regularly in a few countries. For more information on methods, see source]

Country	2000	2005	2010	2015	2017	2018	2019	2020
OBESITY, MEASURED								
United States...................	**30.9**	**(NA)**	**36.1**	**(NA)**	**(NA)**	**(NA)**	**42.8**	**(NA)**
Canada.......................	(NA)	23.7	(NA)	[1] 28.1	26.9	(NA)	24.3	(NA)
China.........................	2.3	3.2	4.5	6.2	(NA)	(NA)	(NA)	(NA)
Colombia......................	(NA)	13.8	16.5	18.7	(NA)	(NA)	(NA)	(NA)
India..........................	1.5	2.0	2.7	3.6	(NA)	(NA)	(NA)	(NA)
Ireland........................	(NA)	(NA)	(NA)	23.0	23.0	(NA)	23.0	(NA)
Japan.........................	2.9	3.9	3.5	3.7	4.4	4.0	4.6	(NA)
Korea, South..................	(NA)	3.5	4.1	5.3	5.4	5.9	5.9	7.4
Latvia.........................	(NA)	(NA)	(NA)	(NA)	(NA)	[1] 24.1	(NA)	[1] 23.9
Mexico........................	24.2	30.2	(NA)	(NA)	(NA)	36.1	(NA)	36.0
New Zealand..................	(NA)	(NA)	(NA)	30.9	32.4	32.5	31.3	31.2
South Africa...................	18.1	20.6	23.3	26.4	(NA)	(NA)	(NA)	(NA)
United Kingdom................	21.2	23.2	26.1	26.9	28.7	27.7	28.0	(NA)
OBESITY, SELF-REPORTED								
United States...................	**21.8**	**25.1**	**28.2**	**30.2**	**31.0**	**31.6**	**32.6**	**33.6**
Brazil.........................	(NA)	(NA)	15.0	17.0	18.9	19.8	20.3	21.5
Canada.......................	(NA)	15.2	17.5	[1] 19.2	19.8	19.7	20.4	21.0
Denmark......................	9.5	11.4	13.4	(NA)	16.8	(NA)	(NA)	(NA)
Estonia.......................	14.1	(NA)	16.9	(NA)	(NA)	19.1	(NA)	20.5
Finland........................	11.2	14.1	15.6	[1] 18.8	[1] 19.0	[1] 20.0	21.0	[1] 23.0
France........................	9.0	(NA)	12.9	(NA)	15.4	(NA)	14.4	(NA)
Germany......................	(NA)	13.6	(NA)	(NA)	16.3	(NA)	18.5	(NA)
Israel [2]......................	(NA)	(NA)	15.7	(NA)	14.7	(NA)	17.7	17.0
Italy..........................	8.6	9.9	10.3	9.8	10.6	10.7	11.0	11.5
Korea, South..................	(NA)	(NA)	2.0	2.8	3.4	4.3	(NA)	(NA)
Netherlands...................	9.4	10.7	11.4	12.8	13.4	14.4	14.1	13.4
Russia........................	17.3	19.4	19.9	22.3	22.4	22.7	22.0	(NA)
Spain.........................	(NA)	(NA)	(NA)	(NA)	16.9	(NA)	(NA)	14.9
Sweden.......................	9.2	10.9	11.3	12.3	13.1	14.1	13.7	14.4

NA Not available. [1] Break in series or difference in methodology. [2] See footnote 1, Table 1358.

Source: Organisation for Economic Co-operation and Development (OECD), 2022, "OECD Health Data: Non-medical Determinants of Health," OECD Health Statistics (database) ©, <dx.doi.org/10.1787/data-00546-en>, accessed July 2022.

Table 1360. Daily Tobacco Consumption by Country and Sex: 2000 to 2020

[Daily smokers as percent of population aged over 15. Covers only tobacco consumed by smoking]

Country	Total 2000	2010	2019	2020	Females 2000	2010	2019	2020	Males 2000	2010	2019	2020
United States	19.1	15.1	10.9	9.4	17.3	13.6	10.0	8.6	21.2	16.7	11.7	10.3
Brazil[1]	(NA)	14.1	9.8	9.5	(NA)	11.7	7.7	7.6	(NA)	16.8	12.3	11.7
Canada	(NA)	16.3	10.3	9.4	(NA)	13.7	8.7	7.6	(NA)	19.0	12.0	11.3
China[1]	27.5	26.2	25.4	25.3	3.0	2.4	2.1	2.1	51.1	49.2	48.0	47.8
Costa Rica	12.5	[1]14.4	8.9	8.4	6.1	[1]9.3	4.9	4.6	18.7	[1]19.4	13.0	12.2
Czechia	(NA)	22.8	18.1	16.6	(NA)	16.5	15.2	12.2	(NA)	29.3	21.1	21.2
Finland	23.4	19.0	[1]13.0	[1]12.0	20.3	15.7	[1]10.0	[1]11.0	27.3	23.2	[1]16.0	[1]14.0
France	[1]30.0	29.7	24.0	25.5	[1]26.4	26.6	20.7	22.0	[1]33.7	33.1	27.5	29.1
Iceland	22.4	14.2	[1]8.2	[1]7.3	22.0	13.9	[1]8.4	[1]7.9	22.8	14.5	[1]8.1	[1]6.7
India[1]	26.9	14.7	8.6	8.1	8.0	3.2	1.5	1.4	44.7	25.4	15.3	14.4
Indonesia[1]	30.2	31.4	32.6	32.6	4.8	3.4	2.6	2.5	55.9	59.5	62.5	62.7
Italy	24.4	23.1	18.6	18.8	17.4	17.1	14.9	15.4	31.9	29.6	22.7	22.5
Korea, South	(NA)	22.9	16.4	15.9	(NA)	5.2	4.4	3.9	(NA)	40.8	28.5	27.8
Luxembourg	(NA)	18.3	16.8	16.9	(NA)	15.7	16.0	16.1	(NA)	20.9	17.6	17.7
Netherlands	32.0	[1]20.9	15.4	14.4	29.0	[1]18.8	13.1	13.1	35.0	[1]23.1	17.7	15.7
New Zealand	25.0	(NA)	12.9	11.9	25.0	(NA)	11.5	11.3	25.0	(NA)	14.4	12.5
Norway	32.0	19.0	9.0	9.0	32.0	19.0	9.0	9.0	31.0	19.0	9.0	9.0
South Africa[1]	22.6	21.0	20.2	20.2	11.2	8.4	6.7	6.5	34.5	34.1	34.5	34.6
Sweden	18.9	13.6	10.4	9.5	21.0	12.5	10.6	8.7	16.8	14.7	10.1	10.2
United Kingdom	27.0	20.0	15.8	14.5	25.0	20.0	13.8	13.7	29.0	21.0	17.7	15.3

NA Not available. [1] Break in series or difference in methodology.

Source: Organisation for Economic Co-operation and Development (OECD), 2022, "OECD Health Data: Non-medical Determinants of Health," OECD Health Statistics (database) ©, <dx.doi.org/10.1787/data-00546-en>, accessed July 2022.

Table 1361. Road Traffic Fatalities by Country: 2000 to 2020

[Fatalities include any person killed immediately or dying within 30 days as a result of an injury accident. For countries that do not apply the threshold of 30 days, conversion coefficients are estimated so that comparisons on the basis of the 30 day-definition can be made]

Country	2000	2010	2015	2019	2020	Country	2000	2010	2015	2019	2020
United States	41,945	32,999	35,485	36,096	[2]38,680	Italy	7,061	4,114	3,428	3,173	2,395
Albania	280	353	270	227	181	Japan	10,410	5,828	4,885	3,920	3,416
Australia	1,628	1,233	1,170	1,196	1,091	Korea, South	10,236	5,505	4,621	3,349	3,081
Austria	976	552	479	416	344	Latvia	588	218	188	135	141
Azerbaijan	596	925	894	821	696	Lithuania	641	299	242	186	176
Belarus	1,594	1,190	664	505	575	Mexico	5,224	[1]4,966	3,547	3,044	(NA)
Belgium	1,470	850	762	644	499	Moldova	406	452	298	277	245
Bulgaria	1,012	776	708	628	463	Netherlands	1,166	640	621	661	610
Canada	2,904	2,238	1,887	[2]1,762	(NA)	New Zealand	462	375	317	350	318
Chile	2,207	2,070	2,136	[1]1,973	1,794	North Macedonia	162	162	148	132	125
China	(NA)	65,225	58,022	62,763	(NA)	Norway	341	208	117	108	93
Croatia	655	426	348	297	237	Poland	6,294	3,907	2,938	2,909	2,491
Czechia	1,486	802	738	618	518	Russia	29,594	26,567	23,114	16,981	16,152
Estonia	204	79	67	52	60	Serbia	1,048	656	601	531	492
Finland	396	272	270	211	[2]222	Slovakia	648	353	310	270	247
France	8,079	3,992	3,461	3,244	2,541	Slovenia	313	138	120	102	80
Georgia	500	685	602	481	450	Spain	5,776	2,478	1,689	1,755	(NA)
Germany	7,503	3,648	3,459	3,046	2,719	Sweden	591	[1]266	259	221	204
Greece	2,037	1,258	793	688	[2]585	Switzerland	592	327	253	187	227
Hungary	1,200	740	644	602	460	Turkey	5,510	4,045	[1]7,530	5,473	4,866
Israel[3]	516	375	356	355	305	United Kingdom	3,580	1,905	1,804	1,808	[2]1,528

NA Not available. [1] Break in series. [2] Estimated or provisional. [3] See footnote 1, Table 1358.

Source: International Transport Forum (ITF) / Organisation for Economic Co-operation and Development (OECD), 2022, "Road accidents," ITF Transport Statistics (database) ©, <doi.org/10.1787/g2g55585-en>, accessed June 2022. See also <itf-oecd.org/>.

Table 1362. Suicide Rates by Sex and Country: 2019

[For 2019 except as noted. Deaths due to intentional self-harm per 100,000 persons. Rates are standardized]

Country	Total	Men	Women	Country	Total	Men	Women
United States	14.7	23.6	6.3	Japan	14.6	21.2	8.3
Australia	13.3	20.4	6.4	Korea, South	25.4	38.0	14.9
Austria	11.4	19.2	4.8	Latvia	14.4	25.0	5.3
Brazil	6.7	11.1	2.7	Lithuania	22.2	41.2	6.8
Canada	10.5	16.2	5.0	Luxembourg	10.9	15.8	6.7
Chile[1]	10.0	17.3	3.3	Mexico	5.7	10.0	1.9
Colombia	5.9	10.2	2.1	Netherlands	10.0	13.9	6.3
Costa Rica	7.8	13.8	2.0	Poland	11.6	21.1	3.0
Czechia	10.7	17.9	4.2	Portugal[1]	8.5	14.1	4.0
Denmark[1]	9.7	14.6	5.1	Russia	11.7	22.2	3.6
Estonia	14.1	24.5	5.3	Slovakia	6.6	12.0	1.9
Germany	9.6	15.3	4.4	Slovenia	17.2	28.5	7.3
Greece	4.6	7.9	1.6	Spain	7.1	11.3	3.4
Hungary	14.8	25.2	6.8	Sweden[1]	12.4	17.5	7.6
Iceland	11.2	17.8	4.1	Switzerland[1]	11.1	16.5	6.3
Ireland[1]	9.4	14.3	4.7	Turkey	4.4	7.0	2.0
Israel[1,2]	6.2	10.2	2.5	United Kingdom	8.5	13.4	3.9

[1] 2018 data. [2] See footnote 1, Table 1358.

Source: Organisation for Economic Co-operation and Development (OECD), 2022, "Health Status," OECD Health Statistics database ©, <dx.doi.org/10.1787/data-00540-en>, accessed July 2022.

Table 1363. Health Expenditures by Country: 1990 to 2021

[In percent. GDP = gross domestic product. Data may be estimated or provisional and subject to breaks in data series or difference in methodology]

Country	Total expenditures on health (percent of GDP)					Public (government) expenditures on health (percent of total)				
	1990	2000	2010	2020	2021 [1]	1990	2000	2010	2020	2021 [1]
United States............	**11.2**	**12.5**	**16.2**	**18.8**	**17.8**	**40.4**	**44.4**	**48.7**	**84.8**	**(NA)**
Australia..................	6.5	7.6	8.4	10.6	(NA)	66.2	68.4	68.6	71.5	(NA)
Austria...................	7.7	9.2	10.2	11.5	12.2	74.4	75.5	74.6	76.5	78.6
Belgium..................	7.1	8.0	10.2	10.8	(NA)	(NA)	74.6	76.3	78.7	(NA)
Canada..................	8.4	8.2	10.7	12.9	11.7	74.3	70.0	69.9	75.0	74.5
Chile....................	(NA)	7.0	6.8	9.8	9.1	(NA)	53.3	59.0	65.1	64.4
Denmark.................	8.0	8.1	10.6	10.5	10.8	82.4	83.1	84.3	84.9	85.4
Estonia..................	(NA)	5.2	6.3	7.8	7.5	(NA)	77.0	76.3	77.2	78.5
Finland..................	7.3	7.1	9.1	9.5	(NA)	80.0	74.1	77.1	79.1	(NA)
France..................	8.0	9.6	11.2	12.2	(NA)	76.0	78.9	76.3	84.7	(NA)
Germany [2].............	8.0	9.9	11.1	12.8	12.8	75.4	78.1	83.2	85.1	86.0
Greece..................	6.1	7.2	9.6	9.5	(NA)	54.1	61.6	68.9	61.8	(NA)
Iceland..................	7.4	8.9	8.4	9.5	9.7	86.2	80.8	79.9	83.3	83.5
Ireland..................	5.6	5.9	10.5	7.1	6.7	73.2	77.5	76.2	78.8	78.4
Israel [3]................	6.5	6.8	7.0	8.3	(NA)	(NA)	63.1	62.8	70.8	(NA)
Italy....................	7.0	7.6	8.9	9.6	9.5	81.3	72.6	78.5	76.1	75.6
Japan...................	5.8	7.0	9.1	11.1	(NA)	77.6	80.4	81.9	83.4	(NA)
Korea, South.............	3.6	3.9	5.9	8.4	8.8	40.1	53.9	60.9	62.6	64.8
Lithuania................	(NA)	6.2	6.8	7.5	7.9	(NA)	68.5	71.7	70.1	70.1
Mexico..................	(NA)	4.4	5.7	6.2	(NA)	(NA)	45.2	50.2	52.9	(NA)
Netherlands..............	7.0	7.7	10.2	11.2	(NA)	71.2	69.0	83.4	84.9	(NA)
New Zealand.............	6.7	7.5	9.6	9.7	(NA)	82.4	78.0	81.2	80.1	(NA)
Norway..................	7.1	7.7	8.9	11.3	10.1	82.8	81.7	84.7	86.0	85.6
Poland..................	4.3	5.3	6.4	6.5	6.6	90.9	68.9	71.7	72.3	72.6
Portugal.................	5.5	8.6	10.0	10.5	11.2	64.9	69.8	66.6	64.5	64.0
Spain...................	6.1	6.8	9.1	10.7	(NA)	78.4	71.4	74.4	73.3	(NA)
Sweden..................	7.2	7.3	8.3	11.5	11.4	79.6	85.5	82.5	85.9	85.6
Switzerland..............	7.6	9.1	9.9	11.8	(NA)	(NA)	58.1	64.3	69.7	(NA)
Turkey..................	2.4	4.6	5.0	4.6	(NA)	59.9	61.7	78.0	78.8	(NA)
United Kingdom...........	5.1	7.2	10.0	12.0	11.9	84.3	76.1	80.4	82.8	82.9

NA Not available. [1] Data are estimated or provisional. [2] Data prior to 1991 are for former West Germany. [3] See footnote 1, Table 1364.

Source: Organisation for Economic Co-operation and Development (OECD), 2022, "Health expenditure and financing: Health expenditure indicators," OECD Health Statistics (database) ©, <dx.doi.org/10.1787/data-00349-en>, accessed July 2022.

Table 1364. Physicians and Inpatient Hospital Care—Selected Countries: 2000 to 2020

[Data may be estimated or provisional and subject to breaks in data series or difference in methodology. See source for details]

Country	Practicing physicians per 1,000 population				Hospital beds per 1,000 population				Average length of stay (days)			
	2000	2010	2019	2020	2000	2010	2019	2020	2000	2010	2019	2020
United States.........	**2.3**	**2.4**	**2.6**	**(NA)**	**3.5**	**3.1**	**2.8**	**(NA)**	**5.8**	**5.4**	**5.4**	**(NA)**
Australia.................	2.5	(NA)	3.8	3.9	4.0	3.8	(NA)	(NA)	6.1	5.0	4.7	(NA)
Austria..................	3.9	4.8	5.3	5.4	8.0	7.7	7.2	7.1	7.8	6.6	6.3	6.4
Belgium..................	2.8	2.9	3.2	3.2	6.7	6.1	5.6	5.5	8.2	7.2	6.5	6.7
Canada..................	2.0	2.3	2.7	2.7	3.8	2.8	2.5	2.6	7.2	7.7	7.7	7.7
Czechia.................	3.4	3.6	4.1	4.1	7.8	7.3	6.6	6.5	7.9	6.6	5.7	5.9
Denmark.................	2.9	3.7	4.3	(NA)	4.3	3.5	2.6	2.6	3.8	(NA)	(NA)	(NA)
Estonia..................	2.9	3.2	3.5	3.5	7.0	5.3	4.5	4.5	7.3	5.5	6.2	6.1
Finland..................	2.5	3.2	(NA)	(NA)	7.5	5.9	3.4	2.8	6.9	7.0	6.2	6.3
France..................	3.0	3.0	3.2	3.2	8.0	6.4	5.8	5.7	5.6	5.8	5.4	5.5
Germany.................	3.3	3.7	4.4	4.5	9.1	8.3	7.9	7.8	10.1	8.1	7.4	7.4
Hungary.................	2.7	2.9	3.5	3.1	8.2	7.2	6.9	6.8	7.1	5.8	5.4	5.3
Iceland..................	3.4	3.6	3.9	(NA)	(NA)	3.6	2.8	2.8	(NA)	5.4	5.5	(NA)
Ireland..................	(NA)	(NA)	3.3	3.5	(NA)	2.7	2.9	2.9	6.4	6.0	6.0	5.7
Israel [1]................	3.5	3.0	3.3	3.3	3.8	3.2	3.0	2.9	5.2	4.8	4.6	4.6
Italy....................	3.4	3.8	4.1	4.0	4.7	3.6	3.2	3.2	7.0	6.7	7.0	7.5
Japan...................	1.9	2.2	(NA)	2.6	14.7	13.5	12.8	12.6	24.8	18.2	16.0	16.4
Korea, South.............	1.3	2.0	2.5	2.5	4.7	8.7	12.4	12.7	11.0	10.0	7.3	7.8
Latvia..................	2.9	3.1	3.3	3.3	8.8	5.7	5.4	5.3	8.5	6.2	5.9	5.9
Lithuania................	3.6	4.0	4.6	4.5	8.8	7.2	6.4	6.0	9.2	7.1	6.4	6.7
Netherlands..............	(NA)	(NA)	3.8	3.8	4.9	4.1	3.0	2.9	9.0	5.6	5.1	5.2
New Zealand.............	2.2	2.6	3.4	3.4	(NA)	2.8	2.5	2.5	4.4	6.1	4.7	(NA)
Norway..................	3.4	4.1	5.0	5.1	(NA)	4.3	3.5	3.4	6.0	6.3	5.9	5.9
Poland..................	2.2	2.2	(NA)	(NA)	(NA)	6.6	6.2	6.2	(NA)	7.3	6.7	6.8
Russia..................	4.6	5.0	4.2	(NA)	11.4	9.4	8.0	(NA)	13.5	10.8	9.1	(NA)
Slovenia.................	2.2	2.4	3.3	3.3	5.4	4.6	4.4	4.3	7.1	5.5	6.6	6.6
Spain...................	3.1	3.8	4.4	4.6	3.7	3.1	3.0	3.0	7.1	6.4	6.0	6.4
Sweden..................	3.0	3.8	4.3	(NA)	3.6	2.7	2.1	2.1	6.6	5.8	5.4	5.3
Switzerland..............	(NA)	3.8	4.4	4.4	6.3	5.2	4.6	4.5	9.3	7.8	6.9	6.9
Turkey..................	(NA)	(NA)	(NA)	(NA)	(NA)	2.7	2.9	3.0	5.6	4.0	4.1	4.5
United Kingdom.......	2.0	2.7	3.0	3.0	4.1	2.9	2.5	2.4	(NA)	6.1	6.2	(NA)

NA Not available. [1] The statistical data for Israel are supplied by and under the responsibility of the relevant Israeli authorities. The use of such data by the OECD is without prejudice as to the status of the Golan Heights, East Jerusalem and Israeli settlements in the West Bank under the terms of international law.

Source: Organisation for Economic Co-Operation and Development (OECD), 2022, "Health care resources," OECD Health Statistics (database) ©, <dx.doi.org/10.1787/data-00541-en>; and "Health care utilisation," OECD Health Statistics (database) ©, <dx.doi.org/10.1787/data-00542-en>; accessed July 2022.

Table 1365. Gross National Income (GNI) by Country: 2020 and 2021

[For total GNI, 86,173,655 represents $86,173,655,000,000. GNI is the sum of value added by all resident producers, plus any product taxes (less subsidies) not included in the valuation of output, plus net receipts of primary income from abroad]

Country	Gross national income [1]				GNI on purchasing power parity basis [2]			
	Total (mil. dol.)		Per capita (dol.)		Total (mil. dol.)		Per capita (dol.)	
	2020	2021	2020	2021	2020	2021	2020	2021
World [3]	86,173,655	94,584,972	11,099	12,070	133,171,473	145,955,524	17,153	18,625
United States	21,261,270	23,374,712	64,140	70,430	21,286,637	23,393,117	64,210	70,480
Algeria	156,597	163,120	3,570	3,660	486,457	524,101	11,090	11,750
Angola	58,358	60,097	1,780	1,770	194,999	205,732	5,930	6,060
Argentina	412,023	460,455	9,080	10,050	917,825	1,060,441	20,230	23,150
Australia	1,379,110	1,461,068	53,680	56,760	1,341,876	1,423,004	52,230	55,290
Austria	431,178	467,571	48,360	52,210	495,985	522,766	55,620	58,370
Bangladesh	385,221	435,531	2,340	2,620	1,028,249	1,157,654	6,240	6,960
Belarus	58,944	64,955	6,280	6,950	178,628	194,948	19,040	20,870
Belgium	528,806	585,266	45,810	50,510	619,359	688,982	53,650	59,460
Brazil	1,658,194	1,651,062	7,800	7,720	3,069,857	3,328,105	14,440	15,550
Bulgaria	66,792	73,940	9,630	10,720	167,089	179,352	24,100	26,000
Canada	1,656,240	1,847,815	43,540	48,310	1,751,692	1,976,965	46,050	51,690
Chile	250,793	288,125	13,120	15,000	449,444	526,677	23,510	27,410
China	14,857,275	16,789,239	10,530	11,890	24,083,403	27,070,110	17,070	19,170
Colombia	296,424	315,732	5,830	6,160	749,671	843,884	14,730	16,460
Costa Rica	58,971	63,252	11,580	12,310	106,818	112,043	20,970	21,800
Cote d'Ivoire	60,138	66,354	2,280	2,450	139,748	155,827	5,300	5,760
Croatia	59,957	66,877	14,810	17,150	119,228	132,168	29,460	33,900
Czechia	236,743	257,628	22,130	24,070	430,714	455,530	40,260	42,560
Denmark	367,414	398,882	63,010	68,110	363,082	390,769	62,260	66,720
Dominican Republic	78,824	90,006	7,270	8,220	185,110	216,139	17,000	19,730
Ecuador	97,796	106,070	5,540	5,930	186,678	205,386	10,580	11,480
Egypt	307,450	365,800	3,000	3,510	1,249,924	1,345,735	12,210	12,910
Ethiopia	102,644	113,593	890	960	276,935	304,913	2,410	2,590
Finland	276,898	297,371	50,080	53,660	286,435	309,992	51,800	55,940
France	2,661,230	2,961,949	39,500	43,880	3,216,213	3,499,765	47,730	51,850
Germany	3,951,937	4,242,859	47,520	51,040	4,687,858	4,961,000	56,370	59,680
Ghana	71,863	74,911	2,310	2,360	180,529	191,106	5,810	6,020
Greece	192,107	214,773	17,950	20,140	297,789	334,996	27,830	31,410
Guatemala	75,624	84,558	4,490	4,940	146,434	163,924	8,690	9,580
Hong Kong, China	363,287	403,648	48,560	54,450	466,972	524,091	62,420	70,700
Hungary	155,523	172,241	15,950	17,740	315,818	346,035	32,390	35,640
India	2,641,485	3,027,515	1,910	2,170	8,883,834	10,059,402	6,440	7,220
Indonesia	1,059,880	1,143,082	3,870	4,140	3,213,895	3,471,169	11,750	12,560
Iraq	200,660	207,345	4,990	5,040	395,615	424,916	9,840	10,320
Ireland	327,793	374,687	65,750	74,520	354,159	399,493	71,040	79,450
Israel	392,679	464,124	42,610	49,560	360,186	412,565	39,090	44,060
Italy	1,924,973	2,109,498	32,380	35,710	2,527,004	2,745,846	42,510	46,490
Japan	5,152,435	5,356,987	40,810	42,620	5,508,392	5,601,433	43,630	44,570
Kazakhstan	163,370	165,772	8,710	8,720	457,782	474,465	24,410	24,970
Kenya	98,674	110,401	1,840	2,010	242,407	272,076	4,510	4,950
Korea, South	1,706,856	1,809,840	32,930	34,980	2,362,369	2,457,443	45,570	47,490
Lithuania	54,835	60,407	19,620	21,610	105,524	115,303	37,760	41,250
Malaysia	342,213	358,367	10,550	10,930	885,470	941,705	27,360	28,730
Mexico	1,100,032	1,221,492	8,530	9,380	2,327,615	2,544,720	18,050	19,540
Morocco	113,274	127,221	3,020	3,350	272,301	304,273	7,260	8,020
Myanmar	72,998	62,725	1,340	1,140	269,850	231,797	4,960	4,230
Netherlands	890,765	988,276	51,070	56,370	1,015,727	1,110,987	58,240	63,360
New Zealand	211,117	232,256	41,480	45,340	223,408	232,781	43,890	45,440
Nigeria	412,805	444,040	2,000	2,100	1,030,033	1,109,693	5,000	5,250
Norway	418,963	454,779	77,880	84,090	350,491	448,039	65,150	82,840
Pakistan	321,732	338,864	1,460	1,500	1,176,778	1,306,015	5,330	5,800
Panama	53,579	61,368	12,420	14,010	111,976	131,028	25,950	29,900
Peru	199,685	217,492	6,060	6,520	382,203	430,315	11,590	12,900
Philippines	375,815	404,238	3,430	3,640	989,559	1,048,915	9,030	9,450
Poland	578,462	629,922	15,260	16,670	1,252,324	1,353,823	33,040	35,830
Portugal	224,573	244,396	21,810	23,730	346,396	365,361	33,640	35,470
Qatar	161,110	167,384	55,920	57,120	253,720	269,849	88,060	92,080
Romania	243,279	270,873	12,630	14,170	610,467	665,510	31,700	34,820
Russia	1,572,764	1,692,598	10,740	11,600	4,278,442	4,668,845	29,210	32,000
Singapore	312,755	349,101	55,010	64,010	490,887	558,723	86,340	102,450
Slovakia	103,284	110,301	18,920	20,250	169,250	176,738	31,000	32,450
South Africa	356,586	386,861	6,010	6,440	779,051	849,292	13,140	14,140
Spain	1,295,797	1,407,504	27,360	29,740	1,798,778	1,939,656	37,980	40,980
Sri Lanka	81,446	84,571	3,720	3,820	281,755	305,431	12,850	13,790
Sweden	562,071	613,362	54,290	58,890	590,201	636,301	57,010	61,090
Switzerland	713,590	785,904	82,620	90,360	597,424	659,800	69,110	75,860
Tanzania	62,822	67,766	1,080	1,140	160,994	174,486	2,780	2,920
Thailand	493,157	507,559	7,070	7,260	1,241,048	1,296,444	17,780	18,530
Turkey	762,521	836,295	9,040	9,830	2,267,051	2,553,209	26,880	30,020
Ukraine	149,174	170,655	3,570	4,120	558,273	573,526	13,370	13,860
United Kingdom	2,681,473	3,055,334	39,970	45,380	3,082,891	3,327,025	45,960	49,420
Uzbekistan	59,724	68,584	1,740	1,960	264,328	297,551	7,720	8,520
Vietnam	329,910	349,344	3,390	3,560	1,013,137	1,084,230	10,410	11,040

[1] Gross national income calculated using the World Bank Atlas conversion factor; for details, see source. [2] For explanation of purchasing power parity (PPP), see headnote, Table 1366. [3] Includes other countries not shown separately.

Source: The World Bank, Washington, DC, "World Development Indicators" database ©, <databank.worldbank.org/source/world-development-indicators>, accessed August 2022.

Table 1366. Real Gross Domestic Product (GDP) Per Capita and Per Employed Persons by Country: 1960 to 2021

[U.S. figures based on the System of National Income and Product Accounts (NIPA) from the Bureau of Economic Analysis. Data for all other countries are based on the 1993 or 2008 United Nations System of National Accounts (SNA). Per capita data based on total resident population. Real GDP is a macroeconomic measure of the size of an economy adjusted for price changes and inflation. Employment data include people serving in the armed forces. Real dollars are calculated based on 2021 Purchasing Power Parities (PPPs). PPPs are currency conversion rates used to convert GDP expressed in different currencies to a common value (U.S. dollars in this case). A PPP for a given country is the number of national currency units needed to buy the specific basket of goods and services that one dollar will buy in the United States. See text, this section]

Country	1960	1970	1980	1990	2000	2010	2015	2016	2017	2018	2019	2020	2021
REAL GDP PER CAPITA (2021 U.S. dollars)													
United States	**21,454**	**28,750**	**35,234**	**44,439**	**55,115**	**59,884**	**64,180**	**64,779**	**65,822**	**67,388**	**68,617**	**65,647**	**69,287**
Canada	18,272	25,319	33,184	38,072	45,536	49,418	52,348	52,276	53,223	53,934	54,164	50,742	52,767
Australia	18,937	25,603	29,511	35,033	43,827	51,298	54,306	54,909	55,275	55,941	56,196	54,242	56,052
Japan	7,281	17,742	24,525	36,124	39,827	41,747	44,307	44,703	45,533	45,894	45,884	43,980	44,840
South Korea	1,961	3,466	6,579	13,919	25,255	37,826	42,703	43,787	45,044	46,133	47,075	46,609	48,339
Singapore	6,358	12,317	24,563	40,967	61,412	85,810	97,948	100,134	104,709	108,023	107,962	103,816	110,657
Austria	15,873	23,735	33,504	41,138	50,653	56,527	57,722	58,127	59,067	60,252	60,876	56,526	58,808
Belgium	15,822	24,149	32,926	39,138	47,348	52,791	54,427	54,839	55,511	56,264	57,163	53,671	56,818
Czechia	(NA)	15,974	22,525	25,891	27,516	36,800	39,925	40,852	42,865	44,082	45,235	42,490	43,923
Denmark	20,162	29,025	35,098	43,000	53,891	55,995	58,281	59,679	60,980	61,882	62,940	61,505	64,128
Finland	13,318	20,471	27,679	36,194	43,835	50,406	49,517	50,772	52,270	52,790	53,382	52,069	53,746
France	15,184	23,420	30,748	37,216	43,858	46,529	47,816	48,159	49,053	49,763	50,507	46,409	49,502
Germany	19,646	27,637	35,987	40,614	47,864	52,888	56,518	57,314	58,631	59,089	59,579	56,810	58,428
Ireland	13,697	19,829	27,318	37,800	57,984	59,163	65,031	65,511	67,591	70,593	72,218	65,268	67,945
Italy	14,642	24,052	32,543	40,373	47,132	46,283	44,427	45,087	45,926	46,448	46,796	42,780	45,876
Netherlands	18,929	27,683	34,109	40,245	52,332	57,424	58,461	59,426	60,796	61,866	62,665	59,949	62,642
Norway	17,547	24,425	36,635	45,483	61,657	66,222	67,964	68,089	69,129	69,442	69,489	68,593	70,902
Spain	7,464	15,356	22,362	29,293	38,198	41,012	41,094	42,303	43,483	44,292	44,854	39,790	41,848
Sweden	18,836	27,875	32,171	38,095	45,270	53,255	56,751	57,203	57,887	58,334	58,893	56,747	59,105
United Kingdom	17,027	21,678	26,427	34,416	42,731	46,280	49,456	50,161	50,928	51,460	52,038	47,014	50,215
REAL GDP PER EMPLOYED PERSON (2021 U.S. dollars)													
United States	**55,602**	**70,748**	**78,271**	**90,870**	**111,767**	**131,192**	**136,281**	**136,430**	**137,358**	**139,465**	**140,590**	**144,077**	**147,259**
Canada	50,013	67,071	74,299	80,851	95,008	99,414	104,514	104,782	105,995	107,531	107,263	107,257	106,996
Australia	46,672	58,562	67,044	73,825	90,871	99,595	107,020	107,581	108,440	108,067	107,758	105,086	109,607
Japan	14,375	33,835	48,587	69,083	76,944	81,486	85,907	85,743	86,274	85,280	84,320	80,941	82,227
South Korea	7,159	11,555	18,229	32,812	55,806	77,994	83,218	84,920	86,569	88,762	89,748	89,706	92,023
Singapore	21,499	39,341	54,194	86,171	117,107	142,654	149,262	153,029	160,466	165,168	164,351	160,890	176,229
Austria	32,728	54,639	72,601	89,247	109,422	116,763	117,681	118,480	119,200	120,153	120,565	114,286	116,997
Belgium	41,256	62,449	85,856	101,430	118,318	128,259	133,135	133,152	133,220	133,684	134,406	126,820	132,488
Czechia	(NA)	31,170	44,629	49,450	58,129	76,478	81,176	81,933	84,854	86,416	88,817	85,080	87,814
Denmark	43,761	59,081	71,487	83,924	104,432	111,435	117,078	118,884	120,434	121,038	121,950	120,271	122,700
Finland	26,788	41,306	56,055	73,115	98,662	108,370	107,527	110,053	112,387	110,887	110,218	109,761	111,305
France	35,098	57,042	74,843	91,604	104,173	112,505	116,053	116,575	117,904	118,921	119,680	111,330	116,957
Germany	38,402	57,005	72,785	81,185	97,556	103,456	107,078	108,115	109,532	109,223	109,377	105,239	108,230
Ireland	35,105	53,043	76,738	109,188	130,532	143,805	152,698	149,995	151,914	155,660	156,898	145,504	146,948
Italy	35,014	64,550	85,682	101,003	117,527	112,658	110,067	109,998	110,545	110,544	110,519	102,669	108,841
Netherlands	47,258	64,522	79,748	88,468	101,619	108,697	112,453	113,183	113,755	113,335	113,334	109,578	113,070
Norway	41,471	58,262	77,312	94,208	119,640	126,895	130,190	131,246	132,781	132,150	131,070	132,181	135,665
Spain	18,517	38,681	66,254	81,797	92,831	98,014	103,260	104,168	104,516	104,604	103,872	96,607	99,215
Sweden	38,547	56,686	62,462	70,891	93,470	111,349	115,780	116,029	116,160	116,541	118,153	116,179	120,224
United Kingdom	36,892	48,542	59,325	73,636	91,942	99,793	103,365	104,177	105,360	105,837	106,427	97,362	105,133

NA Not available.

Source: The Conference Board, New York, NY, "Total Economy Database™," April 2022 ©. Reproduced with permission from The Conference Board, Inc. © 2022, The Conference Board, Inc.

Table 1367. Sectoral Contributions to Gross Value Added: 2020 and 2021

[In percent. According to the 2008 System of National Accounts (SNA) and the International Standard Industrial Classification (ISIC), Revision 4 (2008), with some exceptions, value added is estimated at basic prices and includes financial intermediation services indirectly measured (FISIM). Value added represents an industry's contribution to national GDP and is calculated as the difference between production and intermediate inputs. Value added comprises labor costs, consumption of fixed capital, indirect taxes less subsidies, and net operating surplus and mixed income. Selected data are estimated or provisional; see source for details]

Country	Agriculture [1]		Industry [2]				Services	
			Total		Manufacturing			
	2020	2021	2020	2021	2020	2021	2020	2021
United States [3]	1.1	(NA)	13.9	(NA)	11.2	(NA)	80.4	(NA)
Australia	2.4	(NA)	19.8	(NA)	6.0	(NA)	70.3	(NA)
Austria	1.2	1.2	21.4	21.1	18.1	18.6	70.4	70.3
Belgium	0.7	0.7	16.5	18.1	13.8	14.8	77.6	76.0
Chile [4]	4.5	3.7	26.6	28.6	9.9	9.7	62.2	60.9
Czechia	2.2	2.0	28.1	27.7	23.5	23.2	64.1	64.7
Denmark	1.6	1.0	17.5	16.7	15.2	13.8	75.4	76.8
Estonia	2.5	2.5	19.2	19.6	14.7	14.6	71.6	71.4
Finland	2.8	2.6	20.0	20.6	16.5	16.9	69.4	69.0
France	1.8	1.9	13.2	13.1	10.4	10.0	79.8	79.4
Germany	0.8	0.9	23.5	23.5	20.1	20.2	69.9	69.7
Greece	4.8	4.5	15.2	16.3	10.2	10.5	78.1	77.3
Hungary	4.0	3.9	23.4	24.6	20.7	21.9	66.9	65.0
Indonesia	14.2	13.8	28.6	30.7	20.6	20.1	46.1	44.6
Ireland	1.0	1.1	37.4	38.0	36.1	36.8	59.3	58.8
Italy	2.2	2.2	19.5	20.3	16.4	17.0	73.9	72.6
Japan [5]	1.0	(NA)	23.2	(NA)	19.8	(NA)	69.8	(NA)
Korea, South	2.0	(NA)	29.7	(NA)	27.1	(NA)	62.4	(NA)
Mexico	4.1	(NA)	24.9	(NA)	18.5	(NA)	64.3	(NA)
Netherlands	1.8	1.7	14.7	15.0	12.2	12.2	78.2	78.0
Norway	2.0	1.8	22.6	33.6	7.4	6.1	68.4	58.6
Poland	2.8	2.7	24.4	26.9	18.3	19.9	65.7	63.8
Portugal	2.4	2.5	17.4	17.3	13.6	13.7	75.4	75.2
Slovakia	2.0	2.0	24.1	24.9	19.6	21.6	67.5	67.2
Slovenia	2.4	2.1	27.2	27.8	23.4	24.0	64.4	64.0
Spain	3.4	3.0	16.1	16.9	12.1	12.5	74.2	74.3
Sweden	1.5	1.5	17.5	18.7	13.9	14.5	74.2	73.1
Switzerland	0.7	0.6	20.9	21.4	18.7	19.4	73.3	73.0
Turkey	7.5	6.3	25.6	29.0	21.5	24.6	61.0	59.0
United Kingdom	0.6	0.7	13.1	13.5	9.6	9.7	80.4	79.6

NA Not available. [1] Includes forestry, fishing, and hunting sectors. [2] Includes energy. [3] Value added is estimated at factor cost for U.S. [4] Value added is estimated at producer's prices. [5] Value added is estimated approximately at market prices for Japan. According to 1993 System of National Accounts (SNA).

Source: Organisation for Economic Co-operation and Development (OECD), 2022, "National Accounts at a Glance," OECD National Accounts Statistics (database) ©, <dx.doi.org/10.1787/data-00369-en>, accessed July 2022.

Table 1368. Index of Industrial Production by Country: 2000 to 2021

[Annual averages of monthly data. Industrial production indexes generally measure output in the manufacturing, mining, electric, gas, and water utilities sectors. Minus sign (-) indicates decrease]

Country	Index (2015=100)							Annual percent change				
	2000	2005	2010	2015	2019	2020	2021	2009 to 2010	2014 to 2015	2018 to 2019	2019 to 2020	2020 to 2021
United States	91.9	96.0	90.9	100.0	101.6	94.5	99.2	5.5	-1.4	-0.7	-7.0	4.9
Australia	(NA)	(NA)	(NA)	(NA)	109.8	109.0	109.9	(NA)	(NA)	2.2	-0.7	0.8
Austria	70.1	82.2	90.6	100.0	113.2	106.9	117.6	7.0	2.1	0.3	-5.6	10.0
Belgium	71.2	83.9	97.0	100.0	114.0	109.9	128.5	9.4	-0.7	4.8	-3.5	16.9
Brazil	83.8	97.8	112.2	100.0	95.8	91.5	95.2	10.2	-8.2	-1.1	-4.4	3.9
Canada	96.8	100.0	89.9	100.0	108.8	100.7	105.2	6.0	-0.4	-0.1	-7.5	4.5
Chile	70.1	87.6	88.5	100.0	102.8	100.4	105.8	0.5	0.7	0.8	-2.3	5.3
Czechia	60.5	78.9	87.1	100.0	113.2	105.1	112.4	8.6	4.3	-0.2	-7.2	6.9
Denmark	109.8	115.7	98.6	100.0	111.3	105.2	113.9	2.1	0.1	2.7	-5.5	8.3
Finland	99.9	105.6	106.6	100.0	113.0	109.6	114.1	5.7	-0.9	1.6	-3.0	4.0
France	108.6	110.1	99.9	100.0	103.7	92.9	98.4	4.7	1.7	0.4	-10.4	6.0
Germany	80.4	85.9	90.4	100.0	101.2	91.5	95.4	12.0	1.1	-4.2	-9.6	4.3
Hungary	58.1	76.1	82.2	99.6	115.9	107.8	118.6	10.5	7.0	5.4	-6.9	10.0
India	42.9	[2] 57.8	87.9	100.0	115.3	102.7	115.7	9.7	2.5	0.7	-11.0	12.7
Ireland	42.9	57.2	63.0	100.0	104.0	119.2	138.8	8.5	36.9	7.0	14.5	16.4
Israel [1]	70.1	73.3	91.6	100.0	108.1	110.8	114.8	8.0	2.4	3.9	2.5	3.6
Italy	127.7	121.7	107.8	99.6	105.1	93.6	104.5	7.0	1.0	-1.2	-11.0	11.7
Japan	106.1	108.9	102.8	100.0	101.2	90.9	95.8	15.0	-1.2	-2.6	-10.1	5.4
Korea, South	49.4	66.5	92.5	100.0	106.7	106.4	114.3	16.3	-0.3	0.3	-0.2	7.4
Netherlands	95.9	100.2	106.9	100.0	102.4	99.0	103.6	7.6	-3.4	-0.8	-3.3	4.7
New Zealand	87.0	98.4	97.3	100.0	105.4	101.4	104.5	3.6	1.5	0.7	-3.8	3.1
Norway	121.6	116.4	102.5	100.0	92.5	99.3	101.4	-5.6	1.5	-4.4	7.4	2.1
Poland	47.4	62.0	83.4	100.0	120.9	119.4	136.7	11.2	4.9	4.2	-1.3	14.5
Portugal	132.9	124.2	103.7	100.0	103.9	96.2	99.6	1.0	2.0	-2.2	-7.3	3.5
Russia	57.9	76.5	83.8	100.0	113.1	110.8	116.7	7.2	5.3	3.4	-2.1	5.3
Slovakia	41.0	53.9	82.3	100.0	113.4	103.0	113.7	12.2	6.8	0.5	-9.1	10.4
Spain	124.0	127.1	105.6	100.0	106.1	96.0	103.0	0.8	3.3	0.6	-9.5	7.3
Sweden	101.2	110.0	103.1	100.0	111.5	106.6	114.4	9.5	3.3	2.4	-4.4	7.3
Turkey	43.8	59.6	69.4	100.0	113.3	115.8	134.8	13.1	6.1	-0.6	2.2	16.5
United Kingdom	99.0	103.7	97.5	100.0	107.5	98.5	103.5	-0.8	4.5	3.6	-8.4	5.1

NA Not available. [1] See footnote 1, Table 1364. [2] Break in series.

Source: Organisation for Economic Co-operation and Development (OECD), 2022, "Key short-term indicators," Main Economic Indicators (database) ©, <dx.doi.org/10.1787/data-00039-en>, accessed July 2022.

Table 1369. Selected Indexes of Manufacturing Productivity, Unit Labor Costs, Employment, and Hours Worked by Country: 2000 to 2018

[2010=100. Data for all countries are prepared according to the System of National Accounts (SNA) 2008 or its European counterpart, the European System of Accounts 2010 (ESA 2010). Data refer to all employed persons (including employees, self-employed, and unpaid family workers). Minus sign (-) indicates decrease]

Index	United States	Aus- tralia	Canada	France	Ger- many	Italy	Japan	Nether- lands	South Korea	Swe- den	United King- dom
REAL VALUED ADDED PER HOUR WORKED (PRODUCTIVITY)											
2000	58.3	80.9	91.8	75.0	79.0	90.8	75.7	76.0	48.9	67.6	70.2
2010	100.0	100.0	100.0	100.0	100.0	100.0	100.0	100.0	100.0	100.0	100.0
2015	97.8	105.9	109.0	111.3	106.0	108.2	109.4	109.2	107.6	106.1	101.0
2017	98.7	105.0	113.9	116.2	113.6	112.6	113.1	116.9	118.4	108.4	102.7
2018	100.6	105.8	115.5	117.1	113.6	113.5	113.6	120.4	125.8	110.9	102.0
Average annual percent change:											
2000-2007	6.5	2.9	1.6	3.9	4.0	1.5	4.0	4.4	8.9	5.9	4.7
2010-2017	0.5	0.9	2.1	2.6	3.6	3.0	3.0	2.7	2.9	3.5	1.0
2017-2018	1.9	0.8	1.4	0.7	(Z)	0.8	0.4	3.0	6.3	2.2	-0.6
HOURLY LABOR COSTS (national currency basis)											
2000	72.4	65.2	74.9	73.0	82.2	72.0	101.9	74.6	46.1	70.6	63.7
2010	100.0	100.0	100.0	100.0	100.0	100.0	100.0	100.0	100.0	100.0	100.0
2015	109.8	121.1	114.8	111.9	112.4	111.3	102.7	110.6	117.3	117.4	110.8
2017	114.3	123.2	117.1	116.4	118.1	112.6	105.0	115.9	127.2	121.2	112.3
2018	116.6	127.9	121.3	119.1	120.8	114.7	108.5	118.7	138.5	127.3	116.7
Average annual percent change:											
2000-2007	4.0	5.2	3.6	3.2	2.2	3.0	-0.5	3.5	9.7	4.4	5.1
2010-2017	1.8	2.6	1.9	2.4	2.2	1.9	0.4	1.3	3.5	2.2	2.1
2017-2018	2.1	3.9	3.5	2.3	2.3	1.9	3.3	2.4	8.9	5.0	3.9
REAL HOURLY COMPENSATION, CPI DEFLATED (national currency basis)											
2000	91.7	87.7	91.4	86.5	95.9	89.2	99.2	91.1	63.0	81.9	78.2
2010	100.0	100.0	100.0	100.0	100.0	100.0	100.0	100.0	100.0	100.0	100.0
2015	101.0	108.1	105.7	106.0	104.9	103.6	99.1	101.3	106.8	113.4	99.8
2017	101.6	106.5	104.6	108.9	108.0	103.6	101.0	104.4	112.5	113.8	97.7
2018	101.3	108.5	105.9	109.4	108.6	104.3	103.3	105.1	120.8	117.3	99.2
Average annual percent change:											
2000-2007	1.2	2.0	1.3	1.3	0.6	0.7	-0.1	1.3	6.6	2.8	3.3
2010-2017	0.1	0.4	0.3	1.3	0.9	0.7	(Z)	-0.1	1.6	1.3	(Z)
2017-2018	-0.4	1.9	1.3	0.4	0.5	0.7	2.3	0.7	7.3	3.0	1.6
UNIT LABOR COSTS, (national currency basis)											
2000	124.2	80.7	81.5	97.3	104.0	79.2	134.6	98.2	94.2	104.5	90.7
2010	100.0	100.0	100.0	100.0	100.0	100.0	100.0	100.0	100.0	100.0	100.0
2015	112.3	114.4	105.4	100.5	106.1	102.9	93.9	101.2	109.0	110.7	109.7
2017	115.8	117.3	102.8	100.1	103.9	100.0	92.8	99.2	107.4	111.8	109.4
2018	116.0	120.9	105.0	101.7	106.3	101.1	95.5	98.6	110.1	114.8	114.4
Average annual percent change:											
2000-2007	-2.4	2.3	2.0	-0.7	-1.8	1.5	-4.3	-0.9	0.7	-1.4	0.5
2010-2017	1.3	1.6	-0.1	-0.2	-1.3	-1.0	-2.6	-1.3	0.6	-1.2	1.0
2017-2018	0.2	3.0	2.1	1.6	2.3	1.1	2.8	-0.6	2.5	2.7	4.6
REAL VALUE ADDED PER EMPLOYED PERSON											
2000	58.4	82.8	93.2	75.8	81.2	98.1	76.4	77.1	52.3	67.7	70.8
2010	100.0	100.0	100.0	100.0	100.0	100.0	100.0	100.0	100.0	100.0	100.0
2015	98.8	106.1	108.7	111.4	107.2	107.5	110.8	110.4	104.0	103.8	101.7
2017	99.9	104.3	112.6	114.9	113.8	113.4	114.7	117.9	111.3	108.3	102.9
2018	102.2	104.5	115.5	114.8	113.6	114.3	114.3	121.0	116.5	110.9	101.4
Average annual percent change:											
2000-2007	6.3	2.5	1.4	3.6	3.9	1.3	4.4	4.1	7.8	5.8	4.5
2010-2017	1.0	0.8	2.1	2.6	4.1	3.2	3.9	3.0	2.4	3.9	1.2
2017-2018	2.3	0.3	2.6	0.0	-0.2	0.8	-0.4	2.7	4.7	2.4	-1.4
ALL EMPLOYED PERSONS											
2000	148.8	110.0	129.9	125.8	109.8	109.8	114.7	118.9	103.8	124.5	151.4
2010	100.0	100.0	100.0	100.0	100.0	100.0	100.0	100.0	100.0	100.0	100.0
2015	106.7	89.4	99.7	95.2	105.2	92.0	94.9	95.8	111.0	94.1	101.1
2017	107.7	88.2	100.6	94.3	106.4	93.4	95.6	97.2	110.0	94.6	102.4
2018	109.5	89.8	100.1	94.4	108.2	94.7	97.0	99.1	108.7	95.2	104.2
Average annual percent change:											
2000-2007	-2.7	-1.0	-0.8	-1.4	-0.8	(-Z)	-1.2	-1.4	0.3	-1.2	-4.1
2010-2017	0.6	-1.8	(Z)	-1.3	0.5	-1.3	-0.7	-0.7	1.8	-0.9	(Z)
2017-2018	1.6	1.8	-0.5	0.1	1.7	1.4	1.4	1.9	-1.2	0.6	1.8
HOURS WORKED OF ALL EMPLOYED PERSONS											
2000	149.0	112.7	131.7	127.0	112.8	118.6	115.8	120.6	111.0	124.7	152.5
2010	100.0	100.0	100.0	100.0	100.0	100.0	100.0	100.0	100.0	100.0	100.0
2015	107.8	89.6	99.5	95.3	106.3	91.4	96.1	96.8	107.3	92.1	101.8
2017	109.0	87.6	99.4	93.2	106.5	94.0	97.0	98.1	103.4	94.5	102.6
2018	111.2	88.7	100.0	92.6	108.1	95.4	97.6	99.6	100.6	95.3	103.6
Average annual percent change:											
2000-2007	-2.8	-1.4	-1.0	-1.7	-0.9	-0.2	-0.8	-1.7	-0.7	-1.2	-4.2
2010-2017	1.1	-1.9	0.1	-1.2	1.1	-1.1	0.1	-0.4	1.3	-0.5	0.2
2017-2018	2.0	1.2	0.7	-0.6	1.5	1.4	0.6	1.6	-2.7	0.8	1.0

Z less than 0.05 percent.

Source: The Conference Board, Inc., International Labor Comparisons Program, "International Comparisons of Manufacturing Productivity and Unit Labor Cost Trends, 2018," December 2019, <www.conference-board.org/ilcprogram>. © The Conference Board 2022.

Table 1370. Indexes of Hourly Compensation Costs for Employees in Manufacturing by Country: 2000 to 2016

[United States=100. Compensation costs include pay for time worked (base wages and salaries, overtime pay, bonuses and premiums paid each pay period, and cost of living adjustments), directly-paid benefits (pay for leave time, irregular bonuses, and pay in kind), employer social insurance expenditures (legally required, private, and contractual social benefit costs), and labor-related taxes (minus subsidies). Data are adjusted for exchange rates. Regional averages are trade-weighted to account for differences in countries' relative importance to total world trade in manufactured goods. See source for details]

Area or country	2000	2010	2014	2015	2016	Area or country	2000	2010	2014	2015	2016
United States	**100**	**100**	**100**	**100**	**100**	Hungary	12	24	26	22	22
						Ireland	66	117	117	95	93
ILC economies[1]	**78**	**90**	**93**	**82**	**80**	Israel	49	55	62	58	58
OECD[2]	82	96	97	85	84	Italy	67	97	102	86	83
Europe	82	103	108	91	88	Japan[6]	100	91	73	62	68
Euro Area[3]	83	112	118	98	95	Mexico	14	13	13	12	10
Eastern Europe[4]	13	28	29	25	25	Netherlands	85	111	114	93	89
East Asia ex-Japan[5]	35	44	54	51	50	New Zealand	36	59	73	61	61
Argentina[6]	33	37	48	53	43	Norway	98	165	170	135	125
Australia	67	114	124	102	98	Philippines	4	5	6	6	5
Austria	88	115	123	103	101	Poland	14	24	27	23	22
Belgium	105	146	152	127	121	Portugal	24	35	34	29	28
Brazil	17	29	28	20	20	Singapore	47	56	72	68	69
Canada	73	99	93	81	77	Slovakia	10	31	35	29	30
Czechia	14	33	32	27	27	South Korea	39	51	64	60	59
Denmark	89	139	143	118	116	Spain	50	77	76	62	60
Estonia	10	27	34	29	30	Sweden	94	123	135	110	107
Finland	79	116	122	102	99	Switzerland	108	147	175	161	155
France	85	112	119	99	97	Taiwan[6]	29	24	26	25	25
Germany	101	126	134	112	111	Turkey	(NA)	18	17	15	16
Greece	40	65	52	42	40	United Kingdom	83	83	89	82	73

NA Not available. [1] ILC (International Labor Comparisons) economies refers to the 35 national economies included in ILC compensation comparisons, excluding China and India that are not strictly comparable with each other or with data for other countries. Data for 2000 excludes Turkey. [2] Organisation for Economic Co-operation and Development; see text, this section. Includes only those countries that are also ILC economies. [3] Euro Area includes Austria, Belgium, Estonia, Finland, France, Germany, Greece, Ireland, Italy, the Netherlands, Portugal, Slovakia and Spain. [4] Czechia, Estonia, Hungary, Poland, and Slovakia. [5] South Korea, Philippines, Singapore, and Taiwan. Excludes Japan. [6] Except for Argentina, Japan, and Taiwan, data relate to manufacturing as defined by the International Standard Industrial Classification of All Economic Activities (ISIC) Revision 4.

Source: The Conference Board, Inc., International Labor Comparisons program, "International Comparisons of Hourly Compensation Costs in Manufacturing, 2016," April 2018, <www.conference-board.org/ilcprogram/compensation>. © 2022, The Conference Board, Inc.

Table 1371. Annual Percent Change in Labor Productivity and Hours Worked by Country: 2010 to 2021

[Annual percent change for period shown. Labor productivity growth refers to the growth in gross domestic product (GDP) per hour worked. Data are derived from The Conference Board Total Economy Database. Regional labor productivity growth rates are aggregated using shares in nominal PPP converted GDP; regional hours growth is weighted using total hours shares. Growth rates are the averages of yearly growth rates. Minus sign (-) indicates decrease]

Country	Labor productivity		Total hours worked		Country	Labor productivity		Total hours worked	
	2010-2019	2020-2021	2010-2019	2020-2021		2010-2019	2020-2021	2010-2019	2020-2021
Advanced economies[1]	1.1	1.3	0.8	-1.2	Estonia	2.6	1.7	1.0	0.8
United States	**0.9**	**1.9**	**1.4**	**-0.8**	Hungary	1.2	1.5	1.5	-0.3
Japan	1.1	-0.3	0.1	-1.1	Latvia	3.0	3.8	-0.5	-3.4
					Lithuania	3.1	4.0	0.5	-1.6
European Union (EU-14, old)[2]	0.8	0.3	0.4	-1.4	Malta	1.8	2.6	4.0	-2.4
Austria	0.8	0.8	0.8	-2.0	Poland	3.6	-0.5	0.1	2.1
Belgium	0.6	2.2	1.0	-2.0	Romania	3.6	5.7	-0.5	-4.5
Denmark	1.7	0.6	0.2	0.7	Slovakia	2.5	3.9	0.5	-4.5
Finland	0.8	1.2	0.4	-0.6	Slovenia	1.8	1.5	0.1	0.2
France	0.9	-0.2	0.5	-0.5	European Union (EU-27, enlarged)[4]	1.1	0.5	0.4	-1.2
Germany	1.1	0.7	0.8	-1.6	Addenda:				
Greece	-1.6	0.8	-0.6	-1.6	Other advanced economies[1]	2.1	2.8	0.9	-1.2
Ireland	1.6	-3.3	1.3	1.3	Australia	1.2	1.8	1.4	-0.6
Italy	0.4	0.5	-0.1	-2.0	Canada	1.0	0.7	1.2	-1.1
Luxembourg	-0.1	4.4	2.7	-1.9	Hong Kong	2.5	5.6	0.3	-5.5
Netherlands	0.5	0.7	1.0	-0.1	Iceland	1.1	1.6	1.7	-3.1
Portugal	0.8	0.7	0.0	-2.7	Israel	1.9	3.5	2.2	-0.7
Spain	1.0	-1.0	0.1	-2.2	New Zealand	0.8	2.0	2.4	0.0
Sweden	1.2	1.2	1.4	-0.4	Norway	0.4	1.4	1.0	0.1
European Union (EU-13, new)[3]	2.8	1.5	0.2	-0.8	Singapore	2.9	3.9	1.9	-2.3
Bulgaria	2.7	1.7	-0.6	-1.8	South Korea	2.9	2.7	0.4	-1.1
Croatia	1.9	0.8	-0.7	-0.1	Switzerland	1.3	1.4	0.7	-0.8
Cyprus	0.9	1.6	0.8	-1.5	Taiwan	2.9	5.8	0.7	-0.9
Czechia	1.8	0.4	0.7	-1.7	United Kingdom	0.7	1.2	1.4	-2.4

[1] "Advanced" includes the U.S., EU-27, Japan, and "other advanced" economies. [2] Referring to membership of the European Union until April 30, 2004 (excluding the United Kingdom). [3] Referring to new membership of the European Union as of January 1, 2007. [4] Referring to all 27 current members of the European Union. See text, this section.

Source: The Conference Board, "Total Economy Database™," April 2022 ©. Reproduced with permission from The Conference Board, Inc. © 2022, The Conference Board, Inc.

Table 1372. Comparative Price Levels—Selected OECD Countries: June 2022

[Purchasing power parities (PPPs) are rates of currency conversion that eliminate the differences in price levels between countries. Comparative price levels are defined as the ratios of PPPs for private final consumption to exchange rates. The PPPs are given in national currency units per U.S. dollar. This table should be read vertically. Each column shows the number of specified monetary units needed in each of the countries listed to buy the same representative basket of consumer goods and services. In each case the representative basket costs a hundred units in the country whose currency is specified. For example, in June 2022, an item that costs $1.00 in the United States would cost $1.05 (U.S. dollars) in Australia]

Country	United States (USD)	Australia (AUD)	Canada (CAD)	Chile (Chilean peso)	France (EUR)	Germany (EUR)	Italy (EUR)	Japan (JPY)	Korea (KRW)	Mexico (MXN)	Spain (EUR)	Turkey (TRY)	United Kingdom (GBP)
United States	100	96	99	182	122	125	134	132	139	187	134	359	108
Australia [1]	105	100	104	190	128	131	140	138	146	196	140	376	112
Austria	84	80	84	153	103	105	113	111	117	157	113	302	90
Belgium	85	82	85	155	104	107	114	113	119	160	114	306	92
Canada	101	96	100	183	123	126	135	133	140	188	135	361	108
Chile	55	52	55	100	67	69	74	73	77	103	74	197	59
Colombia	38	37	38	70	47	48	51	51	54	72	51	138	41
Costa Rica	51	49	51	93	62	64	68	67	71	95	68	183	55
Czechia	67	64	66	122	82	84	90	88	93	125	90	240	72
Denmark	104	99	103	189	127	130	139	137	145	194	139	372	111
Estonia	72	69	72	132	89	91	97	96	101	136	97	260	78
Finland	93	89	93	170	114	117	125	124	130	175	125	336	101
France	82	78	81	149	100	102	110	108	114	153	110	294	88
Germany	80	76	79	145	98	100	107	105	111	149	107	287	86
Greece	67	64	67	123	82	85	90	89	94	126	90	242	72
Hungary	46	44	46	84	57	58	62	61	65	87	62	167	50
Iceland	122	117	121	222	149	153	163	161	170	228	164	438	131
Ireland	105	100	104	190	128	131	140	138	146	196	140	376	112
Israel [2]	116	111	115	212	142	146	156	154	162	217	156	417	125
Italy	75	71	74	136	91	94	100	99	104	140	101	268	80
Japan	76	72	75	138	93	95	101	100	105	142	101	272	81
Korea, South	72	69	71	131	88	90	96	95	100	134	96	258	77
Latvia	65	62	65	118	79	81	87	86	91	122	87	233	70
Lithuania	59	57	59	108	73	74	80	79	83	111	80	213	64
Luxembourg	98	93	97	178	120	122	131	129	136	183	131	351	105
Mexico	53	51	53	97	65	67	72	71	75	100	72	192	57
Netherlands [1]	86	82	86	157	106	108	116	114	120	161	116	310	93
New Zealand [1]	99	94	98	180	121	124	132	131	138	185	133	355	106
Norway	104	100	104	190	128	131	140	138	145	195	140	374	112
Poland	47	44	46	85	57	58	62	62	65	87	62	167	50
Portugal	66	63	66	121	81	83	89	88	92	124	89	238	71
Slovakia	70	67	70	128	86	88	94	93	98	132	94	253	76
Slovenia	67	64	66	121	81	83	89	88	93	125	89	239	72
Spain	75	71	74	136	91	93	100	99	104	140	100	268	80
Sweden	91	87	90	165	111	114	122	120	127	170	122	326	98
Switzerland	124	119	123	226	152	156	166	164	173	232	166	446	133
Turkey	28	27	28	51	34	35	37	37	39	52	37	100	30
United Kingdom	93	89	92	169	114	117	125	123	130	174	125	334	100

[1] Estimates based on quarterly consumer prices. [2] The statistical data for Israel are supplied by and under the responsibility of the relevant Israeli authorities. The use of such data by the OECD is without prejudice to the status of the Golan Heights, East Jerusalem and Israeli settlements in the West Bank under the terms of international law.

Source: Organisation for Economic Co-operation and Development (OECD), 2022 "Prices: Comparative Price Levels," Main Economic Indicators (database) ©, <dx.doi.org/10.1787/data-00536-en>, accessed August 2022.

Table 1373. Percent of Consumer Expenditures Spent on Food, Alcohol, and Tobacco Consumed at Home by Selected Country: 2020

Country/territory	Food [1]	Alcoholic beverages and tobacco	Country/territory	Food [1]	Alcoholic beverages and tobacco	Country/territory	Food [1]	Alcoholic beverages and tobacco
United States	**7.1**	**2.0**	Georgia	32.8	3.4	Nigeria	59.1	1.1
Algeria	37.5	1.0	Germany	11.7	3.6	Norway	11.7	4.0
Argentina	23.1	1.9	Ghana	41.6	0.5	Pakistan	40.6	1.1
Australia	10.8	4.5	Greece	17.8	4.9	Peru	26.6	2.5
Austria	9.7	3.1	Honduras	32.1	5.0	Philippines	42.8	1.4
Bahrain	13.1	0.4	Hong Kong	13.8	1.1	Poland	19.1	7.0
Bangladesh	53.4	2.5	Hungary	18.9	8.2	Portugal	18.7	3.7
Belarus	31.9	7.7	India	27.9	2.0	Romania	28.0	5.3
Belgium	12.7	4.0	Indonesia	32.6	7.1	Russia	28.5	7.2
Bolivia	29.3	2.1	Iran	28.4	0.6	Saudi Arabia	20.5	0.7
Bosnia-Herzegovina	28.5	9.9	Iraq	31.9	4.1	Serbia	25.9	8.2
Brazil	17.3	1.6	Ireland	10.3	5.2	Singapore	7.9	1.9
Bulgaria	19.6	5.5	Israel	15.9	2.8	Slovakia	18.7	5.4
Cambodia	42.8	1.9	Italy	16.5	4.4	Slovenia	15.6	4.7
Canada	10.6	4.2	Japan	15.7	2.2	South Africa	21.2	5.1
Chile	17.9	3.3	Jordan	26.9	4.5	South Korea	11.6	1.8
China	21.8	2.9	Kazakhstan	48.7	2.4	Spain	15.0	4.0
Colombia	18.6	3.5	Kenya	58.7	3.6	Sweden	13.1	3.6
Croatia	23.2	6.6	Kuwait	19.7	0.1	Switzerland	10.2	3.5
Czechia	16.6	8.0	Laos	50.5	10.7	Taiwan	13.3	2.5
Denmark	12.6	4.0	Latvia	20.5	7.9	Thailand	24.8	3.2
Dominican Republic	27.5	3.8	Lebanon	21.3	1.2	Tunisia	21.6	3.1
Ecuador	26.3	0.8	Lithuania	24.5	6.4	Turkey	21.3	3.3
Egypt	39.8	4.6	Malaysia	25.2	2.1	Ukraine	41.2	7.0
El Salvador	26.5	0.5	Mexico	27.9	3.8	United Arab Emirates	13.9	0.4
Ethiopia	44.2	3.1	Morocco	34.5	1.5	United Kingdom	9.4	3.7
Finland	13.0	5.0	Netherlands	12.4	3.3	Uruguay	18.9	1.2
France	15.0	4.0	New Zealand	14.1	5.3	Vietnam	31.7	2.2

[1] Includes nonalcoholic beverages.

Source: U.S. Department of Agriculture, Economic Research Service, International Consumer and Food Industry Trends, "Data on expenditures on food and alcoholic beverages in selected countries," <www.ers.usda.gov/topics/international-markets-us-trade/international-consumer-and-food-industry-trends/>, accessed August 2021.

Table 1374. Gross Government Assets and Liabilities as a Percent of GDP by Country: 2010 to 2023

[Percent of nominal gross domestic product. The general government sector is a consolidation of accounts for the central, state, and local governments plus social security]

Country	General government gross financial assets as a percent of GDP				General government gross financial liabilities as a percent of GDP			
	2010	2020	2022	2023 (P)	2010	2020	2022	2023 (P)
United States	**25.3**	**35.4**	**28.5**	**28.5**	**94.9**	**134.1**	**126.1**	**126.8**
Australia	43.7	61.1	58.1	58.1	24.4	66.4	64.0	64.9
Austria	44.9	49.8	49.7	49.7	96.4	112.3	103.5	101.2
Belgium	26.8	40.8	40.0	40.0	108.8	141.6	126.3	127.5
Canada	55.2	97.0	93.4	93.4	86.4	126.9	117.0	116.8
Czechia	38.2	33.5	35.4	35.4	44.6	47.1	52.4	56.0
Denmark	56.7	69.9	59.9	59.9	53.4	58.7	46.0	42.4
Estonia	46.4	42.8	38.6	38.6	11.9	25.4	25.4	23.7
Finland	119.5	149.1	150.3	150.3	55.7	85.0	86.3	92.2
France	45.8	51.7	50.9	50.9	100.1	145.8	139.5	140.3
Germany	41.5	46.3	45.6	44.8	87.4	79.1	79.0	78.1
Greece	37.8	61.5	54.7	52.5	130.9	242.3	213.5	202.8
Hungary	25.7	37.9	34.8	32.8	86.6	97.5	88.1	86.7
Ireland	36.8	25.0	24.8	24.8	84.5	72.3	62.0	60.1
Israel [1]	5.9	4.1	4.1	4.1	70.4	71.7	65.8	64.7
Italy	25.8	32.8	31.6	31.4	125.6	185.5	174.4	172.4
Japan	79.7	113.7	108.6	108.6	181.4	240.9	244.7	244.7
Latvia	40.8	39.1	37.9	37.9	54.1	56.0	60.2	61.0
Lithuania	32.7	34.3	34.0	34.0	45.5	55.5	50.5	51.0
Luxembourg	75.0	83.0	80.7	80.7	27.2	32.3	33.7	34.6
Netherlands	36.1	34.3	32.1	32.1	69.6	69.8	64.6	64.3
New Zealand	35.3	38.4	37.5	37.5	37.0	42.4	47.4	50.5
Poland	34.2	32.2	30.7	30.7	61.7	77.3	67.3	67.0
Portugal	33.4	44.8	40.1	40.1	106.7	157.6	138.1	134.9
Slovakia	19.2	28.4	30.2	30.2	48.5	79.3	81.3	78.2
Slovenia	47.5	69.4	58.0	57.0	47.9	109.7	93.0	92.8
Spain	28.8	40.2	39.4	39.4	67.6	147.6	143.3	140.8
Sweden	70.4	89.6	84.0	80.0	47.3	52.1	46.0	44.1
Switzerland	36.6	60.7	60.3	60.3	42.8	43.1	41.2	40.6
United Kingdom	36.9	39.7	38.1	38.1	89.3	149.1	139.2	138.6

P Projected. [1] See footnote 2, Table 1372.

Source: Organisation for Economic Co-operation and Development (OECD), 2022, "OECD Economic Outlook No. 111 (Edition 2022/1)," OECD Economic Outlook: Statistics and Projections (database) ©, <www.oecd-ilibrary.org/economics/data/oecd-economic-outlook-statistics-and-projections_eo-data-en>, accessed August 2022.

Table 1375. Percent Distribution of Tax Receipts by Country and Tax Type: 2010 to 2020

Country	Taxes on income and profits [2]			Social security contributions			Taxes on goods and services [5]		
	Total [1]	Total [3]	Individual	Corporate	Total [4]	Employees	Employers	Total [3]	General consumption taxes [6]	Taxes on specific goods, services [7]

Country	Total [1]	Taxes on income and profits [2] — Total [3]	Individual	Corporate	Social security contributions — Total [4]	Employees	Employers	Taxes on goods and services [5] — Total [3]	General consumption taxes [6]	Taxes on specific goods, services [7]
United States:										
2010	100.0	42.3	34.8	7.5	26.1	11.6	13.1	18.1	8.4	7.2
2020 [8]	100.0	46.2	41.1	5.1	24.8	11.2	12.3	16.9	8.0	6.8
Canada:										
2010	100.0	46.6	35.0	10.5	14.9	5.9	8.4	24.0	14.0	8.5
2020 [8]	100.0	49.7	36.3	12.3	14.2	5.9	7.9	21.6	13.6	6.7
Chile:										
2010	100.0	38.1	6.8	20.4	6.8	6.6	0.3	51.2	38.5	9.8
2020 [8]	100.0	32.4	10.3	24.3	8.0	7.7	0.3	54.9	41.2	9.4
Czechia:										
2010	100.0	20.2	10.2	10.0	44.8	9.1	28.2	33.8	20.5	11.3
2020 [8]	100.0	21.9	13.5	8.4	46.1	9.6	29.3	31.5	21.6	8.5
France:										
2010	100.0	22.6	17.0	5.5	38.2	9.2	25.9	26.6	17.9	7.6
2020 [8]	100.0	26.2	21.0	5.1	32.7	7.9	22.2	27.0	17.2	8.8
Germany:										
2010	100.0	28.3	24.1	4.2	38.9	16.8	18.2	30.5	19.8	8.8
2020 [8]	100.0	31.3	27.0	4.3	39.7	16.8	19.0	25.7	17.2	6.9
Greece:										
2010	100.0	22.0	12.4	7.9	34.2	18.4	15.8	38.6	22.8	12.3
2019 [9]	100.0	21.6	15.2	5.6	30.8	16.7	14.1	39.9	21.4	12.9
Italy:										
2010	100.0	32.7	26.9	5.5	31.1	5.6	21.5	26.6	14.5	9.4
2020 [8]	100.0	33.0	26.9	4.9	31.5	5.9	21.1	26.9	14.0	9.2
Japan:										
2010	100.0	30.2	18.6	11.6	41.1	17.8	18.6	18.7	9.6	7.2
2019 [9]	100.0	30.8	18.8	12.0	41.1	18.2	19.1	19.7	13.2	5.1
Korea, South:										
2010	100.0	28.0	14.2	13.8	23.3	9.5	10.4	33.7	17.5	15.1
2020 [8]	100.0	30.9	18.8	12.1	28.0	12.1	12.6	24.4	15.1	7.8
Turkey:										
2010	100.0	21.3	14.0	7.3	24.9	9.4	13.7	47.7	21.7	24.1
2020 [8]	100.0	21.9	13.2	8.7	29.7	11.4	16.9	43.0	19.2	22.4
United Kingdom:										
2010	100.0	37.4	28.6	8.9	18.9	7.5	10.9	31.6	19.0	11.2
2020 [8]	100.0	35.9	28.9	7.1	20.9	8.1	12.2	31.0	20.2	9.5

[1] Includes property taxes, employer payroll taxes other than social security contributions, and miscellaneous taxes, not shown separately. [2] Includes taxes on capital gains. [3] Includes other taxes, not shown separately. [4] Includes contributions of self-employed persons, not shown separately. [5] Taxes on the production, extraction, sale, transfer, leasing or delivery of goods, and the rendering of services. [6] Primarily value-added and sales taxes. [7] For example, excise taxes on alcohol, tobacco, and gasoline. [8] Data are provisional/estimates. [9] Data for 2020 are not available.

Source: Organisation for Economic Co-operation and Development (OECD), 2022, "Revenue Statistics: Comparative tables," OECD Tax Statistics (database) ©, <dx.doi.org/10.1787/data-00262-en>, accessed June 2022.

Table 1376. Household Tax Burden by Country: 2021

[As percent of gross wage earnings of the average worker. The tax burden reflects income tax plus employee social security contributions less cash benefits]

Country	Single person without children	One-earner married couple with two children	Country	Single person without children	One-earner married couple with two children
OECD average [1]	24.64	19.60	Israel [3]	19.71	19.71
			Italy	29.63	23.53
United States	**24.81**	**9.94**	Japan	22.30	20.90
Australia	23.23	23.23	Korea, South	15.28	13.35
Austria	33.18	25.91	Latvia	26.49	18.63
Belgium	39.76	28.13	Lithuania	36.49	36.49
Canada	25.07	21.64	Luxembourg	31.93	19.87
Chile	7.00	7.00	Mexico	10.23	10.23
Colombia	(NA)	(NA)	Netherlands	27.49	26.80
Costa Rica	10.50	10.50	New Zealand	19.44	19.44
Czechia	19.60	2.38	Norway	27.63	27.63
Denmark	35.55	31.77	Poland	24.19	19.90
Estonia	17.11	12.74	Portugal	28.02	17.72
Finland	30.80	30.80	Slovakia	23.76	12.85
France [2]	27.78	20.84	Slovenia	34.53	26.72
Germany	37.73	19.31	Spain	21.09	14.04
Greece	22.43	22.95	Sweden	24.52	24.52
Hungary	33.50	24.61	Switzerland	17.86	11.27
Iceland	28.01	21.98	Turkey	29.38	27.54
Ireland	26.66	16.69	United Kingdom	23.67	23.10

NA Not available. [1] As of 2021, the Organisation for Economic Co-operation and Development (OECD) is comprised of the 38 member countries shown. See text, this section. [2] Figures correspond to tax calculations that are based on the tax legislation relating to the income earned in the selected year. [3] See footnote 2, Table 1372.

Source: Organisation for Economic Co-operation and Development (OECD), 2022, "Taxing Wages: Comparative tables," OECD Tax Statistics (database) ©, <dx.doi.org/10.1787/data-00265-en>, accessed June 2022.

Table 1377. Household Net Saving Rates by Country: 2000 to 2020

[As a percentage of household disposable income. Household savings are estimated by subtracting household consumption expenditure from household disposable income, plus the change in net equity of households in pension funds. Households include households plus nonprofit institutions serving households. Net saving rates are measured after deducting consumption of fixed capital (depreciation), with respect to assets used in enterprises operated by households, as well as owner-occupied dwellings. The household saving rate is calculated as the ratio of household savings to household disposable income (plus the change in net equity of households in pension funds). Minus sign (-) indicates an excess of expenditures over income]

Country	2000	2005	2010	2014	2015	2016	2017	2018	2019	2020
United States	4.94	2.97	6.47	7.28	7.78	7.22	7.52	7.88	7.90	17.05
Australia [1]	1.70	-0.73	7.34	7.53	6.01	5.36	4.76	5.46	12.33	15.22
Austria	10.63	11.14	9.59	7.30	6.74	7.82	7.52	7.69	8.51	2 14.45
Belgium	11.45	10.18	9.26	6.41	5.53	5.44	5.37	4.70	5.56	2 13.85
Canada	5.05	1.53	4.27	3.54	4.07	1.62	1.85	0.67	2.02	14.43
Chile	(NA)	11.30	8.95	11.37	9.72	10.21	9.45	9.57	11.90	(NA)
Denmark	-5.69	-4.27	1.84	-2.90	3.91	5.61	6.03	5.42	3.56	5.76
Finland	2.63	0.51	3.27	–	-0.46	-1.39	-0.93	-0.84	0.36	4.73
France	8.67	8.50	10.45	8.86	8.33	8.18	8.37	8.66	2 9.21	2 15.73
Germany	9.33	10.56	10.31	9.84	10.06	10.20	10.64	2 11.32	2 10.82	2 16.07
Greece	(NA)	(NA)	3 -4.12	-13.60	-11.55	-11.06	-14.20	2 -14.70	2 -11.76	2 -4.80
Hungary	4.50	7.52	5.91	7.45	7.28	6.97	8.06	10.83	10.52	2 11.03
Ireland	-2.84	2.60	9.99	3.14	3.77	2.68	6.93	5.77	5.21	21.38
Italy	7.36	8.90	3.93	3.69	2.89	3.00	2.56	2.55	2.38	10.19
Japan	8.07	2.69	3.31	-0.78	0.13	1.95	1.60	1.77	3.25	12.09
Korea	(NA)	4.61	3.18	6.83	9.63	8.66	7.54	7.17	8.13	2 14.11
Latvia	-9.76	-5.18	-1.82	-8.86	-4.74	-3.34	-3.52	-2.04	0.07	9.08
Luxembourg	5.85	5.18	5.49	9.75	7.39	5.96	7.41	6.88	7.88	18.11
Mexico	(NA)	5.98	14.54	14.33	15.35	13.98	13.02	10.23	15.58	20.09
New Zealand [1]	-2.57	-5.79	2.12	-0.26	-0.06	0.31	0.16	1.10	3.11	2 5.54
Norway	3.83	9.32	3.73	7.72	9.75	6.89	6.56	5.91	7.05	14.25
Poland	10.15	1.81	2.78	0.46	0.13	1.72	0.38	-0.70	0.70	6.85
Portugal	6.08	2.76	1.57	-1.42	-1.19	-1.31	-2.24	-2.47	-2.17	2 3.26
Slovakia	4.58	0.81	3.11	0.73	3.16	3.27	2.06	4.76	4.13	5.14
Spain	6.60	4.27	5.06	2.28	3.17	2.97	1.64	1.40	4.21	10.81
Sweden	0.42	2.86	9.80	13.84	12.00	13.43	12.30	13.60	15.72	18.01
United Kingdom	4.14	2.68	6.16	2.51	3.65	0.65	-1.29	-1.50	-1.64	7.48

– Represents or rounds to zero. NA Not available. [1] Data refer to fiscal year. [2] Data are estimates. [3] Break in series.

Source: Organisation for Economic Co-operation and Development (OECD), 2022, "National Accounts at a Glance," OECD National Accounts Statistics (database) ©, <dx.doi.org/10.1787/data-00369-en>, accessed June 2022.

Table 1378. Insurance and Pensions by Country: 2020

[7,059,805 represents $7,059,805,000,000]

Country	Insurance					Pensions [2]	
	Investment assets (mil. U.S. dollars) [1]	Direct gross premiums (percent of GDP)	Total gross premiums (mil. U.S. dollars)		Gross claims payments (mil. U.S. dollars)	Investment assets (mil. U.S. dollars)	Benefits paid (percent of GDP)
			Life	Non-life			
United States	7,059,805	12.5	1,242,994	1,691,835	1,617,697	35,491,205	7.1
Australia	108,803	3.5	21,205	36,192	97,754	1,794,300	6.9
Belgium	421,775	6.1	16,819	17,598	29,815	223,702	0.3
Chile	66,476	3.9	5,956	4,033	7,767	208,482	2.0
Colombia	19,960	3.0	4,201	4,216	4,142	93,053	(NA)
Costa Rica	3,477	2.3	215	1,225	627	21,657	0.9
Czechia	(NA)	2.9	2,229	4,987	3,976	25,347	0.5
Denmark	659,473	11.3	29,832	11,166	28,764	882,109	0.8
Finland	92,352	1.7	4,611	(NA)	4,778	186,741	1.7
France	(NA)	10.1	150,513	152,216	274,227	344,114	(NA)
Germany	2,443,184	7.0	116,213	249,684	251,310	338,469	0.3
Greece	22,789	2.5	2,402	2,287	(NA)	2,016	(NA)
Hungary	10,597	2.5	1,722	2,188	2,165	8,922	0.1
Iceland	1,331	2.5	49	496	405	47,842	6.5
Israel [3]	185,396	4.8	10,546	8,967	13,447	300,489	(NA)
Italy	1,110,769	8.1	115,896	39,855	112,860	256,417	0.4
Korea, South	1,145,840	11.5	101,326	97,453	123,646	560,037	2.6
Latvia	1,694	2.7	275	636	573	7,004	0.2
Lithuania	1,727	2.0	332	759	572	5,723	0.1
Luxembourg	315,714	30.9	21,362	2,812	18,381	2,246	0.2
Mexico	75,763	2.6	12,856	15,446	14,405	(NA)	0.5
Norway	233,675	5.9	11,277	10,054	13,659	(NA)	0.3
Poland	50,629	2.6	5,322	10,944	10,295	48,934	–
Portugal	60,610	4.4	4,901	6,149	11,712	54,606	0.4
Slovakia	9,470	2.7	1,334	1,457	976	16,192	0.1
Slovenia	9,346	5.0	596	2,526	2,015	4,605	0.2
Spain	391,593	5.0	26,559	44,971	54,862	199,627	0.4
Switzerland	497,198	7.6	26,668	42,372	57,211	(NA)	5.7
Turkey	12,325	1.5	2,449	9,765	4,902	(NA)	0.1
United Kingdom	3,000,284	11.4	268,534	112,426	358,114	3,593,710	3.1

NA Not available or not applicable. – Represents or rounds to zero. [1] Includes total investment assets of direct insurance companies (excludes re-insurance). [2] Includes public and private autonomous pension funds of all types (occupational and personal, mandatory and voluntary). [3] See footnote 2, Table 1372.

Source: Organisation for Economic Co-operation and Development (OECD), 2022, "Outstanding investment by direct insurance companies," OECD Insurance Statistics (database) ©, <dx.doi.org/10.1787/data-00326-en>; "Insurance activity indicators," OECD Insurance Statistics (database) ©, <dx.doi.org/10.1787/data-00333-en>; "Gross Claims payments," OECD Insurance Statistics (database) ©, <doi.org/10.1787/data-00328-en>; "Pensions statistics," OECD Pensions Statistics (database) ©, <dx.doi.org/10.1787/data-00517-en>; and "Pensions indicators," OECD Pensions Statistics (database) ©, <dx.doi.org/10.1787/data-00518-en>; accessed August 2022.

[Percent change from previous year. Inflation as measured by the consumer price index reflects the annual percent change in the cost to the average consumer of acquiring a basket of goods and services that may be fixed or adjusted at specified intervals, such as yearly. For general comments concerning the data, see text, this section. For additional qualifications of the data for individual countries, see source. Minus sign (-) indicates decrease]

Country	2010	2015	2019	2020	2021	Country	2010	2015	2019	2020	2021
World [1]	**3.4**	**1.4**	**2.2**	**1.9**	**3.4**	Kenya	4.0	6.6	5.2	5.4	6.1
United States	**1.6**	**0.1**	**1.8**	**1.2**	**4.7**	Korea, South	2.9	0.7	0.4	0.5	2.5
Albania	3.6	3.5	1.4	1.6	2.0	Laos	6.0	1.3	3.3	5.1	3.8
Algeria	3.9	4.8	2.0	2.4	7.2	Lebanon	4.0	-3.7	3.0	84.9	154.8
Australia	2.9	1.5	1.6	0.8	2.9	Malaysia	1.6	2.1	0.7	-1.1	2.5
Austria	1.8	0.9	1.5	1.4	2.8	Mexico	4.2	2.7	3.6	3.4	5.7
Bangladesh	8.1	6.2	5.6	5.7	5.5	Mongolia	10.0	5.7	7.3	3.7	7.1
Belarus	7.7	13.5	5.6	5.5	9.5	Morocco	1.0	1.6	0.3	0.7	1.4
Belgium	2.2	0.6	1.4	0.7	2.4	Netherlands	1.3	0.6	2.6	1.3	2.7
Brazil	5.0	9.0	3.7	3.2	8.3	New Zealand	2.3	0.3	1.6	1.7	3.9
Chile	1.4	4.3	2.6	3.0	4.5	Norway	2.4	2.2	2.2	1.3	3.5
China	3.2	1.4	2.9	2.4	1.0	Pakistan	12.9	2.5	10.6	9.7	9.5
Colombia	2.3	5.0	3.5	2.5	3.5	Philippines	3.8	0.7	2.4	2.4	3.9
Czechia	1.5	0.3	2.8	3.2	3.8	Poland	2.6	-0.9	2.2	3.4	5.1
Denmark	2.3	0.5	0.8	0.4	1.9	Portugal	1.4	0.5	0.3	(-Z)	1.3
Egypt	11.3	10.4	9.2	5.0	5.5	Romania	6.1	-0.6	3.8	2.6	5.1
El Salvador	1.2	-0.7	0.1	-0.4	3.5	Russia	6.8	15.5	4.5	3.4	6.7
France	1.5	(Z)	1.1	0.5	1.6	Saudi Arabia	5.3	1.2	-2.1	3.4	3.1
Germany	1.1	0.5	1.4	0.5	3.1	Singapore	2.8	-0.5	0.6	-0.2	2.3
Ghana	10.7	17.1	7.1	9.9	10.0	South Africa	4.1	4.5	4.1	3.2	4.6
Greece	4.7	-1.7	0.3	-1.2	1.2	Spain	1.8	-0.5	0.7	-0.3	3.1
Haiti	4.8	6.7	18.7	22.8	16.8	Sri Lanka	6.2	3.8	3.5	6.2	7.0
Honduras	4.7	3.2	4.4	3.5	4.5	Sweden	1.2	(-Z)	1.8	0.5	2.2
India	12.0	4.9	3.7	6.6	5.1	Switzerland	0.7	-1.1	0.4	-0.7	0.6
Indonesia	5.1	6.4	3.0	1.9	1.6	Thailand	3.2	-0.9	0.7	-0.8	1.2
Ireland	-0.9	-0.3	0.9	-0.3	2.4	Tunisia	3.3	4.4	6.7	5.6	5.7
Israel	2.7	-0.6	0.8	-0.6	1.5	Turkey	8.6	7.7	15.2	12.3	19.6
Italy	1.5	(Z)	0.6	-0.1	1.9	United Kingdom	2.5	0.4	1.7	1.0	2.5
Japan	-0.7	0.8	0.5	(-Z)	-0.2	Vietnam	9.2	0.6	2.8	3.2	1.8
Jordan	4.8	-0.9	0.8	0.3	1.3	Zimbabwe	3.0	-2.4	255.3	557.2	98.5

Z Less than 0.05 percent. [1] Includes other countries not shown separately.

Source: The World Bank, Washington, DC, World Development Indicators database, "Inflation, consumer prices (annual %)," © <databank.worldbank.org/source/world-development-indicators>, accessed July 2022.

Table 1380. Unemployment Rates by Country: 2000 to 2021

[Annual averages. The standardized unemployment rates shown here are calculated as the number of unemployed persons as a percentage of the civilian labor force. The unemployed are persons of working age who, in the reference period, are without work, are available for work, and have taken specific steps to find work. Selected data are estimated or subject to a break in series, see source for details]

Country	2000	2005	2010	2014	2015	2016	2017	2018	2019	2020	2021
OECD, total [1]	(NA)	(NA)	8.5	7.4	6.9	6.5	5.9	5.5	5.4	7.1	6.1
EU-27 [2]	(NA)	9.6	9.8	10.9	10.0	9.1	8.1	7.3	6.7	7.1	7.0
United States	**4.0**	**5.1**	**9.6**	**6.2**	**5.3**	**4.9**	**4.4**	**3.9**	**3.7**	**8.1**	**5.4**
Australia	6.3	5.0	5.2	6.1	6.1	5.7	5.6	5.3	5.2	6.5	5.1
Austria	3.5	5.6	4.8	5.6	5.7	6.0	5.5	4.8	4.5	5.4	6.2
Belgium	7.0	8.4	8.3	8.5	8.5	7.8	7.1	5.9	5.4	5.5	6.3
Canada	6.8	6.8	8.1	6.9	6.9	7.1	6.4	5.9	5.7	9.6	7.5
Chile	9.7	9.2	8.2	6.5	6.3	6.7	7.0	7.4	7.2	10.8	8.9
Czechia	8.8	7.9	7.3	6.1	5.0	4.0	2.9	2.2	2.0	2.5	2.8
Denmark	4.6	4.8	7.7	6.9	6.3	6.0	5.8	5.1	5.0	5.6	5.0
Estonia	14.6	8.0	16.7	7.4	6.2	6.8	5.8	5.4	4.4	6.8	6.2
Finland	9.8	8.4	8.4	8.7	9.4	8.8	8.6	7.4	6.7	7.8	7.6
France	8.4	8.5	8.9	10.3	10.4	10.0	9.4	9.0	8.4	8.0	7.9
Germany	7.8	11.2	7.0	5.0	4.6	4.1	3.7	3.4	3.1	3.8	3.6
Greece	11.3	10.0	12.7	26.5	24.9	23.5	21.5	19.3	17.3	16.3	14.8
Hungary	6.4	7.2	11.2	7.7	6.8	5.1	4.2	3.7	3.4	4.3	4.0
Ireland	4.3	4.3	14.5	11.9	9.9	8.4	6.7	5.7	5.0	5.6	6.2
Israel [3]	8.8	9.0	6.6	5.9	5.2	4.8	4.2	4.0	3.8	4.3	5.0
Italy	10.6	7.7	8.4	12.7	11.9	11.7	11.2	10.6	10.0	9.2	9.5
Japan	4.7	4.4	5.1	3.6	3.4	3.1	2.8	2.4	2.4	2.8	2.8
Korea	4.4	3.8	3.7	3.5	3.6	3.7	3.7	3.8	3.8	3.9	3.7
Latvia	(NA)	10.0	19.5	10.8	9.9	9.6	8.7	7.4	6.3	8.1	7.5
Lithuania	(NA)	8.3	17.8	10.7	9.1	7.9	7.1	6.2	6.3	8.5	7.1
Luxembourg	(NA)	4.5	4.4	5.9	6.7	6.3	5.5	5.6	5.6	6.8	5.2
Mexico	2.5	3.6	5.3	4.8	4.3	3.9	3.4	3.3	3.5	4.5	4.1
Netherlands	2.9	5.9	5.0	7.4	6.9	6.0	4.8	3.8	3.4	3.8	4.2
New Zealand	6.2	3.8	6.2	5.4	5.4	5.1	4.7	4.3	4.1	4.6	3.8
Norway	3.3	4.4	3.5	3.5	4.3	4.7	4.2	3.8	3.7	4.4	4.4
Poland	16.1	17.8	9.6	9.0	7.5	6.2	4.9	3.8	3.3	3.2	3.4
Portugal	4.0	7.6	10.8	13.9	12.4	11.1	8.9	7.0	6.5	6.8	6.6
Slovakia	18.8	16.3	14.4	13.2	11.5	9.7	8.1	6.5	5.8	6.7	6.8
Spain	13.9	9.2	19.9	24.4	22.1	19.6	17.2	15.3	14.1	15.5	14.8
Sweden	(NA)	7.5	8.6	8.0	7.4	7.0	6.7	6.4	6.8	8.3	8.7
Switzerland	(NA)	(NA)	4.8	4.8	4.8	4.9	4.8	4.7	4.4	4.8	5.1
Turkey	(NA)	(NA)	10.7	9.9	10.2	10.8	10.8	10.9	13.7	13.1	12.0
United Kingdom	5.5	4.8	7.9	6.2	5.4	4.9	4.4	4.1	3.8	4.6	4.5

NA Not available. [1] For OECD membership listing, see Section 30 introduction. [2] European Union as of February 1, 2020. [3] See footnote 2, Table 1372.

Source: Organisation for Economic Co-operation and Development (OECD), 2022, "Annual Labour Force Statistics: Summary tables," OECD Employment and Labour Market Statistics (database) ©, <dx.doi.org/10.1787/data-00286-en>, accessed August 2022.

Table 1381. Labor Force, Employment, and Unemployment by Country: 1990 to 2018

[Labor force and employment in thousands (125,840 represent 125,840,000)]

Country and indicator	1990	2000	2005	2010	2011	2012	2013	2014	2015	2016	2017	2018
LABOR FORCE (1,000s)												
United States	125,840	142,583	149,321	153,889	153,616	154,975	155,389	155,922	157,130	159,187	160,319	162,075
Australia	8,443	9,495	10,400	11,626	11,813	11,976	12,145	12,275	12,517	12,691	12,971	13,283
Canada	14,048	15,634	17,054	18,177	18,350	18,551	18,776	18,857	19,011	19,173	19,384	19,526
France	(NA)	(NA)	26,957	27,925	27,926	28,294	28,376	28,367	28,442	28,596	28,775	28,767
Germany	(NA)	38,342	39,724	40,586	41,045	41,151	41,536	41,778	41,987	42,867	43,017	43,085
Italy	(NA)	(NA)	24,027	24,305	24,425	24,957	25,014	25,247	25,248	25,508	25,684	25,727
Japan	(NA)	(NA)	(NA)	65,526	65,106	64,731	64,913	65,154	65,320	65,856	66,395	67,477
Netherlands	(NA)	(NA)	8,269	8,677	8,674	8,812	8,886	8,846	8,884	8,920	8,994	9,097
Sweden	(NA)	(NA)	(NA)	4,931	4,999	5,040	5,093	5,161	5,204	5,253	5,355	5,435
United Kingdom	(NA)	28,962	30,224	31,637	31,883	32,173	32,435	32,705	32,983	33,288	33,452	33,729
EMPLOYMENT LEVEL (1,000s)												
United States	118,793	136,891	141,730	139,064	139,869	142,469	143,929	146,305	148,834	151,436	153,337	155,761
Australia	7,856	8,899	9,877	11,021	11,213	11,350	11,457	11,531	11,760	11,967	12,247	12,580
Canada	12,961	14,683	16,035	16,889	17,153	17,371	17,630	17,741	17,889	18,026	18,357	18,588
France	(NA)	(NA)	24,636	25,421	25,436	25,617	25,537	25,528	25,560	25,789	26,146	26,227
Germany	(NA)	35,338	35,328	37,757	38,644	38,926	39,355	39,688	40,038	41,092	41,397	41,615
Italy	(NA)	(NA)	22,157	22,256	22,351	22,262	21,948	22,031	22,210	22,502	22,763	22,964
Japan	(NA)	(NA)	(NA)	62,431	62,372	62,245	62,715	63,170	63,463	64,120	64,782	66,088
Netherlands	(NA)	(NA)	7,779	8,241	8,241	8,296	8,239	8,186	8,270	8,381	8,556	8,747
Sweden	(NA)	(NA)	(NA)	4,511	4,614	4,643	4,688	4,756	4,823	4,894	5,003	5,096
United Kingdom	(NA)	27,375	28,760	29,140	29,289	29,601	29,961	30,679	31,202	31,655	31,976	32,349
UNEMPLOYMENT LEVEL (1,000s)												
United States	7,047	5,692	7,591	14,825	13,747	12,506	11,460	9,617	8,296	7,751	6,982	6,314
Australia	587	596	523	605	600	626	688	744	757	724	724	703
Canada	1,087	951	1,019	1,288	1,197	1,180	1,146	1,116	1,122	1,147	1,027	938
France	1,890	2,136	2,321	2,504	2,490	2,677	2,839	2,839	2,882	2,807	2,629	2,540
Germany	(NA)	3,004	4,396	2,829	2,401	2,225	2,181	2,090	1,949	1,775	1,620	1,470
Italy	(NA)	(NA)	1,870	2,049	2,074	2,695	3,066	3,216	3,038	3,006	2,921	2,763
Japan	1,282	2,916	2,479	3,095	2,734	2,486	2,198	1,984	1,857	1,736	1,613	1,389
Netherlands	(NA)	(NA)	490	436	433	516	647	660	614	539	438	350
Sweden	(NA)	(NA)	(NA)	420	385	397	405	405	381	359	352	339
United Kingdom	(NA)	1,587	1,464	2,497	2,594	2,572	2,474	2,026	1,781	1,633	1,476	1,380
UNEMPLOYMENT RATE (percent)												
United States	5.6	4.0	5.1	9.6	8.9	8.1	7.4	6.2	5.3	4.9	4.4	3.9
Australia	6.9	6.3	5.0	5.2	5.1	5.2	5.7	6.1	6.1	5.7	5.6	5.3
Canada	7.7	6.1	6.0	7.1	6.5	6.4	6.1	5.9	5.9	6.0	5.3	4.8
France	(NA)	(NA)	8.6	9.0	8.9	9.5	10.0	10.0	10.1	9.8	9.1	8.8
Germany	(NA)	7.8	11.1	7.0	5.8	5.4	5.3	5.0	4.6	4.1	3.8	3.4
Italy	(NA)	(NA)	7.8	8.4	8.5	10.8	12.3	12.7	12.0	11.8	11.4	10.7
Japan	(NA)	(NA)	(NA)	4.7	4.2	3.8	3.4	3.0	2.8	2.6	2.4	2.1
Netherlands	(NA)	(NA)	5.9	5.0	5.0	5.9	7.3	7.5	6.9	6.0	4.9	3.8
Sweden	(NA)	(NA)	(NA)	8.5	7.7	7.9	8.0	7.8	7.3	6.8	6.6	6.2
United Kingdom	(NA)	5.5	4.8	7.9	8.1	8.0	7.6	6.2	5.4	4.9	4.4	4.1

NA Not available.

Source: The Conference Board, Inc., *Business Cycle Indicators*, 2020. © The Conference Board 2022. For more information see <www.conference-board.org/data/bci.cfm>.

Table 1382. Youth Educational Enrollment and Employment Status by Country: 2019 and 2020

[Percent of total youth population for selected age groups]

Country	2019						2020					
	15 to 29 year olds			20 to 24 year olds			15 to 29 year olds			20 to 24 year olds		
	In education, total	Not in education		In education, total	Not in education		In education, total	Not in education		In education, total	Not in education	
		Employed	Not employed		Employed	Not employed		Employed	Not employed		Employed	Not employed
OECD average....	45.2	41.5	13.3	44.3	40.8	14.9	45.9	39.4	14.8	45.1	38.1	16.8
United States [1] ...	**37.3**	**48.4**	**14.3**	**35.6**	**49.6**	**14.8**	**36.8**	**44.2**	**18.9**	**35.1**	**44.8**	**20.1**
Austria........	44.3	45.5	10.2	38.8	49.6	11.6	44.7	44.1	11.2	39.6	47.7	12.7
Belgium......	28.6	55.4	16.0	51.5	33.9	14.6	31.3	52.5	16.2	55.4	30.7	13.9
Canada......	35.8	50.8	13.4	33.6	52.8	13.6	35.1	45.8	19.0	34.4	45.2	20.4
Colombia.....	33.0	43.3	23.7	24.0	48.6	27.5	31.3	38.8	29.8	22.3	42.8	34.9
Czechia......	45.6	44.4	10.0	47.5	43.3	9.2	46.8	42.1	11.1	48.7	40.6	10.7
Estonia.......	47.2	42.4	10.4	45.4	43.8	10.8	49.4	38.3	12.3	47.5	37.9	14.6
Finland.......	53.7	35.7	10.6	49.8	36.7	13.4	53.5	35.1	11.4	49.7	34.7	15.6
France........	48.4	36.3	15.4	42.7	37.5	19.8	49.5	34.8	15.7	45.3	35.2	19.5
Germany.....	53.4	38.5	8.1	54.8	36.3	8.9	53.0	37.3	9.7	55.7	34.4	10.0
Greece.......	54.5	27.0	18.6	60.2	20.8	19.0	55.0	25.3	19.7	59.8	20.2	19.9
Hungary......	42.3	44.4	13.3	41.0	43.5	15.5	42.0	43.7	14.3	38.4	46.0	15.6
Ireland.......	50.3	38.2	11.4	44.4	42.4	13.2	51.1	36.0	12.8	48.6	37.2	14.1
Italy.........	47.8	29.2	23.1	44.5	29.1	26.4	48.7	27.3	24.0	45.9	26.7	27.4
Lithuania.....	48.4	40.5	11.1	51.4	35.1	13.5	47.2	39.2	13.6	49.7	32.2	18.1
Mexico......	37.6	41.7	20.7	30.8	46.3	22.9	37.9	40.0	22.1	31.4	43.8	24.8
Netherlands..	55.7	37.4	6.9	58.6	34.0	7.4	56.0	36.8	7.2	59.2	32.7	8.2
New Zealand....	38.2	50.5	11.3	30.2	56.7	13.1	38.2	49.5	12.4	30.8	54.6	14.7
Poland........	42.5	45.0	12.5	42.1	43.9	14.0	43.4	43.1	13.5	43.8	40.8	15.4
Portugal......	48.9	40.5	10.6	44.0	41.5	14.5	50.5	36.9	12.6	48.7	35.0	16.3
Slovenia......	52.7	37.9	9.4	55.6	34.8	9.6	54.2	36.0	9.7	58.8	29.2	12.0
Spain........	50.4	31.5	18.1	50.3	28.7	21.1	51.3	28.1	20.7	51.4	24.4	24.2
Sweden......	45.0	43.9	11.1	43.1	45.3	11.5	46.7	41.0	12.3	45.0	41.6	13.4
Switzerland...	49.0	43.3	7.7	48.4	42.4	9.2	50.0	42.5	7.5	49.8	41.1	9.1
United Kingdom....	34.9	52.2	12.9	32.8	52.4	14.8	35.8	50.9	13.2	33.9	50.8	15.3

[1] Age group refers to 16-29 year-olds instead of 15-29 year-olds.

Source: Organisation for Economic Co-operation and Development (OECD), 2022, "Indicator A2: Transition from education to work: Where are today's youth?" Education at a Glance 2021: OECD Indicators, OECD Publishing ©, <doi.org/10.1787/bd3a6fb1-en>, accessed August 2022.

Table 1383. Educational Performance and Attainment by Country: 2018 and 2020

Country	2018			2020		
	Student mean proficiency scores [1]			Educational attainment of adults age 25 to 64 (percent)		
	Reading scale	Mathematics scale	Science scale	Below upper secondary	Upper secondary and vocational	Tertiary [2]
United States..............	**505.4**	**478.2**	**502.4**	**8.3**	**41.7**	**50.1**
Australia....................	502.6	491.4	503.0	16.2	34.4	49.3
Austria.....................	484.4	498.9	489.8	14.3	51.5	34.2
Belgium....................	492.9	508.1	498.8	20.2	37.3	42.4
Canada.....................	520.1	512.0	518.0	7.6	32.5	60.0
Colombia...................	412.3	390.9	413.3	41.2	34.2	24.6
Czechia....................	490.2	499.5	496.8	5.9	69.2	24.9
Denmark....................	501.1	509.4	492.6	[4] 18.4	[4] 41.2	[4] 40.4
France.....................	492.6	495.4	493.0	18.5	41.8	39.7
Germany...................	498.3	500.0	503.0	13.9	54.9	31.3
Greece.....................	457.4	451.4	451.6	23.6	43.7	32.7
Ireland.....................	518.1	499.6	496.1	14.5	35.5	49.9
Israel [3].....................	470.4	463.0	462.2	12.0	37.9	50.1
Italy.......................	476.3	486.6	468.0	37.1	42.7	20.1
Japan......................	503.9	527.0	529.1	(NA)	(NA)	(NA)
Korea, South................	514.1	525.9	519.0	10.6	38.6	50.7
Mexico.....................	420.5	408.8	419.2	58.4	22.2	19.4
Netherlands.................	484.8	519.2	503.4	19.0	38.4	42.6
New Zealand................	505.7	494.5	508.5	19.1	40.8	40.1
Norway.....................	499.5	501.0	490.4	17.5	37.2	45.3
Poland.....................	511.9	515.6	511.0	6.8	60.4	32.9
Portugal....................	491.8	492.5	491.7	44.6	27.2	28.2
Spain......................	(NA)	481.4	483.3	37.1	23.2	39.7
Sweden....................	505.8	502.4	499.4	16.1	39.3	44.6
Switzerland.................	483.9	515.3	495.3	10.7	44.0	45.3
Turkey.....................	465.6	453.5	468.3	[4] 58.3	[4] 19.7	[4] 22.0
United Kingdom.............	503.9	501.8	504.7	18.3	32.3	49.4

NA Not available. [1] Proficiency scores are based on the Program for International Student Assessment (PISA), an international standardized test which takes place in three-year cycles. PISA tests are administered to a nationally representative sample of fifteen-year-old students in each country. [2] Tertiary education entails completion of an advanced course of study or research program leading to an associate's, bachelor's, master's, or doctorate degree, usually 2 years or longer in duration. [3] See footnote 2, Table 1372. [4] Data are for 2019.

Source: Organisation for Economic Co-operation and Development (OECD), 2022, "Education at a glance: Educational Attainment and Labour-force Status," OECD Education Statistics (database) ©, <dx.doi.org/10.1787/889e8641-en>; and "Annex B1. Results (tables)" in PISA 2018 Results (Volume 1), OECD Publishing ©, <doi.org/10.1787/5f07c754-en>; accessed August 2022.

Table 1384. World Supply and Utilization of Major Crops and Livestock: 2010 to 2022

[In millions of units (225.8 represents 225,800,000). For major crops, data are for marketing or trade year ending in year shown, unless otherwise indicated. For livestock and dairy, data are for calendar year]

Commodity	2010	2015	2017	2018	2019	2020	2021	2022 (P)
Wheat:								
Area harvested (hectares)	225.8	221.3	222.3	218.1	215.4	215.5	220.8	222.2
Production (metric tons)	688.1	730.3	756.1	761.6	730.9	761.6	775.7	779.0
Exports (metric tons)	135.3	162.0	185.7	187.0	178.1	194.5	199.4	201.2
Consumption (metric tons)	650.9	701.1	733.8	740.6	732.2	740.3	774.3	787.2
Ending stocks (metric tons)	204.1	225.1	266.3	285.8	282.5	298.2	291.6	279.4
Corn:								
Area harvested (hectares)	158.8	188.8	196.9	193.3	192.7	194.4	199.1	206.5
Production (metric tons)	834.0	1,057.9	1,128.5	1,081.9	1,128.7	1,122.7	1,129.0	1,216.1
Exports (metric tons)	92.7	128.7	143.8	154.4	173.6	175.7	184.2	189.1
Consumption (metric tons)	832.3	975.1	1,064.7	1,095.6	1,131.6	1,133.3	1,145.7	1,181.1
Ending stocks (metric tons)	131.6	279.7	351.9	341.5	322.7	307.5	293.2	310.9
Rice, milled:								
Area harvested (hectares)	155.9	163.2	164.1	163.7	163.1	161.7	165.2	166.6
Production (metric tons)	440.8	483.0	491.8	494.8	498.2	499.2	509.3	513.7
Exports (metric tons)	31.8	43.0	48.7	48.3	43.9	45.4	51.8	52.9
Consumption (metric tons)	435.3	473.4	477.9	481.1	485.0	493.0	499.1	513.7
Ending stocks (metric tons)	97.0	135.9	150.8	163.9	177.2	182.3	188.0	187.3
Coarse grains: [1]								
Area harvested (hectares)	307.8	332.8	338.9	329.9	331.6	335.4	343.7	345.2
Production (metric tons)	1,124.1	1,346.6	1,420.1	1,362.7	1,403.0	1,419.6	1,439.1	1,501.8
Exports (metric tons)	118.8	174.2	185.0	192.0	207.1	214.6	235.4	235.0
Consumption (metric tons)	1,124.6	1,281.8	1,381.8	1,376.7	1,423.9	1,434.3	1,453.8	1,488.2
Ending stocks (metric tons)	182.7	316.0	386.9	373.0	352.1	337.4	322.8	336.3
Oilseeds:								
Area harvested (hectares)	235.8	267.7	269.4	281.2	281.8	280.5	286.2	295.2
Production (metric tons)	447.1	539.1	576.2	583.9	600.8	580.6	606.6	599.0
Exports (metric tons)	107.6	147.5	171.4	177.3	171.7	191.0	191.4	178.6
Consumption (metric tons)	425.3	520.6	555.6	574.7	581.5	601.2	602.3	607.1
Ending stocks (metric tons)	77.7	96.0	109.9	118.2	134.0	112.1	115.1	104.9
Coffee, green:								
Production (60 kg bags)	129.8	153.8	161.1	159.8	176.0	169.0	176.4	167.1
Exports (60 kg bags)	106.3	123.6	132.9	133.6	142.9	138.5	144.4	140.5
Consumption (60 kg bags)	138.9	146.5	154.8	160.4	165.5	161.9	161.9	165.2
Ending stocks (60 kg bags)	28.8	43.1	36.5	32.0	37.1	36.2	37.7	32.7
Sugar, centrifugal:								
Production (metric tons)	153.2	177.6	172.1	194.2	179.2	166.6	181.0	181.2
Exports (metric tons)	48.3	55.0	60.0	65.8	57.8	53.2	62.3	64.3
Consumption (metric tons)	154.1	168.0	169.1	173.9	173.0	171.7	172.7	175.5
Ending stocks (metric tons)	28.0	48.8	42.0	51.7	52.9	48.0	52.0	48.9
Cotton:								
Area harvested (hectares)	30.2	33.8	29.9	33.7	33.3	34.5	31.4	32.3
Production (480 lb. bales)	103.1	119.2	107.3	124.4	118.2	120.0	111.5	116.9
Exports (480 lb. bales)	35.8	36.2	38.1	41.6	41.5	41.1	48.5	45.2
Consumption (480 lb. bales)	119.5	112.5	116.6	123.5	120.5	103.2	121.6	121.5
Ending stocks (480 lb. bales)	46.2	108.0	81.9	82.7	81.4	97.6	88.1	82.9
Beef:								
Beef cow beginning stocks (head)	202.9	200.5	205.0	205.9	205.9	206.0	206.5	208.7
Production (metric tons) [2]	57.0	57.5	56.3	57.7	58.7	57.7	58.1	58.7
Exports (metric tons) [2]	7.4	9.1	10.1	10.6	11.4	11.2	11.4	11.8
Consumption (metric tons) [2]	55.6	55.5	53.9	55.5	56.4	56.1	56.6	56.9
Ending stocks (metric tons) [2]	0.6	0.6	0.5	0.5	0.5	0.6	0.5	0.5
Pork:								
Sow beginning stocks (head)	79.3	76.3	73.6	72.7	66.1	60.4	68.6	68.7
Production (metric tons) [2]	102.9	111.8	111.1	111.9	101.0	95.8	107.7	110.5
Exports (metric tons) [2]	5.9	7.1	9.2	9.4	10.4	12.6	12.2	11.7
Consumption (metric tons) [2]	102.5	111.2	110.3	111.1	99.9	95.1	107.2	109.8
Ending stocks (metric tons) [2]	0.6	0.7	0.6	0.7	0.9	0.7	0.7	0.7
Chicken (meat): [3]								
Beginning stocks (metric tons)	0.5	0.6	0.7	0.8	0.7	0.7	0.7	0.7
Production (metric tons)	79.1	91.9	91.0	92.7	97.4	99.3	100.5	101.0
Exports (metric tons)	9.1	10.6	12.2	12.5	13.1	13.1	13.3	13.4
Consumption (metric tons)	77.3	90.0	88.9	90.3	94.8	96.8	98.1	98.5
Ending stocks (metric tons)	0.5	0.7	0.8	0.7	0.7	0.7	0.7	0.7
Dairy:								
Dairy cows beginning stocks (head)	229.2	237.5	236.0	238.5	240.2	243.0	243.3	244.8
Milk production (metric tons) [4]	441.4	496.0	511.6	522.6	527.7	539.6	544.1	549.4
Milk exports (metric tons) [4]	0.7	1.5	2.9	3.0	3.2	3.3	3.4	3.4
Milk consumption (metric tons) [4]	513.5	584.6	612.4	628.8	634.5	648.8	655.3	663.3

P Preliminary. [1] Coarse grains include corn, barley, sorghum, oats, rye, millet, and mixed grains but exclude trade in barley malt, millet, and mixed grains. [2] Carcass weight equivalent (CWE). [3] Weight in ready-to-eat equivalent meat. [4] Cow's milk only.

Source: U.S. Department of Agriculture, Foreign Agricultural Service, "Production, Supply and Distribution Online," <apps.fas.usda.gov/psdonline/app/index.html#/app/home>, accessed June 2022.

Table 1385. World Crop Production Summary: 2020 to 2022

[In millions of metric tons (775.7 represents 775,700,000). Data are for marketing or trade year. Data for 2021-2022 are preliminary]

Country	Wheat 2020–2021	2021–2022	Coarse grains[1] 2020–2021	2021–2022	Rice (milled) 2020–2021	2021–2022	Oilseeds[2] 2020–2021	2021–2022	Cotton 2020–2021	2021–2022
World	**775.7**	**779.0**	**1,439.1**	**1,501.8**	**509.3**	**513.7**	**606.6**	**599.0**	**111.5**	**116.9**
Total foreign	726.0	734.2	1,066.2	1,103.1	502.1	507.6	482.0	468.5	96.9	99.4
United States	**49.8**	**44.8**	**372.9**	**398.7**	**7.2**	**6.1**	**124.5**	**130.5**	**14.6**	**17.5**
Canada	35.2	21.7	29.6	24.2	–	–	25.9	19.0	–	–
Mexico	3.0	3.3	32.7	33.2	0.2	0.2	0.7	0.9	1.0	1.2
Russia	85.4	75.2	41.4	38.5	0.7	0.7	20.1	23.1	–	–
Ukraine	25.4	33.0	39.6	53.5	–	–	19.9	24.3	–	–
European Union	(3)	(3)	(3)	(3)	(3)	(3)	(3)	(3)	1.7	1.6
China	134.3	136.9	269.1	280.9	148.3	149.0	65.6	62.1	29.5	27.0
India	107.9	109.6	51.4	50.6	124.4	129.7	38.3	41.1	27.6	24.5
Indonesia	–	–	12.6	12.7	34.5	34.4	14.6	15.1	–	–
Pakistan	25.2	27.5	9.4	10.0	8.4	8.7	2.7	3.3	4.5	6.0
Thailand	–	–	5.7	5.4	18.9	19.7	1.0	1.0	–	–
Argentina	17.6	22.2	60.0	62.9	0.8	0.8	51.2	48.4	1.4	1.5
Brazil	6.3	7.7	90.3	120.6	8.0	7.3	143.9	131.1	10.8	12.7
Australia	33.3	36.3	17.1	18.4	0.3	0.5	5.4	8.1	2.8	5.5
South Africa	2.1	2.3	17.8	16.9	–	–	2.7	3.0	0.1	0.1
Turkey	18.3	16.0	15.8	11.6	0.6	0.5	2.9	3.4	2.9	3.8
All others	232.1	242.7	373.9	363.8	156.9	156.2	87.1	84.7	14.6	15.5

– Represents zero. [1] Includes corn, barley, sorghum, oats, rye, millet, and mixed grains. [2] Includes soybean, cottonseed, peanut (in shell), sunflower seed, and rapeseed for individual countries. Copra and palm kernel are added to world totals. [3] Indicates no reported or insignificant production.

Source: U.S. Department of Agriculture, Foreign Agricultural Service, *World Agricultural Production*, June 2022. See also <apps.fas.usda.gov/psdonline/app/index.html#/app/downloads>.

Table 1386. Meat Production by Type and Country: 2020 and 2021

[In thousands of metric tons (57,735 represents 57,735,000). Carcass weight equivalent basis for beef, veal, and pork. Chicken weight based on ready-to-cook equivalent meat]

Country	Beef and veal[1] 2020	2021	Country	Pork 2020	2021	Country	Chicken[2] 2020	2021
World	**57,735**	**58,134**	**World**	**95,767**	**107,730**	**World**	**99,254**	**100,537**
United States	**12,389**	**12,730**	China	36,340	47,500	**United States**	**20,255**	**20,391**
Brazil	10,100	9,500	EU-27[3]	23,219	23,720	China	14,600	14,700
China	6,720	6,980	**United States**	**12,845**	**12,559**	Brazil	13,880	14,500
EU-27[3]	6,882	6,855	Brazil	4,125	4,365	EU-27[3]	11,030	10,830
India	3,760	4,195	Russia	3,611	3,700	Russia	4,680	4,600
Argentina	3,170	3,000	Vietnam	2,467	2,590	Mexico	3,725	3,815
Mexico	2,079	2,150	Canada	2,115	2,120	Thailand	3,250	3,220
Australia	2,125	1,888	Mexico	1,451	1,484	Argentina	2,215	2,290
Canada	1,314	1,420	Korea, South	1,403	1,407	Turkey	2,136	2,246
Russia	1,378	1,380	Japan	1,306	1,318	Colombia	1,685	1,774
Others	7,818	8,036	Others	6,885	6,967	Other	21,798	22,171

[1] May include meat of other bovines. [2] Excludes chicken paws. [3] See footnote 3, Table 1387.

Source: U.S. Department of Agriculture, Foreign Agricultural Service, "Production, Supply and Distribution Online," <apps.fas.usda.gov/psdonline/app/index.html#/app/home>, accessed June 2022.

Table 1387. Meat Consumption by Type and Country: 2020 and 2021

[In thousands of metric tons (56,125 represents 56,125,000). Carcass weight equivalent basis for beef, veal, and pork. Chicken weight based on ready-to-cook equivalent meat]

Country	Beef and veal[1] 2020	2021	Country	Pork 2020	2021	Country	Chicken[2] 2020	2021
World	**56,125**	**56,601**	**World**	**95,075**	**107,193**	**World**	**96,835**	**98,093**
United States	**12,531**	**12,705**	China	41,521	51,726	**United States**	**16,994**	**17,158**
China	9,486	9,987	EU-27[3]	18,203	18,833	China	15,211	15,032
Brazil	7,611	7,242	**United States**	**10,034**	**9,915**	Brazil	10,010	10,280
EU-27[3]	6,518	6,502	Russia	3,468	3,558	EU-27[3]	9,653	9,636
India	2,476	2,798	Brazil	2,949	3,047	Mexico	4,560	4,725
Argentina	2,365	2,270	Vietnam	2,687	2,884	Russia	4,688	4,632
Mexico	1,898	1,959	Japan	2,732	2,760	Japan	2,757	2,838
Russia	1,708	1,628	Mexico	2,052	2,320	Thailand	2,299	2,280
Japan	1,295	1,265	Korea, South	1,976	1,997	Argentina	2,025	2,117
Canada	1,045	1,033	Philippines	1,282	1,457	South Africa	1,918	1,896
Others	9,192	9,212	Others	8,171	8,696	Others	26,720	27,499

[1] May include meat of other bovines. [2] Excludes chicken paws. [3] European Union-27: Austria, Belgium, Bulgaria, Croatia, Cyprus, Czech Republic, Denmark, Estonia, Finland, France, Germany, Greece, Hungary, Ireland, Italy, Latvia, Lithuania, Luxembourg, Malta, Netherlands, Poland, Portugal, Romania, Slovakia, Slovenia, Spain, and Sweden.

Source: U.S. Department of Agriculture, Foreign Agricultural Service, "Production, Supply and Distribution Online," <apps.fas.usda.gov/psdonline/app/index.html#/app/home>, accessed June 2022.

Table 1388. Wheat, Rice, and Corn—Exports and Imports of Leading Countries: 2020 to 2022

[In thousands of metric tons (34,485 represents 34,485,000). Wheat data represent trade years ending in June of year shown; corn data represent trade years ending in September of year shown; rice data represent trade years ending in December of year shown]

Leading country	Exports			Leading country	Imports		
	2020	2021	2022 (P)		2020	2021	2022 (P)
WHEAT				**WHEAT**			
Russia..................	34,485	39,100	33,000	Egypt..................	12,811	12,149	11,750
European Union [1]......	39,788	29,740	29,500	Indonesia..............	10,586	10,649	11,000
Australia...............	10,118	19,720	27,000	China..................	5,376	10,618	9,700
United States..........	**26,390**	**26,702**	**21,750**	Turkey.................	11,087	8,051	9,300
Ukraine................	21,016	16,851	19,000	Algeria................	7,145	7,680	7,800
Argentina..............	13,608	9,597	17,000	Iran...................	2,500	2,200	7,700
Canada.................	22,991	27,723	15,500	Bangladesh.............	6,800	7,200	7,500
India..................	595	3,597	10,000	Brazil.................	7,063	6,359	6,500
Kazakhstan.............	6,888	8,128	7,000	Philippines............	7,065	6,113	6,300
Turkey.................	6,633	6,571	6,500	Nigeria................	5,338	6,586	6,200
RICE				**RICE**			
India..................	14,577	21,238	21,000	China..................	3,200	4,921	5,600
Thailand...............	5,706	6,062	7,000	Philippines............	2,450	2,950	3,000
Vietnam................	6,167	6,272	6,500	Nigeria................	1,800	2,100	2,200
Pakistan...............	3,934	3,928	4,350	European Union [1].....	1,993	1,861	2,100
United States..........	**2,858**	**2,915**	**2,650**	Cote d'Ivoire..........	1,100	1,450	1,450
Burma..................	2,300	1,900	2,300	Saudi Arabia...........	1,613	1,200	1,400
China..................	2,265	2,407	2,250	Nepal..................	980	1,240	1,350
Brazil.................	1,240	782	850	Iraq...................	970	1,280	1,250
Uruguay................	969	704	820	Senegal................	1,050	1,250	1,250
European Union [1]......	543	413	440	Iran...................	1,125	875	1,200
Guyana.................	552	406	440	Malaysia...............	1,220	1,150	1,200
CORN				**CORN**			
United States..........	**46,992**	**68,558**	**62,000**	China..................	7,580	29,512	23,000
Argentina..............	39,917	36,544	42,500	Mexico.................	16,526	16,498	17,500
Brazil.................	34,137	27,492	34,000	European Union [1]......	17,384	14,493	16,000
Ukraine................	28,929	23,864	23,000	Japan..................	15,888	15,479	15,400
European Union [1]......	5,388	3,735	5,500	Korea, South...........	11,882	11,708	11,700
Russia.................	4,072	3,989	4,000	Vietnam................	12,000	11,200	10,600
South Africa...........	2,456	2,751	3,500	Egypt..................	10,432	9,633	9,200
India..................	1,125	3,677	3,300	Iran...................	6,800	7,200	8,500
Burma..................	2,209	2,400	2,450	Colombia...............	5,976	5,795	6,000
Canada.................	712	1,592	1,800	Taiwan.................	4,580	4,386	4,400

P Preliminary. [1] Beginning May 2021 with the release of 2021-2022 data, field crops Production, Supply, and Distribution (PSD) datasets reflect EU-27 (shown in the PSD system as "European Union") and UK separately. Historical data for both EU-27 and the UK are provided for 5 years (2016-2017 through 2020-2021). See footnote 3, Table 1387 for list of EU-27 countries.

Source: U.S. Department of Agriculture, Foreign Agricultural Service, "Production, Supply and Distribution Online," <www.fas.usda.gov/psdonline>, accessed June 2022.

Table 1389. World Production of Major Mineral Commodities: 2017 to 2020

[Units are as noted. Th. represents thousand, mil. represents million, and bil. represents billion]

Commodity	Unit	2017	2018	2019	2020	Leading producers, 2020
MINERAL FUELS						
Coal.................................	mil. short tons	8,416	8,749	8,905	8,488	China, India, Indonesia
Dry natural gas......................	bil. cubic feet	131,072	138,252	142,643	(NA)	United States, Russia, Iran [7]
Natural gas plant liquids.............	mil. barrels [1]	3,870	4,097	4,285	4,363	United States, Saudi Arabia, Canada
Petroleum, crude.....................	mil. barrels [1]	29,657	30,287	29,992	27,743	United States, Russia, Saudi Arabia
NONMETALLIC MINERALS						
Barite...............................	th. metric tons	8,620	8,980	9,020	6,840	China, India, Kazakhstan
Cement, hydraulic....................	mil. metric tons	4,130	4,080	4,190	4,190	China, India, Vietnam
Fluorspar............................	th. metric tons	6,730	7,240	7,460	8,240	China, Mexico, Mongolia
Nitrogen in ammonia.................	mil. metric tons	141	142	145	147	China, Russia, United States
Phosphate rock, marketable..........	mil. metric tons	252	225	224	219	China, Morocco, United States
Potash, marketable..................	mil. metric tons	42	43	42	45	Canada, Russia, Belarus
Salt.................................	mil. metric tons	282	290	283	280	China, United States, India
Sulfur...............................	mil. metric tons	81	82	82	80	China, United States, Russia
METALS						
Aluminum, metal content.............	mil. metric tons	60	64	63	65	China, Russia, India
Bauxite, gross weight................	mil. metric tons	307	340	387	391	Australia, China, Guinea
Chromium (chromite), gross weight...	th. metric tons	43,000	48,200	46,400	37,000	South Africa, Turkey, Kazakhstan
Copper, metal content [2].............	th. metric tons	19,900	20,400	20,400	20,600	Chile, Peru, China
Gold, metal content..................	metric tons	3,260	3,290	3,300	3,030	China, Australia, Russia
Iron ore, gross weight [3].............	mil. metric tons	2,440	2,470	2,450	2,470	Australia, Brazil, China
Lead, metal content [2]...............	th. metric tons	4,900	4,560	4,720	4,380	China, Australia, Peru
Magnesium [4]........................	th. metric tons	1,050	1,000	1,060	1,000	China, Russia, Israel
Manganese ore, metal content........	th. metric tons	18,800	19,400	20,600	18,900	South Africa, Australia, Gabon
Nickel, metal content [2]..............	th. metric tons	2,190	2,400	2,610	2,510	Indonesia, Philippines, Russia
Steel, raw...........................	mil. metric tons	1,730	1,820	1,880	1,860	China, India, Japan
Tantalum concentrates [2].............	Metric tons	1,910	2,100	1,920	2,100	Congo, Dem. Rep. of; Brazil; Nigeria
Tin, metal content [2].................	th. metric tons	341	323	296	264	China, Indonesia, Burma
Titanium (Ilmenite concentrate) [2, 5]....	th. metric tons	10,000	10,800	10,700	8,000	China, South Africa, Mozambique
Tungsten [2, 6]........................	th. metric tons	81	82	84	78	China, Vietnam, Russia
Zinc, metal content [2]...............	th. metric tons	12,300	12,700	12,700	12,000	China, Peru, Australia

NA Not available. [1] 42-gallon barrels. [2] Mine output. [3] Includes iron ore concentrates and agglomerates. [4] Primary production; excludes U.S. production. [5] World production includes U.S. production of rutile and ilmenite. [6] Content of ore and concentrate. [7] Leading producers in 2019.

Source: Mineral fuels, U.S. Energy Information Administration, "International Energy Statistics", <www.eia.gov/international/data/world>, accessed September 2022. Nonmetallic minerals and metals, U.S. Geological Survey, *Mineral Commodity Summaries*, annual; and "Minerals Yearbook - Metals and Minerals," <www.usgs.gov/centers/nmic/minerals-yearbook-metals-and-minerals>, accessed September 2022.

Table 1390. Net Electricity Generation by Energy Source and Country: 2020

[25,561.0 represents 25,561,000,000,000. kWh = kilowatt hours. Ranked for top 40 countries]

Country	Total [1] (bil. kWh)	Amount				Percent distribution			
		Fossil fuels [2]	Hydro-electricity	Nuclear	Non-hydro renew-ables [3]	Fossil fuels [2]	Hydro-electricity	Nuclear	Non-hydro renew-ables [3]
World, total [4].........	**25,651.0**	**15,540.6**	**4,354.4**	**2,637.5**	**3,154.4**	**60.6**	**17.0**	**10.3**	**12.3**
China.................	7,601.2	5,025.8	1,355.2	366.3	865.3	66.1	17.8	4.8	11.4
United States..........	**4,048.7**	**2,426.7**	**285.3**	**789.9**	**552.1**	**59.9**	**7.0**	**19.5**	**13.6**
India.................	1,452.2	1,096.5	155.0	40.4	160.4	75.5	10.7	2.8	11.0
Russia.................	1,026.7	610.0	196.0	215.7	5.6	59.4	19.1	21.0	0.5
Japan.................	889.0	655.1	89.2	43.0	104.3	73.7	10.0	4.8	11.7
Canada.................	630.0	103.9	383.0	92.7	50.6	16.5	60.8	14.7	8.0
Brazil.................	622.0	73.3	409.5	14.1	125.2	11.8	65.8	2.3	20.1
France.................	553.7	44.6	64.8	379.5	66.4	8.0	11.7	68.5	12.0
Korea, South...........	549.9	357.0	7.1	152.3	34.5	64.9	1.3	27.7	6.3
Germany.................	545.2	221.7	24.8	60.9	240.1	40.7	4.5	11.2	44.0
Saudi Arabia...........	344.2	343.7	–	–	0.5	99.9	–	–	0.1
Mexico.................	305.5	231.3	23.1	10.9	40.2	75.7	7.6	3.6	13.2
Iran.................	304.3	269.8	27.7	5.8	1.0	88.7	9.1	1.9	0.3
United Kingdom.........	299.5	113.3	7.6	45.7	133.4	37.8	2.6	15.2	44.5
Turkey.................	293.8	165.0	77.4	–	51.4	56.2	26.3	–	17.5
Taiwan.................	279.1	230.2	6.2	31.4	12.3	82.5	2.2	11.3	4.4
Indonesia..............	272.9	224.6	18.6	–	29.7	82.3	6.8	–	10.9
Italy.................	271.9	152.4	47.7	–	72.4	56.0	17.6	–	26.6
Spain.................	254.0	82.6	33.3	55.8	83.5	32.5	13.1	22.0	32.9
Australia..............	243.3	183.5	15.2	–	44.8	75.4	6.2	–	18.4
South Africa...........	223.2	197.6	5.7	11.6	10.0	88.5	2.5	5.2	4.5
Vietnam.................	206.3	145.9	52.0	–	8.4	70.7	25.2	–	4.1
Thailand...............	176.7	147.2	4.5	–	25.0	83.3	2.6	–	14.1
Sweden.................	160.0	1.5	71.6	47.3	39.7	1.0	44.7	29.5	24.8
Egypt.................	158.0	140.1	12.1	–	5.8	88.7	7.7	–	3.7
Norway.................	153.7	1.8	141.7	–	10.4	1.2	92.2	–	6.7
Poland.................	145.9	116.7	2.9	–	26.6	80.0	2.0	–	18.2
Malaysia...............	145.2	127.0	15.8	–	2.4	87.5	10.9	–	1.7
Argentina..............	137.6	90.6	24.3	10.0	12.8	65.9	17.6	7.3	9.3
Ukraine.................	136.3	51.3	4.9	76.2	4.0	37.6	3.6	55.9	2.9
United Arab Emirates...	124.8	119.5	–	1.6	3.8	95.7	–	1.3	3.0
Netherlands............	117.5	80.3	0.1	3.9	33.3	68.3	–	3.3	28.4
Pakistan...............	117.1	64.7	37.4	9.6	5.4	55.2	31.9	8.2	4.6
Venezuela..............	103.7	31.6	72.0	–	0.1	30.5	69.4	–	0.1
Kazakhstan.............	97.8	86.3	9.9	–	1.6	88.2	10.1	–	1.6
Philippines............	97.5	75.6	7.8	–	14.0	77.6	8.0	–	14.4
Iraq.................	85.7	83.8	1.8	–	0.1	97.8	2.1	–	0.1
Belgium.................	85.3	28.3	0.3	32.6	24.4	33.2	0.3	38.2	28.6
Chile.................	79.9	41.4	20.8	–	17.7	51.9	26.0	–	22.1
Bangladesh.............	75.5	74.4	0.6	–	0.4	98.6	0.8	–	0.6

– Represents or rounds to zero. [1] Electricity generated from fossil fuels, and hydroelectric, nuclear, geothermal, solar, wind, tidal, biomass, and waste energy resources. Includes negative values from hydroelectric pumped storage. [2] Electricity generated from coal, oil, and gas resources. [3] Electricity generated from geothermal, solar, wind, tidal and wave, biomass, and waste resources. [4] Includes countries not shown separately.

Source: U.S. Energy Information Administration, "International Energy Statistics," <www.eia.gov/international/data/world>, accessed May 2022.

Table 1391. World Primary Energy Production by Region and Type: 1980 to 2019

[In quadrillion Btu (296.3 represents 296,300,000,000,000,000). Btu = British thermal unit. For Btu conversion factors, see source]

Region and type	1980	1990	1995	2000	2005	2010	2015	2018	2019
World total...........	**296.3**	**357.6**	**368.3**	**399.6**	**461.0**	**517.9**	**567.8**	**600.8**	**611.1**
REGION									
North America..........	83.0	91.5	95.8	98.4	98.4	102.0	116.9	125.7	130.8
United States [1]...........	**67.1**	**70.7**	**71.1**	**71.3**	**69.4**	**74.9**	**88.3**	**95.8**	**101.4**
Central and South America...........	12.1	16.9	21.5	26.2	28.4	31.2	33.6	32.0	31.2
Europe.,...............	42.9	49.9	50.7	51.5	49.7	46.4	44.0	43.6	42.5
Eurasia [2]...............	61.5	75.5	54.5	55.6	67.8	72.3	76.6	82.8	83.7
Middle East............	42.3	40.9	48.3	57.5	66.3	70.3	83.1	90.0	87.4
Africa.................	17.2	21.4	23.7	27.3	34.0	36.7	32.8	34.3	34.3
Asia and Oceania.......	37.3	61.5	73.9	83.1	116.3	159.0	180.8	192.3	201.1
TYPE OF FUEL									
Petroleum [3]...............	133.1	136.2	141.8	156.4	169.8	171.0	187.4	193.2	192.1
Dry natural gas.........	54.8	75.7	80.3	89.3	102.1	116.9	129.6	144.8	149.4
Coal.................	80.1	99.1	93.0	96.4	125.8	156.2	167.6	168.3	171.8
Nuclear, renewables, and other.......	28.4	46.6	53.2	57.6	63.3	73.7	83.1	94.5	97.7

[1] Includes biomass, geothermal, and solar energy produced in the United States and not used for generating electricity. [2] Prior to 1992, data were for the former U.S.S.R. [3] Includes crude oil, lease condensate, and natural gas plant liquids.

Source: U.S. Energy Information Administration, "International Energy Statistics," <www.eia.gov/international/data/world>, accessed April 2022.

Table 1392. World Primary Energy Consumption by Region and Type: 1980 to 2019

[In quadrillion Btu (292.9 represents 292,900,000,000,000,000). Btu = British thermal unit. For Btu conversion factors, see source]

Region and type	1980	1990	1995	2000	2005	2010	2015	2018	2019
World, total........................	**292.9**	**353.5**	**369.4**	**402.4**	**465.3**	**526.7**	**567.3**	**597.7**	**601.0**
REGION									
North America............................	91.4	99.8	108.4	117.7	120.9	118.9	119.9	124.3	123.4
United States [1]	**78.0**	**84.4**	**90.9**	**98.7**	**100.1**	**97.5**	**97.4**	**101.2**	**100.4**
Central and South America.............	11.0	14.5	17.1	20.9	23.2	26.8	29.2	28.9	28.8
Europe....................................	75.4	79.9	79.2	82.6	87.1	85.3	81.1	83.1	82.2
Eurasia [2]................................	51.6	62.9	43.6	39.7	42.1	44.2	44.4	46.4	46.6
Middle East.............................	5.9	11.0	13.8	17.8	23.5	29.9	35.4	37.4	37.5
Africa.....................................	6.6	9.7	10.7	12.1	14.6	16.9	19.3	20.1	20.6
Asia and Oceania........................	51.0	75.7	96.5	111.7	153.7	204.8	238.0	257.6	262.0
TYPE OF FUEL									
Petroleum [3].............................	132.1	136.1	141.6	156.7	171.6	177.9	189.3	196.9	196.1
Dry natural gas.........................	53.9	75.1	81.3	89.6	102.6	119.4	130.1	143.9	146.9
Coal..	78.7	95.9	93.4	98.7	128.3	157.8	167.6	165.9	164.0
Nuclear, renewables, and other.........	28.3	46.5	53.0	57.4	63.0	72.6	81.5	92.4	95.4

[1] Includes biomass, geothermal, and solar energy consumed in the United States and not used for generating electricity. [2] Prior to 1992, data were for the former U.S.S.R. [3] Includes all refined petroleum products.

Source: U.S. Energy Information Administration, "International Energy Statistics," <www.eia.gov/international/data/world>, accessed April 2022.

Table 1393. Energy Consumption by Country: 2010 to 2019

[In quadrillion Btu (526.73 represents 526,730,000,000,000,000). Btu = British thermal units. Total primary energy consumption includes the consumption of petroleum, dry natural gas, coal, and net nuclear, hydroelectric, and non-hydroelectric renewable electricity. For data qualifications for countries and Btu conversion factors, see source]

Country	Total (quad. Btu)				Country	Total (quad. Btu)			
	2010	2015	2018	2019		2010	2015	2018	2019
World, total [1]........	**526.73**	**567.33**	**597.74**	**601.04**	Kuwait...................	1.40	1.68	1.64	1.61
United States..........	**97.51**	**97.39**	**101.20**	**100.43**	Libya....................	0.90	0.61	0.63	0.60
Algeria...................	1.78	2.35	2.52	2.64	Malaysia.................	2.98	3.33	3.84	3.96
Argentina................	3.58	3.83	3.58	3.55	Mexico...................	7.53	7.80	7.91	7.99
Australia.................	5.65	5.78	6.16	6.39	Morocco..................	0.72	0.81	0.85	0.90
Austria...................	1.49	1.43	1.46	1.52	Netherlands..............	4.28	3.81	3.83	3.82
Azerbaijan...............	0.59	0.62	0.61	0.65	New Zealand.............	0.84	0.89	0.91	0.93
Bahrain..................	0.59	0.69	0.72	0.81	Nigeria..................	0.83	1.57	1.65	1.70
Bangladesh..............	0.97	1.33	1.55	1.62	Norway..................	1.87	1.93	1.91	1.79
Belarus..................	1.12	0.95	1.00	0.97	Oman....................	0.89	1.18	1.35	1.35
Belgium..................	2.82	2.49	2.68	2.69	Pakistan.................	2.59	2.96	3.43	3.43
Brazil....................	11.42	12.56	12.44	12.56	Paraguay................	0.44	0.47	0.51	0.44
Bulgaria.................	0.72	0.79	0.76	0.73	Peru.....................	0.86	1.05	1.14	1.19
Burma...................	0.23	0.38	0.62	0.58	Philippines..............	1.21	1.61	1.94	2.09
Canada..................	13.79	14.71	15.17	14.98	Poland...................	4.11	4.12	4.39	4.29
Chile....................	1.26	1.40	1.54	1.56	Portugal.................	1.11	1.04	1.07	1.05
China....................	111.97	136.92	147.02	151.61	Qatar....................	1.25	1.99	1.96	2.05
Colombia................	1.30	1.64	1.74	1.75	Romania.................	1.45	1.36	1.41	1.39
Czechia.................	1.79	1.70	1.76	1.73	Russia...................	30.29	30.95	33.05	33.25
Denmark.................	0.83	0.72	0.73	0.72	Saudi Arabia.............	8.81	10.65	10.17	10.16
Ecuador.................	0.60	0.69	0.73	0.74	Serbia...................	0.68	0.64	0.67	0.68
Egypt....................	3.51	3.73	4.03	4.02	Singapore................	2.93	3.29	3.74	3.65
Finland..................	1.30	1.19	1.23	1.20	Slovakia.................	0.78	0.71	0.73	0.71
France...................	11.00	10.43	10.30	10.16	South Africa.............	5.62	5.59	5.49	5.65
Germany.................	14.17	13.67	13.86	13.53	Spain....................	6.22	5.61	5.88	5.79
Greece...................	1.36	1.13	1.16	1.16	Sweden..................	2.23	2.16	2.13	2.17
Hong Kong...............	1.34	1.28	1.34	1.28	Switzerland..............	1.31	1.21	1.19	1.21
Hungary.................	1.04	0.98	1.06	1.06	Syria....................	1.03	0.42	0.48	0.43
India....................	22.20	27.18	31.20	31.78	Taiwan..................	4.64	4.69	4.72	3.79
Indonesia................	6.19	6.70	7.72	8.04	Thailand.................	4.41	5.14	5.51	5.34
Iran......................	9.03	10.66	11.89	12.06	Trinidad and Tobago. ..	0.96	0.98	0.74	0.73
Iraq......................	1.36	1.43	2.63	2.48	Turkey...................	4.51	5.77	6.40	6.61
Ireland...................	0.63	0.60	0.66	0.66	Turkmenistan............	1.03	1.76	1.74	1.96
Israel....................	0.94	1.01	0.99	0.97	Ukraine..................	5.16	3.85	3.74	3.48
Italy.....................	7.69	6.78	6.83	6.72	United Arab Emirates...	3.64	4.70	4.60	4.61
Japan....................	21.88	19.74	19.29	18.98	United Kingdom........	9.19	8.36	8.27	8.10
Kazakhstan..............	3.19	3.33	3.40	3.35	Uzbekistan..............	1.94	2.00	1.82	1.90
Korea, North............	0.72	0.34	0.33	0.32	Venezuela...............	3.11	3.06	2.71	2.45
Korea, South............	10.87	11.92	12.44	12.41	Vietnam.................	1.89	2.83	3.63	3.51

[1] Includes countries not shown separately.

Source: U.S. Energy Information Administration, "International Energy Statistics," <www.eia.gov/international/data/world>, accessed April 2022.

Table 1394. World Energy Consumption by Region and Energy Source: 2020, and Projections, 2025 to 2050

[In quadrillion Btu (601.5 represents 601,500,000,000,000,000). Btu = British thermal units. For Btu conversion factors, see source. Energy totals include net imports of coal coke and electricity generated from biomass in the United States. The electricity portion of the national consumption values consists of generation for domestic use plus an adjustment for electricity trade based on a fuel's share of total generation in the exporting country. OECD = Organisation for Economic Co-operation and Development; see text, this section]

| Region and energy source | 2020 | Projections | | | | | | Average annual percent change 2020-2050 |
		2025	2030	2035	2040	2045	2050	
World, total.............	**601.5**	**667.5**	**705.2**	**749.5**	**795.4**	**842.8**	**886.3**	**1.30**
OECD, total [1].............	232.9	248.0	251.3	257.7	263.8	272.0	281.3	0.63
OECD Americas................	118.2	126.0	127.5	130.9	134.6	139.7	145.2	0.69
United States.............	**92.9**	**98.4**	**98.6**	**100.0**	**101.9**	**105.0**	**108.7**	**0.52**
OECD Europe................	77.6	82.1	83.3	85.9	88.0	90.7	94.1	0.65
OECD Asia................	37.2	39.9	40.5	41.0	41.2	41.5	42.0	0.40
Non-OECD, total................	368.6	419.6	453.9	491.7	531.7	570.8	605.1	1.67
Non-OECD Europe and Eurasia......	52.6	54.8	56.9	59.5	61.9	64.1	66.0	0.76
Non-OECD Asia................	230.3	267.2	292.8	320.8	349.4	378.5	402.8	1.88
China................	156.4	169.2	174.6	180.7	187.1	193.5	196.9	0.77
India................	31.5	46.5	59.8	74.4	89.3	105.2	119.8	4.56
Middle East................	35.2	40.3	41.7	43.3	46.1	47.6	48.3	1.06
Africa................	22.9	26.6	29.6	33.2	37.0	41.1	46.0	2.36
Non-OECD Americas................	27.6	30.8	32.9	35.0	37.2	39.5	42.0	1.41
Liquids................	182.4	208.8	215.6	223.4	231.6	240.5	248.5	1.04
Natural gas................	147.3	158.4	166.5	171.4	178.1	185.1	193.2	0.91
Coal................	155.6	157.8	155.8	162.3	168.3	174.4	176.7	0.42
Nuclear................	27.5	30.9	31.7	33.2	33.5	32.7	32.7	0.58
Other................	88.7	111.7	135.6	159.3	183.9	210.1	235.2	3.30

[1] For full membership listing of the Organisation for Economic Co-operation and Development (OECD), see introductory text, this section. For purposes of this report, Costa Rica is included in Non-OECD Americas despite joining the OECD in 2021.

Source: U.S. Energy Information Administration, *International Energy Outlook 2021*, October 2021. See also <www.eia.gov/outlooks/ieo/>.

Table 1395. World Daily Crude Oil Production by Major Producing Country: 1980 to 2021

[In thousands of barrels per day (59,558 barrels represents 59,558,000 barrels). Includes lease condensate. Ranked for top 40 countries, as of most recent year]

Country	1980	1990	2000	2005	2010	2015	2018	2019	2020	2021
World, total [1].............	**59,558**	**60,498**	**68,527**	**73,871**	**74,390**	**80,965**	**82,954**	**82,151**	**75,986**	**77,044**
United States................	**8,597**	**7,355**	**5,822**	**5,184**	**5,484**	**9,446**	**10,964**	**12,248**	**11,308**	**11,185**
Russia................	(X)	(X)	6,479	9,043	9,694	10,253	10,759	10,847	9,865	10,112
Saudi Arabia................	9,900	6,410	8,404	9,550	8,417	10,336	10,598	9,981	9,406	9,313
Canada................	1,435	1,553	1,977	2,369	2,741	3,677	4,343	4,408	4,180	4,459
Iraq................	2,514	2,040	2,571	1,878	2,399	4,055	4,623	4,725	4,088	4,085
China................	2,114	2,774	3,249	3,609	4,078	4,278	3,787	3,825	3,889	3,988
Iran................	1,662	3,088	3,696	4,139	4,080	3,293	4,212	2,933	2,644	3,110
United Arab Emirates.........	1,709	2,117	2,368	2,535	2,570	3,149	3,216	3,487	3,138	3,091
Brazil................	182	631	1,269	1,634	2,055	2,437	2,587	2,788	2,940	2,905
Kuwait................	1,656	1,175	2,078	2,529	2,300	2,859	2,862	2,821	2,545	2,527
Norway................	486	1,630	3,222	2,698	1,871	1,610	1,517	1,437	1,713	1,776
Kazakhstan................	(X)	(X)	718	1,288	1,525	1,653	1,856	1,863	1,757	1,764
Mexico................	1,936	2,553	3,104	3,423	2,621	2,302	1,852	1,704	1,710	1,734
Nigeria................	2,055	1,810	2,165	2,627	2,408	2,171	1,910	1,946	1,775	1,541
Qatar................	472	406	742	978	1,297	1,356	1,308	1,231	1,274	1,304
Libya................	1,787	1,375	1,410	1,651	1,710	464	1,027	1,169	408	1,238
Algeria................	1,106	1,180	1,214	1,692	1,540	1,429	1,259	1,259	1,122	1,133
Angola................	150	475	746	1,239	1,909	1,802	1,593	1,448	1,257	1,127
Oman................	282	685	970	774	865	981	978	972	949	971
United Kingdom................	1,622	1,820	2,275	1,649	1,233	893	1,000	1,026	947	811
Colombia................	126	440	691	526	785	1,003	865	886	781	736
Azerbaijan................	(X)	(X)	280	433	1,035	848	789	767	695	711
Indonesia................	1,577	1,462	1,428	1,059	945	786	770	742	708	659
India................	182	660	646	665	751	761	709	668	627	610
Venezuela................	2,168	2,137	3,155	2,565	2,410	2,489	1,486	877	527	595
Egypt................	595	873	768	623	636	682	639	623	587	561
Malaysia................	283	619	690	726	638	654	653	610	556	511
Argentina................	491	483	761	705	613	532	489	508	480	507
Ecuador................	204	285	395	532	486	543	517	531	479	473
Australia................	380	575	722	456	479	322	284	361	351	334
Congo, Republic of...........	65	165	280	229	340	238	340	330	283	266
Turkmenistan................	(X)	(X)	142	183	178	243	252	227	200	186
Vietnam................	–	50	316	358	299	333	241	222	193	182
Ghana................	2	–	7	6	7	102	173	200	199	180
Thailand................	(Z)	44	110	183	242	248	228	228	202	177
Gabon................	175	270	315	266	246	213	196	202	174	175
Bahrain................	48	42	38	35	182	202	197	197	171	175
South Sudan................	(X)	(X)	(X)	(X)	(X)	153	156	157	163	157
Equatorial Guinea............	–	–	168	363	298	250	172	156	148	133
Guyana................	–	–	–	–	–	–	–	1	74	110

– Represents zero or rounds to zero. X Not applicable. Z Less than 500 barrels. [1] Includes countries not shown separately.

Source: U.S. Energy Information Administration, "International Energy Statistics," <www.eia.gov/international/data/world>, accessed April 2022.

Table 1396. World Dry Natural Gas Production by Major Producing Country: 1980 to 2020

[In billions of cubic feet (53,361 represents 53,361,000,000,000). Ranked for top 30 countries in 2019]

Country	Dry natural gas production								
	1980	1990	2000	2005	2010	2015	2018	2019	2020 (P)
World, total [1]	53,361	73,379	86,770	98,598	113,787	125,719	138,252	142,643	(NA)
United States	19,403	17,810	19,182	18,051	21,316	27,065	30,774	33,899	33,485
Russia	(X)	(X)	19,335	21,224	21,458	21,531	23,576	23,938	22,501
Iran	250	818	2,127	3,655	5,161	6,526	8,148	8,389	(NA)
China	505	508	962	1,763	3,278	4,632	5,839	6,333	(NA)
Canada	2,759	3,849	6,470	6,561	5,876	6,165	6,485	6,312	(NA)
Qatar	184	222	1,028	1,617	4,121	5,794	5,843	5,914	(NA)
Australia	313	723	1,159	1,266	1,859	2,546	4,460	5,065	5,018
Norway	917	976	1,867	3,072	3,756	4,139	4,306	4,057	3,957
Saudi Arabia	334	1,077	1,759	2,516	3,096	3,614	3,928	3,982	4,018
Algeria	411	1,787	2,940	3,151	2,988	2,933	3,335	3,103	(NA)
Turkmenistan	(X)	(X)	1,642	2,225	1,466	2,831	2,874	2,953	(NA)
Malaysia	56	501	1,465	1,977	2,171	2,240	2,582	2,648	(NA)
Indonesia	654	1,602	2,237	2,001	2,917	2,571	2,550	2,368	2,211
Egypt	30	286	646	1,501	2,166	1,565	2,117	2,270	(NA)
United Arab Emirates	200	780	1,355	1,659	1,811	2,125	2,210	2,221	(NA)
Uzbekistan	(X)	(X)	1,992	2,108	2,123	1,967	2,014	2,019	1,659
Nigeria	38	131	440	791	1,024	1,594	1,609	1,635	(NA)
Argentina	280	630	1,321	1,611	1,416	1,285	1,524	1,605	1,455
United Kingdom	1,323	1,754	3,826	3,118	2,111	1,428	1,441	1,386	1,389
Thailand	–	208	658	837	1,278	1,406	1,329	1,357	(NA)
Pakistan	286	482	856	1,088	1,400	1,388	1,361	1,344	(NA)
Oman	28	99	322	705	957	1,057	1,265	1,292	(NA)
Trinidad and Tobago	81	177	493	1,094	1,499	1,306	1,240	1,259	1,091
Netherlands	3,398	2,687	2,572	2,773	3,126	1,907	1,338	1,160	(NA)
India	51	399	719	1,056	1,848	1,103	1,125	1,106	979
Bangladesh	50	162	343	494	711	949	1,040	1,011	(NA)
Mexico	900	903	1,297	1,513	1,769	1,426	999	955	(NA)
Kazakhstan	(X)	(X)	314	428	621	749	895	911	(NA)
Brazil	42	97	257	345	523	829	875	897	(NA)
Azerbaijan	(X)	(X)	200	206	552	636	634	815	(NA)

P Preliminary. NA Not available. X Not applicable. – Represents zero. [1] Includes countries not shown separately.

Source: U.S. Energy Information Administration, "International Energy Statistics," <www.eia.gov/international/data/world>, accessed August 2022.

Table 1397. World Coal Production by Major Producing Country: 1980 to 2020

[In thousands of short tons (4,151,845 represents 4,151,845,000). Coal includes anthracite, bituminous, subbituminous, metallurgical and lignite. Ranked for top 30 countries, as of most recent year]

Country	Coal production								
	1980	1990	2000	2010	2015	2017	2018	2019	2020
World, total [1]	4,151,845	5,184,358	5,125,260	8,197,435	8,668,424	8,381,903	8,711,156	8,846,254	8,377,125
China	683,587	1,189,725	1,525,800	3,779,212	4,129,849	3,884,055	4,076,056	4,239,848	4,236,994
India	121,502	241,899	362,804	578,216	667,491	718,212	765,432	762,938	772,038
Indonesia	627	13,165	93,736	397,343	508,789	508,438	614,839	679,199	621,403
Australia	115,196	226,363	339,020	486,400	574,192	557,470	541,959	564,254	552,910
United States	829,700	1,029,076	1,073,612	1,084,368	896,941	774,609	756,167	706,307	535,434
Russia	(X)	(X)	264,912	329,258	409,701	449,579	476,919	481,701	442,475
South Africa	126,898	189,479	247,917	280,796	282,334	283,431	281,553	284,234	271,728
Germany	(X)	(X)	226,047	202,286	203,612	193,039	186,311	144,749	118,363
Poland	253,517	237,082	178,247	146,257	149,147	139,597	134,432	123,406	110,638
Kazakhstan	(X)	(X)	82,548	122,278	118,299	111,782	118,660	115,216	109,937
Turkey	20,531	52,280	69,741	80,908	64,390	81,679	92,524	95,999	82,066
Colombia	4,590	22,562	42,044	82,021	94,300	99,813	92,907	92,972	54,378
Vietnam	5,732	5,100	12,797	49,422	45,927	42,149	46,720	50,361	52,678
Canada	40,442	75,323	76,239	74,835	68,722	68,517	63,377	61,708	50,890
Mongolia	5,818	7,889	5,715	27,736	26,682	53,071	56,660	61,508	48,331
Serbia	(X)	(X)	(X)	41,861	41,696	43,879	41,501	42,858	43,732
Czechia	(X)	(X)	71,829	60,857	51,168	49,297	48,029	45,088	34,809
Bulgaria	33,304	34,916	29,136	32,413	39,528	37,784	33,359	30,866	24,580
Korea, North	33,367	36,542	24,802	20,765	27,514	21,758	18,164	18,773	17,928
Laos	–	3	253	808	5,284	14,962	17,688	17,003	17,681
Romania	38,762	42,090	32,281	34,312	28,101	28,387	26,066	23,868	16,537
Ukraine	(X)	(X)	68,787	63,558	37,990	26,640	28,940	28,142	15,840
Greece	25,571	57,205	70,423	62,303	50,977	41,592	40,222	30,176	15,269
Philippines	363	1,370	1,491	7,330	8,133	13,153	14,392	16,836	15,159
Thailand	1,681	13,711	19,605	20,126	16,701	17,922	16,372	15,518	14,607
Mexico	3,405	7,642	12,505	16,870	11,769	12,981	12,016	9,843	10,021
Kosovo	(X)	(X)	(X)	9,534	9,084	8,350	8,445	8,888	9,411
Mozambique	–	–	26	79	7,276	16,639	17,742	15,315	7,991
Bosnia and Herzegovina	(X)	(X)	8,200	7,047	6,666	7,861	7,742	7,228	6,815
Hungary	28,688	19,654	15,469	10,045	10,208	8,788	8,706	7,548	6,752

– Represents zero. X Not applicable. [1] Includes other countries not shown separately.

Source: U.S. Energy Information Administration, "International Energy Statistics," <www.eia.gov/international/data/world>, accessed April 2022.

Table 1398. Carbon Dioxide Emissions From Consumption of Fossil Fuels by Country: 1980 to 2019

[In millions of metric tons of carbon dioxide (18,702 represents 18,702,000,000). Ranked for top 25 countries, as of most recent year shown. Includes carbon dioxide emissions from the consumption of petroleum, natural gas, and coal]

Country	1980	1990	2000	2010	2015	2016	2017	2018	2019
World, total [1]	**18,702**	**22,145**	**24,258**	**32,519**	**34,752**	**34,572**	**35,003**	**35,585**	**35,549**
China	1,597	2,417	3,483	9,004	10,427	10,262	10,415	10,609	10,773
United States	**4,756**	**5,038**	**5,889**	**5,594**	**5,262**	**5,169**	**5,131**	**5,277**	**5,144**
India	270	541	886	1,648	2,063	2,109	2,200	2,308	2,315
Russia	(X)	(X)	1,540	1,661	1,690	1,676	1,734	1,798	1,848
Japan	872	1,109	1,233	1,197	1,215	1,204	1,172	1,141	1,103
Germany	(X)	(X)	872	822	788	789	805	782	727
Korea, South	139	264	466	612	662	683	688	703	687
Iran	102	195	303	537	613	590	616	643	646
Canada	423	433	512	571	591	579	601	613	612
Saudi Arabia	107	199	290	497	621	589	584	568	580
Indonesia	72	149	256	409	461	465	482	529	564
South Africa	229	329	393	479	474	471	474	455	470
Mexico	198	274	383	449	465	475	472	456	464
Brazil	188	243	327	410	500	467	476	453	457
Australia	216	280	351	402	393	407	418	411	418
United Kingdom	613	606	570	542	451	428	416	411	398
Turkey	62	128	207	268	351	373	403	398	392
France	472	385	409	388	347	350	356	342	338
Italy	337	421	452	416	349	344	342	340	332
Thailand	34	84	158	258	296	294	301	304	305
Poland	399	365	303	315	305	310	324	320	304
Spain	189	236	316	305	284	285	298	294	281
Taiwan	70	119	238	272	273	281	267	283	279
United Arab Emirates	16	77	128	219	283	286	277	274	276
Kazakhstan	(X)	(X)	172	261	265	266	260	270	264

X Not applicable. [1] Includes other countries not shown separately.

Source: U.S. Energy Information Administration, "International Energy Statistics," <www.eia.gov/international/data/world>, accessed April 2022.

Table 1399. Average Temperatures and Precipitation—Selected International Cities

[In degrees Fahrenheit, except as noted. Data are generally based on a standard 30-year period; for details, see source. Minus sign (-) indicates degrees below zero]

City	January Average high	January Average low	January Warmest	January Coldest	January Average precipitation (inches)	July Average high	July Average low	July Warmest	July Coldest	July Average precipitation (inches)
Amsterdam, Netherlands	41	34	57	3	3.1	69	55	90	39	2.9
Athens, Greece	55	44	70	28	1.9	89	73	108	61	0.2
Baghdad, Iraq	58	38	75	25	1.1	110	78	122	61	–
Bangkok, Thailand	89	71	95	54	0.4	90	78	99	72	6.2
Beijing, China	34	17	54	1	0.2	86	72	104	63	8.8
Berlin, Germany	35	26	58	-11	(NA)	73	56	95	41	(NA)
Bogota, Colombia	66	43	84	27	1.9	64	47	82	32	1.8
Brasilia, Brazil	81	64	95	54	(NA)	79	52	97	37	(NA)
Buenos Aires, Argentina	85	64	104	44	4.2	58	41	88	23	2.3
Cairo, Egypt	65	49	86	32	0.2	93	72	108	63	–
Frankfurt, Germany	38	30	56	-4	1.8	75	57	97	38	2.4
Geneva, Switzerland	39	29	57	-2	2.2	77	56	96	41	2.8
Hong Kong, China	67	58	79	43	1.1	89	81	97	70	14.3
Istanbul, Turkey	46	37	64	16	3.7	82	66	100	50	0.7
Jakarta, Indonesia	83	75	92	72	(NA)	88	74	92	67	(NA)
Karachi, Pakistan	76	55	93	39	0.3	89	83	109	68	3.5
Lagos, Nigeria	82	79	93	64	(NA)	79	76	88	70	(NA)
London, England	45	36	61	15	2.4	72	56	93	45	1.8
Madrid, Spain	51	32	68	14	1.8	90	61	104	46	0.4
Manila, Philippines	86	71	95	61	0.8	88	76	99	70	15.9
Mexico City, Mexico	70	45	86	26	0.3	74	56	86	37	5.1
Montreal, Canada	21	7	52	-31	2.8	79	61	93	43	3.4
Moscow, Russia	21	11	46	-33	1.4	71	55	95	41	3.2
Nairobi, Kenya	77	58	88	45	1.8	71	54	85	43	0.5
New Delhi, India	68	48	85	32	0.9	93	81	111	70	7.9
Paris, France	43	34	59	1	(NA)	75	58	95	41	(NA)
Rio De Janeiro, Brazil	91	74	109	64	5.3	81	64	102	52	1.8
Rome, Italy	55	39	64	19	3.2	83	66	100	55	0.6
Seoul, Korea	33	21	55	-1	(NA)	82	71	97	55	(NA)
Singapore, Singapore	85	73	100	66	9.4	86	76	99	70	5.9
Sydney, Australia	79	65	109	49	4.0	62	44	80	32	2.5
Tel Aviv, Israel	62	46	84	32	(NA)	87	69	100	50	(NA)
Tokyo, Japan	48	35	66	25	2.0	82	71	95	55	5.3
Toronto, Canada	28	15	59	-24	1.9	79	60	99	45	2.8

– Represents zero. NA Not available.

Source: U.S. National Oceanic and Atmospheric Administration, *Climates of the World*. See also <library.noaa.gov/Research-Tools/Subject-Guides/weathersites>.

Table 1400. Telephones, Mobile Cellular Phones, and Internet Use by Country: 2020

[Data from the International Telecommunication Union. For data qualifications for individual countries, see source]

Country	Fixed telephone subscriptions per 100 people [1]	Cellphone subscriptions per 100 people [2]	Internet users (as percent of population) [3]	Country	Fixed telephone subscriptions per 100 people [1]	Cellphone subscriptions per 100 people [2]	Internet users (as percent of population) [3]
World............	**11.6**	**106.2**	**59.9**	Kazakhstan.......	16.5	129.4	85.9
United States....	**30.7**	**106.2**	**90.9**	Kenya.............	0.1	114.2	29.5
Afghanistan.......	0.4	58.3	18.4	Korea, South.....	46.5	137.5	96.5
Albania..........	7.8	91.0	72.2	Latvia............	11.2	108.8	88.9
Argentina........	16.3	121.2	85.5	Lithuania.........	11.8	134.9	83.1
Australia.........	24.3	107.7	89.6	Malaysia.........	23.1	135.1	89.6
Austria..........	42.0	119.0	87.5	Mexico...........	19.0	95.3	72.0
Bangladesh......	0.8	107.0	24.8	Mongolia.........	4.9	133.1	62.5
Belarus..........	46.6	123.9	85.1	Morocco.........	6.4	133.9	84.1
Brazil...........	14.4	96.8	81.3	Netherlands......	28.8	125.0	91.3
Bulgaria.........	12.6	114.4	70.2	Nigeria..........	0.1	99.1	35.5
Canada..........	35.3	85.7	97.0	Norway..........	6.4	107.5	97.0
Chile.............	13.4	131.1	88.3	Oman...........	12.7	133.8	95.2
China............	12.6	119.4	70.4	Pakistan.........	1.3	79.5	25.0
Colombia........	14.2	133.0	69.8	Peru............	7.5	133.4	65.3
Costa Rica.......	11.0	147.5	80.5	Philippines.......	4.3	136.5	49.8
Croatia..........	31.7	106.6	78.3	Poland..........	15.3	130.4	83.2
Cuba............	13.3	58.8	74.0	Portugal.........	51.1	116.3	78.3
Czechia..........	12.5	121.4	81.3	Romania.........	15.7	117.4	78.5
Denmark.........	12.7	125.2	96.5	Russia..........	17.7	163.6	85.0
Egypt............	9.6	93.2	71.9	Saudi Arabia.....	16.5	124.1	97.9
France...........	57.8	111.5	84.8	Serbia..........	37.4	120.2	78.4
Georgia..........	9.7	127.8	72.5	Singapore........	32.3	144.3	92.0
Germany.........	45.7	128.2	89.8	South Africa.....	3.5	161.8	70.0
Ghana...........	1.0	130.2	58.0	Spain...........	41.6	119.0	93.2
Greece..........	48.2	109.5	78.1	Sweden.........	14.6	126.7	94.5
Haiti............	0.1	64.2	34.5	Thailand.........	7.2	166.6	77.8
India............	1.5	83.6	43.0	Tunisia..........	13.0	125.7	71.9
Indonesia........	3.5	130.0	53.7	Turkey..........	14.8	97.4	77.7
Iran.............	34.6	151.9	84.1	Ukraine..........	7.9	129.3	75.0
Israel...........	38.9	141.8	90.1	United Kingdom..	47.2	116.4	94.8
Italy.............	32.4	128.3	70.5	Uruguay..........	35.3	131.0	86.1
Japan............	49.0	154.2	90.2	Vietnam..........	3.3	142.7	70.3

[1] Refers to the sum of active number of analogue fixed telephone lines, voice-over-IP (VoIP) subscriptions, fixed wireless local loop (WLL) subscriptions, ISDN voice-channel equivalents and fixed public payphones. [2] Subscriptions to a public mobile telephone service that provide access to the public switched telephone network (PSTN) using cellular technology. Includes number of postpaid subscriptions and active prepaid accounts. Applies to all mobile cellular subscriptions that offer voice communications. Excludes subscriptions via data cards or USB modems, subscriptions to public mobile data services, private trunked mobile radio, telepoint, radio paging, and telemetry services. [3] Internet users are individuals who have used the internet (from any location) in the last 3 months. The internet can be used via a computer, mobile phone, personal digital assistant, electronic game device, digital TV etc.

Source: The World Bank, Washington, DC, "World Development Indicators" database ©, <databank.worldbank.org/source/world-development-indicators>, accessed August 2022.

Table 1401. Global Telecommunications Indicators: 2000 to 2020

[975 represents 975,000,000. Data are from the International Telecommunication Union]

Indicators	2000	2005	2010	2014	2015	2016	2017	2018	2019	2020
NUMBER (million)										
Fixed telephone subscriptions [1]....................	975	1,244	1,229	1,091	1,046	1,008	984	947	925	901
Mobile cellular subscriptions [2]....................	738	2,206	5,295	6,999	7,182	7,509	7,756	7,855	8,211	8,266
Fixed broadband internet subscriptions [3]........	(NA)	220	532	725	840	917	1,026	1,068	1,142	1,229
PERCENT OF POPULATION										
Internet users [4]......................................	6.7	15.7	28.9	38.1	40.5	43.3	45.8	49.4	54.0	59.9
PER 100 INHABITANTS										
Fixed telephone subscriptions [1]....................	15.9	19.4	17.7	15.0	14.2	13.5	13.1	12.8	12.0	11.6
Mobile cellular subscriptions [2]....................	12.0	33.8	76.2	96.1	97.4	100.7	102.9	105.5	106.6	106.2
Fixed broadband internet subscriptions [3]........	(NA)	3.7	7.8	10.2	11.5	12.4	13.8	14.6	14.9	15.9

NA Not available. [1] Refers to the sum of active number of analogue fixed telephone lines, voice-over-IP (VoIP) subscriptions, fixed wireless local loop (WLL) subscriptions, ISDN voice-channel equivalents and fixed public payphones. [2] Subscriptions to a public mobile telephone service that provide access to the public switched telephone network (PSTN) using cellular technology. Includes number of postpaid subscriptions and active prepaid accounts. Applies to all mobile cellular subscriptions that offer voice communications. Excludes subscriptions via data cards or USB modems, subscriptions to public mobile data services, private trunked mobile radio, telepoint, radio paging, and telemetry services. [3] Refers to fixed subscriptions to high-speed access to the public internet (a TCP/IP connection), at downstream speeds equal to, or greater than, 256 kbit/s. Includes cable modem, DSL, fiber-to-the-home/building, other fixed (wired)-broadband subscriptions, satellite broadband and terrestrial fixed wireless broadband. Excludes subscriptions that have access to data communications (including the internet) via mobile-cellular networks. [4] Internet users are individuals who have used the internet (from any location) in the last 3 months. The internet can be used via a computer, mobile phone, personal digital assistant, electronic game device, digital TV etc.

Source: The World Bank, Washington, DC, "World Development Indicators" database ©, <databank.worldbank.org/source/world-development-indicators>, accessed August 2022.

Table 1402. Patents by Country: 2020

[Includes only U.S. patents granted to residents of areas outside of the United States and its territories. For information on types of patents, see <www.uspto.gov/patents/basics/types-patent-applications>. Countries are in rank order. See also Table 815 and Table 816]

Country	Total	Utility (inventions)	Designs	Plant	Reissue
Total	**205,714**	**187,438**	**17,176**	**801**	**299**
Japan	53,779	51,619	2,050	24	86
China	26,845	21,428	5,399	2	16
Korea, South	23,705	21,977	1,667	0	61
Germany	19,173	17,785	1,282	84	22
Taiwan	13,105	12,141	947	0	17
United Kingdom	8,470	7,418	981	56	15
Canada	7,914	7,274	610	9	21
France	7,614	7,090	482	39	3
India	5,984	5,861	121	0	2
Israel	4,844	4,661	154	26	3
Italy	3,794	3,196	569	26	3
Netherlands	3,417	2,835	205	366	11
Sweden	3,411	3,018	390	0	3
Switzerland	3,252	2,928	324	0	0
Australia	2,330	1,862	428	30	10
Austria	1,608	1,511	96	0	1
Finland	1,552	1,456	90	0	6
Belgium	1,482	1,374	88	19	1
Denmark	1,374	1,180	149	42	3
Spain	1,174	1,030	128	16	0
Singapore	1,112	1,045	65	0	2
Hong Kong	1,011	742	267	0	2
Saudi Arabia	981	974	7	0	0
Ireland	942	916	23	1	2
Norway	763	725	36	0	2
Other countries	6,078	5,392	618	61	7

Source: U.S. Patent and Trademark Office, "General Patent Statistics Reports Available for Viewing," <www.uspto.gov/web/offices/ac/ido/oeip/taf/reports_stco.htm>, accessed March 2022.

Table 1403. Foreign Currency Exchange Rates by Country: 2015 to 2021

[Foreign currency units per U.S. dollar. Data are yearly averages]

Country	Currency	2015	2016	2017	2018	2019	2020	2021
Afghanistan	Afghani	63.65	70.65	71.09	73.60	77.58	76.65	83.48
Algeria	Dinar	104.88	114.43	115.88	117.41	119.40	126.74	135.01
Argentina	Peso	9.62	15.36	17.23	28.11	48.19	70.64	95.10
Australia	Dollar	1.35	1.40	1.36	1.34	1.44	1.45	1.33
Bahrain	Dinar	0.40	0.40	0.40	0.40	0.38	0.38	0.38
Brazil	Real	3.47	3.63	3.32	3.66	3.95	5.15	5.40
Canada	Dollar	1.33	1.38	1.35	1.30	1.33	1.34	1.25
Cayman Islands	Dollar	0.89	0.89	0.88	0.83	0.83	0.83	0.83
China	Yuan	6.49	6.91	7.03	6.62	6.91	6.90	6.45
Denmark	Krone	6.99	7.00	6.86	6.32	6.67	6.54	6.29
Egypt	Pound	8.04	10.46	18.59	17.81	16.81	15.81	15.70
Euro Zone	Euro	0.94	0.94	0.92	0.85	0.89	0.88	0.85
Hong Kong	Dollar	8.06	8.07	8.11	7.84	7.84	7.76	7.77
Hungary	Forint	290.64	293.08	285.58	270.44	290.71	307.77	303.29
Iceland	Krona	137.47	126.26	111.23	116.38	122.57	135.35	126.99
India	Rupee	66.77	69.96	67.81	68.42	70.39	74.10	73.94
Iraq	Dinar	1,231.23	1,236.45	1,241.68	1,193.48	1,191.25	1,197.50	1,460.13
Israel	New Shekel	4.05	4.00	3.75	3.60	3.56	3.44	3.23
Japan	Yen	125.91	113.14	116.67	110.42	109.01	106.73	109.82
Lebanon	Pound	1,588.88	1,593.64	1,593.97	1,511.68	1,510.29	1,510.68	1,519.23
Mexico	Peso	16.51	19.44	19.68	19.23	19.25	21.47	20.28
Morocco	Dirham	10.21	10.28	10.23	9.39	9.61	9.50	9.00
New Zealand	Dollar	1.49	1.49	1.47	1.45	1.52	1.54	1.42
Norway	Kroner	8.39	8.75	8.61	8.14	8.80	9.41	8.60
Qatar	Rial	3.79	3.79	3.85	3.64	3.64	3.64	3.64
Russia	Ruble	63.66	69.69	60.69	62.85	64.69	72.30	73.69
Saudi Arabia	Riyal	3.90	3.90	3.90	3.75	3.75	3.75	3.75
Singapore	Dollar	1.43	1.44	1.44	1.35	1.36	1.38	1.34
South Africa	Rand	13.28	15.32	13.86	13.26	14.45	16.46	14.79
South Korean	Won	1,179.13	1,211.12	1,178.59	1,100.59	1,165.70	1,179.20	1,144.88
Sweden	Krona	8.78	8.91	8.89	8.70	9.46	9.21	8.58
Switzerland	Franc	1.00	1.03	1.02	0.98	0.99	0.94	0.91
Taiwan	Dollar	33.09	33.59	31.68	30.15	30.90	29.46	27.93
Thailand	Baht	35.68	36.78	35.37	32.32	31.03	31.27	32.00
Tunisia	Dinar	2.04	2.24	2.51	2.71	2.93	2.84	2.78
Turkey	New Lira	2.83	3.15	3.79	4.85	5.69	7.03	8.90
United Arab Emirates	Dirham	3.82	3.82	3.82	3.67	3.67	3.67	3.67
United Kingdom	Pound	0.68	0.77	0.81	0.75	0.78	0.78	0.73
Venezuela	Bolivar	6.56	9.45	10.45	131,352.21	248,486.04	236,266.51	2,722.76

Source: U.S. Internal Revenue Service, "Yearly Average Currency Exchange Rates," <www.irs.gov/individuals/international-taxpayers/yearly-average-currency-exchange-rates>, accessed March 2022.

Table 1404. Foreign Stock Market Indices: 1980 to 2021

[As of year end. The DAX-40 index is a total return index that includes dividends, whereas the other foreign indices are price indices that exclude dividends]

Year	London FTSE 100	Tokyo Nikkei 225	Hong Kong Hang Seng	Germany DAX-40	Paris CAC-40	Dow Jones Europe STOXX 50
1980	647	7,116	1,477	481	(X)	(X)
1985	1,413	13,113	1,752	1,366	(X)	(X)
1990	2,144	23,849	3,025	1,398	1,518	835
1995	3,689	19,868	10,073	2,254	1,872	1,538
2000	6,223	13,786	15,096	6,434	5,926	4,557
2005	5,619	16,111	14,876	5,408	4,715	3,349
2010	5,900	10,229	23,035	6,914	3,805	2,586
2011	5,572	8,455	18,434	5,898	3,160	2,370
2012	5,898	10,395	22,657	7,612	3,641	2,578
2013	6,749	16,291	23,306	9,552	4,296	2,919
2014	6,566	17,451	23,605	9,806	4,273	3,004
2015	6,242	19,034	21,914	10,743	4,637	3,100
2016	7,143	19,114	22,001	11,481	4,862	3,011
2017	7,688	22,765	29,919	12,918	5,313	3,178
2018	6,728	20,015	25,846	10,559	4,731	2,760
2019	7,542	23,657	28,190	13,249	5,978	3,403
2020	6,461	27,444	27,231	13,719	5,551	3,108
2021	7,385	28,792	23,398	15,885	7,153	3,818

X Not applicable.

Source: Global Financial Data, Los Angeles, CA ©, <www.globalfinancialdata.com>.

Table 1405. Research and Development (R&D) Expenditures by Sector and Country: 2020

[Total expenditures in millions of dollars (1,648,186 represents $1,648,186,000,000). Gross domestic expenditure on R&D (GERD) may include financing from abroad. Selected data are preliminary or estimated. For methodological information for individual countries, see source. GDP = gross domestic product]

Country	Gross domestic expenditure on R&D (GERD) Total (million current PPP U.S. dollars) [1]	Per capita (current PPP U.S. dollars) [1]	Percent of GDP	Percent of GERD performed by: Business enterprise sector	Higher education sector	Government sector	Private non-profit sector
OECD total [2]	1,648,186	1,209	2.7	71.5	16.4	9.6	2.4
EU-27 [2]	441,996	986	2.2	65.5	22.0	11.7	0.8
United States	**720,872**	**2,183**	**3.5**	**75.3**	**11.3**	**9.5**	**4.0**
Austria	15,896	1,783	3.2	69.3	22.8	7.3	0.6
Belgium	21,311	1,846	3.5	72.8	17.5	8.9	0.8
Canada	30,051	790	1.7	51.0	41.2	7.5	0.4
China	582,805	415	2.4	76.6	7.7	15.7	(NA)
Colombia	2,189	44	0.3	51.6	21.3	6.2	20.8
Czechia	8,863	828	2.0	61.0	21.6	17.1	0.3
Denmark	10,402	1,784	3.0	61.6	34.6	3.4	0.4
Estonia	897	675	1.8	54.9	33.6	9.8	1.6
Finland	8,204	1,483	2.9	67.0	24.6	7.6	0.8
France	74,563	1,100	2.4	66.2	20.2	11.9	1.7
Germany	143,407	1,724	3.1	67.1	18.2	14.7	(NA)
Greece	4,474	418	1.5	46.4	31.3	21.7	0.6
Hungary	5,185	532	1.6	76.5	13.0	9.9	(NA)
Iceland	486	1,325	2.5	67.9	28.7	3.4	(NA)
Ireland	5,735	1,152	1.2	73.8	22.6	3.6	(NA)
Israel [3]	19,780	2,147	5.4	90.3	7.6	1.3	0.7
Italy	38,211	643	1.5	60.9	23.7	13.3	2.0
Japan	174,065	1,385	3.3	78.7	11.7	8.3	1.4
Korea, South	112,868	2,180	4.8	79.1	9.0	10.1	1.8
Latvia	422	222	0.7	30.9	50.2	18.8	(NA)
Lithuania	1,255	449	1.2	47.6	36.7	15.6	(NA)
Luxembourg	838	1,329	1.1	53.8	22.1	24.1	(NA)
Mexico	7,157	56	0.3	21.5	50.9	26.3	1.3
Netherlands	23,716	1,360	2.3	67.3	27.1	5.6	(NA)
Norway	7,677	1,427	2.3	54.3	33.2	12.4	(NA)
Poland	18,089	472	1.4	62.8	35.0	2.0	0.2
Portugal	5,692	553	1.6	57.0	36.0	4.9	2.1
Romania	2,907	150	0.5	59.0	8.8	31.9	0.3
Russia	47,954	327	1.1	56.6	9.8	32.8	0.7
Slovakia	1,560	286	0.9	54.1	26.2	19.7	0.0
Slovenia	1,793	853	2.1	73.3	12.2	13.8	0.7
Spain	25,133	531	1.4	55.6	26.6	17.5	0.3
Sweden	20,099	1,941	3.5	72.3	23.1	4.4	0.1
Taiwan	47,856	2,031	3.6	82.5	7.8	9.6	0.1
Turkey	25,013	300	1.1	64.8	28.4	6.8	(NA)

NA Not available or not applicable. [1] Purchasing power parities (PPPs) are currency conversion rates used to convert different currencies to a common value (U.S. dollars in this case). See introductory text, this section. [2] For full membership listing of the Organisation for Economic Co-operation and Development (OECD) and the European Union-27, see introductory text, this section. [3] The statistical data for Israel are supplied by and under the responsibility of the relevant Israeli authorities. The use of such data by the OECD is without prejudice to the status of the Golan Heights, East Jerusalem and Israeli settlements in the West Bank under the terms of international law.

Source: Organisation for Economic Co-operation and Development (OECD), 2022, "Main Science and Technology Indicators," OECD Science, Technology and R&D Statistics (database) ©, <dx.doi.org/10.1787/data-00182-en>, accessed August 2022.

Table 1406. Development Assistance Outlays by Donor Country: 2020 and 2021

[In millions of current U.S. dollars (162,586 represents $162,586,000,000), except percent. Official development assistance (ODA) includes concessional loans and grants made by donor governments to developing countries and to multilateral institutions such as the United Nations or the World Bank]

Country	2020				2021 (Preliminary)			
	Official development assistance (ODA)		Multi-lateral ODA	Net private grants	Official development assistance (ODA)		Multi-lateral ODA	Net private grants
	Net disburse-ments	Percent of total DAC ODA [1]			Net disburse-ments	Percent of total DAC ODA [1]		
DAC countries total [1]....	162,586	100.0	47,739	45,983	177,637.0	100.0	55,268	(NA)
United States..............	35,396	21.8	5,723	37,859	41,872.1	23.6	9,127	(NA)
Australia.....................	2,869	1.8	550	(NA)	3,444.4	1.9	376	(NA)
Austria......................	1,321	0.8	760	185	1,485.2	0.8	778	(NA)
Belgium.....................	2,376	1.5	1,215	(NA)	2,573.8	1.4	1,384	(NA)
Canada......................	4,871	3.0	1,157	2,407	6,225.7	3.5	1,361	(NA)
Czechia......................	299	0.2	226	(NA)	361.7	0.2	284	(NA)
Denmark.....................	2,641	1.6	954	179	2,867.2	1.6	974	(NA)
Finland......................	1,278	0.8	622	(NA)	1,493.2	0.8	794	(NA)
France.......................	16,013	9.8	5,342	(NA)	16,699.9	9.4	6,330	(NA)
Germany.....................	29,320	18.0	6,591	1,514	31,490.9	17.7	8,538	(NA)
Greece.......................	325	0.2	241	(NA)	263.8	0.1	258	(NA)
Hungary.....................	418	0.3	192	(NA)	455.0	0.3	182	(NA)
Iceland......................	58	(Z)	12	(NA)	71.9	(Z)	13	(NA)
Ireland......................	988	0.6	466	136	1,168.8	0.7	541	(NA)
Italy.........................	4,396	2.7	3,090	28	6,119.3	3.4	3,745	(NA)
Japan........................	13,660	8.4	3,418	606	15,750.0	8.9	4,132	(NA)
Korea, South................	2,293	1.4	499	452	2,986.6	1.7	710	(NA)
Luxembourg.................	452	0.3	146	(NA)	538.9	0.3	154	(NA)
Netherlands.................	5,359	3.3	1,666	1,998	5,287.6	3.0	1,530	(NA)
New Zealand................	530	0.3	96	77	681.0	0.4	101	(NA)
Norway......................	4,196	2.6	1,060	(NA)	4,673.1	2.6	1,173	(NA)
Poland.......................	812	0.5	604	(NA)	940.0	0.5	678	(NA)
Portugal.....................	421	0.3	253	32	437.7	0.2	288	(NA)
Slovakia.....................	141	0.1	104	(NA)	150.7	0.1	115	(NA)
Slovenia.....................	91	0.1	61	(NA)	114.8	0.1	69	(NA)
Spain........................	2,739	1.7	2,003	3	3,251.9	1.8	2,093	(NA)
Sweden......................	6,348	3.9	2,776	(NA)	5,926.6	3.3	1,963	(NA)
Switzerland..................	3,721	2.3	868	507	3,925.9	2.2	947	(NA)
United Kingdom............	19,253	11.8	7,043	(NA)	16,379.3	9.2	6,633	(NA)

Z Less than 0.05 percent. NA Not available. [1] Development Assistance Committee (DAC) of the Organisation for Economic Co-operation and Development (OECD) is comprised of 29 developed countries, shown above, and European Union institutions, not shown separately.

Source: Organisation for Economic Co-operation and Development (OECD), 2022, "Detailed aid statistics: Official and private flows," OECD International Development Statistics (database) ©, <dx.doi.org/10.1787/data-00072-en>, accessed August 2022.

Table 1407. Net Flow of Financial Resources to Developing Countries and Multilateral Organizations by Donor Country: 2000 to 2020

[134,228 represents $134,228,000,000. Net flow covers official and private loans, grants, development assistance, and technical assistance, minus amortization on loans. Military flows are excluded. GNI = gross national income. Minus sign (-) indicates net inflow]

Country	Amount (million dollars)				Percent of GNI			
	2000	2010	2015	2020	2000	2010	2015	2020
DAC countries total [1].............	134,228	512,792	316,043	205,215	0.54	1.25	0.72	0.41
United States.......................	25,252	216,950	38,520	4,809	0.25	1.48	0.21	0.02
Australia................................	1,891	14,531	13,840	2,894	0.51	1.23	1.15	0.22
Austria..................................	1,135	6,372	4,692	-91	0.61	1.70	1.25	-0.02
Belgium.................................	2,281	7,896	3,635	4,185	1.00	1.68	0.79	0.85
Canada..................................	6,483	22,642	3,718	2,742	0.95	1.46	0.24	0.17
Czechia.................................	16	228	263	428	0.03	0.13	0.16	0.18
Denmark................................	2,176	4,794	2,931	3,523	1.39	1.52	0.97	0.96
Finland.................................	1,087	4,312	-48	2,612	0.91	1.78	-0.02	0.96
France..................................	5,557	35,198	1,234	20,721	0.41	1.35	0.05	0.78
Germany................................	12,331	41,637	47,627	44,701	0.66	1.24	1.39	1.14
Greece..................................	229	761	-85	448	0.20	0.26	-0.04	0.24
Hungary................................	(NA)	114	156	3,473	(NA)	0.09	0.13	2.25
Iceland.................................	9	29	40	58	0.10	0.26	0.24	0.27
Ireland.................................	740	2,695	1,228	1,123	0.93	1.57	0.54	0.35
Italy....................................	10,846	9,608	15,621	6,529	1.01	0.47	0.86	0.34
Japan...................................	11,423	48,249	37,908	32,472	0.24	0.86	0.83	0.62
Korea, South..........................	44	11,834	12,318	12,201	0.01	1.17	0.89	0.74
Luxembourg...........................	129	411	363	452	0.73	1.07	0.95	1.03
Netherlands...........................	6,947	13,013	68,160	13,258	1.85	1.67	8.91	1.47
New Zealand..........................	142	426	621	688	0.32	0.32	0.37	0.34
Norway.................................	1,437	5,876	4,565	4,188	0.87	1.41	1.12	1.11
Poland..................................	29	378	499	958	0.02	0.08	0.11	0.17
Portugal................................	4,622	162	520	-520	4.45	0.07	0.27	-0.23
Slovakia................................	6	74	85	164	0.03	0.09	0.10	0.16
Slovenia................................	(NA)	59	156	600	(NA)	0.13	0.37	1.15
Spain...................................	23,471	10,340	22,041	13,878	4.25	0.74	1.84	1.08
Sweden.................................	3,952	5,127	10,365	7,058	1.76	1.10	2.05	1.27
Switzerland............................	1,765	23,444	6,518	3,258	0.64	4.01	0.94	0.45
United Kingdom......................	10,230	25,632	18,553	18,403	0.72	1.12	0.70	0.69

NA Not available. [1] The OECD Development Assistance Committee (DAC) is comprised of the above-listed member countries plus the EU.

Source: Organisation for Economic Co-operation and Development (OECD), 2022, "Detailed aid statistics: Official and private flows," OECD International Development Statistics (database) ©, <dx.doi.org/10.1787/data-00072-en>, accessed August 2022.

Table 1408. External Debt by Developing Country: 2000 to 2020

[In millions of U.S. dollars (9,763 represents $9,763,000,000). Total external debt is debt owed to nonresidents repayable in foreign currency, goods, or services. Total external debt is the sum of public, publicly guaranteed, and private nonguaranteed long-term debt, use of International Monetary Fund (IMF) credit, and short-term debt. Short-term debt includes all debt having an original maturity of one year or less and interest in arrears on long-term debt]

Country	2000	2010	2015	2020	Country	2000	2010	2015	2020
Angola	9,763	26,796	49,254	67,287	Mauritius	967	7,929	10,325	18,527
Argentina	150,063	126,642	177,185	253,760	Mexico	152,558	245,906	426,914	467,512
Bangladesh	15,601	26,572	35,967	67,749	Mongolia	960	5,928	21,953	33,236
Belarus	2,620	28,412	38,258	42,491	Morocco	20,790	27,296	44,376	65,683
Brazil	242,512	352,364	543,397	549,234	Mozambique	6,681	5,936	14,102	20,932
Bulgaria	12,009	50,697	40,379	43,347	Nigeria	33,514	18,822	32,413	70,571
Cambodia	2,108	4,010	9,436	17,562	Pakistan	33,094	63,098	68,599	116,506
China	145,937	742,756	1,333,777	2,349,389	Papua New Guinea	2,325	5,987	20,387	17,971
Colombia	34,329	64,432	113,363	155,172	Paraguay	3,106	15,903	16,362	19,763
Costa Rica	4,692	8,154	23,589	31,288	Peru	28,834	42,154	67,186	73,549
Cote d'Ivoire	12,060	11,703	11,388	25,073	Philippines	58,445	65,350	76,261	98,480
Dominican Republic	4,618	13,499	26,727	44,468	Russia	146,665	417,886	485,704	475,518
Ecuador	17,174	15,377	28,402	56,191	Senegal	3,653	4,943	6,800	17,239
Egypt	29,233	36,775	49,846	131,580	Serbia [1]	11,573	32,907	30,261	38,467
El Salvador	4,535	11,496	15,570	18,334	South Africa	26,669	108,429	124,737	170,767
Ethiopia	5,516	7,286	20,443	30,364	Sri Lanka	9,250	21,684	43,925	56,342
Georgia	1,826	8,790	14,875	20,089	Sudan	16,076	22,323	21,401	22,954
Ghana	6,743	8,365	20,073	31,323	Tanzania	7,200	8,937	18,145	25,538
Guatemala	3,948	15,043	20,378	25,136	Thailand	79,830	106,358	132,186	204,147
India	101,131	290,428	478,826	564,179	Tunisia	11,355	22,666	27,487	41,038
Indonesia	144,049	198,278	307,749	417,532	Turkey	116,799	300,869	399,949	435,889
Jamaica	4,828	14,193	14,134	18,035	Uganda	3,535	2,975	9,571	17,207
Jordan	11,063	16,894	25,598	38,016	Ukraine	13,915	124,527	117,455	129,899
Kazakhstan	12,890	119,151	153,180	162,974	Uzbekistan	4,948	7,981	13,445	32,174
Kenya	6,147	8,862	19,762	38,194	Vietnam	12,841	44,940	77,832	125,045
Lebanon	10,075	47,819	68,219	68,865	Zambia	5,811	4,253	11,779	30,046

[1] Data from 2000 to 2005 are for Serbia and Montenegro. In June 2006, Serbia and Montenegro became separate countries; beginning 2006, data exclude Montenegro.

Source: The World Bank, Washington, DC, "External debt stocks, total," World Development Indicators (database) ©, <databank.worldbank.org/home.aspx>, accessed August 2022.

Table 1409. Foreign Direct Investment Flows in Selected Countries: 2010 to 2021

[In millions of dollars (210,554 represents $210,554,000,000). Data are converted to U.S. dollars using the yearly average exchange rate]

Country	Inflows					Outflows				
	2010	2015	2019	2020	2021	2010	2015	2019	2020	2021
United States	210,544	483,849	237,973	164,396	381,933	296,334	274,486	57,964	264,791	433,613
Australia	36,442	29,584	39,218	20,140	(NA)	19,803	-9,340	9,264	9,168	(NA)
Austria	-21,694	-7,577	-23,615	-13,900	3,712	-14,065	-1,783	-17,211	-4,137	10,782
Belgium	132,604	-70,573	1,751	11,886	25,575	60,335	57,563	-3,372	10,563	45,616
Brazil	77,687	49,961	65,386	28,318	50,367	22,060	-11,643	19,031	-12,935	23,083
Canada	28,399	43,853	50,142	23,174	59,694	34,721	67,467	79,377	46,526	89,901
Chile	(NA)	20,404	12,525	8,386	(NA)	(NA)	15,456	9,278	11,583	(NA)
China	243,703	242,489	187,170	253,096	333,979	57,954	174,391	136,910	153,721	128,037
Costa Rica	1,684	2,752	2,812	1,757	3,324	94	211	117	112	215
Czechia	6,147	465	10,109	9,411	5,805	1,168	2,488	4,128	2,989	5,582
Denmark	-12,559	2,237	-12,869	1,256	5,595	-1,407	7,536	-2,733	8,858	22,417
Estonia	1,509	36	3,184	3,388	989	167	182	1,966	219	1,547
Finland	7,359	2,110	13,455	-1,422	8,927	10,189	-16,080	4,864	5,850	3,626
France	13,891	45,355	28,362	4,862	14,159	48,158	53,206	33,817	45,906	-2,842
Germany	65,646	30,534	52,664	64,442	31,263	125,453	99,003	137,289	60,486	151,671
Greece	330	1,268	5,019	3,205	5,731	1,558	1,578	642	547	926
Hungary	-37,104	-28,167	70,730	97,872	17,065	-41,085	-31,123	70,335	94,959	14,609
Iceland	(NA)	670	-225	-933	174	(NA)	-29	479	-391	19
Indonesia	13,771	16,641	23,883	18,591	20,081	2,664	5,937	3,352	4,448	3,596
Ireland	42,807	217,820	158,489	82,122	15,926	22,350	168,443	34,442	-46,482	62,229
Italy	9,179	19,631	18,145	-23,568	8,486	32,657	21,640	19,786	-1,852	11,757
Japan	-1,252	-2,251	13,724	10,255	24,650	56,276	128,698	232,723	115,716	146,768
Korea, South	8,117	3,076	12,548	(NA)	(NA)	26,821	18,490	50,984	(NA)	(NA)
Latvia	420	741	902	1,011	5,326	20	73	-104	269	3,361
Lithuania	1,020	1,055	3,022	3,484	2,053	42	377	1,746	2,868	663
Luxembourg	222,023	584,875	-174,247	-31,215	-276,423	205,556	703,265	-95,745	-22,818	-182,029
Netherlands	135,774	276,393	-124,474	-170,871	-170,119	210,620	344,599	-81,995	-212,486	-60,795
New Zealand	-61	-311	4,279	3,812	3,482	716	-58	-168	523	-1,876
Norway	17,043	-2,515	17,354	-3,731	(NA)	23,238	30,947	12,973	-2,067	(NA)
Poland	12,799	11,819	13,326	13,650	24,822	6,148	1,928	1,674	1,104	178
Portugal	2,913	7,628	12,360	7,739	8,019	-9,456	5,225	3,638	2,328	-1,440
Russia	31,668	11,858	32,076	10,410	38,240	41,116	27,090	22,024	6,778	63,602
Slovakia	1,770	106	2,511	-1,926	59	946	6	43	235	389
Slovenia	106	1,675	1,463	205	1,517	-19	267	610	508	922
Spain	(NA)	8,557	17,416	12,607	9,776	(NA)	41,917	24,826	34,941	-1,625
Sweden	141	8,449	9,111	18,805	26,972	20,364	13,045	16,104	23,689	20,347
Switzerland	28,750	84,327	-105,797	-162,698	1,016	85,718	91,551	-56,169	-36,150	-19,117
Turkey	9,086	18,978	9,701	7,773	12,177	1,469	4,813	2,969	3,231	4,987
United Kingdom	58,180	39,189	45,445	18,201	27,564	48,075	-66,827	-6,080	-65,388	107,751

NA Not available.

Source: Organisation for Economic Co-operation and Development (OECD), 2022, "Benchmark definition, 4th edition (BMD4): Foreign direct investment: financial flows, main aggregates," OECD International Direct Investment Statistics (database) ©, <dx.doi.org/10.1787/data-00741-en>, accessed June 2022.

Table 1410. International Transaction Balances, Reserve Assets, and Trade in Relation to Gross Domestic Product (GDP) by Country: 2020 and 2021

[In millions of U.S. dollars (-616,087 represents -$616,087,000,000), except as noted. Minus sign (-) indicates deficit]

Country	Current account balance 2020	Current account balance 2021	Reserve assets [1] 2020	Reserve assets [1] 2021	Goods and services trade balance 2020	Goods and services trade balance 2021	Exports as percent of GDP 2020	Exports as percent of GDP 2021	Imports as percent of GDP 2020	Imports as percent of GDP 2021
United States.........	-616,087	-821,645	133,849	240,197	-651,187	(NA)	10.2	(NA)	13.3	(NA)
Albania...............	-1,315	-1,393	4,647	5,471	-2,201	-2,426	22.7	30.6	37.3	43.9
Angola...............	872	8,398	13,782	14,468	10,168	16,557	37.9	37.9	19.0	15.1
Argentina............	3,313	6,800	35,650	36,448	11,826	15,593	16.6	18.3	13.6	15.1
Armenia.............	-479	-511	2,616	3,230	-1,260	-1,102	29.8	35.0	39.7	43.0
Australia.............	35,629	56,691	39,152	53,790	52,160	67,065	24.0	22.2	20.1	17.8
Austria...............	8,160	-2,541	13,416	17,572	12,439	4,316	51.4	56.0	48.6	55.0
Azerbaijan...........	-228	8,292	7,634	8,307	-329	9,151	35.6	46.7	36.4	29.9
Bangladesh..........	1,193	-15,563	42,322	45,348	-20,138	-26,634	10.4	10.7	15.8	17.1
Belarus..............	-259	1,843	4,427	5,302	1,900	3,740	61.0	72.1	57.9	66.6
Belgium..............	4,324	-2,157	19,470	28,566	7,338	8,014	80.0	85.4	78.6	84.0
Belize...............	-128	-166	348	420	-190	-42	43.6	51.5	55.5	53.8
Bolivia...............	-271	815	2,662	2,242	-1,816	-1,362	20.3	27.8	25.2	31.2
Brazil................	-24,492	-27,925	351,519	354,623	10,135	16,386	16.8	20.1	16.1	19.1
Bulgaria.............	-106	-257	35,378	36,798	1,027	866	55.3	63.0	53.9	62.0
Cambodia............	-2,197	-12,339	18,564	17,318	-367	-811	61.0	64.6	62.5	67.6
Canada..............	-29,216	1,217	90,428	106,615	-33,824	3,094	29.4	30.7	31.4	30.5
China................	248,836	317,301	3,238,782	3,313,920	366,145	458,930	18.5	20.0	16.1	17.4
Colombia............	-9,207	-17,833	58,248	57,745	-18,711	-25,006	13.5	16.3	20.4	24.3
Costa Rica...........	-709	-2,106	7,232	6,921	1,843	1,065	31.5	36.1	28.6	34.5
Croatia..............	55	2,251	23,254	28,309	-3,866	-649	42.0	51.4	48.8	52.4
Cyprus..............	-2,509	-2,031	392	797	-623	296	75.8	81.0	78.3	79.9
Czechia.............	4,967	-2,282	165,549	172,999	16,761	8,609	71.0	72.6	64.2	69.5
Denmark.............	28,952	32,957	68,777	78,342	22,970	26,633	54.9	59.6	48.4	52.9
Ecuador.............	2,693	3,060	5,236	6,083	2,324	1,052	21.9	26.2	19.5	25.2
El Salvador..........	203	-1,457	2,999	3,346	-4,525	-7,263	25.5	29.6	43.9	54.8
Estonia..............	-141	-453	1,982	2,357	148	95	71.2	80.5	70.7	80.3
Finland..............	2,268	2,115	10,492	13,876	648	701	35.8	38.9	35.5	38.7
France...............	-49,060	-17,669	76,114	101,703	-53,136	-60,843	27.9	30.0	29.9	32.0
Germany............	274,200	314,087	63,969	99,169	220,217	233,637	43.4	47.5	37.7	41.9
Greece..............	-12,413	-12,694	5,006	7,773	-14,380	-17,137	32.0	40.6	39.6	48.6
Guatemala...........	3,832	2,177	18,044	20,532	-6,247	-10,729	16.9	18.5	25.0	31.0
Haiti.................	216	141	2,480	2,653	-3,208	-4,779	7.7	7.1	29.8	29.9
Honduras............	661	-1,385	8,097	(NA)	-3,677	-6,682	35.1	38.5	50.5	61.9
Hong Kong, China. . . .	24,092	41,356	491,649	496,745	6,622	17,456	176.3	203.9	174.4	199.2
Hungary.............	-1,563	-5,243	39,434	37,954	3,260	1,384	79.0	81.3	76.9	80.6
Iceland..............	184	-708	6,299	6,963	-163	-542	34.2	38.1	35.0	40.3
India................	32,730	-34,648	549,087	594,356	-10,339	-65,052	18.7	20.8	19.1	22.9
Indonesia............	-4,433	3,430	131,139	140,310	16,592	32,011	17.3	21.6	15.7	18.9
Ireland..............	-8,904	70,249	7,098	12,690	94,863	200,847	131.1	134.8	108.8	94.6
Israel................	22,042	22,266	173,292	212,934	18,925	21,387	28.0	29.7	23.4	25.3
Italy.................	72,034	53,095	61,614	84,002	69,313	50,753	29.5	32.7	25.9	30.3
Korea, South..........	75,902	88,302	437,113	457,169	60,212	66,197	36.5	41.7	32.8	38.0
Latvia...............	982	-1,133	4,885	5,102	395	-807	60.4	64.1	59.3	66.2
Lithuania............	4,162	937	4,493	5,239	5,251	2,751	73.5	80.4	64.2	76.2
Luxembourg..........	3,091	4,322	981	2,790	24,270	30,684	204.7	212.1	171.6	176.7
Malaysia.............	14,342	12,904	105,280	114,641	21,711	26,344	61.4	68.9	55.0	61.8
Mexico..............	26,210	-4,866	191,769	200,775	22,257	-19,457	39.6	40.4	37.6	41.9
Montenegro..........	-1,237	-538	2,135	1,982	-1,674	-1,142	26.0	43.0	61.0	62.7
Morocco.............	-1,368	-3,261	34,653	34,354	-8,752	-12,570	34.9	37.3	42.6	46.7
Namibia.............	271	-1,120	2,171	2,764	-975	-2,127	33.5	31.9	42.7	49.3
Nepal................	-84	-5,379	11,077	9,194	-9,130	-12,118	6.8	5.2	34.1	38.6
Netherlands.........	63,655	96,623	16,734	28,630	95,121	112,117	77.9	83.6	67.5	72.6
Norway..............	4,223	73,459	75,259	84,271	-3,042	60,094	32.3	41.6	33.1	29.1
Pakistan.............	-651	-12,262	14,592	19,028	-24,392	-34,473	9.3	10.0	17.4	19.9
Paraguay............	960	311	8,704	9,182	1,459	458	33.6	36.5	29.5	35.3
Peru.................	2,398	-5,273	72,671	(NA)	2,484	5,953	22.4	29.1	21.2	26.4
Philippines...........	11,578	-6,922	98,512	99,462	-28,086	-47,357	25.2	25.7	33.0	37.8
Poland..............	17,319	-3,895	140,316	152,522	40,530	28,295	56.2	60.9	49.4	56.7
Portugal.............	-2,355	-2,848	6,199	10,148	-4,827	-7,483	37.0	42.0	39.1	45.0
Romania.............	-12,535	-19,751	45,889	45,821	-10,824	-16,080	37.2	40.9	41.5	46.5
Russia...............	36,030	122,040	457,018	497,554	75,912	169,713	25.5	30.8	20.4	21.3
Saudi Arabia.........	-22,814	44,324	453,208	454,984	2,034	86,870	26.2	34.8	25.9	24.4
Serbia...............	-2,177	-2,742	14,419	16,431	-4,418	-4,950	48.2	54.4	56.5	62.3
Singapore............	58,139	71,926	362,088	416,101	109,478	124,500	181.7	184.8	150.0	153.5
Slovakia.............	459	-2,220	7,417	7,755	974	-736	85.4	93.9	84.5	94.5
Slovenia.............	3,957	2,073	1,118	2,081	4,944	3,270	77.9	83.5	68.7	78.2
South Africa..........	6,798	15,529	47,387	50,262	14,857	25,803	27.8	31.1	23.4	25.0
Spain................	10,788	13,263	64,168	75,724	18,878	21,529	30.6	34.9	29.2	33.4
Sweden..............	32,947	34,684	50,617	54,696	25,100	27,306	44.6	46.3	39.9	41.9
Switzerland..........	20,308	75,502	1,020,172	1,048,963	66,157	120,167	62.3	69.9	53.6	55.2
Thailand.............	20,279	-10,582	248,743	231,737	26,588	-1,209	51.6	58.2	46.3	58.5
Turkey...............	-35,537	-13,693	49,958	71,046	-27,437	-3,436	28.7	35.4	32.5	35.8
Ukraine..............	5,267	-2,639	27,549	29,383	-2,370	-2,249	38.8	40.8	40.3	41.9
United Kingdom.......	-69,828	-82,534	161,188	176,024	8,149	-40,034	28.4	27.0	28.1	28.3
Uruguay.............	-449	-1,092	16,244	16,957	2,327	3,653	25.1	31.5	20.7	25.3
Uzbekistan...........	-3,007	-4,810	14,687	14,189	-8,058	-11,358	24.3	23.7	37.7	40.1
Zambia..............	2,433	2,352	1,203	2,754	2,582	3,941	46.8	54.6	32.5	36.0

NA Not available. [1] Reserve assets are comprised of special drawing rights and reserve position in International Monetary Fund (IMF), and foreign exchange holdings. Gold holdings are excluded.

Source: The World Bank, Washington, DC, "World Development Indicators" database ©, <data.worldbank.org/data-catalog/world-development-indicators>, accessed August 2022.

Table 1411. International Tourism Arrivals, Expenditures, and Receipts—Leading Countries: 2005 to 2020

[Arrivals at national borders in thousands of non-resident tourists (1,501,611 represents 1,501,611,000). Expenditures and receipts in millions of current U.S. dollars (667,122 represents $667,122,000,000). Receipts are money spent by foreign tourists while traveling inside the country shown and include prepayment for goods or services in destination country. Expenditures are money spent by tourists from a given country of origin while traveling outside their home country. Data exclude receipts and expenditures for international transport. Sources and collection methods differ, thus caution should be used in comparing data across countries]

Country	Arrivals (1,000) [1,2]					Expenditures (mil. dol.)					Receipts (mil. dol.)				
	2005	2010	2015	2019	2020	2005	2010	2015	2019	2020	2005	2010	2015	2019	2020
World [3]	1,501,611	1,755,720	2,071,786	2,403,074	(NA)	667,122	880,221	1,198,775	1,403,687	(NA)	711,944	966,554	1,216,223	1,465,469	(NA)
United States	71,484	162,275	176,865	165,478	45,037	74,111	85,165	102,666	133,285	35,806	93,423	130,315	192,602	199,365	72,812
Australia	5,499	5,790	7,449	9,466	1,828	11,749	22,558	29,190	35,968	6,488	16,750	28,472	34,249	45,729	25,867
Austria	19,952	22,004	26,728	31,884	15,091	9,316	10,120	9,329	11,589	4,903	16,243	18,751	18,292	22,983	13,881
Bahrain	6,313	11,952	9,670	11,061	1,909	414	506	4,342	1,720	(NA)	920	1,362	2,705	3,681	673
Belarus	4,738	5,674	4,386	11,832	3,598	448	622	901	1,123	445	253	440	729	901	355
Bulgaria	7,282	8,374	9,311	12,552	4,973	1,309	826	1,116	1,825	1,048	2,412	3,343	3,139	4,287	1,636
Canada	36,160	25,621	27,555	32,430	(NA)	18,027	29,977	33,961	35,776	12,078	13,655	15,830	20,315	28,018	11,256
China	120,292	133,762	133,820	162,538	30,402	21,759	54,880	249,831	254,621	130,504	29,296	45,814	44,969	35,832	14,233
Croatia	45,762	49,006	55,858	60,021	21,608	754	832	755	1,764	776	7,370	8,069	8,022	11,753	5,569
Czechia	24,747	21,941	29,604	37,202	(NA)	2,405	4,252	4,772	5,889	3,430	4,813	7,172	6,056	7,302	3,632
Denmark	26,927	26,730	28,209	33,093	15,595	6,850	9,082	8,918	10,037	5,636	5,293	5,704	6,685	8,651	3,970
Egypt	8,608	14,731	9,328	13,026	(NA)	1,629	2,240	3,442	3,518	2,509	6,851	12,528	6,065	13,030	4,398
France	185,826	189,826	203,302	217,877	117,109	31,347	38,297	39,521	50,507	27,758	43,937	46,459	58,326	63,424	32,646
Germany	21,500	26,875	34,970	39,563	12,449	74,167	77,566	77,468	93,097	38,752	29,111	34,557	36,895	41,779	22,049
Greece	15,938	(NA)	26,114	34,005	7,406	3,038	2,853	2,259	3,070	898	13,336	12,478	15,665	20,276	5,015
Hong Kong, China	23,359	36,030	59,308	55,913	3,569	13,305	17,357	23,059	26,879	5,520	10,179	21,689	35,795	26,371	2,839
Hungary	36,173	39,904	48,345	61,397	31,641	2,277	2,404	1,830	2,741	1,159	4,120	5,587	5,320	7,283	3,229
India	3,919	5,776	13,284	17,914	(NA)	6,187	10,490	14,838	22,915	12,574	7,493	14,490	21,013	30,720	13,036
Indonesia	5,002	7,003	10,407	16,107	4,053	3,584	6,395	7,292	11,308	1,653	4,522	6,958	10,761	16,911	3,312
Ireland	7,333	7,134	9,528	10,951	(NA)	6,073	7,069	5,704	8,156	2,334	4,781	4,085	4,783	6,417	1,858
Italy	59,230	73,225	81,068	95,399	38,419	22,362	26,902	24,425	30,307	10,858	35,310	38,432	39,433	49,521	20,036
Japan	6,728	8,611	19,737	31,881	4,116	37,565	27,950	15,974	21,277	5,445	12,430	13,224	24,968	46,054	10,597
Korea, South	6,023	8,798	13,232	17,503	2,519	15,406	18,766	25,270	32,739	16,157	5,798	10,263	14,798	20,867	10,528
Macao, China	18,711	24,965	30,715	39,406	5,897	412	800	1,326	1,922	845	6,924	22,276	31,101	40,591	9,360
Malaysia	16,431	24,577	25,721	26,101	4,333	3,711	8,324	10,708	12,385	4,820	8,846	18,152	17,666	19,828	3,004
Mexico	103,146	81,953	87,129	97,406	51,128	7,600	7,255	10,098	9,881	3,475	11,803	11,992	17,734	24,573	10,996
Morocco	6,077	9,752	10,542	13,109	2,802	612	1,203	1,402	2,176	1,113	4,610	6,702	6,260	8,187	3,848
Netherlands	10,012	10,883	15,007	20,129	7,265	13,724	19,044	18,038	20,480	7,029	8,770	11,653	13,171	18,575	9,101
Poland	64,606	58,340	77,743	88,515	(NA)	5,540	8,358	7,701	9,220	5,202	6,304	9,414	10,283	13,704	7,771
Portugal	10,612	6,756	11,723	17,283	4,208	3,049	3,905	3,695	5,729	3,140	7,674	10,004	12,875	20,444	8,835
Romania	5,839	7,498	9,331	12,815	5,023	923	1,637	2,237	5,996	3,022	1,051	1,136	1,841	3,572	1,433
Russia	22,201	22,281	33,729	24,419	6,359	16,972	26,693	34,932	36,152	9,140	5,870	8,830	8,420	10,961	2,854
Saudi Arabia	10,417	13,025	21,834	20,292	(NA)	9,087	21,135	19,346	15,140	8,533	4,626	6,712	10,130	16,431	4,036
Singapore	8,943	11,642	15,232	19,116	2,742	10,070	18,700	23,658	27,324	6,828	6,209	14,178	16,617	20,302	5,189
South Africa	7,518	11,303	13,952	14,797	3,887	3,374	5,595	2,998	3,141	928	7,516	9,085	8,259	8,390	2,607
Spain	92,563	93,744	109,834	126,170	36,410	15,169	16,926	17,207	27,858	8,742	51,959	58,348	62,449	79,611	18,352
Switzerland	7,229	8,628	9,305	11,818	(NA)	9,287	11,805	17,207	18,754	9,546	9,891	14,811	16,929	17,955	9,038
Thailand	11,567	15,936	29,923	39,916	(NA)	3,803	5,627	7,718	12,355	2,865	9,576	20,104	41,246	59,810	14,198
Turkey	21,125	32,997	41,114	51,747	15,971	3,104	5,194	5,368	4,110	1,040	19,191	20,585	26,616	29,829	10,220
Ukraine	20,489	24,114	13,025	13,710	3,382	2,805	3,742	5,101	8,517	4,691	3,125	3,788	1,082	1,620	374
United Kingdom	29,970	30,398	36,792	40,857	11,101	65,798	60,353	68,395	71,516	21,698	32,780	35,168	51,947	52,529	19,098

NA Not available. [1] Tourists who travel to a country other than that in which they have their usual residence for a period not exceeding 12 months and whose main purpose in visiting is other than an activity remunerated from within the country visited. When data on number of tourists are not available, the number of visitors, which includes tourists, same-day visitors, cruise passengers, and crew members, is shown instead. Sources and collection methods for arrivals differ across countries. In some cases data are from border statistics (police, immigration, etc.) and supplemented by border surveys. In other cases data are from tourism accommodation establishments. For some countries number of arrivals is limited to arrivals by air and for others to arrivals staying in hotels. Some countries include arrivals of nationals residing abroad while others do not. Caution should thus be used in comparing arrivals across countries. The data on inbound tourists refer to the number of arrivals, not to the number of people traveling. [2] The World Tourism Organization (UNWTO) has changed the way arrivals are reported. Data are now reported by total arrivals, overnight visitors, or same-day visitors. Previously, data were reported by multiple 'total arrivals' indicators, with a note on whether it was counting visitors or tourists at national borders, tourists at hotels, etc. If there is at least 10 years of data and recent data (within the last 5 years) for a given country, the number reported is total arrivals. If data on total arrivals are insufficient, then data on overnight visitors are reported. If data for overnight visitors are insufficient, then data for same-day visitors are reported. See source for details by individual country. [3] Includes other countries not shown separately.

Source: The World Bank, Washington, DC, "World Development Indicators" database ©, <databank.worldbank.org/source/world-development-indicators>, accessed August 2022.

Table 1412. Military Expenditures as a Percent of GDP by Country: 2019 to 2022

[Data are estimated. Military expenditures compares spending on defense programs for the most recent year available as a percent of gross domestic product (GDP), calculated on an exchange rate basis]

Country	Data as of year	Percent of GDP	Rank [1]	Country	Data as of year	Percent of GDP	Rank [1]
United States	**2021**	**3.6**	**23**	Korea, South	2021	2.6	36
Afghanistan	2019	3.3	27	Kuwait	2021	6.8	3
Albania	2021	1.4	95	Kyrgyzstan	2021	1.7	77
Algeria	2021	5.6	6	Latvia	2021	2.2	52
Angola	2021	1.4	96	Lebanon	2021	3.2	28
Armenia	2021	4.4	14	Lesotho	2021	1.5	91
Australia	2021	2.1	53	Lithuania	2021	2.0	61
Austria	2021	0.9	135	Malaysia	2021	1.0	130
Azerbaijan	2021	5.2	9	Mali	2021	3.5	25
Bahrain	2021	3.6	21	Mauritania	2021	2.4	44
Bangladesh	2021	1.2	113	Mexico	2022	0.8	144
Belarus	2021	1.2	114	Montenegro	2021	1.6	83
Belgium	2021	1.1	121	Morocco	2021	4.5	13
Belize	2021	1.3	104	Mozambique	2021	1.2	117
Bolivia	2021	1.4	97	Namibia	2021	3.0	33
Botswana	2021	3.0	31	Nepal	2021	1.3	108
Brazil	2021	1.3	105	Netherlands	2021	1.5	92
Brunei	2021	3.1	30	New Zealand	2021	1.3	109
Bulgaria	2021	1.6	81	Niger	2021	1.8	71
Burkina Faso	2021	2.4	43	North Macedonia	2021	1.5	93
Burma	2021	3.4	26	Norway	2021	1.7	78
Burundi	2021	2.0	56	Oman	2021	8.0	2
Cambodia	2021	2.5	38	Pakistan	2022	4.0	16
Cameroon	2021	1.0	126	Panama	2021	1.4	102
Canada	2021	1.4	98	Paraguay	2021	1.0	131
Central African Republic	2021	1.8	68	Peru	2021	1.1	123
Chad	2021	2.5	39	Philippines	2021	1.1	124
Chile	2021	2.0	57	Poland	2021	2.3	47
China	2021	1.5	86	Portugal	2021	1.6	84
Colombia	2021	3.0	32	Qatar	2021	4.0	17
Congo, Republic of the	2021	2.5	40	Romania	2021	2.0	62
Cote d'Ivoire	2021	1.1	122	Russia	2021	4.0	18
Croatia	2021	2.2	49	Rwanda	2021	1.4	103
Cuba	2020	4.2	15	Saudi Arabia	2021	6.0	5
Cyprus	2021	2.0	58	Senegal	2021	1.7	79
Czechia	2021	1.4	99	Serbia	2021	1.9	65
Denmark	2021	1.4	100	Seychelles	2021	1.5	94
Djibouti	2019	3.5	24	Singapore	2021	3.2	29
Ecuador	2021	2.0	59	Slovakia	2021	1.7	80
Egypt	2021	1.3	106	Slovenia	2021	1.2	118
El Salvador	2021	1.2	115	Somalia	2019	5.6	7
Equatorial Guinea	2021	1.3	107	South Sudan	2021	2.0	63
Eritrea	2019	10.0	1	Spain	2021	1.0	132
Estonia	2021	2.2	50	Sri Lanka	2021	1.9	66
Eswatini	2021	1.7	74	Sudan	2021	1.0	133
Fiji	2021	1.5	87	Suriname	2019	1.2	119
Finland	2021	2.0	60	Sweden	2021	1.3	110
France	2021	1.9	64	Syria	2019	6.5	4
Gabon	2021	1.7	75	Taiwan	2021	2.1	54
Georgia	2021	1.7	76	Tajikistan	2021	1.2	120
Germany	2021	1.5	88	Tanzania	2021	1.1	125
Greece	2021	3.6	22	Thailand	2021	1.3	111
Guinea	2021	1.5	89	Timor-Leste	2021	1.8	72
Guinea-Bissau	2021	1.8	69	Togo	2021	1.8	73
Guyana	2021	1.0	127	Tonga	2020	2.1	55
Honduras	2021	1.6	82	Trinidad and Tobago	2020	1.0	134
Hungary	2021	1.8	70	Tunisia	2021	3.0	34
India	2021	2.2	51	Turkmenistan	2019	1.9	67
Indonesia	2021	0.8	143	Uganda	2021	2.5	41
Iran	2021	2.3	46	Ukraine	2021	4.0	19
Iraq	2021	3.7	20	United Arab Emirates	2020	5.6	8
Israel	2021	5.0	11	United Kingdom	2021	2.5	42
Italy	2021	1.5	90	Uruguay	2021	2.3	48
Jamaica	2021	1.4	101	Uzbekistan	2019	2.8	35
Japan	2021	1.0	128	Venezuela	2019	5.2	10
Jordan	2021	5.0	12	Vietnam	2021	2.4	45
Kazakhstan	2021	1.0	129	Zambia	2021	1.3	112
Kenya	2021	1.2	116	Zimbabwe	2019	2.6	37

[1] Based on a list of 166 countries for which data is available. Not all countries are shown.

Source: Central Intelligence Agency, The World Factbook, "Country Comparisons, Military and Security," <www.cia.gov/the-world-factbook/references/guide-to-country-comparisons/>, accessed August 2022.

Guide to Sources of Statistics, State Statistical Abstracts, and Foreign Statistical Abstracts

Alphabetically arranged, this guide contains references to important primary sources of statistical information for the United States and other countries. Secondary sources have been included if the information contained in them is presented in a particularly convenient form or if primary sources are not readily available. Nonrecurrent publications presenting compilations or estimates for years later than 2010, or types of data not available in regular series, are also included. Data are also available in press releases.

Valuable information may also be found in state reports and foreign statistical abstracts, which are included at the end of this appendix, and in reports for particular commodities, industries, or similar segments of our economic and social structures, many of which are not included here.

Publications listed under each subject are divided into two main groups: "U.S. Government" and "Nongovernment." The location of the publisher of each report is given except for federal agencies located in Washington, DC. Most federal publications may be purchased from the Superintendent of Documents, U.S. Government Printing Office, Washington, DC, tel. 1-866-512-1800, or at <bookstore.gpo.gov>. In some cases, federal publications may be obtained from the issuing agency.

"Quad." represents "quadrennial," or every four years. "Quin." represents "quinquennial," or every five years. Examples of other internet formats include ebooks, digital maps, XML files, and other kinds of digital files.

Appendix I Table: Sources of Statistics, State Statistical Abstracts, and Foreign Statistical Abstracts

Title	Frequency	Paper	PDF	Excel	HTML	Database or API	Other
U.S. GOVERNMENT							
Administrative Office of the United States Courts							
www.uscourts.gov							
Wiretap Reports	Annual		X	X	X		
Federal Court Management Statistics	Quarterly		X	X	X		
Federal Judicial Caseload Statistics	Annual			X	X		
Judicial Business of the United States Courts	Annual				X		
Statistical Tables for the Federal Judiciary	Semiannual			X			
Agency for International Development							
foreignassistance.gov							
U.S. Overseas Loans and Grants: Obligations and Loan Authorizations	Annual		X			X	X
Army Corps of Engineers							
www.usace.army.mil							
Waterborne Commerce of the United States Waterways and Harbors	Annual		X	X		X	X
Board of Governors of the Federal Reserve System							
www.federalreserve.gov							
Assets and Liabilities of Commercial Banks in the United States H.8	Weekly		X	X		X	X
Consumer Credit G.19	Monthly		X	X	X	X	X
Federal Reserve Bulletin	Periodic	X	X		X		X
Financial Accounts of the United States Z.1	Quarterly		X	X	X	X	X
Foreign Exchange Rates H.10	Weekly			X		X	X
Industrial Production and Capacity Utilization G.17	Monthly		X	X	X	X	X
Money Stock Measures H.6	Monthly			X		X	X
Survey of Consumer Finances	Triennial		X	X		X	X
Bureau of Economic Analysis							
www.bea.gov							
Arts and Cultural Production Satellite Accounts	Ongoing		X	X			
Digital Economy Satellite Account	Ongoing		X	X			
Health Care Satellite Account	Ongoing		X	X			
International Economic Accounts	Ongoing		X	X			
National Economic Accounts	Ongoing		X	X			
Regional Economic Accounts	Ongoing		X	X			
Survey of Current Business	Monthly		X			X	
Travel and Tourism Satellite Accounts	Ongoing		X	X	X		
Bureau of Justice Statistics							
www.bjs.gov							
Background Checks for Firearm Transfers	Periodic		X	X			
Capital Punishment	Annual		X	X			
Census of Problem-Solving Courts	Periodic		X	X			
Census of Publicly Funded Forensic Crime Laboratories	Periodic		X	X			
Census of State and Federal Correctional Facilities	Periodic		X	X			
Federal Justice Statistics	Periodic	X	X	X			
Crimes Against the Elderly, 2003-2013, November 2014	Periodic		X	X			
Criminal Victimization	Annual		X	X			
Federal Law Enforcement Officers	Periodic		X	X			
Felony Defendants in Large Urban Counties, 2009, December 2013	Biennial		X	X			
HIV in Prison and Jail	Quin.		X	X			

See footnotes at end of table.

Appendix I Table: Sources of Statistics, State Statistical Abstracts, and Foreign Statistical Abstracts-Continued.

See headnote on page 893.

Title	Frequency	Paper	PDF	Excel	HTML	Database or API	Other
Homicide in the U.S. Known to Law Enforcement, 1992 to 2011	Periodic		X	X			
Immigration Offenders in the Federal Criminal Justice System, 2010, July 2012	Periodic		X	X			
Indicators of School Crime and Safety	Annual		X	X			
Intimate Partner Violence, 1993-2011, November 2013	Periodic	X	X	X			
Prison and Jail Inmates at Midyear	Annual		X	X			
Jails in Indian Country	Annual		X	X			
Justice Expenditure and Employment Extract Series	Annual		X	X			
Local Police Departments, 2016: Personnel, Policies, and Practices	Periodic		X	X			
Prisoners	Annual		X	X			
Probation and Parole in the United States, 2020	Annual		X	X			
Publicly Funded Forensic Crime Laboratories: Resources and Services, 2014, November 2016	Periodic		X	X			
Prosecutors in State Courts, 2007, December 2011	Periodic		X	X			
Rape and Sexual Assault Among College-Age Females, 1995-2013	Periodic		X	X			
Recidivism of Prisoners Released	Periodic		X	X			
Sheriffs' Offices	Periodic		X	X			
Survey of State Criminal History Information Systems, 2018, November 2020	Biennial		X				
Tribal Crime Data Collection Activities	Annual		X	X			
Victims of Identity Theft	Periodic		X	X			
Bureau of Labor Statistics www.bls.gov							
College Enrollment and Work Activity of High School Graduates	Annual		X		X		
Consumer Expenditure Surveys	Annual		X		X		X
Consumer Price Index (CPI) Databases	Monthly			X		X	
Consumer Price Index (CPI) Detailed Report	Monthly		X				
Contingent and Alternative Employment Arrangements	Periodic		X		X		
Employer Costs for Employee Compensation	Quarterly		X		X		
Employment and Earnings	Monthly				X		
Quarterly Census of Employment and Wages	Quarterly				X		
Employment Characteristics of Families	Annual		X		X		
Employment Cost Index	Quarterly		X		X		
The Employment Situation	Monthly		X		X		
Geographic Profile of Employment and Unemployment	Annual		X	X	X		
Metropolitan Area Employment and Unemployment	Monthly		X		X		
Monthly Labor Review	Monthly		X		X		
National Compensation Survey	Annual		X	X	X		
Occupational Employment and Wages	Annual			X	X		
Occupational Injuries and Illnesses	Annual		X	X	X		
Occupational Projections Data	Biennial			X	X		
Producer Price Index (PPI) Detailed Report	Monthly		X	X			
Productivity and Costs by Industry	Annual		X		X		
Real Earnings	Monthly		X		X		
Regional and State Employment and Unemployment	Monthly		X		X		
Relative Importance of Components in the Consumer Price Indexes	Annual		X	X	X		
U.S. Import and Export Price Indexes	Monthly		X		X		
Union Membership	Annual		X		X		
Usual Weekly Earnings of Wage and Salary Workers	Quarterly		X		X		
Work Experience of the Population	Annual		X		X		
Bureau of Land Management www.blm.gov							
Public Land Statistics	Annual		X				
Census Bureau www.census.gov							
America's Families and Living Arrangements	Annual			X			
Annual Business Survey	Annual			X		X	
Annual Revision of Monthly Retail and Food Services: Sales and Inventories	Annual		X	X			
Annual Revision of Monthly Wholesale Distributors: Sales and Inventories	Annual		X	X			
Annual Survey of Entrepreneurs	Annual			X		X	
Annual Survey of Manufactures	Annual			X		X	
Census of Governments	Quin.		X	X			
Census of Population and Housing Decennial (2020, most recent)	Decennial		X	X		X	
Computer and Internet Access in the United States: 2018	Biennial		X				
Consumer Income and Poverty, P60	Periodic	X	X				
County Business Patterns	Annual		X	X		X	
Current Construction Reports: New Residential Construction and New Residential Sales	Monthly		X	X			
Current Construction Reports: Value of Construction Put in Place, C30	Monthly		X	X			
Current Housing Reports, American Housing Survey for Selected Metropolitan Areas, H170	Biennial					X	
Current Housing Reports, American Housing Survey for the United States, H150	Biennial					X	
Current Housing Reports, Housing Vacancies and Homeownership, H111	Quarterly		X				
Current Housing Reports, Survey of Market Absorption of New Multifamily Units (SOMA)	Quarterly		X	X		X	
Current Housing Reports, Who Can Afford to Buy a Home in 2009, H121	Periodic		X	X			
Current Population Reports (Series P20 and P23)	Periodic		X	X			

See footnotes at end of table.

Appendix I Table: Sources of Statistics, State Statistical Abstracts, and Foreign Statistical Abstracts-Continued.

See headnote on page 893.

Title	Frequency	Paper	PDF	Excel	HTML	Database or API	Other
Economic Census	Quin.			X		X	
Economic Census of Island Areas	Quin.			X			
Fertility of American Women in the United States	Annual		X	X			
Health Insurance Coverage in the United States	Annual		X	X			
Household Economic Studies, P70	Periodic	X	X				
Income and Poverty in the United States	Annual		X	X			
International Data Base	Annual			X		X	
International Population Reports (Series P95)	Periodic		X				
Manufacturing and International Trade Report: 2019	Periodic		X	X			
Manufacturer's Shipments, Inventories, and Orders	Monthly		X	X			
National Survey of Fishing, Hunting, and Wildlife Associated Recreation	Quin.		X				
New York City Housing and Vacancy Survey	Triennial		X	X			
Nonemployer Statistics	Annual			X		X	
Population Estimates and Projections	Annual			X		X	
Quarterly Financial Report for Manufacturing, Mining, and Trade Corporations	Quarterly		X	X			
Service Annual Survey Report	Annual			X			
Survey of Plant Capacity Utilization	Quarterly			X			
U.S. International Trade in Goods and Services (FT900)	Monthly		X	X			
U.S. Trade with Puerto Rico and U.S. Possessions (FT 895)	Annual		X				

Centers for Disease Control and Prevention, Atlanta, Georgia
www.cdc.gov

Title	Frequency	Paper	PDF	Excel	HTML	Database or API	Other
Morbidity and Mortality Weekly Report	Weekly		X		X		
National Immunization Survey (NIS) – Children (19-35 months)	Annual		X				X
Surveillance for Foodborne Disease Outbreaks	Annual		X				

Centers for Medicare and Medicaid Services (CMS)
www.cms.gov

Title	Frequency	Paper	PDF	Excel	HTML	Database or API	Other
CMS Program Statistics	Annual		X	X			
Trustees Report	Annual		X	X			

Central Intelligence Agency
www.cia.gov

Title	Frequency	Paper	PDF	Excel	HTML	Database or API	Other
World Factbook	Annual		X	X	X		X

Coast Guard (See Department of Homeland Security)

Council of Economic Advisers
www.whitehouse.gov/cea

Title	Frequency	Paper	PDF	Excel	HTML	Database or API	Other
Economic Indicators	Monthly	X	X	X			
Economic Report of the President	Annual	X	X	X			

Department of Agriculture, Economic Research Service
www.ers.usda.gov

Title	Frequency	Paper	PDF	Excel	HTML	Database or API	Other
Amber Waves	Monthly						
America's Diverse Family Farms	Annual		X				
Cotton and Wool Yearbook	Annual		X	X			
Feed Grains Yearbook	Annual		X	X			
Food Availability (Per Capita) Data System	Ongoing			X			
Food Expenditures	Annual			X			
Fruit and Tree Nut Yearbook	Annual		X	X			
Household Food Security in the United States	Annual		X				
Oil Crops Yearbook	Annual		X	X			
Rice Yearbook	Annual		X	X			
Situation and Outlook Reports. Issued for: agricultural exports, feed, fruit and tree nuts, livestock and poultry, oil crops, rice, sugar and sweeteners, vegetables, wheat, and world agriculture	Periodic	X	X	X			
Structure and Finances of U.S. Farms: Family Farm Report	Periodic		X				
Sugar and Sweeteners Yearbook	Annual		X	X			
Vegetable and Pulses Yearbook	Annual		X	X			
World Agricultural Supply and Demand Estimates	Monthly		X	X			

Department of Agriculture, Food and Nutrition Service
www.fns.usda.gov

Title	Frequency	Paper	PDF	Excel	HTML	Database or API	Other
Characteristics of Supplemental Nutrition Assistance Program Households	Annual		X				
WIC Participant and Program Characteristics	Biennial	X	X				

Department of Agriculture, Foreign Agricultural Service
www.fas.usda.gov

Title	Frequency	Paper	PDF	Excel	HTML	Database or API	Other
Livestock and Poultry World Markets and Trade	Quarterly		X				

Department of Agriculture, National Agricultural Statistics Service
www.nass.usda.gov

Title	Frequency	Paper	PDF	Excel	HTML	Database or API	Other
Agricultural Chemical Usage	Periodic			X			
Agricultural Statistics	Annual	X	X	X		X	
Catfish Production	Semiannual		X	X			
Cattle	Semiannual		X	X			
Census of Agriculture	Quin.		X	X			
Census of Agriculture: Organic Survey	Periodic		X	X			
Cherry Production	Annual		X	X			
Chickens and Eggs	Monthly		X	X			
Citrus Fruits	Annual		X	X			
Cranberries	Annual		X	X			
Crop Production	Monthly		X	X			
Crop Progress	Weekly		X	X			

See footnotes at end of table.

Title	Frequency	Paper	Internet				
			PDF	Excel	HTML	Database *or API*	Other
Crop Values	Annual		X	X			
Dairy Products	Monthly		X	X			
Farm Labor	Semiannual		X	X			
Farms and Land in Farms	Annual		X	X			
Floriculture Crops	Annual		X				
Agricultural Land Values	Annual		X	X			
Livestock Slaughter	Monthly		X	X			
Meat Animals Production, Disposition, and Income	Annual		X	X			
Milk Production	Monthly		X	X			
Milk Production, Disposition, and Income	Annual		X	X			
Noncitrus Fruits and Nuts	Semiannual		X	X			
Stock Reports. Stocks of grain, peanuts, potatoes, and rice	Periodic		X	X			
Trout Production	Annual		X	X			
Turkey Hatchery	Monthly		X	X			
Turkeys Raised	Annual		X	X			
Usual Planting and Harvesting Dates	Periodic		X	X			
Vegetables	Periodic		X	X			
Weekly Weather and Crop Bulletin	Weekly		X	X			
Winter Wheat and Rye Seedlings	Annual		X	X			
Winter Wheat Seedlings	Annual		X	X			
Department of Agriculture, Natural Resources Conservation Service www.nrcs.usda.gov							
National Resources Inventory	Periodic		X	X			
Department of Defense www.defense.gov							
Base Structure Report: A Summary of the Real Property Inventory	Annual		X				
Demographics Report, Profile of the Military Community	Annual		X			X	
Department of Defense, Defense Manpower Data Center dwp.dmdc.osd.mil/dwp/app/dod-data-reports/workforce-reports							
Personnel Statistics	Periodic		X				X
Department of Defense, Defense Security Cooperation Agency www.dsca.mil/resources/dsca-historical-sales-book							
Historical Sales Book	Annual		X				
Department of Education www.ed.gov							
Annual Report for Federal Student Aid	Annual		X				
Federal Campus-Based Programs Data Book	Annual			X			
Federal Pell Grant Program, End of Year Report	Annual		X	X			
Department of Energy, Oak Ridge National Laboratory tedb.ornl.gov							
Transportation Energy Data Book	Annual		X	X			
Department of Health and Human Services www.hhs.gov							
Health Care Fraud and Abuse Control Program Annual Report	Annual		X				
Profile of Older Americans	Annual		X	X			
Department of Homeland Security www.dhs.gov							
Budget in Brief	Annual		X				
Entry/Exit Overstay Report	Annual		X				
Department of Homeland Security, Coast Guard www.uscg.mil							
State of the Coast Guard	Annual		X				X
Department of Homeland Security, Office of Immigration Statistics www.dhs.gov/immigration-statistics							
Yearbook of Immigration Statistics	Annual		X	X			
Department of Housing and Urban Development www.hud.gov							
National Housing Market Summary	Quarterly		X		X		
Department of Justice www.justice.gov							
Asset Forfeiture Fund Report to Congress	Annual		X		X		
Department of Justice, Bureau of Alcohol, Tobacco, Firearms and Explosives www.atf.gov							
Firearms Commerce in the U.S. [Annual Firearms Manufacturing and Export Report]	Annual		X	X			
Firearms Trace Data (by State)	Annual			X	X		
Department of Labor www.dol.gov							
Agency Financial Report	Annual		X				
Annual Performance Report	Annual		X				
Health Insurance Coverage Bulletin	Periodic		X				X
Retirement Bulletins	Periodic		X	X			X
Department of State www.state.gov							

See footnotes at end of table.

Title	Frequency	Paper	Internet				
			PDF	Excel	HTML	Database *or API*	Other
Country Reports on Terrorism	Annual		X		X		
United States Contributions to International Organizations	Annual		X				
Annex of Statistical Information: Country Reports on Terrorism	Annual		X		X		
Department of Transportation							
www.dot.gov							
Air Travel Consumer Report	Monthly		X				
Annual U.S Domestic Average Itinerary Fare in Current and Constant Dollars	Annual				X		
National Transportation Statistics	Quarterly	X	X	X			
Transportation Statistics Annual Report	Annual		X				
U.S. International Air Passenger and Freight Statistics	Quarterly		X	X			
Department of the Treasury, Alcohol and Tobacco Tax and Trade Bureau							
www.ttb.gov							
Tobacco Products Monthly Statistical Releases	Monthly		X	X			
Department of the Treasury, Bureau of the Fiscal Service							
www.fiscal.treasury.gov							
Combined Statement of Receipts, Outlays, and Balances	Annual		X	X			
Financial Report of the United States Government	Annual	X	X	X			
Monthly Statement of the Public Debt of the United States	Monthly		X	X	X		
Monthly Treasury Statement of Receipts and Outlays of the United States Government	Monthly		X	X			
Treasury Bulletin	Quarterly	X	X				
Department of Veterans Affairs							
www.va.gov							
Annual Benefits Report	Annual		X				
Annual Performance Plan and Report	Annual		X				
Compensation and Pension Data by County	Annual			X			
Employment and Training Administration							
www.dol.gov/agencies/eta							
Unemployment Insurance Weekly Claims	Weekly		X	X	X		
Energy Information Administration							
www.eia.gov							
Annual Coal Report	Annual		X	X			
Annual Energy Outlook	Annual		X	X		X	X
Electric Power Annual	Annual		X	X			
Electric Power Monthly	Monthly		X	X			
Electric Sales, Revenue and Average Price	Annual		X	X			
International Energy Outlook	Annual		X	X			
International Energy Statistics portal	Ongoing		X	X			
Monthly Energy Review	Monthly		X	X			
Petroleum Marketing Monthly	Monthly		X				
Petroleum Supply Annual	Annual		X	X			
Petroleum Supply Monthly	Monthly		X	X			
Quarterly Coal Report	Quarterly		X	X			
Residential Energy Consumption Survey	Quad.		X	X			
State Electricity Profiles	Annual		X	X	X		
State Energy Data System Reports	Annual		X	X	X		
U.S. Crude Oil and Natural Gas Proved Reserves	Annual			X			
Weekly Coal Production	Weekly			X		X	
Environmental Protection Agency							
www.epa.gov							
Air Quality Statistics Report	Annual				X		
Clean Watersheds Needs Survey	Quad.		X	X		X	
Drinking Water Infrastructure Needs Survey and Assessment	Quad.		X				
National Water Quality Inventory Report to Congress	Periodic		X				
Toxics Release Inventory National Analysis	Annual		X	X		X	
UST Performance Measures	Semiannual		X				
Export-Import Bank of the United States							
www.exim.gov							
Annual Report	Annual		X				
Report to the U.S. Congress on Global Export Credit Competition and the Export-Import Bank of the United States	Annual		X				
Farm Credit Administration							
www.fca.gov							
Annual Report on the Farm Credit System	Annual		X				
Federal Bureau of Investigation							
www.fbi.gov/services/cjis/ucr							
Crime in the United States	Annual		X	X			
Hate Crime Statistics	Annual		X	X			
Law Enforcement Officers Killed and Assaulted	Annual		X	X		X	
Federal Communications Commission							
www.fcc.gov							
Annual Assessment of the Status of Competition in the Market for the Delivery of Video Programming	Annual		X				X
International Telecommunications Traffic and Revenue Data Report	Periodically		X	X			
Internet Access Services	Semiannual		X				X
Report on Cable Industry Prices	Periodically		X				
Voice Telephone Services Report	Semiannual		X	X			X

See footnotes at end of table.

Appendix I Table: Sources of Statistics, State Statistical Abstracts, and Foreign Statistical Abstracts-Continued.

See headnote on page 893.

Title	Frequency	Paper	PDF	Excel	HTML	Database or API	Other
Federal Deposit Insurance Corporation							
www.fdic.gov							
Annual Report	Annual		X		X		
FDIC Survey of Unbanked and Underbanked Households	Biennial		X	X	X		
FDIC Quarterly	Quarterly		X	X			
Historical Bank Data	Annual					X	
Quarterly Banking Profile	Quarterly		X	X			
Banking Data & Statistics	Quarterly					X	
Summary of Deposits	Annual				X	X	
Federal Highway Administration							
www.fhwa.dot.gov							
Highway Statistics	Annual		X				X
Federal Railroad Administration							
safetydata.fra.dot.gov/OfficeofSafety/default.aspx							
Railroad Safety Statistics	Annual		X	X	X		X
Forest Service							
www.fs.usda.gov							
Land Areas of the National Forest System	Annual		X		X		
RPA Assessment Tables	Periodic		X	X			
U.S. Timber Production, Trade, Consumption, and Price Statistics	Periodic		X				
General Services Administration							
www.gsa.gov							
Federal Real Property Profile	Annual			X			
Geological Survey							
www.usgs.gov							
Estimated Use of Water in the United States	Quin.		X	X			X
Mineral Commodity Summaries	Annual		X	X			
Mineral Industry Surveys	Periodic		X	X			
Minerals Yearbook	Annual	X	X	X			
Internal Revenue Service							
www.irs.gov/statistics							
Corporation Income Tax Returns	Annual		X	X			
Individual Income Tax Returns	Annual		X	X			
IRS Data Book	Annual		X	X			
Statistics of Income Bulletin	Quarterly		X	X			
International Trade Administration, National Travel and Tourism Office							
www.trade.gov/national-travel-and-tourism-office							
U.S. Travel and Tourism Statistics	Annual	X		X		X	X
International Trade Commission							
www.usitc.gov							
Interactive Tariff and Trade Dataweb	Ongoing					X	X
Recent Trends in U.S. Services Trade	Annual		X			X	
Library of Congress							
www.loc.gov							
Annual Report	Annual		X				
Maritime Administration							
www.maritime.dot.gov							
Annual Report to Congress	Annual		X				
U.S. Waterborne Foreign Trade	Annual			X			
Vessel Calls	Annual			X			
Mine Safety and Health Administration							
www.msha.gov							
Mine Injuries and Worktime	Quarterly		X				
National Aeronautics and Space Administration							
www.nasa.gov							
Annual Procurement Report	Annual		X				
National Center for Education Statistics							
www.nces.ed.gov							
After the Post-9/11 GI Bill: A Profile of Military Service Members and Veterans Enrolled in Undergraduate and Graduate Education	Periodic		X				
Career and Technical Education Programs in Public School Districts	Annual		X				
Characteristics of Private Schools in the United States	Annual		X				
The Condition of Education	Annual		X	X	X		
Digest of Education Statistics	Annual		X	X	X		
Indicators of School Crime and Safety	Annual		X				
National Teacher and Principal Survey	Periodic		X	X	X		
Profile and Financial Aid Estimates of Graduate Students	Quad.		X			X	X
Programs and Services for High School English Learners in Public School Districts	Annual		X				
The Nation's Report Card	Periodic		X	X		X	
Trends in Undergraduate Nonfederal Grant and Scholarship Aid by Demographic and Enrollment Characteristics	Quad.		X			X	X
Trends in Pell Grant Receipt and the Characteristics of Pell Grant Recipients	Quad.		X			X	X
Projections of Education Statistics	Annual		X	X	X		
Status and Trends in the Education of Racial and Ethnic Groups	Irregular		X		X		
Trends in High School Dropout and Completion Rates							

See footnotes at end of table.

Title	Frequency	Paper	PDF	Excel	HTML	Database or API	Other
in the United States	Annual			X	X		
National Center for Health Statistics							
www.cdc.gov/nchs							
Health, United States	Annual		X	X			
National Health and Nutrition Examination Survey	Ongoing		X	X	X		X
National Health Interview Survey	Ongoing		X	X			X
National Health Statistics Reports	Periodic		X				
National Vital Statistics Reports	Periodic		X				
Vital and Health Statistics:							
Series 3: Analytical and Epidemiological Studies	Irregular		X				
Series 11: Health and Nutrition Examination Survey Statistics	Irregular		X				
Series 13: Data on Health Resources Utilization	Irregular		X				
Series 20: Data on Mortality	Irregular		X				
Series 21: Data on Natality, Marriage, and Divorce	Irregular		X				
Series 23: Data from the National Survey of Family Growth	Irregular		X				
National Credit Union Administration							
www.ncua.gov							
Annual Report	Annual		X				
Call Report Quarterly Summary Reports	Quarterly		X	X			X
National Endowment for the Arts							
www.arts.gov							
Annual Report	Annual		X				
Appropriations Request	Annual		X				
National Endowment for the Humanities							
www.neh.gov							
Annual Report	Annual		X				
Appropriations Request	Annual		X				
National Guard Bureau							
www.nationalguard.mil							
Posture Statement	Annual		X				
National Highway Traffic Safety Administration							
www.nhtsa.gov							
Traffic Safety Facts	Annual		X	X	X		
National Oceanic and Atmospheric Administration							
www.noaa.gov							
Climatic Data for the World	Monthly		X			X	X
Comparative Climatic Data	Annual						X
Fisheries of the United States	Annual		X	X		X	
Our Living Oceans	Periodic		X				
Storm Data	Monthly		X	X		X	
Tornado Summaries	Monthly					X	
U.S. Climate Normals	Decennial	X	X	X		X	
National Park Service							
www.nps.gov							
National Park Statistical Abstract	Annual	X	X				
National Science Foundation							
ncsesdata.nsf.gov/home							
Academic Institutional Profiles	Annual			X	X		
Academic Research and Development Expenditures	Annual		X	X			
Characteristics of Doctoral Scientists and Engineers in the United States	Biennial		X	X			
Characteristics of Recent Science/Engineering Graduates	Biennial		X	X			
Doctorate Recipients from U.S. Universities	Annual		X	X			
Federal Funds for Research and Development	Annual		X	X			
Federal Research and Development Funding by Budget Function	Annual		X	X			
Federal Science and Engineering Support to Universities, Colleges, and Nonprofit Institutions	Annual		X	X			
Graduate Students and Postdoctorates in Science and Engineering	Annual		X	X			
National Patterns of Research and Development Resources	Annual		X	X			
Research and Development in Industry	Annual		X	X			
Science and Engineering Degrees	Biennial		X	X			
Science and Engineering Degrees, by Race/Ethnicity of Recipients	Biennial		X	X			
Science and Engineering Doctorate Awards	Annual		X	X			
Science and Engineering Indicators	Biennial		X	X		X	
Science and Engineering State Profiles	Annual		X	X		X	
Scientific and Engineering Research Facilities	Biennial		X	X			
Women, Minorities, and Persons with Disabilities in Science and Engineering	Biennial		X	X			
National Transportation Safety Board							
www.ntsb.gov							
Annual Summary of US Civil Aviation Accidents	Annual		X	X			
Office of Juvenile Justice and Delinquency Prevention							
www.ojjdp.gov							
Highlights of the National Youth Gang Survey	Annual	X	X		X		
Juvenile Arrests	Annual		X	X			
Juvenile Offenders and Victims	Periodic	X	X	X			
Office of Management and Budget							
www.whitehouse.gov/omb							

See footnotes at end of table.

Appendix I Table: Sources of Statistics, State Statistical Abstracts, and Foreign Statistical Abstracts-Continued.

See headnote on page 893.

| Title | Frequency | Paper | Internet | | | | |
			PDF	Excel	HTML	Database or API	Other
The Budget of the United States Government	Annual	X	X	X			
Office of Personnel Management							
www.opm.gov							
Common Characteristics of the Government	Annual		X				
Executive Branch Retirement Statistics	Periodic		X				
Office of the Clerk, U.S. House of Representatives							
www.clerk.house.gov							
Statistics of the Presidential and Congressional Election	Biennial		X				
Patent and Trademark Office							
www.uspto.gov							
All Technologies (Utility Patents)	Annual				X		
Patent Counts by Country/State and Year	Annual				X		
Patenting Trends in the United States	Annual				X		
Railroad Retirement Board							
www.rrb.gov							
Annual Report	Annual		X				
Quarterly Benefit Statistics	Quarterly		X				
Securities and Exchange Commission							
www.sec.gov							
Select SEC and Market Data	Annual		X				
Small Business Administration							
www.sba.gov							
Economic Bulletin	Biannual		X				
Loan Program Performance Reports	Annual		X				
Quarterly Bulletin	Quarterly		X				
Small Business Lending in the United States	Annual		X	X			
Small Business Profiles for States and Territories	Annual		X				
Social Security Administration							
www.ssa.gov							
Annual Statistical Report on the Social Security Disability Insurance Program	Annual		X	X	X		
Annual Statistical Supplement to the Social Security Bulletin	Annual		X	X	X		
Congressional Statistics	Annual		X	X	X		
Fast Facts & Figures about Social Security	Annual		X				
Income of the Population 55 and over	Biennially		X	X	X		
OASDI Beneficiaries by State and County	Annual		X	X	X		
Social Security Bulletin	Quarterly		X				
SSI Annual Statistical Report	Annual		X	X	X		
SSI Recipients by State and County	Annual		X	X	X		
Substance Abuse and Mental Health Services Administration							
www.samhsa.gov							
Behavioral Health Barometer, United States	Annual		X				
National Mental Health Services Survey (N-MHSS)	Annual		X		X		
National Survey on Drug Use and Health (NSDUH)	Annual		X		X		
National Survey on Substance Abuse Treatment Services (N-SSATS)	Annual		X				
U.S. Copyright Office							
www.copyright.gov							
Annual Report	Annual		X				
U.S. Equal Employment Opportunity Commission							
www.eeoc.gov							
Enforcement and Litigation Statistics	Ongoing		X		X		
U.S. Health Resources & Services Administration							
www.hrsa.gov							
Health Center Data Program	Ongoing		X	X	X	X	
U.S. Sentencing Commission							
www.ussc.gov							
Sourcebook of Federal Sentencing Statistics	Annual		X				
NONGOVERNMENT							
Aerospace Industries Association, Arlington, VA							
www.aia-aerospace.org							
Facts & Figures: The U.S. Aerospace & Defense Industry	Annual		X				
Airlines for America, Washington, DC							
www.airlines.org							
American Council of Life Insurers, Washington, DC							
www.acli.com							
Life Insurers Fact Book	Annual		X				
American Dental Association, Chicago, IL							
www.ada.org							
Survey of Dental Practice	Annual						X
American Forest and Paper Association, Washington, DC							
www.afandpa.org							
Monthly Exports/Imports Report	Monthly		X				
Monthly Statistics of Paper, Paperboard and Wood Pulp	Monthly		X				X
Paper Industry Annual Capacity and Fiber Consumption	Annual		X				
Paper Industry Annual Statistical Summary	Annual		X				

See footnotes at end of table.

Title	Frequency	Paper	Internet				
			PDF	Excel	HTML	Database *or API*	Other
American Gas Association, Washington, DC www.aga.org							
Gas Facts	Annual	X	X				
American Iron and Steel Institute, Washington, DC www.steel.org							
Annual Statistical Report	Annual	X	X				
American Osteopathic Association, Chicago, IL www.osteopathic.org							
Osteopathic Medical Profession Report	Annual		X				
American Public Transportation Association, Washington, DC www.apta.com							
Public Transportation Fact Book	Annual		X	X			
American Society for Aesthetic Plastic Surgery www.theaestheticsociety.org							
Cosmetic Surgery National Data Bank Statistics	Annual		X				
Association of American Medical Colleges www.aamc.org							
Physician Specialty Data Report	Biennial		X		X		
State Physician Workforce Data Book	Biennial		X				
Association of American Railroads, Washington, DC www.aar.org							
Analysis of Class I Railroads	Annual	X	X	X			
Freight Commodity Statistics	Annual	X	X	X			
Berman Jewish Data Bank, Storrs, CT www.jewishdatabank.org							
Jewish Population in the United States	Annual		X	X			
Bloomberg BNA, Washington, DC www.bloombergindustry.com							
BNA's Labor and Employment Outlook Report	Annual		X				
BNA's Job Absence and Turnover Report	Quarterly		X				
Directory of U.S. Labor Organizations	Annual	X					
Source Book on Collective Bargaining	Annual	X					
Union Membership and Earnings Data Book	Annual	X					
Brookings Institution, Washington, DC www.brookings.edu							
Vital Statistics on Congress	Biennial		X	X			
Chronicle of Higher Education, Inc., Washington, DC www.chronicle.com							
Almanac of Higher Education	Annual	X	X	X			
College Board, New York, NY www.collegeboard.org							
Suite of Assessments Annual Report	Annual		X				
cmdty® by barchart, Chicago, IL https://www.barchart.com/cmdty							
Commodity Index Report	Monthly						
Commodity Indexes	Ongoing		X	X			
cmdty Yearbook®	Annual	X					
End of Day Data	Daily		X				
Conference Board, New York, NY www.conference-board.org							
Business Cycle Indicators	Monthly		X				X
International Comparisons of Annual Labor Force Statistics	Annual		X				X
International Comparisons of Hourly Compensation Costs for Production Workers in Manufacturing	Annual		X				X
International Comparisons of Manufacturing Productivity and Unit Labor Cost Trends	Annual		X				X
Performance: Productivity, Employment, and Growth in the World's Economies	Irregular		X				
Congressional Quarterly (CQ) Press, Washington, DC https://us.sagepub.com/en-us/nam/cqpress							
America Votes	Biennial	X					X
Council of State Governments, Lexington, KY www.csg.org							
Book of the States	Annual		X				
Dodge Data & Analytics, New York, NY https://www.construction.com							
Construction Potential Bulletins	Monthly		X				
Dow Jones and Company, New York, NY www.dowjones.com							
Wall Street Journal	Daily	X					X
Curated Experiences Group, Fountain Valley, CA www.editorandpublisher.com							
Editor and Publisher	Monthly	X					X
Newspaper Databook	Annual	X					
Edison Electric Institute, Washington, DC							

See footnotes at end of table.

Title	Frequency	Paper	Internet				
			PDF	Excel	HTML	Database or API	Other
www.eei.org							
Statistical Yearbook of the Electric Power Industry	Annual		X				
Euromonitor International, London, England							
www.euromonitor.com							
Consumer Lifestyles in the US	Annual		X				
Federal National Mortgage Association, Washington, DC							
www.fanniemae.com							
Annual Report on Form 10-K	Annual		X				
Food and Agriculture Organization of the United Nations, Rome, Italy							
www.fao.org							
World Fertilizer Trends and Outlook	Annual		X				
FAO Statistical Yearbook: World Food and Agriculture	Annual		X		X		X
FAO Yearbook: Fishery and Aquaculture Statistics	Periodic	X	X				
Yearbook of Forest Products	Annual		X				
General Aviation Manufacturers Association, Washington, DC							
www.gama.aero							
General Aviation Aircraft Shipment Report	Quarterly		X				
General Aviation Manufacturers Association Annual Report	Annual		X				
Giving USA Foundation, Chicago, IL							
www.givingusa.org							
Giving USA	Annual	X	X			X	X
Guttmacher Institute, New York, NY							
www.guttmacher.org							
Perspectives on Sexual and Reproductive Health	Quarterly		X				
Health Forum, an American Hospital Association Company, Chicago, IL							
www.ahadata.com							
AHA Annual Survey Data Base	Annual					X	X
AHA Hospital Statistics	Annual					X	X
IHS Global, Inc., Englewood, CO							
www.janes.com							
IHS Jane's All the World's Aircraft: Development & Production	Annual	X					X
IHS Jane's Defence: C4ISR & Mission Systems	Annual	X					X
IHS Jane's Fighting Ships	Annual	X					X
IHS Jane's Flight Avionics	Annual	X					X
IHS Jane's Land Warfare Platforms: Armoured Fighting Vehicles	Annual	X					X
IHS Jane's Land Warfare Platforms: Logistics, Support & Unmanned	Annual	X					X
IHS Jane's Simulation & Training Systems	Annual	X					X
IHS Jane's Space Systems & Industry	Annual	X					X
IHS Jane's Weapons: Air-Launched	Annual	X					X
IHS Jane's Weapons: Infantry	Annual	X					X
Independent Petroleum Association of America, Washington, DC							
www.ipaa.org							
IPAA Oil & Gas Producing Industry in Your State	Annual	X	X				
U.S. Petroleum Statistics	Annual	X	X				
Information Today, Inc., Medford, NJ							
informationtodayinc.com							
American Library Directory	Annual	X					
Library and Book Trade Almanac (formerly The Bowker Annual)	Annual	X					
Institute for Criminal Justice Ethics, New York, NY							
www.jjay.cuny.edu/artificial-intelligence-and-ethics							
Criminal Justice Ethics	Triannual		X				
Insurance Information Institute, New York, NY							
www.iii.org							
Triple-I Insurance Facts	Annual		X				
Inter-American Development Bank, Washington, DC							
www.iadb.org							
Annual Report	Annual		X				
Development in the Americas	Annual		X				X
International Air Transport Association, Montreal, Canada and Geneva, Switzerland							
www.iata.org							
World Air Transport Statistics	Annual	X	X				X
International City Management Association, Washington, DC							
www.icma.org							
ICMA Chief Administrative Officers Salary & Compensation Survey	Annual		X				
Municipal Year Book	Annual		X				
International Labour Organization, Geneva, Switzerland							
www.ilo.org							
World Employment and Social Outlook	Annual	X	X				
International Monetary Fund, Washington, DC							
www.imf.org							
Annual Report	Annual		X				
Balance of Payments and International Investment Position Statistics	Monthly		X	X		X	X
Direction of Trade Statistics	Quarterly		X	X		X	X

See footnotes at end of table.

Title	Frequency	Paper	PDF	Excel	HTML	Database or API	Other
Government Finance Statistics	Annual			X		X	X
International Financial Statistics	Monthly		X	X		X	X
International Telecommunication Union, Geneva, Switzerland							
www.itu.int/home/index.html							
ITU Yearbook of Statistics	Annual		X				
World Telecommunication/ICT Indicators	Annual	X	X			X	X
Investment Company Institute, Washington, DC							
www.ici.org							
Investment Company Fact Book	Annual		X	X			
Joint Center for Housing Studies of Harvard University, Cambridge, MA							
www.jchs.harvard.edu							
The State of the Nation's Housing	Annual		X	X			X
Media Source, Inc., New York, NY							
www.mediasourceinc.com							
Library Journal	Biweekly	X			X		X
School Library Journal	Monthly	X			X		X
National Academy of Social Insurance, Washington, DC							
www.nasi.org							
Workers Compensation: Benefits, Coverage, and Costs	Annual		X				
National Association of Home Builders, Washington, DC							
www.nahb.org							
HousingEconomics.com (online subscription)	Ongoing						X
National Association of Latino Elected and Appointed Officials, Los Angeles, CA							
www.naleo.org							
National Directory of Latino Elected Officials	Annual		X				
National Association of Realtors, Chicago, IL							
www.nar.realtor							
Economist's Outlook	Daily				X		X
NAR Member Profile	Annual		X				
NAR Profile of Home Buyer and Sellers	Annual		X				
National Association of State Budget Officers, Washington, DC							
www.nasbo.org							
Fiscal Survey of the States	Semiannual	X	X				
State Expenditure Report	Annual	X	X				
National Association of State Park Directors, Raleigh, NC							
www.stateparks.org							
Statistical Report of State Park Operations: Annual Information Exchange	Annual	X	X	X			X
National Catholic Educational Association, Arlington, VA							
www.ncea.org							
The Annual Financial Report	Annual	X					
U.S. Catholic Elementary and Secondary Schools: The Annual Statistical Report on Schools, Enrollment and Staffing	Biennial	X					
National Education Association, Washington, DC							
www.nea.org							
Rankings & Estimates: Rankings of the States and Estimates of School Statistics	Annual		X				
National Fire Protection Association, Quincy, MA							
www.nfpa.org							
National Fire Protection Association (NFPA) Journal	Bimonthly				X		X
National Golf Foundation, Jupiter, FL							
www.ngf.org							
Golf Facilities in the U.S.	Annual						X
National Restaurant Association, Washington, DC							
www.restaurant.org							
Restaurant Industry 2030	Recurring		X				
Restaurant Operations Report	Recurring	X	X				
Restaurant Performance Index	Monthly		X				
Restaurant Trendmapper (online subscription)	Ongoing						X
State of the Industry	Annual		X				
National Safety Council, Itasca, IL							
injuryfacts.nsc.org							
Injury Facts	Annual		X	X	X		
National Sporting Goods Association, Mount Prospect, IL							
www.nsga.org							
Sports Participation in the U.S.	Annual		X				
Organisation for Economic Cooperation and Development, Paris, France							
www.oecd-ilibrary.org							
CO2 Emissions From Fuel Combustion	Annual		X	X			
Coal Information	Annual		X	X			
Digital Economy Outlook	Biennial	X	X		X		
Education at a Glance: OECD Indicators	Annual	X	X		X		
Electricity Information	Annual		X	X			

See footnotes at end of table.

Appendix I Table: Sources of Statistics, State Statistical Abstracts, and Foreign Statistical Abstracts-Continued.

See headnote on page 893.

Title	Frequency	Paper	Internet PDF	Internet Excel	Internet HTML	Internet Database or API	Internet Other
Energy Prices and Taxes	Quarterly		X	X			
Environmental Outlook	Periodic		X	X			
Financial Accounts	Annual	X	X				
Financial Balance Sheets	Annual	X	X				
General Government Accounts	Annual	X	X				
Geographical Distribution of Financial Flows to Developing Countries	Annual	X	X				
International Migration Outlook	Annual	X	X		X		
International Trade by Commodity Statistics	Ongoing		X	X	X		
ITF Transport Outlook	Biennial	X	X	X	X		
Main Economic Indicators	Monthly		X	X			
Main Science and Technology Indicators	Semiannual		X	X	X		
National Accounts at a Glance	Annual	X	X	X	X		
National Accounts of OECD Countries	Annual	X	X	X	X		
Issue 1: Main Aggregates	Annual	X	X	X	X		
Issue 2: Detailed Tables	Annual	X	X	X	X		
Natural Gas Information	Annual		X	X			
Nuclear Energy Data	Annual		X				
OECD Communications Outlook	Biennial	X	X	X	X		
OECD Economic Outlook	Semiannual	X	X	X	X		
OECD Economic Surveys	Periodic		X				
OECD Employment Outlook	Annual		X		X		
OECD Factbook	Annual	X	X	X	X		
OECD-FAO Agricultural Outlook	Annual	X	X	X	X		
OECD Health Statistics	Annual		X				
OECD Insurance Statistics	Annual	X	X	X	X		
OECD International Development Statistics	Annual		X	X	X		
OECD Quarterly International Trade Statistics	Quarterly		X	X	X		
OECD Review of Fisheries: Policies and Summary Statistics	Annual	X	X				
OECD Science, Technology, and Innovation Outlook	Biennial	X	X	X	X		
OECD Science, Technology and R&D Statistics	Ongoing			X			
OECD Society at a Glance	Biennial	X	X	X	X		
OECD Territorial Reviews	Periodic	X	X		X		
Oil Information	Annual		X	X			
Oil, Gas, Coal, and Electricity Quarterly Statistics	Quarterly		X				
Pensions at a Glance	Biennial	X	X	X	X		
PISA (OECD Programme for International Student Assessment)	Periodic						
Quarterly National Accounts	Quarterly		X				
Revenue Statistics	Annual	X	X	X	X		
Taxing Wages	Annual	X	X	X	X		
Uranium: Resources Production and Demand	Biennial		X				
World Energy Balances	Annual		X	X			
World Energy Outlook	Annual		X	X			
World Energy Statistics	Annual		X				
Industrial Endeavor Business Media, Ft. Atkinson, WI industrial.endeavorb2b.com							
Offshore	Monthly	X	X				X
Oil and Gas Journal	Weekly	X	X				X
Pew Research Center www.pewinternet.org							
Book Reading	Periodic		X				X
Home Broadband	Periodic		X				X
Libraries and Learning	Periodic		X				X
Social Media Update	Periodic		X				X
Technology Device Ownership	Periodic		X				X
Teens, Social Media & Technology	Periodic		X				X
PWxyz, LLC, New York, NY www.publishersweekly.com							
Publishers Weekly	Weekly	X					X
Radio Advertising Bureau, Dallas, TX www.rab.com							
Why Radio: Fact Sheets	Ongoing				X		
Regional Airline Association, Washington, DC www.raa.org							
Regional Airlines Association Annual Report	Annual						X
Securities Industry and Financial Markets Association, New York, NY www.sifma.org							
Capital Markets Fact Book	Annual		X	X			
U.S. Foreign Activity Report	Semiannual		X	X			
Skyhorse Publishing, New York, NY www.skyhorsepublishing.com							
The World Almanac and Book of Facts	Annual	X					
Standard and Poor's Financial Services LLC, New York, NY www.spglobal.com/ratings							
Analyst's Handbook	Annual	X					
Corporation Records: Corporate Description	Monthly						X
Corporation Records: Daily News	Daily						X
Daily Stock Price Records	Quarterly						X
United Nations Conference on Trade and Development, Geneva, Switzerland							

See footnotes at end of table.

Appendix I Table: Sources of Statistics, State Statistical Abstracts, and Foreign Statistical Abstracts-Continued.

See headnote on page 893.

Title	Frequency	Paper	PDF	Excel	HTML	Database or API	Other
unctad.org							
Development and Globalization: Facts and Figures	Periodic		X				
Handbook of Statistics	Annual		X				
United Nations Statistics Division, New York, NY							
unstats.un.org/UNSDWebsite							
Demographic Yearbook (Series R)	Annual		X	X			X
Energy Balances and Electricity Profiles (Series W)	Annual	X	X				
Energy Statistics Yearbook (Series J)	Annual	X	X				
Industrial Commodity Statistics Yearbook	Annual	X	X				
International Trade Statistics Yearbook (Series G)	Annual		X				
Monthly Bulletin of Statistics (Series Q)	Monthly		X	X		X	X
National Accounts Statistics: Analysis of Main Aggregates	Annual			X		X	X
National Accounts Statistics: Main Aggregates and Detailed Tables (Series X)	Annual	X	X				
Population and Vital Statistics Report (Series A)	Annual		X				
Statistical Yearbook	Annual		X	X			X
World Statistics Pocketbook (Series V)	Annual		X				
The World's Women	Quin.		X	X		X	X
University of Albany, School of Criminal Justice, Hindelang Criminal Justice Research Center							
www.albany.edu/sourcebook/							
Sourcebook of Criminal Justice Statistics, 2013 (Discontinued)	Annual		X	X	X		
University of Michigan, Institute for Social Research, Inter-University Consortium for Political and Social Research, Ann Arbor, MI							
www.icpsr.umich.edu/icpsrweb/ICPSR/studies/8475							
American National Election Studies Cumulative Data File	Biennial						X
Warren Communications News, Washington, DC							
www.warren-news.com							
Television and Cable Factbook	Ongoing						X
World Bank Group, Washington, DC							
www.worldbank.org							
Atlas of Global Development	Periodic		X				
Global Development Finance	Annual		X				X
The Little Data Book	Annual		X				
World Development Indicators	Annual		X				X
World Health Organization, Geneva, Switzerland							
www.who.int							
World Health Statistics Report	Annual		X	X			
World Trade Organization, Geneva, Switzerland							
www.wto.org							
World Trade Statistical Review	Annual	X	X	X			
STATE STATISTICAL ABSTRACTS FROM UNIVERSITIES							
Pennsylvania State University, Pennsylvania State Data Center, Middletown, PA							
pasdc.hbg.psu.edu							
Pennsylvania Abstract: A Statistical Fact Book	Annual	X		X			X
State University of New York: Nelson A. Rockefeller Institute of Government, Nelson A. Rockefeller Institute of Government, Albany, NY							
www.rockinst.org							
New York State Statistical Yearbook	Annual			X		X	X
University of Florida: Bureau of Economic and Business Research, Gainesville, FL							
www.bebr.ufl.edu							
Florida Statistical Dashboards	Ongoing		X				X
University of Georgia: Selig Center for Economic Growth, Athens, GA							
www.terry.uga.edu/selig							
Georgia Economic Outlook	Annual		X				
University of Kansas: Institute for Policy and Social Research, Lawrence, KS							
ipsr.ku.edu/ksdata/ksah							
Kansas Statistical Abstract	Annual		X	X			
University of Missouri-Columbia: Economic and Policy Analysis Research Center, Columbia, MO							
www.eparc.missouri.edu/publications/archive/archive.html							
Missouri Statistical Data Archive (online)	Ongoing		X				
STATE STATISTICAL ABSTRACT FROM AN ASSOCIATION							
Texas State Historical Association, Austin, TX							
texasalmanac.com							
Texas Almanac	Biennial	X	X				X
STATE STATISTICAL ABSTRACTS FROM STATE AGENCIES							
Hawaii State Department of Business, Economic Development & Tourism, Honolulu, HI							
dbedt.hawaii.gov/economic/databook							

See footnotes at end of table.

Title	Frequency	Paper	Internet				
			PDF	Excel	HTML	Database *or API*	Other
State of Hawaii Data Book	Annual		X				X
Maryland State Data Center, Maryland Department of Planning, Baltimore, MD www.planning.maryland.gov/MSDC/Pages/default.aspx Maryland Statistical Handbook	Periodic		X				
Mississippi Secretary of State www.sos.ms.gov 2016-2020 Mississippi Blue Book	Quad.		X				
South Carolina, Revenue and Fiscal Affairs Office, Columbia, SC rfa.sc.gov/data-research/population-demographics /census-state-data-center South Carolina Census State Data Center	Ongoing			X	X		
INTERNATIONAL STATISTICAL ABSTRACTS FROM A FOREIGN AGENCY							
Austria **Statistik Austria, Vienna** www.statistik.at/en Statistisches Jahrbuch Osterreichs	Annual	X		X		X	
Belgium **Statistics Belgium, Brussels** statbel.fgov.be/en Key Figures	Annual		X	X		X	
Czechia **Czech Statistical Office, Praha** www.czso.cz Statistical Yearbook of the Czech Republic	Annual		X	X			X
Denmark **Statistics Denmark, Copenhagen** www.dst.dk/en Statistical Yearbook (Discontinued)	Annual		X				
Finland **Statistics Finland, Helsinki** www.stat.fi/index_en.html Statistical Yearbook of Finland	Annual		X				X
France **National Institute of Statistics and Economic Studies, Paris** www.insee.fr/en Tableaux de l'Economie Francaise	Annual		X	X	X		X
Germany **Statistisches Bundesamt, Wiesbaden** www.destatis.de/EN/Home/_node.html Statistisches Jahrbuch: Deutschland	Annual		X				
Greece **Hellenic Statistical Authority, Pireus** www.statistics.gr/en/home Greece in Figures	Quarterly		X				
Hungary **Hungarian Central Statistical Office, Budapest** www.ksh.hu/?lang=en Statistical Yearbook of Hungary	Annual	X	X	X			
Ireland **Central Statistics Office, Cork** www.cso.ie/en Statistical Yearbook of Ireland	Annual			X	X		X
Italy **Italian National Institute of Statistics, Rome** www.istat.it/en Annuario Statistico Italiano	Annual	X	X	X			
Japan **Statistics Bureau, Ministry of Internal Affairs and Communications, Tokyo** www.stat.go.jp/english/data/index.html Japan Statistical Yearbook	Annual			X	X		
Korea, South **Statistics Korea, Daejeon** kostat.go.kr/eng Korea Statistical Yearbook	Annual	X					
Luxembourg **Service Central de la Statistique et des Etudes Economiques, Luxembourg** statistiques.public.lu/en.html Luxembourg en Chiffres	Annual		X				
Mexico **Instituto Nacional de Estadística y Geografía, Aguascalientes** en.www.inegi.org.mx							

See footnotes at end of table.

Appendix I Table: Sources of Statistics, State Statistical Abstracts, and Foreign Statistical Abstracts-Continued.

See headnote on page 893.

Title	Frequency	Paper	Internet PDF	Internet Excel	Internet HTML	Internet Database *or API*	Internet Other
Anuario Estadístico y Geográfico de los Estados Unidos Mexicanos	Annual		X	X			
Netherlands **Statistics Netherlands, The Hague** www.cbs.nl/en-gb Trends in the Netherlands	Annual		X				X
New Zealand **Statistics New Zealand, Wellington** www.stats.govt.nz New Zealand Official Yearbook, 2012 (Discontinued)	Biennial		X				
Poland **Central Statistical Office of Poland, Warsaw** www.stat.gov.pl/en/intrastat Concise Statistical Yearbook of Poland Statistical Yearbook of the Republic of Poland	Annual Annual	X X	X X				
Portugal **Statistics Portugal, Lisbon** www.ine.pt Statistical Yearbook of Portugal	Annual		X	X			
Russia **Russian Federation Federal State Statistics Service, Moscow** rosstat.gov.ru Russia in Figures	Annual		X				
Slovakia **Statistical Office of the Slovak Republic, Bratislava** slovak.statistics.sk Statistical Yearbook of the Slovak Republic	Annual	X	X				
Spain **Instituto Nacional de Estadística, Madrid** www.ine.es/en/index.htm Statistical Yearbook of Spain	Annual	X	X	X	X		X
Switzerland **Federal Statistical Office, Neuchâtel** www.bfs.admin.ch/bfs/en/home.html Statistical Yearbook of Switzerland	Annual	X	X				X
Turkey **Turkish Statistical Institute, Ankara** www.tuik.gov.tr/Home/Index Türkiye's Statistics Türkiye in Statistics	Annual Annual	X X	X				
United Kingdom **Office for National Statistics, London** data.gov.uk Annual Abstract of Statistics, 2011 (Discontinued)	Annual				X		

Source: ProQuest research.

Guide to State Statistical Abstracts

This bibliography includes the most recent statistical abstracts for states and island areas published since 2010. For some states, a near equivalent has been listed in substitution for, or in addition to, a statistical abstract. All sources contain statistical tables on a variety of subjects for the state as a whole, its component parts, or both. Internet sites also contain statistical data.

Alabama

University of Alabama, Center for Business and Economic Research, Box 870221, Tuscaloosa, AL 35487-0221. 205-348-6191. Fax: 205-348-2951. Internet site <www.cber.culverhouse.ua.edu>.
Alabama Economic Outlook. Annual. Online.

Alaska

Department of Commerce, Community and Economic Development, P.O. Box 110804, Juneau, AK 99811. 907-465-2510. Fax: 907-465-3767. Internet site <www.commerce.alaska.gov/web/inv>.
The Alaska Economic Performance Report, 2013. Online.
Alaska's Economic Report. Quarterly. Online.

Arizona

University of Arizona, Economic and Business Research Center, Eller College of Management, 1130 East Helen Street, McClelland Hall, Room 103, P.O. Box 210108, Tucson, AZ 85721-0108. 520-621-2155. Internet site <www.azeconomy.org>.
Arizona's Economy. Quarterly. Online.

Arkansas

University of Arkansas at Little Rock, Arkansas Economic Development Institute, 2801 South University Avenue, Little Rock, AR 72204-1099. 501-569-8519. Internet site <www.youraedi.com>.
Arkansas Data Center Online. Online.
Arkansas Personal Income Handbook. Annual. Print and Online.

California

Department of Finance, 915 L Street, Sacramento, CA 95814. 916-445-3274. Internet site <www.dof.ca.gov>.
Finance Bulletin. Monthly. Online.

Colorado

Colorado Department of Local Affairs, Division of Local Government, State Demography Office, 1313 Sherman Street, Room 521, Denver, CO 80203. 303-864-7720. Internet site <demography.dola.colorado.gov>.
State Demography Office Publications and Reports. Online.

Connecticut

CTD Data Collaborative, 10 Constitution Plaza, Hartford, CT 06103. 860-500-1983. Internet site <profiles.ctdata.org>.
Connecticut Town Profiles, 2021. Recurring. Online.

Delaware

Delaware Economic Development Office, 99 Kings Highway, Dover, DE 19901-7305. 302-739-4271. Internet site <www.business.delaware.gov>.
Delaware Data Book, 2017. Online.

District of Columbia

Office of the Chief Technology Officer, 200 I Street SE, Washington, DC 20003. 202-727-2277. Fax: 202-727-6857. Internet site <opendata.dc.gov>.
Open Data Catalog. Online.

Florida

University of Florida, Bureau of Economic and Business Research, P.O. Box 117148, Gainesville, FL 32611. 352-392-0171. Fax: 888-534-2404. Internet site <www.bebr.ufl.edu/>.
Florida Statistical Dashboards. Online.

Georgia

University of Georgia, Terry College of Business, Selig Center for Economic Growth, E201 Ivester Hall, 650 S. Lumpkin Street, Athens, GA 30602-6269. 678-646-9782. Internet site <www.terry.uga.edu/about/selig>.
Georgia Economic Outlook, 2022. Annual. Online.

University of Georgia, Carl Vinson Institute of Government, 201 N. Milledge Avenue, Athens, GA 30602. 706-542-2736. Fax: 706-542-9301. Internet site <www.cviog.uga.edu>.
The Georgia County Guide, 2020. Annual. Print.

Hawaii

Hawaii State Department of Business, Economic Development and Tourism, Research and Economic Analysis Division, Statistics and Data Support Branch, P.O. Box 2359, Honolulu, HI 96804. 808-586-2355. Internet site <www.dbedt.hawaii.gov/economic/databook>.
2021 State of Hawaii Data Book. Annual. Online.

Idaho

University of Idaho Extension, 875 Perimeter Drive. MS 2338, Moscow, ID 83844-2338. 208-885-5883. Fax: 208-885-6654. Internet site <indicatorsidaho.org/>.
Indicators Idaho. Online.

Illinois

University of Illinois, Institute of Government and Public Affairs, MC-037, 1007 W. Nevada Street, Urbana, IL 61801. 217-333-3340. Fax: 217-244-4817. Internet site <www.igpa.uillinois.edu>.

Indiana

Indiana University, Kelley School of Business, Indiana Business Research Center, 1309 E. 10th Street, Suite 4048, Bloomington, IN 47405. 317-274-2147. Internet site <www.stats.indiana.edu>.
STATS Indiana. Online.

Iowa

Iowa State University of Science and Technology: Community Indicators Program, 175 Heady Hall, 518 Farm House Lane, Ames, IA 50011. 515-294-2954. Internet site <www.icip.iastate.edu>.
Community Indicators. Online.

State Library of Iowa, State Data Center, Ola Babcock Miller Building, 1112 East Grand, Des Moines, IA 50319-0233. 800-248-4483. Fax: 515-281-6191. Internet site <www.iowadatacenter.org>.
State Data Center. Online.

Kansas

University of Kansas, Institute for Policy and Social Research, 1541 Lilac Lane, 607 Blake Hall, Lawrence, KS 66045-3129. 785-864-3701. Internet site <www.ipsr.ku.edu/ksdata/ksah>.
Kansas Statistical Abstract, 2021. Online.

Kentucky

Kentucky Cabinet for Economic Development, Old Capitol Annex, 300 West Broadway, Frankfort, KY 40601. 800-626-2930. Fax:502-564-3256. Internet site <www.selectkentucky.com>.

Louisiana

Louisiana State Census Data Center, Office of Electronic Services, 1201 N. Third Street, Suite 2-130, Baton Rouge, LA 70802. 225-219-5987. Fax: 225-219-4994. Internet site <www.louisiana.gov/demographics-and-geography>.

Maine

Department of Administrative and Financial Services, 78 State House Station, Augusta, ME 04330. 207-624-7800. Fax: 207-624-7804. Internet site <www.maine.gov/portal/about_me/statistics.html>.

Maryland

Maryland Department of Planning, 301 W. Preston Street, Suite 1101, Baltimore, MD 21201. 410-767-3219. Internet site <www.planning.maryland.gov/MSDC>.
2020 Maryland Statistical Handbook. Annual. Online.

Massachusetts

Massachusetts State Data Center, University of Massachusetts Donahue Institute, 100 Venture Way, Suite 9, Hadley, MA 01035-9462. 413-545-0001. Fax: 413-545-3420 Internet site <www.donahue.umass.edu/business-groups/economic-public-policy-research/massbenchmarks>.
MassBenchmarks. Online.

Michigan

Michigan Economic Development Corporation, 300 N. Washington Square, Lansing, MI 48913. 1-888-522-0103. Internet site <www.michiganbusiness.org>.

Minnesota

Minnesota Department of Employment and Economic Development, 1st National Bank Building, 332 Minnesota Street, Suite E200, Saint Paul, MN 55101-1351. 800-657-3858. Internet site <www.mn.gov/deed/data>.
Compare Minnesota: Profiles of Minnesota's Economy & Population. Online.
Data Center Online. Online.

Minnesota State Demographic Center, 658 Cedar Street, Room 300, Saint Paul, MN 55155. 651-201-2472. Internet site <mn.gov/admin/demography>.

Mississippi

Mississippi Secretary of State, 401 Mississippi Street, Jackson, MS 39201. 601-359-1350. Internet site <www.sos.ms.gov/communications-publications/2016-2020-mississippi-blue-book>.
2016-2020 Mississippi Blue Book. Quadrennial. Online.

Missouri

University of Missouri—Columbia, Economic and Policy Analysis Research Center, 10 Professional Building, Columbia, MO 65211. 573-882-4805. Internet site <www.eparc.missouri.edu/publications/archive/archive.html>.
Missouri Statistical Data Archive. Online.

Montana

Montana Department of Commerce, Census and Economic Information Center, P.O. Box 200501, 301 S. Park Avenue, Helena, MT 59620-0533. 406-841-2700. Fax: 406-841-2871. Internet site <www.ceic.mt.gov>.

Nebraska

Nebraska Department of Economic Development, P.O. Box 94666, 245 Fallbrook Boulevard, Suite 002, Lincoln, NE 68521-6733. 800-426-6505. Internet site <www.opportunity.nebraska.gov>.

Nevada

Nevada Department of Administration, Budget Division, 209 East Musser Street, Room 200, Carson City, NV 89701-4298. 775-684-0222. Fax: 775-684-0260. Internet site <budget.nv.gov>.

New Hampshire

New Hampshire State Data Center, Governor Hugh J. Gallen State Office Park, Johnson Hall, 3rd Floor, 107 Pleasant Street, Concord, NH 03301-8501. 603-271-1773. Internet site <www.nh.gov/osi/data-center>.
State Data Center. Online.

New Jersey

State of New Jersey Department of Labor and Workforce Development, Bureau of Labor Market Information, 1 John Fitch Plaza, 5th floor, P.O. Box 057, Trenton, NJ 08625-0057. 609-292-2582. Fax: 609-633-9240. Internet site <data.nj.gov/>.
NJOIT Open Data Center. Online.

New Mexico

University of New Mexico, Bureau of Business and Economic Research, 400 Cornell Drive NE, Albuquerque, NM 87131-0001. 505-277-6626. Internet site <bber.unm.edu>.
New Mexico's Economy: Current Situation and Outlook. Annual. Online.

New York

Nelson A. Rockefeller Institute of Government, 411 State Street, Albany, NY 12203-1003. 518-443-5522. Fax: 518-443-5788. Internet site <www.rockinst.org>.
New York State Statistical Yearbook. Annual. Print and Online.

North Carolina

Office of State Budget and Management, MSC 20320, Raleigh, NC 27699-0320. 919-807-4700. Internet site <linc.osbm.nc.gov/pages/home>.
LINC. Online.

North Dakota

University of North Dakota, Nistler College of Business and Public Administration, Gamble Hall Room 110, 293 Centennial Drive, Stop 8098, Grand Forks, ND 58202-8098. 701-777-2135. Fax: 701-777-2019. Internet site <www.business.und.edu>.

Ohio

Office of Research, Ohio Development Services Agency, 77 South High Street, 28th floor, Columbus, OH 43215-6130. 614-466-2116. Internet site <www.devresearch.ohio.gov>.
Reports and Reseach. Online.
Ohio County Trends. Online.

Oklahoma

Oklahoma Office of Management and Enterprise Services, 2401 N. Lincoln Boulevard, Oklahoma City, OK 73105. 405-521-2141. Fax: 405-521-3902. Internet site <data.ok.govl>.
Oklahoma's Open Data. Online.

Oregon

Secretary of State, Archives Division, Archives Bldg., 800 Summer Street NE, Salem, OR 97310. 503-373-0701 ext.1. Fax: 503-373-0953. Internet site <sos.oregon.gov/blue-book/Pages/default.aspx>.
Oregon Blue Book. 2021-2022. Biennial. Online.

Pennsylvania

Pennsylvania State Data Center, Institute of State and Regional Affairs, Penn State Harrisburg, 777 West Harrisburg Pike, Middletown, PA 17057-4898. 717-948-6336. Fax: 717-948-6754. Internet site <pasdc.hbg.psu.edu>.
Pennsylvania Statistical Abstract, 2021. Print and Online.

Rhode Island

Rhode Island Department of Labor and Training, Labor Market Information, 1511 Pontiac Avenue, Cranston, RI 02920. 401-462-8740. Internet site <www.dlt.ri.gov/lmi>.
State and Fiscal Digest, 2021. Online.

South Carolina

South Carolina Revenue and Fiscal Affairs Offices, Data Integration and Analysis Division, 1601 Richland Street, Suite 240, Columbia, SC 29201. 803-898-9940. Internet site <rfa.sc.gov/data-research>.
State Data Center. Online.

South Dakota

South Dakota State University, Census Data Center, Box 504, Brookings, SD 57007. 605-688-4899. Internet site <www.sdstate.edu/school-psychology-sociology-and-rural-studies/census-data-center>.

Tennessee

Tennessee State Data Center, 916 Volunteer Boulevard, 716 Stokely Management Center, Knoxville, TN 37996-0570. 865-974-6070. Internet site <tndata.utk.edu>.

Texas

Texas State Historical Association, 3001 Lake Austin Boulevard, Austin, TX 78703. 512-471-2600. Internet site <texasalmanac.com>.
Texas Almanac, 2022-2023. Biennial. Print and Online.

Texas Demographic Center, Institute for Demographic and Socioeconomic Research (IDSER), 501 W. César E. Chávez Boulevard., San Antonio, TX 78207-4415. 210-458-6543. Fax: 210-458-6541. Internet site <demographics.texas.gov>.

Utah

The University of Utah, Thomas S. Monson Center, 411 East South Temple Street, Salt Lake City, UT 84111. 801-213-8770. Internet site <gardner.utah.edu/economics-and-public-policy/economic-report-to-the-governor/>.
2022 Economic Report to the Governor. Annual. Online.

Vermont

Department of Labor, Labor Market Information, P.O. Box 488, Montpelier, VT 05601-0488. 802-828-4157. Fax: 802-828-4050. Internet site <vtlmi.info/>.
Vermont Economic and Demographic Profile, 2022. Annual. Online.

Virginia

University of Virginia, Weldon Cooper Center for Public Service, 2400 Old Ivy Road, Charlottesville, VA 22903. 434-243-5232. Fax: 434-982-5524. Internet site <coopercenter.org/>.
Virginia Population Estimates. Online.
Virginia Population Projections. Online.

Washington

Washington State Office of Financial Management, Forecasting Division, P.O. Box 43113, Olympia, WA 98504-3113. 360-902-0599. Internet site <ofm.wa.gov/>.
Washington State Data Book, 2019. Biennial. Online.

West Virginia

West Virginia University, John Chambers College of Business and Economics, Bureau of Business and Economic Research, P.O. Box 6527, Morgantown, WV 26506-6025. 304-293-7831. Internet site <business.wvu.edu/research-outreach/bureau-of-business-and-economic-research>.
West Virginia County Data Profile 2020. Annual. Online.
West Virginia Economic Outlook, 2022-2026. Annual. Online.

Wisconsin

Wisconsin Legislative Reference Bureau, One East Main Street, Suite 200, Madison, WI 53703. 608-504-5802. Internet site <legis.wisconsin.gov/lrb>.
2021-2022 Wisconsin Blue Book. Biennial. Print and Online.

Wyoming

Department of Administration and Information, Economic Analysis Division, 2800 Central Avenue, Cheyenne, WY 82002-0060. 307-777-7504. Internet site <eadiv.state.wy.us>.
The Equality State Almanac, 2010. Annual. Online.
Wyoming and County Profiles, 2021. Annual. Online.

American Samoa

Department of Commerce, A.P. Lutali Executive Building, 2nd Floor, Pago Pago, AS 96799. 684-633-5155. Internet site <www.doc.as.gov/resource-center>.
2018 and 2019 Statistical Yearbook. Online.

Guam

Planning and Information Program, Bureau of Statistics and Plans, P.O. Box 2950, Hagatna, GU 96932. 684-633-5155. Internet site <bsp.guam.gov/planning-information-program-2/>.
2020 Guam Statistical Yearbook. Online.
Guam Facts and Figures at a Glance. Online.

Northern Mariana Islands

Central Statistics Division, Department of Commerce P.O. Box 5795 CHRB, Saipan, MP 96950. 670-664-3000. Fax: 670-664-3067. Internet site <ver1.cnmicommerce.com/divisions/central-statistics/report-hub/>.
2017 CNMI Statistical Yearbook. Online.

Puerto Rico

Junta de Planificación. P.O. Box 41119, San Juan, PR 00940-1119. 787-723-6200. Internet site <jp.pr.gov>.
Economic Report to the Governor 2020. Online.

U.S. Virgin Islands

Bureau of Labor Statistics, Department of Labor, 2353 Kronprindsens Gade, St. Thomas, VI 00802. 340-776-3700. Fax: 340-715-5743. Internet site <www.vidol.gov/labor-statistics/>.
Labor Market Information. Online.

Metropolitan and Micropolitan Statistical Areas: Concepts, Components, and Population

The United States Office of Management and Budget (OMB) defines metropolitan and micropolitan statistical areas according to published standards that are applied to U.S. Census Bureau data. The general concept of a metropolitan or micropolitan statistical area is that of a core area containing a substantial population nucleus, together with adjacent communities having a high degree of economic and social integration with that core. Currently defined metropolitan and micropolitan statistical areas are based on application of 2010 standards (which appeared in the Federal Register on June 28, 2010) to 2010 decennial census data. Current metropolitan and micropolitan statistical area delineations were announced by OMB effective March 2020.

Standard definitions of metropolitan areas were first issued in 1949 by the then Bureau of the Budget (predecessor of OMB), under the designation "standard metropolitan area" (SMA). The term was changed to "standard metropolitan statistical area" (SMSA) in 1959 and to "metropolitan statistical area" (MSA) in 1983. The term "metropolitan area" (MA) was adopted in 1990 and referred collectively to metropolitan statistical areas (MSAs), consolidated metropolitan statistical areas (CMSAs), and primary metropolitan statistical areas (PMSAs). The term "core-based statistical area" (CBSA) became effective in 2000 and refers collectively to metropolitan and micropolitan statistical areas.

OMB has been responsible for the official metropolitan areas since they were first defined, except for the period 1977 to 1981, when they were the responsibility of the Office of Federal Statistical Policy and Standards, U.S. Department of Commerce. The standards for defining metropolitan areas were modified in 1958, 1971, 1975, 1980, 1990, 2000, and 2010.

Defining Metropolitan and Micropolitan Statistical Areas—The 2010 standards provide that each CBSA must contain at least one urban area of 10,000 or more population. Each metropolitan statistical area must have at least one urbanized area of 50,000 or more inhabitants. Each micropolitan statistical area must have at least one urban cluster of at least 10,000 but less than 50,000 population.

Under the standards, the county (or counties) in which at least 50 percent of the population resides within urban areas of 10,000 or more population, or that contain at least 5,000 people residing within a single urban area of 10,000 or more population, is identified as a "central county" (counties). Additional "outlying counties" are included in the CBSA if they meet specific requirements of commuting to or from the central counties. Counties or equivalent entities form the geographic "building blocks" for metropolitan and micropolitan statistical areas throughout the United States and Puerto Rico.

If specific criteria are met, a metropolitan statistical area containing a single core with a population of 2.5 million or more may be subdivided to form smaller groupings of counties referred to as "metropolitan divisions."

As of March 2020, there are 384 metropolitan statistical areas and 543 micropolitan statistical areas in the United States. In addition, there are 8 metropolitan statistical areas and 4 micropolitan statistical areas in Puerto Rico.

Principal Cities and Metropolitan and Micropolitan Statistical Area Titles—The largest city in each metropolitan or micropolitan statistical area is designated a "principal city." Additional cities qualify if specific requirements are met concerning population size and employment. The title of each metropolitan or micropolitan statistical area consists of the names of up to three of its principal cities in order of descending population size and the name of each state into which the metropolitan or micropolitan statistical area extends. Titles of metropolitan divisions also typically are based on principal city names, but in certain cases consist of county names.

Defining New England City and Town Areas—Cities and towns are the primary units of local government in the six New England states, where counties, unlike elsewhere, have little or no official governmental functions. The 2010 standards provide for a set of geographic areas that are defined using cities and towns in the New England states. The New England city and town areas (NECTAs) are defined using the same criteria as metropolitan and micropolitan statistical areas and are identified as either metropolitan or micropolitan, based, respectively, on the presence of either an urbanized area of 50,000 or more population or an urban cluster of at least 10,000 but less than 50,000 population. If the specific criteria are met, a NECTA containing a single core with a population of at least 2.5 million may be subdivided to form smaller groupings of cities and towns referred to as New England city and town area divisions.

Changes in Definitions Over Time—Changes in the definitions of these statistical areas since the 1950 census have consisted chiefly of (1) the recognition of new areas as they reached the minimum required city or urbanized area population and (2) the addition of counties (or cities and towns in New England) to existing areas as new decennial census data showed them to qualify.

In some instances, formerly separate areas have been merged, components of an area have been transferred from one area to another, or components have been dropped from an area. The large majority of changes are based on decennial census data; however, Census Bureau data serve as the basis for intercensal updates in specific circumstances.

Because of these historical changes in geographic definitions, users must be cautious in comparing data for these statistical areas from different dates. For some purposes, comparisons of data for areas as defined at given dates may be appropriate; for other purposes, it may be preferable to maintain consistent area definitions. Historical metropolitan area definitions are available for 1950, 1960, 1963, 1970, 1973, 1981, 1983, 1990, 1993, and 1999.

Excluding Tables 21 through 23 in the Population section, Table 629 in the Labor Force section, Table 722 in the Income section, and the tables that follow in this appendix, the tables presenting data for metropolitan areas in this edition of the *Statistical Abstract* may be based on earlier metropolitan area definitions. See the Census Bureau website at <www.census.gov/programs-surveys/metro-micro.html> for information on historical delineations and component counties.

Table A. Metropolitan Statistical Areas and Components—Population: 2021

[In thousands (177 represents 177,000). Population as of July 2021. Metropolitan Statistical Areas delineated by the U.S. Office of Management and Budget as of March 2020. The estimates are developed from a base that incorporates the 2020 Census, Vintage 2020 estimates, and 2020 Demographic Analysis estimates. All Metropolitan Statistical Areas are arranged alphabetically]

Metropolitan Statistical Area ~~Metropolitan Division ~~~~Component county	Population, 2021 (1,000)
Abilene, TX	**177**
Callahan County, TX	14
Jones County, TX	20
Taylor County, TX	143
Akron, OH	**700**
Portage County, OH	162
Summit County, OH	538
Albany, GA	**148**
Dougherty County, GA	85
Lee County, GA	33
Terrell County, GA	9
Worth County, GA	21
Albany-Lebanon, OR	**130**
Linn County, OR	130
Albany-Schenectady-Troy, NY	**899**
Albany County, NY	314
Rensselaer County, NY	160
Saratoga County, NY	237
Schenectady County, NY	158
Schoharie County, NY	30
Albuquerque, NM	**918**
Bernalillo County, NM	674
Sandoval County, NM	151
Torrance County, NM	15
Valencia County, NM	77
Alexandria, LA	**151**
Grant Parish, LA	22
Rapides Parish, LA	129
Allentown-Bethlehem-Easton, PA-NJ	**865**
Warren County, NJ	111
Carbon County, PA	65
Lehigh County, PA	376
Northampton County, PA	314
Altoona, PA	**122**
Blair County, PA	122
Amarillo, TX	**270**
Armstrong County, TX	2
Carson County, TX	6
Oldham County, TX	2
Potter County, TX	117
Randall County, TX	144
Ames, IA	**126**
Boone County, IA	27
Story County, IA	99
Anchorage, AK	**399**
Anchorage Municipality, AK	288
Matanuska-Susitna Borough, AK	111
Ann Arbor, MI	**369**
Washtenaw County, MI	369
Anniston-Oxford, AL	**116**
Calhoun County, AL	116
Appleton, WI	**244**
Calumet County, WI	53
Outagamie County, WI	192
Asheville, NC	**472**
Buncombe County, NC	272
Haywood County, NC	62
Henderson County, NC	117
Madison County, NC	22
Athens-Clarke County, GA	**218**
Clarke County, GA	129
Madison County, GA	31
Oconee County, GA	43
Oglethorpe County, GA	15
Atlanta-Sandy Springs-Alpharetta, GA	**6,144**
Barrow County, GA	87
Bartow County, GA	111
Butts County, GA	26
Carroll County, GA	122
Cherokee County, GA	275
Clayton County, GA	297
Cobb County, GA	767
Coweta County, GA	150
Dawson County, GA	28
DeKalb County, GA	758
Douglas County, GA	146
Fayette County, GA	121
Forsyth County, GA	260
Fulton County, GA	1,065
Gwinnett County, GA	965
Haralson County, GA	31
Heard County, GA	12
Henry County, GA	245
Jasper County, GA	15
Lamar County, GA	19
Meriwether County, GA	21
Morgan County, GA	21
Newton County, GA	115
Paulding County, GA	174
Pickens County, GA	34
Pike County, GA	19
Rockdale County, GA	94
Spalding County, GA	68
Walton County, GA	100
Atlantic City-Hammonton, NJ	**275**
Atlantic County, NJ	275
Auburn-Opelika, AL	**177**
Lee County, AL	177
Augusta-Richmond County, GA-SC	**616**
Burke County, GA	24
Columbia County, GA	160
Lincoln County, GA	8
McDuffie County, GA	22
Richmond County, GA	206
Aiken County, SC	171
Edgefield County, SC	26
Austin-Round Rock-Georgetown, TX	**2,352**
Bastrop County, TX	102
Caldwell County, TX	47
Hays County, TX	255
Travis County, TX	1,305
Williamson County, TX	643
Bakersfield, CA	**918**
Kern County, CA	918
Baltimore-Columbia-Towson, MD	**2,838**
Anne Arundel County, MD	590
Baltimore County, MD	849
Carroll County, MD	174
Harford County, MD	263
Howard County, MD	335
Queen Anne's County, MD	51
Baltimore city, MD	576
Bangor, ME	**153**
Penobscot County, ME	153
Barnstable Town, MA	**232**
Barnstable County, MA	232
Baton Rouge, LA	**872**
Ascension Parish, LA	128
Assumption Parish, LA	21
East Baton Rouge Parish, LA	453
East Feliciana Parish, LA	19
Iberville Parish, LA	30
Livingston Parish, LA	146
Pointe Coupee Parish, LA	20
St. Helena Parish, LA	11
West Baton Rouge Parish, LA	28
West Feliciana Parish, LA	15
Battle Creek, MI	**134**
Calhoun County, MI	134
Bay City, MI	**103**
Bay County, MI	103
Beaumont-Port Arthur, TX	**395**
Hardin County, TX	57
Jefferson County, TX	254
Orange County, TX	85
Beckley, WV	**114**
Fayette County, WV	40
Raleigh County, WV	74
Bellingham, WA	**229**
Whatcom County, WA	229
Bend, OR	**205**
Deschutes County, OR	205
Billings, MT	**187**
Carbon County, MT	11
Stillwater County, MT	9
Yellowstone County, MT	167
Binghamton, NY	**245**
Broome County, NY	197
Tioga County, NY	48
Birmingham-Hoover, AL	**1,114**
Bibb County, AL	22
Blount County, AL	59
Chilton County, AL	45
Jefferson County, AL	668
St. Clair County, AL	93
Shelby County, AL	227
Bismarck, ND	**134**
Burleigh County, ND	99
Morton County, ND	34
Oliver County, ND	2
Blacksburg-Christiansburg, VA	**165**
Giles County, VA	17
Montgomery County, VA	98
Pulaski County, VA	34
Radford city, VA	16
Bloomington, IL	**171**
McLean County, IL	171
Bloomington, IN	**161**
Monroe County, IN	140
Owen County, IN	21
Bloomsburg-Berwick, PA	**83**
Columbia County, PA	65
Montour County, PA	18
Boise City, ID	**795**
Ada County, ID	512
Boise County, ID	8
Canyon County, ID	243
Gem County, ID	20
Owyhee County, ID	12
Boston-Cambridge-Newton, MA-NH	**4,900**
Boston, MA	**2,029**
Norfolk County, MA	725
Plymouth County, MA	533
Suffolk County, MA	771
Cambridge-Newton-Framingham, MA	**2,422**
Essex County, MA	807
Middlesex County, MA	1,615
Rockingham County-Strafford County, NH	**449**
Rockingham County, NH	317
Strafford County, NH	132
Boulder, CO	**330**
Boulder County, CO	330
Bowling Green, KY	**183**
Allen County, KY	21
Butler County, KY	12
Edmonson County, KY	12
Warren County, KY	137
Bremerton-Silverdale-Port Orchard, WA	**274**
Kitsap County, WA	274
Bridgeport-Stamford-Norwalk, CT	**960**
Fairfield County, CT	960
Brownsville-Harlingen, TX	**423**
Cameron County, TX	423
Brunswick, GA	**114**
Brantley County, GA	18
Glynn County, GA	85
McIntosh County, GA	11
Buffalo-Cheektowaga, NY	**1,162**
Erie County, NY	951
Niagara County, NY	212
Burlington, NC	**174**
Alamance County, NC	174
Burlington-South Burlington, VT	**227**
Chittenden County, VT	169
Franklin County, VT	50
Grand Isle County, VT	7
California-Lexington Park, MD	**114**

See footnotes at end of table.

Metropolitan Statistical Area ~~Metropolitan Division ~~~~Component county	Population, 2021 (1,000)
St. Mary's County, MD	114
Canton-Massillon, OH	**401**
Carroll County, OH	27
Stark County, OH	374
Cape Coral-Fort Myers, FL	**788**
Lee County, FL	788
Cape Girardeau, MO-IL	**98**
Alexander County, IL	5
Bollinger County, MO	11
Cape Girardeau County, MO	82
Carbondale-Marion, IL	**133**
Jackson County, IL	53
Johnson County, IL	13
Williamson County, IL	67
Carson City, NV	**59**
Carson City, NV	59
Casper, WY	**80**
Natrona County, WY	80
Cedar Rapids, IA	**275**
Benton County, IA	26
Jones County, IA	21
Linn County, IA	229
Chambersburg-Waynesboro, PA	**156**
Franklin County, PA	156
Champaign-Urbana, IL	**223**
Champaign County, IL	206
Piatt County, IL	17
Charleston, WV	**255**
Boone County, WV	21
Clay County, WV	8
Jackson County, WV	28
Kanawha County, WV	178
Lincoln County, WV	20
Charleston-North Charleston, SC	**813**
Berkeley County, SC	237
Charleston County, SC	413
Dorchester County, SC	163
Charlotte-Concord-Gastonia, NC-SC	**2,701**
Anson County, NC	22
Cabarrus County, NC	231
Gaston County, NC	231
Iredell County, NC	192
Lincoln County, NC	90
Mecklenburg County, NC	1,122
Rowan County, NC	148
Union County, NC	244
Chester County, SC	32
Lancaster County, SC	100
York County, SC	289
Charlottesville, VA	**223**
Albemarle County, VA	114
Fluvanna County, VA	28
Greene County, VA	21
Nelson County, VA	15
Charlottesville city, VA	46
Chattanooga, TN-GA	**568**
Catoosa County, GA	68
Dade County, GA	16
Walker County, GA	69
Hamilton County, TN	369
Marion County, TN	29
Sequatchie County, TN	16
Cheyenne, WY	**101**
Laramie County, WY	101
Chicago-Naperville-Elgin, IL-IN-WI	**9,510**
Chicago-Naperville-Evanston, IL	**7,159**
Cook County, IL	5,173
DuPage County, IL	925
Grundy County, IL	53
McHenry County, IL	311
Will County, IL	697
Elgin, IL	**751**
DeKalb County, IL	100
Kane County, IL	516
Kendall County, IL	135
Gary, IN	**720**
Jasper County, IN	33
Lake County, IN	499

Metropolitan Statistical Area ~~Metropolitan Division ~~~~Component county	Population, 2021 (1,000)
Newton County, IN	14
Porter County, IN	174
Lake County-Kenosha County, IL-WI	**880**
Lake County, IL	711
Kenosha County, WI	169
Chico, CA	**208**
Butte County, CA	208
Cincinnati, OH-KY-IN	**2,260**
Dearborn County, IN	51
Franklin County, IN	23
Ohio County, IN	6
Union County, IN	7
Boone County, KY	137
Bracken County, KY	8
Campbell County, KY	93
Gallatin County, KY	9
Grant County, KY	25
Kenton County, KY	169
Pendleton County, KY	15
Brown County, OH	44
Butler County, OH	390
Clermont County, OH	210
Hamilton County, OH	826
Warren County, OH	247
Clarksville, TN-KY	**328**
Christian County, KY	72
Trigg County, KY	14
Montgomery County, TN	228
Stewart County, TN	14
Cleveland, TN	**128**
Bradley County, TN	110
Polk County, TN	18
Cleveland-Elyria, OH	**2,076**
Cuyahoga County, OH	1,249
Geauga County, OH	96
Lake County, OH	232
Lorain County, OH	316
Medina County, OH	183
Coeur d'Alene, ID	**180**
Kootenai County, ID	180
College Station-Bryan, TX	**272**
Brazos County, TX	237
Burleson County, TX	18
Robertson County, TX	17
Colorado Springs, CO	**763**
El Paso County, CO	738
Teller County, CO	25
Columbia, MO	**213**
Boone County, MO	186
Cooper County, MO	17
Howard County, MO	10
Columbia, SC	**838**
Calhoun County, SC	14
Fairfield County, SC	21
Kershaw County, SC	66
Lexington County, SC	300
Richland County, SC	418
Saluda County, SC	19
Columbus, GA-AL	**328**
Russell County, AL	59
Chattahoochee County, GA	9
Harris County, GA	36
Marion County, GA	7
Muscogee County, GA	206
Stewart County, GA	5
Talbot County, GA	6
Columbus, IN	**82**
Bartholomew County, IN	82
Columbus, OH	**2,151**
Delaware County, OH	221
Fairfield County, OH	161
Franklin County, OH	1,321
Hocking County, OH	28
Licking County, OH	180
Madison County, OH	44
Morrow County, OH	35
Perry County, OH	35
Pickaway County, OH	59
Union County, OH	65
Corpus Christi, TX	**423**
Nueces County, TX	353

Metropolitan Statistical Area ~~Metropolitan Division ~~~~Component county	Population, 2021 (1,000)
San Patricio County, TX	70
Corvallis, OR	**96**
Benton County, OR	96
Crestview-Fort Walton Beach-Destin, FL	**293**
Okaloosa County, FL	213
Walton County, FL	80
Cumberland, MD-WV	**95**
Allegany County, MD	68
Mineral County, WV	27
Dallas-Fort Worth-Arlington, TX	**7,760**
Dallas-Plano-Irving, TX	**5,217**
Collin County, TX	1,109
Dallas County, TX	2,586
Denton County, TX	942
Ellis County, TX	203
Hunt County, TX	103
Kaufman County, TX	158
Rockwall County, TX	116
Fort Worth-Arlington-Grapevine, TX	**2,542**
Johnson County, TX	187
Parker County, TX	157
Tarrant County, TX	2,126
Wise County, TX	72
Dalton, GA	**143**
Murray County, GA	40
Whitfield County, GA	103
Danville, IL	**73**
Vermilion County, IL	73
Daphne-Fairhope-Foley, AL	**239**
Baldwin County, AL	239
Davenport-Moline-Rock Island, IA-IL	**382**
Henry County, IL	49
Mercer County, IL	16
Rock Island County, IL	143
Scott County, IA	174
Dayton-Kettering, OH	**814**
Greene County, OH	168
Miami County, OH	109
Montgomery County, OH	536
Decatur, AL	**157**
Lawrence County, AL	33
Morgan County, AL	124
Decatur, IL	**102**
Macon County, IL	102
Deltona-Daytona Beach-Ormond Beach, FL	**685**
Flagler County, FL	121
Volusia County, FL	564
Denver-Aurora-Lakewood, CO	**2,973**
Adams County, CO	522
Arapahoe County, CO	655
Broomfield County, CO	75
Clear Creek County, CO	9
Denver County, CO	711
Douglas County, CO	369
Elbert County, CO	27
Gilpin County, CO	6
Jefferson County, CO	580
Park County, CO	18
Des Moines-West Des Moines, IA	**719**
Dallas County, IA	104
Guthrie County, IA	11
Jasper County, IA	38
Madison County, IA	17
Polk County, IA	497
Warren County, IA	53
Detroit-Warren-Dearborn, MI	**4,365**
Detroit-Dearborn-Livonia, MI	**1,775**
Wayne County, MI	1,775
Warren-Troy-Farmington Hills, MI	**2,590**
Lapeer County, MI	89
Livingston County, MI	195
Macomb County, MI	877
Oakland County, MI	1,270
St. Clair County, MI	160

See footnotes at end of table.

Table A. Metropolitan Statistical Areas and Components—Population: 2021-Continued.

See headnote on page 915.

Metropolitan Statistical Area ~~Metropolitan Division ~~~~Component county	Population, 2021 (1,000)
Dothan, AL	**152**
Geneva County, AL	27
Henry County, AL	17
Houston County, AL	107
Dover, DE	**184**
Kent County, DE	184
Dubuque, IA	**99**
Dubuque County, IA	99
Duluth, MN-WI	**291**
Carlton County, MN	36
Lake County, MN	11
St. Louis County, MN	199
Douglas County, WI	44
Durham-Chapel Hill, NC	**654**
Chatham County, NC	78
Durham County, NC	326
Granville County, NC	62
Orange County, NC	149
Person County, NC	39
East Stroudsburg, PA	**169**
Monroe County, PA	169
Eau Claire, WI	**173**
Chippewa County, WI	67
Eau Claire County, WI	106
El Centro, CA	**180**
Imperial County, CA	180
Elizabethtown-Fort Knox, KY	**157**
Hardin County, KY	112
Larue County, KY	15
Meade County, KY	30
Elkhart-Goshen, IN	**207**
Elkhart County, IN	207
Elmira, NY	**83**
Chemung County, NY	83
El Paso, TX	**871**
El Paso County, TX	868
Hudspeth County, TX	3
Enid, OK	**62**
Garfield County, OK	62
Erie, PA	**269**
Erie County, PA	269
Eugene-Springfield, OR	**383**
Lane County, OR	383
Evansville, IN-KY	**314**
Posey County, IN	25
Vanderburgh County, IN	180
Warrick County, IN	65
Henderson County, KY	44
Fairbanks, AK	**96**
Fairbanks North Star Borough, AK	96
Fargo, ND-MN	**252**
Clay County, MN	66
Cass County, ND	187
Farmington, NM	**121**
San Juan County, NM	121
Fayetteville, NC	**525**
Cumberland County, NC	336
Harnett County, NC	136
Hoke County, NC	53
Fayetteville-Springdale-Rogers, AR	**561**
Benton County, AR	294
Madison County, AR	17
Washington County, AR	250
Flagstaff, AZ	**145**
Coconino County, AZ	145
Flint, MI	**404**
Genesee County, MI	404
Florence, SC	**199**
Darlington County, SC	63
Florence County, SC	137
Florence-Muscle Shoals, AL	**152**
Colbert County, AL	57
Lauderdale County, AL	94
Fond du Lac, WI	**104**
Fond du Lac County, WI	104
Fort Collins, CO	**363**
Larimer County, CO	363
Fort Smith, AR-OK	**245**

Metropolitan Statistical Area ~~Metropolitan Division ~~~~Component county	Population, 2021 (1,000)
Crawford County, AR	60
Franklin County, AR	17
Sebastian County, AR	128
Sequoyah County, OK	40
Fort Wayne, IN	**423**
Allen County, IN	389
Whitley County, IN	34
Fresno, CA	**1,014**
Fresno County, CA	1,014
Gadsden, AL	**103**
Etowah County, AL	103
Gainesville, FL	**342**
Alachua County, FL	279
Gilchrist County, FL	18
Levy County, FL	44
Gainesville, GA	**207**
Hall County, GA	207
Gettysburg, PA	**104**
Adams County, PA	104
Glens Falls, NY	**127**
Warren County, NY	66
Washington County, NY	61
Goldsboro, NC	**117**
Wayne County, NC	117
Grand Forks, ND-MN	**103**
Polk County, MN	31
Grand Forks County, ND	73
Grand Island, NE	**76**
Hall County, NE	62
Howard County, NE	7
Merrick County, NE	8
Grand Junction, CO	**157**
Mesa County, CO	157
Grand Rapids-Kentwood, MI	**1,092**
Ionia County, MI	67
Kent County, MI	658
Montcalm County, MI	67
Ottawa County, MI	299
Grants Pass, OR	**88**
Josephine County, OR	88
Great Falls, MT	**85**
Cascade County, MT	85
Greeley, CO	**340**
Weld County, CO	340
Green Bay, WI	**329**
Brown County, WI	270
Kewaunee County, WI	21
Oconto County, WI	39
Greensboro-High Point, NC	**779**
Guilford County, NC	542
Randolph County, NC	145
Rockingham County, NC	91
Greenville, NC	**172**
Pitt County, NC	172
Greenville-Anderson, SC	**941**
Anderson County, SC	207
Greenville County, SC	534
Laurens County, SC	68
Pickens County, SC	132
Gulfport-Biloxi, MS	**418**
Hancock County, MS	46
Harrison County, MS	209
Jackson County, MS	144
Stone County, MS	19
Hagerstown-Martinsburg, MD-WV	**298**
Washington County, MD	155
Berkeley County, WV	126
Morgan County, WV	17
Hammond, LA	**135**
Tangipahoa Parish, LA	135
Hanford-Corcoran, CA	**153**
Kings County, CA	153
Harrisburg-Carlisle, PA	**596**
Cumberland County, PA	263
Dauphin County, PA	287
Perry County, PA	46
Harrisonburg, VA	**136**
Rockingham County, VA	84
Harrisonburg city, VA	51

Metropolitan Statistical Area ~~Metropolitan Division ~~~~Component county	Population, 2021 (1,000)
Hartford-East Hartford-Middletown, CT	**1,212**
Hartford County, CT	897
Middlesex County, CT	165
Tolland County, CT	150
Hattiesburg, MS	**173**
Covington County, MS	18
Forrest County, MS	78
Lamar County, MS	65
Perry County, MS	12
Hickory-Lenoir-Morganton, NC	**366**
Alexander County, NC	37
Burke County, NC	88
Caldwell County, NC	80
Catawba County, NC	162
Hilton Head Island-Bluffton, SC	**222**
Beaufort County, SC	192
Jasper County, SC	30
Hinesville, GA	**83**
Liberty County, GA	66
Long County, GA	17
Homosassa Springs, FL	**158**
Citrus County, FL	158
Hot Springs, AR	**100**
Garland County, AR	100
Houma-Thibodaux, LA	**206**
Lafourche Parish, LA	98
Terrebonne Parish, LA	109
Houston-The Woodlands-Sugar Land, TX	**7,207**
Austin County, TX	30
Brazoria County, TX	380
Chambers County, TX	49
Fort Bend County, TX	859
Galveston County, TX	355
Harris County, TX	4,728
Liberty County, TX	98
Montgomery County, TX	649
Waller County, TX	60
Huntington-Ashland, WV-KY-OH	**357**
Boyd County, KY	48
Carter County, KY	26
Greenup County, KY	36
Lawrence County, OH	57
Cabell County, WV	93
Putnam County, WV	57
Wayne County, WV	38
Huntsville, AL	**503**
Limestone County, AL	108
Madison County, AL	395
Idaho Falls, ID	**163**
Bonneville County, ID	128
Butte County, ID	3
Jefferson County, ID	32
Indianapolis-Carmel-Anderson, IN	**2,127**
Boone County, IN	73
Brown County, IN	16
Hamilton County, IN	357
Hancock County, IN	82
Hendricks County, IN	179
Johnson County, IN	164
Madison County, IN	131
Marion County, IN	971
Morgan County, IN	72
Putnam County, IN	37
Shelby County, IN	45
Iowa City, IA	**177**
Johnson County, IA	155
Washington County, IA	22
Ithaca, NY	**105**
Tompkins County, NY	105
Jackson, MI	**160**
Jackson County, MI	160
Jackson, MS	**587**
Copiah County, MS	28
Hinds County, MS	223

See footnotes at end of table.

Table A. Metropolitan Statistical Areas and Components—Population: 2021-Continued.

See headnote on page 915.

Metropolitan Statistical Area ~~*Metropolitan Division* ~~~~*Component county*	Popu-lation, 2021 (1,000)
Holmes County, MS..............	16
Madison County, MS.............	110
Rankin County, MS..............	158
Simpson County, MS.............	26
Yazoo County, MS...............	26
Jackson, TN.....................	**181**
Chester County, TN.............	18
Crockett County, TN............	14
Gibson County, TN..............	51
Madison County, TN.............	99
Jacksonville, FL.................	**1,638**
Baker County, FL...............	29
Clay County, FL................	222
Duval County, FL...............	1,000
Nassau County, FL..............	94
St. Johns County, FL...........	292
Jacksonville, NC.................	**206**
Onslow County, NC..............	206
Janesville-Beloit, WI............	**164**
Rock County, WI................	164
Jefferson City, MO...............	**151**
Callaway County, MO............	45
Cole County, MO................	77
Moniteau County, MO............	15
Osage County, MO...............	13
Johnson City, TN................	**208**
Carter County, TN..............	56
Unicoi County, TN..............	18
Washington County, TN..........	134
Johnstown, PA...................	**132**
Cambria County, PA.............	132
Jonesboro, AR...................	**135**
Craighead County, AR...........	112
Poinsett County, AR............	23
Joplin, MO.......................	**183**
Jasper County, MO..............	123
Newton County, MO..............	59
Kahului-Wailuku-Lahaina, HI....	**164**
Maui County, HI................	164
Kalamazoo-Portage, MI...........	**261**
Kalamazoo County, MI...........	261
Kankakee, IL.....................	**107**
Kankakee County, IL............	107
Kansas City, MO-KS...............	**2,199**
Johnson County, KS.............	613
Leavenworth County, KS.........	82
Linn County, KS................	10
Miami County, KS...............	35
Wyandotte County, KS...........	167
Bates County, MO...............	16
Caldwell County, MO............	9
Cass County, MO................	110
Clay County, MO................	256
Clinton County, MO.............	21
Jackson County, MO.............	717
Lafayette County, MO...........	33
Platte County, MO..............	109
Ray County, MO.................	23
Kennewick-Richland, WA........	**308**
Benton County, WA..............	210
Franklin County, WA............	98
Killeen-Temple, TX...............	**486**
Bell County, TX................	380
Coryell County, TX.............	84
Lampasas County, TX............	22
Kingsport-Bristol, TN-VA........	**309**
Hawkins County, TN.............	57
Sullivan County, TN............	159
Scott County, VA...............	21
Washington County, VA..........	54
Bristol city, VA...............	17
Kingston, NY....................	**183**
Ulster County, NY..............	183
Knoxville, TN....................	**893**
Anderson County, TN............	78
Blount County, TN..............	138
Campbell County, TN............	40
Knox County, TN................	487
Loudon County, TN..............	57
Morgan County, TN..............	21
Roane County, TN...............	54
Union County, TN...............	20
Kokomo, IN.......................	**84**

Metropolitan Statistical Area ~~*Metropolitan Division* ~~~~*Component county*	Popu-lation, 2021 (1,000)
Howard County, IN..............	84
La Crosse-Onalaska, WI-MN....	**139**
Houston County, MN.............	19
La Crosse County, WI...........	120
Lafayette, LA....................	**479**
Acadia Parish, LA..............	57
Iberia Parish, LA..............	69
Lafayette Parish, LA...........	244
St. Martin Parish, LA..........	52
Vermilion Parish, LA...........	57
Lafayette-West Lafayette, IN...	**225**
Benton County, IN..............	9
Carroll County, IN.............	20
Tippecanoe County, IN..........	187
Warren County, IN..............	8
Lake Charles, LA................	**210**
Calcasieu Parish, LA...........	205
Cameron Parish, LA.............	5
Lake Havasu City-Kingman, AZ...................	**218**
Mohave County, AZ..............	218
Lakeland-Winter Haven, FL.....	**754**
Polk County, FL................	754
Lancaster, PA....................	**554**
Lancaster County, PA...........	554
Lansing-East Lansing, MI.......	**540**
Clinton County, MI.............	79
Eaton County, MI...............	109
Ingham County, MI..............	284
Shiawassee County, MI..........	68
Laredo, TX.......................	**268**
Webb County, TX................	268
Las Cruces, NM..................	**222**
Doña Ana County, NM...........	222
Las Vegas-Henderson-Paradise, NV...............	**2,292**
Clark County, NV...............	2,292
Lawrence, KS....................	**119**
Douglas County, KS.............	119
Lawton, OK.......................	**128**
Comanche County, OK............	122
Cotton County, OK..............	5
Lebanon, PA.....................	**143**
Lebanon County, PA.............	143
Lewiston, ID-WA.................	**65**
Nez Perce County, ID...........	42
Asotin County, WA..............	22
Lewiston-Auburn, ME............	**111**
Androscoggin County, ME........	111
Lexington-Fayette, KY...........	**518**
Bourbon County, KY.............	20
Clark County, KY...............	37
Fayette County, KY.............	322
Jessamine County, KY...........	54
Scott County, KY...............	58
Woodford County, KY............	27
Lima, OH.........................	**102**
Allen County, OH...............	102
Lincoln, NE......................	**342**
Lancaster County, NE...........	325
Seward County, NE..............	18
Little Rock-North Little Rock-Conway, AR...........	**751**
Faulkner County, AR............	125
Grant County, AR...............	18
Lonoke County, AR..............	75
Perry County, AR...............	10
Pulaski County, AR.............	398
Saline County, AR..............	125
Logan, UT-ID....................	**152**
Franklin County, ID............	15
Cache County, UT...............	137
Longview, TX....................	**288**
Gregg County, TX...............	124
Harrison County, TX............	69
Rusk County, TX................	53
Upshur County, TX..............	42
Longview, WA....................	**112**
Cowlitz County, WA.............	112
Los Angeles-Long Beach-Anaheim, CA...........12,997	

Metropolitan Statistical Area ~~*Metropolitan Division* ~~~~*Component county*	Popu-lation, 2021 (1,000)
Anaheim-Santa Ana-Irvine, CA.................	**3,168**
Orange County, CA..............	3,168
Los Angeles-Long Beach-Glendale, CA........	**9,830**
Los Angeles County, CA.........	9,830
Louisville/Jefferson County, KY-IN......................	**1,285**
Clark County, IN...............	123
Floyd County, IN...............	80
Harrison County, IN............	40
Washington County, IN..........	28
Bullitt County, KY.............	83
Henry County, KY...............	16
Jefferson County, KY...........	778
Oldham County, KY..............	69
Shelby County, KY..............	48
Spencer County, KY.............	20
Lubbock, TX......................	**325**
Crosby County, TX..............	5
Lubbock County, TX.............	314
Lynn County, TX................	6
Lynchburg, VA...................	**262**
Amherst County, VA.............	31
Appomattox County, VA..........	16
Bedford County, VA.............	80
Campbell County, VA............	55
Lynchburg city, VA.............	79
Macon-Bibb County, GA.........	**234**
Bibb County, GA................	157
Crawford County, GA............	12
Jones County, GA...............	28
Monroe County, GA..............	29
Twiggs County, GA..............	8
Madera, CA......................	**159**
Madera County, CA..............	159
Madison, WI.....................	**683**
Columbia County, WI............	58
Dane County, WI................	564
Green County, WI...............	37
Iowa County, WI................	24
Manchester-Nashua, NH........	**424**
Hillsborough County, NH........	424
Manhattan, KS...................	**134**
Geary County, KS...............	36
Pottawatomie County, KS........	26
Riley County, KS...............	72
Mankato, MN....................	**104**
Blue Earth County, MN..........	69
Nicollet County, MN............	34
Mansfield, OH...................	**125**
Richland County, OH............	125
McAllen-Edinburg-Mission, TX..........................	**880**
Hidalgo County, TX.............	880
Medford, OR.....................	**224**
Jackson County, OR.............	224
Memphis, TN-MS-AR.............	**1,336**
Crittenden County, AR..........	48
DeSoto County, MS..............	189
Marshall County, MS............	34
Tate County, MS................	28
Tunica County, MS..............	10
Fayette County, TN.............	43
Shelby County, TN..............	924
Tipton County, TN..............	61
Merced, CA......................	**286**
Merced County, CA..............	286
Miami-Fort Lauderdale-Pompano Beach, FL....	**6,092**
Fort Lauderdale-Pompano Beach-Sunrise, FL.......	**1,931**
Broward County, FL.............	1,931
Miami-Miami Beach-Kendall, FL........................	**2,663**
Miami-Dade County, FL..........	2,663
West Palm Beach-Boca Raton-Boynton Beach, FL.....	**1,498**
Palm Beach County, FL..........	1,498
Michigan City-La Porte, IN.......	**112**

See footnotes at end of table.

Table A. Metropolitan Statistical Areas and Components—Population: 2021-Continued.

See headnote on page 915.

Metropolitan Statistical Area ~~*Metropolitan Division* ~~~~*Component county*	Popu- lation, 2021 (1,000)
LaPorte County, IN	112
Midland, MI	**83**
Midland County, MI	83
Midland, TX	**173**
Martin County, TX	5
Midland County, TX	168
Milwaukee-Waukesha, WI	**1,566**
Milwaukee County, WI	928
Ozaukee County, WI	92
Washington County, WI	137
Waukesha County, WI	409
Minneapolis-St. **Paul-Bloomington, MN-WI**	**3,691**
Anoka County, MN	367
Carver County, MN	109
Chisago County, MN	57
Dakota County, MN	442
Hennepin County, MN	1,267
Isanti County, MN	42
Le Sueur County, MN	29
Mille Lacs County, MN	27
Ramsey County, MN	543
Scott County, MN	153
Sherburne County, MN	99
Washington County, MN	272
Wright County, MN	145
Pierce County, WI	43
St. Croix County, WI	95
Missoula, MT	**120**
Missoula County, MT	120
Mobile, AL	**428**
Mobile County, AL	413
Washington County, AL	15
Modesto, CA	**553**
Stanislaus County, CA	553
Monroe, LA	**205**
Morehouse Parish, LA	25
Ouachita Parish, LA	159
Union Parish, LA	21
Monroe, MI	**155**
Monroe County, MI	155
Montgomery, AL	**386**
Autauga County, AL	59
Elmore County, AL	89
Lowndes County, AL	10
Montgomery County, AL	227
Morgantown, WV	**141**
Monongalia County, WV	106
Preston County, WV	34
Morristown, TN	**144**
Grainger County, TN	24
Hamblen County, TN	64
Jefferson County, TN	56
Mount Vernon-Anacortes, WA	**131**
Skagit County, WA	131
Muncie, IN	**112**
Delaware County, IN	112
Muskegon, MI	**177**
Muskegon County, MI	177
Myrtle Beach-Conway-North **Myrtle Beach, SC-NC**	**510**
Brunswick County, NC	144
Horry County, SC	366
Napa, CA	**136**
Napa County, CA	136
Naples-Marco Island, FL	**386**
Collier County, FL	386
Nashville-Davidson- **Murfreesboro-Franklin, TN**	**2,012**
Cannon County, TN	15
Cheatham County, TN	42
Davidson County, TN	704
Dickson County, TN	55
Macon County, TN	26
Maury County, TN	105
Robertson County, TN	74
Rutherford County, TN	352
Smith County, TN	20
Sumner County, TN	201
Trousdale County, TN	12

Metropolitan Statistical Area ~~*Metropolitan Division* ~~~~*Component county*	Popu- lation, 2021 (1,000)
Williamson County, TN	256
Wilson County, TN	152
New Bern, NC	**122**
Craven County, NC	101
Jones County, NC	9
Pamlico County, NC	12
New Haven-Milford, CT	**864**
New Haven County, CT	864
New Orleans-Metairie, LA	**1,262**
Jefferson Parish, LA	434
Orleans Parish, LA	377
Plaquemines Parish, LA	23
St. Bernard Parish, LA	44
St. Charles Parish, LA	52
St. James Parish, LA	20
St. John the Baptist Parish, LA	42
St. Tammany Parish, LA	269
New York-Newark-Jersey City, **NY-NJ-PA**	**19,768**
Nassau County-Suffolk **County, NY**	**2,917**
Nassau County, NY	1,391
Suffolk County, NY	1,526
Newark, NJ-PA	**2,273**
Essex County, NJ	855
Hunterdon County, NJ	130
Morris County, NJ	511
Sussex County, NJ	146
Union County, NJ	572
Pike County, PA	60
New Brunswick-Lakewood, **NJ**	**2,501**
Middlesex County, NJ	861
Monmouth County, NJ	645
Ocean County, NJ	649
Somerset County, NJ	346
New York-Jersey City-White **Plains, NY-NJ**	**12,077**
Bergen County, NJ	954
Hudson County, NJ	702
Passaic County, NJ	518
Bronx County, NY	1,425
Kings County, NY	2,641
New York County, NY	1,577
Putnam County, NY	98
Queens County, NY	2,331
Richmond County, NY	493
Rockland County, NY	339
Westchester County, NY	998
Niles, MI	**153**
Berrien County, MI	153
North Port-Sarasota-Bradenton, **FL**	**860**
Manatee County, FL	413
Sarasota County, FL	447
Norwich-New London, CT	**269**
New London County, CT	269
Ocala, FL	**386**
Marion County, FL	386
Ocean City, NJ	**96**
Cape May County, NJ	96
Odessa, TX	**161**
Ector County, TX	161
Ogden-Clearfield, UT	**707**
Box Elder County, UT	60
Davis County, UT	367
Morgan County, UT	13
Weber County, UT	267
Oklahoma City, OK	**1,442**
Canadian County, OK	162
Cleveland County, OK	298
Grady County, OK	56
Lincoln County, OK	34
Logan County, OK	51
McClain County, OK	44
Oklahoma County, OK	799
Olympia-Lacey-Tumwater, WA	**298**
Thurston County, WA	298
Omaha-Council Bluffs, NE-IA	**972**
Harrison County, IA	15

Metropolitan Statistical Area ~~*Metropolitan Division* ~~~~*Component county*	Popu- lation, 2021 (1,000)
Mills County, IA	14
Pottawattamie County, IA	93
Cass County, NE	27
Douglas County, NE	585
Sarpy County, NE	193
Saunders County, NE	23
Washington County, NE	21
Orlando-Kissimmee-Sanford, **FL**	**2,692**
Lake County, FL	396
Orange County, FL	1,423
Osceola County, FL	403
Seminole County, FL	470
Oshkosh-Neenah, WI	**172**
Winnebago County, WI	172
Owensboro, KY	**121**
Daviess County, KY	103
Hancock County, KY	9
McLean County, KY	9
Oxnard-Thousand **Oaks-Ventura, CA**	**840**
Ventura County, CA	840
Palm Bay-Melbourne-Titusville, **FL**	**617**
Brevard County, FL	617
Panama City, FL	**179**
Bay County, FL	179
Parkersburg-Vienna, WV	**89**
Wirt County, WV	5
Wood County, WV	84
Pensacola-Ferry Pass-Brent, **FL**	**516**
Escambia County, FL	322
Santa Rosa County, FL	194
Peoria, IL	**398**
Fulton County, IL	33
Marshall County, IL	12
Peoria County, IL	179
Stark County, IL	5
Tazewell County, IL	130
Woodford County, IL	38
Philadelphia-Camden- **Wilmington, PA-NJ-DE-MD**	**6,229**
Camden, NJ	**1,293**
Burlington County, NJ	464
Camden County, NJ	524
Gloucester County, NJ	304
Montgomery-Bucks-Chester, **PA**	**2,045**
Bucks County, PA	646
Chester County, PA	539
Montgomery County, PA	861
Philadelphia, PA	**2,150**
Delaware County, PA	574
Philadelphia County, PA	1,576
Wilmington, DE-MD-NJ	**741**
New Castle County, DE	572
Cecil County, MD	104
Salem County, NJ	65
Phoenix-Mesa-Chandler, AZ	**4,946**
Maricopa County, AZ	4,497
Pinal County, AZ	450
Pine Bluff, AR	**86**
Cleveland County, AR	8
Jefferson County, AR	66
Lincoln County, AR	13
Pittsburgh, PA	**2,354**
Allegheny County, PA	1,238
Armstrong County, PA	65
Beaver County, PA	167
Butler County, PA	194
Fayette County, PA	127
Washington County, PA	209
Westmoreland County, PA	353
Pittsfield, MA	**129**
Berkshire County, MA	129
Pocatello, ID	**96**
Bannock County, ID	88
Power County, ID	8
Portland-South Portland, ME	**557**

Metropolitan Statistical Area ~~Metropolitan Division ~~~~Component county	Popu- lation, 2021 (1,000)
Cumberland County, ME.	305
Sagadahoc County, ME.	37
York County, ME.	215
Portland-Vancouver-Hillsboro,	
OR-WA.	**2,512**
Clackamas County, OR.	423
Columbia County, OR.	53
Multnomah County, OR.	803
Washington County, OR.	601
Yamhill County, OR.	108
Clark County, WA.	511
Skamania County, WA.	12
Port St. Lucie, FL.	**504**
Martin County, FL.	160
St. Lucie County, FL.	344
Poughkeepsie-Newburgh-	
Middletown, NY.	**702**
Dutchess County, NY.	297
Orange County, NY.	405
Prescott Valley-Prescott, AZ.	**242**
Yavapai County, AZ.	242
Providence-Warwick, RI-MA.	**1,676**
Bristol County, MA.	580
Bristol County, RI.	51
Kent County, RI.	171
Newport County, RI.	85
Providence County, RI.	658
Washington County, RI.	131
Provo-Orem, UT.	**697**
Juab County, UT.	12
Utah County, UT.	685
Pueblo, CO.	**170**
Pueblo County, CO.	170
Punta Gorda, FL.	**195**
Charlotte County, FL.	195
Racine, WI.	**197**
Racine County, WI.	197
Raleigh-Cary, NC.	**1,448**
Franklin County, NC.	72
Johnston County, NC.	227
Wake County, NC.	1,150
Rapid City, SD.	**142**
Meade County, SD.	30
Pennington County, SD.	112
Reading, PA.	**429**
Berks County, PA.	429
Redding, CA.	**182**
Shasta County, CA.	182
Reno, NV.	**498**
Storey County, NV.	4
Washoe County, NV.	493
Richmond, VA.	**1,324**
Amelia County, VA.	13
Charles City County, VA.	7
Chesterfield County, VA.	371
Dinwiddie County, VA.	28
Goochland County, VA.	25
Hanover County, VA.	112
Henrico County, VA.	334
King and Queen County, VA.	7
King William County, VA.	18
New Kent County, VA.	24
Powhatan County, VA.	31
Prince George County, VA.	43
Sussex County, VA.	11
Colonial Heights city, VA.	18
Hopewell city, VA.	23
Petersburg city, VA.	33
Richmond city, VA.	227
Riverside-San	
Bernardino-Ontario, CA.	**4,653**
Riverside County, CA.	2,458
San Bernardino County, CA.	2,195
Roanoke, VA.	**314**
Botetourt County, VA.	34
Craig County, VA.	5
Franklin County, VA.	55
Roanoke County, VA.	97
Roanoke city, VA.	99
Salem city, VA.	25
Rochester, MN.	**227**
Dodge County, MN.	21
Fillmore County, MN.	21

Metropolitan Statistical Area ~~Metropolitan Division ~~~~Component county	Popu- lation, 2021 (1,000)
Olmsted County, MN.	163
Wabasha County, MN.	22
Rochester, NY.	**1,085**
Livingston County, NY.	62
Monroe County, NY.	755
Ontario County, NY.	113
Orleans County, NY.	40
Wayne County, NY.	91
Yates County, NY.	25
Rockford, IL.	**336**
Boone County, IL.	53
Winnebago County, IL.	283
Rocky Mount, NC.	**144**
Edgecombe County, NC.	48
Nash County, NC.	95
Rome, GA.	**99**
Floyd County, GA.	99
Sacramento-Roseville-Folsom,	
CA.	**2,411**
El Dorado County, CA.	193
Placer County, CA.	412
Sacramento County, CA.	1,589
Yolo County, CA.	217
Saginaw, MI.	**190**
Saginaw County, MI.	190
St. Cloud, MN.	**200**
Benton County, MN.	41
Stearns County, MN.	159
St. George, UT.	**191**
Washington County, UT.	191
St. Joseph, MO-KS.	**120**
Doniphan County, KS.	7
Andrew County, MO.	18
Buchanan County, MO.	84
DeKalb County, MO.	11
St. Louis, MO-IL [1]	**2,809**
Bond County, IL.	17
Calhoun County, IL.	4
Clinton County, IL.	37
Jersey County, IL.	21
Macoupin County, IL.	44
Madison County, IL.	264
Monroe County, IL.	35
St. Clair County, IL.	255
Franklin County, MO.	105
Jefferson County, MO.	228
Lincoln County, MO.	62
St. Charles County, MO.	410
St. Louis County, MO.	997
Warren County, MO.	37
St. Louis city, MO.	293
Salem, OR.	**436**
Marion County, OR.	347
Polk County, OR.	89
Salinas, CA.	**437**
Monterey County, CA.	437
Salisbury, MD-DE.	**429**
Sussex County, DE.	248
Somerset County, MD.	25
Wicomico County, MD.	104
Worcester County, MD.	53
Salt Lake City, UT.	**1,263**
Salt Lake County, UT.	1,186
Tooele County, UT.	77
San Angelo, TX.	**122**
Irion County, TX.	2
Sterling County, TX.	1
Tom Green County, TX.	119
San Antonio-New Braunfels,	
TX.	**2,602**
Atascosa County, TX.	50
Bandera County, TX.	22
Bexar County, TX.	2,028
Comal County, TX.	175
Guadalupe County, TX.	177
Kendall County, TX.	47
Medina County, TX.	52
Wilson County, TX.	51
San Diego-Chula	
Vista-Carlsbad, CA.	**3,286**
San Diego County, CA.	3,286

Metropolitan Statistical Area ~~Metropolitan Division ~~~~Component county	Popu- lation, 2021 (1,000)
San Francisco-Oakland-	
Berkeley, CA.	**4,623**
Oakland-Berkeley-Livermore,	
CA.	**2,810**
Alameda County, CA.	1,649
Contra Costa County, CA.	1,161
San Francisco-San	
Mateo-Redwood City, CA.	**1,553**
San Francisco County, CA.	815
San Mateo County, CA.	738
San Rafael, CA.	**260**
Marin County, CA.	260
San Jose-Sunnyvale-Santa	
Clara, CA.	**1,952**
San Benito County, CA.	67
Santa Clara County, CA.	1,886
San Luis Obispo-Paso Robles,	
CA.	**283**
San Luis Obispo County, CA.	283
Santa Cruz-Watsonville, CA.	**268**
Santa Cruz County, CA.	268
Santa Fe, NM.	**155**
Santa Fe County, NM.	155
Santa Maria-Santa Barbara,	
CA.	**446**
Santa Barbara County, CA.	446
Santa Rosa-Petaluma, CA.	**486**
Sonoma County, CA.	486
Savannah, GA.	**410**
Bryan County, GA.	47
Chatham County, GA.	296
Effingham County, GA.	67
Scranton--Wilkes-Barre, PA.	**568**
Lackawanna County, PA.	216
Luzerne County, PA.	326
Wyoming County, PA.	26
Seattle-Tacoma-Bellevue, WA.	**4,012**
Seattle-Bellevue-Kent, WA.	**3,086**
King County, WA.	2,252
Snohomish County, WA.	834
Tacoma-Lakewood, WA.	**926**
Pierce County, WA.	926
Sebastian-Vero Beach, FL.	**164**
Indian River County, FL.	164
Sebring-Avon Park, FL.	**103**
Highlands County, FL.	103
Sheboygan, WI.	**118**
Sheboygan County, WI.	118
Sherman-Denison, TX.	**139**
Grayson County, TX.	139
Shreveport-Bossier City, LA.	**389**
Bossier Parish, LA.	129
Caddo Parish, LA.	233
De Soto Parish, LA.	27
Sierra Vista-Douglas, AZ.	**126**
Cochise County, AZ.	126
Sioux City, IA-NE-SD.	**149**
Woodbury County, IA.	106
Dakota County, NE.	21
Dixon County, NE.	6
Union County, SD.	17
Sioux Falls, SD.	**282**
Lincoln County, SD.	68
McCook County, SD.	6
Minnehaha County, SD.	200
Turner County, SD.	9
South Bend-Mishawaka, IN-MI.	**324**
St. Joseph County, IN.	272
Cass County, MI.	51
Spartanburg, SC.	**336**
Spartanburg County, SC.	336
Spokane-Spokane Valley, WA.	**593**
Spokane County, WA.	546
Stevens County, WA.	47
Springfield, IL.	**207**
Menard County, IL.	12
Sangamon County, IL.	195
Springfield, MA.	**695**
Franklin County, MA.	71
Hampden County, MA.	463

See footnotes at end of table.

Table A. Metropolitan Statistical Areas and Components—Population: 2021-Continued.

See headnote on page 915.

Metropolitan Statistical Area ~~Metropolitan Division ~~~~Component county	Popu-lation, 2021 (1,000)
Hampshire County, MA	162
Springfield, MO	**481**
Christian County, MO	91
Dallas County, MO	17
Greene County, MO	301
Polk County, MO	32
Webster County, MO	40
Springfield, OH	**136**
Clark County, OH	136
State College, PA	**158**
Centre County, PA	158
Staunton, VA	**126**
Augusta County, VA	78
Staunton city, VA	26
Waynesboro city, VA	23
Stockton, CA	**789**
San Joaquin County, CA	789
Sumter, SC	**136**
Clarendon County, SC	31
Sumter County, SC	105
Syracuse, NY	**658**
Madison County, NY	68
Onondaga County, NY	473
Oswego County, NY	117
Tallahassee, FL	**386**
Gadsden County, FL	44
Jefferson County, FL	15
Leon County, FL	293
Wakulla County, FL	35
Tampa-St. Petersburg-Clearwater, FL	**3,220**
Hernando County, FL	201
Hillsborough County, FL	1,478
Pasco County, FL	584
Pinellas County, FL	957
Terre Haute, IN	**185**
Clay County, IN	26
Parke County, IN	16
Sullivan County, IN	21
Vermillion County, IN	15
Vigo County, IN	106
Texarkana, TX-AR	**147**
Little River County, AR	12
Miller County, AR	43
Bowie County, TX	93
The Villages, FL	**136**
Sumter County, FL	136
Toledo, OH	**644**
Fulton County, OH	42
Lucas County, OH	429
Ottawa County, OH	40
Wood County, OH	132
Topeka, KS	**233**
Jackson County, KS	13
Jefferson County, KS	18
Osage County, KS	16
Shawnee County, KS	178
Wabaunsee County, KS	7
Trenton-Princeton, NJ	**386**
Mercer County, NJ	386
Tucson, AZ	**1,052**
Pima County, AZ	1,052
Tulsa, OK	**1,024**
Creek County, OK	72
Okmulgee County, OK	37
Osage County, OK	46
Pawnee County, OK	16
Rogers County, OK	97
Tulsa County, OK	673
Wagoner County, OK	84
Tuscaloosa, AL	**268**
Greene County, AL	8
Hale County, AL	15
Pickens County, AL	19

Metropolitan Statistical Area ~~Metropolitan Division ~~~~Component county	Popu-lation, 2021 (1,000)
Tuscaloosa County, AL	227
Twin Falls, ID	**117**
Jerome County, ID	25
Twin Falls County, ID	92
Tyler, TX	**237**
Smith County, TX	237
Urban Honolulu, HI	**1,001**
Honolulu County, HI	1,001
Utica-Rome, NY	**290**
Herkimer County, NY	60
Oneida County, NY	230
Valdosta, GA	**149**
Brooks County, GA	16
Echols County, GA	4
Lanier County, GA	10
Lowndes County, GA	119
Vallejo, CA	**452**
Solano County, CA	452
Victoria, TX	**98**
Goliad County, TX	7
Victoria County, TX	91
Vineland-Bridgeton, NJ	**154**
Cumberland County, NJ	154
Virginia Beach-Norfolk-Newport News, VA-NC	**1,803**
Camden County, NC	11
Currituck County, NC	30
Gates County, NC	10
Gloucester County, VA	39
Isle of Wight County, VA	39
James City County, VA	80
Mathews County, VA	9
Southampton County, VA	18
York County, VA	71
Chesapeake city, VA	251
Franklin city, VA	8
Hampton city, VA	138
Newport News city, VA	185
Norfolk city, VA	235
Poquoson city, VA	13
Portsmouth city, VA	98
Suffolk city, VA	96
Virginia Beach city, VA	458
Williamsburg city, VA	16
Visalia, CA	**477**
Tulare County, CA	477
Waco, TX	**280**
Falls County, TX	17
McLennan County, TX	263
Walla Walla, WA	**63**
Walla Walla County, WA	63
Warner Robins, GA	**195**
Houston County, GA	167
Peach County, GA	28
Washington-Arlington-Alexandria, DC-VA-MD-WV	**6,356**
Frederick-Gaithersburg-Rockville, MD	**1,335**
Frederick County, MD	280
Montgomery County, MD	1,055
Washington-Arlington-Alexandria, DC-VA-MD-WV	**5,022**
District of Columbia, DC	670
Calvert County, MD	94
Charles County, MD	169
Prince George's County, MD	955
Arlington County, VA	233
Clarke County, VA	15
Culpeper County, VA	54
Fairfax County, VA	1,140
Fauquier County, VA	74
Loudoun County, VA	428
Madison County, VA	14
Prince William County, VA	484

Metropolitan Statistical Area ~~Metropolitan Division ~~~~Component county	Popu-lation, 2021 (1,000)
Rappahannock County, VA	7
Spotsylvania County, VA	144
Stafford County, VA	161
Warren County, VA	41
Alexandria city, VA	155
Fairfax city, VA	24
Falls Church city, VA	14
Fredericksburg city, VA	28
Manassas city, VA	43
Manassas Park city, VA	17
Jefferson County, WV	58
Waterloo-Cedar Falls, IA	**168**
Black Hawk County, IA	130
Bremer County, IA	25
Grundy County, IA	12
Watertown-Fort Drum, NY	**116**
Jefferson County, NY	116
Wausau-Weston, WI	**166**
Lincoln County, WI	29
Marathon County, WI	138
Weirton-Steubenville, WV-OH	**116**
Jefferson County, OH	65
Brooke County, WV	22
Hancock County, WV	29
Wenatchee, WA	**123**
Chelan County, WA	80
Douglas County, WA	44
Wheeling, WV-OH	**138**
Belmont County, OH	66
Marshall County, WV	30
Ohio County, WV	42
Wichita, KS	**648**
Butler County, KS	68
Harvey County, KS	34
Sedgwick County, KS	524
Sumner County, KS	22
Wichita Falls, TX	**149**
Archer County, TX	9
Clay County, TX	10
Wichita County, TX	130
Williamsport, PA	**114**
Lycoming County, PA	114
Wilmington, NC	**292**
New Hanover County, NC	229
Pender County, NC	63
Winchester, VA-WV	**145**
Frederick County, VA	94
Winchester city, VA	28
Hampshire County, WV	23
Winston-Salem, NC	**681**
Davidson County, NC	171
Davie County, NC	44
Forsyth County, NC	386
Stokes County, NC	45
Yadkin County, NC	37
Worcester, MA-CT	**978**
Windham County, CT	116
Worcester County, MA	862
Yakima, WA	**256**
Yakima County, WA	256
York-Hanover, PA	**459**
York County, PA	459
Youngstown-Warren-Boardman, OH-PA	**538**
Mahoning County, OH	227
Trumbull County, OH	201
Mercer County, PA	110
Yuba City, CA	**182**
Sutter County, CA	99
Yuba County, CA	83
Yuma, AZ	**207**
Yuma County, AZ	207

[1] The portion of Sullivan city in Crawford County, Missouri, is legally part of the St. Louis, MO-IL Metropolitan Statistical Area. The estimate shown here for the St. Louis, MO-IL Metropolitan Statistical Area does not include this area.

Source: U.S. Census Bureau, "Metropolitan and Micropolitan Statistical Areas Totals: 2020-2021," <www.census.gov/programs-surveys/popest/data/data-sets.html>.

Table B. Micropolitan Statistical Areas and Components—Population: 2021

[In thousands (42 represents 42,000). Population as of July 2021. Micropolitan Statistical Areas delineated by the U.S. Office of Management and Budget as of March 2020. The estimates are developed from a base that incorporates the 2020 Census, Vintage 2020 estimates, and 2020 Demographic Analysis estimates. All Micropolitan Statistical Areas are arranged alphabetically]

Micropolitan Statistical Area ~~Component county	Population, 2021 (1,000)
Aberdeen, SD	**42**
Brown County, SD	38
Edmunds County, SD	4
Aberdeen, WA	**77**
Grays Harbor County, WA	77
Ada, OK	**38**
Pontotoc County, OK	38
Adrian, MI	**99**
Lenawee County, MI	99
Alamogordo, NM	**69**
Otero County, NM	69
Albemarle, NC	**63**
Stanly County, NC	63
Albert Lea, MN	**31**
Freeborn County, MN	31
Albertville, AL	**98**
Marshall County, AL	98
Alexander City, AL	**51**
Coosa County, AL	10
Tallapoosa County, AL	41
Alexandria, MN	**39**
Douglas County, MN	39
Alice, TX	**49**
Duval County, TX	10
Jim Wells County, TX	39
Alma, MI	**42**
Gratiot County, MI	42
Alpena, MI	**29**
Alpena County, MI	29
Altus, OK	**25**
Jackson County, OK	25
Americus, GA	**34**
Schley County, GA	4
Sumter County, GA	29
Amsterdam, NY	**50**
Montgomery County, NY	50
Andrews, TX	**18**
Andrews County, TX	18
Angola, IN	**35**
Steuben County, IN	35
Arcadia, FL	**34**
DeSoto County, FL	34
Ardmore, OK	**59**
Carter County, OK	48
Love County, OK	10
Arkadelphia, AR	**21**
Clark County, AR	21
Ashland, OH	**52**
Ashland County, OH	52
Ashtabula, OH	**97**
Ashtabula County, OH	97
Astoria, OR	**42**
Clatsop County, OR	42
Atchison, KS	**16**
Atchison County, KS	16
Athens, OH	**62**
Athens County, OH	62
Athens, TN	**54**
McMinn County, TN	54
Athens, TX	**84**
Henderson County, TX	84
Atmore, AL	**37**
Escambia County, AL	37
Auburn, IN	**43**
DeKalb County, IN	43
Auburn, NY	**76**
Cayuga County, NY	76
Augusta-Waterville, ME	**124**
Kennebec County, ME	124
Austin, MN	**40**
Mower County, MN	40
Bainbridge, GA	**29**
Decatur County, GA	29
Baraboo, WI	**66**
Sauk County, WI	66
Bardstown, KY	**47**
Nelson County, KY	47
Barre, VT	**60**
Washington County, VT	60
Bartlesville, OK	**53**
Washington County, OK	53
Batavia, NY	**58**
Genesee County, NY	58
Batesville, AR	**55**
Independence County, AR	38
Sharp County, AR	18
Bay City, TX	**36**
Matagorda County, TX	36
Beatrice, NE	**22**
Gage County, NE	22
Beaver Dam, WI	**89**
Dodge County, WI	89
Bedford, IN	**45**
Lawrence County, IN	45
Beeville, TX	**31**
Bee County, TX	31
Bellefontaine, OH	**46**
Logan County, OH	46
Bemidji, MN	**46**
Beltrami County, MN	46
Bennettsville, SC	**26**
Marlboro County, SC	26
Bennington, VT	**37**
Bennington County, VT	37
Berlin, NH	**31**
Coos County, NH	31
Big Rapids, MI	**40**
Mecosta County, MI	40
Big Spring, TX	**34**
Howard County, TX	34
Big Stone Gap, VA	**39**
Wise County, VA	36
Norton city, VA	4
Blackfoot, ID	**49**
Bingham County, ID	49
Bluefield, WV-VA	**105**
Bland County, VA	6
Tazewell County, VA	40
Mercer County, WV	59
Bluffton, IN	**28**
Wells County, IN	28
Blytheville, AR	**40**
Mississippi County, AR	40
Bogalusa, LA	**45**
Washington Parish, LA	45
Bonham, TX	**37**
Fannin County, TX	37
Boone, NC	**54**
Watauga County, NC	54
Borger, TX	**20**
Hutchinson County, TX	20
Bozeman, MT	**123**
Gallatin County, MT	123
Bradford, PA	**40**
McKean County, PA	40
Brainerd, MN	**98**
Cass County, MN	31
Crow Wing County, MN	67
Branson, MO	**56**
Taney County, MO	56
Breckenridge, CO	**31**
Summit County, CO	31
Brenham, TX	**36**
Washington County, TX	36
Brevard, NC	**33**
Transylvania County, NC	33
Brookhaven, MS	**35**
Lincoln County, MS	35
Brookings, OR	**24**
Curry County, OR	24
Brookings, SD	**35**
Brookings County, SD	35
Brownsville, TN	**18**
Haywood County, TN	18
Brownwood, TX	**38**
Brown County, TX	38
Bucyrus-Galion, OH	**42**
Crawford County, OH	42
Burley, ID	**47**
Cassia County, ID	25
Minidoka County, ID	22
Burlington, IA-IL	**45**
Henderson County, IL	6
Des Moines County, IA	38
Butte-Silver Bow, MT	**35**
Silver Bow County, MT	35
Cadillac, MI	**49**
Missaukee County, MI	15
Wexford County, MI	34
Calhoun, GA	**58**
Gordon County, GA	58
Cambridge, MD	**32**
Dorchester County, MD	32
Cambridge, OH	**38**
Guernsey County, OH	38
Camden, AR	**27**
Calhoun County, AR	5
Ouachita County, AR	22
Campbellsville, KY	**38**
Green County, KY	11
Taylor County, KY	26
Cañon City, CO	**50**
Fremont County, CO	50
Carlsbad-Artesia, NM	**61**
Eddy County, NM	61
Carroll, IA	**21**
Carroll County, IA	21
Cedar City, UT	**61**
Iron County, UT	61
Cedartown, GA	**43**
Polk County, GA	43
Celina, OH	**42**
Mercer County, OH	42
Central City, KY	**31**
Muhlenberg County, KY	31
Centralia, IL	**37**
Marion County, IL	37
Centralia, WA	**84**
Lewis County, WA	84
Charleston-Mattoon, IL	**57**
Coles County, IL	47
Cumberland County, IL	10
Chillicothe, OH	**77**
Ross County, OH	77
Clarksburg, WV	**89**
Doddridge County, WV	8
Harrison County, WV	65
Taylor County, WV	16
Clarksdale, MS	**21**
Coahoma County, MS	21
Clearlake, CA	**69**
Lake County, CA	69
Cleveland, MS	**30**
Bolivar County, MS	30
Clewiston, FL	**40**
Hendry County, FL	40
Clinton, IA	**46**
Clinton County, IA	46
Clovis, NM	**48**
Curry County, NM	48
Coffeyville, KS	**31**
Montgomery County, KS	31
Coldwater, MI	**45**
Branch County, MI	45
Columbus, MS	**58**
Lowndes County, MS	58
Columbus, NE	**34**
Platte County, NE	34
Concord, NH	**155**
Merrimack County, NH	155
Connersville, IN	**23**
Fayette County, IN	23
Cookeville, TN	**116**
Jackson County, TN	12
Overton County, TN	23
Putnam County, TN	81
Coos Bay, OR	**65**
Coos County, OR	65
Cordele, GA	**20**
Crisp County, GA	20
Corinth, MS	**34**
Alcorn County, MS	34
Cornelia, GA	**47**
Habersham County, GA	47
Corning, NY	**93**

See footnotes at end of table.

Micropolitan Statistical Area ~~Component county	Population, 2021 (1,000)
Steuben County, NY	93
Corsicana, TX	**54**
Navarro County, TX	54
Cortland, NY	**46**
Cortland County, NY	46
Coshocton, OH	**37**
Coshocton County, OH	37
Craig, CO	**13**
Moffat County, CO	13
Crawfordsville, IN	**38**
Montgomery County, IN	38
Crescent City, CA	**28**
Del Norte County, CA	28
Crossville, TN	**62**
Cumberland County, TN	62
Cullman, AL	**89**
Cullman County, AL	89
Cullowhee, NC	**58**
Jackson County, NC	43
Swain County, NC	14
Danville, KY	**55**
Boyle County, KY	31
Lincoln County, KY	24
Danville, VA	**102**
Pittsylvania County, VA	60
Danville city, VA	42
Dayton, TN	**33**
Rhea County, TN	33
Decatur, IN	**36**
Adams County, IN	36
Defiance, OH	**38**
Defiance County, OH	38
Del Rio, TX	**48**
Val Verde County, TX	48
Deming, NM	**26**
Luna County, NM	26
DeRidder, LA	**37**
Beauregard Parish, LA	37
Dickinson, ND	**34**
Billings County, ND	1
Stark County, ND	33
Dixon, IL	**34**
Lee County, IL	34
Dodge City, KS	**34**
Ford County, KS	34
Douglas, GA	**52**
Atkinson County, GA	8
Coffee County, GA	43
Dublin, GA	**65**
Johnson County, GA	9
Laurens County, GA	50
Treutlen County, GA	6
DuBois, PA	**80**
Clearfield County, PA	80
Dumas, TX	**21**
Moore County, TX	21
Duncan, OK	**43**
Stephens County, OK	43
Durango, CO	**56**
La Plata County, CO	56
Durant, OK	**47**
Bryan County, OK	47
Dyersburg, TN	**37**
Dyer County, TN	37
Eagle Pass, TX	**58**
Maverick County, TX	58
Easton, MD	**38**
Talbot County, MD	38
Edwards, CO	**56**
Eagle County, CO	56
Effingham, IL	**34**
Effingham County, IL	34
El Campo, TX	**42**
Wharton County, TX	42
El Dorado, AR	**38**
Union County, AR	38
Elizabeth City, NC	**54**
Pasquotank County, NC	41
Perquimans County, NC	13
Elk City, OK	**22**
Beckham County, OK	22
Elkins, WV	**28**

Micropolitan Statistical Area ~~Component county	Population, 2021 (1,000)
Randolph County, WV	28
Elko, NV	**56**
Elko County, NV	54
Eureka County, NV	2
Ellensburg, WA	**45**
Kittitas County, WA	45
Emporia, KS	**35**
Chase County, KS	3
Lyon County, KS	32
Enterprise, AL	**54**
Coffee County, AL	54
Escanaba, MI	**37**
Delta County, MI	37
Española, NM	**40**
Rio Arriba County, NM	40
Eufaula, AL-GA	**27**
Barbour County, AL	25
Quitman County, GA	2
Eureka-Arcata, CA	**136**
Humboldt County, CA	136
Evanston, WY	**21**
Uinta County, WY	21
Fairfield, IA	**16**
Jefferson County, IA	16
Fairmont, MN	**20**
Martin County, MN	20
Fairmont, WV	**56**
Marion County, WV	56
Fallon, NV	**26**
Churchill County, NV	26
Faribault-Northfield, MN	**67**
Rice County, MN	67
Farmington, MO	**68**
St. Francois County, MO	68
Fergus Falls, MN	**60**
Otter Tail County, MN	60
Fernley, NV	**61**
Lyon County, NV	61
Findlay, OH	**75**
Hancock County, OH	75
Fitzgerald, GA	**17**
Ben Hill County, GA	17
Forest City, NC	**65**
Rutherford County, NC	65
Forrest City, AR	**23**
St. Francis County, AR	23
Fort Dodge, IA	**37**
Webster County, IA	37
Fort Leonard Wood, MO	**54**
Pulaski County, MO	54
Fort Madison-Keokuk, IA-IL-MO	**57**
Hancock County, IL	17
Lee County, IA	33
Clark County, MO	7
Fort Morgan, CO	**29**
Morgan County, CO	29
Fort Payne, AL	**72**
DeKalb County, AL	72
Fort Polk South, LA	**48**
Vernon Parish, LA	48
Frankfort, IN	**33**
Clinton County, IN	33
Frankfort, KY	**76**
Anderson County, KY	24
Franklin County, KY	52
Fredericksburg, TX	**27**
Gillespie County, TX	27
Freeport, IL	**44**
Stephenson County, IL	44
Fremont, NE	**37**
Dodge County, NE	37
Fremont, OH	**59**
Sandusky County, OH	59
Gaffney, SC	**56**
Cherokee County, SC	56
Gainesville, TX	**42**
Cooke County, TX	42
Galesburg, IL	**49**
Knox County, IL	49
Gallup, NM	**72**
McKinley County, NM	72

Micropolitan Statistical Area ~~Component county	Population, 2021 (1,000)
Garden City, KS	**42**
Finney County, KS	38
Kearny County, KS	4
Gardnerville Ranchos, NV	**50**
Douglas County, NV	50
Georgetown, SC	**64**
Georgetown County, SC	64
Gillette, WY	**60**
Campbell County, WY	46
Crook County, WY	7
Weston County, WY	7
Glasgow, KY	**55**
Barren County, KY	45
Metcalfe County, KY	10
Glenwood Springs, CO	**80**
Garfield County, CO	62
Pitkin County, CO	17
Gloversville, NY	**53**
Fulton County, NY	53
Granbury, TX	**64**
Hood County, TX	64
Grand Rapids, MN	**45**
Itasca County, MN	45
Grants, NM	**27**
Cibola County, NM	27
Great Bend, KS	**25**
Barton County, KS	25
Greeneville, TN	**71**
Greene County, TN	71
Greensburg, IN	**26**
Decatur County, IN	26
Greenville, MS	**44**
Washington County, MS	44
Greenville, OH	**52**
Darke County, OH	52
Greenwood, MS	**37**
Carroll County, MS	10
Leflore County, MS	28
Greenwood, SC	**69**
Greenwood County, SC	69
Grenada, MS	**21**
Grenada County, MS	21
Guymon, OK	**21**
Texas County, OK	21
Hailey, ID	**26**
Blaine County, ID	25
Camas County, ID	1
Hannibal, MO	**39**
Marion County, MO	29
Ralls County, MO	10
Harrison, AR	**45**
Boone County, AR	38
Newton County, AR	7
Hastings, NE	**31**
Adams County, NE	31
Hays, KS	**29**
Ellis County, KS	29
Heber, UT	**79**
Summit County, UT	43
Wasatch County, UT	36
Helena, MT	**85**
Jefferson County, MT	12
Lewis and Clark County, MT	72
Helena-West Helena, AR	**16**
Phillips County, AR	16
Henderson, NC	**42**
Vance County, NC	42
Hereford, TX	**18**
Deaf Smith County, TX	18
Hermiston-Pendleton, OR	**92**
Morrow County, OR	12
Umatilla County, OR	80
Hillsdale, MI	**46**
Hillsdale County, MI	46
Hilo, HI	**203**
Hawaii County, HI	203
Hobbs, NM	**73**
Lea County, NM	73
Holland, MI	**121**
Allegan County, MI	121
Hood River, OR	**24**
Hood River County, OR	24

Micropolitan Statistical Area ~~Component county	Population, 2021 (1,000)
Hope, AR	**28**
Hempstead County, AR	20
Nevada County, AR	8
Houghton, MI	**39**
Houghton County, MI	37
Keweenaw County, MI	2
Hudson, NY	**62**
Columbia County, NY	62
Huntingdon, PA	**44**
Huntingdon County, PA	44
Huntington, IN	**37**
Huntington County, IN	37
Huntsville, TX	**78**
Walker County, TX	78
Huron, SD	**21**
Beadle County, SD	19
Jerauld County, SD	2
Hutchinson, KS	**61**
Reno County, KS	61
Hutchinson, MN	**37**
McLeod County, MN	37
Indiana, PA	**83**
Indiana County, PA	83
Indianola, MS	**25**
Sunflower County, MS	25
Iron Mountain, MI-WI	**30**
Dickinson County, MI	26
Florence County, WI	5
Jackson, OH	**33**
Jackson County, OH	33
Jackson, WY-ID	**36**
Teton County, ID	12
Teton County, WY	24
Jacksonville, IL	**37**
Morgan County, IL	33
Scott County, IL	5
Jacksonville, TX	**51**
Cherokee County, TX	51
Jamestown, ND	**22**
Stutsman County, ND	22
Jamestown-Dunkirk-Fredonia, NY	**127**
Chautauqua County, NY	127
Jasper, AL	**65**
Walker County, AL	65
Jasper, IN	**56**
Dubois County, IN	44
Pike County, IN	12
Jefferson, GA	**80**
Jackson County, GA	80
Jennings, LA	**32**
Jefferson Davis Parish, LA	32
Jesup, GA	**30**
Wayne County, GA	30
Juneau, AK	**32**
Juneau City and Borough, AK	32
Kalispell, MT	**108**
Flathead County, MT	108
Kapaa, HI	**73**
Kauai County, HI	73
Kearney, NE	**57**
Buffalo County, NE	50
Kearney County, NE	7
Keene, NH	**77**
Cheshire County, NH	77
Kendallville, IN	**47**
Noble County, IN	47
Kennett, MO	**28**
Dunklin County, MO	28
Kerrville, TX	**53**
Kerr County, TX	53
Ketchikan, AK	**14**
Ketchikan Gateway Borough, AK	14
Key West, FL	**82**
Monroe County, FL	82
Kill Devil Hills, NC	**38**
Dare County, NC	38
Kingsville, TX	**31**
Kenedy County, TX	(Z)
Kleberg County, TX	31
Kinston, NC	**55**

Micropolitan Statistical Area ~~Component county	Population, 2021 (1,000)
Lenoir County, NC	55
Kirksville, MO	**29**
Adair County, MO	25
Schuyler County, MO	4
Klamath Falls, OR	**70**
Klamath County, OR	70
Laconia, NH	**64**
Belknap County, NH	64
La Grande, OR	**26**
Union County, OR	26
LaGrange, GA-AL	**104**
Chambers County, AL	35
Troup County, GA	70
Lake City, FL	**70**
Columbia County, FL	70
Lamesa, TX	**12**
Dawson County, TX	12
Laramie, WY	**38**
Albany County, WY	38
Las Vegas, NM	**31**
Mora County, NM	4
San Miguel County, NM	27
Laurel, MS	**83**
Jasper County, MS	16
Jones County, MS	67
Laurinburg, NC	**34**
Scotland County, NC	34
Lawrenceburg, TN	**45**
Lawrence County, TN	45
Lebanon, MO	**36**
Laclede County, MO	36
Lebanon, NH-VT	**223**
Grafton County, NH	92
Sullivan County, NH	44
Orange County, VT	30
Windsor County, VT	58
Levelland, TX	**21**
Hockley County, TX	21
Lewisburg, PA	**43**
Union County, PA	43
Lewisburg, TN	**35**
Marshall County, TN	35
Lewistown, PA	**46**
Mifflin County, PA	46
Lexington, NE	**26**
Dawson County, NE	24
Gosper County, NE	2
Liberal, KS	**22**
Seward County, KS	22
Lincoln, IL	**28**
Logan County, IL	28
Lock Haven, PA	**37**
Clinton County, PA	37
Logansport, IN	**38**
Cass County, IN	38
London, KY	**150**
Clay County, KY	20
Knox County, KY	30
Laurel County, KY	63
Whitley County, KY	37
Los Alamos, NM	**19**
Los Alamos County, NM	19
Ludington, MI	**29**
Mason County, MI	29
Lufkin, TX	**87**
Angelina County, TX	87
Lumberton, NC	**116**
Robeson County, NC	116
Macomb, IL	**27**
McDonough County, IL	27
Madison, IN	**33**
Jefferson County, IN	33
Madisonville, KY	**45**
Hopkins County, KY	45
Magnolia, AR	**23**
Columbia County, AR	23
Malone, NY	**47**
Franklin County, NY	47
Malvern, AR	**33**
Hot Spring County, AR	33
Manitowoc, WI	**82**
Manitowoc County, WI	82

Micropolitan Statistical Area ~~Component county	Population, 2021 (1,000)
Marietta, OH	**59**
Washington County, OH	59
Marinette, WI-MI	**65**
Menominee County, MI	23
Marinette County, WI	42
Marion, IN	**66**
Grant County, IN	66
Marion, NC	**45**
McDowell County, NC	45
Marion, OH	**65**
Marion County, OH	65
Marquette, MI	**66**
Marquette County, MI	66
Marshall, MN	**25**
Lyon County, MN	25
Marshall, MO	**23**
Saline County, MO	23
Marshalltown, IA	**40**
Marshall County, IA	40
Martin, TN	**33**
Weakley County, TN	33
Martinsville, VA	**64**
Henry County, VA	50
Martinsville city, VA	14
Maryville, MO	**21**
Nodaway County, MO	21
Mason City, IA	**50**
Cerro Gordo County, IA	43
Worth County, IA	7
Mayfield, KY	**37**
Graves County, KY	37
Maysville, KY	**17**
Mason County, KY	17
McAlester, OK	**44**
Pittsburg County, OK	44
McComb, MS	**40**
Pike County, MS	40
McMinnville, TN	**42**
Warren County, TN	42
McPherson, KS	**30**
McPherson County, KS	30
Meadville, PA	**83**
Crawford County, PA	83
Menomonie, WI	**46**
Dunn County, WI	46
Meridian, MS	**96**
Clarke County, MS	15
Kemper County, MS	9
Lauderdale County, MS	72
Mexico, MO	**25**
Audrain County, MO	25
Miami, OK	**30**
Ottawa County, OK	30
Middlesborough, KY	**24**
Bell County, KY	24
Milledgeville, GA	**52**
Baldwin County, GA	44
Hancock County, GA	9
Minden, LA	**36**
Webster Parish, LA	36
Mineral Wells, TX	**29**
Palo Pinto County, TX	29
Minot, ND	**77**
McHenry County, ND	5
Renville County, ND	2
Ward County, ND	69
Mitchell, SD	**23**
Davison County, SD	20
Hanson County, SD	4
Moberly, MO	**25**
Randolph County, MO	25
Montrose, CO	**48**
Montrose County, CO	43
Ouray County, CO	5
Morehead City, NC	**69**
Carteret County, NC	69
Morgan City, LA	**48**
St. Mary Parish, LA	48
Moscow, ID	**40**
Latah County, ID	40
Moses Lake, WA	**100**
Grant County, WA	100

See footnotes at end of table.

Table B. Microplitan Statistical Areas and Components—Population: 2021-Continued.

See headnote on page 922.

Micropolitan Statistical Area ~~Component county	Population, 2021 (1,000)	Micropolitan Statistical Area ~~Component county	Population, 2021 (1,000)	Micropolitan Statistical Area ~~Component county	Population, 2021 (1,000)
Moultrie, GA	**46**	St. Landry Parish, LA	82	**Portales, NM**	**19**
Colquitt County, GA	46	**Orangeburg, SC**	**83**	Roosevelt County, NM	19
Mountain Home, AR	**42**	Orangeburg County, SC	83	**Port Angeles, WA**	**78**
Baxter County, AR	42	**Oskaloosa, IA**	**22**	Clallam County, WA	78
Mountain Home, ID	**29**	Mahaska County, IA	22	**Port Lavaca, TX**	**20**
Elmore County, ID	29	**Othello, WA**	**21**	Calhoun County, TX	20
Mount Airy, NC	**71**	Adams County, WA	21	**Portsmouth, OH**	**73**
Surry County, NC	71	**Ottawa, IL**	**147**	Scioto County, OH	73
Mount Gay-Shamrock, WV	**32**	Bureau County, IL	33	**Pottsville, PA**	**143**
Logan County, WV	32	LaSalle County, IL	109	Schuylkill County, PA	143
Mount Pleasant, MI	**65**	Putnam County, IL	6	**Price, UT**	**20**
Isabella County, MI	65	**Ottawa, KS**	**26**	Carbon County, UT	20
Mount Pleasant, TX	**44**	Franklin County, KS	26	**Prineville, OR**	**26**
Camp County, TX	13	**Ottumwa, IA**	**35**	Crook County, OR	26
Titus County, TX	31	Wapello County, IA	35	**Pullman, WA**	**48**
Mount Sterling, KY	**47**	**Owatonna, MN**	**37**	Whitman County, WA	48
Bath County, KY	13	Steele County, MN	37	**Quincy, IL-MO**	**75**
Menifee County, KY	6	**Oxford, MS**	**57**	Adams County, IL	65
Montgomery County, KY	28	Lafayette County, MS	57	Lewis County, MO	10
Mount Vernon, IL	**37**	**Ozark, AL**	**49**	**Raymondville, TX**	**20**
Jefferson County, IL	37	Dale County, AL	49	Willacy County, TX	20
Mount Vernon, OH	**63**	**Paducah, KY-IL**	**98**	**Red Bluff, CA**	**65**
Knox County, OH	63	Massac County, IL	14	Tehama County, CA	65
Murray, KY	**38**	Ballard County, KY	8	**Red Wing, MN**	**48**
Calloway County, KY	38	Livingston County, KY	9	Goodhue County, MN	48
Muscatine, IA	**43**	McCracken County, KY	67	**Rexburg, ID**	**67**
Muscatine County, IA	43	**Pahrump, NV**	**53**	Fremont County, ID	14
Muskogee, OK	**66**	Nye County, NV	53	Madison County, ID	54
Muskogee County, OK	66	**Palatka, FL**	**74**	**Richmond, IN**	**66**
Nacogdoches, TX	**65**	Putnam County, FL	74	Wayne County, IN	66
Nacogdoches County, TX	65	**Palestine, TX**	**58**	**Richmond-Berea, KY**	**109**
Natchez, MS-LA	**47**	Anderson County, TX	58	Estill County, KY	14
Concordia Parish, LA	18	**Pampa, TX**	**22**	Madison County, KY	95
Adams County, MS	29	Gray County, TX	21	**Rio Grande City-Roma, TX**	**66**
Natchitoches, LA	**37**	Roberts County, TX	1	Starr County, TX	66
Natchitoches Parish, LA	37	**Paragould, AR**	**46**	**Riverton, WY**	**39**
Newberry, SC	**38**	Greene County, AR	46	Fremont County, WY	39
Newberry County, SC	38	**Paris, TN**	**32**	**Roanoke Rapids, NC**	**65**
New Castle, IN	**49**	Henry County, TN	32	Halifax County, NC	48
Henry County, IN	49	**Paris, TX**	**50**	Northampton County, NC	17
New Castle, PA	**85**	Lamar County, TX	50	**Rochelle, IL**	**51**
Lawrence County, PA	85	**Parsons, KS**	**20**	Ogle County, IL	51
New Philadelphia-Dover, OH	**93**	Labette County, KS	20	**Rockingham, NC**	**43**
Tuscarawas County, OH	93	**Payson, AZ**	**54**	Richmond County, NC	43
Newport, OR	**51**	Gila County, AZ	54	**Rockport, TX**	**25**
Lincoln County, OR	51	**Pearsall, TX**	**18**	Aransas County, TX	25
Newport, TN	**36**	Frio County, TX	18	**Rock Springs, WY**	**42**
Cocke County, TN	36	**Pecos, TX**	**15**	Sweetwater County, WY	42
New Ulm, MN	**26**	Loving County, TX	(Z)	**Rolla, MO**	**45**
Brown County, MN	26	Reeves County, TX	14	Phelps County, MO	45
Nogales, AZ	**48**	**Pella, IA**	**33**	**Roseburg, OR**	**112**
Santa Cruz County, AZ	48	Marion County, IA	33	Douglas County, OR	112
Norfolk, NE	**48**	**Peru, IN**	**36**	**Roswell, NM**	**65**
Madison County, NE	35	Miami County, IN	36	Chaves County, NM	65
Pierce County, NE	7	**Picayune, MS**	**57**	**Ruidoso, NM**	**20**
Stanton County, NE	6	Pearl River County, MS	57	Lincoln County, NM	20
North Platte, NE	**35**	**Pierre, SD**	**21**	**Russellville, AR**	**84**
Lincoln County, NE	34	Hughes County, SD	18	Pope County, AR	64
Logan County, NE	1	Stanley County, SD	3	Yell County, AR	20
McPherson County, NE	(Z)	**Pinehurst-Southern Pines, NC**	**103**	**Ruston, LA**	**48**
North Vernon, IN	**27**	Moore County, NC	103	Lincoln Parish, LA	48
Jennings County, IN	27	**Pittsburg, KS**	**39**	**Rutland, VT**	**61**
North Wilkesboro, NC	**66**	Crawford County, KS	39	Rutland County, VT	61
Wilkes County, NC	66	**Plainview, TX**	**32**	**Safford, AZ**	**39**
Norwalk, OH	**58**	Hale County, TX	32	Graham County, AZ	39
Huron County, OH	58	**Platteville, WI**	**52**	**St. Marys, GA**	**56**
Oak Harbor, WA	**87**	Grant County, WI	52	Camden County, GA	56
Island County, WA	87	**Plattsburgh, NY**	**80**	**St. Marys, PA**	**31**
Ogdensburg-Massena, NY	**108**	Clinton County, NY	80	Elk County, PA	31
St. Lawrence County, NY	108	**Plymouth, IN**	**46**	**Salem, OH**	**101**
Oil City, PA	**50**	Marshall County, IN	46	Columbiana County, OH	101
Venango County, PA	50	**Point Pleasant, WV-OH**	**54**	**Salina, KS**	**60**
Okeechobee, FL	**40**	Gallia County, OH	29	Ottawa County, KS	6
Okeechobee County, FL	40	Mason County, WV	25	Saline County, KS	54
Olean, NY	**76**	**Ponca City, OK**	**44**	**Sandpoint, ID**	**49**
Cattaraugus County, NY	76	Kay County, OK	44	Bonner County, ID	49
Oneonta, NY	**58**	**Pontiac, IL**	**36**	**Sandusky, OH**	**75**
Otsego County, NY	58	Livingston County, IL	36	Erie County, OH	75
Ontario, OR-ID	**58**	**Poplar Bluff, MO**	**53**	**Sanford, NC**	**64**
Payette County, ID	26	Butler County, MO	42	Lee County, NC	64
Malheur County, OR	32	Ripley County, MO	11	**Sault Ste. Marie, MI**	**37**
Opelousas, LA	**82**			Chippewa County, MI	37

See footnotes at end of table.

Micropolitan Statistical Area ~~Component county	Population, 2021 (1,000)
Sayre, PA	**60**
Bradford County, PA	60
Scottsbluff, NE	**38**
Banner County, NE	1
Scotts Bluff County, NE	36
Sioux County, NE	1
Scottsboro, AL	**53**
Jackson County, AL	53
Scottsburg, IN	**24**
Scott County, IN	24
Searcy, AR	**77**
White County, AR	77
Sedalia, MO	**43**
Pettis County, MO	43
Selinsgrove, PA	**40**
Snyder County, PA	40
Selma, AL	**38**
Dallas County, AL	38
Seneca, SC	**79**
Oconee County, SC	79
Seneca Falls, NY	**34**
Seneca County, NY	34
Sevierville, TN	**100**
Sevier County, TN	100
Seymour, IN	**46**
Jackson County, IN	46
Shawano, WI	**45**
Menominee County, WI	4
Shawano County, WI	41
Shawnee, OK	**73**
Pottawatomie County, OK	73
Shelby, NC	**100**
Cleveland County, NC	100
Shelbyville, TN	**51**
Bedford County, TN	51
Shelton, WA	**68**
Mason County, WA	68
Sheridan, WY	**32**
Sheridan County, WY	32
Show Low, AZ	**108**
Navajo County, AZ	108
Sidney, OH	**48**
Shelby County, OH	48
Sikeston, MO	**38**
Scott County, MO	38
Silver City, NM	**28**
Grant County, NM	28
Snyder, TX	**17**
Scurry County, TX	17
Somerset, KY	**65**
Pulaski County, KY	65
Somerset, PA	**74**
Somerset County, PA	74
Sonora, CA	**56**
Tuolumne County, CA	56
Spearfish, SD	**26**
Lawrence County, SD	26
Spencer, IA	**16**
Clay County, IA	16
Spirit Lake, IA	**18**
Dickinson County, IA	18
Starkville, MS	**62**
Oktibbeha County, MS	52
Webster County, MS	10
Statesboro, GA	**82**
Bulloch County, GA	82
Steamboat Springs, CO	**25**
Routt County, CO	25
Stephenville, TX	**43**
Erath County, TX	43
Sterling, CO	**21**
Logan County, CO	21
Sterling, IL	**55**
Whiteside County, IL	55
Stevens Point, WI	**70**
Portage County, WI	70
Stillwater, OK	**82**
Payne County, OK	82
Storm Lake, IA	**21**
Buena Vista County, IA	21
Sturgis, MI	**61**
St. Joseph County, MI	61
Sulphur Springs, TX	**37**

Micropolitan Statistical Area ~~Component county	Population, 2021 (1,000)
Hopkins County, TX	37
Summerville, GA	**25**
Chattooga County, GA	25
Sunbury, PA	**91**
Northumberland County, PA	91
Susanville, CA	**33**
Lassen County, CA	33
Sweetwater, TX	**15**
Nolan County, TX	15
Tahlequah, OK	**48**
Cherokee County, OK	48
Talladega-Sylacauga, AL	**82**
Talladega County, AL	82
Taos, NM	**35**
Taos County, NM	35
Taylorville, IL	**34**
Christian County, IL	34
The Dalles, OR	**27**
Wasco County, OR	27
Thomaston, GA	**28**
Upson County, GA	28
Thomasville, GA	**46**
Thomas County, GA	46
Tiffin, OH	**55**
Seneca County, OH	55
Tifton, GA	**41**
Tift County, GA	41
Toccoa, GA	**27**
Stephens County, GA	27
Torrington, CT	**185**
Litchfield County, CT	185
Traverse City, MI	**155**
Benzie County, MI	18
Grand Traverse County, MI	96
Kalkaska County, MI	18
Leelanau County, MI	23
Troy, AL	**33**
Pike County, AL	33
Truckee-Grass Valley, CA	**103**
Nevada County, CA	103
Tullahoma-Manchester, TN	**109**
Coffee County, TN	59
Franklin County, TN	43
Moore County, TN	7
Tupelo, MS	**163**
Itawamba County, MS	24
Lee County, MS	83
Pontotoc County, MS	31
Prentiss County, MS	25
Ukiah, CA	**91**
Mendocino County, CA	91
Union, SC	**27**
Union County, SC	27
Union City, TN	**30**
Obion County, TN	30
Urbana, OH	**39**
Champaign County, OH	39
Uvalde, TX	**25**
Uvalde County, TX	25
Van Wert, OH	**29**
Van Wert County, OH	29
Vermillion, SD	**15**
Clay County, SD	15
Vernal, UT	**36**
Uintah County, UT	36
Vernon, TX	**13**
Wilbarger County, TX	13
Vicksburg, MS	**44**
Warren County, MS	44
Vidalia, GA	**36**
Montgomery County, GA	9
Toombs County, GA	27
Vincennes, IN	**36**

Micropolitan Statistical Area ~~Component county	Population, 2021 (1,000)
Knox County, IN	36
Vineyard Haven, MA	**21**
Dukes County, MA	21
Wabash, IN	**31**
Wabash County, IN	31
Wahpeton, ND-MN	**23**
Wilkin County, MN	6
Richland County, ND	17
Wapakoneta, OH	**46**
Auglaize County, OH	46
Warren, PA	**38**
Warren County, PA	38
Warrensburg, MO	**54**
Johnson County, MO	54
Warsaw, IN	**80**
Kosciusko County, IN	80
Washington, IN	**33**
Daviess County, IN	33
Washington, NC	**44**
Beaufort County, NC	44
Washington Court House, OH	**29**
Fayette County, OH	29
Watertown, SD	**35**
Codington County, SD	28
Hamlin County, SD	6
Watertown-Fort Atkinson, WI	**85**
Jefferson County, WI	85
Wauchula, FL	**25**
Hardee County, FL	25
Waycross, GA	**56**
Pierce County, GA	20
Ware County, GA	36
Weatherford, OK	**28**
Custer County, OK	28
West Plains, MO	**40**
Howell County, MO	40
West Point, MS	**19**
Clay County, MS	19
Whitewater, WI	**107**
Walworth County, WI	107
Williston, ND	**38**
Williams County, ND	38
Willmar, MN	**44**
Kandiyohi County, MN	44
Wilmington, OH	**42**
Clinton County, OH	42
Wilson, NC	**78**
Wilson County, NC	78
Winfield, KS	**34**
Cowley County, KS	34
Winnemucca, NV	**18**
Humboldt County, NV	18
Winona, MN	**50**
Winona County, MN	50
Wisconsin Rapids-Marshfield, WI	**74**
Wood County, WI	74
Woodward, OK	**24**
Ellis County, OK	4
Woodward County, OK	20
Wooster, OH	**117**
Wayne County, OH	117
Worthington, MN	**22**
Nobles County, MN	22
Yankton, SD	**23**
Yankton County, SD	23
Zanesville, OH	**86**
Muskingum County, OH	86
Zapata, TX	**14**
Zapata County, TX	14

Z Represents less than 500.

Source: U.S. Census Bureau, "Metropolitan and Micropolitan Statistical Areas Totals: 2020-2021," <www.census.gov/programs-surveys/popest/data/data-sets.html>.

Introduction—The data presented in this *Statistical Abstract* come from not only federal statistical bureaus and other organizations that collect and issue statistics as their principal activity, but also governmental administrative and regulatory agencies, private research organizations, trade associations, insurance companies, health associations, and philanthropic foundations. Consequently, the data vary considerably as to reference periods, definitions of terms and, for ongoing series, the number and frequency of time periods for which data are available.

The statistics presented were obtained and tabulated by various methods. Some statistics are based on complete enumerations or censuses, while others are based on samples. Some information is extracted from records kept for administrative or regulatory purposes (such as school enrollment, hospital records, securities registration, financial accounts, social security records, and income tax returns), while other information is obtained explicitly for statistical purposes through surveys.

Each set of data relates to a group of individuals or units of interest referred to as the *target universe*, or *target population*, or simply as the *universe* or *population*. Tables may present data obtained for all population units, *a census*, or data obtained for only a portion, or *sample*, of the population units.

Prior to data collection, the target universe is clearly defined. For example, if data are to be collected for the universe of households in the United States, it is necessary to define a "household." The target universe may not be completely tractable. Cost and other considerations may restrict data collection to a *survey universe* based on an available list. This list is called a *survey frame, sampling frame,* or *survey sample.*

When data are based on a sample, the sample is usually a scientifically selected *probability sample.* This is a sample selected from a list or sampling frame in such a way that every possible sample has a known chance of selection and usually each unit selected can be assigned a number, greater than zero and less than or equal to one, representing its likelihood or probability of selection.

For large-scale sample surveys, the probability sample of units is often selected as a multistage sample. The first stage of a multistage sample is the selection of a probability sample of large groups of population members, referred to as primary sampling units (PSUs). For example, in a national multistage household sample, PSUs are often counties or groups of counties. The second stage of a multistage sample is the selection, within each PSU selected at the first stage, of smaller groups of population units, referred to as secondary sampling units. In subsequent stages of selection, smaller and smaller nested groups are chosen until the ultimate sample of population units is obtained. To qualify a multistage sample as a probability sample, all stages of sampling must be carried out using probability sampling methods.

Prior to selection at each stage of a multistage (or a single stage) sample, a list of the sampling units or sampling frame for that stage must be obtained. For example, for the first stage of selection of a national household sample, a list of the counties and county groups that form the PSUs must be compiled. For the final stage of selection, lists of households, and sometimes persons within the households, have to be compiled in the field. For surveys of economic entities and for the economic censuses, the U.S. Census Bureau generally uses a frame constructed from the Bureau's Business Register. The Business Register contains all establishments with payroll in the United States, including small single-establishment firms as well as larger firms with multiple establishments.

Wherever the quantities in a table refer to an entire universe but are constructed from data collected in a sample survey, the table quantities are referred to as *sample estimates*. In constructing a sample estimate, an attempt is made to come as close as is feasible to the corresponding universe quantity that would be obtained from a complete census of the universe. Estimates based on a sample will, however, generally differ from the hypothetical census figures. Two classifications of errors are associated with estimates based on sample surveys:

1 *Sampling error*—the error arising from the use of a sample, rather than a census, to estimate population quantities.
2 *Nonsampling error*—those errors arising from nonsampling sources, which can be numerous and varied, depending on the type of survey. Nonsampling errors can include mistakes made in data collection or data processing, misunderstandings of the interviewer or the respondent, and data entry errors.

The particular sample used in a survey is only one of a large number of possible samples of the same size which could have been selected using the same sampling procedure. Estimates derived from the different samples would, in general, differ from each other. The *standard error* (SE) is a measure of the variation among the estimates derived from all possible samples. The standard error is the most commonly used measure of the sampling error of an estimate. Valid estimates of the standard errors of survey estimates can usually be calculated from the data collected in a probability sample. For convenience, the standard error is sometimes expressed as a percent of the estimate and is called the relative standard error (RSE) or *coefficient of variation* (CV). For example, an estimate of 200 units with an estimated standard error of 10 units has an estimated CV of 5 percent.

A sample estimate and an estimate of its standard error or CV can be used to construct interval estimates that have a prescribed confidence that the interval includes the average of the estimates derived from all possible samples with a known probability. To illustrate, if all possible samples were selected under essentially the same general conditions, and using the same sample design, and if an estimate and its estimated standard error were calculated from each sample, then: 1) approximately 68 percent of the intervals from one standard error below the estimate to one standard error above the estimate would include the average estimate derived from all possible samples; 2) approximately 90 percent of the intervals from 1.6 standard errors below the estimate to 1.6 standard errors above the estimate would include the average estimate derived from all possible samples; and 3) approximately 95 percent of the intervals from two standard errors below the estimate to two standard errors above the estimate would include the average estimate derived from all possible samples.

Thus, for a particular sample, one can say with the appropriate level of confidence (e.g., 90 percent or 95 percent) that the average of all possible samples is included in the constructed interval. Example of a confidence interval: an estimate is 200 units with a standard error of 10 units. An approximately 90 percent confidence interval (plus or minus 1.6 standard errors) is from 184 to 216.

All surveys and censuses are subject to nonsampling errors. Nonsampling errors arise from a variety of factors, including total nonresponse (no usable data obtained for a sampled unit), partial or item nonresponse (only a portion of a response may be usable), survey respondents who are unable or unwilling to provide correct information or who have difficulty understanding questions, mistakes in recording, editing and transferring data, errors of collection or processing, and coverage problems (overcoverage and undercoverage of the target universe). Nonresponse errors usually, but not always, result in an understatement of sampling errors and thus an overstatement of the precision of survey estimates. Estimating the magnitude of nonsampling errors would require special experiments or access to independent data. Organizations seldom attempt to measure nonsampling errors. The surveys and censuses described in this appendix are subject to nonsampling error.

Nearly all types of nonsampling errors that affect surveys also occur in complete censuses. Since surveys can be conducted on a smaller scale than censuses, nonsampling errors can presumably be controlled more tightly. Relatively more funds and effort can perhaps be expended toward eliciting responses, detecting and correcting response error, and reducing processing errors. As a result, survey results can sometimes be more accurate than census results.

To reduce nonsampling errors, most surveys use computer-assisted telephone or personal interviewing (CATI or CAPI). The computer-assisted data collection method employs computer software and programs that guide the interviewer through the questionnaire to keep the survey consistent across all respondents, and can automatically route the interviewer to appropriate questions based on answers to previous questions. Computer programs can determine if responses are within an allowable range and check for consistency against other data collected during the interview or even with data from a previous interview. Capturing a survey on a computer also aids in the complete and accurate transfer of data to the organization's data system. Once collected, survey organizations run automated reviews and edits of data, and impute and weight data items. Other steps to reduce nonsampling errors can include designing

questionnaires that are easy to understand and have clear instructions, training personnel in data collection and processing, and conducting audits and other quality control measures. The surveys described below have detailed documentation available online that describes sources of nonsampling error and the many and various efforts they take to reduce nonsampling errors.

Adjustments of sample estimates are often made, frequently for nonresponse, both total and partial. These adjustments are *imputations*. Imputation for total nonresponse is usually made by substituting for the questionnaire responses of the nonrespondents the "average" questionnaire responses of the respondents. These imputations usually are made separately within various groups of sample members, formed by attempting to place respondents and nonrespondents together that have similar characteristics. Imputation for item nonresponse is usually made by substituting for a missing item the response to that item of a respondent having characteristics that are similar to those of the nonrespondent.

For an estimate calculated from a sample survey, the *total error* in the estimate is composed of the sampling error, which can usually be estimated from the sample, and the nonsampling error, which usually cannot be estimated from the sample. The total error present in a population quantity obtained from a complete census is composed of only nonsampling errors. Ideally, estimates of the total error associated with data presented in the *Statistical Abstract* tables would be available; however, due to the unavailability of estimates of nonsampling errors, only estimates of the levels of sampling errors, in terms of estimated standard errors or coefficients of variation, are available. To obtain estimates of the estimated standard errors from the sample of interest, see the source cited at the end of each table.

Source of Additional Material: The Federal Committee on Statistical Methodology (FCSM) is an interagency committee dedicated to improving the quality of federal statistics, online at <www.fcsm.gov/>. See also information available on the Census Bureau website at <www.census.gov/quality/>.

Special Note: Please note that the coronavirus 2019 (COVID-19) pandemic impacted data collection and survey results for many of the sources described below. Users should exercise caution in their use of data collected during the COVID-19 pandemic. See each source's website for more information.

Principal data sources—Beginning below are brief descriptions of over 30 of the sample surveys and censuses that provide a substantial portion of the data contained in this *Statistical Abstract*.

U.S. DEPARTMENT OF AGRICULTURE, National Agricultural Statistics Service

Census of Agriculture

Universes, Frequency, and Types of Data: Complete count of U.S. farms and ranches conducted once every 5 years, with data at the national, state, and county level. The survey includes any place from which $1,000 or more of agricultural products were produced and sold, or normally would have been sold, during the census year. The census collects data on all commodities produced in the U.S. as well as detailed information on land use and ownership, operator characteristics (such as race, gender, age, tenure on farm, and operating arrangement), production practices, and income and expenditures.

Data Collection: The NASS mails out questionnaires to all farmers and ranchers. Producers can return their forms by mail or utilize a census form online. For nonrespondents, NASS sends reminder notices and attempts to contact those producers for a personal interview done over the telephone or in-person. Personal interviewing is conducted for special classes of records in the census operations. Response to the Census of Agriculture is required by federal law. The response rate for the 2012 Census was 74.6 percent, and for the 2017 Census, 71.8 percent.

Data Editing and Imputation: Captured data go through a computer editing process that validates various aspects of the record, and determines whether to accept the value for each data item, or to take corrective action. Imputation is conducted for unreasonable and missing data. NASS may contact a producer to verify information or compare information to existing known data, to ensure the most accurate information. See *Appendix A Census of Agriculture Methodology* for detailed imputation methods.

Methodology: NASS uses capture-recapture methodology, an accepted statistical methodology, to account for undercoverage (farms not reached in the original mailing), nonresponse (people not returning their census questionnaires), and misclassification (whether an operation is correctly classified as a farm or not). Details are in *Appendix A Census of Agriculture Methodology*. The uncertainty these adjustments introduce causes the exact numbers to be unknown; however, the uncertainty can be quantified. This measure of relative reliability is known as the coefficient of variation. Estimates of reliability are available from NASS.

Sources of Additional Material: U.S. Department of Agriculture (NASS), 2017 Census of Agriculture, *Appendix A Census of Agriculture Methodology*, and *Appendix B General Explanation and Census of Agriculture Report Form*, online at <www.nass.usda.gov/Publications/AgCensus/2017/> and <www.nass.usda.gov/AgCensus/>. See also <www.nass.usda.gov/AgCensus/FAQ/2022>.

June Area Survey

Universe, Frequency, and Types of Data: Conducted annually, the June Area survey utilizes an area sampling frame and is designed to account for every acre of land, all agricultural activities, and land uses within segment boundaries. Data are collected from all states except Alaska, on crop acreage, grain stocks, cattle inventory, hog inventory, sheep and goat inventory, land values, farm numbers, sales, and technology use. The survey also serves to measure list incompleteness and is subsampled for multiple frame surveys.

Data Collection and Imputation: A sample of over 9,000 segments, smaller units of a PSU measuring roughly one square mile, is selected from each land use stratum for data collection. All farm operators operating within the boundaries of the selected segments are interviewed. In a given year, approximately 70,000 agricultural and non-agricultural land use tracts are identified within the sampled segments. From that identification, over 30,000 detailed interviews are conducted with farmers operating farms inside the segment boundaries or that have the potential to qualify as a farm. Historically, data collection for the June Area survey was completed entirely by personal interview during the 1st two weeks in June. Beginning in 2021, data collection is conducted by telephone. Operators in selected segments are identified, and an informational packet including an aerial photograph and sample questionnaire is mailed to each prospective respondent. This informational packet helps identify tracts of land operated within the segment boundary. Imputation is based on enumerator observation or data reported by respondents having similar agricultural characteristics.

Data Reliability: Reports presenting data from the June area survey include measures of reliability at the national level for the subject covered in the report.

Sources of Additional Material: U.S. Department of Agriculture, National Agricultural Statistics Service, *Area Frame Design for Agricultural Surveys*, June 2009, online at <www.nass.usda.gov/Publications/Methodology_and_Data_Quality/>; and <www.nass.usda.gov/Surveys/Guide_to_NASS_Surveys/June_Area/>.

Objective Yield Surveys

Universe, Frequency, and Types of Data: Monthly forecasts and end-of-season estimates of planted and harvested acres, yield, and production of winter wheat, corn for grain, soybeans, fall potatoes, and upland cotton. All acres for harvest as grain in the leading producing states are eligible for this survey. Survey samples are selected from participants in the March Crops/Stocks Survey or the June Agricultural Survey, and include only the top producing states that together produce the majority of a given crop in the U.S.

Data Collection: Field work begins April 25 for winter wheat and July 25 for all the other crops. Sample units are visited at the end of each month during the growing season. Enumerators count and measure plant characteristics in sample fields. Sample fruit (ears, pods, bolls, heads, or tubers) is sent to a lab to determine fruit weight, threshed grain weight, and moisture content. A post harvest visit is made to glean fruit left in some sample fields. Production is measured from plots at harvest. Harvest loss is measured from post harvest gleanings. Detailed methods are available in the sources cited below.

Data Reliability: Reliability measures at the national level are provided in reports presenting data from the Objective Yield Surveys.

Sources of Additional Material: U.S. Department of Agriculture, National Agricultural Statistics Service, Statistical Methods Branch, *The Yield Forecasting Program of NASS*, May 2012, online at <www.nass.usda.gov/Publications/Methodology_and_Data_Quality/> and <www.nass.usda.gov/Surveys/Guide_to_NASS_Surveys/Objective_Yield/>.

U.S. BUREAU OF JUSTICE STATISTICS (BJS)

National Crime Victimization Survey (NCVS)

Universe, Frequency, and Types of Data: The NCVS is an annual survey of U.S. household members age 12 and older and is the primary source for information on criminal victimization. Data are obtained from a nationally representative sample of about 240,000 persons in about 150,000 households. Survey excludes victimizations occurring outside of the U.S. The NCVS covers nonfatal personal crime and household property crime victimization, and the characteristics of crimes and victims. Nonfatal personal crimes include rape or sexual assault, robbery, aggravated and simple assault, and personal larceny (purse-snatching, pick-pocketing). Household property crimes include burglary and trespassing, motor vehicle theft, and other types of theft. The survey covers crimes that are both reported and not reported to the police. The survey excludes homicide, arson, and commercial crimes.

Data Collection and Weighting: Eligible household members age 12 and older are interviewed every 6 months for a total of 7 interviews. Households stay in the sample for about 3 1/2 years. New households rotate into the sample on an ongoing basis. Personal interviews are used in the first interview; subsequent interviews are conducted either in person or by telephone. Survey respondents provide information about their crime victimization experiences during the past 6 months, and their personal characteristics. NCVS data include both person and household weights to provide estimates of the population and households represented by each person and each household in the sample. Weights are designed to adjust data to known population totals and to compensate for survey nonresponse and other aspects of the complex sample design. Please note that the 2017 NCVS utilized new household weighting adjustments that resulted in 2017 NCVS household estimates being about 8 percent lower than the previous year. Users should exercise caution when comparing trends in household property crimes over time.

Data Reliability: The *Criminal Victimization* report discusses different methods BJS uses to produce standard errors, including the use of a specialized version of a Balanced Repeated Replication estimation (a type of direct replication variance estimation) using Fay's method, and the use of generalized variance function parameters produced by the Census Bureau for BJS. Estimates and standard errors are also presented in the report, available online; see sources cited below. Detailed documentation is also available online.

Sources of Additional Material: U.S. Bureau of Justice Statistics, *Criminal Victimization*, and the National Crime Victimization Survey website at <bjs.ojp.gov/data-collection/ncvs>.

U.S. BUREAU OF LABOR STATISTICS

Consumer Expenditure Survey (CE)

Universe, Frequency and Types of Data: The Consumer Expenditure Survey (CE) is a nationwide household survey on expenditures for goods and services. The CE also collects information on amount and sources of household income, changes in assets and liabilities, and demographic and economic characteristics of family members. The CE has two components: a quarterly interview survey, and a weekly diary survey. Estimates covering 12-month periods are released annually. Samples are national probability samples of households that are representative of the civilian noninstitutional population. Prior to 2020, sample sizes were 12,000 addresses per calendar quarter for the Interview Survey, and 12,000 addresses per year for the Diary Survey. Beginning 2020, the Interview Survey contacts 13,000 addresses per quarter; usable interviews are obtained from about 5,000 households each quarter. The Diary Survey sample is now 18,000 addresses per year; usable diaries come from about 6,700 households.

Data Collection: Both the Interview Survey and the Diary Survey are conducted primarily by personal visit, with some telephone interviewing. The measurement unit is the set of eligible individuals constituting a consumer unit (CU). The CU is defined as 1) all members in a housing unit who make up a family (includes foster children); 2) a person living alone or sharing a household with others, or living as a roomer in a private home or other lodging (includes hotel or motel), but who is financially independent; or 3) two or more unrelated persons living together who pool their income to make joint expenditure decisions. Students living in university-sponsored housing are also included in the sample as separate consumer units. For the Interview Survey, consumer units are interviewed every three months, for 4 quarters. The Interview Survey collects expenditure data for large and recurring items that respondents can recall for 3 months or longer, such as property, automobiles, major appliances, rent, and insurance. The Diary Survey collects expenditure data for smaller and frequently purchased items such as food and beverages, and household and personal care products and services. Consumer units report expenses for two consecutive 1-week periods. Data for the Interview Survey and the Diary Survey are collected and processed separately.

Data Reliability: BLS adjusts data using imputation, allocation, and time adjustment. Detailed discussion of imputation and allocation methods are available at the source cited below. Consumer Expenditure tables include estimates of standard errors and coefficients of variation for expenditure data.

Sources of Additional Material: Bureau of Labor Statistics website <www.bls.gov/cex/home.htm>; and "BLS Handbook of Methods," <www.bls.gov/opub/hom/cex/home.htm>.

Consumer Price Index (CPI)

Universe, Frequency, and Types of Data: The Consumer Price Index (CPI) is a measure of the average change over time in the prices paid by urban consumers for a market basket of consumer goods and services. The CPI is derived from a monthly survey. The CPI reflects spending patterns of two population groups: all urban consumers (CPI-U), and urban wage earners and clerical workers (CPI-W). The all urban consumer group represents approximately 93 percent of the total U.S. population. The CPI-W population represents about 29 percent of the total U.S. population and is a subset of the CPI-U population. Not included in the CPI are the spending patterns of people living in rural non-metropolitan areas, farm families, Armed Forces personnel, and those in institutions such as prisons and mental hospitals. The BLS calculates CPI indexes for the U.S., the census regions and divisions, urban areas by population size, and selected metropolitan and local areas. The CPI covers over 200 item categories of consumer purchases in eight major groups: food and beverages, housing, apparel, transportation, medical care, recreation, education and communication, and other goods and services. Includes user fees (such as water and sewer services), and sales and excise taxes. The index measures price change from a designed reference date. For most of the CPI-U and the CPI-W, the reference base is 1982-84 equals 100.

Data Collection: Prices of most goods and services are collected by personal visit, telephone, or via the internet. A small portion of data are collected from websites. Data on rent are collected from landlords or tenants. Prices are collected either every month or every other month, depending on the item and its location, for approximately 80,000 items in 75 urban areas across the country from about 6,000 housing units and approximately 22,000 retail and service establishments. The BLS collects rent information every 6 months.

Data Adjustment and Imputation: To account for products disappearing, products replaced with new versions, and new products, the BLS uses a CPI item replacement procedure, making adjustments as necessary. The CPI also uses imputation for missing data. See source cited below for more detailed discussion of these methods and other calcuations.

Data Reliability: The CPI is a statistical estimate that is subject to sampling error because it is based upon a sample of retail prices and not the complete universe of all prices. BLS calculates and publishes estimates of the 1-month, 2-month, 6-month, and 12-month percent change standard errors annually for the CPI-U by expenditure item. These standard error estimates can be used to construct confidence intervals for hypothesis testing. For the latest data, including information on how to use the estimates of standard error, see source cited below and <www.bls.gov/cpi/tables/variance-estimates/home. htm>.

Sources of Additional Material: U.S. Bureau of Labor Statistics, <www.bls.gov/cpi/overview.htm> and "BLS Handbook of Methods," <www.bls.gov/opub/ hom/cpi/>.

Current Employment Statistics (CES) Program

Universe, Frequency, and Types of Data: Monthly survey of over 130,000 businesses and government agencies representing approximately 670,000 worksites drawn from a sampling frame of Unemployment Insurance (UI) tax accounts covering over 10 million establishments, which is about 97 percent of all employment within the scope of the CES. The active CES sample includes approximately one-third of all nonfarm payroll employees in the 50 states, the District of Columbia, Puerto Rico, and the Virgin Islands. A semiannual update is performed each summer to select units from the population of business openings and other units

not previously eligible for selection. The CES collects data on employment, hours, and earnings at detailed industry levels. The CES series are estimates of nonfarm wage and salary jobs, not of employed persons; an individual with 2 jobs is counted twice by the payroll survey. The CES excludes employees in agriculture and private households, and the self-employed.

Data Collection: The BLS uses various collection techniques. Data collection centers (DCCs) perform initial enrollment of each firm via telephone, collect the data for several months, and, where possible, transfer respondents to a self-reporting mode such as touch-tone data entry (TDE), facsimile, or internet collection. Very large, multi-establishment firms are often enrolled via personal visit, and thereafter report data via electronic data interchange (EDI). These firms provide electronic files to BLS that include data from all their worksites. All firms with 1,000 or more employees are asked to participate in the survey, as is a sample of firms across all employment sizes. When firms are rotated into the sample, they are retained for 2 years or more. Each month, respondents extract the employment, hours, and earnings data from their payroll records and submit it to the BLS. Data are collected for the pay period that includes the 12th of each month. BLS staff prepare national estimates of employment, hours, and earnings. State agencies cooperate with the BLS to develop state and metropolitan area estimates.

Microdata Review: The CES program tests all respondent data, collectively known as microdata. These tests, also called microdata screening tests, compare all new data reported by survey respondents to the respondent's historically reported data. Data that fail these microdata screening tests are then reviewed by analysts to determine whether the microdata should be used in the estimation of employment, hours, and earnings. Detailed information is available online under "Technical Notes for the Current Employment Statistics Survey" at <www.bls.gov/web/empsit/ cestn.htm>.

Data Reliability: The magnitude of sampling error, or variance, is directly related to the size of the sample and the percentage of universe coverage achieved by the sample. The establishment survey sample covers over one-third of total universe employment; this yields a relatively small variance on the total nonfarm estimates. Information on measurements of error associated with sample estimates are available online under "Technical Notes for the Current Employment Statistics Survey" at <www.bls.gov/web/empsit/cestn.htm>.

Total Error: The benchmark error is used as a proxy measure of total error for the CES survey, and it represents the difference between two employment estimates derived from separate statistical processes (the CES sample process and the Unemployment Insurance administrative process), and thus reflects the sum of the errors present in each program. Historically, benchmark revisions have been very small for total nonfarm employment, averaging 0.1 percent over the past 10 years.

Sources of Additional Material: U.S. Bureau of Labor Statistics, "BLS Handbook of Methods," Chapter 2,

<www.bls.gov/opub/hom/pdf/ces-20110307.pdf>; and Current Employment Statistics, "Technical Notes," <www.bls.gov/web/empsit/cestn.htm>.

National Compensation Survey (NCS)

Universe, Frequency, and Types of Data: The NCS is a voluntary establishment-based survey that provides comprehensive measures of 1) employer costs for employee compensation, including wages and salaries, and benefits, 2) compensation trends, and 3) the availability of and/or employee participation in employer-provided benefits, with an emphasis on health insurance and retirement benefits. The NCS includes establishments in private industry and in state and local government; major exclusions are workers in federal and quasi-federal agencies, military personnel, agricultural workers, workers in private households, the self-employed, and unpaid workers. The NCS releases data through the quarterly Employment Cost Index and the Employer Costs for Employee Compensation, and annual reports on employee benefits, with data shown by various employer and/or employee characteristics, including industry, occupational group, labor union status, and other characteristics.

Sample Selection: The total sample is selected in two stages, one for establishments, and one for occupations within the sample of establishments. The establishment sample has three rotation groups: one for private industry, one for state and local government, and one for the aerospace industry. Government establishments are rotated approximately every 10 years, and all others are rotated every 3 years (except during the government rotation year). Field economists use a probability selection of occupations method to select jobs to sample, then match employees with those jobs, and classify workers according to their duties rather than specific job title. NCS data releases include the number of establishments and occupations covered in the survey.

Data Collection and Adjustments: BLS field economists use personal visits, mail, telephone, and email, to obtain data from NCS survey respondents; they do not use paper and online surveys, but rather use conversational interviews and descriptive documents. Updated data are collected quarterly. Discussion of weight adjustments and imputation for the various types of data collected is available online at the source cited below.

Data Reliability: NCS uses standard errors to evaluate published series. A discussion of sampling and nonsampling errors, as well as web-based links to more detailed data on the reliability of estimates from the NCS, are available online at <www.bls.gov/opub/hom/ncs/calculation.htm>. Each data product produced using NCS data also provides information on where to access data on measures of reliability.

Sources of Additional Material: Bureau of Labor Statistics, Handbook of Methods, "National Compensation Measures," <www.bls.gov/opub/hom/ncs/home.htm>.

Producer Price Index (PPI)

Universe, Frequency, and Types of Data: Monthly survey of producing companies to determine price changes of all commodities and services produced in the United States for sale in commercial transactions. Price changes are from the perspective of the seller. Covers nearly all industries in the goods-producing sectors (including agriculture, fishing, forestry, mining, and manufacturing), and over 70 percent of the service sector's output as measured by revenue reported in the Economic Census. Domestic production of goods for the military is included, as are goods shipped between establishments owned by the same company. Each month approximately 100,000 prices are solicited from roughly 25,000 establishments. The BLS releases each month about 10,000 PPIs for individual products and groups of products. PPIs are organized into three main sets: (1) Final demand-Intermediate demand (FD-ID) indexes, (2) commodity indexes, and (3) indexes for the net output of industries and their products.

Data Collection: PPIs are constructed using selling prices reported by establishments of all sizes, selected by probability sampling, with the probability of selection proportionate to size. Individual items and transaction terms also are chosen by probability proportionate to size. BLS encourages cooperating companies to supply actual transaction prices at the time of shipment to minimize the use of list prices. Prices submitted by survey respondents are effective on the Tuesday of the week containing the 13th day of the month. The survey is conducted online via the BLS Internet Data Collection Facility. BLS publishes price indexes, not actual prices. All PPIs are subject to monthly revisions up to 4 months after original publication to reflect the availability of late reports and corrections by respondents.

Reference Base: The current standard base period for most commodity-oriented PPI series is 1982, but many indexes that began after 1982 are based on the month of their introduction. The FD-ID indexes typically have a reference base of November 2009 = 100.

Weights, Adjustments, and Variance Estimates: BLS provides extensive documentation for the PPI, including descriptions of PPI weights, quality adjustments for products that change over time, seasonal adjustments, and methodologies for selected industries. Please see sources cited below. The PPI program also began publishing variance estimates in 2016 based on data for 2015. The median absolute value of the percent change is provided as the reference statistic and the corresponding median standard error is provided as the measure of variance. Reports on variance methodology and estimates are available online at <www.bls.gov/ppi/variances/>.

Sources of Additional Material: U.S. Bureau of Labor Statistics, PPI overview available online at <www.bls.gov/ppi/overview.htm>, and documentation online at <www.bls.gov/ppi/methods-overview.htm>.

BOARD OF GOVERNORS OF THE FEDERAL RESERVE SYSTEM

Survey of Consumer Finances (SCF)

Universe, Frequency, and Types of Data: Triennial sample survey of families on their finances. The 2019 Survey of Consumer Finances was the most recent survey available for coverage in this *Statistical Abstract.* The survey collects detailed data on the composition of family balance sheets, income, net worth, debt, and relationships with financial institutions. Data include respondent demographic characteristics. In this survey a given household is divided into a primary economic unit (the family), and everyone else in the household. The primary economic unit is the economically dominant single person or couple (married or cohabitating) and all other persons in the household who are financially interdependent with the economically dominant person or couple. The primary economic unit is used as the reference family. The survey instrument remains generally consistent over the years, but the SCF periodically updates questions and adds new questions to accommodate developments in financial behaviors and related topics.

Sample Design: The SCF employs a sample design consisting of two parts: a standard, geographically based random sample, and a special list sample that oversamples relatively wealthy families under strict rules to provide confidentiality and give potential respondents the right to refuse participation. Weights are used to combine information from the two samples to make estimates for the full population. Of the 5,783 interviews completed for the 2019 SCF, 4,291 were from the area-probability sample, and 1,492 were from the list sample; for 2016, 4,754 were from the area-probability sample, and 1,500 were from the list sample. In 2019, about 60 percent of households selected for the area-probability sample actually completed interviews, down from 65 percent in 2016. The overall response rate in the list sample did not change in 2019 at about one-third.

Data Collection and Imputation: National Opinion Research Center (NORC) at the University of Chicago has collected data for the survey since 1992. The majority of interviews for the SCF are conducted in person. Interviews are conducted via telephone if more convenient for respondents. For the 2019 SCF, about 200 area-probability interviews were conducted via a mixed mode strategy of internet and in-person or telephone interviews. These cases were a test of the feasibility of conducting the SCF on the internet. The SCF uses weighting to adjust for differential nonresponse to the survey. To address missing information on individual questions within the interview, the SCF uses statistical methods to impute missing data; the technique makes multiple estimates of missing data to allow for an estimate of the uncertainty attributable to this type of nonresponse.

Data Reliability: Sampling error is estimated using replication methods. Replication methods draw samples, called replicates, from the set of actual respondents, and compute weights for all cases in each of the replicates. Standard error tables and additional technical documentation are available on the source website.

Sources of Additional Material: Board of Governors of the Federal Reserve System, "Changes in U.S. Family Finances from 2016 to 2019: Evidence from the Survey of Consumer Finances," *Federal Reserve Bulletin*, September 2020, <www.federalreserve.gov/econres/scfindex.htm>.

U.S. CENSUS BUREAU

Economic Census

Universe, Frequency, and Types of Data: Conducted every 5 years to obtain data on number of establishments, number of employees, payroll, measure of output (sales, shipments, receipts, or revenue), and other industry-specific statistics from approximately 4 million businesses of all sizes. Data are shown by North American Industry Classification code. The universe is all establishments with paid employees in most industries (exclusions include agriculture, forestry, fishing and hunting, rail transportation, postal service, schools and colleges, religious organizations, private households, and public administration). The sample frame comes from the Census Bureau's Business Register. All establishments of multi-establishment firms are included; single-establishment firms are included based on certain criteria. (Nonemployer Statistics covers establishments without paid employees; see below.) The most recent Economic Census available for coverage is for 2017. Businesses included in the Economic Census (EC) are required by law under Title 13 (sections 131, 224, and 225) to respond to the survey. Section 9 of the same law makes the information collected confidential. Survey is conducted in the 50 states, District of Columbia, and the 5 Island Areas (American Samoa, Commonwealth of the Northern Mariana Islands, Guam, Puerto Rico, and U.S. Virgin Islands).

Data Collection: Beginning with the 2017 EC, businesses used a secure online portal to respond to the survey. Businesses were mailed instructions for completing the survey online. The Economic Census uses approximately 800 different surveys that are tailored for particular business activities, industries, and industry groups. The EC also includes a non-sampled component; data for selected small single-establishment firms were collected from administrative data from the Census Bureau and other government agencies.

Imputation: Imputation is used for replacing missing data due to nonresponse. The primary sources for obtaining or deriving data for imputation are administrative data from the Census Bureau or other government agency, the establishment's other reported or administrative data, 2012 Census data, and another 2017 survey.

Data Reliability: Estimates of basic data items, such as receipts, sales, payroll, employment, and inventories, included in the 2017 Economic Census First Look and Geographic Area Series publications are computed from all in-scope establishments in the country and therefore are not subject to sampling error. For those establishments that were not sampled or did not respond, missing data items were either imputed or filled in with administrative data from other government agencies.

Sources of Additional Material: U.S. Census Bureau, Economic Census, <www.census.gov/programs-surveys/economic-census.html>.

American Community Survey (ACS)

Universe, Frequency, and Types of Data: The American community Survey is conducted every month, every year. The survey is sent to a sample of about 3.54 million households in the U.S. and 36,000 households in Puerto Rico, per year, to obtain data about demographic, social, economic, and housing characteristics of housing units and the people residing in them. Data covered in the ACS were formerly collected on the long form administered to a portion of households in the Decennial Census. Beginning in 2006, the ACS also includes the group quarter population living in correctional facilities, skilled-nursing homes, military barracks, college residence halls, and other group quarters. Sampling frames are drawn from the Census Bureau's Master Address File.

Sample Selection: Housing unit address sampling is performed twice a year. First-phase of sampling defines the universe for the second stage of sampling through two steps. First, all addresses that were eligible for the second-phase sampling within the past four years are excluded from eligibility. This ensures that no address is in sample more than once in any 5-year period. The second step is to select a 20 percent systematic sample of "new" units, i.e. those units that have never appeared on a previous Master Address File (MAF) extract. All new addresses are systematically assigned to either the current year or to one of four back-samples. This procedure maintains five equal partitions of the universe. The second-phase sampling is done on the current year's partition and results in approximately 3,540,000 housing unit addresses in the U.S. and 36,000 in Puerto Rico.

Group quarter sampling is performed separately from the housing unit sampling. The sampling begins with separating the small (15 persons or fewer) and the large (more than 15 persons) group quarters. The target sampling rate for both groups is a 2.5% sample of the group quarters population. Data are collected from approximately 20,000 group quarters and 195,000 sample residents per year.

Data Collection: The data collection operation for housing units (HUs) consists of four modes: internet, mail, telephone, and personal visit. For most housing units, the first phase includes a mailed request to respond by internet, followed later by an option to complete a paper questionnaire and return it by mail. If no response is received by mail or internet, the Census Bureau follows up with telephone interviewing when a telephone number is available. If a telephone interview is not successful, then the ACS attempts a personal visit and interview. Mailable addresses with neither a response to the mail-out nor a telephone interview are sampled at a rate of 1 in 2, 2 in 5, or 1 in 3 based on the expected rate of completed interviews at the tract level. Unmailable addresses are sampled at a rate of 2 in 3. Those addresses selected through this process are assigned to field representatives (FRs), who visit the addresses, verify their existence, determine their occupancy status, and conduct interviews.

Group quarters: Collection of group quarters data is conducted primarily through FR interviews. Field representatives' methods include completing the questionnaire while speaking to the resident in person or over the telephone, or leaving paper questionnaires for residents to complete for themselves and then pick up later. This last option is used for data collection in federal prisons. If needed, a personal interview can be conducted with a proxy such as a relative or guardian.

Imputation: The Census Bureau uses two principal methods to impute missing or inconsistent data: assignment and allocation. Assignment involves looking at other data as reported by the respondent to fill in missing responses. For example, if sex is unknown but the respondent reported giving birth, the assignment is female. Hot-deck allocation uses a statistical method to supply missing or inconsistent responses from other housing units or survey respondents with similar characteristics.

Data Reliability: All ACS estimates are accompanied by margins of errors or confidence intervals to assist users.

Special Note for 2020 ACS 1-Year Experimental Estimates: Due to the impacts of the coronavirus 2019 (COVID-19) pandemic on data collection, the Census Bureau did not release standard 1-year estimates from the 2020 American Community Survey. The standard 2020 ACS 1-year estimates did not meet statistical quality standards. The ACS collected only two-thirds of the responses that it normally collects, and respondents had significantly different social, economic and housing characteristics compared to nonrespondents. The Census Bureau released experimental 1-year estimates from the 2020 ACS; users should exercise caution in using these data. For more information, see <www.census.gov/programs-surveys/acs/data/experimental-data.html>.

Sources of Additional Material: U.S. Census Bureau, American Community Survey, online at <www.census.gov/programs-surveys/acs/>;and American Community Survey Accuracy of the Data documents available on the internet at <www.census.gov/programs-surveys/acs/methodology.html>.

American Housing Survey (AHS)

Universe, Frequency, and Types of Data: The American Housing Survey is sponsored by the Department of Housing and Urban Development (HUD), and is conducted biennially in odd-numbered years by the Census Bureau to collect data on occupied or vacant housing units in the United States (group quarters are excluded). The AHS provides information on a wide range of "core" housing subjects, including size and composition of the nation's housing inventory, vacancies, fuel usage, physical condition of housing units, characteristics of occupants, equipment breakdowns, home improvements, mortgages and other housing costs, persons eligible for and beneficiaries of assisted housing, home values, and characteristics of recent movers. Beginning 2011, the AHS includes topical supplements that rotate in and out of the survey. The 2019 AHS sample contains 117,422 housing units total, which includes 46,090 housing units from top 15 metropolitan areas, 5,185 units from a HUD-assisted renter oversample, and 31,271 housing units from an additional 10 metro areas.

Data Collection: Census Bureau interviewers visit or telephone the household occupying each housing unit in the sample. For unoccupied units, they obtain information from landlords, rental agents, or neighbors. Housing units participating in the AHS are scientifically selected to represent a cross section of all housing in the nation. The same basic sample of housing units is interviewed every two years until a new sample is selected. The U.S. Census Bureau updates the sample by adding newly constructed housing units and units discovered through coverage improvement efforts. Each housing unit in the AHS sample represents itself and between 450 to 4,000 other units.

Data Reliability: The AHS provides documentation for users to use to calculate sampling errors. See source website under Technical Documentation,

"Accuracy of the Data." The AHS data tool online also provides margins of error along with estimates.

Sources of Additional Material: U.S. Census Bureau, American Housing Survey, Technical Documentation, <www.census.gov/programs-surveys/ahs/tech-documentation.html>; and <www.census.gov/programs-surveys/ahs/about/methodology.html>.

Annual Survey of Public Employment and Payroll, and Census of Governments

Universe, Frequency, and Types of Data: A sample survey is conducted annually except in years ending in '2' and '7', when a census of all state and local governments is done. Covers employees of all agencies of the 50 state governments, the District of Columbia, and about 90,500 local governments (i.e., counties, municipalities, townships, special districts, and school districts). For the annual survey, a sample is selected from the Census of Governments; the typical sample contains approximately 11,500 state and local governments. The survey measures the number of state and local government employees and their gross payrolls for the pay period including March 12. The annual survey provides state and local government data on full-time and part-time employment, full-time equivalent employment, and payroll statistics by governmental function. The census obtains data on how governments are organized, employment and payroll, and government finances. Through 2014, the survey also collected data for federal government employees.

Data Collection: Most state governments provide data from central payroll records for all or most of their agencies and institutions. Data for agencies and institutions for the remaining state governments and all local governments are obtained by an online collection instrument. Some elementary and secondary school system data are supplied by special arrangements with the state government.

Data Editing: Edits are built into the internet data collection instrument and the data entry programs. Post collection edits consist primarily of two types: consistency, and a ratio of the current year's reported value to the value from other years.

Imputation: For general purpose governments, school districts, and special districts not responding to the survey, imputations were based on recent historical data from either a prior year annual survey or the most recent Census of Governments, as available. These data were adjusted by a growth rate that was determined by the growth of units that were similar (in size, geography, and type of government) to the nonrespondent. If no recent historical data were available, imputations were based on the data from a randomly selected donor that was similar to the nonrespondent.

Data Reliability: Census data are not subject to sampling and do not contain sampling error. Data from the annual survey are subject to sampling error. The estimated coefficients of variation (CVs), which are provided for each estimate in data tables available online, are an estimate of this sampling variability. The CVs are expressed as percentages. The CV is the ratio of the standard error to the expectation of the estimate. State government employment and payroll data are not subject to

sampling error. Consequently, state and local government aggregates for individual states are more reliable statistically than the local government only estimates.

Sources of Additional Material: Census Bureau, Annual Survey of Public Employment and Payroll (ASPEP), <www.census.gov/programs-surveys/apes/technical-documentation.html>.

Annual Survey of State and Local Government Finances

Universe, Frequency, and Types of Data: In the years ending in "2" and "7," the Census Bureau conducts a census of the entire universe of all 50 state governments, the District of Columbia, and approximately 90,000 local governments (counties, cities, townships, special districts, and school districts). In intervening years, the Bureau conducts an annual survey of a sample of state and local governments. The survey collects data on government revenue (including taxes, charges, interest, and other earnings), expenditures by function and accounting category, debt, and financial assets by type. Data are published about 20 months after data collection. Revisions are made for the next 2 years.

Data Collection: Data are collected via mail canvass, internet, and central collection from State sources. Collection methods vary by state and type of government. Reviews of government accounting records provide data for most state government agencies and some of the largest and most complex county and municipal governments. Data for local governments in about 27 states are consolidated and submitted by state agencies (central collections), usually as electronic transmissions or mutually developed questionnaires. In some cases, data could be obtained from state Comprehensive Annual Financial Reports.

Data Editing: Edits are built into the internet data collection instrument and data entry programs; edits also occur after data collection. Edits primarily include consistency checks, historical ratio edits, current year ratio edits, and balance checks.

Imputation: Imputations for nonresponding general purpose governments are based on recently reported historical data from either a prior year annual survey or the most recent census, adjusted by a growth rate. If no historical data are available, or the unit has not responded in over five years, data from a randomly selected similar unit are adjusted by the ratio of the populations of the nonresponding and randomly selected donor governments. The imputations for nonresponding special districts are done similarly. If prior year reported data are available, the prior year data for the nonrespondent are adjusted by a growth rate that is determined from reporting units that are similar to the nonrespondent.

Data Reliability: State government financial statistics result from a complete canvass of all state government agencies, and therefore do not have an associated measure of sampling error. Data from local governments come from a sample of local governments and are subject to sampling variability. Data files include the coefficients of variation along with the data.

Annual Survey of Manufactures (ASM)

Universe, Frequency, and Types of Data: The Annual Survey of Manufactures is a sample survey of approximately 50,000 manufacturing establishments conducted annually, except for years ending in '2' and '7' when the survey is included in the Economic Census, for all manufacturing establishments having one or more paid employees. The sample is drawn from the manufacturing portion of the most recent Economic Census available, and, for new establishments, from the Census Bureau's Business Register. The ASM collects data on employment, payroll, worker hours, payroll supplements, cost of materials, select operating expenses, value added by manufacturing, capital expenditures, inventories, and energy consumption. The ASM also covers the value of shipments for approximately 3,500 products.

Data Collection: The ASM mails out instructions for responding to the survey via an online tool. Firms not responding receive follow up mailings and telephone calls. Response is required by law.

Data Editing and Imputation: Data editing first verifies whether an establishment's kind of business or industry classification is valid, then survey responses are evaluated for consistency and validity. The primary sources for imputing data missing due to nonresponse are administrative data, other data reported by the establishment, and data reported in previous surveys or other census surveys. Sampled establishments that did not report product data are assigned products in a hot-deck imputation process. In this process the products from a similar establishment (called the donor) are assigned to the establishment missing the product data (the recipient).

Data Reliability: Statistics for the industry groups and industries, and product shipments include estimated relative standard errors. Relative standard errors vary by industry and product category.

Sources of Additional Material: Census Bureau, Annual Survey of Manufactures Methodology, <www.census.gov/programs-surveys/asm/technical-documentation/methodology.html>.

Decennial Census of Population and Housing

Universe, Frequency, and Types of Data: Mandated by the U.S. Constitution, the Decennial Census has made a complete count of the U.S. population every 10 years since 1790. The data collected by the decennial census are used to apportion the number of seats each state has in the U.S. House of Representatives, as well as to realign congressional districts and determine allocation of federal funding. The Census obtains data on the number and characteristics of people in the United States and its outlying territories, and also counts Federally affiliated Americans overseas. The 2010 and 2020 Censuses asked information on name, gender, age, race, ethnicity, relationship to householder, and whether the respondent owns or rents their home.

Data Collection: Up until the 2020, the Decennial Census was conducted by mail. Census workers, also known as enumerators, conducted personal interviews for households that could not be reached by the U.S. postal service or that did not return their mailed questionnaire. The 2020 Census mailed out invitations to households to complete the census by mail, telephone, or the internet. The Census Bureau employs special operations to count people not living in households, including people living in various group quarters and people experiencing homelessness. See source for more information on these methods. Prior to 2010, the Census used 2 forms of questionnaires; all households had to answer questions on the short form, and a portion of households would receive the long form seeking more detailed information. Beginning 2010, the Census uses a single questionnaire that contains about 9 to 10 questions, with several questions repeated for each member of a household. Detailed information that was asked on the long form questionnaire was moved to the annual American Community Survey.

Imputation: For missing data, the 2010 Census employed count imputation using three general procedures: assignment, allocation, and substitution. For the 2020 Census, the Census Bureau is using imputation procedures for missing characteristics (demographic and housing data) and counts of people. The 2010 Census has imputation procedures outlined in technical documentation. Technical documentation is not yet complete for 2020 Census; imputation procedures are currently described in Census memoranda and blog posts, which are available online.

Coverage Measurement: The Census Bureau uses several methods to assess the quality of data and to provide data on net coverage errors. One such method is the demographic analysis. The demographic analysis collects data from other sources, including vital statistics records, migration data, and Medicare records, to estimate the population size for comparison with official census data. Another method is a post-enumeration survey, an independent survey to measure how many people and housing units were counted correctly and erroneously, or missed by the Decennial Census. Detailed documentation and data from these data quality operations are available through links at the source cited below.

Sources of Additional Material: U.S. Census Bureau's Decennial Census webpage has links to numerous documents, <www.census.gov/programs-surveys/decennial-census.html>. Information is organized by type and by decade.

County Business Patterns

Universe, Frequency, and Types of Data: County Business Patterns is an annual series that contains data on number of establishments, employment during the week of March 12, and first quarter and annual payrolls, by detailed industry and geographic level. Data cover over 6 million single-unit establishments and 1.8 million multi-unit establishments, and are available by geographic area (state, county, and metropolitan areas), 6-digit NAICS industry, legal form of organization (U.S. and state only), and employment size class. Most industries are covered; excluded are crop and animal production; rail transportation; U.S. Postal Service; pension, health, welfare, and vacation funds; trusts, estates, and agency accounts; private households; and public administration. CBP also excludes most establishments reporting government employees.

Data Collection: Most basic data items are extracted from the Census Bureau's Business Register, a database of all known employer companies. The Census Bureau's Report of Organization, formerly the Company Organization Survey, provides individual establishment data for companies that operate 2 or more units (multi-establishment companies). Data for single establishment companies are obtained from various Census Bureau programs such as the Economic Census, Annual Survey of Manufactures, and Current Business Surveys, as well as from administrative records of the Internal Revenue Service, the Social Security Administration, and the Bureau of Labor Statistics.

Data Reliability: Payroll and employment data are obtained from administrative records for single-unit companies and a combination of administrative records and survey-collected data for multi-unit companies. They are not subject to sampling error. Missing employment and payroll data are imputed using averages, or by examing patterns for various time periods.

Noise Infusion: Since reference year 2007, County Business Patterns has used noise infusion to protect the confidentiality of respondent data. Noise infusion is a method of avoiding disclosure in which data values for each establishment are perturbed prior to table creation by applying a random noise multiplier to the magnitude data (i.e., characteristics such as first-quarter payroll, annual payroll, and number of employees) for each establishment. This results in a relatively small change in the vast majority of cell values. See source below for more information.

Sources of Additional Material: U.S. Census Bureau, County Business Patterns, online at <www.census.gov/programs-surveys/cbp/about.html> and <www.census.gov/programs-surveys/cbp/technical-documentation/methodology.html>.

Current Population Survey (CPS)

Universe, Frequency, and Types of Data: Nationwide monthly sample of approximately 60,000 households designed primarily to produce national and state estimates of labor force and other characteristics of the civilian noninstitutionalized population 15 years of age and older, including sex, age, race, marital status, educational attainment, and family structure. In addition to the monthly survey, each March the CPS produces the Annual Social and Economic (ASEC) Supplement, which contains the basic monthly demographic and labor force data covered by the CPS, plus data on numerous additional topics such as work experience, income, health insurance coverage, poverty, receipt of noncash benefits, and geographic mobility.

Data Collection: The CPS uses a multistage probability sample that currently includes 60,000 households from 824 sample areas. Sample size increased in some states to improve data reliability for those

areas on an average annual basis. A continual sample rotation system is used. Households are in sample for 4 months, out for 8 months, and in for 4 more. The Census Bureau field representatives administer the CPS questionnaire across the country through both personal and telephone interviews. One person, usually the person who owns or rents the housing unit, generally responds for all eligible members in a household regarding activities during the prior week (the week including the 12th of the month).

Imputation: The CPS makes imputations for missing data items. The CPS uses 3 imputation methods for item nonresponse: relational imputation, which infers the missing value from other characteristics on the person's record or within the household; longitudinal edits for most of the labor force edits, as appropriate; and "hot deck" allocation, a method of assigning a missing value from a record with similar characteristics, which is the hot deck. Hot decks are defined by variables such as age, race, and sex.

Sampling: Sufficient sample is allocated to maintain, at most, a 1.9 percent coefficient of variation on national monthly estimates of unemployment, assuming a 6 percent unemployment rate. This translates into a change of 0.2 percentage point in the unemployment rate being significant at a 90 percent confidence level. For each of the 50 States and for the District of Columbia, the design maintains a coefficient of variation of at most 8 percent on the annual average estimate of unemployment, assuming a 6 percent unemployment rate.

Sources of Additional Material: U.S. Census Bureau, Current Population Survey, <www.census.gov/programs-surveys/cps/technical-documentation/methodology.html>, and <www.census.gov/programs-surveys/cps/technical-documentation/complete.html>.

Foreign Trade—Export Statistics

Universe, Frequency, and Types of Data: Export statistics cover goods valued at more than $2,500 per commodity shipped by individuals and organizations (including exporters, freight forwarders, and carriers) from the U.S. to other countries. Data are compiled in terms of commodity classification, quantities, values, shipping weights, method of transportation (air or vessel), state of (movement) origin, customs district, customs port, country of destination, and whether contents are domestic goods or reexports. Transactions are classified under approximately 8,000 different products leaving the United States. Data cover about 240 U.S. trading partners. Data are continuously compiled and processed. Documents are collected as shipments depart, and processed on a flow basis. Reports summarize shipments made during calendar months, quarters, and years. Statistics are reported monthly approximately 35 days after the end of the reference month and on a year-to-date basis.

Data Collection: Data consist of a full compilation (i.e., a census) of commodity exports, plus U.S. Census Bureau estimates of low-valued exports and Bureau of Economic Analysis (BEA) estimates of trade in services. Statistics for exported goods transactions are compiled from three sources: Shipper's Export Declaration documents filed with Customs and

Border Protection (CBP) and sent to the U.S. Census Bureau (3 percent of all transactions), comparable data in electronic form submitted directly by exporters and their agents (63 percent), and special computer tapes from Canada for U.S. exports to Canada (34 percent). Estimates are made for low-value exports by country of destination and based on bilateral trade patterns. Statistics for U.S. exports to Canada are based on import documents filed with Canadian agencies and forwarded to the U.S. Census Bureau under a 1987 data exchange agreement. Under this agreement, each country eliminated most cross-border export documents; maintains detailed statistics on cross-border imports; exchanges monthly files of cross-border import statistics; and publishes exchanged statistics in place of previously compiled export statistics.

Data Reliability: The goods data are a complete enumeration of electronic export information (EEI) reported in the automated export system (AES) and are not subject to sampling errors, but they are subject to several types of nonsampling errors. The most significant of these include reporting errors, undocumented shipments, timeliness, data capture errors, and errors in the estimation of low-valued transactions.

Sources of Additional Material: U.S. Census Bureau, Foreign Trade, Guide to Foreign Trade Statistics, <www.census.gov/foreign-trade/guide/sec2.html>.

Foreign Trade—Import Statistics

Universe, Frequency, and Types of Data: The import statistics cover goods valued at more than $2,000 per commodity shipped by individuals and organizations (including importers and customs brokers) into the U.S. from other countries. Data are compiled in terms of commodity classification, quantities, values, shipping weights, methods of transportation (air or vessel), duties collected, unit prices, and market share, country of origin, customs district, customs port, import charges and duties. Commodities are compiled under the Harmonized Tariff Schedules of the United States containing more than 18,000 import commodity codes. Data cover about 240 U.S. trading partners. Data are continuously compiled and processed. Documents are collected as shipments arrive and processed on a flow basis. Reports summarize shipments made during calendar months and years. Statistics are reported monthly approximately 35 days after the end of the reference month and on a year-to-date basis.

Data Collection: A full compilation (i.e., a census) is taken of import shipments, plus U.S. Census Bureau estimates of low-valued imports and Bureau of Economic Analysis (BEA) estimates of trade in services. Statistics for imported goods shipments are compiled from the records filed with Customs and Border Protection (CBP), usually within 10 days after the merchandise enters the United States. Estimates are made for low-value shipments by country of origin based on previous bilateral trade patterns and periodically updated. Statistics for over 95 percent of all commodity transactions are compiled from records filed electronically with CBP and forwarded as computer tape files to the U.S. Census Bureau. Statistics for other transactions are compiled from hard-copy documents filed with CBP and forwarded on a flow basis for U.S. Census Bureau processing.

Data Reliability: The goods data are a complete enumeration of documents collected by the U.S. Customs and Border Protection and are not subject to sampling errors, but they are subject to several types of nonsampling errors. The most significant of these include reporting errors, undocumented shipments, timeliness, data capture errors, and errors in the estimation of low-valued transactions. Other quality issues are described in the source cited below.

Sources of Additional Material: U.S. Census Bureau, Foreign Trade, Guide to Foreign Trade Statistics, <www.census.gov/foreign-trade/guide/sec2.html>.

Monthly and Annual Retail Trade Survey

Universe, Frequency, and Types of Data: The size of the Monthly Retail Trade Survey (MRTS) sample is approximately 13,000 employer firms. Data cover retail store and food service sales, and inventories held by retail stores. Data had historically been available at the national level only, but in September 2020, the Census Bureau began an experimental data product featuring monthly retail sales data by state. See source for more information. The Annual Retail Trade Survey (ARTS) uses a sample of approximately 16,500 employer firms in the retail trade sector and electronic commerce sales, and requests data on sales, sales taxes, inventories, purchases, operating expenses, and other financial items. Annual data are published at the industry level using the North American Industry Classifcation System.

Data Collection and Imputation: Firms for the retail trade surveys come from the Economic Census and the Census Bureau's Business Register. Data are collected by mail questionnaire and the internet, with telephone follow-ups for nonrespondents. Imputation is made for each nonresponse item and each item failing edit checks. For both unit and item nonresponse, a missing value is replaced by a predicted value obtained from an appropriate model for nonresponse. This imputation uses survey data and administrative data as input. In any given month, about a third of monthly retail trade data is imputed. For the annual survey, imputed data amount to about 10 percent for sales and about 12 percent for inventories. Additional information about the imputation rates for published estimates are available upon request.

Data Reliability: Estimated CVs and standard errors are released with monthly reports. Annual data releases include measures of sampling variability.

Sources of Additional Material: Census Bureau, Monthly and Annual Retail Trade, <www.census.gov/retail/mrts/how_surveys_are_collected.html>, and <www.census.gov/programs-surveys/arts/technical-documentation/methodology.html>.

Survey of Construction

Universe, Frequency, and Types of Data: The Survey of Construction provides current national and regional statistics on starts, completions, and characteristics of new, privately-owned single-family and multifamily housing units and on sales of new single-family houses. Data collected include start and completion dates, sales date, sales price (single-family houses only), and the physical characteristics of housing units. Survey data are available monthly and annually for housing starts since 1959, for new home sales since 1963, and for completions since 1968. Reported data are for building or sales activity taking place during the applicable reference period. Monthly data collection begins the first day after the reference month and continues through the 7th working day.

Survey Design: The Survey of Construction includes two parts: the Survey of Use of Permits (SUP), which covers new construction in areas that require a building permit, and the Non-Permit Survey (NP), which covers new construction in areas that do not require a building permit. Less than 2 percent of all new construction takes place in non-permit areas. A multistage probability sample of approximately 900 permit-issuing jurisdictions in the U.S. is selected. Each month in each of these permit offices, field representatives list and select a sample of permits for which to collect data. To obtain data in non-permit areas, a multistage probability sample of over 80 land areas (census tracts or subsections of census tracts) is selected. All roads in these areas are canvassed and data are collected on all new residential construction found. Sampled buildings are followed up until they are completed (and sold, if for sale), or abandoned. Permits for 1- to 4-unit buildings are sampled at an overall rate of 1 in 50. All permits authorizing buildings with 5 or more housing units in the sampled permit offices are selected.

Data Collection and Processing: Data from both parts of SOC are collected by Census field representatives in person or by telephone. For the SUP, Census representatives visit a sample of permit offices and select a sample of permits issued for new housing. These permits are then followed through to see when they are started and completed, and when they are sold for single-family units that are built to be sold. Each project is also surveyed to collect information on characteristics of the structure. For the Non-Permit Survey, roads in sampled non-permit land areas are driven at least once every 3 months to see if there is any new construction. Once new residential construction is found, it is followed up the same as in SUP. Each month, interviews are required for about half of the buildings currently being followed up. Nonresponse/undercoverage adjustment factors are used to account for late reported data. Each month, housing starts, completions, and sales estimates derived from this survey are adjusted by the total numbers of authorized housing units (obtained from the Building Permits Survey) to develop national and regional estimates. Estimates are adjusted to reflect variations by region and type of construction, and to account for late reports and houses started or sold before a permit has been issued. Reported data are seasonally adjusted.

Data Reliability: Data are subject to sampling errors. Estimates of the standard errors have been computed from the sample data for selected statistics. They are presented in the source tables in the form of average relative standard errors (RSEs).

Sources of Additional Material: Census Bureau, Survey of Construction, online at <www.census.gov/construction/nrc/how_the_data_are_collected/soc.html>.

Nonemployer Statistics

Universe, Frequency, and Types of Data: Nonemployer statistics are an annual tabulation of economic data by industry for active businesses without paid employees or payroll, that are subject to federal income taxes, and that have receipts of $1,000 or more ($1 or more for the construction sector). Excluded are corporations and partnerships with over $1 million in receipts (except for service-type industries, maximum is $2 million). Maximum receipts for sole proprietorships depends on industry classification. Most nonemployers are self-employed individuals operating unincorporated businesses (known as sole proprietorships). Data showing the number of firms and receipts by industry are available for the U.S., states, counties, and metropolitan areas. Most types of businesses covered by the Census Bureau's economic statistics programs are included in the nonemployer statistics. Nonemployer statistics exclude crop and animal production; investment funds, trusts, and other financial vehicles; management of companies and enterprises; and public administration.

Data Collection and Processing: The universe of nonemployer firms is created annually in conjunction with identifying the Census Bureau's employer universe. If a business is active but without paid employees, then it becomes part of the potential nonemployer universe. The data are primarily from business income tax returns filed with the Internal Revenue Service and maintained in the Census Bureau's Business Register. The potential nonemployer universe undergoes an analytical review to distinguish nonemployers from employers.

Data Reliability: Data are tabulated from administrative records and are not subject to sampling error. Data are subject to nonsampling errors. The improper inclusion of possible employer establishments in the nonemployer universe is the primary source of nonsampling error.

Noise Infusion: Since reference year 2005, the noise infusion data protection method has been applied to prevent disclosure of receipt cell values. Noise infusion is a method of disclosure avoidance in which values are perturbed prior to table creation by applying a random noise multiplier to the magnitude data (in this case, receipts) independently for each business. Disclosure protection is accomplished in a manner that results in a relatively small change for the vast majority of cell values.

Sources of Additional Material: U. S. Census Bureau, Nonemployer Statistics, <www.census.gov/programs-surveys/nonemployer-statistics/technical-documentation.html>.

Service Annual Survey (SAS)

Universe, Frequency, and Types of Data: The U.S. Census Bureau conducts the Service Annual Survey (SAS) to provide nationwide estimates of revenues and expenses for most traditional service industries. Estimates are summarized by industry classification based on the North American Industry Classification System (NAICS). Service industries covered by the Service Annual Survey include all or part of the following NAICS sectors: Utilities (NAICS 22); Transportation and Warehousing (NAICS 48-49); Information (NAICS 51); Finance and Insurance (NAICS 52); Real Estate and Rental and Leasing (NAICS 53); Professional, Scientific, and Technical Services (NAICS 54); Administrative and Support and Waste Management and Remediation Services (NAICS 56); Educational Services (NAICS 61); Health Care and Social Assistance (NAICS 62); Arts, Entertainment, and Recreation (NAICS 71); Accommodation and Food Services (NAICS 72); and Other Services except Public Administration (NAICS 81). The SAS includes firms of all sizes and covers both taxable firms and firms exempt from federal income taxes.

Data Collection: Questionnaires are mailed in January and request annual data for the prior year. Estimates are published approximately 12 months after the initial survey mailing. The Service Annual Survey estimates are developed from a probability sample of approximately 78,000 employer firms, and administrative records for nonemployers. Service Annual Survey uses a probability sample that is periodically reselected from a universe of firms having paid employees. Updates to the sample are made on a quarterly basis to account for new and closed businesses. Firms without paid employees, or nonemployers, are included in the estimates through imputation and/or administrative records data provided by other federal agencies.

Data Reliability: Estimates are based on a sample and subject to sampling error. The most recent Service Annual Survey results, including coefficients of variations (CVs), can be found on the internet at <www.census.gov/programs-surveys/sas/data/tables.html>. To address the potential bias due to nonresponse, for both unit and item nonresponse a missing value is replaced by a predicted value obtained from an appropriate model for nonresponse. This imputation uses survey data and administrative data as input.

Sources of Additional Material: U.S. Census Bureau, Service Annual Survey, <www.census.gov/programs-surveys/sas/technical-documentation/methodology.html>.

Annual Business Survey

Universe, Frequency, and Types of Data: The survey is conducted by the U.S. Census Bureau and the National Science Foundation's National Center for Science and Engineering Statistics. The survey began in 2017 and replaces several surveys, including the Census Bureau's Survey of Business Owners, and the Annual Survey of Entrepreneurs. The survey covers all nonfarm employers filing 941, 944, or 1120 tax forms with receipts of $1,000 or more. The ABS sampled approximately 850,000 employer businesses in 2018 and approximately 300,000 employer businesses annually 2018-2021. The survey collects data on the number of employer firms, sales and receipts, payroll, and employment by sex, race, ethnicity, and veteran status. Data are tabulated by business owner sex, race, ethnicity, and veteran status. The survey also collects data on research and development, innovation, and

technology, and new topics relevant to the business community. Data are available for the U.S. and by state, metropolitan statistical area, and county, and economic place levels.

Data Collection: Businesses selected for the survey receive an initial letter about the survey and instructions for accessing the survey on the internet. Survey response is required by law. Additional data are collected electronically from the Economic Census and government administrative records, and are combined with survey data. Data results are available by business owner characteristics. Business ownership is defined as having 51 percent or more of the stock or equity in the business and is categorized by sex, race, ethnicity, and veteran status, and firms unclassifiable by sex, race, ethnicity, and veteran status. Businesses could be tabulated in more than one racial group. Historical data and imputation methods were used to adjust for nonresponse.

Noise Infusion: The Annual Business Survey uses noise infusion as the primary method of disclosure avoidance. Noise infusion perturbs data values prior to tabulation by applying a random noise multiplier to all data. For this reason, detailed estimates may not sum to the total for estimates of firm counts. Disclosure protection is accomplished in a manner that causes the vast majority of cell values to be perturbed by, at most, a few percentage points.

Data Reliability: The estimated relative standard errors and estimated standard errors presented in ABS data tables estimate the sampling variability, and thus measure the precision with which an estimate from the particular sample selected for this survey approximates the average result of all possible samples. Relative standard errors and standard errors are applicable only to those published cells in which sample cases are tabulated. A relative standard error is an expression of the standard error as a percent of the quantity being estimated. For the *Characteristics of Businesses* and *Characteristics of Business Owners* datasets, some data are expressed as percentages with standard errors rather than relative standard errors.

Sources of Additional Materials: U.S. Census Bureau, Annual Business Survey, <www.census.gov/programs-surveys/abs.html>, and <www.census.gov/programs-surveys/abs/technical-documentation/methodology.html>

U.S. DEPARTMENT OF EDUCATION, National Center for Education Statistics

Integrated Postsecondary Education Data Survey (IPEDS)

Universe, Frequency, and Types of Data: The IPEDS annually collects institution-level data from postsecondary institutions across the U.S. on tuition and fees, number and types of degrees and certificates conferred, number of students applying and enrolled, number of employees, financial statistics, graduation rates, student outcomes, student financial aid, and academic libraries. The survey consists of 12 components that are administered across the fall, winter, and spring reporting seasons. Submission of data to IPEDS is mandatory for any institution that participates in or is an applicant for participation in any federal financial assistance program authorized by Title IV of the Higher Education Act of 1965. IPEDS response rates for each component are nearly 100 percent. Close to 7,000 institutions participate in the survey each year.

Data Collection: The IPEDS collects data via the internet. As respondents enter data online, the data collection system automatically calculates totals, averages, and percentages, and compares the responses with the previous year's submission for the same institution to ensure the data are consistent. The system also compares data with other related values to ensure consistency of reporting within each survey component and across the data collection program. If data are still missing, analysts conduct imputations to complete the database.

Imputation: Missing data are imputed by using data of similar institutions. With the exception of the Institutional Characteristics component, all items collected in each component were eligible for imputation. Within the Institutional Characteristics component, only cost of attendance and other institutional charges data were eligible for imputation. IPEDS may apply one of three imputation methods for both unit and item nonresponse, depending on the data available. Carry Forward uses data from previous years to substitute for current data, with adjustments to account for yearly changes. The Nearest Neighbor procedure identifies data related to the key statistics of interest for each component (the distance measure), then uses those data to identify a responding institution similar to the nonresponding institution and uses the respondent's data as a substitute for the nonrespondent's missing items. Lastly, for data that cannot be imputed by carry forward or nearest neighbor methods, the Group Median method identifies the median institution that provides values that are missing for another institution.

Edit Procedures: The internet-based survey instrument conducts edit checks to detect major reporting errors. The system can prompt survey respondents to correct errors as they are found. If accurate data fails the edit checks, survey respondents either confirm the response or explain why the data appear to be out of the expected data range. The system requires all edit checks to be confirmed or explained. In some cases, respondents could contact IPEDS for assistance. IPEDS staff also review data for additional errors and contact respondents for verification.

Data Reliability: Data are not subject to sampling error. Data are subject to such nonsampling errors as errors of design, reporting, processing, nonresponse, and imputation.

Sources of Additional Material: U.S. Department of Education, National Center for Education Statistics, IPEDS Survey Methodology, online at <nces.ed.gov/ipeds/ReportYourData/IpedsSurveyMethodology>.

National Household Education Surveys (NHES) Program

Universe, Frequency, and Types of Data: The National Household Education Surveys Program is a system of surveys of the noninstitutionalized civilian population of the United States. NHES surveys have

been conducted periodically since 1991 and have varying universes of interest depending on the particular survey. Some surveys are recurring; others are fielded as 1-time surveys. Currently, the NHES surveys cover young children's care and education before kindergarten, and parent and family involvement in their children's education, which also covers home schooling. A list of past surveys and their collection years are available online at <nces.ed.gov/nhes>. The most recent surveys fielded in 2016 and 2019 include:

1 Early Childhood Program Participation—Surveys of parents of a representative sample of children age 6 and younger not yet enrolled in kindergarten.

2 Parent and Family Involvement in Education—Surveys of parents of a representative sample of children age 3 to 20 who were enrolled in kindergarten through grade 12. Separate questionnaires are administered for children enrolled in public and private schools, and for children who are home schooled.

3 Adult Training and Education Survey—Covers adults age 16 to 65 who are not enrolled in high school, focusing on nondegree credentials and work experience programs (2016 only).

Data Collection: NHES typically fields 2 to 3 topical surveys at a time, although the number has varied across its administration. Surveys are administered in English and in Spanish. From 1991 to 2007, the NHES used telephone interviews to collect data. In 2012, the NHES switched to a mail survey, and samples were developed using household address information for all 50 states and the District of Columbia. The 2016 survey included use of the internet for a small portion of the sample. In 2019, the NHES mailed invitations to participate in the survey and provide responses either by mail or the internet. Both of the 2016 and 2019 NHES samples were selected using a 2-stage address-based sampling frame. Black and Hispanic American households were sampled at a higher rate than other households.

Data Reliability: Reports presenting NHES data include tables on standard errors. Efforts to prevent nonsampling errors include cognitive interviews to assess respondents' knowledge of the survey topics, their comprehension of questions and terms, and the sensitivity of items.

Sources of Additional Material: Please see the NHES website at <nces.ed.gov/nhes>; and technical notes and related methodological information in individual NHES reports available online at <nces.ed.gov/pubsearch/getpubcats.asp?sid=004>.

U.S. DEPARTMENT OF JUSTICE, FEDERAL BUREAU OF INVESTIGATION

Uniform Crime Reporting (UCR) Program

Universe, Frequency, and Types of Data: Monthly reports on the number of criminal offenses that become known to law enforcement agencies. More than 18,000 city, university and college, county, state, tribal, and federal law enforcement agencies are eligible to contribute data to the FBI. Law enforcement agencies tabulate data on violent crimes (murder and nonnegligent manslaughter, rape, robbery, aggravated assault) and property crimes (burglary, larceny-theft, motor vehicle theft, and arson); this group of violent and property crimes are also known as Part I offenses. (Although the FBI classifies arson as a property crime, it does not estimate arson data because of variations in the level of participation by the reporting agencies. Consequently, arson is not included in the property crime estimate.) Also collected are data on persons arrested for Part I and Part II offenses (Part II offenses encompass all crimes, except traffic violations, that are not classified as Part I offenses), law enforcement officers killed or assaulted, annual data on law enforcement personnel, and quarterly data on hate crimes.

Data Collection: The UCR Program consists of four data collections: the National Incident-Based Reporting System (NIBRS), the Summary Reporting System (SRS), the Law Enforcement Officers Killed and Assaulted (LEOKA) Program, and the Hate Crime Statistics Program. The SRS was phased out in 2021; as of January 1, 2021, the UCR program collects all data via the NIBRS only. Law enforcement agencies report data on crimes brought to their attention based on records of all reports of crime received from victims, officers who discover infractions, or other sources, and submit data each month to the FBI either directly or through their state UCR Programs. Data must be prepared in accordance to UCR standards. The UCR program participation is voluntary. Beginning with the 2013 data collections, all data must be submitted electronically, and after July 2013 the UCR Program no longer accepted paper submissions or the electronic submission of documents (i.e., Portable Document Format files).

Data Quality Procedures: The FBI's Crime Statistics Management Unit staff initially review the data to determine adherence to UCR policy, conformance to UCR definitions and principles, and consistency with established statistical methodologies and norms. Before the information is entered into the national database, the CSMU staff use edit functions to ensure that the data meet established standards. If staff find errors or anomalies, they obtain verification and/or correction from the submitting agency or state UCR Program. After data pass through this first series of checks, the data are uploaded into the national database. Data then undergo a series of multi-layered processes to check for reasonableness, quality, and validity. FBI staff contact data contributors to clarify data submissions that do not pass data quality checks.

Sources of Additional Material: U.S. Department of Justice, Federal Bureau of Investigation, <www.fbi.gov/services/cjis/ucr>;*Crime in the United States*, annual, *Hate Crime Statistics*, annual, and *Law Enforcement Officers Killed and Assaulted*, annual, <www.fbi.gov/services/cjis/ucr/publications>. Law Enforcement Resources, <le.fbi.gov/informational-tools/ucr/additional-ucr-resources>. Reports available on FBI's Crime Data Explorer include methodologies, online at <crime-data-explorer.app.cloud.gov/pages/about>.

U.S. INTERNAL REVENUE SERVICE, Statistics of Income (SOI)

Corporation Income Tax Returns

Universe, Frequency, and Types of Data: Annual study of unaudited corporation income tax returns filed by corporations or businesses legally defined as corporations. The IRS Statistics of Income (SOI) Division collects data on corporations by size, industry, and total assets, along with data on business receipts, deductions, liabilities, net income, income tax liability, tax credits, and other financial data. SOI aggregates these data for C corporations and passthrough entities, such as S corporations. The target population consists of all returns of active corporations organized for profit that are required to file one of the 1120 forms that are part of the SOI study. For 2016 to 2019, the survey universe consisted of 6.6 to 6.9 million corporate tax returns, from which each year a sample of over 100,000 returns were selected (the target sample size was approximately 120,000 returns). Tax returns are allocated to sample classes based on type of return, and either size of total assets alone or both size of total assets and a measure of income. Sampling rates for sample classes varied from 0.25 percent to 100 percent. Please note that changes in tax laws affect comparability of data from year to year.

Data Collection and Imputation: Data processing for SOI begins with information already extracted for IRS administrative purposes; over 100 items available from the Business Master File system are checked and corrected as necessary. SOI extracts some 2,500 additional data items from corporate tax returns during processing. After data capture, data go through hundreds of tests for consistency and error resolution. The SOI addresses missing data items and identifies returns excluded from the study. For missing balance sheet items, as of tax year 2012, only the largest returns with incomplete balance sheets are subject to a balance sheet imputation procedure. The IRS's Statistics of Income (SOI) division performs imputation on an ad hoc basis only. For other items, SOI uses various methods to impute data for some certainty returns unavailable for editing, depending on the information available. The data completion process includes identifying returns not eligible for the sample (duplicates and other out-of-scope returns).

Measures of Variability: Estimated coefficients of variation for selected data are published in the Statistics of Income, *Corporation Complete Report*, and are also available with data tables online.

Sources of Additional Material: U.S. Internal Revenue Service, Statistics of Income, *Corporation Income Tax Returns*, <www.irs.gov/statistics/soi-tax-stats-corporation-tax-statistics>.

Individual Income Tax Returns

Universe, Frequency, and Types of Data: Annual study of unaudited individual income tax returns, Forms 1040, 1040A, and 1040EZ, filed by U.S. citizens and residents. New for tax year 2019 is form 1040-SR, for taxpayers born before January 2, 1955. The IRS compiles data on sources of income, adjusted gross income, exemptions, deductions, taxable income, income tax, modified income tax, tax credits, self-employment tax, and tax payments. Data include detail by size of adjustable income and other items. Please note that changes in tax laws affect comparability of data from year to year.

Data Collection and Processing: Data are collected for returns processed during the most recent year available, which mostly includes returns for a single tax year but can also include returns for earlier tax years that were filed and processed during the year of processing. Thus, returns processed in 2020 include mostly returns filed for tax year 2019 but also a few returns for tax year 2018. All returns processed during the year of coverage are subject to sampling except tentative and amended returns. For 2018, 361,501 returns were selected for the study sample out of 154.4 million returns; for 2019, the sample count is 370,894, out of 167.7 million total returns. All tax returns are classified into one of 4 subpopulations, strata, and each strata are sampled at a rate of 0.10 percent to 100 percent. All data are captured and processed electronically. The administrative data and controlling information for each record designated for the sample are loaded into an online submission processing database. Computer data for the selected administrative records are then used to identify inconsistencies, questionable values, and missing values. After the submission processing center review, data are further validated, tested, and balanced. Adjustments and imputations are made for selected items based on prior-year data and other available information.

Measures of Variability: Coefficients of variation and confidence intervals are provided along with selected data tables in the report and online at the website, both indicated below.

Sources of Additional Material: U.S. Internal Revenue Service, Statistics of Income, *Individual Income Tax Returns* (Publication 1304), annual, <www.irs.gov/statistics/soi-tax-stats-individual-income-tax-returns-complete-report-publication-1304>, and <www.irs.gov/statistics/soi-tax-stats-individual-income-tax-return-form-1040-statistics>.

U.S. NATIONAL CENTER FOR HEALTH STATISTICS (NCHS)

National Health Interview Survey (NHIS)

Universe, Frequency, and Types of Data: Since 1957, the NHIS has been a continuous data collection covering the civilian noninstitutional population in the 50 states and the District of Columbia to obtain information on demographic characteristics and various health indicators. The NHIS universe includes residents of households and noninstitutional group quarters (e.g., homeless shelters, group homes). Persons excluded from the universe are those with no fixed household address (e.g., homeless and/or transient persons not residing in shelters), active duty military personnel and civilians living on military bases, persons in long-term care institutions (e.g., nursing homes for the elderly), persons in correctional facilities, and U.S. nationals living in foreign countries. Civilians residing with Armed Forces personnel in non-military housing are eligible to be sampled. The sampling plan is redesigned after every decennial census. A new sampling plan for the 2016–2025 NHIS was designed with results of the 2010 decennial census. Commercial address lists are used as the main source of addresses, supplemented by field listing. Beginning in 2019, the sample is expected to yield 30,000 sample adult and 9,000 sample child completed interviews. The annual sample size can fluctuate depending on funding. Every year the survey collects data on demographic characteristics and selected health topics, including health insurance coverage, chronic conditions, health care access and use,

health-related behaviors, and functioning and disability. Additional topics are covered on a rotating basis within a 3-year period, including mental health, preventive services, chronic pain, sleep, physical activity, and other topics. Please note that the content and structure of the NHIS were redesigned and updated in 2019. Details of the NHIS redesign are available online at <www.cdc.gov/nchs/nhis/about_nhis.htm>.

Data Collection: The U.S. Census Bureau collects data for the NHIS. About 750 interviewers across the country conduct personal face-to-face interviews in respondents' homes; follow-up interviews may be conducted by telephone. Telephone interviews are also used at the request of the respondent, or when travel conditions are difficult. The interview begins with a household roster to ask basic demographic information for everyone in the household. One sample adult from each household is randomly selected to answer detailed questions about his or her health. One sample child, if present, is also randomly selected from each household and an adult knowledgeable and responsible for the child's health answers questions about the child's health. Please note that prior to the 2019 NHIS, the survey also included a separate family questionnaire. Questions at the family level are now included in the sample adult and sample child surveys.

Data Reliability: NHIS Adult and Child Summary Health Statistics datasets found online at <Data.CDC.gov> contain estimates and confidence intervals for all data items. All estimates shown meet the NCHS standards of reliability as specified in *National Center for Health Statistics Data Presentation Standards for Proportions*. Detailed and technical documentation are available online.

Sources of Additional Material: National Center for Health Statistics, National Health Interview Survey, online at <www.cdc.gov/nchs/nhis/shs.htm>,with additional information at <www.cdc.gov/nchs/nhis/about_nhis.htm>. Technical documentation are online at <www.cdc.gov/nchs/nhis/data-questionnaires-documentation.htm>.

National Survey of Family Growth (NSFG)

Universe, Frequency, and Types of Data: The National Survey of Family Growth (NSFG) gathers information on pregnancy and births, marriage and cohabitation, infertility, use of contraception, and general and reproductive health. The NSFG also collects data on sexual behavior and attraction, and sexual orientation. The NSFG began in 1973 as a periodic survey of ever-married women age 15-44 among the civilian noninstitutionalized population. In 1982, the survey covered all women regardless of marital status; in 2002, men were included in the survey; and in 2015 the age range expanded to cover people age 15-49. Periodic surveys were conducted 1973 to 2002. Beginning in 2006, the survey employed continuous interviewing. The most recent NSFG data available come from the 2011 to 2019 interviewing period, which gathered data in 2-year increments, and overall completed approximately 23,000 interviews with women and 19,000 interviews with men.

Data Collection: Survey participation is voluntary. Only one person is interviewed in a selected household. Signed consent is required for minors age 15-17. The NSFG collects data by employing female interviewers to conduct personal interviews using computer-assisted personal interviewing (CAPI). Selected data items are also collected using audio computer-assisted self-interviewing (ACASI). In ACASI, the respondent listens to the questions through headphones, reads them on the screen, or both, and enters the response directly into the computer. This method avoids asking the respondent to give his or her answers to the interviewer, and it has been found to yield more complete reporting of sensitive behaviors.

Imputation: In the NSFG, item imputation is performed on a number of "recoded variables," or "recodes," rather than all of the thousands of variables in the data set. For the 2017-2019 NSFG, most missing recode values were assigned using regression imputation software in which multiple regression was used to predict a value for the case using other variables in the data set as predictors. For each variable with missing data, a regression model was estimated to predict the values for the missing data. In some cases, recodes were imputed using logical imputation, which involved having a subject-matter expert at NCHS examine variables related to the variable in question, and assign a value that was consistent with those other variables. Logical imputation is an educated guess of the true value when there is any ambiguity.

Data Quality: Data releases generally include standard errors. The NSFG utilizes the following to maintain high quality data: 1) questionnaire design work, 2) consistency checks built into the interview to enable the interviewer to resolve problems in the field, 3) evaluation of monthly data files to find and correct survey instrument problems, and 4) extensive interviewer training. The NSFG website provides access to documentation that cover survey design and methods, variance estimation examples, and survey instruments. See "Questionnaires, Datasets, and Related Documentation" online at <www.cdc.gov/nchs/nsfg/nsfg_questionnaires.htm>.

Sources of Additional Material: National Center for Health Statistics, National Survey of Family Growth, online at <www.cdc.gov/nchs/nsfg/about_nsfg.htm>.

National Vital Statistics System

Universe, Frequency, and Types of Data: Annual data on births, deaths, marriages, divorces, and fetal deaths in the United States. Legal authority for the registration of these events resides individually with the 50 States, 2 cities (Washington, DC, and New York City), and 5 territories (Puerto Rico, the Virgin Islands, Guam, American Samoa, and the Commonwealth of the Northern Mariana Islands). These jurisdictions are responsible for maintaining registries of vital events and for issuing copies of birth, marriage, divorce, and death certificates.

Data Collection: Jurisdictions record vital events. Through its Vital Statistics Cooperative Program, NCHS cooperates with state vital statistics offices to develop and recommend standard forms for data collection, model regulations, and procedures to ensure uniform reporting of the events. The National Vital Statistics System uses electronic systems to collect data, including an electronic death reporting system. NVSS is working with states to modernize systems to improve the timeliness and quality of vital statistics data.

Data Reliability: Currently, there is no sampling for these files; the files are based on 100 percent of certificates registered. Generally more than 99 percent of the births and deaths occurring in this country are registered. Reports presenting vital statistics data include technical notes with further information on data sources and where to find information on methods and data reliability.

Sources of Additional Material: U.S. National Center for Health Statistics, National Vital Statistics System, <www.cdc.gov/nchs/nvss/about_nvss.htm>;and individual reports and technical documentation for data of interest available via the NVSS website, <www.cdc.gov/nchs/nvss/index.htm>.

National Highway Traffic Safety Administration (NHTSA)

Fatality Analysis Reporting System (FARS)

Universe, Frequency, and Types of Data: FARS is a census of all fatal motor vehicle traffic crashes that occur throughout the United States, including the District of Columbia and Puerto Rico, on roadways customarily open to the public. The crash must be reported to the state/jurisdiction, and is classified as fatal if a directly related fatality occurs within thirty days of the crash. The FARS database contains descriptions, in a standardized format, of each fatal crash reported. Each crash has over 140 different coded elements that characterize the crash, the vehicles, and the people involved. The specific data elements may be modified slightly each year to conform to changing user needs, vehicle characteristics, and highway safety emphasis areas. Data are in two versions of annual files, with the second report for the year being the final file with additional cases or updates.

Data Collection and Imputation: NHTSA has a cooperative agreement with an agency in each State government to provide specific information in a standard format on fatal crashes occurring in the State. State analysts extract data from state documents and enter the data into a standardized electronic database. State documents include police crash reports, death certificates, state vehicle registration files, coroner/medical examiner reports, emergency medical service reports, and other types of files and records. Each analyst interprets and codes data directly onto an electronic data file. The data are automatically checked when entered for acceptable range values and for consistency, enabling the analyst to make corrections immediately. Several programs continually monitor and improve the completeness and accuracy of the data. The FARS incorporates a sophisticated mathematical multiple imputation procedure to develop a probability distribution of missing blood alcohol concentration (BAC) levels in the database for drivers, pedestrians, and cyclists.

Data Reliability: Since this is census data, there are no sampling errors. Data are dependent on the accuracy of police crash reports and other reports, which may contain errors or omissions that go undetected.

Sources of Additional Material: Fatality Analysis Reporting System (FARS), online at <www.nhtsa.gov/FARS>;and *Fatality Analysis Reporting System Analytical User's Manual, 1975-2020,* online at <crashstats.nhtsa.dot.gov/#!/DocumentTypeList/23>.

Weights and Measures

U.S. Customary/Metric Conversion Table

[Conversions provided in the table are approximate]

Symbol	When you know U.S. customary	Multiply by	To find metric	Symbol
in	inches	2.54	centimeters	cm
ft	feet	30.48	centimeters	cm
yd	yards	0.91	meters	m
mi	miles	1.61	kilometers	km
in^2	square inches	6.45	square centimeters	cm^2
ft^2	square feet	0.09	square meters	m^2
yd^2	square yards	0.84	square meters	m^2
mi^2	square miles	2.59	square kilometers	km^2
	acre	0.41	hectare	ha
oz	ounces	28.35	grams	g
lb	pounds	0.45	kilograms	kg
oz (troy)	troy ounces	31.1	grams	g
	short tons (2,000 lb)	0.91	metric tons	t
	long tons (2,240 lb)	1.02	metric tons	t
fl oz	fluid ounces	29.57	mililiters	mL
c	cups	0.24	liters	L
pt	pints	0.47	liters	L
qt	quarts	0.95	liters	L
gal	gallons	3.79	liters	L
ft^3	cubic feet	0.03	cubic meters	m^3
yd^3	cubic yards	0.76	cubic meters	m^3
°F	degrees Fahrenheit (subtract 32)	0.55	degrees Celsius	°C

Symbol	When you know metric	Multiply by	To find U.S. customary	Symbol
cm	centimeters	0.39	inches	in
cm	centimeters	0.03	feet	ft
m	meters	1.09	yards	yd
km	kilometers	0.62	miles	mi
cm^2	square centimeters	0.16	square inches	in^2
cm^2	square centimeters	10.76	square feet	ft^2
m^2	square meters	1.2	square yards	yd^2
km^2	square kilometers	0.39	square miles	mi^2
ha	hectare	2.47	acre	
g	grams	0.04	ounces	oz
kg	kilograms	2.20	pounds	lb
g	grams	0.04	troy ounces	oz (troy)
t	metric tons	1.1	short tons (2,000 lb)	
t	metric tons	0.98	long tons (2,240 lb)	
mL	mililiters	0.03	fluid ounces	fl oz
L	liters	4.23	cups	c
L	liters	2.11	pints	pt
L	liters	1.06	quarts	qt
L	liters	0.26	gallons	gal
m^3	cubic meters	35.31	cubic feet	ft^3
m^3	cubic meters	1.31	cubic yards	yd^3
°C	degrees Celsius (after multiplying, add 32)	1.8	degrees Fahrenheit	°F

Source: National Institute of Standards and Technology (NIST), Weights and Measures Division. See <www.nist.gov/pml/weights-and-measures/metric-si/unit-conversion>

Index

[NOTE: Index citations refer to **table** numbers, not **page** numbers]

A

Note: Index citations refer to **table** numbers, not **page** numbers

Note: Index citations refer to **table** numbers, not **page** numbers

Note: Index citations refer to **table** numbers, not **page** numbers

Book publishing industry, 776, 1156, 1161, 1164
Bookkeeping. (See Accounting, tax preparation, bookkeeping, and payroll services.)
Books (see also Book publishing industry, Libraries and Reading), 1084, 1164, 1191
Boots. (See Footwear.)
Borders, Canada and Mexico, 411, 1285
Border Patrol activities, 566, 567
Boron, 947, 948
Bosnia and Herzegovina. (See Foreign countries.)
Botox, 196
Botswana. (See Foreign countries.)
Botulism, 200
Bowling, 1268, 1269
Bowling center industry, 1248, 1251
Boxing, 1268
Brazil. (See Foreign countries.)
Bread, 767, 772
Breweries, 1069
Bridges, 1116
Broadband, 1163, 1180, 1181, 1184, 1185, 1401
Broadcasting industry:
    Capital, 818
    Earnings, 667, 792, 1156, 1157
    Employees, 667, 792, 1156, 1157
    Establishments, 792, 1156, 1157
    Finances, 1161
    Gross domestic product, 708
    Multinational companies, 834, 835
    Number of stations, 1163
    Productivity, 675
    Receipts, revenue, 792, 1157, 1161, 1296
Broadway and off-Broadway shows, 1254
Broccoli, 243, 885, 908
Broilers (see also Poultry), 776, 885, 915, 923, 924
Bromine, 947, 948
Brunei. (See Foreign countries.)
Buddhist population. (See Religion.)
Budget, federal:
    Debt, 511
    Outlays, 150, 510, 512, 513, 514
    Receipts, 510, 516
    Tax expenditures, 518
    Taxes, 516
Building construction:
    Earnings, 667
    Employees, 667, 1001
    Occupational safety, 699
Building materials, and garden supplies stores:
    Earnings, 667, 792, 1078
    Electronic commerce, 1073, 1083
    Employees, 667, 792, 1070, 1076, 1078
    Establishments, 792, 1070, 1076, 1077
    Inventories, 1082
    Nonemployers, 1077
    Price indexes, 1010
    Productivity, 675
    Sales, 792, 1063, 1070, 1073, 1077, 1079, 1081, 1082, 1083
Building permits. (See Construction industry, and Housing and housing units.)
Buildings (see also Construction industry, and Housing and housing units):
    Characteristics of, 1047
    Construction value, 1003, 1006, 1007

    Federal, 541
    Fires and property loss, 404, 405, 438
    Floor space, 541, 1047
Bulgaria. (See Foreign countries.)
Bullying, 334, 337
Burglaries, 332, 341, 342, 343, 344, 347, 357, 358
Burkina Faso. (See Foreign countries.)
Burma. (See Foreign countries.)
Burundi. (See Foreign countries.)
Buses and bus transportation. (See Passenger transit industry, and Motor vehicles.)
Business cycles, 824
Business enterprises (see also individual types of business and industry):
    Age of firms, 802
    Age of owner, 796
    American Indian- and Alaska Native- owned businesses, 806, 812
    Asian- owned businesses, 806, 811
    Bankruptcies filed, 813, 814
    Births and deaths of, 804, 857
    Black- owned businesses, 806, 810
    Capital, 818, 819, 820
    Corporations, partnerships, and proprietorships, 782, 784, 785, 786, 1071, 1077
    Digital technology use, 822
    Employees, 673, 794, 795, 799, 800, 801, 803, 804, 808, 809, 810, 811, 812, 833, 857, 1292, 1324, 1325
    Establishments, 673, 792, 793, 794, 795, 796, 797, 800, 801, 804, 806, 1325
    Expansions and contractions, 804
    Finances, 782, 784, 785, 786, 787, 788, 829, 830, 831, 834, 835, 1064, 1065, 1080
    Firms, 799, 800, 801, 804, 807, 808, 809, 810, 811, 812, 1324
    Flow of funds, 1197, 1198
    Foreign investment in the U.S., 1305, 1306, 1307
    Foreign trade, 1324, 1325
    Franchises, 798
    High technology, 857
    Hispanic- owned businesses, 806, 809
    Leading indicators, 825
    Loans to minority- operated small businesses, 805
    Minority- owned, 808, 809, 810, 811, 812
    Multinational companies, 832, 833, 834, 835
    Native Hawaiian, Other Pacific Islander- owned business, 806
    Patents, 815, 816, 1402
    Paycheck Protection Program loans, 823
    Payroll, 794, 795, 799, 800, 801
    Profits, 829, 830, 831, 1064, 1065, 1080
    Sales, shipments, receipts, 793, 807, 808, 809, 810, 811, 812, 1060, 1062, 1063, 1065, 1080, 1324
    Small business, 799, 800, 801, 804, 805
    Startups, 802
    Veteran–owned, 806
    Women- owned businesses, 806, 807
    Work from home, 803
Business management, degrees, 322, 325, 326, 327, 328
Butane, 954
Butter, 244, 772, 921

Note: Index citations refer to **table** numbers, not **page** numbers

C

Cabbage, 243, 908, 913
Cable/pay television services, 767, 1162
Cable and other subscription programming:
  Earnings, 667, 1156
  Employees, 667, 1156, 1157
  Establishments, 1156, 1157
  Finances, 1161, 1172
  Revenue, 1157, 1161, 1172
Cadmium, 948
Cafeterias. (See Food services and drinking places.)
California. (See State data.)
Calves, 885, 915, 916, 919
Cambodia. (See Foreign countries.)
Cameroon. (See Foreign countries.)
Campaigns, fundraising, 476, 477, 478, 479
Campylobacteriosis, 200, 242
Canada, (see also Foreign countries), 408, 411
Cancer (malignancies), 126, 197, 198, 199
  Deaths, 118, 119, 120, 121, 122, 123, 126
Candy, 767
Cantaloupes, 243, 885, 908
Capacity utilization, index, 828
Cape Verde. (See Foreign countries.)
Capital (see also individual industries):
  Banking, 1208, 1209
  Expenditures, 819, 820, 821, 833
  New security issues, 1227
  Residential, 1025
  Services, 674
  Stocks, 818
  Utilities, 994, 999
Capital equipment, producer price indexes, 776
Capital gains, 522, 523
Capital punishment, 395, 396, 397
Carbon dioxide emissions, 424, 425, 972, 1398
Carbohydrate, consumption, 245, 246
Cardiovascular disease. (See Heart disease.)
Carpal tunnel syndrome, 700
Carrots, 243, 885, 908, 913
Cars. (See Automobiles.)
Casinos, 1248, 1251
Catalog and mail order sales, 1077, 1079, 1083, 1084
Catfish, 942
Catholic population. (See Religion.)
Cattle:
  Dairy cows, 914, 917, 920, 921
  Farm marketings, sales, 885, 886, 914
  Imports, 895
  Number on farms, 914, 916, 917, 919, 920
  Prices, 776, 916
  Production, 916, 919
  Slaughter, 919
  Value on farms, 916
Cauliflower, 243, 908
Celery, 243, 908
Cellular and other wireless telecommunications, 1156, 1161, 1173, 1174, 1176, 1177
Cellular telephones, 1176, 1177, 1178, 1179, 1182, 1184, 1186, 1187, 1400, 1401

Cement (see also Nonmetallic mineral product manufacturing), 947, 948
  Earnings, 667
  Employment, 667, 948
  Prices, 776, 948
  Productivity, 675
  World production, 1389
Central African Republic. (See Foreign countries.)
Central America. (See Foreign countries.)
Central and South American population (see also Hispanic or Latino origin population), 37
Cereal and bakery products:
  Expenditures, prices, 727, 731, 732, 767
  Per capita consumption, 244
Cerebrovascular diseases, 118, 119, 120, 121, 122, 123, 125
Certificates of deposit, 1201
Certification and license status of workers, 690
Cesarean section deliveries, 84
Chad. (See Foreign countries.)
Charitable contributions (see also Philanthropy), 528, 531, 615, 616, 617, 618, 619
Charter schools, 284, 285, 286
Cheerleading, 1270
Cheese (see also Dairy products), 244, 772, 921, 1329
Chemical engineering, degrees conferred, 852
Chemical products:
  Foreign trade, 893, 1313, 1321, 1322, 1327, 1328
  Price indexes, 776, 780, 781
  Production, 827
Chemicals manufacturing (see also individual chemicals):
  Capital, 818
  Earnings, 667, 1052, 1059
  Employees, 667, 1050, 1052, 1054, 1059
  Establishments, 1050
  Foreign trade, 780, 781, 1055, 1322
  Gross domestic product, 708, 1048
  Industrial production index, 827
  Inventories, 1061, 1062
  Multinational companies, 832, 834, 835
  Productivity, 675
  Research and development, 842
  Shipments, 1052, 1055, 1061, 1062
  Toxic chemical releases, 431, 432
Chemistry (see also Physical sciences):
  Degrees conferred, 851, 852
  Employment, 649
  Salary offers, 322
Cherries, 243, 885, 909
Chicken pox, 200, 235, 236
Chickens. (See Poultry.)
Chikungunya virus, 200
Child abuse, 390, 391
Child care, 604, 608, 649, 767
  Expenditures for, 608
  Tax credit, 532
Child day care services, 604, 608, 611, 649, 667
Child support, 576, 605, 606
Children (see also Births, Deaths, Marriages, Divorces, and Population):
  Adopted, 46, 77, 607
  Age and/or sex, 7, 8, 9, 10, 12, 17
  Aid, social welfare programs, 574, 576, 577, 579, 596, 597, 599, 600, 602, 603, 605, 606, 609, 611

Note: Index citations refer to **table** numbers, not **page** numbers

ProQuest Statistical Abstract of the United States: 2023

Note: Index citations refer to **table** numbers, not **page** numbers

Computers and electronic product manufacturing:
  Capital, 818
  Earnings, 667, 1052, 1059
  Employees, 667, 1050, 1052, 1054, 1059
  Establishments, 1050
  Foreign trade, 1322, 1327, 1328
  Gross domestic product, 708, 1048
  Industrial production index, 827
  Inventories, 1061, 1062, 1063
  Multinational companies, 834, 835
  Productivity, 675
  Prices, 780
  Research and development, 842
  Shipments, 1052, 1061, 1062, 1063
Concussions, 234, 700
Condensed and evaporated milk, 244
Congestion, traffic, 1141
Congo (Brazzaville). (See Foreign countries.)
Congo (Kinshasa). (See Foreign countries.)
Congress, U.S.:
  Apportionment of, 463
  Asian members, 466
  Bills, acts, resolutions, 468, 469
  Black members, 466
  Campaign finances, 477, 478
  Composition of, 464, 465, 467
  Congressional districts, 462
  Hispanic members, 466
  Seniority, 465
  Time in session, 468
  Women members, 466
  Votes cast, 450, 452, 460, 461, 462
Connecticut. (See State data.)
Construction industry (see also Building
    construction, and Highways):
  Building permits, 1004, 1005
  Capital, 797, 818, 820
  Earnings, 665, 667, 678, 679, 792, 807, 808,
    809, 810, 811, 812, 1002, 1345
  Employees, 652, 653, 654, 656, 665, 666, 667,
    673, 792, 795, 800, 807, 808, 809, 810,
    811, 812, 855, 1001, 1002, 1345
  Establishments, 673, 792, 793, 795, 796, 797,
    800, 806, 807, 808, 809, 810, 811, 812,
    1001, 1002, 1345
  Finances, 786, 1337
  Gross domestic product, 708, 1337
  Hires and separations, 671, 672
  Hours, 665
  Nonemployers, 793
  Occupational safety, 697, 699
  Profits, 831
  Residential, 1004, 1005, 1006, 1007, 1008,
    1009, 1011, 1012
  Shipments, receipts, 786, 792, 793, 807, 808,
    809, 810, 811, 812
  Unions, 702
  Value, of, 1003, 1006, 1007
Construction machinery, manufacturing:
  Earnings, 667, 1052
  Employees, 667, 1052
  Productivity, 675
  Shipments, 1052
Construction materials. (See Building materials.)
Consumers:
  Consumer complaints, 356, 359, 1104

Consumer goods, 215, 776
Credit, 787, 788, 1200, 1202, 1203, 1206, 1215,
  1217, 1218, 1219, 1222
Expenditures:
  Card transactions, 726
  Entertainment, 716, 727, 731, 732, 1260,
    1261
  Education, 716, 727, 731, 732, 777
  Food, 716, 727, 728, 730, 731, 732, 777, 889
  Health insurance, 148, 716
  Housing, 716, 727, 728, 730, 731, 732, 777
  Medical care, 142, 143, 144, 145, 148, 149,
    716, 727, 728, 730, 731, 732, 777
  Metropolitan areas, 728
  Pets, 716, 1260
  Reading material, 716, 727, 731, 732, 777,
    1260, 1261, 1265
  Sporting goods, 777, 1260, 1276
  Telephone service, 1178
  Transportation, 716, 727, 728, 730, 731, 732,
    777
Consumer price indexes, 764, 765, 766, 767
  Foreign countries, 1379
  Medical care, 147, 765, 766, 767
  Purchasing power of the dollar, 764
Consumption. (See individual commodities, and
    Personal consumption expenditures.)
Contraception, use of, 98, 99
Contract employees, 650
Convenience stores. (See Food and beverage
    stores.)
Copper:
  Consumption, 948, 951
  Foreign trade, 948, 951
  Prices, 776, 780, 781, 948, 949
  Production and value, 947, 948, 1389
Copyrights, registration, 817
Corn:
  Acreage, 905, 908, 913, 1384
  Consumption, 243, 244, 1384
  Farm marketings, sales, 885, 886, 913
  Foreign trade, 897, 899, 900, 1321, 1384, 1388
  Genetically engineered, 879
  Prices, 776, 780, 905
  Production, 897, 905, 908, 913, 1384
  Supply and disappearance, 1384
Coronavirus disease 2019 (COVID-19), 117, 118,
  119, 120, 121, 122, 123, 127, 176, 205, 206,
  279, 304, 725, 726, 823
Corporations:
  Bonds, 1226
  Capital, 790
  Dividend payments, 829
  Finances, 782, 783, 784, 785, 786, 788, 789,
    790, 1064, 1065, 1080, 1196, 1197, 1235
  Manufacturing, 1064, 1065
  Nonfinancial, 788
  Philanthropy, 615
  Profits, 782, 829, 830, 831, 1064, 1065, 1080
  Receipts, 782, 786
  Sales, 786, 1064, 1065, 1080
  Taxes:
    Audits, 791
    Corporate income tax, 485, 486, 492, 499,
      501, 516, 534, 791, 829
    Returns, 782, 783, 790

Note: Index citations refer to **table** numbers, not **page** numbers

---

Note: Index citations refer to **table** numbers, not **page** numbers

D

Dairy products (see also individual products):
    Consumer expenditures, 727, 731, 732
    Consumption, 244, 922, 1384
    Farm marketings, sales, 883, 885, 886, 921
    Foreign trade, 891, 895, 898, 922, 1384
    Manufacture, 675, 921, 1052, 1054
    Prices, 772, 776, 888
    Production, 921, 922, 1384
Dance, 1262
Data processing services. (See Computer
    programming and data processing services.)
Dates, 909
Day care. (See Child day care services.)
DAX, German stock index, 1404
Death care services, 667, 675, 716, 767, 1290,
    1291, 1292, 1298
Death penalty, 395, 396, 397
Deaths and death rates (see also Accidents and
    fatalities), 3, 4, 5, 22, 80
    Age and sex, 108, 109, 110, 112, 117, 121, 122,
      124, 125, 126, 128, 129, 130
    American Indian, Alaska Native population, 108,
      109, 110, 119, 124, 128, 129
    Asian population, 108, 109, 110, 119, 124,
      128, 129
    Black, African American population, 108, 109,
      110, 115, 116, 119, 124, 128, 129
    Causes of death, 117, 118, 119, 120, 121, 122,
      123, 124, 125, 126, 128, 129, 130, 131, 132,
      133, 1100
    COVID- 19, 117, 118, 119, 120, 121, 122, 123, 127
    Fetal and neonatal, 113, 114
    Foreign countries, 1357, 1361, 1362
    Heart disease, 118, 119, 120, 121, 122, 123, 124
    Hispanic or Latino origin, 108, 110, 116, 119,
      124, 128, 129
    Industrial, 699
    Infant, 80, 109, 110, 113, 114, 115, 121
    Injuries, 120
    Island areas of the U.S., 115, 1331
    Maternal, 114, 116
    Military deaths, 548, 550
    Race, 108, 109, 110, 114, 115, 119, 124, 128,
      129, 133
    States, 16, 111, 115, 117, 123
    Suicide, 119, 120, 121, 122, 123, 129, 130,
      548, 550, 1362
    Traffic fatalities, 1100, 1129, 1130, 1131, 1133,
      1134, 1136, 1138, 1139, 1140, 1361
    Urban- rural status, 112
    Weather related, 438, 441
    Workers' deaths, 403, 698, 699, 945
Deaths, of businesses, 804
Debit cards, 1215, 1216
Debt (see also Loans and mortgages):
    Consumer, 1206, 1219
    Credit card, 1203, 1204, 1217, 1219
    Credit market, 1198
    Farm, 881
    Federal government, 511
    Foreign countries, 1374, 1408
    Households and families, 1203, 1205
    Individual, 757

    Local government, 489, 504
    Medical, 194
    State and local government, 489, 493, 499, 502,
      1119, 1198
    Student loan debt, 312
Deductions, taxes, 528, 529, 531
    Business, 784, 785, 786, 790
Defense, Department of (see also Army, Air Force,
    Marine Corps, and Navy):
    Budget authority, outlays, 512, 513, 514, 542,
      543
    Expenditures, 140, 143, 146
    Military personnel, 544, 545, 546, 548, 549,
      550, 551
    Military retirees, 547, 576
Deferred Action for Childhood Arrivals (DACA), 559
Defined benefit and contribution plans, 582, 585,
    586, 587, 589, 1197, 1239, 1240, 1241, 1242
Degrees conferred (see also individual fields), 250,
    323, 324, 325, 326, 327, 328, 329, 848, 849,
    850, 851, 852
    Salary offers, 322
Delaware. (See State data.)
Delinquency. (See Juvenile delinquency.)
Dengue fever, 200
Denmark. (See Foreign countries.)
Dentists, 649
    Care visits, 195, 213, 229
    Charges and expenditures for, 139, 141, 142,
      143, 147, 149, 777
    Dental schools, students, and graduates, 329
    Employment, 170, 667
    Offices, 168, 169
Department stores:
    Earnings, 667
    Employees, 667, 1076
    Establishments, 1076
    Inventories, 1082
    Productivity, 675
    Sales, 1079, 1082
Deportations, illegal aliens, 565, 566, 567
Deposit Insurance Fund, 1211
Deposits. (See Banks, commercial.)
Depression, 213, 230, 241
Dermatologists, 171
Development aid (see also Foreign aid), 1406, 1407
Diabetes, 90, 118, 119, 120, 121, 122, 123, 211
Diamonds, 948
Diatomite, 947, 948
Diesel, fuel, 769, 969, 974
Dietitians and nutritionists, 649
Digital economy, 1159, 1160
Direct mail advertising industry, 1294
Directory and mailing list publications industry,
    1156, 1161, 1164
Disabilities:
    Age, 35, 208, 209
    Beneficiaries, 576, 579, 580
    Benefits paid, 579, 580, 581
    Elderly, 35, 208, 209
    Food stamp participants, 602, 603
    Government transfer payments, 573, 574, 575
    Hate crimes, 353, 354
    Labor force status, 625
    Learning, 231

Note: Index citations refer to **table** numbers, not **page** numbers

Note: Index citations refer to **table** numbers, not **page** numbers

Note: Index citations refer to **table** numbers, not **page** numbers

Note: Index citations refer to **table** numbers, not **page** numbers

Employment, 649, 854, 855, 858
  Research and development, 839, 844
  Salary, 322, 858
English, ability to speak, 56, 57, 58, 261, 269, 280
English language and literature, degrees, 325, 326, 327, 328
Entertainment:
  Consumer expenditures, 716, 727, 731, 732, 1261
  Consumer price indexes, 767
  Gaming, 1277
  Personal expenditures, 716, 731, 732, 1260
Environment (see also Pollution):
  Charitable contributions, 615
  Environmental industries, 430
  Volunteers, 614
  Wetlands, 416, 418
Environmental science, 839, 844
Equal Employment Opportunity Commission, 369
Equatorial Guinea. (See Foreign countries.)
Equestrian, 1268, 1269
Eritrea. (See Foreign countries.)
Eskimo population. (See American Indian, Alaska Native population.)
Establishments. (See Business enterprise, and individual industries.)
Estate and gift taxes, 519
Estonia. (See Foreign countries.)
Eswatini. (See Foreign countries.)
Ethane, 954
Ethanol, 974, 1128, 1151
Ethiopia. (See Foreign countries.)
Ethnicities. (See Hispanic or Latino origin population.)
Europe. (See Foreign countries.)
European Union. (See Foreign countries.)
Exchange- traded funds, 1197, 1228
Excise taxes, 516, 519
Executions of prisoners, 395, 396
Exercise, 1266
Exercise equipment, 215
Expectation of life (average lifetime), 103, 104, 105, 106
  Foreign countries, 1357, 1358
  Projections, 103
Expenditures. (See individual subjects.)
Expenditures of state and local government. (See individual governmental units.)
Expenditures of U.S. government, 483, 484, 514, 715, 1311, 1312
  Aid to the arts and humanities, 1255
  Aid to state and local government, 483, 484
  Budget outlays, 150, 510, 512, 513, 514, 515
  COVID- 19 response, 725
  Education. (See Federal aid to education.)
  Food programs, federal, 600, 601
  Health, 139, 140, 141, 142, 143, 484
  Homeland security, 484, 561, 562, 563, 564
  Hospitals, 191
  National defense, 542, 543, 778
  Outlays, 510, 512, 513, 514, 515, 542
  Payrolls, 537
  Price indexes, 778
  Public debt, 511
  Research and development, 836, 837, 838, 839, 840, 841

Schools, 247, 484
Science/space, 859
Veterans benefits. (See Veterans Affairs.)
Exports. (See Foreign trade.)
Express mail, 1154, 1155

F

Fabricated metal product manufacturing:
  Capital, 818
  Earnings, 667, 1052, 1059
  Employees, 667, 1050, 1052, 1054, 1059
  Establishments, 1050
  Foreign trade, 1055, 1322
  Gross domestic product, 708, 1048
  Industrial production index, 827
  Productivity, 675
  Shipments, 1052, 1055, 1061, 1062
  Toxic chemical releases, 432
Fabrics. (See Textile mill products.)
Falls, accidental deaths, 120, 121
Families. (See Households.)
Family and consumer sciences, degrees conferred, 325, 326, 327, 328
Family farms, 865, 867, 873, 874
Farm loans, 1220, 1222
Farms:
  Acreage, 862, 863, 864, 865, 866, 867, 868, 869, 871, 874, 878
    Cropland, 415, 417, 862, 866, 902
    Crops harvested (see also individual crops), 902, 903, 905, 906, 907, 908, 1384
    Farm type, 865, 867, 874
  Agrichemicals, 883, 888, 893
  Agricultural products:
    Exports, 1388
    Foreign countries, production, 1385, 1386
    Market value, 862
    Prices. (See Prices received by farmers.)
    World production, 1384, 1385, 1386
  Assets and liabilities, 881
  Corporate, 865, 868, 874
  Crops (see also individual crops):
    Acreage, 862, 902, 903, 913, 1342
    Fruits and nuts, 909, 910, 913, 1329, 1343
    Income, 885, 886, 887, 1342
    Production, 897, 902, 903, 913, 1384, 1385
    Vegetables, 908, 912, 913
  Debt, 881, 1220
  Expenses, 880, 883
  Family or individual, 865, 867, 873, 1342
  Farm land and buildings value, 867, 868, 869, 881
  Farm operators, farmers, 872
  Farm products sold, marketing receipts, 867, 868, 869, 870, 871, 876, 882, 883, 885, 886, 887
  Farm to school programs, 877
  Fertilizers:
    Farm expenditures for, 883
    Foreign trade, 893, 1321
    Prices, 776, 888
  Government payments to farmers (subsidies), 870, 882, 883, 884, 890

Note: Index citations refer to **table** numbers, not **page** numbers

---

Note: Index citations refer to **table** numbers, not **page** numbers

Note: Index citations refer to **table** numbers, not **page** numbers

Note: Index citations refer to **table** numbers, not **page** numbers

Note: Index citations refer to **table** numbers, not **page** numbers

Note: Index citations refer to **table** numbers, not **page** numbers

Note: Index citations refer to **table** numbers, not **page** numbers

Expenditures, 248, 296
Faculty, 294, 319, 320, 321
Federal funding, 247
Finances, 248, 296, 317
Financial aid, 310, 313, 314, 315, 316
Foreign- born students, 299, 302, 847, 848
Foreign languages, 303
Historically Black Colleges and Universities, 296
Housing population, 71
Libraries, 331
Number, 294, 295, 296
Online course enrollment, 330
Price indexes, 318, 767
Research and development, 836, 838, 844, 845, 1405
Salary offers, college graduates, 322
State appropriations, 317
Tuition and fees, 309, 311, 316
Voluntary financial support, 313, 315, 316
Highways:
  Accidents, 1100, 1129, 1130, 1131, 1132, 1133, 1135, 1137, 1138, 1139, 1140
  Bridge inventory and condition, 1116
  Debt, state and local government, 1119
  Distracted driving, 1133
  Employees, government, 507, 509
  Expenditures:
    Local government, 487, 488, 504
    State and local government, 485, 486, 487, 488, 493
    State government, 487, 488, 499, 502
    U.S. government, 484
  Funding, 1117, 1121, 1122
  Interstate highways, 1115
  Mileage, 1095, 1114, 1115
  Motor fuel consumption, 969, 1127
  Motor fuel tax, 1118, 1122
  Transit savings, 1145
  Types of roads, 1114, 1115
  Value of new construction, 1006, 1007
Hindu population. (See Religions.)
Hispanic or Latino origin population, 6, 8, 9, 12, 13, 19, 36, 37, 42
  Adoption, 607
  Age and/or sex, 6, 8, 9, 12, 37
  AIDS and/or HIV, 202, 203
  Births and birth rates, 81, 82, 83, 84, 86, 87, 88, 91, 92, 93, 94
  Body weight, 226, 227
  Bullying, student, 337, 338
  Business owners, 809
  Cancer, 198
  Child care, 604, 608
  Children, 8, 9, 12, 37, 69, 238
  College enrollment, 270, 288, 295, 297 299, 300, 301, 307, 330
  Congress, members of, 466
  Consumer expenditure, 731
  Contraceptive use, 98, 99
  Criminal victimizations, 348, 353, 357, 361
  Deaths, 108, 110, 116, 119, 124, 127, 128, 129, 133
  Dental care visits, 195, 229
  Degrees conferred, 324, 851
  Disability status, 208, 305

Educational attainment, 36, 37, 256, 257, 258, 259, 288, 297
Elderly, 8, 9, 12, 753
Elected officials, 466, 475
Elections, voter registration and turnout, 453
Families, characteristics, 36, 37, 67, 73
Food stamp participants, 577, 603
Foreign- born populations, 37, 41, 42, 623
Foster care, 607
Grandparents living with grandchildren, 67, 70
Hate crimes, 353
Health insurance coverage, 163, 164, 165
Health and dental care visits, 183, 186, 195
Heart disease, deaths, 119, 124
High school dropouts, 37, 270, 288, 290, 291
Household or family characteristics, 37, 62, 67, 73
Housing, 36, 1031, 1035, 1041, 1043, 1045, 1046
Immunization of children, 236
Income:
  Family, 36, 37, 738, 739, 740
  Household, 733, 734, 736
  Persons, 576, 743, 746, 747
Internet access/use, 1180, 1184, 1185, 1188
Jail inmates, 393, 394
Labor force and employment, 621, 622, 623, 627, 630, 634, 682, 702
  Displaced workers, 646
  Earnings, 259, 506, 682, 687, 690
  Educational attainment, 627, 630, 643, 655, 662
  Employed, 37, 506, 622, 623, 627, 630, 639, 641, 643, 649, 655, 656
  Industry, 656, 1292
  Job search, 658
  Multiple job holders, 641
  Unemployed, 37, 622, 623, 630, 657, 658, 662
  Union membership, 702
Leisure time use, 1266
Life expectancy, 103, 104, 107
Living arrangements, 69
Marital status, 59, 63, 73
Maternal mortality, 116
Minimum wage workers, 687
Murders, 350
Nurses, 649
Occupation, 36, 275, 649, 655
Pension plan coverage, 576
Poverty, 36, 37, 751, 752, 753, 755, 756
Projections, 12, 13
Public assistance, 576, 577, 603, 609
Schools and education:
  Homeschooled, 282
  Parent participation, 269
  Preprimary school, 262, 270
  School enrollment, 253, 270, 288, 299, 300, 630
  Teachers, 275, 276, 277, 278, 649
  Sexual activity and identity, 98, 99
  States, 19
  Suicides, deaths, 119, 129, 550
  Veterans, 558
  Voter registration and turnout, 453, 455
  Weapons in school, 335

Note: Index citations refer to **table** numbers, not **page** numbers

Male householder, 62, 64, 65, 66, 67, 74, 75
Marital status, 62, 64, 66, 73
Married couples with or without own children, 62, 63, 66, 73
Media users, 1162
Mobility (geographic) status, 31
Mortgages, 1045, 1046, 1202, 1203, 1204
Mutual fund ownership, 1236, 1237
Net worth, 760, 761, 762
Native Hawaiian, Other Pacific Islander, 36, 73
Nonfamily, 62, 64
Participation in education, 269
Persons living alone (one- person households), 34, 61, 62, 64, 65
Poverty, 36, 755, 756
Production value, 713
Public assistance to families, 577
Race, 36, 62, 67, 73
Region of householder, 735, 741
Same- sex couple, 73, 75
Savings rate, 1377
Single parent, 62, 66, 67
Size, 40, 62, 64, 65
Stay- at- home parents, 68
Stock ownership, 1201, 1232
Telephones, 1163, 1177
Tenure, 36, 73, 735
Unmarried partners, 73, 74, 75
Wealth, 760, 761
Household work, 691
Housekeeping supplies expenditures, 731, 732
Housing and household operations, price indexes, 767, 768, 777
Housing and housing units (see also Households or families):
Age of housing stocks, 1028
Amenities, 1009, 1038, 1039, 1041
Apartments, 1011, 1019, 1020, 1038, 1039
Appliances, 767
Building permit value, 1004, 1005
Capital, 1025
Condominiums, 1019
Construction:
Apartments completed and rented, 1011, 1020
New units, 1004, 1005, 1008, 1009, 1012
Time to completion, 1012
Value, 1003, 1006, 1007
Consumer expenditures, 716, 727, 728, 730, 731, 732, 1038
Consumer price indexes, 765, 766, 767
Costs, 1034, 1035, 1036
Deficiencies, 1038, 1041
Elderly, 1022, 1032, 1035, 1041
Energy, 968, 970, 971, 973, 975, 988, 992, 1009, 1042, 1043
Fires, and property loss, 404
Floor space, 1009, 1042
Government expenditures, 485, 486, 493, 514, 515
Heating equipment used, 1009, 1028, 1039, 1040
Heating fuel used, 1009, 1040, 1042
Homeless, 612, 613
Hurricanes, 410
Improvements, 1044

Kitchen equipment, 1028, 1038, 1039
Loans and mortgages, 1014, 1045, 1046, 1220, 1221, 1222
Lot size, 1030
Maintenance and repair expenditures, 731, 732
Metropolitan area data, 1018, 1027
Mobile homes, 1016, 1028, 1029, 1038, 1039
New privately owned homes, characteristics, 1009
Ownership, 30, 36, 40, 735, 1021, 1022, 1023, 1024, 1026, 1027, 1028, 1030, 1031, 1032, 1033, 1034, 1035, 1036
Plumbing, 1028, 1039
Price indexes, 765, 766, 767, 768, 1013
Prices, or costs, 1013, 1014, 1015, 1016, 1017, 1018, 1019, 1034, 1035, 1036, 1038
Puerto Rico, 1334
Remodeling, 1044
Rent, rental value, 1020, 1034, 1035, 1037
Rooms, 1030
Sales, 1014, 1017, 1019
Shelters, 612, 613
Square footage, 1009, 1030
State data, 1024, 1026, 1029, 1033, 1036, 1037
Structural type, 1023, 1028, 1029, 1038, 1039
Subsidized, 1011
Supportive, 612
Tenure, 30, 36, 40, 735, 760, 761, 1021, 1022, 1023, 1024, 1026, 1027, 1028, 1030, 1031, 1032, 1033, 1034, 1035, 1036, 1037, 1038, 1041, 1042, 1043, 1334
Transitional, 612
Vacancies, 1021, 1023, 1024, 1026, 1027, 1028, 1030
Value, 760, 762, 1036
Year built, 1009, 1028, 1039, 1042
Housing assistance, 577, 612, 613
Human immunodeficiency virus (HIV) (see also AIDS), 120, 121, 122, 200, 201, 202, 203
Human papillomavirus (HPV), 204
Human services, 612
Hungary. (See Foreign countries.)
Hunger, 216
Hunting and fishing, 925, 1275
Hurricanes, 410, 438, 441
Hydrocarbon gas liquids, 954
Hydroelectric power, 970, 995
Capacity, 984
Consumption, 966, 970, 971
Net generation, 984, 986, 989, 995
Net summer capacity, 984, 987
Production, 966, 984, 1390
Hypertension, 90, 119, 120, 121, 212, 213

I

Ice cream, 244, 772, 921, 1329
Ice hockey, 1267, 1268, 1269
Iceland. (See Foreign countries.)
Idaho. (See State data.)
Identity theft, 356, 359, 360
Illegal aliens, 50, 366, 559, 565, 566, 567
Illinois. (See State data.)
Immigrants (see also Foreign- born population):
Class of admission, 48, 51, 52
Country of birth, 46, 50, 52, 53, 54

Note: Index citations refer to **table** numbers, not **page** numbers

---

Note: Index citations refer to **table** numbers, not **page** numbers

---

Note: Index citations refer to **table** numbers, not **page** numbers

---

Note: Index citations refer to **table** numbers, not **page** numbers

Note: Index citations refer to **table** numbers, not **page** numbers

Toxic chemical releases, 432
Lebanon. (See Foreign countries.)
Legal assistants, 649
Legal services:
  Capital, 818
  Earnings, 667
  Employees, 667, 1291, 1292
  Establishments, 1290, 1291
  Gross domestic product, 708
  Prices, 767
  Receipts, 1290, 1294
Legionellosis, 200
Legislatures, state party composition, 472, 473
Leisure activities, 1258, 1262, 1266
Leisure and hospitality industry:
  Earnings, 667, 679
  Employees, 656, 666, 667
  Hires and separations, 671, 672
  Occupational safety, 699
  Union membership, 702
Lemons, 243, 772, 885, 909
Lesotho. (See Foreign countries.)
Letters (postal), 1154, 1155
Lettuce, 243, 772, 885, 908, 913
Liberal arts degrees conferred, 325, 326, 328
Liberia. (See Foreign countries.)
Libraries and librarians, 1156, 1161, 1189, 1190,
    1191
  Colleges and universities, 331
  Degrees conferred, 326, 327, 328
  Employees, 509, 649, 1189
  Internet access/use, 1189, 1190
  Library visits, 1190
  Resources and services, 1189, 1190, 1191
Libya. (See Foreign countries.)
Liechtenstein. (See Foreign countries.)
Life expectancy, 103, 104, 105, 106, 107, 1357,
    1358
Life insurance:
  Capital, 1244
  Cash value, 1201
  Consumer expenditures, 716, 727, 731, 732
  Establishments, 1244
  Finances, 1197, 1220, 1228, 1235, 1244
  Foreign countries, 1378
  Flow of funds, 1228
  In force, 1243
  Individual Retirement Accounts (IRAs), 1239
  Mortgage loans outstanding, 1220
  Purchases, policies, 1243
  Reserves, 762, 1199, 1200, 1244
  Sales, 1243, 1244
Life sciences, 325, 328, 839, 844, 851, 852, 855
Life tables, 103, 104, 105, 106, 107
Light and power. (See Electric light and power
    industry.)
Lightning, 438
Lime, mineral, 947, 948
Liposuction, 196
Liquor stores. (See Beer, wine, and liquor stores.)
Liquors and beverages:
  Alcoholism treatment, 220
  Consumption, 221
  Government revenues, 485, 486, 492, 499, 500,
    503
  Manufacturing industry, 1069

Listeriosis, 200
Literacy, comparative, 1383
Lithium, 948
Lithuania. (See Foreign countries.)
Liver disease, 119, 120, 121, 122
Livestock and livestock products (see also Animals
    domestic, and individual classes):
  Consumption, 244, 915, 1343, 1384
  Farm marketings, sales, 876, 883, 885, 887, 914,
    1343
  Foreign trade, 891, 895, 898, 900, 915, 1321,
    1322, 1384
  Number on farms, 914, 916, 917, 918, 919, 920
  Prices, 774, 780, 781, 888, 916
  Production, 915, 916, 918, 919, 920, 1384, 1386
  Purchases, 883
  Supply, 915
  Value on farms, 916
Living cost. (See Consumer price indexes and Prices.)
Loans and mortgages (see also Debt):
  Automobile loans, 1204, 1219
  Banks, commercial, 1209, 1222
  Consumer credit, 1200, 1202, 1203, 1204, 1206,
    1209, 1217, 1218, 1219, 1222
  Credit market, flow of funds, 1200
  Credit unions, 1214
  Delinquency rates, 1221, 1222
  Farms. (See Farm mortgage loans.)
  Federal Housing Administration (FHA), 1221
  Foreclosure rates, 1221
  Gross assets, 757
  Home mortgage/equity loans, 757, 1045, 1046,
    1202, 1203, 1204, 1206, 1220
    Applications, denials, 1045
    Delinquency, 1221, 1222
  Installment loans, 1203, 1204
  Life insurance, 1243, 1244
  Minority- operated small businesses, 805
  Mortgage- backed securities, 1226
  Paycheck Protection Program, 823
  Personal loans, 1219
  Savings institutions, 1214
  Student loan debt, 312
  Veterans Administration (VA), 1221
Lobsters, 941
Local and suburban transit. (See Passenger
    transit industry.)
Local government. (See State and local government,
    and individual governmental units.)
Locks, water navigation, 1110
Lodging industries. (See Hotels and other
    lodging places.)
London FTSE 100 stock market index, 1404
Long- term care facilities, 177
Lotteries, 496, 497
Louisiana. (See State data.)
Low birth weight, 89
Lumber (see also Forest products, and Wood
    products manufacturing):
  Consumption, 934, 936
  Foreign trade, 934, 935
  Prices, 776, 938
  Production, 934, 936

Note: Index citations refer to **table** numbers, not **page** numbers

Lung disease. (See Pulmonary or respiratory disease.)
Luxembourg. (See Foreign countries.)
Lyme disease, 200, 201

M

Macadamia nuts, 909
Macedonia. (See Foreign countries.)
Machine tools, 767, 776
Machinery manufacturing:
  Capital, 818
  Earnings, 667, 1052, 1059
  Employees, 667, 1050, 1052, 1054, 1059
  Establishments, 1050
  Foreign trade, 780, 781, 1055, 1313, 1321
  Gross domestic product, 708, 1048
  Industrial production index, 827
  Inventories, 1061, 1062
  Multinational companies, 834, 835
  Price indexes, 780, 781
  Productivity, 675
  Research and development, 842
  Shipments, 1052, 1055, 1061, 1062
  Toxic chemical releases, 432
Madagascar. (See Foreign countries.)
Magnesium, 947, 948, 1389
Magnet schools, 284
Mail, 1154, 1155
Mail order houses (including electronic shopping):
  Earnings, 667, 1078
  Employees, 667, 1076, 1078
  Establishments, 1076, 1077
  Productivity, 675
  Sales, 1077, 1079, 1083, 1084
Maine. (See State data.)
Malaria, 200
Malawi. (See Foreign countries.)
Malaysia. (See Foreign countries.)
Maldives. (See Foreign countries.)
Male householders. (See Households or families.)
Mali. (See Foreign countries.)
Malignant neoplasms. (See Cancer.)
Malt beverages (see also Beverages), 767, 892, 895
Malta. (See Foreign countries.)
Mammography testing, 217
Managed care health plans, 159
Management of companies and enterprises:
  Capital, 818, 820
  Earnings, 667, 678, 807, 808, 809, 810, 811, 812
  Employees, 649, 667, 673, 792, 795, 800, 807, 808, 809, 810, 811, 812, 1289, 1291, 1292
  Establishments, 673, 792, 795, 796, 797, 800, 806, 807, 808, 809, 810, 811, 812, 1289, 1290, 1291
  Finances, 786
  Gross domestic product, 708
  Occupational safety, 697
  Profits, 792, 831
  Sales, receipts, 786, 807, 808, 809, 810, 811, 812, 1289, 1290
Managers. (See Proprietors.)
Mandatory minimum sentencing, 387
Manganese, 948, 951, 1389

Manufacturing industry (see also individual industries):
  Capital, 797, 818, 820
  Construction value, 1006
  Earnings, 665, 667, 678, 679, 792, 807, 808, 809, 810, 811, 812, 1052, 1058, 1059, 1069, 1345
  Economic indicators, 825
  Employees, 654, 656, 665, 666, 667, 673, 792, 795, 800, 807, 808, 809, 810, 811, 812, 853, 1050, 1051, 1052, 1053, 1054, 1057, 1059, 1066, 1067, 1069, 1345
  Establishments, 673, 792, 793, 795, 796, 797, 800, 806, 807, 808, 809, 810, 811, 812, 1050, 1051, 1069, 1345
  Finances, 786, 1064, 1065, 1309, 1337
  Foreign countries, 1369, 1370
  Foreign investments in U.S., 1306, 1307
  Foreign trade, 1055
  Gross domestic product, 708, 712, 1048, 1337
  Hires and separations, 671, 672
  Hours, 665, 1056, 1057
  Industrial production index, 827, 1057
  Inventories, 826, 1060, 1061, 1062, 1063
  Investment abroad, 1309
  Island areas of the United States, 1345
  Multinational companies, 832, 834, 835
  Nonemployers, 793
  Occupational safety, 697, 699
  Research and development, 842
  Robotics, 1049
  Productivity, 675, 676, 827, 828, 1057, 1369
  Profits, 830, 831, 1064, 1065
  Sales, shipments, receipts, 786, 792, 793, 807, 808, 809, 810, 811, 812, 826, 1052, 1053, 1055, 1060, 1061, 1062, 1063, 1064, 1065, 1066, 1067
  State data, 1051, 1053, 1058
  Toxic chemical releases, 432
  Union membership, 702
  Value added, 1052, 1053
Margarine, 772
Marijuana (see also Drugs, illegal), 221, 222, 377, 560
Marine Corps, 545
Marine economy, 420
Marital status, 59, 60, 138
  Asian population, 59, 73
  Black, African American population, 59, 63, 73
  Computer use, 1182
  Couples with or without own household, 62
  Elderly, 33, 60, 73
  Employed persons, 632, 633, 635
  Foreign-born population, 40
  Hispanic origin population, 59, 63
  Householder status, 62, 64
  Internet access, 1182
  Interracial, 63
  Labor force participation rates, 631, 632, 633, 634
  Male householder, 62, 64
  Same-sex couple households, 73, 75
  Unmarried partners, 73, 74, 75
  Women in the labor force, 631, 632, 633, 634

Note: Index citations refer to **table** numbers, not **page** numbers

Marriages (see also Marital status), 80, 134, 135, 136, 137, 138
Married couples. (See Households or families.)
Married persons. (See Marital status.)
Marshall Islands. (See Foreign countries.)
Maryland. (See State data.)
Massachusetts. (See State data.)
Maternal and child health services, expenditures for, 140
Mathematics:
    Degrees conferred, 325, 326, 327, 328, 851, 852
    Employment, 855, 858
    Literacy, 1383
    Research & development, 839, 844
    Salary, 322, 858
    School enrollment, 847
Mauritania. (See Foreign countries.)
Mauritius. (See Foreign countries.)
Measles, 200, 235, 236
Meat and meat products (see also Food manufacturing, and individual meats):
    Consumer expenditures, 727, 731, 732
    Consumption, 244, 915, 1384, 1387
    Farm marketings, 883, 885
    Foreign trade, 891, 892, 898, 900, 915, 1321, 1327, 1328, 1384
    Prices, 767, 772, 774, 781
    Production, 915, 1384, 1386
    Supply, 915
Mechanical engineering, 852
Media (see also individual medium), 1162, 1163, 1170
Medicaid:
    Coverage, recipients, 154, 157, 159, 163, 577
    Expenditures, 143, 144, 146, 157, 160, 574
    Federal budget outlays and payments, 150, 157, 515
    State data, 157, 159
Medical care (see also Health services):
    Debt, 194
    Delay, 195
    Expenditures for, 139, 140, 141, 142, 143, 144, 145, 146, 148, 149, 194, 573, 574, 575, 727, 728, 730, 731, 732, 1363
    Insurance benefits, 140, 141, 144
    Price indexes, consumer, 147, 765, 766, 767, 777
Medical equipment and products:
    Expenditures for, 139, 141, 142, 143, 148, 149
Medical equipment and supplies manufacturing, 667, 675, 1052, 1054, 1055
Medical records, security breaches, 175
Medical research, 140, 141
Medical schools, 329
Medical sciences, employment, 170, 649
Medical services. (See Health services.)
Medicare:
    Ambulatory care visits, 153, 186
    Benefit payments, expenditures, 140, 141, 143, 144, 145, 146, 153, 155, 156, 161, 574
    Certified care providers, 187
    Contributions, 153, 156
    Enrollees, 151, 152, 153, 154, 163
    Federal budget outlays and payments, 150, 156, 161, 514, 515
    Hospital visits, 153, 186
    State data, 151

Trust funds, 156, 517
Medicines (See Drugs and medicines, and Pharmaceutical and medicine manufacturing.)
Meditation, 210
Melons, 243, 908
Membership organizations:
    Earnings, 667
    Employees, 667, 1291, 1292
    Establishments, 1291
    Revenue, 1298
Meningitis, 200
Mental disorders and illness, 230, 231, 233, 241, 366, 700
Mental hospitals, 168, 170, 178, 179, 180, 190, 191
Mercury, 948
Metal detectors, in public schools, 336
Metal ore mining industry, 944, 945, 946
Metals, 947, 948, 951
    Foreign trade, 948, 951, 1321, 1322
    Prices, 776, 780, 781, 948, 949
    Production and value, 946, 947, 948
    Recycling, 427, 428, 429
    Spot market price indexes, 774
    World production, 1389
Metalworking manufacturing, 667, 675, 1052, 1054
Methamphetamine (see also Drugs, illegal), 132, 221, 377, 560
Methane emissions, 424
Metropolitan statistical areas:
    Air quality index, 426
    Airline markets, 1101, 1103
    Civilian labor force, 629
    Commuting, 1147
    Components of change, 22
    Consumer expenditures, 728
    Consumer price index, 766
    Crime, 342
    Housing, 1018, 1027
    Migration, 22
    Personal income, 722
    Population, 21, 22, 23
    Religious adherents, 79
    Science and engineering employment, 856
    States, 23
    Unemployment rate, 629
    Vacancy rates, housing, 1027
Mexican- origin population, 37
    Educational attainment, 37
    Labor force, 37, 622
Mexico. (See Foreign countries.)
Mica:
    Foreign trade (sheet), 948, 951
    Production and value, 947, 948
Michigan. (See State data.)
Microcomputers (See Computers.)
Micronesia, Federated States of. (See Foreign countries.)
Migration, 3, 4, 5, 16, 22, 28, 29, 30, 31, 32, 1354
Military assistance, 552, 1311, 1312
Military manpower, 544, 545, 546, 549
Military expenditures outlays, 542, 543, 1412
Military sciences, degrees conferred, 326, 327
Military services and personnel:
    Casualties, 548
    Pay grades, 546

Note: Index citations refer to **table** numbers, not **page** numbers

---

Note: Index citations refer to **table** numbers, not **page** numbers

---

Note: Index citations refer to **table** numbers, not **page** numbers

Payroll and earnings, 667, 925, 926
Petroleum industry, 953
Sales and revenue, 926
Timber- related industry, 928, 929
Naturalized citizens, 37, 40, 42, 49, 455
Nauru. (See Foreign countries.)
Navy, personnel, 545
Nebraska. (See State data.)
Nectarines, 243, 909
Neonatal deaths (see also Deaths and death rates), 114
Nepal. (See Foreign countries.)
Nephritis, nephrotic syndrome, and nephrosis (see also Kidney disease), 118, 119, 120, 121, 122
Netherlands. (See Foreign countries.)
Neurologists, 171
Nevada. (See State data.)
New Hampshire. (See State data.)
New Jersey. (See State data.)
New Mexico. (See State data.)
New York. (See State data.)
New York Stock Exchange, 1231
New Zealand. (See Foreign countries.)
Newspaper, book, and directory publishers:
Earnings, 667, 1156
Employees, 667, 1156, 1157
Establishments, 1156, 1157
Finances, 1161, 1164
Productivity, 675
Revenue, 1157, 1161, 1164
Newspapers (see also Publishing industry):
Number and circulation, 1165, 1166
Reading, 1162
Recycling, 429
Newsprint, 938, 939
Nicaragua. (See Foreign countries.)
Nickel:
Consumption, 948
Employment, 948
Foreign trade, 948, 951
Prices, 948, 949
Production and value, 947, 948
World production, 1389
Niger. (See Foreign countries.)
Nigeria. (See Foreign countries.)
Niobium, 948, 951
Nitrogen in ammonia, 948, 1389
Nonalcoholic beverages, 731, 732
Nonemployer establishments, 610, 793, 1071, 1077, 1094, 1194, 1245, 1250, 1290
Nonimmigrant admissions, 47
Nonmetallic mineral mining and quarrying, except fuels, 818, 925, 944
Nonmetallic mineral product manufacturing (see also Metals and metal products):
Earnings, 667, 1052, 1059
Employees, 667, 1050, 1052, 1054, 1059
Establishments, 1050
Foreign trade, 1055, 1321, 1322
Gross domestic product, 708, 1048
Productivity, 675, 827
Shipments, receipts, 1052, 1055, 1061, 1062
Toxic chemical releases, 432

Nonprofit organizations, 615, 616, 617, 618, 667, 673, 1298, 1299
North Carolina. (See State data.)
North Dakota. (See State data.)
North Korea. (See Foreign countries.)
Northern Mariana Islands. (See Island areas of the U.S.)
Norway. (See Foreign countries.)
Notifiable diseases, 200
Nuclear power, 981, 982, 983, 986, 987
Capacity, 981, 982
Consumption, 966, 967, 971, 1394
Production, 966, 967, 981, 982, 986, 987, 989, 1390, 1391
Reactors, 981, 982
State data, 982, 989
Nursing and residential care facilities:
Capital, 818
Earnings, 667, 792
Employees, 170, 667, 792
Establishments, 187, 188, 792
Expenditures, 139, 141, 142, 143, 146, 149
Gross domestic product, 708
Medicare utilization, 153
Population, 71, 188
Receipts, 168, 169, 792
Nursing personnel, 173, 182, 649, 651, 653
Nutrients and nutritional intake, 245, 246
Nutritional deficiencies, deaths, 120
Nuts, 244, 885, 898, 900, 909, 910

O

Obesity, 227, 228, 238, 1359
Obstetricians (see also Physicians), 171, 182
Occupational safety, 696, 697, 699, 945
Occupations (see also individual occupations):
American Indian, Alaska Native population, 36
Asian population, 36, 649, 655
Black, African American population, 36, 649, 655
Earnings, 651, 682, 684, 689
Employment, 36, 649, 651, 652, 655, 684
Employment cost index, 685, 773
Hispanic origin population, 36, 649, 655
Island areas of the U.S., 1350
Mobility (geographic) status, 30
Native Hawaiian, Other Pacific Islander population, 36
Retirement and health plan benefits, 694
Self- employed, 640
Science and engineering, 853, 854, 855, 858
Women, 649, 689
Office buildings. (See Commercial buildings.)
Office equipment, 1084
Office supplies, stationery, and gift stores, 667, 675, 1076, 1077, 1078, 1079
Ohio. (See State data.)
Oil. (See Petroleum and products.)
Oil and gas extraction industry:
Capital, 818
Earnings, 667, 792, 925, 926, 944
Employees, 653, 667, 792, 925, 926, 944, 952
Establishments, 792, 925, 926, 952

Note: Index citations refer to **table** numbers, not **page** numbers

---

Note: Index citations refer to **table** numbers, not **page** numbers

Note: Index citations refer to **table** numbers, not **page** numbers

---

Note: Index citations refer to **table** numbers, not **page** numbers

Note: Index citations refer to **table** numbers, not **page** numbers

---

Note: Index citations refer to **table** numbers, not **page** numbers

Q

Qatar. (See Foreign countries.)
Quarries. (See Mining industries.)
Quicksilver (mercury), 948

R

Rabies, 200
Race (See individual race categories.)
Radio broadcasting industry (see also Broadcasting, and Telecommunications):
  Earnings, 667, 1156, 1157
  Employees, 667, 1156, 1157
  Establishments, 1156, 1157
  Finances, 1161, 1171
  Productivity, 675
  Revenue, 1157, 1161, 1171
  Stations, 1163
Radiologists, 171
Radio listening, 1162
Rail transportation industry (see also Railroads):
  Capital, 818
  Earnings, 667
  Employees, 667, 1090, 1091
  Establishments, 1091
  Foreign trade, 1097
  Gross domestic product, 708
  Shipments, 1097, 1098, 1151
Railroad employees' retirement funds, 515, 516, 517, 574
Railroads:
  AMTRAK, 1095, 1096
  Energy consumption, 969
  Mileage owned and operated, 1095
  Occupational safety, 1100
  Passenger traffic and revenue, 1146, 1285
  Shipments, 1097, 1098, 1151
  Vehicles, 1096
Rainfall, selected cities, 1399
Rankings:
  Airport traffic, 1103, 1287
  Amusement parks, 1264
  Cities:
    Commuting, 1148
    Population, 21, 24, 39
    Residential property tax, 495
    Science and engineering employment, 856
  Countries:
    Agricultural exports and imports, 1388
    Consumption of beef, pork, poultry, 1387
    Military expenditures, 1412
    Population, 1353
  Federal R&D obligations to higher education, 845
  Freight gateways, 1315
  Port traffic, 1112, 1113
  State:
    Exports, 1318
    Farm marketings, 887
    Foreign trade, 1318
    Personal income per capita, 720
    Population, 15
    Public elementary/secondary school finances, 264

Rape, 332, 341, 342, 343, 344, 347, 348, 355, 371, 372, 551
Raspberries, 885, 909
Raw materials. (See Crude materials.)
Reading (see also Books, and Libraries), 727, 731, 732, 1258, 1261, 1262, 1265, 1266
  E- book readers, 1265
  Literacy, 1383
Real estate (see also Housing), 758
Real estate and rental and leasing industry:
  Capital, 797, 818, 820
  Earnings, 665, 667, 678, 792, 798, 807, 808, 809, 810, 811, 812, 1193, 1246, 1247
  Electronic commerce, 1296
  Employees, 649, 656, 665, 667, 673, 792, 795, 798, 807, 808, 809, 810, 811, 812, 1193, 1246
  Establishments, 673, 792, 793, 795, 796, 797, 806, 807, 808, 809, 810, 811, 812, 1193, 1245, 1246
  Finances, 786, 1306
  Gross domestic product, 708, 712, 1192
  Hires and separations, 671, 672
  Hours, 665
  Multinational companies, 834, 835
  Nonemployers, 793, 1245
  Occupational safety, 697
  Productivity, 675
  Profits, 831
  Sales, receipts, 786, 792, 793, 807, 808, 809, 810, 811, 812, 1193, 1245
Real estate investment trust (REITs), 1197, 1220
Receipts (see also Tax receipts, and individual industries):
  American Indian, Alaska Native- owned businesses, 812
  Asian- owned businesses, 811
  Black- owned businesses, 810
  Corporations, partnerships, and proprietorships, 782, 783, 784, 785, 786, 790, 1071
  Hispanic- or Latino- owned businesses, 809
  International transactions, 1300
  Minority- owned businesses, 808, 809, 810, 811, 812
  Revenue, government (see also individual governmental units):
    Local governments, 486, 503
    State and local governments combined, 482, 485, 486, 491, 492
    State governments, 486, 499, 500
    Tax collections, 501
    United States government, 485, 510, 516, 519
Recreation (see also Arts, recreation, and travel, and Sports):
  Activities, 1254, 1257, 1258, 1262, 1263, 1264, 1266, 1271, 1274
  Art, 1257, 1258
  Building construction, value, 1006, 1007
  Consumer expenditures, 716, 1260, 1261, 1276
  Consumer price indexes, 767, 777
  Employment and expenditures, government, 507, 509, 514
  Leisure, 1258, 1262, 1266

Note: Index citations refer to **table** numbers, not **page** numbers

---

Note: Index citations refer to **table** numbers, not **page** numbers

Russia. (See Foreign countries.)
Rwanda. (See Foreign countries.)

S

Safety and security measures, 336, 945
Saint Kitts and Nevis. (See Foreign countries.)
Saint Lucia. (See Foreign countries.)
Saint Vincent and the Grenadines. (See Foreign countries.)
Salaries and wages. (See Earnings.)
Sales. (See individual commodities and industries.)
Sales workers, 649
Salmon, 941
Salmonellosis, 200, 242
Salt (common), production/value, 947, 948, 1389
Samoa. (See Foreign countries.)
Samoa, American. (See Island areas of the U.S.)
Samoan population, 1330
San Marino. (See Foreign countries.)
Sand and gravel industry (see also Mining industry), 776, 947
Sanitation. (See Refuse collection, and Sewage treatment.)
Sao Tome and Principe. (See Foreign countries.)
SAT scores, 293
Saudi Arabia. (See Foreign countries.)
Savings:
    Credit unions, 1214
    Deposits, 714, 1200
    Gross savings, sources and uses, 710
    Personal, 710, 717
    Rates, 1377
Savings banks. (See Savings institutions.)
Savings bonds, 1201
Savings institutions:
    Consumer credit, 1218
    Debt held by families, 1204
    Earnings, 1195
    Employees, 1195
    Establishments, 1195, 1209
    Finances, 1196, 1197, 1210, 1211, 1220, 1225
    Individual Retirement Accounts (IRAs), 1239
Saw logs, 934, 935
Saw mills, 925, 928, 929
Scallops, 941
Scenic and sightseeing transportation industry, 667, 1090, 1091, 1092, 1093, 1094
Schools (see also Education):
    Average class size, 283
    Boards, elected officials, 475
    Bullying, 334, 337, 338
    Districts, 480, 481
    Dress code, 336
    Fundraising, 269
    Homeschooling, 282
    Lunch and breakfast programs, 600
    Number, 272, 273, 284, 285, 286, 294, 295
    Parent participation, 269
    Parent Teacher Association (PTA), 269
    Parent Teacher Organization, 269

Safety and security, 336
Special education, 231, 232
Start times, 281
States, 286
Types, 273, 284, 285, 286
Volunteers, 269
Weapons, 335
Science, literacy, 1383
Scientific instruments. (See Instruments.)
Scientific research. (See Research and development.)
Scientists and engineers (see also individual fields):
    Characteristics, 847, 853
    Degrees conferred, 325, 326, 327, 328, 848, 849, 850, 851, 852
    Earnings, 858
    Employment, 649, 855, 856, 858
    Non U.S. citizens, 848
    Occupation, 855
    School enrollment, 847
Scrap metal. (See individual commodities, and Municipal waste and Solid Waste.)
Seafood, 941
Securities (see also individual types of securities):
    Foreign holdings, 1199, 1230, 1300, 1302
    Government, 490, 787, 788, 1199, 1226, 1230
    Held by life insurance, 1244
    Holdings of banks, 787, 788, 1209
    Holdings of individuals and businesses, 1200
    New issues, 1226, 1227
    Prices, indexes, yields, and issues, 1231, 1233
    Sales, stocks and bonds, 1226
    Savings of individuals, 714
    State and local government, 490, 787, 788, 1226
Securities, commodity contracts, and investments industry:
    Capital, 818
    Earnings, 667, 1193, 1195
    Electronic commerce, 1296
    Employees, 667, 1193, 1195
    Establishments, 1193, 1194, 1195
    Finances, 1196, 1197, 1198
    Gross domestic product, 1192
    Nonemployers, 1194
    Receipts, 1193, 1194
Seeds, 883
Self- employed, 639, 640, 855
Semiconductors (see also Computer and electronic product components), 1052, 1327
Senators, U.S., 460, 464, 465, 466, 467, 468
Senegal. (See Foreign countries.)
Septicemia, 119, 120, 121, 122
Serbia. (See Foreign countries.)
Service industries (see also specific sectors):
    Capital, 797, 818, 820
    Earnings, 667, 678, 679, 798, 807, 808, 809, 810, 811, 812, 1289, 1345
    Electronic commerce, 1296
    Employees, 170, 656, 666, 667, 792, 795, 798, 800, 807, 808, 809, 810, 811, 812, 1289, 1291, 1292, 1345
    Establishments, 793, 795, 796, 797, 798, 800, 806, 807, 808, 809, 810, 811, 812, 1289, 1290, 1291, 1345

Note: Index citations refer to **table** numbers, not **page** numbers

---

Note: Index citations refer to **table** numbers, not **page** numbers

Note: Index citations refer to **table** numbers, not **page** numbers

Note: Index citations refer to **table** numbers, not **page** numbers

Note: Index citations refer to **table** numbers, not **page** numbers

Note: Index citations refer to **table** numbers, not **page** numbers

U

Uganda (See Foreign countries.)
Ukraine (See Foreign countries.)
Unemployment. (See Labor force, unemployed workers.)
Unemployment insurance:
  Beneficiaries, 576, 590, 591, 664
  Coverage, workers and earnings, 590, 591
  Government finances, 485, 516, 517
  Payments, 573, 574, 575, 590, 591
Union membership, 701, 702, 703
United Arab Emirates. (See Foreign countries.)
United Kingdom. (See Foreign countries.)
United States securities (see also Debt), 1198, 1199, 1200, 1209, 1226, 1228, 1230, 1233
Universities. (See Education, higher education institutions.)
Unpaid work, 636, 691, 713
Uranium (see also Nuclear power), 947, 963, 983
Urban population (see also Cities, and Metropolitan statistical areas), 23, 26, 79
  Deaths and death rates, 112
Urban transit systems, 1091, 1095, 1145
Uruguay. (See Foreign countries.)
Utah. (See State data.)
Utilities (see also Electric light and power industry and Gas utility industry.):
  Capital, 818, 820, 997, 999
  Consumer expenditures, 716, 727, 728
  Customers and bills, 993, 997, 998
  Earnings, 665, 667, 678, 792, 807, 808, 809, 810, 811, 812, 964, 965
  Electric, 984, 990
  Employees, 656, 665, 667, 792, 795, 807, 808, 809, 810, 811, 812, 964, 965, 1000
  Establishments, 792, 793, 795, 796, 806, 807, 808, 809, 810, 811, 812, 965
  Expense, 994
  Finances, 786, 999
  Gross domestic product, 708
  Gas, 997, 998, 999
  Government employees and payroll, 509
  Hours, 665
  Income, 994
  Industrial production index, 827
  Industry, 792, 964, 965, 990
  Investor owned, 994
  Multinational companies, 834, 835
  Net generation, 990, 993
  Net summer capacity, 984, 989, 990
  Nonemployers, 793
  Occupational safety, 697, 699
  Price indexes, 766, 767
  Productivity, 675
  Profits, 830, 831
  Revenue, 964, 993, 994, 997, 998, 1296
  Sales, receipts, 786, 792, 793, 807, 808, 809, 810, 811, 812, 998
  Sewage treatment, 965, 1000
  State and local government expenditures, 486, 487, 488, 493, 499, 502, 504
  States, 989, 991, 992
  Water, 430, 965
Uzbekistan. (See Foreign countries.)

V

Vacancy rates, housing, 1021, 1023, 1024, 1026, 1027, 1030
Vaccination, 204, 205, 206, 235, 236
Vanadium, 947, 951
Vanuatu. (See Foreign countries.)
Vaping (Electronic cigarette use), 213, 240
Veal (see also Beef, and Meat and meat products), 244, 776, 915, 1386, 1387
Vegetable oils. (See Oils.)
Vegetables (see also individual commodities):
  Acreage, 908, 913
  Consumer expenditures, 727, 731, 732
  Consumption, 243, 912
  Farm marketings, sales, 876, 883, 885, 913
  Foreign trade, 891, 892, 895, 898, 900, 912, 1321, 1329
  Organic, 913
  Prices, 767, 776, 780, 781, 888
  Production, 908, 912, 913
Vehicles. (See Motor vehicles.)
Veneer, wood products, 925, 928, 929, 938
Venezuela. (See Foreign countries.)
Vermiculite, 947, 948
Vermont. (See State data.)
Vessels. (See Ships.)
Veterans:
  Characteristics, 554, 557, 558, 613
  Employment, 536, 624
  Medical care, 150
  Number, 553, 554, 556
  Pensions and other benefits:
    Beneficiaries, 555, 556, 576
    Service- connected compensation, 555, 556
    Disbursements, 542, 556, 574, 575
    Federal aid to state and local governments, 484
    Federal payments, 514, 515, 573, 574, 575
Veterans Affairs, Dept. of:
  Expenditures, 140, 143, 146, 555, 556, 573, 574, 575
  Home loans, 1221
  Mental health treatment facilities, 178, 179
Veterinary services, 1291, 1292, 1294
Vetoed bills, Congressional, 469
Victimizations, criminal, 347, 348, 351, 352, 353, 354, 356, 357, 358, 361, 362, 363
Vietnam. (See Foreign countries.)
Violent crime, (see also Crime), 332, 341, 342, 343, 344, 345, 346, 347, 349, 350, 361, 362, 363, 371, 372
Virgin Islands. (See Island areas of the U.S.)
Virginia. (See State data.)
Virtual schools, 284
Visa holders, doctorates, 848
Visa overstays, 569
Visual and performing arts, degrees, 325, 326, 327, 328
Vital statistics. (See Births and birth rates, Deaths and death rates, Divorces, and Marriages.)
Vitamins, 245
Vocational rehabilitation, 140, 611
Volleyball, 1268, 1269, 1270

Note: Index citations refer to **table** numbers, not **page** numbers

---

Note: Index citations refer to **table** numbers, not **page** numbers

---

Note: Index citations refer to **table** numbers, not **page** numbers

---

Note: Index citations refer to **table** numbers, not **page** numbers